Collins

German

Dictionary

William Collins' dream of knowledge for all began with the publication of his first book in 1819. A self-educated mill worker, he not only enriched millions of lives, but also founded a flourishing publishing house. Today, staying true to this spirit, Collins books are packed with inspiration, innovation, and practical expertise. They place you at the centre of a world of possibility and give you exactly what you need to explore it.

Language is the key to this exploration, and at the heart of Collins Dictionaries is language as it is really used. New words, phrases, and meanings spring up every day, and all of them are captured and analysed by the Collins Word Web. Constantly updated, and with over 2.5 billion entries, this living language resource is unique to our dictionaries.

Words are tools for life. And a Collins Dictionary makes them work for you.

Collins. Do more.

Collins

German

Dictionary

HarperCollins Publishers
Westerhill Road
Bishopbriggs
Glasgow
G64 2QT
Great Britain

Sixth Edition 2010

Reprint 10 9 8 7 6 5 4 3 2

© HarperCollins Publishers 1997, 1999, 2004,
2006, 2007, 2010

ISBN 978-0-00-732316-6

Collins® is a registered trademark of
HarperCollins Publishers Limited

Dictionary text prepared by
Collins in collaboration with the
Langenscheidt Editorial Staff

www.collinslanguage.com

A catalogue record for this book is
available from the British Library

HarperCollins Publishers,
10 East 53rd Street,
New York, NY 10022

COLLINS GERMAN CONCISE DICTIONARY.
Fifth US Edition 2010

ISBN 978-0-06-199862-1

www.harpercollins.com

HarperCollins books may be purchased for
educational, business, or sales promotional
use. For information, please write to:
Special Markets Department,
HarperCollins Publishers,
10 East 53rd Street,
New York, NY 10022

Typeset by Wordcraft, Glasgow

Printed in Italy by
LEGO Spa, Lavis (Trento)

Acknowledgements
We would like to thank those authors and
publishers who kindly gave permission for
copyright material to be used in the Collins
Word Web. We would also like to thank
Times Newspapers Ltd for providing
valuable data.

Inhalt

Contents

GESAMTLEITUNG/PUBLISHING DIRECTOR
Rob Scriven

REDAKTIONELLE LEITUNG/EDITORIAL MANAGEMENT
Gaëlle-Amiot Cadey

LEITENDE REDAKTEURIN/SENIOR EDITOR
Susie Beattie

MITARBEITER/CONTRIBUTIONS FROM
Horst Kopleck, Joyce Littlejohn, Dagmar Förtsch, Hildegard Pesch, Veronika Schnorr,
Gisela Moohan, Ulrike Seeberger, Elspeth Anderson, Val McNulty, Eva Vennebusch,
Robin Sawers, Ilse MacLean, Beate Wengel

DATENVERARBEITUNG/COMPUTING STAFF
Thomas Callan

Einleitung

Sie möchten Englisch lernen oder vielleicht bereits vorhandene Kenntnisse vertiefen. Sie möchten sich auf Englisch ausdrücken, englische Texte lesen oder übersetzen, oder Sie möchten sich ganz einfach mit Englisch sprechenden Menschen unterhalten können. Ganz gleich ob Sie Englisch an der Schule oder an der Universität lernen, in einem Büro oder in einem Unternehmen tätig sind: Sie haben sich den richtigen Begleiter für Ihre Arbeit ausgesucht! Dieses Buch ist der ideale Helfer, wenn Sie sich in englischer Sprache ausdrücken und verständlich machen wollen, ob Sie nun sprechen oder schreiben. Unser Wörterbuch ist ganz bewusst praktisch und modern, es räumt vor allem der Alltagssprache und der Sprache, wie sie Ihnen in Zeitungen und Nachrichten, im Geschäftsleben, im Büro und im Urlaub begegnet, großen Raum ein. Wie in allen unseren Wörterbüchern haben wir das Hauptgewicht auf zeitgenössische Sprache und idiomatische Redewendungen gelegt.

Wie man dieses Buch benutzt

Im Folgenden geben wir einige Erklärungen darüber, wie die Einträge Ihres Wörterbuchs aufgebaut sind. Unser Ziel: Wir wollen Ihnen so viel Information wie möglich bieten, ohne dabei an Klarheit und Verständlichkeit einzubüßen.

Die Wörterbucheinträge

Ein typischer Eintrag in Ihres Wörterbuchs besteht aus folgenden Elementen:

Lautschrift

Wie die meisten modernen Wörterbücher geben wir die Aussprache mit Zeichen an, die zum „internationalen phonetischen Alphabet" gehören. Weiter unten (auf den Seiten xiv) finden Sie eine vollständige Liste der Zeichen, die in diesem System benutzt werden. Die Aussprache englischer Wörter geben wir auf der englisch-deutschen Seite unmittelbar hinter dem jeweiligen Wort in eckigen Klammern an. Die deutsche Aussprache erscheint im deutsch-englischen Teil ebenfalls auf diese Weise unmittelbar hinter den Worteinträgen. Allerdings wird sie nicht immer angegeben, zum Beispiel bei zusammengesetzten Wörtern wie Liebesbrief, deren Bestandteile schon an anderer Stelle im Wörterbuch zu finden sind.

Grammatik-Information

Alle Wörter gehören zu einer der folgenden grammatischen Klassen: Substantiv, Verb, Adjektiv, Pronomen, Artikel, Konjunktion, Präposition, Interjektion, Abkürzung. Substantive können im Deutschen männlich, weiblich oder sächlich sein. Verben können transitiv, intransitiv, reflexiv oder auch unpersönlich sein. Die Wortart folgt auf die Lautschrift und ist in *Kursivschrift* angegeben. Wo bei Übersetzungen eine Geschlechtsangabe erforderlich ist, wird diese ebenfalls in *Kursivschrift* gegeben.

Oft gehören Wörter zu zwei oder mehr grammatischen Klassen. So kann das deutsche Wort gut ein Adjektiv („good") oder auch ein Adverb („well") sein, und das englische Wort spell ist sowohl ein Substantiv („Zauber") als auch ein Verb („schreiben, buchstabieren"). Das Verb reden ist manchmal transitiv, d. h. es hat ein Objekt („sie redet Unsinn"), manchmal intransitiv, d.h. es wird ohne Objekt gebraucht („er redet ständig vom Wetter"). Zur besseren Übersichtlichkeit sind verschiedene Wortarten durch das Symbol ▷ abgegrenzt; alle Beispielsätze werden dann unter den entsprechenden grammatischen Kategorien gegeben.

Bedeutungsunterschiede

Die meisten Wörter haben mehr als eine Bedeutung. So kann z.B. Rad einen Teil eines Autos oder Fahrrads bezeichnen, aber auch ein Wort für das Fahrrad selbst sein. Andere Wörter haben je nach Kontext verschiedene Übersetzungen; so bedeutet das Verb to recede abhängig vom Subjekt des Satzes entweder „zurückgehen" oder „verschwinden". Damit Sie in jedem Zusammenhang immer die richtige Übersetzung finden, haben wir die Einträge nach Bedeutungen eingeteilt: jede Kategorie wird durch einen „Verwendungshinweis" bestimmt, der *kursiv* gedruckt ist und in

Klammern steht. Die beiden Beispiele von oben sehen dann so aus:

> **Rad** *nt* wheel; *(Fahrrad)* bike
> **recede** *vi (tide)* zurückgehen; *(lights etc)* verschwinden

Andere Wörter haben in verschiedenen Sachzusammenhängen unterschiedliche Bedeutungen. Das Wort **Rezept** z. B. bezeichnet eine Koch- oder Backanleitung, bezieht sich in medizinischen Zusammenhängen jedoch auf ärztlich verordnete Medikamente. Wir zeigen Ihnen, welche Übersetzung Sie auswählen sollten, indem wir wieder in Klammern solche Fachgebiete in *kursiven* Buchstaben angeben, mit dem Anfangsbuchstaben großgeschrieben, im vorigen Fall *Koch* als Abkürzung für *Kochen* und *Med* als Abkürzung für *Medizin*:

> **Rezept** *nt (Koch)* recipe; *(Med)* prescription

Sie finden eine Liste aller in diesem Wörterbuch benutzten Abkürzungen für solche Sachgebiete auf den Seiten x–xii.

Übersetzungen

Die meisten deutschen Wörter können mit einem einzigen englischen Wort übersetzt werden und umgekehrt. Aber manchmal gibt es eine solche genaue Entsprechung nicht. In diesen Fällen haben wir eine ungefähre Entsprechung angegeben, gekennzeichnet durch ≈. Dies ist z. B. der Fall bei **Gymnasium** mit den englischen bzw. amerikanischen Äquivalenten „grammar school" und „high school", die aufgrund der unterschiedlichen Ausbildungssysteme lediglich ungefähre Entsprechungen sein können.

> **Gymnasium** *nt* ≈ grammar school *(Brit)*, high school *(US)*

Manchmal kann man nicht einmal ein ungefähres Äquivalent finden. Besonders oft ist das der Fall beim Essen, insbesondere bei lokalen Spezialitäten wie dieser schottischen Speise:

> **haggis** *(Scot) n Gericht aus gehackten Schafsinnereien und Haferschrot, im Schafsmagen gekocht*

Hier wird statt einer Übersetzung (die es einfach gar nicht gibt) eine Erklärung gegeben, die durch *Kursivschrift* als solche kenntlich gemacht ist.

Im Deutschen wissen Sie , in welcher Situation Sie den Ausdruck **ich bin pleite** verwenden würden, wann Sie **ich bin knapp bei Kasse** sagen und wann **ich bin in Geldschwierigkeiten**. Wenn Sie jedoch Englisch verstehen oder selbst sprechen wollen, ist es wichtig zu wissen, welcher Ausdruck etwa höflich ist und welcher nicht. Um Ihnen hierbei zu helfen, haben wir für umgangssprachliche Ausdrücke die Kennzeichnung *(umg)* bzw. *(inf)* verwendet. Besonders anstößige Ausdrücke sind zusätzlich mit einem Ausrufezeichen versehen, also *(umg!)* bzw. *(inf!)*, um den Benutzer zu warnen, diese nur mit großer Vorsicht zu verwenden. Angaben wie *(umg)* oder *(inf)* werden bei Übersetzungen in der Regel nicht wiederholt, wenn das Sprachniveau der Zielsprache dem der Ausgangssprache entspricht.

Schlüsselwörter

Im Text als **SCHLÜSSELWÖRTER** hervorgehobene Einträge, wie etwa **to be** und **to do** und ihre deutschen Entsprechungen **sein** und **machen**, werden als Grundelemente der Sprache besonders ausführlich behandelt.

Landeskundliche Informationen

In vom restlichen Text durch eine senkrechte Reihe schattierter Punkte abgesetzten Artikeln werden landeskundliche Aspekte in deutsch- und englischsprachigen Ländern behandelt. Die Themen umfassen Politik, Ausbildung, Medien und Feiertage, z. B. **Bundestag**, **Abitur**, **BBC** und **Hallowe'en**.

Introduction

You may be starting to learn German, or you may wish to extend your knowledge of the language. Perhaps you want to read and study German books, newspapers and magazines, or perhaps simply have a conversation with German speakers. Whatever the reason, whether you're a student, a tourist or want to use German for business, this is the ideal book to help you understand and communicate. This modern, user-friendly dictionary gives priority to everyday vocabulary and the language of current affairs, business and tourism. As in all Collins dictionaries, the emphasis is firmly placed on contemporary language and expressions.

How to use this Dictionary
You will find below an outline of the way in which information is presented in your dictionary. Our aim is to give you the maximum amount of information whilst still providing a text which is clear and user-friendly.

Entries
A typical entry in your dictionary will be made up of the following elements:

Phonetic transcription
Phonetics appear in square brackets immediately after the headword. They are shown using the International Phonetic Alphabet (IPA), and a complete list of the symbols used in this system can be found on pages xiv and xv.

Grammatical information
All words belong to one of the following parts of speech: noun, verb, adjective, adverb, pronoun, article, conjunction, preposition, exclamation, abbreviation. Nouns can be singular or plural and, in German, masculine, feminine or neuter. Verbs can be transitive, intransitive, reflexive or impersonal. Parts of speech appear in *italics* immediately after the phonetic spelling of the headword. The gender of the translation appears in *italics* immediately following the key element of the translation.

Often a word can have more than one part of speech. Just as the English word **next** can be an adjective or an adverb, the German word **gut** can be an adjective ("good") or an adverb ("well"). In the same way the verb **to walk** is sometimes transitive, i.e. it takes an object ("to walk the dog") and sometimes intransitive, i.e. it doesn't take an object ("to walk to school"). To help you find the meaning you are looking for quickly and for clarity of presentation, the different part of speech categories are separated by an open white triangle ▷.

Meaning divisions
Most words have more than one meaning. Take, for example, **punch** which can be, amongst other things, a blow with the fist or an object used for making holes. Other words are translated differently depending on the context in which they are used. The intransitive verb **to recede**, for example, can be translated by "zurückgehen" or "verschwinden" depending on *what* is receding. To help you select the most appropriate translation in every context, entries are divided according to meaning. Each different meaning is introduced by an "indicator" in *italics* and in brackets. Thus, the examples given above will be shown as follows:

> **punch** n (*blow*) Schlag m; (*tool*) Locher m
> **recede** vi (*tide*) zurückgehen; (*lights etc*) verschwinden

Likewise, some words can have a different meaning when used to talk about a specific subject area or field. For example, **bishop**, which in a religious context means a high-ranking clergyman, is also the name of a chess piece. To show English speakers which translation to use, we have added "subject field labels" in italics with initial capitals and in brackets, in this case (*Rel*) and (*Chess*):

> **bishop** *n* (*Rel*) Bischof *m*; (*Chess*) Läufer *m*

Field labels are often shortened to save space. You will find a complete list of abbreviations used in the dictionary on pages x to xii

Translations

Most English words have a direct translation in German and vice versa, as shown in the examples given above. Sometimes, however, no exact equivalent exists in the target language. In such cases we have given an approximate equivalent, indicated by the sign ≈. Such is the case of **high school**, the German equivalent of which is "Oberschule *f*". This is not an exact translation since the systems of the two countries in question are quite different:

> **high school** *n* ≈ Oberschule *f*

On occasion it is impossible to find even an approximate equivalent. This may be the case, for example, with the names of culinary specialities like this German cake:

> **Streuselkuchen** *m cake with crumble topping*

Here the translation (which doesn't exist) is replaced by an explanation. For increased clarity the explanation, or "gloss", is shown in *italics*.

Register

In English you instinctively know when to say **I'm broke** *or* **I'm a bit short of cash** and when to say **I don't have any money**. When you are trying to understand someone who is speaking German, however, or when you yourself try to speak German, it is especially important to know what is polite and what is less so. To help you with this, we have added the register labels (*umg*) and (*inf*) to colloquial or offensive expressions. Those expressions which are particularly vulgar are also given an exclamation mark (*umg!*) or (*inf!*), warning you to use them with extreme care. Please note that the register labels (*umg*) and (*inf*) are not repeated in the target language when the register of the translation matches that of the word or phrase being translated.

Keywords

Words labelled in the text as KEYWORDS, such as **be** and **do** or their German equivalents **sein** and **machen**, have been given special treatment because they form the basic elements of the language. This extra help will ensure that you know how to use these complex words with confidence.

Cultural information

Entries which appear separated by a column of dots explain aspects of culture in German- and English-speaking countries. Subject areas covered include politics, education, media and national festivals, for example **Bundestag, Abitur, BBC** and **Hallowe'en**.

Abkürzungen

Abbreviations

Abkürzung	*abk, abbr*	abbreviation
Adjektiv	*adj*	adjective
Verwaltung	*Admin*	administration
Adverb	*adv*	adverb
Landwirtschaft	*Agr*	agriculture
Akkusativ	*akk, acc*	accusative
Anatomie	*Anat*	anatomy
Architektur	*Archit*	architecture
Artikel	*art*	article
Kunst	*Art*	
Astrologie	*Astrol*	astrology
Astronomie	*Astron*	astronomy
attributiv	*attrib*	attributive
Kraftfahrzeuge	*Aut*	automobiles
Hilfsverb	*aux*	auxiliary
Luftfahrt	*Aviat*	aviation
Bergbau	*Bergb*	mining
besonders	*bes*	especially
Biologie	*Biol*	biology
Botanik	*Bot*	botany
britisch	*Brit*	British
Kartenspiel	*Cards*	
Chemie	*Chem*	chemistry
Film	*Cine*	cinema
Handel	*Comm*	commerce
Komparativ	*comp*	comparative
Computer	*Comput*	computers
Konjunktion	*conj*	conjunction
Bauwesen	*Constr*	building
zusammengesetztes Wort	*cpd*	compound
Kochen und Backen	*Culin*	cooking
Dativ	*dat*	dative
bestimmt	*def*	definite
diminutiv	*dimin*	diminutive
dekliniert	*dekl*	declined
kirchlich	*Eccl*	ecclesiastical
Volkswirtschaft	*Econ*	economics
Eisenbahn	*Eisenb*	railways
Elektrizität	*Elek, Elec*	electricity
besonders	*esp*	especially
und so weiter	*etc*	et cetera
etwas	*etw*	something
Euphemismus	*euph*	euphemism
Ausruf	*excl*	exclamation
Femininum	*f*	feminine
übertragen	*fig*	figurative
Film	*Film*	cinema
Finanzen	*Fin*	finance
formell	*form*	formal
'phrasal verb', bei dem Partikel und Verb nicht getrennt werden können	*fus*	fused: phrasal verb where the particle cannot be separated from the verb
gehoben	*geh*	elevated

Genitiv	*gen*	genitive
Geografie	*Geog*	geography
Geologie	*Geol*	geology
Geometrie	*Geom*	geometry
Grammatik	*Gram*	grammar
Geschichte	*Hist*	history
scherzhaft	*hum*	humorous
Imperfekt	*imperf*	imperfect
unpersönlich	*impers*	impersonal
unbestimmt	*indef*	indefinite
umgangssprachlich	*inf*	informal
untrennbares Verb	*insep*	inseparable
Interjektion	*interj*	interjection
Interrogativ	*interrog*	interrogative
unveränderlich	*inv*	invariable
unregelmäßig	*irreg*	irregular
jemand	*jd*	somebody
jemandem	*jdm*	(to) somebody
jemanden	*jdn*	somebody
jemandes	*jds*	somebody's
Rechtswesen	*Jur*	law
Kartenspiel	*Karten*	cards
Kochen und Backen	*Koch*	cooking
Komparativ	*komp*	comparative
Konjunktion	*konj*	conjunction
Rechtswesen	*Law*	law
Sprachwissenschaft	*Ling*	linguistics
wörtlich	*lit*	literal
literarisch	*liter*	literary
Literatur	*Liter*	literature
Maskulinum	*m*	masculine
Mathematik	*Math*	mathematics
Medizin	*Med*	medicine
Meteorologie	*Met*	meteorology
Militärwesen	*Mil*	military
Bergbau	*Min*	mining
Musik	*Mus*	music
Substantiv	*n*	noun
nautisch	*Naut*	nautical
Nominativ	*nom*	nominative
norddeutsch	*Nordd*	North Germany
Neutrum	*nt*	neuter
Zahlwort	*num*	numeral
Objekt	*obj*	object
oder	*od*	or
veraltet	*old*	
sich	*o.s.*	oneself
österreichisch	*Österr*	Austria
Parlament	*Parl*	parliament
pejorativ	*pej*	pejorative
Person/persönlich	*pers*	person/personal
Pharmazie	*Pharm*	pharmacy
Fotografie	*Phot*	photography
Physik	*Phys*	physics
Physiologie	*Physiol*	physiology

Plural	*pl*	plural
Politik	*Pol*	politics
possessiv	*poss*	possessive
Partizip Perfekt	*pp*	past participle
Präfix	*präf, pref*	prefix
Präposition	*präp, prep*	preposition
Präsens	*präs, pres*	present
Pronomen	*pron*	pronoun
Psychologie	*Psych*	psychology
Imperfekt	*pt*	past tense
Radio	*Radio*	radio
Eisenbahn	*Rail*	railways
Religion	*Rel*	religion
Relativ-	*rel*	relative
Rundfunk	*Rundf*	broadcasting
jemand (-en, -em)	*sb*	somebody
Schulwesen	*Sch*	school
Naturwissenschaft	*Sci*	science
Schulwesen	*Scol*	school
schottisch	*Scot*	Scottish
Singular	*sing*	singular
Skisport	*Ski*	skiing
etwas	*sth*	something
Süddeutschland	*Südd*	South German
Suffix	*suff*	suffix
Superlativ	*superl*	superlative
Technik	*Tech*	technology
Telekommunikation	*Tel*	telecommunications
Theater	*Theat*	theatre
Fernsehen	*TV*	television
Typografie	*Typ*	typography
umgangssprachlich	*umg*	colloquial
Universität	*Univ*	university
unpersönlich	*unpers*	impersonal
unregelmäßig	*unreg*	irregular
untrennbar	*untr*	inseparable
unveränderlich	*unver*	invariable
(nord)amerikanisch	*US*	(North)American
gewöhnlich	*usu*	usually
und so weiter	*usw*	et cetera
Verb	*vb*	verb
intransitives Verb	*vi*	intransitive verb
reflexives Verb	*vr*	reflexive verb
transitives Verb	*vt*	transitive verb
Wirtschaft	*Wirts*	economy
Zoologie	*Zool*	zoology
zusammengesetztes Wort	*zW*	compound
ungefähre Entsprechung	≈	cultural equivalent
eingetragene Marke	®	registered trademark

German Noun Endings

After many noun entries on the German-English side of the dictionary, you will find two pieces of grammatical information, separated by commas, to help you with the declension of the noun, e.g. -, -n or -(e)s, -e. The first item shows you the genitive singular form, and the second gives the plural form. The hyphen stands for the word itself and the other letters are endings. Sometimes an umlaut is shown over the hyphen, which means an umlaut must be placed on the vowel of the word, e.g.:

DICTIONARY ENTRY	GENITIVE SINGULAR	PLURAL
Mann *m* -(e)s, ˝er	**Mannes** *or* **Manns**	**Männer**
Jacht *f* -, -en	**Jacht**	**Jachten**

This information is not given when the noun has one of the regular German noun endings below, and you should refer to this table in such cases. Similarly, genitive and plural endings are not shown when the German entry is a compound consisting of two or more words which are to be found elsewhere in the dictionary, since the compound form takes the endings of the LAST word of which it is formed, e.g.:

for **Nebenstraße** *see* **Straße**
for **Schneeball** *see* **Ball**

Regular German Noun Endings

NOM	GEN	PL
-ant *m*	-anten	-anten
-anz *f*	-anz	-anzen
-ar *m*	-ar(e)s	-are
-chen *nt*	-chens	-chen
-ei *f*	-ei	-eien
-elle *f*	-elle	-ellen
-ent *m*	-enten	-enten
-enz *f*	-enz	-enzen
-ette *f*	-ette	-etten
-eur *m*	-eurs	-eure
-euse *f*	-euse	-eusen
-heit *f*	-heit	-heiten
-ie *f*	-ie	-ien
-ik *f*	-ik	-iken
-in *f*	-in	-innen
-ine *f*	-ine	-inen
-ion *f*	-ion	-ionen
-ist *m*	-isten	-isten
-ium *nt*	-iums	-ien
-ius *m*	-ius	-iusse
-ive *f*	-ive	-iven
-keit *f*	-keit	-keiten
-lein *nt*	-leins	-lein
-ling *m*	-lings	-linge
-ment *nt*	-ments	-mente
-mus *m*	-mus	-men
-schaft *f*	-schaft	-schaften
-tät *f*	-tät	-täten
-tor *m*	-tors	-toren
-ung *f*	-ung	-ungen
-ur *f*	-ur	-uren

Phonetic Symbols

NB: All vowels sounds are
approximate only.

Lautschrift

NB: Alle Vokallaute sind nur
ungefähre Entsprechungen.

Vowels			Vokale
matt	[a]		
Fahne	[aː]		
Vater	[ər]		
	[ɑː]	calm, part	
	[æ]	sat	
Rendezvous	[ã]		
Chance	[aː]		
	[ãː]	clientele	
Etage	[e]		
Seele, Mehl	[eː]		
Wäsche, Bett	[ɛ]	egg	
zählen	[ɛː]		
Teint	[ɛ̃ː]		
mache	[ə]	above	
	[əː]	burn, earn	
Kiste	[ɪ]	pit, awfully	
Vitamin	[i]		
Ziel	[iː]	peat	
Oase	[o]		
oben	[oː]		
Champignon	[õ]		
Salon	[õː]		
Most	[ɔ]	cot	
	[ɔː]	born, jaw	
ökonomisch	[ø]		
blöd	[øː]		
Göttin	[œ]		
	[ʌ]	hut	
zuletzt	[u]	put	
Mut	[uː]	pool	
Mutter	[ʊ]		
Physik	[y]		
Kübel	[yː]		
Sünde	[ʏ]		

Diphthongs			Diphthonge
Styling	[ai]		
weit	[aɪ]		buy, die, my
umbauen	[au]		house, now
Haus	[aʊ]		
	[eɪ]		pay, mate
	[ɛə]		pair, mare
	[əu]		no, boat
	[ɪə]		mere, shear
Heu, Häuser	[ɔʏ]		
	[ɔɪ]		boy, coin
	[uə]		tour, poor

Consonants			Konsonanten
Ball	[b]		ball
mich	[ç]		
	[tʃ]		child
fern	[f]		field
gern	[g]		good
Hand	[h]		hand
ja	[j]		yet, million
	[dʒ]		just
Kind	[k]		kind, catch
links, Pult	[l]		left, little
matt	[m]		mat
Nest	[n]		nest
lang	[ŋ]		long
Paar	[p]		put
rennen	[r]		run
fast, fassen	[s]		sit
Chef, Stein, Schlag	[ʃ]		shall
Tafel	[t]		tab
	[θ]		thing
	[ð]		this
wer	[v]		very
	[w]		wet
Loch	[x]		loch
fix	[ks]		box
singen	[z]		pods, zip
Zahn	[ts]		
genieren	[ʒ]		measure

Other signs			Andere Zeichen
glottal stop	|		Knacklaut
main stress	[']		Hauptton
long vowel	[:]		Längezeichen

German Irregular Verbs

* with "sein"

INFINITIV	PRÄSENS 2., 3. SINGULAR	PRÄTERITUM	PARTIZIP PERFEKT
abwägen	wägst ab, wägt ab	wog ab	abgewogen
ausbedingen	bedingst aus, bedingt aus	bedang *od* bedingte aus	ausbedungen
backen	bäckst, bäckt	backte *od* buk	gebacken
befehlen	befiehlst, befiehlt	befahl	befohlen
beginnen	beginnst, beginnt	begann	begonnen
beißen	beißt, beißt	biss	gebissen
bergen	birgst, birgt	barg	geborgen
bersten*	birst, birst	barst	geborsten
betrügen	betrügst, betrügt	betrog	betrogen
bewegen	bewegst, bewegt	bewog	bewogen
biegen	biegst, biegt	bog	gebogen
bieten	bietest, bietet	bot	geboten
binden	bindest, bindet	band	gebunden
bitten	bittest, bittet	bat	gebeten
blasen	bläst, bläst	blies	geblasen
bleiben*	bleibst, bleibt	blieb	geblieben
braten	brätst, brät	briet	gebraten
brechen*	brichst, bricht	brach	gebrochen
brennen	brennst, brennt	brannte	gebrannt
bringen	bringst, bringt	brachte	gebracht
denken	denkst, denkt	dachte	gedacht
dreschen	drischst, drischt	drosch	gedroschen
dringen*	dringst, dringt	drang	gedrungen
dürfen	darfst, darf	durfte	gedurft
empfangen	empfängst, empfängt	empfing	empfangen
empfehlen	empfiehlst, empfiehlt	empfahl	empfohlen
empfinden	empfindest, empfindet	empfand	empfunden
erbleichen*	erbleichst, erbleicht	erbleichte	erblichen
erlöschen*	erlischst, erlischt	erlosch	erloschen
erschrecken*	erschrickst, erschrickt	erschrak	erschrocken
erwägen	erwägst, erwägt	erwog	erwogen
essen	isst, isst	aß	gegessen
fahren*	fährst, fährt	fuhr	gefahren
fallen*	fällst, fällt	fiel	gefallen
fangen	fängst, fängt	fing	gefangen
fechten	fichtst, ficht	focht	gefochten
finden	findest, findet	fand	gefunden
flechten	flichtst, flicht	flocht	geflochten
fliegen*	fliegst, fliegt	flog	geflogen
fliehen*	fliehst, flieht	floh	geflohen
fließen*	fließt, fließt	floss	geflossen
fressen	frisst, frisst	fraß	gefressen
frieren	frierst, friert	fror	gefroren
gären*	gärst, gärt	gor	gegoren
gebären	gebierst, gebiert	gebar	geboren
geben	gibst, gibt	gab	gegeben
gedeihen*	gedeihst, gedeiht	gedieh	gediehen
gehen*	gehst, geht	ging	gegangen

INFINITIV	PRÄSENS 2., 3. SINGULAR	PRÄTERITUM	PARTIZIP PERFEKT
gelingen*	–, gelingt	gelang	gelungen
gelten	giltst, gilt	galt	gegolten
genesen*	genest, genest	genas	genesen
genießen	genießt, genießt	genoss	genossen
geraten*	gerätst, gerät	geriet	geraten
geschehen*	–, geschieht	geschah	geschehen
gewinnen	gewinnst, gewinnt	gewann	gewonnen
gießen	gießt, gießt	goss	gegossen
gleichen	gleichst, gleicht	glich	geglichen
gleiten*	gleitest, gleitet	glitt	geglitten
glimmen	glimmst, glimmt	glomm	geglommen
graben	gräbst, gräbt	grub	gegraben
greifen	greifst, greift	griff	gegriffen
haben	hast, hat	hatte	gehabt
halten	hältst, hält	hielt	gehalten
hängen	hängst, hängt	hing	gehangen
hauen	haust, haut	haute	gehauen
heben	hebst, hebt	hob	gehoben
heißen	heißt, heißt	hieß	geheißen
helfen	hilfst, hilft	half	geholfen
kennen	kennst, kennt	kannte	gekannt
klimmen*	klimmst, klimmt	klomm	geklommen
klingen	klingst, klingt	klang	geklungen
kneifen	kneifst, kneift	kniff	gekniffen
kommen*	kommst, kommt	kam	gekommen
können	kannst, kann	konnte	gekonnt
kriechen*	kriechst, kriecht	kroch	gekrochen
laden	lädst, lädt	lud	geladen
lassen	lässt, lässt	ließ	gelassen
laufen*	läufst, läuft	lief	gelaufen
leiden	leidest, leidet	litt	gelitten
leihen	leihst, leiht	lieh	geliehen
lesen	liest, liest	las	gelesen
liegen	liegst, liegt	lag	gelegen
lügen	lügst, lügt	log	gelogen
mahlen	mahlst, mahlt	mahlte	gemahlen
meiden	meidest, meidet	mied	gemieden
melken	melkst, melkt	melkte *od* molk	gemolken
messen	misst, misst	maß	gemessen
misslingen*	–, misslingt	misslang	misslungen
mögen	magst, mag	mochte	gemocht
müssen	musst, muss	musste	gemusst
nehmen	nimmst, nimmt	nahm	genommen
nennen	nennst, nennt	nannte	genannt
pfeifen	pfeifst, pfeift	pfiff	gepfiffen
preisen	preist, preist	pries	gepriesen
quellen*	quillst, quillt	quoll	gequollen
raten	rätst, rät	riet	geraten
reiben	reibst, reibt	rieb	gerieben

INFINITIV	PRÄSENS 2., 3. SINGULAR	PRÄTERITUM	PARTIZIP PERFEKT
reißen*	reißt, reißt	riss	gerissen
reiten*	reitest, reitet	ritt	geritten
rennen*	rennst, rennt	rannte	gerannt
riechen	riechst, riecht	roch	gerochen
ringen	ringst, ringt	rang	gerungen
rinnen*	rinnst, rinnt	rann	geronnen
rufen	rufst, ruft	rief	gerufen
salzen	salzt, salzt	salzte	gesalzen
saufen	säufst, säuft	soff	gesoffen
saugen	saugst, saugt	sog od saugte	-gesogen od gesaugt
schaffen	schaffst, schafft	schuf	geschaffen
schallen	schallst, schallt	scholl	geschollen
scheiden*	scheidest, scheidet	schied	geschieden
scheinen	scheinst, scheint	schien	geschienen
scheißen	scheißt, scheißt	schiss	geschissen
schelten	schiltst, schilt	schalt	gescholten
scheren	scherst, schert	schor	geschoren
schieben	schiebst, schiebt	schob	geschoben
schießen	schießt, schießt	schoss	geschossen
schinden	schindest, schindet	schindete	geschunden
schlafen	schläfst, schläft	schlief	geschlafen
schlagen	schlägst, schlägt	schlug	geschlagen
schleichen*	schleichst, schleicht	schlich	geschlichen
schleifen	schleifst, schleift	schliff	geschliffen
schließen	schließt, schließt	schloss	geschlossen
schlingen	schlingst, schlingt	schlang	geschlungen
schmeißen	schmeißt, schmeißt	schmiss	geschmissen
schmelzen*	schmilzt, schmilzt	schmolz	geschmolzen
schneiden	schneidest, schneidet	schnitt	geschnitten
schreiben	schreibst, schreibt	schrieb	geschrieben
schreien	schreist, schreit	schrie	geschrien
schreiten*	schreitest, schreitet	schritt	geschritten
schweigen	schweigst, schweigt	schwieg	geschwiegen
schwellen*	schwillst, schwillt	schwoll	geschwollen
schwimmen*	schwimmst, schwimmt	schwamm	geschwommen
schwinden*	schwindest, schwindet	schwand	geschwunden
schwingen	schwingst, schwingt	schwang	geschwungen
schwören	schwörst, schwört	schwor	geschworen
sehen	siehst, sieht	sah	gesehen
sein*	bist, ist	war	gewesen
senden	sendest, sendet	sandte	gesandt
singen	singst, singt	sang	gesungen
sinken*	sinkst, sinkt	sank	gesunken
sinnen	sinnst, sinnt	sann	gesonnen
sitzen	sitzt, sitzt	saß	gesessen
sollen	sollst, soll	sollte	gesollt
speien	speist, speit	spie	gespien
spinnen	spinnst, spinnt	spann	gesponnen
sprechen	sprichst, spricht	sprach	gesprochen
sprießen*	sprießt, sprießt	spross	gesprossen
springen*	springst, springt	sprang	gesprungen

INFINITIV	PRÄSENS 2., 3. SINGULAR	PRÄTERITUM	PARTIZIP PERFEKT
stechen	stichst, sticht	stach	gestochen
stecken	steckst, steckt	steckte od stak	gesteckt
stehen	stehst, steht	stand	gestanden
stehlen	stiehlst, stiehlt	stahl	gestohlen
steigen*	steigst, steigt	stieg	gestiegen
sterben*	stirbst, stirbt	starb	gestorben
stinken	stinkst, stinkt	stank	gestunken
stoßen	stößt, stößt	stieß	gestoßen
streichen	streichst, streicht	strich	gestrichen
streiten	streitest, streitet	stritt	gestritten
tragen	trägst, trägt	trug	getragen
treffen	triffst, trifft	traf	getroffen
treiben*	treibst, treibt	trieb	getrieben
treten*	trittst, tritt	trat	getreten
trinken	trinkst, trinkt	trank	getrunken
trügen	trügst, trügt	trog	getrogen
tun	tust, tut	tat	getan
verderben	verdirbst, verdirbt	verdarb	verdorben
verdrießen	verdrießt, verdrießt	verdross	verdrossen
vergessen	vergisst, vergisst	vergaß	vergessen
verlieren	verlierst, verliert	verlor	verloren
verschleißen	verschleißt, verschleißt	verschliss	verschlissen
verschwinden	verschwindest, verschwindet	verschwand	verschwunden
verzeihen	verzeihst, verzeiht	verzieh	verziehen
wachsen*	wächst, wächst	wuchs	gewachsen
wägen	wägst, wägt	wog	gewogen
waschen	wäschst, wäscht	wusch	gewaschen
weben	webst, webt	webte od wob	gewoben
weichen*	weichst, weicht	wich	gewichen
weisen	weist, weist	wies	gewiesen
wenden	wendest, wendet	wandte	gewandt
werben	wirbst, wirbt	warb	geworben
werden*	wirst, wird	wurde	geworden
werfen	wirfst, wirft	warf	geworfen
wiegen	wiegst, wiegt	wog	gewogen
winden	windest, windet	wand	gewunden
wissen	weißt, weiß	wusste	gewusst
wollen	willst, will	wollte	gewollt
wringen	wringst, wringt	wrang	gewrungen
zeihen	zeihst, zeiht	zieh	geziehen
ziehen*	ziehst, zieht	zog	gezogen
zwingen	zwingst, zwingt	zwang	gezwungen

Deutsch–Englisch

German–English

A¹, a [a:] *nt* A, a; **A wie Anton** ≈ A for Andrew, ≈ A for Able (*US*); **das A und O** the be-all and end-all; (*eines Wissensgebietes*) the basics *pl*; **wer A sagt, muss auch B sagen** (*Sprichwort*) in for a penny, in for a pound (*Sprichwort*)

A² *f abk* (= *Autobahn*) ≈ M (*Brit*)

a. *abk* = **am**

à [a:] *präp* (*bes Comm*) at

AA *nt abk* (= *Auswärtiges Amt*) F.O. (*Brit*)

Aachen ['a:xən] (**-s**) *nt* Aachen

Aal [a:l] (**-(e)s, -e**) *m* eel

aalen ['a:lən] (*umg*) *vr*: **sich in der Sonne ~** to bask in the sun

a. a. O. *abk* (= *am angegebenen od angeführten Ort*) loc. cit.

Aas [a:s] (**-es, -e** *od* **Äser**) *nt* carrion; **Aasgeier** *m* vulture

🔵 SCHLÜSSELWORT

ab [ap] *präp+dat* from; **ab Werk** (*Comm*) ex works; **Kinder ab 12 Jahren** children from the age of 12; **ab morgen** from tomorrow; **ab sofort** as of now
▷ *adv* **1** off; **links ab** to the left; **der Knopf ist ab** the button has come off; **ab nach Hause!** off home with you!; **ab durch die Mitte!** (*umg*) beat it!
2 (*zeitlich*): **von da ab** from then on; **von heute ab** from today, as of today
3 (*auf Fahrplänen*): **München ab 12.20** leaving Munich 12.20
4: ab und zu *od* **an** now and then *od* again

abändern ['ap|ɛndərn] *vt*: **~ (in** +*akk*) to alter (to); (*Gesetzentwurf*) to amend (to); (*Strafe, Urteil*) to revise (to)

Abänderung *f* alteration; amendment; revision

Abänderungsantrag *m* (*Parl*) proposed amendment

abarbeiten ['ap|arbaɪtən] *vr* to slave away

Abart ['ap|a:rt] *f* (*Biol*) variety

abartig *adj* abnormal

Abb. *abk* (= *Abbildung*) illus.

Abbau ['apbau] (**-(e)s**) *m* (+*gen*) dismantling; (*Verminderung*) reduction (in); (*Verfall*) decline (in); (*Min*) mining; (*über Tage*) quarrying; (*Chem*) decomposition

abbaubar *adj*: **biologisch ~** biodegradable

abbauen *vt* to dismantle; (*verringern*) to reduce; (*Min*) to mine; to quarry; (*Chem*) to break down; **Arbeitsplätze ~** to make job cuts

Abbaurechte *pl* mineral rights *pl*

abbeißen ['apbaɪsən] *unreg vt* to bite off

abbekommen ['apbəkɔmən] *unreg vt*: **etwas ~** to get some (of it); (*beschädigt werden*) to get damaged; (*verletzt werden*) to get hurt

abberufen ['apbəru:fən] *unreg vt* to recall

Abberufung *f* recall

abbestellen ['apbəʃtɛlən] *vt* to cancel

abbezahlen ['apbətsa:lən] *vt* to pay off

abbiegen ['apbi:gən] *unreg vi* to turn off; (*Straße*) to bend ▷ *vt* to bend; (*verhindern*) to ward off

Abbiegespur *f* turning lane

Abbild ['apbɪlt] *nt* portrayal; (*einer Person*) image, likeness; **abbilden** ['apbɪldən] *vt* to portray; **Abbildung** *f* illustration; (*Schaubild*) diagram

abbinden ['apbɪndən] *unreg vt* (*Med: Arm, Bein etc*) to ligature

Abbitte ['apbɪtə] *f*: **~ leisten** *od* **tun (bei)** to make one's apologies (to)

abblasen ['apbla:zən] *unreg vt* to blow off; (*fig: umg*) to call off

abblättern ['apblɛtərn] *vi* (*Putz, Farbe*) to flake (off)

abblenden ['apblɛndən] *vt* (*Aut*) to dip (*Brit*), dim (*US*) ▷ *vi* to dip (*Brit*) *od* dim (*US*) one's headlights

Abblendlicht ['apblɛntlɪçt] *nt* dipped (*Brit*) *od* dimmed (*US*) headlights *pl*

abblitzen ['apblɪtsən] (*umg*) *vi*: **jdn ~ lassen** to send sb packing

abbrechen ['apbrɛçən] *unreg vt* to break off; (*Gebäude*) to pull down; (*Zelt*) to take down; (*aufhören*) to stop; (*Comput*) to abort ▷ *vi* to break off; to stop; **sich** *dat* **einen ~** (*umg: sich sehr anstrengen*) to bust a gut

abbrennen ['apbrɛnən] *unreg vt* to burn off; (*Feuerwerk*) to let off ▷ *vi* (*Hilfsverb sein*) to burn down; **abgebrannt sein** (*umg*) to be broke

abbringen ['apbrɪŋən] *unreg vt*: **jdn von etw ~** to dissuade sb from sth; **jdn vom Weg ~** to divert sb; **ich bringe den Verschluss nicht ab** (*umg*) I can't get the top off

abbröckeln ['apbrœkəln] *vi* to crumble off *od* away; (*Börse: Preise*) to ease

Abbruch ['apbrʊx] *m* (*von Verhandlungen etc*) breaking off; (*von Haus*) demolition; (*Comput*) abort; **jdm/etw ~ tun** to harm sb/sth; **Abbrucharbeiten** *pl* demolition work *sing*; **abbruchreif** *adj* only fit for demolition

abbrühen ['apbry:ən] *vt* to scald

abbuchen ['apbu:xən] *vt* to debit; (*durch Dauerauftrag*): **~ (von)** to pay by standing order (from)

abbürsten ['apbyrstən] *vt* to brush off

abbüßen ['apby:sən] *vt* (*Strafe*) to serve

ABC-Waffen *pl abk* (= *atomare, biologische und chemische Waffen*) ABC weapons (= atomic, biological and chemical weapons)

abdampfen ['apdampfən] *vi* (*fig: umg: losgehen/-fahren*) to hit the road

abdanken ['apdaŋkən] *vi* to resign; (*König*) to abdicate

Abdankung *f* resignation; abdication

abdecken ['apdɛkən] *vt* to uncover; (*Tisch*) to clear; (*Loch*) to cover

abdichten ['apdɪçtən] *vt* to seal; (*Naut*) to caulk

abdrängen ['apdrɛŋən] *vt* to push off

abdrehen ['apdre:ən] *vt* (*Gas*) to turn off; (*Licht*) to switch off; (*Film*) to shoot ▷ *vi* (*Schiff*) to change course; **jdm den Hals ~** to wring sb's neck

abdriften ['apdrɪftən] *vi* to drift (away)

abdrosseln ['apdrɔsəln] *vt* to throttle; (*Aut*) to stall; (*Produktion*) to cut back

Abdruck ['apdrʊk] *m* (*Nachdrucken*) reprinting; (*Gedrucktes*) reprint; (*Gipsabdruck, Wachsabdruck*) impression; (*Fingerabdruck*) print; **abdrucken** *vt* to print

abdrücken ['apdrʏkən] *vt* to make an impression of; (*Waffe*) to fire; (*umg: Person*) to hug, squeeze ▷ *vr* to leave imprints; (*abstoßen*) to push o.s. away; **jdm die Luft ~** to squeeze all the breath out of sb

abdüsen ['apdy:sən] (*umg*) *vi* to dash *od* whizz off

abebben ['ap|ɛbən] *vi* to ebb away

Abend ['a:bənt] (**-s, -e**) *m* evening; **gegen ~** towards (the) evening; **den ganzen ~ (über)** the whole evening; **zu ~ essen** to have dinner *od* supper; **heute ~** this evening; **Abendanzug** *m* dinner jacket (*Brit*), tuxedo (*US*); **Abendbrot** *nt* supper; **Abendessen** *nt* supper; **abendfüllend** *adj* taking up the whole evening; **Abendgymnasium** *nt* night school; **Abendkasse** *f* (*Theat*) box office; **Abendkleid** *nt* evening gown; **Abendkurs** *m* evening classes *pl*; **Abendland** *nt* West; **abendlich** *adj* evening; **Abendmahl** *nt* Holy Communion; **Abendrot** *nt* sunset

abends *adv* in the evening

Abend- *zW*: **Abendvorstellung** *f* evening performance; **Abendzeitung** *f* evening paper

Abenteuer ['a:bəntɔyər] (**-s, -**) *nt* adventure; (*Liebesabenteuer*) affair; **abenteuerlich** *adj* adventurous; **Abenteuerspielplatz** *m* adventure playground

Abenteurer (**-s, -**) *m* adventurer; **Abenteurerin** *f* adventuress

aber ['a:bər] *konj* but; (*jedoch*) however ▷ *adv*: **oder ~** or else; **bist du ~ braun!** aren't you brown!; **das ist ~ schön** that's really nice; **nun ist ~ Schluss!** now that's enough!; **Aber** *nt* but

Aberglaube ['a:bərglaʊbə] *m* superstition

abergläubisch ['a:bərglɔybɪʃ] *adj* superstitious

aberkennen ['ap|ɛrkɛnən] *unreg vt*: **jdm etw ~** to deprive sb of sth, take sth (away) from sb

Aberkennung *f* taking away

abermalig *adj* repeated

abermals *adv* once again

Abertausend, abertausend ['a:bərtaʊznt] *num*: **Tausend und ~** thousands upon thousands

Abf. *abk* (= *Abfahrt*) dep.

abfahren ['apfa:rən] *unreg vi* to leave, depart ▷ *vt* to take *od* cart away; (*Film*) to start; (*Film, TV: Kamera*) to roll; (*Strecke*) to drive; (*Reifen*) to wear; (*Fahrkarte*) to use; **der Zug ist abgefahren** (*lit*) the train has left; (*fig*) we've/you've *etc* missed the boat; **der Zug fährt um 8.00 von Bremen ab** the train leaves Bremen at 8 o'clock; **jdn ~ lassen** (*umg: abweisen*) to tell sb to get lost; **auf jdn ~** (*umg*) to really go for sb

Abfahrt ['apfa:rt] *f* departure; (*Autobahnabfahrt*) exit; (*Ski*) descent; (*Piste*) run; **Vorsicht bei der ~ des Zuges!** stand clear, the train is about to leave!

Abfahrts- *zW*: **Abfahrtslauf** *m* (*Ski*) downhill; **Abfahrtstag** *m* day of departure; **Abfahrtszeit** *f* departure time

Abfall ['apfal] *m* waste; (*von Speisen etc*) rubbish (*Brit*), garbage (*US*); (*Neigung*) slope; (*Verschlechterung*) decline; **Abfalleimer** *m* rubbish bin (*Brit*), garbage can (*US*)

abfallen *unreg vi* (*lit, fig*) to fall *od* drop off; (*Pol, vom Glauben*) to break away; (*sich neigen*) to fall *od* drop away; **wie viel fällt bei dem Geschäft für mich ab?** (*umg*) how much do I get out of the deal?

abfällig ['apfɛlɪç] *adj* disparaging, deprecatory

Abfallprodukt *nt* (*lit, fig*) waste product

abfangen ['apfaŋən] *unreg vt* to intercept; (*Person*) to catch; (*unter Kontrolle bringen*) to check; (*Aufprall*) to absorb; (*Kunden*) to lure away

Abfangjäger *m* (*Mil*) interceptor

abfärben ['apfɛrbən] *vi* (*lit*) to lose its colour; (*Wäsche*) to run; (*fig*) to rub off

abfassen ['apfasən] *vt* to write, draft

abfeiern ['apfaiərn] (*umg*) *vt*: **Überstunden ~** to take time off in lieu of overtime pay

abfertigen ['apfɛrtɪgən] *vt* to prepare for dispatch, process; (*an der Grenze*) to clear; (*Kundschaft*) to attend to; **jdn kurz ~** to give sb short shrift

Abfertigung *f* preparing for dispatch, processing; clearance; (*Bedienung: von Kunden*) service; (: *von Antragstellern*): **~ von** dealing with

abfeuern ['apfɔyərn] vt to fire
abfinden ['apfɪndən] unreg vt to pay off ▷ vr to come to terms; **sich mit jdm ~/nicht ~** to put up with/not to get on with sb; **er konnte sich nie damit ~, dass ...** he could never accept the fact that ...
Abfindung f (von Gläubigern) payment; (Geld) sum in settlement
abflachen ['apflaxən] vt to level (off), flatten (out) ▷ vi (fig: sinken) to decline
abflauen ['apflauən] vi (Wind, Erregung) to die away, subside; (Nachfrage, Geschäft) to fall od drop off
abfliegen ['apfli:gən] unreg vi to take off ▷ vt (Gebiet) to fly over
abfließen ['apfli:sən] unreg vi to drain away; **ins Ausland ~** (Geld) to flow out of the country
Abflug ['apflu:k] m departure; (Start) take-off
Abflugterminal ['apflu:ktœrmɪnəl] (-s, -s) m departure terminal; **Abflugzeit** f departure time
Abfluss ['apflʊs] m draining away; (Öffnung) outlet; **Abflussrohr** nt drainpipe; (von sanitären Anlagen) wastepipe
abfragen ['apfra:gən] vt to test; (Comput) to call up; **jdn etw ~** to question sb on sth
abfrieren ['apfri:rən] unreg vi: **ihm sind die Füße abgefroren** his feet got frostbitten, he got frostbite in his feet
abfrühstücken ['apfry:ʃtykən] (umg) vt (jdn) to fob off, snub; (Sache) to get through with
Abfuhr ['apfu:r] (-, -en) f removal; (fig) snub, rebuff; **sich dat eine ~ holen** to meet with a rebuff
abführen ['apfy:rən] vt to lead away; (Gelder, Steuern) to pay ▷ vi (Med) to have a laxative effect
Abführmittel nt laxative, purgative
Abfüllanlage f bottling plant
abfüllen ['apfʏlən] vt to draw off; (in Flaschen) to bottle
Abgabe ['apga:bə] f handing in; (von Ball) pass; (Steuer) tax; (einer Erklärung) giving
abgabenfrei adj tax-free
abgabenpflichtig adj liable to tax
Abgabetermin m closing date; (für Dissertation etc) submission date
Abgang ['apgaŋ] m (von Schule) leaving; (Theat) exit; (Med: Ausscheiden) passing; (: Fehlgeburt) miscarriage; (Abfahrt) departure; (der Post, von Waren) dispatch
Abgangszeugnis nt leaving certificate
Abgas ['apga:s] nt waste gas; (Aut) exhaust
Abgasgrenzwert m exhaust emission standard
ABGB nt abk (Österr: = Allgemeines Bürgerliches Gesetzbuch) Civil Code in Austria
abgeben ['apge:bən] unreg vt (Gegenstand) to hand od give in; (Ball) to pass; (Wärme) to give off; (Amt) to hand over; (Schuss) to fire; (Erklärung, Urteil) to give; (darstellen) to make ▷ vr: **sich mit jdm/etw ~** to associate with sb/bother with sth; **„Kinderwagen abzugeben"**

"pram for sale"; **jdm etw ~** (überlassen) to let sb have sth
abgebrannt ['apgəbrant] (umg) adj broke
abgebrüht ['apgəbry:t] (umg) adj (skrupellos) hard-boiled, hardened
abgedroschen ['apgədrɔʃən] adj trite; (Witz) corny
abgefahren ['apgəfa:rən] pp von **abfahren**
abgefeimt ['apgəfaɪmt] adj cunning
abgegeben ['apgəge:bən] pp von **abgeben**
abgegriffen ['apgəgrɪfən] adj (Buch) well-thumbed; (Redensart) trite
abgehackt ['apgəhakt] adj clipped
abgehalftert ['apgəhalftərt] adj (fig: umg) run-down, dead beat
abgehangen ['apgəhaŋən] pp von **abhängen** ▷ adj: **(gut) ~** (Fleisch) well-hung
abgehärtet ['apgəhɛrtət] adj tough, hardy; (fig) hardened
abgehen ['apge:ən] unreg vi to go away, leave; (Theat) to exit; (Post) to go; (Med) to be passed; (sterben) to die; (Knopf etc) to come off; (abgezogen werden) to be taken off; (Straße) to branch off; (abweichen): **von einer Forderung ~** to give up a demand ▷ vt (Strecke) to go od walk along; (Mil: Gelände) to patrol; **von seiner Meinung ~** to change one's opinion; **davon gehen 5% ab** 5% is taken off that; **etw geht jdm ab** (fehlt) sb lacks sth
abgekämpft ['apgəkɛmpft] adj exhausted
abgekartet ['apgəkartət] adj: **ein ~es Spiel** a rigged job
abgeklärt ['apgəklɛ:rt] adj serene, tranquil
abgelegen ['apgəle:gən] adj remote
abgelten ['apgɛltən] unreg vt (Ansprüche) to satisfy
abgemacht ['apgəmaxt] adj fixed; **~!** done!
abgemagert ['apgəma:gərt] adj (sehr dünn) thin; (ausgemergelt) emaciated
abgeneigt ['apgənaɪkt] adj averse
abgenutzt ['apgənʊtst] adj worn, shabby; (Reifen) worn; (fig: Klischees) well-worn
Abgeordnete, r ['apgəɔrdnətə(r)] f(m) elected representative; (von Parlament) member of parliament
Abgesandte, r ['apgəzantə(r)] f(m) delegate; (Pol) envoy
abgeschieden ['apgəʃi:dən] adv (einsam): **~ leben/wohnen** to live in seclusion
abgeschlagen ['apgəʃla:gən] adj (besiegt) defeated; (erschöpft) exhausted, worn-out
abgeschlossen ['apgəʃlɔsən] pp von **abschließen** ▷ adj attrib (Wohnung) self-contained
abgeschmackt ['apgəʃmakt] adj tasteless; **Abgeschmacktheit** f lack of taste; (Bemerkung) tasteless remark
abgesehen ['apgəze:ən] adj: **es auf jdn/etw ~ haben** to be after sb/sth; **~ von ...** apart from ...
abgespannt ['apgəʃpant] adj tired out
abgestanden ['apgəʃtandən] adj stale; (Bier) flat

3

abgestorben ['apgəʃtɔrbən] *adj* numb; (*Biol, Med*) dead

abgestumpft ['apgəʃtʊmpft] *adj* (*gefühllos: Person*) insensitive; (*Gefühle, Gewissen*) dulled

abgetakelt ['apgəta:kəlt] *adj* (*fig*) decrepit, past it

abgetan ['apgəta:n] *adj*: **damit ist die Sache ~** that settles the matter

abgetragen ['apgətra:gən] *adj* worn

abgewinnen ['apgəvɪnən] *unreg vt*: **jdm Geld ~ to** win money from sb; **einer Sache etw/ Geschmack ~** to get sth/pleasure from sth

abgewogen ['apgəvo:gən] *adj* (*Urteil, Worte*) balanced

abgewöhnen ['apgəvø:nən] *vt*: **jdm/sich etw ~** to cure sb of sth/give sth up

abgießen ['apgi:sən] *unreg vt* (*Flüssigkeit*) to pour off

Abglanz ['apglants] *m* (*auch fig*) reflection

abgleiten ['apglaɪtən] *unreg vi* to slip, slide

Abgott ['apgɔt] *m* idol

abgöttisch ['apgœtɪʃ] *adj*: **~ lieben** to idolize

abgrasen ['apgra:zən] *vt* (*Feld*) to graze; (*umg: Thema*) to do to death

abgrenzen ['apgrɛntsən] *vt* (*lit, fig*) to mark off; (*Gelände*) to fence off ▷ *vr*: **sich ~ (gegen)** to dis(as)sociate o.s. (from)

Abgrund ['apgrʊnt] *m* (*lit, fig*) abyss

abgründig ['apgryndɪç] *adj* unfathomable; (*Lächeln*) cryptic

abgrundtief *adj* (*Hass, Verachtung*) profound

abgucken ['apgʊkən] *vt, vi* to copy

Abguss ['apgʊs] *m* (*Kunst, Metallurgie: Vorgang*) casting; (: *Form*) cast

abhaben ['apha:bən] *unreg* (*umg*) *vt* (*abbekommen*): **willst du ein Stück ~?** do you want a bit?

abhacken ['aphakən] *vt* to chop off

abhaken ['apha:kən] *vt* to tick off (*Brit*), check off (*US*)

abhalten ['aphaltən] *unreg vt* (*Versammlung*) to hold; **jdn von etw ~** (*fernhalten*) to keep sb away from sth; (*hindern*) to keep sb from sth

abhandeln ['aphandəln] *vt* (*Thema*) to deal with; **jdm die Waren/10 Euro ~** to do a deal with sb for the goods/beat sb down 10 euros

abhandenkommen [ap'handən-] *vi* to get lost

Abhandlung ['aphandlʊŋ] *f* treatise, discourse

Abhang ['aphaŋ] *m* slope

abhängen ['aphɛŋən] *unreg vt* (*Bild*) to take down; (*Anhänger*) to uncouple; (*Verfolger*) to shake off ▷ *vi* (*Fleisch*) to hang; **von jdm/etw ~** to depend on sb/sth; **das hängt ganz davon ab** it all depends; **er hat abgehängt** (*Tel: umg*) he hung up (on me *etc*)

abhängig ['aphɛŋɪç] *adj*: **~ (von)** dependent (on); **Abhängigkeit** *f*: **Abhängigkeit (von)** dependence (on)

abhärten ['aphɛrtən] *vt* to toughen up ▷ *vr* to toughen (o.s.) up; **sich gegen etw ~** to harden o.s. to sth

abhauen ['aphaʊən] *unreg vt* to cut off; (*Baum*) to cut down ▷ *vi* (*umg*) to clear off *od* out; **hau ab!** beat it!

abheben ['aphe:bən] *unreg vt* to lift (up); (*Karten*) to cut; (*Masche*) to slip; (*Geld*) to withdraw, take out ▷ *vi* (*Flugzeug*) to take off; (*Rakete*) to lift off; (*Karten*) to cut ▷ *vr*: **sich ~ von** to stand out from, contrast with

abheften ['aphɛftən] *vt* (*Rechnungen etc*) to file away; (*Nähen*) to tack, baste

abhelfen ['aphɛlfən] *unreg vi +dat* to remedy

abhetzen ['aphɛtsən] *vr* to wear *od* tire o.s. out

Abhilfe ['aphɪlfə] *f* remedy; **~ schaffen** to put things right

abholen ['apho:lən] *vt* (*Gegenstand*) to fetch, collect; (*Person*) to call for; (*am Bahnhof etc*) to pick up, meet

Abholmarkt *m* cash and carry

abholzen ['aphɔltsən] *vt* (*Wald*) to clear, deforest

abhorchen ['aphɔrçən] *vt* (*Med*) to listen to, sound

abhören ['aphø:rən] *vt* (*Vokabeln*) to test; (*Telefongespräch*) to tap; (*Tonband etc*) to listen to; **abgehört werden** (*umg*) to be bugged

Abhörgerät *nt* bug

abhungern ['aphʊŋərn] *vr*: **sich dat 10 Kilo ~** to lose 10 kilos by going on a starvation diet

Abi ['abi] (**-s, -s**) *nt* (*Sch: umg*) = **Abitur**

Abitur [abi'tu:r] (**-s, -e**) *nt* German school-leaving examination; **≈** A-levels *pl* (*Brit*); (**das**) **~ machen** to take one's school-leaving exam *od* A-levels; *see culture note*

○ **ABITUR**
○
○ The *Abitur* is the German school-leaving
○ examination which is taken at the age of
○ 18 or 19 by pupils at a *Gymnasium*. It is taken
○ in four subjects and is necessary for entry
○ to a university education.

Abiturient, in [abitʊri'ɛnt(ɪn)] *m(f)* candidate for school-leaving certificate

abkämmen ['apkɛmən] *vt* (*Gegend*) to comb, scour

abkanzeln ['apkantsəln] (*umg*) *vt*: **jdn ~** to give sb a dressing-down

abkapseln ['apkapsəln] *vr* to shut *od* cut o.s. off

abkarten ['apkartən] (*umg*) *vt*: **die Sache war von vornherein abgekartet** the whole thing was a put-up job

abkaufen ['apkaʊfən] *vt*: **jdm etw ~** to buy sth from sb

abkehren ['apke:rən] *vt* (*Blick*) to avert, turn away ▷ *vr* to turn away

abklappern ['apklapərn] (*umg*) *vt* (*Kunden*) to call on; (: *Läden, Straße*): **~ nach** to scour (for), comb (for)

abklären ['apklɛ:rən] *vt* (*klarstellen*) to clear up, clarify ▷ *vr* (*sich setzen*) to clarify

Abklatsch ['apklatʃ] (**-es, -e**) *m* (*fig*) (poor) copy

abklemmen ['apklɛmən] *vt* (*Leitung*) to clamp

abklingen ['apklɪŋən] *unreg vi* to die away;

(Rundf) to fade out

abknallen ['apknalən] (umg) vt to shoot down

abknöpfen ['apknœpfən] vt to unbutton; **jdm etw ~** (umg) to get sth off sb

abkochen ['apkɔxən] vt to boil; (keimfrei machen) to sterilize (by boiling)

abkommandieren ['apkɔmandi:rən] vt (Mil: zu Einheit) to post; (zu bestimmtem Dienst): **~ zu** to detail for

abkommen ['apkɔmən] unreg vi to get away; **(vom Thema) ~** to get off the subject, digress; **von der Straße/einem Plan ~** to leave the road/give up a plan

Abkommen (-s, -) nt agreement

abkömmlich ['apkœmlıç] adj available, free

Abkömmling m (Nachkomme) descendant; (fig) adherent

abkönnen ['apkœnən] unreg (umg) vt (mögen): **das kann ich nicht ab** I can't stand it

abkratzen ['apkratsən] vt to scrape off ▷ vi (umg) to kick the bucket

abkriegen ['apkri:gən] (umg) vt = **abbekommen**

abkühlen ['apky:lən] vt to cool down ▷ vr (Mensch) to cool down od off; (Wetter) to get cool; (Zuneigung) to cool

Abkunft ['apkʊnft] (-) f origin, birth

abkürzen ['apkʏrtsən] vt to shorten; (Wort) to abbreviate; **den Weg ~** to take a short cut

Abkürzung f abbreviation; short cut

abladen ['apla:dən] unreg vi to unload ▷ vt to unload; (fig: umg): **seinen Ärger (bei jdm) ~** to vent one's anger (on sb)

Ablage ['apla:gə] f place to keep/put sth; (Aktenablage) filing; (für Akten) tray

ablagern ['apla:gərn] vt to deposit ▷ vr to be deposited ▷ vi to mature

Ablagerung f (abgelagerter Stoff) deposit

ablassen ['aplasən] unreg vt (Wasser, Dampf) to let out od off; (vom Preis) to knock off ▷ vi: **von etw ~** to give sth up, abandon sth

Ablauf m (Abfluss) drain; (von Ereignissen) course; (einer Frist, Zeit) expiry (Brit), expiration (US); **nach ~ des Jahres/dieser Zeit** at the end of the year/this time

Ablaufdatum nt (Österr) expiry date; (von Lebensmitteln) use-by od best-before date

ablaufen ['aplaufən] unreg vi (abfließen) to drain away; (Ereignisse) to happen; (Frist, Zeit, Pass) to expire ▷ vt (Sohlen) to wear (down od out); **~ lassen** (abspulen, abspielen: Platte, Tonband) to play; (Film) to run; **sich** dat **die Beine** od **Hacken nach etw ~** (umg) to walk one's legs off looking for sth; **jdm den Rang ~** to steal a march on sb

Ableben ['aple:bən] nt (form) demise (form)

ablegen ['aple:gən] vt to put od lay down; (Kleider) to take off; (Gewohnheit) to get rid of; (Prüfung) to take, sit (Brit); (Zeugnis) to give; (Schriftwechsel) to file (away); (nicht mehr tragen: Kleidung) to discard, cast off; (Schwur, Eid) to swear ▷ vi (Schiff) to cast off

Ableger (-s, -) m layer; (fig) branch, offshoot

ablehnen ['aple:nən] vt to reject; (missbilligen)

to disapprove of; (Einladung) to decline, refuse ▷ vi to decline, refuse

Ablehnung f rejection; refusal; **auf ~ stoßen** to meet with disapproval

ableisten ['aplaıstən] vt (form: Zeit) to serve

ableiten ['aplaıtən] vt (Wasser) to divert; (deduzieren) to deduce; (Wort) to derive

Ableitung f diversion; deduction; derivation; (Wort) derivative

ablenken ['aplɛŋkən] vt to turn away, deflect; (zerstreuen) to distract ▷ vi to change the subject; **das lenkt ab** (zerstreut) it takes your mind off things; (stört) it's distracting

Ablenkung f deflection; distraction

Ablenkungsmanöver nt diversionary tactic; (um vom Thema abzulenken) red herring

ablesen ['aple:zən] unreg vt to read; **jdm jeden Wunsch von den Augen ~** to anticipate sb's every wish

ableugnen ['aplɔygnən] vt to deny

ablichten ['aplıçtən] vt to photocopy; (fotografieren) to photograph

abliefern ['apli:fərn] vt to deliver; **etw bei jdm/einer Dienststelle ~** to hand sth over to sb/in at an office

Ablieferung f delivery

abliegen ['apli:gən] unreg vi to be some distance away; (fig) to be far removed

ablisten ['aplıstən] vt: **jdm etw ~** to trick od con sb out of sth

ablösen ['aplø:zən] vt (abtrennen) to take off, remove; (in Amt) to take over from; (Fin: Schuld, Hypothek) to pay off, redeem; (Methode, System) to supersede ▷ vr (auch: **einander ablösen**) to take turns; (Fahrer, Kollegen, Wachen) to relieve each other

Ablösung f removal; relieving

abluchsen ['aplʊksən] (umg) vt: **jdm etw ~** to get od wangle sth out of sb

Abluft f (Tech) used air

ABM pl abk (= Arbeitsbeschaffungsmaßnahmen) job-creation scheme

abmachen ['apmaxən] vt to take off; (vereinbaren) to agree; **etw mit sich allein ~** to sort sth out for o.s.

Abmachung f agreement

abmagern ['apma:gərn] vi to get thinner, become emaciated

Abmagerungskur f diet; **eine ~ machen** to go on a diet

Abmarsch ['apmarʃ] m departure; **abmarschbereit** adj ready to start

abmarschieren ['apmarʃi:rən] vi to march off

abmelden ['apmɛldən] vt (Auto) to take off the road; (Telefon) to have disconnected; (Comput) to log off ▷ vr to give notice of one's departure; (im Hotel) to check out; **ein Kind von einer Schule ~** to take a child away from a school; **er/sie ist bei mir abgemeldet** (umg) I don't want anything to do with him/her; **jdn bei der Polizei ~** to register sb's departure with the police

abmessen ['apmɛsən] unreg vt to measure

Abmessung f measurement; (*Ausmaß*) dimension

abmontieren ['apmɔntiːrən] vt to take off; (*Maschine*) to dismantle

ABM-Stelle f *temporary post created as part of a job creation scheme*

abmühen ['apmyːən] vr to wear o.s. out

abnabeln ['apnaːbəln] vt: **jdn ~** (*auch fig*) to cut sb's umbilical cord

abnagen ['apnaːgən] vt to gnaw off; (*Knochen*) to gnaw

Abnäher ['apnɛːər] (**-s, -**) m dart

Abnahme ['apnaːmə] f (*+gen*) removal; (*Comm*) buying; (*Verringerung*) decrease (in)

abnehmen ['apneːmən] unreg vt to take off, remove; (*Führerschein*) to take away; (*Prüfung*) to hold; (*Maschen*) to decrease; (*Hörer*) to lift, pick up; (*begutachten: Gebäude, Auto*) to inspect ▷ vi to decrease; (*schlanker werden*) to lose weight; **jdm etw ~** (*Geld*) to get sth out of sb; (*kaufen: auch umg: glauben*) to buy sth from sb; **kann ich dir etwas ~?** (*tragen*) can I take something for you?; **jdm Arbeit ~** to take work off sb's shoulders; **jdm ein Versprechen ~** to make sb promise sth

Abnehmer (**-s, -**) m purchaser, customer; **viele/wenige ~ finden** (*Comm*) to sell well/badly

Abneigung ['apnaɪgʊŋ] f aversion, dislike

abnicken ['apnɪkən] (*umg*) vt: **etw ~** to nod sth through

abnorm [ap'nɔrm] adj abnormal

abnötigen ['apnøːtɪgən] vt: **jdm etw/Respekt ~** to force sth from sb/gain sb's respect

abnutzen ['apnʊtsən] vt to wear out

Abnutzung f wear (and tear)

Abo ['abo] (**-s, -s**) (*umg*) nt = **Abonnement**

Abonnement [abɔn(ə)'maː] (**-s, -s** *od* **-e**) nt subscription; (*Theaterabonnement*) season ticket

Abonnent, in [abɔ'nɛnt(ɪn)] m(f) subscriber

abonnieren [abɔ'niːrən] vt to subscribe to

abordnen ['apʔɔrdnən] vt to delegate

Abordnung f delegation

Abort [a'bɔrt] (**-(e)s, -e**) m (*veraltet*) lavatory

abpacken ['appakən] vt to pack

abpassen ['appasən] vt (*Person, Gelegenheit*) to wait for; (*warten auf*) to catch; (*jdm auflauern*) to waylay; **etw gut ~** to time sth well

abpausen ['appaʊzən] vt to make a tracing of

abpfeifen ['appfaɪfən] unreg vt, vi (*Sport*): **(das Spiel) ~** to blow the whistle (for the end of the game)

Abpfiff ['appfɪf] m final whistle

abplagen ['applaːgən] vr to struggle (away)

Abprall ['appral] m rebound; (*von Kugel*) ricochet

abprallen ['appralən] vi to bounce off; to ricochet; **an jdm ~** (*fig*) to make no impression on sb

abputzen ['appʊtsən] vt to clean; (*Nase etc*) to wipe

abquälen ['apkvɛːlən] vr to struggle (away)

abrackern ['aprakərn] (*umg*) vr to slave away

abraten ['apraːtən] unreg vi: **jdm von etw ~** to advise sb against sth, warn sb against sth

abräumen ['aprɔymən] vt to clear up *od* away; (*Tisch*) to clear ▷ vi to clear up *od* away

abreagieren ['apreagiːrən] vt: **seinen Zorn (an jdm/etw) ~** to work one's anger off (on sb/sth) ▷ vr to calm down; **seinen Ärger an anderen ~** to take it out on others

abrechnen ['aprɛçnən] vt to deduct, take off ▷ vi (*lit*) to settle up; (*fig*) to get even; **darf ich ~?** would you like your bill (*Brit*) *od* check (*US*) now?

Abrechnung f settlement; (*Rechnung*) bill; (*Aufstellung*) statement; (*Bilanz*) balancing; (*fig: Rache*) revenge; **in ~ stellen** (*form: Abzug*) to deduct; **~ über** +*akk* bill/statement for

Abrechnungszeitraum m accounting period

Abrede ['apreːdə] f: **etw in ~ stellen** to deny *od* dispute sth

abregen ['apreːgən] (*umg*) vr to calm *od* cool down

abreiben ['apraɪbən] unreg vt to rub off; (*säubern*) to wipe; **jdn mit einem Handtuch ~** to towel sb down

Abreibung (*umg*) f (*Prügel*) hiding, thrashing

Abreise ['apraɪzə] f departure

abreisen vi to leave, set off

abreißen ['apraɪsən] unreg vt (*Haus*) to tear down; (*Blatt*) to tear off ▷ vi: **den Kontakt nicht ~ lassen** to stay in touch

abrichten ['aprɪçtən] vt to train

abriegeln ['apriːgəln] vt (*Tür*) to bolt; (*Straße, Gebiet*) to seal off

abringen ['aprɪŋən] unreg vt: **sich** *dat* **ein Lächeln ~** to force a smile

Abriss ['aprɪs] (**-es, -e**) m (*Übersicht*) outline; (*Abbruch*) demolition

abrollen ['aprɔlən] vt (*abwickeln*) to unwind ▷ vi (*vonstattengehen: Programm*) to run; (: *Veranstaltung*) to go off; (: *Ereignisse*) to unfold

Abruf ['apruːf] m: **auf ~** on call

abrufen unreg vt (*Mensch*) to call away; (*Comm: Ware*) to request delivery of; (*Comput*) to recall, retrieve

abrunden ['aprʊndən] vt to round off

abrüsten ['aprʏstən] vi to disarm

Abrüstung f disarmament

abrutschen ['aprʊtʃən] vi to slip; (*Aviat*) to sideslip

Abs. *abk* = **Absender**; (= *Absatz*) par., para

absacken ['apzakən] vi (*sinken*) to sink; (*Boden, Gebäude*) to subside

Absage ['apzaːgə] (**-, -n**) f refusal; (*auf Einladung*) negative reply

absagen vt to cancel, call off; (*Einladung*) to turn down ▷ vi to cry off; (*ablehnen*) to decline; **jdm ~** to tell sb that one can't come

absägen ['apzɛːgən] vt to saw off

absahnen ['apzaːnən] vt (*lit*) to skim; **das Beste für sich ~** (*fig*) to take the cream

Absatz ['apzats] m (*Comm*) sales *pl*; (*Jur*) section; (*Bodensatz*) deposit; (*neuer Abschnitt*) paragraph; (*Treppenabsatz*) landing;

(*Schuhabsatz*) heel; **Absatzflaute** f slump in the market; **Absatzförderung** f sales promotion; **Absatzgebiet** nt (*Comm*) market; sales territory; **Absatzplus** nt increase in sales; **Absatzprognose** f sales forecast; **Absatzschwierigkeiten** pl sales problems pl; **Absatzziffern** pl sales figures pl

absaufen ['apzaʊfən] unreg (*umg*) vi (*ertrinken*) to drown; (: *Motor*) to flood; (: *Schiff etc*) to go down

absaugen ['apzaʊgən] vt (*Flüssigkeit*) to suck out od off; (*Teppich, Sofa*) to hoover®, vacuum

abschaben ['apʃaːbən] vt to scrape off; (*Möhren*) to scrape

abschaffen ['apʃafən] vt to abolish, do away with

Abschaffung f abolition

abschalten ['apʃaltən] vt, vi (*lit: umg*) to switch off

abschattieren ['apʃatiːrən] vt to shade

abschätzen ['apʃɛtsən] vt to estimate; (*Lage*) to assess; (*Person*) to size up

abschätzig ['apʃɛtsɪç] adj disparaging, derogatory

Abschaum ['apʃaʊm] (**-(e)s**) m scum

Abscheu ['apʃɔy] (**-(e)s**) m loathing, repugnance; **abscheuerregend** adj repulsive, loathsome; **abscheulich** adj abominable

abschicken ['apʃɪkən] vt to send off

abschieben ['apʃiːbən] unreg vt to push away; (*Person*) to pack off; (*ausweisen: Ausländer*) to deport; (*fig: Verantwortung, Schuld*): ~ **(auf** +akk**)** to shift (onto)

Abschied ['apʃiːt] (**-(e)s, -e**) m parting; (*von Armee*) discharge; **(von jdm) ~ nehmen** to say goodbye (to sb), take one's leave (of sb); **seinen ~ nehmen** (*Mil*) to apply for discharge; **zum ~** on parting

Abschiedsbrief m farewell letter

Abschiedsfeier f farewell party

abschießen ['apʃiːsən] unreg vt (*Flugzeug*) to shoot down; (*Geschoss*) to fire; (*umg: Minister*) to get rid of

abschirmen ['apʃɪrmən] vt to screen; (*schützen*) to protect ▷ vr (*sich isolieren*): **sich ~ (gegen)** to cut o.s. off (from)

abschlaffen ['apʃlafən] (*umg*) vi to flag

abschlagen ['apʃlaːgən] unreg vt (*abhacken, Comm*) to knock off; (*ablehnen*) to refuse; (*Mil*) to repel

abschlägig ['apʃlɛːgɪç] adj negative; **jdn/etw ~ bescheiden** (*form*) to turn sb/sth down

Abschlagszahlung f interim payment

abschleifen ['apʃlaɪfən] unreg vt to grind down; (*Holzboden*) to sand (down) ▷ vr to wear off

Abschleppdienst m (*Aut*) breakdown service (*Brit*), towing company (*US*)

abschleppen ['apʃlɛpən] vt to (take in) tow

Abschleppseil nt towrope

abschließen ['apʃliːsən] unreg vt (*Tür*) to lock; (*beenden*) to conclude, finish; (*Vertrag, Handel*) to conclude; (*Versicherung*) to take out; (*Wette*) to place ▷ vr (*sich isolieren*) to cut o.s. off; **mit abgeschlossenem Studium** with a degree;

mit der Vergangenheit ~ to break with the past

abschließend adj concluding ▷ adv in conclusion, finally

Abschluss ['apʃlʊs] m (*Beendigung*) close, conclusion; (*Comm: Bilanz*) balancing; (*von Vertrag, Handel*) conclusion; **zum ~** in conclusion; **Abschlussfeier** f (*Sch*) school-leavers' ceremony; **Abschlussprüfer** m accountant; **Abschlussprüfung** f (*Sch*) final examination; (*Univ*) finals pl; **Abschlussrechnung** f final account; **Abschlusszeugnis** nt (*Sch*) leaving certificate, diploma (*US*)

abschmecken ['apʃmɛkən] vt (*kosten*) to taste; (*würzen*) to season

abschmieren ['apʃmiːrən] vt (*Aut*) to grease, lubricate

abschminken ['apʃmɪŋkən] vt: **sich ~** to remove one's make-up

abschmirgeln ['apʃmɪrgəln] vt to sand down

abschnallen ['apʃnalən] vr to unfasten one's seat belt ▷ vi (*umg: nicht mehr folgen können*) to give up; (: *fassungslos sein*) to be staggered

abschneiden ['apʃnaɪdən] unreg vt to cut off ▷ vi **bei etw gut/schlecht ~** (*umg*) to come off well/badly in sth

Abschnitt ['apʃnɪt] m section; (*Mil*) sector; (*Kontrollabschnitt*) counterfoil (*Brit*), stub (*US*); (*Math*) segment; (*Zeitabschnitt*) period

abschnüren ['apʃnyːrən] vt to constrict

abschöpfen ['apʃœpfən] vt to skim off

abschrauben ['apʃraʊbən] vt to unscrew

abschrecken ['apʃrɛkən] vt to deter, put off; (*mit kaltem Wasser*) to plunge into cold water

abschreckend adj deterrent; **~es Beispiel** warning; **eine abschreckende Wirkung haben**, **~ wirken** to act as a deterrent

abschreiben ['apʃraɪbən] unreg vt to copy; (*verloren geben*) to write off; (*Comm*) to deduct; **er ist bei mir abgeschrieben** I'm finished with him

Abschreibung f (*Comm*) deduction; (*Wertverminderung*) depreciation

Abschrift ['apʃrɪft] f copy

abschuften ['apʃʊftən] (*umg*) vr to slog one's guts out (*umg*)

abschürfen ['apʃʏrfən] vt to graze

Abschuss ['apʃʊs] m (*eines Geschützes*) firing; (*Herunterschießen*) shooting down; (*Tötung*) shooting

abschüssig ['apʃʏsɪç] adj steep

Abschussliste f: **er steht auf der ~** (*umg*) his days are numbered

Abschussrampe f launch(ing) pad

abschütteln ['apʃʏtəln] vt to shake off

abschütten ['apʃʏtən] vt (*Flüssigkeit etc*) to pour off

abschwächen ['apʃvɛçən] vt to lessen; (*Behauptung, Kritik*) to tone down ▷ vr to lessen

abschweifen ['apʃvaɪfən] vi to wander; (*Redner*) to digress

Abschweifung f digression

7

abschwellen ['apʃvɛlən] *unreg vi (Geschwulst)* to go down; *(Lärm)* to die down

abschwenken ['apʃvɛŋkən] *vi* to turn away

abschwören ['apʃvøːrən] *unreg vi +dat* to renounce

absehbar ['apzeːbaːr] *adj* foreseeable; **in ~er Zeit** in the foreseeable future; **das Ende ist ~** the end is in sight

absehen *unreg vt (Ende, Folgen)* to foresee ▷ *vi*: **von etw ~** to refrain from sth; *(nicht berücksichtigen)* to leave sth out of consideration; **jdm etw ~** *(erlernen)* to copy sth from sb

abseilen ['apzaɪlən] *vt* to lower down on a rope ▷ *vr (Bergsteiger)* to abseil (down)

Abseits ['apzaɪts] *nt (Sport)* offside; **im ~ stehen** to be offside; **im ~ leben** *(fig)* to live in the shadows

abseits *adv* out of the way ▷ *präp +gen* away from

absenden ['apzɛndən] *unreg vt* to send off, dispatch

Absender *m* sender

Absendung *f* dispatch

absetzbar ['apzɛtsbaːr] *adj (Beamter)* dismissible; *(Waren)* saleable; *(von Steuer)* deductible

absetzen ['apzɛtsən] *vt (niederstellen, aussteigen lassen)* to put down; *(abnehmen; auch Theaterstück)* to take off; *(Comm: verkaufen)* to sell; *(Fin: abziehen)* to deduct; *(entlassen)* to dismiss; *(König)* to depose; *(streichen)* to drop; *(Fußballspiel, Termin)* to cancel; *(hervorheben)* to pick out ▷ *vi*: **er trank das Glas aus, ohne abzusetzen** he emptied his glass in one ▷ *vr (sich entfernen)* to clear off; *(sich ablagern)* to be deposited; **das kann man ~** that is tax-deductible

Absetzung *f (Fin: Abzug)* deduction; *(Entlassung)* dismissal; *(von König)* deposing; *(Streichung)* dropping

absichern ['apzɪçərn] *vt* to make safe; *(schützen)* to safeguard ▷ *vr* to protect o.s.

Absicht ['apzɪçt] *f* intention; **mit ~** on purpose; **absichtlich** *adj* intentional, deliberate

absichtslos *adj* unintentional

absinken ['apzɪŋkən] *unreg vi* to sink; *(Temperatur, Geschwindigkeit)* to decrease

absitzen ['apzɪtsən] *unreg vi* to dismount ▷ *vt (Strafe)* to serve

absolut [apzoˈluːt] *adj* absolute

Absolutheitsanspruch *m* claim to absolute right

Absolutismus [apzoluˈtɪsmʊs] *m* absolutism

Absolvent, in *m(f)*: **die ~en eines Lehrgangs** the students who have completed a course

absolvieren [apzɔlˈviːrən] *vt (Sch)* to complete

absonderlich [apˈzɔndərlɪç] *adj* odd, strange

absondern *vt* to separate; *(ausscheiden)* to give off, secrete ▷ *vr* to cut o.s. off

Absonderung *f* separation; *(Med)* secretion

absorbieren [apzɔrˈbiːrən] *vt (lit, fig)* to absorb

abspalten ['apʃpaltən] *vt* to split off

Abspannung ['apʃpanʊŋ] *f (Ermüdung)* exhaustion

absparen ['apʃpaːrən] *vt*: **sich** *dat* **etw ~** to scrimp and save for sth

abspecken ['apʃpɛkən] *(umg) vt* to shed ▷ *vi* to lose weight

abspeisen ['apʃpaɪzən] *vt (fig)* to fob off

abspenstig ['apʃpɛnstɪç] *adj*: **(jdm) ~ machen** to lure away (from sb)

absperren ['apʃpɛrən] *vt* to block od close off; *(Tür)* to lock

Absperrung *f (Vorgang)* blocking od closing off; *(Sperre)* barricade

abspielen ['apʃpiːlən] *vt (Platte, Tonband)* to play; *(Sport: Ball)* to pass ▷ *vr* to happen; **vom Blatt ~** *(Mus)* to sight-read

absplittern ['apʃplɪtərn] *vt, vi* to chip off

Absprache ['apʃpraːxə] *f* arrangement; **ohne vorherige ~** without prior consultation

absprechen ['apʃprɛçən] *unreg vt (vereinbaren)* to arrange ▷ *vr*: **die beiden hatten sich vorher abgesprochen** they had agreed on what to do/say *etc* in advance; **jdm etw ~** to deny sb sth; *(in Abrede stellen: Begabung)* to dispute sb's sth

abspringen ['apʃprɪŋən] *unreg vi* to jump down/off; *(Farbe, Lack)* to flake off; *(Aviat)* to bale out; *(sich distanzieren)* to back out

Absprung ['apʃprʊŋ] *m* jump; **den ~ schaffen** *(fig)* to make the break *(umg)*

abspulen ['apʃpuːlən] *vt (Kabel, Garn)* to unwind

abspülen ['apʃpyːlən] *vt* to rinse; **Geschirr ~** to wash up *(Brit)*, do the dishes

abstammen ['apʃtamən] *vi* to be descended; *(Wort)* to be derived

Abstammung *f* descent; derivation; **französischer ~** of French extraction od descent

Abstand ['apʃtant] *m* distance; *(zeitlich)* interval; **davon ~ nehmen, etw zu tun** to refrain from doing sth; **~ halten** *(Aut)* to keep one's distance; **~ von etw gewinnen** *(fig)* to distance o.s. from sth; **mit großem ~ führen** to lead by a wide margin; **mit ~ der Beste** by far the best

Abstandssumme *f* compensation

abstatten ['apʃtatən] *vt (form: Dank)* to give; *(: Besuch)* to pay

abstauben ['apʃtaʊbən] *vt, vi* to dust; *(umg: mitgehen lassen)* to help oneself to, pinch; **(den Ball) ~** *(Sport)* to tuck the ball away

Abstauber, in ['apʃtaʊbər(ɪn)] **(-s, -)** *(umg) m(f)* *(Person)* somebody on the make

abstechen ['apʃtɛçən] *unreg vt* to cut; *(Tier)* to cut the throat of ▷ *vi*: **~ gegen** od **von** to contrast with

Abstecher (-s, -) *m* detour

abstecken ['apʃtɛkən] *vt (Fläche)* to mark out; *(Saum)* to pin

abstehen ['apʃteːən] *unreg vi (Ohren, Haare)* to stick out; *(entfernt sein)* to stand away

Absteige *f* cheap hotel

absteigen ['apʃtaɪgən] *unreg vi (vom Rad etc)* to

get off, dismount; **in einem Gasthof ~ to**
put up at an inn; **(in die Zweite Liga) ~ to be**
relegated (to the second division); **auf dem**
~den Ast sein (umg) to be going downhill, be
on the decline

abstellen ['apʃtɛlən] vt (niederstellen) to
put down; (entfernt stellen) to pull out;
(hinstellen: Auto) to park; (ausschalten) to turn
od switch off; (Missstand, Unsitte) to stop;
(abkommandieren) to order off; (ausrichten): **~ auf**
+akk to gear to; **das lässt sich nicht/lässt**
sich ~ nothing/something can be done about
that

Abstellgleis nt siding; **jdn aufs ~ schieben**
(fig) to cast sb aside

Abstellraum m storeroom

abstempeln ['apʃtɛmpəln] vt to stamp; (fig): **~**
zu od **als** to brand as

absterben ['apʃtɛrbən] unreg vi to die;
(Körperteil) to go numb

Abstieg ['apʃtiːk] (**-(e)s, -e**) m descent; (Sport)
relegation; (fig) decline

Abstiegskampf m (Sport) relegation battle

abstimmen ['apʃtɪmən] vi to vote ⊳ vt: **~ (auf**
+akk) (Instrument) to tune (to); (Interessen) to
match (with); (Termine, Ziele) to fit in (with)
⊳ vr to agree

Abstimmung f vote; (geheime Abstimmung)
ballot

abstinent [apstiˈnɛnt] adj (von Alkohol) teetotal

Abstinenz [apstiˈnɛnts] f teetotalism

Abstinenzler, in (**-s, -**) m(f) teetotaller

abstoßen ['apʃtoːsən] unreg vt to push off od
away; (anekeln) to repel; (Comm: Ware, Aktien)
to sell off

abstoßend adj repulsive

abstottern ['apʃtɔtərn] (umg) vt to pay off in
instalments

abstrahieren [apstraˈhiːrən] vt, vi to abstract

abstrakt [apˈstrakt] adj abstract ⊳ adv
abstractly, in the abstract

Abstraktion [apstraktsiˈoːn] f abstraction

Abstraktum [apˈstraktʊm] (**-s, Abstrakta**) nt
abstract concept; (Gram) abstract noun

abstrampeln ['apʃtrampəln] vr (fig: umg) to
sweat (away)

abstreifen ['apʃtraɪfən] vt (abtreten: Schuhe, Füße)
to wipe; (abziehen: Schmuck) to take off, slip off

abstreiten ['apʃtraɪtən] unreg vt to deny

Abstrich ['apʃtrɪç] m (Abzug) cut; (Med) smear;
~e machen to lower one's sights

abstufen ['apʃtuːfən] vt (Hang) to terrace;
(Farben) to shade; (Gehälter) to grade

abstumpfen ['apʃtʊmpfən] vt (lit, fig) to dull,
blunt ⊳ vi to become dulled

Absturz ['apʃtʊrts] m fall; (Aviat) crash

abstürzen ['apʃtʏrtsən] vi to fall; (Aviat) to
crash

absuchen ['apzuːxən] vt to scour, search

absurd [apˈzʊrt] adj absurd

Abszess [apsˈtsɛs] (**-es, -sse**) m abscess

Abt [apt] (**-(e)s, ⸚e**) m abbot

Abt. abk (= Abteilung) dept.

abtasten ['aptastən] vt to feel, probe; (Elek)
to scan; (bei Durchsuchung): **~ (auf** +akk) to frisk
(for)

abtauen ['aptaʊən] vt, vi to thaw; (Kühlschrank)
to defrost

Abtei [apˈtaɪ] (**-, -en**) f abbey

Abteil [apˈtaɪl] (**-(e)s, -e**) nt compartment

abteilen ['aptaɪlən] vt to divide up; (abtrennen)
to divide off

Abteilung f (in Firma, Kaufhaus) department;
(Mil) unit; (in Krankenhaus, Jur) section

Abteilungsleiter, in m(f) head of department;
(in Kaufhaus) department manager(ess)

abtelefonieren ['aptelefoniːrən] (umg) vi to
telephone to say one can't make it

Äbtissin [ɛpˈtɪsɪn] f abbess

abtönen ['aptøːnən] vt (Phot) to tone down

abtöten ['aptøːtən] vt (lit, fig) to destroy, kill
(off); (Nerv) to deaden

abtragen ['aptraːɡən] unreg vt (Hügel, Erde) to
level down; (Essen) to clear away; (Kleider) to
wear out; (Schulden) to pay off

abträglich ['aptrɛːklɪç] adj (+dat) harmful (to)

Abtragung f (Geol) erosion

Abtransport (**-(e)s, -e**) m transportation; (aus
Katastrophengebiet) evacuation

abtransportieren ['aptranspɔrtiːrən] vt to
transport; to evacuate

abtreiben ['aptraɪbən] unreg vt (Boot, Flugzeug)
to drive off course; (Kind) to abort ⊳ vi to be
driven off course; (Frau) to have an abortion

Abtreibung f abortion

Abtreibungsparagraf m abortion law

Abtreibungsversuch m attempted abortion

abtrennen ['aptrɛnən] vt (lostrennen) to detach;
(entfernen) to take off; (abteilen) to separate off

abtreten ['aptreːtən] unreg vt to wear out;
(überlassen) to hand over, cede; (Rechte,
Ansprüche) to transfer ⊳ vi to go off; (zurücktreten)
to step down; **sich** dat **die Füße ~** to wipe
one's feet; **~!** (Mil) dismiss!

Abtritt ['aptrɪt] m (Rücktritt) resignation

abtrocknen ['aptrɔknən] vt to dry ⊳ vi to do the
drying-up

abtropfen ['aptrɔpfən] vi: **etw ~ lassen** to let
sth drain

abtrünnig ['aptrʏnɪç] adj renegade

abtun ['aptuːn] unreg vt to take off; (fig) to
dismiss; **etw kurz ~** to brush sth aside

aburteilen ['apʊrtaɪlən] vt to condemn

abverlangen ['apfɛrlaŋən] vt: **jdm etw ~** to
demand sth from sb

abwägen ['apvɛːɡən] unreg vt to weigh up

abwählen ['apvɛːlən] vt to vote out (of office);
(Sch: Fach) to give up

abwälzen ['apvɛltsən] vt: **~ (auf** +akk) (Schuld,
Verantwortung) to shift (onto); (Arbeit) to unload
(onto); (Kosten) to pass on (to)

abwandeln ['apvandəln] vt to adapt

abwandern ['apvandərn] vi to move away

Abwärme ['apvɛrmə] f waste heat

abwarten ['apvartən] vt to wait for ⊳ vi to
wait; **das Gewitter ~** to wait till the storm is

over; ~ **und Tee trinken** (umg) to wait and
see; **eine ~de Haltung einnehmen** to play a
waiting game

abwärts ['apvɛrts] adv down; **mit ihm/dem
Land geht es** ~ he/the country is going
downhill

Abwasch ['apvaʃ] **(-(e)s)** m washing-up; **du
kannst das auch machen, das ist (dann)
ein** ~ (umg) you could do that as well and kill
two birds with one stone

abwaschen unreg vt (Schmutz) to wash off;
(Geschirr) to wash (up)

Abwasser ['apvasər] **(-s, -wässer)** nt sewage;
Abwasseraufbereitung f sewage treatment;
Abwasserkanal m sewer

abwechseln ['apvɛksəln] vi, vr to alternate;
(Personen) to take turns

abwechselnd adj alternate

Abwechslung f change; (Zerstreuung) diversion;
für ~ **sorgen** to provide entertainment

abwechslungsreich adj varied

Abweg ['apve:k] m: **auf ~e geraten/führen** to
go/lead astray

abwegig ['apve:gɪç] adj wrong; (Verdacht)
groundless

Abwehr ['apve:r] **(-)** f defence; (Schutz)
protection; (Abwehrdienst) counter-intelligence
(service); **auf ~ stoßen** to be repulsed;
abwehren vt to ward off; (Ball) to stop;
abwehrende Geste dismissive gesture;
Abwehrreaktion f (Psych) defence (Brit)
od defense (US) reaction; **Abwehrstoff** m
antibody

abweichen ['apvaiçən] unreg vi to deviate;
(Meinung) to differ; **vom rechten Weg** ~ (fig) to
wander off the straight and narrow

abweichend adj deviant; differing

Abweichler **(-s, -)** m (Pol) maverick

Abweichung f (zeitlich, zahlenmäßig) allowance;
zulässige ~ (Tech) tolerance

abweisen ['apvaizən] unreg vt to turn away;
(Antrag) to turn down; **er lässt sich nicht** ~ he
won't take no for an answer

abweisend adj (Haltung) cold

abwenden ['apvɛndən] unreg vt to avert ▷ vr to
turn away

abwerben ['apvɛrbən] unreg vt: **(jdm)** ~ to woo
away (from sb)

abwerfen ['apvɛrfən] unreg vt to throw off;
(Profit) to yield; (aus Flugzeug) to drop; (Spielkarte)
to discard

abwerten ['apvɛrtən] vt (Fin) to devalue

abwertend adj pejorative

Abwertung f devaluation

abwesend ['apve:zənt] adj absent; (zerstreut)
far away

Abwesenheit ['apve:zənhait] f absence;
durch ~ **glänzen** (ironisch) to be conspicuous
by one's absence

abwickeln ['apvɪkəln] vt to unwind; (Geschäft)
to transact, conclude; (fig: erledigen) to deal
with

Abwicklungskosten ['apvɪkluŋskɔstən] pl

transaction costs pl

abwiegen ['apvi:gən] unreg vt to weigh out

abwimmeln ['apvɪməln] (umg) vt (Person) to get
rid of; (: Auftrag) to get out of

abwinken ['apvɪŋkən] vi to wave it/him etc
aside; (fig: ablehnen) to say no

abwirtschaften ['apvɪrtʃaftən] vi to go
downhill

abwischen ['apvɪʃən] vt to wipe off od away;
(putzen) to wipe

abwracken ['apvrakən] vt (Schiff) to break
(up); **ein abgewrackter Mensch** a wreck (of
a person)

Abwurf ['apvurf] m throwing off; (von Bomben
etc) dropping; (von Reiter, Sport) throw

abwürgen ['apvyrgən] (umg) vt to scotch;
(Motor) to stall; **etw von vornherein** ~ to nip
sth in the bud

abzahlen ['aptsa:lən] vt to pay off

abzählen ['aptse:lən] vt to count (up);
abgezähltes Fahrgeld exact fare

Abzählreim ['aptse:lraim] m counting rhyme
(e.g. eeny meeny miney mo)

Abzahlung f repayment; **auf** ~ **kaufen** to buy
on hire purchase (Brit) od the installment plan
(US)

abzapfen ['aptsapfən] vt to draw off; **jdm Blut**
~ to take blood from sb

abzäunen ['aptsɔynən] vt to fence off

Abzeichen ['aptsaiçən] nt badge; (Orden)
decoration

abzeichnen ['aptsaiçnən] vt to draw, copy;
(unterschreiben) to initial ▷ vr to stand out;
(fig: bevorstehen) to loom

Abziehbild nt transfer

abziehen ['aptsi:ən] unreg vt to take off; (Tier)
to skin; (Bett) to strip; (Truppen) to withdraw;
(subtrahieren) to take away, subtract; (kopieren)
to run off; (Schlüssel) to take out, remove ▷ vi to
go away; (Truppen) to withdraw; (abdrücken) to
pull the trigger, fire

abzielen ['aptsi:lən] vi: ~ **auf** +akk to be aimed
at

Abzocke ['aptsɔkə] (umg) f rip-off

Abzug ['aptsu:k] m departure; (von Truppen)
withdrawal; (Kopie) copy; (Subtraktion)
subtraction; (Betrag) deduction; (Rauchabzug)
flue; (von Waffen) trigger; (Rabatt) discount;
(Korrekturfahne) proof; (Phot) print; **jdm freien**
~ **gewähren** to grant sb safe passage

abzüglich ['aptsy:klɪç] präp +gen less

abzweigen ['aptsvaigən] vi to branch off ▷ vt
to set aside

Abzweigung f junction

Accessoires [aksɛso'a:rs] pl accessories pl

ach [ax] interj oh; ~ **so!** I see!; **mit A~ und
Krach** by the skin of one's teeth; ~ **was** od **wo,
das ist doch nicht so schlimm!** come on
now, it's not that bad!

Achillesferse [a'xɪlɛsfɛrzə] f Achilles heel

Achse ['aksə] **(-, -n)** f axis; (Aut) axle; **auf** ~ **sein**
(umg) to be on the move

Achsel ['aksəl] **(-, -n)** f shoulder; **Achselhöhle**

f armpit; **Achselzucken** *nt* shrug (of one's shoulders)
Achsenbruch *m* (*Aut*) broken axle
Achsenkreuz *nt* coordinate system
Acht¹ [axt] (**-, -en**) *f* eight; (*beim Eislaufen etc*) figure (of) eight
Acht² (**-**) *f* attention; **hab ~** (*Mil*) attention!; **~ geben = achtgeben; sich in ~ nehmen (vor** +*dat*) to be careful (of), watch out (for); **etw außer ~ lassen** to disregard sth
acht *num* eight; **~ Tage** a week
achtbar *adj* worthy
achte, r, s *adj* eighth
Achteck *nt* octagon
Achtel *nt* eighth; **Achtelnote** *f* quaver, eighth note (*US*)
achten *vt* to respect ▷ *vi*: **~ (auf** +*akk*) to pay attention (to); **darauf ~, dass ...** to be careful that ...
ächten ['ɛçtən] *vt* to outlaw, ban
Achterbahn *f* roller coaster
Achterdeck *nt* (*Naut*) afterdeck
achtfach *adj* eightfold
achtgeben *unreg vi*: **~ (auf** +*akk*) to take care (of); (*aufmerksam sein*) to pay attention (to)
achtlos *adj* careless; **viele gehen ~ daran vorbei** many people just pass by without noticing
achtmal *adv* eight times
achtsam *adj* attentive
Achtstundentag *m* eight-hour day
Achtung ['axtʊŋ] *f* attention; (*Ehrfurcht*) respect ▷ *interj* watch out!; (*Mil*) attention!; **alle ~!** good for you/him *etc*!; **~, fertig, los!** ready, steady, go!; **„~ Hochspannung!"** "danger, high voltage"; **„~ Lebensgefahr/Stufe!"** "danger/mind the step!"
Achtungserfolg *m* reasonable success
achtzehn *num* eighteen
achtzig *num* eighty; **Achtziger, in** (**-s, -**) *m(f)* octogenarian
ächzen ['ɛçtsən] *vi*: **~ (vor** +*dat*) to groan (with)
Acker ['akər] (**-s, ⁻**) *m* field; **Ackerbau** *m* agriculture; **Ackerbau und Viehzucht** farming
ackern *vi* to plough; (*umg*) to slog away
a conto [a 'kɔnto] *adv* (*Comm*) on account
A. D. *abk* (= *Anno Domini*) A.D.
a. D. *abk* = **außer Dienst**
a. d. *abk* = **an der** (*bei Ortsnamen*)
ad absurdum [at ap'zʊrdʊm] *adv*: **~ führen** (*Argument etc*) to reduce to absurdity
ADAC (**-**) *m abk* (= *Allgemeiner Deutscher Automobil-Club*) German motoring organization, ≈ AA (*Brit*), AAA (*US*)
ad acta [at 'akta] *adv*: **etw ~ legen** (*fig*) to consider sth finished; (*Frage, Problem*) to consider sth closed
Adam ['a:dam] *m*: **bei ~ und Eva anfangen** (*umg*) to start right from scratch *od* from square one
adaptieren [adap'ti:rən] *vt* to adapt
adäquat [adɛ'kva:t] *adj* (*Belohnung, Übersetzung*)

adequate; (*Stellung, Verhalten*) suitable
addieren [a'di:rən] *vt* to add (up)
Addis Abeba ['adɪs'a:beba] (**-, -s**) *nt* Addis Ababa
Addition [aditsi'o:n] *f* addition
ade *interj* bye!
Adel ['a:dəl] (**-s**) *m* nobility; **~ verpflichtet** noblesse oblige
adelig *adj* noble
Adelsstand *m* nobility
Ader ['a:dər] (**-, -n**) *f* vein; (*fig: Veranlagung*) bent
Adhäsionsverschluss [athɛzi'o:nsfɛrʃlʊs] *m* adhesive seal
Adjektiv ['atjɛkti:f] (**-s, -e**) *nt* adjective
Adler ['a:dlər] (**-s, -**) *m* eagle
adlig *adj* = **adelig**
Admiral [atmi'ra:l] (**-s, -e**) *m* admiral
Admiralität *f* admiralty
adoptieren [adɔp'ti:rən] *vt* to adopt
Adoption [adɔptsi'o:n] *f* adoption
Adoptiveltern *pl* adoptive parents *pl*
Adoptivkind *nt* adopted child
Adr. *abk* (= *Adresse*) add.
Adressant [adrɛ'sant] *m* sender
Adressat [adrɛ'sa:t] (**-en, -en**) *m* addressee
Adressbuch *nt* directory; (*privat*) address book
Adresse [a'drɛsə] (**-, -n**) *f* (*auch Comput*) address; **an der falschen ~ sein** (*umg*) to have gone/come to the wrong person; **absolute ~** absolute address; **relative ~** relative address
adressieren [adrɛ'si:rən] *vt*: **~ (an** +*akk*) to address (to)
Adria ['a:dria] (**-**) *f* Adriatic Sea
Adriatisches Meer [adri'a:tɪʃəs me:r] *nt* (*form*) Adriatic Sea
ADSL *m abk* (= *Asymmetric Digital Subscriber Line*) ADSL
Advent [at'vɛnt] (**-(e)s, -e**) *m* Advent; **der erste ~** the first Sunday in Advent
Advents- *zW*: **Adventskalender** *m* Advent calendar; **Adventskranz** *m* Advent wreath
Adverb [at'vɛrp] *nt* adverb
adverbial [atvɛrbi'a:l] *adj* adverbial
aero- [aero] *präf* aero-
Aerobic [ae'ro:bik] (**-s**) *nt* aerobics *sing*
Affäre [a'fɛ:rə] (**-, -n**) *f* affair; **sich aus der ~ ziehen** (*umg*) to get (o.s.) out of it
Affe ['afə] (**-n, -n**) *m* monkey; (*umg: Kerl*) berk (*Brit*)
Affekt (**-(e)s, -e**) *m*: **im ~ handeln** to act in the heat of the moment
affektiert [afɛk'ti:rt] *adj* affected
Affen- *zW*: **affenartig** *adj* like a monkey; **mit affenartiger Geschwindigkeit** (*umg*) like a flash; **affengeil** (*umg*) *adj* magic, fantastic; **Affenhitze** (*umg*) *f* incredible heat; **Affenliebe** *f*: **Affenliebe (zu)** blind adoration (of); **Affenschande** (*umg*) *f* crying shame; **Affentempo** (*umg*) *nt*: **in** *od* **mit einem Affentempo** at breakneck speed; **Affentheater** (*umg*) *nt*: **ein Affentheater aufführen** to make a fuss
affig ['afɪç] *adj* affected
Afghane [af'ga:nə] (**-n, -n**) *m* Afghan

Afghanin [af'ga:nɪn] f Afghan
afghanisch adj Afghan
Afghanistan [af'ga:nɪsta:n] (-s) nt
Afghanistan
Afrika ['a:frika] (-s) nt Africa
Afrikaans [afri'ka:ns] (-) nt Afrikaans
Afrikaner, in [afri'ka:nər(ɪn)] (-s, -) m(f)
African
afrikanisch adj African
afroamerikanisch ['a:fro|ameri'ka:nɪʃ] adj
Afro-American
After ['aftər] (-s, -) m anus
AG (-) f abk (= Aktiengesellschaft) ≈ plc (Brit), corp.,
inc. (US)
Ägäis [ɛ'gɛ:ɪs] (-) f Aegean (Sea)
Ägäisches Meer nt Aegean Sea
Agent, in [a'gɛnt(ɪn)] m(f) agent
Agententätigkeit f espionage
Agentur [agɛn'tu:r] f agency; **Agenturbericht**
m, **Agenturmeldung** f (news) agency report
Aggregat [agre'ga:t] (-(e)s, -e) nt aggregate;
(Tech) unit; **Aggregatzustand** m (Phys) state
Aggression [agrɛsi'o:n] f aggression
aggressiv [agrɛ'si:f] adj aggressive
Aggressivität [agrɛsivi'tɛ:t] f aggressiveness
Aggressor [a'grɛso:r] (-s, -en) m aggressor
Agitation [agitatsi'o:n] f agitation
Agrarpolitik f agricultural policy
Agrarstaat m agrarian state
AGV f abk (= Arbeitsgemeinschaft der
Verbraucherverbände) consumer groups' association
Ägypten [ɛ'gʏptən] (-s) nt Egypt
Ägypter, in (-s, -) m(f) Egyptian
ägyptisch adj Egyptian
aha [a'ha:] interj aha!
Aha-Erlebnis nt sudden insight
ahd. abk (= althochdeutsch) OHG
Ahn [a:n] (-en, -en) m forebear
ahnden ['a:ndən] vt (geh: Freveltat, Verbrechen) to
avenge; (Übertretung, Verstoß) to punish
ähneln ['ɛ:nəln] vi +dat to be like, resemble ▷ vr
to be alike od similar
ahnen ['a:nən] vt to suspect; (Tod, Gefahr) to
have a presentiment of; **nichts Böses** ~ to be
unsuspecting; **du ahnst es nicht!** you have
no idea!; **davon habe ich nichts geahnt** I
didn't have the slightest inkling of it
Ahnenforschung f genealogy
ähnlich ['ɛ:nlɪç] adj (+dat) similar (to); **das
sieht ihm (ganz) ~!** (umg) that's just like
him!, that's him all over!; **Ähnlichkeit** f
similarity
Ahnung ['a:nʊŋ] f idea, suspicion; (Vorgefühl)
presentiment
ahnungslos adj unsuspecting
Ahorn ['a:hɔrn] (-s, -e) m maple
Ähre ['ɛ:rə] (-, -n) f ear
AHS f abk (Österr. = allgemeinbildende höhere Schule)
≈ secondary school
Aids [e:dz] (-) nt Aids
Airbag ['ɛ:bɛːg] (-s, -s) m (Aut) airbag
Akademie [akade'mi:] f academy
Akademiker, in [aka'de:mikər(ɪn)] (-s, -) m(f)

university graduate
akademisch adj academic
Akazie [a'ka:tsiə] (-, -n) f acacia
Akk. abk = **Akkusativ**
akklimatisieren [aklimati'zi:rən] vr to become
acclimatized
Akkord [a'kɔrt] (-(e)s, -e) m (Mus) chord; **im
~ arbeiten** to do piecework; **Akkordarbeit** f
piecework
Akkordeon [a'kɔrdeɔn] (-s, -s) nt accordion
Akkordlohn m piece wages pl, piece rate
Akkreditiv [akredi'ti:f] (-s, -e) nt (Comm) letter
of credit
Akku ['aku] (-s, -s) (umg) m (Akkumulator) battery
akkurat [aku'ra:t] adj precise; (sorgfältig)
meticulous
Akkusativ ['akuzati:f] (-s, -e) m accusative
(case); **Akkusativobjekt** nt accusative od direct
object
Akne ['aknə] (-, -n) f acne
Akribie [akri'bi:] f (geh) meticulousness
Akrobat, in [akro'ba:t(ɪn)] (-en, -en) m(f)
acrobat
Akt [akt] (-(e)s, -e) m act; (Kunst) nude
Akte ['aktə] (-, -n) f file; **etw zu den ~n legen**
(lit, fig) to file sth away
Akten- zW: **Aktendeckel** m folder; **Aktenkoffer**
m attaché case; **aktenkundig** adj on record;
Aktennotiz f memo(randum); **Aktenordner**
m file; **Aktenschrank** m filing cabinet;
Aktentasche f briefcase; **Aktenzeichen** nt
reference
Aktie ['aktsiə] (-, -n) f share; **wie stehen die
~n?** (hum: umg) how are things?
Aktien- zW: **Aktienbank** f joint-stock
bank; **Aktienemission** f share issue;
Aktiengesellschaft f joint-stock company;
Aktienindex m share index; **Aktienkapital** nt
share capital; **Aktienkurs** m share price
Aktion [aktsi'o:n] f campaign; (Polizeiaktion,
Suchaktion) action
Aktionär, in [aktsio'nɛ:r(ɪn)] (-s, -e) m(f)
shareholder
Aktionismus [aktsio'nɪsmʊs] m (Pol)
actionism
Aktionsradius [aktsi'o:nzra:diʊs] (-, -ien) m
(Aviat, Naut) range; (fig: Wirkungsbereich) scope
aktiv [ak'ti:f] adj active; (Mil) regular; **Aktiv** (-s)
nt (Gram) active (voice)
Aktiva [ak'ti:va] pl assets pl
aktivieren [akti'vi:rən] vt to activate;
(fig: Arbeit, Kampagne) to step up; (Mitarbeiter) to
get moving
Aktivität [aktivi'tɛ:t] f activity
Aktivposten m (lit, fig) asset
Aktivsaldo m (Comm) credit balance
Aktivurlaub m activity holiday
aktualisieren [aktuali'zi:rən] vt (Comput) to
update
Aktualität [aktuali'tɛ:t] f topicality; (einer
Mode) up-to-dateness
aktuell [aktu'ɛl] adj topical; up-to-date; **eine
~e Sendung** (Rundf, TV) a current affairs

programme
Akupunktur [akupuŋkˈtuːər] f acupuncture
Akustik [aˈkʊstɪk] f acoustics pl
akustisch [aˈkʊstɪʃ] adj acoustic; **ich habe dich rein ~ nicht verstanden** I simply didn't catch what you said (properly)
akut [aˈkuːt] adj acute; (Frage) pressing, urgent
AKW nt abk = **Atomkraftwerk**
Akzent [akˈtsɛnt] (-(e)s, -e) m accent; (Betonung) stress; **~e setzen** (fig) to bring out od emphasize the main points; **Akzentverschiebung** f (fig) shift of emphasis
Akzept (-(e)s, -e) nt (Comm: Wechsel) acceptance
akzeptabel [aktsɛpˈtaːbl] adj acceptable
akzeptieren [aktsɛpˈtiːrən] vt to accept
AL f abk (= Alternative Liste) siehe **alternativ**
Alarm [aˈlarm] (-(e)s, -e) m alarm; (Zustand) alert; **~ schlagen** to give od raise the alarm; **Alarmanlage** f alarm system; **alarmbereit** adj standing by; **Alarmbereitschaft** f stand-by
alarmieren [alarˈmiːrən] vt to alarm
Alaska [aˈlaska] (-s) nt Alaska
Albaner, in [alˈbaːnər(ɪn)] (-s, -) m(f) Albanian
Albanien [alˈbaːniən] (-s) nt Albania
albanisch adj Albanian
albern [ˈalbərn] adj silly
Albtraum [ˈalptraʊm] m nightmare
Album [ˈalbʊm] (-s, **Alben**) nt album
Alcopops [ˈalkopɔps] pl alcopops pl
Aleuten [aleˈuːtən] pl Aleutian Islands pl
Alge [ˈalgə] (-, -n) f alga
Algebra [ˈalgebra] (-) f algebra
Algerien [alˈgeːriən] (-s) nt Algeria
Algerier, in (-s, -) m(f) Algerian
algerisch [alˈgeːrɪʃ] adj Algerian
Algier [ˈalʒiːər] (-s) nt Algiers
ALGOL [ˈalgɔl] (-(s)) nt (Comput) ALGOL
alias [ˈaːlias] adv alias
Alibi [ˈaːlibi] (-s, -s) nt alibi
Alimente [aliˈmɛntə] pl alimony sing
Alkohol [ˈalkohɔl] (-s, -e) m alcohol; **unter ~ stehen** to be under the influence (of alcohol); **alkoholarm** adj low alcohol; **Alkoholexzess** m binge drinking; **alkoholfrei** adj non-alcoholic; **Alkoholgehalt** m proof
Alkoholika [alkoˈhoːlika] pl alcoholic drinks pl, liquor (US)
Alkoholiker, in [alkoˈhoːlikər(ɪn)] (-s, -) m(f) alcoholic
alkoholisch adj alcoholic
Alkoholverbot nt ban on alcohol
All [al] (-s) nt universe; (Raumfahrt) space; (außerhalb unseres Sternsystems) outer space
allabendlich adj every evening
allbekannt adj universally known
alle adj siehe **alle(r, s)**
alledem [ˈaləˈdeːm] pron: **bei/trotz** etc **~ with/** in spite of etc all that; **zu ~** moreover
Allee [aˈleː] (-, -n) f avenue
allein [aˈlaɪn] adj, adv alone; (ohne Hilfe) on one's own, by oneself ▷ konj (geh) but, only; **von ~** by oneself/itself; **nicht ~** (nicht nur) not only; **~ schon der Gedanke**

the very od mere thought ..., the thought alone ...; **alleinerziehend** adj single-parent; **Alleinerziehende, r** f(m), **Alleinerzieher,** in m(f) single parent; **Alleingang** m: **im Alleingang** on one's own; **Alleinherrscher,** in m(f) autocrat; **Alleinhersteller, in** m(f) sole manufacturer
alleinig [aˈlaɪnɪç] adj sole
allein- zW: Alleinsein nt being on one's own; (Einsamkeit) loneliness; **alleinstehend** adj single; **Alleinunterhalter, in** m(f) solo entertainer; **Alleinvertretung** f (Comm) sole agency; **Alleinvertretungsvertrag** m (Comm) exclusive agency agreement
allemal [ˈaləˈmaːl] adv (jedes Mal) always; (ohne Weiteres) with no bother; siehe auch **Mal**
allenfalls [ˈalənˈfals] adv at all events; (höchstens) at most

○ SCHLÜSSELWORT

alle, r, s adj **1** (sämtliche) all; **wir alle** all of us; **alle Kinder waren da** all the children were there; **alle Kinder mögen ...** all children like ...; **alle beide** both of us/them; **sie kamen alle** they all came; **alles Gute** all the best; **alles in allem** all in all; **vor allem** above all; **das ist alles andere als ...** that's anything but ...; **es hat alles keinen Sinn mehr** nothing makes sense any more; **was habt ihr alles gemacht?** what did you get up to?
2 (mit Zeit- oder Maßangaben) every; **alle vier Jahre** every four years; **alle fünf Meter** every five metres
▷ pron everything; **alles was er sagt** everything he says, all that he says; **trotz allem** in spite of everything
▷ adv (zu Ende, aufgebraucht) finished; **die Milch ist alle** the milk's all gone, there's no milk left; **etw alle machen** to finish sth up

allerbeste, r, s [ˈalərˈbɛstə(r, s)] adj very best
allerdings [ˈalərˈdɪŋs] adv (zwar) admittedly; (gewiss) certainly
Allergie [alerˈgiː] f allergy
allergisch [aˈlɛrgɪʃ] adj allergic; **auf etw** akk **~ reagieren** to be allergic to sth
allerhand (umg) adj inv all sorts of; **das ist doch ~!** that's a bit much!; **~!** (lobend) good show!
Allerheiligen nt All Saints' Day; see culture note

● **ALLERHEILIGEN**
●
● Allerheiligen (All Saints' Day) is a public
● holiday in Germany and in Austria. It is a
● day in honour of all the saints. Allerseelen
● (All Souls' Day) is celebrated on November
● 2nd in the Roman Catholic Church. It is
● customary to visit cemeteries and place
● lighted candles on the graves of deceased
● relatives and friends.

aller- *zW:* **allerhöchste, r, s** *adj* very highest; **es wird allerhöchste Zeit, dass ...** it's really high time that ...; **allerhöchstens** *adv* at the very most; **allerlei** *adj inv* all sorts of; **allerletzte, r, s** *adj* very last; **der/das ist das Allerletzte** (*umg*) he's/it's the absolute end!; **allerneueste, allerneuste, r, s** *adj* very latest

Allerseelen (-s) *nt* All Soul's Day; *siehe auch* **Allerheiligen; allerseits** *adv* on all sides; **prost allerseits!** cheers everyone!

Allerwelts- *in zW* (*Durchschnitts-*) common; (*nichtssagend*) commonplace

allerwenigste, r, s *adj* very least; **die ~n Menschen wissen das** very few people know that

Allerwerteste, r *m* (*hum*) posterior (*hum*)

alles *pron* everything; *siehe auch* **alle(r, s)**

allesamt *adv* all (of them/us *etc*)

Alleskleber (-s, -) *m* all-purpose adhesive

Allgäu ['algɔʏ] *nt part of the alpine region of Bavaria*

allgegenwärtig *adj* omnipresent, ubiquitous

allgemein ['algəmaɪn] *adj* general ▷ *adv:* **es ist ~ üblich** it's the general rule; **~ verständlich** generally intelligible; **im A~** in general; **im ~en Interesse** in the common interest; **auf ~en Wunsch** by popular request; **Allgemeinbildung** *f* general *od* all-round education; **allgemeingültig** *adj* generally accepted; **Allgemeinheit** *f* (*Menschen*) general public; **Allgemeinheiten** *pl* (*Redensarten*) general remarks *pl*; **Allgemeinwissen** *nt* general knowledge

Allheilmittel [al'haɪlmɪtəl] *nt* cure-all, panacea (*bes fig*)

Alliierte, r [ali'i:rtə(r)] *f(m)* ally

all- *zW:* **alljährlich** *adj* annual; **allmächtig** *adj* all-powerful, omnipotent; **allmählich** *adv* gradually; **es wird allmählich Zeit** (*umg*) it's about time; **Allradantrieb** *m* all-wheel drive; **allseitig** *adj* (*allgemein*) general; (*ausnahmslos*) universal; **Alltag** *m* everyday life; **alltäglich** *adj* daily; (*gewöhnlich*) commonplace; **alltags** *adv* on weekdays; **Alltagskultur** *f* everyday culture

Allüren [a'ly:rən] *pl* odd behaviour (*Brit*) *od* behavior (*US*) *sing*; (*eines Stars etc*) airs and graces *pl*

all- *zW:* **allwissend** *adj* omniscient; **Allzeithoch** *nt* all-time high; **Allzeittief** *nt* all-time low; **allzu** *adv* all too; **allzu gern** (*mögen*) only too much; (*bereitwillig*) only too willingly; **allzu oft** all too often; **allzu viel** too much

Allzweck- ['altsvɛk-] *in zW* all-purpose

Alm [alm] **(-, -en)** *f* alpine pasture

Almosen ['almo:zən] **(-s, -)** *nt* alms *pl*

Alpen ['alpən] *pl* Alps *pl*; **Alpenblume** *f* alpine flower; **Alpenveilchen** *nt* cyclamen; **Alpenvorland** *nt* foothills *pl* of the Alps

Alphabet [alfa'be:t] **(-(e)s, -e)** *nt* alphabet

alphabetisch *adj* alphabetical

alphanumerisch [alfanu'me:rɪʃ] *adj* (*Comput*) alphanumeric

Alptraum ['alptraʊm] *m* = **Albtraum**

 SCHLÜSSELWORT

als [als] *konj* **1** (*zeitlich*) when; (*gleichzeitig*) as; **damals als ...** (in the days) when ...; **gerade als ...** just as ...
2 (*in der Eigenschaft*) than; **als Antwort** as an answer; **als Kind** as a child
3 (*bei Vergleichen*) than; **ich kam später als er** I came later than he (did) *od* later than him; **lieber ... als ...** rather ... than ...; **alles andere als** anything but; **nichts als Ärger** nothing but trouble; **so viel/so weit als möglich** (*bei Vergleichen*) as much/far as possible
4: als ob/wenn as if

alsbaldig [als'baldɪç] *konj:* „**zum ~en Verbrauch bestimmt**" "for immediate use only"

also ['alzo:] *konj* so; (*folglich*) therefore; **~ wie ich schon sagte** well (then), as I said before; **ich komme ~ morgen** so I'll come tomorrow; **~ gut** *od* **schön!** okay then; **~, so was!** well really!; **na ~!** there you are then!

Alt [alt] **(-s, -e)** *m* (*Mus*) alto

alt *adj* old; **ich bin nicht mehr der A~e** I am not the man I was; **alles beim A~en lassen** to leave everything as it was; **ich werde heute nicht ~ (werden)** (*umg*) I won't last long today/tonight *etc*; **~ aussehen** (*fig: umg*) to be in a pickle

Altar [al'ta:r] **(-(e)s, -äre)** *m* altar

alt- *zW:* **Altbau** *m* old building; **Altbauwohnung** *f* flat (*Brit*) *od* apartment (*US*) in an old building; **altbekannt** *adj* well-known; **altbewährt** *adj* (*Methode etc*) well-tried; (*Tradition etc*) long-standing; **Altbier** *nt* top-fermented German dark beer; **alteingesessen** *adj* old-established; **Alteisen** *nt* scrap iron

Altenheim *nt* old people's home

Altenteil ['altəntaɪl] *nt:* **sich aufs ~ setzen** *od* **zurückziehen** (*fig*) to retire from public life

Alter ['altər] **(-s, -)** *nt* age; (*hohes*) old age; **er ist in deinem ~** he's your age; **im ~ von** at the age of

älter ['ɛltər] *adj* (*comp*) older; (*Bruder, Schwester*) elder; (*nicht mehr jung*) elderly

altern ['altərn] *vi* to grow old, age

Alternativ- [altɛrna'ti:f] *in zW* alternative

alternativ *adj:* **A~e Liste** *electoral pact between the Greens and alternative parties*; **~ leben** to live an alternative way of life

Alternative [altɛrna'ti:və] *f* alternative

Alternativ- *zW:* **Alternativmedizin** *f* alternative medicine; **Alternativszene** *f* alternative scene; **Alternativtechnologie** *f* alternative technology

alters ['altərs] *adv* (*geh*): **von ~ od seit ~ (her)** from time immemorial

Alters- *zW:* **Altersarmut** *f* old-age poverty; **altersbedingt** *adj* related to a particular age;

a

caused by old age; **Altersgrenze** f age limit; **flexible Altersgrenze** flexible retirement age; **Altersheim** nt old people's home; **Altersrente** f old age pension; **Altersruhegeld** nt retirement benefit; **altersschwach** adj (Mensch) old and infirm; (Auto, Möbel) decrepit; **Altersversorgung** f provision for old age

Altertum ['altərtuːm] nt antiquity

altertümlich adj (aus dem Altertum) ancient; (veraltet) antiquated

alt- zW: **altgedient** adj long-serving; **Altglas** nt used glass (for recycling), scrap glass; **Altglascontainer** m bottle bank; **althergebracht** adj traditional; **Altherrenmannschaft** f (Sport) team of players over thirty; **altklug** adj precocious; **Altlasten** pl legacy sing of dangerous waste; **Altmaterial** nt scrap; **Altmetall** nt scrap metal; **altmodisch** adj old-fashioned; **Altpapier** nt waste paper; **Altstadt** f old town

Altstimme f alto

Altwarenhändler m second-hand dealer

Altweibersommer m Indian summer

Alu ['aːlu] (umg) abk = **Arbeitslosen- unterstützung; Aluminium**

Alufolie ['aːlufoːliə] f tinfoil

Aluminium [alu'miːniʊm] (-s) nt aluminium, aluminum (US); **Aluminiumfolie** f tinfoil

Alzheimerkrankheit ['altshaɪmər'kraŋkhaɪt] f Alzheimer's disease

am [am] = **an dem; am Sterben** on the point of dying; **am 15. März** on March 15th; **am letzten Sonntag** last Sunday; **am Morgen/ Abend** in the morning/evening; **am besten/ schönsten** best/most beautiful

Amalgam [amal'gaːm] (-s, -e) nt amalgam

Amateur [ama'tøːr] m amateur

Amazonas [ama'tsoːnas] (-) m Amazon (river)

Ambiente [ambi'ɛntə] (-) nt ambience

Ambition [ambitsi'oːn] f: **-en auf etw** akk **haben** to have ambitions of getting sth

Amboss ['ambɔs] (-es, -e) m anvil

ambulant [ambu'lant] adj outpatient

Ameise ['aːmaɪzə] (-, -n) f ant

Ameisenhaufen m anthill

Amerika [a'meːrika] (-s) nt America

Amerikaner [ameri'kaːnər] (-s, -) m American; (Gebäck) flat iced cake; **Amerikanerin** f American

amerikanisch adj American

Ami ['ami] (-s, -s) (umg) m Yank; (Soldat) GI

Amme ['amə] (-, -n) f (veraltet) foster mother; (Nährmutter) wet nurse

Ammenmärchen ['amənmɛːrçən] nt fairy tale od story

Amok ['aːmɔk] m: **~ laufen** to run amok od amuck

Amortisation [amɔrtizatsi'oːn] f amortization

amortisieren [amɔrti'ziːrən] vr to pay for itself

Ampel ['ampəl] (-, -n) f traffic lights pl

amphibisch [am'fiːbɪʃ] adj amphibious

Ampulle [am'pʊlə] (-, -n) f (Behälter) ampoule

amputieren [ampu'tiːrən] vt to amputate

Amsel ['amzəl] (-, -n) f blackbird

Amsterdam [amstər'dam] nt (-s) Amsterdam

Amt [amt] (-(e)s, ⁼er) nt office; (Pflicht) duty; (Tel) exchange; **zum zuständigen ~ gehen** to go to the relevant authority; **von ~s wegen** (auf behördliche Anordnung hin) officially

amtieren [am'tiːrən] vi to hold office; (fungieren): **als ... ~** to act as ...

amtierend adj incumbent

amtlich adj official; **~es Kennzeichen** registration (number), license number (US)

Amtmann (-(e)s, pl **-männer** od **-leute**) m (Verwaltung) senior civil servant

Amtmännin f (Verwaltung) senior civil servant

Amts- zW: **Amtsarzt** m medical officer; **amtsärztlich** adj: **amtsärztlich untersucht werden** to have an official medical examination; **Amtsdeutsch, Amtsdeutsche** nt officialese; **Amtseid** m: **den Amtseid ablegen** to be sworn in, take the oath of office; **Amtsgeheimnis** nt (geheime Sache) official secret; (Schweigepflicht) official secrecy; **Amtsgericht** nt county (Brit) od district (US) court; **Amtsmissbrauch** m abuse of one's position; **Amtsperiode** f term of office; **Amtsperson** f official; **Amtsrichter** m district judge; **Amtsschimmel** m (hum) officialdom; **Amtssprache** f official language; **Amtsstunden** pl office hours pl; **Amtsträger** m office bearer; **Amtswechsel** m change of office; (in Behörde) rotation (in office); **Amtsweg** m: **auf dem Amtsweg** through official channels; **Amtszeit** f period of office

amüsant [amy'zant] adj amusing

Amüsement [amyzə'maː] nt amusement

amüsieren [amy'ziːrən] vt to amuse ▷ vr to enjoy o.s.; **sich über etw** akk **~** to find sth funny; (unfreundlich) to make fun of sth

⊙ SCHLÜSSELWORT

an [an] präp +dat **1** (räumlich: wo?) at; (auf, bei) on; (nahe bei) near; **an diesem Ort** at this place; **an der Wand** on the wall; **zu nahe an etw** too near to sth; **unten am Fluss** down by the river; **Köln liegt am Rhein** Cologne is on the Rhine; **an der gleichen Stelle** at od on the same spot; **jdn an der Hand nehmen** to take sb by the hand; **sie wohnen Tür an Tür** they live next door to one another; **es an der Leber** etc **haben** (umg) to have liver etc trouble

2 (zeitlich: wann?) on; **an diesem Tag** on this day; **an Ostern** at Easter

3: arm an Fett low in fat; **jung an Jahren sein** to be young in years; **an der ganzen Sache ist nichts** there is nothing in it; **an etw sterben** to die of sth; **an (und für) sich** actually

▷ präp +akk **1** (räumlich: wohin?) to; **er ging ans Fenster** he went (over) to the window; **etw an die Wand hängen/schreiben** to hang/write sth on the wall; **an die Arbeit gehen** to get down to work

2 (zeitlich: woran?): **an etw denken** to think of

15

sth

3 (*gerichtet an*) to; **ein Gruß/eine Frage an dich** greetings/a question to you

▷ *adv* **1** (*ungefähr*) about; **an die Hundert** about a hundred; **an die 10 Euro** around 10 euros **2** (*auf Fahrplänen*): **Frankfurt an 18.30** arriving Frankfurt 18.30

3 (*ab*): **von dort/heute an** from there/today onwards

4 (*angeschaltet, angezogen*) on; **an sein** (*umg*) to be on; **das Licht ist an** the light is on; **ohne etwas an** with nothing on; *siehe auch* **am**

analog [ana'lo:k] *adj* analogous

Analogie [analo'gi:] *f* analogy

Analogrechner [ana'lo:krɛçnər] *m* analog computer

Analphabet, in [an|alfa'be:t(ɪn)] (**-en, -en**) *m(f)* illiterate (person)

Analyse [ana'ly:zə] (**-, -n**) *f* analysis

analysieren [analy'zi:rən] *vt* to analyse (*Brit*), analyze (US), analyze US

Anämie [anɛ'mi:] (**-, -n**) *f* anaemia (*Brit*), anemia (US)

Ananas ['ananas] (**-, -** *od* **-se**) *f* pineapple

Anarchie [anar'çi:] *f* anarchy

anarchisch [a'narçɪʃ] *adj* anarchic

Anarchist, in [anar'çɪst(ɪn)] *m(f)* (**-en, -en**) anarchist

Anästhesist, in [an|ɛste'zɪst(ɪn)] (**-en, -en**) *m(f)* anaesthetist (*Brit*), anesthesiologist (US)

Anatomie [anato'mi:] *f* anatomy

anbahnen ['anba:nən] *vr* to open up; (*sich andeuten*) to be in the offing; (*Unangenehmes*) to be looming ▷ *vt* to initiate

Anbahnung *f* initiation

anbändeln ['anbɛndəln] (*umg*) *vi* to flirt

Anbau ['anbaʊ] *m* (*Agr*) cultivation; (*Gebäude*) extension

anbauen *vt* (*Agr*) to cultivate; (*Gebäudeteil*) to build on

Anbaugebiet *nt*: **ein gutes ~ für etw** a good area for growing sth

Anbaumöbel *pl* unit furniture *sing*

anbehalten ['anbəhaltən] *unreg vt* to keep on

anbei [an'baɪ] *adv* enclosed (*form*); **~ schicken wir Ihnen …** please find enclosed …

anbeißen ['anbaɪsən] *unreg vt* to bite into ▷ *vi* (*lit*) to bite; (*fig*) to swallow the bait; **zum A~ aussehen** (*umg*) to look good enough to eat

anbelangen ['anbəlaŋən] *vt* to concern; **was mich anbelangt** as far as I am concerned

anberaumen ['anbəraʊmən] *vt* (*form*) to fix, arrange

anbeten ['anbe:tən] *vt* to worship

Anbetracht ['anbətraxt] *m*: **in ~** +*gen* in view of

Anbetung *f* worship

anbiedern ['anbi:dərn] (*pej*) *vr*: **sich ~ (bei)** to curry favour (with)

anbieten ['anbi:tən] *unreg vt* to offer ▷ *vr* to volunteer; **das bietet sich als Lösung an** that would provide a solution

anbinden ['anbɪndən] *unreg vt* to tie up;

(*verbinden*) to connect

Anblick ['anblɪk] *m* sight

anblicken *vt* to look at

anbraten ['anbra:tən] *unreg vt* (*Fleisch*) to brown

anbrechen ['anbrɛçən] *unreg vt* to start; (*Vorräte*) to break into ▷ *vi* to start; (*Tag*) to break; (*Nacht*) to fall

anbrennen ['anbrɛnən] *unreg vi* to catch fire; (*Koch*) to burn

anbringen ['anbrɪŋən] *unreg vt* to bring; (*Ware*) to sell; (*festmachen*) to fasten; (*Telefon etc*) to install

Anbruch ['anbrʊx] *m* beginning; **~ des Tages** dawn; **~ der Nacht** nightfall

anbrüllen ['anbrylən] *vt* to roar at

Andacht ['andaxt] (**-, -en**) *f* devotion; (*Versenkung*) rapt interest; (*Gottesdienst*) prayers *pl*; (*Ehrfurcht*) reverence

andächtig ['andɛçtɪç] *adj* devout

andauern ['andaʊərn] *vi* to last, go on

andauernd *adj* continual

Anden ['andən] *pl*: **die ~** the Andes *pl*

Andenken ['andɛŋkən] (**-s, -**) *nt* memory; (*Reiseandenken*) souvenir; (*Erinnerungsstück*): **ein ~ (an** +*akk*) a memento (of), a keepsake (from)

andere, r, s *adj* other; (*verschieden*) different; **am ~n Tage** the next day; **ein ~s Mal** another time; **kein ~r** nobody else; **alles ~ als zufrieden** anything but pleased, far from pleased; **von etwas ~m sprechen** to talk about something else; **es blieb mir nichts ~s übrig als selbst hinzugehen** I had no alternative but to go myself; **unter ~m** among other things; **von einem Tag zum ~n** overnight; **sie hat einen ~n** she has someone else

andererseits *adv* on the other hand

andermal *adv*: **ein ~** some other time

ändern ['ɛndərn] *vt* to alter, change ▷ *vr* to change

andernfalls *adv* otherwise

andernorts ['andərn'ɔrts] *adv* elsewhere

anders *adv*: **~ (als)** differently (from); **wer ~?** who else?; **niemand ~** no-one else; **wie nicht ~ zu erwarten** as was to be expected; **wie könnte es ~ sein?** how could it be otherwise?; **ich kann nicht ~** (*kann es nicht lassen*) I can't help it; (*muss leider*) I have no choice; **~ ausgedrückt** to put it another way; **jemand/ irgendwo ~** somebody/somewhere else; **~ aussehen/klingen** to look/sound different; **~ lautend = anderslautend**

andersartig *adj* different

Andersdenkende, r *f(m)* dissident, dissenter

anderseits ['andər'zaɪts] *adv* = **andererseits**

anders- *zW*: **andersfarbig** *adj* of a different colour; **andersgläubig** *adj* of a different faith; **andersherum** *adv* the other way round; **anderslautend** *adj*: **anderslautende Berichte** reports to the contrary; **anderswo** *adv* elsewhere; **anderswoher** *adv* from elsewhere; **anderswohin** *adv* elsewhere

anderthalb ['andərt'halp] *adj* one and a half

Änderung ['ɛndərʊŋ] f alteration, change

Änderungsantrag ['ɛndərʊŋs|antra:k] m (Parl) amendment

anderweitig ['andər'vaɪtɪç] adj other ▷ adv otherwise; (anderswo) elsewhere

andeuten ['andɔytən] vt to indicate; (Wink geben) to hint at

Andeutung f indication; hint

andeutungsweise adv (als Anspielung, Anzeichen) by way of a hint; (als flüchtiger Hinweis) in passing

andichten ['andɪçtən] vt: **jdm etw ~** (umg: Fähigkeiten) to credit sb with sth

Andorra [an'dɔra] (**-s**) nt Andorra

Andorraner, in [andɔ'ra:nər(ɪn)] m(f) Andorran

Andrang ['andraŋ] m crush

andrehen ['andre:ən] vt to turn od switch on; **jdm etw ~** (umg) to unload sth onto sb

androhen ['andro:ən] vt: **jdm etw ~ to** threaten sb with sth

Androhung f: **unter ~ von Gewalt** with the threat of violence

anecken ['an|ɛkən] (umg) vi: **(bei jdm/allen) ~** to rub (sb/everyone) up the wrong way

aneignen ['an|aignən] vt: **sich** dat **etw ~ to** acquire sth; (widerrechtlich) to appropriate sth; (sich mit etw vertraut machen) to learn sth

aneinander [an|aɪ'nandər] adv at/on/to etc one another od each other; **aneinanderfügen** vt to put together; **aneinandergeraten** vi to clash; **aneinanderlegen** vt to put together

anekeln ['an|e:kəln] vt to disgust

Anemone [ane'mo:nə] (**-, -n**) f anemone

anerkannt ['an|ɛrkant] adj recognized, acknowledged

anerkennen ['an|ɛrkɛnən] unreg vt to recognize, acknowledge; (würdigen) to appreciate; **das muss man ~** (zugeben) you can't argue with that; (würdigen) one has to appreciate that

anerkennend adj appreciative

anerkennenswert adj praiseworthy

Anerkennung f recognition, acknowledgement; appreciation

anerzogen ['an|ɛrtso:gən] adj acquired

anfachen ['anfaxən] vt (lit) to fan into flame; (fig) to kindle

anfahren ['anfa:rən] unreg vt to deliver; (fahren gegen) to hit; (Hafen) to put into; (umg) to bawl at ▷ vi to drive up; (losfahren) to drive off

Anfahrt ['anfa:rt] f (Anfahrtsweg, Anfahrtszeit) journey; (Zufahrt) approach

Anfall ['anfal] m (Med) attack; **in einem ~ von** (fig) in a fit of

anfallen unreg vt to attack ▷ vi (Arbeit) to come up; (Produkt, Nebenprodukte) to be obtained; (Zinsen) to accrue; (sich anhäufen) to accumulate; **die ~den Kosten/Reparaturen** the costs/repairs incurred

anfällig ['anfɛlɪç] adj delicate; **~ für etw** prone to sth

Anfang ['anfaŋ] (**-(e)s, -fänge**) m beginning, start; **von ~ an** right from the beginning; **zu ~ at** the beginning; **~ fünfzig** in one's early fifties; **~ Mai/1994** at the beginning of May/1994

anfangen ['anfaŋən] unreg vt to begin, start; (machen) to do ▷ vi to begin, start; **damit kann ich nichts ~** (nützt mir nichts) that's no good to me; (verstehe ich nicht) it doesn't mean a thing to me; **mit dir ist heute (aber) gar nichts anzufangen!** you're no fun at all today!; **bei einer Firma ~ to** start working for a firm

Anfänger, in ['anfɛŋər(ɪn)] (**-s, -**) m(f) beginner

anfänglich ['anfɛŋlɪç] adj initial

anfangs adv at first; **wie ich schon ~ erwähnte** as I mentioned at the beginning; **Anfangsbuchstabe** m initial od first letter; **Anfangsgehalt** nt starting salary; **Anfangsstadium** nt initial stages pl

anfassen ['anfasən] vt to handle; (berühren) to touch ▷ vi to lend a hand ▷ vr to feel

anfechtbar ['anfɛçtba:r] adj contestable

anfechten ['anfɛçtən] unreg vt to dispute; (Meinung, Aussage) to challenge; (Urteil) to appeal against; (beunruhigen) to trouble

anfeinden ['anfaɪndən] vt to treat with hostility

anfertigen ['anfɛrtɪgən] vt to make

anfeuchten ['anfɔyçtən] vt to moisten

anfeuern ['anfɔyərn] vt (fig) to spur on

anflehen ['anfle:ən] vt to implore

anfliegen ['anfli:gən] unreg vt to fly to ▷ vi to fly up

Anflug ['anflu:k] m (Aviat) approach; (Spur) trace

anfordern ['anfɔrdərn] vt to demand; (Comm) to requisition

Anforderung f (+gen) demand (for); (Comm) requisition

Anfrage ['anfra:gə] f inquiry; (Parl) question

anfragen ['anfra:gən] vi to inquire

anfreunden ['anfrɔyndən] vr to make friends; **sich mit etw ~** (fig) to get to like sth

anfügen ['anfy:gən] vt to add; (beifügen) to enclose

anfühlen ['anfy:lən] vt, vr to feel

anführen ['anfy:rən] vt to lead; (zitieren) to quote; (umg: betrügen) to lead up the garden path

Anführer, in (**-s, -**) m(f) leader

Anführung f leadership; (Zitat) quotation

Anführungszeichen pl quotation marks pl, inverted commas pl (Brit)

Angabe ['anga:bə] f statement; (Tech) specification; (umg: Prahlerei) boasting; (Sport) service; **Angaben** pl (Auskunft) particulars pl; **ohne ~ von Gründen** without giving any reasons; **~n zur Person** (form) personal details od particulars

angeben ['ange:bən] unreg vt to give; (anzeigen) to inform on; (bestimmen) to set ▷ vi (umg) to boast; (Sport) to serve

Angeber, in (**-s, -**) (umg) m(f) show-off

Angeberei [ange:bə'raɪ] (umg) f showing off

angeblich ['angəːplıç] *adj* alleged

angeboren ['angəboːrən] *adj* (+dat) inborn, innate (in); (*Med, fig*): ~ **(bei)** congenital (to)

Angebot ['angəboːt] *nt* offer; (*Comm*): ~ **(an** +dat) supply (of); **im** ~ (*umg*) on special offer

angeboten ['angəboːtən] *pp von* **anbieten**

Angebotspreis *m* offer price

angebracht ['angəbraxt] *adj* appropriate

angebrannt ['angəbrant] *adv*: **es riecht hier so** ~ there's a smell of burning here

angebrochen ['angəbrɔxən] *adj* (*Packung, Flasche*) open(ed); **was machen wir mit dem ~en Abend?** (*umg*) what shall we do with the rest of the evening?

angebunden ['angəbundən] *adj*: **kurz** ~ **sein** (*umg*) to be abrupt od curt

angefangen *pp von* **anfangen**

angegeben *pp von* **angeben**

angegossen ['angəgɔsən] *adj*: **wie** ~ **sitzen** to fit like a glove

angegriffen ['angəgrıfən] *adj*: **er wirkt** ~ he looks as if he's under a lot of strain

angehalten ['angəhaltən] *pp von* **anhalten** ▷ *adj*: ~ **sein, etw zu tun** to be required od obliged to do sth

angehaucht ['angəhauxt] *adj*: **links/rechts** ~ **sein** to have left-/right-wing tendencies od leanings

angeheiratet ['angəhairatət] *adj* related by marriage

angeheitert ['angəhaitərt] *adj* tipsy

angehen ['angeːən] *unreg vt* to concern; (*angreifen*) to attack; (*bitten*): **jdn** ~ **(um)** to approach sb (for) ▷ *vi* (*Feuer*) to light; (*umg: beginnen*) to begin; **das geht ihn gar nichts an** that's none of his business; **gegen jdn** ~ (*entgegentreten*) to fight sb; **gegen etw** ~ (*entgegentreten*) to fight sth; (*Missstände, Zustände*) to take measures against sth

angehend *adj* prospective; (*Musiker, Künstler*) budding

angehören ['angəhøːrən] *vi* +dat to belong to

Angehörige, r *f(m)* relative

Angeklagte, r ['angəklaːktə(r)] *f(m)* accused, defendant

angeknackst ['angəknakst] (*umg*) *adj* (*Mensch*) uptight; (: *Selbstbewusstsein*) weakened

angekommen ['angəkɔmən] *pp von* **ankommen**

Angel ['angəl] (-, **-n**) *f* fishing rod; (*Türangel*) hinge; **die Welt aus den ~n heben** (*fig*) to turn the world upside down

Angelegenheit ['angəleːgənhait] *f* affair, matter

angelernt ['angəlɛrnt] *adj* (*Arbeiter*) semi-skilled

Angelhaken *m* fish hook

angeln ['angəln] *vt* to catch ▷ *vi* to fish; **Angeln** (**-s**) *nt* angling, fishing

Angelpunkt *m* crucial od central point; (*Frage*) key od central issue

Angelrute *f* fishing rod

Angelsachse ['angəlzaksə] (**-n, -n**) *m* Anglo-Saxon

Angelsächsin ['angəlzɛksın] *f* Anglo-Saxon

angelsächsisch ['angəlzɛksıʃ] *adj* Anglo-Saxon

Angelschein *m* fishing permit

angemessen ['angəmɛsən] *adj* appropriate, suitable; **eine der Leistung ~e Bezahlung** payment commensurate with the input

angenehm ['angəneːm] *adj* pleasant; ~! (*bei Vorstellung*) pleased to meet you; **das A~e mit dem Nützlichen verbinden** to combine business with pleasure

angenommen ['angənɔmən] *pp von* **annehmen** ▷ *adj* assumed; (*Kind*) adopted; ~, **wir ...** assuming we ...

angepasst ['angəpast] *adj* conformist

angerufen ['angəruːfən] *pp von* **anrufen**

angesäuselt ['angəzɔyzəlt] *adj* tipsy, merry

angeschlagen ['angəʃlaːgən] (*umg*) *adj* (*Mensch, Aussehen, Nerven*) shattered; (*Gesundheit*) poor

angeschlossen ['angəʃlɔsən] *adj* (+dat) affiliated (to od with), associated (with)

angeschmiert ['angəʃmiːrt] (*umg*) *adj* in trouble; **der/die A~e sein** to have been had

angeschrieben ['angəʃriːbən] (*umg*) *adj*: **bei jdm gut/schlecht** ~ **sein** to be in sb's good/bad books

angesehen ['angəzeːən] *pp von* **ansehen** ▷ *adj* respected

Angesicht ['angəzıçt] *nt* (*geh*) face

angesichts ['angəzıçts] *präp* +gen in view of, considering

angespannt ['angəʃpant] *adj* (*Aufmerksamkeit*) close; (*Nerven, Lage*) tense, strained; (*Comm: Markt*) tight, overstretched; (*Arbeit*) hard

Angest. *abk* = **Angestellte(r)**

angestammt ['angəʃtamt] *adj* (*überkommen*) traditional; (*ererbt: Rechte*) hereditary; (: *Besitz*) inherited

Angestellte, r ['angəʃtɛltə(r)] *f(m)* employee; (*Büroangestellte*) white-collar worker

angestrengt ['angəʃtrɛŋt] *adv* as hard as one can

angetan ['angətaːn] *adj*: **von jdm/etw** ~ **sein** to be taken with sb/sth; **es jdm** ~ **haben** to appeal to sb

angetrunken ['angətruŋkən] *adj* inebriated

angewiesen ['angəviːzən] *adj*: **auf jdn/etw** ~ **sein** to be dependent on sb/sth; **auf sich selbst** ~ **sein** to be left to one's own devices

angewöhnen ['angəvøːnən] *vt*: **jdm/sich etw** ~ to accustom sb/become accustomed to sth

Angewohnheit ['angəvoːnhait] *f* habit

angewurzelt ['angəvurtsəlt] *adj*: **wie** ~ **dastehen** to be rooted to the spot

angiften ['angıftən] (*pej: umg*) *vt* to snap at

angleichen ['anglaiçən] *unreg vt, vr* to adjust

Angler ['anglər] (**-s, -**) *m* angler

angliedern ['angliːdərn] *vt*: ~ **(an** +akk) (*Verein, Partei*) to affiliate (to od with); (*Land*) to annex (to)

Anglist, in [an'glıst(ın)] (**-en, -en**) *m(f)* English specialist; (*Student*) English student; (*Professor* *etc*) English lecturer/professor

Angola [aŋ'go:la] (**-s**) *nt* Angola

angreifen ['angraɪfən] *unreg vt* to attack; (*anfassen*) to touch; (*Arbeit*) to tackle; (*beschädigen*) to damage

Angreifer, in (**-s, -**) *m(f)* attacker

angrenzen ['angrɛntsən] *vi*: **an etw** *akk* ~ to border on sth, adjoin sth

Angriff ['angrɪf] *m* attack; **etw in ~ nehmen** to make a start on sth

Angriffsfläche *f*: **jdm/etw eine ~ bieten** (*lit, fig*) to provide sb/sth with a target

angriffslustig *adj* aggressive

Angst [aŋst] (**-, ̈e**) *f* fear; **~ haben (vor** +*dat*) to be afraid *od* scared (of); **~ um jdn/etw haben** to be worried about sb/sth; **jdm ~ einflößen** *od* **einjagen** to frighten sb; **jdm ~ machen** to scare sb; **nur keine ~!** don't be scared;

angst *adj*: **jdm ist angst** sb is afraid *od* scared;

angstfrei *adj* free of fear; **Angsthase** (*umg*) *m* chicken, scaredy-cat

ängstigen ['ɛŋstɪgən] *vt* to frighten ▷ *vr*: **sich ~ (vor** +*dat od* **um)** to worry (o.s.) (about)

ängstlich *adj* nervous; (*besorgt*) worried; (*schüchtern*) timid; **Ängstlichkeit** *f* nervousness

Angstschweiß *m*: **mir brach der ~ aus** I broke out in a cold sweat

angurten ['angʊrtən] *vt, vr* = **anschnallen**

Anh. *abk* (= *Anhang*) app.

anhaben ['anha:bən] *unreg vt* to have on; **er kann mir nichts ~** he can't hurt me

anhaften ['anhaftən] *vi* (*lit*): **~ (an** +*dat*) to stick (to); (*fig*): **~** +*dat* to stick to, stay with

anhalten ['anhaltən] *unreg vt* to stop ▷ *vi* to stop; (*andauern*) to persist; (*werben*): **um die Hand eines Mädchens ~** to ask for a girl's hand in marriage; (**jdm**) **etw ~** to hold sth up (against sb); **jdn zur Arbeit/Höflichkeit ~** to get sb to work/teach sb to be polite

anhaltend *adj* persistent

Anhalter, in (**-s, -**) *m(f)* hitch-hiker; **per ~ fahren** to hitch-hike

Anhaltspunkt *m* clue

anhand [an'hant] *präp* +*gen* with; **~ eines Beispiels** by means of an example

Anhang ['anhaŋ] *m* appendix; (*Comput*) attachment; (*Leute*) family; (*Anhängerschaft*) supporters *pl*

anhängen ['anhɛŋən] *unreg vt* to hang up; (*Wagen*) to couple up; (*Zusatz*) to add (on); (*Comput*) to append; **sich an jdn ~** to attach o.s. to sb; **eine Datei an eine E-Mail ~** (*Comput*) to attach a file to an email; **jdm etw ~** (*umg: nachsagen, anlasten*) to blame sb for sth, blame sth on sb; (: *Verdacht, Schuld*) to pin sth on sb

Anhänger (**-s, -**) *m* supporter; (*Aut*) trailer; (*am Koffer*) tag; (*Schmuck*) pendant; **Anhängerschaft** *f* supporters *pl*

Anhängeschloss *nt* padlock

anhängig *adj* (*Jur*) sub judice; **etw ~ machen** to start legal proceedings over sth

anhänglich *adj* devoted; **Anhänglichkeit** *f* devotion

Anhängsel (**-s, -**) *nt* appendage

anhauen ['anhaʊən] (*umg*) *vt* (*ansprechen*): **jdn ~ (um)** to accost sb (for)

anhäufen ['anhɔyfən] *vt* to accumulate, amass ▷ *vr* to accrue

Anhäufung ['anhɔyfʊŋ] *f* accumulation

anheben ['anhe:bən] *unreg vt* to lift up; (*Preise*) to raise

anheimelnd ['anhaɪməlnt] *adj* comfortable, cosy

anheimstellen [an'haɪmʃtɛlən] *vt*: **jdm etw ~** to leave sth up to sb

anheizen ['anhaɪtsən] *vt* (*Ofen*) to light; (*fig: umg: Wirtschaft*) to stimulate; (*verschlimmern: Krise*) to aggravate

anheuern ['anhɔyərn] *vt, vi* (*Naut, fig*) to sign on *od* up

Anhieb ['anhi:b] *m*: **auf ~** straight off, first go; **es klappte auf ~** it was an immediate success

anhimmeln ['anhɪməln] (*umg*) *vt* to idolize

Anhöhe ['anhø:ə] *f* hill

anhören ['anhø:rən] *vt* to listen to; (*anmerken*) to hear ▷ *vr* to sound

Anhörung *f* hearing

Animierdame [ani'mi:rdamə] *f* nightclub/bar hostess

animieren [ani'mi:rən] *vt* to encourage, urge on

Anis [a'ni:s] (**-es, -e**) *m* aniseed

Ank. *abk* (= *Ankunft*) arr.

ankämpfen ['ankɛmpfən] *vi*: **gegen etw ~** to fight (against) sth; (*gegen Wind, Strömung*) to battle against sth

Ankara ['aŋkara] (**-s**) *nt* Ankara

Ankauf ['ankaʊf] *m*: **~ und Verkauf von ...** we buy and sell ...; **ankaufen** *vt* to purchase, buy

Anker ['aŋkər] (**-s, -**) *m* anchor; **vor ~ gehen** to drop anchor

ankern *vt, vi* to anchor

Ankerplatz *m* anchorage

Anklage ['ankla:gə] *f* accusation; (*Jur*) charge; **gegen jdn ~ erheben** (*Jur*) to bring *od* prefer charges against sb; **Anklagebank** *f* dock

anklagen ['ankla:gən] *vt* to accuse; **jdn (eines Verbrechens) ~** (*Jur*) to charge sb (with a crime)

Anklagepunkt *m* charge

Ankläger, in ['anklɛ:gər(ɪn)] (**-s, -**) *m(f)* accuser

Anklageschrift *f* indictment

anklammern ['anklamərn] *vt* to clip, staple ▷ *vr*: **sich an etw** *akk od dat* **~** to cling to sth

Anklang ['anklaŋ] *m*: **bei jdm ~ finden** to meet with sb's approval

ankleben ['ankle:bən] *vt*: „**Plakate ~ verboten!**" "stick no bills"

Ankleidekabine *f* changing cubicle

ankleiden ['anklaɪdən] *vt, vr* to dress

anklingen ['anklɪŋən] *vi* (*angeschnitten werden*) to be touched (up)on; (*erinnern*): **~ an** +*akk* to be reminiscent of

anklopfen ['anklɔpfən] *vi* to knock

anknipsen ['anknɪpsən] *vt* to switch on; (*Schalter*) to flick

19

anknüpfen ['anknʏpfən] vt to fasten od tie on; (Beziehungen) to establish; (Gespräch) to start up ▷ vi (anschließen): ~ **an** +akk to refer to

Anknüpfungspunkt m link

ankommen ['ankɔmən] unreg vi to arrive; (näher kommen) to approach; (Anklang finden): **bei jdm (gut)** ~ to go down well with sb ▷ vi unpers: **er ließ es auf einen Streit/einen Versuch** ~ he was prepared to argue about it/to give it a try; **es kommt darauf an** it depends; (wichtig sein) that is what matters; **es kommt auf ihn an** it depends on him; **es darauf** ~ **lassen** to let things take their course; **gegen jdn/etw** ~ to cope with sb/sth; **damit kommst du bei ihm nicht an!** you won't get anywhere with him like that

ankreiden ['ankraɪdən] vt (fig): **jdm etw (dick od übel)** ~ to hold sth against sb

ankreuzen ['ankrɔʏtsən] vt to mark with a cross

ankündigen ['ankʏndɪgən] vt to announce

Ankündigung f announcement

Ankunft ['ankʊnft] (-, **-künfte**) f arrival

Ankunftszeit f time of arrival

ankurbeln ['ankʊrbəln] vt (Aut) to crank; (fig) to boost

Anl. abk (= Anlage) enc(l).

anlachen ['anlaxən] vt to smile at; **sich** dat **jdn** ~ (umg) to pick sb up

Anlage ['anla:gə] f disposition; (Begabung) talent; (Park) gardens pl; (Beilage) enclosure; (Tech) plant; (Einrichtung: Mil, Elek) installation(s pl); (Sportanlage etc) facilities pl; (umg: Stereoanlage) (stereo) system; (Fin) investment; (Entwurf) layout; **als** ~ od **in der** ~ **erhalten Sie** ... please find enclosed ...;

Anlageberater, in m(f) investment consultant; **Anlagekapital** nt fixed capital

Anlagenabschreibung f capital allowance

Anlagengeschäft nt investment deal; (Branche) investment banking

Anlagevermögen nt capital assets pl, fixed assets pl

anlangen ['anlaŋən] vi (ankommen) to arrive

Anlass ['anlas] (-es, **-lässe**) m: ~ **(zu)** cause (for); (Ereignis) occasion; **aus** ~ +gen on the occasion of; **zu etw geben** to give rise to sth; **beim geringsten/bei jedem** ~ for the slightest reason/at every opportunity; **etw zum** ~ **nehmen** to take the opportunity of sth

anlassen unreg vt to leave on; (Motor) to start ▷ vr (umg) to start off

Anlasser (-s, -) m (Aut) starter

anlässlich ['anlɛslɪç] präp +gen on the occasion of

anlasten ['anlastən] vt: **jdm etw** ~ to blame sb for sth

Anlauf ['anlaʊf] m run-up; (fig: Versuch) attempt, try

anlaufen unreg vi to begin; (Film) to be showing; (Sport) to run up; (Fenster) to mist up; (Metall) to tarnish ▷ vt to call at; **rot** ~ to turn od go red; **gegen etw** ~ to run into od up against sth;

angelaufen kommen to come running up

Anlauf- zW: **Anlaufstelle** f place to go (with one's problems); **Anlaufzeit** f (fig) time to get going od started

anläuten ['anlɔʏtən] vi to ring

anlegen ['anle:gən] vt to put; (anziehen) to put on; (gestalten) to lay out; (Kartei, Akte) to start; (Comput: Datei) to create; (Geld) to invest ▷ vi to dock; (Naut) to berth; **etw an etw** akk ~ to put sth against od on sth; **ein Gewehr** ~ **(auf** +akk) to aim a weapon (at); **es auf etw** akk ~ to be out for sth/to do sth; **strengere Maßstäbe** ~ **(bei)** to lay down od impose stricter standards (in); **sich mit jdm** ~ (umg) to quarrel with sb

Anlegeplatz m landing place

Anleger, in (-s, -) m(f) (Fin) investor

Anlegestelle f landing place

anlehnen ['anle:nən] vt to lean; (Tür) to leave ajar; **(sich) an etw** akk ~ to lean on od against sth

Anlehnung f (Imitation): **in** ~ **an jdn/etw** following sb/sth

Anlehnungsbedürfnis nt need of loving care

anleiern ['anlaɪərn] vt (umg) vt to get going

Anleihe ['anlaɪə] (-, **-n**) f (Fin) loan; (Wertpapier) bond

anleiten ['anlaɪtən] vt to instruct

Anleitung f instructions pl

anlernen ['anlɛrnən] vt to teach, instruct

anlesen ['anle:zən] unreg vt (aneignen): **sich** dat **etw** ~ to learn sth by reading

Anliegen ['anli:gən] (-s, -) nt matter; (Wunsch) wish

anliegen unreg vi (Kleidung) to cling

anliegend adj adjacent; (beigefügt) enclosed

Anlieger (-s, -) m resident; ~ **frei** no thoroughfare – residents only

anlocken ['anlɔkən] vt to attract; (Tiere) to lure

anlügen ['anly:gən] unreg vt to lie to

Anm. abk (= Anmerkung) n.

anmachen ['anmaxən] vt to attach; (Elektrisches) to put on; (Salat) to dress; **jdn** ~ (umg) to try and pick sb up

anmalen ['anma:lən] vt to paint ▷ vr (pej: schminken) to paint one's face od o.s.

Anmarsch ['anmarʃ] m: **im** ~ **sein** to be advancing; (hum) to be on the way; **im** ~ **sein auf** +akk to be advancing on

anmaßen ['anma:sən] vt: **sich** dat **etw** ~ to lay claim to sth

anmaßend adj arrogant

Anmaßung f presumption

Anmeldeformular ['anmɛldəfɔrmʊla:r] nt registration form

anmelden vt to announce; (geltend machen: Recht, Ansprüche, zu Steuerzwecken) to declare; (Comput) to log on ▷ vr (sich ankündigen) to make an appointment; (polizeilich, für Kurs etc) to register; **ein Gespräch nach Deutschland** ~ (Tel) to book a call to Germany

Anmeldung f announcement; appointment; registration; **nur nach vorheriger** ~ by appointment only

anmerken ['anmɛrkən] vt to observe; (anstreichen) to mark; **jdm seine Verlegenheit** etc ~ to notice sb's embarrassment etc; **sich** dat **nichts ~ lassen** not to give anything away

Anmerkung f note

Anmut ['anmuːt] (-) f grace

anmuten vt (geh): **jdn ~** to appear od seem to sb

anmutig adj charming

annähen ['anːɛːən] vt to sew on

annähern ['anːɛːərn] vr to get closer

annähernd adj approximate; **nicht ~ so viel** not nearly as much

Annäherung f approach

Annäherungsversuch (-, -en) m advances pl

Annahme ['anːaːmə] (-, -n) f acceptance; (Vermutung) assumption; **Annahmestelle** f counter; (für Reparaturen) reception; **Annahmeverweigerung** f refusal

annehmbar ['anːeːmbaːr] adj acceptable

annehmen unreg vt to accept; (Namen) to take; (Kind) to adopt; (vermuten) to suppose, assume ▷ vr (+gen) to take care (of); **jdn an Kindes statt ~** to adopt sb; **angenommen, das ist so** assuming that is so

Annehmlichkeit f comfort

annektieren [anɛkˈtiːrən] vt to annex

anno ['ano] adj: **von ~ dazumal** (umg) from the year dot

Annonce [aˈnõːsə] (-, -n) f advertisement

annoncieren [anõˈsiːrən] vt, vi to advertise

annullieren [anʊˈliːrən] vt to annul

Anode [aˈnoːdə] (-, -n) f anode

anöden ['an|øːdən] (umg) vt to bore stiff

anomal [anoˈmaːl] adj (regelwidrig) unusual, abnormal; (nicht normal) strange, odd

anonym [anoˈnyːm] adj anonymous

Anorak ['anorak] (-s, -s) m anorak

anordnen ['an|ɔrdnən] vt to arrange; (befehlen) to order

Anordnung f arrangement; order; **~en treffen** to give orders

anorganisch ['an|ɔrganɪʃ] adj (Chem) inorganic

anpacken ['anpakən] vt to grasp; (fig) to tackle; **mit ~** to lend a hand

anpassen ['anpasən] vt (Kleidung) to fit; (fig) to adapt ▷ vr to adapt

Anpassung f fitting; adaptation

Anpassungsdruck m pressure to conform (to society)

anpassungsfähig adj adaptable

anpeilen ['anpaɪlən] vt (mit Radar, Funk etc) to take a bearing on; **etw ~** (fig: umg) to have one's sights on sth

Anpfiff ['anpfɪf] m (Sport) (starting) whistle; (Spielbeginn: Fußball etc) kick-off; **einen ~ bekommen** (umg) to get a rocket (Brit)

anpöbeln ['anpøːbəln] vt to abuse; (umg) to pester

Anprall ['anpral] m: **~ gegen** od **an** +akk impact on od against

anprangern ['anpraŋərn] vt to denounce

anpreisen ['anpraɪzən] unreg vt to extol; **sich ~ (als)** to sell o.s. (as); **etw ~** to extol (the virtues

of) sth; **seine Waren ~** to cry one's wares

Anprobe ['anproːbə] f trying on

anprobieren ['anprobiːrən] vt to try on

anpumpen ['anpʊmpən] (umg) vt to borrow from

anquatschen ['ankvatʃən] (umg) vt to speak to; (: Mädchen) to try to pick up

Anrainer ['anraɪnər] (-s, -) m neighbour (Brit), neighbor (US)

anranzen ['anrantsən] (umg) vt: **jdn ~** to tick sb off

anraten ['anraːtən] unreg vt to recommend; **auf A~ des Arztes** etc on the doctor's etc advice od recommendation

anrechnen ['anrɛçnən] vt to charge; (fig) to count; **jdm etw hoch ~** to think highly of sb for sth

Anrecht ['anrɛçt] nt: **~ auf** +akk right (to); **ein ~ auf etw haben** to be entitled to sth, have a right to sth

Anrede ['anreːdə] f form of address

anreden vt to address

anregen ['anreːgən] vt to stimulate; **angeregte Unterhaltung** lively discussion

anregend adj stimulating

Anregung f stimulation; (Vorschlag) suggestion

anreichern ['anraɪçərn] vt to enrich

Anreise ['anraɪzə] f journey there/here

anreisen vi to arrive

anreißen ['anraɪsən] unreg vt (kurz zur Sprache bringen) to touch on

Anreiz ['anraɪts] m incentive

anrempeln ['anrɛmpəln] vt (anstoßen) to bump into; (absichtlich) to jostle

anrennen ['anrɛnən] unreg vi: **gegen etw ~** (gegen Wind etc) to run against sth; (Mil) to storm sth

Anrichte ['anrɪçtə] (-, -n) f sideboard

anrichten vt to serve up; **Unheil ~** to make mischief; **da hast du aber etwas angerichtet!** (umg: verursacht) you've started something there all right!; (: angestellt) you've really made a mess there!

anrüchig ['anrʏçɪç] adj dubious

anrücken ['anrʏkən] vi to approach; (Mil) to advance

Anruf ['anruːf] m call; **Anrufbeantworter** m (telephone) answering machine, answerphone

anrufen unreg vt to call out to; (bitten) to call on; (Tel) to ring up, phone, call

anrühren ['anryːrən] vt to touch; (mischen) to mix

ans [ans] = **an das**

Ansage ['anzaːgə] f announcement

ansagen vt to announce ▷ vr to say one will come

Ansager, in (-s, -) m(f) announcer

ansammeln ['anzaməln] vt to collect ▷ vr to accumulate; (fig: Wut, Druck) to build up

Ansammlung f collection; (Leute) crowd

ansässig ['anzɛsɪç] adj resident

Ansatz ['anzats] m start; (Haaransatz) hairline; (Halsansatz) base; (Verlängerungsstück) extension; (Veranschlagung) estimate; **die ersten Ansätze zu etw** the beginnings of sth; **Ansatzpunkt** m starting point; **Ansatzstück** nt (Tech) attachment

anschaffen ['anʃafən] vt to buy, purchase ▷ vi: **~ gehen** (umg: durch Prostitution) to be on the game; **sich** dat **Kinder ~** (umg) to have children

Anschaffung f purchase

anschalten ['anʃaltən] vt to switch on

anschauen ['anʃauən] vt to look at

anschaulich adj illustrative

Anschauung f (Meinung) view; **aus eigener ~** from one's own experience

Anschauungsmaterial nt illustrative material

Anschein ['anʃain] m appearance; **allem ~ nach** to all appearances; **den ~ haben** to seem, appear

anscheinend adj apparent

anschieben ['anʃi:bən] unreg vt (Fahrzeug) to push

Anschiss ['anʃis] (umg) m: **einen ~ bekommen** to get a telling-off od ticking-off (bes Brit)

Anschlag ['anʃla:k] m notice; (Attentat) attack; (Comm) estimate; (auf Klavier) touch; (auf Schreibmaschine) keystroke; **einem ~ zum Opfer fallen** to be assassinated; **ein Gewehr im ~ haben** (Mil) to have a rifle at the ready; **Anschlagbrett** nt notice board (Brit), bulletin board (US)

anschlagen ['anʃla:gən] unreg vt to put up; (beschädigen) to chip; (Akkord) to strike; (Kosten) to estimate ▷ vi to hit; (wirken) to have an effect; (Glocke) to ring; (Hund) to bark; **einen anderen Ton ~** (fig) to change one's tune; **an etw** akk **~** to hit against sth

anschlagfrei adj: **~er Drucker** non-impact printer

Anschlagzettel m notice

anschleppen ['anʃlɛpən] (umg) vt (unerwünscht mitbringen) to bring along

anschließen ['anʃli:sən] unreg vt to connect up; (Sender) to link up; (in Steckdose) to plug in; (fig: hinzufügen) to add ▷ vi: **an etw** akk **~** (zeitlich) to follow sth ▷ vr: **sich jdm/etw ~** to join sb/sth; (beipflichten) to agree with sb/sth; **sich an etw** akk **~** (angrenzen) to adjoin sth

anschließend adj adjacent; (zeitlich) subsequent ▷ adv afterwards; **~ an** +akk following

Anschluss ['anʃlus] m (Elek, Eisenb, Tel) connection; (weiterer Apparat) extension; (von Wasser etc) supply; (Comput) port; **im ~ an** +akk following; **~ finden** to make friends; **~ bekommen** to get through; **kein ~ unter dieser Nummer** number unobtainable; **den ~ verpassen** (Eisenb etc) to miss one's connection; (fig) to miss the boat

anschmiegen ['anʃmi:gən] vr: **sich an jdn/etw ~** (Kind, Hund) to snuggle od nestle up to od against sb/sth

anschmiegsam ['anʃmi:kza:m] adj affectionate

anschmieren ['anʃmi:rən] vt to smear; (umg) to take in

anschnallen ['anʃnalən] vt to buckle on ▷ vr to fasten one's seat belt

Anschnallpflicht f: **für Kinder besteht ~** children must wear seat belts

anschnauzen ['anʃnautsən] (umg) vt to yell at

anschneiden ['anʃnaidən] unreg vt to cut into; (Thema) to introduce

Anschnitt ['anʃnit] m first slice

anschreiben ['anʃraibən] unreg vt to write (up); (Comm) to charge up; (benachrichtigen) to write to; **bei jdm gut/schlecht angeschrieben sein** to be well/badly thought of by sb, be in sb's good/bad books

anschreien ['anʃraiən] unreg vt to shout at

Anschrift ['anʃrift] f address

Anschriftenliste f mailing list

Anschub m (bei Firmengründung) start-up (funds pl)

Anschuldigung ['anʃuldigʊŋ] f accusation

anschwärzen ['anʃvɛrtsən] vt (fig: umg): **jdn ~ (bei)** to blacken sb's name (with)

anschwellen ['anʃvelən] unreg vi to swell (up)

anschwemmen ['anʃvemən] vt to wash ashore

anschwindeln ['anʃvindəln] (umg) vt to lie to

ansehen ['anze:ən] unreg vt to look at; **jdm etw ~** to see sth (from sb's face); **jdn/etw als etw ~** to look on sb/sth as sth; **~ für** to consider; **(sich** dat**) etw ~** to (have a) look at sth; (Fernsehsendung) to watch sth; (Film, Stück, Sportveranstaltung) to see sth; **etw (mit) ~** to watch sth, see sth happening

Ansehen (-s) nt respect; (Ruf) reputation; **ohne ~ der Person** (Jur) without respect of person

ansehnlich ['anze:nliç] adj fine-looking; (beträchtlich) considerable

anseilen ['anzailən] vt: **jdn/sich ~** to rope sb/o.s. up

an sein ['anzain] siehe **an**

ansetzen ['anzɛtsən] vt (festlegen) to fix; (entwickeln) to develop; (Fett) to put on; (Blätter) to grow; (zubereiten) to prepare ▷ vi (anfangen) to start, begin; (Entwicklung) to set in; (dick werden) to put on weight ▷ vr (Rost etc) to start to develop; **~ an** +akk (anfügen) to fit on to; (anlegen, an Mund etc) to put to; **zu etw ~** to prepare to do sth; **jdn/etw auf jdn/etw ~** to set sb/sth on sb/sth

Ansicht ['anziçt] f (Anblick) sight; (Meinung) view, opinion; **zur ~** on approval; **meiner ~ nach** in my opinion

Ansichtskarte f picture postcard

Ansichtssache f matter of opinion

ansiedeln ['anzi:dəln] vt to settle; (Tierart) to introduce ▷ vr to settle; (Industrie etc) to get established

ansonsten [an'zɔnstən] adv otherwise

anspannen ['anʃpanən] vt to harness; (Muskel) to strain

Anspannung f strain
Anspiel ['anʃpiːl] nt (Sport) start of play
anspielen vt (Sport) to play the ball etc to
▷ vi: **auf etw** akk ~ to refer od allude to sth
Anspielung f: ~ **(auf** +akk) reference (to),
allusion (to)
Ansporn ['anʃpɔrn] **(-(e)s)** m incentive
Ansprache ['anʃpraːxə] f (Rede) address
ansprechen ['anʃprɛçən] unreg vt to speak to;
(bitten, gefallen) to appeal to; (Eindruck machen
auf) to make an impression on ▷ vi: ~ **auf** +akk
(Patient) to respond (to); (Messgerät) to react (to);
jdn auf etw akk **(hin)** ~ to ask sb about sth
ansprechend adj attractive
Ansprechpartner m contact
anspringen ['anʃprɪŋən] unreg vi (Aut) to start
▷ vt (anfallen) to jump; (Raubtier) to pounce (up)
on; (Hund: hochspringen) to jump up at
Anspruch ['anʃprʊx] **(-s, -sprüche)** m (Recht): ~
(auf +akk) claim (to); **den Ansprüchen
gerecht werden** to meet the requirements;
hohe Ansprüche stellen/haben to demand/
expect a lot; **jdn/etw in** ~ **nehmen** to occupy
sb/take up sth
anspruchslos adj undemanding
anspruchsvoll adj demanding; (Comm)
upmarket
anspucken ['anʃpʊkən] vt to spit at
anstacheln ['anʃtaxəln] vt to spur on
Anstalt ['anʃtalt] **(-, -en)** f institution; **~en
machen, etw zu tun** to prepare to do sth
Anstand ['anʃtant] m decency; (Manieren)
(good) manners pl
anständig ['anʃtɛndɪç] adj decent; (umg)
proper; (groß) considerable; **Anständigkeit** f
propriety, decency
anstandshalber ['anʃtantshalbər] adv out of
politeness
anstandslos adv without any ado
anstarren ['anʃtarən] vt to stare at
anstatt [an'ʃtat] präp +gen instead of ▷ konj: ~
etw zu tun instead of doing sth
anstauen ['anʃtauən] vr to accumulate; (Blut in
Adern etc) to congest; (fig: Gefühle) to build up
anstechen ['anʃtɛçən] unreg vt to prick; (Fass)
to tap
anstecken ['anʃtɛkən] vt to pin on; (Ring) to
put od slip on; (Med) to infect; (Pfeife) to light;
(Haus) to set fire to ▷ vr: **ich habe mich bei
ihm angesteckt** I caught it from him ▷ vi (fig)
to be infectious
ansteckend adj infectious
Ansteckung f infection
anstehen ['anʃteːən] unreg vi to queue (up)
(Brit), line up (US); (Verhandlungspunkt) to be on
the agenda
ansteigen ['anʃtaɪgən] unreg vi to rise; (Straße)
to climb
anstelle, an Stelle [an'ʃtɛlə] präp +gen in place
of
anstellen ['anʃtɛlən] vt (einschalten) to turn on;
(Arbeit geben) to employ; (umg: Unfug treiben) to
get up to; (: machen) to do ▷ vr to queue (up)

(Brit), line up (US); (umg) to act; (: sich zieren) to
make a fuss, act up
Anstellung f employment; (Posten) post,
position; ~ **auf Lebenszeit** tenure
ansteuern ['anʃtɔyərn] vt to make od steer od
head for
Anstich ['anʃtɪç] m (von Fass) tapping,
broaching
Anstieg ['anʃtiːk] **(-(e)s, -e)** m climb; (fig: von
Preisen etc) increase
anstiften ['anʃtɪftən] vt (Unglück) to cause; **jdn
zu etw** ~ to put sb up to sth
Anstifter (-s, -) m instigator
Anstiftung f (von Tat) instigation; (von
Mensch): ~ **(zu)** incitement (to)
anstimmen ['anʃtɪmən] vt (Lied) to strike up
(with); (Geschrei) to set up ▷ vi to strike up
Anstoß ['anʃtoːs] m impetus; (Ärgernis) offence
(Brit), offense (US); (Sport) kick-off; **der erste**
~ the initiative; **ein Stein des ~es** (umstrittene
Sache) a bone of contention; ~ **nehmen an** +dat
to take offence at
anstoßen unreg vt to push; (mit Fuß) to kick
▷ vi to knock, bump; (mit der Zunge) to lisp;
(mit Gläsern) to drink a toast; **an etw** akk ~
(angrenzen) to adjoin sth; ~ **auf** +akk to drink (a
toast) to
anstößig ['anʃtøːsɪç] adj offensive, indecent;
Anstößigkeit f indecency, offensiveness
anstrahlen ['anʃtraːlən] vt to floodlight;
(strahlend ansehen) to beam at
anstreben ['anʃtreːbən] vt to strive for
anstreichen ['anʃtraɪçən] unreg vt to paint;
(jdm) etw als Fehler ~ to mark sth wrong
Anstreicher, in (-s, -) m(f) painter
anstrengen ['anʃtrɛŋən] vt to strain;
(strapazieren: jdn) to tire out; (: Patienten) to
fatigue; (Jur) to bring ▷ vr to make an effort;
eine Klage ~ **(gegen)** (Jur) to initiate od
institute proceedings (against)
anstrengend adj tiring
Anstrengung f effort
Anstrich ['anʃtrɪç] m coat of paint
Ansturm ['anʃtʊrm] m rush; (Mil) attack
Ansuchen ['anzuːxən] **(-s, -)** nt request
ansuchen ['anzuːxən] vi: **um etw** ~ to apply
for sth
Antagonismus [antago'nɪsmʊs] m
antagonism
antanzen ['antantsən] (umg) vi to turn od show
up
Antarktis [ant'ʔarktɪs] **(-)** f Antarctic
antarktisch adj Antarctic
antasten ['antastən] vt to touch; (Recht) to
infringe upon; (Ehre) to question
Anteil ['antaɪl] **(-s, -e)** m share; (Mitgefühl)
sympathy; ~ **nehmen an** +dat to share in;
(sich interessieren) to take an interest in; ~ **an**
etw dat **haben** (beitragen) to contribute to sth;
(teilnehmen) to take part in sth
anteilig adj proportionate, proportional
anteilmäßig adj pro rata
Anteilnahme (-) f sympathy

23

Antenne [an'tɛnə] (-, -n) f aerial; (Zool) antenna; **eine/keine ~ für etw haben** (fig: umg) to have a/no feeling for sth

Anthrazit [antra'tsi:t] (-s, -e) m anthracite

Anthropologie [antropolo'gi:] (-) f anthropology

Anti- ['anti] inzW anti; **Antialkoholiker** m teetotaller; **antiautoritär** adj anti-authoritarian; **Antibabypille** f (contraceptive) pill; **Antibiotikum** (-s, -ka) nt antibiotic; **Antiheld** m antihero

antik [an'ti:k] adj antique

Antike (-, -n) f (Zeitalter) ancient world; (Kunstgegenstand) antique

Antikörper m antibody

Antilope [anti'lo:pə] (-, -n) f antelope

Antipathie [antipa'ti:] f antipathy

antippen ['antɪpən] vt to tap; (Pedal, Bremse) to touch; (fig: Thema) to touch on

Antiquariat [antikvari'a:t] (-(e)s, -e) nt secondhand bookshop; **modernes ~** remainder bookshop/department

antiquiert [anti'kvi:rt] (pej) adj antiquated

Antiquitäten [antikvi'tɛ:tən] pl antiques pl; **Antiquitätenhandel** m antique business; **Antiquitätenhändler, in** m(f) antique dealer

Antisemitismus [antizemi'tɪsmʊs] m anti-semitism

antiseptisch [anti'zɛptɪʃ] adj antiseptic

Antiviren- adj (Comput) antivirus; **Antivirensoftware** f antivirus software

Antlitz ['antlɪts] (-es, -e) nt (liter) countenance (liter), face

antörnen ['antœrnən] (umg) vt (Drogen, Musik) to turn on ▷ vi: **... törnt an ...** turns you on

Antrag ['antra:k] (-(e)s, -träge) m proposal; (Parl) motion; (Gesuch) application; **einen ~ auf etw** akk **stellen** to make an application for sth; (Jur etc) to file a petition/claim for sth

Antragsformular nt application form

Antragsgegner, in m(f) (Jur) respondent

Antragsteller, in (-s, -) m(f) claimant; (für Kredit etc) applicant

antreffen ['antrɛfən] unreg vt to meet

antreiben ['antraɪbən] unreg vt to drive on; (Motor) to drive; (anschwemmen) to wash up ▷ vi to be washed up; **jdn zur Eile/Arbeit ~** to urge sb to hurry up/to work

Antreiber (-s, -) (pej) m slave-driver (pej)

antreten ['antre:tən] unreg vt (Amt) to take up; (Erbschaft) to come into; (Beweis) to offer; (Reise) to start, begin ▷ vi to fall in; (Sport) to line up; (zum Dienst) to report; **gegen jdn ~** to play/fight against sb

Antrieb ['antri:p] m (lit, fig) drive; **aus eigenem ~** of one's own accord

Antriebskraft f (Tech) power

antrinken ['antrɪŋkən] unreg vt (Flasche, Glas) to start to drink from; **sich** dat **Mut/einen Rausch ~** to give o.s. Dutch courage/get drunk; **angetrunken sein** to be tipsy

Antritt ['antrɪt] m beginning, commencement; (eines Amts) taking up

antun ['antu:n] unreg vt: **jdm etw ~** to do sth to sb; **sich** dat **Zwang ~** to force o.s.

anturnen ['antœrnən] (umg) vt = **antörnen**

Antwerpen [ant'vɛrpən] (-s) nt Antwerp

Antwort ['antvɔrt] (-, -en) f answer, reply; **um ~ wird gebeten** RSVP

antworten vi to answer, reply

anvertrauen ['anfɛrtrauən] vt: **jdm etw ~** to entrust sb with sth; **sich jdm ~** to confide in sb

anvisieren ['anvizi:rən] vt (fig) to set one's sights on

anwachsen ['anvaksən] unreg vi to grow; (Pflanze) to take root

Anwalt ['anvalt] (-(e)s, -wälte) m solicitor; lawyer; (fig: Fürsprecher) advocate

Anwältin ['anvɛltɪn] f siehe **Anwalt**

Anwalts- zW: **Anwaltshonorar** nt retainer, retaining fee; **Anwaltskammer** f professional association of lawyers, ≈ Law Society (Brit); **Anwaltskosten** pl legal expenses pl

Anwandlung ['anvandlʊŋ] f caprice; **eine ~ von etw** a fit of sth

anwärmen ['anvɛrmən] vt to warm up

Anwärter, in ['anvɛrtər(ɪn)] m(f) candidate

anweisen ['anvaɪzən] unreg vt to instruct; (zuteilen) to assign

Anweisung f instruction; (Comm) remittance; (Postanweisung, Zahlungsanweisung) money order

anwendbar ['anvɛntba:r] adj practicable, applicable

anwenden ['anvɛndən] unreg vt to use, employ; (Gesetz, Regel) to apply

Anwenderprogramm nt (Comput) application program

Anwendersoftware f application package

Anwendung f use; (auch Comput) application, app

anwerfen ['anvɛrfən] unreg vt (Tech) to start up

anwesend ['anve:zənt] adj present; **die A~en** those present

Anwesenheit f presence

Anwesenheitsliste f attendance register

anwidern ['anvi:dərn] vt to disgust

Anwohner, in ['anvo:nər(ɪn)] (-s, -) m(f) resident

Anwuchs ['anvu:ks] m growth

Anzahl ['antsa:l] f: **~ (an** +dat) number (of)

anzahlen vt to pay on account

Anzahlung f deposit, payment on account

anzapfen ['antsapfən] vt to tap

Anzeichen ['antsaiçən] nt sign, indication; **alle ~ deuten darauf hin, dass ...** all the signs are that ...

Anzeige ['antsaɪgə] (-, -n) f (Zeitungsanzeige) announcement; (Werbung) advertisement; (Comput) display; (bei Polizei) report; **gegen jdn ~ erstatten** to report sb (to the police)

anzeigen vt (zu erkennen geben) to show; (bekannt geben) to announce; (bei Polizei) to report

Anzeigenteil m advertisements pl

anzeigepflichtig adj notifiable

Anzeiger m indicator

anzetteln ['antsɛtəln] (umg) vt to instigate
anziehen ['antsi:ən] unreg vt to attract;
(Kleidung) to put on; (Mensch) to dress;
(Schraube, Seil) to pull tight; (Knie) to draw up;
(Feuchtigkeit) to absorb ▷ vr to get dressed
anziehend adj attractive
Anziehung f (Reiz) attraction
Anziehungskraft f power of attraction; (Phys)
force of gravitation
Anzug ['antsu:k] m suit; **im ~ sein** to be
approaching
anzüglich ['antsy:klɪç] adj personal; (anstößig)
offensive; **Anzüglichkeit** f offensiveness;
(Bemerkung) personal remark
anzünden ['antsʏndən] vt to light
Anzünder m lighter
anzweifeln ['antsvaɪfəln] vt to doubt
AOK (-) f abk (= Allgemeine Ortskrankenkasse) siehe
Ortskrankenkasse; see culture note

AOK

The AOK (Allgemeine Ortskrankenkasse)
forms part of a compulsory medical
insurance scheme for people who are not
members of a private scheme. In every
large town there is an independently run
AOK office. Foreign nationals may also
receive help from these offices if they fall
ill while in Germany.

APA f abk (= Austria Presse-Agentur) Austrian news
agency
apart [a'part] adj distinctive
Apartheid [a'pa:rthaɪt] f apartheid
Apartment [a'partmənt] (-s, -s) nt flat (Brit),
apartment (bes US)
Apathie [apa'ti:] f apathy
apathisch [a'pa:tɪʃ] adj apathetic
Apenninen [apɛ'ni:nən] pl Apennines pl
Apfel ['apfəl] (-s, -̈) m apple; **in den sauren
~ beißen** (fig: umg) to swallow the bitter pill;
etw für einen ~ und ein Ei kaufen (umg) to
buy sth dirt cheap od for a song; **Apfelmus** nt
apple purée; (als Beilage) apple sauce; **Apfelsaft**
m apple juice
Apfelsine [apfəl'zi:nə] (-, -n) f orange
Apfeltasche f apple turnover
Apfelwein m strong cider
apl. abk = **außerplanmäßig**
APO, Apo ['a:po] (-) f abk (= außerparlamentarische
Opposition) extraparliamentary opposition; see culture
note

APO

The APO was an extraparliamentary
opposition group formed in West
Germany in the late 1960's by those who
felt that their interests were not being
sufficiently represented in parliament. It
was disbanded in the 1970's. Some of its
members then formed the RAF, a terrorist

organisation. Some formed the Green
Party (die Grünen).

apolitisch ['apoli:tɪʃ] adj non-political,
apolitical
Apostel [a'pɔstəl] (-s, -) m apostle
Apostroph [apo'stro:f] (-s, -e) m apostrophe
Apotheke [apo'te:kə] (-, -n) f chemist's (shop)
(Brit), drugstore (US); see culture note

APOTHEKE

The Apotheke is a pharmacy where
prescribed drugs and other medicines only
available on prescription are sold. It also
sells toiletries. The pharmacist is qualified
to give advice on medicines and treatment.

Apotheker, in (-s, -) m(f) pharmacist,
(dispensing) chemist (Brit), druggist (US)
Appalachen [apa'laxən] pl Appalachian
Mountains pl
Apparat [apa'ra:t] (-(e)s, -e) m piece of
apparatus; (Fotoapparat) camera; (Telefon)
telephone; (Rundf, TV) set; (Verwaltungsapparat,
Parteiapparat) machinery, apparatus; **am ~**
on the phone; (als Antwort) speaking; **am ~
bleiben** to hold the line
Apparatur [apara'tu:r] f apparatus
Appartement [apart(ə)'mãː] (-s, -s) nt flat
(Brit), apartment (bes US)
Appell [a'pɛl] (-s, -e) m (Mil) muster, parade;
(fig) appeal
appellieren [apɛ'li:rən] vi: ~ **(an** +akk) to appeal
(to)
Appetit [ape'ti:t] (-(e)s, -e) m appetite; **guten
~!** enjoy your meal; **appetitlich** adj appetizing;
Appetitlosigkeit f lack of appetite
Applaus [ap'laʊs] (-es, -e) m applause
Appretur [apre'tu:r] f finish;
(Wasserundurchlässigkeit) waterproofing
approbiert [apro'bi:rt] adj (Arzt) registered,
certified
Apr. abk (= April) Apr.
Aprikose [apri'ko:zə] (-, -n) f apricot
April [a'prɪl] (-(s), -e) (pl selten) m April; **jdn in
den ~ schicken** to make an April fool of sb;
siehe auch **September**; **Aprilwetter** nt April
showers pl
apropos [apro'po:] adv by the way, that
reminds me
Aquaplaning [akva'pla:nɪŋ] (-(s)) nt
aquaplaning
Aquarell [akva'rɛl] (-s, -e) nt watercolour (Brit),
watercolor (US)
Aquarium [a'kva:riʊm] nt aquarium
Äquator [ɛ'kva:tɔr] (-s) m equator
Äquivalent [ɛkviva'lɛnt] (-(e)s, -e) nt
equivalent
Ar [a:r] (-s, -e) nt od m (Maß) are (100 m²)
Ära ['ɛːra] (-, **Ären**) f era
Araber, in ['a:rabər(ɪn)] (-s, -) m(f) Arab
Arabien [a'ra:biən] (-s) nt Arabia

arabisch adj Arab; (Arabien betreffend) Arabian; (Sprache) Arabic; **A-er Golf** Arabian Gulf; **A-es Meer** Arabian Sea; **A-e Wüste** Arabian Desert

Arbeit ['arbait] (-, -en) f work; (Stelle) job; (Erzeugnis) piece of work; (wissenschaftliche) dissertation; (Klassenarbeit) test; **Tag der ~** Labour (Brit) od Labor (US) Day; **sich an die ~ machen, an die ~ gehen** to get down to work, start working; **jdm ~ machen** (Mühe) to put sb to trouble; **das war eine ~** that was a hard job

arbeiten vi to work ⊳ vt to make ⊳ vr: **sich nach oben/an die Spitze ~** (fig) to work one's way up/to the top

Arbeiter, in (-s, -) m(f) worker; (ungelernt) labourer (Brit), laborer (US)

Arbeiter- zW: **Arbeiterfamilie** f working-class family; **Arbeiterkammer** f (Österr) Chambers of Labour; **Arbeiterkind** nt child from a working-class family; **Arbeitermitbestimmung** f employee participation; **Arbeiterschaft** f workers pl, labour (Brit) od labor (US) force; **Arbeiterselbstkontrolle** f workers' control; **Arbeiter-und-Bauern-Staat** m (DDR) workers' and peasants' state; **Arbeiterwohlfahrt** f workers' welfare association

Arbeit- zW: **Arbeitgeber** (-s, -) m employer; **Arbeitnehmer** (-s, -) m employee

Arbeitsagentur f job agency

Arbeits- in zW labour (Brit), labor (US); **arbeitsam** adj industrious

Arbeits- zW**: **Arbeitsamt** nt employment exchange, Job Centre (Brit); **Arbeitsaufwand** m expenditure of energy; (Industrie) use of labour (Brit) od labor (US); **Arbeitsbedingungen** pl working conditions pl; **Arbeitsbeschaffung** f (Arbeitsplatzbeschaffung) job creation; **Arbeitserlaubnis** f work permit; **arbeitsfähig** adj fit for work, able-bodied; **Arbeitsgang** m operation; **Arbeitsgemeinschaft** f study group; **Arbeitsgericht** nt industrial tribunal; **arbeitsintensiv** adj labour-intensive (Brit), labor-intensive (US); **Arbeitskonflikt** m industrial dispute; **Arbeitskraft** f worker; **Arbeitskräfte** pl workers pl, labour (Brit), labor (US); **arbeitslos** adj unemployed, out-of-work; **Arbeitslosengeld** nt unemployment benefit; **Arbeitslosenhilfe** f supplementary benefit; **Arbeitslosenunterstützung** f unemployment benefit; **Arbeitslosenversicherung** f compulsory insurance against unemployment; **Arbeitslosigkeit** f unemployment; **Arbeitsmarkt** m job market; **Arbeitsmoral** f attitude to work; (in Betrieb) work climate; **Arbeitsniederlegung** f walkout; **Arbeitsplatte** f (Küche) work-top, work surface; **Arbeitsplatz** m place of work; (Stelle) job; **Arbeitsplatzrechner** m (Comput) work station; **Arbeitsplatzverlust** m job loss; **Arbeitsrecht** nt industrial law; **arbeitsscheu** adj workshy; **Arbeitsschutz** m maintenance of health and safety standards at work; **Arbeitstag** m work(ing) day; **Arbeitsteilung** f division of labour (Brit) od

labor (US); **Arbeitstier** nt (fig: umg) glutton for work, workaholic; **arbeitsunfähig** adj unfit for work; **Arbeitsunfall** m industrial accident; **Arbeitsverhältnis** nt employee-employer relationship; **Arbeitsvermittler**, in m(f): **(privater) Arbeitsvermittler** employment officer, job placement officer; **Arbeitsvermittlung** f (Amt) employment exchange; (privat) employment agency; **Arbeitsvertrag** m contract of employment; **Arbeitszeit** f working hours pl; **Arbeitszeitkonto** nt record of hours worked; **Arbeitszeitmodell** nt model of working hours; **Arbeitszeitregelung** f regulation of working hours; **Arbeitszeitverkürzung** f reduction in working hours; **Arbeitszimmer** nt study

Archäologe [arçɛo'lo:gə] (-n, -n) m arch(a)eologist

Archäologin [arçɛo'lo:gɪn] f arch(a)eologist

Arche ['arçə] (-, -n) f: **die ~ Noah** Noah's Ark

Architekt, in [arçi'tɛkt(ɪn)] (-en, -en) m(f) architect

architektonisch [arçitɛk'to:nɪʃ] adj architectural

Architektur [arçitɛk'tu:r] f architecture

Archiv [ar'çi:f] (-s, -e) nt archive

ARD f archive; see culture note

Arena [a're:na] (-, **Arenen**) f (lit, fig) arena; (Zirkusarena, Stierkampfarena) ring

arg [ark] adj bad, awful ⊳ adv awfully, very; **es zu ~ treiben** to go too far

Argentinien [argɛn'ti:niən] (-s) nt Argentina, the Argentine

Argentinier, in (-s, -) m(f) Argentine, Argentinian (Brit), Argentinean (US)

argentinisch [argɛn'ti:nɪʃ] adj Argentine, Argentinian (Brit), Argentinean (US)

Ärger ['ɛrgər] (-s) m (Wut) anger; (Unannehmlichkeit) trouble; **jdm ~ machen** od **bereiten** to cause sb a lot of trouble od bother; **ärgerlich** adj (zornig) angry; (lästig) annoying, aggravating

ärgern vt to annoy ⊳ vr to get annoyed

Ärgernis (-ses, -se) nt annoyance; (Anstoß) offence (Brit), offense (US), outrage; **öffentliches ~ erregen** to be a public nuisance

arg- zW: **arglistig** adj cunning, insidious;

a

arglistige Täuschung fraud; **arglos** *adj* guileless, innocent; **Arglosigkeit** *f* guilelessness, innocence

Argument [argu'mɛnt] *nt* argument

argumentieren [argumɛn'tiːrən] *vi* to argue

Argusauge ['argʊs|aʊgə] *nt* (*geh*): **mit ~n** eagle-eyed

Argwohn *m* suspicion

argwöhnisch *adj* suspicious

Arie ['aːriə] *f* aria

Aristokrat, in [arɪsto'kraːt(ɪn)] (**-en, -en**) *m(f)* aristocrat

Aristokratie [arɪstokra'tiː] *f* aristocracy

aristokratisch *adj* aristocratic

arithmetisch [arɪt'meːtɪʃ] *adj* arithmetical; **~es Mittel** arithmetic mean

Arkaden [ar'kaːdən] *pl* (*Bogengang*) arcade *sing*

Arktis ['arktɪs] (**-**) *f* Arctic

arktisch *adj* Arctic

arm [arm] *adj* poor; **~ dran sein** (*umg*) to have a hard time of it

Arm (**-(e)s, -e**) *m* arm; (*Flussarm*) branch; **jdn auf den ~ nehmen** (*fig: umg*) to pull sb's leg; **jdm unter die ~e greifen** (*fig*) to help sb out; **einen langen/den längeren ~ haben** (*fig*) to have a lot of/more pull (*umg*) *od* influence

Armatur [arma'tuːr] *f* (*Elek*) armature

Armaturenbrett *nt* instrument panel; (*Aut*) dashboard

Armband *nt* bracelet; **Armbanduhr** *f* (wrist) watch

Arme, r *f(m)* poor man/woman; **die ~n** the poor

Armee [ar'meː] (**-, -n**) *f* army; **Armeekorps** *nt* army corps

Ärmel ['ɛrməl] (**-s, -**) *m* sleeve; **etw aus dem ~ schütteln** (*fig*) to produce sth just like that

Ärmelkanal *m* (English) Channel

Armenien [ar'meːniən] (**-s**) *nt* Armenia

Armenier, in [ar'meːniər(ɪn)] (**-s, -**) *m(f)* Armenian

armenisch [ar'meːnɪʃ] *adj* Armenian

Armenrecht *nt* (*Jur*) legal aid

Armer *m siehe* **Arme(r)**

Armlehne *f* armrest

Armleuchter (*pej: umg*) *m* (*Dummkopf*) twit (*Brit*), fool

ärmlich ['ɛrmlɪç] *adj* poor; **aus ~en Verhältnissen** from a poor family

armselig *adj* wretched, miserable; (*mitleiderregend*) pathetic, pitiful

Armut ['armuːt] (**-**) *f* poverty

Armutsgrenze *f* poverty line

Armutsrisiko *nt* poverty risk

Armutszeugnis *nt* (*fig*): **jdm/sich ein ~ ausstellen** to show sb's/one's shortcomings

Aroma [a'roːma] (**-s, Aromen**) *nt* aroma; **Aromatherapie** *f* aromatherapy

aromatisch [aro'maːtɪʃ] *adj* aromatic

arrangieren [araⁿ'ʒiːrən] *vt* to arrange ▷ *vr* to come to an arrangement

Arrest [a'rɛst] (**-(e)s, -e**) *m* detention

arretieren [are'tiːrən] *vt* (*Tech*) to lock (in place)

arrogant [aro'gant] *adj* arrogant

Arroganz *f* arrogance

Arsch [arʃ] (**-es, ̈-e**) (*umg!*) *m* arse (!); **leck mich am ~!** (*lass mich in Ruhe*) get stuffed! (!), fuck off! (!); **am ~ der Welt** (*umg*) in the back of beyond; **Arschkriecher** (*umg!*) *m* arse licker (!), crawler; **Arschloch** (*umg!*) *nt* (*Mensch*) bastard (!)

Arsen [ar'zeːn] (**-s**) *nt* arsenic

Art [aːrt] *f* (*Weise*) way; (*Sorte*) kind, sort; (*Biol*) species; **eine ~ (von) Frucht** a kind of fruit; **Häuser aller ~** houses of all kinds; **einzig in seiner ~ sein** to be the only one of its kind, be unique; **auf diese ~ und Weise** in this way; **das ist doch keine ~!** that's no way to behave!; **es ist nicht seine ~, das zu tun** it's not like him to do that; **ich mache das auf meine ~** I do that my (own) way; **Schnitzel nach ~ des Hauses** chef's special escalope

arten *vi*: **nach jdm ~** to take after sb; **der Mensch ist so geartet, dass ...** human nature is such that ...

Artenschutz *m* protection of endangered species

Arterie [ar'teːriə] *f* artery

Arterienverkalkung *f* arteriosclerosis

Artgenosse ['aːrtgənɔsə] *m* animal/plant of the same species; (*Mensch*) person of the same type

Arthritis [ar'triːtɪs] (**-, -ritiden**) *f* arthritis

artig ['aːrtɪç] *adj* good, well-behaved

Artikel [ar'tiːkəl] (**-s, -**) *m* article

Artillerie [artɪlə'riː] *f* artillery

Artischocke [arti'ʃɔkə] (**-, -n**) *f* artichoke

Artistik [ar'tɪstɪk] (**-**) *f* artistry; (*Zirkus-/Varietékunst*) circus/variety performing

Arznei [aːrts'naɪ] *f* medicine; **Arzneimittel** *nt* medicine, medicament

Arzt [aːrtst] (**-es, ̈-e**) *m* doctor; **praktischer ~** general practitioner, GP

Ärztekammer *f* ≈ General Medical Council (*Brit*), State Medical Board of Registration (*US*)

Arzthelferin *f* doctor's assistant

Ärztin ['ɛːrtstɪn] *f* woman doctor; *siehe auch* **Arzt**

ärztlich ['ɛːrtstlɪç] *adj* medical

Arztpraxis *f* doctor's practice; (*Räume*) doctor's surgery (*Brit*) *od* office (*US*)

As [as] (**-ses, -se**) *nt* (*Mus*) A flat; *siehe auch* **Ass**

Asbest [as'bɛst] (**-(e)s, -e**) *m* asbestos

Asche ['aʃə] (**-, -n**) *f* ash

Aschen- *zW*: **Aschenbahn** *f* cinder track; **Aschenbecher** *m* ashtray; **Aschenbrödel** *nt* (*Liter, fig*) Cinderella; **Aschenputtel** *nt* (*Liter, fig*) Cinderella

Aschermittwoch *m* Ash Wednesday

Aserbaidschan [azɛrbaɪ'dʒaːn] (**-s**) *nt* Azerbaijan

aserbaidschanisch *adj* Azerbaijani

Asiat, in [azi'aːt(ɪn)] (**-en, -en**) *m(f)* Asian

asiatisch *adj* Asian, Asiatic

Asien ['aːziən] (**-s**) *nt* Asia

asozial ['azotsia:l] *adj* antisocial; *(Familie)* asocial

Asoziale, r *(pej) f(m) dekl wie adj* antisocial person; **Asoziale** *pl* antisocial elements

Aspekt [as'pɛkt] (**-(e)s, -e**) *m* aspect

Asphalt [as'falt] (**-(e)s, -e**) *m* asphalt

asphaltieren [asfal'ti:rən] *vt* to asphalt

Asphaltstraße *f* asphalt road

aß *etc* [a:s] *vb siehe* **essen**

Ass [as] (**-es, -e**) *nt* ace

Ass. *abk* = **Assessor**

Assekurant, in [aseku'rant(ın)] (**-en, -en**) *m(f)* underwriter

Assemblersprache [ə'sɛmblərʃpra:xə] *f (Comput)* assembly language

Assessor, in [a'sɛsɔr, -'so:rın] (**-s, -en**) *m(f) graduate civil servant who has completed his/her traineeship*

Assistent, in [asıs'tɛnt(ın)] *m(f)* assistant

Assistenzarzt [asıs'tentsa:rtst] *m* houseman *(Brit)*, intern *(US)*

Assoziation [asotsiatsi'o:n] *f* association

assoziieren [asotsi'i:rən] *vt (geh)* to associate

Ast [ast] (**-(e)s, ̈-e**) *m* branch; **sich** *dat* **einen ~ lachen** *(umg)* to double up (with laughter)

AStA ['asta] (**-(s), -(s)**) *m abk* (= *Allgemeiner Studentenausschuss*) *students' association*

ästhetisch [ɛs'te:tıʃ] *adj* aesthetic *(Brit)*, esthetic *(US)*

Asthma ['astma] (**-s**) *nt* asthma

Asthmatiker, in [ast'ma:tikər(ın)] (**-s, -**) *m(f)* asthmatic

astrein ['astraın] *adj (fig: umg: moralisch einwandfrei)* straight, on the level; (: *echt*) genuine; *(prima)* fantastic

Astrologe [astro'lo:gə] (**-n, -n**) *m* astrologer

Astrologie [astrolo'gi:] *f* astrology

Astrologin *f* astrologer

Astronaut, in [astro'naʊt(ın)] (**-en, -en**) *m(f)* astronaut

Astronautik *f* astronautics

Astronom, in [astro'no:m(ın)] (**-en, -en**) *m(f)* astronomer

Astronomie [astrono'mi:] *f* astronomy

ASU *f abk* (= *Arbeitsgemeinschaft selbstständiger Unternehmer*) *association of private traders*; (= *Abgassonderuntersuchung*) *exhaust emission test*

ASW *f abk* (= *außersinnliche Wahrnehmung*) ESP

Asyl [a'zy:l] (**-s, -e**) *nt* asylum; *(Heim)* home; *(Obdachlosenasyl)* shelter

Asylant, in [azy'lant(ın)] (**-en, -en**) *m(f)* person seeking (political) asylum

Asylrecht *nt (Pol)* right of (political) asylum

A.T. *abk* (= *Altes Testament*) O.T.

Atelier [atəli'e:] (**-s, -s**) *nt* studio

Atem ['a:təm] (**-s**) *m* breath; **den ~ anhalten** to hold one's breath; **außer ~** out of breath; **jdn in ~ halten** to keep sb in suspense *od* on tenterhooks; **das verschlug mir den ~** it took my breath away; **einen langen/den längeren ~ haben** to have a lot of staying power; **atemberaubend** *adj* breathtaking;

atemlos *adj* breathless; **Atempause** *f* breather; **Atemwege** *pl (Anat)* respiratory tract; **Atemzug** *m* breath

Atheismus [ate'ısmʊs] *m* atheism

Atheist, in *m(f)* atheist; **atheistisch** *adj* atheistic

Athen [a'te:n] (**-s**) *nt* Athens

Athener, in (**-s, -**) *m(f)* Athenian

Äther ['ɛ:tər] (**-s, -**) *m* ether

Äthiopien [ɛti'o:piən] (**-s**) *nt* Ethiopia

Äthiopier, in (**-s, -**) *m(f)* Ethiopian

äthiopisch *adj* Ethiopian

Athlet, in [at'le:t(ın)] (**-en, -en**) *m(f)* athlete

Athletik *f* athletics *sing*

Atlantik [at'lantık] (**-s**) *m* Atlantic

atlantisch *adj* Atlantic; **der A~e Ozean** the Atlantic Ocean

Atlas ['atlas] (**- *od* -ses, -se** *od* **Atlanten**) *m* atlas; **Atlasgebirge** *nt* Atlas Mountains *pl*

atmen ['a:tmən] *vt, vi* to breathe

Atmosphäre [atmo'sfɛ:rə] (**-, -n**) *f* atmosphere

atmosphärisch *adj* atmospheric

Atmung ['a:tmʊŋ] *f* respiration

Ätna ['ɛ:tna] (**-(s)**) *m* Etna

Atom [a'to:m] (**-s, -e**) *nt* atom

atomar [ato'ma:r] *adj* atomic, nuclear; *(Drohung)* nuclear

Atom- *zW:* **Atombombe** *f* atom bomb; **Atomenergie** *f* nuclear *od* atomic energy; **Atomgegner** *m:* **Atomgegner sein** to be antinuclear; **Atomkern** *m* atomic nucleus; **Atomkraft** *f* nuclear power; **Atomkraftwerk** *nt* nuclear power station; **Atomkrieg** *m* nuclear *od* atomic war; **Atomlobby** *f* nuclear lobby; **Atommacht** *f* nuclear *od* atomic power; **Atommeiler** *m* nuclear reactor; **Atommüll** *m* nuclear waste; **Atomphysik** *f* nuclear physics *sing*; **Atompilz** *m* mushroom cloud; **Atomsperrvertrag** *m (Pol)* nuclear nonproliferation treaty; **Atomsprengkopf** *m* nuclear *od* atomic warhead; **Atomstrom** *m electricity generated by nuclear power*; **Atomtest** *m* nuclear test; **Atomtestgelände** *nt* nuclear testing range; **Atomwaffen** *pl* nuclear *od* atomic weapons *pl*; **atomwaffenfrei** *adj (Zone)* nuclear-free; **Atomwirtschaft** *f* nuclear industry; **Atomzeitalter** *nt* atomic age

Attachment [ə'tɛtʃmɛnt] *nt (Comput)* attachment

Attacke [a'takə] (**-, -n**) *f (Angriff)* attack

Attentat [atɛn'ta:t] (**-(e)s, -e**) *nt:* **~ (auf** +*akk*) (attempted) assassination (of)

Attentäter, in [atɛn'tɛ:tər(ın)] (**-s, -**) *m(f)* (would-be) assassin

Attest [a'tɛst] (**-(e)s, -e**) *nt* certificate

Attraktion [atraktsi'o:n] *f* attraction

attraktiv [atrak'ti:f] *adj* attractive

Attrappe [a'trapə] (**-, -n**) *f* dummy; **bei ihr ist alles ~** everything about her is false

Attribut [atri'bu:t] (**-(e)s, -e**) *nt (Gram)* attribute

At-Zeichen ['attsaıçən] *nt (Comput)* at symbol

ätzen ['ɛtsən] *vi* to be caustic

ätzend *adj (lit: Säure)* corrosive; *(Geruch)* pungent; *(fig: umg: furchtbar)* dreadful, horrible

○ SCHLÜSSELWORT

auch [aʊx] *adv* **1** (*ebenfalls*) also, too, as well; **das ist auch schön** that's nice too *od* as well; **er kommt — ich auch** he's coming — so am I *od* me too; **auch nicht** not ... either; **ich auch nicht** nor I, me neither; **oder auch** or; **auch das noch!** not that as well!; **nicht nur ..., sondern auch ...** not only ... but also ...
2 (*selbst, sogar*) even; **auch wenn das Wetter schlecht ist** even if the weather is bad; **ohne auch nur zu fragen** without even asking **3** (*wirklich*) really; **du siehst müde aus — bin ich auch** you look tired — (so) I am; **so sieht es auch aus** (and) that's what it looks like
4 (*auch immer*): **wer auch** whoever; **was auch** whatever; **wozu auch?** (*emphatisch*) whatever for?; **wie dem auch sei** be that as it may; **wie sehr er sich auch bemühte** however much he tried

Audienz [aʊdi'ents] (**-**, **-en**) *f* (*bei Papst, König etc*) audience
Audimax [aʊdi'maks] *nt* (*Univ: umg*) main lecture hall
audiovisuell [aʊdiovizu'ɛl] *adj* audiovisual
Auditorium [aʊdi'to:riʊm] *nt* (*Hörsaal*) lecture hall; (*geh: Zuhörerschaft*) audience

○ SCHLÜSSELWORT

auf [aʊf] *präp +dat* (*wo?*) on; **auf dem Tisch** on the table; **auf der Reise** on the way; **auf der Post/dem Fest** at the post office/party; **auf der Straße** on the road; **auf dem Land/ der ganzen Welt** in the country/the whole world; **was hat es damit auf sich?** what does it mean?
▷ *präp +akk* **1** (*wohin?*) on(to); **auf den Tisch** on(to) the table; **auf die Post gehen** to go to the post office; **auf das Land** into the country; **etw auf einen Zettel schreiben** to write sth on a piece of paper; **auf eine Tasse Kaffee/eine Zigarette(nlänge)** for a cup of coffee/a smoke; **die Nacht (von Montag) auf Dienstag** Monday night; **auf einen Polizisten kommen 1.000 Bürger** there is one policeman to every 1,000 citizens
2: **auf Deutsch** in German; **auf Lebenszeit** for my/his lifetime; **bis auf ihn** except for him; **auf einmal** at once; **auf seinen Vorschlag (hin)** at his suggestion
▷ *adv* **1** (*offen*) open; **auf sein** to be open; **das Fenster ist auf** the window is open
2 (*hinauf*) up; **auf und ab** up and down; **auf und davon** up and away; **auf!** (*los!*) come on!; **von klein auf** from childhood onwards **3** (*aufgestanden*) up; **auf sein** (*Person*) to be up; **ist er schon auf?** is he up yet?
▷ *konj*: **auf dass** (so) that

aufarbeiten ['aʊf|arbaɪtən] *vt* (*erledigen: Korrespondenz etc*) to catch up with
aufatmen ['aʊf|a:tmən] *vi* to heave a sigh of relief
aufbahren ['aʊfba:rən] *vt* to lay out
Aufbau ['aʊfbaʊ] *m* (*Bauen*) building, construction; (*Struktur*) structure; (*aufgebautes Teil*) superstructure
aufbauen ['aʊfbaʊən] *vt* to erect, build (up); (*Existenz*) to make; (*gestalten*) to construct; (*gründen*) ~ **(auf** *+dat*) to found (on), base (on) ▷ *vr*: **sich vor jdm** ~ to draw o.s. up to one's full height in front of sb
aufbäumen ['aʊfbɔymən] *vr* to rear; (*fig*) to revolt, rebel
aufbauschen ['aʊfbaʊʃən] *vt* to puff out; (*fig*) to exaggerate
aufbegehren ['aʊfbəge:rən] *vi* (*geh*) to rebel
aufbehalten ['aʊfbəhaltən] *unreg vt* to keep on
aufbekommen ['aʊfbəkɔmən] *unreg* (*umg*) *vt* (*öffnen*) to get open; (: *Hausaufgaben*) to be given
aufbereiten ['aʊfbəraɪtən] *vt* to process; (*Trinkwasser*) to purify; (*Text etc*) to work up
Aufbereitungsanlage *f* processing plant
aufbessern ['aʊfbɛsərn] *vt* (*Gehalt*) to increase
aufbewahren ['aʊfbəva:rən] *vt* to keep; (*Gepäck*) to put in the left-luggage office
Aufbewahrung *f* (safe)keeping; (*Gepäckaufbewahrung*) left-luggage office (*Brit*), baggage check (*US*); **jdm etw zur** ~ **geben** to give sb sth for safekeeping
Aufbewahrungsort *m* storage place
aufbieten ['aʊfbi:tən] *unreg vt* (*Kraft*) to summon (up); (*Armee, Polizei*) to mobilize
Aufbietung *f*: **unter** ~ **aller Kräfte ...** summoning (up) all his/her *etc* strength ...
aufbinden ['aʊfbɪndən] *unreg vt*: **lass dir doch so etwas nicht** ~ (*fig*) don't fall for that
aufblähen ['aʊfblɛ:ən] *vr* to blow out; (*Segel*) to billow out; (*Med*) to become swollen; (*fig: pej*) to puff o.s. up
aufblasen ['aʊfbla:zən] *unreg vt* to blow up, inflate ▷ *vr* (*umg*) to become big-headed
aufbleiben ['aʊfblaɪbən] *unreg vi* (*Laden*) to remain open; (*Person*) to stay up
aufblenden ['aʊfblɛndən] *vt* (*Scheinwerfer*) to turn on full beam
aufblicken ['aʊfblɪkən] *vi* to look up; ~ **zu** (*lit*) to look up at; (*fig*) to look up to
aufblühen ['aʊfbly:ən] *vi* to blossom; (*fig*) to blossom, flourish
aufblühend *adj* (*Comm*) booming
aufbocken ['aʊfbɔkən] *vt* (*Auto*) to jack up
aufbrauchen ['aʊfbraʊxən] *vt* to use up
aufbrausen ['aʊfbraʊzən] *vi* (*fig*) to flare up
aufbrausend *adj* hot-tempered
aufbrechen ['aʊfbrɛçən] *unreg vt* to break open, to prise (*Brit*) *od* pry (*US*) open ▷ *vi* to burst open; (*gehen*) to start, set off
aufbringen ['aʊfbrɪŋən] *unreg vt* (*öffnen*) to open; (*in Mode*) to bring into fashion; (*beschaffen*) to procure; (*Fin*) to raise; (*ärgern*) to irritate; **Verständnis für etw** ~ to be able to

understand sth

Aufbruch ['aʊfbrʊx] *m* departure

aufbrühen ['aʊfbryːən] *vt* (*Tee*) to make

aufbrummen ['aʊfbrʊmən] (*umg*) *vt*: **jdm die Kosten** ~ to land sb with the costs

aufbürden ['aʊfbʏrdən] *vt*: **jdm etw** ~ to burden sb with sth

aufdecken ['aʊfdɛkən] *vt* to uncover; (*Spielkarten*) to show

aufdrängen ['aʊfdrɛŋən] *vt*: **jdm etw** ~ to force sth on sb ▷ *vr*: **sich jdm** ~ to intrude on sb

aufdrehen ['aʊfdreːən] *vt* (*Wasserhahn etc*) to turn on; (*Ventil*) to open; (*Schraubverschluss*) to unscrew; (*Radio etc*) to turn up; (*Haar*) to put in rollers

aufdringlich ['aʊfdrɪŋlɪç] *adj* pushy; (*Benehmen*) obtrusive; (*Parfüm*) powerful

aufeinander [aʊf|aɪ'nandər] *adv* on top of one another; (*schießen*) at each other; (*warten*) for one another; (*vertrauen*) each other; **Aufeinanderfolge** *f* succession, series; **aufeinanderfolgen** *vi* to follow one another; **aufeinanderfolgend** *adj* consecutive; **aufeinanderlegen** *vt* to lay on top of one another; **aufeinanderprallen** *vi* (*Autos etc*) to collide; (*Truppen, Meinungen*) to clash

Aufenthalt ['aʊf|ɛnthalt] *m* stay; (*Verzögerung*) delay; (*Eisenb: Halten*) stop; (*Ort*) haunt

Aufenthalts- *zW*: **Aufenthaltserlaubnis** *f*, **Aufenthaltsgenehmigung** *f* residence permit; **Aufenthaltsraum** *m* day room; (*in Betrieb*) recreation room

auferlegen ['aʊf|ɛrleːgən] *vt*: (**jdm**) ~ to impose (upon sb)

auferstehen ['aʊf|ɛrʃteːən] *unreg vi untr* to rise from the dead

Auferstehung *f* resurrection

aufessen ['aʊf|ɛsən] *unreg vt* to eat up

auffahren ['aʊffaːrən] *unreg vi* (*herankommen*) to draw up; (*hochfahren*) to jump up; (*wütend werden*) to flare up; (*in den Himmel*) to ascend ▷ *vt* (*Kanonen, Geschütz*) to bring up; ~ **auf** +*akk* (*Auto*) to run *od* crash into

auffahrend *adj* hot-tempered

Auffahrt *f* (*Hausauffahrt*) drive; (*Autobahnauffahrt*) slip road (*Brit*), entrance ramp (*US*)

Auffahrunfall *m* pile-up

auffallen ['aʊffalən] *unreg vi* to be noticeable; **angenehm/unangenehm** ~ to make a good/ bad impression; **jdm** ~ (*bemerkt werden*) to strike sb

auffallend *adj* striking

auffällig ['aʊffɛlɪç] *adj* conspicuous, striking

auffangen ['aʊffaŋən] *unreg vt* to catch; (*Funkspruch*) to intercept; (*Preise*) to peg; (*abfangen: Aufprall etc*) to cushion, absorb

Auffanglager *nt* reception camp

auffassen ['aʊffasən] *vt* to understand, comprehend; (*auslegen*) to see, view

Auffassung *f* (*Meinung*) opinion; (*Auslegung*) view, conception; (*auch*: **Auffassungsgabe**)

grasp

auffindbar ['aʊffɪntbaːr] *adj* to be found

aufflammen ['aʊfflamən] *vi* (*lit, fig: Feuer, Unruhen etc*) to flare up

auffliegen ['aʊffliːgən] *unreg vi* to fly up; (*umg: Rauschgiftring etc*) to be busted

auffordern ['aʊffɔrdərn] *vt* to challenge; (*befehlen*) to call upon, order; (*bitten*) to ask

Aufforderung *f* (*Befehl*) order; (*Einladung*) invitation

aufforsten ['aʊffɔrstən] *vt* (*Gebiet*) to reafforest; (*Wald*) to restock

auffrischen ['aʊffrɪʃən] *vt* to freshen up; (*Kenntnisse*) to brush up; (*Erinnerungen*) to reawaken ▷ *vi* (*Wind*) to freshen

aufführen ['aʊffyːrən] *vt* (*Theat*) to perform; (*in einem Verzeichnis*) to list, specify ▷ *vr* (*sich benehmen*) to behave; **einzeln** ~ to itemize

Aufführung *f* (*Theat*) performance; (*Liste*) specification

auffüllen ['aʊffʏlən] *vt* to fill up; (*Vorräte*) to replenish; (*Öl*) to top up

Aufgabe ['aʊfgaːbə] (**-, -n**) *f* task; (*Sch*) exercise; (*Hausaufgabe*) homework; (*Verzicht*) giving up; (*von Gepäck*) registration; (*von Post*) posting; (*von Inserat*) insertion; **sich** *dat* **etw zur** ~ **machen** to make sth one's job *od* business

aufgabeln ['aʊfgaːbəln] *vt* (*fig: umg: jdn*) to pick up; (*: Sache*) to get hold of

Aufgabenbereich *m* area of responsibility

Aufgang ['aʊfgaŋ] *m* ascent; (*Sonnenaufgang*) rise; (*Treppe*) staircase

aufgeben ['aʊfgeːbən] *unreg vt* (*verzichten auf*) to give up; (*Paket*) to send, post; (*Gepäck*) to register; (*Bestellung*) to give; (*Inserat*) to insert; (*Rätsel, Problem*) to set ▷ *vi* to give up

aufgeblasen ['aʊfgəblaːzən] *adj* (*fig*) puffed up, self-important

Aufgebot ['aʊfgəboːt] *nt* supply; (*von Kräften*) utilization; (*Eheaufgebot*) banns *pl*

aufgedonnert ['aʊfgədɔnərt] (*pej: umg*) *adj* tarted up

aufgedreht ['aʊfgədreːt] (*umg*) *adj* excited

aufgedunsen ['aʊfgədʊnzən] *adj* swollen, puffed up

aufgegeben ['aʊfgeːgeːbən] *pp von* **aufgeben**

aufgehen ['aʊfgeːən] *unreg vi* (*Sonne, Teig*) to rise; (*sich öffnen*) to open; (*Theat: Vorhang*) to go up; (*Knopf, Knoten etc*) to come undone; (*klar werden*) to become clear; (*Math*) to come out exactly; ~ (**in** +*dat*) (*sich widmen*) to be absorbed (in); **in Rauch/Flammen** ~ to go up in smoke/flames

aufgeilen ['aʊfgaɪlən] (*umg*) *vt* to turn on ▷ *vr* to be turned on

aufgeklärt ['aʊfgəklɛːrt] *adj* enlightened; (*sexuell*) knowing the facts of life

aufgekratzt ['aʊfgəkratst] (*umg*) *adj* in high spirits, full of beans

aufgelaufen ['aʊfgəlaʊfən] *adj*: ~**e Zinsen** *pl* accrued interest *sing*

Aufgeld *nt* premium

aufgelegt ['aʊfgəleːkt] *adj*: **gut/schlecht** ~

sein to be in a good/bad mood; **zu etw ~ sein** to be in the mood for sth

aufgenommen ['aʊfgənɔmən] *pp von* **aufnehmen**

aufgeregt ['aʊfgəreːkt] *adj* excited

aufgeschlossen ['aʊfgəʃlɔsən] *adj* open, open-minded

aufgeschmissen ['aʊfgəfmɪsən] (*umg*) *adj* in a fix, stuck

aufgeschrieben ['aʊfgəfriːbən] *pp von* **aufschreiben**

aufgestanden ['aʊfgəftandən] *pp von* **aufstehen**

aufgetakelt ['aʊfgətaːkəlt] *adj* (*fig: umg*) dressed up to the nines

aufgeweckt ['aʊfgəvɛkt] *adj* bright, intelligent

aufgießen ['aʊfgiːsən] *unreg vt* (*Wasser*) to pour over; (*Tee*) to infuse

aufgliedern ['aʊfgliːdərn] *vr:* **sich ~ (in** +*akk*) to (sub)divide (into), break down (into)

aufgreifen ['aʊfgraɪfən] *unreg vt* (*Thema*) to take up; (*Verdächtige*) to pick up, seize

aufgrund, auf Grund [aʊfgrʊnt] *präp* +*gen:* **~ von** on the basis of; (*wegen*) because of

Aufgussbeutel ['aʊfgʊsbɔʏtəl] *m* sachet (containing coffee/herbs *etc*) for brewing; (*Teebeutel*) tea bag

aufhaben ['aʊfhaːbən] *unreg vt* (*Hut etc*) to have on; (*Arbeit*) to have to do

aufhalsen ['aʊfhalzən] (*umg*) *vt:* **jdm etw ~** to saddle *od* lumber sb with sth

aufhalten ['aʊfhaltən] *unreg vt* (*Person*) to detain; (*Entwicklung*) to check; (*Tür, Hand*) to hold open; (*Augen*) to keep open ▷ *vr* (*wohnen*) to live; (*bleiben*) to stay; **jdn (bei etw) ~** (*abhalten, stören*) to hold *od* keep sb back (from sth); **sich über etw/jdn ~** to go on about sth/sb; **sich mit etw ~** to waste time over sth; **sich bei etw ~** (*sich befassen*) to dwell on sth

aufhängen ['aʊfhɛŋən] *unreg vt* (*Wäsche*) to hang up; (*Menschen*) to hang ▷ *vr* to hang o.s.

Aufhänger (-s, -) *m* (*am Mantel*) hook; (*fig*) peg

Aufhängung *f* (*Tech*) suspension

aufheben ['aʊfheːbən] *unreg vt* (*hochheben*) to raise, lift; (*Sitzung*) to wind up; (*Urteil*) to annul; (*Gesetz*) to repeal, abolish; (*aufbewahren*) to keep; (*ausgleichen*) to offset, make up for ▷ *vr* to cancel itself out; **viel A~(s) machen (von)** to make a fuss (about); **bei jdm gut aufgehoben sein** to be well looked after at sb's

aufheitern ['aʊfhaɪtərn] *vt, vr* (*Himmel, Miene*) to brighten; (*Mensch*) to cheer up

Aufheiterungen *pl* (*Met*) bright periods *pl*

aufheizen ['aʊfhaɪtsən] *vt:* **die Stimmung ~** to stir up feelings

aufhelfen ['aʊfhɛlfən] *unreg vi* (*lit: beim Aufstehen*): **jdm ~** to help sb up

aufhellen ['aʊfhɛlən] *vt, vr* to clear up; (*Farbe, Haare*) to lighten

aufhetzen ['aʊfhɛtsən] *vt* to stir up

aufheulen ['aʊfhɔʏlən] *vi* to howl; (*Sirene*) to (start to) wail; (*Motor*) to (give a) roar

aufholen ['aʊfhoːlən] *vt* to make up ▷ *vi* to catch up

aufhorchen ['aʊfhɔrçən] *vi* to prick up one's ears

aufhören ['aʊfhøːrən] *vi* to stop; **~, etw zu tun** to stop doing sth

aufkaufen ['aʊfkaʊfən] *vt* to buy up

aufklappen ['aʊfklapən] *vt* to open; (*Verdeck*) to fold back

aufklären ['aʊfklɛːrən] *vt* (*Geheimnis etc*) to clear up; (*Person*) to enlighten; (*sexuell*) to tell the facts of life to; (*Mil*) to reconnoitre ▷ *vr* to clear up

Aufklärung *f* (*von Geheimnis*) clearing up; (*Unterrichtung, Zeitalter*) enlightenment; (*sexuell*) sex education; (*Mil, Aviat*) reconnaissance

Aufklärungsarbeit *f* educational work

aufkleben ['aʊfkleːbən] *vt* to stick on

Aufkleber (-s, -) *m* sticker

aufknöpfen ['aʊfknœpfən] *vt* to unbutton

aufkochen ['aʊfkɔxən] *vt* to bring to the boil

aufkommen ['aʊfkɔmən] *unreg vi* (*Wind*) to come up; (*Zweifel, Gefühl*) to arise; (*Mode*) to start; **für jdn/etw ~** to be liable *od* responsible for sb/sth; **für den Schaden ~** to pay for the damage; **endlich kam Stimmung auf** at last things livened up

aufkreuzen ['aʊfkrɔʏtsən] (*umg*) *vi* (*erscheinen*) to turn *od* show up

aufkündigen ['aʊfkʏndɪgən] *vt* (*Vertrag etc*) to terminate

aufladen ['aʊflaːdən] *unreg vt* to load ▷ *vr* (*Batterie etc*) to be charged; (*neu aufladen*) to be recharged; **jdm/sich etw ~** (*fig*) to saddle sb/o.s. with sth

Auflage ['aʊflaːgə] *f* edition; (*Zeitung*) circulation; (*Bedingung*) condition; **jdm etw zur ~ machen** to make sth a condition for sb

Auflagehöhe, Auflagenhöhe *f* (*von Buch*) number of copies published; (*von Zeitung*) circulation

auflassen ['aʊflasən] *unreg* (*umg*) *vt* (*offen*) to leave open; (: *aufgesetzt*) to leave on; **die Kinder länger ~** to let the children stay up (longer)

auflauern ['aʊflaʊərn] *vi:* **jdm ~** to lie in wait for sb

Auflauf ['aʊflaʊf] *m* (*Koch*) pudding; (*Menschenauflauf*) crowd

auflaufen *unreg vi* (*auf Grund laufen: Schiff*) to run aground; **jdn ~ lassen** (*umg*) to drop sb in it

Auflaufform *f* (*Koch*) ovenproof dish

aufleben ['aʊfleːbən] *vi* to revive

auflegen ['aʊfleːgən] *vt* to put on; (*Hörer*) to put down; (*Typ*) to print ▷ *vi* (*Tel*) to hang up

auflehnen ['aʊfleːnən] *vt* to lean on ▷ *vr* to rebel

Auflehnung *f* rebellion

auflesen ['aʊfleːzən] *unreg vt* to pick up

aufleuchten ['aʊflɔʏçtən] *vi* to light up

aufliegen ['aʊfliːgən] *unreg vi* to lie on; (*Comm*) to be available

auflisten ['aʊflɪstən] *vt* (*auch Comput*) to list

auflockern ['aʊflɔkərn] vt to loosen; (fig: Eintönigkeit etc) to liven up; (entspannen, zwangloser machen) to make relaxed; (Atmosphäre) to make more relaxed, ease

auflösen ['aʊflø:zən] vt to dissolve; (Missverständnis) to sort out; (Konto) to close; (Firma) to wind up; (Haushalt) to break up; **in Tränen aufgelöst sein** to be in tears

Auflösung f dissolving; (fig) solution; (Bildschirm) resolution

aufmachen ['aʊfmaxən] vt to open; (Kleidung) to undo; (zurechtmachen) to do up ▷ vr to set out

Aufmacher m (Presse) lead

Aufmachung f (Kleidung) outfit, get-up; (Gestaltung) format

aufmerksam ['aʊfmɛrkza:m] adj attentive; **auf etw** akk ~ **werden** to become aware of sth; **jdn auf etw** akk ~ **machen** to point sth out to sb; **(das ist) sehr ~ von Ihnen** (zuvorkommend) (that's) most kind of you; **Aufmerksamkeit** f attention, attentiveness; (Geschenk) token (gift)

aufmöbeln ['aʊfmø:bəln] (umg) vt (Gegenstand) to do up; (: beleben) to buck up, pep up

aufmucken ['aʊfmʊkən] (umg) vi: ~ **gegen** to protest at od against

aufmuntern ['aʊfmʊntərn] vt (ermutigen) to encourage; (erheitern) to cheer up

aufmüpfig ['aʊfmʏpfɪç] (umg) adj rebellious

Aufnahme ['aʊfna:mə] (-, -n) f reception; (Beginn) beginning; (in Verein etc) admission; (in Liste etc) inclusion; (Notieren) taking down; (Phot) shot; (auf Tonband etc) recording; **Aufnahmeantrag** m application for membership od admission; **aufnahmefähig** adj receptive; **Aufnahmeleiter** m (Film) production manager; (Rundf, TV) producer; **Aufnahmeprüfung** f entrance test; **Aufnahmestopp** m (für Flüchtlinge etc) freeze on immigration

aufnehmen ['aʊfne:mən] unreg vt to receive; (hochheben) to pick up; (beginnen) to take up; (in Verein etc) to admit; (in Liste etc) to include; (fassen) to hold; (begreifen) to take in, grasp; (beim Stricken: Maschen) to increase, make; (notieren) to take down; (fotografieren) to photograph; (auf Tonband, Platte) to record; (Fin: leihen) to take out; **es mit jdm ~ können** to be able to compete with sb

aufnötigen ['aʊfnø:tɪgən] vt: **jdm etw ~** to force sth on sb

aufoktroyieren ['aʊf|ɔktroaji:rən] vt: **jdm etw ~** (geh) to impose od force sth on sb

aufopfern ['aʊf|ɔpfərn] vt to sacrifice ▷ vr to sacrifice o.s.

aufopfernd adj selfless

aufpassen ['aʊfpasən] vi (aufmerksam sein) to pay attention; **auf jdn/etw ~** to look after od watch sb/sth; **aufgepasst!** look out!

Aufpasser, in (-s, -) (pej) m(f) (Aufseher, Spitzel) spy, watchdog; (Beobachter) supervisor; (Wächter) guard

aufpflanzen ['aʊfpflantsən] vr: **sich vor jdm ~** to plant o.s. in front of sb

aufplatzen ['aʊfplatsən] vi to burst open

aufplustern ['aʊfplu:stərn] vr (Vogel) to ruffle (up) its feathers; (Mensch) to puff o.s. up

aufprägen ['aʊfprɛ:gən] vt: **jdm/etw seinen Stempel ~** (fig) to leave one's mark on sb/sth

Aufprall ['aʊfpral] (-(e)s, -e) m impact

aufprallen vi to hit, strike

Aufpreis ['aʊfpraɪs] m extra charge

aufpumpen ['aʊfpʊmpən] vt to pump up

aufputschen ['aʊfpʊtʃən] vt (aufhetzen) to inflame; (erregen) to stimulate

Aufputschmittel nt stimulant

aufraffen ['aʊfrafən] vr to rouse o.s.

aufräumen ['aʊfrɔʏmən] vt, vi (Dinge) to clear away; (Zimmer) to tidy up

Aufräumungsarbeiten pl clearing-up operations pl

aufrecht ['aʊfrɛçt] adj (lit, fig) upright

aufrechterhalten unreg vt to maintain

aufregen ['aʊfre:gən] vt to excite; (ärgerlich machen) to irritate, annoy; (nervös machen) to make nervous; (beunruhigen) to disturb ▷ vr to get excited

aufregend adj exciting

Aufregung f excitement

aufreiben ['aʊfraɪbən] unreg vt (Haut) to rub raw; (erschöpfen) to exhaust; (Mil: völlig vernichten) to wipe out, annihilate

aufreibend adj strenuous

aufreihen ['aʊfraɪən] vt (in Linie) to line up; (Perlen) to string

aufreißen ['aʊfraɪsən] unreg vt (Umschlag) to tear open; (Augen) to open wide; (Tür) to throw open; (Straße) to take up; (umg: Mädchen) to pick up

Aufreißer (-s, -) m (Person) smooth operator

aufreizen ['aʊfraɪtsən] vt to incite, stir up

aufreizend adj exciting, stimulating

aufrichten ['aʊfrɪçtən] vt to put up, erect; (moralisch) to console ▷ vr to rise; (moralisch): **sich ~ (an** +dat) to take heart (from); **sich im Bett ~** to sit up in bed

aufrichtig ['aʊfrɪçtɪç] adj sincere; honest; **Aufrichtigkeit** f sincerity

aufrollen ['aʊfrɔlən] vt (zusammenrollen) to roll up; (Kabel) to coil od wind up; siehe auch **wiederaufrollen**

aufrücken ['aʊfrʏkən] vi to move up; (beruflich) to be promoted

Aufruf ['aʊfru:f] m summons; (zur Hilfe) call; (des Namens) calling out

aufrufen unreg vt (Namen) to call out; (auffordern): **jdn ~ (zu)** to call upon sb (for); **einen Schüler ~** to ask a pupil (to answer) a question

Aufruhr ['aʊfru:r] (-(e)s, -e) m uprising, revolt; **in ~ sein** to be in uproar

Aufrührer, in (-s, -) m(f) rabble-rouser

aufrührerisch ['aʊfry:rərɪʃ] adj rebellious

aufrunden ['aʊfrʊndən] vt (Summe) to round up

aufrüsten ['aʊfrʏstən] vt, vi to arm

Aufrüstung f rearmament

aufrütteln ['aʊfrʏtəln] vt (lit, fig) to shake up

aufs [aʊfs] = **auf das**

aufsagen ['aʊfzaːɡən] vt (Gedicht) to recite; (geh: Freundschaft) to put an end to

aufsammeln ['aʊfzaməln] vt to gather up

aufsässig ['aʊfzɛsɪç] adj rebellious

Aufsatz ['aʊfzats] m (Geschriebenes) essay, composition; (auf Schrank etc) top

aufsaugen ['aʊfzaʊɡən] unreg vt to soak up

aufschauen ['aʊfʃaʊən] vi to look up

aufscheuchen ['aʊfʃɔyçən] vt to scare, startle

aufschichten ['aʊfʃɪçtən] vt to stack, pile up

aufschieben ['aʊfʃiːbən] unreg vt to push open; (verzögern) to put off, postpone

Aufschlag ['aʊfʃlaːk] m (Ärmelaufschlag) cuff; (Jackenaufschlag) lapel; (Hosenaufschlag) turn-up (Brit), cuff (US); (Aufprall) impact; (Preisaufschlag) surcharge; (Tennis) service

aufschlagen ['aʊfʃlaːɡən] unreg vt (öffnen) to open; (verwunden) to cut; (hochschlagen) to turn up; (aufbauen: Zelt, Lager) to pitch, erect; (Wohnsitz) to take up ▷ vi (aufprallen) to hit; (teurer werden) to go up; (Tennis) to serve; **schlagt Seite 111 auf** open your books at page 111

aufschließen ['aʊfʃliːsən] unreg vt to open up, unlock ▷ vi (aufrücken) to close up

Aufschluss ['aʊfʃlʊs] m information

aufschlüsseln ['aʊfʃlʏsəln] vt: ~ **(nach)** to break down (into); (klassifizieren) to classify (according to)

aufschlussreich adj informative, illuminating

aufschnappen ['aʊfʃnapən] vt (umg) to pick up ▷ vi to fly open

aufschneiden ['aʊfʃnaɪdən] unreg vt to cut open; (Brot) to cut up; (Med: Geschwür) to lance ▷ vi (umg) to brag

Aufschneider (-s, -) m boaster, braggart

Aufschnitt ['aʊfʃnɪt] m (slices of) cold meat

aufschnüren ['aʊfʃnyːrən] vt to unlace; (Paket) to untie

aufschrauben ['aʊfʃraʊbən] vt (festschrauben) to screw on; (lösen) to unscrew

aufschrecken ['aʊfʃrɛkən] vt to startle ▷ vi (unreg) to start up

Aufschrei ['aʊfʃraɪ] m cry

aufschreiben ['aʊfʃraɪbən] unreg vt to write down

aufschreien unreg vi to cry out

Aufschrift ['aʊfʃrɪft] f (Inschrift) inscription; (Etikett) label

Aufschub ['aʊfʃuːp] (-(e)s, -schübe) m delay, postponement; **jdm ~ gewähren** to grant sb an extension

aufschürfen ['aʊfʃʏrfən] vt: **sich** dat **die Haut/ das Knie ~** to graze od scrape o.s./one's knee

aufschütten ['aʊfʃʏtən] vt (Flüssigkeit) to pour on; (Kohle) to put on (the fire); (Damm, Deich) to throw up; **Kaffee ~** to make coffee

aufschwatzen ['aʊfʃvatsən] (umg) vt: **jdm etw ~** to talk sb into (getting/having etc) sth

Aufschwung ['aʊfʃvʊŋ] m (Elan) boost; (wirtschaftlich) upturn, boom; (Sport: an Gerät) mount

aufsehen ['aʊfzeːən] unreg vi to look up; ~ **zu** (lit) to look up at; (fig) to look up to; **Aufsehen** (-s) nt sensation, stir; **aufsehenerregend** adj sensational

Aufseher, in (-s, -) m(f) guard; (im Betrieb) supervisor; (Museumsaufseher) attendant; (Parkaufseher) keeper

auf sein ['aʊfzaɪn] siehe **auf**

aufseiten, auf Seiten [aʊfˈzaɪtn] präp+gen: ~ **von** on the part of

aufsetzen ['aʊfzɛtsən] vt to put on; (Flugzeug) to put down; (Dokument) to draw up ▷ vr to sit upright ▷ vi (Flugzeug) to touch down

Aufsicht ['aʊfzɪçt] f supervision; **die ~ haben** to be in charge; **bei einer Prüfung ~ führen** to invigilate (Brit) od supervise an exam

Aufsichtsrat m board (of directors)

aufsitzen ['aʊfzɪtsən] unreg vi (aufgerichtet sitzen) to sit up; (aufs Pferd, Motorrad) to mount, get on; (Schiff) to run aground; **jdn ~ lassen** (umg) to stand sb up; **jdm ~** (umg) to be taken in by sb

aufspalten ['aʊfʃpaltən] vt to split

aufspannen ['aʊfʃpanən] vt (Netz, Sprungtuch) to stretch od spread out; (Schirm) to put up, open

aufsparen ['aʊfʃpaːrən] vt to save (up)

aufsperren ['aʊfʃpɛrən] vt to unlock; (Mund) to open wide; **die Ohren ~** (umg) to prick up one's ears

aufspielen ['aʊfʃpiːlən] vr to show off; **sich als etw ~** to try to come on as sth

aufspießen ['aʊfʃpiːsən] vt to spear

aufspringen ['aʊfʃprɪŋən] unreg vi (hochspringen) to jump up; (sich öffnen) to spring open; (Hände, Lippen) to become chapped; ~ **auf** +akk to jump onto

aufspüren ['aʊfʃpyːrən] vt to track down, trace

aufstacheln ['aʊfʃtaxəln] vt to incite

aufstampfen ['aʊfʃtampfən] vi: **mit dem Fuß ~** to stamp one's foot

Aufstand ['aʊfʃtant] m insurrection, rebellion

aufständisch ['aʊfʃtɛndɪʃ] adj rebellious, mutinous

aufstauen ['aʊfʃtaʊən] vr to collect; (fig: Ärger) to be bottled up

aufstechen ['aʊfʃtɛçən] unreg vt to prick open, puncture

aufstecken ['aʊfʃtɛkən] vt to stick on; (mit Nadeln) to pin up; (umg) to give up

aufstehen ['aʊfʃteːən] unreg vi to get up; (Tür) to be open; **da musst du früher** od **eher ~!** (fig: umg) you'll have to do better than that!

aufsteigen ['aʊfʃtaɪɡən] unreg vi (hochsteigen) to climb; (Rauch) to rise; ~ **auf** +akk to get onto; **in jdm ~** (Hass, Verdacht, Erinnerung etc) to well up in sb

Aufsteiger (-s, -) m (Sport) promoted team; **(sozialer) ~** social climber

aufstellen ['aʊfʃtɛlən] vt (aufrecht stellen) to put up; (Maschine) to install; (aufreihen) to line up; (Kandidaten) to nominate; (Forderung, Behauptung) to put forward; (formulieren: Programm etc) to draw up;

(leisten: Rekord) to set up

Aufstellung *f* *(Sport)* line-up; *(Liste)* list

Aufstieg ['aʊfʃtiːk] **(-(e)s, -e)** *m* *(auf Berg)* ascent; *(Fortschritt)* rise; *(beruflich, Sport)* promotion

Aufstiegschance *f* prospect of promotion

aufstöbern ['aʊfʃtøːbərn] *vt* *(Wild)* to start, flush; *(umg: entdecken)* to run to earth

aufstocken ['aʊfʃtɔkən] *vt* *(Vorräte)* to build up

aufstoßen ['aʊfʃtoːsən] *unreg vt* to push open ▷ *vi* to belch

aufstrebend ['aʊfʃtreːbənd] *adj* ambitious; *(Land)* striving for progress

Aufstrich ['aʊfʃtrɪç] *m* spread

aufstülpen ['aʊfʃtʏlpən] *vt* *(Ärmel)* to turn up; *(Hut)* to put on

aufstützen ['aʊfʃtʏtsən] *vt* *(Körperteil)* to prop, lean; *(Person)* to prop up ▷ *vr*: **sich ~ auf** *+akk* to lean on

aufsuchen ['aʊfzuːxən] *vt* *(besuchen)* to visit; *(konsultieren)* to consult

auftakeln ['aʊftaːkəln] *vt* *(Naut)* to rig (out) ▷ *vr* *(pej: umg)* to deck o.s. out

Auftakt ['aʊftakt] *m* *(Mus)* upbeat; *(fig)* prelude

auftanken ['aʊftaŋkən] *vi* to get petrol *(Brit) od* gas *(US)* ▷ *vt* to refuel

auftauchen ['aʊftaʊxən] *vi* to appear; *(gefunden werden, kommen)* to turn up; *(aus Wasser etc)* to emerge; *(U-Boot)* to surface; *(Zweifel)* to arise

auftauen ['aʊftaʊən] *vt* to thaw ▷ *vi* to thaw; *(fig)* to relax

aufteilen ['aʊftaɪlən] *vt* to divide up; *(Raum)* to partition

Aufteilung *f* division; partition

auftischen ['aʊftɪʃən] *vt* to serve (up); *(fig)* to tell

Auftr. *abk* = **Auftrag**

Auftrag ['aʊftraːk] **(-(e)s, -träge)** *m* order; *(Anweisung)* commission; *(Aufgabe)* mission; **etw in ~ geben (bei)** to order/commission sth (from); **im ~ von** on behalf of; **im ~ od i. A. J. Burnett** *pp* J. Burnett

auftragen ['aʊftraːgən] *unreg vt* *(Essen)* to serve; *(Farbe)* to put on; *(Kleidung)* to wear out ▷ *vi* *(dick machen)*: **die Jacke trägt auf** the jacket makes one look fat; **jdm etw ~** to tell sb sth; **dick ~** *(umg)* to exaggerate

Auftraggeber, in **(-s, -)** *m(f)* client; *(Comm)* customer

Auftragsbestätigung *f* confirmation of order

auftreiben ['aʊftraɪbən] *unreg (umg) vt* *(beschaffen)* to raise

auftrennen ['aʊftrɛnən] *vt* to undo

auftreten ['aʊftreːtən] *unreg vt* to kick open ▷ *vi* to appear; *(mit Füßen)* to tread; *(sich verhalten)* to behave; *(fig: eintreten)* to occur; *(Schwierigkeiten etc)* to arise; **als Vermittler** *etc* to act as intermediary *etc*; **geschlossen ~** to put up a united front

Auftreten **(-s)** *nt* *(Vorkommen)* appearance; *(Benehmen)* behaviour *(Brit)*, behavior *(US)*

Auftrieb ['aʊftriːp] *m* *(Phys)* buoyancy, lift; *(fig)* impetus

Auftritt ['aʊftrɪt] *m* *(des Schauspielers)* entrance;

(lit, fig: Szene) scene

auftrumpfen ['aʊftrʊmpfən] *vi* to show how good one is; *(mit Bemerkung)* to crow

auftun ['aʊftuːn] *unreg vt* to open ▷ *vr* to open up

auftürmen ['aʊftʏrmən] *vr* *(Gebirge etc)* to tower up; *(Schwierigkeiten)* to pile *od* mount up

aufwachen ['aʊfvaxən] *vi* to wake up

aufwachsen ['aʊfvaksən] *unreg vi* to grow up

Aufwand ['aʊfvant] **(-(e)s)** *m* expenditure; *(Kosten)* expense; *(Luxus)* show; **bitte, keinen ~!** please don't go out of your way

aufwändig ['aʊfvɛndɪç] *adj, adv* costly

Aufwandsentschädigung *f* expense allowance

aufwärmen ['aʊfvɛrmən] *vt* to warm up; *(alte Geschichten)* to rake up

aufwarten ['aʊfvartən] *vi* *(zu bieten haben)*: **mit etw ~** to offer sth

aufwärts ['aʊfvɛrts] *adv* upwards; **es geht ~** things are looking up; **Aufwärtsentwicklung** *f* upward trend

aufwecken ['aʊfvɛkən] *vt* to wake(n) up

aufweichen ['aʊfvaɪçən] *vt* to soften; *(Brot)* to soak

aufweisen ['aʊfvaɪzən] *unreg vt* to show

aufwenden ['aʊfvɛndən] *unreg vt* to expend; *(Geld)* to spend; *(Sorgfalt)* to devote

aufwendig ['aʊfvɛndɪç] *adj, adv* costly

aufwerfen ['aʊfvɛrfən] *unreg vt* *(Fenster etc)* to throw open; *(Probleme)* to throw up, raise ▷ *vr*: **sich zu etw ~** to make o.s. out to be sth

aufwerten ['aʊfvɛrtən] *vt* *(Fin)* to revalue; *(fig)* to raise in value

Aufwertung *f* revaluation

aufwickeln ['aʊfvɪkəln] *vt* *(aufrollen)* to roll up; *(umg: Haar)* to put in curlers; *(lösen)* to untie

aufwiegeln ['aʊfviːgəln] *vt* to stir up, incite

aufwiegen ['aʊfviːgən] *unreg vt* to make up for

Aufwind ['aʊfvɪnt] *m* up-current; **neuen ~ bekommen** *(fig)* to get new impetus

aufwirbeln ['aʊfvɪrbəln] *vt* to whirl up; **Staub ~** *(fig)* to create a stir

aufwischen ['aʊfvɪʃən] *vt* to wipe up

aufwühlen ['aʊfvyːlən] *vt* *(lit: Erde, Meer)* to churn (up); *(Gefühle)* to stir

aufzählen ['aʊftsɛːlən] *vt* to count out

aufzeichnen ['aʊftsaɪçnən] *vt* to sketch; *(schriftlich)* to jot down; *(auf Band)* to record

Aufzeichnung *f* *(schriftlich)* note; *(Tonbandaufzeichnung, Filmaufzeichnung)* recording

aufzeigen ['aʊftsaɪgən] *vt* to show, demonstrate

aufziehen ['aʊftsiːən] *unreg vt* *(hochziehen)* to raise, draw up; *(öffnen)* to pull open; *(: Reißverschluss)* to undo; *(Gardinen)* to draw (back); *(Uhr)* to wind; *(großziehen: Kinder)* to raise, bring up; *(Tiere)* to rear; *(umg: necken)* to tease; *(: veranstalten)* to set up; *(: Fest)* to arrange ▷ *vi* *(Gewitter, Wolken)* to gather

Aufzucht ['aʊftsʊxt] *f* *(das Großziehen)* rearing, raising

Aufzug ['aʊftsuːk] *m* (*Fahrstuhl*) lift (*Brit*), elevator (*US*); (*Aufmarsch*) procession, parade; (*Kleidung*) get-up; (*Theat*) act
aufzwingen ['aʊftsvɪŋən] *unreg vt*: **jdm etw ~** to force sth upon sb
Aug. *abk* (*= August*) Aug.
Augapfel ['aʊk|apfəl] *m* eyeball; (*fig*) apple of one's eye
Auge ['aʊgə] (**-s, -n**) *nt* eye; (*Fettauge*) globule of fat; **unter vier ~n** in private; **vor aller ~n** in front of everybody, for all to see; **jdn/ etw mit anderen ~n (an)sehen** to see sb/ sth in a different light; **ich habe kein ~ zugetan** I didn't sleep a wink; **ein ~/beide ~n zudrücken** (*umg*) to turn a blind eye; **jdn/ etw aus den ~n verlieren** to lose sight of sb/ sth; (*fig*) to lose touch with sb/sth; **etw ins ~ fassen** to contemplate sth; **das kann leicht ins ~ gehen** (*fig: umg*) it might easily go wrong
Augenarzt *m* eye specialist, ophthalmologist
Augenblick *m* moment; **im ~** at the moment; **im ersten ~** for a moment; **augenblicklich** *adj* (*sofort*) instantaneous; (*gegenwärtig*) present
Augen- *zW*: **Augenbraue** *f* eyebrow; **Augenhöhe** *f*: **in Augenhöhe** at eye level; **Augenmerk** *nt* (*Aufmerksamkeit*) attention; **Augenschein** *m*: **jdn/etw in Augenschein nehmen** to have a close look at sb/sth; **augenscheinlich** *adj* obvious; **Augenweide** *f* sight for sore eyes; **Augenwischerei** *f* (*fig*) eye-wash; **Augenzeuge** *m* eye witness; **Augenzeugin** *f* eye witness
August [aʊˈɡʊst] (**-(e)s** *od* **-, -e**) (*pl selten*) *m* August; *siehe auch* **September**
Auktion [aʊktsiˈoːn] *f* auction
Auktionator [aʊktsioˈnaːtɔr] *m* auctioneer
Aula ['aʊla] (**-, Aulen** *od* **-s**) *f* assembly hall
Aus [aʊs] (**-**) *nt* (*Sport*) outfield; **ins ~ gehen** to go out

○ SCHLÜSSELWORT

aus [aʊs] *präp +dat* **1** (*räumlich*) out of; (*von ... her*) from; **er ist aus Berlin** he's from Berlin; **aus dem Fenster** out of the window
2 (*gemacht/hergestellt aus*) made of; **ein Herz aus Stein** a heart of stone
3 (*auf Ursache deutend*) out of; **aus Mitleid** out of sympathy; **aus Erfahrung** from experience; **aus Spaß** for fun
4: **aus ihr wird nie etwas** she'll never get anywhere
▷ *adv* **1** (*zu Ende*) finished, over; **aus sein** to be over; **es ist aus mit ihm** he is finished, he has had it; **aus und vorbei** over and done with
2 (*ausgeschaltet, ausgezogen*) off; **aus sein** to be out; **Licht aus!** lights out!
3 (*in Verbindung mit von*): **von Rom aus** from Rome; **vom Fenster aus** out of the window; **von sich aus** (*selbstständig*) of one's own accord; **von mir aus** as far as I'm concerned
4: **aus und ein gehen** to come and go; (*bei*

jdm) to visit frequently; **weder aus noch ein wissen** to be at one's wits' end; **auf etw** *akk* **aus sein** to be after sth

ausarbeiten ['aʊs|arbaɪtən] *vt* to work out
ausarten ['aʊs|artən] *vi* to degenerate; (*Kind*) to become overexcited
ausatmen ['aʊs|aːtmən] *vi* to breathe out
ausbaden ['aʊsbaːdən] (*umg*) *vt*: **etw ~ müssen** to carry the can for sth
Ausbau ['aʊsbaʊ] *m* extension, expansion; removal
ausbauen *vt* to extend, expand; (*herausnehmen*) to take out, remove
ausbaufähig *adj* (*fig*) worth developing
ausbedingen ['aʊsbədɪŋən] *unreg vt*: **sich** *dat* **etw ~** to insist on sth
ausbeißen ['aʊsbaɪsən] *unreg vr*: **sich** *dat* **an etw** *dat* **die Zähne ~** (*fig*) to have a tough time of it with sth
ausbessern ['aʊsbɛsərn] *vt* to mend, repair
Ausbesserungsarbeiten *pl* repair work *sing*
ausbeulen ['aʊsbɔylən] *vt* to beat out
Ausbeute ['aʊsbɔytə] *f* yield; (*Gewinn*) profit, gain; (*Fische*) catch
ausbeuten *vt* to exploit; (*Min*) to work
ausbezahlen ['aʊsbətsaːlən] *vt* (*Geld*) to pay out
ausbilden ['aʊsbɪldən] *vt* to educate; (*Lehrling, Soldat*) to instruct, train; (*Fähigkeiten*) to develop; (*Geschmack*) to cultivate
Ausbilder, in (**-s, -**) *m(f)* instructor, instructress
Ausbildung *f* education; training, instruction; development; cultivation; **er ist noch in der ~** he's still a trainee; he hasn't finished his education
Ausbildungs- *zW*: **Ausbildungsförderung** *f* (provision of) grants for students and trainees; (*Stipendium*) grant; **Ausbildungsplatz** *m* (*Stelle*) training vacancy
ausbitten ['aʊsbɪtən] *unreg vt*: **sich** *dat* **etw ~** (*geh: erbitten*) to ask for sth; (*verlangen*) to insist on sth
ausblasen ['aʊsblaːzən] *unreg vt* to blow out; (*Ei*) to blow
ausbleiben ['aʊsblaɪbən] *unreg vi* (*Personen*) to stay away, not come; (*Ereignisse*) to fail to happen, not happen; **es konnte nicht ~, dass ...** it was inevitable that ...
ausblenden ['aʊsblɛndən] *vt, vi* (*TV etc*) to fade out
Ausblick ['aʊsblɪk] *m* (*lit, fig*) prospect, outlook, view
ausbomben ['aʊsbɔmbən] *vt* to bomb out
ausbooten ['aʊsboːtən] (*umg*) *vt* (*jdn*) to kick *od* boot out
ausbrechen ['aʊsbrɛçən] *unreg vi* to break out ▷ *vt* to break off; **in Tränen/Gelächter ~** to burst into tears/out laughing
Ausbrecher, in (**-s, -**) (*umg*) *m(f)* (*Gefangener*) escaped prisoner, escapee
ausbreiten ['aʊsbraɪtən] *vt* to spread (out); (*Arme*) to stretch out ▷ *vr* to spread; **sich über**

ein Thema ~ to expand od enlarge on a topic
ausbrennen ['aʊsbrɛnən] unreg vt to scorch; (Wunde) to cauterize ▷ vi to burn out
ausbringen ['aʊsbrɪŋən] unreg vt (ein Hoch) to propose
Ausbruch ['aʊsbrʊx] m outbreak; (von Vulkan) eruption; (Gefühlsausbruch) outburst; (von Gefangenen) escape
ausbrüten ['aʊsbry:tən] vt (lit, fig) to hatch
Ausbuchtung ['aʊsbʊxtʊŋ] f bulge; (Küste) cove
ausbügeln ['aʊsby:gəln] vt to iron out; (umg: Fehler, Verlust) to make good
ausbuhen ['aʊsbu:ən] vt to boo
Ausbund ['aʊsbʊnt] m: **ein ~ an** od **von Tugend/Sparsamkeit** a paragon of virtue/a model of thrift
ausbürgern ['aʊsbyrgərn] vt to expatriate
ausbürsten ['aʊsbyrstən] vt to brush out
Ausdauer ['aʊsdaʊər] f stamina; (Beharrlichkeit) perseverance
ausdauernd adj persevering
ausdehnen ['aʊsde:nən] vt, vr (räumlich) to expand; (zeitlich, auch Gummi) to stretch; (Nebel, fig: Macht) to extend
ausdenken ['aʊsdɛŋkən] unreg vt (zu Ende denken) to think through; **sich** dat **etw ~** to think sth up; **das ist nicht auszudenken** (unvorstellbar) it's inconceivable
ausdiskutieren ['aʊsdɪskuti:rən] vt to talk out
ausdrehen ['aʊsdre:ən] vt to turn od switch off
Ausdruck ['aʊsdrʊk] (**-s, -drücke**) m expression, phrase; (Kundgabe, Gesichtsausdruck) expression; (Fachausdruck) term; (Comput) hard copy; **mit dem ~ des Bedauerns** (form) expressing regret
ausdrucken vt (Text) to print out
ausdrücken ['aʊsdrʏkən] vt (auch vr: formulieren, zeigen) to express; (Zigarette) to put out; (Zitrone) to squeeze
ausdrücklich adj express, explicit
Ausdrucks- zW: **Ausdrucksfähigkeit** f expressiveness; (Gewandtheit) articulateness; **ausdruckslos** adj expressionless, blank; **ausdrucksvoll** adj expressive; **Ausdrucksweise** f mode of expression
Ausdünstung ['aʊsdʏnstʊŋ] f (Dampf) vapour (Brit), vapor (US); (Geruch) smell
auseinander [aʊs|aɪ'nandər] adv (getrennt) apart; **weit ~** far apart
auseinander- zW: **auseinanderbringen** unreg vt to separate; **auseinanderfallen** unreg vi to fall apart; **auseinandergehen** unreg vi (Menschen) to separate; (Meinungen) to differ; (Gegenstand) to fall apart; (umg: dick werden) to put on weight; **auseinanderhalten** unreg vt to tell apart; **auseinanderklaffen** vi to gape open; (fig: Meinungen) to be far apart, diverge (wildly); **auseinanderlaufen** unreg vi (Menge) to disperse; (umg: sich trennen) to break up; **auseinanderleben** vr to drift apart; **auseinandernehmen** unreg vt to take to pieces, dismantle; **auseinanderschreiben** unreg vt to

write as separate words; **auseinandersetzen** unreg vt to set forth, explain ▷ vr (sich verständigen) to come to terms, settle; (sich befassen) to concern o.s.; **sich mit jdm auseinandersetzen** to talk with sb; (sich streiten) to argue with sb; **Auseinandersetzung** f argument
auserkoren ['aʊs|ɛrko:rən] adj (liter) chosen, selected
auserlesen ['aʊs|ɛrle:zən] adj select, choice
ausersehen ['aʊs|ɛrze:ən] unreg vt (geh): **dazu ~ sein, etw zu tun** to be chosen to do sth
ausfahrbar adj extendable; (Antenne, Fahrgestell) retractable
ausfahren ['aʊsfa:rən] unreg vi to drive out; (Naut) to put out (to sea) ▷ vt to take out; (Aut) to drive flat out; (ausliefern: Waren) to deliver; **ausgefahrene Wege** rutted roads
Ausfahrt f (des Zuges etc) leaving, departure; (Autobahnausfahrt, Garagenausfahrt) exit, way out; (Spazierfahrt) drive, excursion
Ausfall ['aʊsfal] m loss; (Nichtstattfinden) cancellation; (das Versagen: Tech, Med) failure; (von Motor) breakdown; (Produktionsstörung) stoppage; (Mil) sortie; (Fechten) lunge; (radioaktiv) fallout
ausfallen ['aʊsfalən] unreg vi (Zähne, Haare) to fall od come out; (nicht stattfinden) to be cancelled; (wegbleiben) to be omitted; (Person) to drop out; (Lohn) to be stopped; (nicht funktionieren) to break down; (Resultat haben) to turn out; **wie ist das Spiel ausgefallen?** what was the result of the game?; **die Schule fällt morgen aus** there's no school tomorrow
ausfallend adj impertinent
Ausfallstraße f arterial road
Ausfallzeit f (Maschine) downtime
ausfegen ['aʊsfe:gən] vt to sweep out
ausfeilen ['aʊsfaɪlən] vt to file out; (Stil) to polish up
ausfertigen ['aʊsfɛrtɪgən] vt (form) to draw up; (Rechnung) to make out; **doppelt ~** to duplicate
Ausfertigung f (form) drawing up; making out; (Exemplar) copy; **in doppelter/dreifacher ~** in duplicate/triplicate
ausfindig ['aʊsfɪndɪç] adj: **~ machen** to discover
ausfliegen ['aʊsfli:gən] unreg vi to fly away ▷ vt to fly out; **sie sind ausgeflogen** (umg) they're out
ausfließen ['aʊsfli:sən] unreg vi: **~ (aus)** (herausfließen) to flow out (of); (auslaufen: Öl etc) to leak (out of); (Eiter etc) to be discharged (from)
ausflippen ['aʊsflɪpən] (umg) vi to freak out
Ausflucht ['aʊsflʊxt] (**-, -flüchte**) f excuse
Ausflug ['aʊsflu:k] m excursion, outing
Ausflügler, in ['aʊsfly:klər(ɪn)] (**-s, -**) m(f) tripper (Brit), excursionist (US)
Ausfluss ['aʊsflʊs] m outlet; (Med) discharge
ausfragen ['aʊsfra:gən] vt to interrogate, question
ausfransen ['aʊsfranzən] vi to fray

ausfressen ['aʊsfrɛsən] *unreg* (*umg*) *vt* (*anstellen*) to be up to

Ausfuhr ['aʊsfuːr] (**-**, **-en**) *f* export, exportation; (*Ware*) export ▷ *in zW* export

ausführbar ['aʊsfyːrbaːr] *adj* feasible; (*Comm*) exportable

ausführen ['aʊsfyːrən] *vt* (*verwirklichen*) to carry out; (*Person*) to take out; (*Hund*) to take for a walk; (*Comm*) to export; (*erklären*) to give details of; **die ~de Gewalt** (*Pol*) the executive

Ausfuhrgenehmigung *f* export licence

ausführlich *adj* detailed ▷ *adv* in detail; **Ausführlichkeit** *f* detail

Ausführung *f* execution, performance; (*von Waren*) design; (*von Thema*) exposition; (*Durchführung*) completion; (*Herstellungsart*) version; (*Erklärung*) explanation

Ausfuhrzoll *m* export duty

ausfüllen ['aʊsfʏlən] *vt* to fill up; (*Fragebogen etc*) to fill in; (*Beruf*) to be fulfilling for; **jdn (ganz) ~** (*Zeit in Anspruch nehmen*) to take (all) sb's time

Ausg. *abk* (= *Ausgabe*) ed.

Ausgabe ['aʊsgaːbə] *f* (*Geld*) expenditure, outlay; (*Aushändigung*) giving out; (*Schalter*) counter; (*Ausführung*) version; (*Buch*) edition; (*Nummer*) issue

Ausgang ['aʊsgaŋ] *m* way out, exit; (*Ende*) end; (*Ausgangspunkt*) starting point; (*Ergebnis*) result; (*Ausgehtag*) free time, time off; **ein Unfall mit tödlichem ~** a fatal accident; **kein ~** no exit

Ausgangs- *zW*: **Ausgangsbasis** *f* starting point; **Ausgangspunkt** *m* starting point; **Ausgangssperre** *f* curfew

ausgeben ['aʊsgeːbən] *unreg vt* (*Geld*) to spend; (*austeilen*) to issue, distribute; (*Comput*) to output ▷ *vr*: **sich für etw/jdn ~** to pass o.s. off as sth/sb; **ich gebe heute Abend einen aus** (*umg*) it's my treat this evening

ausgebeult ['aʊsgəbɔʏlt] *adj* (*Kleidung*) baggy; (*Hut*) battered

ausgebucht ['aʊsgəbuːxt] *adj* fully booked

Ausgeburt ['aʊsgəbuːrt] (*pej*) *f* (*der Fantasie etc*) monstrous product *od* invention

ausgedehnt ['aʊsgədeːnt] *adj* (*breit, groß, fig: weitreichend*) extensive; (*Spaziergang*) long; (*zeitlich*) lengthy

ausgedient ['aʊsgədiːnt] *adj* (*Soldat*) discharged; (*verbraucht*) no longer in use; **~ haben** to have come to the end of its useful life

ausgefallen ['aʊsgəfalən] *adj* (*ungewöhnlich*) exceptional

ausgefuchst ['aʊsgəfʊkst] (*umg*) *adj* clever; (*listig*) crafty

ausgegangen ['aʊsgəgaŋən] *pp von* **ausgehen**

ausgeglichen ['aʊsgəglɪçən] *adj* (well-) balanced; **Ausgeglichenheit** *f* balance; (*von Mensch*) even-temperedness

Ausgehanzug *m* good suit

ausgehen ['aʊsgeːən] *unreg vi* (*auch Feuer, Ofen, Licht*) to go out; (*zu Ende gehen*) to come to an end; (*Benzin*) to run out; (*Haare, Zähne*) to fall *od* come out; (*Strom*) to go off; (*Resultat haben*) to

turn out; (*spazieren gehen*) to go (out) for a walk; (*abgeschickt werden: Post*) to be sent off; **mir ging das Benzin aus** I ran out of petrol (*Brit*) *od* gas (*US*); **auf etw** *akk* **~** to aim at sth; **von etw ~** (*wegführen*) to lead away from sth; (*herrühren*) to come from sth; (*zugrunde legen*) to proceed from sth; **wir können davon ~, dass ...** we can proceed from the assumption that ..., we can take as our starting point that ...; **leer ~** to get nothing; **schlecht ~** to turn out badly

ausgehungert ['aʊsgəhʊŋərt] *adj* starved; (*abgezehrt: Mensch etc*) emaciated

Ausgehverbot *nt* curfew

ausgeklügelt ['aʊsgəklyːgəlt] *adj* ingenious

ausgekocht ['aʊsgəkɔxt] (*pej: umg*) *adj* (*durchtrieben*) cunning; (*fig*) out-and-out

ausgelassen ['aʊsgəlasən] *adj* boisterous, high-spirited, exuberant; **Ausgelassenheit** *f* boisterousness, high spirits *pl*, exuberance

ausgelastet ['aʊsgəlastət] *adj* fully occupied

ausgeleiert ['aʊsgəlaɪərt] *adj* worn; (*Gummiband*) stretched

ausgelernt ['aʊsgəlɛrnt] *adj* trained, qualified

ausgemacht ['aʊsgəmaxt] *adj* settled; (*umg: Dummkopf etc*) out-and-out, downright; **es gilt als ~, dass ...** it is settled that ...; **es war eine ~e Sache, dass ...** it was a foregone conclusion that ...

ausgemergelt ['aʊsgəmɛrgəlt] *adj* (*Gesicht*) emaciated, gaunt

ausgenommen ['aʊsgənɔmən] *konj* except; **Anwesende sind ~** present company excepted

ausgepowert ['aʊsgəpoːvərt] *adj*: **~ sein** (*umg*) to be tired, be exhausted

ausgeprägt ['aʊsgəprɛːkt] *adj* prominent; (*Eigenschaft*) distinct

ausgerechnet ['aʊsgərɛçnət] *adv* just, precisely; **~ du** you of all people; **~ heute** today of all days

ausgeschlossen ['aʊsgəʃlɔsən] *pp von* **ausschließen** ▷ *adj* (*unmöglich*) impossible, out of the question; **es ist nicht ~, dass ...** it cannot be ruled out that ...

ausgeschnitten ['aʊsgəʃnɪtən] *adj* (*Kleid*) low-necked

ausgesehen ['aʊsgəzeːən] *pp von* **aussehen**

ausgesprochen ['aʊsgəʃprɔxən] *adj* (*Faulheit, Lüge etc*) out-and-out; (*unverkennbar*) marked ▷ *adv* decidedly

ausgestorben ['aʊsgəʃtɔrbən] *adj* (*Tierart*) extinct; (*fig*) deserted

ausgewogen ['aʊsgəvoːgən] *adj* balanced; (*Maß*) equal

ausgezeichnet ['aʊsgətsaɪçnət] *adj* excellent

ausgiebig ['aʊsgiːbɪç] *adj* (*Gebrauch*) full, good; (*Essen*) generous, lavish; **~ schlafen** to have a good sleep

ausgießen ['aʊsgiːsən] *unreg vt* (*aus einem Behälter*) to pour out; (*Behälter*) to empty; (*weggießen*) to pour away

Ausgleich ['aʊsglaɪç] (**-(e)s**, **-e**) *m* balance; (*von Fehler, Mangel*) compensation; (*Sport*): **den ~ erzielen** to equalize; **zum ~ +gen** in order to offset sth; **das ist ein guter ~** (*entspannend*) that's very relaxing

ausgleichen ['aʊsglaɪçən] *unreg vt* to balance (out); (*Konflikte*) to reconcile; (*Höhe*) to even up ▷ *vi* (*Sport*) to equalize; **~de Gerechtigkeit** poetic justice

Ausgleichssport *m* keep-fit activity

Ausgleichstor *nt* equalizer

ausgraben ['aʊsgraːbən] *unreg vt* to dig up; (*Leichen*) to exhume; (*fig*) to unearth

Ausgrabung *f* excavation

ausgrenzen ['aʊsgrɛntsən] *vt* to shut out, separate

Ausgrenzung *f* shut-out, separation

Ausguck ['aʊsgʊk] *m* look-out

Ausguss ['aʊsgʊs] *m* (*Spüle*) sink; (*Abfluss*) outlet; (*Tülle*) spout

aushaben ['aʊshaːbən] *unreg* (*umg*) *vt* (*Kleidung*) to have taken off; (*Buch*) to have finished

aushalten ['aʊshaltən] *unreg vt* to bear, stand; (*umg: Geliebte*) to keep ▷ *vi* to hold out; **das ist nicht zum A~** that is unbearable; **sich von jdm ~ lassen** to be kept by sb

aushandeln ['aʊshandəln] *vt* to negotiate

aushändigen ['aʊshɛndɪgən] *vt*: **jdm etw ~** to hand sth over to sb

Aushang ['aʊshaŋ] *m* notice

aushängen ['aʊshɛŋən] *unreg vt* (*Meldung*) to put up; (*Fenster*) to take off its hinges ▷ *vi* to be displayed ▷ *vr* to hang out

Aushängeschild *nt* (shop) sign; (*fig*): **als ~ für etw dienen** to promote sth

ausharren ['aʊsharən] *vi* to hold out

aushäusig ['aʊshɔʏzɪç] *adj* gallivanting around, on the tiles

ausheben ['aʊsheːbən] *unreg vt* (*Erde*) to lift out; (*Grube*) to hollow out; (*Tür*) to take off its hinges; (*Diebesnest*) to clear out; (*Mil*) to enlist

aushecken ['aʊshɛkən] (*umg*) *vt* to concoct, think up

aushelfen ['aʊshɛlfən] *unreg vi*: **jdm ~** to help sb out

Aushilfe ['aʊshɪlfə] *f* help, assistance; (*Person*) (temporary) worker

Aushilfs- *zW*: **Aushilfskraft** *f* temporary worker; **Aushilfslehrer, in** *m(f)* supply teacher; **aushilfsweise** *adv* temporarily, as a stopgap

aushöhlen ['aʊshøːlən] *vt* to hollow out; (*fig: untergraben*) to undermine

ausholen ['aʊshoːlən] *vi* to swing one's arm back; (*zur Ohrfeige*) to raise one's hand; (*beim Gehen*) to take long strides; **zum Gegenschlag ~** (*lit, fig*) to prepare for a counter-attack

aushorchen ['aʊshɔrçən] *vt* to sound out, pump

aushungern ['aʊshʊŋərn] *vt* to starve out

auskennen ['aʊskɛnən] *unreg vr* to know a lot; (*an einem Ort*) to know one's way about; (*in Fragen etc*) to be knowledgeable; **man kennt sich bei ihm nie aus** you never know where you are with him

auskippen ['aʊskɪpən] *vt* to empty

ausklammern ['aʊsklamərn] *vt* (*Thema*) to exclude, leave out

Ausklang ['aʊsklaŋ] *m* (*geh*) end

ausklappbar ['aʊsklapbaːr] *adj*: **dieser Tisch ist ~** this table can be opened out

auskleiden ['aʊsklaɪdən] *vr* (*geh*) to undress ▷ *vt* (*Wand*) to line

ausklingen ['aʊsklɪŋən] *unreg vi* to end; (*Ton, Lied*) to die away; (*Fest*) to come to an end

ausklinken ['aʊsklɪŋkən] *vt* (*Bomben*) to release ▷ *vi* (*umg*) to flip one's lid

ausklopfen ['aʊsklɔpfən] *vt* (*Teppich*) to beat; (*Pfeife*) to knock out

auskochen ['aʊskɔxən] *vt* to boil; (*Med*) to sterilize

auskommen ['aʊskɔmən] *unreg vi*: **mit jdm ~** to get on with sb; **mit etw ~** to get by with sth; **Auskommen (-s)** *nt*: **sein Auskommen haben** to get by; **mit ihr ist kein Auskommen** she's impossible to get on with

auskosten ['aʊskɔstən] *vt* to enjoy to the full

auskramen ['aʊskraːmən] (*umg*) *vt* to dig out, unearth; (*fig: alte Geschichten etc*) to bring up

auskratzen ['aʊskratsən] *vt* (*auch Med*) to scrape out

auskugeln ['aʊskuːgəln] *vr*: **sich** *dat* **den Arm ~** to dislocate one's arm

auskundschaften ['aʊskʊntʃaftən] *vt* to spy out; (*Gebiet*) to reconnoitre (*Brit*), reconnoiter (*US*)

Auskunft ['aʊskʊnft] (**-, -künfte**) *f* information; (*nähere*) details *pl*, particulars *pl*; (*Stelle*) information office; (*Tel*) inquiries; **jdm ~ erteilen** to give sb information

auskuppeln ['aʊskʊpəln] *vi* to disengage the clutch

auskurieren ['aʊskuriːrən] (*umg*) *vt* to cure

auslachen ['aʊslaxən] *vt* to laugh at, mock

ausladen ['aʊslaːdən] *unreg vt* to unload; (*umg: Gäste*) to cancel an invitation to ▷ *vi* (*Äste*) to spread

ausladend *adj* (*Gebärden, Bewegung*) sweeping

Auslage ['aʊslaːgə] *f* shop window (display)

Auslagen *pl* outlay *sing*, expenditure *sing*

Ausland ['aʊslant] *nt* foreign countries *pl*; **im ~** abroad; **ins ~** abroad

Ausländer, in ['aʊslɛndər(ɪn)] (**-s, -**) *m(f)* foreigner

Ausländerfeindlichkeit *f* hostility to foreigners, xenophobia

ausländisch *adj* foreign

Auslands- *zW*: **Auslandsaufenthalt** *m* stay abroad; **Auslandsgespräch** *nt* international call; **Auslandskorrespondent, in** *m(f)* foreign correspondent; **Auslandsreise** *f* trip abroad; **Auslandsschutzbrief** *m* international travel cover; **Auslandsvertretung** *f* agency abroad; (*von Firma*) foreign branch

auslassen ['aʊslasən] *unreg vt* to leave out; (*Wort etc*) to omit; (*Fett*) to melt; (*Kleidungsstück*) to let out ▷ *vr*: **sich über etw** *akk* **~** to speak one's mind about sth; **seine Wut** *etc* **an jdm ~** to vent one's rage *etc* on sb

Auslassung f omission
Auslassungszeichen nt apostrophe
auslasten ['aʊslastən] vt (Fahrzeug) to make full use of; (Maschine) to use to capacity; (jdn) to occupy fully
Auslauf ['aʊslaʊf] m (für Tiere) run; (Ausfluss) outflow, outlet
auslaufen unreg vi to run out; (Behälter) to leak; (Naut) to put out (to sea); (langsam aufhören) to run down
Ausläufer ['aʊslɔyfər] m (von Gebirge) spur; (Pflanze) runner; (Met: von Hoch) ridge; (: von Tief) trough
ausleeren ['aʊsle:rən] vt to empty
auslegen ['aʊsle:gən] vt (Waren) to lay out; (Köder) to put down; (Geld) to lend; (bedecken) to cover; (Text etc) to interpret
Ausleger (-s, -) m (von Kran etc) jib, boom
Auslegung f interpretation
Ausleihe ['aʊslaɪə] (-, -n) f issuing; (Stelle) issue desk
ausleihen ['aʊslaɪən] unreg vt (verleihen) to lend; **sich** dat etw ~ to borrow sth
auslernen ['aʊslɛrnən] vi (Lehrling) to finish one's apprenticeship; **man lernt nie aus** (Sprichwort) you live and learn
Auslese ['aʊsle:zə] (-, -n) f selection; (Elite) elite; (Wein) choice wine
auslesen ['aʊsle:zən] unreg vt to select; (umg: zu Ende lesen) to finish
ausliefern ['aʊsli:fərn] vt to hand over; (Comm) to deliver ▷ vr: **sich jdm** ~ to give o.s. up to sb; **~ (an** +akk) to deliver (up) (to), hand over (to); (an anderen Staat) to extradite (to); **jdm/etw ausgeliefert sein** to be at the mercy of sb/sth
Auslieferungsabkommen nt extradition treaty
ausliegen ['aʊsli:gən] unreg vi (zur Ansicht) to be displayed; (Zeitschriften etc) to be available (to the public); (Liste) to be up
auslöschen ['aʊslœʃən] vt to extinguish; (fig) to wipe out, obliterate
auslosen ['aʊslo:zən] vt to draw lots for
auslösen ['aʊsløːzən] vt (Explosion, Schuss) to set off; (hervorrufen) to cause, produce; (Gefangene) to ransom; (Pfand) to redeem
Auslöser (-s, -) m trigger; (Phot) release; (Anlass) cause
ausloten ['aʊslo:tən] vt (Naut: Tiefe) to sound; (fig geh) to plumb
ausmachen ['aʊsmaxən] vt (Licht, Radio) to turn off; (Feuer) to put out; (entdecken) to make out; (vereinbaren) to agree; (beilegen) to settle; (Anteil darstellen, betragen) to represent; (bedeuten) to matter; **das macht ihm nichts aus** it doesn't matter to him; **macht es Ihnen etwas aus, wenn ...?** would you mind if ...?
ausmalen ['aʊsma:lən] vt to paint; (fig) to describe; **sich** dat etw ~ to imagine sth
Ausmaß ['aʊsma:s] nt dimension; (fig) scale
ausmerzen ['aʊsmɛrtsən] vt to eliminate
ausmessen ['aʊsmɛsən] unreg vt to measure
ausmisten ['aʊsmɪstən] vt (Stall) to muck out;

(fig: umg: Schrank etc) to tidy out; (: Zimmer) to clean out
ausmustern ['aʊsmʊstərn] vt (Maschine, Fahrzeug etc) to take out of service; (Mil: entlassen) to invalid out
Ausnahme ['aʊsna:mə] (-, -n) f exception; **eine ~ machen** to make an exception; **Ausnahmeerscheinung** f exception, one-off example; **Ausnahmefall** m exceptional case; **Ausnahmezustand** m state of emergency
ausnahmslos adv without exception
ausnahmsweise adv by way of exception, for once
ausnehmen ['aʊsne:mən] unreg vt to take out, remove; (Tier) to gut; (Nest) to rob; (umg: Geld abnehmen) to clean out; (ausschließen) to make an exception of ▷ vr to look, appear
ausnehmend adj exceptional
ausnüchtern ['aʊsnyçtərn] vt, vi to sober up
Ausnüchterungszelle f drying-out cell
ausnutzen ['aʊsnʊtsən] vt (Zeit, Gelegenheit) to use, turn to good account; (Einfluss) to use; (Mensch, Gutmütigkeit) to exploit
auspacken ['aʊspakən] vt to unpack ▷ vi (umg: alles sagen) to talk
auspfeifen ['aʊspfaɪfən] unreg vt to hiss/boo at
ausplaudern ['aʊsplaʊdərn] vt (Geheimnis) to blab
ausposaunen ['aʊspozaʊnən] (umg) vt to tell the world about
ausprägen ['aʊspre:gən] vr (Begabung, Charaktereigenschaft) to reveal od show itself
auspressen ['aʊsprɛsən] vt (Saft, Schwamm etc) to squeeze out; (Zitrone etc) to squeeze
ausprobieren ['aʊsprobi:rən] vt to try (out)
Auspuff ['aʊspʊf] (-(e)s, -e) m (Tech) exhaust; **Auspuffrohr** nt exhaust (pipe); **Auspufftopf** m (Aut) silencer (Brit), muffler (US)
ausquartieren ['aʊskvarti:rən] vt to move out
ausquetschen ['aʊskvɛtʃən] vt (Zitrone etc) to squeeze; (umg: ausfragen) to grill; (: aus Neugier) to pump
ausradieren ['aʊsradi:rən] vt to erase, rub out
ausrangieren ['aʊsraˈʒi:rən] (umg) vt to chuck out; (Maschine, Auto) to scrap
ausrauben ['aʊsraʊbən] vt to rob
ausräumen ['aʊsrɔymən] vt (Dinge) to clear away; (Schrank, Zimmer) to empty; (Bedenken) to put aside
ausrechnen ['aʊsrɛçnən] vt to calculate, reckon
Ausrechnung f calculation, reckoning
Ausrede ['aʊsre:də] f excuse
ausreden ['aʊsre:dən] vi to have one's say ▷ vt: **jdm etw** ~ to talk sb out of sth; **er hat mich nicht mal ~ lassen** he didn't even let me finish (speaking)
ausreichen ['aʊsraɪçən] vi to suffice, be enough
ausreichend adj sufficient, adequate; (Sch) adequate
Ausreise ['aʊsraɪzə] f departure; **bei der ~** when leaving the country; **Ausreiseerlaubnis**

f exit visa

ausreisen ['aʊsraɪzən] vi to leave the country

ausreißen ['aʊsraɪsən] unreg vt to tear od
pull out ▷ vi (Riss bekommen) to tear; (umg)
to make off, scram; **er hat sich** dat **kein
Bein ausgerissen** (umg) he didn't exactly
overstrain himself

ausrenken ['aʊsrɛŋkən] vt to dislocate

ausrichten ['aʊsrɪçtən] vt (Botschaft) to deliver;
(Gruß) to pass on; (Hochzeit etc) to arrange;
(in gerade Linie bringen) to get in a straight
line; (angleichen) to bring into line; (Typ etc)
to justify; **etwas/nichts bei** jdm ~ to get
somewhere/nowhere with sb; **jdm etw** ~ to
take a message for sb; **ich werde es ihm** ~ I'll
tell him

ausrotten ['aʊsrɔtən] vt to stamp out,
exterminate

ausrücken ['aʊsrʏkən] vi (Mil) to move
off; (Feuerwehr, Polizei) to be called out;
(umg: weglaufen) to run away

Ausruf ['aʊsruːf] m (Schrei) cry, exclamation;
(Verkünden) proclamation

ausrufen unreg vt to cry out, exclaim; to call
out; **jdn** ~ **(lassen)** (über Lautsprecher etc) to
page sb

Ausrufezeichen nt exclamation mark

ausruhen ['aʊsruːən] vt, vi, vr to rest

ausrüsten ['aʊsrʏstən] vt to equip, fit out

Ausrüstung f equipment

ausrutschen ['aʊsrʊtʃən] vi to slip

Ausrutscher (-s, -) (umg) m (lit, fig) slip

Aussage ['aʊszaːgə] (-, -n) f (Jur) statement;
der Angeklagte/Zeuge verweigerte die ~
the accused/witness refused to give evidence

aussagekräftig adj expressive, full of
expression

aussagen ['aʊszaːgən] vt to say, state ▷ vi (Jur)
to give evidence

Aussatz ['aʊszats] (-es) m (Med) leprosy

aussaugen ['aʊszaʊgən] vt (Saft etc) to suck
out; (Wunde) to suck the poison out of;
(fig: ausbeuten) to drain dry

ausschalten ['aʊsʃaltən] vt to switch off; (fig)
to eliminate

Ausschank ['aʊsʃaŋk] (-(e)s, -schänke) m
dispensing, giving out; (Comm) selling; (Theke)
bar

Ausschankerlaubnis f licence (Brit), license
(US)

Ausschau ['aʊsʃaʊ] f: ~ **halten (nach)** to look
out (for), watch (for)

ausschauen vi: ~ **(nach)** to look out (for), be on
the look-out (for)

ausscheiden ['aʊsʃaɪdən] unreg vt (aussondern)
to take out; (Med) to excrete ▷ vi: ~ **(aus)** to
leave; (aus einem Amt) to retire (from); (Sport)
to be eliminated (from), be knocked out (of);
er scheidet für den Posten aus he can't be
considered for the job

Ausscheidung f (Aussondern) removal; (Med)
excretion; (Sport) elimination

ausschenken ['aʊsʃɛŋkən] vt to pour out; (am

Ausschank) to serve

ausscheren ['aʊsʃeːrən] vi (Fahrzeug) to leave
the line od convoy; (zum Überholen) to pull out

ausschildern ['aʊsʃɪldərn] vt to signpost

ausschimpfen ['aʊsʃɪmpfən] vt to scold, tell off

ausschlachten ['aʊsʃlaxtən] vt (Auto) to
cannibalize; (fig) to make a meal of

ausschlafen ['aʊsʃlaːfən] unreg vi, vr to sleep late
▷ vt to sleep off; **ich bin nicht ausgeschlafen**
I didn't have od get enough sleep

Ausschlag ['aʊsʃlaːk] m (Med) rash;
(Pendelausschlag) swing; (von Nadel) deflection;
den ~ **geben** (fig) to tip the balance

ausschlagen ['aʊsʃlaːgən] unreg vt to knock out;
(auskleiden) to deck out; (verweigern) to decline
▷ vi (Pferd) to kick out; (Bot) to sprout; (Zeiger) to
be deflected

ausschlaggebend adj decisive

ausschließen ['aʊsʃliːsən] unreg vt to shut od
lock out; (Sport) to disqualify; (Fehler, Möglichkeit
etc) to rule out; (fig) to exclude; **ich will mich
nicht** ~ myself not excepted

ausschließlich adj exclusive ▷ adv exclusively
▷ präp+gen excluding, exclusive of

ausschlüpfen ['aʊsʃlʏpfən] vi to slip out; (aus
Ei, Puppe) to hatch out

Ausschluss ['aʊsʃlʊs] m exclusion; **unter** ~
der Öffentlichkeit stattfinden to be closed
to the public; (Jur) to be held in camera

ausschmücken ['aʊsʃmʏkən] vt to decorate;
(fig) to embellish

ausschneiden ['aʊsʃnaɪdən] unreg vt to cut out;
(Büsche) to trim

Ausschnitt ['aʊsʃnɪt] m (Teil) section; (von Kleid)
neckline; (Zeitungsausschnitt) cutting (Brit),
clipping (US); (aus Film etc) excerpt

ausschöpfen ['aʊsʃœpfən] vt to ladle out; (fig)
to exhaust; **Wasser** etc **aus etw** ~ to ladle
water etc out of sth

ausschreiben ['aʊsʃraɪbən] unreg vt (ganz
schreiben) to write out (in full); (Scheck, Rechnung
etc) to write (out); (Stelle, Wettbewerb etc) to
announce, advertise

Ausschreibung f (Bekanntmachung: von Wahlen)
calling; (: von Stelle) advertising

Ausschreitung ['aʊsʃraɪtʊŋ] f excess

Ausschuss ['aʊsʃʊs] m committee, board;
(Abfall) waste, scraps pl; (Comm: auch:
Ausschussware) reject

ausschütten ['aʊsʃʏtən] vt to pour out; (Eimer)
to empty; (Geld) to pay ▷ vr to shake (with
laughter)

Ausschüttung f (Fin) distribution

ausschwärmen ['aʊsʃvɛrmən] vi (Bienen,
Menschen) to swarm out; (Mil) to fan out

ausschweifend ['aʊsʃvaɪfənt] adj (Leben)
dissipated, debauched; (Fantasie) extravagant

Ausschweifung f excess

ausschweigen ['aʊsʃvaɪgən] unreg vr to keep
silent

ausschwitzen ['aʊsʃvɪtsən] vt to sweat out

aussehen ['aʊszeːən] unreg vi to look; **gut** ~
to look good/well; **wie siehts aus?** (umg: wie

stehts?) how's things?; **das sieht nach nichts aus** that doesn't look anything special; **es sieht nach Regen aus** it looks like rain; **es sieht schlecht aus** things look bad; **Aussehen (-s)** *nt* appearance

aus sein ['aussaɪn] *siehe* **aus**

außen ['aʊsən] *adv* outside; *(nach außen)* outwards; **~ ist es rot** it's red (on the) outside

Außen- *zW:* **Außenantenne** *f* outside aerial; **Außenarbeiten** *pl* work *sing* on the exterior; **Außenaufnahme** *f* outdoor shot; **Außenbezirk** *m* outlying district; **Außenbordmotor** *m* outboard motor

aussenden ['aʊszɛndən] *unreg vt* to send out, emit

Außen- *zW:* **Außendienst** *m* outside *od* field service; *(von Diplomat)* foreign service; **Außenhandel** *m* foreign trade; **Außenminister** *m* foreign minister; **Außenministerium** *nt* foreign office; **Außenpolitik** *f* foreign policy; **Außenseite** *f* outside; **Außenseiter, in (-s, -)** *m(f)* outsider; **Außenspiegel** *m (Aut)* outside mirror; **Außenstände** *pl (bes Comm)* outstanding debts *pl*, arrears *pl*; **Außenstehende, r** *f(m)* outsider; **Außenstelle** *f* branch; **Außenwelt** *f* outside world

außer ['aʊsər] *präp +dat (räumlich)* out of; *(abgesehen von)* except ▷ *konj (ausgenommen)* except; **~ Gefahr sein** to be out of danger; **~ Zweifel** beyond any doubt; **~ Betrieb** out of order; **~ sich** *dat* **sein/geraten** to be beside o.s.; **~ Dienst** retired; **~ Landes** abroad; **~ wenn** unless; **~ dass** except; **außeramtlich** *adj* unofficial, private

außerdem *konj* besides, in addition ▷ *adv* anyway

außerdienstlich *adj* private

äußere, r, s ['ɔysərə(r,s)] *adj* outer, external; **Äußere, s** *nt* exterior; *(fig: Aussehen)* outward appearance

außer- *zW:* **außerehelich** *adj* extramarital; **außergewöhnlich** *adj* unusual; **außerhalb** *präp +gen* outside ▷ *adv* outside; **außerirdisch** *adj* extraterrestrial; **Außerkraftsetzung** *f* repeal

äußerlich *adj* external; **rein ~ betrachtet** on the face of it; **Äußerlichkeit** *f (fig)* triviality; *(Oberflächlichkeit)* superficiality; *(Formalität)* formality

äußern *vt* to utter, express; *(zeigen)* to show ▷ *vr* to give one's opinion; *(sich zeigen)* to show itself

außer- *zW:* **außerordentlich** *adj* extraordinary; **außerplanmäßig** *adj* unscheduled; **außersinnlich** *adj:* **außersinnliche Wahrnehmung** extrasensory perception

äußerst ['ɔysərst] *adv* extremely, most

außerstande, außer Stande [aʊsər'ʃtandə] *adv (nicht in der Lage)* not in a position; *(nicht fähig)* unable

Äußerste, s *nt:* **bis zum ~n gehen** to go to extremes

äußerste, r, s *adj* utmost; *(räumlich)* farthest;

(Termin) last possible; *(Preis)* highest; **mein ~s Angebot** my final offer

äußerstenfalls *adv* if the worst comes to the worst

Äußerung *f (Bemerkung)* remark, comment; *(Behauptung)* statement; *(Zeichen)* expression

aussetzen ['aʊszɛtsən] *vt (Kind, Tier)* to abandon; *(Boote)* to lower; *(Belohnung)* to offer; *(Urteil, Verfahren)* to postpone ▷ *vi (aufhören)* to stop; *(Pause machen)* to have a break; **jdn/sich einer Sache** *dat* **~** to lay sb/o.s. open to sth; **jdm/etw ausgesetzt sein** to be exposed to sb/sth; **was haben Sie daran auszusetzen?** what's your objection to it?; **an jdm/etw etwas ~** to find fault with sb/sth

Aussicht ['aʊszɪçt] *f* view; *(in Zukunft)* prospect; **in ~ sein** to be in view; **etw in ~ haben** to have sth in view; **jdm etw in ~ stellen** to promise sb sth

Aussichts- *zW:* **aussichtslos** *adj* hopeless; **Aussichtspunkt** *m* viewpoint; **aussichtsreich** *adj* promising; **Aussichtsturm** *m* observation tower

Aussiedler, in ['aʊszi:dlər(ɪn)] **(-s, -)** *m(f)* *(Auswanderer)* emigrant; *see culture note*

○ **AUSSIEDLER**
○
○ *Aussiedler* are people of German origin from
○ East and South-East Europe who have
○ resettled in Germany. Many come from
○ the former Soviet Union. They are given
○ free German language tuition and receive
○ financial help. The number of *Aussiedler*
○ increased dramatically in the early 1990s.

aussöhnen ['aʊszø:nən] *vt* to reconcile ▷ *vr* *(einander)* to become reconciled; **sich mit jdm/ etw ~** to reconcile o.s. with sb/to sth

Aussöhnung *f* reconciliation

aussondern ['aʊszɔndərn] *vt* to separate off, select

aussorgen ['aʊszɔrgən] *vi:* **ausgesorgt haben** to have no more money worries

aussortieren ['aʊszɔrti:rən] *vt* to sort out

ausspannen ['aʊsʃpanən] *vt* to spread *od* stretch out; *(Pferd)* to unharness; *(umg: Mädchen)*: **jdm jdn ~** to steal sb from sb ▷ *vi* to relax

aussparen ['aʊsʃpa:rən] *vt* to leave open

aussperren ['aʊsʃpɛrən] *vt* to lock out

Aussperrung *f (Industrie)* lock-out

ausspielen ['aʊsʃpi:lən] *vt (Karte)* to lead; *(Geldprämie)* to offer as a prize ▷ *vi (Karten)* to lead; **ausgespielt haben** to be finished; **jdn gegen jdn ~** to play sb off against sb

Ausspielung *f (im Lotto)* draw

ausspionieren ['aʊsʃpioni:rən] *vt (Pläne etc)* to spy out; *(Person)* to spy on

Aussprache ['aʊsʃpra:xə] *f* pronunciation; *(Unterredung)* (frank) discussion

aussprechen ['aʊsʃprɛçən] *unreg vt* to pronounce; *(zu Ende sprechen)* to speak; *(äußern)* to say, express ▷ vr (*sich äußern*): **sich ~ (über +akk)** to speak (about); (*sich anvertrauen*) to unburden o.s. (about *od* on); (*diskutieren*) to discuss ▷ vi (*zu Ende sprechen*) to finish speaking; **der Regierung das Vertrauen ~** to pass a vote of confidence in the government

Ausspruch ['aʊsʃprʊx] m remark; (*geflügeltes Wort*) saying

ausspucken ['aʊsʃpʊkən] vt to spit out ▷ vi to spit

ausspülen ['aʊsʃpyːlən] vt to wash out; (*Mund*) to rinse

ausstaffieren ['aʊsʃtafiːrən] vt to equip, kit out; (*Zimmer*) to furnish

Ausstand ['aʊsʃtant] m strike; **in den ~ treten** to go on strike; **seinen ~ geben** to hold a leaving party

ausstatten ['aʊsʃtatən] vt (*Zimmer etc*) to furnish; **jdn mit etw ~** to equip sb *od* kit sb out with sth

Ausstattung f (Ausstatten) provision; (*Kleidung*) outfit; (*Aussteuer*) dowry; (*Aufmachung*) make-up; (*Einrichtung*) furnishing

ausstechen ['aʊsʃteçən] unreg vt (*Torf, Kekse*) to cut out; (*Augen*) to gouge out; (*übertreffen*) to outshine

ausstehen ['aʊsʃteːən] unreg vt to stand, endure ▷ vi (*noch nicht da sein*) to be outstanding

aussteigen ['aʊsʃtaɪgən] unreg vi to get out, alight; **alles ~!** (*von Schaffner*) all change!; **aus der Gesellschaft ~** to drop out (of society)

Aussteiger, in (*umg*) m(f) dropout

ausstellen ['aʊsʃtɛlən] vt to exhibit, display; (*umg: ausschalten*) to switch off; (*Rechnung etc*) to make out; (*Pass, Zeugnis*) to issue

Aussteller, in m(f) (*auf Messe*) exhibitor; (*von Scheck*) drawer

Ausstellung f exhibition; (*Fin*) drawing up; (*einer Rechnung*) making out; (*eines Passes etc*) issuing

Ausstellungsdatum nt date of issue

Ausstellungsstück nt (*in Ausstellung*) exhibit; (*in Schaufenster etc*) display item

aussterben ['aʊsʃtɛrbən] unreg vi to die out; **Aussterben** nt extinction

Aussteuer ['aʊsʃtɔʏər] f dowry

aussteuern ['aʊsʃtɔʏərn] vt (*Verstärker*) to adjust

Ausstieg ['aʊsʃtiːk] (**-(e)s, -e**) m (*Ausgang*) exit; **~ aus der Atomenergie** abandonment of nuclear energy

ausstopfen ['aʊsʃtɔpfən] vt to stuff

ausstoßen ['aʊsʃtoːsən] unreg vt (*Luft, Rauch*) to give off, emit; (*aus Verein etc*) to expel, exclude; (*herstellen: Teile, Stückzahl*) to turn out, produce

ausstrahlen ['aʊsʃtraːlən] vt, vi to radiate; (*Rundf*) to broadcast

Ausstrahlung f radiation; (*fig*) charisma

ausstrecken ['aʊsʃtrɛkən] vt, vr to stretch out

ausstreichen ['aʊsʃtraɪçən] unreg vt to cross out; (*glätten*) to smooth out

ausstreuen ['aʊsʃtrɔʏən] vt to scatter; (*fig: Gerücht*) to spread

ausströmen ['aʊsʃtrøːmən] vi (*Gas*) to pour out, escape ▷ vt to give off; (*fig*) to radiate

aussuchen ['aʊszuːxən] vt to select, pick out

Austausch ['aʊstaʊʃ] m exchange; **austauschbar** adj exchangeable

austauschen vt to exchange, swop

Austauschmotor m replacement engine; (*gebraucht*) factory-reconditioned engine

Austauschstudent, in m(f) exchange student

austeilen ['aʊstaɪlən] vt to distribute, give out

Auster ['aʊstər] (**-, -n**) f oyster

austoben ['aʊstoːbən] vr (*Kind*) to run wild; (*Erwachsene*) to let off steam; (*sich müde machen*) to tire o.s. out

austragen ['aʊstraːgən] unreg vt (*Post*) to deliver; (*Streit etc*) to decide; (*Wettkämpfe*) to hold; **ein Kind ~** (*nicht abtreiben*) to have a child

Austräger ['aʊstrɛːgər] m delivery boy; (*Zeitungsausträger*) newspaper boy

Austragungsort m (*Sport*) venue

Australien [aʊsˈtraːliən] (**-s**) nt Australia

Australier, in (**-s, -**) m(f) Australian

australisch adj Australian

austreiben ['aʊstraɪbən] unreg vt to drive out, expel; (*Teufel etc*) to exorcize; **jdm etw ~** to cure sb of sth; (*bes durch Schläge*) to knock sth out of sb

austreten ['aʊstreːtən] unreg vi (*zur Toilette*) to be excused ▷ vt (*Feuer*) to tread out, trample; (*Schuhe*) to wear out; (*Treppe*) to wear down; **aus etw ~** to leave sth

austricksen ['aʊstrɪksən] (*umg*) vt (*Sport, fig*) to trick

austrinken ['aʊstrɪŋkən] unreg vt (*Glas*) to drain; (*Getränk*) to drink up ▷ vi to finish one's drink, drink up

Austritt ['aʊstrɪt] m emission; (*aus Verein, Partei etc*) retirement, withdrawal

austrocknen ['aʊstrɔknən] vt, vi to dry up

austüfteln ['aʊstʏftəln] (*umg*) vt to work out; (*ersinnen*) to think up

ausüben ['aʊsʔyːbən] vt (*Beruf*) to practise (*Brit*), practice (*US*), carry out; (*innehaben: Amt*) to hold; (*Funktion*) to perform; (*Einfluss*) to exert; **einen Reiz auf jdn ~** to hold an attraction for sb; **eine Wirkung auf jdn ~** to have an effect on sb

Ausübung f practice, exercise; **in ~ seines Dienstes/seiner Pflicht** (*form*) in the execution of his duty

ausufern ['aʊsʔuːfərn] vi (*fig*) to get out of hand; (*Konflikt etc*): **~ (zu)** to escalate (into)

Ausverkauf ['aʊsfɛrkaʊf] m sale; (*fig: Verrat*) sell-out

ausverkaufen vt to sell out; (*Geschäft*) to sell up

ausverkauft adj (*Karten, Artikel*) sold out; (*Theat: Haus*) full

auswachsen ['aʊsvaksən] unreg vi: **das ist (ja) zum A~** (*umg*) it's enough to drive you mad

Auswahl ['aʊsvaːl] f: **eine ~ (an +dat)** a selection (of), a choice (of)

auswählen ['aʊsvɛːlən] vt to select, choose

Auswahlmöglichkeit f choice

Auswanderer ['aʊsvandərər] **(-s, -)** *m* emigrant

Auswanderin ['aʊsvandərɪn] *f* emigrant

auswandern *vi* to emigrate

Auswanderung *f* emigration

auswärtig ['aʊsvɛrtɪç] *adj (nicht am/vom Ort)* out-of-town; *(ausländisch)* foreign; **das A~e Amt** the Foreign Office *(Brit)*, the State Department *(US)*

auswärts ['aʊsvɛrts] *adv* outside; *(nach außen)* outwards; **~ essen** to eat out; **Auswärtsspiel** *nt* away game

auswaschen ['aʊsvaʃən] *unreg vt* to wash out; *(spülen)* to rinse (out)

auswechseln ['aʊsvɛksəln] *vt* to change, substitute

Ausweg ['aʊsveːk] *m* way out; **der letzte ~** the last resort; **ausweglos** *adj* hopeless

ausweichen ['aʊsvaɪçən] *unreg vi:* **jdm/etw ~** *(lit)* to move aside *od* make way for sb/sth; *(fig)* to sidestep sb/sth; **jdm/einer Begegnung ~** to avoid sb/a meeting

ausweichend *adj* evasive

Ausweichmanöver *nt* evasive action

ausweinen ['aʊsvaɪnən] *vr* to have a (good) cry

Ausweis ['aʊsvaɪs] **(-es, -e)** *m* identity card; passport; *(Mitgliedsausweis, Bibliotheksausweis etc)* card; **~, bitte** your papers, please

ausweisen ['aʊsvaɪzən] *unreg vt* to expel, banish ▷ *vr* to prove one's identity

Ausweis- *zW:* **Ausweiskarte** *f* identity papers *pl*; **Ausweiskontrolle** *f* identity check; **Ausweispapiere** *pl* identity papers *pl*

Ausweisung *f* expulsion

ausweiten ['aʊsvaɪtən] *vt* to stretch

auswendig ['aʊsvɛndɪç] *adv* by heart; **~ lernen** to learn by heart

auswerfen ['aʊsvɛrfən] *unreg vt (Anker, Netz)* to cast

auswerten ['aʊsvɛrtən] *vt* to evaluate

Auswertung *f* evaluation, analysis; *(Nutzung)* utilization

auswickeln ['aʊsvɪkəln] *vt (Paket, Bonbon etc)* to unwrap

auswirken ['aʊsvɪrkən] *vr* to have an effect

Auswirkung *f* effect

auswischen ['aʊsvɪʃən] *vt* to wipe out; **jdm eins ~** *(umg)* to put one over on sb

Auswuchs ['aʊsvuːks] *m (out)*growth; *(fig)* product; *(Missstand, Übersteigerung)* excess

auswuchten ['aʊsvʊxtən] *vt (Aut)* to balance

auszacken ['aʊstsakən] *vt (Stoff etc)* to pink

auszahlen ['aʊstsaːlən] *vt (Lohn, Summe)* to pay out; *(Arbeiter)* to pay off; *(Miterben)* to buy out ▷ *vr (sich lohnen)* to pay

auszählen ['aʊstsɛːlən] *vt (Stimmen)* to count; *(Boxen)* to count out

auszeichnen ['aʊstsaɪçnən] *vt* to honour *(Brit)*, honor *(US)*; *(Mil)* to decorate; *(Comm)* to price ▷ *vr* to distinguish o.s.; **der Wagen zeichnet sich durch ... aus** one of the car's main features is ...

Auszeichnung *f* distinction; *(Comm)* pricing;

(Ehrung) awarding of decoration; *(Ehre)* honour *(Brit)*, honor *(US)*; *(Orden)* decoration; **mit ~** with distinction

ausziehen ['aʊstsiːən] *unreg vt (Kleidung)* to take off; *(Haare, Zähne, Tisch etc)* to pull out ▷ *vr* to undress ▷ *vi (aufbrechen)* to leave; *(aus Wohnung)* to move out

Auszubildende, r ['aʊstsʊbɪldəndə(r)] *f(m)* trainee; *(als Handwerker)* apprentice

Auszug ['aʊstsuːk] *m (aus Wohnung)* removal; *(aus Buch etc)* extract; *(Kontoauszug)* statement; *(Ausmarsch)* departure

autark [aʊˈtark] *adj* self-sufficient *(auch fig)*; *(Comm)* autarkical

Auto ['aʊto] **(-s, -s)** *nt* (motor-)car, automobile *(US)*; **mit dem ~ fahren** to go by car; **~ fahren** to drive

Autoatlas *m* road atlas

Autobahn *f* motorway *(Brit)*, expressway *(US)*; *see culture note*

AUTOBAHN

Autobahn is the German for a motorway. In the former West Germany there is an widespread network but in the former DDR the motorways are somewhat less extensive. There is no overall speed limit but a limit of 130 km per hour is recommended and there are lower mandatory limits on certain stretches of road. As yet there are no tolls payable on German Autobahns.

Autobahndreieck *nt* motorway *(Brit) od* expressway *(US)* junction

Autobahnkreuz *nt* motorway *(Brit) od* expressway *(US)* intersection

Autobahnzubringer *m* motorway feeder *od* access road

Autobiografie [aʊtobiograˈfiː] *f* autobiography

Auto- *zW:* **Autobombe** *f* car bomb; **Autobus** *m* bus; *(Reisebus)* coach *(Brit)*, bus *(US)*; **Autofähre** *f* car ferry; **Autofahrer, in** *m(f)* motorist, driver; **Autofahrt** *f* drive; **Autofriedhof** *(umg)* *m* car dump

autogen [aʊtoˈgeːn] *adj* autogenous; **~es Training** *(Psych)* relaxation through self-hypnosis

Autogramm [aʊtoˈgram] *nt* autograph

Automat (-en, -en) *m* machine

Automatik [aʊtoˈmaːtɪk] *f* automatic mechanism *(auch fig)*; *(Gesamtanlage)* automatic system; *(Aut)* automatic transmission

automatisch *adj* automatic

Automatisierung [aʊtomatiˈziːrʊŋ] *f* automation

Automobilausstellung [aʊtoموˈbiːlaʊsʃtɛlʊŋ] *f* motor show

autonom [aʊtoˈnoːm] *adj* autonomous

Autopsie [aʊtɔˈpsiː] *f* post-mortem, autopsy

Autor ['aʊtɔr] **(-s, -en)** *m* author

Autoradio | Azubi

Auto- zW: **Autoradio** nt car radio; **Autoreifen** m car tyre (Brit) od tire (US); **Autoreisezug** m motorail train; **Autorennen** nt motor race; (Sportart) motor racing

Autorin [au'to:rɪn] f author(ess)

autoritär [autori'tɛ:r] adj authoritarian

Autorität f authority

Auto- zW: **Autoschalter** m drive-in bank (counter); **Autotelefon** nt car phone; **Autounfall** m car od motor accident;

Autoverleih m, **Autovermietung** f car hire (Brit) od rental (US)

AvD (-) m abk (= Automobilclub von Deutschland) German motoring organization, ≈ AA (Brit), AAA (US)

Axt [akst] (-, ¨e) f axe (Brit), ax (US)

AZ, Az. abk (= Aktenzeichen) ref.

Azoren [a'tso:rən] pl (Geog) Azores pl

Azteke [ats'te:kə] (-n, -n) m Aztec

Azubi [a'tsu:bi] (-s, -s) (umg) f(m) abk = **Auszubildende(r)**

Bb

B¹, b [be:] *nt* (*letter*) B, b; **B wie Bertha** = B for Benjamin, B for Baker (US); **B-Dur/b-Moll** (the key of) B flat major/minor

B² [be:] *f abk* = **Bundesstraße**

Baby ['be:bi] (**-s, -s**) *nt* baby; **Babyausstattung** *f* layette; **Babyklappe** *f* anonymous drop-off point for unwanted babies; **Babyraum** *m* (*Flughafen etc*) nursing room; **babysitten** *vi* to babysit; **Babysitter** ['be:bisɪtər] (**-s, -**) *m* baby-sitter; **Babyspeck** (*umg*) *m* puppy fat

Bach [bax] (**-(e)s, ̈-e**) *m* stream, brook

Backblech *nt* baking tray

Backbord (**-(e)s, -e**) *nt* (*Naut*) port

Backe (**-, -n**) *f* cheek

backen ['bakən] *unreg vt, vi* to bake; **frisch/ knusprig gebackenes Brot** fresh/crusty bread

Backenbart *m* sideboards *pl*

Backenzahn *m* molar

Bäcker, in ['bɛkər(ɪn)] (**-s, -**) *m(f)* baker

Bäckerei [bɛkə'raɪ] *f* bakery; (*Bäckerladen*) baker's (shop)

Bäckerjunge *m* (*Lehrling*) baker's apprentice

Back- *zW*: **Backfisch** *m* fried fish; (*veraltet*) teenager; **Backform** *f* baking tin (*Brit*) *od* pan (US); **Backhähnchen** *nt* fried chicken in breadcrumbs; **Backobst** *nt* dried fruit; **Backofen** *m* oven; **Backpflaume** *f* prune; **Backpulver** *nt* baking powder; **Backstein** *m* brick

bäckt [bɛkt] *vb siehe* **backen**

Bad [ba:t] (**-(e)s, ̈-er**) *nt* bath; (*Schwimmen*) bathing; (*Ort*) spa

Bade- *zW*: **Badeanstalt** *f* swimming pool; **Badeanzug** *m* bathing suit; **Badehose** *f* bathing *od* swimming trunks *pl*; **Badekappe** *f* bathing cap; **Bademantel** *m* bath(ing) robe; **Bademeister** *m* swimming pool attendant

baden ['ba:dən] *vi* to bathe, have a bath ▷ *vt* to bath; **~ gehen** (*fig: umg*) to come a cropper

Bade- *zW*: **Badeort** *m* spa; **Badesachen** *pl* swimming things *pl*; **Badetuch** *nt* bath towel; **Badewanne** *f* bath(tub); **Badezimmer** *nt* bathroom

baff [baf] *adj*: **~ sein** (*umg*) to be flabbergasted

BAföG, Bafög [ba:føk] *nt abk* = **Bundesausbildungsförderungsgesetz**; *see culture note*

BAG (**-**) *nt abk* (= *Bundesarbeitsgericht*) German industrial tribunal

Bagatelle [baga'tɛlə] (**-, -n**) *f* trifle

Bagdad ['bakdat] (**-s**) *nt* Baghdad

Bagger ['bagər] (**-s, -**) *m* excavator; (*Naut*) dredger

baggern *vt, vi* (*Naut*) to dredge

Baggersee *m* (flooded) gravel pit

Bahamas [ba'ha:mas] *pl*: **die ~** the Bahamas *pl*

Bahn [ba:n] (**-, -en**) *f* railway (*Brit*), railroad (US); (*Weg*) road, way; (*Spur*) lane; (*Rennbahn*) track; (*Astron*) orbit; (*Stoffbahn*) length; **mit der ~** by train *od* rail/tram; **frei ~** (*Comm*) carriage free to station of destination; **jdm/ etw die ~ ebnen** (*fig*) to clear the way for sb/ sth; **von der rechten ~ abkommen** to stray from the straight and narrow; **jdn aus der ~ werfen** (*fig*) to shatter sb; **Bahnbeamte, r** *m* railway (*Brit*) *od* railroad (US) official; **bahnbrechend** *adj* pioneering; **Bahnbrecher, in** (**-s, -**) *m(f)* pioneer; **Bahndamm** *m* railway embankment

bahnen *vt*: **sich einen Weg ~** to clear a way

Bahnfahrt *f* railway (*Brit*) *od* railroad (US) journey

Bahnhof *m* station; **auf dem ~** at the station; **ich verstehe nur ~** (*hum: umg*) it's all Greek to me

Bahnhofshalle *f* station concourse

Bahnhofsmission *f* charitable organization for helping rail travellers; *see culture note*

railway stations in most big cities to which
people in need of advice and help can go.

Bahnhofswirtschaft f station restaurant
Bahn- zW: **bahnlagernd** adj (Comm) to
be collected from the station; **Bahnlinie**
f (railway (Brit) od railroad (US)) line;
Bahnschranke f level (Brit) od grade (US)
crossing barrier; **Bahnsteig** m platform;
Bahnsteigkarte f platform ticket;
Bahnstrecke f railway (Brit) od railroad (US)
line; **Bahnübergang** m level (Brit) od grade
(US) crossing; **beschrankter Bahnübergang**
crossing with gates; **unbeschrankter**
Bahnübergang unguarded crossing;
Bahnwärter m signalman
Bahrain [baˈraɪn] (-s) nt Bahrain
Bahre [ˈbaːrə] (-, -n) f stretcher
Baiser [bɛˈzeː] (-s, -s) nt meringue
Baisse [ˈbɛːsə] (-, -n) f (Börse) fall; (plötzlich)
slump
Bajonett [bajoˈnɛt] (-(e)s, -e) nt bayonet
Bakelit® [bakeˈliːt] (-s) nt Bakelite®
Bakterien [bakˈteːriən] pl bacteria pl
Balance [baˈlãːsə] (-, -n) f balance, equilibrium
balancieren vt, vi to balance
bald [balt] adv (zeitlich) soon; (beinahe) almost;
~ ... ~ ... now ... now ...; ~ **darauf** soon
afterwards; **bis ~!** see you soon
baldig [ˈbaldɪç] adj early, speedy
baldmöglichst adv as soon as possible
Baldrian [ˈbaldriaːn] (-s, -e) m valerian
Balearen [baleˈaːrən] pl: **die ~** the Balearics pl
Balg [balk] (-(e)s, -er) (pej: umg) m od nt (Kind)
brat
balgen [ˈbalgən] vr: **sich ~ (um)** to scrap (over)
Balkan [ˈbalkaːn] m: **der ~** the Balkans pl
Balken [ˈbalkən] (-s, -) m beam; (Tragbalken)
girder; (Stützbalken) prop
Balkon [balˈkõː] (-s, -s od -e) m balcony; (Theat)
(dress) circle
Ball [bal] (-(e)s, -e) m ball; (Tanz) dance, ball
Ballade [baˈlaːdə] (-, -n) f ballad
Ballast [ˈbalast] (-(e)s, -e) m ballast; (fig)
weight, burden; **Ballaststoffe** pl (Med)
roughage sing
Ballen [ˈbalən] (-s, -) m bale; (Anat) ball
ballen vt (formen) to make into a ball; (Faust) to
clench ▷ vr to build up; (Menschen) to gather
ballern [ˈbalərn] (umg) vi to shoot, fire
Ballett [baˈlɛt] (-(e)s, -e) nt ballet;
Balletttänzer, in m(f) ballet dancer
Ballistik [baˈlɪstɪk] f ballistics sing
Balljunge m ball boy
Ballkleid nt evening dress
Ballon [baˈlõː] (-s, -s od -e) m balloon
Ballspiel nt ball game
Ballung [ˈbaluŋ] f concentration; (von Energie)
build-up
Ballungs- zW: **Ballungsgebiet** nt,
Ballungsraum m conurbation;
Ballungszentrum nt centre (Brit) od center (US)
(of population, industry etc)

Balsam [ˈbalzaːm] (-s, -e) m balsam; (fig) balm
Balte [ˈbaltə] (-n, -n) m Balt; **er ist ~** he comes
from the Baltic
Baltikum [ˈbaltikum] (-s) nt: **das ~** the Baltic
States pl
baltisch adj Baltic attrib
Balz [balts] (-, -en) f (Paarungsspiel) courtship
display; (Paarungszeit) mating season
Bambus [ˈbambus] (-ses, -se) m bamboo;
Bambusrohr nt bamboo cane
Bammel [ˈbaməl] (-s) (umg) m: **(einen) ~ vor**
jdm/etw haben to be scared of sb/sth
banal [baˈnaːl] adj banal
Banalität [banaliˈtɛːt] f banality
Banane [baˈnaːnə] (-, -n) f banana
Bananenschale f banana skin
Bananenstecker m jack plug
Banause [baˈnauzə] (-n, -n) m philistine
Band¹ [bant] (-(e)s, -e) m (Buchband) volume;
das spricht Bände that speaks volumes
Band² [bant] (-(e)s, -er) nt (Stoffband) ribbon, tape;
(Fließband) production line; (Fassband) hoop;
(Zielband, Tonband) tape; (Anat) ligament; **etw**
auf ~ aufnehmen to tape sth; **am laufenden**
~ (umg) non-stop
Band³ (-(e)s, -e) nt (Freundschaftsband etc) bond
Band⁴ [bɛnt] (-, -s) f band, group
band etc [bant] vb siehe **binden**
Bandage [banˈdaːʒə] (-, -n) f bandage
bandagieren vt to bandage
Bandbreite f (von Meinungen etc) range
Bande [ˈbandə] (-, -n) f band; (Straßenbande)
gang
bändigen [ˈbɛndɪgən] vt (Tier) to tame; (Trieb,
Leidenschaft) to control, restrain
Bandit [banˈdiːt] (-en, -en) m bandit
Band- zW: **Bandmaß** nt tape measure;
Bandnudeln pl tagliatelle pl; **Bandsäge**
f band saw; **Bandscheibe** f (Anat) disc;
Bandscheibenschaden m slipped disc;
Bandwurm m tapeworm
bange [ˈbaŋə] adj scared; (besorgt) anxious;
jdm wird es ~ sb is becoming scared; **jdm B~**
machen to scare sb; **Bangemacher** (-s, -) m
scaremonger
bangen vi: **um jdn/etw ~** to be anxious od
worried about sb/sth
Bangkok [ˈbaŋkɔk] (-s) nt Bangkok
Bangladesch [baŋglaˈdɛʃ] (-s) nt Bangladesh
Banjo [ˈbanjo, ˈbɛndʒo] (-s, -s) nt banjo
Bank¹ [baŋk] (-, -e) f (Sitzbank) bench; (Sandbank
etc) (sand)bank, (sand)bar; **etw auf die lange**
~ schieben (umg) to put sth off
Bank² (-, -en) f (Geldbank) bank; **bei der ~** at the
bank; **Geld auf der ~ haben** to have money
in the bank; **Bankanweisung** f banker's
order; **Bankautomat** m cash dispenser;
Bankbeamte, r m bank clerk; **Bankeinlage** f
(bank) deposit
Bankett [baŋˈkɛt] (-(e)s, -e) nt (Essen) banquet;
(Straßenrand) verge (Brit), shoulder (US)
Bank- zW: **Bankfach** nt (Schließfach) safe-
deposit box; **Bankgebühr** f bank charge;

b

Bankgeheimnis *nt* confidentiality in banking

Bankier [baŋki'e:] **(-s, -s)** *m* banker

Bank- *zW:* **Bankkonto** *nt* bank account; **Bankleitzahl** *f* bank code number; **Banknote** *f* banknote; **Bankraub** *m* bank robbery

bankrott [baŋ'krɔt] *adj* bankrupt; **Bankrott (-(e)s, -e)** *m* bankruptcy; **Bankrott machen** to go bankrupt; **den Bankrott anmelden** *od* **erklären** to declare o.s. bankrupt; **Bankrotterklärung** *f* (*lit*) declaration of bankruptcy; (*fig: umg*) declaration of failure

Banküberfall *m* bank raid

Bann [ban] **(-(e)s, -e)** *m* (*Hist*) ban; (*Kirchenbann*) excommunication; (*fig: Zauber*) spell; **bannen** *vt* (*Geister*) to exorcize; (*Gefahr*) to avert; (*bezaubern*) to enchant; (*Hist*) to banish

Banner (-s, -) *nt* banner, flag

Bar [ba:r] **(-, -s)** *f* bar

bar *adj* (*+gen*) (*unbedeckt*) bare; (*frei von*) lacking (in); (*offenkundig*) utter, sheer; **~e(s) Geld** cash; **etw (in) ~ bezahlen** to pay sth (in) cash; **etw für ~e Münze nehmen** (*fig*) to take sth at face value; **~ aller Hoffnung** (*liter*) devoid of hope, completely without hope

Bär [bε:r] **(-en, -en)** *m* bear; **jdm einen ~en aufbinden** (*umg*) to have sb on

Baracke [ba'rakə] **(-, -n)** *f* hut

barbarisch [bar'ba:rɪʃ] *adj* barbaric, barbarous

Barbestand *m* money in hand

Bardame *f* barmaid

Bärenhunger (*umg*) *m*: **einen ~ haben** to be famished

bärenstark (*umg*) *adj* strapping, strong as an ox; (*fig*) terrific

barfuß *adj* barefoot

barg *etc* [bark] *vb siehe* **bergen**

Bargeld *nt* cash, ready money

bargeldlos *adj* non-cash; **~er Zahlungsverkehr** non-cash *od* credit transactions *pl*

barhäuptig *adj* bareheaded

Barhocker *m* bar stool

Bariton ['ba:ritɔn] *m* baritone

Barkauf *m* cash purchase

Barkeeper ['ba:rki:pər] **(-s, -)** *m* barman, bartender

Barkredit *m* cash loan

Barmann (-(e)s, pl -männer) *m* barman

barmherzig [barm'hɛrtsɪç] *adj* merciful, compassionate; **Barmherzigkeit** *f* mercy, compassion

Barock [ba'rɔk] **(-s** *od* **-)** *nt od m* baroque

Barometer [baro'me:tər] **(-s, -)** *nt* barometer; **das ~ steht auf Sturm** (*fig*) there's a storm brewing

Baron [ba'ro:n] **(-s, -e)** *m* baron

Baronesse [baro'nɛsə] **(-, -n)** *f* baroness

Baronin *f* baroness

Barren ['barən] **(-s, -)** *m* parallel bars *pl*; (*Goldbarren*) ingot

Barriere [bari'ε:rə] **(-, -n)** *f* barrier

Barrikade [bari'ka:də] **(-, -n)** *f* barricade

Barsch [barʃ] **(-(e)s, -e)** *m* perch

barsch [barʃ] *adj* brusque, gruff; **jdn ~ anfahren** to snap at sb

Barschaft *f* ready money

Barscheck *m* open *od* uncrossed cheque (*Brit*), open check (*US*)

barst *etc* [barst] *vb siehe* **bersten**

Bart [ba:rt] **(-(e)s, ⸚e)** *m* beard; (*Schlüsselbart*) bit

bärtig ['bε:rtɪç] *adj* bearded

Barvermögen *nt* liquid assets *pl*

Barzahlung *f* cash payment

Basar [ba'za:r] **(-s, -e)** *m* bazaar

Base ['ba:zə] **(-, -n)** *f* (*Chem*) base; (*Cousine*) cousin

Basel ['ba:zəl] **(-s)** *nt* Basle

Basen *pl von* **Base; Basis**

basieren [ba'zi:rən] *vt* to base ▷ *vi* to be based

Basilikum [ba'zi:likʊm] **(-s)** *nt* basil

Basis ['ba:zɪs] **(-, *pl* Basen)** *f* basis; (*Archit, Mil, Math*) base; **~ und Überbau** (*Pol, Soziologie*) foundation and superstructure; **die ~** (*umg*) the grass roots

basisch ['ba:zɪʃ] *adj* (*Chem*) alkaline

Basisgruppe *f* action group

Baske ['baskə] **(-n, -n)** *m* Basque

Baskenland *nt* Basque region

Baskenmütze *f* beret

Baskin *f* Basque

Bass [bas] **(-es, ⸚e)** *m* bass

Bassin [ba'sɛ̃:] **(-s, -s)** *nt* pool

Bassist [ba'sɪst] *m* bass

Bassschlüssel *m* bass clef

Bassstimme *f* bass voice

Bast [bast] **(-(e)s, -e)** *m* raffia

basta ['basta] *interj*: **(und damit) ~!** (and) that's that!

basteln ['bastəln] *vt* to make ▷ *vi* to do handicrafts; **an etw** *dat* **~** (*an etw herumbasteln*) to tinker with sth

Bastler ['bastlər] **(-s, -)** *m* do-it-yourselfer; (*handwerklich*) handicrafts enthusiast

BAT *m abk* (*= Bundesangestelltentarif*) German salary scale for employees

bat *etc* [ba:t] *vb siehe* **bitten**

Bataillon [batal'joːn] **(-s, -e)** *nt* battalion

Batist [ba'tɪst] **(-(e)s, -e)** *m* batiste

Batterie [batə'ri:] *f* battery

Bau [baʊ] **(-(e)s)** *m* (*Bauen*) building, construction; (*Aufbau*) structure; (*Körperbau*) frame; (*Baustelle*) building site; (*pl Baue: Tierbau*) hole, burrow; (*: Min*) working(s); (*pl Bauten: Gebäude*) building; **sich im ~ befinden** to be under construction; **Bauarbeiten** *pl* (*Straßenbau*) roadworks *pl* (*Brit*), roadwork *sing* (*US*); building *od* construction work *sing*; **Bauarbeiter** *m* building worker

Bauch [baʊx] **(-(e)s, Bäuche)** *m* belly; (*Anat*) stomach, abdomen; **sich** *dat* **(vor Lachen) den ~ halten** (*umg*) to split one's sides (laughing); **mit etw auf den ~ fallen** (*umg*) to come a cropper with sth; **Bauchansatz** *m* beginning of a paunch; **Bauchfell** *nt* peritoneum

bauchig *adj* bulging

Bauch- *zW:* **Bauchlandung** *f:* **eine Bauchlandung machen** (*fig*) to experience a failure, to flop; **Bauchmuskel** *m* abdominal muscle; **Bauchnabel** *m* navel, belly-button (*umg*); **Bauchredner** *m* ventriloquist; **Bauchschmerzen** *pl* stomachache *sing*; **Bauchspeicheldrüse** *f* pancreas; **Bauchtanz** *m* belly dance; belly dancing; **Bauchweh** *nt* stomachache

Baudrate [baʊtˈraːtə] *f* (*Comput*) baud rate

bauen [ˈbaʊən] *vt* to build; (*Tech*) to construct; (*umg: verursachen: Unfall*) to cause ▷ *vi* to build; **auf jdn/etw** ~ to depend upon sb/sth; **da hast du Mist gebaut** (*umg*) you really messed that up

Bauer¹ [ˈbaʊər] (**-n** *od* **-s, -n**) *m* farmer; (*Schach*) pawn

Bauer² (**-s, -**) *nt od m* (*Vogelbauer*) cage

Bäuerchen [ˈbɔʏərçən] *nt* (*Kindersprache*) burp

Bäuerin [ˈbɔʏərɪn] *f* farmer; (*Frau des Bauern*) farmer's wife

bäuerlich *adj* rustic

Bauern- *zW:* **Bauernbrot** *nt* black bread; **Bauernfängerei** *f* deception, confidence trick(s); **Bauernfrühstück** *nt* bacon and potato omelette (*Brit*) *od* omelet (*US*); **Bauernhaus** *nt* farmhouse; **Bauernhof** *m* farm; **Bauernschaft** *f* farming community; **Bauernschläue** *f* native cunning, craftiness, shrewdness

Bau- *zW:* **baufällig** *adj* dilapidated; **Baufälligkeit** *f* dilapidation; **Baufirma** *f* construction firm; **Bauführer** *m* site foreman; **Baugelände** *nt* building site; **Baugenehmigung** *f* building permit; **Baugerüst** *nt* scaffolding; **Bauherr** *m* client (*of construction firm*); **Bauingenieur** *m* civil engineer

Bauj. *abk* = **Baujahr**

Bau- *zW:* **Baujahr** *nt* year of construction; (*von Auto*) year of manufacture; **Baukasten** *m* box of bricks; **Bauklötzchen** *nt* (building) block; **Baukosten** *pl* construction costs *pl*; **Bauland** *nt* building land; **Bauleute** *pl* building workers *pl*; **baulich** *adj* structural; **Baulöwe** *m* building speculator; **Baulücke** *f* undeveloped building plot

Baum [baʊm] (**-(e)s,** *pl* **Bäume**) *m* tree; **heute könnte ich Bäume ausreißen** I feel full of energy today

Baumarkt *m* DIY superstore

baumeln [ˈbaʊməln] *vi* to dangle

bäumen [ˈbɔʏmən] *vr* to rear (up)

Baum- *zW:* **Baumgrenze** *f* tree line; **Baumschule** *f* nursery; **Baumstamm** *m* tree trunk; **Baumstumpf** *m* tree stump; **Baumwolle** *f* cotton

Bau- *zW:* **Bauplan** *m* architect's plan; **Bauplatz** *m* building site; **Bausachverständige, r** *f(m)* quantity surveyor; **Bausatz** *m* construction kit

Bausch [baʊʃ] (**-(e)s,** *pl* **Bäusche**) *m* (*Wattebausch*) ball, wad; **in ~ und Bogen** (*fig*) lock, stock, and barrel

bauschen *vt, vi, vr* to puff out

bauschig *adj* baggy, wide

Bau- *zW:* **bausparen** *vi untr* to save with a building society (*Brit*) *od* a building and loan association (*US*); **Bausparkasse** *f* building society (*Brit*), building and loan association (*US*); **Bausparvertrag** *m* savings contract with a building society (*Brit*) *od* building and loan association (*US*); **Baustein** *m* building stone, freestone; **Baustelle** *f* building site; **Baustil** *m* architectural style; **bautechnisch** *adj* in accordance with building *od* construction methods; **Bauteil** *nt* prefabricated part (of building); **Bauten** *pl von* **Bau**; **Bauunternehmer** *m* contractor, builder; **Bauweise** *f* (method of) construction; **Bauwerk** *nt* building; **Bauzaun** *m* hoarding

b. a. W. *abk* (= *bis auf Weiteres*) until further notice

Bayer, in [ˈbaɪər(ɪn)] (**-n, -n**) *m(f)* Bavarian

bayerisch, bayrisch *adj* Bavarian

Bayern *nt* Bavaria

Bazillus [baˈtsɪlʊs] (**-,** *pl* **Bazillen**) *m* bacillus

Bd. *abk* (= *Band*) vol.

Bde. *abk* (= *Bände*) vols.

beabsichtigen [bəˈʔapzɪçtɪɡən] *vt* to intend

beachten [bəˈʔaxtən] *vt* to take note of; (*Vorschrift*) to obey; (*Vorfahrt*) to observe

beachtenswert *adj* noteworthy

beachtlich *adj* considerable

Beachtung *f* notice, attention, observation; **jdm keine ~ schenken** to take no notice of sb

Beamte, r [bəˈʔamtə(r)] (**-n, -n**) *m* official; (*Staatsbeamte*) civil servant; (*Bankbeamte etc*) employee

Beamtenlaufbahn *f:* **die ~ einschlagen** to enter the civil service

Beamtenverhältnis *nt:* **im ~ stehen** to be a civil servant

beamtet *adj* (*form*) appointed on a permanent basis (*by the state*)

Beamtin *f siehe* **Beamte(r)**

beängstigend [bəˈʔɛŋstɪɡənt] *adj* alarming

beanspruchen [bəˈʔanʃpruxən] *vt* to claim; (*Zeit, Platz*) to take up, occupy; **jdn ~** to take up sb's time; **etw stark ~** to put sth under a lot of stress

beanstanden [bəˈʔanʃtandən] *vt* to complain about, object to; (*Rechnung*) to query

Beanstandung *f* complaint

beantragen [bəˈʔantraːɡən] *vt* to apply for, ask for

beantworten [bəˈʔantvɔrtən] *vt* to answer

Beantwortung *f* reply

bearbeiten [bəˈʔarbaɪtən] *vt* to work; (*Material*) to process; (*Thema*) to deal with; (*Land*) to cultivate; (*Chem*) to treat; (*Buch*) to revise; (*umg: beeinflussen wollen*) to work on

Bearbeitung *f* processing; cultivation; treatment; revision; **die ~ meines Antrags hat lange gedauert** it took a long time to deal with my claim

Bearbeitungsgebühr *f* handling charge

beatmen [bə'|a:tmən] *vt*: **jdn künstlich ~** to give sb artificial respiration

Beatmung [bə'|a:tmʊŋ] *f* respiration

beaufsichtigen [bə'|aʊfzɪçtɪgən] *vt* to supervise

Beaufsichtigung *f* supervision

beauftragen [bə'|aʊftra:gən] *vt* to instruct; **jdn mit etw ~** to entrust sb with sth

Beauftragte, r *f(m)* representative

bebauen [bə'baʊən] *vt* to build on; (*Agr*) to cultivate

beben ['be:bən] *vi* to tremble, shake; **Beben (-s, -)** *nt* earthquake

bebildern [bə'bɪldərn] *vt* to illustrate

Becher ['bɛçər] (**-s, -**) *m* mug; (*ohne Henkel*) tumbler

bechern ['bɛçərn] (*umg*) *vi* (*trinken*) to have a few (drinks)

Becken ['bɛkən] (**-s, -**) *nt* basin; (*Mus*) cymbal; (*Anat*) pelvis

Bedacht [bə'daxt] *m*: **mit ~** (*vorsichtig*) prudently, carefully; (*absichtlich*) deliberately

bedacht *adj* thoughtful, careful; **auf etw** *akk* **~ sein** to be concerned about sth

bedächtig [bə'dɛçtɪç] *adj* (*umsichtig*) thoughtful, reflective; (*langsam*) slow, deliberate

bedanken [bə'daŋkən] *vr*: **sich (bei jdm) ~** to say thank you (to sb); **ich bedanke mich herzlich** thank you very much

Bedarf [bə'darf] (**-(e)s**) *m* need; (*Bedarfsmenge*) requirements *pl*; (*Comm*) demand; supply; **alles für den häuslichen ~** all household requirements; **je nach ~** according to demand; **bei ~** if necessary; **~ an etw** *dat* **haben** to be in need of sth

Bedarfs- *zW*: **Bedarfsartikel** *m* requisite; **Bedarfsdeckung** *f* satisfaction of sb's needs; **Bedarfsfall** *m* case of need; **Bedarfshaltestelle** *f* request stop

bedauerlich [bə'daʊərlɪç] *adj* regrettable

bedauern [bə'daʊərn] *vt* to be sorry for; (*bemitleiden*) to pity; **wir ~, Ihnen mitteilen zu müssen, ...** we regret to have to inform you ...; **Bedauern (-s)** *nt* regret

bedauernswert *adj* (*Zustände*) regrettable; (*Mensch*) pitiable, unfortunate

bedecken [bə'dɛkən] *vt* to cover

bedeckt *adj* covered; (*Himmel*) overcast

bedenken [bə'dɛŋkən] *unreg vt* to think over, consider; **ich gebe zu ~, dass ...** (*geh*) I would ask you to consider that ...; **Bedenken (-s, -)** *nt* (*Überlegen*) consideration; (*Zweifel*) doubt; (*Skrupel*) scruple; **mir kommen Bedenken** I am having second thoughts

bedenklich *adj* doubtful; (*bedrohlich*) dangerous, risky

Bedenkzeit *f* time to consider; **zwei Tage ~** two days to think about it

bedeuten [bə'dɔʏtən] *vt* to mean; to signify; (*wichtig sein*) to be of importance; **das bedeutet nichts Gutes** that means trouble

bedeutend *adj* important; (*beträchtlich*) considerable

bedeutsam *adj* significant; (*vielsagend*) meaningful

Bedeutung *f* meaning; significance; (*Wichtigkeit*) importance

bedeutungslos *adj* insignificant, unimportant

bedeutungsvoll *adj* momentous, significant

bedienen [bə'di:nən] *vt* to serve; (*Maschine*) to work, operate ▷ *vr* (*beim Essen*) to help o.s.; (*gebrauchen*): **sich jds/einer Sache ~** to make use of sb/sth; **werden Sie schon bedient?** are you being served?; **damit sind Sie sehr gut bedient** that should serve you very well; **ich bin bedient!** (*umg*) I've had enough

Bedienung *f* service; (*Kellner etc*) waiter/waitress; (*Zuschlag*) service (charge); (*von Maschinen*) operation

Bedienungsanleitung *f* operating instructions *pl*

bedingen [bə'dɪŋən] *vt* (*voraussetzen*) to demand, involve; (*verursachen*) to cause, occasion

bedingt *adj* limited; (*Straferlass*) conditional; (*Reflex*) conditioned; **(nur) ~ gelten** to be (only) partially valid; **~ geeignet** suitable up to a point

Bedingung *f* condition; (*Voraussetzung*) stipulation; **mit** *od* **unter der ~, dass ...** on condition that ...; **zu günstigen ~en** (*Comm*) on favourable (*Brit*) *od* favorable (*US*) terms

Bedingungsform *f* (*Gram*) conditional

bedingungslos *adj* unconditional

bedrängen [bə'drɛŋən] *vt* to pester, harass

Bedrängnis [bə'drɛŋnɪs] *f* (*seelisch*) distress, torment

Bedrängung *f* trouble

bedrohen [bə'dro:ən] *vt* to threaten

bedrohlich *adj* ominous, threatening

Bedrohung *f* threat, menace

bedrucken [bə'drʊkən] *vt* to print on

bedrücken [bə'drykən] *vt* to oppress, trouble

bedürfen [bə'dyrfən] *unreg vi +gen* (*geh*) to need, require; **ohne dass es eines Hinweises bedurft hätte, ...** without having to be asked ...

Bedürfnis [bə'dyrfnɪs] (**-ses, -se**) *nt* need; **das ~ nach etw haben** to need sth; **Bedürfnisanstalt** *f* (*form*) public convenience (*Brit*), comfort station (*US*); **bedürfnislos** *adj* frugal, modest

bedürftig *adj* in need, poor, needy

Beefsteak ['bi:fste:k] (**-s, -s**) *nt* steak; **deutsches ~** hamburger

beehren [bə'|e:rən] *vt* (*geh*) to honour (*Brit*), honor (*US*); **wir ~ uns ...** we have pleasure in ...

beeilen [bə'|aɪlən] *vr* to hurry

beeindrucken [bə'|aɪndrʊkən] *vt* to impress, make an impression on

beeinflussen [bə'|aɪnflʊsən] *vt* to influence

Beeinflussung *f* influence

beeinträchtigen [bə'|aɪntrɛçtɪgən] *vt* to affect adversely; (*Sehvermögen*) to impair; (*Freiheit*) to

49

infringe upon

beenden [bə'|ɛndən], **beendigen** [bə'|ɛndɪgən] vt to end, finish, terminate

Beendung, Beendigung f end(ing), finish(ing)

beengen [bə'|ɛŋən] vt to cramp; (fig) to hamper, inhibit; **~de Kleidung** restricting clothing

beengt adj cramped; (fig) stifled

beerben [bə'|ɛrbən] vt to inherit from

beerdigen [bə'|e:rdɪgən] vt to bury

Beerdigung f funeral, burial

Beerdigungsunternehmer m undertaker

Beere ['be:rə] (-, -n) f berry; (Traubenbeere) grape

Beerenauslese f wine made from specially selected grapes

Beet [be:t] (-(e)s, -e) nt (Blumenbeet) bed

befähigen [bə'fɛ:ɪgən] vt to enable

befähigt adj (begabt) talented; (fähig): ~ **(für)** capable (of)

Befähigung f capability; (Begabung) talent, aptitude; **die ~ zum Richteramt** the qualifications to become a judge

befahl etc [bə'fa:l] vb siehe **befehlen**

befahrbar [bə'fa:rba:r] adj passable; (Naut) navigable; **nicht ~ sein** (Straße, Weg) to be closed (to traffic); (wegen Schnee etc) to be impassable

befahren [bə'fa:rən] unreg vt to use, drive over; (Naut) to navigate ▷ adj used

befallen [bə'falən] unreg vt to come over

befangen [bə'faŋən] adj (schüchtern) shy, self-conscious; (voreingenommen) bias(s)ed; **Befangenheit** f shyness; bias

befassen [bə'fasən] vr to concern o.s.

Befehl [bə'fe:l] (-(e)s, -e) m command, order; (Comput) command; **auf ~ handeln** to act under orders; **zu ~, Herr Hauptmann!** (Mil) yes, sir; **den ~ haben** od **führen (über** +akk) to be in command (of)

befehlen unreg vt to order ▷ vi to give orders; **jdm etw ~** to order sb to do sth; **du hast mir gar nichts zu ~** I won't take orders from you

befehligen vt to be in command of

Befehls- zW: **Befehlsempfänger** m subordinate; **Befehlsform** f (Gram) imperative; **Befehlshaber** (-s, -) m commanding officer; **Befehlsnotstand** m (Jur) obligation to obey orders; **Befehlsverweigerung** f insubordination

befestigen [bə'fɛstɪgən] vt to fasten; (stärken) to strengthen; (Mil) to fortify; **~ an** +dat to fasten to

Befestigung f fastening; strengthening; (Mil) fortification

Befestigungsanlage f fortification

befeuchten [bə'fɔʏçtən] vt to damp(en), moisten

befinden [bə'fɪndən] unreg vr to be; (sich fühlen) to feel ▷ vt: **jdn/etw für** od **als etw ~** to deem sb/sth to be sth ▷ vi: **~ (über** +akk) to decide (on), adjudicate (on)

Befinden (-s) nt health, condition; (Meinung)

view, opinion

beflecken [bə'flɛkən] vt (lit) to stain; (fig geh: Ruf, Ehre) to besmirch

befliegen [bə'fli:gən] unreg vt (Strecke) to fly

beflügeln [bə'fly:gəln] vt (geh) to inspire

befohlen [bə'fo:lən] pp von **befehlen**

befolgen [bə'fɔlgən] vt to comply with, follow

befördern [bə'fœrdərn] vt (senden) to transport, send; (beruflich) to promote; **etw mit der Post/per Bahn ~** to send sth by post/by rail

Beförderung f transport; promotion

Beförderungskosten pl transport costs pl

befragen [bə'fra:gən] vt to question; (um Stellungnahme bitten): **~ (über** +akk) to consult (about)

Befragung f poll

befreien [bə'fraɪən] vt to set free; (erlassen) to exempt

Befreier, in (-s, -) m(f) liberator

befreit adj (erleichtert) relieved

Befreiung f liberation, release; (Erlassen) exemption

Befreiungs- zW: **Befreiungsbewegung** f liberation movement; **Befreiungskampf** m struggle for liberation; **Befreiungsversuch** m escape attempt

befremden [bə'frɛmdən] vt to surprise; (unangenehm) to disturb; **Befremden** (-s) nt surprise, astonishment

befreunden [bə'frɔʏndən] vr to make friends; (mit Idee etc) to acquaint o.s.

befreundet adj friendly; **wir sind schon lange (miteinander) ~** we have been friends for a long time

befriedigen [bə'fri:dɪgən] vt to satisfy

befriedigend adj satisfactory

Befriedigung f satisfaction, gratification

befristet [bə'frɪstət] adj limited; (Arbeitsverhältnis, Anstellung) temporary

befruchten [bə'frʊxtən] vt to fertilize; (fig) to stimulate

Befruchtung f: **künstliche ~** artificial insemination

Befugnis [bə'fu:knɪs] (-, -se) f authorization, powers pl

befugt adj authorized, entitled

befühlen [bə'fy:lən] vt to feel, touch

Befund [bə'fʊnt] (-(e)s, -e) m findings pl; (Med) diagnosis; **ohne ~** (Med) (results) negative

befürchten [bə'fʏrçtən] vt to fear

Befürchtung f fear, apprehension

befürworten [bə'fy:rvɔrtən] vt to support, speak in favour (Brit) od favor (US) of

Befürworter, in (-s, -) m(f) supporter, advocate

Befürwortung f support(ing), favouring (Brit), favoring (US)

begabt [bə'ga:pt] adj gifted

Begabung [bə'ga:bʊŋ] f talent, gift

begann etc [bə'gan] vb siehe **beginnen**

begatten [bə'gatən] vr to mate ▷ vt to mate od pair (with)

begeben [bə'ge:bən] unreg vr (gehen) to proceed; (geschehen) to occur; **sich ~ nach** od

zu to proceed to(wards); **sich in ärztliche Behandlung ~** to undergo medical treatment; **sich in Gefahr ~** to expose o.s. to danger; **Begebenheit** f occurrence

begegnen [bə'ge:gnən] vi: **jdm ~** to meet sb; (behandeln) to treat; **Blicke ~ sich** eyes meet

Begegnung f meeting; (Sport) match

begehen [bə'ge:ən] unreg vt (Straftat) to commit; (Weg etc) to use, negotiate; (geh: feiern) to celebrate

begehren [bə'ge:rən] vt to desire

begehrenswert adj desirable

begehrt adj in demand; (Junggeselle) eligible

begeistern [bə'gaɪstərn] vt to fill with enthusiasm; (inspirieren) to inspire ▷ vr: **sich für etw ~** to get enthusiastic about sth; **er ist für nichts zu ~** he's not interested in doing anything

begeistert adj enthusiastic

Begeisterung f enthusiasm

Begierde [bə'gi:rdə] (-, -n) f desire, passion

begierig [bə'gi:rɪç] adj eager, keen; (voll Verlangen) hungry, greedy

begießen [bə'gi:sən] unreg vt to water; (mit Fett: Braten etc) to baste; (mit Alkohol) to drink to

Beginn [bə'gɪn] **(-(e)s)** m beginning; **zu ~** at the beginning

beginnen unreg vt, vi to start, begin

beglaubigen [bə'glaʊbɪgən] vt to countersign; (Abschrift) to authenticate; (Echtheit, Übersetzung) to certify

Beglaubigung f countersignature

Beglaubigungsschreiben nt credentials pl

begleichen [bə'glaɪçən] unreg vt to settle, pay; **mit Ihnen habe ich noch eine Rechnung zu ~** (fig) I've a score to settle with you

begleiten [bə'glaɪtən] vt to accompany; (Mil) to escort

Begleiter, in (-s, -) m(f) companion; (zum Schutz) escort; (Mus) accompanist

Begleit- zW: **Begleiterscheinung** f side effect; **Begleitmusik** f accompaniment; **Begleitpapiere** pl (Comm) accompanying documents pl; **Begleitschiff** nt escort vessel; **Begleitschreiben** nt covering letter; **Begleitumstände** pl attendant circumstances

Begleitung f company; (Mil) escort; (Mus) accompaniment

beglücken [bə'glʏkən] vt to make happy, delight

beglückwünschen [bə'glʏkvʏnʃən] vt: **~ (zu)** to congratulate (on)

begnadet [bə'gna:dət] adj gifted

begnadigen [bə'gna:dɪgən] vt to pardon

Begnadigung f pardon

begnügen [bə'gny:gən] vr: **sich ~ mit** to be satisfied with, content o.s. with

Begonie [bə'go:niə] f begonia

begonnen [bə'gɔnən] pp von **beginnen**

begossen [bə'gɔsən] pp von **begießen** ▷ adj: **er stand da wie ein ~er Pudel** (umg) he looked so sheepish

begraben [bə'gra:bən] unreg vt to bury;

(aufgeben: Hoffnung) to abandon; (beenden: Streit etc) to end; **dort möchte ich nicht ~ sein** (umg) I wouldn't like to be stuck in that hole

Begräbnis [bə'grɛ:pnɪs] **(-ses, -se)** nt burial, funeral

begradigen [bə'gra:dɪgən] vt to straighten (out)

begreifen [bə'graɪfən] unreg vt to understand, comprehend

begreiflich [bə'graɪflɪç] adj understandable; **ich kann mich ihm nicht ~ machen** I can't make myself clear to him

begrenzen [bə'grɛntsən] vt (beschränken): **~ (auf +akk)** to restrict (to), limit (to)

Begrenztheit [bə'grɛntsthaɪt] f limitation, restriction; (fig) narrowness

Begriff [bə'grɪf] **(-(e)s, -e)** m concept, idea; **im ~ sein, etw zu tun** to be about to do sth; **sein Name ist mir ein/kein ~** his name means something/doesn't mean anything to me; **du machst dir keinen ~ (davon)** you've no idea; **für meine ~e** in my opinion; **schwer von ~** (umg) slow on the uptake

Begriffsbestimmung f definition

begriffsstutzig adj slow-witted, dense

begrub etc [bə'gru:p] vb siehe **begraben**

begründen [bə'grʏndən] vt (Gründe geben) to justify; **etw näher ~** to give specific reasons for sth

Begründer, in (-s, -) m(f) founder

begründet adj well-founded, justified; **sachlich ~** founded on fact

Begründung f justification, reason

begrünen [bə'gry:nən] vt to plant with greenery

begrüßen [bə'gry:sən] vt to greet, welcome

begrüßenswert adj welcome

Begrüßung f greeting, welcome

begünstigen [bə'gʏnstɪgən] vt (Person) to favour (Brit), favor (US); (Sache) to further, promote

Begünstigte, r f(m) beneficiary

begutachten [bə'gu:t|axtən] vt to assess; (umg: ansehen) to have a look at

begütert [bə'gy:tərt] adj wealthy, well-to-do

begütigend adj (Worte etc) soothing; **~ auf jdn einreden** to calm sb down

behaart [bə'ha:rt] adj hairy

behäbig [bə'hɛ:bɪç] adj (dick) portly, stout; (geruhsam) comfortable

behaftet [bə'haftət] adj: **mit etw ~ sein** to be afflicted by sth

behagen [bə'ha:gən] vi: **das behagt ihm nicht** he does not like it; **Behagen (-s)** nt comfort, ease; **mit Behagen essen** to eat with relish

behaglich [bə'ha:klɪç] adj comfortable, cosy; **Behaglichkeit** f comfort, cosiness

behält [bə'hɛlt] vb siehe **behalten**

behalten [bə'haltən] unreg vt to keep, retain; (im Gedächtnis) to remember; **~ Sie (doch) Platz!** please don't get up!

Behälter [bə'hɛltər] **(-s, -)** m container,

51

receptacle

behämmert [bə'hɛmərt] (umg) adj screwy, crazy

behandeln [bə'handəln] vt to treat; (Thema) to deal with; (Maschine) to handle; **der ~de Arzt** the doctor in attendance

Behändigkeit [bə'hɛndɪçkaɪt] f agility, quickness

Behandlung f treatment; (von Maschine) handling

behängen [bə'hɛŋən] vt to decorate

beharren [bə'harən] vi: **auf etw** dat ~ to stick od keep to sth

beharrlich [bə'harlıç] adj (ausdauernd) steadfast, unwavering; (hartnäckig) tenacious, dogged; **Beharrlichkeit** f steadfastness; tenacity

behaupten [bə'hauptən] vt to claim, assert, maintain; (sein Recht) to defend ▷ vr to assert o.s.; **von jdm ~, dass ...** to say (of sb) that ...; **sich auf dem Markt ~** to establish itself on the market

Behauptung f claim, assertion

Behausung [bə'hauzʊŋ] f dwelling, abode; (armselig) hovel

beheben [bə'he:bən] unreg vt (beseitigen) to remove; (Missstände) to remedy; (Schaden) to repair; (Störung) to clear

beheimatet [bə'haima:tət] adj: ~ **(in** +dat) domiciled (at/in); (Tier, Pflanze) native (to)

beheizen [bə'haitsən] vt to heat

Behelf [bə'hɛlf] **(-(e)s, -e)** m expedient, makeshift; **behelfen** unreg vr: **sich mit etw behelfen** to make do with sth

behelfsmäßig adj improvised, makeshift; (vorübergehend) temporary

behelligen [bə'hɛlıgən] vt to trouble, bother

Behendigkeit [bə'hɛndıçkaɪt] f siehe **Behändigkeit**

beherbergen [bə'hɛrbɛrgən] vt (lit, fig) to house

beherrschen [bə'hɛrʃən] vt (Volk) to rule, govern; (Situation) to control; (Sprache, Gefühle) to master ▷ vr to control o.s.

beherrscht adj controlled; **Beherrschtheit** f self-control

Beherrschung f rule; control; mastery; **die ~ verlieren** to lose one's temper

beherzigen [bə'hɛrtsıgən] vt to take to heart

beherzt adj spirited, brave

behielt etc [bə'hi:lt] vb siehe **behalten**

behilflich [bə'hılflıç] adj helpful; **jdm ~ sein (bei)** to help sb (with)

behindern [bə'hındərn] vt to hinder, impede

Behinderte, r f(m) disabled person

Behinderung f hindrance; (Körperbehinderung) handicap

Behörde [bə'hø:rdə] **(-, -n)** f authorities pl; (Amtsgebäude) office(s pl)

behördlich [bə'hø:rtlıç] adj official

behüten [bə'hy:tən] vt to guard; **jdn vor etw** dat ~ to preserve sb from sth

behütet adj (Jugend etc) sheltered

behutsam [bə'hu:tza:m] adj cautious, careful; **man muss es ihr ~ beibringen** it will have

to be broken to her gently; **Behutsamkeit** f caution, carefulness

 SCHLÜSSELWORT

bei [baɪ] präp +dat **1** (nahe bei) near; (zum Aufenthalt) at, with; (unter, zwischen) among; **bei München** near Munich; **bei uns** at our place; **beim Friseur** at the hairdresser's; **bei seinen Eltern wohnen** to live with one's parents; **bei einer Firma arbeiten** to work for a firm; **etw bei sich haben** to have sth on one; **jdn bei sich haben** to have sb with one; **bei Goethe** in Goethe; **beim Militär** in the army **2** (zeitlich) at, on; (während) during; (Zustand, Umstand) in; **bei Nacht** at night; **bei Nebel** in fog; **bei Regen** if it rains; **bei solcher Hitze** in such heat; **bei meiner Ankunft** on my arrival; **bei der Arbeit** when I'm etc working; **beim Fahren** while driving; **bei offenem Fenster schlafen** to sleep with the window open; **bei Feuer Scheibe einschlagen** in case of fire break glass; **bei seinem Talent** with his talent

beibehalten ['baɪbəhaltən] unreg vt to keep, retain

Beibehaltung f keeping, retaining

Beiblatt ['baɪblat] nt supplement

beibringen ['baɪbrıŋən] unreg vt (Beweis, Zeugen) to bring forward; (Gründe) to adduce; **jdm etw ~** (zufügen) to inflict sth on sb; (zu verstehen geben) to make sb understand sth; (lehren) to teach sb sth

Beichte ['baɪçtə] f confession

beichten vt to confess ▷ vi to go to confession

Beichtgeheimnis nt secret of the confessional

Beichtstuhl m confessional

beide ['baɪdə] pron, adj both; **meine ~n Brüder** my two brothers, both my brothers; **die ersten ~n** the first two; **wir ~** we two; **einer von ~n** one of the two; **alles ~s** both (of them); **~ Mal** both times

beider- zW: **beiderlei** adj inv of both; **beidseitig** adj mutual, reciprocal; **beiderseits** adv mutually ▷ präp +gen on both sides of

beidhändig ['baɪthɛndıç] adj ambidextrous

beidrehen ['baɪdre:ən] vi to heave to

beidseitig ['baɪtzaɪtıç] adj (auf beiden Seiten) on both sides

beieinander [baɪaɪ'nandər] adv together; **gut ~ sein** (umg: gesundheitlich) to be in good shape; (: geistig) to be all there

Beifahrer, in ['baɪfa:rər(ın)] **(-s, -)** m(f) passenger; **Beifahrerairbag** m (Aut) passenger airbag; **Beifahrersitz** m passenger seat

Beifall ['baɪfal] **(-(e)s)** m applause; (Zustimmung) approval; **~ heischend** fishing for applause/approval

beifällig ['baɪfɛlıç] adj approving; (Kommentar) favourable (Brit), favorable (US)

Beifilm ['baɪfılm] m supporting film

beifügen ['baɪfy:gən] *vt* to enclose
Beigabe ['baɪga:bə] *f* addition
beige ['be:ʒ] *adj* beige
beigeben ['baɪge:bən] *unreg vt* (*zufügen*) to add; (*mitgeben*) to give ▷ *vi*: **klein ~** (*nachgeben*) to climb down
Beigeschmack ['baɪgəʃmak] *m* aftertaste
Beihilfe ['baɪhɪlfə] *f* aid, assistance; (*Studienbeihilfe*) grant; (*Jur*) aiding and abetting; **wegen ~ zum Mord** (*Jur*) because of being an accessory to the murder
beikommen ['baɪkɔmən] *unreg vi* +*dat* to get at; (*einem Problem*) to deal with
Beil [baɪl] (-(e)s, -e) *nt* axe (Brit), ax (US), hatchet
Beilage ['baɪla:gə] *f* (*Buchbeilage etc*) supplement; (*Koch*) accompanying vegetables; (*getrennt serviert*) side dish
beiläufig ['baɪlɔyfɪç] *adj* casual, incidental ▷ *adv* casually, by the way
beilegen ['baɪle:gən] *vt* (*hinzufügen*) to enclose, add; (*beimessen*) to attribute, ascribe; (*Streit*) to settle
beileibe [baɪ'laɪbə] *adv*: **~ nicht** by no means
Beileid ['baɪlaɪt] *nt* condolence, sympathy; **herzliches ~** deepest sympathy
beiliegend ['baɪli:gənt] *adj* (*Comm*) enclosed
beim [baɪm] = **bei dem**
beimessen ['baɪmɛsən] *unreg vt* to attribute, ascribe
Bein [baɪn] (-(e)s, -e) *nt* leg; **jdm ein ~ stellen** (*lit, fig*) to trip sb up; **wir sollten uns auf die ~e machen** (*umg*) we ought to be making tracks; **jdm ~e machen** (*umg: antreiben*) to make sb get a move on; **die ~e in die Hand nehmen** (*umg*) to take to one's heels; **sich** *dat* **die ~e in den Bauch stehen** (*umg*) to stand about until one is fit to drop; **etw auf die ~e stellen** (*fig*) to get sth off the ground
beinah [baɪ'na:], **beinahe** [baɪ'na:ə] *adv* almost, nearly
Beinbruch *m* fracture of the leg; **das ist kein ~** (*fig: umg*) it could be worse
beinhalten [bə'ɪnhaltən] *vt* to contain
beipflichten ['baɪpflɪçtən] *vi*: **jdm/etw ~** to agree with sb/sth
Beiprogramm ['baɪprogram] *nt* supporting programme (Brit) *od* program (US)
Beirat ['baɪra:t] *m* advisory council; (*Elternbeirat*) parents' council
beirren [bə'ɪrən] *vt* to confuse, muddle; **sich nicht ~ lassen** not to let o.s. be confused
Beirut [baɪ'ru:t] (-s) *nt* Beirut
beisammen [baɪ'zamən] *adv* together; **beisammenhaben** *unreg vt*: **er hat (sie) nicht alle beisammen** (*umg*) he's not all there; **Beisammensein** (-s) *nt* get-together
Beischlaf ['baɪʃla:f] *m* (*Jur*) sexual intercourse
Beisein ['baɪzaɪn] (-s) *nt* presence
beiseite [baɪ'zaɪtə] *adv* to one side, aside; (*stehen*) on one side, aside; **Spaß ~!** joking apart!; **beiseitelegen** *vt* (*sparen*) to put by; **beiseiteschaffen** *vt* to get rid of

beisetzen ['baɪzɛtsən] *vt* to bury
Beisetzung *f* funeral
Beisitzer, in ['baɪzɪtsər(ɪn)] (-s, -) *m(f)* (*Jur*) assessor; (*bei Prüfung*) observer
Beispiel ['baɪʃpi:l] (-(e)s, -e) *nt* example; **mit gutem ~ vorangehen** to set a good example; **sich** *dat* **an jdm ein ~ nehmen** to take sb as an example; **zum ~** for example; **beispielhaft** *adj* exemplary; **beispiellos** *adj* unprecedented
beispielsweise *adv* for instance, for example
beispringen ['baɪʃprɪŋən] *unreg vi* +*dat* to come to the aid of
beißen ['baɪsən] *unreg vt, vi* to bite; (*stechen: Rauch, Säure*) to burn ▷ *vr* (*Farben*) to clash
beißend *adj* biting, caustic; (*Geruch*) pungent, sharp; (*fig*) sarcastic
Beißzange ['baɪstsaŋə] *f* pliers *pl*
Beistand ['baɪʃtant] (-(e)s, -̈e) *m* support, help; (*Jur*) adviser; **jdm ~ leisten** to give sb assistance/one's support
beistehen ['baɪʃte:ən] *unreg vi*: **jdm ~** to stand by sb
Beistelltisch ['baɪʃtɛltɪʃ] *m* occasional table
beisteuern ['baɪʃtɔyərn] *vt* to contribute
beistimmen ['baɪʃtɪmən] *vi* +*dat* to agree with
Beistrich ['baɪʃtrɪç] *m* comma
Beitrag ['baɪtra:k] (-(e)s, -̈e) *m* contribution; (*Zahlung*) fee, subscription; (*Versicherungsbeitrag*) premium; **einen ~ zu etw leisten** to make a contribution to sth
beitragen ['baɪtra:gən] *unreg vt, vi*: **~ (zu)** to contribute (to); (*mithelfen*) to help (with)
Beitrags- *zW*: **beitragsfinanziert** *adj* financed by fees/contributions; **beitragsfrei** *adj* non-contributory; **beitragspflichtig** *adj* contributory; **beitragspflichtig sein** (*Mensch*) to have to pay contributions; **Beitragszahler, in** *m(f)* contributor
beitreten ['baɪtre:tən] *unreg vi* +*dat* to join
Beitritt ['baɪtrɪt] *m* joining; membership
Beitrittserklärung *f* declaration of membership
Beitrittsland *nt* (*zu EU etc*) acceding country
Beiwagen ['baɪva:gən] *m* (*Motorradbeiwagen*) sidecar; (*Straßenbahnbeiwagen*) extra carriage
beiwohnen ['baɪvo:nən] *vi* (*geh*): **einer Sache** *dat* **~** to attend *od* be present at sth
Beiwort ['baɪvɔrt] *nt* adjective
Beize ['baɪtsə] (-, -n) *f* (*Holzbeize*) stain; (*Koch*) marinade
beizeiten [baɪ'tsaɪtən] *adv* in time
bejahen [bə'ja:ən] *vt* (*Frage*) to say yes to, answer in the affirmative; (*gutheißen*) to agree with
bejahrt [bə'ja:rt] *adj* elderly, advanced in years
bejammern [bə'jamərn] *vt* to lament, bewail
bejammernswert *adj* lamentable
bekakeln [bə'ka:kəln] (*umg*) *vt* to discuss
bekam *etc* [bə'kam] *vb siehe* **bekommen**
bekämpfen [bə'kɛmpfən] *vt* (*Gegner*) to fight; (*Seuche*) to combat ▷ *vr* to fight
Bekämpfung *f*: **~ (+*gen*)** fight (against),

struggle (against)

bekannt [bə'kant] *adj* (well-)known; (*nicht fremd*) familiar; **~ geben** to announce publicly; **mit jdm ~ sein** to know sb; **~ machen** to announce; **jdn mit jdm ~ machen** to introduce sb to sb; **sich mit etw ~ machen** to familiarize o.s. with sth; **das ist mir ~** I know that; **es/sie kommt mir ~ vor** it/she seems familiar; **durch etw ~ werden** to become famous because of sth

Bekannte, r *f(m)* friend, acquaintance

Bekanntenkreis *m* circle of friends

bekanntermaßen *adv* as is known

bekannt- *zW*: **Bekanntgabe** *f* announcement; **Bekanntheitsgrad** *m* degree of fame; **bekanntlich** *adv* as is well known, as you know; **Bekanntmachung** *f* publication; (*Anschlag etc*) announcement; **Bekanntschaft** *f* acquaintance

bekehren [bə'ke:rən] *vt* to convert ▷ *vr* to be *od* become converted

Bekehrung *f* conversion

bekennen [bə'kɛnən] *unreg vt* to confess; (*Glauben*) to profess ▷ *vr*: **sich zu jdm/etw ~** to declare one's support for sb/sth; **Farbe ~** (*umg*) to show where one stands

Bekenntnis [bə'kɛntnɪs] **(-ses, -se)** *nt* admission, confession; (*Religion*) confession, denomination; **ein ~ zur Demokratie ablegen** to declare one's belief in democracy; **Bekenntnisschule** *f* denominational school

beklagen [bə'kla:gən] *vt* to deplore, lament ▷ *vr* to complain

beklagenswert *adj* lamentable, pathetic; (*Mensch*) pitiful; (*Zustand*) deplorable; (*Unfall*) terrible

beklatschen [bə'klatʃən] *vt* to applaud, clap

bekleben [bə'kle:bən] *vt*: **etw mit Bildern ~** to stick pictures onto sth

bekleckern [bə'klɛkərn] (*umg*) *vt* to stain

bekleiden [bə'klaɪdən] *vt* to clothe; (*Amt*) to occupy, fill

Bekleidung *f* clothing; (*form: eines Amtes*) tenure

Bekleidungsindustrie *f* clothing industry, rag trade (*umg*)

beklemmen [bə'klɛmən] *vt* to oppress

Beklemmung *f* oppressiveness; (*Gefühl der Angst*) feeling of apprehension

beklommen [bə'kləmən] *adj* anxious, uneasy; **Beklommenheit** *f* anxiety, uneasiness

bekloppt [bə'kləpt] (*umg*) *adj* (*Mensch*) crazy; (: *Sache*) lousy

beknackt [bə'knakt] (*umg*) *adj* = **bekloppt**

beknien [bə'kni:ən] (*umg*) *vt* (*jdn*) to beg

bekommen [bə'kəmən] *unreg vt* to get, receive; (*Kind*) to have; (*Zug*) to catch, get ▷ *vi*: **jdm ~** to agree with sb; **es mit jdm zu tun ~** to get into trouble with sb; **wohl bekomms!** your health!

bekömmlich [bə'kœmlɪç] *adj* easily digestible

beköstigen [bə'kœstɪgən] *vt* to cater for

bekräftigen [bə'krɛftɪgən] *vt* to confirm, corroborate

Bekräftigung *f* corroboration

bekreuzigen [bə'krɔʏtsɪgən] *vr* to cross o.s.

bekritteln [bə'krɪtəln] *vt* to criticize, pick holes in

bekümmern [bə'kʏmərn] *vt* to worry, trouble

bekunden [bə'kʊndən] *vt* (*sagen*) to state; (*zeigen*) to show

belächeln [bə'lɛçəln] *vt* to laugh at

beladen [bə'la:dən] *unreg vt* to load

Belag [bə'la:k] **(-(e)s, ¨e)** *m* covering, coating; (*Brotbelag*) spread; (*auf Pizza, Brot*) topping; (*auf Tortenboden, zwischen Brotscheiben*) filling; (*Zahnbelag*) tartar; (*auf Zunge*) fur; (*Bremsbelag*) lining

belagern [bə'la:gərn] *vt* to besiege

Belagerung *f* siege

Belagerungszustand *m* state of siege

belämmert [bəlɛmərt] (*umg*) *adj* sheepish

Belang [bə'laŋ] **(-(e)s)** *m* importance

Belange *pl* interests *pl*, concerns *pl*

belangen *vt* (*Jur*) to take to court

belanglos *adj* trivial, unimportant

Belanglosigkeit *f* triviality

belassen [bə'lasən] *unreg vt* (*in Zustand, Glauben*) to leave; (*in Stellung*) to retain; **es dabei ~** to leave it at that

Belastbarkeit *f* (*von Brücke, Aufzug*) load-bearing capacity; (*von Menschen, Nerven*) ability to take stress

belasten [bə'lastən] *vt* (*lit*) to burden; (*fig: bedrücken*) to trouble, worry; (*Comm: Konto*) to debit; (*Jur*) to incriminate ▷ *vr* to weigh o.s. down; (*Jur*) to incriminate o.s.; **etw (mit einer Hypothek) ~** to mortgage sth

belastend *adj* (*Jur*) incriminating

belästigen [bə'lɛstɪgən] *vt* to annoy, pester

Belästigung *f* annoyance, pestering; (*körperlich*) molesting

Belastung [bə'lastʊŋ] *f* (*lit*) load; (*fig: Sorge etc*) weight; (*Comm*) charge, debit(ing); (*mit Hypothek*): **~ (+gen)** mortgage (on); (*Jur*) incriminating evidence

Belastungs- *zW*: **Belastungsmaterial** *nt* (*Jur*) incriminating evidence; **Belastungsprobe** *f* capacity test; (*fig*) test; **Belastungszeuge** *m* witness for the prosecution

belaubt [bə'laʊpt] *adj*: **dicht ~ sein** to have thick foliage

belaufen [bə'laʊfən] *unreg vr*: **sich ~ auf** +*akk* to amount to

belauschen [bə'laʊʃən] *vt* to eavesdrop on

beleben [bə'le:bən] *vt* (*anregen*) to liven up; (*Konjunktur, jds Hoffnungen*) to stimulate

belebt [bə'le:pt] *adj* (*Straße*) crowded

Beleg [bə'le:k] **(-(e)s, -e)** *m* (*Comm*) receipt; (*Beweis*) documentary evidence, proof; (*Beispiel*) example

belegen [bə'le:gən] *vt* to cover; (*Kuchen, Brot*) to spread; (*Platz*) to reserve, book; (*Kurs, Vorlesung*) to register for; (*beweisen*) to verify, prove

Belegschaft *f* personnel, staff

belegt *adj* (*Zunge*) furred; (*Stimme*) hoarse; (*Zimmer*) occupied; **~e Brote** open sandwiches

belehren [bə'le:rən] *vt* to instruct, teach; **jdn**

eines Besseren ~ to teach sb better; **er ist nicht zu** ~ he won't be told
Belehrung f instruction
beleibt [bə'laɪpt] adj stout, corpulent
beleidigen [bə'laɪdɪgən] vt to insult; to offend
beleidigt adj insulted; (gekränkt) offended; **die ~e Leberwurst spielen** (umg) to be in a huff
Beleidigung f insult; (Jur) slander; (: schriftlich) libel
beleihen [bə'laɪən] unreg vt (Comm) to lend money on
belemmert [bə'lɛmərt] (umg) adj siehe **belämmert**
belesen [bə'le:zən] adj well-read
beleuchten [bə'lɔʏçtən] vt to light, illuminate; (fig) to throw light on
Beleuchter, in (-s, -) m(f) lighting technician
Beleuchtung f lighting, illumination
beleumdet [bə'lɔʏmdət] adj: **gut/schlecht ~ sein** to have a good/bad reputation
beleumundet [bə'lɔʏmʊndət] adj = **beleumdet**
Belgien ['bɛlgiən] (-s) nt Belgium
Belgier, in (-s, -) m(f) Belgian
belgisch adj Belgian
Belgrad ['bɛlgra:t] (-s) nt Belgrade
belichten [bə'lɪçtən] vt to expose
Belichtung f exposure
Belichtungsmesser m exposure meter
Belieben [bə'li:bən] nt: **(ganz) nach** ~ (just) as you wish
belieben vi unpers (geh): **wie es Ihnen beliebt** as you wish
beliebig [bə'li:bɪç] adj any you like, as you like; **~ viel** as much as you like; **in ~er Reihenfolge** in any order whatever; **ein ~es Thema** any subject you like od want
beliebt [bə'li:pt] adj popular; **sich bei jdm ~ machen** to make o.s. popular with sb; **Beliebtheit** f popularity
beliefern [bə'li:fərn] vt to supply
Belize [be'li:z] (-s) nt Belize
bellen ['bɛlən] vi to bark
Belletristik [bɛle'trɪstɪk] f fiction and poetry
belohnen [bə'lo:nən] vt to reward
Belohnung f reward
Belüftung [bə'lʏftʊŋ] f ventilation
belügen [bə'ly:gən] unreg vt to lie to, deceive
belustigen [bə'lʊstɪgən] vt to amuse
Belustigung f amusement
bemächtigen [bə'mɛçtɪgən] vr: **sich einer Sache** gen ~ to take possession of sth, seize sth
bemalen [bə'ma:lən] vt to paint ▷ vr (pej: schminken) to put on one's war paint (umg)
bemängeln [bə'mɛŋəln] vt to criticize
bemannen [bə'manən] vt to man
Bemannung f manning; (Naut, Aviat etc) crew
bemänteln [bə'mɛntəln] vt to cloak, hide
bemerkbar adj perceptible, noticeable; **sich ~ machen** (Person) to make od get o.s. noticed; (Unruhe) to become noticeable
bemerken [bə'mɛrkən] vt (wahrnehmen) to notice, observe; (sagen) to say, mention; **nebenbei bemerkt** by the way

bemerkenswert adj remarkable, noteworthy
Bemerkung f remark, comment; (schriftlich) comment, note
bemitleiden [bə'mɪtlaɪdən] vt to pity
bemittelt [bə'mɪtəlt] adj well-to-do, well-off
bemühen [bə'my:ən] vr to take trouble; **sich um eine Stelle** ~ to try to get a job
bemüht adj: **(darum) ~ sein, etw zu tun** to endeavour (Brit) od endeavor (US) to do sth
Bemühung f trouble, pains pl, effort
bemüßigt [bə'my:sɪçt] adj: **sich ~ fühlen/sehen** (geh) to feel called upon
bemuttern [bə'mʊtərn] vt to mother
benachbart [bə'naxba:rt] adj neighbouring (Brit), neighboring (US)
benachrichtigen [bə'na:xrɪçtɪgən] vt to inform
Benachrichtigung f notification
benachteiligen [bə'na:xtaɪlɪgən] vt to (put at a) disadvantage, victimize
benehmen [bə'ne:mən] unreg vr to behave; **Benehmen** (-s) nt behaviour (Brit), behavior (US); **kein Benehmen haben** not to know how to behave
beneiden [bə'naɪdən] vt to envy
beneidenswert adj enviable
Beneluxländer ['be:nelʊkslɛndər] pl Benelux (countries pl)
Beneluxstaaten pl Benelux (countries pl)
benennen [bə'nɛnən] unreg vt to name
Bengel ['bɛŋəl] (-s, -) m (little) rascal od rogue
Benimm [bə'nɪm] (-s) (umg) m manners pl
Benin [be'ni:n] (-s) nt Benin
benommen [bə'nɔmən] adj dazed
benoten [bə'no:tən] vt to mark
benötigen [bə'nø:tɪgən] vt to need
benutzen [bə'nʊtsən] vt to use
benützen [bə'nʏtsən] vt to use
Benutzer, in (-s, -) m(f) user; **benutzerdefiniert** adj (Comput) user-defined; **benutzerfreundlich** adj user-friendly; **Benutzerkonto** nt (Comput) user account; **Benutzername** m username
Benutzung f utilization, use; **jdm etw zur ~ überlassen** to put sth at sb's disposal
Benzin [bɛnt'si:n] (-s, -e) nt (Aut) petrol (Brit), gas(oline) (US); **Benzineinspritzanlage** f (Aut) fuel injection system; **Benzinkanister** m petrol (Brit) od gas (US) can; **Benzintank** m petrol (Brit) od gas (US) tank; **Benzinuhr** f petrol (Brit) od gas (US) gauge
beobachten [bə'|o:baxtən] vt to observe
Beobachter, in (-s, -) m(f) observer; (eines Unfalls) witness; (Presse, TV) correspondent
Beobachtung f observation
beordern [bə'|ɔrdərn] vt: **jdn zu sich ~** to send for sb
bepacken [bə'pakən] vt to load, pack
bepflanzen [bə'pflantsən] vt to plant
bequatschen [bə'kvatʃən] (umg) vt (überreden) to persuade; **etw ~** to talk sth over
bequem [bə'kve:m] adj comfortable; (Ausrede) convenient; (Person) lazy, indolent
bequemen [bə'kve:mən] vr: **sich ~, etw zu**

tun to condescend to do sth

Bequemlichkeit f convenience, comfort; (Faulheit) laziness, indolence

Ber. abk = **Bericht; Beruf**

berät [bə'rɛːt] vb siehe **beraten**

beraten [bə'raːtən] unreg vt to advise; (besprechen) to discuss, debate ▷ vr to consult; **gut/schlecht ~ sein** to be well/ill advised; **sich ~ lassen** to get advice

beratend adj consultative; **jdm ~ zur Seite stehen** to act in an advisory capacity to sb

Berater, in (-s, -) m(f) adviser; **Beratervertrag** m consultancy contract

beratschlagen [bə'raːtʃlaːgən] vi to deliberate, confer ▷ vt to deliberate on, confer about

Beratung f advice; (Besprechung) consultation

Beratungsstelle f advice centre (Brit) od center (US)

berauben [bə'raʊbən] vt to rob

berauschen [bə'raʊʃən] vt (lit, fig) to intoxicate

berauschend adj: **das war nicht sehr ~** (ironisch) that wasn't very exciting

berechenbar [bə'rɛçənbaːr] adj calculable; (Verhalten) predictable

berechnen [bə'rɛçnən] vt to calculate; (Comm: anrechnen) to charge

berechnend adj (Mensch) calculating, scheming

Berechnung f calculation; (Comm) charge

berechtigen [bə'rɛçtɪgən] vt to entitle; (bevollmächtigen) to authorize; (fig) to justify

berechtigt [bə'rɛçtɪçt] adj justifiable, justified

Berechtigung f authorization; (fig) justification

bereden [bə'reːdən] vt (besprechen) to discuss; (überreden) to persuade ▷ vr to discuss

beredt [bə'reːt] adj eloquent

Bereich [bə'raɪç] (-(e)s, -e) m (Bezirk) area; (Ressort, Gebiet) sphere; **im ~ des Möglichen liegen** to be within the bounds of possibility

bereichern [bə'raɪçərn] vt to enrich ▷ vr to get rich; **sich auf Kosten anderer ~** to feather one's nest at the expense of other people

Bereifung [bə'raɪfʊŋ] f (set of) tyres (Brit) od tires (US) pl; (Vorgang) fitting with tyres (Brit) od tires (US)

bereinigen [bə'raɪnɪgən] vt to settle

bereisen [bə'raɪzən] vt to travel through; (Comm: Gebiet) to travel, cover

bereit [bə'raɪt] adj ready, prepared; **zu etw ~ sein** to be ready for sth; **sich ~ erklären** to declare o.s. willing; **(sich) ~ machen** to prepare, to get ready

bereiten vt to prepare, make ready; (Kummer, Freude) to cause; **einer Sache** dat **ein Ende ~** to put an end to sth

bereit- zW: **bereithalten** unreg vt to keep in readiness; **bereitlegen** vt to lay out; **bereitmachen** vt, vr siehe **bereit**

bereits adv already

bereit- zW: **Bereitschaft** f readiness; (Polizei) alert; **in Bereitschaft sein** to be on the alert od on stand-by; **Bereitschaftsarzt** m

doctor on call; (im Krankenhaus) duty doctor; **Bereitschaftsdienst** m emergency service; **bereitstehen** unreg vi (Person) to be prepared; (Ding) to be ready; **bereitstellen** vt (Kisten, Pakete etc) to put ready; (Geld etc) to make available; (Truppen, Maschinen) to put at the ready

Bereitung f preparation

bereitwillig adj willing, ready; **Bereitwilligkeit** f willingness, readiness

bereuen [bə'rɔʏən] vt to regret

Berg [bɛrk] (-(e)s, -e) m mountain; (kleiner) hill; **mit etw hinterm ~ halten** (fig) to keep quiet about sth; **über alle ~e sein** to be miles away; **da stehen einem ja die Haare zu ~e** it's enough to make your hair stand on end; **bergab** adv downhill; **bergan** adv uphill; **Bergarbeiter** m miner; **bergauf** adv uphill; **Bergbahn** f mountain railway (Brit) od railroad (US); **Bergbau** m mining

bergen ['bɛrgən] unreg vt (retten) to rescue; (Ladung) to salvage; (enthalten) to contain

Bergführer m mountain guide

Berggipfel m mountain top, peak, summit

bergig ['bɛrgɪç] adj mountainous, hilly

Berg- zW: **Bergkamm** m crest, ridge; **Bergkette** f mountain range; **Bergkristall** m rock crystal; **Bergmann** (-(e)s, pl **-leute**) m miner; **Bergnot** f: **in Bergnot sein/geraten** to be in/get into difficulties while climbing; **Bergpredigt** f (Rel) Sermon on the Mount; **Bergrettungsdienst** m mountain rescue service; **Bergrutsch** m landslide; **Bergschuh** m walking boot; **Bergsteigen** nt mountaineering; **Bergsteiger, in** m(f) mountaineer, climber; **Berg-und-Tal-Bahn** f big dipper, roller-coaster

Bergung ['bɛrgʊŋ] f (von Menschen) rescue; (von Material) recovery; (Naut) salvage

Bergwacht f mountain rescue service

Bergwerk nt mine

Bericht [bə'rɪçt] (-(e)s, -e) m report, account; **berichten** vt, vi to report; **Berichterstatter** (-s, -) m reporter, (newspaper) correspondent; **Berichterstattung** f reporting

berichtigen [bə'rɪçtɪgən] vt to correct

Berichtigung f correction

berieseln [bə'riːzəln] vt to spray with water

Berieselung f watering; **die dauernde ~ mit Musik ...** (fig) the constant stream of music ...

Berieselungsanlage f sprinkler (system)

Beringmeer ['beːrɪŋmeːr] nt Bering Sea

beritten [bə'rɪtən] adj mounted

Berlin [bɛr'liːn] (-s) nt Berlin

Berliner¹ adj attrib Berlin

Berliner² (-s, -) m (Person) Berliner; (Koch) jam doughnut

Berlinerin f Berliner

berlinerisch (umg) adj (Dialekt) Berlin attr

Bermudas [bɛr'muːdas] pl: **auf den ~ in Bermuda**

Bern [bɛrn] (-s) nt Berne

Bernhardiner [bɛrnhar'diːnər] (-s, -) m Saint

Bernard (dog)

Bernstein ['bɛrnʃtaɪn] *m* amber

bersten ['bɛrstən] *unreg vi* to burst, split

berüchtigt [bə'rʏçtɪçt] *adj* notorious, infamous

berücksichtigen [bə'rʏkzɪçtɪgən] *vt* to consider, bear in mind

Berücksichtigung *f* consideration; **in** *od* **unter ~ der Tatsache, dass ...** in view of the fact that ...

Beruf [bə'ru:f] *(-(e)s, -e) m* occupation, profession; (*Gewerbe*) trade; **was sind Sie von ~?** what is your occupation *etc*?, what do you do for a living?; **seinen ~ verfehlt haben** to have missed one's vocation

berufen *unreg vt* (*in Amt*): **jdn in etw** *akk* **~** to appoint sb to sth ▷ *vr*: **sich auf jdn/etw ~** to refer *od* appeal to sb/sth ▷ *adj* competent, qualified; (*ausersehen*): **zu etw ~ sein** to have a vocation for sth

beruflich *adj* professional; **sie ist ~ viel unterwegs** she is away a lot on business

Berufs- *zW*: **Berufsakademie** *f* college of advanced vocational studies; **Berufsausbildung** *f* vocational *od* professional training; **berufsbedingt** *adj* occupational; **Berufsberater** *m* careers adviser; **Berufsberatung** *f* vocational guidance; **Berufsbezeichnung** *f* job description; **Berufseinsteiger**, in *m(f)* first-time employee; **Berufserfahrung** *f* (professional) experience; **Berufsfeuerwehr** *f* fire service; **Berufsgeheimnis** *nt* professional secret; **Berufskrankheit** *f* occupational disease; **Berufskriminalität** *f* professional crime; **Berufsleben** *nt* professional life; **im Berufsleben stehen** to be working *od* in employment; **berufsmäßig** *adj* professional; **Berufsperspektive** *f* job *od* career prospects *pl*; **Berufsrisiko** *nt* occupational hazard; **Berufsschule** *f* vocational *od* trade school; **Berufssoldat** *m* professional soldier, regular; **Berufssportler** *m* professional (sportsman); **berufstätig** *adj* employed; **berufsunfähig** *adj* unable to work (at one's profession); **Berufsunfall** *m* occupational accident; **Berufsverbot** *nt*: **jdm Berufsverbot erteilen** to ban sb from his/her profession; (*einem Arzt, Anwalt*) to strike sb off; **Berufsverkehr** *m* commuter traffic; **Berufswahl** *f* choice of a job

Berufung *f* vocation, calling; (*Ernennung*) appointment; (*Jur*) appeal; **~ einlegen** to appeal; **unter ~ auf etw** *akk* (*form*) with reference to sth

Berufungsgericht *nt* appeal court, court of appeal

beruhen [bə'ru:ən] *vi*: **auf etw** *dat* **~** to be based on sth; **etw auf sich ~ lassen** to leave sth at that; **das beruht auf Gegenseitigkeit** the feeling is mutual

beruhigen [bə'ru:ɪgən] *vt* to calm, pacify, soothe ▷ *vr* (*Mensch*) to calm (o.s.) down; (*Situation*) to calm down

beruhigend *adj* (*Gefühl, Wissen*) reassuring;

(*Worte*) comforting; (*Mittel*) tranquillizing

Beruhigung *f* reassurance; (*der Nerven*) calming; **zu jds ~** to reassure sb

Beruhigungsmittel *nt* sedative

Beruhigungspille *f* tranquillizer

berühmt [bə'ry:mt] *adj* famous; **das war nicht ~** (*umg*) it was nothing to write home about; **berühmt-berüchtigt** *adj* infamous, notorious; **Berühmtheit** *f* (*Ruf*) fame; (*Mensch*) celebrity

berühren [bə'ry:rən] *vt* to touch; (*gefühlsmäßig bewegen*) to affect; (*flüchtig erwähnen*) to mention, touch on ▷ *vr* to meet, touch; **von etw peinlich berührt sein** to be embarrassed by sth

Berührung *f* contact

Berührungsbildschirm *m* (*Tech*) touch screen

berührungsempfindlich *adj* touch-sensitive

Berührungspunkt *m* point of contact

bes. *abk* (*= besonders*) esp

besagen [bə'za:gən] *vt* to mean

besagt *adj* (*form*): *Tag etc*) in question

besaiten [bə'zaɪtən] *vt*: **neu ~** (*Instrument*) to restring

besänftigen [bə'zɛnftɪgən] *vt* to soothe, calm

besänftigend *adj* soothing

Besänftigung *f* soothing, calming

besaß *etc* [bə'za:s] *vb siehe* **besitzen**

besät [bə'zɛ:t] *adj* covered; (*mit Blättern etc*) strewn

Besatz [bə'zats] *(-es, -̈e) m* trimming, edging

Besatzung *f* garrison; (*Naut, Aviat*) crew

Besatzungsmacht *f* occupying power

Besatzungszone *f* occupied zone

besaufen [bə'zaʊfən] *unreg* (*umg*) *vr* to get drunk *od* stoned

beschädigen [bə'ʃɛ:dɪgən] *vt* to damage

Beschädigung *f* damage; (*Stelle*) damaged spot

beschaffen [bə'ʃafən] *vt* to get, acquire ▷ *adj* constituted; **so ~ sein wie ...** to be the same as ...; **Beschaffenheit** *f* constitution, nature; **je nach Beschaffenheit der Lage** according to the situation

Beschaffung *f* acquisition

beschäftigen [bə'ʃɛftɪgən] *vt* to occupy; (*beruflich*) to employ; (*innerlich*): **jdn ~** to be on sb's mind ▷ *vr* to occupy *od* concern o.s.

beschäftigt *adj* busy, occupied; (*angestellt*): (**bei einer Firma**) **~** employed (by a firm)

Beschäftigung *f* (*Beruf*) employment; (*Tätigkeit*) occupation; (*geistige Beschäftigung*) preoccupation; **einer ~ nachgehen** (*form*) to be employed

Beschäftigungsprogramm *nt* employment scheme

Beschäftigungstherapie *f* occupational therapy

beschämen [bə'ʃɛ:mən] *vt* to put to shame

beschämend *adj* shameful; (*Hilfsbereitschaft*) shaming

beschämt *adj* ashamed

beschatten [bə'ʃatən] *vt* to shade; (*Verdächtige*) to shadow

beschaulich [bə'ʃaʊlɪç] adj contemplative; (Leben, Abend) quiet, tranquil

Bescheid [bə'ʃaɪt] (-(e)s, -e) m information; (Weisung) directions pl; **~ wissen (über** +akk) to be well-informed (about); **ich weiß ~** I know; **jdm ~ geben** od **sagen** to let sb know; **jdm ordentlich ~ sagen** (umg) to tell sb where to go

bescheiden [bə'ʃaɪdən] unreg vr to content o.s. ▷ vt: **etw abschlägig ~** (form) to turn sth down ▷ adj modest; **Bescheidenheit** f modesty

bescheinen [bə'ʃaɪnən] unreg vt to shine on

bescheinigen [bə'ʃaɪnɪgən] vt to certify; (bestätigen) to acknowledge; **hiermit wird bescheinigt, dass ...** this is to certify that ...

Bescheinigung f certificate; (Quittung) receipt

bescheißen [bə'ʃaɪsən] unreg (umg!) vt to cheat

beschenken [bə'ʃɛŋkən] vt to give presents to

bescheren [bə'ʃeːrən] vt: **jdm etw ~** to give sb sth as a present; **jdn ~** to give presents to sb

Bescherung f giving of presents; (umg) mess; **da haben wir die ~!** (umg) what did I tell you!

bescheuert [bə'ʃɔʏɐt] (umg) adj stupid

beschichten [bə'ʃɪçtən] vt (Tech) to coat, cover

beschießen [bə'ʃiːsən] unreg vt to shoot od fire at

beschildern [bə'ʃɪldərn] vt to signpost

beschimpfen [bə'ʃɪmpfən] vt to abuse

Beschimpfung f abuse, insult

beschirmen [bə'ʃɪrmən] vt (geh: beschützen) to shield

Beschiss [bə'ʃɪs] (-es) (umg) m: **das ist ~** that is a cheat

beschiss etc vb siehe **bescheißen**

beschissen pp von **bescheißen** ▷ adj (umg!) bloody awful, lousy

Beschlag [bə'ʃlaːk] (-(e)s, -e) m (Metallband) fitting; (auf Fenster) condensation; (auf Metall) tarnish; finish; (Hufeisen) horseshoe; **jdn/etw in ~ nehmen** od **mit ~ belegen** to monopolize sb/sth

beschlagen [bə'ʃlaːgən] unreg vt to cover; (Pferd) to shoe; (Fenster, Metall) to cover ▷ vi, vr (Fenster etc) to mist over; **~ sein (in** od **auf** +dat) to be well versed (in)

beschlagnahmen vt to seize, confiscate

Beschlagnahmung f confiscation

beschleunigen [bə'ʃlɔʏnɪgən] vt to accelerate, speed up ▷ vi (Aut) to accelerate

Beschleunigung f acceleration

beschließen [bə'ʃliːsən] unreg vt to decide on; (beenden) to end, close

beschlossen [bə'ʃlɔsən] pp von **beschließen** ▷ adj (entschieden) decided, agreed; **das ist ~e Sache** that's been settled

Beschluss [bə'ʃlʊs] (-es, -e) m decision, conclusion; (Ende) close, end; **einen ~ fassen** to pass a resolution

beschlussfähig adj: **~ sein** to have a quorum

Beschlusslage f policy position

beschmieren [bə'ʃmiːrən] vt (Wand) to bedaub

beschmutzen [bə'ʃmʊtsən] vt to dirty, soil

beschneiden [bə'ʃnaɪdən] unreg vt to cut; (stutzen) to trim; (: Strauch) to prune; (Rel) to circumcise

beschnuppern [bə'ʃnʊpərn] vr (Hunde) to sniff each other; (fig: umg) to size each other up

beschönigen [bə'ʃøːnɪgən] vt to gloss over; **~der Ausdruck** euphemism

beschränken [bə'ʃrɛŋkən] vt, vr: **(sich) ~ (auf** +akk) to limit od restrict (o.s.) (to)

beschrankt [bə'ʃraŋkt] adj (Bahnübergang) with barrier

beschränkt [bə'ʃrɛŋkt] adj confined, narrow; (Mensch) limited, narrow-minded; (pej: geistig) dim; **Gesellschaft mit ~er Haftung** limited company (Brit), corporation (US); **Beschränktheit** f narrowness

Beschränkung f limitation

beschreiben [bə'ʃraɪbən] unreg vt to describe; (Papier) to write on

Beschreibung f description

beschrieb etc [bə'ʃriːp] vb siehe **beschreiben**

beschrieben [bə'ʃriːbən] pp von **beschreiben**

beschriften [bə'ʃrɪftən] vt to mark, label

Beschriftung f lettering

beschuldigen [bə'ʃʊldɪgən] vt to accuse

Beschuldigung f accusation

beschummeln [bə'ʃʊməln] (umg) vt, vi to cheat

Beschuss [bə'ʃʊs] m: **jdn/etw unter ~ nehmen** (Mil) to (start to) bombard od shell sb/sth; (fig) to attack sb/sth; **unter ~ geraten** (lit, fig) to come into the firing line

beschützen [bə'ʃʏtsən] vt: **~ (vor** +dat) to protect (from)

Beschützer, in (-s, -) m(f) protector

Beschützung f protection

beschwatzen [bə'ʃvatsən] (umg) vt (überreden) to talk over

Beschwerde [bə'ʃveːrdə] (-, -n) f complaint; (Mühe) hardship; (Industrie) grievance; **Beschwerden** pl (Leiden) trouble; **~ einlegen** (form) to lodge a complaint; **beschwerdefrei** adj fit and healthy; **Beschwerdefrist** f (Jur) period of time during which an appeal may be lodged

beschweren [bə'ʃveːrən] vt to weight down; (fig) to burden ▷ vr to complain

beschwerlich adj tiring, exhausting

beschwichtigen [bə'ʃvɪçtɪgən] vt to soothe, pacify

Beschwichtigung f soothing, calming

beschwindeln [bə'ʃvɪndəln] vt (betrügen) to cheat; (belügen) to fib to

beschwingt [bə'ʃvɪŋt] adj cheery, in high spirits

beschwipst [bə'ʃvɪpst] adj tipsy

beschwören [bə'ʃvøːrən] unreg vt (Aussage) to swear to; (anflehen) to implore; (Geister) to conjure up

beseelen [bə'zeːlən] vt to inspire

besehen [bə'zeːən] unreg vt to look at; **genau ~** to examine closely

beseitigen [bə'zaɪtɪgən] vt to remove

Beseitigung f removal

Besen ['beːzən] (-s, -) m broom; (pej: umg: Frau) old bag; **ich fresse einen ~, wenn das stimmt** (umg) if that's right, I'll eat my hat;

Besenstiel m broomstick

besessen [bə'zesən] adj possessed; (von einer Idee etc): ~ **(von)** obsessed (with)

besetzen [bə'zetsən] vt (Haus, Land) to occupy; (Platz) to take, fill; (Posten) to fill; (Rolle) to cast; (mit Edelsteinen) to set

besetzt adj full; (Tel) engaged, busy; (Platz) taken; (WC) engaged; **Besetztzeichen** nt engaged tone (Brit), busy signal (US)

Besetzung f occupation; (von Stelle) filling; (von Rolle) casting; (die Schauspieler) cast; **zweite ~** (Theat) understudy

besichtigen [bə'zıçtıgən] vt to visit, look at

Besichtigung f visit

besiedeln vt: **dicht/dünn besiedelt** densely/ thinly populated

Besiedelung [bə'zi:dəluŋ], **Besiedlung** [bə'zi:dluŋ] f population

besiegeln [bə'zi:gəln] vt to seal

besiegen [bə'zi:gən] vt to defeat, overcome

Besiegte, r [bə'zi:ktə(r)] f(m) loser

besinnen [bə'zınən] unreg vr (nachdenken) to think, reflect; (erinnern) to remember; **sich anders ~** to change one's mind

besinnlich adj contemplative

Besinnung f consciousness; **bei/ohne ~ sein** to be conscious/unconscious; **zur ~ kommen** to recover consciousness; (fig) to come to one's senses

besinnungslos adj unconscious; (fig) blind

Besitz [bə'zıts] (-es) m possession; (Eigentum) property; **Besitzanspruch** m claim of ownership; (Jur) title; **besitzanzeigend** adj (Gram) possessive

besitzen unreg vt to possess, own; (Eigenschaft) to have

Besitzer, in (-s, -) m(f) owner, proprietor

Besitz- zW: **Besitzergreifung** f seizure; **Besitznahme** f seizure; **Besitztum** nt (Grundbesitz) estate(s pl), property; **Besitzurkunde** f title deeds pl

besoffen [bə'zɔfən] (umg) adj sozzled

besohlen [bə'zo:lən] vt to sole

Besoldung [bə'zɔlduŋ] f salary, pay

besondere, r, s [bə'zɔndərə(r, s)] adj special; (eigen) particular; (gesondert) separate; (eigentümlich) peculiar

Besonderheit f peculiarity

besonders adv especially, particularly; (getrennt) separately; **das Essen/der Film war nicht ~** the food/film was nothing special od out of the ordinary; **wie gehts dir? — nicht ~** how are you? — not too hot

besonnen [bə'zɔnən] adj sensible, level-headed; **Besonnenheit** f level-headedness

besorgen [bə'zɔrgən] vt (beschaffen) to acquire; (kaufen) to purchase; (erledigen: Geschäfte) to deal with; (sich kümmern um) to take care of; **es jdm ~** (umg) to sort sb out

Besorgnis (-, -se) f anxiety, concern; **besorgniserregend** adj alarming, worrying

besorgt [bə'zɔrkt] adj anxious, worried; **Besorgtheit** f anxiety, worry

Besorgung f acquisition; (Kauf) purchase; (Einkauf): **~en machen** to do some shopping

bespannen [bə'ʃpanən] vt (mit Saiten, Fäden) to string

bespielbar adj (Rasen etc) playable

bespielen [bə'ʃpi:lən] vt (Tonband, Kassette) to make a recording on

bespitzeln [bə'ʃpıtsəln] vt to spy on

besprechen [bə'ʃprɛçən] unreg vt to discuss; (Tonband etc) to record, speak onto; (Buch) to review ▷ vr to discuss, consult

Besprechung f meeting, discussion; (von Buch) review

bespringen [bə'ʃprıŋən] unreg vt (Tier) to mount, cover

bespritzen [bə'ʃprıtsən] vt to spray; (beschmutzen) to spatter

besser ['besər] adj better; **nur ein ~er ...** just a glorified ...; **~e Leute** a better class of people; **es geht ihm ~** he feels better; siehe auch **besserstehen**

bessern vt to make better, improve ▷ vr to improve; (Mensch) to reform

besserstehen unreg vr (umg) to be better off

Besserung f improvement; **auf dem Weg(e) der ~ sein** to be getting better, be improving; **gute ~!** get well soon!

Besserwisser, in (-s, -) m(f) know-all (Brit), know-it-all (US)

Bestand [bə'ʃtant] (-(e)s, ̈-e) m (Fortbestehen) duration, continuance; (Kassenbestand) amount, balance; (Vorrat) stock; **eiserner ~** iron rations pl; **~ haben, von ~ sein** to last long, endure

bestand etc vb siehe **bestehen**

bestanden pp von **bestehen** ▷ adj: **nach ~er Prüfung** after passing the exam

beständig [bə'ʃtendıç] adj (ausdauernd) constant (auch fig); (Wetter) settled; (Stoffe) resistant; (Klagen etc) continual

Bestandsaufnahme f stocktaking

Bestandsüberwachung f stock control, inventory control

Bestandteil m part, component; (Zutat) ingredient; **sich in seine ~e auflösen** to fall to pieces

bestärken [bə'ʃterkən] vt: **jdn in etw** dat **~** to strengthen od confirm sb in sth

bestätigen [bə'ʃte:tıgən] vt to confirm; (anerkennen, Comm) to acknowledge; **jdn (im Amt) ~** to confirm sb's appointment

Bestätigung f confirmation; acknowledgement

bestatten [bə'ʃtatən] vt to bury

Bestatter (-s, -) m undertaker

Bestattung f funeral

Bestattungsinstitut nt undertaker's (Brit), mortician's (US)

bestäuben [bə'ʃtɔybən] vt to powder, dust; (Pflanze) to pollinate

beste, r, s ['bestə(r, s)] adj best; **sie singt am ~n** she sings best; **so ist es am ~n** it's best that way; **am ~n gehst du gleich** you'd better go at once; **jdn zum B~n haben** to pull sb's leg; **einen Witz** etc **zum B~n geben** to tell a joke etc; **aufs B~** in the best possible way; **zu jds B~n** for the benefit of sb; **es steht nicht zum B~n** it does not look too promising

bestechen [bə'ʃtɛçən] unreg vt to bribe
 ▷ vi (Eindruck machen): **(durch etw)** ~ to be impressive (because of sth)

bestechend adj (Schönheit, Eindruck) captivating; (Angebot) tempting

bestechlich adj corruptible; **Bestechlichkeit** f corruptibility

Bestechung f bribery, corruption

Bestechungsgelder pl bribe sing

Bestechungsversuch m attempted bribery

Besteck [bə'ʃtɛk] **(-(e)s, -e)** nt knife, fork and spoon, cutlery; (Med) set of instruments; **Besteckkasten** m cutlery canteen

bestehen [bə'ʃteːən] unreg vi to exist; (andauern) to last ▷ vt (Probe, Prüfung) to pass; (Kampf) to win; ~ **bleiben** to last, endure; (Frage, Hoffnung) to remain; **die Schwierigkeit/das Problem besteht darin, dass ...** the difficulty/problem lies in the fact that ..., the difficulty/problem is that ...; ~ **auf** +dat to insist on; ~ **aus** to consist of; **Bestehen** nt: **seit Bestehen der Firma** ever since the firm came into existence od has existed

bestehlen [bə'ʃteːlən] unreg vt to rob

besteigen [bə'ʃtaɪɡən] unreg vt to climb, ascend; (Pferd) to mount; (Thron) to ascend

Bestellbuch nt order book

bestellen [bə'ʃtɛlən] vt to order; (kommen lassen) to arrange to see; (nominieren) to name; (Acker) to cultivate; (Grüße, Auftrag) to pass on; **wie bestellt und nicht abgeholt** (hum: umg) like orphan Annie; **er hat nicht viel/nichts zu ~** he doesn't have much/any say here; **ich bin für 10 Uhr bestellt** I have an appointment for od at 10 o'clock; **es ist schlecht um ihn bestellt** (fig) he is in a bad way

Bestell- zW: **Bestellformular** nt purchase order; **Bestellnummer** f order number; **Bestellschein** m order coupon

Bestellung f (Comm) order; (Bestellen) ordering; (Ernennung) nomination, appointment

bestenfalls ['bɛstən'fals] adv at best

bestens ['bɛstəns] adv very well

besteuern [bə'ʃtɔʏɐn] vt to tax

bestialisch [bɛsti'aːlɪʃ] (umg) adj awful, beastly

besticken [bə'ʃtɪkən] vt to embroider

Bestie ['bɛstiə] f (lit, fig) beast

bestimmen [bə'ʃtɪmən] vt (Regeln) to lay down; (Tag, Ort) to fix; (prägen) to characterize; (ausersehen) to mean; (ernennen) to appoint; (definieren) to define; (veranlassen) to induce ▷ vi: **du hast hier nicht zu ~** you don't make the decisions here; **er kann über sein Geld allein ~** it is up to him what he does with his money

bestimmend adj (Faktor, Einfluss) determining, decisive

bestimmt adj (entschlossen) firm; (gewiss)

certain, definite; (Artikel) definite ▷ adv (gewiss) definitely, for sure; **suchen Sie etwas B~es?** are you looking for anything in particular?; **Bestimmtheit** f certainty; **in** od **mit aller Bestimmtheit** quite categorically

Bestimmung f (Verordnung) regulation; (Festsetzen) determining; (Verwendungszweck) purpose; (Schicksal) fate; (Definition) definition

Bestimmungs- zW: **Bestimmungsbahnhof** m (Eisenb) destination; **bestimmungsgemäß** adj as agreed; **Bestimmungshafen** m (port of) destination; **Bestimmungsort** m destination

Bestleistung f best performance

bestmöglich adj best possible

Best.-Nr. abk = **Bestellnummer**

bestrafen [bə'ʃtraːfən] vt to punish

Bestrafung f punishment

bestrahlen [bə'ʃtraːlən] vt to shine on; (Med) to treat with X-rays

Bestrahlung f (Med) X-ray treatment, radiotherapy

Bestreben [bə'ʃtreːbən] **(-s)** nt endeavour (Brit), endeavor (US), effort

bestrebt [bə'ʃtreːpt] adj: ~ **sein, etw zu tun** to endeavour (Brit) od endeavor (US) to do sth

Bestrebung [bə'ʃtreːbʊŋ] f = **Bestreben**

bestreichen [bə'ʃtraɪçən] unreg vt (Brot) to spread

bestreiken [bə'ʃtraɪkən] vt (Industrie) to black; **die Fabrik wird zur Zeit bestreikt** there's a strike on in the factory at the moment

bestreiten [bə'ʃtraɪtən] unreg vt (abstreiten) to dispute; (finanzieren) to pay for, finance; **er hat das ganze Gespräch allein bestritten** he did all the talking

bestreuen [bə'ʃtrɔʏən] vt to sprinkle, dust; (Straße) to (spread with) grit

Bestseller ['bɛstsɛlər] **(-s, -)** m best-seller

bestürmen [bə'ʃtʏrmən] vt (mit Fragen, Bitten etc) to overwhelm, swamp

bestürzen [bə'ʃtʏrtsən] vt to dismay

bestürzt adj dismayed

Bestürzung f consternation

Bestzeit f (bes Sport) best time

Besuch [bə'zuːx] **(-(e)s, -e)** m visit; (Person) visitor; **einen ~ bei jdm machen** to pay sb a visit od call; ~ **haben** to have visitors; **bei jdm auf** od **zu ~ sein** to be visiting sb

besuchen vt to visit; (Sch etc) to attend; **gut besucht** well-attended

Besucher, in (-s, -) m(f) visitor, guest

Besuchserlaubnis f permission to visit

Besuchszeit f visiting hours pl

besudeln [bə'zuːdəln] vt (Wände) to smear; (fig: Namen, Ehre) to sully

betagt [bə'taːkt] adj aged

betasten [bə'tastən] vt to touch, feel

betätigen [bə'tɛːtɪɡən] vt (bedienen) to work, operate ▷ vr to involve o.s.; **sich politisch ~** to be involved in politics; **sich als etw ~** to work as sth

Betätigung f activity; (beruflich) occupation; (Tech) operation

betäuben [bə'tɔybən] vt to stun; (fig: Gewissen) to still; (Med) to anaesthetize (Brit), anesthetize (US); **ein ~der Duft** an overpowering smell

Betäubung f (Narkose): **örtliche ~** local anaesthetic (Brit) od anesthetic (US)

Betäubungsmittel nt anaesthetic (Brit), anesthetic (US)

Bete ['be:tə] (-, -n) f: **Rote ~** beetroot (Brit), beet (US)

beteiligen [bə'taɪlɪɡən] vr: **sich (an etw** dat) **~** to take part (in sth), participate (in sth); (an Geschäft: finanziell) to have a share (in sth) ▷ vt: **jdn (an etw** dat) **~** to give sb a share od interest (in sth); **sich an den Unkosten ~** to contribute to the expenses

Beteiligung f participation; (Anteil) share, interest; (Besucherzahl) attendance

Beteiligungsgesellschaft f associated company

beten ['be:tən] vi to pray ▷ vt (Rosenkranz) to say

beteuern [bə'tɔyərn] vt to assert; (Unschuld) to protest; **jdm etw ~** to assure sb of sth

Beteuerung f assertion; protestation; assurance

Beton [be'tõ:] (-s, -s) m concrete

betonen [bə'to:nən] vt to stress

betonieren [beto'ni:rən] vt to concrete

Betonmischmaschine f concrete mixer

betont [bə'to:nt] adj (Höflichkeit) emphatic, deliberate; (Kühle, Sachlichkeit) pointed

Betonung f stress, emphasis

betören [bə'tø:rən] vt to beguile

Betr. abk = **Betreff**

betr. abk (= betreffend, betreffs) re

Betracht [bə'traxt] m: **in ~ kommen** to be concerned od relevant; **nicht in ~ kommen** to be out of the question; **etw in ~ ziehen** to consider sth; **außer ~ bleiben** not to be considered

betrachten vt to look at; (fig) to consider, look at

Betrachter, in (-s, -) m(f) onlooker

beträchtlich [bə'trɛçtlɪç] adj considerable

Betrachtung f (Ansehen) examination; (Erwägung) consideration; **über etw** akk **~en anstellen** to reflect on od contemplate sth

betraf etc [bə'tra:f] vb siehe **betreffen**

Betrag [bə'tra:k] (-(e)s, -̈e) m amount, sum; **~ erhalten** (Comm) sum received

betragen [bə'tra:ɡən] unreg vt to amount to ▷ vr to behave

Betragen (-s) nt behaviour (Brit), behavior (US); (bes in Zeugnis) conduct

beträgt [bə'trɛ:kt] vb siehe **betragen**

betrat etc [bə'tra:t] vb siehe **betreten**

betrauen [bə'trauən] vt: **jdn mit etw ~** to entrust sb with sth

betrauern [bə'trauərn] vt to mourn

beträufeln [bə'trɔyfəln] vt: **den Fisch mit Zitrone ~** to sprinkle lemon juice on the fish

Betreff m: **~: Ihr Schreiben vom ...** re od reference your letter of ...

betreffen [bə'trɛfən] unreg vt to concern, affect; **was mich betrifft** as for me

betreffend adj relevant, in question

betreffs [bə'trɛfs] präp+gen concerning, regarding

betreiben [bə'traɪbən] unreg vt (ausüben) to practise (Brit), practice (US); (Politik) to follow; (Studien) to pursue; (vorantreiben) to push ahead; (Tech: antreiben) to drive; **auf jds B~** akk **hin** (form) at sb's instigation

Betreiberfirma [bə'traɪbərfɪrma] f operating company

betreten [bə'tre:tən] unreg vt to enter; (Bühne etc) to step onto ▷ adj embarrassed; „**B~ verboten"** "keep off/out"

betreuen [bə'trɔyən] vt to look after

Betreuer, in (-s, -) m(f) carer; (Kinderbetreuer) child-minder

Betreuung f: **er wurde mit der ~ der Gruppe beauftragt** he was put in charge of the group

Betrieb (-(e)s, -e) m (Firma) firm, concern; (Anlage) plant; (Tätigkeit) operation; (Treiben) bustle; (Verkehr) traffic; **außer ~ sein** to be out of order; **in ~ sein** to be in operation; **eine Maschine in/außer ~ setzen** to start a machine up/stop a machine; **eine Maschine/Fabrik in ~ nehmen** to put a machine/factory into operation; **in den Geschäften herrscht großer ~** the shops are very busy; **er hält den ganzen ~ auf** (umg) he's holding everything up

betrieb etc [bə'tri:p] vb siehe **betreiben**

betrieben [bə'tri:bən] pp von **betreiben**

betrieblich adj company attr ▷ adv (regeln) within the company

Betriebs- zW: **Betriebsanleitung** f operating instructions pl; **Betriebsausflug** m firm's outing; **Betriebsausgaben** pl revenue expenditure sing; **betriebseigen** adj company attr; **Betriebsergebnis** nt trading od operating result; **Betriebserlaubnis** f operating permission/licence (Brit) od license (US); **betriebsfähig** adj in working order; **Betriebsferien** pl company holidays pl (Brit) od vacation sing (US); **Betriebsführung** f management; **Betriebsgeheimnis** nt trade secret; **Betriebskapital** nt capital employed; **Betriebsklima** nt (working) atmosphere; **Betriebskosten** pl running costs; **Betriebsleitung** f management; **Betriebsrat** m workers' council; **Betriebsrente** f company pension; **betriebssicher** adj safe, reliable; **Betriebsstoff** m fuel; **Betriebsstörung** f breakdown; **Betriebssystem** nt (Comput) operating system; **Betriebsunfall** m industrial accident; **Betriebswirt** m management expert; **Betriebswirtschaft** f business management

betrifft [bə'trɪft] vb siehe **betreffen**

betrinken [bə'trɪŋkən] unreg vr to get drunk

betritt [bə'trɪt] vb siehe **betreten**

betroffen [bə'trɔfən] pp von **betreffen** ▷ adj (bestürzt) amazed, perplexed; **von etw ~**

werden *od* **sein** to be affected by sth
betrüben [bə'try:bən] *vt* to grieve
betrübt [bə'try:pt] *adj* sorrowful, grieved
Betrug (-(e)s) *m* deception; (*Jur*) fraud
betrug *etc* [bə'tru:k] *vb siehe* **betragen**
betrügen [bə'try:gən] *unreg vt* to cheat; (*Jur*) to
  defraud; (*Ehepartner*) to be unfaithful to ▷ *vr* to
  deceive o.s.
Betrüger, in (-**s, -**) *m(f)* cheat, deceiver
betrügerisch *adj* deceitful; (*Jur*) fraudulent; **in**
  ~er Absicht with intent to defraud
betrunken [bə'trʊŋkən] *adj* drunk
Betrunkene, r *f(m)* drunk
Bett [bɛt] (-**(e)s, -en**) *nt* bed; **im ~** in bed; **ins** *od*
  zu ~ gehen to go to bed; **Bettbezug** *m* duvet
  cover; **Bettdecke** *f* blanket; (*Daunenbettdecke*)
  quilt; (*Überwurf*) bedspread
bettelarm ['bɛtəl|arm] *adj* very poor, destitute
Bettelei [bɛtə'laɪ] *f* begging
Bettelmönch *m* mendicant *od* begging monk
betteln *vi* to beg
betten *vt* to make a bed for
Bett- *zW:* **Betthupferl** (*Südd*) *nt* bedtime sweet;
  bettlägerig *adj* bedridden; **Bettlaken** *nt*
  sheet; **Bettlektüre** *f* bedtime reading
Bettler, in ['bɛtlər(ɪn)] (-**s, -**) *m(f)* beggar
Bett- *zW:* **Bettnässer (-s, -)** *m* bedwetter;
  Bettschwere (*umg*) *f:* **die nötige**
  Bettschwere haben/bekommen to be/
  get tired enough to sleep; **Betttuch** *nt* sheet;
  Bettvorleger *m* bedside rug; **Bettwäsche**
  f bedclothes *pl*, bedding; **Bettzeug** *nt* =
  Bettwäsche
betucht [bə'tu:xt] (*umg*) *adj* well-to-do
betulich [bə'tu:lɪç] *adj* (*übertrieben besorgt*)
  fussing *attr*; (*Redeweise*) twee
betupfen [bə'tʊpfən] *vt* to dab; (*Med*) to swab
Beugehaft ['bɔygəhaft] *f* (*Jur*) coercive
  detention
beugen ['bɔygən] *vt* to bend; (*Gram*) to inflect
  ▷ *vr* (+*dat*) (*sich fügen*) to bow (to)
Beule ['bɔylə] (-**, -n**) *f* bump
beunruhigen [bə'|ʊnru:ɪgən] *vt* to disturb,
  alarm ▷ *vr* to become worried
Beunruhigung *f* worry, alarm
beurkunden [bə'|u:rkʊndən] *vt* to attest, verify
beurlauben [bə'|u:rlaʊbən] *vt* to give leave
  od holiday to (*Brit*), grant vacation to (*US*);
  beurlaubt sein to have leave of absence;
  (*suspendiert sein*) to have been relieved of one's
  duties
beurteilen [bə'|ʊrtaɪlən] *vt* to judge; (*Buch etc*)
  to review
Beurteilung *f* judgement; (*von Buch etc*) review;
  (*Note*) mark
Beute ['bɔytə] (-) *f* booty, loot; (*von Raubtieren*
  etc) prey
Beutel (-s, -) *m* bag; (*Geldbeutel*) purse;
  (*Tabaksbeutel*) pouch
bevölkern [bə'fœlkərn] *vt* to populate
Bevölkerung *f* population
Bevölkerungs- *zW:* **Bevölkerungsexplosion** *f*
  population explosion; **Bevölkerungsschicht** *f*

social stratum; **Bevölkerungsstatistik** *f* vital
  statistics *pl*
bevollmächtigen [bə'fɔlmɛçtɪgən] *vt* to
  authorize
Bevollmächtigte, r *f(m)* authorized agent
Bevollmächtigung *f* authorization
bevor [bə'fo:r] *konj* before; **bevormunden**
  vt untr to dominate; **bevorstehen** *unreg*
  vi: (**jdm**) **bevorstehen** to be in store (for sb);
  bevorstehend *adj* imminent, approaching;
  bevorzugen *vt untr* to prefer; **bevorzugt**
  [bə'fo:rtsu:kt] *adv:* **etw bevorzugt abfertigen**
  etc to give sth priority; **Bevorzugung** *f*
  preference
bewachen [bə'vaxən] *vt* to watch, guard
bewachsen [bə'vaksən] *adj* overgrown
Bewachung *f* (*Bewachen*) guarding; (*Leute*)
  guard, watch
bewaffnen [bə'vafnən] *vt* to arm
Bewaffnung *f* (*Vorgang*) arming; (*Ausrüstung*)
  armament, arms *pl*
bewahren [bə'va:rən] *vt* to keep; **jdn vor jdm/**
  etw ~ to save sb from sb/sth; (**Gott**) **bewahre!**
  (*umg*) heaven *od* God forbid!
bewähren [bə've:rən] *vr* to prove o.s.;
  (*Maschine*) to prove its worth
bewahrheiten [bə'va:rhaɪtən] *vr* to come true
bewährt *adj* reliable
Bewährung *f* (*Jur*) probation; **ein Jahr**
  Gefängnis mit ~ a suspended sentence of one
  year with probation
Bewährungs- *zW:* **Bewährungsfrist** *f* (period
  of) probation; **Bewährungshelfer** *m* probation
  officer; **Bewährungsprobe** *f:* **etw einer**
  Bewährungsprobe *dat* **unterziehen** to put
  sth to the test
bewaldet [bə'valdət] *adj* wooded
bewältigen [bə'vɛltɪgən] *vt* to overcome;
  (*Arbeit*) to finish; (*Portion*) to manage;
  (*Schwierigkeiten*) to cope with
bewandert [bə'vandərt] *adj* expert,
  knowledgeable
Bewandtnis [bə'vantnɪs] *f:* **damit hat es**
  folgende ~ the fact of the matter is this
bewarb *etc* [bə'varp] *vb siehe* **bewerben**
bewässern [bə'vɛsərn] *vt* to irrigate
Bewässerung *f* irrigation
bewegen [bə've:gən] *vt, vr* to move; **der Preis**
  bewegt sich um die 50 Euro the price is
  about 50 euros; **jdn zu etw ~** to induce sb to
  do sth
Beweggrund *m* motive
beweglich *adj* movable, mobile; (*flink*) quick
bewegt [bə've:kt] *adj* (*Leben*) eventful; (*Meer*)
  rough; (*ergriffen*) touched
Bewegung *f* movement, motion; (*innere*)
  emotion; (*körperlich*) exercise; **sich** *dat* **~**
  machen to take exercise
Bewegungsfreiheit *f* freedom of movement;
  (*fig*) freedom of action
bewegungslos *adj* motionless
Beweis [bə'vaɪs] (-**es, -e**) *m* proof; (*Zeichen*) sign;
  Beweisaufnahme *f* (*Jur*) taking *od* hearing of

evidence; **beweisbar** *adj* provable
beweisen *unreg vt* to prove; (*zeigen*) to show;
was zu ~ war QED
Beweis- *zW:* **Beweisführung** *f* reasoning;
(*Jur*) presentation of one's case; **Beweiskraft**
f weight, conclusiveness; **beweiskräftig**
adj convincing, conclusive; **Beweislast** *f*
(*Jur*) onus, burden of proof; **Beweismittel** *nt*
evidence; **Beweisnot** *f* (*Jur*) lack of evidence;
Beweisstück *nt* exhibit
bewenden [bə'vɛndən] *vi:* **etw dabei ~ lassen**
to leave sth at that
bewerben [bə'vɛrbən] *unreg vr:* **sich ~ (um)** to
apply (for)
Bewerber, in (-s, -) *m(f)* applicant
Bewerbung *f* application
Bewerbungsfrist *f* application deadline
Bewerbungsmappe *f*, **Bewerbungs-
unterlagen** *pl* application documents *pl*
bewerkstelligen [bə'vɛrkʃtɛligən] *vt* to
manage, accomplish
bewerten [bə've:rtən] *vt* to assess
bewies *etc* [bə'vi:s] *vb siehe* **beweisen**
bewiesen [bə'vi:zən] *pp von* **beweisen**
bewilligen [bə'viligən] *vt* to grant, allow
Bewilligung *f* granting
bewirbt [bə'virpt] *vb siehe* **bewerben**
bewirken [bə'virkən] *vt* to cause, bring about
bewirten [bə'virtən] *vt* to entertain
bewirtschaften [bə'virtʃaftən] *vt* to manage
Bewirtung *f* hospitality; **die ~ so vieler Gäste**
catering for so many guests
bewog *etc* [bə'vo:k] *vb siehe* **bewegen**
bewogen [bə'vo:gən] *pp von* **bewegen**
bewohnbar *adj* inhabitable
bewohnen [bə'vo:nən] *vt* to inhabit, live in
Bewohner, in (-s, -) *m(f)* inhabitant; (*von Haus*)
resident
bewölkt [bə'vœlkt] *adj* cloudy, overcast
Bewölkung *f* clouds *pl*
Bewölkungsauflockerung *f* break-up of the
cloud
beworben [bə'vɔrbən] *pp von* **bewerben**
Bewunderer, in (-s, -) *m(f)* admirer
bewundern [bə'vundərn] *vt* to admire
bewundernswert *adj* admirable, wonderful
Bewunderung *f* admiration
bewusst [bə'vust] *adj* conscious; (*absichtlich*)
deliberate; **jdm etw ~ machen** to make sb
conscious of sth; **sich** *dat* **etw ~ machen** to
realize sth; **sich** *dat* **einer Sache** *gen* **~ sein** to
be aware of sth; **bewusstlos** *adj* unconscious;
Bewusstlosigkeit *f* unconsciousness; **bis
zur Bewusstlosigkeit** (*umg*) ad nauseam;
Bewusstsein *nt* consciousness; **bei
Bewusstsein** conscious; **im Bewusstsein,
dass ...** in the knowledge that ...
Bewusstseins- *zW:* **Bewusstseinsbildung**
f (*Pol*) shaping of political ideas;
bewusstseinserweiternd
adj: **bewusstseinserweiternde
Drogen** mind-expanding drugs;
Bewusstseinserweiterung *f* consciousness

raising
Bez. *abk* = **Bezirk**
bez. *abk* (= *bezüglich*) re.
bezahlen [bə'tsa:lən] *vt* to pay (for); **es macht
sich bezahlt** it will pay
Bezahlfernsehen *nt* pay TV
Bezahlung *f* payment; **ohne/gegen** *od* **für ~**
without/for payment
bezaubern [bə'tsaubərn] *vt* to enchant, charm
bezeichnen [bə'tsaiçnən] *vt* (*kennzeichnen*) to
mark; (*nennen*) to call; (*beschreiben*) to describe;
(*zeigen*) to show, indicate
bezeichnend *adj:* **~ (für)** characteristic (of),
typical (of)
Bezeichnung *f* (*Zeichen*) mark, sign;
(*Beschreibung*) description; (*Ausdruck*)
expression, term
bezeugen [bə'tsɔygən] *vt* to testify to
bezichtigen [bə'tsiçtigən] *vt* (+*gen*) to accuse
(of)
Bezichtigung *f* accusation
beziehen [bə'tsi:ən] *unreg vt* (*mit Überzug*) to
cover; (*Haus, Position*) to move into; (*Standpunkt*)
to take up; (*erhalten*) to receive; (*Zeitung*) to
subscribe to, take ▷ *vr* (*Himmel*) to cloud over;
die Betten frisch ~ to change the beds; **etw
auf jdn/etw ~** to relate sth to sb/sth; **sich ~
auf** +*akk* to refer to
Beziehung *f* (*Verbindung*) connection;
(*Zusammenhang*) relation; (*Verhältnis*)
relationship; (*Hinsicht*) respect;
diplomatische ~en diplomatic relations;
seine ~en spielen lassen to pull strings;
in jeder ~ in every respect; **~en haben**
(*vorteilhaft*) to have connections *od* contacts
Beziehungskiste (*umg*) *f* relationship
beziehungsweise *adv* or; (*genauer gesagt*) that
is, or rather; (*im anderen Fall*) and ... respectively
beziffern [bə'tsifərn] *vt* (*angeben*): **~ auf** +*akk* *od*
mit to estimate at
Bezirk [bə'tsirk] **(-(e)s, -e)** *m* district
bezirzen [bə'tsirtsən] (*umg*) *vt* to bewitch
bezogen [bə'tso:gən] *pp von* **beziehen**
Bezogene, r [bə'tso:gənə(r)] *f(m)* (*von Scheck etc*)
drawee
Bezug [bə'tsu:k] **(-(e)s, ¨e)** *m* (*Hülle*) covering;
(*Comm*) ordering; (*Gehalt*) income, salary;
(*Beziehung*): **~ (zu)** relationship (to); **in ~ auf**
+*akk* with reference to; **mit** *od* **unter ~ auf**
+*akk* regarding; (*form*) with reference to; **~
nehmen auf** +*akk* to refer to
bezüglich [bə'tsy:kliç] *präp* +*gen* concerning,
referring to ▷ *adj* concerning; (*Gram*) relative
Bezugnahme *f:* **~ (auf** +*akk*) reference (to)
Bezugs- *zW:* **Bezugsperson** *f:* **die wichtigste
Bezugsperson des Kleinkindes** the person
to whom the small child relates most closely;
Bezugspreis *m* retail price; **Bezugsquelle** *f*
source of supply
bezuschussen [bə'tsu:ʃusən] *vt* to subsidize
bezwecken [bə'tsvɛkən] *vt* to aim at
bezweifeln [bə'tsvaifəln] *vt* to doubt
bezwingen [bə'tsviŋən] *unreg vt* to conquer;

(Feind) to defeat, overcome

bezwungen [bə'tsvʊŋən] *pp von* **bezwingen**

Bf. *abk* = **Bahnhof; Brief**

BfA (-) *f abk* (= *Bundesversicherungsanstalt für Angestellte*) Federal insurance company for employees

BfV (-) *nt abk* (= *Bundesamt für Verfassungsschutz*) Federal Office for Protection of the Constitution

BG (-) *f abk* (= *Berufsgenossenschaft*) professional association

BGB (-) *nt abk* (= *Bürgerliches Gesetzbuch*) siehe **bürgerlich**

BGH (-) *m abk* (= *Bundesgerichtshof*) Federal Supreme Court

BGS (-) *m abk* = **Bundesgrenzschutz**

BH (-**s**, -(**s**)) *m abk* (= *Büstenhalter*) bra

Bhf. *abk* = **Bahnhof**

BI *f abk* = **Bürgerinitiative**

Biathlon ['bi:atlɔn] (-**s**, -**s**) *nt* biathlon

bibbern ['bɪbərn] (*umg*) *vi* (*vor Kälte*) to shiver

Bibel ['bi:bəl] (-, -**n**) *f* Bible

bibelfest *adj* well versed in the Bible

Biber ['bi:bər] (-**s**, -) *m* beaver

Biberbettuch *nt* flannelette sheet

Bibliografie [bibliogra'fi:] *f* bibliography

Bibliothek [biblio'te:k] (-, -**en**) *f* (*auch Comput*) library

Bibliothekar, in [bibliote'ka:r(ɪn)] (-**s**, -**e**) *m(f)* librarian

biblisch ['bi:blɪʃ] *adj* biblical

bieder ['bi:dər] *adj* upright, worthy; (*pej*) conventional; (*Kleid etc*) plain

Biedermann (-(**e**)**s**, *pl* -**männer**) (*pej*) *m* (*geh*) petty bourgeois

biegbar ['bi:kba:r] *adj* flexible

Biege *f*: **die ~ machen** (*umg*) to buzz off, split

biegen ['bi:gən] *unreg* *vt, vr* to bend ▷ *vi* to turn; **sich vor Lachen ~** (*fig*) to double up with laughter; **auf B~ oder Brechen** (*umg*) by hook or by crook

biegsam ['bi:kza:m] *adj* supple

Biegung *f* bend, curve

Biene ['bi:nə] (-, -**n**) *f* bee; (*veraltet: umg: Mädchen*) bird (*Brit*), chick (*bes US*)

Bienen- *zW*: **Bienenhonig** *m* honey; **Bienenkorb** *m* beehive; **Bienenstich** *m* (*Koch*) sugar-and-almond coated cake filled with custard or cream; **Bienenstock** *m* beehive; **Bienenwachs** *nt* beeswax

Bier [bi:r] (-(**e**)**s**, -**e**) *nt* beer; **zwei ~, bitte!** two beers, please; **Bierbauch** (*umg*) *m* beer belly; **Bierbrauer** *m* brewer; **Bierdeckel** *m* beer mat; **Bierfilz** *m* beer mat; **Bierkrug** *m* beer mug; **Bierschinken** *m* ham sausage; **Bierseidel** *nt* beer mug; **Bierwurst** *f* ham sausage

Biest [bi:st] (-(**e**)**s**, -**er**) (*pej: umg*) *nt* (*Mensch*) (little) wretch; (*Frau*) bitch (!)

biestig *adj* beastly

bieten ['bi:tən] *unreg* *vt* to offer; (*bei Versteigerung*) to bid ▷ *vr* (*Gelegenheit*): **sich jdm ~** to present itself to sb; **sich dat etw ~ lassen** to put up with sth

Bigamie [biga'mi:] *f* bigamy

Bikini [bi'ki:ni] (-**s**, -**s**) *m* bikini

Bilanz [bi'lants] *f* balance; (*fig*) outcome; **eine ~ aufstellen** to draw up a balance sheet; **~ ziehen (aus)** to take stock (of); **Bilanzprüfer** *m* auditor

bilateral ['bi:latera:l] *adj* bilateral; **~er Handel** bilateral trade; **~es Abkommen** bilateral agreement

Bild [bɪlt] (-(**e**)**s**, -**er**) *nt* (*lit, fig*) picture; photo; (*Spiegelbild*) reflection; (*fig: Vorstellung*) image, picture; **ein ~ machen** to take a photo *od* picture; **im ~e sein (über** +*akk*) to be in the picture (about); **Bildauflösung** *f* (*TV, Comput*) resolution; **Bildband** *m* illustrated book; **Bildbericht** *m* pictorial report; **Bildbeschreibung** *f* (*Sch*) description of a picture; **Bilddatei** *f* picture file

bilden ['bɪldən] *vt* to form; (*erziehen*) to educate; (*ausmachen*) to constitute ▷ *vr* to arise; (*durch Lesen etc*) to improve one's mind; (*erziehen*) to educate o.s.

bildend *adj*: **die ~e Kunst** art

Bilderbuch *nt* picture book

Bilderrahmen *m* picture frame

Bild- *zW*: **Bildfläche** *f* screen; (*fig*) scene; **von der Bildfläche verschwinden** (*fig: umg*) to disappear (from the scene); **bildhaft** *adj* (*Sprache*) vivid; **Bildhauer** *m* sculptor; **bildhübsch** *adj* lovely, pretty as a picture; **bildlich** *adj* figurative; pictorial; **sich** *dat* **etw bildlich vorstellen** to picture sth in one's mind's eye

Bildnis ['bɪltnɪs] *nt* (*liter*) portrait

Bild- *zW*: **Bildplatte** *f* videodisc; **Bildröhre** *f* (*TV*) cathode ray tube; **Bildschirm** *m* (*TV, Comput*) screen; **Bildschirmgerät** *nt* (*Comput*) visual display unit, VDU; **Bildschirmschoner** (-**s**, -) *m* (*Comput*) screen saver; **Bildschirmtext** *m* teletext; ≈ Ceefax®, Oracle®; **bildschön** *adj* lovely

Bildtelefon *nt* videophone

Bildung ['bɪldʊŋ] *f* formation; (*Wissen, Benehmen*) education

Bildungs- *zW*: **Bildungsgang** *m* school (and university/college) career; **Bildungsgut** *nt* cultural heritage; **Bildungslücke** *f* gap in one's education; **Bildungspolitik** *f* educational policy; **Bildungsroman** *m* (*Liter*) Bildungsroman, novel relating hero's intellectual/ spiritual development; **Bildungsurlaub** *m* educational holiday; **Bildungsweg** *m*: **auf dem zweiten Bildungsweg** through night school/the Open University *etc*; **Bildungswesen** *nt* education system

Bildweite *f* (*Phot*) distance

Bildzuschrift *f* reply enclosing photograph

Billard ['bɪljart] (-**s**, -**e**) *nt* billiards; **Billardball** *m* billiard ball; **Billardkugel** *f* billiard ball

billig ['bɪlɪç] *adj* cheap; (*gerecht*) fair, reasonable; **~e Handelsflagge** flag of convenience; **~es Geld** cheap/easy money

billigen ['bɪlɪgən] *vt* to approve of; **etw stillschweigend ~** to condone sth

billigerweise *adv* (*veraltet*) in all fairness,

reasonably

Billig- zW: **Billigflieger** m, **Billigfluglinie** f cheap od low-cost airline; **Billigladen** m discount store; **Billigpreis** m low price; **Billigprodukt** nt low-price product

Billigung f approval

Billion [bɪliˈoːn] f billion (Brit), trillion (US)

bimmeln [ˈbɪməln] vi to tinkle

Bimsstein [ˈbɪmsʃtaɪn] m pumice stone

bin [bɪn] vb siehe **sein**

binär [biˈnɛːr] adj binary; **Binärzahl** f binary number

Binde [ˈbɪndə] (-, -n) f bandage; (Armbinde) band; (Med) sanitary towel (Brit) od napkin (US); **sich** dat **einen hinter die ~ gießen** od **kippen** (umg) to put a few drinks away

Binde- zW: **Bindeglied** nt connecting link; **Bindehautentzündung** f conjunctivitis; **Bindemittel** nt binder

binden unreg vt to bind, tie ▷ vr (sich verpflichten): **sich ~ (an** +akk) to commit o.s. (to)

bindend adj binding; (Zusage) definite; **~ für** binding on

Bindestrich m hyphen

Bindewort nt conjunction

Bindfaden m string; **es regnet Bindfäden** (umg) it's sheeting down

Bindung f bond, tie; (Ski) binding

binnen [ˈbɪnən] präp (+dat od gen) within; **Binnenhafen** m inland harbour (Brit) od harbor (US); **Binnenhandel** m internal trade; **Binnenmarkt** m home market; **Europäischer Binnenmarkt** single European market; **Binnennachfrage** f domestic demand

Binse [ˈbɪnzə] (-, -n) f rush, reed; **in die ~n gehen** (fig: umg) to be a wash-out

Binsenwahrheit f truism

Bio- [bio-] zW: bio-, organic

Biografie [biograˈfiː] f biography

Bioladen [ˈbiolaːdən] m health food shop (Brit) od store (US); see culture note

● **BIOLADEN**

● A Bioladen is a shop which specializes in
● selling environmentally-friendly products
● such as phosphate-free washing powders,
● recycled paper and organically-grown
● vegetables.

Biologe [bioˈloːgə] (-n, -n) m biologist

Biologie [bioloˈgiː] f biology

Biologin f biologist

biologisch [bioˈloːgɪʃ] adj biological; **~e Vielfalt** biodiversity; **~e Uhr** biological clock

Bio- [bio-] zW: **Biosphäre** f biosphere; **Biotechnik** [bioˈtɛçnɪk] f biotechnology; **Bioterrorismus** m bioterrorism; **Biotreibstoff** [ˈbioːtraɪpʃtɔf] m biofuel

birgt [bɪrkt] vb siehe **bergen**

Birke [ˈbɪrkə] (-, -n) f birch

Birma [ˈbɪrma] (-s) nt Burma

Birnbaum m pear tree

Birne [ˈbɪrnə] (-, -n) f pear; (Elek) (light) bulb

birst [bɪrst] vb siehe **bersten**

 SCHLÜSSELWORT

bis [bɪs] adv, präp +akk **1** (zeitlich) till, until; (bis spätestens) by; **Sie haben bis Dienstag Zeit** you have until od till Tuesday; **bis zum Wochenende** up to od until the weekend; (spätestens) by the weekend; **bis Dienstag muss es fertig sein** it must be ready by Tuesday; **bis wann ist das fertig?** when will that be finished?; **bis auf Weiteres** until further notice; **bis in die Nacht** into the night; **bis bald!/gleich!** see you later/soon

2 (räumlich) (up) to; **ich fahre bis Köln** I'm going as far as Cologne; **bis an unser Grundstück** (right od up) to our plot; **bis hierher** this far; **bis zur Straße kommen** to get as far as the road

3 (bei Zahlen, Angaben) up to; **bis zu** up to; **Gefängnis bis zu 8 Jahren** a maximum of 8 years' imprisonment

4: bis auf etw akk (außer) except sth; (einschließlich) including sth

▷ konj **1** (mit Zahlen) to; **10 bis 20** 10 to 20

2 (zeitlich) till, until; **bis es dunkel wird** till od until it gets dark; **von ... bis ...** from ... to ...

Bisamratte [ˈbiːzamratə] f muskrat (beaver)

Bischof [ˈbɪʃɔf] (-s, ̈-e) m bishop

bischöflich [ˈbɪʃøːflɪç] adj episcopal

bisexuell [bizɛksuˈɛl] adj bisexual

bisher [bɪsˈheːr] adv till now, hitherto

bisherig [bɪsˈheːrɪç] adj till now

Biskaya [bɪsˈkaˈya] f: **Golf von ~** Bay of Biscay

Biskuit [bɪsˈkviːt] (-(e)s, -s od -e) m od nt biscuit; **Biskuitgebäck** nt sponge cake(s); **Biskuitteig** m sponge mixture

bislang [bɪsˈlaŋ] adv hitherto

Biss (-es, -e) m bite

biss etc [bɪs] vb siehe **beißen**

bisschen [ˈbɪsçən] adj, adv bit

Bissen [ˈbɪsən] (-s, -) m bite, morsel; **sich** dat **jeden ~ vom** od **am Munde absparen** to watch every penny one spends

bissig [ˈbɪsɪç] adj (Hund) snappy; vicious; (Bemerkung) cutting, biting; **„Vorsicht, ~er Hund"** "beware of the dog"

bist [bɪst] vb siehe **sein**

bisweilen [bɪsˈvaɪlən] adv at times, occasionally

Bit [bɪt] (-(s), -(s)) nt (Comput) bit

Bittbrief m petition

Bitte [ˈbɪtə] (-, -n) f request; **auf seine ~ hin** at his request; **bitte** interj please; (als Antwort auf Dank) you're welcome; **wie bitte?** (I beg your) pardon?; **bitte schön!** it was a pleasure; **bitte schön?** (in Geschäft) can I help you?; **na bitte!** there you are!

bitten unreg vt to ask ▷ vi (einladen): **ich lasse ~** would you ask him/her etc to come in now?; **~ um** to ask for; **aber ich bitte dich!** not at all;

ich bitte darum (form) if you wouldn't mind; **ich muss doch (sehr) ~!** well I must say!

bittend adj pleading, imploring

bitter ['bɪtər] adj bitter; (Schokolade) plain; **etw ~ nötig haben** to be in dire need of sth; **bitterböse** adj very angry; **bitterernst** adj: **damit ist es mir bitterernst** I am deadly serious od in deadly earnest; **Bitterkeit** f bitterness; **bitterlich** adj bitter ▷ adv bitterly

Bittsteller, in (-s, -) m(f) petitioner

Biwak ['bi:vak] (-s, -s od -e) nt bivouac

Bj. abk = **Baujahr**

Blabla [bla:'bla:] (-s) (umg) nt waffle

blähen ['blɛ:ən] vt, vr to swell, blow out ▷ vi (Speisen) to cause flatulence od wind

Blähungen pl (Med) wind sing

blamabel [bla'ma:bəl] adj disgraceful

Blamage [bla'ma:ʒə] (-, -n) f disgrace

blamieren [bla'mi:rən] vr to make a fool of o.s., disgrace o.s. ▷ vt to let down, disgrace

blank [blaŋk] adj bright; (unbedeckt) bare; (sauber) clean, polished; (umg: ohne Geld) broke; (offensichtlich) blatant

blanko ['blaŋko] adv blank; **Blankoscheck** m blank cheque (Brit) od check (US); **Blankovollmacht** f carte blanche

Bläschen ['blɛ:sçən] nt bubble; (Med) small blister

Blase ['bla:zə] (-, -n) f bubble; (Med) blister; (Anat) bladder

Blasebalg m bellows pl

blasen unreg vt, vi to blow; **zum Aufbruch ~** (fig) to say it's time to go

Blasenentzündung f cystitis

Bläser, in ['blɛ:zər(ɪn)] (-s, -) m(f) (Mus) wind player; **die ~** the wind (section)

blasiert [bla'zi:rt] (pej) adj (geh) blasé

Blas- zW: **Blasinstrument** nt wind instrument; **Blaskapelle** f brass band; **Blasmusik** f brass band music

blass [blas] adj pale; (Ausdruck) weak, insipid; (fig: Ahnung, Vorstellung) faint, vague; **~ vor Neid werden** to go green with envy

Blässe ['blɛsə] (-) f paleness, pallor

Blatt [blat] (-(e)s, ¨er) nt leaf; (von Papier) sheet; (Zeitung) newspaper; (Karten) hand; **vom ~ singen/spielen** to sight-read; **kein ~ vor den Mund nehmen** not to mince one's words

blättern ['blɛtərn] vi: **in etw** dat **~** to leaf through sth

Blätterteig m flaky od puff pastry

Blattlaus f greenfly, aphid

blau [blaʊ] adj blue; (umg) drunk, stoned; (Koch) boiled; (Auge) black; **~er Fleck** bruise; **mit einem ~en Auge davonkommen** (fig) to get off lightly; **~er Brief** (Sch) letter telling parents a child may have to repeat a year; **er wird sein ~es Wunder erleben** (umg) he won't know what's hit him; **blauäugig** adj blue-eyed; **Blaubeere** f bilberry

Blaue nt: **Fahrt ins ~** mystery tour; **das ~ vom Himmel (herunter) lügen** (umg) to tell a pack of lies

blau- zW: **Blauhelm** (umg) m UN Soldier; **Blaukraut** nt red cabbage; **Blaulicht** nt flashing blue light; **blaumachen** (umg) vi to skive off work; **Blaupause** f blueprint; **Blausäure** f prussic acid; **Blaustrumpf** m (fig) bluestocking

Blech [blɛç] (-(e)s, -e) nt tin, sheet metal; (Backblech) baking tray; **~ reden** (umg) to talk rubbish od nonsense; **Blechbläser** pl the brass (section); **Blechbüchse** f tin, can; **Blechdose** f tin, can

blechen (umg) vt, vi to pay

Blechschaden m (Aut) damage to bodywork

Blechtrommel f tin drum

blecken ['blɛkən] vt: **die Zähne ~** to bare od show one's teeth

Blei [blaɪ] (-(e)s, -e) nt lead

Bleibe (-, -n) f roof over one's head

bleiben unreg vi to stay, remain; **bitte, ~ Sie doch sitzen** please don't get up; **wo bleibst du so lange?** what's keeping you?; **das bleibt unter uns** (fig) that's (just) between ourselves; **~ lassen** (aufgeben) to give up; **etw ~ lassen** (unterlassen) to give sth a miss

bleich [blaɪç] adj faded, pale; **bleichen** vt to bleach; **Bleichgesicht** (umg) nt (blasser Mensch) pasty-face

bleiern adj leaden

Blei- zW: **bleifrei** adj lead-free; **Bleigießen** nt New Year's Eve fortune-telling using lead shapes; **bleihaltig** adj: **bleihaltig sein** to contain lead; **Bleistift** m pencil; **Bleistiftabsatz** m stiletto heel (Brit), spike heel (US); **Bleistiftspitzer** m pencil sharpener; **Bleivergiftung** f lead poisoning

Blende ['blɛndə] (-, -n) f (Phot) aperture; (: Einstellungsposition) f-stop

blenden vt to blind, dazzle; (fig) to hoodwink

blendend (umg) adj grand; **~ aussehen** to look smashing

Blender (-s, -) m con-man

blendfrei ['blɛntfraɪ] adj (Glas) non-reflective

Blick [blɪk] (-(e)s, -e) m (kurz) glance, glimpse; (Anschauen) look, gaze; (Aussicht) view; **Liebe auf den ersten ~** love at first sight; **den ~ senken** to look down; **den bösen ~ haben** to have the evil eye; **einen (guten) ~ für etw haben** to have an eye for sth; **mit einem ~** at a glance

blicken vi to look; **das lässt tief ~** that's very revealing; **sich ~ lassen** to put in an appearance

Blick- zW: **Blickfang** m eye-catcher; **Blickfeld** nt range of vision (auch fig); **Blickkontakt** m visual contact; **Blickpunkt** m: **im Blickpunkt der Öffentlichkeit stehen** to be in the public eye

blieb etc [bli:p] vb siehe **bleiben**

blies etc [bli:s] vb siehe **blasen**

blind [blɪnt] adj blind; (Glas etc) dull; (Alarm) false; **~er Passagier** stowaway

Blinddarm m appendix; **Blinddarmentzündung** f appendicitis

Blindenhund m guide dog
Blindenschrift f braille
Blind- zW: **Blindgänger** m (Mil, fig) dud; **Blindheit** f blindness; **mit Blindheit geschlagen sein** (fig) to be blind; **blindlings** adv blindly; **Blindschleiche** f slow worm; **blindschreiben** unreg vi to touch-type
blinken ['blɪŋkən] vi to twinkle, sparkle; (Licht) to flash, signal; (Aut) to indicate ▷ vt to flash, signal
Blinker (**-s, -**) m (Aut) indicator
Blinklicht nt (Aut) indicator
blinzeln ['blɪntsəln] vi to blink, wink
Blitz [blɪts] (**-es, -e**) m (flash of) lightning; **wie ein ~ aus heiterem Himmel** (fig) like a bolt from the blue; **Blitzableiter** m lightning conductor; (fig) vent od safety valve for feelings; **blitzen** vi (aufleuchten) to glint, shine; **es blitzt** (Met) there's a flash of lightning; **Blitzgerät** nt (Phot) flash(gun); **Blitzlicht** nt flashlight; **blitzsauber** adj spick and span; **blitzschnell** adj, adv as quick as a flash; **Blitzwürfel** m (Phot) flashcube
Block [blɔk] (**-(e)s, ̈-e**) m (lit, fig) block; (von Papier) pad; (Pol: Staatenblock) bloc; (Fraktion) faction
Blockade [blɔ'ka:də] (**-, -n**) f blockade
Block- zW: **Blockbuchstabe** m block letter od capital; **Blockflöte** f recorder; **blockfrei** adj (Pol) non-aligned; **Blockhaus** nt log cabin; **Blockhütte** f log cabin
blockieren [blɔ'ki:rən] vt to block ▷ vi (Räder) to jam
Block- zW: **Blockschokolade** f cooking chocolate; **Blockschrift** f block letters pl; **Blockstunde** f double period
blöd [blø:t] adj silly, stupid
blödeln ['blø:dəln] (umg) vi to fool around
Blödheit f stupidity
Blödian ['blø:dian] (**-(e)s, -e**) (umg) m idiot
blöd- zW: **Blödmann** (**-(e)s,** pl **-männer**) (umg) m idiot; **Blödsinn** m nonsense; **blödsinnig** adj silly, idiotic
Blog (**-s, -s**) nt (Comput) blog; **bloggen** vi to blog; **Blogging** nt blogging
blöken ['blø:kən] vi (Schaf) to bleat
blond [blɔnt] adj blond(e), fair-haired
Blondine [blɔn'di:nə] f blonde

○ SCHLÜSSELWORT

bloß [blo:s] adj **1** (unbedeckt) bare; (nackt) naked; **mit der bloßen Hand** with one's bare hand; **mit bloßem Auge** with the naked eye
2 (alleinig: nur) mere; **der bloße Gedanke** the very thought; **bloßer Neid** sheer envy
▷ adv only, merely; **lass das bloß!** just don't do that!; **wie ist das bloß passiert?** how on earth did that happen?

Blöße ['blø:sə] (**-, -n**) f bareness; nakedness; (fig) weakness; **sich** dat **eine ~ geben** (fig) to lay o.s. open to attack

bloßlegen vt to expose
bloßstellen vt to show up
blühen ['bly:ən] vi (lit) to bloom, be in bloom; (fig) to flourish; (umg: bevorstehen): (**jdm**) **~ to be** in store (for sb)
blühend adj: **wie das ~e Leben aussehen** to look the very picture of health
Blume ['blu:mə] (**-, -n**) f flower; (von Wein) bouquet; **jdm etw durch die ~ sagen** to say sth in a roundabout way to sb
Blumen- zW: **Blumenbeet** nt flower bed; **Blumengeschäft** nt flower shop, florist's; **Blumenkasten** m window box; **Blumenkohl** m cauliflower; **Blumenstrauß** m bouquet, bunch of flowers; **Blumentopf** m flowerpot; **Blumenzwiebel** f bulb
Bluse ['blu:zə] (**-, -n**) f blouse
Blut [blu:t] (**-(e)s**) nt (lit, fig) blood; **(nur) ruhig ~** keep your shirt on (umg); **jdn/sich bis aufs ~ bekämpfen** to fight sb/fight bitterly; **~ stillend** styptic; **blutarm** adj anaemic (Brit), anemic (US); (fig) penniless; **Blutbahn** f bloodstream; **Blutbank** f blood bank; **blutbefleckt** adj bloodstained; **Blutbild** nt blood count; **Blutbuche** f copper beech; **Blutdruck** m blood pressure
Blüte ['bly:tə] (**-, -n**) f blossom; (fig) prime
Blutegel ['blu:t|e:gəl] m leech
bluten vi to bleed
Blütenstaub m pollen
Bluter (**-s, -**) m (Med) haemophiliac (Brit), hemophiliac (US)
Bluterguss m haemorrhage (Brit), hemorrhage (US); (auf Haut) bruise
Blütezeit f flowering period; (fig) prime
Blutgerinnsel nt blood clot
Blutgruppe f blood group
blutig adj bloody; (umg: Anfänger) absolute; (: Ernst) deadly
Blut- zW: **blutjung** adj very young; **Blutkonserve** f unit od pint of stored blood; **Blutkörperchen** nt blood corpuscle; **Blutprobe** f blood test; **blutrünstig** adj bloodthirsty; **Blutschande** f incest; **Blutsenkung** f (Med): **eine Blutsenkung machen** to test the sedimentation rate of the blood; **Blutspender** m blood donor; **blutstillend** adj styptic; **Blutsturz** m haemorrhage (Brit), hemorrhage (US)
blutsverwandt adj related by blood
Blutübertragung f blood transfusion
Blutung f bleeding, haemorrhage (Brit), hemorrhage (US)
Blut- zW: **blutunterlaufen** adj suffused with blood; (Augen) bloodshot; **Blutvergießen** nt bloodshed; **Blutvergiftung** f blood poisoning; **Blutwurst** f black pudding; **Blutzuckerspiegel** m blood sugar level
BLZ abk = **Bankleitzahl**
BMX-Rad nt BMX
BND (**-s, -**) m abk = **Bundesnachrichtendienst**
Bö (**-, -en**) f squall
Bock [bɔk] (**-(e)s, ̈-e**) m buck, ram; (Gestell)

b

67

trestle, support; (*Sport*) buck; **alter ~** (*umg*) old goat; **den ~ zum Gärtner machen** (*fig*) to choose the worst possible person for the job; **einen ~ schießen** (*fig: umg*) to (make a) boob; **~ haben, etw zu tun** (*umg: Lust*) to fancy doing sth

Bockbier *nt* bock (beer) (*type of strong beer*)

bocken ['bɔkən] (*umg*) *vi* (*Auto, Mensch*) to play up

Bocksbeutel *m* wide, rounded (*dumpy*) bottle containing Franconian wine

Bockshorn *nt*: **sich von jdm ins ~ jagen lassen** to let sb upset one

Bocksprung *m* leapfrog; (*Sport*) vault

Bockwurst *f* bockwurst (*large frankfurter*)

Boden ['boːdən] (**-s, ⁼**) *m* ground; (*Fußboden*) floor; (*Meeresboden, Fassboden*) bottom; (*Speicher*) attic; **den ~ unter den Füßen verlieren** (*lit*) to lose one's footing; (*fig: in Diskussion*) to get out of one's depth; **ich hätte (vor Scham) im ~ versinken können** (*fig*) I was so ashamed, I wished the ground would swallow me up; **am ~ zerstört sein** (*umg*) to be shattered; **etw aus dem ~ stampfen** (*fig*) to conjure sth up out of nothing; (*Häuser*) to build overnight; **auf dem ~ der Tatsachen bleiben** (*fig: Grundlage*) to stick to the facts; **zu ~ fallen** to fall to the ground; **festen ~ unter den Füßen haben** to be on firm ground, be on terra firma; **Bodenkontrolle** *f* (*Raumfahrt*) ground control; **bodenlos** *adj* bottomless; (*umg*) incredible; **Bodenpersonal** *nt* (*Aviat*) ground personnel *pl*, ground staff; **Bodensatz** *m* dregs *pl*, sediment; **Bodenschätze** *pl* mineral wealth *sing*

Bodensee ['boːdənzeː] *m*: **der ~** Lake Constance

Bodenturnen *nt* floor exercises *pl*

Böe (**-, -n**) *f* squall

bog etc [boːk] *vb siehe* **biegen**

Bogen ['boːgən] (**-s, -**) *m* (*Biegung*) curve; (*Archit*) arch; (*Waffe, Mus*) bow; (*Papier*) sheet; **den ~ heraushaben** (*umg*) to have got the hang of it; **einen großen ~ um jdn/etw machen** (*meiden*) to give sb/sth a wide berth; **jdn in hohem ~ hinauswerfen** (*umg*) to fling sb out; **Bogengang** *m* arcade; **Bogenschütze** *m* archer

Bohle ['boːlə] (**-, -n**) *f* plank

Böhme ['bøːmə] (**-n, -n**) *m* Bohemian

Böhmen (**-s**) *nt* Bohemia

Böhmin *f* Bohemian woman

böhmisch ['bøːmɪʃ] *adj* Bohemian; **das sind für mich ~e Dörfer** (*umg*) that's all Greek to me

Bohne ['boːnə] (**-, -n**) *f* bean; **blaue ~** (*umg*) bullet; **nicht die ~** not one little bit

Bohnen- *zW*: **Bohnenkaffee** *m* real coffee; **Bohnenstange** *f* (*fig: umg*) beanpole; **Bohnenstroh** *nt*: **dumm wie Bohnenstroh** (*umg*) as thick as two (short) planks

bohnern *vt* to wax, polish

Bohnerwachs *nt* floor polish

bohren ['boːrən] *vt* to bore; (*Loch*) to drill ▷ *vi* to drill; (*fig: drängen*) to keep on; (*peinigen: Schmerz, Zweifel etc*) to gnaw; **nach Öl/Wasser ~** drill for oil/water; **in der Nase ~** to pick one's nose

Bohrer (**-s, -**) *m* drill

Bohr- *zW*: **Bohrinsel** *f* oil rig; **Bohrmaschine** *f* drill; **Bohrturm** *m* derrick

Boiler ['bɔylər] (**-s, -**) *m* water heater

Boje ['boːjə] (**-, -n**) *f* buoy

Bolivianer, in [boliviˈaːnər(ɪn)] (**-s, -**) *m(f)* Bolivian

Bolivien [boˈliːviən] *nt* Bolivia

bolivisch [boˈliːvɪʃ] *adj* Bolivian

Bollwerk ['bɔlvɛrk] *nt* (*lit, fig*) bulwark

Bolschewismus [bɔlʃeˈvɪsmʊs] (**-**) *m* Bolshevism

Bolzen ['bɔltsən] (**-s, -**) *m* bolt

bombardieren [bɔmbarˈdiːrən] *vt* to bombard; (*aus der Luft*) to bomb

Bombe ['bɔmbə] (**-, -n**) *f* bomb; **wie eine ~ einschlagen** to come as a (real) bombshell

Bomben- *zW*: **Bombenalarm** *m* bomb scare; **Bombenangriff** *m* bombing raid; **Bombenanschlag** *m* bomb attack; **Bombenerfolg** (*umg*) *m* huge success; **Bombengeschäft** (*umg*) *nt*: **ein Bombengeschäft machen** to do a roaring trade; **bombensicher** (*umg*) *adj* dead certain

bombig (*umg*) *adj* great, super

Bon [bɔŋ] (**-s, -s**) *m* voucher; (*Kassenzettel*) receipt

Bonbon [bõˈbõː] (**-s, -s**) *nt od m* sweet

Bonn [bɔn] (**-s**) *nt* Bonn

Bonus [ˈboːnʊs] (**-, -se**) *m* bonus

Bonusmeile *f* bonus mile

Bonuszahlung *f* bonus payment

Bonze ['bɔntsə] (**-n, -n**) *m* big shot (*umg*)

Bonzenviertel (*umg*) *nt* posh quarter (*of town*)

Boot [boːt] (**-(e)s, -e**) *nt* boat

Bord [bɔrt] (**-(e)s, -e**) *m* (*Aviat, Naut*) board ▷ *nt* (*Brett*) shelf; **über ~ gehen** to go overboard; (*fig*) to go by the board; **an ~** on board

Bordell [bɔrˈdɛl] (**-s, -e**) *nt* brothel

Bordstein *m* kerb(stone) (*Brit*), curb(stone) (*US*)

borgen ['bɔrgən] *vt* to borrow; **jdm etw ~** to lend sb sth

Borneo ['bɔrneo] (**-s**) *nt* Borneo

borniert [bɔrˈniːrt] *adj* narrow-minded

Börse ['bœːrzə] (**-, -n**) *f* stock exchange; (*Geldbörse*) purse

Börsen- *zW*: **Börsenmakler** *m* stockbroker; **börsennotiert** *adj*: **börsennotierte Firma** listed company; **Börsennotierung** *f* quotation (on the stock exchange)

Borste ['bɔrstə] (**-, -n**) *f* bristle

Borte ['bɔrtə] (**-, -n**) *f* edging; (*Band*) trimming

bös [bøːs] *adj* = **böse**; **bösartig** *adj* malicious; (*Med*) malignant

Böschung ['bœʃʊŋ] *f* slope; (*Uferböschung etc*) embankment

böse ['bøːzə] *adj* bad, evil; (*zornig*) angry; **das war nicht ~ gemeint** I/he *etc* didn't mean it nastily

Bösewicht (*umg*) *m* baddy

boshaft ['boːshaft] *adj* malicious, spiteful

Bosheit f malice, spite
Bosnien ['bɔsniən] (-s) nt Bosnia
Bosnien-Herzegowina ['bɔsniənhɛrtsə-'goːviːna] (-s) nt Bosnia-Herzegovina
Bosnier, in (-s, -) m(f) Bosnian
bosnisch adj Bosnian
Boss [bɔs] (-es, -e) (umg) m boss
böswillig ['bøːsvɪlɪç] adj malicious
bot etc [boːt] vb siehe **bieten**
Botanik [bo'taːnɪk] f botany
botanisch [bo'taːnɪʃ] adj botanical
Bote ['boːtə] (-n, -n) m messenger
Botengang m errand
Botenjunge m errand boy
Botin ['boːtɪn] f messenger
Botschaft f message, news; (Pol) embassy;
die Frohe ~ the Gospel; **Botschafter (-s, -)** m ambassador
Botswana [bɔ'tsvaːna] (-s) nt Botswana
Bottich ['bɔtɪç] (-(e)s, -e) m vat, tub
Bouillon [bʊ'ljõː] (-, -s) f consommé
Boulevard- [bulə'vaːr] zW: **Boulevardblatt** (umg) nt tabloid; **Boulevardpresse** f tabloid press; **Boulevardstück** nt light play/comedy
Boutique [bu'tiːk] (-, -n) f boutique
Bowle ['boːlə] (-, -n) f punch
Bowlingbahn ['boːlɪŋbaːn] f bowling alley
Box [bɔks] f (Lautsprecherbox) speaker
boxen vi to box
Boxer (-s, -) m boxer
Boxhandschuh m boxing glove
Boxkampf m boxing match
Boykott [bɔy'kɔt] (-(e)s, -s) m boycott
boykottieren [bɔykɔ'tiːrən] vt to boycott
BR abk (= Bayerischer Rundfunk) German radio station
brach etc [braːx] vb siehe **brechen**
brachial [braxi'aːl] adj: **mit ~er Gewalt** by brute force
brachliegen ['braːxliːgən] unreg vi (lit, fig) to lie fallow
brachte etc ['braxtə] vb siehe **bringen**
Branche ['brãː ʃə] (-, -n) f line of business
Branchenführer, in m(f) market leader
Branchenverzeichnis nt trade directory
Brand [brant] (-(e)s, ̈-e) m fire; (Med) gangrene
Brandanschlag m arson attack
branden ['brandən] vi to surge; (Meer) to break
Brandenburg ['brandənbʊrk] (-s) nt Brandenburg
Brandherd m source of the fire
brandmarken vt to brand; (fig) to stigmatize
brandneu (umg) adj brand-new
Brand- zW: **Brandsalbe** f ointment for burns; **Brandsatz** m incendiary device; **Brandstifter** m arsonist, fire-raiser; **Brandstiftung** f arson
Brandung f surf
Brandwunde f burn
brannte etc ['brantə] vb siehe **brennen**
Branntwein ['brantvaɪn] m brandy; **Branntweinsteuer** f tax on spirits
Brasilianer, in [brazili'aːnər(ɪn)] (-s, -) m(f) Brazilian
brasilianisch adj Brazilian

Brasilien [bra'ziːliən] nt Brazil
brät [brɛt] vb siehe **braten**
Bratapfel m baked apple
braten ['braːtən] unreg vt to roast; (in Pfanne) to fry; **Braten (-s, -)** m roast, joint; **den Braten riechen** (umg) to smell a rat, suss something
Brat- zW: **Brathähnchen** nt (Südd, Österr) roast chicken; **Brathendl** nt roast chicken; **Brathuhn** nt roast chicken; **Bratkartoffeln** pl fried/roast potatoes pl; **Bratpfanne** f frying pan; **Bratrost** m grill
Bratsche ['braːtʃə] (-, -n) f viola
Bratspieß m spit
Bratwurst f grilled sausage
Brauch [braʊx] (-(e)s, pl **Bräuche**) m custom
brauchbar adj usable, serviceable; (Person) capable
brauchen vt (bedürfen) to need; (müssen) to have to; (verwenden) to use; **wie lange braucht man, um ...?** how long does it take to ...?
Brauchtum nt customs pl, traditions pl
Braue ['braʊə] (-, -n) f brow
brauen ['braʊən] vt to brew
Brauerei [braʊə'raɪ] f brewery
braun [braʊn] adj brown; (von Sonne) tanned; **~ gebrannt** tanned; (pej) Nazi
Bräune ['brɔynə] (-, -n) f brownness; (Sonnenbräune) tan
bräunen vt to make brown; (Sonne) to tan
Braunkohle f brown coal
Braunschweig ['braʊnʃvaɪk] (-s) nt Brunswick
Brause ['braʊzə] (-, -n) f shower; (von Gießkanne) rose; (Getränk) lemonade
brausen vi to roar; (auch vr: duschen) to take a shower
Brausepulver nt lemonade powder
Brausetablette f lemonade tablet
Braut [braʊt] (-, pl **Bräute**) f bride; (Verlobte) fiancée
Bräutigam ['brɔytɪgam] (-s, -e) m bridegroom; (Verlobter) fiancé
Braut- zW: **Brautjungfer** f bridesmaid; **Brautkleid** nt wedding dress; **Brautpaar** nt bride and bridegroom, bridal pair
brav [braːf] adj (artig) good; (ehrenhaft) worthy, honest; (bieder: Frisur, Kleid) plain; **sei schön ~!** be a good boy/girl
BRD (-) f abk (= Bundesrepublik Deutschland) FRG; **die alte ~** former West Germany; see culture note

● **BRD**

● The BRD (Bundesrepublik Deutschland) is
● the official name for the Federal Republic
● of Germany. It comprises 16 Länder (see
● Land). It was the name given to the former
● West Germany as opposed to East Germany
● (the DDR). The two Germanies were
● reunited on 3rd October 1990.

Brechbohne f French bean
Brecheisen nt crowbar

brechen *unreg vt, vi* to break; (*Licht*) to refract; (*speien*) to vomit; **die Ehe ~** to commit adultery; **mir bricht das Herz** it breaks my heart; **~d voll sein** to be full to bursting

Brechmittel *nt*: **er/das ist das reinste ~** (*umg*) he/it makes me feel ill

Brechreiz *m* nausea

Brechung *f* (*des Lichts*) refraction

Brei [braɪ] (**-(e)s, -e**) *m* (*Masse*) pulp; (*Koch*) gruel; (*Haferbrei*) porridge (*Brit*), oatmeal (*US*); (*für Kinder, Kranke*) mash; **um den heißen ~ herumreden** (*umg*) to beat about the bush

breit [braɪt] *adj* broad; (*bei Maßangabe*) wide; **die ~e Masse** the masses *pl* ▷ *adv*: **ein ~ gefächertes Angebot** a wide range; **Breitband** *nt* (*Comput*) broadband; **Breitbandanschluss** *m* (*Comput*) broadband connection; **breitbeinig** *adj* with one's legs apart

Breite (**-, -n**) *f* breadth; (*bei Maßangabe*) width; (*Geog*) latitude

breiten *vt*: **etw über etw** *akk* **~** to spread sth over sth

Breitengrad *m* degree of latitude

Breitensport *m* popular sport

breit- *zW*: **breitmachen** *unreg* (*umg*) *vr* to spread o.s. out; **breitschlagen** *unreg* (*umg*) *vt*: **sich breitschlagen lassen** to let o.s. be talked round; **breitschulterig, breitschultrig** *adj* broad-shouldered; **breittreten** *unreg* (*umg*) *vt* to go on about; **Breitwandfilm** *m* wide-screen film

Bremen ['breːmən] (**-s**) *nt* Bremen

Bremsbelag *m* brake lining

Bremse ['bremzə] (**-, -n**) *f* brake; (*Zool*) horsefly

bremsen *vi* to brake, apply the brakes ▷ *vt* (*Auto*) to brake; (*fig*) to slow down ▷ *vr*: **ich kann mich ~** (*umg*) not likely!

Brems- *zW*: **Bremsflüssigkeit** *f* brake fluid; **Bremslicht** *nt* brake light; **Bremspedal** *nt* brake pedal; **Bremsschuh** *m* brake shoe; **Bremsspur** *f* tyre (*Brit*) *od* tire (*US*) marks *pl*; **Bremsweg** *m* braking distance

brennbar *adj* inflammable; **leicht ~** highly inflammable

Brennelement *nt* fuel element

brennen ['brɛnən] *unreg vi* to burn, to be on fire; (*Licht, Kerze etc*) to burn ▷ *vt* (*Holz etc*) to burn; (*Ziegel, Ton*) to fire; (*Kaffee*) to roast; (*Branntwein*) to distil; **wo brennts denn?** (*fig*: *umg*) what's the panic?; **darauf ~, etw zu tun** to be dying to do sth

Brenn- *zW*: **Brennmaterial** *nt* fuel; **Brennnessel** *f* nettle; **Brennofen** *m* kiln; **Brennpunkt** *m* (*Math, Optik*) focus; **Brennspiritus** *m* methylated spirits *pl*; **Brennstoff** *m* liquid fuel

brenzlig ['brɛntslɪç] *adj* smelling of burning, burnt; (*fig*) precarious

Bresche ['brɛʃə] (**-, -n**) *f*: **in die ~ springen** (*fig*) to step into the breach

Bretagne [bre'tanjə] *f*: **die ~** Brittany

Bretone [bre'toːnə] (**-n, -n**) *m* Breton

Bretonin [bre'toːnɪn] *f* Breton

Brett [brɛt] (**-(e)s, -er**) *nt* board, plank; (*Bord*) shelf; (*Spielbrett*) board; **Bretter** *pl* (*Ski*) skis *pl*; (*Theat*) boards *pl*; **Schwarzes ~** notice board; **er hat ein ~ vor dem Kopf** (*umg*) he's really thick

brettern (*umg*) *vi* to speed

Bretterzaun *m* wooden fence

Brezel ['breːtsəl] (**-, -n**) *f* pretzel

bricht [brɪçt] *vb siehe* **brechen**

Brief [briːf] (**-(e)s, -e**) *m* letter; **Briefbeschwerer** (**-s, -**) *m* paperweight; **Briefdrucksache** *f* circular; **Brieffreund, in** *m(f)* pen friend, pen-pal; **Briefkasten** *m* letter box; (*Comput*) mailbox; **Briefkopf** *m* letterhead; **brieflich** *adj, adv* by letter; **Briefmarke** *f* postage stamp; **Brieföffner** *m* letter opener; **Briefpapier** *nt* notepaper; **Briefqualität** *f* (*Comput*) letter quality; **Brieftasche** *f* wallet; **Brieftaube** *f* carrier pigeon; **Briefträger** *m* postman; **Briefumschlag** *m* envelope; **Briefwahl** *f* postal vote; **Briefwechsel** *m* correspondence

briet *etc* [briːt] *vb siehe* **braten**

Brigade [bri'gaːdə] (**-, -n**) *f* (*Mil*) brigade; (*DDR*) (work) team *od* group

Brikett [bri'kɛt] (**-s, -s**) *nt* briquette

brillant [brɪl'jant] *adj* (*fig*) sparkling, brilliant; **Brillant** (**-en, -en**) *m* brilliant, diamond

Brille ['brɪlə] (**-, -n**) *f* spectacles *pl*; (*Schutzbrille*) goggles *pl*; (*Toilettenbrille*) (toilet) seat

Brillenschlange *f* (*hum*) four-eyes

Brillenträger, in *m(f)*: **er ist ~** he wears glasses

bringen ['brɪŋən] *unreg vt* to bring; (*mitnehmen, begleiten*) to take; (*einbringen: Profit*) to bring in; (*veröffentlichen*) to publish; (*Theat, Film*) to show; (*Rundf, TV*) to broadcast; (*in einen Zustand versetzen*) to get; (*umg: tun können*) to manage; **jdn dazu ~, etw zu tun** to make sb do sth; **jdn zum Lachen/Weinen ~** to make sb laugh/cry; **es weit ~** to do very well, get far; **jdn nach Hause ~** to take sb home; **jdn um etw ~** to make sb lose sth; **jdn auf eine Idee ~** to give sb an idea

brisant [bri'zant] *adj* (*fig*) controversial

Brisanz [bri'zants] *f* (*fig*) controversial nature

Brise ['briːzə] (**-, -n**) *f* breeze

Brite ['briːtə] (**-n, -n**) *m* Briton, Britisher (*US*); **die ~n** the British

Britin *f* Briton, Britisher (*US*)

britisch ['briːtɪʃ] *adj* British; **die B~en Inseln** the British Isles

bröckelig ['brœkəlɪç] *adj* crumbly

Brocken ['brɔkən] (**-s, -**) *m* piece, bit; (*Felsbrocken*) lump of rock; **ein paar ~ Spanisch** a smattering of Spanish; **ein harter ~** (*umg*) a tough nut to crack

brodeln ['broːdəln] *vi* to bubble

Brokat [bro'kaːt] (**-(e)s, -e**) *m* brocade

Brokkoli ['brɔkoli] *pl* broccoli

Brombeere ['brɔmbeːrə] *f* blackberry, bramble (*Brit*)

bronchial [brɔnçi'aːl] *adj* bronchial

Bronchien ['brɔnçiən] *pl* bronchial tubes *pl*

Bronchitis [brɔn'çi:tɪs] **(-, -tiden)** f bronchitis

Bronze ['brõ:sə] **(-, -n)** f bronze

Brosame ['bro:za:mə] **(-, -n)** f crumb

Brosche ['brɔʃə] **(-, -n)** f brooch

Broschüre [brɔ'ʃy:rə] **(-, -n)** f pamphlet

Brot [bro:t] **(-(e)s, -e)** nt bread; (*Brotlaib*) loaf; **das ist ein hartes ~** (*fig*) that's a hard way to earn one's living

Brötchen ['brø:tçən] nt roll; **kleine ~ backen** (*fig*) to set one's sights lower; **Brötchengeber** m (*hum*) employer, provider (*hum*)

brotlos ['bro:tlo:s] adj (*Person*) unemployed; (*Arbeit etc*) unprofitable

Brotzeit (*Südd*) f (*Pause*) ≈ tea break

browsen ['brauzən] vi (*Comput*) to browse

BRT abk (= *Bruttoregistertonne*) GRT

Bruch [brux] **(-(e)s, ¨e)** m break; (*zerbrochene Stelle*) break; (*fig*) split, breach; (*Med: Eingeweidebruch*) rupture, hernia; (*Beinbruch etc*) fracture; (*Math*) fraction; **zu ~ gehen** to get broken; **sich einen ~ heben** to rupture o.s.; **Bruchbude** (*umg*) f shack

brüchig ['brʏçɪç] adj brittle, fragile

Bruch- zW: **Bruchlandung** f crash landing; **Bruchschaden** m breakage; **Bruchstelle** f break; (*von Knochen*) fracture; **Bruchstrich** m (*Math*) line; **Bruchstück** nt fragment; **Bruchteil** m fraction

Brücke ['brʏkə] **(-, -n)** f bridge; (*Teppich*) rug; (*Turnen*) crab

Bruder ['bru:dər] **(-s, ¨)** m brother; **unter Brüdern** (*umg*) between friends

brüderlich adj brotherly; **Brüderlichkeit** f fraternity

Brudermord m fratricide

Brüderschaft f brotherhood, fellowship; **~ trinken** to agree to use the familiar "du" (*over a drink*)

Brühe ['bry:ə] **(-, -n)** f broth, stock; (*pej*) muck

brühwarm ['bry:'varm] (*umg*) adj: **er hat das sofort ~ weitererzählt** he promptly spread it around

Brühwürfel m stock cube (*Brit*), bouillon cube (*US*)

brüllen ['brʏlən] vi to bellow, roar

Brummbär m grumbler

brummeln ['bruməln] vt, vi to mumble

brummen ['brumən] vi (*Bär, Mensch etc*) to growl; (*Insekt, Radio*) to buzz; (*Motor*) to roar; (*murren*) to grumble ▷ vt to growl; **jdm brummt der Kopf** sb's head is buzzing

Brummer ['brumər] **(-s, -)** (*umg*) m (*Lastwagen*) juggernaut

brummig (*umg*) adj grumpy

Brummschädel (*umg*) m thick head

brünett [brʏ'nɛt] adj brunette, brown-haired

Brunnen ['brunən] **(-s, -)** m fountain; (*tief*) well; (*natürlich*) spring; **Brunnenkresse** f watercress

Brunst [brunst] f (*von männlichen Tieren*) rut; (*von weiblichen Tieren*) heat; **Brunstzeit** f rutting season

brüsk [brʏsk] adj abrupt, brusque

brüskieren [brʏs'ki:rən] vt to snub

Brüssel ['brʏsəl] **(-s)** nt Brussels

Brust [brust] **(-, ¨e)** f breast; (*Männerbrust*) chest; **einem Kind die ~ geben** to breast-feed (*Brit*) od nurse (*US*) a baby

brüsten ['brʏstən] vr to boast

Brust- zW: **Brustfellentzündung** f pleurisy; **Brustkasten** m chest; **Brustkorb** m (*Anat*) thorax; **Brustschwimmen** nt breast-stroke; **Brustton** m: **im Brustton der Überzeugung** in a tone of utter conviction

Brüstung ['brʏstʊŋ] f parapet

Brustwarze f nipple

Brut [bru:t] **(-, -en)** f brood; (*Brüten*) hatching

brutal [bru'ta:l] adj brutal; **Brutalität** f brutality

Brutapparat m incubator

brüten ['bry:tən] vi (*auch fig*) to brood; **~de Hitze** oppressive od stifling heat

Brüter (-s, -) m (*Tech*): **Schneller ~** fast-breeder (reactor)

Brutkasten m incubator

Brutstätte f (+gen) (*lit, fig*) breeding ground (for)

brutto ['bruto] adv gross; **Bruttoeinkommen** nt gross salary; **Bruttogehalt** nt gross salary; **Bruttogewicht** nt gross weight; **Bruttogewinn** m gross profit; **Bruttoinlandsprodukt** nt gross domestic product; **Bruttolohn** m gross wages pl; **Bruttosozialprodukt** nt gross national product

brutzeln ['brutsəln] (*umg*) vi to sizzle away ▷ vt to fry (up)

Btx abk **= Bildschirmtext**

Bub [bu:p] **(-en, -en)** m boy, lad

Bube ['bu:bə] **(-n, -n)** m (*Schurke*) rogue; (*Karten*) jack

Bubikopf m bobbed hair

Buch [bu:x] **(-(e)s, ¨er)** nt book; (*Comm*) account book; **er redet wie ein ~** (*umg*) he never stops talking; **ein ~ mit sieben Siegeln** (*fig*) a closed book; **über etw** akk **~ führen** to keep a record of sth; **zu ~(e) schlagen** to make a significant difference, tip the balance; **Buchbinder** m bookbinder; **Buchdrucker** m printer

Buche (-, -n) f beech tree

buchen vt to book; (*Betrag*) to enter; **etw als Erfolg ~** to put sth down as a success

Bücherbord ['by:çər-] nt bookshelf

Bücherbrett nt bookshelf

Bücherei [by:çə'raɪ] f library

Bücherregal nt bookshelves pl, bookcase

Bücherschrank m bookcase

Bücherwurm (*umg*) m bookworm

Buchfink ['bu:xfɪŋk] m chaffinch

Buch- zW: **Buchführung** f book-keeping, accounting; **Buchhalter, in (-s, -)** m(f) book-keeper; **Buchhandel** m book trade; **im Buchhandel erhältlich** available in bookshops; **Buchhändler, in** m(f) bookseller; **Buchhandlung** f bookshop; **Buchprüfung** f audit; **Buchrücken** m spine

Büchse ['bʏksə] (-, -n) f tin, can; (Holzbüchse) box; (Gewehr) rifle
Büchsenfleisch nt tinned meat
Büchsenöffner m tin od can opener
Buchstabe (-ns, -n) m letter (of the alphabet)
buchstabieren [bu:xʃta'bi:rən] vt to spell
buchstäblich ['bu:xʃte:plɪç] adj literal
Buchstütze f book end
Bucht ['bʊxt] (-, -en) f bay
Buchung ['bu:xʊŋ] f booking; (Comm) entry
Buchweizen m buckwheat
Buchwert m book value
Buckel ['bʊkəl] (-s, -) m hump; **er kann mir den ~ runterrutschen** (umg) he can (go and) take a running jump
buckeln (pej) vi to bow and scrape
bücken ['bʏkən] vr to bend; **sich nach etw ~** to bend down od stoop to pick sth up
Bückling ['bʏklɪŋ] m (Fisch) kipper; (Verbeugung) bow
Budapest ['bu:dapest] (-s) nt Budapest
buddeln ['budəln] (umg) vi to dig
Bude ['bu:də] (-, -n) f booth, stall; (umg) digs pl (Brit) od place (US); **jdm die ~ einrennen** (umg) to pester sb; **Leben in die ~ bringen** to liven up the place
Budget [bʏ'dʒe:] (-s, -s) nt budget
Büfett [bʏ'fɛt] (-s, -s) nt (Anrichte) sideboard; (Geschirrschrank) dresser; **kaltes ~** cold buffet
Büffel ['bʏfəl] (-s, -) m buffalo
büffeln ['bʏfəln] (umg) vi to swot, cram ▷ vt (Lernstoff) to swot up
Bug [bu:k] (-(e)s, -e) m (Naut) bow; (Aviat) nose
Bügel ['by:gəl] (-s, -) m (Kleiderbügel) hanger; (Steigbügel) stirrup; (Brillenbügel) arm; **Bügelbrett** nt ironing board; **Bügeleisen** nt iron; **Bügelfalte** f crease; **bügelfrei** adj non-iron; (Hemd) drip-dry
bügeln vt, vi to iron
Buhmann ['bu:man] (umg) m bogeyman
Bühne ['by:nə] (-, -n) f stage
Bühnenbild nt set, scenery
Buhruf ['bu:ru:f] m boo
buk etc [bu:k] vb (veraltet) siehe **backen**
Bukarest ['bu:karest] (-s) nt Bucharest
Bulette [bu'lɛtə] f meatball
Bulgare [bʊl'ga:rə] (-n, -n) m Bulgarian
Bulgarien (-s) nt Bulgaria
Bulgarin f Bulgarian
bulgarisch adj Bulgarian
Bulimie [buli'mi:] f (Med) bulimia
Bull- zW: **Bullauge** nt (Naut) porthole; **Bulldogge** f bulldog; **Bulldozer** ['bʊldo:zər] (-s, -) m bulldozer
Bulle (-n, -n) m bull; **die ~n** (pej: umg) the fuzz sing, the cops
Bullenhitze (umg) f sweltering heat
Bummel ['bʊməl] (-s, -) m stroll; (Schaufensterbummel) window-shopping (expedition)
Bummelant [bʊmə'lant] m slowcoach
Bummelei [bʊmə'laɪ] f wandering; dawdling; skiving

bummeln vi to wander, stroll; (trödeln) to dawdle; (faulenzen) to skive (Brit), loaf around
Bummelstreik m go-slow (Brit), slowdown (US)
Bummelzug m slow train
Bummler, in ['bʊmlər(ɪn)] (-s, -) m(f) (langsamer Mensch) dawdler (Brit), slowpoke (US); (Faulenzer) idler, loafer
bumsen ['bʊmzən] vi (schlagen) to thump; (prallen, stoßen) to bump, bang; (umg: koitieren) to bonk ▷ vt (Brit)
Bund¹ [bʊnt] (-(e)s, ̈e) m (Freundschaftsbund etc) bond; (Organisation) union; (Pol) confederacy; (Hosenbund, Rockbund) waistband; **den ~ fürs Leben schließen** to take the marriage vows
Bund² [bʊnt] (-(e)s, -e) nt bunch; (Strohbund) bundle
Bündchen ['bʏntçən] nt ribbing; (Ärmelbündchen) cuff
Bündel (-s, -) nt bundle, bale
bündeln vt to bundle
Bundes- ['bʊndəs] in zW Federal; **Bundesagentur** f: **Bundesagentur für Arbeit** ≈ Department of Employment; **Bundesbahn** f: **die Deutsche Bundesbahn** German Federal Railways pl; **Bundesbank** f Federal Bank, Bundesbank; **Bundesbürger** m German citizen; (vor 1990) West German citizen; **Bundesgebiet** nt Federal territory; **Bundesgerichtshof** m Federal Supreme Court; **Bundesgrenzschutz** m Federal Border Guard; **Bundeshauptstadt** f Federal capital; **Bundeshaushalt** m (Pol) National Budget; **Bundeskanzler** m Federal Chancellor; see culture note

● **BUNDESKANZLER**

● The Bundeskanzler, head of the German
● government, is elected for 4 years and
● determines government guidelines. He
● is formally proposed by the Bundespräsident
● but needs a majority in parliament to be
● elected to office.

Bundes- zW: **Bundesland** nt state, Land; **Bundesliga** f (Sport) national league; **Bundesministerium** nt Federal Ministry; **Bundesnachrichtendienst** m Federal Intelligence Service; **Bundespost** f (früher): **die (Deutsche) Bundespost** the (German) Federal Post (Office); **Bundespräsident** m see culture note

● **BUNDESPRÄSIDENT**
●
● The Bundespräsident is the head of state of
● the Federal Republic of Germany who is
● elected every 5 years by the members of the
● Bundestag and by delegates of the Landtage
● (regional parliaments). His role is that of
● a figurehead who represents Germany at
● home and abroad. He can only be elected
● twice.

Bundesrat *m see culture note*

Bundes- *zW*: **Bundesrechnungshof** *m* Federal Audit Office; **Bundesregierung** *f* Federal Government; **Bundesrepublik** *f* Federal Republic (of Germany); **Bundesstaat** *m* Federal state; **Bundesstraße** *f* Federal Highway, main road; **Bundestag** *m see culture note*

Bundes- *zW*: **Bundestagsabgeordnete, r** *f(m)* member of the German Parliament; **Bundestagswahl** *f* (Federal) parliamentary elections *pl*; **Bundesverfassungsgericht** *nt* Federal Constitutional Court; **Bundeswehr** *f* German (of (vor 1990) West German Armed Forces *pl*; *see culture note*

Bundfaltenhose *f* pleated trousers *pl*
Bundhose *f* knee breeches *pl*
bündig ['byndıç] *adj* (*kurz*) concise
Bündnis ['byntnıs] (**-ses, -se**) *nt* alliance
Bunker ['buŋkər] (**-s, -**) *m* bunker; (*Luftschutzbunker*) air-raid shelter
bunt [bunt] *adj* coloured (*Brit*), colored (*US*);

(*gemischt*) mixed; **jdm wird es zu ~** it's getting too much for sb; **Buntstift** *m* coloured (*Brit*) *od* colored (*US*) pencil, crayon
Bürde ['byrdə] (**-, -n**) *f* (*lit, fig*) burden
Burg [burk] (**-, -en**) *f* castle, fort
Bürge ['byrgə] (**-n, -n**) *m* guarantor
bürgen *vi* to vouch; **für jdn ~** (*fig*) to vouch for sb; (*Fin*) to stand surety for sb
Bürger, in (**-s, -**) *m(f)* citizen; member of the middle class; **bürgerfreundlich** *adj* citizen-friendly; **Bürgerinitiative** *f* citizen's initiative; **Bürgerkrieg** *m* civil war; **bürgerlich** *adj* (*Rechte*) civil; (*Klasse*) middle-class; (*pej*) bourgeois; **bürgerliches Gesetzbuch** Civil Code; **Bürgermeister** *m* mayor; **Bürgerrecht** *nt* civil rights *pl*; **Bürgerrechtler, in** *m(f)* civil rights campaigner; **Bürgerschaft** *f* population, citizens *pl*; **Bürgerschaftswahl** *f* metropolitan council election; **Bürgerschreck** *m* bogey of the middle classes; **Bürgersteig** *m* pavement (*Brit*), sidewalk (*US*); **Bürgertum** *nt* citizens *pl*; **Bürgerversicherung** *f* citizens' insurance; **Bürgerwehr** *f* vigilantes *pl*
Burgfriede, Burgfrieden *m* (*fig*) truce
Bürgin *f* guarantor
Bürgschaft *f* surety; **~ leisten** to give security
Burgunder (**-s, -**) *m* (*Wein*) burgundy
Büro [by'ro:] (**-s, -s**) *nt* office; **Büroangestellte, r** *f(m)* office worker; **Büroklammer** *f* paper clip; **Bürokraft** *f* (office) clerk
Bürokrat [byro'kra:t] (**-en, -en**) *m* bureaucrat
Bürokratie [byrokra'ti:] *f* bureaucracy
bürokratisch *adj* bureaucratic
Bürokratismus *m* red tape
Büroschluss *m* office closing time
Büroturm *m* office tower
Bursch ['burʃ(ə)] (**-en, -en**) *m* = **Bursche**
Bursche (**-n, -n**) *m* lad, fellow; (*Diener*) servant
Burschenschaft *f* student fraternity
burschikos [burʃi'ko:s] *adj* (*jungenhaft*) (tom) boyish; (*unbekümmert*) casual
Bürste ['byrstə] (**-, -n**) *f* brush
bürsten *vt* to brush
Bus [bus] (**-ses, -se**) *m* bus
Busch [buʃ] (**-(e)s, ̈e**) *m* bush, shrub; **bei jdm auf den ~ klopfen** (*umg*) to sound sb out
Büschel ['byʃəl] (**-s, -**) *nt* tuft
buschig *adj* bushy
Busen ['bu:zən] (**-s, -**) *m* bosom; (*Meerbusen*) inlet, bay; **Busenfreund, in** *m(f)* bosom friend
Bushaltestelle *f* bus stop
Buslinie *f* bus route
Bussard ['busart] (**-s, -e**) *m* buzzard
Buße ['bu:sə] (**-, -n**) *f* atonement, penance; (*Geld*) fine
büßen ['by:sən] *vi* to do penance, atone ▷ *vt* to atone for
Bußgeld *nt* fine
Buß- und Bettag *m* day of prayer and repentance
Büste ['bystə] (**-, -n**) *f* bust
Büstenhalter *m* bra
Butan [bu'ta:n] (**-s**) *nt* butane

b

73

Büttenrede | bzw.

Büttenrede [ˈbʏtənreːdə] f carnival speech
Butter [ˈbʊtər] (-) f butter; **alles (ist) in ~** (umg)
everything is fine od hunky-dory; **Butterberg**
(umg) m butter mountain; **Butterblume** f
buttercup; **Butterbrot** nt (piece of) bread
and butter; **Butterbrotpapier** nt greaseproof
paper; **Buttercremetorte** f gateau with
buttercream filling; **Butterdose** f butter
dish; **Butterkeks** m ≈ Rich Tea® biscuit;
Buttermilch f buttermilk; **butterweich** adj

soft as butter; (fig: umg) soft
Butzen [ˈbʊtsən] (-s, -) m core
BVG nt abk (= Betriebsverfassungsgesetz)
≈ Industrial Relations Act; =
Bundesverfassungsgericht
b. w. abk (= bitte wenden) p.t.o
Byte [baɪt] (-s, -s) nt (Comput) byte
Bz. abk = **Bezirk**
bzgl. abk (= bezüglich) re.
bzw. abk = **beziehungsweise**

C¹, c [tse:] *nt* C, c; **C wie Cäsar** ≈ C for Charlie
C² [tse:] *abk* (= *Celsius*) C
ca. [ka] *abk* (= *circa*) approx.
Cabriolet [kabrio'le:] (**-s, -s**) *nt* (*Aut*) convertible
Café [ka'fe:] (**-s, -s**) *nt* café
Cafeteria [kafete'ri:a] (**-, -s**) *f* cafeteria
cal *abk* (= *Kalorie*) cal
Calais [ka'lɛ:] (**-'**) *nt*: **die Straße von ~** the Straits of Dover
Callcenter ['kɔ:lsɛntər] *nt* call centre (*Brit*), call center (*US*)
Camcorder (**-s, -**) *m* camcorder
campen ['kɛmpən] *vi* to camp
Camper, in (**-s, -**) *m(f)* camper
Camping ['kɛmpɪŋ] (**-s**) *nt* camping; **Campingbus** *m* camper; **Campingplatz** *m* camp(ing) site
Caravan ['karavan] (**-s, -s**) *m* caravan
Cargo ['kargo] (**-s, -s**) *m* (*Comm*) cargo
Cäsium ['tsɛ:zium] *nt* caesium (*Brit*), cesium (*US*)
ccm *abk* (= *Kubikzentimeter*) cm³
CD *f abk* (= *Compact Disc*) CD; **CD-Brenner** *m* CD burner; **CD-ROM** (**-, -s**) *f* CD-ROM; **CD-Spieler** *m* CD player
CDU [tse:de:'|u:] (**-**) *f abk* (= *Christlich-Demokratische Union (Deutschlands)*) Christian Democratic Union; *see culture note*

⬤ **CDU**

⬤ The CDU (Christlich-Demokratische
⬤ Union) is a Christian and conservative
⬤ political party founded in 1945. It operates
⬤ in all the *Länder* apart from Bavaria where
⬤ its sister party the CSU is active. In the
⬤ *Bundestag* the two parties form a coalition.
⬤ It is the second largest party in Germany
⬤ after the SPD, the Social Democratic Party.

Celli *pl von* **Cello**
Cellist, in [tʃe'lɪst(ɪn)] *m(f)* cellist
Cello ['tʃelo] (**-s, -s** *od* **Celli**) *nt* cello
Celsius ['tsɛlziʊs] *m* Celsius
Cent [(t)sɛnt] (**-(s), -(s)**) *m* cent
Ces [tsɛs] (**-, -**) *nt* (*Mus*) C flat
ces [tsɛs] (**-, -**) *nt* (*Mus*) C flat
Ceylon ['tsaɪlɔn] (**-s**) *nt* Ceylon

Chamäleon [ka'mɛ:leɔn] (**-s, -s**) *nt* chameleon
Champagner [ʃam'panjər] (**-s, -**) *m* champagne
Champignon ['ʃampɪnjõ] (**-s, -s**) *m* button mushroom
Chance ['ʃã:s(ə)] (**-, -n**) *f* chance, opportunity
chancengleich *adj* with equal opportunities
Chancengleichheit *f* equality of opportunity
Chaos ['ka:ɔs] (**-**) *nt* chaos
Chaot, in [ka'o:t(ɪn)] (**-en, -en**) *m(f)* (*Pol: pej*) anarchist (*pej*)
chaotisch [ka'o:tɪʃ] *adj* chaotic
Charakter [ka'raktər] (**-s, -e**) *m* character; **charakterfest** *adj* of firm character
charakterisieren [karakteri'zi:rən] *vt* to characterize
Charakteristik [karakte'rɪstɪk] *f* characterization
charakteristisch [karakte'rɪstɪʃ] *adj*: **~ (für)** characteristic (of), typical (of)
Charakter- *zW*: **charakterlos** *adj* unprincipled; **Charakterlosigkeit** *f* lack of principle; **Charakterschwäche** *f* weakness of character; **Charakterstärke** *f* strength of character; **Charakterzug** *m* characteristic, trait
charmant [ʃar'mant] *adj* charming
Charme [ʃarm] (**-s**) *m* charm
Charta ['karta] (**-, -s**) *f* charter
Charterflug ['tʃartərflu:k] *m* charter flight
Chartermaschine ['tʃartərmaʃi:nə] *f* charter plane
chartern ['tʃartərn] *vt* to charter
Chassis [ʃa'si:] (**-, -**) *nt* chassis
Chatroom ['tʃɛtru:m] *m* (*Comput*) chatroom
Chauffeur [ʃo'fø:r] *m* chauffeur
Chaussee [ʃo'se:] (**-, -n**) *f* (*veraltet*) high road
Chauvi ['ʃovi] (**-s, -s**) (*umg*) *m* male chauvinist
Chauvinismus [ʃovi'nɪsmʊs] *m* chauvinism
Chauvinist [ʃovi'nɪst] *m* chauvinist
checken ['tʃɛkən] *vt* (*überprüfen*) to check; (*umg: verstehen*) to get
Chef, in [ʃɛf(ɪn)] (**-s, -s**) *m(f)* head; (*umg*) boss; **Chefarzt** *m* senior consultant; **Chefetage** *f* executive floor; **Chefredakteur** *m* editor-in-chief; **Chefsekretärin** *f* personal assistant/secretary; **Chefvisite** *f* (*Med*) consultant's round
Chemie [çe'mi:] (**-**) *f* chemistry; **Chemiefaser** *f*

man-made fibre (*Brit*) *od* fiber (*US*)

Chemikalie [çemi'ka:liə] *f* chemical

Chemiker, in ['çe:mikər(ın)] (**-s, -**) *m(f)* (industrial) chemist

chemisch ['çe:mıʃ] *adj* chemical; **~e Reinigung** dry cleaning

Chemotherapie [çemotera'pi:] *f* chemotherapy

chic [ʃık] *adj inv* stylish, chic

Chicorée [ʃiko're:] (**-s**) *f od m* chicory

Chiffre ['ʃıfrə] (**-, -n**) *f* (*Geheimzeichen*) cipher; (*in Zeitung*) box number

Chiffriermaschine [ʃı'fri:rmaʃi:nə] *f* cipher machine

Chile ['tʃi:le] (**-s**) *nt* Chile

Chilene [tʃi'le:nə] (**-n, -n**) *m* Chilean

Chilenin [tʃi'le:nın] *f* Chilean

chilenisch *adj* Chilean

China ['çi:na] (**-s**) *nt* China

Chinakohl *m* Chinese leaves *pl*

Chinese [çi'ne:zə] (**-n, -n**) *m* Chinaman, Chinese

Chinesin *f* Chinese woman

chinesisch *adj* Chinese

Chinin [çi'ni:n] (**-s**) *nt* quinine

Chipkarte ['tʃıpkartə] *f* smart card

Chips [tʃıps] *pl* crisps *pl* (*Brit*), chips *pl* (*US*)

Chirurg, in [çi'rʊrg(ın)] (**-en, -en**) *m(f)* surgeon

Chirurgie [çirʊr'gi:] *f* surgery

chirurgisch *adj* surgical; **ein ~er Eingriff** surgery

Chlor [klo:r] (**-s**) *nt* chlorine

Chloroform [kloro'fɔrm] (**-s**) *nt* chloroform

chloroformieren [klorofor'mi:rən] *vt* to chloroform

Chlorophyll [kloro'fʏl] (**-s**) *nt* chlorophyll

Cholera ['ko:lera] (**-**) *f* cholera

Choleriker, in [ko'le:rikər(ın)] (**-s, -**) *m(f)* hot-tempered person

cholerisch [ko'le:rıʃ] *adj* choleric

Cholesterin [koleste'ri:n] (**-s**) *nt* cholesterol; **Cholesterinspiegel** [koleste'ri:nʃpi:gəl] *m* cholesterol level

Chor [ko:r] (**-(e)s, ̈e**) *m* choir; (*Musikstück, Theat*) chorus

Choral [ko'ra:l] (**-s, -äle**) *m* chorale

Choreograf, in [koreo'gra:f(ın)] (**-en, -en**) *m(f)* choreographer

Choreografie [koreogra'fi:] *f* choreography

Chorgestühl *nt* choir stalls *pl*

Chorknabe *m* choirboy

Chose ['ʃo:zə] (**-, -n**) (*umg*) *f* (*Angelegenheit*) thing

Chr. *abk* = **Christus; Chronik**

Christ [krıst] (**-en, -en**) *m* Christian; **Christbaum** *m* Christmas tree

Christenheit *f* Christendom

Christentum (**-s**) *nt* Christianity

Christin *f* Christian

Christkind *nt* ≈ Father Christmas; (*Jesus*) baby Jesus

christlich *adj* Christian

Christus (**Christi**) *m* Christ; **Christi Himmelfahrt** Ascension Day

Chrom [kro:m] (**-s**) *nt* (*Chem*) chromium; chrome

Chromosom [kromo'zo:m] (**-s, -en**) *nt* (*Biol*) chromosome

Chronik ['kro:nık] *f* chronicle

chronisch *adj* chronic

Chronologie [kronolo'gi:] *f* chronology

chronologisch *adj* chronological

Chrysantheme [kryzan'te:mə] (**-, -n**) *f* chrysanthemum

CIA ['si:aı'eı] (**-**) *f od m abk* (= *Central Intelligence Agency*) CIA

circa ['tsırka] *adv* (round) about

Cis [tsıs] (**-, -**) *nt* (*Mus*) C sharp

cis [tsıs] (**-, -**) *nt* (*Mus*) C sharp

City ['sıti] (**-, -s**) *f* city centre (*Brit*); **in der ~ in** the city centre (*Brit*), downtown (*US*); **die ~ von Berlin** the (city) centre of Berlin (*Brit*), downtown Berlin (*US*)

clean [kli:n] *adj* (*Drogen*: *umg*) off drugs

clever ['klɛvər] *adj* clever; (*gerissen*) crafty

Clique ['klıkə] (**-, -n**) *f* set, crowd

Clou [klu:] (**-s, -s**) *m* (*von Geschichte*) (whole) point; (*von Show*) highlight, high spot

Clown [klaʊn] (**-s, -s**) *m* clown

cm *abk* (= *Zentimeter*) cm.

Cockpit ['kɔkpıt] (**-s, -s**) *nt* cockpit

Cocktail ['kɔkte:l] (**-s, -s**) *m* cocktail

Code [ko:t] (**-s, -s**) *m* code

Cola ['ko:la] (**-(s), -s**) *nt od f* Coke®

Collier [kɔli'e:] (**-s, -s**) *nt* necklet, necklace

Comicheft ['kɔmıkhɛft] *nt* comic

Computer [kɔm'pju:tər] (**-s, -**) *m* computer; **computergesteuert** *adj* computer-controlled; **computergestützt** *adj* computer-based; **computergestütztes Design** computer-aided design; **Computerkriminalität** *f* computer crime; **Computerspiel** *nt* computer game; **Computerspieler, in** *m* (*f*) (*Comput*) gamer; **Computertechnik** *f* computer technology

Conférencier [kõfera˜si'e:] (**-s, -s**) *m* compère

Container [kɔn'te:nər] (**-s, -**) *m* container; **Containerschiff** *nt* container ship

Contergankind [kɔntɛr'gankınt] (*umg*) *nt* thalidomide child

Cookie ['kuki] (**-s, -s**) (*Comput*) cookie

cool [ku:l] (*umg*) *adj* (*gefasst*) cool

Cord [kɔrt] (**-(e)s, -e** *od* **-s**) *m* corduroy

Cornichon [kɔrni'ʃõ:] (**-s, -s**) *nt* gherkin

Couch [kaʊtʃ] (**-, -es** *od* **-en**) *f* couch; **Couchgarnitur** ['kaʊtʃgarni'tu:r] *f* three-piece suite

Couleur [ku'lø:r] (**-s, -s**) *f* (*geh*) kind, sort

Coupé [ku'pe:] (**-s, -s**) *nt* (*Aut*) coupé, sports version

Coupon [ku'põ:, ku'pɔŋ] (**-s, -s**) *m* coupon, voucher; (*Stoffcoupon*) length of cloth

Courage [ku'ra:ʒə] (**-**) *f* courage

Cousin [ku'zɛ̃:] (**-s, -s**) *m* cousin

Cousine [ku'zi:nə] (**-, -n**) *f* cousin

Crack [krɛk] (-) *nt* (*Droge*) crack
Creme [krɛːm] (-, -s) *f* (*lit, fig*) cream; (*Schuhcreme*) polish; (*Koch*) mousse;
  cremefarben *adj* cream(-coloured (*Brit*) *od* -colored (*US*))
cremig ['kreːmɪç] *adj* creamy
Crux [krʊks] (-) *f* = **Krux**
CSU [tseː|ɛs'|uː] (-) *f abk* (= *Christlich-Soziale Union*) Christian Social Union; *see culture note*

- **c s u**
-
- The CSU (Christlich-Soziale Union) is a
- party founded in 1945 in Bavaria. Like its

- sister party the CDU it is a Christian, right-
- wing party.

CT-Scanner [tseː'teːskenər] *m* CT scanner
Curriculum [kʊ'riːkulʊm] (-s, -cula) *nt* (*geh*) curriculum
Curry ['kari] (-s) *m od nt* curry powder;
  Currypulver ['karipʊlfər] *nt* curry powder;
  Currywurst *f* curried sausage
Cursor ['køːrsər] (-s) *m* (*Comput*) cursor;
  Cursortaste *f* cursor key
Cutter, in ['katər(ɪn)] (-s, -) *m(f)* (*Film*) editor
CVJM [tseː'faʊjɔt'|ɛm] (-) *m abk* (= *Christlicher Verein Junger Männer*) YMCA

Dd

D, d [de:] *nt* D, d; **D wie Dora** = D for David, D for Dog (*US*)

D. *abk* = **Doktor** (*der evangelischen Theologie*)

 SCHLÜSSELWORT

da [da:] *adv* **1** (*örtlich*) there; (*hier*) here; **da draußen** out there; **da sein** to be there; **ein Arzt, der immer für seine Patienten da ist** a doctor who always has time for his patients; **da bin ich** here I am; **da hast du dein Geld** (there you are,) there's your money; **da, wo** where; **ist noch Milch da?** is there any milk left?

2 (*zeitlich*) then; (*folglich*) so; **es war niemand im Zimmer, da habe ich ...** there was nobody in the room, so I ...

3: **da haben wir Glück gehabt** we were lucky there; **was gibts denn da zu lachen?** what's so funny about that?; **da kann man nichts machen** there's nothing one can do (in a case like that)

▷ *konj* (*weil*) as, since

d. Ä. *abk* (= *der Ältere*) Sen., sen.

DAAD (**-**) *m abk* (= *Deutscher Akademischer Austauschdienst*) German Academic Exchange Service

dabehalten *unreg vt* to keep

dabei [da'baɪ] *adv* (*räumlich*) close to it; (*noch dazu*) besides; (*zusammen mit*) with them/it *etc*; (*zeitlich*) during this; (*obwohl doch*) but, however; **~ sein** (*anwesend*) to be present; (*beteiligt*) to be involved; **ich bin ~!** count me in!; **was ist schon ~?** what of it?; **es ist doch nichts ~, wenn ...** it doesn't matter if ...; **bleiben wir ~** let's leave it at that; **es soll nicht ~ bleiben** this isn't the end of it; **es bleibt ~** that's settled; **das Dumme/Schwierige ~** the stupid/difficult part of it; **er war gerade ~ zu gehen** he was just leaving; **hast du ~ etwas gelernt?** did you learn anything from it?; **~ darf man nicht vergessen, dass ...** it shouldn't be forgotten that ...; **die ~ entstehenden Kosten** the expenses arising from this; **es kommt doch nichts ~ heraus** nothing will come of it; **ich finde gar nichts ~** I don't see any harm in it; **dabeistehen** *unreg vi* to stand around

Dach [dax] (**-(e)s, ̈er**) *nt* roof; **unter ~ und Fach sein** (*abgeschlossen*) to be in the bag (*umg*); (*Vertrag, Geschäft*) to be signed and sealed; (*in Sicherheit*) to be safe; **jdm eins aufs ~ geben** (*umg: ausschimpfen*) to give sb a (good) talking to; **Dachboden** *m* attic, loft; **Dachdecker** (**-s, -**) *m* slater, tiler; **Dachfenster** *nt* skylight; (*ausgestellt*) dormer window; **Dachfirst** *m* ridge of the roof; **Dachgepäckträger** *m* (*Aut*) roof rack; **Dachgeschoss** *nt* attic storey (*Brit*) *od* story (*US*); (*oberster Stock*) top floor *od* storey (*Brit*) *od* story (*US*); **Dachluke** *f* skylight; **Dachpappe** *f* roofing felt; **Dachrinne** *f* gutter

Dachs [daks] (**-es, -e**) *m* badger

Dachschaden (*umg*) *m*: **einen ~ haben** to have a screw loose

dachte *etc* ['daxtə] *vb siehe* **denken**

Dach- *zW*: **Dachterrasse** *f* roof terrace; **Dachverband** *m* umbrella organization; **Dachziegel** *m* roof tile

Dackel ['dakəl] (**-s, -**) *m* dachshund

dadurch [da'dʊrç] *adv* (*räumlich*) through it; (*durch diesen Umstand*) thereby, in that way; (*deshalb*) because of that, for that reason

▷ *konj*: **~, dass** because

dafür [da'fy:r] *adv* for it; (*anstatt*) instead; (*zum Ausgleich*): **in Latein ist er schlecht, ~ kann er gut Fußball spielen** he's bad at Latin but he makes up for it at football; **er ist bekannt ~** he is well-known for that; **was bekomme ich ~?** what will I get for it?; **~ ist er immer zu haben** he never says no to that; **~ bin ich ja hier** that's what I'm here for; **er kann nichts ~ (, dass ...)** he can't help it (that ...); **Dafürhalten** (**-s**) *nt* (*geh*): **nach meinem Dafürhalten** in my opinion

DAG *f abk* (= *Deutsche Angestellten-Gewerkschaft*) Clerical and Administrative Workers' Union

dagegen [da'ge:gən] *adv* against it; (*im Vergleich damit*) in comparison with it; (*bei Tausch*) for it ▷ *konj* however; **haben Sie etwas ~, wenn ich rauche?** do you mind if I smoke?; **ich habe nichts ~** I don't mind; **ich war ~** I was against it; **ich hätte nichts ~ (einzuwenden)** that's okay by me; **~ kann man nichts tun** one can't do anything about it; **dagegenhalten** *unreg vt* (*vergleichen*) to compare with it; (*entgegnen*) to put forward as an objection

daheim [da'haɪm] adv at home; **bei uns** ~ back home; **Daheim** (**-s**) nt home

daher [da'he:r] adv (räumlich) from there; (Ursache) from that ▷ konj (deshalb) that's why; **das kommt ~, dass ...** that is because ...; ~ **kommt er auch** that's where he comes from too; ~ **die Schwierigkeiten** that's what is causing the difficulties; **dahergelaufen** adj: **jeder dahergelaufene Kerl** any Tom, Dick or Harry; **daherreden** vi to talk away ▷ vt to say without thinking

dahin [da'hɪn] adv (räumlich) there; (zeitlich) then; (vergangen) gone; **ist es noch weit bis ~?** is there still far to go?; ~ **gehend** on this matter; **das tendiert** ~ it is tending towards that; **er bringt es noch ~, dass ich ...** he'll make me ...; **dahingegen** konj on the other hand; **dahingehen** unreg vi (Zeit) to pass; **dahingestellt** adv: **dahingestellt bleiben** to remain to be seen; **etw dahingestellt sein lassen** to leave sth open od undecided; **dahinschleppen** vr (lit: sich fortbewegen) to drag o.s. along; (fig: Verhandlungen, Zeit) to drag on; **dahinschmelzen** vi to be enthralled

dahinten [da'hɪntən] adv over there

dahinter [da'hɪntər] adv behind it; **sich ~ klemmen** od **knien** (umg) to put one's back into it; ~ **kommen** (umg) to find out

dahinvegetieren [da'hɪnvege'ti:rən] vi to vegetate

Dahlie ['da:liə] (**-, -n**) f dahlia

DAK (**-**) f abk (= Deutsche Angestellten-Krankenkasse) health insurance company for employees

Dakar ['dakar] (**-s**) nt Dakar

dalassen ['da:lasən] unreg vt to leave (behind)

dalli ['dali] (umg) adv: ~, ~! on (Brit) od at (US) the double!

damalig ['da:ma:lɪç] adj of that time, then

damals ['da:ma:ls] adv at that time, then

Damaskus [da'maskʊs] nt Damascus

Damast [da'mast] (**-(e)s, -e**) m damask

Dame ['da:mə] (**-, -n**) f lady; (Schach, Karten) queen; (Spiel) draughts (Brit), checkers (US)

Damen- zW: **Damenbesuch** m lady visitor od visitors; **Damenbinde** f sanitary towel (Brit) od napkin (US); **damenhaft** adj ladylike; **Damensattel** m: **im Damensattel reiten** to ride side-saddle; **Damenwahl** f ladies' excuse-me

Damespiel nt draughts (Brit), checkers (US)

damit [da'mɪt] adv with it; (begründend) by that ▷ konj in order that od to; **was meint er ~?** what does he mean by that?; **was soll ich ~?** what am I meant to do with that?; **muss er denn immer wieder ~ ankommen?** must he keep on about it?; **was ist ~?** what about it?; **genug ~!** that's enough!; ~ **basta!** and that's that!; ~ **eilt es nicht** there's no hurry

dämlich ['dɛ:mlɪç] (umg) adj silly, stupid

Damm [dam] (**-(e)s, ̈-e**) m dyke (Brit), dike (US); (Staudamm) dam; (Hafendamm) mole; (Bahndamm, Straßendamm) embankment

dämmen ['dɛmən] vt (Wasser) to dam up;

(Schmerzen) to keep back

dämmerig adj dim, faint

Dämmerlicht nt twilight; (abends) dusk; (Halbdunkel) half-light

dämmern ['dɛmərn] vi (Tag) to dawn; (Abend) to fall; **es dämmerte ihm, dass ...** (umg) it dawned on him that ...

Dämmerung f twilight; (Morgendämmerung) dawn; (Abenddämmerung) dusk

Dämmerzustand m (Halbschlaf) dozy state; (Bewusstseinstrübung) semi-conscious state

Dämmung f insulation

Dämon ['dɛ:mɔn] (**-s, -en**) m demon

dämonisch [dɛ'mo:nɪʃ] adj demonic

Dampf [dampf] (**-(e)s, ̈-e**) m steam; (Dunst) vapour (Brit), vapor (US); **jdm ~ machen** (umg) to make sb get a move on; ~ **ablassen** (lit, fig) to let off steam; **dampfen** vi to steam

dämpfen ['dɛmpfən] vt (Koch) to steam; (bügeln) to iron with a damp cloth; (mit Dampfbügeleisen) to steam iron; (fig) to dampen, subdue

Dampfer ['dampfər] (**-s, -**) m steamer; **auf dem falschen ~ sein** (fig) to have got the wrong idea

Dämpfer (**-s, -**) m (Mus: bei Klavier) damper; (bei Geige, Trompete) mute; **er hat einen ~ bekommen** (fig) it dampened his spirits

Dampf- zW: **Dampfkochtopf** m pressure cooker; **Dampfmaschine** f steam engine; **Dampfschiff** nt steamship; **Dampfwalze** f steamroller

Damwild ['damvɪlt] nt fallow deer

danach [da'na:x] adv after that; (zeitlich) afterwards; (gemäß) accordingly; (laut diesem) according to which od that; **mir war nicht ~ (zumute)** I didn't feel like it; **er griff schnell ~** he grabbed at it; ~ **kann man nicht gehen** you can't go by that; **er sieht ~ aus** he looks it

Däne ['dɛ:nə] (**-n, -n**) m Dane, Danish man/boy

daneben [da'ne:bən] adv beside it; (im Vergleich) in comparison; ~ **sein** (umg) to be completely confused; **danebenbenehmen** unreg vr to misbehave; **danebengehen** unreg vi to miss; (Plan) to fail; **danebengreifen** unreg vi to miss; (fig: mit Schätzung etc) to be wide of the mark

Dänemark ['dɛ:nəmark] (**-s**) nt Denmark

Dänin ['dɛ:nɪn] f Dane, Danish woman od girl

dänisch adj Danish

Dank [daŋk] (**-(e)s**) m thanks pl; **vielen od schönen** ~ many thanks; **jdm ~ sagen** to thank sb; **mit (bestem) ~ zurück!** many thanks for the loan; **dank** präp (+dat od gen) thanks to; **dankbar** adj grateful; (Aufgabe) rewarding; (haltbar) hard-wearing; **Dankbarkeit** f gratitude

danke interj thank you, thanks; ~ **schön** od **sehr** thank you very much

danken vi +dat to thank; **nichts zu ~!** don't mention it; ~**d erhalten/ablehnen** to receive/decline with thanks

dankenswert adj (Arbeit) worthwhile; (Bemühung) kind

Dank- zW: **Dankgottesdienst** m service of

thanksgiving; **danksagen** *vi* to express one's thanks; **Dankschreiben** *nt* letter of thanks

dann [dan] *adv* then; ~ **und wann** now and then; ~ **eben nicht** well, in that case (there's no more to be said); **erst ~, wenn ...** only when ...; ~ **erst recht nicht!** in that case no way (*umg*)

dannen ['danən] *adv*: **von ~** (*liter: weg*) away

daran [da'ran] *adv* on it; (*stoßen*) against it; **es liegt ~, dass ...** the cause of it is that ...; **gut/schlecht ~ sein** to be well/badly off; **das Beste/Dümmste ~** the best/stupidest thing about it; **ich war nahe ~, zu ...** I was on the point of ...; **im Anschluss ~** (*zeitlich: danach anschließend*) following that *od* this; **wir können nichts ~ machen** we can't do anything about it; **es ist nichts ~** (*ist nicht fundiert*) there's nothing in it; (*ist nichts Besonderes*) it's nothing special; **er ist ~ gestorben** he died from *od* of it; **darangehen** *unreg vi* to start; **daranmachen** (*umg*) *vr*: **sich daranmachen, etw zu tun** to set about doing sth; **daransetzen** *vt* to stake; **er hat alles darangesetzt, von Glasgow wegzukommen** he has done his utmost to get away from Glasgow

darauf [da'rauf] *adv* (*räumlich*) on it; (*zielgerichtet*) towards it; (*danach*) afterwards; ~ **folgend** following; **es kommt ganz ~ an, ob ...** it depends whether ...; **seine Behauptungen stützen sich ~, dass ...** his claims are based on the supposition that ...; **wie kommst du ~?** what makes you think that?; **die Tage ~** the days following *od* thereafter; **am Tag ~** the next day; **darauffolgend** *adj* (*Tag, Jahr*) next, following; **daraufhin** *adv* (*im Hinblick darauf*) in this respect; (*aus diesem Grund*) as a result; **wir müssen es daraufhin prüfen, ob ...** we must test it to see whether ...; **darauflegen** *vt* to lay *od* put on top

daraus [da'raus] *adv* from it; **was ist ~ geworden?** what became of it?; ~ **geht hervor, dass ...** this means that ...

darbieten ['da:rbi:tən] *vt* (*vortragen: Lehrstoff*) to present ▷ *vr* to present itself

Darbietung *f* performance

Dardanellen [darda'nɛlən] *pl* Dardanelles *pl*

darein- *präf* = **drein-**

Daressalam [daresa'la:m] *nt* Dar-es-Salaam

darf [darf] *vb siehe* **dürfen**

darin [da'rɪn] *adv* in (there), in it; **der Unterschied liegt ~, dass ...** the difference is that ...

darlegen ['da:rle:gən] *vt* to explain, expound, set forth

Darlegung *f* explanation

Darlehen, Darlehn (-s, -) *nt* loan

Darm [darm] (**-(e)s, ⸚e**) *m* intestine; (*Wurstdarm*) skin; **Darmausgang** *m* anus; **Darmgrippe** *f* gastric influenza

darstellen ['da:rʃtɛlən] *vt* (*abbilden, bedeuten*) to represent; (*Theat*) to act; (*beschreiben*) to describe ▷ *vr* to appear to be

Darsteller, in (-s, -) *m(f)* actor, actress

darstellerisch *adj*: **eine ~e Höchstleistung** a magnificent piece of acting

Darstellung *f* portrayal, depiction

darüber [da'ry:bər] *adv* (*räumlich*) over/above it; (*fahren*) over it; (*mehr*) more; (*währenddessen*) meanwhile; (*sprechen, streiten*) about it; ~ **hinweg sein** (*fig*) to have got over it; ~ **hinaus** over and above that; ~ **geht nichts** there's nothing like it; **seine Gedanken ~** his thoughts about *od* on it; ~ **liegen** (*fig*) to be higher

darum [da'rʊm] *adv* (*räumlich*) round it ▷ *konj* that's why; ~ **herum** round about (it); **er bittet ~** he is pleading for it; **es geht ~, dass ...** the thing is that ...; ~ **geht es mir/geht es mir nicht** that's my point/that's not the point for me; **er würde viel ~ geben, wenn ...** he would give a lot to ...; *siehe auch* **drum**

darunter [da'rʊntər] *adv* (*räumlich*) under it; (*dazwischen*) among them; (*weniger*) less; **ein Stockwerk ~** one floor below (it); **was verstehen Sie ~?** what do you understand by that?; ~ **kann ich mir nichts vorstellen** that doesn't mean anything to me; ~ **fallen** to be included; ~ **mischen** (*Mehl*) to mix in; **sich ~ mischen** to mingle; ~ **setzen** (*Unterschrift*) to put to it

das [das] *pron* that ▷ *def art* the; *siehe auch* **der**; ~ **heißt** that is; ~ **und ~** such and such

Dasein ['da:zain] **(-s)** *nt* (*Leben*) life; (*Anwesenheit*) presence; (*Bestehen*) existence

da sein *unreg vi siehe* **da**

Daseinsberechtigung *f* right to exist

Daseinskampf *m* struggle for survival

dass [das] *konj* that

dasselbe [das'zɛlbə] *nt pron* the same

dastehen ['da:ʃte:ən] *unreg vi* to stand there; (*fig*): **gut/schlecht ~** to be in a good/bad position; **allein ~** to be on one's own

Dat. *abk* = **Dativ**

Datei [da'tai] *f* (*Comput*) file; **Dateimanager** *m* file manager; **Dateiname** *m* file name; **Dateiverwaltung** *f* file management

Daten ['da:tən] *pl* (*Comput*) data; (*Angaben*) data *pl*, particulars; *siehe auch* **Datum**; **Datenabgleich** *m* data comparison; **Datenautobahn** *f* information (super) highway; **Datenbank** *f* database; **Datendiebstahl** *m* (*Wirts, Comput*) data theft; **Datenerfassung** *f* data capture; **Datenleitung** *f* data line; **Datenmüll** *m* (*aus dem Internet*) Internet buildup; (*auf Festplatte*) hard disk clutter; **Datennetz** *nt* data network; **Datensatz** *m* record; **Datenschutz** *m* data protection; **Datensichtgerät** *nt* visual display unit, VDU; **Datenträger** *m* data carrier; **Datenübertragung** *f* data transmission; **Datenverarbeitung** *f* data processing; **Datenverarbeitungsanlage** *f* data processing equipment, DP equipment

datieren [da'ti:rən] *vt* to date

Dativ ['daːtiːf] (**-s, -e**) m dative; **Dativobjekt** nt (Gram) indirect object

dato ['daːto] adv: **bis ~** (Comm: umg) to date

Dattel ['datəl] (**-, -n**) f date

Datum ['daːtʊm] (**-s, Daten**) nt date; **das heutige ~** today's date

Datumsgrenze f (Geog) (international) date line

Dauer ['daʊər] (**-, -n**) f duration; (gewisse Zeitspanne) length; (Bestand, Fortbestehen) permanence; **es war nur von kurzer ~** it didn't last long; **auf die ~** in the long run; (auf längere Zeit) indefinitely; **Dauerauftrag** m standing order; **dauerhaft** adj lasting, durable; **Dauerhaftigkeit** f durability; **Dauerkarte** f season ticket; **Dauerlauf** m long-distance run

dauern vi to last; **es hat sehr lang gedauert, bis er ...** it took him a long time to ...

dauernd adj constant

Dauer- zW: **Dauerobst** nt fruit suitable for storing; **Dauerredner** (pej) m long-winded speaker; **Dauerregen** m continuous rain; **Dauerschlaf** m prolonged sleep; **Dauerstellung** f permanent position; **Dauerwelle** f perm, permanent wave; **Dauerwurst** f German salami; **Dauerzustand** m permanent condition

Daumen ['daʊmən] (**-s, -**) m thumb; **jdm die ~ drücken** od **halten** to keep one's fingers crossed for sb; **über den ~ peilen** to guess roughly; **Daumenlutscher** m thumb-sucker

Daune ['daʊnə] (**-, -n**) f down

Daunendecke f down duvet

davon [da'fɔn] adv of it; (räumlich) away; (weg von) away from it; (Grund) because of it; (mit Passiv) by it; **das kommt ~!** that's what you get; **~ abgesehen** apart from that; **wenn wir einmal ~ absehen, dass ...** if for once we overlook the fact that ...; **~ sprechen/ wissen** to talk/know of od about it; **was habe ich ~?** what's the point?; **~ betroffen werden** to be affected by it; **davongehen** unreg vi to leave, go away; **davonkommen** unreg vi to escape; **davonlassen** unreg vt: **die Finger davonlassen** (umg) to keep one's hands od fingers off (it); **davonlaufen** unreg vi to run away; **davonmachen** vr to make off; **davontragen** unreg vt to carry off; (Verletzung) to receive

davor [da'foːr] adv (räumlich) in front of it; (zeitlich) before (that); **~ warnen** to warn about it

dazu [da'tsuː] adv (legen, stellen) by it; (essen) with it; **und ~ noch** and in addition; **ein Beispiel/seine Gedanken ~** one example for/his thoughts on this; **wie komme ich denn ~?** why should I?; **... aber ich bin nicht ~ gekommen** ... but I didn't get around to it; **das Recht ~** the right to do it; **~ bereit sein, etw zu tun** to be prepared to do sth; **~ fähig sein** to be capable of it; **sich ~ äußern** to say something on it; **dazugehören** vi to belong

to it; **das gehört dazu** (versteht sich von selbst) it's all part of it; **es gehört schon einiges dazu, das zu tun** it takes a lot to do that; **dazugehörig** adj appropriate; **dazukommen** unreg vi (Ereignisse) to happen too; (an einen Ort) to come along; **kommt noch etwas dazu?** will there be anything else?; **dazulernen** vt: **schon wieder was dazugelernt!** you learn something new every day!; **dazumal** ['daːtsumaːl] adv in those days; **dazutun** unreg vt to add; **er hat es ohne dein Dazutun geschafft** he managed it without your doing etc anything

dazwischen [da'tsvɪʃən] adv in between; (zusammen mit) among them; **der Unterschied ~** the difference between them; **dazwischenfahren** unreg vi (eingreifen) to intervene; **dazwischenfunken** (umg) vi (eingreifen) to put one's oar in; **dazwischenkommen** unreg vi (hineingeraten) to get caught up in it; **es ist etwas dazwischengekommen** something (has) cropped up; **dazwischenreden** vi (unterbrechen) to interrupt; (sich einmischen) to interfere; **dazwischentreten** unreg vi to intervene

DB f abk (= Deutsche Bahn) German railways

DBP f abk (früher) = **Deutsche Bundespost**

DDR (**-**) f abk (früher: = Deutsche Demokratische Republik) GDR; see culture note

> **DDR**
>
> The DDR (Deutsche Demokratische Republik) was the name by which the former Communist German Democratic Republic was known. It was founded in 1949 from the Soviet-occupied zone. After the building of the Berlin Wall in 1961 it was virtually sealed off from the West until mass demonstrations and demands for reform forced the opening of the borders in 1989. It then merged in 1990 with the BRD.

DDT® nt abk DDT

Dealer, in ['diːlər(ɪn)] (**-s, -**) (umg) m(f) pusher

Debatte [de'batə] (**-, -n**) f debate; **das steht hier nicht zur ~** that's not the issue

debattieren [deba'tiːrən] vt to debate

Debet ['deːbɛt] (**-s, -s**) nt (Fin) debits pl

Debüt [de'byː] (**-s, -s**) nt debut

dechiffrieren [deʃɪ'friːrən] vt to decode; (Text) to decipher

Deck [dɛk] (**-(e)s, -s** od **-e**) nt deck; **an ~ gehen** to go on deck

Deckbett nt feather quilt

Deckblatt nt (Schutzblatt) cover

Decke (**-, -n**) f cover; (Bettdecke) blanket; (Tischdecke) tablecloth; (Zimmerdecke) ceiling; **unter einer ~ stecken** to be hand in glove; **an die ~ gehen** to hit the roof; **mir fällt die ~ auf den Kopf** (fig) I feel really claustrophobic

Deckel (**-s, -**) m lid; **du kriegst gleich eins auf**

den ~ (umg) you're going to catch it

Deckelung f capping

decken vt to cover ▷ vr to coincide ▷ vi to lay the table; **mein Bedarf ist gedeckt** I have all I need; (fig) I've had enough; **sich an einen gedeckten Tisch setzen** (fig) to be handed everything on a plate

Deckmantel m: **unter dem ~ von** under the guise of

Deckname m assumed name

Deckung f (das Schützen) covering; (Schutz) cover; (Sport) defence (Brit), defense (US); (Übereinstimmen) agreement; **zur ~ seiner Schulden** to meet his debts

deckungsgleich adj congruent

Decoder m (TV) decoder

de facto [de: 'fakto] adv de facto

Defekt [de'fɛkt] (-(e)s, -e) m fault, defect; **defekt** adj faulty

defensiv [defen'si:f] adj defensive

Defensive f: **jdn in die ~ drängen** to force sb onto the defensive

definieren [defi'ni:rən] vt to define

Definition [definitsi'o:n] f definition

definitiv [defini'ti:f] adj definite

Defizit ['de:fitsɪt] (-s, -e) nt deficit

defizitär [defitsi'tɛ:r] adj: **eine ~e Haushaltspolitik führen** to follow an economic policy which can only lead to deficit

Deflation [deflatsi'o:n] f (Econ) deflation

deflationär [deflatsio'nɛ:r] adj deflationary

deftig ['dɛftɪç] adj (Essen) large; (Witz) coarse

Degen ['de:gən] (-s, -) m sword

degenerieren [degene'ri:rən] vi to degenerate

degradieren [degra'di:rən] vt to degrade

dehnbar ['de:nba:r] adj elastic; (fig: Begriff) loose; **Dehnbarkeit** f elasticity; looseness

dehnen vt, vr to stretch

Dehnung f stretching

Deich [daɪç] (-(e)s, -e) m dyke (Brit), dike (US)

Deichsel ['daɪksəl] (-, -n) f shaft

deichseln vt (fig: umg) to wangle

dein [daɪn] pron your; (adjektivisch): **herzliche Grüße, D~e Elke** with best wishes, yours od (herzlicher) love, Elke

deine, r, s poss pron yours

deiner gen von **du** pron of you

deinerseits adv on your part

deinesgleichen pron people like you

deinetwegen ['daɪnət've:gən] adv (für dich) for your sake; (wegen dir) on your account

deinetwillen ['daɪnət'vɪlən] adv: **um ~ = deinetwegen**

deinige pron: **der/die/das D~** yours

dekadent [deka'dɛnt] adj decadent

Dekadenz f decadence

Dekan [de'ka:n] (-s, -e) m dean

deklassieren [dekla'si:rən] vt (Soziologie: herabsetzen) to downgrade; (Sport: übertreffen) to outclass

Deklination [deklinatsi'o:n] f declension

deklinieren [dekli'ni:rən] vt to decline

Dekolleté, Dekolletee [dekɔl'te:] (-s, -s) nt

low neckline

dekomprimieren vt (Comput) to decompress

Dekor [de'ko:r] (-s, -s od -e) m od nt decoration

Dekorateur, in [dekora'tø:r(ɪn)] m(f) window dresser

Dekoration [dekoratsi'o:n] f decoration; (in Laden) window dressing

dekorativ [dekora'ti:f] adj decorative

dekorieren [deko'ri:rən] vt to decorate; (Schaufenster) to dress

Dekostoff ['de:koʃtɔf] m (Textil) furnishing fabric

Dekret [de'kre:t] (-(e)s, -e) nt decree

Delegation [delegatsi'o:n] f delegation

delegieren [dele'gi:rən] vt: **~ (an +akk)** to delegate (to)

Delegierte, r f(m) delegate

Delfin [dɛl'fi:n] (-s, -e) m dolphin

Delfinschwimmen nt butterfly (stroke)

Delhi ['de:lɪ] (-s) nt Delhi

delikat [deli'ka:t] adj (zart, heikel) delicate; (köstlich) delicious

Delikatesse [delika'tɛsə] (-, -n) f delicacy

Delikatessengeschäft nt delicatessen (shop)

Delikt [de'lɪkt] (-(e)s, -e) nt (Jur) offence (Brit), offense (US)

Delinquent [delɪŋ'kvɛnt] m (geh) offender

Delirium [de'li:riʊm] nt: **im ~ sein** to be delirious; (umg: betrunken) to be paralytic

Delle ['dɛlə] (-, -n) (umg) f dent

Delphin etc [dɛl'fi:n] (-s, -e) m = **Delfin** etc

Delta ['dɛlta] (-s, -s) nt delta

dem [de(:)m] art dat von **der; das; wie ~ auch sei** be that as it may

Demagoge [dema'go:gə] (-n, -n) m demagogue

Demarkationslinie [demarkatsi'o:nzli:niə] f demarcation line

Dementi [de'mɛnti] (-s, -s) nt denial

dementieren [demɛn'ti:rən] vt to deny

dem- zW: **dementsprechend** adj appropriate ▷ adv correspondingly; (demnach) accordingly; **demgemäß** adv accordingly; **demnach** adv accordingly; **demnächst** adv shortly

Demo ['de:mo] (-s, -s) (umg) f demo

Demografie [demogra'fi:] f demography

Demokrat, in [demo'kra:t(ɪn)] (-en, -en) m(f) democrat

Demokratie [demokra'ti:] f democracy; **Demokratieverständnis** nt understanding of (the meaning of) democracy

demokratisch adj democratic

demokratisieren [demokrati'zi:rən] vt to democratize

demolieren [demo'li:rən] vt to demolish

Demonstrant, in [demɔn'strant(ɪn)] m(f) demonstrator

Demonstration [demɔnstratsi'o:n] f demonstration

demonstrativ [demɔnstra'ti:f] adj demonstrative; (Protest) pointed

demonstrieren [demɔn'stri:rən] vt, vi to demonstrate

Demontage [demɔn'ta:ʒə] (-, -n) f (lit, fig)

dismantling

demontieren [demɔn'ti:rən] *vt* (*lit, fig*) to dismantle; (*Räder*) to take off

demoralisieren [demorali'zi:rən] *vt* to demoralize

Demoskopie [demosko'pi:] *f* public opinion research

demselben *dat von* **derselbe; dasselbe**

Demut ['de:mu:t] (-) *f* humility

demütig ['de:my:tɪç] *adj* humble

demütigen ['de:my:tɪgən] *vt* to humiliate

Demütigung *f* humiliation

demzufolge ['de:mtsu'fɔlgə] *adv* accordingly

den [de(:)n] *art akk von* **der**

denen ['de:nən] *pron dat pl von* **der; die; das**

Denk- *zW:* **Denkanstoß** *m:* **jdm Denkanstöße geben** to give sb food for thought; **Denkart** *f* mentality; **denkbar** *adj* conceivable

denken ['dɛŋkən] *unreg vi* to think ▷ *vt:* **für jdn/etw gedacht sein** to be intended *od* meant for sb/sth ▷ *vr* (*vorstellen*): **das kann ich mir ~** I can imagine; (*beabsichtigen*): **sich** *dat* **etw bei etw ~** to mean sth by sth; **wo ~ Sie hin!** what an idea!; **ich denke schon** I think so; **an jdn/etw ~** to think of sb/sth; **daran ist gar nicht zu ~** that's (quite) out of the question; **ich denke nicht daran, das zu tun** there's no way I'm going to do that (*umg*)

Denken (-s) *nt* thinking

Denker, in (-s, -) *m(f)* thinker; **das Volk der Dichter und ~** the nation of poets and philosophers

Denk- *zW:* **Denkfähigkeit** *f* intelligence; **denkfaul** *adj* mentally lazy; **Denkfehler** *m* logical error; **Denkhorizont** *m* mental horizon

Denkmal (-s, "-er) *nt* monument; **Denkmalschutz** *m:* **etw unter Denkmalschutz stellen** to classify sth as a historical monument

Denk- *zW:* **Denkpause** *f:* **eine Denkpause einlegen** to have a break to think things over; **Denkschrift** *f* memorandum; **Denkvermögen** *nt* intellectual capacity; **denkwürdig** *adj* memorable; **Denkzettel** *m:* **jdm einen Denkzettel verpassen** to teach sb a lesson

denn [dɛn] *konj* for; (*konzessiv*): **es sei ~, (dass)** unless ▷ *adv* then; (*nach Komparativ*) than

dennoch ['dɛnnɔx] *konj* nevertheless ▷ *adv:* **und ~, ...** and yet ...

denselben *akk von* **derselbe** ▷ *dat von* **dieselben**

Denunziant, in [denʊntsi'ant(ɪn)] *m(f)* informer

denunzieren [denʊn'tsi:rən] *vt* to inform against

Deospray ['de:oʃpreɪ] *nt od m* deodorant spray

Depesche [de'pɛʃə] (-, -n) *f* dispatch

deplatziert [depla'tsi:rt] *adj* out of place

Deponent, in [depo'nɛnt(ɪn)] *m(f)* depositor

Deponie *f* dump, disposal site

deponieren [depo'ni:rən] *vt* (*Comm*) to deposit

deportieren [depɔr'ti:rən] *vt* to deport

Depot [de'po:] (-s, -s) *nt* warehouse; (*Busdepot, Eisenb*) depot; (*Bankdepot*) strongroom (*Brit*),

safe (*US*)

Depp [dɛp] (-en, -en) *m* (*Dialekt: pej*) twit

Depression [deprɛsi'o:n] *f* depression

depressiv *adj* depressive; (*Fin*) depressed

deprimieren [depri'mi:rən] *vt* to depress

der [de(:)r] (*f* **die**, *nt* **das**, *gen* **des, der, des**, *dat* **dem, der, dem**, *akk* **den**) *def art* the; **der Rhein** the Rhine; **der Klaus** (*umg*) Klaus; **die Frau** (*im Allgemeinen*) women; **der Tod/das Leben** death/life; **der Fuß des Berges** the foot of the hill; **gib es der Frau** give it to the woman; **er hat sich** *dat* **die Hand verletzt** he has hurt his hand

▷ *rel pron* (*bei Menschen*) who, that; (*bei Tieren, Sachen*) which, that; **der Mann, den ich gesehen habe** the man who *od* whom *od* that I saw

▷ *demon pron* he/she/it; (*jener, dieser*) that; (*pl*) those; **der/die war es** it was him/her; **der mit der Brille** the one with the glasses; **ich will den (da)** I want that one

derart ['de:r'a:rt] *adv* (*Art und Weise*) in such a way; (*Ausmaß: vor adj*) so; (: *vor vb*) so much

derartig *adj* such, this sort of

derb [dɛrp] *adj* sturdy; (*Kost*) solid; (*grob*) coarse; **Derbheit** *f* sturdiness; solidity; coarseness

deren ['de:rən] *rel pron* (*gen sing von die*) whose; (*von Sachen*) of which; (*gen pl von der, die, das*) their; whose; of whom

derentwillen ['de:rənt'vɪlən] *adv:* **um ~** (*rel*) for whose sake; (*von Sachen*) for the sake of which

dergestalt *adv* (*geh*): **~, dass ...** in such a way that ...

der- *zW:* **dergleichen** *pron* such; (*substantivisch*): **er tat nichts dergleichen** he did nothing of the kind; **und dergleichen (mehr)** and suchlike; **derjenige** *pron* he; she; it; (*rel*) the one (who); that (which); **dermaßen** *adv* to such an extent, so; **derselbe** *m pron* the same; **derweil** *adv* in the meantime; **derzeit** *adv* (*jetzt*) at present, at the moment; **derzeitig** *adj* present, current; (*damalig*) then

des [dɛs] *art gen von* **der**

Des [dɛs] (-) *nt* (*Mus: auch:* **des**) D flat

Deserteur [dezɛr'tø:r] *m* deserter

desertieren [dezɛr'ti:rən] *vi* to desert

desgl. *abk* = **desgleichen**

desgleichen ['dɛs'glaɪçən] *pron* the same

deshalb ['dɛs'halp] *adv, konj* therefore, that's why

Design [di'zaɪn] (-s, -s) *nt* design

designiert [dezi'gni:rt] *adj attrib:* **der ~e Vorsitzende/Nachfolger** the chairman designate/prospective successor

Desinfektion [dezɪnfɛktsi'o:n] *f* disinfection

Desinfektionsmittel *nt* disinfectant

desinfizieren [dezɪnfi'tsi:rən] *vt* to disinfect

Desinteresse [dɛs|ɪntə'rɛsə] (-s) *nt:* **~ (an +**dat**)**

lack of interest (in)
desinteressiert [dɛs|ɪntərɛ'siːrt] *adj*
uninterested
desselben *gen von* **derselbe; dasselbe**
dessen ['dɛsən] *pron gen von* **der; das;** ~
ungeachtet nevertheless, regardless
Dessert [dɛ'seːr] (**-s, -s**) *nt* dessert
Dessin [dɛ'sɛ̃ː] (**-s, -s**) *nt* (*Textil*) pattern, design
Destillation [dɛstɪlatsi'oːn] *f* distillation
destillieren [dɛstɪ'liːrən] *vt* to distil
desto ['dɛsto] *adv* all *od* so much the; ~ **besser**
all the better
destruktiv [destrʊk'tiːf] *adj* destructive
deswegen ['dɛs've:gən] *konj* therefore, hence
Detail [de'taɪ] (**-s, -s**) *nt* detail
detaillieren [deta'jiːrən] *vt* to specify, give
details of
Detektiv [detɛk'tiːf] (**-s, -e**) *m* detective;
Detektivroman *m* detective novel
Detektor [de'tɛktɔr] *m* (*Tech*) detector
Detonation [detonatsi'oːn] *f* explosion, blast
Deut *m*: (**um**) **keinen** ~ not one iota *od* jot
deuten ['dɔʏtən] *vt* to interpret; (*Zukunft*) to
read ▷ *vi*: ~ (**auf** +*akk*) to point (to *od* at)
deutlich *adj* clear; (*Unterschied*) distinct; **jdm**
etw ~ **zu verstehen geben** to make sth
perfectly clear *od* plain to sb; **Deutlichkeit** *f*
clarity; distinctness
deutsch [dɔʏtʃ] *adj* German; **-e Schrift**
Gothic script; **auf D~** in German; **auf gut**
D~ (gesagt) (*fig*: *umg*) ≈ in plain English; **D~e**
Demokratische Republik (*Hist*) German
Democratic Republic
Deutsche, r *f(m)*: **er ist ~r** he is (a) German
Deutschland *nt* Germany; **Deutschlandlied**
nt German national anthem; **Deutschlandpolitik**
f home *od* domestic policy; (*von fremdem Staat*)
policy towards Germany
deutschsprachig *adj* (*Bevölkerung, Gebiete*)
German-speaking; (*Zeitung, Ausgabe*) German-
language; (*Literatur*) German
deutschstämmig *adj* of German origin
Deutung *f* interpretation
Devise [de'viːzə] (**-, -n**) *f* motto, device;
Devisen *pl* (*Fin*) foreign currency *od* exchange
Devisenausgleich *m* foreign exchange offset
Devisenkontrolle *f* exchange control
Dez. *abk* (= *Dezember*) Dec.
Dezember [de'tsɛmbər] (**-(s), -**) *m* December;
siehe auch **September**
dezent [de'tsɛnt] *adj* discreet
Dezentralisation [detsɛntralizatsi'oːn] *f*
decentralization
Dezernat [detser'naːt] (**-(e)s, -e**) *nt* (*Verwaltung*)
department
Dezibel [detsi'bɛl] (**-s, -**) *nt* decibel
dezidiert [detsi'diːrt] *adj* firm, determined
dezimal [detsi'maːl] *adj* decimal;
Dezimalbruch *m* decimal (fraction);
Dezimalsystem *nt* decimal system
dezimieren [detsi'miːrən] *vt* (*fig*) to decimate
▷ *vr* to be decimated
DFB *m abk* (= *Deutscher Fußball-Bund*) German

Football Association
DFG *f abk* (= *Deutsche Forschungsgemeinschaft*)
German Research Council
DGB *m abk* (= *Deutscher Gewerkschaftsbund*) ≈ TUC
dgl. *abk* = **dergleichen**
d. h. *abk* (= *das heißt*) i.e.
Di. *abk* = **Dienstag**
Dia ['diːa] (**-s, -s**) *nt* = **Diapositiv**
Diabetes [dia'beːtɛs] (**-, -**) *m* (*Med*) diabetes
Diabetiker, in [dia'be:tikər(ɪn)] (**-s, -**) *m(f)*
diabetic
Diagnose [dia'gnoːzə] (**-, -n**) *f* diagnosis
diagnostizieren [diagnɔsti'tsiːrən] *vt, vi*
(*Med, fig*) to diagnose
diagonal [diago'naːl] *adj* diagonal
Diagonale (**-, -n**) *f* diagonal
Diagramm [dia'gram] *nt* diagram
Diakonie [diako'niː] *f* (*Rel*) social welfare work
Dialekt [dia'lɛkt] (**-(e)s, -e**) *m* dialect;
Dialektausdruck *m* dialect expression *od*
word; **dialektfrei** *adj* without an accent
dialektisch *adj* dialectal; (*Logik*) dialectical
Dialog [dia'loːk] (**-(e)s, -e**) *m* dialogue
Diamant [dia'mant] *m* diamond
Diapositiv [diapozi'tiːf] (**-s, -e**) *nt* (*Phot*) slide,
transparency
Diaprojektor *m* slide projector
Diät [di'ɛːt] (**-**) *f* diet; **Diäten** *pl* (*Pol*) allowance
sing; ~ **essen** to eat according to a diet; (**nach**
einer) ~ **leben** to be on a special diet
dich [dɪç] *akk von* **du** ▷ *pron* you ▷ *re, pron* yourself
dicht [dɪçt] *adj* dense; (*Nebel*) thick; (*Gewebe*)
close; (*undurchlässig*) (water)tight; (*fig*) concise;
(*umg*: *zu*) shut, closed ▷ *adv*: ~ **an/bei** close
to; **er ist nicht ganz** ~ (*umg*) he's crackers;
~ **machen** to make watertight/airtight; ~
hintereinander right behind one another; ~
bevölkert densely *od* heavily populated; *siehe*
auch **dichtmachen**
Dichte (**-, -n**) *f* density; thickness; closeness;
(water)tightness; (*fig*) conciseness
dichten *vt* (*dicht machen*) to make watertight; to
seal; (*Naut*) to caulk; (*Liter*) to compose, write
▷ *vi* (*Liter*) to compose, write
Dichter, in (**-s, -**) *m(f)* poet; (*Autor*) writer;
dichterisch *adj* poetical; **dichterische**
Freiheit poetic licence (*Brit*) *od* license (*US*)
dichthalten *unreg* (*umg*) *vi* to keep one's mouth
shut
dichtmachen (*umg*) *vt* (*Geschäft*) to wind up
▷ *vi* (*Person*) to close one's mind; *siehe auch*
dicht
Dichtung *f* (*Tech*) washer; (*Aut*) gasket;
(*Gedichte*) poetry; (*Prosa*) (piece of) writing; ~
und Wahrheit (*fig*) fact and fantasy
dick [dɪk] *adj* thick; (*fett*) fat; **durch** ~ **und**
dünn through thick and thin; **Dickdarm** *m*
(*Anat*) colon
Dicke (**-, -n**) *f* thickness; fatness
dickfellig *adj* thick-skinned
dickflüssig *adj* viscous
Dickicht (**-s, -e**) *nt* thicket
dick- *zW*: **Dickkopf** *m* mule; **Dickmilch** *f* soured

milk; **Dickschädel** m = **Dickkopf**
die [di:] *def art* the; *siehe auch* **der**
Dieb, in [di:p, 'di:bɪn] **(-(e)s, -e)** m(f) thief;
haltet den ~! stop thief!; **diebisch** *adj*
thieving; *(umg)* immense; **Diebstahl** m theft;
diebstahlsicher *adj* theft-proof
diejenige ['di:je:nɪgə] *pron siehe* **derjenige**
Diele ['di:lə] **(-, -n)** f (Brett) board; (Flur) hall,
lobby; (Eisdiele) ice-cream parlour (Brit) od
parlor (US)
dienen ['di:nən] vi: **(jdm)** ~ to serve (sb); **womit
kann ich Ihnen ~?** what can I do for you?; (in
Geschäft) can I help you?
Diener (-s, -) m servant; *(umg: Verbeugung)* bow;
Dienerin f (maid)servant
dienern vi (fig): ~ **(vor** +dat) to bow and scrape
(to)
Dienerschaft f servants pl
dienlich *adj* useful, helpful
Dienst [di:nst] **(-(e)s, -e)** m service; (Arbeit,
Arbeitszeit) work; ~ **am Kunden** customer
service; **jdm zu ~en stehen** to be at sb's
disposal; **außer ~** retired; ~ **haben** to be on
duty; ~ **habend** = **diensthabend**; ~ **tuend**
= **diensttuend**; **der öffentliche ~** the civil
service
Dienstag m Tuesday; **am ~** on Tuesday; ~ **in
acht Tagen** od **in einer Woche** a week on
Tuesday, Tuesday week; ~ **vor einer Woche**
od **acht Tagen** a week (ago) last Tuesday
dienstags *adv* on Tuesdays
Dienst- zW: **Dienstalter** nt length of service;
dienstbeflissen *adj* zealous; **Dienstbote**
m servant; **Dienstboteneingang** m
tradesmen's od service entrance; **diensteifrig**
adj zealous; **dienstfrei** *adj* off duty;
Dienstgebrauch m (Mil, Verwaltung): **nur
für den Dienstgebrauch** for official use
only; **Dienstgeheimnis** nt professional
secret; **Dienstgespräch** nt business call;
Dienstgrad m rank; **diensthabend** *adj* (Arzt,
Offizier) on duty; **Dienstleistung** f service;
Dienstleistungsbereich m service sector od
industry; **Dienstleistungsbetrieb** m service
industry business; **Dienstleistungsgewerbe**
nt service industries pl; **Dienstleistungssektor**
m service sector od industry; **dienstlich** *adj*
official; (Angelegenheiten) business attrib;
Dienstmädchen nt domestic servant;
Dienstplan m duty rota; **Dienstreise**
f business trip; **Dienststelle** f office;
diensttuend *adj* on duty; **Dienstvorschrift** f
service regulations pl; **Dienstwagen** m (von
Beamten) official car; **Dienstweg** m official
channels pl; **Dienstzeit** f office hours pl; (Mil)
period of service
diesbezüglich *adj* (Frage) on this matter
diese, r, s *pron* this (one) ▷ *adj* this; ~ **Nacht**
tonight
Diesel ['di:zəl] **(-s)** m (Kraftstoff) diesel fuel
dieselbe [di:'zɛlbə] f pron the same
dieselben [di:'zɛlbən] pl pron the same
Dieselöl ['di:zəlø:l] nt diesel oil

diesig *adj* drizzly
dies- zW: **diesjährig** *adj* this year's; **diesmal** *adv*
this time; **Diesseits (-)** nt this life; **diesseits**
präp +gen on this side
Dietrich ['di:trɪç] **(-s, -e)** m picklock
Diffamierungskampagne
[dɪfa'mi:rʊŋskampanjə] f smear campaign
differential etc [dɪferɛntsi'a:l] *adj* = **differenzial**
etc
Differenz [dɪfe'rɛnts] f difference;
Differenzbetrag m difference, balance
differenzial [dɪferɛntsi'a:l] *adj* differential;
Differenzialgetriebe nt differential gear;
Differenzialrechnung f differential calculus
differenzieren [dɪferɛn'tsi:rən] vt to
make distinctions in ▷ vi: ~ **(bei)** to make
distinctions (in)
differenziert *adj* complex
diffus [dɪ'fu:s] *adj* (Gedanken etc) confused
Digital- [digi'ta:l-] zW: **Digitalanzeige** f
digital display; **Digitalfernsehen** nt digital
TV; **Digitalrechner** m digital computer;
Digitaluhr f digital watch
Diktafon, Diktaphon [dɪkta'fo:n] nt
dictaphone®
Diktat [dɪk'ta:t] **(-(e)s, -e)** nt dictation;
(fig: Gebot) dictate; (Pol) diktat, dictate
Diktator [dɪk'ta:tor] m dictator; **diktatorisch**
[-a'to:rɪʃ] *adj* dictatorial
Diktatur [dɪkta'tu:r] f dictatorship
diktieren [dɪk'ti:rən] vt to dictate
Diktion [dɪktsi'o:n] f style
Dilemma [di'lɛma] **(-s, -s** od **-ta)** nt dilemma
Dilettant [dile'tant] m dilettante, amateur;
dilettantisch *adj* dilettante
Dimension [dimɛnzi'o:n] f dimension
DIN f abk (= Deutsche Industrie-Norm) German
Industrial Standard; ~ **A4** A4
Ding [dɪŋ] **(-(e)s, -e)** nt thing; object; **das ist
ein ~ der Unmöglichkeit** that is totally
impossible; **guter ~e sein** to be in good
spirits; **so wie die ~e liegen, nach Lage
der ~e** as things are; **es müsste nicht mit
rechten ~en zugehen, wenn ...** it would be
more than a little strange if ...; **ein krummes
~ drehen** to commit a crime; to do something
wrong; **dingfest** *adj*: **jdn dingfest machen** to
arrest sb; **dinglich** *adj* real, concrete
Dings (-) (umg) nt thingummyjig (Brit)
Dingsbums ['dɪŋsbʊms] **(-)** (umg) nt
thingummybob (Brit)
Dingsda (-) (umg) nt thingummyjig (Brit)
Dinosaurier [dino'zaʊriər] m dinosaur
Diözese [diø'tse:zə] **(-, -n)** f diocese
Diphtherie [dɪfte'ri:] f diphtheria
Dipl.-Ing. abk = **Diplom-Ingenieur**
Diplom [di'plo:m] **(-(e)s, -e)** nt diploma;
(Hochschulabschluss) degree; **Diplomarbeit** f
dissertation
Diplomat [diplo'ma:t] **(-en, -en)** m diplomat
Diplomatie [diploma'ti:] f diplomacy
diplomatisch [diplo'ma:tɪʃ] *adj* diplomatic
Diplom-Ingenieur m academically qualified

engineer

dir [diːr] *dat von* **du** ▷ *pron* (to) you

direkt [diˈrɛkt] *adj* direct; **~ fragen** to ask outright *od* straight out

Direktion [dirɛktsiˈoːn] *f* management; (*Büro*) manager's office

Direktmandat *nt* (*Pol*) direct mandate

Direktor, in *m(f)* director; (*von Hochschule*) principal; (*von Schule*) principal, head (teacher) (*Brit*)

Direktorium [dirɛkˈtoːriʊm] *nt* board of directors

Direktübertragung *f* live broadcast

Direktverkauf *m* direct selling

Dirigent, in [diriˈɡɛnt(ɪn)] *m(f)* conductor

dirigieren [diriˈɡiːrən] *vt* to direct; (*Mus*) to conduct

Dirne [ˈdɪrnə] (-, -n) *f* prostitute

Dis [dɪs] (-, -) *nt* (*Mus*) D sharp

dis [dɪs] (-, -) *nt* (*Mus*) D sharp

Disco [ˈdɪsko] (-, -s) *f* disco

Disharmonie [dɪsharmoˈniː] *f* (*lit, fig*) discord

Diskette [dɪsˈkɛtə] *f* disk, diskette

Diskettenlaufwerk *nt* disk drive

Disko [ˈdɪsko] (-, -s) *f* disco

Diskont [dɪsˈkɔnt] (-s, -e) *m* discount; **Diskontsatz** *m* rate of discount

Diskothek [dɪskoˈteːk] (-, -en) *f* disco(theque)

diskreditieren [dɪskrediˈtiːrən] *vt* (*geh*) to discredit

Diskrepanz [dɪskreˈpants] *f* discrepancy

diskret [dɪsˈkreːt] *adj* discreet

Diskretion [dɪskretsiˈoːn] *f* discretion; **strengste ~ wahren** to preserve the strictest confidence

diskriminieren [dɪskrimiˈniːrən] *vt* to discriminate against

Diskriminierung *f*: **~ (von)** discrimination (against)

Diskussion [dɪskusiˈoːn] *f* discussion; **zur ~ stehen** to be under discussion

Diskussionsbeitrag *m* contribution to the discussion

Diskuswerfen [ˈdɪskʊsvɛrfən] *nt* throwing the discus

diskutabel [dɪskuˈtaːbəl] *adj* debatable

diskutieren [dɪskuˈtiːrən] *vt, vi* to discuss; **darüber lässt sich ~** that sounds like something we could talk about

disponieren [dɪspoˈniːrən] *vi* (*geh: planen*) to make arrangements

Disposition [dɪspozitsiˈoːn] *f* (*geh: Verfügung*): **jdm zur** *od* **zu jds ~ stehen** to be at sb's disposal

disqualifizieren [dɪskvalifiˈtsiːrən] *vt* to disqualify

dissen [ˈdɪsən] (*umg*) *vt* to slag off (*Brit*), to diss (*esp US*)

Dissertation [dɪsɛrtatsiˈoːn] *f* dissertation; doctoral thesis

Dissident, in [dɪsiˈdɛnt(ɪn)] *m(f)* dissident

Distanz [dɪsˈtants] *f* distance; (*fig: Abstand, Entfernung*) detachment; (*Zurückhaltung*) reserve

distanzieren [dɪstanˈtsiːrən] *vr*: **sich von jdm/etw ~** to dissociate o.s. from sb/sth

distanziert *adj* (*Verhalten*) distant

Distel [ˈdɪstəl] (-, -n) *f* thistle

Disziplin [dɪstsiˈpliːn] (-, -en) *f* discipline

Disziplinarverfahren [dɪstsipliˈnarfɛrfaːrən] *nt* disciplinary proceedings *pl*

dito [ˈdiːto] *adv* (*hum, Comm*) ditto

Diva [ˈdiːva] (-, -s) *f* star; (*Film*) screen goddess

divers [diˈvɛrs] *adj* various

Diverses *pl* sundries *pl*; „**~**" "miscellaneous"

Dividende [diviˈdɛndə] (-, -n) *f* dividend

dividieren [diviˈdiːrən] *vt*: **~ (durch)** to divide (by)

d. J. *abk* (= *der Jüngere*) jun.

Djakarta [dʒaˈkarta] *nt* Jakarta

DJH *nt abk* (= *Deutsches Jugendherbergswerk*) German Youth Hostel Association

DKP *f abk* (= *Deutsche Kommunistische Partei*) German Communist Party

DLV *m abk* (= *Deutscher Leichtathletik-Verband*) German track and field association

DM *f abk* (*Hist*: = *Deutsche Mark*) DM

d. M. *abk* (= *dieses Monats*) inst.

D-Mark [ˈdeːmark] (-, -) *f* (*Hist*) deutschmark

DNS *f abk* (= *Desoxyribo(se)nukleinsäure*) DNA

Do. *abk* = **Donnerstag**

 SCHLÜSSELWORT

doch [dɔx] *adv* **1** (*dennoch*) after all; (*sowieso*) anyway; **er kam doch noch** he came after all; **du weißt es ja doch besser** you know more about it (than I do) anyway; **es war doch ganz interessant** it was actually quite interesting; **und doch, ... and yet ...**

2 (*als bejahende Antwort*) yes I do/it does *etc*; **das ist nicht wahr — doch!** that's not true — yes it is!

3 (*auffordernd*): **komm doch** do come; **lass ihn doch** just leave him; **nicht doch!** oh no!

4: **sie ist doch noch so jung** but she's still so young; **Sie wissen doch, wie das ist** you know how it is(, don't you?); **wenn doch** if only

▷ *konj* (*aber*) but; (*trotzdem*) all the same; **und doch hat er es getan** but still he did it

Docht [dɔxt] (-(e)s, -e) *m* wick

Dock [dɔk] (-s, -s *od* -e) *nt* dock; **Dockgebühren** *pl* dock dues *pl*

Dogge [ˈdɔɡə] (-, -n) *f* bulldog; **Deutsche ~** Great Dane

Dogma [ˈdɔɡma] (-s, -men) *nt* dogma

dogmatisch [dɔˈɡmaːtɪʃ] *adj* dogmatic

Dohle [ˈdoːlə] (-, -n) *f* jackdaw

Doktor [ˈdɔktɔr] (-s, -en) *m* doctor; **den ~ machen** (*umg*) to do a doctorate *od* Ph.D.

Doktorand, in [dɔktoˈrant (-dɪn)] (-en, -en) *m(f)* Ph.D. student

Doktor- *zW*: **Doktorarbeit** *f* doctoral thesis; **Doktortitel** *m* doctorate; **Doktorvater** *m* supervisor

doktrinär [dɔktriˈnɛːr] *adj* doctrinal; *(stur)* doctrinaire

Dokument [dokuˈmɛnt] *nt* document

Dokumentar- *zW:* **Dokumentarbericht** *m* documentary; **Dokumentarfilm** *m* documentary (film); **dokumentarisch** *adj* documentary; **Dokumentarspiel** *nt* docudrama

Dokumentationszentrum *nt* documentation centre *(Brit)* od center *(US)*

dokumentieren [dokumɛnˈtiːrən] *vt* to document; *(fig: zu erkennen geben)* to reveal, show

Dolch [dɔlç] **(-(e)s, -e)** *m* dagger; **Dolchstoß** *m* *(bes fig)* stab

dolmetschen [ˈdɔlmɛtʃən] *vt, vi* to interpret

Dolmetscher, in **(-s, -)** *m(f)* interpreter

Dolomiten [doloˈmiːtən] *pl (Geog):* **die ~** the Dolomites *pl*

Dom [doːm] **(-(e)s, -e)** *m* cathedral

Domäne [doˈmɛːnə] **(-, -n)** *f (fig)* domain, province

dominieren [domiˈniːrən] *vt* to dominate ▷ *vi* to predominate

Dominikanische Republik [dominiˈkaːnɪʃərepuˈbliːk] *f* Dominican Republic

Dompfaff [ˈdoːmpfaf] **(-en, -en)** *m* bullfinch

Dompteur [dɔmpˈtøːr] *m (Zirkus)* trainer

Dompteuse [dɔmpˈtøːzə] *f (Zirkus)* trainer

Donau [ˈdoːnaʊ] *f:* **die ~** the Danube

Donner [ˈdɔnər] **(-s, -)** *m* thunder; **wie vom ~ gerührt** *(fig)* thunderstruck

donnern *vi unpers* to thunder ▷ *vt (umg)* to slam, crash

Donnerschlag *m* thunderclap

Donnerstag *m* Thursday; *siehe auch* **Dienstag**

Donnerwetter *nt* thunderstorm; *(fig)* dressing-down ▷ *interj* good heavens!; *(anerkennend)* my word!

doof [doːf] *(umg) adj* daft, stupid

Dopingkontrolle [ˈdɔpɪŋkɔntrɔlə] *f (Sport)* dope check

Doppel [ˈdɔpəl] **(-s, -)** *nt* duplicate; *(Sport)* doubles; **Doppelband** *m (von doppeltem Umfang)* double-sized volume; *(zwei Bände)* two volumes *pl*; **Doppelbett** *nt* double bed; **doppelbödig** *adj (fig)* ambiguous; **doppeldeutig** *adj* ambiguous; **Doppelfenster** *nt* double glazing; **Doppelgänger, in** **(-s, -)** *m(f)* double; **doppelklicken** *vi* to double-click; **Doppelkorn** *m type of schnapps*; **Doppelpunkt** *m* colon; **doppelseitig** *adj* double-sided; *(Lungenentzündung)* double; **doppelseitige Anzeige** double-page advertisement; **doppelsinnig** *adj* ambiguous; **Doppelstecker** *m* two-way adaptor; **Doppelstunde** *f (Sch)* double period

doppelt *adj* double; *(Comm: Buchführung)* double-entry; *(Staatsbürgerschaft)* dual ▷ *adv:* **die Karte habe ich ~** I have two of these cards; **~ gemoppelt** *(umg)* saying the same thing twice over; **in ~er Ausführung** in duplicate

Doppel- *zW:* **Doppelverdiener** *pl* two-income

family; **Doppelzentner** *m* 100 kilograms; **Doppelzimmer** *nt* double room

Dorf [dɔrf] **(-(e)s, ¨er)** *nt* village; **Dorfbewohner** *m* villager

dörflich [ˈdœrflɪç] *adj* village *attrib*

Dorn[1] [dɔrn] **(-(e)s, -en)** *m (Bot)* thorn; **das ist mir ein ~ im Auge** *(fig)* it's a thorn in my flesh

Dorn[2] [dɔrn] **(-(e)s, -e)** *m (Schnallendorn)* tongue, pin

dornig *adj* thorny

Dornröschen *nt* Sleeping Beauty

dörren [ˈdœrən] *vt* to dry

Dörrobst [ˈdœroːpst] *nt* dried fruit

dort [dɔrt] *adv* there; **~ drüben** over there; **dorther** *adv* from there; **dorthin** *adv* (to) there

dortig *adj* of that place; in that town

Dose [ˈdoːzə] **(-, -n)** *f* box; *(Blechdose)* tin, can; **in ~n** *(Konserven)* canned, tinned *(Brit)*

Dosen *pl von* **Dose**; **Dosis**

dösen [ˈdøːzən] *(umg) vi* to doze

Dosenmilch *f* evaporated milk

Dosenöffner *m* tin *(Brit)* od can opener

Dosenpfand *nt* deposit on drink cans; *(allgemein: Einwegpfand)* deposit on drink cans and disposable bottles

dosieren [doˈziːrən] *vt (lit, fig)* to measure out

Dosis [ˈdoːzɪs] **(-, Dosen)** *f* dose

Dotierung [doˈtiːrʊŋ] *f* endowment; *(von Posten)* remuneration

Dotter [ˈdɔtər] **(-s, -)** *m* egg yolk

Double [ˈduːbəl] **(-s, -s)** *nt (Film etc)* stand-in

Download [ˈdaʊnloːd] *m (Comput)* download

downloaden [ˈdaʊnloːdən] *vti (Comput)* to download

Downsyndrom *nt no pl (Med)* Down's Syndrome

Doz. *abk* = **Dozent(in)**

Dozent, in [doˈtsɛnt(ɪn)] **(-en, -en)** *m(f):* **~ (für)** lecturer (in), professor (of) *(US)*

dpa *f abk (= Deutsche Presse-Agentur)* German Press Agency

Dr. *abk* = **Doktor**

Drache [ˈdraxə] **(-n, -n)** *m (Tier)* dragon

Drachen **(-s, -)** *m* kite; **einen ~ steigen lassen** to fly a kite; **drachenfliegen** *vi* to hang-glide; **Drachenfliegen** *nt (Sport)* hang-gliding

Dragee, Dragée [draˈʒeː] **(-s, -s)** *nt (Pharm)* dragee, sugar-coated pill

Draht [draːt] **(-(e)s, ¨e)** *m* wire; **auf ~ sein** to be on the ball; **Drahtesel** *m (hum)* trusty bicycle; **Drahtgitter** *nt* wire grating; **drahtlos** *adj* cordless; *(Telefon)* mobile; **Drahtseil** *nt* cable; **Nerven wie Drahtseile** *(umg)* nerves of steel; **Drahtseilbahn** *f* cable railway; **Drahtzange** *f* pliers *pl*; **Drahtzieher, in** *m(f) (fig)* wire-puller

Drall *m (fig: Hang)* tendency; **einen ~ nach links haben** *(Aut)* to pull to the left

drall [dral] *adj* strapping; *(Frau)* buxom

Drama [ˈdraːma] **(-s, Dramen)** *nt* drama

Dramatiker, in [draˈmaːtikər(ɪn)] **(-s, -)** *m(f)* dramatist

dramatisch [draˈmaːtɪʃ] *adj* dramatic

Dramaturg, in [dramaˈtʊrk (-gɪn)] **(-en, -en)**

m(f) artistic director; *(TV)* drama producer

dran [dran] *(umg) adv (an der Reihe)*: **jetzt bist du ~** it's your turn now; **früh/spät ~ sein** to be early/late; **ich weiß nicht, wie ich (bei ihm) ~ bin** I don't know where I stand (with him); *siehe auch* **daran**; **dranbleiben** *unreg (umg) vi* to stay close; *(am Apparat)* to hang on

Drang (**-(e)s, ~**) *m (Trieb)* urge, yearning; *(Druck)* pressure; **~ nach etw** *od* yearning for

drang *etc* [draŋ] *vb siehe* **dringen**

drängeln ['drɛŋəln] *vt, vi* to push, jostle

drängen ['drɛŋən] *vt (schieben)* to push, press; *(antreiben)* to urge ▷ *vi (eilig sein)* to be urgent; *(Zeit)* to press; **auf etw** *akk* **~** to press for sth

drangsalieren [draŋza'li:rən] *vt* to pester, plague

dranhalten *(umg) vr* to get a move on

drankommen *(umg: unreg: vi (an die Reihe kommen)* to have one's turn; *(Sch: beim Melden)* to be called; *(Frage, Aufgabe etc)* to come up

drannehmen *(umg: unreg: vt (Schüler)* to ask

drastisch ['drastɪʃ] *adj* drastic

drauf [drauf] *(umg) adv*: **~ und dran sein, etw zu tun** to be on the point of doing sth; *siehe auch* **darauf**; **Draufgänger** (**-s, -**) *m* daredevil; **draufgehen** *unreg vi (verbraucht werden)* to be used up; *(kaputtgehen)* to be smashed up; **draufhaben** *(umg) unreg vt*: **etw draufhaben** *(können)* to be able to do sth just like that; *(Kenntnisse)* to be well up on sth; **draufzahlen** *vi (fig: Einbußen erleiden)* to pay the price

draußen ['drausən] *adv* outside, out-of-doors

Drechsler, in ['drɛkslər(ɪn)] (**-s, -**) *m(f)* (wood) turner

Dreck [drɛk] (**-(e)s**) *m* mud, dirt; **~ am Stecken haben** *(fig)* to have a skeleton in the cupboard; **das geht ihn einen ~ an** *(umg)* that's none of his business

dreckig *adj* dirty, filthy; **es geht mir ~** *(umg)* I'm in a bad way

Dreckskerl *(umg!) m* dirty swine *(!)*

Dreh [dre:] *m*: **den ~ raushaben** *od* **weghaben** *(umg)* to have got the hang of it

Dreh- *zW*: **Drehachse** *f* axis of rotation; **Dreharbeiten** *pl (Film)* shooting *sing*; **Drehbank** *f* lathe; **drehbar** *adj* revolving; **Drehbuch** *nt (Film)* script

drehen *vt* to turn, rotate; *(Zigaretten)* to roll; *(Film)* to shoot ▷ *vi* to turn, rotate ▷ *vr* to turn; *(handeln von)*: **sich um etw ~** to be about sth; **ein Ding ~** *(umg)* to play a prank

Dreher, in (**-s, -**) *m(f)* lathe operator

Dreh- *zW*: **Drehorgel** *f* barrel organ; **Drehort** *m (Film)* location; **Drehscheibe** *f (Eisenb)* turntable; **Drehtür** *f* revolving door

Drehung *f (Rotation)* rotation; *(Umdrehung, Wendung)* turn

Dreh- *zW*: **Drehwurm** *(umg) m*: **einen Drehwurm haben/bekommen** to be/ become dizzy; **Drehzahl** *f* rate of revolution; **Drehzahlmesser** *m* rev(olution) counter

drei [drai] *num* three; **~ viertel** three quarters; **aller guten Dinge sind ~!**

(Sprichwort) all good things come in threes!; *(nach zwei missglückten Versuchen)* third time lucky!; **Dreieck** *nt* triangle; **dreieckig** *adj* triangular; **Dreiecksverhältnis** *nt* eternal triangle; **dreieinhalb** *num* three and a half; **Dreieinigkeit** [-'|ainiçkait] *f* Trinity

dreierlei *adj inv* of three kinds

drei- *zW*: **dreifach** *adj* triple, treble ▷ *adv* three times; **die dreifache Menge** three times the amount; **Dreifaltigkeit** *f* trinity; **Dreifuß** *m* tripod; *(Schemel)* three-legged stool; **Dreigangschaltung** *f* three-speed gear; **dreihundert** *num* three hundred; **Dreikäsehoch** *(umg) m* tiny tot; **Dreikönigsfest** *nt* Epiphany; **dreimal** *adv* three times, thrice; **dreimalig** *adj* three times

dreinblicken ['drainblikən] *vi*: **traurig** *etc* **~** to look sad *etc*

dreinreden ['drainre:dən] *vi*: **jdm ~** *(dazwischenreden)* to interrupt sb; *(sich einmischen)* to interfere with sb

Dreirad *nt* tricycle

Dreisprung *m* triple jump

dreißig ['draisiç] *num* thirty

dreist [draist] *adj* bold, audacious

Dreistigkeit *f* boldness, audacity

drei- *zW*: **Dreiviertelstunde** *f* three-quarters of an hour; **Dreivierteltakt** *m*: **im Dreivierteltakt** in three-four time; **dreizehn** *num* thirteen; **jetzt schlägts dreizehn!** *(umg)* that's a bit much

dreschen ['drɛʃən] *unreg vt* to thresh; **Skat ~** *(umg)* to play skat

Dresden ['dre:sdən] (**-s**) *nt* Dresden

dressieren [drɛ'si:rən] *vt* to train

Dressur [drɛ'su:r] *f* training; *(für Dressurreiten)* dressage

Dr. h. c. *abk* (= *Doktor honoris causa*) honorary doctor

driften ['driftən] *vi (Naut, fig)* to drift

Drillbohrer *m* light drill

drillen ['drilən] *vt (bohren)* to drill, bore; *(Mil)* to drill; *(fig)* to train; **auf etw** *akk* **gedrillt sein** *(fig: umg)* to be practised *(Brit)* od practiced *(US)* at doing sth

Drilling *m* triplet

drin [drin] *(umg) adv*: **bis jetzt ist noch alles ~** everything is still quite open; *siehe auch* **darin**

dringen ['driŋən] *unreg vi (Wasser, Licht, Kälte)*: **~ (durch/in** +*akk*) to penetrate (through/into); **auf etw** *akk* **~** to insist on sth; **in jdn ~** *(geh)* to entreat sb

dringend ['drinənt] *adj* urgent; **~ empfehlen** to recommend strongly

dringlich ['drinliç] *adj* = **dringend**

Dringlichkeit *f* urgency

Dringlichkeitsstufe *f* priority; **~ 1** top priority

drinnen ['drinən] *adv* inside, indoors

drinstecken ['drinʃtɛkən] *(umg) vi*: **da steckt eine Menge Arbeit drin** a lot of work has gone into it

drischt [driʃt] *vb siehe* **dreschen**

dritt *adv*: **wir kommen zu ~** three of us are

coming together

dritte, r, s *adj* third; **D~ Welt** Third World; **im Beisein D~r** in the presence of a third party

Drittel (-s, -) *nt* third

drittens *adv* thirdly

drittklassig *adj* third-rate, third-class

Dr. jur. *abk* (= *Doktor der Rechtswissenschaften*) ≈ L.L.D.

DRK (-) *nt abk* (= *Deutsches Rotes Kreuz*) ≈ R.C.

Dr. med. *abk* (= *Doktor der Medizin*) ≈ M.D.

droben ['dro:bən] *adv* above, up there

Droge ['dro:gə] **(-, -n)** *f* drug

dröge ['drøgə] (*Nordd*) *adj* boring

Drogen- *zW*: **drogenabhängig** *adj* addicted to drugs; **Drogenhändler, in** *m(f)* peddler, pusher; **drogensüchtig** *adj* addicted to drugs

Drogerie [drogə'ri:] *f* chemist's shop (*Brit*), drugstore (*US*); *see culture note*

○ **DROGERIE**
○
○ The *Drogerie* as opposed to the *Apotheke* sells
○ medicines not requiring a prescription.
○ It tends to be cheaper and also sells
○ cosmetics, perfume and toiletries.

Drogist, in [dro'gɪst(ɪn)] *m(f)* pharmacist, chemist (*Brit*)

Drohbrief *m* threatening letter

drohen ['dro:ən] *vi*: **(jdm) ~** to threaten (sb)

Drohgebärde *f* (*lit, fig*) threatening gesture

Drohne ['dro:nə] **(-, -n)** *f* drone

dröhnen ['drø:nən] *vi* (*Motor*) to roar; (*Stimme, Musik*) to ring, resound

Drohung ['dro:ʊŋ] *f* threat

drollig ['drɔlɪç] *adj* droll

Drops [drɔps] **(-, -)** *m od nt* fruit drop

drosch *etc* [drɔʃ] *vb siehe* **dreschen**

Droschke ['drɔʃkə] **(-, -n)** *f* cab

Droschkenkutscher *m* cabman

Drossel ['drɔsəl] **(-, -n)** *f* thrush

drosseln ['drɔsəln] *vt* (*Motor etc*) to throttle; (*Heizung*) to turn down; (*Strom, Tempo, Produktion etc*) to cut down

Dr. phil. *abk* (= *Doktor der Geisteswissenschaften*) ≈ Ph.D.

Dr. theol. *abk* (= *Doktor der Theologie*) ≈ D.D.

drüben ['dry:bən] *adv* over there, on the other side

drüber ['dry:bər] (*umg*) *adv* = **darüber**

Druck [drʊk] **(-(e)s, -e)** *m* (*Zwang, Phys*) pressure; (*Typ: Vorgang*) printing; (: *Produkt*) print; (*fig: Belastung*) burden, weight; **~ hinter etw** *akk* **machen** to put some pressure on sth; **Druckbuchstabe** *m* block letter; **in Druckbuchstaben schreiben** to print

Drückeberger ['drʏkəbɛrgər] **(-s, -)** *m* shirker, dodger

drucken ['drʊkən] *vt, vi* (*Typ, Comput*) to print

drücken ['drʏkən] *vt* (*Knopf, Hand*) to press; (*zu eng sein*) to pinch; (*fig: Preise*) to keep down; (: *belasten*) to oppress, weigh down ▷ *vi* to press; to pinch ▷ *vr*: **sich vor etw** *dat* **~** to get out of

(doing) sth; **jdm etw in die Hand ~** to press sth into sb's hand

drückend *adj* oppressive; (*Last, Steuern*) heavy; (*Armut*) grinding; (*Wetter, Hitze*) oppressive, close

Drucker (-s, -) *m* printer

Drücker (-s, -) *m* button; (*Türdrücker*) handle; (*Gewehrdrücker*) trigger; **am ~ sein** *od* **sitzen** (*fig: umg*) to be the key person; **auf den letzten ~** (*fig: umg*) at the last minute

Druckerei [drʊkə'raɪ] *f* printing works, press

Druckerschwärze *f* printer's ink

Druck- *zW*: **Druckfahne** *f* galley(-proof); **Druckfehler** *m* misprint; **Druckknopf** *m* press stud (*Brit*), snap fastener; **Druckkopf** *m* printhead; **Druckluft** *f* compressed air; **Druckmittel** *nt* leverage; **druckreif** *adj* ready for printing, passed for press; (*fig*) polished; **Drucksache** *f* printed matter; **Druckschrift** *f* printing; (*gedrucktes Werk*) pamphlet; **Drucktaste** *f* push button; **Druckwelle** *f* shock wave

drum [drʊm] (*umg*) *adv* around; **mit allem D~ und Dran** with all the bits and pieces *pl*; (*Mahlzeit*) with all the trimmings *pl*

Drumherum *nt* trappings *pl*

drunten ['drʊntən] *adv* below, down there

Drüse ['dry:zə] **(-, -n)** *f* gland

DSB (-) *m abk* (= *Deutscher Sportbund*) German Sports Association

Dschungel ['dʒʊŋəl] **(-s, -)** *m* jungle

DSD *nt abk* (= *Duales System Deutschland*) German waste collection and recycling service; *see culture note*

○ **DSD**
○
○ The *DSD* (Duales System Deutschland)
○ is a scheme introduced in Germany for
○ separating domestic refuse into two types
○ so as to reduce environmental damage.
○ Normal refuse is disposed of in the usual
○ way by burning or dumping at land-fill
○ sites; packets and containers with a green
○ spot (*Grüner Punkt*) imprinted on them are
○ kept separate and are then collected for
○ recycling.

dt. *abk* = **deutsch**

DTC (-) *m abk* (= *Deutscher Touring Automobil Club*) German motoring organization

DTP (-) *nt abk* (= *Desktop publishing*) DTP

Dtzd. *abk* (= *Dutzend*) doz.

du [du:] *pron* you; **mit jdm per du sein** to be on familiar terms with sb; **Du** *nt*: **jdm das Du anbieten** to suggest that sb uses "du", suggest that sb uses the familiar form of address

Dübel ['dy:bəl] **(-s, -)** *m* plug; (*Holzdübel*) dowel

dübeln ['dy:bəln] *vt, vi* to plug

Dublin ['dablɪn] *nt* Dublin

ducken ['dʊkən] *vt* (*Kopf*) to duck; (*fig*) to take down a peg or two ▷ *vr* to duck

Duckmäuser ['dʊkmɔyzər] **(-s, -)** *m* yes-man

Dudelsack ['du:dəlzak] *m* bagpipes *pl*

Duell [du'ɛl] (**-s, -e**) *nt* duel

Duett [du'ɛt] (**-(e)s, -e**) *nt* duet

Duft [dʊft] (**-(e)s, ̈-e**) *m* scent, odour (*Brit*), odor (*US*); **duften** *vi* to smell, be fragrant

duftig *adj* (*Stoff, Kleid*) delicate, diaphanous; (*Muster*) fine

Duftnote *f* (*von Parfüm*) scent

dulden ['dʊldən] *vt* to suffer; (*zulassen*) to tolerate ▷ *vi* to suffer

duldsam *adj* tolerant

dumm [dʊm] *adj* stupid; **das wird mir zu ~** that's just too much; **der D~e sein** to be the loser; **der ~e August** (*umg*) the clown; **du willst mich wohl für ~ verkaufen** you must think I'm stupid; **sich ~ und dämlich reden** (*umg*) to talk till one is blue in the face; **so etwas D~es** how stupid; what a nuisance; **dummdreist** *adj* impudent

dummerweise *adv* stupidly

Dummheit *f* stupidity; (*Tat*) blunder, stupid mistake

Dummkopf *m* blockhead

dumpf [dʊmpf] *adj* (*Ton*) hollow, dull; (*Luft*) close; (*Erinnerung, Schmerz*) vague; **Dumpfheit** *f* hollowness, dullness; closeness; vagueness

dumpfig *adj* musty

Dumpingpreis ['dampɪŋpraɪs] *m* give-away price

Düne ['dy:nə] (**-, -n**) *f* dune

Dung [dʊŋ] (**-(e)s**) *m* manure

düngen ['dyŋən] *vt* to fertilize

Dünger (**-s, -**) *m* fertilizer; (*Dung*) manure

dunkel ['dʊŋkəl] *adj* dark; (*Stimme*) deep; (*Ahnung*) vague; (*rätselhaft*) obscure; (*verdächtig*) dubious, shady; **im D~n tappen** (*fig*) to grope in the dark

Dünkel ['dyŋkəl] (**-s**) *m* self-conceit; **dünkelhaft** *adj* conceited

Dunkelheit *f* darkness; (*fig*) obscurity; **bei Einbruch der ~** at nightfall

Dunkelkammer *f* (*Phot*) dark room

dunkeln *vi unpers* to grow dark

Dunkelziffer *f* estimated number of unnotified cases

dünn [dʏn] *adj* thin ▷ *adv*: **~ gesät** scarce; **Dünndarm** *m* small intestine; **dünnflüssig** *adj* watery, thin; **Dünnheit** *f* thinness; **Dünnschiss** (*umg*) *m* the runs

Dunst [dʊnst] (**-es, ̈-e**) *m* vapour (*Brit*), vapor (*US*); (*Wetter*) haze; **Dunstabzugshaube** *f* extractor hood

dünsten ['dʏnstən] *vt* to steam

Dunstglocke *f* haze; (*Smog*) pall of smog

dunstig ['dʊnstɪç] *adj* vaporous; (*Wetter*) hazy, misty

düpieren [dy'pi:rən] *vt* to dupe

Duplikat [dupli'ka:t] (**-(e)s, -e**) *nt* duplicate

Dur [du:r] (**-, -**) *nt* (*Mus*) major

 SCHLÜSSELWORT

durch [dʊrç] *präp +akk* **1** (*hindurch*) through; **durch den Urwald** through the jungle; **durch die ganze Welt reisen** to travel all over the world

2 (*mittels*) through, by (means of); (*aufgrund*) due to, owing to; **Tod durch Herzschlag/ den Strang** death from a heart attack/by hanging; **durch die Post** by post; **durch seine Bemühungen** through his efforts

▷ *adj* **1** (*hindurch*) through; **die ganze Nacht durch** all through the night; **den Sommer durch** during the summer; **8 Uhr durch** past 8 o'clock; **durch und durch** completely; **das geht mir durch und durch** that goes right through me

2 (*Koch: umg: durchgebraten*) done; (**gut**) **durch** well-done

durcharbeiten *vt, vi* to work through ▷ *vr*: **sich durch etw ~** to work one's way through sth

durchatmen *vi* to breathe deeply

durchaus [dʊrç'aus] *adv* completely; (*unbedingt*) definitely; **~ nicht** (*in verneinten Sätzen: als Verstärkung*) by no means; (*: als Antwort*) not at all; **das lässt sich ~ machen** that sounds feasible; **ich bin ~ Ihrer Meinung** I quite *od* absolutely agree with you

durchbeißen *unreg vt* to bite through ▷ *vr* (*fig*) to battle on

durchblättern *vt* to leaf through

Durchblick ['dʊrçblɪk] *m* view; (*fig*) comprehension; **den ~ haben** (*fig: umg*) to know what's what

durchblicken *vi* to look through; (*umg: verstehen*): (**bei etw**) **~** to understand (sth); **etw ~ lassen** (*fig*) to hint at sth

Durchblutung [dʊrç'blu:tʊŋ] *f* circulation (of blood)

durchbohren *vt untr* to bore through, pierce

durchboxen ['dʊrçbɔksən] *vr* (*fig: umg*): **sich (durch etw) ~** to fight one's way through (sth)

durchbrechen¹ ['dʊrçbrɛçən] *unreg vt, vi* to break

durchbrechen² [dʊrç'brɛçən] *unreg vt untr* (*Schranken*) to break through

durchbrennen *unreg vi* (*Draht, Sicherung*) to burn through; (*umg*) to run away

durchbringen *unreg vt* to get through; (*Geld*) to squander ▷ *vr* to make a living

Durchbruch ['dʊrçbrʊx] *m* (*Öffnung*) opening; (*Mil*) breach; (*von Gefühlen etc*) eruption; (*der Zähne*) cutting; (*fig*) breakthrough; **zum ~ kommen** to break through

durchdacht [dʊrç'daxt] *adj* well thought-out

durchdenken *unreg vt untr* to think out

durch- *zW*: **durchdiskutieren** *vt* to talk over, discuss; **durchdrängen** *vr* to force one's way through; **durchdrehen** *vt* (*Fleisch*) to mince ▷ *vi* (*umg*) to crack up

durchdringen¹ ['dʊrçdrɪŋən] *unreg vi* to penetrate, get through

durchdringen² [dʊrç'drɪŋən] *unreg vt untr* to penetrate

durchdringend *adj* piercing; (*Kälte, Wind*) biting; (*Geruch*) pungent

durchdrücken ['dʊrçdrʏkən] vt (durch Presse) to press through; (Creme, Teig) to pipe; (fig: Gesetz, Reformen etc) to push through; (seinen Willen) to get; (Knie, Kreuz etc) to straighten

durcheinander [dʊrç|aɪ'nandər] adv in a mess, in confusion; (verwirrt) confused; **Durcheinander** (-s) nt (Verwirrung) confusion; (Unordnung) mess; **durcheinanderbringen** vt to mess up; (verwirren) to confuse; **durcheinanderreden** vi to talk at the same time; **durcheinandertrinken** vi to mix one's drinks; **durcheinanderwerfen** vt to muddle up

durch- zW: **durchfahren** unreg vi: **er ist bei Rot durchgefahren** he jumped the lights ▷ vt: **die Nacht durchfahren** to travel through the night; **Durchfahrt** f transit; (Verkehr) thoroughfare; **Durchfahrt bitte freihalten!** please keep access free; **Durchfahrt verboten!** no through road; **Durchfall** m (Med) diarrhoea (Brit), diarrhea (US); **durchfallen** unreg vi to fall through; (in Prüfung) to fail; **durchfinden** unreg vr to find one's way through; **durchfliegen** unreg (umg) vi (in Prüfung): (durch etw od in etw dat) **durchfliegen** to fail (sth); **Durchflug** m: **Passagiere auf dem Durchflug** transit passengers

durchforschen vt untr to explore

durchforsten [dʊrç'fɔrstən] vt untr (fig: Akten etc) to go through

durchfragen vr to find one's way by asking

durchfressen unreg vr to eat one's way through

durchführbar adj feasible, practicable

durchführen ['dʊrçfy:rən] vt to carry out; (Gesetz) to implement; (Kursus) to run

Durchführung f execution, performance

Durchgang ['dʊrçɡaŋ] m passage(way); (bei Produktion, Versuch) run; (Sport) round; (bei Wahl) ballot; ~ **verboten** no thoroughfare

durchgängig ['dʊrçɡɛŋɪç] adj universal, general

Durchgangs- zW: **Durchgangshandel** m transit trade; **Durchgangslager** nt transit camp; **Durchgangsstadium** nt transitory stage; **Durchgangsverkehr** m through traffic

durchgeben ['dʊrçɡe:bən] unreg vt (Rundf, TV: Hinweis, Wetter) to give; (Lottozahlen) to announce

durchgefroren ['dʊrçɡəfro:rən] adj (See) completely frozen; (Mensch) frozen stiff

durchgehen ['dʊrçɡe:ən] unreg vt (behandeln) to go over od through ▷ vi to go through; (ausreißen: Pferd) to break loose; (Mensch) to run away; **mein Temperament ging mit mir durch** my temper got the better of me; **jdm etw ~ lassen** to let sb get away with sth

durchgehend adj (Zug) through; (Öffnungszeiten) continuous

durchgeschwitzt ['dʊrçɡəʃvɪtst] adj soaked in sweat

durch- zW: **durchgreifen** unreg vi to take strong action; **durchhalten** unreg vi to last out ▷ vt to keep up; **Durchhaltevermögen**

nt staying power; **durchhängen** unreg vi (lit, fig) to sag; **durchhecheln** (umg) vt to gossip about; **durchkommen** unreg vi to get through; (überleben) to pull through

durchkreuzen vt untr to thwart, frustrate

durchlassen unreg vt (Person) to let through; (Wasser) to let in

durchlässig adj leaky

Durchlaucht ['dʊrçlaʊxt] (-, -en) f: **(Euer) ~** Your Highness

Durchlauf ['dʊrçlaʊf] m (Comput) run

durchlaufen unreg vt untr (Schule, Phase) to go through

Durchlauferhitzer (-s, -) m continuous-flow water heater

Durchlaufzeit f (Comput) length of the run

durch- zW: **durchleben** vt untr (Zeit) to live od go through; (Jugend, Gefühl) to experience; **durchlesen** unreg vt to read through; **durchleuchten** vt untr to X-ray; **durchlöchern** vt untr to perforate; (mit Löchern) to punch holes in; (mit Kugeln) to riddle; **durchmachen** vt to go through; **die Nacht durchmachen** to make a night of it

Durchmarsch m march through

Durchmesser (-s, -) m diameter

durchnässen vt untr to soak (through)

durch- zW: **durchnehmen** unreg vt to go over; **durchnummerieren** vt to number consecutively; **durchorganisieren** vt to organize down to the last detail; **durchpausen** vt to trace; **durchpeitschen** vt (lit) to whip soundly; (fig: Gesetzentwurf, Reform) to force through

durchqueren [dʊrç'kve:rən] vt untr to cross

durch- zW: **durchrechnen** vt to calculate; **durchregnen** vi unpers: **es regnet durchs Dach durch** the rain is coming through the roof; **Durchreiche** (-, -n) f (serving) hatch, pass-through (US); **Durchreise** f transit; **auf der Durchreise** passing through; (Güter) in transit; **Durchreisevisum** nt transit visa; **durchringen** unreg vr to make up one's mind finally; **durchrosten** vi to rust through; **durchrutschen** vi: **(durch etw) durchrutschen** (lit) to slip through (sth); (bei Prüfung) to scrape through (sth)

durchs [dʊrçs] = **durch das**

Durchsage ['dʊrçza:ɡə] f intercom od radio announcement

Durchsatz ['dʊrçzats] m (Produktion, Comput) throughput

durchschauen¹ ['dʊrçʃaʊən] vt, vi (lit) to look od see through

durchschauen² [dʊrç'ʃaʊən] vt untr (Person, Lüge) to see through

durchscheinen ['dʊrçʃaɪnən] unreg vi to shine through

durchscheinend adj translucent

durchschlafen ['dʊrçʃla:fən] unreg vi to sleep through

Durchschlag ['dʊrçʃla:k] m (Doppel) carbon copy; (Sieb) strainer

durchschlagen unreg vt (entzweischlagen) to split (in two); (sieben) to sieve ▷ vi (zum Vorschein kommen) to emerge, come out ▷ vr to get by

durchschlagend adj resounding; **(eine) ~e Wirkung haben** to be totally effective

Durchschlagpapier nt flimsy; (Kohlepapier) carbon paper

Durchschlagskraft f (von Geschoss) penetration; (fig: von Argument) decisiveness

durch- zW: **durchschlängeln** vr (durch etw: Mensch) to thread one's way through; **durchschlüpfen** vi to slip through; **durchschneiden** unreg vt to cut through

Durchschnitt ['dʊrçʃnɪt] m (Mittelwert) average; **über/unter dem ~** above/below average; **im ~** on average; **durchschnittlich** adj average ▷ adv on average; **durchschnittlich begabt/ groß** etc of average ability/height etc

Durchschnitts- zW: **Durchschnittsgeschwindigkeit** f average speed; **Durchschnittsmensch** m average man, man in the street; **Durchschnittswert** m average

durch- zW: **Durchschrift** f copy; **Durchschuss** m (Loch) bullet hole; **durchschwimmen** unreg vt untr to swim across; **durchsegeln** (umg) vi (nicht bestehen): **durch** od **bei etw durchsegeln** to fail od flunk (umg) (sth); **durchsehen** unreg vt to look through

durchsetzen[1] ['dʊrçzɛtsən] vt to enforce ▷ vr (Erfolg haben) to succeed; (sich behaupten) to get one's way; **seinen Kopf ~** to get one's own way

durchsetzen[2] [dʊrç'zɛtsən] vt untr to mix

Durchsicht ['dʊrçzɪçt] f looking through, checking

durchsichtig adj transparent; **Durchsichtigkeit** f transparency

durch- zW: **durchsickern** vi to seep through; (fig) to leak out; **durchsieben** vt to sieve; **durchsitzen** unreg vt (Sessel etc) to wear out (the seat of); **durchspielen** vt to go od run through; **durchsprechen** unreg vt to talk over; **durchstehen** unreg vt to live through; **Durchstehvermögen** nt endurance, staying power; **durchstellen** vt (Tel) to put through; **durchstöbern** [-'ʃtøːbərn] vt untr to ransack, search through; **durchstoßen** unreg vt, vi to break through (auch Mil); **durchstreichen** unreg vt to cross out; **durchstylen** vt to ponce up (umg); **durchsuchen** vt untr to search; **Durchsuchung** f search; **Durchsuchungsbefehl** m search warrant; **durchtrainieren** vt (Sportler, Körper): **gut durchtrainiert** in superb condition; **durchtränken** vt untr to soak; **durchtreten** unreg vt (Pedal) to step on; (Starter) to kick; **durchtrieben** adj cunning, wily; **durchwachsen** adj (lit: Speck) streaky; (fig: mittelmäßig) so-so

Durchwahl ['dʊrçvaːl] f (Tel) direct dialling; (bei Firma) extension

durch- zW: **durchweg** adv throughout, completely; **durchwursteln** (umg) vr to muddle through; **durchzählen** vt to count ▷ vi to count od number off; **durchzechen** vt untr: **eine durchzechte Nacht** a night of drinking; **durchziehen** unreg vt (Faden) to draw through ▷ vi to pass through; **eine Sache durchziehen** to finish off sth; **durchzucken** vt untr to shoot od flash through; **Durchzug** m (Luft) draught (Brit), draft (US); (von Truppen, Vögeln) passage; **durchzwängen** vt, vr to squeeze od force through

 SCHLÜSSELWORT

dürfen ['dʏrfən] unreg vi **1** (Erlaubnis haben) to be allowed to; **ich darf das** I'm allowed to (do that); **darf ich?** may I?; **darf ich ins Kino?** can od may I go to the cinema?; **es darf geraucht werden** you may smoke

2 (in Verneinungen): **er darf das nicht** he's not allowed to (do that); **das darf nicht geschehen** that must not happen; **da darf sie sich nicht wundern** that shouldn't surprise her; **das darf doch nicht wahr sein!** that can't be true!

3 (in Höflichkeitsformeln): **darf ich Sie bitten, das zu tun?** may od could I ask you to do that?; **wir freuen uns, Ihnen mitteilen zu dürfen** we are pleased to be able to tell you; **was darf es sein?** what can I get for you?

4 (können): **das dürfen Sie mir glauben** you can believe me

5 (Möglichkeit): **das dürfte genug sein** that should be enough; **es dürfte Ihnen bekannt sein, dass ...** as you will probably know ...

durfte etc ['dʊrftə] vb siehe **dürfen**

dürftig ['dʏrftɪç] adj (ärmlich) needy, poor; (unzulänglich) inadequate

dürr [dʏr] adj dried-up; (Land) arid; (mager) skinny

Dürre (-, -n) f aridity; (Zeit) drought

Durst [dʊrst] (-(e)s) m thirst; **~ haben** to be thirsty; **einen über den ~ getrunken haben** (umg) to have had one too many

durstig adj thirsty

Durststrecke f hard times pl

Dusche ['dʊʃə] (-, -n) f shower; **das war eine kalte ~** (fig) that really brought him/her etc down with a bump

duschen vi, vr to have a shower

Duschgelegenheit f shower facilities pl

Düse ['dyːzə] (-, -n) f nozzle; (Flugzeugdüse) jet

Dusel ['duːzəl] (umg) m: **da hat er (einen) ~ gehabt** he was lucky

Düsen- zW: **Düsenantrieb** m jet propulsion; **Düsenflugzeug** nt jet (plane); **Düsenjäger** m jet fighter

Dussel ['dʊsəl] (-s, -) (umg) m twit, berk

Düsseldorf ['dʏsəldɔrf] nt Dusseldorf

dusselig ['dʊsəlɪç], **dusslig** ['dʊslɪç] (umg) adj stupid

düster ['dy:stər] *adj* dark; (*Gedanken, Zukunft*) gloomy; **Düsterkeit** *f* darkness, gloom; gloominess

Dutzend ['dʊtsənt] (**-s, -e**) *nt* dozen; **~(e) Mal** a dozen times; **Dutzendware** (*pej*) *f* (cheap) mass-produced item; **dutzendweise** *adv* by the dozen

duzen ['du:tsən] *vt* to address with the familiar "du" form ▷ *vr* to address each other with the familiar "du" form; *siehe auch* **siezen**; *see culture note*

● **DUZEN/SIEZEN**

●
● There are two different forms of address
● in German: du and Sie. *Duzen* means
● addressing someone as "du" and *siezen*
● means addressing someone as "Sie". "Du"

● is used to address children, family and
● close friends. Students almost always use
● "du" to each other. "Sie" is used for all
● grown-ups and older teenagers.

Duzfreund *m* good friend

DVD (**-, -s**) *f abk* (= *Digital Versatile Disc*) DVD

Dynamik [dy'na:mɪk] *f* (*Phys*) dynamics; (*fig: Schwung*) momentum; (*von Mensch*) dynamism

dynamisch [dy'na:mɪʃ] *adj* (*lit, fig*) dynamic; (*rentendynamisch*) index-linked

Dynamit [dyna'mi:t] (**-s**) *nt* dynamite

Dynamo [dy'na:mo] (**-s, -s**) *m* dynamo

dz *abk* = **Doppelzentner**

D-Zug ['de:tsu:k] *m* through train; **ein alter Mann ist doch kein ~** (*umg*) I am going as fast as I can

d

Ee

E¹, e [eː] *nt* E, e; **E wie Emil** = E for Edward, E for Easy (*US*)

E² [eː] *abk* = **Eilzug; Europastraße**

Ebbe ['ɛbə] (**-, -n**) *f* low tide; **~ und Flut** ebb and flow

eben ['eːbən] *adj* level; (*glatt*) smooth ▷ *adv* just; (*bestätigend*) exactly; **das ist ~ so** that's just the way it is; **mein Bleistift war doch ~ noch da** my pencil was there (just) a minute ago; **~ deswegen** just because of that

Ebenbild *nt*: **das genaue ~ seines Vaters** the spitting image of his father

ebenbürtig *adj*: **jdm ~ sein** to be sb's peer

Ebene (**-, -n**) *f* plain; (*Math, Phys*) plane; (*fig*) level

eben- *zW*: **ebenerdig** *adj* at ground level; **ebenfalls** *adv* likewise; **Ebenheit** *f* levelness; (*Glätte*) smoothness; **Ebenholz** *nt* ebony; **ebenso** *adv* just as; **ebenso gut** just as well; **ebenso oft** just as often; **ebenso viel** just as much; **ebenso weit** just as far; **ebenso wenig** just as little

Eber ['eːbər] (**-s, -**) *m* boar

Eberesche *f* mountain ash, rowan

ebnen ['eːbnən] *vt* to level; **jdm den Weg ~** (*fig*) to smooth the way for sb

Echo ['ɛço] (**-s, -s**) *nt* echo; (**bei jdm**) **ein lebhaftes ~ finden** (*fig*) to meet with a lively response (from sb)

Echolot ['ɛçoloːt] *nt* (*Naut*) echo-sounder, sonar

Echse ['ɛksə] (**-, -n**) *f* (*Zool*) lizard

echt [ɛçt] *adj* genuine; (*typisch*) typical; **ich hab ~ keine Zeit** (*umg*) I really don't have any time; **Echtheit** *f* genuineness

Eckball ['ɛkbal] *m* corner (kick)

Ecke ['ɛkə] (**-, -n**) *f* corner; (*Math*) angle; **gleich um die ~** just around the corner; **an allen ~n und Enden sparen** (*umg*) to pinch and scrape; **jdn um die ~ bringen** (*umg*) to bump sb off; **mit jdm um ein paar ~n herum verwandt sein** (*umg*) to be distantly related to sb, be sb's second cousin twice removed (*hum*)

eckig *adj* angular

Eckzahn *m* eye tooth

Eckzins *m* (*Fin*) minimum lending rate

Ecstasy ['ɛkstəsɪ] *nt* (*Droge*) ecstasy

Ecuador [ekua'doːr] (**-s**) *nt* Ecuador

edel ['eːdəl] *adj* noble; **Edelganove** *m* gentleman criminal; **Edelgas** *nt* rare gas; **Edelmetall** *nt* rare metal; **Edelstein** *m* precious stone

Edinburg, Edinburgh ['eːdɪnbʊrk] *nt* Edinburgh

EDV (**-**) *f abk* (= *elektronische Datenverarbeitung*) EDP

EEG (**-**) *nt abk* (= *Elektroenzephalogramm*) EEG

Efeu ['eːfɔʏ] (**-s**) *m* ivy

Effeff [ɛf'ɛf] (**-**) (*umg*) *nt*: **etw aus dem ~ können** to be able to do sth standing on one's head

Effekt [ɛ'fɛkt] (**-(e)s, -e**) *m* effect

Effekten [ɛ'fɛktən] *pl* stocks *pl*; **Effektenbörse** *f* Stock Exchange

Effekthascherei [ɛfɛkthaʃə'raɪ] *f* sensationalism

effektiv [ɛfɛk'tiːf] *adj* effective, actual

Effet [ɛ'feː] (**-s**) *m* spin

EG (**-**) *f abk* (= *Europäische Gemeinschaft*) EC

egal [e'gaːl] *adj* all the same; **das ist mir ganz ~** it's all the same to me

egalitär [egali'tɛːr] *adj* (*geh*) egalitarian

Egge ['ɛgə] (**-, -n**) *f* (*Agr*) harrow

Egoismus [ego'ɪsmʊs] *m* selfishness, egoism

Egoist, in *m(f)* egoist; **egoistisch** *adj* selfish, egoistic

egozentrisch [ego'tsɛntrɪʃ] *adj* egocentric, self-centred (*Brit*), self-centered (*US*)

eh [eː] *adv*: **seit eh und je** for ages, since the year dot (*umg*); **ich komme eh nicht dazu** I won't get around to it anyway

e. h. *abk* = **ehrenhalber**

Ehe ['eːə] (**-, -n**) *f* marriage; **die ~ eingehen** (*form*) to enter into matrimony; **sie leben in wilder ~** (*veraltet*) they are living in sin

ehe *konj* before

Ehe- *zW*: **Ehebrecher** (**-s, -**) *m* adulterer; **Ehebrecherin** *f* adulteress; **Ehebruch** *m* adultery; **Ehefrau** *f* wife; **Eheleute** *pl* married couple *pl*; **ehelich** *adj* matrimonial; (*Kind*) legitimate

ehemalig *adj* former

ehemals *adv* formerly

Ehe- *zW*: **Ehemann** *m* married man; (*Partner*) husband; **Ehepaar** *nt* married couple; **Ehepartner** *m* husband; **Ehepartnerin** *f* wife

eher ['eːər] *adv* (*früher*) sooner; (*lieber*) rather, sooner; (*mehr*) more; **nicht ~ als** not before;

umso ~, als the more so because
Ehe- zW: **Ehering** m wedding ring;
Ehescheidung f divorce; **Eheschließung** f
marriage; **Ehestand** m: **in den Ehestand**
treten (form) to enter into matrimony
eheste, r, s ['eːəstə(r, s)] adj (früheste) first,
earliest; **am ~n** (am liebsten) soonest; (meist)
most; (am wahrscheinlichsten) most probably
Ehevermittlung f (Büro) marriage bureau
Eheversprechen nt (Jur) promise to marry
ehrbar ['eːrbaːr] adj honourable (Brit),
honorable (US), respectable
Ehre (-, -n) f honour (Brit), honor (US); **etw in**
~n halten to treasure od cherish sth
ehren vt to honour (Brit), honor (US)
Ehren- zW: **ehrenamtlich** adj honorary;
Ehrenbürgerrecht nt: **die Stadt verlieh**
ihr das Ehrenbürgerrecht she was given
the freedom of the city; **Ehrengast** m guest
of honour (Brit) od honor (US); **ehrenhaft**
adj honourable (Brit), honorable (US);
ehrenhalber adv: **er wurde ehrenhalber**
zum Vorsitzenden auf Lebenszeit ernannt
he was made honorary president for life;
Ehrenmann m man of honour (Brit) od honor
(US); **Ehrenmitglied** nt honorary member;
Ehrenplatz m place of honour (Brit) od
honor (US); **Ehrenrechte** pl civic rights pl;
ehrenrührig adj defamatory; **Ehrenrunde** f
lap of honour (Brit) od honor (US); **Ehrensache**
f point of honour (Brit) od honor (US);
Ehrensache! (umg) you can count on me;
Ehrentag m (Geburtstag) birthday; (großer
Tag) big day; **ehrenvoll** adj honourable (Brit),
honorable (US); **Ehrenwort** nt word of honour
(Brit) od honor (US); **Urlaub auf Ehrenwort**
parole
Ehr- zW: **ehrerbietig** adj respectful; **Ehrfurcht**
f awe, deep respect; **Ehrfurcht gebietend**
awesome; (Stimme) authoritative; **Ehrgefühl**
nt sense of honour (Brit) od honor (US); **Ehrgeiz**
m ambition; **ehrgeizig** adj ambitious; **ehrlich**
adj honest; **ehrlich verdientes Geld** hard-
earned money; **ehrlich gesagt ...** quite
frankly od honestly ...; **Ehrlichkeit** f honesty;
ehrlos adj dishonourable (Brit), dishonorable
(US)
Ehrung f honour(ing) (Brit), honor(ing) (US)
ehrwürdig adj venerable
Ei [aɪ] **(-(e)s, -er)** nt egg; **Eier** pl (umg!: Hoden)
balls pl (!); **jdn wie ein rohes Ei behandeln**
(fig) to handle sb with kid gloves; **wie aus**
dem Ei gepellt aussehen (umg) to look spruce
ei interj well, well; (beschwichtigend) now, now
Eibe ['aɪbə] **(-, -n)** f (Bot) yew
Eichamt ['aɪç|amt] nt Office of Weights and
Measures
Eiche (-, -n) f oak (tree)
Eichel (-, -n) f acorn; (Karten) club; (Anat) glans
eichen vt to calibrate
Eichhörnchen nt squirrel
Eichmaß nt standard
Eichung f standardization

Eid [aɪt] **(-(e)s, -e)** m oath; **eine Erklärung**
an ~es statt abgeben (Jur) to make a solemn
declaration
Eidechse ['aɪdɛksə] **(-, -n)** f lizard
eidesstattlich adj: **~e Erklärung** affidavit
Eid- zW: **Eidgenosse** m Swiss;
Eidgenossenschaft f: **Schweizerische**
Eidgenossenschaft Swiss Confederation;
eidlich adj (sworn) upon oath
Eidotter nt egg yolk
Eier- zW: **Eierbecher** m egg cup; **Eierkuchen** m
pancake; (Omelett) omelette (Brit), omelet (US);
Eierlikör m advocaat
eiern ['aɪərn] (umg) vi to wobble
Eier- zW: **Eierschale** f eggshell; **Eierstock** m
ovary; **Eieruhr** f egg timer
Eifel ['aɪfəl] **(-)** f Eifel (Mountains)
Eifer ['aɪfər] **(-s)** m zeal, enthusiasm; **mit**
großem ~ bei der Sache sein to put one's
heart into it; **im ~ des Gefechts** (fig) in the
heat of the moment; **Eifersucht** f jealousy;
eifersüchtig adj: **eifersüchtig (auf** +akk)
jealous (of)
eifrig ['aɪfrɪç] adj zealous, enthusiastic
Eigelb ['aɪgɛlp] **(-(e)s, -e** od **-)** nt egg yolk
eigen ['aɪgən] adj own; (eigenartig) peculiar;
(ordentlich) particular; (übergenau) fussy; **ich**
möchte kurz in ~er Sache sprechen I would
like to say something on my own account;
mit dem ihm ~en Lächeln with that smile
peculiar to him; **sich** dat **etw zu ~ machen** to
make sth one's own; **Eigenart** f (Besonderheit)
peculiarity; (Eigenschaft) characteristic;
eigenartig adj peculiar; **Eigenbau** m: **er fährt**
ein Fahrrad Marke Eigenbau (hum: umg)
he rides a home-made bike; **Eigenbedarf** m
one's own requirements pl; **Eigenbrötler,**
in (**-s, -**) m(f) loner, lone wolf; (komischer
Kauz) oddball (umg); **Eigengewicht** nt dead
weight; **eigenhändig** adj with one's own
hand; **Eigenheim** nt owner-occupied house;
Eigenheit f peculiarity; **Eigeninitiative**
f initiative of one's own; **Eigenkapital** nt
personal capital; (von Firma) company capital;
Eigenlob nt self-praise; **eigenmächtig** adj
high-handed; (eigenverantwortlich) taken/
done etc on one's own authority; (unbefugt)
unauthorized; **Eigenname** m proper name;
Eigennutz m self-interest
eigens adv expressly, on purpose
eigen- zW: **Eigenschaft** f quality, property,
attribute; **Eigenschaftswort** nt adjective;
Eigensinn m obstinacy; **eigensinnig** adj
obstinate; **eigenständig** adj independent;
Eigenständigkeit f independence
eigentlich adj actual, real ▷ adv actually,
really; **was willst du ~ hier?** what do you
want here anyway?
eigen- zW: **Eigentor** nt own goal; **Eigentum** nt
property; **Eigentümer, in** (**-s, -**) m(f) owner,
proprietor; **eigentümlich** adj peculiar;
Eigentümlichkeit f peculiarity
Eigentumsdelikt nt (Jur: Diebstahl) theft

Eigentumswohnung f freehold flat
Eigenvorsorge f private provision (for retirement etc)
eigenwillig adj with a mind of one's own
eignen ['aɪɡnən] vr to be suited
Eignung f suitability
Eignungsprüfung f aptitude test
Eignungstest (-(e)s, -s od **-e)** m aptitude test
Eilbote m courier; **per** od **durch ~n** express
Eilbrief m express letter
Eile (-) f haste; **es hat keine ~** there's no hurry
Eileiter ['aɪlaɪtər] m (Anat) Fallopian tube
eilen vi (Mensch) to hurry; (dringend sein) to be urgent
eilends adv hastily
Eilgut nt express goods pl, fast freight (US)
eilig adj hasty, hurried; (dringlich) urgent; **es ~ haben** to be in a hurry
Eil- zW: **Eiltempo** nt: **etw im Eiltempo machen** to do sth in a rush; **Eilzug** m fast stopping train; **Eilzustellung** f special delivery
Eimer ['aɪmər] **(-s, -)** m bucket, pail; **im ~ sein** (umg) to be up the spout
ein, e ['aɪn(ə)] num one ▷ indef art a, an
  ▷ adv: **nicht ~ noch aus wissen** not to know what to do; **E~/Aus** (an Geräten) on/off; **er ist ihr E~ und Alles** he means everything to her; **er geht bei uns ~ und aus** he is always round at our place
einander [aɪ'nandər] pron one another, each other
einarbeiten ['aɪn|arbaɪtən] vr: **sich (in etw** akk) **~** to familiarize o.s. (with sth)
Einarbeitungszeit f training period
einarmig ['aɪn|armɪç] adj one-armed
einäschern ['aɪn|ɛʃərn] vt (Leichnam) to cremate; (Stadt etc) to reduce to ashes
einatmen ['aɪn|a:tmən] vt, vi to inhale, breathe in
einäugig ['aɪn|ɔyɡɪç] adj one-eyed
Einbahnstraße ['aɪnba:nʃtrasə] f one-way street
Einband ['aɪnbant] m binding, cover
einbändig ['aɪnbɛndɪç] adj one-volume
einbauen ['aɪnbauən] vt to build in; (Motor) to install, fit
Einbau- zW: **Einbauküche** f (fully-)fitted kitchen; **Einbaumöbel** pl built-in furniture sing; **Einbauschrank** m fitted cupboard
einbegriffen ['aɪnbəɡrɪfən] adj included, inclusive
einbehalten ['aɪnbəhaltən] unreg vt to keep back
einberufen unreg vt to convene; (Mil) to call up (Brit), draft (US)
Einberufung f convocation; call-up (Brit), draft (US)
Einberufungsbefehl m, **Einberufungsbescheid** m (Mil) call-up (Brit) od draft (US) papers pl
einbetten ['aɪnbɛtən] vt to embed
Einbettzimmer nt single room
einbeziehen ['aɪnbətsi:ən] unreg vt to include

einbiegen ['aɪnbi:ɡən] unreg vi to turn
einbilden ['aɪnbɪldən] vr: **sich** dat **etw ~** to imagine sth; **sich** dat **viel auf etw** akk **~:** stolz sein) to be conceited about sth
Einbildung f imagination; (Dünkel) conceit
Einbildungskraft f imagination
einbinden ['aɪnbɪndən] unreg vt to bind (up)
einbläuen ['aɪnblɔyən] (umg) vt: **jdm etw ~** to hammer sth into sb
einblenden ['aɪnblɛndən] vt to fade in
Einblick ['aɪnblɪk] m insight; **~ in die Akten nehmen** to examine the files; **jdm ~ in etw** akk **gewähren** to allow sb to look at sth
einbrechen ['aɪnbrɛçən] unreg vi (einstürzen) to fall in; (Einbruch verüben) to break in; **bei ~der Dunkelheit** at nightfall
Einbrecher (-s, -) m burglar
einbringen ['aɪnbrɪŋən] unreg vt to bring in; (Geld, Vorteil) to yield; (mitbringen) to contribute; **das bringt nichts ein** (fig) it's not worth it
einbrocken ['aɪnbrɔkən] (umg) vt: **jdm/sich etwas ~** to land sb/o.s. in it
Einbruch ['aɪnbrʊx] m (Hauseinbruch) break-in, burglary; (des Winters) onset; (Einsturz, Fin) collapse; (Mil: in Front) breakthrough; **bei ~ der Nacht** at nightfall
einbruchssicher adj burglar-proof
Einbuchtung ['aɪnbʊxtʊŋ] f indentation; (Bucht) inlet, bay
einbürgern ['aɪnbʏrɡərn] vt to naturalize
  ▷ vr to become adopted; **das hat sich so eingebürgert** that's become a custom
Einbürgerung f naturalization
Einbuße ['aɪnbu:sə] f loss, forfeiture
einbüßen ['aɪnby:sən] vt to lose, forfeit
einchecken ['aɪntʃɛkən] vt, vi to check in
eincremen ['aɪnkre:mən] vt to put cream on
eindämmen ['aɪndɛmən] vt (Fluss) to dam; (fig) to check, contain
eindecken ['aɪndɛkən] vr: **sich ~ (mit)** to lay in stocks (of) ▷ vt (umg: überhäufen): **mit Arbeit eingedeckt sein** to be inundated with work
eindeutig ['aɪndɔytɪç] adj unequivocal
eindeutschen ['aɪndɔytʃən] vt (Fremdwort) to Germanize
eindösen ['aɪndø:zən] (umg) vi to doze off
eindringen ['aɪndrɪŋən] unreg vi: **~ (in** +akk) to force one's way in(to); (in Haus) to break in(to); (in Land) to invade; (Gas, Wasser) to penetrate; **auf jdn ~** (mit Bitten) to pester sb
eindringlich adj forcible, urgent; **ich habe ihn ~ gebeten ...** I urged him ...
Eindringling m intruder
Eindruck ['aɪndrʊk] m impression
eindrücken ['aɪndrʏkən] vt to press in
eindrucksfähig adj impressionable
eindrucksvoll adj impressive
eine, r, s pron one; (jemand) someone; **wie kann ~r nur so dumm sein!** how could anybody be so stupid!; **es kam ~s zum anderen** it was (just) one thing after another; **sich** dat **~n genehmigen** (umg) to have a quick one
einebnen ['aɪn|e:bnən] vt (lit) to level (off); (fig)

to level out

Einehe ['aɪn|e:ə] f monogamy

eineiig ['aɪn|aɪç] adj (Zwillinge) identical

eineinhalb ['aɪn|aɪn'halp] num one and a half

einengen ['aɪn|ɛŋən] vt to confine, restrict

Einer ['aɪnər] (-) m (Math) unit; (Ruderboot) single scull

Einerlei ['aɪnər'laɪ] (-s) nt monotony; **einerlei** adj (gleichartig) the same kind of; **es ist mir einerlei** it is all the same to me

einerseits adv on the one hand

einfach ['aɪnfax] adj simple; (nicht mehrfach) single ▷ adv simply; **Einfachheit** f simplicity

einfädeln ['aɪnfɛ:dəln] vt (Nadel) to thread; (fig) to contrive

einfahren ['aɪnfa:rən] unreg vt to bring in; (Barriere) to knock down; (Auto) to run in ▷ vi to drive in; (Zug) to pull in; (Min) to go down

Einfahrt f (Vorgang) driving in; pulling in; (Min) descent; (Ort) entrance; (von Autobahn) slip road (Brit); entrance ramp (US)

Einfall ['aɪnfal] m (Idee) idea, notion; (Lichteinfall) incidence; (Mil) raid

einfallen unreg vi (einstürzen) to fall in, collapse; (Licht) to fall; (Mil) to raid; (einstimmen): ~ (**in** +akk) to join in (with); **etw fällt jdm ein** sth occurs to sb; **das fällt mir gar nicht ein!** I wouldn't dream of it; **sich** dat **etwas ~ lassen** to have a good idea; **dabei fällt mir mein Onkel ein, der ...** that reminds me of my uncle who ...; **es fällt mir jetzt nicht ein** I can't think of it od it won't come to me at the moment

einfallslos adj unimaginative

einfallsreich adj imaginative

einfältig ['aɪnfɛltɪç] adj simple(-minded)

Einfaltspinsel ['aɪnfaltspɪnzəl] (umg) m simpleton

Einfamilienhaus [aɪnfa'mi:liənhaus] nt detached house

einfangen ['aɪnfaŋən] unreg vt to catch

einfarbig ['aɪnfarbɪç] adj all one colour (Brit) od color (US); (Stoff etc) self-coloured (Brit), self-colored (US)

einfassen ['aɪnfasən] vt (Edelstein) to set; (Beet, Stoff) to edge

Einfassung f setting; border

einfetten ['aɪnfɛtən] vt to grease

einfinden ['aɪnfɪndən] unreg vr to come, turn up

einfliegen ['aɪnfli:gən] unreg vt to fly in

einfließen ['aɪnfli:sən] unreg vi to flow in

einflößen ['aɪnflø:sən] vt: **jdm etw ~** (lit) to give sb sth; (fig) to instil sth into sb

Einfluss ['aɪnflʊs] m influence; **~ nehmen** to bring an influence to bear; **Einflussbereich** m sphere of influence; **einflussreich** adj influential

einflüstern ['aɪnflʏstərn] vt: **jdm etw ~** to whisper sth to sb; (fig) to insinuate sth to sb

einförmig ['aɪnfœrmɪç] adj uniform; (eintönig) monotonous; **Einförmigkeit** f uniformity; monotony

einfrieren ['aɪnfri:rən] unreg vi to freeze (in) ▷ vt

to freeze; (Pol: Beziehungen) to suspend

einfügen ['aɪnfy:gən] vt to fit in; (zusätzlich) to add; (Comput) to insert

einfühlen ['aɪnfy:lən] vr: **sich in jdn ~** to empathize with sb

einfühlsam ['aɪnfy:lza:m] adj sensitive

Einfühlungsvermögen nt empathy; **mit großem ~** with a great deal of sensitivity

Einfuhr ['aɪnfu:r] (-) f import; **Einfuhrartikel** m imported article

einführen ['aɪnfy:rən] vt to bring in; (Mensch, Sitten) to introduce; (Ware) to import; **jdn in sein Amt ~** to install sb (in office)

Einfuhr- zW: **Einfuhrgenehmigung** f import permit; **Einfuhrkontingent** nt import quota; **Einfuhrsperre** f ban on imports; **Einfuhrstopp** m ban on imports

Einführung f introduction

Einführungspreis m introductory price

Einfuhrzoll m import duty

einfüllen ['aɪnfʏlən] vt to pour in

Eingabe ['aɪnga:bə] f petition; (Dateneingabe) input; **~/Ausgabe** (Comput) input/output

Eingang ['aɪngaŋ] m entrance; (Comm: Ankunft) arrival; (Sendung) post; **wir bestätigen den ~ Ihres Schreibens vom ...** we acknowledge receipt of your letter of the ...

eingängig ['aɪngɛŋɪç] adj catchy

eingangs adv at the outset ▷ präp +gen at the outset of

Eingangs- zW: **Eingangsbestätigung** f acknowledgement of receipt; **Eingangshalle** f entrance hall; **Eingangsstempel** m (Comm) receipt stamp

eingeben ['aɪnge:bən] unreg vt (Arznei) to give; (Daten etc) to enter; (Gedanken) to inspire

eingebettet ['aɪngəbetət] adj: **in** od **zwischen Hügeln ~** nestling among the hills

eingebildet ['aɪngəbɪldət] adj imaginary; (eitel) conceited; **~er Kranker** hypochondriac

Eingeborene, r ['aɪngəbo:rənə(r)] f(m) native

Eingebung f inspiration

eingedenk ['aɪngədɛŋk] präp +gen bearing in mind

eingefahren ['aɪngəfa:rən] adj (Verhaltensweise) well-worn

eingefallen ['aɪngəfalən] adj (Gesicht) gaunt

eingefleischt ['aɪngəflaɪʃt] adj inveterate; **~er Junggeselle** confirmed bachelor

eingefroren ['aɪngəfro:rən] adj frozen

eingehen ['aɪnge:ən] unreg vi (Aufnahme finden) to come in; (Sendung, Geld) to be received; (Tier, Pflanze) to die; (Firma) to fold; (schrumpfen) to shrink ▷ vt (abmachen) to enter into; (Wette) to make; **auf etw** akk **~** to go into sth; **auf jdn ~** to respond to sb; **jdm ~** (verständlich sein) to be comprehensible to sb; **auf einen Vorschlag/Plan ~** (zustimmen) to go along with a suggestion/plan; **bei dieser Hitze/ Kälte geht man ja ein!** (umg) this heat/cold is just too much!

eingehend adj in-depth, thorough

eingekeilt ['aɪngəkaɪlt] adj hemmed in; (fig)

trapped

eingekesselt ['aɪŋɡəkɛsəlt] *adj*: ~ **sein** to be encircled *od* surrounded

Eingemachte, s ['aɪŋɡəma:xtə(s)] *nt* preserves *pl*

eingemeinden ['aɪŋɡəmaɪndən] *vt* to incorporate

eingenommen ['aɪŋɡənɔmən] *adj*: ~ **(von)** fond (of), partial (to); ~ **(gegen)** prejudiced (against)

eingeschnappt ['aɪŋɡəʃnapt] (*umg*) *adj* cross; ~ **sein** to be in a huff

eingeschrieben ['aɪŋɡəʃri:bən] *adj* registered

eingeschworen ['aɪŋɡəʃvo:rən] *adj* confirmed; (*Gemeinschaft*) close

eingesessen ['aɪŋɡəzɛsən] *adj* old-established

eingespannt ['aɪŋɡəʃpant] *adj* busy

eingespielt ['aɪŋɡəʃpi:lt] *adj*: **aufeinander ~ sein** to be in tune with each other

Eingeständnis ['aɪŋɡəʃtɛntnɪs] *nt* admission, confession

eingestehen ['aɪŋɡəʃte:ən] *unreg vt* to confess

eingestellt ['aɪŋɡəʃtɛlt] *adj*: **ich bin im Moment nicht auf Besuch ~** I'm not prepared for visitors

eingetragen ['aɪŋɡətra:ɡən] *adj* (*Comm*) registered; **~er Gesellschaftssitz** registered office; **~es Warenzeichen** registered trademark

Eingeweide ['aɪŋɡəvaɪdə] (**-s, -**) *nt* innards *pl*, intestines *pl*

Eingeweihte, r ['aɪŋɡəvaɪtə(r)] *f(m)* initiate

eingewöhnen ['aɪŋɡəvø:nən] *vr*: **sich ~ (in** +*dat*) to settle down (in)

eingezahlt ['aɪŋɡətsa:lt] *adj*: **~es Kapital** paid-up capital

eingießen ['aɪŋgi:sən] *unreg vt* to pour (out)

eingleisig ['aɪŋɡlaɪzɪç] *adj* single-track; **er denkt sehr ~** (*fig*) he's completely single-minded

eingliedern ['aɪŋɡli:dərn] *vt*: ~ **(in** +*akk*) to integrate (into) ▷ *vr*: **sich ~ (in** +*akk*) to integrate o.s. (into)

eingraben ['aɪŋɡra:bən] *unreg vt* to dig in ▷ *vr* to dig o.s. in; **dieses Erlebnis hat sich seinem Gedächtnis eingegraben** this experience has engraved itself on his memory

eingreifen ['aɪŋɡraɪfən] *unreg vi* to intervene, interfere; (*Zahnrad*) to mesh

Eingreiftruppe *f* (*Mil*) strike force

eingrenzen ['aɪŋɡrɛntsən] *vt* to enclose; (*fig: Problem*) to delimit

Eingriff ['aɪŋɡrɪf] *m* intervention, interference; (*Operation*) operation

einhaken ['aɪnha:kən] *vt* to hook in ▷ *vr*: **sich bei jdm ~** to link arms with sb ▷ *vi* (*sich einmischen*) to intervene

Einhalt ['aɪnhalt] *m*: ~ **gebieten** +*dat* to put a stop to

einhalten *unreg vt* (*Regel*) to keep ▷ *vi* to stop

einhämmern ['aɪnhɛmərn] *vt*: **jdm etw ~** (*fig*) to hammer sth into sb

einhandeln ['aɪnhandəln] *vt*: **etw gegen** *od*

für etw ~ to trade sth for sth

einhändig ['aɪnhendɪç] *adj* one-handed

einhändigen ['aɪnhendɪɡən] *vt* to hand in

einhängen ['aɪnhɛŋən] *vt* to hang; (*Telefon: auch vi*) to hang up; **sich bei jdm ~** to link arms with sb

einheimisch ['aɪnhaɪmɪʃ] *adj* native

Einheimische, r *f(m)* local

einheimsen (*umg*) *vt* to bring home

einheiraten ['aɪnhaɪra:tən] *vi*: **in einen Betrieb ~** to marry into a business

Einheit ['aɪnhaɪt] *f* unity; (*Maß, Mil*) unit; **eine geschlossene ~ bilden** to form an integrated whole; **einheitlich** *adj* uniform

Einheits- *zW*: **Einheitsfront** *f* (*Pol*) united front; **Einheitsliste** *f* (*Pol*) single *od* unified list of candidates; **Einheitspreis** *m* uniform price

einheizen ['aɪnhaɪtsən] *vi*: **jdm (tüchtig) ~** (*umg: die Meinung sagen*) to make things hot for sb

einhellig ['aɪnhɛlɪç] *adj* unanimous ▷ *adv* unanimously

einholen ['aɪnho:lən] *vt* (*Tau*) to haul in; (*Fahne, Segel*) to lower; (*Vorsprung aufholen*) to catch up with; (*Verspätung*) to make up; (*Rat, Erlaubnis*) to ask ▷ *vi* (*einkaufen*) to buy, shop

Einhorn ['aɪnhɔrn] *nt* unicorn

einhüllen ['aɪnhʏlən] *vt* to wrap up

einhundert ['aɪn'hʊndərt] *num* one hundred

einig ['aɪnɪç] *adj* (*vereint*) united; **sich** *dat* ~ **sein** to be in agreement; ~ **werden** to agree

einige, r, s *adj, pron* some ▷ *pl* some; (*mehrere*) several; **mit Ausnahme ~r weniger** with a few exceptions; **vor ~n Tagen** the other day, a few days ago; **dazu ist noch ~s zu sagen** there are still one or two things to say about that; ~ **Mal** a few times

einigen *vt* to unite ▷ *vr*: **sich (auf etw** *akk*) ~ to agree (on sth)

einigermaßen *adv* somewhat; (*leidlich*) reasonably

einiges *pron siehe* **einige(r, s)**

einiggehen *unreg vi* to agree

Einigkeit *f* unity; (*Übereinstimmung*) agreement

Einigung *f* agreement; (*Vereinigung*) unification

einimpfen ['aɪn|ɪmpfən] *vt*: **jdm etw ~** to inoculate sb with sth; (*fig*) to impress sth upon sb

einjagen ['aɪnja:ɡən] *vt*: **jdm Furcht/einen Schrecken ~** to give sb a fright

einjährig ['aɪnjɛ:rɪç] *adj* of *od* for one year; (*Alter*) one-year-old; (*Pflanze*) annual

einkalkulieren ['aɪnkalkuli:rən] *vt* to take into account, allow for

einkassieren ['aɪnkasi:rən] *vt* (*Geld, Schulden*) to collect

Einkauf ['aɪnkaʊf] *m* purchase; (*Comm: Abteilung*) purchasing (department)

einkaufen *vt* to buy ▷ *vi* to shop; ~ **gehen** to go shopping

Einkäufer, in ['aɪnkɔʏfər(ɪn)] *m(f)* (*Comm*) buyer

Einkaufs- *zW*: **Einkaufsbummel** *m*: **einen**

Einkaufsbummel machen to go on a shopping spree; **Einkaufskorb** m shopping basket; **Einkaufsleiter, in** m(f) (Comm) chief buyer; **Einkaufsnetz** nt string bag; **Einkaufspreis** m cost price, wholesale price; **Einkaufswagen** m trolley (Brit), cart (US); **Einkaufszentrum** nt shopping centre

einkehren ['aɪnke:rən] vi (geh: Ruhe, Frühling) to come; **in einem Gasthof** ~ to (make a) stop at an inn

einkerben ['aɪnkɛrbən] vt to notch

einklagen ['aɪnkla:gən] vt (Schulden) to sue for (the recovery of)

einklammern ['aɪnklamərn] vt to put in brackets, bracket

Einklang ['aɪnklaŋ] m harmony

einkleiden ['aɪnklaɪdən] vt to clothe; (fig) to express

einklemmen ['aɪnklɛmən] vt to jam

einknicken ['aɪnknɪkən] vt (Papier) to fold ▷ vi (Knie) to give way

einkochen ['aɪnkɔxən] vt to boil down; (Obst) to preserve, bottle

Einkommen ['aɪnkɔmən] (-s, -) nt income

einkommensschwach adj low-income attrib

einkommensstark adj high-income attrib

Einkommensteuer, Einkommensteuer f income tax; **Einkommensteuererklärung, Einkommensteuererklärung** f income tax return

Einkommensverhältnisse pl (level of) income sing

einkreisen ['aɪnkraɪzən] vt to encircle

einkriegen ['aɪnkri:gən] (umg) vr: **sie konnte sich gar nicht mehr darüber ~, dass …** she couldn't get over the fact that …

Einkünfte ['aɪnkʏnftə] pl income sing, revenue sing

einladen ['aɪnla:dən] unreg vt (Person) to invite; (Gegenstände) to load; **jdn ins Kino ~** to take sb to the cinema

Einladung f invitation

Einlage ['aɪnla:gə] f (Programmeinlage) interlude; (Spareinlage) deposit; (Fin: Kapitaleinlage) investment; (Schuheinlage) insole; (Fußstütze) support; (Zahneinlage) temporary filling; (Koch) noodles, vegetables etc (in clear soup)

einlagern ['aɪnla:gərn] vt to store

Einlass ['aɪnlas] (-es, -e) m admission; **jdm ~ gewähren** to admit sb

einlassen unreg vt to let in; (einsetzen) to set in ▷ vr: **sich mit jdm/auf etw** akk ~ to get involved with sb/sth; **sich auf einen Kompromiss ~** to agree to a compromise; **ich lasse mich auf keine Diskussion ein** I'm not having any discussion about it

Einlauf ['aɪnlaʊf] m arrival; (von Pferden) finish; (Med) enema

einlaufen unreg vi to arrive, come in; (Sport) to finish; (Wasser) to run in; (Stoff) to shrink ▷ vt (Schuhe) to break in ▷ vr (Sport) to warm up; (Motor, Maschine) to run in; **jdm das Haus ~** to invade sb's house; **in den Hafen ~** to enter

the harbour

einläuten ['aɪnlɔytən] vt (neues Jahr) to ring in; (Sport: Runde) to sound the bell for

einleben ['aɪnle:bən] vr to settle down

Einlegearbeit f inlay

einlegen ['aɪnle:gən] vt (einfügen: Blatt, Sohle) to insert; (Koch) to pickle; (in Holz etc) to inlay; (Geld) to deposit; (Pause) to have; (Protest) to make; (Veto) to use; (Berufung) to lodge; **ein gutes Wort bei jdm ~** to put in a good word with sb

Einlegesohle f insole

einleiten ['aɪnlaɪtən] vt to introduce, start; (Geburt) to induce

Einleitung f introduction; induction

einlenken ['aɪnlɛŋkən] vi (fig) to yield, give way

einlesen ['aɪnle:zən] unreg vr: **sich in ein Gebiet ~** to get into a subject ▷ vt: **etw in etw** +akk ~ (Daten) to feed sth into sth

einleuchten ['aɪnlɔyçtən] vi: (jdm) ~ to be clear od evident (to sb)

einleuchtend adj clear

einliefern ['aɪnli:fərn] vt: ~ **(in** +akk) to take (into); **jdn ins Krankenhaus ~** to admit sb to hospital

Einlieferungsschein m certificate of posting

einlochen ['aɪnlɔxən] (umg) vt (einsperren) to lock up

einlösen ['aɪnlø:zən] vt (Scheck) to cash; (Schuldschein, Pfand) to redeem; (Versprechen) to keep

einmachen ['aɪnmaxən] vt to preserve

Einmachglas nt bottling jar

einmal ['aɪnma:l] adv once; (erstens) first of all, firstly; (später) one day; **nehmen wir ~ an** just let's suppose; **noch ~** once more; **nicht ~** not even; **auf ~** all at once; **es war ~** once upon a time there was/were; ~ **ist keinmal** (Sprichwort) once doesn't count; **waren Sie schon ~ in Rom?** have you ever been to Rome?

Einmaleins nt multiplication tables pl; (fig) ABC, basics pl

einmalig adj unique; (einmal geschehend) single; (prima) fantastic

Einmalzahlung f one-off payment

Einmannbetrieb m one-man business

Einmannbus m one-man-operated bus

Einmarsch ['aɪnmarʃ] m entry; (Mil) invasion

einmarschieren vi to march in

einmengen ['aɪnmɛŋən] vr: **sich (in etw** +akk) ~ to interfere (with sth)

einmieten ['aɪnmi:tən] vr: **sich bei jdm ~** to take lodgings with sb

einmischen ['aɪnmɪʃən] vr: **sich (in etw** +akk) ~ to interfere (with sth)

einmotten ['aɪnmɔtən] vt (Kleider etc) to put in mothballs

einmünden ['aɪnmʏndən] vi: ~ **in** +akk (subj: Fluss) to flow od run into, join; (: Straße: in Platz) to run into; (: in andere Straße) to run into, join

einmütig ['aɪnmy:tɪç] adj unanimous

einnähen ['aɪnnɛ:ən] vt (enger machen) to take in

99

Einnahme ['aɪnnaːmə] (-, -n) f (Geld) takings pl, revenue; (von Medizin) taking; (Mil) capture, taking; **~n und Ausgaben** income and expenditure; **Einnahmeausfall** f (Wirts) drop in takings od revenue; (von Staat) revenue shortfall; **Einnahmequelle** f source of income

einnehmen ['aɪnneːmən] unreg vt to take; (Stellung, Raum) to take up; **~ für/gegen** to persuade in favour of/against

einnehmend adj charming

einnicken ['aɪnnɪkən] vi to nod off

einnisten ['aɪnnɪstən] vr to nest; (fig) to settle o.s.

Einöde ['aɪn|øːdə] (-, -n) f desert, wilderness

einordnen ['aɪn|ɔrdnən] vt to arrange, fit in ▷ vr to adapt; (Aut) to get in(to) lane

einpacken ['aɪnpakən] vt to pack (up)

einparken ['aɪnparkən] vt, vi to park

einpauken ['aɪnpaʊkən] (umg) vt: **jdm etw ~** to drum sth into sb

einpendeln ['aɪnpɛndəln] vr to even out

einpennen ['aɪnpɛnən] (umg) vi to drop off

einpferchen ['aɪnpfɛrçən] vt to pen in; (fig) to coop up

einpflanzen ['aɪnpflantsən] vt to plant; (Med) to implant

einplanen ['aɪnplaːnən] vt to plan for

einprägen ['aɪnprɛːgən] vt to impress, imprint; (beibringen): **jdm etw ~** to impress sth on sb; **sich** dat **etw ~** to memorize sth

einprägsam ['aɪnprɛːkzaːm] adj easy to remember; (Melodie) catchy

einprogrammieren ['aɪnprogramiːrən] vt (Comput) to feed in

einprügeln ['aɪnpryːgəln] (umg) vt: **jdm etw ~** to din sth into sb

einquartieren ['aɪnkvartiːrən] vt (Mil) to billet; **Gäste bei Freunden ~** to put visitors up with friends

einrahmen ['aɪnraːmən] vt to frame

einrasten ['aɪnrastən] vi to engage

einräumen ['aɪnrɔymən] vt (ordnend) to put away; (überlassen: Platz) to give up; (zugestehen) to admit, concede

einrechnen ['aɪnrɛçnən] vt to include; (berücksichtigen) to take into account

einreden ['aɪnreːdən] vt: **jdm/sich etw ~** to talk sb/o.s. into believing sth ▷ vi: **auf jdn ~** to keep on and on at sb

Einreibemittel nt liniment

einreiben ['aɪnraɪbən] unreg vt to rub in

einreichen ['aɪnraɪçən] vt to hand in; (Antrag) to submit

einreihen ['aɪnraɪən] vt (einordnen, einfügen) to put in; (klassifizieren) to classify ▷ vr (Auto) to get in lane; **etw in etw** akk **~** to put sth into sth

Einreise ['aɪnraɪzə] f entry; **Einreisebestimmungen** pl entry regulations pl; **Einreiseerlaubnis** f entry permit; **Einreisegenehmigung** f entry permit

einreisen ['aɪnraɪzən] vi: **in ein Land ~** to enter a country

Einreiseverbot nt refusal of entry

Einreisevisum nt entry visa

einreißen ['aɪnraɪsən] unreg vt (Papier) to tear; (Gebäude) to pull down ▷ vi to tear; (Gewohnheit werden) to catch on

einrenken ['aɪnrɛŋkən] vt (Gelenk, Knie) to put back in place; (fig: umg) to sort out ▷ vr (fig: umg) to sort itself out

einrichten ['aɪnrɪçtən] vt (Haus) to furnish; (schaffen) to establish, set up; (arrangieren) to arrange; (möglich machen) to manage ▷ vr (in Haus) to furnish one's house; **sich ~ (auf** +akk) (sich vorbereiten) to prepare o.s. (for); (sich anpassen) to adapt (to)

Einrichtung f (Wohnungseinrichtung) furnishings pl; (öffentliche Anstalt) organization; (Dienste) service; (Laboreinrichtung etc) equipment; (Gewohnheit): **zur ständigen ~ werden** to become an institution

Einrichtungsgegenstand m item of furniture

einrosten ['aɪnrɔstən] vi to get rusty

einrücken ['aɪnrykən] vi (Mil: Soldat) to join up; (: in Land) to move in ▷ vt (Anzeige) to insert; (Zeile, Text) to indent

Eins [aɪns] (-, -en) f one; **eins** num one; **es ist mir alles eins** it's all one to me; **eins zu eins** (Sport) one all; **eins a** (umg) first-rate

einsalzen ['aɪnzaltsən] vt to salt

einsam ['aɪnzaːm] adj lonely, solitary; **~e Klasse/Spitze** (umg: hervorragend) absolutely fantastic; **Einsamkeit** f loneliness, solitude

einsammeln ['aɪnzaməln] vt to collect

Einsatz ['aɪnzats] m (Teil) insert; (an Kleid) insertion; (Tischeinsatz) leaf; (Verwendung) use, employment; (Spieleinsatz) stake; (Risiko) risk; (Mil) operation; (Mus) entry; **im ~** in action; **etw unter ~ seines Lebens tun** to risk one's life to do sth; **Einsatzbefehl** m order to go into action; **einsatzbereit** adj ready for action; **Einsatzkommando** nt (Mil) task force

einschalten ['aɪnʃaltən] vt (Elek) to switch on; (einfügen) to insert; (Pause) to make; (Aut: Gang) to engage; (Anwalt) to bring in ▷ vr (dazwischentreten) to intervene

Einschaltquote f (TV) viewing figures pl

einschärfen ['aɪnʃɛrfən] vt: **jdm etw ~** to impress sth on sb

einschätzen ['aɪnʃɛtsən] vt to estimate, assess ▷ vr to rate o.s.

einschenken ['aɪnʃɛŋkən] vt to pour out

einscheren ['aɪnʃeːrən] vi to get back (into lane)

einschicken ['aɪnʃɪkən] vt to send in

einschieben ['aɪnʃiːbən] unreg vt to push in; (zusätzlich) to insert; **eine Pause ~** to have a break

einschiffen ['aɪnʃɪfən] vt to ship ▷ vr to embark, go on board

einschl. abk (= einschließlich) inc.

einschlafen ['aɪnʃlaːfən] unreg vi to fall asleep, go to sleep; (fig: Freundschaft) to peter out

einschläfern ['aɪnʃlɛːfərn] vt (schläfrig machen) to make sleepy; (Gewissen) to soothe; (narkotisieren) to give a soporific to; (töten: Tier) to put to sleep

einschläfernd *adj* (*Med*) soporific; (*langweilig*) boring; (*Stimme*) lulling

Einschlag ['aɪnʃlaːk] *m* impact; (*Aut*) lock; (*fig: Beimischung*) touch, hint

einschlagen ['aɪnʃlaːgən] *unreg vt* to knock in; (*Fenster*) to smash, break; (*Zähne, Schädel*) to smash in; (*Steuer*) to turn; (*kürzer machen*) to take up; (*Ware*) to pack, wrap up; (*Weg, Richtung*) to take ▷ *vi* to hit; (*sich einigen*) to agree; (*Anklang finden*) to work, succeed; **es muss irgendwo eingeschlagen haben** something must have been struck by lightning; **gut ~** (*umg*) to go down well, be a big hit; **auf jdn ~** to hit sb

einschlägig ['aɪnʃlɛːgɪç] *adj* relevant; **er ist ~ vorbestraft** (*Jur*) he has a previous conviction for a similar offence

einschleichen ['aɪnʃlaɪçən] *unreg vr* (*in Haus, fig: Fehler*) to creep in, steal in; (*in Vertrauen*) to worm one's way in

einschleppen ['aɪnʃlɛpən] *vt* (*fig: Krankheit etc*) to bring in

einschleusen ['aɪnʃlɔyzən] *vt:* **~ (in +***akk***)** to smuggle in(to)

einschließen ['aɪnʃliːsən] *unreg vt* (*Kind*) to lock in; (*Häftling*) to lock up; (*Gegenstand*) to lock away; (*Bergleute*) to cut off; (*umgeben*) to surround; (*Mil*) to encircle; (*fig*) to include, comprise ▷ *vr* to lock o.s. in

einschließlich *adv* inclusive ▷ *präp +gen* inclusive of, including

einschmeicheln ['aɪnʃmaɪçəln] *vr:* **sich (bei jdn) ~** to ingratiate o.s. (with sb)

einschmuggeln ['aɪnʃmʊgəln] *vt:* **~ (in +***akk***)** to smuggle in(to)

einschnappen ['aɪnʃnapən] *vi* (*Tür*) to click to; (*fig*) to be touchy; **eingeschnappt sein** to be in a huff

einschneidend ['aɪnʃnaɪdənt] *adj* incisive

einschneien ['aɪnʃnaɪən] *vi:* **eingeschneit sein** to be snowed in

Einschnitt ['aɪnʃnɪt] *m* (*Med*) incision; (*im Tal, Gebirge*) cleft; (*im Leben*) decisive point

einschnüren ['aɪnʃnyːrən] *vt* (*einengen*) to cut into; **dieser Kragen schnürt mir den Hals ein** this collar is strangling me

einschränken ['aɪnʃrɛŋkən] *vt* to limit, restrict; (*Kosten*) to cut down, reduce ▷ *vr* to cut down (on expenditure); **~d möchte ich sagen, dass ...** I'd like to qualify that by saying ...

einschränkend *adj* restrictive

Einschränkung *f* restriction, limitation; reduction; (*von Behauptung*) qualification

Einschreibbrief, Einschreibebrief *m* registered (*Brit*) *od* certified (*US*) letter

einschreiben ['aɪnʃraɪbən] *unreg vt* to write in; (*Post*) to send by registered (*Brit*) *od* certified (*US*) mail ▷ *vr* to register; (*Univ*) to enrol; **Einschreiben** *nt* registered (*Brit*) *od* certified (*US*) letter

einschreiten ['aɪnʃraɪtən] *unreg vi* to step in,

intervene; **~ gegen** to take action against

Einschub ['aɪnʃuːp] (**-(e)s, -̈e**) *m* insertion

einschüchtern ['aɪnʃʏçtərn] *vt* to intimidate

Einschüchterung ['aɪnʃʏçtərʊŋ] *f* intimidation

einschulen ['aɪnʃuːlən] *vt:* **eingeschult werden** (*Kind*) to start school

einschweißen ['aɪnʃvaɪsən] *vt* (*in Plastik*) to shrink-wrap; (*Tech*): **etw in etw** *akk* **~** to weld sth into sth

einschwenken ['aɪnʃvɛŋkən] *vi:* **~ (in +***akk***)** to turn *od* swing in(to)

einsehen ['aɪnzeːən] *unreg vt* (*prüfen*) to inspect; (*Fehler etc*) to recognize; (*verstehen*) to see; **das sehe ich nicht ein** I don't see why; **Einsehen (-s)** *nt* understanding; **ein Einsehen haben** to show understanding

einseifen ['aɪnzaɪfən] *vt* to soap, lather; (*fig: umg*) to take in, con

einseitig ['aɪnzaɪtɪç] *adj* one-sided; (*Pol*) unilateral; (*Ernährung*) unbalanced; (*Diskette*) single-sided; **Einseitigkeit** *f* one-sidedness

einsenden ['aɪnzɛndən] *unreg vt* to send in

Einsender, in (**-s, -**) *m(f)* sender, contributor

Einsendeschluss *m* closing date (for entries)

Einsendung *f* sending in

einsetzen ['aɪnzɛtsən] *vt* to put (in); (*in Amt*) to appoint, install; (*Geld*) to stake; (*verwenden*) to use; (*Mil*) to employ ▷ *vi* (*beginnen*) to set in; (*Mus*) to enter, come in ▷ *vr* to work hard; **sich für jdn/etw ~** to support sb/sth; **ich werde mich dafür ~, dass ...** I will do what I can to see that ...

Einsicht ['aɪnzɪçt] *f* insight; (*in Akten*) look, inspection; **zu der ~ kommen, dass ...** to come to the conclusion that ...

einsichtig *adj* (*Mensch*) judicious; **jdm etw ~ machen** to make sb understand *od* see sth

Einsichtnahme (-, -n) *f* (*form*) perusal; **„zur ~"** "for attention"

einsichtslos *adj* unreasonable

einsichtsvoll *adj* understanding

Einsiedler ['aɪnziːdlər] (**-s, -**) *m* hermit

einsilbig ['aɪnzɪlbɪç] *adj* (*lit, fig*) monosyllabic; **Einsilbigkeit** *f* (*fig*) taciturnity

einsinken ['aɪnzɪŋkən] *unreg vi* to sink in

Einsitzer ['aɪnzɪtsər] (**-s, -**) *m* single-seater

einspannen ['aɪnʃpanən] *vt* (*Werkstück, Papier*) to put (in), insert; (*Pferde*) to harness; (*umg: Person*) to rope in; **jdn für seine Zwecke ~** to use sb for one's own ends

einsparen ['aɪnʃpaːrən] *vt* to save, economize on; (*Kosten*) to cut down on; (*Posten*) to eliminate

Einsparung *f* saving

einspeichern ['aɪnʃpaɪçərn] *vt:* **etw (in etw** *akk*) **~** (*Comput*) to feed sth in(to sth)

einsperren ['aɪnʃpɛrən] *vt* to lock up

einspielen ['aɪnʃpiːlən] *vr* (*Sport*) to warm up ▷ *vt* (*Film: Geld*) to bring in; (*Instrument*) to play in; **sich aufeinander ~** to become attuned to each other; **gut eingespielt** running smoothly

einsprachig ['aɪnʃpraːxɪç] *adj* monolingual

einspringen ['aɪnʃprɪŋən] *unreg vi* (*aushelfen*) to stand in; (*mit Geld*) to help out

einspritzen ['aɪnʃprɪtsən] *vt* to inject

Einspritzmotor *m* (*Aut*) injection engine

Einspruch ['aɪnʃprʊx] *m* protest, objection; **~ einlegen** (*Jur*) to file an objection

Einspruchsfrist *f* (*Jur*) period for filing an objection

Einspruchsrecht *nt* veto

einspurig ['aɪnʃpuːrɪç] *adj* single-lane; (*Eisenb*) single-track

einst [aɪnst] *adv* once; (*zukünftig*) one *od* some day

Einstand ['aɪnʃtant] *m* (*Tennis*) deuce; (*Antritt*) entrance (to office); **er hat gestern seinen ~ gegeben** yesterday he celebrated starting his new job

einstechen ['aɪnʃtɛçən] *unreg vt* to pierce

einstecken ['aɪnʃtɛkən] *vt* to stick in, insert; (*Brief*) to post, mail (*US*); (*Elek: Stecker*) to plug in; (*Geld*) to pocket; (*mitnehmen*) to take; (*überlegen sein*) to put in the shade; (*hinnehmen*) to swallow

einstehen ['aɪnʃteːən] *unreg vi*: **für jdn ~** to vouch for sb; **für etw ~** to guarantee sth, vouch for sth; (*Ersatz leisten*) to make good sth

einsteigen ['aɪnʃtaɪgən] *unreg vi* to get in *od* on; (*in Schiff*) to go on board; (*sich beteiligen*) to come in; (*hineinklettern*) to climb in; **~!** (*Eisenb etc*) all aboard!

Einsteiger(-s, -) (*umg*) *m* beginner

einstellbar *adj* adjustable

einstellen ['aɪnʃtɛlən] *vt* (*in Firma*) to employ, take on; (*aufhören*) to stop; (*Geräte*) to adjust; (*Kamera etc*) to focus; (*Sender, Radio*) to tune in to; (*unterstellen*) to put ▷ *vi* to take on staff/ workers ▷ *vr* (*anfangen*) to set in; (*kommen*) to arrive; **Zahlungen ~** to suspend payment; **etw auf etw** *akk* **~** to adjust sth to sth; to focus sth on sth; **sich auf jdn/etw ~** to adapt to sb/ prepare o.s. for sth

einstellig *adj* (*Zahl*) single-digit

Einstellplatz *m* (*auf Hof*) carport; (*in Großgarage*) (covered) parking space

Einstellung *f* (*Aufhören*) suspension, cessation; (*von Gerät*) adjustment; (*von Kamera etc*) focusing; (*von Arbeiter etc*) appointment; (*Haltung*) attitude

Einstellungsgespräch *nt* interview

Einstellungsstopp *m* halt in recruitment

Einstieg ['aɪnʃtiːk] *m* (**-(e)s, -e**) entry; (*fig*) approach; (*von Bus, Bahn*) door; **kein ~** exit only

einstig ['aɪnstɪç] *adj* former

einstimmen ['aɪnʃtɪmən] *vi* to join in ▷ *vt* (*Mus*) to tune; (*in Stimmung bringen*) to put in the mood

einstimmig *adj* unanimous; (*Mus*) for one voice; **Einstimmigkeit** *f* unanimity

einstmalig *adj* former

einstmals *adv* once, formerly

einstöckig ['aɪnʃtœkɪç] *adj* two-storeyed (*Brit*), two-storied (*US*)

einstöpseln ['aɪnʃtœpsəln] *vt*: **etw (in etw**

+akk) ~: *Elek*) to plug sth in(to sth)

einstudieren ['aɪnʃtudiːrən] *vt* to study, rehearse

einstufen ['aɪnʃtuːfən] *vt* to classify

Einstufung *f*: **nach seiner ~ in eine höhere Gehaltsklasse** after he was put on a higher salary grade

einstündig ['aɪnʃtʏndɪç] *adj* one-hour *attrib*

einstürmen ['aɪnʃtʏrmən] *vi*: **auf jdn ~** to rush at sb; (*Eindrücke*) to overwhelm sb

Einsturz ['aɪnʃtʊrts] *m* collapse

einstürzen ['aɪnʃtʏrtsən] *vi* to fall in, collapse; **auf jdn ~** (*fig*) to overwhelm sb

Einsturzgefahr *f* danger of collapse

einstweilen *adv* meanwhile; (*vorläufig*) temporarily, for the time being

einstweilig *adj* temporary; **~e Verfügung** (*Jur*) temporary *od* interim injunction

eintägig ['aɪntɛːgɪç] *adj* one-day

Eintagsfliege ['aɪntaːksfliːgə] *f* (*Zool*) mayfly; (*fig*) nine-day wonder

eintauchen ['aɪntaʊxən] *vt* to immerse, dip in ▷ *vi* to dive

eintauschen ['aɪntaʊʃən] *vt* to exchange

eintausend ['aɪntaʊzənt] *num* one thousand

einteilen ['aɪntaɪlən] *vt* (*in Teile*) to divide (up); (*Menschen*) to assign

einteilig *adj* one-piece

eintönig ['aɪntøːnɪç] *adj* monotonous; **Eintönigkeit** *f* monotony

Eintopf ['aɪntɔpf] *m* stew

Eintopfgericht ['aɪntɔpfgərɪçt] *nt* stew

Eintracht ['aɪntraxt] (**-**) *f* concord, harmony

einträchtig ['aɪntrɛçtɪç] *adj* harmonious

Eintrag ['aɪntraːk] (**-(e)s, ⸚e**) *m* entry; **amtlicher ~** entry in the register

eintragen ['aɪntraːgən] *unreg vt* (*in Buch*) to enter; (*Profit*) to yield ▷ *vr* to put one's name down; **jdm etw ~** to bring sb sth

einträglich ['aɪntrɛːklɪç] *adj* profitable

Eintragung *f*: **~ (in** *+akk*) entry (in)

eintreffen ['aɪntrɛfən] *unreg vi* to happen; (*ankommen*) to arrive; (*fig: wahr werden*) to come true

eintreiben ['aɪntraɪbən] *unreg vt* (*Geldbeträge*) to collect

eintreten ['aɪntreːtən] *unreg vi* (*hineingehen*) to enter; (*sich ereignen*) to occur ▷ *vt* (*Tür*) to kick open; **in etw** *akk* **~** to enter sth; (*in Klub, Partei*) to join sth; **für jdn/etw ~** to stand up for sb/ sth

eintrichtern ['aɪntrɪçtərn] (*umg*) *vt*: **jdm etw ~** to drum sth into sb

Eintritt ['aɪntrɪt] *m* (*Betreten*) entrance; (*in Klub etc*) joining; **~ frei** admission free; „**~ verboten"** "no admittance"; **bei ~ der Dunkelheit** at nightfall

Eintritts- *zW*: **Eintrittsgeld** *nt* admission charge; **Eintrittskarte** *f* (admission) ticket; **Eintrittspreis** *m* admission charge

eintrocknen ['aɪntrɔknən] *vi* to dry up

eintrudeln ['aɪntruːdəln] (*umg*) *vi* to drift in

eintunken ['aɪntʊŋkən] *vt* (*Brot*): **etw in etw**

akk ~ to dunk sth in sth

einüben ['aın|y:bən] *vt* to practise (*Brit*), practice (*US*), drill

einverleiben ['aınferlaıbən] *vt* to incorporate; (*Gebiet*) to annex; **sich** *dat* **etw** ~ (*fig: geistig*) to assimilate sth

Einvernehmen ['aınferne:mən] (**-s, -**) *nt* agreement, understanding

einverstanden ['aınferʃtandən] *interj* agreed ▷ *adj*: ~ **sein** to agree, be agreed; **sich mit etw** ~ **erklären** to give one's agreement to sth

Einverständnis ['aınferʃtentnıs] (**-ses**) *nt* understanding; (*gleiche Meinung*) agreement; **im ~ mit jdm handeln** to act with sb's consent

Einwand ['aınvant] (**-(e)s, ¨e**) *m* objection; **einen ~ erheben** to raise an objection

Einwanderer ['aınvandərər] *m* immigrant

Einwanderin *f* immigrant

einwandern *vi* to immigrate

Einwanderung *f* immigration

einwandfrei *adj* perfect; **etw ~ beweisen** to prove sth beyond doubt

einwärts ['aınverts] *adv* inwards

Einwegflasche ['aınve:gflaʃə] *f* non-returnable bottle

Einwegpfand *nt* deposit on non-returnables

Einwegspritze *f* disposable (hypodermic) syringe

einweichen ['aınvaıçən] *vt* to soak

einweihen ['aınvaıən] *vt* (*Kirche*) to consecrate; (*Brücke*) to open; (*Gebäude*) to inaugurate; (*Person*): **in etw** *akk* ~ to initiate in sth; **er ist eingeweiht** (*fig*) he knows all about it

Einweihung *f* consecration; opening; inauguration; initiation

einweisen ['aınvaızən] *unreg vt* (*in Amt*) to install; (*in Arbeit*) to introduce; (*in Anstalt*) to send; (*in Krankenhaus*): ~ **(in** +*akk*) to admit (to)

Einweisung *f* installation; introduction; sending

einwenden ['aınvendən] *unreg vt*: **etwas ~ gegen** to object to, oppose

einwerfen ['aınverfən] *unreg vt* to throw in; (*Brief*) to post; (*Geld*) to put in, insert; (*Fenster*) to smash; (*äußern*) to interpose

einwickeln ['aınvıkəln] *vt* to wrap up; (*fig: umg*) to outsmart

einwilligen ['aınvılıgən] *vi*: **(in etw** *akk*) ~ to consent (to sth), agree (to sth)

Einwilligung *f* consent

einwirken ['aınvırkən] *vi*: **auf jdn/etw** ~ to influence sb/sth

Einwirkung *f* influence

Einwohner, in ['aınvo:nər(ın)] (**-s, -**) *m(f)* inhabitant; **Einwohnermeldeamt** *nt* registration office; **sich beim Einwohnermeldeamt (an)melden** ≈ to register with the police; **Einwohnerschaft** *f* population, inhabitants *pl*

Einwurf ['aınvʊrf] *m* (*Öffnung*) slot; (*Einwand*) objection; (*Sport*) throw-in

Einzahl ['aıntsa:l] *f* singular

einzahlen *vt* to pay in

Einzahlung *f* payment; (*auf Sparkonto*) deposit

einzäunen ['aıntsɔynən] *vt* to fence in

einzeichnen ['aıntsaıçnən] *vt* to draw in

Einzel ['aıntsəl] (**-s, -**) *nt* (*Tennis*) singles *pl*

Einzel- *zW*: **Einzelaufstellung** *f* (*Comm*) itemized list; **Einzelbett** *nt* single bed; **Einzelblattzuführung** *f* sheet feed; **Einzelfall** *m* single instance, individual case; **Einzelgänger, in** *m(f)* loner; **Einzelhaft** *f* solitary confinement; **Einzelhandel** *m* retail trade; **im Einzelhandel erhältlich** available retail; **Einzelhandelsgeschäft** *nt* retail outlet; **Einzelhandelspreis** *m* retail price; **Einzelhändler** *m* retailer; **Einzelheit** *f* particular, detail; **Einzelkind** *nt* only child

Einzeller ['aıntsɛlər] (**-s, -**) *m* (*Biol*) single-celled organism

einzeln *adj* single; (*von Paar*) odd ▷ *adv* singly; ~ **angeben** to specify; **E~e** some (people), a few (people); **der/die E~e** the individual; **das E~e** the particular; **ins E~e gehen** to go into detail(s); **etw im E~en besprechen** to discuss sth in detail; ~ **aufführen** to list separately *od* individually; **bitte ~ eintreten** please come in one (person) at a time

Einzelteil *nt* individual part; (*Ersatzteil*) spare part; **etw in seine ~e zerlegen** to take sth to pieces, dismantle sth

Einzelzimmer *nt* single room

einziehen ['aıntsi:ən] *unreg vt* to draw in, take in; (*Kopf*) to duck; (*Fühler, Antenne, Fahrgestell*) to retract; (*Steuern, Erkundigungen*) to collect; (*Mil*) to call up, draft (*US*); (*aus dem Verkehr ziehen*) to withdraw; (*konfiszieren*) to confiscate ▷ *vi* to move in; (*Friede, Ruhe*) to come; (*Flüssigkeit*): ~ **(in** +*akk*) to soak in(to)

einzig ['aıntsıç] *adj* only; (*ohnegleichen*) unique ▷ *adv*: ~ **und allein** solely; **das E~e** the only thing; **der/die E~e** the only one; **kein ~es Mal** not once, not one single time; **kein E~er** nobody, not a single person; **einzigartig** *adj* unique

Einzug ['aıntsu:k] *m* entry, moving in

Einzugsauftrag *m* (*Fin*) direct debit

Einzugsbereich *m* catchment area

Einzugsverfahren *nt* (*Fin*) direct debit

Eis [aıs] (**-es, -**) *nt* ice; (*Speiseeis*) ice cream; ~ **am Stiel** ice lolly (*Brit*), popsicle® (*US*); **Eisbahn** *f* ice *od* skating rink; **Eisbär** *m* polar bear; **Eisbecher** *m* sundae; **Eisbein** *nt* pig's trotters *pl*; **Eisberg** *m* iceberg; **Eisbeutel** *m* ice pack; **Eiscafé** *nt* = **Eisdiele**

Eischnee ['aıʃne:] *m* (*Koch*) beaten white of egg

Eisdecke *f* sheet of ice

Eisdiele *f* ice-cream parlour (*Brit*) *od* parlor (*US*)

Eisen ['aızən] (**-s, -**) *nt* iron; **zum alten ~ gehören** (*fig*) to be on the scrap heap

Eisenbahn *f* railway, railroad (*US*); **es ist (aller)höchste ~** (*umg*) it's high time; **Eisenbahner** (**-s, -**) *m* railwayman, railway employee, railroader (*US*); **Eisenbahnnetz** *nt* rail network; **Eisenbahnschaffner** *m*

railway guard, (railroad) conductor (US);
Eisenbahnüberführung f footbridge;
Eisenbahnübergang m level crossing, grade
crossing (US); **Eisenbahnwagen** m railway
od railroad (US) carriage; **Eisenbahnwaggon**,
Eisenbahnwagon (*Güterwagen*) goods wagon
Eisen- zW: **Eisenerz** nt iron ore; **eisenhaltig**
adj containing iron; **Eisenmangel** m
iron deficiency; **Eisenwarenhandlung** f
ironmonger's (Brit), hardware store (US)
eisern ['aɪzərn] adj iron; (*Gesundheit*) robust;
(*Energie*) unrelenting; (*Reserve*) emergency;
der E~e Vorhang the Iron Curtain; **in etw**
dat ~ **sein** to be adamant about sth; **er ist ~
bei seinem Entschluss geblieben** he stuck
firmly to his decision
Eis- zW: **Eisfach** nt freezer compartment,
icebox; **eisfrei** adj clear of ice; **eisgekühlt** adj
chilled; **Eishockey** nt ice hockey
eisig ['aɪzɪç] adj icy
Eis- zW: **Eiskaffee** m iced coffee; **eiskalt** adj icy
cold; **Eiskunstlauf** m figure skating; **Eislaufen**
nt ice-skating; **Eisläufer** m ice-skater; **Eismeer**
nt: **Nördliches/Südliches Eismeer** Arctic/
Antarctic Ocean; **Eispickel** m ice-axe (Brit),
ice-ax (US)
Eisprung ['aɪʃprʊŋ] m ovulation
Eis- zW: **Eisschießen** nt ≈ curling; **Eisscholle**
f ice floe; **Eisschrank** m fridge, icebox (US);
Eisstadion nt ice od skating rink; **Eiswürfel** m
ice cube; **Eiszapfen** m icicle; **Eiszeit** f Ice Age
eitel ['aɪtəl] adj vain; **Eitelkeit** f vanity
Eiter ['aɪtər] (**-s**) m pus
eiterig adj suppurating
eitern vi to suppurate
Ei- zW: **Eiweiß** (**-es, -e**) nt white of an egg;
(*Chem*) protein; **Eiweißgehalt** m protein
content; **Eizelle** f ovum
EKD f abk (= *Evangelische Kirche in Deutschland*)
German Protestant Church
Ekel[1] ['eːkəl] (**-s**) m nausea, disgust; **vor jdm/
etw einen ~ haben** to loathe sb/sth
Ekel[2] ['eːkəl] (**-s, -**) (umg) nt (*Mensch*) nauseating
person
ekelerregend adj nauseating, disgusting
ekelhaft adj, **ekelig** adj nauseating,
disgusting
ekeln vt to disgust ▷ vr: **sich vor etw** dat ~ to be
disgusted at sth; **es ekelt ihn** he is disgusted
EKG (**-**) nt abk (= *Elektrokardiogramm*) ECG
Eklat [e'klaː] (**-s**) m (geh: *Aufsehen*) sensation
eklig adj nauseating, disgusting
Ekstase [ɛk'staːzə] (**-, -n**) f ecstasy; **jdn in ~
versetzen** to send sb into ecstasies
Ekzem [ɛk'tseːm] (**-s, -e**) nt (*Med*) eczema
Elan [e'lãː] (**-s**) m élan
elastisch [e'lastɪʃ] adj elastic
Elastizität [elastitsi'tɛːt] f elasticity
Elbe ['ɛlbə] f (*Fluss*) Elbe
Elch [ɛlç] (**-(e)s, -e**) m elk
Elefant [ele'fant] m elephant; **wie ein ~ im
Porzellanladen** (umg) like a bull in a china
shop

elegant [ele'gant] adj elegant
Eleganz [ele'gants] f elegance
Elektrifizierung [elɛktrifi'tsiːrʊŋ] f
electrification
Elektriker [e'lɛktrikər] (**-s, -**) m electrician
elektrisch [e'lɛktrɪʃ] adj electric
elektrisieren [elɛktri'ziːrən] vt (lit, fig) to
electrify; (*Mensch*) to give an electric shock to
▷ vr to get an electric shock
Elektrizität [elɛktritsi'tɛːt] f electricity
Elektrizitätswerk nt electric power station
Elektroartikel [e'lɛktro|artɪkəl] m electrical
appliance
Elektrode [elɛk'troːdə] (**-, -n**) f electrode
Elektro- zW: **Elektrogerät** nt electrical
appliance; **Elektroherd** m electric
cooker; **Elektrokardiogramm** nt (*Med*)
electrocardiogram
Elektrolyse [elɛktro'lyːzə] (**-, -n**) f electrolysis
Elektromotor m electric motor
Elektron [e'lɛktrɔn] (**-s, -en**) nt electron
Elektronengehirn, Elektronenhirn nt
electronic brain
Elektronenrechner m computer
Elektronik [elɛk'troːnɪk] f electronics sing;
(*Teile*) electronics pl
elektronisch adj electronic; **~e Post** electronic
mail
Elektro- zW: **Elektrorasierer** (**-s, -**) m electric
razor; **Elektroschock** m (*Med*) electric shock,
electroshock; **Elektrotechniker** m electrician;
(*Ingenieur*) electrical engineer
Element [ele'mɛnt] (**-s, -e**) nt element; (*Elek*)
cell, battery
elementar [elemɛn'taːr] adj elementary;
(*naturhaft*) elemental; **Elementarteilchen** nt
(*Phys*) elementary particle
Elend ['eːlɛnt] (**-(e)s**) nt misery; **da kann man
das heulende ~ kriegen** (umg) it's enough to
make you scream; **elend** adj miserable; **mir
ist ganz elend** I feel really awful
elendiglich ['eːlɛndɪklɪç] adv miserably; **~
zugrunde gehen** to come to a wretched end
Elendsviertel nt slum
elf [ɛlf] num eleven; **Elf** (**-, en**) f (*Sport*) eleven
Elfe (**-, -n**) f elf
Elfenbein nt ivory; **Elfenbeinküste** f Ivory
Coast
Elfmeter m (*Sport*) penalty (kick)
Elfmeterschießen nt (*Sport*) penalty shoot-out
eliminieren [elimi'niːrən] vt to eliminate
elitär [eli'tɛːr] adj elitist ▷ adv in an elitist
fashion
Elite [e'liːtə] (**-, -n**) f elite
Elixier [elɪ'ksiːr] (**-s, -e**) nt elixir
Ellbogen m = **Ellenbogen**
Elle ['ɛlə] (**-, -n**) f ell; (*Maß*) ≈ yard
Ellenbogen m elbow; **die ~ gebrauchen** (umg)
to be pushy; **Ellenbogenfreiheit** f (fig) elbow
room; **Ellenbogengesellschaft** f dog-eat-dog
society
Ellipse [ɛ'lɪpsə] (**-, -n**) f ellipse
E-Lok ['eːlɔk] (**-**) f abk (= *elektrische Lokomotive*)

electric locomotive *od* engine
Elsass ['ɛlzas] *nt:* **das ~** Alsace
Elsässer ['ɛlzɛsər] *adj* Alsatian
Elsässer, in (**-s, -**) *m(f)* Alsatian, inhabitant of Alsace
elsässisch *adj* Alsatian
Elster ['ɛlstər] (**-, -n**) *f* magpie
elterlich *adj* parental
Eltern ['ɛltərn] *pl* parents *pl;* **nicht von schlechten ~ sein** (*umg*) to be quite something; **Elternabend** *m* (*Sch*) parents' evening; **Elternhaus** *nt* home; **elternlos** *adj* orphaned; **Elternsprechtag** *m* open day (for parents); **Elternteil** *m* parent
Email [e'maːj] (**-s, -s**) *nt* enamel
E-Mail ['iːmeːl] (**-, -s**) *f* email; **E-Mail-Adresse** *f* email address
e-mailen ['iːmeːlən] *vt* to email
emaillieren [ema'jiːrən] *vt* to enamel
Emanze (**-, -n**) (*pej*) *f* women's libber (*umg*)
Emanzipation [emantsipatsi'oːn] *f* emancipation
emanzipieren [emantsi'piːrən] *vt* to emancipate
Embargo [ɛm'bargo] (**-s, -s**) *nt* embargo
Embryo ['ɛmbryo] (**-s, -s** *od* **-nen**) *m* embryo
Embryonenforschung *f* embryo research
Emigrant, in [emi'grant(ɪn)] *m(f)* emigrant
Emigration [emigratsi'oːn] *f* emigration
emigrieren [emi'griːrən] *vi* to emigrate
Emissionen *pl* emissions *pl*
emissionsarm [emɪsi'oːnsarm] *adj* low in emissions
Emissionshandel *m* emissions trading
Emissionskurs *m* (*Aktien*) issued price
EMNID *m abk* (*= Erforschung, Meinung, Nachrichten, Informationsdienst*) opinion poll organization
emotional [emotsio'naːl] *adj* emotional; (*Ausdrucksweise*) emotive
emotionsgeladen [emotsi'oːnsgəla:dən] *adj* emotionally-charged
Empf. *abk* = **Empfänger**
empfahl *etc* [ɛm'pfaːl] *vb siehe* **empfehlen**
empfand *etc* [ɛm'pfant] *vb siehe* **empfinden**
Empfang [ɛm'pfaŋ] (**-(e)s, ⁻e**) *m* reception; (*Erhalten*) receipt; **in ~ nehmen** to receive; (**zahlbar**) **nach** *od* **bei ~** *+gen* (payable) on receipt (of)
empfangen *unreg vt* to receive ▷ *vi* (*schwanger werden*) to conceive
Empfänger, in [ɛm'pfɛŋər(ɪn)] (**-s, -**) *m(f)* receiver; (*Comm*) addressee, consignee; **~ unbekannt** (*auf Briefen*) not known at this address
empfänglich *adj* receptive, susceptible
Empfängnis (**-, -se**) *f* conception; **empfängnisverhütend** *adj:* **empfängnisverhütende Mittel** contraceptives *pl;* **Empfängnisverhütung** *f* contraception
Empfangs- *zW:* **Empfangsbestätigung** *f* (acknowledgement of) receipt; **Empfangschef** *m* (*von Hotel*) head porter; **Empfangsdame** *f* receptionist; **Empfangsschein** *m* receipt;

Empfangsstörung *f* (*Rundf, TV*) interference; **Empfangszimmer** *nt* reception room
empfehlen [ɛm'pfeːlən] *unreg vt* to recommend ▷ *vr* to take one's leave
empfehlenswert *adj* recommendable
Empfehlung *f* recommendation; **auf ~ von** on the recommendation of
Empfehlungsschreiben *nt* letter of recommendation
empfiehlt [ɛm'pfiːlt] *vb siehe* **empfehlen**
empfinden [ɛm'pfɪndən] *unreg vt* to feel; **etw als Beleidigung ~** to find sth insulting; **Empfinden** (**-s**) *nt:* **meinem Empfinden nach** to my mind
empfindlich *adj* sensitive; (*Stelle*) sore; (*reizbar*) touchy; **deine Kritik hat ihn ~ getroffen** your criticism cut him to the quick; **Empfindlichkeit** *f* sensitiveness; (*Reizbarkeit*) touchiness
empfindsam *adj* sentimental; (*Mensch*) sensitive
Empfindung *f* feeling, sentiment
empfindungslos *adj* unfeeling, insensitive
empfing *etc* [ɛm'pfɪŋ] *vb siehe* **empfangen**
empfohlen [ɛm'pfoːlən] *pp von* **empfehlen** ▷ *adj:* **~er Einzelhandelspreis** recommended retail price
empfunden [ɛm'pfʊndən] *pp von* **empfinden**
empor [ɛm'poːr] *adv* up, upwards
emporarbeiten *vr* (*geh*) to work one's way up
Empore [ɛm'poːrə] (**-, -n**) *f* (*Archit*) gallery
empören [ɛm'pøːrən] *vt* to make indignant; to shock ▷ *vr* to become indignant
empörend *adj* outrageous
emporkommen *unreg vi* to rise; (*vorankommen*) to succeed
Emporkömmling *m* upstart, parvenu
empört *adj:* **~ (über** *+akk***)** indignant (at), outraged (at)
Empörung *f* indignation
emsig ['ɛmzɪç] *adj* diligent, busy
End- ['ɛnt] *in zW* final; **Endauswertung** *f* final analysis; **Endbahnhof** *m* terminus; **Endbetrag** *m* final amount
Ende ['ɛndə] (**-s, -n**) *nt* end; **am ~** at the end; (*schließlich*) in the end; **am ~ sein** to be at the end of one's tether; **~ Dezember** at the end of December; **zu ~ sein** to be finished; **zu ~ gehen** to come to an end; **zu ~ führen** to finish (off); **letzten ~s** in the end, at the end of the day; **ein böses ~ nehmen** to come to a bad end; **ich bin mit meiner Weisheit am ~** I'm at my wits' end; **er wohnt am ~ der Welt** (*umg*) he lives at the back of beyond
Endeffekt *m:* **im ~** (*umg*) when it comes down to it
enden *vi* to end
Endergebnis *nt* final result
endgültig *adj* final, definite
Endivie [ɛn'diːviə] *f* endive
End- *zW:* **Endkunde** *m* end customer *od* consumer; **Endlager** *nt* permanent waste disposal site; **Endlagerung** *f* permanent

disposal; **endlich** adj final; (Math) finite
▷ adv finally; **endlich!** at last!; **hör endlich damit auf!** will you stop that!; **endlos** adj endless; **Endlospapier** nt continuous paper; **Endprodukt** nt end od final product; **Endspiel** nt final(s); **Endspurt** m (Sport) final spurt; **Endstation** f terminus
Endung f ending
Endverbraucher m consumer, end-user
Energie [enɛr'gi:] f energy; **Energieaufwand** m energy expenditure; **Energiebedarf** m energy requirement; **Energieeinsparung** f energy saving; **Energiegewinnung** f generation of energy; **energielos** adj lacking in energy, weak; **Energiequelle** f source of energy; **Energieversorgung** f supply of energy; **Energiewirtschaft** f energy industry
energisch [e'nɛrgɪʃ] adj energetic; ~ **durchgreifen** to take vigorous od firm action
eng [ɛŋ] adj narrow; (Kleidung) tight; (fig: Horizont) narrow, limited; (Freundschaft, Verhältnis) close; ~ **an etw** dat close to sth; **in die ~ere Wahl kommen** to be short-listed (Brit)
Engadin ['ɛŋgadi:n] (-s) nt: **das** ~ the Engadine
Engagement [ãgaʒə'mãː] (-s, -s) nt engagement; (Verpflichtung) commitment
engagieren [ãga'ʒi:rən] vt to engage ▷ vr to commit o.s.; **ein engagierter Schriftsteller** a committed writer
Enge ['ɛŋə] (-, -n) f (lit, fig) narrowness; (Landenge) defile; (Meerenge) straits pl; **jdn in die ~ treiben** to drive sb into a corner
Engel ['ɛŋəl] (-s, -) m angel; **engelhaft** adj angelic; **Engelmacher, in** (-s, -) (umg) m(f) backstreet abortionist
Engelsgeduld f: **sie hat eine ~** she has the patience of a saint
Engelszungen pl: **(wie) mit ~ reden** to use all one's own powers of persuasion
engherzig adj petty
engl. abk = **englisch**
England ['ɛŋlant] nt England
Engländer ['ɛŋlɛndər] (-s, -) m Englishman; English boy; **die Engländer** pl the English, the Britishers (US); **Engländerin** f Englishwoman; English girl
englisch ['ɛŋlɪʃ] adj English
engmaschig ['ɛŋmaʃɪç] adj close-meshed
Engpass m defile, pass; (fig: Verkehr) bottleneck
en gros [ã'gro] adv wholesale
engstirnig ['ɛŋʃtɪrnɪç] adj narrow-minded
Enkel ['ɛŋkəl] (-s, -) m grandson; **Enkelin** f granddaughter; **Enkelkind** nt grandchild
en masse [ã'mas] adv en masse
enorm [e'nɔrm] adj enormous; (umg: herrlich, kolossal) tremendous
en passant [ãpa'sã] adv en passant, in passing
Ensemble [ã'sãbəl] (-s, -s) nt ensemble
entarten [ɛnt'|a:rtən] vi to degenerate
entbehren [ɛnt'be:rən] vt to do without, dispense with
entbehrlich adj superfluous

Entbehrung f privation; **~en auf sich** akk **nehmen** to make sacrifices
entbinden [ɛnt'bɪndən] unreg vt (+gen) to release (from); (Med) to deliver ▷ vi (Med) to give birth
Entbindung f release; (Med) delivery, birth
Entbindungsheim nt maternity hospital
Entbindungsstation f maternity ward
entblößen [ɛnt'blø:sən] vt to denude, uncover; (berauben): **einer Sache** gen **entblößt** deprived of sth
entbrennen [ɛnt'brɛnən] unreg vi (liter: Kampf, Streit) to flare up; (: Liebe) to be aroused
entdecken [ɛnt'dɛkən] vt to discover; **jdm etw ~** to disclose sth to sb
Entdecker, in (-s, -) m(f) discoverer
Entdeckung f discovery
Ente ['ɛntə] (-, -n) f duck; (fig) canard, false report; (Aut) Citroën 2CV, deux-chevaux
entehren [ɛnt'|e:rən] vt to dishonour (Brit), dishonor (US), disgrace
enteignen [ɛnt'|aɪgnən] vt to expropriate; (Besitzer) to dispossess
enteisen [ɛnt'|aɪzən] vt to de-ice; (Kühlschrank) to defrost
enterben [ɛnt'|ɛrbən] vt to disinherit
Enterhaken ['ɛntərha:kən] m grappling iron od hook
entfachen [ɛnt'faxən] vt to kindle
entfallen [ɛnt'falən] unreg vi to drop, fall; (wegfallen) to be dropped; **jdm ~** (vergessen) to slip sb's memory; **auf jdn ~** to be allotted to sb
entfalten [ɛnt'faltən] vt to unfold; (Talente) to develop ▷ vr to open; (Mensch) to develop one's potential
Entfaltung f unfolding; (von Talenten) development
entfernen [ɛnt'fɛrnən] vt to remove; (hinauswerfen) to expel ▷ vr to go away, retire, withdraw
entfernt adj distant ▷ adv: **nicht im E~esten!** not in the slightest!; **weit davon ~ sein, etw zu tun** to be far from doing sth
Entfernung f distance; (Wegschaffen) removal; **unerlaubte ~ von der Truppe** absence without leave
Entfernungsmesser m (Phot) rangefinder
entfesseln [ɛnt'fesəln] vt (fig) to arouse
entfetten [ɛnt'fɛtən] vt to take the fat from
entflammen [ɛnt'flamən] vt (fig) to (a)rouse ▷ vi to burst into flames; (fig: Streit) to flare up; (: Leidenschaft) to be (a)roused od inflamed
entfremden [ɛnt'frɛmdən] vt to estrange, alienate
Entfremdung f estrangement, alienation
entfrosten [ɛnt'frɔstən] vt to defrost
Entfroster (-s, -) m (Aut) defroster
entführen [ɛnt'fy:rən] vt to abduct, kidnap; (Flugzeug) to hijack
Entführer (-s, -) m kidnapper (Brit), kidnaper (US); hijacker
Entführung f abduction, kidnapping (Brit), kidnaping (US); hijacking
entgegen [ɛnt'ge:gən] präp +dat contrary to,

against ▷ *adv* towards; **entgegenbringen** *unreg*
vt to bring; *(fig)*: **jdm etw entgegenbringen**
to show sb sth; **entgegengehen** *unreg* *vi* +*dat*
to go to meet, go towards; **Schwierigkeiten**
entgegengehen to be heading for difficulties;
entgegengesetzt *adj* opposite; *(widersprechend)*
opposed; **entgegenhalten** *unreg* *vt* *(fig)*: **einer**
Sache *dat* **entgegenhalten, dass ...** to
object to sth that ...; **Entgegenkommen** *nt*
obligingness; **entgegenkommen** *unreg* *vi*
+*dat* to come towards, approach; *(fig)*: **jdm**
entgegenkommen to accommodate
sb; **das kommt unseren Plänen sehr**
entgegen that fits in very well with our
plans; **entgegenkommend** *adj* obliging;
entgegenlaufen *unreg* *vi* +*dat* to run
towards *od* to meet; *(fig)* to run counter to;
Entgegennahme *f* *(form: Empfang)* receipt;
(Annahme) acceptance; **entgegennehmen**
unreg *vt* to receive, accept; **entgegensehen**
unreg *vi* +*dat* to await; **entgegensetzen** *vt* to
oppose; **dem habe ich entgegenzusetzen,**
dass ... against that I'd like to say that ...;
jdm/etw Widerstand entgegensetzen to
put up resistance to sb/sth; **entgegenstehen**
unreg *vi*: **dem steht nichts entgegen** there's
no objection to that; **entgegentreten** *unreg* *vi*
+*dat* *(lit)* to step up to; *(fig)* to oppose, counter;
entgegenwirken *vi* +*dat* to counteract
entgegnen [ɛnt'ge:gnən] *vt* to reply, retort
Entgegnung *f* reply, retort
entgehen [ɛnt'ge:ən] *unreg* *vi* *(fig)*: **jdm** ~ to
escape sb's notice; **sich** *dat* **etw** ~ **lassen** to
miss sth
entgeistert [ɛnt'gaɪstərt] *adj* thunderstruck
Entgelt [ɛnt'gɛlt] (**-(e)s, -e**) *nt* remuneration
entgelten *unreg* *vt*: **jdm etw** ~ to repay sb for
sth
entgleisen [ɛnt'glaɪzən] *vi* *(Eisenb)* to be
derailed; *(fig: Person)* to misbehave; ~ **lassen**
to derail
Entgleisung *f* derailment; *(fig)* faux pas, gaffe
entgleiten [ɛnt'glaɪtən] *unreg* *vi*: **jdm** ~ to slip
from sb's hand
entgräten [ɛnt'grɛːtən] *vt* to fillet, bone
Enthaarungsmittel [ɛnt'haːrʊŋsmɪtəl] *nt*
depilatory
enthält [ɛnt'hɛlt] *vb siehe* **enthalten**
enthalten [ɛnt'haltən] *unreg* *vt* to contain ▷ *vr*
+*gen* to abstain from, refrain from; **sich (der**
Stimme) ~ to abstain
enthaltsam [ɛnt'haltzaːm] *adj* abstinent,
abstemious; **Enthaltsamkeit** *f* abstinence
enthärten [ɛnt'hɛrtən] *vt* *(Wasser)* to soften;
(Metall) to anneal
enthaupten [ɛnt'hauptən] *vt* to decapitate;
(als Hinrichtung) to behead
enthäuten [ɛnt'hɔytən] *vt* to skin
entheben [ɛnt'heːbən] *unreg* *vt*: **jdn einer**
Sache *gen* ~ to relieve sb of sth
enthemmen [ɛnt'hɛmən] *vt*: **jdn** ~ to free sb
from his/her inhibitions
enthielt *etc* [ɛnt'hiːlt] *vb siehe* **enthalten**

enthüllen [ɛnt'hʏlən] *vt* to reveal, unveil
Enthüllung *f* revelation; *(von Skandal)* exposure
Enthusiasmus [ɛntuzi'asmʊs] *m* enthusiasm
entjungfern [ɛnt'jʊŋfərn] *vt* to deflower
entkalken [ɛnt'kalkən] *vt* to decalcify
entkernen [ɛnt'kɛrnən] *vt* *(Kernobst)* to core;
(Steinobst) to stone
entkleiden [ɛnt'klaɪdən] *vt, vr* *(geh)* to undress
entkommen [ɛnt'kɔmən] *unreg* *vi* to get away,
escape; **jdm/etw** *od* **aus etw** ~ to get away *od*
escape from sb/sth
entkorken [ɛnt'kɔrkən] *vt* to uncork
entkräften [ɛnt'krɛftən] *vt* to weaken,
exhaust; *(Argument)* to refute
entkrampfen [ɛnt'krampfən] *vt* *(fig)* to relax,
ease
entladen [ɛnt'laːdən] *unreg* *vt* to unload; *(Elek)*
to discharge ▷ *vr* *(Gewehr, Elek)* to discharge;
(Ärger etc) to vent itself
entlang [ɛnt'laŋ] *präp* (+*akk od dat*) along ▷ *adv*
along; ~ **dem Fluss, den Fluss entlang** along
the river; **hier** ~ this way; **entlanggehen** *unreg*
vi to walk along
entlarven [ɛnt'larfən] *vt* to unmask, expose
entlassen [ɛnt'lasən] *unreg* *vt* to discharge;
(Arbeiter) to dismiss; *(nach Stellenabbau)* to make
redundant
entlässt [ɛnt'lɛst] *vb siehe* **entlassen**
Entlassung *f* discharge; dismissal; **es gab 20**
~**en** there were 20 redundancies
Entlassungswelle *f* wave of redundancies *od*
job losses
Entlassungszeugnis *nt* *(Sch)* school-leaving
certificate
entlasten [ɛnt'lastən] *vt* to relieve; *(Arbeit*
abnehmen) to take some of the load off;
(Angeklagte) to exonerate; *(Konto)* to clear
Entlastung *f* relief; *(Comm)* crediting
Entlastungszeuge *m* defence *(Brit)* *od* defense
(US) witness
Entlastungszug *m* relief train
entledigen [ɛnt'leːdɪgən] *vr*: **sich jds/einer**
Sache ~ to rid o.s. of sb/sth
entleeren [ɛnt'leːrən] *vt* to empty; *(Darm)* to
evacuate
entlegen [ɛnt'leːgən] *adj* remote
entließ *etc* [ɛnt'liːs] *vb siehe* **entlassen**
entlocken [ɛnt'lɔkən] *vt*: **jdm etw** ~ to elicit
sth from sb
entlohnen *vt* to pay; *(fig)* to reward
entlüften [ɛnt'lʏftən] *vt* to ventilate
entmachten [ɛnt'maxtən] *vt* to deprive of
power
entmenscht [ɛnt'mɛnʃt] *adj* inhuman, bestial
entmilitarisiert [ɛntmilitari'ziːrt] *adj*
demilitarized
entmündigen [ɛnt'mʏndɪgən] *vt* to certify;
(Jur) to (legally) incapacitate, declare incapable
of managing one's own affairs
entmutigen [ɛnt'muːtɪgən] *vt* to discourage
Entnahme [ɛnt'naːmə] (**-, -n**) *f* removal,
withdrawal
Entnazifizierung [ɛntnatsifi'tsiːrʊŋ] *f*

e

107

denazification

entnehmen [ɛntˈneːmən] *unreg vt +dat* to take out of, take from; *(folgern)* to infer from; **wie ich Ihren Worten entnehme,** ... I gather from what you say that ...

entpuppen [ɛntˈpʊpən] *vr (fig)* to reveal o.s., turn out; **sich als etw ~** to turn out to be sth

entrahmen [ɛntˈraːmən] *vt* to skim

entreißen [ɛntˈraɪsən] *unreg vt*: **jdm etw ~** to snatch sth (away) from sb

entrichten [ɛntˈrɪçtən] *vt (form)* to pay

entrosten [ɛntˈrɔstən] *vt* to derust

entrüsten [ɛntˈrʏstən] *vt* to incense, outrage ▷ *vr* to be filled with indignation

entrüstet *adj* indignant, outraged

Entrüstung *f* indignation

Entsafter [ɛntˈzaftər] **(-s, -)** *m* juice extractor

entsagen [ɛntˈzaːgən] *vi +dat* to renounce

entschädigen [ɛntˈʃɛːdɪgən] *vt* to compensate

Entschädigung *f* compensation

entschärfen [ɛntˈʃɛrfən] *vt* to defuse; *(Kritik)* to tone down

Entscheid [ɛntˈʃaɪt] **(-(e)s, -e)** *m (form)* decision

entscheiden *unreg vt, vi, vr* to decide; **darüber habe ich nicht zu ~** that is not for me to decide; **sich für jdn/etw ~** to decide in favour of sb/sth; to decide on sb/sth

entscheidend *adj* decisive, *(Stimme)* casting; **das E~e** the decisive *od* deciding factor

Entscheidung *f* decision; **wie ist die ~ ausgefallen?** which way did the decision go?

Entscheidungs- *zW*: **Entscheidungsbefugnis** *f* decision-making powers *pl*; **entscheidungsfähig** *adj* capable of deciding; **Entscheidungsspiel** *nt* play-off; **Entscheidungsträger** *m* decision-maker

entschied *etc* [ɛntˈʃiːt] *vb siehe* **entscheiden**

entschieden [ɛntˈʃiːdən] *pp von* **entscheiden** ▷ *adj* decided; *(entschlossen)* resolute; **das geht ~ zu weit** that's definitely going too far; **Entschiedenheit** *f* firmness, determination

entschlacken [ɛntˈʃlakən] *vt (Med: Körper)* to purify

entschließen [ɛntˈʃliːsən] *unreg vr* to decide; **sich zu nichts ~ können** to be unable to make up one's mind; **kurz entschlossen** straight away

Entschließungsantrag *m (Pol)* resolution proposal

entschloss *etc* [ɛntˈʃlɔs] *vb siehe* **entschließen**

entschlossen [ɛntˈʃlɔsən] *pp von* **entschließen** ▷ *adj* determined, resolute; **Entschlossenheit** *f* determination

entschlüpfen [ɛntˈʃlʏpfən] *vi* to escape, slip away; *(fig: Wort etc)* to slip out

Entschluss [ɛntˈʃlʊs] *m* decision; **aus eigenem ~ handeln** to act on one's own initiative; **es ist mein fester ~** it is my firm intention

entschlüsseln [ɛntˈʃlʏsəln] *vt* to decipher; *(Funkspruch)* to decode

entschlussfreudig *adj* decisive

Entschlusskraft *f* determination, decisiveness

entschuldbar [ɛntˈʃʊltbaːr] *adj* excusable

entschuldigen [ɛntˈʃʊldɪgən] *vt* to excuse ▷ *vr* to apologize ▷ *vi*: **~ Sie (bitte)!** excuse me; *(Verzeihung)* sorry; **jdn bei jdm ~** to make sb's excuses *od* apologies to sb; **sich ~ lassen** to send one's apologies

entschuldigend *adj* apologetic

Entschuldigung *f* apology; *(Grund)* excuse; **jdn um ~ bitten** to apologize to sb; **~!** excuse me; *(Verzeihung)* sorry

entschwefeln [ɛntˈʃveːfəln] *vt* to desulphurize

Entschwefelungsanlage *f* desulphurization plant

entschwinden [ɛntˈʃvɪndən] *unreg vi* to disappear

entsetzen [ɛntˈzɛtsən] *vt* to horrify ▷ *vr* to be horrified *od* appalled; **Entsetzen (-s)** *nt* horror, dismay

entsetzlich *adj* dreadful, appalling

entsetzt *adj* horrified

entsichern [ɛntˈzɪçərn] *vt* to release the safety catch of

entsinnen [ɛntˈzɪnən] *unreg vr +gen* to remember

entsorgen [ɛntˈzɔrgən] *vt*: **eine Stadt ~** to dispose of a town's refuse and sewage

Entsorgung *f* waste disposal; *(von Chemikalien)* disposal

entspannen [ɛntˈʃpanən] *vt, vr (Körper)* to relax; *(Pol: Lage)* to ease

Entspannung *f* relaxation, rest; *(Pol)* détente

Entspannungspolitik *f* policy of détente

Entspannungsübungen *pl* relaxation exercises *pl*

entspr. *abk* = **entsprechend**

entsprach *etc* [ɛntˈʃprax] *vb siehe* **entsprechen**

entsprechen [ɛntˈʃprɛçən] *unreg vi +dat* to correspond to; *(Anforderungen, Wünschen)* to meet, comply with

entsprechend *adj* appropriate ▷ *adv* accordingly ▷ *präp +dat*: **er wird seiner Leistung ~ bezahlt** he is paid according to output

entspricht [ɛntˈʃprɪçt] *vb siehe* **entsprechen**

entspringen [ɛntˈʃprɪŋən] *unreg vi (+dat)* to spring (from)

entsprochen [ɛntˈʃprɔxən] *pp von* **entsprechen**

entstaatlichen [ɛntˈʃtaːtlɪçən] *vt* to denationalize

entstammen [ɛntˈʃtamən] *vi +dat* to stem *od* come from

entstand *etc* [ɛntˈʃtant] *vb siehe* **entstehen**

entstanden [ɛntˈʃtandən] *pp von* **entstehen**

entstehen [ɛntˈʃteːən] *unreg vi*: **~ (aus** *od* **durch)** to arise (from), result (from); **wir wollen nicht den Eindruck ~ lassen,** ... we don't want to give rise to the impression that ...; **für ~den** *od* **entstandenen Schaden** for damages incurred

Entstehung *f* genesis, origin

entstellen [ɛntˈʃtɛlən] *vt* to disfigure; *(Wahrheit)* to distort

Entstellung *f* distortion; disfigurement

entstören [ɛntˈʃtøːrən] *vt (Rundf)* to eliminate

interference from; (Aut) to suppress
enttäuschen [ɛntˈtɔʏʃən] vt to disappoint
Enttäuschung f disappointment
entwachsen [ɛntˈvaksən] unreg vi +dat to
outgrow, grow out of; (geh: herauswachsen aus) to
spring from
entwaffnen [ɛntˈvafnən] vt (lit, fig) to disarm
entwaffnend adj disarming
Entwarnung [ɛntˈvarnʊŋ] f all clear (signal)
entwässern [ɛntˈvɛsərn] vt to drain
Entwässerung f drainage
entweder [ɛntˈveːdər] konj either; ~ ... oder ...
either ... or ...
entweichen [ɛntˈvaɪçən] unreg vi to escape
entweihen [ɛntˈvaɪən] unreg vt to desecrate
entwenden [ɛntˈvɛndən] unreg vt to purloin,
steal
entwerfen [ɛntˈvɛrfən] unreg vt (Zeichnung) to
sketch; (Modell) to design; (Vortrag, Gesetz etc)
to draft
entwerten [ɛntˈveːrtən] vt to devalue;
(stempeln) to cancel
Entwerter (-s, -) m (ticket-)cancelling (Brit) od
canceling (US) machine
entwickeln [ɛntˈvɪkəln] vt to develop (auch
Phot); (Mut, Energie) to show, display ▷ vr to
develop
Entwickler (-s, -) m developer
Entwicklung [ɛntˈvɪklʊŋ] f development;
(Phot) developing; **in der** ~ at the development
stage; (Jugendliche etc) still developing
Entwicklungs- zW: **Entwicklungsabschnitt**
m stage of development; **Entwicklungshelfer**,
in m(f) VSO worker (Brit), Peace Corps worker
(US); **Entwicklungshilfe** f aid for developing
countries; **Entwicklungsjahre** pl adolescence
sing; **Entwicklungsland** nt developing country;
Entwicklungszeit f period of development;
(Phot) developing time
entwirren [ɛntˈvɪrən] vt to disentangle
entwischen [ɛntˈvɪʃən] vi to escape
entwöhnen [ɛntˈvøːnən] vt to wean;
(Süchtige): **(einer Sache** dat od **von etw)** ~ to
cure (of sth)
Entwöhnung f weaning; cure, curing
entwürdigend [ɛntˈvʏrdɪgənt] adj degrading
Entwurf [ɛntˈvʊrf] m outline, design;
(Vertragsentwurf, Konzept) draft
entwurzeln [ɛntˈvʊrtsəln] vt to uproot
entziehen [ɛntˈtsiːən] unreg vt (+dat) to
withdraw (from), take away (from);
(Flüssigkeit) to draw (from), extract (from) ▷ vr
(+dat) to escape (from); (jds Kenntnis) to be
outside od beyond; (der Pflicht) to shirk (from);
sich jds Blicken ~ to be hidden from sight
Entziehung f withdrawal
Entziehungsanstalt f drug addiction/
alcoholism treatment centre (Brit) od center
(US)
Entziehungskur f treatment for drug
addiction/alcoholism
entziffern [ɛntˈtsɪfərn] vt to decipher;
(Funkspruch) to decode

entzücken [ɛntˈtsʏkən] vt to delight;
Entzücken (-s) nt delight
entzückend adj delightful, charming
Entzug [ɛntˈtsuːk] (-(e)s) m (einer Lizenz etc, Med)
withdrawal
Entzugserscheinung f withdrawal symptom
entzündbar adj: **leicht** ~ highly inflammable;
(fig) easily roused
entzünden [ɛntˈtsʏndən] vt to light, set light
to; (fig, Med) to inflame; (Streit) to spark off ▷ vr
(lit, fig) to catch fire; (Streit) to start; (Med) to
become inflamed
Entzündung f (Med) inflammation
entzwei [ɛntˈtsvaɪ] adv in two; broken;
entzweibrechen unreg vt, vi to break in two
entzweien vt to set at odds ▷ vr to fall out
entzweigehen unreg vi to break (in two)
Enzian [ˈɛntsiaːn] (-s, -e) m gentian
Enzyklika [ɛnˈtsyːklika] (-, -liken) f (Rel)
encyclical
Enzyklopädie [ɛntsyklopɛˈdiː] f encyclop(a)
edia
Enzym [ɛnˈtsyːm] (-s, -e) nt enzyme
Epen pl von **Epos**
Epidemie [epideˈmiː] f epidemic
Epilepsie [epilɛpˈsiː] f epilepsy
episch [ˈeːpɪʃ] adj epic
Episode [epiˈzoːdə] (-, -n) f episode
Epoche [eˈpɔxə] (-, -n) f epoch;
epochemachend adj epoch-making
Epos [ˈeːpɔs] (-, **Epen**) nt epic (poem)
Equipe [eˈkɪp] (-, -n) f team
er [eːr] pron he; it
erachten [ɛrˈʔaxtən] vt (geh): ~ **für** od **als** to
consider (to be); **meines E~s** in my opinion
erarbeiten [ɛrˈʔarbaɪtən] vt to work for,
acquire; (Theorie) to work out
Erbanlage [ˈɛrp|anlaːgə] f hereditary factor(s
pl)
erbarmen [ɛrˈbarmən] vr (+gen) to have pity od
mercy (on) ▷ vt: **er sieht zum E~ aus** he's a
pitiful sight; **Herr, erbarme dich (unser)!**
Lord, have mercy (upon us)!; **Erbarmen (-s)**
nt pity
erbärmlich [ɛrˈbɛrmlɪç] adj wretched, pitiful;
Erbärmlichkeit f wretchedness
Erbarmungs- zW: **erbarmungslos** adj
pitiless, merciless; **erbarmungsvoll** adj
compassionate; **erbarmungswürdig** adj
pitiable, wretched
erbauen [ɛrˈbaʊən] vt to build, erect; (fig)
to edify; **er ist von meinem Plan nicht
besonders erbaut** (umg) he isn't particularly
enthusiastic about my plan
Erbauer (-s, -) m builder
erbaulich adj edifying
Erbauung f construction; (fig) edification
erbberechtigt adj entitled to inherit
erbbiologisch adj: **~es Gutachten** (Jur) blood
test (to establish paternity)
Erbe¹ [ˈɛrbə] (-n, -n) m heir; **jdn zum** od **als ~n
einsetzen** to make sb one's/sb's heir
Erbe² [ˈɛrbə] (-s) nt inheritance; (fig) heritage

e

109

erben vt to inherit; (umg: geschenkt bekommen) to get, be given

erbeuten [ɛr'bɔʏtən] vt to carry off; (Mil) to capture

Erb- zW: **Erbfaktor** m gene; **Erbfehler** m hereditary defect; **Erbfeind** m traditional od arch enemy; **Erbfolge** f (line of) succession

Erbin f heiress

erbitten [ɛr'bɪtən] unreg vt to ask for, request

erbittern [ɛr'bɪtərn] vt to embitter; (erzürnen) to incense

erbittert [ɛr'bɪtərt] adj (Kampf) fierce, bitter

erblassen [ɛr'blasən] vi to (turn) pale

Erblasser, in ['ɛrblasər(ɪn)] (-s, -) m(f) (Jur) person who leaves an inheritance

erbleichen [ɛr'blaɪçən] unreg vi to (turn) pale

erblich ['ɛrplɪç] adj hereditary; **er/sie ist ~ (vor)belastet** it runs in the family

erblichen pp von **erbleichen**

erblicken [ɛr'blɪkən] vt to see; (erspähen) to catch sight of

erblinden [ɛr'blɪndən] vi to go blind

Erbmasse ['ɛrpmasə] f estate; (Biol) genotype

erbosen [ɛr'boːzən] vt (geh) to anger ▷ vr to grow angry

erbrechen [ɛr'brɛçən] unreg vt, vr to vomit

Erbrecht nt hereditary right; (Gesetze) law of inheritance

Erbschaft f inheritance, legacy

Erbschaftssteuer f estate od death duties pl

Erbschleicher, in ['ɛrpʃlaɪçər(ɪn)] (-s, -) m(f) legacy-hunter

Erbse ['ɛrpsə] (-, -n) f pea

Erb- zW: **Erbstück** nt heirloom; **Erbsünde** f (Rel) original sin; **Erbteil** nt inherited trait; (Jur) (portion of) inheritance

Erd- zW: **Erdachse** f earth's axis; **Erdapfel** (Österr) m potato; **Erdatmosphäre** f earth's atmosphere; **Erdbahn** f orbit of the earth; **Erdbeben** nt earthquake; **Erdbeere** f strawberry; **Erdboden** m ground; **etw dem Erdboden gleichmachen** to level sth, raze sth to the ground

Erde (-, -n) f earth; **zu ebener ~** at ground level; **auf der ganzen ~** all over the world; **du wirst mich noch unter die ~ bringen** (umg) you'll be the death of me yet

erden vt (Elek) to earth

erdenkbar [ɛr'dɛŋkbaːr] adj conceivable; **sich** dat **alle ~e Mühe geben** to take the greatest (possible) pains

erdenklich [ɛr'dɛŋklɪç] adj = **erdenkbar**

Erdg. abk = **Erdgeschoss**

Erd- zW: **Erdgas** nt natural gas; **Erdgeschoss** nt ground floor (Brit), first floor (US); **Erdkunde** f geography; **Erdnuss** f peanut; **Erdoberfläche** f surface of the earth; **Erdöl** nt (mineral) oil; **Erdölfeld** nt oilfield; **Erdölindustrie** f oil industry; **Erdreich** nt soil, earth

erdreisten [ɛr'draɪstən] vr to dare, have the audacity (to do sth)

erdrosseln [ɛr'drɔsəln] vt to strangle, throttle

erdrücken [ɛr'drʏkən] vt to crush; **~de**

Übermacht/~des Beweismaterial overwhelming superiority/evidence

Erd- zW: **Erdrutsch** m landslide; **Erdstoß** m (seismic) shock; **Erdteil** m continent

erdulden [ɛr'dʊldən] vt to endure, suffer

ereifern [ɛr'|aɪfərn] vr to get excited

ereignen [ɛr'|aɪgnən] vr to happen

Ereignis [ɛr'|aɪgnɪs] (-ses, -se) nt event; **ereignislos** adj uneventful; **ereignisreich** adj eventful

Eremit [ere'miːt] (-en, -en) m hermit

erfahren [ɛr'faːrən] unreg vt to learn, find out; (erleben) to experience ▷ adj experienced

Erfahrung f experience; **~en sammeln** to gain experience; **etw in ~ bringen** to learn od find out sth

Erfahrungsaustausch m exchange of experiences

erfahrungsgemäß adv according to experience

erfand etc [ɛr'fant] vb siehe **erfinden**

erfassen [ɛr'fasən] vt to seize; (fig: einbeziehen) to include, register; (verstehen) to grasp

erfinden [ɛr'fɪndən] unreg vt to invent; **frei erfunden** completely fictitious

Erfinder, in (-s, -) m(f) inventor; **erfinderisch** adj inventive

Erfindung f invention

Erfindungsgabe f inventiveness

Erfolg [ɛr'fɔlk] (-(e)s, -e) m success; (Folge) result; **~ versprechend** promising; **viel ~!** good luck!

erfolgen [ɛr'fɔlgən] vi to follow; (sich ergeben) to result; (stattfinden) to take place; (Zahlung) to be effected; **nach erfolgter Zahlung** when payment has been made

Erfolg- zW: **erfolglos** adj unsuccessful; **Erfolglosigkeit** f lack of success; **erfolgreich** adj successful

Erfolgserlebnis nt feeling of success, sense of achievement

erfolgversprechend adj siehe **Erfolg**

erforderlich adj requisite, necessary

erfordern [ɛr'fɔrdərn] vt to require, demand

Erfordernis (-ses, -se) nt requirement, prerequisite

erforschen [ɛr'fɔrʃən] vt (Land) to explore; (Problem) to investigate; (Gewissen) to search

Erforscher, in (-s, -) m(f) explorer; investigator

Erforschung f exploration; investigation; searching

erfragen [ɛr'fraːgən] vt to inquire, ascertain

erfreuen [ɛr'frɔʏən] vr: **sich ~ an** +dat to enjoy ▷ vt to delight; **sich einer Sache** gen **~** (geh) to enjoy sth; **sehr erfreut!** (form: bei Vorstellung) pleased to meet you!

erfreulich [ɛr'frɔʏlɪç] adj pleasing, gratifying

erfreulicherweise adv happily, luckily

erfrieren [ɛr'friːrən] unreg vi to freeze (to death); (Glieder) to get frostbitten; (Pflanzen) to be killed by frost

erfrischen [ɛr'frɪʃən] vt to refresh

Erfrischung f refreshment

Erfrischungsraum *m* snack bar, cafeteria

erfüllen [ɛr'fʏlən] *vt* (*Raum etc*) to fill; (*fig: Bitte etc*) to fulfil (*Brit*), fulfill (*US*) ▷ *vr* to come true; **ein erfülltes Leben** a full life

Erfüllung *f*: **in ~ gehen** to be fulfilled

erfunden [ɛr'fʊndən] *pp von* **erfinden**

ergab *etc* [ɛr'ga:p] *vb siehe* **ergeben**

ergänzen [ɛr'gɛntsən] *vt* to supplement, complete ▷ *vr* to complement one another

Ergänzung *f* completion; (*Zusatz*) supplement

ergattern [ɛr'gatərn] (*umg*) *vt* to get hold of, hunt up

ergaunern [ɛr'gaʊnərn] (*umg*) *vt*: **sich** *dat* **etw ~** to get hold of sth by underhand methods

ergeben [ɛr'ge:bən] *unreg vt* to yield, produce ▷ *vr* to surrender; (*folgen*) to result ▷ *adj* devoted; (*demütig*) humble; **sich einer Sache** *dat* **~** (*sich hingeben*) to give o.s. up to sth, yield to sth; **es ergab sich, dass unsere Befürchtungen ...** it turned out that our fears ...; **dem Trunk ~** addicted to drink; **Ergebenheit** *f* devotion; humility

Ergebnis [ɛr'ge:pnɪs] (**-ses, -se**) *nt* result; **zu einem ~ kommen** to come to *od* reach a conclusion; **ergebnislos** *adj* without result, fruitless; **ergebnislos bleiben** *od* **verlaufen** to come to nothing

ergehen [ɛr'ge:ən] *unreg vi* (*form*) to be issued, go out ▷ *vi unpers*: **es ergeht ihm gut/schlecht** he's faring *od* getting on well/badly ▷ *vr*: **sich in etw** *dat* **~** to indulge in sth; **etw über sich** *akk* **~ lassen** to put up with sth; **sich (in langen Reden) über ein Thema ~** (*fig*) to hold forth at length on sth

ergiebig [ɛr'gi:bɪç] *adj* productive

ergo ['ɛrgo] *konj* therefore, ergo (*liter, hum*)

Ergonomie [ɛrgono'mi:] *f* ergonomics *pl*

ergötzen [ɛr'gœtsən] *vt* to amuse, delight

ergrauen [ɛr'graʊən] *vi* to turn *od* go grey (*Brit*) *od* gray (*US*)

ergreifen [ɛr'graɪfən] *unreg vt* (*lit, fig*) to seize; (*Beruf*) to take up; (*Maßnahmen*) to resort to; (*rühren*) to move; **er ergriff das Wort** he began to speak

ergreifend *adj* moving, affecting

ergriff *etc* [ɛr'grɪf] *vb siehe* **ergreifen**

ergriffen *pp von* **ergreifen** ▷ *adj* deeply moved

Ergriffenheit *f* emotion

ergründen [ɛr'gryndən] *vt* (*Sinn etc*) to fathom; (*Ursache, Motive*) to discover

Erguss [ɛr'gʊs] (**-es, ̈e**) *m* discharge; (*fig*) outpouring, effusion

erhaben [ɛr'ha:bən] *adj* (*lit*) raised, embossed; (*fig*) exalted, lofty; **über etw** *akk* **~ sein** to be above sth

Erhalt *m*: **bei** *od* **nach ~** on receipt

erhält [ɛr'hɛlt] *vb siehe* **erhalten**

erhalten [ɛr'haltən] *unreg vt* to receive; (*bewahren*) to preserve, maintain; **das Wort ~** to receive permission to speak; **jdn am Leben ~** to keep sb alive; **gut ~** in good condition

erhältlich [ɛr'hɛltlɪç] *adj* obtainable, available

Erhaltung *f* maintenance, preservation

erhängen [ɛr'hɛŋən] *vt, vr* to hang

erhärten [ɛr'hɛrtən] *vt* to harden; (*These*) to substantiate, corroborate

erhaschen [ɛr'haʃən] *vt* to catch

erheben [ɛr'he:bən] *unreg vt* to raise; (*Protest, Forderungen*) to make; (*Fakten*) to ascertain ▷ *vr* to rise (up); **sich über etw** *akk* **~** to rise above sth

erheblich [ɛr'he:plɪç] *adj* considerable

erheitern [ɛr'haɪtərn] *vt* to amuse, cheer (up)

Erheiterung *f* exhilaration; **zur allgemeinen ~** to everybody's amusement

erhellen [ɛr'hɛlən] *vt* (*lit, fig*) to illuminate; (*Geheimnis*) to shed light on ▷ *vr* (*Fenster*) to light up; (*Himmel, Miene*) to brighten (up); (*Gesicht*) to brighten up

erhielt *etc* [ɛr'hi:lt] *vb siehe* **erhalten**

erhitzen [ɛr'hɪtsən] *vt* to heat ▷ *vr* to heat up; (*fig*) to become heated *od* aroused

erhoffen [ɛr'hɔfən] *vt* to hope for; **was erhoffst du dir davon?** what do you hope to gain from it?

erhöhen [ɛr'hø:ən] *vt* to raise; (*verstärken*) to increase; **erhöhte Temperatur haben** to have a temperature

Erhöhung *f* (*Gehalt*) increment

erholen [ɛr'ho:lən] *vr* to recover; (*entspannen*) to have a rest; (*fig: Preise, Aktien*) to rally, pick up

erholsam *adj* restful

Erholung *f* recovery; relaxation, rest

erholungsbedürftig *adj* in need of a rest, run-down

Erholungsgebiet *nt* holiday (*Brit*) *od* vacation (*US*) area

Erholungsheim *nt* convalescent home

erhören [ɛr'hø:rən] *vt* (*Gebet etc*) to hear; (*Bitte etc*) to yield to

Erika ['e:rika] (**-, Eriken**) *f* heather

erinnern [ɛr'|ɪnərn] *vt*: **~ (an +***akk***)** to remind (of) ▷ *vr*: **sich (an etw** *akk***) ~** to remember (sth)

Erinnerung *f* memory; (*Andenken*) reminder; **Erinnerungen** *pl* (*Lebenserinnerung*) reminiscences *pl*; (*Liter*) memoirs *pl*; **jdn/ etw in guter ~ behalten** to have pleasant memories of sb/sth

Erinnerungsschreiben *nt* (*Comm*) reminder

Erinnerungstafel *f* commemorative plaque

Eritrea [eri'tre:a] (**-s**) *nt* Eritrea

erkalten [ɛr'kaltən] *vi* to go cold, cool (down)

erkälten [ɛr'kɛltən] *vr* to catch cold; **sich** *dat* **die Blase ~** to catch a chill in one's bladder

erkältet *adj* with a cold; **~ sein** to have a cold

Erkältung *f* cold

erkämpfen [ɛr'kɛmpfən] *vt* to win, secure

erkannt [ɛr'kant] *pp von* **erkennen**

erkannte *etc vb siehe* **erkennen**

erkennbar *adj* recognizable

erkennen [ɛr'kɛnən] *unreg vt* to recognize; (*sehen, verstehen*) to see; **jdm zu ~ geben, dass ...** to give sb to understand that ...

erkenntlich *adj*: **sich ~ zeigen** to show one's appreciation; **Erkenntlichkeit** *f* gratitude; (*Geschenk*) token of one's gratitude

Erkenntnis (-, -se) f knowledge; (das Erkennen) recognition; (Einsicht) insight; **zur ~ kommen** to realize

Erkennung f recognition

Erkennungsdienst m police records department

Erkennungsmarke f identity disc

Erker ['ɛrkər] (-s, -) m bay; **Erkerfenster** nt bay window

erklärbar adj explicable

erklären [ɛr'klɛ:rən] vt to explain; (Rücktritt) to announce; (Politiker, Pressesprecher etc) to say; **ich kann mir nicht ~, warum ... I** can't understand why ...

erklärlich adj explicable; (verständlich) understandable

erklärt adj attrib (Gegner etc) professed, avowed; (Favorit, Liebling) acknowledged

Erklärung f explanation; (Aussage) declaration

erklecklich [ɛr'klɛklɪç] adj considerable

erklimmen [ɛr'klɪmən] unreg vt to climb to

erklingen [ɛr'klɪŋən] unreg vi to resound, ring out

erklomm etc [ɛr'klɔm] vb siehe **erklimmen**

erklommen pp von **erklimmen**

erkranken [ɛr'kraŋkən] vi: **~ (an** +dat) to be taken ill (with); (Organ, Pflanze, Tier) to become diseased (with)

Erkrankung f illness

erkunden [ɛr'kʊndən] vt to find out, ascertain; (bes Mil) to reconnoitre (Brit), reconnoiter (US)

erkundigen vr: **sich ~ (nach)** to inquire (about); **ich werde mich ~** I'll find out

Erkundigung f inquiry; **~en einholen** to make inquiries

Erkundung f (Mil) reconnaissance, scouting

erlahmen [ɛr'la:mən] vi to tire; (nachlassen) to flag, wane

erlangen [ɛr'laŋən] vt to attain, achieve

Erlass [ɛr'las] (-es, -e) m decree; (Aufhebung) remission

erlassen unreg vt (Verfügung) to issue; (Gesetz) to enact; (Strafe) to remit; **jdm etw ~** to release sb from sth

erlauben [ɛr'laʊbən] vt to allow, permit
▷ vr: **sich** dat **etw ~** (Zigarette, Pause) to permit o.s. sth; (Bemerkung, Verschlag) to venture sth; (sich leisten) to afford sth; **jdm etw ~** to allow od permit sb (to do) sth; **~ Sie?** may I?; **~ Sie mal!** do you mind!; **was ~ Sie sich (eigentlich)!** how dare you!

Erlaubnis [ɛr'laʊpnɪs] (-, -se) f permission

erläutern [ɛr'lɔʏtərn] vt to explain

Erläuterung f explanation; **zur ~ in** explanation

Erle ['ɛrlə] (-, -n) f alder

erleben [ɛr'le:bən] vt to experience; (Zeit) to live through; (miterleben) to witness; (noch miterleben) to live to see; **so wütend habe ich ihn noch nie erlebt** I've never seen od known him so furious

Erlebnis [ɛr'le:pnɪs] (-ses, -se) nt experience

erledigen [ɛr'le:dɪgən] vt to take care of, deal

with; (Antrag etc) to process; (umg: erschöpfen) to wear out; (ruinieren) to finish; (umbringen) to do in ▷ vr: **das hat sich erledigt** that's all settled; **das ist erledigt** that's taken care of, that's been done; **ich habe noch einiges in der Stadt zu ~** I've still got a few things to do in town

erledigt (umg) adj (erschöpft) shattered, done in; (: ruiniert) finished, ruined

erlegen [ɛr'le:gən] vt to kill

erleichtern [ɛr'laɪçtərn] vt to make easier; (fig: Last) to lighten; (lindern, beruhigen) to relieve

erleichtert adj relieved; **~ aufatmen** to breathe a sigh of relief

Erleichterung f facilitation; lightening; relief

erleiden [ɛr'laɪdən] unreg vt to suffer, endure

erlernbar adj learnable

erlernen [ɛr'lɛrnən] vt to learn, acquire

erlesen [ɛr'le:zən] adj select, choice

erleuchten [ɛr'lɔʏçtən] vt to illuminate; (fig) to inspire

Erleuchtung f (Einfall) inspiration

erliegen [ɛr'li:gən] unreg vi +dat (lit, fig) to succumb to; (einem Irrtum) to be the victim of; **zum E~ kommen** to come to a standstill

erlischt [ɛr'lɪʃt] vb siehe **erlöschen**

erlogen [ɛr'lo:gən] adj untrue, made-up

Erlös [ɛr'lø:s] (-es, -e) m proceeds pl

erlosch etc [ɛr'lɔʃ] vb siehe **erlöschen**

erlöschen [ɛr'lœʃən] unreg vi (Feuer) to go out; (Interesse) to cease, die; (Vertrag, Recht) to expire; **ein erloschener Vulkan** an extinct volcano

erlösen [ɛr'lø:zən] vt to redeem, save

Erlöser (-s, -) m (Rel) Redeemer; (Befreier) saviour (Brit), savior (US)

Erlösung f release; (Rel) redemption

ermächtigen [ɛr'mɛçtɪgən] vt to authorize, empower

Ermächtigung f authorization

ermahnen [ɛr'ma:nən] vt to admonish, exhort

Ermahnung f admonition, exhortation

Ermangelung [ɛr'maŋəlʊŋ], **Ermanglung** [ɛr'maŋlʊŋ] f: **in Ermang(e)lung** +gen because of the lack of

ermäßigen [ɛr'mɛsɪgən] vt to reduce

Ermäßigung f reduction

ermessen [ɛr'mɛsən] unreg vt to estimate, gauge; **Ermessen** (-s) nt estimation; discretion; **in jds Ermessen** dat **liegen** to lie within sb's discretion; **nach meinem Ermessen** in my judgement

Ermessensfrage f matter of discretion

ermitteln [ɛr'mɪtəln] vt to determine; (Täter) to trace ▷ vi: **gegen jdn ~** to investigate sb

Ermittlung [ɛr'mɪtlʊŋ] f determination; (Polizeiermittlung) investigation; **~en anstellen (über** +akk) to make inquiries (about)

Ermittlungsverfahren nt (Jur) preliminary proceedings pl

ermöglichen [ɛr'mø:klɪçən] vt (+dat) to make possible (for)

ermorden [ɛr'mɔrdən] vt to murder

Ermordung f murder

ermüden [ɛrˈmyːdən] vt to tire; (Tech) to fatigue ▷ vi to tire

ermüdend adj tiring; (fig) wearisome

Ermüdung f fatigue

Ermüdungserscheinung f sign of fatigue

ermuntern [ɛrˈmʊntərn] vt to rouse; (ermutigen) to encourage; (beleben) to liven up; (aufmuntern) to cheer up

ermutigen [ɛrˈmuːtɪɡən] vt to encourage

ernähren [ɛrˈnɛːrən] vt to feed, nourish; (Familie) to support ▷ vr to support o.s., earn a living; **sich ~ von** to live on

Ernährer, in (-s, -) m(f) breadwinner

Ernährung f nourishment; (Med) nutrition; (Unterhalt) maintenance

ernennen [ɛrˈnɛnən] unreg vt to appoint

Ernennung f appointment

erneuern [ɛrˈnɔʏərn] vt to renew; (restaurieren) to restore; (renovieren) to renovate

Erneuerung f renewal; restoration; renovation

erneut adj renewed, fresh ▷ adv once more

erniedrigen [ɛrˈniːdrɪɡən] vt to humiliate, degrade

Ernst [ɛrnst] (-es) m seriousness; **das ist mein ~** I'm quite serious; **im ~** in earnest; **~ machen mit etw** to put sth into practice; **ernst** adj serious ▷ adv: **es steht ernst um ihn** things don't look too good for him; **ernst gemeint** meant in earnest, serious; **Ernstfall** m emergency; **ernsthaft** adj serious; **Ernsthaftigkeit** f seriousness; **ernstlich** adj serious

Ernte [ˈɛrntə] (-, -n) f harvest; **Erntedankfest** nt harvest festival

ernten vt to harvest; (Lob etc) to earn

ernüchtern [ɛrˈnʏçtərn] vt to sober up; (fig) to bring down to earth

Ernüchterung f sobering up; (fig) disillusionment

Eroberer [ɛrˈʔobərər] (-s, -) m conqueror

erobern vt to conquer

Eroberung f conquest

eröffnen [ɛrˈʔœfnən] vt to open ▷ vr to present itself; **jdm etw ~** (geh) to disclose sth to sb

Eröffnung f opening

Eröffnungsansprache f inaugural od opening address

Eröffnungsfeier f opening ceremony

erogen [ɛroˈɡeːn] adj erogenous

erörtern [ɛrˈʔœrtərn] vt to discuss (in detail)

Erörterung f discussion

Erotik [eˈroːtɪk] f eroticism

erotisch adj erotic

Erpel [ˈɛrpəl] (-s, -) m drake

erpicht [ɛrˈpɪçt] adj: **~ (auf** +akk) keen (on)

erpressen [ɛrˈprɛsən] vt (Geld etc) to extort; (jdn) to blackmail

Erpresser (-s, -) m blackmailer

Erpressung f blackmail; extortion

erproben [ɛrˈproːbən] vt to test; **erprobt** tried and tested

erraten [ɛrˈraːtən] unreg vt to guess

errechnen [ɛrˈrɛçnən] vt to calculate, work out

erregbar [ɛrˈreːkbaːr] adj excitable; (reizbar) irritable; **Erregbarkeit** f excitability; irritability

erregen [ɛrˈreːɡən] vt to excite; (sexuell) to arouse; (ärgern) to infuriate; (hervorrufen) to arouse, provoke ▷ vr to get excited od worked up

Erreger (-s, -) m causative agent

Erregtheit f excitement; (Beunruhigung) agitation

Erregung f excitement; (sexuell) arousal

erreichbar adj accessible, within reach

erreichen [ɛrˈraɪçən] vt to reach; (Zweck) to achieve; (Zug) to catch; **wann kann ich Sie morgen ~?** when can I get in touch with you tomorrow?; **vom Bahnhof leicht zu ~** within easy reach of the station

errichten [ɛrˈrɪçtən] vt to erect, put up; (gründen) to establish, set up

erringen [ɛrˈrɪŋən] unreg vt to gain, win

erröten [ɛrˈrøːtən] vi to blush, flush

Errungenschaft [ɛrˈrʊŋənʃaft] f achievement; (umg: Anschaffung) acquisition

Ersatz [ɛrˈzats] (-es) m substitute; replacement; (Schadenersatz) compensation; (Mil) reinforcements pl; **als ~ für jdn einspringen** to stand in for sb; **Ersatzbefriedigung** f vicarious satisfaction; **Ersatzdienst** m (Mil) alternative service; **Ersatzkasse** f private health insurance; **Ersatzmann** m replacement; (Sport) substitute; **Ersatzmutter** f substitute mother; **ersatzpflichtig** adj liable to pay compensation; **Ersatzreifen** m (Aut) spare tyre (Brit) od tire (US); **Ersatzteil** nt spare (part); **ersatzweise** adv as an alternative

ersaufen [ɛrˈzaʊfən] unreg (umg) vi to drown

ersäufen [ɛrˈzɔʏfən] vt to drown

erschaffen [ɛrˈʃafən] unreg vt to create

erscheinen [ɛrˈʃaɪnən] unreg vi to appear

Erscheinung f appearance; (Geist) apparition; (Gegebenheit) phenomenon; (Gestalt) figure; **in ~ treten** (Merkmale) to appear; (Gefühle) to show themselves

Erscheinungsform f manifestation

Erscheinungsjahr nt (von Buch) year of publication

erschien etc [ɛrˈʃiːn] vb siehe **erscheinen**

erschienen pp von **erscheinen**

erschießen [ɛrˈʃiːsən] unreg vt to shoot (dead)

erschlaffen [ɛrˈʃlafən] vi to go limp; (Mensch) to become exhausted

erschlagen [ɛrˈʃlaːɡən] unreg vt to strike dead ▷ adj (umg: todmüde) worn out, dead beat (umg)

erschleichen [ɛrˈʃlaɪçən] unreg vt to obtain by stealth od dubious methods

erschließen [ɛrˈʃliːsən] unreg vt (Gebiet, Absatzmarkt) to develop, open up; (Bodenschätze) to tap

erschlossen [ɛrˈʃlɔsən] adj (Gebiet) developed

erschöpfen [ɛrˈʃœpfən] vt to exhaust

erschöpfend adj exhaustive, thorough

erschöpft adj exhausted

113

Erschöpfung f exhaustion
erschossen [ɛrˈʃɔsən] (umg) adj: **(völlig) ~ sein** to be whacked, be dead (beat)
erschrak etc [ɛrˈʃraːk] vb siehe **erschrecken²**
erschrecken¹ [ɛrˈʃrɛkən] vt to startle, frighten
erschrecken² [ɛrˈʃrɛkən] unreg vi to be frightened od startled
erschreckend adj alarming, frightening
erschrickt [ɛrˈʃrɪkt] vb siehe **erschrecken²**
erschrocken [ɛrˈʃrɔkən] pp von **erschrecken²** ▷ adj frightened, startled
erschüttern [ɛrˈʃʏtərn] vt to shake; (ergreifen) to move deeply; **ihn kann nichts ~** he always keeps his cool (umg)
erschütternd adj shattering
Erschütterung f (des Bodens) tremor; (tiefe Ergriffenheit) shock
erschweren [ɛrˈʃveːrən] vt to complicate; **~de Umstände** (Jur) aggravating circumstances; **es kommt noch ~d hinzu, dass ...** to compound matters ...
erschwindeln [ɛrˈʃvɪndəln] vt to obtain by fraud
erschwinglich [ɛrˈʃvɪŋlɪç] adj affordable
ersehen [ɛrˈzeːən] unreg vt: **aus etw ~, dass ...** to gather from sth that ...
ersehnt [ɛrˈzeːnt] adj longed-for
ersetzbar adj replaceable
ersetzen [ɛrˈzɛtsən] vt to replace; **jdm Unkosten** etc **~** to pay sb's expenses etc
ersichtlich [ɛrˈzɪçtlɪç] adj evident, obvious
ersparen [ɛrˈʃpaːrən] vt (Ärger etc) to spare; (Geld) to save; **ihr blieb auch nichts erspart** she was spared nothing
Ersparnis (-, **-se**) f saving
ersprießlich [ɛrˈʃpriːslɪç] adj profitable, useful; (angenehm) pleasant

🔵 **SCHLÜSSELWORT**

erst [eːrst] adv **1** first; **mach erst (ein)mal die Arbeit fertig** finish your work first; **wenn du das erst (ein)mal hinter dir hast** once you've got that behind you
2 (nicht früher als, nur) only; (nicht bis) not till; **erst gestern** only yesterday; **erst morgen** not until tomorrow; **erst als** only when, not until; **wir fahren erst später** we're not going until later; **er ist (gerade) erst angekommen** he's only just arrived
3: **wäre er doch erst zurück!** if only he were back!; **da fange ich erst gar nicht an** I simply won't bother to begin; **jetzt erst recht!** that just makes me all the more determined; **da gings erst richtig los** then things really got going

erstarren [ɛrˈʃtarən] vi to stiffen; (vor Furcht) to grow rigid; (Materie) to solidify
erstatten [ɛrˈʃtatən] vt (Unkosten) to refund; **Anzeige gegen jdn ~** to report sb; **Bericht ~** to make a report
Erstattung f (von Unkosten) reimbursement

Erstaufführung [ˈeːrstˌaʊffyːrʊŋ] f first performance
erstaunen [ɛrˈʃtaʊnən] vt to astonish ▷ vi to be astonished; **Erstaunen** (**-s**) nt astonishment
erstaunlich adj astonishing
Erstausgabe f first edition
erstbeste, r, s adj first that comes along
erste, r, s adj first; **als E~s** first of all; **in ~r Linie** first and foremost; **fürs E~** for the time being; **E~ Hilfe** first aid; **das ~ Mal** the first time
erstechen [ɛrˈʃtɛçən] unreg vt to stab (to death)
erstehen [ɛrˈʃteːən] unreg vt to buy ▷ vi to (a)rise
ersteigen [ɛrˈʃtaɪɡən] unreg vt to climb, ascend
ersteigern [ɛrˈʃtaɪɡərn] vt to buy at an auction
erstellen [ɛrˈʃtɛlən] vt to erect, build
erstens adv firstly, in the first place
erstere, r, s pron (the) former; **der/die/das E~** the former
ersticken [ɛrˈʃtɪkən] vt (lit, fig) to stifle; (Mensch) to suffocate; (Flammen) to smother ▷ vi (Mensch) to suffocate; (Feuer) to be smothered; **mit erstickter Stimme** in a choked voice; **in Arbeit ~** to be snowed under with work
Erstickung f suffocation
erst- zW: **erstklassig** adj first-class; **Erstkommunion** f first communion; **erstmalig** adj first; **erstmals** adv for the first time; **erstrangig** adj first-rate
erstrebenswert [ɛrˈʃtreːbənsveːrt] adj desirable, worthwhile
erstrecken [ɛrˈʃtrɛkən] vr to extend, stretch
Erststimme f first vote; see culture note

⚪ **ERSTSTIMME/ZWEITSTIMME**

The Erststimme and Zweitstimme (first and second vote) system is used to elect MPs to the Bundestag. Each elector is given two votes. The first is to choose a candidate in his constituency; the candidate with the most votes is elected MP. The second is to choose a party. All the second votes in each Land are counted and a proportionate number of MP's from each party is sent to the Bundestag.

Ersttagsbrief m first-day cover
Ersttagsstempel m first-day (date) stamp
erstunken [ɛrˈʃtʊŋkən] adj: **das ist ~ und erlogen** (umg) that's a pack of lies
Erstwähler (**-s**, **-**) m first-time voter
ersuchen [ɛrˈzuːxən] vt to request
ertappen [ɛrˈtapən] vt to catch, detect
erteilen [ɛrˈtaɪlən] vt to give
ertönen [ɛrˈtøːnən] vi to sound, ring out
Ertrag [ɛrˈtraːk] (**-(e)s**, **-̈e**) m yield; (Gewinn) proceeds pl
ertragen unreg vt to bear, stand
erträglich [ɛrˈtrɛːklɪç] adj tolerable, bearable
ertragreich adj (Geschäft) profitable, lucrative
ertrank etc [ɛrˈtraŋk] vb siehe **ertrinken**
ertränken [ɛrˈtrɛŋkən] vt to drown

erträumen [ɛr'trɔʏmən] *vt*: **sich** *dat* **etw ~** to dream of sth, imagine sth

ertrinken [ɛr'trɪŋkən] *unreg vi* to drown; **Ertrinken (-s)** *nt* drowning

ertrunken [ɛr'trʊŋkən] *pp von* **ertrinken**

erübrigen [ɛr'|y:brɪgən] *vt* to spare ▷ *vr* to be unnecessary

erwachen [ɛr'vaxən] *vi* to awake; **ein böses E~** (*fig*) a rude awakening

erwachsen [ɛr'vaksən] *adj* grown-up ▷ *vi unreg*: **daraus erwuchsen ihm Unannehmlichkeiten** that caused him some trouble

Erwachsene, r *f(m)* adult

Erwachsenenbildung *f* adult education

erwägen [ɛr'vɛ:gən] *unreg vt* to consider

Erwägung *f* consideration; **etw in ~ ziehen** to take sth into consideration

erwähnen [ɛr'vɛ:nən] *vt* to mention

erwähnenswert *adj* worth mentioning

Erwähnung *f* mention

erwarb *etc* [ɛr'varp] *vb siehe* **erwerben**

erwärmen [ɛr'vɛrmən] *vt* to warm, heat ▷ *vr* to get warm, warm up; **sich ~ für** to warm to

erwarten [ɛr'vartən] *vt* to expect; (*warten auf*) to wait for; **etw kaum ~ können** to hardly be able to wait for sth

Erwartung *f* expectation; **in ~ Ihrer baldigen Antwort** (*form*) in anticipation of your early reply

erwartungsgemäß *adv* as expected

erwartungsvoll *adj* expectant

erwecken [ɛr'vɛkən] *vt* to rouse, awake; **den Anschein ~** to give the impression; **etw zu neuem Leben ~** to resurrect sth

erwehren [ɛr'veːrən] *vr* + *gen* (*geh*) to fend off, ward off; (*des Lachens etc*) to refrain from

erweichen [ɛr'vaɪçən] *vt* to soften; **sich nicht ~ lassen** to be unmoved

erweisen [ɛr'vaɪzən] *unreg vt* to prove ▷ *vr*: **sich ~ als** to prove to be; **jdm einen Gefallen/ Dienst ~** to do sb a favour/service; **sich jdm gegenüber dankbar ~** to show one's gratitude to sb

erweitern [ɛr'vaɪtərn] *vt, vr* to widen, enlarge; (*Geschäft*) to expand; (*Med*) to dilate; (*fig: Kenntnisse*) to broaden; (*Macht*) to extend

Erweiterung *f* expansion

Erwerb [ɛr'vɛrp] **(-(e)s, -e)** *m* acquisition; (*Beruf*) trade

erwerben [ɛr'vɛrbən] *unreg vt* to acquire; **er hat sich** *dat* **große Verdienste um die Firma erworben** he has done great service for the firm

Erwerbs- *zW*: **erwerbsfähig** *adj* (*form*) capable of gainful employment; **Erwerbsgesellschaft** *f* acquisitive society; **erwerbslos** *adj* unemployed; **Erwerbsquelle** *f* source of income; **erwerbstätig** *adj* (gainfully) employed; **erwerbsunfähig** *adj* unable to work

erwidern [ɛr'viːdərn] *vt* to reply; (*vergelten*) to return

Erwiderung *f*: **in ~ Ihres Schreibens vom ...**

(*form*) in reply to your letter of the ...

erwiesen [ɛr'viːzən] *adj* proven

erwirbt [ɛr'vɪrpt] *vb siehe* **erwerben**

erwirtschaften [ɛr'vɪrtʃaftən] *vt* (*Gewinn etc*) to make by good management

erwischen [ɛr'vɪʃən] (*umg*) *vt* to catch, get; **ihn hats erwischt!** (*umg: verliebt*) he's got it bad; (*: krank*) he's got it; **kalt ~** (*umg*) to catch off-balance

erworben [ɛr'vɔrbən] *pp von* **erwerben**

erwünscht [ɛr'vʏnʃt] *adj* desired

erwürgen [ɛr'vʏrgən] *vt* to strangle

Erz [eːrts] **(-es, -e)** *nt* ore

erzählen [ɛr'tsɛːlən] *vt, vi* to tell; **dem werd ich was ~!** (*umg*) I'll have something to say to him; **~de Dichtung** narrative fiction

Erzähler, in [ɛr'tsɛːlɐ, -] *m(f)* narrator

Erzählung *f* story, tale

Erzbischof *m* archbishop

Erzengel *m* archangel

erzeugen [ɛr'tsɔʏgən] *vt* to produce; (*Strom*) to generate

Erzeuger (-s, -) *m* producer; **Erzeugerpreis** *m* manufacturer's price

Erzeugnis (-ses, -se) *nt* product, produce

Erzeugung *f* production; generation

Erzfeind *m* arch enemy

erziehbar *adj*: **ein Heim für schwer ~e Kinder** a home for difficult children

erziehen [ɛr'tsiːən] *unreg vt* to bring up; (*bilden*) to educate, train

Erzieher, in [ɛr'tsiːɐ, -] *m(f)* educator; (*in Kindergarten*) nursery school teacher

Erziehung *f* bringing up; (*Bildung*) education

Erziehungs- *zW*: **Erziehungsberechtigte, r** *f(m)* parent, legal guardian; **Erziehungsgeld** *nt* payment for new parents; **Erziehungsheim** *nt* community home; **Erziehungsurlaub** *m* leave for a new parent

erzielen [ɛr'tsiːlən] *vt* to achieve, obtain; (*Tor*) to score

erzkonservativ ['ɛrtskɔnzɛrva'tiːf] *adj* ultraconservative

erzog *etc* [ɛr'tsoːk] *vb siehe* **erziehen**

erzogen [ɛr'tsoːgən] *pp von* **erziehen**

erzürnen [ɛr'tsʏrnən] *vt* (*geh*) to anger, incense

erzwingen [ɛr'tsvɪŋən] *unreg vt* to force, obtain by force

Es [ɛs] **(-)** *nt* (*Mus: Dur*) E flat

es [ɛs] *nom, akk pron* it

Esche ['ɛʃə] **(-, -n)** *f* ash

Esel ['eːzəl] **(-s, -)** *m* donkey, ass; **ich ~!** (*umg*) silly me!

Eselsbrücke *f* (*Gedächtnishilfe*) mnemonic, aide-mémoire

Eselsohr *nt* dog-ear

Eskalation [ɛskalatsi'oːn] *f* escalation

eskalieren [ɛska'liːrən] *vt, vi* to escalate

Eskimo ['ɛskimo] **(-s, -s)** *m* eskimo

Eskorte [ɛs'kɔrtə] **(-, -n)** *f* (*Mil*) escort

eskortieren [ɛskɔr'tiːrən] *vt* (*geh*) to escort

Espenlaub ['ɛspənlaʊp] *nt*: **zittern wie ~** to shake like a leaf

115

essbar ['ɛsbaːr] adj eatable, edible

Essecke f dining area

essen ['esən] unreg vt, vi to eat; ~ **gehen** (auswärts) to eat out; ~ **Sie gern Äpfel?** do you like apples?; **Essen (-s, -)** nt (Mahlzeit) meal; (Nahrung) food; **Essen auf Rädern** meals on wheels

Essens- zW: **Essensausgabe** f serving of meals; (Stelle) serving counter; **Essensmarke** f meal voucher; **Essenszeit** f mealtime

Essgeschirr nt dinner service

Essig ['ɛsɪç] (-s, -e) m vinegar; **damit ist es ~** (umg) it's all off; **Essiggurke** f gherkin

Esskastanie f sweet chestnut

Essl. abk (= Esslöffel) tbsp.

Ess- zW: **Esslöffel** m tablespoon; **Esstisch** m dining table; **Esswaren** pl foodstuffs pl; **Esszimmer** nt dining room

Establishment [ɪs'tæblɪʃmənt] (-s, -s) nt establishment

Este ['eːstə] (-n, -n) m, **Estin** f Estonian

Estland ['eːstlant] nt Estonia

estnisch ['eːstnɪʃ] adj Estonian

Estragon ['ɛstragɔn] (-s) m tarragon

Estrich ['ɛstrɪç] (-s, -e) m stone/clay etc floor

etablieren [eta'bliːrən] vr to establish o.s.; (Comm) to set up

Etage [e'taːʒə] (-, -n) f floor, storey (Brit), story (US)

Etagenbetten pl bunk beds pl

Etagenwohnung f flat (Brit), apartment (US)

Etappe [e'tapə] (-, -n) f stage

etappenweise adv step by step, stage by stage

Etat [e'taː] (-s, -s) m budget; **Etatjahr** nt financial year; **Etatposten** m budget item

etc abk (= et cetera) etc.

etepetete [eːtəpe'teːtə] (umg) adj fussy

Ethik ['eːtɪk] f ethics sing

ethisch ['eːtɪʃ] adj ethical

ethnisch ['ɛtnɪʃ] adj ethnic; **~e Säuberung** ethnic cleansing

Etikett [eti'kɛt] (-(e)s, -e) nt (lit, fig) label

Etikette f etiquette, manners pl

Etikettenschwindel m (Pol): **es ist reinster ~, wenn ...** it is just playing od juggling with names if ...

etikettieren [etike'tiːrən] vt to label

etliche, r, s ['ɛtlɪçə(r, s)] adj quite a lot of ▷ pron pl some, quite a few; **~s** quite a lot

Etüde [e'tyːdə] (-, -n) f (Mus) étude

Etui [ɛt'viː] (-s, -s) nt case

etwa ['ɛtva] adv (ungefähr) about; (vielleicht) perhaps; (beispielsweise) for instance; (entrüstet, erstaunt): **hast du ~ schon wieder kein Geld dabei?** don't tell me you haven't got any money again! ▷ adv (zur Bestätigung): **Sie kommen doch, oder ~ nicht?** you are coming, aren't you?; **nicht ~** by no means; **willst du ~ schon gehen?** (surely) you don't want to go already?

etwaig ['ɛtvaɪç] adj possible

etwas pron something; (fragend, verneinend) anything; (ein wenig) a little ▷ adv a little; **er**

kann ~ he's good; **Etwas** nt: **das gewisse Etwas** that certain something

Etymologie [etymolo'giː] f etymology

EU [eː'|uː] (-) f abk (= Europäische Union) EU

euch [ɔʏç] pron (akk von ihr) you; yourselves; (dat von ihr) (to/for) you ▷ re, pron yourselves

euer ['ɔʏər] pron gen von **ihr** of you ▷ adj your

EU-Erweiterung f enlargement of the EU

EU-Kommissar, in m(f) EU commissioner

EU-Kommission f EU commission

Eule ['ɔʏlə] (-, -n) f owl

EU-Osterweiterung f eastward expansion of the EU

Euphemismus [ɔʏfe'mɪsmʊs] m euphemism

Eurasien [ɔʏ'raːziən] nt Eurasia

Euratom [ɔʏra'toːm] f abk (= Europäische Atomgemeinschaft) Euratom

eure, r, s ['ɔʏrə(r, s)] pron yours

eurerseits adv on your part

euresgleichen pron people like you

euretwegen ['ɔʏrət'veːgən] adv (für euch) for your sakes; (wegen euch) on your account

euretwillen ['ɔʏrət'vɪlən] adv: **um ~ =** **euretwegen**

eurige pron: **der/die/das E~** (geh) yours

Euro ['ɔʏro] (-, -s) m (Fin) euro

Eurocent m euro cent

Eurokrat [ɔʏro'kraːt] (-en, -en) m eurocrat

Europa [ɔʏ'roːpa] (-s) nt Europe

Europäer, in [ɔʏro'pɛːər(ɪn)] (-s, -) m(f) European

europäisch adj European; **das E~e Parlament** the European Parliament; **E~e Union** European Union; **E~e (Wirtschafts)gemeinschaft** European (Economic) Community, Common Market

Europa- zW: **Europameister** m European champion; **Europarat** m Council of Europe; **Europastraße** f Euroroute

Euter ['ɔʏtər] (-s, -) nt udder

Euthanasie [ɔʏtana'ziː] f euthanasia

EU-Verfassung f EU constitution

E. V., e. V. abk (= eingetragener Verein) registered association

ev. abk = **evangelisch**

evakuieren [evaku'iːrən] vt to evacuate

evangelisch [evaŋ'geːlɪʃ] adj Protestant

Evangelium [evaŋ'geːliʊm] nt Gospel

Evaskostüm nt: **im ~** in her birthday suit

eventuell [evɛntu'ɛl] adj possible ▷ adv possibly, perhaps

Evolution [evolutsi'oːn] f evolution

Evolutionstheorie f theory of evolution

evtl. abk = **eventuell**

EWG [eːve'geː] (-) f abk (früher: = Europäische Wirtschaftsgemeinschaft) EEC

ewig ['eːvɪç] adj eternal ▷ adv: **auf ~** forever; **ich habe Sie ~ lange nicht gesehen** (umg) I haven't seen you for ages; **Ewigkeit** f eternity; **bis in alle Ewigkeit** forever

EWS (-) nt abk (= Europäisches Währungssystem) EMS

EWU (-) f abk (= Europäische Währungsunion) EMU

ex [ɛks] (*umg*) *adv*: **etw ex trinken** to drink sth down in one

exakt [ɛ'ksakt] *adj* exact

exaltiert [ɛksal'tiːrt] *adj* exaggerated, effusive

Examen [ɛ'ksaːmən] (**-s, -** *od* **Examina**) *nt* examination

Examensarbeit *f* dissertation

Exekutionskommando [ɛksekutsi'oːnskɔmando] *nt* firing squad

Exekutive [ɛkseku'tiːvə] *f* executive

Exempel [ɛ'ksɛmpəl] (**-s, -**) *nt* example; **die Probe aufs ~ machen** to put it to the test

Exemplar [ɛksɛm'plaːr] (**-s, -e**) *nt* specimen; (*Buchexemplar*) copy; **exemplarisch** *adj* exemplary

exerzieren [ɛksɛr'tsiːrən] *vi* to drill

Exhibitionist [ɛkshibitsio'nɪst] *m* exhibitionist

Exil [ɛ'ksiːl] (**-s, -e**) *nt* exile

existentiell [ɛksɪstɛntsi'ɛl] *adj* = **existenziell**

Existenz [ɛksɪs'tɛnts] *f* existence; (*Unterhalt*) livelihood, living; (*pej: Mensch*) character; **Existenzberechtigung** *f* right to exist; **Existenzgrundlage** *f* basis of one's livelihood

existenziell [ɛksɪstɛntsi'ɛl] *adj*: **von ~er Bedeutung** of vital significance

Existenzkampf *m* struggle for existence

Existenzminimum (**-s, -ma**) *nt* subsistence level

existieren [ɛksɪs'tiːrən] *vi* to exist

exkl. *abk* = **exklusive**

exklusiv [ɛksklu'ziːf] *adj* exclusive; **Exklusivbericht** *m* (*Presse*) exclusive report

exklusive [ɛksklu'ziːvə] *präp+gen* exclusive of, not including ▷ *adv* exclusive of, excluding

Exkursion [ɛkskʊrzi'oːn] *f* (*study*) trip

Exmatrikulation [ɛksmatrikulatsi'oːn] *f* (*Univ*): **bei seiner ~** when he left university

exorzieren [ɛksɔr'tsiːrən] *vt* to exorcize

exotisch [ɛ'ksoːtɪʃ] *adj* exotic

expandieren [ɛkspan'diːrən] *vi* (*Econ*) to expand

Expansion [ɛkspanzi'oːn] *f* expansion

expansiv [ɛkspan'ziːf] *adj* expansionist; (*Wirtschaftszweige*) expanding

Expedition [ɛkspeditsi'oːn] *f* expedition; (*Comm*) forwarding department

Experiment [ɛksperi'mɛnt] *nt* experiment

experimentell [ɛksperimɛn'tɛl] *adj* experimental

experimentieren [ɛksperimɛn'tiːrən] *vi* to experiment

Experte [ɛks'pɛrtə] (**-n, -n**) *m* expert, specialist; **Expertenkommission** *f* think tank; **Expertenmeinung** *f* expert opinion

Expertin [ɛks'pɛrtɪn] *f* expert, specialist

explodieren [ɛksplo'diːrən] *vi* to explode

Explosion [ɛksplozi'oːn] *f* explosion

explosiv [ɛksplo'ziːf] *adj* explosive

Exponent [ɛkspo'nɛnt] *m* exponent

exponieren [ɛkspo'niːrən] *vt*: **an exponierter Stelle stehen** to be in an exposed position

Export [ɛks'pɔrt] (**-(e)s, -e**) *m* export

Exportartikel *m* export

Exporteur [ɛkspɔr'tøːr] *m* exporter

Exporthandel *m* export trade

Exporthaus *nt* export house

exportieren [ɛkspɔr'tiːrən] *vt* to export

Exportkaufmann *m* exporter

Exportland *nt* exporting country

Exportvertreter *m* export agent

Exportwirtschaft *f* export business *od* sector

Expressgut [ɛks'prɛsgut] *nt* express goods *pl od* freight

Expressionismus [ɛksprɛsio'nɪsmʊs] *m* expressionism

Expresszug *m* express (train)

extra ['ɛkstra] *adj inv* (*umg: gesondert*) separate; (*besondere*) extra ▷ *adv* (*gesondert*) separately; (*speziell*) specially; (*absichtlich*) on purpose; (*vor Adjektiven, zusätzlich*) extra; **Extra** (**-s, -s**) *nt* extra; **Extraausgabe** *f* special edition; **Extrablatt** *nt* special edition

Extrakt [ɛks'trakt] (**-(e)s, -e**) *m* extract

Extratour *f* (*fig: umg*): **sich** *dat* **~en leisten** to do one's own thing

extravagant [ɛkstrava'gant] *adj* extravagant; (*Kleidung*) flamboyant

Extrawurst (*umg*) *f* (*Sonderwunsch*): **er will immer eine ~ (gebraten haben)** he always wants something different

Extrem [ɛks'treːm] (**-s, -e**) *nt* extreme; **extrem** *adj* extreme; **Extremfall** *m* extreme (case)

Extremist, in *m(f)* extremist

Extremistenerlass [ɛkstre'mɪstən|ɛrlas] *m* law(s) governing extremism

extremistisch [ɛkstre'mɪstɪʃ] *adj* (*Pol*) extremist

Extremitäten [ɛkstremi'tɛːtən] *pl* extremities *pl*

extrovertiert [ɛkstrovɛr'tiːrt] *adj* extrovert

Exzellenz [ɛkstsɛ'lɛnts] *f* excellency

exzentrisch [ɛks'tsɛntrɪʃ] *adj* eccentric

Exzess [ɛks'tsɛs] (**-es, -e**) *m* excess

F, f¹ [εf] (-, -) *nt* F, f; **F wie Friedrich** ≈ F for Frederick, F for Fox (US); **nach Schema F** (*umg*) in the usual old way

f² *abk* (= *feminin*) fem.

Fa. *abk* (= *Firma*) co.

Fabel ['faːbəl] (-, -n) *f* fable; **fabelhaft** *adj* fabulous, marvellous (*Brit*), marvelous (*US*)

Fabrik [faˈbriːk] *f* factory; **Fabrikanlage** *f* plant; (*Gelände*) factory premises *pl*

Fabrikant [fabriˈkant] *m* (*Hersteller*) manufacturer; (*Besitzer*) industrialist

Fabrikarbeiter, in *m(f)* factory worker

Fabrikat [fabriˈkaːt] (-(e)s, -e) *nt* product; (*Marke*) make

Fabrikation [fabriːkatsiˈoːn] *f* manufacture, production

Fabrikbesitzer *m* factory owner

Fabrikgelände *nt* factory site

fabrizieren [fabriˈtsiːrən] *vt* (*geistiges Produkt*) to produce; (*Geschichte*) to concoct, fabricate

Fach [fax] (-(e)s, ¨er) *nt* compartment; (*in Schrank, Regal etc*) shelf; (*Sachgebiet*) subject; **ein Mann/eine Frau vom ~** an expert; **Facharbeiter** *m* skilled worker; **Facharzt** *m* (medical) specialist; **Fachausdruck** *m* technical term; **Fachbereich** *m* (special) field; (*Univ*) school, faculty; **Fachbuch** *nt* reference book

Fächer ['fɛçər] (-s, -) *m* fan

Fach- *zW:* **Fachfrau** *f* expert; **Fachgebiet** *nt* (special) field; **Fachgeschäft** *nt* specialist shop (*Brit*) *od* store (*US*); **Fachhändler** *m* stockist; **Fachhochschule** *f* college; **Fachidiot** (*umg*) *m* narrow-minded specialist; **Fachkraft** *f* qualified employee; **Fachkräftemangel** *m* lack of skilled *od* qualified personnel; **Fachkreise** *pl:* **in Fachkreisen** among experts; **fachkundig** *adj* expert, specialist; **Fachlehrer** *m* specialist subject teacher; **fachlich** *adj* technical; (*beruflich*) professional; **Fachmann** (-(e)s, *pl* **-leute**) *m* expert; **fachmännisch** *adj* professional; **Fachrichtung** *f* subject area; **Fachschule** *f* technical college; **fachsimpeln** *vi* to talk shop; **fachspezifisch** *adj* technical; **Fachverband** *m* trade association; **Fachwelt** *f* profession; **Fachwerk** *nt* timber frame; **Fachwerkhaus** *nt* half-timbered house

Fackel ['fakəl] (-, -n) *f* torch

fackeln (*umg*) *vi* to dither

Fackelzug *m* torchlight procession

fad, fade *adj* insipid; (*langweilig*) dull; (*Essen*) tasteless

Faden ['faːdən] (-s, ¨) *m* thread; **der rote ~** (*fig*) the central theme; **alle Fäden laufen hier zusammen** this is the nerve centre (*Brit*) *od* center (*US*) of the whole thing; **Fadennudeln** *pl* vermicelli *sing*; **fadenscheinig** *adj* (*lit, fig*) threadbare

Fagott [faˈgɔt] (-(e)s, -e) *nt* bassoon

fähig ['fɛːɪç] *adj:* **~ (zu** *od* +*gen*) capable (of); able (to); **zu allem ~ sein** to be capable of anything; **Fähigkeit** *f* ability

Fähnchen ['fɛːnçən] *nt* pennon, streamer

fahnden ['faːndən] *vi:* **~ nach** to search for

Fahndung *f* search

Fahndungsliste *f* list of wanted criminals, wanted list

Fahne ['faːnə] (-, -n) *f* flag; standard; **mit fliegenden ~n zu jdm/etw überlaufen** to go over to sb/sth; **eine ~ haben** (*umg*) to smell of drink

Fahnenflucht *f* desertion

Fahrausweis *m* (*form*) ticket

Fahrbahn *f* carriageway (*Brit*), roadway

fahrbar *adj:* **~er Untersatz** (*hum*) wheels *pl*

Fähre ['fɛːrə] (-, -n) *f* ferry

fahren ['faːrən] *unreg vt* to drive; (*Rad*) to ride; (*befördern*) to drive, take; (*Rennen*) to drive in ▷ *vi* (*sich bewegen*) to go; (*Schiff*) to sail; (*abfahren*) to leave; **mit dem Auto/Zug ~** to go *od* travel by car/train; **mit dem Aufzug ~** to take the lift, ride the elevator (*US*); **links/rechts ~** to drive on the left/right; **gegen einen Baum ~** to drive *od* go into a tree; **die U-Bahn fährt alle fünf Minuten** the underground goes *od* runs every five minutes; **mit der Hand ~ über** +*akk* to pass one's hand over; **(bei etw) gut/schlecht ~** (*zurechtkommen*) to do well/badly (with sth); **was ist (denn) in dich ge~?** what's got (*Brit*) *od* gotten (*US*) into you?; **einen ~ lassen** (*umg*) to fart (!)

fahrend *adj:* **~es Volk** travelling people

Fahrer, in ['faːrər(ɪn)] (-s, -) *m(f)* driver; **Fahrerflucht** *f* hit-and-run driving

Fahr- *zW:* **Fahrgast** *m* passenger; **Fahrgeld** *nt* fare; **Fahrgelegenheit** *f* transport; **Fahrgestell**

nt chassis; (*Aviat*) undercarriage

fahrig ['faːrɪç] *adj* nervous; (*unkonzentriert*) distracted

Fahr- *zW:* **Fahrkarte** *f* ticket; **Fahrkartenausgabe** *f* ticket office; **Fahrkartenautomat** *m* ticket machine; **Fahrkartenschalter** *m* ticket office

fahrlässig *adj* negligent; **~e Tötung** manslaughter; **Fahrlässigkeit** *f* negligence

Fahr- *zW:* **Fahrlehrer** *m* driving instructor; **Fahrplan** *m* timetable; **fahrplanmäßig** *adj* (*Eisenb*) scheduled; **Fahrpraxis** *f* driving experience; **Fahrpreis** *m* fare; **Fahrprüfung** *f* driving test; **Fahrrad** *nt* bicycle; **Fahrradweg** *m* cycle path; **Fahrrinne** *f* (*Naut*) shipping channel, fairway; **Fahrschein** *m* ticket; **Fahrschule** *f* driving school; **Fahrschüler** *m* learner (driver); **Fahrspur** *f* lane; **Fahrstuhl** *m* lift (*Brit*), elevator (*US*); **Fahrstunde** *f* driving lesson

Fahrt [faːrt] (**-, -en**) *f* journey; (*kurz*) trip; (*Aut*) drive; (*Geschwindigkeit*) speed; **gute ~!** safe journey!; **volle ~ voraus!** (*Naut*) full speed ahead!

fährt [fɛːrt] *vb siehe* **fahren**

fahrtauglich ['faːrtaʊklɪç] *adj* fit to drive

Fährte ['fɛːrtə] (**-, -n**) *f* track, trail; **jdn auf eine falsche ~ locken** (*fig*) to put sb off the scent

Fahrtenschreiber *m* tachograph

Fahrtkosten *pl* travelling expenses *pl*

Fahrtrichtung *f* course, direction

Fahr- *zW:* **fahrtüchtig** ['faːrtʏçtɪç] *adj* fit to drive; **Fahrverhalten** *nt* (*von Fahrer*) behaviour (*Brit*) *od* behavior (*US*) behind the wheel; (*von Wagen*) road performance; **Fahrzeug** *nt* vehicle; **Fahrzeughalter** (**-s, -**) *m* owner of a vehicle; **Fahrzeugpapiere** *pl* vehicle documents *pl*

Faible ['fɛːbl] (**-s, -s**) *nt* (*geh*) liking; (*Schwäche*) weakness; (*Vorliebe*) penchant

fair [fɛːr] *adj* fair

Fäkalien [fɛ'kaːliən] *pl* faeces *pl*

Faksimile [fak'ziːmile] (**-s, -s**) *nt* facsimile

faktisch ['faktɪʃ] *adj* actual

Faktor *m* factor

Faktum (**-s, -ten**) *nt* fact

fakturieren [faktuˈriːrən] *vt* (*Comm*) to invoice

Fakultät [fakʊlˈtɛːt] *f* faculty

Falke ['falkə] (**-n, -n**) *m* falcon

Falklandinseln ['falklantˈɪnzəln] *pl* Falkland Islands, Falklands

Fall [fal] (**-(e)s, ⁻e**) *m* (*Sturz*) fall; (*Sachverhalt, Jur, Gram*) case; **auf jeden ~, auf alle Fälle** in any case; (*bestimmt*) definitely; **gesetzt den ~ sein** (*umg*) to be sb's cup of tea; **klarer ~!** (*umg*) sure thing!, you bet!; **das mache ich auf keinen ~** there's no way I'm going to do that

Falle (**-, -n**) *f* trap; (*umg*: *Bett*) bed; **jdm eine ~ stellen** to set a trap for sb

fallen *unreg vi* to fall; (*im Krieg*) to fall, be killed; **etw ~ lassen** to drop sth; (*Bemerkung*) to make

sth; (*Plan*) to abandon sth, to drop sth

fällen ['fɛlən] *vt* (*Baum*) to fell; (*Urteil*) to pass

fällig ['fɛlɪç] *adj* due; (*Wechsel*) mature(d); **längst ~** long overdue; **Fälligkeit** *f* (*Comm*) maturity

Fallobst *nt* fallen fruit, windfall

falls *adv* in case, if

Fall- *zW:* **Fallschirm** *m* parachute; **Fallschirmjäger** *m* paratrooper; **Fallschirmspringer, in** *m(f)* parachutist; **Fallschirmtruppe** *f* paratroops *pl*; **Fallstrick** *m* (*fig*) trap, snare; **Fallstudie** *f* case study

fällt [fɛlt] *vb siehe* **fallen**

Falltür *f* trap door

fallweise *adv* from case to case

falsch [falʃ] *adj* false; (*unrichtig*) wrong; **ein ~es Spiel (mit jdm) treiben** to play (sb) false; **etw ~ verstehen** to misunderstand sth, get sth wrong; *siehe auch* **falschliegen**

fälschen ['fɛlʃən] *vt* to forge

Fälscher, in (**-s, -**) *m(f)* forger

Falschgeld *nt* counterfeit money

Falschheit *f* falsity, falseness; (*Unrichtigkeit*) wrongness

fälschlich *adj* false

fälschlicherweise *adv* mistakenly

falschliegen *unreg vi* to be wrong; **~ bei/mit** to be wrong about/in

Falschmeldung *f* (*Presse*) false report

Fälschung *f* forgery

fälschungssicher *adj* forgery-proof

Faltblatt *nt* leaflet; (*in Zeitschrift etc*) insert

Fältchen ['fɛltçən] *nt* crease, wrinkle

Falte ['faltə] (**-, -n**) *f* (*Knick*) fold, crease; (*Hautfalte*) wrinkle; (*Rockfalte*) pleat

falten *vt* to fold; (*Stirn*) to wrinkle

faltenlos *adj* without folds; without wrinkles

Faltenrock *m* pleated skirt

Falter ['faltər] (**-s, -**) *m* (*Tagfalter*) butterfly; (*Nachtfalter*) moth

faltig ['faltɪç] *adj* (*Haut*) wrinkled; (*Rock usw*) creased

falzen ['faltsən] *vt* (*Papierbogen*) to fold

Fam. *abk* = **Familie**

familiär [familiˈɛːr] *adj* familiar

Familie [faˈmiːliə] *f* family; **~ Otto Francke** (*als Anschrift*) Mr & Mrs Otto Francke and family; **zur ~ gehören** to be one of the family

Familien- *zW:* **Familienanschluss** *m:* **Unterkunft mit Familienanschluss** accommodation where one is treated as one of the family; **Familienkreis** *m* family circle; **Familienmitglied** *nt* member of the family; **Familienname** *m* surname; **Familienpackung** *f* family(-size) pack; **Familienplanung** *f* family planning; **Familienstand** *m* marital status; **Familienunternehmen** *nt* family business; **Familienvater** *m* head of the family; **Familienverhältnisse** *pl* family circumstances *pl*

Fanatiker, in [faˈnaːtikər(ɪn)] (**-s, -**) *m(f)* fanatic

fanatisch *adj* fanatical

Fanatismus [fana'tɪsmʊs] *m* fanaticism

fand *etc* [fant] *vb siehe* **finden**

Fang [faŋ] **(-(e)s, ⸚e)** *m* catch; (*Jagen*) hunting; (*Kralle*) talon, claw

fangen *unreg vt* to catch ▷ *vr* to get caught; (*Flugzeug*) to level out; (*Mensch: nicht fallen*) to steady o.s.; (*fig*) to compose o.s.; (*in Leistung*) to get back on form

Fangfrage *f* catch *od* trick question

Fanggründe *pl* fishing grounds *pl*

fängt [fɛŋkt] *vb siehe* **fangen**

Fantasie [fanta'zi:] *f* imagination; **in seiner ~** in his mind; **Fantasiegebilde** *nt* (*Einbildung*) figment of the imagination; **fantasielos** *adj* unimaginative

fantasieren [fanta'zi:rən] *vi* to fantasize; (*Med*) to be delirious

fantasievoll *adj* imaginative

Fantast [fan'tast] **(-en, -en)** *m* dreamer

fantastisch *adj* fantastic

Farb- *zW*: **Farbabzug** *m* coloured (*Brit*) *od* colored (*US*) print; **Farbaufnahme** *f* colour (*Brit*) *od* color (*US*) photograph; **Farbband** *nt* typewriter ribbon

Farbe ['fa:rbə] **(-, -n)** *f* colour (*Brit*), color (*US*); (*zum Malen etc*) paint; (*Stofffarbe*) dye; (*Karten*) suit

farbecht ['farp|ɛçt] *adj* colourfast (*Brit*), colorfast (*US*)

färben ['fɛrbən] *vt* to colour (*Brit*), color (*US*); (*Stoff, Haar*) to dye

farben- *zW*: **farbenblind** *adj* colour-blind (*Brit*), color-blind (*US*); **farbenfroh** *adj* colourful (*Brit*), colorful (*US*); **farbenprächtig** *adj* colourful (*Brit*), colorful (*US*)

Farbfernsehen *nt* colour (*Brit*) *od* color (*US*) television

Farbfilm *m* colour (*Brit*) *od* color (*US*) film

Farbfoto *nt* colour (*Brit*) *od* color (*US*) photo

farbig *adj* coloured (*Brit*), colored (*US*)

Farbige, r *f(m)* coloured (*Brit*) *od* colored (*US*) person

Farb- *zW*: **Farbkasten** *m* paintbox; **farblos** *adj* colourless (*Brit*), colorless (*US*); **Farbstift** *m* coloured (*Brit*) *od* colored (*US*) pencil; **Farbstoff** *m* dye; (*Lebensmittelfarb*) (artificial) colouring (*Brit*) *od* coloring (*US*); **Farbton** *m* hue, tone

Färbung ['fɛrbʊŋ] *f* colouring (*Brit*), coloring (*US*); (*Tendenz*) bias

Farn [farn] **(-(e)s, -e)** *m* fern; (*Adlerfarn*) bracken

Farnkraut [farn] *nt* = **Farn**

Färöer [fɛ'rø:ər] *pl* Faeroe Islands *pl*

Fasan [fa'za:n] **(-(e)s, -e(n))** *m* pheasant

Fasching ['faʃɪŋ] **(-s, -e** *od* **-s)** *m* carnival

Faschismus [fa'ʃɪsmʊs] *m* fascism

Faschist, in *m(f)* fascist

faschistisch [fa'ʃɪstɪʃ] *adj* fascist

faseln ['fa:zəln] *vi* to talk nonsense, drivel

Faser ['fa:zər] **(-, -n)** *f* fibre

Fass [fas] **(-es, ⸚er)** *nt* vat, barrel; (*für Öl*) drum; **Bier vom ~** draught beer; **ein ~ ohne Boden** (*fig*) a bottomless pit

Fassade [fa'sa:də] *f* (*lit, fig*) façade

fassbar *adj* comprehensible

Fassbier *nt* draught beer

fassen ['fasən] *vt* (*ergreifen*) to grasp, take; (*inhaltlich*) to hold; (*Entschluss etc*) to take; (*verstehen*) to understand; (*Ring etc*) to set; (*formulieren*) to formulate, phrase ▷ *vr* to calm down; **nicht zu ~** unbelievable; *siehe auch* **kurzfassen**

fasslich ['faslɪç] *adj* comprehensible

Fasson [fa'sõ:] **(-, -s)** *f* style; (*Art und Weise*) way; **aus der ~ geraten** (*lit*) to lose its shape

Fassung ['fasʊŋ] *f* (*Umrahmung*) mounting; (*Lampenfassung*) socket; (*Wortlaut*) version; (*Beherrschung*) composure; **jdn aus der ~ bringen** to upset sb; **völlig außer ~ geraten** to lose all self-control

fassungslos *adj* speechless

Fassungsvermögen *nt* capacity; (*Verständnis*) comprehension

fast [fast] *adv* almost, nearly; **~ nie** hardly ever

fasten ['fastən] *vi* to fast; **Fasten (-s)** *nt* fasting; **Fastenzeit** *f* Lent

Fastnacht *f* Shrovetide carnival

faszinieren [fastsi'ni:rən] *vt* to fascinate

fatal [fa'ta:l] *adj* fatal; (*peinlich*) embarrassing

fauchen ['fauxən] *vt, vi* to hiss

faul [faul] *adj* rotten; (*Person*) lazy; (*Ausreden*) lame; **daran ist etwas ~** there's something fishy about it

faulen *vi* to rot

faulenzen ['faulɛntsən] *vi* to idle

Faulenzer, in [**-s, -**) *m(f)* idler, loafer

Faulheit *f* laziness

faulig *adj* putrid

Fäulnis ['fɔylnɪs] **(-)** *f* decay, putrefaction

Faulpelz (*umg*) *m* lazybones *sing*

Faust ['faust] **(-, Fäuste)** *f* fist; **das passt wie die ~ aufs Auge** (*passt nicht*) it's all wrong; **auf eigene ~** (*fig*) on one's own initiative

Fäustchen ['fɔystçən] *nt*: **sich** *dat* **ins ~ lachen** to laugh up one's sleeve

faustdick (*umg*) *adj*: **er hat es ~ hinter den Ohren** he's a crafty one

Fausthandschuh *m* mitten

Faustregel *f* rule of thumb

Favorit, in [favo'ri:t(ɪn)] **(-en, -en)** *m(f)* favourite (*Brit*), favorite (*US*)

Fax [faks] **(-, -e)** *nt* fax; **faxen** *vt* to fax

Faxen ['faksən] *pl*: **~ machen** to fool around

Fazit ['fa:tsɪt] **(-s, -s** *od* **-e)** *nt*: **wenn wir aus diesen vier Jahren das ~ ziehen** if we take stock of these four years

FCKW (-s, -s) *m abk* (= *Fluorchlorkohlenwasserstoff*) CFC

FdH (*umg*) *abk* (= *Friss die Hälfte*) eat less

FDP, F.D.P. *f abk* (= *Freie Demokratische Partei*) Free Democratic Party; *see culture note*

● **FDP**

○ The FDP (Freie Demokratische Partei) was
○ founded in 1948 and is Germany's centre
○ party. It is a liberal party which has formed

governing coalitions with both the SPD and the CDU/CSU at times, both in the regions and in the *Bundestag*.

Feb. *abk* (= *Februar*) Feb.

Februar ['fe:brua:r] (**-(s), -e**) (*pl selten*) *m* February; *siehe auch* **September**

fechten ['fɛçtən] *unreg vi* to fence

Feder ['fe:dər] (**-, -n**) *f* feather; (*Schreibfeder*) pen nib; (*Tech*) spring; **in den ~n liegen** (*umg*) to be/stay in bed; **Federball** *m* shuttlecock; **Federballspiel** *nt* badminton; **Federbett** *nt* continental quilt; **federführend** *adj* (*Behörde*): **federführend (für)** in overall charge (of); **Federhalter** *m* pen; **federleicht** *adj* light as a feather; **Federlesen** *nt*: **nicht viel Federlesens mit jdm/etw machen** to make short work of sb/sth

federn *vi* (*nachgeben*) to be springy; (*sich bewegen*) to bounce ▷ *vt* to spring

Federung *f* suspension

Federvieh *nt* poultry

Federweiße, r *m* new wine

Federzeichnung *f* pen-and-ink drawing

Fee [fe:] (**-, -n**) *f* fairy

feenhaft ['fe:ənhaft] *adj* (*liter*) fairylike

Fegefeuer ['fe:gəfɔyər] *nt* purgatory

fegen ['fe:gən] *vt* to sweep

fehl [fe:l] *adj*: **~ am Platz** *od* **Ort** out of place; **Fehlanzeige** (*umg*) *f* dead loss

fehlen *vi* to be wanting *od* missing; (*abwesend sein*) to be absent ▷ *vi unpers*: **es fehlte nicht viel und ich hätte ihn verprügelt** I almost hit him; **etw fehlt jdm** sb lacks sth; **du fehlst mir** I miss you; **was fehlt ihm?** what's wrong with him?; **der/das hat mir gerade noch gefehlt!** (*ironisch*) he/that was all I needed; **weit gefehlt!** (*fig*) you're way out! (*umg*); (*ganz im Gegenteil*) far from it!; **mir ~ die Worte** words fail me; **wo fehlt es?** what's the trouble?, what's up? (*umg*)

Fehlentscheidung *f* wrong decision

Fehlentwicklung *f* mistake

Fehler (**-s, -**) *m* mistake, error; (*Mangel, Schwäche*) fault; **ihr ist ein ~ unterlaufen** she's made a mistake; **Fehlerbeseitigung** *f* (*Comput*) debugging; **fehlerfrei** *adj* faultless; without any mistakes; **fehlerhaft** *adj* incorrect; faulty; **fehlerlos** *adj* = **fehlerfrei**; **Fehlermeldung** *f* (*Comput*) error message; **Fehlersuchprogramm** *nt* (*Comput*) debugger

fehl- *zW*: **Fehlgeburt** *f* miscarriage; **fehlgehen** *unreg vi* to go astray; **Fehlgriff** *m* blunder; **Fehlkonstruktion** *f*: **eine Fehlkonstruktion sein** to be badly designed; **Fehlleistung** *f*: **freudsche Fehlleistung** Freudian slip; **Fehlschlag** *m* failure; **fehlschlagen** *unreg vi* to fail; **Fehlschluss** *m* wrong conclusion; **Fehlstart** *m* (*Sport*) false start; **Fehltritt** *m* false move; (*fig*) blunder, slip; (: *Affäre*) indiscretion; **Fehlurteil** *nt* miscarriage of justice; **Fehlzündung** *f* (*Aut*) misfire, backfire

Feier ['faɪər] (**-, -n**) *f* celebration; **Feierabend**

m time to stop work; **Feierabend machen** to stop, knock off; **was machst du am Feierabend?** what are you doing after work?; **jetzt ist Feierabend!** that's enough!

feierlich *adj* solemn; **das ist ja nicht mehr ~** (*umg*) that's beyond a joke; **Feierlichkeit** *f* solemnity; **Feierlichkeiten** *pl* festivities *pl*

feiern *vt, vi* to celebrate

Feiertag *m* holiday

feig *adj* cowardly

Feige ['faɪgə] (**-, -n**) *f* fig

feige *adj* cowardly

Feigheit *f* cowardice

Feigling *m* coward

Feile ['faɪlə] (**-, -n**) *f* file

feilen *vt, vi* to file

feilschen ['faɪlʃən] *vi* to haggle

fein [faɪn] *adj* fine; (*vornehm*) refined; (*Gehör etc*) keen; **~!** great!; **er ist ~ raus** (*umg*) he's sitting pretty; **sich ~ machen** to get all dressed up

Feind, in [faɪnt, 'faɪndɪn] (**-(e)s, -e**) *m(f)* enemy; **Feindbild** *nt* concept of an/the enemy; **feindlich** *adj* hostile; **Feindschaft** *f* enmity; **feindselig** *adj* hostile; **Feindseligkeit** *f* hostility

Fein- *zW*: **feinfühlend** *adj* sensitive; **feinfühlig** *adj* sensitive; **Feingefühl** *nt* delicacy, tact; **Feinheit** *f* fineness; refinement; keenness; **Feinkostgeschäft** *nt* delicatessen (shop), deli; **Feinschmecker** (**-s, -**) *m* gourmet; **Feinwaschmittel** *nt* mild(-action) detergent

feist [faɪst] *adj* fat

feixen ['faɪksən] (*umg*) *vi* to smirk

Feld [fɛlt] (**-(e)s, -er**) *nt* field; (*Schach*) square; (*Sport*) pitch; **Argumente ins ~ führen** to bring arguments to bear; **das ~ räumen** (*fig*) to bow out; **Feldarbeit** *f* (*Agr*) work in the fields; (*Geog etc*) fieldwork; **Feldblume** *f* wild flower; **Feldherr** *m* commander; **Feldjäger** *pl* (*Mil*) the military police; **Feldlazarett** *nt* (*Mil*) field hospital; **Feldsalat** *m* lamb's lettuce; **Feldstecher** *m* (pair of) binoculars *pl od* field glasses *pl*

Feld-Wald-und-Wiesen- (*umg*) *in zW* common-or-garden

Feld- *zW*: **Feldwebel** (**-s, -**) *m* sergeant; **Feldweg** *m* path; **Feldzug** *m* (*lit, fig*) campaign

Felge ['fɛlgə] (**-, -n**) *f* (wheel) rim

Felgenbremse *f* caliper brake

Fell [fɛl] (**-(e)s, -e**) *nt* fur; coat; (*von Schaf*) fleece; (*von toten Tieren*) skin; **ein dickes ~ haben** to be thick-skinned, have a thick skin; **ihm sind die ~e weggeschwommen** (*fig*) all his hopes were dashed

Fels [fɛls] (**-en, -en**) *m* = **Felsen**

Felsen ['fɛlzən] (**-s, -**) *m* rock; (*Klippe*) cliff; **felsenfest** *adj* firm

felsig *adj* rocky

Felsspalte *f* crevice

Felsvorsprung *m* ledge

feminin [femi'ni:n] *adj* feminine; (*pej*) effeminate

Feministin [femi'nɪstɪn] *f* feminist

Fenchel ['fɛnçəl] (**-s**) m fennel

Fenster ['fɛnstər] (**-s, -**) nt window; **weg vom ~** (umg) out of the game, finished; **Fensterbrett** nt windowsill; **Fensterladen** m shutter; **Fensterleder** nt chamois, shammy (leather); **Fensterplatz** m window seat; **Fensterputzer** (**-s, -**) m window cleaner; **Fensterscheibe** f windowpane; **Fenstersims** m windowsill

Ferien ['fe:riən] pl holidays pl, vacation (US); **die großen ~** the summer holidays (Brit), the long vacation (US Univ); **~ haben** to be on holiday; **Ferienhaus** nt holiday home; **Ferienkurs** m holiday course; **Ferienreise** f holiday; **Ferienwohnung** f holiday flat (Brit), vacation apartment (US); **Ferienzeit** f holiday period

Ferkel ['fɛrkəl] (**-s, -**) nt piglet

fern [fɛrn] adj, adv far-off, distant; **~ von hier** a long way (away) from here; siehe auch **fernhalten, fernliegen; Fernbedienung** f remote control; **fernbleiben** unreg vi: **fernbleiben (von** od **+dat)** to stay away (from)

Ferne (**-, -n**) f distance

ferner adj, adv further; (weiterhin) in future; **unter „~ liefen" rangieren** (umg) to be an also-ran

fern- zW: **Fernfahrer** m long-distance lorry (Brit) od truck driver; **Fernflug** m long-distance flight; **Ferngespräch** nt long-distance call (Brit), toll call (US); **ferngesteuert** adj remote-controlled; (Rakete) guided; **Fernglas** nt binoculars pl; **fernhalten** unreg vt to keep away; **Fernkopie** f fax; **Fernkopierer** m fax machine; **Fernkurs, Fernkursus** m correspondence course; **Fernlenkung** f remote control; **Fernlicht** nt (Aut): **mit Fernlicht fahren** to drive on full beam; **fernliegen** unreg vi: **jdm fernliegen** to be far from sb's mind

Fernmelde- in zW telecommunications; (Mil) signals

fern- zW: **Fernost aus/in Fernost** from/in the Far East; **fernöstlich** adj Far Eastern attrib; **Fernrohr** nt telescope; **Fernschreiben** nt telex; **Fernschreiber** m teleprinter; **fernschriftlich** adj by telex

Fernsehapparat m television (set)

Fernsehduell nt TV duel od debate

fernsehen ['fɛrnze:ən] unreg vi to watch television; **Fernsehen** (**-s**) nt television; **im Fernsehen** on television

Fernseher (**-s, -**) m television (set)

Fernseh- zW: **Fernsehgebühr** f television licence (Brit) od license (US) fee; **Fernsehgerät** nt television set; **Fernsehprogramm** nt (Kanal) channel, station (US); (Sendung) programme (Brit), program (US); (Fernsehzeitschrift) (television) programme (Brit) od program (US) guide; **Fernsehsendung** f television programme (Brit) od program (US); **Fernsehüberwachungsanlage** f closed-circuit television; **Fernsehzuschauer** m (television) viewer

Fern- zW: **Fernsprecher** m telephone;

Fernsprechzelle f telephone box (Brit) od booth (US); **Fernsteuerung** f remote control

Fernstudium nt multimedia course, = Open University course (Brit); see culture note

Fernverkehr m long-distance traffic

Fernweh nt wanderlust

Ferse ['fɛrzə] (**-, -n**) f heel

Fersengeld nt: **~ geben** to take to one's heels

fertig ['fɛrtıç] adj (bereit) ready; (beendet) finished; (gebrauchsfertig) ready-made; **~ ausgebildet** fully qualified; **mit jdm/etw ~ werden** to cope with sb/sth; **mit den Nerven ~ sein** to be at the end of one's tether; **~ bringen** od **machen** (beenden) to finish; **sich ~ machen** to get ready; **~ essen/lesen** to finish eating/reading; **~ stellen** to complete; **Fertigbau** m prefab(ricated house)

fertigbringen unreg vt (fähig sein) to manage, be capable of; (beenden) to finish

fertigen ['fɛrtıgən] vt to manufacture

Fertig- zW: **Fertiggericht** nt ready-to-serve meal; **Fertighaus** nt prefab(ricated house); **Fertigkeit** f skill; **fertigmachen** (umg) vt (Person) to finish; (körperlich) to exhaust; (moralisch) to get down; siehe auch **fertig**; **fertigstellen** vt to complete

Fertigung f production

Fertigungs- in zW production; **Fertigungsstraße** f production line

Fertigware f finished product

fertigwerden unreg vi siehe **fertig**

fesch [fɛʃ] (umg) adj (modisch) smart; (: hübsch) attractive

Fessel ['fɛsəl] (**-, -n**) f fetter

fesseln vt to bind; (mit Fesseln) to fetter; (fig) to grip; **ans Bett gefesselt** (fig) confined to bed

fesselnd adj gripping

Fest [fɛst] (**-(e)s, -e**) nt (Feier) celebration; (Party) party; **man soll die ~e feiern wie sie fallen** (Sprichwort) make hay while the sun shines

fest adj firm; (Nahrung) solid; (Gehalt) regular; (Gewebe, Schuhe) strong, sturdy; (Freund(in)) steady ▷ adv (schlafen) soundly; **~ angestellt** employed on a permanent basis; **~ entschlossen sein** to be absolutely determined; **~ umrissen** clearcut; **~e Kosten** (Comm) fixed costs pl

Festbeleuchtung f illumination

festbinden unreg vt to tie, fasten

festbleiben *unreg vi* to stand firm
Festessen *nt* banquet
festfahren *unreg vr* to get stuck
Festgeldkonto *nt* time-deposit account
festhalten *unreg vt* to seize, hold fast; (*Ereignis*) to record ▷ *vr:* **sich ~ (an** +*dat*) to hold on (to)
festigen *vt* to strengthen
Festigkeit *f* strength
fest- *zW:* **festklammern** *vr:* **sich festklammern (an** +*dat*) to cling on (to); **festklemmen** *vt* to wedge fast; **Festkomma** *nt* (*Comput*) fixed point; **Festland** *nt* mainland; **festlegen** *vt* to fix ▷ *vr* to commit o.s.; **jdn auf etw** *akk* **festlegen** (*festnageln*) to tie sb (down) to sth; (*verpflichten*) to commit sb to sth
festlich *adj* festive
fest- *zW:* **festliegen** *unreg vi* (*Fin: Geld*) to be tied up; **festmachen** *vt* to fasten; (*Termin etc*) to fix; **festnageln** *vt:* **jdn festnageln (auf** +*akk*) (*fig: umg*) to pin sb down (to); **Festnahme** (**-, -n**) *f* capture; **festnehmen** *unreg vt* to capture, arrest; **Festnetztelefon** *nt* fixed-line phone; **Festplatte** *f* (*Comput*) hard disk; **Festpreis** *m* (*Comm*) fixed price
Festrede *f* speech, address
festschnallen *vt* to strap down ▷ *vr* to fasten one's seat belt
festsetzen *vt* to fix, settle
Festspiel *nt* festival
fest- *zW:* **feststehen** *unreg vi* to be certain; **feststellbar** *adj* (*herauszufinden*) ascertainable; **feststellen** *vt* to establish; (*sagen*) to remark; (*Tech*) to lock (fast); **Feststellung** *f:* **die Feststellung machen, dass ...** to realize that ...; (*bemerken*) to remark *od* observe that ...; **Festtag** *m* holiday
Festung *f* fortress
festverzinslich *adj* fixed-interest *attrib*
Festwertspeicher *m* (*Comput*) read-only memory
Festzelt *nt* marquee
Fête ['fɛːtə] (**-, -n**) *f* party
Fett [fɛt] (**-(e)s, -e**) *nt* fat, grease; **fett** *adj* fat; (*Essen etc*) greasy; **fett gedruckt** bold-type; **fettarm** *adj* low fat; **fetten** *vt* to grease; **Fettfleck** *m* grease spot *od* stain; **fettfrei** *adj* fat-free; **Fettgehalt** *m* fat content; **fettig** *adj* greasy, fatty; **Fettnäpfchen** *nt:* **ins Fettnäpfchen treten** to put one's foot in it; **Fettpolster** *nt* (*hum: umg*): **Fettpolster haben** to be well-padded
Fetzen ['fɛtsən] (**-s, -**) *m* scrap; **..., dass die ~ fliegen** (*umg*) ... like mad
feucht [fɔʏçt] *adj* damp; (*Luft*) humid; **feuchtfröhlich** *adj* (*hum*) boozy
Feuchtigkeit *f* dampness; humidity
Feuchtigkeitscreme *f* moisturizer
feudal [fɔʏˈdaːl] *adj* (*Pol, Hist*) feudal; (*umg*) plush
Feuer ['fɔʏər] (**-s, -**) *nt* fire; (*zum Rauchen*) a light; (*fig: Schwung*) spirit; **für jdn durchs ~ gehen** to go through fire and water for sb; **~ und Flamme (für etw) sein** (*umg*) to be

dead keen (on sth); **~ für etw/jdn fangen** (*fig*) to develop a great interest in sth/sb; **Feueralarm** *m* fire alarm; **Feuereifer** *m* zeal; **feuerfest** *adj* fireproof; **Feuergefahr** *f* danger of fire; **bei Feuergefahr** in the event of fire; **feuergefährlich** *adj* inflammable; **Feuerleiter** *f* fire escape ladder; **Feuerlöscher** (**-s, -**) *m* fire extinguisher; **Feuermelder** (**-s, -**) *m* fire alarm
feuern *vt, vi* (*lit, fig*) to fire
Feuer- *zW:* **feuerpolizeilich** *adj* (*Bestimmungen*) laid down by the fire authorities; **Feuerprobe** *f* acid test; **feuerrot** *adj* fiery red
Feuersbrunst *f* (*geh*) conflagration
Feuer- *zW:* **Feuerschlucker** *m* fire-eater; **Feuerschutz** *m* (*Vorbeugung*) fire prevention; (*Mil: Deckung*) covering fire; **feuersicher** *adj* fireproof; **Feuerstein** *m* flint; **Feuerstelle** *f* fireplace; **Feuertreppe** *f* fire escape; **Feuerversicherung** *f* fire insurance; **Feuerwaffe** *f* firearm; **Feuerwehr** *f* fire brigade; **Feuerwehrauto** *nt* fire engine; **Feuerwerk** *nt* fireworks *pl*; **Feuerwerkskörper** *m* firework; **Feuerzangenbowle** *f* red wine punch containing rum which has been flamed off; **Feuerzeug** *nt* (cigarette) lighter
Feuilleton [fœjəˈtõː] (**-s, -s**) *nt* (*Presse*) feature section; (*Artikel*) feature (article)
feurig ['fɔʏrɪç] *adj* fiery
Fiche [fiːʃ] (**-s, -s**) *m od nt* (micro)fiche
ficht [fɪçt] *vb siehe* **fechten**
Fichte ['fɪçtə] (**-, -n**) *f* spruce
ficken ['fɪkən] (*umg!*) *vt, vi* to fuck (!)
fickerig ['fɪkərɪç], **fickrig** ['fɪkrɪç] (*umg*) *adj* fidgety
fidel [fiˈdeːl] (*umg*) *adj* jolly
Fidschi-Inseln, Fidschiinseln ['fɪdʒi|ɪnzəln] *pl* Fiji Islands
Fieber ['fiːbər] (**-s, -**) *nt* fever, temperature; (*Krankheit*) fever; **~ haben** to have a temperature; **fieberhaft** *adj* feverish; **Fiebermesser** *m* thermometer; **Fieberthermometer** *nt* thermometer
fiel *etc* [fiːl] *vb siehe* **fallen**
fies [fiːs] (*umg*) *adj* nasty
Figur [fiˈɡuːr] (**-, -en**) *f* figure; (*Schachfigur*) chessman, chess piece; **eine gute/schlechte/ traurige ~ abgeben** to cut a good/poor/sorry figure
fiktiv [fɪkˈtiːf] *adj* fictitious
Filet [fiˈleː] (**-s, -s**) *nt* (*Koch*) fillet; (*Rinderfilet*) fillet steak; (*zum Braten*) piece of sirloin *od* tenderloin (*US*)
Filiale [filiˈaːlə] (**-, -n**) *f* (*Comm*) branch
Filipino [fili'piːno] (**-s, -s**) *m* Filipino
Film [fɪlm] (**-(e)s, -e**) *m* film, movie (*bes US*); **da ist bei mir der ~ gerissen** (*umg*) I had a mental blackout; **Filmaufnahme** *f* shooting
Filmemacher, in *m(f)* film-maker
filmen *vt, vi* to film
Film- *zW:* **Filmfestspiele** *pl* film festival *sing*; **Filmkamera** *f* cine-camera; **Filmriss** (*umg*) *m* mental blackout; **Filmschauspieler, in** *m(f)* film *od* movie (*bes US*) actor, film *od* movie

actress; **Filmverleih** m film distributors pl;
Filmvorführgerät nt cine-projector

Filter ['fɪltər] **(-s, -)** m filter; **Filterkaffee** m
filter od drip (US) coffee; **Filtermundstück** nt
filter tip

filtern vt to filter

Filterpapier nt filter paper

Filz [fɪlts] **(-es, -e)** m felt

filzen vt (umg) to frisk ▷ vi (Wolle) to mat

Filzstift m felt-tip (pen)

Fimmel ['fɪməl] **(-s, -)** (umg) m: **du hast wohl
einen ~!** you're crazy!

Finale [fi'na:lə] **(-s, -(s))** nt finale; (Sport) final(s
pl)

Finanz [fi'nants] f finance; **Finanzen** pl
finances pl; **das übersteigt meine ~en**
that's beyond my means; **Finanzamt** nt ≈
Inland Revenue Office (Brit), Internal Revenue
Office (US); **Finanzbeamte, r** f(m) revenue
officer; **Finanzdienstleister, in** m(f) (Bank etc)
financial services provider

finanziell [finantsi'ɛl] adj financial

finanzieren [finan'tsi:rən] vt to finance, to
fund

Finanzierung f financing, funding

Finanz- zW: **Finanzminister** m ≈ Chancellor
of the Exchequer (Brit), Minister of
Finance; **finanzschwach** adj financially
weak; **Finanzwesen** nt financial system;
Finanzwirtschaft f public finances pl

finden ['fɪndən] unreg vt to find; (meinen) to
think ▷ vr to be (found); (sich fassen) to compose
o.s. ▷ vi: **ich finde schon allein hinaus** I
can see myself out; **ich finde nichts dabei,
wenn ...** I don't see what's wrong if ...; **das
wird sich ~** things will work out

Finder, in (-s, -) m(f) finder; **Finderlohn** m
reward (for the finder)

findig adj resourceful

fing etc [fɪŋ] vb siehe **fangen**

Finger ['fɪŋər] **(-s, -)** m finger; **mit ~n auf jdn
zeigen** (fig) to look askance at sb; **das kann
sich jeder an den (fünf) ~n abzählen** (umg)
it sticks out a mile; **sich** dat **etw aus den ~n
saugen** to conjure sth up; **lange ~ machen**
(umg) to be light-fingered; **Fingerabdruck**
m fingerprint; **Fingerhandschuh** m glove;
Fingerhut m thimble; (Bot) foxglove;
Fingernagel m fingernail; **Fingerring** m ring;
Fingerspitze f fingertip; **Fingerspitzengefühl**
nt sensitivity; **Fingerzeig** (-(e)s, -e) m hint,
pointer

fingieren [fɪŋ'gi:rən] vt to feign

fingiert adj made-up, fictitious

Fink ['fɪŋk] **(-en, -en)** m finch

Finne ['fɪnə] **(-n, -n)** m Finn

Finnin ['fɪnɪn] f Finn

finnisch adj Finnish

Finnland nt Finland

finster ['fɪnstər] adj dark, gloomy; (verdächtig)
dubious; (verdrossen) grim; (Gedanke) dark; **jdn
~ ansehen** to give sb a black look; **Finsternis**
(-) f darkness, gloom

Finte ['fɪntə] **(-, -n)** f feint, trick

Firlefanz ['fɪrləfants] (umg) m (Kram) frippery;
(Albernheit): **mach keinen ~** don't clown
around

Firma (-, **-men**) f firm; **die ~ dankt** (hum) much
obliged (to you)

Firmen- zW: **Firmeninhaber** m proprietor
(of firm); **Firmenregister** nt register of
companies; **Firmenschild** nt (shop) sign;
Firmenübernahme f takeover; **Firmenwagen**
m company car; **Firmenzeichen** nt trademark

Firmung f (Rel) confirmation

Firnis ['fɪrnɪs] **(-ses, -se)** m varnish

Fis [fɪs] **(-, -)** nt (Mus) F sharp

Fisch [fɪʃ] **-(e)s, -e)** m fish; **Fische** pl (Astrol)
Pisces sing; **das sind kleine ~e** (fig: umg) that's
child's play; **Fischbestand** m fish population

fischen vt, vi to fish

Fischer (-s, -) m fisherman

Fischerei [fɪʃə'raɪ] f fishing, fishery

Fisch- zW: **Fischfang** m fishing; **Fischgeschäft**
nt fishmonger's (shop); **Fischgräte** f
fishbone; **Fischgründe** pl fishing grounds pl,
fisheries pl; **Fischstäbchen** nt fish finger (Brit),
fish stick (US); **Fischzucht** f fish-farming;
Fischzug m catch of fish

Fisimatenten [fizima'tɛntən] (umg) pl
(Ausflüchte) excuses pl; (Umstände) fuss sing

Fiskus ['fɪskus] m (fig: Staatskasse) Treasury

fit [fɪt] adj fit

Fitness ['fɪtnəs] nt fitness

Fitnesstrainer, in m(f) fitness trainer,
personal trainer

Fittich ['fɪtɪç] **(-(e)s, -e)** m (liter): **jdn unter
seine ~e nehmen** (hum) to take sb under one's
wing

fix [fɪks] adj (flink) quick; (Person) alert, smart;
~e Idee obsession, idée fixe; **~ und fertig**
finished; (erschöpft) done in; **jdn ~ und fertig
machen** (umg) to drive sb mad

fixen (umg) vi (Drogen spritzen) to fix

Fixer, in ['fɪksər(ɪn)] (umg) m(f) junkie (inf);
Fixerstube (umg) f junkies' centre (inf)

fixieren [fɪ'ksi:rən] vt to fix; (anstarren) to stare
at; **er ist zu stark auf seine Mutter fixiert**
(Psych) he has a mother fixation

Fixkosten pl (Comm) fixed costs pl

FKK abk = **Freikörperkultur**

flach [flax] adj flat; (Gefäß) shallow; **auf dem
~en Land** in the middle of the country

Fläche ['flɛçə] **(-, -n)** f area; (Oberfläche) surface

Flächeninhalt m surface area

Flach- zW: **flachfallen** unreg (umg) vi to fall
through; **Flachheit** f flatness; shallowness;
Flachland nt lowland; **flachliegen** unreg (umg)
vi to be laid up; **Flachmann** **-(e)s, pl -männer)**
(umg) m hip flask

flachsen ['flaksən] (umg) vi to kid around

flackern ['flakərn] vi to flare, flicker

Fladen ['fla:dən] **(-s, -)** m (Koch) round flat
dough-cake; (umg: Kuhfladen) cowpat

Flagge ['flagə] **(-, -n)** f flag; **~ zeigen** (fig) to
nail one's colours to the mast

flaggen vi to fly flags od a flag

flagrant [fla'grant] adj flagrant; **in ~i** red-handed

Flak [flak] **(-s, -)** f (= Flug(zeug)abwehrkanone) anti-aircraft gun; (Einheit) anti-aircraft unit

flambieren [flam'bi:rən] vt (Koch) to flambé

Flame ['fla:mə] **(-n, -n)** m Fleming

Flämin ['flɛ:mɪn] f Fleming

flämisch ['flɛ:mɪʃ] adj Flemish

Flamme ['flamə] **(-, -n)** f flame; **in ~n stehen/ aufgehen** to be in/go up in flames

Flandern ['flandərn] nt Flanders sing

Flanell [fla'nɛl] **(-s, -e)** m flannel

Flanke ['flaŋkə] **(-, -n)** f flank; (Sport: Seite) wing

Flasche ['flaʃə] **(-, -n)** f bottle; (umg: Versager) wash-out; **zur ~ greifen** (fig) to hit the bottle

Flaschen- zW: **Flaschenbier** nt bottled beer; **Flaschenöffner** m bottle opener; **Flaschenwein** m bottled wine; **Flaschenzug** m pulley

flatterhaft adj flighty, fickle

flattern ['flatərn] vi to flutter

flau [flaʊ] adj (Brise, Comm) slack; **jdm ist ~ (im Magen)** sb feels queasy

Flaum [flaʊm] **(-(e)s)** m (Feder) down

flauschig ['flaʊʃɪç] adj fluffy

Flausen ['flaʊzən] pl silly ideas pl; (Ausflüchte) weak excuses pl

Flaute ['flaʊtə] **(-, -n)** f calm; (Comm) recession

Flechte ['flɛçtə] **(-, -n)** f (Med) dry scab; (Bot) lichen

flechten unreg vt to plait; (Kranz) to twine

Fleck [flɛk] **(-(e)s, -e)** m (Schmutzfleck) stain; (Farbfleck) patch; (Stelle) spot; **nicht vom ~ kommen** (lit, fig) not to get any further; **sich nicht vom ~ rühren** not to budge; **vom ~ weg** straight away

Fleckchen nt: **ein schönes ~ (Erde)** a lovely little spot

Flecken **(-s, -)** m = **Fleck**; **fleckenlos** adj spotless; **Fleckenmittel** nt stain remover; **Fleckenwasser** nt stain remover

fleckig adj marked; (schmutzig) stained

Fledermaus ['fle:dərmaʊs] f bat

Flegel ['fle:gəl] **(-s, -)** m flail; (Person) lout; **flegelhaft** adj loutish, unmannerly; **Flegeljahre** pl adolescence sing

flegeln vr to loll, sprawl

flehen ['fle:ən] vi (geh) to implore

flehentlich adj imploring

Fleisch ['flaɪʃ] **(-(e)s)** nt flesh; (Essen) meat; **sich dat od akk ins eigene ~ schneiden** to cut off one's nose to spite one's face (Sprichwort); **es ist mir in ~ und Blut übergegangen** it has become second nature to me; **Fleischbrühe** f meat stock

Fleischer **(-s, -)** m butcher

Fleischerei [flaɪʃə'raɪ] f butcher's (shop)

fleischig adj fleshy

Fleisch- zW: **Fleischkäse** m meat loaf; **fleischlich** adj carnal; **Fleischpastete** f meat pie; **Fleischsalat** m diced meat salad with mayonnaise; **Fleischvergiftung** f food poisoning (from meat); **Fleischwolf** m mincer; **Fleischwunde** f flesh wound; **Fleischwurst** f pork sausage

Fleiß ['flaɪs] **(-es)** m diligence, industry; **ohne ~ kein Preis** (Sprichwort) success never comes easily

fleißig adj diligent, industrious; **~ studieren/ arbeiten** to study/work hard

flektieren [flɛk'ti:rən] vt to inflect

flennen ['flɛnən] (umg) vi to cry, blubber

fletschen ['flɛtʃən] vt (Zähne) to show

Fleurop® ['flɔʏrɔp] f ≈ Interflora®

flexibel [flɛ'ksi:bəl] adj flexible

Flexibilität [flɛksibili'tɛ:t] f flexibility

flicht [flɪçt] vb siehe **flechten**

Flicken ['flɪkən] **(-s, -)** m patch

flicken vt to mend

Flickschusterei ['flɪkʃu:stəraɪ] f: **das ist ~** that's a patch-up job

Flieder ['fli:dər] **(-s, -)** m lilac

Fliege ['fli:gə] **(-, -n)** f fly; (Schlips) bow tie; **zwei ~n mit einer Klappe schlagen** (Sprichwort) to kill two birds with one stone; **ihn stört die ~ an der Wand** every little thing irritates him

fliegen unreg vt, vi to fly; **auf jdn/etw ~** (umg) to be mad about sb/sth; **aus der Kurve ~** to skid off the bend; **aus der Firma ~** (umg) to get the sack

fliegend adj attrib flying; **~e Hitze** hot flushes pl

Fliegengewicht nt (Sport, fig) flyweight

Fliegenklatsche ['fli:gənklatʃə] f fly-swat

Fliegenpilz m fly agaric

Flieger **(-s, -)** m flier, airman; **Fliegeralarm** m air-raid warning

fliehen ['fli:ən] unreg vi to flee

Fliehkraft ['fli:kraft] f centrifugal force

Fliese ['fli:zə] **(-, -n)** f tile

Fließband ['fli:sbant] nt assembly od production line; **am ~ arbeiten** to work on the assembly od production line; **Fließbandarbeit** f production-line work; **Fließbandproduktion** f assembly-line production

fließen unreg vi to flow

fließend adj flowing; (Rede, Deutsch) fluent; (Übergang) smooth

Fließ- zW: **Fließheck** nt fastback; **Fließkomma** nt (Comput) ≈ floating point; **Fließpapier** nt blotting paper (Brit), fleece paper (US)

Flimmerkasten (umg) m (Fernsehen) box

Flimmerkiste (umg) f (Fernsehen) box

flimmern ['flɪmərn] vi to glimmer; **es flimmert mir vor den Augen** my head's swimming

flink [flɪŋk] adj nimble, lively; **mit etw ~ bei der Hand sein** to be quick (off the mark) with sth; **Flinkheit** f nimbleness, liveliness

Flinte ['flɪntə] **(-, -n)** f shotgun; **die ~ ins Korn werfen** to throw in the sponge

Flirt [flœrt] **(-s, -s)** m flirtation; **einen ~ (mit jdm) haben** flirt (with sb)

flirten ['flɪrtən] vi to flirt

Flittchen (*pej: umg*) *nt* floozy
Flitter (**-s**, **-**) *m* (*Flitterschmuck*) sequins *pl*
Flitterwochen *pl* honeymoon *sing*
flitzen ['flɪtsən] *vi* to flit
Flitzer (**-s**, **-**) (*umg*) *m* (*Auto*) sporty car
floaten ['floːtən] *vt*, *vi* (*Fin*) to float
flocht *etc* [flɔxt] *vb siehe* **flechten**
Flocke ['flɔkə] (**-**, **-n**) *f* flake
flockig *adj* flaky
flog *etc* [floːk] *vb siehe* **fliegen**
Floh [floː] (**-(e)s**, **ˮe**) *m* flea; **jdm einen ~ ins Ohr setzen** (*umg*) to put an idea into sb's head
floh *etc* *vb siehe* **fliehen**
Flohmarkt *m* flea market
Flora ['floːra] (**-**, **-ren**) *f* flora
Florenz [floˈrɛnts] *nt* Florence
florieren [floˈriːrən] *vi* to flourish
Florist, in *m(f)* florist
Floskel ['flɔskəl] (**-**, **-n**) *f* set phrase; **floskelhaft** *adj* cliché-ridden, stereotyped
Floß [floːs] (**-es**, **ˮe**) *nt* raft
floss *etc* [flɔs] *vb siehe* **fließen**
Flosse ['flɔsə] (**-**, **-n**) *f* fin; (*Taucherflosse*) flipper; (*umg: Hand*) paw
Flöte ['fløːtə] (**-**, **-n**) *f* flute; (*Blockflöte*) recorder
flöten gehen ['fløːtəngeːən] (*umg*) *unreg vi* to go for a burton
Flötist, in [fløːtɪst(ɪn)] *m(f)* flautist, flutist (*bes US*)
flott [flɔt] *adj* lively; (*elegant*) smart; (*Naut*) afloat
Flotte (**-**, **-n**) *f* fleet
Flottenstützpunkt *m* naval base
flottmachen *vt* (*Schiff*) to float off; (*Auto, Fahrrad etc*) to put back on the road
Flöz [fløːts] (**-es**, **-e**) *nt* layer, seam
Fluch [fluːx] (**-(e)s**, **ˮe**) *m* curse; **fluchen** *vi* to curse, swear
Flucht [flʊxt] (**-**, **-en**) *f* flight; (*Fensterflucht*) row; (*Reihe*) range; (*Zimmerflucht*) suite; (*geglückt*) flight, escape; **jdn/etw in die ~ schlagen** to put sb/sth to flight
fluchtartig *adj* hasty
flüchten ['flʏçtən] *vi* to flee ▷ *vr* to take refuge
Fluchthilfe *f*: **~ leisten** to aid an escape
flüchtig *adj* fugitive; (*Chem*) volatile; (*oberflächlich*) cursory; (*eilig*) fleeting; **~er Speicher** (*Comput*) volatile memory; **jdn ~ kennen** to have met sb briefly; **Flüchtigkeit** *f* transitoriness; volatility; cursoriness; **Flüchtigkeitsfehler** *m* careless slip
Flüchtling *m* refugee
Flüchtlingslager *nt* refugee camp
Flucht- *zW*: **Fluchtversuch** *m* escape attempt; **Fluchtweg** *m* escape route
Flug [fluːk] (**-(e)s**, **ˮe**) *m* flight; **im ~** airborne, in flight; **wie im ~(e)** (*fig*) in a flash; **Flugabwehr** *f* anti-aircraft defence; **Flugbahn** *f* flight path; (*Kreisbahn*) orbit; **Flugbegleiter, in** *m(f)* (*Aviat*) flight attendant; **Flugblatt** *nt* pamphlet
Flügel ['flyːgəl] (**-s**, **-**) *m* wing; (*Mus*) grand piano; **Flügeltür** *f* double door

flugfähig *adj* able to fly; (*Flugzeug: in Ordnung*) airworthy
Fluggast *m* airline passenger
flügge ['flʏgə] *adj* (fully-)fledged; **~ werden** (*lit*) to be able to fly; (*fig*) to leave the nest
Flug- *zW*: **Fluggeschwindigkeit** *f* flying *od* air speed; **Fluggesellschaft** *f* airline (company); **Flughafen** *m* airport; **Flughöhe** *f* altitude (of flight); **Flugkarte** *f* airline ticket; **Fluglotse** *m* air traffic *od* flight controller; **Flugplan** *m* flight schedule; **Flugplatz** *m* airport; (*klein*) airfield; **Flugreise** *f* flight
flugs [flʊks] *adv* speedily
Flug- *zW*: **Flugsand** *m* drifting sand; **Flugschein** *m* pilot's licence (*Brit*) *od* license (*US*); **Flugschreiber** *m* flight recorder; **Flugschrift** *f* pamphlet; **Flugsteig** *m* gate; **Flugstrecke** *f* air route; **Flugverkehr** *m* air traffic; **Flugwesen** *nt* aviation
Flugzeug (**-(e)s**, **-e**) *nt* plane, aeroplane (*Brit*), airplane (*US*); **Flugzeugentführung** *f* hijacking of a plane; **Flugzeughalle** *f* hangar; **Flugzeugträger** *m* aircraft carrier
fluktuieren [flʊktuˈiːrən] *vi* to fluctuate
Flunder ['flʊndər] (**-**, **-n**) *f* flounder
flunkern ['flʊŋkərn] *vi* to fib, tell stories
Fluor ['fluːɔr] (**-s**) *nt* fluorine
Flur[1] [fluːr] (**-(e)s**, **-e**) *m* hall; (*Treppenflur*) staircase
Flur[2] [fluːr] (**-**, **-en**) *f* (*geh*) open fields *pl*; **allein auf weiter ~ stehen** (*fig*) to be out on a limb
Fluss [flʊs] (**-es**, **ˮe**) *m* river; (*Fließen*) flow; **im ~ sein** (*fig*) to be in a state of flux; **etw in ~ bringen** *akk* to get sth moving; **flussab, flussabwärts** *adv* downstream; **flussauf, flussaufwärts** *adv* upstream; **Flussdiagramm** *nt* flow chart
flüssig ['flʏsɪç] *adj* liquid; (*Stil*) flowing; **~es Vermögen** (*Comm*) liquid assets *pl*; **Flüssigkeit** *f* liquid; (*Zustand*) liquidity; **flüssigmachen** *vt* (*Geld*) to make available
Flussmündung *f* estuary
Flusspferd *nt* hippopotamus
flüstern ['flʏstərn] *vt*, *vi* to whisper
Flüsterpropaganda *f* whispering campaign
Flut [fluːt] (**-**, **-en**) *f* (*lit, fig*) flood; (*Gezeiten*) high tide; **fluten** *vi* to flood; **Flutlicht** *nt* floodlight
flutschen ['flʊtʃən] (*umg*) *vi* (*rutschen*) to slide; (*funktionieren*) to go well
Flutwelle *f* tidal wave
fl. W. *abk* (= *fließendes Wasser*) running water
focht *etc* [fɔxt] *vb siehe* **fechten**
föderativ [føderaˈtiːf] *adj* federal
Fohlen ['foːlən] (**-s**, **-**) *nt* foal
Föhn [føːn] (**-(e)s**, **-e**) *m* foehn, *warm dry alpine wind*; (*Haartrockner*) hairdryer
föhnen *vt* to blow-dry
Föhre ['føːrə] (**-**, **-n**) *f* Scots pine
Folge ['fɔlgə] (**-**, **-n**) *f* series, sequence; (*Fortsetzung*) instalment (*Brit*), installment (*US*); (*TV, Rundf*) episode; (*Auswirkung*) result; **in rascher ~** in quick succession; **etw zur ~ haben** to result in sth; **~n haben** to have

consequences; **einer Sache** dat ~ **leisten** to comply with sth; **Folgeerscheinung** f result, consequence

folgen vi+dat to follow ▷ vi (gehorchen) to obey; **jdm ~ können** (fig) to follow od understand sb; **daraus folgt, dass ...** it follows from this that ...

folgend adj following; **im F-en** in the following; (schriftlich) below

folgendermaßen ['fɔlɡəndər'ma:sən] adv as follows, in the following way

folgenreich adj momentous

folgenschwer adj momentous

folgerichtig adj logical

folgern vt: ~ **(aus)** to conclude (from)

Folgerung f conclusion

folgewidrig adj illogical

folglich ['fɔlklɪç] adv consequently

folgsam ['fɔlkza:m] adj obedient

Folie ['fo:liə] (-, -n) f foil

Folienschweißgerät nt shrink-wrap machine

Folklore ['fɔlklo:ər] (-) f folklore

Folter ['fɔltər] (-, -n) f torture; (Gerät) rack; **jdn auf die ~ spannen** (fig) to keep sb on tenterhooks

foltern vt to torture

Fön® [fø:n] (-(e)s, -e) m hairdryer

Fonds [fõ:] (-, -) m (lit, fig) fund; (Fin: Schuldverschreibung) government bond; **Fondsmanager, in** m(f) fund manager

fönen vt siehe **föhnen**

Fono-, fono- in zW = **Phono-, phono-**

Fontäne [fɔn'tɛ:nə] (-, -n) f fountain

foppen ['fɔpən] vt to tease

forcieren [fɔr'si:rən] vt to push; (Tempo) to force; (Konsum, Produktion) to push od force up

Förderband ['fœrdərbant] nt conveyor belt

Förderer (-s, -) m patron

Fördergebiet nt development area

Förderin f patroness

Förderkorb m pit cage

Förderleistung f (Min) output

förderlich adj beneficial

fordern ['fɔrdərn] vt to demand; (fig: kosten: Opfer) to claim; (: herausfordern) to challenge

fördern ['fœrdərn] vt to promote; (unterstützen) to help; (Kohle) to extract; (finanziell: Projekt) to sponsor; (jds Talent, Neigung) to encourage, foster

Förderplattform f production platform

Förderstufe f (Sch) first stage of secondary school where abilities are judged

Förderturm m (Min) winding tower; (auf Bohrstelle) derrick

Forderung ['fɔrdəruŋ] f demand

Förderung ['fœrdəruŋ] f promotion; help; extraction

Forelle [fo'rɛlə] f trout

Form [fɔrm] (-, -en) f shape; (Gestaltung) form; (Gussform) mould; (Backform) baking tin; **in ~ von** in the shape of; **in ~ sein** to be in good form od shape; **die ~ wahren** to observe the proprieties; **in aller ~** formally

formal [fɔr'ma:l] adj formal; (Besitzer, Grund) technical

formalisieren [fɔrmali'zi:rən] vt to formalize

Formalität [fɔrmali'tɛ:t] f formality; **alle ~en erledigen** to go through all the formalities

Format [fɔr'ma:t] (-(e)s, -e) nt format; (fig) quality

formatieren [fɔrma'ti:rən] vt (Text, Diskette) to format

Formation [fɔrmatsi'o:n] f formation

formbar adj malleable

Formblatt nt form

Formel (-, -n) f formula; (von Eid etc) wording; (Floskel) set phrase; **formelhaft** adj (Sprache, Stil) stereotyped

formell [fɔr'mɛl] adj formal

formen vt to form, shape

Formfehler m faux pas, gaffe; (Jur) irregularity

Formfleisch nt pressed meat

formieren [fɔr'mi:rən] vt to form ▷ vr to form up

förmlich ['fœrmlɪç] adj formal; (umg) real; **Förmlichkeit** f formality

formlos adj shapeless; (Benehmen etc) informal; (Antrag) unaccompanied by a form od any forms

Formsache f formality

Formular [fɔrmu'la:r] (-s, -e) nt form

formulieren [fɔrmu'li:rən] vt to formulate

Formulierung f wording

formvollendet adj perfect; (Vase etc) perfectly formed

forsch [fɔrʃ] adj energetic, vigorous

forschen [fɔrʃən] vi to search; (wissenschaftlich) to (do) research; ~ **nach** to search for

forschend adj searching

Forscher (-s, -) m research scientist; (Naturforscher) explorer

Forschung ['fɔrʃuŋ] f research; ~ **und Lehre** research and teaching; ~ **und Entwicklung** research and development

Forschungsreise f scientific expedition

Forst [fɔrst] (-(e)s, -e) m forest; **Forstarbeiter** m forestry worker

Förster ['fœrstər] (-s, -) m forester; (für Wild) gamekeeper

Forstwesen nt forestry

Forstwirtschaft f forestry

fort [fɔrt] adv away; (verschwunden) gone; (vorwärts) on; **und so ~** and so on; **in einem ~** incessantly; **fortbestehen** unreg vi to continue to exist; **fortbewegen** vt, vr to move away; **fortbilden** vr to continue one's education; **Fortbildung** f further education; **fortbleiben** unreg vi to stay away; **fortbringen** unreg vt to take away; **Fortdauer** f continuance; **fortdauernd** adj continuing; (in der Vergangenheit) continued ▷ adv constantly, continuously; **fortfahren** unreg vi to depart; (fortsetzen) to go on, continue; **fortführen** vt to continue, carry on; **Fortgang** m (Verlauf) progress; (Weggang): **Fortgang (aus)** departure (from); **fortgehen** unreg vi to go away;

fortgeschritten adj advanced; **fortkommen** unreg vi to get on; (wegkommen) to get away; **fortkönnen** unreg vi to be able to get away; **fortlassen** vt (auslassen) to leave out, omit; (weggehen lassen): **jdn fortlassen** to let sb go; **fortlaufend** adj: **fortlaufend nummeriert** consecutively numbered; **fortmüssen** unreg vi to have to go; **fortpflanzen** vr to reproduce; **Fortpflanzung** f reproduction

FORTRAN ['fɔrtran] nt FORTRAN

Forts. abk = **Fortsetzung**

fortschaffen vt to remove

fortschreiten unreg vi to advance

Fortschritt ['fɔrtʃrɪt] m advance; **~e machen** to make progress; **dem ~ dienen** to further progress; **fortschrittlich** adj progressive

fortschrittsgläubig adj believing in progress

fort- zW: **fortsetzen** vt to continue; **Fortsetzung** f continuation; (folgender Teil) instalment (Brit), installment (US); **Fortsetzung folgt** to be continued; **Fortsetzungsroman** m serialized novel; **fortwährend** adj incessant, continual; **fortwirken** vi to continue to have an effect; **fortziehen** unreg vt to pull away ▷ vi to move on; (umziehen) to move away

Foto ['fo:to] (-s, -s) nt photo(graph); **ein ~ machen** to take a photo(graph); **Fotoalbum** nt photograph album; **Fotoapparat** m camera; **Fotograf, in** (-en, -en) m(f) photographer; **Fotografie** f photography; (Bild) photograph; **fotografieren** vt to photograph ▷ vi to take photographs; **Fotohandy** nt camera phone; **Fotokopie** f photocopy; **fotokopieren** vt to photocopy; **Fotokopierer** m photocopier; **Fotokopiergerät** nt photocopier

Foul [faʊl] (-s, -s) nt foul

Foyer [foa'je:] (-s, -s) nt foyer; (in Hotel) lobby, foyer

FPÖ (-) f abk (= Freiheitliche Partei Österreichs) Austrian Freedom Party

Fr. abk (= Frau) Mrs, Ms

Fracht [fraxt] (-, -en) f freight; (Naut) cargo; (Preis) carriage; **~ zahlt Empfänger** (Comm) carriage forward; **Frachtbrief** m consignment note, waybill

Frachter (-s, -) m freighter

Fracht- zW: **frachtfrei** adj (Comm) carriage paid od free; **Frachtgut** nt freight; **Frachtkosten** pl (Comm) freight charges pl

Frack [frak] (-(e)s, ̈-e) m tails pl, tail coat

Frage ['fra:gə] (-, -n) f question; **jdm eine ~ stellen** to ask sb a question, put a question to sb; **das ist gar keine ~, das steht außer ~** there's no question about it; siehe auch **infrage**; **Fragebogen** m questionnaire

fragen vt, vi to ask ▷ vr to wonder; **nach Arbeit/Post ~** to ask whether there is/was any work/mail; **da fragst du mich zu viel** (umg) I really couldn't say; **nach** od **wegen** (umg) **jdn ~** to ask for sb; (nach jds Befinden) to ask after sb; **ohne lange zu ~** without asking a lot of questions

Fragerei [fra:gə'raɪ] f questions pl

Fragestunde f (Parl) question time

Fragezeichen nt question mark

fraglich adj questionable, doubtful; (betreffend) in question

fraglos adv unquestionably

Fragment [fra'gmɛnt] nt fragment

fragmentarisch [fragmɛn'ta:rɪʃ] adj fragmentary

fragwürdig ['fra:kvʏrdɪç] adj questionable, dubious

Fraktion [fraktsi'o:n] f parliamentary party

Fraktionsvorsitzende, r f(m) (Pol) party whip

Fraktionszwang m requirement to obey the party whip

Franchisekette ['frɛnʃaɪskɛtə] f franchise chain

frank [fraŋk] adj frank, candid

Franken¹ ['fraŋkən] nt Franconia

Franken² ['fraŋkən] (-, -) m: **(Schweizer) ~** (Swiss) Franc

Frankfurt ['fraŋkfʊrt] (-s) nt Frankfurt

Frankfurter, in m(f) native of Frankfurt ▷ adj Frankfurt; **Frankfurter Würstchen** pl frankfurters

frankieren [fraŋ'ki:rən] vt to stamp, frank

Frankiermaschine f franking machine

fränkisch ['fraŋkɪʃ] adj Franconian

franko adv carriage paid; (Post) post-paid

Frankreich ['fraŋkraɪç] (-s) nt France

Franse ['franzə] (-, -n) f fringe

fransen vi to fray

franz. abk = **französisch**

Franzbranntwein m alcoholic liniment

Franzose [fran'tso:zə] (-n, -n) m Frenchman; French boy

Französin [fran'tsø:zɪn] f Frenchwoman; French girl

französisch adj French; **~es Bett** double bed

Fräse ['frɛ:zə] (-, -n) f (Werkzeug) milling cutter; (für Holz) moulding cutter

Fraß (-es, -e) (pej: umg) m (Essen) muck

fraß etc [fra:s] vb siehe **fressen**

Fratze ['fratsə] (-, -n) f grimace; **eine ~ schneiden** to pull od make a face

Frau [fraʊ] (-, -en) f woman; (Ehefrau) wife; (Anrede) Mrs, Ms; **~ Doktor** Doctor

Frauen- zW: **Frauenarzt** m gynaecologist (Brit), gynecologist (US); **Frauenbewegung** f feminist movement; **frauenfeindlich** adj anti-women, misogynous; **Frauenhaus** nt women's refuge; **Frauenquote** f recommended proportion of women (employed); **Frauenrechtlerin** f feminist; **Frauenzentrum** nt women's advice centre; **Frauenzimmer** (pej) nt female, broad (US)

Fräulein ['frɔʏlaɪn] nt young lady; (Anrede) Miss; (Verkäuferin) assistant (Brit), sales clerk (US); (Kellnerin) waitress

fraulich ['fraʊlɪç] adj womanly

frech [frɛç] adj cheeky, impudent; **~ wie Oskar sein** (umg) to be a little monkey; **Frechdachs** m cheeky monkey; **Frechheit** f cheek, impudence; **sich** dat **(einige) Frechheiten erlauben** to be a bit cheeky (bes Brit) od fresh (bes US)

Fregatte [fre'gatə] (-, -n) f frigate

frei [fraɪ] adj free; (Stelle) vacant; (Mitarbeiter) freelance; (Geld) available; (unbekleidet) bare; **aus ~en Stücken** od **~em Willen** of one's own free will; **~ nach ...** based on ...; **für etw ~e Fahrt geben** (fig) to give sth the go-ahead; **der Film ist ~ ab 16 (Jahren)** the film may be seen by people of 16 years (of age) and over; **unter ~em Himmel** in the open (air); **morgen/Mittwoch ist ~** tomorrow/Wednesday is a holiday; „Zimmer ~" "vacancies"; **auf ~er Strecke** (Eisenb) between stations; (Aut) on the road; **~er Wettbewerb** fair/open competition; **~ Haus** (Comm) carriage paid; **~ Schiff** (Comm) free on board; **~e Marktwirtschaft** free market economy; **von etw ~ sein** to be free of sth; **im F~en** in the open air; **~ halten** (Ausfahrt etc) to keep free; **~ sprechen** to talk without notes; **Freibad** nt open-air swimming pool; **freibekommen** unreg vt: **jdn/einen Tag freibekommen** to get sb freed/get a day off; **freiberuflich** adj self-employed; **Freibetrag** m tax allowance

Freier (-s, -) m suitor

Frei- zW: **Freiexemplar** nt free copy; **freigeben** unreg vt: **etw zum Verkauf freigeben** to allow sth to be sold on the open market; **freigebig** adj generous; **Freigebigkeit** f generosity; **Freihafen** m free port; **freihalten** unreg vt (bezahlen) to pay for; siehe auch **frei**; **Freihandel** m free trade; **Freihandelszone** f free trade area; **freihändig** adv (fahren) with no hands

Freiheit f freedom; **sich** dat **die ~ nehmen, etw zu tun** to take the liberty of doing sth; **freiheitlich** adj liberal; (Verfassung) based on the principle of liberty; (Demokratie) free

Freiheits- zW: **Freiheitsberaubung** f (Jur) wrongful deprivation of personal liberty; **Freiheitsdrang** m urge/desire for freedom; **Freiheitskampf** m fight for freedom; **Freiheitskämpfer, in** m(f) freedom fighter; **Freiheitsrechte** pl civil liberties pl; **Freiheitsstrafe** f prison sentence

frei- zW: **freiheraus** adv frankly; **Freikarte** f free ticket; **freikaufen** vt: **jdn/sich freikaufen** to buy sb's/one's freedom; **freikommen** unreg vi to get free; **Freikörperkultur** f nudism; **freilassen** unreg vt to (set) free; **Freilauf** m freewheeling; **freilaufend** adj (Hühner) free-range; **freilegen** vt to expose; **freilich** adv certainly, admittedly; **ja freilich!** yes of course; **Freilichtbühne** f open-air theatre; **freimachen** vt (Post) to frank ▷ vr to arrange to be free; **Tage freimachen** to take days off; **sich freimachen** (beim Arzt) to take one's clothes off, strip; **Freimaurer** m Mason, Freemason

freimütig ['fraɪmyːtɪç] adj frank, honest

Frei- zW: **freinehmen** vt: **sich** dat **einen Tag freinehmen** to take a day off;

Freiraum m: **Freiraum (zu)** (fig) freedom (for); **freischaffend** adj attrib freelance; **Freischaltcode** m (Tel) connecting od enabling code; **Freischärler (-s, -)** m guerrilla; **freischwimmen** vr (fig) to learn to stand on one's own two feet; **freisetzen** vt (Energien) to release; **freisinnig** adj liberal; **Freisprechanlage** f hands-free (headset); (im Auto) hands-free (car kit); **freisprechen** unreg vt: **freisprechen (von)** to acquit (of); **Freispruch** m acquittal; **freistehen** unreg vi: **es steht dir frei, das zu tun** you are free to do so; **das steht Ihnen völlig frei** that is completely up to you; **freistellen** vt: **jdm etw freistellen** to leave sth (up) to sb; **Freistoß** m free kick; **Freistunde** f free hour; (Sch) free period

Freitag m Friday; siehe auch **Dienstag**

freitags adv on Fridays

Frei- zW: **Freitod** m suicide; **Freiübungen** pl (physical) exercises pl; **Freiumschlag** m reply-paid envelope; **Freiwild** nt (fig) fair game; **freiwillig** adj voluntary; **Freiwillige, r** f(m) volunteer; **Freizeichen** nt (Tel) ringing tone; **Freizeit** f spare od free time; **Freizeitgestaltung** f organization of one's leisure time; **freizügig** adj liberal, broad-minded; (mit Geld) generous

fremd [frɛmt] adj (unvertraut) strange; (ausländisch) foreign; (nicht eigen) someone else's; **etw ist jdm ~** sth is foreign to sb; **ich bin hier ~** I'm a stranger here; **sich ~ fühlen** to feel like a stranger; **fremdartig** adj strange

Fremde (-) f (liter): **die ~** foreign parts pl

Fremde, r f(m) stranger; (Ausländer) foreigner

Fremden- zW: **Fremdenführer** m (tourist) guide; (Buch) guide (book); **Fremdenlegion** f foreign legion; **Fremdenverkehr** m tourism; **Fremdenzimmer** nt guest room

fremd- zW: **fremdgehen** unreg (umg) vi to be unfaithful; **Fremdkapital** nt loan capital; **Fremdkörper** m foreign body; **fremdländisch** adj foreign; **Fremdling** m stranger; **Fremdsprache** f foreign language; **Fremdsprachenkorrespondentin** f bilingual secretary; **fremdsprachig** adj attrib foreign-language; **Fremdwort** nt foreign word

frenetisch [fre'neːtɪʃ] adj frenetic

Frequenz [fre'kvɛnts] f (Rundf) frequency

Fresse (-, -n) (umg!) f (Mund) gob; (Gesicht) mug

fressen ['frɛsən] unreg vt, vi to eat ▷ vr: **sich satt ~** to gorge o.s.; **einen Narren an jdm/etw ge~ haben** to dote on sb/sth

Freude ['frɔydə] (-, -n) f joy, delight; **~ an etw** dat **haben** to get od derive pleasure from sth; **jdm eine ~ machen** od **bereiten** to make sb happy

Freudenhaus nt (veraltet) house of ill repute

Freudentanz m: **einen ~ aufführen** to dance with joy

freudestrahlend adj beaming with delight

freudig adj joyful, happy

freudlos adj joyless

freuen ['frɔʏən] vt unpers to make happy od pleased ▷ vr to be glad od happy; **sich auf etw** akk ~ to look forward to sth; **sich über etw** akk ~ to be pleased about sth; **sich zu früh** ~ to get one's hopes up too soon

Freund ['frɔʏnt] **(-(e)s, -e)** m friend; (Liebhaber) boyfriend; **ich bin kein ~ von so etwas** I'm not one for that sort of thing; **Freundin** f friend; (Liebhaberin) girlfriend; **freundlich** adj kind, friendly; **bitte recht freundlich!** smile please!; **würden Sie bitte so freundlich sein und das tun?** would you be so kind as to do that?; **freundlicherweise** adv kindly; **Freundlichkeit** f friendliness, kindness; **Freundschaft** f friendship; **freundschaftlich** adj friendly

Frevel ['fre:fəl] **(-s, -)** m: ~ **(an +**dat**)** crime od offence (against); **frevelhaft** adj wicked

Frieden ['fri:dən] **(-s, -)** m peace; **im ~ in** peacetime; ~ **schließen** to make one's peace; (Pol) to make peace; **um des lieben ~s willen** (umg) for the sake of peace and quiet; **ich traue dem ~ nicht** (umg) something (fishy) is going on

Friedens- zW: **Friedensbewegung** f peace movement; **Friedensrichter** m justice of the peace; **Friedensschluss** m peace agreement; **Friedenstruppe** f peace-keeping force; **Friedensverhandlungen** pl peace negotiations pl; **Friedensvertrag** m peace treaty; **Friedenszeit** f peacetime

fried- zW: **friedfertig** adj peaceable; **Friedhof** m cemetery; **friedlich** adj peaceful; **etw auf friedlichem Wege lösen** to solve sth by peaceful means

frieren ['fri:rən] unreg vi to freeze ▷ vt unpers to freeze ▷ vi unpers: **heute Nacht hat es gefroren** it was below freezing last night; **ich friere, es friert mich** I am freezing, I'm cold; **wie ein Schneider ~** (umg) to be od get frozen to the marrow

Fries [fri:s] **(-es, -e)** m (Archit) frieze

Friese ['fri:zə] **(-n, -n)** m Fri(e)sian

Friesin ['fri:zɪn] f Fri(e)sian

frigid, frigide adj frigid

Frikadelle [frika'dɛlə] f meatball

frisch [frɪʃ] adj fresh; (lebhaft) lively; ~ **gestrichen!** wet paint!; **sich ~ machen** to freshen (o.s.) up; **jdn auf ~er Tat ertappen** to catch sb red-handed od in the act

Frische(-) f freshness; liveliness; **in alter ~** (umg) as always

Frischhaltebeutel m airtight bag

Frischhaltefolie f clingfilm

frischweg adv (munter) straight out

Friseur [fri'zø:r] m hairdresser

Friseuse [fri'zø:zə] f hairdresser

frisieren [fri'zi:rən] vt (Haar) to do; (fig: Abrechnung) to fiddle, doctor ▷ vr to do one's hair; **jdn ~, jdm das Haar ~** to do sb's hair

Frisiersalon m hairdressing salon

Frisiertisch m dressing table

Frisör [fri'zø:r] **(-s, -e)** m **= Friseur**

frisst [frɪst] vb siehe **fressen**

Frist [frɪst] **(-, -en)** f period; (Termin) deadline; **eine ~ einhalten/verstreichen lassen** to meet a deadline/let a deadline pass; (bei Rechnung) to pay/not to pay within the period stipulated; **jdm eine ~ von vier Tagen geben** to give sb four days' grace

fristen vt (Dasein) to lead; (kümmerlich) to eke out

Fristenlösung f abortion law (permitting abortion in the first three months)

fristgerecht adj within the period stipulated

fristlos adj (Entlassung) instant

Frisur [fri'zu:r] f hairdo, hairstyle

Fritteuse [fri'tø:zə] **(-, -n)** f chip pan (Brit), deep fat fryer

frittieren [fri'ti:rən] vt to deep fry

frivol [fri'vo:l] adj frivolous

Frl. abk (= Fräulein) Miss

froh [fro:] adj happy, cheerful; **ich bin ~, dass ...** I'm glad that ...

fröhlich ['frø:lɪç] adj merry, happy; **Fröhlichkeit** f merriment, gaiety

frohlocken vi (geh) to rejoice; (pej) to gloat

Frohsinn m cheerfulness

fromm [frɔm] adj pious, good; (Wunsch) idle

Frömmelei [frœmə'laɪ] f false piety

Frömmigkeit f piety

frönen ['frø:nən] vi +dat to indulge in

Fronleichnam [fro:n'laɪçna:m] **(-(e)s)** m Corpus Christi

Front [frɔnt] **(-, -en)** f front; **klare ~en schaffen** (fig) to clarify the position

frontal [frɔn'ta:l] adj frontal; **Frontalangriff** m frontal attack

fror etc [fro:r] vb siehe **frieren**

Frosch [frɔʃ] **(-(e)s, ̈-e)** m frog; (Feuerwerk) squib; **sei kein ~!** (umg) be a sport!; **Froschmann** m frogman; **Froschperspektive** f: **etw aus der Froschperspektive sehen** to get a worm's-eye view of sth; **Froschschenkel** m frog's leg

Frost [frɔst] **(-(e)s, ̈-e)** m frost; **frostbeständig** adj frost-resistant; **Frostbeule** f chilblain

frösteln ['frœstəln] vi to shiver

frostig adj frosty

Frostschutzmittel nt anti-freeze

Frottee, Frotté [fro'te:] **(-(s), -s)** nt od m towelling

frottieren [frɔ'ti:rən] vt to rub, towel

Frottierhandtuch nt towel

Frottiertuch nt towel

frotzeln ['frɔtsəln] (umg) vt, vi to tease

Frucht [frʊxt] **(-, ̈-e)** f (lit, fig) fruit; (Getreide) corn; (Embryo) foetus; **fruchtbar** adj fruitful, fertile; **Fruchtbarkeit** f fertility; **Fruchtbecher** m fruit sundae

Früchtchen ['frʏçtçən] (umg) nt (Tunichtgut) good-for-nothing

fruchten vi to be of use

fruchtlos adj fruitless

Fruchtsaft m fruit juice

früh [fry:] adj, adv early; **heute ~** this morning;

von ~ auf from an early age; **Frühaufsteher (-s, -)** m early riser; **Frühdienst** m: **Frühdienst haben** to be on early shift

Frühe (-) f early morning; **in aller ~** at the crack of dawn

früher adj earlier; (ehemalig) former ▷ adv formerly; **~ war das anders** that used to be different; **~ oder später** sooner or later

frühestens adv at the earliest

Frühgeburt f premature birth; (Kind) premature baby

Frühjahr nt spring

Frühjahrsmüdigkeit f springtime lethargy

Frühjahrsputz m spring-cleaning

Frühling m spring; **im ~** in spring

früh- zW: **frühreif** adj precocious; **Frührentner** m person who has retired early; **Frühschicht** f early shift; **Frühschoppen** m morning/lunchtime drink; **Frühsport** m early morning exercise; **Frühstück** nt breakfast; **frühstücken** vi to (have) breakfast; **Frühwarnsystem** nt early warning system; **frühzeitig** adj early; (vorzeitig) premature

Frust (-(e)s) (umg) m frustration

frustrieren [frus'tri:rən] vt to frustrate

frz. abk = **französisch**

FSV abk (= Fußball-Sportverein) F.C.

FU (-) f abk (= Freie Universität Berlin) Berlin University

Fuchs [fuks] **(-es, ⁻e)** m fox

fuchsen (umg) vt to rile, annoy ▷ vr to be annoyed

Füchsin ['fʏksɪn] f vixen

fuchsteufelswild adj hopping mad

Fuchtel ['fuxtl] **(-, -n)** f (fig: umg): **unter jds ~** under sb's control od thumb

fuchteln ['fuxtəln] vi to gesticulate wildly

Fuge ['fu:gə] **(-, -n)** f joint; (Mus) fugue

fügen ['fy:gən] vt to place, join ▷ vr unpers to happen ▷ vr: **sich ~ (in** +akk) to be obedient (to); (anpassen) to adapt o.s. (to)

fügsam ['fy:kza:m] adj obedient

fühlbar adj perceptible, noticeable

fühlen ['fy:lən] vt, vi, vr to feel

Fühler (-s, -) m feeler

Fühlung f: **mit jdm in ~ bleiben/stehen** to stay/be in contact od touch with sb

fuhr etc [fu:r] vb siehe **fahren**

Fuhre (-, -n) f (Ladung) load

führen ['fy:rən] vt to lead; (Geschäft) to run; (Name) to bear; (Buch) to keep; (im Angebot haben) to stock ▷ vi to lead ▷ vr to behave; **was führt Sie zu mir?** (form) what brings you to me?; **Geld/seine Papiere bei sich ~** (form) to carry money/one's papers on one's person; **das führt zu nichts** that will come to nothing

Führer, in ['fy:rər(ɪn)] **(-s, -)** m(f) leader; (Fremdenführer) guide; **Führerhaus** nt cab; **Führerschein** m driving licence (Brit), driver's license (US); **den Führerschein machen** (Aut) to learn to drive; (die Prüfung ablegen) to take one's (driving) test; **Führerscheinentzug** m disqualification from driving

Fuhrmann ['fu:rman] **(-(e)s, pl -leute)** m carter

Führung ['fy:rʊŋ] f leadership; (eines Unternehmens) management; (Mil) command; (Benehmen) conduct; (Museumsführung) conducted tour

Führungs- zW: **Führungskraft** f executive; **Führungsstab** m (Mil) command; (Comm) top management; **Führungsstil** m management style; **Führungszeugnis** nt certificate of good conduct

Fuhrunternehmen nt haulage business

Fuhrwerk nt cart

Fülle ['fʏlə] **(-)** f wealth, abundance

Füllen (-s, -) nt foal

füllen vt to fill; (Koch) to stuff ▷ vr to fill (up)

Füller (-s, -) m fountain pen

Füllfederhalter m fountain pen

Füllgewicht nt (Comm) weight at time of packing; (auf Dosen) net weight

füllig ['fʏlɪç] adj (Mensch) corpulent, portly; (Figur) ample

Füllung f filling; (Holzfüllung) panel

fummeln ['fʊməln] (umg) vi to fumble

Fund [fʊnt] **(-(e)s, -e)** m find

Fundament [fʊnda'mɛnt] nt foundation

fundamental adj fundamental

Fundamentalismus m fundamentalism

Fundbüro nt lost property office, lost and found (US)

Fundgrube f (fig) treasure trove

fundieren [fʊn'di:rən] vt to back up

fundiert adj sound

fündig ['fʏndɪç] adj (Min) rich; **~ werden** to make a strike; (fig) to strike it lucky

Fundsachen pl lost property sing

fünf [fʏnf] num five; **seine ~ Sinne beisammen haben** to have all one's wits about one; **~(e) gerade sein lassen** (umg) to turn a blind eye; **fünfhundert** num five hundred; **fünfjährig** adj (Frist, Plan) five-year; (Kind) five-year-old; **Fünfkampf** m pentathlon

Fünfprozentklausel f (Parl) clause debarring parties with less than 5% of the vote from Parliament; see culture note

> ● **FÜNFPROZENTKLAUSEL**
>
> ● The Fünfprozentklausel is a rule in German
> ● Federal elections whereby only those
> ● parties who collect at least 5% of the second
> ● vote (Zweitstimme) receive a parliamentary
> ● seat. This is to avoid the parliament being
> ● made up of a large number of very small
> ● parties which, in the Weimar Republic, led
> ● to political instability.

Fünftagewoche f five-day week

fünfte, r, s adj fifth

Fünftel (-s, -) nt fifth

fünfzehn num fifteen

fünfzig num fifty

fungieren [fʊŋ'gi:rən] vi to function; (Person) to act

Funk [fʊŋk] **(-s)** m radio, wireless (Brit old);

Funkausstellung f radio and television exhibition

Funke (**-ns, -n**) m (lit, fig) spark

funkeln vi to sparkle

funkelnagelneu (umg) adj brand-new

Funken (**-s, -**) m = **Funke**

funken vt to radio

Funker (**-s, -**) m radio operator

Funk- zW: **Funkgerät** nt radio set; **Funkhaus** nt broadcasting centre; **Funkkolleg** nt educational radio broadcasts pl; **Funkrufempfänger** m (Telec) pager, paging device; **Funkspot** m advertisement on the radio; **Funksprechgerät** nt radio telephone; **Funkspruch** m radio signal; **Funkstation** f radio station; **Funkstille** f (fig) ominous silence; **Funkstreife** f police radio patrol; **Funktaxi** nt radio taxi; **Funktelefon** nt cell phone; **Funktelefonnetz** nt radio telephone network

Funktion [fʊŋktsiˈoːn] f function; **in ~ treten/sein** to come into/be in operation

Funktionär, in [fʊŋktsioˈnɛːr(ɪn)] (**-s, -e**) m(f) functionary, official

funktionieren [fʊŋktsioˈniːrən] vi to work, function

Funktions- zW: **Funktionsbekleidung** f functional wear; **funktionsfähig** adj working; **Funktionstaste** f (Comput) function key; **funktionstüchtig** adj in working order

Funzel [fʊntsəl] (**-, -n**) (umg) f dim lamp

für [fyːr] präp +akk for; **was ~** what kind of sort of; **~s Erste** for the moment; **was Sie da sagen, hat etwas ~ sich** there's something in what you're saying; **Tag ~ Tag** day after day; **Schritt ~ Schritt** step by step; **das F~ und Wider** the pros and cons pl; **Fürbitte** f intercession

Furche [fʊrçə] (**-, -n**) f furrow

furchen vt to furrow

Furcht [fʊrçt] (**-**) f fear; **furchtbar** adj terrible, awful

fürchten [ˈfʏrçtən] vt to be afraid of, fear
  ▷ vr: **sich ~ (vor** +dat) to be afraid (of)

fürchterlich adj awful

furchtlos adj fearless

furchtsam adj timorous

füreinander [fyːrʔaɪˈnandər] adv for each other

Furie [ˈfuːriə] (**-, -n**) f (Mythologie) fury; (fig) hellcat

Furnier [fʊrˈniːr] (**-s, -e**) nt veneer

Furore [fuˈroːrə] f od nt: **~ machen** (umg) to cause a sensation

fürs [fyːrs] = **für das**

Fürsorge [ˈfyːrzɔrgə] f care; (Sozialfürsorge) welfare; **von der ~ leben** to live on social security (Brit) od welfare (US); **Fürsorgeamt** nt welfare office

Fürsorger, in (**-s, -**) m(f) welfare worker

Fürsorgeunterstützung f social security

(Brit), welfare benefit (US)

fürsorglich adj caring

Fürsprache f recommendation; (um Gnade) intercession

Fürsprecher m advocate

Fürst [fʏrst] (**-en, -en**) m prince

Fürstentum nt principality

Fürstin f princess

fürstlich adj princely

Furt [fʊrt] (**-**) f ford

Furunkel [fuˈrʊŋkəl] (**-s, -**) nt od m boil

Fürwort [ˈfyːrvɔrt] nt pronoun

furzen [ˈfʊrtsən] (umg!) vi to fart (!)

Fusion [fuziˈoːn] f amalgamation; (von Unternehmen) merger; (von Atomkernen, Zellen) fusion

fusionieren [fuzioˈniːrən] vt to amalgamate

Fuß [fuːs] (**-es, ⁻e**) m foot; (von Glas, Säule etc) base; (von Möbel) leg; **zu ~** on foot; **bei ~!** heel!; **jdm etw vor die Füße werfen** (lit) to throw sth at sb; (fig) to tell sb to keep sth; **(festen) ~ fassen** (lit, fig) to gain a foothold; (sich niederlassen) to settle down; **mit jdm auf gutem ~ stehen** to be on good terms with sb; **auf großem ~ leben** to live the high life

Fußball m football; **Fußballplatz** m football pitch; **Fußballspiel** nt football match; **Fußballspieler** m footballer (Brit), football player (US); **Fußballtoto** m od nt football pools pl

Fußboden m floor; **Fußbodenheizung** f underfloor heating

Fußbremse f (Aut) foot brake

fusselig [ˈfʊsəlɪç] adj: **sich** dat **den Mund ~ reden** (umg) to talk till one is blue in the face

fusseln [ˈfʊsəln] vi (Stoff, Kleid etc) to go bobbly (umg)

fußen vi: **~ auf** +dat to rest on, be based on

Fuß- zW: **Fußende** nt foot; **Fußgänger, in** (**-s, -**) m(f) pedestrian; **Fußgängerüberführung** f pedestrian bridge; **Fußgängerzone** f pedestrian precinct; **Fußleiste** f skirting board (Brit), baseboard (US); **Fußnagel** m toenail; **Fußnote** f footnote; **Fußpfleger** m chiropodist; **Fußpilz** m (Med) athlete's foot; **Fußspur** f footprint; **Fußstapfen** (**-s, -**) m: **in jds Fußstapfen treten** (fig) to follow in sb's footsteps; **Fußtritt** m kick; (Spur) footstep; **Fußvolk** nt (fig): **das Fußvolk** the rank and file; **Fußweg** m footpath

futsch [fʊtʃ] (umg) adj (weg) gone, vanished

Futter [ˈfʊtər] (**-s, -**) nt fodder, feed; (Stoff) lining

Futteral [fʊtəˈraːl] (**-s, -e**) nt case

futtern [ˈfʊtərn] vi (hum: umg) to stuff o.s. ▷ vt to scoff

füttern [ˈfʏtərn] vt to feed; (Kleidung) to line; **„F~ verboten"** "do not feed the animals"

Futur [fuˈtuːr] (**-s, -e**) nt future

Gg

G, g¹ [ge:] *nt* G, g; **G wie Gustav** = G for George; **G-8** *f abk* (*Pol*) (= *Group of Eight*) G8; **G-20** *f abk* (*Pol*) (= *Group of Twenty*) G20

g² *abk* (*Österr*) = **Groschen**; (= **Gramm**) g

gab *etc* [ga:p] *vb siehe* **geben**

Gabe ['ga:bə] (-, -n) *f* gift

Gabel ['ga:bəl] (-, -n) *f* fork; (*Tel*) rest, cradle; **Gabelfrühstück** *nt* mid-morning light lunch; **gabeln** *vr* to fork; **Gabelstapler** (-s, -) *m* fork-lift truck; **Gabelung** *f* fork

Gabentisch ['ga:bəntɪʃ] *m* table for Christmas or birthday presents

Gabun [ga'bu:n] *nt* Gabon

gackern ['gakərn] *vi* to cackle

gaffen ['gafən] *vi* to gape

Gag [gɛk] (-s, -s) *m* (*Filmgag*) gag; (*Werbegag*) gimmick

Gage ['ga:ʒə] (-, -n) *f* fee

gähnen ['gɛ:nən] *vi* to yawn; **~de Leere** total emptiness

GAL (-) *f abk* (= *Grün-Alternative Liste*) electoral pact of Greens and alternative parties

galant [ga'lant] *adj* gallant, courteous

Galavorstellung *f* (*Theat*) gala performance

Galerie [galə'ri:] *f* gallery

Galgen ['galgən] (-s, -) *m* gallows *pl*; **Galgenfrist** *f* respite; **Galgenhumor** *m* macabre humour (*Brit*) *od* humor (*US*); **Galgenstrick** (*umg*) *m*, **Galgenvogel** (*umg*) *m* gallows bird

Galionsfigur [gali'o:nsfigu:r] *f* figurehead

gälisch ['gɛ:lɪʃ] *adj* Gaelic

Galle ['galə] (-, -n) *f* gall; (*Organ*) gall bladder; **jdm kommt die ~ hoch** sb's blood begins to boil

Galopp [ga'lɔp] (-s, -s *od* -e) *m* gallop; **im ~** (*lit*) at a gallop; (*fig*) at top speed

galoppieren [galɔ'pi:rən] *vi* to gallop

galt *etc* [galt] *vb siehe* **gelten**

galvanisieren [galvani'zi:rən] *vt* to galvanize

Gamasche [ga'maʃə] (-, -n) *f* gaiter; (*kurz*) spat

Gameboy® ['ge:mbɔʏ] *m* games console

Gamer, in ['ge:mər] (-s, -) *m(f)* (*Comput*) gamer

Gameshow ['ge:mʃo:] (-, -s) *f* game show

Gammastrahlen ['gamaʃtra:lən] *pl* gamma rays *pl*

gamm(e)lig ['gam(ə)lɪç] (*umg*) *adj* (*Kleidung*) tatty

gammeln ['gaməln] (*umg*) *vi* to loaf about

Gammler, in ['gamlər(ɪn)] (-s, -) *m(f)* dropout

Gämse ['gɛmzə] (-, -n) *f* chamois

Gang¹ [gaŋ] (-(e)s, ⸚e) *m* walk; (*Botengang*) errand; (*Gangart*) gait; (*Abschnitt eines Vorgangs*) operation; (*Essensgang, Ablauf*) course; (*Flur etc*) corridor; (*Durchgang*) passage; (*Aut, Tech*) gear; (*in Kirche, Theat, Aviat*) aisle; **den ersten ~ einlegen** to engage first (gear); **einen ~ machen/tun** to go on an errand/for a walk; **den ~ nach Canossa antreten** (*fig*) to eat humble pie; **seinen gewohnten ~ gehen** (*fig*) to run its usual course; **in ~ bringen** to start up; (*fig*) to get off the ground; **in ~ sein** to be in operation; (*fig*) to be under way

Gang² [gɛŋ] (-, -s) *f* gang

gang *adj*: **~ und gäbe** usual, normal

Gangart *f* way of walking, walk, gait; (*von Pferd*) gait; **eine härtere ~ einschlagen** (*fig*) to apply harder tactics

gangbar *adj* passable; (*Methode*) practicable

Gängelband ['gɛŋəlbant] *nt*: **jdn am ~ halten** (*fig*) to spoon-feed sb

gängeln *vt* to spoonfeed; **jdn ~** to treat sb like a child

gängig ['gɛŋɪç] *adj* common, current; (*Ware*) in demand, selling well

Gangschaltung *f* gears *pl*

Gangway ['gæŋweɪ] *f* (*Naut*) gangway; (*Aviat*) steps *pl*

Ganove [ga'no:və] (-n, -n) (*umg*) *m* crook

Gans [gans] (-, ⸚e) *f* goose

Gänse- *zW*: **Gänseblümchen** *nt* daisy; **Gänsebraten** *m* roast goose; **Gänsefüßchen** (*umg*) *pl* inverted commas *pl* (*Brit*), quotes *pl*; **Gänsehaut** *f* goose pimples *pl*; **Gänsemarsch** *m*: **im Gänsemarsch** in single file

Gänserich (-s, -e) *m* gander

ganz [gants] *adj* whole; (*vollständig*) complete ▷ *adv* quite; (*völlig*) completely; (*sehr*) really; (*genau*) exactly; **~ Europa** all Europe; **im (Großen und) G~en genommen** on the whole, all in all; **etw wieder ~ machen** to mend sth; **sein ~es Geld** all his money; **~ gewiss!** absolutely!; **ein ~ klein wenig** just a tiny bit; **das mag ich ~ besonders gern(e)** I'm particularly fond of that; **sie ist ~ die Mutter** she's just *od* exactly like her mother; **~ und gar nicht** not at all

Ganze, s *nt*: **es geht ums ~** everything's at

stake; **aufs ~ gehen** to go for the lot

Ganzheitsmethode ['gantshaitsmeto:də] f (Sch) look-and-say method

gänzlich ['gɛntslɪç] adj complete, entire ▷ adv completely, entirely

ganztägig ['gantstɛ:gɪç] adj all-day attrib

ganztags adv (arbeiten) full time; **Ganztagsschule** f all-day school; **Ganztagsstelle** f full-time job

gar [ga:r] adj cooked, done ▷ adv quite; ~ **nicht/nichts/keiner** not/nothing/nobody at all; ~ **nicht schlecht** not bad at all; ~ **kein Grund** no reason whatsoever od at all; **er wäre ~ zu gern noch länger geblieben** he would really have liked to stay longer

Garage [ga'ra:ʒə] (-, -n) f garage

Garantie [garan'ti:] f guarantee; **das fällt noch unter die ~** that's covered by the guarantee

garantieren vt to guarantee

garantiert adv guaranteed; (umg) I bet

Garantieschein m guarantee

Garaus ['ga:raus] (umg) m: **jdm den ~ machen** to do sb in

Garbe ['garbə] (-, -n) f sheaf; (Mil) burst of fire

Garde ['gardə] (-, -n) f guard(s); **die alte ~** the old guard

Garderobe [gardə'ro:bə] (-, -n) f wardrobe; (Abgabe) cloakroom (Brit), checkroom (US); (Kleiderablage) hall stand; (Theat: Umkleideraum) dressing room

Garderobenfrau f cloakroom attendant

Garderobenständer m hall stand

Gardine [gar'di:nə] (-, -n) f curtain

Gardinenpredigt (umg) f: **jdm eine ~ halten** to give sb a talking-to

Gardinenstange f curtain rail; (zum Ziehen) curtain rod

garen ['ga:rən] vt, vi (Koch) to cook

gären ['gɛ:rən] unreg vi to ferment

Garn [garn] (-(e)s, -e) nt thread; (Häkelgarn, fig) yarn

Garnele [gar'ne:lə] (-, -n) f shrimp, prawn

garnieren [gar'ni:rən] vt to decorate; (Speisen) to garnish

Garnison [garni'zo:n] (-, -en) f garrison

Garnitur [garni'tu:r] f (Satz) set; (Unterwäsche) set of (matching) underwear; **erste ~** (fig) top rank; **zweite ~** second rate

garstig ['garstɪç] adj nasty, horrid

Garten ['gartən] (-s, -̈) m garden; **Gartenarbeit** f gardening; **Gartenbau** m horticulture; **Gartenfest** nt garden party; **Gartengerät** nt gardening tool; **Gartenhaus** nt summerhouse; **Gartenkresse** f cress; **Gartenlaube** f (Gartenhäuschen) summerhouse; **Gartenlokal** nt beer garden; **Gartenschere** f pruning shears pl; **Gartentür** f garden gate; **Gartenzaun** m garden fence; **Gartenzwerg** m garden gnome; (pej: umg) squirt

Gärtner, in ['gɛrtnər(ɪn)] (-s, -) m(f) gardener

Gärtnerei [gɛrtnə'raɪ] f nursery; (Gemüsegärtnerei) market garden (Brit), truck farm (US)

gärtnern vi to garden

Gärung ['gɛ:rʊŋ] f fermentation

Gas [ga:s] (-es, -e) nt gas; ~ **geben** (Aut) to accelerate, step on the gas

Gas- zW: **Gasflasche** f bottle of gas, gas canister; **gasförmig** adj gaseous; **Gashahn** m gas tap; **Gasherd** m gas cooker; **Gaskocher** m gas cooker; **Gasleitung** f gas pipeline; **Gasmaske** f gas mask; **Gaspedal** nt accelerator, gas pedal (US); **Gaspistole** f gas pistol

Gasse ['gasə] (-, -n) f lane, alley

Gassenhauer (-s, -) (veraltet: umg) m popular melody

Gassenjunge m street urchin

Gast [gast] (-es, -̈e) m guest; **bei jdm zu ~ sein** to be sb's guest(s); **Gastarbeiter** m foreign worker

Gäste- zW: **Gästebett** nt spare bed; **Gästebuch** nt visitors' book; **Gästezimmer** nt guest room

Gast- zW: **gastfreundlich** adj hospitable; **Gastfreundlichkeit** f hospitality; **Gastfreundschaft** f hospitality; **Gastgeber, in** (-s, -) m(f) host(ess); **Gasthaus** nt hotel, inn; **Gasthof** m hotel, inn; **Gasthörer, in** m(f) (Univ) observer, auditor (US)

gastieren [gas'ti:rən] vi (Theat) to (appear as a) guest

Gast- zW: **Gastland** nt host country; **gastlich** adj hospitable; **Gastlichkeit** f hospitality; **Gastrolle** f (Theat) guest role; **eine Gastrolle spielen** to make a guest appearance

Gastronomie [gastrono'mi:] f (form: Gaststättengewerbe) catering trade

gastronomisch [gastro'no:mɪʃ] adj gastronomic(al)

Gast- zW: **Gastspiel** nt (Sport) away game; **ein Gastspiel geben** (Theat) to give a guest performance; (fig) to put in a brief appearance; **Gaststätte** f restaurant; (Trinklokal) pub; **Gastwirt** m innkeeper; **Gastwirtschaft** f hotel, inn; **Gastzimmer** nt guest room

Gas- zW: **Gasvergiftung** f gas poisoning; **Gasversorgung** f (System) gas supply; **Gaswerk** nt gasworks sing od pl; **Gaszähler** m gas meter

Gatte ['gatə] (-n, -n) m (form) husband, spouse; **die ~n** husband and wife

Gatter ['gatər] (-s, -) nt grating; (Tür) gate

Gattin f (form) wife, spouse

Gattung ['gatʊŋ] f (Biol) genus; (Sorte) kind

GAU [gau] m abk (= größter anzunehmender Unfall) MCA, maximum credible accident

Gaudi ['gaudi] (Südd, Österr: umg) nt od f fun

Gaukler ['gauklər] (-s, -) m (liter) travelling entertainer; (Zauberkünstler) conjurer, magician

Gaul [gaul] (-(e)s, **Gäule**) m (pej) m nag

Gaumen ['gaumən] (-s, -) m palate

Gauner ['gaunər] (-s, -) m rogue

Gaunerei [gaunə'raɪ] f swindle

Gaunersprache f underworld jargon

Gaze ['ga:zə] (-, -n) f gauze

Geäst [gə'ɛst] nt branches pl

geb. *abk* = **geboren**

Gebäck [gə'bɛk] **(-(e)s, -e)** *nt* (*Kekse*) biscuits *pl* (*Brit*); cookies *pl* (*US*); (*Teilchen*) pastries *pl*

gebacken [gə'bakən] *pp von* **backen**

Gebälk [gə'bɛlk] **(-(e)s)** *nt* timberwork

gebannt [gə'bant] *adj* spellbound

gebar *etc* [gə'baːr] *vb siehe* **gebären**

Gebärde [gə'bɛːrdə] **(-, -n)** *f* gesture

gebärden *vr* to behave

Gebaren [gə'baːrən] **(-s)** *nt* behaviour (*Brit*), behavior (*US*); (*Geschäftsgebaren*) conduct

gebären [gə'bɛːrən] *unreg vt* to give birth to

Gebärmutter *f* uterus, womb

Gebäude [gə'bɔʏdə] **(-s, -)** *nt* building; **Gebäudekomplex** *m* (building) complex; **Gebäudereinigung** *f* (*das Reinigen*) commercial cleaning; (*Firma*) cleaning contractors *pl*

Gebein [gə'baɪn] **(-(e)s, -e)** *nt* bones *pl*

Gebell [gə'bɛl] **(-(e)s)** *nt* barking

geben ['geːbən] *unreg vt, vi* to give; (*Karten*) to deal ▷ *vt unpers*: **es gibt** there is/are; there will be ▷ *vr* (*sich verhalten*) to behave, act; (*aufhören*) to abate; **jdm etw ~** to give sb sth *od* sth to sb; **in die Post ~** to post; **das gibt keinen Sinn** that doesn't make sense; **er gibt Englisch** he teaches English; **viel/nicht viel auf etw** *akk* **~** to set great store/not much store by sth; **etw von sich ~** (*Laute etc*) to utter; **ein Wort gab das andere** one angry word led to another; **ein gutes Beispiel ~** to set a good example; **~ Sie mir bitte Herrn Braun** (*Tel*) can I speak to Mr Braun please?; **ein Auto in Reparatur ~** to have a car repaired; **was gibts?** what's the matter?, what's up?; **was gibts zum Mittagessen?** what's for lunch?; **das gibts doch nicht!** that's impossible!; **sich geschlagen ~** to admit defeat; **das wird sich schon ~** that'll soon sort itself out

Geberkonferenz ['geːbər-] *f* (*Pol*) donor conference

Gebet [gə'beːt] **(-(e)s, -e)** *nt* prayer; **jdn ins ~ nehmen** (*fig*) to take sb to task

gebeten [gə'beːtən] *pp von* **bitten**

gebeugt [gə'bɔʏkt] *adj* (*Haltung*) stooped; (*Kopf*) bowed; (*Schultern*) sloping

gebiert [gə'biːrt] *vb siehe* **gebären**

Gebiet [gə'biːt] **(-(e)s, -e)** *nt* area; (*Hoheitsgebiet*) territory; (*fig*) field

gebieten *unreg vt* to command, demand

Gebieter **(-s, -)** *m* master; (*Herrscher*) ruler; **Gebieterin** *f* mistress; **gebieterisch** *adj* imperious

Gebietshoheit *f* territorial sovereignty

Gebilde [gə'bɪldə] **(-s, -)** *nt* object, structure

gebildet *adj* cultured, educated

Gebimmel [gə'bɪməl] **(-s)** *nt* (continual) ringing

Gebirge [gə'bɪrgə] **(-s, -)** *nt* mountains *pl*

gebirgig *adj* mountainous

Gebirgs- *zW*: **Gebirgsbahn** *f* railway crossing a mountain range; **Gebirgskette** *f*, **Gebirgszug** *m* mountain range

Gebiss [gə'bɪs] **(-es, -e)** *nt* teeth *pl*; (*künstlich*) dentures *pl*

gebissen *pp von* **beißen**

Gebläse [gə'blɛːzə] **(-s, -)** *nt* fan, blower

geblasen [gə'blaːzən] *pp von* **blasen**

geblichen [gə'blɪçən] *pp von* **bleichen**

geblieben [gə'bliːbən] *pp von* **bleiben**

geblümt [gə'blyːmt] *adj* flowered; (*Stil*) flowery

Geblüt [gə'blyːt] **(-(e)s)** *nt* blood, race

gebogen [gə'boːgən] *pp von* **biegen**

geboren [gə'boːrən] *pp von* **gebären** ▷ *adj* born; (*Frau*) née; **wo sind Sie ~?** where were you born?

geborgen [gə'bɔrgən] *pp von* **bergen** ▷ *adj* secure, safe

geborsten [gə'bɔrstən] *pp von* **bersten**

Gebot **(-(e)s, -e)** *nt* (*Gesetz*) law; (*Rel*) commandment; (*bei Auktion*) bid; **das ~ der Stunde** the needs of the moment

gebot *etc* [gə'boːt] *vb siehe* **gebieten**

geboten [gə'boːtən] *pp von* **bieten; gebieten** ▷ *adj* (*geh: ratsam*) advisable; (*: notwendig*) necessary; (*: dringend geboten*) imperative

Gebr. *abk* (= *Gebrüder*) Bros., bros.

gebracht [gə'braxt] *pp von* **bringen**

gebrannt [gə'brant] *pp von* **brennen** ▷ *adj*: **ein ~es Kind scheut das Feuer** (*Sprichwort*) once bitten twice shy (*Sprichwort*)

gebraten [gə'braːtən] *pp von* **braten**

Gebräu [gə'brɔʏ] **(-(e)s, -e)** *nt* brew, concoction

Gebrauch [gə'braux] **(-(e)s, Gebräuche)** *m* use; (*Sitte*) custom; **zum äußerlichen/innerlichen ~** for external use/to be taken internally

gebrauchen *vt* to use; **er/das ist zu nichts zu ~** he's/that's (of) no use to anybody

gebräuchlich [gə'brɔʏçlɪç] *adj* usual, customary

Gebrauchs- *zW*: **Gebrauchsanweisung** *f* directions *pl* for use; **Gebrauchsartikel** *m* article of everyday use; **gebrauchsfertig** *adj* ready for use; **Gebrauchsgegenstand** *m* commodity

gebraucht [gə'brauxt] *adj* used; **Gebrauchtwagen** *m* second-hand *od* used car

gebrechlich [gə'brɛçlɪç] *adj* frail; **Gebrechlichkeit** *f* frailty

gebrochen [gə'brɔxən] *pp von* **brechen**

Gebrüder [gə'bryːdər] *pl* brothers *pl*

Gebrüll [gə'brʏl] **(-(e)s)** *nt* (*von Mensch*) yelling; (*von Löwe*) roar

gebückt [gə'bʏkt] *adj*: **eine ~e Haltung** a stoop

Gebühr [gə'byːr] **(-, -en)** *f* charge; (*Postgebühr*) postage *no pl*; (*Honorar*) fee; **zu ermäßigter ~** at a reduced rate; **~ (be)zahlt Empfänger** postage to be paid by addressee; **nach ~** suitably; **über ~** excessively

gebühren *vi* (*geh*): **jdm ~** to be sb's due *od* due to sb ▷ *vr* to be fitting

gebührend *adj* (*verdient*) due; (*angemessen*) suitable

Gebühren- *zW*: **Gebühreneinheit** *f* (*Tel*) tariff unit; **Gebührenerlass** *m* remission of fees; **Gebührenermäßigung** *f* reduction of fees; **gebührenfrei** *adj* free of charge;

Gebührenmanager *m* tariff meter;
gebührenpflichtig *adj* subject to charges;
gebührenpflichtige Verwarnung (*Jur*) fine
gebunden [gə'bʊndən] *pp von* **binden**
▷ *adj*: **vertraglich ~ sein** to be bound by
contract
Geburt [gə'buːrt] (-, -en) *f* birth; **das war eine
schwere ~!** (*fig*: *umg*) that took some doing
Geburten- *zW*: **Geburtenkontrolle** *f* birth
control; **Geburtenregelung** *f* birth control;
Geburtenrückgang *m* drop in the birth rate;
geburtenschwach *adj* (*Jahrgang*) with a low
birth rate; **Geburtenziffer** *f* birth rate
gebürtig [gə'byrtɪç] *adj* born in, native of; **~e
Schweizerin** native of Switzerland, Swiss-
born woman
Geburts- *zW*: **Geburtsanzeige** *f* birth notice;
Geburtsdatum *nt* date of birth; **Geburtsfehler**
m congenital defect; **Geburtshelfer** *m* (*Arzt*)
obstetrician; **Geburtshelferin** *f* (*Ärztin*)
obstetrician; (*Hebamme*) midwife; **Geburtshilfe** *f* (*als Fach*) obstetrics *sing*; (*von Hebamme*)
midwifery; **Geburtsjahr** *nt* year of birth;
Geburtsort *m* birthplace; **Geburtstag** *m*
birthday; **herzlichen Glückwunsch zum
Geburtstag!** happy birthday!, many happy
returns (of the day)!; **Geburtsurkunde** *f* birth
certificate
Gebüsch [gə'byʃ] (-(e)s, -e) *nt* bushes *pl*
gedacht [gə'daxt] *pp von* **denken; gedenken**
gedachte *etc vb siehe* **gedenken**
Gedächtnis [gə'dɛçtnɪs] (-ses, -se) *nt* memory;
wenn mich mein ~ nicht trügt if my
memory serves me right; **Gedächtnisfeier** *f*
commemoration; **Gedächtnishilfe** *f* memory
aid, mnemonic; **Gedächtnisschwund** *m* loss
of memory; **Gedächtnisverlust** *m* amnesia
gedämpft [gə'dɛmpft] *adj* (*Geräusch*) muffled;
(*Farben, Instrument, Stimmung*) muted; (*Licht,
Freude*) subdued
Gedanke [gə'daŋkə] (-ns, -n) *m* thought; (*Idee,
Plan, Einfall*) idea; (*Konzept*) concept; **sich über
etw** *akk* **~n machen** to think about sth; **jdn
auf andere ~n bringen** to make sb think
about other things; **etw ganz in ~n** *dat* **tun**
to do sth without thinking; **auf einen ~n
kommen** to have *od* get an idea
Gedanken- *zW*: **Gedankenaustausch** *m*
exchange of ideas; **Gedankenfreiheit**
f freedom of thought; **gedankenlos**
adj thoughtless; **Gedankenlosigkeit** *f*
thoughtlessness; **Gedankensprung** *m*
mental leap; **Gedankenstrich** *m* dash;
Gedankenübertragung *f* thought
transference, telepathy; **gedankenverloren**
adj lost in thought; **gedankenvoll** *adj*
thoughtful
Gedärme [gə'dɛrmə] *pl* intestines *pl*
Gedeck [gə'dɛk] (-(e)s, -e) *nt* cover(ing); (*Menü*)
set meal; **ein ~ auflegen** to lay a place
gedeckt *adj* (*Farbe*) muted
Gedeih *m*: **auf ~ und Verderb** for better or for
worse

gedeihen [gə'daɪən] *unreg vi* to thrive, prosper;
die Sache ist so weit gediehen, dass ... the
matter has reached the point *od* stage where ...
gedenken [gə'dɛŋkən] *unreg vi* +*gen* (*geh*: *denken
an*) to remember; (*beabsichtigen*) to intend;
Gedenken *nt*: **zum Gedenken an jdn** in
memory *od* remembrance of sb
Gedenk- *zW*: **Gedenkfeier** *f* commemoration;
Gedenkminute *f* minute's silence;
Gedenkstätte *f* memorial; **Gedenktag** *m*
remembrance day
Gedicht [gə'dɪçt] (-(e)s, -e) *nt* poem
gediegen [gə'diːgən] *adj* (*gut*) quality;
(*Mensch*) reliable; (*rechtschaffen*) honest;
Gediegenheit *f* quality; reliability; honesty
gedieh *etc* [gə'diː] *vb siehe* **gedeihen**
gediehen *pp von* **gedeihen**
gedr. *abk* = **gedruckt**
Gedränge [gə'drɛŋə] (-s) *nt* crush, crowd; **ins ~
kommen** (*fig*) to get into difficulties
gedrängt *adj* compressed; **~ voll** packed
gedroschen [gə'drɔʃən] *pp von* **dreschen**
gedruckt [gə'drʊkt] *adj* printed; **lügen wie ~**
(*umg*) to lie left, right and centre
gedrungen [gə'drʊŋən] *pp von* **dringen** ▷ *adj*
thickset, stocky
Geduld [gə'dʊlt] (-) *f* patience; **mir reißt die
~, ich verliere die ~** my patience is wearing
thin, I'm losing my patience
gedulden [gə'dʊldən] *vr* to be patient
geduldig *adj* patient
Geduldsprobe *f* trial of (one's) patience
gedungen [gə'dʊŋən] (*pej*) *adj* (*geh*: *Mörder*)
hired
gedunsen [gə'dʊnzən] *adj* bloated
gedurft [gə'dʊrft] *pp von* **dürfen**
geehrt [gə'|eːrt] *adj*: **Sehr ~e Damen und
Herren!** Ladies and Gentlemen!; (*in Briefen*)
Dear Sir or Madam
geeignet [gə'|aɪgnət] *adj* suitable; **im ~en
Augenblick** at the right moment
Gefahr [gə'faːr] (-, -en) *f* danger; **~ laufen,
etw zu tun** to run the risk of doing sth; **auf
eigene ~** at one's own risk; **außer ~** (*nicht
gefährdet*) not in danger; (*nicht mehr gefährdet*)
out of danger; (*Patienten*) off the danger list
gefährden [gə'fɛːrdən] *vt* to endanger
gefahren [gə'faːrən] *pp von* **fahren**
Gefahren- *zW*: **Gefahrenquelle** *f* source
of danger; **Gefahrenschwelle** *f* threshold
of danger; **Gefahrenstelle** *f* danger spot;
Gefahrenzulage *f* danger money
gefährlich [gə'fɛːrlɪç] *adj* dangerous
Gefährte [gə'fɛːrtə] (-n, -n) *m* companion
Gefährtin [gə'fɛːrtɪn] *f* companion
Gefälle [gə'fɛlə] (-s, -) *nt* (*von Land, Straße*) slope;
(*Neigungsgrad*) gradient; **starkes ~!** steep hill
Gefallen¹ [gə'falən] (-s, -) *m* favour; **jdm etw
zu ~ tun** to do sth to please sb
Gefallen² [gə'falən] (-s) *nt* pleasure; **an etw** *dat*
~ finden to derive pleasure from sth; **an jdm
~ finden** to take to sb
gefallen *pp von* **fallen; gefallen** ▷ *vi* (*unreg*): **jdm**

~ to please sb; **er/es gefällt mir** I like him/ it; **das gefällt mir an ihm** that's one thing I like about him; **sich** *dat* **etw ~ lassen** to put up with sth

Gefallene, r *m* soldier killed in action

gefällig [gə'fɛlɪç] *adj* (*hilfsbereit*) obliging; (*erfreulich*) pleasant; **sonst noch etwas ~?** (*veraltet, ironisch*) will there be anything else?; **Gefälligkeit** *f* favour (*Brit*), favor (*US*); helpfulness; **etw aus Gefälligkeit tun** to do sth as a favour (*Brit*) *od* favor (*US*)

gefälligst (*umg*) *adv* kindly; **sei ~ still!** will you kindly keep your mouth shut!

gefällt [gə'fɛlt] *vb siehe* **gefallen**

gefangen [gə'faŋən] *pp von* **fangen** ▷ *adj* captured; (*fig*) captivated; **~ halten** to keep prisoner; **~ nehmen** to capture

Gefangene, r *f(m)* prisoner, captive

Gefangenenlager *nt* prisoner-of-war camp

Gefangen- *zW:* **Gefangennahme** (-, -n) *f* capture; **Gefangenschaft** *f* captivity

Gefängnis [gə'fɛŋnɪs] (-ses, -se) *nt* prison; **zwei Jahre ~ bekommen** to get two years' imprisonment; **Gefängnisstrafe** *f* prison sentence; **Gefängniswärter** *m* prison warder (*Brit*) *od* guard

gefärbt [gə'fɛrpt] *adj* (*fig: Bericht*) biased; (*Lebensmittel*) coloured (*Brit*), colored (*US*)

Gefasel [gə'faːzəl] (-s) *nt* twaddle, drivel

Gefäß [gə'fɛːs] (-es, -e) *nt* vessel (*auch Anat*), container

gefasst [gə'fast] *adj* composed, calm; **auf etw** *akk* **~ sein** to be prepared *od* ready for sth; **er kann sich auf etwas ~ machen** (*umg*) I'll give him something to think about

Gefecht [gə'fɛçt] (-(e)s, -e) *nt* fight; (*Mil*) engagement; **jdn/etw außer ~ setzen** (*lit, fig*) to put sb/sth out of action

gefedert [gə'feːdərt] *adj* (*Matratze*) sprung

gefeiert [gə'faɪərt] *adj* celebrated

gefeit [gə'faɪt] *adj:* **gegen etw ~ sein** to be immune to sth

gefestigt [gə'fɛstɪçt] *adj* (*Charakter*) steadfast

Gefieder [gə'fiːdər] (-s, -) *nt* plumage, feathers *pl*

gefiedert *adj* feathered

gefiel *etc* [gə'fiːl] *vb siehe* **gefallen**

Geflecht [gə'flɛçt] (-(e)s, -e) *nt* (*lit, fig*) network

gefleckt [gə'flɛkt] *adj* spotted; (*Blume, Vogel*) speckled

Geflimmer [gə'flɪmər] (-s) *nt* shimmering; (*Film, TV*) flicker(ing)

geflissentlich [gə'flɪsəntlɪç] *adj* intentional ▷ *adv* intentionally

geflochten [gə'flɔxtən] *pp von* **flechten**

geflogen [gə'floːgən] *pp von* **fliegen**

geflohen [gə'floːən] *pp von* **fliehen**

geflossen [gə'flɔsən] *pp von* **fließen**

Geflügel [gə'flyːgəl] (-s) *nt* poultry

Geflügelpest *f* poultry plague

geflügelt *adj:* **~e Worte** familiar quotations

Geflüster [gə'flʏstər] (-s) *nt* whispering

gefochten [gə'fɔxtən] *pp von* **fechten**

Gefolge [gə'fɔlgə] (-s, -) *nt* retinue

Gefolgschaft [gə'fɔlkʃaft] *f* following

Gefolgsmann (-(e)s, *pl* **-leute**) *m* follower

gefragt [gə'fraːkt] *adj* in demand

gefräßig [gə'frɛːsɪç] *adj* voracious

Gefreite, r [gə'fraɪtə(r)] *m* (*Mil*) lance corporal (*Brit*), private first class (*US*); (*Naut*) able seaman (*Brit*), seaman apprentice (*US*); (*Aviat*) aircraftman (*Brit*), airman first class (*US*)

gefressen [gə'frɛsən] *pp von* **fressen** ▷ *adj:* **den hab(e) ich ~** (*umg*) I'm sick of him

gefrieren [gə'friːrən] *unreg vi* to freeze

Gefrier- *zW:* **Gefrierfach** *nt* freezer compartment; **Gefrierfleisch** *nt* frozen meat; **gefriergetrocknet** *adj* freeze-dried; **Gefrierpunkt** *m* freezing point; **Gefrierschutzmittel** *nt* antifreeze; **Gefriertruhe** *f* deep-freeze

gefror *etc* [gə'froːr] *vb siehe* **gefrieren**

gefroren *pp von* **frieren, gefrieren**

Gefüge [gə'fyːgə] (-s, -) *nt* structure

gefügig *adj* submissive; (*gehorsam*) obedient

Gefühl [gə'fyːl] (-(e)s, -e) *nt* feeling; **etw im ~ haben** to have a feel for sth; **gefühllos** *adj* unfeeling; (*Glieder*) numb

Gefühls- *zW:* **gefühlsbetont** *adj* emotional; **Gefühlsduselei** [-duːzə'laɪ] (*pej*) *f* mawkishness; **Gefühlsleben** *nt* emotional life; **gefühlsmäßig** *adj* instinctive; **Gefühlsmensch** *m* emotional person

gefühlvoll *adj* (*empfindsam*) sensitive; (*ausdrucksvoll*) expressive; (*liebevoll*) loving

gefüllt [gə'fʏlt] *adj* (*Koch*) stuffed; (*Pralinen*) with soft centres

gefunden [gə'fʊndən] *pp von* **finden** ▷ *adj:* **das war ein ~es Fressen für ihn** that was handing it to him on a plate

gegangen [gə'gaŋən] *pp von* **gehen**

gegeben [gə'geːbən] *pp von* **geben** ▷ *adj* given; **zu ~er Zeit** in due course

gegebenenfalls [gə'geːbənənfals] *adv* if need be

🔘 SCHLÜSSELWORT

gegen ['geːgən] *präp* +*akk* **1** against; **nichts gegen jdn haben** to have nothing against sb; **X gegen Y** (*Sport, Jur*) X versus Y; **ein Mittel gegen Schnupfen** something for colds

2 (*in Richtung auf*) towards; **gegen Osten** to(wards) the east; **gegen Abend** towards evening; **gegen einen Baum fahren** to drive into a tree

3 (*ungefähr*) round about; **gegen 3 Uhr** around 3 o'clock

4 (*gegenüber*) towards; (*ungefähr*) around; **gerecht gegen alle** fair to all

5 (*im Austausch für*) for; **gegen bar** for cash; **gegen Quittung** against a receipt

6 (*verglichen mit*) compared with

Gegen- *zW:* **Gegenangriff** *m* counter-attack; **Gegenbesuch** *m* return visit; **Gegenbeweis** *m*

counter-evidence

Gegend ['ge:gənt] (-, -en) f area, district

Gegen- zW: **Gegendarstellung** f (Presse) reply; **gegeneinander** adv against one another; **Gegenfahrbahn** f opposite carriageway; **gegenfinanzieren** vt to counterfinance; **Gegenfinanzierung** f financing of state expenditure by means of cuts, tax increases etc; **Gegenfrage** f counterquestion; **Gegengewicht** nt counterbalance; **Gegengift** nt antidote; **Gegenkandidat** m rival candidate; **gegenläufig** adj contrary; **Gegenleistung** f service in return; **Gegenlichtaufnahme** f back lit photograph; **Gegenliebe** f requited love; (fig: Zustimmung) approval; **Gegenmaßnahme** f countermeasure; **Gegenmittel** nt: **Gegenmittel (gegen)** (Med) antidote (to); **Gegenprobe** f cross-check

Gegensatz(-es, ̈e) m contrast; **Gegensätze überbrücken** to overcome differences

gegensätzlich adj contrary, opposite; (widersprüchlich) contradictory

Gegen- zW: **Gegenschlag** m counter-attack; **Gegenseite** f opposite side; (Rückseite) reverse; **gegenseitig** adj mutual, reciprocal; **sich gegenseitig helfen** to help each other; **in gegenseitigem Einverständnis** by mutual agreement; **Gegenseitigkeit** f reciprocity; **Gegenspieler** m opponent; **Gegensprechanlage** f (two-way) intercom; **Gegenstand** m object; **gegenständlich** adj objective, concrete; (Kunst) representational; **gegenstandslos** adj (überflüssig) irrelevant; (grundlos) groundless; **Gegenstimme** f vote against; **Gegenstoß** m counterblow; **Gegenstück** nt counterpart; **Gegenteil** nt opposite; **im Gegenteil** on the contrary; **das Gegenteil bewirken** to have the opposite effect; (Mensch) to achieve the exact opposite; **ganz im Gegenteil** quite the reverse; **ins Gegenteil umschlagen** to swing to the other extreme; **gegenteilig** adj opposite, contrary; **ich habe nichts Gegenteiliges gehört** I've heard nothing to the contrary

gegenüber [ge:gən'|y:bər] präp +dat opposite; (zu) to(wards); (in Bezug auf) with regard to; (im Vergleich zu) in comparison with; (angesichts) in the face of ▷ adv opposite; **mir ~ hat er das nicht geäußert** he didn't say that to me; **Gegenüber (-s, -)** nt person opposite; (bei Kampf) opponent; (bei Diskussion) opposite number; **gegenüberliegen** unreg vr to face each other; **gegenüberstehen** unreg vr to be opposed (to each other); **gegenüberstellen** vt to confront; (fig) to contrast; **Gegenüberstellung** f confrontation; (fig) contrast; (: Vergleich) comparison; **gegenübertreten** unreg vi +dat to face

Gegen- zW: **Gegenveranstaltung** f counter-meeting; **Gegenverkehr** m oncoming traffic; **Gegenvorschlag** m counterproposal

Gegenwart ['ge:gənvart] f present; **in ~ von** in the presence of

gegenwärtig adj present ▷ adv at present; **das ist mir nicht mehr ~** that has slipped my mind

gegenwartsbezogen adj (Roman etc) relevant to present times

Gegen- zW: **Gegenwert** m equivalent; **Gegenwind** m headwind; **Gegenwirkung** f reaction; **gegenzeichnen** vt to countersign; **Gegenzug** m countermove; (Eisenb) corresponding train in the other direction

gegessen [gə'gɛsən] pp von **essen**

geglichen [gə'glɪçən] pp von **gleichen**

gegliedert [gə'gli:dərt] adj jointed; (fig) structured

geglitten [gə'glɪtən] pp von **gleiten**

geglommen [gə'gləmən] pp von **glimmen**

geglückt [gə'glʏkt] adj (Feier) successful; (Überraschung) real

Gegner, in ['gɛgnər(ɪn)] (-s, -) m(f) opponent; **gegnerisch** adj opposing; **Gegnerschaft** f opposition

gegolten [gə'gɔltən] pp von **gelten**

gegoren [gə'go:rən] pp von **gären**

gegossen [gə'gɔsən] pp von **gießen**

gegr. abk (=gegründet) estab.

gegraben [gə'gra:bən] pp von **graben**

gegriffen [gə'grɪfən] pp von **greifen**

Gehabe [gə'ha:bə] (-s) (umg) nt affected behaviour (Brit) od behavior (US)

gehabt [gə'ha:pt] pp von **haben**

Gehackte, s [ge'haktə(s)] nt mince(d meat) (Brit), ground meat (US)

Gehalt¹ [gə'halt] (-(e)s, -e) m content

Gehalt² [gə'halt] (-(e)s, ̈er) nt salary

gehalten [gə'haltən] pp von **halten** ▷ adj: **~ sein, etw zu tun** (form) to be required to do sth

Gehalts- zW: **Gehaltsabrechnung** f salary statement; **Gehaltsempfänger** m salary earner; **Gehaltserhöhung** f salary increase; **Gehaltsklasse** f salary bracket; **Gehaltskonto** nt current account (Brit), checking account (US); **Gehaltszulage** f salary increment

gehaltvoll [gə'haltfɔl] adj (Speise, Buch) substantial

gehandicapt, gehandikapt [gə'hɛndikɛpt] adj handicapped

gehangen [gə'haŋən] pp von **hängen**

geharnischt [gə'harnɪʃt] adj (fig) forceful, sharp

gehässig [gə'hɛsɪç] adj spiteful, nasty; **Gehässigkeit** f spite(fulness)

gehäuft [gə'hɔyft] adj (Löffel) heaped

Gehäuse [gə'hɔyzə] (-s, -) nt case; (Radiogehäuse, Uhrgehäuse) casing; (von Apfel etc) core

gehbehindert ['ge:bəhɪndərt] adj disabled

Gehege [gə'he:gə] (-s, -) nt enclosure, preserve; **jdm ins ~ kommen** (fig) to poach on sb's preserve

geheim [gə'haɪm] adj secret; (Dokumente) classified; **streng ~** top secret; **~ halten** to keep secret; **Geheimdienst** m secret service, intelligence service; **Geheimfach** nt secret compartment

Geheimnis (**-ses, -se**) nt secret; (rätselhaftes Geheimnis) mystery; **Geheimniskrämer** m mystery-monger; **geheimnisvoll** adj mysterious

Geheim- zW: **Geheimnummer** f (Tel) secret number; **Geheimpolizei** f secret police; **Geheimrat** m privy councillor; **Geheimratsecken** pl: **er hat Geheimratsecken** he is going bald at the temples; **Geheimschrift** f code, secret writing; **Geheimtipp** m (personal) tip

Geheiß [gə'haɪs] (**-es**) nt (geh) command; **auf jds ~** akk at sb's bidding

geheißen [gə'haɪsən] pp von **heißen**

gehemmt [gə'hɛmt] adj inhibited

gehen ['ge:ən] unreg vi (auch Auto, Uhr) to go; (zu Fuß gehen) to walk; (funktionieren) to work; (Teig) to rise ▷ vt to go; to walk ▷ vi unpers: **wie geht es dir?** how are you od things?; **~ nach** (Fenster) to face; **in sich** akk **~** to think things over; **nach etw ~** (urteilen) to go by sth; **sich ~ lassen** to lose one's self-control; (nachlässig sein) to let o.s. go; **wie viele Leute ~ in deinen Wagen?** how many people can you get in your car?; **nichts geht über** +akk ... there's nothing to beat ..., there's nothing better than ...; **schwimmen/schlafen ~** to go swimming/to bed; **in die Tausende ~** to run into (the) thousands; **mir/ihm geht es gut** I'm/he's (doing) fine; **geht das?** is that possible?; **gehts noch?** can you manage?; **es geht** not too bad, O.K.; **das geht nicht** that's not on; **es geht um etw** it concerns sth, it's about sth; **lass es dir gut ~** look after yourself, take care of yourself; **so geht das, das geht so** that/this is how it's done; **darum geht es (mir) nicht** that's not the point; (spielt keine Rolle) that's not important to me; **morgen geht es nicht** tomorrow's no good; **wenn es nach mir ginge** ... if it were od was up to me ...

gehetzt [gə'hɛtst] adj harassed

geheuer [gə'hɔʏər] adj: **nicht ~** eerie; (fragwürdig) dubious

Geheul [gə'hɔʏl] (**-(e)s**) nt howling

Gehilfe [gə'hɪlfə] (**-n, -n**) m assistant

Gehilfin [gə'hɪlfɪn] f assistant

Gehirn [gə'hɪrn] (**-(e)s, -e**) nt brain; **Gehirnerschütterung** f concussion; **Gehirnschlag** m stroke; **Gehirnwäsche** f brainwashing

gehoben [gə'ho:bən] pp von **heben** ▷ adj: **~er Dienst** professional and executive levels of the civil service

geholfen [gə'hɔlfən] pp von **helfen**

Gehör [gə'hø:r] (**-(e)s**) nt hearing; **musikalisches ~** ear; **absolutes ~** perfect pitch; **~ finden** to gain a hearing; **jdm ~ schenken** to give sb a hearing

gehorchen [gə'hɔrçən] vi +dat to obey

gehören [gə'hø:rən] vi to belong ▷ vr unpers to be right od proper; **das gehört nicht zur Sache** that's irrelevant; **dazu gehört (schon)** einiges od **etwas** that takes some doing (umg); **er gehört ins Bett** he should be in bed

gehörig adj proper; **~ zu** od +dat (geh) belonging to

gehörlos adj (form) deaf

gehorsam [gə'ho:rza:m] adj obedient; **Gehorsam** (**-s**) m obedience

Gehörsinn m sense of hearing

Gehsteig ['ge:ʃtaɪk] m, **Gehweg** ['ge:vɛk] m pavement (Brit), sidewalk (US)

Geier ['gaɪər] (**-s, -**) m vulture; **weiß der ~!** (umg) God knows

geifern ['gaɪfərn] vi to slaver; (fig) to be bursting with venom

Geige ['gaɪgə] (**-, -n**) f violin; **die erste/zweite ~ spielen** (lit) to play first/second violin; (fig) to call the tune/play second fiddle

Geiger, in (**-s, -**) m(f) violinist

Geigerzähler m geiger counter

geil [gaɪl] adj randy (Brit), horny (US); (pej: lüstern) lecherous; (umg: gut) fantastic

Geisel ['gaɪzəl] (**-, -n**) f hostage; **Geiselnahme** (**-**) f taking of hostages

Geißel ['gaɪsəl] (**-, -n**) f scourge, whip

geißeln vt to scourge

Geist [gaɪst] (**-(e)s, -er**) m spirit; (Gespenst) ghost; (Verstand) mind; **von allen guten ~ern verlassen sein** (umg) to have taken leave of one's senses; **hier scheiden sich die ~er** this is the parting of the ways; **den** od **seinen ~ aufgeben** to give up the ghost

Geister- zW: **Geisterfahrer** (umg) m ghost-driver (US), person driving in the wrong direction; **geisterhaft** adj ghostly; **Geisterhand** f: **wie von Geisterhand** as if by magic

Geistes- zW: **geistesabwesend** adj absent-minded; **Geistesakrobat** m mental acrobat; **Geistesblitz** m brain wave; **Geistesgegenwart** f presence of mind; **geistesgegenwärtig** adj quick-witted; **geistesgestört** adj mentally disturbed; (stärker) (mentally) deranged; **Geisteshaltung** f mental attitude; **geisteskrank** adj mentally ill; **Geisteskranke, r** f(m) mentally ill person; **Geisteskrankheit** f mental illness; **Geistesstörung** f mental disturbance; **Geistesverfassung** f frame of mind; **Geisteswissenschaften** pl arts (subjects) pl; **Geisteszustand** m state of mind; **jdn auf seinen Geisteszustand untersuchen** to give sb a psychiatric examination

geistig adj intellectual; (Psych) mental; (Getränke) alcoholic; **~ behindert** mentally handicapped; **~-seelisch** mental and spiritual

geistlich adj spiritual; (religiös) religious; **Geistliche, r** m clergyman; **Geistlichkeit** f clergy

geist- zW: **geistlos** adj uninspired, dull; **geistreich** adj intelligent; (witzig) witty; **geisttötend** adj soul-destroying; **geistvoll** adj intellectual; (weise) wise

Geiz [gaɪts] (**-es**) m miserliness, meanness; **geizen** vi to be miserly; **Geizhals** m miser

g

geizig adj miserly, mean
Geizkragen m miser
gekannt [gə'kant] pp von **kennen**
Gekicher [gə'kıçər] (**-s**) nt giggling
Geklapper [gə'klapər] (**-s**) nt rattling
Geklimper [gə'klımpər] (**-s**) (umg) nt (Klaviergeklimper) tinkling; (: stümperhaft) plonking; (von Geld) jingling
geklungen [gə'kluŋən] pp von **klingen**
geknickt [gə'knıkt] adj (fig) dejected
gekniffen [gə'knıfən] pp von **kneifen**
gekommen [gə'kɔmən] pp von **kommen**
gekonnt [gə'kɔnt] pp von **können** ▷ adj skilful (Brit), skillful (US)
Gekritzel [gə'krıtsəl] (**-s**) nt scrawl, scribble
gekrochen [gə'krɔxən] pp von **kriechen**
gekünstelt [ge'kynstəlt] adj artificial; (Sprache, Benehmen) affected
Gel [ge:l] (**-s, -e**) nt gel
Gelaber [gə'la:bər], **Gelabere** [gə'la:bərə] (**-s**) (umg) nt prattle
Gelächter [gə'lɛçtər] (**-s, -**) nt laughter; **in ~ ausbrechen** to burst out laughing
gelackmeiert [gə'lakmaıərt] (umg) adj conned
geladen [ge'la:dən] pp von **laden** ▷ adj loaded; (Elek) live; (fig) furious
Gelage [gə'la:gə] (**-s, -**) nt feast, banquet
gelagert [gə'la:gərt] adj: **in anders/ähnlich ~en Fällen** in different/similar cases
gelähmt [gə'lɛ:mt] adj paralysed
Gelände [gə'lɛndə] (**-s, -**) nt land, terrain; (von Fabrik, Sportgelände) grounds pl; (Baugelände) site; **Geländefahrzeug** nt cross-country vehicle; **geländegängig** adj able to go cross-country; **Geländelauf** m cross-country race
Geländer [gə'lɛndər] (**-s, -**) nt railing; (Treppengeländer) banister(s)
gelang etc vb siehe **gelingen**
gelangen [gə'laŋən] vi: **~ an** +akk od **zu** to reach; (erwerben) to attain; **in jds Besitz** akk **~** to come into sb's possession; **in die richtigen/falschen Hände ~** to fall into the right/wrong hands
gelangweilt adj bored
gelassen [gə'lasən] pp von **lassen** ▷ adj calm; (gefasst) composed; **Gelassenheit** f calmness; composure
Gelatine [ʒela'ti:nə] f gelatine
gelaufen [gə'laufən] pp von **laufen**
geläufig [gə'lɔyfıç] adj (üblich) common; **das ist mir nicht ~** I'm not familiar with that; **Geläufigkeit** f commonness; familiarity
gelaunt [gə'launt] adj: **schlecht/gut ~** in a bad/good mood; **wie ist er ~?** what sort of mood is he in?
Geläut [gə'lɔyt] (**-(e)s**) nt ringing; (Läutwerk) chime
Geläute (**-s**) nt ringing
gelb [gɛlp] adj yellow; (Ampellicht) amber (Brit), yellow (US); **~e Seiten** Yellow Pages; **gelblich** adj yellowish
Gelbsucht f jaundice
Geld [gɛlt] (**-(e)s, -er**) nt money; **etw zu ~**

machen to sell sth off; **er hat ~ wie Heu** (umg) he's stinking rich; **am ~ hängen** od **kleben** to be tight with money; **staatliche/ öffentliche ~er** state/public funds pl od money; **Geldadel** m: **der Geldadel** the moneyed aristocracy; (hum: die Reichen) the rich; **Geldanlage** f investment; **Geldautomat** m cash dispenser; **Geldautomatenkarte** f cash card; **Geldbeutel** m purse; **Geldbörse** f purse; **Geldeinwurf** m slot; **Geldgeber** (**-s, -**) m financial backer; **geldgierig** adj avaricious; **Geldinstitut** nt financial institution; **Geldmittel** pl capital sing, means pl; **Geldquelle** f source of income; **Geldschein** m banknote; **Geldschrank** m safe, strongbox; **Geldstrafe** f fine; **Geldstück** nt coin; **Geldverlegenheit** f: **in Geldverlegenheit sein/kommen** to be/run short of money; **Geldverleiher** m moneylender; **Geldwäsche** f money-laundering; **Geldwechsel** m exchange (of money); **„Geldwechsel"** "bureau de change"; **Geldwert** m cash value; (Fin: Kaufkraft) currency value
geleckt [gə'lɛkt] adj: **wie ~ aussehen** to be neat and tidy
Gelee [ʒe'le:] (**-s, -s**) nt od m jelly
gelegen [gə'le:gən] pp von **liegen** ▷ adj situated; (passend) convenient, opportune; **etw kommt jdm ~** sth is convenient for sb; **mir ist viel/ nichts daran ~** (wichtig) it matters a great deal/doesn't matter to me
Gelegenheit [gə'le:gənhaıt] f opportunity; (Anlass) occasion; **bei ~** some time (or other); **bei jeder ~** at every opportunity
Gelegenheits- zW: **Gelegenheitsarbeit** f casual work; **Gelegenheitsarbeiter** m casual worker; **Gelegenheitskauf** m bargain
gelegentlich [gə'le:gəntlıç] adj occasional ▷ adv occasionally; (bei Gelegenheit) some time (or other) ▷ präp +gen on the occasion of
gelehrig [gə'le:rıç] adj quick to learn
gelehrt [gə'le:rt] adj learned; **Gelehrte, r** f(m) scholar; **Gelehrtheit** f scholarliness
Geleise [gə'laızə] (**-s, -**) nt = **Gleis**
Geleit [gə'laıt] (**-(e)s, -e**) nt escort; **freies** od **sicheres ~** safe conduct; **geleiten** vt to escort; **Geleitschutz** m escort
Gelenk [gə'lɛŋk] (**-(e)s, -e**) nt joint
gelenkig adj supple
gelernt [gə'lɛrnt] adj skilled
gelesen [gə'le:zən] pp von **lesen**
Geliebte f sweetheart; (Liebhaberin) mistress
Geliebte, r m sweetheart; (Liebhaber) lover
geliefert [gə'li:fərt] adj: **ich bin ~** (umg) I've had it
geliehen [gə'li:ən] pp von **leihen**
gelind [gə'lınt] adj = **gelinde**
gelinde [gə'lındə] adj (geh) mild; **~ gesagt** to put it mildly
gelingen [gə'lıŋən] unreg vi to succeed; **die Arbeit gelingt mir nicht** I'm not doing very well with this work; **es ist mir gelungen, etw zu tun** I succeeded in doing sth; **Gelingen**

nt (geh: Glück) success; (: erfolgreiches Ergebnis) successful outcome

gelitten [gə'lɪtən] pp von **leiden**

gellen ['gɛlən] vi to shrill

gellend adj shrill, piercing

geloben [gə'lo:bən] vt, vi to vow, swear; **das Gelobte Land** (Rel) the Promised Land

gelogen [gə'lo:gən] pp von **lügen**

gelten ['gɛltən] unreg vt (wert sein) to be worth ▷ vi (gültig sein) to be valid; (erlaubt sein) to be allowed ▷ vb unpers (geh): **es gilt, etw zu tun** it is necessary to do sth; **was gilt die Wette?** do you want a bet?; **das gilt nicht!** that doesn't count!; (nicht erlaubt) that's not allowed; **etw gilt bei jdm viel/wenig** sb values sth highly/ doesn't value sth very highly; **jdm viel/ wenig ~** to mean a lot/not mean much to sb; **jdm ~** (gemünzt sein auf) to be meant for od aimed at sb; **etw ~ lassen** to accept sth; **für diesmal lasse ichs ~** I'll let it go this time; **als** od **für etw ~** to be considered to be sth; **jdm** od **für jdn ~** (betreffen) to apply to sb

geltend adj (Preise) current; (Gesetz) in force; (Meinung) prevailing; **etw ~ machen** to assert sth; **sich ~ machen** to make itself/o.s. felt; **einen Einwand ~ machen** to raise an objection

Geltung ['gɛltʊŋ] f: **~ haben** to have validity; **sich/etw** dat **~ verschaffen** to establish o.s./ sth; **etw zur ~ bringen** to show sth to its best advantage; **zur ~ kommen** to be seen/heard etc to its best advantage

Geltungsbedürfnis nt desire for admiration

geltungssüchtig adj craving admiration

Gelübde [gə'lʏpdə] (-s, -) nt vow

gelungen [gə'lʊŋən] pp von **gelingen** ▷ adj successful

Gem. abk = **Gemeinde**

gemächlich [gə'mɛ:çlɪç] adj leisurely

gemacht [gə'ma:xt] adj (gewollt, gekünstelt) false, contrived; **ein ~er Mann sein** to be made

Gemahl [gə'ma:l] (-(e)s, -e) m (geh, form) spouse, husband

gemahlen [gə'ma:lən] pp von **mahlen**

Gemahlin f (geh, form) spouse, wife

Gemälde [gə'mɛ:ldə] (-s, -) nt picture, painting

gemasert [gə'ma:zərt] adj (Holz) grained

gemäß [gə'mɛ:s] präp +dat in accordance with ▷ adj +dat appropriate to

gemäßigt adj moderate; (Klima) temperate

Gemauschel [gə'maʊʃəl] (-s) (umg) nt scheming

Gemecker [gə'mɛkər] (-s) nt (von Ziegen) bleating; (umg: Nörgelei) moaning

gemein [gə'maɪn] adj common; (niederträchtig) mean; **etw ~ haben (mit)** to have sth in common (with)

Gemeinde [gə'maɪndə] (-, -n) f district; (Bewohner) community; (Pfarrgemeinde) parish; (Kirchengemeinde) congregation; **Gemeindeabgaben** pl rates and local taxes pl; **Gemeindebau** m (Österr) subsidized housing; (Gebäude) subsidized house;

Gemeindeordnung f by(e) laws pl, ordinances pl (US); **Gemeinderat** m district council; (Mitglied) district councillor; **Gemeindeschwester** f district nurse (Brit); **Gemeindesteuer** f local rates pl; **Gemeindeverwaltung** f local administration; **Gemeindevorstand** m local council; **Gemeindewahl** f local election

Gemein- zW: **Gemeineigentum** nt common property; **gemeingefährlich** adj dangerous to the public; **Gemeingut** nt public property; **Gemeinheit** f (Niedertracht) meanness; **das war eine Gemeinheit** that was a mean thing to do/to say; **gemeinhin** adv generally; **Gemeinkosten** pl overheads pl; **Gemeinnutz** m public good; **gemeinnützig** adj of benefit to the public; (wohltätig) charitable; **Gemeinplatz** m commonplace, platitude; **gemeinsam** adj joint, common (auch Math) ▷ adv together; **gemeinsame Sache mit jdm machen** to be in cahoots with sb; **der Gemeinsame Markt** the Common Market; **gemeinsames Konto** joint account; **etw gemeinsam haben** to have sth in common; **Gemeinsamkeit** f common ground; **Gemeinschaft** f community; **in Gemeinschaft mit** jointly od together with; **eheliche Gemeinschaft** (Jur) matrimony; **Gemeinschaft Unabhängiger Staaten** Commonwealth of Independent States; **gemeinschaftlich** adj = **gemeinsam**; **Gemeinschaftsantenne** f party aerial (Brit) od antenna (US); **Gemeinschaftsarbeit** f teamwork; **Gemeinschaftsbesitz** m collective ownership; **Gemeinschaftserziehung** f coeducation; **Gemeinschaftskunde** f social studies pl; **Gemeinschaftsraum** m common room; **Gemeinschaftswährung** f common od single currency; (innerhalb der EU) single European currency; **Gemeinsinn** m public spirit; **gemeinverständlich** adj generally comprehensible; **Gemeinwesen** nt community; **Gemeinwohl** nt common good

Gemenge [gə'mɛŋə] (-s, -) nt mixture; (Handgemenge) scuffle

gemessen [gə'mɛsən] pp von **messen** ▷ adj measured

Gemetzel [gə'mɛtsəl] (-s, -) nt slaughter, carnage

gemieden [gə'mi:dən] pp von **meiden**

Gemisch [gə'mɪʃ] (-es, -e) nt mixture

gemischt adj mixed

gemocht [gə'mɔxt] pp von **mögen**

gemolken [gə'mɔlkən] pp von **melken**

Gemse ['gɛmzə] (-, -n) f siehe **Gämse**

Gemunkel [gə'mʊŋkəl] (-s) nt gossip

Gemurmel [gə'mʊrməl] (-s) nt murmur(ing)

Gemüse [gə'my:zə] (-s, -) nt vegetables pl; **Gemüsegarten** m vegetable garden; **Gemüsehändler** m greengrocer (Brit), vegetable dealer (US); **Gemüseplatte** f (Koch): **eine Gemüseplatte** assorted vegetables

gemusst [gə'mʊst] pp von **müssen**

g

141

gemustert [gə'mʊstərt] *adj* patterned

Gemüt [gə'my:t] (**-(e)s, -er**) *nt* disposition, nature; *(fig: Mensch)* person; **sich** *dat* **etw zu ~e führen** *(umg)* to indulge in sth; **die ~er erregen** to arouse strong feelings; **wir müssen warten, bis sich die ~er beruhigt haben** we must wait until feelings have cooled down

gemütlich *adj* comfortable, cosy; *(Person)* good-natured; **wir verbrachten einen ~en Abend** we spent a very pleasant evening; **Gemütlichkeit** *f* comfortableness, cosiness; amiability

Gemüts- *zW:* **Gemütsbewegung** *f* emotion; **gemütskrank** *adj* emotionally disturbed; **Gemütsmensch** *m* sentimental person; **Gemütsruhe** *f* composure; **in aller Gemütsruhe** *(umg)* (as) cool as a cucumber; *(gemächlich)* at a leisurely pace; **Gemütszustand** *m* state of mind

gemütvoll *adj* warm, tender

Gen [geːn] (**-s, -e**) *nt* gene

Gen. *abk* = **Genossenschaft**; (= *Genitiv*) gen.

gen. *abk* (= *genannt*) named, called

genannt [gə'nant] *pp von* **nennen**

genas *etc* [gə'naːs] *vb siehe* **genesen**

genau [gə'nau] *adj* exact, precise ▷ *adv* exactly, precisely; **etw ~ nehmen** to take sth seriously; **~ genommen** strictly speaking; **G~eres** further details *pl*; **etw ~ wissen** to know sth for certain; **~ auf die Minute, auf die Minute genau** exactly on time

Genauigkeit *f* exactness, accuracy

genauso [gə'nauzoː] *adv (vor Adjektiv)* just as; *(allein stehend)* just *od* exactly the same

genehm [gə'neːm] *adj* agreeable, acceptable

genehmigen *vt* to approve, authorize; **sich** *dat* **etw ~** to indulge in sth

Genehmigung *f* approval, authorization

geneigt [gə'naikt] *adj (geh)* well-disposed, willing; **~ sein, etw zu tun** to be inclined to do sth

Genera *pl von* **Genus**

General [gene'raːl] (**-s, -e** *od* **ẅe**) *m* general; **Generaldirektor** *m* chairman (Brit), president (US); **Generalkonsulat** *nt* consulate general; **Generalprobe** *f* dress rehearsal; **Generalsekretär** *m* secretary-general; **Generalstabskarte** *f* ordnance survey map; **Generalstreik** *m* general strike; **generalüberholen** *vt* to overhaul thoroughly; **Generalvertretung** *f* sole agency

Generation [generatsi'oːn] *f* generation

Generationskonflikt *m* generation gap

Generator [gene'raːtɔr] *m* generator, dynamo

generell [genə'rɛl] *adj* general

genesen [ge'neːzən] *unreg vi (geh)* to convalesce, recover

Genesende, r *f(m)* convalescent

Genesung *f* recovery, convalescence

Genetik [ge'neːtɪk] *f* genetics

genetisch [ge'neːtɪʃ] *adj* genetic

Genf ['gɛnf] (**-s**) *nt* Geneva

Genfer *adj attrib:* **der ~ See** Lake Geneva; **die ~ Konvention** the Geneva Convention

genial [geni'aːl] *adj* brilliant

Genialität [geniali'tɛːt] *f* brilliance, genius

Genick [gə'nɪk] (**-(e)s, -e**) *nt* (back of the) neck; **jdm/etw das ~ brechen** *(fig)* to finish sb/sth; **Genickstarre** *f* stiff neck

Genie [ʒe'niː] (**-s, -s**) *nt* genius

genieren [ʒe'niːrən] *vr* to be embarrassed ▷ *vt* to bother; **geniert es Sie, wenn ...?** do you mind if ...?

genießbar *adj* edible; *(trinkbar)* drinkable

genießen [gə'niːsən] *unreg vt* to enjoy; *(essen)* to eat; *(trinken)* to drink; **er ist heute nicht zu ~** *(umg)* he is unbearable today

Genießer, in (**-s, -**) *m(f)* connoisseur; *(des Lebens)* pleasure-lover; **genießerisch** *adj* appreciative ▷ *adv* with relish

Genitalien [geni'taːliən] *pl* genitals *pl*

Genitiv ['geːnitiːf] *m* genitive

Genmais *m* GM maize

genmanipuliert *adj* genetically modified

genommen [gə'nɔmən] *pp von* **nehmen**

genoss *etc* [gə'nɔs] *vb siehe* **genießen**

Genosse [gə'nɔsə] (**-n, -n**) *m* comrade *(bes Pol)*, companion

genossen *pp von* **genießen**

Genossenschaft *f* cooperative (association)

Genossin [gə'nɔsɪn] *f* comrade *(bes Pol)*, companion

genötigt [gə'nøːtɪçt] *adj:* **sich ~ sehen, etw zu tun** to feel obliged to do sth

Genre [ʒãːrə] (**-s, -s**) *nt* genre

Gent [gɛnt] (**-s**) *nt* Ghent

Gentechnik *f*, **Gentechnologie** *f* gene technology

Genua ['geːnua] (**-s**) *nt* Genoa

genug [gə'nuːk] *adv* enough; **jetzt ist(s) aber ~!** that's enough!

Genüge [gə'nyːgə] *f:* **jdm/etw ~ tun** *od* **leisten** to satisfy sb/sth; **etw zur ~ kennen** to know sth well enough; *(abwertender)* to know sth only too well

genügen *vi* to be enough; *(den Anforderungen etc)* to satisfy; **jdm ~** to be enough for sb

genügend *adj* enough, sufficient; *(befriedigend)* satisfactory

genügsam [gə'nyːkzaːm] *adj* modest, easily satisfied; **Genügsamkeit** *f* moderation

Genugtuung [gə'nuːktuːʊŋ] *f* satisfaction

Genus ['geːnʊs] (**-, Genera**) *nt (Gram)* gender

Genuss [gə'nʊs] (**-es, ẅe**) *m* pleasure; *(Zusichnehmen)* consumption; **etw mit ~ essen** to eat sth with relish; **in den ~ von etw kommen** to receive the benefit of sth

genüsslich [gə'nʏslɪç] *adv* with relish

Genussmittel *pl* (semi-)luxury items *pl*

geöffnet [gə'œfnət] *adj* open

Geograf [geo'graːf] (**-en, -en**) *m* geographer

Geografie [geogra'fiː] *f* geography

Geografin *f* geographer

geografisch *adj* geographical

Geologe [geo'loːgə] (**-n, -n**) *m* geologist

Geologie [geolo:'gi:] f geology
Geologin f geologist
Geometrie [geome'tri:] f geometry
geordnet [gə'ɔrdnət] adj: **in ~en Verhält-nissen leben** to live a well-ordered life
Georgien [ge'ɔrgiən] (**-s**) nt Georgia
Gepäck [gə'pɛk] (**-(e)s**) nt luggage, baggage; **mit leichtem ~ reisen** to travel light; **Gepäckabfertigung** f luggage desk/office; **Gepäckannahme** f (Bahnhof) baggage office; (Flughafen) baggage check-in; **Gepäckaufbewahrung** f left-luggage office (Brit), baggage check (US); **Gepäckausgabe** f (Bahnhof) baggage office; (Flughafen) baggage reclaim; **Gepäcknetz** nt luggage rack; **Gepäckschein** m luggage od baggage ticket; **Gepäckstück** nt piece of baggage; **Gepäckträger** m porter; (Fahrrad) carrier; **Gepäckwagen** m luggage van (Brit), baggage car (US)
Gepard ['ge:part] (**-(e)s, -e**) m cheetah
gepfeffert [gə'pfɛfərt] (umg) adj (Preise) steep; (Fragen, Prüfung) tough; (Kritik) biting
gepfiffen [gə'pfɪfən] pp von **pfeifen**
gepflegt [gə'pfle:kt] adj well-groomed; (Park etc) well looked after; (Atmosphäre) sophisticated; (Ausdrucksweise, Sprache) cultured
Gepflogenheit [gə'pflo:gənhaɪt] f (geh) custom
Geplapper [gə'plapər] (**-s**) nt chatter
Geplauder [gə'plaʊdər] (**-s**) nt chat(ting)
Gepolter [gə'pɔltər] (**-s**) nt din
gepr. abk (= geprüft) tested
gepriesen [gə'pri:zən] pp von **preisen**
gequält [gə'kvɛ:lt] adj (Lächeln) forced; (Miene, Ausdruck) pained; (Gesang, Stimme) strained
Gequatsche [gə'kvatʃə] (**-s**) (pej: umg) nt gabbing; (Blödsinn) twaddle
gequollen [gə'kvɔlən] pp von **quellen**
Gerade [gə'ra:də] (**-n, -n**) f straight line

○ SCHLÜSSELWORT

gerade [gə'ra:də] adj straight; (aufrecht) upright; **eine gerade Zahl** an even number
▷ adv **1** (genau) just, exactly; (speziell) especially; **gerade deshalb** that's just od exactly why; **das ist es ja gerade!** that's just it; **gerade du** you especially; **warum gerade ich?** why me (of all people)?; **jetzt gerade nicht!** not now!; **gerade neben** right next to; **nicht gerade schön** not exactly beautiful; **gerade biegen** to straighten out; **gerade stehen** (aufrecht) to stand up straight
2 (eben, soeben) just; **er wollte gerade aufstehen** he was just about to get up; **da wir gerade von Geld sprechen ...** talking of money ...; **gerade erst** only just; **gerade noch** (only) just

gerade- zW: **geradeaus** adv straight ahead; **geradebiegen** unreg vt (fig) to straighten out; **geradeheraus** adv straight out, bluntly
gerädert [gə'rɛ:dərt] adj: **wie ~ sein, sich wie**

~ **fühlen** to be od feel (absolutely) whacked (umg)
geradeso adv just so; **~ dumm** etc just as stupid etc; **~ wie** just as
geradestehen unreg vi: **für jdn/etw ~** (fig) to answer od be answerable for sb/sth
geradezu adv (beinahe) virtually, almost
geradlinig adj straight
gerammelt [gə'raməlt] adv: **~ voll** (umg) (jam-)packed
Geranie [gɛ'ra:niə] f geranium
gerannt [gə'rant] pp von **rennen**
Gerät [gə'rɛ:t] (**-(e)s, -e**) nt device; (Apparat) gadget; (elektrisches Gerät) appliance; (Werkzeug) tool; (Sport) apparatus; (Zubehör) equipment no pl
gerät [gə'rɛ:t] vb siehe **geraten**
geraten [gə'ra:tən] unreg pp von **raten; geraten** ▷ vi (gedeihen) to thrive; (gelingen): **(jdm) ~** to turn out well (for sb); (zufällig gelangen): **~ in** +akk to get into; **gut/schlecht ~** to turn out well/badly; **an jdn ~** to come across sb; **an den Richtigen/Falschen ~** to come to the right/wrong person; **in Angst ~** to get frightened; **nach jdm ~** to take after sb
Geräteturnen nt apparatus gymnastics
Geratewohl [gəra:tə'vo:l] nt: **aufs ~** on the off chance; (bei Wahl) at random
geraum [gə'raʊm] adj: **seit ~er Zeit** for some considerable time
geräumig [gə'rɔymɪç] adj roomy
Geräusch [gə'rɔyʃ] (**-(e)s, -e**) nt sound; (unangenehm) noise; **geräuscharm** adj quiet; **Geräuschkulisse** f background noise; (Film, Rundf, TV) sound effects pl; **geräuschlos** adj silent; **Geräuschpegel** m sound level; **geräuschvoll** adj noisy
gerben ['gɛrbən] vt to tan
Gerber (**-s, -**) m tanner
Gerberei [gɛrbə'raɪ] f tannery
gerecht [gə'rɛçt] adj just, fair; **jdm/etw ~ werden** to do justice to sb/sth; **gerechtfertigt** adj justified
Gerechtigkeit f justice, fairness
Gerechtigkeits- zW: **Gerechtigkeitsfanatiker** m justice fanatic; **Gerechtigkeitsgefühl** nt sense of justice; **Gerechtigkeitssinn** m sense of justice
Gerede [gə're:də] (**-s**) nt talk; (Klatsch) gossip
geregelt [gə're:gəlt] adj (Arbeit, Mahlzeiten) regular; (Leben) well-ordered
gereizt [gə'raɪtst] adj irritable; **Gereiztheit** f irritation
Gericht [gə'rɪçt] (**-(e)s, -e**) nt court; (Essen) dish; **jdn/einen Fall vor ~ bringen** to take sb/a case to court; **mit jdm ins ~ gehen** (fig) to judge sb harshly; **über jdn zu ~ sitzen** to sit in judgement on sb; **das Jüngste ~** the Last Judgement; **gerichtlich** adj judicial, legal ▷ adv judicially, legally; **ein gerichtliches Nachspiel haben** to finish up in court; **gerichtlich gegen jdn vorgehen** to take legal proceedings against sb

g

143

Gerichts- zW: **Gerichtsakten** pl court records pl; **Gerichtsbarkeit** f jurisdiction; **Gerichtshof** m court (of law); **Gerichtskosten** pl (legal) costs pl; **gerichtsmedizinisch** adj forensic medical attrib; **Gerichtssaal** m courtroom; **Gerichtsstand** m court of jurisdiction; **Gerichtsverfahren** nt legal proceedings pl; **Gerichtsverhandlung** f court proceedings pl; **Gerichtsvollzieher** m bailiff

gerieben [gə'riːbən] pp von **reiben** ▷ adj grated; (umg: schlau) smart, wily

geriet etc [gə'riːt] vb siehe **geraten**

gering [gə'rɪŋ] adj slight, small; (niedrig) low; (Zeit) short ▷ adv: ~ **achten** to think little of; **geringfügig** adj slight, trivial; **geringfügig Beschäftigte** ≈ part-time workers pl; **geringschätzig** adj disparaging; **Geringschätzung** f disdain

geringste, r, s adj slightest, least; **nicht im G~n** not in the least od slightest

Geringverdiener, in m(f) low-income earner

gerinnen [gə'rɪnən] unreg vi to congeal; (Blut) to clot; (Milch) to curdle

Gerinnsel [gə'rɪnzəl] (**-s, -**) nt clot

Gerippe [gə'rɪpə] (**-s, -**) nt skeleton

gerissen [gə'rɪsən] pp von **reißen** ▷ adj wily, smart

geritten [gə'rɪtən] pp von **reiten**

geritzt [gə'rɪtst] (umg) adj: **die Sache ist ~** everything's fixed up od settled

Germanist, in [gɛrma'nɪst(ɪn)] m(f) Germanist, German specialist; (Student) German student

Germanistik f German (studies pl)

gern [gɛrn] adv willingly, gladly; **(aber) ~!** of course!; ~ **mögen** to like; **etw ~ tun** to like doing sth; ~ **geschehen!** you're welcome!, not at all!; **ein ~ gesehener Gast** a welcome visitor; **ich hätte** od **möchte ~ ...** I would like ...; siehe auch **gernhaben**

gerne ['gɛrnə] adv = **gern**

Gernegroß (**-, -e**) m show-off; **gernhaben** unreg vt to like; **du kannst mich mal gernhaben!** (umg) (you can) go to hell!

gerochen [gə'rɔxən] pp von **riechen**

Geröll [gə'rœl] (**-(e)s, -e**) nt scree

geronnen [gə'rɔnən] pp von **rinnen; gerinnen**

Gerste ['gɛrstə] (**-, -n**) f barley

Gerstenkorn nt (im Auge) stye

Gerte ['gɛrtə] (**-, -n**) f switch, rod

gertenschlank adj willowy

Geruch [gə'rʊx] (**-(e)s, ̈-e**) m smell, odour (Brit), odor (US); **geruchlos** adj odourless (Brit), odorless (US)

Geruchssinn m sense of smell

Gerücht [gə'rʏçt] (**-(e)s, -e**) nt rumour (Brit), rumor (US)

geruchtilgend adj deodorant

gerufen [gə'ruːfən] pp von **rufen**

geruhen [gə'ruːən] vi to deign

geruhsam [gə'ruːzaːm] adj peaceful; (Spaziergang etc) leisurely

Gerümpel [gə'rʏmpəl] (**-s**) nt junk

gerungen [gə'rʊŋən] pp von **ringen**

Gerüst [gə'rʏst] (**-(e)s, -e**) nt (Baugerüst) scaffold(ing); (fig) framework

Ges. abk (= Gesellschaft) Co., co.

gesalzen [gə'zaltsən] pp von **salzen** ▷ adj (fig: umg: Preis, Rechnung) steep, stiff

gesamt [gə'zamt] adj whole, entire; (Kosten) total; (Werke) complete; **im G~en** all in all; **Gesamtauflage** f gross circulation; **Gesamtausgabe** f complete edition; **Gesamtbetrag** m total (amount); **gesamtdeutsch** adj all-German; **Gesamteindruck** m general impression; **Gesamtheit** f totality, whole

Gesamthochschule f polytechnic (Brit); see culture note

◉ GESAMTHOCHSCHULE

A Gesamthochschule is an institution combining several different kinds of higher education organizations eg. a university, teacher training college and institute of applied science. Students can study for various degrees within the same subject area and it is easier to change course than it is in an individual institution.

Gesamt- zW: **Gesamtmasse** f (Comm) total assets pl; **Gesamtnachfrage** f (Comm) composite demand; **Gesamtschaden** m total damage

Gesamtschule f ≈ comprehensive school; see culture note

◉ GESAMTSCHULE

The Gesamtschule is a comprehensive school teaching pupils who have different aims. Traditionally pupils would go to one of three different schools, the Gymnasium, Realschule or Hauptschule, depending on ability. The Gesamtschule seeks to avoid the elitist element prevalent in many Gymnasium, but in Germany these schools are still very controversial. Many parents still prefer the traditional system.

Gesamtwertung f (Sport) overall placings pl

gesandt pp von **senden**

Gesandte, r [gə'zantə(r)] f(m) envoy

Gesandtschaft [gə'zantʃaft] f legation

Gesang [gə'zaŋ] (**-(e)s, ̈-e**) m song; (Singen) singing; **Gesangbuch** nt (Rel) hymn book

Gesäß [gə'zɛːs] (**-es, -e**) nt seat, bottom

gesättigt [gə'zɛtɪçt] adj (Chem) saturated

gesch. abk (= geschieden) div.

Geschädigte, r [gə'ʃɛːdɪçtə(r)] f(m) victim

geschaffen [gə'ʃafən] pp von **schaffen**

Geschäft [gə'ʃɛft] (**-(e)s, -e**) nt business; (Laden) shop; (Geschäftsabschluss) deal; **mit jdm ins ~ kommen** to do business with sb; **dabei**

hat er ein ~ gemacht he made a profit by it; **im ~** at work; (*im Laden*) in the shop; **sein ~ verrichten** to do one's business (*euph*)

Geschäftemacher m wheeler-dealer

geschäftig adj active, busy; (*pej*) officious

geschäftlich adj commercial ▷ adv on business; **~ unterwegs** away on business

Geschäfts- zW: **Geschäftsabschluss** m business deal od transaction; **Geschäftsaufgabe** f closure of a/the business; **Geschäftsauflösung** f closure of a/the business; **Geschäftsbedingungen** pl terms of business; **Geschäftsbereich** m (*Parl*) responsibilities pl; **Minister ohne Geschäftsbereich** minister without portfolio; **Geschäftsbericht** m financial report; **Geschäftsbeziehungen** pl business relations; **Geschäftscomputer** m business computer; **Geschäftsessen** nt business lunch; **Geschäftsführer** m manager; (*Klub*) secretary; **Geschäftsgeheimnis** nt trade secret; **Geschäftsinhaber** m owner; **Geschäftsjahr** nt financial year; **Geschäftslage** f business conditions pl; **Geschäftsleitung** f management; **Geschäftsmann** (**-(e)s**, pl **-leute**) m businessman; **geschäftsmäßig** adj businesslike; **Geschäftsordnung** f standing orders pl; **eine Frage zur Geschäftsordnung** a question on a point of order; **Geschäftspartner** m partner; **Geschäftsreise** f business trip; **Geschäftsschluss** m closing time; **Geschäftssinn** m business sense; **Geschäftsstelle** f office(s pl), place of business; **geschäftstüchtig** adj business-minded; **Geschäftsviertel** nt shopping centre (*Brit*) od center (*US*); (*Banken etc*) business quarter, commercial district; **Geschäftswagen** m company car; **Geschäftswesen** nt business; **Geschäftszeit** f business hours pl; **Geschäftszweig** m branch (of a business)

geschah etc [gəˈʃa:] vb siehe **geschehen**

geschehen [gəˈʃe:ən] unreg vi to happen; **das geschieht ihm (ganz) recht** it serves him (jolly well (*umg*)) right; **was soll mit ihm/damit ~?** what is to be done with him/it?; **es war um ihn ~** that was the end of him

gescheit [gəˈʃaɪt] adj clever; (*vernünftig*) sensible

Geschenk [gəˈʃɛŋk] (**-(e)s**, **-e**) nt present, gift; **Geschenkartikel** m gift; **Geschenkgutschein** m gift voucher; **Geschenkpackung** f gift pack; **Geschenksendung** f gift parcel

Geschichte [gəˈʃɪçtə] (**-**, **-n**) f story; (*Sache*) affair; (*Historie*) history

Geschichtenerzähler m storyteller

geschichtlich adj historical; (*bedeutungsvoll*) historic

Geschichtsfälschung f falsification of history

Geschichtsschreiber m historian

Geschick [gəˈʃɪk] (**-(e)s**, **-e**) nt skill; (*geh: Schicksal*) fate

Geschicklichkeit f skill, dexterity

Geschicklichkeitsspiel nt game of skill

geschickt adj skilful (*Brit*), skillful (*US*); (*taktisch*) clever; (*beweglich*) agile

geschieden [gəˈʃi:dən] pp von **scheiden** ▷ adj divorced

geschieht [gəˈʃi:t] vb siehe **geschehen**

geschienen [gəˈʃi:nən] pp von **scheinen**

Geschirr [gəˈʃɪr] (**-(e)s**, **-e**) nt crockery; (*Küchengeschirr*) pots and pans pl; (*Pferdegeschirr*) harness; **Geschirrspülmaschine** f dishwasher; **Geschirrtuch** nt tea towel (*Brit*), dishtowel (*US*)

geschissen [gəˈʃɪsən] pp von **scheißen**

geschlafen [gəˈʃla:fən] pp von **schlafen**

geschlagen [gəˈʃla:gən] pp von **schlagen**

geschlaucht [gəˈʃlaʊxt] adv: **~ sein** (*umg*) to be exhausted od knackered

Geschlecht [gəˈʃlɛçt] (**-(e)s**, **-er**) nt sex; (*Gram*) gender; (*Gattung*) race; (*Abstammung*) lineage; **geschlechtlich** adj sexual

Geschlechts- zW: **Geschlechtskrankheit** f sexually-transmitted disease; **geschlechtsreif** adj sexually mature; **geschlechtsspezifisch** adj (*Soziologie*) sex-specific; **Geschlechtsteil** nt od m genitals pl; **Geschlechtsverkehr** m sexual intercourse; **Geschlechtswort** nt (*Gram*) article

geschlichen [gəˈʃlɪçən] pp von **schleichen**

geschliffen [gəˈʃlɪfən] pp von **schleifen**

geschlossen [gəˈʃlɔsən] pp von **schließen** ▷ adj: **~e Gesellschaft** (*Fest*) private party ▷ adv: **~ hinter jdm stehen** to stand solidly behind sb; **~e Ortschaft** built-up area

geschlungen [gəˈʃlʊŋən] pp von **schlingen**

Geschmack [gəˈʃmak] (**-(e)s**, **-̈e**) m taste; **nach jds ~** to sb's taste; **je nach ~** to one's own taste; **an etw** dat **finden** to (come to) like sth; **er hat einen guten ~** (*fig*) he has good taste; **geschmacklos** adj tasteless; (*fig*) in bad taste

Geschmacks- zW: **Geschmackssache** f matter of taste; **Geschmackssinn** m sense of taste; **Geschmacksverirrung** f: **unter Geschmacksverirrung leiden** (*ironisch*) to have no taste

geschmackvoll adj tasteful

Geschmeide [gəˈʃmaɪdə] (**-s**, **-**) nt jewellery (*Brit*), jewelry (*US*)

geschmeidig adj supple; (*formbar*) malleable

Geschmeiß nt vermin pl

Geschmiere [gəˈʃmi:rə] (**-s**) nt scrawl; (*Bild*) daub

geschmissen [gəˈʃmɪsən] pp von **schmeißen**

geschmolzen [gəˈʃmɔltsən] pp von **schmelzen**

Geschnetzelte, s [gəˈʃnɛtsəltə(s)] nt (*Koch*) meat cut into strips and stewed to produce a thick sauce

geschnitten [gəˈʃnɪtən] pp von **schneiden**

geschoben [gəˈʃo:bən] pp von **schieben**

geschollen [gəˈʃɔlən] pp von **schallen**

gescholten [gəˈʃɔltən] pp von **schelten**

Geschöpf [gəˈʃœpf] (**-(e)s**, **-e**) nt creature

geschoren [gəˈʃo:rən] pp von **scheren**

Geschoss [gəˈʃɔs] (**-es**, **-e**) nt, **Geschoß** [gəˈʃo:s] (**-sses**, **-sse**) (*Österr*) nt (*Mil*) projectile; (*Rakete*) missile; (*Stockwerk*) floor

geschossen [gəˈʃɔsən] pp von **schießen**

g

145

geschraubt [gəˈʃraʊpt] adj stilted, artificial

Geschrei [gəˈʃraɪ] (-s) nt cries pl, shouting; (fig: Aufheben) noise, fuss

geschrieben [gəˈʃriːbən] pp von **schreiben**

geschrieen [gəˈʃriːən], geschrien [gəˈʃriːn] pp von **schreien**

geschritten [gəˈʃrɪtən] pp von **schreiten**

geschunden [gəˈʃʊndən] pp von **schinden**

Geschütz [gəˈʃʏts] (-es, -e) nt gun, piece of artillery; **ein schweres ~ auffahren** (fig) to bring out the big guns; **Geschützfeuer** nt artillery fire, gunfire

geschützt adj protected; (Winkel, Ecke) sheltered

Geschw. abk = **Geschwister**

Geschwader [gəˈʃvaːdər] (-s, -) nt (Naut) squadron; (Aviat) group

Geschwafel [gəˈʃvaːfəl] (-s) nt silly talk

Geschwätz [gəˈʃvɛts] (-es) nt chatter; (Klatsch) gossip

geschwätzig adj talkative; **Geschwätzigkeit** f talkativeness

geschweige [gəˈʃvaɪgə] adv: **~ (denn)** let alone, not to mention

geschwiegen [gəˈʃviːgən] pp von **schweigen**

geschwind [gəˈʃvɪnt] adj quick, swift

Geschwindigkeit [gəˈʃvɪndɪçkaɪt] f speed, velocity

Geschwindigkeits- zW: **Geschwindig-keitsbegrenzung** f, **Geschwindigkeitsbeschränkung** f speed limit; **Geschwindigkeitsmesser** m (Aut) speedometer; **Geschwindigkeitsüberschreitung** f speeding

Geschwister [gəˈʃvɪstər] pl brothers and sisters pl

geschwollen [gəˈʃvɔlən] pp von **schwellen** ▷ adj pompous

geschwommen [gəˈʃvɔmən] pp von **schwimmen**

geschworen [gəˈʃvoːrən] pp von **schwören**

Geschworene, r f(m) juror; **die Geschworenen** pl the jury

Geschwulst [gəˈʃvʊlst] (-, ⁻e) f growth, tumour

geschwunden [gəˈʃvʊndən] pp von **schwinden**

geschwungen [gəˈʃvʊŋən] pp von **schwingen** ▷ adj curved

Geschwür [gəˈʃvyːr] (-(e)s, -e) nt ulcer; (Furunkel) boil

gesehen [gəˈzeːən] pp von **sehen**

Geselle [gəˈzɛlə] (-n, -n) m fellow; (Handwerksgeselle) journeyman

gesellen vr: **sich zu jdm ~** to join sb

Gesellenbrief m articles pl

Gesellenprüfung f examination to become a journeyman

gesellig adj sociable; **~es Beisammensein** get-together; **Geselligkeit** f sociability

Gesellschaft f society; (Begleitung, Comm) company; (Abendgesellschaft etc) party; (pej) crowd (umg); (Kreis von Menschen) group of people; **in schlechte ~ geraten** to get into bad company; **geschlossene ~** private party;

jdm ~ leisten to keep sb company

Gesellschafter, in [gəˈzɛlʃaftər] (-s, -) m(f) shareholder; (Partner) partner

gesellschaftlich adj social

Gesellschafts- zW: **Gesellschaftsanzug** m evening dress; **gesellschaftsfähig** adj socially acceptable; **Gesellschaftsordnung** f social structure; **Gesellschaftsreise** f group tour; **Gesellschaftsschicht** f social stratum; **Gesellschaftssystem** nt social system

gesessen [gəˈzɛsən] pp von **sitzen**

Gesetz [gəˈzɛts] (-es, -e) nt law; (Parl) act; (Satzung, Regel) rule; **vor dem ~** in (the eyes of the) law; **nach dem ~** under the law; **das oberste ~ (der Wirtschaft** etc**)** the golden rule (of industry etc); **Gesetzblatt** nt law gazette; **Gesetzbuch** nt statute book; **Gesetzentwurf** m bill

Gesetzeshüter m (ironisch) guardian of the law

Gesetzesvorlage f bill

Gesetz- zW: **gesetzgebend** adj legislative; **Gesetzgeber** (-s, -) m legislator; **Gesetzgebung** f legislation; **gesetzlich** adj legal, lawful; **Gesetzlichkeit** f legality, lawfulness; **gesetzlos** adj lawless; **gesetzmäßig** adj lawful

gesetzt adj (Mensch) sedate ▷ konj: **~ den Fall ...** assuming (that) ...

gesetzwidrig adj illegal; (unrechtmäßig) unlawful

ges. gesch. abk (= gesetzlich geschützt) reg.

Gesicht [gəˈzɪçt] (-(e)s, -er) nt face; **das Zweite ~** second sight; **das ist mir nie zu ~ gekommen** I've never laid eyes on that; **jdm zu ~ bekommen** to clap eyes on sb; **jdm etw ins ~ sagen** to tell sb sth to his face; **sein wahres ~ zeigen** to show (o.s. in) one's true colours; **jdm wie aus dem ~ geschnitten sein** to be the spitting image of sb

Gesichts- zW: **Gesichtsausdruck** m (facial) expression; **Gesichtsfarbe** f complexion; **Gesichtspackung** f face pack; **Gesichtspunkt** m point of view; **Gesichtswasser** nt face lotion; **Gesichtszüge** pl features pl

Gesindel [gəˈzɪndəl] (-s) nt rabble

gesinnt [gəˈzɪnt] adj disposed, minded

Gesinnung [gəˈzɪnʊŋ] f disposition; (Ansicht) views pl

Gesinnungs- zW: **Gesinnungsgenosse** m like-minded person; **Gesinnungslosigkeit** f lack of conviction; **Gesinnungsschnüffelei** (pej) f: **Gesinnungsschnüffelei betreiben** to pry into people's political convictions; **Gesinnungswandel** m change of opinion

gesittet [gəˈzɪtət] adj well-mannered

gesoffen [gəˈzɔfən] pp von **saufen**

gesogen [gəˈzoːgən] pp von **saugen**

gesollt [gəˈzɔlt] pp von **sollen**

gesondert [gəˈzɔndərt] adj separate

gesonnen [gəˈzɔnən] pp von **sinnen**

gespalten [gəˈʃpaltən] adj (Bewusstsein) split; (Lippe) cleft

Gespann [gəˈʃpan] (-(e)s, -e) nt team; (umg) couple

gespannt adj tense, strained; (neugierig) curious; (begierig) eager; **ich bin ~, ob** I wonder if od whether; **auf etw/jdn ~ sein** to look forward to sth/to meeting sb; **ich bin ~ wie ein Flitzebogen** (hum: umg) I'm on tenterhooks

Gespenst [gə'ʃpɛnst] **(-(e)s, -er)** nt ghost; (fig: Gefahr) spectre (Brit), specter (US); **~er sehen** (fig: umg) to imagine things

gespensterhaft, gespenstisch adj ghostly

gespieen [gəʃpi:ən], **gespien** [gəʃpi:n] pp von **speien**

gespielt [gə'ʃpi:lt] adj feigned

gesponnen [gəʃpɔnən] pp von **spinnen**

Gespött [gə'ʃpœt] **(-(e)s)** nt mockery; **zum ~ werden** to become a laughing stock

Gespräch [gə'ʃprɛːç] **(-(e)s, -e)** nt conversation; (Diskussion) discussion; (Anruf) call; **zum ~ werden** to become a topic of conversation; **ein ~ unter vier Augen** a confidential od private talk; **mit jdm ins ~ kommen** to get into conversation with sb; (fig) to establish a dialogue with sb

gesprächig adj talkative; **Gesprächigkeit** f talkativeness

Gesprächs- zW: **Gesprächseinheit** f (Tel) unit; **Gesprächsgegenstand** m topic; **Gesprächspartner** m: **mein Gesprächspartner bei den Verhandlungen** my opposite number at the talks; **Gesprächsstoff** m topics pl; **Gesprächsthema** nt subject od topic (of conversation)

gesprochen [gə'ʃprɔxən] pp von **sprechen**

gesprossen [gəʃprɔsən] pp von **sprießen**

gesprungen [gə'ʃprʊŋən] pp von **springen**

Gespür [gə'ʃpy:r] **(-s)** nt feeling

gest. abk (=gestorben) dec.

Gestalt [gə'ʃtalt] **(-, -en)** f form, shape; (Person) figure; (Liter: pej: Mensch) character; **in ~ von** in the form of; **~ annehmen** to take shape

gestalten vt (formen) to shape, form; (organisieren) to arrange, organize ▷ vr: **sich ~ (zu)** to turn out (to be); **etw interessanter** etc **~** to make sth more interesting etc

Gestaltung f formation; organization

gestanden [gəʃtandən] pp von **stehen; gestehen**

geständig [gə'ʃtɛndɪç] adj: **~ sein** to have confessed

Geständnis [gə'ʃtɛntnɪs] **(-ses, -se)** nt confession

Gestank [gə'ʃtaŋk] **(-(e)s)** m stench

gestatten [gə'ʃtatən] vt to permit, allow; **~ Sie?** may I?; **sich** dat **~, etw zu tun** to take the liberty of doing sth

Geste ['gɛstə] **(-, -n)** f gesture

Gesteck [gə'ʃtɛk] **(-(e)s, -e)** nt flower arrangement

gestehen [gə'ʃteːən] unreg vt to confess; **offen gestanden** quite frankly

Gestein [gə'ʃtaɪn] **(-(e)s, -e)** nt rock

Gestell [gə'ʃtɛl] **(-(e)s, -e)** nt stand; (Regal) shelf; (Bettgestell, Brillengestell) frame

gestellt adj (unecht) posed

gestern ['gɛstərn] adv yesterday; **~ Abend/Morgen** yesterday evening/morning; **er ist nicht von ~** (umg) he wasn't born yesterday

gestiefelt [gə'ʃti:fəlt] adj: **der G~e Kater** Puss-in-Boots

gestiegen [gə'ʃti:gən] pp von **steigen**

Gestik (-) f gestures pl

gestikulieren [gɛstiku'li:rən] vi to gesticulate

Gestirn [gə'ʃtɪrn] **(-(e)s, -e)** nt star

gestoben [gə'ʃto:bən] pp von **stieben**

Gestöber [gə'ʃtø:bər] **(-s, -)** nt flurry; (länger) blizzard

gestochen [gə'ʃtɔxən] pp von **stechen** ▷ adj (Handschrift) clear, neat

gestohlen [gə'ʃto:lən] pp von **stehlen** ▷ adj: **der/das kann mir ~ bleiben** (umg) he/it can go hang

gestorben [gə'ʃtɔrbən] pp von **sterben**

gestört [gə'ʃtø:rt] adj disturbed; (Rundfunkempfang) poor, with a lot of interference

gestoßen [gə'ʃto:sən] pp von **stoßen**

Gestotter [gə'ʃtɔtər] **(-s)** nt stuttering, stammering

Gesträuch [gə'ʃtrɔyç] **(-(e)s, -e)** nt shrubbery, bushes pl

gestreift [gə'ʃtraɪft] adj striped

gestrichen [gə'ʃtrɪçən] pp von **streichen** ▷ adj: **~ voll** (genau voll) level; (sehr voll) full to the brim; **ein ~er Teelöffel voll** a level teaspoon(ful)

gestrig ['gɛstrɪç] adj yesterday's

gestritten [gə'ʃtrɪtən] pp von **streiten**

Gestrüpp [gə'ʃtrʏp] **(-(e)s, -e)** nt undergrowth

gestunken [gə'ʃtʊŋkən] pp von **stinken**

Gestüt [gə'ʃty:t] **(-(e)s, -e)** nt stud farm

Gesuch [gə'zu:x] **(-(e)s, -e)** nt petition; (Antrag) application

gesucht adj (begehrt) sought after

gesund [gə'zʊnt] adj healthy; **wieder ~ werden** to get better; **~ und munter** hale and hearty; **Gesundheit** f health; (Sportlichkeit, fig) healthiness; **Gesundheit!** bless you!; **bei guter Gesundheit** in good health; **gesundheitlich** adj health attrib, physical ▷ adv physically; **wie geht es Ihnen gesundheitlich?** how's your health?

Gesundheits- zW: **Gesundheitsamt** nt public health department; **Gesundheitsapostel** m (ironisch) health freak (umg); **Gesundheitsfarm** f health farm; **Gesundheitsfürsorge** f health care; **Gesundheitsreform** f health service reforms pl; **Gesundheitsrisiko** nt health hazard; **gesundheitsschädlich** adj unhealthy; **Gesundheitssystem** nt health (care) system; **Gesundheitswesen** nt health service; **Gesundheitszeugnis** nt health certificate; **Gesundheitszustand** m state of health

gesundschreiben unreg vt: **jdn ~** to certify sb (as) fit

gesungen [gə'zʊŋən] pp von **singen**

gesunken [gə'zʊŋkən] pp von **sinken**

getan [gə'ta:n] pp von **tun** ▷ adj: **nach ~er**

Arbeit when the day's work is done

Getier [gə'ti:ər] (**-(e)s, -e**) *nt* (*Tiere, bes Insekten*) creatures *pl*; (*einzelnes*) creature

Getöse [gə'tø:zə] (**-s**) *nt* din, racket

getragen [gə'tra:gən] *pp von* **tragen**

Getränk [gə'treŋk] (**-(e)s, -e**) *nt* drink

Getränkeautomat *m* drinks machine *od* dispenser

Getränkekarte *f* (*in Café*) list of beverages; (*in Restaurant*) wine list

getrauen [gə'traʊən] *vr* to dare

Getreide [gə'traɪdə] (**-s, -**) *nt* cereal, grain; **Getreidespeicher** *m* granary

getrennt [gə'trɛnt] *adj* separate; ~ **leben** to be separated, live apart

getreten [gə'tre:tən] *pp von* **treten**

getreu [gə'trɔʏ] *adj* faithful

Getriebe [gə'tri:bə] (**-s, -**) *nt* (*Leute*) bustle; (*Aut*) gearbox

getrieben *pp von* **treiben**

Getriebeöl *nt* transmission oil

getroffen [gə'trɔfən] *pp von* **treffen**

getrogen [gə'tro:gən] *pp von* **trügen**

getrost [gə'tro:st] *adv* confidently; ~ **sterben** to die in peace; **du kannst dich ~ auf ihn verlassen** you need have no fears about relying on him

getrunken [gə'trʊŋkən] *pp von* **trinken**

Getto ['gɛto] (**-s, -s**) *nt* ghetto

Gettoblaster ['gɛtobla:stər] (**-s, -s**) *m* ghettoblaster

Getue [gə'tu:ə] (**-s**) *nt* fuss

Getümmel [gə'tʏməl] (**-s**) *nt* turmoil

geübt [gə'y:pt] *adj* experienced

GEW (**-**) *f abk* (= *Gewerkschaft Erziehung und Wissenschaft*) *union of employees in education and science*

Gew. *abk* = **Gewerkschaft**

Gewächs [gə'vɛks] (**-es, -e**) *nt* growth; (*Pflanze*) plant

gewachsen [gə'vaksən] *pp von* **wachsen** ▷ *adj*: **jdm/etw ~ sein** to be sb's equal/equal to sth

Gewächshaus *nt* greenhouse

gewagt [gə'va:kt] *adj* daring, risky

gewählt [gə'vɛ:lt] *adj* (*Sprache*) refined, elegant

gewahr [gə'va:r] *adj*: **eine** *od* **einer Sache** *gen* ~ **werden** to become aware of sth

Gewähr [gə'vɛ:r] (**-**) *f* guarantee; **keine ~ übernehmen für** to accept no responsibility for; **die Angabe erfolgt ohne ~** this information is supplied without liability

gewähren *vt* to grant; (*geben*) to provide; **jdn ~ lassen** not to stop sb

gewährleisten *vt* to guarantee

Gewährleistungspflicht *f* warranty obligation

Gewahrsam [gə'va:rza:m] (**-s, -e**) *m* safekeeping; (*Polizeigewahrsam*) custody

Gewährsmann *m* informant, source

Gewährung *f* granting

Gewalt [gə'valt] (**-, -en**) *f* power; (*große Kraft*) force; (*Gewalttaten*) violence; **mit aller ~**

with all one's might; **die ausübende/ gesetzgebende/richterliche ~** the executive/ legislature/judiciary; **elterliche ~** parental authority; **höhere ~** acts/an act of God; **Gewaltanwendung** *f* use of force

Gewaltenteilung *f* separation of powers

Gewaltherrschaft *f* tyranny

gewaltig *adj* tremendous; (*Irrtum*) huge; **sich ~ irren** to be very much mistaken

Gewalt- *zW*: **gewaltlos** *adj* non-violent ▷ *adv* without force/violence; **Gewaltmarsch** *m* forced march; **Gewaltmonopol** *nt* monopoly on the use of force; **gewaltsam** *adj* forcible; **gewalttätig** *adj* violent; **Gewaltverbrechen** *nt* crime of violence; **Gewaltverzicht** *m* non-aggression

Gewand [gə'vant] (**-(e)s, "-er**) *nt* garment

gewandt [gə'vant] *pp von* **wenden** ▷ *adj* deft, skilful (*Brit*), skillful (*US*); (*erfahren*) experienced; **Gewandtheit** *f* dexterity, skill

gewann *etc* [gə'van] *vb siehe* **gewinnen**

gewaschen [gə'vaʃən] *pp von* **waschen**

Gewässer [gə'vɛsər] (**-s, -**) *nt* waters *pl*

Gewebe [gə've:bə] (**-s, -**) *nt* (*Stoff*) fabric; (*Biol*) tissue

Gewehr [gə've:r] (**-(e)s, -e**) *nt* (*Flinte*) rifle; (*Schrotbüchse*) shotgun; **Gewehrlauf** *m* rifle barrel; barrel of a shotgun

Geweih [gə'vaɪ] (**-(e)s, -e**) *nt* antlers *pl*

Gewerbe [gə'vɛrbə] (**-s, -**) *nt* trade, occupation; **Handel und ~** trade and industry; **fahrendes ~** mobile trade; *siehe auch* **gewerbetreibend**; **Gewerbeaufsichtsamt** *nt* ≈ factory inspectorate; **Gewerbepark** *m* trading estate, business park; **Gewerbeschein** *m* trading licence; **Gewerbeschule** *f* technical school

gewerbetreibend *adj* carrying on a trade

gewerblich *adj* industrial

gewerbsmäßig *adj* professional

Gewerbszweig *m* line of trade

Gewerkschaft [gə'vɛrkʃaft] *f* trade *od* labor (*US*) union

Gewerkschafter, Gewerkschaftler, in *m(f)* trade *od* labor (*US*) unionist

gewerkschaftlich *adj*: **wir haben uns ~ organisiert** we organized ourselves into a union

Gewerkschaftsbund *m* federation of trade *od* labor (*US*) unions, ≈ Trades Union Congress (*Brit*), Federation of Labor (*US*)

gewesen [gə've:zən] *pp von* **sein**

gewichen [gə'vɪçən] *pp von* **weichen**

Gewicht [gə'vɪçt] (**-(e)s, -e**) *nt* weight; (*fig*) importance

gewichten *vt* to evaluate

Gewichtheben (**-s**) *nt* (*Sport*) weight-lifting

gewichtig *adj* weighty

Gewichtsklasse *f* (*Sport*) weight (category)

gewieft [gə'vi:ft] (*umg*) *adj* shrewd, cunning

gewiesen [gə'vi:zən] *pp von* **weisen**

gewillt [gə'vɪlt] *adj* willing, prepared

Gewimmel [gə'vɪməl] (**-s**) *nt* swarm; (*Menge*) crush

Gewinde [gə'vɪndə] (-s, -) nt (Kranz) wreath; (von Schraube) thread

Gewinn [gə'vɪn] (-(e)s, -e) m profit; (bei Spiel) winnings pl; ~ **bringend** profitable; **etw mit ~ verkaufen** to sell sth at a profit; **aus etw ~ schlagen** (umg) to make a profit out of sth; **Gewinnanteil** m (Comm) dividend; **Gewinnausschüttung** f prize draw; **Gewinnbeteiligung** f profit-sharing; **gewinnbringend** adj profitable; **Gewinnchancen** pl (beim Wetten) odds pl; **Gewinneinbruch** m slump in profits

gewinnen unreg vt to win; (erwerben) to gain; (Kohle, Öl) to extract ▷ vi to win; (profitieren) to gain; **jdn (für etw) ~** to win sb over (to sth); **an etw** dat **~** to gain in sth

gewinnend adj winning, attractive

Gewinner, in (-s, -) m(f) winner

Gewinn- zW: **Gewinnmitnahme** f profit-taking; **Gewinnnummer** f winning number; **Gewinnspanne** f profit margin; **Gewinnsucht** f love of gain; **Gewinn- und Verlustrechnung** f profit and loss account

Gewinnung f (von Kohle etc) mining; (von Zucker etc) extraction

Gewinnwarnung f (Comm) profit warning

Gewirr [gə'vɪr] (-(e)s, -e) nt tangle; (von Straßen) maze

gewiss [gə'vɪs] adj certain ▷ adv certainly; **in ~em Maße** to a certain extent

Gewissen [gə'vɪsən] (-s, -) nt conscience; **jdm ins ~ reden** to have a serious talk with sb; **gewissenhaft** adj conscientious; **Gewissenhaftigkeit** f conscientiousness; **gewissenlos** adj unscrupulous

Gewissens- zW: **Gewissensbisse** pl pangs of conscience pl, qualms pl; **Gewissensfrage** f matter of conscience; **Gewissensfreiheit** f freedom of conscience; **Gewissenskonflikt** m moral conflict

gewissermaßen [gəvɪsər'ma:sən] adv more or less, in a way

Gewissheit f certainty; **sich** dat **~ verschaffen** to find out for certain

gewisslich adv surely

Gewitter [gə'vɪtər] (-s, -) nt thunderstorm

gewittern vi unpers: **es gewittert** there's a thunderstorm

gewitterschwül adj sultry and thundery

Gewitterwolke f thundercloud; (fig: umg) storm cloud

gewitzt [gə'vɪtst] adj shrewd, cunning

gewoben [gə'vo:bən] pp von **weben**

gewogen [gə'vo:gən] pp von **wiegen** ▷ adj (+dat) well-disposed (towards)

gewöhnen [gə'vø:nən] vt: **jdn an etw** akk **~** to accustom sb to sth; (erziehen zu) to teach sb sth ▷ vr: **sich an etw** akk **~** to get used od accustomed to sth

Gewohnheit [gə'vo:nhaɪt] f habit; (Brauch) custom; **aus ~** from habit; **zur ~ werden** to become a habit; **sich** dat **etw zur ~ machen** to make a habit of sth

Gewohnheits- in zW habitual; **Gewohnheitsmensch** m creature of habit; **Gewohnheitsrecht** nt common law; **Gewohnheitstier** (umg) nt creature of habit

gewöhnlich [gə'vø:nlɪç] adj usual; (durchschnittlich) ordinary; (pej) common; **wie ~** as usual

gewohnt [gə'vo:nt] adj usual; **etw ~ sein** to be used to sth

Gewöhnung f: **~ (an** +akk) getting accustomed (to); (das Angewöhnen) training (in)

Gewölbe [gə'vœlbə] (-s, -) nt vault

gewollt [gə'vɔlt] pp von **wollen** ▷ adj forced, artificial

gewonnen [gə'vɔnən] pp von **gewinnen**

geworben [gə'vɔrbən] pp von **werben**

geworden [gə'vɔrdən] pp von **werden**

geworfen [gə'vɔrfən] pp von **werfen**

gewrungen [gə'vrʊŋən] pp von **wringen**

Gewühl [gə'vy:l] (-(e)s) nt throng

gewunden [gə'vʊndən] pp von **winden**

gewunken [gə'vʊŋkən] pp von **winken**

Gewürz [gə'vyrts] (-es, -e) nt spice; (Pfeffer, Salz) seasoning; **Gewürzgurke** f pickled gherkin; **Gewürznelke** f clove

gewusst [gə'vʊst] pp von **wissen**

gez. abk (= gezeichnet) signed

gezackt [gə'tsakt] adj (Fels) jagged; (Blatt) serrated

gezähnt [gə'tsɛnt] adj serrated, toothed

gezeichnet [gə'tsaɪçnət] adj marked

Gezeiten [gə'tsaɪtən] pl tides pl

Gezeter [gə'tse:tər] (-s) nt nagging

gezielt [gə'tsi:lt] adj (Frage, Maßnahme) specific; (Hilfe) well-directed; (Kritik) pointed

geziemen [gə'tsi:mən] vr unpers to be fitting

geziemend adj proper

geziert [gə'tsi:rt] adj affected; **Geziertheit** f affectation

gezogen [gə'tso:gən] pp von **ziehen**

Gezwitscher [gə'tsvɪtʃər] (-s) nt twitter(ing), chirping

gezwungen [gə'tsvʊŋən] pp von **zwingen** ▷ adj forced; (Atmosphäre) strained

gezwungenermaßen adv of necessity; **etw ~ tun** to be forced to do sth, do sth of necessity

GG abk = **Grundgesetz**

ggf. abk = **gegebenenfalls**

Ghetto ['geto] (-s, -s) nt = **Getto**

Gibraltar [gi'braltar] (-s) nt Gibraltar

gibst [gi:pst] vb siehe **geben**

gibt vb siehe **geben**

Gicht [gɪçt] (-) f gout; **gichtisch** adj gouty

Giebel ['gi:bəl] (-s, -) m gable; **Giebeldach** nt gable(d) roof; **Giebelfenster** nt gable window

Gier [gi:r] (-) f greed

gierig adj greedy

Gießbach m torrent

gießen ['gi:sən] unreg vt to pour; (Blumen) to water; (Metall) to cast; (Wachs) to mould ▷ vi unpers: **es gießt in Strömen** it's pouring down

Gießerei [gi:sə'raɪ] f foundry

Gießkanne f watering can

Gift [gɪft] (-(e)s, -e) nt poison; **das ist ~ für ihn** (umg) that is very bad for him; **darauf kannst du ~ nehmen** (umg) you can bet your life on it; **giftgrün** adj bilious green

giftig adj poisonous; (fig: boshaft) venomous

Giftler, in ['gɪftlər] m(f) (Österr: umg) junkie

Gift- zW: **Giftmüll** m toxic waste; **Giftpilz** m poisonous toadstool; **Giftstoff** m toxic substance; **Giftwolke** f poisonous cloud; **Giftzahn** m fang; **Giftzwerg** (umg) m spiteful little devil

Gigabyte ['gɪgabaɪt] nt (Comput) gigabyte

Gilde ['gɪldə] (-, -n) f guild

gilt [gɪlt] vb siehe **gelten**

ging etc [gɪŋ] vb siehe **gehen**

Ginseng ['gɪnzɛŋ] (-s, -s) m ginseng

Ginster ['gɪnstər] (-s, -) m broom

Gipfel ['gɪpfəl] (-s, -) m summit, peak; (fig) height; **das ist der ~!** (umg) that's the limit!; **Gipfelkonferenz** f (Pol) summit conference

gipfeln vi to culminate

Gipfeltreffen nt summit (meeting)

Gips [gɪps] (-es, -e) m plaster; (Med) plaster (of Paris); **Gipsabdruck** m plaster cast; **Gipsbein** (umg) nt leg in plaster; **gipsen** vt to plaster; **Gipsfigur** f plaster figure; **Gipsverband** m plaster (cast)

Giraffe [gi'rafə] (-, -n) f giraffe

Girlande [gɪr'landə] (-, -n) f garland

Giro ['ʒi:ro] (-s, -s) nt giro; **Girokonto** nt current account (Brit), checking account (US)

girren ['gɪrən] vi to coo

Gis [gɪs] (-, -) nt (Mus) G sharp

Gischt [gɪʃt] (-(e)s, -e) m od f spray, foam

Gitarre [gi'tarə] (-, -n) f guitar

Gitter ['gɪtər] (-s, -) nt grating, bars pl; (für Pflanzen) trellis; (Zaun) railing(s); **Gitterbett** nt cot (Brit), crib (US); **Gitterfenster** nt barred window; **Gitterzaun** m railing(s)

Glacéhandschuh, Glaceehandschuh [gla'se:hantʃu:] m kid glove

Gladiole [gladi'o:lə] (-, -n) f gladiolus

Glanz [glants] (-es) m shine, lustre (Brit), luster (US); (fig) splendour (Brit), splendor (US); **Glanzabzug** m (Phot) glossy od gloss print

glänzen ['glɛntsən] vi to shine (also fig), gleam

glänzend adj shining; (fig) brilliant; **wir haben uns ~ amüsiert** we had a marvellous od great time

Glanz- zW: **Glanzlack** m gloss (paint); **Glanzleistung** f brilliant achievement; **glanzlos** adj dull; **Glanzstück** nt pièce de résistance; **Glanzzeit** f heyday

Glas [gla:s] (-es, ¨er) nt glass; (Brillenglas) lens sing; **zwei ~ Wein** two glasses of wine; **Glasbläser** m glass blower; **Glaser** (-s, -) m glazier; **Glasfaser** f fibreglass (Brit), fiberglass (US); **Glasfaserkabel** nt optical fibre (Brit) od fiber (US) cable

Glasgow ['gla:sgoʊ] nt Glasgow

glasieren [gla'zi:rən] vt to glaze

glasig adj glassy; (Zwiebeln) transparent

glasklar adj crystal clear

Glasscheibe f pane

Glasur [gla'zu:r] f glaze; (Koch) icing, frosting (bes US)

glatt [glat] adj smooth; (rutschig) slippery; (Absage) flat; (Lüge) downright; (Haar) straight; (Med: Bruch) clean; (pej: allzu gewandt) smooth, slick ▷ adv: **~ rasiert** (Mann, Kinn) clean-shaven; **~ streichen** to smooth out; siehe auch **glattgehen**

Glätte ['glɛtə] (-, -n) f smoothness; slipperiness

Glatteis nt (black) ice; „**Vorsicht ~!**" "danger, black ice!"; **jdn aufs ~ führen** (fig) to take sb for a ride

glätten vt to smooth out

glattgehen unreg vi to go smoothly

Glatze ['glatsə] (-, -n) f bald head; **eine ~ bekommen** to go bald

glatzköpfig adj bald

Glaube ['glaʊbə] (-ns, -n) m: **~ (an +akk)** faith (in); (Überzeugung) belief (in); **den ~n an jdn/ etw verlieren** to lose faith in sb/sth

glauben vt, vi to believe; (meinen) to think; **jdm ~** to believe sb; **~ an** +akk to believe in; **jdm (etw) aufs Wort ~** to take sb's word (for sth); **wers glaubt, wird selig** (ironisch) a likely story

Glaubens- zW: **Glaubensbekenntnis** nt creed; **Glaubensfreiheit** f religious freedom; **Glaubensgemeinschaft** f religious sect; (christliche) denomination

glaubhaft ['glaʊbhaft] adj credible; **jdm etw ~ machen** to satisfy sb of sth

Glaubhaftigkeit f credibility

gläubig ['glɔʏbɪç] adj (Rel) devout; (vertrauensvoll) trustful; **Gläubige, r** f(m) believer; **die Gläubigen** pl the faithful

Gläubiger, in f(m) creditor

glaubwürdig ['glaʊbvʏrdɪç] adj credible; (Mensch) trustworthy; **Glaubwürdigkeit** f credibility; trustworthiness

gleich [glaɪç] adj equal; (identisch) (the) same, identical ▷ adv equally; (sofort) straight away; (bald) in a minute; (räumlich): **~ hinter dem Haus** just behind the house; (zeitlich): **~ am Anfang** at the very beginning; **es ist mir ~** it's all the same to me; **zu ~en Teilen** in equal parts; **das ~e, aber nicht dasselbe Auto** a similar car, but not the same one; **ganz ~ wer/was** etc no matter who/what etc; **2 mal 2 ~ 4** 2 times 2 is od equals 4; **bis ~!** see you soon!; **wie war doch ~ Ihr Name?** what was your name again?; **es ist ~ drei Uhr** it's very nearly three o'clock; **~ gesinnt** like-minded; **~ lautend** identical; **sie sind ~ groß** they are the same size; **~ nach/an** right after/at; **gleichaltrig** adj of the same age; **gleichartig** adj similar; **gleichbedeutend** adj synonymous; **gleichberechtigt** adj with equal rights; **Gleichberechtigung** f equal rights pl; **gleichbleibend** adj constant; **bei gleichbleibendem Gehalt** when one's salary stays the same

gleichen unreg vi: **jdm/etw ~** to be like sb/sth

▷ *vr* to be alike

gleichermaßen *adv* equally

gleich- *zW:* **gleichfalls** *adv* likewise; **danke gleichfalls!** the same to you; **Gleichförmigkeit** *f* uniformity; **gleichgestellt** *adj:* **rechtlich gleichgestellt** equal in law; **Gleichgewicht** *nt* equilibrium, balance; **jdm aus dem Gleichgewicht bringen** to throw sb off balance; **gleichgültig** *adj* indifferent; (*unbedeutend*) unimportant; **Gleichgültigkeit** *f* indifference; (*Industrie*) parity; **Gleichheitsprinzip** *nt* principle of equality; **Gleichheitszeichen** *nt* (*Math*) equals sign; **gleichkommen** *unreg vi +dat* to be equal to; **gleichlautend** *adj* identical; **Gleichmacherei** *f* egalitarianism, levelling down (*pej*); **gleichmäßig** *adj* even, equal; **Gleichmut** *m* equanimity

Gleichnis (**-ses, -se**) *nt* parable

gleich- *zW:* **gleichrangig** *adj* (*Probleme etc*) equally important; **gleichrangig (mit)** (*Beamte etc*) equal in rank (to), at the same level (as); **gleichsam** *adv* as it were; **gleichschalten** (*pej*) *vt* to bring into line; **Gleichschritt** *m:* **im Gleichschritt, marsch!** forward march!; **gleichsehen** *unreg vi:* **jdm gleichsehen** to be *od* look like sb; **gleichstellen** *vt* (*rechtlich etc*) to treat as equal; **Gleichstrom** *m* (*Elek*) direct current; **gleichtun** *unreg vi:* **es jdm gleichtun** to match sb

Gleichung *f* equation

gleich- *zW:* **gleichviel** *adv* no matter; **gleichwertig** *adj* of the same value; (*Leistung, Qualität*) equal; (*Gegner*) evenly matched; **gleichwohl** *adv* (*geh*) nevertheless; **gleichzeitig** *adj* simultaneous

Gleis [glaɪs] (**-es, -e**) *nt* track, rails *pl*; (*am Bahnhof*) platform (Brit), track (US)

gleißend ['glaɪsənt] *adj* glistening, gleaming

gleiten *unreg vi* to glide; (*rutschen*) to slide

gleitend ['glaɪtənt] *adj:* **~e Arbeitszeit** flexible working hours *pl*, flex(i)time

Gleit- *zW:* **Gleitflug** *m* glide; **Gleitklausel** *f* (*Comm*) escalator clause; **Gleitkomma** *nt* floating point; **Gleitzeit** *f* flex(i)time

Gletscher ['glɛtʃər] (**-s, -**) *m* glacier; **Gletscherspalte** *f* crevasse

glich *etc* [glɪç] *vb siehe* **gleichen**

Glied [gliːt] (**-(e)s, -er**) *nt* member; (*Arm, Bein*) limb; (*Penis*) penis; (*von Kette*) link; (*Mil*) rank(s); **der Schreck steckt ihr noch in den ~ern** she is still shaking with the shock

gliedern *vt* to organize, structure

Gliederreißen *nt* rheumatic pains *pl*

Gliederschmerz *m* rheumatic pains *pl*

Gliederung *f* structure, organization

Gliedmaßen *pl* limbs *pl*

glimmen ['glɪmən] *unreg vi* to glow

Glimmer (**-s, -**) *m* (*Mineral*) mica

Glimmstängel (*umg*) *m* fag (Brit), butt (US)

glimpflich ['glɪmpflɪç] *adj* mild, lenient; **~ davonkommen** to get off lightly

glitschig ['glɪtʃɪç] (*umg*) *adj* slippery, slippy

glitt *etc* [glɪt] *vb siehe* **gleiten**

glitzern ['glɪtsərn] *vi* to glitter; (*Stern*) to twinkle

global [glo'baːl] *adj* (*weltweit*) global, worldwide; (*ungefähr, pauschal*) general

Globalisierung [globalɪ'ziːrʊŋ] *f* globalization; **Globalisierungsfalle** *f* globalization trap

Globus ['gloːbʊs] (**- *od* -ses, Globen** *od* **-se**) *m* globe

Glöckchen ['glœkçən] *nt* (little) bell

Glocke ['glɔkə] (**-, -n**) *f* bell; **etw an die große ~ hängen** (*fig*) to shout sth from the rooftops

Glocken- *zW:* **Glockengeläut** *nt* peal of bells; **Glockenschlag** *m* stroke of the bell; (*von Uhr*) chime; **Glockenspiel** *nt* chime(s); (*Mus*) glockenspiel; **Glockenturm** *m* belfry, bell-tower

glomm *etc* [glɔm] *vb siehe* **glimmen**

Glorie ['gloːriə] *f* glory; (*von Heiligen*) halo

glorreich ['gloːrraɪç] *adj* glorious

Glossar [glɔ'saːr] (**-s, -e**) *nt* glossary

Glosse ['glɔsə] (**-, -n**) *f* comment

Glotze (**-, -n**) (*umg*) *f* gogglebox (Brit), TV set

glotzen ['glɔtsən] (*umg*) *vi* to stare

Glück [glʏk] (**-(e)s**) *nt* luck, fortune; (*Freude*) happiness; **~ haben** to be lucky; **viel ~** good luck; **zum ~** fortunately; **ein ~!** how lucky!, what a stroke of luck!; **auf gut ~** (*aufs Geratewohl*) on the off-chance; (*unvorbereitet*) trusting to luck; (*wahllos*) at random; **sie weiß noch nichts von ihrem ~** (*ironisch*) she doesn't know anything about it yet; **er kann von ~ sagen, dass ...** he can count himself lucky that ...; **Glückauf** *nt:* „**Glückauf**" (*Bergleute*) (cry of) "good luck"

Glucke (**-, -n**) *f* (*Bruthenne*) broody hen; (*mit Jungen*) mother hen

glücken *vi* to succeed; **es glückte ihm, es zu bekommen** he succeeded in getting it

gluckern ['glʊkərn] *vi* to glug

glücklich *adj* fortunate; (*froh*) happy ▷ *adv* happily; (*umg: endlich, zu guter Letzt*) finally, eventually

glücklicherweise *adv* fortunately

glücklos *adj* luckless

Glücksbringer (**-s, -**) *m* lucky charm

glückselig [glʏk'zeːlɪç] *adj* blissful

Glücks- *zW:* **Glücksfall** *m* stroke of luck; **Glückskind** *nt* lucky person; **Glückspilz** *m* lucky beggar (*umg*); **Glückssache** *f* matter of luck; **Glücksspiel** *nt* game of chance; **Glücksstern** *m* lucky star; **Glückssträhne** *f* lucky streak

glückstrahlend *adj* radiant (with happiness)

Glückszahl *f* lucky number

Glückwunsch *m:* **~ (zu)** congratulations *pl* (on), best wishes *pl* (on)

Glühbirne *f* light bulb

glühen ['glyːən] *vi* to glow

glühend *adj* glowing; (*heiß glühend: Metall*) red-hot; (*Hitze*) blazing; (*fig: leidenschaftlich*) ardent; (: *Hass*) burning; (*Wangen*) flushed, burning

Glüh- *zW:* **Glühfaden** *m* (*Elek*) filament;

Glühwein *m* mulled wine; **Glühwürmchen** *nt* glow-worm

Glut [glu:t] (-, -en) *f* (*Röte*) glow; (*Feuersglut*) fire; (*Hitze*) heat; (*fig*) ardour (*Brit*), ardor (*US*)

GmbH (-, -s) *f abk* (= *Gesellschaft mit beschränkter Haftung*) ≈ Ltd. (*Brit*), plc (*Brit*), Inc. (*US*)

Gnade ['gna:də] (-, -n) *f* (*Gunst*) favour (*Brit*), favor (*US*); (*Erbarmen*) mercy; (*Milde*) clemency; **~ vor Recht ergehen lassen** to temper justice with mercy

gnaden *vi*: **(dann) gnade dir Gott!** (then) God help you *od* heaven have mercy on you!

Gnaden- *zW*: **Gnadenbrot** *nt*: **jdm/einem Tier das Gnadenbrot geben** to keep sb/an animal in his/her/its old age; **Gnadenfrist** *f* reprieve; **Gnadengesuch** *nt* petition for clemency; **gnadenlos** *adj* merciless; **Gnadenstoß** *m* coup de grâce

gnädig ['gnɛ:dɪç] *adj* gracious; (*voll Erbarmen*) merciful; **~e Frau** (*form*) madam, ma'am

Gockel ['gɔkəl] (-s, -) *m* (*bes Südd*) cock

Gold [gɔlt] (-(e)s) *nt* gold; **nicht mit ~ zu bezahlen** *od* **aufzuwiegen sein** to be worth one's weight in gold; **golden** *adj* golden; **goldene Worte** words of wisdom; **der Tanz ums Goldene Kalb** (*fig*) the worship of Mammon; **Goldfisch** *m* goldfish; **Goldgrube** *f* gold mine; **Goldhamster** *m* (golden) hamster

goldig ['gɔldɪç] *adj* (*fig: umg*) sweet, cute

Gold- *zW*: **Goldregen** *m* laburnum; (*fig*) riches *pl*; **goldrichtig** (*umg*) *adj* dead right; **Goldschmied** *m* goldsmith; **Goldschnitt** *m* gilt edging; **Goldstandard** *m* gold standard; **Goldstück** *nt* piece of gold; (*fig: umg*) treasure; **Goldwaage** *f*: **jedes Wort auf die Goldwaage legen** (*fig*) to weigh one's words; **Goldwährung** *f* gold standard

Golf¹ [gɔlf] (-(e)s, -e) *m* gulf; **der (Persische) ~** the Gulf

Golf² [gɔlf] (-s) *nt* golf; **Golfplatz** *m* golf course; **Golfschläger** *m* golf club; **Golfspieler** *m* golfer

Golfstaaten *pl*: **die ~** the Gulf States *pl*

Golfstrom *m* (*Geog*) Gulf Stream

Gondel ['gɔndəl] (-, -n) *f* gondola; (*von Seilbahn*) cable car

gondeln (*umg*) *vi*: **durch die Welt ~** to go globetrotting

Gong [gɔŋ] (-s, -s) *m* gong; (*bei Boxkampf etc*) bell

gönnen ['gœnən] *vt*: **jdm etw ~** not to begrudge sb sth; **sich** *dat* **etw ~** to allow o.s. sth

Gönner (-s, -) *m* patron; **gönnerhaft** *adj* patronizing; **Gönnerin** *f* patroness; **Gönnermiene** *f* patronizing air

googeln ['gu:gəln] *vi* (*Comput: umg*) to google®

gor *etc* [go:r] *vb siehe* **gären**

Gorilla [go'rɪla] (-s, -s) *m* gorilla; (*umg: Leibwächter*) heavy

goss *etc* [gɔs] *vb siehe* **gießen**

Gosse ['gɔsə] (-, -n) *f* gutter

Gote ['go:tə] (-n, -n) *m* Goth

Gotik ['go:tɪk] *f* (*Kunst*) Gothic (style); (*Epoche*) Gothic period

Gotin ['go:tɪn] *f* Goth

Gott [gɔt] (-es, ̈er) *m* god; (*als Name*) God; **um ~es Willen!** for heaven's sake!; **~ sei Dank!** thank God!; **grüß ~!** (*bes Südd, Österr*) hello, good morning/afternoon/evening; **den lieben ~ einen guten Mann sein lassen** (*umg*) to take things as they come; **ein Bild für die Götter** (*hum: umg*) a sight for sore eyes; **das wissen die Götter** (*umg*) God (only) knows; **über ~ und die Welt reden** (*fig*) to talk about everything under the sun; **wie ~ in Frankreich leben** (*umg*) to be in clover

Götterspeise *f* (*Koch*) jelly (*Brit*), jello (*US*)

Gottes- *zW*: **Gottesdienst** *m* service; **gottesfürchtig** *adj* god-fearing; **Gotteshaus** *nt* place of worship; **Gotteskrieger, in** *m(f)* religious terrorist; **Gotteslästerung** *f* blasphemy

Gottheit *f* deity

Göttin ['gœtɪn] *f* goddess

göttlich *adj* divine

Gott- *zW*: **gottlob** *interj* thank heavens!; **gottlos** *adj* godless; **gottverdammt** *adj* goddamn(ed); **gottverlassen** *adj* godforsaken; **Gottvertrauen** *nt* trust in God

Götze ['gœtsə] (-n, -n) *m* idol

Grab [gra:p] (-(e)s, ̈er) *nt* grave

grabbeln ['grabəln] (*Nordd: umg*) *vt* to rummage

Graben ['gra:bən] (-s, ̈) *m* ditch; (*Mil*) trench

graben *unreg* *vt* to dig

Grabesstille *f* (*liter*) deathly hush

Grab- *zW*: **Grabmal** *nt* monument; (*Grabstein*) gravestone; **Grabrede** *f* funeral oration; **Grabstein** *m* gravestone

gräbt *vb siehe* **graben**

Gracht [graxt] (-, -en) *f* canal

Grad [gra:t] (-(e)s, -e) *m* degree; **im höchsten ~(e)** extremely; **Verbrennungen ersten ~es** (*Med*) first-degree burns; **Gradeinteilung** *f* graduation; **gradlinig** *adj* straight; **gradweise** *adv* gradually

Graf [gra:f] (-en, -en) *m* count, earl (*Brit*)

Grafik ['gra:fɪk] (-, -en) *f* (*Comput, Tech*) graphics; (*Art*) graphic arts *pl*

Grafiker, in ['gra:fɪkər(ɪn)] (-s, -) *m(f)* graphic artist; (*Illustrator*) illustrator

Gräfin ['grɛ:fɪn] *f* countess

grafisch *adj* ['gra:fɪʃ] ▷ *adj* graphic; **~e Darstellung** graph

Grafschaft *f* county

Grahambrot ['gra:hambro:t] *nt* type of wholemeal (*Brit*) *od* whole-wheat (*US*) bread

Gralshüter ['gra:lzhy:tər] (-s, -) *m* (*fig*) guardian

Gram [gra:m] (-(e)s) *m* (*geh*) grief, sorrow

grämen ['grɛ:mən] *vr* to grieve; **sich zu Tode ~** to die of grief *od* sorrow

Gramm [gram] (-s, -e) *nt* gram(me)

Grammatik [gra'matɪk] *f* grammar

grammatisch *adj* grammatical

Grammofon, Grammophon [gramo'fo:n] (-s, -e) *nt* gramophone

Granat [gra'na:t] (-(e)s, -e) *m* (*Stein*) garnet; **Granatapfel** *m* pomegranate

Granate (-, -n) f (Mil) shell; (Handgranate) grenade

grandios [gran'dio:s] adj magnificent, superb

Granit [gra'ni:t] (-s, -e) m granite; **auf ~ beißen (bei ...)** to bang one's head against a brick wall (with ...)

grantig ['grantɪç] (umg) adj grumpy

Graphik etc ['gra:fɪk] = **Grafik** etc

grapschen ['grapʃən] (umg) vt, vi to grab; **(sich dat) etw ~** to grab sth

Gras [gra:s] (-es, ⁻er) nt grass; (auch umg: Marihuana) grass; **über etw** akk **~ wachsen lassen** (fig) to let the dust settle on sth; **grasen** vi to graze; **Grashalm** m blade of grass

grasig adj grassy

Grasnarbe f turf

grassieren [gra'si:rən] vi to be rampant, rage

grässlich ['grɛslɪç] adj horrible

Grat [gra:t] (-(e)s, -e) m ridge

Gräte ['grɛ:tə] (-, -n) f fish-bone

Gratifikation [gratifikatsi'o:n] f bonus

gratis ['gra:tɪs] adj, adv free (of charge); **Gratisprobe** f free sample

Grätsche ['grɛ:tʃə] (-, -n) f (Sport) straddle

Gratulant, in [gratu'lant(ɪn)] m(f) well-wisher

Gratulation [gratulatsi'o:n] f congratulation(s)

gratulieren [gratu'li:rən] vi: **jdm (zu etw) ~** to congratulate sb (on sth); **(ich) gratuliere!** congratulations!

Gratwanderung f (fig) tightrope walk

grau [grau] adj grey (Brit), gray (US); **der ~e Alltag** drab reality; **~ meliert** grey-flecked (Brit), gray-flecked (US); **Graubrot** nt = **Mischbrot**

Gräuel ['grɔʏəl] (-s, -) m horror; (Gräueltat) atrocity; **etw ist jdm ein ~** sb loathes sth; **Gräuelpropaganda** f atrocity propaganda; **Gräueltat** f atrocity

Grauen (-s) nt horror

grauen vi (Tag) to dawn ▷ vi unpers: **es graut jdm vor etw** sb dreads sth, sb is afraid of sth ▷ vr: **sich ~ vor** to dread

grauenhaft, grauenvoll adj horrible

grauhaarig adj grey-haired (Brit), gray-haired (US)

gräulich ['grɔʏlɪç] adj horrible

Graupelregen ['graupəlre:gən] m sleet

Graupelschauer m sleet

Graupen ['graupən] pl pearl barley sing

grausam ['grauza:m] adj cruel; **Grausamkeit** f cruelty

Grausen ['grauzən] (-s) nt horror; **da kann man das kalte ~ kriegen** (umg) it's enough to give you the creeps

grausen vb = **grauen**

Grauzone f (fig) grey (Brit) od gray (US) area

gravieren [gra'vi:rən] vt to engrave

gravierend adj grave

Grazie ['gra:tsiə] f grace

graziös [gratsi'ø:s] adj graceful

Greencard, Green Card ['gri:nka:əd] (-, -s) f green card

greifbar adj tangible, concrete; **in ~er Nähe** within reach

greifen ['graɪfən] unreg vt (nehmen) to grasp; (grapschen) to seize, grab ▷ vi (nicht rutschen, einrasten) to grip; **nach etw ~** to reach for sth; **um sich ~** (fig) to spread; **zu etw ~** (fig) to turn to sth; **diese Zahl ist zu niedrig gegriffen** (fig) this figure is too low; **aus dem Leben gegriffen** taken from life

Greifer (-s, -) m (Tech) grab

Greifvogel m bird of prey

Greis [graɪs] (-es, -e) m old man

Greisenalter nt old age

greisenhaft adj very old

Greisin ['graɪzɪn] f old woman

grell [grɛl] adj harsh

Gremium ['gre:miʊm] nt body; (Ausschuss) committee

Grenadier [grena'di:ər] (-s, -e) m (Mil: Infanterist) infantryman

Grenzbeamte, r m frontier official

Grenze (-, -n) f border; (zwischen Grundstücken, fig) boundary; (Staatsgrenze) frontier; (Schranke) limit; **über die ~ gehen/fahren** to cross the border; **hart an der ~ des Erlaubten** bordering on the limits of what is permitted

grenzen vi: **~ an** +akk to border on

grenzenlos adj boundless

Grenz- zW: **Grenzfall** m borderline case; **Grenzgänger** m (Arbeiter) international commuter (across a local border); **Grenzgebiet** nt (lit, fig) border area; **Grenzkosten** pl marginal cost sing; **Grenzlinie** f boundary; **Grenzübergang** m frontier crossing; **Grenzwert** m limit; **Grenzzwischenfall** m border incident

Gretchenfrage ['gre:tçənfra:gə] f (fig) crunch question, sixty-four-thousand-dollar question (umg)

Greuel etc ['grɔʏəl] siehe **Gräuel**

greulich ['grɔʏlɪç] siehe **gräulich**

Grieche ['gri:çə] (-n, -n) m Greek

Griechenland nt Greece

Griechin ['gri:çɪn] f Greek

griechisch adj Greek

griesgrämig ['gri:sgrɛ:mɪç] adj grumpy

Grieß [gri:s] (-es, -e) m (Koch) semolina; **Grießbrei** m cooked semolina

Griff [grɪf] (-(e)s, -e) m grip; (Vorrichtung) handle; (das Greifen): **der ~ nach etw** reaching for sth; **jdn/etw in den ~ bekommen** (fig) to gain control of sb/sth; **etw in den ~ bekommen** (geistig) to get a grasp of sth

griff etc vb siehe **greifen**

griffbereit adj handy

Griffel ['grɪfəl] (-s, -) m slate pencil; (Bot) style

griffig ['grɪfɪç] adj (Fahrbahn etc) that has a good grip; (fig: Ausdruck) useful, handy

Grill [grɪl] (-s, -s) m grill; (Aut) grille

Grille ['grɪlə] (-, -n) f cricket; (fig) whim

grillen vt to grill

Grimasse [gri'masə] (-, -n) f grimace; **~n schneiden** to make faces

g

grimmig adj furious; (heftig) fierce, severe
grinsen ['grɪnzən] vi to grin; (höhnisch) to smirk
Grippe ['grɪpə] (-, -n) f influenza, flu
Grips [grɪps] (-es, -e) (umg) m sense
grob [gro:p] adj coarse, gross; (Fehler, Verstoß)
gross; (brutal, derb) rough; (unhöflich) ill-
mannered; ~ **geschätzt** at a rough estimate;
Grobheit f coarseness; (Beschimpfung) coarse
expression
Grobian ['gro:biaːn] (-s, -e) m ruffian
grobknochig adj large-boned
groggy ['grɔgɪ] adj (Boxen) groggy;
(umg: erschöpft) bushed
grölen ['grøːlən] (pej) vt, vi to bawl
Groll [grɔl] (-(e)s) m resentment; **grollen** vi
(Donner) to rumble; **grollen (mit** od +dat) **to**
bear ill will (towards)
Grönland ['grøːnlant] (-s) nt Greenland
Grönländer, in (-s, -) m(f) Greenlander
Groschen ['grɔʃən] (-s, -) (umg) m 10-pfennig
piece; (Österr) groschen; (fig) penny, cent (US);
Groschenroman (pej) m cheap od dime (US)
novel
groß [gro:s] adj big, large; (hoch) tall; (Freude,
Werk) great ▷ adv greatly; **im G~en und**
Ganzen on the whole; **wie ~ bist du?** how tall
are you?; **die G~en** (Erwachsene) the grown-
ups; **mit etw ~ geworden sein** to have grown
up with sth; **die G~en Seen** the Great Lakes
pl; **~en Hunger haben** to be very hungry; **~e**
Mode sein to be all the fashion; **~ angelegt**
large-scale, on a large scale; **~ und breit**
(fig: umg) at great od enormous length; siehe
auch **großschreiben**; **Großabnehmer** m (Comm)
bulk buyer; **Großalarm** m red alert; **großartig**
adj great, splendid; **Großaufnahme** f (Film)
close-up; **Großbritannien** (-s) nt (Great)
Britain; **Großbuchstabe** m capital (letter)
Größe ['grøːsə] (-, -n) f size; (Länge) height; (fig)
greatness; **eine unbekannte ~** (lit, fig) an
unknown quantity
Groß- zW: **Großeinkauf** m bulk purchase;
Großeinsatz m: **Großeinsatz der Polizei**
etc large-scale operation by the police etc;
Großeltern pl grandparents pl
Größenordnung f scale; (Größe) magnitude;
(Math) order (of magnitude)
großenteils adv for the most part
Größen- zW: **Größenunterschied** m difference
in size; **Größenwahn** m, **Größenwahnsinn** m
megalomania, delusions pl of grandeur
Groß- zW: **Großformat** nt large size;
Großhandel m wholesale trade;
Großhandelspreisindex m wholesale-
price index; **Großhändler** m wholesaler;
großherzig adj generous; **Großhirn** nt
cerebrum; **Großindustrielle, r** f(m) major
industrialist; **großkotzig** (umg) adj show-
offish, bragging; **Großkundgebung** f mass
rally; **Großmacht** f great power; **Großmaul**
m braggart; **Großmut** (-) f magnanimity;
großmütig adj magnanimous; **Großmutter** f
grandmother; **Großraum** m: **der Großraum**

München the Munich area od conurbation,
Greater Munich; **Großraumbüro** nt open-
plan office; **Großrechner** m mainframe;
Großreinemachen nt thorough cleaning, ≈
spring cleaning; **großschreiben** unreg vt: **ein**
Wort großschreiben to write a word with a
capital; **großgeschrieben werden** (umg) to
be stressed; **Großschreibung** f capitalization;
großspurig adj pompous; **Großstadt** f city
größte, r, s [grøːstə(r, s)] adj superl von **groß**
größtenteils adv for the most part
Groß- zW: **Großtuer** (-s, -) m boaster; **großtun**
unreg vi to boast; **Großvater** m grandfather;
Großverbraucher m (Comm) heavy user;
Großverdiener m big earner; **Großwild** nt big
game; **großziehen** unreg vt to raise; **großzügig**
adj generous; (Planung) on a large scale
grotesk [gro'tɛsk] adj grotesque
Grotte ['grɔtə] (-, -n) f grotto
grub etc [gru:p] vb siehe **graben**
Grübchen ['gryːpçən] nt dimple
Grube ['gruːbə] (-, -n) f pit; (Bergwerk) mine
grübeln ['gryːbəln] vi to brood
Grubenarbeiter m miner
Grubengas nt firedamp
Grübler ['gryːblər] (-s, -) m brooder; **grüblerisch**
adj brooding, pensive
Gruft [gruft] (-, ⁻e) f tomb, vault
grün [gryːn] adj green; (ökologisch) green;
(Pol): **die G~en** the Greens; **~e Minna** (umg)
Black Maria (Brit), paddy wagon (US); **~e Welle**
phased traffic lights; **~e Versicherungskarte**
(Aut) green card; **sich ~ und blau** od **gelb**
ärgern (umg) to be furious; **auf keinen ~en**
Zweig kommen (fig: umg) to get nowhere;
jdm ~es Licht geben to give sb the green
light; **Grünanlage** f park
Grund [grunt] (-(e)s, ⁻e) m ground; (von
See, Gefäß) bottom; (fig) reason; **von ~ auf**
entirely, completely; **aus gesundheitlichen**
etc **Gründen** for health etc reasons; **im ~e**
genommen basically; **ich habe ~ zu der**
Annahme, dass ... I have reason to believe
that ...; **einer Sache** dat **auf den ~ gehen** (fig)
to get to the bottom of sth; **in ~ und Boden**
(fig) utterly, thoroughly; siehe auch **aufgrund**;
zugrunde; **Grundausbildung** f basic
training; **Grundbedeutung** f basic meaning;
Grundbedingung f fundamental condition;
Grundbegriff m basic concept; **Grundbesitz**
m land(ed property), real estate; **Grundbuch**
nt land register; **grundehrlich** adj thoroughly
honest
gründen [grʏndən] vt to found ▷ vr: **sich ~ auf**
+akk to be based on; **~ auf** +akk to base on
Gründer, in (-s, -) m(f) founder
Grund- zW: **grundfalsch** adj utterly wrong;
Grundgebühr f basic charge; **Grundgedanke**
m basic idea; **Grundgesetz** nt constitution
Grundierung [grʊnˈdiːrʊŋ] f (Farbe) primer
Grund- zW: **Grundkapital** nt nominal capital;
Grundkurs m basic course; **Grundlage** f
foundation; **jeder Grundlage** gen **entbehren**

to be completely unfounded; **grundlegend** adj fundamental

gründlich adj thorough; **jdm ~ die Meinung sagen** to give sb a piece of one's mind

Grund- zW: **grundlos** adj (fig) groundless; **Grundmauer** f foundation wall; **Grundnahrungsmittel** nt basic food(stuff)

Gründonnerstag m Maundy Thursday

Grund- zW: **Grundordnung** f: **die freiheitlich-demokratische Grundordnung** (Brd Pol) the German constitution based on democratic liberty; **Grundrechenart** f basic arithmetical operation; **Grundrecht** nt basic od constitutional right; **Grundregel** f basic od ground rule; **Grundriss** m plan; (fig) outline; **Grundsatz** m principle; **grundsätzlich** adj fundamental; (Frage) of principle ▷ adv fundamentally; (prinzipiell) on principle; **das ist grundsätzlich verboten** it is absolutely forbidden; **Grundsatzurteil** nt judgement that establishes a principle

Grundschule f primary (Brit) od elementary school; see culture note

GRUNDSCHULE

The Grundschule is a primary school which children attend for 4 years from the age of 6 to 10. There are no formal examinations in the Grundschule but parents receive a report on their child's progress twice a year. Many children attend a Kindergarten from 3-6 years before going to the Grundschule, but no formal instruction takes place in the Kindergarten.

Grund- zW: **Grundsicherung** f (Wirts) guaranteed minimum income; **Grundstein** m foundation stone; **Grundsteuer** f rates pl; **Grundstück** nt plot (of land); (Anwesen) estate; **Grundstücksmakler** m estate agent (Brit), realtor® (US); **Grundstufe** f first stage; (Sch) ≈ junior (Brit) od grade (US) school

Gründung f foundation

Gründungsurkunde f (Comm) certificate of incorporation

Gründungsversammlung f (Aktiengesellschaft) statutory meeting

Grund- zW: **grundverschieden** adj utterly different; **Grundwasser** nt ground water; **Grundwasserspiegel** m water table, ground-water level; **Grundzug** m characteristic; **etw in seinen Grundzügen darstellen** to outline (the essentials of) sth

Grüne(-n) nt: **im ~n** in the open air; **ins ~ fahren** to go to the country

Grüne, r f(m) (Pol) Ecologist, Green; **die Grünen** pl (als Partei) the Greens; see culture note

DIE GRÜNEN

Die Grünen is the name given to the Green or ecological party in Germany which was founded in 1980. Since 1993 they have been allied with the originally East German party, Bündnis 90.

GRÜNER PUNKT

The Grüner Punkt is the green spot symbol which appears on packaging, indicating that the packaging should not be thrown into the normal household refuse but kept separate to be recycled through the DSD system. The recycling is financed by licences bought by the manufacturer from the DSD and the cost of this is often passed on to the consumer.

Grün- zW: **Grünkohl** m kale; **Grünschnabel** m greenhorn; **Grünspan** m verdigris; **Grünstreifen** m central reservation

grunzen ['gruntsən] vi to grunt

Gruppe ['grupə] (-, -n) f group

Gruppen- zW: **Gruppenarbeit** f teamwork; **Gruppendynamik** f group dynamics pl; **Gruppentherapie** f group therapy; **gruppenweise** adv in groups

gruppieren [gru'piːrən] vt, vr to group

Gruselfilm m horror film

gruselig adj creepy

gruseln ['gruːzəln] vi unpers: **es gruselt jdm vor etw** sth gives sb the creeps ▷ vr to have the creeps

Gruß [gruːs] (-es, ⁻e) m greeting; (Mil) salute; **viele Grüße** best wishes; **Grüße an** +akk regards to; **einen (schönen) ~ an Ihre Frau!** (geh) my regards to your wife; **mit freundlichen Grüßen** (als Briefformel) Yours sincerely

grüßen ['gryːsən] vt to greet; (Mil) to salute; **jdn von jdm ~** to give sb sb's regards; **jdn ~ lassen** to send sb one's regards

Grütze ['grʏtsə] (-, -n) f (Brei) gruel; **rote ~** (type of) red fruit jelly

Guatemala [guate'maːla] (-s) nt Guatemala

Guayana [gua'jaːna] (-s) nt Guyana

gucken ['gʊkən] vi to look

Guckloch nt peephole

Guinea [gi'neːa] (-s) nt Guinea

Gulasch ['guːlaʃ] (-(e)s, -e) nt goulash

gültig ['gʏltɪç] adj valid; **~ werden** to become valid; (Gesetz, Vertrag) to come into effect; (Münze) to become legal tender; **Gültigkeit** f validity; **Gültigkeitsdauer** f period of validity

Gummi ['gʊmi] (-s, -s) nt od m rubber; (Gummiharze) gum; (umg: Kondom) rubber, Durex®; (Gummiband) rubber od elastic band; (Hosengummi) elastic; **Gummiband** nt rubber od elastic band; **Gummibärchen** nt jelly baby; **Gummigeschoss** nt rubber bullet; **Gummiknüppel** m rubber truncheon; **Gummiparagraf** m ambiguous od meaningless law od statute; **Gummistiefel** m rubber boot, wellington (boot) (Brit); **Gummistrumpf** m elastic stocking;

Gummizelle f padded cell

Gunst [gʊnst] (-) f favour (Brit), favor (US); *siehe auch* **zugunsten**

günstig ['gʏnstɪç] *adj* favourable (Brit), favorable (US); (*Angebot, Preis etc*) reasonable, good; **bei ~er Witterung** weather permitting; **im ~sten Fall(e)** with luck

Gurgel ['gʊrgəl] (-, -n) f throat

gurgeln *vi* to gurgle; (*im Rachen*) to gargle

Gurke ['gʊrkə] (-, -n) f cucumber; **saure ~** pickled cucumber, gherkin

Gurt [gʊrt] (-(e)s, -e) m belt

Gurtanlegepflicht f (*form*) obligation to wear a safety belt in vehicles

Gürtel ['gʏrtəl] (-s, -) m belt; (*Geog*) zone; **Gürtelreifen** m radial tyre; **Gürtelrose** f shingles *sing od pl*

GUS [ge:|uː'|ɛs] f abk (= *Gemeinschaft Unabhängiger Staaten*) CIS

Guss [gʊs] (-es, ·"e) m casting; (*Regenguss*) downpour; (*Koch*) glazing; **Gusseisen** nt cast iron

Gut [guːt] (-(e)s, ·"er) nt (*Besitz*) possession; (*Landgut*) estate; **Güter** pl (*Waren*) goods pl

SCHLÜSSELWORT

gut *adj* good; **das ist gut gegen** *od* **für** (*umg*) **Husten** it's good for coughs; **sei so gut (und) gib mir das** would you mind giving me that; **dafür ist er sich zu gut** he wouldn't stoop to that sort of thing; **das ist ja alles gut und schön, aber ...** that's all very well but ...; **du bist gut!** (*umg*) you're a fine one!; **alles Gute** all the best; **also gut** all right then

▷ *adv* well; **gut gehen** to work, come off; **es geht jdm gut** sb's doing fine; **das ist noch einmal gut gegangen** it turned out all right; **gut gehend** thriving; **gut gelaunt** cheerful, in a good mood; **gut gemeint** well meant; **du hast es gut!** you've got it made!; **gut situiert** well-off; **gut unterrichtet** well-informed; **gut, aber ...** OK, but ...; **(na) gut, ich komme** all right, I'll come; **gut drei Stunden** a good three hours; **das kann gut sein** that may well be; **gut und gern** easily; **lass es gut sein** that'll do; *siehe auch* **guttun**

Gut- zW: **Gutachten** (-s, -) nt report; **Gutachter** (-s, -) m expert; **Gutachterkommission** f quango; **gutartig** adj good-natured; (*Med*) benign; **gutbürgerlich** adj (*Küche*) (good) plain; **Gutdünken** nt: **nach Gutdünken** at one's discretion

Güte ['gyːtə] (-) f goodness, kindness;

(*Qualität*) quality; **ach du liebe** *od* **meine ~!** (*umg*) goodness me!; **Güteklasse** f (*Comm*) grade; **Güteklasseneinteilung** f (*Comm*) grading

Güter- zW: **Güterabfertigung** f (*Eisenb*) goods office; **Güterbahnhof** m goods station; **Gütertrennung** f (*Jur*) separation of property; **Güterverkehr** m freight traffic; **Güterwagen** m goods waggon (Brit), freight car (US); **Güterzug** m goods train (Brit), freight train (US)

Gütesiegel nt (*Comm*) stamp of quality

gut- zW: **gutgläubig** adj trusting; **Guthaben** (-s) nt credit; **guthaben** unreg vt: **30 Euro (bei jdm) guthaben** to be in credit (with sb) to the tune of 30 euros; **gutheißen** unreg vt to approve (of); **gutherzig** adj kind(-hearted)

gütig ['gyːtɪç] adj kind

gütlich ['gyːtlɪç] adj amicable

gut- zW: **gutmachen** vt (*in Ordnung bringen*: *Fehler*) to put right, correct; (*Schaden*) to make good; **gutmütig** adj good-natured; **Gutmütigkeit** f good nature

Gutsbesitzer, in m(f) landowner

Gut- zW: **Gutschein** m voucher; **gutschreiben** unreg vt to credit; **Gutschrift** f credit

Gutsherr m squire

Gutshof m estate

guttun unreg vi: **jdm ~** to do sb good

Gutverdienende, r f(m) high-income earner

gutwillig adj willing

Gymnasiallehrer, in [gʏmnaziˈaːllɛːrər(ɪn)] m(f) ≈ grammar school teacher (Brit), high school teacher (US)

Gymnasium [gʏmˈnaːziʊm] nt ≈ grammar school (Brit), high school (US); *see culture note*

GYMNASIUM

The *Gymnasium* is a selective secondary school. There are nine years of study at a *Gymnasium* leading to the *Abitur* which gives access to higher education. Pupils who successfully complete six years automatically gain the *mittlere Reife*.

Gymnastik [gʏmˈnastɪk] f exercises pl, keep-fit; **~ machen** to do keep-fit (exercises)/ gymnastics

Gynäkologe [gʏnɛkoˈloːgə] (-n, -n) m gynaecologist (Brit), gynecologist (US)

Gynäkologin [gʏnɛkoˈloːgɪn] f gynaecologist (Brit), gynecologist (US)

Hh

H, h [haː] *nt* H, h; (*Mus*) B; **H wie Heinrich** ≈ H for Harry, H for How (*US*)

ha *abk* = **Hektar**

Haag [haːk] (**-s**) *m*: **Den ~** The Hague

Haar [haːr] (**-(e)s, -e**) *nt* hair; **um ein ~** nearly; **~e auf den Zähnen haben** to be a tough customer; **sich die ~e raufen** (*umg*) to tear one's hair; **sich** *dat* **in die ~e kriegen** (*umg*) to quarrel; **das ist an den ~en herbeigezogen** that's rather far-fetched; **Haaransatz** *m* hairline; **Haarbürste** *f* hairbrush

haaren *vi, vr* to lose hair

Haaresbreite *f*: **um ~** by a hair's-breadth

Haarfestiger (**-s, -**) *m* setting lotion

haargenau *adv* precisely

haarig *adj* hairy; (*fig*) nasty

Haar- *zW*: **Haarklammer** *f*, **Haarklemme** *f* hair grip (*Brit*), barrette (*US*); **haarklein** *adv* in minute detail; **haarlos** *adj* hairless; **Haarnadel** *f* hairpin; **haarscharf** *adv* (*beobachten*) very sharply; (*verfehlen*) by a hair's breadth; **Haarschnitt** *m* haircut; **Haarschopf** *m* head of hair; **Haarsieb** *nt* fine sieve; **Haarspalterei** *f* hair-splitting; **Haarspange** *f* hair slide; **haarsträubend** *adj* hair-raising; **Haarteil** *nt* hairpiece; **Haarwaschmittel** *nt* shampoo; **Haarwasser** *nt* hair lotion

Hab [haːp] *nt*: **~ und Gut** possessions *pl*, belongings *pl*, worldly goods *pl*

Habe [haːbə] (**-**) *f* property

haben [haːbən] *unreg vt, hilfsverb* to have ▷ *vr unpers*: **und damit hat es sich** (*umg*) and that's that; **Hunger/Angst ~** to be hungry/afraid; **da hast du 10 Mark** there's 10 Marks; **die ~s (ja)** (*umg*) they can afford it; **Ferien ~** to be on holiday; **es am Herzen ~** (*umg*) to have heart trouble; **sie ist noch zu ~** (*umg*: *nicht verheiratet*) she's still single; **für etw zu ~ sein** to be keen on sth; **sie werden schon merken, was sie an ihm ~** they'll see how valuable he is; **haste was, biste was** (*Sprichwort*) money brings status; **wie gehabt!** some things don't change; **das hast du jetzt davon** now see what's happened; **woher hast du das?** where did you get that from?; **was hast du denn?** what's the matter (with you)?; **ich habe zu tun** I'm busy

Haben (**-s, -**) *nt* (*Comm*) credit

Habenseite *f* (*Comm*) credit side

Habgier *f* avarice

habgierig *adj* avaricious

habhaft *adj*: **jds/einer Sache ~ werden** (*geh*) to get hold of sb/sth

Habicht [haːbɪçt] (**-(e)s, -e**) *m* hawk

Habilitation [habilitatsiˈoːn] *f* (*Lehrberechtigung*) postdoctoral lecturing qualification

Habseligkeiten [haːpzeːlɪçkaɪtən] *pl* belongings *pl*

Habsucht [haːpzʊxt] *f* greed

Hachse [haksə] (**-, -n**) *f* (*Koch*) knuckle

Hackbraten *m* meat loaf

Hackbrett *nt* chopping board; (*Mus*) dulcimer

Hacke [hakə] (**-, -n**) *f* hoe; (*Ferse*) heel

hacken *vt* to hack, chop; (*Erde*) to hoe

Hacker [hakər] (**-s, -**) *m* (*Comput*) hacker

Hackfleisch *nt* mince, minced meat, ground meat (*US*)

Hackordnung *f* (*lit, fig*) pecking order

Häcksel [hɛksəl] (**-s**) *m od nt* chopped straw, chaff

hadern [haːdərn] *vi* (*geh*): **~ mit** to quarrel with; (*unzufrieden sein*) to be at odds with

Hafen [haːfən] (**-s, -̈**) *m* harbour, harbor (*US*), port; (*fig*) haven; **Hafenanlagen** *pl* docks *pl*; **Hafenarbeiter** *m* docker; **Hafendamm** *m* jetty, mole; **Hafengebühren** *pl* harbo(u)r dues *pl*; **Hafenstadt** *f* port

Hafer [haːfər] (**-s, -**) *m* oats *pl*; **ihn sticht der ~** (*umg*) he is feeling his oats; **Haferbrei** *m* porridge (*Brit*), oatmeal (*US*); **Haferflocken** *pl* rolled oats *pl* (*Brit*), oatmeal (*US*); **Haferschleim** *m* gruel

Haff [haf] (**-s, -s** *od* **-e**) *nt* lagoon

Haft [haft] (**-**) *f* custody; **Haftanstalt** *f* detention centre (*Brit*) *od* center (*US*); **haftbar** *adj* liable, responsible; **Haftbefehl** *m* warrant (for arrest); **einen Haftbefehl gegen jdn ausstellen** to issue a warrant for sb's arrest

haften *vi* to stick, cling; **~ für** to be liable *od* responsible for; **für Garderobe kann nicht gehaftet werden** all articles are left at owner's risk; **~ bleiben (an** +*dat*) to stick (to)

Häftling [hɛftlɪŋ] *m* prisoner

Haft- *zW*: **Haftpflicht** *f* liability; **Haftpflichtversicherung** *f* third party insurance; **Haftrichter** *m* magistrate

Haftschalen pl contact lenses pl

Haftung f liability

Hagebutte ['ha:gəbʊtə] (-, -n) f rose hip

Hagedorn m hawthorn

Hagel ['ha:gəl] (-s) m hail; **Hagelkorn** nt hailstone; (Med) eye cyst

hageln vi unpers to hail

Hagelschauer m (short) hailstorm

hager ['ha:gər] adj gaunt

Häher ['hɛ:ər] (-s, -) m jay

Hahn [ha:n] (-(e)s, ⸚e) m cock; (Wasserhahn) tap, faucet (US); (Abzug) trigger; ~ **im Korb sein** (umg) to be cock of the walk; **danach kräht kein ~ mehr** (umg) no one cares two hoots about that any more

Hähnchen ['hɛ:nçən] nt cockerel; (Koch) chicken

Hai ['haɪ], **Haifisch** ['haɪfɪʃ] (-(e)s, -e) m shark

Haiti [ha'i:ti] (-s) nt Haiti

Häkchen ['hɛ:kçən] nt small hook

Häkelarbeit f crochet work

häkeln ['hɛ:kəln] vt to crochet

Häkelnadel f crochet hook

Haken ['ha:kən] (-s, -) m hook; (fig) catch; **einen ~ schlagen** to dart sideways; **Hakenkreuz** nt swastika; **Hakennase** f hooked nose

halb [halp] adj half ▷ adv (beinahe) almost; ~ **eins** half past twelve; ~ **offen** half-open; **ein ~es Dutzend** half a dozen; **nichts H~es und nichts Ganzes** neither one thing nor the other; **(noch) ein ~es Kind sein** to be scarcely more than a child; **das ist ~ so schlimm** it's not as bad as all that; **mit jdm ~e-halbe machen** (umg) to go halves with sb

halb- zW: **Halbblut** nt (Tier) crossbreed; **Halbbruder** m half-brother; **Halbdunkel** nt semi-darkness

halber ['halbər] präp +gen (wegen) on account of; (für) for the sake of

Halb- zW: **halbfett** adj medium fat; **Halbfinale** nt semi-final; **Halbheit** f half-measure; **halbherzig** adj half-hearted

halbieren [hal'bi:rən] vt to halve

Halb- zW: **Halbinsel** f peninsula; **halbjährlich** adj half-yearly; **Halbkreis** m semicircle; **Halbkugel** f hemisphere; **halblang** adj: **nun mach mal halblang!** (umg) now wait a minute!; **halblaut** adv in an undertone; **Halbleiter** m (Phys) semiconductor; **halbmast** adv at half-mast; **Halbmond** m half-moon; (fig) crescent; **Halbpension** f half-board (Brit), European plan (US); **Halbschuh** m shoe; **Halbschwester** f half-sister; **halbseiden** adj (lit) fifty per cent silk; (fig: Dame) fast; (: homosexuell) gay; **halbseitig** adj (Anzeige) half-page; **Halbstarke**, r f(m) hooligan, rowdy; **halbtags** adv: **halbtags arbeiten** to work part-time; **Halbtagsarbeit** f part-time work; **Halbtagskraft** f part-time worker; **Halbton** m half-tone; (Mus) semitone; **halbtrocken** adj medium-dry; **Halbwaise** f child/person who has lost one parent; **halbwegs** adv half-

way; **halbwegs besser** more or less better; **Halbwelt** f demimonde; **Halbwertzeit** f half-life; **Halbwüchsige**, r f(m) adolescent; **Halbzeit** f (Sport) half; (Pause) half-time

Halde ['haldə] f tip; (Schlackenhalde) slag heap

half etc [half] vb siehe **helfen**

Hälfte ['hɛlftə] (-, -n) f half; **um die ~ steigen** to increase by half

Halfter¹ ['halftər] (-s, -) m od nt (für Tiere) halter

Halfter² ['halftər] (-, -n od -s, -) f od nt (Pistolenhalfter) holster

Hall [hal] (-(e)s, -e) m sound

Halle ['halə] (-, -n) f hall; (Aviat) hangar

hallen vi to echo, resound

Hallen- in zW indoor; **Hallenbad** nt indoor swimming pool

hallo [ha'lo:] interj hallo

Halluzination [halutsinatsi'o:n] f hallucination

Halm ['halm] (-(e)s, -e) m blade, stalk

Hals [hals] (-es, ⸚e) m neck; (Kehle) throat; **sich** dat **nach jdm/etw den ~ verrenken** (umg) to crane one's neck to see sb/sth; **jdm um den ~ fallen** to fling one's arms around sb's neck; **aus vollem ~(e)** at the top of one's voice; ~ **über Kopf** in a rush; **jdn auf dem** od **am ~ haben** (umg) to be lumbered od saddled with sb; **das hängt mir zum ~ raus** (umg) I'm sick and tired of it; **sie hat es in den falschen ~ bekommen** (falsch verstehen) she took it wrongly; **Halsabschneider** (pej: umg) m shark; **Halsband** nt (Hundehalsband) collar; **halsbrecherisch** adj (Tempo) breakneck; (Fahrt) hair-raising; **Halskette** f necklace; **Halskrause** f ruff; **Hals-Nasen-Ohren-Arzt** m ear, nose and throat specialist; **Halsschlagader** f carotid artery; **Halsschmerzen** pl sore throat sing; **halsstarrig** adj stubborn, obstinate; **Halstuch** nt scarf; **Hals- und Beinbruch** interj good luck; **Halsweh** nt sore throat; **Halswirbel** m cervical vertebra

Halt [halt] (-(e)s, -e) m stop; (fester Halt) hold; (innerer Halt) stability; ~!, **halt!** stop!, halt!; ~ **machen** to stop

hält [hɛlt] vb siehe **halten**

Halt- zW: **haltbar** adj durable; (Lebensmittel) non-perishable; (Mil, fig) tenable; **haltbar bis 6.11.** use by 6 Nov.; **Haltbarkeit** f durability; (non-)perishability; tenability; (von Lebensmitteln) shelf life; **Haltbarkeitsdatum** nt best-before date

halten ['haltən] unreg vt to keep; (festhalten) to hold ▷ vi to hold; (frisch bleiben) to keep; (stoppen) to stop ▷ vr (frisch bleiben) to keep; (sich behaupten) to hold out; **den Mund ~** (umg) to keep one's mouth shut; ~ **für** to regard as; ~ **von** to think of; **das kannst du ~ wie du willst** that's completely up to you; **der Film hält nicht, was er verspricht** the film doesn't live up to expectations; **davon halt(e) ich nichts** I don't think much of it; **zu jdm ~** to stand od stick by sb; **an sich** akk ~ to restrain o.s.; **auf sich** akk ~ (auf Äußeres achten) to take a pride in o.s.; **er hat sich gut gehalten** (umg) he's well-preserved; **sich an ein Versprechen** ~ to keep a promise; **sich rechts/links** ~ to keep to the right/left

Halter ['haltər] (-s, -) m (Halterung) holder

Haltestelle f stop

Halteverbot nt: **absolutes** ~ no stopping; **eingeschränktes** ~ no waiting; **hier ist** ~ you cannot stop here

haltlos adj unstable

Haltlosigkeit f instability

haltmachen vi to stop

Haltung f posture; (fig) attitude; (Selbstbeherrschung) composure; ~ **bewahren** to keep one's composure

Halunke [ha'lʊŋkə] (-n, -n) m rascal

Hamburg ['hambʊrk] (-s) nt Hamburg

Hamburger (-s, -) m (Koch) burger, hamburger

Hamburger, in (-s, -) m(f) native of Hamburg

Hameln ['ha:məln] nt Hamelin

hämisch ['hɛ:mɪʃ] adj malicious

Hammel ['haməl] (-s, " od -) m wether; **Hammelfleisch** nt mutton; **Hammelkeule** f leg of mutton

Hammelsprung m (Parl) division

Hammer ['hamər] (-s, ") m hammer; **das ist ein** ~! (umg: unerhört) that's absurd!

hämmern ['hɛmərn] vt, vi to hammer

Hammondorgel ['hæmənd|ɔrgəl] f electric organ

Hämorrhoiden [hɛmɔroˈiːdən], **Hämorriden** [hɛmɔˈriːdən] pl piles pl, haemorrhoids pl (Brit); hemorrhoids pl (US)

Hampelmann ['hampəlman] m (lit, fig) puppet

Hamster ['hamstər] (-s, -) m hamster

Hamsterei [hamstə'raɪ] f hoarding

Hamsterer (-s, -) m hoarder

hamstern vi to hoard

Hand [hant] (-, "e) f hand; **etw zur** ~ **haben** to have sth to hand; (Ausrede, Erklärung) to have sth ready; **jdm zur** ~ **gehen** to lend sb a helping hand; **zu Händen von jdm** for the attention of sb; **in festen Händen sein** to be spoken for; **die** ~ **für jdn ins Feuer legen** to vouch for sb; **hinter vorgehaltener** ~ on the quiet; ~ **aufs Herz** cross your heart; **jdn auf Händen tragen** to cherish sb; **bei etw die** od **seine** ~ **im Spiel haben** to have a hand in sth; **eine** ~ **wäscht die andere** (Sprichwort) if you scratch my back I'll scratch yours; **das hat weder** ~ **noch Fuß** that doesn't make sense; **das liegt auf der** ~ (umg) that's obvious; **unter der** ~ secretly; (verkaufen) privately; siehe auch **anhand**; **Handarbeit** f manual work; (Nadelarbeit) needlework; **Handarbeiter** m manual worker; **Handball** m handball; **Handbesen** m brush; **Handbetrieb** m: **mit Handbetrieb** hand-operated; **Handbewegung** f gesture; **Handbibliothek** f (in Bibliothek) reference section; (auf Schreibtisch) reference books pl; **Handbremse** f handbrake; **Handbuch** nt handbook, manual

Händedruck m handshake

Händeklatschen nt clapping, applause

Handel[1] ['handəl] (-s) m trade; (Geschäft) transaction; **im** ~ **sein** to be on the market; **(mit jdm)** ~ **treiben** to trade (with sb); **etw in den** ~ **bringen/aus dem** ~ **ziehen** to put sth on/take sth off the market

Handel[2] (-s, ") m quarrel

handeln ['handəln] vi to trade; (tätig werden) to act ▷ vr unpers: **sich** ~ **um** to be a question of, be about; ~ **von** to be about; **ich lasse mit mir** ~ I'm open to persuasion; (in Bezug auf Preis) I'm open to offers

Handeln (-s) nt action

handelnd adj: **die** ~**en Personen in einem Drama** the characters in a drama

Handels- zW: **Handelsbank** f merchant bank (Brit), commercial bank; **Handelsbilanz** f balance of trade; **aktive/passive Handelsbilanz** balance of trade surplus/deficit; **Handelsdelegation** f trade mission; **handelseinig** adj: **mit jdm handelseinig werden** to conclude a deal with sb; **Handelsgesellschaft** f commercial company; **Handelskammer** f chamber of commerce; **Handelsklasse** f grade; **Handelsmarine** f merchant navy; **Handelsmarke** f trade name; **Handelsname** m trade name; **Handelsrecht** nt commercial law; **Handelsregister** nt register of companies; **Handelsreisende, r** f(m) = **Handlungsreisende(r)** commercial traveller; **Handelssanktionen** pl trade sanctions pl; **Handelsschule** f business school; **Handelsspanne** f gross margin, mark-up; **Handelssperre** f trade embargo; **handelsüblich** adj customary; **Handelsvertreter** m sales representative; **Handelsvertretung** f trade mission; **Handelsware** f commodity

händeringend ['hɛndərɪŋənd] adv wringing one's hands; (fig) imploringly

Hand- zW: **Handfeger** (-s, -) m brush; **Handfertigkeit** f dexterity; **handfest** adj hefty; **Handfläche** f palm od flat (of one's hand); **handgearbeitet** adj handmade; **Handgelenk** nt wrist; **aus dem Handgelenk** (umg: ohne Mühe) effortlessly; (: improvisiert) off the cuff; **Handgemenge** nt scuffle; **Handgepäck** nt hand baggage od luggage; **handgeschrieben** adj handwritten; **Handgranate** f hand grenade; **handgreiflich** adj palpable; **handgreiflich werden** to become violent; **Handgriff** m flick of the wrist; **Handhabe** f: **ich habe gegen ihn keine Handhabe** (fig) I have no hold on him; **handhaben** unreg vt untr to handle; **Handkarren** m handcart; **Handkäse** m strong-smelling, round German cheese; **Handkuss** m kiss on the hand; **Handlanger** (-s, -) m odd-job man, handyman; (fig: Untergeordneter) dogsbody

Händler ['hɛndlər] (-s, -) m trader, dealer

handlich ['hantlɪç] adj handy

Handlung ['handlʊŋ] f action; (Tat) act; (in

Buch) plot; (*Geschäft*) shop

Handlungs- zW: **Handlungsablauf** m plot; **Handlungsbevollmächtigte,** r f(m) authorized agent; **handlungsfähig** adj (*Regierung*) able to act; (*Jur*) empowered to act; **Handlungsfreiheit** f freedom of action; **handlungsorientiert** adj action-orientated; **Handlungsreisende,** r f(m) commercial traveller (*Brit*), traveling salesman (*US*); **Handlungsvollmacht** f proxy; **Handlungsweise** f manner of dealing

Hand- zW: **Handpflege** f manicure; **Handschelle** f handcuff; **Handschlag** m handshake; **keinen Handschlag tun** not to do a stroke (of work); **Handschrift** f handwriting; (*Text*) manuscript; **handschriftlich** adj handwritten ▷ adv (*korrigieren, einfügen*) by hand; **Handschuh** m glove; **Handschuhfach** nt (*Aut*) glove compartment; **Handtasche** f handbag (*Brit*), pocket book (*US*), purse (*US*); **Handtuch** nt towel; **Handumdrehen** nt: **im Handumdrehen** (*fig*) in the twinkling of an eye

Handwerk nt trade, craft; **jdm das ~ legen** (*fig*) to put a stop to sb's game

Handwerker (-s, -) m craftsman, artisan; **wir haben seit Wochen die ~ im Haus** we've had workmen in the house for weeks

Handwerkskammer f trade corporation

Handwerkszeug nt tools pl

Handwörterbuch nt concise dictionary

Handy ['hɛndi] (-s, -s) nt (*Tel*) mobile (phone) (*Brit*), cellphone (*US*)

Handzeichen nt signal; (*Geste*) sign; (*bei Abstimmung*) show of hands

Handzettel m leaflet, handbill

Hanf [hanf] (-(e)s) m hemp

Hang [haŋ] (-(e)s, ¨e) m inclination; (*Abhang*) slope

Hänge- ['hɛŋə] in zW hanging; **Hängebrücke** f suspension bridge; **Hängematte** f hammock

Hängen ['hɛŋən] nt: **mit ~ und Würgen** (*umg*) by the skin of one's teeth

hängen unreg vi to hang ▷ vt: **~ (an** +akk) **to** hang (on(to)); **an jdm ~** (*fig*) to be attached to sb; **~ bleiben** to be caught; (*fig*) to remain, stick; **~ bleiben an** +dat to catch od get caught on; **es bleibt ja doch alles an mir ~** (*fig: umg*) in the end it's all down to me anyhow; **~ lassen** (*vergessen*) to leave behind; **sich ~ lassen** to let o.s. go; **den Kopf ~ lassen** (*fig*) to be downcast; **die ganze Sache hängt an ihm** it all depends on him; **sich ~ an** +akk to hang on to, cling to

hängend adj: **mit ~er Zunge kam er angelaufen** (*fig*) he came running up panting

Hängeschloss nt padlock

Hanglage f: **in ~** situated on a slope

Hannover [ha'no:fər] (-s) nt Hanover

Hannoveraner, in [hanovə'ra:nər(ɪn)] (-s, -) m(f) Hanoverian

hänseln ['hɛnzəln] vt to tease

Hansestadt ['hanzəʃtat] f Hanseatic od Hanse town

Hanswurst [hans'vʊrst] (-(e)s, -e od -würste) m clown

Hantel ['hantəl] (-, -n) f (*Sport*) dumb-bell

hantieren [han'ti:rən] vi to work, be busy; **mit etw ~** to handle sth

hapern ['ha:pərn] vi unpers: **es hapert an etw** dat there is a lack of sth

Happen ['hapən] (-s, -) m mouthful

happig ['hapɪç] (*umg*) adj steep

Harfe ['harfə] (-, -n) f harp

Harke ['harkə] (-, -n) f rake

harken vt, vi to rake

harmlos ['harmlo:s] adj harmless

Harmlosigkeit f harmlessness

Harmonie [harmo'ni:] f harmony

harmonieren vi to harmonize

Harmonika [har'mo:nika] (-, -s) f (*Ziehharmonika*) concertina

harmonisch [har'mo:nɪʃ] adj harmonious

Harmonium [har'mo:niʊm] (-s, -nien od -s) nt harmonium

Harn ['harn] (-(e)s, -e) m urine; **Harnblase** f bladder

Harnisch ['harnɪʃ] (-(e)s, -e) m armour, armor (*US*); **jdn in ~ bringen** to infuriate sb; **in ~ geraten** to become angry

Harpune [har'pu:nə] (-, -n) f harpoon

harren ['harən] vi: **~ auf** +akk to wait for

Harsch [harʃ] (-(e)s) m frozen snow

harschig adj (*Schnee*) frozen

hart [hart] adj hard; (*fig*) harsh ▷ adv: **das ist ~ an der Grenze** that's almost going too far; **~e Währung** hard currency; **~ bleiben** to stand firm; **~ gekocht** hard-boiled; **~ gesotten** (*Ei*) hard-boiled; **es geht ~ auf ~** it's a tough fight

Härte ['hɛrtə] (-, -n) f hardness; (*fig*) harshness; **soziale ~n** social hardships; **Härtefall** m case of hardship; (*umg: Mensch*) hardship case; **Härteklausel** f hardship clause

härten vt, vr to harden

hart- zW: **Hartfaserplatte** f hardboard, fiberboard (*US*); **hartgesotten** adj (*Kerl*) tough, hard-boiled; **hartherzig** adj hard-hearted; **hartnäckig** adj stubborn; **Hartnäckigkeit** f stubbornness

Harz[1] [ha:rts] (-es, -e) nt resin

Harz[2] (-es) m (*Geog*) Harz Mountains pl

Haschee [ha'ʃe:] (-s, -s) nt hash

haschen ['haʃən] vt to catch, snatch ▷ vi (*umg*) to smoke hash

Haschisch ['haʃɪʃ] (-) nt hashish

Hase ['ha:zə] (-n, -n) m hare; **falscher ~** (*Koch*) meat loaf; **wissen, wie der ~ läuft** (*fig: umg*) to know which way the wind blows; **mein Name ist ~(, ich weiß von nichts)** I don't know anything about anything

Haselnuss ['ha:zəlnʊs] f hazelnut

Hasenfuß m coward

Hasenscharte f harelip

Haspel (-, -n) f reel, bobbin; (*Winde*) winch

Hass [has] (-es) m hate, hatred; **einen ~ (auf**

jdn) **haben** (umg: Wut) to be really mad (with sb)

hassen ['hasən] vt to hate; **etw ~ wie die Pest** (umg) to detest sth

hassenswert adj hateful

hässlich ['hɛslɪç] adj ugly; (gemein) nasty; **Hässlichkeit** f ugliness; nastiness

Hassliebe f love-hate relationship

Hast [hast] (-) f haste

hast vb siehe **haben**

hasten vi, vr to rush

hastig adj hasty

hat [hat] vb siehe **haben**

hätscheln ['hɛtʃəln] vt to pamper; (zärtlich) to cuddle

hatte etc ['hatə] vb siehe **haben**

hätte etc ['hɛtə] vb siehe **haben**

Haube ['haʊbə] (-, -n) f hood; (Mütze) cap; (Aut) bonnet (Brit), hood (US); **unter der ~ sein/ unter die ~ kommen** (hum) to be/get married

Hauch [haʊx] (-(e)s, -e) m breath; (Lufthauch) breeze; (fig) trace; **hauchdünn** adj extremely thin; (Scheiben) wafer-thin; (fig: Mehrheit) extremely narrow; **hauchen** vi to breathe; **hauchfein** adj very fine

Haue ['haʊə] (-, -n) f hoe; (Pickel) pick; (umg) hiding

hauen unreg vt to hew, cut; (umg) to thrash

Hauer ['haʊər] (-s, -) m (Min) face-worker

Häufchen ['hɔyfçən] nt: **ein ~ Unglück** od **Elend** a picture of misery

Haufen ['haʊfən] (-s, -) m heap; (Leute) crowd; **ein ~ (Bücher)** (umg) loads od a lot (of books); **auf einem ~** in one heap; **etw über den ~ werfen** (umg: verwerfen) to chuck sth out; **jdn über den ~ rennen** od **fahren** etc (umg) to knock sb down

häufen ['hɔyfən] vt to pile up ▷ vr to accumulate

haufenweise adv in heaps; in droves; **etw ~ haben** to have piles of sth

häufig ['hɔyfɪç] adj frequent ▷ adv frequently; **Häufigkeit** f frequency

Haupt [haʊpt] (-(e)s, Häupter) nt head; (Oberhaupt) chief ▷ in zW main; **Hauptakteur** m (lit, fig) leading light; (pej) main figure; **Hauptaktionär** m major shareholder; **Hauptbahnhof** m central station; **hauptberuflich** adv as one's main occupation; **Hauptbuch** nt (Comm) ledger; **Hauptdarsteller, in** m(f) leading actor, leading actress; **Haupteingang** m main entrance; **Hauptfach** nt (Sch, Univ) main subject, major (US); **etw im Hauptfach studieren** to study sth as one's main subject, major in sth (US); **Hauptfilm** m main film; **Hauptgericht** nt main course; **Hauptgeschäftsstelle** f head office; **Hauptgeschäftszeit** f peak (shopping) period; **Hauptgewinn** m first prize; **einer der Hauptgewinne** one of the main prizes; **Hauptleitung** f mains pl

Häuptling ['hɔyptlɪŋ] m chief(tain)

Haupt- zW: **Hauptmahlzeit** f main meal; **Hauptmann** (-(e)s, pl -leute) m (Mil) captain; **Hauptnahrungsmittel** nt staple food; **Hauptperson** f (im Roman usw) main character; (fig) central figure; **Hauptpostamt** nt main post office; **Hauptquartier** nt headquarters pl; **Hauptrolle** f leading part; **Hauptsache** f main thing; **in der Hauptsache** in the main, mainly; **hauptsächlich** adj chief ▷ adv chiefly; **Hauptsaison** f peak od high season; **Hauptsatz** m main clause; **Hauptschlagader** f aorta; **Hauptschlüssel** m master key

Hauptschule f ≈ secondary modern (school) (Brit), junior high (school) (US); see culture note

○ **HAUPTSCHULE**
○
○ The Hauptschule is a non-selective school
○ which pupils attend after the Grundschule.
○ They complete five years of study and most
○ go on to do some training in a practical
○ subject or trade.

Haupt- zW: **Hauptsendezeit** f (TV) prime time; **Hauptstadt** f capital; **Hauptstraße** f main street; **Hauptverkehrsstraße** f (in Stadt) main street; (Durchgangsstraße) main thoroughfare; (zwischen Städten) main highway, trunk road (Brit); **Hauptverkehrszeit** f rush hour; **Hauptversammlung** f general meeting; **Hauptwohnsitz** m main place of residence; **Hauptwort** nt noun

hau ruck ['hau 'rʊk] interj heave-ho

Haus [haʊs] (-es, Häuser) nt house; **nach ~e** home; **zu ~e** at home; **fühl dich wie zu ~e!** make yourself at home!; **ein Freund des ~es** a friend of the family; **~ halten** (sparen) to economize; **wir liefern frei ~** (Comm) we offer free delivery; **das erste ~ am Platze** (Hotel) the best hotel in town; **Hausangestellte** f domestic servant; **Hausarbeit** f housework; (Sch) homework; **Hausarrest** m (im Internat) detention; (Jur) house arrest; **Hausarzt** m family doctor; **Hausaufgabe** f (Sch) homework; **Hausbesetzung** f squat; **Hausbesitzer** m house-owner; **Hausbesuch** m home visit; (von Arzt) house call

Häuschen ['hɔysçən] nt: **ganz aus dem ~ sein** (fig: umg) to be out of one's mind (with excitement/fear etc)

Haus zW: **Hausdurchsuchung** f police raid; **Hausdurchsuchungsbefehl** m search warrant

Hauseigentümer m house-owner

hausen ['haʊzən] vi to live (in poverty); (pej) to wreak havoc

Häuser- zW: **Häuserblock** m block (of houses); **Häusermakler** m estate agent (Brit), real estate agent (US); **Häuserreihe** f, **Häuserzeile** f row of houses; (aneinandergebaut) terrace (Brit)

Haus- zW: **Hausfrau** f housewife; **Hausfreund** m family friend; (umg) lover; **Hausfriedensbruch** m (Jur) trespass (in sb's house); **Hausgebrauch** m: **für den**

Hausgebrauch (*Gerät*) for domestic *od* household use; **hausgemacht** *adj* home-made; **Hausgemeinschaft** *f* household (community); **Haushalt** *m* household; (*Pol*) budget; **haushalten** *unreg vi* (*old*) to keep house; (*sparen*) to economize; **Haushälterin** *f* housekeeper

Haushalts- *zW*: **Haushaltsauflösung** *f* dissolution of the household; **Haushaltsbuch** *nt* housekeeping book; **Haushaltsdebatte** *f* (*Parl*) budget debate; **Haushaltsgeld** *nt* housekeeping (money); **Haushaltsgerät** *nt* domestic appliance; **Haushaltshilfe** *f* domestic *od* home help; **Haushaltsjahr** *nt* (*Pol, Wirts*) financial *od* fiscal year; **Haushaltsperiode** *f* budget period; **Haushaltsplan** *m* budget

Haus- *zW*: **Haushaltung** *f* housekeeping; **Hausherr** *m* host; (*Vermieter*) landlord; **haushoch** *adv*: **haushoch verlieren** to lose by a mile

hausieren [hau'zi:rən] *vi* to peddle

Hausierer (-s, -) *m* pedlar (*Brit*), peddler (*US*)

hausintern ['haus|ɪntɛrn] *adj* internal company *attrib*

häuslich ['hɔyslɪç] *adj* domestic; **sich irgendwo ~ einrichten** *od* **niederlassen** to settle in somewhere; **Häuslichkeit** *f* domesticity

Hausmacherart ['hausmaxər|a:rt] *f*: **Wurst** *etc* **nach ~** home-made-style sausage *etc*

Haus- *zW*: **Hausmann (-(e)s,** *pl* **-männer)** *m* (*den Haushalt versorgender Mann*) househusband; **Hausmarke** *f* (*eigene Marke*) own brand; (*bevorzugte Marke*) favourite (*Brit*) *od* favorite (*US*) brand; **Hausmeister** *m* caretaker, janitor; **Hausmittel** *nt* household remedy; **Hausnummer** *f* house number; **Hausordnung** *f* house rules *pl*; **Hausputz** *m* house cleaning; **Hausratversicherung** *f* (household) contents insurance; **Hausschlüssel** *m* front-door key; **Hausschuh** *m* slipper; **Hausschwamm** *m* dry rot

Hausse ['ho:sə] **(-, -n)** *f* (*Wirts*) boom; (*Börse*) bull market; **~ an** +*dat* boom in

Haus- *zW*: **Haussegen** *m*: **bei ihnen hängt der Haussegen schief** (*hum*) they're a bit short on domestic bliss; **Hausstand** *m*: **einen Hausstand gründen** to set up house *od* home; **Haussuchung** *f* = **Hausdurchsuchung**; **Haussuchungsbefehl** *m* = **Hausdurchsuchungsbefehl**; **Haustier** *nt* domestic animal; **Haustür** *f* front door; **Hausverbot** *nt*: **jdm Hausverbot erteilen** to ban sb from the house; **Hausverwalter** *m* property manager; **Hausverwaltung** *f* property management; **Hauswirt** *m* landlord; **Hauswirtschaft** *f* domestic science; **Haus-zu-haus-Verkauf** *m* door-to-door selling

Haut [haut] **(-, Häute)** *f* skin; (*Tierhaut*) hide; **mit ~ und Haar(en)** (*umg*) completely; **aus der ~ fahren** (*umg*) to go through the roof; **Hautarzt** *m* skin specialist, dermatologist

häuten ['hɔytən] *vt* to skin ▷ *vr* to shed one's skin

hauteng *adj* skintight

Hautfarbe *f* complexion

Hautkrebs *m* (*Med*) skin cancer

Havanna [ha'vana] **(-s)** *nt* Havana

Haxe ['haksə] **(-, -n)** *f* = **Hachse**

Hbf. *abk* = **Hauptbahnhof**

H-Bombe ['ha:bɔmbə] *f abk* H-bomb

HDTV *abk* (= *high definition television: hochauflösendes Fernsehen*) HDTV

Hebamme ['he:p|amə] *f* midwife

Hebel ['he:bəl] **(-s, -)** *m* lever; **alle ~ in Bewegung setzen** (*umg*) to move heaven and earth; **am längeren ~ sitzen** (*umg*) to have the whip hand

heben ['he:bən] *unreg vt* to raise, lift; (*steigern*) to increase; **einen ~ gehen** (*umg*) to go for a drink

Hebräer, in [he'brɛ:ər(ɪn)] **(-s, -)** *m(f)* Hebrew

hebräisch [he'brɛ:ɪʃ] *adj* Hebrew

Hebriden [he'bri:dən] *pl*: **die ~** the Hebrides *pl*

hecheln ['hɛçəln] *vi* (*Hund*) to pant

Hecht [hɛçt] **(-(e)s, -e)** *m* pike; **Hechtsprung** *m* (*beim Schwimmen*) racing dive; (*beim Turnen*) forward dive; (*Fussball*: *umg*) dive

Heck [hɛk] **(-(e)s, -e)** *nt* stern; (*von Auto*) rear

Hecke ['hɛkə] **(-, -n)** *f* hedge

Heckenrose *f* dog rose

Heckenschütze *m* sniper

Heck- *zW*: **Heckfenster** *nt* (*Aut*) rear window; **Heckklappe** *f* tailgate; **Heckmotor** *m* rear engine

heda ['he:da] *interj* hey there

Heer [he:r] **(-(e)s, -e)** *nt* army

Hefe ['he:fə] **(-, -n)** *f* yeast

Heft [hɛft] **(-(e)s, -e)** *nt* exercise book; (*Zeitschrift*) number; (*von Messer*) haft; **jdm das ~ aus der Hand nehmen** (*fig*) to seize control *od* power from sb

Heftchen *nt* (*Fahrkartenheftchen*) book of tickets; (*Briefmarkenheftchen*) book of stamps

heften *vt*: **~ (an** +*akk*) to fasten (to); (*nähen*) to tack (on (to)); (*mit Heftmaschine*) to staple *od* fasten (to) ▷ *vr*: **sich an jds Fersen** *od* **Sohlen ~** (*fig*) to dog sb's heels

Hefter (-s, -) *m* folder

heftig *adj* fierce, violent; **Heftigkeit** *f* fierceness, violence

Heft- *zW*: **Heftklammer** *f* staple; **Heftmaschine** *f* stapling machine; **Heftpflaster** *nt* sticking plaster; **Heftzwecke** *f* drawing pin (*Brit*), thumb tack (*US*)

hegen ['he:gən] *vt* to nurse; (*fig*) to harbour (*Brit*), harbor (*US*), foster

Hehl [he:l] *m od nt*: **kein(en) ~ aus etw machen** to make no secret of sth

Hehler (-s, -) *m* receiver (of stolen goods), fence

Heide¹ ['haidə] **(-, -n)** *f* heath, moor; (*Heidekraut*) heather

Heide² ['haidə] **(-n, -n)** *m* heathen, pagan

Heidekraut *nt* heather

Heidelbeere *f* bilberry

Heiden- *zW*: **Heidenangst** (*umg*) *f*: **eine**

Heidenangst vor etw/jdm haben to be scared stiff of sth/sb; **Heidenarbeit** (*umg*) *f* real slog; **heidenmäßig** (*umg*) *adj* terrific; **Heidentum** *nt* paganism

Heidin *f* heathen, pagan

heidnisch ['haɪdnɪʃ] *adj* heathen, pagan

heikel ['haɪkəl] *adj* awkward, thorny; (*wählerisch*) fussy

Heil [haɪl] **(-(e)s)** *nt* well-being; (*Seelenheil*) salvation ▷ *interj* hail; **Ski/Petri ~!** good skiing/fishing!

heil *adj* in one piece, intact; **mit ~er Haut davonkommen** to escape unscathed; **die ~e Welt** an ideal world (*without problems etc*)

Heiland (-(e)s, -e) *m* saviour (*Brit*), savior (*US*)

Heil- *zW:* **Heilanstalt** *f* nursing home; (*für Sucht- oder Geisteskranke*) home; **Heilbad** *nt* (*Bad*) medicinal bath; (*Ort*) spa; **heilbar** *adj* curable

Heilbutt ['haɪlbʊt] **(-s, -e)** *m* halibut

heilen *vt* to cure ▷ *vi* to heal; **als geheilt entlassen werden** to be discharged with a clean bill of health

heilfroh *adj* very relieved

Heilgymnastin *f* physiotherapist

heilig ['haɪlɪç] *adj* holy; **jdm ~ sein** (*lit, fig*) to be sacred to sb; **die H~e Schrift** the Holy Scriptures *pl*; **es ist mein ~er Ernst** I am deadly serious; *siehe auch* **heiligsprechen**; **Heiligabend** *m* Christmas Eve

Heilige, r *f(m)* saint

heiligen *vt* to sanctify, hallow; **der Zweck heiligt die Mittel** the end justifies the means

Heiligenschein *m* halo

Heiligkeit *f* holiness

heiligsprechen *unreg vt* to canonize

Heiligtum *nt* shrine; (*Gegenstand*) relic

Heilkunde *f* medicine

heillos *adj* unholy; (*Schreck*) terrible

Heil- *zW:* **Heilmittel** *nt* remedy; **Heilpraktiker, in (-s, -)** *m(f)* non-medical practitioner; **heilsam** *adj* (*fig*) salutary

Heilsarmee *f* Salvation Army

Heilung *f* cure

heim [haɪm] *adv* home

Heim (-(e)s, -e) *nt* home; (*Wohnheim*) hostel

Heimarbeit *f* (*Industrie*) homework, outwork

Heimat ['haɪmaːt] **(-, -en)** *f* home (town/country *etc*); **Heimatfilm** *m* sentimental film *in idealized regional setting*; **Heimatkunde** *f* (*Sch*) local history; **Heimatland** *nt* homeland; **heimatlich** *adj* native, home *attrib*; (*Gefühle*) nostalgic; **heimatlos** *adj* homeless; **Heimatmuseum** *nt* local history museum; **Heimatort** *m* home town *od* area; **Heimatvertriebene, r** *f(m)* displaced person

heimbegleiten *vt* to accompany home

Heimchen *nt:* **~ (am Herd)** (*pej: Frau*) housewife

Heimcomputer *m* home computer

heimelig ['haɪməlɪç] *adj* homely

Heim- *zW:* **heimfahren** *unreg vi* to drive *od* go home; **Heimfahrt** *f* journey home; **Heimgang** *m* return home; (*Tod*) decease;

heimgehen *unreg vi* to go home; (*sterben*) to pass away; **heimisch** *adj* (*gebürtig*) native; **sich heimisch fühlen** to feel at home; **Heimkehr (-, -en)** *f* homecoming; **heimkehren** *vi* to return home; **Heimkind** *nt* child brought up in a home; **heimkommen** *unreg vi* to come home; **Heimleiter** *m* warden of a home/hostel

heimlich *adj* secret ▷ *adv:* **~, still und leise** (*umg*) quietly, on the quiet; **Heimlichkeit** *f* secrecy; **Heimlichtuerei** *f* secrecy

Heim- *zW:* **Heimreise** *f* journey home; **Heimspiel** *nt* home game; **heimsuchen** *vt* to afflict; (*Geist*) to haunt; **heimtückisch** *adj* malicious; **heimwärts** *adv* homewards; **Heimweg** *m* way home; **Heimweh** *nt* homesickness; **Heimweh haben** to be homesick; **Heimwerker** *m* handyman; **heimzahlen** *vt:* **jdm etw heimzahlen** to pay back sb for sth

Heini ['haɪni] **(-s, -s)** *m:* **blöder ~** (*umg*) silly idiot

Heirat ['haɪraːt] **(-, -en)** *f* marriage; **heiraten** *vt, vi* to marry

Heirats- *zW:* **Heiratsantrag** *m* proposal (of marriage); **Heiratsanzeige** *f* (*Annonce*) advertisement for a marriage partner; **Heiratsschwindler** *m* person who makes a marriage proposal under false pretences; **Heiratsurkunde** *f* marriage certificate

heiser ['haɪzər] *adj* hoarse; **Heiserkeit** *f* hoarseness

heiß [haɪs] *adj* hot; (*Thema*) hotly disputed; (*Diskussion, Kampf*) heated, fierce; (*Begierde, Liebe, Wunsch*) burning; **es wird nichts so ~ gegessen, wie es gekocht wird** (*Sprichwort*) things are never as bad as they seem; **~er Draht** hot line; **~es Eisen** (*fig: umg*) hot potato; **~es Geld** hot money; **~ ersehnt** longed for; **~ umstritten** hotly debated; **jdn/etw ~ und innig lieben** to love sb/sth madly; **heißblütig** *adj* hot-blooded

heißen ['haɪsən] *unreg vi* to be called; (*bedeuten*) to mean ▷ *vt* to command; (*nennen*) to name ▷ *vi unpers:* **es heißt hier ...** it says here ...; **es heißt, dass ...** they say that ...; **wie ~ Sie?** what's your name?; **... und wie sie alle ~ ...** and the rest of them; **das will schon etwas ~** that's quite something; **jdn willkommen ~** to bid sb welcome; **das heißt** that is; (*mit anderen Worten*) that is to say

Heiß- *zW:* **Heißhunger** *m* ravenous hunger; **heißlaufen** *unreg vi, vr* to overheat; **Heißluft** *f* hot air; **Heißwasserbereiter** *m* water heater

heiter ['haɪtər] *adj* cheerful; (*Wetter*) bright; **aus ~em Himmel** (*fig*) out of the blue; **Heiterkeit** *f* cheerfulness; (*Belustigung*) amusement

heizbar *adj* heated; (*Raum*) with heating; **leicht ~** easily heated

Heizdecke *f* electric blanket

heizen *vt* to heat

Heizer (-s, -) *m* stoker

Heiz- *zW:* **Heizgerät** *nt* heater; **Heizkörper**

m radiator; **Heizöl** *nt* fuel oil; **Heizsonne** *f* electric fire

Heizung *f* heating

Heizungsanlage *f* heating system

Hektar [hɛk'taːr] (**-s, -e**) *nt od m* hectare

Hektik [['hɛktɪk]] *f* hectic rush; (*von Leben etc*) hectic pace

hektisch ['hɛktɪʃ] *adj* hectic

Hektoliter [hɛkto'liːtər] *m od nt* hectolitre (*Brit*), hectoliter (*US*)

Held [hɛlt] (**-en, -en**) *m* hero; **heldenhaft** ['hɛldənhaft] *adj* heroic; **Heldin** *f* heroine

helfen ['hɛlfən] *unreg vi* to help; (*nützen*) to be of use ▷ *vb unpers*: **es hilft nichts, du musst ...** it's no use, you'll have to ...; **jdm (bei etw)** ~ to help sb (with sth); **sich** *dat* **zu ~ wissen** to be resourceful; **er weiß sich** *dat* **nicht mehr zu ~** he's at his wits' end

Helfer, in (**-s, -**) *m(f)* helper, assistant

Helfershelfer *m* accomplice

Helgoland ['hɛlgolant] (**-s**) *nt* Heligoland

hell [hɛl] *adj* clear; (*Licht, Himmel*) bright; (*Farbe*) light; **~es Bier** ≈ lager; **von etw ~ begeistert sein** to be very enthusiastic about sth; **es wird** ~ it's getting light; **hellblau** *adj* light blue; **hellblond** *adj* ash-blond

Helle (**-**) *f* clearness; brightness

Heller (**-s, -**) *m* (*Hist*) farthing; **auf ~ und Pfennig** (down) to the last penny

hellhörig *adj* keen of hearing; (*Wand*) poorly soundproofed

hellicht ['hɛllɪçt] *adj siehe* **helllicht**

Helligkeit *f* clearness; brightness; lightness

helllicht ['hɛllɪçt] *adj*: **am ~en Tage** in broad daylight

hell- *zW*: **Hellraumprojektor** *m* (*Schweiz*) overhead projector; **hellsehen** *vi*: **hellsehen können** to be clairvoyant; **Hellseher, in** *m(f)* clairvoyant; **hellwach** *adj* wide-awake

Helm ['hɛlm] (**-(e)s, -e**) *m* helmet

Helsinki ['hɛlzɪŋki] (**-s**) *nt* Helsinki

Hemd [hɛmt] (**-(e)s, -en**) *nt* shirt; (*Unterhemd*) vest; **Hemdbluse** *f* blouse

Hemdenknopf *m* shirt button

hemdsärmelig *adj* shirt-sleeved; (*fig: umg: salopp*) pally; (*Ausdrucksweise*) casual

Hemisphäre [hemi'sfɛːrə] *f* hemisphere

hemmen ['hɛmən] *vt* to check, hold up; **gehemmt sein** to be inhibited

Hemmschuh *m* (*fig*) impediment

Hemmung *f* check; (*Psych*) inhibition; (*Bedenken*) scruple

hemmungslos *adj* unrestrained, without restraint

Hengst [hɛŋst] (**-es, -e**) *m* stallion

Henkel ['hɛŋkəl] (**-s, -**) *m* handle; **Henkelkrug** *m* jug; **Henkelmann** (*umg*) *m* (*Gefäß*) canteen

henken ['hɛŋkən] *vt* to hang

Henker (**-s, -**) *m* hangman

Henne ['hɛnə] (**-, -n**) *f* hen

Hepatitis [hepa'tiːtɪs] *f* (**-, Hepatitiden**) hepatitis

○ SCHLÜSSELWORT

her [heːr] *adv* **1** (*Richtung*): **komm her zu mir** come here (to me); **von England her** from England; **von weit her** from a long way away; **her damit!** hand it over!; **wo bist du her?** where do you come from?; **wo hat er das her?** where did he get that from?; **hinter jdm/etw her sein** to be after sb/sth

2 (*Blickpunkt*): **von der Form her** as far as the form is concerned

3 (*zeitlich*): **das ist 5 Jahre her** that was 5 years ago; **ich kenne ihn von früher her** I know him from before

herab [hɛ'rap] *adv* down, downward(s); **herabhängen** *unreg vi* to hang down; **herablassen** *unreg vt* to let down ▷ *vr* to condescend; **herablassend** *adj* condescending; **Herablassung** *f* condescension; **herabsehen** *unreg vi*: **herabsehen (auf** +*akk*) to look down (on); **herabsetzen** *vt* to lower, reduce; (*fig*) to belittle, disparage; **zu stark herabgesetzten Preisen** at greatly reduced prices; **Herabsetzung** *f* reduction; disparagement; **herabstufen** *vt* to downgrade; **herabstürzen** *vi* to fall off; (*Felsbrocken*) to fall down; **von etw herabstürzen** to fall off sth; to fall down from sth; **herabwürdigen** *vt* to belittle, disparage

heran [hɛ'ran] *adv*: **näher ~!** come closer!; **~ zu mir!** come up to me!; **heranbilden** *vt* to train; **heranbringen** *unreg vt*: **heranbringen (an** +*akk*) to bring up (to); **heranfahren** *unreg vi*: **heranfahren (an** +*akk*) to drive up (to); **herangehen** *unreg vi*: **an etw** *akk* **herangehen** (*an Problem, Aufgabe*) to tackle sth; **herankommen** *unreg vi*: (**an jdn/etw**) **herankommen** to approach (sb/sth), come near ((to) sb/sth); **er lässt alle Probleme an sich herankommen** he always adopts a wait-and-see attitude; **heranmachen** *vr*: **sich an jdn heranmachen** to make up to sb; (*umg*) to approach sb; **heranwachsen** *unreg vi* to grow up; **Heranwachsende, r** *f(m)* adolescent; **heranwinken** *vt* to beckon over; (*Taxi*) to hail; **heranziehen** *unreg vt* to pull nearer; (*aufziehen*) to raise; (*ausbilden*) to train; (*zu Hilfe holen*) to call in; (*Literatur*) to consult; **etw zum Vergleich heranziehen** to use sth by way of comparison; **jdn zu etw heranziehen** to call upon sb to help in sth

herauf [hɛ'rauf] *adv* up, upward(s), up here; **heraufbeschwören** *unreg vt* to conjure up, evoke; **heraufbringen** *unreg vt* to bring up; **heraufsetzen** *vt* to increase; **heraufziehen** *unreg vt* to draw *od* pull up ▷ *vi* to approach; (*Sturm*) to gather

heraus [hɛ'raus] *adv* out; **nach vorn ~ wohnen** to live at the front (of the house); **aus dem Gröbsten ~ sein** to be over the worst; **~ mit der Sprache!** out with it!; **herausarbeiten** *vt* to work out; **herausbekommen** *unreg vt* to get out; (fig) to find od figure out; (Wechselgeld) to get back; **herausbringen** unreg vt to bring out; (Geheimnis) to elicit; **jdn/etw ganz groß herausbringen** (umg) to give sb/sth a big build-up; **aus ihm war kein Wort herauszubringen** they couldn't get a single word out of him; **herausfinden** unreg vt to find out; **herausfordern** vt to challenge; (provozieren) to provoke; **Herausforderung** f challenge; provocation; **herausgeben** unreg vt to give up, surrender; (Geld) to give back; (Buch) to edit; (veröffentlichen) to publish ▷ vi (Wechselgeld geben): **können Sie (mir) herausgeben?** can you give me change?; **Herausgeber** (-s, -) m editor; (Verleger) publisher; **herausgehen** unreg vi: **aus sich herausgehen** to come out of one's shell; **heraushalten** unreg vr: **sich aus etw heraushalten** to keep out of sth; **heraushängen** unreg vt, vi to hang out; **herausholen** vt: **herausholen (aus)** to get out (of); **heraushören** vt (wahrnehmen) to hear; (fühlen): **heraushören (aus)** to detect (in); **herauskehren** vt (fig): **den Vorgesetzten herauskehren** to act the boss; **herauskommen** unreg vi to come out; **dabei kommt nichts heraus** nothing will come of it; **er kam aus dem Staunen nicht heraus** he couldn't get over his astonishment; **es kommt auf dasselbe heraus** it comes (down) to the same thing; **herausnehmen** unreg vt to take out; **sich** dat **Freiheiten herausnehmen** to take liberties; **Sie nehmen sich zu viel heraus** you're going too far; **herausputzen** vt: **sich herausputzen** to get dressed up; **herausreden** vr to talk one's way out of it (umg); **herausreißen** unreg vt to tear out; (Zahn, Baum) to pull out; **herausrücken** vt (Geld) to fork out, hand over; **mit etw herausrücken** (fig) to come out with sth; **herausrutschen** vi to slip out; **herausschlagen** unreg vt to knock out; (fig) to obtain; **herausstellen** vr: **sich herausstellen (als)** to turn out (to be); **das muss sich erst herausstellen** that remains to be seen; **herausstrecken** vt to stick out; **heraussuchen** vt: **sich** dat **jdn/etw heraussuchen** to pick out sb/ sth; **heraustreten** unreg vi: **heraustreten (aus)** to come out (of); **herauswachsen** unreg vi: **herauswachsen aus** to grow out of; **herauswinden** unreg vr (fig): **sich aus etw herauswinden** to wriggle out of sth; **herauswollen** vi: **nicht mit etw herauswollen** (umg: sagen wollen) to not want to come out with sth; **herausziehen** unreg vt to pull out, extract

herb [hɛrp] adj (slightly) bitter, acid; (Wein) dry; (fig: schmerzlich) bitter; (: streng) stern, austere

herbei [hɛrˈbaɪ] adv (over) here; **herbeiführen** vt to bring about; **herbeischaffen** vt to procure; **herbeisehnen** vt to long for; **herbemühen** [ˈheːrbəmyːən] vr to take the

trouble to come

Herberge [ˈhɛrbɛrgə] (-, -n) f (Jugendherberge etc) hostel

Herbergsmutter f warden

Herbergsvater m warden

herbitten unreg vt to ask to come (here)

herbringen unreg vt to bring here

Herbst [hɛrpst] (-(e)s, -e) m autumn, fall (US); **im** ~ in autumn, in the fall (US); **herbstlich** adj autumnal

Herd [heːrt] (-(e)s, -e) m cooker; (fig, Med) focus, centre (Brit), center (US)

Herde [ˈheːrdə] (-, -n) f herd; (Schafherde) flock

Herdentrieb m (lit, fig: pej) herd instinct

Herdplatte f (von Elektroherd) hotplate

herein [heˈraɪn] adv in (here), here; ~! come in!; **hereinbitten** unreg vt to ask in; **hereinbrechen** unreg vi to set in; **hereinbringen** unreg vt to bring in; **hereindürfen** unreg vi to have permission to enter; **Hereinfall** m letdown; **hereinfallen** unreg vi to be caught, be taken in; **hereinfallen auf** +akk to fall for; **hereinkommen** unreg vi to come in; **hereinlassen** unreg vt to admit; **hereinlegen** vt: **jdn hereinlegen** to take sb in; **hereinplatzen** vi to burst in; **hereinschneien** (umg) vi to drop in; **hereinspazieren** vi: **hereinspaziert!** come right in!

her- zW: **Herfahrt** f journey here; **herfallen** unreg vi: **herfallen über** +akk to fall upon; **Hergang** m course of events, circumstances pl; **hergeben** unreg vt to give, hand (over); **sich zu etw hergeben** to lend one's name to sth; **das Thema gibt viel/nichts her** there's a lot/nothing to this topic; **hergebracht** adj: **in hergebrachter Weise** in the traditional way; **hergehen** unreg vi: **hinter jdm hergehen** to follow sb; **es geht hoch her** there are a lot of goings-on; **herhaben** unreg (umg) vt: **wo hat er das her?** where did he get that from?; **herhalten** unreg vt to hold out; **herhalten müssen** (umg) to have to suffer; **herhören** vi to listen; **hör mal her!** listen here!

Hering [ˈheːrɪŋ] (-s, -e) m herring; (Zeltpflock) (tent) peg

herkommen unreg vi to come; **komm mal her!** come here!

herkömmlich adj traditional

Herkunft (-, -künfte) f origin

Herkunftsland nt (Comm) country of origin

her- zW: **herlaufen** unreg vi: **herlaufen hinter** +dat to run after; **herleiten** vr to derive; **hermachen** vr: **sich hermachen über** +akk to set about od upon ▷ vt (umg): **viel hermachen** to look impressive

Hermelin [hɛrməˈliːn] (-s, -e) m od nt ermine

hermetisch [hɛrˈmeːtɪʃ] adj hermetic; ~ **abgeriegelt** completely sealed off

her- zW: **hernach** adv afterwards; **hernehmen** unreg vt: **wo soll ich das hernehmen?** where am I supposed to get that from?; **hernieder** adv down

Heroin [heroˈiːn] (-s) nt heroin; **heroinsüchtig**

h

adj addicted to heroin; **Heroinsüchtige, r** *f(m)* heroin addict

heroisch [he'ro:ɪʃ] *adj* heroic

Herold ['he:rɔlt] **(-(e)s, -e)** *m* herald

Herpes [['hɛrpɛs]] *m* (-) *(Med)* herpes

Herr [hɛr] **(-(e)n, -en)** *m* master; *(Mann)* gentleman; *(adliger, Rel)* Lord; *(vor Namen)* Mr; **mein ~!** sir!; **meine ~en!** gentlemen!; **Lieber ~ A, Sehr geehrter ~ A** *(in Brief)* Dear Mr A; **„~en"** *(Toilette)* "gentlemen" *(Brit)*, "men's room" *(US)*; **die ~en der Schöpfung** *(hum: Männer)* the gentlemen

Herrchen *(umg)* *nt (von Hund)* master

Herren- *zW:* **Herrenbekanntschaft** *f* gentleman friend; **Herrenbekleidung** *f* menswear; **Herrenbesuch** *m* gentleman visitor *od* visitors; **Herrendoppel** *nt* men's doubles; **Herreneinzel** *nt* men's singles; **herrenlos** *adj* ownerless; **Herrenmagazin** *nt* men's magazine

Herrgott *m:* **~ noch mal!** *(umg)* damn it all!

Herrgottsfrühe *f:* **in aller ~** *(umg)* at the crack of dawn

herrichten ['he:rrɪçtən] *vt* to prepare

Herrin *f* mistress

herrisch *adj* domineering

herrje [hɛr'je:] *interj* goodness gracious!

herrjemine [hɛr'je:mine] *interj* goodness gracious!

herrlich *adj* marvellous *(Brit)*, marvelous *(US)*, splendid; **Herrlichkeit** *f* splendour *(Brit)*, splendor *(US)*, magnificence

Herrschaft *f* power, rule; *(Herr und Herrin)* master and mistress; **meine ~en!** ladies and gentlemen!

herrschen ['hɛrʃən] *vi* to rule; *(bestehen)* to prevail, be; **hier ~ ja Zustände!** things are in a pretty state round here!

Herrscher, in **(-s, -)** *m(f)* ruler

Herrschsucht *f* domineeringness

her- *zW:* **herrühren** *vi* to arise, originate; **hersagen** *vt* to recite; **hersehen** *unreg* *vi:* **hinter jdm/etw hersehen** to follow sb/ sth with one's eyes

her sein *siehe* **her**

her- *zW:* **herstammen** *vi* to descend *od* come from; **herstellen** *vt* to make, manufacture; *(zustande bringen)* to establish; **Hersteller (-s, -)** *m* manufacturer; **Herstellung** *f* manufacture; **Herstellungskosten** *pl* manufacturing costs *pl*; **hertragen** *unreg* *vt:* **etw hinter jdm hertragen** to carry sth behind sb

herüber [hɛ'ry:bər] *adv* over (here), across

herum [he'rʊm] *adv* about, (a)round; **um etw ~** around sth; **herumärgern** *vr:* **sich herumärgern (mit)** to get annoyed (with); **herumblättern** *vi:* **herumblättern in** +*dat* to browse *od* flick through; **herumdoktern** *(umg)* *vi* to fiddle *od* tinker about; **herumdrehen** *vt:* **jdm das Wort im Mund herumdrehen** to twist sb's words; **herumdrücken** *vr* *(vermeiden):* **sich um etw herumdrücken** to dodge sth; **herumfahren** *unreg* *vi* to travel around; *(mit Auto)* to drive around; *(sich rasch*

umdrehen) to spin (a)round; **herumführen** *vt* to show around; **herumgammeln** *(umg)* *vi* to bum around; **herumgehen** *unreg* *vi (herumspazieren)* to walk about; **um etw herumgehen** to walk *od* go round sth; **etw herumgehen lassen** to circulate sth; **herumhacken** *vi (fig: umg):* **auf jdm herumhacken** to pick on sb; **herumirren** *vi* to wander about; **herumkommen** *unreg* *(umg)* *vi:* **um etw herumkommen** to get out of sth; **er ist viel herumgekommen** he has been around a lot; **herumkriegen** *vt* to bring *od* talk round; **herumlungern** *vi* to lounge about; *(umg)* to hang around; **herumquälen** *vr:* **sich mit Rheuma herumquälen** to be plagued by rheumatism; **herumreißen** *unreg* *vt* to swing around (hard); **herumschlagen** *unreg* *vr:* **sich mit etw herumschlagen** *(umg)* to tussle with sth; **herumschleppen** *vt:* **etw mit sich herumschleppen** *(Sorge, Problem)* to be troubled by sth; *(Krankheit)* to have sth; **herumsprechen** *unreg* *vr* to get around, be spread; **herumstochern** *(umg)* *vi:* **im Essen herumstochern** to pick at one's food; **herumtreiben** *unreg* *vi, vr* to drift about; **Herumtreiber, in (-s, -)** *(pej)* *m(f)* tramp; **herumziehen** *unreg* *vi, vr* to wander about

herunter [he'rʊntər] *adv* downward(s), down (there); **mit den Nerven/der Gesundheit ~ sein** *(umg)* to be at the end of one's tether/be run-down; **herunterbrechen** *unreg* *vt (Zahlen, Kalkulation)* to break down; **herunterfahren** *unreg* *vti (Comput, Tech)* to shut down; **heruntergekommen** *adj* run-down; **herunterhandeln** *(umg)* *vt (Preis)* to beat down; **herunterhängen** *unreg* *vi* to hang down; **herunterholen** *vt* to bring down; **herunterkommen** *unreg* *vi* to come down; *(fig)* to come down in the world; **herunterladbar** *adj (Comput)* downloadable; **herunterladen** *unreg* *vt (Comput)* to download; **herunterleiern** *(umg)* *vt* to reel off; **heruntermachen** *vt* to take down; *(schlechtmachen)* to run down, knock; **herunterputzen** *(umg)* *vt:* **jdn herunterputzen** to tear sb off a strip; **herunterspielen** *vt* to play down; **herunterwirtschaften** *(umg)* *vt* to bring to the brink of ruin

hervor [hɛr'fo:r] *adv* out, forth; **hervorbrechen** *unreg* *vi* to burst forth, break out; **hervorbringen** *unreg* *vt* to produce; *(Wort)* to utter; **hervorgehen** *unreg* *vi* to emerge, result; **daraus geht hervor, dass ...** from this it follows that ...; **hervorheben** *unreg* *vt* to stress; *(als Kontrast)* to set off; **hervorragend** *adj* excellent; *(lit)* projecting; **hervorrufen** *unreg* *vt* to cause, give rise to; **hervorstechen** *unreg* *vi (lit, fig)* to stand out; **hervorstoßen** *unreg* *vt (Worte)* to gasp (out); **hervortreten** *unreg* *vi* to come out; **hervortun** *unreg* *vr* to distinguish o.s.; *(umg: sich wichtigtun)* to show off; **sich mit etw hervortun** to show off sth

Herz [hɛrts] **(-ens, -en)** *nt* heart; *(Karten: Farbe)*

hearts pl; **mit ganzem ~en** wholeheartedly; **etw auf dem ~en haben** to have sth on one's mind; **sich** dat **etw zu ~en nehmen** to take sth to heart; **du sprichst mir aus dem ~en** that's just what I feel; **es liegt mir am ~en** I am very concerned about it; **seinem ~en Luft machen** to give vent to one's feelings; **sein ~ an jdn/etw hängen** to commit o.s. heart and soul to sb/sth; **ein ~ und eine Seele sein** to be the best of friends; **jdn/etw auf ~ und Nieren prüfen** to examine sb/sth very thoroughly; **Herzanfall** m heart attack; **Herzbeschwerden** pl heart trouble sing

herzen vt to caress, embrace

Herzenslust f: **nach ~** to one's heart's content

Herz- zW: **herzergreifend** adj heart-rending; **herzerweichend** adj heartrending; **Herzfehler** m heart defect; **herzhaft** adj hearty

herziehen ['heːrtsiːən] vi: **über jdn/etw ~** (umg) to pull sb/sth to pieces (fig)

Herz- zW: **Herzinfarkt** m heart attack; **Herzklappe** f (heart) valve; **Herzklopfen** nt palpitation; **herzkrank** adj suffering from a heart condition

herzlich adj cordial ▷ adv (sehr): **~ gern!** with the greatest of pleasure!; **~en Glückwunsch** congratulations pl; **~e Grüße** best wishes; **Herzlichkeit** f cordiality

herzlos adj heartless; **Herzlosigkeit** f heartlessness

Herzog ['hertsoːk] (-(e)s, ⁻e) m duke; **Herzogin** f duchess; **herzoglich** adj ducal; **Herzogtum** nt duchy

Herz- zW: **Herzschlag** m heartbeat; (Med) heart attack; **Herzschrittmacher** m pacemaker; **herzzerreißend** adj heartrending

Hesse ['hesə] (-n, -n) m Hessian

Hessen ['hesən] (-s) nt Hesse

Hessin f Hessian

hessisch adj Hessian

heterogen [hetero'geːn] adj heterogeneous

heterosexuell [heterozeksu'el] adj heterosexual

Hetze ['hetsə] f (Eile) rush

hetzen vt to hunt; (verfolgen) to chase ▷ vi (eilen) to rush; **jdn/etw auf jdn/etw ~** to set sb/sth on sb/sth; **~ gegen** to stir up feeling against; **~ zu** to agitate for

Hetzerei [hetsə'raɪ] f agitation; (Eile) rush

Hetzkampagne ['hetskampanjə] f smear campaign

Heu [hɔy] (-(e)s) nt hay; **Heuboden** m hayloft

Heuchelei [hɔyçə'laɪ] f hypocrisy

heucheln ['hɔyçəln] vt to pretend, feign ▷ vi to be hypocritical

Heuchler, in [hɔyçlər(ɪn)] (-s, -) m(f) hypocrite; **heuchlerisch** adj hypocritical

Heuer ['hɔyər] (-, -n) f (Naut) pay

heuer adv this year

heuern ['hɔyərn] vt to sign on, hire

Heugabel f pitchfork

Heuhaufen m haystack

heulen ['hɔylən] vi to howl; (weinen) to cry; **das**

~de Elend bekommen to get the blues

heurig ['hɔyrɪç] adj this year's

Heuschnupfen m hay fever

Heuschrecke f grasshopper; (in heißen Ländern) locust

heute ['hɔytə] adv today; **~ Abend/früh** this evening/morning; **~ Morgen** this morning; **~ in einer Woche** a week today, today week; **von ~ auf morgen** (fig: plötzlich) overnight, from one day to the next; **das H~** today

heutig ['hɔytɪç] adj today's; **unser ~es Schreiben** (Comm) our letter of today('s date)

heutzutage ['hɔyttsuːtaːgə] adv nowadays

Hexe ['heksə] (-, -n) f witch

hexen vi to practise witchcraft; **ich kann doch nicht ~** I can't work miracles

Hexen- zW: **Hexenhäuschen** nt gingerbread house; **Hexenkessel** m (lit, fig) cauldron; **Hexenmeister** m wizard; **Hexenschuss** m lumbago

Hexerei [heksə'raɪ] f witchcraft

HG f abk = **Handelsgesellschaft**

Hg. abk (= Herausgeber) ed.

hg. abk (= herausgegeben) ed.

HGB (-) nt abk (= Handelsgesetzbuch) statutes of commercial law

Hieb (-(e)s, -e) m blow; (Wunde) cut, gash; (Stichelei) cutting remark; **~e bekommen** to get a thrashing

hieb etc [hiːp] vb (veraltet) siehe **hauen**

hieb- und stichfest adj (fig) watertight

hielt etc [hiːlt] vb siehe **halten**

hier [hiːr] adv here; **~ spricht Dr. Müller** (Tel) this is Dr Müller (speaking); **er ist von ~** he's a local (man); siehe auch **hierbehalten; hierbleiben; hierlassen**

Hierarchie [hierar'çiː] f hierarchy

hier- zW: **hierauf** adv thereupon; (danach) after that; **hieraus** adv: **hieraus folgt, dass ...** from this it follows that ...; **hierbehalten** unreg vt to keep here; **hierbei** adv (bei dieser Gelegenheit) on this occasion; **hierbleiben** unreg vi to stay here; **hierdurch** adv by this means; (örtlich) through here; **hierher** adv this way, here; **hierher gehören** to belong here; (fig: relevant sein) to be relevant; **hierlassen** unreg vt to leave here; **hiermit** adv hereby; **hiermit erkläre ich ...** (form) I hereby declare ...; **hiernach** adv hereafter; **hiervon** adv about this, hereof; **hiervon abgesehen** apart from this; **hierzu** adv (dafür) for this; (dazu) with this; (außerdem) in addition to this, moreover; (zu diesem Punkt) about this; **hierzulande, hier zu Lande** adv in this country

hiesig ['hiːzɪç] adj of this place, local

hieß etc [hiːs] vb siehe **heißen**

Hi-Fi-Anlage ['haɪfianlaːgə] f hi-fi set od system

Hightechindustrie ['haɪtekɪndʊs'triː] f high tech od hi-tech industry

Hilfe ['hɪlfə] (-, -n) f help; (für Notleidende) aid; **Erste ~** first aid; **jdm ~ leisten** to help sb; **~!** help!; **Hilfeleistung** f: **unterlassene**

Hilfeleistung (*Jur*) denial of assistance;
Hilfestellung f (*Sport*, *fig*) support
Hilf- zW: **hilflos** *adj* helpless; **Hilflosigkeit** f
helplessness; **hilfreich** *adj* helpful
Hilfs- zW: **Hilfsaktion** f relief action, relief
measures pl; **Hilfsarbeiter** m labourer (*Brit*),
laborer (*US*); **hilfsbedürftig** *adj* needy;
hilfsbereit *adj* ready to help; **Hilfskraft**
f assistant, helper; **Hilfsmittel** nt aid;
Hilfsschule f school for backward children;
Hilfszeitwort nt auxiliary verb
hilft [hɪlft] vb siehe **helfen**
Himalaja [hi'ma:laja] (-s) m: **der ~** the
Himalayas pl
Himbeere ['hɪmbeːrə] (-, -n) f raspberry
Himmel ['hɪməl] (-s, -) m sky; (*Rel*) heaven; **um
~s willen** (*umg*) for Heaven's sake; **zwischen
~ und Erde** in midair; **himmelangst** *adj*: **es
ist mir himmelangst** I'm scared to death;
Himmelbett nt four-poster bed; **himmelblau**
adj sky-blue
Himmelfahrt f Ascension
Himmelfahrtskommando nt (*Mil*: *umg*)
suicide squad; (*Unternehmen*) suicide mission
Himmelreich nt (*Rel*) Kingdom of Heaven
himmelschreiend *adj* outrageous
Himmelsrichtung f direction; **die vier ~en**
the four points of the compass
himmelweit *adj*: **ein ~er Unterschied** a world
of difference
himmlisch ['hɪmlɪʃ] *adj* heavenly

⭕ SCHLÜSSELWORT

hin [hɪn] *adv* **1** (*Richtung*): **hin und zurück**
there and back; **einmal London hin und
zurück** a return to London (*Brit*), a roundtrip
ticket to London (*US*); **hin und her** to and fro;
etw hin und her überlegen to turn sth over
and over in one's mind; **bis zur Mauer hin**
up to the wall; **wo ist er hin?** where has he
gone?; **nichts wie hin!** (*umg*) let's go then!;
nach außen hin (*fig*) outwardly; **Geld hin,
Geld her** money or no money
2 (*auf ... hin*): **auf meine Bitte hin** at my
request; **auf seinen Rat hin** on the basis
of his advice; **auf meinen Brief hin** on the
strength of my letter
3: **hin sein** (*umg*: *kaputt sein*) to have had it;
(*Ruhe*) to be gone; **mein Glück ist hin** my
happiness has gone; **hin und wieder** (every)
now and again

hinab [hɪ'nap] *adv* down; **hinabgehen** unreg vi
to go down; **hinabsehen** unreg vi to look down
hinarbeiten ['hɪnarbaɪtən] vi: **auf etw** akk **~**
(*auf Ziel*) to work towards sth
hinauf [hɪ'naʊf] *adv* up; **hinaufarbeiten** vr to
work one's way up; **hinaufsteigen** unreg vi to
climb
hinaus [hɪ'naʊs] *adv* out; **hinten/vorn ~**
at the back/front; **darüber ~** over and
above this; **auf Jahre ~** for years to come;

hinausbefördern vt to kick od throw out;
hinausfliegen unreg (*umg*) vi to be kicked out;
hinausführen vi: **über etw** akk **hinausführen**
(*lit*, *fig*) to go beyond sth; **hinausgehen** unreg
vi to go out; **hinausgehen über** +akk to
exceed; **hinauslaufen** unreg vi to run out;
hinauslaufen auf +akk to come to, amount
to; **hinausschieben** unreg vt to put off,
postpone; **hinausschießen** unreg vi: **über das
Ziel hinausschießen** (*fig*) to overshoot the
mark; **hinauswachsen** unreg vi: **er wuchs
über sich selbst hinaus** he surpassed
himself; **hinauswerfen** unreg vt to throw
out; **hinauswollen** vi to want to go out; **hoch
hinauswollen** to aim high; **hinauswollen
auf** +akk to drive at, get at; **hinausziehen**
unreg vt to draw out ▷ vr to be protracted;
hinauszögern vt to delay, put off ▷ vr to be
delayed, be put off
hinbekommen unreg (*umg*) vt: **das hast du gut
~** you've made a good job of it
hinblättern (*umg*) vt (*Geld*) to fork out
Hinblick ['hɪnblɪk] m: **in** od **im ~ auf** +akk in
view of
hinderlich ['hɪndərlɪç] *adj* awkward; **jds
Karriere** dat **~ sein** to be a hindrance to sb's
career
hindern vt to hinder, hamper; **jdn an etw** dat
~ to prevent sb from doing sth
Hindernis (-ses, -se) nt obstacle; **Hindernislauf**
m, **Hindernisrennen** nt steeplechase
Hinderungsgrund m obstacle
hindeuten ['hɪndɔʏtən] vi: **~ auf** +akk to point
to
Hinduismus [hɪndu'ɪsmʊs] m Hinduism
hindurch [hɪn'dʊrç] *adv* through; across;
(*zeitlich*) over
hindürfen [hɪn'dʏrfən] unreg vi: **~ (zu)** to be
allowed to go (to)
hinein [hɪ'naɪn] *adv* in; **bis tief in die Nacht
~** well into the night; **hineinfallen** unreg vi
to fall in; **hineinfallen in** +akk to fall into;
hineinfinden unreg vr (*fig*: *sich vertraut machen*)
to find one's feet; (*sich abfinden*) to come to
terms with it; **hineingehen** unreg vi to go
in; **hineingehen in** +akk to go into, enter;
hineingeraten unreg vi: **hineingeraten
in** +akk to get into; **hineinknien** vr
(*fig*: *umg*): **sich in etw** akk **hineinknien** to
get into sth; **hineinlesen** unreg vt: **etw in
etw** akk **hineinlesen** to read sth into sth;
hineinpassen vi to fit in; **hineinpassen in**
+akk to fit into; **hineinprügeln** vt: **etw in
jdn hineinprügeln** to cudgel sth into sb;
hineinreden vi: **jdm hineinreden** to interfere
in sb's affairs; **hineinstecken** vt: **Geld/Arbeit
in etw** akk **hineinstecken** to put money/
some work into sth; **hineinsteigern** vr to get
worked up; **hineinversetzen** vr: **sich in jdn
hineinversetzen** to put o.s. in sb's position;
hineinziehen unreg vt: **hineinziehen (in** +akk)
to pull in (to); **jdn in etw hineinziehen** (*in
Konflikt*, *Gespräch*) to draw sb into sth

hin- zW: **hinfahren** unreg vi to go; to drive ▷ vt to take; to drive; **Hinfahrt** f journey there; **hinfallen** unreg vi to fall down; **hinfällig** adj frail, decrepit; (Regel etc) unnecessary; **hinfliegen** unreg vi to fly there; (umg: hinfallen) to fall over; **Hinflug** m outward flight

hing etc [hɪŋ] vb siehe **hängen**

hin- zW: **Hingabe** f devotion; **mit Hingabe tanzen/singen** etc (fig) to dance/sing etc with abandon; **hingeben** unreg vr+dat to give o.s. up to, devote o.s. to; **hingebungsvoll** ['hɪŋgəbʊŋsfɔl] adv (begeistert) with abandon; (lauschen) raptly

hingegen [hɪn'ge:gən] konj however

hin- zW: **hingehen** unreg vi to go; (Zeit) to pass; **gehst du auch hin?** are you going too?; **hingerissen** adj: **hingerissen sein** to be enraptured; **hin- und hergerissen sein** (fig) to be torn; **ich bin ganz hin- und hergerissen** (ironisch) that's absolutely great; **hinhalten** unreg vt to hold out; (warten lassen) to put off, stall; **Hinhaltetaktik** f stalling od delaying tactics pl

hinhauen ['hɪnhaʊən] unreg (umg) vi (klappen) to work; (ausreichen) to do

hinhören ['hɪnhø:rən] vi to listen

hinken ['hɪŋkən] vi to limp; (Vergleich) to be unconvincing

hin- zW: **hinkommen** unreg (umg) vi (auskommen) to manage; (: ausreichen, stimmen) to be right; **hinlänglich** adj adequate ▷ adv adequately; **hinlegen** vt to put down ▷ vr to lie down; **sich der Länge nach hinlegen** (umg) to fall flat; **hinnehmen** unreg vt (fig) to put up with, take; **hinreichen** vi to be adequate ▷ vt: **jdm etw hinreichen** to hand sb sth; **hinreichend** adj adequate; (genug) sufficient; **Hinreise** f journey out; **hinreißen** unreg vt to carry away, enrapture; **sich hinreißen lassen, etw zu tun** to get carried away and do sth; **hinreißend** adj (Landschaft, Anblick) enchanting; (Schönheit, Mensch) captivating; **hinrichten** vt to execute; **Hinrichtung** f execution; **hinsehen** unreg vi: **bei genauerem Hinsehen** on closer inspection

hin sein ['hɪnzaɪn] siehe **hin**

hin- zW: **hinsetzen** vr to sit down; **Hinsicht** f: **in mancher** od **gewisser Hinsicht** in some respects od ways; **hinsichtlich** präp+gen with regard to; **hinsollen** (umg) vi: **wo soll ich/das Buch hin?** where do I/does the book go?; **Hinspiel** nt (Sport) first leg; **hinstellen** vt to put (down) ▷ vr to place o.s.

hintanstellen [hɪnt'|anʃtɛlən] vt (fig) to ignore

hinten ['hɪntən] adv behind; (rückwärtig) at the back; **~ und vorn** (fig: betrügen) left, right and centre; **das reicht ~ und vorn nicht** that's nowhere near enough; **hintendran** (umg) adv at the back; **hintenherum** adv round the back; (fig) secretly

hinter ['hɪntər] präp (+dat od akk) behind; (: nach) after; **~ jdm her sein** to be after sb; **~ die Wahrheit kommen** to get to the truth; **sich ~**

jdn stellen (fig) to support sb; **etw ~ sich** dat **haben** (zurückgelegt haben) to have got through sth; **sie hat viel ~ sich** she has been through a lot; **Hinterachse** f rear axle; **Hinterbänkler** (-s, -) m (Pol: pej) backbencher; **Hinterbein** nt hind leg; **sich auf die Hinterbeine stellen** to get tough; **Hinterbliebene, r** f(m) surviving relative; **hinterdrein** adv afterwards

hintere, r, s adj rear, back

hinter- zW: **hintereinander** adv one after the other; **zwei Tage hintereinander** two days running; **hinterfotzig** (umg) adj underhanded; **hinterfragen** vt untr to analyse; **Hintergedanke** m ulterior motive; **hintergehen** unreg vt untr to deceive; **Hintergrund** m background; **hintergründig** adj cryptic, enigmatic; **Hintergrundprogramm** nt (Comput) background program; **Hinterhalt** m ambush; **etw im Hinterhalt haben** to have sth in reserve; **hinterhältig** adj underhand, sneaky; **hinterher** adv afterwards, after; **er ist hinterher, dass ...** (fig) he sees to it that ...; **Hinterhof** m back yard; **Hinterkopf** m back of one's head; **Hinterland** nt hinterland; **hinterlassen** unreg vt untr to leave; **Hinterlassenschaft** f (testator's) estate; **hinterlegen** vt untr to deposit; **Hinterlegungsstelle** f depository; **Hinterlist** f cunning, trickery; (Handlung) trick, dodge; **hinterlistig** adj cunning, crafty; **Hintermann** (-(e)s, pl -männer) m person behind; **die Hintermänner des Skandals** the men behind the scandal

Hintern ['hɪntərn] (-s, -) (umg) m bottom, backside; **jdm den ~ versohlen** to smack sb's bottom

hinter- zW: **Hinterrad** nt back wheel; **Hinterradantrieb** m (Aut) rear-wheel drive; **hinterrücks** adv from behind; **Hinterteil** nt behind; **Hintertreffen** nt: **ins Hintertreffen kommen** to lose ground; **hintertreiben** unreg vt untr to prevent, frustrate; **Hintertreppe** f back stairs pl; **Hintertür** f back door; (fig: Ausweg) escape, loophole; **Hinterwäldler** (-s, -) (umg) m backwoodsman, hillbilly (bes US); **hinterziehen** unreg vt untr (Steuern) to evade (paying)

hintun ['hɪntu:n] unreg (umg) vt: **ich weiß nicht, wo ich ihn ~ soll** (fig) I can't (quite) place him

hinüber [hɪ'ny:bər] adv across, over; **hinübergehen** unreg vi to go over od across

hinunter [hɪ'nʊntər] adv down; **hinunterbringen** unreg vt to take down; **hinunterschlucken** (lit, fig) to swallow; **hinunterspülen** vt to flush away; (Essen, Tablette) to wash down; (fig: Ärger) to soothe; **hinuntersteigen** unreg vi to descend

Hinweg ['hɪnve:k] m journey out

hinweg- ['hɪn'vɛk] zW: **hinweggehen** unreg vi: **über etw** akk **hinweggehen** (fig) to pass over sth; **hinweghelfen** unreg vi: **jdm**

h

über etw akk **hinweghelfen** to help sb to get over sth; **hinwegkommen** unreg vi (fig): **über etw** akk **hinwegkommen** to get over sth; **hinwegsehen** unreg vi: **darüber hinwegsehen, dass** ... to overlook the fact that ...; **hinwegsetzen** vr: **sich hinwegsetzen über** +akk to disregard

Hinweis ['hɪnvaɪs] (-es, -e) m (Andeutung) hint; (Anweisung) instruction; (Verweis) reference; **sachdienliche ~e** relevant information

hinweisen unreg vi: **~ auf** +akk to point to; (verweisen) to refer to; **darauf ~, dass** ... to point out that ...; (anzeigen) to indicate that ...

Hinweisschild nt sign

Hinweistafel f sign

hinwerfen unreg vt to throw down; **eine hingeworfene Bemerkung** a casual remark

hinwirken vi: **auf etw** akk **~** to work towards sth

Hinz [hɪnts] m: **~ und Kunz** (umg) every Tom, Dick and Harry

hinziehen unreg vr (fig) to drag on

hinzielen vi: **~ auf** +akk to aim at

hinzu [hɪn'tsuː] adv in addition; **hinzufügen** vt to add; **Hinzufügung** f: **unter Hinzufügung von etw** (form) by adding sth; **hinzukommen** unreg vi: **es kommt noch hinzu, dass** ... there is also the fact that ...; **hinzuziehen** unreg vt to consult

Hiobsbotschaft ['hiːɔpsboˑtʃaft] f bad news

Hirn [hɪrn] (-(e)s, -e) nt brain(s); **Hirngespinst** (-(e)s, -e) nt fantasy; **Hirnhautentzündung** f (Med) meningitis; **hirntot** adj braindead; **hirnverbrannt** adj (umg) harebrained

Hirsch [hɪrʃ] (-(e)s, -e) m stag

Hirse ['hɪrzə] (-, -n) f millet

Hirt ['hɪrt] (-en, -en) m, **Hirte** (-n, -n) m herdsman; (Schafhirt, fig) shepherd

Hirtin f herdswoman; (Schafhirtin) shepherdess

hissen ['hɪsən] vt to hoist

Historiker [hɪs'toːrikər] (-s, -) m historian

historisch [hɪs'toːrɪʃ] adj historical

Hit [hɪt] (-s, -s) (umg) m (Mus, fig) hit; **Hitparade** f hit parade

Hitze ['hɪtsə] (-) f heat; **hitzebeständig** adj heat-resistant; **Hitzefrei** (-) nt: **Hitzefrei haben** to have time off school/work because of excessive heat; **Hitzewelle** f heat wave

hitzig adj hot-tempered; (Debatte) heated

Hitz- zW: **Hitzkopf** m hothead; **hitzköpfig** adj fiery, hot-headed; **Hitzschlag** m heatstroke

HIV-negativ adj HIV-negative

HIV-positiv adj HIV-positive

hl. abk = **heilig**

H-Milch ['haːmɪlç] f long-life milk, UHT milk

HNO-Arzt m ENT specialist

hob etc [hoːp] vb siehe **heben**

Hobby ['hɔbi] (-s, -s) nt hobby

Hobel ['hoːbəl] (-s, -) m plane; **Hobelbank** f carpenter's bench

hobeln vt, vi to plane

Hobelspäne pl wood shavings pl

hoch [hoːx] (attrib **hohe(r, s)**) adj high ▷ adv: **~**

achten to respect; **~ begabt = hochbegabt**; **~ dotiert** highly paid; **~ entwickelt** (Kultur, Land) highly developed; (Geräte, Methoden) sophisticated; **wenn es ~ kommt** (umg) at (the) most, at the outside; **das ist mir zu ~** (umg) that's above my head; **ein hohes Tier** (umg) a big fish; **es ging ~ her** (umg) we/they etc had a whale of a time; **~ und heilig versprechen** to promise faithfully; siehe auch **hochempfindlich; hochgestellt**

Hoch (-s, -s) nt (Ruf) cheer; (Met, fig) high

hoch- zW: **Hochachtung** f respect, esteem; **mit vorzüglicher Hochachtung** (form: Briefschluss) yours faithfully; **hochachtungsvoll** adv yours faithfully; **hochaktuell** adj highly topical; **Hochamt** nt high mass; **hocharbeiten** vr to work one's way up; **hochbegabt** adj extremely gifted, aged; **hochbetagt** adj very old, aged; **Hochbetrieb** m intense activity; (Comm) peak time; **Hochbetrieb haben** to be at one's od its busiest; **hochbringen** unreg vt to bring up; **Hochburg** f stronghold; **Hochdeutsch** nt High German; **Hochdruck** m high pressure; **Hochebene** f plateau; **hochempfindlich** adj highly sensitive; (Film) high-speed; **hocherfreut** adj highly delighted; **hochfahren** unreg vi (erschreckt) to jump; (Comput, Tech) to start up; **hochfliegend** adj ambitious; (fig) high-flown; **Hochform** f top form; **Hochgebirge** nt high mountains pl; **Hochgefühl** nt elation; **hochgehen** unreg (umg) vi (explodieren) to blow up; (Bombe) to go off; **Hochgenuss** m great od special treat; (großes Vergnügen) great pleasure; **hochgeschlossen** adj (Kleid etc) high-necked; **hochgestellt** adj (fig: Persönlichkeit) high-ranking; **Hochglanz** m high polish; (Phot) gloss; **hochgradig** adj intense, extreme; **hochhalten** unreg vt to hold up; (fig) to uphold, cherish; **Hochhaus** nt multi-storey building; **hochheben** unreg vt to lift (up); **hochkant** adv: **jdn hochkant hinauswerfen** (fig: umg) to chuck sb out on his/her ear; **hochkommen** unreg vi (nach oben) to come up; (fig: gesund werden) to get back on one's feet; (beruflich, gesellschaftlich) to come up in the world; **Hochkonjunktur** f boom; **hochkrempeln** vt to roll up; **Hochland** nt highlands pl; **hochleben** vi: **jdn hochleben lassen** to give sb three cheers; **Hochleistungssport** m competitive sport; **hochmodern** adj very modern, ultra-modern; **Hochmut** m pride; **hochmütig** adj proud, haughty; **hochnäsig** adj stuck-up, snooty; **hochnehmen** unreg vt to pick up; **jdn hochnehmen** (umg: verspotten) to pull sb's leg; **Hochofen** m blast furnace; **hochprozentig** adj (Alkohol) strong; **Hochrechnung** f projected result; **Hochsaison** f high season; **Hochschätzung** f high esteem

Hochschulabschluss m degree

Hochschulbildung f higher education

Hochschule f college; (Universität) university

Hochschulreife f: **er hat (die) ~ ≈** he's got

his A-levels (*Brit*), he's graduated from high school (*US*)

hoch- *zW:* **hochschwanger** *adj* heavily pregnant, well advanced in pregnancy; **Hochseefischerei** *f* deep-sea fishing; **Hochsitz** *m* (*Jagd*) (raised) hide; **Hochsommer** *m* middle of summer; **Hochspannung** *f* high tension; **hochspielen** *vt* (*fig*) to blow up; **Hochsprache** *f* standard language; **hochspringen** *unreg vi* to jump up; **Hochsprung** *m* high jump

höchst [høːçst] *adv* highly, extremely

Hochstapler ['hoːxstaːplər] (**-s, -**) *m* swindler

höchste, r, s *adj* highest; (*äußerste*) extreme; **die ~ Instanz** (*Jur*) the supreme court of appeal

höchstens *adv* at the most

Höchst- *zW:* **Höchstform** *f* (*Sport*) top form; **Höchstgeschwindigkeit** *f* maximum speed; **Höchstgrenze** *f* upper limit

Hochstimmung *f* high spirits *pl*

Höchst- *zW:* **Höchstleistung** *f* best performance; (*bei Produktion*) maximum output; **höchstpersönlich** *adv* personally, in person; **Höchstpreis** *m* maximum price; **Höchststand** *m* peak; **höchstwahrscheinlich** *adv* most probably

Hoch- *zW:* **Hochtechnologie** *f* high technology; **hochtechnologisch** *adj* high-tech; **Hochtemperaturreaktor** *m* high-temperature reactor; **Hochtour** *f:* **auf Hochtouren laufen** *od* **arbeiten** to be working flat out; **hochtrabend** *adj* pompous; **Hoch- und Tiefbau** *m* structural and civil engineering; **Hochverrat** *m* high treason; **Hochwasser** *nt* high water; (*Überschwemmung*) floods *pl*; **hochwertig** *adj* high-class, first-rate; **Hochwürden** *m* Reverend; **Hochzahl** *f* (*Math*) exponent

Hochzeit ['hɔxtsaɪt] (**-, -en**) *f* wedding; **man kann nicht auf zwei ~en tanzen** (*Sprichwort*) you can't have your cake and eat it

Hochzeitsreise *f* honeymoon

Hochzeitstag *m* wedding day; (*Jahrestag*) wedding anniversary

hochziehen *unreg vt* (*Rollladen, Hose*) to pull up; (*Brauen*) to raise

Hocke ['hɔkə] (**-, -n**) *f* squatting position; (*beim Turnen*) squat vault; (*beim Skilaufen*) crouch

hocken ['hɔkən] *vi, vr* to squat, crouch

Hocker (**-s, -**) *m* stool

Höcker ['hœkər] (**-s, -**) *m* hump

Hockey ['hɔki] (**-s**) *nt* hockey

Hoden [['hoːdən]] (**-s, -**) *m* testicle

Hodensack *m* scrotum

Hof [hoːf] (**-(e)s, ̈e**) *m* (*Hinterhof*) yard; (*Bauernhof*) farm; (*Königshof*) court; **einem Mädchen den ~ machen** (*veraltet*) to court a girl

hoffen ['hɔfən] *vi:* **~ (auf** +*akk*) to hope (for)

hoffentlich *adv* I hope, hopefully

Hoffnung ['hɔfnʊŋ] *f* hope; **jdm ~en machen** to raise sb's hopes; **sich** *dat* **~en machen** to have hopes; **sich** *dat* **keine ~en machen** not to hold out any hope(s)

Hoffnungs- *zW:* **hoffnungslos** *adj* hopeless; **Hoffnungslosigkeit** *f* hopelessness; **Hoffnungsschimmer** *m* glimmer of hope; **hoffnungsvoll** *adj* hopeful

höflich ['høːflɪç] *adj* courteous, polite; **Höflichkeit** *f* courtesy, politeness

hohe, r, s ['hoːə(r, s)] *adj siehe* **hoch**

Höhe ['høːə] (**-, -n**) *f* height; (*Anhöhe*) hill; **nicht auf der ~ sein** (*fig: umg*) to feel below par; **ein Scheck in ~ von ...** a cheque (*Brit*) *od* check (*US*) for the amount of ...; **das ist doch die ~** (*fig: umg*) that's the limit; **er geht immer gleich in die ~** (*umg*) he always flares up; **auf der ~ der Zeit sein** to be up-to-date

Hoheit ['hoːhaɪt] *f* (*Pol*) sovereignty; (*Titel*) Highness

Hoheits- *zW:* **Hoheitsgebiet** *nt* sovereign territory; **Hoheitsgewalt** *f* (*national*) jurisdiction; **Hoheitsgewässer** *nt* territorial waters *pl*; **Hoheitszeichen** *nt* national emblem

Höhen- *zW:* **Höhenangabe** *f* altitude reading; (*auf Karte*) height marking; **Höhenflug** *m:* **geistiger Höhenflug** intellectual flight; **Höhenlage** *f* altitude; **Höhenluft** *f* mountain air; **Höhenmesser** *m* altimeter; **Höhensonne** *f* sun lamp; **Höhenunterschied** *m* difference in altitude; **Höhenzug** *m* mountain chain

Höhepunkt *m* climax; (*des Lebens*) high point

höher *adj, adv* higher

hohl [hoːl] *adj* hollow; (*umg: dumm*) hollow(-headed)

Höhle ['høːlə] (**-, -n**) *f* cave; hole; (*Mundhöhle*) cavity; (*fig, Zool*) den

Hohl- *zW:* **Hohlheit** *f* hollowness; **Hohlkreuz** *nt* (*Med*) hollow back; **Hohlmaß** *nt* measure of volume; **Hohlraum** *m* hollow space; (*Gebäude*) cavity; **Hohlsaum** *m* hemstitch; **Hohlspiegel** *m* concave mirror

Hohn [hoːn] (**-(e)s**) *m* scorn; **das ist der reinste ~** it's sheer mockery

höhnen ['høːnən] *vt* to taunt, scoff at

höhnisch *adj* scornful, taunting

Hokuspokus [hoːkʊs'poːkʊs] (**-**) *m* (*Zauberformel*) hey presto; (*fig: Täuschung*) hocus-pocus

hold [hɔlt] *adj* charming, sweet

holen ['hoːlən] *vt* to get, fetch; (*Atem*) to take; **jdn/etw ~ lassen** to send for sb/sth; **sich** *dat* **eine Erkältung ~** to catch a cold

Holland ['hɔlant] (**-s**) *nt* Holland

Holländer ['hɔlandər] (**-s, -**) *m* Dutchman

Holländerin *f* Dutchwoman, Dutch girl

holländisch *adj* Dutch

Hölle ['hœlə] (**-, -n**) *f* hell; **ich werde ihm die ~ heißmachen** (*umg*) I'll give him hell

Höllenangst *f:* **eine ~ haben** to be scared to death

Höllenlärm *m* infernal noise (*umg*)

höllisch ['hœlɪʃ] *adj* hellish, infernal

Hologramm [holo'gram] (**-s, -e**) *nt* hologram

holperig ['hɔlpərɪç] *adj* rough, bumpy

holpern ['hɔlpərn] *vi* to jolt

Holunder [ho'lʊndər] (**-s, -**) *m* elder

Holz [hɔlts] **(-es, ¨er)** nt wood; **aus ~ made** of wood, wooden; **aus einem anderen/ demselben ~ geschnitzt sein** (fig) to be cast in a different/the same mould; **gut ~!** (Kegeln) have a good game!; **Holzbläser** m woodwind player

hölzern ['hœltsərn] adj (lit, fig) wooden

Holz- zW: **Holzfäller (-s, -)** m lumberjack, woodcutter; **Holzfaserplatte** f (wood) fibreboard (Brit) od fiberboard (US); **holzfrei** adj (Papier) wood-free

holzig adj woody

Holz- zW: **Holzklotz** m wooden block; **Holzkohle** f charcoal; **Holzkopf** m (fig: umg) blockhead, numbskull; **Holzscheit** nt log; **Holzschuh** m clog; **Holzweg** m (fig) wrong track; **Holzwolle** f fine wood shavings pl; **Holzwurm** m woodworm

Homecomputer ['houmkɔm'pju:tər] **(-s, -)** m home computer

Homepage ['houm'pa:gə] nt (Comput) home page

Homo-Ehe ['ho:mo|e:ə] (umg) f gay marriage

homogen [homo'ge:n] adj homogenous

Homöopath [homøo'pa:t] **(-en, -en)** m homeopath

Homöopathie [homøopa'ti:] f homeopathy, homeopathic medicine

homosexuell [homozɛksu'ɛl] adj homosexual

Honduras [hɔn'du:ras] **(-)** nt Honduras

Hongkong [hɔŋ'kɔŋ] **(-s)** nt Hong Kong

Honig ['ho:nɪç] **(-s, -e)** m honey; **Honiglecken** nt (fig): **das ist kein Honiglecken** it's no picnic; **Honigmelone** f honeydew melon; **Honigwabe** f honeycomb

Honorar [hono'ra:r] **(-s, -e)** nt fee

Honoratioren [honoratsi'o:rən] pl dignitaries

honorieren [hono'ri:rən] vt to remunerate; (Scheck) to honour (Brit), honor (US)

Hopfen ['hɔpfən] **(-s, -)** m hops pl; **bei ihm ist ~ und Malz verloren** (umg) he's a dead loss

hoppla ['hɔpla] interj whoops

hopsen ['hɔpsən] vi to hop

hörbar adj audible

horch [hɔrç] interj listen

horchen vi to listen; (pej) to eavesdrop

Horcher (-s, -) m listener; eavesdropper

Horde ['hɔrdə] **(-, -n)** f horde

hören ['hø:rən] vt, vi to hear; **auf jdn/etw ~** to listen to sb/sth; **ich lasse von mir ~** I'll be in touch; **etwas/nichts von sich ~ lassen** to get/not to get in touch; **Hören** nt: **es verging ihm Hören und Sehen** (umg) he didn't know whether he was coming or going

Hörensagen nt: **vom ~** from hearsay

Hörer (-s, -) m (Rundf) listener; (Univ) student; (Telefonhörer) receiver

Hörfunk m radio

Hörgerät nt hearing aid

hörig ['hø:rɪç] adj: **sie ist ihm (sexuell) ~** he has (sexual) power over her

Horizont [hori'tsɔnt] **(-(e)s, -e)** m horizon; **das geht über meinen ~** (fig) that is beyond me

horizontal [horitsɔ'ta:l] adj horizontal

Hormon [hɔr'mo:n] **(-s, -e)** nt hormone

Hörmuschel f (Tel) earpiece

Horn [hɔrn] **(-(e)s, ¨er)** nt horn; **ins gleiche** od **in jds ~ blasen** to chime in; **sich** dat **die Hörner abstoßen** (umg) to sow one's wild oats; **Hornbrille** f horn-rimmed spectacles pl

Hörnchen ['hœrnçən] nt (Gebäck) croissant

Hornhaut f horny skin; (des Auges) cornea

Hornisse [hɔr'nɪsə] **(-, -n)** f hornet

Hornochs, Hornochse m (fig: umg) blockhead, idiot

Horoskop [horo'sko:p] **(-s, -e)** nt horoscope

Hör- zW: **Hörrohr** nt ear trumpet; (Med) stethoscope; **Hörsaal** m lecture room; **Hörspiel** nt radio play

Hort [hɔrt] **(-(e)s, -e)** m hoard; (Sch) nursery school; **horten** vt to hoard

Hörweite f: **in/außer ~** within/out of hearing od earshot

Hose ['ho:ze] **(-, -n)** f trousers pl, pants pl (US); **in die ~ gehen** (umg) to be a complete flop

Hosen- zW: **Hosenanzug** m trouser suit, pantsuit (US); **Hosenboden** m: **sich auf den Hosenboden setzen** (umg) to get stuck in; **Hosenrock** m culottes pl; **Hosentasche** f trouser pocket; **Hosenträger** pl braces pl (Brit), suspenders pl (US)

Hostie ['hɔstiə] f (Rel) host

Hotel [ho'tɛl] **(-s, -s)** nt hotel; **Hotelfach** nt hotel management; **Hotel garni** nt bed and breakfast hotel

Hotelier [hoteli'e:] **(-s, -s)** m hotelier

Hotspot ['hɔtspɔt] m (wireless) hotspot

Hr. abk (= Herr) Mr

Hrsg. abk (= Herausgeber) ed.

hrsg. abk (= herausgegeben) ed.

HTML abk (= Hyper Text Markup Language) HTML

Hub [hu:p] **(-(e)s, ¨e)** m lift; (Tech) stroke

hüben ['hy:bən] adv on this side, over here; **~ und drüben** on both sides

Hubraum m (Aut) cubic capacity

hübsch [hypʃ] adj pretty, nice; **immer ~ langsam!** (umg) nice and easy

Hubschrauber (-s, -) m helicopter

Hucke ['hukə] **(-, -n)** f: **jdm die ~ vollhauen** (umg) to give sb a good hiding

huckepack ['hukəpak] adv piggy-back, pick-a-back

hudeln ['hu:dəln] vi to be sloppy

Huf ['hu:f] **(-(e)s, -e)** m hoof; **Hufeisen** nt horseshoe; **Hufnagel** m horseshoe nail

Hüfte ['hyftə] **(-, -n)** f hip

Hüftgürtel m girdle

Hüfthalter m girdle

Huftier nt hoofed animal, ungulate

Hügel ['hy:gəl] **(-s, -)** m hill

hügelig, hüglig adj hilly

Huhn [hu:n] **(-(e)s, ¨er)** nt hen; (Koch) chicken; **da lachen ja die Hühner** (umg) it's enough to make a cat laugh; **er sah aus wie ein gerupftes ~** (umg) he looked as if he'd been dragged through a hedge backwards

Hühnchen ['hy:nçən] *nt* young chicken; **mit jdm ein ~ zu rupfen haben** (*umg*) to have a bone to pick with sb
Hühner- *zW:* **Hühnerauge** *nt* corn; **Hühnerbrühe** *f* chicken broth; **Hühnerklein** *nt* (*Koch*) chicken trimmings *pl*
Huld [hʊlt] (-) *f* favour (*Brit*), favor (*US*)
huldigen ['hʊldɪgən] *vi:* **jdm ~** to pay homage to sb
Huldigung *f* homage
Hülle ['hylə] (-, -n) *f* cover(ing); (*Zellophanhülle*) wrapping; **in ~ und Fülle** galore; **die ~n fallen lassen** (*fig*) to strip off
hüllen *vt:* **~ (in** +*akk*) to cover (with); to wrap (in)
Hülse ['hylzə] (-, -n) *f* husk, shell
Hülsenfrucht *f* pulse
human [hu'ma:n] *adj* humane
humanistisch [huma'nɪstɪʃ] *adj:* **~es Gymnasium** *secondary school with bias on Latin and Greek*
humanitär [humani'tɛ:r] *adj* humanitarian
Humanität *f* humanity
Humanmedizin *f* (human) medicine
Hummel ['hʊməl] (-, -n) *f* bumblebee
Hummer ['hʊmər] (-s, -) *m* lobster
Humor [hu'mo:r] (-s, -e) *m* humour (*Brit*), humor (*US*); **~ haben** to have a sense of humo(u)r; **Humorist**, in *m(f)* humorist; **humoristisch** *adj* humorous; **humorlos** *adj* humourless; **humorvoll** *adj* humorous
humpeln ['hʊmpəln] *vi* to hobble
Humpen ['hʊmpən] (-s, -) *m* tankard
Humus ['hu:mʊs] (-) *m* humus
Hund [hʊnt] (-(e)s, -e) *m* dog; **auf den ~ kommen, vor die Hunde gehen** (*fig: umg*) to go to the dogs; **~e, die bellen, beißen nicht** (*Sprichwort*) empty vessels make most noise (*Sprichwort*); **er ist bekannt wie ein bunter ~** (*umg*) everybody knows him
Hunde- *zW:* **hundeelend** (*umg*) *adj:* **mir ist hundeelend** I feel lousy; **Hundehütte** *f* (dog) kennel; **Hundekuchen** *m* dog biscuit; **Hundemarke** *f* dog licence disc, dog tag (*US*); **hundemüde** (*umg*) *adj* dog-tired
hundert ['hʊndərt] *num* hundred; **Hundert** (-s, -e) *nt* hundred; **Hunderte von Menschen** hundreds of people
Hunderter (-s, -) *m* hundred; (*umg: Geldschein*) hundred (euro/pound/dollar *etc* note)
hundert- *zW:* **Hundertjahrfeier** *f* centenary; **Hundertmeterlauf** *m* (*Sport*): **der/ein Hundertmeterlauf** the/a hundred metres (*Brit*) *od* meters (*US*) *sing*; **hundertprozentig** *adj, adv* one hundred per cent
hundertste, r, s *adj* hundredth; **von H~n ins Tausendste kommen** (*fig*) to get carried away
Hundesteuer *f* dog licence (*Brit*) *od* license (*US*) fee
Hundewetter (*umg*) *nt* filthy weather
Hündin ['hʏndɪn] *f* bitch
Hüne ['hy:nə] (-n, -n) *m:* **ein ~ von Mensch** a giant of a man

Hünengrab *nt* megalithic tomb
Hunger ['hʊŋər] (-s) *m* hunger; **~ haben** to be hungry; **ich sterbe vor ~** (*umg*) I'm starving; **Hungerlohn** *m* starvation wages *pl*
hungern *vi* to starve
Hungersnot *f* famine
Hungerstreik *m* hunger strike
Hungertuch *nt:* **am ~ nagen** (*fig*) to be starving
hungrig ['hʊŋrɪç] *adj* hungry
Hunsrück ['hʊnsrʏk] *m* Hunsruck (Mountains *pl*)
Hupe ['hu:pə] (-, -n) *f* horn
hupen *vi* to hoot, sound one's horn
hupfen ['hʊpfən] *vi* to hop, jump; **das ist gehupft wie gesprungen** (*umg*) it's six of one and half a dozen of the other
hüpfen ['hʏpfən] *vi* = **hupfen**
Hupkonzert (*umg*) *nt* hooting (of car horns)
Hürde ['hʏrdə] (-, -n) *f* hurdle; (*für Schafe*) pen
Hürdenlauf *m* hurdling
Hure ['hu:rə] (-, -n) *f* whore
Hurensohn (*pej: umg!*) *m* bastard (!), son of a bitch (!)
hurra [hʊ'ra:] *interj* hurray, hurrah
hurtig ['hʊrtɪç] *adj* brisk, quick ▷ *adv* briskly, quickly
huschen ['hʊʃən] *vi* to flit, scurry
Husten ['hu:stən] (-s) *m* cough; **husten** *vi* to cough; **auf etw** *akk* **husten** (*umg*) not to give a damn for sth; **Hustenanfall** *m* coughing fit; **Hustenbonbon** *m od nt* cough drop; **Hustensaft** *m* cough mixture
Hut¹ [hu:t] (-(e)s, -e) *m* hat; **unter einen ~ bringen** (*umg*) to reconcile; (*Termine etc*) to fit in
Hut² [hu:t] (-) *f* care; **auf der ~ sein** to be on one's guard
hüten ['hy:tən] *vt* to guard ▷ *vr* to watch out; **das Bett/Haus ~** to stay in bed/indoors; **sich ~ zu** to take care not to; **sich ~ vor** +*dat* to beware of; **ich werde mich ~!** not likely!
Hutschnur *f:* **das geht mir über die ~** (*umg*) that's going too far
Hütte ['hʏtə] (-, -n) *f* hut; (*Holzhütte, Blockhütte*) cabin; (*Eisenhütte*) forge; (*umg: Wohnung*) pad; (*Tech: Hüttenwerk*) iron and steel works
Hüttenindustrie *f* iron and steel industry
Hüttenkäse *m* cottage cheese
Hüttenwerk *nt* iron and steel works
hutzelig ['hʊtsəlɪç] *adj* shrivelled
Hyäne [hy'ɛ:nə] (-, -n) *f* hyena
Hyazinthe [hya'tsɪntə] (-, -n) *f* hyacinth
Hydrant [hy'drant] *m* hydrant
hydraulisch [hy'draʊlɪʃ] *adj* hydraulic
Hydrierung [hy'dri:rʊŋ] *f* hydrogenation
Hygiene [hygi'e:nə] (-) *f* hygiene
hygienisch [hygi'e:nɪʃ] *adj* hygienic
Hymne ['hʏmnə] (-, -n) *f* hymn, anthem
hyper- ['hypɛr] *präf* hyper-
Hypnose [hyp'no:zə] (-, -n) *f* hypnosis
hypnotisch *adj* hypnotic
Hypnotiseur [hypnoti'zø:r] *m* hypnotist
hypnotisieren [hypnoti|zi:rən] *vt* to

h

Hypotenuse | hysterisch

hypnotize
Hypotenuse [[hypote'nu:zə]] (-, -n) *f*
hypotenuse
Hypothek [hypo'te:k] (-, -en) *f* mortgage; **eine
~ aufnehmen** to raise a mortgage; **etw mit
einer ~ belasten** to mortgage sth

Hypothese [hypo'te:zə] (-, -n) *f* hypothesis
hypothetisch [hypo'te:tɪʃ] *adj* hypothetical
Hysterie [hyste'ri:] *f* hysteria
hysterisch [hys'te:rɪʃ] *adj* hysterical; **einen
~en Anfall bekommen** (*fig*) to have
hysterics

I i

I, i [iː] *nt* I, i; **I wie Ida** ≈ I for Isaac, I for Item (US); **das Tüpfelchen auf dem i** (*fig*) the final touch

i. *abk* = **in; im**

i. A. *abk* (= *im Auftrag*) p.p.

iberisch [iˈbeːrɪʃ] *adj* Iberian; **die I~e Halbinsel** the Iberian Peninsula

IC (-) *m abk* = **Intercityzug**

ICE *m abk* (= *Intercity-Expresszug*) inter-city train

ich [ɪç] *pron* I; **~ bins!** it's me!; **Ich (-(s), -(s))** *nt* self; (*Psych*) ego; **Ichform** *f* first person; **Ichroman** *m* novel in the first person

Ideal [ideˈaːl] (-s, -e) *nt* ideal; **ideal** *adj* ideal; **Idealfall** *m*: **im Idealfall** ideally

Idealismus [ideaˈlɪsmʊs] *m* idealism

Idealist, in *m(f)* idealist

idealistisch *adj* idealistic

Idealvorstellung *f* ideal

Idee [iˈdeː] (-, -n) *f* idea; (*ein wenig*) shade, trifle; **jdn auf die ~ bringen, etw zu tun** to give sb the idea of doing sth

ideell [ideˈɛl] *adj* ideal

identifizieren [ɪdɛntifiˈtsiːrən] *vt* to identify

identisch [iˈdɛntɪʃ] *adj* identical

Identität [ɪdɛntiˈtɛːt] *f* identity

Ideologe [ideoˈloːgə] (-n, -n) *m* ideologist

Ideologie [ideoloˈgiː] *f* ideology

Ideologin [ideoˈloːgɪn] *f* ideologist

ideologisch [ideoˈloːgɪʃ] *adj* ideological

idiomatisch [idioˈmaːtɪʃ] *adj* idiomatic

Idiot [idiˈoːt] (-en, -en) *m* idiot

Idiotenhügel *m* (*hum: umg*) beginners' *od* nursery slope

idiotensicher (*umg*) *adj* foolproof

Idiotin *f* idiot

idiotisch *adj* idiotic

Idol [iˈdoːl] *nt* (-s, -e) idol

idyllisch [iˈdʏlɪʃ] *adj* idyllic

IG *abk* (= *Industriegewerkschaft*) industrial trade union

IGB (-) *m abk* (= *Internationaler Gewerkschaftsbund*) International Trades Union Congress

Igel [ˈiːgəl] (-s, -) *m* hedgehog

igitt [iˈgɪt], **igittigitt** [iˈgɪtiˈgɪt] *interj* ugh!

Iglu [ˈiːglu] (-s, -s) *m od nt* igloo

Ignorant [ɪgnoˈrant] (-en, -en) *m* ignoramus

ignorieren [ɪgnoˈriːrən] *vt* to ignore

IHK *f abk* = **Industrie- und Handelskammer**

ihm [iːm] *pron dat von* **er, es** (to) him, (to) it; **es**
ist ~ nicht gut he doesn't feel well

ihn [iːn] *pron akk von* **er** him; (*bei Tieren, Dingen*) it

ihnen [ˈiːnən] *pron dat pl von* **sie** (to) them; (*nach Präpositionen*) them

Ihnen *pron dat von* **Sie** (to) you; (*nach Präpositionen*) you

 SCHLÜSSELWORT

ihr [iːr] *pron* **1** (*nom pl*) you; **ihr seid es** it's you
2 (*dat von sie*) (to) her; (*bei Tieren, Dingen*) (to) it; **gib es ihr** give it to her; **er steht neben ihr** he is standing beside her
▷ *poss pron* **1** (*sing*) her; (*: bei Tieren, Dingen*) its; **ihr Mann** her husband
2 (*pl*) their; **die Bäume und ihre Blätter** the trees and their leaves

Ihr *poss pron* your

Ihre, r, s *poss pron* yours; **tun Sie das ~** (*geh*) you do your bit

ihre, r, s *poss pron* hers; (*eines Tieres*) its; (*von mehreren*) theirs; **sie taten das I~** (*geh*) they did their bit

ihrer [ˈiːrər] *pron gen sing von* **sie** of her; (*pl*) of them

Ihrer *pron gen von* **Sie** of you

Ihrerseits *adv* for your part

ihrerseits *adv* for her/their part

ihresgleichen *pron* people like her/them; (*von Dingen*) others like it; **eine Frechheit, die ~ sucht!** an incredible cheek!

ihretwegen *adv* (*für sie*) for her/its/their sake; (*wegen ihr, ihnen*) on her/its/their account; **sie sagte, ~ könnten wir gehen** she said that, as far as she was concerned, we could go

ihretwillen *adv*: **um ~** for her/its/their sake

ihrige [ˈiːrɪgə] *pron*: **der/die/das ~** *od* **Ihrige** hers; its; theirs

i. J. *abk* (= *im Jahre*) in (the year)

Ikone [iˈkoːnə] (-, -n) *f* icon

IKRK *nt abk* (= *Internationales Komitee vom Roten Kreuz*) ICRC

illegal [ˈɪlegaːl] *adj* illegal

illegitim [ˈɪlegitiːm] *adj* illegitimate

Illusion [ɪluziˈoːn] *f* illusion; **sich** *dat* **~en machen** to delude o.s.

illusorisch [ɪluˈzoːrɪʃ] *adj* illusory

Illustration [ɪlʊstratsi'oːn] f illustration
illustrieren [ɪlʊs'triːrən] vt to illustrate
Illustrierte (-n, -n) f picture magazine
Iltis ['ɪltɪs] (-ses, -se) m polecat
im [ɪm] = **in dem** präp: **etw im Liegen/Stehen
tun** do sth lying down/standing up
IM (-s, no pl) nt abk IM (= instant messaging)
Image ['ɪmɪtʃ] (-(s), -s) nt image;
Imagekampagne ['ɪmɪtʃkampanjə] f
image-building campaign; **Imagepflege**
['ɪmɪtʃpfleːgə] (umg) f image-building;
Imageschaden f damage to one's image
imaginär [imagi'nɛːr] adj imaginary
Imbiss ['ɪmbɪs] (-es, -e) m snack; **Imbisshalle**
f snack bar; **Imbissstand** m, **Imbissstube** f
snack bar
Imissionswert [imisi'oːnsveːrt] m pollution
count
imitieren [imi'tiːrən] vt to imitate
Imker ['ɪmkər] (-s, -) m beekeeper
immanent [ɪma'nɛnt] adj inherent, intrinsic
Immatrikulation [ɪmatrikulatsi'oːn] f (Univ)
registration
immatrikulieren [ɪmatriku'liːrən] vi, vr to
register
immer ['ɪmər] adv always; **~ wieder** again
and again; **etw ~ wieder tun** to keep on
doing sth; **~ noch** still; **~ noch nicht** still
not; **für ~** forever; **~ wenn ich ...** every time
I ...; **~ schöner** more and more beautiful; **~
trauriger** sadder and sadder; **was/wer (auch)
~** whatever/whoever; **immerhin** adv all the
same; **immerzu** adv all the time
Immigrant, in [ɪmi'grant(ɪn)] m(f) immigrant
Immobilien [ɪmo'biːliən] pl real property (Brit),
real estate (US); (in Zeitungsannoncen) property
sing; **Immobilienhändler, Immobilienmakler**
m estate agent (Brit), realtor (US)
immun [ɪ'muːn] adj immune
immunisieren [ɪmuni'ziːrən] vt to
immunize
Immunität [ɪmu:ni'tɛːt] f immunity
Immunschwäche f immunodeficiency
Immunsystem nt immune system
Imperativ (-s, -e) m imperative
Imperfekt ['ɪmpɛrfɛkt] (-s, -e) nt imperfect
(tense)
Imperialismus [ɪmperia'lɪsmʊs] m
imperialism
Imperialist [ɪmperia'lɪst] m imperialist;
imperialistisch adj imperialistic
impfen ['ɪmpfən] vt to vaccinate
Impf- zW: **Impfpass** m vaccination card;
Impfschutz m protection given by
vaccination; **Impfstoff** m vaccine; **Impfung**
f vaccination; **Impfzwang** m compulsory
vaccination
implizieren [ɪmpli'tsiːrən] vt to imply
imponieren [ɪmpo'niːrən] vi +dat to impress
Import [ɪm'pɔrt] (-(e)s, -e) m import
Importeur [ɪmpɔr'tøːr] (-s, -e) m importer
importieren [ɪmpɔr'tiːrən] vt to import
imposant [ɪmpo'zant] adj imposing

impotent ['ɪmpotɛnt] adj impotent
Impotenz ['ɪmpotɛnts] f impotence
imprägnieren [ɪmprɛ'gniːrən] vt to (water)
proof
Impressionismus [ɪmpresio'nɪsmʊs] m
impressionism
Impressum [ɪm'prɛsʊm] (-s, -ssen) nt imprint
Improvisation [ɪmprovizatsi'oːn] f
improvisation
improvisieren [ɪmprovi'ziːrən] vt, vi to
improvise
Impuls [ɪm'pʊls] (-es, -e) m impulse; **etw aus
einem ~ heraus tun** to do sth on impulse
impulsiv [ɪmpʊl'ziːf] adj impulsive
imstande, im Stande [ɪm'ʃtandə] adj: **~ sein**
to be in a position; (fähig) to be able; **er ist zu
allem ~** he's capable of anything

 SCHLÜSSELWORT

in [ɪn] präp +akk **1** (räumlich: wohin) in, into; **in die
Stadt** into town; **in die Schule gehen** to go
to school; **in die Hunderte gehen** to run into
(the) hundreds
2 (zeitlich): **bis ins 20. Jahrhundert** into od up
to the 20th century
▷ präp +dat **1** (räumlich: wo) in; **in der Stadt** in
town; **in der Schule sein** to be at school; **es
in sich haben** (umg: Text) to be tough; (: Drink)
to have quite a kick
2 (zeitlich: wann): **in diesem Jahr** this year;
(in jenem Jahr) in that year; **heute in zwei
Wochen** two weeks today

inaktiv ['ɪn|aktiːf] adj inactive; (Mitglied) non-
active
Inangriffnahme [ɪn'|angrɪfnaːmə] (-, -n) f
(form) commencement
Inanspruchnahme [ɪn'|anʃprʊxnaːmə] (-, -n)
f: **~** (+gen) demands pl (on); **im Falle einer
~ der Arbeitslosenunterstützung** (form)
where unemployment benefit has been
sought
inbegr. abk (= inbegriffen) enc.
Inbegriff ['ɪnbəgrɪf] m embodiment,
personification
inbegriffen adv included
Inbetriebnahme [ɪnbə'triːpnaːmə] (-, -n) f
(form) commissioning; (von Gebäude, U-Bahn etc)
inauguration
inbrünstig ['ɪnbrʏnstɪç] adj ardent
indem [ɪn'deːm] konj while; **~ man etw macht**
(dadurch) by doing sth
Inder, in ['ɪndər(ɪn)] (-s, -) m(f) Indian
indes [ɪn'dɛs], **indessen** [ɪn'dɛsən] adv
meanwhile ▷ konj while
Index ['ɪndɛks] (-(es), -e od **Indizes**) m: **auf dem
~ stehen** (fig) to be banned; **Indexzahl** f index
number
Indianer, in [ɪndi'a:nər(ɪn)] (-s, -) m(f)
(American) Indian
indianisch adj (American) Indian
Indien ['ɪndiən] (-s) nt India

indigniert [ɪndɪˈgniːrt] *adj* indignant
Indikation [ɪndikatsiˈoːn] *f*: **medizinische/ soziale** ~ medical/social grounds *pl* for the termination of pregnancy
Indikativ [ˈɪndikatiːf] **(-s, -e)** *m* indicative
indirekt [ˈɪndirɛkt] *adj* indirect; **~e Steuer** indirect tax
indisch [ˈɪndɪʃ] *adj* Indian; **I~er Ozean** Indian Ocean
indiskret [ˈɪndɪskreːt] *adj* indiscreet
Indiskretion [ɪndɪskretsiˈoːn] *f* indiscretion
indiskutabel [ˈɪndɪskutaːbəl] *adj* out of the question
indisponiert [ˈɪndɪsponiːrt] *adj* (*geh*) indisposed
Individualist [ɪndividuaˈlɪst] *m* individualist
Individualität [ɪndividualiˈtɛt] *f* individuality
Individualtourismus *m* individual tourism
individuell [ɪndividuˈɛl] *adj* individual; **etw ~ gestalten** to give sth a personal note
Individuum [ɪndiˈviːduʊm] **(-s, -duen)** *nt* individual
Indiz [ɪnˈdiːts] **(-es, -ien)** *nt* (*Jur*) clue; **~ (für)** sign (of)
Indizes [ˈɪnditseːz] *pl von* **Index**
Indizienbeweis *m* circumstantial evidence
indizieren [ɪndiˈtsiːrən] *vt, vi* (*Comput*) to index
Indochina [ˈɪndoˈçiːna] **(-s)** *nt* Indochina
indogermanisch [ˈɪndogɛrmaːnɪʃ] *adj* Indo-Germanic, Indo-European
indoktrinieren [ɪndɔktriˈniːrən] *vt* to indoctrinate
Indonesien [ɪndoˈneːziən] **(-s)** *nt* Indonesia
Indonesier, in **(-s, -)** *m(f)* Indonesian
indonesisch [ɪndoˈneːzɪʃ] *adj* Indonesian
Indossament [ɪndɔsaˈmɛnt] *nt* (*Comm*) endorsement
Indossant [ɪndɔˈsant] *m* endorser
Indossat [ɪndɔˈsaːt] **(-en, -en)** *m* endorsee
indossieren *vt* to endorse
industrialisieren [ɪndʊstriali'ziːrən] *vt* to industrialize
Industrialisierung *f* industrialization
Industrie [ɪndʊsˈtriː] *f* industry; **in der ~ arbeiten** to be in industry; **Industriegebiet** *nt* industrial area; **Industriegelände** *nt* industrial *od* trading estate; **Industriekaufmann** *m* industrial manager
industriell [ɪndʊstriˈɛl] *adj* industrial; **~e Revolution** industrial revolution
Industrielle, r *f(m)* industrialist
Industrie- *zW*: **Industriestaat** *m* industrial nation; **Industrie- und Handelskammer** *f* chamber of industry and commerce; **Industriezone** *f* (*bes Österr, Schweiz*) industrial zone; **Industriezweig** *m* branch of industry
ineinander [ɪnʔaɪˈnandər] *adv* in(to) one another *od* each other; **~ übergehen** to merge (into each other)
ineinandergreifen *unreg vi* (*lit*) to interlock; (*Zahnräder*) to mesh; (*fig: Ereignisse etc*) to overlap
Infanterie [ɪnfantəˈriː] *f* infantry
Infarkt [ɪnˈfarkt] **(-(e)s, -e)** *m* coronary (thrombosis)

Infektion [ɪnfɛktsiˈoːn] *f* infection
Infektionsherd *m* focus of infection
Infektionskrankheit *f* infectious disease
Infinitiv [ˈɪnfinitiːf] **(-s, -e)** *m* infinitive
infizieren [ɪnfiˈtsiːrən] *vt* to infect ▷ *vr*: **sich (bei jdm)** ~ to be infected (by sb)
in flagranti [ɪn flaˈgranti] *adv* in the act, red-handed
Inflation [ɪnflatsiˈoːn] *f* inflation
inflationär [ɪnflatsioˈnɛːr] *adj* inflationary
inflationsbereinigt *adj* inflation-adjusted
Inflationsrate *f* rate of inflation
inflatorisch [ɪnflaˈtoːrɪʃ] *adj* inflationary
Info [ˈɪnfo] **(-s, -s)** (*umg*) *nt* (information) leaflet
Infobrief [ˈɪnfo-] *m* info letter
infolge [ɪnˈfɔlgə] *präp* +*gen* as a result of, owing to; **infolgedessen** *adv* consequently
Informatik [ɪnfɔrˈmaːtɪk] *f* information studies *pl*
Informatiker, in **(-s, -)** *m(f)* computer scientist
Information [ɪnfɔrmatsiˈoːn] *f* information *no pl*; **Informationen** *pl* (*Comput*) data; **zu Ihrer ~** for your information
Informationsabruf *m* (*Comput*) information retrieval
Informationsgesellschaft *f* information society
Informationstechnik *f* information technology
informativ [ɪnfɔrmaˈtiːf] *adj* informative
informieren [ɪnfɔrˈmiːrən] *vt*: **~ (über** +*akk*) to inform (about) ▷ *vr*: **sich ~ (über** +*akk*) to find out (about)
Infotelefon *nt* information line
infrage, in Frage [ɪnˈfraːgə] *adv*: **etw ~ stellen** to question sth; **~ kommend** possible; (*Bewerber*) worth considering; **nicht ~ kommen** to be out of the question
Infrastruktur [ˈɪnfraʃtrʊktuːr] *f* infrastructure
Infusion [ɪnfuziˈoːn] *f* infusion
Ing. *abk* = **Ingenieur**
Ingenieur [ɪnʒeniˈøːr] *m* engineer; **Ingenieurschule** *f* school of engineering
Ingwer [ˈɪŋvər] **(-s)** *m* ginger
Inh. *abk* (= *Inhaber(in)*) prop.; (= *Inhalt*) cont.
Inhaber, in [ˈɪnhaːbər(ɪn)] **(-s, -)** *m(f)* owner; (*Comm*) proprietor; (*Hausinhaber*) occupier; (*Lizenzinhaber*) licensee, holder; (*Fin*) bearer
inhaftieren [ɪnhafˈtiːrən] *vt* to take into custody
inhalieren [ɪnhaˈliːrən] *vt, vi* to inhale
Inhalt [ˈɪnhalt] **(-(e)s, -e)** *m* contents *pl*; (*eines Buchs etc*) content; (*Math: Flächen*) area; (*: Rauminhalt*) volume; **inhaltlich** *adj* as regards content
Inhalts- *zW*: **Inhaltsangabe** *f* summary; **Inhaltslos** *adj* empty; **Inhaltsreich** *adj* full; **Inhaltsverzeichnis** *nt* table of contents; (*Comput*) directory
inhuman [ˈɪnhumaːn] *adj* inhuman
initialisieren [initsiaːliˈziːrən] *vt* (*Comput*) to initialize
Initialisierung *f* (*Comput*) initialization

177

Initiative [initsia'ti:və] *f* initiative; **die ~ ergreifen** to take the initiative

Initiator, in [initsi'a:tɔr, -'to:rɪn] *m(f)* (geh) initiator

Injektion [ɪnjɛktsi'o:n] *f* injection

injizieren [ɪnji'tsi:rən] *vt* to inject; **jdm etw ~** to inject sb with sth

Inka ['ɪŋka] **(-(s), -s)** *f(m)* Inca

Inkaufnahme [ɪn'kaʊfna:mə] *f (form)*: **unter ~ finanzieller Verluste** accepting the inevitable financial losses

inkl. *abk* (= *inklusive*) inc.

inklusive [ɪnklu'zi:və] *präp +gen* inclusive of ▷ *adv* inclusive

Inklusivpreis *m* all-in rate

inkognito [ɪn'kɔgnito] *adv* incognito

inkonsequent ['ɪnkɔnzekvɛnt] *adj* inconsistent

inkorrekt ['ɪnkɔrɛkt] *adj* incorrect

Inkrafttreten [ɪn'kraftre:tən] **(-s)** *nt* coming into force

Inkubationszeit [ɪnkubatsi'o:nstsaɪt] *f (Med)* incubation period

Inland ['ɪnlant] **(-(e)s)** *nt* (*Geog*) inland; (*Pol, Comm*) home (country); **im ~ und Ausland** at home and abroad; **Inlandflug** *m* domestic flight

Inlandsporto *nt* inland postage

inmitten [ɪn'mɪtən] *präp +gen* in the middle of; **~ von** amongst

innehaben ['ɪnəha:bən] *unreg vt* to hold

innehalten ['ɪnəhaltən] *unreg vi* to pause, stop

innen ['ɪnən] *adv* inside; **nach ~** inwards; **von ~** from the inside; **Innenarchitekt** *m* interior designer; **Innenaufnahme** *f* indoor photograph; **Innenbahn** *f* (*Sport*) inside lane; **Innendienst** *m*: **im Innendienst sein** to work in the office; **Inneneinrichtung** *f* (interior) furnishings *pl*; **Innenleben** *nt* (*seelisch*) emotional life; (*umg: körperlich*) insides *pl*; **Innenminister** *m* minister of the interior, Home Secretary (*Brit*); **Innenpolitik** *f* domestic policy; **innenpolitisch** *adj* relating to domestic policy, domestic; **Innenstadt** *f* town *od* city centre (*Brit*) *od* center (*US*)

innerbetrieblich *adj* in-house; **etw ~ regeln** to settle sth within the company

innerdeutsch *adj*: **~e(r) Handel** domestic trade in Germany

Innere, s *nt* inside; (*Mitte*) centre (*Brit*), center (*US*); (*fig*) heart

innere, r, s *adj* inner; (*im Körper, inländisch*) internal

Innereien [ɪnə'raɪən] *pl* innards *pl*

inner- *zW*: **innerhalb** *adv* within; (*räumlich*) inside ▷ *prep +dat* within; inside; **innerlich** *adj* internal; (*geistig*) inward; **Innerlichkeit** *f* (*Liter*) inwardness; **innerparteilich** *adj*: **innerparteiliche Demokratie** democracy (with)in the party structure

Innerste, s *nt* heart; **bis ins ~ getroffen** hurt to the quick

innerste, r, s *adj* innermost

innewohnen ['ɪnəvo:nən] *vi +dat* (*geh*) to be inherent in

innig ['ɪnɪç] *adj* profound; (*Freundschaft*) intimate; **mein ~ster Wunsch** my dearest wish

Innovation [ɪnovatsi'o:n] *f* innovation

Innung ['ɪnʊŋ] *f* (trade) guild; **du blamierst die ganze ~** (*hum: umg*) you are letting the whole side down

inoffiziell ['ɪnǀofitsiɛl] *adj* unofficial

ins [ɪns] **= in das**

Insasse ['ɪnzasə] **(-n, -n)** *m*, **Insassin** *f* (*einer Anstalt*) inmate; (*Aut*) passenger

insbesondere [ɪnsbə'zɔndərə] *adv* (e)specially

Inschrift ['ɪnʃrɪft] *f* inscription

Insekt [ɪn'zɛkt] **(-(e)s, -en)** *nt* insect

Insektenvertilgungsmittel *nt* insecticide

Insel ['ɪnzəl] **(-, -n)** *f* island

Inserat [ɪnze'ra:t] **(-(e)s, -e)** *nt* advertisement

Inserent [ɪnze'rɛnt] *m* advertiser

inserieren [ɪnze'ri:rən] *vt, vi* to advertise

insgeheim [ɪnsgə'haɪm] *adv* secretly

insgesamt [ɪnsgə'zamt] *adv* altogether, all in all

Insiderhandel ['ɪnsaɪdər-] *m* insider dealing *od* trading

Insidertipp ['ɪnsaɪdər-] *m* insider tip

insofern [ɪnzo'fɛrn] *adv* in this respect ▷ *konj* if; (*deshalb*) (and) so; **~ als** in so far as

insolvent ['ɪnzɔlvɛnt] *adj* bankrupt, insolvent

Insolvenz ['ɪnzɔlvɛnts] *f* (*Comm*) insolvency; **Insolvenzantrag** *m* application for insolvency proceedings; **Insolvenzverfahren** *nt* insolvency proceedings *pl*; **Insolvenzverwalter, in** *m(f)* official receiver

insoweit *adv, konj* **= insofern**

in spe [ɪn'ʃpe:] (*umg*) *adj*: **unser Schwiegersohn ~** our son-in-law to be, our future son-in-law

Inspektion [ɪnspɛktsi'o:n] *f* inspection; (*Aut*) service

Inspektor, in [ɪn'spɛktɔr, -'to:rɪn] **(-s, -en)** *m(f)* inspector

Inspiration [ɪnspiratsi'o:n] *f* inspiration

inspirieren [ɪnspi'ri:rən] *vt* to inspire; **sich von etw ~ lassen** to get one's inspiration from sth

inspizieren [ɪnspi'tsi:rən] *vt* to inspect

Installateur [ɪnstala'tø:r] *m* plumber; (*Elektroinstallateur*) electrician

installieren [ɪnsta'li:rən] *vt* to install (*auch fig, Comput*)

Instandhaltung [ɪn'ʃtanthaltʊŋ] *f* maintenance

inständig [ɪn'ʃtɛndɪç] *adj* urgent; **~ bitten** to beg

Instandsetzung *f* overhaul; (*eines Gebäudes*) restoration

Instant Messaging ['ɪnstənt'mɛsɪdʒɪŋ] **(-, -)** *nt* instant messaging

Instanz [ɪn'stants] *f* authority; (*Jur*) court; **Verhandlung in erster/zweiter ~** first/ second court case

Instanzenweg *m* official channels *pl*
Instinkt [ɪn'stɪŋkt] **(-(e)s, -e)** *m* instinct
instinktiv [ɪnstɪŋk'tiːf] *adj* instinctive
Institut [ɪnsti'tuːt] **(-(e)s, -e)** *nt* institute
Institution [ɪnstitutsi'oːn] *f* institution
Instrument [ɪnstru'mɛnt] *nt* instrument
Insulin [ɪnzu'liːn] **(-s)** *nt* insulin
inszenieren [ɪnstse'niːrən] *vt* to direct; *(fig)* to stage-manage
Inszenierung *f* production
intakt [ɪn'takt] *adj* intact
Integralrechnung [ɪnte'graːlrɛçnʊŋ] *f* integral calculus
Integration [ɪntegratsi'oːn] *f* integration
integrieren [ɪnte'griːrən] *vt* to integrate; **integrierte Gesamtschule** comprehensive school *(Brit)*
Integrität [ɪntegri'tɛːt] *f* integrity
Intellekt [ɪntɛ'lɛkt] **(-(e)s)** *m* intellect
intellektuell [ɪntɛlɛktu'ɛl] *adj* intellectual
Intellektuelle, r *f(m)* intellectual
intelligent [ɪntɛli'gɛnt] *adj* intelligent
Intelligenz [ɪntɛli'gɛnts] *f* intelligence; *(Leute)* intelligentsia *pl*; **Intelligenzquotient** *m* IQ, intelligence quotient
Intendant [ɪntɛn'dant] *m* director
Intensität [ɪntɛnzi'tɛːt] *f* intensity
intensiv [ɪntɛn'ziːf] *adj* intensive
intensivieren [ɪntɛnzi'viːrən] *vt* to intensify
Intensivkurs *m* intensive course
Intensivstation *f* intensive care unit
interaktiv *adj* *(Comput)* interactive
Intercityzug [ɪntər'sɪtitsuːk] *m* inter-city train
interessant [ɪntere'sant] *adj* interesting; **sich ~ machen** to attract attention
interessanterweise *adv* interestingly enough
Interesse [ɪnte'resə] **(-s, -n)** *nt* interest; **~ haben an** +*dat* to be interested in
Interessengebiet *nt* field of interest
Interessengegensatz *m* clash of interests
Interessent, in [ɪntere'sɛnt(ɪn)] *m(f)* interested party; **es haben sich mehrere ~en gemeldet** several people have shown interest
interessieren [ɪntere'siːrən] *vt*: **jdn (für etw** *od* **an etw** *dat***) ~** to interest sb (in sth) ▷ *vr*: **sich ~ für** to be interested in
interessiert *adj*: **politisch ~** interested in politics
Interkontinentalrakete [ɪntərkɔntinen'taːlrakeːtə] *f* intercontinental missile
interkulturell *adj* intercultural
intern [ɪn'tɛrn] *adj* internal
Internat [ɪntɛr'naːt] **(-(e)s, -e)** *nt* boarding school
international [ɪntɛrnatsio'naːl] *adj* international
Internatsschüler, in *m(f)* boarder
Internet ['ɪntɛrnɛt] **(-s)** *nt*: **das ~** the internet; **ins Internet stellen** to put on the internet; **Internetanbieter, in** *m(f)* internet provider; **internetbasiert** *adj* internet-based; **internetbasierte Anwendung** internet-based application; **Internetcafé** *nt* internet

café; **Internethändler, in** *m(f)* online trader *od* dealer; **Internethandy** *nt* mobile phone with internet access, smartphone; **Internetportal** *nt* web *od* internet portal; **Internetseite** *f* web page
internieren [ɪntɛr'niːrən] *vt* to intern
Internierungslager *nt* internment camp
Internist, in *m(f)* internist
Interpol ['ɪntərpoːl] **(-)** *f abk* (= *Internationale Polizei*) Interpol
Interpret [ɪntər'preːt] **(-en, -en)** *m*: **Lieder verschiedener ~en** songs by various singers
Interpretation [ɪntərpretatsi'oːn] *f* interpretation
interpretieren [ɪntɛrpre'tiːrən] *vt* to interpret
Interpretin *f siehe* **Interpret**
Interpunktion [ɪntɛrpʊŋktsi'oːn] *f* punctuation
Intervall [ɪntɛr'val] **(-s, -e)** *nt* interval
intervenieren [ɪntɛrve'niːrən] *vi* to intervene
Interview [ɪntər'vjuː] **(-s, -s)** *nt* interview; **interviewen** [-'vjuːən] *vt* to interview
intim [ɪn'tiːm] *adj* intimate; **Intimbereich** *m* *(Anat)* genital area
Intimität [ɪntimi'tɛːt] *f* intimacy
Intimsphäre *f*: **jds ~ verletzen** to invade sb's privacy
intolerant ['ɪntolerant] *adj* intolerant
intransitiv ['ɪntranzitiːf] *adj* (Gram) intransitive
Intrige [ɪn'triːgə] **(-, -n)** *f* intrigue, plot
intrinsisch [ɪn'trɪnzɪʃ] *adj*: **~er Wert** intrinsic value
introvertiert [ɪntrover'tiːrt] *adj*: **~ sein** to be an introvert
intuitiv [ɪntui'tiːf] *adj* intuitive
intus ['ɪntʊs] *adj*: **etw ~ haben** *(umg: Wissen)* to have got sth into one's head; *(Essen, Trinken)* to have got sth down one *(umg)*
Invalide [ɪnva'liːdə] **(-n, -n)** *m* disabled person, invalid
Invalidenrente *f* disability pension
Invasion [ɪnvazi'oːn] *f* invasion
Inventar [ɪnvɛn'taːr] **(-s, -e)** *nt* inventory; *(Comm)* assets and liabilities *pl*
Inventur [ɪnvɛn'tuːr] *f* stocktaking; **~ machen** to stocktake
investieren [ɪnvɛs'tiːrən] *vt* to invest
investiert *adj*: **~es Kapital** capital employed
Investition [ɪnvɛstitsi'oːn] *f* investment
Investitionszulage *f* investment grant
Investmentgesellschaft [ɪn'vɛstmɛntgəzɛlʃaft] *f* unit trust
inwiefern [ɪnvi'fɛrn] *adv* how far, to what extent
inwieweit [ɪnvi'vait] *adv* how far, to what extent
Inzest [ɪn'tsɛst] **(-(e)s, -e)** *m* incest *no pl*
inzwischen [ɪn'tsvɪʃən] *adv* meanwhile
IOK *nt abk* (= *Internationales Olympisches Komitee*) IOC
Ion [i'oːn] **(-s, -en)** *nt* ion
ionisch [i'oːnɪʃ] *adj* Ionian; **I~es Meer** Ionian

179

Sea

IP abk (Comput: = Internet Protocol) IP
IQ m abk (= Intelligenzquotient) IQ
i. R. abk (= im Ruhestand) retd
IRA f abk (= Irisch-Republikanische Armee) IRA
Irak [i'ra:k] (-s) m: (der) ~ Iraq
Iraker, in (-s, -) m(f) Iraqi
irakisch adj Iraqi
Iran [i'ra:n] (-s) m: (der) ~ Iran
Iraner, in (-s, -) m(f) Iranian
iranisch adj Iranian
irdisch ['ɪrdɪʃ] adj earthly; **den Weg alles I~en
gehen** to go the way of all flesh
Ire ['i:rə] (-n, -n) m Irishman; **die ~n** the Irish
irgend ['ɪrgənt] adv at all; **wann/was/wer ~**
whenever/whatever/whoever; **irgendein,
e, s** adj some, any; **haben Sie (sonst) noch
irgendeinen Wunsch?** is there anything
else you would like?; **irgendeine, r, s** pron
(Person) somebody; (Ding) something; (fragend,
verneinend) anybody/anything; **ich will nicht
bloß irgendein(e)s** I don't want any old
one; **irgendeinmal** adv sometime or other;
(fragend) ever; **irgendetwas** pron something;
(fragend, verneinend) anything; **irgendjemand**
pron somebody; (fragend, verneinend) anybody;
irgendwann adv sometime; **irgendwer** (umg)
pron somebody; (fragend, verneinend) anybody;
irgendwie adv somehow; **irgendwo** adv
somewhere (Brit), someplace (US); (fragend,
verneinend, bedingend) anywhere (Brit), any place
(US); **irgendwohin** adv somewhere (Brit),
someplace (US); (fragend, verneinend, bedingend)
anywhere (Brit), any place (US)
Irin ['i:rɪn] f Irishwoman; Irish girl
Iris ['i:rɪs] (-, -) f iris
irisch adj Irish; **I~e See** Irish Sea
IRK nt abk (= Internationales Rotes Kreuz) IRC
Irland ['ɪrlant] (-s) nt Ireland; (Republik Irland)
Eire
Irländer ['ɪrlɛndər] (-s, -) m = **Ire; Irländerin** f
= **Irin**
Ironie [iro'ni:] f irony
ironisch [i'ro:nɪʃ] adj ironic(al)
irre ['ɪrə] adj crazy, mad; **~ gut** (umg) way out
(umg); **Irre, r** f(m) lunatic; **irreführen** vt to
mislead; **Irreführung** f fraud
irrelevant ['ɪrelevant] adj: **~ (für)** irrelevant
(for od to)
irremachen vt to confuse
irren vi to be mistaken; (umherirren) to wander,
stray ▷ vr to be mistaken; **jeder kann**

sich mal ~ anyone can make a mistake;
Irrenanstalt f (veraltet) lunatic asylum;
Irrenhaus nt: **hier geht es zu wie im
Irrenhaus** (umg) this place is an absolute
madhouse
Irrfahrt ['ɪrfaːrt] f wandering
irrig ['ɪrɪç] adj incorrect, wrong
irritieren [ɪri'ti:rən] vt (verwirren) to confuse,
muddle; (ärgern) to irritate
Irr- zW: **Irrlicht** nt will-o'-the-wisp; **Irrsinn** m
madness; **so ein Irrsinn, das zu tun!** what
a crazy thing to do!; **irrsinnig** adj mad, crazy;
(umg) terrific; **irrsinnig komisch** incredibly
funny; **Irrtum** (-s, -tümer) m mistake, error;
im Irrtum sein to be wrong od mistaken;
Irrtum! wrong!; **irrtümlich** adj mistaken
ISBN f abk (= Internationale Standardbuchnummer)
ISBN
Ischias ['ɪʃias] (-) m od nt sciatica
ISDN-Anlage [i:|esdeː'|en-] m (Tel) ISDN
connection
Islam ['ɪslam] (-s) m Islam
islamisch [ɪs'la:mɪʃ] adj Islamic
Island ['i:slant] (-s) nt Iceland
Isländer, in ['i:slɛndər(ɪn)] (-s, -) m(f) Icelander
isländisch adj Icelandic
Isolation [izolatsi'o:n] f isolation; (Elek)
insulation; (von Häftlingen) solitary
confinement
Isolator [izo'la:tɔr] m insulator
Isolierband nt insulating tape
isolieren [izo'li:rən] vt to isolate; (Elek) to
insulate
Isolierstation f (Med) isolation ward
Isolierung f isolation; (Elek) insulation
Israel ['ɪsraeːl] (-s) nt Israel
Israeli[1] [ɪsra'e:li] (-(s), -s) m Israeli
Israeli[2] [ɪsra'e:li] (-, -(s)) f Israeli
israelisch adj Israeli
isst [ɪst] vb siehe **essen**
ist [ɪst] vb siehe **sein**
Istanbul ['ɪstambuːl] (-s) nt Istanbul
Istbestand m (Geld) cash in hand; (Waren)
actual stock
Italien [i'ta:liən] (-s) nt Italy
Italiener, in [itali'e:nər(ɪn)] (-s, -) m(f) Italian
italienisch adj Italian; **die ~e Schweiz** Italian-
speaking Switzerland
i. V., I. V. abk (= in Vertretung) on behalf of; (= in
Vollmacht) by proxy
IWF m abk (= Internationaler Währungsfonds)
IMF

Jj

J, j [jɔt] *nt* J, j; **J wie Julius** ≈ J for Jack, J for Jig (US)

ja [jaː] *adv* **1** yes; **haben Sie das gesehen? — ja** did you see it? — yes(, I did); **ich glaube ja** (yes) I think so; **zu allem Ja und Amen sagen** (*umg*) to accept everything without question **2** (*fragend*) really; **ich habe gekündigt — ja?** I've quit — have you?; **du kommst, ja?** you're coming, aren't you?

3: sei ja vorsichtig do be careful; **Sie wissen ja, dass ...** as you know, ...; **tu das ja nicht!** don't do that!; **sie ist ja erst fünf** (after all) she's only five; **Sie wissen ja, wie das so ist** you know how it is; **ich habe es ja gewusst** I just knew it; **ja, also ...** well you see ...

Jacht [jaxt] (-, **-en**) *f* yacht
Jacke ['jakə] (-, **-n**) *f* jacket; (*Wolljacke*) cardigan
Jacketkrone ['dʒɛ'kɪtkroːnə] *f* (*Zahnkrone*) jacket crown
Jackett [ʒa'kɛt] (-s, -s *od* -e) *nt* jacket
Jagd [jaːkt] (-, **-en**) *f* hunt; (*Jagen*) hunting; **Jagdbeute** *f* kill; **Jagdflugzeug** *nt* fighter; **Jagdgewehr** *nt* sporting gun; **Jagdhund** *m* hunting dog; **Jagdschein** *m* hunting licence (*Brit*) *od* license (US); **Jagdwurst** *f* smoked sausage
jagen ['jaːɡən] *vi* to hunt; (*eilen*) to race ▷ *vt* to hunt; (*wegjagen*) to drive (off); (*verfolgen*) to chase; **mit diesem Essen kannst du mich ~** (*umg*) I wouldn't touch that food with a barge pole (*Brit*) *od* ten-foot pole (US)
Jäger ['jɛːɡər] (-s, -) *m* hunter; **Jägerin** *f* huntress, huntswoman; **Jägerlatein** (*umg*) *nt* hunters' tales *pl*; **Jägerschnitzel** *nt* (*Koch*) cutlet *served with mushroom sauce*
jäh [jɛː] *adj* abrupt, sudden; (*steil*) steep, precipitous; **jählings** *adv* abruptly
Jahr [jaːr] (-(e)s, -e) *nt* year; **im ~(e) 1066** in (the year) 1066; **die Sechzigerjahre** *od* **sechziger ~e** the sixties *pl*; **mit dreißig ~en** at the age of thirty; **in den besten ~en sein** to be in the prime of (one's) life; **nach ~ und Tag** after (many) years; **zwischen den ~en** (*umg*) between Christmas and New Year; **jahraus**

adv: **jahraus, jahrein** year in, year out; **Jahrbuch** *nt* annual, year book
jahrelang *adv* for years
Jahres- *zW*: **Jahresabonnement** *nt* annual subscription; **Jahresabschluss** *m* end of the year; (*Comm*) annual statement of account; **Jahresbeitrag** *m* annual subscription; **Jahresbericht** *m* annual report; **Jahreshauptversammlung** *f* (*Comm*) annual general meeting, AGM; **Jahreskarte** *f* annual season ticket; **Jahrestag** *m* anniversary; **Jahresumsatz** *m* (*Comm*) yearly turnover; **Jahreswechsel** *m* turn of the year; **Jahreszahl** *f* date, year; **Jahreszeit** *f* season
Jahr- *zW*: **Jahrgang** *m* age group; (*von Wein*) vintage; **er ist Jahrgang 1950** he was born in 1950; **Jahrhundert** *nt* century; **Jahrhundertfeier** *f* centenary; **Jahrhundertwende** *f* turn of the century
jährlich ['jɛːrlɪç] *adj, adv* yearly; **zweimal ~** twice a year
Jahr- *zW*: **Jahrmarkt** *m* fair; **Jahrtausend** *nt* millennium; **Jahrzehnt** *nt* decade
Jähzorn ['jɛːtsɔrn] *m* hot temper
jähzornig *adj* hot-tempered
Jalousie [ʒalu'ziː] *f* venetian blind
Jamaika [ja'maɪka] (-s) *nt* Jamaica
Jammer ['jamər] (-s) *m* misery; **es ist ein ~, dass ...** it is a crying shame that ...
jämmerlich ['jɛmərlɪç] *adj* wretched, pathetic; **Jämmerlichkeit** *f* wretchedness
jammern *vi* to wail ▷ *vt unpers*: **es jammert mich** it makes me feel sorry
jammerschade *adj*: **es ist ~** it is a crying shame
Jan. *abk* (= *Januar*) Jan.
Januar ['janua:r] (-(s), -e) (*pl selten*) *m* January; *siehe auch* **September**
Japan ['ja:pan] (-s) *nt* Japan
Japaner, in [ja'pa:nər(ɪn)] (-s, -) *m(f)* Japanese
japanisch *adj* Japanese
Jargon [ʒar'ɡõ:] (-s, -s) *m* jargon
Jasager ['ja:za:ɡər] (-s, -) (*pej*) *m* yes man
Jastimme *f* vote in favour (*Brit*) *od* favor (US) (of)
jäten ['jɛːtən] *vt, vi* to weed
Jauche ['jauxə] *f* liquid manure; **Jauchegrube** *f* cesspool, cesspit
jauchzen ['jauxtsən] *vi* to rejoice, shout (with

joy)

Jauchzer (-s, -) m shout of joy
jaulen ['jaʊlən] vi to howl
Jause ['jaʊzə] (Österr) f snack
jawohl adv yes (of course)
Jawort nt consent; **jdm das ~ geben** to consent to marry sb; (bei Trauung) to say "I do"
Jazz [dʒæz] (-) m jazz; **Jazzkeller** m jazz club

⬤ SCHLÜSSELWORT

je [je:] adv 1 (jemals) ever; **hast du so was je gesehen?** did you ever see anything like it?
2 (jeweils) every, each; **sie zahlten je 15 Euro** they paid 15 euros each
▷ konj 1: **je nach** depending on; **je nachdem** it depends; **je nachdem, ob ...** depending on whether ...
2: **je eher, desto** od **umso besser** the sooner the better; **je länger, je lieber** the longer the better

Jeans [dʒiːnz] pl jeans pl; **Jeansanzug** m denim suit
jede, r, s ['je:də(r, s)] adj (einzeln) each; (von zweien) either; (jede von allen) every ▷ indef pron (einzeln) each (one); (jede von allen) everyone, everybody; **ohne ~ Anstrengung** without any effort; **~r Zweite** every other (one); **~s Mal** every time, each time
jedenfalls adv in any case
jedermann pron everyone; **das ist nicht ~s Sache** it's not everyone's cup of tea
jederzeit adv at any time
jedoch [je'dɔx] adv however
jeher ['je:he:r] adv: **von ~** all along
jein [jaɪn] adv (hum) yes no
jemals ['je:maːls] adv ever
jemand ['je:mant] indef pron someone, somebody; (bei Fragen, bedingenden Sätzen, Negation) anyone, anybody
Jemen ['je:mən] (-s) m Yemen
Jemenit, in [jeme'niːt(ɪn)] (-en, -en) m(f) Yemeni
jemenitisch adj Yemeni
Jenaer Glas® ['je:naərglaːs] nt heatproof glass, ≈ Pyrex®
jene, r, s ['je:nə(r, s)] adj that; (pl) those ▷ pron that one; (pl) those; (der Vorherige, die Vorherigen) the former
jenseits ['je:nzaɪts] adv on the other side ▷ präp +gen on the other side of, beyond; **Jenseits** nt: **das Jenseits** the hereafter, the beyond; **jdn ins Jenseits befördern** (umg) to send sb to kingdom come
Jesus ['je:zʊs] (Jesu) m Jesus; **~ Christus** Jesus Christ
jetten ['dʒɛtən] (umg) vi to jet (inf)
jetzig ['jɛtsɪç] adj present
jetzt [jɛtst] adv now; **~ gleich** right now
jeweilig adj respective; **die ~e Regierung** the government of the day
jeweils adv: **~ zwei zusammen** two at a time;

zu ~ 10 Euro at 10 euros each; **~ das Erste** the first each time; **~ am Monatsletzten** on the last day of each month
Jg. abk = **Jahrgang**
Jh. abk (= Jahrhundert) cent.
jiddisch ['jɪdɪʃ] adj Yiddish
Job [dʒɔp] (-s, -s) (umg) m job
jobben ['dʒɔbən] (umg) vi to work, have a job
Jobcenter ['dʒɔpsɛntər] nt job centre (Brit) od center
Jobmaschine ['dʒɔp-] f (umg) job-creation machine
Joch [jɔx] (-(e)s, -e) nt yoke
Jochbein nt cheekbone
Jockey, Jockei ['dʒɔke] (-s, -s) m jockey
Jod [joːt] (-(e)s) nt iodine
jodeln ['joːdəln] vi to yodel
joggen ['dʒɔgən] vi to jog
Joghurt, Jogurt ['joːgʊrt] (-s, -s) m od nt yog(h)urt
Johannisbeere [jo'hanɪsbeːrə] f: **Rote ~** redcurrant; **Schwarze ~** blackcurrant
johlen ['joːlən] vi to yell
Joint [dʒɔɪnt] (-s, -s) (umg) m joint
Joint Venture ['dʒɔɪntventʃər] (-, -s) nt joint venture
Jolle ['jɔlə] (-, -n) f dinghy
Jongleur [ʒõ'gløːr] (-s, -e) m juggler
jonglieren [ʒõ'gliːrən] vi to juggle
Joppe ['jɔpə] (-, -n) f jacket
Jordanien [jɔr'daːniən] (-s) nt Jordan
Jordanier, in (-s, -) m(f) Jordanian
jordanisch adj Jordanian
Journalismus [ʒʊrna'lɪsmʊs] m journalism
Journalist, in [ʒʊrna'lɪst(ɪn)] m(f) journalist; **journalistisch** adj journalistic
Jubel ['juːbəl] (-s) m rejoicing; **~, Trubel, Heiterkeit** laughter and merriment; **Jubeljahr** nt: **alle Jubeljahre (einmal)** (umg) once in a blue moon
jubeln vi to rejoice
Jubilar, in [jubi'laːr(ɪn)] (-s, -e) m(f) person celebrating an anniversary
Jubiläum [jubi'lɛːʊm] (-s, Jubiläen) nt jubilee; (Jahrestag) anniversary
jucken ['jʊkən] vi to itch ▷ vt: **es juckt mich am Arm** my arm is itching; **das juckt mich** that's itchy; **das juckt mich doch nicht** (umg) I don't care
Juckpulver nt itching powder
Juckreiz m itch
Judaslohn ['juːdaslʊoːn] m (liter) blood money
Jude ['juːdə] (-n, -n) m Jew
Juden- zW: **Judenstern** m star of David; **Judentum** (-s) nt (die Juden) Jewry; **Judenverfolgung** f persecution of the Jews
Jüdin ['jyːdɪn] f Jewess
jüdisch adj Jewish
Judo ['juːdo] (-(s)) nt judo
Jugend ['juːgənt] (-) f youth; **Jugendamt** nt youth welfare department; **jugendfrei** adj suitable for young people; (Film) U(-certificate), G (US); **Jugendherberge** f

youth hostel; **Jugendhilfe** f youth welfare scheme; **Jugendkriminalität** f juvenile crime; **jugendlich** adj youthful; **Jugendliche, r** f(m) teenager, young person; **Jugendliebe** f (Geliebte(r)) love of one's youth; **Jugendrichter** m juvenile court judge; **Jugendschutz** m protection of children and young people; **Jugendstil** m (Kunst) Art Nouveau; **Jugendstrafanstalt** f youth custody centre (Brit); **Jugendsünde** f youthful misdeed; **Jugendzentrum** nt youth centre (Brit) od center (US)

Jugoslawe [jugo'slaːvə] (**-n, -n**) m Yugoslav

Jugoslawien [jugo'slaːviən] (**-s**) nt Yugoslavia

Jugoslawin [jugo'slaːvɪn] f Yugoslav

jugoslawisch adj Yugoslav(ian)

Juli ['juːli] (**-(s), -s**) (pl selten) m July; siehe auch **September**

jun. abk (= junior) jun.

jung [jʊŋ] adj young

Junge (**-n, -n**) m boy, lad ▷ nt young animal; (pl) **young** pl

Jünger ['jʏŋər] (**-s, -**) m disciple

jünger adj younger

Jungfer (**-, -n**) f: **alte ~** old maid

Jungfernfahrt f maiden voyage

Jung- zW: **Jungfrau** f virgin; (Astrol) Virgo; **Junggeselle** m bachelor; **Junggesellin** f bachelor girl; (älter) single woman

Jüngling ['jʏŋlɪŋ] m youth

Jungsozialist m (Brd Pol) Young Socialist

jüngst [jʏŋst] adv lately, recently

jüngste, r, s adj youngest; (neueste) latest; **das J~ Gericht** the Last Judgement; **der J~ Tag** Doomsday, the Day of Judgement

Jungwähler, in m(f) young voter

Juni ['juːni] (**-(s), -s**) (pl selten) m June; siehe auch **September**

Junior ['juːnior] (**-s, -en**) m junior

Junta ['xʊnta] (**-, -ten**) f (Pol) junta

jur. abk = **juristisch**

Jura ['juːra] no art (Univ) law

Jurist, in [ju'rɪst(ɪn)] m(f) jurist, lawyer; (Student) law student; **juristisch** adj legal

Juso ['juːzo] (**-s, -s**) m abk = **Jungsozialist**

just [jʊst] adv just

Justiz [jus'tiːts] (**-**) f justice; **Justizbeamte, r** m judicial officer; **Justizirrtum** m miscarriage of justice; **Justizminister** m minister of justice; **Justizmord** m judicial murder

Juwel [ju'veːl] (**-s, -en**) m od nt jewel

Juwelier [juve'liːr] (**-s, -e**) m jeweller (Brit), jeweler (US); **Juweliergeschäft** nt jeweller's (Brit) od jeweler's (US) (shop)

Jux [jʊks] (**-es, -e**) m joke, lark; **etw aus ~ tun/ sagen** (umg) to do/say sth in fun

jwd [jɔtveːˈdeː] adv (hum) in the back of beyond

j

Kk

K, k [ka:] *nt* K, k; **K wie Kaufmann** ≈ K for King
Kabarett [kaba'rɛt] (**-s, -e** *od* **-s**) *nt* cabaret;
  Kabarettist, in [kabarɛ'tɪst(ɪn)] *m(f)* cabaret
  artiste
Kabel ['ka:bəl] (**-s, -**) *nt* (*Elek*) wire; (*stark*) cable;
  Kabelanschluss *m*: **~anschluss haben** to have
  cable television; **Kabelfernsehen** *nt* cable
  television
Kabeljau ['ka:bəljaʊ] (**-s, -e** *od* **-s**) *m* cod
kabeln *vt, vi* to cable
Kabelsalat (*umg*) *m* tangle of cable
Kabine [ka'bi:nə] *f* cabin; (*Zelle*) cubicle
Kabinett [kabi'nɛt] (**-s, -e**) *nt* (*Pol*) cabinet;
  (*kleines Zimmer*) small room ▷ *m* high-quality
  German white wine
Kabriolett [kabrio'lɛt] (**-s, -s**) *nt* (*Aut*)
  convertible
Kachel ['kaxəl] (**-, -n**) *f* tile
kacheln *vt* to tile
Kachelofen *m* tiled stove
Kacke ['kakə] (**-, -n**) (*umg!*) *f* crap (!)
Kadaver [ka'da:vər] (**-s, -**) *m* carcass
Kader ['ka:dər] (**-s, -**) *m* (*Mil, Pol*) cadre; (*Sport*)
  squad; (*DDR, Schweiz: Fachleute*) group of
  specialists; **Kaderschmiede** *f* (*Pol: umg*)
  institution for the training of cadre personnel
Kadett [ka'dɛt] (**-en, -en**) *m* cadet
Käfer ['kɛ:fər] (**-s, -**) *m* beetle
Kaff [kaf] (**-s, -s**) (*umg*) *nt* dump, hole
Kaffee ['kafe] (**-s, -s**) *m* coffee; **zwei ~, bitte!**
  two coffees, please; **das ist kalter ~** (*umg*)
  that's old hat; **Kaffeekanne** *f* coffeepot;
  Kaffeeklatsch *m*, **Kaffeekränzchen** *nt*
  coffee circle; **Kaffeelöffel** *m* coffee spoon;
  Kaffeemaschine *f* coffee maker; **Kaffeemühle**
  f coffee grinder; **Kaffeesatz** *m* coffee grounds
  pl; **Kaffeetante** *f* (*hum*) coffee addict; (*in Café*)
  old biddy; **Kaffeewärmer** *m* cosy (*for coffeepot*)
Käfig ['kɛ:fɪç] (**-s, -e**) *m* cage
kahl [ka:l] *adj* bald; **~ fressen** to strip bare;
  ~ geschoren shaven, shorn; **Kahlheit** *f*
  baldness; **kahlköpfig** *adj* bald-headed;
  Kahlschlag *m* (*in Wald*) clearing
Kahn [ka:n] (**-(e)s, ̈e**) *m* boat, barge
Kai [kaɪ] (**-s, -e** *od* **-s**) *m* quay
Kairo ['kaɪro] (**-s**) *nt* Cairo
Kaiser ['kaɪzər] (**-s, -**) *m* emperor; **Kaiserin** *f*
  empress; **kaiserlich** *adj* imperial; **Kaiserreich**
  nt empire; **Kaiserschmarren** ['kaizərʃmarən]
  m (*Koch*) sugared, *cut-up pancake with raisins*;
  Kaiserschnitt *m* (*Med*) Caesarean (*Brit*) *od*
  Cesarean (*US*) (section)
Kajak ['ka:jak] (**-s, -s**) *m or nt* kayak
Kajüte [ka'jy:tə] (**-, -n**) *f* cabin
Kakao [ka'ka:o] (**-s, -s**) *m* cocoa; **jdn durch
  den ~ ziehen** (*umg: veralbern*) to make fun of sb;
  (*: boshaft reden*) to run sb down
Kakerlak ['ka:kərlak] (**-en, -en**) *m* cockroach
Kaktee [kak'te:ə] (**-, -n**) *f* cactus
Kaktus ['kaktʊs] (**-, -se**) *m* cactus
Kalabrien [ka'la:briən] (**-s**) *nt* Calabria
Kalauer ['ka:laʊər] (**-s, -**) *m* corny joke;
  (*Wortspiel*) corny pun
Kalb [kalp] (**-(e)s, ̈er**) *nt* calf; **kalben** ['kalbən]
  vi to calve; **Kalbfleisch** *nt* veal
Kalbsleder *nt* calf(skin)
Kalender [ka'lɛndər] (**-s, -**) *m* calendar;
  (*Taschenkalender*) diary
Kali ['ka:li] (**-s, -s**) *nt* potash
Kaliber [ka'li:bər] (**-s, -**) *nt* (*lit, fig*) calibre (*Brit*),
  caliber (*US*)
Kalifornien [kali'fɔrniən] (**-s**) *nt* California
Kalk [kalk] (**-(e)s, -e**) *m* lime; (*Biol*) calcium;
  Kalkstein *m* limestone
Kalkül [kal'ky:l] (**-s, -e**) *m od nt* (*geh*) calculation
Kalkulation [kalkulatsi'o:n] *f* calculation
Kalkulator [kalku'la:tɔr] *m* cost accountant
kalkulieren [kalku'li:rən] *vt* to calculate
kalkuliert *adj*: **~es Risiko** calculated risk
Kalkutta [kal'kʊta] (**-s**) *nt* Calcutta
Kalorie [kalo'ri:] (**-, -n**) *f* calorie
kalorienarm *adj* low-calorie
kalt [kalt] *adj* cold; **mir ist (es) ~** I am cold;
  ~e Platte cold meat; **der K~e Krieg** the Cold
  War; **etw ~ stellen** to chill, to put sth to chill;
  die Wohnung kostet ~ 500 Euro the flat
  costs 500 euros without heating; **~ bleiben**
  to be unmoved; **~ lächelnd** (*ironisch*) cool as
  you please; **kaltblütig** *adj* cold-blooded; (*ruhig*)
  cool; **Kaltblütigkeit** *f* cold-bloodedness;
  coolness
Kälte ['kɛltə] (**-**) *f* coldness; (*Wetter*) cold;
  Kälteeinbruch *m* cold spell; **Kältegrad** *m*
  degree of frost *od* below zero; **Kältewelle** *f* cold
  spell
kalt- *zW*: **kaltherzig** *adj* cold-hearted;

kaltmachen (*umg*) *vt* to do in; **Kaltmiete** *f* rent exclusive of heating; **Kaltschale** *f* (*Koch*) cold *sweet soup*; **kaltschnäuzig** *adj* cold, unfeeling; **kaltstellen** *vt* (*fig*) to leave out in the cold

Kalzium ['kaltsiʊm] (**-s**) *nt* calcium

kam *etc* [kaːm] *vb siehe* **kommen**

Kambodscha [kamˈbɔdʒa] *nt* Cambodia

Kamel [kaˈmeːl] (**-(e)s, -e**) *nt* camel

Kamera ['kamera] (**-, -s**) *f* camera

Kamerad, in [kaməˈraːt, -ˈraːdɪn] (**-en, -en**) *m(f)* comrade, friend; **Kameradschaft** *f* comradeship; **kameradschaftlich** *adj* comradely

Kamera- *zW*: **Kameraführung** *f* camera work; **Kameramann** (**-(e)s**, *pl* **-männer**) *m* cameraman; **Kamerarekorder** *m* camcorder; **Kameratelefon** *nt* cameraphone

Kamerun ['kaməruːn] (**-s**) *nt* Cameroon

Kamille [kaˈmɪlə] (**-, -n**) *f* camomile

Kamillentee *m* camomile tea

Kamin [kaˈmiːn] (**-s, -e**) *m* (*außen*) chimney; (*innen*) fireside; (*Feuerstelle*) fireplace; **Kaminfeger** (**-s, -**) *m* chimney sweep; **Kaminkehrer** (**-s, -**) *m* chimney sweep

Kamm [kam] (**-(e)s, ̈-e**) *m* comb; (*Bergkamm*) ridge; (*Hahnenkamm*) crest; **alle/alles über einen ~ scheren** (*fig*) to lump everyone/everything together

kämmen ['kɛmən] *vt* to comb

Kammer ['kamər] (**-, -n**) *f* chamber; (*Zimmer*) small bedroom; **Kammerdiener** *m* valet; **Kammerjäger** *m* (*Schädlingsbekämpfer*) pest controller; **Kammermusik** *f* chamber music; **Kammerzofe** *f* chambermaid

Kammstück *nt* (*Koch*) shoulder

Kampagne [kamˈpanjə] (**-, -n**) *f* campaign

Kampf [kampf] (**-(e)s, ̈-e**) *m* fight, battle; (*Wettbewerb*) contest; (*fig: Anstrengung*) struggle; **jdm/etw den ~ ansagen** (*fig*) to declare war on sb/sth; **kampfbereit** *adj* ready for action

kämpfen ['kɛmpfən] *vi* to fight; **ich habe lange mit mir ~ müssen, ehe ...** I had a long battle with myself before ...

Kampfer ['kampfər] (**-s**) *m* camphor

Kämpfer, in (**-s, -**) *m(f)* fighter, combatant

Kampf- *zW*: **Kampfflugzeug** *nt* fighter (aircraft); **Kampfgeist** *m* fighting spirit; **Kampfhandlung** *f* action; **Kampfkunst** *f* martial arts *pl*; **kampflos** *adj* without a fight; **kampflustig** *adj* pugnacious; **Kampfplatz** *m* battlefield; (*Sport*) arena, stadium; **Kampfrichter** *m* (*Sport*) referee; **Kampfsport** *m* martial art

Kampuchea [kampuˈtʃeːa] (**-s**) *nt* Kampuchea

Kanada ['kanada] (**-s**) *nt* Canada

Kanadier, in [kaˈnaːdiər(ɪn)] (**-s, -**) *m(f)* Canadian

kanadisch [kaˈnaːdɪʃ] *adj* Canadian

Kanal [kaˈnaːl] (**-s, Kanäle**) *m* (*Fluss*) canal; (*Rinne*) channel; (*für Abfluss*) drain; **der ~** (*auch: der Ärmelkanal*) the (English) Channel

Kanalinseln *pl* Channel Islands *pl*

Kanalisation [kanalizatsi'oːn] *f* sewage system

kanalisieren [kanaliˈziːrən] *vt* to provide with a sewage system; (*fig: Energie etc*) to channel

Kanaltunnel *m* Channel Tunnel

Kanarienvogel [kaˈnaːriənfoːgəl] *m* canary

Kanarische Inseln [kaˈnaːrɪʃəˈɪnzəln] *pl* Canary Islands *pl*, Canaries *pl*

Kandare [kanˈdaːrə] (**-, -n**) *f*: **jdn an die ~ nehmen** (*fig*) to take sb in hand

Kandidat, in [kandiˈdaːt(ɪn)] (**-en, -en**) *m(f)* candidate; **jdn als ~en aufstellen** to nominate sb

Kandidatur [kandidaˈtuːr] *f* candidature, candidacy

kandidieren [kandiˈdiːrən] *vi* (*Pol*) to stand, run

kandiert [kanˈdiːrt] *adj* (*Frucht*) candied

Kandis ['kandɪs], **Kandiszucker** ['kandɪstsʊkər] (**-**) *m* rock candy

Känguru ['kɛŋguru] (**-s, -s**) *nt* kangaroo

Kaninchen [kaˈniːnçən] *nt* rabbit

Kanister [kaˈnɪstər] (**-s, -**) *m* can, canister

kann [kan] *vb siehe* **können**

Kännchen ['kɛnçən] *nt* pot; (*für Milch*) jug

Kanne ['kanə] (**-, -n**) *f* (*Krug*) jug; (*Kaffeekanne*) pot; (*Milchkanne*) churn; (*Gießkanne*) watering can

Kannibale [kaniˈbaːlə] (**-n, -n**) *m* cannibal

kannte *etc* ['kantə] *vb siehe* **kennen**

Kanon ['kaːnɔn] (**-s, -s**) *m* canon

Kanone [kaˈnoːnə] (**-, -n**) *f* gun; (*Hist*) cannon; (*fig: Mensch*) ace; **das ist unter aller ~** (*umg*) that defies description

Kanonenfutter (*umg*) *nt* cannon fodder

Kant. *abk* = **Kanton**

Kantate [kanˈtaːtə] (**-, -n**) *f* cantata

Kante ['kantə] (**-, -n**) *f* edge; **Geld auf die hohe ~ legen** (*umg*) to put money by

kantig ['kantɪç] *adj* (*Holz*) edged; (*Gesicht*) angular

Kantine [kanˈtiːnə] *f* canteen

Kanton [kanˈtoːn] (**-s, -e**) *m* canton

Kantor ['kantɔr] *m* choirmaster

Kanu ['kaːnu] (**-s, -s**) *nt* canoe

Kanzel ['kantsəl] (**-, -n**) *f* pulpit; (*Aviat*) cockpit

Kanzlei [kantsˈlai] *f* chancery; (*Büro*) chambers *pl*

Kanzler, in ['kantslər] (**-s, -**) *m(f)* chancellor

Kanzlerkandidatur *f* candidacy for the chancellorship

Kap [kap] (**-s, -s**) *nt* cape; **das ~ der guten Hoffnung** the Cape of Good Hope

Kapazität [kapatsiˈtɛːt] *f* capacity; (*Fachmann*) authority

Kapelle [kaˈpɛlə] *f* (*Gebäude*) chapel; (*Mus*) band

Kapellmeister, in *m(f)* director of music; (*Mil, von Tanzkapelle etc*) bandmaster, bandleader

Kaper ['kaːpər] (**-, -n**) *f* caper

kapern *vt* to capture

kapieren [kaˈpiːrən] (*umg*) *vt, vi* to understand

Kapital [kapiˈtaːl] (**-s, -e** *od* **-ien**) *nt* capital; **aus etw ~ schlagen** (*pej: lit, fig*) to make capital out of sth; **Kapitalanlage** *f*

k

investment; **Kapitalaufwand** m capital expenditure; **Kapitalertrag** m capital gains pl; **Kapitalertragssteuer** f capital gains tax; **Kapitalflucht** f flight of capital; **Kapitalgesellschaft** f (Comm) joint-stock company; **Kapitalgüter** pl capital goods pl; **kapitalintensiv** adj capital-intensive

Kapitalismus [kapita'lɪsmʊs] m capitalism

Kapitalist [kapita'lɪst] m capitalist

kapitalistisch adj capitalist

Kapital- zW: **kapitalkräftig** adj wealthy; **Kapitalmarkt** m money market; **kapitalschwach** adj financially weak; **kapitalstark** adj financially strong; **Kapitalverbrechen** nt serious crime; (mit Todesstrafe) capital crime

Kapitän [kapi'tɛːn] (-s, -e) m captain

Kapitel [ka'pɪtəl] (-s, -) nt chapter; **ein trauriges ~** (Angelegenheit) a sad story

Kapitulation [kapitulatsi'oːn] f capitulation

kapitulieren [kapitu'liːrən] vi to capitulate

Kaplan [ka'plaːn] (-s, **Kapläne**) m chaplain

Kappe ['kapə] (-, -n) f cap; (Kapuze) hood; **das nehme ich auf meine ~** (fig: umg) I'll take the responsibility for that

kappen vt to cut

Kapsel ['kapsəl] (-, -n) f capsule

Kapstadt ['kapʃtat] nt Cape Town

kaputt [ka'pʊt] (umg) adj smashed, broken; (Person) exhausted, knackered; **etw ~ machen/schlagen** to break/smash sth; **der Fernseher ist ~** the TV's not working; **ein ~er Typ** a bum; siehe auch **kaputtmachen**; **kaputtgehen** unreg vi to break; (Schuhe) to fall apart; (Firma) to go bust; (Stoff) to wear out; (sterben) to cop it (umg); **kaputtlachen** vr to laugh o.s. silly; **kaputtmachen** vt to break; (Mensch) to exhaust, wear out; **kaputtschlagen** unreg vt to smash

Kapuze [ka'puːtsə] (-, -n) f hood

Karabiner [kara'biːnər] (-s, -) m (Gewehr) carbine

Karacho [ka'raxo] (-s) nt: **mit ~** (umg) hell for leather

Karaffe [ka'rafə] (-, -n) f carafe; (geschliffen) decanter

Karambolage [karambo'laːʒə] (-, -n) f (Zusammenstoß) crash

Karamell [kara'mɛl] (-s) m caramel; **Karamellbonbon** m od nt toffee

Karat [ka'raːt] (-(e)s, -e) nt carat

Karate (-s) nt karate

Karawane [kara'vaːnə] (-, -n) f caravan

Kardinal [kardi'naːl] (-s, **Kardinäle**) m cardinal; **Kardinalfehler** m cardinal error; **Kardinalzahl** f cardinal number

Karenzzeit [ka'rɛntstsait] f waiting period

Karfreitag [kaːr'fraitaːk] m Good Friday

karg [kark] adj scanty, poor; (Mahlzeit) meagre (Brit), meager (US); **etw ~ bemessen** to be mean with sth; **Kargheit** f poverty, scantiness; meagreness (Brit), meagerness (US)

kärglich ['kɛrklɪç] adj poor, scanty

Kargo ['kargo] (-s, -s) m (Comm) cargo

Karibik [ka'riːbɪk] (-) f: **die ~** the Caribbean

karibisch adj Caribbean; **das K~e Meer** the Caribbean Sea

kariert [ka'riːrt] adj (Stoff) checked (Brit), checkered (US); (Papier) squared; **~ reden** (umg) to talk rubbish od nonsense

Karies ['kaːries] (-) f caries

Karikatur [karika'tuːr] f caricature; **Karikaturist, in** [karikatu:'rɪst(ɪn)] m(f) cartoonist

karikieren [kari'kiːrən] vt to caricature

karitativ [karita'tiːf] adj charitable

Karneval ['karnəval] (-s, -e od -s) m carnival; see culture note

KARNEVAL

Karneval is the name given to the days immediately before Lent when people gather to sing, dance, eat, drink and generally make merry before the fasting begins. Rosenmontag, the day before Shrove Tuesday, is the most important day of Karneval on the Rhine. Most firms take a day's holiday on that day to enjoy the parades and revelry. In South Germany Karneval is called "Fasching".

Karnickel [kar'nɪkəl] (-s, -) (umg) nt rabbit

Kärnten ['kɛrntən] (-s) nt Carinthia

Karo ['kaːro] (-s, -s) nt square; (Karten) diamonds; **Karoass** nt ace of diamonds

Karosse [ka'rɔsə] (-, -n) f coach, carriage

Karosserie [karɔsə'riː] f (Aut) body(work)

Karotte [ka'rɔtə] (-, -n) f carrot

Karpaten [kar'paːtən] pl Carpathians pl

Karpfen ['karpfən] (-s, -) m carp

Karre ['karə] (-, -n) f = **Karren**

Karree [ka'reː] (-s, -s) nt: **einmal ums ~ gehen** (umg) to walk around the block

karren ['karən] vt to cart, transport; **Karren** (-s, -) m cart, barrow; **den Karren aus dem Dreck ziehen** (umg) to get things sorted out

Karriere [kari'ɛːrə] (-, -n) f career; **~ machen** to get on, get to the top; **Karrieremacher, in** m(f) careerist

Karsamstag [kaːr'zamstaːk] m Easter Saturday

Karst [karst] (-s, -e) m (Geog, Geol) karst, barren landscape

Karte ['kartə] (-, -n) f card; (Landkarte) map; (Speisekarte) menu; (Eintrittskarte, Fahrkarte) ticket; **mit offenen ~n spielen** (fig) to put one's cards on the table; **alles auf eine ~ setzen** to put all one's eggs in one basket

Kartei [kar'tai] f card index; **Karteikarte** f index card; **Karteileiche** (umg) f sleeping od non-active member; **Karteischrank** m filing cabinet

Kartell [kar'tɛl] (-s, -e) nt cartel; **Kartellamt** nt monopolies commission; **Kartellgesetzgebung** f anti-trust legislation

Karten- zW: **Kartenhaus** nt (lit, fig) house of cards; **Kartenlegen** nt fortune-telling (using cards); **Kartenspiel** nt card game; (Karten) pack (Brit) od deck (US) of cards; **Kartentelefon** nt cardphone; **Kartenvorverkauf** m advance sale of tickets

Kartoffel [kar'tɔfəl] (-, -n) f potato; **Kartoffelbrei** m mashed potatoes pl; **Kartoffelchips** pl potato crisps pl (Brit), potato chips pl (US); **Kartoffelpüree** nt mashed potatoes pl; **Kartoffelsalat** m potato salad

Karton [kar'tõ:] (-s, -s) m cardboard; (Schachtel) cardboard box

kartoniert [karto'ni:rt] adj hardback

Karussell [karʊ'sɛl] (-s, -s) nt roundabout (Brit), merry-go-round

Karwoche ['ka:rvɔxə] f Holy Week

Karzinom [kartsi'no:m] (-s, -e) nt (Med) carcinoma

Kasachstan [kazaxs'ta:n] (-s) nt (Geog) Kazakhstan

Kaschemme [ka'ʃɛmə] (-, -n) f dive

kaschieren [ka'ʃi:rən] vt to conceal, cover up

Kaschmir ['kaʃmi:r] (-s) nt (Geog) Kashmir

Käse ['kɛ:zə] (-s, -) m cheese; (umg: Unsinn) rubbish, twaddle; **Käseblatt** (umg) nt (local) rag; **Käseglocke** f cheese cover; **Käsekuchen** m cheesecake

Kaserne [ka'zɛrnə] (-, -n) f barracks pl

Kasernenhof m parade ground

käsig ['kɛ:zɪç] adj (fig: umg: Gesicht, Haut) pasty, pale; (vor Schreck) white; (lit) cheesy

Kasino [ka'zi:no] (-s, -s) nt club; (Mil) officers' mess; (Spielkasino) casino

Kaskoversicherung ['kaskofɛrzɪçərʊŋ] f (Aut: Teilkaskoversicherung) ≈ third party, fire and theft insurance; (: Vollkaskoversicherung) fully comprehensive insurance

Kasper ['kaspər] (-s, -) m Punch; (fig) clown

Kasperletheater ['kaspərlətea:tər], **Kasperltheater** ['kaspərltea:tər] nt Punch and Judy (show)

Kaspisches Meer ['kaspɪʃəs'me:r] nt Caspian Sea

Kasse ['kasə] (-, -n) f (Geldkasten) cashbox; (in Geschäft) till, cash register; (Kinokasse, Theaterkasse etc) box office; (Krankenkasse) health insurance; (Sparkasse) savings bank; **die ~ führen** to be in charge of the money; **jdn zur ~ bitten** to ask sb to pay up; **~ machen** to count the money; **getrennte ~ führen** to pay separately; **an der ~** (in Geschäft) at the (cash) desk; **gut bei ~ sein** to be in the money

Kasseler ['kasələr] (-s, -) nt lightly smoked pork loin

Kassen- zW: **Kassenarzt** m ≈ National Health doctor (Brit), ≈ panel doctor (US); **Kassenbestand** m cash balance; **Kassenführer** m (Comm) cashier; **Kassenpatient** m ≈ National Health patient (Brit); **Kassenprüfung** f audit; **Kassenschlager** (umg) m (Theat etc) box-office hit; (: Ware) big seller; **Kassensturz** m: **Kassensturz machen** to check one's money; **Kassenwart** m (von Klub

etc) treasurer; **Kassenzettel** m sales slip

Kasserolle [kasə'rɔlə] (-, -n) f casserole

Kassette [ka'sɛtə] f small box; (Tonband, Phot) cassette; (Comput) cartridge, cassette; (Bücherkassette) case

Kassettenrekorder (-s, -) m cassette recorder

Kassiber [ka'si:bər] (-s, -) m (in Gefängnis) secret message

kassieren [ka'si:rən] vt (Gelder etc) to collect; (umg: wegnehmen) to take (away) ▷ vi: **darf ich ~?** would you like to pay now?

Kassierer, in [ka'si:rər(ɪn)] (-s, -) m(f) cashier; (von Klub) treasurer

Kastanie [kas'ta:niə] f chestnut

Kastanienbaum m chestnut tree

Kästchen ['kɛstçən] nt small box, casket

Kaste ['kastə] (-, -n) f caste

Kasten ['kastən] (-s, ⸚) m box (auch Sport), case; (Truhe) chest; **er hat was auf dem ~** (umg) he's brainy; **Kastenform** f (Koch) (square) baking tin (Brit) od pan (US); **Kastenwagen** m van

kastrieren [kas'tri:rən] vt to castrate

Kat (-, -s) m abk (Aut) = **Katalysator**

katalanisch [kata'la:nɪʃ] adj Catalan

Katalog [kata'lo:k] (-(e)s, -e) m catalogue (Brit), catalog (US)

katalogisieren [katalogi'zi:rən] vt to catalogue (Brit), catalog (US)

Katalysator [kataly'za:tɔr] m (lit, fig) catalyst; (Aut) catalytic converter; **~-Auto** vehicle fitted with a catalytic converter

Katapult [kata'pʊlt] (-(e)s, -e) nt or m catapult

katapultieren [katapʊl'ti:rən] vt to catapult ▷ vr to catapult o.s.; (Pilot) to eject

Katar ['ka:tar] nt Qatar

Katarrh, Katarr [ka'tar] (-s, -e) m catarrh

Katasteramt [ka'tastəramt] nt land registry

katastrophal [katastro'fa:l] adj catastrophic

Katastrophe [kata'stro:fə] (-, -n) f catastrophe, disaster

Katastrophen- zW: **Katastrophenalarm** m emergency alert; **Katastrophengebiet** nt disaster area; **Katastrophenmedizin** f medical treatment in disasters; **Katastrophenmeldung** f news of a/the catastrophe; **Katastrophenschutz** m disaster control

Katechismus [katɛ'çɪsmʊs] m catechism

Kategorie [katego'ri:] f category

kategorisch [kate'go:rɪʃ] adj categorical

kategorisieren [kategori'zi:rən] vt to categorize

Kater ['ka:tər] (-s, -) m tomcat; (umg) hangover; **Katerfrühstück** nt breakfast (of pickled herring etc) to cure a hangover

kath. abk = **katholisch**

Katheder [ka'te:dər] (-s, -) nt (Sch) teacher's desk; (Univ) lectern

Kathedrale [kate'dra:lə] (-, -n) f cathedral

Katheter [ka'te:tər] (-s, -) m (Med) catheter

Kathode [ka'to:də] (-, -n) f cathode

Katholik, in [kato'li:k(ɪn)] (-en, -en) m(f) Catholic

k

katholisch [ka'to:lɪʃ] *adj* Catholic

Katholizismus [katoli'tsɪsmʊs] *m* Catholicism

Katode [ka'to:də] (-, -n) *f* = **Kathode**

katzbuckeln ['katsbʊkəln] (*pej: umg*) *vi* to bow and scrape

Kätzchen ['kɛtsçən] *nt* kitten

Katze ['katsə] (-, -n) *f* cat; **die ~ im Sack kaufen** to buy a pig in a poke; **für die Katz** (*umg*) in vain, for nothing

Katzen- *zW*: **Katzenauge** *nt* cat's-eye (*Brit*); (*am Fahrrad*) rear light; **Katzenjammer** (*umg*) *m* hangover; **Katzenmusik** *f* (*fig*) caterwauling; **Katzensprung** (*umg*) *m* stone's throw, short distance; **Katzentür** *f* cat flap; **Katzenwäsche** *f* a lick and a promise

Kauderwelsch ['kaʊdərvɛlʃ] (-(s)) *nt* jargon; (*umg*) double Dutch (*Brit*)

kauen ['kaʊən] *vt, vi* to chew

kauern ['kaʊərn] *vi* to crouch

Kauf [kaʊf] (-(e)s, **Käufe**) *m* purchase, buy; (*Kaufen*) buying; **ein guter ~** a bargain; **etw in ~ nehmen** to put up with sth

kaufen *vt* to buy; **dafür kann ich mir nichts ~** (*ironisch*) what use is that to me!

Käufer, in ['kɔʏfər(ɪn)] (-s, -) *m(f)* buyer

Käuferverhalten *nt* buying habits *pl*

Kauf- *zW*: **Kauffrau** *f* businesswoman; (*Einzelhandelskauffrau*) shopkeeper; **kauffreudig** *adj* consumerist; **Kaufhaus** *nt* department store; **Kaufkraft** *f* purchasing power; **Kaufladen** *m* shop, store

käuflich ['kɔʏflɪç] *adj* purchasable, for sale; (*pej*) venal ▷ *adv*: **~ erwerben** to purchase

Kauf- *zW*: **Kauflust** *f* desire to buy things; (*Börse*) buying; **kauflustig** *adj* interested in buying; **Kaufmann** (-(e)s, *pl* **-leute**) *m* businessman; (*Einzelhandelskaufmann*) shopkeeper; **kaufmännisch** *adj* commercial; **kaufmännischer Angestellter** clerk; **Kaufpreis** *m* purchase price; **kaufsüchtig** *adj*: **kaufsüchtig sein** to be a shopaholic (*umg*); **Kaufvertrag** *m* bill of sale; **Kaufwillige, r** *f(m)* potential buyer; **Kaufzurückhaltung** *f* consumer reticence; **Kaufzwang** *m*: **kein/ ohne Kaufzwang** no/without obligation

Kaugummi ['kaʊgʊmi] *m* chewing gum

Kaukasus ['kaʊkazʊs] *m*: **der ~** the Caucasus

Kaulquappe ['kaʊlkvapə] (-, -n) *f* tadpole

kaum [kaʊm] *adv* hardly, scarcely; **wohl ~, ich glaube ~** I hardly think so

Kausalzusammenhang [kaʊ'za:ltsuzamənhaŋ] *m* causal connection

Kaution [kaʊtsi'o:n] *f* deposit; (*Jur*) bail

Kautschuk ['kaʊtʃʊk] (-s, -e) *m* India rubber

Kauz [kaʊts] (-es, **Käuze**) *m* owl; (*fig*) queer fellow

Kavalier [kava'li:r] (-s, -e) *m* gentleman

Kavaliersdelikt *nt* peccadillo

Kavallerie [kavalə'ri:] *f* cavalry

Kavallerist [kavalə'rɪst] *m* cavalryman

Kaviar ['ka:viar] *m* caviar

KB *nt abk* (= *Kilobyte*) KB, kbyte

Kcal *abk* (= *Kilokalorie*) kcal

keck [kɛk] *adj* daring, bold; **Keckheit** *f* daring, boldness

Kegel ['ke:gəl] (-s, -) *m* skittle; (*Math*) cone; **Kegelbahn** *f* skittle alley, bowling alley; **kegelförmig** *adj* conical

kegeln *vi* to play skittles

Kehle ['ke:lə] (-, -n) *f* throat; **er hat das in die falsche ~ bekommen** (*lit*) it went down the wrong way; (*fig*) he took it the wrong way; **aus voller ~** at the top of one's voice

Kehl- *zW*: **Kehlkopf** *m* larynx; **Kehlkopfkrebs** *m* cancer of the throat; **Kehllaut** *m* guttural

Kehre ['ke:rə] (-, -n) *f* turn(ing), bend

kehren *vt, vi* (*wenden*) to turn; (*mit Besen*) to sweep; **sich an etw** *dat* **nicht ~** not to heed sth; **in sich** *akk* **gekehrt** (*versunken*) pensive; (*verschlossen*) introspective, introverted

Kehricht (-s) *m* sweepings *pl*

Kehr- *zW*: **Kehrmaschine** *f* sweeper; **Kehrreim** *m* refrain; **Kehrseite** *f* reverse, other side; (*ungünstig*) wrong *od* bad side; **die Kehrseite der Medaille** the other side of the coin

kehrtmachen *vi* to turn about, about-turn

Kehrtwendung *f* about-turn

keifen ['kaɪfən] *vi* to scold, nag

Keil [kaɪl] (-(e)s, -e) *m* wedge; (*Mil*) arrowhead; **keilen** *vt* to wedge ▷ *vr* to fight

Keilerei [kaɪlə'raɪ] (*umg*) *f* punch-up

Keilriemen *m* (*Aut*) fan belt

Keim [kaɪm] (-(e)s, -e) *m* bud; (*Med, fig*) germ; **etw im ~ ersticken** to nip sth in the bud

keimen *vi* to germinate

Keim- *zW*: **keimfrei** *adj* sterile; **keimtötend** *adj* antiseptic, germicidal; **Keimzelle** *f* (*fig*) nucleus

kein ['kaɪn], **keine** ['kaɪnə] *pron* none ▷ *adj* no, not any; **~e schlechte Idee** not a bad idea; **~e Stunde/drei Monate** (*nicht einmal*) less than an hour/three months

keine, r, s *indef pron* no one, nobody; (*von Gegenstand*) none

keinerlei ['kaɪnər'laɪ] *adj attrib* no ... whatever

keinesfalls *adv* on no account

keineswegs *adv* by no means

keinmal *adv* not once

Keks [ke:ks] (-es, -e) *m od nt* biscuit (*Brit*), cookie (*US*)

Kelch [kɛlç] (-(e)s, -e) *m* cup, goblet, chalice

Kelle ['kɛlə] (-, -n) *f* ladle; (*Maurerkelle*) trowel

Keller ['kɛlər] (-s, -) *m* cellar; **Kellerassel** (-, -n) *f* woodlouse

Kellerei [kɛlə'raɪ] *f* wine cellars *pl*; (*Firma*) wine producer

Kellergeschoss *nt* basement

Kellerwohnung *f* basement flat (*Brit*) *od* apartment (*US*)

Kellner, in ['kɛlnər(ɪn)] (-s, -) *m(f)* waiter, waitress

kellnern (*umg*) *vi* to work as a waiter/waitress (*Brit*), wait on tables (*US*)

Kelte ['kɛltə] (-n, -n) *m* Celt

Kelter (-, -n) *f* winepress; (*Obstkelter*) press

keltern ['kɛltərn] *vt* to press

Keltin ['kɛltɪn] f (female) Celt
keltisch adj Celtic
Kenia ['ke:nia] (-s) nt Kenya
kennen ['kɛnən] unreg vt to know; **~ Sie sich schon?** do you know each other (already)?; **kennst du mich noch?** do you remember me?
kennenlernen vt to get to know ▷ vr to get to know each other; (zum ersten Mal) to meet
Kenner, in (-s, -) m(f): **~ (von** od **+gen)** connoisseur (of); expert (on)
Kennkarte f identity card
kenntlich adj distinguishable, discernible; **etw ~ machen** to mark sth
Kenntnis (-, -se) f knowledge no pl; **etw zur ~ nehmen** to note sth; **von etw ~ nehmen** to take notice of sth; **jdn in ~ setzen** to inform sb; **über ~se von etw verfügen** to be knowledgeable about sth
Kenn- zW: **Kennwort** nt (Chiffre) code name; (Losungswort) password, code word; **Kennzeichen** nt mark, characteristic; **(amtliches/polizeiliches) Kennzeichen** (Aut) number plate (Brit), license plate (US); **kennzeichnen** vt untr to characterize; **kennzeichnenderweise** adv characteristically; **Kennziffer** f (code) number; (Comm) reference number
kentern ['kɛntərn] vi to capsize
Keramik [ke'ra:mɪk] (-, -en) f ceramics pl, pottery; (Gegenstand) piece of ceramic work od pottery
Kerbe ['kɛrbə] (-, -n) f notch, groove
Kerbel (-s, -) m chervil
kerben vt to notch
Kerbholz nt: **etw auf dem ~ haben** to have done sth wrong
Kerker ['kɛrkər] (-s, -) m prison
Kerl [kɛrl] (-s, -e) (umg) m chap, bloke (Brit), guy; **du gemeiner ~!** you swine!
Kern [kɛrn] (-(e)s, -e) m (Obstkern) pip, stone; (Nusskern) kernel; (Atomkern) nucleus; (fig) heart, core; **Kernenergie** f nuclear energy; **Kernfach** nt (Sch) core subject; **Kernfamilie** f nuclear family; **Kernforschung** f nuclear research; **Kernfrage** f central issue; **Kernfusion** f nuclear fusion; **Kerngehäuse** nt core; **kerngesund** adj thoroughly healthy, fit as a fiddle
kernig adj robust; (Ausspruch) pithy
Kern- zW: **Kernkompetenz** f core competence; **Kernkraftwerk** nt nuclear power station; **Kernland** f heartland; **kernlos** adj seedless, pipless; **Kernphysik** f nuclear physics sing; **Kernreaktion** f nuclear reaction; **Kernreaktor** m nuclear reactor; **Kernschmelze** f meltdown; **Kernseife** f washing soap; **Kernspaltung** f nuclear fission; **Kernstück** nt (fig) main item; (von Theorie etc) central part, core; **Kernwaffen** pl nuclear weapons pl; **kernwaffenfrei** adj nuclear-free; **Kernzeit** f core time
Kerze ['kɛrtsə] (-, -n) f candle; (Zündkerze) plug
Kerzen- zW: **kerzengerade** adj straight as a die; **Kerzenhalter** m candlestick;

Kerzenständer m candleholder
kess [kɛs] adj saucy
Kessel ['kɛsəl] (-s, -) m kettle; (von Lokomotive etc) boiler; (Mulde) basin; (Geog) depression; (Mil) encirclement; **Kesselstein** m scale, fur (Brit); **Kesseltreiben** nt (fig) witch-hunt
Kette ['kɛtə] (-, -n) f chain; **jdn an die ~ legen** (fig) to tie sb down
ketten vt to chain
Ketten- zW: **Kettenfahrzeug** nt tracked vehicle; **Kettenhund** m watchdog; **Kettenkarussell** nt merry-go-round (with gondolas on chains); **Kettenladen** m chain store; **Kettenrauchen** nt chain smoking; **Kettenreaktion** f chain reaction
Ketzer, in ['kɛtsər(ɪn)] (-s, -) m(f) heretic; **Ketzerei** [kɛtsə'raɪ] f heresy; **ketzerisch** adj heretical
keuchen ['kɔʏçən] vi to pant, gasp
Keuchhusten m whooping cough
Keule ['kɔʏlə] (-, -n) f club; (Koch) leg
Keulung ['kɔʏlʊŋ] f cull, culling
keusch [kɔʏʃ] adj chaste; **Keuschheit** f chastity
Kfm. abk = **Kaufmann**
kfm. abk = **kaufmännisch**
Kfz (-(s), -(s)) f abk = **Kraftfahrzeug**
KG (-, -s) f abk = **Kommanditgesellschaft**
kg abk (= Kilogramm) kg
kHz abk (= Kilohertz) kHz
Kibbuz [kɪ'bu:ts] (-, **Kibbuzim** od **-e**) m kibbutz
kichern ['kɪçərn] vi to giggle
kicken ['kɪkən] vt, vi (Fußball) to kick
kidnappen ['kɪtnɛpən] vt to kidnap
Kidnapper, in (-s, -) m(f) kidnapper
Kiebitz ['ki:bɪts] (-es, -e) m peewit
Kiefer[1] ['ki:fər] (-s, -) m jaw
Kiefer[2] ['ki:fər] (-, -n) f pine
Kiefernholz nt pine(wood)
Kiefernzapfen m pine cone
Kieferorthopäde m orthodontist
Kieker ['ki:kər] (-s, -) m: **jdn auf dem ~ haben** (umg) to have it in for sb
Kiel [ki:l] (-(e)s, -e) m (Federkiel) quill; (Naut) keel; **Kielwasser** nt wake
Kieme ['ki:mə] (-, -n) f gill
Kies [ki:s] (-es, -e) m gravel; (umg: Geld) money, dough
Kiesel ['ki:zəl] (-s, -) m pebble; **Kieselstein** m pebble
Kiesgrube f gravel pit
Kiesweg m gravel path
Kiew ['ki:ɛf] (-s) nt Kiev
kiffen ['kɪfən] (umg) vt to smoke pot od grass
Kilimandscharo [kiliman'dʒa:ro] (-s) m Kilimanjaro
Killer ['kɪlər] (-s, -) (umg) m killer, murderer; (gedungener) hit man; **Killerin** (umg) f killer, female murderer, murderess
Kilo ['ki:lo] (-s, -(s)) nt kilo; **Kilobyte** [kilo'baɪt] nt (Comput) kilobyte; **Kilogramm** [kilo'gram] nt kilogram
Kilometer [kilo'me:tər] m kilometre (Brit), kilometer (US); **Kilometerfresser** (umg)

m long-haul driver; **Kilometergeld** *nt* ≈ mileage (allowance); **Kilometerstand** *m* ≈ mileage; **Kilometerstein** *m* ≈ milestone; **Kilometerzähler** *m* ≈ mileometer

Kilowatt [kilo'vat] *nt* kilowatt

Kimme ['kɪmə] (-, -n) *f* notch; (*Gewehr*) back sight

Kind [kɪnt] (-(e)s, -er) *nt* child; **sich freuen wie ein ~** to be as pleased as Punch; **mit ~ und Kegel** (*hum: umg*) with the whole family; **von ~ auf** from childhood

Kinderarzt *m* paediatrician (*Brit*), pediatrician (*US*)

Kinderbett *nt* cot (*Brit*), crib (*US*)

Kinderei [kɪndə'raɪ] *f* childishness

Kindererziehung *f* bringing up of children; (*durch Schule*) education of children

kinderfeindlich *adj* anti-children; (*Architektur, Planung*) not catering for children

Kinderfreibetrag *m* child allowance

Kindergarten *m* nursery school; *see culture note*

⬤ **KINDERGARTEN**

A *Kindergarten* is a nursery school for children aged between 3 and 6 years. The children sing, play and do handicrafts. They are not taught the three Rs at this stage. Most Kindergartens are financed by the town or the church and not by the state. Parents pay a monthly contribution towards the cost.

Kinder- *zW*: **Kindergärtner, in** *m(f)* nursery-school teacher; **Kindergeld** *nt* child benefit (*Brit*); **Kinderheim** *nt* children's home; **Kinderkrankheit** *f* childhood illness; **Kinderladen** *m* (alternative) playgroup; **Kinderlähmung** *f* polio(myelitis); **kinderleicht** *adj* childishly easy; **kinderlieb** *adj* fond of children; **Kinderlied** *nt* nursery rhyme; **kinderlos** *adj* childless; **Kindermädchen** *nt* nursemaid; **Kinderpflegerin** *f* child minder; **kinderreich** *adj* with a lot of children; **Kinderschuh** *m*: **es steckt noch in den Kinderschuhen** (*fig*) it's still in its infancy; **Kinderspiel** *nt* child's play; **ein Kinderspiel sein** to be a doddle; **Kinderstube** *f*: **eine gute Kinderstube haben** to be well-mannered; **Kindertagesstätte** *f* day-nursery; **Kinderteller** *m* children's dish; **Kinderwagen** *m* pram (*Brit*), baby carriage (*US*); **Kinderzimmer** *nt* child's/children's room; (*für Kleinkinder*) nursery

Kindes- *zW*: **Kindesalter** *nt* infancy; **Kindesbeine** *pl*: **von Kindesbeinen an** from early childhood; **Kindesmisshandlung** *f* child abuse

Kind- *zW*: **kindgemäß** *adj* suitable for a child *od* children; **Kindheit** *f* childhood; **kindisch** *adj* childish; **kindlich** *adj* childlike

kindsköpfig *adj* childish

Kinkerlitzchen ['kɪŋkərlɪtsçən] (*umg*) *pl* knick-

knacks *pl*

Kinn [kɪn] (-(e)s, -e) *nt* chin; **Kinnhaken** *m* (*Boxen*) uppercut; **Kinnlade** *f* jaw

Kino ['kiːno] (-s, -s) *nt* cinema (*Brit*), movies (*US*); **Kinobesucher** *m*, **Kinogänger** *m* cinema-goer (*Brit*), movie-goer (*US*); **Kinoprogramm** *nt* film programme (*Brit*), movie program (*US*)

Kiosk [ki'ɔsk] (-(e)s, -e) *m* kiosk

Kippe ['kɪpə] (-, -n) *f* (*umg*) cigarette end; **auf der ~ stehen** (*fig*) to be touch and go

kippen *vi* to topple over, overturn ▷ *vt* to tilt

Kipper ['kɪpər] (-s, -) *m* (*Aut*) tipper, dump(er) truck

Kippschalter *m* rocker switch

Kirche ['kɪrçə] (-, -n) *f* church

Kirchen- *zW*: **Kirchenchor** *m* church choir; **Kirchendiener** *m* churchwarden; **Kirchenfest** *nt* church festival; **Kirchenlied** *nt* hymn; **Kirchenschiff** *nt* (*Längsschiff*) nave; (*Querschiff*) transept; **Kirchensteuer** *f* church tax; **Kirchentag** *m* church congress

Kirch- *zW*: **Kirchgänger, in** (-s, -) *m(f)* churchgoer; **Kirchhof** *m* churchyard; **kirchlich** *adj* ecclesiastical; **Kirchturm** *m* church tower, steeple; **Kirchweih** *f* fair, kermis (*US*)

Kirgistan ['kɪrgistaːn] (-s) *nt* (*Geog*) Kirghizia

Kirmes ['kɪrmɛs] (-, -sen) *f* (*Dialekt*) fair, kermis (*US*)

Kirschbaum ['kɪrʃbaʊm] *m* cherry tree; (*Holz*) cherry (wood)

Kirsche ['kɪrʃə] (-, -n) *f* cherry; **mit ihm ist nicht gut ~n essen** (*fig*) it's best not to tangle with him

Kirschtorte *f*: **Schwarzwälder ~** Black Forest Gateau

Kirschwasser *nt* kirsch

Kissen ['kɪsən] (-s, -) *nt* cushion; (*Kopfkissen*) pillow; **Kissenbezug** *m* pillow case

Kiste ['kɪstə] (-, -n) *f* box; (*Truhe*) chest; (*umg: Bett*) sack; (: *Fernsehen*) box (*Brit*), tube (*US*)

Kita ['kɪta] *f abk* = **Kindertagesstätte**

Kitsch [kɪtʃ] (-(e)s) *m* trash

kitschig *adj* trashy

Kitt [kɪt] (-(e)s, -e) *m* putty

Kittchen (*umg*) *nt* clink

Kittel (-s, -) *m* overall; (*von Arzt, Laborant etc*) (white) coat

kitten *vt* to putty; (*fig*) to patch up

Kitz [kɪts] (-es, -e) *nt* kid; (*Rehkitz*) fawn

kitzelig ['kɪtsəlɪç] *adj* (*lit, fig*) ticklish

kitzeln *vt, vi* to tickle

Kiwi ['kiːvi] (-, -s) *f* kiwi fruit

KKW (-, -s) *nt abk* = **Kernkraftwerk**

Kl. *abk* (= *Klasse*) cl.

Klacks [klaks] (-es, -e) (*umg*) *m* (*von Kartoffelbrei, Sahne*) dollop; (*von Senf, Farbe etc*) blob

Kladde ['kladə] (-, -n) *f* rough book; (*Block*) scribbling pad

klaffen ['klafən] *vi* to gape

kläffen ['klɛfən] *vi* to yelp

Klage ['klaːgə] (-, -n) *f* complaint; (*Jur*) action; **eine ~ gegen jdn einreichen** *od* **erheben** to

institute proceedings against sb; **Klagelied**
nt: **ein Klagelied über jdn/etw anstimmen**
(fig) to complain about sb/sth; **Klagemauer**
f: **die Klagemauer** the Wailing Wall
klagen vi (wehklagen) to lament, wail; (sich
beschweren) to complain; (Jur) to take legal
action; **jdm sein Leid/seine Not ~** to pour
out one's sorrow/distress to sb
Kläger, in ['klɛːɡər(ɪn)] (**-s, -**) m(f) (Jur: im
Zivilrecht) plaintiff; (: im Strafrecht) prosecuting
party; (: in Scheidung) petitioner
Klageschrift f (Jur) charge; (bei Scheidung)
petition
kläglich ['klɛːklɪç] adj wretched
Klamauk [kla'maʊk] (**-s**) m (Alberei)
tomfoolery; (im Theater) slapstick
Klamm [klam] (**-, -en**) f ravine
klamm adj (Finger) numb; (feucht) damp
Klammer ['klamər] (**-, -n**) f clamp; (in Text)
bracket; (Büroklammer) clip; (Wäscheklammer)
peg (Brit), pin (US); (Zahnklammer) brace; **~ auf/
zu** open/close brackets
klammern vr: **sich ~ an** +akk to cling to
klammheimlich [klam'haɪmlɪç] (umg) adj
secret ▷ adv on the quiet
Klamotte [kla'mɔtə] (**-, -n**) f (pej: Film
etc) rubbishy old film etc; **Klamotten** pl
(umg: Kleider) clothes pl; (: Zeug) stuff
Klampfe ['klampfə] (**-, -n**) (umg) f guitar
klang etc [klaŋ] vb siehe **klingen**
Klang (**-(e)s, ⁻e**) m sound
klangvoll adj sonorous
Klappbett nt folding bed
Klappe ['klapə] (**-, -n**) f valve; (an Oboe etc) key;
(Film) clapperboard; (Ofenklappe) damper;
(umg: Mund) trap; **die ~ halten** to shut one's
trap
klappen vi (Geräusch) to click; (Sitz etc) to tip
▷ vt to tip ▷ vi unpers to work; **hat es mit den
Karten/dem Job geklappt?** did you get the
tickets/job O.K.?
Klappentext m blurb
Klapper ['klapər] (**-, -n**) f rattle
klapperig adj run-down, worn-out
klappern vi to clatter, rattle
Klapperschlange f rattlesnake
Klapperstorch m stork; **er glaubt noch an
den ~** he still thinks babies are found under
the gooseberry bush
Klapp- zW: **Klappmesser** nt jackknife;
Klapprad nt collapsible od folding bicycle;
Klappstuhl m folding chair; **Klapptisch** m
folding table
Klaps [klaps] (**-es, -e**) m slap; **einen ~ haben**
(umg) to have a screw loose; **klapsen** vt to slap
klar [klaːr] adj clear; (Naut) ready to sail; (Mil)
ready for action; **bei ~em Verstand sein** to
be in full possession of one's faculties; **sich
dat im K~en sein über** +akk to be clear about;
ins K~e kommen to get clear; **~ sehen** to see
clearly; **sich** dat **über etw** akk **~ werden** to get
sth clear in one's mind
Kläranlage f sewage plant; (von Fabrik)

purification plant
Klare, r (umg) m schnapps
klären vt (Flüssigkeit) to purify; (Probleme) to
clarify ▷ vr to clear (itself) up
Klarheit f clarity; **sich** dat **~ über etw** akk
verschaffen to get sth straight
Klarinette [klari'nɛtə] f clarinet
klar- zW: **klarkommen** unreg (umg) vi: **mit
jdm/etw klarkommen** to be able to cope
with sb/sth; **klarlegen** vt to clear up, explain;
klarmachen vt (Schiff) to get ready for sea;
jdm etw klarmachen to make sth clear to sb;
Klarsichtfolie f transparent film; **klarstellen**
vt to clarify; **Klartext** m: **im Klartext** in clear;
(fig: umg) ≈ in plain English
Klärung ['klɛːrʊŋ] f purification; clarification
Klärungsbedarf m need for clarification
Klasse ['klasə] (**-, -n**) f class; (Sch) class, form;
(auch: **Steuerklasse**) bracket; (Güterklasse) grade
klasse (umg) adj smashing
Klassen- zW: **Klassenarbeit** f test;
Klassenbewusstsein nt class-consciousness;
Klassenbuch nt (Sch) (class) register;
Klassengesellschaft f class society;
Klassenkamerad, in m(f) classmate;
Klassenkampf m class conflict; **Klassenlehrer,
in** m(f) class teacher; **klassenlos** adj classless;
Klassensprecher, in m(f) class spokesperson;
Klassenziel nt: **das Klassenziel nicht
erreichen** (Sch) not to reach the required
standard (for the year); (fig) not to make the
grade; **Klassenzimmer** nt classroom
klassifizieren [klasifi'tsiːrən] vt to classify
Klassifizierung f classification
Klassik ['klasɪk] f (Zeit) classical period; (Stil)
classicism; **Klassiker** (**-s, -**) m classic
klassisch adj (lit, fig) classical
Klassizismus [klasi'tsɪsmʊs] m classicism
Klatsch [klatʃ] (**-(e)s, -e**) m smack, crack;
(Gerede) gossip; **Klatschbase** f gossip(monger)
klatschen vi (tratschen) to gossip; (Beifall spenden)
to applaud, to clap ▷ vt: **(jdm) Beifall ~** to
applaud od clap (sb)
Klatsch- zW: **Klatschmohn** m (corn) poppy;
klatschnass adj soaking wet; **Klatschspalte**
f gossip column; **Klatschtante** (pej: umg) f
gossip(monger)
klauben ['klaʊbən] vt to pick
Klaue ['klaʊə] (**-, -n**) f claw; (umg: Schrift) scrawl
klauen vt to claw; (umg) to pinch
Klause ['klaʊzə] (**-, -n**) f cell; (von Mönch)
hermitage
Klausel ['klaʊzəl] (**-, -n**) f clause; (Vorbehalt)
proviso
Klausur [klaʊ'zuːr] f seclusion; **Klausurarbeit** f
examination paper
Klaviatur [klavia'tuːr] f keyboard
Klavier [kla'viːr] (**-s, -e**) nt piano;
Klavierauszug m piano score
Klebeband nt adhesive tape
Klebemittel nt glue
kleben ['kleːbən] vt, vi: **~ (an** +akk) to stick (to);
jdm eine ~ (umg) to belt sb one

Klebezettel m gummed label
klebrig adj sticky
Klebstoff m glue
Klebstreifen m adhesive tape
kleckern ['klɛkərn] vi to slobber
Klecks [klɛks] (**-es, -e**) m blot, stain; **klecksen** vi to blot; (pej) to daub
Klee [kle:] (**-s**) m clover; **jdn/etw über den grünen ~ loben** (fig) to praise sb/sth to the skies; **Kleeblatt** nt cloverleaf; (fig) trio
Kleid [klaɪt] (**-(e)s, -er**) nt garment; (Frauenkleid) dress; **Kleider** pl clothes pl
kleiden ['klaɪdən] vt to clothe, dress ▷ vr to dress; **jdn ~** to suit sb
Kleider- zW: **Kleiderbügel** m coat hanger; **Kleiderbürste** f clothes brush; **Kleiderschrank** m wardrobe; **Kleiderständer** m coat-stand
kleidsam adj becoming
Kleidung f clothing
Kleidungsstück nt garment
Kleie ['klaɪə] (**-, -n**) f bran
klein [klaɪn] adj little, small; **haben Sie es nicht ~er?** haven't you got anything smaller?; **ein ~es Bier, ein K~es** (umg) ≈ half a pint, ≈ a half; **von ~ an** od **auf** (von Kindheit an) from childhood; (von Anfang an) from the very beginning; **das ~ere Übel** the lesser evil; **sein Vater war (ein) ~er Beamter** his father was a minor civil servant; **~ anfangen** to start off in a small way; **~ geschrieben werden** (umg) to count for (very) little; **~ hacken** to chop up; **~ schneiden** to chop up; **Kleinanzeige** f small ad (Brit), want ad (US); **Kleinanzeigen** pl classified advertising sing; **Kleinarbeit** f: **in zäher/mühseliger Kleinarbeit** with rigorous/painstaking attention to detail; **Kleinasien** nt Asia Minor; **Kleinbürgertum** nt petite bourgeoisie; **Kleinbus** m minibus
Kleine, r f(m) little one
klein- zW: **Kleinfamilie** f small family, nuclear family (Soziologie); **Kleinformat** nt small size; **im Kleinformat** small-scale; **Kleingedruckte, s** nt small print; **Kleingeld** nt small change; **das nötige Kleingeld haben** (fig) to have the wherewithal (umg); **kleingläubig** adj of little faith; **kleinhacken** vt to chop up; **Kleinholz** nt firewood; **Kleinholz aus jdm machen** to make mincemeat of sb
Kleinigkeit f trifle; **wegen** od **bei jeder ~ for** the slightest reason; **eine ~ essen** to have a bite to eat
klein- zW: **kleinkariert** adj: **kleinkariert denken** to think small; **Kleinkind** nt infant; **Kleinkram** m details pl; **Kleinkredit** m personal loan; **kleinkriegen** (umg) vt (gefügig machen) to bring into line; (unterkriegen) to get down; (körperlich) to tire out; **kleinlaut** adj dejected, quiet; **kleinlich** adj petty, paltry; **Kleinlichkeit** f pettiness, paltriness; **kleinmütig** adj fainthearted
Kleinod ['klaɪno:t] (**-s, -odien**) nt gem; (fig) treasure
klein- zW: **Kleinrechner** m minicomputer;

kleinschneiden unreg vt to chop up;
kleinschreiben unreg vt: **ein Wort kleinschreiben** to write a word with a small initial letter; **Kleinschreibung** f use of small initial letters; **Kleinstadt** f small town; **kleinstädtisch** adj provincial
kleinstmöglich adj smallest possible
Kleinwagen m small car
Kleister ['klaɪstər] (**-s, -**) m paste
kleistern vt to paste
Klemme ['klɛmə] (**-, -n**) f clip; (Med) clamp; (fig) jam; **in der ~ sitzen** od **sein** (fig: umg) to be in a fix
klemmen vt (festhalten) to jam; (quetschen) to pinch, nip ▷ vr to catch o.s.; (sich hineinzwängen) to squeeze o.s. ▷ vi (Tür) to stick, jam; **sich hinter jdn/etw ~** to get on to sb/get down to sth
Klempner ['klɛmpnər] (**-s, -**) m plumber
Kleptomanie [klɛptoma'ni:] f kleptomania
Kleriker ['kle:rikər] (**-s, -**) m cleric
Klerus ['kle:rʊs] (**-**) m clergy
Klette ['klɛtə] (**-, -n**) f burr; **sich wie eine ~ an jdn hängen** to cling to sb like a limpet
Kletterer ['klɛtərər] (**-s, -**) m climber
Klettergerüst nt climbing frame
klettern vi to climb
Kletterpflanze f creeper
Kletterseil nt climbing rope
Klettverschluss m Velcro® fastener
klicken ['klɪkən] vi to click
Klient, in [kli'ɛnt(ɪn)] m(f) client
Klima ['kli:ma] (**-s, -s** od **-te**) nt climate; **Klimaanlage** f air conditioning
Klimaschutz m climate protection; **Klimaschutzabkommen** nt agreement on climate change
klimatisieren [klimati'zi:rən] vt to air-condition
klimatisiert adj air-conditioned
Klimawechsel m change of air
Klimawandel m climate change#
Klimbim [klɪm'bɪm] (**-s**) (umg) m odds and ends pl
klimpern ['klɪmpərn] vi to tinkle; (auf Gitarre) to strum
Klinge ['klɪŋə] (**-, -n**) f blade, sword; **jdn über die ~ springen lassen** (fig: umg) to allow sb to run into trouble
Klingel ['klɪŋəl] (**-, -n**) f bell; **Klingelbeutel** m collection bag; **Klingelknopf** m bell push
klingeln vi to ring; **es hat geklingelt** (an Tür) somebody just rang the doorbell, the doorbell just rang
Klingelton m ringtone
klingen ['klɪŋən] unreg vi to sound; (Gläser) to clink
Klinik ['kli:nɪk] f clinic
klinisch ['kli:nɪʃ] adj clinical
Klinke ['klɪŋkə] (**-, -n**) f handle
Klinker ['klɪŋkər] (**-s, -**) m clinker
Klippe ['klɪpə] (**-, -n**) f cliff; (im Meer) reef; (fig) hurdle

klippenreich adj rocky

klipp und klar ['klɪp|ʊntklaːr] adj clear and concise

Klips [klɪps] (-es, -e) m clip; (Ohrklips) earring

klirren ['klɪrən] vi to clank, jangle; (Gläser) to clink; **~de Kälte** biting cold

Klischee [klɪ'ʃeː] (-s, -s) nt (Druckplatte) plate, block; (fig) cliché; **Klischeevorstellung** f stereotyped idea

Klitoris ['kliːtorɪs] (-, -) f clitoris

Klo [kloː] (-s, -s) (umg) nt loo (Brit), john (US)

Kloake [klo'aːkə] (-, -n) f sewer

klobig ['kloːbɪç] adj clumsy

Klon [kloːn] (-s, -e) m clone

Klonschaf nt cloned sheep

Klopapier (umg) nt toilet paper

klopfen ['klɔpfən] vi to knock; (Herz) to thump ▷ vt to beat; **es klopft** somebody's knocking; **jdm auf die Finger ~** (lit, fig) to give sb a rap on the knuckles; **jdm auf die Schulter ~** to tap sb on the shoulder

Klopfer (-s, -) m (Teppichklopfer) beater; (Türklopfer) knocker

Klöppel ['klœpəl] (-s, -) m (von Glocke) clapper

klöppeln vi to make lace

Klops [klɔps] (-es, -e) m meatball

Klosett [klo'zɛt] (-s, -e od -s) nt lavatory, toilet; **Klosettbrille** f toilet seat; **Klosettpapier** nt toilet paper

Kloß [kloːs] (-es, ̈-e) m (Erdkloß) clod; (im Hals) lump; (Koch) dumpling

Kloster ['kloːstər] (-s, ̈-) nt (Männerkloster) monastery; (Frauenkloster) convent; **ins ~ gehen** to become a monk/nun

klösterlich ['klœstərlɪç] adj monastic; convent

Klotz [klɔts] (-es, ̈-e) m log; (Hackklotz) block; **jdm ein ~ am Bein sein** (fig) to be a millstone round sb's neck

Klub [klʊp] (-s, -s) m club; **Klubjacke** f blazer; **Klubsessel** m easy chair

Kluft [klʊft] (-, ̈-e) f cleft, gap; (Geog) chasm; (Uniform) uniform; (umg: Kleidung) gear

klug [kluːk] adj clever, intelligent; **ich werde daraus nicht ~** I can't make head or tail of it; **Klugheit** f cleverness, intelligence; **Klugscheißer** (umg) m smart-ass

Klümpchen ['klʏmpçən] nt clot, blob

klumpen ['klʊmpən] vi to go lumpy, clot

Klumpen (-s, -) m (Koch) lump; (Erdklumpen) clod; (Blutklumpen) clot; (Goldklumpen) nugget

Klumpfuß ['klʊmpfuːs] m club foot

Klüngel ['klʏŋəl] (-s, -) (umg) m (Clique) clique

Klunker ['klʊŋkər] (-s, -) (umg) m (Schmuck) rock(s pl)

km abk (= Kilometer) km

km/h abk (= Kilometer pro Stunde) km/h

knabbern ['knabərn] vt, vi to nibble; **an etw** dat **~** (fig: umg) to puzzle over sth

Knabe ['knaːbə] (-n, -n) m boy

knabenhaft adj boyish

Knäckebrot ['knɛkəbroːt] nt crispbread

knacken ['knakən] vi (lit, fig) to crack ▷ vt (umg: Auto) to break into

knackfrisch (umg) adj oven-fresh, crispy-fresh

knackig adj crisp

Knacks [knaks] (-es, -e) m: **einen ~ weghaben** (umg) to be uptight about sth

Knackwurst f type of frankfurter

Knall [knal] (-(e)s, -e) m bang; (Peitschenknall) crack; **~ auf Fall** just like that; **einen ~ haben** (umg) to be crazy od crackers; **Knallbonbon** nt cracker; **Knalleffekt** m surprise effect, spectacular effect; **knallen** vi to bang; to crack ▷ vt: **jdm eine knallen** (umg) to clout sb; **Knallfrosch** m jumping jack; **knallhart** (umg) adj really hard; (: Worte) hard-hitting; (: Film) brutal; (: Porno) hardcore; **Knallkopf** (umg) m dickhead; **knallrot** adj bright red

knapp [knap] adj tight; (Geld) scarce; (kurz) short; (Mehrheit, Sieg) narrow; (Sprache) concise; **meine Zeit ist ~ bemessen** I am short of time; **mit ~er Not** only just; siehe auch **knapphalten**

Knappe (-n, -n) m (Edelmann) young knight

knapphalten unreg vt: **jdn (mit etw) ~** to keep sb short (of sth)

Knappheit f tightness; scarcity; conciseness

Knarre ['knarə] (-, -n) (umg) f (Gewehr) shooter

knarren vi to creak

Knast [knast] (-(e)s) (umg) m clink, can (US)

Knatsch [knaːtʃ] (-es) (umg) m trouble

knattern ['knatərn] vi to rattle; (Maschinengewehr) to chatter

Knäuel ['knɔʏəl] (-s, -) m od nt (Wollknäuel) ball; (Menschenknäuel) knot

Knauf [knaʊf] (-(e)s, Knäufe) m knob; (Schwertknauf) pommel

Knauser ['knaʊzər] (-s, -) m miser

knauserig adj miserly

knausern vi to be mean

knautschen ['knaʊtʃən] vt, vi to crumple

Knebel ['kneːbəl] (-s, -) m gag

knebeln vt to gag; (Naut) to fasten

Knecht [knɛçt] (-(e)s, -e) m servant; (auf Bauernhof) farm labourer (Brit) od laborer (US)

knechten vt to enslave

Knechtschaft f servitude

kneifen ['knaɪfən] unreg vt to pinch ▷ vi to pinch; (sich drücken) to back out; **vor etw** dat **~** to dodge sth

Kneifzange f pliers pl; (kleine) pincers pl

Kneipe ['knaɪpə] (-, -n) (umg) f pub (Brit), bar, saloon (US)

Kneippkur ['knaɪpkuːr] f Kneipp cure, type of hydropathic treatment combined with diet, rest etc

Knete ['kneːtə] (umg) f (Geld) dough

kneten vt to knead; (Wachs) to mould (Brit), mold (US)

Knetgummi m od nt Plasticine®

Knetmasse f Plasticine®

Knick [knɪk] (-(e)s, -e) m (Sprung) crack; (Kurve) bend; (Falte) fold

knicken vt, vi (springen) to crack; (brechen) to break; (Papier) to fold; **„nicht ~!"** "do not bend"; **geknickt sein** to be downcast

k

193

Knicks [knɪks] (**-es, -e**) *m* curts(e)y; **knicksen** *vi* to curts(e)y

Knie [kni:] (**-s, -**) *nt* knee; **in die ~ gehen** to kneel; (*fig*) to be brought to one's knees; **Kniebeuge** (**-, -n**) *f* knee bend; **Kniefall** *m* genuflection; **Kniegelenk** *nt* knee joint; **Kniekehle** *f* back of the knee

knien *vi* to kneel ▷ *vr*: **sich in die Arbeit ~** (*fig*) to get down to (one's) work

Kniescheibe *f* kneecap

Kniestrumpf *m* knee-length sock

kniff *etc* [knɪf] *vb siehe* **kneifen**

Kniff (**-(e)s, -e**) *m* (*Zwicken*) pinch; (*Falte*) fold; (*fig*) trick, knack

kniffelig *adj* tricky

knipsen ['knɪpsən] *vt* (*Fahrkarte*) to punch; (*Phot*) to take a snap of, snap ▷ *vi* (*Phot*) to take snaps/a snap

Knirps [knɪrps] (**-es, -e**) *m* little chap; **er hat einen neuen ~® gekauft** he has bought a new Knirps® (*folding umbrella*)

knirschen ['knɪrʃən] *vi* to crunch; **mit den Zähnen ~** to grind one's teeth

knistern ['knɪstərn] *vi* to crackle; (*Papier, Seide*) to rustle

Knitterfalte *f* crease

knitterfrei *adj* non-crease

knittern *vi* to crease

knobeln ['kno:bəln] *vi* (*würfeln*) to play dice; (*um eine Entscheidung*) to toss for it

Knoblauch ['kno:plaux] (**-(e)s**) *m* garlic

Knöchel ['knœçəl] (**-s, -**) *m* knuckle; (*Fußknöchel*) ankle

Knochen ['knɔxən] (**-s, -**) *m* bone; **Knochenarbeit** (*umg*) *f* hard work; **Knochenbau** *m* bone structure; **Knochenbruch** *m* fracture; **Knochengerüst** *nt* skeleton; **Knochenmark** *nt* bone marrow

knöchern ['knœçərn] *adj* bone

knochig ['knɔxɪç] *adj* bony

Knödel ['knø:dəl] (**-s, -**) *m* dumpling

Knolle ['knɔlə] (**-, -n**) *f* bulb

Knopf [knɔpf] (**-(e)s, ̈e**) *m* button; **Knopfdruck** *m* touch of a button

knöpfen ['knœpfən] *vt* to button

Knopfloch *nt* buttonhole

Knorpel ['knɔrpəl] (**-s, -**) *m* cartilage, gristle

knorpelig *adj* gristly

knorrig ['knɔrɪç] *adj* gnarled, knotted

Knospe ['knɔspə] (**-, -n**) *f* bud

knospen *vi* to bud

knoten ['kno:tən] *vt* to knot; **Knoten** (**-s, -**) *m* knot; (*Haar*) bun; (*Bot*) node; (*Med*) lump

Knotenpunkt *m* junction

knuffen ['knʊfən] (*umg*) *vt* to cuff

Knüller ['knʏlər] (**-s, -**) (*umg*) *m* hit; (*Reportage*) scoop

knüpfen ['knʏpfən] *vt* to tie; (*Teppich*) to knot; (*Freundschaft*) to form

Knüppel ['knʏpəl] (**-s, -**) *m* cudgel; (*Polizeiknüppel*) baton, truncheon; (*Aviat*) (joy)stick; **jdm ~ zwischen die Beine werfen** (*fig*) to put a spoke in sb's wheel; **knüppeldick**

(*umg*) *adj* very thick; (*fig*) thick and fast; **Knüppelschaltung** *f* (*Aut*) floor-mounted gear change

knurren ['knʊrən] *vi* (*Hund*) to snarl, growl; (*Magen*) to rumble; (*Mensch*) to mutter

knusperig ['knʊspərɪç], **knusprig** ['knʊsprɪç] *adj* crisp; (*Keks*) crunchy

knutschen ['knu:tʃən] (*umg*) *vt* to snog with ▷ *vi, vr* to snog

k. o. *adj* (*Sport*) knocked out; (*fig: umg*) whacked

Koalition [koalitsi'o:n] *f* coalition

Koalitionsabsprache *f* coalition agreement

koalitionsfähig *f* in a position to form a coalition

Kobalt ['ko:balt] (**-s**) *nt* cobalt

Kobold ['ko:bɔlt] (**-(e)s, -e**) *m* imp

Kobra ['ko:bra] (**-, -s**) *f* cobra

Koch [kɔx] (**-(e)s, ̈e**) *m* cook; **Kochbuch** *nt* cookery book, cookbook; **kochecht** *adj* (*Farbe*) fast

kochen *vi* to cook; (*Wasser*) to boil ▷ *vt* (*Essen*) to cook; **er kochte vor Wut** (*umg*) he was seething; **etw auf kleiner Flamme ~** to simmer sth over a low heat

Kocher (**-s, -**) *m* stove, cooker

Köcher ['kœçər] (**-s, -**) *m* quiver

Kochgelegenheit *f* cooking facilities *pl*

Köchin ['kœçɪn] *f* cook

Koch- *zW*: **Kochkunst** *f* cooking; **Kochlöffel** *m* kitchen spoon; **Kochnische** *f* kitchenette; **Kochplatte** *f* hotplate; **Kochsalz** *nt* cooking salt; **Kochtopf** *m* saucepan, pot; **Kochwäsche** *f* washing that can be boiled

Kode [ko:t] (**-s, -s**) *m* code

Köder ['kø:dər] (**-s, -**) *m* bait, lure

ködern *vt* to lure, entice

Koexistenz [koeksɪs'tɛnts] *f* coexistence

Koffein [kɔfe'i:n] (**-s**) *nt* caffeine; **koffeinfrei** *adj* decaffeinated

Koffer ['kɔfər] (**-s, -**) *m* suitcase; (*Schrankkoffer*) trunk; **die ~ packen** (*lit, fig*) to pack one's bags; **Kofferkuli** *m* (luggage) trolley (*Brit*), cart (*US*); **Kofferradio** *nt* portable radio; **Kofferraum** *m* (*Aut*) boot (*Brit*), trunk (*US*)

Kognak ['kɔnjak] (**-s, -s**) *m* brandy, cognac

Kohl [ko:l] (**-(e)s, -e**) *m* cabbage

Kohldampf (*umg*) *m*: **~ haben** to be famished

Kohle ['ko:lə] (**-, -n**) *f* coal; (*Holzkohle*) charcoal; (*Chem*) carbon; (*umg: Geld*) die **~n stimmen** the money's right; **Kohlehydrat** (**-(e)s, -e**) *nt* carbohydrate; **Kohlekraftwerk** *nt* coal-fired power station

kohlen ['ko:lən] (*umg*) *vi* to tell white lies

Kohlen- *zW*: **Kohlenbergwerk** *nt* coal mine, pit, colliery (*Brit*); **Kohlendioxid** (**-(e)s, -e**) *nt* carbon dioxide; **Kohlengrube** *f* coal mine, pit; **Kohlenhändler** *m* coal merchant, coalman; **Kohlensäure** *f* carbon dioxide; **ein Getränk ohne Kohlensäure** a non-fizzy *od* still drink; **Kohlenstoff** *m* carbon

Kohlepapier *nt* carbon paper

Köhler ['kø:lər] (**-s, -**) *m* charcoal burner

Kohlestift *m* charcoal pencil

Kohlezeichnung f charcoal drawing
Kohl- zW: **kohlpechrabenschwarz, kohlrabenschwarz** adj (Haar) jet-black; (Nacht) pitch-black; **Kohlrübe** f turnip; **kohlschwarz** adj coal-black
Koitus ['ko:ɪtʊs] (-, -od -**se**) m coitus
Koje ['ko:jə] (-, -n) f cabin; (Bett) bunk
Kokain [koka'i:n] (-s) nt cocaine
kokett [ko'kɛt] adj coquettish, flirtatious
kokettieren [koke'ti:rən] vi to flirt
Kokosnuss ['ko:kɔsnʊs] f coconut
Koks [ko:ks] (-es, -e) m coke
Kolben ['kɔlbən] (-s, -) m (Gewehrkolben) butt; (Keule) club; (Chem) flask; (Tech) piston; (Maiskolben) cob
Kolchose [kɔl'ço:zə] (-, -n) f collective farm
Kolik ['ko:lɪk] f colic, gripe
Kollaborateur, in [kɔlabora'tø:r(ɪn)] m(f) (Pol) collaborator
Kollaps [kɔ'laps] (-es, -e) m collapse
Kolleg [kɔl'e:k] (-s, -s od -**ien**) nt lecture course
Kollege [kɔ'le:gə] (-n, -n) m colleague
kollegial [kɔlegi'a:l] adj cooperative
Kollegin [kɔ'le:gɪn] f colleague
Kollegium nt board; (Sch) staff
Kollekte [kɔ'lɛktə] (-, -n) f (Rel) collection
Kollektion [kɔlɛktsi'o:n] f collection; (Sortiment) range
kollektiv [kɔlɛk'ti:f] adj collective
Koller ['kɔlər] (-s, -) (umg) m (Anfall) funny mood; (Wutanfall) rage; (Tropenkoller, Gefängniskoller) madness
kollidieren [kɔli'di:rən] vi to collide; (zeitlich) to clash
Kollier [kɔli'e:] (-s, -s) nt = **Collier**
Kollision [kɔlizi'o:n] f collision; (zeitlich) clash
Kollisionskurs m: **auf ~ gehen** (fig) to be heading for trouble
Köln [kœln] (-s) nt Cologne
Kölnischwasser nt eau de Cologne
kolonial [koloni'a:l] adj colonial; **Kolonialmacht** f colonial power; **Kolonialwarenhändler** m grocer
Kolonie [kolo'ni:] f colony
kolonisieren [koloni'zi:rən] vt to colonize
Kolonist, in [kolo'nɪst(ɪn)] m(f) colonist
Kolonne [ko'lɔnə] (-, -n) f column; (von Fahrzeugen) convoy
Koloss [ko'lɔs] (-es, -e) m colossus
kolossal [kolo'sa:l] adj colossal
Kolumbianer, in [kolʊmbi'a:nər(ɪn)] m(f) Columbian
kolumbianisch adj Columbian
Kolumbien [ko'lʊmbiən] (-s) nt Columbia
Koma ['ko:ma] (-s, -s od -**ta**) nt (Med) coma
Kombi ['kɔmbi] (-s, -s) m (Aut) estate (car) (Brit), station wagon (US)
Kombination [kɔmbinatsi'o:n] f combination; (Vermutung) conjecture; (Hemdhose) combinations pl; (Aviat) flying suit
Kombinationsschloss nt combination lock
kombinieren [kɔmbi'ni:rən] vt to combine ▷ vi to deduce, work out; (vermuten) to guess

Kombiwagen m (Aut) estate (car) (Brit), station wagon (US)
Kombizange f (pair of) pliers
Komet [ko'me:t] (-en, -en) m comet
kometenhaft adj (fig: Aufstieg) meteoric
Komfort [kɔm'fo:r] (-s) m luxury; (von Möbel etc) comfort; (von Wohnung) amenities pl; (von Auto) luxury features pl; (von Gerät) extras pl
komfortabel [kɔmfɔr'ta:bəl] adj comfortable
Komik ['ko:mɪk] f humour (Brit), humor (US), comedy; **Komiker** (-s, -) m comedian
komisch ['ko:mɪʃ] adj funny; **mir ist so ~** (umg) I feel funny od strange od odd; **komischerweise** ['ko:mɪʃər'vaɪzə] adv funnily enough
Komitee [komi'te:] (-s, -s) nt committee
Komm. abk (= Kommission) comm.
Komma ['kɔma] (-s, -s od -**ta**) nt comma; (Math) decimal point; **fünf ~ drei** five point three
Kommandant [kɔman'dant] m commander, commanding officer
Kommandeur [kɔman'dø:r] m commanding officer
kommandieren [kɔman'di:rən] vt to command ▷ vi to command; (Befehle geben) to give orders
Kommanditgesellschaft [kɔman'di:tgəzɛlʃaft] f limited partnership
Kommando [kɔ'mando] (-s, -s) nt command, order; (Truppe) detachment, squad; **auf ~** to order; **Kommandobrücke** f (Naut) bridge; **Kommandowirtschaft** f command economy
kommen ['kɔmən] unreg vi to come; (näher kommen) to approach; (passieren) to happen; (gelangen, geraten) to get; (Blumen, Zähne, Tränen etc) to appear; (in die Schule, ins Gefängnis etc) to go; **was kommt diese Woche im Kino?** what's on at the cinema this week? ▷ vi unpers: **es kam eins zum anderen** one thing led to another; **~ lassen** to send for; **in Bewegung ~** to start moving; **jdn besuchen ~** to come and visit sb; **das kommt davon!** see what happens?; **du kommst mir gerade recht** (ironisch) you're just what I need; **das kommt in den Schrank** that goes in the cupboard; **an etw** akk **~ (berühren)** to touch sth; (sich verschaffen) to get hold of sth; **auf etw** akk **~ (sich erinnern)** to think of sth; (sprechen über) to get onto sth; **das kommt auf die Rechnung** that goes onto the bill; **hinter etw** akk **~ (herausfinden)** to find sth out; **zu sich ~** to come round od to; **zu etw ~** to acquire sth; **um etw ~** to lose sth; **nichts auf jdn/etw ~ lassen** to have nothing said against sb/sth; **jdm frech ~** to get cheeky with sb; **auf jeden vierten kommt ein Platz** there's one place to every fourth person; **mit einem Anliegen ~** to have a request (to make); **wer kommt zuerst?** who's first?; **wer zuerst kommt, mahlt zuerst** (Sprichwort) first come first served; **unter ein Auto ~** to be run over by a car; **das kommt zusammen auf 20 Euro** that comes to 20 euros altogether; **und so kam es, dass ...** and that is how it happened that ...;

daher kommt es, dass ... that's why ...

Kommen (-s) *nt* coming

kommend *adj* (*Jahr, Woche, Generation*) coming; (*Ereignisse, Mode*) future; (*Trend*) upcoming; **(am) ~en Montag** next Monday

Kommentar [kɔmɛn'taːr] *m* commentary; **kein ~** no comment; **kommentarlos** *adj* without comment

Kommentator [kɔmɛn'taːtɔr] *m* (*TV*) commentator

kommentieren [kɔmɛn'tiːrən] *vt* to comment on; **kommentierte Ausgabe** annotated edition

kommerziell [kɔmɛrtsi'ɛl] *adj* commercial

Kommilitone [kɔmili'toːnə] (**-n, -n**) *m*, **Kommilitonin** *f* fellow student

Kommiss [kɔ'mɪs] (**-es**) *m* (life in the) army

Kommissar [kɔmɪ'saːr] *m* police inspector

Kommissbrot *nt* army bread

Kommission [kɔmɪsi'oːn] *f* (*Comm*) commission; (*Ausschuss*) committee; **in ~ geben** to give (to a dealer) for sale on commission

Kommode [kɔ'moːdə] (**-, -n**) *f* (chest of) drawers

kommunal [kɔmu'naːl] *adj* local; (*von Stadt*) municipal; **Kommunalabgaben** *pl* local rates and taxes *pl*; **Kommunalpolitik** *f* local government politics; **Kommunalverwaltung** *f* local government; **Kommunalwahlen** *pl* local (government) elections *pl*

Kommune [kɔ'muːnə] (**-, -n**) *f* commune

Kommunikation [kɔmunɪkatsi'oːn] *f* communication

Kommunikator, in [kɔmuni'kaːtɔr, -'toːrɪn] *m(f)* communicator

Kommunikee [kɔmyni'keː] (**-s, -s**) *nt* = **Kommuniqué**

Kommunion [kɔmuni'oːn] *f* communion

Kommuniqué [kɔmyni'keː] (**-s, -s**) *nt* communiqué

Kommunismus [kɔmu'nɪsmʊs] *m* communism

Kommunist, in [kɔmu'nɪst(ɪn)] *m(f)* communist; **kommunistisch** *adj* communist

kommunizieren [kɔmuni'tsiːrən] *vi* to communicate; (*Eccl*) to receive communion

Komödiant [komødi'ant] *m* comedian; **Komödiantin** *f* comedienne

Komödie [ko'møːdiə] *f* comedy; **~ spielen** (*fig*) to put on an act

Kompagnon [kɔmpan'jõː] (**-s, -s**) *m* (*Comm*) partner

kompakt [kɔm'pakt] *adj* compact

Kompaktanlage *f* (*Rundf*) audio system

Kompanie [kɔmpa'niː] *f* company

Komparativ ['kɔmparatiːf] (**-s, -e**) *m* comparative

Kompass ['kɔmpas] (**-es, -e**) *m* compass

kompatibel [kɔmpa'tiːbəl] *adj* (*auch Comput*) compatible

Kompatibilität [kɔmpatibili'tɛːt] *f* (*auch Comput*) compatibility

kompensieren [kɔmpɛn'ziːrən] *vt* to compensate for, offset

kompetent [kɔmpe'tɛnt] *adj* competent

Kompetenz *f* competence, authority; **Kompetenzstreitigkeiten** *pl* dispute over respective areas of responsibility; **Kompetenzverteilung** *f* distribution of powers; **Kompetenzzentrum** *f* competence centre (*Brit*) *od* center (*US*)

komplett [kɔm'plɛt] *adj* complete

komplex [kɔm'plɛks] *adj* complex; **Komplex** (**-es, -e**) *m* complex

Komplikation [kɔmplikatsi'oːn] *f* complication

Kompliment [kɔmpli'mɛnt] *nt* compliment

Komplize [kɔm'pliːtsə] (**-n, -n**) *m* accomplice

komplizieren [kɔmpli'tsiːrən] *vt* to complicate

kompliziert *adj* complicated; (*Med: Bruch*) compound

Komplizin [kɔm'pliːtsɪn] *f* accomplice

Komplott [kɔm'plɔt] (**-(e)s, -e**) *nt* plot

komponieren [kɔmpo'niːrən] *vt* to compose

Komponist, in [kɔmpo'nɪst(ɪn)] *m(f)* composer

Komposition [kɔmpozitsi'oːn] *f* composition

Kompost [kɔm'pɔst] (**-(e)s, -e**) *m* compost; **Komposthaufen** *m* compost heap

Kompott [kɔm'pɔt] (**-(e)s, -e**) *nt* stewed fruit

Kompresse [kɔm'prɛsə] (**-, -n**) *f* compress

Kompressor [kɔm'prɛsɔr] *m* compressor

Kompromiss [kɔmpro'mɪs] (**-es, -e**) *m* compromise; **einen ~ schließen** to compromise; **kompromissbereit** *adj* willing to compromise; **Kompromisslösung** *f* compromise solution

kompromittieren [kɔmprɔmɪ'tiːrən] *vt* to compromise

Kondensation [kɔndɛnzatsi'oːn] *f* condensation

Kondensator [kɔndɛn'zaːtɔr] *m* condenser

kondensieren [kɔndɛn'ziːrən] *vt* to condense

Kondensmilch *f* condensed milk

Kondensstreifen *m* vapour (*Brit*) *od* vapor (*US*) trail

Kondition [kɔnditsi'oːn] *f* condition, shape; (*Durchhaltevermögen*) stamina

Konditionalsatz [kɔnditsio'naːlzats] *m* conditional clause

Konditionstraining *nt* fitness training

Konditor [kɔn'diːtɔr] *m* pastry-cook

Konditorei [kɔndito'raɪ] *f* cake shop; (*mit Café*) café

kondolieren [kɔndo'liːrən] *vi*: **jdm ~** to condole with sb, offer sb one's condolences

Kondom [kɔn'doːm] (**-s, -e**) *m or nt* condom

Konfektion [kɔnfɛktsi'oːn] *f* (production of) ready-to-wear *od* off-the-peg clothing

Konfektionsgröße *f* clothes size

Konfektionskleidung *f* ready-to-wear *od* off-the-peg clothing

Konferenz [kɔnfe'rɛnts] *f* conference; (*Besprechung*) meeting; **Konferenzschaltung** *f* (*Tel*) conference circuit; (*Rundf, TV*) television *od* radio link-up

konferieren [kɔnfe'riːrən] *vi* to confer; to have a meeting

Konfession [kɔnfɛsi'oːn] *f* religion; *(christlich)* denomination; **konfessionell** [-'nɛl] *adj* denominational

Konfessions- *zW:* **konfessionsgebunden** *adj* denominational; **konfessionslos** *adj* non-denominational; **Konfessionsschule** *f* denominational school

Konfetti [kɔn'fɛti] *(-(s))* *nt* confetti

Konfiguration [kɔnfiguratsi'oːn] *f* (Comput) configuration

Konfirmand, in [kɔnfɪr'mant, -'mandɪn] *m(f)* candidate for confirmation

Konfirmation [kɔnfɪrmatsi'oːn] *f* (Eccl) confirmation

konfirmieren [kɔnfɪr'miːrən] *vt* to confirm

konfiszieren [kɔnfɪs'tsiːrən] *vt* to confiscate

Konfitüre [kɔnfi'tyːrə] *(-, -n)* *f* jam

Konflikt [kɔn'flɪkt] *(-(e)s, -e)* *m* conflict; **Konfliktherd** *m* (Pol) centre (Brit) od center (US) of conflict; **Konfliktstoff** *m* cause of conflict

konform [kɔn'fɔrm] *adj* concurring; **~ gehen** to be in agreement

Konfrontation [kɔnfrɔntatsi'oːn] *f* confrontation

konfrontieren [kɔnfrɔn'tiːrən] *vt* to confront

konfus [kɔn'fuːs] *adj* confused

Kongo ['kɔŋgo] *(-(s))* *m* Congo

Kongress [kɔn'grɛs] *(-es, -e)* *m* congress

Kongruenz [kɔŋgru'ɛnts] *f* agreement, congruence

König ['køːnɪç] *(-(e)s, -e)* *m* king

Königin ['køːnɪgɪn] *f* queen

königlich *adj* royal ▷ *adv:* **sich ~ amüsieren** *(umg)* to have the time of one's life

Königreich *nt* kingdom

Königtum ['køːnɪçtuːm] *(-(e)s, -tümer)* *nt* kingship; *(Reich)* kingdom

konisch ['koːnɪʃ] *adj* conical

Konj. *abk* (= Konjunktiv) conj.

Konjugation [kɔnjugatsi'oːn] *f* conjugation

konjugieren [kɔnju'giːrən] *vt* to conjugate

Konjunktion [kɔnjʊŋktsi'oːn] *f* conjunction

Konjunktiv ['kɔnjʊŋktiːf] *(-s, -e)* *m* subjunctive

Konjunktur [kɔnjʊŋk'tuːr] *f* economic situation; *(Hochkonjunktur)* boom; **steigende/ fallende ~** upward/downward economic trend; **Konjunkturbarometer** *nt* economic indicators *pl;* **Konjunktureinbruch** *nt* economic slump; **Konjunkturklima** *nt* economic climate; **Konjunkturloch** *nt* temporary economic dip; **Konjunkturpolitik** *f* policies aimed at preventing economic fluctuations

konkav [kɔn'kaːf] *adj* concave

konkret [kɔn'kreːt] *adj* concrete

Konkurrent, in [kɔnkʊ'rɛnt(ɪn)] *m(f)* competitor

Konkurrenz [kɔnkʊ'rɛnts] *f* competition; **jdm ~ machen** (Comm, fig) to compete with sb; **konkurrenzfähig** *adj* competitive; **Konkurrenzkampf** *m* competition; *(umg)* rat race

konkurrieren [kɔnkʊ'riːrən] *vi* to compete

Konkurs [kɔn'kʊrs] *(-es, -e)* *m* bankruptcy; **in ~ gehen** to go into receivership; **~ machen** *(umg)* to go bankrupt; **Konkursverfahren** *nt* bankruptcy proceedings *pl;* **Konkursverwalter** *m* receiver; *(von Gläubigern bevollmächtigt)* trustee

 SCHLÜSSELWORT

können ['kœnən] *(pt* **konnte,** *pp* **gekonnt** *od (als Hilfsverb)* **können)** *vt, vi* **1** to be able to; **ich kann es machen** I can do it, I am able to do it; **ich kann es nicht machen** I can't do it, I'm not able to do it; **ich kann nicht ...** I can't ..., I cannot ...; **was können Sie?** what can you do?; **ich kann nicht mehr** I can't go on; **ich kann nichts dafür** I can't help it; **du kannst mich (mal)!** *(umg)* get lost!

2 *(wissen, beherrschen)* to know; **können Sie Deutsch?** can you speak German?; **er kann gut Englisch** he speaks English well; **sie kann keine Mathematik** she can't do mathematics

3 *(dürfen)* to be allowed to; **kann ich gehen?** can I go?; **könnte ich ...?** could I ...?; **kann ich mit?** *(umg)* can I come with you?

4 *(möglich sein):* **Sie könnten recht haben** you may be right; **das kann sein** that's possible; **kann sein** maybe

Können *(-s)* *nt* ability

Könner *(-s, -)* *m* expert

Konnossement [kɔnɔsə'mɛnt] *nt* (Export) bill of lading

konnte *etc* ['kɔntə] *vb siehe* **können**

konsequent [kɔnze'kvɛnt] *adj* consistent; **ein Ziel ~ verfolgen** to pursue an objective single-mindedly

Konsequenz [kɔnze'kvɛnts] *f* consistency; *(Folgerung)* conclusion; **die ~en tragen** to take the consequences; **(aus etw) die ~en ziehen** to take the appropriate steps

konservativ [kɔnzɛrva'tiːf] *adj* conservative

Konservatorium [kɔnzɛrva'toːriʊm] *nt* academy of music, conservatory

Konserve [kɔn'zɛrvə] *(-, -n)* *f* tinned (Brit) od canned food

Konservenbüchse *f,* **Konservendose** *f* tin (Brit), can

konservieren [kɔnzɛr'viːrən] *vt* to preserve

Konservierung *f* preservation

Konservierungsstoff *m* preservative

Konsole [kɔnzo'leː] *f* games console

konsolidiert [kɔnzoli'diːrt] *adj* consolidated

Konsolidierung *f* consolidation

Konsonant [kɔnzo'nant] *m* consonant

Konsortium [kɔn'zɔrtsiʊm] *nt* consortium, syndicate

konspirativ [kɔnspira'tiːf] *adj:* **~e Wohnung** conspirators' hideaway

konstant [kɔn'stant] *adj* constant

Konstellation [kɔnstɛlatsi'oːn] *f* constellation;

k

(fig) line-up; *(von Faktoren etc)* combination

Konstitution [kɔnstitutsiˈoːn] *f* constitution

konstitutionell [kɔnstitutsioˈnɛl] *adj* constitutional

konstruieren [kɔnstruˈiːrən] *vt* to construct

Konstrukteur, in [kɔnstrʊkˈtøːr(ɪn)] *m(f)* designer

Konstruktion [kɔnstrʊktsiˈon] *f* construction

Konstruktionsfehler *m (im Entwurf)* design fault; *(im Aufbau)* structural defect

konstruktiv [kɔnstrʊkˈtiːf] *adj* constructive

Konsul [ˈkɔnzʊl] **(-s, -n)** *m* consul

Konsulat [kɔnzuˈlaːt] **(-(e)s, -e)** *nt* consulate

konsultieren [kɔnzʊlˈtiːrən] *vt* to consult

Konsum¹ [kɔnˈzuːm] **(-s)** *m* consumption

Konsum² [ˈkɔnzuːm] **(-s, -s)** *m (Genossenschaft)* cooperative society; *(Laden)* cooperative store, co-op *(umg)*

Konsumartikel *m* consumer article

Konsument [kɔnzuˈmɛnt] *m* consumer

konsumfreudig *f* consumption-oriented, consumerist

Konsumgesellschaft *f* consumer society

konsumieren [kɔnzuˈmiːrən] *vt* to consume

Konsumtempel *m* temple of consumerism

Konsumterror *m* pressures *pl* of a materialistic society

Konsumzwang *m* compulsion to buy

Kontakt [kɔnˈtakt] **(-(e)s, -e)** *m* contact; **mit jdm ~ aufnehmen** to get in touch with sb; **Kontaktanzeige** *f* lonely hearts ad; **kontaktarm** *adj* unsociable; **kontaktfreudig** *adj* sociable

kontaktieren [kɔntakˈtiːrən] *vt* to contact

Kontakt- *zW:* **Kontaktlinsen** *pl* contact lenses *pl*; **Kontaktmann** **(-(e)s, *pl* -männer)** *m (Agent)* contact; **Kontaktsperre** *f* ban on visits and letters *(to a prisoner)*

Konterfei [ˈkɔntərfaɪ] **(-s, -s)** *nt* likeness, portrait

kontern [ˈkɔntɛrn] *vt, vi* to counter

Konterrevolution [ˈkɔntɛrrevolutsioːn] *f* counter-revolution

Kontinent [kɔntiˈnɛnt] *m* continent

Kontingent [kɔntɪŋˈgɛnt] **(-(e)s, -e)** *nt* quota; *(Truppenkontingent)* contingent

kontinuierlich [kɔntinuˈiːrlɪç] *adj* continuous

Kontinuität [kɔntinuiˈtɛːt] *f* continuity

Konto [ˈkɔnto] **(-s, Konten)** *nt* account; **das geht auf mein ~** *(umg: ich bin schuldig)* I am to blame for this; *(ich zahle)* this is on me *(umg)*; **Kontoauszug** *m* statement (of account); **Kontoinhaber, in** *m(f)* account holder

Kontor [kɔnˈtoːr] **(-s, -e)** *nt* office

Kontorist, in [kɔntoˈrɪst(ɪn)] *m(f)* clerk, office worker

Kontostand *m* bank balance

kontra [ˈkɔntra] *präp +akk* against; *(Jur)* versus

Kontra **(-s, -s)** *nt (Karten)* double; **jdm ~ geben** *(fig)* to contradict sb

Kontrabass *m* double bass

Kontrahent [-ˈhɛnt] *m* contracting party; *(Gegner)* opponent

Kontrapunkt *m* counterpoint

Kontrast [kɔnˈtrast] **(-(e)s, -e)** *m* contrast

Kontrollabschnitt *m (Comm)* counterfoil, stub

Kontrollampe [kɔnˈtrɔllampə] *f siehe* **Kontrolllampe**

Kontrolle [kɔnˈtrɔlə] **(-, -n)** *f* control, supervision; *(Passkontrolle)* passport control

Kontrolleur [kɔntrɔˈløːr] *m* inspector

kontrollieren [kɔntrɔˈliːrən] *vt* to control, supervise; *(nachprüfen)* to check

Kontrolllampe [kɔnˈtrɔllampə] *f* pilot lamp; *(Aut: für Ölstand etc)* warning light

Kontrollturm *m* control tower

Kontroverse [kɔntroˈvɛrzə] **(-, -n)** *f* controversy

Kontur [kɔnˈtuːr] *f* contour

Konvention [kɔnvɛntsiˈoːn] *f* convention

Konventionalstrafe [kɔnvɛntsioˈnaːlʃtraːfə] *f* penalty *od* fine *(for breach of contract)*

konventionell [kɔnvɛntsioˈnɛl] *adj* conventional

Konversation [kɔnvɛrzatsiˈoːn] *f* conversation

Konversationslexikon *nt* encyclopaedia

konvex [kɔnˈvɛks] *adj* convex

Konvoi [ˈkɔnvɔy] **(-s, -s)** *m* convoy

Konzentrat [kɔntsɛnˈtraːt] **(-s, -e)** *nt* concentrate

Konzentration [kɔntsɛntratsiˈoːn] *f* concentration

Konzentrationsfähigkeit *f* power of concentration

Konzentrationslager *nt* concentration camp

konzentrieren [kɔntsɛnˈtriːrən] *vt, vr* to concentrate

konzentriert *adj* concentrated ▷ *adv (zuhören, arbeiten)* intently

Konzept [kɔnˈtsɛpt] **(-(e)s, -e)** *nt* rough draft; *(Plan, Programm)* plan; *(Begriff, Vorstellung)* concept; **jdn aus dem ~ bringen** to confuse sb; **Konzeptpapier** *nt* rough paper

Konzern [kɔnˈtsɛrn] **(-s, -e)** *m* combine

Konzert [kɔnˈtsɛrt] **(-(e)s, -e)** *nt* concert; *(Stück)* concerto; **Konzertsaal** *m* concert hall

Konzession [kɔntsɛsiˈoːn] *f* licence *(Brit)*, license *(US)*; *(Zugeständnis)* concession; **die ~ entziehen** *+dat: Comm)* to disenfranchise

Konzessionär [kɔntsɛsioˈnɛːr] **(-s, -e)** *m* concessionaire

konzessionieren [kɔntsɛsioˈniːrən] *vt* to license

Konzil [kɔnˈtsiːl] **(-s, -e *od* -ien)** *nt* council

konzipieren [kɔntsiˈpiːrən] *vt* to conceive; *(entwerfen)* to design

kooperativ [koˌopəraˈtiːf] *adj* cooperative

kooperieren [koˌopeˈriːrən] *vi* to cooperate

koordinieren [koˌɔrdiˈniːrən] *vt* to coordinate

Kopenhagen [koːpənˈhaːgən] **(-s)** *nt* Copenhagen

Kopf [kɔpf] **(-(e)s, ⁻e)** *m* head; **~ hoch!** chin up!; **~ an Kopf** shoulder to shoulder; *(Sport)* neck and neck; **pro ~** per person *od* head; **~ oder Zahl?** heads or tails?; **jdm den ~ waschen** *(fig: umg)* to give sb a piece of one's mind; **jdm über den ~ wachsen** *(lit)* to outgrow sb; (fig: Sorgen etc) to be more than sb can cope with; **jdn vor den ~ stoßen** to antagonize sb; **sich** dat **an den ~ fassen** (fig) to be speechless; **sich** dat **über etw** akk **den ~ zerbrechen** to rack one's brains over sth; **sich** dat **etw durch den ~ gehen lassen** to think about sth; **sich** dat **etw aus dem ~ schlagen** to put sth out of one's mind; **... und wenn du dich auf den ~ stellst!** (umg) ... no matter what you say/do!; **er ist nicht auf den ~ gefallen** he's no fool; **Kopfbahnhof** m terminus station; **Kopfbedeckung** f headgear

Köpfchen ['kœpfçən] nt: **~ haben** to be brainy
köpfen ['kœpfən] vt to behead; (Baum) to lop; (Ei) to take the top off; (Ball) to head
Kopf- zW: **Kopfende** nt head; **Kopfhaut** f scalp; **Kopfhörer** m headphone; **Kopfkissen** nt pillow; **kopflastig** adj (fig) completely rational; **kopflos** adj panic-stricken; **Kopflosigkeit** f panic; **kopfrechnen** vi to do mental arithmetic; **Kopfsalat** m lettuce; **kopfscheu** adj: **jdn kopfscheu machen** to intimidate sb; **Kopfschmerzen** pl headache sing; **Kopfsprung** m header, dive; **Kopfstand** m headstand; **Kopfsteinpflaster** nt: **eine Straße mit Kopfsteinpflaster** a cobbled street; **Kopfstütze** f headrest; (im Auto) head restraint; **Kopftuch** nt headscarf; **kopfüber** adv head-first; **Kopfweh** nt headache; **Kopfzerbrechen** nt: **jdm Kopfzerbrechen machen** to give sb a lot of headaches
Kopie [ko'pi:] f copy
kopieren [ko'pi:rən] vt to copy
Kopierer (-s, -) m (photo)copier
Kopilot, in ['ko:pilo:t(ɪn)] m(f) co-pilot
Koppel¹ ['kɔpəl] (-, -n) f (Weide) enclosure
Koppel² ['kɔpəl] (-s, -) nt (Gürtel) belt
koppeln vt to couple
Koppelung f coupling
Koppelungsmanöver nt docking manoeuvre (Brit) od maneuver (US)
Koralle [ko'ralə] (-, -n) f coral
Korallenkette f coral necklace
Korallenriff nt coral reef
Korb [kɔrp] (-(e)s, ⁻e) m basket; **jdm einen ~ geben** (fig) to turn sb down; **Korbball** m basketball
Körbchen ['kœrpçən] nt (von Büstenhalter) cup
Korbstuhl m wicker chair
Kord [kɔrt] (-(e)s, -e od -s) m = **Cord**
Kordel ['kɔrdəl] (-, -n) f cord, string
Korea [ko're:a] (-s) nt Korea
Koreaner, in (-s, -) m(f) Korean
Korfu ['kɔrfu] (-s) nt Corfu
Korinthe [ko'rɪntə] (-, -n) f currant
Korinthenkacker [ko'rɪntənkakər] (-s, -) (umg) m fusspot, hair-splitter
Kork [kɔrk] (-(e)s, -e) m cork
Korken (-s, -) m stopper, cork; **Korkenzieher** (-s, -) m corkscrew
Korn¹ [kɔrn] (-(e)s, ⁻er) nt corn, grain
Korn² [kɔrn] (-(e)s, -e) nt (Gewehr) sight; **etw aufs ~ nehmen** (fig: umg) to hit out at sth

Korn³ [kɔrn] (-, -s) m (Kornbranntwein) corn schnapps
Kornblume f cornflower
Körnchen ['kœrnçən] nt grain, granule
körnig ['kœrnɪç] adj granular, grainy
Kornkammer f granary
Körnung ['kœrnʊŋ] f (Tech) grain size; (Phot) granularity
Körper ['kœrpər] (-s, -) m body; **Körperbau** m build; **körperbehindert** adj disabled; **Körpergeruch** m body odour (Brit) od odor (US); **Körpergewicht** nt weight; **Körpergröße** f height; **Körperhaltung** f carriage, deportment; **körperlich** adj physical; **körperliche Arbeit** manual work; **Körperpflege** f personal hygiene; **Körperschaft** f corporation; **Körperschaft des öffentlichen Rechts** public corporation od body; **Körperschaftssteuer** f corporation tax; **Körpersprache** f body language; **Körperteil** m part of the body; **Körperverletzung** f (Jur): **schwere Körperverletzung** grievous bodily harm
Korps [ko:r] (-, -) nt (Mil) corps; (Univ) students' club
korpulent [kɔrpu'lɛnt] adj corpulent
korrekt [kɔ'rɛkt] adj correct; **Korrektheit** f correctness
Korrektor, in [kɔ'rɛktɔr, -'to:rɪn] (-s, -) m(f) proofreader
Korrektur [kɔrɛk'tu:r] f (eines Textes) proofreading; (Text) proof; (Sch) marking, correction; **(bei etw) ~ lesen** to proofread (sth); **Korrekturfahne** f (Typ) proof
Korrespondent, in [kɔrɛspɔn'dɛnt(ɪn)] m(f) correspondent
Korrespondenz [kɔrɛspɔn'dɛnts] f correspondence; **Korrespondenzqualität** f (Drucker) letter quality
korrespondieren [kɔrɛspɔn'di:rən] vi to correspond
Korridor ['kɔrido:r] (-s, -e) m corridor
korrigieren [kɔri'gi:rən] vt to correct; (Meinung, Einstellung) to change
Korrosion [kɔrozi'o:n] f corrosion
Korrosionsschutz m corrosion protection
korrumpieren [kɔrʊm'pi:rən] vt (auch Comput) to corrupt
korrupt [kɔ'rʊpt] adj corrupt
Korruption [kɔrʊptsi'o:n] f corruption
Korsett [kɔr'zɛt] (-(e)s, -e) nt corset
Korsika ['kɔrzika] (-s) nt Corsica
Koseform ['ko:zəfɔrm] f pet form
kosen vt to caress ▷ vi to bill and coo
Kosename m pet name
Kosewort nt term of endearment
Kosmetik [kɔs'me:tɪk] f cosmetics pl
Kosmetikerin f beautician
kosmetisch adj cosmetic; (Chirurgie) plastic
kosmisch ['kɔsmɪʃ] adj cosmic
Kosmonaut [kɔsmo'naʊt] (-en, -en) m cosmonaut
Kosmopolit [kɔsmopo'li:t] (-en, -en) m

k

cosmopolitan; **kosmopolitisch** [-po'li:tiʃ] *adj* cosmopolitan

Kosmos ['kɔsmɔs] (-) *m* cosmos

Kost [kɔst] (-) *f* (*Nahrung*) food; (*Verpflegung*) board; ~ **und Logis** board and lodging

kostbar *adj* precious; (*teuer*) costly, expensive; **Kostbarkeit** *f* preciousness; costliness, expensiveness; (*Wertstück*) treasure

Kosten *pl* cost(s); (*Ausgaben*) expenses *pl*; **auf ~ von** at the expense of; **auf seine ~ kommen** (*fig*) to get one's money's worth

kosten *vt* to cost; (*versuchen*) to taste ▷ *vi* to taste; **koste es, was es wolle** whatever the cost

Kosten- *zW:* **Kostenanschlag** *m* estimate; **kostendeckend** *adj* cost-effective; **Kostenerstattung** *f* reimbursement of expenses; **Kostenkontrolle** *f* cost control; **kostenlos** *adj* free (of charge); **Kosten-Nutzen-Analyse** *f* cost-benefit analysis; **kostenpflichtig** *adj:* **ein Auto kostenpflichtig abschleppen** to tow away a car at the owner's expense; **Kostenstelle** *f* (*Comm*) cost centre (*Brit*) *od* center (*US*); **Kostenvoranschlag** *m* (costs) estimate

Kostgeld *nt* board

köstlich ['kœstlıç] *adj* precious; (*Einfall*) delightful; (*Essen*) delicious; **sich ~ amüsieren** to have a marvellous time

Kostprobe *f* taste; (*fig*) sample

kostspielig *adj* expensive

Kostüm [kɔs'ty:m] (-s, -e) *nt* costume; (*Damenkostüm*) suit; **Kostümfest** *nt* fancy-dress party

kostümieren [kɔsty'mi:rən] *vt, vr* to dress up

Kostümprobe *f* (*Theat*) dress rehearsal

Kostümverleih *m* costume agency

Kot [ko:t] (-(e)s) *m* excrement

Kotelett [kotə'lɛt] (-(e)s, -e *od* -s) *nt* cutlet, chop

Koteletten *pl* sideboards *pl* (*Brit*), sideburns *pl* (*US*)

Köter ['kø:tər] (-s, -) *m* cur

Kotflügel *m* (*Aut*) wing

kotzen ['kɔtsən] (*umg!*) *vi* to puke (!), throw up; **das ist zum K~** it makes you sick

KP (-, -s) *f abk* (= *Kommunistische Partei*) C.P.

KPÖ (-) *f abk* (= *Kommunistische Partei Österreichs*) Austrian Communist Party

Kr. *abk* = **Kreis**

Krabbe ['krabə] (-, -n) *f* shrimp

krabbeln *vi* to crawl

Krach [krax] (-(e)s, -s *od* -e) *m* crash; (*andauernd*) noise; (*umg: Streit*) quarrel, argument; ~ **schlagen** to make a fuss; **krachen** *vi* to crash; (*beim Brechen*) to crack ▷ *vr* (*umg*) to argue, quarrel

krächzen ['krɛçtsən] *vi* to croak

Kräcker ['krɛkər] (-s, -) *m* (*Koch*) cracker

kraft [kraft] *präp +gen* by virtue of

Kraft (-, ¨e) *f* strength; (*von Stimme, fig*) power, force; (*Arbeitskraft*) worker; **mit vereinten Kräften werden wir ...** if we combine our

efforts we will ...; **nach (besten) Kräften** to the best of one's abilities; **außer ~ sein** (*Jur: Geltung*) to be no longer in force; **in ~ treten** to come into effect

Kraft- *zW:* **Kraftaufwand** *m* effort; **Kraftausdruck** *m* swearword; **Kraftbrühe** *f* beef tea

Kräfteverhältnis ['krɛftəferheltnıs] *nt* (*Pol*) balance of power; (*von Mannschaften etc*) relative strength

Kraftfahrer *m* motor driver

Kraftfahrzeug *nt* motor vehicle; **Kraftfahrzeugbrief** *m* (*Aut*) logbook (*Brit*), motor-vehicle registration certificate (*US*); **Kraftfahrzeugschein** *m* (*Aut*) car licence (*Brit*) *od* license (*US*); **Kraftfahrzeugsteuer** *f* ≈ road tax

kräftig ['krɛftıç] *adj* strong; (*Suppe, Essen*) nourishing; **kräftigen** ['krɛftıgən] *vt* to strengthen

Kraft- *zW:* **kraftlos** *adj* weak; powerless; (*Jur*) invalid; **Kraftmeierei** (*umg*) *f showing off of physical strength*; **Kraftprobe** *f* trial of strength; **Kraftrad** *nt* motorcycle; **Kraftstoff** *m* fuel; **Krafttraining** *nt* weight training; **kraftvoll** *adj* vigorous; **Kraftwagen** *m* motor vehicle; **Kraftwerk** *nt* power station; **Kraftwerker** *m* power station worker

Kragen ['kra:gən] (-s, -) *m* collar; **da ist mir der ~ geplatzt** (*umg*) I blew my top; **es geht ihm an den ~** (*umg*) he's in for it; **Kragenweite** *f* collar size; **das ist nicht meine Kragenweite** (*fig: umg*) that's not my cup of tea

Krähe ['krɛ:ə] (-, -n) *f* crow

krähen *vi* to crow

krakeelen [kra'ke:lən] (*umg*) *vi* to make a din

krakelig ['kra:kəlıç] (*umg*) *adj* (*Schrift*) scrawly, spidery

Kralle ['kralə] (-, -n) *f* claw; (*Vogelkralle*) talon

krallen *vt* to clutch; (*krampfhaft*) to claw

Kram [kra:m] (-(e)s) *m* stuff, rubbish; **den ~ hinschmeißen** (*umg*) to chuck the whole thing; **kramen** *vi* to rummage; **Kramladen** (*pej*) *m* small shop

Krampf [krampf] (-(e)s, ¨e) *m* cramp; (*zuckend*) spasm; (*Unsinn*) rubbish; **Krampfader** *f* varicose vein; **krampfhaft** *adj* convulsive; (*fig: Versuche*) desperate

Kran [kra:n] (-(e)s, ¨e) *m* crane; (*Wasserkran*) tap (*Brit*), faucet (*US*)

Kranich ['kra:nıç] (-s, -e) *m* (*Zool*) crane

krank [kraŋk] *adj* ill, sick; **das macht mich ~!** (*umg*) it gets on my nerves!, it drives me round the bend!; **sich ~ stellen** to pretend to be ill, malinger

Kranke, r *f(m)* sick person, invalid; (*Patient*) patient

kränkeln ['krɛŋkəln] *vi* to be in bad health

kranken ['kraŋkən] *vi:* **an etw** *dat* ~ (*fig*) to suffer from sth

kränken ['krɛŋkən] *vt* to hurt

Kranken- *zW:* **Krankenbericht** *m* medical

report; **Krankenbesuch** m visit to a sick person; **Krankengeld** nt sick pay; **Krankengeschichte** f medical history; **Krankengymnastik** f physiotherapy; **Krankenhaus** nt hospital; **Krankenkasse** f health insurance; **Krankenpfleger** m orderly; (mit Schwesternausbildung) male nurse; **Krankenpflegerin** f nurse; **Krankenschein** m medical insurance certificate; **Krankenschwester** f nurse; **Krankenversicherung** f health insurance; **Krankenwagen** m ambulance

krankfeiern (umg) vi to be off sick; (vortäuschend) to skive (Brit)

krankhaft adj diseased; (Angst etc) morbid; **sein Geiz ist schon ~** his meanness is almost pathological

Krankheit f illness; disease; **nach langer schwerer ~** after a long serious illness

Krankheitserreger m disease-causing agent

kränklich ['krɛŋklɪç] adj sickly

krankmelden vr to let one's boss etc know that one is ill; (telefonisch) to phone in sick; (bes Mil) to report sick

krankschreiben unreg vt to give sb a medical certificate; (bes Mil) to put sb on the sick list

Kränkung f insult, offence (Brit), offense (US)

Kranz [krants] (-es, "e) m wreath, garland

Kränzchen ['krɛntsçən] nt small wreath; (fig: Kaffeekränzchen) coffee circle

Krapfen ['krapfən] (-s, -) m fritter; (Berliner) doughnut (Brit), donut (US)

krass [kras] adj crass; (Unterschied) extreme

Krater ['kra:tər] (-s, -) m crater

Kratzbürste ['kratsbyrstə] f (fig) crosspatch

Krätze ['krɛtsə] f (Med) scabies sing

kratzen ['kratsən] vt, vi to scratch; (abkratzen): **etw von etw ~** to scrape sth off sth

Kratzer (-s, -) m scratch; (Werkzeug) scraper

Kraul [kraʊl] (-s) nt (auch: **Kraulschwimmen**) crawl; **kraulen** vi (schwimmen) to do the crawl ▷ vt (streicheln) to tickle

kraus [kraʊs] adj crinkly; (Haar) frizzy; (Stirn) wrinkled

Krause ['kraʊzə] (-, -n) f frill, ruffle

kräuseln ['krɔʏzəln] vt (Haar) to make frizzy; (Stoff) to gather; (Stirn) to wrinkle ▷ vr (Haar) to go frizzy; (Stirn) to wrinkle; (Wasser) to ripple

Kraut [kraʊt] (-(e)s, **Kräuter**) nt plant; (Gewürz) herb; (Gemüse) cabbage; **dagegen ist kein ~ gewachsen** (fig) there's nothing anyone can do about that; **ins ~ schießen** (lit) to run to seed; (fig) to get out of control; **wie ~ und Rüben** (umg) extremely untidy

Kräutertee ['krɔʏtərte:] m herb tea

Krawall [kra'val] (-s, -e) m row, uproar

Krawatte [kra'vatə] (-, -n) f tie

kreativ [krea'ti:f] adj creative

Kreativität [kreativi'tɛːt] f creativity

Kreatur [krea'tuːr] f creature

Krebs [kre:ps] (-es, -e) m crab; (Med) cancer; (Astrol) Cancer; **krebserregend** adj carcinogenic; **krebskrank** adj suffering from

cancer; **krebskrank sein** to have cancer; **Krebskranke, r** f(m) cancer victim; (Patient) cancer patient; **krebsrot** adj red as a lobster

Kredit [kre'diːt] (-(e)s, -e) m credit; (Darlehen) loan; (fig) standing; **Kreditdrosselung** f credit squeeze; **kreditfähig** adj creditworthy; **Kreditgrenze** f credit limit; **Kredithai** (umg) m loan-shark; **Kreditkarte** f credit card; **Kreditkonto** nt credit account; **Kreditpolitik** f lending policy; **kreditwürdig** adj creditworthy; **Kreditwürdigkeit** f creditworthiness, credit status

Kreide ['kraɪdə] (-, -n) f chalk; **bei jdm (tief) in der ~ stehen** to be (deep) in debt to sb; **kreidebleich** adj as white as a sheet

Kreis [kraɪs] (-es, -e) m circle; (Stadtkreis etc) district; **im ~ gehen** (lit, fig) to go round in circles; **(weite) ~e ziehen** (fig) to have (wide) repercussions; **weite ~e der Bevölkerung** wide sections of the population; **eine Feier im kleinen ~e** a celebration for a few close friends and relatives

kreischen ['kraɪʃən] vi to shriek, screech

Kreisel ['kraɪzəl] (-s, -) m top; (Verkehrskreisel) roundabout (Brit), traffic circle (US)

kreisen ['kraɪzən] vi to spin; (fig: Gedanken, Gespräch): **~ um** to revolve around

Kreis- zW: **kreisförmig** adj circular; **Kreislauf** m (Med) circulation; (fig: der Natur etc) cycle; **Kreislaufkollaps** m circulatory collapse; **Kreislaufstörungen** pl circulation trouble sing; **Kreissäge** f circular saw

Kreißsaal ['kraɪsza:l] m delivery room

Kreisstadt f ≈ county town

Kreisverkehr m roundabout (Brit), traffic circle (US)

Krematorium [krema'to:riʊm] nt crematorium

Kreml ['kre:ml] (-s) m: **der ~** the Kremlin

Krempe ['krɛmpə] (-, -n) f brim

Krempel (-s) (umg) m rubbish

krepieren [kre'pi:rən] (umg) vi (sterben) to die, kick the bucket

Krepp [krɛp] (-s, -s od -e) m crêpe

Krepppapier nt crêpe paper

Kreppsohle f crêpe sole

Kresse ['krɛsə] (-, -n) f cress

Kreta ['kre:ta] (-s) nt Crete

Kreter, in [kre:tər(ɪn)] (-s, -) m(f) Cretan

kretisch adj Cretan

kreuz [krɔʏts] adj: **~ und quer** all over

Kreuz (-es, -e) nt cross; (Anat) small of the back; (Karten) clubs; (Mus) sharp; (Autobahnkreuz) intersection; **zu ~e kriechen** (fig) to eat humble pie, eat crow (US); **jdn aufs ~ legen** to throw sb on his back; (fig: umg) to take sb for a ride

kreuzen vt to cross ▷ vr to cross; (Meinungen etc) to clash ▷ vi (Naut) to cruise; **die Arme ~** to fold one's arms

Kreuzer (-s, -) m (Schiff) cruiser

Kreuz- zW: **Kreuzfahrt** f cruise; **Kreuzfeuer** nt (fig): **im Kreuzfeuer stehen** to be caught in

k

the crossfire; **Kreuzgang** m cloisters pl
kreuzigen vt to crucify
Kreuzigung f crucifixion
Kreuzotter f adder
Kreuzschmerzen pl backache sing
Kreuzung f (Verkehrskreuzung) crossing,
junction; (Züchtung) cross
Kreuz- zW: **kreuzunglücklich** adj absolutely
miserable; **Kreuzverhör** nt cross-
examination; **ins Kreuzverhör nehmen**
to cross-examine; **Kreuzweg** m crossroads;
(Rel) Way of the Cross; **Kreuzworträtsel** nt
crossword puzzle; **Kreuzzeichen** nt sign of the
cross; **Kreuzzug** m crusade
kribbelig ['krɪbəlɪç], **kribblig** ['krɪblɪç] (umg) adj
fidgety; (kribbelnd) tingly
kribbeln ['krɪbəln] vi (jucken) to itch; (prickeln)
to tingle
kriechen ['kri:çən] unreg vi to crawl, creep; (pej)
to grovel, crawl
Kriecher (-s, -) m crawler
kriecherisch adj grovelling (Brit), groveling
(US)
Kriechspur f crawler lane (Brit)
Kriechtier nt reptile
Krieg [kri:k] (-(e)s, -e) m war; ~ **führen (mit** od
gegen) to wage war (on)
kriegen ['kri:gən] (umg) vt to get
Krieger (-s, -) m warrior; **Kriegerdenkmal** nt
war memorial; **kriegerisch** adj warlike
Kriegführung f warfare
Kriegs- zW: **Kriegsbeil** nt: **das**
Kriegsbeil begraben (fig) to bury the
hatchet; **Kriegsbemalung** f war paint;
Kriegsdienstverweigerer m conscientious
objector; **Kriegserklärung** f declaration
of war; **Kriegsfuß** m: **mit jdm/etw auf**
Kriegsfuß stehen to be at loggerheads with
sb/not to get on with sth; **Kriegsgefangene,**
r f(m) prisoner of war; **Kriegsgefangenschaft**
f captivity; **Kriegsgericht** nt court-martial;
Kriegsrat m council of war; **Kriegsrecht**
nt (Mil) martial law; **Kriegsschauplatz**
m theatre (Brit) od theater (US) of war;
Kriegsschiff nt warship; **Kriegsschuld** f war
guilt; **Kriegsverbrecher** m war criminal;
Kriegsversehrte, r f(m) person disabled in the
war; **Kriegszustand** m state of war
Krim [krɪm] f: **die ~** the Crimea
Krimi ['kri:mi] (-s, -s) (umg) m thriller
kriminal [krimi'na:l] adj criminal;
Kriminalbeamte, r m detective; **Kriminalfilm**
m crime thriller od movie (esp US)
Kriminalität [kriminali'tɛːt] f criminality
Kriminalpolizei f ≈ Criminal Investigation
Department (Brit), ≈ Federal Bureau of
Investigation (US)
Kriminalroman m detective story
kriminell [kri:mi'nɛl] adj criminal
Kriminelle, r f(m) criminal
Krimskrams ['krɪmskrams] (-es) (umg) m odds
and ends pl
Kringel ['krɪŋəl] (-s, -) m (der Schrift) squiggle;

(Koch) ring
kringelig adj: **sich ~ lachen** (umg) to kill o.s.
laughing
Kripo ['kri:po] (-, -s) f abk (= Kriminalpolizei) ≈ CID
(Brit), ≈ FBI (US)
Krippe ['krɪpə] (-, -n) f manger, crib;
(Kinderkrippe) crèche
Krippenspiel nt nativity play
Krippentod m cot death
Krise ['kri:zə] (-, -n) f crisis
kriseln vi: **es kriselt** there's a crisis looming,
there is trouble brewing
Krisen- zW: **krisenfest** adj stable; **Krisenherd**
m flash point; trouble spot; **Krisenstab** m
action od crisis committee
Kristall[1] [krɪs'tal] (-s, -e) m crystal
Kristall[2] (-s) nt (Glas) crystal; **Kristallzucker** m
refined sugar crystals pl
Kriterium [kri'te:riʊm] nt criterion
Kritik [kri'ti:k] f criticism; (Zeitungskritik)
review, write-up; **an jdm/etw ~ üben** to
criticize sb/sth; **unter aller ~ sein** (umg) to be
beneath contempt
Kritiker, in ['kri:tikər(ɪn)] (-s, -) m(f) critic
kritiklos adj uncritical
kritisch ['kri:tɪʃ] adj critical
kritisieren [kriti'zi:rən] vt, vi to criticize
kritteln ['krɪtəln] vi to find fault, carp
kritzeln ['krɪtsəln] vt, vi to scribble, scrawl
Kroate [kro'a:tə] (-n, -n) m Croat
Kroatien [kro'a:tsiən] (-s) nt Croatia
Kroatin f Croat
kroatisch adj Croatian
kroch etc [krɔx] vb siehe **kriechen**
Krokodil [kroko'di:l] (-s, -e) nt crocodile
Krokodilstränen pl crocodile tears pl
Krokus ['kro:kʊs] (-, od -se) m crocus
Krone ['kro:nə] (-, -n) f crown; (Baumkrone) top;
einen in der ~ haben (umg) to be tipsy
krönen ['krø:nən] vt to crown
Kron- zW: **Kronkorken** m bottle top;
Kronleuchter m chandelier; **Kronprinz** m
crown prince
Krönung ['krø:nʊŋ] f coronation
Kronzeuge m (Jur) person who turns
Queen's/King's (Brit) od State's (US) evidence;
(Hauptzeuge) principal witness
Kropf [krɔpf] (-(e)s, ̈-e) m (Med) goitre (Brit),
goiter (US); (von Vogel) crop
Krösus ['krø:zʊs] (-ses, -se) m: **ich bin doch**
kein ~ (umg) I'm not made of money
Kröte ['krø:tə] (-, -n) f toad; **Kröten** pl
(umg: Geld) pennies pl
Krs. abk = **Kreis**
Krücke ['krʏkə] (-, -n) f crutch
Krug [kru:k] (-(e)s, ̈-e) m jug; (Bierkrug) mug
Krümel ['kry:məl] (-s, -) m crumb
krümeln vt, vi to crumble
krumm [krʊm] adj (lit, fig) crooked; (kurvig)
curved; **keinen Finger ~ machen** (umg) not to
lift a finger; **ein ~es Ding drehen** (umg) to do
something crooked; siehe auch **krummnehmen;**
krummbeinig adj bandy-legged

krümmen ['krʏmːən] vt to bend ▷ vr to bend, curve

krummlachen (umg) vr to laugh o.s. silly; **sich krumm- und schieflachen** to fall about laughing

krummnehmen unreg (umg) vt: **jdm etw ~** (umg) to take sth amiss

Krümmung f bend, curve

Krüppel ['krʏpəl] (**-s, -**) m cripple

Kruste ['krʊstə] (**-, -n**) f crust

Krux [krʊks] (**-**) f (Schwierigkeit) trouble, problem

Kruzifix [krutsi'fɪks] (**-es, -e**) nt crucifix

Kt. abk = **Kanton**

Kto. abk (= Konto) a/c

Kuba ['ku:ba] (**-s**) nt Cuba

Kubaner, in [ku'ba:nər(ɪn)] (**-s, -**) m(f) Cuban

kubanisch [ku'ba:nɪʃ] adj Cuban

Kübel ['ky:bəl] (**-s, -**) m tub; (Eimer) pail

Kubik- [ku'bi:k] in zW cubic; **Kubikmeter** m cubic metre (Brit) od meter (US)

Küche ['kʏçə] (**-, -n**) f kitchen; (Kochen) cooking, cuisine

Kuchen ['ku:xən] (**-s, -**) m cake; **Kuchenblech** nt baking tray; **Kuchenform** f baking tin (Brit) od pan (US); **Kuchengabel** f pastry fork

Küchen- zW: **Küchengerät** nt kitchen utensil; (elektrisch) kitchen appliance; **Küchenherd** m cooker, stove; **Küchenmaschine** f food processor; **Küchenmesser** nt kitchen knife; **Küchenschabe** f cockroach; **Küchenschrank** m kitchen cabinet

Kuchenteig m cake mixture

Kuckuck ['kʊkʊk] (**-s, -e**) m cuckoo; (umg: Siegel des Gerichtsvollziehers) bailiff's seal (for distraint of goods); **das weiß der ~** heaven (only) knows

Kuckucksuhr f cuckoo clock

Kuddelmuddel ['kʊdəlmʊdəl] (**-s**) (umg) m od nt mess

Kufe ['ku:fə] (**-, -n**) f (Fasskufe) vat; (Schlittenkufe) runner; (Aviat) skid

Kugel ['ku:gəl] (**-, -n**) f ball; (Math) sphere; (Mil) bullet; (Erdkugel) globe; (Sport) shot; **eine ruhige ~ schieben** (umg) to have a cushy number; **kugelförmig** adj spherical; **Kugelkopf** m (Schreibmaschine) golf ball; **Kugelkopfschreibmaschine** f golf-ball typewriter; **Kugellager** nt ball bearing

kugeln vt to roll; (Sport) to bowl ▷ vr (vor Lachen) to double up

Kugel- zW: **kugelrund** adj (Gegenstand) round; (umg: Person) tubby; **Kugelschreiber** m ball-point (pen), Biro®; **kugelsicher** adj bulletproof; **Kugelstoßen** (**-s**) nt shot put

Kuh [ku:] (**-, -̈e**) f cow; **Kuhdorf** (pej: umg) nt one-horse town; **Kuhhandel** (pej: umg) m horse-trading; **Kuhhaut** f: **das geht auf keine Kuhhaut** (fig: umg) that's absolutely incredible

kühl [ky:l] adj (lit, fig) cool; **Kühlanlage** f refrigeration plant

Kühle (**-**) f coolness

kühlen vt to cool

Kühler (**-s, -**) m (Aut) radiator; **Kühlerhaube** f (Aut) bonnet (Brit), hood (US)

Kühl- zW: **Kühlflüssigkeit** f coolant; **Kühlhaus** nt cold-storage depot; **Kühlraum** m cold-storage chamber; **Kühlschrank** m refrigerator; **Kühltasche** f cool bag; **Kühltruhe** f freezer

Kühlung f cooling

Kühlwagen m (Lastwagen, Eisenb) refrigerator van

Kühlwasser nt coolant

kühn [ky:n] adj bold, daring; **Kühnheit** f boldness

Kuhstall m cow-shed

k. u. k. abk (= kaiserlich und königlich) imperial and royal

Küken ['ky:kən] (**-s, -**) nt chicken; (umg: Nesthäkchen) baby of the family

kulant [ku'lant] adj obliging

Kulanz [ku'lants] f accommodating attitude, generousness

Kuli ['ku:li] (**-s, -s**) m coolie; (umg: Kugelschreiber) Biro®

kulinarisch [kuli'na:rɪʃ] adj culinary

Kulisse [ku'lɪsə] (**-, -n**) f scene

Kulissenschieber, in m(f) stagehand

Kulleraugen ['kʊləraʊgən] (umg) pl wide eyes pl

kullern ['kʊlərn] vi to roll

Kult [kʊlt] (**-(e)s, -e**) m worship, cult; **mit etw ~ treiben** to make a cult out of sth

kultivieren [kʊlti'vi:rən] vt to cultivate

kultiviert adj cultivated, refined

Kultstätte f place of worship

Kultstatus m: **~ haben/genießen** to have/ enjoy cult status

Kultur [kʊl'tu:r] f culture; (Lebensform) civilization; (des Bodens) cultivation; **Kulturbanause** (umg) m philistine, low-brow; **Kulturbetrieb** m culture industry; **Kulturbeutel** m toilet bag (Brit), washbag

kulturell [kʊltu'rɛl] adj cultural

Kulturfilm m documentary film

Kulturhauptstadt f: **Europäische ~** European City of Culture

Kulturteil m (von Zeitung) arts section

Kultusminister ['kʊltʊsmɪnɪstər] m minister of education and the arts

Kümmel ['kʏməl] (**-s, -**) m caraway seed; (Branntwein) kümmel

Kummer ['kʊmər] (**-s**) m grief, sorrow

kümmerlich ['kʏmərlɪç] adj miserable, wretched

kümmern vr: **sich um jdn ~** to look after sb ▷ vt to concern; **sich um etw ~** to see to sth; **das kümmert mich nicht** that doesn't worry me

Kumpan, in [kʊm'pa:n(ɪn)] (**-s, -e**) m(f) mate; (pej) accomplice

Kumpel ['kʊmpəl] (**-s, -**) (umg) m mate

kündbar ['kʏntba:r] adj redeemable, recallable; (Vertrag) terminable

Kunde¹ ['kʊndə] (**-n, -n**) m customer

Kunde² ['kʊndə] (**-, -n**) f (Botschaft) news

Kunden- zW: **Kundenberatung** f customer

advisory service; **Kundendienst** *m* after-sales service; **Kundenfang** (*pej*) *m*: **auf Kundenfang sein** to be touting for customers; **Kundenfänger** *m* tout (*umg*); **Kundenkonto** *nt* charge account; **Kundenkreis** *m* customers *pl*, clientele; **kundenorientiert** *m* customer-oriented; **Kundenservice** *f* customer service; **Kundenwerbung** *f* publicity (*aimed at attracting custom or customers*)

Kund- *zW*: **Kundgabe** *f* announcement; **kundgeben** *unreg vt* to announce; **Kundgebung** *f* announcement; (*Versammlung*) rally

kundig *adj* expert, experienced

kündigen ['kʏndɪgən] *vi* to give in one's notice ▷ *vt* to cancel; **jdm ~** to give sb his notice; **zum 1. April ~** to give one's notice for April 1st; (*Mieter*) to give notice for April 1st; (*bei Mitgliedschaft*) to cancel one's membership as of April 1st; (**jdm**) **die Stellung ~** to give (sb) notice; **sie hat ihm die Freundschaft gekündigt** she has broken off their friendship

Kündigung *f* notice

Kündigungsfrist *f* period of notice

Kündigungsschutz *m* protection against wrongful dismissal

Kundin *f* customer

Kundschaft *f* customers *pl*, clientele

Kundschafter (-s, -) *m* spy; (*Mil*) scout

künftig ['kʏnftɪç] *adj* future ▷ *adv* in future

Kunst [kʊnst] **(-, ⁻e)** *f* (*auch Sch*) art; (*Können*) skill; **das ist doch keine ~** it's easy; **mit seiner ~ am Ende sein** to be at one's wits' end; **das ist eine brotlose ~** there's no money in that; **Kunstakademie** *f* academy of art; **Kunstdruck** *m* art print; **Kunstdünger** *m* artificial manure; **Kunsterziehung** *f* (*Sch*) art; **Kunstfaser** *f* synthetic fibre (*Brit*) *od* fiber (*US*); **Kunstfehler** *m* professional error; (*weniger ernst*) slip; **Kunstfertigkeit** *f* skilfulness (*Brit*), skillfulness (*US*); **Kunstflieger** *m* stunt flyer; **kunstgerecht** *adj* skilful (*Brit*), skillful (*US*); **Kunstgeschichte** *f* history of art; **Kunstgewerbe** *nt* arts and crafts *pl*; **Kunstgriff** *m* trick, knack; **Kunsthändler** *m* art dealer; **Kunstharz** *nt* artificial resin; **Kunstleder** *nt* artificial leather

Künstler, in ['kʏnstlər(ɪn)] **(-s, -)** *m(f)* artist; **künstlerisch** *adj* artistic; **Künstlername** *m* pseudonym; (*von Schauspieler*) stage name; **Künstlerpech** (*umg*) *nt* hard luck

künstlich ['kʏnstlɪç] *adj* artificial; **~e Intelligenz** (*Comput*) artificial intelligence; **sich ~ aufregen** (*umg*) to get all worked up about nothing

Kunst- *zW*: **Kunstsammler** *m* art collector; **Kunstseide** *f* artificial silk; **Kunststoff** *m* synthetic material; **Kunststopfen (-s)** *nt* invisible mending; **Kunststück** *nt* trick; **das ist kein Kunststück** (*fig*) there's nothing to it; **Kunstturnen** *nt* gymnastics *sing*; **kunstvoll** *adj* artistic; **Kunstwerk** *nt* work of art

kunterbunt ['kʊntərbʊnt] *adj* higgledy-piggledy

Kupee [ku'pe:] **(-s, -s)** *nt* = **Coupé**

Kupfer ['kʊpfər] **(-s, -)** *nt* copper; **Kupfergeld** *nt* coppers *pl*

kupfern *adj* copper ▷ *vt* (*fig*: *umg*) to plagiarize, copy, imitate

Kupferstich *m* copperplate engraving

Kupon [ku'põ:] **(-s, -s)** *m* = **Coupon**

Kuppe ['kʊpə] **(-, -n)** *f* (*Bergkuppe*) top; (*Fingerkuppe*) tip

Kuppel (-, -n) *f* cupola, dome

Kuppelei [kʊpə'laɪ] *f* (*Jur*) procuring

kuppeln *vi* (*Jur*) to procure; (*Aut*) to operate *od* use the clutch ▷ *vt* to join

Kuppler ['kʊplər] **(-s, -)** *m* procurer; **Kupplerin** *f* procuress

Kupplung *f* (*auch Tech*) coupling; (*Aut etc*) clutch; **die ~ (durch)treten** to disengage the clutch

Kur [ku:r] **(-, -en)** *f* (*im Kurort*) (health) cure, (course of) treatment; (*Schlankheitskur*) diet; **eine ~ machen** to take a cure (in a health resort)

Kür [kʏ:r] **(-, -en)** *f* (*Sport*) free exercises *pl*

Kuratorium [kura'to:riʊm] *nt* (*Vereinigung*) committee

Kurbel ['kʊrbəl] **(-, -n)** *f* crank, winder; (*Aut*) starting handle; **Kurbelwelle** *f* crankshaft

Kürbis ['kʏrbɪs] **(-ses, -se)** *m* pumpkin; (*exotisch*) gourd

Kurde ['kʊrdə] **(-n, -n)** *m*, **Kurdin** *f* Kurd

Kurfürst ['ku:rfʏrst] *m* Elector, electoral prince

Kurgast *m* visitor (to a health resort)

Kurier [ku'ri:r] **(-s, -e)** *m* courier, messenger

kurieren [ku'ri:rən] *vt* to cure

kurios [kuri'o:s] *adj* curious, odd

Kuriosität [kuriozi'te:t] *f* curiosity

Kur- *zW*: **Kurkonzert** *nt* concert (*at a health resort*); **Kurort** *m* health resort; **Kurpfuscher** *m* quack

Kurs [kʊrs] **(-es, -e)** *m* course; (*Fin*) rate; **hoch im ~ stehen** (*fig*) to be highly thought of; **einen ~ besuchen** *od* **mitmachen** to attend a class; **harter/weicher ~** (*Pol*) hard/soft line; **Kursänderung** *f* (*lit, fig*) change of course; **Kursbuch** *nt* timetable

Kürschner, in ['kʏrʃnər(ɪn)] **(-s, -)** *m(f)* furrier

kursieren [kʊr'zi:rən] *vi* to circulate

kursiv *adv* in italics

Kursnotierung *f* quotation

Kursus ['kʊrzʊs] **(-, Kurse)** *m* course

Kurswagen *m* (*Eisenb*) through carriage

Kurswert *m* (*Fin*) market value

Kurtaxe *f* spa tax (*paid by visitors*)

Kurve ['kʊrvə] **(-, -n)** *f* curve; (*Straßenkurve*) bend; (*statistisch, Fieberkurve etc*) graph; **die ~ nicht kriegen** (*umg*) not to get around to it

kurvenreich *adj*: „**~e Strecke**" "bends"

kurvig *adj* (*Straße*) bendy

kurz [kʊrts] *adj* short ▷ *adv*: **~ und bündig** concisely; **zu ~ kommen** to come off badly; **den Kürzeren ziehen** to get the worst of it; **~ und gut** in short; **über ~ oder lang** sooner or

later; **eine Sache ~ abtun** to dismiss sth out of hand; **~ gefasst** concise; **darf ich mal ~ stören?** could I just interrupt for a moment?; *siehe auch* **kurzfassen; kurzhalten; kurztreten**
Kurzarbeit f short-time work; *see culture note*

⬤ **KURZARBEIT**
⬤
⬤
⬤ *Kurzarbeit* is the term used to describe a
⬤ shorter working week made necessary by
⬤ a lack of work. It has been introduced in
⬤ recent years as a preferable alternative to
⬤ redundancy. It has to be approved by the
⬤ Arbeitsamt, the job centre, which pays
⬤ some compensation to the worker for loss
⬤ of pay.

kurzärmelig, kurzärmlig *adj* short-sleeved
kurzatmig *adj* (*fig*) feeble, lame; (*Med*) short-winded
Kürze ['kʏrtsə] (**-, -n**) f shortness, brevity
kürzen *vt* to cut short; (*in der Länge*) to shorten; (*Gehalt*) to reduce
kurzerhand ['kʊrtsər'hant] *adv* without further ado; (*entlassen*) on the spot
kurz- *zW:* **kurzfassen** *vr* to be brief; **Kurzfassung** f shortened version; **kurzfristig** *adj* short-term; **kurzfristige Verbindlichkeiten** current liabilities *pl*; **Kurzgeschichte** f short story; **kurzhalten** *unreg vt* to keep short; **kurzlebig** *adj* short-lived
kürzlich ['kʏrtslıç] *adv* lately, recently
Kurz- *zW:* **Kurzmeldung** f news flash; **Kurzparker** m short-stay parker; **Kurzschluss** m (*Elek*) short circuit; **Kurzschlusshandlung** f (*fig*) rash action; **Kurzschrift** f shorthand;

kurzsichtig *adj* short-sighted; **Kurzstrecken-** *in zW* short-range; **Kurzstreckenläufer, in** m(f) sprinter; **kurztreten** *unreg vi* (*fig: umg*) to go easy; **kurzum** *adv* in a word
Kürzung f cutback
Kurzwaren *pl* haberdashery (*Brit*), notions *pl* (US)
Kurzwelle f short wave
kuschelig *adj* cuddly
kuscheln ['kʊʃəln] *vr* to snuggle up
kuschen ['kʊʃən] *vi, vr* (*Hund etc*) to get down; (*fig*) to knuckle under
Kusine [ku'zi:nə] f cousin
Kuss [kʊs] (**-es, ̈-e**) m kiss
küssen ['kʏsən] *vt, vr* to kiss
Küste ['kʏstə] (**-, -n**) f coast, shore
Küsten- *zW:* **Küstengewässer** *pl* coastal waters *pl*; **Küstenschiff** *nt* coaster; **Küstenwache** f coastguard (station)
Küster ['kʏstər] (**-s, -**) m sexton, verger
Kutsche ['kʊtʃə] (**-, -n**) f coach, carriage
Kutscher (**-s, -**) m coachman
kutschieren [kʊ'tʃiːrən] *vi:* **durch die Gegend ~** (*umg*) to drive around
Kutte ['kʊtə] (**-, -n**) f cowl
Kuvert [ku'vɛrt] (**-s, -e** *od* **-s**) *nt* envelope; (*Gedeck*) cover
Kuwait [ku'vait] (**-s**) *nt* Kuwait
KV *abk* (*Mus:* = *Köchelverzeichnis*): **KV 280** K. (number) 280
KW *abk* (= *Kurzwelle*) SW
kW *abk* (= *Kilowatt*) kW
Kybernetik [kybɛr'ne:tık] f cybernetics *sing*
kybernetisch [kybɛr'ne:tıʃ] *adj* cybernetic
KZ (**-s, -s**) *nt abk* = **Konzentrationslager**

k

L l

L, l¹ [ɛl] *nt* L, l; **L wie Ludwig** ≈ L for Lucy, ≈ L for Love (*US*)

l² [ɛl] *abk* (= *Liter*) l

laben ['la:bən] *vt* to refresh ▷ *vr* to refresh o.s.; (*fig*): **sich an etw** *dat* ~ to relish sth

labern ['la:bərn] (*umg*) *vi* to prattle (on) ▷ *vt* to talk

labil [la'bi:l] *adj* (*physisch: Gesundheit*) delicate; (: *Kreislauf*) poor; (*psychisch*) unstable

Labor [la'bo:r] (**-s, -e** *od* **-s**) *nt* lab(oratory)

Laborant, in [labo'rant(ın)] *m(f)* lab(oratory) assistant

Laboratorium [labora'to:riʊm] *nt* lab(oratory)

Labyrinth [laby'rınt] (**-s, -e**) *nt* labyrinth

Lache ['laxə] (**-, -n**) *f* (*Wasser*) pool, puddle; (*umg: Gelächter*) laugh

lächeln ['lɛçəln] *vi* to smile; **Lächeln (-s)** *nt* smile

lachen ['laxən] *vi* to laugh; **mir ist nicht zum L~ (zumute)** I'm in no laughing mood; **dass ich nicht lache!** (*umg*) don't make me laugh!; **das wäre doch gelacht** it would be ridiculous; **Lachen** *nt*: **dir wird das Lachen schon noch vergehen!** you'll soon be laughing on the other side of your face

Lacher (-s, -) *m*: **die ~ auf seiner Seite haben** to have the last laugh

lächerlich ['lɛçərlıç] *adj* ridiculous; **Lächerlichkeit** *f* absurdity

Lach- *zW*: **Lachgas** *nt* laughing gas; **lachhaft** *adj* laughable; **Lachkrampf** *m*: **einen Lachkrampf bekommen** to go into fits of laughter

Lachs [laks] (**-es, -e**) *m* salmon

Lachsalve ['laxzalvə] *f* burst *od* roar of laughter

Lachsschinken *m* smoked, rolled fillet of ham

Lack [lak] (**-(e)s, -e**) *m* lacquer, varnish; (*von Auto*) paint

lackieren [la'ki:rən] *vt* to varnish; (*Auto*) to spray

Lackierer [la'ki:rər] (**-s, -**) *m* varnisher

Lackleder *nt* patent leather

Lackmus ['lakmʊs] (**-**) *m od nt* litmus

Lade ['la:də] (**-, -n**) *f* box, chest; **Ladebaum** *m* derrick; **Ladefähigkeit** *f* load capacity; **Ladefläche** *f* load area; **Ladegewicht** *nt* tonnage; **Ladehemmung** *f*: **das Gewehr hat Ladehemmung** the gun is jammed

Laden ['la:dən] (**-s, -̈**) *m* shop; (*Fensterladen*) shutter; (*umg: Betrieb*) outfit; **der ~ läuft** (*umg*) business is good

laden ['la:dən] *unreg vt* (*Lasten, Comput*) to load; (*Jur*) to summon; (*einladen*) to invite; **eine schwere Schuld auf sich** *akk* ~ to place o.s. under a heavy burden of guilt

Laden- *zW*: **Ladenaufsicht** *f* shopwalker (*Brit*), floorwalker (*US*); **Ladenbesitzer** *m* shopkeeper; **Ladendieb** *m* shoplifter; **Ladendiebstahl** *m* shoplifting; **Ladenhüter** (**-s, -**) *m* unsaleable item; **Ladenöffnungszeit** *f* shop opening hours *pl*; **Ladenpreis** *m* retail price; **Ladenschluss** *m*, **Ladenschlusszeit** *f* closing time; **Ladentisch** *m* counter

Laderampe *f* loading ramp

Laderaum *m* (*Naut*) hold

lädieren [lɛ'di:rən] *vt* to damage

lädt [lɛ:t] *vb siehe* **laden**

Ladung ['la:dʊŋ] *f* (*Last*) cargo, load; (*Beladen*) loading; (*Jur*) summons; (*Einladung*) invitation; (*Sprengladung*) charge

lag *etc* [la:k] *vb siehe* **liegen**

Lage ['la:gə] (**-, -n**) *f* position, situation; (*Schicht*) layer; **in der ~ sein** to be in a position; **eine gute/ruhige ~ haben** to be in a good/peaceful location; **Herr der ~ sein** to be in control of the situation; **Lagebericht** *m* report; (*Mil*) situation report; **Lagebeurteilung** *f* situation assessment

lagenweise *adv* in layers

Lager ['la:gər] (**-s, -**) *nt* camp; (*Comm*) warehouse; (*Schlaflager*) bed; (*von Tier*) lair; (*Tech*) bearing; **etw auf ~ haben** to have sth in stock; **Lagerarbeiter** *m* storehand; **Lagerbestand** *m* stocks *pl*; **Lagerfeuer** *nt* camp fire; **Lagergeld** *nt* storage (charges *pl*); **Lagerhaus** *nt* warehouse, store

Lagerist, in [la:gə'rıst(ın)] *m(f)* storeman, storewoman

lagern ['la:gərn] *vi* (*Dinge*) to be stored; (*Menschen*) to camp; (*auch vr: rasten*) to lie down ▷ *vt* to store; (*betten*) to lay down; (*Maschine*) to bed

Lager- *zW*: **Lagerraum** *m* storeroom; (*in Geschäft*) stockroom; **Lagerschuppen** *m* store shed; **Lagerstätte** *f* resting place

Lagerung *f* storage

Lagune [la'gu:nə] **(-, -n)** f lagoon

lahm [la:m] adj lame; (umg: langsam, langweilig) dreary, dull; (Geschäftsgang) slow, sluggish; **eine ~e Ente sein** (umg) to have no zip; siehe auch **lahmlegen**; **lahmarschig** ['la:m|arʃɪç] (umg) adj bloody od damn (!) slow

lahmen vi to be lame, limp

lähmen ['lɛːmən], **lahmlegen** vt to paralyse (Brit), paralyze (US)

Lähmung f paralysis

Lahn [la:n] **(-)** f (Fluss) Lahn

Laib [laɪp] **(-s, -e)** m loaf

Laich [laɪç] **(-(e)s, -e)** m spawn; **laichen** vi to spawn

Laie ['laɪə] **(-n, -n)** m layman; (fig, Theat) amateur

laienhaft adj amateurish

Lakai [la'kaɪ] **(-en, -en)** m lackey

Laken ['la:kən] **(-s, -)** nt sheet

Lakritze [la'krɪtsə] **(-, -n)** f liquorice

lala ['la'la] (umg) adv: **so ~** so-so, not too bad

lallen vt, vi to slur; (Baby) to babble

Lama ['la:ma] **(-s, -s)** nt llama

Lamelle [la'mɛlə] f lamella; (Elek) lamina; (Tech) plate

lamentieren [lamɛn'tiːrən] vi to lament

Lametta [la'mɛta] **(-s)** nt tinsel

Lamm [lam] **(-(e)s, ⸚er)** nt lamb; **Lammfell** nt lambskin; **lammfromm** adj like a lamb; **Lammwolle** f lambswool

Lampe ['lampə] **(-, -n)** f lamp

Lampenfieber nt stage fright

Lampenschirm m lampshade

Lampion [lampi'õː] **(-s, -s)** m Chinese lantern

Land [lant] **(-(e)s, ⸚er)** nt land; (Nation, nicht Stadt) country; (Bundesland) state; **auf dem ~(e)** in the country; **an ~ gehen** to go ashore; **endlich sehe ich ~** (fig) at last I can see the light at the end of the tunnel; **einen Auftrag an ~ ziehen** (umg) to land an order; **aus aller Herren Länder** from all over the world; siehe auch **hierzulande**; see culture note

LAND

A Land (plural Länder) is a member state of the BRD. There are 16 Länder, namely Baden-Württemberg, Bayern, Berlin, Brandenburg, Bremen, Hamburg, Hessen, Mecklenburg-Vorpommern, Niedersachsen, Nordrhein-Westfalen, Rheinland-Pfalz, Saarland, Sachsen, Sachsen-Anhalt, Schleswig-Holstein and Thüringen. Each Land has its own parliament and constitution.

Landarbeiter m farm od agricultural worker

Landbesitz m landed property

Landbesitzer m landowner

Landbahn f runway

Landeerlaubnis f permission to land

landeinwärts [lant'|aɪnvɛrts] adv inland

landen ['landən] vt, vi to land; **mit deinen**

Komplimenten kannst du bei mir nicht ~ your compliments won't get you anywhere with me

Ländereien [lɛndə'raɪən] pl estates pl

Länderspiel nt international (match)

Landes- zW: **Landesfarben** pl national colours pl (Brit) od colors pl (US); **Landesgrenze** f (national) frontier; (von Bundesland) state boundary; **Landesinnere, s** nt inland region; **Landeskind** nt native of a German state; **Landeskunde** f regional studies pl; **Landestracht** f national costume; **landesüblich** adj customary; **Landesverrat** m high treason; **Landesverweisung** f banishment; **Landeswährung** f national currency; **landesweit** adj countrywide

Landeverbot nt refusal of permission to land

Land- zW: **Landflucht** f emigration to the cities; **Landgut** nt estate; **Landhaus** nt country house; **Landkarte** f map; **Landkreis** m administrative region; **landläufig** adj customary

ländlich ['lɛntlɪç] adj rural

Land- zW: **Landrat** m head of administration of a Landkreis; **Landschaft** f countryside; (Kunst) landscape; **die politische Landschaft** the political scene; **landschaftlich** adj scenic; (Besonderheiten) regional

Landsmann **(-(e)s,** pl **-leute)** m compatriot, fellow countryman

Landsmännin f compatriot, fellow countrywoman

Land- zW: **Landstraße** f country road; **Landstreicher (-s, -)** m tramp; **Landstrich** m region; **Landtag** m (Pol) regional parliament

Landung ['landʊŋ] f landing

Landungs- zW: **Landungsboot** nt landing craft; **Landungsbrücke** f jetty, pier; **Landungsstelle** f landing place

Landurlaub m shore leave

Landvermesser m surveyor

landw. abk (= landwirtschaftlich) agricultural

Land- zW: **Landwirt** m farmer; **Landwirtschaft** f agriculture; **Landwirtschaft betreiben** to farm; **Landzunge** f spit

lang [laŋ] adj long; (umg: Mensch) tall ▷ adv: **~ anhaltender Beifall** prolonged applause; **~ ersehnt** longed-for; **hier wird mir die Zeit nicht ~** I won't get bored here; **er machte ein ~es Gesicht** his face fell; **~ und breit** at great length; **langatmig** adj long-winded

lange adv for a long time; (dauern, brauchen) a long time; **~ nicht so ...** not nearly as ...; **wenn der das schafft, kannst du das schon ~** if he can do it, you can do it easily

Länge ['lɛŋə] **(-, -n)** f length; (Geog) longitude; **etw der ~ nach falten** to fold sth lengthways; **etw in die ~ ziehen** to drag sth out (umg); **der ~ nach hinfallen** to fall flat (on one's face)

langen ['laŋən] vi (ausreichen) to do, suffice; (fassen): **~ nach** to reach for; **es langt mir** I've had enough; **jdm eine ~** (umg) to give sb a clip on the ear

207

Längengrad m longitude
Längenmaß nt linear measure
Langeweile f boredom
lang- zW: **langfristig** adj long-term ▷ adv in the long term; (planen) for the long term; **langfristige Verbindlichkeiten** long-term liabilities pl; **langjährig** adj (Freundschaft, Gewohnheit) long-standing; (Erfahrung, Verhandlungen) many years of; (Mitarbeiter) of many years' standing; **Langlauf** m (Ski) cross-country skiing; **langlebig** adj long-lived; **langlebige Gebrauchsgüter** consumer durables pl
länglich adj longish
Langmut f forbearance, patience
langmütig adj forbearing
längs [lɛŋs] präp (+gen od dat) along ▷ adv lengthways
langsam adj slow; **immer schön ~!** (umg) easy does it!; **ich muss jetzt ~ gehen** I must be getting on my way; **~ (aber sicher) reicht es mir** I've just about had enough; **Langsamkeit** f slowness
Langschläfer m late riser
Langspielplatte f long-playing record
längsseit, längsseits adv alongside ▷ präp +gen alongside
längst [lɛŋst] adv: **das ist ~ fertig** that was finished a long time ago, that has been finished for a long time
längste, r, s adj longest
Langstrecken- in zw long-distance; **Langstreckenflugzeug** nt long-range aircraft
Languste [laŋ'gʊstə] (-, -n) f crayfish, crawfish (US)
lang- zW: **langweilen** vt untr to bore ▷ vr untr to be od get bored; **Langweiler** (-s, -) m bore; **langweilig** adj boring, tedious; **Langwelle** f long wave; **langwierig** adj lengthy, long-drawn-out
Lanze ['lantsə] (-, -n) f lance
Lanzette [lan'tsɛtə] f lancet
Laos ['la:ɔs] (-) nt Laos
Laote [la'o:tə] (-n, -n) m, **Laotin** f Laotian
laotisch [la'o:tɪʃ] adj Laotian
lapidar [lapi'da:r] adj terse, pithy
Lappalie [la'pa:liə] f trifle
Lappe ['lapə] (-n, -n) m Lapp, Laplander
Lappen (-s, -) m cloth, rag; (Anat) lobe; **jdm durch die ~ gehen** (umg) to slip through sb's fingers
läppern ['lɛpərn] (umg) vr unpers: **es läppert sich zusammen** it (all) mounts up
Lappin ['lapɪn] f Lapp, Laplander
läppisch ['lɛpɪʃ] adj foolish
Lappland ['laplant] (-s) nt Lapland
Lappländer, in ['laplɛndər(ɪn)] (-s, -) m(f) Lapp, Laplander
lappländisch adj Lapp
Lapsus ['lapsʊs] (-, -) m slip
Laptop ['lɛptɔp] (-s, -s) m laptop
Lärche ['lɛrçə] (-, -n) f larch
Lärm [lɛrm] (-(e)s) m noise; **Lärmbelästigung** f noise nuisance; **Lärmemission** f noise emission; (stärker) noise pollution; **lärmen** vi to be noisy, make a noise
Larve ['larfə] (-, -n) f mask; (Biol) larva
las etc [la:s] vb siehe **lesen**
Lasagne [la'zanjə] pl lasagne sing
lasch [laʃ] adj slack; (Geschmack) tasteless
Lasche ['laʃə] (-, -n) f (Schuhlasche) tongue; (Eisenb) fishplate
Laser ['le:zər] (-s, -) m laser; **Laserdrucker** m laser printer

 SCHLÜSSELWORT

lassen ['lasən] (pt **ließ**, pp **gelassen** od (als Hilfsverb) **lassen**) vt **1** (unterlassen) to stop; (momentan) to leave; **lass das (sein)!** don't (do it)!; (hör auf) stop it!; **lass mich!** leave me alone!; **lassen wir das!** let's leave it; **er kann das Trinken nicht lassen** he can't stop drinking; **tu, was du nicht lassen kannst!** if you must, you must!
2 (zurücklassen) to leave; **etw lassen, wie es ist** to leave sth (just) as it is
3 (erlauben) to let, allow; **lass ihn doch** let him; **jdn ins Haus lassen** to let sb into the house; **das muss man ihr lassen** (zugestehen) you've got to grant her that
▷ vi: **lass mal, ich mache das schon** leave it, I'll do it
▷ hilfsverb **1** (veranlassen): **etw machen lassen** to have od get sth done; **jdn etw machen lassen** to get sb to do sth; (durch Befehl usw) to make sb do sth; **er ließ mich warten** he kept me waiting; **mein Vater wollte mich studieren lassen** my father wanted me to study; **sich** dat **etw schicken lassen** to have sth sent (to one)
2 (zulassen): **jdn etw wissen lassen** to let sb know sth; **das Licht brennen lassen** to leave the light on; **einen Bart wachsen lassen** to grow a beard; **lass es dir gut gehen!** take care of yourself!
3: lass uns gehen let's go
▷ vr: **das lässt sich machen** that can be done; **es lässt sich schwer sagen** it's difficult to say

lässig ['lɛsɪç] adj casual; **Lässigkeit** f casualness
lässlich ['lɛslɪç] adj pardonable, venial
lässt [lɛst] vb siehe **lassen**
Last [last] (-, -en) f load; (Traglast) burden; (Naut, Aviat) cargo; (meist pl: Gebühr) charge; **jdm zur ~ fallen** to be a burden to sb; **Lastauto** nt lorry (Brit), truck
lasten vi: **~ auf** +dat to weigh on
Lastenaufzug m hoist, goods lift (Brit) od elevator (US)
Lastenausgleichsgesetz nt law on financial compensation for losses suffered in WWII
Laster ['lastər] (-s, -) nt vice ▷ m (umg) lorry (Brit), truck
Lästerer ['lɛstərər] (-s, -) m mocker;

(*Gotteslästerer*) blasphemer

lasterhaft *adj* immoral

lästerlich *adj* scandalous

lästern ['lɛstərn] *vt, vi* (*Gott*) to blaspheme; (*schlecht sprechen*) to mock

Lästerung f jibe; (*Gotteslästerung*) blasphemy

lästig ['lɛstɪç] *adj* troublesome, tiresome; **(jdm)** ~ **werden** to become a nuisance (to sb); (*zum Ärgernis werden*) to get annoying (to sb)

Last- *zW:* **Lastkahn** m barge; **Lastkraftwagen** m heavy goods vehicle; **Lastschrift** f debiting; (*Eintrag*) debit item; **Lasttier** nt beast of burden; **Lastträger** m porter; **Lastwagen** m lorry (*Brit*), truck; **Lastzug** m truck and trailer

Latein [la'taɪn] (**-s**) nt Latin; **mit seinem ~ am Ende sein** (*fig*) to be stumped (*umg*); **Lateinamerika** nt Latin America; **lateinamerikanisch** *adj* Latin-American; **lateinisch** *adj* Latin

latent [la'tɛnt] *adj* latent

Laterne [la'tɛrnə] (**-, -n**) f lantern; (*Straßenlaterne*) lamp, light

Laternenpfahl m lamppost

Latinum [la'ti:nʊm] (**-s**) nt: **kleines/großes ~** = Latin O-/A-level exams (*Brit*)

Latrine [la'tri:nə] f latrine

Latsche ['latʃə] (**-, -n**) f dwarf pine

Latschen ['la:tʃən] (*umg*) m (*Hausschuh*) slipper; (*pej: Schuh*) worn-out shoe

latschen (*umg*) vi (*gehen*) to wander, go; (*lässig*) to slouch

Latte ['latə] (**-, -n**) f lath; (*Sport*) goalpost; (*quer*) crossbar

Lattenzaun m lattice fence

Latz [lats] (**-es, ⁻e**) m bib; (*Hosenlatz*) front flap

Lätzchen ['lɛtsçən] nt bib

Latzhose f dungarees pl

lau [lau] *adj* (*Nacht*) balmy; (*Wasser*) lukewarm; (*fig: Haltung*) half-hearted

Laub [laup] (**-(e)s**) nt foliage; **Laubbaum** m deciduous tree

Laube ['laubə] (**-, -n**) f arbour (*Brit*), arbor (*US*); (*Gartenhäuschen*) summerhouse

Laub- *zW:* **Laubfrosch** m tree frog; **Laubsäge** f fretsaw; **Laubwald** m deciduous forest

Lauch [laux] (**-(e)s, -e**) m leek

Lauer ['lauər] f: **auf der ~ sein** *od* **liegen** to lie in wait

lauern vi to lie in wait; (*Gefahr*) to lurk

Lauf [lauf] (**-(e)s, Läufe**) m run; (*Wettlauf*) race; (*Entwicklung, Astron*) course; (*Gewehrlauf*) barrel; **im ~e des Gesprächs** during the conversation; **sie ließ ihren Gefühlen freien ~** she gave way to her feelings; **einer Sache** *dat* **ihren ~ lassen** to let sth take its course; **Laufbahn** f career; **eine Laufbahn einschlagen** to embark on a career; **Laufbursche** m errand boy

laufen ['laufən] *unreg* vi to run; (*umg: gehen*) to walk; (*Uhr*) to go; (*funktionieren*) to work; (*Elektrogerät: eingeschaltet sein*) to be on; (*gezeigt werden: Film, Stück*) to be on; (*Bewerbung, Antrag*) to be under consideration ▷ vt to run; **es lief**

mir eiskalt über den Rücken a chill ran up my spine; **ihm läuft die Nase** he's got a runny nose; ~ **lassen** (*Person*) to let go; **die Dinge ~ lassen** to let things slide; **die Sache ist ge~** (*umg*) it's in the bag; **das Auto läuft auf meinen Namen** the car is in my name; **Ski/Schlittschuh/Rollschuh** *etc* ~ to ski/ skate/rollerskate *etc*

laufend *adj* running; (*Monat, Ausgaben*) current; **auf dem L~en sein/halten** to be/keep up to date; **am ~en Band** (*fig*) continuously; **~e Nummer** serial number; (*von Konto*) number; **~e Kosten** running costs *pl*

Läufer ['lɔyfər] (**-s, -**) m (*Teppich, Sport*) runner; (*Fußball*) half-back; (*Schach*) bishop

Lauferei [laufə'raɪ] (*umg*) f running about

Läuferin f (*Sport*) runner

Lauf- *zW:* **lauffähig** *adj* (*Comput*): **das Programm is unter Windows lauffähig** the program can be run under Windows; **Lauffeuer** nt: **sich wie ein Lauffeuer verbreiten** to spread like wildfire; **Laufkundschaft** f passing trade; **Laufmasche** f run, ladder (*Brit*); **Laufpass** m: **jdm den Laufpass geben** (*umg*) to give sb his/ her marching orders; **Laufschritt** m: **im Laufschritt** at a run; **Laufstall** m playpen; **Laufsteg** m catwalk

läuft [lɔyft] *vb siehe* **laufen**

Lauf- *zW:* **Laufwerk** nt running gear; (*Comput*) drive; **Laufzeit** f (*von Wechsel, Vertrag*) period of validity; (*von Maschine*) life; **Laufzettel** m circular

Lauge ['laugə] (**-, -n**) f soapy water; (*Chem*) alkaline solution

Laune ['launə] (**-, -n**) f mood, humour (*Brit*), humor (*US*); (*Einfall*) caprice; (*schlechte Laune*) temper

launenhaft *adj* capricious, changeable

launisch *adj* moody

Laus [laus] (**-, Läuse**) f louse; **ihm ist (wohl) eine ~ über die Leber gelaufen** (*umg*) something's biting him; **Lausbub** m rascal, imp

Lauschangriff m: ~ **(gegen)** bugging operation (on)

lauschen ['lauʃən] vi to eavesdrop, listen in

Lauscher, in (**-s, -**) m(f) eavesdropper

lauschig ['lauʃɪç] *adj* snug

Lausejunge (*umg*) m little devil; (*wohlwollend*) rascal

lausen ['lauzən] vt to delouse

lausig ['lauzɪç] (*umg*) *adj* lousy; (*Kälte*) perishing ▷ *adv* awfully

laut [laut] *adj* loud ▷ *adv* loudly; (*lesen*) aloud ▷ *präp* (+*gen od dat*) according to

Laut (**-(e)s, -e**) m sound

Laute ['lautə] (**-, -n**) f lute

lauten ['lautən] vi to say; (*Urteil*) to be

läuten ['lɔytən] vt, vi to ring, sound; **er hat davon (etwas) ~ hören** (*umg*) he has heard something about it

lauter ['lautər] *adj* (*Wasser*) clear, pure;

(*Wahrheit, Charakter*) honest ▷ *adj inv* (*Freude, Dummheit etc*) sheer ▷ *adv* (*nur*) nothing but, only; **Lauterkeit** *f* purity; honesty, integrity
läutern ['lɔʏtərn] *vt* to purify
Läuterung *f* purification
laut- zW: **lauthals** *adv* at the top of one's voice; **lautlos** *adj* noiseless, silent; **lautmalend** *adj* onomatopoeic; **Lautschrift** *f* phonetics *pl*; **Lautsprecher** *m* loudspeaker; **Lautsprecheranlage** *f*: **öffentliche Lautsprecheranlage** public-address *od* PA system; **Lautsprecherwagen** *m* loudspeaker van; **lautstark** *adj* vociferous; **Lautstärke** *f* (*Rundf*) volume
lauwarm ['lauvarm] *adj* (*lit, fig*) lukewarm
Lava ['la:va] (**-, Laven**) *f* lava
Lavendel [la'vɛndəl] (**-s, -**) *m* lavender
Lawine [la'vi:nə] *f* avalanche
Lawinengefahr *f* danger of avalanches
lax [laks] *adj* lax
Layout, Lay-out ['le:|aut] (**-s, -s**) *nt* layout
Lazarett [latsa'rɛt] (**-(e)s, -e**) *nt* (*Mil*) hospital, infirmary
Ldkrs. *abk* = **Landkreis**
leasen ['li:zən] *vt* to lease
Leasing ['li:zɪŋ] (**-s, -s**) *nt* (*Comm*) leasing
Lebehoch *nt* three cheers *pl*
Lebemann (**-(e)s, *pl* -männer**) *m* man about town
Leben ['le:bən] (**-s, -**) *nt* life; **am ~ sein/ bleiben** to be/stay alive; **ums ~ kommen** to die; **etw ins ~ rufen** to bring sth into being; **seines ~s nicht mehr sicher sein** to fear for one's life; **etw für sein ~ gern tun** to love doing sth
leben *vt, vi* to live
lebend *adj* living; **~es Inventar** livestock
lebendig [le'bɛndɪç] *adj* living, alive; (*lebhaft*) lively; **Lebendigkeit** *f* liveliness
Lebens- zW: **Lebensabend** *m* old age; **Lebensalter** *nt* age; **Lebensanschauung** *f* philosophy of life; **Lebensart** *f* way of life; **lebensbejahend** *adj* positive; **Lebensdauer** *f* life (span); (*von Maschine*) life; **Lebenserfahrung** *f* experience of life; **Lebenserwartung** *f* life expectancy; **lebensfähig** *adj* able to live; **lebensfroh** *adj* full of the joys of life; **Lebensgefahr** *f*: **Lebensgefahr!** danger!; **in Lebensgefahr** critically *od* dangerously ill; **lebensgefährlich** *adj* dangerous; (*Krankheit, Verletzung*) critical; **Lebensgefährte** *m*: **ihr Lebensgefährte** the man she lives with; **Lebensgefährtin** *f*: **seine Lebensgefährtin** the woman he lives with; **Lebensgröße** *f*: **in Lebensgröße** life-size(d); **Lebenshaltungskosten** *pl* cost of living *sing*; **Lebensinhalt** *m* purpose in life; **Lebensjahr** *nt* year of life; **Lebenskünstler** *m* master in the art of living; **Lebenslage** *f* situation in life; **lebenslänglich** *adj* (*Strafe*) for life; **Lebenslauf** *m* curriculum vitae, CV; **lebenslustig** *adj* cheerful, lively; **Lebensmittel** *pl* food *sing*; **Lebensmittelgeschäft** *nt*

grocer's; **Lebensmittelvergiftung** *f* food poisoning; **lebensmüde** *adj* tired of life; **Lebenspartnerschaft** *f* long-term relationship; **eingetragene Lebenspartnerschaft** registered *or* civil (*Brit*) partnership; **Lebensqualität** *f* quality of life; **Lebensraum** *m* (*Pol*) Lebensraum; (*Biol*) biosphere; **Lebensretter** *m* lifesaver; **Lebensstandard** *m* standard of living; **Lebensstellung** *f* permanent post; **Lebensstil** *m* life style; **Lebensunterhalt** *m* livelihood; **Lebensversicherung** *f* life insurance; **Lebenswandel** *m* way of life; **Lebensweise** *f* way of life, habits *pl*; **Lebensweisheit** *f* maxim; (*Lebenserfahrung*) wisdom; **Lebenswichtig** *adj* vital; **Lebenszeichen** *nt* sign of life; **Lebenszeit** *f* lifetime; **Beamter auf Lebenszeit** permanent civil servant
Leber ['le:bər] (**-, -n**) *f* liver; **frei** *od* **frisch von der ~ weg reden** (*umg*) to speak out frankly; **Leberfleck** *m* mole; **Leberkäse** *m* ≈ meat loaf; **Lebertran** *m* cod-liver oil; **Leberwurst** *f* liver sausage
Lebewesen *nt* creature
Lebewohl *nt* farewell, goodbye
leb- zW: **lebhaft** *adj* lively, vivacious; **Lebhaftigkeit** *f* liveliness, vivacity; **Lebkuchen** *m* gingerbread; **leblos** *adj* lifeless; **Lebtag** *m* (*fig*): **das werde ich mein Lebtag nicht vergessen** I'll never forget that as long as I live; **Lebzeiten** *pl*: **zu jds Lebzeiten** (*Leben*) in sb's lifetime
lechzen ['lɛçtsən] *vi*: **nach etw ~** to long for sth
leck [lɛk] *adj* leaky, leaking; **Leck** (**-(e)s, -e**) *nt* leak
lecken[1] *vi* (*Loch haben*) to leak
lecken[2] *vt, vi* (*schlecken*) to lick
lecker ['lɛkər] *adj* delicious, tasty; **Leckerbissen** *m* dainty morsel; **Leckermaul** *nt*: **ein Leckermaul sein** to enjoy one's food
led. *abk* = **ledig**
Leder ['le:dər] (**-s, -**) *nt* leather; (*umg: Fußball*) ball; **Lederhose** *f* leather trousers *pl*; (*von Tracht*) leather shorts *pl*
ledern *adj* leather
Lederwaren *pl* leather goods *pl*
ledig ['le:dɪç] *adj* single; **einer Sache** *gen* **~ sein** to be free of sth; **lediglich** *adv* merely, solely
leer [le:r] *adj* empty; (*Blick*) vacant; **~ gefegt** (*Straße*) deserted; **~ stehend** empty
Leere (**-**) *f* emptiness; (**eine**) **gähnende ~** a gaping void
leeren *vt* to empty ▷ *vr* to (become) empty
Leer- zW: **Leergewicht** *nt* unladen weight; **Leergut** *nt* empties *pl*; **Leerlauf** *m* (*Aut*) neutral; **Leertaste** *f* (*Schreibmaschine*) space-bar
Leerung *f* emptying; (*Post*) collection
legal [le'ga:l] *adj* legal, lawful
legalisieren [legali'zi:rən] *vt* to legalize
Legalität [legali'tɛ:t] *f* legality; (**etwas**) **außerhalb der ~** (*euph*) (slightly) outside the law
Legasthenie [legaste'ni:] *f* dyslexia

Legastheniker, in [legas'te:nikər(ɪn)] (**-s, -**) *m(f)* dyslexic

Legebatterie *f* laying battery

legen ['le:gən] *vt* to lay, put, place; (*Ei*) to lay ▷ *vr* to lie down; (*fig*) to subside; **sich ins Bett ~** to go to bed

Legende [le'gɛndə] (**-, -n**) *f* legend

leger [le'ʒɛːr] *adj* casual

legieren [le'gi:rən] *vt* to alloy

Legierung *f* alloy

Legislative [legɪsla'ti:və] *f* legislature

Legislaturperiode [legɪsla'tu:rperio:də] *f* parliamentary (*Brit*) *od* congressional (*US*) term

legitim [legi'ti:m] *adj* legitimate

Legitimation [legiti:matsi'o:n] *f* legitimation

legitimieren [legiti'mi:rən] *vt* to legitimate ▷ *vr* to prove one's identity

Legitimität [legitimi'tɛ:t] *f* legitimacy

Lehm [le:m] (**-(e)s, -e**) *m* loam

lehmig *adj* loamy

Lehne ['le:nə] (**-, -n**) *f* arm; (*Rückenlehne*) back

lehnen *vt, vr* to lean

Lehnstuhl *m* armchair

Lehr- *zW:* **Lehramt** *nt* teaching profession; **Lehrbefähigung** *f* teaching qualification; **Lehrbrief** *m* indentures *pl*; **Lehrbuch** *nt* textbook

Lehre ['le:rə] (**-, -n**) *f* teaching, doctrine; (*beruflich*) apprenticeship; (*moralisch*) lesson; (*Tech*) gauge; **bei jdm in die ~ gehen** to serve one's apprenticeship with sb

lehren *vt* to teach

Lehrer, in (**-s, -**) *m(f)* teacher; **Lehrerausbildung** *f* teacher training; **Lehrerkollegium** *nt* teaching staff; **Lehrerzimmer** *nt* staff room

Lehr- *zW:* **Lehrgang** *m* course; **Lehrgeld** *nt:* **Lehrgeld für etw zahlen müssen** (*fig*) to pay dearly for sth; **Lehrjahre** *pl* apprenticeship *sing*; **Lehrkraft** *f* (*form*) teacher; **Lehrling** *m* apprentice; trainee; **Lehrmittel** *nt* teaching aid; **Lehrplan** *m* syllabus; **Lehrprobe** *f* demonstration lesson, crit (*umg*); **lehrreich** *adj* instructive; **Lehrsatz** *m* proposition; **Lehrstelle** *f* apprenticeship; **Lehrstuhl** *m* chair; **Lehrzeit** *f* apprenticeship

Leib [laɪp] (**-(e)s, -er**) *m* body; **halt ihn mir vom ~!** keep him away from me!; **etw am eigenen ~(e) spüren** to experience sth for o.s.

leiben ['laɪbən] *vi:* **wie er leibt und lebt** to a T (*umg*)

Leibes- *zW:* **Leibeserziehung** *f* physical education; **Leibeskräfte** *pl:* **aus Leibeskräften schreien** *etc* to shout *etc* with all one's might; **Leibesübung** *f* physical exercise; **Leibesvisitation** *f* body search

Leibgericht *nt* favourite (*Brit*) *od* favorite (*US*) meal

Leib- *zW:* **leibhaftig** *adj* personified; (*Teufel*) incarnate; **leiblich** *adj* bodily; (*Vater etc*) natural; **Leibrente** *f* life annuity; **Leibwache** *f* bodyguard

Leiche ['laɪçə] (**-, -n**) *f* corpse; **er geht über ~n**

(*umg*) he'd stick at nothing

Leichen- *zW:* **Leichenbeschauer** (**-s, -**) *m* doctor conducting a post-mortem; **Leichenhalle** *f* mortuary; **Leichenhemd** *nt* shroud; **Leichenträger** *m* bearer; **Leichenwagen** *m* hearse

Leichnam ['laɪçna:m] (**-(e)s, -e**) *m* corpse

leicht [laɪçt] *adj* light; (*einfach*) easy ▷ *adv:* **~ zerbrechlich** very fragile; **es sich** *dat* **~ machen** to make things easy for o.s.; (*nicht gewissenhaft sein*) to take the easy way out; **~ verletzt** slightly injured; **nichts ~er als das!** nothing (could be) simpler!; *siehe auch* **leichtfallen; leichtnehmen; Leichtathletik** *f* athletics *sing;* **leichtfallen** *unreg vi:* **jdm leichtfallen** to be easy for sb; **leichtfertig** *adj* thoughtless; **leichtgläubig** *adj* gullible, credulous; **Leichtgläubigkeit** *f* gullibility, credulity; **leichthin** *adv* lightly

Leichtigkeit *f* easiness; **mit ~** with ease

leicht- *zW:* **leichtlebig** *adj* easy-going; **Leichtmatrose** *m* ordinary seaman; **Leichtmetall** *nt* light alloy; **leichtnehmen** *unreg vt* to take lightly; **Leichtsinn** *m* carelessness; **sträflicher Leichtsinn** criminal negligence; **leichtsinnig** *adj* careless

Leid [laɪt] (**-(e)s**) *nt* grief, sorrow; **jdm sein ~ klagen** to tell sb one's troubles

leid *adj:* **etw ~ haben** *od* **sein** to be tired of sth; *siehe auch* **leidtun**

leiden ['laɪdən] *unreg vt* to suffer; (*erlauben*) to permit ▷ *vi* to suffer; **jdn/etw nicht ~ können** not to be able to stand sb/sth; **Leiden** (**-s, -**) *nt* suffering; (*Krankheit*) complaint

Leidenschaft *f* passion; **leidenschaftlich** *adj* passionate

Leidens- *zW:* **Leidensgenosse** *m*, **Leidensgenossin** *f* fellow sufferer; **Leidensgeschichte** *f:* **die Leidensgeschichte (Christi)** (*Rel*) Christ's Passion

leider ['laɪdər] *adv* unfortunately; **ja, ~** yes, I'm afraid so; **~ nicht** I'm afraid not

leidig ['laɪdɪç] *adj* miserable, tiresome

leidlich ['laɪtlɪç] *adj* tolerable ▷ *adv* tolerably

Leidtragende, r *f(m)* bereaved; (*Benachteiligter*) one who suffers

leidtun *unreg vi:* **es tut mir/ihm leid** I am/he is sorry; **er/das tut mir leid** I am sorry for him/about it; **sie kann einem ~** you can't help feeling sorry for her

Leidwesen *nt:* **zu jds ~** to sb's dismay

Leier ['laɪər] (**-, -n**) *f* lyre; (*fig*) old story

Leierkasten *m* barrel organ

leiern *vt* (*Kurbel*) to turn; (*umg: Gedicht*) to rattle off ▷ *vi* (*drehen*): **~ an** +*dat* to crank

Leih- *zW:* **Leiharbeit** *f* subcontracted labour; **Leiharbeiter, in** *m(f)* subcontracted worker; **Leihbibliothek** *f*, **Leihbücherei** *f* lending library

leihen ['laɪən] *unreg vt* to lend; **sich** *dat* **etw ~** to borrow sth

Leih- *zW:* **Leihgabe** *f* loan; **Leihgebühr** *f* hire charge; **Leihhaus** *nt* pawnshop;

Leim | Lette

Leihmutter f surrogate mother; **Leihschein** m pawn ticket; (in der Bibliothek) borrowing slip; **Leihunternehmen** nt hire service; (Arbeitsmarkt) temp service; **Leihwagen** m hired car (Brit), rental car (US); **leihweise** adv on loan

Leim [laɪm] (-(e)s, -e) m glue; **jdm auf den ~ gehen** to be taken in by sb; **leimen** vt to glue

Leine ['laɪnə] (-, -n) f line, cord; (Hundeleine) leash, lead; ~ **ziehen** (umg) to clear out

Leinen (-s, -) nt linen; (grob, segeltuchartig) canvas; (als Bucheinband) cloth

leinen adj linen

Lein- zW: **Leinsamen** m linseed; **Leintuch** nt linen cloth; (Bettuch) sheet; **Leinwand** f (Kunst) canvas; (Film) screen

leise ['laɪzə] adj quiet; (sanft) soft, gentle; **mit ~r Stimme** in a low voice; **nicht die ~ste Ahnung haben** not to have the slightest (idea)

Leisetreter (pej: umg) m pussyfoot(er)

Leiste ['laɪstə] (-, -n) f ledge; (Zierleiste) strip; (Anat) groin

leisten ['laɪstən] vt (Arbeit) to do; (Gesellschaft) to keep; (Ersatz) to supply; (vollbringen) to achieve; **sich** dat **etw ~** to allow o.s. sth; (sich gönnen) to treat o.s. to sth; **sich** dat **etw ~ können** to be able to afford sth

Leistenbruch m (Med) hernia, rupture

Leistung f performance; (gute) achievement; (eines Motors) power; (von Krankenkasse etc) benefit; (Zahlung) payment

Leistungs- zW: **Leistungsabfall** m (in Bezug auf Qualität) drop in performance; (in Bezug auf Quantität) drop in productivity; **Leistungsbeurteilung** f performance appraisal; **Leistungsdruck** m pressure; **leistungsfähig** adj efficient; **Leistungsfähigkeit** f efficiency; **Leistungsgesellschaft** f meritocracy; **Leistungskurs** m (Sch) set; **Leistungskürzung** f reduction of benefit; **leistungsorientiert** adj performance-orientated; **Leistungsprinzip** nt achievement principle; **Leistungssport** m competitive sport; **Leistungszulage** f productivity bonus

Leitartikel m leader

Leitbild nt model

leiten ['laɪtən] vt to lead; (Firma) to manage; (in eine Richtung) to direct; (Elek) to conduct; **sich von jdm/etw ~ lassen** (lit, fig) to (let o.s.) be guided by sb/sth

leitend adj leading; (Gedanke, Idee) dominant; (Stellung, Position) managerial; (Ingenieur, Beamter) in charge; (Phys) conductive; **~er Angestellter** executive

Leiter[1] ['laɪtər] (-s, -) m leader, head; (Elek) conductor

Leiter[2] ['laɪtər] (-, -n) f ladder

Leiterin f leader, head

Leiterplatte f (Comput) circuit board

Leit- zW: **Leitfaden** m guide; **Leitfähigkeit** f conductivity; **Leitgedanke** m central idea;

Leitmotiv nt leitmotiv; **Leitplanke** f crash barrier; **Leitspruch** m motto

Leitung f (Führung) direction; (Film, Theat etc) production; (von Firma) management; directors pl; (Wasserleitung) pipe; (Kabel) cable; **eine lange ~ haben** to be slow on the uptake; **da ist jemand in der ~** (umg) there's somebody else on the line

Leitungs- zW: **Leitungsdraht** m wire; **Leitungsmast** m telegraph pole; **Leitungsrohr** nt pipe; **Leitungswasser** nt tap water

Leitwerk nt (Aviat) tail unit

Leitzins f (Fin) base rate

Lektion [lɛktsi'oːn] f lesson; **jdm eine ~ erteilen** (fig) to teach sb a lesson

Lektor, in ['lɛktɔr, lɛk'toːrɪn] m(f) (Univ) lector; (Verlag) editor

Lektüre [lɛk'tyːrə] (-, -n) f (Lesen) reading; (Lesestoff) reading matter

Lende ['lɛndə] (-, -n) f loin

Lendenbraten m roast sirloin

Lendenstück nt fillet

lenkbar ['lɛŋkbaːr] adj (Fahrzeug) steerable; (Kind) manageable

lenken vt to steer; (Kind) to guide; (Gespräch) to lead; ~ **auf** +akk (Blick, Aufmerksamkeit) to direct at; (Verdacht) to throw on(to); (: auf sich) to draw onto

Lenkrad nt steering wheel

Lenkstange f handlebars pl

Lenkung f steering; (Führung) direction

Lenz [lɛnts] (-es, -e) m (liter) spring; **sich** dat **einen (faulen) ~ machen** (umg) to laze about, swing the lead

Leopard [leo'part] (-en, -en) m leopard

Lepra ['leːpra] (-) f leprosy; **Leprakranke, r** f(m) leper

Lerche ['lɛrçə] (-, -n) f lark

lernbegierig adj eager to learn

lernbehindert adj educationally handicapped (Brit) od handicaped (US)

lernen vt to learn ▷ vi: **er lernt bei der Firma Braun** he's training at Braun's

Lernhilfe f educational aid

lesbar ['leːsbaːr] adj legible

Lesbierin ['lɛsbiərɪn] f lesbian

lesbisch adj lesbian

Lese ['leːzə] (-, -n) f (Weinlese) harvest

Lesebuch nt reading book, reader

lesen unreg vt to read; (ernten) to gather, pick ▷ vi to read; **~/schreiben** (Comput) to read/write

Leser, in (-s, -) m(f) reader

Leseratte ['leːzəratə] (umg) f bookworm

Leser- zW: **Leserbrief** m reader's letter; **„Leserbriefe"** "letters to the editor"; **Leserkreis** m readership; **leserlich** adj legible

Lese- zW: **Lesesaal** m reading room; **Lesestoff** m reading material; **Lesezeichen** nt bookmark; **Lesezirkel** m magazine club

Lesotho [le'zoːto] (-s) nt Lesotho

Lesung ['leːzʊŋ] f (Parl) reading; (Eccl) lesson

lethargisch [le'targɪʃ] adj (Med, fig) lethargic

Lette ['lɛtə] (-n, -n) m, **Lettin** f Latvian

lettisch *adj* Latvian
Lettland ['lɛtlant] (-s) *nt* Latvia
Letzt *f*: **zu guter ~** finally, in the end
letzte, r, s ['lɛtstə(r, s)] *adj* last; (*neueste*) latest;
  der L~ Wille the last will and testament; **bis
  zum L~n** to the utmost; **zum ~n Mal** for the
  last time; **in ~r Zeit** recently
Letzte, s *nt*: **das ist ja das ~!** (*umg*) that really
  is the limit!
letztens *adv* lately
letztere, r, s *adj* the latter
letztlich *adv* in the end
Leuchte ['lɔʏçtə] (-, -n) *f* lamp, light;
  (*umg: Mensch*) genius
leuchten *vi* to shine, gleam
Leuchter (-s, -) *m* candlestick
Leucht- *zW*: **Leuchtfarbe** *f* fluorescent colour
  (*Brit*) *od* color (*US*); **Leuchtfeuer** *nt* beacon;
  Leuchtkäfer *m* glow-worm; **Leuchtkugel**
  f flare; **Leuchtpistole** *f* flare pistol;
  Leuchtrakete *f* flare; **Leuchtreklame** *f* neon
  sign; **Leuchtröhre** *f* strip light; **Leuchtturm**
  m lighthouse; **Leuchtzifferblatt** *nt* luminous
  dial
leugnen ['lɔʏgnən] *vt, vi* to deny
Leugnung *f* denial
Leukämie [lɔʏkɛ'mi:] *f* leukaemia (*Brit*),
  leukemia (*US*)
Leukoplast® [lɔʏko'plast] (-(e)s, -e) *nt*
  Elastoplast®
Leumund ['lɔʏmʊnt] (-(e)s, -e) *m* reputation
Leumundszeugnis *nt* character reference
Leute ['lɔʏtə] *pl* people *pl*; **kleine ~** (*fig*)
  ordinary people; **etw unter die ~ bringen**
  (*umg: Gerücht etc*) to spread sth around
Leutnant ['lɔʏtnant] (-s, -s *od* -e) *m* lieutenant
leutselig ['lɔʏtze:lɪç] *adj* affable; **Leutseligkeit**
  f affability
Leviten [le'vi:tən] *pl*: **jdm die ~ lesen** (*umg*) to
  haul sb over the coals
lexikalisch [lɛksi'ka:lɪʃ] *adj* lexical
Lexikografie [lɛksikogra'fi:] *f* lexicography
Lexikon ['lɛksikɔn] (-s, **Lexiken** *od* **Lexika**) *nt*
  encyclopedia
lfd. *abk* = **laufend**
Libanese [liba'ne:zə] (-n, -n) *m*, **Libanesin** *f*
  Lebanese
libanesisch *adj* Lebanese
Libanon ['li:banɔn] (-s) *m*: **der ~** the Lebanon
Libelle [li'bɛlə] (-, -n) *f* dragonfly; (*Tech*) spirit
  level
liberal [libe'ra:l] *adj* liberal
Liberale, r *f(m)* (*Pol*) Liberal
Liberalisierung [liberali'zi:rʊŋ] *f*
  liberalization
Liberalismus [libera'lɪsmʊs] *m* liberalism
Liberia [li'be:ria] (-s) *nt* Liberia
Liberianer, in [liberi'a:nər(ɪn)] (-s, -) *m(f)*
  Liberian
liberianisch *adj* Liberian
Libero ['li:bero] (-s, -s) *m* (*Fussball*) sweeper
Libyen ['li:byən] (-s) *nt* Libya
Libyer, in (-s, -) *m(f)* Libyan

libysch *adj* Libyan
Licht [lɪçt] (-(e)s, -er) *nt* light; **~ machen**
  (*anschalten*) to turn on a light; (*anzünden*) to
  light a candle *etc*; **mir geht ein ~ auf** it's
  dawned on me; **jdn hinters ~ führen** (*fig*) to
  lead sb up the garden path
licht *adj* light, bright
Licht- *zW*: **Lichtbild** *nt* photograph; (*Dia*)
  slide; **Lichtblick** *m* cheering prospect;
  lichtempfindlich *adj* sensitive to light
lichten ['lɪçtən] *vt* to clear; (*Anker*) to weigh ▷ *vr*
  (*Nebel*) to clear; (*Haar*) to thin
lichterloh ['lɪçtər'lo:] *adv*: **~ brennen** to blaze
Licht- *zW*: **Lichtgeschwindigkeit** *f* speed
  of light; **Lichtgriffel** *m* (*Comput*) light pen;
  Lichthupe *f* flashing of headlights; **Lichtjahr**
  nt light year; **Lichtmaschine** *f* dynamo;
  Lichtmess (-) *f* Candlemas; **Lichtpause** *f*
  photocopy; (*bei Blaupausverfahren*) blueprint;
  Lichtschalter *m* light switch; **lichtscheu** *adj*
  averse to light; (*fig: Gesindel*) shady
Lichtung *f* clearing, glade
Lid [li:t] (-(e)s, -er) *nt* eyelid; **Lidschatten** *m*
  eyeshadow
lieb [li:p] *adj* dear; **(viele) ~e Grüße, Deine
  Silvia** love, Silvia; **Liebe Anna, ~er Klaus!** ...
  Dear Anna and Klaus, ...; **am ~sten lese ich
  Kriminalromane** best of all I like detective
  novels; **den ~en langen Tag** (*umg*) all the
  livelong day; **sich bei jdm ~ Kind machen**
  (*pej*) to suck up to sb (*umg*); **~ gewinnen** to get
  fond of; **~ haben** to love; (*weniger stark*) to be
  (very) fond of
liebäugeln ['li:plɔʏgəln] *vi untr*: **mit dem
  Gedanken ~, etw zu tun** to toy with the idea
  of doing sth
Liebe ['li:bə] (-, -n) *f* love; **liebebedürftig**
  adj: **liebebedürftig sein** to need love
Liebelei *f* flirtation
lieben ['li:bən] *vt* to love; (*weniger stark*) to like;
  etw ~d gern tun to love to do sth
liebens- *zW*: **liebenswert** *adj*
  loveable; **liebenswürdig** *adj* kind;
  liebenswürdigerweise *adv* kindly;
  Liebenswürdigkeit *f* kindness
lieber ['li:bər] *adv* rather, preferably; **ich gehe
  ~ nicht** I'd rather not go; **ich trinke ~ Wein
  als Bier** I prefer wine to beer; **bleib ~ im Bett**
  you'd better stay in bed
Liebes- *zW*: **Liebesbrief** *m* love letter;
  Liebesdienst *m* good turn; **Liebeskummer**
  m: **Liebeskummer haben** to be lovesick;
  Liebespaar *nt* courting couple, lovers *pl*;
  Liebesroman *m* romantic novel
liebevoll *adj* loving
lieb- *zW*: **Liebhaber, in** (-s, -) *m(f)* lover;
  (*Sammler*) collector; **Liebhaberei** *f* hobby;
  liebkosen *vt untr* to caress; **lieblich** *adj* lovely,
  charming; (*Duft, Wein*) sweet
Liebling *m* darling
Lieblings- *in zw* favourite (*Brit*), favorite (*US*)
lieblos *adj* unloving
Liebschaft *f* love affair

213

Liechtenstein ['lıçtənʃtaın] (-s) nt Liechtenstein

Lied [li:t] (-(e)s, -er) nt song; (Eccl) hymn; **davon kann ich ein ~ singen** (fig) I could tell you a thing or two about that (umg)

Liederbuch nt songbook; (Rel) hymn book

liederlich ['li:dərlıç] adj slovenly; (Lebenswandel) loose, immoral; **Liederlichkeit** f slovenliness; immorality

lief etc [li:f] vb siehe **laufen**

Lieferant [li:fə'rant] m supplier

Lieferanteneingang m tradesmen's entrance; (von Warenhaus etc) goods entrance

lieferbar adj (vorrätig) available

Lieferbedingungen pl terms of delivery

Lieferfrist f delivery period

liefern ['li:fərn] vt to deliver; (versorgen mit) to supply; (Beweis) to produce

Lieferschein m delivery note

Liefertermin m delivery date

Lieferung f delivery; (Versorgung) supply

Lieferwagen m (delivery) van, panel truck (US)

Lieferzeit f delivery period; **~ 6 Monate** delivery six months

Liege ['li:gə] (-, -n) f bed; (Campingliege) camp bed (Brit), cot (US); **Liegegeld** nt (Hafen, Flughafen) demurrage

liegen ['li:gən] unreg vi to lie; (sich befinden) to be (situated); **mir liegt nichts/viel daran** it doesn't matter to me/it matters a lot to me; **es liegt bei Ihnen, ob ...** it rests with you whether ...; **Sprachen ~ mir nicht** languages are not my line; **woran liegt es?** what's the cause?; **so, wie die Dinge jetzt ~** as things stand at the moment; **an mir soll es nicht ~, wenn die Sache schiefgeht** it won't be my fault if things go wrong; **~ bleiben** (Person) to stay in bed; (nicht aufstehen) to stay lying down; (Ding) to be left (behind); (nicht ausgeführt werden) to be left (undone); **~ lassen** (vergessen) to leave behind; **Liegenschaft** f real estate

Liege- zW: **Liegeplatz** m (auf Schiff, in Zug etc) berth; (Ankerplatz) moorings pl; **Liegesitz** m (Aut) reclining seat; **Liegestuhl** m deck chair; **Liegestütz** m (Sport) press-up (Brit), push-up (US); **Liegewagen** m (Eisenb) couchette car; **Liegewiese** f lawn (for sunbathing)

lieh etc [li:] vb siehe **leihen**

ließ etc [li:s] vb siehe **lassen**

liest [li:st] vb siehe **lesen**

Lift [lıft] (-(e)s, -e od -s) m lift

Liga ['li:ga] (-, Ligen) f (Sport) league

liieren [li'i:rən] vt: **liiert sein** (Firmen etc) to be working together; (ein Verhältnis haben) to have a relationship

Likör [li'kø:r] (-s, -e) m liqueur

lila ['li:la] adj inv purple; **Lila** (-s, -s) nt (Farbe) purple

Lilie ['li:liə] f lily

Liliputaner, in [lilipu'ta:nər(ın)] (-s, -) m(f) midget

Limit ['lımıt] (-s, -s od -e) nt limit; (Fin) ceiling

Limonade [limo'na:də] (-, -n) f lemonade

lind [lınt] adj gentle, mild

Linde ['lındə] (-, -n) f lime tree, linden

lindern ['lındərn] vt to alleviate, soothe

Linderung f alleviation

lindgrün adj lime green

Lineal [line'a:l] (-s, -e) nt ruler

linear [line'a:r] adj linear

Linguist, in [lıŋgu'ıst(ın)] m(f) linguist

Linguistik f linguistics sing

Linie ['li:niə] f line; **in erster ~** first and foremost; **auf die ~ achten** to watch one's figure; **fahren Sie mit der ~ 2** take the number 2 (bus etc)

Linien- zW: **Linienblatt** nt ruled sheet; **Linienbus** m service bus; **Linienflug** m scheduled flight; **Linienrichter** m (Sport) linesman; **linientreu** adj loyal to the (party) line

linieren [li'ni:rən], **liniieren** [lini'i:rən] vt to line

Link [lıŋk] (-s, -s) m (Comput) link

Linke ['lıŋkə] (-, -n) f left side; left hand; (Pol) left

Linke, r f(m) (Pol) left-winger, leftie (pej)

linke, r, s adj left; **~ Masche** purl

linkisch adj awkward, gauche

links adv left; to od on the left; **~ von mir** on od to my left; **~ von der Mitte** left of centre; **jdn ~ liegen lassen** (fig: umg) to ignore sb; **das mache ich mit ~** (umg) I can do that with my eyes shut; **Linksabbieger** m motorist/vehicle turning left; **Linksaußen** (-s, -) m (Sport) outside left; **Linkshänder, in** (-s, -) m(f) left-handed person; **Linkskurve** f left-hand bend; **linkslastig** adj: **linkslastig sein** to list od lean to the left; **linksradikal** adj (Pol) radically left-wing; **Linksrutsch** m (Pol) swing to the left; **Linkssteuerung** f (Aut) left-hand drive; **Linksverkehr** m driving on the left

Linse ['lınzə] (-, -n) f lentil; (optisch) lens

linsen (umg) vi to peek

Lippe ['lıpə] (-, -n) f lip

Lippenbekenntnis nt lip service

Lippenstift m lipstick

Liquidation [likvidatsi'o:n] f liquidation

Liquidationswert m break-up value

liquid [lik'vi:t], **liquide** [lik'vi:də] adj (Firma) solvent

Liquidator [likvi'da:tər] m liquidator

liquidieren [likvi'di:rən] vt to liquidate

Liquidität [likvidi'te:t] f liquidity

lispeln ['lıspəln] vi to lisp

Lissabon ['lısabon] nt Lisbon

List [lıst] (-, -en) f cunning; (Plan) trick, ruse; **mit ~ und Tücke** (umg) with a lot of coaxing

Liste ['lıstə] (-, -n) f list

Listenplatz m (Pol) place on the party list

Listenpreis m list price

listig adj cunning, sly

Litanei [lita'naı] f litany

Litauen ['li:tauən] (-s) nt Lithuania

Litauer, in (-s, -) m(f) Lithuanian

litauisch adj Lithuanian

Liter ['li:tər] (**-s, -**) *m od nt* litre (*Brit*), liter (*US*)
literarisch [lite'ra:rɪʃ] *adj* literary
Literatur [litera'tu:r] *f* literature;
  Literaturpreis *m* award *od* prize for literature;
  Literaturwissenschaft *f* literary studies *pl*
literweise ['li:tərvaɪzə] *adv* (*lit*) by the litre (*Brit*)
  od liter (*US*); (*fig*) by the gallon
Litfaßsäule ['lɪtfaszɔylə] *f* advertising (*Brit*) *od*
  advertizing (*US*) pillar
Lithografie [litogra'fi:] *f* lithography
litt *etc* [lɪt] *vb siehe* **leiden**
Liturgie [litʊr'gi:] *f* liturgy
liturgisch [li'tʊrgɪʃ] *adj* liturgical
Litze ['lɪtsə] (**-, -n**) *f* braid; (*Elek*) flex
live [laɪf] *adj, adv* (*Rundf, TV*) live
Livree [li'vre:] (**-, -n**) *f* livery
Lizenz [li'tsɛnts] *f* licence (*Brit*), license
  (*US*); **Lizenzausgabe** *f* licensed edition;
  Lizenzgebühr *f* licence fee; (*im Verlagswesen*)
  royalty
Lkw, LKW (**-(s), -(s)**) *m abk* = **Lastkraftwagen**
Lkw-Maut, LKW-Maut *f* toll for trucks
Lob [lo:p] (**-(e)s**) *nt* praise
Lobby ['lɔbi] (**-, -s**) *f* lobby
loben ['lo:bən] *vt* to praise; **das lob ich mir**
  that's what I like (to see/hear *etc*)
lobenswert *adj* praiseworthy
löblich ['lø:plɪç] *adj* praiseworthy, laudable
Loblied *nt*: **ein ~ auf jdn/etw singen** to sing
  sb's/sth's praises
Lobrede *f* eulogy
Loch [lɔx] (**-(e)s, ̈-er**) *nt* hole; **lochen** *vt* to
  punch holes in; **Locher** (**-s, -**) *m* punch
löcherig ['lœçərɪç] *adj* full of holes
löchern (*umg*) *vt*: **jdn ~** to pester sb with
  questions
Loch- *zW*: **Lochkarte** *f* punch card; **Lochzange**
  f punch
Locke ['lɔkə] (**-, -n**) *f* lock, curl
locken *vt* to entice; (*Haare*) to curl
lockend *adj* tempting
Lockenwickler (**-s, -**) *m* curler
locker ['lɔkər] *adj* loose; (*Kuchen, Schaum*)
  light; (*umg*) cool; **lockerlassen** *unreg vi*: **nicht**
  lockerlassen not to let up
lockern *vt* to loosen ▷ *vr* (*Atmosphäre*) to get
  more relaxed
Lockerungsübung *f* loosening-up exercise;
  (*zum Warmwerden*) limbering-up exercise
lockig ['lɔkɪç] *adj* curly
Lockmittel *nt* lure
Lockruf *m* call
Lockung *f* enticement
Lockvogel *m* decoy, bait; **Lockvogelangebot** *nt*
  (*Comm*) loss leader
Lodenmantel ['lo:dənmantəl] *m* thick woollen
  coat
lodern ['lo:dərn] *vi* to blaze
Löffel ['lœfəl] (**-s, -**) *m* spoon
löffeln *vt* to spoon
löffelweise *adv* by the spoonful
log *etc* [lo:k] *vb siehe* **lügen**
Logarithmentafel [loga'rɪtməntaː:fəl] *f*

log(arithm) tables *pl*
Logarithmus [loga'rɪtmʊs] *m* logarithm
Loge ['lo:ʒə] (**-, -n**) *f* (*Theat*) box; (*Freimaurerloge*)
  (masonic) lodge; (*Pförtnerloge*) office
logieren [lo'ʒi:rən] *vi* to lodge, stay
Logik ['lo:gɪk] *f* logic
Logis [lo'ʒi:] (**-, -**) *nt*: **Kost und ~** board and
  lodging
logisch ['lo:gɪʃ] *adj* logical; (*umg: selbstverständ-*
  lich): **gehst du auch hin?** — **~** are you going
  too? — of course
logo ['logo] (*umg*) *interj* obvious!
Logopäde [logo'pɛ:də] (**-n, -n**) *m* speech
  therapist
Logopädin [logo'pɛ:dɪn] *f* speech therapist
Lohn [lo:n] (**-(e)s, ̈-e**) *m* reward; (*Arbeitslohn*)
  pay, wages *pl*; **Lohnabrechnung** *f* wages slip;
  Lohnausfall *m* loss of earnings; **Lohnbüro**
  nt wages office; **Lohndiktat** *nt* wage
  dictate; **Lohndumping** *nt* wage dumping;
  Lohnempfänger *m* wage earner
lohnen ['lo:nən] *vt* (*liter*): **jdm etw ~** to reward
  sb for sth ▷ *vr unpers* to be worth it
lohnend *adj* worthwhile
Lohn- *zW*: **Lohnerhöhung** *f* wage increase,
  pay rise; **Lohnforderung** *f* wage claim;
  Lohnfortzahlung *f* continued payment of
  wages; **Lohnfortzahlungsgesetz** *nt law on*
  continued payment of wages; **Lohngefälle** *nt* wage
  differential; **Lohnkosten** *pl* labour (*Brit*) *od*
  labor (*US*) costs; **Lohnpolitik** *f* wages policy;
  Lohnrunde *f* pay round; **Lohnsteuer** *f* income
  tax; **Lohnsteuerjahresausgleich** *m* income
  tax return; **Lohnsteuerkarte** *f* (income) tax
  card; **Lohnstopp** *m* pay freeze; **Lohnstreifen** *m*
  pay slip; **Lohntüte** *f* pay packet
Lok [lɔk] (**-, -s**) *f abk* (= *Lokomotive*) loco (*umg*)
lokal [lo'ka:l] *adj* local
Lokal (**-(e)s, -e**) *nt* pub(lic house) (*Brit*)
Lokalblatt (*umg*) *nt* local paper
lokalisieren [lokali'zi:rən] *vt* to localize
Lokalisierung *f* localization
Lokalität [lokali'tɛ:t] *f* locality; (*Raum*)
  premises *pl*
Lokal- *zW*: **Lokalpresse** *f* local press; **Lokalteil**
  m (*Zeitung*) local section; **Lokaltermin** *m* (*Jur*)
  visit to the scene of the crime
Lokomotive [lokomo'ti:və] (**-, -n**) *f* locomotive
Lokomotivführer *m* engine driver (*Brit*),
  engineer (*US*)
lol *abk* (*Internet, Tel*) lol (= *Lautes Lachen*) laugh
  out loud
Lombardei [lɔmbar'daɪ] *f* Lombardy
London ['lɔndɔn] (**-s**) *nt* London
Londoner *adj attrib* London
Londoner, in (**-s, -**) *m(f)* Londoner
Lorbeer ['lɔrbe:r] (**-s, -en**) *m* (*lit, fig*) laurel;
  Lorbeerblatt *nt* (*Koch*) bay leaf
Lore ['lo:rə] (**-, -n**) *f* (*Min*) truck
Los [lo:s] (**-es, -e**) *nt* (*Schicksal*) lot, fate; (*in der*
  Lotterie) lottery ticket; **das große ~ ziehen**
  (*lit, fig*) to hit the jackpot; **etw durch das ~**
  entscheiden to decide sth by drawing lots

I

los adj loose ▷ adv: ~! go on!; **etw ~ sein** to be rid of sth; **was ist ~?** what's the matter?; **dort ist nichts/viel ~** there's nothing/a lot going on there; **ich bin mein ganzes Geld ~** (umg) I'm cleaned out; **irgendwas ist mit ihm ~** there's something wrong with him; **wir wollen früh ~** we want to be off early; **nichts wie ~!** let's get going; **losbinden** unreg vt to untie; **losbrechen** unreg vi (Sturm, Gewitter) to break

losch etc [lɔʃ] vb siehe **löschen**

Löschblatt ['lœʃblat] nt sheet of blotting paper

löschen ['lœʃən] vt (Feuer, Licht) to put out, extinguish; (Durst) to quench; (Comm) to cancel; (Tonband) to erase; (Fracht) to unload; (Comput) to delete; (Tinte) to blot ▷ vi (Feuerwehr) to put out a fire; (Papier) to blot

Lösch- zW: **Löschfahrzeug** nt fire engine; **Löschgerät** nt fire extinguisher; **Löschpapier** nt blotting paper; **Löschtaste** f (Comput) delete key

Löschung f extinguishing; (Comm) cancellation; (Fracht) unloading

lose ['loːzə] adj loose

Lösegeld nt ransom

losen ['loːzən] vi to draw lots

lösen ['løːzən] vt to loosen; (Handbremse) to release; (Husten, Krampf) to ease; (Rätsel etc) to solve; (Verlobung) to call off; (Chem) to dissolve; (Partnerschaft) to break up; (Fahrkarte) to buy ▷ vr (aufgehen) to come loose; (Schuss) to go off; (Zucker etc) to dissolve; (Problem, Schwierigkeit) to (re)solve itself

los- zW: **losfahren** unreg vi to leave; **losgehen** unreg vi to set out; (anfangen) to start; (Bombe) to go off; **jetzt gehts los!** here we go!; **nach hinten losgehen** (umg) to backfire; **auf jdn losgehen** to go for sb; **loskaufen** vt (Gefangene, Geiseln) to pay ransom for; **loskommen** unreg vi (sich befreien) to free o.s.; **von etw loskommen** to get away from sth; **loslassen** unreg vt (Seil etc) to let go of; **der Gedanke lässt mich nicht mehr los** the thought haunts me; **loslaufen** unreg vi to run off; **loslegen** (umg) vi: **nun leg mal los und erzähl(e) ...** now come on and tell me/us ...

löslich ['løːslɪç] adj soluble; **Löslichkeit** f solubility

loslösen vt to free ▷ vr: **sich (von etw) ~** to detach o.s. (from sth)

losmachen vt to loosen; (Boot) to unmoor ▷ vr to get free

Losnummer f ticket number

los- zW: **lossagen** vr: **sich von jdm/etw lossagen** to renounce sb/sth; **losschießen** unreg vi: **schieß los!** (fig: umg) fire away!; **losschrauben** vt to unscrew; **lossprechen** unreg vt to absolve; **losstürzen** vi: **auf jdn/etw losstürzen** to pounce on sb/sth

Losung ['loːzʊŋ] f watchword, slogan

Lösung ['løːzʊŋ] f (Lockermachen) loosening; (eines Rätsels, Chem) solution

Lösungsmittel nt solvent

loswerden unreg vt to get rid of

losziehen unreg vi (sich aufmachen) to set out; **gegen jdn ~** (fig) to run sb down

Lot [loːt] (-(e)s, -e) nt plumbline; (Math) perpendicular; **im ~** vertical; (fig) on an even keel; **die Sache ist wieder im ~** things have been straightened out; **loten** vt to plumb, sound

löten ['løːtən] vt to solder

Lothringen ['loːtrɪŋən] (-s) nt Lorraine

Lötkolben m soldering iron

Lotse ['loːtsə] (-n, -n) m pilot; (Aviat) air traffic controller

lotsen vt to pilot; (umg) to lure

Lotterie [lɔtə'riː] f lottery

Lotterleben ['lɔtərleːbən] (umg) nt dissolute life

Lotto ['lɔto] (-s, -s) nt ≈ National Lottery

Lottozahlen pl winning Lotto numbers pl

Löwe ['løːvə] (-n, -n) m lion; (Astrol) Leo

Löwen- zW: **Löwenanteil** m lion's share; **Löwenmaul** nt, **Löwenmäulchen** nt antirrhinum, snapdragon; **Löwenzahn** m dandelion

Löwin ['løːvɪn] f lioness

loyal [loa'jaːl] adj loyal

Loyalität [loajali'tɛːt] f loyalty

LP (-, -s) f abk (= Langspielplatte) LP

LSD (-(s)) nt abk (= Lysergsäurediäthylamid) LSD

lt. abk = **laut**

Luchs [lʊks] (-es, -e) m lynx

Lücke ['lʏkə] (-, -n) f gap; (Gesetzeslücke) loophole; (in Versorgung) break

Lücken- zW: **Lückenbüßer** (-s, -) m stopgap; **lückenhaft** adj full of gaps; (Versorgung) deficient; **lückenlos** adj complete

lud etc [luːt] vb siehe **laden**

Luder ['luːdər] (-s, -) (pej) nt (Frau) hussy; (bedauernswert) poor wretch

Luft [lʊft] (-, -̈e) f air; (Atem) breath; **die ~ anhalten** (lit) to hold one's breath; **seinem Herzen ~ machen** to get everything off one's chest; **in der ~ liegen** to be in the air; **dicke ~** (umg) a bad atmosphere; **(frische) ~ schnappen** (umg) to get some fresh air; **in die ~ fliegen** (umg) to explode; **diese Behauptung ist aus der ~ gegriffen** this statement is (a) pure invention; **die ~ ist rein** (umg) the coast is clear; **jdn an die (frische) ~ setzen** (umg) to show sb the door; **er ist ~ für mich** I'm not speaking to him; **jdn wie ~ behandeln** to ignore sb; **Luftangriff** m air raid; **Luftaufnahme** f aerial photo; **Luftballon** m balloon; **Luftblase** f air bubble; **Luftbrücke** f airlift; **luftdicht** adj airtight; **Luftdruck** m atmospheric pressure; **luftdurchlässig** adj pervious to air

lüften ['lʏftən] vt to air; (Hut) to lift, raise ▷ vi to let some air in

Luft- zW: **Luftfahrt** f aviation; **Luftfeuchtigkeit** f humidity; **Luftfracht** f air cargo; **luftgekühlt** adj air-cooled; **Luftgewehr** nt air rifle

luftig adj (Ort) breezy; (Raum) airy; (Kleider)

summery

Luft- zW: **Luftkissenfahrzeug** nt hovercraft; **Luftkrieg** m war in the air, aerial warfare; **Luftkurort** m health resort; **luftleer** adj: **luftleerer Raum** vacuum; **Luftlinie** f: **in der Luftlinie** as the crow flies; **Luftloch** nt air hole; (Aviat) air pocket; **Luftmatratze** f Lilo® (Brit), air mattress; **Luftpirat** m hijacker; **Luftpost** f airmail; **Luftpumpe** f (für Fahrrad) (bicycle) pump; **Luftraum** m air space; **Luftröhre** f (Anat) windpipe; **Luftschlange** f streamer; **Luftschloss** nt (fig) castle in the air; **Luftschutz** m anti-aircraft defence (Brit) od defense (US); **Luftschutzbunker** m, **Luftschutzkeller** m air-raid shelter; **Luftsprung** m (fig): **einen Luftsprung machen** to jump for joy

Lüftung ['lʏftʊŋ] f ventilation

Luft- zW: **Luftveränderung** f change of air; **Luftverkehr** m air traffic; **Luftverschmutzung** f air pollution; **Luftwaffe** f air force; **Luftweg** m: **etw auf dem Luftweg befördern** to transport sth by air; **Luftzufuhr** f air supply; **Luftzug** m draught (Brit), draft (US)

Lüge ['ly:gə] (-, -n) f lie; **jdn/etw ~n strafen** to give the lie to sb/sth

lügen ['ly:gən] unreg vi to lie; **wie gedruckt ~** (umg) to lie like mad

Lügendetektor ['ly:gəndetɛktɔr] m lie detector

Lügner, in (-s, -) m(f) liar

Luke ['lu:kə] (-, -n) f hatch; (Dachluke) skylight

lukrativ [lukra'ti:f] adj lucrative

Lümmel ['lʏməl] (-s, -) m lout

lümmeln vr to lounge (about)

Lump [lʊmp] (-en, -en) m scamp, rascal

lumpen ['lʊmpən] vt: **sich nicht ~ lassen** not to be mean

Lumpen (-s, -) m rag

Lumpensammler m rag and bone man

lumpig ['lʊmpɪç] adj shabby; **~e 10 Euro** (umg) 10 measly euros

Lüneburger Heide ['ly:nəbʊrgər 'haɪdə] f Lüneburg Heath

Lunge ['lʊŋə] (-, -n) f lung

Lungen- zW: **Lungenentzündung** f pneumonia; **lungenkrank** adj suffering from a lung disease; **Lungenkrankheit** f lung disease

lungern ['lʊŋərn] vi to hang about

Lunte ['lʊntə] (-, -n) f fuse; **~ riechen** to smell a rat

Lupe ['lu:pə] (-, -n) f magnifying glass; **unter die ~ nehmen** (fig) to scrutinize

lupenrein adj (lit: Edelstein) flawless

Lupine [lu'pi:nə] f lupin

Lurch [lʊrç] (-(e)s, -e) m amphibian

Lust [lʊst] (-, ^-e) f joy, delight; (Neigung) desire; (sexuell) lust (pej); **~ haben zu** od **auf etw** akk/ **etw zu tun** to feel like sth/doing sth; **hast du ~?** how about it?; **er hat die ~ daran verloren** he has lost all interest in it; **je nach ~ und Laune** just depending on how I od you etc feel; **lustbetont** adj pleasure-orientated

lüstern ['lʏstərn] adj lustful, lecherous

Lustgefühl nt pleasurable feeling

Lustgewinn m pleasure

lustig ['lʊstɪç] adj (komisch) amusing, funny; (fröhlich) cheerful; **sich über jdn/etw ~ machen** to make fun of sb/sth

Lüstling m lecher

Lust- zW: **lustlos** adj unenthusiastic; **Lustmord** m sex(ual) murder; **Lustprinzip** nt (Psych) pleasure principle; **Lustspiel** nt comedy; **lustwandeln** vi to stroll about

luth. abk = **lutherisch**

Lutheraner, in [lʊtə'ra:nər(ɪn)] m(f) Lutheran

lutherisch ['lʊtərɪʃ] adj Lutheran

lutschen ['lʊtʃən] vt, vi to suck; **am Daumen ~** to suck one's thumb

Lutscher (-s, -) m lollipop

Luxemburg ['lʊksəmbʊrk] (-s) nt Luxembourg

Luxemburger, in ['lʊksəmbʊrgər(ɪn)] (-s, -) m(f) citizen of Luxembourg, Luxembourger

luxemburgisch adj Luxembourgian

luxuriös [lʊksuri'ø:s] adj luxurious

Luxus ['lʊksʊs] (-) m luxury; **Luxusartikel** pl luxury goods pl; **Luxusausführung** f de luxe model; **Luxusdampfer** m luxury cruise ship; **Luxushotel** nt luxury hotel; **Luxussteuer** f tax on luxuries

LVA (-) f abk (= Landesversicherungsanstalt) county insurance company

LW abk (= Langwelle) LW

Lycra ['ly:kra] (-(s)) no pl nt Lycra®

Lymphe ['lʏmfə] (-, -n) f lymph

Lymphknoten m lymph(atic) gland

lynchen ['lʏnçən] vt to lynch

Lynchjustiz f lynch law

Lyrik ['ly:rɪk] f lyric poetry; **Lyriker, in** (-s, -) m(f) lyric poet

lyrisch ['ly:rɪʃ] adj lyrical

Mm

M, m¹ [ɛm] *nt* M, m; **M wie Martha** ≈ M for Mary, ≈ M for Mike (US)
m² *abk* (= *Meter*) m; (= *männlich*) m.
M. *abk* = **Monat**
MA. *abk* = **Mittelalter**
Maat [maːt] (**-s, -e** *od* **-en**) *m* (*Naut*) (ship's) mate
Machart *f* make
machbar *adj* feasible
Machbarkeitsstudie *f* feasibility study
Mache (-) (*umg*) *f* show, sham; **jdn in der ~ haben** to be having a go at sb

O SCHLÜSSELWORT

machen ['maxən] *vt* **1** to do; **was machst du da?** what are you doing there?; **das ist nicht zu machen** that can't be done; **was machen Sie (beruflich)?** what do you do for a living?; **mach, dass du hier verschwindest!** (you just) get out of here!; **mit mir kann mans ja machen!** (*umg*) the things I put up with!; **das lässt er nicht mit sich machen** he won't stand for that; **eine Prüfung machen** to take an exam
2 (*herstellen*) to make; **das Radio leiser machen** to turn the radio down; **aus Holz gemacht** made of wood; **das Essen machen** to get the meal; **Schluss machen** to finish (off)
3 (*verursachen, bewirken*) to make; **jdm Angst machen** to make sb afraid; **das macht die Kälte** it's the cold that does that
4 (*ausmachen*) to matter; **das macht nichts** that doesn't matter; **die Kälte macht mir nichts** I don't mind the cold
5 (*kosten: ergeben*) to be; **3 und 5 macht 8** 3 and 5 is *od* are 8; **was** *od* **wie viel macht das?** how much does that come to?
6: was macht die Arbeit? how's the work going?; **was macht dein Bruder?** how is your brother doing?; **das Auto machen lassen** to have the car done; **machs gut!** take care!; (*viel Glück*) good luck!
▷ *vi*: **mach schnell!** hurry up!; **mach schon!** come on!; **jetzt macht sie auf große Dame** (*umg*) she's playing the lady now; **lass mich mal machen** (*umg*) let me do it; (*ich bringe das in*

Ordnung) I'll deal with it; **groß/klein machen** (*umg: Notdurft*) to do a big/little job; **sich** *dat* **in die Hose machen** to wet o.s.; **ins Bett machen** to wet one's bed; **das macht müde** it makes you tired; **in etw** *dat* **machen** to be *od* deal in sth
▷ *vr* to come along (nicely); **sich an etw** *akk* **machen** to set about sth; **sich verständlich machen** to make o.s. understood; **sich** *dat* **viel aus jdm/etw machen** to like sb/sth; **mach dir nichts daraus** don't let it bother you; **sich auf den Weg machen** to get going; **sich an etw** *akk* **machen** to set about sth

Machenschaften *pl* wheelings and dealings *pl*
Macher (**-s, -**) (*umg*) *m* man of action
Macho ['matʃo] (*umg*) *adj* macho
Macho (**-s, -s**) (*umg*) *m* macho type
Macht [maxt] (**-, ̈-e**) *f* power; **mit aller ~** with all one's might; **an der ~ sein** to be in power; **alles in unserer ~ Stehende** everything in our power; **Machtergreifung** *f* seizure of power; **Machthaber** (**-s, -**) *m* ruler
mächtig ['mɛçtɪç] *adj* powerful, mighty; (*umg: ungeheuer*) enormous
Macht- *zW*: **machtlos** *adj* powerless; **Machtprobe** *f* trial of strength; **Machtstellung** *f* position of power; **Machtwort** *nt*: **ein Machtwort sprechen** to lay down the law
Machwerk *nt* work; (*schlechte Arbeit*) botched job
Macke ['makə] (**-, -n**) (*umg*) *f* (*Tick, Knall*) quirk; (*Fehler*) fault
Macker (**-s, -**) (*umg*) *m* fellow, guy
MAD (-) *m abk* (= *Militärischer Abschirmdienst*) ≈ MI5 (*Brit*); ≈ CIA (US)
Madagaskar [mada'gaskar] (**-s**) *nt* Madagascar
Mädchen ['mɛːtçən] *nt* girl; **ein ~ für alles** (*umg*) a dogsbody; (*im Büro etc*) a girl Friday; **mädchenhaft** *adj* girlish; **Mädchenname** *m* maiden name
Made ['maːdə] (**-, -n**) *f* maggot
Madeira¹ [ma'deːra] (**-s**) *nt* (*Geog*) Madeira
Madeira² (**-s, -s**) *m* (*Wein*) Madeira
Mädel ['mɛːdl] (**-s, -(s)**) *nt* (*Dialekt*) lass, girl
madig ['maːdɪç] *adj* maggoty; **madigmachen** *vt*: **jdm etw madigmachen** to spoil sth for sb

Madrid [ma'drɪt] (**-s**) *nt* Madrid

mag [ma:k] *vb siehe* **mögen**

Mag. *abk* = **Magister**

Magazin [maga'tsi:n] (**-s, -e**) *nt* (*Zeitschrift, am Gewehr*) magazine; (*Lager*) storeroom; (*Bibliotheksmagazin*) stockroom

Magd [ma:kt] (**-, ⁻e**) *f* maid(servant)

Magen ['ma:gən] (**-s, - *od* ⁻**) *m* stomach; **jdm auf den ~ schlagen** (*umg*) to upset sb's stomach; (*fig*) to upset sb; **sich** *dat* **den ~ verderben** to upset one's stomach; **Magenbitter** *m* bitters *pl*; **Magengeschwür** *nt* stomach ulcer; **Magenschmerzen** *pl* stomach-ache *sing*; **Magenverstimmung** *f* stomach upset

mager ['ma:gər] *adj* lean; (*dünn*) thin; **Magerkeit** *f* leanness; thinness; **Magermilch** *f* skimmed milk; **Magerquark** *m* low-fat soft cheese; **Magersucht** *f* (*Med*) anorexia; **magersüchtig** *adj* anorexic

Magie [ma'gi:] *f* magic

Magier ['ma:giər] (**-s, -**) *m* magician

magisch ['ma:gɪʃ] *adj* magical

Magister [ma'gɪstər] (**-s, -**) *m* (*Univ*) M.A., Master of Arts

Magistrat [magɪs'tra:t] (**-(e)s, -e**) *m* municipal authorities *pl*

Magnat [ma'gna:t] (**-en, -en**) *m* magnate

Magnet [ma'gne:t] (**-s *od* -en, -en**) *m* magnet; **Magnetbahn** *f* magnetic railway; **Magnetband** *nt* (*Comput*) magnetic tape; **magnetisch** *adj* magnetic

magnetisieren [magneti'zi:rən] *vt* to magnetize

Magnetnadel *f* magnetic needle

Magnettafel *f* magnetic board

Mahagoni [maha'go:ni] (**-s**) *nt* mahogany

Mähdrescher (**-s, -**) *m* combine (harvester)

mähen ['mɛ:ən] *vt, vi* to mow

Mahl [ma:l] (**-(e)s, -e**) *nt* meal

mahlen *unreg vt* to grind

Mahlstein *m* grindstone

Mahlzeit *f* meal ▷ *interj* enjoy your meal!

Mahnbrief *m* reminder

Mähne ['mɛ:nə] (**-, -n**) *f* mane

mahnen ['ma:nən] *vt* to remind; (*warnend*) to warn; (*wegen Schuld*) to demand payment from; **jdn zur Eile/Geduld** *etc* **~** (*auffordern*) to urge sb to hurry/be patient *etc*

Mahn- *zW*: **Mahngebühr** *f* reminder fee; **Mahnmal** *nt* memorial; **Mahnschreiben** *nt* reminder

Mahnung *f* admonition, warning; (*Mahnbrief*) reminder

Mähre ['mɛ:rə] (**-, -n**) *f* mare

Mähren ['mɛ:rən] (**-s**) *nt* Moravia

Mai [maɪ] (**-(e)s, -e**) (*pl selten*) *m* May; *siehe auch* **September**; **Maibaum** *m* maypole; **Maibowle** *f* white wine punch (*flavoured with woodruff*); **Maiglöckchen** *nt* lily of the valley; **Maikäfer** *m* cockchafer

Mail [me:l] (**-, -s**) *f* (*Comput*) email

Mailand ['maɪlant] (**-s**) *nt* Milan

Main [maɪn] (**-(e)s**) *m* (*Fluss*) Main

Mais [maɪs] (**-es, -e**) *m* maize, corn (*US*); **Maiskolben** *m* corncob

Majestät [majɛs'tɛ:t] *f* majesty

majestätisch *adj* majestic

Majestätsbeleidigung *f* lese-majesty

Majonäse [majo'nɛ:zə] (**-, -n**) *f* mayonnaise

Major [ma'jo:r] (**-s, -e**) *m* (*Mil*) major; (*Aviat*) squadron leader

Majoran [majo'ra:n] (**-s, -e**) *m* marjoram

makaber [ma'ka:bər] *adj* macabre

Makedonien [make'do:niən] (**-s**) *nt* Macedonia

makedonisch *adj* Macedonian

Makel ['ma:kəl] (**-s, -**) *m* blemish; (*moralisch*) stain; **ohne ~** flawless; **makellos** *adj* immaculate, spotless

mäkeln ['mɛ:kəln] *vi* to find fault

Make-up [me:k'|ap] (**-s, -s**) *nt* make-up; (*flüssig*) foundation

Makkaroni [maka'ro:ni] *pl* macaroni *sing*

Makler [ma'kl:ɔr] (**-s, -**) *m* broker; (*Grundstücksmakler*) estate agent (*Brit*), realtor (*US*); **Maklergebühr** *f* broker's commission, brokerage

Makrele [ma'kre:lə] (**-, -n**) *f* mackerel

Makro- *in zw* macro-

Makrone [ma'kro:nə] (**-, -n**) *f* macaroon

Makroökonomie *f* macroeconomics *sing*

Mal [ma:l] (**-(e)s, -e**) *nt* mark, sign; (*Zeitpunkt*) time; **ein für alle ~** once and for all; **mit einem ~(e)** all of a sudden; **das erste ~** the first time; **jedes ~** every time, each time; **zum letzten ~** for the last time; **ein paar ~** a few times

mal *adv* times

-mal *suff* -times

Malaie [ma'laɪə] (**-n, -n**) *m*, **Malaiin** *f* Malay

malaiisch *adj* Malayan

Malawi [ma'la:vi] (**-s**) *nt* Malawi

Malaysia [ma'laɪzia] (**-s**) *nt* Malaysia

Malaysier, in (**-s, -**) *m(f)* Malaysian

malaysisch *adj* Malaysian

Malediven [male'di:vən] *pl*: **die ~** the Maldive Islands

malen *vt, vi* to paint

Maler (**-s, -**) *m* painter

Malerei [ma:lə'raɪ] *f* painting

malerisch *adj* picturesque

Malkasten *m* paintbox

Mallorca [ma'jɔrka, ma'lɔrka] (**-s**) *nt* Majorca

Mallorquiner, in [majɔr'ki:nər(ɪn), malɔr'ki:nər(ɪn)] (**-s, -**) *m(f)* Majorcan

mallorquinisch *adj* Majorcan

malnehmen *unreg vt, vi* to multiply

Malta ['malta] (**-s**) *nt* Malta

Malteser, in [mal'te:zər(ɪn)] (**-s, -**) *m(f)* Maltese

Malteser-Hilfsdienst *m* ≈ St. John's Ambulance Brigade (*Brit*)

maltesisch *adj* Maltese

malträtieren [maltrɛ'ti:rən] *vt* to ill-treat, maltreat

Malz [malts] (**-es**) *nt* malt; **Malzbonbon** *nt or m* cough drop; **Malzkaffee** *m* coffee substitute made

219

from malt barley

Mama ['mamaː] (**-, -s**) (*umg*) f mum(my) (*Brit*), mom(my) (*US*)

Mami ['mami] (**-, -s**) f = **Mama**

Mammografie [mamɔgra'fiː] f (*Med*) mammography

Mammut ['mamʊt] (**-s, -e** *od* **-s**) nt mammoth ▷ *in zw* mammoth, giant; **Mammutanlagen** pl (*Industrie*) mammoth plants

mampfen ['mampfən] (*umg*) vt, vi to munch, chomp

man [man] *pron* one, you, people pl; **~ hat mir gesagt ...** I was told ...

managen ['mɛnɪdʒən] vt to manage; **ich manage das schon!** (*umg*) I'll fix it somehow!

Manager, in (**-s, -**) m(f) manager

manch [manç] *pron*: **~ ein(e) ...** many a ...; **~ eine(r)** many a person

manche, r, s *adj* many a; (*pl*) a number of ▷ *pron* some

mancherlei [mançər'laɪ] *adj inv* various ▷ *pron* a variety of things

manchmal *adv* sometimes

Mandant, in [man'dant(ɪn)] m(f) (*Jur*) client

Mandarine [manda'riːnə] f mandarin, tangerine

Mandat [man'daːt] (**-(e)s, -e**) nt mandate; **sein ~ niederlegen** (*Parl*) to resign one's seat

Mandel ['mandəl] (**-, -n**) f almond; (*Anat*) tonsil; **Mandelentzündung** f tonsillitis

Mandschurei (-) [mandʒu'raɪ] f: **die ~** Manchuria

Manege [ma'nɛːʒə] (**-, -n**) f ring, arena

Mangel[1] ['maŋəl] (**-, -n**) f mangle; **durch die ~ drehen** (*fig: umg*) to put through it; (*Prüfling etc*) to put through the mill

Mangel[2] ['maŋəl] (**-s, ⁻**) m lack; (*Knappheit*) shortage; (*Fehler*) defect, fault; **~ an** +*dat* shortage of

Mängelbericht ['mɛŋəlbərɪçt] m list of faults

Mangelerscheinung f deficiency symptom

mangelhaft *adj* poor; (*fehlerhaft*) defective, faulty; (*Schulnote*) unsatisfactory

mangeln vi *unpers*: **es mangelt jdm an etw** *dat* sb lacks sth ▷ *vt* (*Wäsche*) to mangle

mangels *präp* +*gen* for lack of

Mangelware f scarce commodity

Manie [ma'niː] f mania

Manier [ma'niːr] (-) f manner; (*Stil*) style; (*pej*) mannerism

Manieren pl manners pl; (*pej*) mannerisms pl

manieriert [mani'riːrt] *adj* mannered, affected

manierlich *adj* well-mannered

Manifest [mani'fɛst] (**-es, -e**) nt manifesto

Maniküre [mani'kyːrə] (**-, -n**) f manicure

maniküren vt to manicure

Manipulation [manipulatsi'oːn] f manipulation; (*Trick*) manoeuvre (*Brit*), maneuver (*US*)

manipulieren [manipu'liːrən] vt to manipulate

Manko ['maŋko] (**-s, -s**) nt deficiency; (*Comm*) deficit

Mann [man] (**-(e)s, ⁻er** *od* (*Naut*) **Leute**) m man; (*Ehemann*) husband; (*Naut*) hand; **pro ~** per head; **mit ~ und Maus untergehen** to go down with all hands; (*Passagierschiff*) to go down with no survivors; **seinen ~ stehen** to hold one's own; **etw an den ~ bringen** (*umg*) to get rid of sth; **einen kleinen ~ im Ohr haben** (*hum: umg*) to be crazy

Männchen ['mɛnçən] nt little man; (*Tier*) male; **~ machen** (*Hund*) to (sit up and) beg

Mannequin [manə'kɛ̃ː] (**-s, -s**) nt fashion model

Männersache ['mɛnərzaxə] f (*Angelegenheit*) man's business; (*Arbeit*) man's job

mannigfaltig ['manɪçfaltɪç] *adj* various, varied; **Mannigfaltigkeit** f variety

männlich ['mɛnlɪç] *adj* (*Biol*) male; (*fig, Gram*) masculine

Mannsbild nt (*veraltet: pej*) fellow

Mannschaft f (*Sport, fig*) team; (*Naut, Aviat*) crew; (*Mil*) other ranks pl

Mannschaftsgeist m team spirit

Mannsleute (*umg*) pl menfolk pl

Mannweib (*pej*) nt mannish woman

Manometer [mano'meːtər] nt (*Tech*) pressure gauge; **~!** (*umg*) wow!

Manöver [ma'nøːvər] (**-s, -**) nt manoeuvre (*Brit*), maneuver (*US*)

manövrieren [manø'vriːrən] vt, vi to manoeuvre (*Brit*), maneuver (*US*)

Mansarde [man'zardə] (**-, -n**) f attic

Manschette [man'ʃɛtə] f cuff; (*Papiermanschette*) paper frill; (*Tech*) sleeve

Manschettenknopf m cufflink

Mantel ['mantəl] (**-s, ⁻**) m coat; (*Tech*) casing, jacket; **Manteltarif** m general terms of employment; **Manteltarifvertrag** m general agreement on conditions of employment

Manuskript [manu'skrɪpt] (**-(e)s, -e**) nt manuscript

Mappe ['mapə] (**-, -n**) f briefcase; (*Aktenmappe*) folder

Marathonlauf ['maːratɔnlaʊf] m marathon

Märchen ['mɛːrçən] nt fairy tale; **märchenhaft** *adj* fabulous; **Märchenprinz** m prince charming

Marder ['mardər] (**-s, -**) m marten

Margarine [marga'riːnə] f margarine

Marge ['marʒə] (**-, -n**) f (*Comm*) margin

Maria [ma'riːa] (-) f Mary

Marienbild nt picture of the Virgin Mary

Marienkäfer m ladybird

Marihuana [marihu'aːna] (**-s**) nt marijuana

Marinade [mari'naːdə] (**-, -n**) f (*Koch*) marinade; (*Soße*) mayonnaise-based sauce

Marine [ma'riːnə] f navy; **marineblau** *adj* navy-blue

marinieren [mari'niːrən] vt to marinate

Marionette [mario'nɛtə] f puppet

Mark[1] [mark] (**-, -**) f (*Hist: Geld*) mark

Mark[2] [mark] (**-(e)s**) nt (*Knochenmark*) marrow; **jdn bis ins ~ treffen** (*fig*) to cut sb to the quick; **jdm durch ~ und Bein gehen** to go right through sb

markant [mar'kant] *adj* striking

Marke ['markə] (-, -n) *f* mark; (*Warensorte*) brand; (*Fabrikat*) make; (*Rabattmarke, Briefmarke*) stamp; (*Essen(s)marke*) luncheon voucher; (*aus Metall etc*) token, disc

Marken- *zW*: **Markenartikel** *m* proprietary article; **markenbewusst** *adj* brand conscious; **Markenbutter** *f* best quality butter; **Markenkleidung** *f* designer clothes; **Markenzeichen** *nt* trademark

Marketing ['markətɪŋ] (-s) *nt* marketing

markieren [mar'ki:rən] *vt* to mark; (*umg*) to act ▷ *vi* (*umg*) to act it

Markierung *f* marking

markig ['markɪç] *adj* (*fig*) pithy

Markise [mar'ki:zə] (-, -n) *f* awning

Markstück *nt* (*Hist*) one-mark piece

Markt [markt] (-(e)s, ̈e) *m* market; **Marktanalyse** *f* market analysis; **Marktanteil** *m* market share; **marktfähig** *adj* marketable; **Marktforschung** *f* market research; **marktgängig** *adj* marketable; **marktgerecht** *adj* geared to market requirements; **Marktlücke** *f* gap in the market; **Marktmacht** *f* market power; **Marktplatz** *m* market place; **Marktpotenzial, Marktpotential** *nt* market potential; **Marktpreis** *m* market price; **Marktwert** *m* market value; **Marktwirtschaft** *f* market economy; **marktwirtschaftlich** *adj* free enterprise

Marmelade [marmə'la:də] (-, -n) *f* jam

Marmor ['marmor] (-s, -e) *m* marble

marmorieren [marmo'ri:rən] *vt* to marble

Marmorkuchen *m* marble cake

marmorn *adj* marble

Marokkaner, in [marɔ'ka:nər(ɪn)] (-s, -) *m(f)* Moroccan

marokkanisch *adj* Moroccan

Marokko [ma'rɔko] (-s) *nt* Morocco

Marone [ma'ro:nə] (-, -n) *f* chestnut

Marotte [ma'rɔtə] (-, -n) *f* fad, quirk

Marsch¹ [marʃ] (-, -en) *f* marsh

Marsch² (-(e)s, ̈e) *m* march; **jdm den ~ blasen** (*umg*) to give sb a rocket; **marsch!** *interj* march!; **marsch ins Bett!** off to bed with you!

Marschbefehl *m* marching orders *pl*

marschbereit *adj* ready to move

marschieren [mar'ʃi:rən] *vi* to march

Marschverpflegung *f* rations *pl*; (*Mil*) field rations *pl*

Marseille [mar'sɛ:j] (-s) *nt* Marseilles

Marsmensch ['marsmɛnʃ] *m* Martian

Marter ['martər] (-, -n) *f* torment

martern *vt* to torture

Martinshorn ['marti:nshɔrn] *nt* siren (*of police etc*)

Märtyrer, in ['mɛrtyrər(ɪn)] (-s, -) *m(f)* martyr

Martyrium [mar'ty:riʊm] *nt* (*fig*) ordeal

Marxismus [mar'ksɪsmʊs] *m* Marxism

März [mɛrts] (-(es), -e) (*pl selten*) *m* March; *siehe auch* **September**

Marzipan [martsi'pa:n] (-s, -e) *nt* marzipan

Masche ['maʃə] (-, -n) *f* mesh; (*Strickmasche*) stitch; **das ist die neueste ~** that's the latest dodge; **durch die ~n schlüpfen** to slip through the net

Maschendraht *m* wire mesh

maschenfest *adj* runproof

Maschine [ma'ʃi:nə] *f* machine; (*Motor*) engine; **~ schreiben** to type

maschinell [maʃi'nɛl] *adj* machine(-), mechanical

Maschinen- *zW*: **Maschinenausfallzeit** *f* machine downtime; **Maschinenbauer** *m* mechanical engineer; **Maschinenführer** *m* machinist; **maschinengeschrieben** *adj* typewritten; **Maschinengewehr** *nt* machine gun; **maschinenlesbar** *adj* (*Comput*) machine-readable; **Maschinenpistole** *f* submachine gun; **Maschinenraum** *m* plant room; (*Naut*) engine room; **Maschinensaal** *m* machine shop; **Maschinenschaden** *m* mechanical fault; **Maschinenschlosser** *m* fitter; **Maschinenschrift** *f* typescript; **Maschinensprache** *f* (*Comput*) machine language

Maschinerie [maʃinə'ri:] *f* (*fig*) machinery

Maschinist, in [maʃi'nɪst(ɪn)] *m(f)* engineer

Maser ['ma:zər] (-, -n) *f* grain

Masern *pl* (*Med*) measles *sing*

Maserung *f* grain(ing)

Maske ['maskə] (-, -n) *f* mask

Maskenball *m* fancy-dress ball

Maskenbildner, in *m(f)* make-up artist

Maskerade [maskə'ra:də] *f* masquerade

maskieren [mas'ki:rən] *vt* to mask; (*verkleiden*) to dress up ▷ *vr* to disguise o.s., dress up

Maskottchen [mas'kɔtçən] *nt* (lucky) mascot

Maskulinum [masku'li:nʊm] (-s, **Maskulina**) *nt* (*Gram*) masculine noun

Masochist [mazɔ'xɪst] (-en, -en) *m* masochist

Maß¹ [ma:s] (-es, -e) *nt* measure; (*Mäßigung*) moderation; (*Grad*) degree, extent; **über alle ~en** (*liter*) extremely, beyond measure; **~ halten = maßhalten; mit zweierlei ~ messen** (*fig*) to operate a double standard; **sich** *dat* **etw nach ~ anfertigen lassen** to have sth made to measure *od* order (*US*); **in besonderem ~e** especially; **das ~ ist voll** (*fig*) that's enough (of that)

Maß² (-, -(e)) *f* litre (*Brit*) *od* liter (*US*) of beer

maß *etc vb siehe* **messen**

Massage [ma'sa:ʒə] (-, -n) *f* massage

Massaker [ma'sa:kər] (-s, -) *nt* massacre

Maßanzug *m* made-to-measure suit

Maßarbeit *f* (*fig*) neat piece of work

Masse ['masə] (-, -n) *f* mass; **eine ganze ~** (*umg*) a great deal

Maßeinheit *f* unit of measurement

Massen- *zW*: **Massenartikel** *m* mass-produced article; **Massenblatt** *nt* tabloid; **Massengrab** *nt* mass grave; **massenhaft** *adj* masses of; **Massenmedien** *pl* mass media *pl*; **Massenproduktion** *f* mass production; **Massenveranstaltung** *f* mass meeting;

Massenvernichtungswaffen pl weapons of mass destruction; **Massenware** f mass-produced article; **massenweise** adv in huge numbers

Masseur [ma'søːr] m masseur

Masseuse [ma'søːzə] f masseuse

Maß- zW: **maßgebend** adj authoritative; **maßgebende Kreise** influential circles; **maßgeblich** adj definitive; **maßgeschneidert** adj (Anzug) made-to-measure, made-to-order (US), custom attrib (US); **maßhalten** unreg vi to exercise moderation

massieren [ma'siːrən] vt to massage; (Mil) to mass

massig ['masıç] adj massive; (umg) a massive amount of

mäßig ['mɛːsıç] adj moderate; **mäßigen** ['mɛːsıgən] vt to restrain, moderate; **sein Tempo mäßigen** to slacken one's pace; **Mäßigkeit** f moderation

massiv [ma'siːf] adj solid; (fig) heavy, rough; **~ werden** (umg) to turn nasty; **Massiv (-s, -e)** nt massif

Maß- zW: **Maßkrug** m tankard; **maßlos** adj (Verschwendung, Essen, Trinken) excessive, immoderate; (Enttäuschung, Ärger etc) extreme; **Maßnahme (-, -n)** f measure, step; **maßregeln** vt untr to reprimand

Maßstab m rule, measure; (fig) standard; (Geog) scale; **als ~ dienen** to serve as a model

maßstabgetreu, maßstabsgetreu adj (true) to scale

maßvoll adj moderate

Mast [mast] **(-(e)s, -e(n))** m mast; (Elek) pylon

Mastdarm m rectum

mästen ['mɛstən] vt to fatten

masturbieren [mastʊr'biːrən] vi to masturbate

Material [materi'aːl] **(-s, -ien)** nt material(s); **Materialfehler** m material defect

Materialismus [materia'lısmʊs] m materialism

Materialist, in m(f) materialist; **materialistisch** adj materialistic

Materialkosten pl cost sing of materials

Materialprüfung f material(s) control

Materie [ma'teːriə] f matter, substance

materiell [materi'ɛl] adj material

Mathe ['matə] (-) f (Sch: umg) maths (Brit), math (US)

Mathematik [matema'tiːk] f mathematics sing; **Mathematiker, in** [mate'ma:tıkər(ın)] **(-s, -)** m(f) mathematician

mathematisch [mate'ma:tıʃ] adj mathematical

Matjeshering ['matjəshe:rıŋ] (umg) m salted young herring

Matratze [ma'tratsə] **(-, -n)** f mattress

Matrixdrucker m dot-matrix printer

Matrixzeichen nt matrix character

Matrize [ma'triːtsə] **(-, -n)** f matrix; (zum Abziehen) stencil

Matrose [ma'tro:zə] **(-n, -n)** m sailor

Matsch [matʃ] **(-(e)s)** m mud; (Schneematsch) slush

matschig adj muddy; slushy

matt [mat] adj weak; (glanzlos) dull; (Phot) matt; (Schach) mate; **jdn ~ setzen** (lit) to checkmate sb; siehe auch **mattsetzen**; **Matt (-s, -s)** nt (Schach) checkmate

Matte ['matə] **(-, -n)** f mat; **auf der ~ stehen** (am Arbeitsplatz etc) to be in

Mattigkeit f weakness; dullness

Mattscheibe f (TV) screen; **~ haben** (umg) to be not quite with it

mattsetzen vt (fig) to checkmate

Matura [ma'tu:ra] (-) (Österr, Schweiz) f = **Abitur**

Mätzchen ['mɛtsçən] (umg) nt antics pl; **~ machen** to fool around

mau [mau] (umg) adj poor, bad

Mauer ['mauər] **(-, -n)** f wall; **Mauerblümchen** (umg) nt (fig) wallflower

mauern vi to build, lay bricks ▷ vt to build

Mauer- zW: **Mauerschwalbe** f swift; **Mauersegler** m swift; **Mauerwerk** nt brickwork; (Stein) masonry

Maul [maul] **(-(e)s, Mäuler)** nt mouth; **ein loses** od **lockeres ~ haben** (umg: frech sein) to be an impudent so-and-so; (: indiskret sein) to be a blabbermouth; **halts ~!** (umg) shut your face! (!); **darüber werden sich die Leute das ~ zerreißen** (umg) that will start people's tongues wagging; **dem Volk** od **den Leuten aufs ~ schauen** (umg) to listen to what ordinary people say; **maulen** (umg) vi to grumble; **Maulesel** m mule; **Maulkorb** m muzzle; **Maulsperre** f lockjaw; **Maultier** nt mule; **Maul- und Klauenseuche** f (Tiere) foot-and-mouth disease

Maulwurf m mole

Maulwurfshaufen m molehill

Maurer ['maurər] **(-s, -)** m bricklayer; **pünktlich wie die ~** (hum) super-punctual

Mauretanien [maurə'ta:niən] **(-s)** nt Mauritania

Maus [maus] **(-, Mäuse)** f (auch Comput) mouse; **Mäuse** pl (umg: Geld) bread sing, dough sing

mauscheln ['mauʃəln] (umg) vt, vi (manipulieren) to fiddle

mäuschenstill ['mɔʏsçən'ʃtıl] adj very quiet

Mausefalle f mousetrap

mausen vt (umg) to pinch ▷ vi to catch mice

mausern vr to moult (Brit), molt (US)

mausetot adj stone dead

mausgesteuert adj (Comput) mouse-driven

Mausklick [mausklık] nt (Comput) (mouse) click

Maut [maut] **(-, -en)** f toll; **Mautsystem** nt toll system

max. abk (= maximal) max.

maximal [maksi'ma:l] adj maximum

Maxime [ma'ksi:mə] **(-, -n)** f maxim

maximieren [maksi'mi:rən] vt to maximize

Maximierung f (Wirts) maximization

Maximum ['maksimʊm] **(-s, Maxima)** nt maximum

Mayonnaise [majɔ'nɛːzə] **(-, -n)** f mayonnaise

Mazedonien [matse'do:niən] (**-s**) *nt* Macedonia

Mäzen [mɛ'tse:n] (**-s, -e**) *m* (*gen*) patron, sponsor

MdB *nt abk* (= *Mitglied des Bundestages*) member of the Bundestag, ≈ MP

MdL *nt abk* (= *Mitglied des Landtages*) member of the Landtag

m. E. *abk* (= *meines Erachtens*) in my opinion

Mechanik [me'ça:nɪk] *f* mechanics *sing*; (*Getriebe*) mechanics *pl*; **Mechaniker** (**-s, -**) *m* mechanic, engineer

mechanisch *adj* mechanical

Mechanisierung *f* mechanization

Mechanismus [meça'nɪsmʊs] *m* mechanism

meckern ['mɛkərn] *vi* to bleat; (*umg*) to moan

Mecklenburg ['me:klənbʊrk] (**-s**) *nt* Mecklenburg

Mecklenburg-Vorpommern (**-s**) *nt* (state of) Mecklenburg-Vorpommern

Medaille [me'daljə] (**-, -n**) *f* medal

Medaillon [medal'jõ:] (**-s, -s**) *nt* (*Schmuck*) locket

Medien ['me:diən] *pl* media *pl*; **Medienbericht** *m* (*meist pl*) media report; **Medienberichten zufolge** according to reports in the media; **Medienforschung** *f* media research; **Mediengesellschaft** *f* media society; **Medienmogul** *m* media mogul; **medienübergreifend** *adj* cross-media *attrib*; **Medienvielfalt** *f* mixture of media

Medikament [medika'mɛnt] *nt* medicine

Meditation [meditatsi'o:n] *f* meditation

meditieren [medi'ti:rən] *vi* to meditate

Medium ['me:diʊm] *nt* medium

Medizin [medi'tsi:n] (**-, -en**) *f* medicine

Mediziner, in (**-s, -**) *m(f)* doctor; (*Univ*) medic (*umg*)

medizinisch *adj* medical; **~-technische Assistentin** medical assistant

Meer [me:r] (**-(e)s, -e**) *nt* sea; **am ~(e)** by the sea; **ans ~ fahren** to go to the sea(side); **Meerbusen** *m* bay, gulf; **Meerenge** *f* straits *pl*

Meeres- *zW:* **Meeresfrüchte** *pl* seafood; **Meeresklima** *nt* maritime climate; **Meeresspiegel** *m* sea level

Meer- *zW:* **Meerjungfrau** *f* mermaid; **Meerrettich** *m* horseradish; **Meerschweinchen** *nt* guinea pig; **Meerwasser** *nt* sea water

Mega-, mega- [mega-] *in zw* mega-; **Megabyte** [mega'baɪt] *nt* megabyte; **Megafon, Megaphon** [mega'fo:n] (**-s, -e**) *nt* megaphone; **Megawatt** [mega'vat] *nt* megawatt

Mehl [me:l] (**-(e)s, -e**) *nt* flour

mehlig *adj* floury

Mehlschwitze *f* (*Koch*) roux

mehr [me:r] *adv* more; **nie ~** never again, nevermore (*liter*); **es war niemand ~ da** there was no one left; **nicht ~ lange** not much longer; **Mehraufwand** *m* additional expenditure; **Mehrbelastung** *f* excess load; (*fig*) additional burden; **mehrdeutig** *adj* ambiguous

mehrere *indef pron* several; (*verschiedene*) various; **~s** several things

mehrfach *adj* multiple; (*wiederholt*) repeated

Mehrheit *f* majority

Mehrheitsprinzip *nt* principle of majority rule

Mehrheitswahlrecht *nt* first-past-the-post voting system

mehr- *zW:* **mehrjährig** *adj attrib* of several years; **Mehrkosten** *pl* additional costs *pl*; **mehrmalig** *adj* repeated; **mehrmals** *adv* repeatedly; **Mehrparteiensystem** *nt* multi-party system; **Mehrplatzsystem** *nt* (*Comput*) multi-user system; **Mehrprogrammbetrieb** *m* (*Comput*) multiprogramming; **mehrsprachig** *adj* multilingual; **mehrstimmig** *adj* for several voices; **mehrstimmig singen** to harmonize; **Mehrwegflasche** *f* returnable bottle; **Mehrwertsteuer** *f* value added tax, VAT; **Mehrzahl** *f* majority; (*Gram*) plural

Mehrzweck- *in zw* multipurpose

meiden ['maɪdən] *unreg vt* to avoid

Meile ['maɪlə] (**-, -n**) *f* mile; **das riecht man drei ~n gegen den Wind** (*umg*) you can smell that a mile off

Meilenstein *m* milestone

meilenweit *adj* for miles

mein [maɪn] *pron* my

meine, r, s *poss pron* mine

Meineid ['maɪn|aɪt] *m* perjury

meinen ['maɪnən] *vt* to think; (*sagen*) to say; (*sagen wollen*) to mean ▷ *vi* to think; **wie Sie ~!** as you wish; **damit bin ich gemeint** that refers to me; **das will ich ~** I should think so

meiner *gen von* **ich** ▷ *pron* of me

meinerseits *adv* for my part

meinesgleichen ['maɪnəs'glaɪçən] *pron* people like me

meinetwegen ['maɪnət've:gən] *adv* (*für mich*) for my sake; (*wegen mir*) on my account; (*von mir aus*) as far as I'm concerned; (*ich habe nichts dagegen*) I don't care *od* mind

meinetwillen ['maɪnət'vɪlən] *adv:* **um ~ =** **meinetwegen**

meinige *pron:* **der/die/das ~** *od* **Meinige** mine

meins [maɪns] *pron* mine

Meinung ['maɪnʊŋ] *f* opinion; **meiner ~ nach** in my opinion; **einer ~ sein** to think the same; **jdm die ~ sagen** to give sb a piece of one's mind

Meinungs- *zW:* **Meinungsaustausch** *m* exchange of views; **Meinungsbildungsprozess** *f* opinion-forming process; **Meinungsforscher, in** *m(f)* pollster; **Meinungsforschungsinstitut** *nt* opinion research institute; **Meinungsfreiheit** *f* freedom of speech; **Meinungsumfrage** *f* opinion poll; **Meinungsverschiedenheit** *f* difference of opinion

Meise ['maɪzə] (**-, -n**) *f* tit(mouse); **eine ~ haben** (*umg*) to be crackers

Meißel ['maɪsəl] (**-s, -**) *m* chisel

meißeln *vt* to chisel

meist [maɪst] *adj* most ▷ *adv* mostly;

223

Meistbegünstigungsklausel f (Comm) most-favoured-nation clause; **meistbietend** adj: **meistbietend versteigern** to sell to the highest bidder

meiste, r, s superl von **viel**

meistens adv mostly

Meister ['maɪstər] (-s, -) m master; (Sport) champion; **seinen ~ machen** to take one's master craftsman's diploma; **es ist noch kein ~ vom Himmel gefallen** (Sprichwort) no one is born an expert; **Meisterbrief** m master craftsman's diploma; **meisterhaft** adj masterly

Meisterin f (auf einem Gebiet) master, expert; (Sport) (woman) champion

meistern vt to master; **sein Leben ~** to come to grips with one's life

Meister- zW: **Meisterschaft** f mastery; (Sport) championship; **Meisterstück** nt masterpiece; **Meisterwerk** nt masterpiece

meistgekauft adj attrib best-selling

Mekka ['mɛka] (-s, -s) nt (Geog, fig) Mecca

Melancholie [melaŋko'li:] f melancholy

melancholisch [melaŋ'ko:lɪʃ] adj melancholy

Meldebehörde f registration authorities pl

Meldefrist f registration period

melden vt to report; (registrieren) to register ▷ vr to report; to register; (Sch) to put one's hand up; (freiwillig) to volunteer; (auf etw, am Telefon) to answer; **nichts zu ~ haben** (umg) to have no say; **wen darf ich ~?** who shall I say (is here)?; **sich ~ bei** to report to; to register with; **sich auf eine Anzeige ~** to answer an advertisement; **es meldet sich niemand** there's no answer; **sich zu Wort ~** to ask to speak

Meldepflicht f obligation to register with the police

Meldestelle f registration office

Meldung ['mɛldʊŋ] f announcement; (Bericht) report

meliert [me'li:rt] adj mottled, speckled

melken ['mɛlkən] unreg vt to milk

Melodie [melo'di:] f melody, tune

melodisch [me'lo:dɪʃ] adj melodious, tuneful

melodramatisch [melodra'ma:tɪʃ] adj (auch fig) melodramatic

Melone [me'lo:nə] (-, -n) f melon; (Hut) bowler (hat)

Membran [mɛm'bra:n] (-, -en) f (Tech) diaphragm; (Anat) membrane

Memme ['mɛmə] (-, -n) (umg) f cissy, yellow-belly

Memoiren [memo'a:rən] pl memoirs pl

Menge ['mɛŋə] (-, -n) f quantity; (Menschenmenge) crowd; (große Anzahl) lot (of); **jede ~** (umg) masses pl, loads pl

mengen vt to mix ▷ vr: **sich ~ in** +akk to meddle with

Mengen- zW: **Mengeneinkauf** m bulk buying; **Mengenlehre** f (Math) set theory; **Mengenrabatt** m bulk discount

Menorca [me'nɔrka] (-s) nt Menorca

Mensa ['mɛnza] (-, -s od **Mensen**) f (Univ) refectory (Brit), commons (US)

Mensch [mɛnʃ] (-en, -en) m human being, man; (Person) person; **kein ~** nobody; **ich bin auch nur ein ~!** I'm only human; **~ ärgere dich nicht** nt (Spiel) ludo

Menschen- zW: **Menschenalter** nt generation; **Menschenfeind** m misanthrope; **menschenfreundlich** adj philanthropical; **Menschengedenken** nt: **der kälteste Winter seit Menschengedenken** the coldest winter in living memory; **Menschenhandel** m slave trade; (Jur) trafficking in human beings; **Menschenkenner** m judge of human nature; **Menschenkenntnis** f knowledge of human nature; **menschenleer** adj deserted; **Menschenliebe** f philanthropy; **Menschenmasse** f crowd (of people); **Menschenmenge** f crowd (of people); **menschenmöglich** adj humanly possible; **Menschenrechte** pl human rights pl; **menschenscheu** adj shy; **Menschenschlag** (umg) m kind of people; **Menschenseele** f: **keine Menschenseele** (fig) not a soul

Menschenkind interj good heavens!

Menschen- zW: **menschenunwürdig** adj degrading; **Menschenverachtung** f contempt for human beings od of mankind; **Menschenverstand** m: **gesunder Menschenverstand** common sense; **Menschenwürde** f human dignity; **menschenwürdig** adj (Behandlung) humane; (Unterkunft) fit for human habitation

Mensch- zW: **Menschheit** f humanity, mankind; **menschlich** adj human; (human) humane; **Menschlichkeit** f humanity

Menstruation [mɛnstruatsi'o:n] f menstruation

Mentalität [mɛntali'tɛ:t] f mentality

Menü [me'ny:] (-s, -s) nt (auch Comput) menu; **Menüführung** f (Comput) menu assistance; **menügesteuert** adj (Comput) menu-driven

Merkblatt nt instruction sheet od leaflet

merken ['mɛrkən] vt to notice; **sich dat etw ~** to remember sth; **sich dat eine Autonummer ~** to make a (mental) note of a licence (Brit) od license (US) number

merklich adj noticeable

Merkmal nt sign, characteristic

merkwürdig adj odd

meschugge [me'ʃʊgə] (umg) adj nuts, meshuga (US)

Mess- zW: **Messband** nt tape measure; **messbar** adj measurable; **Messbecher** m measuring cup

Messbuch nt missal

Messdiener m (Rel) server, acolyte (form)

Messe ['mɛsə] (-, -n) f fair; (Eccl) mass; (Mil) mess; **auf der ~** at the fair; **Messegelände** nt exhibition centre (Brit) od center (US)

messen unreg vt to measure ▷ vr to compete

Messer (-s, -) nt knife; **auf des ~s Schneide stehen** (fig) to hang in the balance; **jdm**

ins offene ~ laufen (fig) to walk into a trap; **messerscharf** adj (fig): **messerscharf schließen** to conclude with incredible logic (ironisch); **Messerspitze** f knife point; (in Rezept) pinch; **Messerstecherei** f knife fight
Messestadt f (town with an) exhibition centre (Brit) od center (US)
Messestand m exhibition stand
Messgerät nt measuring device, gauge
Messgewand nt chasuble
Messing ['mɛsɪŋ] (-s) nt brass
Messstab m (Aut: Ölmessstab etc) dipstick
Messung f (das Messen) measuring; (von Blutdruck) taking; (Messergebnis) measurement
Messwert m measurement; (Ableseergebnis) reading
Metall [me'tal] (-s, -e) nt metal; **die ~ verarbeitende Industrie** the metal-processing industry; **metallen** adj metallic; **metallisch** adj metallic
Metallurgie [metalʊr'gi:] f metallurgy
Metapher [me'tafər] (-, -n) f metaphor
metaphorisch [meta'fo:rɪʃ] adj metaphorical
Metaphysik [metafy'zi:k] f metaphysics sing
Metastase [meta'sta:zə] (-, -n) f (Med) secondary growth
Meteor [mete'o:r] (-s, -e) m meteor
Meteorologe [meteoro'lo:gə] (-n, -n) m meteorologist
Meter ['me:tər] (-s, -) m od nt metre (Brit), meter (US); **in 500 ~ Höhe** at a height of 500 metres; **Metermaß** nt tape measure; **Meterware** f (Textil) piece goods
Methode [me'to:də] (-, -n) f method
Methodik [me'to:dɪk] f methodology
methodisch [me'to:dɪʃ] adj methodical
Metier [meti'e:] (-s, -s) nt (hum) job, profession
metrisch ['me:trɪʃ] adj metric, metrical
Metropole [metro'po:lə] (-, -n) f metropolis
Mettwurst ['mɛtvʊrst] f (smoked) sausage
Metzger ['mɛtsgər] (-s, -) m butcher
Metzgerei [mɛtsgə'raɪ] f butcher's (shop)
Meuchelmord ['mɔʏçəlmɔrt] m assassination
Meute ['mɔʏtə] (-, -n) f pack
Meuterei [mɔʏtə'raɪ] f mutiny
meutern vi to mutiny
Mexikaner, in [mɛksi'ka:nər(ɪn)] (-s, -) m(f) Mexican
mexikanisch adj Mexican
Mexiko ['mɛksiko] (-s) nt Mexico
MEZ abk (= mitteleuropäische Zeit) C.E.T.
MFG abk = **Mitfahrgelegenheit**
MfG abk (= mit freundlichen Grüßen) (with) best wishes
MG (-(s), -(s)) nt abk = **Maschinengewehr**
mg abk (= Milligramm) mg
mhd. abk (= mittelhochdeutsch) MHG
MHz abk (= Megahertz) MHz
Mi. abk = **Mittwoch**
miauen [mi'aʊən] vi to miaow
mich [mɪç] akk von **ich** ▷ pron me; (reflexiv) myself
mickerig ['mɪkərɪç], **mickrig** ['mɪkrɪç] (umg)

adj pathetic; (altes Männchen) puny
mied etc [mi:t] vb siehe **meiden**
Miederwaren ['mi:dərva:rən] pl corsetry sing
Mief [mi:f] (-s) (umg) m fug; (muffig) stale air; (Gestank) stink, pong (Brit)
miefig (umg) adj smelly, pongy (Brit)
Miene ['mi:nə] (-, -n) f look, expression; **gute ~ zum bösen Spiel machen** to grin and bear it
Mienenspiel nt facial expressions pl
mies [mi:s] (umg) adj lousy
Miese ['mi:zə] (umg) pl: **in den ~n sein** to be in the red
Miesmacher, in (umg) m(f) killjoy
Mietauto nt hired car (Brit), rental car (US)
Miete ['mi:tə] (-, -n) f rent; **zur ~ wohnen** to live in rented accommodation od accommodations (US)
mieten vt to rent; (Auto) to hire (Brit), rent
Mieter, in (-s, -) m(f) tenant; **Mieterschutz** m rent control
Mietshaus nt tenement, block of flats (Brit) od apartments (US)
Miet- zW: **Mietverhältnis** nt tenancy; **Mietvertrag** m tenancy agreement; **Mietwagen** m = **Mietauto**; **Mietwucher** m the charging of exorbitant rent(s)
Mieze ['mi:tsə] (-, -n) (umg) f (Katze) pussy; (Mädchen) chick, bird (Brit)
Migräne [mi'grɛ:nə] (-, -n) f migraine
migrieren [mi'gri:rən] vi to migrate
Mikado [mi'ka:do] (-s) nt (Spiel) pick-a-stick
Mikro- ['mi:kro] in zw micro-
Mikrobe [mi'kro:bə] (-, -n) f microbe
Mikro- zW: **Mikrochip** m microchip; **Mikrocomputer** m microcomputer; **Mikrofiche** m od nt microfiche; **Mikrofilm** m microfilm
Mikrofon [mikro'fo:n] (-s, e) nt microphone
Mikroökonomie f microeconomics pl
Mikrophon [mikro'fo:n] (-s, -e) nt microphone
Mikroprozessor (-s, -oren) m microprocessor
Mikroskop [mikro'sko:p] (-s, -e) nt microscope; **mikroskopisch** adj microscopic
Mikrowelle ['mi:krovɛlə] f microwave
Mikrowellenherd m microwave (oven)
Milbe ['mɪlbə] (-, -n) f mite
Milch [mɪlç] (-) f milk; (Fischmilch) milt, roe; **Milchdrüse** f mammary gland; **Milchglas** nt frosted glass
milchig adj milky
Milch- zW: **Milchkaffee** m white coffee; **Milchmixgetränk** nt milk shake; **Milchpulver** nt powdered milk; **Milchstraße** f Milky Way; **Milchtüte** f milk carton; **Milchzahn** m milk tooth
mild [mɪlt] adj mild; (Richter) lenient; (freundlich) kind, charitable
Milde ['mɪldə] (-, -n) f mildness; leniency
mildern vt to mitigate, soften; (Schmerz) to alleviate; **~de Umstände** extenuating circumstances
Milieu [mili'ø:] (-s, -s) nt background, environment; **milieugeschädigt** adj

m

225

maladjusted
militant [mili'tant] *adj* militant
Militär [mili'tɛːr] **(-s)** *nt* military, army;
  Militärdienst *m* military service;
  Militäreinsatz *m* use of troops;
  (*Kampfhandlung*) military action; **Militärgericht**
  nt military court; **militärisch** *adj* military
Militarismus [milita'rɪsmʊs] *m* militarism
militaristisch *adj* militaristic
Militärpflicht *f* (compulsory) military service
Mill. *abk* (= *Million(en)*) m
Milli- *in zw* milli-
Milliardär, in [mɪliar'dɛːr(ɪn)] **(-s, -e)** *m(f)*
  multimillionaire
Milliarde [mɪli'ardə] **(-, -n)** *f* milliard, billion
  (*bes US*); **Milliardengrab** *nt* (*fig*) money burner,
  white elephant
Millimeter *m* millimetre (*Brit*), millimeter (*US*);
  Millimeterpapier *nt* graph paper
Million [mɪli'oːn] **(-, -en)** *f* million
Millionär, in [mɪlio'nɛːr(ɪn)] **(-s, -e)** *m(f)*
  millionaire
millionenschwer (*umg*) *adj* worth a few
  million
Milz [mɪlts] **(-, -en)** *f* spleen
Mimik ['miːmɪk] *f* mime
Mimose [mi'moːzə] **(-, -n)** *f* mimosa; (*fig*)
  sensitive person
minder ['mɪndər] *adj* inferior ▷ *adv* less;
  minderbegabt *adj* less able; **minderbemittelt**
  adj: **geistig minderbemittelt** (*ironisch*)
  intellectually challenged
Minderheit *f* minority
Minderheitsbeteiligung *f* (*Aktien*) minority
  interest
Minderheitsregierung *f* minority
  government
minderjährig *adj* minor; **Minderjährige, r** *f(m)*
  minor; **Minderjährigkeit** *f* minority
mindern *vt, vr* to decrease, diminish
minderqualifiziert *adj* less qualified;
  Minderqualifizierte, r *f(m)* less qualified
  person
Minderung *f* decrease
minder- *zW*: **minderwertig** *adj* inferior;
  Minderwertigkeitsgefühl *nt* inferiority
  complex; **Minderwertigkeitskomplex (-es, -e)**
  m inferiority complex
Mindestalter *nt* minimum age
Mindestbetrag *m* minimum amount
mindeste, r, s *adj* least
mindestens *adv* at least
Mindest- *zW*: **Mindestlohn** *m* minimum
  wage; **Mindestmaß** *nt* minimum;
  Mindeststand *m* (*Comm*) minimum stock;
  Mindeststudiendauer *nt* (*Österr*) minimum
  length of study; **Mindestumtausch** *m*
  minimum obligatory exchange
Mine ['miːnə] **(-, -n)** *f* mine; (*Bleistiftmine*) lead;
  (*Kugelschreibermine*) refill
Minenfeld *nt* minefield
Minensuchboot *nt* minesweeper
Mineral [mine'raːl] **(-s, -e** *od* **-ien)** *nt* mineral;

mineralisch *adj* mineral; **Mineralölsteuer**
  f tax on oil and petrol (*Brit*) *od* gasoline (*US*);
  Mineralwasser *nt* mineral water
Miniatur [minia'tuːr] *f* miniature
Minigolf ['mɪniɡɔlf] *nt* miniature golf
minimal [mini'maːl] *adj* minimal
Minimum ['miːnimʊm] **(-s, Minima)** *nt*
  minimum
Minirock ['mɪnirɔk] *m* miniskirt
Minister, in [mi'nɪstər(ɪn)] **(-s, -)** *m(f)* (*Pol*)
  minister
ministeriell [minɪsteri'ɛl] *adj* ministerial
Ministerium [minɪs'teːriʊm] *nt* ministry
Ministerpräsident, in *m(f)* prime minister
Minna ['mɪna] *f*: **jdn zur ~ machen** (*umg*) to
  give sb a piece of one's mind
minus ['miːnʊs] *adv* minus; **Minus (-, -)**
  nt deficit; **Minuspol** *m* negative pole;
  Minuszeichen *nt* minus sign
Minute [mi'nuːtə] **(-, -n)** *f* minute; **auf die ~**
  (genau *od* **pünktlich)** (right) on the dot
Minutenzeiger *m* minute hand
Mio. *abk* (= *Million(en)*) m
mir [miːr] *dat von* **ich** ▷ *pron* (to) me; **von ~ aus!**
  I don't mind; **wie du ~, so ich dir** (*Sprichwort*)
  tit for tat (*umg*); (*als Drohung*) I'll get my own
  back; **~ nichts, dir nichts** just like that
Mirabelle [mira'bɛlə] *f* mirabelle, *small yellow*
  plum
Misch- *zW*: **Mischbatterie** *f* mixer tap;
  Mischbrot *nt* *bread made from more than one kind of*
  flour; **Mischehe** *f* mixed marriage
mischen *vt* to mix; (*Comput: Datei, Text*) to
  merge; (*Karten*) to shuffle ▷ *vi* (*Karten*) to
  shuffle
Misch- *zW*: **Mischfinanzierung** *m* (*Wirts*) mixed
  financing; **Mischkonzern** *m* conglomerate;
  Mischling *m* half-caste; **Mischmasch** (*umg*) *m*
  hotchpotch; (*Essen*) concoction; **Mischpult** *nt*
  (*Rundf, TV*) mixing panel
Mischung *f* mixture
Mischwald *m* mixed (deciduous and
  coniferous) woodland
miserabel [mizə'raːbəl] (*umg*) *adj* lousy;
  (*Gesundheit*) wretched; (*Benehmen*) dreadful
Misere [mi'zeːrə] **(-, -n)** *f* (*von Leuten, Wirtschaft*
  etc) plight; (*von Hunger, Krieg etc*) misery,
  miseries *pl*
Miss- *zW*: **missachten** *vt untr* to disregard;
  Missachtung *f* disregard; **Missbehagen**
  nt uneasiness; (*Missfallen*) discontent;
  Missbildung *f* deformity; **missbilligen** *vt untr*
  to disapprove of; **Missbilligung** *f* disapproval;
  Missbrauch *m* abuse; (*falscher Gebrauch*)
  misuse; **missbrauchen** *vt untr* to abuse; to
  misuse; (*vergewaltigen*) to assault; **jdn zu** *od*
  für etw missbrauchen to use sb for *od* to do
  sth; **missdeuten** *vt untr* to misinterpret
missen *vt* to do without; (*Erfahrung*) to miss
Misserfolg *m* failure
Missernte *f* crop failure
Missetat ['mɪsətaːt] *f* misdeed
Missetäter *m* criminal; (*umg*) scoundrel

Miss- zW: **missfallen** unreg vi untr: **jdm missfallen** to displease sb; **Missgeburt** f freak; (fig) failure; **Missgeschick** nt misfortune; **missglücken** vi untr to fail; **jdm missglückt etw** sb does not succeed with sth; **missgönnen** vt untr: **jdm etw missgönnen** to (be)grudge sb sth; **Missgriff** m mistake; **Missgunst** f envy; **missgünstig** adj envious; **misshandeln** vt untr to ill-treat; **Misshandlung** f ill-treatment; **Misshelligkeit** f: **Misshelligkeiten haben** to be at variance

Mission [mɪsiˈoːn] f mission

Missionar, in [mɪsioˈnaːr(ɪn)] m(f) missionary

Missklang m discord

Misskredit m discredit

misslang etc [mɪsˈlaŋ] vb siehe **misslingen**

missliebig adj unpopular

misslingen [mɪsˈlɪŋən] unreg vi untr to fail; **Misslingen** (-s) nt failure

misslungen [mɪsˈlʊŋən] pp von **misslingen**

Miss- zW: **Missmut** m bad temper; **missmutig** adj cross; **missraten** unreg vi untr to turn out badly ▷ adj ill-bred; **Missstand** m deplorable state of affairs; **Missstimmung** f discord; (Missmut) ill feeling

misst vb siehe **messen**

Miss- zW: **misstrauen** vi untr to mistrust; **Misstrauen** (-s) nt: **Misstrauen (gegenüber)** distrust (of), suspicion (of); **Misstrauensantrag** m (Pol) motion of no confidence; **Misstrauensvotum** nt (Pol) vote of no confidence; **misstrauisch** adj distrustful, suspicious; **Missverhältnis** nt disproportion; **missverständlich** adj unclear; **Missverständnis** nt misunderstanding; **missverstehen** unreg vt untr to misunderstand

Misswahl [ˈmɪsvaːl] f beauty contest

Misswirtschaft f mismanagement

Mist [mɪst] m (-(e)s) m dung; (umg) rubbish; **~!** (umg) blast!; **das ist nicht auf seinem ~ gewachsen** (umg) he didn't think that up himself

Mistel (-, -n) f mistletoe

Mist- zW: **Mistgabel** f pitchfork (used for shifting manure); **Misthaufen** m dungheap; **Miststück** (umg!) nt, **Mistvieh** (umg!) nt (Mann) bastard (!); (Frau) bitch (!)

mit [mɪt] präp +dat with; (mittels) by ▷ adv along, too; **~ der Bahn** by train; **~ dem nächsten Flugzeug/Bus kommen** to come on the next plane/bus; **~ Bleistift schreiben** to write in pencil; **~ Verlust** at a loss; **er ist ~ der Beste in der Gruppe** he is among the best in the group; **wie wärs ~ einem Bier?** (umg) how about a beer?; **~ 10 Jahren** at the age of 10; **wollen Sie ~?** do you want to come along?

Mitarbeit [ˈmitarbaɪt] f cooperation; **mitarbeiten** vi: **mitarbeiten (an** +dat) to cooperate (on), collaborate (on)

Mitarbeiter, in m(f) (an Projekt) collaborator; (Kollege) colleague; (Angestellter) member of staff ▷ pl staff; **Mitarbeiterstab** m staff

mit- zW: **mitbekommen** unreg vt to get od be given; (umg: verstehen) to get; **mitbestimmen** vi: **(bei etw) mitbestimmen** to have a say (in sth) ▷ vt to have an influence on; **Mitbestimmung** f participation in decision-making; (Pol) determination; **mitbringen** unreg vt to bring along; **Mitbringsel** [ˈmɪtbrɪŋzəl] (-s, -) nt (Geschenk) small present; (Andenken) souvenir; **Mitbürger, in** m(f) fellow citizen; **mitdenken** unreg vi to follow; **du hast ja mitgedacht!** good thinking!; **mitdürfen** unreg vi: **wir durften nicht mit** we weren't allowed to go along; **Miteigentümer** m joint owner

miteinander [mɪtaɪˈnandər] adv together, with one another

miterleben vt to see, witness

Mitesser [ˈmɪtɛsər] (-s, -) m blackhead

mit- zW: **mitfahren** unreg vi: **(mit jdm) mitfahren** to go (with sb); (auf Reise auch) to go od travel (with sb); **Mitfahrzentrale** f agency for arranging lifts; **Mitfahrgelegenheit** f lift; **mitfühlen** vi: **mit jdm/etw mitfühlen** to sympathize with sb/sth; **mitfühlend** adj sympathetic; **mitführen** vt (Papiere, Ware etc) to carry (with one); (Fluss) to carry along; **mitgeben** unreg vt to give; **Mitgefühl** nt sympathy; **mitgehen** unreg vi to go od come along; **etw mitgehen lassen** (umg) to pinch sth; **mitgenommen** adj done in, in a bad way; **Mitgift** f dowry

Mitglied [ˈmɪtgliːt] nt member

Mitgliedsbeitrag m membership fee, subscription

Mitgliedschaft f membership

mit- zW: **mithaben** unreg vt: **etw mithaben** to have sth (with one); **mithalten** unreg vi to keep up; **mithelfen** vi unreg to help, lend a hand; **bei etw mithelfen** to help with sth; **Mithilfe** f help, assistance; **mithören** vt to listen in to; **mitkommen** unreg vi to come along; (verstehen) to keep up, follow; **Mitläufer** m hanger-on; (Pol) fellow traveller

Mitleid nt sympathy; (Erbarmen) compassion

Mitleidenschaft f: **in ~ ziehen** to affect

mitleidig adj sympathetic

mitleidslos adj pitiless, merciless

mit- zW: **mitmachen** vt to join in, take part in; (umg: einverstanden sein): **da macht mein Chef nicht mit** my boss won't go along with that; **Mitmensch** m fellow man; **mitmischen** (umg) vi (sich beteiligen): **mitmischen (in** +dat od **bei)** to be involved (in); (sich einmischen) to interfere (in); **mitnehmen** unreg vt to take along od away; (anstrengen) to wear out, exhaust; **mitgenommen aussehen** to look the worse for wear; **mitreden** vi (Meinung äußern): **(bei etw) mitreden** to join in (sth); (mitbestimmen) to have a say (in sth) ▷ vt: **Sie haben hier nichts mitzureden** this is none of your concern; **mitreißen** vt unreg to sweep away; (fig: begeistern) to carry away; **mitreißend** adj (Rhythmus) infectious; (Reden) rousing; (Film,

m

227

Fußballspiel) thrilling, exciting
mitsamt [mɪt'zamt] *präp* +*dat* together with
mitschneiden *vt unreg* to record
Mitschnitt ['mɪtʃnɪt] (-(e)s, -e) *m* recording
mitschreiben *unreg vt* to write *od* take down ▷ *vi* to take notes
Mitschuld *f* complicity
mitschuldig *adj*: ~ **(an** +*dat*) implicated (in); (*an Unfall*) partly responsible (for)
Mitschuldige, r *f(m)* accomplice
mit- *zW*: **Mitschüler, in** *m(f)* schoolmate; **mitspielen** *vi* to join in, take part; **er hat ihr übel** *od* **hart mitgespielt** (*Schaden zufügen*) he has treated her badly; **Mitspieler, in** *m(f)* partner; **Mitspracherecht** *nt* voice, say
Mittag ['mɪtaːk] (-(e)s, -e) *m* midday, noon, lunchtime; **morgen** ~ tomorrow at lunchtime *od* noon; ~ **machen** to take one's lunch hour; **(zu)** ~ **essen** to have lunch; **Mittagessen** *nt* lunch, dinner
mittags *adv* at lunchtime *od* noon
Mittags- *zW*: **Mittagspause** *f* lunch break; **Mittagsruhe** *f* period of quiet (after lunch); (*in Geschäft*) midday closing; **Mittagsschlaf** *m* early afternoon nap, siesta; **Mittagszeit** *f*: **während** *od* **in der Mittagszeit** at lunchtime
Mittäter, in ['mɪtɛːtər(ɪn)] *m(f)* accomplice
Mitte ['mɪtə] (-, -n) *f* middle; **aus unserer** ~ from our midst
mitteilen ['mɪttaɪlən] *vt*: **jdm etw** ~ to inform sb of sth, communicate sth to sb ▷ *vr*: **sich (jdm)** ~ to communicate (with sb)
mitteilsam *adj* communicative
Mitteilung *f* communication; **jdm (eine)** ~ **von etw machen** (*form*) to inform sb of sth; (*bekannt geben*) to announce sth to sb
Mitteilungsbedürfnis *nt* need to talk to other people
Mittel ['mɪtəl] (-s, -) *nt* means; (*Methode*) method; (*Math*) average; (*Med*) medicine; **kein** ~ **unversucht lassen** to try everything; **als letztes** ~ as a last resort; **ein** ~ **zum Zweck** a means to an end; **Mittelalter** *nt* Middle Ages *pl*; **mittelalterlich** *adj* medieval; **Mittelamerika** *nt* Central America (and the Caribbean); **mittelamerikanisch** *adj* Central American; **mittelbar** *adj* indirect; **Mittelding** *nt* (*Mischung*) cross; **Mitteleuropa** *nt* Central Europe; **Mitteleuropäer, in** *m(f)* Central European; **mitteleuropäisch** *adj* Central European; **mittelfristig** *adj* (*Finanzplanung, Kredite*) medium-term; **Mittelgebirge** *nt* low mountain range; **mittelgroß** *adj* medium-sized; **mittellos** *adj* without means; **Mittelmaß** *nt*: **das (gesunde) Mittelmaß** the happy medium; **mittelmäßig** *adj* mediocre, middling; **Mittelmäßigkeit** *f* mediocrity; **Mittelmeer** *nt* Mediterranean (Sea); **mittelprächtig** *adj* not bad; **Mittelpunkt** *m* centre (*Brit*), center (*US*); **im Mittelpunkt stehen** to be centre-stage
mittels *präp* +*gen* by means of

Mittelschicht *f* middle class
Mittelsmann (-(e)s, *pl* **Mittelsmänner** *od* **Mittelsleute**) *m* intermediary
Mittel- *zW*: **Mittelstand** *m* middle class; **Mittelstreckenrakete** *f* medium-range missile; **Mittelstreifen** *m* central reservation (*Brit*), median strip (*US*); **Mittelstufe** *f* (*Sch*) middle school (*Brit*), junior high (*US*); **Mittelstürmer** *m* centre forward; **Mittelweg** *m* middle course; **Mittelwelle** *f* (*Rundf*) medium wave; **Mittelwert** *m* average value, mean
mitten ['mɪtən] *adv* in the middle; ~ **auf der Straße/in der Nacht** in the middle of the street/night; **mittendrin** *adv* (right) in the middle of it; **mittendurch** *adv* (right) through the middle
Mitternacht ['mɪtərnaxt] *f* midnight
mittlere, r, s ['mɪtlərə(r, s)] *adj* middle; (*durchschnittlich*) medium, average; **der M~ Osten** the Middle East; ~**s Management** middle management; ~ **Reife**; *see culture note*

mittlerweile ['mɪtlər'vaɪlə] *adv* meanwhile
Mittwoch ['mɪtvɔx] (-(e)s, -e) *m* Wednesday; *siehe auch* **Dienstag**
mittwochs *adv* on Wednesdays
mitunter [mɪt'|ʊntər] *adv* occasionally, sometimes
mit- *zW*: **mitverantwortlich** *adj* also responsible; **mitverdienen** *vi* to (go out to) work as well; **Mitverfasser** *m* co-author; **Mitverschulden** *nt* contributory negligence; **mitwirken** *vi*: **(bei etw) mitwirken** to contribute (to sth); (*Theat*) to take part (in sth); **Mitwirkende, r** *f(m)*: **die Mitwirkenden** (*Theat*) the cast; **Mitwirkung** *f* contribution; participation; **unter Mitwirkung von** with the help of; **Mitwisser** (-s, -) *m*: **Mitwisser (einer Sache** *gen*) **sein** to be in the know (about sth); **jdn zum Mitwisser machen** to tell sb (all) about it
Mixer ['mɪksər] (-s, -) *m* (*Barmixer*) cocktail waiter; (*Küchenmixer*) blender; (*Rührmaschine, Rundf, TV*) mixer
ml *abk* (= *Milliliter*) ml
mm *abk* (= *Millimeter*) mm
MMS® *m* (= *Multimedia Messaging Service*) MMS
Mnemonik [mne'moːnɪk] *f* mnemonic
Mo. *abk* = **Montag**
mobben ['mɔbən] *vt* to bully (at work)
Mobbing ['mɔbɪŋ] (-s) *nt* workplace bullying
Möbel ['møːbəl] (-s, -) *nt* (piece of) furniture;

Möbelpacker m removal man (*Brit*), (furniture) mover (*US*); **Möbelwagen** m furniture *od* removal van (*Brit*), moving van (*US*)

mobil [mo'bi:l] *adj* mobile; (*Internet, Tel*) ~**e Internetnutzung** mobile internet use; ~**es Internet** mobile web; (*Mil*) mobilized

Mobilfunk m cellular telephone service

Mobiliar [mobili'a:r] (**-s, -e**) *nt* movable assets *pl*

mobilisieren [mobili'zi:rən] *vt* (*Mil*) to mobilize

Mobilmachung f mobilization

Mobiltelefon *nt* (*Telec*) mobile phone

möbl. *abk* = **möbliert**

möblieren [mø'bli:rən] *vt* to furnish; **möbliert wohnen** to live in furnished accommodation

mochte *etc* ['mɔxtə] *vb siehe* **mögen**

Möchtegern- ['mœçtəgɛrn] *in zw* (*ironisch*) would-be

Modalität [modali'tɛ:t] f (*von Plan, Vertrag etc*) arrangement

Mode ['mo:də] (**-, -n**) f fashion; **Modefarbe** f in colour (*Brit*) *od* color (*US*); **Modeheft** *nt* fashion magazine; **Modejournal** *nt* fashion magazine

Modell [mo'dɛl] (**-s, -e**) *nt* model; **Modelleisenbahn** f model railway; (*als Spielzeug*) train set; **Modellfall** m textbook case

modellieren [modɛ'li:rən] *vt* to model

Modellversuch m (*bes Sch*) pilot scheme

Modem ['mo:dɛm] (**-s, -s**) *nt* (*Comput*) modem

Modenschau f fashion show

Modepapst m high priest of fashion

Moder ['mo:dər] (**-s**) m mustiness; (*Schimmel*) mildew

moderat [mode'ra:t] *adj* moderate

Moderator, in [mode'ra:tɔr, -a'to:rɪn] m(f) presenter

moderieren [mode'ri:rən] *vt, vi* (*Rundf, TV*) to present

modern [mo'dɛrn] *adj* modern; (*modisch*) fashionable

modernisieren [modɛrni'zi:rən] *vt* to modernize

Mode- *zW*: **Modeschmuck** m fashion jewellery (*Brit*) *od* jewelry (*US*); **Modeschöpfer, in** m(f) fashion designer; **Modewort** *nt* fashionable word

modifizieren [modifi'tsi:rən] *vt* to modify

modisch ['mo:dɪʃ] *adj* fashionable

Modul ['mo:dʊl] (**-s, -n**) *nt* (*Comput*) module

Modus ['mo:dʊs] (**-, Modi**) m way; (*Gram*) mood; (*Comput*) mode

Mofa ['mo:fa] (**-s, -s**) *nt* (= *Motorfahrrad*) small moped

Mogadischu (**-s**) [moga'dɪʃu] *nt* Mogadishu

mogeln ['mo:gəln] (*umg*) *vi* to cheat

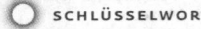
SCHLÜSSELWORT

mögen ['mø:gən] (*pt* **mochte**, *pp* **gemocht** *od* (*als Hilfsverb*) **mögen**) *vt, vi* to like; **magst du/mögen Sie ihn?** do you like him?; **ich möchte ...** I would like ..., I'd like ...; **er möchte in die Stadt** he'd like to go into town; **ich möchte nicht, dass du ...** I wouldn't like you to ...; **ich mag nicht mehr** I've had enough; (*bin am Ende*) I can't take any more; **man möchte meinen, dass ...** you would think that ...

▷ *hilfsverb* to like to; (*wollen*) to want; **möchtest du etwas essen?** would you like something to eat?; **sie mag nicht bleiben** she doesn't want to stay; **das mag wohl sein** that may very well be; **was mag das heißen?** what might that mean?; **Sie möchten zu Hause anrufen** could you please call home?

möglich ['mø:klɪç] *adj* possible; **er tat sein M~stes** he did his utmost

möglicherweise *adv* possibly

Möglichkeit f possibility; **nach ~** if possible

möglichst *adv* as ... as possible

Mohikaner [mohi'ka:nər] (**-s, -**) m: **der letzte ~** (*hum: umg*) the very last one

Mohn [mo:n] (**-(e)s, -e**) m (*Mohnblume*) poppy; (*Mohnsamen*) poppy seed

Möhre ['mø:rə] (**-, -n**) f carrot

Mohrenkopf ['mo:rənkɔpf] m *chocolate-covered marshmallow*

Mohrrübe f carrot

mokieren [mo'ki:rən] *vr*: **sich über etw** *akk* ~ to make fun of sth

Mokka ['mɔka] (**-s**) m mocha, *strong coffee*

Moldau ['mɔldaʊ] f: **die** ~ the Vltava

Moldawien [mɔl'da:viən] (**-s**) *nt* Moldavia

moldawisch *adj* Moldavian

Mole ['mo:lə] (**-, -n**) f (*Naut*) mole

Molekül [mole'ky:l] (**-s, -e**) *nt* molecule

molk *etc* [mɔlk] *vb siehe* **melken**

Molkerei [mɔlkə'raɪ] f dairy; **Molkereibutter** f blended butter

Moll [mɔl] (**-, -**) *nt* (*Mus*) minor (key)

mollig *adj* cosy; (*dicklich*) plump

Molotowcocktail ['mo:lotɔfkɔkte:l] m Molotov cocktail

Moment [mo'mɛnt] (**-(e)s, -e**) m moment ▷ *nt* factor, element; **im** ~ at the moment; ~ **mal!** just a minute!; **im ersten** ~ for a moment

momentan [momɛn'ta:n] *adj* momentary ▷ *adv* at the moment

Monaco [mo'nako, 'mo:nako] (**-s**) *nt* Monaco

Monarch [mo'narç] (**-en, -en**) m monarch

Monarchie [monar'çi:] f monarchy

Monat ['mo:nat] (**-(e)s, -e**) m month; **sie ist im sechsten ~ (schwanger)** she's five months pregnant; **was verdient er im ~?** how much does he earn a month?

monatelang *adv* for months

monatlich *adj* monthly

Monats- *zW*: **Monatsblutung** f menstrual period; **Monatskarte** f monthly ticket; **Monatsrate** f monthly instalment (*Brit*) *od* installment (*US*)

Mönch [mœnç] (**-(e)s, -e**) m monk

Mond [moːnt] (**-(e)s, -e**) m moon; **auf** od **hinter dem ~ leben** (umg) to be behind the times; **Mondfähre** f lunar (excursion) module; **Mondfinsternis** f eclipse of the moon; **mondhell** adj moonlit; **Mondlandung** f moon landing; **Mondschein** m moonlight; **Mondsonde** f moon probe

Monegasse [moneˈgasə] (**-n, -n**) m Monegasque

Monegassin [moneˈgasɪn] f Monegasque

monegassisch adj Monegasque

Monetarismus [monetaˈrɪsmʊs] m (Econ) monetarism

Monetarist m monetarist

Moneten [moˈneːtən] (umg) pl (Geld) bread sing, dough sing

Mongole [mɔŋˈgoːlə] (**-n, -n**) m Mongolian, Mongol

Mongolei [mɔŋgoˈlaɪ] f: **die ~** Mongolia

Mongolin f Mongolian, Mongol

mongolisch [mɔŋˈgoːlɪʃ] adj Mongolian

mongoloid [mɔŋgoloˈiːt] adj (Med) mongoloid

monieren [moˈniːrən] vt to complain about ▷ vi to complain

Monitor [ˈmoːnitɔr] m (Bildschirm) monitor

Mono- [mono] in zw mono

monogam [monoˈgaːm] adj monogamous

Monogamie [monogaˈmiː] f monogamy

Monolog [monoˈloːk] (**-s, -e**) m monologue

Monopol (**-s, -e**) nt monopoly

monopolisieren [monopoliˈziːrən] vt to monopolize

Monopolstellung f monopoly

monoton [monoˈtoːn] adj monotonous

Monotonie [monotoˈniː] f monotony

Monstrum [ˈmɔnstrʊm] (**-s, Monstren**) nt (lit, fig) monster; **ein ~ von einem/einer ...** a hulking great ...

Monsun [mɔnˈzuːn] (**-s, -e**) m monsoon

Montag [ˈmoːntaːk] (**-(e)s, -e**) m Monday; siehe auch **Dienstag**

Montage [mɔnˈtaːʒə] (**-, -n**) f (Phot etc) montage; (Tech) assembly; (Einbauen) fitting

montags adv on Mondays

Montanindustrie [mɔnˈtaːnɪndʊstriː] f coal and steel industry

Montblanc [mõˈblãː] m Mont Blanc

Monte Carlo [ˈmɔntə ˈkarlo] (**-s**) nt Monte Carlo

Montenegro [mɔnteˈneːgro] (**-s**) nt Montenegro

Monteur [mɔnˈtøːr] m fitter, assembly man

montieren [mɔnˈtiːrən] vt to assemble, set up

Montur [mɔnˈtuːr] (umg) f (Spezialkleidung) gear, rig-out

Monument [monuˈmɛnt] nt monument

monumental [monumɛnˈtaːl] adj monumental

Moor [moːr] (**-(e)s, -e**) nt moor; **Moorbad** nt mud bath

Moos [moːs] (**-es, -e**) nt moss

Moped [ˈmoːpɛt] (**-s, -s**) nt moped

Mops [mɔps] (**-es, ̈e**) m (Hund) pug

Moral [moˈraːl] (**-, -en**) f morality; (einer Geschichte) moral; (Disziplin: von Volk, Soldaten) morale; **Moralapostel** m upholder of moral standards; **moralisch** adj moral; **einen** od **den moralischen haben** (umg) to have (a fit of) the blues

Moräne [moˈrɛːnə] (**-, -n**) f moraine

Morast [moˈrast] (**-(e)s, -e**) m morass, mire **morastig** adj boggy

Mord [mɔrt] (**-(e)s, -e**) m murder; **dann gibt es ~ und Totschlag** (umg) there'll be hell to pay; **Mordanschlag** m murder attempt

Mörder [ˈmœrdər] (**-s, -**) m murderer; **Mörderin** f murderess

mörderisch adj (fig: schrecklich) dreadful, terrible; (Preise) exorbitant; (Konkurrenzkampf) cut-throat ▷ adv (umg: entsetzlich) dreadfully, terribly

Mordkommission f murder squad

Mords- zW: **Mordsding** (umg) nt whopper; **Mordsglück** (umg) nt amazing luck; **Mordskerl** (umg) m (verwegen) hell of a guy; **mordsmäßig** (umg) adj terrific, enormous; **Mordsschreck** (umg) m terrible fright

Mord- zW: **Mordverdacht** m suspicion of murder; **Mordversuch** m murder attempt; **Mordwaffe** f murder weapon

morgen [ˈmɔrgən] adv tomorrow; **bis ~!** see you tomorrow!; **~ in acht Tagen** a week (from) tomorrow; **~ um diese Zeit** this time tomorrow; **~ früh** tomorrow morning; **Morgen** (**-s, -**) m morning; (Maß) ≈ acre; **am Morgen** in the morning; **guten Morgen!** good morning!

Morgen- zW: **Morgengrauen** nt dawn, daybreak; **Morgenmantel** m dressing gown; **Morgenrock** m dressing gown; **Morgenrot** nt, **Morgenröte** f dawn

morgens adv in the morning; **von ~ bis abends** from morning to night

Morgenstunde f: **Morgenstund(e) hat Gold im Mund(e)** (Sprichwort) the early bird catches the worm (Sprichwort)

morgig [ˈmɔrgɪç] adj tomorrow's; **der ~e Tag** tomorrow

Morphium [ˈmɔrfiʊm] nt morphine

morsch [mɔrʃ] adj rotten

Morsealphabet [ˈmɔrzəˌalfabeːt] nt Morse code

morsen vi to send a message by Morse code

Mörser [ˈmœrzər] (**-s, -**) m mortar (auch Mil)

Mörtel [ˈmœrtəl] (**-s, -**) m mortar

Mosaik [mozaˈiːk] (**-s, -en** od **-e**) nt mosaic

Mosambik [mozamˈbiːk] (**-s**) nt Mozambique

Moschee [mɔˈʃeː] (**-, -n**) f mosque

Mosel[1] [ˈmoːzəl] f (Geog) Moselle

Mosel[2] (**-s, -**) m (auch: **Moselwein**) Moselle (wine)

mosern [ˈmoːzərn] (umg) vi to gripe, bellyache

Moskau [ˈmɔskau] (**-s**) nt Moscow

Moskauer adj Moscow attrib

Moskauer, in (**-s, -**) m(f) Muscovite

Moskito [mɔsˈkiːto] (**-s, -s**) m mosquito

Moslem ['mɔslɛm] (**-s, -s**) m Muslim
moslemisch [mɔs'le:mɪʃ] adj Muslim
Most [mɔst] (**-(e)s, -e**) m (unfermented) fruit juice; (Apfelwein) cider
Motel [mo'tɛl] (**-s, -s**) nt motel
Motiv [mo'ti:f] (**-s, -e**) nt motive; (Mus) theme
Motivation [motivatsi'o:n] f motivation
motivieren [moti'vi:rən] vt to motivate
Motivierung f motivation
Motor ['mo:tɔr] (**-s, -en**) m engine; (bes Elek) motor; **Motorboot** nt motorboat
Motorenöl nt engine oil
Motorhaube f (Aut) bonnet (Brit), hood (US)
motorisch adj (Physiologie) motor attrib
motorisieren [motori'zi:rən] vt to motorize
Motor- zW: **Motorrad** nt motorcycle; **Motorradfahrer** m motorcyclist; **Motorroller** m motor scooter; **Motorschaden** m engine trouble od failure; **Motorsport** m motor sport
Motte ['mɔtə] (**-, -n**) f moth
Motten- zW: **mottenfest** adj mothproof; **Mottenkiste** f: **etw aus der Mottenkiste hervorholen** (fig) to dig sth out; **Mottenkugel** f mothball
Motto ['mɔto] (**-s, -s**) nt motto
motzen ['mɔtsən] (umg) vi to grouse, beef
Mountainbike nt mountain bike
Möwe ['møːvə] (**-, -n**) f seagull
MP (-) f abk = **Maschinenpistole**
MP3 abk (Comput) MP3
MP3-Spieler m (Comput) MP3 player
Mrd. abk = **Milliarde(n)**
MS abk (= Motorschiff) motor vessel, MV; (= multiple Sklerose) MS
MTA (**-, -s**) f abk (= medizinisch-technische Assistentin) medical assistant
mtl. abk = **monatlich**
Mucke ['mʊkə] (**-, -n**) f (meist pl) caprice; (von Ding) snag, bug; **seine ~n haben** to be temperamental
Mücke ['mʏkə] (**-, -n**) f midge, gnat; **aus einer ~ einen Elefanten machen** (umg) to make a mountain out of a molehill
Muckefuck ['mʊkəfʊk] (**-s**) (umg) m coffee substitute
mucken vi: **ohne zu ~** without a murmur
Mückenstich m midge od gnat bite
Mucks [mʊks] (**-es, e**) m: **keinen ~ sagen** not to make a sound; (nicht widersprechen) not to say a word
mucksen (umg) vr to budge; (Laut geben) to open one's mouth
mucksmäuschenstill ['mʊks'mɔʏsçənʃtɪl] (umg) adj (as) quiet as a mouse
müde ['myːdə] adj tired; **nicht ~ werden, etw zu tun** never to tire of doing something
Müdigkeit f tiredness; **nur keine ~ vorschützen!** (umg) don't (you) tell me you're tired!
Muff [mʊf] (**-(e)s, -e**) m (Handwärmer) muff
Muffel (**-s, -**) (umg) m killjoy, sourpuss
muffig adj (Luft) musty
Mühe ['myːə] (**-, -n**) f trouble, pains pl; **mit**

Müh(e) und Not with great difficulty; **sich** dat **~ geben** to go to a lot of trouble; **mühelos** adj effortless, easy
muhen ['muːən] vi to low, moo
mühevoll adj laborious, arduous
Mühle ['myːlə] (**-, -n**) f mill; (Kaffeemühle) grinder; (Mühlespiel) nine men's morris
Mühlrad nt millwheel
Mühlstein m millstone
Mühsal (**-, -e**) f tribulation
mühsam adj arduous, troublesome ▷ adv with difficulty
mühselig adj arduous, laborious
Mulatte [mu'latə] (**-, -n**) m mulatto
Mulattin f mulatto
Mulde ['mʊldə] (**-, -n**) f hollow, depression
Mull [mʊl] (**-(e)s, -e**) m thin muslin
Müll [mʏl] (**-(e)s**) m refuse, rubbish, garbage (US); **Müllabfuhr** f refuse od garbage (US) collection; (Leute) dustmen pl (Brit), garbage collectors pl (US); **Mülladeplatz** m rubbish dump; **Müllbeutel** m bin liner (Brit), trashcan liner (US)
Mullbinde f gauze bandage
Mülldeponie f waste disposal site, rubbish tip
Mülleimer m rubbish bin (Brit), garbage can (US)
Müller (**-s, -**) m miller
Müll- zW: **Müllhalde** f, **Müllhaufen** m rubbish od garbage (US) heap; **Müllmann** (**-(e)s**, pl **Müllmänner**) (umg) m dustman (Brit), garbage collector (US); **Müllsack** m rubbish od garbage (US) bag; **Müllschlucker** m waste (Brit) od garbage (US) disposal unit; **Mülltonne** f dustbin (Brit), trashcan (US); **Müllverbrennung** f rubbish od garbage (US) incineration; **Müllverbrennungsanlage** f incinerator, incinerating plant; **Müllwagen** m dustcart (Brit), garbage truck (US)
mulmig ['mʊlmɪç] adj rotten; (umg) uncomfortable; **jdm ist ~** sb feels funny
Multi ['mʊlti] (**-s, -s**) (umg) m multinational (organization)
multi- in zW multi; **multilateral** adj: **multilateraler Handel** multilateral trade; **multinational** adj multinational; **multinationaler Konzern** multinational organization
multiple Sklerose [mʊl'tiːplə skle'roːzə] f multiple sclerosis
multiplizieren [mʊltipli'tsiːrən] vt to multiply
Mumie ['muːmiə] f (Leiche) mummy
Mumm [mʊm] (**-s**) (umg) m gumption, nerve
Mumps [mʊmps] (-) m od f mumps sing
München ['mʏnçən] nt Munich
Münchener, Münchner, in (**-s, -**) m(f) person from Munich
Mund [mʊnt] (**-(e)s, ̈er**) m mouth; **den ~ aufmachen** (fig: seine Meinung sagen) to speak up; **sie ist nicht auf den ~ gefallen** (umg) she's never at a loss for words; **Mundart** f dialect
Mündel ['mʏndəl] (**-s, -**) nt (Jur) ward

münden ['mʏndən] vi: **in etw** akk ~ to flow into sth

Mund- zW: **mundfaul** adj uncommunicative; **mundgerecht** adj bite-sized; **Mundgeruch** m bad breath; **Mundharmonika** f mouth organ

mündig ['mʏndɪç] adj of age; **Mündigkeit** f majority

mündlich ['mʏntlɪç] adj oral; ~**e Prüfung** oral (exam); ~**e Verhandlung** (Jur) hearing; **alles Weitere** ~! let's talk about it more when I see you

Mund- zW: **Mundraub** m (Jur) theft of food for personal consumption; **Mundstück** nt mouthpiece; (von Zigarette) tip; **mundtot** adj: **jdn mundtot machen** to muzzle sb

Mündung ['mʏndʊŋ] f estuary; (von Fluss, Rohr etc) mouth; (Gewehrmündung) muzzle

Mund- zW: **Mundwasser** nt mouthwash; **Mundwerk** nt: **ein großes Mundwerk haben** to have a big mouth; **Mundwinkel** m corner of the mouth; **Mund-zu-mund-Beatmung** f mouth-to-mouth resuscitation

Munition [munitsi'o:n] f ammunition

Munitionslager nt ammunition dump

munkeln ['mʊŋkəln] vi to whisper, mutter; **man munkelt, dass** ... there's a rumour (Brit) od rumor (US) that ...

Münster ['mʏnstər] (-**s,** -) nt minster

munter ['mʊntər] adj lively; (wach) awake; (aufgestanden) up and about; **Munterkeit** f liveliness

Münzanstalt f mint

Münzautomat m slot machine

Münze ['mʏntsə] (-, -**n**) f coin

münzen vt to coin, mint; **auf jdn gemünzt sein** to be aimed at sb

Münzfernsprecher ['mʏntsfɛrnʃprɛçər] m callbox (Brit), pay phone (US)

Münzwechsler m change machine

mürb ['mʏrb], **mürbe** ['mʏrbə] adj (Gestein) crumbly; (Holz) rotten; (Gebäck) crisp; **jdn** ~(**e**) **machen** to wear sb down

Mürbeteig, Mürbteig m shortcrust pastry

Murmel ['mʊrməl] (-, -**n**) f marble

murmeln vt, vi to murmur, mutter

Murmeltier ['mʊrməlti:r] nt marmot; **schlafen wie ein** ~ to sleep like a log

murren ['mʊrən] vi to grumble, grouse

mürrisch ['mʏrɪʃ] adj sullen

Mus [mu:s] (-**es,** -**e**) nt purée

Muschel ['mʊʃəl] (-, -**n**) f mussel; (Muschelschale) shell; (Telefonmuschel) receiver

Muse ['mu:zə] (-, -**n**) f muse

Museum [mu'ze:ʊm] (-**s, Museen**) nt museum

museumsreif adj: ~ **sein** to be almost a museum piece

Musik [mu'zi:k] f music; (Kapelle) band

musikalisch [muzi'ka:lɪʃ] adj musical

Musikbox f jukebox

Musiker, in [mu'zikər(ɪn)] (-**s,** -) m(f) musician

Musik- zW: **Musikhochschule** f music school; **Musikinstrument** nt musical instrument; **Musikkapelle** f band; **Musikstück** nt piece of music; **Musikstunde** f music lesson

musisch ['mu:zɪʃ] adj artistic

musizieren [muzi'tsi:rən] vi to make music

Muskat [mʊs'ka:t] (-(e)**s, -e**) m nutmeg

Muskel ['mʊskəl] (-**s, -n**) m muscle; **Muskeldystrophie** f muscular dystrophy; **Muskelkater** m: **einen Muskelkater haben** to be stiff; **Muskelpaket** (umg) nt muscleman; **Muskelzerrung** (umg) f pulled muscle

Muskulatur [mʊskula'tu:r] f muscular system

muskulös [mʊsku'lø:s] adj muscular

Müsli ['my:sli] (-**s, -**) nt muesli

Muss [mʊs] (-) nt necessity, must

muss vb siehe **müssen**

Muße ['mu:sə] (-) f leisure

O SCHLÜSSELWORT

müssen ['mʏsən] (pt **musste,** pp **gemusst** od (als Hilfsverb) **müssen**) vi **1** (Zwang) must (nur im Präsens), to have to; **ich muss es tun** I must do it, I have to do it; **ich musste es tun** I had to do it; **er muss es nicht tun** he doesn't have to do it; **muss ich?** must I?, do I have to?; **wann müsst ihr zur Schule?** when do you have to go to school?; **der Brief muss heute noch zur Post** the letter must be posted (Brit) od mailed (US) today; **er hat gehen müssen** he (has) had to go; **muss das sein?** is that really necessary?; **wenn es (unbedingt) sein muss** if it's absolutely necessary; **ich muss mal** (umg) I need to go to the loo (Brit) od bathroom (US)

2 (sollen): **das musst du nicht tun!** you oughtn't to od shouldn't do that; **das müsstest du eigentlich wissen** you ought to od you should know that; **Sie hätten ihn fragen müssen** you should have asked him

3: **es muss geregnet haben** it must have rained; **es muss nicht wahr sein** it needn't be true

Mussheirat (umg) f shotgun wedding

müßig ['my:sɪç] adj idle; **Müßiggang** m idleness

musst [mʊst] vb siehe **müssen**

musste etc ['mʊstə] vb siehe **müssen**

Muster ['mʊstər] (-**s, -**) nt model; (Dessin) pattern; (Probe) sample; ~ **ohne Wert** free sample; **Musterbeispiel** nt classic example; **mustergültig** adj exemplary; **musterhaft** adj exemplary

mustern vt (betrachten, Mil) to examine; (Truppen) to inspect

Musterprozess m test case

Musterschüler m model pupil

Musterung f (von Stoff) pattern; (Mil) inspection

Mut [mu:t] m courage; **nur** ~! cheer up!; **jdm** ~ **machen** to encourage sb; ~ **fassen** to pluck up courage

mutig adj courageous

mutlos adj discouraged, despondent

mutmaßen *vt untr* to conjecture ▷ *vi untr* to conjecture
mutmaßlich ['mu:tma:slɪç] *adj* presumed ▷ *adv* probably
Mutprobe *f* test of courage
Mutter¹ ['mʊtər] (-, -n) *f* (*Schraubenmutter*) nut
Mutter² ['mʊtər] (-, ⸚) *f* mother;
Mutterfreuden *pl* the joys *pl* of motherhood; **Muttergesellschaft** *f* (*Comm*) parent company; **Mutterkuchen** *m* (*Anat*) placenta; **Mutterland** *nt* mother country; **Mutterleib** *m* womb
mütterlich ['mʏtərlɪç] *adj* motherly
mütterlicherseits *adv* on the mother's side
Mutter- *zW:* **Mutterliebe** *f* motherly love; **Muttermal** *nt* birthmark; **Muttermilch** *f* mother's milk
Mutterschaft *f* motherhood
Mutterschaftsgeld *nt* maternity benefit
Mutterschaftsurlaub *m* maternity leave

Mutter- *zW:* **Mutterschutz** *m* maternity regulations *pl*; **mutterseelenallein** *adj* all alone; **Muttersprache** *f* native language; **Muttertag** *m* Mother's Day
Mutti (-, -s) (*umg*) *f* mum(my) (*Brit*), mom(my) (*US*)
mutwillig ['mu:tvɪlɪç] *adj* deliberate
Mütze ['mʏtsə] (-, -n) *f* cap
MV *f abk* (= *Mitgliederversammlung*) general meeting
MW *abk* (= *Mittelwelle*) MW
MwSt, Mw.-St. *abk* (= *Mehrwertsteuer*) VAT
mysteriös [mʏsteri'øːs] *adj* mysterious
Mystik ['mʏstɪk] *f* mysticism
Mystiker, in (-s, -) *m(f)* mystic
mystisch ['mʏstɪʃ] *adj* mystical; (*rätselhaft*) mysterious
Mythologie [mytolo'giː] *f* mythology
Mythos ['myːtɔs] (-, **Mythen**) *m* myth

m

Nn

N¹, n [ɛn] *nt* N, n; **N wie Nordpol** ≈ N for Nellie, N for Nan (US)

N² [ɛn] *abk* (= *Norden*) N

na [na] *interj* well; **na gut** (*umg*) all right, OK; **na also!** (well,) there you are (then)!; **na so was!** well, I never!; **na und?** so what?

Nabel ['na:bəl] (**-s, -**) *m* navel; **der ~ der Welt** (*fig*) the hub of the universe; **Nabelschnur** *f* umbilical cord

 SCHLÜSSELWORT

nach [na:x] *präp +dat* **1** (*örtlich*) to; **nach Berlin** to Berlin; **nach links/rechts** (to the) left/right; **nach oben/hinten** up/back; **er ist schon nach London abgefahren** he has already left for London

2 (*zeitlich*) after; **einer nach dem anderen** one after the other; **nach Ihnen!** after you!; **zehn (Minuten) nach drei** ten (minutes) past *od* after (US) three

3 (*gemäß*) according to; **nach dem Gesetz** according to the law; **die Uhr nach dem Radio stellen** to put a clock right by the radio; **ihrer Sprache nach (zu urteilen)** judging by her language; **dem Namen nach** judging by his/her name; **nach allem, was ich weiß** as far as I know

▷ *adv*: **ihm nach!** after him!; **nach und nach** gradually, little by little; **nach wie vor** still

nachäffen ['na:x|ɛfən] *vt* to ape
nachahmen ['na:x|a:mən] *vt* to imitate
nachahmenswert *adj* exemplary
Nachahmung *f* imitation; **etw zur ~ empfehlen** to recommend sth as an example
Nachbar, in ['naxba:r(ɪn)] (**-s, -n**) *m(f)* neighbour (*Brit*), neighbor (US); **Nachbarhaus** *nt*: **im Nachbarhaus** next door; **nachbarlich** *adj* neighbourly (*Brit*), neighborly (US); **Nachbarschaft** *f* neighbourhood (*Brit*), neighborhood (US); **Nachbarstaat** *m* neighbouring (*Brit*) *od* neighboring (US) state
nach- *zW*: **Nachbehandlung** *f* (*Med*) follow-up treatment; **nachbestellen** *vt* to order again; **Nachbestellung** *f* (*Comm*) repeat order; **nachbeten** (*pej*: *umg*) *vt* to repeat parrot-fashion; **nachbezahlen** *vt* to pay; (*später*) to pay later; **nachbilden** *vt* to copy; **Nachbildung** *f* imitation, copy; **nachblicken** *vi* to look *od* gaze after; **nachdatieren** *vt* to postdate

nachdem [na:x'de:m] *konj* after; (*weil*) since; **je ~ (ob)** it depends (whether)

nach- *zW*: **nachdenken** *unreg vi*: **über etw** *akk* **nachdenken** to think about sth; **darüber darf man gar nicht nachdenken** it doesn't bear thinking about; **Nachdenken** *nt* reflection, meditation; **nachdenklich** *adj* thoughtful, pensive; **nachdenklich gestimmt sein** to be in a thoughtful mood

Nachdruck ['na:xdrʊk] *m* emphasis; (*Typ*) reprint, reproduction; **besonderen ~ darauf legen, dass ...** to stress *od* emphasize particularly that ...

nachdrücklich ['na:xdrʏklɪç] *adj* emphatic; **~ auf etw** *dat* **bestehen** to insist firmly (up) on sth

nacheifern ['na:x|aɪfərn] *vi*: **jdm ~** to emulate sb

nacheinander [na:x|aɪ'nandər] *adv* one after the other; **kurz ~** shortly after each other; **drei Tage ~** three days running, three days on the trot (*umg*)

nachempfinden ['na:x|ɛmpfɪndən] *unreg vt*: **jdm etw ~** to feel sth with sb

nacherzählen ['na:x|ɛrtsɛ:lən] *vt* to retell
Nacherzählung *f* reproduction (of a story)
Nachf. *abk* = **Nachfolger**
Nachfahr ['na:xfa:r] (**-en, -en**) *m* descendant
Nachfolge ['na:xfɔlgə] *f* succession; **die/jds ~ antreten** to succeed/succeed sb
nachfolgen *vi* (*lit*): **jdm/etw ~** to follow sb/sth
nachfolgend *adj* following
Nachfolger, in (**-s, -**) *m(f)* successor
nachforschen *vt, vi* to investigate
Nachforschung *f* investigation; **~en anstellen** to make enquiries
Nachfrage ['na:xfra:gə] *f* inquiry; (*Comm*) demand; **es besteht eine rege ~** (*Comm*) there is a great demand; **danke der ~** (*form*) thank you for your concern; (*umg*) nice of you to ask; **nachfragemäßig** *adj* according to demand
nachfragen *vi* to inquire
nach- *zW*: **nachfühlen** *vt* = **nachempfinden**; **nachfüllen** *vt* to refill; **nachgeben** *unreg vi* to give way, yield

Nachgebühr f surcharge; (*Post*) excess postage
Nachgeburt f afterbirth
nachgehen ['na:xge:ən] *unreg vi* (+*dat*) to follow; (*erforschen*) to inquire (into); (*Uhr*) to be slow; **einer geregelten Arbeit ~** to have a steady job
Nachgeschmack ['na:xgəʃmak] *m* aftertaste
nachgiebig ['na:xgi:bɪç] *adj* soft, accommodating; **Nachgiebigkeit** f softness
nachgrübeln ['na:xgry:bəln] *vi:* **über etw** akk **~** to think about sth; (*sich Gedanken machen*) to ponder on sth
nachgucken ['na:xgʊkən] *vt, vi* = **nachsehen**
nachhaken ['na:xha:kən] (*umg*) *vi* to dig deeper
Nachhall ['na:xhal] *m* resonance
nachhallen *vi* to resound
nachhaltig ['na:xhaltɪç] *adj* lasting; (*Widerstand*) persistent
nachhängen ['na:xhɛŋən] *unreg vi:* **seinen Erinnerungen ~** to lose o.s. in one's memories
nachhause *adv* home
Nachhauseweg [na:x'haʊzəve:k] *m* way home
nachhelfen ['na:xhɛlfən] *unreg vi:* **jdm ~** to help *od* assist sb; **er hat dem Glück ein bisschen nachgeholfen** he engineered himself a little luck
nachher [na:x'he:r] *adv* afterwards; **bis ~** see you later!
Nachhilfe ['na:xhɪlfə] f (*auch:* **Nachhilfe-unterricht**) extra (private) tuition
Nachhinein ['na:xhɪnaɪn] *adv:* **im ~** afterwards; (*rückblickend*) in retrospect
Nachholbedarf *m:* **einen ~ an etw** dat **haben** to have a lot of sth to catch up on
nachholen ['na:xho:lən] *vt* to catch up with; (*Versäumtes*) to make up for
Nachkomme ['na:xkɔmə] (**-n, -n**) *m* descendant
nachkommen *unreg vi* to follow; (*einer Verpflichtung*) to fulfil; **Sie können Ihr Gepäck ~ lassen** you can have your luggage sent on (after)
Nachkommenschaft f descendants *pl*
Nachkriegs- ['na:xkri:ks] *in zw* postwar; **Nachkriegszeit** f postwar period
Nach- *zW:* **Nachlass** (**-es, -lässe**) *m* (*Comm*) discount, rebate; (*Erbe*) estate; **nachlassen** *unreg vt* (*Strafe*) to remit; (*Summe*) to take off; (*Schulden*) to cancel ▷ *vi* to decrease, ease off; (*Sturm*) to die down; (*schlechter werden*) to deteriorate; **er hat nachgelassen** he has got worse; **nachlässig** *adj* negligent, careless; **Nachlässigkeit** f negligence, carelessness; **Nachlasssteuer** f death duty; **Nachlassverwalter** *m* executor
nachlaufen ['na:xlaʊfən] *unreg vi:* **jdm ~** to run after *od* chase sb
nachliefern ['na:xli:fərn] *vt* (*später liefern*) to deliver at a later date; (*zuzüglich liefern*) to make a further delivery of
nachlösen ['na:xlø:zən] *vi* to pay on the train/ when one gets off; (*zur Weiterfahrt*) to pay the extra

nachm. *abk* (= *nachmittags*) p.m.
nachmachen ['na:xmaxən] *vt* to imitate, copy; (*fälschen*) to counterfeit; **jdm etw ~** to copy sth from sb; **das soll erst mal einer ~!** I'd like to see anyone else do that!
Nachmieter, in ['na:xmi:tər(ɪn)] *m(f):* **wir müssen einen ~ finden** we have to find someone to take over the flat *etc*
Nachmittag ['na:xmɪta:k] *m* afternoon; **am ~** in the afternoon; **gestern/heute ~** yesterday/ this afternoon
nachmittags *adv* in the afternoon
Nachmittagsvorstellung f matinée (performance)
Nachn. *abk* = **Nachnahme**
Nachnahme (**-, -n**) f cash on delivery (*Brit*), collect on delivery (*US*); **per ~** C.O.D.
Nachname *m* surname
Nachporto *nt* excess postage
nachprüfbar ['na:xpry:fba:r] *adj* verifiable
nachprüfen ['na:xpry:fən] *vt* to check, verify
nachrechnen ['na:xrɛçnən] *vt* to check
Nachrede ['na:xre:də] f: **üble ~** (*Jur*) defamation of character
nachreichen ['na:xraɪçən] *vt* to hand in later
Nachricht ['na:xrɪçt] (**-, -en**) f (piece of) news *sing*; (*Mitteilung*) message
Nachrichten *pl* news *sing*; **Nachrichtenagentur** f news agency; **Nachrichtendienst** *m* (*Mil*) intelligence service; **Nachrichtensatellit** *m* (tele)communications satellite; **Nachrichtensperre** f news blackout; **Nachrichtensprecher, in** *m(f)* newsreader; **Nachrichtentechnik** f telecommunications *sing*
nachrücken ['na:xrʏkən] *vi* to move up
Nachruf ['na:xru:f] *m* obituary (notice)
nachrüsten ['na:xrʏstən] *vt* (*Kraftwerk etc*) to modernize; (*Auto etc*) to refit; (*Waffen*) to keep up to date ▷ *vi* (*Mil*) to deploy new arms
nachsagen ['na:xza:gən] *vt* to repeat; **jdm etw ~** to say sth of sb; **das lasse ich mir nicht ~!** I'm not having that said of me!
Nachsaison ['na:xzɛzõ:] f off season
nachschenken ['na:xʃɛŋkən] *vt, vi:* **darf ich Ihnen noch (etwas) ~?** may I top up your glass?
nachschicken ['na:xʃɪkən] *vt* to forward
nachschlagen ['na:xʃla:gən] *unreg vt* to look up ▷ *vi:* **jdm ~** to take after sb
Nachschlagewerk *nt* reference book
Nachschlüssel *m* master key
nachschmeißen ['na:xʃmaɪsən] *unreg* (*umg*) *vt:* **das ist ja nachgeschmissen!** it's a real bargain!
Nachschrift ['na:xʃrɪft] f postscript
Nachschub ['na:xʃu:p] *m* supplies *pl*; (*Truppen*) reinforcements *pl*
nachsehen ['na:xze:ən] *unreg vt* (*prüfen*) to check ▷ *vi* (*erforschen*) to look and see; **jdm etw ~** to forgive sb sth; **jdm ~** to gaze after sb
Nachsehen *nt:* **das ~ haben** to be left empty-handed

n

235

nachsenden ['na:xzɛndən] *unreg vt* to send on, forward

Nachsicht ['na:xzɪçt] (-) *f* indulgence, leniency

nachsichtig *adj* indulgent, lenient

Nachsilbe ['na:xzɪlbə] *f* suffix

nachsitzen ['na:xzɪtsən] *unreg vi* (*Sch*) to be kept in

Nachsorge ['na:xzɔrgə] *f* (*Med*) aftercare

Nachspann ['na:xʃpan] *m* credits *pl*

Nachspeise ['na:xʃpaɪzə] *f* dessert, sweet (*Brit*)

Nachspiel ['na:xʃpi:l] *nt* epilogue; (*fig*) sequel

nachspionieren ['na:xʃpioni:rən] (*umg*) *vi*: **jdm ~** to spy on sb

nachsprechen ['na:xʃprɛçən] *unreg vt*: **(jdm) ~** to repeat (after sb)

nächst [nɛ:çst] *präp +dat* (*räumlich*) next to; (*außer*) apart from; **nächstbeste, r, s** *adj* first that comes along; (*zweitbeste*) next-best

Nächste, r, s *f(m)* neighbour (*Brit*), neighbor (*US*)

nächste, r, s *adj* next; (*nächstgelegen*) nearest; **aus ~r Nähe** from close by; (*betrachten*) at close quarters; **Ende ~n Monats** at the end of next month; **am ~n Tag** (the) next day; **bei ~r Gelegenheit** at the earliest opportunity; **in ~r Zeit** some time soon; **der ~ Angehörige** the next of kin

nachstehen ['na:xʃte:ən] *unreg vi*: **jdm in nichts ~** to be sb's equal in every way

nachstehend *adj attrib* following

nachstellen ['na:xʃtɛlən] *vi*: **jdm ~** to follow sb; (*aufdringlich umwerben*) to pester sb

Nächstenliebe *f* love for one's fellow men

nächstens *adv* shortly, soon

nächstliegend *adj* (*lit*) nearest; (*fig*) obvious

nächstmöglich *adj* next possible

nachsuchen ['na:xzu:xən] *vi*: **um etw ~** to ask *od* apply for sth

Nacht [naxt] (-, -̈e) *f* night; **gute ~!** good night!; **heute ~** tonight; **in der ~** at night; **in der ~ auf Dienstag** during Monday night; **in der ~ vom 12. zum 13. April** during the night of April 12th to 13th; **über ~** (*auch fig*) overnight; **bei ~ und Nebel** (*umg*) at dead of night; **sich** *dat* **die ~ um die Ohren schlagen** (*umg*) to stay up all night; (*mit Feiern, arbeiten*) to make a night of it

Nachtdienst *m* night duty

Nachteil ['na:xtaɪl] *m* disadvantage; **im ~ sein** to be at a disadvantage

nachteilig *adj* disadvantageous

Nachtfalter *m* moth

Nachthemd *nt* (*Herrennachthemd*) nightshirt; nightdress (*Brit*), nightgown

Nachtigall ['naxtɪgal] (-, -en) *f* nightingale

Nachtisch ['na:xtɪʃ] *m* = **Nachspeise**

Nachtleben *nt* night life

nächtlich ['nɛçtlɪç] *adj* nightly

Nacht- *zW*: **Nachtlokal** *nt* night club; **Nachtmensch** ['naxtmɛnʃ] *m* night person; **Nachtportier** *m* night porter

nach- *zW*: **Nachtrag** ['na:xtra:k] (-(e)s, -träge) *m* supplement; **nachtragen** *unreg*

vt (*zufügen*) to add; **jdm etw nachtragen** to carry sth after sb; (*fig*) to hold sth against sb; **nachtragend** *adj* resentful; **nachträglich** *adj* later, subsequent; (*zusätzlich*) additional ▷ *adv* later, subsequently; (*zusätzlich*) additionally; **nachtrauern** *vi*: **jdm/etw nachtrauern** to mourn the loss of sb/sth

Nachtruhe ['naxtru:ə] *f* sleep

nachts *adv* by night

Nachtschicht *f* night shift

Nachtschwester *f* night nurse

nachtsüber *adv* during the night

Nacht- *zW*: **Nachttarif** *m* off-peak tariff; **Nachttisch** *m* bedside table; **Nachttopf** *m* chamber pot; **Nachtwache** *f* night watch; (*im Krankenhaus*) night duty; **Nachtwächter** *m* night watchman

Nach- *zW*: **Nachuntersuchung** *f* checkup; **nachvollziehen** *unreg vt* to understand, comprehend; **nachwachsen** *unreg vi* to grow again; **Nachwahl** *f* ≈ by-election (*bes Brit*); **Nachwehen** *pl* afterpains *pl*; (*fig*) aftereffects *pl*; **nachweinen** *vi +dat* to mourn ▷ *vt*: **dieser Sache** *dat* **weine ich keine Träne nach** I won't shed any tears over that

Nachweis ['na:xvaɪs] (-es, -e) *m* proof; **den ~ für etw erbringen** *od* **liefern** to furnish proof of sth; **nachweisbar** *adj* provable, demonstrable; **nachweisen** ['na:xvaɪzən] *unreg vt* to prove; **jdm etw nachweisen** to point sth out to sb; **nachweislich** *adj* evident, demonstrable

nach- *zW*: **Nachwelt** *f*: **die Nachwelt** posterity; **nachwinken** *vi*: **jdm nachwinken** to wave after sb; **nachwirken** *vi* to have aftereffects; **Nachwirkung** *f* aftereffect; **Nachwort** *nt* appendix; **Nachwuchs** *m* offspring; (*beruflich etc*) new recruits *pl*; **nachzahlen** *vt, vi* to pay extra; **nachzählen** *vt* to count again; **Nachzahlung** *f* additional payment; (*zurückdatiert*) back pay

nachziehen ['na:xtsi:ən] *unreg vt* (*Linie*) to go over; (*Lippen*) to paint; (*Augenbrauen*) to pencil in; (*hinterherziehen*): **etw ~** to drag sth behind one

Nachzügler (-s, -) *m* straggler

Nackedei ['nakədaɪ] (-(e)s, -e *od* -s) *m* (*hum: umg: Kind*) little bare monkey

Nacken ['nakən] (-s, -) *m* nape of the neck; **jdm im ~ sitzen** (*umg*) to breathe down sb's neck

nackt [nakt] *adj* naked; (*Tatsachen*) plain, bare; **Nacktheit** *f* nakedness; **Nacktkultur** *f* nudism

Nadel ['na:dəl] (-, -n) *f* needle; (*Stecknadel*) pin; **Nadelbaum** *m* conifer; **Nadelkissen** *nt* pincushion; **Nadelöhr** *nt* eye of a needle; **Nadelwald** *m* coniferous forest

Nagel ['na:gəl] (-s, -̈) *m* nail; **sich** *dat* **etw unter den ~ reißen** (*umg*) to pinch sth; **etw an den ~ hängen** (*fig*) to chuck sth in (*umg*); **Nägel mit Köpfen machen** (*umg*) to do the job properly; **Nagelbürste** *f* nailbrush; **Nagelfeile** *f* nailfile; **Nagelhaut** *f* cuticle;

Nagellack *m* nail varnish (*Brit*) *od* polish;
Nagellackentferner (**-s, -**) *m* nail polish remover
nageln *vt, vi* to nail
nagelneu *adj* brand-new
Nagelschere *f* nail scissors *pl*
nagen ['naːgən] *vt, vi* to gnaw
Nagetier ['naːgətiːr] *nt* rodent
nah *adj* = **nahe**
Nahaufnahme *f* close-up
Nahe *f* (*Fluss*) Nahe
nahe *adj* (*räumlich*) near(by); (*Verwandte*) near, close; (*Freunde*) close; (*zeitlich*) near, close
  ▷ *adv:* **von nah und fern** from near and far
  ▷ *präp+dat* near (to), close to; **von N~m** at close quarters; **der N~ Osten** the Middle East; **jdm ~ kommen** to get close to sb; **~ stehend** close; **jdm zu ~ treten** (*fig*) to offend sb; **mit jdm ~ verwandt sein** to be closely related to sb; *siehe auch* **naheliegen; nahestehen** *etc*
Nähe ['nɛːə] (**-**) *f* nearness, proximity; (*Umgebung*) vicinity; **in der ~** close by; at hand; **aus der ~** from close to
nahebei *adv* nearby
nahebringen *unreg vt* (*fig*): **jdm etw ~** to bring sth home to sb
nahegehen *unreg vi* (*fig*): **jdm ~** to grieve sb
nahelegen *vi* (*fig*): **jdm etw ~** to suggest sth to sb
naheliegen *unreg vi* (*fig*) to be obvious; **der Verdacht liegt nahe, dass ...** it seems reasonable to suspect that ...; **~d** obvious
nahen *vi, vr* to approach, draw near
nähen ['nɛːən] *vt, vi* to sew
näher *adj* nearer; (*Erklärung, Erkundigung*) more detailed ▷ *adv* nearer; in greater detail; **~ kommen** to get closer; **ich kenne ihn nicht ~** I don't know him well
Nähere, s *nt* details *pl*, particulars *pl*
Näherei [nɛːə'raɪ] *f* sewing, needlework
Naherholungsgebiet *nt* recreational area (*close to a centre of population*)
Näherin *f* seamstress
nähern *vr* to approach
Näherungswert *m* approximate value
nahestehen *unreg vi* (*fig*): **jdm ~** to be close to sb; **einer Sache ~** to sympathize with sth
nahezu *adv* nearly
Nähgarn *nt* thread
Nahkampf *m* hand-to-hand fighting
Nähkasten *m* workbox, sewing basket
nahm *etc* [naːm] *vb siehe* **nehmen**
Nähmaschine *f* sewing machine
Nähnadel *f* (sewing) needle
Nahost [naːˈɔst] *m*: **aus ~** from the Middle East
Nährboden *m* (*lit*) fertile soil; (*fig*) breeding ground
nähren ['nɛːrən] *vt* to feed ▷ *vr* (*Person*) to feed o.s.; (*Tier*) to feed; **er sieht gut genährt aus** he looks well fed
Nährgehalt ['nɛːrgəhalt] *m* nutritional value
nahrhaft ['naːrhaft] *adj* (*Essen*) nourishing
Nährstoffe *pl* nutrients *pl*

Nahrung ['naːrʊŋ] *f* food; (*fig*) sustenance
Nahrungs- *zW:* **Nahrungsaufnahme** *f:* **die Nahrungsaufnahme verweigern** to refuse food; **Nahrungskette** *f* food chain; **Nahrungsmittel** *nt* food(stuff); **Nahrungsmittelindustrie** *f* food industry; **Nahrungssuche** *f* search for food
Nährwert *m* nutritional value
Naht [naːt] (**-, ⁻e**) *f* seam; (*Med*) suture; (*Tech*) join; **aus allen Nähten platzen** (*umg*) to be bursting at the seams; **nahtlos** *adj* seamless; **nahtlos ineinander übergehen** to follow without a gap
Nahverkehr *m* local traffic
Nahverkehrszug *m* local train
Nähzeug *nt* sewing kit, sewing things *pl*
Nahziel *nt* immediate objective
naiv [naˈiːf] *adj* naïve
Naivität [naivivˈtɛːt] *f* naïveté, naïvety
Name ['naːmə] (**-ns, -n**) *m* name; **im ~n von** on behalf of; **dem ~n nach müsste sie Deutsche sein** judging by her name she must be German; **die Dinge beim ~n nennen** (*fig*) to call a spade a spade; **ich kenne das Stück nur dem ~n nach** I've heard of the play but that's all
namens *adv* by the name of
Namensänderung *f* change of name
Namenstag *m* name day, saint's day; *see culture note*

● **NAMENSTAG**
●
● In Catholic areas of Germany the *Namenstag*
● is often a more important celebration than
● a birthday. It is the day dedicated to the
● saint after whom a person is called, and
● on that day the person receives presents
● and invites relatives and friends round to
● celebrate.

---

namentlich ['naːməntlɪç] *adj* by name ▷ *adv* particularly, especially
namhaft ['naːmhaft] *adj* (*berühmt*) famed, renowned; (*beträchtlich*) considerable; **~ machen** to name, identify
Namibia [naˈmiːbia] (**-s**) *nt* Namibia
nämlich ['nɛːmlɪç] *adv* that is to say, namely; (*denn*) since; **der/die/das N~e** the same
nannte *etc* ['nantə] *vb siehe* **nennen**
nanu [naˈnuː] *interj* well I never!
Napalm ['naːpalm] (**-s**) *nt* napalm
Napf [napf] (**-(e)s, ⁻e**) *m* bowl, dish; **Napfkuchen** *m* ≈ ring-shaped pound cake
Narbe ['narbə] (**-, -n**) *f* scar
narbig ['narbɪç] *adj* scarred
Narkose [narˈkoːzə] (**-, -n**) *f* anaesthetic (*Brit*), anesthetic (*US*)
Narr [nar] (**-en, -en**) *m* fool; **jdn zum ~en halten** to make a fool of sb; **narren** *vt* to fool
Narrenfreiheit *f:* **sie hat bei ihm ~** he gives her (a) free rein
narrensicher *adj* foolproof

n

Narrheit f foolishness
Närrin ['nɛrɪn] f fool
närrisch adj foolish, crazy; **die ~en Tage** Fasching and the period leading up to it
Narzisse [nar'tsɪsə] (-, -n) f narcissus
narzisstisch [nar'tsɪstɪʃ] adj narcissistic
NASA ['na:za] (-) f abk (= National Aeronautics and Space Administration) NASA
naschen ['naʃən] vt to nibble; (heimlich) to eat secretly ▷ vi to nibble sweet things; **~ von** od **an** +dat to nibble at
naschhaft adj sweet-toothed
Nase ['na:zə] (-, -n) f nose; **sich** dat **die ~ putzen** to wipe one's nose; (sich schnäuzen) to blow one's nose; **jdm auf der ~ herumtanzen** (umg) to play sb up; **jdm etw vor der ~ wegschnappen** (umg) to just beat sb to sth; **die ~ vollhaben** (umg) to have had enough; **jdm etw auf die ~ binden** (umg) to tell sb all about sth; (immer) **der ~ nachgehen** (umg) to follow one's nose; **jdn an der ~ herumführen** (als Täuschung) to lead sb by the nose; (als Scherz) to pull sb's leg
Nasen- zW: **Nasenbluten** (-s) nt nosebleed; **Nasenloch** nt nostril; **Nasenrücken** m bridge of the nose; **Nasentropfen** pl nose drops pl
naseweis adj pert, cheeky; (neugierig) nosey
Nashorn ['na:shɔrn] nt rhinoceros
nass [nas] adj wet
Nassauer ['nasaʊər] (-s, -) (umg) m scrounger
Nässe ['nɛsə] (-) f wetness
nässen vt to wet
nasskalt adj wet and cold
Nassrasur f wet shave
Nation [natsi'o:n] f nation
national [natsio'na:l] adj national; **Nationalelf** f international (football) team; **Nationalfeiertag** m national holiday; **Nationalhymne** f national anthem
nationalisieren [natsionali'zi:rən] vt to nationalize
Nationalisierung f nationalization
Nationalismus [natsiona'lɪsmʊs] m nationalism
nationalistisch [natsiona'lɪstɪʃ] adj nationalistic
Nationalität [natsionali'tɛ:t] f nationality
National- zW: **Nationalmannschaft** f international team; **Nationalsozialismus** m National Socialism; **Nationalsozialist** m National Socialist
NATO, Nato ['na:to] (-) f abk: **die ~** NATO
Natrium ['na:triʊm] (-s) nt sodium
Natron ['na:trɔn] (-s) nt soda
Natter ['natər] (-, -n) f adder
Natur [na'tu:r] f nature; (körperlich) constitution; (freies Land) countryside; **das geht gegen meine ~** it goes against the grain
Naturalien [natu'ra:liən] pl natural produce sing; **in ~** in kind
Naturalismus [natura'lɪsmʊs] m naturalism
Naturell [natu'rɛl] (-s, -e) nt temperament, disposition

Natur- zW: **Naturerscheinung** f natural phenomenon od event; **naturfarben** adj natural-coloured (Brit) od -colored (US); **Naturforscher** m natural scientist; **Naturfreak** (-s, -s) (umg) m back-to-nature freak; **naturgemäß** adj natural; **Naturgeschichte** f natural history; **Naturgesetz** nt law of nature; **naturgetreu** adj true to life; **Naturheilverfahren** nt natural cure; **Naturkatastrophe** f natural disaster; **Naturkostladen** m health food shop; **Naturkunde** f natural history; **Naturlehrpfad** m nature trail
natürlich [na'ty:rlɪç] adj natural ▷ adv naturally; **eines ~en Todes sterben** to die of natural causes
natürlicherweise [na'ty:rlɪçər'vaɪzə] adv naturally, of course
Natürlichkeit f naturalness
Natur- zW: **Naturprodukt** nt natural product; **naturrein** adj natural, pure; **Naturschutz** m: **unter Naturschutz stehen** to be legally protected; **Naturschutzgebiet** nt nature reserve (BRIT), national park (US); **Naturtalent** nt natural prodigy; **naturverbunden** adj nature-loving; **Naturwissenschaft** f natural science; **Naturwissenschaftler** m scientist; **Naturzustand** m natural state
Nautik ['naʊtɪk] f nautical science, navigation
nautisch ['naʊtɪʃ] adj nautical
Navelorange ['na:vəlorã:ʒə] f navel orange
Navigation [navigatsi'o:n] f navigation
Navigationsfehler m navigational error
Navigationsinstrumente pl navigation instruments pl
Nazi ['na:tsi] (-s, -s) m Nazi
NB abk (= nota bene) NB
n. Br. abk (= nördlicher Breite) northern latitude
NC m abk (= numerus clausus) siehe **Numerus**
Nchf. abk = **Nachfolger**
n. Chr. abk (= nach Christus) A.D.
NDR (-) m abk (= Norddeutscher Rundfunk) North German Radio
Neapel [ne'a:pəl] (-s) nt Naples
Neapolitaner, in [neapoli'ta:nər(ɪn)] (-s, -) m(f) Neapolitan
neapolitanisch [neapoli'ta:nɪʃ] adj Neapolitan
Nebel ['ne:bəl] (-s, -) m fog, mist
nebelig adj foggy, misty
Nebel- zW: **Nebelleuchte** f (Aut) rear fog-light; **Nebelscheinwerfer** m fog-lamp; **Nebelschlussleuchte** f (Aut) rear fog-light
neben ['ne:bən] präp +akk next to ▷ präp +dat next to; (außer) apart from, besides; **Nebenan** [ne:bən'an] adv next door; **Nebenanschluss** m (Tel) extension; **Nebenausgaben** pl incidental expenses pl; **nebenbei** [ne:bən'baɪ] adv at the same time; (außerdem) additionally; (beiläufig) incidentally; **nebenbei bemerkt** od **gesagt** by the way, incidentally; **Nebenberuf** m second occupation; **er ist im Nebenberuf ...** he has a second job as a ...; **Nebenbeschäftigung** f sideline; (Zweitberuf)

extra job; **Nebenbuhler, in** (**-s, -**) *m(f)* rival;
nebeneinander [ne:bənaɪ'nandər] *adv* side by
side; **nebeneinanderlegen** *vt* to put next to
each other; **Nebeneingang** *m* side entrance;
Nebeneinkünfte *pl*, **Nebeneinnahmen**
pl supplementary income *sing*;
Nebenerscheinung *f* side effect; **Nebenfach**
nt subsidiary subject; **Nebenfluss** *m* tributary;
Nebengeräusch *nt* (*Rundf*) atmospherics
pl, interference; **Nebenhandlung** *f* (*Liter*)
subplot; **nebenher** [ne:bən'he:r] *adv* (*zusätzlich*)
besides; (*gleichzeitig*) at the same time;
(*daneben*) alongside; **nebenherfahren** *unreg vi*
to drive alongside; **Nebenkläger** *m* (*Jur*) joint
plaintiff; **Nebenkosten** *pl* extra charges *pl*,
extras *pl*; **Nebenmann** (**-(e)s,** *pl* **-männer**)
m: **Ihr Nebenmann** the person next to you;
Nebenprodukt *nt* by-product; **Nebenrolle**
f minor part; **Nebensache** *f* trifle, side
issue; **nebensächlich** *adj* minor, peripheral;
Nebensaison *f* low season; **Nebensatz** *m*
(*Gram*) subordinate clause; **nebenstehend**
adj: **nebenstehende Abbildung** illustration
opposite; **Nebenstraße** *f* side street;
Nebenstrecke *f* (*Eisenb*) branch *od* local
line; **Nebenverdienst** *m* secondary income;
Nebenzimmer *nt* adjoining room
neblig ['ne:blɪç] *adj* = **nebelig**
nebst [ne:pst] *präp* +*dat* together with
Necessaire [nese'sɛ:r] (**-s, -s**) *nt* (*Nähnecessaire*)
needlework box; (*Nagelnecessaire*) manicure
case
Neckar ['nɛkar] (**-s**) *m* (*Fluss*) Neckar
necken ['nɛkən] *vt* to tease
Neckerei [nɛkə'raɪ] *f* teasing
neckisch *adj* coy; (*Einfall, Lied*) amusing
nee [ne:] (*umg*) *adv* no, nope
Neffe ['nɛfə] (**-n, -n**) *m* nephew
negativ ['ne:gati:f] *adj* negative; **Negativ** (**-s,
-e**) *nt* (*Phot*) negative
Neger ['ne:gər] (**-s, -**) (*pej*) *m* negro (*pej*); **Negerin**
(*pej*) *f* negress (*pej*)
negieren [ne'gi:rən] *vt* (*bestreiten*) to deny;
(*verneinen*) to negate
nehmen ['ne:mən] *unreg vt, vi* to take; **etw zu
sich ~** to take sth, partake of sth (*liter*); **jdm
etw ~** to take sth (away) from sb; **sich ernst
~** to take o.s. seriously; **~ Sie sich doch bitte**
help yourself; **man nehme ...** (*Koch*) take ...;
wie mans nimmt depending on your point
of view; **die Mauer nimmt einem die ganze
Sicht** the wall blocks the whole view; **er ließ
es sich** *dat* **nicht ~, es persönlich zu tun** he
insisted on doing it himself
Nehrung ['ne:rʊŋ] *f* (*Geog*) spit (of land)
Neid [naɪt] (**-(e)s**) *m* envy
Neidhammel (*umg*) *m* envious person
neidisch *adj* envious, jealous
Neige (**-, -n**) *f* (*geh: Ende*): **die Vorräte gehen
zur ~** the provisions are fast becoming
exhausted
neigen ['naɪgən] *vt* to incline, lean; (*Kopf*) to
bow ▷ *vi*: **zu etw ~** to tend to sth

Neigung *f* (*des Geländes*) slope; (*Tendenz*)
tendency, inclination; (*Vorliebe*) liking;
(*Zuneigung*) affection
Neigungswinkel *m* angle of inclination
nein [naɪn] *adv* no
Nelke ['nɛlkə] (**-, -n**) *f* carnation, pink;
(*Gewürznelke*) clove
nennen ['nɛnən] *unreg vt* to name; (*mit Namen*)
to call; **das nenne ich Mut!** that's what I call
courage!
nennenswert *adj* worth mentioning
Nenner (**-s, -**) *m* denominator; **etw auf einen
~ bringen** (*lit, fig*) to reduce sth to a common
denominator
Nennung *f* naming
Nennwert *m* nominal value; (*Comm*) par
neokonservativ *adj* neo-conservative, neo-con
(*umg*)
neoliberal *adj* neo-liberal, neo-lib (*umg*)
Neon ['ne:ɔn] (**-s**) *nt* neon
Neonazi [neo'na:tsi] *m* Neonazi
Neon- zW: Neonlicht *nt* neon light;
Neonreklame *f* neon sign; **Neonröhre** *f* neon
tube
Nepal ['ne:pal] (**-s**) *nt* Nepal
Nepp [nɛp] (**-s**) (*umg*) *m*: **der reinste ~** daylight
robbery, a rip-off
Nerv [nɛrf] (**-s, -en**) *m* nerve; **die ~en sind
mit ihm durchgegangen** he lost control, he
snapped (*umg*); **jdm auf die ~en gehen** to get
on sb's nerves
nerven (*umg*) *vt*: **jdn ~** to get on sb's nerves
Nerven- zW: Nervenaufreibend *adj*
nerve-racking; **Nervenbündel** *nt* bundle
of nerves; **Nervengas** *nt* (*Mil*) nerve
gas; **Nervenheilanstalt** *f* psychiatric
hospital; **Nervenklinik** *f* psychiatric clinic;
nervenkrank *adj* mentally ill; **Nervensäge**
(*umg*) *f* pain (in the neck); **Nervenschwäche**
f neurasthenia; **Nervensystem** *nt* nervous
system; **Nervenzusammenbruch** *m* nervous
breakdown
nervig ['nɛrvɪç] (*umg*) *adj* exasperating,
annoying
nervös [nɛr'vø:s] *adj* nervous
Nervosität [nɛrvozi'tɛ:t] *f* nervousness
nervtötend *adj* nerve-racking; (*Arbeit*) soul-
destroying
Nerz [nɛrts] (**-es, -e**) *m* mink
Nessel ['nɛsəl] (**-, -n**) *f* nettle; **sich in die ~n
setzen** (*fig: umg*) to put o.s. in a spot
Nessessär [nese'sɛ:r] (**-s, -s**) *nt* = **Necessaire**
Nest [nɛst] (**-(e)s, -er**) *nt* nest; (*umg: Ort*) dump;
(*fig: Bett*) bed; (: *Schlupfwinkel*) hide-out, lair;
da hat er sich ins warme ~ gesetzt (*umg*)
he's got it made; **Nestbeschmutzung** (*pej*) *f*
running-down (*umg*) *od* denigration (of one's
family/country)
nesteln *vi*: **an etw** +*dat* **~** to fumble *od* fiddle
about with sth
Nesthäkchen ['nɛsthɛ:kçən] *nt* baby of the
family
Netiquette [netɪ'kɛtə] (**-, no pl**) *f* (*Internet*)

Netiquette

nett [nɛt] *adj* nice; **sei so ~ und räum auf!** would you mind clearing up?

netterweise ['nɛtər'vaɪzə] *adv* kindly

netto *adv* net; **Nettoeinkommen** *nt* net income; **Nettogewicht** *nt* net weight; **Nettogewinn** *m* net profit; **Nettogewinnspanne** *f* net margin; **Nettolohn** *m* take-home pay; **Nettozahler** *m* (*Land etc*) net contributor

Netz [nɛts] (**-es, -e**) *nt* net; (*Gepäcknetz*) rack; (*Einkaufsnetz*) string bag; (*Spinnennetz*) web; (*System, Comput*) network; (*Stromnetz*) mains *sing od pl*; **das soziale ~** the social security network; **jdm ins ~ gehen** (*fig*) to fall into sb's trap; **Netzanbieter** *m* (*Comput*) Internet provider; **Netzanschluss** *m* mains connection; **Netzbetreiber** *m* (*Comput*) Internet provider; **Netzcomputer** *m* network computer; **Netzhaut** *f* retina; **Netzkarte** *f* (*Eisenb*) runabout ticket (*Brit*); **Netzplantechnik** *f* network analysis; **Netzspannung** *f* mains voltage; **Netzwerken** *nt* (social) networking; **Netzzugang** *m* (*Comput*) network access

neu [nɔʏ] *adj* new; (*Sprache, Geschichte*) modern; **der/die N~e** the new person, the newcomer; **seit N~estem** (since) recently; **~ schreiben** to rewrite, write again; **auf ein N~es!** (*Aufmunterung*) let's try again; **was gibts N~es?** (*umg*) what's the latest?; **von N~em** (*von vorn*) from the beginning; (*wieder*) again; **sich ~ einkleiden** to buy o.s. a new set of clothes; **~ eröffnet** newly-opened; (*wieder geöffnet*) reopened; **Neuankömmling** *m* newcomer; **Neuanschaffung** *f* new purchase *od* acquisition; **neuartig** *adj* new kind of; **Neuauflage** *f* new edition; **Neuausgabe** *f* new edition; **Neubau** (**-(e)s, -ten**) *m* new building; **Neubauwohnung** *f* newly-built flat; **Neubearbeitung** *f* revised edition; (*das Neubearbeiten*) revision, reworking; **Neudruck** *m* reprint; **Neuemission** *f* (*Aktien*) new issue

neuerdings *adv* (*kürzlich*) (since) recently; (*von Neuem*) again

Neuerscheinung *f* (*Buch*) new publication; (*Schallplatte*) new release

Neuerung *f* innovation, new departure

Neufassung *f* revised version

Neufundland [nɔʏ'fʊntlant] *nt* Newfoundland; **Neufundländer, in** (**-s, -**) *m(f)* Newfoundlander; **neufundländisch** *adj* Newfoundland *attrib*

neugeboren *adj* newborn; **sich wie ~ fühlen** to feel (like) a new man/woman

Neugier *f* curiosity

Neugierde (**-**) *f*: **aus ~** out of curiosity

neugierig *adj* curious

Neuguinea [nɔʏgi'neːa] (**-s**) *nt* New Guinea

Neuheit *f* novelty; (*neuartige Ware*) new thing

Neuigkeit *f* news *sing*

neu- *zW*: **Neujahr** *nt* New Year; **Neuland** *nt* virgin land; (*fig*) new ground; **neulich** *adv* recently, the other day; **Neuling** *m*

novice; **neumodisch** *adj* fashionable; (*pej*) newfangled; **Neumond** *m* new moon

neun [nɔʏn] *num* nine; **Neun** (**-, -en**) *f* nine; **ach du grüne Neune!** (*umg*) well I'm blowed!

neunmalklug *adj* (*ironisch*) smart-aleck *attrib*

neunzehn *num* nineteen

neunzig *num* ninety

Neuregelung, Neureglung *f* adjustment

neureich *adj* nouveau riche; **Neureiche, r** *f(m)* nouveau riche

Neurologie [nɔʏrolo'giː] *f* neurology

neurologisch [nɔʏro'loːgɪʃ] *adj* neurological

Neurose [nɔʏ'roːzə] (**-, -n**) *f* neurosis

Neurotiker, in [nɔʏ'roːtikər(ɪn)] (**-s, -**) *m(f)* neurotic

neurotisch *adj* neurotic

Neu- *zW*: **Neuschnee** *m* fresh snow; **Neuseeland** [nɔʏ'zeːlant] *nt* New Zealand; **Neuseeländer, in** (**-s, -**) *m(f)* New Zealander; **neuseeländisch** *adj* New Zealand *attrib*; **neusprachlich** *adj*: **neusprachliches Gymnasium** grammar school (*Brit*) *od* high school (*bes US*) stressing modern languages

neutral [nɔʏ'traːl] *adj* neutral

neutralisieren [nɔʏtrali'ziːrən] *vt* to neutralize

Neutralität [nɔʏtrali'tɛːt] *f* neutrality

Neutron ['nɔʏtrɔn] (**-s, -en**) *nt* neutron

Neutrum ['nɔʏtrʊm] (**-s, Neutra** *od* **Neutren**) *nt* neuter

Neu- *zW*: **Neuwert** *m* purchase price; **neuwertig** *adj* as new; **Neuzeit** *f* modern age; **neuzeitlich** *adj* modern, recent

N. H. *abk* (= *Normalhöhenpunkt*) normal peak (level)

nhd. *abk* (= *neuhochdeutsch*) NHG

Nicaragua [nika'raːgua] (**-s**) *nt* Nicaragua; **Nicaraguaner, in** [nikaragu'aːnər(ɪn)] (**-s, -**) *m(f)* Nicaraguan; **nicaraguanisch** [nikaragu'aːnɪʃ] *adj* Nicaraguan

 SCHLÜSSELWORT

nicht [nɪçt] *adv* **1** (*Verneinung*) not; **er ist es nicht** it's not him, it isn't him; **nicht rostend** stainless; **er raucht nicht** (*gerade*) isn't smoking; (*gewöhnlich*) he doesn't smoke; **ich kann das nicht — ich auch nicht** I can't do it — neither *od* nor can I; **es regnet nicht mehr** it's not raining any more; **nicht mehr als** no more than

2 (*Bitte, Verbot*): **nicht!** don't!, no!; **nicht berühren!** do not touch!; **nicht doch!** don't!

3 (*rhetorisch*): **du bist müde, nicht (wahr)?** you're tired, aren't you?; **das ist schön, nicht (wahr)?** it's nice, isn't it?

4: was du nicht sagst! the things you say!
▷ *präf* non-

Nicht- *zW*: **Nichtachtung** *f* disregard; **Nichtanerkennung** *f* repudiation; **Nichtangriffspakt** *m* non-aggression pact

Nichte ['nɪçtə] (**-, -n**) *f* niece

Nicht- *zW*: **Nichteinhaltung** *f* (*+gen*) non-

compliance (with); **Nichteinmischung** f
(*Pol*) nonintervention; **Nichtgefallen** nt: **bei**
Nichtgefallen (zurück) if not satisfied
(return)

nichtig ['nɪçtɪç] adj (*ungültig*) null, void; (*wertlos*)
futile; **Nichtigkeit** f nullity, invalidity;
(*Sinnlosigkeit*) futility

Nichtraucher m nonsmoker; **ich bin ~** I don't
smoke

nichts [nɪçts] pron nothing; **~ ahnend**
unsuspecting; **~ sagend** meaningless; **~ als**
nothing but; **~ da!** (*ausgeschlossen*) nothing
doing (*umg*); **~ wie raus/hin** etc (*umg*) let's get
out/over there etc (on the double); **für ~ und**
wieder nichts for nothing at all; **Nichts (-s)** nt
nothingness; (*pej: Person*) nonentity

Nichtschwimmer (-s, -) m nonswimmer

nichts- zW: **nichtsdestotrotz** adv
notwithstanding (*form*), nonetheless;
nichtsdestoweniger adv nevertheless;
Nichtsnutz (-es, -e) m good-for-nothing;
nichtsnutzig adj worthless, useless;
nichtssagend adj meaningless; **Nichtstun (-s)**
nt idleness

Nichtzutreffende, s nt: **~s (bitte) streichen**
(please) delete as applicable

Nickel ['nɪkəl] **(-s)** nt nickel; **Nickelbrille** f
metal-rimmed glasses pl

nicken ['nɪkən] vi to nod

Nickerchen ['nɪkərçən] nt nap; **ein ~ machen**
(*umg*) to have forty winks

Nicki ['nɪki] **(-s, -s)** m velours pullover

nie [niː] adv never; **~ wieder** od **mehr** never
again; **~ und nimmer** never ever; **fast ~**
hardly ever

nieder ['niːdər] adj low; (*gering*) inferior ▷ adv
down; **niederdeutsch** adj (*Ling*) Low-German;
Niedergang m decline; **niedergedrückt** adj
depressed; **niedergehen** unreg vi to descend;
(*Aviat*) to come down; (*Regen*) to fall; (*Boxer*) to
go down; **niedergeschlagen** adj depressed,
dejected; **Niedergeschlagenheit** f depression,
dejection; **Niederkunft** f (*veraltet*) delivery,
giving birth; **Niederlage** f defeat

Niederlande ['niːdərlandə] pl: **die ~** the
Netherlands pl

Niederländer, in ['niːdərlɛndər(ɪn)] **(-s, -)** m(f)
Dutchman, Dutchwoman

niederländisch adj Dutch, Netherlands attrib

nieder- zW: **niederlassen** unreg vr (*sich*
setzen) to sit down; (*an Ort*) to settle (down);
(*Arzt, Rechtsanwalt*) to set up in practice;
Niederlassung f settlement; (*Comm*) branch;
niederlegen vt to lay down; (*Arbeit*) to stop;
(*Amt*) to resign; **niedermachen** vt to mow
down; **Niederösterreich** nt Lower Austria;
Niederrhein m Lower Rhine; **niederrheinisch**
adj Lower Rhine attrib; **Niedersachsen** nt
Lower Saxony; **Niederschlag** m (*Chem*)
precipitate; (*Bodensatz*) sediment; (*Met*)
precipitation (*form*), rainfall; (*Boxen*)
knockdown; **radioaktiver Niederschlag**
(radioactive) fallout; **niederschlagen** unreg

vt (*Gegner*) to beat down; (*Gegenstand*) to
knock down; (*Augen*) to lower; (*Jur: Prozess*) to
dismiss; (*Aufstand*) to put down ▷ vr (*Chem*) to
precipitate; **sich in etw** dat **niederschlagen**
(*Erfahrungen etc*) to find expression in
sth; **niederschlagsfrei** ['niːdərʃlaːksfraɪ]
adj dry, without precipitation (*form*);
niederschmetternd adj (*Nachricht,*
Ergebnis) shattering; **niederschreiben**
unreg vt to write down; **Niederschrift** f
transcription; **niedertourig** adj (*Motor*)
low-revving; **niederträchtig** adj base, mean;
Niederträchtigkeit f despicable od malicious
behaviour

Niederung f (*Geog*) depression

niederwalzen ['niːdərvaltsən] vt: **jdn/etw ~**
(*umg*) to mow sb/sth down

niederwerfen ['niːdərvɛrfən] unreg vt to throw
down; (*fig*) to overcome; (*Aufstand*) to suppress

niedlich ['niːtlɪç] adj sweet, nice, cute

niedrig ['niːdrɪç] adj low; (*Stand*) lowly,
humble; (*Gesinnung*) mean

Niedriglohnsektor m low-wage sector

niemals ['niːmaːls] adv never

niemand ['niːmant] pron nobody, no-one

Niemandsland ['niːmantslant] nt no-man's-
land

Niere ['niːrə] **(-, -n)** f kidney; **künstliche ~**
kidney machine

Nierenentzündung f kidney infection

nieseln ['niːzəln] vi to drizzle

Nieselregen m drizzle

niesen ['niːzən] vi to sneeze

Niespulver nt sneezing powder

Niet [niːt] **(-(e)s, -e)** m (*Tech*) rivet

Niete ['niːtə] **(-, -n)** f (*Tech*) rivet; (*Los*) blank;
(*Reinfall*) flop; (*Mensch*) failure

nieten vt to rivet

Nietenhose f (pair of) studded jeans pl

niet- und nagelfest (*umg*) adj nailed down

Niger¹ ['niːgər] **(-s)** nt (*Staat*) Niger

Niger² ['niːgər] **(-s)** m (*Fluss*) Niger

Nigeria [ni'geːria] **(-s)** nt Nigeria; **Nigerianer,**
in [nigeri'aːnər(ɪn)] m(f) Nigerian;
nigerianisch [nige'riːanɪʃ] adj Nigerian

Nihilismus [nihi'lɪsmʊs] m nihilism

Nihilist [nihi'lɪst] m nihilist; **nihilistisch** adj
nihilistic

Nikolaus ['niːkolaʊs] **(-, -e** od (*hum: umg*) **-läuse)**
m ≈ Santa Claus, ≈ Father Christmas

Nikosia [niko'ziːa] **(-s)** nt Nicosia

Nikotin [niko'tiːn] **(-s)** nt nicotine; **nikotinarm**
adj low-nicotine

Nil [niːl] **(-s)** m Nile; **Nilpferd** nt hippopotamus

Nimbus ['nɪmbʊs] **(-, -se)** m (*Heiligenschein*) halo;
(*fig*) aura

nimmersatt ['nɪmərzat] adj insatiable;
Nimmersatt (-(e)s, -e) m glutton

Nimmerwiedersehen (*umg*) nt: **auf ~!** I never
want to see you again

nimmt [nɪmt] vb siehe **nehmen**

nippen ['nɪpən] vt, vi to sip

Nippes ['nɪpəs] pl knick-knacks pl, bric-a-brac

sing

Nippsachen ['nɪpzaxən] *pl* knick-knacks *pl*

nirgends ['nɪrgənts] *adv* nowhere; **überall und ~** here, there and everywhere

nirgendwo ['nɪrgəntvo] *adv* = **nirgends**

nirgendwohin *adv* nowhere

Nische ['niːʃə] (-, -n) *f* niche

nisten ['nɪstən] *vi* to nest

Nitrat [ni'traːt] (-(e)s, -e) *nt* nitrate

Niveau [ni'voː] (-s, -s) *nt* level; **diese Schule hat ein hohes ~** this school has high standards; **unter meinem ~** beneath me

Nivellierung [nive'liːrʊŋ] *f* (*Ausgleichung*) levelling out

nix [nɪks] (*umg*) *pron* = **nichts**

Nixe ['nɪksə] (-, -n) *f* water nymph

Nizza ['nɪtsa] (-s) *nt* Nice

n. J. *abk* (= *nächsten Jahres*) next year

n. M. *abk* (= *nächsten Monats*) next month

NN *abk* (= *Normalnull*) m.s.l.

N. N. *abk* = **NN**

NO *abk* (= *Nordost*) NE

no. *abk* (= *netto*) net

nobel ['noːbəl] *adj* (*großzügig*) generous; (*elegant*) posh (*umg*)

Nobelpreis [no'bɛlpraɪs] *m* Nobel prize; **Nobelpreisträger, in** *m(f)* Nobel prize winner

⭕ **SCHLÜSSELWORT**

noch [nɔx] *adv* **1** (*weiterhin*) still; **noch nicht** not yet; **noch nie** never (yet); **noch immer** *od* **immer noch** still; **bleiben Sie doch noch** stay a bit longer; **ich gehe kaum noch aus** I hardly go out any more

2 (*in Zukunft*) still, yet; (*irgendwann einmal*) one day; **das kann noch passieren** that might still happen; **er wird noch kommen** he'll come (yet); **das wirst du noch bereuen** you'll come to regret it (one day)

3 (*nicht später als*): **noch vor einer Woche** only a week ago; **noch am selben Tag** the very same day; **noch im 19. Jahrhundert** as late as the 19th century; **noch heute** today

4 (*zusätzlich*): **wer war noch da?** who else was there?; **noch (ein)mal** once more, again; **noch dreimal** three more times; **noch einer** another one; **und es regnete auch noch** on top of that it was raining

5 (*bei Vergleichen*): **noch größer** even bigger; **das ist noch besser** that's better still; **und wenn es noch so schwer ist** however hard it is

6: Geld noch und noch heaps (and heaps) of money; **sie hat noch und noch versucht, ...** she tried again and again to ...

▷ *konj*: **weder A noch B** neither A nor B

nochmal, nochmals *adv siehe* **noch**

nochmalig *adj* repeated

Nockenwelle ['nɔkənvɛlə] *f* camshaft

NOK *nt abk* (= *Nationales Olympisches Komitee*)

National Olympic Committee

Nom. *abk* = **Nominativ**

Nominalwert [nomi'naːlveːrt] *m* (*Fin*) nominal *od* par value

Nominativ ['noːminatiːf] (-s, -e) *m* nominative

nominell [nomi'nɛl] *adj* nominal

nominieren [nomi'niːrən] *vt* to nominate

Nonne ['nɔnə] (-, -n) *f* nun

Nonnenkloster *nt* convent

Nonplusultra [nɔnplʊs'|ʊltra] (-s) *nt* ultimate

Non-Profit-Unternehmen, **Nonprofitunternehmen** [nɔn'prɔfit-] *nt* non-profit company

Nord [nɔrt] (-s) *m* north; **Nordafrika** ['nort'|aːfrika] *nt* North Africa; **Nordamerika** *nt* North America; **nordamerikanisch** ['nɔrt|ameri'kaːnɪʃ] *adj* North American

nordd. *abk* = **norddeutsch**

norddeutsch *adj* North German

Norddeutschland *nt* North(ern) Germany

Norden ['nɔrdən] *m* north

Nord- *zW*: **Nordengland** *nt* the North of England; **Nordirland** *nt* Northern Ireland, Ulster; **nordisch** *adj* northern; **nordische Kombination** (*Ski*) nordic combination; **Nordkap** *nt* North Cape; **Nordkorea** ['nɔrtko're:a] *nt* North Korea

nördlich ['nœrtlɪç] *adj* northerly, northern ▷ *präp* +*gen* (to the) north of; **der ~e Polarkreis** the Arctic Circle; **N~es Eismeer** Arctic Ocean; **~ von** north of

Nord- *zW*: **Nordlicht** *nt* northern lights *pl*, aurora borealis; **Nord-Ostsee-Kanal** *m* Kiel Canal; **Nordpol** *m* North Pole; **Nordpolargebiet** *nt* Arctic (Zone)

Nordrhein-Westfalen ['nɔrtraɪnvɛst'faːlən] (-s) *nt* North Rhine-Westphalia

Nordsee *f* North Sea

nordwärts *adv* northwards

Nörgelei [nœrgə'laɪ] *f* grumbling

nörgeln *vi* to grumble

Nörgler, in (-s, -) *m(f)* grumbler

Norm [nɔrm] (-, -en) *f* norm; (*Leistungssoll*) quota; (*Größenvorschrift*) standard (specification)

normal [nɔr'maːl] *adj* normal; **bist du noch ~?** (*umg*) have you gone mad?; **Normalbenzin** *nt* two-star petrol (*Brit veraltet*), regular gas (*US*)

normalerweise *adv* normally

Normalfall *m*: **im ~** normally

Normalgewicht *nt* normal weight; (*genormt*) standard weight

normalisieren [nɔrmali'ziːrən] *vt* to normalize ▷ *vr* to return to normal

Normalzeit *f* (*Geog*) standard time

Normandie [nɔrman'diː] *f* Normandy

normen *vt* to standardize

Norwegen ['nɔrveːgən] (-s) *nt* Norway

Norweger, in (-s, -) *m(f)* Norwegian

norwegisch *adj* Norwegian

Nostalgie [nɔstal'giː] *f* nostalgia

Not [noːt] (-, ̈-e) *f* need; (*Mangel*) want; (*Mühe*) trouble; (*Zwang*) necessity; **~ leidend** needy;

zur ~ if necessary; (*gerade noch*) just about; **wenn** ~ **am Mann ist** if you/they *etc* are short (*umg*); (*im Notfall*) in an emergency; **er hat seine liebe** ~ **mit ihr/damit** he really has problems with her/it; **in seiner** ~ in his hour of need

Notar, in [no'taːr(ɪn)] (**-s, -e**) *m(f)* notary; **notariell** *adj* notarial; **notariell beglaubigt** attested by a notary

Not- *zW*: **Notarzt** *m* doctor on emergency call; **Notausgang** *m* emergency exit; **Notbehelf** *m* stopgap; **Notbremse** *f* emergency brake; **Notdienst** *m*: **Notdienst haben** (*Apotheke*) to be open 24 hours; (*Arzt*) to be on call; **notdürftig** *adj* scanty; (*behelfsmäßig*) makeshift; **sich notdürftig verständigen können** to be able to communicate to some extent

Note ['noːtə] (**-, -n**) *f* note; (*Sch*) mark (*Brit*), grade (*US*); **Noten** *pl* (*Mus*) music *sing*; **eine persönliche** ~ a personal touch

Noten- *zW*: **Notenbank** *f* issuing bank; **Notenblatt** *nt* sheet of music; **Notenschlüssel** *m* clef; **Notenständer** *m* music stand

Not- *zW*: **Notfall** *m* (case of) emergency; **notfalls** *adv* if need be; **notgedrungen** *adj* necessary, unavoidable; **etw notgedrungen machen** to be forced to do sth; **Notgroschen** ['noːtɡrɔʃən] *m* nest egg

notieren [no'tiːrən] *vt* to note; (*Comm*) to quote **Notierung** *f* (*Comm*) quotation

nötig ['nøːtɪç] *adj* necessary ▷ *adv* (*dringend*): **etw** ~ **brauchen** to need sth urgently; **etw** ~ **haben** to need sth; **das habe ich nicht** ~! I can do without that!

nötigen *vt* to compel, force; **nötigenfalls** *adv* if necessary

Nötigung *f* compulsion, coercion (*Jur*)

Notiz [no'tiːts] (**-, -en**) *f* note; (*Zeitungsnotiz*) item; ~ **nehmen** to take notice; **Notizblock** *m* notepad; **Notizbuch** *nt* notebook; **Notizzettel** *m* piece of paper

Not- *zW*: **Notlage** *f* crisis, emergency; **notlanden** *vi* to make a forced *od* emergency landing; **Notlandung** *f* forced *od* emergency landing; **Notlösung** *f* temporary solution; **Notlüge** *f* white lie

notorisch [no'toːrɪʃ] *adj* notorious

Not- *zW*: **Notruf** *m* emergency call; **Notrufsäule** *f* emergency telephone; **notschlachten** *vt* (*Tiere*) to destroy; **Notstand** *m* state of emergency; **Notstandsgebiet** *nt* (*wirtschaftlich*) depressed area; (*bei Katastrophen*) disaster area; **Notstandsgesetz** *nt* emergency law; **Notunterkunft** *f* emergency accommodation; **Notverband** *m* emergency dressing; **Notwehr** (**-**) *f* self-defence; **notwendig** *adj* necessary; **Notwendigkeit** *f* necessity; **Notzucht** *f* rape

Nov. *abk* (*= November*) Nov.

Novelle [no'vɛlə] (**-, -n**) *f* novella; (*Jur*) amendment

November [no'vɛmbər] (**-(s), -**) *m* November;

siehe auch **September**

Novum ['noːvʊm] (**-s, Nova**) *nt* novelty

NPD (**-**) *f abk* (*= Nationaldemokratische Partei Deutschlands*) National Democratic Party

Nr. *abk* (*= Nummer*) no.

NRW *abk* = **Nordrhein-Westfalen**

NS *abk* = **Nachschrift; Nationalsozialismus**

NS- *in zw* Nazi

N. T. *abk* (*= Neues Testament*) N.T.

Nu [nuː] *m*: **im Nu** in an instant

Nuance [ny'ãːsə] (**-, -n**) *f* nuance; (*Kleinigkeit*) shade

nüchtern ['nʏçtərn] *adj* sober; (*Magen*) empty; (*Urteil*) prudent; **Nüchternheit** *f* sobriety

Nudel ['nuːdəl] (**-, -n**) *f* noodle; (*umg: Mensch: dick*) dumpling; ((*: komisch*) character; **Nudelholz** *nt* rolling pin

Nugat ['nuːgat] (**-s, -s**) *m od nt* nougat

nuklear [nukle'aːr] *adj attrib* nuclear

null [nʊl] *num* zero; (*Fehler*) no; ~ **Uhr** midnight; **in** ~ **Komma nichts** (*umg*) in less than no time; **die Stunde** ~ the new starting point; **gleich** ~ **sein** to be absolutely nil; ~ **und nichtig** null and void; **Null** (**-, -en**) *f* nought, zero; (*pej: Mensch*) dead loss; **nullachtfünfzehn** (*umg*) *adj* run-of-the-mill; **Nulldiät** *f* starvation diet; **Nulllösung** *f* (*Pol*) zero option; **Nullpunkt** *m* zero; **auf dem Nullpunkt** at zero; **Nulltarif** *m* (*für Verkehrsmittel*) free travel; **zum Nulltarif** free of charge

numerieren [nume'riːrən] *vt siehe* **nummerieren**

numerisch [nu'meːrɪʃ] *adj* numerical; **~es Tastenfeld** (*Comput*) numeric pad

Numerus ['nuːmerʊs] (**-, Numeri**) *m* (*Gram*) number; ~ **clausus** (*Univ*) restricted entry

Nummer ['nʊmər] (**-, -n**) *f* number; **auf** ~ **sicher gehen** (*umg*) to play (it) safe

nummerieren [nume'riːrən] *vt* to number

Nummern- *zW*: **Nummernkonto** *nt* numbered bank account; **Nummernscheibe** *f* telephone dial; **Nummernschild** *nt* (*Aut*) number *od* license (*US*) plate

nun [nuːn] *adv* now ▷ *interj* well

nur [nuːr] *adv* just, only; **nicht** ~ ..., **sondern auch** ... not only ... but also ...; **alle,** ~ **ich nicht** everyone but me; **ich hab das** ~ **so gesagt** I was just talking

Nürnberg ['nʏrnbɛrk] (**-s**) *nt* Nuremberg

nuscheln ['nʊʃəln] (*umg*) *vt, vi* to mutter, mumble

Nuss [nʊs] (**-, -̈e**) *f* nut; **eine doofe** ~ (*umg*) a stupid twit; **eine harte** ~ a hard nut (to crack); **Nussbaum** *m* walnut tree; **Nussknacker** (**-s, -**) *m* nutcracker

Nüster ['nyːstər] (**-, -n**) *f* nostril

Nutte ['nʊtə] (**-, -n**) *f* tart (*Brit*), hooker (*US*)

nutz [nʊts] *adj* = **nütze; nutzbar** *adj*: **nutzbar machen** to utilize; **Nutzbarmachung** *f* utilization; **nutzbringend** *adj* profitable; **etw nutzbringend anwenden** to use sth to good effect, put sth to good use

nütze ['nʏtsə] *adj*: **zu nichts ~ sein** to be useless

nutzen *vi* to be of use ▷ *vt*: **(zu etw) ~** to use (for sth); **was nutzt es?** what's the use?, what use is it?; **Nutzen (-s)** *m* usefulness; *(Gewinn)* profit; **von Nutzen** useful

nützen *vt, vi* = **nutzen**

Nutz- *zW*: **Nutzfahrzeug** *nt* farm od military vehicle etc; *(Comm)* commercial vehicle; **Nutzfläche** *f* us(e)able floor space; *(Agr)* productive land; **Nutzlast** *f* maximum load, payload

nützlich ['nʏtslɪç] *adj* useful; **Nützlichkeit** *f* usefulness

Nutz- *zW*: **nutzlos** *adj* useless; *(unnötig)* needless; **Nutzlosigkeit** *f* uselessness; **Nutznießer (-s, -)** *m* beneficiary

Nutzung *f (Gebrauch)* use; *(das Ausnutzen)* exploitation

NW *abk (= Nordwest)* NW

Nylon ['naɪlɔn] **(-s)** *nt* nylon

Nymphe ['nʏmfə] **(-, -n)** *f* nymph

Oo

O¹, o [o:] *nt* O, o; **O wie Otto** = O for Olive, = O for Oboe (*US*)

O² [o:] *abk* (= *Osten*) E

o. Ä. *abk* (= *oder Ähnliche(s)*) or similar

Oase [o'a:zə] (**-, -n**) *f* oasis

OB (**-s, -s**) *m abk* = **Oberbürgermeister**

ob [ɔp] *konj* if, whether; **ob das wohl wahr ist?** can that be true?; **ob ich (nicht) lieber gehe?** maybe I'd better go; **(so) tun als ob** (*umg*) to pretend; **und ob!** you bet!

Obacht ['o:baxt] *f*: ~ **geben** to pay attention

Obdach ['ɔpdax] (**-(e)s**) *nt* shelter, lodging; **obdachlos** *adj* homeless; **Obdachlosenasyl** *nt* hostel *od* shelter for the homeless; **Obdachlosenheim** *nt* = **Obdachlosenasyl**; **Obdachlose, r** *f(m)* homeless person

Obduktion [ɔpduktsi'o:n] *f* postmortem

obduzieren [ɔpdu'tsi:rən] *vt* to do a postmortem on

O-Beine ['o:baɪnə] *pl* bow *od* bandy legs *pl*

oben ['o:bən] *adv* above; (*in Haus*) upstairs; (*am oberen Ende*) at the top; ~ **erwähnt**, ~ **genannt** above-mentioned; **nach** ~ up; **von** ~ down; **siehe** ~ see above; **ganz** ~ right at the top; ~ **ohne** topless; **die Abbildung** ~ **links** *od* **links oben** the illustration in the top left-hand corner; **jdn von** ~ **herab behandeln** to treat sb condescendingly; **jdn von** ~ **bis unten ansehen** to look sb up and down; **Befehl von** ~ orders from above; **die da** ~ (*umg: die Vorgesetzten*) the powers that be; **oben'an** *adv* at the top; **oben'auf** *adv* up above, on the top ▷ *adj* (*munter*) in form; **oben'drein** *adv* into the bargain; **oben'hin** *adv* cursorily, superficially

Ober ['o:bər] (**-s, -**) *m* waiter

Ober- *zW*: **Oberarm** *m* upper arm; **Oberarzt** *m* senior physician; **Oberaufsicht** *f* supervision; **Oberbayern** *nt* Upper Bavaria; **Oberbefehl** *m* supreme command; **Oberbefehlshaber** *m* commander-in-chief; **Oberbegriff** *m* generic term; **Oberbekleidung** *f* outer clothing; **Oberbett** *nt* quilt; **Oberbürgermeister** *m* lord mayor; **Oberdeck** *nt* upper *od* top deck

obere, r, s *adj* upper; **die O~n** the bosses; (*Eccl*) the superiors; **die ~n Zehntausend** (*umg*) high society

Ober- *zW*: **Oberfläche** *f* surface; **oberflächlich** *adj* superficial; **bei oberflächlicher Betrachtung** at a quick glance; **jdn (nur) oberflächlich kennen** to know sb (only) slightly; **Obergeschoss** *nt* upper storey *od* story (*US*); **im zweiten Obergeschoss** on the second floor (*Brit*), on the third floor (*US*); **oberhalb** *adv* above ▷ *präp* +*gen* above; **Oberhand** *f* (*fig*): **die Oberhand gewinnen (über** +*akk*) to get the upper hand (over); **Oberhaupt** *nt* head, chief; **Oberhaus** *nt* (*in Großbritannien*) upper house, House of Lords; **Oberhemd** *nt* shirt; **Oberherrschaft** *f* supremacy, sovereignty

Oberin *f* matron; (*Eccl*) Mother Superior

Ober- *zW*: **oberirdisch** *adj* above ground; (*Leitung*) overhead; **Oberitalien** *nt* Northern Italy; **Oberkellner** *m* head waiter; **Oberkiefer** *m* upper jaw; **Oberkommando** *nt* supreme command; **Oberkörper** *m* upper part of body; **Oberlauf** *m*: **am Oberlauf des Rheins** in the upper reaches of the Rhine; **Oberleitung** *f* (*Elek*) overhead cable; **Oberlicht** *nt* skylight; **Oberlippe** *f* upper lip; **Oberösterreich** *nt* Upper Austria; **Oberprima** *f* (*früher*) *final year of German secondary school*; **Oberschenkel** *m* thigh; **Oberschicht** *f* upper classes *pl*; **Oberschule** *f* grammar school (*Brit*), high school (*US*); **Oberschwester** *f* (*Med*) matron; **Oberseite** *f* top (side); **Obersekunda** *f* (*früher*) *seventh year of German secondary school*

Oberst ['o:bərst] (**-en** *od* **-s, -en** *od* **-e**) *m* colonel

oberste, r, s *adj* very top, topmost

Ober- *zW*: **Oberstübchen** (*umg*) *nt*: **er ist nicht ganz richtig im Oberstübchen** he's not quite right up top; **Oberstufe** *f* upper school; **Oberteil** *nt* upper part; **Obertertia** *f* (*früher*) *fifth year of German secondary school*; **Oberwasser** *nt*: **Oberwasser haben/bekommen** to be/get on top of (of things); **Oberweite** *f* bust *od* chest measurement

obgleich [ɔp'glaɪç] *konj* although

Obhut ['ɔphu:t] (**-**) *f* care, protection; **in jds** ~ *dat* **sein** to be in sb's care

obig ['o:bɪç] *adj* above

Objekt [ɔp'jɛkt] (**-(e)s, -e**) *nt* object

objektiv [ɔpjɛk'ti:f] *adj* objective

Objektiv (**-s, -e**) *nt* lens *sing*

Objektivität [ɔpjɛktivi'tɛ:t] *f* objectivity

Oblate [o'bla:tə] (**-, -n**) *f* (*Gebäck*) wafer; (*Eccl*) host

obligatorisch [obliga'to:rɪʃ] *adj* compulsory, obligatory

Oboe [o'bo:ə] (-, -n) *f* oboe

Obrigkeit ['o:brɪçkaɪt] *f* (*Behörden*) authorities *pl*, administration; (*Regierung*) government

Obrigkeitsdenken *nt* acceptance of authority

obschon [ɔp'ʃo:n] *konj* although

Observatorium [ɔpzɛrva'to:riʊm] *nt* observatory

obskur [ɔps'ku:r] *adj* obscure; (*verdächtig*) dubious

Obst [o:pst] (-(e)s) *nt* fruit; **Obstbau** *m* fruit-growing; **Obstbaum** *m* fruit tree; **Obstgarten** *m* orchard; **Obsthändler** *m* fruiterer (Brit), fruit merchant; **Obstkuchen** *m* fruit tart; **Obstsaft** *m* fruit juice; **Obstsalat** *m* fruit salad

obszön [ɔps'tsø:n] *adj* obscene

Obszönität [ɔpstøni'tɛ:t] *f* obscenity

Obus ['o:bʊs] (-ses, -se) (*umg*) *m* trolleybus

obwohl [ɔp'vo:l] *konj* although

Ochse ['ɔksə] (-n, -n) *m* ox; (*umg: Dummkopf*) twit; **er stand da wie der ~ vorm Berg** (*umg*) he stood there utterly bewildered

ochsen (*umg*) *vt, vi* to cram, swot (Brit)

Ochsenschwanzsuppe *f* oxtail soup

Ochsenzunge *f* ox tongue

Ocker ['ɔkər] (-s, -) *m od nt* ochre (Brit), ocher (US)

öd [ø:t(ə)] *adj* = **öde**

öde *adj* (*Land*) waste, barren; (*fig*) dull; **~ und leer** dreary and desolate

Öde (-, -n) *f* desert, waste(land); (*fig*) tedium

oder ['o:dər] *konj* or; **entweder ... ~** either ... or; **du kommst doch, ~?** you're coming, aren't you?

Ofen ['o:fən] (-s, ⸚) *m* oven; (*Heizofen*) fire, heater; (*Kohleofen*) stove; (*Hochofen*) furnace; (*Herd*) cooker, stove; **jetzt ist der ~ aus** (*umg*) that does it!; **Ofenrohr** *nt* stovepipe

offen ['ɔfən] *adj* open; (*aufrichtig*) frank; (*Stelle*) vacant; (*Bein*) ulcerated; (*Haare*) loose; **~er Wein** wine by the carafe *od* glass; **auf ~er Strecke** (*Straße*) on the open road; (*Eisenb*) between stations; **Tag der ~en Tür** open day (Brit), open house (US); **~e Handelsgesellschaft** (*Comm*) general *od* ordinary (US) partnership; **~ bleiben** (*Fenster*) to stay open; **~ halten** to keep open; **~ lassen** to leave open; **~ stehen** to be open; **seine Meinung ~ sagen** to speak one's mind; **ein ~es Wort mit jdm reden** to have a frank talk with sb; **~ gesagt** to be honest; *siehe auch* **offenbleiben; offenstehen**

offenbar *adj* obvious; (*vermutlich*) apparently

offenbaren [ɔfən'ba:rən] *vt* to reveal, manifest

Offenbarung *f* (*Rel*) revelation

Offenbarungseid *m* (*Jur*) oath of disclosure

Offen- *zW*: **offenbleiben** *unreg vi* (*fig: Frage, Entscheidung*) to remain open; *siehe auch* **offen**; **Offenheit** *f* candour (Brit), candor (US), frankness; **offenherzig** *adj* candid, frank; (*hum: Kleid*) revealing; **Offenherzigkeit** *f*

frankness; **offenkundig** *adj* well-known; (*klar*) evident; **offensichtlich** *adj* evident, obvious

offensiv [ɔfɛn'zi:f] *adj* offensive

Offensive (-, -n) *f* offensive

offenstehen *unreg vi* (*fig: Rechnung*) to be unpaid; **es steht Ihnen offen, es zu tun** you are at liberty to do it; **die (ganze) Welt steht ihm offen** he has the (whole) world at his feet; *siehe auch* **offen**

öffentlich ['œfəntlɪç] *adj* public; **die ~e Hand** (central/local) government; **Anstalt des ~en Rechts** public institution; **Ausgaben der ~en Hand** public spending *sing*

Öffentlichkeit *f* (*Leute*) public; (*einer Versammlung etc*) public nature; **in aller ~** in public; **an die ~ dringen** to reach the public ear; **unter Ausschluss der ~** in secret; (*Jur*) in camera

Öffentlichkeitsarbeit *f* public relations work

öffentlich-rechtlich *adj attrib* (under) public law

offerieren [ɔfe'ri:rən] *vt* to offer

Offerte [ɔ'fɛrtə] (-, -n) *f* offer

offiziell [ɔfitsi'ɛl] *adj* official

Offizier [ɔfi'tsi:r] (-s, -e) *m* officer

Offizierskasino *nt* officers' mess

öffnen ['œfnən] *vt, vr* to open; **jdm die Tür ~** to open the door for sb

Öffner ['œfnər] (-s, -) *m* opener

Öffnung ['œfnʊŋ] *f* opening

Öffnungsklausel *f* (*Jur*) escape clause; (*fig: Schlupfloch*) loophole

Öffnungszeiten *pl* opening times *pl*

Offsetdruck ['ɔfsɛtdrʊk] *m* offset (printing)

oft [ɔft] *adv* often

öfter ['œftər] *adv* more often *od* frequently; **des Öfteren** quite frequently; **~ mal was Neues** (*umg*) variety is the spice of life (*Sprichwort*)

öfters *adv* often, frequently

oftmals *adv* often, frequently

o. G. *abk* (= *ohne Gewähr*) without liability

OHG *f abk* (= *offene Handelsgesellschaft*) *siehe* **offen**

ohne ['o:nə] *präp +akk, konj* without; **das Darlehen ist ~ Weiteres bewilligt worden** the loan was granted without any problem; **das kann man nicht ~ Weiteres voraussetzen** you can't just assume that automatically; **das ist nicht ~** (*umg*) it's not bad; **~ Weiteres** without a second thought; (*sofort*) immediately; **ohnedies** *adv* anyway; **ohneeinander** [o:nəʔaɪ'nandər] *adv* without each other; **ohnegleichen** *adj* unsurpassed, without equal; **ohnehin** *adv* anyway, in any case; **es ist ohnehin schon spät** it's late enough already

Ohnmacht ['o:nmaxt] *f* faint; (*fig*) impotence; **in ~ fallen** to faint

ohnmächtig ['o:nmɛçtɪç] *adj* in a faint, unconscious; (*fig*) weak, impotent; **sie ist ~** she has fainted; **ohnmächtige Wut, ~er Zorn** helpless rage; **einer Sache** *dat* **~ gegenüberstehen** to be helpless in the face of sth

Ohr [oːr] (**-(e)s, -en**) nt ear; (Gehör) hearing; **sich aufs ~ legen** od **hauen** (umg) to kip down; **jdm die ~en lang ziehen** (umg) to tweak sb's ear(s); **jdm in den ~en liegen** to keep on at sb; **jdn übers ~ hauen** (umg) to pull a fast one on sb; **auf dem ~ bin ich taub** (fig) nothing doing (umg); **schreib es dir hinter die ~en** (umg) will you (finally) get that into your (thick) head!; **bis über die** od **beide ~en verliebt sein** to be head over heels in love; **viel um die ~en haben** (umg) to have a lot on (one's plate); **halt die ~en steif!** keep a stiff upper lip!

Öhr [øːr] (**-(e)s, -e**) nt eye

Ohren- zW: **Ohrenarzt** m ear specialist; **ohrenbetäubend** adj deafening; **Ohrensausen** nt (Med) buzzing in one's ears; **Ohrenschmalz** nt earwax; **Ohrenschmerzen** pl earache sing; **Ohrenschützer** (**-s, -**) m earmuff

Ohr- zW: **Ohrfeige** f slap on the face; (als Strafe) box on the ears; **ohrfeigen** vt untr: **jdn ohrfeigen** to slap sb's face; to box sb's ears; **ich könnte mich selbst ohrfeigen, dass ich das gemacht habe** I could kick myself for doing that; **Ohrläppchen** nt ear lobe; **Ohrringe** pl earrings pl; **Ohrwurm** m earwig; (Mus) catchy tune

o. J. abk (= ohne Jahr) no year given

okkupieren [ɔku'piːrən] vt to occupy

Öko- ['øko-] in zw eco-, ecological; **Ökofonds** ['øːkofõ:] m eco-fund, green fund; **Ökoladen** ['øːkola:dən] m wholefood shop

Ökologie [økolo'giː] f ecology

ökologisch [øko'loːgɪʃ] adj ecological, environmental

Ökonometrie [økonome'triː] f econometrics pl

Ökonomie [økono'miː] f economy; (als Wissenschaft) economics sing

ökonomisch [øko'noːmɪʃ] adj economical

Öko- zW: **Ökopax** [øko'paks] (**-en, -e**) (umg) m environmentalist; **Ökostrom** m green electricity; **Ökosystem** ['øːkozyste:m] nt ecosystem

Okt. abk (= Oktober) Oct.

Oktan [ɔk'ta:n] (**-s, -e**) nt octane; **Oktanzahl** f octane rating

Oktave [ɔk'ta:və] (**-, -n**) f octave

Oktober [ɔk'to:bər] (**-(s), -**) m October; siehe auch **September**

Oktoberfest nt see culture note

○ **OKTOBERFEST**

○ The annual October beer festival, the
○ Oktoberfest, takes place in Munich on a huge
○ field where beer tents, roller coasters and
○ many other amusements are set up. People
○ sit at long wooden tables, drink beer from
○ enormous litre beer mugs, eat pretzels and
○ listen to brass bands. It is a great attraction
○ for tourists and locals alike.

ökumenisch [øku'me:nɪʃ] adj ecumenical

Öl [øːl] (**-(e)s, -e**) nt oil; **auf Öl stoßen** to strike oil

Öl- zW: **Ölbaum** m olive tree; **ölen** vt to oil; (Tech) to lubricate; **wie ein geölter Blitz** (umg) like greased lightning; **Ölfarbe** f oil paint; **Ölfeld** nt oilfield; **Ölfilm** m film of oil; **Ölheizung** f oil-fired central heating

ölig adj oily

Oligopol [oligo'po:l] (**-s, -e**) nt oligopoly

oliv [o'li:f] adj olive-green

Olive [o'li:və] (**-, -n**) f olive

Olivenöl nt olive oil

Öljacke f oilskin jacket

oll [ɔl] (umg) adj old; **das sind ~e Kamellen** that's old hat

Öl- zW: **Ölmessstab** m dipstick; **Ölpest** f oil pollution; **Ölplattform** f oil rig; **Ölsardine** f sardine; **Ölscheich** m oil sheik; **Ölstand** m oil level; **Ölstandanzeiger** m (Aut) oil level indicator; **Öltanker** m oil tanker; **Ölteppich** m oil slick

Ölung f oiling; (Eccl) anointment; **die Letzte ~** Extreme Unction

Ölwanne f (Aut) sump (Brit), oil pan (US)

Ölwechsel m oil change

Olymp [o'lʏmp] (**-s**) m (Berg) Mount Olympus

Olympiade [olʏmpi'a:də] (**-, -n**) f Olympic Games pl

Olympiasieger, in [o'lʏmpiazi:gər(ɪn)] m(f) Olympic champion

olympisch [o'lʏmpɪʃ] adj Olympic

Ölzeug nt oilskins pl

Oma ['o:ma] (**-, -s**) (umg) f granny

Oman [o'ma:n] (**-s**) nt Oman

Omelett [ɔm(ə)'lɛt] (**-(e)s, -s**) nt omelette (Brit), omelet (US)

Omelette [ɔm(ə)'lɛt] f = **Omelett**

Omen ['o:mɛn] (**-s, -** od **Omina**) nt omen

Omnibus ['ɔmnibʊs] m (omni)bus

Onanie [ona'ni:] f masturbation

onanieren vi to masturbate

ondulieren [ɔndu'li:rən] vt, vi to crimp

Onkel ['ɔŋkəl] (**-s, -**) m uncle

online ['ɔnlaɪn] adj (Comput) on-line

Onlineauktion f on-line auction

Onlinedienst m (Comput) on-line service

OP m abk = **Operationssaal**

Opa ['o:pa] (**-s, -s**) (umg) m grandpa

Opal [o'pa:l] (**-s, -e**) m opal

Oper ['o:pər] (**-, -n**) f opera; (Opernhaus) opera house

Operation [operatsi'o:n] f operation

Operationssaal m operating theatre (Brit) od theater (US)

operativ [opəra'ti:f] adv (Med): **eine Geschwulst ~ entfernen** to remove a growth by surgery

Operette [ope'rɛtə] f operetta

operieren [ope'ri:rən] vt, vi to operate; **sich ~ lassen** to have an operation

Opern- zW: **Opernglas** nt opera glasses pl; **Opernhaus** nt opera house; **Opernsänger, in** m(f) opera singer

Opfer ['ɔpfər] (**-s, -**) nt sacrifice; (Mensch)

o

victim; **Opferbereitschaft** f readiness to make sacrifices
opfern vt to sacrifice
Opferstock m (Eccl) offertory box
Opferung f sacrifice; (Eccl) offertory
Opium ['o:piʊm] (-s) nt opium
opponieren [ɔpo'ni:rən] vi: **gegen jdn/etw ~** to oppose sb/sth
opportun [ɔpɔr'tu:n] adj opportune;
Opportunismus [-'nɪsmʊs] m opportunism;
Opportunist, in [-'nɪst(ɪn)] m(f) opportunist
Opposition [ɔpozitsi'o:n] f opposition
oppositionell [ɔpozitsio:'nɛl] adj opposing
Oppositionsführer m leader of the opposition
optieren [ɔp'ti:rən] vi (Pol: form): **~ für** to opt for
Optik ['ɔptɪk] f optics sing
Optiker, in (-s, -) m(f) optician
optimal [ɔpti'ma:l] adj optimal, optimum
Optimismus [ɔpti'mɪsmʊs] m optimism
Optimist, in [ɔpti'mɪst(ɪn)] m(f) optimist;
optimistisch adj optimistic
optisch ['ɔptɪʃ] adj optical; **~e Täuschung** optical illusion
Orakel [o'ra:kəl] (-s, -) nt oracle
Orange [o'rã:ʒə] (-, -n) f orange; **orange** adj orange
Orangeade [orã'ʒa:də] (-, -n) f orangeade
Orangeat [orã'ʒa:t] (-s, -e) nt candied peel
Orangen- zW: **Orangenmarmelade** f marmalade; **Orangensaft** m orange juice;
Orangenschale f orange peel
Oratorium [ora'to:riʊm] nt (Mus) oratorio
Orchester [ɔr'kɛstər] (-s, -) nt orchestra
Orchidee [ɔrçi'de:ə] (-, -n) f orchid
Orden ['ɔrdən] (-s, -) m (Eccl) order; (Mil) decoration
Ordensgemeinschaft f religious order
Ordensschwester f nun
ordentlich ['ɔrdəntlɪç] adj (anständig) decent, respectable; (geordnet) tidy, neat; (umg: annehmbar) not bad; (: tüchtig) real, proper; (Leistung) reasonable; **~es Mitglied** full member; **~er Professor** (full) professor; **eine ~e Tracht Prügel** a proper hiding; **~ arbeiten** to be a thorough and precise worker;
Ordentlichkeit f respectability; tidiness
Order (-, -s od -n) f (Comm: Auftrag) order
ordern vt (Comm) to order
Ordinalzahl [ɔrdi'na:ltsa:l] f ordinal number
ordinär [ɔrdi'nɛ:r] adj common, vulgar
Ordinarius [ɔrdi'na:riʊs] (-, **Ordinarien**) m (Univ): ~ **(für)** professor (of)
ordnen ['ɔrdnən] vt to order, put in order
Ordner (-s, -) m steward; (Comm) file
Ordnung f order; (Ordnen) ordering; (Geordnetsein) tidiness; **geht in ~** (umg) that's all right od OK (umg); **~ schaffen, für ~ sorgen** to put things in order, tidy things up; **jdn zur ~ rufen** to call sb to order; **bei ihm muss alles seine ~ haben** (räumlich) he has to have everything in its proper place; (zeitlich) he has to do everything according to a fixed schedule; **das Kind braucht seine ~** the child needs a

routine
Ordnungs- zW: **Ordnungsamt** nt ≈ town clerk's office; **ordnungsgemäß** adj proper, according to the rules; **ordnungshalber** adv as a matter of form; **Ordnungsliebe** f tidiness, orderliness; **Ordnungsstrafe** f fine; **ordnungswidrig** adj contrary to the rules, irregular; **Ordnungswidrigkeit** f infringement (of law or rule); **Ordnungszahl** f ordinal number
ORF (-) m abk (= Österreichischer Rundfunk)
Organ [ɔr'ga:n] (-s, -e) nt organ; (Stimme) voice
Organisation [ɔrganizatsi'o:n] f organization
Organisationstalent nt organizing ability; (Person) good organizer
Organisator [ɔrgani'za:tɔr] m organizer
organisch [ɔr'ga:nɪʃ] adj organic; (Erkrankung, Leiden) physical
organisieren [ɔrgani'zi:rən] vt to organize, arrange; (umg: beschaffen) to acquire ▷ vr to organize
Organismus [ɔrga'nɪsmʊs] m organism
Organist [ɔrga'nɪst] m organist
Organspender m donor (of an organ)
Organspenderausweis m donor card
Organverpflanzung f transplantation (of an organ)
Orgasmus [ɔr'gasmʊs] m orgasm
Orgel ['ɔrgəl] (-, -n) f organ; **Orgelpfeife** f organ pipe; **wie die Orgelpfeifen stehen** to stand in order of height
Orgie ['ɔrgiə] f orgy
Orient ['o:rient] (-s) m Orient, east; **der Vordere ~** the Near East
Orientale [o:rien'ta:lə] (-n, -n) m Oriental
Orientalin [o:rien'ta:lɪn] f Oriental
orientalisch adj oriental
orientieren [o:rien'ti:rən] vt (örtlich) to locate; (fig) to inform ▷ vr to find one's way od bearings; (fig) to inform o.s.
Orientierung [o:rien'ti:rʊŋ] f orientation; (fig) information; **die ~ verlieren** to lose one's bearings
Orientierungssinn m sense of direction
Orientierungsstufe m see culture note

○ **ORIENTIERUNGSSTUFE**
○
○   The Orientierungsstufe is the name given
○   to the first two years spent in a Realschule
○   or Gymnasium, during which a child is
○   assessed as to his or her suitability for the
○   school. At the end of the two years it may
○   be decided to transfer the child to a school
○   more suited to his or her ability.

original [origi'na:l] adj original; ~ **Meißener Porzellan** genuine Meissen porcelain; **Original (-s, -e)** nt original; (Mensch) character; **Originalausgabe** f first edition; **Originalfassung** f original version
Originalität [originali'tɛ:t] f originality
Originalübertragung f live broadcast
originell [origi'nɛl] adj original

Orkan [ɔr'kaːn] (**-(e)s, -e**) m hurricane; **orkanartig** adj (Wind) gale-force; (Beifall) thunderous

Orkneyinseln ['ɔːknɪ|ɪnzəln] pl Orkney Islands pl, Orkneys pl

Ornament [ɔrna'mɛnt] nt decoration, ornament

ornamental [ɔrnamɛn'taːl] adj decorative, ornamental

Ornithologe [ɔrnito'loːgə] (**-n, -n**) m ornithologist

Ornithologin [ɔrnito'loːgɪn] f ornithologist

Ort¹ [ɔrt] (**-(e)s, -e**) m place; **an ~ und Stelle** on the spot; **am ~** in the place; **am angegebenen ~** in the place quoted, loc. cit.; **~ der Handlung** (Theat) scene of the action; **das ist höheren ~(e)s entschieden worden** (hum: form) the decision came from above

Ort² [ɔrt] (**-(e)s, ̈-er**) m: **vor ~** at the (coal) face; (auch fig) on the spot

Örtchen ['œrtçən] (umg) nt loo (Brit), john (US)

orten vt to locate

orthodox [ɔrto'dɔks] adj orthodox

Orthografie [ɔrtogra'fiː] f spelling, orthography

orthografisch [ɔrto'graːfɪʃ] adj orthographic

Orthopäde [ɔrto'pɛːdə] (**-n, -n**) m orthopaedic (Brit) od orthopedic (US) specialist, orthopaedist (Brit), orthopedist (US)

Orthopädie [ɔrtopɛ'diː] f orthopaedics sing (Brit), orthopedics sing (US)

orthopädisch adj orthopaedic (Brit), orthopedic (US)

örtlich ['œrtlɪç] adj local; **jdn ~ betäuben** to give sb a local anaesthetic (Brit) od anesthetic (US); **Örtlichkeit** f locality; **sich mit den Örtlichkeiten vertraut machen** to get to know the place

Ortsangabe f (name of the) town; **ohne ~** (Buch) no place of publication indicated

ortsansässig adj local

Ortschaft f village, small town; **geschlossene ~** built-up area

Orts- zW: **ortsfremd** adj nonlocal; **Ortsfremde, r** f(m) stranger; **Ortsgespräch** nt local (phone) call; **Ortsgruppe** f local branch od group; **Ortskenntnis** f: **(gute) Ortskenntnisse haben** to know one's way around (well); **Ortskrankenkasse** f: **Allgemeine Ortskrankenkasse** compulsory medical insurance scheme; **ortskundig** adj familiar with the place; **ortskundig sein** to know one's way around; **Ortsname** m place name; **Ortsnetz** nt (Tel) local telephone exchange area; **Ortsnetzkennzahl** f (Tel) dialling (Brit) od area (US) code; **Ortsschild** nt place name sign; **Ortssinn** m sense of direction; **Ortstarif** m (Tel) charge for local calls; **Ortsvorschriften** pl by(e)-laws pl; **Ortszeit** f local time; **Ortszuschlag** m (local) weighting allowance

Ortung f locating

öS. abk (= österreichischer Schilling)

Öse ['øːzə] (**-, -n**) f loop; (an Kleidung) eye

Oslo ['ɔslo] (**-s**) nt Oslo

Ossi ['ɔsi] (**-s, -s**) (umg) m East German; see culture note

öst. abk (= österreichisch) Aust.

Ost- zW: **Ostafrika** nt East Africa; **ostdeutsch** adj East German; **Ostdeutsche, Ostdeutscher** f(m) East German; **Ostdeutschland** nt (Pol: früher) East Germany; (Geog) Eastern Germany

Osten (**-s**) m east; **der Ferne ~** the Far East; **der Nahe ~** the Middle East, the Near East

ostentativ [ɔstɛnta'tiːf] adj pointed, ostentatious

Oster- zW: **Osterei** nt Easter egg; **Osterfest** nt Easter; **Osterglocke** f daffodil; **Osterhase** m Easter bunny; **Osterinsel** f Easter Island; **Ostermarsch** m Easter demonstration; **Ostermontag** m Easter Monday

Ostern (**-s, -**) nt Easter; **frohe** od **fröhliche ~!** Happy Easter!; **zu ~** at Easter

Österreich ['øːstəraɪç] (**-s**) nt Austria

Österreicher, in (**-s, -**) m(f) Austrian

österreichisch adj Austrian

Ostersonntag m Easter Day od Sunday

Osteuropa nt East(ern) Europe

osteuropäisch adj East European

östlich ['œstlɪç] adj eastern, easterly

Östrogen [œstro'geːn] (**-s, -e**) nt oestrogen (Brit), estrogen (US)

Ost- zW: **Ostsee** f Baltic Sea; **ostwärts** adv eastwards; **Ostwind** m east wind

oszillieren [ɔstsɪ'liːrən] vi to oscillate

Otter¹ ['ɔtər] (**-s, -**) m otter

Otter² ['ɔtər] (**-, -n**) f (Schlange) adder

ÖTV (**-**) f abk (= Gewerkschaft öffentliche Dienste, Transport und Verkehr) ≈ Transport and General Workers' Union

Ouvertüre [uvɛr'tyːrə] (**-, -n**) f overture

oval [o'vaːl] adj oval

Ovation [ovatsi'oːn] f ovation

Overall ['oʊvərɔːl] (**-s, -s**) m (Schutzanzug) overalls pl

ÖVP (**-**) f abk (= Österreichische Volkspartei) Austrian People's Party

Ovulation [ovulatsi'oːn] f ovulation

Oxid, Oxyd [ɔ'ksyːt] (**-(e)s, -e**) nt oxide

oxidieren, oxydieren [ɔksy'diːrən] vt, vi to oxidize

Oxidierung, Oxydierung f oxidization

Ozean ['oːtseaːn] (**-s, -e**) m ocean; **Ozeandampfer** m (ocean-going) liner

Ozeanien [otse'aːniən] (**-s**) nt Oceania

ozeanisch [otse'aːnɪʃ] adj oceanic; (Sprachen) Oceanic

Ozeanriese (umg) m ocean liner

Ozon [o'tsoːn] (**-s**) nt ozone; **Ozonloch** nt hole in the ozone layer; **Ozonschicht** f ozone layer

○

Pp

P, p [pe:] *nt* P, p; **P wie Peter** ≈ P for Peter

P. *abk* = **Pastor; Pater**

Paar [pa:r] (**-(e)s, -e**) *nt* pair; (*Liebespaar*) couple

paar *adj inv:* **ein ~ a** few; (*zwei oder drei*) a couple of; *siehe auch* **paarmal**

paaren *vt, vr* (*Tiere*) to mate, pair

Paar- *zW:* **Paarhufer** *pl* (*Zool*) cloven-hoofed animals *pl;* **Paarlauf** *m* pair skating; **paarmal** *adv:* **ein paarmal** a few times

Paarung *f* combination; (*von Tieren*) mating

paarweise *adv* in pairs; in couples

Pacht [paxt] (**-, -en**) *f* lease; (*Entgelt*) rent; **pachten** *vt* to lease; **du hast das Sofa doch nicht für dich gepachtet** (*umg*) don't hog the sofa

Pächter, in ['pɛçtər(ɪn)] (**-s, -**) *m(f)* leaseholder; tenant

Pachtvertrag *m* lease

Pack¹ [pak] (**-(e)s, -e** *od* **ⁱe**) *m* bundle, pack

Pack² [pak] (**-(e)s**) (*pej*) *nt* mob, rabble

Päckchen ['pɛkçən] *nt* small package; (*Zigaretten*) packet; (*Postpäckchen*) small parcel

Packeis *nt* pack ice

Packen (**-s, -**) *m* bundle; (*fig: Menge*) heaps (of); **packen** *vt, vi* (*auch Comput*) to pack; (*fassen*) to grasp, seize; (*umg: schaffen*) to manage; (*fig: fesseln*) to grip; **packen wirs!** (*umg: gehen*) let's go

Packer, in (**-s, -**) *m(f)* packer

Packesel *m* pack mule; (*fig*) packhorse

Packpapier *nt* brown paper, wrapping paper

Packung *f* packet; (*Pralinenpackung*) box; (*Med*) compress

Packzettel *m* (*Comm*) packing slip

Pädagoge [pɛda'go:gə] (**-n, -n**) *m* educationalist

Pädagogik *f* education

Pädagogin [pɛda'go:gɪn] *f* educationalist

pädagogisch *adj* educational, pedagogical; **~e Hochschule** college of education

Paddel ['padəl] (**-s, -**) *nt* paddle; **Paddelboot** *nt* canoe

paddeln *vi* to paddle

pädophil [pɛdo'fi:l] *adj* paedophile (*Brit*), pedophile (*US*)

Pädophilie [pɛdofi'li:] *f* paedophilia (*Brit*), pedophilia (*US*)

paffen ['pafən] *vt, vi* to puff

Page ['pa:ʒə] (**-n, -n**) *m* page(boy)

Pagenkopf *m* pageboy cut

paginieren [pagi'ni:rən] *vt* to paginate

Paginierung *f* pagination

Paillette [paɪ'jɛtə] *f* sequin

Paket [pa'ke:t] (**-(e)s, -e**) *nt* packet; (*Postpaket*) parcel; **Paketannahme** *f* parcels office; **Paketausgabe** *f* parcels office; **Paketkarte** *f* dispatch note; **Paketpost** *f* parcel post; **Paketschalter** *m* parcels counter

Pakistan ['pa:kɪsta:n] (**-s**) *nt* Pakistan

Pakistaner, in [pakɪs'ta:nər(ɪn)] (**-s, -**) *m(f)* Pakistani

Pakistani [pakɪs'ta:ni] (**-(s), -(s)**) *m* Pakistani

pakistanisch *adj* Pakistani

Pakt [pakt] (**-(e)s, -e**) *m* pact

Paläontologie [palɛɔntolo'gi:] *f* palaeontology (*Brit*), paleontology (*US*)

Palast [pa'last] (**-es, Paläste**) *m* palace

Palästina [palɛ'sti:na] (**-s**) *nt* Palestine

Palästinenser, in [palɛsti'nɛnzər(ɪn)] (**-s, -**) *m(f)* Palestinian

palästinensisch *adj* Palestinian

Palaver [pa'la:vər] (**-s, -**) *nt* (*auch fig: umg*) palaver

Palette [pa'lɛtə] *f* palette; (*fig*) range; (*Ladepalette*) pallet

Palme ['palmə] (**-, -n**) *f* palm (tree); **jdn auf die ~ bringen** (*umg*) to make sb see red

Palmsonntag *m* Palm Sunday

Pampelmuse ['pampəlmu:zə] (**-, -n**) *f* grapefruit

pampig ['pampɪç] (*umg*) *adj* (*frech*) fresh

Panama ['panama] (**-s**) *nt* Panama; **Panamakanal** *m* Panama Canal

Panflöte ['pa:nflø:tə] *f* panpipes *pl*, Pan's pipes *pl*

panieren [pa'ni:rən] *vt* (*Koch*) to coat with egg and breadcrumbs

Paniermehl [pa'ni:rme:l] *nt* breadcrumbs *pl*

Panik ['pa:nɪk] *f* panic; **nur keine ~!** don't panic!; **in ~ ausbrechen** to panic; **Panikkäufe** *pl* panic buying *sing*; **Panikmache** (*umg*) *f* panicmongering

panisch ['pa:nɪʃ] *adj* panic-stricken

Panne ['panə] (**-, -n**) *f* (*Aut etc*) breakdown; (*Missgeschick*) slip; **uns ist eine ~ passiert** we've boobed (*Brit*) (*umg*) *od* goofed (*US*) (*umg*)

Pannendienst *m* breakdown service
Pannenhilfe *f* breakdown service
Panorama [pano'ra:ma] (**-s, -men**) *nt* panorama
panschen ['panʃən] *vi* to splash about ▷ *vt* to water down
Panther, Panter ['pantər] (**-s, -**) *m* panther
Pantoffel [pan'tɔfəl] (**-s, -n**) *m* slipper; **Pantoffelheld** (*umg*) *m* henpecked husband
Pantomime [panto'mi:mə] (**-, -n**) *f* mime
Panzer ['pantsər] (**-s, -**) *m* armour (*Brit*), armor (*US*); (*fig*) shield; (*Platte*) armo(u)r plate; (*Fahrzeug*) tank; **Panzerfaust** *f* bazooka; **Panzerglas** *nt* bulletproof glass; **Panzergrenadier** *m* armoured (*Brit*) *od* armored (*US*) infantryman
panzern *vt* to armour (*Brit*) *od* armor (*US*) plate ▷ *vr* (*fig*) to arm o.s.
Panzerschrank *m* strongbox
Panzerwagen *m* armoured (*Brit*) *od* armored (*US*) car
Papa [pa'pa:] (**-s, -s**) (*umg*) *m* dad(dy), pa
Papagei [papa'gaɪ] (**-s, -en**) *m* parrot
Papier [pa'pi:r] (**-s, -e**) *nt* paper; (*Wertpapier*) share; **Papiere** *pl* (identity) papers *pl*; (*Urkunden*) documents *pl*; **seine ~e bekommen** (*entlassen werden*) to get one's cards; **Papierfabrik** *f* paper mill; **Papiergeld** *nt* paper money; **Papierkorb** *m* wastepaper basket; **Papierkram** (*umg*) *m* bumf (*Brit*) (*umg*); **Papierkrieg** *m* red tape; **Papiertüte** *f* paper bag; **Papiervorschub** *m* (*Drucker*) paper advance
Pappbecher *m* paper cup
Pappdeckel (**-, -n**) *m* cardboard
Pappe ['papə] *f* cardboard; **das ist nicht von ~** (*umg*) that is really something
Pappeinband *m* pasteboard
Pappel (**-, -n**) *f* poplar
pappen (*umg*) *vt, vi* to stick
Pappenheimer *pl*: **ich kenne meine ~** (*umg*) I know you lot/that lot (inside out)
Pappenstiel (*umg*) *m*: **keinen ~ wert sein** not to be worth a thing; **für einen ~ bekommen** to get for a song
papperlapapp [papərla'pap] *interj* rubbish!
pappig *adj* sticky
Pappmaschee, Pappmaché [papma'ʃe:] (**-s, -s**) *nt* papier-mâché
Pappteller *m* paper plate
Paprika ['paprika] (**-s, -s**) *m* (*Gewürz*) paprika; (*Paprikaschote*) pepper; **Paprikaschote** *f* pepper; **gefüllte Paprikaschoten** stuffed peppers
Papst [pa:pst] (**-(e)s, ̈-e**) *m* pope
päpstlich ['pɛ:pstlɪç] *adj* papal; **~er als der Papst sein** to be more Catholic than the Pope
Parabel [pa'ra:bəl] (**-, -n**) *f* parable; (*Math*) parabola
Parabolantenne [para'bo:l|antɛnə] *f* (*TV*) satellite dish
Parade [pa'ra:də] (**-, -n**) *f* (*Mil*) parade, review; (*Sport*) parry; **Paradebeispiel** *nt* prime example; **Parademarsch** *m* march past;

Paradeschritt *m* goose step
Paradies [para'di:s] (**-es, -e**) *nt* paradise; **paradiesisch** *adj* heavenly
Paradox [para'dɔks] (**-es, -e**) *nt* paradox; **paradox** *adj* paradoxical
Paraffin [para'fi:n] (**-s, -e**) *nt* (*Chem: Paraffinöl*) paraffin (*Brit*), kerosene (*US*); (*Paraffinwachs*) paraffin wax
Paragraf [para'gra:f] (**-en, -en**) *m* paragraph; (*Jur*) section
Paragrafenreiter (*umg*) *m* pedant
Paraguay [paragu'a:i] (**-s**) *nt* Paraguay
Paraguayer, in [para'gua:jər(ɪn)] (**-s, -**) *m(f)* Paraguayan
paraguayisch *adj* Paraguayan
parallel [para'le:l] *adj* parallel; **~ schalten** (*Elek*) to connect in parallel
Parallele (**-, -n**) *f* parallel
Parameter [pa'ra:metər] *m* parameter
paramilitärisch [paramili'tɛ:rɪʃ] *adj* paramilitary
Paranuss ['pa:ranʊs] *f* Brazil nut
paraphieren [para'fi:rən] *vt* (*Vertrag*) to initial
Parasit [para'zi:t] (**-en, -en**) *m* (*lit, fig*) parasite
parat [pa'ra:t] *adj* ready
Pärchen ['pe:rçən] *nt* couple
Parcours [par'ku:r] (**-, -**) *m* showjumping course; (*Sportart*) showjumping
Pardon [par'dõ:] (**-s**) (*umg*) *m od nt*: **~!** (*Verzeihung*) sorry!; **kein ~ kennen** to be ruthless
Parfüm [par'fy:m] (**-s, -s** *od* **-e**) *nt* perfume
Parfümerie [parfymə'ri:] *f* perfumery
Parfümflasche *f* scent bottle
parfümieren [parfy'mi:rən] *vt* to scent, perfume
parieren [pa'ri:rən] *vt* to parry ▷ *vi* (*umg*) to obey
Paris [pa'ri:s] (**-**) *nt* Paris
Pariser [pa'ri:zər] (**-s, -**) *m* Parisian; (*umg: Kondom*) rubber ▷ *adj attrib* Parisian, Paris *attrib*
Pariserin *f* Parisian
Parität [pari'tɛ:t] *f* parity; **paritätisch** *adj*: **paritätische Mitbestimmung** equal representation
Pariwert ['pa:rive:rt] *m* par value, parity
Park [park] (**-s, -s**) *m* park
Parka ['parka] (**-(s), -s**) *m* parka
Parkanlage *f* park; (*um Gebäude*) grounds *pl*
Parkbucht *f* parking bay
parken *vt, vi* to park; **„P~ verboten!"** "No Parking"
Parkett [par'kɛt] (**-(e)s, -e**) *nt* parquet (floor); (*Theat*) stalls *pl* (*Brit*), orchestra (*US*); **Parketthandel** *m* (*Fin*) floor trading
Park- *zW*: **Parkhaus** *nt* multistorey car park; **Parklücke** *f* parking space; **Parkplatz** *m* car park, parking lot (*US*); parking place; **Parkscheibe** *f* parking disc; **Parkuhr** *f* parking meter; **Parkverbot** *nt* parking ban
Parlament [parla'mɛnt] *nt* parliament
Parlamentarier [parlamɛn'ta:riər] (**-s, -**) *m* parliamentarian

parlamentarisch *adj* parliamentary

Parlaments- *zW:* **Parlamentsausschuss** *m* parliamentary committee; **Parlamentsbeschluss** *m* vote of parliament; **Parlamentsferien** *pl* recess *sing;* **Parlamentsmitglied** *nt* Member of Parliament (*Brit*), Congressman (*US*); **Parlamentssitzung** *f* sitting (of parliament)

Parodie [paro'diː] *f* parody

parodieren *vt* to parody

Parodontose [parodɔn'toːzə] (**-, -n**) *f* shrinking gums *pl*

Parole [pa'roːlə] (**-, -n**) *f* password; (*Wahlspruch*) motto

Partei [par'taɪ] *f* party; (*im Mietshaus*) tenant, party (*form*); **für jdn ~ ergreifen** to take sb's side; **Parteibuch** *nt* party membership book; **Parteiführung** *f* party leadership; **Parteigenosse** *m* party member; **parteiisch** *adj* partial, bias(s)ed; **parteilich** *adj* party *attrib;* **Parteilinie** *f* party line; **parteilos** *adj* neutral; **Parteinahme** (**-, -n**) *f* partisanship; **parteipolitisch** *adj* party political; **Parteiprogramm** *nt* (party) manifesto; **Parteitag** *m* party conference; **Parteivorsitzende, r** *f(m)* party leader

Parterre [par'tɛr] (**-s, -s**) *nt* ground floor; (*Theat*) stalls *pl* (*Brit*), orchestra (*US*)

Partie [par'tiː] *f* part; (*Spiel*) game; (*Ausflug*) outing; (*Mann, Frau*) catch; (*Comm*) lot; **mit von der ~ sein** to join in

partiell [partsi'ɛl] *adj* partial

Partikel [par'tiːkəl] (**-, -n**) *f* particle

Partisan, in [parti'zaːn(ɪn)] (**-s** *od* **-en, -en**) *m(f)* partisan

Partitur [parti'tuːr] *f* (*Mus*) score

Partizip [parti'tsiːp] (**-s, -ien**) *nt* participle; **~ Präsens/Perfekt** (*Gram*) present/past participle

Partner, in ['partnər(ɪn)] (**-s, -**) *m(f)* partner; **Partnerschaft** *f* partnership; (*Städtepartnerschaft*) twinning; **partnerschaftlich** *adj* as partners; **Partnerstadt** *f* twin town (*Brit*)

partout [par'tuː] *adv:* **er will ~ ins Kino gehen** he insists on going to the cinema

Party ['paːrti] (**-, -s**) *f* party

Parzelle [par'tsɛlə] *f* plot, lot

Pascha ['paʃa] (**-s, -s**) *m:* **wie ein ~** like Lord Muck (*Brit*) (*umg*)

Pass [pas] (**-es, ̈-e**) *m* pass; (*Ausweis*) passport

passabel [pa'saːbəl] *adj* passable, reasonable

Passage [pa'saːʒə] (**-, -n**) *f* passage; (*Ladenstraße*) arcade

Passagier [pasa'ʒiːr] (**-s, -e**) *m* passenger; **Passagierdampfer** *m* passenger steamer; **Passagierflugzeug** *nt* airliner

Passah ['pasa], **Passahfest** ['pasafɛst] *nt* (Feast of the) Passover

Passamt *nt* passport office

Passant, in [pa'sant(ɪn)] *m(f)* passer-by

Passbild *nt* passport photo(graph)

passé, passee [pa'seː] *adj:* **diese Mode ist längst ~** this fashion went out long ago

passen ['pasən] *vi* to fit; (*auf Frage, Karten*) to pass; **~ zu** (*Farbe etc*) to go with; **Sonntag passt uns nicht** Sunday is no good for us; **die Schuhe ~ (mir) gut** the shoes are a good fit (for me); **zu jdm ~** (*Mensch*) to suit sb; **das passt mir nicht** that doesn't suit me; **er passt nicht zu dir** he's not right for you; **das könnte dir so ~!** (*umg*) you'd like that, wouldn't you?

passend *adj* suitable; (*zusammenpassend*) matching; (*angebracht*) fitting; (*Zeit*) convenient; **haben Sie es ~?** (*Geld*) have you got the right money?

Passfoto *nt* passport photo(graph)

passierbar [pa'siːrbaːr] *adj* passable; (*Fluss, Kanal*) negotiable

passieren *vt* to pass; (*durch Sieb*) to strain ▷ *vi* (*Hilfsverb sein*) to happen; **es ist ein Unfall passiert** there has been an accident

Passierschein *m* pass, permit

Passion [pasi'oːn] *f* passion

passioniert [pasio'niːrt] *adj* enthusiastic, passionate

Passionsfrucht *f* passion fruit

Passionsspiel *nt* Passion Play

Passionszeit *f* Passiontide

passiv ['pasiːf] *adj* passive; **~es Rauchen** passive smoking; **Passiv** (**-s, -e**) *nt* passive

Passiva [pa'siːva] *pl* (*Comm*) liabilities *pl*

Passivität [pasivi'tɛːt] *f* passiveness

Passivposten *m* (*Comm*) debit entry

Pass- *zW:* **Passkontrolle** *f* passport control; **Passstelle** *f* passport office; **Passstraße** *f* (mountain) pass; **Passzwang** *m* requirement to carry a passport

Paste ['pastə] (**-, -n**) *f* paste

Pastell [pas'tɛl] (**-(e)s, -e**) *nt* pastel; **Pastellfarbe** *f* pastel colour (*Brit*) *od* color (*US*); **pastellfarben** *adj* pastel-colo(u)red

Pastete [pas'teːtə] (**-, -n**) *f* pie; (*Pastetchen*) vol-au-vent; (: *ungefüllt*) vol-au-vent case

pasteurisieren [pastøri'ziːrən] *vt* to pasteurize

Pastor ['pastɔr] *m* vicar; pastor, minister

Pate ['paːtə] (**-n, -n**) *m* godfather; **bei etw ~ gestanden haben** (*fig*) to be the force behind sth

Patenkind *nt* godchild

Patenstadt *f* twin town (*Brit*)

patent [pa'tɛnt] *adj* clever

Patent [pa'tɛnt] (**-(e)s, -e**) *nt* patent; (*Mil*) commission; **etw als** *od* **zum ~ anmelden** to apply for a patent on sth

Patentamt *nt* patent office

patentieren [patɛn'tiːrən] *vt* to patent

Patent- *zW:* **Patentinhaber** *m* patentee; **Patentlösung** *f* (*fig*) patent remedy; **Patentschutz** *m* patent right; **Patenturkunde** *f* letters patent *pl*

Pater ['paːtər] (**-s, -** *od* **Patres**) *m* Father

Paternoster [patər'nɔstər] (**-s, -**) *m* (*Aufzug*) paternoster

pathetisch [pa'teːtɪʃ] *adj* emotional

Pathologe [pato'lo:gə] (**-n, -n**) *m* pathologist
Pathologin [pato'lo:gɪn] *f* pathologist
pathologisch *adj* pathological
Pathos ['pa:tɔs] (**-**) *nt* pathos
Patience [pasi'ã:s] (**-, -n**) *f*: **~n legen** to play patience
Patient, in [patsi'ɛnt(ɪn)] *m(f)* patient
Patin ['pa:tɪn] *f* godmother
Patriarch [patri'arç] (**-en, -en**) *m* patriarch
patriarchalisch [patriar'ça:lɪʃ] *adj* patriarchal
Patriot, in [patri'o:t(ɪn)] (**-en, -en**) *m(f)* patriot;
   patriotisch *adj* patriotic
Patriotismus [patrio:'tɪsmʊs] *m* patriotism
Patron [pa'tro:n] (**-s, -e**) *m* patron; (*Eccl*) patron saint
Patrone (**-, -n**) *f* cartridge
Patronenhülse *f* cartridge case
Patronin *f* patroness; (*Eccl*) patron saint
Patrouille [pa'trʊljə] (**-, -n**) *f* patrol
patrouillieren [patrʊl'ji:rən] *vi* to patrol
patsch [patʃ] *interj* splash!
Patsche (**-, -n**) (*umg*) *f* (*Händchen*) paw;
   (*Fliegenpatsche*) swat; (*Feuerpatsche*) beater;
   (*Bedrängnis*) mess, jam
patschen *vi* to smack, slap; (*im Wasser*) to splash
patschnass *adj* soaking wet
Patt [pat] (**-s, -s**) *nt* (*lit, fig*) stalemate
patzen ['patsən] (*umg*) *vi* to boob (*Brit*), goof (*US*)
patzig ['patsɪç] (*umg*) *adj* cheeky, saucy
Pauke ['paʊkə] (**-, -n**) *f* kettledrum; **auf die ~ hauen** to live it up; **mit ~n und Trompeten durchfallen** (*umg*) to fail dismally
pauken *vt, vi* (*Sch*) to swot (*Brit*), cram
Pauker (**-s, -**) (*umg*) *m* teacher
pausbäckig ['paʊsbɛkɪç] *adj* chubby-cheeked
pauschal [paʊ'ʃa:l] *adj* (*Kosten*) inclusive;
   (*einheitlich*) flat-rate *attrib*; (*Urteil*) sweeping;
   die Werkstatt berechnet ~ pro Inspektion 130 Euro the garage has a flat rate of 130 euros per service
Pauschale (**-, -n**) *f* flat rate; (*vorläufig geschätzter Betrag*) estimated amount
Pauschal- *zW*: **Pauschalgebühr** *f* flat rate;
   Pauschalpreis *m* all-in price; **Pauschalreise** *f* package tour; **Pauschalsumme** *f* lump sum;
   Pauschalversicherung *f* comprehensive insurance
Pause ['paʊzə] (**-, -n**) *f* break; (*Theat*) interval;
   (*das Innehalten*) pause; (*Mus*) rest; (*Kopie*) tracing
pausen *vt* to trace
Pausen- *zW*: **Pausenbrot** *nt* sandwich (*to eat at break*); **Pausenhof** *m* playground, schoolyard (*US*); **pausenlos** *adj* nonstop; **Pausenzeichen** *nt* (*Rundf*) call sign; (*Mus*) rest
pausieren [paʊ'si:rən] *vi* to make a break
Pauspapier ['paʊspapi:r] *nt* tracing paper
Pavian ['pa:via:n] (**-s, -e**) *m* baboon
Paybackkarte ['pe:bɛkkartə] *f* loyalty card
Pay-per-Click ['pe:pərklɪk] (**-s**) *nt* pay-per-click
Pazifik [pa'tsi:fɪk] (**-s**) *m* Pacific
pazifisch *adj* Pacific; **der P~e Ozean** the Pacific (Ocean)

Pazifist, in [patsi'fɪst(ɪn)] *m(f)* pacifist;
   pazifistisch *adj* pacifist
PC *m abk* (= *Personal Computer*) PC
PDA *m abk* (*Comput*: = *personal digital assistant*) PDA
PDS *f abk* (= *Partei des Demokratischen Sozialismus*) German Socialist Party; *see culture note*

> ◉ **PDS**
> ◉
> ◉
> ◉ The PDS (Partei des Demokratischen
> ◉ Sozialismus) was founded in 1989 as the
> ◉ successor of the SED, the former East
> ◉ German Communist Party. Its aims are the
> ◉ establishment of a democratic socialist
> ◉ society and to hold a position in the
> ◉ German political scene left of the SPD.

Pech [pɛç] (**-s, -e**) *nt* pitch; (*fig*) bad luck; **~ haben** to be unlucky; **die beiden halten zusammen wie ~ und Schwefel** (*umg*) the two are inseparable; **~ gehabt!** (*umg*);
   pechschwarz *adj* pitch-black; **Pechsträhne** (*umg*) *f* unlucky patch; **Pechvogel** (*umg*) *m* unlucky person
Pedal [pe'da:l] (**-s, -e**) *nt* pedal; **in die ~e treten** to pedal (hard)
Pedant [pe'dant] *m* pedant
Pedanterie [pedantə'ri:] *f* pedantry
pedantisch *adj* pedantic
Peddigrohr ['pɛdɪçro:r] *nt* cane
Pediküre [pedi'ky:rə] (**-, -n**) *f* (*Fußpflege*) pedicure; (*Fußpflegerin*) chiropodist
Pegel ['pe:gəl] (**-s, -**) *m* water gauge;
   (*Geräuschpegel*) noise level; **Pegelstand** *m* water level
peilen ['paɪlən] *vt* to get a fix on; **die Lage ~** (*umg*) to see how the land lies
Pein [paɪn] (**-**) *f* agony, suffering
peinigen *vt* to torture; (*plagen*) to torment
peinlich *adj* (*unangenehm*) embarrassing, awkward, painful; (*genau*) painstaking; **in seinem Zimmer herrschte ~e Ordnung** his room was meticulously tidy; **er vermied es ~st, davon zu sprechen** he was at pains not to talk about it; **Peinlichkeit** *f* painfulness, awkwardness; (*Genauigkeit*) scrupulousness
Peitsche ['paɪtʃə] (**-, -n**) *f* whip
peitschen *vt* to whip; (*Regen*) to lash
Peitschenhieb *m* lash
Pekinese [peki'ne:zə] (**-n, -n**) *m* Pekinese, peke (*umg*)
Peking ['pe:kɪŋ] (**-s**) *nt* Peking
Pelikan ['pe:lika:n] (**-s, -e**) *m* pelican
Pelle ['pɛlə] (**-, -n**) *f* skin; **der Chef sitzt mir auf der ~** (*umg*) I've got the boss on my back
pellen *vt* to skin, peel
Pellkartoffeln *pl* jacket potatoes *pl*
Pelz [pɛlts] (**-es, -e**) *m* fur
Pendel ['pɛndəl] (**-s, -**) *nt* pendulum
pendeln *vi* (*schwingen*) to swing (to and fro); (*Zug, Fähre etc*) to shuttle; (*Mensch*) to commute; (*fig*) to fluctuate
Pendelverkehr *m* shuttle service;

P

(*Berufsverkehr*) commuter traffic

Pendler, in ['pɛndlər(ɪn)] (**-s**, **-**) *m(f)* commuter

penetrant [pene'trant] *adj* sharp; (*Person*) pushing; **das schmeckt/riecht ~ nach Knoblauch** it has a very strong taste/smell of garlic

penibel [pe'niːbəl] *adj* pernickety (*Brit*) (*umg*), persnickety (*US*) (*umg*), precise

Penis ['peːnɪs] (**-**, **-se**) *m* penis

Pennbruder ['pɛnbruːdər] (*umg*) *m* tramp (*Brit*), hobo (*US*)

Penne (**-**, **-n**) (*umg*) *f* (*Sch*) school

pennen (*umg*) *vi* to kip

Penner (**-s**, **-**) (*pej: umg*) *m* tramp (*Brit*), hobo (*US*)

Pension [pɛnzi'oːn] *f* (*Geld*) pension; (*Ruhestand*) retirement; (*für Gäste*) boarding house, guesthouse; **halbe/volle ~** half/full board; **in ~ gehen** to retire

Pensionär, in [pɛnzio'nɛːr(ɪn)] (**-s**, **-e**) *m(f)* pensioner

Pensionat (**-(e)s**, **-e**) *nt* boarding school

pensionieren [pɛnzio'niːrən] *vt* to pension (off); **sich ~ lassen** to retire

pensioniert *adj* retired

Pensionierung *f* retirement

Pensions- *zW*: **pensionsberechtigt** *adj* entitled to a pension; **Pensionsfonds** *m* pension fund; **Pensionsgast** *m* boarder, paying guest; **pensionsreif** (*umg*) *adj* ready for retirement

Pensum ['pɛnzʊm] (**-s**, **Pensen**) *nt* quota; (*Sch*) curriculum

Peperoni [pepe'roːni] *pl* chillies *pl*

per [pɛr] *präp +akk* by, per; (*pro*) per; (*bis*) by; **~ Adresse** (*Comm*) care of, c/o; **mit jdm ~ du sein** (*umg*) to be on first-name terms with sb

Perfekt ['pɛrfɛkt] (**-(e)s**, **-e**) *nt* perfect

perfekt [pɛr'fɛkt] *adj* perfect; (*abgemacht*) settled; **die Sache ~ machen** to clinch the deal; **der Vertrag ist ~** the contract is all settled

perfektionieren [pɛrfɛktsio'niːrən] *vt* to perfect

Perfektionismus [pɛrfɛktsio'nɪsmʊs] *m* perfectionism

perforieren [pɛrfo'riːrən] *vt* to perforate

Pergament [perga'mɛnt] *nt* parchment; **Pergamentpapier** *nt* greaseproof paper (*Brit*), wax(ed) paper (*US*)

Pergola ['pɛrgola] (**-**, **Pergolen**) *f* pergola, arbour (*Brit*), arbor (*US*)

Periode [peri'oːdə] (**-**, **-n**) *f* period; **0,33 ~** 0.33 recurring

periodisch [peri'oːdɪʃ] *adj* periodic; (*dezimal*) recurring

Peripherie [perife'riː] *f* periphery; (*um Stadt*) outskirts *pl*; (*Math*) circumference; **Peripheriegerät** *nt* (*Comput*) peripheral

Perle ['pɛrlə] (**-**, **-n**) *f* (*lit, fig*) pearl; (*Glasperle, Holzperle, Tropfen*) bead; (*veraltet: umg: Hausgehilfin*) maid

perlen *vi* to sparkle; (*Tropfen*) to trickle

Perlenkette *f* pearl necklace

Perlhuhn *nt* guinea fowl

Perlmutt ['pɛrlmʊt] (**-s**) *nt* mother-of-pearl

Perlon® ['pɛrlɔn] (**-s**) *nt* ≈ nylon

Perlwein *m* sparkling wine

perplex [pɛr'plɛks] *adj* dumbfounded

Perser ['pɛrzər] (**-s**, **-**) *m* (*Person*) Persian; (*umg: Teppich*) Persian carpet

Perserin *f* Persian

Persianer [pɛrzi'aːnər] (**-s**, **-**) *m* Persian lamb (coat)

Persien ['pɛrziən] (**-s**) *nt* Persia

Persiflage [pɛrzi'flaːʒə] (**-**, **-n**) *f*: **~** (*+gen od* **auf** *+akk*) pastiche (of), satire (on)

persisch *adj* Persian; **P~er Golf** Persian Gulf

Person [pɛr'zoːn] (**-**, **-en**) *f* person; (*pej: Frau*) female; **sie ist Köchin und Haushälterin in einer ~** she is cook and housekeeper rolled into one; **ich für meine ~** personally I

Personal [pɛrzo'naːl] (**-s**) *nt* personnel; (*Bedienung*) servants *pl*; **Personalabbau** *m* staff cuts *pl*; **Personalakte** *f* personal file; **Personalangaben** *pl* particulars *pl*; **Personalausweis** *m* identity card; **Personalbogen** *m* personal record; **Personalbüro** *nt* personnel (department); **Personalchef** *m* personnel manager; **Personal Computer** *m* personal computer

Personalien [pɛrzo'naːliən] *pl* particulars *pl*

Personalität [pɛrzonali'tɛːt] *f* personality

Personal- *zW*: **Personalkosten** *pl* staff costs; **Personalmangel** *m* staff shortage; **Personalpronomen** *nt* personal pronoun; **Personalreduzierung** *f* staff reduction

personell [pɛrzo'nɛl] *adj* staff *attrib*; **-e Veränderungen** changes in personnel

Personen- *zW*: **Personenaufzug** *m* lift, elevator (*US*); **Personenbeschreibung** *f* (personal) description; **Personengedächtnis** *nt* memory for faces; **Personengesellschaft** *f* partnership; **Personenkraftwagen** *m* private motorcar, automobile (*US*); **Personenkreis** *m* group of people; **Personenkult** *m* personality cult; **Personennahverkehr** *m*: **öffentlicher Personennahverkehr** local public transport; **Personenschaden** *m* injury to persons; **Personenverkehr** *m* passenger services *pl*; **Personenwaage** *f* scales *pl*; **Personenzug** *m* stopping train; passenger train

personifizieren [pɛrzonifi'tsiːrən] *vt* to personify

persönlich [pɛr'zøːnlɪç] *adj* personal ▷ *adv* in person; personally; (*auf Briefen*) private (and confidential); **~ haften** (*Comm*) to be personally liable; **Persönlichkeit** *f* personality; **Persönlichkeiten des öffentlichen Lebens** public figures

Perspektive [pɛrspɛk'tiːvə] *f* perspective; **das eröffnet ganz neue ~n für uns** that opens new horizons for us

Pers. Ref. *abk* (= *Persönlicher Referent*) personal representative

Peru [pe'ruː] (**-s**) *nt* Peru

Peruaner, in [peru'aːnər(ɪn)] (**-s**, **-**) *m(f)* Peruvian

peruanisch adj Peruvian
Perücke [pe'rykə] (-, -n) f wig
pervers [pɛr'vɛrs] adj perverse
Perversität [pɛrvɛrzi'tɛːt] f perversity
Pessar [pɛ'saːr] (-s, -e) nt pessary; (zur Empfängnisverhütung) cap, diaphragm
Pessimismus [pɛsi'mɪsmʊs] m pessimism
Pessimist, in [pɛsi'mɪst(ɪn)] m(f) pessimist; **pessimistisch** adj pessimistic
Pest [pɛst] (-) f plague; **jdn/etw wie die ~ hassen** (umg) to loathe (and detest) sb/sth
Petersilie [petər'ziːliə] f parsley
Petrochemie [petro'çe'miː] f petrochemistry
Petrodollar [petro'dɔlar] m petrodollar
Petroleum [pe'troːleʊm] (-s) nt paraffin (Brit), kerosene (US)
petzen [ˈpɛtsən] (umg) vi to tell tales; **er petzt immer** he always tells
Pf. (Hist) abk = **Pfennig**
Pfad [pfaːt] (-(e)s, -e) m path; **Pfadfinder** m Boy Scout; **er ist bei den Pfadfindern** he's in the (Boy) Scouts; **Pfadfinderin** f Girl Guide
Pfaffe [ˈpfafə] (-n, -n) (pej) m cleric, parson
Pfahl [pfaːl] (-(e)s, -̈e) m post, stake; **Pfahlbau** m pile dwelling
Pfalz [pfalts] (-, -en) f (Geog) Palatinate
Pfälzer, in [ˈpfɛltsər(ɪn)] (-s, -) m(f) person from the Palatinate
pfälzisch adj Palatine, of the (Rhineland) Palatinate
Pfand [pfant] (-(e)s, -̈er) nt pledge, security; (Flaschenpfand) deposit; (im Spiel) forfeit; (fig: der Liebe etc) pledge; **Pfandbrief** m bond
pfänden [ˈpfɛndən] vt to seize, impound
Pfänderspiel nt game of forfeits
Pfand- zW: **Pfandhaus** nt pawnshop; **Pfandleiher** (-s, -) m pawnbroker; **Pfandrecht** nt lien; **Pfandschein** m pawn ticket
Pfändung [ˈpfɛndʊŋ] f seizure, distraint (form)
Pfanne [ˈpfanə] (-, -n) f (frying) pan; **jdn in die ~ hauen** (umg) to tear a strip off sb
Pfannkuchen m pancake; (Berliner) doughnut (Brit), donut (US)
Pfarrei [pfar'raɪ] f parish
Pfarrer (-s, -) m priest; (evangelisch) vicar; (von Freikirchen) minister
Pfarrhaus nt vicarage
Pfau [pfaʊ] (-(e)s, -en) m peacock
Pfauenauge nt peacock butterfly
Pfd. abk (= Pfund) ≈ lb.
Pfeffer [ˈpfɛfər] (-s, -) m pepper; **er soll bleiben, wo der ~ wächst!** (umg) he can take a running jump; **Pfefferkorn** nt peppercorn; **Pfefferkuchen** m gingerbread; **Pfefferminz** (-es, -e) nt peppermint; **Pfefferminze** f peppermint (plant); **Pfeffermühle** f pepper mill
pfeffern vt to pepper; (umg: werfen) to fling; **gepfefferte Preise/Witze** steep prices/spicy jokes
Pfeife [ˈpfaɪfə] (-, -n) f whistle; (Tabakpfeife, Orgelpfeife) pipe; **nach jds ~ tanzen** to dance to sb's tune

pfeifen unreg vt, vi to whistle; **auf dem letzten Loch ~** (umg: erschöpft sein) to be on one's last legs; (: finanziell) to be on one's beam ends; **ich pfeif(e) drauf!** (umg) I don't give a damn!; **Pfeifenstopfer** m tamper
Pfeifer (-s, -) m piper
Pfeifkonzert nt catcalls pl
Pfeil [pfaɪl] (-(e)s, -e) m arrow
Pfeiler [ˈpfaɪlər] (-s, -) m pillar, prop; (Brückenpfeiler) pier
Pfennig [ˈpfɛnɪç] (-(e)s, -e) m (Hist) pfennig (one hundredth of a mark); **Pfennigabsatz** m stiletto heel; **Pfennigfuchser** (-s, -) (umg) m skinflint
pferchen [ˈpfɛrçən] vt to cram, pack
Pferd [pfeːrt] (-(e)s, -e) nt horse; **wie ein ~ arbeiten** (umg) to work like a Trojan; **mit ihm kann man ~e stehlen** (umg) he's a great sport; **auf das falsche/richtige ~ setzen** (lit, fig) to back the wrong/right horse
Pferde- zW: **Pferdeäpfel** pl horse droppings pl od dung sing; **Pferdefuß** m: **die Sache hat aber einen Pferdefuß** there's just one snag; **Pferderennen** nt horse-race; (Sportart) horse-racing; **Pferdeschwanz** m (Frisur) ponytail; **Pferdestall** m stable; **Pferdestärke** f horsepower
Pfiff (-(e)s, -e) m whistle; (Kniff) trick
pfiff etc [pfɪf] vb siehe **pfeifen**
Pfifferling [ˈpfɪfərlɪŋ] m yellow chanterelle; **keinen ~ wert** not worth a thing
pfiffig adj smart
Pfingsten [ˈpfɪŋstən] (-, -) nt Whitsun
Pfingstrose f peony
Pfingstsonntag m Whit Sunday, Pentecost (Rel)
Pfirsich [ˈpfɪrzɪç] (-s, -e) m peach
Pflanze [ˈpflantsə] (-, -n) f plant
pflanzen vt to plant ▷ vr (umg) to plonk o.s.
Pflanzenfett nt vegetable fat
Pflanzenschutzmittel nt pesticide
pflanzlich adj vegetable
Pflanzung f plantation
Pflaster [ˈpflastər] (-s, -) nt plaster; (Straßenpflaster) pavement (Brit), sidewalk (US); **ein teures ~** (umg) a pricey place; **ein heißes ~** a dangerous od unsafe place; **pflastermüde** adj dead on one's feet
pflastern vt to pave
Pflasterstein m paving stone
Pflaume [ˈpflaʊmə] (-, -n) f plum; (umg: Mensch) twit (Brit)
Pflaumenmus nt plum jam
Pflege [ˈpfleːgə] (-, -n) f care; (von Idee) cultivation; (Krankenpflege) nursing; **jdn/etw in ~ nehmen** to look after sb/sth; **in ~ sein** (Kind) to be fostered out; **pflegebedürftig** adj needing care; **Pflegeeltern** pl foster parents pl; **Pflegefall** m case for nursing; **Pflegegeld** nt (für Pflegekinder) boarding-out allowance; (für Kranke) attendance allowance; **Pflegeheim** nt nursing home; **Pflegekind** nt foster child; **pflegeleicht** adj easy-care; **Pflegemutter** f foster mother

pflegen vt to look after; (Kranke) to nurse; (Beziehungen) to foster ▷ vi (gewöhnlich tun): **sie pflegte zu sagen** she used to say

Pfleger (-s, -) m (im Krankenhaus) orderly; (voll qualifiziert) male nurse; **Pflegerin** f nurse

Pflegesatz m hospital and nursing charges pl

Pflegevater m foster father

Pflegeversicherung f geriatric care insurance

Pflicht [pflɪçt] (-, -en) f duty; (Sport) compulsory section; **Rechte und ~en** rights and responsibilities; **pflichtbewusst** adj conscientious; **Pflichtbewusstsein** nt sense of duty; **Pflichtfach** nt (Sch) compulsory subject; **Pflichtgefühl** nt sense of duty; **pflichtgemäß** adj dutiful; **pflichtvergessen** adj irresponsible; **Pflichtversicherung** f compulsory insurance

Pflock [pflɔk] (-(e)s, ̈-e) m peg; (für Tiere) stake

pflog etc [pflo:k] vb (veraltet) siehe **pflegen**

pflücken ['pflʏkən] vt to pick

Pflug [pflu:k] (-(e)s, ̈-e) m plough (Brit), plow (US)

pflügen ['pfly:gən] vt to plough (Brit), plow (US)

Pflugschar f ploughshare (Brit), plowshare (US)

Pforte ['pfɔrtə] (-, -n) f (Tor) gate

Pförtner ['pfœrtnər] (-s, -) m porter, doorkeeper, doorman

Pförtnerin f doorkeeper, porter

Pfosten ['pfɔstən] (-s, -) m post; (senkrechter Balken) upright

Pfote ['pfo:tə] (-, -n) f paw; (umg: Schrift) scrawl

Pfropf [pfrɔpf] (-(e)s, -e) m (Flaschenpfropf) stopper; (Blutpfropf) clot

Pfropfen (-s, -) m = **Pfropf**

pfropfen vt (stopfen) to cram; (Baum) to graft; **gepfropft voll** crammed full

pfui [pfʊɪ] interj ugh!; (na na) tut tut!; (Buhruf) boo!; **~ Teufel!** (umg) ugh!, yuck!

Pfund [pfʊnt] (-(e)s) nt (Gewicht, Fin) pound; **das ~ sinkt** sterling od the pound is falling

pfundig (umg) adj great

Pfundskerl ['pfʊntskɛrl] (umg) m great guy

pfundweise adv by the pound

pfuschen ['pfʊʃən] vi to bungle; (einen Fehler machen) to slip up

Pfuscher, in ['pfʊʃər(ɪn)] (-s, -) (umg) m(f) sloppy worker; (Kurpfuscher) quack

Pfuscherei [pfʊʃə'raɪ] (umg) f sloppy work; (Kurpfuscherei) quackery

Pfütze ['pfʏtsə] (-, -n) f puddle

PH (-, -s) f abk = **pädagogische Hochschule**

Phänomen [fɛno'me:n] (-s, -e) nt phenomenon; **phänomenal** [-'na:l] adj phenomenal

Phantasie etc [fanta'zi:] = **Fantasie** etc

phantasieren [fanta'zi:rən] vi = **fantasieren**

phantasievoll adj = **fantasievoll**

Phantast [fan'tast] (-en, -en) m = **Fantast**

phantastisch adj = **fantastisch**

Phantom [fan'to:m] (-s, -e) nt (Trugbild) phantom; **einem ~ nachjagen** (fig) to tilt at windmills; **Phantombild** nt Identikit® picture

Pharisäer [fari'zɛ:ər] (-s, -) m (lit, fig) pharisee

Pharmazeut, in [farma'tsɔʏt(ɪn)] (-en, -en) m(f) pharmacist

pharmazeutisch adj pharmaceutical

Pharmazie f pharmacy, pharmaceutics sing

Phase ['fa:zə] (-, -n) f phase

Philanthrop [filan'tro:p] (-en, -en) m philanthropist; **philanthropisch** adj philanthropic

Philatelist, in [filate'lɪst(ɪn)] (-en, -en) m(f) philatelist

Philharmoniker [fɪlhar'mo:nikər] (-s, -) m: **die ~** the philharmonic (orchestra) sing

Philippine [fɪlɪ'pi:nə] (-n, -n) m Filipino

Philippinen pl Philippines pl, Philippine Islands pl

Philippinin f Filipino

philippinisch adj Filipino

Philologe [filo'lo:gə] (-n, -n) m philologist

Philologie [filolo'gi:] f philology

Philologin f philologist

Philosoph, in [filo'zo:f(ɪn)] (-en, -en) m(f) philosopher

Philosophie [filozo'fi:] f philosophy

philosophieren [filozo'fi:rən] vi: **~ (über +akk)** to philosophize (about)

philosophisch adj philosophical

Phlegma ['flɛgma] (-s) nt lethargy

phlegmatisch [flɛ'gma:tɪʃ] adj lethargic

Phobie [fo'bi:] f: **~ (vor +dat)** phobia (about)

Phonetik [fo'ne:tɪk] f phonetics sing

phonetisch adj phonetic

Phonotypistin [fonoty'pɪstɪn] f audiotypist

Phosphat [fos'fa:t] (-(e)s, -e) nt phosphate

Phosphor ['fɔsfɔr] (-s) m phosphorus

phosphoreszieren [fɔsfɔres'tsi:rən] vt to phosphoresce

Photo etc ['fo:to] = **Foto** etc

Phrase ['fra:zə] (-, -n) f phrase; (pej) hollow phrase; **~n dreschen** (umg) to churn out one cliché after another

pH-Wert [pe:'ha:ve:rt] m pH value

Physik [fy'zi:k] f physics sing

physikalisch [fyzi'ka:lɪʃ] adj of physics

Physiker, in ['fy:zikər(ɪn)] (-s, -) m(f) physicist

Physikum ['fy:zikʊm] (-s) nt (Univ) preliminary examination in medicine

Physiologe [fyzio'lo:gə] (-n, -n) m physiologist

Physiologie [fyziolo'gi:] f physiology

Physiologin f physiologist

physisch ['fy:zɪʃ] adj physical

Pianist, in [pia'nɪst(ɪn)] m(f) pianist

Piccolo ['pɪkolo] (-s, -s) m trainee waiter; (auch: **Piccoloflasche**) quarter bottle of champagne; (Mus: auch: **Piccoloflöte**) piccolo

picheln ['pɪçəln] (umg) vi to booze

Pickel ['pɪkəl] (-s, -) m pimple; (Werkzeug) pickaxe; (Bergpickel) ice axe

pickelig, picklig adj pimply

picken ['pɪkən] vt to peck ▷ vi: **~ (nach)** to peck (at)

Picknick ['pɪknɪk] (-s, -e od -s) nt picnic; **~ machen** to have a picnic

piekfein ['pi:k'faɪn] (umg) adj posh
Piemont [pie'mɔnt] (-s) nt Piedmont
piepen ['pi:pən] vi to chirp; (Funkgerät etc) to bleep; **bei dir piepts wohl!** (umg) are you off your head?; **es war zum P~!** (umg) it was a scream!
piepsen ['pi:psən] vi = **piepen**
Piepser (umg) m pager, paging device
Piepsstimme f squeaky voice
Piepton m bleep
Pier [pi:ər] (-s, -s od -e) m jetty, pier
piesacken ['pi:zakən] (umg) vt to torment
Pietät [pie'tɛːt] f piety; reverence; **pietätlos** adj impious, irreverent
Pigment [pɪg'mɛnt] (-(e)s, -e) nt pigment
Pik [pi:k] (-s, -s) nt (Karten) spades; **einen ~ auf jdn haben** (umg) to have it in for sb
pikant [pi'kant] adj spicy, piquant; (anzüglich) suggestive
Pike (-, -n) f: **etw von der ~ auf lernen** (fig) to learn sth from the bottom up
pikiert [pi'ki:rt] adj offended
Pikkolo ['pɪkolo] (-s, -s) m = **Piccolo**
Piktogramm [pɪkto'gram] nt pictogram
Pilger, in ['pɪlgər(ɪn)] (-s, -) m(f) pilgrim; **Pilgerfahrt** f pilgrimage
pilgern vi to make a pilgrimage; (umg: gehen) to wend one's way
Pille ['pɪlə] (-, -n) f pill
Pilot, in [pi'lo:t(ɪn)] (-en, -en) m(f) pilot; **Pilotenschein** m pilot's licence (Brit) od license (US)
Pils [pɪls] (-, -) nt Pilsener (lager)
Pilsener [pɪlzənər], **Pilsner** [pɪlznər] (-s, -) nt Pilsner (lager)
Pilz [pɪlts] (-es, -e) m fungus; (essbar) mushroom; (giftig) toadstool; **wie ~e aus dem Boden schießen** (fig) to mushroom; **Pilzkrankheit** f fungal disease
Pimmel ['pɪməl] (-s, -) (umg) m (Penis) willie
pingelig ['pɪŋəliç] (umg) adj fussy
Pinguin ['pɪŋgui:n] (-s, -e) m penguin
Pinie ['pi:niə] f pine
Pinkel (-s, -) (umg) m: **ein feiner** od **vornehmer ~** a swell, Lord Muck (Brit) (umg)
pinkeln ['pɪŋkəln] (umg) vi to pee
Pinnwand ['pɪnvant] f pinboard
Pinsel ['pɪnzəl] (-s, -) m paintbrush
pinseln (umg) vt, vi to paint; (pej: malen) to daub
Pinte ['pɪntə] (-, -n) (umg) f (Lokal) boozer (Brit)
Pinzette [pɪn'tsɛtə] f tweezers pl
Pionier [pio'ni:r] (-s, -e) m pioneer; (Mil) sapper, engineer; **Pionierarbeit** f pioneering work; **Pionierunternehmen** nt pioneer company
Pipi [pi'pi:] (-s, -s) nt od m (Kindersprache) wee(-wee)
Pirat [pi'ra:t] (-en, -en) m pirate
Piratensender m pirate radio station
Pirsch [pɪrʃ] (-) f stalking
PISA-Studie ['pi:za-] f (Sch) PISA study
pissen ['pɪsən] (umg!) vi to (have a) piss (!); (regnen) to piss down (!)

Pistazie [pɪs'ta:tsiə] (-, -n) f pistachio
Piste ['pɪstə] (-, -n) f (Ski) run, piste; (Aviat) runway
Pistole [pɪs'to:lə] (-, -n) f pistol; **wie aus der ~ geschossen** (fig) like a shot; **jdm die ~ auf die Brust setzen** (fig) to hold a pistol to sb's head
pitschenass ['pɪtʃə'nas], **pitschnass** ['pɪtʃnas] (umg) adj soaking (wet)
Pizza ['pɪtsa] (-, -s) f pizza
PKW, Pkw ['pe:ka:ve:] (-(s), -(s)) m abk = **Personenkraftwagen**
Pl. abk (= Plural) pl.; (= Platz) Sq.
Plackerei [plakə'raɪ] f drudgery
plädieren [plɛ'di:rən] vi to plead
Plädoyer [plɛdoa'je:] (-s, -s) nt speech for the defence; (fig) plea
Plage ['pla:gə] (-, -n) f plague; (Mühe) nuisance; **Plagegeist** m pest, nuisance
plagen vt to torment ▷ vr to toil, slave
Plagiat [plagi'a:t] (-(e)s, -e) nt plagiarism
Plakat [pla'ka:t] (-(e)s, -e) nt poster; (aus Pappe) placard
plakativ [plaka'ti:f] adj striking, bold
Plakatwand f hoarding, billboard (US)
Plakette [pla'kɛtə] (-, -n) f (Abzeichen) badge; (Münze) commemorative coin; (an Wänden) plaque
Plan [pla:n] (-(e)s, ̈-e) m plan; (Karte) map; **Pläne schmieden** to make plans; **nach ~ verlaufen** to go according to plan; **jdn auf den ~ rufen** (fig) to bring sb into the arena
Plane (-, -n) f tarpaulin
planen vt to plan; (Mord etc) to plot
Planer, in (-s, -) m(f) planner
Planet [pla'ne:t] (-en, -en) m planet
Planetenbahn f orbit (of a planet)
planieren [pla'ni:rən] vt to level off
Planierraupe f bulldozer
Planke ['plaŋkə] (-, -n) f plank
Plänkelei [plɛŋkə'laɪ] f skirmish(ing)
plänkeln ['plɛŋkəln] vi to skirmish
Plankton ['plaŋktɔn] (-s) nt plankton
planlos adj (Vorgehen) unsystematic; (Umherlaufen) aimless
planmäßig adj according to plan; (methodisch) systematic; (Eisenb) scheduled
Planschbecken, Plantschbecken ['planʃbekən] nt paddling pool
planschen, plantschen vi to splash
Plansoll nt output target
Planstelle f post
Plantage [plan'ta:ʒə] (-, -n) f plantation
Planung f planning
Planwagen m covered wagon
Planwirtschaft f planned economy
Plappermaul (umg) nt (Kind) chatterbox
plappern ['plapərn] vi to chatter
plärren ['plɛrən] vi (Mensch) to cry, whine; (Radio) to blare
Plasma ['plasma] (-s, **Plasmen**) nt plasma
Plastik¹ ['plastɪk] f sculpture
Plastik² ['plastɪk] (-s) nt (Kunststoff) plastic; **Plastikfolie** f plastic film; **Plastikgeschoss** nt

p

plastic bullet; **Plastiktüte** f plastic bag
Plastilin [plasti'li:n] (**-s**) nt Plasticine®
plastisch ['plastıʃ] adj plastic; **stell dir das ~ vor!** just picture it!
Platane [pla'ta:nə] (**-, -n**) f plane (tree)
Platin ['pla:ti:n] (**-s**) nt platinum
Platitüde [plati'ty:də] (**-, -n**) f platitude
platonisch [pla'to:nıʃ] adj platonic
platsch [platʃ] interj splash!
platschen vi to splash
plätschern ['pletʃərn] vi to babble
platschnass adj drenched
platt [plat] adj flat; (umg: überrascht) flabbergasted; (fig: geistlos) flat, boring; **einen P~en haben** to have a flat (umg), have a flat tyre (Brit) od tire (US)
plattdeutsch adj Low German
Platte (**-, -n**) f (Speisenplatte, Phot, Tech) plate; (Steinplatte) flag; (Kachel) tile; (Schallplatte) record; **kalte ~** cold dish; **die ~ kenne ich schon** (umg) I've heard all that before
Plätteisen nt iron
plätten vt, vi to iron
Platten- zW: **Plattenleger** (**-s, -**) m paver; **Plattenspieler** m record player; **Plattenteller** m turntable
Plattform f platform; (fig: Grundlage) basis
Plattfuß m flat foot; (Reifen) flat tyre (Brit) od tire (US)
Plattitüde [plati'ty:də] (**-, -n**) f platitude
Platz [plats] (**-es, ̈-e**) m place; (Sitzplatz) seat; (Raum) space, room; (in Stadt) square; (Sportplatz) playing field; **~ machen** to get out of the way; **~ nehmen** to take a seat; **jdm ~ machen** to make room for sb; **~ sparend** space-saving; **auf ~ zwei** in second place; **fehl am ~e sein** to be out of place; **seinen ~ behaupten** to stand one's ground; **das erste Hotel am ~** the best hotel in town; **auf die Plätze, fertig, los!** (beim Sport) on your marks, get set, go!; **einen Spieler vom ~ stellen** od **verweisen** (Sport) to send a player off; **Platzangst** f (Med) agoraphobia; (umg) claustrophobia; **Platzangst haben/bekommen** (umg) to feel/get claustrophobic; **Platzanweiser, in** (**-s, -**) m(f) usher(ette)
Plätzchen ['pletsçən] nt spot; (Gebäck) biscuit
platzen vi (Hilfsverb sein) to burst; (Bombe) to explode; (Naht, Hose, Haut) to split; (umg: scheitern: Geschäft) to fall through; (: Freundschaft) to break up; (: Theorie, Verschwörung) to collapse; (: Wechsel) to bounce; **vor Wut ~** (umg) to be bursting with anger
platzieren [pla'tsi:rən] vt to place ▷ vr (Sport) to be placed; (Tennis) to be seeded; (umg: sich setzen, stellen) to plant o.s.
Platz- zW: **Platzkarte** f seat reservation; **Platzkonzert** nt open-air concert; **Platzmangel** m lack of space; **Platzpatrone** f blank cartridge; **Platzregen** m downpour; **platzsparend** adj space-saving; **Platzverweis** m sending-off; **Platzwart** m (Sport) groundsman (Brit), groundskeeper (US);

Platzwunde f cut
Plauderei [plaudə'raı] f chat, conversation
plaudern ['plaudərn] vi to chat, talk
Plausch [plauʃ] (**-(e)s, -e**) (umg) m chat
plausibel [plau'zi:bəl] adj plausible
Play-back, Playback ['pleıbæk] (**-s, -s**) nt (Verfahren: Schallplatte) double-tracking; (TV) miming
plazieren [pla'tsi:rən] vt siehe **platzieren**
Plebejer, in [ple'be:jər(ın)] (**-s, -**) m(f) plebeian
plebejisch [ple'be:jıʃ] adj plebeian
pleite ['plaıtə] (umg) adj broke; **Pleite** (**-, -n**) f bankruptcy; (umg: Reinfall) flop; **Pleite machen** to go bust
Pleitegeier (umg) m (drohende Pleite) vulture; (Bankrotteur) bankrupt
plemplem [plɛm'plɛm] (umg) adj nuts
Plenarsitzung [ple'na:rzıtsʊŋ] f plenary session
Plenum ['ple:nʊm] (**-s, Plenen**) nt plenum
Pleuelstange ['plɔyəlʃtaŋə] f connecting rod
Plissee [plı'se:] (**-s, -s**) nt pleat
Plombe ['plɔmbə] (**-, -n**) f lead seal; (Zahnplombe) filling
plombieren [plɔm'bi:rən] vt to seal; (Zahn) to fill
Plotter ['plɔtər] (**-s, -s**) m (Comput) plotter
plötzlich ['plœtslıç] adj sudden ▷ adv suddenly; **~er Kindstod** SIDS
Pluderhose ['plu:dərho:zə] f harem trousers pl
plump [plʊmp] adj clumsy; (Hände) coarse; (Körper) shapeless; **~e Annäherungsversuche** very obvious advances
plumpsen (umg) vi to plump down, fall
Plumpsklo, Plumpsklosett (umg) nt earth closet
Plunder ['plʊndər] (**-s**) m junk, rubbish
Plundergebäck nt flaky pastry
plündern ['plʏndərn] vt to plunder; (Stadt) to sack ▷ vi to plunder
Plünderung ['plʏndərʊŋ] f plundering, sack, pillage
Plural ['plu:ra:l] (**-s, -e**) m plural; **im ~ stehen** to be (in the) plural
pluralistisch [plura'lıstıʃ] adj pluralistic
plus [plʊs] adv plus; **mit ~ minus null abschließen** (Comm) to break even; **Plus** (**-, -**) nt plus; (Fin) profit; (Vorteil) advantage
Plüsch [ply:ʃ] (**-(e)s, -e**) m plush; **Plüschtier** nt ≈ soft toy
Plus- zW: **Pluspol** m (Elek) positive pole; **Pluspunkt** m (Sport) point; (fig) point in sb's favour; **Plusquamperfekt** nt pluperfect
Plutonium [plu'to:nium] (**-s**) nt plutonium
PLZ abk = **Postleitzahl**
Pneu [pnɔy] (**-s, -s**) m abk (= Pneumatik) tyre (Brit), tire (US)
Po [po:] (**-s, -s**) (umg) m bum (Brit), fanny (US)
Pöbel ['pø:bəl] (**-s**) m mob, rabble
Pöbelei [pø:bə'laı] f vulgarity
pöbelhaft adj low, vulgar
pochen ['pɔxən] vi to knock; (Herz) to pound; **auf etw** akk **~** (fig) to insist on sth

Pocken ['pɔkən] *pl* smallpox *sing*

Pockenimpfung, Pockenschutzimpfung *f* smallpox vaccination

Podcast ['pɔtka:st] (**-s, -s**) *m* podcast

Podest [po'dɛst] (**-(e)s, -e**) *nt od m* (*Sockel, fig*) pedestal; (*Podium*) platform

Podium ['po:diʊm] *nt* podium

Podiumsdiskussion *f* panel discussion

Poesie [poe'zi:] *f* poetry

Poet [po'e:t] (**-en, -en**) *m* poet; **poetisch** *adj* poetic

Pointe [po'ɛ̃:tə] (**-, -n**) *f* point; (*eines Witzes*) punch line

pointiert [poɛ̃'ti:rt] *adj* trenchant, pithy

Pokal [po'ka:l] (**-s, -e**) *m* goblet; (*Sport*) cup; **Pokalspiel** *nt* cup tie

Pökelfleisch ['pø:kəlflaɪʃ] *nt* salt meat

pökeln *vt* (*Fleisch, Fisch*) to pickle, salt

Poker ['po:kər] (**-s**) *nt* poker

pokern ['po:kərn] *vi* to play poker

Pol [po:l] (**-s, -e**) *m* pole; **der ruhende ~** (*fig*) the calming influence

pol. *abk* = **politisch; polizeilich**

polar [po'la:r] *adj* polar

polarisieren [polari'zi:rən] *vt, vr* to polarize

Polarkreis *m* polar circle; **nördlicher/ südlicher ~** Arctic/Antarctic Circle

Polarstern *m* Pole Star

Pole ['po:lə] (**-n, -n**) *m* Pole

Polemik [po'le:mɪk] *f* polemics *sing*

polemisch *adj* polemical

polemisieren [polemi'zi:rən] *vi* to polemicize

Polen ['po:lən] (**-s**) *nt* Poland

Polente (**-**) (*veraltet: umg*) *f* cops *pl*

Police [po'li:s(ə)] (**-, -n**) *f* insurance policy

Polier [po'li:r] (**-s, -e**) *m* foreman

polieren *vt* to polish

Poliklinik [poli'kli:nɪk] *f* outpatients (department) *sing*

Polin *f* Pole, Polish woman

Politesse [poli'tɛsə] (**-, -n**) *f* (*Frau*) ≈ traffic warden (*Brit*)

Politik [poli'ti:k] *f* politics *sing*; (*eine bestimmte*) policy; **in die ~ gehen** to go into politics; **eine ~ verfolgen** to pursue a policy

Politiker, in [po'li:tikər(ɪn)] (**-s, -**) *m(f)* politician

politisch [po'li:tɪʃ] *adj* political

politisieren [politi'zi:rən] *vi* to talk politics ▷ *vt* to politicize; **jdn ~ to** make sb politically aware

Politur [poli'tu:r] *f* polish

Polizei [poli'tsaɪ] *f* police; **Polizeiaufsicht** *f*: **unter Polizeiaufsicht stehen** to have to report regularly to the police; **Polizeibeamte, r** *m* police officer; **polizeilich** *adj* police *attrib*; **sich polizeilich melden** to register with the police; **polizeiliches Führungszeugnis** *certificate of "no criminal record" issued by the police*; **Polizeipräsidium** *nt* police headquarters *pl*; **Polizeirevier** *nt* police station; **Polizeispitzel** *m* police spy, informer; **Polizeistaat** *m* police state; **Polizeistreife** *f* police patrol;

Polizeistunde *f* closing time; **Polizeiwache** *f* police station; **Polizeiwidrig** *adj* illegal

Polizist, in [poli'tsɪst(ɪn)] (**-en, -en**) *m(f)* policeman/-woman

Pollen ['pɔlən] (**-s, -**) *m* pollen

poln. *abk* = **polnisch**

polnisch ['pɔlnɪʃ] *adj* Polish

Polohemd ['po:lohɛmt] *nt* polo shirt

Polster ['pɔlstər] (**-s, -**) *nt* cushion; (*Polsterung*) upholstery; (*in Kleidung*) padding; (*fig: Geld*) reserves *pl*; **Polsterer** (**-s, -**) *m* upholsterer; **Polstergarnitur** *f* three-piece suite; **Polstermöbel** *pl* upholstered furniture *sing*

polstern *vt* to upholster; (*Kleidung*) to pad; **sie ist gut gepolstert** (*umg*) she's well padded; (: *finanziell*) she's not short of the odd penny

Polsterung *f* upholstery

Polterabend ['pɔltəra:bənt] *m* party on the eve of a wedding

poltern *vi* (*Krach machen*) to crash; (*schimpfen*) to rant

Polygamie [polyga'mi:] *f* polygamy

Polynesien [poly'ne:ziən] (**-s**) *nt* Polynesia

Polynesier, in [poly'ne:ziər(ɪn)] (**-s, -**) *m(f)* Polynesian

polynesisch *adj* Polynesian

Polyp [po'ly:p] (**-en, -en**) *m* polyp; (*umg*) cop; **Polypen** *pl* (*Med*) adenoids *pl*

Polytechnikum [poly'tɛçnikʊm] (**-s, Polytechnika**) *nt* polytechnic, poly (*umg*)

Pomade [po'ma:də] *f* pomade

Pommern ['pɔmərn] (**-s**) *nt* Pomerania

Pommes frites [pɔm'frɪt] *pl* chips *pl* (*Brit*), French fried potatoes *pl* (*Brit*), French fries *pl* (*US*)

Pomp [pɔmp] (**-(e)s**) *m* pomp

pompös [pɔm'pø:s] *adj* grandiose

Pontius ['pɔntsius] *m*: **von ~ zu Pilatus** from pillar to post

Pony ['pɔni] (**-s, -s**) *m* (*Frisur*) fringe (*Brit*), bangs *pl* (*US*) ▷ *nt* (*Pferd*) pony

Pop [pɔp] (**-s**) *m* (*Mus*) pop; (*Kunst*) pop art

Popelin [popə'li:n] (**-s, -e**) *m* poplin

Popeline (**-, -n**) *f* poplin

Popkonzert *nt* pop concert

Popmusik *f* pop music

Popo [po'po:] (**-s, -s**) (*umg*) *m* bottom, bum (*Brit*)

populär [popu'lɛ:r] *adj* popular

Popularität [populari'tɛ:t] *f* popularity

populärwissenschaftlich *adj* popular science

Pore ['po:rə] (**-, -n**) *f* pore

Porno ['pɔrno] (**-s, no pl**) (*umg*) *m* porn

Pornografie [pɔrnogra'fi:] *f* pornography

pornografisch [pɔrno'gra:fɪʃ] *adj* pornographic

porös [po'rø:s] *adj* porous

Porree ['pɔre] (**-s, -s**) *m* leek

Portal [pɔr'ta:l] (**-s, -e**) *nt* portal

Portefeuille [pɔrt(ə)'fø:j] (**-s, -s**) *nt* (*Pol, Fin*) portfolio

Portemonnaie [pɔrtmɔ'nɛ:] (**-s, -s**) *nt* purse

Portier [pɔrti'e:] (**-s, -s**) *m* porter; (*Pförtner*) porter, doorkeeper, doorman

Portion [pɔrtsi'o:n] *f* portion, helping;

P

(*umg*: *Anteil*) amount; **eine halbe ~** (*fig*: *umg*: *Person*) a half-pint; **eine ~ Kaffee** a pot of coffee

Portmonee [pɔrtmɔ'neː] (**-s, -s**) *nt* purse

Porto ['pɔrto] (**-s, -s** *od* **Porti**) *nt* postage; **~ zahlt Empfänger** postage paid; **portofrei** *adj* post-free, (postage) prepaid

Porträt [pɔr'trɛː] (**-s, -s**) *nt* portrait

porträtieren [pɔrtrɛ'tiːrən] *vt* to paint (a portrait of); (*fig*) to portray

Portugal ['pɔrtugal] (**-s**) *nt* Portugal

Portugiese [pɔrtu'giːzə] (**-n, -n**) *m* Portuguese

Portugiesin *f* Portuguese

portugiesisch *adj* Portuguese

Portwein ['pɔrtvaɪn] *m* port

Porzellan [pɔrtsɛ'laːn] (**-s, -e**) *nt* china, porcelain; (*Geschirr*) china

Posaune [po'zaʊnə] (**-, -n**) *f* trombone

Pose ['poːzə] (**-, -n**) *f* pose

posieren [po'ziːrən] *vi* to pose

Position [pozitsi'oːn] *f* position; (*Comm*: *auf Liste*) item

Positionslichter *pl* navigation lights *pl*

Positionspapier *nt* position paper

positiv ['poːzitiːf] *adj* positive; **~ zu etw stehen** to be in favour (*Brit*) *od* favor (*US*) of sth; **Positiv** (**-s, -e**) *nt* (*Phot*) positive

Positur [pozi'tuːr] *f* posture, attitude; **sich in ~ setzen** *od* **stellen** to adopt a posture

Posse ['pɔsə] (**-, -n**) *f* farce

possessiv ['pɔsɛsiːf] *adj* possessive; **Possessiv** (**-s, -e**) *nt*, **Possessivpronomen** *nt* possessive pronoun

possierlich [pɔ'siːrlɪç] *adj* funny

Post [pɔst] (**-, -en**) *f* post (office); (*Briefe*) post, mail; **ist ~ für mich da?** are there any letters for me?; **mit getrennter ~** under separate cover; **etw auf die ~ geben** to post (*Brit*) *od* mail sth; **auf die** *od* **zur ~ gehen** to go to the post office; **Postamt** *nt* post office; **Postanweisung** *f* postal order (*Brit*), money order; **Postbote** *m* postman (*Brit*), mailman (*US*)

Posten (**-s, -**) *m* post, position; (*Comm*) item; (: *Warenmenge*) quantity, lot; (*auf Liste*) entry; (*Mil*) sentry; (*Streikposten*) picket; **~ beziehen** to take up one's post; **nicht ganz auf dem ~ sein** (*nicht gesund sein*) to be off-colour (*Brit*) *od* off-color (*US*)

posten ['poːstən] *vt* (*ins Internet*) to post

Poster ['poːstər] (**-s, -(s)**) *nt* poster

Postf. *abk* (= *Postfach*) PO Box

Post- *zW*: **Postfach** *nt* post office box; **Postkarte** *f* postcard; **postlagernd** *adv* poste restante; **Postleitzahl** *f* postal code

postmodern [pɔstmo'dɛrn] *adj* postmodern

Post- *zW*: **Postscheckkonto** *nt* Post Office Giro account (*Brit*); **Postsparbuch** *nt* post office savings book (*Brit*); **Postsparkasse** *f* post office savings bank; **Poststempel** *m* postmark; **postwendend** *adv* by return (of post); **Postwertzeichen** *nt* (*form*) postage stamp; **Postwurfsendung** *f* direct mail advertising

potent [po'tɛnt] *adj* potent; (*fig*) high-powered

Potential [potɛntsi'aːl] (**-s, -e**) *nt* = **Potenzial**

potentiell [potɛntsi'ɛl] *adj* = **potenziell**

Potenz [po'tɛnts] *f* power; (*eines Mannes*) potency

Potenzial [potɛntsi'aːl] (**-s, -e**) *nt* potential

potenziell [potɛntsi'ɛl] *adj* potential

potenzieren [potɛn'tsiːrən] *vt* (*Math*) to raise to the power of

Potpourri ['pɔtpuri] (**-s, -s**) *nt*: **~ (aus)** (*Mus*) medley (of); (*fig*) assortment (of)

Pott [pɔt] (**-(e)s, ̈-e**) (*umg*) *m* pot; **potthässlich** (*umg*) *adj* ugly as sin

pp., ppa. *abk* (= *per procura*) p.p.

Präambel [prɛ'|ambəl] (**-, -n**) *f* (+*gen*) preamble (to)

Pracht [praxt] (**-**) *f* splendour (*Brit*), splendor (*US*), magnificence; **es ist eine wahre ~** it's (really) marvellous; **Prachtexemplar** *nt* beauty (*umg*); (*fig*: *Mensch*) fine specimen

prächtig ['prɛçtiç] *adj* splendid

Prachtstück *nt* showpiece

prachtvoll *adj* splendid, magnificent

prädestinieren [prɛdɛsti'niːrən] *vt* to predestine

Prädikat [prɛdi'kaːt] (**-(e)s, -e**) *nt* title; (*Gram*) predicate; (*Zensur*) distinction; **Wein mit ~** special quality wine

Prag [praːk] (**-s**) *nt* Prague

prägen ['prɛːgən] *vt* to stamp; (*Münze*) to mint; (*Ausdruck*) to coin; (*Charakter*) to form; (*kennzeichnen*: *Stadtbild*) to characterize; **das Erlebnis prägte ihn** the experience left its mark on him

prägend *adj* having a forming *od* shaping influence

pragmatisch [pra'gmaːtɪʃ] *adj* pragmatic

prägnant [prɛ'gnant] *adj* concise, terse

Prägnanz *f* conciseness, terseness

Prägung ['prɛːgʊŋ] *f* minting; forming; (*Eigenart*) character, stamp

prahlen ['praːlən] *vi* to boast, brag

Prahlerei [praːlə'raɪ] *f* boasting

prahlerisch *adj* boastful

Praktik ['praktɪk] *f* practice

praktikabel [praktɪ'kaːbəl] *adj* practicable

Praktikant, in [praktɪ'kant(ɪn)] *m(f)* trainee

Praktikum (**-s, Praktika** *od* **Praktiken**) *nt* practical training

praktisch ['praktɪʃ] *adj* practical, handy; **~er Arzt** general practitioner; **~es Beispiel** concrete example

praktizieren [praktɪ'tsiːrən] *vt, vi* to practise (*Brit*), practice (*US*)

Praline [pra'liːnə] *f* chocolate

prall [pral] *adj* firmly rounded; (*Segel*) taut; (*Arme*) plump; (*Sonne*) blazing

prallen *vi* to bounce, rebound; (*Sonne*) to blaze

prallvoll *adj* full to bursting; (*Brieftasche*) bulging

Prämie ['prɛːmiə] *f* premium; (*Belohnung*) award, prize

prämienbegünstigt *adj* with benefit of premiums

prämiensparen vi to save in a bonus scheme
prämieren [prɛˈmiːrən] vt to give an award to
Pranger [ˈpraŋər] **(-s, -)** m (Hist) pillory; **jdn an den ~ stellen** (fig) to pillory sb
Pranke [ˈpraŋkə] **(-, -n)** f (Tierpranke: umg: Hand) paw
Präparat [prɛpaˈraːt] **(-(e)s, -e)** nt (Biol) preparation; (Med) medicine
präparieren vt (konservieren) to preserve; (Med: zerlegen) to dissect
Präposition [prɛpozitsiˈoːn] f preposition
Prärie [prɛˈriː] f prairie
Präs. abk = **Präsens; Präsident**
Präsens [ˈprɛːzɛns] **(-)** nt present tense
präsent adj: **etw ~ haben** to have sth at hand
präsentieren [prɛzɛnˈtiːrən] vt to present
Präsenzbibliothek f reference library
Präservativ [prɛzɛrvaˈtiːf] **(-s, -e)** nt condom, sheath
Präsident, in [prɛziˈdɛnt(ɪn)] m(f) president; **Präsidentschaft** f presidency; **Präsidentschaftskandidat** m presidential candidate
Präsidium [prɛˈziːdiʊm] nt presidency, chairmanship; (Polizeipräsidium) police headquarters pl
prasseln [ˈprasəln] vi (Feuer) to crackle; (Hagel) to drum; (Wörter) to rain down
prassen [ˈprasən] vi to live it up
Präteritum [prɛˈteːritʊm] **(-s, Präterita)** nt preterite
Pratze [ˈpratsə] **(-, -n)** f paw
Präventiv- [prɛvɛnˈtiːf] in zw preventive
Praxis [ˈpraksɪs] **(-, Praxen)** f practice; (Erfahrung) experience; (Behandlungsraum) surgery; (von Anwalt) office; **die ~ sieht anders aus** the reality is different; **ein Beispiel aus der ~** an example from real life
Präzedenzfall [prɛtseˈdɛntsfal] m precedent
präzis [prɛˈtsiːs] adj precise
Präzision [prɛtsiziˈoːn] f precision
PR-Chef m PR officer
predigen [ˈpreːdɪgən] vt, vi to preach
Prediger (-s, -) m preacher
Predigt [ˈpreːdɪçt] **(-, -en)** f sermon
Preis [praɪs] **(-es, -e)** m price; (Siegespreis) prize; (Auszeichnung) award; **um keinen ~** not at any price; **um jeden ~** at all costs; **Preisangebot** nt quotation; **Preisausschreiben** nt competition; **Preisbindung** f price-fixing; **Preisbrecher** m (Firma) undercutter
Preiselbeere f cranberry
preisempfindlich adj price-sensitive
preisen [ˈpraɪzən] unreg vt to praise; **sich glücklich ~** (geh) to count o.s. lucky
Preis- zW: **Preisentwicklung** f price trend; **Preiserhöhung** f price increase; **Preisfrage** f question of price; (Wettbewerb) prize question
preisgeben unreg vt to abandon; (opfern) to sacrifice; (zeigen) to expose
Preis- zW: **Preisgefälle** nt price gap; **preisgekrönt** adj prizewinning; **Preisgericht** nt jury; **preisgünstig** adj inexpensive;

Preisindex m price index; **Preiskrieg** m price war; **Preislage** f price range; **preislich** adj price attr, in price; **Preisliste** f price list, tariff; **Preisnachlass** m discount; **Preisschild** nt price tag; **Preisspanne** f price range; **Preissturz** m slump; **Preisträger** m prizewinner; **preiswert** adj inexpensive
prekär [preˈkɛːr] adj precarious
Prellbock [ˈprɛlbɔk] m buffers pl
prellen vt to bruise; (fig) to cheat, swindle
Prellung f bruise
Premiere [prəmiˈɛːrə] **(-, -n)** f premiere
Premierminister, in [prəmiˈeːmɪnɪstər(ɪn)] m(f) prime minister, premier
Presse [ˈprɛsə] **(-, -n)** f press; **Presseagentur** f press od news agency; **Presseausweis** m press pass; **Presseerklärung** f press release; **Pressefreiheit** f freedom of the press; **Pressekonferenz** f press conference; **Pressemeldung** f press report
pressen vt to press
Presse- zW: **Pressesprecher, in** m(f) spokesperson, press officer; **Pressestelle** f press office; **Presseverlautbarung** f press release
pressieren [prɛˈsiːrən] vi to be in a hurry; **es pressiert** it's urgent
Pressluft [ˈprɛslʊft] f compressed air; **Pressluftbohrer** m pneumatic drill
Prestige [prɛsˈtiːʒə] **(-s)** nt prestige; **Prestigeverlust** m loss of prestige
Preuße [ˈprɔʏsə] **(-n, -n)** m Prussian
Preußen (-s) nt Prussia
Preußin f Prussian
preußisch adj Prussian
prickeln [ˈprɪkəln] vi to tingle; (kitzeln) to tickle; (Bläschen bilden) to sparkle, bubble ▷ vt to tickle
pries etc [priːs] vb siehe **preisen**
Priester [ˈpriːstər] **(-s, -)** m priest
Priesterin f priestess
Priesterweihe f ordination (to the priesthood)
Prima [ˈpriːma] **(-, Primen)** f (früher) eighth and ninth year of German secondary school
prima adj inv first-class, excellent
primär [priˈmɛːr] adj primary; **Primärdaten** pl primary data pl
Primel [ˈpriːməl] **(-, -n)** f primrose
primitiv [primiˈtiːf] adj primitive
Primzahl [ˈpriːmtsaːl] f prime (number)
Prinz [prɪnts] **(-en, -en)** m prince
Prinzessin [prɪnˈtsɛsɪn] f princess
Prinzip [prɪnˈtsiːp] **(-s, -ien)** nt principle; **aus ~** on principle; **im ~** in principle
prinzipiell [prɪntsiˈpiɛl] adj on principle
prinzipienlos adj unprincipled
Priorität [prioriˈtɛːt] f priority; **Prioritäten** pl (Comm) preference shares pl, preferred stock sing (US); **~en setzen** to establish one's priorities
Prise [ˈpriːzə] **(-, -n)** f pinch
Prisma [ˈprɪsma] **(-s, Prismen)** nt prism
privat [priˈvaːt] adj private; **jdn ~ sprechen** to speak to sb in private; **Privatbesitz** m private

P

property; **Privatdozent** m outside lecturer; **Privatfernsehen** nt commercial television; **Privatgespräch** nt private conversation; (am Telefon) private call

privatisieren [privati'ziːrən] vt to privatize

Privatschule f private school

Privatvorsorge f (fürs Alter) private pension scheme; (für Gesundheit) health insurance scheme

Privatwirtschaft f private sector

Privileg [privi'leːk] (-(e)s, -ien) nt privilege

Pro [proː] (-) nt pro

pro präp +akk per; ~ **Stück** each, apiece

Probe ['proːbə] (-, -n) f test; (Teststück) sample; (Theat) rehearsal; **jdn auf die ~ stellen** to put sb to the test; **er ist auf ~ angestellt** he's employed for a probationary period; **zur ~** to try out; **Probebohrung** f (Öl) exploration well; **Probeexemplar** nt specimen copy; **Probefahrt** f test drive; **Probelauf** m trial run

proben vt to try; (Theat) to rehearse

Probe- zW: **Probestück** nt specimen; **probeweise** adv on approval; **Probezeit** f probation period

probieren [pro'biːrən] vt to try; (Wein, Speise) to taste, sample ▷ vi to try; to taste

Problem [pro'bleːm] (-s, -e) nt problem; **vor einem ~ stehen** to be faced with a problem

Problematik [proble:'maːtɪk] f problem

problematisch [proble:'maːtɪʃ] adj problematic

problemlos adj problem-free

Problemstellung f way of looking at a problem

Produkt [pro'dʊkt] (-(e)s, -e) nt product; (Agr) produce no pl

Produktentwicklung f product development

Produktion [prodʊktsi'oːn] f production

Produktionsleiter m production manager

Produktionsstätte f (Halle) shop floor

produktiv [prodʊk'tiːf] adj productive

Produktivität [prodʊktivi'tɛːt] f productivity

Produzent [produ'tsɛnt] m manufacturer; (Film) producer

produzieren [produ'tsiːrən] vt to produce ▷ vr to show off

Prof. [prof] abk (= Professor) Prof

profan [pro'faːn] adj (weltlich) secular, profane; (gewöhnlich) mundane

professionell [profesio'nɛl] adj professional

Professor, in [pro'fɛsɔr, profɛ'soːrɪn] m(f) professor; (Österr: Gymnasiallehrer) grammar school teacher (Brit), high school teacher (US)

Professur [profɛ'suːr] f: ~ **(für)** chair (of)

Profi ['proːfi] (-s, -s) m abk (= Professional) pro

Profil [pro'fiːl] (-s, -e) nt profile; (fig) image; (Querschnitt) cross section; (Längsschnitt) vertical section; (von Reifen, Schuhsohle) tread

profilieren [profi'liːrən] vr to create an image for o.s.

Profilsohle f sole with a tread

Profit [pro'fiːt] (-(e)s, -e) m profit

profitgeil adj (umg) profit-greedy

profitieren [profi'tiːrən] vi: ~ **(von)** to profit

(from)

Profitmacherei (umg) f profiteering

pro forma adv as a matter of form

Pro-forma-Rechnung f pro forma invoice

Prognose [pro'gnoːzə] (-, -n) f prediction, prognosis

Programm [pro'gram] (-s, -e) nt programme (Brit), program (US); (Comput) program; (TV: Sender) channel; (Kollektion) range; **nach ~** as planned; **Programmfehler** m (Comput) bug; **programmgemäß** adj according to plan; **Programmhinweis** m (Rundf, TV) programme (Brit) od program (US) announcement

programmieren [progra'miːrən] vt to programme (Brit), program (US); (Comput) to program; **auf etw** akk **programmiert sein** (fig) to be geared to sth

Programmierer, in (-s, -) m(f) programmer

Programmiersprache f (Comput) programming language

Programmierung f (Comput) programming

Programmvorschau f preview; (Film) trailer

progressiv [progrɛ'siːf] adj progressive

Projekt [pro'jɛkt] (-(e)s, -e) nt project

Projektleiter, in m(f) project manager(ess)

Projektor [pro'jɛktɔr] m projector

projizieren [proji'tsiːrən] vt to project

proklamieren [prokla'miːrən] vt to proclaim

Pro-Kopf-Einkommen nt per capita income

Prokura [pro'kuːra] (-, **Prokuren**) f (form) power of attorney

Prokurist, in [proku'rɪst(ɪn)] m(f) attorney

Prolet [pro'leːt] (-en, -en) m prole, pleb

Proletariat [proletari'aːt] (-(e)s, -e) nt proletariat

Proletarier [prole'taːriər] (-s, -) m proletarian

Prolog [pro'loːk] (-(e)s, -e) m prologue

Promenade [promə'naːdə] (-, -n) f promenade

Promenadenmischung f (hum) mongrel

Promille [pro'mɪlə] (-(s), -) (umg) nt alcohol level; **Promillegrenze** f legal (alcohol) limit

prominent [promi'nɛnt] adj prominent

Prominenz [promi'nɛnts] f VIPs pl

Promoter [pro'moːtər] (-s, -) m promoter

Promotion [promotsi'oːn] f doctorate, Ph.D.

promovieren [promo'viːrən] vi to receive a doctorate etc

prompt [prɔmpt] adj prompt

Pronomen [pro'noːmɛn] (-s, -) nt pronoun

Propaganda [propa'ganda] (-) f propaganda

propagieren [propa'giːrən] vt to propagate

Propangas [pro'paːngaːs] nt propane gas

Propeller [pro'pɛlər] (-s, -) m propeller

proper ['prɔpər] (umg) adj neat, tidy

Prophet, in [pro'feːt(ɪn)] (-en, -en) m(f) prophet(ess)

prophezeien [profe'tsaɪən] vt to prophesy

Prophezeiung f prophecy

prophylaktisch [profy'laktɪʃ] adj prophylactic (form), preventive

Proportion [proportsi'oːn] f proportion

proportional [proportsio'naːl] adj proportional; **Proportionalschrift** f (Comput) proportional printing

proportioniert [proportsio'ni:rt] *adj*: **gut/ schlecht** ~ well/badly proportioned

Proporz [pro'ports] (**-es, -e**) *m* proportional representation

Prosa ['pro:za] (-) *f* prose

prosaisch [pro'za:ıʃ] *adj* prosaic

prosit ['pro:zıt] *interj* cheers!; ~ **Neujahr!** happy New Year!

Prospekt [pro'spɛkt] (**-(e)s, -e**) *m* leaflet, brochure

prost [pro:st] *interj* cheers!

Prostata ['prostata] (-) *f* prostate gland

Prostituierte [prostitu'i:rtə] (**-n, -n**) *f* prostitute

Prostitution [prostitutsi'o:n] *f* prostitution

prot. [prot] *abk* = **protestantisch**

Protektionismus [protɛktsio'nısmʊs] *m* protectionism

Protektorat [protɛkto'ra:t] (**-(e)s, -e**) *nt* (*Schirmherrschaft*) patronage; (*Schutzgebiet*) protectorate

Protest [pro'tɛst] (**-(e)s, -e**) *m* protest

Protestant, in [protɛs'tant(ın)] *m(f)* Protestant; **protestantisch** *adj* Protestant

Protestbewegung *f* protest movement

protestieren [protɛs'ti:rən] *vi* to protest

Protestkundgebung *f* (protest) rally

Protestpartei *f* protest party

Prothese [pro'te:zə] (**-, -n**) *f* artificial limb; (*Zahnprothese*) dentures *pl*

Protokoll [proto'kɔl] (**-s, -e**) *nt* register; (*Niederschrift*) record; (*von Sitzung*) minutes *pl*; (*diplomatisch*) protocol; (*Polizeiprotokoll*) statement; (*Strafzettel*) ticket; (**das**) ~ **führen** (*bei Sitzung*) to take the minutes; (*bei Gericht*) to make a transcript of the proceedings; **etw zu** ~ **geben** to have sth put on record; (*bei Polizei*) to say sth in one's statement; **Protokollführer** *m* secretary; (*Jur*) clerk (of the court)

protokollieren [protoko'li:rən] *vt* to take down; (*Bemerkung*) to enter in the minutes

Proton ['pro:tɔn] (**-s, -en**) *nt* proton

Prototyp *m* prototype

Protz ['prots] (**-es, -e**) *m* swank; **protzen** *vi* to show off

protzig *adj* ostentatious

Proviant [provi'ant] (**-s, -e**) *m* provisions *pl*, supplies *pl*

Provinz [pro'vınts] (**-, -en**) *f* province; **das ist finsterste** ~ (*pej*) it's a cultural backwater

provinziell [provın'tsiɛl] *adj* provincial

Provision [provizi'o:n] *f* (*Comm*) commission

provisorisch [provi'zo:rıʃ] *adj* provisional

Provisorium [provi'zo:rium] (**-s, -ien**) *nt* provisional arrangement

Provokation [provokatsi'o:n] *f* provocation

provokativ [provoka'ti:f] *adj* provocative, provoking

provokatorisch [provoka'to:rıʃ] *adj* provocative, provoking

provozieren [provo'tsi:rən] *vt* to provoke

Proz. *abk* (= *Prozent*) pc

Prozedur [protse'du:r] *f* procedure; (*pej*) carry-on; **die** ~ **beim Zahnarzt** the ordeal at the dentist's

Prozent [pro'tsɛnt] (**-(e)s, -e**) *nt* per cent, percentage; **Prozentrechnung** *f* percentage calculation; **Prozentsatz** *m* percentage

prozentual [protsɛntu'a:l] *adj* percentage *attrib*

Prozess [pro'tsɛs] (**-es, -e**) *m* trial, case; (*Vorgang*) process; **es zum** ~ **kommen lassen** to go to court; **mit jdm/etw kurzen** ~ **machen** (*fig: umg*) to make short work of sb/sth; **Prozessanwalt** *m* barrister, counsel; **Prozessführung** *f* handling of a case

prozessieren [protse'si:rən] *vi*: ~ (**mit**) to bring an action (against), go to law (with *od* against)

Prozession [protsesi'o:n] *f* procession

Prozesskosten *pl* (legal) costs *pl*

prüde ['pry:də] *adj* prudish

Prüderie [pry:də'ri:] *f* prudery

prüfen ['pry:fən] *vt* to examine, test; (*nachprüfen*) to check; (*erwägen*) to consider; (*Geschäftsbücher*) to audit; (*mustern*) to scrutinize

Prüfer, in (**-s, -**) *m(f)* examiner

Prüfling *m* examinee

Prüfstein *m* touchstone

Prüfung *f* (*Sch, Univ*) examination, exam; (*Überprüfung*) checking; **eine** ~ **machen** to take *od* sit (*Brit*) an exam(ination); **durch eine** ~ **fallen** to fail an exam(ination)

Prüfungs- *zW*: **Prüfungsausschuss** *m* examining board; **Prüfungskommission** *f* examining board; **Prüfungsordnung** *f* exam(ination) regulations *pl*

Prügel ['pry:gəl] (**-s, -**) *m* cudgel ⊳ *pl* beating *sing*

Prügelei [pry:gə'laı] *f* fight

Prügelknabe *m* scapegoat

prügeln *vt* to beat ⊳ *vr* to fight

Prügelstrafe *f* corporal punishment

Prunk [prʊŋk] (**-(e)s**) *m* pomp, show; **prunkvoll** *adj* splendid, magnificent

prusten ['pru:stən] (*umg*) *vi* to snort

PS *abk* (= *Pferdestärke*) hp; (= *Postskript(um)*) PS

Psalm [psalm] (**-s, -en**) *m* psalm

pseudo- [psɔʏdo] *in zw* pseudo

Psychiater [psy'çia:tər] (**-s, -**) *m* psychiatrist

Psychiatrie [psyçia'tri:] *f* psychiatry

psychiatrisch [psy'çia:trıʃ] *adj* psychiatric; ~**e Klinik** mental *od* psychiatric hospital

psychisch ['psy:çıʃ] *adj* psychological; ~ **gestört** emotionally *od* psychologically disturbed

Psychoanalyse [psyçoana'ly:zə] *f* psychoanalysis

Psychologe [psyço'lo:gə] (**-n, -n**) *m* psychologist

Psychologie *f* psychology

Psychologin *f* psychologist

psychologisch *adj* psychological

Psychotherapie *f* psychotherapy

PTT (*Schweiz*) *abk* (= *Post, Telefon, Telegraf*) postal and telecommunication services

Pubertät [pubɛr'tɛ:t] *f* puberty

publik [pu'bli:k] *adj*: ~ **werden** to become

263

public knowledge

Publikum ['pu:blikʊm] (-s) nt audience; (Sport) crowd; **das ~ in dieser Bar ist sehr gemischt** you get a very mixed group of people using this bar

Publikumserfolg m popular success

Publikumsverkehr m: „**heute kein ~**" "closed today for public business"

publizieren [publi'tsi:rən] vt to publish

Pudding ['pʊdɪŋ] (-s, -e od -s) m blancmange; **Puddingpulver** nt custard powder

Pudel ['pu:dəl] (-s, -) m poodle; **das also ist des ~s Kern** (fig) that's what it's really all about

pudelwohl (umg) adj: **sich ~ fühlen** to feel on top of the world

Puder ['pu:dər] (-s, -) m powder; **Puderdose** f powder compact

pudern vt to powder

Puderzucker m icing sugar (Brit), confectioner's sugar (US)

Puerto Ricaner, in [puɛrtori'ka:nər(ɪn)] (-s, -) m(f) Puerto Rican

puerto-ricanisch adj Puerto Rican

Puerto Rico [pu'ɛrto'ri:ko] (-s) nt Puerto Rico

Puff¹ [pʊf] (-(e)s, -e) m (Wäschepuff) linen basket; (Sitzpuff) pouf

Puff² (-(e)s, -e) (umg) m (Stoß) push

Puff³ (-s, -s) (umg) m od nt (Bordell) brothel

Puffer (-s, -) m (auch Comput) buffer; **Pufferspeicher** m (Comput) cache; **Pufferstaat** m buffer state; **Pufferzone** f buffer zone

Puffreis m puffed rice

Pulle ['pʊlə] (-, -n) (umg) f bottle; **volle ~ fahren** (umg) to drive flat out

Pulli ['pʊli] (-s, -s) (umg) m sweater, jumper (Brit)

Pullover [pʊ'lo:vər] (-s, -) m sweater, jumper (Brit)

Pullunder [pʊ'lʊndər] (-s, -) m slipover

Puls [pʊls] (-es, -e) m pulse; **Pulsader** f artery; **sich** dat **die Pulsader(n) aufschneiden** to slash one's wrists

pulsieren [pʊl'zi:rən] vi to throb, pulsate

Pult [pʊlt] (-(e)s, -e) nt desk

Pulver ['pʊlfər] (-s, -) nt powder; **Pulverfass** nt powder keg; **(wie) auf einem Pulverfass sitzen** (fig) to be sitting on (top of) a volcano

pulverig adj powdery

pulverisieren [pʊlveri'zi:rən] vt to pulverize

Pulverkaffee m instant coffee

Pulverschnee m powdery snow

pummelig ['pʊmәlɪç] adj chubby

Pump (-(e)s) (umg) m: **auf ~ kaufen** to buy on tick (Brit) od credit

Pumpe ['pʊmpə] (-, -n) f pump; (umg: Herz) ticker

pumpen vt to pump; (umg) to lend; (: entleihen) to borrow

Pumphose f knickerbockers pl

puncto ['pʊŋkto] präp +gen: **in ~ X** where X is concerned

Punkt [pʊŋkt] (-(e)s, -e) m point; (bei Muster) dot; (Satzzeichen) full stop, period (bes US); **~ 12**

Uhr at 12 o'clock on the dot; **nun mach aber mal einen ~!** (umg) come off it!; **punktgleich** adj (Sport) level

punktieren [pʊŋk'ti:rən] vt to dot; (Med) to aspirate

pünktlich ['pʏŋktlɪç] adj punctual; **Pünktlichkeit** f punctuality

Punkt- zW: **Punktmatrix** f dot matrix; **Punktrichter** m (Sport) judge; **Punktsieg** m victory on points; **Punktwertung** f points system; **Punktzahl** f score

Punsch [pʊnʃ] (-(e)s, -e) m (hot) punch

Pupille [pu'pɪlə] (-, -n) f (im Auge) pupil

Puppe ['pʊpə] (-, -n) f doll; (Marionette) puppet; (Insektenpuppe) pupa, chrysalis; (Schaufensterpuppe, Übungspuppe) dummy; (umg: Mädchen) doll, bird (bes Brit)

Puppen- zW: **Puppenhaus** nt doll's house, dollhouse (US); **Puppenspieler** m puppeteer; **Puppenstube** f (single-room) doll's house od dollhouse (US); **Puppentheater** nt puppet theatre (Brit) od theater (US); **Puppenwagen** m doll's pram

pupsen ['pu:psən] (umg) vi to make a rude noise/smell

pur [pu:r] adj pure; (völlig) sheer; (Whisky) neat

Püree [py're:] (-s, -s) nt purée; (Kartoffelpüree) mashed potatoes pl

Purpur ['pʊrpʊr] (-s) m crimson

Purzelbaum ['pʊrtsəlbaʊm] m somersault

purzeln vi to tumble

Puste ['pu:stə] (-) (umg) f puff; (fig) steam

Pusteblume (umg) f dandelion

Pustel ['pʊstəl] (-, -n) f pustule

pusten ['pu:stən] (umg) vi to puff

Pute ['pu:tə] (-, -n) f turkey hen

Puter (-s, -) m turkey cock; **puterrot** adj scarlet

Putsch [pʊtʃ] (-(e)s, -e) m revolt, putsch; **putschen** vi to revolt; **Putschist** m rebel; **Putschversuch** m attempted coup (d'état)

Putte ['pʊtə] (-, -n) f (Kunst) cherub

Putz [pʊts] (-es) m (Mörtel) plaster, roughcast; **eine Mauer mit ~ verkleiden** to roughcast a wall

putzen vt to clean; (Nase) to wipe, blow ▷ vr to clean o.s.; (veraltet: sich schmücken) to dress o.s. up

Putzfrau f cleaning lady, charwoman (Brit)

putzig adj quaint, funny

Putzlappen m cloth

putzmunter (umg) adj full of beans

Putz- zW: **Putztag** m cleaning day; **Putzteufel** (umg) m maniac for housework; **Putzzeug** nt cleaning things pl

Puzzle ['pasəl] (-s, -s) nt jigsaw (puzzle)

PVC [pe:fau'tse:] (-(s)) nt abk PVC

Pygmäe [pʏ'gmɛ:ə] (-n, -n) m Pygmy

Pyjama [pi'dʒa:ma] (-s, -s) m pyjamas pl (Brit), pajamas pl (US)

Pyramide [pyra'mi:də] (-, -n) f pyramid

Pyrenäen [pyre'nɛ:ən] pl: **die ~** the Pyrenees pl

Python ['py:tɔn] (-s, -s) m python; **Pythonschlange** f python

Qq

Q, q [ku:] *nt* Q, q; **Q wie Quelle** = Q for Queen
qcm *abk* (= *Quadratzentimeter*) cm²
qkm *abk* (= *Quadratkilometer*) km²
qm *abk* (= *Quadratmeter*) m²
quabbelig ['kvabəlıç], **quabblig** ['kvablıç] *adj* wobbly; (*Frosch*) slimy
Quacksalber ['kvakzalbər] (**-s, -**) *m* quack (doctor)
Quader ['kva:dər] (**-s, -**) *m* square stone block; (*Math*) cuboid
Quadrat [kva'dra:t] (**-(e)s, -e**) *nt* square; **quadratisch** *adj* square; **Quadratlatschen** *pl* (*hum*: *umg*: *Schuhe*) clodhoppers *pl*; **Quadratmeter** *m* square metre (*Brit*) *od* meter (*US*)
quadrieren [kva'dri:rən] *vt* to square
quaken ['kva:kən] *vi* to croak; (*Ente*) to quack
quäken ['kvɛ:kən] *vi* to screech
quäkend *adj* screeching
Quäker, in (**-s, -**) *m(f)* Quaker
Qual [kva:l] (**-, -en**) *f* pain, agony; (*seelisch*) anguish; **er machte ihr das Leben zur ~** he made her life a misery
quälen ['kvɛ:lən] *vt* to torment ⊳ *vr* (*sich abmühen*) to struggle; (*geistig*) to torment o.s.; **~de Ungewissheit** agonizing uncertainty
Quälerei [kvɛ:lə'raı] *f* torture, torment
Quälgeist (*umg*) *m* pest
Qualifikation [kvalifikatsi'o:n] *f* qualification
qualifizieren [kvalifi'tsi:rən] *vt* to qualify; (*einstufen*) to label ⊳ *vr* to qualify
qualifiziert *adj* (*Arbeiter, Nachwuchs*) qualified; (*Arbeit*) professional; (*Pol*: *Mehrheit*) requisite
Qualität [kvali'tɛ:t] *f* quality; **von ausgezeichneter ~** (of) top quality
qualitativ [kvalita'ti:f] *adj* qualitative
Qualitätskontrolle *f* quality control
Qualitätsstandard *m* quality standard
Qualitätsware *f* article of high quality
Qualle ['kvalə] (**-, -n**) *f* jellyfish
Qualm [kvalm] (**-(e)s**) *m* thick smoke
qualmen *vt, vi* to smoke
qualvoll ['kva:lfɔl] *adj* painful; (*Schmerzen*) excruciating, agonizing
Quantensprung *m* quantum leap
Quantentheorie ['kvantənteori:] *f* quantum theory
Quantität [kvanti'tɛ:t] *f* quantity

quantitativ [kvantita'ti:f] *adj* quantitative
Quantum ['kvantom] (**-s, Quanten**) *nt* quantity, amount
Quarantäne [karan'tɛ:nə] (**-, -n**) *f* quarantine
Quark¹ [kvark] (**-s**) *m* curd cheese, quark; (*umg*) rubbish
Quark² [kvark] (**-s, -s**) *nt* (*Phys*) quark
Quarta ['kvarta] (**-, Quarten**) *f* (*früher*) third year of German secondary school
Quartal [kvar'ta:l] (**-s, -e**) *nt* quarter (year); **Kündigung zum ~** quarterly notice date
Quartett [kvar'tɛt] (**-(e)s, -e**) *nt* (*Mus*) quartet; (*Karten*) set of four cards; (: *Spiel*) = happy families
Quartier [kvar'ti:r] (**-s, -e**) *nt* accommodation (*Brit*), accommodations *pl* (*US*); (*Mil*) quarters *pl*; (*Stadtquartier*) district
Quarz [kva:rts] (**-es, -e**) *m* quartz
quasi ['kva:zi] *adv* virtually ⊳ *präf* quasi
quasseln ['kvasəln] (*umg*) *vi* to natter
Quaste ['kvastə] (**-, -n**) *f* (*Troddel*) tassel; (*von Pinsel*) bristles *pl*
Quästur [kvɛs'tu:r] *f* (*Univ*) bursary
Quatsch [kvatʃ] (**-es**) (*umg*) *m* rubbish, hogwash; **hört doch endlich auf mit dem ~!** stop being so stupid!; **~ machen** to mess about
quatschen *vi* to chat, natter
Quatschkopf (*umg*) *m* (*pej*: *Schwätzer*) windbag; (*Dummkopf*) twit (*Brit*)
Quecksilber ['kvɛkzɪlbər] *nt* mercury
Quelle ['kvɛlə] (**-, -n**) *f* spring; (*eines Flusses, Comput*) source; **an der ~ sitzen** (*fig*) to be well placed; **aus zuverlässiger ~** from a reliable source
quellen *vi* (*hervorquellen*) to pour *od* gush forth; (*schwellen*) to swell
Quellenangabe *f* reference
Quellsprache *f* source language
Quengelei [kvɛŋə'laı] (*umg*) *f* whining
quengelig (*umg*) *adj* whining
quengeln (*umg*) *vi* to whine
quer [kve:r] *adv* crossways, diagonally; (*rechtwinklig*) at right angles; **~ gestreift** horizontally striped; **~ auf dem Bett** across the bed; *siehe auch* **querlegen**; **Querbalken** *m* crossbeam; **Querdenker** *m* maverick
Quere ['kve:rə] (**-**) *f*: **jdm in die ~ kommen** to cross sb's path

q

quer- ZW: **querfeldein** adv across country; **Querfeldeinrennen** nt cross-country; (mit Motorrädern) motocross; (Radrennen) cyclocross; **Querflöte** f flute; **Querformat** nt oblong format; **Querkopf** m awkward customer; **querlegen** vr (fig: umg) to be awkward; **Querschiff** nt transept; **Querschläger** (umg) m ricochet; **Querschnitt** m cross section; **querschnittsgelähmt** adj paraplegic, paralysed below the waist; **Querschnittslähmung** f paraplegia; **Querstraße** f intersecting road; **Querstrich** m (horizontal) stroke od line; **Quersumme** f (Math) sum of digits of a number; **Quertreiber** (-s, -) m obstructionist

Querulant, in [kveru'lant(ɪn)] (-en, -en) m(f) grumbler

Querverbindung f connection, link

Querverweis m cross-reference

quetschen ['kvɛtʃən] vt to squash, crush; (Med) to bruise ▷ vr (sich klemmen) to be caught; (sich zwängen) to squeeze (o.s.)

Quetschung f bruise, contusion (form)

Queue [køː] (-s, -s) nt (Billiard) cue

quicklebendig ['kvɪkle'bɛndɪç] (umg) adj (Kind) lively, active; (ältere Person) spry

quieken ['kviːkən] vi to squeak

quietschen ['kviːtʃən] vi to squeak

quietschvergnügt ['kviːtʃfɛrgnyːkt] (umg) adj happy as a sandboy

quillt [kvɪlt] vb siehe **quellen**

Quinta ['kvɪnta] (-, **Quinten**) f (früher) second year in German secondary school

Quintessenz ['kvɪntesɛnts] f quintessence

Quintett [kvɪn'tet] (-(e)s, -e) nt quintet

Quirl [kvɪrl] (-(e)s, -e) m whisk

quirlig ['kvɪrlɪç] adj lively, frisky

quitt [kvɪt] adj quits, even

Quitte (-, -n) f quince

quittieren [kvɪ'tiːrən] vt to give a receipt for; (Dienst) to leave

Quittung f receipt; **er hat seine ~ bekommen** he's paid the penalty od price

Quiz [kvɪs] (-, -) nt quiz

quoll etc [kvɔl] vb siehe **quellen**

Quote ['kvoːtə] (-, -n) f proportion; (Rate) rate

Quotenbringer m (TV: umg) ratings booster

Quotenregelung f quota system (for ensuring adequate representation of women)

Quotierung [kvo'tiːruŋ] f (Comm) quotation

Rr

R¹, r nt R, r; **R wie Richard** ≈ R for Robert, R for Roger (US).

R², **r** abk (= Radius) r.

r. abk (= rechts) r.

Rabatt [ra'bat] (-(e)s, -e) m discount

Rabatte (-, -n) f flower bed, border

Rabattmarke f trading stamp

Rabatz [ra'bats] (-es) (umg) m row, din

Rabe ['ra:bə] (-n, -n) m raven

Rabenmutter f bad mother

rabenschwarz adj pitch-black

rabiat [rabi'a:t] adj furious

Rache ['raxə] (-) f revenge, vengeance

Rachen (-s, -) m throat

rächen ['rɛçən] vt to avenge, revenge ▷ vr to take (one's) revenge; **das wird sich ~** you'll pay for that

Rachitis [ra'xi:tɪs] (-) f rickets sing

Rachsucht f vindictiveness

rachsüchtig adj vindictive

Racker ['rakər] (-s, -) m rascal, scamp

Rad [ra:t] (-(e)s, ̈-er) nt wheel; (Fahrrad) bike; **~ fahren** to cycle; **unter die Räder kommen** (umg) to fall into bad ways; **das fünfte ~ am Wagen sein** (umg) to be in the way

Radar ['ra:da:r] (-s) m od nt radar; **Radarfalle** f speed trap; **Radarkontrolle** f radar-controlled speed check

Radau [ra'dau] (-s) (umg) m row; **~ machen** to kick up a row; (Unruhe stiften) to cause trouble

Raddampfer m paddle steamer

radebrechen ['ra:dəbrɛçən] vi untr: **Deutsch** etc **~ to speak broken German** etc

radeln vi (Hilfsverb sein) to cycle

Rädelsführer ['rɛ:dəlsfy:rər] (-s, -) m ringleader

Rad- zW: **Radfahrer** m cyclist; (pej: umg) crawler; **Radfahrweg** m cycle track od path

radieren [ra'di:rən] vt to rub out, erase; (Art) to etch

Radiergummi m rubber (Brit), eraser (bes US)

Radierung f etching

Radieschen [ra'di:sçən] nt radish

radikal [radi'ka:l] adj radical; **~ gegen etw vorgehen** to take radical steps against sth

Radikale, r f(m) radical

Radikalisierung [radikali'zi:rʊŋ] f radicalization

Radikalkur (umg) f drastic remedy

Radio ['ra:dio] (-s, -s) nt radio, wireless (bes Brit); **im ~** on the radio; **radioaktiv** adj radioactive; **radioaktiver Niederschlag** (radioactive) fallout; **Radioaktivität** f radioactivity; **Radioapparat** m radio (set); **Radiorekorder** m radio-cassette recorder

Radium ['ra:diʊm] (-s) nt radium

Radius ['ra:diʊs] (-, **Radien**) m radius

Radkappe f (Aut) hub cap

Radler, in (-s, -) m(f) cyclist

Rad- zW: **Radrennbahn** f cycling (race)track; **Radrennen** nt cycle race; (Sportart) cycle racing; **Radsport** m cycling

RAF f abk (= Rote Armee Fraktion) Red Army Faction

raffen ['rafən] vt to snatch, pick up; (Stoff) to gather (up); (Geld) to pile up, rake in; (umg: verstehen) to catch on to

Raffgier f greed, avarice

Raffinade [rafi'na:də] f refined sugar

Raffinesse [rafi'nɛsə] (-) f (Feinheit) refinement; (Schlauheit) cunning

raffinieren [rafi'ni:rən] vt to refine

raffiniert adj crafty, cunning; (Zucker) refined

Rage ['ra:ʒə] (-) f (Wut) rage, fury

ragen ['ra:gən] vi to tower, rise

Rahm [ra:m] (-s) m cream

Rahmen (-s, -) m frame(work); **aus dem ~ fallen** to go too far; **im ~ des Möglichen** within the bounds of possibility; **rahmen** vt to frame; **Rahmenhandlung** f (Liter) background story; **Rahmenplan** m outline plan; **Rahmenrichtlinien** pl guidelines pl

rahmig adj creamy

räkeln ['rɛ:kln] vr = **rekeln**

Rakete [ra'ke:tə] (-, -n) f rocket; **ferngelenkte ~** guided missile

Raketenstützpunkt m missile base

Rallye ['rali] (-, -s) f rally

rammdösig ['ramdø:zıç] (umg) adj giddy, dizzy

rammen ['ramən] vt to ram

Rampe ['rampə] (-, -n) f ramp

Rampenlicht nt (Theat) footlights pl; **sie möchte immer im ~ stehen** (fig) she always wants to be in the limelight

ramponieren [rampo'ni:rən] (umg) vt to damage

r

Ramsch [ramʃ] (-(e)s, -e) *m* junk

ran [ran] (*umg*) *adv* = **heran**

Rand [rant] (-(e)s, ⸚er) *m* edge; (*von Brille, Tasse etc*) rim; (*Hutrand*) brim; (*auf Papier*) margin; (*Schmutzrand, unter Augen*) ring; (*fig*) verge, brink; **außer ~ und Band** wild; **am ~e bemerkt** mentioned in passing; **am ~e der Stadt** on the outskirts of the town; **etw am ~e miterleben** to experience sth from the sidelines

randalieren [randa'li:rən] *vi* to (go on the) rampage

Rand- *zW:* **Randbemerkung** *f* marginal note; (*fig*) odd comment; **Randerscheinung** *f* unimportant side effect, marginal phenomenon; **Randfigur** *f* minor figure; **Randgebiet** *nt* (*Geog*) fringe; (*Pol*) border territory; (*fig*) subsidiary; **Randstreifen** *m* (*der Straße*) verge (*Brit*), berm (*US*); (*der Autobahn*) hard shoulder (*Brit*), shoulder (*US*); **randvoll** *adj* full to the brim

rang *etc* [raŋ] *vb siehe* **ringen**

Rang (-(e)s, ⸚e) *m* rank; (*Stand*) standing; (*Wert*) quality; (*Theat*) circle; **ein Mann ohne ~ und Namen** a man without any standing; **erster/zweiter ~** dress/upper circle

Rangabzeichen *nt* badge of rank

Rangälteste, r *m* senior officer

rangeln ['raŋəln] (*umg*) *vi* to scrap; (*um Posten*): ~ **(um)** to wrangle (for)

Rangfolge *f* order of rank (*bes MIL*)

Rangierbahnhof [rãʒi:rba:nho:f] *m* marshalling yard

rangieren *vt* (*Eisenb*) to shunt, switch (*US*) ▷ *vi* to rank, be classed

Rangiergleis *nt* siding

Rangliste *f* (*Sport*) ranking list, rankings *pl*

Rangordnung *f* hierarchy; (*Mil*) rank

Rangunterschied *m* social distinction; (*Mil*) difference in rank

rank [raŋk] *adj:* ~ **und schlank** (*liter*) slender and supple

Ranke ['raŋkə] (-, -n) *f* tendril, shoot

Ränke ['rɛŋkə] *pl* intrigues *pl*

ranken ['raŋkən] *vr* to trail, grow; **sich um etw ~** to twine around sth

Ränkeschmied *m* (*liter*) intriguer

ränkevoll *adj* scheming

ranklotzen ['ranklɔtsən] (*umg*) *vi* to put one's nose to the grindstone

ranlassen *unreg* (*umg*) *vt:* **jdn ~** to let sb have a go

rann *etc* [ran] *vb siehe* **rinnen**

rannte *etc* ['rantə] *vb siehe* **rennen**

Ranzen ['rantsən] (-s, -) *m* satchel; (*umg: Bauch*) belly, gut

ranzig ['rantsɪç] *adj* rancid

Rappe ['rapə] (-n, -n) *m* black horse

Rappel ['rapəl] (-s, -) (*umg*) *m* (*Fimmel*) craze; (*Wutanfall*): **einen ~ kriegen** to throw a fit

Rappen ['rapən] (-s, -) (*Schweiz*) *m* (*Geld*) centime, rappen

Raps [raps] (-es, -e) *m* (*Bot*) rape; **Rapsöl** *nt* rapeseed oil

rar [ra:r] *adj* rare; *siehe auch* **rarmachen**

Rarität [rari'tɛ:t] *f* rarity; (*Sammelobjekt*) curio

rarmachen (*umg*) *vr* to stay away

rasant [ra'zant] *adj* quick, rapid

rasch [raʃ] *adj* quick

rascheln *vi* to rustle

rasen ['ra:zən] *vi* to rave; (*sich schnell bewegen*) to race

Rasen (-s, -) *m* grass; (*gepflegt*) lawn

rasend *adj* furious; ~**e Kopfschmerzen** a splitting headache

Rasen- *zW:* **Rasenmäher** (-s, -) *m* lawnmower; **Rasenmähmaschine** *f* lawnmower; **Rasenplatz** *m* lawn; **Rasensprenger** *m* (lawn) sprinkler

Raserei [ra:zə'raɪ] *f* raving, ranting; (*Schnelle*) reckless speeding

Rasier- *zW:* **Rasierapparat** *m* shaver; **Rasiercreme** *f* shaving cream; **rasieren** *vt, vr* to shave; **Rasierklinge** *f* razor blade; **Rasiermesser** *nt* razor; **Rasierpinsel** *m* shaving brush; **Rasierseife** *f* shaving soap *od* stick; **Rasierwasser** *nt* aftershave

raspeln ['raspəln] *vt* to grate; (*Holz*) to rasp

Rasse ['rasə] (-, -n) *f* race; (*Tierrasse*) breed; **Rassehund** *m* thoroughbred dog

Rassel (-, -n) *f* rattle

rasseln *vi* to rattle, clatter

Rassenhass *m* race *od* racial hatred

Rassentrennung *f* racial segregation

rassig ['rasɪç] *adj* (*Pferd, Auto*) sleek; (*Frau*) vivacious; (*Wein*) spirited, lively

Rassismus [ra'sɪsmʊs] (-) *m* racialism, racism

rassistisch [ra'sɪstɪʃ] *adj* racialist, racist

Rast [rast] (-, -en) *f* rest; **rasten** *vi* to rest

Raster ['rastər] (-s, -) *m* (*Archit*) grid; (*Phot: Gitter*) screen; (*TV*) raster; (*fig*) framework

Rast- *zW:* **Rasthaus** *nt* (*Aut*) service area, services *pl*; **Rasthof** *m* (motorway) motel; (*mit Tankstelle*) service area (*with a motel*); **rastlos** *adj* tireless; (*unruhig*) restless; **Rastplatz** *m* (*Aut*) lay-by (*Brit*); **Raststätte** *f* service area, services *pl*

Rasur [ra'zu:r] *f* shave; (*das Rasieren*) shaving

Rat [ra:t] (-(e)s, -schläge) *m* (piece of) advice; **jdm mit ~ und Tat zur Seite stehen** to support sb in (both) word and deed; **sich ~ suchend an jdn wenden** to turn to sb for advice; **(sich** *dat*) **keinen ~ wissen** not to know what to do; *siehe auch* **zurate**

rät [rɛ:t] *vb siehe* **raten**

Rate (-, -n) *f* instalment (*Brit*), installment (*US*); **auf ~n kaufen** to buy on hire purchase (*Brit*) *od* on the installment plan (*US*); **in ~n zahlen** to pay in instalments (*Brit*) *od* installments (*US*)

raten *unreg vt, vi* to guess; (*empfehlen*): **jdm ~** to advise sb; **dreimal darfst du ~** I'll give you three guesses (*auch ironisch*)

ratenweise *adv* by instalments (*Brit*) *od* installments (*US*)

Ratenzahlung *f* hire purchase (*Brit*),

installment plan (US)
Ratespiel nt guessing game; (TV) quiz; (: *Beruferaten etc*) panel game
Ratgeber (-s, -) m adviser
Rathaus nt town hall; (*einer Großstadt*) city hall (*bes US*)
ratifizieren [ratifi'tsi:rən] vt to ratify
Ratifizierung f ratification
Ration [ratsi'o:n] f ration
rational [ratsio'na:l] adj rational
rationalisieren [ratsionali'zi:rən] vt to rationalize
rationell [ratsio'nɛl] adj efficient
rationieren [ratsio'ni:rən] vt to ration
ratlos adj at a loss, helpless
Ratlosigkeit f helplessness
rätoromanisch [retoro'ma:nıʃ] adj Rhaetian
ratsam adj advisable
Ratschlag m (piece of) advice
Rätsel ['rɛ:tsəl] (-s, -) nt puzzle; (*Worträtsel*) riddle; **vor einem ~ stehen** to be baffled; **rätselhaft** adj mysterious; **es ist mir rätselhaft** it's a mystery to me; **rätseln** vi to puzzle; **Rätselraten** nt guessing game
Ratsherr m councillor (*Brit*), councilor (US)
Ratskeller m town-hall restaurant
Ratte ['ratə] (-, -n) f rat
Rattenfänger (-s, -) m rat-catcher
rattern ['ratərn] vi to rattle, clatter
rau [rau] adj rough, coarse; (*Wetter*) harsh; **in ~en Mengen** (*umg*) by the ton, galore
Raub [raup] (-(e)s) m robbery; (*Beute*) loot, booty; **Raubbau** m overexploitation; **Raubdruck** m pirate(d) edition
raubeinig adj rough-and-ready
rauben ['raubən] vt to rob; (*jdn*) to kidnap, abduct
Räuber ['rɔybər] (-s, -) m robber; **räuberisch** adj thieving
Raub- zW: **Raubfisch** m predatory fish; **raubgierig** adj rapacious; **Raubkassette** f pirate cassette; **Raubmord** m robbery with murder; **Raubtier** nt predator; **Raubüberfall** m robbery with violence; **Raubvogel** m bird of prey
Rauch [raux] (-(e)s) m smoke; **Rauchabzug** m smoke outlet
rauchen vt, vi to smoke; **mir raucht der Kopf** (*fig*) my head's spinning; **„R~ verboten"** "no smoking"
Raucher, in (-s, -) m(f) smoker; **Raucherabteil** nt (*Eisenb*) smoker
räuchern ['rɔyçərn] vt to smoke, cure
Räucherspeck m ≈ smoked bacon
Räucherstäbchen nt joss stick
Rauch- zW: **Rauchfahne** f smoke trail; **Rauchfang** m chimney hood; **Rauchfleisch** nt smoked meat
rauchig adj smoky
Rauchschwaden pl drifts of smoke pl
räudig ['rɔydıç] adj mangy
rauf [rauf] (*umg*) adv = **herauf; hinauf**
Raufasertapete f woodchip paper

Raufbold (-(e)s, -e) m thug, hooligan
raufen vt (*Haare*) to pull out ▷ vi, vr to fight
Rauferei [raufə'rai] f brawl, fight
rauflustig adj ready for a fight, pugnacious
rauh etc siehe **rau** etc
rauhaarig adj wire-haired
Raum [raum] (-(e)s, **Räume**) m space; (*Zimmer, Platz*) room; (*Gebiet*) area; **~ sparend** space-saving; **eine Frage im ~ stehen lassen** to leave a question unresolved; **Raumausstatter, in** m(f) interior decorator
räumen ['rɔymən] vt to clear; (*Wohnung, Platz*) to vacate, move out of; (*verlassen: Gebäude, Gebiet*) to evacuate; (*wegbringen*) to shift, move; (*in Schrank etc*) to put away
Raum- zW: **Raumfähre** f space shuttle; **Raumfahrer** m astronaut; (*sowjetisch*) cosmonaut; **Raumfahrt** f space travel
Räumfahrzeug ['rɔymfa:rtsɔyk] nt bulldozer; (*für Schnee*) snow-clearer
Rauminhalt m cubic capacity, volume
Raumkapsel f space capsule
räumlich ['rɔymlıç] adj spatial; **Räumlichkeiten** pl premises pl
Raum- zW: **Raummangel** m lack of space; **Raummaß** nt unit of volume; cubic measurement; **Raummeter** m cubic metre (*Brit*) od meter (US); **Raumnot** f shortage of space; **Raumordnung** f environmental planning; **Raumpflegerin** f cleaner; **Raumschiff** nt spaceship; **Raumschifffahrt** f space travel; **Raumstation** f space station; **Raumtransporter** m space shuttle
Räumung ['rɔymuŋ] f clearing (away); (*von Haus etc*) vacating; (*wegen Gefahr*) evacuation; (*unter Zwang*) eviction
Räumungs- zW: **Räumungsbefehl** m eviction order; **Räumungsklage** f action for eviction; **Räumungsverkauf** m clearance sale
raunen ['raunən] vt, vi to whisper
Raupe ['raupə] (-, -n) f caterpillar; (*Raupenkette*) (caterpillar) track
Raupenschlepper m caterpillar tractor
Raureif ['raurai̯f] m hoarfrost
raus [raus] (*umg*) adv = **heraus; hinaus**
Rausch [rauʃ] (-(e), pl **Räusche**) m intoxication; **einen ~ haben** to be drunk
rauschen vi (*Wasser*) to rush; (*Baum*) to rustle; (*Radio etc*) to hiss; (*Mensch*) to sweep, sail
rauschend adj (*Beifall*) thunderous; (*Fest*) sumptuous
Rauschgift nt drug; **Rauschgifthandel** m drug traffic; **Rauschgifthändler, in** m(f) drug trafficker; **Rauschgiftsüchtige, r** f(m) drug addict
rausfliegen unreg (*umg*) vi to be chucked out
räuspern ['rɔyspərn] vr to clear one's throat
Rausschmeißer ['rausʃmaisər] (-s, -) (*umg*) m bouncer
Raute ['rautə] (-, -n) f diamond; (*Math*) rhombus
rautenförmig adj rhombic
Razzia ['ratsia] (-, **Razzien**) f raid

r

269

Reagenzglas [rea'gɛntsglaːs] *nt* test tube
reagieren [rea'giːrən] *vi*: ~ **(auf** +*akk*) to react (to)
Reaktion [reaktsi'oːn] *f* reaction
reaktionär [reaktsio'nɛːr] *adj* reactionary
Reaktionsfähigkeit *f* reactions *pl*
Reaktionsgeschwindigkeit *f* speed of reaction
Reaktor [re'aktɔr] *m* reactor; **Reaktorkern** *m* reactor core; **Reaktorunglück** *nt* nuclear accident
real [re'aːl] *adj* real, material; **Realeinkommen** *nt* real income
realisierbar [reali'ziːrbaːr] *adj* practicable, feasible
Realismus [rea'lɪsmʊs] *m* realism
Realist, in [rea'lɪst(ɪn)] *m(f)* realist; **realistisch** *adj* realistic
Realität [reali'tɛːt] *f* reality; **Realitäten** *pl* (*Gegebenheiten*) facts *pl*
realitätsfremd *adj* out of touch with reality
Realpolitik *f* political realism
Realschule *f* ≈ middle school (*Brit*), junior high school (*US*); *see culture note*

Realzeit *f* real time
Rebe ['reːbə] (**-, -n**) *f* vine
Rebell, in [re'bɛl(ɪn)] (**-en, -en**) *m(f)* rebel
rebellieren [rebɛ'liːrən] *vi* to rebel
Rebellion [rebɛli'oːn] *f* rebellion
rebellisch [re'bɛlɪʃ] *adj* rebellious
Rebensaft *m* wine
Reb- [rep] *zW*: **Rebhuhn** *nt* partridge; **Reblaus** *f* vine pest; **Rebstock** *m* vine
Rechen ['rɛçən] (**-s, -**) *m* rake; **rechen** *vt, vi* to rake
Rechen- *zW*: **Rechenaufgabe** *f* sum, mathematical problem; **Rechenfehler** *m* miscalculation; **Rechenmaschine** *f* adding machine
Rechenschaft *f* account; **jdm über etw** *akk* ~ **ablegen** to account to sb for sth; **jdn zur ~ ziehen (für)** to call sb to account (for *od* over); **jdm ~ schulden** to be accountable to sb
Rechenschaftsbericht *m* report
Rechenschieber *m* slide rule
Rechenzentrum *nt* computer centre (*Brit*) *od* center (*US*)
recherchieren [reʃɛr'ʃiːrən] *vt, vi* to investigate
rechnen ['rɛçnən] *vt, vi* to calculate; (*veranschlagen*) to estimate, reckon; **jdn/etw zu etw ~** to count sb/sth among sth; **~ mit** to reckon with; **~ auf** +*akk* to count on

Rechnen *nt* arithmetic; (*bes Sch*) sums *pl*
Rechner (-s, -) *m* calculator; (*Comput*) computer; **rechnerfern** *adj* (*Comput*) remote; **rechnerisch** *adj* arithmetical
Rechnung *f* calculation(s); (*Comm*) bill (*Brit*), check (*US*); **auf eigene ~** on one's own account; **(jdm) etw in ~ stellen** to charge (sb) for sth; **jdm/etw ~ tragen** to take sb/sth into account
Rechnungs- *zW*: **Rechnungsbuch** *nt* account book; **Rechnungshof** *m* ≈ Auditor-General's office (*Brit*), audit division (*US*); **Rechnungsjahr** *nt* financial year; **Rechnungsprüfer** *m* auditor; **Rechnungsprüfung** *f* audit(ing)
recht [rɛçt] *adj* right ▷ *adv* (*vor Adjektiv*) really, quite; **das ist mir ~** that suits me; **jetzt erst ~** now more than ever; **alles, was ~ ist** (*empört*) fair's fair; (*anerkennend*) you can't deny it; **nach dem R~en sehen** to see that everything's O.K.; **~ haben** to be right; **jdm ~ geben** to agree with sb, admit that sb is right; **du kommst gerade ~, um ...** you're just in time to ...; **gehe ich ~ in der Annahme, dass ...?** am I correct in assuming that ...?; **~ herzlichen Dank** thank you very much indeed
Recht (-(e)s, -e) *nt* right; (*Jur*) law; **~ sprechen** to administer justice; **mit** *od* **zu ~** rightly, justly; **von ~s wegen** by rights; **zu seinem ~ kommen** (*lit*) to gain one's rights; (*fig*) to come into one's own; **gleiches ~ für alle!** equal rights for all!
Rechte *f* right (hand); (*Pol*) Right
Rechte, r, s *f(m)* (*Pol*) right-winger ▷ *nt* right thing; **etwas/nichts ~s** something/nothing proper
rechte, r, s *adj* right; (*Pol*) right-wing
recht- *zW*: **Rechteck (-(e)s, -e)** *nt* rectangle; **rechteckig** *adj* rectangular; **rechtfertigen** *vt untr* to justify ▷ *vr untr* to justify o.s.; **Rechtfertigung** *f* justification; **rechthaberisch** *adj* dogmatic; **rechtlich** *adj* legal, lawful; **rechtlich nicht zulässig** not permissible in law, illegal; **rechtmäßig** *adj* legal, lawful
rechts [rɛçts] *adv* on *od* to the right; **~ stehen** *od* **sein** (*Pol*) to be right-wing; **~ stricken** to knit (plain); **Rechtsabbieger (-s, -)** *m*: **die Spur für Rechtsabbieger** the right-hand turn-off lane; **Rechtsanspruch** *m*: **einen Rechtsanspruch auf etw** *akk* **haben** to be legally entitled to sth; **Rechtsanwalt** *m*, **Rechtsanwältin** *f* lawyer, barrister; **Rechtsaußen (-, -)** *m* (*Sport*) outside right; **Rechtsbeistand** *m* legal adviser
rechtschaffen *adj* upright
Rechtschreibung *f* spelling
Rechts- *zW*: **Rechtsdrehung** *f* clockwise rotation; **Rechtsextremismus** *m* right-wing extremism; **Rechtsextremist** *m* right-wing extremist; **Rechtsfall** *m* (law) case; **Rechtsfrage** *f* legal question; **rechtsgültig**

adj legally valid; **Rechtshänder, in (-s, -)**
m(f) right-handed person; **rechtskräftig** *adj*
valid, legal; **Rechtskurve** *f* right-hand bend;
Rechtslage *f* legal position; **rechtslastig** *adj*
listing to the right; (*fig*) leaning to the right;
Rechtspflege *f* administration of justice;
Rechtspfleger *m official with certain judicial
powers*
Rechtsprechung ['rɛçtʃprɛçʊŋ] *f*
(*Gerichtsbarkeit*) jurisdiction; (*richterliche
Tätigkeit*) dispensation of justice
Rechts- *zW*: **rechtsradikal** *adj* (*Pol*) extreme
right-wing; **Rechtsschutz** *m* legal protection;
Rechtsspruch *m* verdict; **Rechtsstaat** *m* state
under the rule of law; **Rechtsstreit** *m* lawsuit;
Rechtstitel *m* title; **rechtsverbindlich**
adj legally binding; **Rechtsverkehr** *m*
driving on the right; **Rechtsweg** *m*: **der
Rechtsweg ist ausgeschlossen** ≈ the judges'
decision is final; **rechtswidrig** *adj* illegal;
Rechtswissenschaft *f* jurisprudence
rechtwinklig *adj* right-angled
rechtzeitig *adj* timely ▷ *adv* in time
Reck [rɛk] (**-(e)s, -e**) *nt* horizontal bar
recken *vt, vr* to stretch
recyceln [riː'saɪkəln] *vt* to recycle
Recycling [riː'saɪklɪŋ] (**-s**) *nt* recycling
Red. *abk* = **Redaktion**; (= *Redakteur(in)*) ed
Redakteur, in [redak'tøːr(ɪn)] *m(f)* editor
Redaktion [redaktsi'oːn] *f* editing; (*Leute*)
editorial staff; (*Büro*) editorial office(s *pl*)
Redaktionsschluss *m* time of going to press;
(*Einsendeschluss*) copy deadline
Rede ['reːdə] (**-, -n**) *f* speech; (*Gespräch*) talk;
jdn zur ~ stellen to take sb to task; **eine
~ halten** to make a speech; **das ist nicht
der ~ wert** it's not worth mentioning;
davon kann keine ~ sein it's out of the
question; **Redefreiheit** *f* freedom of speech;
redegewandt *adj* eloquent
Reden (**-s**) *nt* talking, speech
reden *vi* to talk, speak ▷ *vt* to say; (*Unsinn
etc*) to talk; (**viel) von sich ~ machen** to
become (very much) a talking point; **darüber
lässt sich ~** that's a possibility; (*über Preis,
Bedingungen*) I think we could discuss that;
er lässt mit sich ~ he could be persuaded;
(*in Bezug auf Preis*) he's open to offers;
(*gesprächsbereit*) he's open to discussion
Redensart *f* set phrase
Redeschwall *m* torrent of words
Redewendung *f* expression, idiom
redlich ['reːtlɪç] *adj* honest; **Redlichkeit** *f*
honesty
Redner, in (-s, -) *m(f)* speaker, orator
redselig ['reːtzeːlɪç] *adj* talkative, loquacious;
Redseligkeit *f* talkativeness, loquacity
redundant [redʊn'dant] *adj* redundant
Redundanz [redʊn'dants] (**-**) *f* redundancy
reduzieren [redu'tsiːrən] *vt* to reduce
Reduzierung *f* reduction
Reede ['reːdə] (**-, -n**) *f* protected anchorage
Reeder (-s, -) *m* shipowner

Reederei [reːdə'raɪ] *f* shipping line *od* firm
reell [re'ɛl] *adj* fair, honest; (*Preis*) fair;
(*Comm*: *Geschäft*) sound; (*Math*) real
Reetdach ['reːtdax] *nt* thatched roof
Ref. *abk* = **Referendar(in); Referent(in)**
Referat [refe'raːt] (**-(e)s, -e**) *nt* report; (*Vortrag*)
paper; (*Gebiet*) section; (*Verwaltung*: *Ressort*)
department; **ein ~ halten** to present a
seminar paper
Referendar, in [referɛn'daːr(ɪn)] *m(f)* trainee
(in civil service); (*Studienreferendar*) trainee
teacher; (*Gerichtsreferendar*) articled clerk
Referendum [refe'rɛndʊm] (**-s, Referenden**) *nt*
referendum
Referent, in [refe'rɛnt(ɪn)] *m(f)* speaker;
(*Berichterstatter*) reporter; (*Sachbearbeiter*) expert
Referenz [refe'rɛnts] *f* reference
referieren [refe'riːrən] *vi*: **~ über** +*akk* to speak
od talk on
reflektieren [reflɛk'tiːrən] *vt, vi* to reflect; **~
auf** +*akk* to be interested in
Reflex [re'flɛks] (**-es, -e**) *m* reflex;
Reflexbewegung *f* reflex action
reflexiv [reflɛ'ksiːf] *adj* (*Gram*) reflexive
Reform [re'fɔrm] (**-, -en**) *f* reform
Reformation [reformatsi'oːn] *f* reformation
Reformator [refɔr'maːtɔr] *m* reformer;
reformatorisch *adj* reformatory, reforming
reform- *zW*: **reformbedürftig** *adj* in need of
reform; **reformfreudig** *adj* avid for reform;
Reformhaus *nt* health food shop
reformieren [refɔr'miːrən] *vt* to reform
Refrain [rə'frɛ̃ː] (**-s, -s**) *m* refrain, chorus
Reg. *abk* (= *Regierungs-*) gov.; (= *Register*) reg
Regal [re'gaːl] (**-s, -e**) *nt* (book)shelves *pl*,
bookcase; (*Typ*) stand, rack
Regatta [re'gata] (**-, Regatten**) *f* regatta
Reg.-Bez. *abk* = **Regierungsbezirk**
rege ['reːgə] *adj* lively, active; (*Geschäft*) brisk
Regel ['reːgəl] (**-, -n**) *f* rule; (*Med*) period; **in
der ~** as a rule; **nach allen ~n der Kunst** (*fig*)
thoroughly; **sich** *dat* **etw zur ~ machen** to
make a habit of sth; **regellos** *adj* irregular,
unsystematic; **regelmäßig** *adj* regular;
Regelmäßigkeit *f* regularity
regeln *vt* to regulate, control; (*Angelegenheit*)
to settle ▷ *vr*: **sich von selbst ~** to take care
of itself; **gesetzlich geregelt sein** to be laid
down by law
regelrecht *adj* proper, thorough
Regelung *f* regulation; settlement
regelwidrig *adj* irregular, against the rules
regen ['reːgən] *vt* to move ▷ *vr* to move, stir
Regen (-s, -) *m* rain; **vom ~ in die Traufe
kommen** (*Sprichwort*) to jump out of the frying
pan into the fire (*Sprichwort*)
Regenbogen *m* rainbow; **Regenbogenhaut**
f (*Anat*) iris; **Regenbogenpresse** *f* trashy
magazines *pl*
regenerieren [regene'riːrən] *vr* (*Biol*) to
regenerate; (*fig*) to revitalize *od* regenerate o.s.
od itself; (*nach Anstrengung, Schock etc*) to recover
Regen- *zW*: **Regenguss** *m* downpour;

r

Regenmantel *m* raincoat, mac(kintosh);
Regenmenge *f* rainfall; **Regenschauer** *m*
shower (of rain); **Regenschirm** *m* umbrella
Regent, in [re'gɛnt(ɪn)] *m(f)* regent
Regentag *m* rainy day
Regentropfen *m* raindrop
Regentschaft *f* regency
Regen- zW: **Regenwald** *m* (Geog) rain forest;
Regenwetter *nt*: **er macht ein Gesicht wie**
drei od **sieben Tage Regenwetter** (umg)
he's got a face as long as a month of Sundays;
Regenwurm *m* earthworm; **Regenzeit** *f* rainy
season, rains *pl*
Regie [re'ʒi:] *f* (Film etc) direction; (Theat)
production; **unter der ~ von** directed od
produced by; **Regieanweisung** *f* (stage)
direction
regieren [re'gi:rən] *vt, vi* to govern, rule
Regierung *f* government; (Monarchie) reign; **an**
die ~ kommen to come to power
Regierungs- zW: **Regierungsbezirk** *m* ≈ county
(Brit, US), ≈ region (Scot); **Regierungserklärung**
f inaugural speech; (in Großbritannien) Queen's/
King's Speech; **Regierungsmannschaft** *f*
government team; **Regierungssprecher** *m*
government spokesman; **Regierungsvorlage**
f government bill; **Regierungswechsel** *m*
change of government; **Regierungszeit** *f*
period in government; (von König) reign
Regiment [regi'mɛnt] (**-s, -er**) *nt* regiment
Region [regi'o:n] *f* region
Regionalplanung [regio'na:lpla:nʊŋ] *f*
regional planning
Regionalprogramm *nt* (Rundf, TV) regional
programme (Brit) od program (US)
Regisseur, in [reʒɪ'sø:r(ɪn)] *m(f)* director;
(Theat) (stage) producer
Register [re'gɪstər] (**-s, -**) *nt* register; (in Buch)
table of contents, index; **alle ~ ziehen** (fig)
to pull out all the stops; **Registerführer** *m*
registrar
Registratur [regɪstra'tu:r] *f* registry, records
office
registrieren [regɪs'tri:rən] *vt* to register;
(umg: zur Kenntnis nehmen) to note
Registrierkasse *f* cash register
Regler ['re:glər] (**-s, -**) *m* regulator, governor
reglos ['re:klo:s] *adj* motionless
regnen ['re:gnən] *vi unpers* to rain ▷ *vt unpers*: **es**
regnet Glückwünsche congratulations
are pouring in; **es regnet in Strömen** it's
pouring (with rain)
regnerisch *adj* rainy
Regress [re'grɛs] (**-es, -e**) *m* (Jur) recourse,
redress; **Regressanspruch** *m* (Jur) claim for
compensation
regsam ['re:kza:m] *adj* active
regulär [regu'lɛ:r] *adj* regular
regulieren [regu'li:rən] *vt* to regulate; (Comm)
to settle; **sich von selbst ~** to be self-
regulating
Regulierungsbehörde [regu'li:rəʊŋsbəhø:rdə]
f regulatory body od authority

Regung ['re:gʊŋ] *f* motion; (Gefühl) feeling,
impulse
regungslos *adj* motionless
Reh [re:] (**-(e)s, -e**) *nt* deer; (weiblich) roe deer
rehabilitieren [rehabili'ti:rən] *vt* to
rehabilitate; (Ruf, Ehre) to vindicate ▷ *vr* to
rehabilitate (form) od vindicate o.s.
Rehabilitierung *f* rehabilitation
Reh- zW: **Rehbock** *m* roebuck; **Rehbraten** *m*
roast venison; **Rehkalb** *nt* fawn; **Rehkitz** *nt*
fawn
Reibach ['raɪbax] (**-s**) *m*: **einen ~ machen**
(umg) to make a killing
Reibe ['raɪbə] (**-, -n**) *f* grater
Reibeisen ['raɪp|aɪzən] *nt* grater
Reibekuchen *m* (Koch) ≈ potato waffle
reiben *unreg* *vt* to rub; (Koch) to grate
Reiberei [raɪbə'raɪ] *f* friction *no pl*
Reibfläche *f* rough surface
Reibung *f* friction
reibungslos *adj* smooth; **~ verlaufen** to go off
smoothly
Reich [raɪç] (**-(e)s, -e**) *nt* empire, kingdom; (fig)
realm; **das Dritte ~** the Third Reich
reich *adj* rich ▷ *adv*: **eine ~ ausgestattete**
Bibliothek a well-stocked library
reichen *vi* to reach; (genügen) to be enough
od sufficient ▷ *vt* to hold out; (geben) to
pass, hand; (anbieten) to offer; **so weit das**
Auge reicht as far as the eye can see; **jdm ~**
(genügen) to be enough od sufficient for sb; **mir**
reichts! I've had enough!
reich- zW: **reichhaltig** *adj* ample, rich;
reichlich *adj* ample, plenty of; **Reichtum** (**-s,**
-tümer) *m* wealth; **Reichweite** *f* range; **jd ist**
in Reichweite sb is nearby
reif [raɪf] *adj* ripe; (Mensch, Urteil) mature; **für**
etw ~ sein (umg) to be ready for sth
Reif¹ (**-(e)s**) *m* hoarfrost
Reif² (**-(e)s, -e**) *m* (Ring) ring, hoop
Reife (**-**) *f* ripeness; maturity; **mittlere ~**
(Sch) first public examination in secondary school, ≈
O-Levels *pl* (Brit)
Reifen (**-s, -**) *m* ring, hoop; (Fahrzeugreifen) tyre
(Brit), tire (US)
reifen *vi* to mature; (Obst) to ripen
Reifen- zW: **Reifendruck** *m* tyre (Brit) od tire
(US) pressure; **Reifenpanne** *f* puncture, flat;
Reifenprofil *nt* tyre (Brit) od tire (US) tread;
Reifenschaden *m* puncture, flat
Reifeprüfung *f* school-leaving exam
Reifezeugnis *nt* school-leaving certificate
reiflich ['raɪflɪç] *adj* thorough, careful
Reihe ['raɪə] (**-, -n**) *f* row; (von Tagen
etc: umg: Anzahl) series *sing*; **eine ganze ~ (von)**
(unbestimmte Anzahl) a whole lot (of); **der ~**
nach in turn; **er ist an der ~** it's his turn; **an**
die ~ kommen to have one's turn; **außer der**
~ out of turn; (ausnahmsweise) out of the usual
way of things; **aus der ~ tanzen** (fig: umg) to
be different; (gegen Konventionen verstoßen) to
step out of line; **ich kriege heute nichts auf**
die ~ I can't get my act together today

reihen vt to set in a row; to arrange in series; (Perlen) to string

Reihen- zW: **Reihenfolge** f sequence; **alphabetische Reihenfolge** alphabetical order; **Reihenhaus** nt terraced (Brit) od row (US) house; **Reihenuntersuchung** f mass screening; **reihenweise** adv (in Reihen) in rows; (fig: in großer Anzahl) by the dozen

Reiher (-s, -) m heron

reihum [raɪˈʊm] adv: **etw ~ gehen lassen** to pass sth around

Reim [raɪm] **(-(e)s, -e)** m rhyme; **sich** dat **einen ~ auf etw** akk **machen** (umg) to make sense of sth; **reimen** vt to rhyme

rein¹ [raɪn] (umg) adv = **herein; hinein**

rein² [raɪn] adj pure; (sauber) clean ▷ adv purely; **~ waschen** to clear o.s.; **das ist die ~ste Freude/der ~ste Hohn** etc it's pure od sheer joy/mockery etc; **etw ins R~e schreiben** to make a fair copy of sth; **etw ins R~e bringen** to clear sth up; **~en Tisch machen** (fig) to get things straight; **~ unmöglich** (umg: ganz, völlig) absolutely impossible

Rein- in zw (Comm) net(t)

Reinemachefrau f cleaning lady, charwoman (Brit)

reineweg (umg) adv completely, absolutely

rein- zW: **Reinfall** (umg) m let-down; (Misserfolg) flop; **reinfallen** vi: **auf jdn/etw reinfallen** to be taken in by sb/sth; **Reingewinn** m net profit; **Reinheit** f purity; cleanness

reinigen [ˈraɪnɪɡən] vt to clean; (Wasser) to purify

Reiniger (-s, -) m cleaner

Reinigung f cleaning; purification; (Geschäft) cleaner's; **chemische ~** dry-cleaning; (Geschäft) dry-cleaner's

Reinigungsmittel nt cleansing agent

rein- zW: **reinlich** adj clean; **Reinlichkeit** f cleanliness; **Reinmachefrau** f = **Reinemachefrau; reinrassig** adj pedigree; **reinreiten** unreg vt: **jdn reinreiten** to get sb into a mess; **Reinschrift** f fair copy; **Reinvermögen** nt net assets pl

reinweg (umg) adv = **reineweg**

Reis¹ [raɪs] **(-es, -e)** m rice

Reis² [raɪs] **(-es, -er)** nt twig, sprig

Reise [ˈraɪzə] **(-, -n)** f journey; (Schiffsreise) voyage; **Reisen** pl travels pl; **gute ~!** bon voyage!, have a good journey!; **auf ~n sein** to be away (travelling (Brit) od traveling (US)); **er ist viel auf ~n** he does a lot of travelling (Brit) od traveling (US); **Reiseandenken** nt souvenir; **Reiseapotheke** f first-aid kit; **Reisebericht** m account of one's journey; (Buch) travel story; (Film) travelogue (Brit), travelog (US); **Reisebüro** nt travel agency; **Reisediplomatie** f shuttle diplomacy; **Reiseerleichterungen** pl easing sing of travel restrictions; **reisefertig** adj ready to start; **Reisefieber** nt (fig) travel nerves pl; **Reiseführer** m guide(book); (Mensch) (travel) guide; **Reisegepäck** nt luggage; **Reisegesellschaft** f party of travellers (Brit)

od travelers (US); **Reisekosten** pl travelling (Brit) od traveling (US) expenses pl; **Reiseleiter** m courier; **Reiselektüre** f reading for the journey; **Reiselust** f wanderlust

reisen vi to travel; **~ nach** to go to

Reisende, r f(m) traveller (Brit), traveler (US)

Reise- zW: **Reisepass** m passport; **Reisepläne** pl plans pl for a od the journey; **Reiseproviant** m provisions pl for the journey; **Reiseroute** f itinerary; **Reisescheck** m traveller's cheque (Brit), traveler's check (US); **Reiseschreibmaschine** f portable typewriter; **Reisetasche** f travelling (Brit) od traveling (US) bag od case; **Reisethrombose** f deep vein thrombosis, economy-class syndrome (umg); **Reiseveranstalter** m tour operator; **Reiseverkehr** m tourist od holiday traffic; **Reisewetter** nt holiday weather; **Reiseziel** nt destination

Reisig [ˈraɪzɪç] **(-s)** nt brushwood

Reißaus m: **~ nehmen** to run away, flee

Reißbrett nt drawing board; **Reißbrettstift** m drawing pin (Brit), thumbtack (US)

reißen [ˈraɪsən] unreg vt to tear; (ziehen) to pull, drag; (Witz) to crack ▷ vi to tear; to pull, drag; **etw an sich ~** to snatch sth up; (fig) to take sth over; **sich um etw ~** to scramble for sth; **wenn alle Stricke ~** (fig: umg) if the worst comes to the worst; siehe auch **hingerissen**

Reißen nt (Gewichtheben: Disziplin) snatch; (umg: Gliederreißen) ache

reißend adj (Fluss) torrential; (Comm) rapid; **~en Absatz finden** to sell like hot cakes (umg)

Reißer (-s, -) (umg) m thriller; **reißerisch** adj sensational

Reiß- zW: **Reißleine** f (Aviat) ripcord; **Reißnagel** m drawing pin (Brit), thumbtack (US); **Reißschiene** f T-square; **Reißverschluss** m zip (fastener) (Brit), zipper (US); **Reißwolf** m shredder; **durch den Reißwolf geben** (Dokumente) to shred; **Reißzeug** nt geometry set; **Reißzwecke** f = **Reißnagel**

reiten [ˈraɪtən] unreg vt, vi to ride

Reiter (-s, -) m rider; (Mil) cavalryman, trooper

Reiterei [raɪtəˈraɪ] f cavalry

Reiterin f rider

Reit- zW: **Reithose** f riding breeches pl; **Reitpferd** nt saddle horse; **Reitschule** f riding school; **Reitstiefel** m riding boot; **Reitturnier** nt horse show; **Reitweg** m bridle path; **Reitzeug** nt riding outfit

Reiz [raɪts] **(-es, -e)** m stimulus; (angenehm) charm; (Verlockung) attraction

reizbar adj irritable; **Reizbarkeit** f irritability

reizen vt to stimulate; (unangenehm) to irritate; (verlocken) to appeal to, attract; (Karten) to bid ▷ vi: **zum Widerspruch ~** to invite contradiction

reizend adj charming

Reiz- zW: **Reizgas** nt tear gas, CS gas; **Reizhusten** m chesty cough; **reizlos** adj unattractive; **reizvoll** adj attractive; **Reizwäsche** f sexy underwear; **Reizwort** nt

r

emotive word

rekapitulieren [rekapitu'liːrən] *vt* to recapitulate

rekeln ['reːkəln] *vr* to stretch out; (*lümmeln*) to lounge *od* loll about

Reklamation [reklamatsi'oːn] *f* complaint

Reklame [re'klaːmə] (-, -n) *f* advertising; (*Anzeige*) advertisement; **mit etw ~ machen** (*pej*) to show off about sth; **für etw ~ machen** to advertise sth; **Reklametrommel** *f*: **die Reklametrommel für jdn/etw rühren** (*umg*) to beat the (big) drum for sb/sth; **Reklamewand** *f* notice (*Brit*) *od* bulletin (*US*) board

reklamieren [rekla'miːrən] *vi* to complain ▷ *vt* to complain about; (*zurückfordern*) to reclaim

rekonstruieren [rekɔnstru'iːrən] *vt* to reconstruct

Rekonvaleszenz [rekɔnvalɛs'tsɛnts] *f* convalescence

Rekord [re'kɔrt] (-(e)s, -e) *m* record; **Rekordleistung** *f* record performance

Rekrut [re'kruːt] (-en, -en) *m* recruit

rekrutieren [rekru'tiːrən] *vt* to recruit ▷ *vr* to be recruited

Rektor ['rɛktɔr] *m* (*Univ*) rector, vice-chancellor; (*Sch*) head teacher (*Brit*), principal (*US*)

Rektorat [rɛktɔ'raːt] (-(e)s, -e) *nt* rectorate, vice-chancellorship; headship (*Brit*), principalship (*US*); (*Zimmer*) rector's *etc* office

Rektorin [rɛk'toːrɪn] *f* (*Sch*) head teacher (*Brit*), principal (*US*)

Rel. *abk* (= *Religion*) rel.

Relais [rə'lɛː] (-, -) *nt* relay

Relation [relatsi'oːn] *f* relation

relativ [rela'tiːf] *adj* relative

Relativität [relativi'tɛːt] *f* relativity

Relativpronomen *nt* (*Gram*) relative pronoun

relevant [rele'vant] *adj* relevant

Relevanz *f* relevance

Relief [reli'ɛf] (-s, -s) *nt* relief

Religion [religi'oːn] *f* religion

Religions- *zW*: **Religionsfreiheit** *f* freedom of worship; **Religionslehre** *f* religious education; **Religionsunterricht** *m* religious education

religiös [religi'øːs] *adj* religious

Relikt [re'lɪkt] (-(e)s, -e) *nt* relic

Reling ['reːlɪŋ] (-, -s) *f* (*Naut*) rail

Reliquie [re'liːkviə] *f* relic

Reminiszenz [reminɪs'tsɛnts] *f* reminiscence, recollection

Remis [rə'miː] (-, - *od* -en) *nt* (*Schach, Sport*) draw

Remittende [remɪ'tɛndə] (-, -n) *f* (*Comm*) return

Remittent *m* (*Fin*) payee

remittieren *vt* (*Comm: Waren*) to return; (*Geld*) to remit

Remmidemmi ['rɛmi'dɛmi] (-s) *nt* (*umg*) (*Krach*) row, rumpus; (*Trubel*) rave-up

Remoulade [remu'laːdə] (-, -n) *f* remoulade

rempeln ['rɛmpəln] (*umg*) *vt* to jostle, elbow; (*Sport*) to barge into; (*foulen*) to push

Ren [reːn, rɛn] (-s, -s *od* -e) *nt* reindeer

Renaissance [rənɛ'sãːs] (-, -n) *f* (*Hist*) renaissance; (*fig*) revival, rebirth

Rendezvous [rãde'vuː] (-, -) *nt* rendezvous

Rendite [rɛn'diːtə] (-, -n) *f* (*Fin*) yield, return on capital

Rennbahn *f* racecourse; (*Aut*) circuit, racetrack

rennen ['rɛnən] *unreg vt, vi* to run, race; **um die Wette ~** to have a race; **Rennen** (-s, -) *nt* running; (*Wettbewerb*) race; **das Rennen machen** (*lit, fig*) to win (the race)

Renner (-s, -) (*umg*) *m* winner, worldbeater

Renn- *zW*: **Rennfahrer** *m* racing driver (*Brit*), race car driver (*US*); **Rennpferd** *nt* racehorse; **Rennplatz** *m* racecourse; **Rennrad** *nt* racing cycle; **Rennsport** *m* racing; **Rennwagen** *m* racing car (*Brit*), race car (*US*)

renommiert [renɔ'miːrt] *adj*: **~ (wegen)** renowned (for), famous (for)

renovieren [reno'viːrən] *vt* to renovate

Renovierung *f* renovation

rentabel [rɛn'taːbəl] *adj* profitable, lucrative

Rentabilität [rɛntabili'tɛːt] *f* profitability

Rente ['rɛntə] (-, -n) *f* pension

Renten- *zW*: **Rentenbasis** *f* annuity basis; **Rentenempfänger** *m* pensioner; **Rentenpapier** *nt* (*Fin*) fixed-interest security; **Rentenversicherung** *f* pension scheme; **Rentenversicherungsträger** *m* pension provider

Rentier ['rɛntiːr] *nt* reindeer

rentieren [rɛn'tiːrən] *vi, vr* to pay, be profitable; **das rentiert (sich) nicht** it's not worth it

Rentner, in ['rɛntnər(ɪn)] (-s, -) *m(f)* pensioner

Reparation [reparatsi'oːn] *f* reparation

Reparatur [repara'tuːr] *f* repairing; repair; **etw in ~ geben** to have sth repaired; **reparaturbedürftig** *adj* in need of repair; **Reparaturwerkstatt** *f* repair shop; (*Aut*) garage

reparieren [repa'riːrən] *vt* to repair

Repertoire [reperto'aːr] (-s, -s) *nt* repertoire

Reportage [repɔr'taːʒə] (-, -n) *f* report

Reporter, in [re'pɔrtər(ɪn)] (-s, -) *m(f)* reporter, commentator

Repräsentant, in [reprɛzɛn'tant(ɪn)] *m(f)* representative

repräsentativ [reprɛzɛnta'tiːf] *adj* representative; (*Geschenk etc*) prestigious; **die ~en Pflichten eines Botschafters** the social duties of an ambassador

repräsentieren [reprɛzɛn'tiːrən] *vt* to represent ▷ *vi* to perform official duties

Repressalien [repre'saːliən] *pl* reprisals *pl*

reprivatisieren [reprivati'ziːrən] *vt* to denationalize

Reprivatisierung *f* denationalization

Reproduktion [reprodʊktsi'oːn] *f* reproduction

reproduzieren [reprodu'tsiːrən] *vt* to reproduce

Reptil [rɛp'tiːl] (-s, -ien) *nt* reptile

Republik [repu'bliːk] *f* republic

Republikaner [republi'ka:nər] **(-s, -)** *m* republican

republikanisch *adj* republican

Requisiten *pl* (*Theat*) props *pl*, properties *pl* (*form*)

Reservat [rezɛr'va:t] **(-(e)s, -e)** *nt* reservation

Reserve [re'zɛrvə] **(-, -n)** *f* reserve; **jdn aus der ~ locken** to bring sb out of his/her shell; **Reserverad** *nt* (*Aut*) spare wheel; **Reservespieler** *m* reserve; **Reservetank** *m* reserve tank

reservieren [rezɛr'vi:rən] *vt* to reserve

reserviert *adj* (*Platz, Mensch*) reserved

Reservist [rezɛr'vɪst] *m* reservist

Reservoir [rezɛrvo'a:r] **(-s, -e)** *nt* reservoir

Residenz [rezi'dɛnts] *f* residence, seat

residieren [rezi'di:rən] *vi* to reside

Resignation [rezɪgnatsi'o:n] *f* resignation

resignieren [rezɪ'gni:rən] *vi* to resign

resolut [rezo'lu:t] *adj* resolute

Resolution [rezolutsi'o:n] *f* resolution; (*Bittschrift*) petition

Resonanz [rezo'nants] *f* (*lit, fig*) resonance; **Resonanzboden** *m* sounding board; **Resonanzkasten** *m* soundbox

Resopal® [rezo'pa:l] **(-s)** *nt* Formica®

resozialisieren [rezotsiali'zi:rən] *vt* to rehabilitate

Resozialisierung *f* rehabilitation

Respekt [rɛ'spɛkt] **(-(e)s)** *m* respect; (*Angst*) fear; **bei allem ~ (vor jdm/etw)** with all due respect (to sb/for sth)

respektabel [rɛspɛk'ta:bəl] *adj* respectable

respektieren [rɛspɛk'ti:rən] *vt* to respect

respektlos *adj* disrespectful

Respektsperson *f* person commanding respect

respektvoll *adj* respectful

Ressentiment [rɛsãti'mãː] **(-s, -s)** *nt* resentment

Ressort [rɛ'so:r] **(-s, -s)** *nt* department; **in das ~ von jdm fallen** (*lit, fig*) to be sb's department

Ressourcen [rɛ'sʊrsən] *pl* resources *pl*

Rest [rɛst] **(-(e)s, -e)** *m* remainder, rest; (*Überrest*) remains *pl*; **Reste** *pl* (*Comm*) remnants *pl*; **das hat mir den ~ gegeben** (*umg*) that finished me off

Restaurant [rɛsto'rãː] **(-s, -s)** *nt* restaurant

Restauration [rɛstaʊratsi'o:n] *f* restoration

restaurieren [rɛstaʊ'ri:rən] *vt* to restore

Restaurierung *f* restoration

Rest- *zW*: **Restbetrag** *m* remainder, outstanding sum; **Restlaufzeit** *f* (*Wirts*) unexpired term; **restlich** *adj* remaining; **restlos** *adj* complete; **Restmüll** *m* non-recyclable waste; **Restposten** *m* (*Comm*) remaining stock

Resultat [rezʊl'ta:t] **(-(e)s, -e)** *nt* result

Retorte [re'tɔrtə] **(-, -n)** *f* retort; **aus der ~** (*umg*) synthetic

Retortenbaby *nt* test-tube baby

retour [re'tu:r] *adv* (*veraltet*) back

Retouren *pl* (*Waren*) returns *pl*

retten ['rɛtən] *vt* to save, rescue ▷ *vr* to escape; **bist du noch zu ~?** (*umg*) are you out of your mind?; **sich vor etw** *dat* **nicht mehr ~ können** (*fig*) to be swamped with sth

Retter, in **(-s, -)** *m(f)* rescuer, saviour (*Brit*), savior (*US*)

Rettich ['rɛtɪç] **(-s, -e)** *m* radish

Rettung *f* rescue; (*Hilfe*) help; **seine letzte ~** his last hope

Rettungs- *zW*: **Rettungsaktion** *f* rescue operation; **Rettungsboot** *nt* lifeboat; **Rettungsdienst** *m* rescue service; **Rettungsgürtel** *m* lifebelt, life preserver (*US*); **rettungslos** *adj* hopeless; **Rettungsring** *m* = **Rettungsgürtel**; **Rettungsschwimmer** *m* lifesaver; (*am Strand*) lifeguard; **Rettungswagen** *m* ambulance

Return-Taste [ri'tø:rntastə] *f* (*Comput*) return key

retuschieren [retu'ʃi:rən] *vt* (*Phot*) to retouch

Reue ['rɔyə] **(-)** *f* remorse; (*Bedauern*) regret

reuen *vt*: **es reut ihn** he regrets it, he is sorry about it

reuig ['rɔyɪç] *adj* penitent

reumütig *adj* remorseful; (*Sünder*) contrite

Reuse ['rɔyzə] **(-, -n)** *f* fish trap

Revanche [re'vãːʃə] **(-, -n)** *f* revenge; (*Sport*) return match

revanchieren [revã'ʃi:rən] *vr* (*sich rächen*) to get one's own back, have one's revenge; (*erwidern*) to reciprocate, return the compliment

Revers [re've:r] **(-, -)** *nt or m* lapel

revidieren [revi'di:rən] *vt* to revise; (*Comm*) to audit

Revier [re'vi:r] **(-s, -e)** *nt* district; (*Min: Kohlenrevier*) (coal)mine; (*Jagdrevier*) preserve; (*Polizeirevier*) police station, station house (*US*); (*Dienstbereich*) beat (*Brit*), precinct (*US*); (*Mil*) sick bay

Revision [revizi'o:n] *f* revision; (*Comm*) auditing; (*Jur*) appeal

Revisionsverhandlung *f* appeal hearing

Revisor [re'vi:zɔr] **(-s, -en)** *m* (*Comm*) auditor

Revolte [re'vɔltə] **(-, -n)** *f* revolt

Revolution [revolutsi'o:n] *f* revolution

revolutionär [revolutsio'nɛ:r] *adj* revolutionary

Revolutionär, in [revolutsio'nɛ:r(ɪn)] **(-s, -e)** *m(f)* revolutionary

revolutionieren [revolutsio'ni:rən] *vt* to revolutionize

Revoluzzer [revo'lʊtsər] **(-s, -)** (*pej*) *m* would-be revolutionary

Revolver [re'vɔlvər] **(-s, -)** *m* revolver

Revue [rə'vy:] **(-, -n)** *f*: **etw ~ passieren lassen** (*fig*) to pass sth in review

Reykjavik ['raɪkjavi:k] **(-s)** *nt* Reykjavik

Rezensent [retsɛn'zɛnt] *m* reviewer, critic

rezensieren [retsɛn'zi:rən] *vt* to review

Rezension *f* review

Rezept [re'tsɛpt] **(-(e)s, -e)** *nt* (*Koch*) recipe; (*Med*) prescription

Rezeption [retsɛptsi'o:n] *f* (*von Hotel: Empfang*)

r

275

reception

rezeptpflichtig *adj* available only on prescription

Rezession [retsɛsiˈoːn] *f* (*Fin*) recession

rezitieren [retsiˈtiːrən] *vt* to recite

R-Gespräch [ˈɛrɡəʃprɛːç] *nt* (*Tel*) reverse charge call (*Brit*), collect call (*US*)

Rh *abk* (= *Rhesus(faktor) positiv*) Rh positive

rh *abk* (= *Rhesus(faktor) negativ*) Rh negative

Rhabarber [raˈbarbər] (**-s**) *m* rhubarb

Rhein [raɪn] (**-(e)s**) *m* Rhine

rhein. *abk* = **rheinisch**

Rheingau *m* wine-growing area along the Rhine

Rheinhessen *nt* wine-growing area along the Rhine

rheinisch *adj attrib* Rhenish, Rhineland

Rheinland *nt* Rhineland

Rheinländer, in *m(f)* Rhinelander

Rheinland-Pfalz *nt* Rhineland-Palatinate

Rhesusfaktor [ˈreːzusfaktɔr] *m* rhesus factor

Rhetorik [reˈtoːrɪk] *f* rhetoric

rhetorisch [reˈtoːrɪʃ] *adj* rhetorical

Rheuma [ˈrɔʏma] (**-s**) *nt* rheumatism

Rheumatismus [rɔʏmaˈtɪsmʊs] *m* rheumatism

Rhinozeros [riˈnoːtserɔs] (**-** *od* **-ses, -se**) *nt* rhinoceros; (*umg: Dummkopf*) fool

Rhld. *abk* = **Rheinland**

Rhodesien [roˈdeːziən] (**-s**) *nt* Rhodesia

Rhodos [ˈroːdɔs] (**-**) *nt* Rhodes

rhythmisch [ˈrʏtmɪʃ] *adj* rhythmical

Rhythmus *m* rhythm

RIAS [ˈriːas] (**-**) *m abk* (= *Rundfunk im amerikanischen Sektor (Berlin)*) broadcasting station in the former American sector of Berlin

Richtantenne [ˈrɪçt|antɛnə] (**-, -n**) *f* directional aerial (*bes Brit*) *od* antenna

richten [ˈrɪçtən] *vt* to direct; (*Waffe*) to aim; (*einstellen*) to adjust; (*instand setzen*) to repair; (*zurechtmachen*) to prepare, get ready; (*adressieren: Briefe, Anfragen*) to address; (*Bitten, Forderungen*) to make; (*in Ordnung bringen*) to do, fix; (*bestrafen*) to pass judgement on ▷ *vr*: **sich ~ nach** to go by; **~ an** +*akk* to direct at; (*fig*) to direct to; (*Briefe etc*) to address to; (*Bitten etc*) to make to; **~ auf** +*akk* to aim at; **wir ~ uns ganz nach unseren Kunden** we are guided entirely by our customers' wishes

Richter, in (**-s, -**) *m(f)* judge; **sich zum ~ machen** (*fig*) to set (o.s.) up in judgement; **richterlich** *adj* judicial

Richtgeschwindigkeit *f* recommended speed

richtig *adj* right, correct; (*echt*) proper ▷ *adv* correctly, right; (*umg: sehr*) really; **der/die R~e** the right one *od* person; **das R~e** the right thing; **die Uhr geht ~** the clock is right; **Richtigkeit** *f* correctness; **das hat schon seine Richtigkeit** it's right enough; **richtigstellen** *vt* to correct; **Richtigstellung** *f* correction, rectification

Richt- *zW*: **Richtlinie** *f* guideline; **Richtpreis** *m* recommended price; **Richtschnur** *f* (*fig: Grundsatz*) guiding principle

Richtung *f* direction; (*Tendenz*) tendency, orientation; **in jeder ~** each way

Richtungstaste *f* arrow key

Richtungsstreit *m* (*Pol*) factional dispute

richtungweisend *adj*: **~ sein** to point the way (ahead)

rieb *etc* [riːp] *vb siehe* **reiben**

riechen [ˈriːçən] *unreg vt, vi* to smell; **an etw** *dat* **~** to smell sth; **es riecht nach Gas** there's a smell of gas; **ich kann das/ihn nicht ~** (*umg*) I can't stand it/him; **das konnte ich doch nicht ~!** (*umg*) how was I (supposed) to know?

Riecher (**-s, -**) *m*: **einen guten** *od* **den richtigen ~ für etw haben** (*umg*) to have a nose for sth

Ried [riːt] (**-(e)s, -e**) *nt* reed; (*Moor*) marsh

rief *etc* [riːf] *vb siehe* **rufen**

Riege [ˈriːɡə] (**-, -n**) *f* team, squad

Riegel [ˈriːɡəl] (**-s, -**) *m* bolt, bar; **einer Sache** *dat* **einen ~ vorschieben** (*fig*) to clamp down on sth

Riemen [ˈriːmən] (**-s, -**) *m* strap; (*Gürtel, Tech*) belt; (*Naut*) oar; **sich am ~ reißen** (*fig: umg*) to get a grip on o.s.; **Riemenantrieb** *m* belt drive

Riese [ˈriːzə] (**-n, -n**) *m* giant

rieseln *vi* to trickle; (*Schnee*) to fall gently

Riesen- *zW*: **Riesenerfolg** *m* enormous success; **Riesengebirge** *nt* (*Geog*) Sudeten Mountains *pl*; **riesengroß** *adj*, **riesenhaft** *adj* colossal, gigantic, huge; **Riesenrad** *nt* big *od* Ferris wheel; **Riesenschritt** *m*: **sich mit Riesenschritten nähern** (*fig*) to be drawing on apace; **Riesenslalom** *m* (*Ski*) giant slalom

riesig [ˈriːzɪç] *adj* enormous, huge, vast

Riesin *f* giantess

riet *etc* [riːt] *vb siehe* **raten**

Riff [rɪf] (**-(e)s, -e**) *nt* reef

rigoros [riɡoˈroːs] *adj* rigorous

Rille [ˈrɪlə] (**-, -n**) *f* groove

Rind [rɪnt] (**-(e)s, -er**) *nt* ox; (*Kuh*) cow; (*Koch*) beef; **Rinder** *pl* cattle *pl*; **vom ~** beef

Rinde [ˈrɪndə] (**-, -n**) *f* rind; (*Baumrinde*) bark; (*Brotrinde*) crust

Rinderbraten *m* roast beef

Rinderwahn [ˈrɪndərvaːn] *m* mad cow disease

Rindfleisch *nt* beef

Rindvieh *nt* cattle *pl*; (*umg*) blockhead, stupid oaf

Ring [rɪŋ] (**-(e)s, -e**) *m* ring; **Ringbuch** *nt* ring binder

ringeln [ˈrɪŋəln] *vt* (*Pflanze*) to (en)twine; (*Schwanz etc*) to curl ▷ *vr* to go curly, curl; (*Rauch*) to curl up(wards)

Ringelnatter *f* grass snake

Ringeltaube *f* wood pigeon

ringen *unreg vi* to wrestle; **nach** *od* **um etw ~** to struggle for sth; **Ringen** (**-s**) *nt* wrestling

Ringer (**-s, -**) *m* wrestler

Ring- *zW*: **Ringfinger** *m* ring finger; **ringförmig** *adj* ring-shaped; **Ringkampf** *m* wrestling bout; **Ringrichter** *m* referee

rings *adv*: **~ um** round; **ringsherum** *adv* round about

Ringstraße *f* ring road

ringsum, ringsumher *adv (rundherum)* round about; *(überall)* all round
Rinne ['rɪnə] **(-, -n)** *f* gutter, drain
rinnen *unreg vi* to run, trickle
Rinnsal (-s, -e) *nt* trickle of water
Rinnstein *m* gutter
Rippchen ['rɪpçən] *nt* small rib; cutlet
Rippe ['rɪpə] **(-, -n)** *f* rib
Rippen- *zW:* **Rippenfellentzündung** *f* pleurisy; **Rippenspeer** *m od nt (Koch):* **Kasseler Rippenspeer** *slightly cured pork spare rib;* **Rippenstoß** *m* dig in the ribs
Risiko ['ri:ziko] **(-s, -s** *od* **Risiken)** *nt* risk; **risikobehaftet** *adj* fraught with risk; **Risikoinvestition** *f* sunk cost
riskant [rɪs'kant] *adj* risky, hazardous
riskieren [rɪs'ki:rən] *vt* to risk
riss *etc* [rɪs] *vb siehe* **reißen**
Riss (-es, -e) *m* tear; *(in Mauer, Tasse etc)* crack; *(in Haut)* scratch; *(Tech)* design
rissig ['rɪsɪç] *adj* torn; cracked; scratched
ritt *etc* [rɪt] *vb siehe* **reiten**
Ritt (-(e)s, -e) *m* ride
Ritter (-s, -) *m* knight; **jdn zum ~ schlagen** to knight sb; **arme ~** *pl (Koch) sweet French toast, made with bread soaked in milk;* **ritterlich** *adj* chivalrous; **Ritterschlag** *m* knighting; **Rittertum (-s)** *nt* chivalry; **Ritterzeit** *f* age of chivalry
rittlings *adv* astride
Ritual [ritu'a:l] **(-s, -e** *od* **-ien)** *nt (lit, fig)* ritual
rituell [ritu'ɛl] *adj* ritual
Ritus ['ri:tʊs] **(-, Riten)** *m* rite
Ritze ['rɪtsə] **(-, -n)** *f* crack, chink
ritzen *vt* to scratch; **die Sache ist geritzt** *(umg)* it's all fixed up
Rivale [ri'va:lə] **(-n, -n)** *m,* **Rivalin** *f* rival
rivalisieren [rivali'zi:rən] *vi:* **mit jdm ~ to** compete with sb
Rivalität [rivali'tɛːt] *f* rivalry
Riviera [rivi'eːra] **(-)** *f* Riviera
Rizinusöl ['riːtsinʊs|øːl] *nt* castor oil
r.-k. *abk (= römisch-katholisch)* R.C.
Robbe ['rɔbə] **(-, -n)** *f* seal
robben ['rɔbən] *vi (Hilfsverb sein: auch Mil)* to crawl *(using elbows)*
Robbenfang *m* seal hunting
Robe ['roːbə] **(-, -n)** *f* robe
Roboter ['rɔbɔtər] **(-s, -)** *m* robot; **Robotertechnik** *f* robotics *sing*
Robotik ['rɔbɔtɪk] *f* robotics *sing*
robust [ro'bʊst] *adj (Mensch, Gesundheit)* robust; *(Material)* tough
roch *etc* [rɔx] *vb siehe* **riechen**
Rochade [rɔ'xa:də] **(-, -n)** *f (Schach):* **die kleine/ große ~** castling king's side/queen's side
röcheln ['rœçəln] *vi* to wheeze; *(Sterbender)* to give the death rattle
Rock¹ [rɔk] **(-(e)s, ⁓e)** *m* skirt; *(Jackett)* jacket; *(Uniformrock)* tunic
Rock² [rɔk] **(-(s), -(s))** *m (Mus)* rock; **Rockmusik** *f* rock music
Rockzipfel *m:* **an Mutters ~ hängen** *(umg)* to

cling to (one's) mother's skirts
Rodel ['roːdəl] **(-s, -)** *m* toboggan; **Rodelbahn** *f* toboggan run
rodeln *vi* to toboggan
roden ['roːdən] *vt, vi* to clear
Rogen ['roːgən] **(-s, -)** *m* roe
Roggen ['rɔgən] **(-s, -)** *m* rye; **Roggenbrot** *nt* rye bread; *(Vollkornbrot)* black bread
roh [roː] *adj* raw; *(Mensch)* coarse, crude; **~e Gewalt** brute force; **Rohbau** *m* shell of a building; **Roheisen** *nt* pig iron; **Rohfassung** *f* rough draft; **Rohkost** *f* raw fruit and vegetables *pl;* **Rohling** *m* ruffian; **Rohmaterial** *nt* raw material; **Rohöl** *nt* crude oil
Rohr [roːr] **(-(e)s, -e)** *nt* pipe, tube; *(Bot)* cane; *(Schilf)* reed; *(Gewehrrohr)* barrel; **Rohrbruch** *m* burst pipe
Röhre ['røːrə] **(-, -n)** *f* tube, pipe; *(Rundf etc)* valve; *(Backröhre)* oven
Rohr- *zW:* **Rohrgeflecht** *nt* wickerwork; **Rohrleger (-s, -)** *m* plumber; **Rohrleitung** *f* pipeline; **Rohrpost** *f* pneumatic post; **Rohrspatz** *m:* **schimpfen wie ein Rohrspatz** *(umg)* to curse and swear; **Rohrstock** *m* cane; **Rohrstuhl** *m* basket chair; **Rohrzucker** *m* cane sugar
Rohseide *f* raw silk
Rohstoff *m* raw material
Rokoko ['rokoko] **(-s)** *nt* rococo
Rolladen *m siehe* **Rollladen**
Rollbahn *f (Aviat)* runway
Rollbrett *nt* skateboard
Rolle ['rɔlə] **(-, -n)** *f* roll; *(Theat, Soziologie)* role; *(Garnrolle etc)* reel, spool; *(Walze)* roller; *(Wäscherolle)* mangle, wringer; **bei** *od* **in etw** *dat* **eine ~ spielen** to play a part in sth; **aus der ~ fallen** *(fig)* to forget o.s.; **keine ~ spielen** not to matter
rollen *vi* to roll; *(Aviat)* to taxi ▷ *vt* to roll; *(Wäsche)* to mangle, put through the wringer; **den Stein ins R~ bringen** *(fig)* to start the ball rolling
Rollen- *zW:* **Rollenbesetzung** *f (Theat)* cast; **Rollenkonflikt** *m (Psych)* role conflict; **Rollenspiel** *nt* role-play; **Rollentausch** *m* exchange of roles; *(Soziologie)* role reversal
Roller (-s, -) *m* scooter; *(Welle)* roller
Roll- *zW:* **Rollfeld** *nt* runway; **Rollkragen** *m* roll *od* polo neck; **Rollladen** *m* shutter; **Rollmops** *m* pickled herring
Rollo ['rɔlo] **(-, -s)** *nt* (roller) blind
Roll- *zW:* **Rollschrank** *m* roll-fronted cupboard; **Rollschuh** *m* roller skate; **Rollschuhlaufen** *nt* roller skating; **Rollsplitt** *m* grit; **Rollstuhl** *m* wheelchair; **Rolltreppe** *f* escalator
Rom [roːm] **(-s)** *nt* Rome; **das sind Zustände wie im alten ~** *(umg: unmoralisch)* it's disgraceful; *(: primitiv)* it's medieval *(umg)*
röm. *abk =* **römisch**
Roman [ro'ma:n] **(-s, -e)** *m* novel; **(jdm) einen ganzen ~ erzählen** *(umg)* to give (sb) a long rigmarole; **Romanheft** *nt* pulp novel
romanisch *adj (Volk, Sprache)* Romance; *(Kunst)*

r

Romanesque

Romanistik [roma'nɪstɪk] f (Univ) Romance languages and literature

Romanschreiber m novelist

Romanschriftsteller m novelist

Romantik [ro'mantɪk] f romanticism

Romantiker, in (-s, -) m(f) romanticist

romantisch adj romantic

Romanze [ro'mantsə] (-, -n) f romance

Römer ['rø:mər] (-s, -) m wineglass; (Mensch) Roman; **Römertopf®** m (Koch) = (chicken) brick

römisch ['rø:mɪʃ] adj Roman; **römisch-katholisch** adj Roman Catholic

röm.-kath. abk (= römisch-katholisch) R.C.

Rommé, Rommee [rɔ'me:] (-s, -s) nt rummy

röntgen ['rœntgən] vt to X-ray; **Röntgenaufnahme** f X-ray; **Röntgenbild** nt X-ray; **Röntgenstrahlen** pl X-rays pl

rosa ['ro:za] adj inv pink, rose(-coloured)

Rose ['ro:zə] (-, -n) f rose

Rosé [ro'ze:] (-s, -s) m rosé

Rosenkohl m Brussels sprouts pl

Rosenkranz m rosary

Rosenmontag m Monday of Shrovetide; siehe auch **Karneval**

Rosette [ro'zɛtə] f rosette

rosig ['ro:zɪç] adj rosy

Rosine [ro'zi:nə] (-, -n) f raisin; **(große) ~n im Kopf haben** (umg) to have big ideas

Rosmarin ['ro:smari:n] (-s) m rosemary

Ross [rɔs] (-es, -e) nt horse, steed; **auf dem hohen ~ sitzen** (fig) to be on one's high horse; **Rosskastanie** f horse chestnut; **Rosskur** (umg) f kill-or-cure remedy

Rost [rɔst] (-(e)s, -e) m rust; (Gitter) grill, gridiron; (Bettrost) springs pl; **Rostbraten** m roast(ed) meat, roast; **Rostbratwurst** f grilled od barbecued sausage

rosten vi to rust

rösten ['rø:stən] vt to roast; (Brot) to toast

rostfrei adj (Stahl) stainless

rostig adj rusty

Röstkartoffeln pl fried potatoes pl

Rostschutz m rustproofing

rot [ro:t] adj red; **~ werden, einen roten Kopf bekommen** to blush, go red; **die R~e Armee** the Red Army; **das R~e Kreuz** the Red Cross; **das R~e Meer** the Red Sea

Rotation [rotatsi'o:n] f rotation

rot- zW: **rotbäckig** adj red-cheeked; **Rotbarsch** m rosefish; **rotblond** adj strawberry blond

Röte ['rø:tə] (-) f redness

Röteln pl German measles sing

röten vt, vr to redden

rothaarig adj red-haired

rotieren [ro'ti:rən] vi to rotate

Rot- zW: **Rotkäppchen** nt Little Red Riding Hood; **Rotkehlchen** nt robin; **Rotkohl** m red cabbage; **Rotkraut** nt red cabbage; **rotsehen** (umg: unreg) vi to see red, to become angry; **Rotstift** m red pencil; **Rotwein** m red wine

Rotz [rɔts] (-es, -e) (umg) m snot; **rotzfrech** (umg) adj cocky; **rotznäsig** (umg) adj snotty-nosed

Rouge [ru:ʒ] (-s, -s) nt rouge

Roulade [ru'la:də] (-, -n) f (Koch) beef olive

Roulette, Roulett [ru'lɛt] (-s, -s) nt roulette

Route ['ru:tə] (-, -n) f route

Routine [ru'ti:nə] f experience; (Gewohnheit) routine

routiniert [ruti'ni:ərt] adj experienced

Rowdy ['raʊdɪ] (-s, -s) m hooligan; (zerstörerisch) vandal; (lärmend) rowdy (type)

Ruanda [ru'anda] nt Rwanda

ruandisch adj Rwandan

rubbeln ['rʊbəln] (umg) vt, vi to rub

Rübe ['ry:bə] (-, -n) f turnip; **Gelbe ~** carrot; **Rote ~** beetroot (Brit), beet (US)

Rübenzucker m beet sugar

Rubin [ru'bi:n] (-s, -e) m ruby

Rubrik [ru'bri:k] f heading; (Spalte) column

Ruck [rʊk] (-(e)s, -e) m jerk, jolt; **sich** dat **einen ~ geben** (fig: umg) to make an effort

ruck adv: **das geht ~, zuck** it won't take a second

Rückantwort f reply, answer; **um ~ wird gebeten** please reply

ruckartig adj: **er stand ~ auf** he shot to his feet

Rück- zW: **Rückbesinnung** f recollection; **rückbezüglich** adj reflexive; **Rückblende** f flashback; **rückblenden** vi to flash back; **Rückblick** m: **im Rückblick auf etw** akk looking back on sth; **rückblickend** adj retrospective ▷ adv in retrospect; **rückdatieren** vt to backdate

Rücken (-s, -) m back; (Bergrücken) ridge; **jdm in den ~ fallen** (fig) to stab sb in the back

rücken vt, vi to move

Rücken- zW: **Rückendeckung** f backing; **Rückenlage** f supine position; **Rückenlehne** f back (of chair); **Rückenmark** nt spinal cord; **Rückenschwimmen** nt backstroke; **Rückenstärkung** f (fig) moral support; **Rückenwind** m following wind

Rück- zW: **Rückerstattung** f return, restitution; **Rückfahrkarte** f return ticket (Brit), round-trip ticket (US); **Rückfahrt** f return journey; **Rückfall** m relapse; **rückfällig** adj relapsed; **rückfällig werden** to relapse; **Rückflug** m return flight; **Rückfrage** f question; **nach Rückfrage bei der zuständigen Behörde** ... after checking this with the appropriate authority ...; **rückfragen** vi to inquire; (nachprüfen) to check; **Rückführung** f (von Menschen) repatriation, return; **Rückgabe** f return; **gegen Rückgabe (+gen)** on return (of); **Rückgang** m decline, fall; **rückgängig** adj: **etw rückgängig machen** (widerrufen) to undo sth; (Bestellung) to cancel sth; **Rückgewinnung** f recovery; (von Land, Gebiet) reclaiming; (aus verbrauchten Stoffen) recycling

Rückgrat nt spine, backbone

Rück- zW: **Rückgriff** m recourse; **Rückhalt** m backing; (Einschränkung) reserve; **rückhaltlos**

adj unreserved; **Rückhand** *f* (*Sport*) backhand;
rückkaufbar *adj* redeemable; **Rückkehr**
(-**,**) *f* return; **Rückkoppelung** *f* feedback;
Rücklage *f* reserve, savings *pl*; **Rücklauf**
m reverse running; (*beim Tonband*) rewind;
(*von Maschinenteil*) return travel; **rückläufig**
adj declining, falling; **eine rückläufige
Entwicklung** a decline; **Rücklicht** *nt*
rear light; **rücklings** *adv* from behind;
(*rückwärts*) backwards; **Rücknahme** *f* (*Univ*)
reregistration; **Rücknahme** (-**, -n**) *f* taking
back; **Rückporto** *nt* return postage; **Rückreise**
f return journey; (*Naut*) home voyage; **Rückruf**
m recall

Rucksack ['rʊkzak] *m* rucksack

Rück- *zW*: **Rückschau** *f* reflection;
rückschauend *adj* = **rückblickend**; **Rückschlag**
m setback; **Rückschluss** *m* conclusion;
Rückschritt *m* retrogression; **rückschrittlich**
adj reactionary; (*Entwicklung*) retrograde;
Rückseite *f* back; (*von Münze etc*) reverse;
siehe Rückseite see over(leaf); **rücksetzen** *vt*
(*Comput*) to reset

Rücksicht *f* consideration; ~ **nehmen auf** +*akk*
to show consideration for; **Rücksichtnahme** *f*
consideration

rücksichtslos *adj* inconsiderate; (*Fahren*)
reckless; (*unbarmherzig*) ruthless

Rücksichtslosigkeit *f* lack of consideration;
(*beim Fahren*) recklessness; (*Unbarmherzigkeit*)
ruthlessness

rücksichtsvoll *adj* considerate

Rück- *zW*: **Rücksitz** *m* back seat; **Rückspiegel**
m (*Aut*) rear-view mirror; **Rückspiel** *nt* return
match; **Rücksprache** *f* further discussion
od talk; **Rücksprache mit jdm nehmen**
to confer with sb; **Rückstand** *m* arrears *pl*;
(*Verzug*) delay; **rückständig** *adj* backward,
out-of-date; (*Zahlungen*) in arrears; **Rückstau**
m (*Aut*) tailback (*Brit*), line of cars; **Rückstoß**
m recoil; **Rückstrahler** (-**s, -**) *m* rear reflector;
Rückstrom *m* (*von Menschen, Fahrzeugen*) return;
Rücktaste *f* (*an Schreibmaschine*) backspace key;
Rücktritt *m* resignation; **Rücktrittbremse**
f backpedal brake; **Rücktrittsklausel** *f*
(*Vertrag*) escape clause; **Rückvergütung** *f*
repayment; (*Comm*) refund; **rückversichern**
vt, vi to reinsure ▷ *vr* to check (up *od* back);
Rückversicherung *f* reinsurance; **rückwärtig**
adj rear; **rückwärts** *adv* backward(s), back;
Rückwärtsgang *m* (*Aut*) reverse gear; **im
Rückwärtsgang fahren** to reverse; **Rückweg**
m return journey, way back; **rückwirkend**
adj retroactive; **Rückwirkung** *f* repercussion;
**eine Zahlung mit Rückwirkung
vom ...** a payment backdated to ...; **eine
Gesetzesänderung mit Rückwirkung
vom ...** an amendment made retrospective
to ...; **Rückzahlung** *f* repayment; **Rückzieher**
(*umg*) *m*: **einen Rückzieher machen** to back
out; **Rückzug** *m* retreat; **Rückzugsgefecht** *nt*
(*Mil, fig*) rearguard action

rüde ['ry:də] *adj* blunt, gruff

Rüde (-**n, -n**) *m* male dog

Rudel ['ru:dəl] (-**s, -**) *nt* pack; (*von Hirschen*) herd

Ruder ['ru:dər] (-**s, -**) *nt* oar; (*Steuer*) rudder; **das
~ fest in der Hand haben** (*fig*) to be in control
of the situation; **Ruderboot** *nt* rowing boat;
Ruderer (-**s, -**) *m* rower, oarsman

rudern *vt, vi* to row; **mit den Armen** ~ (*fig*) to
flail one's arms about

Ruf [ru:f] (-**(e)s, -e**) *m* call, cry; (*Ansehen*)
reputation; (*Univ: Berufung*) offer of a chair

rufen *unreg vt, vi* to call; (*ausrufen*) to cry; **um
Hilfe** ~ to call for help; **das kommt mir wie
ge~** that's just what I needed

Rüffel ['ryfəl] (-**s, -**) (*umg*) *m* telling-off, ticking-
off

Ruf- *zW*: **Rufmord** *m* character assassination;
Rufname *m* usual (first) name; **Rufnummer**
f (tele)phone number; **Rufsäule** *f* (*für
Taxi*) telephone; (*an Autobahn*) emergency
telephone; **Rufzeichen** *nt* (*Rundf*) call sign;
(*Tel*) ringing tone

Rüge ['ry:gə] (-**, -n**) *f* reprimand, rebuke

rügen *vt* to reprimand

Ruhe ['ru:ə] (-) *f* rest; (*Ungestörtheit*) peace,
quiet; (*Gelassenheit, Stille*) calm; (*Schweigen*)
silence; ~! be quiet!, silence!; **angenehme ~!**
sleep well!; ~ **bewahren** to stay cool *od* calm;
das lässt ihm keine ~ he can't stop thinking
about it; **sich zur ~ setzen** to retire; **die ~
weghaben** (*umg*) to be unflappable; **immer
mit der ~** (*umg*) don't panic; **die letzte ~
finden** (*liter*) to be laid to rest; **Ruhelage** *f* (*von
Mensch*) reclining position; (*Med: bei Bruch*)
immobile position; **ruhelos** *adj* restless

ruhen *vi* to rest; (*Verkehr*) to cease; (*Arbeit*) to
stop, cease; (*Waffen*) to be laid down; (*begraben
sein*) to lie, be buried

Ruhe- *zW*: **Ruhepause** *f* break; **Ruheplatz**
m resting place; **Ruhestand** *m* retirement;
Ruhestätte *f*: **letzte Ruhestätte** final
resting place; **Ruhestörung** *f* breach of the
peace; **Ruhetag** *m* closing day

ruhig ['ru:ɪç] *adj* quiet; (*bewegungslos*) still;
(*Hand*) steady; (*gelassen, friedlich*) calm;
(*Gewissen*) clear; **tu das** ~ feel free to do that;
etw ~ mit ansehen (*gleichgültig*) to stand by
and watch sth; **du könntest ~ mal etwas für
mich tun!** it's about time you did something
for me!

Ruhm [ru:m] (-**(e)s**) *m* fame, glory

rühmen ['ry:mən] *vt* to praise ▷ *vr* to boast

rühmlich *adj* praiseworthy; (*Ausnahme*) notable

ruhmlos *adj* inglorious

ruhmreich *adj* glorious

Ruhr [ru:r] (-) *f* dysentery

Rührei ['ry:r|aɪ] *nt* scrambled egg

rühren *vt* (*lit, fig*) to move, stir (*auch Koch*) ▷ *vr*
(*lit, fig*) to move, stir ▷ *vi*: ~ **von** to come *od* stem
from; ~ **an** +*akk* to touch; (*fig*) to touch on

rührend *adj* touching, moving; **das ist ~ von
Ihnen** that is sweet of you

Ruhrgebiet *nt* Ruhr (area)

rührig *adj* active, lively

rührselig *adj* sentimental, emotional
Rührung *f* emotion
Ruin [ru'iːn] (**-s**) *m* ruin; **vor dem ~ stehen** to be on the brink *od* verge of ruin
Ruine (**-, -n**) *f* (*lit, fig*) ruin
ruinieren [rui'niːrən] *vt* to ruin
rülpsen ['rʏlpsən] *vi* to burp, belch
Rum [rʊm] (**-s, -s**) *m* rum
rum (*umg*) *adv* = **herum**
Rumäne [ru'mɛːnə] (**-n, -n**) *m* Romanian
Rumänien (**-s**) *nt* Romania
Rumänin *f* Romanian
rumänisch *adj* Romanian
rumfuhrwerken ['rʊmfuːrvɛrkən] (*umg*) *vt* to bustle around
Rummel ['rʊməl] (**-s**) (*umg*) *m* hurly-burly; (*Jahrmarkt*) fair; **Rummelplatz** *m* fairground, fair
rumoren [ru'moːrən] *vi* to be noisy, make a noise
Rumpelkammer ['rʊmpəlkamər] *f* junk room
rumpeln *vi* to rumble; (*holpern*) to jolt
Rumpf [rʊmpf] (**-(e)s, ̈-e**) *m* trunk, torso; (*Aviat*) fuselage; (*Naut*) hull
rümpfen ['rʏmpfən] *vt* (*Nase*) to turn up
Rumtopf *m* *soft fruit in rum*
rund [rʊnt] *adj* round ▷ *adv* (*etwa*) around; **~ um etw** round sth; **jetzt gehts ~** (*umg*) this is where the fun starts; **wenn er das erfährt, gehts ~** (*umg*) there'll be a to-do when he finds out; **Rundbogen** *m* Norman *od* Romanesque arch; **Rundbrief** *m* circular
Runde ['rʊndə] (**-, -n**) *f* round; (*in Rennen*) lap; (*Gesellschaft*) circle; **die ~ machen** to do the rounds; (*herumgegeben werden*) to be passed round; **über die ~n kommen** (*Sport, fig*) to pull through; **eine ~ spendieren** *od* **schmeißen** (*umg: Getränke*) to stand a round
runden *vt* to make round ▷ *vr* (*fig*) to take shape
rund- *zW*: **runderneuert** *adj* (*Reifen*) remoulded (*Brit*), remolded (*US*); **Rundfahrt** *f* (round) trip; **Rundfrage** *f*: **Rundfrage (unter** +*dat*) survey (of)
Rundfunk ['rʊntfʊŋk] (**-(e)s**) *m* broadcasting; (*bes Hörfunk*) radio; (*Rundfunkanstalt*) broadcasting corporation; **im ~** on the radio; **Rundfunkanstalt** *f* broadcasting corporation; **Rundfunkempfang** *m* reception; **Rundfunkgebühr** *f* licence (*Brit*), license (*US*); **Rundfunkgerät** *nt* radio set; **Rundfunksendung** *f* broadcast, radio programme (*Brit*) *od* program (*US*)
Rund- *zW*: **Rundgang** *m* (*Spaziergang*) walk; (*von Wachmann*) rounds *pl*; (*von Briefträger etc*) round; (*zur Besichtigung*): **Rundgang (durch)** tour (of); **rundheraus** *adv* straight out, bluntly;

rundherum *adv* all round; (*fig: umg: völlig*) totally; **rundlich** *adj* plump, rounded; **Rundreise** *f* round trip; **Rundschreiben** *nt* (*Comm*) circular; **rundum** *adv* all around; (*fig*) completely
Rundung *f* curve, roundness
rundweg *adv* straight out
runter ['rʊntər] (*umg*) *adv* = **herunter; hinunter; runterwürgen** (*umg*) *vt* (*Ärger*) to swallow
Runzel ['rʊntsəl] (**-, -n**) *f* wrinkle
runzelig, runzlig *adj* wrinkled
runzeln *vt* to wrinkle; **die Stirn ~** to frown
Rüpel ['ryːpəl] (**-s, -**) *m* lout; **rüpelhaft** *adj* loutish
rupfen ['rʊpfən] *vt* to pluck
Rupfen (**-s, -**) *m* sackcloth
ruppig ['rʊpɪç] *adj* rough, gruff
Rüsche ['ryːʃə] (**-, -n**) *f* frill
Ruß [ruːs] (**-es**) *m* soot
Russe ['rʊsə] (**-n, -n**) *m* Russian
Rüssel ['rʏsəl] (**-s, -**) *m* snout; (*Elefantenrüssel*) trunk
rußen *vi* to smoke; (*Ofen*) to be sooty
rußig *adj* sooty
Russin *f* Russian
russisch *adj* Russian; **~e Eier** (*Koch*) egg(s) mayonnaise
Russland (**-s**) *nt* Russia
rüsten ['rʏstən] *vt, vi, vr* to prepare; (*Mil*) to arm
rüstig ['rʏstɪç] *adj* sprightly, vigorous; **Rüstigkeit** *f* sprightliness, vigour (*Brit*), vigor (*US*)
rustikal [rʊsti'kaːl] *adj*: **sich ~ einrichten** to furnish one's home in a rustic style
Rüstung ['rʏstʊŋ] *f* preparation; (*Mil*) arming; (*Ritterrüstung*) armour (*Brit*), armor (*US*); (*Waffen etc*) armaments *pl*
Rüstungs- *zW*: **Rüstungsgegner** *m* opponent of the arms race; **Rüstungsindustrie** *f* armaments industry; **Rüstungskontrolle** *f* arms control; **Rüstungswettlauf** *m* arms race
Rüstzeug *nt* tools *pl*; (*fig*) capacity
Rute ['ruːtə] (**-, -n**) *f* rod, switch
Rutsch [rʊtʃ] (**-(e)s, -e**) *m* slide; (*Erdrutsch*) landslide; **guten ~!** (*umg*) have a good New Year!; **Rutschbahn** *f* slide
rutschen *vi* to slide; (*ausrutschen*) to slip; **auf dem Stuhl hin und her ~** to fidget around on one's chair
rutschfest *adj* non-slip
rutschig *adj* slippery
rütteln ['rʏtəln] *vt, vi* to shake, jolt; **daran ist nicht zu ~** (*fig: umg: an Grundsätzen*) there's no doubt about that
Rüttelschwelle *f* (*Aut*) rumble strips *pl*

Ss

S¹, s¹ [ɛs] *nt* S, s; **S wie Samuel** ≈ S for Sugar
S² [ɛs] *abk* (= *Süden*) S; (= *Seite*) p; (= *Schilling*) S
s² *abk* (= *Sekunde*) sec.; (= *siehe*) v., vid.
Sa. *abk* = **Samstag**
SA (-) *f abk* (= *Sturmabteilung*) SA
s. a. *abk* (= *siehe auch*) see also
Saal [zaːl] (**-(e)s, Säle**) *m* hall; (*für Sitzungen etc*) room
Saarland ['zaːrlant] (**-s**) *nt* Saarland
Saat [zaːt] (**-, -en**) *f* seed; (*Pflanzen*) crop; (*Säen*) sowing; **Saatgut** *nt* seed(s *pl*)
Sabbat ['zabat] (**-s, -e**) *m* sabbath
sabbern ['zabərn] (*umg*) *vi* to dribble
Säbel ['zɛːbəl] (**-s, -**) *m* sabre (*Brit*), saber (*US*); **Säbelrasseln** *nt* sabre-rattling
Sabotage [zabo'taːʒə] (**-, -n**) *f* sabotage
sabotieren [zabo'tiːrən] *vt* to sabotage
Saccharin, Sacharin [zaxa'riːn] (**-s**) *nt* saccharin
Sachanlagen ['zaxˌanlaːgən] *pl* tangible assets *pl*
Sachbearbeiter, in *m(f)*: **~ (für)** (*Beamter*) official in charge (of)
Sachbuch *nt* non-fiction book
sachdienlich *adj* relevant, helpful
Sache ['zaxə] (**-, -n**) *f* thing; (*Angelegenheit*) affair, business; (*Frage*) matter; (*Pflicht*) task; (*Thema*) subject; (*Jur*) case; (*Aufgabe*) job; (*Ideal*) cause; (*umg*: *km/h*): **mit 60/100 ~n** ≈ at 40/60 (mph); **ich habe mir die ~ anders vorgestellt** I had imagined things differently; **er versteht seine ~** he knows what he's doing; **das ist so eine ~** (*umg*) it's a bit tricky; **mach keine ~n!** (*umg*) don't be daft!; **bei der ~ bleiben** (*bei Diskussion*) to keep to the point; **bei der ~ sein** to be with it (*umg*); **das ist ~ der Polizei** this is a matter for the police; **zur ~** to the point; **das ist eine runde ~** that's well-balanced *od* rounded-off
Sachertorte ['zaxərtɔrtə] *f* rich chocolate cake, sachertorte
Sach- *zW*: **sachgemäß** *adj* appropriate, suitable; **Sachkenntnis** *f* (*in Bezug auf Wissensgebiet*) knowledge of the/his *etc* subject; (*in Bezug auf Sachlage*) knowledge of the facts; **sachkundig** *adj* (well-)informed; **sich sachkundig machen** to inform oneself; **Sachlage** *f* situation, state of affairs;

Sachleistung *f* payment in kind; **sachlich** *adj* matter-of-fact; (*Kritik etc*) objective; (*Irrtum, Angabe*) factual; **bleiben Sie bitte sachlich** don't get carried away (*umg*); (*nicht persönlich werden*) please stay objective
sächlich ['zɛxlɪç] *adj* neuter
Sachregister *nt* subject index
Sachschaden *m* material damage
Sachse ['zaksə] (**-n, -n**) *m* Saxon
Sachsen (**-s**) *nt* Saxony; **Sachsen-Anhalt** (**-s**) *nt* Saxony Anhalt
Sächsin ['zɛksɪn] *f* Saxon
sächsisch ['zɛksɪʃ] *adj* Saxon
sacht, sachte *adv* softly, gently
Sach- *zW*: **Sachverhalt** (**-(e)s, -e**) *m* facts *pl* (of the case); **sachverständig** *adj* (*Urteil*) expert; (*Publikum*) informed; **Sachverständige, r** *f(m)* expert; **Sachzwang** *m* force of circumstances
Sack [zak] (**-(e)s, ̈e**) *m* sack; (*aus Papier, Plastik*) bag; (*Anat, Zool*) sac; (*umg!: Hoden*) balls *pl* (!); (: *Kerl, Bursche*) bastard (!); **mit ~ und Pack** (*umg*) with bag and baggage
sacken *vi* to sag, sink
Sackgasse *f* cul-de-sac, dead-end street (*US*)
Sackhüpfen *nt* sack race
Sadismus [za'dɪsmʊs] *m* sadism
Sadist, in [za'dɪst(ɪn)] *m(f)* sadist; **sadistisch** *adj* sadistic
Sadomasochismus [zadomazɔ'xɪsmʊs] *m* sadomasochism
säen ['zɛːən] *vt, vi* to sow; **dünn gesät** (*fig*) thin on the ground, few and far between
Safari [za'faːri] (**-, -s**) *f* safari
Safe [zeːf] (**-s, -s**) *m od nt* safe
Saft [zaft] (**-(e)s, ̈e**) *m* juice; (*Bot*) sap; **ohne ~ und Kraft** (*fig*) wishy-washy (*umg*), effete
saftig *adj* juicy; (*Grün*) lush; (*umg: Rechnung, Ohrfeige*) hefty; (*Brief, Antwort*) hard-hitting
Saftladen (*pej: umg*) *m* rum joint
saftlos *adj* dry
Sage ['zaːgə] (**-, -n**) *f* saga
Säge ['zɛːgə] (**-, -n**) *f* saw; **Sägeblatt** *nt* saw blade; **Sägemehl** *nt* sawdust
sagen ['zaːgən] *vt, vi*: **(jdm etw) ~** to say (sth to sb), tell (sb sth); **unter uns gesagt** between you and me (and the gatepost (*hum umg*)); **lass dir das gesagt sein** take it from me; **das hat nichts zu ~** that doesn't mean anything; **sagt**

S

dir der Name etwas? does the name mean anything to you?; **das ist nicht gesagt** that's by no means certain; **sage und schreibe** (whether you) believe it or not

sägen vt, vi to saw; (hum: umg: schnarchen) to snore, saw wood (US)

sagenhaft adj legendary; (umg) great, smashing

sagenumwoben adj legendary

Sägespäne pl wood shavings pl

Sägewerk nt sawmill

sah etc [za:] vb siehe **sehen**

Sahara [za'ha:ra] f Sahara (Desert)

Sahne ['za:nə] (-) f cream

Saison [zɛ'zõ:] (-, -s) f season

saisonal [zɛzo'na:l] adj seasonal

Saisonarbeiter m seasonal worker

saisonbedingt adj seasonal

Saite ['zaɪtə] (-, -n) f string; **andere ~n aufziehen** (umg) to get tough

Saiteninstrument nt string(ed) instrument

Sakko ['zako] (-s, -s) m od nt jacket

Sakrament [zakra'mɛnt] nt sacrament

Sakristei [zakrɪs'taɪ] f sacristy

Salami [za'la:mi] (-, -s) f salami

Salat [za'la:t] (-(e)s, -e) m salad; (Kopfsalat) lettuce; **da haben wir den ~!** (umg) now we're in a fine mess!; **Salatbesteck** nt salad servers pl; **Salatplatte** f salad; **Salatsoße** f salad dressing

Salbe ['zalbə] (-, -n) f ointment

Salbei ['zalbaɪ] (-s) m sage

salben vt to anoint

Salbung f anointing

salbungsvoll adj unctuous

saldieren [zal'di:rən] vt (Comm) to balance

Saldo ['zaldo] (-s, **Salden**) m balance; **Saldoübertrag** m balance brought od carried forward; **Saldovortrag** m balance brought od carried forward

Säle ['zɛ:lə] pl von **Saal**

Salmiak [zalmi'ak] (-s) m sal ammoniac; **Salmiakgeist** m liquid ammonia

Salmonellen [zalmo'nɛlən] pl salmonellae pl

Salon [za'lɔŋ, za'lõ:] (-s, -s) m salon; **Salonlöwe** m lounge lizard

salopp [za'lɔp] adj casual; (Manieren) slovenly; (Sprache) slangy

Salpeter [zal'pe:tər] (-s) m saltpetre (Brit), saltpeter (US); **Salpetersäure** f nitric acid

Salto ['zalto] (-s, -s od **Salti**) m somersault

Salut [za'lu:t] (-(e)s, -e) m salute

salutieren [zalu'ti:rən] vi to salute

Salve ['zalvə] (-, -n) f salvo

Salz [zalts] (-es, -e) nt salt; **salzarm** adj (Koch) low-salt; **Salzbergwerk** nt salt mine

salzen unreg vt to salt

salzig adj salty

Salz- zW: **Salzkartoffeln** pl boiled potatoes pl; **Salzsäule** f: **zur Salzsäule erstarren** (fig) to stand rooted to the spot; **Salzsäure** f hydrochloric acid; **Salzstange** f pretzel stick; **Salzstreuer** m salt cellar; **Salzwasser** nt salt

water

Sambia ['zambia] (-s) nt Zambia

sambisch adj Zambian

Samen ['za:mən] (-s, -) m seed; (Anat) sperm; **Samenbank** f sperm bank; **Samenhandlung** f seed shop

sämig ['zɛ:mɪç] adj thick, creamy

Sammel- zW: **Sammelanschluss** m (Tel) private (branch) exchange; (von Privathäusern) party line; **Sammelantrag** m composite motion; **Sammelband** m anthology; **Sammelbecken** nt reservoir; (fig): **Sammelbecken (von)** melting pot (for); **Sammelbegriff** m collective term; **Sammelbestellung** f collective order; **Sammelbüchse** f collecting tin; **Sammelmappe** f folder

sammeln vt to collect ▷ vr to assemble, gather; (sich konzentrieren) to collect one's thoughts

Sammelname m collective term

Sammelnummer f (Tel) private exchange number, switchboard number

Sammelsurium [zaməl'zu:riʊm] nt hotchpotch (Brit), hodgepodge (US)

Sammler, in (-s, -) m(f) collector

Sammlung ['zamlʊŋ] f collection; (Konzentration) composure

Samstag ['zamsta:k] m Saturday; siehe auch **Dienstag**

samstags adv (on) Saturdays

samt [zamt] präp +dat (along) with, together with; **~ und sonders** each and every one (of them); **Samt** (-(e)s, -e) m velvet; **in Samt und Seide** (liter) in silks and satins

Samthandschuh m: **jdn mit ~en anfassen** (umg) to handle sb with kid gloves

sämtlich ['zɛmtlɪç] adj (alle) all (the); (vollständig) complete; **Schillers ~e Werke** the complete works of Schiller

Sanatorium [zana'to:riʊm] nt sanatorium (Brit), sanitarium (US)

Sand [zant] (-(e)s, -e) m sand; **das/die gibts wie ~ am Meer** (umg) there are piles of it/heaps of them; **im ~e verlaufen** to peter out

Sandale [zan'da:lə] (-, -n) f sandal

Sandbank f sandbank

Sandelholz ['zandəlhɔlts] (-es) nt sandalwood

sandig ['zandɪç] adj sandy

Sand- zW: **Sandkasten** m sandpit; **Sandkastenspiele** pl (Mil) sand-table exercises pl; (fig) tactical manoeuvrings pl (Brit) od maneuverings pl (US); **Sandkuchen** m Madeira cake; **Sandmann** m, **Sandmännchen** nt (in Geschichten) sandman; **Sandpapier** nt sandpaper; **Sandstein** m sandstone; **sandstrahlen** vt, vi untr to sandblast

sandte etc ['zantə] vb siehe **senden**

Sanduhr f hourglass; (Eieruhr) egg timer

sanft [zanft] adj soft, gentle; **sanftmütig** adj gentle, meek

sang etc [zaŋ] vb siehe **singen**

Sänger, in ['zɛŋər(ɪn)] (-s, -) m(f) singer

sang-und klanglos (umg) adv without any ado, quietly

Sani ['zani] (-s, -s) (umg) m = **Sanitäter**

sanieren [za'ni:rən] vt to redevelop; (Betrieb) to make financially sound; (Haus) to renovate ▷ vr to line one's pockets; (Unternehmen) to become financially sound

Sanierung f redevelopment; renovation

sanitär [zani'tɛ:r] adj sanitary; **~e Anlagen** sanitation sing

Sanitäter [zani'tɛ:tər] (-s, -) m first-aid attendant; (in Krankenwagen) ambulance man; (Mil) (medical) orderly

Sanitätsauto nt ambulance

sank etc [zaŋk] vb siehe **sinken**

Sanktion [zaŋktsi'o:n] f sanction

sanktionieren [zaŋktsio'ni:rən] vt to sanction

sann etc [zan] vb siehe **sinnen**

Saphir ['za:fi:r] (-s, -e) m sapphire

Sarde ['zardə] (-n, -n) m Sardinian

Sardelle [zar'dɛlə] f anchovy

Sardine [zar'di:nə] f sardine

Sardinien [zar'di:niən] (-s) nt Sardinia

Sardinier, in (-s, -) m(f) Sardinian

sardinisch adj Sardinian

sardisch adj Sardinian

Sarg [zark] (-(e)s, ̈e) m coffin; **Sargnagel** (umg) m (Zigarette) coffin nail

Sarkasmus [zar'kasmʊs] m sarcasm

sarkastisch [zar'kastɪʃ] adj sarcastic

SARS, Sars [zars] abk (= Schweres Akutes Respiratorisches Syndrom) SARS

saß etc [zas] vb siehe **sitzen**

Satan ['za:tan] (-s, -e) m Satan; (fig) devil

Satansbraten m (hum: umg) young devil

Satellit [zate'li:t] (-en, -en) m satellite

Satelliten- zW: **Satellitenantenne** f satellite dish; **Satellitenfernsehen** nt satellite television; **Satellitenfoto** nt satellite picture; **Satellitenschüssel** f satellite dish; **Satellitenstation** f space station

Satin [za'tɛ̃:] (-s, -s) m satin

Satire [za'ti:rə] (-, -n) f: **~ (auf** +akk) satire (on)

Satiriker [za'ti:rikər] (-s, -) m satirist

satirisch [za'ti:rɪʃ] adj satirical

satt [zat] adj full; (Farbe) rich, deep; (blasiert, übersättigt) well-fed; (selbstgefällig) smug; **jdn/ etw ~ sein** to be fed-up with sb/sth; **sich ~ essen** to eat one's fill; **~ machen** to be filling; siehe auch **satthaben; satthören; sattsehen**

Sattel ['zatəl] (-s, ̈) m saddle; (Berg) ridge; **sattelfest** adj (fig) proficient

satteln vt to saddle

Sattelschlepper m articulated lorry (Brit), artic (Brit umg), semitrailer (US), semi (US umg)

Satteltasche f saddlebag; (Gepäcktasche am Fahrrad) pannier

satthaben unreg vt: **jdn/etw ~** to be fed up with sb/sth

satthören vr: **sich ~ an** +dat to hear enough of

sättigen ['zɛtɪgən] vt to satisfy; (Chem) to saturate

Sattler (-s, -) m saddler; (Polsterer) upholsterer

sattsehen unreg vt: **sich ~ an** +dat to see enough of

Satz [zats] (-es, ̈e) m (Gram) sentence; (Nebensatz, Adverbialsatz) clause; (Theorem) theorem; (der gesetzte Text) type; (Mus) movement; (Comput) record; (Briefmarken, Zusammengehöriges, Tennis) set; (Kaffeesatz) grounds pl; (Bodensatz) dregs pl; (Spesensatz) allowance; (Comm) rate; (Sprung) jump; **Satzbau** m sentence construction; **Satzgegenstand** m (Gram) subject; **Satzlehre** f syntax; **Satzteil** m constituent (of a sentence)

Satzung f statute, rule; (Firma) (memorandum and) articles of association

satzungsgemäß adj statutory

Satzzeichen nt punctuation mark

Sau [zaʊ] (-, **Säue**) f sow; (umg) dirty pig; **die ~ rauslassen** (fig: umg) to let it all hang out

sauber ['zaʊbər] adj clean; (anständig) honest, upstanding; (umg: großartig) fantastic, great; (: ironisch) fine; **~ sein** (Kind) to be (potty-) trained; (Hund etc) to be house-trained; **~ halten** to keep clean; **~ machen** to clean; **Sauberkeit** f cleanness; (einer Person) cleanliness

säuberlich ['zɔybərlɪç] adv neatly

säubern vt to clean; (Pol etc) to purge

Säuberung f cleaning; purge

Säuberungsaktion f cleaning-up operation; (Pol) purge

saublöd (umg) adj bloody (Brit!) od damn (!) stupid

Saubohne f broad bean

Sauce ['zo:sə] (-, -n) f = **Soße**

Sauciere [zosi'e:rə] (-, -n) f sauce boat

Saudi- [zaʊdi-] zW: **Saudi-Araber, in** m(f) Saudi; **Saudi-Arabien** (-s) nt Saudi Arabia; **saudi-arabisch** adj Saudi(-Arabian)

sauer ['zaʊər] adj sour; (Chem) acid; (umg) cross; **saurer Regen** acid rain; **~ werden** (Milch, Sahne) to go sour, turn; **jdm das Leben ~ machen** to make sb's life a misery; **Sauerbraten** m braised beef (marinaded in vinegar), sauerbraten (US)

Sauerei [zaʊə'raɪ] (umg) f rotten state of affairs, scandal; (Schmutz etc) mess; (Unanständigkeit) obscenity

Sauerkirsche f sour cherry

Sauerkraut (-(e)s) nt sauerkraut, pickled cabbage

säuerlich ['zɔyərlıç] adj sourish, tart

Sauer- zW: **Sauermilch** f sour milk; **Sauerstoff** m oxygen; **Sauerstoffgerät** nt breathing apparatus; **Sauerteig** m leaven

saufen ['zaʊfən] unreg (umg) vt, vi to drink, booze; **wie ein Loch ~** (umg) to drink like a fish

Säufer, in ['zɔyfər(ın)] (-s, -) (umg) m(f) boozer, drunkard

Sauferei [zaʊfə'raɪ] f drinking, boozing; (Saufgelage) booze-up

Saufgelage (pej: umg) nt drinking bout, booze-up

säuft [zɔyft] vb siehe **saufen**

saugen ['zaʊgən] unreg vt, vi to suck

S

säugen ['zɔygən] vt to suckle

Sauger ['zaʊgər] (**-s, -**) m dummy (Brit), pacifier (US); (auf Flasche) teat; (Staubsauger) vacuum cleaner, hoover® (Brit)

Säugetier nt mammal

saugfähig adj absorbent

Säugling m infant, baby

Säuglingsschwester f infant nurse

Sau- zW: **Sauhaufen** (umg) m bunch of layabouts; **saukalt** (umg) adj bloody (Brit!) od damn (!) cold; **Sauklaue** (umg) f scrawl

Säule ['zɔylə] (**-, -n**) f column, pillar

Säulengang m arcade

Saum [zaʊm] (**-(e)s, Säume**) m hem; (Naht) seam

saumäßig (umg) adj lousy ▷ adv lousily

säumen ['zɔymən] vt to hem; to seam ▷ vi to delay, hesitate

säumig ['zɔymɪç] adj (geh: Schuldner) defaulting; (Zahlung) outstanding, overdue

Sauna ['zaʊna] (**-, -s**) f sauna

Säure ['zɔyrə] (**-, -n**) f acid; (Geschmack) sourness, acidity; **säurebeständig** adj acid-proof

Saure-Gurken-Zeit (-) f (hum: umg) bad time od period; (in den Medien) silly season

säurehaltig adj acidic

Saurier ['zaʊriər] (**-s, -**) m dinosaur

Saus [zaʊs] (**-es**) m: **in ~ und Braus leben** to live like a lord

säuseln ['zɔyzəln] vi to murmur; (Blätter) to rustle ▷ vt to murmur

sausen ['zaʊzən] vi to blow; (umg: eilen) to rush; (Ohren) to buzz; **etw ~ lassen** (umg) not to bother with sth

Sau- zW: **Saustall** (umg) m pigsty; **Sauwetter** (umg) nt bloody (Brit!) od damn (!) awful weather; **sauwohl** (umg) adj: **ich fühle mich sauwohl** I feel bloody (Brit!) od really good

Saxofon, Saxophon [zakso'foːn] (**-s, -e**) nt saxophone

SB abk = **Selbstbedienung**

S-Bahn f abk (= Schnellbahn) high-speed suburban railway or railroad (US)

SBB abk (= Schweizerische Bundesbahnen) Swiss Railways

s. Br. abk (= südlicher Breite) southern latitude

Schabe ['ʃaːbə] (**-, -n**) f cockroach

schaben vt to scrape

Schaber (**-s, -**) m scraper

Schabernack (**-(e)s, -e**) m trick, prank

schäbig ['ʃɛːbɪç] adj shabby; (Mensch) mean; **Schäbigkeit** f shabbiness

Schablone [ʃa'bloːnə] (**-, -n**) f stencil; (Muster) pattern; (fig) convention

schablonenhaft adj stereotyped, conventional

Schach [ʃax] (**-s, -s**) nt chess; (Stellung) check; **im ~ stehen** to be in check; **jdn in ~ halten** (fig) to stall sb; **Schachbrett** nt chessboard

schachern (pej) vi: **um etw ~** to haggle over sth

Schach- zW: **Schachfigur** f chessman; **schachmatt** adj checkmate; **jdn schachmatt setzen** (lit) to (check)mate sb; (fig) to snooker

sb (umg); **Schachpartie** f game of chess; **Schachspiel** nt game of chess

Schacht [ʃaxt] (**-(e)s, -̈e**) m shaft

Schachtel (**-, -n**) f box; (pej: Frau) bag, cow (Brit); **Schachtelsatz** m complicated od multi-clause sentence

Schachzug m (auch fig) move

schade ['ʃaːdə] adj a pity od shame ▷ interj (what a) pity od shame; **sich** dat **für etw zu ~ sein** to consider o.s. too good for sth; **um sie ist es nicht ~** she's no great loss

Schädel ['ʃɛːdəl] (**-s, -**) m skull; **einen dicken ~ haben** (fig: umg) to be stubborn; **Schädelbruch** m fractured skull

Schaden (**-s, -̈**) m damage; (Verletzung) injury; (Nachteil) disadvantage; **zu ~ kommen** to suffer; (physisch) to be injured; **jdm ~ zufügen** to harm sb

schaden ['ʃaːdən] vi +dat to hurt; **einer Sache ~** to damage sth

Schaden- zW: **Schadenersatz** m compensation, damages pl; **Schadenersatz leisten** to pay compensation; **Schadenersatzanspruch** m claim for compensation; **schadenersatzpflichtig** adj liable for damages; **Schadenfreiheitsrabatt** m (Versicherung) no-claim(s) bonus; **Schadenfreude** f malicious delight; **schadenfroh** adj gloating

schadhaft ['ʃaːthaft] adj faulty, damaged

schädigen ['ʃɛːdɪgən] vt to damage; (Person) to do harm to, harm

Schädigung f damage; harm

schädlich adj: **~ (für)** harmful (to); **Schädlichkeit** f harmfulness

Schädling m pest

Schädlingsbekämpfungsmittel nt pesticide

schadlos ['ʃaːtloːs] adj: **sich ~ halten an** +dat to take advantage of

Schadstoff (**-(e)s, -e**) m pollutant; **schadstoffarm** adj low in pollutants; **schadstoffhaltig** adj containing pollutants

Schaf [ʃaːf] (**-(e)s, -e**) nt sheep; (umg: Dummkopf) twit (Brit), dope; **Schafbock** m ram

Schäfchen ['ʃɛːfçən] nt lamb; **sein ~ ins Trockene bringen** (Sprichwort) to see o.s. all right (umg); **Schäfchenwolken** pl cirrus clouds pl

Schäfer ['ʃɛːfər] (**-s, -**) m shepherd; **Schäferhund** m Alsatian (dog) (Brit), German shepherd (dog) (US); **Schäferin** f shepherdess

Schaffen ['ʃafən] (**-s**) nt (creative) activity

schaffen¹ unreg vt to create; (Platz) to make; **sich** dat **etw ~** to get o.s. sth; **dafür ist er wie ge-** he's just made for it

schaffen² ['ʃafən] vt (erreichen) to manage, do; (erledigen) to finish; (Prüfung) to pass; (transportieren) to take ▷ vi (tun) to do; (umg: arbeiten) to work; **das ist nicht zu ~** that can't be done; **das hat mich geschafft** it took it out of me; (nervlich) it got on top of me; **ich habe damit nichts zu ~** that has nothing to do with me; **jdm (schwer) zu ~**

machen (zusetzen) to cause sb (a lot of) trouble; (bekümmern) to worry sb (a lot); **sich** dat **an etw** dat **zu ~ machen** to busy o.s. with sth
Schaffensdrang m energy; (von Künstler) creative urge
Schaffenskraft f creativity
Schaffner, in [ˈʃafnər(ɪn)] (-s, -) m(f) (Busschaffner) conductor, conductress; (Eisenb) guard (Brit), conductor (US)
Schaffung f creation
Schafskäse m sheep's od ewe's milk cheese
Schaft [ʃaft] (-(e)s, ̈-e) m shaft; (von Gewehr) stock; (von Stiefel) leg; (Bot) stalk; (von Baum) tree trunk; **Schaftstiefel** m high boot
Schakal [ʃaˈkaːl] (-s, -e) m jackal
Schäker, in [ˈʃɛːkər(ɪn)] (-s, -) m(f) flirt; (Witzbold) joker
schäkern vi to flirt; to joke
Schal [ʃaːl] (-s, -s od -e) m scarf
schal adj flat; (fig) insipid
Schälchen [ˈʃɛːlçən] nt bowl
Schale [ˈʃaːlə] (-, -n) f skin; (abgeschält) peel; (Nussschale, Muschelschale, Eierschale) shell; (Geschirr) dish, bowl; **sich in ~ werfen** (umg) to get dressed up
schälen [ˈʃɛːlən] vt to peel; to shell ▷ vr to peel
Schalk [ʃalk] (-s, -e od ̈-e) m (veraltet) joker
Schall [ʃal] (-(e)s, -e) m sound; **Name ist ~ und Rauch** what's in a name?; **schalldämmend** adj sound-deadening; **Schalldämpfer** m (Aut) silencer (Brit), muffler (US); **schalldicht** adj soundproof
schallen vi to (re)sound
schallend adj resounding, loud
Schall- zW: **Schallgeschwindigkeit** f speed of sound; **Schallgrenze** f sound barrier; **Schallmauer** f sound barrier; **Schallplatte** f record
schalt etc [ʃalt] vb siehe **schelten**
Schaltbild nt circuit diagram
Schaltbrett nt switchboard
schalten [ˈʃaltən] vt to switch, turn ▷ vi (Aut) to change (gear); (umg: begreifen) to catch on; (reagieren) to react; **in Reihe/parallel ~** (Elek) to connect in series/in parallel; **~ und walten** to do as one pleases
Schalter (-s, -) m counter; (an Gerät) switch; **Schalterbeamte, r** m counter clerk; **Schalterstunden** pl hours of business pl
Schalt- zW: **Schalthebel** m switch; (Aut) gear lever (Brit), gearshift (US); **Schaltjahr** nt leap year; **Schaltknüppel** m (Aut) gear lever (Brit), gearshift (US); **Schaltkreis** m (switching) circuit; **Schaltplan** m circuit diagram; **Schaltpult** nt control desk; **Schaltstelle** f (fig) coordinating point; **Schaltuhr** f time switch
Schaltung f switching; (Elek) circuit; (Aut) gear change
Scham [ʃaːm] (-) f shame; (Schamgefühl) modesty; (Organe) private parts pl
schämen [ˈʃɛːmən] vr to be ashamed
Scham- zW: **Schamgefühl** nt sense of shame;

Schamhaare pl pubic hair sing; **schamhaft** adj modest; bashful; **Schamlippen** pl labia pl, lips pl of the vulva; **schamlos** adj shameless; (unanständig) indecent; (Lüge) brazen, barefaced
Schampus [ˈʃampʊs] (-, no pl) (umg) m champagne, champers (Brit)
Schande [ˈʃandə] (-) f disgrace; **zu meiner ~ muss ich gestehen, dass ...** to my shame I have to admit that ...
schänden [ˈʃɛndən] vt to violate
Schandfleck [ˈʃantflɛk] m: **er war der ~ der Familie** he was the disgrace of his family
schändlich [ˈʃɛntlɪç] adj disgraceful, shameful; **Schändlichkeit** f disgracefulness, shamefulness
Schandtat (umg) f escapade, shenanigan
Schändung f violation, defilement
Schänke [ˈʃɛŋkə] (-, -n) f = **Schenke**
Schank- zW: **Schankerlaubnis** f, **Schankkonzession** f (publican's) licence (Brit), excise license (US); **Schanktisch** m bar
Schanze [ˈʃantsə] (-, -n) f (Mil) fieldwork, earthworks pl; (Sprungschanze) ski jump
Schar [ʃaːr] (-, -en) f band, company; (Vögel) flock; (Menge) crowd; **in ~en** in droves
Scharade [ʃaˈraːdə] (-, -n) f charade
scharen vr to assemble, rally
scharenweise adv in droves
scharf [ʃarf] adj sharp; (Verstand, Augen) keen; (Kälte, Wind) biting; (Protest) fierce; (Ton) piercing, shrill; (Essen) hot, spicy; (Munition) live; (Maßnahmen) severe; (Bewachung) close, tight; (Geruch, Geschmack) pungent, acrid; (umg: geil) randy (Brit), horny; (Film) sexy, blue attrib; **~ nachdenken** to think hard; **~ aufpassen/zuhören** to pay close attention/ listen closely; **etw ~ einstellen** (Bild, Diaprojektor etc) to bring sth into focus; **mit ~em Blick** (fig) with penetrating insight; **auf etw** akk **~ sein** (umg) to be keen on sth; **~e Sachen** (umg) hard stuff
Scharfblick m (fig) penetration
Schärfe [ˈʃɛrfə] (-, -n) f sharpness; (Strenge) rigour (Brit), rigor (US); (an Kamera, Fernsehen) focus
schärfen vt to sharpen
Schärfentiefe f (Phot) depth of focus
Scharf- zW: **scharfmachen** (umg) vt to stir up; **Scharfrichter** m executioner; **Scharfschießen** nt shooting with live ammunition; **Scharfschütze** m marksman, sharpshooter; **Scharfsinn** m astuteness, shrewdness; **scharfsinnig** adj astute, shrewd
Scharlach [ˈʃarlax] (-s, -e) m scarlet; (Krankheit) scarlet fever; **Scharlachfieber** nt scarlet fever
Scharlatan [ˈʃarlatan] (-s, -e) m charlatan
Scharmützel [ʃarˈmʏtsəl] (-s, -) nt skirmish
Scharnier [ʃarˈniːr] (-s, -e) nt hinge
Schärpe [ˈʃɛrpə] (-, -n) f sash
scharren [ˈʃarən] vt, vi to scrape, scratch
Scharte [ˈʃartə] (-, -n) f notch, nick; (Berg) wind gap
schartig [ˈʃartɪç] adj jagged

S

Schaschlik ['ʃaʃlɪk] (-s, -s) *m od nt* (shish) kebab
Schatten ['ʃatən] (-s, -) *m* shadow; (*schattige Stelle*) shade; **jdn/etw in den ~ stellen** (*fig*) to put sb/sth in the shade; **Schattenbild** *nt* silhouette; **schattenhaft** *adj* shadowy
Schattenmorelle (-, -n) *f* morello cherry
Schatten- *zW:* **Schattenriss** *m* silhouette; **Schattenseite** *f* shady side; (*von Planeten*) dark side; (*fig: Nachteil*) drawback; **Schattenwirtschaft** *f* black economy
schattieren [ʃa'tiːrən] *vt, vi* to shade
Schattierung *f* shading
schattig ['ʃatɪç] *adj* shady
Schatulle [ʃa'tʊlə] (-, -n) *f* casket; (*Geldschatulle*) coffer
Schatz [ʃats] (-es, ̈e) *m* treasure; (*Person*) darling; **Schatzamt** *nt* treasury
schätzbar ['ʃɛtsbaːr] *adj* assessable
Schätzchen *nt* darling, love
schätzen *vt* (*abschätzen*) to estimate; (*Gegenstand*) to value; (*würdigen*) to value, esteem; (*vermuten*) to reckon; **etw zu ~ wissen** to appreciate sth; **sich glücklich ~** to consider o.s. lucky; **~ lernen** to learn to appreciate
Schatzkammer *f* treasure chamber *od* vault
Schatzmeister *m* treasurer
Schätzung *f* estimate; estimation; valuation; **nach meiner ~ ...** I reckon that ...
schätzungsweise *adv* (*ungefähr*) approximately; (*so vermutet man*) it is thought
Schätzwert *m* estimated value
Schau [ʃaʊ] (-) *f* show; (*Ausstellung*) display, exhibition; **etw zur ~ stellen** to make a show of sth, show sth off; **eine ~ abziehen** (*umg*) to put on a show; **Schaubild** *nt* diagram
Schauder ['ʃaʊdər] (-s, -) *m* shudder; (*wegen Kälte*) shiver; **schauderhaft** *adj* horrible
schaudern *vi* to shudder; (*wegen Kälte*) to shiver
schauen ['ʃaʊən] *vi* to look; **da schau her!** well, well!
Schauer ['ʃaʊər] (-s, -) *m* (*Regenschauer*) shower; (*Schreck*) shudder; **Schauergeschichte** *f* horror story; **schauerlich** *adj* horrific, spine-chilling; **Schauermärchen** (*umg*) *nt* horror story
Schaufel ['ʃaʊfəl] (-, -n) *f* shovel; (*Kehrichtschaufel*) dustpan; (*von Turbine*) vane; (*Naut*) paddle; (*Tech*) scoop
schaufeln *vt* to shovel; (*Grab, Grube*) to dig ▷ *vi* to shovel
Schaufenster *nt* shop window; **Schaufensterauslage** *f* window display; **Schaufensterbummel** *m* window-shopping (expedition); **Schaufensterdekorateur, in** *m(f)* window dresser; **Schaufensterpuppe** *f* display dummy
Schaugeschäft *nt* show business
Schaukasten *m* showcase
Schaukel ['ʃaʊkəl] (-, -n) *f* swing
schaukeln *vi* to swing, rock ▷ *vt* to rock; **wir werden das Kind** *od* **das schon ~** (*fig: umg*) we'll manage it
Schaukelpferd *nt* rocking horse
Schaukelstuhl *m* rocking chair

Schaulustige, r ['ʃaʊlʊstɪgə(r)] *f(m)* onlooker
Schaum [ʃaʊm] (-(e)s, **Schäume**) *m* foam; (*Seifenschaum*) lather; (*von Getränken*) froth; (*von Bier*) head; **Schaumbad** *nt* bubble bath
schäumen ['ʃɔʏmən] *vi* to foam
Schaumgummi *m* foam (rubber)
schaumig *adj* frothy, foamy
Schaum- *zW:* **Schaumkrone** *f* whitecap; **Schaumschläger** *m* (*fig*) windbag; **Schaumschlägerei** *f* (*fig: umg*) hot air; **Schaumstoff** *m* foam material; **Schaumwein** *m* sparkling wine
Schauplatz *m* scene
Schauprozess *m* show trial
schaurig *adj* horrific, dreadful
Schauspiel *nt* spectacle; (*Theat*) play
Schauspieler, in *m(f)* actor, actress; **schauspielerisch** *adj* (*Können, Leistung*) acting
schauspielern *vi untr* to act
Schauspielhaus *nt* playhouse, theatre (*Brit*), theater (*US*)
Schauspielschule *f* drama school
Schausteller ['ʃaʊʃtɛlər] (-s, -) *m* person who owns or runs a fairground ride/sideshow etc
Scheck [ʃɛk] (-s, -s) *m* cheque (*Brit*), check (*US*); **Scheckbuch** *nt*, **Scheckheft** *nt* cheque book (*Brit*), check book (*US*)
scheckig *adj* dappled, piebald
Scheckkarte *f* cheque (*Brit*) *od* check (*US*) card, banker's card
scheel [ʃeːl] (*umg*) *adj* dirty; **jdn ~ ansehen** to give sb a dirty look
scheffeln ['ʃɛfəln] *vt* to amass
Scheibe ['ʃaɪbə] (-, -n) *f* disc (*Brit*), disk (*US*); (*Brot etc*) slice; (*Glasscheibe*) pane; (*Mil*) target; (*Eishockey*) puck; (*Töpferscheibe*) wheel; (*umg: Schallplatte*) disc (*Brit*), disk (*US*); **von ihm könntest du dir eine ~ abschneiden** (*fig: umg*) you could take a leaf out of his book
Scheiben- *zW:* **Scheibenbremse** *f* (*Aut*) disc brake; **Scheibenkleister** *interj* (*euph: umg*) sugar!; **Scheibenwaschanlage** *f* (*Aut*) windscreen (*Brit*) *od* windshield (*US*) washers *pl*; **Scheibenwischer** *m* (*Aut*) windscreen (*Brit*) *od* windshield (*US*) wiper
Scheich [ʃaɪç] (-s, -e *od* -s) *m* sheik(h)
Scheide ['ʃaɪdə] (-, -n) *f* sheath; (*Anat*) vagina
scheiden *unreg vt* to separate; (*Ehe*) to dissolve ▷ *vi* to depart; (*sich trennen*) to part ▷ *vr* (*Wege*) to divide; (*Meinungen*) to diverge; **sich ~ lassen** to get a divorce; **von dem Moment an waren wir (zwei) geschiedene Leute** (*umg*) after that it was the parting of the ways for us; **aus dem Leben ~** to depart this life
Scheideweg *m* (*fig*) crossroads *sing*
Scheidung *f* (*Ehescheidung*) divorce; **die ~ einreichen** to file a petition for divorce
Scheidungsgrund *m* grounds *pl* for divorce
Scheidungsklage *f* divorce suit
Schein [ʃaɪn] (-(e)s, -e) *m* light; (*Anschein*) appearance; (*Geldschein*) (bank)note; (*Bescheinigung*) certificate; **den ~ wahren** to keep up appearances; **etw zum ~ tun**

to pretend to do sth, make a pretence (Brit) od pretense (US) of doing sth; **scheinbar** adj apparent

scheinen unreg vi to shine; (Anschein haben) to seem

Schein- zW: **scheinheilig** adj hypocritical; **Scheintod** m apparent death; **Scheinwerfer** (**-s, -**) m floodlight; (Theat) spotlight; (Suchscheinwerfer) searchlight; (Aut) headlight

Scheiß [ʃaɪs] (**-, no pl**) (umg) m bullshit (!)

Scheiß- ['ʃaɪs-] (umg) in zw bloody (Brit!); **Scheißdreck** (umg!) m shit (!), crap (!); **das geht dich einen Scheißdreck an** it's got bugger-all to do with you (!)

Scheiße ['ʃaɪsə] (**-**) (umg!) f shit (!)

scheißegal (umg!) adj: **das ist mir doch ~!** I don't give a shit (!)

scheißen (umg!) vi to shit (!)

scheißfreundlich (pej: umg) adj as nice as pie (ironisch)

Scheißkerl (umg!) m bastard (!), son-of-a-bitch (US!)

Scheit [ʃaɪt] **-(e)s, -e** od **-er**) nt log

Scheitel ['ʃaɪtəl] (**-s, -**) m top; (Haar) parting (Brit), part (US)

scheiteln vt to part

Scheitelpunkt m zenith, apex

Scheiterhaufen ['ʃaɪtərhaufən] m (funeral) pyre; (Hist: zur Hinrichtung) stake

scheitern ['ʃaɪtərn] vi to fail

Schelle ['ʃɛlə] (**-, -n**) f small bell

schellen vi to ring; **es hat geschellt** the bell has gone

Schellfisch ['ʃɛlfɪʃ] m haddock

Schelm [ʃɛlm] (**-(e)s, -e**) m rogue

Schelmenroman m picaresque novel

schelmisch adj mischievous, roguish

Schelte ['ʃɛltə] (**-, -n**) f scolding

schelten unreg vt to scold

Schema ['ʃeːma] (**-s, -s** od **-ta**) nt scheme, plan; (Darstellung) schema; **nach ~ F** quite mechanically

schematisch [ʃeˈmaːtɪʃ] adj schematic; (pej) mechanical

Schemel ['ʃeːməl] (**-s, -**) m (foot)stool

schemenhaft adj shadowy

Schenke (**-, -n**) f tavern, inn

Schenkel ['ʃɛŋkəl] (**-s, -**) m thigh; (Math: von Winkel) side

schenken ['ʃɛŋkən] vt (lit, fig) to give; (Getränk) to pour; **ich möchte nichts geschenkt haben!** (lit) I don't want any presents!; (fig: bevorzugt werden) I don't want any special treatment!; **sich** dat **etw ~** (umg) to skip sth; **jdm etw ~** (erlassen) to let sb off sth; **ihm ist nie etwas geschenkt worden** (fig) he never had it easy; **das ist geschenkt!** (billig) that's a giveaway!; (nichts wert) that's worthless!

Schenkung f gift

Schenkungsurkunde f deed of gift

scheppern ['ʃɛpərn] (umg) vi to clatter

Scherbe ['ʃɛrbə] (**-, -n**) f broken piece, fragment; (archäologisch) potsherd

Schere ['ʃeːrə] (**-, -n**) f scissors pl; (groß) shears pl; (Zool) pincer; (von Hummer, Krebs etc) pincer, claw; **eine ~** a pair of scissors

scheren unreg vt to cut; (Schaf) to shear; (stören) to bother ▷ vr (sich kümmern) to care; **scher dich (zum Teufel)!** get lost!

Scherenschleifer (**-s, -**) m knife grinder

Scherenschnitt m silhouette

Schererei [ʃeːrəˈraɪ] (umg) f bother, trouble

Scherflein ['ʃɛrflaɪn] nt mite, bit

Scherz [ʃɛrts] (**-es, -e**) m joke; fun; **scherzen** vi to joke; (albern) to banter; **Scherzfrage** f conundrum; **scherzhaft** adj joking, jocular

Scheu [ʃɔy] (**-**) f shyness; (Ehrfurcht) awe; (Angst): **~ (vor +dat)** fear (of)

scheu [ʃɔy] adj shy

Scheuche (**-, -n**) f scarecrow

scheuchen ['ʃɔyçən] vt to scare (off)

scheuen vr: **sich ~ vor** +dat to be afraid of, shrink from ▷ vt to shun ▷ vi (Pferd) to shy; **weder Mühe noch Kosten ~** to spare neither trouble nor expense

Scheuer ['ʃɔyər] (**-, -n**) f barn

Scheuer- zW: **Scheuerbürste** f scrubbing brush; **Scheuerlappen** m floorcloth (Brit), scrubbing rag (US); **Scheuerleiste** f skirting board

scheuern vt to scour; (mit Bürste) to scrub ▷ vr: **sich** akk **(wund) ~** to chafe o.s.; **jdm eine ~** (umg) to clout sb one

Scheuklappe f blinker

Scheune ['ʃɔynə] (**-, -n**) f barn

Scheunendrescher (**-s, -**) m: **er frisst wie ein ~** (umg) he eats like a horse

Scheusal ['ʃɔyzaːl] (**-s, -e**) nt monster

scheußlich ['ʃɔyslɪç] adj dreadful, frightful; **Scheußlichkeit** f dreadfulness

Schi [ʃiː] m = **Ski**

Schicht [ʃɪçt] (**-, -en**) f layer; (Klasse) class, level; (in Fabrik etc) shift; **Schichtarbeit** f shift work

schichten vt to layer, stack

Schichtwechsel m change of shifts

schick [ʃɪk] adj = **chic**

schicken vt to send ▷ vr: **sich ~ (in** +akk) to resign o.s. (to) ▷ vb unpers (anständig sein) to be fitting

Schickeria [ʃɪkəˈriːa] f (ironisch) in-people pl

Schicki ['ʃɪkɪ], **Schickimicki** ['ʃɪkɪˈmɪkɪ] (**-s, -s**) (umg) m trendy

schicklich adj proper, fitting

Schicksal (**-s, -e**) nt fate

schicksalhaft adj fateful

Schicksalsschlag m great misfortune, blow

Schickse ['ʃɪksə] (**-, -n**) (umg) f floozy, shiksa (US)

Schiebedach nt (Aut) sunroof, sunshine roof

schieben ['ʃiːbən] unreg vt (auch Drogen) to push; (Schuld) to put; (umg: handeln mit) to traffic in; **die Schuld auf jdn ~** to put the blame on (to) sb; **etw vor sich** dat **her ~** (fig) to put sth off

Schieber (**-s, -**) m slide; (umg) pusher; (Person) profiteer; (umg: Schwarzhändler) black marketeer; (: Waffenschieber) gunrunner;

(: *Drogenschieber*) pusher
Schiebetür f sliding door
Schieblehre f (*Math*) calliper (*Brit*) od caliper (*US*) rule
Schiebung f fiddle; **das war doch ~** (*umg*) that was rigged od a fix
schied etc [ʃiːt] vb siehe **scheiden**
Schieds- zW: **Schiedsgericht** nt court of arbitration; **Schiedsmann** (**-(e)s,** pl **-männer**) m arbitrator; **Schiedsrichter** m referee, umpire; (*Schlichter*) arbitrator; **schiedsrichtern** vi untr to referee, umpire; to arbitrate; **Schiedsspruch** m (arbitration) award; **Schiedsverfahren** nt arbitration
schief [ʃiːf] adj crooked; (*Ebene*) sloping; (*Turm*) leaning; (*Winkel*) oblique; (*Blick*) wry; (*Vergleich*) distorted ▷ adv crookedly; (*ansehen*) askance; **auf die ~e Bahn geraten** (*fig*) to leave the straight and narrow; **etw ~ stellen** to slope sth; siehe auch **schiefgehen; schiefliegen**
Schiefer ['ʃiːfər] (**-s,** -) m slate; **Schieferdach** nt slate roof; **Schiefertafel** f (child's) slate
schiefgehen (*umg: unreg*) vi to go wrong; **es wird schon ~!** (*hum*) it'll be OK
schieflachen (*umg*) vr to kill o.s. laughing
schiefliegen (*umg: unreg*) vi to be wrong, be on the wrong track (*umg*)
schielen ['ʃiːlən] vi to squint; **nach etw ~** (*fig*) to eye sth up
schien etc [ʃiːn] vb siehe **scheinen**
Schienbein nt shinbone
Schiene ['ʃiːnə] f rail; (*Med*) splint
schienen vt to put in splints
Schienenbus m railcar
Schienenstrang m (*Eisenb etc*) (section of) track
schier [ʃiːr] adj pure; (*fig*) sheer ▷ adv nearly, almost
Schießbude f shooting gallery
Schießbudenfigur (*umg*) f clown, ludicrous figure
schießen ['ʃiːsən] unreg vi to shoot; (*Salat etc*) to run to seed ▷ vt to shoot; (*Ball*) to kick; (*Geschoss*) to fire; **~ auf** +akk to shoot at; **aus dem Boden ~** (*lit, fig*) to spring od sprout up; **jdm durch den Kopf ~** (*fig*) to flash through sb's mind
Schießerei [ʃiːsəˈraɪ] f shoot-out, gun battle
Schieß- zW: **Schießgewehr** nt (*hum*) gun; **Schießhund** m: **wie ein Schießhund aufpassen** (*umg*) to watch like a hawk; **Schießplatz** m firing range; **Schießpulver** nt gunpowder; **Schießscharte** f embrasure; **Schießstand** m rifle od shooting range
Schiff [ʃɪf] (**-(e)s,** -e) nt ship, vessel; (*Kirchenschiff*) nave
Schiffahrt f siehe **Schifffahrt**
Schiff- zw**: **schiffbar** adj navigable; **Schiffbau** m shipbuilding; **Schiffbruch** m shipwreck; **Schiffbruch erleiden** (*lit*) to be shipwrecked; (*fig*) to fail; (*Unternehmen*) to founder; **schiffbrüchig** adj shipwrecked
Schiffchen nt small boat; (*Weben*) shuttle; (*Mütze*) forage cap

Schiffer (**-s,** -) m boatman, sailor; (*von Lastkahn*) bargee
Schiff- zW: **Schifffahrt** f shipping; (*Reise*) voyage; **Schifffahrtslinie** f shipping route; **Schiffschaukel** f swing boat
Schiffs- zW: **Schiffsjunge** m cabin boy; **Schiffskörper** m hull; **Schiffsladung** f cargo, shipload; **Schiffsplanke** f gangplank; **Schiffsschraube** f ship's propeller
Schiit [ʃiˈiːt] (**-en, -en**) m Shiite; **schiitisch** adj Shiite
Schikane [ʃiˈkaːnə] (**-, -n**) f harassment; dirty trick; **mit allen ~n** with all the trimmings; **das hat er aus reiner ~ gemacht** he did it out of sheer bloody-mindedness
schikanieren [ʃikaˈniːrən] vt to harass; (*Ehepartner*) to mess around; (*Mitschüler*) to bully
schikanös [ʃikaˈnøːs] adj (*Mensch*) bloody-minded; (*Maßnahme etc*) harassing
Schild[1] [ʃɪlt] (**-(e)s, -e**) m shield; (*Mützenschild*) peak, visor; **etwas im ~e führen** to be up to something
Schild[2] [ʃɪlt] (**-(e)s, -er**) nt sign; (*Namensschild*) nameplate; (*an Monument, Haus, Grab*) plaque; (*Etikett*) label
Schildbürger m duffer, blockhead
Schilddrüse f thyroid gland
schildern ['ʃɪldərn] vt to describe; (*Menschen etc*) to portray; (*skizzieren*) to outline
Schilderung f description; portrayal
Schildkröte f tortoise; (*Wasserschildkröte*) turtle
Schildkrötensuppe f turtle soup
Schilf [ʃɪlf] (**-(e)s, -e**) nt, **Schilfrohr** nt (*Pflanze*) reed; (*Material*) reeds pl, rushes pl
Schillerlocke ['ʃɪlərlɔkə] f (*Gebäck*) cream horn; (*Räucherfisch*) strip of smoked rock salmon
schillern ['ʃɪlərn] vi to shimmer
schillernd adj iridescent; (*fig: Charakter*) enigmatic
Schilling ['ʃɪlɪŋ] (**-s, -** od (*Schillingstücke*) **-e**) (*Österr*) m schilling
schilt [ʃɪlt] vb siehe **schelten**
Schimmel ['ʃɪməl] (**-s, -**) m mould (*Brit*), mold (*US*); (*Pferd*) white horse
schimmelig adj mouldy (*Brit*), moldy (*US*)
schimmeln vi to go mouldy (*Brit*) od moldy (*US*)
Schimmer ['ʃɪmər] (**-s**) m glimmer; **keinen (blassen) ~ von etw haben** (*umg*) not to have the slightest idea about sth
schimmern vi to glimmer; (*Seide, Perlen*) to shimmer
schimmlig adj = **schimmelig**
Schimpanse [ʃɪmˈpanzə] (**-n, -n**) m chimpanzee
Schimpf [ʃɪmpf] (**-(e)s, -e**) m disgrace; **mit ~ und Schande** in disgrace
schimpfen vi (*sich beklagen*) to grumble; (*fluchen*) to curse
Schimpfkanonade f barrage of abuse
Schimpfwort nt term of abuse
Schindel ['ʃɪndəl] (**-, -n**) f shingle
schinden ['ʃɪndən] unreg vt to maltreat, drive

too hard ▷ *vr*: **sich ~ (mit)** to sweat and strain (at), toil away (at); **Eindruck ~** (*umg*) to create an impression

Schinder **(-s, -)** *m* knacker; (*fig*) slave driver

Schinderei [ʃɪndəˈraɪ] *f* grind, drudgery

Schindluder [ˈʃɪntluːdər] *nt*: **mit etw ~ treiben** to muck *od* mess sth about; (*Vorrecht*) to abuse sth

Schinken [ˈʃɪŋkən] **(-s, -)** *m* ham; (*gekocht und geräuchert*) gammon; (*pej: umg: Theaterstück etc*) hackneyed and clichéd play *etc*; **Schinkenspeck** *m* bacon

Schippe [ˈʃɪpə] **(-, -n)** *f* shovel; **jdn auf die ~ nehmen** (*fig: umg*) to pull sb's leg

schippen *vt* to shovel

Schirm [ʃɪrm] **(-(e)s, -e)** *m* (*Regenschirm*) umbrella; (*Sonnenschirm*) parasol, sunshade; (*Wandschirm, Bildschirm*) screen; (*Lampenschirm*) (lamp)shade; (*Mützenschirm*) peak; (*Pilzschirm*) cap; **Schirmbildaufnahme** *f* X-ray; **Schirmherr, in** *m(f)* patron(ess); **Schirmherrschaft** *f* patronage; **Schirmmütze** *f* peaked cap; **Schirmständer** *m* umbrella stand

Schiss *m*: **~ haben** (*umg*) to be shit scared (!)

schiss *etc* [ʃɪs] *vb siehe* **scheißen**

schizophren [ʃitsoˈfreːn] *adj* schizophrenic

Schizophrenie [ʃitsofreˈniː] *f* schizophrenia

schlabbern [ˈʃlabərn] (*umg*) *vt, vi* to slurp

Schlacht [ʃlaxt] **(-, -en)** *f* battle

schlachten *vt* to slaughter, kill

Schlachtenbummler (*umg*) *m* visiting football fan

Schlachter **(-s, -)** *m* butcher

Schlacht- *zW*: **Schlachtfeld** *nt* battlefield; **Schlachtfest** *nt country feast at which freshly slaughtered meat is served*; **Schlachthaus** *nt*, **Schlachthof** *m* slaughterhouse, abattoir (*Brit*); **Schlachtopfer** *nt* sacrifice; (*Mensch*) human sacrifice; **Schlachtplan** *m* battle plan; (*fig*) plan of action; **Schlachtruf** *m* battle cry, war cry; **Schlachtschiff** *nt* battleship; **Schlachtvieh** *nt* animals *pl* kept for meat

Schlacke [ˈʃlakə] **(-, -n)** *f* slag

schlackern (*umg*) *vi* to tremble; (*Kleidung*) to hang loosely, be baggy; **mit den Ohren ~** (*fig*) to be (left) speechless

Schlaf [ʃlaːf] **(-(e)s)** *m* sleep; **um seinen ~ kommen** *od* **gebracht werden** to lose sleep; **Schlafanzug** *m* pyjamas *pl* (*Brit*), pajamas *pl* (*US*)

Schläfchen [ˈʃlɛːfçən] *nt* nap

Schläfe **(-, -n)** *f* (*Anat*) temple

schlafen *unreg vi* to sleep; (*umg: nicht aufpassen*) to be asleep; **~ gehen** to go to bed; **bei jdm ~** to stay overnight with sb; **Schlafengehen** *nt* going to bed

Schlafenszeit *f* bedtime

Schläfer, in [ˈʃlɛːfər(ɪn)] **(-s, -)** *m(f)* sleeper

schlaff [ʃlaf] *adj* slack; (*Haut*) loose; (*Muskeln*) flabby; (*energielos*) limp; (*erschöpft*) exhausted; **Schlaffheit** *f* slackness; looseness; flabbiness; limpness; exhaustion

Schlafgelegenheit *f* place to sleep

Schlafittchen [ʃlaˈfɪtçən] (*umg*) *nt*: **jdn am** *od* **beim ~ nehmen** to take sb by the scruff of the neck

Schlaf- *zW*: **Schlafkrankheit** *f* sleeping sickness; **Schlaflied** *nt* lullaby; **schlaflos** *adj* sleepless; **Schlaflosigkeit** *f* sleeplessness, insomnia; **Schlafmittel** *nt* sleeping drug; (*fig, ironisch*) soporific; **Schlafmütze** (*umg*) *f* dope

schläfrig [ˈʃlɛːfrɪç] *adj* sleepy

Schlaf- *zW*: **Schlafrock** *m* dressing gown; **Apfel im Schlafrock** baked apple in puff pastry; **Schlafsaal** *m* dormitory; **Schlafsack** *m* sleeping bag

schläft [ʃlɛːft] *vb siehe* **schlafen**

Schlaf- *zW*: **Schlaftablette** *f* sleeping pill; **schlaftrunken** *adj* drowsy, half-asleep; **Schlafwagen** *m* sleeping car, sleeper; **schlafwandeln** *vi untr* to sleepwalk; **Schlafwandler, in** **(-s, -)** *m(f)* sleepwalker; **Schlafzimmer** *nt* bedroom

Schlag [ʃlaːk] **(-(e)s, ̈-e)** *m* (*lit, fig*) blow; (*auch Med*) stroke; (*Pulsschlag, Herzschlag*) beat; (*Elek*) shock; (*Blitzschlag*) bolt, stroke; (*Glockenschlag*) chime; (*Autotür*) car door; (*umg: Portion*) helping; (: *Art*) kind, type; **Schläge** *pl* (*Tracht Prügel*) beating *sing*; **~ acht Uhr** (*umg*) on the stroke of eight; **mit einem ~** all at once; **~ auf Schlag** in rapid succession; **die haben keinen ~ getan** (*umg*) they haven't done a stroke (of work); **ich dachte, mich trifft der ~** (*umg*) I was thunderstruck; **vom gleichen ~ sein** to be cast in the same mould (*Brit*) *od* mold (*US*); (*pej*) to be tarred with the same brush; **ein ~ ins Wasser** (*umg*) a wash-out; **Schlagabtausch** *m* (*Boxen*) exchange of blows; (*fig*) (verbal) exchange; **Schlagader** *f* artery; **Schlaganfall** *m* stroke; **schlagartig** *adj* sudden, without warning; **Schlagbaum** *m* barrier; **Schlagbohrer** *m* percussion drill

Schlägel [ˈʃlɛːgl] **(-s, -)** *m* drumstick; (*Hammer*) hammer

schlagen [ˈʃlaːgən] *unreg vt* to strike, hit; (*wiederholt schlagen, besiegen*) to beat; (*Glocke*) to ring; (*Stunde*) to strike; (*Kreis, Bogen*) to describe; (*Purzelbaum*) to do; (*Sahne*) to whip; (*Schlacht*) to fight; (*einwickeln*) to wrap ▷ *vi* to strike, hit; to beat; to ring; to strike ▷ *vr* to fight; **um sich ~** to lash out; **ein Ei in die Pfanne ~** to crack an egg into the pan; **eine ge~e Stunde** a full hour; **na ja, ehe ich mich ~ lasse!** (*hum: umg*) I suppose you could twist my arm; **nach jdm ~** (*fig*) to take after sb; **sich gut ~** (*fig*) to do well; **sich nach links/Norden ~** to strike out to the left/(for the) north; **sich auf jds Seite** *akk* **~** to side with sb; (*die Fronten wechseln*) to go over to sb

schlagend *adj* (*Beweis*) convincing; **~e Wetter** (*Min*) firedamp

Schlager [ˈʃlaːgər] **(-s, -)** *m* (*Mus, fig*) hit

Schläger [ˈʃlɛːgər] **(-s, -)** *m* brawler; (*Sport*) bat; (*Tennis etc*) racket; (*Golf*) club; (*Hockeyschläger*) hockey stick

Schlägerei [ʃlɛːgəˈraɪ] f fight, punch-up
Schlagersänger m pop singer
Schlägertyp (umg) m thug
Schlag- zW: **schlagfertig** adj quick-witted;
Schlagfertigkeit f ready wit, quickness of
repartee; **Schlaginstrument** nt percussion
instrument; **Schlagkraft** f (lit, fig) power;
(Mil) strike power; (Boxen) punch(ing power);
schlagkräftig adj powerful; (Beweise) clear-
cut; **Schlagloch** nt pothole; **Schlagobers** (-, -)
(Österr) nt, **Schlagrahm** m, **Schlagsahne**
f (whipped) cream; **Schlagseite** f (Naut)
list; **Schlagstock** m (form) truncheon (Brit),
nightstick (US)
schlägt [ʃlɛːkt] vb siehe **schlagen**
Schlag- zW: **Schlagwort** nt slogan, catch
phrase; **Schlagzeile** f headline; **Schlagzeilen
machen** (umg) to hit the headlines;
Schlagzeug nt drums pl; (in Orchester)
percussion; **Schlagzeuger** (-s, -) m drummer;
percussionist
schlaksig [ˈʃlaːksɪç] (umg) adj gangling, gawky
Schlamassel [ʃlaˈmasəl] (-s, -) (umg) m mess
Schlamm [ʃlam] (-(e)s, -e) m mud
schlammig adj muddy
Schlampe [ˈʃlampə] (-, -n) (umg) f slattern, slut
schlampen (umg) vi to be sloppy
Schlamperei [ʃlampəˈraɪ] (umg) f disorder,
untidiness; (schlechte Arbeit) sloppy work
schlampig (umg) adj slovenly, sloppy
schlang etc [ʃlaŋ] vb siehe **schlingen**
Schlange [ˈʃlaŋə] (-, -n) f snake;
(Menschenschlange) queue (Brit), line (US); ~
stehen to (form a) queue (Brit), stand in line
(US); **eine falsche ~** a snake in the grass
schlängeln [ˈʃlɛŋəln] vr to twist, wind; (Fluss)
to meander
Schlangen- zW: **Schlangenbiss** m snake
bite; **Schlangengift** nt snake venom;
Schlangenlinie f wavy line
schlank [ʃlaŋk] adj slim, slender; **Schlankheit** f
slimness, slenderness; **Schlankheitskur** f diet
schlapp [ʃlap] adj limp; (locker) slack;
(umg: energielos) listless; (nach Krankheit etc)
run-down
Schlappe (-, -n) (umg) f setback
Schlappen (-s, -) (umg) m slipper
schlapp- zW: **Schlappheit** f limpness;
slackness; **Schlapphut** m slouch hat;
schlappmachen (umg) vi to wilt, droop;
Schlappschwanz (pej: umg) m weakling, softy
Schlaraffenland [ʃlaˈrafənlant] nt land of milk
and honey
schlau [ʃlaʊ] adj crafty, cunning; **ich werde
nicht ~ aus ihm** I don't know what to make of
him; **Schlauberger** (-s, -) (umg) m clever Dick
Schlauch [ʃlaʊx] (-(e)s, **Schläuche**) m hose;
(in Reifen) inner tube; (umg: Anstrengung) grind;
auf dem ~ stehen (umg) to be in a jam od fix;
Schlauchboot nt rubber dinghy
schlauchen (umg) vt to tell on, exhaust
schlauchlos adj (Reifen) tubeless
Schläue [ˈʃlɔʏə] (-) f cunning

Schlaufe [ˈʃlaʊfə] (-, -n) f loop; (Aufhänger)
hanger
Schlauheit f cunning
Schlaukopf m clever Dick
Schlawiner [ʃlaˈviːnər] (-s, -) m (hum: umg)
villain, rogue
schlecht [ʃlɛçt] adj bad; (ungenießbar) bad, off
(Brit) ▷ adv: **jdm geht es ~** sb is in a bad way;
heute geht es ~ today is not very convenient;
er kann ~ Nein sagen he finds it hard to
say no, he can't say no; **jdm ist ~** sb feels
sick od ill; **~ und recht** after a fashion; **auf
jdn ~ zu sprechen sein** not to have a good
word to say for sb; **er hat nicht ~ gestaunt**
(umg) he wasn't half surprised; siehe auch
schlechtmachen
schlechterdings adv simply
Schlecht- zW: **Schlechtheit** f badness;
schlechthin adv simply; **der Dramatiker
schlechthin** THE playwright
Schlechtigkeit f badness; (Tat) bad deed
schlechtmachen vt to run down, denigrate
schlecken [ˈʃlɛkən] vt, vi to lick
Schlegel [ˈʃleːgəl] (-s, -) m (Koch) leg; siehe auch
Schlägel
schleichen [ˈʃlaɪçən] unreg vi to creep, crawl
schleichend adj creeping; (Krankheit, Gift)
insidious
Schleichweg m: **auf ~en** (fig) on the quiet
Schleichwerbung f: **eine ~** a plug
Schleie [ˈʃlaɪə] (-, -n) f tench
Schleier [ˈʃlaɪər] (-s, -) m veil; **Schleiereule**
f barn owl; **schleierhaft** (umg) adj: **jdm
schleierhaft sein** to be a mystery to sb
Schleife [ˈʃlaɪfə] (-, -n) f (auch Comput) loop;
(Band) bow; (Kranzschleife) ribbon
schleifen¹ vt to drag; (Mil: Festung) to raze ▷ vi
to drag; **die Kupplung ~ lassen** (Aut) to slip
the clutch
schleifen² unreg vt to grind; (Edelstein) to cut;
(Mil: Soldaten) to drill
Schleifmaschine f sander; (in Fabrik) grinding
machine
Schleifstein m grindstone
Schleim [ʃlaɪm] (-(e)s, -e) m slime; (Med)
mucus; (Koch) gruel; **Schleimhaut** f mucous
membrane
schleimig adj slimy
schlemmen [ˈʃlɛmən] vi to feast
Schlemmer, in (-s, -) m(f) gourmet, bon vivant
Schlemmerei [ʃlɛməˈraɪ] f feasting
schlendern [ˈʃlɛndərn] vi to stroll
Schlendrian [ˈʃlɛndriaːn] (-(e)s) m sloppy way
of working
Schlenker [ˈʃlɛŋkər] (-s, -) m swerve
schlenkern vt, vi to swing, dangle
Schleppe [ˈʃlɛpə] (-, -n) f train
schleppen vt to drag; (Auto, Schiff) to tow;
(tragen) to lug
schleppend adj dragging; (Bedienung,
Abfertigung) sluggish, slow
Schlepper (-s, -) m tractor; (Schiff) tug
Schleppkahn m (canal) barge

Schlepptau *nt* towrope; **jdn ins ~ nehmen** (*fig*) to take sb in tow

Schlesien ['ʃleːziən] (**-s**) *nt* Silesia

Schlesier, in (**-s, -**) *m(f)* Silesian

schlesisch *adj* Silesian

Schleswig-Holstein ['ʃleːsvɪçˈhɔlʃtaɪn] (**-s**) *nt* Schleswig-Holstein

Schleuder ['ʃlɔʏdər] (**-, -n**) *f* catapult; (*Wäscheschleuder*) spin-dryer; (*Zentrifuge*) centrifuge; **Schleuderhonig** *m* extracted honey

schleudern *vt* to hurl; (*Wäsche*) to spin-dry ▷ *vi* (*Aut*) to skid; **ins S~ kommen** (*Aut*) to go into a skid; (*fig: umg*) to run into trouble

Schleuder- *zW*: **Schleuderpreis** *m* give-away price; **Schleudersitz** *m* (*Aviat*) ejector seat; (*fig*) hot seat; **Schleuderware** *f* cut-price (*Brit*) *od* cut-rate (*US*) goods *pl*

schleunig ['ʃlɔʏnɪç] *adj* prompt, speedy; (*Schritte*) quick

schleunigst *adv* straight away

Schleuse ['ʃlɔʏzə] (**-, -n**) *f* lock; (*Schleusentor*) sluice

schleusen *vt* (*Schiffe*) to pass through a lock, lock; (*Wasser*) to channel; (*Menschen*) to filter; (*fig: heimlich*) to smuggle

Schlich (**-(e)s, -e**) *m* dodge, trick; **jdm auf die ~e kommen** to get wise to sb

schlich *etc* [ʃlɪç] *vb siehe* **schleichen**

schlicht [ʃlɪçt] *adj* simple, plain

schlichten *vt* to smooth; (*beilegen*) to settle; (*Streit: vermitteln*) to mediate, arbitrate

Schlichter, in (**-s, -**) *m(f)* mediator, arbitrator

Schlichtheit *f* simplicity, plainness

Schlichtung *f* settlement; arbitration

Schlick [ʃlɪk] (**-(e)s, -e**) *m* mud; (*Ölschlick*) slick

schlief *etc* [ʃliːf] *vb siehe* **schlafen**

Schließe ['ʃliːsə] (**-, -n**) *f* fastener

schließen ['ʃliːsən] *unreg vt* to close, shut; (*beenden*) to close; (*Freundschaft, Bündnis, Ehe*) to enter into; (*Comput: Datei*) to close; (*folgern*): **~ (aus)** to infer (from) ▷ *vi, vr* to close, shut; **auf etw** *akk* **~ lassen** to suggest sth; **jdn/etw in sein Herz ~** to take sb/sth to one's heart; **etw in sich ~** to include sth; **„geschlossen"** "closed"

Schließfach *nt* locker

schließlich *adv* finally; (*schließlich doch*) after all

Schliff (**-(e)s, -e**) *m* cut(ting); (*fig*) polish; **einer Sache den letzten ~ geben** (*fig*) to put the finishing touch(es) to sth

schliff *etc* [ʃlɪf] *vb siehe* **schleifen**

schlimm [ʃlɪm] *adj* bad; **das war ~** that was terrible; **das ist halb so ~!** that's not so bad!; **schlimmer** *adj* worse; **schlimmste, r, s** *adj* worst

schlimmstenfalls *adv* at (the) worst

Schlinge ['ʃlɪŋə] (**-, -n**) *f* loop; (*an Galgen*) noose; (*Falle*) snare; (*Med*) sling

Schlingel (**-s, -**) *m* rascal

schlingen *unreg vt* to wind ▷ *vi* (*essen*) to bolt one's food, gobble

schlingern *vi* to roll

Schlingpflanze *f* creeper

Schlips [ʃlɪps] (**-es, -e**) *m* tie, necktie (*US*); **sich auf den ~ getreten fühlen** (*fig: umg*) to feel offended

Schlitten ['ʃlɪtən] (**-s, -**) *m* sledge, sled; (*Pferdeschlitten*) sleigh; **mit jdm ~ fahren** (*umg*) to give sb a rough time; **Schlittenbahn** *f* toboggan run; **Schlittenfahren** (**-s**) *nt* tobogganing

schlittern ['ʃlɪtərn] *vi* to slide; (*Wagen*) to skid

Schlittschuh ['ʃlɪtʃuː] *m* skate; **~ laufen** to skate; **Schlittschuhbahn** *f* skating rink; **Schlittschuhläufer** *m* skater

Schlitz [ʃlɪts] (**-es, -e**) *m* slit; (*für Münze*) slot; (*Hosenschlitz*) flies *pl*; **schlitzäugig** *adj* slant-eyed; **schlitzen** *vt* to slit; **Schlitzohr** *nt* (*fig*) sly fox

schlohweiß ['ʃloːvaɪs] *adj* snow-white

Schlokal *nt* gourmet restaurant

Schloss (**-es, -̈er**) *nt* lock, padlock; (*an Schmuck etc*) clasp; (*Bau*) castle; (*Palast*) palace; **ins ~ fallen** to lock (itself)

schloss *etc* [ʃlɔs] *vb siehe* **schließen**

Schlosser ['ʃlɔsər] (**-s, -**) *m* (*Autoschlosser*) fitter; (*für Schlüssel etc*) locksmith

Schlosserei [ʃlɔsəˈraɪ] *f* metal(working) shop

Schlosshund *m*: **heulen wie ein ~** to howl one's head off

Schlot [ʃloːt] (**-(e)s, -e**) *m* chimney; (*Naut*) funnel

schlottern ['ʃlɔtərn] *vi* to shake; (*vor Angst*) to tremble; (*Kleidung*) to be baggy

Schlucht [ʃlʊxt] (**-, -en**) *f* gorge, ravine

schluchzen ['ʃlʊxtsən] *vi* to sob

Schluck [ʃlʊk] (**-(e)s, -e**) *m* swallow; (*größer*) gulp; (*kleiner*) sip; (*ein bisschen*) drop

Schluckauf (**-s**) *m* hiccups *pl*

schlucken *vt* to swallow; (*umg: Alkohol, Benzin*) to guzzle; (*: verschlingen*) to swallow up ▷ *vi* to swallow

Schlucker (**-s, -**) (*umg*) *m*: **armer ~** poor devil

Schluckimpfung *f* oral vaccination

schluderig ['ʃluːdərɪç], **schludrig** ['ʃluːdrɪç] (*umg*) *adj* slipshod

schludern ['ʃluːdərn] (*umg*) *vi* to do slipshod work

schlug *etc* [ʃluːk] *vb siehe* **schlagen**

Schlummer ['ʃlʊmər] (**-s**) *m* slumber

schlummern *vi* to slumber

Schlund [ʃlʊnt] (**-(e)s, -̈e**) *m* gullet; (*fig*) jaw

schlüpfen ['ʃlʏpfən] *vi* to slip; (*Vogel etc*) to hatch (out)

Schlüpfer ['ʃlʏpfər] (**-s, -**) *m* panties *pl*, knickers *pl*

Schlupfloch ['ʃlʊpflɔx] *nt* hole; (*Versteck*) hide-out; (*fig*) loophole

schlüpfrig ['ʃlʏpfrɪç] *adj* slippery; (*fig*) lewd; **Schlüpfrigkeit** *f* slipperiness; lewdness

Schlupfwinkel *m* hiding place; (*fig*) quiet corner

schlurfen ['ʃlʊrfən] *vi* to shuffle

schlürfen ['ʃlʏrfən] *vt, vi* to slurp

Schluss [ʃlʊs] (**-es, -̈e**) *m* end; (*Schlussfolgerung*)

S

conclusion; **am ~** at the end; **~ für heute!** that'll do for today; **~ jetzt!** that's enough now!; **~ machen mit** to finish with

Schlüssel ['ʃlʏsəl] **(-s, -)** m (lit, fig) key; (Schraubschlüssel) spanner, wrench; (Mus) clef; **Schlüsselbein** nt collarbone; **Schlüsselblume** f cowslip, primrose; **Schlüsselbund** m bunch of keys; **Schlüsselerlebnis** nt (Psych) crucial experience; **Schlüsselkind** nt latchkey child; **Schlüsselloch** nt keyhole; **Schlüsselposition** f key position; **Schlüsselwort** nt safe combination; (Comput) keyword

Schlussfolgerung f conclusion, inference

Schlussformel f (in Brief) closing formula; (bei Vertrag) final clause

schlüssig ['ʃlʏsɪç] adj conclusive; **sich** dat **(über etw** akk**) ~ sein** to have made up one's mind (about sth)

Schluss- zW: **Schlusslicht** nt rear light (Brit), taillight (US); (fig) tail ender; **Schlussstrich** m (fig) final stroke; **einen Schlussstrich unter etw** akk **ziehen** to consider sth finished; **Schlussverkauf** m clearance sale; **Schlusswort** nt concluding words pl

Schmach [ʃmaːx] **(-)** f disgrace, ignominy

schmachten ['ʃmaxtən] vi to languish; **nach jdm ~** to pine for sb

schmächtig ['ʃmɛçtɪç] adj slight

schmachvoll adj ignominious, humiliating

schmackhaft ['ʃmakhaft] adj tasty; **jdm etw ~ machen** (fig) to make sth palatable to sb

schmähen ['ʃmɛːən] vt to abuse, revile

schmählich adj ignominious, shameful

Schmähung f abuse

schmal [ʃmaːl] adj narrow; (Person, Buch etc) slender, slim; (karg) meagre (Brit), meager (US); **schmalbrüstig** adj narrow-chested

schmälern ['ʃmɛːlərn] vt to diminish; (fig) to belittle

Schmalfilm m cine (Brit) od movie (US) film

Schmalspur f narrow gauge

Schmalspur- (pej) in zw small-time

Schmalz [ʃmalts] **(-es, -e)** nt dripping; (Schweineschmalz) lard; (fig) sentiment, schmaltz

schmalzig adj (fig) schmaltzy, slushy

schmarotzen [ʃmaˈrɔtsən] vi (Biol) to be parasitic; (fig) to sponge

Schmarotzer (-s, -) m (auch fig) parasite

Schmarren ['ʃmarən] **(-s, -)** m (Österr) small pieces of pancake; (fig) rubbish, tripe

schmatzen ['ʃmatsən] vi to eat noisily

Schmaus [ʃmaʊs] **(-es, Schmäuse)** m feast; **schmausen** vi to feast

schmecken ['ʃmɛkən] vt, vi to taste; **es schmeckt ihm** he likes it; **schmeckt es Ihnen?** is it good?, are you enjoying your food od meal?; **das schmeckt nach mehr!** (umg) it's very moreish (hum); **es sich ~ lassen** to tuck in

Schmeichelei [ʃmaɪçəˈlaɪ] f flattery

schmeichelhaft ['ʃmaɪçəlhaft] adj flattering

schmeicheln vi to flatter

Schmeichler, in (-s, -) m(f) flatterer

schmeißen ['ʃmaɪsən] unreg (umg) vt to throw, chuck; (spendieren): **eine Runde** od **Lage ~** to stand a round

Schmeißfliege f bluebottle

Schmelz [ʃmɛlts] **(-es, -e)** m enamel; (Glasur) glaze; (von Stimme) melodiousness; **schmelzbar** adj fusible

schmelzen unreg vt to melt; (Erz) to smelt ▷ vi to melt

Schmelz- zW: **Schmelzhütte** f smelting works pl; **Schmelzkäse** m cheese spread; (in Scheiben) processed cheese; **Schmelzofen** m melting furnace; (für Erze) smelting furnace; **Schmelzpunkt** m melting point; **Schmelztiegel** m (lit, fig) melting pot; **Schmelzwasser** nt melted snow

Schmerbauch ['ʃmeːrbaʊx] (umg) m paunch, potbelly

Schmerz [ʃmɛrts] **(-es, -en)** m pain; (Trauer) grief no pl; **~en haben** to be in pain; **schmerzempfindlich** adj sensitive to pain

schmerzen vt, vi to hurt

Schmerzensgeld nt compensation

Schmerz- zW: **schmerzhaft** adj painful; **schmerzlich** adj painful; **schmerzlindernd** adj pain-relieving; **schmerzlos** adj painless; **Schmerzmittel** nt painkiller, analgesic; **schmerzstillend** adj pain-killing, analgesic; **Schmerztablette** f pain-killing tablet

Schmetterling ['ʃmetərlɪŋ] m butterfly

Schmetterlingsstil m (Schwimmen) butterfly stroke

schmettern ['ʃmetərn] vt to smash; (Melodie) to sing loudly, bellow out ▷ vi to smash (SPORT); (Trompete) to blare

Schmied [ʃmiːt] **(-(e)s, -e)** m blacksmith

Schmiede ['ʃmiːdə] **(-, -n)** f smithy, forge; **Schmiedeeisen** nt wrought iron

schmieden vt to forge; (Pläne) to devise, concoct

schmiegen ['ʃmiːgən] vt to press, nestle ▷ vr: **sich ~ an** +akk to cuddle up to, nestle up to

schmiegsam ['ʃmiːkzaːm] adj flexible, pliable

Schmiere ['ʃmiːrə] f grease; (Theat) greasepaint, make-up; (pej: schlechtes Theater) fleapit; **~ stehen** (umg) to be the look-out

schmieren vt to smear; (ölen) to lubricate, grease; (bestechen) to bribe ▷ vi (schreiben) to scrawl; **es läuft wie geschmiert** it's going like clockwork; **jdm eine ~** (umg) to clout sb one

Schmierenkomödiant (pej) m ham (actor)

Schmier- zW: **Schmierfett** nt grease; **Schmierfink** m messy person; **Schmiergeld** nt bribe; **Schmierheft** nt jotter

schmierig adj greasy

Schmiermittel nt lubricant

Schmierseife f soft soap

schmilzt [ʃmɪltst] vb siehe **schmelzen**

Schminke ['ʃmɪŋkə] **(-, -n)** f make-up

schminken vt, vr to make up

schmirgeln ['ʃmɪrgəln] vt to sand (down)

Schmirgelpapier (**-s**) *nt* emery paper
Schmiss (**-es, -e**) *m* (*Narbe*) duelling (*Brit*) *od*
dueling (*US*) scar; (*veraltet: Schwung*) dash, élan
schmiss *etc* [ʃmɪs] *vb siehe* **schmeißen**
Schmöker [ˈʃmøːkər] (**-s, -**) (*umg*) *m* (trashy)
old book
schmökern *vi* to bury o.s. in a book; (*umg*) to
browse
schmollen [ˈʃmɔlən] *vi* to pout; (*gekränkt*) to
sulk
schmollend *adj* sulky
Schmollmund *m* pout
schmolz *etc* [ʃmɔlts] *vb siehe* **schmelzen**
Schmorbraten *m* stewed *od* braised meat
schmoren [ˈʃmoːrən] *vt* to braise
Schmu [ʃmuː] (**-s**) (*umg*) *m* cheating
Schmuck [ʃmʊk] (**-(e)s, -e**) *m* jewellery (*Brit*),
jewelry (*US*); (*Verzierung*) decoration
schmücken [ˈʃmʏkən] *vt* to decorate
Schmuck- *zW:* **schmucklos** *adj* unadorned,
plain; **Schmucklosigkeit** *f* simplicity;
Schmucksachen *pl* jewels *pl*, jewellery *sing*
(*Brit*), jewelry *sing* (*US*); **Schmuckstück** *nt* (*Ring
etc*) piece of jewellery (*Brit*) *od* jewelry (*US*);
(*fig: Prachtstück*) gem
schmuddelig [ˈʃmʊdəlɪç], **schmuddlig**
[ˈʃmʊdlɪç] *adj* messy; (*schmutzig*) dirty;
(*schmierig, unsauber*) filthy
Schmuggel [ˈʃmʊgəl] (**-s**) *m* smuggling
schmuggeln *vt, vi* to smuggle
Schmuggelware *f* contraband
Schmuggler, in (**-s, -**) *m(f)* smuggler
schmunzeln [ˈʃmʊntsəln] *vi* to smile benignly
schmusen [ˈʃmuːzən] *vi* (*zärtlich sein*) to
cuddle; **mit jdm ~** to cuddle sb
Schmutz [ʃmʊts] (**-es**) *m* dirt; (*fig*) filth;
schmutzen *vi* to get dirty; **Schmutzfink** *m*
filthy creature; **Schmutzfleck** *m* stain
schmutzig *adj* dirty; **~e Wäsche waschen** (*fig*)
to wash one's dirty linen in public
Schnabel [ˈʃnaːbəl] (**-s, ⁻**) *m* beak, bill; (*Ausguss*)
spout; (*umg: Mund*) mouth; **reden, wie einem
der ~ gewachsen ist** to say exactly what
comes into one's head; (*unaffektiert*) to talk
naturally
schnacken [ˈʃnakən] (*Nordd: umg*) *vi* to chat
Schnake [ˈʃnaːkə] (**-, -n**) *f* crane fly; (*Stechmücke*)
gnat
Schnalle [ˈʃnalə] (**-, -n**) *f* buckle; (*an Handtasche,
Buch*) clasp
schnallen *vt* to buckle
schnalzen [ˈʃnaltsən] *vi* to snap; (*mit Zunge*) to
click
Schnäppchen [ˈʃnɛpçən] (*umg*) *nt* bargain, snip
schnappen [ˈʃnapən] *vt* to grab, catch;
(*umg: ergreifen*) to snatch ▷ *vi* to snap
Schnappschloss *nt* spring lock
Schnappschuss *m* (*Phot*) snapshot
Schnaps [ʃnaps] (**-es, ⁻e**) *m* schnapps;
(*umg: Branntwein*) spirits *pl*; **Schnapsidee** (*umg*) *f*
crackpot idea; **Schnapsleiche** (*umg*) *f* drunk
schnarchen [ˈʃnarçən] *vi* to snore
schnattern [ˈʃnatərn] *vi* to chatter; (*zittern*) to
shiver
schnauben [ˈʃnaʊbən] *vi* to snort ▷ *vr* to blow
one's nose
schnaufen [ˈʃnaʊfən] *vi* to puff, pant
Schnaufer (**-s, -**) (*umg*) *m* breath
Schnauzbart [ˈʃnaʊtsbaːrt] *m* moustache (*Brit*),
mustache (*US*)
Schnauze (**-, -n**) *f* snout, muzzle; (*Ausguss*)
spout; (*umg*) gob; **auf die ~ fallen** (*fig*) to come
a cropper (*umg*); **etw frei nach ~ machen** to
do sth any old how
schnäuzen [ˈʃnɔʏtsn] *vr* to blow one's nose
Schnecke [ˈʃnɛkə] (**-, -n**) *f* snail; (*Nacktschnecke*)
slug; (*Koch: Gebäck*) ≈ Chelsea bun; **jdn zur ~
machen** (*umg*) to give sb a real bawling out
Schneckenhaus *nt* snail's shell
Schneckentempo (*umg*) *nt:* **im ~** at a snail's
pace
Schnee [ʃneː] (**-s**) *m* snow; (*Eischnee*) beaten egg
white; **~ von gestern** old hat; water under the
bridge; **Schneeball** *m* snowball; **Schneebesen**
m (*Koch*) whisk; **Schneefall** *m* snowfall;
Schneeflocke *f* snowflake; **Schneegestöber** *nt*
snowstorm; **Schneeglöckchen** *nt* snowdrop;
Schneegrenze *f* snowline; **Schneekette**
f (*Aut*) snow chain; **Schneemann** *m:* **sich
freuen wie ein Schneekönig** to be as
pleased as Punch; **Schneemann** *m* snowman;
Schneepflug *m* snowplough (*Brit*), snowplow
(*US*); **Schneeregen** *m* sleet; **Schneeschmelze**
f thaw; **Schneetreiben** *nt* driving snow;
Schneewehe *f* snowdrift; **Schneewittchen** *nt*
Snow White
Schneid [ʃnaɪt] (**-(e)s**) (*umg*) *m* pluck
Schneidbrenner (**-s, -**) *m* (*Tech*) oxyacetylene
cutter
Schneide [ˈʃnaɪdə] (**-, -n**) *f* edge; (*Klinge*) blade
schneiden *unreg* *vt* to cut; (*Film, Tonband*) to
edit; (*kreuzen*) to cross, intersect ▷ *vr* to cut
o.s.; (*umg: sich täuschen*): **da hat er sich aber
geschnitten!** he's very much mistaken; **die
Luft ist zum S~** (*fig: umg*) the air is very bad
schneidend *adj* cutting
Schneider (**-s, -**) *m* tailor; **frieren wie ein ~**
(*umg*) to be frozen to the marrow; **aus dem ~
sein** (*fig*) to be out of the woods
Schneiderei [ʃnaɪdəˈraɪ] *f* tailor's shop; (*einer
Schneiderin*) dressmaker's shop
Schneiderin *f* dressmaker
schneidern *vt* to make ▷ *vi* to be a tailor
Schneidersitz (**-es**) *m:* **im ~ sitzen** to sit cross-
legged
Schneidezahn *m* incisor
schneidig *adj* dashing; (*mutig*) plucky
schneien [ˈʃnaɪən] *vi* to snow; **jdm ins Haus ~**
(*umg: Besuch*) to drop in on sb; (: *Rechnung, Brief*)
to come in the post (*Brit*) *od* mail (*US*)
Schneise [ˈʃnaɪzə] (**-, -n**) *f* (*Waldschneise*) clearing
schnell [ʃnɛl] *adj* quick, fast ▷ *adv* quick(ly),
fast; **das ging ~** that was quick; **Schnellboot**
nt speedboat
Schnelle (**-**) *f:* **etw auf die ~ machen** to do sth
in a rush

S

293

schnellen *vi* to shoot

Schnellgericht *nt* (*Jur*) summary court; (*Koch*) convenience food

Schnellhefter *m* loose-leaf binder

Schnelligkeit *f* speed

Schnell- *zW*: **Schnellimbiss** *m* (*Essen*) (quick) snack; (*Raum*) snack bar; **Schnellkochtopf** *m* (*Dampfkochtopf*) pressure cooker; **Schnellreinigung** *f* express cleaner's

schnellstens *adv* as quickly as possible

Schnellstraße *f* expressway

Schnellzug *m* fast *od* express train

schneuzen ['ʃnɔytsən] *vr siehe* **schnäuzen**

Schnickschnack ['ʃnɪkʃnak] (**-(e)s**) (*umg*) *m* twaddle

Schnippchen ['ʃnɪpçən] *nt*: **jdm ein ~ schlagen** to play a trick on sb

schnippeln ['ʃnɪpəln] (*umg*) *vt* to snip; (*mit Messer*) to hack ▷ *vi*: **~ an** +*dat* to snip at; to hack at

schnippen ['ʃnɪpən] *vi*: **mit den Fingern ~** to snap one's fingers

schnippisch ['ʃnɪpɪʃ] *adj* sharp-tongued

Schnipsel ['ʃnɪpsəl] (**-s, -**) (*umg*) *m od nt* scrap; (*Papierschnipsel*) scrap of paper

Schnitt (**-(e)s, -e**) *m* cut(ting); (*Schnittpunkt*) intersection; (*Querschnitt*) (cross) section; (*Durchschnitt*) average; (*Schnittmuster*) pattern; (*Ernte*) crop; (*an Buch*) edge; (*umg: Gewinn*) profit; **~:** L. Schwarz (*Film*) editor – L. Schwarz; **im ~** on average

schnitt *etc* [ʃnɪt] *vb siehe* **schneiden**

Schnittblumen *pl* cut flowers *pl*

Schnittbohnen *pl* French *od* green beans *pl*

Schnitte (**-, -n**) *f* slice; (*belegt*) sandwich

schnittfest *adj* (*Tomaten*) firm

Schnittfläche *f* section

schnittig ['ʃnɪtɪç] *adj* smart; (*Auto, Formen*) stylish

Schnitt- *zW*: **Schnittlauch** *m* chive; **Schnittmuster** *nt* pattern; **Schnittpunkt** *m* (point of) intersection; **Schnittstelle** *f* (*Comput*) interface; **Schnittwunde** *f* cut

Schnitzarbeit *f* wood carving

Schnitzel (**-s, -**) *nt* scrap; (*Koch*) escalope; **Schnitzeljagd** *f* paperchase

schnitzen ['ʃnɪtsən] *vt* to carve

Schnitzer (**-s, -**) *m* carver; (*umg*) blunder

Schnitzerei [ʃnɪtsəˈraɪ] *f* wood carving

schnodderig ['ʃnɔdərɪç] (*umg*) *adj* snotty

schnöde ['ʃnøːdə] *adj* base, mean

Schnorchel ['ʃnɔrçəl] (**-s, -**) *m* snorkel

schnorcheln *vi* to go snorkelling

Schnörkel ['ʃnœrkəl] (**-s, -**) *m* flourish; (*Archit*) scroll

schnorren ['ʃnɔrən] *vt, vi* to cadge (*Brit*)

Schnorrer (**-s, -**) (*umg*) *m* cadger (*Brit*)

Schnösel ['ʃnøːzəl] (**-s, -**) (*umg*) *m* snotty(-nosed) little upstart

schnuckelig ['ʃnʊkəlɪç] (*umg*) *adj* (*gemütlich*) snug, cosy; (*Person*) sweet

schnüffeln ['ʃnʏfəln] *vi* to sniff; (*fig: umg: spionieren*) to snoop around;

Schnüffeln *nt* (*von Klebstoff etc*) glue-sniffing *etc*

Schnüffler, in (**-s, -**) *m(f)* snooper

Schnuller ['ʃnʊlər] (**-s, -**) *m* dummy (*Brit*), pacifier (*US*)

Schnulze ['ʃnʊltsə] (**-, -n**) (*umg*) *f* schmaltzy film/book/song

Schnupfen ['ʃnʊpfən] (**-s, -**) *m* cold

Schnupftabak *m* snuff

schnuppe ['ʃnʊpə] (*umg*) *adj*: **jdm ~ sein** to be all the same to sb

schnuppern ['ʃnʊpərn] *vi* to sniff

Schnur [ʃnuːr] (**-, ̈-e**) *f* string; (*Kordel*) cord; (*Elek*) flex

Schnürchen ['ʃnyːrçən] *nt*: **es läuft** *od* **klappt (alles) wie am ~** everything's going like clockwork

schnüren ['ʃnyːrən] *vt* to tie

schnurgerade *adj* straight (as a die *od* an arrow)

Schnurrbart ['ʃnʊrbaːrt] *m* moustache (*Brit*), mustache (*US*)

schnurren ['ʃnʊrən] *vi* to purr; (*Kreisel*) to hum

Schnürschuh *m* lace-up (shoe)

Schnürsenkel *m* shoelace

schnurstracks *adv* straight (away); **~ auf jdn/ etw zugehen** to make a beeline for sb/sth (*umg*)

schob *etc* [ʃoːp] *vb siehe* **schieben**

Schock [ʃɔk] (**-(e)s, -e**) *m* shock; **unter ~ stehen** to be in (a state of) shock

schocken (*umg*) *vt* to shock

Schocker (**-s, -**) (*umg*) *m* shocking film/novel, shocker

schockieren *vt* to shock, outrage

Schöffe ['ʃœfə] (**-n, -n**) *m* lay magistrate

Schöffengericht *nt* magistrates' court

Schöffin *f* lay magistrate

Schokolade [ʃokoˈlaːdə] (**-, -n**) *f* chocolate

scholl *etc* [ʃɔl] *vb siehe* **schallen**

Scholle ['ʃɔlə] (**-, -n**) *f* clod; (*Eisscholle*) ice floe; (*Fisch*) plaice

Scholli ['ʃɔlɪ] (*umg*) *m*: **mein lieber ~!** (*drohend*) now look here!

 SCHLÜSSELWORT

schon [ʃoːn] *adv* **1** (*bereits*) already; **er ist schon da** he's there/here already, he's already there/here; **ist er schon da?** is he there/here yet?; **warst du schon einmal dort?** have you ever been there?; **ich war schon einmal dort** I've been there before; **das war schon immer so** that has always been the case; **hast du schon gehört?** have you heard?; **schon 1920** as early as 1920; **schon vor 100 Jahren** as far back as 100 years ago; **er wollte schon die Hoffnung aufgeben, als …** he was just about to give up hope when …; **wartest du schon lange?** have you been waiting (for) long?; **wie schon so oft** as so often (before); **was, schon wieder?** what – again?

2 (*bestimmt*) all right; **du wirst schon sehen** you'll see (all right); **das wird schon noch**

gut gehen that should turn out OK (in the end)
3 (*bloß*) just; **allein schon das Gefühl ...** just the very feeling ...; **schon der Gedanke** the mere *od* very thought; **wenn ich das schon höre** I only have to hear that
4 (*einschränkend*): **ja schon, aber ...** yes (well), but ...
5: **das ist schon möglich** that's quite possible; **schon gut** OK; **du weißt schon** you know; **komm schon** come on; **hör schon auf damit!** will you stop that!; **was macht das schon, wenn ...?** what does it matter if ...?; **und wenn schon!** (*umg*) so what?

schön [ʃøːn] *adj* beautiful; (*Mann*) handsome; (*nett*) nice ▷ *adv*: **sich ganz ~ ärgern** to be very angry; **da hast du etwas S~es angerichtet** you've made a fine *od* nice mess; **sich ~ machen** to make o.s. look nice; **~e Grüße** best wishes; **~en Dank** (many) thanks; **~ weich/warm** nice and soft/warm
schonen ['ʃoːnən] *vt* to look after; (*jds Nerven*) to spare; (*Gegner, Kind*) to be easy on; (*Teppich, Füße*) to save ▷ *vr* to take it easy
schonend *adj* careful, gentle; **jdm etw ~ beibringen** to break sth to sb gently
Schoner ['ʃoːnər] (**-s, -**) *m* (*Naut*) schooner; (*Sesselschoner*) cover
Schönfärberei *f* (*fig*) glossing things over
Schonfrist *f* period of grace
Schöngeist *m* cultured person, aesthete (*Brit*), esthete (*US*)
Schönheit *f* beauty
Schönheits- *zW*: **Schönheitsfehler** *m* blemish, flaw; **Schönheitsoperation** *f* cosmetic surgery; **Schönheitswettbewerb** *m* beauty contest
Schonkost (**-**) *f* light diet
Schönschrift *f*: **in ~** in one's best (hand) writing
schöntun *unreg vi*: **jdm ~** (*schmeicheln*) to flatter *od* soft-soap sb, play up to sb
Schonung *f* good care; (*Nachsicht*) consideration; (*Forst*) plantation of young trees
schonungslos *adj* ruthless, harsh
Schonzeit *f* close season
Schopf [ʃɔpf] (**-(e)s, -̈e**) *m*: **eine Gelegenheit beim ~ ergreifen** *od* **fassen** to seize *od* grasp an opportunity with both hands
schöpfen ['ʃœpfən] *vt* to scoop; (*Suppe*) to ladle; (*Mut*) to summon up; (*Luft*) to breathe in; (*Hoffnung*) to find
Schöpfer (**-s, -**) *m* creator; (*Gott*) Creator; (*umg: Schöpfkelle*) ladle; **schöpferisch** *adj* creative
Schöpfkelle *f* ladle
Schöpflöffel *m* skimmer, scoop
Schöpfung *f* creation
Schoppen ['ʃɔpən] (**-s, -**) *m* (*Glas Wein*) glass of wine; **Schoppenwein** *m* wine by the glass
schor *etc* [ʃoːr] *vb siehe* **scheren**

Schorf [ʃɔrf] (**-(e)s, -e**) *m* scab
Schorle ['ʃɔrlə] (**-, -n**) *f* spritzer, *wine and soda water or lemonade*
Schornstein ['ʃɔrnʃtaɪn] *m* chimney; (*Naut*) funnel; **Schornsteinfeger** (**-s, -**) *m* chimney sweep
Schose ['ʃoːzə] (**-, -n**) *f* = **Chose**
Schoß (**-es, -̈e**) *m* lap; (*Rockschoß*) coat tail; **im ~e der Familie** in the bosom of one's family
schoss *etc* [ʃɔs] *vb siehe* **schießen**
Schoßhund *m* lapdog
Schössling ['ʃœslɪŋ] *m* (*Bot*) shoot
Schote ['ʃoːtə] (**-, -n**) *f* pod
Schotte ['ʃɔtə] (**-n, -n**) *m* Scot, Scotsman
Schottenrock ['ʃɔtənrɔk] *m* kilt; (*für Frauen*) tartan skirt
Schotter ['ʃɔtər] (**-s**) *m* gravel; (*im Straßenbau*) road metal; (*Eisenb*) ballast
Schottin ['ʃɔtɪn] *f* Scot, Scotswoman
schottisch ['ʃɔtɪʃ] *adj* Scottish, Scots; **das ~e Hochland** the Scottish Highlands *pl*
Schottland (**-s**) *nt* Scotland
schraffieren [ʃra'fiːrən] *vt* to hatch
schräg [ʃrɛːk] *adj* slanting; (*schief, geneigt*) sloping; (*nicht gerade od parallel*) oblique ▷ *adv*: **~ gedruckt** in italics; **etw ~ stellen** to put sth at an angle; **~ gegenüber** diagonally opposite
Schräge ['ʃrɛːɡə] (**-, -n**) *f* slant
Schräg- *zW*: **Schrägkante** *f* bevelled (*Brit*) *od* beveled (*US*) edge; **Schrägschrift** *f* italics *pl*; **Schrägstreifen** *m* bias binding; **Schrägstrich** *m* oblique stroke
Schramme ['ʃramə] (**-, -n**) *f* scratch
schrammen *vt* to scratch
Schrank [ʃraŋk] (**-(e)s, -̈e**) *m* cupboard (*Brit*), closet (*US*); (*Kleiderschrank*) wardrobe
Schranke (**-, -n**) *f* barrier; (*fig: Grenze*) limit; (*: Hindernis*) barrier; **jdn in seine ~n (ver)weisen** (*fig*) to put sb in his place
schrankenlos *adj* boundless; (*zügellos*) unrestrained
Schrankenwärter *m* (*Eisenb*) level-crossing (*Brit*) *od* grade-crossing (*US*) attendant
Schrankkoffer *m* wardrobe trunk
Schrankwand *f* wall unit
Schraube ['ʃraʊbə] (**-, -n**) *f* screw
schrauben *vt* to screw; **etw in die Höhe ~** (*fig: Preise, Rekorde*) to push sth up; (*: Ansprüche*) to raise sth
Schraubenschlüssel *m* spanner (*Brit*), wrench (*US*)
Schraubenzieher (**-s, -**) *m* screwdriver
Schraubstock ['ʃraʊpʃtɔk] *m* (*Tech*) vice (*Brit*), vise (*US*)
Schrebergarten ['ʃreːbərɡartən] *m* allotment (*Brit*)
Schreck [ʃrɛk] (**-(e)s, -e**) *m* fright; **o ~ lass nach!** (*hum: umg*) for goodness' sake!
Schrecken (**-s, -**) *m* terror; (*Schreck*) fright; **schrecken** *vt* to frighten, scare ▷ *vi*: **aus dem Schlaf schrecken** to be startled out of one's sleep
schreckensbleich *adj* as white as a sheet *od*

S

ghost

Schreckensherrschaft f (reign of) terror

Schreck- zW: **Schreckgespenst** nt nightmare; **schreckhaft** adj jumpy, easily frightened; **schrecklich** adj terrible, dreadful; **schrecklich gerne!** (umg) I'd absolutely love to; **Schreckschraube** (pej: umg) f (old) battle-axe; **Schreckschuss** m shot fired in the air; **Schrecksekunde** f moment of shock

Schrei [ʃraɪ] (-(e)s, -e) m scream; (Ruf) shout; **der letzte ~** (umg) the latest thing, all the rage

Schreibbedarf m writing materials pl, stationery

Schreibblock m writing pad

schreiben ['ʃraɪbən] unreg vt to write; (mit Schreibmaschine) to type out; (berichten: Zeitung etc) to say; (buchstabieren) to spell ▷ vi to write; to type; to say; to spell ▷ vr: **wie schreibt sich das?** how is that spelt?; **Schreiben** (-s, -) nt letter, communication

Schreiber, in (-s, -) m(f) writer; (Büroschreiber) clerk

Schreib- zW: **schreibfaul** adj lazy about writing letters; **Schreibfehler** m spelling mistake; **Schreibkraft** f typist; **Schreibmaschine** f typewriter; **Schreibpapier** nt notepaper; **Schreibschrift** f running handwriting; (Typ) script; **Schreibschutz** m (Comput) write-protect; **Schreibstube** f orderly room; **Schreibtisch** m desk; **Schreibtischtäter** m wire od string puller

Schreibung f spelling

Schreib- zW: **Schreibunterlage** f pad; **Schreibwaren** pl stationery sing; **Schreibwarengeschäft** nt stationer's (shop) (Brit), stationery store (US); **Schreibweise** f spelling; (Stil) style; **schreibwütig** adj crazy about writing; **Schreibzentrale** f typing pool; **Schreibzeug** nt writing materials pl

schreien ['ʃraɪən] unreg vt, vi to scream; (rufen) to shout; **es war zum S~** (umg) it was a scream od a hoot; **nach etw ~** (fig) to cry out for sth

schreiend adj (fig) glaring; (: Farbe) loud

Schreihals (umg) m (Baby) bawler; (Unruhestifter) noisy troublemaker

Schreikrampf m screaming fit

Schreiner ['ʃraɪnər] (-s, -) m joiner; (Zimmermann) carpenter; (Möbelschreiner) cabinetmaker

Schreinerei [ʃraɪnəˈraɪ] f joiner's workshop

schreiten ['ʃraɪtən] unreg vi to stride

schrie etc [ʃriː] vb siehe **schreien**

Schrieb (-(e)s, -e) (umg) m missive (hum)

schrieb etc [ʃriːp] vb siehe **schreiben**

Schrift [ʃrɪft] (-, -en) f writing; (Handschrift) handwriting; (Schriftart) script; (Typ) typeface; (Buch) work; **Schriftart** f (Handschrift) script; (Typ) typeface; **Schriftbild** nt script; (Comput) typeface; **Schriftdeutsch** nt written German; **Schrifterkennung** f optical character recognition, OCR; **Schriftführer** m secretary; **schriftlich** adj written ▷ adv in writing; **das kann ich Ihnen schriftlich geben** (fig: umg)

I can tell you that for free; **Schriftprobe** f (Handschrift) specimen of one's handwriting; **Schriftsatz** m (Typ) fount (Brit), font (US); **Schriftsetzer** m compositor; **Schriftsprache** f written language

Schriftsteller, in (-s, -) m(f) writer; **schriftstellerisch** adj literary

Schrift- zW: **Schriftstück** nt document; **Schriftverkehr** m correspondence; **Schriftwechsel** m correspondence

schrill [ʃrɪl] adj shrill; **schrillen** vi (Stimme) to sound shrilly; (Telefon) to ring shrilly

Schritt (-(e)s, -e) m step; (Gangart) walk; (Tempo) pace; (von Hose) crotch, crutch (Brit); **auf ~ und Tritt** (lit, fig) wherever od everywhere one goes; „**~ fahren**" "dead slow"; **mit zehn ~en Abstand** at a distance of ten paces; **den ersten ~ tun** (fig) to make the first move; (: etw beginnen) to take the first step

schritt etc [ʃrɪt] vb siehe **schreiten**

Schritt- zW: **Schrittmacher** m pacemaker; **Schritttempo** nt: **im Schritttempo** at a walking pace; **schrittweise** adv gradually, little by little

schroff [ʃrɔf] adj steep; (zackig) jagged; (fig) brusque; (ungeduldig) abrupt

schröpfen ['ʃrœpfən] vt (fig) to fleece

Schrot [ʃroːt] (-(e)s, -e) m od nt (Blei) (small) shot; (Getreide) coarsely ground grain, groats pl; **Schrotflinte** f shotgun

Schrott [ʃrɔt] (-(e)s, -e) m scrap metal; **ein Auto zu ~ fahren** to write off a car; **Schrotthändler** m scrap merchant; **Schrotthaufen** m scrap heap; **schrottreif** adj ready for the scrap heap; **Schrottwert** m scrap value

schrubben ['ʃrubən] vt to scrub

Schrubber (-s, -) m scrubbing brush

Schrulle ['ʃrulə] (-, -n) f eccentricity, quirk

schrullig adj cranky

schrumpfen ['ʃrumpfən] vi (Hilfsverb sein) to shrink; (Apfel) to shrivel; (Leber, Niere) to atrophy

Schub [ʃuːp] (-(e)s, ̈-e) m (Stoß) push, shove; (Gruppe, Anzahl) batch; **Schubfach** nt drawer; **Schubkarren** m wheelbarrow; **Schublade** f drawer

Schubs [ʃuːps] (-es, -e) (umg) m shove, push; **schubsen** (umg) vt, vi to shove, push

schüchtern ['ʃʏçtərn] adj shy; **Schüchternheit** f shyness

schuf etc [ʃuːf] vb siehe **schaffen**

Schuft [ʃʊft] (-(e)s, -e) m scoundrel

schuften (umg) vi to graft, slave away

Schuh [ʃuː] (-(e)s, -e) m shoe; **jdm etw in die ~e schieben** (fig: umg) to put the blame for sth on sb; **wo drückt der ~?** (fig) what's troubling you?; **Schuhband** nt shoelace; **Schuhcreme** f shoe polish; **Schuhgröße** f shoe size; **Schuhlöffel** m shoehorn; **Schuhmacher** m shoemaker; **Schuhwerk** nt footwear

Schukosteckdose® ['ʃukoʃtɛkdoːzə] f safety socket

Schukostecker® *m* safety plug

Schul- *zW:* **Schulaufgaben** *pl* homework *sing;* **Schulbank** *f:* **die Schulbank drücken** (*umg*) to go to school; **Schulbehörde** *f* education authority; **Schulbesuch** *m* school attendance; **Schulbuch** *nt* schoolbook; **Schulbuchverlag** *m* educational publisher

Schuld [ʃʊlt] (**-, -en**) *f* guilt; (*Fin*) debt; (*Verschulden*) fault; ~ **haben (an** +*dat*) to be to blame (for); **jdm (die)** ~ **geben, jdm die** ~ **zuschieben** to blame sb; **ich bin mir keiner** ~ **bewusst** I'm not aware of having done anything wrong; ~ **und Sühne** crime and punishment; **ich stehe tief in seiner** ~ (*fig*) I'm deeply indebted to him; ~**en machen** to run up debts; *siehe auch* **zuschulden**; **schuld** *adj:* **schuld sein (an** +*dat*) to be to blame (for); **er ist schuld** it's his fault

schuldbewusst *adj* (*Mensch*) feeling guilty; (*Miene*) guilty

schulden [ˈʃʊldən] *vt* to owe

schuldenfrei *adj* free from debt

Schuldgefühl *nt* feeling of guilt

schuldhaft *adj* (*Jur*) culpable

Schuldienst (**-(e)s**) *m* (school)teaching

schuldig *adj* (*gebührend*) due; **an etw** *dat* ~ **sein** to be guilty of sth; **jdm etw** ~ **sein** *od* **bleiben** to owe sb sth; **jdn** ~ **sprechen** to find sb guilty; ~ **geschieden sein** to be the guilty party in a divorce; **Schuldigkeit** *f* duty

schuldlos *adj* innocent, blameless

Schuldner, in (**-s, -**) *m(f)* debtor

Schuld- *zW:* **Schuldprinzip** *nt* (*Jur*) principle of the guilty party; **Schuldschein** *m* promissory note, IOU; **Schuldspruch** *m* verdict of guilty

Schule [ˈʃuːlə] (**-, -n**) *f* school; **auf** *od* **in der** ~ at school; **in die** ~ **kommen/gehen** to start school/go to school; ~ **machen** (*fig*) to become the accepted thing

schulen *vt* to train, school

Schüler, in [ˈʃyːlər(ɪn)] (**-s, -**) *m(f)* pupil; **Schülerausweis** *m* (school) student card; **Schülerlotse** *m* pupil acting as a road-crossing warden; **Schülermitverwaltung** *f* school *od* student council

Schul- *zW:* **Schulferien** *pl* school holidays *pl* (*Brit*) *od* vacation *sing* (*US*); **Schulfernsehen** *nt* schools' *od* educational television; **schulfrei** *adj:* **die Kinder haben morgen schulfrei** the children don't have to go to school tomorrow; **Schulfunk** *m* schools' broadcasts *pl;* **Schulgeld** *nt* school fees *pl,* tuition (*US*); **Schulheft** *nt* exercise book; **Schulhof** *m* playground, schoolyard

schulisch [ˈʃuːlɪʃ] *adj* (*Leistungen, Probleme*) at school; (*Angelegenheiten*) school *attrib*

Schul- *zW:* **Schuljahr** *nt* school year; **Schuljunge** *m* schoolboy; **Schulkind** *nt* schoolchild; **Schulleiter** *m* headmaster (*bes* Brit), principal; **Schulleiterin** *f* headmistress (*bes* Brit), principal; **Schulmädchen** *nt* schoolgirl; **Schulmedizin** *f* orthodox medicine; **Schulpflicht** *f* compulsory school

attendance; **schulpflichtig** *adj* of school age; **Schulreife** *f:* **die Schulreife haben** to be ready to go to school; **Schulschiff** *nt* (*Naut*) training ship; **Schulsprecher, in** *m(f)* head boy/girl (*Brit*); **Schulstunde** *f* period, lesson; **Schultasche** *f* school bag

Schulter [ˈʃʊltər] (**-, -n**) *f* shoulder; **auf die leichte** ~ **nehmen** to take lightly; **Schulterblatt** *nt* shoulder blade

schultern *vt* to shoulder

Schultüte *f* bag of sweets given to children on the first day at school

Schulung *f* education, schooling

Schul- *zW:* **Schulverweigerer, in** *m(f)* school refuser; **Schulweg** *m* way to school; **Schulwesen** *nt* educational system; **Schulzeugnis** *nt* school report

schummeln [ˈʃʊməln] (*umg*) *vi:* **(bei etw)** ~ to cheat (at sth)

schummerig [ˈʃʊmərɪç], **schummrig** [ˈʃʊmrɪç] *adj* (*Beleuchtung*) dim; (*Raum*) dimly-lit

Schund (**-(e)s**) *m* trash, garbage

schund *etc* [ʃʊnt] *vb siehe* **schinden**

Schundroman *m* trashy novel

Schupo [ˈʃuːpo] (**-s, -s**) *m abk* (*veraltet:* = *Schutzpolizist*) cop

Schuppe [ˈʃʊpə] (**-, -n**) *f* scale; **Schuppen** *pl* (*Haarschuppen*) dandruff

Schuppen (**-s, -**) *m* shed; (*umg: übles Lokal*) dive; *siehe auch* **Schuppe**

schuppen *vt* to scale ▷ *vr* to peel

schuppig [ˈʃʊpɪç] *adj* scaly

Schur [ʃuːr] (**-, -en**) *f* shearing

Schüreisen *nt* poker

schüren [ˈʃyːrən] *vt* to rake; (*fig*) to stir up

schürfen [ˈʃʏrfən] *vt, vi* to scrape, scratch; (*Min*) to prospect; to dig

Schürfung *f* abrasion; (*Min*) prospecting

Schürhaken *m* poker

Schurke [ˈʃʊrkə] (**-n, -n**) *m* rogue

Schurwolle *f:* **„reine ~"** "pure new wool"

Schurz [ʃʊrts] (**-es, -e**) *m* apron

Schürze [ˈʃʏrtsə] (**-, -n**) *f* apron

Schürzenjäger (*umg*) *m* philanderer, one for the girls

Schuss [ʃʊs] (**-es, -"e**) *m* shot; (*Fussball*) kick; (*Spritzer: von Wein, Essig etc*) dash; (*Weben*) weft; **(gut) in** ~ **sein** (*umg*) to be in good shape *od* nick; (*Mensch*) to be in form; **etw in** ~ **halten** to keep sth in good shape; **weitab vom** ~ **sein** (*fig: umg*) to be miles from where the action is; **der goldene** ~ ≈ a lethal dose of a drug; **ein** ~ **in den Ofen** (*umg*) a complete waste of time, a failure; **Schussbereich** *m* effective range

Schüssel [ˈʃʏsəl] (**-, -n**) *f* bowl, basin; (*Servierschüssel, umg: Satellitenschüssel*) dish; (*Waschschüssel*) basin

schusselig [ˈʃʊsəlɪç] (*umg*) *adj* (*zerstreut*) scatterbrained, muddle-headed (*umg*)

Schuss- *zW:* **Schusslinie** *f* line of fire; **Schussverletzung** *f* bullet wound; **Schusswaffe** *f* firearm; **Schusswaffengebrauch** *m* (*form*) use of firearms; **Schusswechsel** m exchange of shots; **Schussweite** f range (of fire)

Schuster [ˈʃuːstər] (-s, -) m cobbler, shoemaker

Schutt [ʃʊt] (-(e)s) m rubbish; (Bauschutt) rubble; „~ abladen verboten" "no tipping"; **Schuttabladeplatz** m refuse dump

Schüttelfrost m shivering

schütteln [ˈʃʏtəln] vt to shake ▷ vr to shake o.s.; **sich vor Kälte ~** to shiver with cold; **sich vor Ekel ~** to shudder with od in disgust

schütten [ˈʃʏtən] vt to pour; (Zucker, Kies etc) to tip; (verschütten) to spill ▷ vi unpers to pour (down)

schütter adj (Haare) sparse, thin

Schutthalde f dump

Schutthaufen m heap of rubble

Schutz [ʃʊts] (-es) m protection; (Unterschlupf) shelter; **jdn in ~ nehmen** to stand up for sb; **Schutzanzug** m overalls pl; **schutzbedürftig** adj in need of protection; **Schutzbefohlene**, **r** f(m) charge; **Schutzblech** nt mudguard; **Schutzbrief** m (international) travel cover; **Schutzbrille** f goggles pl

Schütze [ˈʃʏtsə] (-n, -n) m gunman; (Gewehrschütze) rifleman; (Scharfschütze, Sportschütze) marksman; (Astrol) Sagittarius

schützen [ˈʃʏtsən] vt to protect ▷ vr to protect o.s.; **(sich) ~ vor** +dat od **gegen** to protect (o.s.) from od against; **gesetzlich geschützt** registered; **urheberrechtlich geschützt** protected by copyright; **vor Nässe ~!** keep dry

Schützenfest nt fair featuring shooting matches

Schutzengel m guardian angel

Schützen- zW: **Schützengraben** m trench; **Schützenhilfe** f (fig) support; **Schützenverein** m shooting club

Schutz- zW: **Schutzgebiet** nt protectorate; (Naturschutzgebiet) reserve; **Schutzgebühr** f (token) fee; **Schutzhaft** f protective custody; **Schutzheilige**, **r** f(m) patron saint; **Schutzhelm** m safety helmet; **Schutzimpfung** f immunization

Schützling [ˈʃʏtslɪŋ] m protégé; (bes Kind) charge

Schutz- zW: **schutzlos** adj defenceless (Brit), defenseless (US); **Schutzmann** (-(e)s, pl **-leute** od **-männer**) m policeman; **Schutzmarke** f trademark; **Schutzmaßnahme** f precaution; **Schutzpatron** m patron saint; **Schutzschirm** m (Tech) protective screen; **Schutzumschlag** m (book) jacket; **Schutzverband** m (Med) protective bandage od dressing; **Schutzvorrichtung** f safety device

Schw. abk = **Schwester**

schwabbelig [ˈʃvab(ə)lɪç] (umg) adj (Körperteil) flabby; (: Gelee) wobbly

Schwabe [ˈʃvaːbə] (-n, -n) m Swabian

Schwaben (-s) nt Swabia

Schwäbin [ˈʃveːbɪn] f Swabian

schwäbisch [ˈʃveːbɪʃ] adj Swabian

schwach [ʃvax] adj weak, feeble; (Gedächtnis, Gesundheit) poor; (Hoffnung) faint; **~ werden** to weaken; **das ist ein ~es Bild** (umg) od **eine**

~e Leistung (umg) that's a poor show; **ein ~er Trost** cold od small comfort; **mach mich nicht ~!** (umg) don't say that!; **auf ~en Beinen** od **Füßen stehen** (fig) to be on shaky ground; (: Theorie) to be shaky

Schwäche [ˈʃveçə] (-, -n) f weakness

schwächen vt to weaken

schwach- zW: **Schwachheit** f weakness; **Schwachkopf** (umg) m dimwit, idiot; **schwachköpfig** adj silly, daft (Brit)

schwächlich adj weakly, delicate

Schwächling m weakling

Schwach- zW: **Schwachsinn** m (Med) mental deficiency, feeble-mindedness (veraltet); (umg: Quatsch) rubbish; (fig: umg: unsinnige Tat) idiocy; **schwachsinnig** adj mentally deficient; (Idee) idiotic; **Schwachstelle** f weak point; **Schwachstrom** m weak current

Schwächung [ˈʃveçʊŋ] f weakening

Schwaden [ˈʃvaːdən] (-s, -) m cloud

schwafeln [ˈʃvaːfəln] (umg) vi to blather, drivel; (in einer Prüfung) to waffle

Schwager [ˈʃvaːgər] (-s, ⁻) m brother-in-law

Schwägerin [ˈʃveːgərɪn] f sister-in-law

Schwalbe [ˈʃvalbə] (-, -n) f swallow

Schwall [ʃval] (-(e)s, -e) m surge; (Worte) flood, torrent

Schwamm (-(e)s, ⁻e) m sponge; (Pilz) fungus; **~ drüber!** (umg) (let's) forget it!

schwamm etc [ʃvam] vb siehe **schwimmen**

schwammig adj spongy; (Gesicht) puffy; (vage: Begriff) woolly (Brit), wooly (US)

Schwan [ʃvaːn] (-(e)s, ⁻e) m swan

schwand etc [ʃvant] vb siehe **schwinden**

schwanen vi unpers: **jdm schwant es** sb has a foreboding od forebodings; **jdm schwant etwas** sb senses something might happen

schwang etc [ʃvaŋ] vb siehe **schwingen**

schwanger [ˈʃvaŋər] adj pregnant

schwängern [ˈʃvɛŋərn] vt to make pregnant

Schwangerschaft f pregnancy

Schwangerschaftsabbruch m termination of pregnancy, abortion

Schwank [ʃvaŋk] (-(e)s, ⁻e) m funny story; (Liter) merry od comical tale; (Theat) farce

schwanken vi to sway; (taumeln) to stagger, reel; (Preise, Zahlen) to fluctuate; (zögern) to hesitate; (Überzeugung etc) to begin to waver; **ins S~ kommen** (Baum, Gebäude etc) to start to sway; (Preise, Kurs etc) to start to fluctuate od vary

Schwankung f fluctuation

Schwanz [ʃvants] (-es, ⁻e) m tail; (umg!: Penis) prick (!); **kein ~** (umg) not a (blessed) soul

schwänzen [ˈʃvɛntsən] (umg) vt (Stunde, Vorlesung) to skip ▷ vi to play truant

Schwänzer [ˈʃvɛntsər] (-s, -) (umg) m truant

schwappen [ˈʃvapən] vi (überschwappen) to splash, slosh

Schwarm [ʃvarm] (-(e)s, ⁻e) m swarm; (umg) heart-throb, idol

schwärmen [ˈʃvɛrmən] vi to swarm; **~ für** to be mad od wild about

Schwärmerei [ʃvɛrməˈraɪ] f enthusiasm
schwärmerisch adj impassioned, effusive
Schwarte [ˈʃvartə] (-, -n) f hard skin;
(Speckschwarte) rind; (umg: Buch) tome (hum)
Schwartenmagen (-s) m (Koch) brawn
schwarz [ʃvarts] adj black; (umg: ungesetzlich)
illicit; (: katholisch) Catholic, Papist (pej); (Pol)
Christian Democrat; **ins S~e treffen** (lit,
fig) to hit the bull's-eye; **das S~e Brett** the
notice (Brit) od bulletin (US) board; **~e Liste**
blacklist; **~es Loch** black hole; **das S~e Meer**
the Black Sea; **S~er Peter** (Karten) children's
card game; **jdm den ~en Peter zuschieben**
(fig: die Verantwortung abschieben) to pass the
buck to sb (umg); **dort wählen alle ~** they all
vote conservative there; **in den ~en Zahlen**
in the black; siehe auch **schwarzärgern;**
schwarzmalen; schwarzsehen;
Schwarzarbeit f illicit work, moonlighting;
Schwarzarbeiter m moonlighter;
schwarzärgern vr to get extremely annoyed;
Schwarzbrot nt (Pumpernickel) black bread,
pumpernickel; (braun) brown rye bread
Schwärze [ˈʃvɛrtsə] (-, -n) f blackness; (Farbe)
blacking; (Druckerschwärze) printer's ink
Schwarze, r f(m) (Neger) black; (umg: Katholik)
Papist; (Pol: umg) Christian Democrat
schwärzen vt to blacken
Schwarz- zW: **schwarzfahren** unreg vi to
travel without paying; (ohne Führerschein) to
drive without a licence (Brit) od license (US);
Schwarzfahrer m (Bus etc) fare dodger (umg);
Schwarzhandel m black market (trade);
Schwarzhändler m black-market operator;
schwarzhören vi to listen to the radio without
a licence (Brit) od license (US)
schwärzlich [ˈʃvɛrtslɪç] adj blackish, darkish
Schwarz- zW: **schwarzmalen** vi to be
pessimistic; **Schwarzmarkt** m black market;
schwarzsehen vi unreg (TV) to watch TV
without a licence (Brit) od license (US); (umg) to
see the gloomy side of things; **Schwarzseher**
m pessimist; (TV) viewer without a licence
(Brit) od license (US); **Schwarzwald** m Black
Forest; **Schwarzwälder Kirschtorte** f Black
Forest gâteau; **schwarz-weiß, schwarzweiß**
adj black and white; **Schwarzweiß-** in zw black
and white; **Schwarzwurzel** f (Koch) salsify
Schwatz [ʃvats] (-es, -e) m chat
schwatzen [ˈʃvatsən] vi to chat; (schnell,
unaufhörlich) to chatter; (über belanglose Dinge) to
prattle; (Unsinn reden) to blether (umg)
schwätzen [ˈʃvɛtsən] vi = **schwatzen**
Schwätzer, in [ˈʃvɛtsər(ɪn)] (-s, -) m(f)
chatterbox; (Schwafler) gasbag (umg);
(Klatschbase) gossip
schwatzhaft adj talkative, gossipy
Schwebe [ˈʃveːbə] f: **in der ~** (fig) in abeyance;
(Jur, Comm) pending
Schwebebahn f overhead railway (Brit) od
railroad (US)
Schwebebalken m (Sport) beam
schweben vi to drift, float; (hoch) to soar;

(unentschieden sein) to be in the balance; **es
schwebte mir vor Augen** (Bild) I saw it in my
mind's eye
schwebend adj (Tech, Chem) suspended; (fig)
undecided, unresolved; **~es Verfahren** (Jur)
pending case
schwed. abk = **schwedisch**
Schwede [ˈʃveːdə] (-n, -n) m Swede
Schweden (-s) nt Sweden
Schwedin [ˈʃveːdɪn] f Swede
schwedisch adj Swedish
Schwefel [ˈʃveːfəl] (-s) m sulphur (Brit), sulfur
(US); **Schwefeldioxid** nt sulphur dioxide
schwefelig adj sulphurous (Brit), sulfurous (US)
Schwefelsäure f sulphuric (Brit) od sulfuric
(US) acid
Schweif [ʃvaɪf] (-(e)s, -e) m tail
schweifen vi to wander, roam
Schweigegeld nt hush money
Schweigeminute f one minute('s) silence
schweigen [ˈʃvaɪɡən] unreg vi to be silent; (still
sein) to keep quiet; **kannst du ~?** can you keep
a secret?; **ganz zu ~ von ...** to say nothing
of ...; **Schweigen (-s)** nt silence
schweigend adj silent
Schweigepflicht f pledge of secrecy; (von
Anwalt etc) requirement of confidentiality
schweigsam [ˈʃvaɪkzaːm] adj silent; (als
Charaktereigenschaft) taciturn; **Schweigsamkeit**
f silence; taciturnity
Schwein [ʃvaɪn] (-(e)s, -e) nt pig; (fig: umg)
(good) luck; **kein ~** (umg) nobody, not a single
person
Schweine- zW: **Schweinebraten** m joint of
pork; (gekocht) roast pork; **Schweinefleisch**
nt pork; **Schweinegeld** (umg) nt: **ein
Schweinegeld** a packet; **Schweinegrippe** f
swine flu; **Schweinehund** (umg) m stinker,
swine
Schweinerei [ʃvaɪnəˈraɪ] f mess; (Gemeinheit)
dirty trick; **so eine ~!** (umg) how disgusting!
Schweineschmalz nt dripping; (als Kochfett)
lard
Schweinestall m pigsty
schweinisch adj filthy
Schweinsleder nt pigskin
Schweinsohr nt pig's ear; (Gebäck) (kidney-
shaped) pastry
Schweiß [ʃvaɪs] (-es) m sweat, perspiration;
Schweißband nt sweatband
Schweißbrenner(-s, -) m (Tech) welding torch
schweißen vt, vi to weld
Schweißer(-s, -) m welder
Schweiß- zW: **Schweißfüße** pl sweaty feet pl;
Schweißnaht f weld; **schweißnass** adj sweaty
Schweiz [ʃvaɪts] f: **die ~** Switzerland
schweiz. abk = **schweizerisch**
Schweizer [ˈʃvaɪtsər] (-s, -) m Swiss ▷ adj attrib
Swiss; **Schweizerdeutsch** nt Swiss German;
Schweizerin f Swiss; **schweizerisch** adj Swiss
schwelen [ˈʃveːlən] vi to smoulder (Brit),
smolder (US)
schwelgen [ˈʃvɛlɡən] vi to indulge o.s.; **~ in**

299

+*dat* to indulge in

Schwelle [ˈʃvɛlə] (**-, -n**) *f* (*auch fig*) threshold; (*Eisenb*) sleeper (*Brit*), tie (*US*)

schwellen *unreg vi* to swell

Schwellenland *nt* threshold country

Schwellung *f* swelling

Schwemme [ˈʃvɛmə] *f*: **eine ~ an** +*dat* a glut of

schwemmen [ˈʃvɛmən] *vt* (*treiben: Sand etc*) to wash

Schwengel [ˈʃvɛŋəl] (**-s, -**) *m* pump handle; (*Glockenschwengel*) clapper

Schwenk [ʃvɛŋk] (**-(e)s, -s**) *m* (*Film*) pan, panning shot

Schwenkarm *m* swivel arm

schwenkbar *adj* swivel-mounted

schwenken *vt* to swing; (*Kamera*) to pan; (*Fahne*) to wave; (*Kartoffeln*) to toss; (*abspülen*) to rinse ▷ *vi* to turn, swivel; (*Mil*) to wheel

Schwenkung *f* turn; (*Mil*) wheel

schwer [ʃveːr] *adj* heavy; (*schwierig*) difficult, hard; (*schlimm*) serious, bad ▷ *adv* (*sehr*) very (much); (*verletzt etc*) seriously, badly; **~ erziehbar** maladjusted; **jdm/sich etw ~ machen** to make sth difficult for sb/o.s.; **~ verdaulich** indigestible; (*fig*) heavy; **~ verdient** (*Geld*) hard-earned; **~ verletzt** seriously *od* badly injured; **~ verwundet** seriously wounded; **~ erkältet sein** to have a heavy cold; **er lernt ~** he's a slow learner; **er ist ~ in Ordnung** (*umg*) he's a good bloke (*Brit*) *od* guy; **~ hören** to be hard of hearing; *siehe auch* **schwerfallen; schwernehmen; schwertun; schwerwiegend; Schwerarbeiter** *m* labourer (*Brit*), laborer (*US*); **Schwerbehinderte, r** *f(m)*, **Schwerbeschädigte, r** *f(m)* (*veraltet*) severely handicapped person

Schwere (**-, -n**) *f* weight; heaviness; (*Phys*) gravity; **schwerelos** *adj* weightless; **Schwerelosigkeit** *f* weightlessness

schwer- *zW*: **schwerfallen** *unreg vi*: **jdm schwerfallen** to be difficult for sb; **schwerfällig** *adj* (*auch Stil*) ponderous; (*Gang*) clumsy, awkward; (*Verstand*) slow; **Schwergewicht** *nt* heavyweight; (*fig*) emphasis; **schwergewichtig** *adj* heavyweight; **schwerhörig** *adj* hard of hearing; **Schwerindustrie** *f* heavy industry; **Schwerkraft** *f* gravity; **Schwerkranke, r** *f(m)* person who is seriously ill; **schwerlich** *adv* hardly; **Schwermetall** *nt* heavy metal; **schwermütig** *adj* melancholy; **schwernehmen** *unreg vt* to take to heart; **Schwerpunkt** *m* centre (*Brit*) *od* center (*US*) of gravity; (*fig*) emphasis, crucial point; **Schwerpunktstreik** *m* pinpoint strike; **schwerreich** (*umg*) *adj attrib* stinking rich

Schwert [ʃveːrt] (**-(e)s, -er**) *nt* sword; **Schwertlilie** *f* iris

schwer- *zW*: **schwertun** *unreg vr*: **sich** *dat od akk* **schwertun** to have difficulties; **Schwerverbrecher** *m* criminal; **Schwerverletzte, r** *f(m)* serious casualty;

schwerwiegend *adj* weighty, important

Schwester [ˈʃvɛstər] (**-, -n**) *f* sister; (*Med*) nurse; **schwesterlich** *adj* sisterly

schwieg *etc* [ʃviːk] *vb siehe* **schweigen**

Schwieger- *zW*: **Schwiegereltern** *pl* parents-in-law *pl*; **Schwiegermutter** *f* mother-in-law; **Schwiegersohn** *m* son-in-law; **Schwiegertochter** *f* daughter-in-law; **Schwiegervater** *m* father-in-law

Schwiele [ˈʃviːlə] (**-, -n**) *f* callus

schwierig [ˈʃviːrɪç] *adj* difficult, hard; **Schwierigkeit** *f* difficulty; **Schwierigkeitsgrad** *m* degree of difficulty

schwillt [ʃvɪlt] *vb siehe* **schwellen**

Schwimmbad *nt* swimming baths *pl*

Schwimmbecken *nt* swimming pool

schwimmen *unreg vi* to swim; (*treiben, nicht sinken*) to float; (*fig: unsicher sein*) to be all at sea; **im Geld ~** (*umg*) to be rolling in money; **mir schwimmt es vor den Augen** I feel dizzy

Schwimmer (**-s, -**) *m* swimmer; (*Angeln*) float

Schwimmerin *f* swimmer

Schwimm- *zW*: **Schwimmflosse** *f* (*von Taucher*) flipper; **Schwimmhaut** *f* (*Ornithologie*) web; **Schwimmlehrer** *m* swimming instructor; **Schwimmsport** *m* swimming; **Schwimmweste** *f* life jacket

Schwindel [ˈʃvɪndəl] (**-s**) *m* dizziness; (*Betrug*) swindle, fraud; (*Zeug*) stuff; **in ~ erregender Höhe** at a dizzy height; **schwindelfrei** *adj* free from giddiness

schwindeln *vi* (*umg: lügen*) to fib; **mir schwindelt** I feel dizzy; **jdm schwindelt es** sb feels dizzy

schwinden [ˈʃvɪndən] *unreg vi* to disappear; (*Kräfte*) to fade, fail; (*sich verringern*) to decrease

Schwindler (**-s, -**) *m* swindler; (*Hochstapler*) con man, fraud; (*Lügner*) liar

schwindlig *adj* dizzy; **mir ist ~** I feel dizzy

Schwindsucht *f* (*veraltet*) consumption

schwingen [ˈʃvɪŋən] *unreg vt* to swing; (*Waffe etc*) to brandish ▷ *vi* to swing; (*vibrieren*) to vibrate; (*klingen*) to sound

Schwinger (**-s, -**) *m* (*Boxen*) swing

Schwingtor *nt* up-and-over door

Schwingtür *f* swing door(s *pl*) (*Brit*), swinging door(s *pl*) (*US*)

Schwingung *f* vibration; (*Phys*) oscillation

Schwips [ʃvɪps] (**-es, -e**) *m*: **einen ~ haben** to be tipsy

schwirren [ˈʃvɪrən] *vi* to buzz

Schwitze [ˈʃvɪtsə] (**-, -n**) *f* (*Koch*) roux

schwitzen *vi* to sweat, perspire

schwofen [ˈʃvoːfən] (*umg*) *vi* to dance

schwoll *etc* [ʃvɔl] *vb siehe* **schwellen**

schwören [ˈʃvøːrən] *unreg vt, vi* to swear; **auf jdn/etw ~** (*fig*) to swear by sb/sth

schwul [ʃvuːl] (*umg*) *adj* gay, queer (*pej*)

schwül [ʃvyːl] *adj* sultry, close

Schwule, r (*umg*) *m* gay, queer (*pej*), fag (*US pej*)

Schwüle (**-**) *f* sultriness, closeness

Schwulität [ʃvuliˈtɛːt] (*umg*) *f* trouble, difficulty

Schwulst [ʃvʊlst] (**-(e)s**) m bombast

schwülstig ['ʃvʏlstɪç] adj pompous

Schwund [ʃvʊnt] (**-(e)s**) m (+gen) decrease (in), decline (in), dwindling (of); (Med) atrophy; (Schrumpfen) shrinkage

Schwung [ʃvʊŋ] (**-(e)s**, **-̈e**) m swing; (Triebkraft) momentum; (fig: Energie) verve, energy; (umg: Menge) batch; **in ~ sein** (fig) to be in full swing; **~ in die Sache bringen** (umg) to liven things up; **schwunghaft** adj brisk, lively; **Schwungrad** nt flywheel; **schwungvoll** adj vigorous

Schwur (**-(e)s**, **-̈e**) m oath

schwur etc [ʃvuːr] vb siehe **schwören**

Schwurgericht nt court with a jury

SDR (**-**) m abk (= Süddeutscher Rundfunk) South German Radio

sechs [zɛks] num six; **Sechseck** nt hexagon; **sechshundert** num six hundred

sechste, r, s adj sixth

Sechstel ['zɛkstəl] (**-s**, **-**) nt sixth

sechzehn ['zɛçtseːn] num sixteen

sechzig ['zɛçtsɪç] num sixty

See¹ [zeː] (**-**, **-n**) f sea; **an der ~** by the sea, at the seaside; **in ~ stechen** to put to sea; **auf hoher ~** on the high seas

See² [zeː] (**-s**, **-n**) m lake

See- zW: **Seebad** nt seaside resort; **Seebär** m (hum: umg) seadog; (Zool) fur seal; **Seefahrt** f seafaring; (Reise) voyage; **seefest** adj (Mensch) not subject to seasickness; **Seegang** m (motion of the) sea; **Seegras** nt seaweed; **Seehund** m seal; **Seeigel** m sea urchin; **Seekarte** f chart; **seekrank** adj seasick; **Seekrankheit** f seasickness; **Seelachs** m rock salmon

Seele ['zeːlə] (**-**, **-n**) f soul; (Mittelpunkt) life and soul; **jdm aus der ~ sprechen** to express exactly what sb feels; **das liegt mir auf der ~** it weighs heavily on my mind; **eine ~ von Mensch** an absolute dear

Seelen- zW: **Seelenamt** nt (Rel) requiem; **Seelenfriede, Seelenfrieden** m peace of mind; **Seelenheil** nt salvation of one's soul; (fig) spiritual welfare; **Seelenruhe** f: **in aller Seelenruhe** calmly; (kaltblütig) as cool as you please; **seelenruhig** adv calmly

Seeleute ['zeːlɔʏtə] pl seamen pl

Seel- zW: **seelisch** adj mental; (Rel) spiritual; (Belastung) emotional; **Seelsorge** f pastoral duties pl; **Seelsorger** (**-s**, **-**) m clergyman

See- zW: **Seemacht** f naval power; **Seemann** (**-(e)s**, pl **-leute**) m seaman, sailor; **Seemeile** f nautical mile

Seengebiet ['zeːəngəbiːt] nt lakeland district

See- zW: **Seenot** f: **in Seenot** (Schiff etc) in distress; **Seepferd, Seepferdchen** nt sea horse; **Seeräuber** m pirate; **Seerecht** nt maritime law; **Seerose** f waterlily; **Seestern** m starfish; **Seetang** m seaweed; **seetüchtig** adj seaworthy; **Seeversicherung** f marine insurance; **Seeweg** m sea route; **auf dem Seeweg** by sea; **Seezunge** f sole

Segel ['zeːgəl] (**-s**, **-**) nt sail; **mit vollen ~n** under full sail od canvas; (fig) with gusto; **die ~ streichen** (fig) to give in; **Segelboot** nt yacht; **Segelfliegen** (**-s**) nt gliding; **Segelflieger** m glider pilot; **Segelflugzeug** nt glider

segeln vt, vi to sail; **durch eine Prüfung ~** (umg) to flop in an exam, fail (in) an exam

Segel- zW: **Segelschiff** nt sailing vessel; **Segelsport** m sailing; **Segeltuch** nt canvas

Segen ['zeːgən] (**-s**, **-**) m blessing

segensreich adj beneficial

Segler ['zeːglər] (**-s**, **-**) m sailor, yachtsman; (Boot) sailing boat

Seglerin f yachtswoman

segnen ['zeːgnən] vt to bless

sehen ['zeːən] unreg vt, vi to see; (in bestimmte Richtung) to look; (Fernsehsendung) to watch; **sieht man das?** does it show?; **da sieht man(s) mal wieder!** that's typical!; **du siehst das nicht richtig** you've got it wrong; **so ge~** looked at in this way; **sich ~ lassen** to put in an appearance, appear; **das neue Rathaus kann sich ~ lassen** the new town hall is certainly something to be proud of; **siehe oben/unten** see above/below; **da kann man mal ~** that just shows (you) od just goes to show (umg); **mal ~!** we'll see!; **darauf ~, dass ...** to make sure (that) ...; **jdn kommen ~** to see sb coming

sehenswert adj worth seeing

Sehenswürdigkeiten pl sights pl (of a town)

Seher (**-s**, **-**) m seer

Sehfehler m sight defect

Sehkraft f (eye)sight

Sehne ['zeːnə] (**-**, **-n**) f sinew; (an Bogen) string

sehnen vr: **sich ~ nach** to long od yearn for

Sehnenscheidenentzündung f (Med) tendinitis

Sehnerv m optic nerve

sehnig adj sinewy

sehnlich adj ardent

Sehnsucht f longing

sehnsüchtig adj longing; (Erwartung) eager

sehnsuchtsvoll adv longingly, yearningly

sehr [zeːr] adv (vor adj, adv) very; (mit Verben) a lot, (very) much; **zu ~** too much; **er ist ~ dafür/dagegen** he is all for it/very much against it; **wie ~ er sich auch bemühte ...** however much he tried ...

Sehvermögen ['zeːfɛrmøːgən] (**-s**) nt powers pl of vision

seicht [zaɪçt] adj (lit, fig) shallow

seid [zaɪt] vb siehe **sein**

Seide ['zaɪdə] (**-**, **-n**) f silk

Seidel (**-s**, **-**) nt tankard, beer mug

seiden adj silk; **Seidenpapier** nt tissue paper

seidig ['zaɪdɪç] adj silky

Seife ['zaɪfə] (**-**, **-n**) f soap

Seifen- zW: **Seifenblase** f soap bubble; (fig) bubble; **Seifenlauge** f soapsuds pl; **Seifenschale** f soap dish; **Seifenschaum** m lather

seifig ['zaɪfɪç] adj soapy

S

seihen ['zaɪən] *vt* to strain, filter
Seil [zaɪl] (**-(e)s, -e**) *nt* rope; (*Kabel*) cable;
Seilbahn *f* cable railway; **Seilhüpfen** (**-s**)
nt skipping; **Seilspringen** (**-s**) *nt* skipping;
Seiltänzer, in *m(f)* tightrope walker; **Seilzug**
m tackle

 SCHLÜSSELWORT

sein [zaɪn] (*pt* **war**, *pp* **gewesen**) *vi* **1** to be; **ich
bin** I am; **du bist** you are; **er/sie/es ist** he/
she/it is; **wir sind/ihr seid/sie sind** we/
you/they are; **wir waren** we were; **wir sind
gewesen** we have been
2: seien Sie nicht böse don't be angry; **sei so
gut und …** be so kind as to …; **das wäre gut**
that would *od* that'd be a good thing; **wenn
ich Sie wäre** if I were *od* was you; **das wärs**
that's all, that's it; **morgen bin ich in Rom**
tomorrow I'll *od* I will *od* I shall be in Rome;
waren Sie mal in Rom? have you ever been
to Rome?
3: wie ist das zu verstehen? how is that to
be understood?; **er ist nicht zu ersetzen**
he cannot be replaced; **mit ihr ist nicht zu
reden** you can't talk to her
4: mir ist kalt I'm cold; **mir ist, als hätte
ich ihn früher schon einmal gesehen** I've a
feeling I've seen him before; **was ist?** what's
the matter?, what is it?; **ist was?** is something
the matter?; **es sei denn(, dass …)** unless …;
wie dem auch sei be that as it may; **wie wäre
es mit …?** how *od* what about …?; **etw sein
lassen** (*aufhören*) to stop (doing) sth; (*nicht
tun*) to drop sth, leave sth; **lass das sein!** stop
that!; **es ist an dir, zu … …** it's up to you to …;
was sind Sie (beruflich)? what do you do?;
das kann schon sein that may well be
▷ *pron* his; (*bei Dingen*) its

Sein (**-s**) *nt*: **~ oder Nichtsein** to be or not to be
seine, r, s *poss pron* his; its; **er ist gut ~ zwei
Meter** (*umg*) he's a good two metres (*Brit*)
od meters (*US*); **die S~n** (*geh*) his family, his
people; **jedem das S~** to each his own
seiner *gen von* **er; es** ▷ *pron* of him; of it
seinerseits *adv* for his part
seinerzeit *adv* in those days, formerly
seinesgleichen *pron* people like him
seinetwegen *adv* (*für ihn*) for his sake; (*wegen
ihm*) on his account; (*von ihm aus*) as far as he is
concerned
seinetwillen *adv*: **um ~ = seinetwegen**
seinige *pron*: **der/die/das ~** his
Seismograf [zaɪsmo'graːf] (**-en, -en**) *m*
seismograph
seit [zaɪt] *präp +dat* since; (*Zeitdauer*) for, in (*bes
US*) ▷ *konj* since; **er ist ~ einer Woche hier** he
has been here for a week; **~ Langem** for a long
time; **seitdem** *adv, konj* since
Seite ['zaɪtə] (**-, -n**) *f* side; (*Buchseite*) page;
(*Mil*) flank; **~ an Seite** side by side; **jdm zur
~ stehen** (*fig*) to stand by sb's side; **jdn zur ~**

nehmen to take sb aside; **auf der einen ~ …,
auf der anderen (~) …** on the one hand …, on
the other (hand) …; **einer Sache** *dat* **die beste
~ abgewinnen** to make the best *od* most of sth;
siehe auch **aufseiten; vonseiten**
Seiten- *zW*: **Seitenairbag** *m* (*Aut*) side-impact
airbag; **Seitenansicht** *f* side view; **Seitenhieb**
m (*fig*) passing shot, dig; **seitenlang** *adj* several
pages long, going on for pages; **Seitenruder** *nt*
(*Aviat*) rudder
seitens *präp +gen* on the part of
Seiten- *zW*: **Seitenschiff** *nt* aisle; **Seitensprung**
m extramarital escapade; **Seitenstechen**
nt (a) stitch; **Seitenstraße** *f* side road;
Seitenstreifen *m* (*der Straße*) verge (*Brit*),
berm (*US*); (*der Autobahn*) hard shoulder
(*Brit*), shoulder (*US*); **seitenverkehrt** *adj* the
wrong way round; **Seitenwagen** *m* sidecar;
Seitenwind *m* crosswind; **Seitenzahl** *f* page
number; (*Gesamtzahl*) number of pages
seit- *zW*: **seither** [zaɪt'heːr] *adv, konj* since
(then); **seitlich** *adv* on one/the side ▷ *adj* side
attrib; **seitwärts** *adv* sideways
sek, Sek. *abk* (= **Sekunde**) sec.
Sekretär [zekre'tɛːr] *m* secretary; (*Möbel*)
bureau
Sekretariat [zekretari'aːt] (**-(e)s, -e**) *nt*
secretary's office, secretariat
Sekretärin *f* secretary
Sekt [zɛkt] (**-(e)s, -e**) *m* sparkling wine
Sekte (**-, -n**) *f* sect
Sektor ['zɛktor] *m* sector; (*Sachgebiet*) field
Sekunda [ze'kʊnda] (**-, Sekunden**) *f*
(*Sch: früher: Untersekunda/Obersekunda*) sixth/
seventh year of German secondary school
sekundär [zekʊn'dɛːr] *adj* secondary;
Sekundärliteratur *f* secondary literature
Sekunde [ze'kʊnda] (**-, -n**) *f* second
Sekunden- *zW*: **Sekundenkleber** *m* superglue;
Sekundenschnelle *f*: **in Sekundenschnelle**
in a matter of seconds; **Sekundenzeiger** *m*
second hand
sel. *abk* = **selig**
selber ['zɛlbər] *demon pron* = **selbst**;
Selbermachen *nt* do-it-yourself, DIY (*Brit*);
(*von Kleidern etc*) making one's own
Selbst [zɛlpst] (**-**) *nt* self

 SCHLÜSSELWORT

selbst [zɛlpst] *pron* **1: ich/er/wir selbst** I
myself/he himself/we ourselves; **sie ist die
Tugend selbst** she's virtue itself; **er braut
sein Bier selbst** he brews his own beer; **das
muss er selbst wissen** it's up to him; **wie
gehts? — gut, und selbst?** how are things? —
fine, and yourself?
2 (*ohne Hilfe*) alone, on my/his/one's *etc* own;
von selbst by itself; **er kam von selbst**
he came of his own accord; **selbst ist der
Mann/die Frau!** self-reliance is the name of
the game (*umg*); **selbst gemacht** home-made;
selbst gestrickt hand-knitted; (*umg: Methode*

etc) homespun, amateurish; **selbst verdientes Geld** money one has earned o.s. ▷ *adv* even; **selbst wenn** even if; **selbst Gott** even God (himself)

Selbstachtung *f* self-respect
selbständig *etc* ['zɛlpʃtɛndɪç] *adj* = **selbstständig** *etc*
Selbst- *zW:* **Selbstanzeige** *f:* **Selbstanzeige erstatten** to come forward oneself; **der Dieb hat Selbstanzeige erstattet** the thief has come forward; **Selbstauslöser** *m* (*Phot*) delayed-action shutter release; **Selbstbedienung** *f* self-service; **Selbstbedienungsmentalität** *f* self-service mentality; **Selbstbefriedigung** *f* masturbation; (*fig*) self-gratification; **Selbstbeherrschung** *f* self-control; **Selbstbestätigung** *f* self-affirmation; **selbstbewusst** *adj* self-confident; (*selbstsicher*) self-assured; **Selbstbewusstsein** *nt* self-confidence; **Selbstbildnis** *nt* self-portrait; **Selbsterhaltung** *f* self-preservation; **Selbsterkenntnis** *f* self-knowledge; **Selbstfahrer** *m* (*Aut*): **Autovermietung für Selbstfahrer** self-drive car hire (*Brit*) *od* rental; **selbstgefällig** *adj* smug, self-satisfied; **selbstgerecht** *adj* self-righteous; **Selbstgespräch** *nt* conversation with o.s.; **selbstgewiss** *adj* confident; **selbstherrlich** *adj* high-handed; (*selbstgerecht*) self-satisfied; **Selbsthilfe** *f* self-help; **zur Selbsthilfe greifen** to take matters into one's own hands; **selbstklebend** *adj* self-adhesive; **Selbstkostenpreis** *m* cost price; **selbstlos** *adj* unselfish, selfless; **Selbstmord** *m* suicide; **Selbstmordanschlag** *m* suicide attack; **Selbstmordattentäter, in** *m(f)* suicide bomber; **Selbstmörder, in** *m(f)* (*Person*) suicide; **selbstmörderisch** *adj* suicidal; **selbstsicher** *adj* self-assured; **Selbstsicherheit** *f* self-assurance; **selbstständig** ['zɛlpstʃtɛndɪç] *adj* independent; **sich selbstständig machen** (*beruflich*) to set up on one's own, start one's own business; **Selbstständigkeit** *f* independence; **Selbststudium** *nt* private study; **selbstsüchtig** *adj* selfish; **selbsttätig** *adj* automatic; **Selbstüberwindung** *f* willpower; **selbstvergessen** *adj* absent-minded; (*Blick*) faraway; **selbstverschuldet** *adj*: **wenn der Unfall selbstverschuldet ist** if there is personal responsibility for the accident; **Selbstversorger** *m*: **Selbstversorger sein** to be self-sufficient *od* self-reliant; **Urlaub für Selbstversorger** self-catering holiday
selbstverständlich *adj* obvious ▷ *adv* naturally; **ich halte das für ~** I take that for granted
Selbstverständlichkeit *f* (*Unbefangenheit*) naturalness; (*natürliche Voraussetzung*) matter of course
Selbst- *zW:* **Selbstverständnis** *nt:* **nach**

seinem eigenen Selbstverständnis as he sees himself; **Selbstverteidigung** *f* self-defence (*Brit*), self-defense (*US*); **Selbstvertrauen** *nt* self-confidence; **Selbstverwaltung** *f* autonomy, self-government; **Selbstwählferndienst** *m* (*Tel*) automatic dialling service, subscriber trunk dialling (*Brit*), STD (*Brit*), direct distance dialing (*US*); **Selbstwertgefühl** *nt* feeling of one's own worth *od* value, self-esteem; **selbstzufrieden** *adj* self-satisfied; **Selbstzweck** *m* end in itself

selig ['zeːlɪç] *adj* happy, blissful; (*Rel*) blessed; (*tot*) late; **Seligkeit** *f* bliss
Sellerie ['zɛlərɪː] (**-s, -(s)** *od* **-, -n**) *m od f* celery
selten ['zɛltən] *adj* rare ▷ *adv* seldom, rarely; **Seltenheit** *f* rarity; **Seltenheitswert** (**-(e)s**) *m* rarity value
Selterswasser ['zɛltərsvasər] *nt* soda water
seltsam ['zɛltzaːm] *adj* curious, strange
seltsamerweise *adv* curiously, strangely
Seltsamkeit *f* strangeness
Semester [ze'mɛstər] (**-s, -**) *nt* semester; **ein älteres ~** a senior student
Semi- [zemi] *in zw* semi-
Semikolon [-'koːlɔn] (**-s, -s**) *nt* semicolon
Seminar [zemi'naːr] (**-s, -e**) *nt* seminary; (*Kurs*) seminar; (*Univ: Ort*) department building
semitisch [ze'miːtɪʃ] *adj* Semitic
Semmel ['zɛməl] (**-, -n**) *f* roll; **Semmelbrösel**, **Semmelbröseln** *pl* breadcrumbs *pl*; **Semmelknödel** (*Südd, Österr*) *m* bread dumpling
sen. *abk* (= *senior*) sen.
Senat [ze'naːt] (**-(e)s, -e**) *m* senate
Sendebereich *m* transmission range
Sendefolge *f* (*Serie*) series
senden¹ *unreg vt* to send
senden² *vt, vi* (*Rundf, TV*) to transmit, broadcast
Sendenetz *nt* network
Sendepause *f* (*Rundf, TV*) interval
Sender (**-s, -**) *m* station; (*Anlage*) transmitter
Sende- *zW:* **Sendereihe** *f* series (of broadcasts); **Sendeschluss** *m* (*Rundf, TV*) closedown; **Sendestation** *f* transmitting station; **Sendestelle** *f* transmitting station; **Sendezeit** *f* broadcasting time, air time
Sendung ['zɛndʊŋ] *f* consignment; (*Aufgabe*) mission; (*Rundf, TV*) transmission; (*Programm*) programme (*Brit*), program (*US*)
Senegal ['zeːnegal] (**-s**) *nt* Senegal
Senf [zɛnf] (**-(e)s, -e**) *m* mustard; **seinen ~ dazugeben** (*umg*) to put one's oar in; **Senfkorn** *nt* mustard seed
sengen ['zɛŋən] *vt* to singe ▷ *vi* to scorch
senil [ze'niːl] (*pej*) *adj* senile
Senior ['zeːnɪɔr] (**-s, -en**) *m* (*Rentner*) senior citizen; (*Geschäftspartner*) senior partner
Seniorenpass [zeni'oːrənpas] *m* senior citizen's travel pass (*Brit*)
Senkblei ['zɛŋkblaɪ] *nt* plumb
Senke (**-, -n**) *f* depression
Senkel (**-s, -**) *m* (shoe)lace

S

303

senken vt to lower; (Kopf) to bow; (Tech) to sink ▷ vr to sink; (Stimme) to drop

Senk- zW: **Senkfuß** m flat foot; **Senkgrube** f cesspit; **senkrecht** adj vertical, perpendicular; **Senkrechte** f perpendicular; **Senkrechtstarter** m (Aviat) vertical takeoff plane; (fig: Person) high-flier

Senner, in ['zɛnər(ɪn)] (-s, -) m(f) (Alpine) dairyman, dairymaid

Sensation [zɛnzatsi'oːn] f sensation

sensationell [zɛnzatsio'nɛl] adj sensational

Sensationsblatt nt sensational paper

Sensationssucht f sensationalism

Sense ['zɛnzə] (-, -n) f scythe; **dann ist ~!** (umg) that's the end!

sensibel [zɛn'ziːbəl] adj sensitive

sensibilisieren [zɛnzibili'ziːrən] vt to sensitize

Sensibilität [zɛnzibili'tɛːt] f sensitivity

sentimental [zɛntimɛn'taːl] adj sentimental

Sentimentalität [zɛntimɛntali'tɛːt] f sentimentality

separat [zepa'raːt] adj separate; (Wohnung, Zimmer) self-contained

Sept. abk (= September) Sept.

September [zɛp'tɛmbər] (-(s), -) m September; **im ~** in September; **im Monat ~** in the month of September; **heute ist der zweite ~** today is the second of September od September second (US); (geschrieben) today is 2nd September; **in diesem ~** this September; **Anfang/Ende/ Mitte ~** at the beginning/end/in the middle of September

septisch ['zɛptɪʃ] adj septic

sequentiell [zekvɛntsi'ɛl] adj = **sequenziell**

Sequenz [ze'kvɛnts] f sequence

sequenziell [zekvɛntsi'ɛl] adj (Comput) sequential; **~er Zugriff** sequential access

Serbe ['zɛrbə] (-n, -n) m Serbian

Serbien (-s) nt Serbia; **~ und Montenegro** Serbia and Montenegro

Serbin f Serbian

serbisch adj Serbian

Serbokroatisch, e nt Serbo-Croat

Serie ['zeːriə] f series

seriell [zeri'ɛl] adj (Comput) serial; **~e Daten** serial data pl; **~er Anschluss** serial port; **~er Drucker** serial printer

Serien- zW: **Serienanfertigung** f, **Serienherstellung** f series production; **serienmäßig** adj (Ausstattung) standard; (Herstellung) series attrib ▷ adv (herstellen) in series; **Seriennummer** f serial number; **serienweise** adv in series

seriös [zeri'øːs] adj serious; (anständig) respectable

Serpentine [zɛrpɛn'tiːnə] f hairpin (bend)

Serum ['zeːrʊm] (-s, Seren) nt serum

Service[1] [zɛr'viːs] (-(s), -) nt (Gläserservice) set; (Geschirr) service

Service[2] ['sɐːvɪs] (-, -s) m (Comm, Sport) service

servieren [zɛr'viːrən] vt, vi to serve

Serviererin [zɛr'viːrərɪn] f waitress

Servierwagen m trolley

Serviette [zɛrvi'ɛtə] f napkin, serviette

Servolenkung f power steering

Servomotor m servo motor

Servus ['zɛrvʊs] (Österr, Südd) interj hello; (beim Abschied) goodbye, so long (umg)

Sesam ['zeːzam] (-s, -s) m sesame

Sessel ['zɛsəl] (-s, -) m armchair; **Sessellift** m chairlift

sesshaft ['zɛshaft] adj settled; (ansässig) resident

Set [zɛt] (-s, -s) nt od m set; (Deckchen) tablemat

setzen ['zɛtsən] vt to put, place, set; (Baum etc) to plant; (Segel, Typ) to set ▷ vr (Platz nehmen) to sit down; (Kaffee, Tee) to settle ▷ vi to leap; (wetten) to bet; (Typ) to set; **jdm ein Denkmal ~** to build a monument to sb; **sich zu jdm ~** to sit with sb

Setzer ['zɛtsər] (-s, -) m (Typ) typesetter

Setzerei [zɛtsə'raɪ] f caseroom; (Firma) typesetting firm

Setz- zW: **Setzkasten** m (Typ) case; (an Wand) ornament shelf; **Setzling** m young plant; **Setzmaschine** f (Typ) typesetting machine

Seuche ['zɔʏçə] (-, -n) f epidemic

Seuchengebiet nt infected area

seufzen ['zɔʏftsən] vt, vi to sigh

Seufzer ['zɔʏftsər] (-s, -) m sigh

Sex [zɛks] (-(es)) m sex

Sexta ['zɛksta] (-, Sexten) f (früher) first year of German secondary school

Sexualerziehung [zɛksu'aːlɛrtsiːʊŋ] f sex education

Sexualität [zɛksuali'tɛːt] f sex, sexuality

Sexual- zW: **Sexualkunde** [zɛksu'aːlkʊndə] f sex education; **Sexualleben** nt sex life; **Sexualobjekt** nt sex object

sexuell [zɛksu'ɛl] adj sexual

Seychellen [ze'ʃɛlən] pl Seychelles pl

sezieren [ze'tsiːrən] vt to dissect

SFB (-) m abk (= Sender Freies Berlin) Radio Free Berlin

Sfr, sFr. abk (= Schweizer Franken) sfr

Shampoo [ʃam'puː] (-s, -s) nt shampoo

Shetlandinseln ['ʃɛtlant|ɪnzəln] pl Shetland, Shetland Isles pl

Shorts [ʃɔːrts] pl shorts pl

Showmaster ['ʃoːmaːstər] (-s, -) m compère, MC

siamesisch [zia'meːzɪʃ] adj: **~e Zwillinge** Siamese twins

Siamkatze f Siamese (cat)

Sibirien [zi'biːriən] (-s) nt Siberia

sibirisch adj Siberian

🔵 SCHLÜSSELWORT

sich [zɪç] pron 1 (akk): **er/sie/es ... sich** he/ she/it ... himself/herself/itself; **sie** pl/ **man ... sich** they/one ...themselves/oneself; **Sie ... sich** you ... yourself/yourselves pl; **sich wiederholen** to repeat oneself/itself

2 (dat): **er/sie/es ... sich** he/she/it ... to himself/herself/itself; **sie** pl/**man ... sich**

they/one ... to themselves/oneself; **Sie ... sich** you ... to yourself/yourselves *pl*; **sie hat sich einen Pullover gekauft** she bought herself a jumper; **sich die Haare waschen** to wash one's hair

3 (*mit Präposition*): **haben Sie Ihren Ausweis bei sich?** do you have your pass on you?; **er hat nichts bei sich** he's got nothing on him; **sie bleiben gern unter sich** they keep themselves to themselves

4 (*einander*) each other, one another; **sie bekämpfen sich** they fight each other *od* one another

5: **dieses Auto fährt sich gut** this car drives well; **hier sitzt es sich gut** it's good to sit here

Sichel ['zɪçəl] (**-, -n**) *f* sickle; (*Mondsichel*) crescent

sicher ['zɪçər] *adj* safe; (*gewiss*) certain; (*Hand, Job*) steady; (*zuverlässig*) secure, reliable; (*selbstsicher*) confident; (*Stellung*) secure ▷ *adv* (*natürlich*): **du hast dich ~ verrechnet** you must have counted wrongly; **vor jdm/etw ~ sein** to be safe from sb/sth; **sich** *dat* **einer Sache/jds ~ sein** to be sure of sth/sb; **~ ist sicher** you can't be too sure

sichergehen *unreg vi* to make sure

Sicherheit ['zɪçərhaɪt] *f* safety; (*auch Fin*) security; (*Gewissheit*) certainty; (*Selbstsicherheit*) confidence; **die öffentliche ~** public security; **~ im Straßenverkehr** road safety; **~ leisten** (*Comm*) to offer security

Sicherheits- *zW*: **Sicherheitsabstand** *m* safe distance; **Sicherheitsbestimmungen** *pl* safety regulations *pl*; (*betrieblich, Pol etc*) security controls *pl*; **Sicherheitseinrichtungen** *pl* security equipment *sing*, security devices *pl*; **Sicherheitsglas** *nt* safety glass; **Sicherheitsgurt** *m* seat belt; **sicherheitshalber** *adv* to be on the safe side; **Sicherheitsnadel** *f* safety pin; **Sicherheitsrat** *m* Security Council; **Sicherheitsschloss** *nt* safety lock; **Sicherheitsspanne** *f* (*Comm*) margin of safety; **Sicherheitsverschluss** *m* safety clasp; **Sicherheitsvorkehrung** *f* safety precaution

sicherlich *adv* certainly, surely

sichern *vt* to secure; (*schützen*) to protect; (*Bergsteiger etc*) to belay; (*Waffe*) to put the safety catch on; (*Comput: Daten*) to back up; **jdm/sich etw ~** to secure sth for sb/for o.s.

sicherstellen *vt* to impound; (*garantieren*) to guarantee

Sicherung *f* (*Sichern*) securing; (*Vorrichtung*) safety device; (*an Waffen*) safety catch; (*Elek*) fuse; **da ist (bei) ihm die ~ durchgebrannt** (*fig: umg*) he blew a fuse

Sicherungskopie *f* backup copy

Sicht [zɪçt] (**-**) *f* sight; (*Aussicht*) view; (*Sehweite*) visibility; **auf** *od* **nach ~** (*Fin*) at sight; **auf lange ~** on a long-term basis; **sichtbar** *adj* visible; **Sichtbarkeit** *f* visibility

sichten *vt* to sight; (*auswählen*) to sort out;

(*ordnen*) to sift through

Sicht- *zW*: **sichtlich** *adj* evident, obvious; **Sichtverhältnisse** *pl* visibility *sing*; **Sichtvermerk** *m* visa; **Sichtweite** *f* visibility; **außer Sichtweite** out of sight

sickern ['zɪkərn] *vi* (*Hilfsverb sein*) to seep; (*in Tropfen*) to drip

Sie [zi:] *nom, akk pron* you

sie *pron* (*sing: nom*) she; (: *akk*) her; (*pl: nom*) they; (: *akk*) them

Sieb [zi:p] (**-(e)s, -e**) *nt* sieve; (*Koch*) strainer; (*Gemüsesieb*) colander

sieben¹ ['zi:bən] *vt* to sieve, sift; (*Flüssigkeit*) to strain ▷ *vi*: **bei der Prüfung wird stark gesiebt** (*fig: umg*) the exam will weed a lot of people out

sieben² ['zi:bən] *num* seven; **Siebengebirge** *nt*: **das Siebengebirge** the Seven Mountains *pl* (*near Bonn*); **siebenhundert** *num* seven hundred; **Siebenmeter** *m* (*Sport*) penalty; **Siebensachen** *pl* belongings *pl*; **Siebenschläfer** *m* (*Zool*) dormouse

siebte, r, s ['zi:ptə(r, s)] *adj* seventh

Siebtel (**-s, -**) *nt* seventh

siebzehn ['zi:ptse:n] *num* seventeen

siebzig ['zi:ptsɪç] *num* seventy

siedeln ['zi:dəln] *vi* to settle

sieden ['zi:dən] *vt, vi* to boil

Siedepunkt *m* boiling point

Siedler (**-s, -**) *m* settler

Siedlung *f* settlement; (*Häusersiedlung*) housing estate (*Brit*) *od* development (*US*)

Sieg [zi:k] (**-(e)s, -e**) *m* victory

Siegel ['zi:gəl] (**-s, -**) *nt* seal; **Siegellack** *m* sealing wax; **Siegelring** *m* signet ring

siegen ['zi:gən] *vi* to be victorious; (*Sport*) to win; **über jdn/etw ~** (*fig*) to triumph over sb/sth; (*in Wettkampf*) to beat sb/sth

Sieger, in (**-s, -**) *m(f)* victor; (*Sport etc*) winner; **Siegerehrung** *f* (*Sport*) presentation ceremony

siegessicher *adj* sure of victory

Siegeszug *m* triumphal procession

siegreich *adj* victorious

siehe ['zi:ə] *imperativ* see; (*siehe da*) behold

siehst [zi:st], **sieht** [zi:t] *vb siehe* **sehen**

Siel [zi:l] (**-(e)s, -e**) *nt od m* (*Schleuse*) sluice; (*Abwasserkanal*) sewer

siezen ['zi:tsən] *vt* to address as "Sie"; *siehe auch* **duzen**

Signal [zɪ'gna:l] (**-s, -e**) *nt* signal; **Signalanlage** *f* signals *pl*, set of signals

signalisieren [zɪgnali'zi:rən] *vt* (*lit, fig*) to signal

Signatur [zɪgna'tu:r] *f* signature; (*Bibliothekssignatur*) shelf mark

Silbe ['zɪlbə] (**-, -n**) *f* syllable; **er hat es mit keiner ~ erwähnt** he didn't say a word about it

Silber ['zɪlbər] (**-s**) *nt* silver; **Silberbergwerk** *nt* silver mine; **Silberblick** *m*: **einen Silberblick haben** to have a slight squint; **Silberhochzeit** *f* silver wedding

silbern *adj* silver

305

Silberpapier nt silver paper
Silhouette [zilu'ɛtə] f silhouette
Silikonchip [zili'ko:ntʃɪp] m silicon chip
Silo ['zi:lo] (**-s, -s**) nt od m silo
Silvester [zɪl'vɛstər] (**-s, -**) m or nt New Year's Eve, Hogmanay (Scot); see culture note

Simbabwe [zɪm'ba:bvə] (**-s**) nt Zimbabwe
SIM-Karte ['zɪm-] f SIM card
simpel ['zɪmpəl] adj simple; **Simpel** (**-s, -**) (umg) m simpleton
Sims [zɪms] (**-es, -e**) nt od m (Kaminsims) mantelpiece; (Fenstersims) (window)sill
simsen ['zɪmsən] (umg) vti to text
Simulant, in [zimu'lant(ɪn)] (**-en, -en**) m(f) malingerer
simulieren [zimu'li:rən] vt to simulate; (vortäuschen) to feign ▷ vi to feign illness
simultan [zimul'ta:n] adj simultaneous; **Simultandolmetscher** m simultaneous interpreter
sind [zɪnt] vb siehe **sein**
Sinfonie [zɪnfo'ni:] f symphony
Singapur ['zɪŋgapu:r] (**-s**) nt Singapore
singen ['zɪŋən] unreg vt, vi to sing
Single[1] ['sɪŋgəl] (**-s, -s**) m (Alleinlebender) single person
Single[2] ['sɪŋgəl] (**-, -s**) f (Mus) single
Singsang m (Gesang) monotonous singing
Singstimme f vocal part
Singular ['zɪŋgula:r] m singular
Singvogel ['zɪŋfo:gəl] m songbird
sinken ['zɪŋkən] unreg vi to sink; (Boden, Gebäude) to subside; (Fundament) to settle; (Preise etc) to fall, go down; **den Mut/die Hoffnung ~ lassen** to lose courage/hope
Sinn [zɪn] (**-(e)s, -e**) m mind; (Wahrnehmungssinn) sense; (Bedeutung) sense, meaning; **im ~e des Gesetzes** according to the spirit of the law; **~ für etw** sense of sth; **im ~e des Verstorbenen** in accordance with the wishes of the deceased; **von ~en sein** to be out of one's mind; **das ist nicht der ~ der Sache** that is not the point; **das hat keinen ~** there is no point in that; **Sinnbild** nt symbol; **sinnbildlich** adj symbolic
sinnen unreg vi to ponder; **auf etw** akk **~ to** contemplate sth; **über etw** akk **~ to** reflect on sth
Sinnenmensch m sensualist
Sinnes- zW: **Sinnesorgan** nt sense organ; **Sinnestäuschung** f illusion; **Sinneswandel** m change of mind

sinngemäß adj faithful; (Wiedergabe) in one's own words
sinnig adj apt; (ironisch) clever
Sinn- zW: **sinnlich** adj sensual, sensuous; (Wahrnehmung) sensory; **Sinnlichkeit** f sensuality; **sinnlos** adj senseless, meaningless; **sinnlos betrunken** blind drunk; **Sinnlosigkeit** f senselessness, meaninglessness; **sinnverwandt** adj synonymous; **sinnvoll** adj meaningful; (vernünftig) sensible
Sinologe [zino'lo:gə] (**-n, -n**) m Sinologist
Sinologie f Sinology
Sinologin f Sinologist
Sintflut ['zɪntflu:t] f Flood; **nach uns die ~** (umg) it doesn't matter what happens after we've gone; **sintflutartig** adj: **sintflutartige Regenfälle** torrential rain sing
Sinus ['zi:nʊs] (**-, -** od **-se**) m (Anat) sinus; (Math) sine
Siphon [zi'fõ:] (**-s, -s**) m siphon
Sippe ['zɪpə] (**-, -n**) f (extended) family; (umg: Verwandtschaft) clan
Sippschaft ['zɪpʃaft] (pej) f tribe; (Bande) gang
Sirene [zi're:nə] (**-, -n**) f siren
Sirup ['zi:rʊp] (**-s, -e**) m syrup
Sit-in [sɪt'ɪn] (**-(s), -s**) nt: **ein ~ machen** to stage a sit-in
Sitte ['zɪtə] (**-, -n**) f custom; **Sitten** pl morals pl; **was sind denn das für ~n?** what sort of way is that to behave?
Sitten- zW: **Sittenpolizei** f vice squad; **Sittenstrolch** (umg) m sex fiend; **Sittenwächter** m (ironisch) guardian of public morals; **sittenwidrig** adj (form) immoral
Sittich ['zɪtɪç] (**-(e)s, -e**) m parakeet
Sitt- zW: **sittlich** adj moral; **Sittlichkeit** f morality; **Sittlichkeitsverbrechen** nt sex offence (Brit) od offense (US); **sittsam** adj modest, demure
Situation [zituatsi'o:n] f situation
situiert [zitu'i:rt] adj: **gut ~ sein** to be well off
Sitz [zɪts] (**-es, -e**) m seat; (von Firma, Verwaltung) headquarters pl; **der Anzug hat einen guten ~** the suit sits well
sitzen unreg vi to sit; (Bemerkung, Schlag) to strike home; (Gelerntes) to have sunk in; (umg: im Gefängnis sitzen) to be inside; **locker ~** to be loose; **einen ~ haben** (umg) to have had one too many; **er sitzt im Kultusministerium** (umg: sein) he's in the Ministry of Education; **~ bleiben** to remain seated; (Sch) to have to repeat a year; **auf etw** dat **~ bleiben** to be lumbered with sth; **~ lassen** (Sch) to keep down a year; (Mädchen) to jilt; (Wartenden) to stand up; **etw auf sich** dat **~ lassen** to take sth lying down
sitzend adj (Tätigkeit) sedentary
Sitz- zW: **Sitzfleisch** (umg) nt: **Sitzfleisch haben** to be able to sit still; **Sitzgelegenheit** f seats pl; **Sitzordnung** f seating plan; **Sitzplatz** m seat; **Sitzstreik** m sit-down strike
Sitzung f meeting

Sizilianer, in [zitsili'a:nər(ɪn)] (-**s,** -) *m(f)*
  Sicilian
sizilianisch *adj* Sicilian
Sizilien [zi'tsi:liən] (-**s**) *nt* Sicily
Skala ['ska:la] (-, **Skalen**) *f* scale; (*fig*) range
Skalpell [skal'pɛl] (-**s,** -**e**) *nt* scalpel
skalpieren [skal'pi:rən] *vt* to scalp
Skandal [skan'da:l] (-**s,** -**e**) *m* scandal
skandalös [skanda'løːs] *adj* scandalous
Skandinavien [skandi'na:viən] (-**s**) *nt*
  Scandinavia
Skandinavier, in (-**s,** -) *m(f)* Scandinavian
skandinavisch *adj* Scandinavian
Skat [ska:t] (-**(e)s,** -**e** *od* -**s**) *m* (*Karten*) skat
Skateboard ['ske:tbɔːrd] (-**s,** -**s**) *nt* skateboard;
  skateboarden *vi* to skateboard
Skelett [ske'lɛt] (-**(e)s,** -**e**) *nt* skeleton
Skepsis ['skɛpsɪs] (-) *f* scepticism (*Brit*),
  skepticism (*US*)
skeptisch ['skɛptɪʃ] *adj* sceptical (*Brit*), skeptical
  (*US*)
Ski [ʃiː] (-**s,** -**er**) *m* ski; ~ **laufen** *od* **fahren** to
  ski; **Skifahrer** *m* skier; **Skihütte** *f* ski hut;
  Skiläufer *m* skier; **Skilehrer** *m* ski instructor;
  Skilift *m* ski lift; **Skispringen** *nt* ski
  jumping; **Skistiefel** *m* ski boot; **Skistock** *m*
  ski pole
Skizze ['skɪtsə] (-, -**n**) *f* sketch
skizzieren [skɪ'tsi:rən] *vt* to sketch; (*fig: Plan*
  etc) to outline ▷ *vi* to sketch
Sklave ['skla:və] (-**n,** -**n**) *m* slave
Sklaventreiber (-**s,** -) (*pej*) *m* slave-driver
Sklaverei [skla:və'raɪ] *f* slavery
Sklavin *f* slave
sklavisch *adj* slavish
Skonto ['skɔnto] (-**s,** -**s**) *nt od m* discount
Skorpion [skɔrpi'oːn] (-**s,** -**e**) *m* scorpion;
  (*Astrol*) Scorpio
Skrupel ['skru:pəl] (-**s,** -) *m* scruple; **skrupellos**
  adj unscrupulous
Skulptur [skʊlp'tu:r] *f* sculpture
skurril [skʊ'ri:l] *adj* (*geh*) droll, comical
Skype® (*Internet, Tel*) *nt* Skype®
skypen (*Internet, Tel*) *vt* to skype
Slalom ['sla:lɔm] (-**s,** -**s**) *m* slalom
Slawe ['sla:və] (-**n,** -**n**) *m* Slav
Slawin *f* Slav
slawisch *adj* Slavonic, Slavic
Slip [slɪp] (-**s,** -**s**) *m* (pair of) briefs *pl*
Slowakei [slova'kaɪ] *f* Slovakia
slowakisch *adj* Slovak
Slowenien [slo've:niən] (-**s**) *nt* Slovenia
slowenisch *adj* Slovene
Smaragd [sma'rakt] (-**(e)s,** -**e**) *m* emerald
Smoking ['smo:kɪŋ] (-**s,** -**s**) *m* dinner jacket
  (*Brit*), tuxedo (*US*)
SMS (-, -) *f abk* (= *Short Message Service*) SMS;
  jdm eine ~ schicken to send sb a text; **SMS-**
  Nachricht *f* text message
Snob [snɔp] (-**s,** -**s**) *m* snob
Snowboard ['snɔːbɔːrd] (-**s,** -**s**) *nt* snowboard;
  snowboarden *vi* to snowboard
So. *abk* = **Sonntag**

SO *abk* (= *Südost(en)*) SE

 SCHLÜSSELWORT

so [zoː] *adv* **1** (*so sehr*) so; **so groß/schön** *etc* so
  big/nice *etc*; **so groß/schön wie ...** as big/
  nice as ...; **das hat ihn so geärgert, dass ...**
  that annoyed him so much that ...
  2 (*auf diese Weise*) like this; **so genannt** so-
  called; **mach es nicht so** don't do it like that;
  so oder so (in) one way or the other; **... oder**
  so something (like that); **und so weiter** and
  so on; **so viel (wie)** as much as; **rede nicht**
  so viel don't talk so much; **so weit sein** to
  be ready; **so weit wie** *od* **als möglich** as far
  as possible; **ich bin so weit zufrieden** by
  and large I'm quite satisfied; **es ist bald so**
  weit it's nearly time; **so wenig (wie)** no more
  (than), not any more (than); **so wenig wie**
  möglich as little as possible; **so ein ...** such
  a ...; **so einer wie ich** somebody like me; **so**
  (et)was something like this/that; **na so was!**
  well I never!; **das ist gut so** that's fine; **sie ist**
  nun einmal so that's just the way she is; **das**
  habe ich nur so gesagt I didn't really mean it
  3 (*umg: umsonst*): **ich habe es so bekommen** I
  got it for nothing
  4 (*als Füllwort: nicht übersetzt*): **so mancher** a
  number of people *pl*
  ▷ *konj*: **so wie es jetzt ist** as things are at the
  moment; *siehe auch* **sodass**
  ▷ *interj*: **so?** really?; **so, das wärs** right, that's
  it then

s. o. *abk* (= *siehe oben*) see above
sobald [zo'balt] *konj* as soon as
Söckchen [zœkçən] *nt* ankle sock
Socke ['zɔkə] (-, -**n**) *f* sock; **sich auf die ~n**
  machen (*umg*) to get going
Sockel ['zɔkəl] (-**s,** -) *m* pedestal, base
sodass [zo'das] *konj* so that
Sodawasser ['zoːdavasər] *nt* soda water
Sodbrennen ['zoːtbrɛnən] (-**s**) *nt* heartburn
Sodomie [zodo'mi:] *f* bestiality
soeben [zo'|eːbən] *adv* just (now)
Sofa ['zoːfa] (-**s,** -**s**) *nt* sofa
Sofabett *nt* sofa bed, bed settee
sofern [zo'fɛrn] *konj* if, provided (that)
soff *etc* [zɔf] *vb siehe* **saufen**
Softeis ['zɔft|aɪs] (-**es**) *nt* soft ice-cream
Softie ['zɔfti:] (-**s,** -**s**) (*umg*) *m* softy
Software ['zɔftwɛːər] (-, -**s**) *f* software;
  softwarekompatibel *adj* software compatible
Sog ['zoːk] (-**(e)s,** -**e**) *m* suction; (*von Strudel*) vortex;
  (*fig*) maelstrom
sog *etc* [zoːk] *vb siehe* **saugen**
sog. *abk* = **sogenannt**

307

sogar [zoˈgaːr] *adv* even

sogenannt [ˈzoːgənant] *adj attrib* so-called

sogleich [zoˈglaɪç] *adv* straight away, at once

Sogwirkung *f* suction; *(fig)* knock-on effect

Sohle [ˈzoːlə] **(-, -n)** *f (Fußsohle)* sole; *(Talsohle etc)* bottom; *(Min)* level; **auf leisen ~n** *(fig)* softly, noiselessly

Sohn [zoːn] **(-(e)s, ⁻e)** *m* son

Sojasoße [ˈzoːjazoːsə] *f* soy *od* soya sauce

solang, solange *konj* as *od* so long as

Solar- [zoˈlaːr] *in zw* solar; **Solarenergie** *f* solar energy

Solarium [zoˈlaːriʊm] *nt* solarium

Solbad [ˈzoːlbaːt] *nt* saltwater bath

solch [zɔlç] *adj inv* such

solche, r, s *adj* such; **ein ~r Mensch** such a person

Sold [zɔlt] **(-(e)s, -e)** *m* pay

Soldat [zɔlˈdaːt] **(-en, -en)** *m* soldier; **soldatisch** *adj* soldierly

Söldner [ˈzœldnər] **(-s, -)** *m* mercenary

Sole [ˈzoːlə] **(-, -n)** *f* brine, salt water

Solei [ˈzoːlaɪ] *nt* pickled egg

Soli [ˈzoːli] *pl von* **Solo**

solid [zoˈliːd], **solide** [zoˈliːdə] *adj* solid; *(Arbeit, Wissen)* sound; *(Leben, Person)* staid, respectable

solidarisch [zoliˈdaːrɪʃ] *adj* in *od* with solidarity; **sich ~ erklären** to declare one's solidarity

solidarisieren [zolidariˈziːrən] *vr:* **sich ~ mit** to show (one's) solidarity with

Solidarität [zolidariˈtɛːt] *f* solidarity

Solidaritätsstreik *m* sympathy strike

Solist, in [zoˈlɪst(ɪn)] *m(f) (Mus)* soloist

Soll [zɔl] **(-(s), -(s))** *nt (Fin)* debit (side); *(Arbeitsmenge)* quota, target; **~ und Haben** debit and credit

soll *vb siehe* **sollen**

 SCHLÜSSELWORT

sollen [ˈzɔlən] *(pt* **sollte***, pp* **gesollt** *od (als Hilfsverb)* **sollen)** *hilfsverb* **1** *(Pflicht, Befehl)* be supposed to; **du hättest nicht gehen sollen** you shouldn't have gone, you oughtn't to have gone; **er sollte eigentlich morgen kommen** he was supposed to come tomorrow; **soll ich?** shall I?; **soll ich dir helfen?** shall I help you?; **sag ihm, er soll warten** tell him he's to wait; **was soll ich machen?** what should I do?; **mir soll es gleich sein** it's all the same to me; **er sollte sie nie wiedersehen** he was never to see her again

2 *(Vermutung):* **sie soll verheiratet sein** she's said to be married; **was soll das heißen?** what's that supposed to mean?; **man sollte glauben, dass ...** you would think that ...; **sollte das passieren, ...** if that should happen ...

▷ *vt, vi:* **was soll das?** what's all this about *od* in aid of?; **das sollst du nicht** you shouldn't do that; **was solls?** what the hell!

sollte etc [ˈzɔltə] *vb siehe* **sollen**

Solo [ˈzoːlo] **(-s, -s** *od* **Soli)** *nt* solo

solo *adv (Mus)* solo; *(fig: umg)* on one's own, alone

solvent [zɔlˈvɛnt] *adj (Fin)* solvent

Solvenz [zɔlˈvɛnts] *f (Fin)* solvency

Somalia [zoˈmaːlia] **(-s)** *nt* Somalia

somit [zoˈmɪt] *konj* and so, therefore

Sommer [ˈzɔmər] **(-s, -)** *m* summer; **~ wie Winter** all year round; **Sommerferien** *pl* summer holidays *pl (Brit) od* vacation *sing (US)*; *(Jur, Parl)* summer recess *sing*; **sommerlich** *adj* summer *attrib*; *(sommerartig)* summery; **Sommerloch** *nt* silly season; **Sommerreifen** *m* normal tyre *(Brit) od* tire *(US)*; **Sommerschlussverkauf** *m* summer sale; **Sommersemester** *nt (Univ)* summer semester *(bes US)*, ≈ summer term *(Brit)*; **Sommersprossen** *pl* freckles *pl*; **Sommerzeit** *f* summertime

Sonate [zoˈnaːtə] **(-, -n)** *f* sonata

Sonde [ˈzɔndə] **(-, -n)** *f* probe

Sonder- [ˈzɔndər] *in zw* special; **Sonderanfertigung** *f* special model; **Sonderangebot** *nt* special offer; **Sonderausgabe** *f* special edition; **sonderbar** *adj* strange, odd; **Sonderbeauftragte, r** *f(m)* *(Pol)* special emissary; **Sonderbeitrag** *m* (special) feature; **Sonderfahrt** *f* special trip; **Sonderfall** *m* special case; **sondergleichen** *adj inv* without parallel, unparalleled; **eine Frechheit sondergleichen** the height of cheek; **sonderlich** *adj* particular; *(außergewöhnlich)* remarkable; *(eigenartig)* peculiar; **Sonderling** *m* eccentric; **Sondermarke** *f* special issue (stamp); **Sondermüll** *m* dangerous waste

sondern *konj* but ▷ *vt* to separate; **nicht nur ..., ~ auch** not only ..., but also

Sonder- *zW:* **Sonderpreis** *m* special price; **Sonderregelung** *f* special provision; **Sonderschule** *f* special school; **Sondervergünstigungen** *pl* perquisites *pl*, perks *pl (bes Brit)*; **Sonderwünsche** *pl* special requests *pl*; **Sonderzug** *m* special train

sondieren [zɔnˈdiːrən] *vt* to suss out; *(Gelände)* to scout out

Sonett [zoˈnɛt] **(-(e)s, -e)** *nt* sonnet

Sonnabend [ˈzɔnˌaːbənt] *m* Saturday; *siehe auch* **Dienstag**

Sonne [ˈzɔnə] **(-, -n)** *f* sun; **an die ~ gehen** to go out in the sun

sonnen *vr* to sun o.s.; **sich in etw** *dat* **~** *(fig)* to bask in sth

Sonnen- *zW:* **Sonnenaufgang** *m* sunrise; **sonnenbaden** *vi* to sunbathe; **Sonnenblume** *f* sunflower; **Sonnenbrand** *m* sunburn; **Sonnenbrille** *f* sunglasses *pl*; **Sonnencreme** *f* suntan lotion; **Sonnenenergie** *f* solar energy; **Sonnenfinsternis** *f* solar eclipse; **Sonnenfleck** *m* sunspot; **sonnengebräunt** *adj* suntanned; **sonnenklar** *adj* crystal-clear; **Sonnenkollektor** *m* solar panel; **Sonnenkraftwerk** *nt* solar

power station; **Sonnenmilch** f suntan lotion;
Sonnenöl nt suntan oil; **Sonnenschein** m
sunshine; **Sonnenschirm** m sunshade;
Sonnenschutzmittel nt sunscreen;
Sonnenstich m sunstroke; **du hast wohl
einen Sonnenstich!** (hum: umg) you
must have been out in the sun too long!;
Sonnensystem nt solar system; **Sonnenuhr**
f sundial; **Sonnenuntergang** m sunset;
Sonnenwende f solstice
sonnig ['zɔnɪç] adj sunny
Sonntag ['zɔnta:k] m Sunday; siehe auch
Dienstag
sonntäglich adj attrib: ~ **gekleidet** dressed in
one's Sunday best
sonntags adv (on) Sundays
Sonntagsdienst m: ~ **haben** (Apotheke) to be
open on Sundays
Sonntagsfahrer (pej) m Sunday driver
sonst [zɔnst] adv otherwise; (mit pron, in Fragen)
else; (zu anderer Zeit) at other times; (gewöhnlich)
usually, normally ▷ konj otherwise; **er denkt,
er ist ~ wer** (umg) he thinks he's somebody
special; ~ **gehts dir gut?** (ironisch: umg) are
you feeling okay?; **wenn ich Ihnen ~ noch
behilflich sein kann** if I can help you in
any other way; ~ **noch etwas?** anything
else?; ~ **nichts** nothing else; ~ **jemand**
(umg) anybody (at all); **da kann ja ~ was
passieren** (umg) anything could happen; ~
wo (umg) somewhere else; ~ **woher** (umg) from
somewhere else; ~ **wohin** (umg) somewhere
else
sonstig adj other; „**S~es**" "other"
sooft [zo'ɔft] konj whenever
Sopran [zo'pra:n] (-s, -e) m soprano (voice)
Sopranistin [zopra'nɪstɪn] f soprano (singer)
Sorge ['zɔrgə] (-, -n) f care, worry; **dafür ~
tragen, dass ...** (geh) to see to it that ...
sorgen vi: **für jdn ~** to look after sb ▷ vr: **sich ~
(um)** to worry (about); **für etw ~** to take care
of od see to sth; **dafür ~, dass ...** to see to it
that ...; **dafür ist gesorgt** that's taken care of
Sorgen- zW: **sorgenfrei** adj carefree;
Sorgenkind nt problem child; **sorgenvoll** adj
troubled, worried
Sorgerecht (-(e)s) nt custody (of a child)
Sorgfalt ['zɔrkfalt] (-) f care(fulness); **viel ~
auf etw** akk **verwenden** to take a lot of care
over sth
sorgfältig adj careful
sorglos adj careless; (ohne Sorgen) carefree
sorgsam adj careful
Sorte ['zɔrtə] (-, -n) f sort; (Warensorte) brand;
Sorten pl (Fin) foreign currency sing
sortieren [zɔr'ti:rən] vt to sort (out); (Comput)
to sort
Sortiermaschine f sorting machine
Sortiment [zɔrti'mɛnt] nt assortment
SOS [ɛs|o:'|ɛs] nt abk SOS
sosehr [zo'ze:r] konj as much as
soso [zo'zo:] interj: ~**!** I see!; (erstaunt) well, well!;
(drohend) well!

Soße ['zo:sə] (-, -n) f sauce; (Bratensoße) gravy
Souffleur [zu'flø:r] m prompter
Souffleuse [zu'flø:zə] f prompter
soufflieren [zu'fli:rən] vt, vi to prompt
soundso ['zo:|ʊnt'zo:] adv: ~ **lange** for such and
such a time
soundsovielte, r, s adj: **am S~n** (Datum) on
such and such a date
Souterrain [zutɛ'rɛ̃:] (-s, -s) nt basement
Souvenir [zuvə'ni:r] (-s, -s) nt souvenir
souverän [zuvə'rɛ:n] adj sovereign; (überlegen)
superior; (fig) supremely good
soviel [zo'fi:l] konj as far as
sowenig [zo've:nɪç] konj however little
sowie [zo'vi:] konj (sobald) as soon as; (ebenso) as
well as
sowieso [zovi'zo:] adv anyway
Sowjetbürger m (früher) Soviet citizen
sowjetisch [zɔ'vjɛtɪʃ] adj (früher) Soviet
Sowjet- zW (früher): **Sowjetrepublik** f Soviet
Republic; **Sowjetrusse** m Soviet Russian;
Sowjetunion f Soviet Union
sowohl [zo'vo:l] konj: ~ **... als** od **wie auch ...**
both ... and ...
soz. abk = **sozial**; **sozialistisch**
sozial [zotsi'a:l] adj social; ~ **eingestellt**
public-spirited; ~ **verträglich** socially
acceptable; **~er Wohnungsbau** public-sector
housing (programme); **Sozialabgaben** pl National
Insurance contributions pl (Brit), Social
Security contributions pl (US); **Sozialamt** nt
(social) welfare office; **Sozialarbeiter** m social
worker; **Sozialberuf** m caring profession;
Sozialdemokrat m social democrat;
Sozialhilfe f welfare (aid)
Sozialisation [zotsializatsi'o:n] f (Psych,
Soziologie) socialization
sozialisieren [zotsiali'zi:rən] vt to socialize
Sozialismus [zotsia'lɪsmʊs] m socialism
Sozialist, in [zotsia'lɪst(ɪn)] m(f) socialist
sozialistisch adj socialist
Sozial- zW: **Sozialkunde** f social studies
sing; **Sozialleistungen** pl social security
contributions (from the state and employer);
Sozialplan m redundancy payments
scheme; **Sozialpolitik** f social welfare policy;
Sozialprodukt nt (gross od net) national
product; **Sozialstaat** m welfare state;
Sozialversicherung f national insurance
(Brit), social security (US); **sozialverträglich**
adj siehe **sozial**; **Sozialwohnung** f ≈ council flat
(Brit), state-subsidized apartment; see culture
note

- **SOZIALWOHNUNG**

- A Sozialwohnung is a council house or flat
- let at a fairly low rent to people on low
- income. They are built from public funds.
- People applying for a Sozialwohnung have
- to prove their entitlement.

S

Soziologe [zotsio'lo:gə] (**-n, -n**) *m* sociologist
Soziologie [zotsio'lo:gi:] *f* sociology
Soziologin [zotsio'lo:gɪn] *f* sociologist
soziologisch [zotsio'lo:gɪʃ] *adj* sociological
Sozius ['zo:tsiʊs] (**-, -se**) *m* (*Comm*) partner; (*Motorrad*) pillion rider; **Soziussitz** *m* pillion (seat)
sozusagen [zotsu'za:gən] *adv* so to speak
Spachtel ['ʃpaxtəl] (**-s, -**) *m* spatula
spachteln *vt* (*Mauerfugen, Ritzen*) to fill (in) ▷ *vi* (*umg: essen*) to tuck in
Spagat [ʃpa'ga:t] (**-s, -e**) *m od nt* splits *pl*
Spaghetti, Spagetti [ʃpa'gɛti] *pl* spaghetti *sing*
spähen ['ʃpɛ:ən] *vi* to peep, peek
Spalier [ʃpa'li:r] (**-s, -e**) *nt* (*Gerüst*) trellis; (*Leute*) guard of honour (*Brit*) *od* honor (*US*); **~ stehen, ein ~ bilden** to form a guard of honour (*Brit*) *od* honor (*US*)
Spalt [ʃpalt] (**-(e)s, -e**) *m* crack; (*Türspalt*) chink; (*fig: Kluft*) split
Spalte (**-, -n**) *f* crack, fissure; (*Gletscherspalte*) crevasse; (*in Text*) column
spalten *vt, vr* (*lit, fig*) to split
Spaltung *f* splitting
Spam [spɛm] (**-s, -s**) *nt* (*Comput*) spam; **Spamfilter** *m* spam filter *od* blocker
spammen ['spɛmən] *vt, vi* to spam
Span [ʃpa:n] (**-(e)s, ̈e**) *m* shaving
Spanferkel *nt* sucking pig
Spange ['ʃpaŋə] (**-, -n**) *f* clasp; (*Haarspange*) hair slide; (*Schnalle*) buckle; (*Armspange*) bangle
Spaniel ['ʃpa:niəl] (**-s, -s**) *m* spaniel
Spanien ['ʃpa:niən] (**-s**) *nt* Spain
Spanier, in (**-s, -**) *m(f)* Spaniard
spanisch *adj* Spanish; **das kommt mir ~ vor** (*umg*) that seems odd to me; **~e Wand** (folding) screen
Spann (**-(e)s, -e**) *m* instep
spann *etc* [ʃpan] *vb siehe* **spinnen**
Spannbeton (**-s**) *m* prestressed concrete
Spanne (**-, -n**) *f* (*Zeitspanne*) space; (*Differenz*) gap; *siehe auch* **Spann**
spannen *vt* (*straffen*) to tighten, tauten; (*befestigen*) to brace ▷ *vi* to be tight
spannend *adj* exciting, gripping; **machs nicht so ~!** (*umg*) don't keep me *etc* in suspense!
Spanner (**-s, -**) (*umg*) *m* (*Voyeur*) peeping Tom
Spannkraft *f* elasticity; (*fig*) energy
Spannung *f* tension; (*Elek*) voltage; (*fig*) suspense; (*unangenehm*) tension
Spannungsgebiet *nt* (*Pol*) flashpoint, area of tension
Spannungsprüfer *m* voltage detector
Spannweite *f* (*von Flügeln, Aviat*) (wing)span
Spanplatte *f* chipboard
Sparbuch *nt* savings book
Sparbüchse *f* moneybox
sparen ['ʃpa:rən] *vt, vi* to save; **sich** *dat* **etw ~** to save o.s. sth; (*Bemerkung*) to keep sth to o.s.; **mit etw ~** to be sparing with sth; **an etw** *dat* **~** to economize on sth
Sparer, in (**-s, -**) *m(f)* (*bei Bank etc*) saver
Sparflamme *f* low flame; **auf ~** (*fig: umg*) just ticking over
Spargel ['ʃpargəl] (**-s, -**) *m* asparagus
Spar- *zW:* **Spargroschen** *m* nest egg; **Sparkasse** *f* savings bank; **Sparkonto** *nt* savings account
spärlich ['ʃpɛ:rlɪç] *adj* meagre (*Brit*), meager (*US*); (*Bekleidung*) scanty; (*Beleuchtung*) poor
Spar- *zW:* **Sparmaßnahme** *f* economy measure; **Sparpackung** *f* economy size; **sparsam** *adj* economical, thrifty; **sparsam im Verbrauch** economical; **Sparsamkeit** *f* thrift, economizing; **Sparschwein** *nt* piggy bank
Sparte ['ʃpartə] (**-, -n**) *f* field; (*Comm*) line of business; (*Presse*) column
Sparvertrag *m* savings agreement
Spaß [ʃpa:s] (**-es, ̈e**) *m* joke; (*Freude*) fun; **~ muss sein** there's no harm in a joke; **jdm ~ machen** to be fun (for sb); **spaßen** *vi* to joke; **mit ihm ist nicht zu spaßen** you can't take liberties with him
spaßeshalber *adv* for the fun of it
spaßig *adj* funny, droll
Spaß- *zW:* **Spaßmacher** *m* joker, funny man; **Spaßverderber** (**-s, -**) *m* spoilsport; **Spaßvogel** *m* joker
Spastiker, in ['ʃpastikər(ɪn)] *m(f)* (*Med*) spastic
spät [ʃpɛ:t] *adj, adv* late; **heute Abend wird es ~** it'll be a late night tonight
Spaten ['ʃpa:tən] (**-s, -**) *m* spade; **Spatenstich** *m:* **den ersten Spatenstich tun** to turn the first sod
Spätentwickler *m* late developer
später *adj, adv* later; **an ~ denken** to think of the future; **bis ~!** see you later!
spätestens *adv* at the latest
Spätlese *f* late vintage
Spatz [ʃpats] (**-en, -en**) *m* sparrow
spazieren [ʃpa'tsi:rən] *vi* (*Hilfsverb sein*) to stroll; **~ fahren** to go for a drive; **~ gehen** to go for a walk
Spazier- *zW:* **Spaziergang** *m* walk; **einen Spaziergang machen** to go for a walk; **Spaziergänger, in** *m(f)* stroller; **Spazierstock** *m* walking stick; **Spazierweg** *m* path, walk
SPD (**-**) *f abk* (= *Sozialdemokratische Partei Deutschlands*) German Social Democratic Party; *see culture note*

● **SPD**

● The SPD (Sozialdemokratische Partei
Deutschlands), the German Social
Democratic Party, was newly formed in
1945. It is the largest political party in
Germany.

Specht [ʃpeçt] (**-(e)s, -e**) *m* woodpecker
Speck [ʃpɛk] (**-(e)s, -e**) *m* bacon; **mit ~ fängt man Mäuse** (*Sprichwort*) you need a sprat to catch a mackerel; **ran an den ~** (*umg*) let's get stuck in
Spediteur [ʃpedi'tø:r] *m* carrier; (*Möbelspediteur*) furniture remover
Spedition [ʃpeditsi'o:n] *f* carriage;

(*Speditionsfirma*) road haulage contractor; (*Umzugsfirma*) removal (*Brit*) *od* moving (*US*) firm

Speer [ʃpeːr] (**-(e)s, -e**) *m* spear; (*Sport*) javelin; **Speerwerfen** *nt*: **das Speerwerfen** throwing the javelin

Speiche [ʃpaɪçə] (**-, -n**) *f* spoke

Speichel [ʃpaɪçəl] (**-s**) *m* saliva, spit(tle); **Speichellecker** (*pej: umg*) *m* bootlicker

Speicher [ʃpaɪçər] (**-s, -**) *m* storehouse; (*Dachspeicher*) attic, loft; (*Kornspeicher*) granary; (*Wasserspeicher*) tank; (*Tech*) store; (*Comput*) memory; **Speicherauszug** *m* (*Comput*) dump

speichern *vt* (*auch Comput*) to store

speien [ʃpaɪən] *unreg vt, vi* to spit; (*erbrechen*) to vomit; (*Vulkan*) to spew

Speise [ʃpaɪzə] (**-, -n**) *f* food; **kalte und warme ~n** hot and cold meals; **Speiseeis** *nt* ice-cream; **Speisefett** *nt* cooking fat; **Speisekammer** *f* larder, pantry; **Speisekarte** *f* menu

speisen *vt* to feed; to eat ▷ *vi* to dine

Speise- *zW*: **Speiseöl** *nt* salad oil; (*zum Braten*) cooking oil; **Speiseröhre** *f* (*Anat*) gullet, oesophagus (*Brit*), esophagus (*US*); **Speisesaal** *m* dining room; **Speisewagen** *m* dining car; **Speisezettel** *m* menu

Spektakel [ʃpɛkˈtaːkəl] (**-s, -**) *m* (*umg: Lärm*) row ▷ *nt* (**-s, -**) spectacle

spektakulär [ʃpɛktakuˈlɛːr] *adj* spectacular

Spektrum [ʃpɛktrʊm] (**-s, -tren**) *nt* spectrum

Spekulant, in [ʃpekuˈlant(ɪn)] *m(f)* speculator

Spekulation [ʃpekulatsiˈoːn] *f* speculation

Spekulatius [ʃpekuˈlaːtsiʊs] (**-, -**) *m* spiced biscuit (*Brit*) *od* cookie (*US*)

spekulieren [ʃpekuˈliːrən] *vi* (*fig*) to speculate; **auf etw** *akk* **~** to have hopes of sth

Spelunke [ʃpeˈlʊŋkə] (**-, -n**) *f* dive

spendabel [ʃpɛnˈdaːbəl] (*umg*) *adj* generous, open-handed

Spende [ʃpɛndə] (**-, -n**) *f* donation

spenden *vt* to donate, give; **Spendenkonto** *nt* donations account; **Spendenwaschanlage** *f* donation-laundering organization

Spender, in (**-s, -**) *m(f)* donator; (*Med*) donor

spendieren [ʃpɛnˈdiːrən] *vt* to pay for, buy; **jdm etw ~** to treat sb to sth, stand sb sth

Sperling [ʃpɛrlɪŋ] *m* sparrow

Sperma [ʃpɛrma] (**-s, Spermen**) *nt* sperm

sperrangelweit [ʃpɛrˈaŋəlˈvaɪt] *adj* wide-open

Sperrbezirk *m* no-go area

Sperre (**-, -n**) *f* barrier; (*Verbot*) ban; (*Polizeisperre*) roadblock

sperren [ʃpɛrən] *vt* to block; (*Comm: Konto*) to freeze; (*Comput: Daten*) to disable; (*Sport*) to suspend, bar; (*: vom Ball*) to obstruct; (*einschließen*) to lock; (*verbieten*) to ban ▷ *vr* to baulk, jibe, jib

Sperr- *zW*: **Sperrfeuer** *nt* (*Mil, fig*) barrage; **Sperrfrist** *f* (*auch Jur*) waiting period; (*Sport*) (period of) suspension; **Sperrgebiet** *nt* prohibited area; **Sperrgut** *nt* bulky freight; **Sperrholz** *nt* plywood

sperrig *adj* bulky

Sperr- *zW*: **Sperrkonto** *nt* blocked account; **Sperrmüll** *m* bulky refuse; **Sperrsitz** *m* (*Theat*) stalls *pl* (*Brit*), orchestra (*US*); **Sperrstunde** *f* closing time; **Sperrzeit** *f* closing time; **Sperrzone** *f* exclusion zone

Spesen [ʃpeːzən] *pl* expenses *pl*; **Spesenabrechnung** *f* expense account

Spessart [ʃpɛsart] (**-s**) *m* Spessart (Mountains *pl*)

Spezi [ʃpeːtsi] (**-s, -s**) (*umg*) *m* pal, mate (*Brit*)

Spezial- [ʃpetsiˈaːl] *in zw* special; **Spezialausbildung** *f* specialized training

spezialisieren [ʃpetsialiˈziːrən] *vr* to specialize

Spezialisierung *f* specialization

Spezialist, in [ʃpetsiaˈlɪst(ɪn)] *m(f)*: **~ (für)** specialist (in)

Spezialität [ʃpetsialiˈtɛːt] *f* speciality (*Brit*), specialty (*US*)

speziell [ʃpetsiˈɛl] *adj* special

Spezifikation [ʃpetsifikatsiˈoːn] *f* specification

spezifisch [ʃpeˈtsiːfɪʃ] *adj* specific

Sphäre [ʃfɛːrə] (**-, -n**) *f* sphere

spicken [ʃpɪkən] *vt* to lard ▷ *vi* (*Sch*) to copy, crib

Spickzettel *m* (*Sch: umg*) crib

spie *etc* [ʃpiː] *vb siehe* **speien**

Spiegel [ʃpiːgəl] (**-s, -**) *m* mirror; (*Wasserspiegel*) level; (*Mil*) tab; **Spiegelbild** *nt* reflection; **spiegelbildlich** *adj* reversed

Spiegelei [ʃpiːgəlˌaɪ] *nt* fried egg

spiegeln *vt* to mirror, reflect ▷ *vr* to be reflected ▷ *vi* to gleam; (*widerspiegeln*) to be reflective

Spiegelreflexkamera *f* reflex camera

Spiegelschrift *f* mirror writing

Spiegelung *f* reflection

spiegelverkehrt *adj* in mirror image

Spiel [ʃpiːl] (**-(e)s, -e**) *nt* game; (*Schauspiel*) play; (*Tätigkeit*) play(ing); (*Karten*) pack (*Brit*), deck (*US*); (*Tech*) (free) play; **leichtes ~ (bei** *od* **mit jdm) haben** to have an easy job of it (with sb); **die Hand** *od* **Finger im ~ haben** to have a hand in affairs; **jdn/etw aus dem ~ lassen** to leave sb/sth out of it; **auf dem ~(e) stehen** to be at stake; **Spielautomat** *m* gambling machine; (*zum Geldgewinnen*) fruit machine (*Brit*); **Spielbank** *f* casino; **Spieldose** *f* musical box (*Brit*), music box (*US*)

spielen *vt, vi* to play; (*um Geld*) to gamble; (*Theat*) to perform, act; **was wird hier gespielt?** (*umg*) what's going on here?

spielend *adv* easily

Spieler, in (**-s, -**) *m(f)* player; (*um Geld*) gambler

Spielerei [ʃpiːləˈraɪ] *f* (*Kinderspiel*) child's play

spielerisch *adj* playful; (*Leichtigkeit*) effortless; **~es Können** skill as a player; (*Theat*) acting ability

Spiel- *zW*: **Spielfeld** *nt* pitch, field; **Spielfilm** *m* feature film; **Spielgeld** *nt* (*Einsatz*) stake; (*unechtes Geld*) toy money; **Spielkarte** *f* playing card; **Spielkonsole** *f* play console; **Spielmannszug** *m* (brass) band; **Spielplan** *m* (*Theat*) programme (*Brit*), program (*US*); **Spielplatz** *m* playground; **Spielraum** *m*

S

311

room to manoeuvre (Brit) od maneuver (US); scope; **Spielregel** f (lit, fig) rule of the game; **Spielsachen** pl toys pl; **Spielshow** f gameshow; **Spielstand** m score; **Spielstraße** f play street; **Spielsucht** f addiction to gambling; **Spielverderber** (-s, -) m spoilsport; **Spielwaren** pl toys pl; **Spielzeit** f (Saison) season; (Spieldauer) playing time; **Spielzeug** nt toy; (Spielsachen) toys pl

Spieß [ʃpiːs] (-es, -e) m spear; (Bratspieß) spit; (Mil: umg) sarge; **den ~ umdrehen** (fig) to turn the tables; **wie am ~(e) schreien** (umg) to squeal like a stuck pig; **Spießbraten** m joint roasted on a spit

Spießbürger (-s, -) m bourgeois

Spießer (-s, -) m bourgeois

Spikes [spaɪks] pl (Sport) spikes pl; (Aut) studs pl; **Spikesreifen** m studded tyre (Brit) od tire (US)

Spinat [ʃpiˈnaːt] (-(e)s, -e) m spinach

Spind [ʃpɪnt] (-(e)s, -e) m od nt locker

spindeldürr [ˈʃpɪndəlˈdyr] (pej) adj spindly, thin as a rake

Spinne [ˈʃpɪnə] (-, -n) f spider; **spinnefeind** (umg) adj: **sich** od **einander** dat **spinnefeind sein** to be deadly enemies

spinnen unreg vt to spin ▷ vi (umg) to talk rubbish; (verrückt) to be crazy od mad; **ich denk ich spinne** (umg) I don't believe it

Spinnengewebe nt cobweb

Spinner, in (-s, -) m(f) (fig: umg) screwball, crackpot

Spinnerei [ʃpɪnəˈraɪ] f spinning mill

Spinn- zW: **Spinngewebe** nt cobweb; **Spinnrad** nt spinning wheel; **Spinnwebe** f cobweb

Spion [ʃpiˈoːn] (-s, -e) m spy; (in Tür) spyhole

Spionage [ʃpioˈnaːʒə] (-) f espionage; **Spionageabwehr** f counterintelligence; **Spionagesatellit** m spy satellite

spionieren [ʃpioˈniːrən] vi to spy

Spionin f (woman) spy

Spirale [ʃpiˈraːlə] (-, -n) f spiral; (Med) coil

Spirituosen [ʃpirituˈoːzən] pl spirits pl

Spiritus [ˈʃpiːritʊs] (-, -se) m (methylated) spirits pl; **Spirituskocher** m spirit stove

Spitz [ʃpɪts] (-es, -e) m (Hund) spitz

spitz adj pointed; (Winkel) acute; (fig: Zunge) sharp; (: Bemerkung) caustic

Spitz- zW: **spitzbekommen** unreg vt: **etw spitzbekommen** (umg) to get wise to sth; **Spitzbogen** m pointed arch; **Spitzbube** m rogue

Spitze (-, -n) f point, tip; (Bergspitze) peak; (Bemerkung) taunt; (fig: Stichelei) dig; (erster Platz) lead, top; (meist pl: Gewebe) lace; **etw auf die ~ treiben** to carry sth too far

spitze adj inv ugt: prima! great

Spitzel (-s, -) m police informer

spitzen vt to sharpen; (Lippen, Mund) to purse; (lit, fig: Ohren) to prick up

Spitzen- in zw top; **Spitzenleistung** f top performance; **Spitzenlohn** m top wages pl; **Spitzenmarke** f brand leader; **spitzenmäßig** adj really great; **Spitzenposition** f leading

position; **Spitzenreiter** m (Sport) leader; (fig: Kandidat) front runner; (Ware) top seller; (Schlager) number one; **Spitzensportler** m top-class sportsman; **Spitzenverband** m leading organization; **Spitzenverdiener, in** m(f) top earner

Spitzer (-s, -) m sharpener

spitzfindig adj (over)subtle

Spitzmaus f shrew

Spitzname m nickname

Spleen [ʃpliːn] (-s, -e od -s) m (Angewohnheit) crazy habit; (Idee) crazy idea; (Fimmel) obsession

Splitt [ʃplɪt] (-s, -e) m stone chippings pl; (Streumittel) grit

Splitter (-s, -) m splinter; **Splittergruppe** f (Pol) splinter group; **splitternackt** adj stark naked

SPÖ (-) f abk (= Sozialistische Partei Österreichs) Austrian Socialist Party

sponsern [ˈʃpɔnzərn] vt to sponsor

Sponsor [ˈʃpɔnzɔr] (-s, -en) m sponsor

spontan [ʃpɔnˈtaːn] adj spontaneous

sporadisch [ʃpoˈraːdɪʃ] adj sporadic

Sporen [ˈʃpoːrən] pl (auch Bot, Zool) spurs pl

Sport [ʃpɔrt] (-(e)s, -e) m sport; (fig) hobby; **treiben Sie ~?** do you do any sport?; **Sportabzeichen** nt sports certificate; **Sportartikel** pl sports equipment sing; **Sportfest** nt sports gala; (Sch) sports day (Brit); **Sportgeist** m sportsmanship; **Sporthalle** f sports hall; **Sportklub** m sports club; **Sportlehrer** m games od P.E. teacher

Sportler, in (-s, -) m(f) sportsman, sportswoman

Sport- zW: **sportlich** adj sporting; (Mensch) sporty; (durchtrainiert) athletic; (Kleidung) smart but casual; **Sportmedizin** f sports medicine; **Sportplatz** m playing od sports field; **Sportschuh** m sports shoe; (sportlicher Schuh) casual shoe

Sportsfreund m (fig: umg) buddy

Sport- zW: **Sportverein** m sports club; **Sportwagen** m sports car; **Sportzeug** nt sports gear

Spot [spɔt] (-s, -s) m commercial, advertisement

Spott [ʃpɔt] (-(e)s) m mockery, ridicule; **spottbillig** adj dirt-cheap; **spotten** vi to mock; **spotten über** +akk to mock (at), ridicule; **das spottet jeder Beschreibung** that simply defies description

spöttisch [ˈʃpœtɪʃ] adj mocking

Spottpreis m ridiculously low price

sprach etc [ʃpraːx] vb siehe **sprechen**

sprachbegabt adj good at languages

Sprache (-, -n) f language; **heraus mit der ~!** (umg) come on, out with it!; **zur ~ kommen** to be mentioned; **in französischer ~** in French

Sprachenschule f language school

Sprach- zW: **Sprachfehler** m speech defect; **Sprachfertigkeit** f fluency; **Sprachführer** m phrase book; **Sprachgebrauch** m (linguistic) usage; **Sprachgefühl** nt feeling for language;

Sprachkenntnisse pl: **mit englischen Sprachkenntnissen** with a knowledge of English; **Sprachkurs** m language course; **Sprachlabor** nt language laboratory; **sprachlich** adj linguistic; **sprachlos** adj speechless; **Sprachrohr** nt megaphone; (fig) mouthpiece; **Sprachstörung** f speech disorder; **Sprachwissenschaft** f linguistics sing

sprang etc [ʃpraŋ] vb siehe **springen**

Spray [spre:] (**-s, -s**) m od nt spray; **Spraydose** f aerosol (can), spray

sprayen vt, vi to spray

Sprechanlage f intercom

Sprechblase f speech balloon

sprechen [ˈʃprɛçən] unreg vi to speak, talk ▷ vt to say; (Sprache) to speak; (Person) to speak to; **mit jdm ~** to speak od talk to sb; **das spricht für ihn** that's a point in his favour; **frei ~** to extemporize; **nicht gut auf jdn zu ~ sein** to be on bad terms with sb; **es spricht vieles dafür, dass ...** there is every reason to believe that ...; **hier spricht man Spanisch** Spanish spoken; **wir ~ uns noch!** you haven't heard the last of this!

Sprecher, in (**-s, -**) m(f) speaker; (für Gruppe) spokesman, spokeswoman; (Rundf, TV) announcer

Sprech- zW: **Sprechfunkgerät** nt radio telephone; **Sprechrolle** f speaking part; **Sprechstunde** f consultation (hour); (von Arzt) (doctor's) surgery (Brit); **Sprechstundenhilfe** f (doctor's) receptionist; **Sprechzimmer** nt consulting room, surgery (Brit)

spreizen [ˈʃpraɪtsən] vt to spread ▷ vr to put on airs

Sprengarbeiten pl blasting operations pl

sprengen [ˈʃprɛŋən] vt to sprinkle; (mit Sprengstoff) to blow up; (Gestein) to blast; (Versammlung) to break up

Spreng- zW: **Sprengkopf** m warhead; **Sprengladung** f explosive charge; **Sprengsatz** m explosive device; **Sprengstoff** m explosive(s pl); **Sprengstoffanschlag** m bomb attack

Spreu [ʃprɔy] (**-**) f chaff

spricht [ʃprɪçt] vb siehe **sprechen**

Sprichwort nt proverb

sprichwörtlich adj proverbial

sprießen [ˈʃpriːsən] vi (aus der Erde) to spring up; (Knospen) to shoot

Springbrunnen m fountain

springen [ˈʃprɪŋən] unreg vi to jump, leap; (Glas) to crack; (mit Kopfsprung) to dive; **etw ~ lassen** (umg) to fork out sth

springend adj: **der ~e Punkt** the crucial point

Springer (**-s, -**) m jumper; (Schach) knight

Springreiten nt show jumping

Springseil nt skipping rope

Sprinkler [ˈʃprɪŋklər] (**-s, -**) m sprinkler

Sprit [ʃprɪt] (**-(e)s, -e**) m (umg) petrol (Brit), gas(oline) (US), fuel

Spritzbeutel m icing bag

Spritze [ˈʃprɪtsə] (**-, -n**) f syringe; (Injektion)

injection; (an Schlauch) nozzle

spritzen vt to spray; (Wein) to dilute with soda water/lemonade; (Med) to inject ▷ vi to splash; (heißes Fett) to spit; (herausspritzen) to spurt; (aus einer Tube etc) to squirt; (Med) to give injections

Spritzer (**-s, -**) m (Farbspritzer, Wasserspritzer) splash

Spritzpistole f spray gun

Spritztour (umg) f spin

spröde [ˈʃprøːdə] adj brittle; (Person) reserved; (Haut) rough

Spross (**-es, -e**) m shoot

spross etc [ʃprɔs] vb siehe **sprießen**

Sprosse [ˈʃprɔsə] (**-, -n**) f rung

Sprossenwand f (Sport) wall bars pl

Sprössling [ˈʃprœslɪŋ] m offspring no pl

Spruch [ʃprʊx] (**-(e)s, -̈e**) m saying, maxim; (Jur) judgement; **Sprüche klopfen** (umg) to talk fancy; **Spruchband** nt banner

Sprüchemacher [ˈʃprʏçəmaxər] (umg) m patter-merchant

spruchreif adj: **die Sache ist noch nicht ~** it's not definite yet

Sprudel [ˈʃpruːdəl] (**-s, -**) m mineral water; (süß) lemonade

sprudeln vi to bubble

Sprüh- zW: **Sprühdose** f aerosol (can); **sprühen** vi to spray; (fig) to sparkle ▷ vt to spray; **Sprühregen** m drizzle

Sprung [ʃprʊŋ] (**-(e)s, -̈e**) m jump; (schwungvoll, fig: Gedankensprung) leap; (Riss) crack; **immer auf dem ~ sein** (umg) to be always on the go; **jdm auf die Sprünge helfen** (wohlwollend) to give sb a (helping) hand; **auf einen ~ bei jdm vorbeikommen** (umg) to drop in to see sb; **damit kann man keine großen Sprünge machen** (umg) you can't exactly live it up on that; **Sprungbrett** nt springboard; **Sprungfeder** f spring; **sprunghaft** adj erratic; (Aufstieg) rapid; **Sprungschanze** f ski jump; **Sprungturm** m diving platform

Spucke [ˈʃpʊkə] (**-**) f spit

spucken vt, vi to spit; **in die Hände ~** (fig) to roll up one's sleeves

Spucknapf m spittoon

Spucktüte f sickbag

Spuk [ʃpuːk] (**-(e)s, -e**) m haunting; (fig) nightmare; **spuken** vi to haunt; **hier spukt es** this place is haunted

Spülbecken [ˈʃpyːlbɛkən] nt sink

Spule [ˈʃpuːlə] (**-, -n**) f spool; (Elek) coil

Spüle [ˈʃpyːlə] (**-, -n**) f (kitchen) sink

spülen vt to rinse; (Geschirr) to wash, do; (Toilette) to flush ▷ vi to rinse; to wash up (Brit), do the dishes; to flush; **etw an Land ~** to wash sth ashore

Spül- zW: **Spülmaschine** f dishwasher; **Spülmittel** nt washing-up liquid (Brit), dish-washing liquid; **Spülstein** m sink

Spülung f rinsing; (Wasserspülung) flush; (Med) irrigation

Spund [ʃpʊnt] (**-(e)s, -e**) m: **junger ~**

(*veraltet*: *umg*) young pup

Spur [ʃpuːr] **(-, -en)** *f* trace; (*Fußspur, Radspur, Tonbandspur*) track; (*Fährte*) trail; (*Fahrspur*) lane; **jdm auf die ~ kommen** to get onto sb; **(seine) ~en hinterlassen** (*fig*) to leave its mark; **keine ~** (*umg*) not/nothing at all

spürbar *adj* noticeable, perceptible

spuren (*umg*) *vi* to obey; (*sich fügen*) to toe the line

spüren ['ʃpyːrən] *vt* to feel; **etw zu ~ bekommen** (*lit*) to feel sth; (*fig*) to feel the (full) force of sth

Spurenelement *nt* trace element

Spurensicherung *f* securing of evidence

Spürhund *m* tracker dog; (*fig*) sleuth

spurlos *adv* without (a) trace; **~ an jdm vorübergehen** to have no effect on sb

Spurt [ʃpʊrt] **(-(e)s, -s** *od* **-e)** *m* spurt

spurten *vi* (*Hilfsverb sein*: *Sport*) to spurt; (*umg*: *rennen*) to sprint

sputen ['ʃpuːtən] *vr* to make haste

Squash [skvɔʃ] **(-)** *nt* (*Sport*) squash

SS (-) *f abk* (= *Schutzstaffel*) SS ▷ *nt abk* = **Sommersemester**

s. S. *abk* (= *siehe Seite*) see p.

SSV *abk* = **Sommerschlussverkauf**

st *abk* (= *Stunde*) h.

St. *abk* (= *Stück*; (= *Stunde*) h.; (= *Sankt*) St

Staat [ʃtaːt] **(-(e)s, -en)** *m* state; (*Prunk*) show; (*Kleidung*) finery; **mit etw ~ machen** to show off *od* parade sth

staatenlos *adj* stateless

staatl. *abk* = **staatlich**

staatlich *adj* state *attrib*; state-run ▷ *adv*: **~ geprüft** state-certified

Staats- *zW*: **Staatsaffäre** *f* (*lit*) affair of state; (*fig*) major operation; **Staatsangehörige, r** *f(m)* national; **Staatsangehörigkeit** *f* nationality; **Staatsanleihe** *f* government bond; **Staatsanwalt** *m* public prosecutor; **Staatsbürger** *m* citizen; **Staatsbürgerschaft** *f* nationality; **doppelte Staatsbürgerschaft** dual nationality; **Staatsdienst** *m* civil service; **staatseigen** *adj* state-owned; **Staatseigentum** *nt* public ownership; **Staatsexamen** *nt* (*Univ*) degree; **staatsfeindlich** *adj* subversive; **Staatsgeheimnis** *nt* (*lit, fig hum*) state secret; **Staatshaushalt** *m* budget; **Staatskosten** *pl* public expenses *pl*; **Staatsmann (-(e)s, *pl* -männer)** *m* statesman; **staatsmännisch** *adj* statesmanlike; **Staatsoberhaupt** *nt* head of state; **Staatsschuld** *f* (*Fin*) national debt; **Staatssekretär** *m* secretary of state; **Staatsstreich** *m* coup (d'état); **Staatsverschuldung** *f* national debt

Stab [ʃtaːp] **(-(e)s, ¨e)** *m* rod; (*für Stabhochsprung*) pole; (*für Staffellauf*) baton; (*Gitterstab*) bar; (*Menschen*) staff; (*von Experten*) panel

Stäbchen ['ʃtɛːpçən] *nt* (*Essstäbchen*) chopstick

Stabhochsprung *m* pole vault

stabil [ʃtaˈbiːl] *adj* stable; (*Möbel*) sturdy

Stabilisator [ʃtabiliˈzaːtɔr] *m* stabilizer

stabilisieren [ʃtabiliˈziːrən] *vt* to stabilize

Stabilisierung *f* stabilization

Stabilität [ʃtabiliˈtɛːt] *f* stability

Stabreim *m* alliteration

Stabsarzt *m* (*Mil*) captain in the medical corps

stach *etc* [ʃtaːx] *vb siehe* **stechen**

Stachel ['ʃtaxəl] **(-s, -n)** *m* spike; (*von Tier*) spine; (*von Insekten*) sting; **Stachelbeere** *f* gooseberry; **Stacheldraht** *m* barbed wire

stachelig, stachlig *adj* prickly

Stachelschwein *nt* porcupine

Stadion ['ʃtaːdiɔn] **(-s, Stadien)** *nt* stadium

Stadium ['ʃtaːdiʊm] *nt* stage, phase

Stadt [ʃtat] **(-, ¨e)** *f* town; (*Großstadt*) city; (*Stadtverwaltung*) (town/city) council; **Stadtbad** *nt* municipal swimming baths *pl*; **stadtbekannt** *adj* known all over town; **Stadtbezirk** *m* municipal district

Städtchen ['ʃtɛːtçən] *nt* small town

Städtebau (-(e)s) *m* town planning

Städter, in (-s, -) *m(f)* town/city dweller, townie

Stadtgespräch *nt*: **(das) ~ sein** to be the talk of the town

Stadtguerilla *f* urban guerrilla

städtisch *adj* municipal; (*nicht ländlich*) urban

Stadt- *zW*: **Stadtkasse** *f* town/city treasury; **Stadtkern** *m* = **Stadtzentrum**; **Stadtkreis** *m* town/city borough; **Stadtmauer** *f* city wall(s *pl*); **Stadtmitte** *f* town/city centre (*Brit*) *od* center (*US*); **Stadtpark** *m* municipal park; **Stadtplan** *m* street map; **Stadtrand** *m* outskirts *pl*; **Stadtrat** *m* (*Behörde*) (town/city) council; **Stadtstreicher** *m* street vagrant; **Stadtstreicherin** *f* bag lady; **Stadtteil** *m* district, part of town; **Stadtverwaltung** *f* (*Behörde*) municipal authority; **Stadtviertel** *m* district *od* part of a town; **Stadtzentrum** *nt* town/city centre (*Brit*) *od* center (*US*)

Staffel ['ʃtafəl] **(-, -n)** *f* rung; (*Sport*) relay (team); (*Aviat*) squadron

Staffelei [ʃtafəˈlaɪ] *f* easel

Staffellauf *m* relay race

staffeln *vt* to graduate

Staffelung *f* graduation

Stagnation [ʃtagnatsiˈoːn] *f* stagnation

stagnieren [ʃtaˈgniːrən] *vi* to stagnate

Stahl (-(e)s, ¨e) *m* steel

stahl *etc* [ʃtaːl] *vb siehe* **stehlen**

Stahlhelm *m* steel helmet

stak *etc* [ʃtaːk] *vb siehe* **stecken**

Stall [ʃtal] **(-(e)s, ¨e)** *m* stable; (*Kaninchenstall*) hutch; (*Schweinestall*) sty; (*Hühnerstall*) henhouse

Stallung *f* stables *pl*

Stamm [ʃtam] **(-(e)s, ¨e)** *m* (*Baumstamm*) trunk; (*Menschenstamm*) tribe; (*Gram*) stem; (*Bakterienstamm*) strain; **Stammaktie** *f* ordinary share, common stock (*US*); **Stammbaum** *m* family tree; (*von Tier*) pedigree; **Stammbuch** *nt* book of family events with legal documents

stammeln *vt, vi* to stammer

stammen *vi*: **~ von** *od* **aus** to come from

Stamm- zW: **Stammform** f base form; **Stammgast** m regular (customer); **Stammhalter** m son and heir

stämmig ['ʃtɛmɪç] adj sturdy; (Mensch) stocky; **Stämmigkeit** f sturdiness; stockiness

Stamm- zW: **Stammkapital** nt (Fin) ordinary share od common stock (US) capital; **Stammkunde** m, **Stammkundin** f regular (customer); **Stammlokal** nt favourite (Brit) od favorite (US) café/restaurant etc; (Kneipe) local (Brit); **Stammplatz** m usual seat; **Stammtisch** m (Tisch in Gasthaus) table reserved for the regulars; **Stammzelle** f stem cell; **embryonale Stammzellen** embryonic stem cells

stampfen ['ʃtampfən] vi to stamp; (stapfen) to tramp ▷ vt (mit Stampfer) to mash

Stampfer (-s, -) m (Stampfgerät) masher

Stand (-(e)s, ̈e) m position; (Wasserstand, Benzinstand etc) level; (Zählerstand etc) reading; (Stehen) standing position; (Zustand) state; (Spielstand) score; (Messestand etc) stand; (Klasse) class; (Beruf) profession; **bei jdm** od **gegen jdn einen schweren ~ haben** (fig) to have a hard time of it with sb; **etw auf den neuesten ~ bringen** to bring sth up to date; siehe auch **außerstande; imstande; zustande**

stand etc [ʃtant] vb siehe **stehen**

Standard ['ʃtandart] (-s, -s) m standard; **Standardausführung** f standard design

standardisieren [ʃtandardi'ziːrən] vt to standardize

Standarte (-, -n) f (Mil, Pol) standard

Standbild nt statue

Ständchen ['ʃtɛntçən] nt serenade

Ständer (-s, -) m stand

Standes- zW: **Standesamt** nt registry office (Brit), city/county clerk's office (US); **standesamtlich** adj: **standesamtliche Trauung** registry office wedding (Brit), civil marriage ceremony; **Standesbeamte, r** m registrar; **Standesbewusstsein** nt status consciousness; **Standesdünkel** m snobbery; **standesgemäß** adj, adv according to one's social position; **Standesunterschied** m social difference

Stand- zW: **standfest** adj (Tisch, Leiter) stable, steady; (fig) steadfast; **standhaft** adj steadfast; **Standhaftigkeit** f steadfastness; **standhalten** unreg vi: **(jdm/etw) standhalten** to stand firm (against sb/sth), resist (sb/sth)

ständig ['ʃtɛndɪç] adj permanent; (ununterbrochen) constant, continual

Stand- zW: **Standlicht** nt sidelights pl (Brit), parking lights pl (US); **Standort** m location; (Mil) garrison; **Standpauke** (umg) f: **jdm eine Standpauke halten** to give sb a lecture; **Standpunkt** m standpoint; **standrechtlich** adj: **standrechtlich erschießen** to put before a firing squad; **Standspur** f (Aut) hard shoulder (Brit), berm (US)

Stange ['ʃtaŋə] (-, -n) f stick; (Stab) pole; (Querstange) bar; (Zigaretten) carton; **von der ~** (Comm) off the peg (Brit) od rack (US); **eine ~**

Geld quite a packet; **jdm die ~ halten** (umg) to stick up for sb; **bei der ~ bleiben** (umg) to stick at od to sth

Stängel ['ʃtɛŋl] (-s, -) m stalk; **vom ~ fallen** (umg: überrascht sein) to be staggered

Stangenbohne f runner bean

Stangenbrot nt French bread; (Laib) French stick (loaf)

stank etc [ʃtaŋk] vb siehe **stinken**

stänkern ['ʃtɛŋkərn] (umg) vi to stir things up

Stanniol [ʃtani'oːl] (-s, -e) nt tinfoil

Stanze ['ʃtantsə] (-, -n) f stanza; (Tech) stamp

stanzen vt to stamp; (Löcher) to punch

Stapel ['ʃtaːpəl] (-s, -) m pile; (Naut) stocks pl; **Stapellauf** m launch

stapeln vt to pile (up)

Stapelverarbeitung f (Comput) batch processing

stapfen ['ʃtapfən] vi to trudge, plod

Star¹ [ʃtaːr] (-(e)s, -e) m starling; **grauer/grüner ~** (Med) cataract/glaucoma

Star² [ʃtaːr] (-s, -s) m (Filmstar etc) star

starb etc [ʃtarp] vb siehe **sterben**

stark [ʃtark] adj strong; (heftig, groß) heavy; (Maßangabe) thick; (umg: hervorragend) great ▷ adv very; (beschädigt etc) badly; (vergrößert, verkleinert) greatly; **das ist ein ~es Stück!** (umg) that's a bit much!; **er ist ~ erkältet** he has a bad cold; siehe auch **starkmachen**

Stärke ['ʃtɛrkə] (-, -n) f strength (auch fig); heaviness; thickness; (von Mannschaft) size; (Wäschestärke, Koch) starch; **Stärkemehl** nt (Koch) thickening agent

stärken vt (lit, fig) to strengthen; (Wäsche) to starch; (Selbstbewusstsein) to boost; (Gesundheit) to improve; (erfrischen) to fortify ▷ vi to be fortifying; **~des Mittel** tonic

starkmachen vr: **sich für etw ~** (umg) to stand up for sth

Starkstrom m heavy current

Stärkung ['ʃtɛrkʊŋ] f strengthening; (Essen) refreshment

Stärkungsmittel nt tonic

starr [ʃtar] adj stiff; (unnachgiebig) rigid; (Blick) staring

starren vi to stare; **~ vor** +dat od **von** (voll von) to be covered in; (Waffen) to be bristling with; **vor sich akk hin ~** to stare straight ahead

starr- zW: **Starrheit** f rigidity; **starrköpfig** adj stubborn; **Starrsinn** m obstinacy

Start [ʃtart] (-(e)s, -e) m start; (Aviat) takeoff; **Startautomatik** f (Aut) automatic choke; **Startbahn** f runway; **starten** vi to start; (Aviat) to take off ▷ vt to start; **Starter** (-s, -) m starter; **Starterlaubnis** f takeoff clearance; **Starthilfe** f (Aviat) rocket-assisted takeoff; (fig) initial aid; **jdm Starthilfe geben** to help sb get off the ground; **Starthilfekabel** nt jump leads pl (Brit), jumper cables pl (US); **startklar** adj (Aviat) clear for takeoff; (Sport) ready to start; **Startkommando** nt (Sport) starting signal; **Startzeichen** nt start signal

Stasi ['ʃtaːzi] (-) (umg) f abk

(*früher:* = *Staatssicherheitsdienst der DDR*) Stasi; *see culture note*

● **STASI**
●
● *Stasi*, an abbreviation of
● Staatssicherheitsdienst, the DDR
● secret service, was founded in 1950 and
● disbanded in 1989. The Stasi organized
● an extensive spy network of full-time
● and part-time workers who often held
● positions of trust in both the DDR and the
● BRD. They held personal files on 6 million
● people.

Station [ʃtatsi'oːn] *f* station; (*Krankenstation*) hospital ward; (*Haltestelle*) stop; ~ **machen** to stop off

stationär [ʃtatsio'nɛːr] *adj* stationary; (*Med*) in-patient *attrib*

stationieren [ʃtatsio'niːrən] *vt* to station; (*Atomwaffen etc*) to deploy

Stations- *zW:* **Stationsarzt** *m* ward doctor; **Stationsärztin** *f* ward doctor; **Stationsvorsteher** *m* (*Eisenb*) stationmaster

statisch ['ʃtaːtɪʃ] *adj* static

Statist, in [ʃta'tɪst(ɪn)] *m(f)* (*Film*) extra; (*Theat*) supernumerary

Statistik *f* statistic; (*Wissenschaft*) statistics *sing*

Statistiker, in (**-s, -**) *m(f)* statistician

statistisch *adj* statistical

Stativ [ʃta'tiːf] (**-s, -e**) *nt* tripod

statt *konj* instead of ▷ *präp* (+*dat od gen*) instead of

stattdessen *adv* instead

Stätte ['ʃtɛtə] (**-, -n**) *f* place

statt- *zW:* **stattfinden** *unreg vi* to take place; **statthaft** *adj* admissible; **Statthalter** *m* governor; **stattlich** *adj* imposing, handsome; (*Bursche*) strapping; (*Sammlung*) impressive; (*Familie*) large; (*Summe*) handsome

Statue ['ʃtaːtuə] (**-, -n**) *f* statue

Statur [ʃta'tuːr] *f* build

Status ['ʃtaːtʊs] (**-, -**) *m* status; **Statussymbol** *nt* status symbol

Statuten [ʃta'tuːtən] *pl* by(e)-law(s *pl*)

Stau [ʃtaʊ] (**-(e)s, -e**) *m* blockage; (*Verkehrsstau*) (traffic) jam

Staub [ʃtaʊp] (**-(e)s**) *m* dust; ~ **saugen** to vacuum; ~ **wischen** to dust; **sich aus dem ~ machen** (*umg*) to clear off

stauben ['ʃtaʊbən] *vi* to be dusty

Staubfaden *m* (*Bot*) stamen

staubig ['ʃtaʊbɪç] *adj* dusty

Staub- *zW:* **Staublappen** *m* duster; **Staublunge** *f* (*Med*) dust on the lung; **staubsaugen** (*pp* **staubgesaugt**) *vi untr* to vacuum; **Staubsauger** *m* vacuum cleaner; **Staubtuch** *nt* duster

Staudamm *m* dam

Staude ['ʃtaʊdə] (**-, -n**) *f* shrub

stauen ['ʃtaʊən] *vt* (*Wasser*) to dam up; (*Blut*) to stop the flow of ▷ *vr* (*Wasser*) to become

dammed up; (*Verkehr, Med*) to become congested; (*Menschen*) to collect together; (*Gefühle*) to build up

staunen ['ʃtaʊnən] *vi* to be astonished; **da kann man nur noch** ~ it's just amazing; **Staunen** (**-s**) *nt* amazement

Stausee ['ʃtaʊzeː] *m* reservoir; artificial lake

Stauung ['ʃtaʊʊŋ] *f* (*von Wasser*) damming-up; (*von Blut, Verkehr*) congestion

Std. *abk* (= *Stunde*) h.

stdl. *abk* = **stündlich**

Steak [ʃteːk] (**-s, -s**) *nt* steak

Stechen ['ʃtɛçən] (**-s, -**) *nt* (*Sport*) play-off; (*Springreiten*) jump-off; (*Schmerz*) sharp pain

stechen *unreg vt* (*mit Nadel etc*) to prick; (*mit Messer*) to stab; (*mit Finger*) to poke; (*Biene etc*) to sting; (*Mücke*) to bite; (*Karten*) to take; (*Kunst*) to engrave; (*Torf, Spargel*) to cut ▷ *vi* (*Sonne*) to beat down; (*mit Stechkarte*) to clock in ▷ *vr:* **sich** *akk od dat* **in den Finger** ~ to prick one's finger; **es sticht** it is prickly; **in See** ~ to put to sea

stechend *adj* piercing, stabbing; (*Geruch*) pungent

Stech- *zW:* **Stechginster** *m* gorse; **Stechkarte** *f* clocking-in card; **Stechmücke** *f* gnat; **Stechpalme** *f* holly; **Stechuhr** *f* time clock

Steck- *zW:* **Steckbrief** *m* "wanted" poster; **steckbrieflich** *adv:* **steckbrieflich gesucht werden** to be wanted; **Steckdose** *f* (wall) socket

stecken ['ʃtɛkən] *vt* to put; (*einführen*) to insert; (*Nadel*) to stick; (*Pflanzen*) to plant; (*beim Nähen*) to pin ▷ *vi* (*auch unreg*) to be; (*festsitzen*) to be stuck; (*Nadeln*) to stick; **etw in etw** *akk* ~ (*umg: Geld, Mühe*) to put sth into sth; (: *Zeit*) to devote sth to sth; **der Schlüssel steckt** the key is in the lock; **wo steckt er?** where has he got to?; **zeigen, was in einem steckt** to show what one is made of; ~ **bleiben** to get stuck; ~ **lassen** to leave in

Steckenpferd *nt* hobbyhorse

Stecker (**-s, -**) *m* (*Elek*) plug

Steck- *zW:* **Stecknadel** *f* pin; **Steckrübe** *f* swede, turnip; **Steckschlüssel** *m* box spanner (*Brit*) *od* wrench (*US*); **Steckzwiebel** *f* bulb

Steg [ʃteːk] (**-(e)s, -e**) *m* small bridge; (*Anlegesteg*) landing stage

Stegreif *m:* **aus dem** ~ just like that

Stehaufmännchen ['ʃteː|aʊfmɛnçən] *nt* (*Spielzeug*) tumbler

stehen ['ʃteːən] *unreg vi* to stand; (*sich befinden*) to be; (*in Zeitung*) to say; (*angehalten haben*) to have stopped ▷ *vi unpers:* **es steht schlecht um ...** things are bad for ... ▷ *vr:* **sich gut/ schlecht** ~ to be well-off/badly off; **zu jdm/ etw** ~ to stand by sb/sth; **jdm** ~ to suit sb; **ich tue, was in meinen Kräften steht** I'll do everything I can; **es steht 2:1 für München** the score is 2-1 to Munich; **mit dem Dativ** ~ (*Gram*) to take the dative; **auf Betrug steht eine Gefängnisstrafe** the penalty for fraud is imprisonment; **wie** ~ **Sie dazu?** what are your views on that?; **wie stehts?** how are things?;

(*Sport*) what's the score?; **wie steht es damit?** how about it?; ~ **bleiben** (*Uhr*) to stop; (*Zeit*) to stand still; (*Auto, Zug*) to stand; (*Fehler*) to stay as it is; (*Verkehr, Produktion etc*) to come to a standstill *od* stop; ~ **lassen** to leave; (*Bart*) to grow; **alles ~ und liegen lassen** to drop everything

stehend *adj attrib* (*Fahrzeug*) stationary; (*Gewässer*) stagnant; (*ständig: Heer*) regular

Stehlampe *f* standard lamp (*Brit*), floor lamp (*US*)

stehlen ['ʃteːlən] *unreg vt* to steal

Stehplatz *m*: **ein ~ kostet 15 Euro** a standing ticket costs 15 euros

Stehvermögen *nt* staying power, stamina

Steiermark ['ʃtaɪrmark] *f*: **die ~** Styria

steif [ʃtaɪf] *adj* stiff; **~ und fest auf etw** *dat* **beharren** to insist stubbornly on sth

Steifftier® ['ʃtaɪftiːr] *nt* soft toy animal

Steifheit *f* stiffness

Steigbügel ['ʃtaɪkbyːgəl] *m* stirrup

Steigeisen *nt* crampon

steigen *unreg vi* to rise; (*klettern*) to climb ▷ *vt* (*Treppen, Stufen*) to climb (up); **das Blut stieg ihm in den Kopf** the blood rushed to his head; **~ in** +*akk*/**auf** +*akk* to get in/on

Steiger (**-s, -**) *m* (*Min*) pit foreman

steigern *vt* to raise; (*Gram*) to compare ▷ *vi* (*Auktion*) to bid ▷ *vr* to increase

Steigerung *f* raising; (*Gram*) comparison

Steigung *f* incline, gradient, rise

steil [ʃtaɪl] *adj* steep; **Steilhang** *m* steep slope; **Steilpass** *m* (*Sport*) through ball

Stein [ʃtaɪn] (**-(e)s, -e**) *m* stone; (*in Uhr*) jewel; **mir fällt ein ~ vom Herzen!** (*fig*) that's a load off my mind!; **bei jdm einen ~ im Brett haben** (*fig: umg*) to be well in with sb; **jdm ~e in den Weg legen** to make things difficult for sb; **Steinadler** *m* golden eagle; **steinalt** *adj* ancient; **Steinbock** *m* (*Astrol*) Capricorn; **Steinbruch** *m* quarry

steinern *adj* (made of) stone; (*fig*) stony

Stein- *zW*: **Steinerweichen** *nt*: **zum Steinerweichen weinen** to cry heartbreakingly; **Steingarten** *m* rockery; **Steingut** *nt* stoneware; **steinhart** *adj* hard as stone

steinig *adj* stony

steinigen *vt* to stone

Stein- *zW*: **Steinkohle** *f* mineral coal; **Steinmetz** (**-es, -e**) *m* stonemason; **steinreich** (*umg*) *adj* stinking rich; **Steinschlag** *m*: **„Achtung Steinschlag"** "danger – falling stones"; **Steinwurf** *m* (*fig*) stone's throw; **Steinzeit** *f* Stone Age

Steiß [ʃtaɪs] (**-es, -e**) *m* rump; **Steißbein** *nt* (*Anat*) coccyx

Stelle ['ʃtɛlə] (**-, -n**) *f* place; (*Arbeit*) post, job; (*Amt*) office; (*Abschnitt*) passage; (*Textstelle, bes beim Zitieren*) reference; **drei ~n hinter dem Komma** (*Math*) three decimal places; **eine freie** *od* **offene ~** a vacancy; **an dieser ~** in this place, here; **an anderer ~** elsewhere;

nicht von der ~ kommen not to make any progress; **auf der ~** (*fig: sofort*) on the spot; *siehe auch* **anstelle**

stellen *vt* to put; (*Uhr etc*) to set; (*zur Verfügung stellen*) to supply; (*fassen: Dieb*) to apprehend; (*Antrag, Forderung*) to make; (*Aufnahme*) to pose; (*arrangieren: Szene*) to arrange ▷ *vr* (*sich aufstellen*) to stand; (*sich einfinden*) to present o.s.; (*bei Polizei*) to give o.s. up; (*vorgeben*) to pretend (to be); **das Radio lauter/leiser ~** to turn the radio up/down; **auf sich** *akk* **selbst gestellt sein** (*fig*) to have to fend for o.s.; **sich hinter jdn/etw ~** (*fig*) to support sb/sth; **sich einer Herausforderung ~** to take up a challenge; **sich zu etw ~** to have an opinion of sth

Stellen- *zW*: **Stellenangebot** *nt* offer of a post; (*in Zeitung*): **„Stellenangebote"** "vacancies"; **Stellenanzeige** *f* job advertisement *od* ad (*umg*); **Stellengesuch** *nt* application for a post; **„Stellengesuche"** "situations wanted"; **Stellenmarkt** *m* job market; (*in Zeitung*) appointments section; **Stellennachweis** *m* employment agency; **Stellenvermittlung** *f* employment agency; **stellenweise** *adv* in places; **Stellenwert** *m* (*fig*) status

Stellung *f* position; (*Mil*) line; **~ nehmen zu** to comment on

Stellungnahme *f* comment

stellungslos *adj* unemployed

stellv. *abk* = **stellvertretend**

Stell- *zW*: **stellvertretend** *adj* deputy *attrib*, acting *attrib*; **Stellvertreter** *m* (*von Amts wegen*) deputy, representative; **Stellwerk** *nt* (*Eisenb*) signal box

Stelze ['ʃtɛltsə] (**-, -n**) *f* stilt

stelzen (*umg*) *vi* to stalk

Stemmbogen *m* (*Ski*) stem turn

Stemmeisen *nt* crowbar

stemmen ['ʃtɛmən] *vt* to lift (up); (*drücken*) to press; **sich ~ gegen** (*fig*) to resist, oppose

Stempel ['ʃtɛmpəl] (**-s, -**) *m* stamp; (*Poststempel*) postmark; (*Tech: Prägestempel*) die; (*Bot*) pistil; **Stempelgebühr** *f* stamp duty; **Stempelkissen** *nt* inkpad

stempeln *vt* to stamp; (*Briefmarke*) to cancel ▷ *vi* (*umg: Stempeluhr betätigen*) to clock in/out; **~ gehen** (*umg*) to be *od* go on the dole (*Brit*) *od* on welfare (*US*)

Stengel ['ʃtɛŋəl] (**-s, -**) *m siehe* **Stängel**

Steno ['ʃteno] (*umg*) *f* shorthand; **Stenograf, in** [-graːf(ɪn)] *m(f)* (*im Büro*) shorthand secretary; **Stenografie** [-graˈfiː] *f* shorthand; **stenografieren** [-graˈfiːrən] *vt, vi* to write (in) shorthand; **Stenogramm** [-ˈgram] *nt* text in shorthand; **Stenotypist, in** [-tyˈpɪst(ɪn)] *m(f)* shorthand typist (*Brit*), stenographer (*US*)

Steppdecke *f* quilt

Steppe (**-, -n**) *f* steppe

steppen ['ʃtɛpən] *vt* to stitch ▷ *vi* to tap-dance

Stepptanz *m* tap-dance

Sterbe- *zW*: **Sterbebett** *nt* deathbed; **Sterbefall** *m* death; **Sterbehilfe** *f* euthanasia; **Sterbekasse** *f* death benefit fund

S

sterben ['ʃtɛrbən] *unreg vi* to die; **an einer Krankheit/Verletzung** ~ to die of an illness/from an injury; **er ist für mich gestorben** (*fig: umg*) he might as well be dead
Sterben *nt*: **im ~ liegen** to be dying
sterbenslangweilig (*umg*) *adj* deadly boring
Sterbenswörtchen (*umg*) *nt*: **er hat kein ~ gesagt** he didn't say a word
Sterbeurkunde *f* death certificate
sterblich ['ʃtɛrplıç] *adj* mortal; **Sterblichkeit** *f* mortality; **Sterblichkeitsziffer** *f* death rate
stereo- ['steːreo] *in zw* stereo(-); **Stereoanlage** *f* stereo unit; **stereotyp** *adj* stereotyped
steril [ʃteˈriːl] *adj* sterile
sterilisieren [ʃteriliˈziːrən] *vt* to sterilize
Sterilisierung *f* sterilization
Stern [ʃtɛrn] (**-(e)s, -e**) *m* star; **das steht (noch) in den ~en** (*fig*) it's in the lap of the gods; **Sternbild** *nt* constellation; **Sternchen** *nt* asterisk; **Sternenbanner** *nt* Stars and Stripes *sing*; **sternhagelvoll** (*umg*) *adj* legless; **Sternschnuppe** (**-, -n**) *f* meteor, falling star; **Sternstunde** *f* historic moment; **Sternwarte** *f* observatory; **Sternzeichen** *nt* (*Astrol*) sign of the zodiac
stet [ʃteːt] *adj* steady
Stethoskop [ʃtetoˈskoːp] (**-(e)s, -e**) *nt* stethoscope
stetig *adj* constant, continual; (*Math: Funktion*) continuous
stets *adv* continually, always
Steuer¹ ['ʃtɔʏər] (**-s, -**) *nt* (*Naut*) helm; (*Steuerruder*) rudder; (*Aut*) steering wheel; **am ~ sitzen** (*Aut*) to be at the wheel; (*Aviat*) to be at the controls
Steuer² (**-, -n**) *f* tax
Steuer- *zW*: **Steuerbefreiung** *f* tax exemption; **steuerbegünstigt** *adj* (*Investitionen, Hypothek*) tax-deductible; (*Waren*) taxed at a lower rate; **Steuerberater,** *in* *m(f)* tax consultant; **Steuerbescheid** *m* tax assessment; **Steuerbord** *nt* starboard; **Steuererhöhung** *f* tax increase; **Steuererklärung** *f* tax return; **steuerfrei** *adj* tax-free; **Steuerfreibetrag** *m* tax allowance; **Steuerhinterziehung** *f* tax evasion; **Steuerjahr** *nt* fiscal *od* tax year; **Steuerkarte** *f* tax notice; **Steuerklasse** *f* tax group; **Steuerknüppel** *m* control column; (*Aviat, Comput*) joystick; **steuerlich** *adj* tax *attrib*; **Steuermann** (**-(e)s,** *pl* **-männer** *od* **-leute**) *m* helmsman
steuern *vt* to steer; (*Flugzeug*) to pilot; (*Entwicklung, Tonstärke*) to control ▷ *vi* to steer; (*in Flugzeug etc*) to be at the controls; (*bei Entwicklung etc*) to be in control
Steuer- *zW*: **Steuernummer** *f* ≈ National Insurance Number (*Brit*), ≈ Social Security Number (*US*); **Steuerparadies** *nt* tax haven; **steuerpflichtig** *adj* taxable; (*Person*) liable to pay tax; **Steuerprogression** *f* progressive taxation; **Steuerprüfung** *f* tax inspector's investigation; **Steuerrad** *nt* steering wheel; **Steuerrückvergütung** *f* tax rebate;

Steuersenkung *f* tax cut
Steuerung *f* steering (*auch AUT*), piloting; control; (*Vorrichtung*) controls *pl*; **automatische ~** (*Aviat*) autopilot; (*Tech*) automatic steering (device)
Steuer- *zW*: **Steuervergünstigung** *f* tax relief; **Steuerzahler** *m* taxpayer; **Steuerzuschlag** *m* additional tax
Steward ['stjuːərt] (**-s, -s**) *m* steward
Stewardess ['stjuːərdɛs] (**-, -en**) *f* stewardess
StGB (**-s**) *nt abk* = **Strafgesetzbuch**
stibitzen [ʃtiˈbıtsən] (*umg*) *vt* to pilfer, pinch (*umg*)
Stich [ʃtıç] (**-(e)s, -e**) *m* (*Insektenstich*) sting; (*Messerstich*) stab; (*beim Nähen*) stitch; (*Färbung*) tinge; (*Karten*) trick; (*Art*) engraving; (*fig*) pang; **ein ~ ins Rote** a tinge of red; **einen ~ haben** (*umg: Esswaren*) to be bad *od* off (*Brit*); (*: Mensch: verrückt sein*) to be nuts; **jdn im ~ lassen** to leave sb in the lurch
Stichel (**-s, -**) *m* engraving tool, style
Stichelei [ʃtıçəˈlaı] *f* jibe, taunt
sticheln *vi* (*fig*) to jibe; (*pej: umg*) to make snide remarks
Stich- *zW*: **Stichflamme** *f* tongue of flame; **stichhaltig** *adj* valid; (*Beweis*) conclusive; **Stichprobe** *f* spot check
sticht [ʃtıçt] *vb siehe* **stechen**
Stichtag *m* qualifying date
Stichwahl *f* final ballot
Stichwort *nt* (*pl* **-worte**) cue; (*: für Vortrag*) note (*pl* **-wörter**) (*in Wörterbuch*) headword; **Stichwortkatalog** *m* classified catalogue (*Brit*) *od* catalog (*US*); **Stichwortverzeichnis** *nt* index
Stichwunde *f* stab wound
sticken ['ʃtıkən] *vt, vi* to embroider
Stickerei [ʃtıkəˈraı] *f* embroidery
stickig *adj* stuffy, close
Stickstoff (**-(e)s**) *m* nitrogen
stieben ['ʃtiːbən] *vi* (*geh: sprühen*) to fly
Stief- ['ʃtiːf] *in zw* step-
Stiefel ['ʃtiːfəl] (**-s, -**) *m* boot; (*Trinkgefäß*) large boot-shaped beer glass
Stief- *zW*: **Stiefkind** *nt* stepchild; (*fig*) Cinderella; **Stiefmutter** *f* stepmother; **Stiefmütterchen** *nt* pansy; **stiefmütterlich** *adj* (*fig*): **jdn/etw stiefmütterlich behandeln** to pay little attention to sb/sth; **Stiefvater** *m* stepfather
stieg *etc* [ʃtiːk] *vb siehe* **steigen**
Stiege ['ʃtiːgə] (**-, -n**) *f* staircase
Stieglitz ['ʃtiːglıts] (**-es, -e**) *m* goldfinch
stiehlt [ʃtiːlt] *vb siehe* **stehlen**
Stiel [ʃtiːl] (**-(e)s, -e**) *m* handle; (*Bot*) stalk
Stielaugen *pl* (*fig: umg*): **er machte ~** his eyes (nearly) popped out of his head
Stier (**-(e)s, -e**) *m* bull; (*Astrol*) Taurus
stier [ʃtiːr] *adj* staring, fixed
stieren *vi* to stare
Stierkampf *m* bullfight
stieß *etc* [ʃtiːs] *vb siehe* **stoßen**
Stift [ʃtıft] (**-(e)s, -e**) *m* peg; (*Nagel*) tack; (*Buntstift*) crayon; (*Bleistift*) pencil;

(*umg*: *Lehrling*) apprentice (boy)

stiften *vt* to found; (*Unruhe*) to cause; (*spenden*) to contribute; **~ gehen** to hop it

Stifter, in (**-s, -**) *m(f)* founder

Stiftung *f* donation; (*Organisation*) foundation

Stiftzahn *m* post crown

Stil [ʃtiːl] (**-(e)s, -e**) *m* style; (*Eigenart*) way, manner; **Stilblüte** *f* howler; **Stilbruch** *m* stylistic incongruity

stilistisch [ʃti'lɪstɪʃ] *adj* stylistic

still [ʃtɪl] *adj* quiet; (*unbewegt*) still; (*heimlich*) secret; **ich dachte mir im S~en** I thought to myself; **er ist ein ~es Wasser** he's a deep one; **~er Teilhaber** (*Comm*) sleeping (*Brit*) *od* silent (*US*) partner; **der S~e Ozean** the Pacific (Ocean); **~ stehen** (*unbewegt*) to stand still

Stille (**-, -n**) *f* quietness; stillness; **in aller ~** quietly

Stilleben *nt siehe* **Stillleben**

Stillegung *f siehe* **Stilllegung**

stillen *vt* to stop; (*befriedigen*) to satisfy; (*Säugling*) to breast-feed

still- *zW*: **stillgestanden** *interj* attention!; **Stillhalteabkommen** *nt* (*Fin, fig*) moratorium; **stillhalten** *unreg vi* to keep still; **Stillleben** *nt* still life; **stilllegen** *vt* to close down; **Stilllegung** *f* (*Betrieb*) shut-down, closure; **stillliegen** *unreg vi* (*außer Betrieb sein*) to be shut down; (*lahmgelegt sein*) to be at a standstill; **Stillschweigen** *nt* silence; **stillschweigen** *unreg vi* to be silent; **stillschweigend** *adj* silent; (*Einverständnis*) tacit ▷ *adv* silently; tacitly; **Stillstand** *m* standstill; **stillstehen** *unreg vi* to stand still

Stilmöbel *pl* reproduction *od* (*antik*) period furniture *sing*

stilvoll *adj* stylish

Stimm- *zW*: **Stimmabgabe** *f* voting; **Stimmbänder** *pl* vocal cords *pl*; **stimmberechtigt** *adj* entitled to vote; **Stimmbruch** *m*: **er ist im Stimmbruch** his voice is breaking

Stimme [ʃtɪmə] (**-, -n**) *f* voice; (*Wahlstimme*) vote; (*Mus: Rolle*) part; **mit leiser/lauter ~** in a soft/loud voice; **seine ~ abgeben** to vote

stimmen *vi* (*richtig sein*) to be right; (*wählen*) to vote ▷ *vt* (*Instrument*) to tune; **stimmt so!** that's all right; **für/gegen etw ~** to vote for/against sth; **jdn traurig ~** to make sb feel sad

Stimmen- *zW*: **Stimmengewirr** *nt* babble of voices; **Stimmengleichheit** *f* tied vote; **Stimmenmehrheit** *f* majority (of votes)

Stimm- *zW*: **Stimmenthaltung** *f* abstention; **Stimmgabel** *f* tuning fork; **stimmhaft** *adj* voiced

stimmig *adj* harmonious

Stimm- *zW*: **stimmlos** *adj* (*Ling*) unvoiced; **Stimmrecht** *nt* right to vote; **stimmrechtslos** *adj*: **stimmrechtslose Aktien** "A" shares

Stimmung *f* mood; (*Atmosphäre*) atmosphere; (*Moral*) morale; **in ~ kommen** to liven up; **~ gegen/für jdn/etw machen** to stir up (public) opinion against/in favour of sb/sth

Stimmungs- *zW*: **Stimmungskanone** (*umg*) *f* life and soul of the party; **Stimmungsmache** (*pej*) *f* cheap propaganda; **stimmungsvoll** *adj* (*Atmosphäre*) enjoyable; (*Gedicht*) full of atmosphere

Stimmzettel *m* ballot paper

stinken [ʃtɪŋkən] *unreg vi* to stink; **die Sache stinkt mir** (*umg*) I'm fed-up to the back teeth (with it)

Stink- *zW*: **stinkfaul** (*umg*) *adj* bone-lazy; **stinklangweilig** (*umg*) *adj* deadly boring; **Stinktier** *nt* skunk; **Stinkwut** (*umg*) *f*: **eine Stinkwut (auf jdn) haben** to be livid (with sb)

Stipendium [ʃti'pɛndiʊm] *nt* grant; (*als Auszeichnung*) scholarship

Stippvisite [ʃtɪpvi'ziːtə] (*umg*) *f* flying visit

stirbt [ʃtɪrpt] *vb siehe* **sterben**

Stirn [ʃtɪrn] (**-, -en**) *f* forehead, brow; (*Frechheit*) impudence; **die ~ haben zu ...** to have the nerve to ...; **Stirnband** *nt* headband; **Stirnhöhle** *f* sinus; **Stirnrunzeln** (**-s**) *nt* frown

stob *etc* [ʃtoːp] *vb siehe* **stieben**

stöbern [ʃtøːbərn] *vi* to rummage

stochern [ʃtɔxərn] *vi* to poke (about)

Stock[1] [ʃtɔk] (**-(e)s, ⁻e**) *m* stick; (*Rohrstock*) cane; (*Zeigestock*) pointer; (*Bot*) stock; **über ~ und Stein** up hill and down dale

Stock[2] [ʃtɔk] (**-(e)s, - od -werke**) *m* storey (*Brit*), story (*US*); **im ersten ~** on the first (*Brit*) *od* second (*US*) floor

stock- *in zw* (*vor adj: umg*) completely

Stöckelschuh [ʃtœkəlʃuː] *m* stiletto-heeled shoe

stocken *vi* to stop, pause; (*Arbeit, Entwicklung*) to make no progress; (*im Satz*) to break off; (*Verkehr*) to be held up

stockend *adj* halting

stockfinster (*umg*) *adj* pitch-dark

Stockholm [ʃtɔkhɔlm] (**-s**) *nt* Stockholm

stocksauer (*umg*) *adj* pissed-off (!)

stocktaub *adj* stone-deaf

Stockung *f* stoppage

Stockwerk *nt* storey (*Brit*), story (*US*), floor

Stoff [ʃtɔf] (**-(e)s, -e**) *m* (*Gewebe*) material, cloth; (*Materie*) matter; (*von Buch etc*) subject (matter); (*umg: Rauschgift*) dope

Stoffel (**-s, -**) (*pej: umg*) *m* lout, boor

Stoff- *zW*: **stofflich** *adj* with regard to subject matter; **Stoffrest** *m* remnant; **Stofftier** *nt* soft toy; **Stoffwechsel** *m* metabolism

stöhnen [ʃtøːnən] *vi* to groan

stoisch [ʃtoːɪʃ] *adj* stoical

Stola [ʃtoːla] (**-, Stolen**) *f* stole

Stollen [ʃtɔlən] (**-s, -**) *m* (*Min*) gallery; (*Koch*) stollen, *cake eaten at Christmas*; (*von Schuhen*) stud

stolpern [ʃtɔlpərn] *vi* to stumble, trip; (*fig: zu Fall kommen*) to come a cropper (*umg*)

stolz [ʃtɔlts] *adj* proud; (*imposant: Bauwerk*) majestic; (*ironisch: Preis*) princely; **Stolz** (**-es**) *m* pride

stolzieren [ʃtɔl'tsiːrən] *vi* to strut

stopfen [ʃtɔpfən] *vt* (*hineinstopfen*) to stuff;

319

(*nähen*) to darn ▷ vi (*Med*) to cause constipation; **jdm das Maul ~** (*umg*) to silence sb

Stopfgarn nt darning thread

Stopp [ʃtɔp] (**-s, -s**) m stop, halt; (*Lohnstopp*) freeze

Stoppel ['ʃtɔpəl] (**-, -n**) f stubble

stoppen vt to stop; (*mit Uhr*) to time ▷ vi to stop

Stoppschild nt stop sign

Stoppuhr f stopwatch

Stöpsel ['ʃtœpsəl] (**-s, -**) m plug; (*für Flaschen*) stopper

Stör [ʃtøːr] (**-(e)s, -e**) m sturgeon

Störaktion f disruptive action

störanfällig adj susceptible to interference od breakdown

Storch [ʃtɔrç] (**-(e)s, ̈-e**) m stork

Store [ʃtoːr] (**-s, -s**) m net curtain

stören ['ʃtøːrən] vt to disturb; (*behindern, Rundf*) to interfere with ▷ vr: **sich an etw** dat **~** to let sth bother one ▷ vi to get in the way; **was mich an ihm/daran stört** what I don't like about him/it; **stört es Sie, wenn ich rauche?** do you mind if I smoke?; **ich möchte nicht ~** I don't want to be in the way

störend adj disturbing, annoying

Störenfried (**-(e)s, -e**) m troublemaker

Störfall m (*in Kraftwerk etc*) malfunction, accident

stornieren [ʃtɔr'niːrən] vt (*Comm: Auftrag*) to cancel; (: *Buchungsfehler*) to reverse

Storno ['ʃtɔrno] (**-s**) m od nt (*Comm: von Buchungsfehler*) reversal; (: *von Auftrag*) cancellation (*Brit*), cancelation (*US*)

störrisch ['ʃtœrɪʃ] adj stubborn, perverse

Störsender m jammer, jamming transmitter

Störung f disturbance; interference; (*Tech*) fault; (*Med*) disorder

Störungsstelle f (*Tel*) faults service

Stoß [ʃtoːs] (**-es, ̈-e**) m (*Schub*) push; (*leicht*) poke; (*Schlag*) blow; (*mit Schwert*) thrust; (*mit Ellbogen*) nudge; (*mit Fuß*) kick; (*Erdstoß*) shock; (*Haufen*) pile; **seinem Herzen einen ~ geben** to pluck up courage; **Stoßdämpfer** m shock absorber

Stößel ['ʃtøːsəl] (**-s, -**) m pestle; (*Aut: Ventilstößel*) tappet

stoßen unreg vt (*mit Druck*) to shove, push; (*mit Schlag*) to knock, bump; (*mit Ellbogen*) to nudge; (*mit Fuß*) to kick; (*mit Schwert*) to thrust; (*anstoßen: Kopf etc*) to bump; (*zerkleinern*) to pulverize ▷ vr to get a knock ▷ vi: **~ an** od **auf** +akk to bump into; (*finden*) to come across; (*angrenzen*) to be next to; **sich ~ an** +dat (*fig*) to take exception to; **zu jdm ~** to meet up with sb

Stoßgebet nt quick prayer

Stoßstange f (*Aut*) bumper

stößt [ʃtøːst] vb siehe **stoßen**

Stoß- zW: **Stoßverkehr** m rush-hour traffic; **Stoßzahn** m tusk; **Stoßzeit** f (*im Verkehr*) rush hour; (*in Geschäft etc*) peak period

Stotterer (**-s, -**) m stutterer

Stotterin f stutterer

stottern ['ʃtɔtərn] vt, vi to stutter

Stövchen ['ʃtøːfçən] nt (teapot- *etc*) warmer

StPO abk = **Strafprozessordnung**

Str. abk (= *Straße*) St.

stracks [ʃtraks] adv straight

Straf- zW: **Strafanstalt** f penal institution; **Strafarbeit** f (*Sch*) lines pl, punishment exercise; **Strafbank** f (*Sport*) penalty bench; **strafbar** adj punishable; **sich strafbar machen** to commit an offence (*Brit*) od offense (*US*); **Strafbarkeit** f criminal nature

Strafe ['ʃtraːfə] (**-, -n**) f punishment; (*Jur*) penalty; (*Gefängnisstrafe*) sentence; (*Geldstrafe*) fine; **... bei ~ verboten** ... forbidden; **100 Dollar ~ zahlen** to pay a $100 fine; **er hat seine ~ weg** (*umg*) he's had his punishment

strafen vt, vi to punish; **mit etw gestraft sein** to be cursed with sth

strafend adj attrib punitive; (*Blick*) reproachful

straff [ʃtraf] adj tight; (*streng*) strict; (*Stil etc*) concise; (*Haltung*) erect

straffällig ['ʃtraːffɛlɪç] adj: **~ werden** to commit a criminal offence (*Brit*) od offense (*US*)

straffen vt to tighten

Straf- zW: **straffrei** adj: **straffrei ausgehen** to go unpunished; **Strafgefangene, r** f(m) prisoner, convict; **Strafgesetzbuch** nt penal code; **Strafkolonie** f penal colony

sträflich ['ʃtrɛːflɪç] adj criminal ▷ adv (*vernachlässigen etc*) criminally

Sträfling m convict

Straf- zW: **Strafmandat** nt ticket; **Strafmaß** nt sentence; **strafmildernd** adj mitigating; **Strafporto** nt excess postage (charge); **Strafpredigt** f severe lecture; **Strafprozessordnung** f code of criminal procedure; **Strafraum** m (*Sport*) penalty area; **Strafrecht** nt criminal law; **strafrechtlich** adj criminal; **Strafstoß** m (*Sport*) penalty (kick); **Straftat** f punishable act; **strafversetzen** vt untr (*Beamte*) to transfer for disciplinary reasons; **Strafvollzug** m penal system; **Strafzettel** (*umg*) m ticket

Strahl [ʃtraːl] (**-(e)s, -en**) m ray, beam; (*Wasserstrahl*) jet

strahlen vi (*Kernreaktor*) to radiate; (*Sonne, Licht*) to shine; (*fig*) to beam

Strahlenbehandlung f radiotherapy

Strahlenbelastung f (effects of) radiation

strahlend adj (*Wetter*) glorious; (*Lächeln, Schönheit*) radiant

Strahlen- zW: **Strahlendosis** f radiation dose; **strahlengeschädigt** adj suffering from radiation damage; **Strahlenopfer** nt victim of radiation; **Strahlenschutz** m radiation protection; **Strahlentherapie** f radiotherapy

Strahlung f radiation

Strähnchen ['ʃtrɛːnçən] pl strands (of hair); (*gefärbt*) highlights

Strähne ['ʃtrɛːnə] (**-, -n**) f strand

strähnig adj (*Haar*) straggly

stramm [ʃtram] adj tight; (*Haltung*) erect; (*Mensch*) robust; **strammstehen** unreg vi (*Mil*) to stand to attention

Strampelhöschen nt rompers pl
strampeln ['ʃtrampəln] vi to kick (about),
fidget
Strand [ʃtrant] (-(e)s, ̈e) m shore;
(Meeresstrand) beach; **am ~** on the beach;
Strandbad nt open-air swimming pool;
(Badeort) bathing resort
stranden ['ʃtrandən] vi to run aground;
(fig: Mensch) to fail
Strandgut nt flotsam and jetsam
Strandkorb m beach chair
Strang [ʃtraŋ] (-(e)s, ̈e) m (Nervenstrang,
Muskelstrang) cord; (Schienenstrang) track; **über
die Stränge schlagen** to run riot (umg); **an
einem ~ ziehen** (fig) to act in concert
strangulieren [ʃtraŋguˈliːrən] vt to strangle
Strapaze [ʃtraˈpaːtsə] (-, -n) f strain
strapazieren [ʃtrapaˈtsiːrən] vt (Material) to
be hard on, punish; (jdn) to be a strain on;
(erschöpfen) to wear out, exhaust
strapazierfähig adj hard-wearing
strapaziös [ʃtrapatsiˈøːs] adj exhausting,
tough
Straßburg ['ʃtraːsburk] (-s) nt Strasbourg
Straße ['ʃtraːsə] (-, -n) f road; (in Stadt, Dorf)
street; **auf der ~** in the street; **auf der ~
liegen** (fig: umg) to be out of work; **auf die ~
gesetzt werden** (umg) to be turned out (onto
the streets)
Straßen- zW: **Straßenbahn** f tram (Brit),
streetcar (US); **Straßenbauarbeiten** pl
roadworks pl (Brit), roadwork sing (US);
Straßenbeleuchtung f street lighting;
Straßenfeger (-s, -) m roadsweeper;
Straßenglätte f slippery road surface;
Straßenjunge (pej) m street urchin;
Straßenkarte f road map; **Straßenkehrer**
(-s, -) m roadsweeper; **Straßenkind** nt child
of the streets; **Straßenkreuzer** (umg) m
limousine; **Straßenmädchen** nt streetwalker;
Straßenrand m road side; **Straßensperre**
f roadblock; **Straßenüberführung** f
footbridge; **Straßenverkehr** m road traffic;
Straßenverkehrsordnung f Highway Code
(Brit); **Straßenzustandsbericht** m road report
Stratege [ʃtraˈteːgə] (-n, -n) m strategist
Strategie [ʃtrateˈgiː] f strategy
strategisch adj strategic
Stratosphäre [ʃtratoˈsfɛːrə] (-) f stratosphere
sträuben ['ʃtrɔybən] vt to ruffle ▷ vr to bristle;
(Mensch): **sich (gegen etw) ~** to resist (sth)
Strauch [ʃtraux] (-(e)s, Sträucher) m bush,
shrub
straucheln ['ʃtrauxəln] vi to stumble, stagger
Strauß¹ [ʃtraus] (-es, Sträuße) m (Blumenstrauß)
bouquet, bunch
Strauß² [ʃtraus] (-es, -e) m ostrich
Strebe ['ʃtreːbə] (-, -n) f strut
Strebebalken m buttress
streben vi to strive, endeavour (Brit), endeavor
(US); **~ nach** to strive for; **~ zu** od **nach** (sich
bewegen) to make for
Strebepfeiler m buttress

Streber (-s, -) m (pej) pushy person; (Sch) swot
(Brit)
strebsam adj industrious; **Strebsamkeit** f
industry
Strecke ['ʃtrɛkə] (-, -n) f stretch; (Entfernung)
distance; (Eisenb, Math) line; **auf der ~ Paris-
Brüssel** on the way from Paris to Brussels;
auf der ~ bleiben (fig) to fall by the wayside;
zur ~ bringen (Jagd) to bag
strecken vt to stretch; (Waffen) to lay down;
(Koch) to eke out ▷ vr to stretch (o.s.)
streckenweise adv in parts
Streich [ʃtraiç] (-(e)s, -e) m trick, prank; (Hieb)
blow; **jdm einen ~ spielen** (Person) to play a
trick on sb
streicheln vt to stroke
streichen unreg vt (berühren) to stroke; (auftragen)
to spread; (anmalen) to paint; (durchstreichen) to
delete; (nicht genehmigen) to cancel; (Schulden) to
write off; (Zuschuss etc) to cut ▷ vi (berühren) to
brush past; (schleichen) to prowl; **etw glatt ~** to
smooth sth (out)
Streicher pl (Mus) strings pl
Streich- zW: **Streichholz** nt match;
Streichholzschachtel f matchbox;
Streichinstrument nt string(ed) instrument;
Streichkäse m cheese spread
Streifband nt wrapper; **Streifbandzeitung** f
newspaper sent at printed paper rate
Streife (-, -n) f patrol
streifen ['ʃtraifən] vt (leicht berühren) to brush
against, graze; (Blick) to skim over; (Thema,
Problem) to touch on; (abstreifen) to take off ▷ vi
(gehen) to roam
Streifen (-s, -) m (Linie) stripe; (Stück) strip;
(Film) film
Streifendienst m patrol duty
Streifenwagen m patrol car
Streifschuss m graze, grazing shot
Streifzug m scouting trip; (Bummel)
expedition; (fig: kurzer Überblick): **~ (durch)** brief
survey (of)
Streik [ʃtraik] (-(e)s, -s) m strike; **in den
~ treten** to come out on strike, strike;
Streikbrecher m blackleg (Brit), strikebreaker;
streiken vi to strike; **der Computer
streikt** the computer's packed up (umg), the
computer's on the blink (umg); **da streike
ich** (umg) I refuse!; **Streikkasse** f strike fund;
Streikmaßnahmen pl industrial action sing;
Streikposten m (peaceful) picket
Streit [ʃtrait] (-(e)s, -e) m argument;
(Auseinandersetzung) dispute
streiten unreg vi, vr to argue; to dispute;
darüber lässt sich ~ that's debatable
Streitfrage f point at issue
Streitgespräch nt debate
streitig adj: **jdm etw ~ machen** to dispute
sb's right to sth; **Streitigkeiten** pl quarrel sing,
dispute sing
Streit- zW: **Streitkräfte** pl (Mil) armed
forces pl; **streitlustig** adj quarrelsome;
Streitpunkt m contentious issue; **Streitsucht**

S

f quarrelsomeness

streng [ʃtrɛŋ] *adj* severe; (*Lehrer, Maßnahme*) strict; (*Geruch etc*) sharp; **~ geheim** top-secret; **~ genommen** strictly speaking; **~ verboten!** strictly prohibited

Strenge (-) f severity; strictness; sharpness

strenggläubig *adj* strict

strengstens *adv* strictly

Stress [ʃtrɛs] **(-es, -e)** *m* stress

stressen *vt* to put under stress

stressfrei *adj* without stress

stressig *adj* stressful

Streu [ʃtrɔy] **(-, -en)** f litter, bed of straw

streuen *vt* to strew, scatter, spread ▷ *vi* (*mit Streupulver*) to grit; (*mit Salz*) to put down salt

Streuer (-s, -) *m* shaker; (*Salzstreuer*) cellar; (*Pfefferstreuer*) pot

Streufahrzeug *nt* gritter (*Brit*), sander

streunen *vi* to roam about; (*Hund, Katze*) to stray

Streupulver (-s) *nt* grit *od* sand for road

Streuselkuchen ['ʃtrɔyzəlku:xən] *m cake with crumble topping*

Streuung f dispersion; (*Statistik*) mean variation; (*Phys*) scattering

Strich (-(e)s, -e) *m* (*Linie*) line; (*Federstrich, Pinselstrich*) stroke; (*von Geweben*) nap; (*von Fell*) pile; (*Querstrich*) dash; (*Schrägstrich*) oblique, slash (*bes US*); **einen ~ machen durch** (*lit*) to cross out; (*fig*) to foil; **jdm einen ~ durch die Rechnung machen** to thwart *od* foil sb's plans; **einen ~ unter etw** *akk* **machen** (*fig*) to forget sth; **nach ~ und Faden** (*umg*) good and proper; **auf den ~ gehen** (*umg*) to walk the streets; **jdm gegen den ~ gehen** to rub sb up the wrong way

strich *etc* [ʃtrɪç] *vb siehe* **streichen**

Strichcode *m* bar code (*Brit*), universal product code (*US*)

Stricheinteilung f calibration

stricheln ['ʃtrɪçəln] *vt:* **eine gestrichelte Linie** a broken line

Strich- *zW:* **Strichjunge** (*umg*) *m* male prostitute; **Strichkode** *m* = **Strichcode**; **Strichmädchen** *nt* streetwalker; **Strichpunkt** *m* semicolon; **strichweise** *adv* here and there; **strichweise Regen** (*Met*) rain in places

Strick [ʃtrɪk] **(-(e)s, -e)** *m* rope; **jdm aus etw einen ~ drehen** to use sth against sb

stricken *vt, vi* to knit

Strick- *zW:* **Strickjacke** f cardigan; **Strickleiter** f rope ladder; **Stricknadel** f knitting needle; **Strickwaren** *pl* knitwear *sing*

striegeln ['ʃtri:gəln] (*umg*) *vr* to spruce o.s. up

Strieme ['ʃtri:mə] **(-, -n)** f weal

strikt [ʃtrɪkt] *adj* strict

Strippe ['ʃtrɪpə] **(-, -n)** f (*Tel: umg*): **jdn an der ~ haben** to have sb on the line

Stripper, in (-s, -) *m(f)* stripper

stritt *etc* [ʃtrɪt] *vb siehe* **streiten**

strittig ['ʃtrɪtɪç] *adj* disputed, in dispute

Stroh [ʃtro:] **(-(e)s)** *nt* straw; **Strohblume** f everlasting flower; **Strohdach** *nt* thatched

roof; **strohdumm** (*umg*) *adj* thick; **Strohfeuer** *nt:* **ein Strohfeuer sein** (*fig*) to be a passing fancy; **Strohhalm** *m* (drinking) straw; **Strohmann (-(e)s,** *pl* **-männer)** *m* (*Comm*) dummy; **Strohwitwe** f grass widow; **Strohwitwer** *m* grass widower

Strolch [ʃtrɔlç] **(-(e)s, -e)** (*pej*) *m* rogue, rascal

Strom [ʃtro:m] **(-(e)s, ¨e)** *m* river; (*fig*) stream; (*Elek*) current; **unter ~ stehen** (*Elek*) to be live; (*fig*) to be excited; **der Wein floss in Strömen** the wine flowed like water; **in Strömen regnen** to be pouring with rain; **stromabwärts** *adv* downstream; **Stromanschluss** *m:* **Stromanschluss haben** to be connected to the electricity mains; **stromaufwärts** *adv* upstream; **Stromausfall** *m* power failure

strömen [ʃtrø:mən] *vi* to stream, pour

Strom- *zW:* **Stromkabel** *nt* electric cable; **Stromkreis** *m* (electrical) circuit; **stromlinienförmig** *adj* streamlined; **Stromnetz** *nt* power supply system; **Stromrechnung** f electricity bill; **Stromschnelle** f rapids *pl*; **Stromsperre** f power cut; **Stromstärke** f amperage

Strömung ['ʃtrø:mʊŋ] f current

Stromzähler *m* electricity meter

Strophe ['ʃtro:fə] **(-, -n)** f verse

strotzen ['ʃtrɔtsən] *vi:* **~ vor** +*dat od* **von** to abound in, be full of

Strudel ['ʃtru:dəl] **(-s, -)** *m* whirlpool, vortex; (*Koch*) strudel

strudeln *vi* to swirl, eddy

Struktur [ʃtrʊk'tu:r] f structure

strukturell [ʃtrʊktu'rɛl] *adj* structural

strukturieren [ʃtrʊktu'ri:rən] *vt* to structure

Strumpf [ʃtrʊmpf] **(-(e)s, ¨e)** *m* stocking; **Strumpfband** *nt* garter; **Strumpfhalter** *m* suspender (*Brit*), garter (*US*); **Strumpfhose** f (pair of) tights *pl* (*Brit*) *od* pantihose *pl* (*US*)

Strunk [ʃtrʊŋk] **(-(e)s, ¨e)** *m* stump

struppig ['ʃtrʊpɪç] *adj* shaggy, unkempt

Stube ['ʃtu:bə] **(-, -n)** f room; **die gute ~** (*veraltet*) the parlour (*Brit*) *od* parlor (*US*)

Stuben- *zW:* **Stubenarrest** *m* confinement to one's room; (*Mil*) confinement to quarters; **Stubenfliege** f (common) housefly; **Stubenhocker** (*umg*) *m* stay-at-home; **stubenrein** *adj* house-trained

Stuck [ʃtʊk] **(-(e)s)** *m* stucco

Stück [ʃtʏk] **(-(e)s, -e)** *nt* piece; (*etwas*) bit; (*Theat*) play; **am ~** in one piece; **das ist ein starkes ~!** (*umg*) that's a bit much!; **große ~e auf jdn halten** to think highly of sb; **Stückarbeit** f piecework

Stuckateur [ʃtʊka'tø:r] *m* (ornamental) plasterer

Stück- *zw**:* **Stückgut** *nt* (*Eisenb*) parcel service; **Stückkosten** *pl* unit cost *sing*; **Stücklohn** *m* piecework rates *pl*; **stückweise** *adv* bit by bit, piecemeal; (*Comm*) individually; **Stückwerk** *nt* bits and pieces *pl*

Student, in [ʃtu'dɛnt(ɪn)] *m(f)* student

Studenten- zW: **Studentenausweis** m student card; **Studentenfutter** nt nuts and raisins pl; **Studentenwerk** nt student administration; **Studentenwohnheim** nt hall of residence (Brit), dormitory (US)

studentisch adj student attrib

Studie ['ʃtuːdiə] f study

Studien- zW: **Studienberatung** f course guidance service; **Studienbuch** nt (Univ) book in which the courses one has attended are entered; **Studienfahrt** f study trip; **Studienplatz** m university place; **Studienrat** m, **Studienrätin** f teacher at a secondary (Brit) od high (US) school; **Studienreform** f university course reform; **Studienzeitverkürzung** f shortening of the course of studies

studieren [ʃtuˈdiːrən] vt, vi to study; **bei jdm ~** to study under sb

Studio ['ʃtuːdio] (-s, -s) nt studio

Studium ['ʃtuːdiʊm] nt studies pl

Stufe ['ʃtuːfə] (-, -n) f step; (Entwicklungsstufe) stage; (Niveau) level

Stufen- zW: **Stufenheck** nt (Aut) notchback; **Stufenleiter** f (fig) ladder; **stufenlos** adj (Tech) infinitely variable; **stufenlos verstellbar** continuously adjustable; **Stufenplan** m graduated plan; **Stufenschnitt** m (Frisur) layered cut; **stufenweise** adv gradually

Stuhl [ʃtuːl] (-(e)s, ̈e) m chair; **zwischen zwei Stühlen sitzen** (fig) to fall between two stools

Stuhlgang m bowel movement

Stukkateur [ʃtʊkaˈtøːr] m siehe **Stuckateur**

stülpen ['ʃtʏlpən] vt (bedecken) to put; **etw über etw** akk **~** to put sth over sth; **den Kragen nach oben ~** to turn up one's collar

stumm [ʃtʊm] adj silent; (Med) dumb

Stummel (-s, -) m stump; (Zigarettenstummel) stub

Stummfilm m silent film (Brit) od movie (US)

Stümper, in ['ʃtʏmpər(ɪn)] (-s, -) m(f) incompetent, duffer; **stümperhaft** adj bungling, incompetent

stümpern (umg) vi to bungle

Stumpf [ʃtʊmpf] (-(e)s, ̈e) m stump; **etw mit ~ und Stiel ausrotten** to eradicate sth root and branch

stumpf adj blunt; (teilnahmslos, glanzlos) dull; (Winkel) obtuse

Stumpfsinn -(e)s) m tediousness

stumpfsinnig adj dull

Stunde ['ʃtʊndə] (-, -n) f hour; (Augenblick, Zeitpunkt) time; (Sch) lesson, period (Brit); **~ um Stunde** hour after hour; **80 Kilometer in der ~ ≈ 50** miles per hour

stunden vt: **jdm etw ~** to give sb time to pay sth

Stunden- zW: **Stundengeschwindigkeit** f average speed (per hour); **Stundenkilometer** pl kilometres (Brit) od kilometers (US) per hour; **stundenlang** adj for hours; **Stundenlohn** m hourly wage; **Stundenplan** m timetable; **stundenweise** adv by the hour; (stündlich) every hour

stündlich ['ʃtʏntlɪç] adj hourly

Stunk [ʃtʊŋk] (-s, no pl) m: **~ machen** (umg) to kick up a stink

stupide [ʃtuˈpiːdə] adj mindless

Stups [ʃtʊps] (-es, -e) (umg) m push

stupsen vt to nudge

Stupsnase f snub nose

stur [ʃtuːr] adj obstinate, stubborn; (Nein, Arbeiten) dogged; **er fuhr ~ geradeaus** he just carried straight on; **sich ~ stellen, auf ~ stellen** (umg) to dig one's heels in; **ein ~er Bock** (umg) a pig-headed fellow

Sturm [ʃtʊrm] (-(e)s, ̈e) m storm; (Wind) gale; (Mil etc) attack, assault; **~ läuten** to keep one's finger on the doorbell; **gegen etw ~ laufen** (fig) to be up in arms against sth

stürmen ['ʃtʏrmən] vi (Wind) to blow hard, to rage; (rennen) to storm ▷ vt (Mil, fig) to storm ▷ vi unpers: **es stürmt** there's a gale blowing

Stürmer (-s, -) m (Sport) forward

sturmfrei adj (Mil) unassailable; **eine ~e Bude** (umg) a room free from disturbance

stürmisch adj stormy; (fig) tempestuous; (Entwicklung) rapid; (Liebhaber) passionate; (Beifall) tumultuous; **nicht so ~** take it easy

Sturm- zW: **Sturmschritt** m (Mil, fig): **im Sturmschritt** at the double; **Sturmwarnung** f gale warning; **Sturmwind** m gale

Sturz [ʃtʊrts] (-es, ̈e) m fall; (Pol) overthrow; (in Temperatur, Preis) drop

stürzen ['ʃtʏrtsən] vt (werfen) to hurl; (Pol) to overthrow; (umkehren) to overturn ▷ vr to rush; (hineinstürzen) to plunge ▷ vi (Aviat) to dive; (rennen) to dash; **jdn ins Unglück ~** to bring disaster upon sb; **„nicht ~"** "this side up"; **sich auf jdn/etw ~** to pounce on sb/sth; **sich in Unkosten ~** to go to great expense

Sturzflug m nose dive

Sturzhelm m crash helmet

Stuss [ʃtʊs] (-es) (umg) m nonsense, rubbish

Stute ['ʃtuːtə] (-, -n) f mare

Stuttgart ['ʃtʊtgart] (-s) nt Stuttgart

Stützbalken m brace, joist

Stütze ['ʃtʏtsə] (-, -n) f support; (Hilfe) help; **die ~n der Gesellschaft** the pillars of society

stutzen ['ʃtʊtsən] vt to trim; (Ohr, Schwanz) to dock; (Flügel) to clip ▷ vi to hesitate; (argwöhnisch werden) to become suspicious

stützen vt (lit, fig) to support; (Ellbogen etc) to prop up ▷ vr: **sich auf jdn/etw ~** (lit) to lean on sb/sth; (Beweise, Theorie) to be based on sb/sth

stutzig adj perplexed, puzzled; (misstrauisch) suspicious

Stützmauer f supporting wall

Stützpunkt m point of support; (von Hebel) fulcrum; (Mil, fig) base

Stützungskäufe pl (Fin) support buying sing

StVO abk = **Straßenverkehrsordnung**

stylen ['staɪlən] vt to style; (Wohnung) to design

Styling ['staɪlɪŋ] (-s, no pl) nt styling

Styropor® [ʃtyroˈpoːr] (-s) nt (expanded) polystyrene

S

s. u. *abk* (= *siehe unten*) see below

Suaheli [zua'he:li] (**-(s)**) *nt* Swahili

Subjekt [zʊp'jɛkt] (**-(e)s, -e**) *nt* subject; (*pej: Mensch*) character (*umg*)

subjektiv [zʊpjɛk'ti:f] *adj* subjective

Subjektivität [zʊpjɛktivi'tɛ:t] *f* subjectivity

Subkultur ['zʊpkʊltu:r] *f* subculture

sublimieren [zubli'mi:rən] *vt* (*Chem, Psych*) to sublimate

Submissionsangebot [zʊpmɪsi'o:ns|angəbo:t] *nt* sealed-bid tender

Subroutine ['zʊpruti:nə] *f* (*Comput*) subroutine

Subskription [zʊpskrɪptsi'o:n] *f* subscription

Substantiv ['zʊpstanti:f] (**-s, -e**) *nt* noun

Substanz [zʊp'stants] *f* substance; **von der ~ zehren** to live on one's capital

subtil [zʊp'ti:l] *adj* subtle

subtrahieren [zʊptra'hi:rən] *vt* to subtract

subtropisch ['zʊptro:pɪʃ] *adj* subtropical

Subunternehmer *m* subcontractor

Subvention [zʊpvɛntsi'o:n] *f* subsidy

subventionieren [zʊpvɛntsio'ni:rən] *vt* to subsidize

subversiv [zʊpvɛr'zi:f] *adj* subversive

Suchaktion *f* search

Suchdienst *m* missing persons tracing service

Suche (**-, -n**) *f* search

suchen ['zu:xən] *vt* to look for, seek; (*versuchen*) to try ▷ *vi* to seek, search; **du hast hier nichts zu ~** you have no business being here; **nach Worten ~** to search for words; (*sprachlos sein*) to be at a loss for words; **such!** (*zu Hund*) seek!, find!; **~ und ersetzen** (*Comput*) search and replace

Sucher (**-s, -**) *m* seeker, searcher; (*Phot*) viewfinder

Suchmaschine *f* (*Comput*) search engine

Suchmeldung *f* missing *od* wanted person announcement

Suchscheinwerfer *m* searchlight

Sucht [zʊxt] (**-, ¨e**) *f* mania; (*Med*) addiction; **Suchtdroge** *f* addictive drug; **suchterzeugend** *adj* addictive

süchtig ['zʏçtɪç] *adj* addicted

Süchtige, r *f(m)* addict

Süd [zy:t] (**-(e)s**) *m* south; **Südafrika** *nt* South Africa; **Südamerika** *nt* South America

Sudan [zu'da:n] (**-s**) *m*: **der ~** the Sudan

Sudanese [zuda'ne:zə] (**-n, -n**) *m* Sudanese

Sudanesin *f* Sudanese

südd. *abk* = **süddeutsch**

süddeutsch *adj* South German

Süddeutschland *nt* South(ern) Germany

Süden ['zy:dən] (**-s**) *m* south

Süd- *zW:* **Südeuropa** *nt* Southern Europe; **Südfrüchte** *pl* Mediterranean fruit; **Südkorea** *nt* South Korea; **südländisch** *adj* southern; (*italienisch, spanisch etc*) Latin; **südlich** *adj* southern; **südlich von** (to the) south of; **Südostasien** *nt* South-East Asia; **Südpol** *m* South Pole; **Südpolarmeer** *nt* Antarctic Ocean; **Südsee** *f* South Seas *pl*, South Pacific; **Südtirol** *nt* South Tyrol; **südwärts** *adv* southwards;

Südwestafrika *nt* South West Africa, Namibia

Sueskanal ['zu:eskana:l] (**-s**) *m* Suez Canal

Suff [zʊf] *m*: **etw im ~ sagen** (*umg*) to say sth while under the influence

süffig ['zʏfɪç] *adj* (*Wein*) very drinkable

süffisant [zʏfi'zant] *adj* smug

suggerieren [zʊge'ri:rən] *vt* to suggest

Suggestivfrage [zʊgɛs'ti:ffra:gə] *f* leading question

suhlen ['zu:lən] *vr* (*lit, fig*) to wallow

Sühne ['zy:nə] (**-, -n**) *f* atonement, expiation

sühnen *vt* to atone for, expiate

Sühnetermin *m* (*Jur*) conciliatory hearing

Suite ['svi:tə] *f* suite

Sulfat [zʊl'fa:t] (**-(e)s, -e**) *nt* sulphate (*Brit*), sulfate (*US*)

Sultan ['zʊltan] (**-s, -e**) *m* sultan

Sultanine [zʊlta'ni:nə] *f* sultana

Sülze ['zʏltsə] (**-, -n**) *f* brawn (*Brit*), headcheese (*US*); (*Aspik*) aspic

summarisch [zʊ'ma:rɪʃ] *adj* summary

Sümmchen ['zʏmçən] *nt*: **ein hübsches ~** a tidy sum

Summe (**-, -n**) *f* sum, total

summen *vi* to buzz ▷ *vt* (*Lied*) to hum

Summer (**-s, -**) *m* buzzer

summieren [zʊ'mi:rən] *vt* to add up ▷ *vr* to mount up

Sumpf [zʊmpf] (**-(e)s, ¨e**) *m* swamp, marsh

sumpfig *adj* marshy

Sund [zʊnt] (**-(e)s, -e**) *m* sound, straits *pl*

Sünde ['zʏndə] (**-, -n**) *f* sin

Sünden- *zW:* **Sündenbock** *m* (*fig*) scapegoat; **Sündenfall** *m* (*Rel*) Fall; **Sündenregister** *nt* (*fig*) list of sins

Sünder, in (**-s, -**) *m(f)* sinner

sündhaft *adj* (*lit*) sinful; (*fig: umg: Preise*) wicked

sündigen ['zʏndɪgən] *vi* to sin; (*hum*) to indulge; **~ an** +*dat* to sin against

Super ['zu:pər] (**-s**) *nt* (*Benzin*) four-star (petrol) (*Brit*), premium (*US*)

super (*umg*) *adj* super ▷ *adv* incredibly well

Superlativ ['zu:pərlati:f] (**-s, -e**) *m* superlative

Supermarkt *m* supermarket

Superstar *m* superstar

Suppe ['zʊpə] (**-, -n**) *f* soup; (*mit Einlage*) broth; (*klare Brühe*) bouillon; (*fig: umg: Nebel*) peasouper (*Brit*), pea soup (*US*); **jdm die ~ versalzen** (*umg*) to put a spoke in sb's wheel

Suppen- *zW:* **Suppenfleisch** *nt* meat for making soup; **Suppengrün** *nt* herbs and vegetables for making soup; **Suppenkasper** (*umg*) *m* poor eater; **Suppenteller** *m* soup plate

Surfbrett ['zø:rfbrɛt] *nt* surfboard

surfen ['zø:rfən] *vi* to surf

Surfer, in *m(f)* surfer

Surrealismus [zʊrea'lɪsmʊs] *m* surrealism

surren ['zʊrən] *vi* to buzz; (*Insekt*) to hum

Surrogat [zʊro'ga:t] (**-(e)s, -e**) *nt* substitute, surrogate

suspekt [zʊs'pɛkt] *adj* suspect

suspendieren [zʊspɛn'di:rən] *vt*: **~ (von)** to suspend (from)

Suspendierung f suspension
süß [zyːs] adj sweet
Süße (-) f sweetness
süßen vt to sweeten
Süßholz nt: ~ **raspeln** (fig) to turn on the blarney
Süßigkeit f sweetness; (Bonbon etc) sweet (Brit), candy (US)
süß- zW: **süßlich** adj sweetish; (fig) sugary; **süßsauer** adj sweet-and-sour; (fig: gezwungen: Lächeln) forced; (Gurken etc) pickled; (Miene) artificially friendly; **Süßspeise** f pudding, sweet (Brit); **Süßstoff** m sweetener; **Süßwaren** pl confectionery sing; **Süßwasser** nt fresh water
SV (-) m abk = **Sportverein**
SW abk (= Südwest(en)) SW
Swasiland ['svaːzilant] (-s) nt Swaziland
SWF (-) m abk (früher: = Südwestfunk) South West German Radio
Sylvester [zylˈvɛstər] (-s, -) nt = **Silvester**
Symbol [zymˈboːl] (-s, -e) nt symbol
Symbolik f symbolism
symbolisch adj symbolic(al)
symbolisieren [zymboliˈziːrən] vt to symbolize
Symmetrie [zymeˈtriː] f symmetry; **Symmetrieachse** f symmetric axis
symmetrisch [zyˈmeːtrɪʃ] adj symmetrical
Sympathie [zympaˈtiː] f liking; sympathy; **er hat sich** dat **alle ~(n) verscherzt** he has turned everyone against him; **Sympathiekundgebung** f demonstration of support; **Sympathiestreik** m sympathy strike
Sympathisant, in m(f) sympathizer
sympathisch [zymˈpaːtɪʃ] adj likeable, congenial; **er ist mir ~** I like him
sympathisieren [zympatiˈziːrən] vi to sympathize
Symphonie [zymfoˈniː] f = **Sinfonie**
Symptom [zympˈtoːm] (-s, -e) nt symptom
symptomatisch [zymptoˈmaːtɪʃ] adj symptomatic
Synagoge [zynaˈgoːgə] (-, -n) f synagogue
synchron [zynˈkroːn] adj synchronous; **Synchrongetriebe** nt synchromesh gearbox (Brit) od transmission (US)
synchronisieren [zynkroniˈziːrən] vt to synchronize; (Film) to dub
Synchronschwimmen nt synchronized swimming
Syndikat [zyndiˈkaːt] (-(e)s, -e) nt combine, syndicate
Syndrom [zynˈdroːm] (-s, -e) nt syndrome
Synkope [zynˈkoːpə] (-, -n) f (Mus) syncopation
Synode [zyˈnoːdə] (-, -n) f (Rel) synod
Synonym [zynoˈnyːm] (-s, -e) nt synonym; **synonym** adj synonymous
Syntax ['zyntaks] (-, -en) f syntax
Synthese [zynˈteːzə] (-, -n) f synthesis
synthetisch adj synthetic
Syphilis ['zyːfilɪs] (-) f syphilis
Syrer, in ['zyːrər(ɪn)] (-s, -) m(f) Syrian
Syrien (-s) nt Syria
syrisch adj Syrian
System [zysˈteːm] (-s, -e) nt system; **Systemanalyse** f systems analysis; **Systemanalytiker, in** m(f) systems analyst
Systematik f system
systematisch [zysteˈmaːtɪʃ] adj systematic
systematisieren [zystematiˈziːrən] vt to systematize
System- zW: **Systemkritiker** m critic of the system; **Systemplatte** f (Comput) system disk; **Systemvoraussetzung** f (meist pl) system requirement; **Systemzwang** m obligation to conform (to the system)
Szenarium [stseˈnaːriʊm] nt scenario
Szene ['stseːnə] (-, -n) f scene; **sich in der ~ auskennen** (umg) to know the scene; **sich in ~ setzen** to play to the gallery
Szenenwechsel m scene change
Szenerie [stseneˈriː] f scenery

S

325

Tt

T, t¹ [te:] *nt* T, t; **T wie Theodor** ≈ T for Tommy
t² *abk* (= Tonne) t
Tabak ['ta:bak] (**-s, -e**) *m* tobacco; **Tabakladen**
m tobacconist's (*Brit*), tobacco store (*US*)
tabellarisch [tabɛ'la:rɪʃ] *adj* tabular
Tabelle (**-, -n**) *f* table
Tabellenführer *m* (*Sport*) top of the table,
league leader
Tabernakel [tabɛr'na:kəl] (**-s, -**) *nt* tabernacle
Tabl. *abk* = **Tablette(n)**
Tablett (**-(e)s, -s** *od* **-e**) *nt* tray
Tablette [ta'blɛtə] (**-, -n**) *f* tablet, pill
Tabu [ta'bu:] (**-s, -s**) *nt* taboo
tabuisieren [tabui'zi:rən] *vt* to make taboo
Tabulator [tabu'la:tɔr] *m* tabulator, tab (*umg*)
tabulieren *vt* to tab
Tacho ['taxo] (**-s, -s**) (*umg*) *m* speedo (*Brit*)
Tachometer [taxo'me:tər] (**-s, -**) *m* (*Aut*)
speedometer
Tadel ['ta:dəl] (**-s, -**) *m* censure, scolding;
(*Fehler*) fault; (*Makel*) blemish; **tadellos** *adj*
faultless, irreproachable
tadeln *vt* to scold
tadelnswert *adj* blameworthy
Tadschikistan [ta'dʒi:kista:n] (**-s**) *nt* Tajikistan
Tafel ['ta:fəl] (**-, -n**) *f* (*form: festlicher Speisetisch,*
Math) table; (*Festmahl*) meal; (*Anschlagtafel*)
board; (*Wandtafel*) blackboard; (*Schiefertafel*)
slate; (*Gedenktafel*) plaque; (*Illustration*) plate;
(*Schalttafel*) panel; (*Schokoladentafel etc*) bar;
tafelfertig *adj* ready to serve
täfeln ['tɛ:fəln] *vt* to panel
Tafelöl *nt* cooking oil; salad oil
Täfelung *f* panelling (*Brit*), paneling (*US*)
Tafelwasser *nt* table water
Taft [taft] (**-(e)s, -e**) *m* taffeta
Tag [ta:k] (**-(e)s, -e**) *m* day; (*Tageslicht*) daylight;
am ~ during the day; **für** *od* **auf ein paar**
~**e** for a few days; **in den** ~ **hinein leben** to
take each day as it comes; **bei** ~**(e)** (*ankommen*)
while it's light; (*arbeiten, reisen*) during the day;
unter ~**e** (*Min*) underground; **über** ~**e** (*Min*)
on the surface; **an den** ~ **kommen** to come to
light; **er legte großes Interesse an den** ~ he
showed great interest; **auf den** ~ **(genau)** to
the day; **auf seine alten** ~**e** at his age; **guten**
~**!** good morning/afternoon!; *siehe auch* **zutage**;
tagaus *adv*: **tagaus, tagein** day in, day out;

Tagdienst *m* day duty
Tage- *zW*: **Tagebau** *m* (*Min*) open-cast mining;
Tagebuch *nt* diary; **Tagedieb** *m* idler;
Tagegeld *nt* daily allowance; **tagelang** *adv*
for days
tagen *vi* to sit, meet ▷ *vi unpers*: **es tagt** dawn
is breaking
Tages- *zW*: **Tagesablauf** *m* daily routine;
Tagesanbruch *m* dawn; **Tagesausflug** *m* day
trip; **Tagesdecke** *f* bedspread; **Tagesfahrt** *f*
day trip; **Tageskarte** *f* (*Eintrittskarte*) day ticket;
(*Speisekarte*) menu of the day; **Tageskasse** *f*
(*Comm*) day's takings *pl*; (*Theat*) box office;
Tageslicht *nt* daylight; **Tagesmutter** *f* child
minder; **Tagesordnung** *f* agenda; **an der**
Tagesordnung sein (*fig*) to be the order of the
day; **Tagesrückfahrkarte** *f* day return (ticket);
Tagessatz *m* daily rate; **Tagesschau** *f* (*TV*)
television news (programme (*Brit*) *od* program
(*US*)); **Tagesstätte** *f* day nursery (*Brit*), daycare
center (*US*); **Tageswert** *m* (*Fin*) present value;
Tageszeit *f* time of day; **zu jeder Tages- und**
Nachtzeit at all hours of the day and night;
Tageszeitung *f* daily (paper)
tägl. *abk* = **täglich**
täglich ['tɛ:klɪç] *adj, adv* daily; **einmal** ~ once
a day
tags [ta:ks] *adv*: ~ **darauf** *od* **danach** the next
od following day; **tagsüber** *adv* during the day
tagtäglich *adj* daily ▷ *adv* every (single) day
Tagung *f* conference
Tagungsort *m* venue (of a conference)
Tahiti [ta'hi:ti] (**-s**) *nt* Tahiti
Taifun [taɪ'fu:n] (**-s, -e**) *m* typhoon
Taille ['taljə] (**-, -n**) *f* waist
tailliert [ta'ji:rt] *adj* waisted, gathered at the
waist
Taiwan ['taɪvan] (**-s**) *nt* Taiwan
Takel ['ta:kəl] (**-s, -**) *nt* tackle
takeln ['ta:kəln] *vt* to rig
Takt [takt] (**-(e)s, -e**) *m* tact; (*Mus*) time;
Taktgefühl *nt* tact
Taktik *f* tactics *pl*
Taktiker, in *m(f)* tactician
taktisch *adj* tactical
Takt- *zW*: **taktlos** *adj* tactless; **Taktlosigkeit**
f tactlessness; **Taktstock** *m* (conductor's)
baton; **Taktstrich** *m* (*Mus*) bar (line); **taktvoll**

adj tactful

Tal [taːl] (**-(e)s, ̈-er**) *nt* valley

Talar [taˈlaːr] (**-s, -e**) *m* (*Jur*) robe; (*Univ*) gown

Talbrücke *f* bridge over a valley

Talent [taˈlɛnt] (**-(e)s, -e**) *nt* talent

talentiert [talɛnˈtiːrt] *adj* talented, gifted

Talfahrt *f* descent; (*fig*) decline

Talg [talk] (**-(e)s, -e**) *m* tallow

Talgdrüse *f* sebaceous gland

Talisman [ˈtaːlɪsman] (**-s, -e**) *m* talisman

Tal- *zW*: **Talsohle** *f* bottom of a valley; **Talsperre** *f* dam; **talwärts** *adv* down to the valley

Tamburin [tambuˈriːn] (**-s, -e**) *nt* tambourine

Tamile [taˈmiːlə] (**-n, -n**) *m*, **Tamilin** *f* Tamil

tamilisch *adj* Tamil

Tampon [ˈtampɔn] (**-s, -s**) *m* tampon

Tamtam [tamˈtam] (**-s, -s**) *nt* (*Mus*) tomtom; (*umg: Wirbel*) fuss, ballyhoo; (*Lärm*) din

Tang [taŋ] (**-(e)s, -e**) *m* seaweed

Tangente [taŋˈgɛntə] (**-, -n**) *f* tangent

Tanger [ˈtaŋər] (**-s**) *nt* Tangier(s)

tangieren [taŋˈgiːrən] *vt* (*Problem*) to touch on; (*fig*) to affect

Tank [taŋk] (**-s, -s**) *m* tank

tanken *vt* (*Wagen etc*) to fill up with petrol (*Brit*) *od* gas (*US*); (*Benzin etc*) to fill up with; (*Aviat*) to (re)fuel; (*umg: frische Luft, neue Kräfte*) to get ▷ *vi* to fill up (with petrol *od* gas); to (re)fuel

Tanker (**-s, -**) *m* tanker

Tank- *zW*: **Tanklaster** *m* tanker; **Tankschiff** *nt* tanker; **Tankstelle** *f* petrol (*Brit*) *od* gas (*US*) station; **Tankuhr** *f* fuel gauge; **Tankverschluss** *m* fuel cap; **Tankwart** *m* petrol pump (*Brit*) *od* gas station (*US*) attendant

Tanne [ˈtanə] (**-, -n**) *f* fir

Tannenbaum *m* fir tree

Tannenzapfen *m* fir cone

Tansania [tanˈzaːnia] (**-s**) *nt* Tanzania

Tante [ˈtantə] (**-, -n**) *f* aunt; **Tante-Emma-Laden** (*umg*) *m* corner shop

Tantieme [tãtiˈeːmə] (**-, -n**) *f* fee; (*für Künstler etc*) royalty

Tanz [tants] (**-es, ̈-e**) *m* dance

tänzeln [ˈtɛntsəln] *vi* to dance along

tanzen *vt, vi* to dance

Tänzer, in (**-s, -**) *m(f)* dancer

Tanz- *zW*: **Tanzfläche** *f* (dance) floor; **Tanzlokal** *nt* café/restaurant with dancing; **Tanzschule** *f* dancing school

Tapet [taˈpeːt] (*umg*) *nt*: **etw aufs ~ bringen** to bring sth up

Tapete [taˈpeːtə] (**-, -n**) *f* wallpaper

Tapetenwechsel *m* (*fig*) change of scenery

tapezieren [tapeˈtsiːrən] *vt* to (wall)paper

Tapezierer (**-s, -**) *m* (interior) decorator

tapfer [ˈtapfər] *adj* brave; **sich ~ schlagen** (*umg*) to put on a brave show; **Tapferkeit** *f* courage, bravery

tappen [ˈtapən] *vi* to walk uncertainly *od* clumsily; **im Dunkeln ~** (*fig*) to grope in the dark

täppisch [ˈtɛpɪʃ] *adj* clumsy

Tara [ˈtaːra] (**-, Taren**) *f* tare

Tarantel [taˈrantəl] (**-, -n**) *f*: **wie von der ~ gestochen** as if stung by a bee

Tarif [taˈriːf] (**-s, -e**) *m* tariff, (scale of) fares/ charges; **nach/über/unter ~ bezahlen** to pay according to/above/below the (union) rate(s); **Tarifautonomie** *f* free collective bargaining; **Tarifgruppe** *f* grade; **tariflich** *adj* agreed, union; **Tariflohn** *m* standard wage rate; **Tarifordnung** *f* wage *od* salary scale; **Tarifpartner** *m*: **die Tarifpartner** union and management; **Tarifvereinbarung** *f* labour (*Brit*) *od* labor (*US*) agreement; **Tarifverhandlungen** *pl* collective bargaining *sing*; **Tarifvertrag** *m* pay agreement

tarnen [ˈtarnən] *vt* to camouflage; (*Person, Absicht*) to disguise

Tarnfarbe *f* camouflage paint

Tarnmanöver *nt* (*lit, fig*) feint, covering ploy

Tarnung *f* camouflaging; disguising

Tarock [taˈrɔk] (**-s, s**) *m od nt* tarot

Tasche [ˈtaʃə] (**-, -n**) *f* pocket; (*Handtasche*) handbag; **in die eigene ~ wirtschaften** to line one's own pockets; **jdm auf der ~ liegen** (*umg*) to live off sb

Taschen- *zW*: **Taschenbuch** *nt* paperback; **Taschendieb** *m* pickpocket; **Taschengeld** *nt* pocket money; **Taschenlampe** *f* (electric) torch, flashlight (*US*); **Taschenmesser** *nt* penknife; **Taschenrechner** *m* pocket calculator; **Taschenspieler** *m* conjurer; **Taschentuch** *nt* handkerchief

Tasmanien [tasˈmaːniən] (**-s**) *nt* Tasmania

Tasse [ˈtasə] (**-, -n**) *f* cup; **er hat nicht alle ~n im Schrank** (*umg*) he's not all there

Tastatur [tastaˈtuːr] *f* keyboard

Taste [ˈtastə] (**-, -n**) *f* push-button control; (*an Schreibmaschine*) key

tasten *vt* to feel, touch; (*drücken*) to press ▷ *vi* to feel, grope ▷ *vr* to feel one's way

Tastentelefon *nt* push-button telephone

Tastsinn *m* sense of touch

Tat (**-, -en**) *f* act, deed, action; **in der ~** indeed, as a matter of fact; **etw in die ~ umsetzen** to put sth into action

tat *etc* [taːt] *vb siehe* **tun**

Tatbestand *m* facts *pl* of the case

Tatendrang *m* energy

tatenlos *adj* inactive

Täter, in [ˈtɛːtər(ɪn)] (**-s, -**) *m(f)* perpetrator, culprit; **Täterschaft** *f* guilt

tätig *adj* active; **~er Teilhaber** active partner; **in einer Firma ~ sein** to work for a firm

tätigen *vt* (*Comm*) to conclude; (*geh: Einkäufe, Anruf*) to make

Tätigkeit *f* activity; (*Beruf*) occupation

Tätigkeitsbereich *m* field of activity

tatkräftig *adj* energetic; (*Hilfe*) active

tätlich *adj* violent; **Tätlichkeit** *f* violence; **es kam zu Tätlichkeiten** there were violent scenes

Tatort (**-(e)s, -e**) *m* scene of the crime

tätowieren [tɛtoˈviːrən] *vt* to tattoo

Tätowierung f tattooing; (*Ergebnis*) tattoo
Tatsache f fact; **jdn vor vollendete ~n stellen** to present sb with a fait accompli
Tatsachenbericht m documentary (report)
tatsächlich *adj* actual ▷ *adv* really
tatverdächtig *adj* suspected
Tatze ['tatsə] (-, -n) f paw
Tau[1] [taʊ] (-(e)s, -e) *nt* rope
Tau[2] (-(e)s) *m* dew
taub [taʊp] *adj* deaf; (*Nuss*) hollow; **sich ~ stellen** to pretend not to hear
Taube ['taʊbə] (-, -n) f (*Zool*) pigeon; (*fig*) dove
Taubenschlag m dovecote; **hier geht es zu wie im ~** (*fig: umg*) it's like Waterloo Station here (*Brit*), it's like Grand Central Station here (*US*)
Taubheit f deafness
taubstumm *adj* deaf-mute
tauchen ['taʊxən] *vt* to dip ▷ *vi* to dive; (*Naut*) to submerge
Taucher (-s, -) m diver; **Taucheranzug** m diving suit
Tauchsieder (-s, -) m portable immersion heater
Tauchstation f: **auf ~ gehen** (*U-Boot*) to dive
tauen ['taʊən] *vt, vi* to thaw ▷ *vi unpers*: **es taut** it's thawing
Taufbecken *nt* font
Taufe ['taʊfə] (-, -n) f baptism
taufen *vt* to baptize; (*nennen*) to christen
Tauf- *zW*: **Taufname** m Christian name; **Taufpate** m godfather; **Taufpatin** f godmother; **Taufschein** m certificate of baptism
taugen ['taʊgən] *vi* to be of use; **~ für** to do *od* be good for; **nicht ~** to be no good *od* useless
Taugenichts (-es, -e) m good-for-nothing
tauglich ['taʊklɪç] *adj* suitable; (*Mil*) fit (for service); **Tauglichkeit** f suitability; fitness
Taumel ['taʊməl] (-s) m dizziness; (*fig*) frenzy
taumelig *adj* giddy, reeling
taumeln *vi* to reel, stagger
Taunus ['taʊnʊs] (-) m Taunus (Mountains *pl*)
Tausch [taʊʃ] (-(e)s, -e) m exchange; **einen guten/schlechten ~ machen** to get a good/bad deal
tauschen *vt* to exchange, swap ▷ *vi*: **ich möchte nicht mit ihm ~** I wouldn't like to be in his place
täuschen ['tɔʏʃən] *vt* to deceive ▷ *vi* to be deceptive ▷ *vr* to be wrong; **wenn mich nicht alles täuscht** unless I'm completely wrong
täuschend *adj* deceptive
Tauschhandel m barter
Täuschung f deception; (*optisch*) illusion
Täuschungsmanöver *nt* (*Sport*) feint; (*fig*) ploy
tausend ['taʊzənt] *num* a *od* one thousand;
Tausend (-, -en) f (*Zahl*) thousand
Tausender (-s, -) m (*Geldschein*) thousand
Tausendfüßler (-s, -) m centipede
Tau- *zW*: **Tautropfen** m dew drop; **Tauwetter** *nt* thaw; **Tauziehen** *nt* tug-of-war
Taxe ['taksə] (-, -n) f taxi, cab

Taxi ['taksi] (-(s), -(s)) *nt* taxi, cab
taxieren [ta'ksi:rən] *vt* (*Preis, Wert*) to estimate; (*Haus, Gemälde*) to value; (*mustern*) to look up and down
Taxi- *zW*: **Taxifahrer** m taxi driver; **Taxistand** m taxi rank (*Brit*) *od* stand (*US*)
Tb, Tbc f *abk* (= *Tuberkulose*) TB
Teamarbeit ['ti:m|arbaɪt] f teamwork
Technik ['tɛçnɪk] f technology; (*Methode, Kunstfertigkeit*) technique
Techniker, in (-s -) m(f) technician
technisch *adj* technical; **~e Hochschule** ≈ polytechnic
Technologie [tɛçnolo'gi:] f technology
technologisch [tɛçno'lo:gɪʃ] *adj* technological
Techtelmechtel [tɛçtəl'mɛçtəl] (-s, -) (*umg*) *nt* (*Liebschaft*) affair, carry-on
TEE *abk* (= *Trans-Europ-Express*) Trans-Europe-Express
Tee [te:] (-s, -s) m tea; **Teebeutel** m tea bag; **Teekanne** f teapot; **Teelicht** *nt* night-light; **Teelöffel** m teaspoon; **Teemischung** f blend of tea
Teer [te:r] (-(e)s, -e) m tar; **teeren** *vt* to tar
Teesieb *nt* tea strainer
Teewagen m tea trolley
Teflon® ['teflo:n] (-s) *nt* Teflon®
Teheran ['te:həra:n] (-s) *nt* Teheran
Teich [taɪç] (-(e)s, -e) m pond
Teig [taɪk] (-(e)s, -e) m dough
teigig ['taɪgɪç] *adj* doughy
Teigwaren *pl* pasta *sing*
Teil [taɪl] (-(e)s, -e) m *od nt* part; (*Anteil*) share ▷ *nt* (*Bestandteil*) component, part; (*Ersatzteil*) spare (part); **zum ~** partly; **ich für mein(en) ~ ...** I, for my part ...; **sich** *dat* **sein ~ denken** (*umg*) to draw one's own conclusions; **er hat sein(en) ~ dazu beigetragen** he did his bit *od* share; **teilbar** *adj* divisible; **Teilbetrag** m instalment (*Brit*), installment (*US*); **Teilchen** *nt* (atomic) particle
teilen *vt* to divide; (*mit jdm*) to share ▷ *vr* to divide; (*in Gruppen*) to split up
Teil- *zW*: **teilentrahmt** *adj* semi-skimmed; **Teilgebiet** *nt* (*Bereich*) branch; (*räumlich*) area; **teilhaben** *unreg vi*: **an etw** *dat* **teilhaben** to share in sth; **Teilhaber** (-s, -) m partner; **Teilkaskoversicherung** f third party, fire and theft insurance
Teilnahme (-, -n) f participation; (*Mitleid*) sympathy; **jdm seine herzliche ~ aussprechen** to offer sb one's heartfelt sympathy
teilnahmslos *adj* disinterested, apathetic
teilnehmen *unreg vi*: **an etw** *dat* **~** to take part in sth
Teilnehmer, in (-s, -) m(f) participant
teils *adv* partly
Teilschaden m partial loss
Teilstrecke f stage; (*von Straße*) stretch; (*bei Bus etc*) fare stage
Teilung f division
Teil- *zW*: **teilweise** *adv* partially, in part;

Teilzahlung f payment by instalments (Brit) od installments (US); **Teilzeitarbeit** f part-time job od work; **Teilzeitbasis** f: **auf Teilzeitbasis arbeiten** to work part-time; **Teilzeitmodell** nt part-time working arrangements

Teint [tɛ̃:] (**-s, -s**) m complexion

Telearbeit ['te:learbaɪt] f teleworking

Telebanking ['te:lebɛŋkɪŋ] (**-s**) nt telebanking

Telebrief ['te:lebri:f] m facsimile, fax

Telefax ['te:lefaks] (**-**) nt telefax

Telefon [tele'fo:n] (**-s, -e**) nt (tele)phone; **ans ~ gehen** to answer the phone; **Telefonamt** nt telephone exchange; **Telefonanruf** m (tele) phone call

Telefonat [telefo'na:t] (**-(e)s, -e**) nt (tele)phone call

Telefon- zW: **Telefonbuch** nt (tele) phone directory; **Telefongebühr** f call charge; (Grundgebühr) (tele)phone rental; **Telefongespräch** nt (tele)phone call; **Telefonhäuschen** (umg) nt = **Telefonzelle**

telefonieren [telefo'ni:rən] vi to (tele)phone; **bei jdm ~** to use sb's phone; **mit jdm ~** to speak to sb on the phone

telefonisch [tele'fo:nɪʃ] adj telephone; (Benachrichtigung) by telephone; **ich bin ~ zu erreichen** I can be reached by phone

Telefonist, in [telefo'nɪst(ɪn)] m(f) telephonist

Telefon- zW: **Telefonkarte** f phone card; **Telefonnummer** f (tele)phone number; **Telefonseelsorge** f: **die Telefonseelsorge** ≈ the Samaritans; **Telefonverbindung** f telephone connection; **Telefonzelle** f telephone box (Brit) od booth (US), callbox (Brit); **Telefonzentrale** f telephone exchange

Telegraf [tele'gra:f] (**-en, -en**) m telegraph

Telegrafenleitung f telegraph line

Telegrafenmast m telegraph pole

Telegrafie [telegra'fi:] f telegraphy

telegrafieren [telegra'fi:rən] vt, vi to telegraph, cable, wire

telegrafisch [tele'gra:fɪʃ] adj telegraphic; **jdm ~ Geld überweisen** to cable sb money

Telegramm [tele'gram] (**-s, -e**) nt telegram, cable; **Telegrammadresse** f telegraphic address; **Telegrammformular** nt telegram form

Telekolleg ['te:ləkɔlɛk] nt ≈ Open University (Brit)

Teleobjektiv ['te:ləʔɔpjɛkti:f] nt telephoto lens

Telepathie [telepa'ti:] f telepathy

telepathisch [tele'pa:tɪʃ] adj telepathic

Teleskop [tele'sko:p] (**-s, -e**) nt telescope

Telespiel nt video game

Telex ['te:lɛks] (**-, -(e)**) nt telex

Teller ['tɛlər] (**-s, -**) m plate

Tempel ['tɛmpəl] (**-s, -**) m temple

Temperafarbe ['tɛmperafarbə] f distemper

Temperament [tɛmpera'mɛnt] nt temperament; (Schwung) vivacity, vitality; **sein ~ ist mit ihm durchgegangen** he went over the top; **temperamentlos** adj spiritless; **temperamentvoll** adj high-spirited, lively

Temperatur [tɛmpera'tu:r] f temperature; **erhöhte ~ haben** to have a temperature

Tempo¹ ['tɛmpo] (**-s, -s**) nt speed, pace; **~! get a move on!**

Tempo² ['tɛmpo] (**-s, Tempi**) nt (Mus) tempo; **das ~ angeben** (fig) to set the pace; **Tempolimit** nt speed limit

temporär [tɛmpo'rɛ:r] adj temporary

Tempotaschentuch® nt paper handkerchief

Tendenz [tɛn'dɛnts] f tendency; (Absicht) intention

tendenziell [tɛndɛntsi'ɛl] adj: **nur ~e Unterschiede** merely differences in emphasis

tendenziös [tɛndɛntsi'ø:s] adj bias(s)ed, tendentious

tendieren [tɛn'di:rən] vi: **zu etw ~** to show a tendency to(wards) sth, incline to(wards) sth

Teneriffa [tene'rɪfa] (**-s**) nt Tenerife

Tenne ['tɛnə] (**-, -n**) f threshing floor

Tennis ['tɛnɪs] (**-**) nt tennis; **Tennisplatz** m tennis court; **Tennisschläger** m tennis racket; **Tennisspieler** m tennis player

Tenor [te'no:r] (**-s, ̈e**) m tenor

Teppich ['tɛpɪç] (**-s, -e**) m carpet; **Teppichboden** m wall-to-wall carpeting; **Teppichkehrmaschine** f carpet sweeper; **Teppichklopfer** m carpet beater

Termin [tɛr'mi:n] (**-s, -e**) m (Zeitpunkt) date; (Frist) deadline; (Arzttermin etc) appointment; (Jur: Verhandlung) hearing; **sich** dat **einen ~ geben lassen** to make an appointment; **termingerecht** adj on schedule

terminieren [tɛrmi'ni:rən] vt (befristen) to limit; (festsetzen) to set a date for

Terminkalender m diary, appointments book

Terminologie [tɛrminolo'gi:] f terminology

Termite [tɛr'mi:tə] (**-, -n**) f termite

Terpentin [tɛrpɛn'ti:n] (**-s, -e**) nt turpentine, turps sing

Terrain [tɛ'rɛ̃:] (**-s, -s**) nt land, terrain; (fig) territory; **das ~ sondieren** (Mil) to reconnoitre the terrain; (fig) to see how the land lies

Terrasse [tɛ'rasə] (**-, -n**) f terrace

Terrine [tɛ'ri:nə] f tureen

territorial [tɛritori'a:l] adj territorial

Territorium [tɛri'to:riʊm] nt territory

Terror ['tɛrɔr] (**-s**) m terror; (Terrorherrschaft) reign of terror; **blanker ~** sheer terror; **Terroranschlag** m terrorist attack

terrorisieren [tɛrori'zi:rən] vt to terrorize

Terrorismus [tɛro'rɪsmʊs] m terrorism

Terrorist, in m(f) terrorist

terroristisch adj terrorist attr

Terrornetz(werk) nt terrorist network

Terrororganisation f terrorist organization

Terrorzelle f terrorist cell

Tertia ['tɛrtsia] (**-, Tertien**) f (Sch: früher: Untertertia/Obertertia) fourth/fifth year of German secondary school

Terz [tɛrts] (**-, -en**) f (Mus) third

Terzett [tɛr'tsɛt] (**-(e)s, -e**) nt (Mus) trio

Tesafilm® ['te:zafɪlm] m Sellotape® (Brit), Scotch tape® (US)

t

Test [tɛst] (-s, -s) m test
Testament [tɛsta'mɛnt] nt will, testament; (Rel) Testament; **Altes/Neues** ~ Old/New Testament
testamentarisch [tɛstamɛn'taːrɪʃ] adj testamentary
Testamentsvollstrecker, in (-s, -) m(f) executor (of a will)
Testat [tɛs'taːt] (-(e)s, -e) nt certificate
Testator [tɛs'taːtɔr] m testator
Test- zW: **Testbild** nt (TV) test card; **testen** vt to test; **Testfall** m test case; **Testperson** f subject (of a test); **Teststoppabkommen** nt nuclear test ban agreement
Tetanus ['teːtanʊs] (-) m tetanus; **Tetanusimpfung** f (anti-)tetanus injection
teuer ['tɔyər] adj dear, expensive; **teures Geld** good money; **das wird ihn ~ zu stehen kommen** (fig) that will cost him dear
Teuerung f increase in prices
Teuerungszulage f cost-of-living bonus
Teufel ['tɔyfəl] (-s, -) m devil; **den ~ an die Wand malen** (schwarzmalen) to imagine the worst; (Unheil heraufbeschwören) to tempt fate od providence; **in ~s Küche kommen** to get into a mess; **jdn zum ~ jagen** (umg) to send sb packing
Teufelei [tɔyfə'laɪ] f devilment
Teufels- zW: **Teufelsaustreibung** f exorcism; **Teufelsbrut** (umg) f devil's brood; **Teufelskreis** m vicious circle
teuflisch ['tɔyflɪʃ] adj fiendish, diabolic
Text [tɛkst] (-(e)s, -e) m text; (Liedertext) words pl; (: von Schlager) lyrics pl; **Textdichter** m songwriter; **texten** vi to write the words
textil [tɛks'tiːl] adj textile; **Textilbranche** f textile trade
Textilien pl textiles pl
Textilindustrie f textile industry
Textilwaren pl textiles pl
Text- zW: **Textnachrichten** pl (Tel) text messaging; **Textstelle** f passage; **Textverarbeitungssystem** nt word processor
TH (-, -s) f abk (= technische Hochschule) siehe **technisch**
Thailand ['taɪlant] (-s) nt Thailand
Thailänder, in ['taɪlɛndər(ɪn)] (-s, -) m(f) Thai
Theater [te'aːtər] (-s, -) nt theatre (Brit), theater (US); (umg) fuss; **(ein) ~ machen** to make a (big) fuss; **~ spielen** to act; (fig) to put on an act; **Theaterbesucher** m playgoer; **Theaterkasse** f box office; **Theaterstück** nt (stage) play
theatralisch [tea'traːlɪʃ] adj theatrical
Theke ['teːkə] (-, -n) f (Schanktisch) bar; (Ladentisch) counter
Thema ['teːma] (-s, Themen od -ta) nt (Leitgedanke, Mus) theme; topic, subject; **beim ~ bleiben/vom ~ abschweifen** to stick to/ wander off the subject
thematisch [te'maːtɪʃ] adj thematic
Themenkreis m topic
Themenpark m theme park

Themse ['tɛmzə] f: **die** ~ the Thames
Theologe [teo'loːgə] (-n, -n) m theologian
Theologie [teolo'giː] f theology
Theologin f theologian
theologisch [teo'loːgɪʃ] adj theological
Theoretiker, in [teo're:tikər(ɪn)] (-s, -) m(f) theorist
theoretisch adj theoretical; **~ gesehen** in theory, theoretically
Theorie [teo'riː] f theory
Therapeut [tera'pɔyt] (-en, -en) m therapist
therapeutisch adj therapeutic
Therapie [tera'piː] f therapy
Thermalbad [tɛr'maːlbaːt] nt thermal bath; (Badeort) thermal spa
Thermalquelle f thermal spring
Thermometer [tɛrmo'meːtər] (-s, -) nt thermometer
Thermosflasche® ['tɛrmɔsflaʃə] f Thermos® flask
Thermostat [tɛrmo'staːt] (-(e)s od -en, -e(n)) m thermostat
These ['teːzə] (-, -n) f thesis
Thrombose [trɔm'boːzə] (-, -n) f thrombosis
Thron [troːn] (-(e)s, -e) m throne; **Thronbesteigung** f accession (to the throne)
thronen vi to sit enthroned; (fig) to sit in state
Thronerbe m heir to the throne
Thronfolge f succession (to the throne)
Thunfisch ['tuːnfɪʃ] m tuna (fish)
Thüringen ['tyːrɪŋən] (-s) nt Thuringia
Thymian ['tyːmiaːn] (-s, -e) m thyme
Tibet ['tiːbɛt] (-s) nt Tibet
Tick [tɪk] (-(e)s, -s) m tic; (Eigenart) quirk; (Fimmel) craze
ticken vi to tick; **nicht richtig ~** (umg) to be off one's rocker
Ticket ['tɪkət] (-s, -s) nt ticket
tief [tiːf] adj deep; (tiefsinnig) profound; (Ausschnitt, Ton) low; **~er Teller** soup plate; **~ greifend** far-reaching; **~ schürfend** profound; **bis ~ in die Nacht hinein** late into the night; **Tief** (-s, -s) nt (Met) depression; (fig) low; **Tiefbau** m civil engineering (at or below ground level); **Tiefdruck** m (Met) low pressure
Tiefe (-, -n) f depth
Tiefebene ['tiːfˌeːbənə] f plain
Tiefenpsychologie f depth psychology
Tiefenschärfe f (Phot) depth of focus
tief- zW: **tiefernst** adj very grave od solemn; **Tiefflug** m low-level od low-altitude flight; **Tiefgang** m (Naut) draught (Brit), draft (US); (geistig) depth; **Tiefgarage** f underground car park (Brit) od parking lot (US); **tiefgekühlt** adj frozen; **Tiefkühlfach** nt freezer compartment; **Tiefkühlkost** f frozen food; **Tiefkühltruhe** f freezer, deep freeze (US); **Tieflader** (-s, -) m low-loader; **Tiefland** nt lowlands pl; **Tiefparterre** f basement; **Tiefpunkt** m low point; (fig) low ebb; **Tiefschlag** m (Boxen, fig) blow below the belt; **Tiefsee** f deep parts of the sea; **Tiefsinn** m profundity; **tiefsinnig** adj profound; (umg) melancholy; **Tiefstand**

m low level; **tiefstapeln** *vi* to be overmodest; **Tiefstart** *m* (*Sport*) crouch start

Tiefstwert *m* minimum *od* lowest value

Tiegel ['ti:gəl] (**-s, -**) *m* saucepan; (*Chem*) crucible

Tier [ti:r] (**-(e)s, -e**) *nt* animal; **Tierarzt** *m*, **Tierärztin** *f* vet(erinary surgeon) (*Brit*), veterinarian (*US*); **Tierfreund** *m* animal lover; **Tiergarten** *m* zoo, zoological gardens *pl*; **Tierhandlung** *f* pet shop (*Brit*) *od* store (*US*); **tierisch** *adj* animal *attrib*; (*lit, fig*) brutish; (*fig: Ernst etc*) deadly; **Tierkreis** *m* zodiac; **Tierkunde** *f* zoology; **tierlieb** *adj*, **tierliebend** *adj* fond of animals; **Tierquälerei** *f* cruelty to animals; **Tierreich** *nt* animal kingdom; **Tierschutz** *m* protection of animals; **Tierschutzverein** *m* society for the prevention of cruelty to animals; **Tierversuch** *m* animal experiment; **Tierwelt** *f* animal kingdom

Tiger ['ti:gər] (**-s, -**) *m* tiger; **Tigerin** *f* tigress

tilgen ['tɪlgən] *vt* to erase; (*Sünden*) to expiate; (*Schulden*) to pay off

Tilgung *f* erasing, blotting out; expiation; repayment

Tilgungsfonds *m* (*Comm*) sinking fund

tingeln ['tɪŋgəln] (*umg*) *vi* to appear in small night clubs

Tinktur [tɪŋk'tu:r] *f* tincture

Tinte ['tɪntə] (**-, -n**) *f* ink

Tinten- *zW:* **Tintenfass** *nt* inkwell; **Tintenfisch** *m* cuttlefish; (*achtarmig*) octopus; **Tintenfleck** *m* ink stain *od* blot; **Tintenstift** *m* indelible pencil; **Tintenstrahldrucker** *m* ink-jet printer

Tipp [tɪp] (**-s, -s**) *m* (*Sport, Börse*) tip; (*Andeutung*) hint; (*an Polizei*) tip-off

tippen ['tɪpən] *vi* to tap, touch; (*umg: schreiben*) to type; (*im Lotto etc*) to bet ▷ *vt* to type; to bet; **auf jdn ~** (*umg: raten*) to tip sb, put one's money on sb (*fig*)

Tippfehler (*umg*) *m* typing error

Tippse (**-, -n**) (*umg*) *f* typist

tipptopp ['tɪp'tɔp] (*umg*) *adj* tiptop

Tippzettel *m* (*pools*) coupon

Tirade [ti'ra:də] (**-, -n**) *f* tirade

Tirol [ti'ro:l] (**-s**) *nt* the Tyrol

Tiroler, in (**-s, -**) *m(f)* Tyrolese, Tyrolean

tirolerisch *adj* Tyrolese, Tyrolean

Tisch [tɪʃ] (**-(e)s, -e**) *m* table; **bitte zu ~!** lunch *od* dinner is served; **bei ~** at table; **vor/nach ~** before/after eating; **unter den ~ fallen** (*fig*) to be dropped; **Tischdecke** *f* tablecloth

Tischler (**-s, -**) *m* carpenter, joiner

Tischlerei [tɪʃlə'raɪ] *f* joiner's workshop; (*Arbeit*) carpentry, joinery

Tischlerhandwerk *nt* cabinetmaking

tischlern *vi* to do carpentry *etc*

Tisch- *zW:* **Tischnachbar** *m* neighbour (*Brit*) *od* neighbor (*US*) (at table); **Tischrechner** *m* desk calculator; **Tischrede** *f* after-dinner speech; **Tischtennis** *nt* table tennis; **Tischtuch** *nt* tablecloth

Titel ['ti:təl] (**-s, -**) *m* title; **Titelanwärter** *m* (*Sport*) challenger; **Titelbild** *nt* cover (picture); (*von Buch*) frontispiece; **Titelgeschichte** *f* headline story; **Titelrolle** *f* title role; **Titelseite** *f* cover; (*Buchtitel*) title page; **Titelverteidiger** *m* defending champion, title holder

Titte ['tɪtə] (**-, -n**) (*umg*) *f* (*weibliche Brust*) boob, tit (*umg*)

titulieren [titu'li:rən] *vt* to entitle; (*anreden*) to address

tja [tja] *interj* well!

Toast [to:st] (**-(e)s, -s** *od* **-e**) *m* toast

toasten *vi* to drink a toast ▷ *vt* (*Brot*) to toast; **auf jdn ~** to toast sb, drink a toast to sb

Toaster (**-s, -**) *m* toaster

toben ['to:bən] *vi* to rage; (*Kinder*) to romp about

tob- *zW:* **Tobsucht** *f* raving madness; **tobsüchtig** *adj* maniacal; **Tobsuchtsanfall** *m* maniacal fit

Tochter ['tɔxtər] (**-, ̈ -**) *f* daughter; **Tochtergesellschaft** *f* subsidiary (company)

Tod [to:t] (**-(e)s, -e**) *m* death; **zu ~e betrübt sein** to be in the depths of despair; **eines natürlichen/gewaltsamen ~es sterben** to die of natural causes/die a violent death; **todernst** (*umg*) *adj* deadly serious ▷ *adv* in dead earnest

Todes- *zW:* **Todesangst** *f* mortal fear; **Todesängste ausstehen** (*umg*) to be scared to death; **Todesanzeige** *f* obituary (notice); **Todesfall** *m* death; **Todeskampf** *m* death throes *pl*; **Todesopfer** *nt* death, casualty, fatality; **Todesqualen** *pl*: **Todesqualen ausstehen** (*fig*) to suffer agonies; **Todesstoß** *m* deathblow; **Todesstrafe** *f* death penalty; **Todestag** *m* anniversary of death; **Todesursache** *f* cause of death; **Todesurteil** *nt* death sentence; **Todesverachtung** *f* utter disgust

Todfeind *m* deadly *od* mortal enemy

todkrank *adj* dangerously ill

tödlich ['tø:tlɪç] *adj* fatal; (*Gift*) deadly, lethal

tod- *zW:* **todmüde** *adj* dead tired; **todschick** (*umg*) *adj* smart, classy; **todsicher** (*umg*) *adj* absolutely *od* dead certain; **Todsünde** *f* deadly sin; **todtraurig** *adj* extremely sad

Tofu ['to:fu] (**-(s)**) *m* tofu

Togo ['to:go] (**-s**) *nt* Togo

Toilette [toa'lɛtə] *f* toilet, lavatory (*Brit*), john (*US*); (*Frisiertisch*) dressing table; (*Kleidung*) outfit; **auf die ~ gehen/auf der ~ sein** to go to/be in the toilet

Toiletten- *zW:* **Toilettenartikel** *pl* toiletries *pl*, toilet articles *pl*; **Toilettenpapier** *nt* toilet paper; **Toilettentisch** *m* dressing table

toi, toi, toi ['tɔy'tɔy'tɔy] (*umg*) *interj* good luck; (*unberufen*) touch wood

Tokio ['to:kjo] (**-s**) *nt* Tokyo

tolerant [tole'rant] *adj* tolerant

Toleranz *f* tolerance

tolerieren [tole'ri:rən] *vt* to tolerate

toll [tɔl] *adj* mad; (*Treiben*) wild; (*umg*) terrific

tollen vi to romp

toll- zW: **Tollheit** f madness, wildness; **Tollkirsche** f deadly nightshade; **tollkühn** adj daring; **Tollwut** f rabies

Tomate [to'ma:tə] (-, -n) f tomato; **du treulose ~!** (umg) you're a fine friend!

Tomatenmark (-(e)s) nt tomato purée

Tombola ['tɔmbola] (-, -s od **Tombolen**) f tombola

Ton¹ [to:n] (-(e)s, -e) m (Erde) clay

Ton² [to:n] (-(e)s, ̈-e) m (Laut) sound; (Mus) note; (Redeweise) tone; (Farbton, Nuance) shade; (Betonung) stress; **keinen ~ herausbringen** not to be able to say a word; **den ~ angeben** (Mus) to give an A; (fig: Mensch) to set the tone; **Tonabnehmer** m pick-up; **tonangebend** adj leading; **Tonarm** m pick-up arm; **Tonart** f (musical) key; **Tonband** nt tape; **Tonbandaufnahme** f tape recording; **Tonbandgerät** nt tape recorder

tönen ['tø:nən] vi to sound ▷ vt to shade; (Haare) to tint

tönern ['tø:nərn] adj clay

Ton- zW: **Tonfall** m intonation; **Tonfilm** m sound film; **Tonhöhe** f pitch

Tonikum (-s, -ika) nt (Med) tonic

Ton- zW: **Toningenieur** m sound engineer; **Tonkopf** m recording head; **Tonkünstler** m musician; **Tonleiter** f (Mus) scale; **tonlos** adj soundless

Tonne ['tɔnə] (-, -n) f barrel; (Maß) ton

Ton- zW: **Tonspur** f soundtrack; **Tontaube** f clay pigeon; **Tonwaren** pl pottery sing, earthenware sing

Topf [tɔpf] (-(e)s, ̈-e) m pot; **alles in einen ~ werfen** (fig) to lump everything together; **Topfblume** f pot plant

Töpfer, in ['tœpfər(ɪn)] (-s, -) m(f) potter

Töpferei [tœpfə'raɪ] f (Töpferware) pottery; (Werkstatt) pottery, potter's workshop

töpfern vi to do pottery

Töpferscheibe f potter's wheel

topfit ['tɔp'fɪt] adj in top form

Topflappen m ovencloth

topografisch [topo'gra:fɪʃ] adj topographic

topp [tɔp] interj O.K.

Tor¹ [to:r] (-en, -en) m fool

Tor² (-(e)s, -e) nt gate; (Sport) goal; **Torbogen** m archway; **Toreinfahrt** f entrance gate

Toresschluss m: **(kurz) vor ~** right at the last minute

Torf [tɔrf] (-(e)s) m peat; **Torfstechen** nt peat-cutting

Torheit f foolishness; (törichte Handlung) foolish deed

Torhüter (-s, -) m goalkeeper

töricht ['tø:rɪçt] adj foolish

torkeln ['tɔrkəln] vi to stagger, reel

torpedieren [tɔrpe'di:rən] vt (lit, fig) to torpedo

Torpedo [tɔr'pe:do] (-s, -s) m torpedo

Torschlusspanik ['to:rʃlʊspa:nɪk] (umg) f (von Unverheirateten) fear of being left on the shelf

Torte ['tɔrtə] (-, -n) f cake; (Obsttorte) flan, tart

Tortenguss m glaze

Tortenheber m cake slice

Tortur [tɔr'tu:r] f ordeal

Torverhältnis nt goal average

Torwart (-(e)s, -e) m goalkeeper

tosen ['to:zən] vi to roar

Toskana [tɔs'ka:na] f Tuscany

tot [to:t] adj dead; **er war auf der Stelle ~** he died instantly; **~ geboren** stillborn; **sich ~ stellen** to pretend to be dead; **der ~e Winkel** the blind spot; **einen ~en Punkt haben** to be at one's lowest; **das T~e Meer** the Dead Sea

total [to'ta:l] adj total; **Totalausverkauf** m clearance sale

totalitär [totali'tɛ:r] adj totalitarian

Totaloperation f extirpation; (von Gebärmutter) hysterectomy

Totalschaden m (Aut) complete write-off

totarbeiten vr to work o.s. to death

totärgern (umg) vr to get really annoyed

Tote, r f(m) dead person

töten ['tø:tən] vt, vi to kill

Toten- zW: **Totenbett** nt deathbed; **totenblass** adj deathly pale, white as a sheet; **Totengräber (-s, -)** m gravedigger; **Totenhemd** nt shroud; **Totenkopf** m skull; **Totenmesse** f requiem mass; **Totenschein** m death certificate; **Totenstille** f deathly silence; **Totentanz** m danse macabre; **Totenwache** f wake

tot- zW: **totfahren** unreg vt to run over; **totkriegen** (umg) vt: **nicht totzukriegen sein** to go on for ever; **totlachen** (umg) vr to laugh one's head off

Toto ['to:to] (-s, -s) m od nt ≈ pools pl

tot- zW: **totsagen** vt: **jdn totsagen** to say that sb is dead; **Totschlag** m (Jur) manslaughter, second degree murder (US); **totschlagen** unreg vt (lit, fig) to kill; **Totschläger** m (Waffe) cosh (Brit), blackjack (US); **totschweigen** unreg vt to hush up; **tottreten** unreg vt to trample to death

Tötung ['tø:tʊŋ] f killing

Touchscreen ['tatʃskri:n] m (Tech) touch screen; **Touchscreen-Handy** nt touch screen mobile; **Touchscreen-Technologie** f touch screen technology

toupieren [tu'pi:rən] vt to backcomb

Tour [tu:r] (-, -en) f tour, trip; (Umdrehung) revolution; (Verhaltensart) way; **auf ~en kommen** (Aut) to reach top speed; (fig) to get into top gear; **auf vollen ~en laufen** (lit) to run at full speed; (fig) to be in full swing; **auf die krumme ~** by dishonest means; **in einer ~** incessantly

Tourenzahl f number of revolutions

Tourenzähler m rev counter

Tourismus [tu'rɪsmʊs] m tourism

Tourist, in m(f) tourist

Touristenklasse f tourist class

Touristik [tu'rɪstɪk] f tourism

touristisch adj tourist attr

Tournee [tur'ne:] (-, -s od -n) f (Theat etc) tour;

auf ~ gehen to go on tour
Trab [tra:p] (**-(e)s**) m trot; **auf ~ sein** (umg) to be on the go
Trabant [tra'bant] m satellite
Trabantenstadt f satellite town
traben ['tra:bən] vi to trot
Tracht [traxt] (**-, -en**) f (Kleidung) costume, dress; **eine ~ Prügel** a sound thrashing
trachten vi to strive, endeavour (Brit), endeavor (US); **danach ~, etw zu tun** to strive to do sth; **jdm nach dem Leben ~** to seek to kill sb
trächtig ['trɛçtıç] adj (Tier) pregnant
Tradition [traditsi'o:n] f tradition
traditionell [traditsio'nɛl] adj traditional
traf etc [tra:f] vb siehe **treffen**
Tragbahre f stretcher
tragbar adj (Gerät) portable; (Kleidung) wearable; (erträglich) bearable
träge ['trɛ:gə] adj sluggish, slow; (Phys) inert
tragen ['tra:gən] unreg vt to carry; (Kleidung, Brille) to wear; (Namen, Früchte) to bear; (erdulden) to endure ▷ vi (schwanger sein) to be pregnant; (Eis) to hold; **schwer an etw** dat ~ (lit) to have a job carrying sth; (fig) to find sth hard to bear; **zum T~ kommen** to come to fruition; (nützlich werden) to come in useful
tragend adj (Säule, Bauteil) load-bearing; (Idee, Motiv) fundamental
Träger ['trɛ:gər] (**-s, -**) m carrier; wearer; bearer; (Ordensträger) holder; (an Kleidung) (shoulder) strap; (Körperschaft etc) sponsor; (Holzträger, Betonträger) (supporting) beam; (Stahlträger, Eisenträger) girder; (Tech: Stütze von Brücken etc) support
Trägerin f (Person) siehe **Träger**
Träger- zW: **Trägerkleid** nt pinafore dress (Brit), jumper (US); **Trägerrakete** f launch vehicle; **Trägerrock** m skirt with shoulder straps
Tragetasche f carrier bag (Brit), carry-all (US)
Trag- zW: **Tragfähigkeit** f load-bearing capacity; **Tragfläche** f (Aviat) wing; **Tragflügelboot** nt hydrofoil
Trägheit ['trɛ:khait] f laziness; (Phys) inertia
Tragik ['tra:gık] f tragedy
tragikomisch [tragi'ko:mıʃ] adj tragi-comic
tragisch adj tragic; **etw ~ nehmen** (umg) to take sth to heart
Traglast f load
Tragödie [tra'gø:diə] f tragedy
trägt [trɛ:kt] vb siehe **tragen**
Tragweite f range; (fig) scope; **von großer ~ sein** to have far-reaching consequences
Tragwerk nt wing assembly
Trainer, in ['trɛ:nər(ın)] (**-s, -**) m(f) (Sport) trainer, coach; (Fussball) manager
trainieren [trɛ'ni:rən] vt to train; (Übung) to practise (Brit), practice (US) ▷ vi to train; **Fußball ~** to do football practice
Training (-s, -s) nt training
Trainingsanzug m track suit
Trakt [trakt] (**-(e)s, -e**) m (Gebäudeteil) section; (Flügel) wing

Traktat [trak'ta:t] (**-(e)s, -e**) m od nt (Abhandlung) treatise; (Flugschrift, religiöse Schrift) tract
traktieren (umg) vt (schlecht behandeln) to maltreat; (quälen) to torment
Traktor ['traktɔr] m tractor; (von Drucker) tractor feed
trällern ['trɛlərn] vt, vi to warble; (Vogel) to trill, warble
trampeln ['trampəln] vt to trample; (abschütteln) to stamp ▷ vi to stamp
Trampelpfad m track, path
Trampeltier nt (Zool) (Bactrian) camel; (fig: umg) clumsy oaf
trampen ['trɛmpən] vi to hitchhike
Tramper, in [trɛmpər(ın)] (**-s, -**) m(f) hitchhiker
Trampolin [trampo'li:n] (**-s, -e**) nt trampoline
Tranchierbesteck nt pair of carvers, carvers pl
tranchieren [trã'ʃi:rən] vt to carve
Träne ['trɛ:nə] (**-, -n**) f tear
tränen vi to water
Tränengas nt tear gas
tranig ['tra:nıç] (umg) adj slow, sluggish
trank etc [traŋk] vb siehe **trinken**
Tränke ['trɛŋkə] (**-, -n**) f watering place
tränken vt (nass machen) to soak; (Tiere) to water
Transaktion [trans|aktsi'o:n] f transaction
Transchierbesteck nt = **Tranchierbesteck**
transchieren vt = **tranchieren**
Transformator [transfɔr'ma:tɔr] m transformer
Transfusion [transfuzi'o:n] f transfusion
Transistor [tran'zıstɔr] m transistor
transitiv ['tranziti:f] adj transitive
Transitverkehr [tran'zi:tfɛrke:r] m transit traffic
transparent [transpa'rɛnt] adj transparent; **Transparent** (**-(e)s, -e**) nt (Bild) transparency; (Spruchband) banner
transpirieren [transpi'ri:rən] vi to perspire
Transplantation [transplantatsi'o:n] f transplantation; (Hauttransplantation) graft(ing)
Transport [trans'pɔrt] (**-(e)s, -e**) m transport; (Fracht) consignment, shipment; **transportfähig** adj moveable
transportieren [transpɔr'ti:rən] vt to transport
Transport- zW: **Transportkosten** pl transport charges pl, carriage sing; **Transportmittel** nt means sing of transport; **Transportunternehmen** nt carrier
transsexuell [transzɛksu'ɛl] adj transsexual
transsig ['tra:nzu:zıç] (umg) adj sluggish
Transvestit [transvɛs'ti:t] (**-en, -en**) m transvestite
Trapez [tra'pe:ts] (**-es, -e**) nt trapeze; (Math) trapezium
Trara [tra'ra:] (**-s**) nt: **mit viel ~ (um)** (fig: umg) with a great hullabaloo (about)
trat etc [tra:t] vb siehe **treten**
Tratsch [tra:tʃ] (**-(e)s**) (umg) m gossip
tratschen ['tra:tʃən] (umg) vi to gossip

Tratte ['tratə] (-, -n) f (Fin) draft
Traube ['traʊbə] (-, -n) f grape; (ganze Frucht) bunch (of grapes)
Traubenlese f grape harvest
Traubenzucker m glucose
trauen ['traʊən] vi +dat to trust ▷ vr to dare ▷ vt to marry; **jdm/etw ~** to trust sb/sth
Trauer ['traʊər] (-) f sorrow; (für Verstorbenen) mourning; **Trauerfall** m death, bereavement; **Trauerfeier** f funeral service; **Trauerflor** (-s, -e) m black ribbon; **Trauergemeinde** f mourners pl; **Trauermarsch** m funeral march
trauern vi to mourn; **um jdn ~** to mourn (for) sb
Trauer- zW: **Trauerrand** m black border; **Trauerspiel** nt tragedy; **Trauerweide** f weeping willow
Traufe ['traʊfə] (-, -n) f eaves pl
träufeln ['trɔyfəln] vt, vi to drip
traulich ['traʊlɪç] adj cosy, intimate
Traum [traʊm] (-(e)s, Träume) m dream; **aus der ~!** it's all over!
Trauma (-s, -men) nt trauma
traumatisieren [traʊmatiˈziːrən] vt to traumatize
Traumbild nt vision
Traumdeutung f interpretation of dreams
träumen ['trɔymən] vt, vi to dream; **das hätte ich mir nicht ~ lassen** I'd never have thought it possible
Träumer, in (-s, -) m(f) dreamer
Träumerei [trɔyməˈraɪ] f dreaming
träumerisch adj dreamy
traumhaft adj dreamlike; (fig) wonderful
Traumtänzer m dreamer
traurig ['traʊrɪç] adj sad; **Traurigkeit** f sadness
Trauring m wedding ring
Trauschein m marriage certificate
Trauung f wedding ceremony
Trauzeuge m witness (to a marriage)
treffen ['trɛfən] unreg vt to strike, to hit; (Bemerkung) to hurt; (begegnen) to meet; (Entscheidung etc) to make; (Maßnahmen) to take ▷ vi to hit ▷ vr to meet; **er hat es gut getroffen** he did well; **er fühlte sich getroffen** he took it personally; **~ auf** +akk to come across, meet; **es traf sich, dass ...** it so happened that ...; **es trifft sich gut** it's convenient
Treffen (-s, -) nt meeting
treffend adj pertinent, apposite
Treffer (-s, -) m hit; (Tor) goal; (Los) winner
trefflich adj excellent
Treffpunkt m meeting place
Treibeis nt drift ice
treiben ['traɪbən] unreg vt to drive; (Studien etc) to pursue; (Sport) to do, go in for ▷ vi (Schiff etc) to drift; (Pflanzen) to sprout; (Koch: aufgehen) to rise; (Medikamente) to be diuretic; **die ~de Kraft** (fig) the driving force; **Handel mit etw/jdm ~** to trade in sth/with sb; **es zu weit ~** to go too far; **Unsinn ~** to fool around; **Treiben** (-s) nt activity

Treib- zW: **Treibgut** nt flotsam and jetsam; **Treibhaus** nt greenhouse; **Treibhauseffekt** m greenhouse effect; **Treibhausgas** nt greenhouse gas; **Treibjagd** f shoot (in which game is sent up); (fig) witchhunt; **Treibsand** m quicksand; **Treibstoff** m fuel
Trend [trɛnt] (-s, -s) m trend; **Trendwende** f new trend
trennbar adj separable
trennen ['trɛnən] vt to separate; (teilen) to divide ▷ vr to separate; **sich ~ von** to part with
Trennschärfe f (Rundf) selectivity
Trennung f separation
Trennungsstrich m hyphen
Trennwand f partition (wall)
treppab adv downstairs
treppauf adv upstairs
Treppe ['trɛpə] (-, -n) f stairs pl, staircase; (im Freien) steps pl; **eine ~** a staircase, a flight of stairs od steps; **sie wohnt zwei ~n hoch/höher** she lives two flights up/higher up
Treppengeländer nt banister
Treppenhaus nt staircase
Tresen ['treːzən] (-s, -) m (Theke) bar; (Ladentisch) counter
Tresor [treˈzoːr] (-s, -e) m safe
Tretboot nt pedal boat, pedalo
treten ['treːtən] unreg vi to step; (Tränen, Schweiß) to appear ▷ vt (mit Fußtritt) to kick; (niedertreten) to tread, trample; **~ nach** to kick at; **~ in** +akk to step in(to); **in Verbindung ~** to get in contact; **in Erscheinung ~** to appear; **der Fluss trat über die Ufer** the river overflowed its banks; **in Streik ~** to go on strike
Treter ['treːtər] (umg) pl (Schuhe) casual shoes pl
Tretmine f (Mil) (anti-personnel) mine
Tretmühle f (fig) daily grind
treu [trɔy] adj faithful, true; **treudoof** (umg) adj naïve
Treue (-) f loyalty, faithfulness
Treuhand (umg) f, **Treuhandanstalt** f trustee organization (overseeing the privatization of former GDR state-owned firms)
Treuhandanstalt f see culture note

Treuhänder (-s, -) m trustee
Treuhandgesellschaft f trust company
treu- zW: **treuherzig** adj innocent; **treulich** adv faithfully; **treulos** adj faithless; **treulos an**

jdm handeln to fail sb
Triathlon ['triːatlɔn] (**-s**, **-s**) nt triathlon
Tribüne [tri'byːnə] (**-**, **-n**) f grandstand; (Rednertribüne) platform
Tribut [tri'buːt] (**-(e)s**, **-e**) m tribute
Trichter ['trɪçtər] (**-s**, **-**) m funnel; (Bombentrichter) crater
Trick [trɪk] (**-s**, **-e** od **-s**) m trick; **Trickfilm** m cartoon
Trieb (**-(e)s**, **-e**) m urge, drive; (Neigung) inclination; (Bot) shoot
trieb etc [triːp] vb siehe **treiben**
Trieb- zW: **Triebfeder** f (fig) motivating force; **triebhaft** adj impulsive; **Triebkraft** f (fig) drive; **Triebtäter** m sex offender; **Triebwagen** m (Eisenb) railcar; **Triebwerk** nt engine
triefen ['triːfən] vi to drip
trifft [trɪft] vb siehe **treffen**
triftig ['trɪftɪç] adj convincing; (Grund etc) good
Trigonometrie [trigonome'triː] f trigonometry
Trikot [tri'koː] (**-s**, **-s**) nt vest; (Sport) shirt ▷ m (Gewebe) tricot
Triller ['trɪlər] (**-s**, **-**) m (Mus) trill
trillern vi to trill, warble
Trillerpfeife f whistle
Trilogie [trilo'giː] f trilogy
Trimester [tri'mɛstər] (**-s**, **-**) nt term
Trimm-Aktion f keep-fit campaign
Trimm-dich-Pfad m keep-fit trail
trimmen vt (Hund) to trim; (umg: Mensch, Tier) to teach, train ▷ vr to keep fit
trinkbar adj drinkable
trinken ['trɪŋkən] unreg vt, vi to drink
Trinker, in (**-s**, **-**) m(f) drinker
Trink- zW: **trinkfest** adj: **ich bin nicht sehr trinkfest** I can't hold my drink very well; **Trinkgeld** nt tip; **Trinkhalle** f (Kiosk) refreshment kiosk; **Trinkhalm** m (drinking) straw; **Trinkmilch** f milk; **Trinkspruch** m toast; **Trinkwasser** nt drinking water
Trio ['triːo] (**-s**, **-s**) nt trio
trippeln ['trɪpəln] vi to toddle
Tripper ['trɪpər] (**-s**, **-**) m gonorrhoea (Brit), gonorrhea (US)
trist [trɪst] adj dreary, dismal; (Farbe) dull
tritt [trɪt] vb siehe **treten**
Tritt (**-(e)s**, **-e**) m step; (Fußtritt) kick
Trittbrett nt (Eisenb) step; (Aut) running board
Trittleiter f stepladder
Triumph [tri'ʊmf] (**-(e)s**, **-e**) m triumph; **Triumphbogen** m triumphal arch
triumphieren [triʊm'fiːrən] vi to triumph; (jubeln) to exult
trivial [trivi'aːl] adj trivial; **Trivialliteratur** f light fiction
trocken ['trɔkən] adj dry; **sich ~ rasieren** to use an electric razor; **Trockenautomat** m tumble dryer; **Trockendock** nt dry dock; **Trockeneis** nt dry ice; **Trockenelement** nt dry cell; **Trockenhaube** f hair-dryer; **Trockenheit** f dryness; **trockenlegen** vt (Sumpf) to drain; (Kind) to put a clean nappy (Brit) od diaper (US)

on; **Trockenmilch** f dried milk; **Trockenzeit** f (Jahreszeit) dry season
trocknen vt, vi to dry
Trockner (**-s**, **-**) m dryer
Troddel ['trɔdəl] (**-**, **-n**) f tassel
Trödel ['trøːdəl] (**-s**) (umg) m junk; **Trödelmarkt** m flea market
trödeln (umg) vi to dawdle
Trödler (**-s**, **-**) m secondhand dealer
Trog (**-(e)s**, **-̈e**) m trough
trog etc [troːk] vb siehe **trügen**
trollen ['trɔlən] (umg) vr to push off
Trommel ['trɔməl] (**-**, **-n**) f drum; **die ~ rühren** (fig: umg) to drum up support; **Trommelfell** nt eardrum; **Trommelfeuer** nt drumfire, heavy barrage
trommeln vt, vi to drum
Trommelrevolver m revolver
Trommelwaschmaschine f tumble-action washing machine
Trommler, in ['trɔmlər(ɪn)] (**-s**, **-**) m(f) drummer
Trompete [trɔm'peːtə] (**-**, **-n**) f trumpet
Trompeter (**-s**, **-**) m trumpeter
Tropen ['troːpən] pl tropics pl; **tropenbeständig** adj suitable for the tropics; **Tropenhelm** m topee, sun helmet
Tropf¹ [trɔpf] (**-(e)s**, **-̈e**) (umg) m rogue; **armer ~** poor devil
Tropf² (**-(e)s**) (umg) m (Med: Infusion) drip (umg); **am ~ hängen** to be on a drip
tröpfeln ['trœpfəln] vi to drip, trickle
Tropfen (**-s**, **-**) m drop; **ein guter** od **edler ~** a good wine; **ein ~ auf den heißen Stein** (fig: umg) a drop in the ocean
tropfen vt, vi to drip ▷ vi unpers: **es tropft** a few raindrops are falling
tropfenweise adv in drops
tropfnass adj dripping wet
Tropfsteinhöhle f stalactite cave
Trophäe [tro'fɛːə] (**-**, **-n**) f trophy
tropisch ['troːpɪʃ] adj tropical
Trost [troːst] (**-es**) m consolation, comfort; **trostbedürftig** adj in need of consolation
trösten ['trøːstən] vt to console, comfort
Tröster, in (**-s**, **-**) m(f) comfort(er)
tröstlich adj comforting
trost- zW: **trostlos** adj bleak; (Verhältnisse) wretched; **Trostpflaster** nt (fig) consolation; **Trostpreis** m consolation prize; **trostreich** adj comforting
Tröstung ['trøːstʊŋ] f comfort, consolation
Trott [trɔt] (**-(e)s**, **-e**) m trot; (Routine) routine
Trottel (**-s**, **-**) (umg) m fool, dope
trotten vi to trot
Trottoir [trɔto'aːr] (**-s**, **-s** od **-e**) nt (veraltet) pavement (Brit), sidewalk (US)
trotz [trɔts] präp (+gen od dat) in spite of
Trotz (**-es**) m pig-headedness; **etw aus ~ tun** to do sth just to show them; **jdm zum ~ in** defiance of sb
Trotzalter nt obstinate phase
trotzdem adv nevertheless ▷ konj although

trotzen vi +dat to defy; (der Kälte, dem Klima etc) to withstand; (der Gefahr) to brave; (trotzig sein) to be awkward

trotzig adj defiant; (Kind) difficult, awkward

Trotzkopf m obstinate child

Trotzreaktion f fit of pique

trüb [try:p] adj dull; (Flüssigkeit, Glas) cloudy; (fig) gloomy; **~e Tasse** (umg) drip

Trubel ['tru:bəl] (-s) m hurly-burly

trüben ['try:bən] vt to cloud ▷ vr to become clouded

Trübheit f dullness; cloudiness; gloom

Trübsal (-, -e) f distress; **~ blasen** (umg) to mope

trüb- zW: **trübselig** adj sad, melancholy; **Trübsinn** m depression; **trübsinnig** adj depressed, gloomy

trudeln ['tru:dəln] vi (Aviat) to (go into a) spin

Trüffel ['tryfəl] (-, -n) f truffle

Trug (-(e)s) m (liter) deception; (der Sinne) illusion

trug etc [tru:k] vb siehe **tragen**

trügen ['try:gən] unreg vt to deceive ▷ vi to be deceptive; **wenn mich nicht alles trügt** unless I am very much mistaken

trügerisch adj deceptive

Trugschluss ['tru:gʃlʊs] m false conclusion

Truhe ['tru:ə] (-, -n) f chest

Trümmer ['trymər] pl wreckage sing; (Bautrümmer) ruins pl; **Trümmerfeld** nt expanse of rubble od ruins; (fig) scene of devastation; **Trümmerfrauen** pl (German) women who cleared away the rubble after the war; **Trümmerhaufen** m heap of rubble

Trumpf [trʊmpf] (-(e)s, ̈-e) m (lit, fig) trump; **trumpfen** vt, vi to trump

Trunk [trʊŋk] (-(e)s, ̈-e) m drink

trunken adj intoxicated; **Trunkenbold** (-(e)s, -e) m drunkard; **Trunkenheit** f intoxication; **Trunkenheit am Steuer** drink-driving

Trunksucht f alcoholism

Trupp [trʊp] (-s, -s) m troop

Truppe (-, -n) f troop; (Waffengattung) force; (Schauspieltruppe) troupe; **nicht von der schnellen ~ sein** (umg) to be slow

Truppen pl troops pl; **Truppenabbau** m cutback in troop numbers; **Truppenführer** m (military) commander; **Truppenteil** m unit; **Truppenübungsplatz** m training area

Trust [trast] (-(e)s, -e od -s) m trust

Truthahn ['tru:tha:n] m turkey

Tschad [tʃat] (-s) m: **der ~** Chad

Tscheche ['tʃɛçə] (-n, -n) m, **Tschechin** f Czech

tschechisch adj Czech; **die T~e Republik** the Czech Republic

Tschechoslowakei [tʃɛçoslova:'kai] f (früher): **die ~** Czechoslovakia

tschüss [tʃʏs] (umg) interj cheerio (Brit), so long (US)

T-Shirt ['ti:ʃə:t] (-s, -s) nt T-shirt

TU (-) f abk (= technische Universität) ≈ polytechnic

Tuba ['tu:ba] (-, **Tuben**) f (Mus) tuba

Tube ['tu:bə] (-, -n) f tube

Tuberkulose [tubɛrku'lo:zə] (-, -n) f tuberculosis

Tuch [tu:x] (-(e)s, ̈-er) nt cloth; (Halstuch) scarf; (Kopftuch) (head)scarf; (Handtuch) towel; **Tuchfühlung** f physical contact

tüchtig ['tʏçtɪç] adj efficient; (fähig) able, capable; (umg: kräftig) good, sound; **etwas T~es lernen/werden** (umg) to get a proper training/job; **Tüchtigkeit** f efficiency; ability

Tücke ['tʏkə] (-, -n) f (Arglist) malice; (Trick) trick; (Schwierigkeit) difficulty, problem; **seine ~n haben** to be temperamental

tückisch adj treacherous; (böswillig) malicious

tüfteln ['tʏftəln] (umg) vi to puzzle; (basteln) to fiddle about

Tugend ['tu:gənt] (-, -en) f virtue; **tugendhaft** adj virtuous

Tüll [tʏl] (-s, -e) m tulle

Tülle (-, -n) f spout

Tulpe ['tʊlpə] (-, -n) f tulip

tummeln ['tʊməln] vr to romp (about); (sich beeilen) to hurry

Tummelplatz m play area; (fig) hotbed

Tumor ['tu:mɔr] (-s, -e) m tumour (Brit), tumor (US)

Tümpel ['tʏmpəl] (-s, -) m pond

Tumult [tu'mʊlt] (-(e)s, -e) m tumult

tun [tu:n] unreg vt (machen) to do; (legen) to put ▷ vi to act ▷ vr: **es tut sich etwas/viel** something/a lot is happening; **jdm etw ~** to do sth to sb; **etw tut es auch** sth will do; **das tut nichts** that doesn't matter; **das tut nichts zur Sache** that's neither here nor there; **du kannst ~ und lassen, was du willst** you can do as you please; **so ~, als ob** to act as if; **zu ~ haben** (beschäftigt sein) to be busy, have things od something to do

Tünche ['tʏnçə] (-, -n) f whitewash

tünchen vt to whitewash

Tunesien [tu'ne:ziən] (-s) nt Tunisia

Tunesier, in [-] m(f) Tunisian

tunesisch adj Tunisian

Tunfisch m = **Thunfisch**

Tunke ['tʊŋkə] (-, -n) f sauce

tunken vt to dip, dunk

tunlichst ['tu:nlıçst] adv if at all possible; **~ bald** as soon as possible

Tunnel ['tʊnəl] (-s, -s od -) m tunnel

Tunte ['tʊntə] (-, -n) (pej: umg) f fairy (pej)

Tüpfel ['tʏpfəl] (-s, -) m dot; **Tüpfelchen** nt (small) dot

tüpfeln ['tʏpfəln] vt to dab

tupfen ['tʊpfən] vt to dab; (mit Farbe) to dot; **Tupfen** (-, -) m dot, spot

Tupfer (-s, -) m swab

Tür [ty:r] (-, -en) f door; **an die ~ gehen** to answer the door; **zwischen ~ und Angel** in passing; **Weihnachten steht vor der ~** (fig) Christmas is just around the corner; **mit der ~ ins Haus fallen** (umg) to blurt it od things out; **Türangel** f (door) hinge

Turbine [tʊr'bi:nə] f turbine

turbulent [tʊrbu'lɛnt] adj turbulent

Türke ['tyrkə] (**-n, -n**) *m* Turk
Türkei [tyr'kaɪ] *f*: **die** ~ Turkey
Türkin *f* Turk
Türkis [tyr'ki:s] (**-es, -e**) *m* turquoise; **türkis** *adj* turquoise
türkisch *adj* Turkish
Türklinke *f* door handle
Turm [tʊrm] (**-(e)s, ̈-e**) *m* tower; (*Kirchturm*) steeple; (*Sprungturm*) diving platform; (*Schach*) castle, rook
türmen ['tyrmən] *vr* to tower up ▷ *vt* to heap up ▷ *vi* (*umg*) to scarper, bolt
Turmuhr *f* clock (on a tower); (*Kirchturmuhr*) church clock
Turnanzug *m* gym costume
turnen ['tʊrnən] *vi* to do gymnastic exercises; (*herumklettern*) to climb about; (*Kind*) to romp ▷ *vt* to perform; **Turnen** (**-s**) *nt* gymnastics *sing*; (*Sch*) physical education, P.E.
Turner, in (**-s, -**) *m(f)* gymnast
Turnhalle *f* gym(nasium)
Turnhose *f* gym shorts *pl*
Turnier [tʊr'ni:r] (**-s, -e**) *nt* tournament
Turn- *zW*: **Turnlehrer, in** *m(f)* gym *od* PE teacher; **Turnschuh** *m* gym shoe; **Turnstunde** *f* gym *od* PE lesson
Turnus ['tʊrnʊs] (**-, -se**) *m* rota; **im** ~ in rotation
Turnverein *m* gymnastics club
Turnzeug *nt* gym kit
Türöffner *m* buzzer
turteln ['tʊrtəln] (*umg*) *vi* to bill and coo; (*fig*) to whisper sweet nothings
Tusch [tʊʃ] (**-(e)s, -e**) *m* (*Mus*) flourish
Tusche ['tʊʃə] (**-, -n**) *f* Indian ink
tuscheln ['tʊʃəln] *vt, vi* to whisper
Tuschkasten *m* paintbox
Tussi ['tʊsɪ] (**-, -s**) (*umg*) *f* (*Frau, Freundin*) bird (*Brit*), chick (*US*)

tust [tu:st] *vb siehe* **tun**
tut [tu:t] *vb siehe* **tun**
Tüte ['ty:tə] (**-, -n**) *f* bag; **in die** ~ **blasen** (*umg*) to be breathalyzed; **das kommt nicht in die** ~**!** (*umg*) no way!
tuten ['tu:tən] *vi* (*Aut*) to hoot (*Brit*), honk (*US*); **von T**~ **und Blasen keine Ahnung haben** (*umg*) not to have a clue
TÜV [tyf] *m abk* (= *Technischer Überwachungs-Verein*) ≈ MOT (*Brit*); **durch den** ~ **kommen** (*Aut*) to pass its test *od* MOT (*Brit*); *see culture note*

◉ **TÜV**
◉
◉ The TÜV (Technischer
◉ Überwachungsverein) is the organization
◉ responsible for checking the safety of
◉ machinery, particularly vehicles. Cars over
◉ three years old have to be examined every
◉ two years for their safety and for their
◉ exhaust emissions. The TÜV is the German
◉ equivalent of the MOT.

TV (**-**) *nt abk* (= *Television*) TV ▷ *m abk* = **Turnverein**
Twen [tvɛn] (**-(s), -s**) *m person in his/her twenties*
Twitter® ['tvɪtər] *nt* Twitter®
Typ [ty:p] (**-s, -en**) *m* type
Type (**-, -n**) *f* (*Typ*) type
Typhus ['ty:fʊs] (**-**) *m* typhoid (fever)
typisch ['ty:pɪʃ] *adj*: ~ (**für**) typical (of)
Tyrann [ty'ran] (**-en, -en**) *m(f)* tyrant
Tyrannei [tyra'naɪ] *f* tyranny
Tyrannin *f* tyrant
tyrannisch *adj* tyrannical
tyrannisieren [tyrani'zi:rən] *vt* to tyrannize
tyrrhenisch [ty're:nɪʃ] *adj* Tyrrhenian; **T**~**es Meer** Tyrrhenian Sea

t

Uu

U, u [uː] *nt* U, u; **U wie Ulrich** ≈ U for Uncle
u. *abk* = **und**
u. a. *abk* (= *und andere(s)*) and others; (= *unter anderem*) amongst other things
u. Ä. *abk* (= *und Ähnliche(s)*) and similar
u. A. w. g. *abk* (= *um Antwort wird gebeten*) R.S.V.P.
U-Bahn ['uːbaːn] *f abk* (= *Untergrundbahn*) underground (*Brit*), subway (*US*)
übel ['yːbəl] *adj* bad; **jdm ist ~** sb feels sick; **~ gelaunt** bad-tempered, sullen; **jdm eine Bemerkung** *etc* **~ nehmen** to be offended at sb's remark *etc*; *siehe auch* **übelwollend**; Übel (**-s, -**) *nt* evil; (*Krankheit*) disease; **zu allem Übel ...** to make matters worse ...; **Übelkeit** *f* nausea; **Übelstand** *m* bad state of affairs; **Übeltäter** *m* wrongdoer; **übelwollend** *adj* malevolent
üben ['yːbən] *vt, vi, vr* to practise (*Brit*), practice (*US*); (*Gedächtnis, Muskeln*) to exercise; **Kritik an etw** *dat* **~** to criticize sth

 SCHLÜSSELWORT

über ['yːbər] *präp +dat* **1** (*räumlich*) over, above; **zwei Grad über null** two degrees above zero
2 (*zeitlich*) over; **über der Arbeit einschlafen** to fall asleep over one's work
▷ *präp +akk* **1** (*räumlich*) over; (*hoch über*) above; (*quer über*) across; **er lachte über das ganze Gesicht** he was beaming all over his face; **Macht über jdn haben** to have power over sb
2 (*zeitlich*) over; **über Weihnachten** over Christmas; **über kurz oder lang** sooner or later
3 (*auf dem Wege*) via; **nach Köln über Aachen** to Cologne via Aachen; **ich habe es über die Auskunft erfahren** I found out from information
4 (*betreffend*) about; **ein Buch über ...** a book about *od* on ...; **über jdn/etw lachen** to laugh about *od* at sb/sth; **ein Scheck über 200 Euro** a cheque for 200 euros
5: Fehler über Fehler mistake after mistake
▷ *adv* **1** (*mehr als*) over, more than; **Kinder über 12 Jahren** children over *od* above 12 years of age; **sie liebt ihn über alles** she loves him more than anything
2: über und über over and over; **den ganzen**

Tag/die ganze Zeit über all day long/all the time; **jdm in etw** *dat* **über sein** to be superior to sb in sth

überall [yːbər'|al] *adv* everywhere; **überallhin** *adv* everywhere
überaltert [yːbər'|altərt] *adj* obsolete
Überangebot ['yːbər|angəboːt] *nt*: **~ (an +**dat) surplus (of)
überanstrengen [yːbər'|anʃtrɛŋən] *vt untr* to overexert ▷ *vr untr* to overexert o.s.
überantworten [yːbər'|antvɔrtən] *vt untr* to hand over, deliver (up)
überarbeiten [yːbər'|arbaɪtən] *vt untr* to revise, rework ▷ *vr untr* to overwork (o.s.)
überaus ['yːbər|aus] *adv* exceedingly
überbacken [yːbər'bakən] *unreg vt untr* to put in the oven/under the grill
Überbau ['yːbərbau] *m* (*Gebäude, Philosophie*) superstructure
überbeanspruchen ['yːbərbə|anʃpruxən] *vt untr* (*Menschen, Körper, Maschine*) to overtax
überbelichten ['yːbərbəlɪçtən] *vt untr* (*Phot*) to overexpose
Überbesetzung ['yːbərbəzɛtsuŋ] *f* overmanning
überbewerten ['yːbərbəveːrtən] *vt untr* (*fig*) to overrate; (*Äußerungen*) to attach too much importance to
überbieten [yːbər'biːtən] *unreg vt untr* to outbid; (*übertreffen*) to surpass; (*Rekord*) to break ▷ *vr untr*: **sich in etw** *dat* **(gegenseitig) ~** to vie with each other in sth
Überbleibsel ['yːbərblaɪpsəl] (**-s, -**) *nt* residue, remainder
Überblick ['yːbərblɪk] *m* view; (*fig: Darstellung*) survey, overview; (*Fähigkeit*): **~ (über +**akk) overall view (of), grasp (of); **den ~ verlieren** to lose track (of things); **sich einen ~ verschaffen** to get a general idea
überblicken [yːbər'blɪkən] *vt untr* to survey; (*fig*) to see; (: *Lage etc*) to grasp
überbringen [yːbər'brɪŋən] *unreg vt untr* to deliver, hand over
Überbringer(-s, -) *m* bearer
Überbringung *f* delivery
überbrücken [yːbər'brʏkən] *vt untr* to bridge
Überbrückung *f*: **100 Euro zur ~** 100 euros to

tide me/him *etc* over
Überbrückungskredit *m* bridging loan
überbuchen ['y:bərbu:xən] *vt* to overbook
überdauern [y:bər'dauərn] *vt untr* to outlast
überdenken [y:bər'dɛŋkən] *unreg vt untr* to think over
überdies [y:bər'di:s] *adv* besides
überdimensional ['y:bərdimɛnziona:l] *adj* oversize
Überdosis ['y:bərdo:zɪs] *f* overdose, OD (*umg*); (*zu große Zumessung*) excessive amount
überdrehen [y:bər'dre:ən] *vt untr* (*Uhr etc*) to overwind
überdreht *adj*: ~ **sein** (*fig*) to be hyped up, be overexcited
Überdruck ['y:bərdrʊk] *m* (*Tech*) excess pressure
Überdruss ['y:bərdrʊs] (**-es**) *m* weariness; **bis zum** ~ ad nauseam
überdrüssig ['y:bərdrysɪç] *adj +gen* tired of, sick of
überdurchschnittlich ['y:bərdʊrçʃnɪtlɪç] *adj* above-average ▷ *adv* exceptionally
übereifrig ['y:bər|aɪfrɪç] *adj* overzealous
übereignen [y:bər'|aɪgnən] *vt untr*: **jdm etw** ~ (*geh*) to make sth over to sb
übereilen [y:bər'|aɪlən] *vt untr* to hurry
übereilt *adj* (over)hasty
übereinander [y:bər|aɪ'nandər] *adv* one upon the other; (*sprechen*) about each other
übereinanderschlagen *unreg vt* (*Arme*) to fold; (*Beine*) to cross
übereinkommen [y:bər|'aɪnkɔmən] *unreg vi* to agree
Übereinkunft [y:bər|'aɪnkʊnft] (**-, -künfte**) *f* agreement
übereinstimmen [y:bər|'aɪnʃtɪmən] *vi* to agree; (*Angaben, Messwerte etc*) to tally; (*mit Tatsachen*) to fit
Übereinstimmung *f* agreement
überempfindlich ['y:bər|ɛmpfɪntlɪç] *adj* hypersensitive
überfahren¹ ['y:bərfa:rən] *unreg vt* to take across ▷ *vi* to cross, go across
überfahren² [y:bər'fa:rən] *unreg vt untr* (*Aut*) to run over; (*fig*) to walk all over
Überfahrt ['y:bərfa:rt] *f* crossing
Überfall ['y:bərfal] *m* (*Banküberfall, Mil*) raid; (*auf jdn*) assault
überfallen [y:bər'falən] *unreg vt untr* to attack; (*Bank*) to raid; (*besuchen*) to drop in on, descend (up)on
überfällig ['y:bərfɛlɪç] *adj* overdue
Überfallkommando *nt* flying squad
überfliegen [y:bər'fli:gən] *unreg vt untr* to fly over, overfly; (*Buch*) to skim through
Überflieger *m* (*fig*) high-flier
überflügeln [y:bər'fly:gəln] *vt untr* to outdo
Überfluss ['y:bərflʊs] *m*: ~ **(an** +*dat*) (*super*) abundance (of), excess (of); **zu allem** *od* **zum** ~ (*unnötigerweise*) superfluously; (*obendrein*) to crown it all (*umg*); **Überflussgesellschaft** *f* affluent society

überflüssig ['y:bərflʏsɪç] *adj* superfluous
überfluten [y:bər'flu:tən] *vt untr* (*lit*) to flood; (*fig*) to flood, inundate
überfordern [y:bər'fɔrdərn] *vt untr* to demand too much of; (*Kräfte etc*) to overtax
überfragt [y:bər'fra:kt] *adj*: **da bin ich** ~ there you've got me, you've got me there
überführen¹ ['y:bərfy:rən] *vt* to transfer; (*Leiche etc*) to transport
überführen² [y:bər'fy:rən] *vt untr* (*Täter*) to have convicted
Überführung *f* (*siehe vbs*) transfer; transport; conviction; (*Brücke*) bridge, overpass
überfüllt [y:bər'fʏlt] *adj* overcrowded; (*Kurs*) oversubscribed
Übergabe ['y:bərga:bə] *f* handing over; (*Mil*) surrender
Übergang ['y:bərgaŋ] *m* crossing; (*Wandel, Überleitung*) transition
Übergangs- *zW*: **Übergangserscheinung** *f* transitory phenomenon; **Übergangsfinanzierung** *f* (*Fin*) accommodation; **übergangslos** *adj* without a transition; **Übergangslösung** *f* provisional solution, stopgap; **Übergangsstadium** *nt* state of transition; **Übergangszeit** *f* transitional period
übergeben [y:bər'ge:bən] *unreg vt untr* to hand over; (*Mil*) to surrender ▷ *vr untr* to be sick; **dem Verkehr** ~ to open to traffic
übergehen¹ ['y:bərge:ən] *unreg vi* (*Besitz*) to pass; (*zum Feind etc*) to go over, defect; (*überwechseln*): **(zu etw)** ~ to go on (to sth); ~ **in** +*akk* to turn into
übergehen² [y:bər'ge:ən] *unreg vt untr* to pass over, omit
übergeordnet ['y:bərgə|ɔrdnət] *adj* (*Behörde*) higher
Übergepäck ['y:bərgəpɛk] *nt* excess baggage
übergeschnappt ['y:bərgəʃnapt] (*umg*) *adj* crazy
Übergewicht ['y:bərgəvɪçt] *nt* excess weight; (*fig*) preponderance
übergießen [y:bər'gi:sən] *unreg vt untr* to pour over; (*Braten*) to baste
überglücklich ['y:bərglʏklɪç] *adj* overjoyed
übergreifen ['y:bərgraɪfən] *unreg vi*: ~ **(auf** +*akk*) (*auf Rechte etc*) to encroach (on); (*Feuer, Streik, Krankheit etc*) to spread (to); **ineinander** ~ to overlap
übergroß ['y:bərgro:s] *adj* outsize, huge
Übergröße ['y:bərgrø:sə] *f* oversize
überhaben ['y:bərha:bən] *unreg* (*umg*) *vt* to be fed up with
überhandnehmen [y:bər'hant-] *unreg vi* to gain the ascendancy
überhängen ['y:bərhɛŋən] *unreg vi* to overhang
überhäufen [y:bər'hɔyfən] *vt untr*: **jdn mit Geschenken/Vorwürfen** ~ to heap presents/reproaches on sb
überhaupt [y:bər'haupt] *adv* at all; (*im Allgemeinen*) in general; (*besonders*) especially; ~ **nicht** not at all; **wer sind Sie** ~**?** who do you

u

think you are?

überheblich [y:bər'he:plɪç] *adj* arrogant;
Überheblichkeit *f* arrogance

überhöht [y:bər'hø:t] *adj* (*Forderungen, Preise*)
exorbitant, excessive

überholen [y:bər'ho:lən] *vt untr* to overtake;
(*Tech*) to overhaul

Überholspur *f* overtaking lane

überholt *adj* out-of-date, obsolete

Überholverbot [y:bər'ho:lfɛrbo:t] *nt*
overtaking (*Brit*) *od* passing ban

überhören [y:bər'hø:rən] *vt untr* to not hear;
(*absichtlich*) to ignore; **das möchte ich
überhört haben!** (I'll pretend) I didn't hear
that!

Über-Ich, Überich ['y:bər|ɪç] (**-s**) *nt* superego

überirdisch ['y:bər|ɪrdɪʃ] *adj* supernatural,
unearthly

überkapitalisieren ['y:bərkapitali'zi:rən] *vt
untr* to overcapitalize

überkochen ['y:bərkɔxən] *vi* to boil over

überkompensieren ['y:bərkɔmpɛnzi:rən] *vt
untr* to overcompensate for

überladen [y:bər'ladən] *unreg vt untr* to overload
▷ *adj* (*fig*) cluttered

überlassen [y:bər'lasən] *unreg vt untr*: **jdm etw
~** to leave sth to sb ▷ *vr untr*: **sich einer Sache
dat ~** to give o.s. over to sth; **das bleibt Ihnen
~** that's up to you; **jdn sich *dat* selbst ~** to
leave sb to his/her own devices

überlasten [y:bər'lastən] *vt untr* to overload;
(*jdn*) to overtax

überlaufen¹ ['y:bərlaufən] *unreg vi* (*Flüssigkeit*) to
flow over; (*zum Feind etc*) to go over, defect

überlaufen² [y:bər'laufən] *unreg vt untr* (*Schauer
etc*) to come over ▷ *adj* overcrowded; **~ sein** to
be inundated *od* besieged

Überläufer ['y:bərlɔyfər] *m* deserter

überleben [y:bər'le:bən] *vt untr* to survive

Überlebende, r *f(m)* survivor

überlebensgroß [y:bər'le:bənsgro:s] *adj* larger-than-life

überlegen [y:bər'le:gən] *vt untr* to consider ▷ *adj*
superior; **ich habe es mir anders** *od* **noch
einmal überlegt** I've changed my mind;
Überlegenheit *f* superiority

Überlegung *f* consideration, deliberation

überleiten ['y:bərlaɪtən] *vt* (*Abschnitt etc*): **~ in**
+*akk* to link up with

überlesen [y:bər'le:zən] *unreg vt untr* (*übersehen*)
to overlook, miss

überliefern [y:bər'li:fərn] *vt untr* to hand down,
transmit

Überlieferung *f* tradition; **schriftliche ~en**
(written) records

überlisten [y:bər'lɪstən] *vt untr* to outwit

überm ['y:bərm] = **über dem**

Übermacht ['y:bərmaxt] *f* superior force,
superiority

übermächtig ['y:bərmeçtɪç] *adj* superior (in
strength); (*Gefühl etc*) overwhelming

übermannen [y:bər'manən] *vt untr* to overcome

Übermaß ['y:bərma:s] *nt*: **~ (an** +*dat*) excess (of)

übermäßig ['y:bərme:sɪç] *adj* excessive

Übermensch ['y:bərmɛnʃ] *m* superman;
übermenschlich *adj* superhuman

übermitteln [y:bər'mɪtəln] *vt untr* to convey

übermorgen ['y:bərmɔrgən] *adv* the day after
tomorrow

Übermüdung [y:bər'my:dʊŋ] *f* overtiredness

Übermut ['y:bərmu:t] *m* exuberance

übermütig ['y:bərmy:tɪç] *adj* exuberant, high-
spirited; **~ werden** to get overconfident

übernächste, r, s ['y:bərnɛ:çstə(r, s)] *adj*
next ... but one; (*Woche, Jahr etc*) after next

übernachten [y:bər'naxtən] *vi untr*: **(bei jdm) ~**
to spend the night (at sb's place)

übernächtigt [y:bər'nɛçtɪçt] *adj* sleepy, tired

Übernachtung *f*: **~ mit Frühstück** bed and
breakfast

Übernahme ['y:bərna:mə] (**-, -n**) *f* taking
over *od* on; (*von Verantwortung*) acceptance;
Übernahmeangebot *nt* takeover bid

übernatürlich ['y:bərnaty:rlɪç] *adj*
supernatural

übernehmen [y:bər'ne:mən] *unreg vt untr* to
take on, accept; (*Amt, Geschäft*) to take over ▷ *vr
untr* to take on too much; (*sich überanstrengen*)
to overdo it

überparteilich ['y:bərpartaɪlɪç] *adj* (*Zeitung*)
independent; (*Amt, Präsident etc*) above party
politics

überprüfen [y:bər'pry:fən] *vt untr* to examine,
check; (*Pol: jdn*) to screen

Überprüfung *f* examination

überqueren [y:bər'kve:rən] *vt untr* to cross

überragen [y:bər'ra:gən] *vt untr* to tower above;
(*fig*) to surpass

überragend *adj* outstanding; (*Bedeutung*)
paramount

überraschen [y:bər'raʃən] *vt untr* to surprise

Überraschung *f* surprise

überreden [y:bər're:dən] *vt untr* to persuade;
jdn zu etw ~ to talk sb into sth

Überredungskunst *f* powers *pl* of persuasion

überregional ['y:bərregiona:l] *adj* national;
(*Zeitung, Sender*) nationwide

überreichen [y:bər'raɪçən] *vt untr* to hand over;
(*feierlich*) to present

überreichlich *adj* (more than) ample

überreizt [y:bər'raɪtst] *adj* overwrought

Überreste ['y:bərrɛstə] *pl* remains *pl*, remnants
pl

überrumpeln [y:bər'rumpəln] *vt untr* to take by
surprise; (*umg: überwältigen*) to overpower

überrunden [y:bər'rundən] *vt untr* (*Sport*) to lap

übers ['y:bərs] = **über das**

übersättigen [y:bər'zɛtɪgən] *vt untr* to satiate

Überschall- ['y:bərʃal] *in zw* supersonic;
Überschallflugzeug *nt* supersonic jet;
Überschallgeschwindigkeit *f* supersonic
speed

überschatten [y:bər'ʃatən] *vt untr* to
overshadow

überschätzen [y:bər'ʃɛtsən] *vt untr, vr untr* to
overestimate

überschaubar [yːbərˈʃaʊbaːr] *adj* (*Plan*) easily comprehensible, clear

überschäumen [ˈyːbərʃɔʏmən] *vi* to froth over; (*fig*) to bubble over

überschlafen [yːbərˈʃlaːfən] *unreg vt untr* (*Problem*) to sleep on

Überschlag [ˈyːbərʃlaːk] *m* (*Fin*) estimate; (*Sport*) somersault

überschlagen¹ [yːbərˈʃlaːgən] *unreg vt untr* (*berechnen*) to estimate; (*auslassen: Seite*) to omit ▷ *vr untr* to somersault; (*Stimme*) to crack; (*Aviat*) to loop the loop ▷ *adj* lukewarm, tepid

überschlagen² [ˈyːbərʃlaːgən] *unreg vt* (*Beine*) to cross; (*Arme*) to fold ▷ *vi* (*Hilfsverb sein: Wellen*) to break; (: *Funken*) to flash over; **in etw** *akk* **~** (*Stimmung etc*) to turn into sth

überschnappen [ˈyːbərʃnapən] *vi* (*Stimme*) to crack; (*umg: Mensch*) to flip one's lid

überschneiden [yːbərˈʃnaɪdən] *unreg vr untr* (*lit, fig*) to overlap; (*Linien*) to intersect

überschreiben [yːbərˈʃraɪbən] *unreg vt untr* to provide with a heading; (*Comput*) to overwrite; **jdm etw ~** to transfer od make over sth to sb

überschreiten [yːbərˈʃraɪtən] *unreg vt untr* to cross over; (*fig*) to exceed; (*verletzen*) to transgress

Überschrift [ˈyːbərʃrɪft] *f* heading, title

überschuldet [yːbərˈʃʊldət] *adj* heavily in debt; (*Grundstück*) heavily mortgaged

Überschuss [ˈyːbərʃʊs] *m*: **~ (an** +*dat*) surplus (of)

überschüssig [ˈyːbərʃʏsɪç] *adj* surplus, excess

überschütten [yːbərˈʃʏtən] *vt untr*: **jdn/etw mit etw ~** (*lit*) to pour sth over sb/sth; **jdn mit etw ~** (*fig*) to shower sb with sth

Überschwang [ˈyːbərʃvaŋ] *m* exuberance

überschwänglich [ˈyːbərʃvɛŋlɪç] *adj* effusive; **Überschwänglichkeit** *f* effusion

überschwappen [ˈyːbərʃvapən] *vi* to splash over

überschwemmen [yːbərˈʃvɛmən] *vt untr* to flood

Überschwemmung *f* flood

überschwenglich [ˈyːbərʃvɛŋlɪç] *adj siehe* **überschwänglich**

Übersee [ˈyːbərzeː] *f*: **nach/in ~** overseas

überseeisch *adj* overseas

übersehbar [yːbərˈzeːbaːr] *adj* (*fig: Folgen, Zusammenhänge etc*) clear; (*Kosten, Dauer etc*) assessable

übersehen [yːbərˈzeːən] *unreg vt untr* to look (out) over; (*fig: Folgen*) to see, get an overall view of; (: *nicht beachten*) to overlook

übersenden [yːbərˈzɛndən] *unreg vt untr* to send, forward

übersetzen¹ [yːbərˈzɛtsən] *vt untr, vi untr* to translate

übersetzen² [ˈyːbərzɛtsən] *vi* (*Hilfsverb sein*) to cross

Übersetzer, in [yːbərˈzɛtsər(ɪn)] **(-s, -)** *m(f)* translator

Übersetzung [yːbərˈzɛtsʊŋ] *f* translation; (*Tech*) gear ratio

Übersicht [ˈyːbərzɪçt] *f* overall view; (*Darstellung*) survey; **die ~ verlieren** to lose track; **übersichtlich** *adj* clear; (*Gelände*) open; **Übersichtlichkeit** *f* clarity, lucidity

übersiedeln¹ [ˈyːbərziːdəln] *vi* to move

übersiedeln² [yːbərˈziːdəln] *vi untr* to move

überspannen [yːbərˈʃpanən] *vt untr* (*zu sehr spannen*) to overstretch; (*überdecken*) to cover

überspannt *adj* eccentric; (*Idee*) wild, crazy; **Überspanntheit** *f* eccentricity

überspielen [yːbərˈʃpiːlən] *vt untr* (*verbergen*) to cover (up); (*übertragen: Aufnahme*) to transfer

überspitzt [yːbərˈʃpɪtst] *adj* exaggerated

überspringen [yːbərˈʃprɪŋən] *unreg vt untr* to jump over; (*fig*) to skip

übersprudeln [ˈyːbərʃpruːdəln] *vi* to bubble over

überstehen¹ [yːbərˈʃteːən] *unreg vt untr* to overcome, get over; (*Winter etc*) to survive, get through

überstehen² [ˈyːbərʃteːən] *unreg vi* to project

übersteigen [yːbərˈʃtaɪgən] *unreg vt untr* to climb over; (*fig*) to exceed

übersteigert [yːbərˈʃtaɪgərt] *adj* excessive

überstimmen [yːbɛrˈʃtɪmən] *vt untr* to outvote

überstrapazieren [ˈyːbərʃtrapatsiːrən] *vt untr* to wear out ▷ *vr* to wear o.s. out

überstreifen [ˈyːbərʃtraɪfən] *vt*: **(sich** *dat*) **etw ~** to slip sth on

überströmen¹ [yːbərˈʃtrøːmən] *vt untr*: **von Blut überströmt sein** to be streaming with blood

überströmen² [ˈyːbərʃtrøːmən] *vi* (*lit, fig*): **~ (vor** +*dat*) to overflow (with)

Überstunden [ˈyːbərʃtʊndən] *pl* overtime *sing*

überstürzen [yːbərˈʃtʏrtsən] *vt untr* to rush ▷ *vr untr* to follow (one another) in rapid succession

überstürzt *adj* (over)hasty

übertariflich [ˈyːbərtarifliç] *adj, adv* above the agreed od union rate

übertölpeln [yːbərˈtœlpln] *vt untr* to dupe

übertönen [yːbərˈtøːnən] *vt untr* to drown (out)

Übertrag [ˈyːbərtraːk] **(-(e)s, -träge)** *m* (*Comm*) amount brought forward

übertragbar [yːbərˈtraːkbaːr] *adj* transferable; (*Med*) infectious

übertragen [yːbərˈtraːgən] *unreg vt untr* to transfer; (*Rundf*) to broadcast; (*anwenden: Methode*) to apply; (*übersetzen*) to render; (*Krankheit*) to transmit ▷ *vr untr* to spread ▷ *adj* figurative; **~ auf** +*akk* to transfer to; to apply to; **sich ~ auf** +*akk* to spread to; **jdm etw ~** to assign sth to sb; (*Verantwortung etc*) to give sb sth od sth to sb

Übertragung *f* (*siehe vb*) transference; broadcast; rendering; transmission

übertreffen [yːbərˈtrɛfən] *unreg vt untr* to surpass

übertreiben [yːbərˈtraɪbən] *unreg vt untr* to exaggerate; **man kann es auch ~** you can overdo things

Übertreibung *f* exaggeration

u

341

übertreten[1] [y:bər'tre:tən] *unreg vt untr* to cross; (*Gebot etc*) to break

übertreten[2] ['y:bərtre:tən] *unreg vi* (*über Linie, Gebiet*) to step (over); (*Sport*) to overstep; (*zu anderem Glauben*) to be converted; **~ (in** +*akk*)**:** *Pol*) to go over (to)

Übertretung [y:bər'tre:tʊŋ] *f* violation, transgression

übertrieben [y:bər'tri:bən] *adj* exaggerated, excessive

Übertritt ['y:bərtrɪt] *m* (*zu anderem Glauben*) conversion; (*bes zu anderer Partei*) defection

übertrumpfen [y:bər'trʊmpfən] *vt untr* to outdo; (*Karten*) to overtrump

übertünchen [y:bər'tʏnçən] *vt untr* to whitewash; (*fig*) to cover up, whitewash

übervölkert [y:bər'fœlkərt] *adj* overpopulated

übervoll ['y:bərfɔl] *adj* overfull

übervorteilen [y:bər'fɔrtaɪlən] *vt untr* to dupe, cheat

überwachen [y:bər'vaxən] *vt untr* to supervise; (*Verdächtigen*) to keep under surveillance

Überwachung *f* supervision; surveillance

überwältigen [y:bər'vɛltɪgən] *vt untr* to overpower

überwältigend *adj* overwhelming

überwechseln ['y:bərvɛksəln] *vi*: **~ (in** +*akk*) to move (to); (*zu Partei etc*): **~ (zu)** to go over (to)

überweisen [y:bər'vaɪzən] *unreg vt untr* to transfer; (*Patienten*) to refer

Überweisung *f* transfer; (*von Patient*) referral

überwerfen[1] ['y:bərvɛrfən] *unreg vt* (*Kleidungsstück*) to put on; (*sehr rasch*) to throw on

überwerfen[2] [y:bər'vɛrfən] *unreg vr untr*: **sich (mit jdm) ~** to fall out (with sb)

überwiegen [y:bər'vi:gən] *unreg vi untr* to predominate

überwiegend *adj* predominant

überwinden [y:bər'vɪndən] *unreg vt untr* to overcome ▷ *vr untr*: **sich ~, etw zu tun** to make an effort to do sth, bring o.s. to do sth

Überwindung *f* overcoming; (*Selbstüberwindung*) effort of will

überwintern [y:bər'vɪntərn] *vi untr* to (spend the) winter; (*umg: Winterschlaf halten*) to hibernate

Überwurf ['y:bərvʊrf] *m* wrap

Überzahl ['y:bərtsa:l] *f* superior numbers *pl*, superiority; **in der ~ sein** to be numerically superior

überzählig ['y:bərtsɛ:lɪç] *adj* surplus

überzeugen [y:bər'tsɔygən] *vt untr* to convince

überzeugend *adj* convincing

überzeugt *adj attrib* (*Anhänger etc*) dedicated; (*Vegetarier*) strict; (*Christ, Moslem*) devout

Überzeugung *f* conviction; **zu der ~ gelangen, dass ...** to become convinced that ...

Überzeugungskraft *f* power of persuasion

überziehen[1] ['y:bərtsi:ən] *unreg vt* to put on

überziehen[2] [y:bər'tsi:ən] *unreg vt untr* to cover; (*Konto*) to overdraw; (*Redezeit etc*) to overrun

▷ *vr untr* (*Himmel*) to cloud over; **ein Bett frisch ~** to change a bed, change the sheets (on a bed)

Überziehungskredit *m* overdraft

überzüchten [y:bər'tsʏçtən] *vt untr* to overbreed

Überzug ['y:bərtsu:k] *m* cover; (*Belag*) coating

üblich ['y:plɪç] *adj* usual; **allgemein ~ sein** to be common practice

U-Boot ['u:bo:t] *nt* U-boat, submarine

übrig ['y:brɪç] *adj* remaining; **die Übrigen** the others; **das Übrige** the rest; **im Übrigen** besides; **~ bleiben** to remain, be left (over); **~ lassen** to leave (over); **einiges/ viel zu wünschen ~ lassen** (*umg*) to leave something/a lot to be desired; *siehe auch* **übrighaben**

übrigens ['y:brɪgəns] *adv* besides; (*nebenbei bemerkt*) by the way

übrighaben *unreg vi*: **für jdn etwas ~** (*umg*) to be fond of sb

Übung ['y:bʊŋ] *f* practice; (*Turnübung, Aufgabe etc*) exercise; **~ macht den Meister** (*Sprichwort*) practice makes perfect

Übungsarbeit *f* (*Sch*) mock test

Übungsplatz *m* training ground; (*Mil*) drill ground

u. d. M. *abk* (= *unter dem Meeresspiegel*) below sea level

ü. d. M. *abk* (= *über dem Meeresspiegel*) above sea level

u. E. *abk* (= *unseres Erachtens*) in our opinion

Ufer ['u:fər] (**-s, -**) *nt* bank; (*Meeresufer*) shore; **Uferbefestigung** *f* embankment

uferlos *adj* endless; (*grenzenlos*) boundless; **ins U~e gehen** (*Kosten*) to go up and up; (*Debatte etc*) to go on forever

UFO, Ufo ['u:fo] (**-(s), -s**) *nt abk* (= *unbekanntes Flugobjekt*) UFO, ufo

Uganda [u'ganda] (**-s**) *nt* Uganda

Ugander, in (**-s, -**) *m(f)* Ugandan

ugandisch *adj* Ugandan

U-Haft ['u:haft] *f abk* = **Untersuchungshaft**

Uhr [u:r] (**-, -en**) *f* clock; (*Armbanduhr*) watch; **wie viel ~ ist es?** what time is it?; **um wie viel ~?** at what time?; **1 ~** 1 o'clock; **20 ~** 8 o'clock, 20.00 (twenty hundred) hours; **Uhrband** *nt* watchstrap; **Uhrengehäuse, Uhrgehäuse** *nt* clock case; watch case; **Uhrkette** *f* watch chain; **Uhrmacher** *m* watchmaker; **Uhrwerk** *nt* (*auch fig*) clockwork mechanism; **Uhrzeiger** *m* hand; **Uhrzeigersinn** *m*: **im Uhrzeigersinn** clockwise; **entgegen dem Uhrzeigersinn** anticlockwise; **Uhrzeit** *f* time (of day)

Uhu ['u:hu] (**-s, -s**) *m* eagle owl

Ukraine [ukra'i:nə] *f* Ukraine

Ukrainer, in [ukra'i:nər(ɪn)] (**-s, -**) *m(f)* Ukrainian

ukrainisch *adj* Ukrainian

UKW *abk* (= *Ultrakurzwelle*) VHF

Ulk [ʊlk] (**-s, -e**) *m* lark

ulkig ['ʊlkɪç] *adj* funny

Ulme ['ʊlmə] (**-, -n**) *f* elm

Ulster ['ʊlstər] (**-s**) *nt* Ulster

Ultimatum [ʊlti'maːtʊm] (**-s, Ultimaten**) *nt* ultimatum; **jdm ein ~ stellen** to give sb an ultimatum

Ultra- *zW:* **Ultrakurzwelle** *f* very high frequency; **Ultraleichtflugzeug** *nt* microlight; **Ultraschall** *m* (*Phys*) ultrasound; **ultraviolett** *adj* ultraviolet

○ SCHLÜSSELWORT

um [ʊm] *präp +akk* **1** (*um herum*) (a)round; **um Weihnachten** around Christmas; **er schlug um sich** he hit about him

2 (*mit Zeitangabe*) at; **um acht (Uhr)** at eight (o'clock)

3 (*mit Größenangabe*) by; **etw um 4 cm kürzen** to shorten sth by 4 cm; **um 10% teurer** 10% more expensive; **um vieles besser** better by far; **um nichts besser** not in the least bit better; *siehe auch* **umso**

4: **der Kampf um den Titel** the battle for the title; **um Geld spielen** to play for money; **es geht um das Prinzip** it's a question of principle; **Stunde um Stunde** hour after hour; **Auge um Auge** an eye for an eye

▷ *präp +gen:* **um ... willen** for the sake of ...; **um Gottes willen** for goodness *od* (*stärker*) God's sake

▷ *konj:* **um ... zu** (in order) to ...; **zu klug, um zu ...** too clever to ...; *siehe auch* **umso**

▷ *adv* **1** (*ungefähr*) about; **um (die) 30 Leute** about *od* around 30 people

2 (*vorbei*): **die zwei Stunden sind um** the two hours are up

umadressieren ['ʊm|adrɛsiːrən] *vt untr* to readdress

umändern ['ʊm|ɛndərn] *vt* to alter

Umänderung *f* alteration

umarbeiten ['ʊm|arbaɪtən] *vt* to remodel; (*Buch etc*) to revise, rework

umarmen [ʊm'|armən] *vt untr* to embrace

Umbau ['ʊmbaʊ] (**-(e)s, -e** *od* **-ten**) *m* reconstruction, alteration(s *pl*)

umbauen ['ʊmbaʊən] *vt* to rebuild, reconstruct

umbenennen ['ʊmbənɛnən] *unreg vt untr* to rename

umbesetzen ['ʊmbəzɛtsən] *vt untr* (*Theat*) to recast; (*Mannschaft*) to change; (*Posten, Stelle*) to find someone else for

umbiegen ['ʊmbiːgən] *unreg vt* to bend (over)

umbilden ['ʊmbɪldən] *vt* to reorganize; (*Pol: Kabinett*) to reshuffle

umbinden[1] ['ʊmbɪndən] *unreg vt* (*Krawatte etc*) to put on

umbinden[2] [ʊm'bɪndən] *unreg vt untr:* **etw mit etw ~** to tie sth round sth

umblättern ['ʊmblɛtərn] *vt* to turn over

umblicken ['ʊmblɪkən] *vr* to look around

umbringen ['ʊmbrɪŋən] *unreg vt* to kill

Umbruch ['ʊmbrʊx] *m* radical change; (*Typ*) make-up (into page)

umbuchen ['ʊmbuːxən] *vi* to change one's reservation *od* flight *etc* ▷ *vt* to change

umdenken ['ʊmdɛŋkən] *unreg vi* to adjust one's views

umdisponieren ['ʊmdɪsponiːrən] *vi untr* to change one's plans

umdrängen [ʊm'drɛŋən] *vt untr* to crowd round

umdrehen ['ʊmdreːən] *vt* to turn (round); (*Hals*) to wring ▷ *vr* to turn (round); **jdm den Arm ~** to twist sb's arm

Umdrehung *f* turn; (*Phys*) revolution, rotation

umeinander [ʊm|aɪ'nandər] *adv* round one another; (*füreinander*) for one another

umerziehen ['ʊm|ɛrtsiːən] *unreg vt* (*Pol: euph*): **jdn (zu etw) ~** to re-educate sb (to become sth)

umfahren[1] ['ʊmfaːrən] *unreg vt* to run over

umfahren[2] [ʊm'faːrən] *unreg vt untr* to drive round; (*die Welt*) to sail round

umfallen ['ʊmfalən] *unreg vi* to fall down *od* over; (*fig: umg: nachgeben*) to give in

Umfang ['ʊmfaŋ] *m* extent; (*von Buch*) size; (*Reichweite*) range; (*Fläche*) area; (*Math*) circumference; **in großem ~** on a large scale; **umfangreich** *adj* extensive; (*Buch etc*) voluminous

umfassen [ʊm'fasən] *vt untr* to embrace; (*umgeben*) to surround; (*enthalten*) to include

umfassend *adj* comprehensive; (*umfangreich*) extensive

Umfeld ['ʊmfɛlt] *nt:* **zum ~ von etw gehören** to be associated with sth

umformatieren ['ʊmfɔrmatiːrən] *vt untr* (*Comput*) to reformat

umformen ['ʊmfɔrmən] *vi* to transform

Umformer (**-s, -**) *m* (*Elek*) converter

umformulieren ['ʊmfɔrmuliːrən] *vt untr* to redraft

Umfrage ['ʊmfraːgə] *f* poll; **~ halten** to ask around

umfüllen ['ʊmfʏlən] *vt* to transfer; (*Wein*) to decant

umfunktionieren ['ʊmfʊŋktsioniːrən] *vt untr* to convert

Umgang ['ʊmgaŋ] *m* company; (*mit jdm*) dealings *pl*; (*Behandlung*) dealing

umgänglich ['ʊmgɛŋlɪç] *adj* sociable

Umgangs- *zW:* **Umgangsformen** *pl* manners *pl*; **Umgangssprache** *f* colloquial language; **umgangssprachlich** *adj* colloquial

umgeben [ʊm'geːbən] *unreg vt untr* to surround

Umgebung *f* surroundings *pl*; (*Milieu*) environment; (*Personen*) people in one's circle; **in der näheren/weiteren ~ Münchens** on the outskirts/in the environs of Munich

umgehen[1] ['ʊmgeːən] *unreg vi* to go (a)round; **im Schlosse ~** to haunt the castle; **mit jdm/ etw ~ können** to know how to handle sb/ sth; **mit jdm grob** *etc* **~** to treat sb roughly *etc*; **mit Geld sparsam ~** to be careful with one's money

umgehen² [ʊm'ge:ən] *unreg vt untr* to bypass; (*Mil*) to outflank; (*Gesetz, Vorschrift etc*) to circumvent; (*vermeiden*) to avoid

umgehend *adj* immediate

Umgehung *f* (*siehe vb*) bypassing; outflanking; circumvention; avoidance

Umgehungsstraße *f* bypass

umgekehrt ['ʊmɡəke:rt] *adj* reverse(d); (*gegenteilig*) opposite ▷ *adv* the other way around; **und ~** and vice versa

umgestalten ['ʊmɡəʃtaltən] *vt untr* to alter; (*reorganisieren*) to reorganize; (*umordnen*) to rearrange

umgewöhnen ['ʊmɡəvø:nən] *vr* to readapt

umgraben ['ʊmɡra:bən] *unreg vt* to dig up

umgruppieren ['ʊmɡrʊpi:rən] *vt untr* to regroup

Umhang ['ʊmhaŋ] *m* wrap, cape

umhängen ['ʊmhɛŋən] *vt* (*Bild*) to hang somewhere else; **jdm etw ~** to put sth on sb

Umhängetasche *f* shoulder bag

umhauen ['ʊmhaʊən] *vt* to fell; (*fig*) to bowl over

umher [ʊm'he:r] *adv* about, around; **umhergehen** *unreg vi* to walk about; **umherirren** *vi* to wander around; (*Blick, Augen*) to roam about; **umherreisen** *vi* to travel about; **umherschweifen** *vi* to roam about; **umherziehen** *unreg vi* to wander from place to place

umhinkönnen [ʊm'hɪnkœnən] *unreg vi*: **ich kann nicht umhin, das zu tun** I can't help doing it

umhören ['ʊmhø:rən] *vr* to ask around

umkämpfen [ʊm'kɛmpfən] *vt untr* (*Entscheidung*) to dispute; (*Wahlkreis, Sieg*) to contest

Umkehr ['ʊmke:r] (-) *f* turning back; (*Änderung*) change

umkehren *vi* to turn back; (*fig*) to change one's ways ▷ *vt* to turn round, reverse; (*Tasche etc*) to turn inside out; (*Gefäß etc*) to turn upside down

umkippen ['ʊmkɪpən] *vt* to tip over ▷ *vi* to overturn; (*umg: ohnmächtig werden*) to keel over; (*fig: Meinung ändern*) to change one's mind

umklammern [ʊm'klamərn] *vt untr* (*mit Händen*) to clasp; (*festhalten*) to cling to

umklappen ['ʊmklapən] *vt* to fold down

Umkleidekabine ['ʊmklaɪdəkabi:nə] *f* changing cubicle (*Brit*), dressing room (*US*)

Umkleideraum ['ʊmklaɪdəraʊm] *m* changing room; (*US: Theat*) dressing room

umknicken ['ʊmknɪkən] *vt* (*Ast*) to snap; (*Papier*) to fold (over) ▷ *vi*: **mit dem Fuß ~** to twist one's ankle

umkommen ['ʊmkɔmən] *unreg vi* to die, perish; (*Lebensmittel*) to go bad

Umkreis ['ʊmkraɪs] *m* neighbourhood (*Brit*), neighborhood (*US*); **im ~ von** within a radius of

umkreisen [ʊm'kraɪzən] *vt untr* to circle (round); (*Satellit*) to orbit

umkrempeln ['ʊmkrɛmpəln] *vt* to turn up;

(*mehrmals*) to roll up; (*umg: Betrieb*) to shake up

umladen ['ʊmla:dən] *unreg vt* to transfer, reload

Umlage ['ʊmla:ɡə] *f* share of the costs

Umlauf *m* (*Geldumlauf*) circulation; (*von Gestirn*) revolution; (*Schreiben*) circular; **in ~ bringen** to circulate; **Umlaufbahn** *f* orbit

umlaufen ['ʊmlaʊfən] *unreg vi* to circulate

Umlaufkapital *nt* working capital

Umlaufvermögen *nt* current assets *pl*

Umlaut ['ʊmlaʊt] *m* umlaut

umlegen ['ʊmle:ɡən] *vt* to put on; (*verlegen*) to move, shift; (*Kosten*) to share out; (*umkippen*) to tip over; (*umg: töten*) to bump off

umleiten ['ʊmlaɪtən] *vt* to divert

Umleitung *f* diversion

umlernen ['ʊmlɛrnən] *vi* to learn something new; (*fig*) to adjust one's views

umliegend ['ʊmli:ɡənt] *adj* surrounding

ummelden ['ʊmmɛldən] *vt, vr*: **jdn/sich ~** to notify (the police of) a change in sb's/one's address

Umnachtung [ʊm'naxtʊŋ] *f* mental derangement

umorganisieren ['ʊmˌɔrɡanizi:rən] *vt untr* to reorganize

umpflanzen ['ʊmpflantsən] *vt* to transplant

umquartieren ['ʊmkvarti:rən] *vt untr* to move; (*Truppen*) to requarter

umrahmen [ʊm'ra:mən] *vt untr* to frame

umranden [ʊm'randən] *vt untr* to border, edge

umräumen ['ʊmrɔʏmən] *vt* (*anders anordnen*) to rearrange ▷ *vi* to rearrange things, move things around

umrechnen ['ʊmrɛçnən] *vt* to convert

Umrechnung *f* conversion

Umrechnungskurs *m* rate of exchange

umreißen [ʊm'raɪsən] *unreg vt untr* to outline

umrennen ['ʊmrɛnən] *unreg vt* to (run into and) knock down

umringen [ʊm'rɪŋən] *vt untr* to surround

Umriss ['ʊmrɪs] *m* outline

umrühren ['ʊmry:rən] *vt, vi* to stir

umrüsten ['ʊmrʏstən] *vt* (*Tech*) to adapt; (*Mil*) to re-equip; **~ auf** +*akk* to adapt to

ums [ʊms] = **um das**

umsatteln ['ʊmzatəln] (*umg*) *vi* to change one's occupation, switch jobs

Umsatz ['ʊmzats] *m* turnover; **Umsatzbeteiligung** *f* commission; **Umsatzeinbuße** *f* loss of profit; **Umsatzsteuer** *f* turnover tax

umschalten ['ʊmʃaltən] *vt* to switch ▷ *vi* to push/pull a lever; (*auf anderen Sender*): **~ (auf** +*akk*) to change over (to); (*Aut*): **~ in** +*akk* to change (*Brit*) *od* shift into; **„wir schalten jetzt um nach Hamburg"** "and now we go over to Hamburg"

Umschalttaste *f* shift key

Umschau *f* look(ing) round; **~ halten nach** to look around for

umschauen ['ʊmʃaʊən] *vr* to look round

Umschlag ['ʊmʃla:k] *m* cover; (*Buchumschlag*)

jacket, cover; (*Med*) compress; (*Briefumschlag*) envelope; (*Gütermenge*) volume of traffic; (*Wechsel*) change; (*von Hose*) turn-up (*Brit*), cuff (*US*)

umschlagen ['ʊmʃlaːgən] *unreg vi* to change; (*Naut*) to capsize ▷ *vt* to knock over; (*Ärmel*) to turn up; (*Seite*) to turn over; (*Waren*) to transfer

Umschlag- *zW*: **Umschlaghafen** *m* port of transshipment; **Umschlagplatz** *m* (*Comm*) distribution centre (*Brit*) *od* center (*US*); **Umschlagseite** *f* cover page

umschlingen [ʊm'ʃlɪŋən] *unreg vt untr* (*Pflanze*) to twine around; (*jdn*) to embrace

umschreiben[1] ['ʊmʃraɪbən] *unreg vt* (*neu umschreiben*) to rewrite; (*übertragen*) to transfer; **~ auf** +*akk* to transfer to

umschreiben[2] [ʊm'ʃraɪbən] *unreg vt untr* to paraphrase; (*abgrenzen*) to circumscribe, define

Umschuldung ['ʊmʃʊldʊŋ] *f* rescheduling (of debts)

umschulen ['ʊmʃuːlən] *vt* to retrain; (*Kind*) to send to another school

umschwärmen [ʊm'ʃvɛrmən] *vt untr* to swarm round; (*fig*) to surround, idolize

Umschweife ['ʊmʃvaɪfə] *pl*: **ohne ~** without beating about the bush, straight out

umschwenken ['ʊmʃvɛnkən] *vi* (*Kran*) to swing out; (*fig*) to do an about-turn (*Brit*) *od* about-face (*US*); (*Wind*) to veer

Umschwung ['ʊmʃvʊŋ] *m* (*Gymnastik*) circle; (*fig: ins Gegenteil*) change (around)

umsegeln [ʊm'zeːgəln] *vt untr* to sail around; (*Erde*) to circumnavigate

umsehen ['ʊmzeːən] *unreg vr* to look around *od* about; (*suchen*): **sich ~ (nach)** to look out (for); **ich möchte mich nur mal ~** (*in Geschäft*) I'm just looking

umseitig ['ʊmzaɪtɪç] *adv* overleaf

umsetzen ['ʊmzɛtsən] *vt* (*Waren*) to turn over ▷ *vr* (*Schüler*) to change places; **etw in die Tat ~** to translate sth into action

Umsicht ['ʊmzɪçt] *f* prudence, caution

umsichtig *adj* prudent, cautious

umsiedeln ['ʊmziːdəln] *vt* to resettle

Umsiedler, in (**-s, -**) *m(f)* resettler

umso ['ʊmzo] *konj*: **~ besser/schlimmer** so much the better/worse; **~ mehr, als …** all the more considering …

umsonst [ʊm'zɔnst] *adv* in vain; (*gratis*) for nothing

umspringen ['ʊmʃprɪŋən] *unreg vi* to change; **mit jdm ~** to treat sb badly

Umstand ['ʊmʃtant] *m* circumstance; **Umstände** *pl* (*fig: Schwierigkeiten*) fuss *sing*; **in anderen Umständen sein** to be pregnant; **Umstände machen** to go to a lot of trouble; **den Umständen entsprechend** much as one would expect (under the circumstances); **die näheren Umstände** further details; **unter Umständen** possibly; **mildernde Umstände** (*Jur*) extenuating circumstances

umständehalber *adv* owing to circumstances

umständlich ['ʊmʃtɛntlɪç] *adj* (*Methode*)

cumbersome, complicated; (*Ausdrucksweise, Erklärung*) long-winded; (*ungeschickt*) ponderous; **etw ~ machen** to make heavy weather of (doing) sth

Umstandskleid *nt* maternity dress

Umstandswort *nt* adverb

umstehend ['ʊmʃteːənt] *adj attrib* (*umseitig*) overleaf; **die U~en** *pl* the bystanders *pl*

Umsteigekarte *f* transfer ticket

umsteigen ['ʊmʃtaɪgən] *unreg vi* (*Eisenb*) to change; (*fig: umg*): **~ (auf** +*akk*) to change over (to), switch (over) (to)

umstellen[1] ['ʊmʃtɛlən] *vt* (*an anderen Ort*) to change round, rearrange; (*Tech*) to convert ▷ *vr*: **sich ~ (auf** +*akk*) to adapt o.s. (to)

umstellen[2] [ʊm'ʃtɛlən] *vt untr* to surround

Umstellung *f* change; (*Umgewöhnung*) adjustment; (*Tech*) conversion

umstimmen ['ʊmʃtɪmən] *vt* (*Mus*) to retune; **jdn ~** to make sb change his mind

umstoßen ['ʊmʃtoːsən] *unreg vt* (*lit*) to overturn; (*Plan etc*) to change, upset

umstritten [ʊm'ʃtrɪtən] *adj* disputed; (*fraglich*) controversial

Umsturz ['ʊmʃtʊrts] *m* overthrow

umstürzen ['ʊmʃtʏrtsən] *vt* (*umwerfen*) to overturn ▷ *vi* to collapse, fall down; (*Wagen*) to overturn

umstürzlerisch *adj* revolutionary

Umtausch ['ʊmtaʊʃ] *m* exchange; **diese Waren sind vom ~ ausgeschlossen** these goods cannot be exchanged

umtauschen *vt* to exchange

Umtriebe ['ʊmtriːbə] *pl* machinations *pl*, intrigues *pl*

umtun ['ʊmtuːn] *unreg vr*: **sich nach etw ~** to look for sth

umverteilen ['ʊmfɛrtaɪlən] *vt untr* to redistribute

umwälzend ['ʊmvɛltsənt] *adj* (*fig*) radical; (*Veränderungen*) sweeping; (*Ereignisse*) revolutionary

Umwälzung *f* (*fig*) radical change

umwandeln ['ʊmvandəln] *vt* to change, convert; (*Elek*) to transform

umwechseln ['ʊmvɛksəln] *vt* to change

Umweg ['ʊmveːk] *m* detour; (*fig*) roundabout way

Umwelt ['ʊmvɛlt] *f* environment; **Umweltallergie** *f* environmental allergy; **Umweltauto** (*umg*) *nt* environment-friendly vehicle; **Umweltbelastung** *f* environmental pollution; **Umweltbewusstsein** *nt* environmental awareness; **umweltfreundlich** *adj* environment-friendly; **Umweltkrankheit** *f* environmental illness; **Umweltkriminalität** *f* crimes *pl* against the environment; **Umweltministerium** *nt* Ministry of the Environment; **umweltschädlich** *adj* harmful to the environment; **Umweltschutz** *m* environmental protection; **Umweltschützer** (**-s, -**) *m* environmentalist; **Umweltverschmutzung** *f* pollution (of

u

the environment); **umweltverträglich**
adj not harmful to the environment;
Umweltverträglichkeit f ecofriendliness
umwenden ['ʊmvɛndən] unreg vt, vr to turn
(round)
umwerben [ʊm'vɛrbən] unreg vt untr to court,
woo
umwerfen ['ʊmvɛrfən] unreg vt (lit) to upset,
overturn; (Mantel) to throw on; (fig: erschüttern)
to upset, throw
umwerfend (umg) adj fantastic
umziehen ['ʊmtsi:ən] unreg vt, vr to change ▷ vi
to move
umzingeln [ʊm'tsɪŋəln] vt untr to surround,
encircle
Umzug ['ʊmtsu:k] m procession;
(Wohnungsumzug) move, removal
UN pl abk (= United Nations): **die UN** the UN sing
un- zW: **unabänderlich** adj irreversible,
unalterable; **unabänderlich feststehen**
to be absolutely certain; **unabdingbar**
adj indispensable, essential; (Recht)
inalienable; **unabhängig** adj independent;
Unabhängigkeit f independence;
unabkömmlich adj indispensable; **zur Zeit**
unabkömmlich not free at the moment;
unablässig adj incessant, constant;
unabsehbar adj immeasurable; (Folgen)
unforeseeable; (Kosten) incalculable;
unabsichtlich adj unintentional;
unabwendbar adj inevitable
unachtsam ['ʊn|axtza:m] adj careless;
Unachtsamkeit f carelessness
un- zW: **unanfechtbar** adj indisputable;
unangebracht adj uncalled-for;
unangefochten adj unchallenged;
(Testament, Wahlkandidat, Urteil) uncontested;
unangemeldet adj unannounced;
(Besucher) unexpected; **unangemessen** adj
inadequate; **unangenehm** adj unpleasant;
(peinlich) embarrassing; **unangepasst**
adj nonconformist; **Unannehmlichkeit** f
inconvenience; **Unannehmlichkeiten** pl
trouble sing; **unansehnlich** adj unsightly;
unanständig adj indecent, improper;
Unanständigkeit f indecency, impropriety;
unantastbar adj inviolable, sacrosanct
unappetitlich ['ʊn|apeti:tlɪç] adj unsavoury
(Brit), unsavory (US)
Unart ['ʊn|a:rt] f bad manners pl;
(Angewohnheit) bad habit
unartig adj naughty, badly behaved
un- zW: **unaufdringlich** adj unobtrusive;
(Parfüm) discreet; (Mensch) unassuming;
unauffällig adj unobtrusive; (Kleidung)
inconspicuous; **unauffindbar** adj not to be
found; **unaufgefordert** adj unsolicited ▷ adv
unasked, spontaneously; **unaufgefordert**
zugesandte Manuskripte unsolicited
manuscripts; **unaufhaltsam** adj irresistible;
unaufhörlich adj incessant, continuous;
unaufmerksam adj inattentive; **unaufrichtig**
adj insincere

un- zW: **unausbleiblich** adj inevitable,
unavoidable; **unausgeglichen** adj
volatile; **unausgegoren** adj immature;
(Idee, Plan) half-baked; **unausgesetzt** adj
incessant, constant; **unausgewogen**
adj unbalanced; **unaussprechlich** adj
inexpressible; **unausstehlich** adj intolerable;
unausweichlich adj inescapable, ineluctable
unbändig ['ʊnbɛndɪç] adj extreme, excessive
unbarmherzig ['ʊnbarmhɛrtsɪç] adj pitiless,
merciless
unbeabsichtigt ['ʊnbə|apzɪçtɪçt] adj
unintentional
unbeachtet ['ʊnbə|axtət] adj unnoticed;
(Warnung) ignored
unbedacht ['ʊnbədaxt] adj rash
unbedarft ['ʊnbədarft] (umg) adj clueless
unbedenklich ['ʊnbədɛŋklɪç] adj unhesitating;
(Plan) unobjectionable ▷ adv without
hesitation
unbedeutend ['ʊnbədɔytənt] adj
insignificant, unimportant; (Fehler) slight
unbedingt ['ʊnbədɪŋt] adj unconditional ▷ adv
absolutely; **musst du ~ gehen?** do you really
have to go?; **nicht ~** not necessarily
unbefangen ['ʊnbəfaŋən] adj impartial,
unprejudiced; (ohne Hemmungen) uninhibited;
Unbefangenheit f impartiality;
uninhibitedness
unbefriedigend ['ʊnbəfri:dɪgənt] adj
unsatisfactory
unbefriedigt ['ʊnbəfri:dɪçt] adj unsatisfied;
(unzufrieden) dissatisfied; (unerfüllt) unfulfilled
unbefristet ['ʊnbəfrɪstət] adj permanent
unbefugt ['ʊnbəfu:kt] adj unauthorized; **U-en**
ist der Eintritt verboten no admittance to
unauthorized persons
unbegabt ['ʊnbəga:pt] adj untalented
unbegreiflich [ʊnbə'graɪflɪç] adj inconceivable
unbegrenzt ['ʊnbəgrɛntst] adj unlimited
unbegründet ['ʊnbəgrʏndət] adj unfounded
Unbehagen ['ʊnbəha:gən] nt discomfort
unbehaglich ['ʊnbəha:klɪç] adj uncomfortable;
(Gefühl) uneasy
unbeherrscht ['ʊnbəhɛrʃt] adj uncontrolled;
(Mensch) lacking self-control
unbeholfen ['ʊnbəhɔlfən] adj awkward,
clumsy; **Unbeholfenheit** f awkwardness,
clumsiness
unbeirrt ['ʊnbə|ɪrt] adj imperturbable
unbekannt ['ʊnbəkant] adj unknown; **~e**
Größe (Math, fig) unknown quantity
unbekannterweise adv: **grüß(e) sie ~ von**
mir give her my regards although I don't
know her
unbekümmert ['ʊnbəkʏmərt] adj
unconcerned
unbelehrbar [ʊnbə'le:rba:r] adj fixed in one's
views; (Rassist etc) dyed-in-the-wool attrib
unbeliebt ['ʊnbəli:pt] adj unpopular;
Unbeliebtheit f unpopularity
unbemannt ['ʊnbəmant] adj (Raumflug)
unmanned; (Flugzeug) pilotless

unbemerkt ['ʊnbəmɛrkt] *adj* unnoticed
unbenommen [ʊnbə'nɔmən] *adj (form):* **es bleibt** *od* **ist Ihnen ~, zu ...** you are at liberty to ...
unbequem ['ʊnbəkveːm] *adj (Stuhl)* uncomfortable; *(Mensch)* bothersome; *(Regelung)* inconvenient
unberechenbar [ʊnbə'rɛçənbaːr] *adj* incalculable; *(Mensch, Verhalten)* unpredictable
unberechtigt ['ʊnbərɛçtɪçt] *adj* unjustified; *(nicht erlaubt)* unauthorized
unberücksichtigt [ʊnbə'rʏkzɪçtɪçt] *adj:* **etw ~ lassen** not to consider sth
unberufen [ʊnbə'ruːfən] *interj* touch wood!
unberührt ['ʊnbəryːrt] *adj* untouched; *(Natur)* unspoiled; **sie ist noch ~** she is still a virgin
unbeschadet [ʊnbə'ʃaːdət] *präp+gen (form)* regardless of
unbescheiden ['ʊnbəʃaɪdən] *adj* presumptuous
unbescholten ['ʊnbəʃɔltən] *adj* respectable; *(Ruf)* spotless
unbeschrankt ['ʊnbəʃraŋkt] *adj (Bahnübergang)* unguarded
unbeschränkt [ʊnbə'ʃrɛŋkt] *adj* unlimited
unbeschreiblich [ʊnbə'ʃraɪplɪç] *adj* indescribable
unbeschwert ['ʊnbəʃveːrt] *adj (sorgenfrei)* carefree; *(Melodien)* light
unbesehen [ʊnbə'zeːən] *adv* indiscriminately; *(ohne es anzusehen)* without looking at it
unbesonnen ['ʊnbəzɔnən] *adj* unwise, rash, imprudent
unbesorgt ['ʊnbəzɔrkt] *adj* unconcerned; **Sie können ganz ~ sein** you can set your mind at rest
unbespielt ['ʊnbəʃpiːlt] *adj (Kassette)* blank
unbest. *abk* = **unbestimmt**
unbeständig ['ʊnbəʃtɛndɪç] *adj (Mensch)* inconstant; *(Wetter)* unsettled; *(Lage)* unstable
unbestechlich [ʊnbə'ʃtɛçlɪç] *adj* incorruptible
unbestimmt ['ʊnbəʃtɪmt] *adj* indefinite; *(Zukunft)* uncertain; **Unbestimmtheit** *f* vagueness
unbestritten ['ʊnbəʃtrɪtən] *adj* undisputed
unbeteiligt [ʊnbə'taɪlɪçt] *adj* unconcerned; *(uninteressiert)* indifferent
unbeugsam ['ʊnbɔʏkzaːm] *adj* stubborn, inflexible; *(Wille)* unbending
unbewacht ['ʊnbəvaxt] *adj* unguarded, unwatched
unbewaffnet ['ʊnbəvafnət] *adj* unarmed
unbeweglich ['ʊnbəveːklɪç] *adj* immovable
unbewegt *adj* motionless; *(fig: unberührt)* unmoved
unbewohnt ['ʊnbəvoːnt] *adj (Gegend)* uninhabited; *(Haus)* unoccupied
unbewusst ['ʊnbəvʊst] *adj* unconscious
unbezahlbar [ʊnbə'tsaːlbaːr] *adj* prohibitively expensive; *(fig)* priceless; *(nützlich)* invaluable
unbezahlt ['ʊnbətsaːlt] *adj* unpaid
unblutig ['ʊnbluːtɪç] *adj* bloodless
unbrauchbar ['ʊnbrauxbaːr] *adj (nutzlos)*

useless; *(Gerät)* unusable; **Unbrauchbarkeit** *f* uselessness
unbürokratisch ['ʊnbyrokraːtɪʃ] *adj* without any red tape
und [ʊnt] *konj* and; **~ so weiter** and so on
Undank ['ʊndaŋk] *m* ingratitude; **undankbar** *adj* ungrateful; **Undankbarkeit** *f* ingratitude
undefinierbar [ʊndefi'niːrbaːr] *adj* indefinable
undenkbar ['ʊn'dɛŋkbaːr] *adj* inconceivable
undeutlich ['ʊndɔʏtlɪç] *adj* indistinct; *(Schrift)* illegible; *(Ausdrucksweise)* unclear
undicht ['ʊndɪçt] *adj* leaky
undifferenziert ['ʊndɪfərɛntsiːrt] *adj* simplistic
Unding ['ʊndɪŋ] *nt* absurdity
unduldsam ['ʊnduldsaːm] *adj* intolerant
un- *zW:* **undurchdringlich** *adj (Urwald)* impenetrable; *(Gesicht)* inscrutable; **undurchführbar** *adj* impracticable; **undurchlässig** *adj* impervious; *(wasserundurchlässig)* waterproof, impermeable; **undurchschaubar** *adj* inscrutable; **undurchsichtig** *adj* opaque; *(Motive)* obscure; *(fig: pej: Mensch, Methoden)* devious
uneben ['ʊn|eːbən] *adj* uneven
unecht ['ʊn|ɛçt] *adj* artificial, fake; *(pej: Freundschaft, Lächeln)* false
unehelich ['ʊn|eːəlɪç] *adj* illegitimate
uneigennützig ['ʊn|aɪɡənnʏtsɪç] *adj* unselfish
uneinbringlich ['ʊn|aɪn'brɪŋlɪç] *adj:* **~e Forderungen** *(Comm)* bad debts *pl*
uneingeschränkt ['ʊn|aɪŋɡəʃrɛŋkt] *adj* absolute, total; *(Rechte, Handel)* unrestricted; *(Zustimmung)* unqualified
uneinig ['ʊn|aɪnɪç] *adj* divided; **~ sein** to disagree; **Uneinigkeit** *f* discord, dissension
uneinnehmbar [ʊn|aɪn'neːmbaːr] *adj* impregnable
uneins ['ʊn|aɪns] *adj* at variance, at odds
unempfänglich ['ʊn|ɛmpfɛŋlɪç] *adj:* **~ (für)** not susceptible (to)
unempfindlich ['ʊn|ɛmpfɪntlɪç] *adj* insensitive; **Unempfindlichkeit** *f* insensitivity
unendlich ['ʊn|ɛntlɪç] *adj* infinite ▷ *adv* endlessly; *(fig: sehr)* terribly; **Unendlichkeit** *f* infinity
un- *zW:* **unentbehrlich** *adj* indispensable; **unentgeltlich** *adj* free (of charge); **unentschieden** *adj* undecided; **unentschieden enden** *(Sport)* to end in a draw; **unentschlossen** *adj* undecided; *(entschlusslos)* irresolute; **unentwegt** *adj* unswerving; *(unaufhörlich)* incessant
un- *zW:* **unerbittlich** *adj* unyielding, inexorable; **unerfahren** *adj* inexperienced; **unerfreulich** *adj* unpleasant; **Unerfreuliches** *(schlechte Nachrichten)* bad news *sing*; *(Übles)* bad things *pl*; **unerfüllt** *adj* unfulfilled; **unergiebig** *adj (Quelle, Thema)* unproductive; *(Ernte, Nachschlagewerk)* poor; **unergründlich** *adj* unfathomable; **unerheblich** *adj* unimportant; **unerhört** *adj* unheard-of; *(unverschämt)* outrageous; *(Bitte)* unanswered;

347

unerlässlich *adj* indispensable; **unerlaubt** *adj* unauthorized; **unerledigt** *adj* unfinished; (*Post*) unanswered; (*Rechnung*) outstanding; (*schwebend*) pending; **unermesslich** *adj* immeasurable, immense; **unermüdlich** *adj* indefatigable; **unersättlich** *adj* insatiable; **unerschlossen** *adj* (*Land*) undeveloped; (*Boden*) unexploited; (*Vorkommen, Markt*) untapped; **unerschöpflich** *adj* inexhaustible; **unerschrocken** *adj* intrepid, courageous; **unerschütterlich** *adj* unshakeable; **unerschwinglich** *adj* (*Preis*) prohibitive; **unersetzlich** *adj* irreplaceable; **unerträglich** *adj* unbearable; (*Frechheit*) insufferable; **unerwartet** *adj* unexpected; **unerwünscht** *adj* undesirable, unwelcome; **unerzogen** *adj* ill-bred, rude

unfähig ['ʊnfɛːɪç] *adj* incapable; (*attrib*) incompetent; **zu etw ~ sein** to be incapable of sth; **Unfähigkeit** *f* inability; incompetence

unfair ['ʊnfɛːr] *adj* unfair

Unfall ['ʊnfal] *m* accident; **Unfallflucht** *f* hit-and-run (driving); **Unfallopfer** *nt* casualty; **Unfallstation** *f* emergency ward; **Unfallstelle** *f* scene of the accident; **Unfallversicherung** *f* accident insurance; **Unfallwagen** *m* car involved in an accident; (*umg: Rettungswagen*) ambulance

unfassbar [ʊn'fasbaːr] *adj* inconceivable

unfehlbar [ʊn'feːlbaːr] *adj* infallible ⊳ *adv* without fail; **Unfehlbarkeit** *f* infallibility

unfertig ['ʊnfɛrtɪç] *adj* unfinished, incomplete; (*Mensch*) immature

unflätig ['ʊnflɛːtɪç] *adj* rude

unfolgsam ['ʊnfɔlkzaːm] *adj* disobedient

unförmig ['ʊnfœrmɪç] *adj* (*formlos*) shapeless; (*groß*) cumbersome; (*Füße, Nase*) unshapely

unfrankiert ['ʊnfraŋkiːrt] *adj* unfranked

unfrei ['ʊnfraɪ] *adj* not free

unfreiwillig *adj* involuntary

unfreundlich ['ʊnfrɔʏntlɪç] *adj* unfriendly; **Unfreundlichkeit** *f* unfriendliness

Unfriede ['ʊnfriːdə], **Unfrieden** ['ʊnfriːdən] *m* dissension, strife

unfruchtbar ['ʊnfrʊxtbaːr] *adj* infertile; (*Gespräche*) fruitless; **Unfruchtbarkeit** *f* infertility; fruitlessness

Unfug ['ʊnfuːk] (**-s**) *m* (*Benehmen*) mischief; (*Unsinn*) nonsense; **grober ~** (*Jur*) gross misconduct

Ungar, in ['ʊŋar(ɪn)] (**-n, -n**) *m(f)* Hungarian; **ungarisch** *adj* Hungarian

Ungarn (**-s**) *nt* Hungary

ungeachtet ['ʊŋgə|axtət] *präp +gen* notwithstanding

ungeahndet ['ʊŋgə|aːndət] *adj* (*Jur*) unpunished

ungeahnt ['ʊŋgə|aːnt] *adj* unsuspected, undreamt-of

ungebeten ['ʊŋgəbeːtən] *adj* uninvited

ungebildet ['ʊŋgəbɪldət] *adj* uncultured; (*ohne Bildung*) uneducated

ungeboren ['ʊŋgəboːrən] *adj* unborn

ungebräuchlich ['ʊŋgəbrɔʏçlɪç] *adj* unusual, uncommon

ungebraucht ['ʊŋgəbrauxt] *adj* unused

ungebührlich ['ʊŋgəbyːrlɪç] *adj*: **sich ~ aufregen** to get unduly excited

ungebunden ['ʊŋgəbʊndən] *adj* (*Buch*) unbound; (*Leben*) (fancy-)free; (*ohne festen Partner*) unattached; (*Pol*) independent

ungedeckt ['ʊŋgədɛkt] *adj* (*schutzlos*) unprotected; (*Scheck*) uncovered

Ungeduld ['ʊŋgədʊlt] *f* impatience

ungeduldig ['ʊŋgədʊldɪç] *adj* impatient

ungeeignet ['ʊŋgə|aɪgnət] *adj* unsuitable

ungefähr ['ʊŋgəfɛːr] *adj* rough, approximate ⊳ *adv* roughly, approximately; **so ~!** more or less!; **das kommt nicht von ~** that's hardly surprising

ungefährlich ['ʊŋgəfɛːrlɪç] *adj* not dangerous, harmless

ungehalten ['ʊŋgəhaltən] *adj* indignant

ungeheuer ['ʊŋgəhɔʏər] *adj* huge ⊳ *adv* (*umg*) enormously; **Ungeheuer** (**-s, -**) *nt* monster; **ungeheuerlich** [ʊŋgə'hɔʏərlɪç] *adj* monstrous

ungehindert ['ʊŋgəhɪndərt] *adj* unimpeded

ungehobelt ['ʊŋgəhoːbəlt] *adj* (*fig*) uncouth

ungehörig ['ʊŋgəhøːrɪç] *adj* impertinent, improper; **Ungehörigkeit** *f* impertinence

ungehorsam ['ʊŋgəhoːrzaːm] *adj* disobedient; **Ungehorsam** *m* disobedience

ungeklärt ['ʊŋgəklɛːrt] *adj* not cleared up; (*Rätsel*) unsolved; (*Abwasser*) untreated

ungekürzt ['ʊŋgəkyrtst] *adj* not shortened; (*Film*) uncut

ungeladen ['ʊŋgəlaːdən] *adj* not loaded; (*Elek*) uncharged; (*Gast*) uninvited

ungelegen ['ʊŋgəleːgən] *adj* inconvenient; **komme ich (Ihnen) ~?** is this an inconvenient time for you?

ungelernt ['ʊŋgəlɛrnt] *adj* unskilled

ungelogen ['ʊŋgəloːgən] *adv* really, honestly

ungemein ['ʊŋgəmaɪn] *adj* immense

ungemütlich ['ʊŋgəmyːtlɪç] *adj* uncomfortable; (*Person*) disagreeable; **er kann ~ werden** he can get nasty

ungenau ['ʊŋgənau] *adj* inaccurate

Ungenauigkeit *f* inaccuracy

ungeniert ['ʊnʒeniːrt] *adj* free and easy; (*bedenkenlos, taktlos*) uninhibited ⊳ *adv* without embarrassment, freely

ungenießbar ['ʊŋgəniːsbaːr] *adj* inedible; (*nicht zu trinken*) undrinkable; (*umg*) unbearable

ungenügend ['ʊŋgənyːgənt] *adj* insufficient, inadequate; (*Sch*) unsatisfactory

ungenutzt ['ʊŋgənʊtst] *adj*: **eine Chance ~ lassen** to miss an opportunity

ungepflegt ['ʊŋgəpfleːkt] *adj* (*Garten etc*) untended; (*Person*) unkempt; (*Hände*) neglected

ungerade ['ʊŋgəraːdə] *adj* odd, uneven (*US*)

ungerecht ['ʊŋgərɛçt] *adj* unjust

ungerechtfertigt *adj* unjustified

Ungerechtigkeit *f* unfairness, injustice

ungeregelt ['ʊŋgəreːgəlt] *adj* irregular

ungereimt ['ʊŋgəraɪmt] *adj* (*Verse*) unrhymed;

(fig) inconsistent

ungern ['ʊngɛrn] *adv* unwillingly, reluctantly

ungerufen ['ʊngəru:fən] *adj* without being called

ungeschehen ['ʊngəʃe:ən] *adj:* ~ **machen** to undo

Ungeschicklichkeit ['ʊngəʃɪklɪçkaɪt] *f* clumsiness

ungeschickt *adj* awkward, clumsy

ungeschliffen ['ʊngəʃlɪfən] *adj (Edelstein)* uncut; *(Messer etc)* blunt; *(fig: Benehmen)* uncouth

ungeschmälert ['ʊngəʃmɛ:lərt] *adj* undiminished

ungeschminkt ['ʊngəʃmɪŋkt] *adj* without make-up; *(fig)* unvarnished

ungeschoren ['ʊngəʃo:rən] *adj:* **jdn ~ lassen** *(umg)* to spare sb; *(ungestraft)* to let sb off

ungesetzlich ['ʊngəzɛtslɪç] *adj* illegal

ungestempelt ['ʊngəʃtɛmpəlt] *adj (Briefmarke)* unfranked, mint

ungestört ['ʊngəʃtø:rt] *adj* undisturbed

ungestraft ['ʊngəʃtra:ft] *adv* with impunity

ungestüm ['ʊngəʃty:m] *adj* impetuous; **Ungestüm (-(e)s)** *nt* impetuosity

ungesund ['ʊngəzʊnt] *adj* unhealthy

ungetrübt ['ʊngətry:pt] *adj* clear; *(fig)* untroubled; *(Freude)* unalloyed

Ungetüm ['ʊngəty:m] **(-(e)s, -e)** *nt* monster

ungeübt ['ʊngəˈy:pt] *adj* unpractised *(Brit)*, unpracticed *(US)*; *(Mensch)* out of practice

ungewiss ['ʊngəvɪs] *adj* uncertain; **Ungewissheit** *f* uncertainty

ungewöhnlich ['ʊngəvø:nlɪç] *adj* unusual

ungewohnt ['ʊngəvo:nt] *adj* unusual

ungewollt ['ʊngəvɔlt] *adj* unintentional

Ungeziefer ['ʊngətsi:fər] **(-s)** *nt* vermin *pl*

ungezogen ['ʊngətso:gən] *adj* rude, impertinent; **Ungezogenheit** *f* rudeness, impertinence

ungezwungen ['ʊngətsvʊŋən] *adj* natural, unconstrained

ungläubig ['ʊnglɔʏbɪç] *adj* unbelieving; **ein ~er Thomas** a doubting Thomas; **die U~en** the infidel(s *pl*)

unglaublich [ʊn'glaʊplɪç] *adj* incredible

unglaubwürdig ['ʊnglaʊpvʏrdɪç] *adj* untrustworthy, unreliable; *(Geschichte)* improbable; **sich ~ machen** to lose credibility

ungleich ['ʊnglaɪç] *adj* dissimilar; *(Mittel, Waffen)* unequal ▷ *adv* incomparably; **ungleichartig** *adj* different; **Ungleichbehandlung** *f (von Frauen, Ausländern)* unequal treatment; **Ungleichheit** *f* dissimilarity; inequality; **ungleichmäßig** *adj* uneven; *(Atemzüge, Gesichtszüge, Puls)* irregular

Unglück ['ʊnglʏk] *nt* misfortune; *(Pech)* bad luck; *(Unglücksfall)* calamity, disaster; *(Verkehrsunglück)* accident; **zu allem ~** to make matters worse; **unglücklich** *adj* unhappy; *(erfolglos)* unlucky; *(unerfreulich)* unfortunate; **unglücklicherweise** *adv* unfortunately; **unglückselig** *adj* calamitous; *(Person)* unfortunate

Unglücksfall *m* accident, mishap

Unglücksrabe *(umg)* *m* unlucky thing

Ungnade ['ʊngna:də] *f:* **bei jdm in ~ fallen** to fall out of favour *(Brit) od* favor *(US)* with sb

ungültig ['ʊngʏltɪç] *adj* invalid; **etw für ~ erklären** to declare sth null and void; **Ungültigkeit** *f* invalidity

ungünstig ['ʊngʏnstɪç] *adj* unfavourable *(Brit)*, unfavorable *(US)*; *(Termin)* inconvenient; *(Augenblick, Wetter)* bad; *(nicht preiswert)* expensive

ungut ['ʊngu:t] *adj (Gefühl)* uneasy; **nichts für ~!** no offence!

unhaltbar ['ʊnhaltba:r] *adj* untenable

unhandlich ['ʊnhantlɪç] *adj* unwieldy

Unheil ['ʊnhaɪl] *nt* evil; *(Unglück)* misfortune; **~ anrichten** to cause mischief; **~ bringend** fatal, fateful

unheilbar [ʊn'haɪlbar] *adj* incurable

unheilvoll *adj* disastrous

unheimlich ['ʊnhaɪmlɪç] *adj* weird, uncanny ▷ *adv (umg)* tremendously; **das/er ist mir ~** it/he gives me the creeps *(umg)*

unhöflich ['ʊnhø:flɪç] *adj* impolite; **Unhöflichkeit** *f* impoliteness

unhörbar [ʊn'hø:rba:r] *adj* silent; *(Frequenzen)* inaudible

unhygienisch ['ʊnhygie:nɪʃ] *adj* unhygienic

Uni ['ʊni] **(-, -s)** *(umg)* *f* university

uni ['yni:] *adj* self-coloured *(Brit)*, self-colored *(US)*

Uniform [uni'fɔrm] **(-, -en)** *f* uniform

uniformiert [unifɔr'mi:rt] *adj* uniformed

Unikum ['u:nɪkʊm] **(-s, -s** *od* **Unika)** *(umg)* *nt* real character

uninteressant ['ʊn|ɪntɛresant] *adj* uninteresting

uninteressiert ['ʊn|ɪntərɛ'si:rt] *adj:* ~ **(an** +*dat*) uninterested (in), not interested (in)

Union [uni'o:n] *f* union

Unionsparteien *pl (BRD Pol)* CDU and CSU parties *pl*

universal [univɛr'za:l] *adj* universal

universell [univɛr'zɛl] *adj* universal

Universität [univɛrzi'tɛ:t] *f* university; **auf die ~ gehen, die ~ besuchen** to go to university

Universum [uni'vɛrzʊm] **(-s)** *nt* universe

unkenntlich ['ʊnkɛntlɪç] *adj* unrecognizable; **Unkenntlichkeit** *f:* **bis zur Unkenntlichkeit** beyond recognition

Unkenntnis ['ʊnkɛntnɪs] *f* ignorance

unklar ['ʊnkla:r] *adj* unclear; **im U~en sein über** +*akk* to be in the dark about; **Unklarheit** *f* unclarity; *(Unentschiedenheit)* uncertainty

unklug ['ʊnklu:k] *adj* unwise

unkompliziert ['ʊnkɔmplitsi:rt] *adj* straightforward, uncomplicated

unkontrolliert ['ʊnkɔntrɔli:rt] *adj* unchecked

unkonzentriert ['ʊnkɔntsɛntri:rt] *adj* lacking in concentration

Unkosten ['ʊnkɔstən] *pl* expense(s *pl*); **sich in**

u

349

~ stürzen (*umg*) to go to a lot of expense

Unkraut ['ʊnkraʊt] *nt* weed; weeds *pl*; **~ vergeht nicht** (*Sprichwort*) it would take more than that to finish me/him *etc* off; **Unkrautvertilgungsmittel** *nt* weedkiller

unlängst ['ʊnlɛŋst] *adv* not long ago

unlauter ['ʊnlaʊtər] *adj* unfair

unleserlich ['ʊnleːzərlɪç] *adj* illegible

unleugbar ['ʊnlɔʏkbaːr] *adj* undeniable, indisputable

unlogisch ['ʊnloːɡɪʃ] *adj* illogical

unlösbar [ʊn'løːsbar] *adj* insoluble

unlöslich [ʊn'løːslɪç] *adj* insoluble

Unlust ['ʊnlʊst] *f* lack of enthusiasm

unlustig *adj* unenthusiastic ▷ *adv* without enthusiasm

unmännlich ['ʊnmɛnlɪç] *adj* unmanly

Unmasse ['ʊnmasə] (*umg*) *f* load

unmäßig ['ʊnmɛːsɪç] *adj* immoderate

Unmenge ['ʊnmɛŋə] *f* tremendous number, vast number

Unmensch ['ʊnmɛnʃ] *m* ogre, brute; **unmenschlich** *adj* inhuman, brutal; (*ungeheuer*) awful

unmerklich [ʊn'mɛrklɪç] *adj* imperceptible

unmissverständlich ['ʊnmɪsfɛrʃtɛntlɪç] *adj* unmistakable

unmittelbar ['ʊnmɪtəlbaːr] *adj* immediate; **~er Kostenaufwand** direct expense

unmöbliert ['ʊnmøbliːrt] *adj* unfurnished

unmöglich ['ʊnmøːklɪç] *adj* impossible; **ich kann es ~ tun** I can't possibly do it; **~ aussehen** (*umg*) to look ridiculous; **Unmöglichkeit** *f* impossibility

unmoralisch ['ʊnmoraːlɪʃ] *adj* immoral

unmotiviert ['ʊnmotiviːrt] *adj* unmotivated

unmündig ['ʊnmʏndɪç] *adj* (*minderjährig*) underage

Unmut ['ʊnmuːt] *m* ill humour (*Brit*) *od* humor (*US*)

unnachahmlich ['ʊnnaːx|aːmlɪç] *adj* inimitable

unnachgiebig ['ʊnnaːxɡiːbɪç] *adj* unyielding

unnahbar [ʊn'naːbaːr] *adj* unapproachable

unnatürlich ['ʊnnatyːrlɪç] *adj* unnatural

unnormal ['ʊnnɔrmaːl] *adj* abnormal

unnötig ['ʊnnøːtɪç] *adj* unnecessary

unnötigerweise *adv* unnecessarily

unnütz ['ʊnnʏts] *adj* useless

UNO ['uːno] *f abk* (= *United Nations Organization*): **die ~** the UN

unordentlich ['ʊn|ɔrdəntlɪç] *adj* untidy

Unordnung ['ʊn|ɔrdnʊŋ] *f* disorder; (*Durcheinander*) mess

unorganisiert ['ʊn|ɔrganiziːrt] *adj* disorganized

unparteiisch ['ʊnpartaɪʃ] *adj* impartial

Unparteiische, r *f(m)* umpire; (*Fussball*) referee

unpassend ['ʊnpasənt] *adj* inappropriate; (*Zeit*) inopportune

unpässlich ['ʊnpɛslɪç] *adj* unwell

unpersönlich ['ʊnpɛrzøːnlɪç] *adj* impersonal

unpolitisch ['ʊnpoliːtɪʃ] *adj* apolitical

unpraktisch ['ʊnpraktɪʃ] *adj* impractical, unpractical

unproduktiv ['ʊnprodʊktiːf] *adj* unproductive

unproportioniert ['ʊnprɔpɔrtsioniːrt] *adj* out of proportion

unpünktlich ['ʊnpʏnktlɪç] *adj* unpunctual

unqualifiziert ['ʊnkvalifitsiːrt] *adj* unqualified; (*Äußerung*) incompetent

unrasiert ['ʊnraziːrt] *adj* unshaven

Unrat ['ʊnraːt] *m* (*geh*) filth

unrationell ['ʊnratsionɛl] *adj* inefficient

unrecht ['ʊnrɛçt] *adj* wrong; **das ist mir gar nicht so ~** I don't really mind; **~ haben** to be wrong; **Unrecht** *nt* wrong; **zu Unrecht** wrongly; **nicht zu Unrecht** not without good reason; **im Unrecht sein** to be wrong

unrechtmäßig *adj* unlawful, illegal

unredlich ['ʊnraːtlɪç] *adj* dishonest; **Unredlichkeit** *f* dishonesty

unreell ['ʊnreɛl] *adj* unfair; (*unredlich*) dishonest; (*Preis*) unreasonable

unregelmäßig ['ʊnreːɡəlmɛːsɪç] *adj* irregular; **Unregelmäßigkeit** *f* irregularity

unreif ['ʊnraɪf] *adj* (*Obst*) unripe; (*fig*) immature

Unreife *f* immaturity

unrein ['ʊnraɪn] *adj* not clean; (*Ton, Gedanken, Taten*) impure; (*Atem, Haut*) bad

unrentabel ['ʊnrɛntaːbəl] *adj* unprofitable

unrichtig ['ʊnrɪçtɪç] *adj* incorrect, wrong

Unruh ['ʊnruː] (**-, -en**) *f* (*von Uhr*) balance

Unruhe (**-, -n**) *f* unrest; **Unruheherd** *m* trouble spot; **Unruhestifter** *m* troublemaker

unruhig *adj* restless; (*nervös*) fidgety; (*belebt*) noisy; (*Schlaf*) fitful; (*Zeit etc, Meer*) troubled

unrühmlich ['ʊnryːmlɪç] *adj* inglorious

uns [ʊns] *pron akk, dat von* **wir** us; (*reflexiv*) ourselves

unsachgemäß ['ʊnzaxɡəmɛːs] *adj* improper

unsachlich ['ʊnzaxlɪç] *adj* not to the point, irrelevant; (*persönlich*) personal

unsagbar [ʊn'zaːkbaːr] *adj* indescribable

unsäglich [ʊn'zɛːklɪç] *adj* indescribable

unsanft ['ʊnzanft] *adj* rough

unsauber ['ʊnzaʊbər] *adj* (*schmutzig*) dirty; (*fig*) crooked; (: *Klang*) impure

unschädlich ['ʊnʃɛːtlɪç] *adj* harmless; **jdn/etw ~ machen** to render sb/sth harmless

unscharf ['ʊnʃarf] *adj* indistinct; (*Bild etc*) out of focus, blurred

unschätzbar [ʊn'ʃɛtsbaːr] *adj* incalculable; (*Hilfe*) invaluable

unscheinbar [ʊn'ʃaɪnbaːr] *adj* insignificant; (*Aussehen, Haus etc*) unprepossessing

unschlagbar [ʊn'ʃlaːkbaːr] *adj* invincible

unschlüssig ['ʊnʃlʏsɪç] *adj* undecided

unschön ['ʊnʃøːn] *adj* unsightly; (*lit, fig: Szene*) ugly; (*Vorfall*) unpleasant

Unschuld ['ʊnʃʊlt] *f* innocence

unschuldig ['ʊnʃʊldɪç] *adj* innocent

Unschuldsmiene *f* innocent expression

unschwer ['ʊnʃveːr] *adv* easily, without difficulty

unselbstständig ['ʊnzɛlpstʃtɛndɪç],

unselbständig ['ʊnzɛlpʃtɛndɪç] *adj* dependent, over-reliant on others

unselig ['ʊnzeːlɪç] *adj* unfortunate; (*verhängnisvoll*) ill-fated

unser ['ʊnzər] *poss pron* our ▷ *pron gen von* **wir** of us

unsere, r, s *poss pron* ours; **wir tun das U~** (*geh*) we are doing our bit

unsereiner *pron* the likes of us

unsereins *pron* the likes of us

unsererseits ['ʊnzərər'zaɪts] *adv* on our part

unseresgleichen *pron* the likes of us

unserige, r, s *poss pron*: **der/die/das U~** ours

unseriös ['ʊnzeriøːs] *adj* (*unehrlich*) not straight, untrustworthy

unserseits ['ʊnzər'zaɪts] *adv* = **unsererseits**

unsertwegen ['ʊnzərt've:gən] *adv* (*für uns*) for our sake; (*wegen uns*) on our account

unsertwillen ['ʊnzərt'vɪlən] *adv*: **um ~ =** **unsertwegen**

unsicher ['ʊnzɪçər] *adj* uncertain; (*Mensch*) insecure; **die Gegend ~ machen** (*fig: umg*) to knock about the district; **Unsicherheit** *f* uncertainty; insecurity

unsichtbar ['ʊnzɪçtbaːr] *adj* invisible; **Unsichtbarkeit** *f* invisibility

Unsinn ['ʊnzɪn] *m* nonsense

unsinnig *adj* nonsensical

Unsitte ['ʊnzɪtə] *f* deplorable habit

unsittlich ['ʊnzɪtlɪç] *adj* indecent; **Unsittlichkeit** *f* indecency

unsolide ['ʊnzoliːdə] *adj* (*Mensch, Leben*) loose; (*Firma*) unreliable

unsozial ['ʊnzotsiaːl] *adj* (*Verhalten*) antisocial; (*Politik*) unsocial

unsportlich ['ʊnʃpɔrtlɪç] *adj* not sporty; (*Verhalten*) unsporting

unsre *etc* ['ʊnzrə] *poss pron* = **unsere** *etc*; *siehe auch* **unser**

unsrige, r, s ['ʊnzrɪgə(r, s)] *poss pron* = **unserige**

unsterblich ['ʊnʃtɛrplɪç] *adj* immortal; **Unsterblichkeit** *f* immortality

unstet ['ʊnʃteːt] *adj* (*Mensch*) restless; (*wankelmütig*) changeable; (*Leben*) unsettled

Unstimmigkeit ['ʊnʃtɪmɪçkaɪt] *f* inconsistency; (*Streit*) disagreement

Unsumme ['ʊnzʊmə] *f* vast sum

unsympathisch ['ʊnzʏmpaːtɪʃ] *adj* unpleasant; **er ist mir ~** I don't like him

untadelig ['ʊnta:dəlɪç], **untadlig** ['ʊnta:dlɪç] *adj* impeccable; (*Mensch*) beyond reproach

Untat ['ʊnta:t] *f* atrocity

untätig ['ʊntɛ:tɪç] *adj* idle

untauglich ['ʊntaʊklɪç] *adj* unsuitable; (*Mil*) unfit; **Untauglichkeit** *f* unsuitability; unfitness

unteilbar [ʊn'taɪlbaːr] *adj* indivisible

unten ['ʊntən] *adv* below; (*im Haus*) downstairs; (*an der Treppe etc*) at the bottom; **~ genannt** undermentioned; **siehe ~** see below; **nach ~** down; **~ am Berg** *etc* at the bottom of the mountain *etc*; **er ist bei mir ~ durch** (*umg*) I'm through with him; **untenan** *adv*

(*am unteren Ende*) at the far end; (*lit, fig*) at the bottom

 SCHLÜSSELWORT

unter ['ʊntər] *präp +dat* **1** (*räumlich*) under; (*drunter*) underneath, below
2 (*zwischen*) among(st); **sie waren unter sich** they were by themselves; **einer unter ihnen** one of them; **unter anderem** among other things; **unter der Hand** secretly; (*verkaufen*) privately
▷ *präp +akk* under, below
▷ *adv* (*weniger als*) under; **Mädchen unter 18 Jahren** girls under *od* less than 18 (years of age)

Unter- *zW*: **Unterabteilung** *f* subdivision; **Unterarm** *m* forearm; **unterbelegt** *adj* (*Kurs*) under-subscribed; (*Hotel etc*) not full

unterbelichten ['ʊntərbəlɪçtən] *vt untr* (*Phot*) to underexpose

Unterbeschäftigung ['ʊntərbəʃɛːftɪgʊŋ] *f* underemployment

unterbesetzt ['ʊntərbəzɛtst] *adj* understaffed

Unterbewusstsein ['ʊntərbəvʊstzaɪn] *nt* subconscious

unterbezahlt ['ʊntərbətsaːlt] *adj* underpaid

unterbieten [ʊntər'biːtən] *unreg vt untr* (*Comm*) to undercut; (*fig*) to surpass

unterbinden [ʊntər'bɪndən] *unreg vt untr* to stop, call a halt to

unterbleiben [ʊntər'blaɪbən] *unreg vi untr* (*aufhören*) to stop; (*versäumt werden*) to be omitted

Unterbodenschutz [ʊntər'boːdənʃʊts] *m* (*Aut*) underseal

unterbrechen [ʊntər'brɛçən] *unreg vt untr* to interrupt

Unterbrechung *f* interruption

unterbreiten [ʊntər'braɪtən] *vt untr* (*Plan*) to present

unterbringen ['ʊntərbrɪŋən] *unreg vt* (*in Koffer*) to stow; (*in Zeitung*) to place; (*Person: in Hotel etc*) to accommodate, put up; (*: beruflich*): **~ (bei)** to fix up (with)

unterbuttern ['ʊntərbʊtərn] (*umg*) *vt* (*zuschießen*) to throw in; (*unterdrücken*) to ride roughshod over

unterdessen [ʊntər'dɛsən] *adv* meanwhile

Unterdruck ['ʊntərdrʊk] *m* (*Tech*) below atmospheric pressure

unterdrücken [ʊntər'drʏkən] *vt untr* to suppress; (*Leute*) to oppress

untere, r, s ['ʊntərə(r, s)] *adj* lower

untereinander [ʊntər'aɪ'nandər] *adv* (*gegenseitig*) each other; (*miteinander*) among themselves *etc*

unterentwickelt ['ʊntər'ɛntvɪkəlt] *adj* underdeveloped

unterernährt ['ʊntər'ɛrnɛːrt] *adj* undernourished

Unterernährung *f* malnutrition

Unterfangen [ʊntər'faŋən] *nt* undertaking

u

Unterführung | Unterprogramm

Unterführung [ʊntərˈfyːrʊŋ] f subway, underpass

Untergang [ˈʊntərgaŋ] m (down)fall, decline; (Naut) sinking; (von Gestirn) setting; **dem ~ geweiht sein** to be doomed

untergeben [ʊntərˈgeːbən] adj subordinate

Untergebene, r f(m) subordinate

untergehen [ˈʊntərgeːən] unreg vi to go down; (Sonne) to set, go down; (Staat) to fall; (Volk) to perish; (Welt) to come to an end; (im Lärm) to be drowned

untergeordnet [ˈʊntərgəˌɔrdnət] adj (Dienststelle) subordinate; (Bedeutung) secondary

Untergeschoss [ˈʊntərgəʃɔs] nt basement

Untergewicht [ˈʊntərgəvɪçt] nt: **(10 Kilo) ~ haben** to be (10 kilos) underweight

untergliedern [ʊntərˈgliːdərn] vt untr to subdivide

untergraben [ʊntərˈgraːbən] unreg vt untr to undermine

Untergrund [ˈʊntərgrʊnt] m foundation; (Pol) underground; **Untergrundbahn** f underground (Brit), subway (US); **Untergrundbewegung** f underground (movement)

unterhaken [ˈʊntərhaːkən] vr: **sich bei jdm ~** to link arms with sb

unterhalb [ˈʊntərhalp] präp+gen below ▷ adv below; **~ von** below

Unterhalt [ˈʊntərhalt] m maintenance; **seinen ~ verdienen** to earn one's living

unterhalten [ʊntərˈhaltən] unreg vt untr to maintain; (belustigen) to entertain; (versorgen) to support; (Geschäft, Kfz) to run; (Konto) to have ▷ vr untr to talk; (sich belustigen) to enjoy o.s.

unterhaltend, unterhaltsam [ʊntərˈhaltzaːm] adj entertaining

Unterhaltskosten pl maintenance costs pl

Unterhaltszahlung f maintenance payment

Unterhaltung f maintenance; (Belustigung) entertainment, amusement; (Gespräch) talk

Unterhaltungskosten pl running costs pl

Unterhaltungsmusik f light music

Unterhändler [ˈʊntərhɛntlər] m negotiator

Unterhaus [ˈʊntərhaus] nt House of Commons (Brit), House of Representatives (US), Lower House

Unterhemd [ˈʊntərhɛmt] nt vest (Brit), undershirt (US)

unterhöhlen [ʊntərˈhøːlən] vt untr (lit, fig) to undermine

Unterholz [ˈʊntərhɔlts] nt undergrowth

Unterhose [ˈʊntərhoːzə] f underpants pl

unterirdisch [ˈʊntərˌɪrdɪʃ] adj underground

unterjubeln [ˈʊntərjuːbəln] (umg) vt: **jdm etw ~** to palm sth off on sb

unterkapitalisiert [ˈʊntərkapitaliˈziːrt] adj undercapitalized

unterkellern [ʊntərˈkɛlərn] vt untr to build with a cellar

Unterkiefer [ˈʊntərkiːfər] m lower jaw

unterkommen [ˈʊntərkɔmən] unreg vi to find

shelter; (Stelle finden) to find work; **das ist mir noch nie untergekommen** I've never met with that; **bei jdm ~** to stay at sb's (place)

unterkriegen [ˈʊntərkriːgən] (umg) vt: **sich nicht ~ lassen** not to let things get one down

unterkühlt [ʊntərˈkyːlt] adj (Mensch) affected by hypothermia; (fig: Mensch, Atmosphäre) cool

Unterkunft [ˈʊntərkʊnft] (-, -künfte) f accommodation (Brit), accommodations pl (US); **~ und Verpflegung** board and lodging

Unterlage [ˈʊntərlaːgə] f foundation; (Beleg) document; (Schreibunterlage etc) pad

unterlassen [ʊntərˈlasən] unreg vt untr (versäumen) to fail to do; (sich enthalten) to refrain from

unterlaufen [ʊntərˈlaufən] unreg vi untr to happen ▷ adj: **mit Blut ~** suffused with blood; (Augen) bloodshot; **mir ist ein Fehler ~** I made a mistake

unterlegen¹ [ˈʊntərleːgən] vt to lay od put under

unterlegen² [ʊntərˈleːgən] adj inferior; (besiegt) defeated

Unterleib [ˈʊntərlaip] m abdomen

unterliegen [ʊntərˈliːgən] unreg vi untr +dat to be defeated od overcome (by); (unterworfen sein) to be subject (to)

Unterlippe [ˈʊntərlɪpə] f bottom od lower lip

unterm = **unter dem**

untermalen [ʊntərˈmaːlən] vt untr (mit Musik) to provide with background music

Untermalung f: **musikalische ~** background music

untermauern [ʊntərˈmauərn] vt untr (Gebäude, fig) to underpin

Untermiete [ˈʊntərmiːtə] f subtenancy; **bei jdm zur ~ wohnen** to rent a room from sb

Untermieter, in m(f) lodger

untern = **unter den**

unternehmen [ʊntərˈneːmən] unreg vt untr to do; (durchführen) to undertake; (Versuch, Reise) to make; **Unternehmen (-s, -)** nt undertaking, enterprise (auch COMM); (Firma) business

unternehmend adj enterprising, daring

Unternehmensberater m management consultant

Unternehmensplanung f corporate planning, management planning

Unternehmer, in [ʊntərˈneːmər(ɪn)] (-s, -) m(f) (business) employer; (alten Stils) entrepreneur; **Unternehmerverband** m employers' association

Unternehmungsgeist m spirit of enterprise

unternehmungslustig adj enterprising

Unteroffizier [ˈʊntərˌɔfitsiːr] m noncommissioned officer, NCO

unterordnen [ˈʊntərˌɔrdnən] vt: **~ (+dat)** to subordinate (to)

Unterordnung f subordination

Unterprima [ˈʊntərpriːma] f (früher) eighth year of German secondary school

Unterprogramm [ˈʊntərprogram] nt (Comput) subroutine

Unterredung [ʊntərˈreːdʊŋ] f discussion, talk
Unterricht [ˈʊntərɪçt] (-**(e)s**) m teaching; (Stunden) lessons pl; **jdm ~ (in etw** dat**) geben** to teach sb (sth)
unterrichten [ʊntərˈrɪçtən] vt untr to instruct; (Sch) to teach ▷ vr untr: **sich ~ (über** +akk) to inform o.s. (about), obtain information (about)
Unterrichts- zW: **Unterrichtsgegenstand** m topic, subject; **Unterrichtsmethode** f teaching method; **Unterrichtsstoff** m teaching material; **Unterrichtsstunde** f lesson; **Unterrichtszwecke** pl: **zu Unterrichtszwecken** for teaching purposes
Unterrock [ˈʊntərrɔk] m petticoat, slip
unters = **unter das**
untersagen [ʊntərˈzaːgən] vt untr to forbid; **jdm etw ~** to forbid sb to do sth
Untersatz [ˈʊntərzats] m mat; (für Blumentöpfe etc) base
unterschätzen [ʊntərˈʃɛtsən] vt untr to underestimate
unterscheiden [ʊntərˈʃaɪdən] unreg vt untr to distinguish ▷ vr untr to differ
Unterscheidung f (Unterschied) distinction; (Unterscheiden) differentiation
Unterschenkel [ˈʊntərʃɛŋkəl] m lower leg
Unterschicht [ˈʊntərʃɪçt] f lower class
unterschieben [ˈʊntərʃiːbən] unreg vt (fig): **jdm etw ~** to foist sth on sb
Unterschied [ˈʊntərʃiːt] (-**(e)s, -e**) m difference, distinction; **im ~ zu** as distinct from; **unterschiedlich** adj varying, differing; (diskriminierend) discriminatory
unterschiedslos adv indiscriminately
unterschlagen [ʊntərˈʃlaːgən] unreg vt untr to embezzle; (verheimlichen) to suppress
Unterschlagung f embezzlement; (von Briefen, Beweis) withholding
Unterschlupf [ˈʊntərʃlʊpf] (-**(e)s, -schlüpfe**) m refuge
unterschlüpfen [ˈʊntərʃlʏpfən] (umg) vi to take cover od shelter; (Versteck finden): (**bei jdm**) **~** to hide out (at sb's) (umg)
unterschreiben [ʊntərˈʃraɪbən] unreg vt untr to sign
Unterschrift [ˈʊntərʃrɪft] f signature; (Bildunterschrift) caption
unterschwellig [ˈʊntərʃvɛlɪç] adj subliminal
Unterseeboot [ˈʊntərzeːboːt] nt submarine
Unterseite [ˈʊntərzaɪtə] f underside
Untersekunda [ˈʊntərzekʊnda] f (früher) sixth year of German secondary school
Untersetzer [ˈʊntərzɛtsər] m tablemat; (für Gläser) coaster
untersetzt [ʊntərˈzɛtst] adj stocky
unterste, r, s [ˈʊntərstə(r, s)] adj lowest, bottom
unterstehen¹ [ʊntərˈʃteːən] unreg vi untr+dat to be under ▷ vr untr to dare
unterstehen² [ˈʊntərʃteːən] unreg vi to shelter
unterstellen¹ [ʊntərˈʃtɛlən] vt untr to subordinate; (fig) to impute; **jdm/etw**

unterstellt sein to be under sb/sth; (in Firma) to report to sb/sth
unterstellen² [ˈʊntərʃtɛlən] vt (Auto) to garage, park ▷ vr to take shelter
Unterstellung f (falsche Behauptung) misrepresentation; (Andeutung) insinuation
unterstreichen [ʊntərˈʃtraɪçən] unreg vt untr (lit, fig) to underline
Unterstufe [ˈʊntərʃtuːfə] f lower grade
unterstützen [ʊntərˈʃtʏtsən] vt untr to support
Unterstützung f support, assistance
untersuchen [ʊntərˈzuːxən] vt untr (Med) to examine; (Polizei) to investigate; **sich ärztlich ~ lassen** to have a medical (Brit) od physical (US) (examination), have a check-up
Untersuchung f examination; investigation, inquiry
Untersuchungs- zW: **Untersuchungsausschuss** m committee of inquiry; **Untersuchungsergebnis** nt (Jur) findings pl; (Med) result of an examination; **Untersuchungshaft** f custody; **in Untersuchungshaft sein** to be remanded in custody; **Untersuchungsrichter** m examining magistrate
Untertagebau [ʊntərˈtaːgəbau] m underground mining
Untertan [ˈʊntərtaːn] (-**s, -en**) m subject
untertänig [ˈʊntərtɛːnɪç] adj submissive, humble
Untertasse [ˈʊntərtasə] f saucer
untertauchen [ˈʊntərtauxən] vi to dive; (fig) to disappear, go underground
Unterteil [ˈʊntərtaɪl] nt od m lower part, bottom
unterteilen [ʊntərˈtaɪlən] vt untr to divide up
Untertertia [ˈʊntərtertsia] f (früher) fourth year of German secondary school
Untertitel [ˈʊntərtiːtəl] m subtitle; (für Bild) caption
unterwandern [ʊntərˈvandərn] vt untr to infiltrate
Unterwäsche [ˈʊntərvɛʃə] f underwear
unterwegs [ʊntərˈveːks] adv on the way; (auf Reisen) away
unterweisen [ʊntərˈvaɪzən] unreg vt untr to instruct
Unterwelt [ˈʊntərvɛlt] f (lit, fig) underworld
unterwerfen [ʊntərˈvɛrfən] unreg vt untr to subject; (Volk) to subjugate ▷ vr untr to submit
unterwürfig [ʊntərˈvʏrfɪç] adj obsequious
unterzeichnen [ʊntərˈtsaɪçnən] vt untr to sign
Unterzeichner m signatory
unterziehen [ʊntərˈtsiːən] unreg vt untr+dat to subject ▷ vr untr+dat to undergo; (einer Prüfung) to take
Untiefe [ˈʊntiːfə] f shallow
Untier [ˈʊntiːr] nt monster
untragbar [ʊnˈtraːkbaːr] adj intolerable, unbearable
untreu [ˈʊntrɔy] adj unfaithful; **sich** dat **selbst ~ werden** to be untrue to o.s.
Untreue f unfaithfulness

u

untröstlich [ʊn'trø:stlɪç] *adj* inconsolable

Untugend ['ʊntu:gənt] *f* vice; *(Angewohnheit)* bad habit

un- *zW*: **unüberbrückbar** *adj (fig: Gegensätze etc)* irreconcilable; *(Kluft)* unbridgeable; **unüberlegt** *adj* ill-considered ▷ *adv* without thinking; **unübersehbar** *adj (Schaden etc)* incalculable; *(Menge)* vast, immense; *(auffällig: Fehler etc)* obvious; **unübersichtlich** *adj (Gelände)* broken; *(Kurve)* blind; *(System, Plan)* confused; **unübertroffen** *adj* unsurpassed

un- *zW*: **unumgänglich** *adj* indispensable, vital; **unumstößlich** *adj (Tatsache)* incontrovertible; *(Entschluss)* irrevocable; **unumstritten** *adj* undisputed; **unumwunden** [-ʊm'vʊndən] *adj* candid ▷ *adv* straight out

ununterbrochen ['ʊn|ʊntərbrɔxən] *adj* uninterrupted

un- *zW*: **unveränderlich** *adj* unchangeable; **unverantwortlich** *adj* irresponsible; *(unentschuldbar)* inexcusable; **unverarbeitet** *adj (lit, fig)* raw; **unveräußerlich** [-fɛr'ɔysərlich] *adj* inalienable; *(Besitz)* unmarketable; **unverbesserlich** *adj* incorrigible; **unverbindlich** *adj* not binding; *(Antwort)* curt ▷ *adv (Comm)* without obligation; **unverbleit** [-fɛrblaɪt] *adj (Benzin)* unleaded; **unverblümt** [-fɛr'bly:mt] *adj* plain, blunt ▷ *adv* plainly, bluntly; **unverdaulich** *adj* indigestible; **unverdorben** *adj* unspoilt; **unverdrossen** *adj* undeterred; *(unermüdlich)* untiring; **unvereinbar** *adj* incompatible; **unverfälscht** [-fɛrfɛlʃt] *adj (auch fig)* unadulterated; *(Dialekt)* pure; *(Natürlichkeit)* unaffected; **unverfänglich** *adj* harmless; **unverfroren** *adj* impudent; **unvergänglich** *adj* immortal; *(Eindruck, Erinnerung)* everlasting; **unvergessen** *adj* unforgettable; **unvergleichlich** *adj* unique, incomparable; **unverhältnismäßig** *adv* disproportionately; *(übermäßig)* excessively; **unverheiratet** *adj* unmarried; **unverhofft** *adj* unexpected; **unverhohlen** [-fɛrho:lən] *adj* open, unconcealed; **unverkäuflich** *adj*: „**unverkäuflich**" "not for sale"; **unverkennbar** *adj* unmistakable; **unverletzlich** *adj (fig: Rechte)* inviolable; *(lit)* invulnerable; **unverletzt** *adj* uninjured; **unvermeidlich** *adj* unavoidable; **unvermittelt** *adj (plötzlich)* sudden, unexpected; **Unvermögen** *nt* inability; **unvermutet** *adj* unexpected; **unvernünftig** *adj* foolish; **unverrichtet** *adj*: **unverrichteter Dinge** empty-handed; **unverschämt** *adj* impudent; **Unverschämtheit** *f* impudence, insolence; **unverschuldet** *adj* occurring through no fault of one's own; **unversehens** *adv* all of a sudden; **unversehrt** [-fɛrze:rt] *adj* uninjured; **unversöhnlich** *adj* irreconcilable; **Unverstand** *m* lack of judgement; *(Torheit)* folly; **unverständlich** *adj* unintelligible; **unversucht** *adj*: **nichts unversucht lassen** to try everything; **unverträglich** *adj* quarrelsome; *(Meinungen, Med)* incompatible;

unverwechselbar *adj* unmistakable, distinctive; **unverwüstlich** *adj* indestructible; *(Mensch)* irrepressible; **unverzeihlich** *adj* unpardonable; **unverzinslich** *adj* interest-free; **unverzüglich** [-fɛr'tsy:klɪç] *adj* immediate; **unvollendet** *adj* unfinished; **unvollkommen** *adj* imperfect; **unvollständig** *adj* incomplete; **unvorbereitet** *adj* unprepared; **unvoreingenommen** *adj* unbiased; **unvorhergesehen** *adj* unforeseen; **unvorsichtig** *adj* careless, imprudent; **unvorstellbar** *adj* inconceivable; **unvorteilhaft** *adj* disadvantageous

unwahr ['ʊnva:r] *adj* untrue; **unwahrhaftig** *adj* untruthful; **Unwahrheit** *f* untruth; **die Unwahrheit sagen** not to tell the truth; **unwahrscheinlich** *adj* improbable, unlikely ▷ *adv (umg)* incredibly; **Unwahrscheinlichkeit** *f* improbability, unlikelihood

unwegsam ['ʊnve:kza:m] *adj (Gelände etc)* rough

unweigerlich [ʊn'vaɪgərlɪç] *adj* unquestioning ▷ *adv* without fail

unweit ['ʊnvaɪt] *präp +gen* not far from ▷ *adv* not far

Unwesen ['ʊnve:zən] *nt* nuisance; *(Unfug)* mischief; **sein ~ treiben** to wreak havoc; *(Mörder etc)* to be at large

unwesentlich *adj* inessential, unimportant; **~ besser** marginally better

Unwetter ['ʊnvɛtər] *nt* thunderstorm

unwichtig ['ʊnvɪçtɪç] *adj* unimportant

un- *zW*: **unwiderlegbar** *adj* irrefutable; **unwiderruflich** *adj* irrevocable; **unwiderstehlich** [-vi:dər'ʃte:lɪç] *adj* irresistible

unwiederbringlich [ʊnvi:dər'brɪŋlɪç] *adj (geh)* irretrievable

Unwille ['ʊnvɪlə], **Unwillen** ['ʊnvɪlən] *m* indignation

unwillig *adj* indignant; *(widerwillig)* reluctant

unwillkürlich ['ʊnvɪlky:rlɪç] *adj* involuntary ▷ *adv* instinctively; *(lachen)* involuntarily

unwirklich ['ʊnvɪrklɪç] *adj* unreal

unwirksam ['ʊnvɪrkza:m] *adj* ineffective

unwirsch ['ʊnvɪrʃ] *adj* cross, surly

unwirtlich ['ʊnvɪrtlɪç] *adj* inhospitable

unwirtschaftlich ['ʊnvɪrtʃaftlɪç] *adj* uneconomical

unwissend ['ʊnvɪsənt] *adj* ignorant

Unwissenheit *f* ignorance

unwissenschaftlich *adj* unscientific

unwissentlich *adv* unwittingly, unknowingly

unwohl ['ʊnvo:l] *adj* unwell, ill; **Unwohlsein** (**-s**) *nt* indisposition

unwürdig ['ʊnvʏrdɪç] *adj* unworthy

Unzahl ['ʊntsa:l] *f*: **eine ~ von ...** a whole host of ...

unzählig [ʊn'tsɛ:lɪç] *adj* innumerable, countless

unzeitgemäß ['ʊntsaɪtgəmɛ:s] *adj (altmodisch)* old-fashioned

un- *zW*: **unzerbrechlich** *adj* unbreakable; **unzerreißbar** *adj* untearable; **unzerstörbar** *adj* indestructible; **unzertrennlich** adj inseparable

Unzucht ['ʊntsʊxt] f sexual offence

unzüchtig ['ʊntsʏçtɪç] adj immoral

un- zW: **unzufrieden** adj dissatisfied;
Unzufriedenheit f discontent; **unzugänglich**
adj (Gegend) inaccessible; (Mensch)
inapproachable; **unzulänglich** adj inadequate;
unzulässig adj inadmissible; **unzumutbar**
adj unreasonable; **unzurechnungsfähig** adj
irresponsible; **jdn für unzurechnungsfähig
erklären lassen** (Jur) to have sb certified
(insane); **unzusammenhängend** adj
disconnected; (Äußerung) incoherent;
unzustellbar adj: **falls unzustellbar, bitte
an Absender zurück** if undelivered, please
return to sender; **unzutreffend** adj incorrect;
„nzutreffendes bitte streichen" "delete as
applicable"; **unzuverlässig** adj unreliable

unzweckmäßig ['ʊntsvɛkmɛːsɪç] adj (nicht
ratsam) inadvisable; (unpraktisch) impractical;
(ungeeignet) unsuitable

unzweideutig ['ʊntsvaɪdɔytɪç] adj
unambiguous

unzweifelhaft ['ʊntsvaɪfəlhaft] adj
indubitable

üppig ['ʏpɪç] adj (Frau) curvaceous; (Essen)
sumptuous, lavish; (Vegetation) luxuriant,
lush; (Haar) thick

Ur- ['uːr] in zw original

Urabstimmung ['uːr|apʃtɪmʊŋ] f ballot

Ural [u'raːl] (**-s**) m: **der ~** the Ural mountains pl,
the Urals pl; **Uralgebirge** nt Ural mountains

uralt ['uːr|alt] adj ancient, very old

Uran [u'raːn] (**-s**) nt uranium

Uraufführung f first performance

urbar adj: **die Wüste/Land ~ machen** to
reclaim the desert/cultivate land

Urdu ['ʊrdu] (**-**) nt Urdu

Ur- zW: **Ureinwohner** m original inhabitant;
Ureltern pl ancestors pl; **Urenkel, in** m(f)
great-grandchild; **Urfassung** f original
version; **Urgroßmutter** f great-grandmother;
Urgroßvater m great-grandfather

Urheber (**-s, -**) m originator; (Autor) author;
Urheberrecht nt: **Urheberrecht (an
+dat)** copyright (on); **urheberrechtlich**
adv: **urheberrechtlich geschützt**
copyright

urig ['uːrɪç] (umg) adj (Mensch, Atmosphäre)
earthy

Urin [u'riːn] (**-s, -e**) m urine

urkomisch adj incredibly funny

Urkunde f document; (Kaufurkunde) deed

urkundlich ['uːrkʊntlɪç] adj documentary

URL f abk (= uniform resource locator) URL

Urlader m (Comput) bootstrap

Urlaub ['uːrlaʊp] (**-(e)s, -e**) m holiday(s pl) (Brit),
vacation (US); (Mil etc) leave; **Urlauber** (**-s, -**) m
holiday-maker (Brit), vacationer (US)

Urlaubs- zW: **Urlaubsgeld** nt holiday (Brit) od
vacation (US) money; **Urlaubsort** m holiday
(Brit) od vacation (US) resort; **urlaubsreif** adj in
need of a holiday (Brit) od vacation (US)

Urmensch m primitive man

Urne ['ʊrnə] (**-, -n**) f urn; **zur ~ gehen** to go to
the polls

urplötzlich ['uːr'plœtslɪç] (umg) adv all of a
sudden

Ursache ['uːrzaxə] f cause; **keine ~!** (auf
Dank) don't mention it, you're welcome; (auf
Entschuldigung) that's all right

ursächlich ['uːrzɛçlɪç] adj causal

Urschrei ['uːrʃraɪ] m (Psych) primal scream

Ursprung ['uːrʃprʊŋ] m origin, source; (von
Fluss) source

ursprünglich ['uːrʃprʏŋlɪç] adj original ▷ adv
originally

Ursprungsland nt (Comm) country of origin

Ursprungszeugnis nt certificate of origin

Urteil ['ʊrtaɪl] (**-s, -e**) nt opinion; (Jur) sentence,
judgement; **sich** dat **ein ~ über etw** akk
erlauben to pass judgement on sth; **ein ~
über etw** akk **fällen** to pass judgement on sth;
urteilen vi to judge

Urteilsbegründung f (Jur) opinion

Urteilsspruch m sentence; verdict

Uruguay [uru'gua:i] (**-s**) nt Uruguay

Uruguayer, in (**-s, -**) m(f) Uruguayan

uruguayisch adj Uruguayan

Ur- zW: **Urwald** m jungle; **urwüchsig** adj
natural; (Landschaft) unspoilt; (Humor) earthy;
Urzeit f prehistoric times pl

USA [uːˈɛsˈaː] pl abk: **die ~** the USA sing

USB abk (= universal serial bus) USB

Usbekistan [ʊsˈbeːkistaːn] (**-s**) nt Uzbekistan

usw. abk (= und so weiter) etc.

Utensilien [utɛn'ziːliən] pl utensils pl

Utopie [uto'piː] f pipe dream

utopisch [u'toːpɪʃ] adj utopian

u. U. abk (= unter Umständen) possibly

UV abk (= ultraviolett) U.V.

u. v. a. abk (= und viele(s) andere) and much/
many more

u. v. a. m. abk (= und viele(s) andere mehr) and
much/many more

u. W. abk (= unseres Wissens) to our knowledge

Ü-Wagen m (Rundf, TV) outside broadcast
vehicle

uzen ['uːtsən] (umg) vt, vi to tease, kid

u. zw. abk = **und zwar**

355

V¹, v [faʊ] *nt* V, v; **V wie Viktor** ≈ V for Victor
V² [faʊ] *abk* (= *Volt*) v
VAE *pl abk* (= *Vereinigte Arabische Emirate*) UAE
vag, vage *adj* vague
Vagina [va'giːna] (-, **Vaginen**) *f* vagina
Vakuum ['vaːkuʊm] (-s, **Vakua** *od* **Vakuen**)
    nt vacuum; **vakuumverpackt** *adj* vacuum-
    packed
Vandalismus [vanda'lɪsmʊs] *m* vandalism
Vanille [va'nɪljə] (-) *f* vanilla; **Vanillezucker** *m*
    vanilla sugar
Vanillinzucker *m* vanilla sugar
variabel [vari'aːbəl] *adj*: **variable Kosten**
    variable costs
Variable [vari'aːblə] (-, **-n**) *f* variable
Variante [vari'antə] (-, **-n**) *f*: **~ (zu)** variant (on)
Variation [variatsi'oːn] *f* variation
variieren [vari'iːrən] *vt, vi* to vary
Vase ['vaːzə] (-, **-n**) *f* vase
Vater ['faːtər] (-s, ⸚) *m* father; **~ Staat** (*umg*)
    the State; **Vaterland** *nt* native country; (*bes
    Deutschland*) Fatherland; **Vaterlandsliebe** *f*
    patriotism
väterlich ['fɛːtərlɪç] *adj* fatherly
väterlicherseits *adv* on the father's side
Vaterschaft *f* paternity
Vaterschaftsklage *f* paternity suit
Vaterstelle *f*: **~ bei jdm vertreten** to take the
    place of sb's father
Vaterunser (-s, -) *nt* Lord's Prayer
Vati ['faːti] (-s, **-s**) (*umg*) *m* dad(dy)
Vatikan [vati'kaːn] (-s) *m* Vatican
V-Ausschnitt ['faʊˌaʊsʃnɪt] *m* V-neck
VB *abk* (= *Verhandlungsbasis*) o.i.r.o.
v. Chr. *abk* (= *vor Christus*) B.C.
Vegetarier, in [vege'taːriər(ɪn)] (-s, -) *m(f)*
    vegetarian
vegetarisch *adj* vegetarian
Vegetation [vegetatsi'oːn] *f* vegetation
vegetativ [vegeta'tiːf] *adj* (*Biol*) vegetative;
    (*Med*) autonomic
vegetieren [vege'tiːrən] *vi* to vegetate; (*kärglich
    leben*) to eke out a bare existence
Vehikel [ve'hiːkəl] (-s, -) (*pej: umg*) *nt*
    boneshaker
Veilchen ['faɪlçən] *nt* violet; (*umg: blaues Auge*)
    shiner, black eye
Velours (-, -) *nt* suede; **Veloursleder** *nt* suede

Vene ['veːnə] (-, **-n**) *f* vein
Venedig [ve'neːdɪç] (-s) *nt* Venice
Venezianer, in [venetsi'aːnər(ɪn)] (-s, -) *m(f)*
    Venetian
venezianisch [venetsi'aːnɪʃ] *adj* Venetian
Venezolaner, in [venetsoˈlaːnər(ɪn)] (-s, -) *m(f)*
    Venezuelan
venezolanisch *adj* Venezuelan
Venezuela [venetsu'eːla] (-s) *nt* Venezuela
Ventil [vɛn'tiːl] (-s, **-e**) *nt* valve
Ventilator [vɛnti'laːtɔr] *m* ventilator
verabreden [fɛrˈapreːdən] *vt* to arrange;
    (*Termin*) to agree upon ▷ *vr* to arrange to
    meet; **sich (mit jdm)** ~ to arrange to meet
    (sb); **schon verabredet sein** to have a prior
    engagement (*form*), have something else on
Verabredung *f* arrangement; (*Treffen*)
    appointment; **ich habe eine** ~ I'm meeting
    somebody
verabreichen [fɛrˈapraɪçən] *vt* (*Tracht Prügel
    etc*) to give; (*Arznei*) to administer (*form*)
verabscheuen [fɛrˈapʃɔʏən] *vt* to detest,
    abhor
verabschieden [fɛrˈapʃiːdən] *vt* (*Gäste*) to say
    goodbye to; (*entlassen*) to discharge; (*Gesetz*) to
    pass ▷ *vr*: **sich** ~ **(von)** to take one's leave (of)
Verabschiedung *f* (*von Beamten etc*) discharge;
    (*von Gesetz*) passing
verachten [fɛrˈaxtən] *vt* to despise; **nicht zu**
    ~ (*umg*) not to be scoffed at
verächtlich [fɛrˈɛçtlɪç] *adj* contemptuous;
    (*verachtenswert*) contemptible; **jdn** ~ **machen**
    to run sb down
Verachtung *f* contempt; **jdn mit** ~ **strafen** to
    treat sb with contempt
veralbern [fɛrˈalbərn] (*umg*) *vt* to make fun of
verallgemeinern [fɛrˈalgəmaɪnərn] *vt* to
    generalize
Verallgemeinerung *f* generalization
veralten [fɛrˈaltən] *vi* to become obsolete *od*
    out-of-date
Veranda [ve'randa] (-, **Veranden**) *f* veranda
veränderlich [fɛrˈɛndərlɪç] *adj* variable;
    (*Wetter*) changeable; **Veränderlichkeit** *f*
    variability; changeability
verändern *vt, vr* to change
Veränderung *f* change; **eine berufliche** ~ a
    change of job

verängstigen [fɛr'|ɛŋstɪgən] vt (erschrecken) to frighten; (einschüchtern) to intimidate

verankern [fɛr'|aŋkərn] vt (Naut, Tech) to anchor; (fig): ~ (**in** +dat) to embed (in)

veranlagen [fɛr'|anla:gən] vt: **etw ~ (mit)** to assess sth (at)

veranlagt adj: **praktisch ~ sein** to be practically-minded; **zu** od **für etw ~ sein** to be cut out for sth

Veranlagung f disposition, aptitude

veranlassen [fɛr'|anlasən] vt to cause; **Maßnahmen ~** to take measures; **sich veranlasst sehen** to feel prompted; **etw ~** to arrange for sth; (befehlen) to order sth

Veranlassung f cause; motive; **auf jds ~ akk (hin)** at sb's instigation

veranschaulichen [fɛr'|anʃaʊlɪçən] vt to illustrate

veranschlagen [fɛr'|anʃla:gən] vt to estimate

veranstalten [fɛr'|anʃtaltən] vt to organize, arrange

Veranstalter, in (-s, -) m(f) organizer; (Comm: von Konzerten etc) promoter

Veranstaltung f (Veranstalten) organizing; (Veranstaltetes) event; (feierlich, öffentlich) function

verantworten [fɛr'|antvortən] vt to accept responsibility for; (Folgen etc) to answer for ▷ vr to justify o.s.; **etw vor jdm ~** to answer to sb for sth

verantwortlich adj responsible

Verantwortung f responsibility; **jdn zur ~ ziehen** to call sb to account

verantwortungs- zW: **verantwortungsbewusst** adj responsible; **Verantwortungsgefühl** nt sense of responsibility; **verantwortungslos** adj irresponsible; **verantwortungsvoll** adj responsible

verarbeiten [fɛr'|arbaɪtən] vt to process; (geistig) to assimilate; (Erlebnis etc) to digest; **etw zu etw ~** to make sth into sth; **~de Industrie** processing industries pl

verarbeitet adj: **gut ~** (Kleid etc) well finished

Verarbeitung f processing; assimilation

verärgern [fɛr'|ɛrgərn] vt to annoy

verarmen [fɛr'|armən] vi (lit, fig) to become impoverished

verarschen [fɛr'|arʃən] (umg!) vt: **jdn ~** to take the mickey out of sb

verarzten [fɛr'|a:rtstən] vt to fix up (umg)

verausgaben [fɛr'|aʊsga:bən] vr to run out of money; (fig) to exhaust o.s.

veräußern [fɛr'|ɔʏsərn] vt (form: verkaufen) to dispose of

Verb [vɛrp] (-s, -en) nt verb

Verb. abk (= Verband) assoc.

Verband [fɛr'bant] (-(e)s, ⁻e) m (Med) bandage, dressing; (Bund) association, society; (Mil) unit

verband etc vb siehe **verbinden**

Verband- zW: **Verbandkasten**, **Verbandskasten** m medicine chest, first-aid box; **Verbandpäckchen**, **Verbandspäckchen**

nt gauze bandage; **Verbandstoff** m bandage, dressing material; **Verbandzeug** nt bandage, dressing material

verbannen [fɛr'banən] vt to banish

Verbannung f exile

verbarrikadieren [fɛrbarika'di:rən] vt to barricade ▷ vr to barricade o.s. in

verbauen [fɛr'baʊən] vt: **sich** dat **alle Chancen ~** to spoil one's chances

verbergen [fɛr'bɛrgən] unreg vt, vr: **(sich) ~ (vor** +dat**)** to hide (from)

verbessern [fɛr'bɛsərn] vt to improve; (berichtigen) to correct ▷ vr to improve; to correct o.s.

verbessert adj revised; improved; **eine neue, ~e Auflage** a new revised edition

Verbesserung f improvement; correction

verbeugen [fɛr'bɔʏgən] vr to bow

Verbeugung f bow

verbiegen [fɛr'bi:gən] unreg vi to bend

verbiestert [fɛr'bi:stərt] (umg) adj crotchety

verbieten [fɛr'bi:tən] unreg vt to forbid; (amtlich) to prohibit; (Zeitung, Partei) to ban; **jdm etw ~** to forbid sb to do sth

verbilligen [fɛr'bɪlɪgən] vt to reduce (the price of) ▷ vr to become cheaper, go down

verbinden [fɛr'bɪndən] unreg vt to connect; (kombinieren) to combine; (Med) to bandage ▷ vr to combine (auch CHEM), join (together); **jdm die Augen ~** to blindfold sb

verbindlich [fɛr'bɪntlɪç] adj binding; (freundlich) obliging; **~ zusagen** to accept definitely; **Verbindlichkeit** f obligation; (Höflichkeit) civility; **Verbindlichkeiten** pl (Jur) obligations pl; (Comm) liabilities pl

Verbindung f connection; (Zusammensetzung) combination; (Chem) compound; (Univ) club; (Tel: Anschluss) line; **mit jdm in ~ stehen** to be in touch od contact with sb; **~ mit jdm aufnehmen** to contact sb

Verbindungsmann (-(e)s, pl **-männer** od **-leute**) m intermediary; (Agent) contact

verbissen [fɛr'bɪsən] adj grim; (Arbeiter) dogged; **Verbissenheit** f grimness; doggedness

verbitten [fɛr'bɪtən] unreg vt: **sich** dat **etw ~** not to tolerate sth, not to stand for sth

verbittern [fɛr'bɪtərn] vt to embitter ▷ vi to get bitter

verblassen [fɛr'blasən] vi to fade

Verbleib [fɛr'blaɪp] (-(e)s) m whereabouts

verbleiben [fɛr'blaɪbən] unreg vi to remain; **wir sind so verblieben, dass wir …** we agreed to …

verbleit [fɛr'blaɪt] adj leaded

Verblendung [fɛr'blɛndʊŋ] f (fig) delusion

verblöden [fɛr'blø:dən] vi (Hilfsverb sein) to get stupid

verblüffen [fɛr'blʏfən] vt to amaze; (verwirren) to baffle

Verblüffung f stupefaction

verblühen [fɛr'bly:ən] vi to wither, fade

verbluten [fɛr'blu:tən] vi to bleed to death

357

verbohren [fɛr'boːrən] (*umg*) *vr*: **sich in etw** *akk* ~ to become obsessed with sth

verbohrt *adj* (*Haltung*) stubborn, obstinate

verborgen [fɛr'bɔrgən] *adj* hidden; **~e Mängel** latent defects *pl*

Verbot [fɛr'boːt] (**-(e)s, -e**) *nt* prohibition, ban

verboten *adj* forbidden; **Rauchen ~!** no smoking; **er sah ~ aus** (*umg*) he looked a real sight

verbotenerweise *adv* though it is forbidden

Verbotsschild *nt* prohibitory sign

verbrämen [fɛr'brɛːmən] *vt* (*fig*) to gloss over; (*Kritik*): ~ **(mit)** to veil (in)

Verbrauch [fɛr'braux] (**-(e)s**) *m* consumption

verbrauchen *vt* to use up; **der Wagen verbraucht 10 Liter Benzin auf 100 km** the car does 10 kms to the litre (*Brit*) *od* liter (*US*)

Verbraucher, in (**-s, -**) *m(f)* consumer; **Verbrauchermarkt** *m* hypermarket; **verbrauchernah** *adj* consumer-friendly; **Verbraucherschutz** *m* consumer protection; **Verbraucherverband** *m* consumer council

Verbrauchsgüter *pl* consumer goods *pl*

verbraucht *adj* used up, finished; (*Luft*) stale; (*Mensch*) worn-out

Verbrechen (**-s, -**) *nt* crime

Verbrecher, in (**-s, -**) *m(f)* criminal; **verbrecherisch** *adj* criminal; **Verbrecherkartei** *f* file of offenders, ≈ rogues' gallery; **Verbrechertum** (**-s**) *nt* criminality

verbreiten [fɛr'braɪtən] *vt* to spread; (*Licht*) to shed; (*Wärme, Ruhe*) to radiate ▷ *vr* to spread; **eine (weit) verbreitete Ansicht** a widely held opinion; **sich über etw** *akk* ~ to expound on sth

verbreitern [fɛr'braɪtərn] *vt* to broaden

Verbreitung *f* spread(ing); shedding; radiation

verbrennbar *adj* combustible

verbrennen [fɛr'brɛnən] *unreg vt* to burn; (*Leiche*) to cremate; (*versengen*) to scorch; (*Haar*) to singe; (*verbrühen*) to scald

Verbrennung *f* burning; (*in Motor*) combustion; (*von Leiche*) cremation

Verbrennungsanlage *f* incineration plant

Verbrennungsmotor *m* internal-combustion engine

verbriefen [fɛr'briːfən] *vt* to document

verbringen [fɛr'brɪŋən] *unreg vt* to spend

Verbrüderung [fɛr'bryːdərʊŋ] *f* fraternization

verbrühen [fɛr'bryːən] *vt* to scald

verbuchen [fɛr'buːxən] *vt* (*Fin*) to register; (*Erfolg*) to enjoy; (*Misserfolg*) to suffer

verbummeln [fɛr'bʊməln] (*umg*) *vt* (*verlieren*) to lose; (*Zeit*) to waste, fritter away; (*Verabredung*) to miss

verbunden [fɛr'bʊndən] *adj* connected; **jdm ~ sein** to be obliged *od* indebted to sb; **ich/er** etc **war falsch ~** (*Tel*) it was a wrong number

verbünden [fɛr'byndən] *vr* to form an alliance

Verbundenheit *f* bond, relationship

Verbündete, r *f(m)* ally

Verbundglas [fɛr'bʊntglaːs] *nt* laminated glass

verbürgen [fɛr'bʏrgən] *vr*: **sich ~ für** to vouch for; **ein verbürgtes Recht** an established right

verbüßen [fɛr'byːsən] *vt*: **eine Strafe ~** to serve a sentence

verchromt [fɛr'kroːmt] *adj* chromium-plated

Verdacht [fɛr'daxt] (**-(e)s**) *m* suspicion; ~ **schöpfen (gegen jdn)** to become suspicious (of sb); **jdn in ~ haben** to suspect sb; **es besteht ~ auf Krebs** *akk* cancer is suspected

verdächtig *adj* suspicious

verdächtigen [fɛr'dɛçtɪgən] *vt* to suspect

Verdächtigung *f* suspicion

verdammen [fɛr'damən] *vt* to damn, condemn

Verdammnis (**-**) *f* perdition, damnation

verdammt (*umg*) *adj, adv* damned; ~ **noch mal!** bloody hell (!), damn (!)

verdampfen [fɛr'dampfən] *vt, vi* (*vi Hilfsverb sein*) to vaporize; (*Koch*) to boil away

verdanken [fɛr'daŋkən] *vt*: **jdm etw ~** to owe sb sth

verdarb etc [fɛr'darp] *vb siehe* **verderben**

verdattert [fɛr'datərt] (*umg*) *adj, adv* flabbergasted

verdauen [fɛr'dauən] *vt* (*lit, fig*) to digest ▷ *vi* (*lit*) to digest

verdaulich [fɛr'daulɪç] *adj* digestible; **das ist schwer ~** that is hard to digest

Verdauung *f* digestion

Verdauungsspaziergang *m* constitutional

Verdauungsstörung *f* indigestion

Verdeck [fɛr'dɛk] (**-(e)s, -e**) *nt* (*Aut*) soft top; (*Naut*) deck

verdecken *vt* to cover (up); (*verbergen*) to hide

verdenken [fɛr'dɛŋkən] *unreg vt*: **jdm etw ~** to blame sb for sth, hold sth against sb

verderben [fɛr'dɛrbən] *unreg vt* to spoil; (*schädigen*) to ruin; (*moralisch*) to corrupt ▷ *vi* (*Essen*) to spoil, rot; (*Mensch*) to go to the bad; **es mit jdm ~** to get into sb's bad books

Verderben (**-s**) *nt* ruin

verderblich *adj* (*Einfluss*) pernicious; (*Lebensmittel*) perishable

verderbt *adj* (*veraltet*) depraved; **Verderbtheit** *f* depravity

verdeutlichen [fɛr'dɔytlɪçən] *vt* to make clear

verdichten [fɛr'dɪçtən] *vt* (*Phys, fig*) to compress ▷ *vr* to thicken; (*Verdacht, Eindruck*) to deepen

verdienen [fɛr'diːnən] *vt* to earn; (*moralisch*) to deserve ▷ *vi* (*Gewinn machen*): ~ **(an** +*dat*) to make (a profit) (on)

Verdienst [fɛr'diːnst] (**-(e)s, -e**) *m* earnings *pl* ▷ *nt* merit; (*Dank*) credit; (*Leistung*): ~ **(um)** service (to), contribution (to); **verdienstvoll** *adj* commendable

verdient [fɛr'diːnt] *adj* well-earned; (*Person*) of outstanding merit; (*Lohn, Strafe*) rightful; **sich um etw ~ machen** to do a lot for sth

verdirbst [fɛr'dɪrpst] *vb siehe* **verderben**

verdirbt [fɛr'dɪrpt] *vb siehe* **verderben**

verdonnern [fɛr'dɔnərn] (*umg*) *vt* (*zu Haft* etc): ~ **(zu)** to sentence (to); **jdn zu etw ~** to order sb

to do sth
verdoppeln [fɛrˈdɔpəln] *vt* to double
Verdoppelung, Verdopplung *f* doubling
verdorben [fɛrˈdɔrbən] *pp von* **verderben** ▷ *adj*
spoilt; *(geschädigt)* ruined; *(moralisch)* corrupt
verdorren [fɛrˈdɔrən] *vi* to wither
verdrängen [fɛrˈdrɛŋən] *vt* to oust; *(auch Phys)*
to displace; *(Psych)* to repress
Verdrängung *f* displacement; *(Psych)*
repression
verdrehen [fɛrˈdreːən] *vt (lit, fig)* to twist;
(Augen) to roll; **jdm den Kopf ~** *(fig)* to turn
sb's head
verdreht *(umg) adj* crazy; *(Bericht)* confused
verdreifachen [fɛrˈdraɪfaxən] *vt* to treble
verdrießen [fɛrˈdriːsən] *unreg vt* to annoy
verdrießlich [fɛrˈdriːslɪç] *adj* peevish, annoyed
verdross *etc* [fɛrˈdrɔs] *vb siehe* **verdrießen**
verdrossen [fɛrˈdrɔsən] *pp von* **verdrießen** ▷ *adj*
cross, sulky
verdrücken [fɛrˈdrʏkən] *(umg) vt* to put away,
eat ▷ *vr* to disappear
Verdruss [fɛrˈdrʊs] **(-es, -e)** *m* frustration; **zu
jds ~** to sb's annoyance
verduften [fɛrˈdʊftən] *vi* to evaporate; *(umg)* to
disappear
verdummen [fɛrˈdʊmən] *vt* to make stupid
▷ *vi* to grow stupid
verdunkeln [fɛrˈdʊŋkəln] *vt* to darken; *(fig)* to
obscure ▷ *vr* to darken
Verdunkelung, Verdunklung *f* blackout; *(fig)*
obscuring
verdünnen [fɛrˈdʏnən] *vt* to dilute
Verdünner (-s, -) *m* thinner
verdünnisieren [fɛrdʏniˈziːrən] *(umg) vr* to
make o.s. scarce
verdunsten [fɛrˈdʊnstən] *vi* to evaporate
verdursten [fɛrˈdʊrstən] *vi* to die of thirst
verdutzt [fɛrˈdʊtst] *adj* nonplussed *(Brit)*,
nonplused *(US)*, taken aback
verebben [fɛrˈʔɛbən] *vi* to subside
veredeln [fɛrˈʔeːdəln] *vt (Metalle, Erdöl)* to
refine; *(Fasern)* to finish; *(Bot)* to graft
verehren [fɛrˈʔeːrən] *vt* to venerate, worship
(auch REL); **jdm etw ~** to present sb with sth
Verehrer, in (-s, -) *m(f)* admirer, worshipper
(Brit), worshiper *(US)*
verehrt *adj* esteemed; **(sehr) ~e Anwesende/
verehrtes Publikum** Ladies and Gentlemen
Verehrung *f* respect; *(Rel)* worship
vereidigen [fɛrˈʔaɪdɪgən] *vt* to put on oath; **jdn
auf etw** *akk* **~** to make sb swear on sth
Vereidigung *f* swearing in
Verein [fɛrˈʔaɪn] **(-(e)s, -e)** *m* club, association;
ein wohltätiger ~ a charity
vereinbar *adj* compatible
vereinbaren [fɛrˈʔaɪnbaːrən] *vt* to agree upon
Vereinbarkeit *f* compatibility
Vereinbarung *f* agreement
vereinfachen [fɛrˈʔaɪnfaxən] *vt* to simplify
Vereinfachung *f* simplification
vereinheitlichen [fɛrˈʔaɪnhaɪtlɪçən] *vt* to
standardize

vereinigen [fɛrˈʔaɪnɪgən] *vt, vr* to unite
vereinigt *adj* united; **Vereinigte Arabische
Emirate** *pl* United Arab Emirates; **Vereinigtes
Königreich** *nt* United Kingdom; **Vereinigte
Staaten** *pl* United States
Vereinigung *f* union; *(Verein)* association
vereinnahmen [fɛrˈʔaɪnnaːmən] *vt (geh)* to
take; **jdn ~** *(fig)* to make demands on sb
vereinsamen [fɛrˈʔaɪnzaːmən] *vi* to become
lonely
vereint [fɛrˈʔaɪnt] *adj* united; **Vereinte
Nationen** *pl* United Nations
vereinzelt [fɛrˈʔaɪntsəlt] *adj* isolated
vereisen [fɛrˈʔaɪzən] *vi* to freeze, ice over ▷ *vt*
(Med) to freeze
vereiteln [fɛrˈʔaɪtəln] *vt* to frustrate
vereitern [fɛrˈʔaɪtərn] *vi* to suppurate, fester
Verelendung [fɛrˈʔeːlɛndʊŋ] *f*
impoverishment
verenden [fɛrˈʔɛndən] *vi* to perish, die
verengen [fɛrˈʔɛŋən] *vr* to narrow
vererben [fɛrˈʔɛrbən] *vt* to bequeath; *(Biol)* to
transmit ▷ *vr* to be hereditary
vererblich [fɛrˈʔɛrplɪç] *adj* hereditary
Vererbung *f* bequeathing; *(Biol)* transmission;
das ist ~ *(umg)* it's hereditary
verewigen [fɛrˈʔeːvɪgən] *vt* to immortalize ▷ *vr*
(umg) to leave one's name
Verf. *abk* = **Verfasser**
verfahren [fɛrˈfaːrən] *unreg vi* to act ▷ *vr* to get
lost ▷ *adj* tangled; **~ mit** to deal with
Verfahren (-s, -) *nt* procedure; *(Tech)* process;
(Jur) proceedings *pl*
Verfahrenstechnik *f (Methode)* process
Verfahrensweise *f* procedure
Verfall [fɛrˈfal] **(-(e)s)** *m* decline; *(von Haus)*
dilapidation; *(Fin)* expiry
verfallen *unreg vi* to decline; *(Haus)* to be falling
down; *(Fin)* to lapse ▷ *adj (Gebäude)* dilapidated,
ruined; *(Karten, Briefmarken)* invalid; *(Strafe)*
lapsed; *(Pass)* expired; **~ in** *+akk* to lapse into; **~
auf** *+akk* to hit upon; **einem Laster ~ sein** to
be addicted to a vice; **jdm völlig ~ sein** to be
completely under sb's spell
Verfallsdatum *nt* expiry date; *(der Haltbarkeit)*
best-before date
verfänglich [fɛrˈfɛŋlɪç] *adj* awkward, tricky;
(Aussage, Beweismaterial etc) incriminating;
(gefährlich) dangerous
verfärben [fɛrˈfɛrbən] *vr* to change colour *(Brit)*
od color *(US)*
verfassen [fɛrˈfasən] *vt* to write; *(Gesetz,
Urkunde)* to draw up
Verfasser, in (-s, -) *m(f)* author, writer
Verfassung *f* constitution *(auch POL)*;
(körperlich) state of health; *(seelisch)* state of
mind; **sie ist in guter/schlechter ~** she is in
good/bad shape
Verfassungs- *zW:* **verfassungsfeindlich** *adj*
anticonstitutional; **Verfassungsgericht** *nt*
constitutional court; **verfassungsmäßig**
adj constitutional; **Verfassungsschutz** *m*
(Aufgabe) defence of the constitution; *(Amt)*

V

office responsible for defending the constitution; **Verfassungsschützer, in** *m(f)* defender of the constitution; **verfassungswidrig** *adj* unconstitutional

verfaulen [fɛrˈfaʊlən] *vi* to rot

verfechten [fɛrˈfɛçtən] *unreg vt* to defend; (*Lehre*) to advocate

Verfechter, in [fɛrˈfɛçtər(ɪn)] (**-s, -**) *m(f)* champion; defender

verfehlen [fɛrˈfeːlən] *vt* to miss; **das Thema ~** to be completely off the subject

verfehlt *adj* unsuccessful; (*unangebracht*) inappropriate; **etw für ~ halten** to regard sth as mistaken

Verfehlung *f* (*Vergehen*) misdemeanour (*Brit*), misdemeanor (*US*); (*Sünde*) transgression

verfeinern [fɛrˈfaɪnərn] *vt* to refine

Verfettung [fɛrˈfɛtʊŋ] *f* (*von Organ, Muskeln*) fatty degeneration

verfeuern [fɛrˈfɔʏərn] *vt* to burn; (*Munition*) to fire; (*umg*) to use up

verfilmen [fɛrˈfɪlmən] *vt* to film, make a film of

Verfilmung *f* film (version)

Verfilzung [fɛrˈfɪltsʊŋ] *f* (*fig: von Firmen, Parteien*) entanglements *pl*

verflachen [fɛrˈflaxən] *vi* to flatten out; (*fig: Diskussion*) to become superficial

verfliegen [fɛrˈfliːgən] *unreg vi* to evaporate; (*Zeit*) to pass, fly ▷ *vr* to stray (*past*)

verflixt [fɛrˈflɪkst] (*umg*) *adj, adv* darned

verflossen [fɛrˈflɔsən] *adj* past, former

verfluchen [fɛrˈfluːxən] *vt* to curse

verflüchtigen [fɛrˈflʏçtɪgən] *vr* to evaporate; (*Geruch*) to fade

verflüssigen [fɛrˈflʏsɪgən] *vr* to become liquid

verfolgen [fɛrˈfɔlgən] *vt* to pursue; (*gerichtlich*) to prosecute; (*grausam, bes Pol*) to persecute

Verfolger, in (**-s, -**) *m(f)* pursuer

Verfolgte, r *f(m)* (*politisch*) victim of persecution

Verfolgung *f* pursuit; persecution; **strafrechtliche ~** prosecution

Verfolgungswahn *m* persecution mania

verfrachten [fɛrˈfraxtən] *vt* to ship

verfremden [fɛrˈfrɛmdən] *vt* to alienate, distance

verfressen [fɛrˈfrɛsən] (*umg*) *adj* greedy

verfrüht [fɛrˈfryːt] *adj* premature

verfügbar *adj* available

verfügen [fɛrˈfyːgən] *vt* to direct, order ▷ *vr* to proceed ▷ *vi*: **~ über** +*akk* to have at one's disposal; **über etw** *akk* **frei ~ können** to be able to do as one wants with sth

Verfügung *f* direction, order; (*Jur*) writ; **zur ~** at one's disposal; **jdm zur ~ stehen** to be available to sb

Verfügungsgewalt *f* (*Jur*) right of disposal

verführen [fɛrˈfyːrən] *vt* to tempt; (*sexuell*) to seduce; (*die Jugend, das Volk etc*) to lead astray

Verführer *m* tempter; seducer

Verführerin *f* temptress; seductress

verführerisch *adj* seductive

Verführung *f* seduction; (*Versuchung*) temptation

Vergabe [fɛrˈgaːbə] *f* (*von Arbeiten*) allocation; (*von Stipendium, Auftrag etc*) award

vergällen [fɛrˈgɛlən] *vt* (*geh*): **jdm die Freude/ das Leben ~** to spoil sb's fun/sour sb's life

vergaloppieren [fɛrgalɔˈpiːrən] (*umg*) *vr* (*sich irren*) to be on the wrong track

vergammeln [fɛrˈgaməln] (*umg*) *vi* to go to seed; (*Nahrung*) to go off; (*Zeit*) to waste

vergangen [fɛrˈgaŋən] *adj* past; **Vergangenheit** *f* past; **Vergangenheitsbewältigung** *f* coming to terms with the past

vergänglich [fɛrˈgɛŋlɪç] *adj* transitory; **Vergänglichkeit** *f* transitoriness, impermanence

vergasen [fɛrˈgaːzən] *vt* to gasify; (*töten*) to gas

Vergaser (**-s, -**) *m* (*Aut*) carburettor (*Brit*), carburetor (*US*)

vergaß *etc* [fɛrˈgaːs] *vb siehe* **vergessen**

vergeben [fɛrˈgeːbən] *unreg vt* to forgive; (*weggeben*) to give away; (*fig: Chance*) to throw away; (*Auftrag, Preis*) to award; (*Studienplätze, Stellen*) to allocate; **jdm (etw) ~** to forgive sb (sth); **~ an** +*akk* to award to; to allocate to; **~ sein** to be occupied; (*umg: Mädchen*) to be spoken for

vergebens *adv* in vain

vergeblich [fɛrˈgeːplɪç] *adv* in vain ▷ *adj* vain, futile

Vergebung *f* forgiveness

vergegenwärtigen [fɛrgeːgənˈvɛrtɪgən] *vr*: **sich** *dat* **etw ~** to visualize sth; (*erinnern*) to recall sth

vergehen [fɛrˈgeːən] *unreg vi* to pass by od away ▷ *vr* to commit an offence (*Brit*) od offense (*US*); **vor Angst ~** to be scared to death; **jdm vergeht etw** sb loses sth; **sich an jdm ~** to (sexually) assault sb; **Vergehen** (**-s, -**) *nt* offence (*Brit*), offense (*US*)

vergeigen [fɛrˈgaɪgən] (*umg*) *vt* to cock up

vergeistigt [fɛrˈgaɪstɪçt] *adj* spiritual

vergelten [fɛrˈgɛltən] *unreg vt*: **jdm etw ~** to pay sb back for sth, repay sb for sth

Vergeltung *f* retaliation, reprisal

Vergeltungsmaßnahme *f* retaliatory measure

Vergeltungsschlag *m* (*Mil*) reprisal

vergesellschaften [fɛrgəˈzɛlʃaftən] *vt* (*Pol*) to nationalize

vergessen [fɛrˈgɛsən] *unreg vt* to forget; **Vergessenheit** *f* oblivion; **in Vergessenheit geraten** to fall into oblivion

vergesslich [fɛrˈgɛslɪç] *adj* forgetful; **Vergesslichkeit** *f* forgetfulness

vergeuden [fɛrˈgɔʏdən] *vt* to squander, waste

vergewaltigen [fɛrgəˈvaltɪgən] *vt* to rape; (*fig*) to violate

Vergewaltigung *f* rape

vergewissern [fɛrgəˈvɪsərn] *vr* to make sure; **sich einer Sache** *gen od* **über etw** *akk* **~** to make sure of sth

vergießen [fɛrˈgiːsən] *unreg vt* to shed
vergiften [fɛrˈgɪftən] *vt* to poison
Vergiftung *f* poisoning
vergilbt [fɛrˈgɪlpt] *adj* yellowed
Vergissmeinnicht [fɛrˈgɪsmaɪnnɪçt] (**-(e)s, -e**) *nt* forget-me-not
vergisst [fɛrˈgɪst] *vb siehe* **vergessen**
vergittert [fɛrˈgɪtərt] *adj*: **~e Fenster** barred windows
verglasen [fɛrˈglaːzən] *vt* to glaze
Vergleich [fɛrˈglaɪç] (**-(e)s, -e**) *m* comparison; (*Jur*) settlement; **einen ~ schließen** (*Jur*) to reach a settlement; **in keinem ~ zu etw stehen** to be out of all proportion to sth; **im ~ mit** *od* **zu** compared with *od* to; **vergleichbar** *adj* comparable
vergleichen *unreg vt* to compare ▷ *vr* (*Jur*) to reach a settlement
vergleichsweise *adv* comparatively
verglühen [fɛrˈglyːən] *vi* (*Feuer*) to die away; (*Draht*) to burn out; (*Raumkapsel, Meteor etc*) to burn up
vergnügen [fɛrˈgnyːgən] *vr* to enjoy *od* amuse o.s.; **Vergnügen** (**-s, -**) *nt* pleasure; **das war ein teures Vergnügen** (*umg*) that was an expensive bit of fun; **viel Vergnügen!** enjoy yourself!
vergnüglich *adj* enjoyable
vergnügt [fɛrˈgnyːkt] *adj* cheerful
Vergnügung *f* pleasure, amusement
Vergnügungs- *zW*: **Vergnügungspark** *m* amusement park; **vergnügungssüchtig** *adj* pleasure-loving; **Vergnügungsviertel** *nt* entertainments district
vergolden [fɛrˈgɔldən] *vt* to gild
vergönnen [fɛrˈgœnən] *vt* to grant
vergöttern [fɛrˈgœtərn] *vt* to idolize
vergraben [fɛrˈgraːbən] *unreg vt* to bury
vergrämt [fɛrˈgrɛːmt] *adj* (*Gesicht*) troubled
vergreifen [fɛrˈgraɪfən] *unreg vr*: **sich an jdm ~** to lay hands on sb; **sich an etw** *dat* **~** to misappropriate sth; **sich im Ton ~** to say the wrong thing
vergriffen [fɛrˈgrɪfən] *adj* (*Buch*) out of print; (*Ware*) out of stock
vergrößern [fɛrˈgrøːsərn] *vt* to enlarge; (*mengenmäßig*) to increase; (*Lupe*) to magnify
Vergrößerung *f* enlargement; increase; magnification
Vergrößerungsglas *nt* magnifying glass
vergünstigt *adj* (*Lage*) improved; (*Preis*) reduced
Vergünstigung [fɛrˈgʏnstɪgʊŋ] *f* concession; (*Vorteil*) privilege
vergüten [fɛrˈgyːtən] *vt*: **jdm etw ~** to compensate sb for sth; (*Arbeit, Leistung*) to pay sb for sth
Vergütung *f* compensation; payment
verh. *abk* = **verheiratet**
verhaften [fɛrˈhaftən] *vt* to arrest
Verhaftete, r *f(m)* prisoner
Verhaftung *f* arrest
verhallen [fɛrˈhalən] *vi* to die away
verhalten [fɛrˈhaltən] *unreg vr* (*Sache*) to be,

stand; (*sich benehmen*) to behave; (*Math*) to be in proportion to ▷ *vr unpers*: **wie verhält es sich damit?** (*wie ist die Lage?*) how do things stand?; (*wie wird das gehandhabt?*) how do you go about it? ▷ *adj* restrained; **sich ruhig ~** to keep quiet; (*sich nicht bewegen*) to keep still; **wenn sich das so verhält ...** if that is the case ...;
Verhalten (**-s**) *nt* behaviour (*Brit*), behavior (*US*)
Verhaltens- *zW*: **Verhaltensforschung** *f* behavioural (*Brit*) *od* behavioral (*US*) science; **verhaltensgestört** *adj* disturbed; **Verhaltensmaßregel** *f* rule of conduct
Verhältnis [fɛrˈhɛltnɪs] (**-ses, -se**) *nt* relationship; (*Liebesverhältnis*) affair; (*Math*) proportion, ratio; (*Einstellung*): **~ (zu)** attitude (to); **Verhältnisse** *pl* (*Umstände*) conditions *pl*; **aus was für ~sen kommt er?** what sort of background does he come from?; **für klare ~se sorgen, klare ~se schaffen** to get things straight; **über seine ~se leben** to live beyond one's means; **verhältnismäßig** *adj* relative, comparative ▷ *adv* relatively, comparatively; **Verhältniswahl** *f* proportional representation; **Verhältniswahlrecht** *nt* (system of) proportional representation
verhandeln [fɛrˈhandəln] *vi* to negotiate; (*Jur*) to hold proceedings ▷ *vt* to discuss; (*Jur*) to hear; **über etw** *akk* **~** to negotiate sth *od* about sth
Verhandlung *f* negotiation; (*Jur*) proceedings *pl*; **~en führen** to negotiate
Verhandlungspaket *nt* (*Comm*) package deal
Verhandlungstisch *m* negotiating table
verhangen [fɛrˈhaŋən] *adj* overcast
verhängen [fɛrˈhɛŋən] *vt* (*fig*) to impose, inflict
Verhängnis [fɛrˈhɛŋnɪs] (**-ses, -se**) *nt* fate; **jdm zum ~ werden** to be sb's undoing; **verhängnisvoll** *adj* fatal, disastrous
verharmlosen [fɛrˈharmloːzən] *vt* to make light of, play down
verharren [fɛrˈharən] *vi* to remain; (*hartnäckig*) to persist
verhärten [fɛrˈhɛrtən] *vr* to harden
verhaspeln [fɛrˈhaspəln] (*umg*) *vr* to get into a muddle *od* tangle
verhasst [fɛrˈhast] *adj* odious, hateful
verhätscheln [fɛrˈhɛːtʃəln] *vt* to spoil, pamper
Verhau [fɛrˈhaʊ] (**-(e)s, -e**) *m* (*zur Absperrung*) barrier; (*Käfig*) coop
verhauen *unreg* (*umg*) *vt* (*verprügeln*) to beat up; (*Prüfung etc*) to muff
verheben [fɛrˈheːbən] *unreg vr* to hurt o.s. lifting sth
verheerend [fɛrˈheːrənt] *adj* disastrous, devastating
verhehlen [fɛrˈheːlən] *vt* to conceal
verheilen [fɛrˈhaɪlən] *vi* to heal
verheimlichen [fɛrˈhaɪmlɪçən] *vt*: **(jdm) etw ~** to keep sth secret (from sb)
verheiratet [fɛrˈhaɪraːtət] *adj* married
verheißen [fɛrˈhaɪsən] *unreg vt*: **jdm etw ~** to

V

361

promise sb sth

verheißungsvoll adj promising

verheizen [fɛrˈhaɪtsən] vt to burn, use as fuel

verhelfen [fɛrˈhɛlfən] unreg vi: **jdm zu etw ~** to help sb to get sth

verherrlichen [fɛrˈhɛrlɪçən] vt to glorify

verheult [fɛrˈhɔylt] adj (Augen, Gesicht) puffy (from crying)

verhexen [fɛrˈhɛksən] vt to bewitch; **es ist wie verhext** it's jinxed

verhindern [fɛrˈhɪndərn] vt to prevent; **verhindert sein** to be unable to make it; **das lässt sich leider nicht ~** it can't be helped, unfortunately; **ein verhinderter Politiker** (umg) a would-be politician

Verhinderung f prevention

verhöhnen [fɛrˈhøːnən] vt to mock, sneer at

verhohnepipeln [fɛrˈhoːnəpiːpəln] (umg) vt to send up (Brit), ridicule

verhökern [fɛrˈhøːkərn] (umg) vt to turn into cash

Verhör [fɛrˈhøːr] (-(e)s, -e) nt interrogation; (gerichtlich) (cross-)examination

verhören vt to interrogate; to (cross-)examine ▷ vr to mishear

verhüllen [fɛrˈhʏlən] vt to veil; (Haupt, Körperteil) to cover

verhungern [fɛrˈhʊŋərn] vi to starve, die of hunger

verhunzen [fɛrˈhʊntsən] (umg) vt to ruin

verhüten [fɛrˈhyːtən] vt to prevent, avert

Verhütung f prevention

Verhütungsmittel nt contraceptive

verifizieren [verifiˈtsiːrən] vt to verify

verinnerlichen [fɛrˈɪnərlɪçən] vt to internalize

verirren [fɛrˈɪrən] vr to get lost, lose one's way; (fig) to go astray; (Tier, Kugel) to stray

verjagen [fɛrˈjaːgən] vt to drive away od out

verjähren [fɛrˈjɛːrən] vi to come under the statute of limitations; (Anspruch) to lapse

Verjährungsfrist f limitation period

verjubeln [fɛrˈjuːbəln] (umg) vt (Geld) to blow

verjüngen [fɛrˈjʏŋən] vt to rejuvenate ▷ vr to taper

verkabeln [fɛrˈkaːbəln] vt (TV) to link up to the cable network

Verkabelung f (TV) linking up to the cable network

verkalken [fɛrˈkalkən] vi to calcify; (umg) to become senile

verkalkulieren [fɛrkalkuˈliːrən] vr to miscalculate

verkannt [fɛrˈkant] adj unappreciated

verkatert [fɛrˈkaːtərt] (umg) adj hung over

Verkauf [fɛrˈkaʊf] m sale; **zum ~ stehen** to be up for sale

verkaufen vt, vi to sell; **„zu ~"** "for sale"

Verkäufer, in [fɛrˈkɔyfər(ɪn)] (-s, -) m(f) seller; (im Außendienst) salesman, saleswoman; (in Laden) shop assistant (Brit), sales clerk (US)

verkäuflich [fɛrˈkɔyflɪç] adj saleable

Verkaufs- zW: **Verkaufsabteilung** f sales department; **Verkaufsautomat** m slot

machine; **Verkaufsbedingungen** pl (Comm) terms and conditions of sale; **Verkaufskampagne** f sales drive; **Verkaufsleiter** m sales manager; **verkaufsoffen** adj: **verkaufsoffener Samstag** Saturday on which the shops are open all day; **Verkaufsschlager** m big seller; **Verkaufsstelle** f outlet; **Verkauftüchtigkeit** f salesmanship

Verkehr [fɛrˈkeːr] (-s, -e) m traffic; (Umgang, bes sexuell) intercourse; (Umlauf) circulation; **aus dem ~ ziehen** to withdraw from service; **für den ~ freigeben** (Straße etc) to open to traffic; (Transportmittel) to bring into service

verkehren vi (Fahrzeug) to ply, run ▷ vt, vr to turn, transform; **~ mit** to associate with; **mit jdm brieflich** od **schriftlich ~** (form) to correspond with sb; **bei jdm ~** to visit sb regularly

Verkehrs- zW: **Verkehrsampel** f traffic lights pl; **Verkehrsamt** nt tourist (information) office; **Verkehrsaufkommen** nt volume of traffic; **verkehrsberuhigt** adj traffic-calmed; **Verkehrsberuhigung** f traffic-calming; **Verkehrsbetriebe** pl transport services pl; **Verkehrsdelikt** nt traffic offence (Brit) od violation (US); **Verkehrserziehung** f road safety training; **verkehrsgünstig** adj convenient; **Verkehrsinsel** f traffic island; **Verkehrsknotenpunkt** m traffic junction; **Verkehrsmittel** nt: **öffentliche/private Verkehrsmittel** public/private transport sing; **Verkehrsschild** nt road sign; **verkehrssicher** adj (Fahrzeug) roadworthy; **Verkehrssicherheit** f road safety; **Verkehrsstockung** f traffic jam, stoppage; **Verkehrssünder** (umg) m traffic offender; **Verkehrsteilnehmer** m road user; **verkehrstüchtig** adj (Fahrzeug) roadworthy; (Mensch) fit to drive; **Verkehrsunfall** m traffic accident; **Verkehrsverein** m tourist information office; **verkehrswidrig** adj contrary to traffic regulations; **Verkehrszeichen** nt road sign

verkehrt adj wrong; (umgekehrt) the wrong way round

verkennen [fɛrˈkɛnən] unreg vt to misjudge; (unterschätzen) to underestimate

Verkettung [fɛrˈkɛtʊŋ] f: **eine ~ unglücklicher Umstände** an unfortunate chain of events

verklagen [fɛrˈklaːgən] vt to take to court

verklappen [fɛrˈklapən] vt to dump (at sea)

verklären [fɛrˈklɛːrən] vt to transfigure; **verklärt lächeln** to smile radiantly

verklausulieren [fɛrklaʊzuˈliːrən] vt (Vertrag) to hedge in with (restrictive) clauses

verkleben [fɛrˈkleːbən] vt to glue up, stick ▷ vi to stick together

verkleiden [fɛrˈklaɪdən] vt to disguise; (kostümieren) to dress up; (Schacht, Tunnel) to line; (vertäfeln) to panel; (Heizkörper) to cover in ▷ vr to disguise o.s.; to dress up

Verkleidung f disguise; (Archit) panelling (Brit), paneling (US)

verkleinern [fɛr'klaɪnərn] vt to make smaller, reduce in size

verklemmt [fɛr'klɛmt] adj (fig) inhibited

verklickern [fɛr'klɪkərn] (umg) vt: **jdm etw ~** to make sth clear to sb

verklingen [fɛr'klɪŋən] unreg vi to die away

verknacksen [fɛr'knaksən] (umg) vt: **sich dat den Fuß ~** to twist one's ankle

verknallen [fɛr'knalən] (umg) vr: **sich in jdn ~** to fall for sb

verkneifen [fɛr'knaɪfən] (umg) vt: **sich dat etw ~** to stop o.s. from doing sth; **ich konnte mir das Lachen nicht ~** I couldn't help laughing

verknöchert [fɛr'knœçərt] adj (fig) fossilized

verknüpfen [fɛr'knʏpfən] vt to tie (up), knot; (fig) to connect

Verknüpfung f connection

verkochen [fɛr'kɔxən] vt, vi (Flüssigkeit) to boil away

verkohlen [fɛr'ko:lən] vi to carbonize ▷ vt to carbonize; (umg): **jdn ~** to have sb on

verkommen [fɛr'kɔmən] unreg vi to deteriorate, decay; (Mensch) to go downhill, come down in the world ▷ adj (moralisch) dissolute, depraved; **Verkommenheit** f depravity

verkorksen [fɛr'kɔrksən] (umg) vt to ruin, mess up

verkörpern [fɛr'kœrpərn] vt to embody, personify

verköstigen [fɛr'kœstɪgən] vt to feed

verkrachen [fɛr'kraxən] (umg) vr: **sich (mit jdm) ~** to fall out (with sb)

verkracht (umg) adj (Leben) ruined

verkraften [fɛr'kraftən] vt to cope with

verkrampfen [fɛr'krampfən] vr (Muskeln) to go tense

verkrampft [fɛr'krampft] adj (fig) tense

verkriechen [fɛr'kri:çən] unreg vr to creep away, creep into a corner

verkrümeln [fɛr'kry:məln] (umg) vr to disappear

verkrümmt [fɛr'krʏmt] adj crooked

Verkrümmung f bend, warp; (Anat) curvature

verkrüppelt [fɛr'krʏpəlt] adj crippled

verkrustet [fɛr'krʊstət] adj encrusted

verkühlen [fɛr'ky:lən] vr to get a chill

verkümmern [fɛr'kʏmərn] vi to waste away; **emotionell/geistig ~** to become emotionally/intellectually stunted

verkünden [fɛr'kʏndən] vt to proclaim; (Urteil) to pronounce

verkündigen [fɛr'kʏndɪgən] vt to proclaim; (ironisch) to announce; (Evangelium) to preach

verkuppeln [fɛr'kʊpəln] vt: **jdn an jdn ~** (Zuhälter) to procure sb for sb

verkürzen [fɛr'kʏrtsən] vt to shorten; (Wort) to abbreviate; **sich dat die Zeit ~** to while away the time; **verkürzte Arbeitszeit** shorter working hours pl

Verkürzung f shortening; abbreviation

Verl. abk (= Verlag) publ.

verladen [fɛr'la:dən] unreg vt to load

Verlag [fɛr'la:k] (-(e)s, -e) m publishing firm

verlagern [fɛr'la:gərn] vt, vr (lit, fig) to shift

Verlagsanstalt f publishing firm

Verlagswesen nt publishing

verlangen [fɛr'laŋən] vt to demand; (wollen) to want ▷ vi: **~ nach** to ask for; **Sie werden am Telefon verlangt** you are wanted on the phone; **~ Sie Herrn X** ask for Mr X; **Verlangen** (-s, -) nt: **Verlangen (nach)** desire (for); **auf jds Verlangen** akk **(hin)** at sb's request

verlängern [fɛr'lɛŋərn] vt to extend; (länger machen) to lengthen; (zeitlich) to prolong; (Pass, Abonnement etc) to renew; **ein verlängertes Wochenende** a long weekend

Verlängerung f extension; (Sport) extra time

Verlängerungsschnur f extension cable

verlangsamen [fɛr'laŋza:mən] vt, vr to decelerate, slow down

Verlass [fɛr'las] m: **auf ihn/das ist kein ~** he/it cannot be relied upon

verlassen [fɛr'lasən] unreg vt to leave ▷ vr: **sich ~ auf** +akk to depend on ▷ adj desolate; (Mensch) abandoned; **einsam und ~** so all alone; **Verlassenheit** f loneliness (Brit), lonesomeness (US)

verlässlich [fɛr'leslɪç] adj reliable

Verlauf [fɛr'laʊf] m course; **einen guten/schlechten ~ nehmen** to go well/badly

verlaufen unreg vi (zeitlich) to pass; (Farben) to run ▷ vr to get lost; (Menschenmenge) to disperse

Verlautbarung f announcement

verlauten [fɛr'laʊtən] vi: **etw ~ lassen** to disclose sth; **wie verlautet** as reported

verleben [fɛr'le:bən] vt to spend

verlebt [fɛr'le:pt] adj dissipated, worn-out

verlegen [fɛr'le:gən] vt to move; (verlieren) to mislay; (Kabel, Fliesen etc) to lay; (Buch) to publish; (verschieben): **~ (auf** +akk**)** to postpone (until) ▷ vr: **sich auf etw** akk **~** to resort to sth ▷ adj embarrassed; **nicht ~ um** never at a loss for; **Verlegenheit** f embarrassment; (Situation) difficulty, scrape

Verleger [fɛr'le:gər] (-s, -) m publisher

verleiden [fɛr'laɪdən] vt: **jdm etw ~** to put sb off sth

Verleih [fɛr'laɪ] (-(e)s, -e) m hire service; (das Verleihen) renting (out), hiring (out) (Brit); (Filmverleih) distribution

verleihen unreg vt: **etw (an jdn) ~** to lend sth (to sb), lend (sb) sth; (gegen Gebühr) to rent (sth to sb), hire sth (out) (to sb) (Brit); (Kraft, Anschein) to confer sth (on sb), bestow sth (on sb); (Preis, Medaille) to award sth (to sb), award (sb) sth

Verleiher (-s, -) m hire (Brit) od rental firm; (von Filmen) distributor; (von Büchern) lender

Verleihung f lending; (von Kraft etc) bestowal; (von Preis) award

verleiten [fɛr'laɪtən] vt to lead astray; **~ zu** to talk into, tempt into

verlernen [fɛr'lernən] vt to forget, unlearn

verlesen [fɛr'le:zən] unreg vt to read out; (aussondern) to sort out ▷ vr to make a mistake in reading

V

363

verletzbar *adj* vulnerable
verletzen [fɛr'lɛtsən] *vt* (*lit, fig*) to injure, hurt; (*Gesetz etc*) to violate
verletzend *adj* (*fig: Worte*) hurtful
verletzlich *adj* vulnerable
Verletzte, r *f(m)* injured person
Verletzung *f* injury; (*Verstoß*) violation, infringement
verleugnen [fɛr'lɔygnən] *vt* to deny; (*Menschen*) to disown; **er lässt sich immer (vor ihr) ~** he always pretends not to be there (when she calls)
Verleugnung *f* denial
verleumden [fɛr'lɔymdən] *vt* to slander; (*schriftlich*) to libel
verleumderisch *adj* slanderous; libellous (*Brit*), libelous (*US*)
Verleumdung *f* slander; libel
verlieben *vr*: **sich ~ (in** +*akk*) to fall in love (with)
verliebt [fɛr'li:pt] *adj* in love; **Verliebtheit** *f* being in love
verlieren [fɛr'li:rən] *unreg vt, vi* to lose ▷ *vr* to get lost; (*verschwinden*) to disappear; **das/er hat hier nichts verloren** (*umg*) that/he has no business to be here
Verlierer, in (**-s, -**) *m(f)* loser
Verlies [fɛr'li:s] (**-es, -e**) *nt* dungeon
verloben [fɛr'lo:bən] *vr*: **sich ~ (mit)** to get engaged (to); **verlobt sein** to be engaged
Verlobte, r [fɛr'lo:ptə(r)] *f(m)*: **mein ~r** my fiancé; **meine ~** my fiancée
Verlobung *f* engagement
verlocken [fɛr'lɔkən] *vt* to entice, lure
verlockend *adj* (*Angebot, Idee*) tempting
Verlockung *f* temptation, attraction
verlogen [fɛr'lo:gən] *adj* untruthful; (*Komplimente, Versprechungen*) false; (*Moral, Gesellschaft*) hypocritical; **Verlogenheit** *f* untruthfulness
verlor *etc* [fɛr'lo:r] *vb siehe* **verlieren**
verloren *pp von* **verlieren** ▷ *adj* lost; (*Eier*) poached; **der ~e Sohn** the prodigal son; **auf ~em Posten kämpfen** *od* **stehen** to be fighting a losing battle; **etw ~ geben** to give sth up for lost; **~ gehen** to get lost; **an ihm ist ein Sänger ~ gegangen** he would have made a (good) singer
verlöschen [fɛr'lœʃən] *vi* (*Hilfsverb sein*) to go out; (*Inschrift, Farbe, Erinnerung*) to fade
verlosen [fɛr'lo:zən] *vt* to raffle (off), draw lots for
Verlosung *f* raffle, lottery
verlottern [fɛr'lɔtərn] (*umg*) *vi* to go to the dogs
verludern [fɛr'lu:dərn] (*umg*) *vi* to go to the dogs
Verlust [fɛr'lʊst] (**-(e)s, -e**) *m* loss; (*Mil*) casualty; **mit ~ verkaufen** to sell at a loss; **Verlustanzeige** *f* "lost" notice; **Verlustgeschäft** *nt*: **das war ein Verlustgeschäft** I/he *etc* made a loss; **Verlustzeit** *f* (*Industrie*) waiting time
vermachen [fɛr'maxən] *vt* to bequeath, leave

Vermächtnis [fɛr'mɛçtnɪs] (**-ses, -se**) *nt* legacy
vermählen [fɛr'mɛ:lən] *vr* to marry
Vermählung *f* wedding, marriage
vermarkten [fɛr'marktən] *vt* to market; (*fig: Persönlichkeit*) to promote
Vermarktung [fɛr'marktʊŋ] *f* marketing
vermasseln [fɛr'masəln] (*umg*) *vt* to mess up
vermehren [fɛr'me:rən] *vt, vr* to multiply; (*Menge*) to increase
Vermehrung *f* multiplying; increase
vermeiden [fɛr'maidən] *unreg vt* to avoid
vermeidlich *adj* avoidable
vermeintlich [fɛr'maintlɪç] *adj* supposed
vermengen [fɛr'mɛŋən] *vt* to mix; (*fig*) to mix up, confuse
Vermenschlichung [fɛr'mɛnʃlɪçʊŋ] *f* humanization
Vermerk [fɛr'mɛrk] (**-(e)s, -e**) *m* note; (*in Ausweis*) endorsement
vermerken *vt* to note
vermessen [fɛr'mɛsən] *unreg vt* to survey ▷ *vr* (*falsch messen*) to measure incorrectly ▷ *adj* presumptuous, bold; **Vermessenheit** *f* presumptuousness
Vermessung *f* survey(ing)
Vermessungsamt *nt* land survey(ing) office
Vermessungsingenieur *m* land surveyor
vermiesen [fɛr'mi:zən] (*umg*) *vt* to spoil
vermieten [fɛr'mi:tən] *vt* to let (*Brit*), rent (out); (*Auto*) to hire out, rent
Vermieter, in (**-s, -**) *m(f)* landlord, landlady
Vermietung *f* letting, renting (out); (*von Autos*) hiring (out), rental
vermindern [fɛr'mindərn] *vt, vr* to lessen, decrease
Verminderung *f* reduction
verminen [fɛr'mi:nən] *vt* to mine
vermischen [fɛr'mɪʃən] *vt, vr* to mix; (*Teesorten etc*) to blend; **vermischte Schriften** miscellaneous writings
vermissen [fɛr'mɪsən] *vt* to miss; **vermisst sein, als vermisst gemeldet sein** to be reported missing; **wir haben dich bei der Party vermisst** we didn't see you at the party
Vermisste, r *f(m)* missing person
Vermisstenanzeige *f* missing persons report
vermitteln [fɛr'mitəln] *vi* to mediate ▷ *vt* to arrange; (*Gespräch*) to connect; (*Stelle*) to find; (*Gefühl, Bild, Idee etc*) to convey; (*Wissen*) to impart; **~de Worte** conciliatory words; **jdm etw ~** to help sb to obtain sth; (*Stelle*) to find sth for sb
Vermittler, in [fɛr'mitlər(ɪn)] (**-s, -**) *m(f)* (*Comm*) agent; (*Schlichter*) mediator
Vermittlung *f* procurement; (*Stellenvermittlung*) agency; (*Tel*) exchange; (*Schlichtung*) mediation
Vermittlungsgebühr *f* commission
vermögen [fɛr'mø:gən] *unreg vt* to be capable of; **~ zu** to be able to; **Vermögen** (**-s, -**) *nt* wealth; (*Fähigkeit*) ability; **mein ganzes Vermögen besteht aus ...** my entire assets consist of ...; **ein Vermögen kosten** to cost a fortune

vermögend adj wealthy

Vermögens- zW: **Vermögenssteuer** f property tax; wealth tax; **Vermögenswert** m asset; **vermögenswirksam** adj: **sein Geld vermögenswirksam anlegen** to invest one's money profitably; **vermögenswirksame Leistungen** employers' contributions to tax-deductible savings scheme

vermummen [fɛr'mʊmən] vr to wrap up (warm); (sich verkleiden) to disguise

Vermummungsverbot (-(e)s) nt law against disguising o.s. at demonstrations

vermurksen [fɛr'mʊrksən] (umg) vt to make a mess of

vermuten [fɛr'muːtən] vt to suppose; (argwöhnen) to suspect

vermutlich adj supposed, presumed ▷ adv probably

Vermutung f supposition; suspicion; **die ~ liegt nahe, dass ...** there are grounds for assuming that ...

vernachlässigen [fɛr'naːxlɛsɪɡən] vt to neglect ▷ vr to neglect o.s. od one's appearance

Vernachlässigung f neglect

vernarben [fɛr'narbən] vi to heal up

vernarren [fɛr'narən] (umg) vr: **in jdn/etw vernarrt sein** to be crazy about sb/sth

vernaschen [fɛr'naʃən] vt (Geld) to spend on sweets; (umg: Mädchen, Mann) to make it with

vernehmen [fɛr'neːmən] unreg vt to hear, perceive; (erfahren) to learn; (Jur) to (cross-)examine; (Polizei) to question; **Vernehmen** nt: **dem Vernehmen nach** from what I/we etc hear

vernehmlich adj audible

Vernehmung f (cross-)examination

vernehmungsfähig adj in a condition to be (cross-)examined

verneigen [fɛr'naɪɡən] vr to bow

verneinen [fɛr'naɪnən] vt (Frage) to answer in the negative; (ablehnen) to deny; (Gram) to negate

verneinend adj negative

Verneinung f negation

vernichten [fɛr'nɪçtən] vt to destroy, annihilate

vernichtend adj (fig) crushing; (Blick) withering; (Kritik) scathing

Vernichtung f destruction, annihilation

Vernichtungsschlag m devastating blow

verniedlichen [fɛr'niːtlɪçən] vt to play down

Vernunft [fɛr'nʊnft] (-) f reason; **~ annehmen** to see reason; **Vernunftehe** f, **Vernunftheirat** f marriage of convenience

vernünftig [fɛr'nʏnftɪç] adj sensible, reasonable

Vernunftmensch m rational person

veröden [fɛr'|øːdən] vi to become desolate ▷ vt (Med) to remove

veröffentlichen [fɛr'|œfəntlɪçən] vt to publish

Veröffentlichung f publication

verordnen [fɛr'|ɔrdnən] vt (Med) to prescribe

Verordnung f order, decree; (Med) prescription

verpachten [fɛr'paxtən] vt to lease (out)

verpacken [fɛr'pakən] vt to pack; (verbrauchergerecht) to package; (einwickeln) to wrap

Verpackung f packing; packaging; wrapping

verpassen [fɛr'pasən] vt to miss; **jdm eine Ohrfeige ~** (umg) to give sb a clip round the ear

verpatzen [fɛr'patsən] (umg) vt to spoil, mess up

verpennen [fɛr'pɛnən] (umg) vi, vt to oversleep

verpesten [fɛr'pɛstən] vt to pollute

verpetzen [fɛr'pɛtsən] (umg) vt: **jdn ~ (bei)** to tell on sb (to)

verpfänden [fɛr'pfɛndən] vt to pawn; (Jur) to mortgage

verpfeifen [fɛr'pfaɪfən] unreg (umg) vt: **jdn ~ (bei)** to grass on sb (to)

verpflanzen [fɛr'pflantsən] vt to transplant

Verpflanzung f transplanting; (Med) transplant

verpflegen [fɛr'pfleːɡən] vt to feed, cater for (Brit)

Verpflegung f catering; (Kost) food; (in Hotel) board

verpflichten [fɛr'pflɪçtən] vt to oblige, bind; (anstellen) to engage ▷ vr to undertake; (Mil) to sign on ▷ vi to carry obligations; **jdm verpflichtet sein** to be under an obligation to sb; **sich zu etw ~** to commit o.s. to doing sth; **jdm zu Dank verpflichtet sein** to be obliged to sb

verpflichtend adj (Zusage) binding

Verpflichtung f obligation; (Aufgabe) duty

verpfuschen [fɛr'pfʊʃən] (umg) vt to bungle, make a mess of

verplanen [fɛr'plaːnən] vt (Zeit) to book up; (Geld) to budget

verplappern [fɛr'plapərn] (umg) vr to open one's big mouth

verplempern [fɛr'plɛmpərn] (umg) vt to waste

verpönt [fɛr'pøːnt] adj: **~ (bei)** frowned upon (by)

verprassen [fɛr'prasən] vt to squander

verprügeln [fɛr'pryːɡəln] (umg) vt to beat up

verpuffen [fɛr'pʊfən] vi to (go) pop; (fig) to fall flat

Verputz [fɛr'pʊts] m plaster; (Rauputz) roughcast; **verputzen** vt to plaster; (umg: Essen) to put away

verqualmen [fɛr'kvalmən] vt (Zimmer) to fill with smoke

verquollen [fɛr'kvɔlən] adj swollen; (Holz) warped

verrammeln [fɛr'raməln] vt to barricade

Verrat [fɛr'raːt] **(-(e)s)** m treachery; (Pol) treason; **~ an jdm üben** to betray sb

verraten unreg vt to betray; (fig: erkennen lassen) to show; (Geheimnis) to divulge ▷ vr to give o.s. away

Verräter, in [fɛr'rɛːtər(ɪn)] **(-s, -)** m(f) traitor, traitress; **verräterisch** adj treacherous

verrauchen [fɛr'raʊxən] vi (fig: Zorn) to blow over

V

365

verrechnen [fɛrˈrɛçnən] *vt*: ~ **mit** to set off against ▷*vr* to miscalculate

Verrechnung *f*: **nur zur** ~ (*auf Scheck*) a/c payee only

Verrechnungsscheck *m* crossed cheque (*Brit*)

verregnet [fɛrˈreːgnət] *adj* rainy, spoilt by rain

verreisen [fɛrˈraɪzən] *vi* to go away (on a journey); **er ist geschäftlich verreist** he's away on business

verreißen [fɛrˈraɪsən] *unreg vt* to pull to pieces

verrenken [fɛrˈrɛŋkən] *vt* to contort; (*Med*) to dislocate; **sich** *dat* **den Knöchel** ~ to sprain one's ankle

Verrenkung *f* contortion; (*Med*) dislocation

verrennen [fɛrˈrɛnən] *unreg vr*: **sich in etw** *akk* ~ to get stuck on sth

verrichten [fɛrˈrɪçtən] *vt* (*Arbeit*) to do, perform

verriegeln [fɛrˈriːgəln] *vt* to bolt

verringern [fɛrˈrɪŋərn] *vt* to reduce ▷*vr* to decrease

Verringerung *f* reduction; decrease

verrinnen [fɛrˈrɪnən] *unreg vi* to run out *od* away; (*Zeit*) to elapse

Verriss [fɛrˈrɪs] *m* slating review

verrohen [fɛrˈroːən] *vi* to become brutalized

verrosten [fɛrˈrɔstən] *vi* to rust

verrotten [fɛrˈrɔtən] *vi* to rot

verrucht [fɛrˈruːxt] *adj* despicable; (*verrufen*) disreputable

verrücken [fɛrˈrʏkən] *vt* to move, shift

verrückt *adj* crazy, mad; **Verrückte**, **r** *f(m)* lunatic; **Verrücktheit** *f* madness, lunacy

Verruf [fɛrˈruːf] *m*: **in** ~ **geraten/bringen** to fall/bring into disrepute

verrufen *adj* disreputable

verrutschen [fɛrˈrʊtʃən] *vi* to slip

Vers [fɛrs] **(-es, -e)** *m* verse

versacken [fɛrˈzakən] *vi* (*lit*) to sink; (*fig: umg: herunterkommen*) to go downhill; (: *lange zechen*) to get involved in a booze-up (*Brit*) *od* a drinking spree

versagen [fɛrˈzaːgən] *vt*: **jdm/sich etw** ~ to deny sb/o.s. sth ▷*vi* to fail; **Versagen (-s)** *nt* failure; **menschliches Versagen** human error

Versager (-s, -) *m* failure

versalzen [fɛrˈzaltsən] *vt* to put too much salt in; (*fig*) to spoil

versammeln [fɛrˈzaməln] *vt, vr* to assemble, gather

Versammlung *f* meeting, gathering

Versammlungsfreiheit *f* freedom of assembly

Versand [fɛrˈzant] **(-(e)s)** *m* dispatch; (*Versandabteilung*) dispatch department; **Versandbahnhof** *m* dispatch station; **Versandhaus** *nt* mail-order firm; **Versandkosten** *pl* transport(ation) costs *pl*; **Versandweg** *m*: **auf dem Versandweg** by mail order

versäumen [fɛrˈzɔʏmən] *vt* to miss; (*Pflicht*) to neglect; (*Zeit*) to lose

Versäumnis (-ses, -se) *nt* neglect; (*Unterlassung*) omission

verschachern [fɛrˈʃaxərn] (*umg*) *vt* to sell off

verschachtelt [fɛrˈʃaxtəlt] *adj* (*Satz*) complex

verschaffen [fɛrˈʃafən] *vt*: **jdm/sich etw** ~ to get *od* procure sth for sb/o.s.

verschämt [fɛrˈʃɛːmt] *adj* bashful

verschandeln [fɛrˈʃandəln] (*umg*) *vt* to spoil

verschanzen [fɛrˈʃantsən] *vr*: **sich hinter etw** *dat* ~ to dig in behind sth; (*fig*) to take refuge behind sth

verschärfen [fɛrˈʃɛrfən] *vt* to intensify; (*Lage*) to aggravate; (*strenger machen: Kontrollen, Gesetze*) to tighten up ▷*vr* to intensify; to become aggravated; to become tighter

Verschärfung *f* intensification; (*der Lage*) aggravation; (*von Kontrollen etc*) tightening

verscharren [fɛrˈʃarən] *vt* to bury

verschätzen [fɛrˈʃɛtsən] *vr* to miscalculate

verschenken [fɛrˈʃɛŋkən] *vt* to give away

verscherzen [fɛrˈʃɛrtsən] *vt*: **sich** *dat* **etw** ~ to lose sth, throw sth away

verscheuchen [fɛrˈʃɔʏçən] *vt* to frighten away

verschicken [fɛrˈʃɪkən] *vt* to send off; (*Sträfling*) to transport

verschieben [fɛrˈʃiːbən] *unreg vt* to shift; (*Eisenb*) to shunt; (*Termin*) to postpone; (*umg: Waren, Devisen*) to traffic in

Verschiebung *f* shift, displacement; shunting; postponement

verschieden [fɛrˈʃiːdən] *adj* different; **das ist ganz** ~ (*wird verschieden gehandhabt*) that varies, that just depends; **sie sind** ~ **groß** they are of different sizes; **verschiedenartig** *adj* various, of different kinds; **zwei so verschiedenartige** ... two such differing ...; **Verschiedene** *pron pl* various people; various things *pl*; **Verschiedenes** *pron* various things *pl*; **etwas Verschiedenes** something different; **Verschiedenheit** *f* difference

verschiedentlich *adv* several times

verschiffen [fɛrˈʃɪfən] *vt* to ship; (*Sträfling*) to transport

verschimmeln [fɛrˈʃɪməln] *vi* (*Nahrungsmittel*) to go mouldy (*Brit*) *od* moldy (*US*); (*Leder, Papier etc*) to become mildewed

verschlafen [fɛrˈʃlaːfən] *unreg vt* to sleep through; (*fig: versäumen*) to miss ▷*vi, vr* to oversleep ▷*adj* sleepy

Verschlag [fɛrˈʃlaːk] *m* shed

verschlagen [fɛrˈʃlaːgən] *unreg vt* to board up; (*Tennis*) to hit out of play; (*Buchseite*) to lose ▷*adj* cunning; **jdm den Atem** ~ to take sb's breath away; **an einen Ort** ~ **werden** to wind up in a place

verschlampen [fɛrˈʃlampən] *vi* (*Hilfsverb sein: Mensch*) to go to seed (*umg*) ▷*vt* to lose, mislay

verschlechtern [fɛrˈʃlɛçtərn] *vt* to make worse ▷*vr* to deteriorate, get worse; (*gehaltlich*) to take a lower-paid job

Verschlechterung *f* deterioration

Verschleierung [fɛrˈʃlaɪərʊŋ] *f* veiling; (*fig*) concealment; (*Mil*) screening

Verschleierungstaktik *f* smoke-screen tactics

pl

Verschleiß [fɛrˈʃlaɪs] **(-es, -e)** *m* wear and tear

verschleißen *unreg vt, vi, vr* to wear out

verschleppen [fɛrˈʃlɛpən] *vt* to carry off, abduct; *(zeitlich)* to drag out, delay; *(verbreiten: Seuche)* to spread

verschleudern [fɛrˈʃlɔydərn] *vt* to squander; *(Comm)* to sell dirt-cheap

verschließbar *adj* lockable

verschließen [fɛrˈʃliːsən] *unreg vt* to lock
▷ *vr:* **sich einer Sache** *dat* ~ to close one's mind to sth

verschlimmern [fɛrˈʃlɪmərn] *vt* to make worse, aggravate ▷ *vr* to get worse, deteriorate

Verschlimmerung *f* deterioration

verschlingen [fɛrˈʃlɪŋən] *unreg vt* to devour, swallow up; *(Fäden)* to twist

verschliss *etc* [fɛrˈʃlɪs] *vb siehe* **verschleißen**

verschlissen [fɛrˈʃlɪsən] *pp von* **verschleißen**
▷ *adj* worn(-out)

verschlossen [fɛrˈʃlɔsən] *adj* locked; *(fig)* reserved; *(schweigsam)* tight-lipped;
Verschlossenheit *f* reserve

verschlucken [fɛrˈʃlʊkən] *vt* to swallow ▷ *vr* to choke

Verschluss [fɛrˈʃlʊs] *m* lock; *(von Kleid etc)* fastener; *(Phot)* shutter; *(Stöpsel)* plug; **unter ~ halten** to keep under lock and key

verschlüsseln [fɛrˈʃlʏsəln] *vt* to encode

verschmachten [fɛrˈʃmaxtən] *vi:* ~ **(vor** +*dat)* to languish (for); **vor Durst** ~ to be dying of thirst

verschmähen [fɛrˈʃmɛːən] *vt* to scorn

verschmelzen [fɛrˈʃmɛltsən] *unreg vt, vi* to merge, blend

verschmerzen [fɛrˈʃmɛrtsən] *vt* to get over

verschmiert [fɛrˈʃmiːrt] *adj (Hände)* smeary; *(Schminke)* smudged

verschmitzt [fɛrˈʃmɪtst] *adj* mischievous

verschmutzen [fɛrˈʃmʊtsən] *vt* to soil; *(Umwelt)* to pollute

Verschmutzung *f* pollution

verschnaufen [fɛrˈʃnaʊfən] *(umg) vi, vr* to have a breather

verschneiden [fɛrˈʃnaɪdən] *vt (Whisky etc)* to blend

verschneit [fɛrˈʃnaɪt] *adj* covered in snow, snowed up

Verschnitt [fɛrˈʃnɪt] *m (von Whisky etc)* blend

verschnörkelt [fɛrˈʃnœrkəlt] *adj* ornate

verschnupft [fɛrˈʃnʊpft] *(umg) adj:* ~ **sein** to have a cold; *(beleidigt)* to be peeved *(umg)*

verschnüren [fɛrˈʃnyːrən] *vt* to tie up

verschollen [fɛrˈʃɔlən] *adj* lost, missing

verschonen [fɛrˈʃoːnən] *vt:* **jdn mit etw** ~ **to** spare sb sth; **von etw verschont bleiben** to escape sth

verschönern [fɛrˈʃøːnərn] *vt* to decorate; *(verbessern)* to improve

verschossen [fɛrˈʃɔsən] *adj:* ~ **sein** *(fig: umg)* to be in love

verschränken [fɛrˈʃrɛŋkən] *vt* to cross; *(Arme)* to fold

verschreckt [fɛrˈʃrɛkt] *adj* frightened, scared

verschreiben [fɛrˈʃraɪbən] *unreg vt (Papier)* to use up; *(Med)* to prescribe ▷ *vr* to make a mistake (in writing); **sich einer Sache** *dat* ~ to devote o.s. to sth

verschrieen [fɛrˈʃriːən], **verschrien** [fɛrˈʃriːn] *adj* notorious

verschroben [fɛrˈʃroːbən] *adj* eccentric, odd

verschrotten [fɛrˈʃrɔtən] *vt* to scrap

verschüchtert [fɛrˈʃʏçtərt] *adj* subdued, intimidated

verschulden [fɛrˈʃʊldən] *vt* to be guilty of ▷ *vi (in Schulden geraten)* to get into debt;
Verschulden (-s) *nt* fault

verschuldet *adj* in debt

Verschuldung *f* debts *pl*

verschütten [fɛrˈʃʏtən] *vt* to spill; *(zuschütten)* to fill; *(unter Trümmern)* to bury

verschwand *etc* [fɛrˈʃvant] *vb siehe* **verschwinden**

verschweigen [fɛrˈʃvaɪgən] *unreg vt* to keep secret; **jdm etw** ~ to keep sth from sb

verschwenden [fɛrˈʃvɛndən] *vt* to squander

Verschwender, in (-s, -) *m(f)* spendthrift;
verschwenderisch *adj* wasteful; *(Leben)* extravagant

Verschwendung *f* waste

verschwiegen [fɛrˈʃviːgən] *adj* discreet; *(Ort)* secluded; **Verschwiegenheit** *f* discretion; seclusion; **zur Verschwiegenheit verpflichtet** bound to secrecy

verschwimmen [fɛrˈʃvɪmən] *unreg vi* to grow hazy, become blurred

verschwinden [fɛrˈʃvɪndən] *unreg vi* to disappear, vanish; **verschwinde!** clear off! *(umg)*; **Verschwinden (-s)** *nt* disappearance

verschwindend *adj (Anzahl, Menge)* insignificant

verschwitzen [fɛrˈʃvɪtsən] *vt* to stain with sweat; *(umg)* to forget

verschwitzt *adj (Kleidung)* sweat-stained; *(Mensch)* sweaty

verschwommen [fɛrˈʃvɔmən] *adj* hazy, vague

verschworen [fɛrˈʃvoːrən] *adj (Gesellschaft)* sworn

verschwören [fɛrˈʃvøːrən] *unreg vr* to conspire, plot

Verschwörer, in (-s, -) *m(f)* conspirator

Verschwörung *f* conspiracy, plot

verschwunden [fɛrˈʃvʊndən] *pp von* **verschwinden** ▷ *adj* missing

versehen [fɛrˈzeːən] *unreg vt* to supply, provide; *(Pflicht)* to carry out; *(Amt)* to fill; *(Haushalt)* to keep ▷ *vr (fig)* to make a mistake; **ehe er (es) sich ~ hatte …** before he knew it …; **Versehen (-s, -)** *nt* oversight; **aus Versehen** by mistake

versehentlich *adv* by mistake

Versehrte, r [fɛrˈzeːrtə(r)] *f(m)* disabled person

verselbstständigen [fɛrˈzɛlpstʃtɛndɪgən], **verselbständigen** [fɛrˈzɛlpʃtɛndɪgən] *vr* to become independent

versenden [fɛrˈzɛndən] *unreg vt* to send; *(Comm)* to forward

V

367

versengen [fɛrˈzɛŋən] *vt* to scorch; (*Feuer*) to singe; (*umg: verprügeln*) to wallop

versenken [fɛrˈzɛŋkən] *vt* to sink ▷ *vr*: **sich ~ in** +*akk* to become engrossed in

versessen [fɛrˈzɛsən] *adj*: **~ auf** +*akk* mad about, hellbent on

versetzen [fɛrˈzɛtsən] *vt* to transfer; (*verpfänden*) to pawn; (*umg: vergeblich warten lassen*) to stand up; (*nicht geradlinig anordnen*) to stagger; (*Sch: in höhere Klasse*) to move up ▷ *vr*: **sich in jdn** *od* **in jds Lage ~** to put o.s. in sb's place; **jdm einen Tritt/Schlag ~** to kick/hit sb; **etw mit etw ~** to mix sth with sth; **jdm einen Stich ~** (*fig*) to cut sb to the quick, wound sb (deeply); **jdn in gute Laune ~** to put sb in a good mood

Versetzung *f* transfer; **seine ~ ist gefährdet** (*Sch*) he's in danger of having to repeat a year

verseuchen [fɛrˈzɔʏçən] *vt* to contaminate

Versicherer (**-s, -**) *m* insurer; (*bei Schiffen*) underwriter

versichern [fɛrˈzɪçərn] *vt* to assure; (*mit Geld*) to insure ▷ *vr*: **sich ~** +*gen* to make sure of

Versicherte, r *f(m)* insured

Versicherung *f* assurance; insurance

Versicherungs- *zW*: **Versicherungsbeitrag** *m* insurance premium; (*bei staatlicher Versicherung etc*) social security contribution; **Versicherungsgesellschaft** *f* insurance company; **Versicherungsnehmer** (**-s, -**) *m* (*form*) insured, policy holder; **Versicherungspolice** *f* insurance policy; **Versicherungsschutz** *m* insurance cover; **Versicherungssumme** *f* sum insured; **Versicherungsträger** *m* insurer

versickern [fɛrˈzɪkərn] *vi* to seep away; (*fig: Interesse etc*) to peter out

versiegeln [fɛrˈziːgəln] *vt* to seal (up)

versiegen [fɛrˈziːgən] *vi* to dry up

versiert [vɛrˈziːrt] *adj*: **in etw** *dat* **~ sein** to be experienced *od* well versed in sth

versilbert [fɛrˈzɪlbərt] *adj* silver-plated

versinken [fɛrˈzɪŋkən] *unreg vi* to sink; **ich hätte im Boden** *od* **vor Scham ~ mögen** I wished the ground would swallow me up

versinnbildlichen [fɛrˈzɪnbɪltlɪçən] *vt* to symbolize

Version [vɛrziˈoːn] *f* version

Versmaß [ˈfɛrsmaːs] *nt* metre (*Brit*), meter (*US*)

versohlen [fɛrˈzoːlən] (*umg*) *vt* to belt

versöhnen [fɛrˈzøːnən] *vt* to reconcile ▷ *vr* to become reconciled

versöhnlich *adj* (*Ton, Worte*) conciliatory; (*Ende*) happy

Versöhnung *f* reconciliation

versonnen [fɛrˈzɔnən] *adj* (*Gesichtsausdruck*) pensive, thoughtful; (*träumerisch: Blick*) dreamy

versorgen [fɛrˈzɔrgən] *vt* to provide, supply; (*Familie etc*) to look after ▷ *vr* to look after o.s.

Versorger, in (**-s, -**) *m(f)* (*Ernährer*) provider, breadwinner; (*Belieferer*) supplier

Versorgung *f* provision; (*Unterhalt*) maintenance; (*Altersversorgung etc*) benefit, assistance

Versorgungs- *zW*: **Versorgungsamt** *nt* pension office; **Versorgungsbetrieb** *m* public utility; **Versorgungsnetz** *nt* (*Wasserversorgung etc*) (supply) grid; (*von Waren*) supply network

verspannen [fɛrˈʃpanən] *vr* (*Muskeln*) to tense up

verspäten [fɛrˈʃpɛːtən] *vr* to be late

verspätet *adj* late

Verspätung *f* delay; **~ haben** to be late; **mit zwanzig Minuten ~** twenty minutes late

versperren [fɛrˈʃpɛrən] *vt* to bar, obstruct

verspielen [fɛrˈʃpiːlən] *vt, vi* to lose; (**bei jdm**) **verspielt haben** to have had it (as far as sb is concerned)

verspielt [fɛrˈʃpiːlt] *adj* playful

versponnen [fɛrˈʃpɔnən] *adj* crackpot

verspotten [fɛrˈʃpɔtən] *vt* to ridicule, scoff at

versprach *etc* [fɛrˈʃprax] *vb siehe* **versprechen**

versprechen [fɛrˈʃprɛçən] *unreg vt* to promise ▷ *vr* (*etwas Nichtgemeintes sagen*) to make a slip of the tongue; **sich** *dat* **etw von etw ~** to expect sth from sth; **Versprechen** (**-s, -**) *nt* promise

Versprecher (**-s, -**) (*umg*) *m* slip (of the tongue)

verspricht [fɛrˈʃprɪçt] *vb siehe* **versprechen**

verspüren [fɛrˈʃpyːrən] *vt* to feel, be conscious of

verstaatlichen [fɛrˈʃtaːtlɪçən] *vt* to nationalize

verstaatlicht *adj*: **~er Industriezweig** nationalized industry

Verstaatlichung *f* nationalization

Verstand [fɛrˈʃtant] *m* intelligence; (*Intellekt*) mind; (*Fähigkeit zu denken*) reason; **den ~ verlieren** to go out of one's mind; **über jds ~** *akk* **gehen** to be beyond sb

verstand *etc vb siehe* **verstehen**

verstanden [fɛrˈʃtandən] *pp von* **verstehen**

verstandesmäßig *adj* rational

verständig [fɛrˈʃtɛndɪç] *adj* sensible

verständigen [fɛrˈʃtɛndɪgən] *vt* to inform ▷ *vr* to communicate; (*sich einigen*) to come to an understanding

Verständigkeit *f* good sense

Verständigung *f* communication; (*Benachrichtigung*) informing; (*Einigung*) agreement

verständlich [fɛrˈʃtɛntlɪç] *adj* understandable, comprehensible; (*hörbar*) audible; **sich ~ machen** to make o.s. understood; (*sich klar ausdrücken*) to make o.s. clear

verständlicherweise *adv* understandably (enough)

Verständlichkeit *f* clarity, intelligibility

Verständnis (**-ses, -se**) *nt* understanding; **für etw kein ~ haben** to have no understanding *od* sympathy for sth; (*für Kunst etc*) to have no appreciation of sth; **verständnislos** *adj* uncomprehending; **verständnisvoll** *adj* understanding, sympathetic

verstärken [fɛrˈʃtɛrkən] *vt* to strengthen; (*Ton*) to amplify; (*erhöhen*) to intensify ▷ *vr* to intensify

Verstärker (**-s, -**) *m* amplifier

Verstärkung f strengthening; (*Hilfe*) reinforcements pl; (*von Ton*) amplification

verstaubt [fɛrˈʃtaʊpt] adj dusty; (*fig: Ansichten*) fuddy-duddy (*umg*)

verstauchen [fɛrˈʃtaʊxən] vt to sprain

verstauen [fɛrˈʃtaʊən] vt to stow away

Versteck [fɛrˈʃtɛk] **(-(e)s, -e)** nt hiding (place)

verstecken vt, vr to hide

versteckt adj hidden; (*Tür*) concealed; (*fig: Lächeln, Blick*) furtive; (*Andeutung*) veiled

verstehen [fɛrˈʃteːən] unreg vt, vi to understand; (*können, beherrschen*) to know ▷ vr (*auskommen*) to get on; **das ist nicht wörtlich zu ~** that isn't to be taken literally; **das versteht sich von selbst** that goes without saying; **die Preise ~ sich einschließlich Lieferung** prices are inclusive of delivery; **sich auf etw** akk **~** to be an expert at sth

versteifen [fɛrˈʃtaɪfən] vt to stiffen, brace ▷ vr (*fig*): **sich ~ auf** +akk to insist on

versteigen [fɛrˈʃtaɪgən] unreg vr: **sie hat sich zu der Behauptung verstiegen, dass ...** she presumed to claim that ...

versteigern [fɛrˈʃtaɪgərn] vt to auction

Versteigerung f auction

verstellbar adj adjustable, variable

verstellen [fɛrˈʃtɛlən] vt to move, shift; (*Uhr*) to adjust; (*versperren*) to block; (*fig*) to disguise ▷ vr to pretend, put on an act

Verstellung f pretence (*Brit*), pretense (*US*)

versteuern [fɛrˈʃtɔʏərn] vt to pay tax on; **zu ~** taxable

verstiegen [fɛrˈʃtiːgən] adj exaggerated

verstimmt [fɛrˈʃtɪmt] adj out of tune; (*fig*) cross, put out; (: *Magen*) upset

Verstimmung f (*fig*) disgruntled state, peevishness

verstockt [fɛrˈʃtɔkt] adj stubborn; **Verstocktheit** f stubbornness

verstohlen [fɛrˈʃtoːlən] adj stealthy

verstopfen [fɛrˈʃtɔpfən] vt to block, stop up; (*Med*) to constipate

Verstopfung f obstruction; (*Med*) constipation

verstorben [fɛrˈʃtɔrbən] adj deceased, late

Verstorbene, r f(m) deceased

verstört [fɛrˈʃtøːrt] adj (*Mensch*) distraught

Verstoß [fɛrˈʃtoːs] m: **~ (gegen)** infringement (of), violation (of)

verstoßen unreg vt to disown, reject ▷ vi: **~ gegen** to offend against

Verstrebung [fɛrˈʃtreːbʊŋ] f (*Strebebalken*) support(ing beam)

verstreichen [fɛrˈʃtraɪçən] unreg vt to spread ▷ vi to elapse; (*Zeit*) to pass (by); (*Frist*) to expire

verstreuen [fɛrˈʃtrɔʏən] vt to scatter (about)

verstricken [fɛrˈʃtrɪkən] vt (*fig*) to entangle, ensnare ▷ vr: **sich ~ in** +akk to get entangled in

verströmen [fɛrˈʃtrøːmən] vt to exude

verstümmeln [fɛrˈʃtʏmɛln] vt to maim, mutilate (*auch fig*)

verstummen [fɛrˈʃtʊmən] vi to go silent; (*Lärm*) to die away

Versuch [fɛrˈzuːx] **(-(e)s, -e)** m attempt; (*Chem*

etc) experiment; **das käme auf einen ~ an** we'll have to have a try

versuchen vt to try; (*verlocken*) to tempt ▷ vr: **sich an etw** dat **~** to try one's hand at sth

Versuchs- zW: **Versuchsanstalt** f research institute; **Versuchsbohrung** f experimental drilling; **Versuchskaninchen** nt guinea pig; **Versuchsobjekt** nt test object; (*fig: Mensch*) guinea pig; **Versuchsreihe** f series of experiments; **versuchsweise** adv tentatively

Versuchung f temptation

versumpfen [fɛrˈzʊmpfən] vi (*Gebiet*) to become marshy; (*fig: umg*) to go to pot; (*lange zechen*) to get involved in a booze-up (*Brit*) od drinking spree (*US*)

versündigen [fɛrˈzʏndɪgən] vr (*geh*): **sich an jdm/etw ~** to sin against sb/sth

versunken [fɛrˈzʊŋkən] adj sunken; **~ sein in** +akk to be absorbed od engrossed in; **Versunkenheit** f absorption

versüßen [fɛrˈzyːsən] vt: **jdm etw ~** (*fig*) to make sth more pleasant for sb

vertagen [fɛrˈtaːgən] vt, vi to adjourn

Vertagung f adjournment

vertauschen [fɛrˈtaʊʃən] vt to exchange; (*versehentlich*) to mix up; **vertauschte Rollen** reversed roles

verteidigen [fɛrˈtaɪdɪgən] vt to defend ▷ vr to defend o.s.; (*vor Gericht*) to conduct one's own defence (*Brit*) od defense (*US*)

Verteidiger, in (-s, -) m(f) defender; (*Anwalt*) defence (*Brit*) od defense (*US*) lawyer

Verteidigung f defence (*Brit*), defense (*US*)

Verteidigungsfähigkeit f ability to defend

Verteidigungsminister m Minister of Defence (*Brit*), Defense Secretary (*US*)

verteilen [fɛrˈtaɪlən] vt to distribute; (*Rollen*) to assign; (*Salbe*) to spread

Verteiler (-s, -) m (*Comm, Aut*) distributor

Verteilung f distribution

Verteuerung [fɛrˈtɔʏərʊŋ] f increase in price

verteufeln [fɛrˈtɔʏfəln] vt to condemn

verteufelt (*umg*) adj awful, devilish ▷ adv awfully, devilishly

vertiefen [fɛrˈtiːfən] vt to deepen; (*Sch*) to consolidate ▷ vr: **sich in etw** akk **~** to become engrossed od absorbed in sth

Vertiefung f depression

vertikal [vɛrtiˈkaːl] adj vertical

vertilgen [fɛrˈtɪlgən] vt to exterminate; (*umg*) to eat up, consume

Vertilgungsmittel nt weedkiller; (*Insektenvertilgungsmittel*) pesticide

vertippen [fɛrˈtɪpən] vr to make a typing mistake

vertonen [fɛrˈtoːnən] vt to set to music; (*Film* etc) to add a soundtrack to

vertrackt [fɛrˈtrakt] adj awkward, tricky, complex

Vertrag [fɛrˈtraːk] **(-(e)s, ̈-e)** m contract, agreement; (*Pol*) treaty

vertragen [fɛrˈtraːgən] unreg vt to tolerate, stand ▷ vr to get along; (*sich aussöhnen*)

369

to become reconciled; **viel ~ können**
(*umg: Alkohol*) to be able to hold one's drink;
sich mit etw ~ (*Nahrungsmittel, Farbe*) to go
with sth; (*Aussage, Verhalten*) to be consistent
with sth

vertraglich *adj* contractual

verträglich [fɛr'trɛ:klɪç] *adj* good-natured;
(*Speisen*) easily digested; (*Med*) easily tolerated;
Verträglichkeit f good nature; digestibility

Vertrags- *zW:* **Vertragsbruch** *m* breach
of contract; **vertragsbrüchig** *adj* in
breach of contract; **vertragsfähig** *adj* (*Jur*)
competent to contract; **vertragsmäßig** *adj*,
adv (as) stipulated, according to contract;
Vertragspartner *m* party to a contract;
Vertragsspieler *m* (*Sport*) player under
contract; **vertragswidrig** *adj, adv* contrary to
contract

vertrauen [fɛr'trauən] *vi:* **jdm ~** to trust
sb; **~ auf** +*akk* to rely on; **Vertrauen** (**-s**) *nt*
confidence; **jdn ins Vertrauen ziehen** to
take sb into one's confidence; **Vertrauen
zu jdm fassen** to gain confidence in sb;
vertrauenerweckend *adj* inspiring trust

Vertrauens- *zW:* **Vertrauensmann** (**-(e)
s**, *pl* **-männer** *od* **-leute**) *m* intermediary;
Vertrauenssache f (*vertrauliche Angelegenheit*)
confidential matter; (*Frage des Vertrauens*)
question of trust; **vertrauensselig** *adj*
trusting; **vertrauensvoll** *adj* trustful;
Vertrauensvotum *nt* (*Parl*) vote of confidence;
vertrauenswürdig *adj* trustworthy

vertraulich [fɛr'traʊlɪç] *adj* familiar; (*geheim*)
confidential; **Vertraulichkeit** f familiarity;
confidentiality

verträumt [fɛr'trɔymt] *adj* dreamy; (*Städtchen
etc*) sleepy

vertraut [fɛr'traʊt] *adj* familiar; **sich mit dem
Gedanken ~ machen, dass ...** to get used to
the idea that ...

Vertraute, r f(m) confidant(e), close friend

Vertrautheit f familiarity

vertreiben [fɛr'traɪbən] *unreg vt* to drive away;
(*aus Land*) to expel; (*Comm*) to sell; (*Zeit*) to pass

Vertreibung f expulsion

vertretbar *adj* justifiable; (*Theorie, Argument*)
tenable

vertreten [fɛr'tre:tən] *unreg vt* to represent;
(*Ansicht*) to hold, advocate; (*ersetzen*) to replace;
(*Kollegen*) to cover for; (*Comm*) to be the agent
for; **sich** *dat* **die Beine ~** to stretch one's legs

Vertreter, in (**-s, -**) *m(f)* representative;
(*Verfechter*) advocate; (*Comm: Firma*) agent;
Vertreterprovision f agent's commission

Vertretung f representation; advocacy; **die ~
übernehmen (für)** to stand in (for)

Vertretungsstunde f (*Sch*) cover lesson

Vertrieb [fɛr'tri:p] (**-(e)s, -e**) *m* marketing; **den
~ für eine Firma haben** to have the (selling)
agency for a firm

Vertriebene, r [fɛr'tri:bənə(r)] *f(m)* exile

Vertriebskosten *pl* marketing costs *pl*

vertrocknen [fɛr'trɔknən] *vi* to dry up

vertrödeln [fɛr'trø:dəln] (*umg*) *vt* to fritter
away

vertrösten [fɛr'trø:stən] *vt* to put off

vertun [fɛr'tu:n] *unreg vt* to waste ▷ *vr* (*umg*) to
make a mistake

vertuschen [fɛr'tʊʃən] *vt* to hush *od* cover up

verübeln [fɛr'|y:bəln] *vt:* **jdm etw ~** to be cross
od offended with sb on account of sth

verüben [fɛr'|y:bən] *vt* to commit

verulken [fɛr'|ʊlkən] (*umg*) *vt* to make fun of

verunglimpfen [fɛr'|ʊnɡlɪmpfən] *vt* to
disparage

verunglücken [fɛr'|ʊnɡlʏkən] *vi* to have an
accident; (*fig: umg: misslingen*) to go wrong;
tödlich ~ to be killed in an accident

Verunglückte, r f(m) accident victim

verunreinigen [fɛr'|ʊnraɪnɪɡən] *vt* to soil;
(*Umwelt*) to pollute

verunsichern [fɛr'|ʊnzɪçərn] *vt* to rattle (*fig*)

verunstalten [fɛr'|ʊnʃtaltən] *vt* to disfigure;
(*Gebäude etc*) to deface

veruntreuen [fɛr'|ʊntrɔyən] *vt* to embezzle

verursachen [fɛr'|u:rzaxən] *vt* to cause

verurteilen [fɛr'|u:rtaɪlən] *vt* to condemn; (*zu
Strafe*) to sentence; (*für schuldig befinden*): **jdn ~
(für)** to convict sb (of)

Verurteilung f condemnation; (*Jur*) sentence;
conviction

vervielfachen [fɛr'fi:lfaxən] *vt* to multiply

vervielfältigen [fɛr'fi:lfɛltɪɡən] *vt* to
duplicate, copy

Vervielfältigung f duplication, copying

vervollkommnen [fɛr'fɔlkɔmnən] *vt* to perfect

vervollständigen [fɛr'fɔlʃtɛndɪɡən] *vt* to
complete

verw. *abk* = **verwitwet**

verwachsen [fɛr'vaksən] *adj* (*Mensch*)
deformed; (*verkümmert*) stunted; (*überwuchert*)
overgrown

verwackeln [fɛr'vakəln] *vt* (*Foto*) to blur

verwählen [fɛr'vɛ:lən] *vr* (*Tel*) to dial the wrong
number

verwahren [fɛr'va:rən] *vt* to keep (safe) ▷ *vr* to
protest

verwahrlosen *vi* to become neglected;
(*moralisch*) to go to the bad

verwahrlost *adj* neglected; (*moralisch*)
wayward

Verwahrung f (*von Geld etc*) keeping; (*von Täter*)
custody, detention; **jdn in ~ nehmen** to take
sb into custody

verwaist [fɛr'vaɪst] *adj* orphaned

verwalten [fɛr'valtən] *vt* to manage; (*Behörde*)
to administer

Verwalter, in (**-s, -**) *m(f)* administrator;
(*Vermögensverwalter*) trustee

Verwaltung f management; administration

Verwaltungs- *zW:* **Verwaltungsapparat**
m administrative machinery;
Verwaltungsbezirk *m* administrative district;
Verwaltungsgericht *nt* Administrative Court

verwandeln [fɛr'vandəln] *vt* to change,
transform ▷ *vr* to change

Verwandlung f change, transformation
verwandt [fɛr'vant] adj: ~ **(mit)** related (to);
geistig ~ sein (fig) to be kindred spirits
Verwandte, r f(m) relative, relation
Verwandtschaft f relationship; (Menschen)
relatives pl, relations pl; (fig) affinity
verwarnen [fɛr'varnən] vt to caution
Verwarnung f caution
verwaschen [fɛr'vaʃən] adj faded; (fig) vague
verwässern [fɛr'vɛsərn] vt to dilute, water
down
verwechseln [fɛr'vɛksəln] vt: ~ **mit** to confuse
with; **zum V~ ähnlich** as like as two peas
Verwechslung f confusion, mixing up; **das**
muss eine ~ sein there must be some mistake
verwegen [fɛr've:gən] adj daring, bold;
Verwegenheit f daring, audacity, boldness
verwehren [fɛr've:rən] vt (geh): **jdm etw ~** to
refuse od deny sb sth
Verwehung [fɛr've:ʊŋ] f (Schneeverwehung)
snowdrift; (Sandverwehung) sanddrift
verweichlichen [fɛr'vaɪçlɪçən] vt to
mollycoddle
verweichlicht adj effeminate, soft
verweigern [fɛr'vaɪgərn] vt: **jdm etw ~** to
refuse sb sth; **den Gehorsam/die Aussage ~**
to refuse to obey/testify
Verweigerung f refusal
verweilen [fɛr'vaɪlən] vi to stay; (fig): ~ **bei** to
dwell on
verweint [fɛr'vaɪnt] adj (Augen) swollen with
tears od with crying; (Gesicht) tear-stained
Verweis [fɛr'vaɪs] (-es, -e) m reprimand,
rebuke; (Hinweis) reference
verweisen [fɛr'vaɪzən] unreg vt to refer; **jdn**
auf etw akk/**an jdn ~** (hinweisen) to refer sb to
sth/sb; **jdn vom Platz** od **des Spielfeldes ~**
(Sport) to send sb off; **jdn von der Schule ~** to
expel sb (from school); **jdn des Landes ~** to
deport sb
Verweisung f reference; (Landesverweisung)
deportation
verwelken [fɛr'vɛlkən] vi to fade; (Blumen) to
wilt
verweltlichen [fɛr'vɛltlɪçən] vt to secularize
verwendbar [fɛr'vɛndbaːr] adj usable
verwenden [fɛr'vɛndən] unreg vt to use; (Mühe,
Zeit, Arbeit) to spend ▷ vr to intercede
Verwendung f use
Verwendungsmöglichkeit f (possible) use
verwerfen [fɛr'vɛrfən] unreg vt to reject;
(Urteil) to quash; (kritisieren: Handlungsweise) to
condemn
verwerflich [fɛr'vɛrflɪç] adj reprehensible
verwertbar adj usable
verwerten [fɛr've:rtən] vt to utilize
Verwertung f utilization
verwesen [fɛr've:zən] vi to decay
Verwesung f decomposition
verwickeln [fɛr'vɪkəln] vt to tangle (up); (fig) to
involve ▷ vr to get tangled (up); **jdn ~ in** +akk
to involve sb in, get sb involved in; **sich ~ in**
+akk to get involved in

verwickelt adj involved
Verwicklung f entanglement, complication
verwildern [fɛr'vɪldərn] vi to run wild
verwildert adj wild; (Garten) overgrown; (jds
Aussehen) unkempt
verwinden [fɛr'vɪndən] unreg vt to get over
verwirken [fɛr'vɪrkən] vt (geh) to forfeit
verwirklichen [fɛr'vɪrklɪçən] vt to realize, put
into effect
Verwirklichung f realization
verwirren [fɛr'vɪrən] vt to tangle (up); (fig) to
confuse
Verwirrspiel nt confusing tactics pl
Verwirrung f confusion
verwischen [fɛr'vɪʃən] vt (verschmieren)
to smudge; (lit, fig: Spuren) to cover over;
(fig: Erinnerungen) to blur
verwittern [fɛr'vɪtərn] vi to weather
verwitwet [fɛr'vɪtvət] adj widowed
verwöhnen [fɛr'vø:nən] vt to spoil, pamper
Verwöhnung f spoiling, pampering
verworfen [fɛr'vɔrfən] adj depraved;
Verworfenheit f depravity
verworren [fɛr'vɔrən] adj confused
verwundbar [fɛr'vʊntbaːr] adj vulnerable
verwunden [fɛr'vʊndən] vt to wound
verwunderlich [fɛr'vʊndərlɪç] adj surprising;
(stärker) astonishing
verwundern vt to astonish ▷ vr: **sich ~ über**
+akk to be astonished at
Verwunderung f astonishment
Verwundete, r f(m) injured person; **die ~n** the
injured; (Mil) the wounded
Verwundung f wound, injury
verwünschen [fɛr'vʏnʃən] vt to curse
verwurzelt [fɛr'vʊrtsəlt] adj: **(fest) in etw** dat
od **mit etw ~** (fig) deeply rooted in sth
verwüsten [fɛr'vy:stən] vt to devastate
Verwüstung f devastation
Verz. abk = **Verzeichnis**
verzagen [fɛr'tsa:gən] vi to despair
verzagt [fɛr'tsa:kt] adj disheartened
verzählen [fɛr'tsɛ:lən] vr to miscount
verzahnen [fɛr'tsa:nən] vt to dovetail;
(Zahnräder) to cut teeth in
verzapfen [fɛr'tsapfən] (umg) vt: **Unsinn ~** to
talk nonsense
verzaubern [fɛr'tsaʊbərn] vt (lit) to cast a spell
on; (fig: jdn) to enchant
verzehren [fɛr'tse:rən] vt to consume
verzeichnen [fɛr'tsaɪçnən] vt to list;
(Niederlage, Verlust) to register
Verzeichnis (-ses, -se) nt list, catalogue (Brit),
catalog (US); (in Buch) index; (Comput) directory
verzeihen [fɛr'tsaɪən] unreg vt, vi to forgive;
jdm etw ~ to forgive sb (for) sth; ~ **Sie!** excuse
me!
verzeihlich adj pardonable
Verzeihung f forgiveness, pardon; ~! sorry!,
excuse me!; **(jdn) um ~ bitten** to apologize
(to sb)
verzerren [fɛr'tsɛrən] vt to distort; (Sehne,
Muskel) to strain, pull

V

verzetteln [fɛrˈtsɛtəln] vr to waste a lot of time

Verzicht [fɛrˈtsɪçt] **(-(e)s, -e)** m: **~ (auf** +akk**)** renunciation (of); **verzichten** vi: **verzichten auf** +akk to forego, give up

verziehen [fɛrˈtsiːən] unreg vi (Hilfsverb sein) to move ▷ vt to put out of shape; (Kind) to spoil; (Pflanzen) to thin out ▷ vr to go out of shape; (Gesicht) to contort; (verschwinden) to disappear; **verzogen** (Vermerk) no longer at this address; **keine Miene ~** not to turn a hair; **das Gesicht ~** to pull a face

verzieren [fɛrˈtsiːrən] vt to decorate

Verzierung f decoration

verzinsen [fɛrˈtsɪnzən] vt to pay interest on

verzinslich adj: **(fest)~ sein** to yield (a fixed rate of) interest

verzogen [fɛrˈtsoːɡən] adj (Kind) spoilt; siehe auch **verziehen**

verzögern [fɛrˈtsøːɡərn] vt to delay

Verzögerung f delay

Verzögerungstaktik f delaying tactics pl

verzollen [fɛrˈtsɔlən] vt to pay duty on; **haben Sie etwas zu ~?** have you anything to declare?

verzücken [fɛrˈtsʏkən] vt to send into ecstasies, enrapture

Verzug [fɛrˈtsuːk] m delay; (Fin) arrears pl; **mit etw in ~ geraten** to fall behind with sth

verzweifeln [fɛrˈtsvaɪfəln] vi to despair

verzweifelt adj desperate

Verzweiflung f despair

verzweigen [fɛrˈtsvaɪɡən] vr to branch out

verzwickt [fɛrˈtsvɪkt] (umg) adj awkward, complicated

Vesper [ˈfɛspər] **(-, -n)** f vespers pl

Vesuv [veˈzuːf] **(-(s))** m Vesuvius

Veto [ˈveːto] **(-s, -s)** nt veto

Vetter [ˈfɛtər] **(-s, -n)** m cousin

vgl. abk (= vergleiche) cf

v. H. abk (= vom Hundert) pc

VHS **(-)** f abk = **Volkshochschule**

Viadukt [viaˈdʊkt] **(-(e)s, -e)** m viaduct

Vibrator [viˈbraːtɔr] m vibrator

vibrieren [viˈbriːrən] vi to vibrate

Video [ˈviːdeo] **(-s, -s)** nt video; **Videoaufnahme** f video (recording); **Videokamera** f video camera; **Videorekorder** m video recorder; **Videospiel** nt video game; **Videotext** m teletext

Vieh [fiː] **(-(e)s)** nt cattle pl; (Nutztiere) livestock; (umg: Tier) animal; **viehisch** adj bestial; **Viehzucht** f (live)stock od cattle breeding

viel [fiːl] adj a lot of, much ▷ adv a lot, much; **in ~em** in many respects; **noch (ein)mal so ~** (Zeit etc) as much (time etc) again; **einer zu ~** one too many; **~ zu wenig** much too little; **~ beschäftigt** very busy; **~ geprüft** (hum) sorely tried; **~ sagend** significant; **~ versprechend** promising; **viele** pl a lot of, many; **gleich viele (Angestellte/Anteile** etc**)** the same number (of employees/shares etc)

vielerlei adj a great variety of

vielerorts adv in many places

viel- zW: **vielfach** adj, adv many times; **auf vielfachen Wunsch** at the request of many people; **Vielfache, s** nt (Math) multiple; **um ein Vielfaches** many times over; **Vielfalt (-)** f variety; **vielfältig** adj varied, many-sided; **Vielfraß** m glutton

vielleicht [fiˈlaɪçt] adv perhaps; (in Bitten) by any chance; **du bist ~ ein Idiot!** (umg) you really are an idiot!

viel- zW: **vielmal, vielmals** adv many times; **danke vielmals** many thanks; **ich bitte vielmals um Entschuldigung!** I do apologize!; **vielmehr** adv rather, on the contrary; **vielsagend** adj significant; **vielschichtig** adj (fig) complex; **vielseitig** adj many-sided; (Ausbildung) all-round attr; (Interessen) varied; (Mensch, Gerät) versatile; **vielversprechend** adj promising; **Völkerstaat** m multinational state

vier [fiːr] num four; **alle ~e von sich strecken** (umg) to stretch out; **Vierbeiner** m (hum) four-legged friend; **Viereck (-(e)s, -e)** nt four-sided figure; (gleichseitig) square; **viereckig** adj four-sided; square; **vierhundert** num four hundred; **vierkant** adj, adv (Naut) square; **vierköpfig** adj: **eine vierköpfige Familie** a family of four; **Viermächteabkommen** nt four-power agreement

viert adj: **wir gingen zu ~** four of us went

Viertaktmotor m four-stroke engine

vierte, r, s [ˈfiːrtə(r, s)] adj fourth

vierteilen vt to quarter

Viertel [ˈfɪrtəl] **(-s, -)** nt quarter; **ein ~ Leberwurst** a quarter of liver sausage; **Viertelfinale** nt quarter finals pl; **Vierteljahr** nt three months pl, quarter (COMM, FIN); **Vierteljahresschrift** f quarterly; **vierteljährlich** adj quarterly; **Viertelnote** f crotchet (Brit), quarter note (US); **Viertelstunde** f quarter of an hour

vier- zW: **viertürig** adj four-door attr; **Vierwaldstättersee** m Lake Lucerne; **vierzehn** [ˈfɪrtseːn] num fourteen; **in vierzehn Tagen** in a fortnight (Brit), in two weeks (US); **vierzehntägig** adj fortnightly; **vierzehnte, r, s** adj fourteenth

vierzig [ˈfɪrtsɪç] num forty; **Vierzigstundenwoche** f forty-hour week

Vierzimmerwohnung f four-room flat (Brit) od apartment (US)

Vietnam [viɛtˈnam] **(-s)** nt Vietnam

Vietnamese [viɛtnaˈmeːzə] **(-n, -n)** m, **Vietnamesin** f Vietnamese

vietnamesisch adj Vietnamese

Vikar [viˈkaːr] **(-s, -e)** m curate

Villa [ˈvɪla] **(-, Villen)** f villa

Villenviertel nt (prosperous) residential area

violett [vioˈlɛt] adj violet

Violinbogen m violin bow

Violine [vioˈliːnə] **(-, -n)** f violin

Violinkonzert nt violin concerto

Violinschlüssel m treble clef

virtuell [vɪrtuˈɛl] adj (Comput) virtual; **~e Realität** virtual reality

virtuos [vɪrtu'oːs] *adj* virtuoso *attrib*
Virtuose [vɪrtu'oːzə] (**-n, -n**) *m* virtuoso
Virtuosin [vɪrtu'oːzɪn] *f* virtuoso
Virtuosität [vɪrtuozi'tɛt] *f* virtuosity
Virus ['viːrʊs] (**-, Viren**) *m od nt* (*also Comput*) virus
Virus- *in zw* viral: **Virusinfektion** *f* virus infection
Visage [vi'zaːʒə] (**-, -n**) (*pej*) *f* face, (ugly) mug (*umg*)
Visagist, in [viza'ʒɪst(ɪn)] *m(f)* make-up artist
vis-à-vis, vis-a-vis [viza'viː] *adv* (*veraltet*): ~ **(von)** opposite (to) ▷ *präp +dat* opposite (to)
Visier [vi'ziːr] (**-s, -e**) *nt* gunsight; (*am Helm*) visor
Vision [vizi'oːn] *f* vision
Visite [vi'ziːtə] (**-, -n**) *f* (*Med*) visit
Visitenkarte *f* visiting card
visuell [vizu'ɛl] *adj* visual
Visum ['viːzʊm] (**-s, Visa** *od* **Visen**) *nt* visa; **Visumzwang** *m* obligation to hold a visa
vital [vi'taːl] *adj* lively, full of life; (*lebenswichtig*) vital
Vitamin [vita'miːn] (**-s, -e**) *nt* vitamin; **Vitaminmangel** *m* vitamin deficiency
Vitrine [vi'triːnə] (**-, -n**) *f* (*Schrank*) glass cabinet; (*Schaukasten*) showcase, display case
Vivisektion [vivizɛktsi'oːn] *f* vivisection
Vize ['fiːtsə] *m* (*umg*) number two; (: *Vizemeister*) runner-up ▷ *in zw* vice-
v. J. *abk* (= *vorigen Jahres*) of the previous *od* last year
Vlies [fliːs] (**-es, -e**) *nt* fleece
v. M. *abk* (= *vorigen Monats*) ult.
V-Mann *m abk* = **Verbindungsmann; Vertrauensmann**
VN *pl abk* (= *Vereinte Nationen*) UN
VO *abk* = **Verordnung**
Vogel ['foːɡəl] (**-s, ⁻**) *m* bird; **einen ~ haben** (*umg*) to have bats in the belfry; **den ~ abschießen** (*umg*) to surpass everyone (*ironisch*); **Vogelbauer** *nt* birdcage; **Vogelbeerbaum** *m* rowan (tree); **Vogeldreck** *m* bird droppings *pl*; **Vogelperspektive** *f* bird's-eye view; **Vogelschau** *f* bird's-eye view; **Vogelscheuche** *f* scarecrow; **Vogelschutzgebiet** *nt* bird sanctuary; **Vogel-Strauß-Politik** *f* head-in-the-sand policy
Vogesen [vo'ɡeːzən] *pl* Vosges *pl*
Voicemail ['vɔɪsmeːl] *f* (*Tel*) voice mail
Vokabel [vo'kaːbəl] (**-, -n**) *f* word
Vokabular [vokabu'laːr] (**-s, -e**) *nt* vocabulary
Vokal [vo'kaːl] (**-s, -e**) *m* vowel
Volk [fɔlk] (**-(e)s, ⁻er**) *nt* people; (*Nation*) nation; **etw unters ~ bringen** (*Nachricht*) to spread sth
Völker- *zW*: **Völkerbund** *m* League of Nations; **Völkerkunde** *f* ethnology; **Völkermord** *m* genocide; **Völkerrecht** *nt* international law; **völkerrechtlich** *adj* according to international law; **Völkerverständigung** *f* international understanding; **Völkerwanderung** *f* migration

Volks- *zW*: **Volksabstimmung** *f* referendum; **Volksarmee** *f* People's Army; **Volksbegehren** *nt* petition for a referendum; **Volksdeutsche, r** *f(m) dekl wie adj* ethnic German; **volkseigen** *adj* (*DDR*) nationally-owned; **Volksfeind** *m* enemy of the people; **Volksfest** *nt* popular festival; (*Jahrmarkt*) fair
Volkshochschule *f* adult education classes *pl*; *see culture note*

VOLKSHOCHSCHULE

The *Volkshochschule* (VHS) is an institution which offers Adult Education classes. No set qualifications are necessary to attend. For a small fee adults can attend both vocational and non-vocational classes in the day-time or evening.

Volks- *zW*: **Volkslauf** *m* fun run; **Volkslied** *nt* folk song; **Volksmund** *m* vernacular; **Volkspolizei** *f* (*DDR*) People's Police; **Volksrepublik** *f* people's republic; **Volksschule** *f* ≈ primary school (*Brit*), ≈ elementary school (*US*); **Volksseuche** *f* epidemic; **Volksstamm** *m* tribe; **Volksstück** *nt* folk play in dialect; **Volkstanz** *m* folk dance; **Volkstrauertag** *m* ≈ Remembrance Day (*Brit*), ≈ Memorial Day (*US*); **volkstümlich** *adj* popular; **Volkswirtschaft** *f* national economy; (*Fach*) economics *sing*, political economy; **Volkswirtschaftler** *m* economist; **Volkszählung** *f* (national) census
voll [fɔl] *adj* full ▷ *adv* fully; (*Tafel*) to cover (with writing); **jdn für ~ nehmen** (*umg*) to take sb seriously; **aus dem V~en schöpfen** to draw on unlimited resources; **in ~er Größe** (*Bild*) life-size(d); (*bei plötzlicher Erscheinung etc*) large as life; ~ **sein** (*umg: satt*) to be full (up); (: *betrunken*) to be plastered; ~ **und ganz** completely; *siehe auch* **vollmachen; vollschreiben; volltanken**
vollauf [fɔl'|aʊf] *adv* amply; ~ **zu tun haben** to have quite enough to do
voll- *zW*: **Vollbad** *nt* (proper) bath; **Vollbart** *m* full beard; **Vollbeschäftigung** *f* full employment; **Vollbesitz** *m*: **im Vollbesitz** +*gen* in full possession of; **Vollblut** *nt* thoroughbred; **vollblütig** *adj* full-blooded; **Vollbremsung** *f* emergency stop; **vollbringen** *unreg vt untr* to accomplish; **Volldampf** *m* (*Naut*): **mit Volldampf** at full steam; **vollenden** *vt untr* to finish, complete; **vollendet** *adj* (*vollkommen*) perfect; (*Tänzer etc*) accomplished; **vollends** *adv* completely; **Vollendung** *f* completion
voller *adj* fuller; ~ **Flecken/Ideen** full of stains/ideas
Völlerei [fœlə'raɪ] *f* gluttony
Volleyball ['vɔliːbal] (**-(e)s**) *m* volleyball
voll- *zW*: **vollfett** *adj* full-fat; **Vollgas** *nt*: **mit Vollgas** at full throttle; **Vollgas geben** to step on it
völlig ['fœlɪç] *adj* complete ▷ *adv* completely

V

voll- *zW*: **volljährig** *adj* of age; **Vollkaskoversicherung** *f* fully comprehensive insurance; **vollkommen** *adj* perfect; (*völlig*) complete, absolute; **Vollkommenheit** *f* perfection; **Vollkornbrot** *nt* wholemeal (*Brit*) *od* whole-wheat (*US*) bread; **volllaufen** *unreg vi*: **etw volllaufen lassen** to fill sth up; **vollmachen** *vt* to fill (up); **Vollmacht** *f* authority, power of attorney; **Vollmatrose** *m* able-bodied seaman; **Vollmilch** *f* full-cream milk; **Vollmond** *m* full moon; **Vollnarkose** *f* general anaesthetic (*Brit*) *od* anesthetic (*US*); **Vollpension** *f* full board; **vollschlank** *adj* plump, stout; **vollschreiben** *unreg vt* (*Heft, Seite*) to fill; **vollständig** *adj* complete; **vollstrecken** *vt untr* to execute; **volltanken** *vt*, *vi* to fill up; **Volltreffer** *m* (*lit, fig*) bull's-eye; **Vollversammlung** *f* general meeting; **Vollwaise** *f* orphan; **vollwertig** *adj* full *attrib*; (*Stellung*) equal; **Vollwertkost** *f* wholefoods *pl*; **vollzählig** *adj* complete; (*anwesend*) in full number; **vollziehen** *unreg vt untr* to carry out ▷ *vr untr* to happen; **Vollzug** *m* execution

Volontär, in [volɔnˈtɛːr(ɪn)] (**-s, -e**) *m(f)* trainee

Volt [vɔlt] (**-od -(e)s, -**) *nt* volt

Volumen [voˈluːmən] (**-s, -od Volumina**) *nt* volume

vom [fɔm] = **von dem**

◯ **SCHLÜSSELWORT**

von [fɔn] *präp +dat* **1** (*Ausgangspunkt*) from; **von ... bis** from ... to; **von morgens bis abends** from morning till night; **von ... nach ...** from ... to ...; **von ... an** from ...; **von ... aus** from ...; **von dort aus** from there; **etw von sich aus tun** to do sth of one's own accord; **von mir aus** (*umg*) if you like, I don't mind; **von wo/wann ...?** where/when ... from?

2 (*Ursache, im Passiv*) by; **ein Gedicht von Schiller** a poem by Schiller; **von etw müde** tired from sth

3 (*als Genitiv*) of; **ein Freund von mir** a friend of mine; **nett von dir** nice of you; **jeweils zwei von zehn** two out of every ten

4 (*über*) about; **er erzählte vom Urlaub** he talked about his holiday

5: von wegen! (*umg*) no way!

voneinander *adv* from each other

vonseiten, von Seiten [fɔnˈzaɪtn] *präp +gen* on the part of

vonstattengehen [fɔnˈʃtatən-] *unreg vi* to proceed, go

◯ **SCHLÜSSELWORT**

vor [foːr] *präp +dat* **1** (*räumlich*) in front of

2 (*zeitlich, Reihenfolge*) before; **ich war vor ihm da** I was there before him; **X kommt vor Y** X comes before Y; **vor zwei Tagen** two days ago; **5 (Minuten) vor 4** 5 (minutes) to 4; **vor**

Kurzem a little while ago

3 (*Ursache*) with; **vor Wut/Liebe** with rage/ love; **vor Hunger sterben** to die of hunger; **vor lauter Arbeit** because of work

4: vor allem, vor allen Dingen above all ▷ *präp +akk* (*räumlich*) in front of; **vor sich hin summen** to hum to oneself ▷ *adv*: **vor und zurück** backwards and forwards

Vor- *zW*: **Vorabdruck** *m* preprint; **Vorabend** *m* evening before, eve; **Vorahnung** *f* presentiment, premonition

voran [foˈran] *adv* before, ahead; **voranbringen** *unreg vt* to make progress with; **vorangehen** *unreg vi* to go ahead; **einer Sache** *dat* **vorangehen** to precede sth; **vorangehend** *adj* previous; **vorankommen** *unreg vi* to make progress, come along

Voranschlag [ˈfoːr|anʃlaːk] *m* estimate

voranstellen [foˈranʃtɛlən] *vt +dat* to put in front (of); (*fig*) to give precedence (over)

Vorarbeiter [ˈfoːr|arbaɪtər] *m* foreman

voraus [foˈraʊs] *adv* ahead; (*zeitlich*) in advance; **jdm ~ sein** to be ahead of sb; **im V~** in advance; **vorausbezahlen** *vt* to pay in advance; **vorausgehen** *unreg vi* to go (on) ahead; (*fig*) to precede; **voraushaben** *unreg vt*: **jdm etw voraushaben** to have the edge on sb in sth; **Voraussage** *f* prediction; **voraussagen** *vt* to predict; **vorausgehen** *unreg vi* to foresee; **voraussetzen** *vt* to assume; (*sicher annehmen*) to take for granted; (*erfordern: Kenntnisse, Geduld*) to require, demand; **vorausgesetzt, dass ...** provided that ...; **Voraussetzung** *f* requirement, prerequisite; **unter der Voraussetzung, dass ...** on condition that ...; **Voraussicht** *f* foresight; **aller Voraussicht nach** in all probability; **in der Voraussicht, dass ...** anticipating that ...; **voraussichtlich** *adv* probably; **Vorauszahlung** *f* advance payment

Vorbau [ˈfoːrbaʊ] (**-(e)s, -ten**) *m* porch; (*Balkon*) balcony

vorbauen [ˈfoːrbaʊən] *vt* to build up in front ▷ *vi +dat* to take precautions (against)

Vorbedacht [ˈfoːrbədaxt] *m*: **mit/ohne ~** (*Überlegung*) with/without due consideration; (*Absicht*) intentionally/unintentionally

Vorbedingung [ˈfoːrbədɪŋʊŋ] *f* precondition

Vorbehalt [ˈfoːrbəhalt] *m* reservation, proviso; **unter dem ~, dass ...** with the reservation that ...

vorbehalten *unreg vt*: **sich/jdm etw ~** to reserve sth (for o.s.)/for sb; **alle Rechte ~** all rights reserved

vorbehaltlich *präp +gen* (*form*) subject to

vorbehaltlos *adj* unconditional ▷ *adv* unconditionally

vorbei [fɔrˈbaɪ] *adv* by, past; **aus und ~** over and done with; **damit ist es nun ~** that's all over now; **vorbeibringen** *unreg* (*umg*) *vt* to drop off; **vorbeigehen** *unreg vi* to pass by, go past; **vorbeikommen** unreg vi: **bei jdm vorbeikommen** to drop od call in on sb; **vorbeireden** vi: **an etw** dat **vorbeireden** to talk around sth

vorbelastet ['fo:rbəlastət] adj (fig) handicapped (Brit), handicaped (US)

Vorbemerkung ['fo:rbəmɛrkʊŋ] f introductory remark

vorbereiten ['fo:rbəraɪtən] vt to prepare

Vorbereitung f preparation

vorbestellen ['fo:rbəʃtɛlən] vt to book (in advance), reserve

Vorbestellung f advance booking

vorbestraft ['fo:rbəʃtraft] adj previously convicted, with a record

Vorbeugehaft f preventive custody

vorbeugen ['fo:rbɔygən] vt, vr to lean forward ▷ vi +dat to prevent

vorbeugend adj preventive

Vorbeugung f prevention; **zur ~ gegen** for the prevention of

Vorbild ['fo:rbɪlt] nt model; **sich** dat **jdn zum ~ nehmen** to model o.s. on sb; **vorbildlich** adj model, ideal

Vorbildung ['fo:rbɪldʊŋ] f educational background

Vorbote ['fo:rbo:tə] m (fig) herald

vorbringen ['fo:rbrɪŋən] unreg vt to voice; (Meinung etc) to advance, state; (umg: nach vorne) to bring to the front

vordatieren ['fo:rdati:rən] vt (Schreiben) to postdate

Vorder- zW: **Vorderachse** f front axle; **Vorderansicht** f front view; **Vorderasien** nt Near East

vordere, r, s adj front

Vorder- zW: **Vordergrund** m foreground; **im Vordergrund stehen** (fig) to be to the fore; **Vordergrundprogramm** nt (Comput) foreground program; **vorderhand** adv for the present; **Vordermann** (-**(e)s**, pl -**männer**) m man in front; **jdn auf Vordermann bringen** (umg) to get sb to shape up; **Vorderseite** f front (side); **Vordersitz** m front seat

vorderste, r, s adj front

vordrängen ['fo:rdrɛŋən] vr to push to the front

vordringen ['fo:rdrɪŋən] unreg vi: **bis zu jdm/ etw ~** to get as far as sb/sth

vordringlich adj urgent

Vordruck ['fo:rdrʊk] m form

vorehelich ['fo:r|e:əlɪç] adj premarital

voreilig ['fo:r|aɪlɪç] adj hasty, rash; **~e Schlüsse ziehen** to jump to conclusions

voreinander [fo:r|aɪ'nandər] adv (räumlich) in front of each other; (einander gegenüber) face to face

voreingenommen ['fo:r|aɪngənɔmən] adj bias(s)ed; **Voreingenommenheit** f bias

voreingestellt ['fo:r|aɪngəʃtɛlt] adj: **~er Parameter** (Comput) default (parameter)

vorenthalten ['fo:r|ɛnthaltən] unreg vt: **jdm etw ~** to withhold sth from sb

Vorentscheidung ['fo:r|ɛntʃaɪdʊŋ] f preliminary decision

vorerst ['fo:r|e:rst] adv for the moment od present

Vorfahr ['fo:rfa:r] (-**en**, -**en**) m ancestor

vorfahren unreg vi to drive (on) ahead; (vors Haus etc) to drive up

Vorfahrt f (Aut) right of way; **„~ (be)achten"** "give way" (Brit), "yield" (US)

Vorfahrts- zW: **Vorfahrtsregel** f rule of right of way; **Vorfahrtsschild** nt "give way" (Brit) od "yield" (US) sign; **Vorfahrtsstraße** f major road

Vorfall ['fo:rfal] m incident

vorfallen unreg vi to occur

Vorfeld ['fo:rfɛlt] nt (fig): **im ~ (+gen)** in the run-up (to)

Vorfilm ['fo:rfɪlm] m short

vorfinden ['fo:rfɪndən] unreg vt to find

Vorfreude ['fo:rfrɔydə] f anticipation

vorfühlen ['fo:rfy:lən] vi (fig) to put out feelers

vorführen ['fo:rfy:rən] vt to show, display; (Theaterstück, Kunststücke): **(jdm) etw ~** to perform sth (to od in front of sb); **dem Gericht ~** to bring before the court

Vorgabe ['fo:rga:bə] f (Sport) handicap

Vorgang ['fo:rgaŋ] m (Ereignis) event; (Ablauf) course of events; (Chem etc) process

Vorgänger, in ['fo:rgɛŋər(ɪn)] (-**s**, -) m(f) predecessor

vorgaukeln ['fo:rgaukəln] vt: **jdm etw ~** to lead sb to believe in sth

vorgeben ['fo:rge:bən] unreg vt to pretend, use as a pretext; (Sport) to give an advantage od a start of

Vorgebirge ['fo:rgəbɪrgə] nt foothills pl

vorgefasst ['fo:rgəfast] adj preconceived

vorgefertigt ['fo:rgəfɛrtɪçt] adj prefabricated

Vorgefühl ['fo:rgəfy:l] nt anticipation; (etwas Böses) presentiment

vorgehen ['fo:rge:ən] unreg vi (voraus) to go (on) ahead; (nach vorn) to go forward; (handeln) to act, proceed; (Uhr) to be fast; (Vorrang haben) to take precedence; (passieren) to go on

Vorgehen (-s) nt action

Vorgehensweise f proceedings pl

vorgerückt ['fo:rgərʏkt] adj (Stunde) late; (Alter) advanced

Vorgeschichte ['fo:rgəʃɪçtə] f prehistory; (von Fall, Krankheit) past history

Vorgeschmack ['fo:rgəʃmak] m foretaste

Vorgesetzte, r ['fo:rgəzɛtstə(r)] f(m) superior

vorgestern ['fo:rgɛstərn] adv the day before yesterday; **von ~** (fig) antiquated

vorgreifen ['fo:rgraɪfən] unreg vi +dat to anticipate; **jdm ~** to forestall sb

vorhaben ['fo:rha:bən] unreg vt to intend; **hast du schon was vor?** have you got anything on?

Vorhaben (-s, -) nt intention

Vorhalle ['fo:rhalə] f (Diele) entrance hall; (von Parlament) lobby

vorhalten ['fo:rhaltən] unreg vt to hold od put up ▷ vi to last; **jdm etw ~** to reproach sb for

v

sth

Vorhaltung f reproach

Vorhand ['foːrhant] f forehand

vorhanden [foːr'handən] adj existing; (erhältlich) available; **Vorhandensein (-s)** nt existence, presence

Vorhang ['foːrhaŋ] m curtain

Vorhängeschloss ['foːrhɛŋəʃlɔs] nt padlock

Vorhaut ['foːrhaʊt] f (Anat) foreskin

vorher [foːr'heːr] adv before(hand); **vorherbestimmen** vt (Schicksal) to preordain; **vorhergehen** unreg vi to precede

vorherig [foːr'heːrɪç] adj previous

Vorherrschaft ['foːrhɛrʃaft] f predominance, supremacy

vorherrschen vi to predominate

vorher- ** zW: **Vorhersage f forecast; **vorhersagen** vt to forecast, predict; **vorhersehbar** adj predictable; **vorhersehen** unreg vt to foresee

vorhin [foːr'hɪn] adv not long ago, just now

Vorhinein ['foːrhɪnaɪn] adv: **im ~** beforehand

Vorhof ['foːrhoːf] m forecourt

vorig ['foːrɪç] adj previous, last

Vorjahr ['foːrjaːr] nt previous year, year before

vorjährig ['foːrjɛːrɪç] adj of the previous year

vorjammern ['foːrjamərn] vt, vi: **jdm (etwas) ~** to moan to sb (about sth)

Vorkämpfer, in ['foːrkɛmpfər(ɪn)] m(f) pioneer

Vorkaufsrecht ['foːrkaʊfsrɛçt] nt option to buy

Vorkehrung ['foːrkeːrʊŋ] f precaution

Vorkenntnis ['foːrkɛntnɪs] f previous knowledge

vorknöpfen ['foːrknœpfən] vt (fig: umg): **sich** dat **jdn ~** to take sb to task

vorkommen ['foːrkɔmən] unreg vi to come forward; (geschehen, sich finden) to occur; (scheinen) to seem (to be); **so was soll ~!** that's life!; **sich** dat **dumm** etc **~** to feel stupid etc

Vorkommen nt occurrence; (Min) deposit

Vorkommnis ['foːrkɔmnɪs] **(-ses, -se)** nt occurrence

**Vorkriegs- ** ['foːrkriːks] in zw pre-war

vorladen ['foːrlaːdən] unreg vt (bei Gericht) to summons

Vorladung f summons

Vorlage ['foːrlaːgə] f model, pattern; (das Vorlegen) presentation; (von Beweismaterial) submission; (Gesetzesvorlage) bill; (Sport) pass

vorlassen ['foːrlasən] unreg vt to admit; (überholen lassen) to let pass; (vorgehen lassen) to allow to go in front

Vorlauf ['foːrlaʊf] m (preliminary) heat (of running event)

Vorläufer m forerunner

vorläufig ['foːrlɔyfɪç] adj temporary; (provisorisch) provisional

vorlaut ['foːrlaʊt] adj impertinent, cheeky

Vorleben ['foːrleːbən] nt past (life)

vorlegen ['foːrleːgən] vt to put in front, present; (Beweismaterial etc) to produce, submit; **jdm etw ~** to put sth before sb

Vorleger (-s, -) m mat

Vorleistung ['foːrlaɪstʊŋ] f (Fin: Vorausbezahlung) advance (payment); (Vorarbeit) preliminary work; (Pol) prior concession

vorlesen ['foːrleːzən] unreg vt to read (out)

Vorlesung f (Univ) lecture

Vorlesungsverzeichnis nt lecture timetable

vorletzte, r, s ['foːrlɛtstə(r, s)] adj last but one, penultimate

Vorliebe ['foːrliːbə] f preference, special liking; **etw mit ~ tun** to particularly like doing sth

vorliebnehmen [foːr'liːp-] unreg vi: **~ mit** to make do with

vorliegen ['foːrliːgən] unreg vi to be (here); **etw liegt jdm vor** sb has sth; **etw liegt gegen jdn vor** sb is charged with sth

vorliegend adj present, at issue

vorm. abk (= vormittags) a.m.; (= vormals) formerly

vormachen ['foːrmaxən] vt: **jdm etw ~** to show sb how to do sth; **jdm etwas ~** (fig) to fool sb; **mach mir doch nichts vor** don't try and fool me

Vormachtstellung ['foːrmaxtʃtɛlʊŋ] f supremacy

vormals ['foːrmals] adv formerly

Vormarsch ['foːrmarʃ] m advance

vormerken ['foːrmɛrkən] vt to book; (notieren) to make note of; (bei Bestellung) to take an order for

Vormittag ['foːrmɪtaːk] m morning; **am ~** in the morning

vormittags adv in the morning, before noon

Vormund ['foːrmʊnt] **(-(e)s, -e** od **-münder)** m guardian

vorn [fɔrn] adv in front; **von ~ anfangen** to start at the beginning; **nach ~** to the front; **er betrügt sie von ~ bis hinten** he deceives her right, left and centre

Vorname ['foːrnaːmə] m first od Christian name

vornan [fɔrn'an] adv at the front

vorne ['fɔrnə] = **vorn**

vornehm ['foːrneːm] adj distinguished; (Manieren etc) refined; (Kleid) elegant; **in ~en Kreisen** in polite society

vornehmen unreg vt (fig) to carry out; **sich** dat **etw ~** to start on sth; (beschließen) to decide to do sth; **sich** dat **zu viel ~** to take on too much; **sich** dat **jdn ~** to tell sb off

vornehmlich adv chiefly, specially

vorneweg ['fɔrnəvɛk], **vornweg** ['fɔrnvɛk] adv in front; (als Erstes) first

vornherein ['fɔrnhɛraɪn] adv: **von ~** from the start

Vorort ['foːr|ɔrt] m suburb; **Vorortzug** m commuter train

vorprogrammiert ['foːrprogramiːrt] adj (Erfolg, Antwort) automatic

Vorrang ['foːrraŋ] m precedence, priority

vorrangig adj of prime importance, primary

Vorrat ['foːrraːt] m stock, supply; **solange der ~ reicht** (Comm) while stocks last

vorrätig ['foːrrɛːtɪç] adj in stock

Vorratskammer f store cupboard; (für Lebensmittel) larder

Vorraum m anteroom; (Büro) outer office

vorrechnen ['fo:rrɛçnən] vt: **jdm etw ~** to calculate sth for sb; (als Kritik) to point sth out to sb

Vorrecht ['fo:rrɛçt] nt privilege

Vorrede ['fo:rre:də] f introductory speech; (Theat) prologue (Brit), prolog (US)

Vorrichtung ['fo:rrɪçtʊŋ] f device, gadget

vorrücken ['fo:rrʏkən] vi to advance ▷ vt to move forward

Vorruhestand ['fo:rru:əʃtant] m early retirement

Vorrunde ['fo:rrʊndə] f (Sport) preliminary round

Vors. abk = **Vorsitzende(r)**

vorsagen ['fo:rza:gən] vt to recite; (Sch: zuflüstern) to tell secretly, prompt

Vorsaison ['fo:rzɛzõ:] f early season, low season

Vorsatz ['fo:rzats] m intention; (Jur) intent; **einen ~ fassen** to make a resolution

vorsätzlich ['fo:rzɛtslɪç] adj intentional; (Jur) premeditated ▷ adv intentionally

Vorschau ['fo:rʃaʊ] f (Rundf, TV) (programme (Brit) od program (US)) preview; (Film) trailer

Vorschein ['fo:rʃaɪn] m: **zum ~ kommen** (lit: sichtbar werden) to appear; (fig: entdeckt werden) to come to light

vorschieben ['fo:rʃi:bən] unreg vt to push forward; (vor etw) to push across; (fig) to put forward as an excuse; **jdn ~** to use sb as a front

vorschießen ['fo:rʃi:sən] unreg (umg) vt: **jdm Geld ~** to advance sb money

Vorschlag ['fo:rʃla:k] m suggestion, proposal

vorschlagen ['fo:rʃla:gən] unreg vt to suggest, propose

Vorschlaghammer m sledgehammer

vorschnell ['fo:rʃnɛl] adj hasty, too quick

vorschreiben ['fo:rʃraɪbən] unreg vt (Dosis) to prescribe; (befehlen) to specify; **(jdm) etw ~** (lit) to write sth out (for sb); **ich lasse mir nichts ~** I won't be dictated to

Vorschrift ['fo:rʃrɪft] f regulation(s pl), rule(s pl); (Anweisungen) instruction(s pl); **jdm ~en machen** to give sb orders; **Dienst nach ~** work-to-rule (Brit), slowdown (US)

vorschriftsmäßig adv as per regulations/instructions

Vorschub ['fo:rʃu:p] m: **jdm/einer Sache ~ leisten** to encourage sb/sth

Vorschule ['fo:rʃu:lə] f nursery school

vorschulisch ['fo:rʃu:lɪʃ] adj preschool attr

Vorschuss ['fo:rʃʊs] m advance

vorschützen ['fo:rʃʏtsən] vt to put forward as a pretext; (Unwissenheit) to plead

vorschweben ['fo:rʃve:bən] vi: **jdm schwebt etw vor** sb has sth in mind

vorsehen ['fo:rze:ən] unreg vt to provide for; (planen) to plan ▷ vr to take care, be careful

Vorsehung f providence

vorsetzen ['fo:rzɛtsən] vt to move forward; (davor setzen): **~ vor** +akk to put in front of; (anbieten): **jdm etw ~** to offer sb sth

Vorsicht ['fo:rzɪçt] f caution, care; **~!** look out!, take care!; (auf Schildern) caution!, danger!; **~ Stufe!** mind the step!; **etw mit ~ genießen** (umg) to take sth with a pinch of salt

vorsichtig adj cautious, careful

vorsichtshalber adv just in case

Vorsichtsmaßnahme f precaution

Vorsilbe ['fo:rzɪlbə] f prefix

vorsintflutlich ['fo:rzɪntflu:tlɪç] (umg) adj antiquated

Vorsitz ['fo:rzɪts] m chair(manship); **den ~ führen** to chair the meeting

Vorsitzende, r f(m) chairman/-woman, chair(person)

Vorsorge ['fo:rzɔrgə] f precaution(s pl); (Fürsorge) provision(s pl)

vorsorgen vi: **~ für** to make provision(s pl) for

Vorsorgeuntersuchung ['fo:rzɔrgə|ʊntər-zu:xʊŋ] f medical check-up

vorsorglich ['fo:rzɔrklɪç] adv as a precaution

Vorspann ['fo:rʃpan] m (Film, TV) opening credits pl; (Presse) opening paragraph

vorspannen vt (Pferde) to harness

Vorspeise ['fo:rʃpaɪzə] f hors d'œuvre, starter

Vorspiegelung ['fo:rʃpi:gəlʊŋ] f: **das ist (eine) ~ falscher Tatsachen** it's all sham

Vorspiel ['fo:rʃpi:l] nt prelude; (bei Geschlechtsverkehr) foreplay

vorspielen vt: **jdm etw ~** (Mus) to play sth to sb; (Theat) to act sth to sb; (fig) to act out a sham of sth in front of sb

vorsprechen ['fo:rʃprɛçən] unreg vt to say out loud; (vortragen) to recite ▷ vi (Theat) to audition; **bei jdm ~** to call on sb

vorspringend ['fo:rʃprɪŋənt] adj projecting; (Nase, Kinn) prominent

Vorsprung ['fo:rʃprʊŋ] m projection; (Felsvorsprung) ledge; (fig) advantage, start

Vorstadt ['fo:rʃtat] f suburbs pl

Vorstand ['fo:rʃtant] m executive committee; (Comm) board (of directors); (Person) director; (Leiter) head

Vorstandssitzung f (von Firma) board meeting

Vorstandsvorsitzende, r f(m) chairperson

vorstehen ['fo:rʃte:ən] unreg vi to project; **einer Sache** dat ~ (fig) to be the head of sth

Vorsteher, in (-s, -) m(f) (von Abteilung) head; (von Gefängnis) governor; (Bahnhofsvorsteher) stationmaster

vorstellbar adj conceivable

vorstellen ['fo:rʃtɛlən] vt to put forward; (vor etw) to put in front; (bekannt machen) to introduce; (darstellen) to represent ▷ vr to introduce o.s.; (bei Bewerbung) to go for an interview; **sich** dat **etw ~** to imagine sth; **stell dir das nicht so einfach vor** don't think it's so easy

Vorstellung f (Bekanntmachen) introduction; (Theat etc) performance; (Gedanke) idea

Vorstellungsgespräch nt interview

Vorstellungsvermögen nt powers of

V

Vorstoß | v. u. z.

imagination *pl*

Vorstoß ['foːrʃtoːs] *m* advance; *(fig: Versuch)* attempt

vorstoßen *unreg vt, vi* to push forward

Vorstrafe ['foːrʃtraːfə] *f* previous conviction

vorstrecken ['foːrʃtrɛkən] *vt* to stretch out; *(Geld)* to advance

Vorstufe ['foːrʃtuːfə] *f* first step(s *pl*)

Vortag ['foːrtak] *m*: **am ~ einer Sache** *gen* on the day before sth

Vortal ['foːrtaːl] *nt* (*Comput*) vortal

vortasten ['foːrtastən] *vr*: **sich langsam zu etw ~** to approach sth carefully

vortäuschen ['foːrtɔyʃən] *vt* to pretend, feign

Vortäuschung *f*: **unter ~ falscher Tatsachen** under false pretences (*Brit*) *od* pretenses (*US*)

Vorteil ['foːrtaɪl] (**-s, -e**) *m*: **~ (gegenüber)** advantage (over); **im ~ sein** to have the advantage; **die Vor- und Nachteile** the pros and cons; **vorteilhaft** *adj* advantageous; *(Kleider)* flattering; *(Geschäft)* lucrative

Vortr. *abk* = **Vortrag**

Vortrag ['foːrtraːk] (**-(e)s, Vorträge**) *m* talk, lecture; *(Vortragsart)* delivery; *(von Gedicht)* rendering; *(Comm)* balance carried forward; **einen ~ halten** to give a lecture *od* talk

vortragen ['foːrtraːgən] *unreg vt* to carry forward *(auch COMM)*; *(fig)* to recite; *(Rede)* to deliver; *(Lied)* to perform; *(Meinung etc)* to express

Vortragsabend *m* lecture evening; *(mit Musik)* recital; *(mit Gedichten)* poetry reading

Vortragsreihe *f* series of lectures

vortrefflich [foːr'trɛflɪç] *adj* excellent

vortreten ['foːrtreːtən] *unreg vi* to step forward; *(Augen etc)* to protrude

Vortritt ['foːrtrɪt] *m*: **jdm den ~ lassen** *(lit, fig)* to let sb go first

vorüber [fo'ryːbər] *adv* past, over; **vorübergehen** *unreg vi* to pass (by); **vorübergehen an** *+dat (fig)* to pass over; **vorübergehend** *adj* temporary, passing

Voruntersuchung ['foːr|ʊntɐzuːxʊŋ] *f (Med)* preliminary examination; *(Jur)* preliminary investigation

Vorurteil ['foːr|ʊrtaɪl] *nt* prejudice

vorurteilsfrei *adj* unprejudiced, open-minded

Vorverkauf ['foːrfɛrkaʊf] *m* advance booking

Vorverkaufsstelle *f* advance booking office

vorverlegen ['foːrfɛrleːgən] *vt (Termin)* to bring forward

Vorw. *abk* = **Vorwort**

vorwagen ['foːrvaːgən] *vr* to venture forward

Vorwahl ['foːrvaːl] *f* preliminary election; *(Tel)* dialling (*Brit*) *od* area (*US*) code

Vorwand ['foːrvant] (**-(e)s, Vorwände**) *m* pretext

Vorwarnung ['foːrvarnʊŋ] *f* (advance) warning

vorwärts ['foːrvɛrts] *adv* forward; **~!** (*umg*) let's go!; *(Mil)* forward march!; *siehe auch* **vorwärtsgehen; vorwärtskommen;**
Vorwärtsgang *m (Aut etc)* forward gear; **vorwärtsgehen** *unreg vi* to progress; **vorwärtskommen** *unreg vi* to get on, make progress

Vorwäsche *f* prewash

Vorwaschgang *m* prewash

vorweg [foːr'vɛk] *adv* in advance; **Vorwegnahme** (**-, -n**) *f* anticipation; **vorwegnehmen** *unreg vt* to anticipate

vorweisen ['foːrvaɪzən] *unreg vt* to show, produce

vorwerfen ['foːrvɛrfən] *unreg vt*: **jdm etw ~** to reproach sb for sth, accuse sb of sth; **sich** *dat* **nichts vorzuwerfen haben** to have nothing to reproach o.s. with; **das wirft er mir heute noch vor** he still holds it against me; **Tieren/Gefangenen etw ~** *(lit)* to throw sth down for the animals/prisoners

vorwiegend ['foːrviːgənt] *adj* predominant ▷ *adv* predominantly

vorwitzig *adj* saucy, cheeky

Vorwort ['foːrvɔrt] (**-(e)s, -e**) *nt* preface

Vorwurf ['foːrvʊrf] (**-(e)s, ̈e**) *m* reproach; **jdm/sich Vorwürfe machen** to reproach sb/o.s.

vorwurfsvoll *adj* reproachful

Vorzeichen ['foːrtsaɪçən] *nt (Omen)* omen; *(Med)* early symptom; *(Math)* sign

vorzeigen ['foːrtsaɪgən] *vt* to show, produce

Vorzeit ['foːrtsaɪt] *f* prehistoric times *pl*

vorzeitig *adj* premature

vorziehen ['foːrtsiːən] *unreg vt* to pull forward; *(Gardinen)* to draw; *(zuerst behandeln, abfertigen)* to give priority to; *(lieber haben)* to prefer

Vorzimmer ['foːrtsɪmər] *nt* anteroom; *(Büro)* outer office

Vorzug ['foːrtsuːk] *m* preference; *(gute Eigenschaft)* merit, good quality; *(Vorteil)* advantage; *(Eisenb)* relief train; **einer Sache** *dat* **den ~ geben** *(form)* to prefer sth; *(Vorrang geben)* to give sth precedence

vorzüglich [foːr'tsyːklɪç] *adj* excellent, first-rate

Vorzugsaktien *pl* preference shares (*Brit*), preferred stock (*US*)

vorzugsweise *adv* preferably; *(hauptsächlich)* chiefly

Votum ['voːtʊm] (**-s, Voten**) *nt* vote

Voyeur [voa'jøːr] (**-s, -e**) *m* voyeur; **Voyeurismus** [voajøˈrɪsmʊs] *m* voyeurism

v. T. *abk* (= *vom Tausend*) per thousand

vulgär [vʊlˈgɛːr] *adj* vulgar

Vulkan [vʊlˈkaːn] (**-s, -e**) *m* volcano; **Vulkanausbruch** *m* volcanic eruption

vulkanisieren [vʊlkaniˈziːrən] *vt* to vulcanize

v. u. Z. *abk* (= *vor unserer Zeitrechnung*) B.C.

W, w [veː] *nt* W, w; **W wie Wilhelm** ≈ W for William

W. *abk* (= *West(en)*) W

w. *abk* = **wenden; werktags; westlich;** (= *weiblich*) f

Waage ['vaːgə] **(-, -n)** *f* scales *pl*; (*Astrol*) Libra; **sich** *dat* **die ~ halten** (*fig*) to balance one another; **waagerecht** *adj* horizontal

Waagschale *f* (scale) pan; **(schwer) in die ~ fallen** (*fig*) to carry weight

wabbelig ['vabəlɪç], **wabblig** ['vablɪç] *adj* wobbly

Wabe ['vaːbə] **(-, -n)** *f* honeycomb

wach [vax] *adj* awake; (*fig*) alert; **~ werden** to wake up

Wachablösung *f* changing of the guard; (*Mensch*) relief guard; (*fig: Regierungswechsel*) change of government

Wache (-, -n) *f* guard, watch; **~ halten** to keep watch; **~ stehen** *od* **schieben** (*umg*) to be on guard (duty)

wachen *vi* to be awake; (*Wache halten*) to keep watch; **bei jdm ~** to sit up with sb

wachhabend *adj attrib* duty

Wachhund *m* watchdog, guard dog; (*fig*) watchdog

Wacholder [va'xɔldər] **(-s, -)** *m* juniper

wachrütteln ['vaxrɣtəln] *vt* (*fig*) to (a)rouse

Wachs [vaks] **(-es, -e)** *nt* wax

wachsam ['vaxzaːm] *adj* watchful, vigilant, alert; **Wachsamkeit** *f* vigilance

wachsen[1] *unreg vi* to grow

wachsen[2] *vt* (*Skier*) to wax

Wachsfigurenkabinett *nt* waxworks (exhibition)

Wachsmalstift, Wachsstift *m* wax crayon

wächst [vekst] *vb siehe* **wachsen**[1]

Wachstuch ['vakstuːx] *nt* oilcloth

Wachstum ['vakstuːm] **(-s)** *nt* growth

Wachstums- *zW*: **Wachstumsbranche** *f* growth industry; **Wachstumsgrenze** *f* limits of growth; **wachstumshemmend** *adj* growth-inhibiting; **Wachstumsrate** *f* growth rate; **Wachstumsschmerzen** *pl* growing pains; **Wachstumsstörung** *f* disturbance of growth

Wachtel ['vaxtəl] **(-, -n)** *f* quail

Wächter ['veçtər] **(-s, -)** *m* guard; (*Parkwächter*) warden, keeper; (*Museumswächter*,

Parkplatzwächter) attendant

Wachtmeister *m* officer

Wachtposten *m* guard, sentry

Wachtturm, Wachturm *m* watchtower

Wach- und Schließgesellschaft *f* security corps

wackelig *adj* shaky, wobbly; **auf ~en Beinen stehen** to be wobbly on one's legs; (*fig*) to be unsteady

Wackelkontakt *m* loose connection

wackeln *vi* to shake; (*fig: Position*) to be shaky; **mit den Hüften/dem Schwanz ~** to wiggle one's hips/wag its tail

wacker ['vakər] *adj* valiant, stout; **sich ~ schlagen** (*umg*) to put up a brave fight

wacklig *adj* = **wackelig**

Wade ['vaːdə] **(-, -n)** *f* (*Anat*) calf

Waffe ['vafə] **(-, -n)** *f* weapon; **jdn mit seinen eigenen ~n schlagen** (*fig*) to beat sb at his own game

Waffel ['vafəl] **(-, -n)** *f* waffle; (*Eiswaffel*) wafer

Waffen- *zW*: **Waffengewalt** *f*: **mit Waffengewalt** by force of arms; **Waffenlager** *nt* (*von Armee*) ordnance depot; (*von Terroristen*) cache; **Waffenschein** *m* firearms *od* gun licence (*Brit*), firearms license (*US*); **Waffenschmuggel** *m* gunrunning, arms smuggling; **Waffenstillstand** *m* armistice, truce

Wagemut ['vaːgəmuːt] *m* daring

Wagen ['vaːgən] **(-s, -)** *m* vehicle; (*Auto*) car, automobile (*US*); (*Eisenb*) car, carriage (*Brit*); (*Pferdewagen*) wag(g)on, cart

wagen *vt* to venture, dare

Wagen- *zW*: **Wagenführer** *m* driver; **Wagenheber (-s, -)** *m* jack; **Wagenpark** *m* fleet of cars; **Wagenrückholtaste** *f* (*Schreibmaschine*) carriage return (key); **Wagenrücklauf** *m* carriage return

Waggon [va'gõː] **(-s, -s)** *m* wag(g)on; (*Güterwaggon*) goods van (*Brit*), freight truck (*US*)

waghalsig ['vaːkhalzɪç] *adj* foolhardy

Wagnis ['vaːknɪs] **(-ses, -se)** *nt* risk

Wagon (-s, -s) *m* = **Waggon**

Wahl [vaːl] **(-, -en)** *f* choice; (*Pol*) election; **erste ~** (*Qualität*) top quality; (*Gemüse, Eier*) grade one; **zweite ~** (*Comm*) seconds *pl*; **aus freier ~** of one's own free choice; **wer die ~ hat, hat die Qual** (*Sprichwort*) he is *od* you are *etc* spoilt for choice; **die ~ fiel auf ihn** he was chosen; **sich zur ~ stellen** (*Pol etc*) to stand (*Brit*) *od* run (for parliament *etc*)

wählbar *adj* eligible

Wahl- *zW*: **wahlberechtigt** *adj* entitled to vote; **Wahlbeteiligung** *f* poll, turnout; **Wahlbezirk** *m* (*Pol*) ward

wählen ['vɛ:lən] *vt* to choose; (*Pol*) to elect, vote for; (*Tel*) to dial ▷ *vi* to choose; (*Pol*) to vote; (*Tel*) to dial

Wähler, in (-s, -) *m(f)* voter; **Wählerabwanderung** *f* voter drift; **wählerisch** *adj* fastidious, particular; **Wählerschaft** *f* electorate

Wahl- *zW*: **Wahlfach** *nt* optional subject; **wahlfrei** *adj*: **wahlfreier Zugriff** (*Comput*) random access; **Wahlgang** *m* ballot; **Wahlgeschenk** *nt* pre-election vote-catching gimmick; **Wahlheimat** *f* country of adoption; **Wahlhelfer** *m* (*im Wahlkampf*) election assistant; (*bei der Wahl*) polling officer; **Wahlkabine** *f* polling booth; **Wahlkampf** *m* election campaign; **Wahlkreis** *m* constituency; **Wahlleiter** *m* returning officer; **Wahlliste** *f* electoral register; **Wahllokal** *nt* polling station; **wahllos** *adv* at random; (*nicht wählerisch*) indiscriminately; **Wahlrecht** *nt* franchise; **allgemeines Wahlrecht** universal franchise; **das aktive Wahlrecht** the right to vote; **das passive Wahlrecht** eligibility (for political office); **Wahlspruch** *m* motto; **Wahlurne** *f* ballot box; **wahlweise** *adv* alternatively

Wählzeichen *nt* (*Tel*) dialling tone (*Brit*), dial tone (*US*)

Wahn [va:n] **(-(e)s)** *m* delusion; **Wahnsinn** *m* madness; **wahnsinnig** *adj* insane, mad ▷ *adv* (*umg*) incredibly; **wahnwitzig** *adj* crazy *attrib* ▷ *adv* terribly

wahr [va:r] *adj* true; **da ist (et)was W~es dran** there's some truth in that

wahren *vt* to maintain, keep

während ['vɛ:rən] *vi* to last

während *präp +gen* during ▷ *konj* while; **währenddessen** *adv* meanwhile

wahr- *zW*: **wahrhaben** *unreg vt*: **etw nicht wahrhaben wollen** to refuse to admit sth; **wahrhaft** *adv* (*tatsächlich*) truly; **wahrhaftig** *adj* true, real ▷ *adv* really

Wahrheit *f* truth; **die ~ sagen** to tell the truth

wahrheitsgetreu *adj* (*Bericht*) truthful; (*Darstellung*) faithful

wahrnehmen *unreg vt* to perceive; (*Frist*) to observe; (*Veränderungen etc*) to be aware of; (*Gelegenheit*) to take; (*Interessen, Rechte*) to look after

Wahrnehmung *f* perception; observing; awareness; taking; looking after

wahrsagen *vi* to predict the future, tell fortunes

Wahrsager *m* fortune-teller

wahrscheinlich [va:r'ʃaınlıç] *adj* probable ▷ *adv* probably; **Wahrscheinlichkeit** *f* probability; **aller Wahrscheinlichkeit nach** in all probability

Währung ['vɛ:rʊŋ] *f* currency

Währungs- *zW*: **Währungseinheit** *f* monetary unit; **Währungspolitik** *f* monetary policy; **Währungsraum** *m* currency area; **Währungsreserven** *pl* official reserves *pl*; **Währungsunion** *f* monetary union

Wahrzeichen *nt* (*Gebäude, Turm etc*) symbol; (*von Stadt, Verein*) emblem

Waise ['vaızə] **(-, -n)** *f* orphan

Waisen- *zW*: **Waisenhaus** *nt* orphanage; **Waisenkind** *nt* orphan; **Waisenknabe** *m*: **gegen dich ist er ein Waisenknabe** (*umg*) he's no match for you; **Waisenrente** *f* orphan's allowance

Wal [va:l] **(-(e)s, -e)** *m* whale

Wald [valt] **(-(e)s, ⁻er)** *m* wood(s *pl*); (*groß*) forest; **Waldbrand** *m* forest fire

Wäldchen ['vɛltçən] *nt* copse, grove

Waldhorn *nt* (*Mus*) French horn

waldig ['valdıç] *adj* wooded

Wald- *zW*: **Waldlehrpfad** *m* nature trail; **Waldmeister** *m* (*Bot*) woodruff; **Waldsterben** *nt* loss of trees due to pollution

Wald- und Wiesen- (*umg*) *in zw* common-or-garden

Waldweg *m* woodland *od* forest path

Wales [weılz] *nt* Wales

Walfang ['va:lfaŋ] *m* whaling

Walfisch ['valfıʃ] *m* whale

Waliser, in [va'li:zər(ın)] **(-s, -)** *m(f)* Welshman, Welshwoman

walisisch *adj* Welsh

Walkman® ['wɔ:kman] **(-s)** *m* Walkman®, personal stereo

Wall [val] **(-(e)s, ⁻e)** *m* embankment; (*Bollwerk*) rampart

wallfahren *vi untr* to go on a pilgrimage

Wallfahrer, in *m(f)* pilgrim

Wallfahrt *f* pilgrimage

Wallis ['valıs] **(-)** *nt*: **das ~** Valais

Wallone [va'lo:nə] **(-n, -n)** *m*, **Wallonin** *f* Walloon

Walnuss ['valnʊs] *f* walnut

Walross ['valrɔs] *nt* walrus

walten ['valtən] *vi* (*geh*): **Vernunft ~ lassen** to let reason prevail

Walzblech (-(e)s) *nt* sheet metal

Walze ['valtsə] **(-, -n)** *f* (*Gerät*) cylinder; (*Fahrzeug*) roller

walzen *vt* to roll (out)

wälzen ['vɛltsən] *vt* to roll (over); (*Bücher*) to hunt through; (*Probleme*) to deliberate on ▷ *vr* to wallow; (*vor Schmerzen*) to roll about; (*im Bett*) to toss and turn

Walzer ['valtsər] **(-s, -)** *m* waltz

Wälzer ['vɛltsər] **(-s, -)** (*umg*) *m* tome

Wampe ['vampə] **(-, -n)** (*umg*) *f* paunch

Wand (-, ⁻e) *f* wall; (*Trennwand*) partition; (*Bergwand*) precipice; (*Felswand*) (rock) face; (*fig*)

barrier; **weiß wie die ~** as white as a sheet;
jdn an die ~ spielen to put sb in the shade;
(Sport) to outplay sb
wand *etc* [vant] *vb siehe* **winden**
Wandel ['vandəl] **(-s)** *m* change; **wandelbar** *adj*
changeable, variable
Wandelhalle *f* foyer
wandeln *vt, vr* to change ▷ *vi (gehen)* to walk
Wanderausstellung *f* touring exhibition
Wanderbühne *f* touring theatre *(Brit) od*
theater *(US)*
Wanderer (-s, -) *m* hiker, rambler
Wanderin *f* hiker, rambler
Wanderkarte *f* hiker's map
Wanderlied *nt* hiking song
wandern *vi* to hike; *(Blick)* to wander;
(Gedanken) to stray; *(umg: in den Papierkorb etc)*
to land
Wanderpreis *m* challenge trophy
Wanderschaft *f* travelling *(Brit)*, traveling *(US)*
Wanderung *f* walk, hike; *(von Tieren, Völkern)*
migration
Wanderweg *m* trail, (foot)path
Wandgemälde *nt* mural
Wandlung *f* change; *(völlige Umwandlung)*
transformation; *(Rel)* transubstantiation
Wand- *zW:* **Wandmalerei** *f* mural
painting; **Wandschirm** *m* (folding) screen;
Wandschrank *m* cupboard
wandte *etc* ['vantə] *vb siehe* **wenden**
Wandteppich *m* tapestry
Wandverkleidung *f* panelling
Wange ['vaŋə] **(-, -n)** *f* cheek
wankelmütig ['vaŋkəlmy:tıç] *adj* fickle,
inconstant
wanken ['vaŋkən] *vi* to stagger; *(fig)* to waver
wann [van] *adv* when; **seit ~ bist/hast du ...?**
how long have you been/have you had ...?
Wanne ['vanə] **(-, -n)** *f* tub
Wanze ['vantsə] **(-, -n)** *f (Abhörgerät, Zool)* bug
WAP *nt abk (Comput: = Wireless Application Protocol)*
WAP
WAP-Handy *nt* WAP phone
Wappen ['vapən] **(-s, -)** *nt* coat of arms, crest;
Wappenkunde *f* heraldry
wappnen *vr (fig)* to prepare o.s.; **gewappnet**
sein to be forearmed
war *etc* [va:r] *vb siehe* **sein**
warb *etc* [varp] *vb siehe* **werben**
Ware ['va:rə] **(-, -n)** *f* ware; **Waren** *pl* goods *pl*
wäre *etc* ['vɛ:rə] *vb siehe* **sein**
Waren- *zW:* **Warenbestand** *m* stock;
Warenhaus *nt* department store; **Warenlager**
nt stock, store; **Warenmuster** *nt* sample;
Warenprobe *f* sample; **Warenrückstände** *pl*
backlog *sing*; **Warensendung** *f* trade sample
(sent by post); **Warenzeichen** *nt* trademark
warf *etc* [varf] *vb siehe* **werfen**
warm [varm] *adj* warm; *(Essen)* hot;
(umg: homosexuell) queer; **mir ist ~** I'm warm;
mit jdm ~ werden *(umg)* to get close to
sb; **~ laufen** *(Aut)* to warm up; *siehe auch*
warmhalten

Wärme ['vɛrmə] **(-, -n)** *f* warmth; **10 Grad ~** 10
degrees above zero
wärmen *vt, vr* to warm (up), heat (up)
Wärmflasche *f* hot-water bottle
warm- *zW:* **Warmfront** *f (Met)* warm
front; **warmhalten** *unreg vt:* **sich** *dat*
jdn warmhalten: *(fig)* to keep in with
sb; **warmherzig** *adj* warm-hearted;
Warmwassertank *m* hot-water tank
Warnblinkanlage *f (Aut)* hazard warning
lights *pl*
Warndreieck *nt* warning triangle
warnen ['varnən] *vt* to warn
Warnstreik *m* token strike
Warnung *f* warning
Warschau ['varʃau] **(-s)** *nt* Warsaw;
Warschauer Pakt *m* Warsaw Pact
Warte (-, -n) *f* observation point; *(fig)*
viewpoint
warten ['vartən] *vi* to wait ▷ *vt (Auto, Maschine)*
to service; **~ auf** *+akk* to wait for; **auf sich ~**
lassen to take a long time; **warte mal!** wait
a minute!; *(überlegend)* let me see; **mit dem**
Essen auf jdn ~ to wait for sb before eating
Wärter, in ['vɛrtər(ın)] **(-s, -)** *m(f)* attendant
Wartesaal *m (Eisenb)* waiting room
Wartezimmer *nt* waiting room
Wartung *f (von Auto, Maschine)* servicing; **~ und**
Instandhaltung maintenance
warum [va'rum] *adv* why; **~ nicht gleich so!**
that's better
Warze ['vartsə] **(-, -n)** *f* wart
was [vas] *pron* what; *(umg: etwas)* something;
das, ~ ... that which ...; **~ für ...?** what sort *od*
kind of ...?
Wasch- *zW:* **Waschanlage** *f (für Autos)* car
wash; **waschbar** *adj* washable; **Waschbecken**
nt washbasin
Wäsche ['vɛʃə] **(-, -n)** *f* wash(ing); *(Bettwäsche)*
linen; *(Unterwäsche)* underwear; **dumm aus**
der ~ gucken *(umg)* to look stupid
waschecht *adj (Farbe)* fast; *(fig)* genuine
Wäsche- *zW:* **Wäscheklammer** *f* clothes peg
(Brit), clothespin *(US)*; **Wäschekorb** *m* dirty
clothes basket; **Wäscheleine** *f* washing line
(Brit), clothes line *(US)*
waschen ['vaʃən] *unreg vt, vi* to wash ▷ *vr* to
(have a) wash; **sich** *dat* **die Hände ~** to wash
one's hands; **~ und legen** *(Haare)* to shampoo
and set
Wäscherei [vɛʃə'raı] *f* laundry
Wäscheschleuder *f* spin-dryer
Wasch- *zW:* **Waschgang** *m* stage of the
washing programme *(Brit) od* program *(US)*;
Waschküche *f* laundry room; **Waschlappen**
m face cloth *od* flannel *(Brit)*, washcloth *(US)*;
(umg) softy; **Waschmaschine** *f* washing
machine; **Waschmittel** *nt* detergent;
Waschpulver *nt* washing powder;
Waschsalon *m* Launderette® *(Brit)*,
Laundromat® *(US)*
wäscht [vɛʃt] *vb siehe* **waschen**
Waschtisch *m* washstand

W

Washington ['wɔʃɪŋtən] (**-s**) nt Washington
Wasser[1] ['vasər] (**-s, -**) nt water; **~ abstoßend**
water-repellent; **dort wird auch nur mit
~ gekocht** (fig) they're no different from
anybody else (there); **ins ~ fallen** (fig) to fall
through; **mit allen ~n gewaschen sein** (umg)
to be a shrewd customer; **~ lassen** (euph) to
pass water; **jdm das ~ abgraben** (fig) to take
the bread from sb's mouth
Wasser[2] (**-s, -**) nt (Flüssigkeit) water; (Med)
lotion; (Parfüm) cologne; (Mineralwasser)
mineral water
Wässerchen nt: **er sieht aus, als ob er kein ~
trüben könnte** he looks as if butter wouldn't
melt in his mouth
Wasser- zW: **wasserdicht** adj watertight;
(Stoff, Uhr) waterproof; **Wasserfall** m waterfall;
Wasserfarbe f watercolour (Brit), watercolor
(US); **wassergekühlt** adj (Aut) water-cooled;
Wassergraben m (Sport) water jump; (um Burg)
moat; **Wasserhahn** m tap, faucet (US)
wässerig ['vɛsərɪç] adj watery
Wasser- zW: **Wasserkessel** m kettle; (Tech)
boiler; **Wasserkraftwerk** nt hydroelectric
power station; **Wasserleitung** f water pipe;
(Anlagen) plumbing; **Wassermann** m (Astrol)
Aquarius
wassern vi to land on the water
wässern ['vɛsərn] vt, vi to water
Wasser- zW: **Wasserscheide** f watershed;
wasserscheu adj afraid of water;
Wasserschutzpolizei f (auf Flüssen) river
police; (im Hafen) harbour (Brit) od harbor
(US) police; (auf der See) coastguard service;
Wasserski nt water-skiing; **Wasserspiegel** m
(Oberfläche) surface of the water; (Wasserstand)
water level; **Wasserstand** m water level;
Wasserstoff m hydrogen; **Wasserstoffbombe**
f hydrogen bomb; **Wasserverbrauch** m water
consumption; **Wasserwaage** f spirit level;
Wasserwelle f shampoo and set; **Wasserwerfer**
(**-s, -**) m water cannon; **Wasserwerk** nt
waterworks; **Wasserzeichen** nt watermark
waten ['va:tən] vi to wade
watscheln ['va:tʃəln] vi to waddle
Watt[1] [vat] (**-(e)s, -en**) nt mud flats pl
Watt[2] (**-s, -**) nt (Elek) watt
Watte (**-, -n**) f cotton wool (Brit), absorbent
cotton (US)
Wattenmeer (**-(e)s**) nt mud flats pl
Wattestäbchen nt cotton(-wool) swab
wattieren [va'ti:rən] vt to pad
WC [ve:'tse:] (**-s, -s**) nt abk (= Wasserklosett) WC
Web [wɛb] nt (Comput): **das ~** the Web; **im ~** on
the Web
Webadresse f (= URL, Internet-Adresse) web
address
weben ['ve:bən] unreg vt to weave
Weber, in (**-s, -**) m(f) weaver
Weberei [ve:bə'raɪ] f (Betrieb) weaving mill
Webpage ['wɛbpa:gə] nt web page
Webseite ['wɛbzaɪtə] f Web page, web site
Webstuhl ['ve:pʃtu:l] m loom

Wechsel ['vɛksəl] (**-s, -**) m change;
(Geldwechsel) exchange; (Comm) bill of
exchange; **Wechselbäder** pl alternating
hot and cold baths pl; **Wechselbeziehung**
f correlation; **Wechselforderungen** pl
(Comm) bills receivable pl; **Wechselgeld**
nt change; **wechselhaft** adj (Wetter)
variable; **Wechselinhaber** m bearer;
Wechseljahre pl change of life, menopause;
in die Wechseljahre kommen to start the
change; **Wechselkurs** m rate of exchange;
Wechselkursmechanismus m Exchange Rate
Mechanism, ERM
wechseln vt to change; (Blicke) to exchange ▷ vi
to change; (einander ablösen) to alternate
wechselnd adj changing; (Stimmungen)
changeable; (Winde, Bewölkung) variable
Wechsel- zW: **wechselseitig** adj reciprocal;
Wechselsprechanlage f two-way intercom;
Wechselstrom m alternating current;
Wechselstube f currency exchange, bureau
de change; **Wechselverbindlichkeiten** pl bills
payable pl; **wechselweise** adv alternately;
Wechselwirkung f interaction
wecken ['vɛkən] vt to wake (up); (fig) to arouse;
(Bedarf) to create; (Erinnerungen) to revive
Wecker (**-s, -**) m alarm clock; **jdm auf den ~
fallen** (umg) to get on sb's nerves
Weckglas® nt preserving jar
Weckruf m (Tel) alarm call
wedeln ['ve:dəln] vi (mit Schwanz) to wag; (mit
Fächer) to fan; (Ski) to wedel
weder ['ve:dər] konj neither; **~ ... noch ...**
neither ... nor ...
Weg [ve:k] (**-(e)s, -e**) m way; (Pfad) path; (Route)
route; **sich auf den ~ machen** to be on one's
way; **jdm aus dem ~ gehen** to keep out of
sb's way; **jdm nicht über den ~ trauen** (fig)
not to trust sb an inch; **den ~ des geringsten
Widerstandes gehen** to follow the line of
least resistance; **etw in die ~e leiten** to
arrange sth; **jdm Steine in den ~ legen** (fig)
to put obstacles in sb's way; siehe auch **zuwege**
weg [vɛk] adv away, off; **über etw** akk **~ sein**
to be over sth; **er war schon ~** he had already
left; **nichts wie** od **nur ~ von hier!** let's get
out of here!; **~ damit!** (mit Schere etc) put it/
them away!; **Finger ~!** hands off!
Wegbereiter (**-s, -**) m pioneer
wegblasen unreg vt to blow away; **wie
weggeblasen sein** (fig) to have vanished
wegbleiben unreg vi to stay away; **mir bleibt
die Spucke weg!** (umg) I am absolutely
flabbergasted!
wegen ['ve:gən] (umg) präp +gen od +dat because
of; **von ~!** you must be joking!
weg- zW: **wegfahren** unreg vi to drive
away; (abfahren) to leave; **Wegfahrsperre**
f (Aut): **(elektronische) Wegfahrsperre**
(electronic) immobilizer; **wegfallen** unreg vi to
be left out; (Ferien, Bezahlung) to be cancelled;
(aufhören) to cease; **weggehen** unreg vi to go
away, leave; (umg: Ware) to sell; **weghören** vi

to turn a deaf ear; **wegjagen** *vt* to chase away; **wegkommen** *unreg vi*: **(bei etw) gut/schlecht wegkommen** (*umg*) to come off well/badly (with sth); **weglassen** *unreg vt* to leave out; **weglaufen** *unreg vi* to run away *od* off; **das läuft (dir) nicht weg!** (*fig hum*) that can wait; **weglegen** *vt* to put aside; **wegmachen** (*umg*) *vt* to get rid of; **wegmüssen** *unreg* (*umg*) *vi* to have to go; **wegnehmen** *unreg vt* to take away

Wegrand ['veːkrant] *m* wayside

weg- *zW*: **wegräumen** *vt* to clear away; **wegschaffen** *vt* to clear away; **wegschließen** *unreg vt* to lock away; **wegschnappen** *vt*: **(jdm) etw wegschnappen** to snatch sth away (from sb); **wegstecken** *vt* to put away; (*umg*: *verkraften*) to cope with; **wegtreten** *unreg vi* (*Mil*): **wegtreten!** dismiss!; **geistig weggetreten sein** (*umg*: *geistesabwesend*) to be away with the fairies; **wegtun** *unreg vt* to put away

wegweisend ['veːgvaɪzənt] *adj* pioneering *attrib*, revolutionary

Wegweiser ['veːgvaɪzər] **(-s, -)** *m* road sign, signpost; (*fig: Buch etc*) guide

Wegwerf- ['vɛkvɛrf] *in zw* disposable

weg- *zW*: **wegwerfen** *unreg vt* to throw away; **wegwerfend** *adj* disparaging; **Wegwerfgesellschaft** *f* throw-away society; **wegwollen** *unreg vi* (*verreisen*) to want to go away; **wegziehen** *unreg vi* to move away

weh [veː] *adj* sore

Wehe ['veːə] **(-, -n)** *f* drift

wehe *interj*: **~, wenn du ...** you'll regret it if you ...; **~ dir!** you dare!

Wehen *pl* (*Med*) contractions *pl*; **in den ~ liegen** to be in labour (*Brit*) *od* labor (*US*)

wehen *vt*, *vi* to blow; (*Fahnen*) to flutter

weh- *zW*: **wehklagen** *vi untr* to wail; **wehleidig** *adj* oversensitive to pain; (*jammernd*) whiny, whining; **Wehmut** *f* melancholy; **wehmütig** *adj* melancholy

Wehr¹ [veːr] **(-(e)s, -e)** *nt* weir

Wehr² [veːr] **(-, -en)** *f* (*Feuerwehr*) fire brigade (*Brit*) *od* department (*US*) ▷ *in zw* defence (*Brit*), defense (*US*); **sich zur ~ setzen** to defend o.s.

Wehrdienst *m* military service; *see culture note*

⬤ **WEHRDIENST**

⬤ *Wehrdienst* is military service which is
⬤ still compulsory in Germany. All young
⬤ men receive their call-up papers at 18 and
⬤ all who are pronounced physically fit
⬤ are required to spend ten months in the
⬤ *Bundeswehr*. Conscientious objectors are
⬤ allowed to do *Zivildienst* as an alternative,
⬤ on attending a hearing and presenting
⬤ their case.

Wehrdienstverweigerer *m* ≈ conscientious objector

wehren *vr* to defend o.s.

Wehr- *zW*: **wehrlos** *adj* defenceless (*Brit*), defenseless (*US*); **jdm wehrlos ausgeliefert sein** to be at sb's mercy; **Wehrmacht** *f* armed forces *pl*; **Wehrpflicht** *f* conscription; **wehrpflichtig** *adj* liable for military service; **Wehrübung** *f* reserve duty training exercise

wehtun ['veːtuːn] *unreg vt*: **jdm/sich ~** to hurt sb/o.s.

Wehwehchen (*umg*) *nt* (minor) complaint

Weib [vaɪp] **(-(e)s, -er)** *nt* woman, female (*pej*)

Weibchen *nt* (*Ehefrau*) little woman; (*Zool*) female

weibisch ['vaɪbɪʃ] *adj* effeminate

weiblich *adj* feminine

weich [vaɪç] *adj* soft; (*Ei*) soft-boiled; **~e Währung** soft currency

Weiche **(-, -n)** *f* (*Eisenb*) points *pl*; **die ~n stellen** (*lit*) to switch the points; (*fig*) to set the course

weichen *unreg vi* to yield, give way; **(nicht) von jdm** *od* **von jds Seite ~** (not) to leave sb's side

Weichensteller **(-s, -)** *m* pointsman

weich- *zW*: **Weichheit** *f* softness; **Weichkäse** *m* soft cheese; **weichlich** *adj* soft, namby-pamby; **Weichling** *m* wimp; **Weichspüler** **(-s, -)** *m* fabric conditioner; **Weichteile** *pl* soft parts *pl*; **Weichtier** *nt* mollusc (*Brit*), mollusk (*US*)

Weide ['vaɪdə] **(-, -n)** *f* (*Baum*) willow; (*Gras*) pasture

weiden *vi* to graze ▷ *vr*: **sich an etw** *dat* **~** to delight in sth

Weidenkätzchen *nt* willow catkin

weidlich ['vaɪtlɪç] *adv* thoroughly

weigern ['vaɪgərn] *vr* to refuse

Weigerung ['vaɪgərʊŋ] *f* refusal

Weihe ['vaɪə] **(-, -n)** *f* consecration; (*Priesterweihe*) ordination

weihen *vt* to consecrate; (*widmen*) to dedicate; **dem Untergang geweiht** (*liter*) doomed

Weiher **(-s, -)** *m* pond

Weihnachten **(-)** *nt* Christmas; **fröhliche ~!** happy *od* merry Christmas!; **weihnachten** *vi unpers*: **es weihnachtet sehr** (*poetisch, ironisch*) Christmas is very much in evidence

weihnachtlich *adj* Christmas(sy)

Weihnachts- *zW*: **Weihnachtsabend** *m* Christmas Eve; **Weihnachtsbaum** *m* Christmas tree; **Weihnachtsgeld** *nt* Christmas bonus; **Weihnachtsgeschenk** *nt* Christmas present; **Weihnachtslied** *nt* Christmas carol; **Weihnachtsmann** *m* Father Christmas (*Brit*), Santa Claus

Weihnachtsmarkt *m* Christmas fair; *see culture note*

W

⬤ **WEIHNACHTSMARKT**

⬤ The *Weihnachtsmarkt* is a market held in
⬤ most large towns in Germany in the weeks
⬤ prior to Christmas. People visit it to buy
⬤ presents, toys and Christmas decorations,
⬤ and to enjoy the festive atmosphere. Food
⬤ and drink associated with the Christmas
⬤ festivities can also be eaten and drunk

there, for example, gingerbread and
mulled wine.

Weihnachtstag *m*: **(erster)** ~ Christmas day;
zweiter ~ Boxing Day (*Brit*)
Weihwasser *nt* holy water
weil [vaɪl] *konj* because
Weile ['vaɪlə] (-) *f* while, short time
Weiler ['vaɪlər] **(-s, -)** *m* hamlet
Weimarer Republik ['vaɪmarər repu'bliːk] *f*
Weimar Republic
Wein [vaɪn] **(-(e)s, -e)** *m* wine; (*Pflanze*) vine;
jdm reinen ~ einschenken (*fig*) to tell sb
the truth; **Weinbau** *m* cultivation of vines;
Weinbauer *m* wine-grower; **Weinbeere** *f* grape;
Weinberg *m* vineyard; **Weinbergschnecke** *f*
snail; **Weinbrand** *m* brandy
weinen *vt, vi* to cry; **das ist zum W~** it's
enough to make you cry *od* weep
weinerlich *adj* tearful
Wein- *zW*: **Weingegend** *f* wine-growing area;
Weingeist *m* (ethyl) alcohol; **Weinglas** *nt*
wine glass; **Weingut** *nt* wine-growing estate;
Weinkarte *f* wine list
Weinkrampf *m* crying fit
Wein- *zW*: **Weinlese** *f* vintage; **Weinprobe** *f*
wine tasting; **Weinrebe** *f* vine; **weinrot** *adj*
(*Farbe*) claret; **Weinstein** *m* tartar; **Weinstock**
m vine; **Weinstube** *f* wine bar; **Weintraube**
f grape
weise ['vaɪzə] *adj* wise
Weise (-, -n) *f* manner, way; (*Lied*) tune; **auf
diese** ~ in this way
Weise, r *f(m)* wise man, wise woman, sage
weisen *unreg vt* to show; **etw (weit) von sich ~**
(*fig*) to reject sth (emphatically)
Weisheit ['vaɪshaɪt] *f* wisdom
Weisheitszahn *m* wisdom tooth
weismachen ['vaɪsmaxən] *vt*: **er wollte uns
~, …** he would have us believe that …
weiß[1] [vaɪs] *vb siehe* **wissen**
weiß[2] *adj* white; **Weißblech** *nt* tin plate;
Weißbrot *nt* white bread; **weißen** *vt* to
whitewash; **Weißglut** *f* (*Tech*) incandescence;
jdn zur Weißglut bringen (*fig*) to make sb
see red; **Weißkohl** *m* (white) cabbage
Weißrussland *nt* B(y)elorussia
weißt [vaɪst] *vb siehe* **wissen**
Weißwandtafel *f* whiteboard; **interaktive ~**
interactive whiteboard
Weiß- *zW*: **Weißwaren** *pl* linen *sing*; **Weißwein**
m white wine; **Weißwurst** *f* veal sausage
Weisung ['vaɪzʊŋ] *f* instruction
weit [vaɪt] *adj* wide; (*Begriff*) broad; (*Reise,
Wurf*) long ▷ *adv* far; **~ blickend** far-seeing;
~ hergeholt far-fetched; **~ reichend** (*fig*)
far-reaching; **~ verbreitet** widespread; **~
verzweigt = weitverzweigt; in ~er Ferne**
in the far distance; **wie ~ ist es …?** how far
is it …?; **das geht zu ~** that's going too far;
~ und breit for miles around; **~ gefehlt!** far
from it!; **es so ~ bringen, dass …** to bring
it about that …; **~ zurückliegen** to be far

behind; **von W~em** from a long way off;
weitab *adv*: **weitab von** far (away) from;
weitaus *adv* by far; **Weitblick** *m* (*fig*) far-
sightedness; **weitblickend** *adj* far-seeing
Weite (-, -n) *f* width; (*Raum*) space; (*von
Entfernung*) distance
weiten *vt, vr* to widen
weiter ['vaɪtər] *adj* wider; (*zusätzlich*) further
▷ *adv* further; **wenn es ~ nichts ist, …** well,
if that's all (it is), …; **das hat ~ nichts zu
sagen** that doesn't really matter; **immer
~** on and on; (*Anweisung*) keep on (going);
~ nichts/niemand nothing/nobody
else; **weiterarbeiten** *vi* to go on working;
weiterbilden *vr* to continue one's studies;
Weiterbildung *f* further education
Weitere, s *nt* further details *pl*; **bis auf ~s** for
the time being; **ohne ~s** without further ado,
just like that
weiter- *zW*: **weiterempfehlen** *unreg vt* to
recommend (to others); **weitererzählen**
vt (*Geheimnis*) to pass on; **Weiterfahrt** *f*
continuation of the journey; **weiterführend**
adj (*Schule*) secondary (*Brit*), high (*US*);
weitergehen *unreg vi* to go on; **weiterhin**
adv: **etw weiterhin tun** to go on doing
sth; **weiterkommen** *unreg vi*: **nicht
weiterkommen** (*fig*) to be bogged down;
weiterleiten *vt* to pass on; **weitermachen** *vt,
vi* to continue; **weiterreisen** *vi* to continue
one's journey; **weitersagen** *vt*: **nicht
weitersagen!** don't tell anyone!; **weitersehen**
unreg vi: **dann sehen wir weiter** then
we'll see; **weiterverarbeiten** *vt* to process;
weiterwissen *unreg vi*: **nicht (mehr)
weiterwissen** (*verzweifelt sein*) to be at one's
wits' end
weit- *zW*: **weitgehend** *adj* considerable ▷ *adv*
largely; **weithin** *adv* widely; (*weitgehend*)
to a large extent; **weitläufig** *adj* (*Gebäude*)
spacious; (*Erklärung*) lengthy; (*Verwandter*)
distant; **weitreichend** *adj* (*fig*) far-reaching;
weitschweifig *adj* long-winded; **weitsichtig**
adj (*lit*) long-sighted (*Brit*), far-sighted
(*US*); (*fig*) far-sighted; **Weitsprung** *m* long
jump; **weitverbreitet** *adj* widespread;
weitverzweigt *adj* (*Straßensystem*) extensive;
Weitwinkelobjektiv *nt* (*Phot*) wide-angle lens
Weizen ['vaɪtsən] **(-s, -)** *m* wheat; **Weizenbier**
nt light, fizzy wheat beer; **Weizenkeime** *pl* (*Koch*)
wheatgerm *sing*
welch [vɛlç] *pron*: **~ ein(e) …** what a …

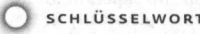

SCHLÜSSELWORT

welche, r, s *interrog pron* which; **welcher von
beiden?** which (one) of the two?; **welchen
hast du genommen?** which (one) did you
take?; **welche Freude!** what joy!
▷ *indef pron* some; (*in Fragen*) any; **ich habe
welche** I have some; **haben Sie welche?** do
you have any?
▷ *rel pron* (*bei Menschen*) who; (*bei Sachen*) which,

that; **welche(r, s) auch immer** whoever/whichever/whatever

welk [vɛlk] adj withered; **welken** vi to wither
Wellblech nt corrugated iron
Welle ['vɛlə] (-, -n) f wave; (Tech) shaft; **(hohe) ~n schlagen** (fig) to create (quite) a stir
Wellen- zW: **Wellenbereich** m waveband; **Wellenbrecher** m breakwater; **Wellengang** m: **starker Wellengang** heavy sea(s) od swell; **Wellenlänge** f (lit, fig) wavelength; **mit jdm auf einer Wellenlänge sein** (fig) to be on the same wavelength as sb; **Wellenlinie** f wavy line
Wellensittich m budgerigar
Wellpappe f corrugated cardboard
Welpe ['vɛlpə] (-n, -n) m pup, whelp; (von Wolf etc) cub
Welt [vɛlt] (-, -en) f world; **aus der ~ schaffen** to eliminate; **in aller ~** all over the world; **vor aller ~** in front of everybody; **auf die ~ kommen** to be born; **Weltall** nt universe; **Weltanschauung** f philosophy of life; **weltberühmt** adj world-famous; **weltbewegend** adj world-shattering; **Weltbild** nt conception of the world; (jds Ansichten) philosophy
Weltenbummler, in m(f) globetrotter
Weltergewicht ['vɛltərɡəvɪçt] nt (Sport) welterweight
weltfremd adj unworldly
Weltgesundheitsorganisation f World Health Organization
Welt- zW: **weltgewandt** adj sophisticated; **Weltkirchenrat** m World Council of Churches; **Weltkrieg** m world war; **weltlich** adj worldly; (nicht kirchlich) secular; **Weltliteratur** f world literature; **Weltmacht** f world power; **weltmännisch** adj sophisticated; **Weltmeister** m world champion; **Weltmeisterschaft** f world od world's (US) championship; (Fussball etc) World Cup; **Weltrang** m: **von Weltrang** world-famous; **Weltraum** m space; **Weltraumforschung** f space research; **Weltraumstation** f space station; **Weltreise** f trip round the world; **Weltruf** m worldwide reputation; **Weltsicherheitsrat** m (Pol) United Nations Security Council; **Weltstadt** f metropolis; **Weltuntergang** m (lit, fig) end of the world; **weltweit** adj worldwide; **Weltwirtschaft** f world economy; **Weltwirtschaftskrise** f world economic crisis; **Weltwunder** nt wonder of the world
wem [ve:m] dat von **wer** ▷ pron to whom
wen [ve:n] akk von **wer** ▷ pron whom
Wende ['vɛndə] (-, -n) f turn; (Veränderung) change; **die ~** (Pol) (the) reunification (of Germany); **Wendekreis** m (Geog) tropic; (Aut) turning circle
Wendeltreppe f spiral staircase
wenden unreg vt, vi, vr to turn; **bitte ~!** please turn over; **sich an jdn ~** to go/come to sb
Wendepunkt m turning point

wendig adj (lit, fig) agile; (Auto etc) manoeuvrable (Brit), maneuverable (US)
Wendung f turn; (Redewendung) idiom
wenig ['ve:nɪç] adj, adv little; **ein ~** a little; **er hat zu ~ Geld** he doesn't have enough money; **ein Exemplar zu ~** one copy too few
wenige ['ve:nɪɡə] pl few pl; **in ~n Tagen** in (just) a few days
weniger adj less; (mit pl) fewer ▷ adv less
Wenigkeit f trifle; **meine ~** (umg) little me
wenigste, r, s adj least
wenigstens adv at least
wenn [vɛn] konj if; (zeitlich) when; **~ auch ...** even if ...; **~ ich doch ...** if only I ...; **~ wir erst die neue Wohnung haben** once we get the new flat
Wenn nt: **ohne ~ und Aber** unequivocally
wennschon adv: **na ~!** so what?; **~, dennschon!** in for a penny, in for a pound!
wer [ve:r] pron who
Werbe- zW: **Werbeagentur** f advertising agency; **Werbeaktion** f advertising campaign; **Werbeantwort** f business reply card; **Werbebanner** nt banner; **Werbefernsehen** nt commercial television; **Werbefilm** m promotional film; **Werbegeschenk** nt promotional gift, freebie (umg); (zu Gekauftem) free gift; **Werbegrafiker, in** m(f) commercial artist; **Werbekampagne** f advertising campaign
werben ['vɛrbən] unreg vt to win; (Mitglied) to recruit ▷ vi to advertise; **um jdn/etw ~** to try to win sb/sth; **für jdn/etw ~** to promote sb/sth
Werbe- zW: **Werbespot** m commercial; **Werbetexter** (-s, -) m copywriter; **Werbetrommel** f: **die Werbetrommel (für etw) rühren** (umg) to beat the big drum (for sth); **werbewirksam** adj: **werbewirksam sein** to be good publicity
Werbung f advertising; (von Mitgliedern) recruitment; (TV etc: Werbeblock) commercial break; **~ um jdn/etw** promotion of sb/sth
Werbungskosten pl professional od business expenses pl
Werdegang ['ve:rdəɡaŋ] m development; (beruflich) career

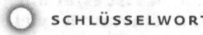

SCHLÜSSELWORT

werden ['ve:rdən] unreg (pt **wurde**, pp **geworden** od **(bei Passiv) worden**) vi to become; **was ist aus ihm/aus der Sache geworden?** what became of him/it?; **es ist nichts/gut geworden** it came to nothing/turned out well; **es wird Nacht/Tage** it's getting dark/light; **es wird bald ein Jahr, dass ...** it's almost a year since ...; **er wird am 8. Mai 36** he will be 36 on the 8th May; **mir wird kalt** I'm getting cold; **mir wird schlecht** I feel ill; **Erster werden** to come od be first; **das muss anders werden** that will have to change; **rot/zu Eis werden** to turn red/to ice; **was willst**

w

du (mal) werden? what do you want to be?;
die Fotos sind gut geworden the photos
turned out well
▷ *hilfsverb* **1** (*bei Futur*): **er wird es tun** he will *od*
he'll do it; **er wird das nicht tun** he will not
od he won't do it; **es wird gleich regnen** it's
going to rain any moment
2 (*bei Konjunktiv*): **ich würde** ... I would ...; **er**
würde gern ... he would *od* he'd like to ...; **ich**
würde lieber ... I would *od* I'd rather ...
3 (*bei Vermutung*): **sie wird in der Küche sein**
she will be in the kitchen
4 (*bei Passiv*): **gebraucht werden** to be used; **er**
ist erschossen worden he has *od* he's been shot;
mir wurde gesagt, dass ... I was told that ...

werdend *adj*: **~e Mutter** expectant mother
werfen ['vɛrfən] *unreg vt* to throw ▷ *vi* (*Tier*) to
have its young; **„nicht ~"** "handle with care"
Werft [vɛrft] (**-, -en**) *f* shipyard; (*für Flugzeuge*)
hangar
Werk [vɛrk] (**-(e)s, -e**) *nt* work; (*Tätigkeit*) job;
(*Fabrik, Mechanismus*) works *pl*; **ans ~ gehen** to
set to work; **das ist sein ~** this is his doing; **ab**
~ (*Comm*) ex works
werkeln ['vɛrkəln] (*umg*) *vi* to potter about
(*Brit*), putter around (*US*)
Werken (**-s**) *nt* (*Sch*) handicrafts *pl*
Werkschutz *m* works security service
Werksgelände *nt* factory premises *pl*
Werk- *zW*: **Werkstatt** (**-, -stätten**) *f* workshop;
(*Aut*) garage; **Werkstoff** *m* material;
Werkstudent *m* self-supporting student;
Werktag *m* working day; **werktags** *adv*
on working days; **werktätig** *adj* working;
Werkzeug *nt* tool; **Werkzeugkasten** *m*
toolbox; **Werkzeugmaschine** *f* machine tool;
Werkzeugschrank *m* tool chest
Wermut ['veːrmuːt] (**-(e)s, -s**) *m* wormwood;
(*Wein*) vermouth
Wermutstropfen *m* (*fig*) drop of bitterness
Wert [veːrt] (**-(e)s, -e**) *m* worth; (*Fin*) value; **~**
legen auf +*akk* to attach importance to; **es hat**
doch keinen ~ it's useless; **im ~e von** to the
value of
wert [veːrt] *adj* worth; (*geschätzt*) dear; (*würdig*)
worthy; **das ist nichts/viel ~** it's not worth
anything/it's worth a lot; **das ist es/er mir ~**
it's/he's worth that to me; **ein Auto ist viel ~**
(*nützlich*) a car is very useful
Wertangabe *f* declaration of value
wertbeständig *adj* stable in value
werten *vt* to rate; (*beurteilen*) to judge; (*Sport: als*
gültig werten) to allow; **~ als** to rate as; to judge
to be
Wert- *zW*: **Wertgegenstand** *m* article of
value; **wertlos** *adj* worthless; **Wertlosigkeit**
f worthlessness; **Wertmaßstab** *m* standard;
▷ **Wertpapier** *nt* security; **faule Wertpapiere**
toxic asset(s); **Wertsteigerung** *f* appreciation
Wertung *f* (*Sport*) score
Wert- *zW*: **wertvoll** *adj* valuable;
Wertvorstellung *f* moral concept;

Wertzuwachs *m* appreciation
Wesen ['veːzən] (**-s, -**) *nt* (*Geschöpf*) being;
(*Natur, Character*) nature
wesentlich *adj* significant; (*beträchtlich*)
considerable; **im W~en** essentially; (*im Großen*)
in the main
weshalb [vɛs'halp] *adv* why
Wespe ['vɛspə] (**-, -n**) *f* wasp
wessen ['vɛsən] *gen von* **wer** ▷ *pron* whose
Wessi ['vɛsɪ] (**-s, -s**) (*umg*) *m* West German; *see*
culture note

West- *zW*: **westdeutsch** *adj* West German;
Westdeutsche, r *f(m)* West German;
Westdeutschland *nt* (*Pol: früher*) West
Germany; (*Geog*) Western Germany
Weste ['vɛstə] (**-, -n**) *f* waistcoat, vest (*US*); **eine**
reine ~ haben (*fig*) to have a clean slate
Westen (**-s**) *m* west
Westentasche *f*: **etw wie seine ~ kennen**
(*umg*) to know sth like the back of one's hand
Westerwald ['vɛstərvalt] (**-s**) *m* Westerwald
(Mountains *pl*)
Westeuropa *nt* Western Europe
westeuropäisch ['vɛst|ɔʏro'pɛːɪʃ] *adj* West(ern)
European; **~e Zeit** Greenwich Mean Time
Westfale [vɛst'faːlə] (**-n, -n**) *m* Westphalian
Westfalen (**-s**) *nt* Westphalia
Westfälin [vɛst'fɛːlɪn] *f* Westphalian
westfälisch *adj* Westphalian
Westindien ['vɛst|ɪndiən] (**-s**) *nt* West Indies *pl*
westindisch *adj* West Indian; **die W~en**
Inseln the West Indies
west- *zW*: **westlich** *adj* western ▷ *adv* to
the west; **Westmächte** *pl* (*Pol: früher*): **die**
Westmächte the Western powers *pl*;
westwärts *adv* westwards
weswegen [vɛs've:gən] *adv* why
wett [vɛt] *adj* even; **~ sein** to be quits
Wettbewerb *m* competition
Wettbewerbsbeschränkung *f* restraint of
trade
wettbewerbsfähig *adj* competitive
Wette (**-, -n**) *f* bet, wager; **um die ~ laufen** to
run a race (with each other)
Wetteifer *m* rivalry
wetteifern *vi untr*: **mit jdm um etw ~** to
compete with sb for sth
wetten ['vɛtən] *vt, vi* to bet; **so haben wir**
nicht gewettet! that's not part of the
bargain!
Wetter ['vɛtər] (**-s, -**) *nt* weather; (*Min*)
air; **Wetteramt** *nt* meteorological office;
Wetteraussichten *pl* weather outlook

sing; **Wetterbericht** m weather report;
Wetterdienst m meteorological service;
wetterfest adj weatherproof; **wetterfühlig**
adj sensitive to changes in the weather;
Wetterkarte f weather chart; **Wetterlage** f
(weather) situation
wettern ['vɛtərn] vi to curse and swear
Wetter- zW: **Wetterumschlag** m sudden
change in the weather; **Wettervorhersage**
f weather forecast; **Wetterwarte** f weather
station; **wetterwendisch** adj capricious
Wett- zW: **Wettkampf** m contest; **Wettlauf**
m race; **ein Wettlauf mit der Zeit** a race
against time
wettmachen vt to make good
Wett- zW: **Wettrüsten** nt arms race; **Wettspiel**
nt match; **Wettstreit** m contest
wetzen ['vɛtsən] vt to sharpen ▷ vi (umg) to
scoot
WEU f abk (= Westeuropäische Union) WEU
WEZ abk (= westeuropäische Zeit) GMT
WG abk = **Wohngemeinschaft**
Whisky ['vɪski] (**-s, -s**) m whisky (Brit), whiskey
(US, Ireland)
WHO (-) f abk (= World Health Organization) WHO
wich etc [vɪç] vb siehe **weichen**
wichsen ['vɪksən] vt (Schuhe) to polish ▷ vi
(umg!: onanieren) to jerk od toss off (!)
Wichser (umg!) m wanker (!)
Wicht [vɪçt] (**-(e)s, -e**) m titch; (pej) worthless
creature
wichtig adj important; **sich selbst/etw (zu)**
~ nehmen to take o.s./sth (too) seriously;
Wichtigkeit f importance; **Wichtigtuer, in**
(pej) m(f) pompous ass (umg)
Wicke ['vɪkə] (**-, -n**) f (Bot) vetch; (Gartenwicke)
sweet pea
wickeln ['vɪkəln] vt to wind; (Haare) to set;
(Kind) to change; **da bist du schief gewickelt!**
(fig: umg) you're very much mistaken; **jdn/etw**
in etw akk **~** to wrap sb/sth in sth
Wickeltisch m baby's changing table
Widder ['vɪdər] (**-s, -**) m ram; (Astrol) Aries
wider ['vi:dər] präp +akk against
widerfahren unreg vi untr: **jdm ~** to happen to sb
Widerhaken ['vi:dərha:kən] m barb
Widerhall ['vi:dərhal] m echo; **keinen ~**
(bei jdm) finden (Interesse) to meet with no
response (from sb)
widerlegen vt untr to refute
widerlich ['vi:dərlɪç] adj disgusting, repulsive;
Widerlichkeit f repulsiveness
widerrechtlich adj unlawful
Widerrede f contradiction; **keine ~!** don't
argue!
Widerruf ['vi:dərru:f] m retraction;
countermanding; **bis auf ~** until revoked
widerrufen unreg vt untr to retract; (Anordnung)
to revoke; (Befehl) to countermand
Widersacher, in ['vi:dərzaxər(ɪn)] (**-s, -**) m(f)
adversary
widersetzen vr untr: **sich jdm ~** to oppose sb;
(der Polizei) to resist sb; **sich einer Sache ~ to**

oppose sth; (einem Befehl) to refuse to comply
with sth
widerspenstig ['vi:dərʃpɛnstɪç] adj wilful (Brit),
willful (US); **Widerspenstigkeit** f wilfulness
(Brit), willfulness (US)
widerspiegeln ['vi:dərʃpi:gəln] vt to reflect
widersprechen unreg vi untr: **jdm ~** to
contradict sb
widersprechend adj contradictory
Widerspruch ['vi:dərʃprʊx] m contradiction;
ein ~ in sich a contradiction in terms
widersprüchlich ['vi:dərʃprʏçlɪç] adj
contradictory, inconsistent
widerspruchslos adv without arguing
Widerstand ['vi:dərʃtant] m resistance; **der**
Weg des geringsten ~es the line of least
resistance; **jdm/etw ~ leisten** to resist sb/sth
Widerstands- zW: **Widerstandsbewegung**
f resistance (movement); **widerstandsfähig**
adj resistant, tough; **widerstandslos** adj
unresisting
widerstehen unreg vi untr: **jdm/etw ~** to
withstand sb/sth
widerstreben vi untr: **es widerstrebt mir, so**
etwas zu tun I am reluctant to do anything
like that
widerstrebend adj reluctant; (gegensätzlich)
conflicting
Wider- zW: **Widerstreit** m conflict;
widerwärtig adj nasty, horrid; **Widerwille**
m: **Widerwille (gegen)** aversion (to);
(Abneigung) distaste (for); (Widerstreben)
reluctance; **widerwillig** adj unwilling,
reluctant; **Widerworte** pl answering back sing
Widget ['vɪdʒɪt] nt (Comput) widget
widmen ['vɪtmən] vt to dedicate ▷ vr to devote
o.s.
Widmung f dedication
widrig ['vi:drɪç] adj (Umstände) adverse; (Mensch)
repulsive

SCHLÜSSELWORT

wie [vi:] adv how; **wie groß/schnell?** how
big/fast?; **wie viel** how much; **wie viel**
Menschen how many people; **wie wärs?** how
about it?; **wie wärs mit einem Whisky?**
(umg) how about a whisky?; **wie nennt man**
das? what is that called?; **wie ist er?** what's
he like?; **wie gut du das kannst!** you're very
good at it; **wie bitte?** pardon? (Brit), pardon
me? (US); (entrüstet) I beg your pardon!; **und**
wie! and how!
▷ konj **1** (bei Vergleichen): **so schön wie ...** as
beautiful as ...; **wie ich schon sagte** as I said;
wie noch nie as never before; **wie du** like you;
singen wie ein ... to sing like a ...; **wie (zum**
Beispiel) such as (for example)
2 (zeitlich): **wie er das hörte, ging er** when he
heard that he left; **er hörte, wie der Regen**
fiel he heard the rain falling

wieder ['vi:dər] adv again; **~ da sein** to be back

(again); **gehst du schon ~?** are you off again?; **~ ein(e)** ... another ...; **das ist auch ~ wahr** that's true enough; **da sieht man mal ~** ... it just shows ...; **~ finden**, **~ gutmachen** *etc* = **wiederfinden, wiedergutmachen** *etc*

wieder- *zW*: **Wiederaufbau** [-'|aufbau] *m* rebuilding; **wiederaufbereiten** *vt* to recycle; (*Atommüll*) to reprocess; **Wiederaufbereitungsanlage** *f* reprocessing plant; **Wiederaufnahme** [-'|aufnaːmə] *f* resumption; **wiederaufnehmen** *unreg vt* to resume; (*Gedanken, Hobby*) to take up again; (*Thema*) to revert to; (*Jur: Verfahren*) to reopen; **wiederaufrollen** *vt* (*Fall, Prozess*) to reopen; **wiederbekommen** *unreg vt* to get back; **wiederbeleben** *unreg vt* to revive; **wiederbeschreibbar** *adj* (*CD, DVD*) rewritable; **wiederbringen** *unreg vt* to bring back; **wiedererkennen** *unreg vt* to recognize; **Wiedererstattung** *f* reimbursement; **wiederfinden** *unreg vt* (*fig: Selbstachtung etc*) to regain

Wiedergabe *f* (*von Rede, Ereignis*) account; (*Wiederholung*) repetition; (*Darbietung*) performance; (*Reproduktion*) reproduction; **Wiedergabegerät** *nt* playback unit

wieder- *zW*: **wiedergeben** *unreg vt* (*zurückgeben*) to return; (*Erzählung etc*) to repeat; (*Gefühle etc*) to convey; **Wiedergeburt** *f* rebirth; **wiedergutmachen** *vt* to make up for; (*Fehler*) to put right; **Wiedergutmachung** *f* reparation; **wiederherstellen** *vt* (*Gesundheit, Gebäude, Ruhe*) to restore

wiederholen *vt untr* to repeat

wiederholt *adj*: **zum ~en Male** once again

Wiederholung *f* repetition

Wiederholungstäter, in *m(f)* (*Jur*) second-time offender; (*mehrmalig*) persistent offender

wieder- *zW*: **Wiederhören** *nt*: **auf Wiederhören** (*Tel*) goodbye; **wiederkäuen** *vi* to ruminate ▷ *vt* to ruminate; (*fig: umg*) to go over again and again; **Wiederkehr (-)** *f* return; (*von Vorfall*) repetition, recurrence; **wiederkehrend** *adj* recurrent; **Wiederkunft (-, ⸚e)** *f* return; **wiedersehen** *unreg vt* to see again; **auf Wiedersehen** goodbye; **wiederum** *adv* again; (*seinerseits etc*) in turn; (*andererseits*) on the other hand; **wiedervereinigen** *vt* to reunite; **Wiedervereinigung** *f* reunification; **Wiederverkäufer** *m* distributor; **Wiederwahl** *f* re-election

Wiege ['viːɡə] (**-, -n**) *f* cradle

wiegen¹ *vt* (*schaukeln*) to rock; (*Kopf*) to shake

wiegen² *unreg vt, vi* to weigh; **schwer ~** (*fig*) to carry a lot of weight; (*Irrtum*) to be serious

wiehern ['viːərn] *vi* to neigh, whinny

Wien [viːn] (**-s**) *nt* Vienna

Wiener, in (-s, -) *m(f)* Viennese ▷ *adj attrib* Viennese; **~ Schnitzel** Wiener schnitzel

wies *etc* [viːs] *vb siehe* **weisen**

Wiese ['viːzə] (**-, -n**) *f* meadow

Wiesel ['viːzəl] (**-s, -**) *nt* weasel; **schnell** *od* **flink wie ein ~** quick as a flash

wieso [viˈzoː] *adv* why

wievielmal [viˈfiːlmaːl] *adv* how often

wievielte, r, s *adj*: **zum ~n Mal?** how many times?; **den W~n haben wir?** what's the date?; **an ~r Stelle?** in what place?; **der ~ Besucher war er?** how many visitors were there before him?

wieweit [viˈvaɪt] *adv* to what extent

Wi-Fi ['waɪfi, 'waɪfai] *nt* Wi-Fi

Wikinger ['viːkɪŋər] (**-s, -**) *m* Viking

wild [vɪlt] *adj* wild; **~er Streik** unofficial strike; **in ~er Ehe leben** (*veraltet, hum*) to live in sin; **~ entschlossen** (*umg*) dead set

Wild (-(e)s) *nt* game

Wild- *zW*: **Wildbahn** *f*: **in freier Wildbahn** in the wild; **Wildbret** *nt* game; (*von Rotwild*) venison; **Wilddieb** *m* poacher

Wilde, r ['vɪldə(r)] *f(m)* savage

wildern ['vɪldərn] *vi* to poach

wild- *zW*: **Wildfang** *m* little rascal; **wildfremd** (*umg*) *adj* quite strange *od* unknown; **Wildheit** *f* wildness; **Wildleder** *nt* suede

Wildnis (-, -se) *f* wilderness

Wild- *zW*: **Wildschwein** *nt* (wild) boar; **Wildwechsel** *m*: **„Wildwechsel“** "wild animals"; **Wildwestroman** *m* western

will [vɪl] *vb siehe* **wollen**

Wille ['vɪlə] (**-ns, -n**) *m* will; **jdm seinen ~n lassen** to let sb have his own way; **seinen eigenen ~n haben** to be self-willed

willen *präp +gen*: **um ...** **~** for the sake of ...

willenlos *adj* weak-willed

willens *adj* (*geh*): **~ sein** to be willing

willensstark *adj* strong-willed

willentlich ['vɪləntlɪç] *adj* wilful (*Brit*), willful (*US*), deliberate

willig *adj* willing

willkommen [vɪl'kɔmən] *adj* welcome; **jdn ~ heißen** to welcome sb; **herzlich ~ (in +dat)** welcome (to); **Willkommen (-s, -)** *nt* welcome

willkürlich *adj* arbitrary; (*Bewegung*) voluntary

willst [vɪlst] *vb siehe* **wollen**

Wilna ['vɪlna] (**-s**) *nt* Vilnius

wimmeln ['vɪməln] *vi*: **~ (von)** to swarm (with)

wimmern ['vɪmərn] *vi* to whimper

Wimper ['vɪmpər] (**-, -n**) *f* eyelash; **ohne mit der ~ zu zucken** (*fig*) without batting an eyelid

Wimperntusche *f* mascara

Wind [vɪnt] (**-(e)s, -e**) *m* wind; **den Mantel** *od* **das Fähnchen nach dem ~ hängen** to trim one's sails to the wind; **etw in den ~ schlagen** to turn a deaf ear to sth

Windbeutel *m* cream puff; (*fig*) windbag

Winde ['vɪndə] (**-, -n**) *f* (*Tech*) winch, windlass; (*Bot*) bindweed

Windel ['vɪndəl] (**-, -n**) *f* nappy (*Brit*), diaper (*US*)

windelweich *adj*: **jdn ~ schlagen** (*umg*) to beat the living daylights out of sb

winden¹ ['vɪndən] *vi unpers* to be windy

winden² *unreg vt* to wind; (*Kranz*) to weave; (*entwinden*) to twist ▷ *vr* to wind; (*Person*) to writhe; (*fig: ausweichen*) to try to wriggle out

Windenergie *f* wind power

Windeseile f: **sich in** od **mit ~ verbreiten** to spread like wildfire

Windhose f whirlwind

Windhund m greyhound; (Mensch) fly-by-night

windig ['vɪndɪç] adj windy; (fig) dubious

Wind- zW: **Windjacke** f windcheater, windbreaker (US); **Windkanal** m (Tech) wind tunnel; **Windkraft** f wind power; **Windkraftanlage** f wind power station; **Windmühle** f windmill; **gegen Windmühlen (an)kämpfen** (fig) to tilt at windmills; **Windpark** m wind farm

Windpocken pl chickenpox sing

Wind- zW: **Windrose** f (Naut) compass card; (Met) wind rose; **Windschatten** m lee; (von Fahrzeugen) slipstream; **Windschutzscheibe** f (Aut) windscreen (Brit), windshield (US); **Windstärke** f wind force; **windstill** adj (Tag) windless; **es ist windstill** there's no wind; **Windstille** f calm; **Windstoß** m gust of wind; **Windsurfen** nt windsurfing

Windung f (von Weg, Fluss etc) meander; (von Schlange, Spule) coil; (von Schraube) thread

Wink [vɪŋk] (-(e)s, -e) m (mit Kopf) nod; (mit Hand) wave; (Tipp, Hinweis) hint; **ein ~ mit dem Zaunpfahl** a broad hint

Winkel ['vɪŋkəl] (-s, -) m (Math) angle; (Gerät) set square; (in Raum) corner; **Winkeladvokat** (pej) m incompetent lawyer; **Winkelmesser** m protractor; **Winkelzug** m: **mach keine Winkelzüge** stop evading the issue

winken ['vɪŋkən] vt, vi to wave; **dem Sieger winkt eine Reise nach Italien** the (lucky) winner will receive a trip to Italy

winseln ['vɪnzəln] vi to whine

Winter ['vɪntər] (-s, -) m winter; **Wintergarten** m conservatory; **winterlich** adj wintry; **Winterreifen** m winter tyre (Brit) od tire (US); **Winterschlaf** m (Zool) hibernation; **Winterschlussverkauf** m winter sale; **Wintersemester** nt (Univ) winter semester (bes US), ≈ autumn term (Brit); **Winterspiele** pl: **(Olympische) Winterspiele** Winter Olympics pl; **Wintersport** m winter sports pl

Winzer, in ['vɪntsər(ɪn)] (-s, -) m(f) winegrower

winzig ['vɪntsɪç] adj tiny

Wipfel ['vɪpfəl] (-s, -) m treetop

Wippe ['vɪpə] (-, -n) f seesaw

wir [viːr] pron we; **~ alle** all of us, we all

Wirbel ['vɪrbəl] (-s, -) m whirl, swirl; (Trubel) hurly-burly; (Aufsehen) fuss; (Anat) vertebra; **~ um jdn/etw machen** to make a fuss about sb/sth

wirbellos adj (Zool) invertebrate

wirbeln vi to whirl, swirl

Wirbel- zW: **Wirbelsäule** f spine; **Wirbeltier** nt vertebrate; **Wirbelwind** m whirlwind

wirbst vb siehe **werben**

wirbt [vɪrpt] vb siehe **werben**

wird [vɪrt] vb siehe **werden**

wirfst vb siehe **werfen**

wirft [vɪrft] vb siehe **werfen**

wirken ['vɪrkən] vi to have an effect; (erfolgreich sein) to work; (scheinen) to seem ▷ vt (Wunder) to work; **etw auf sich** akk **~ lassen** to take sth in

wirklich ['vɪrklɪç] adj real; **Wirklichkeit** f reality; **wirklichkeitsgetreu** adj realistic

wirksam ['vɪrkzaːm] adj effective; **Wirksamkeit** f effectiveness

Wirkstoff m active substance

Wirkung ['vɪrkʊŋ] f effect

Wirkungs- zW: **Wirkungsbereich** m field (of activity od interest etc); (Domäne) domain; **wirkungslos** adj ineffective; **wirkungslos bleiben** to have no effect; **wirkungsvoll** adj effective

wirr [vɪr] adj confused; (unrealistisch) wild; (Haare etc) tangled

Wirren pl disturbances pl

Wirrwarr ['vɪrvar] (-s) m disorder, chaos; (von Stimmen) hubbub; (von Fäden, Haaren etc) tangle

Wirsing ['vɪrzɪŋ], **Wirsingkohl** ['vɪrzɪŋkoːl] (-s) m savoy cabbage

wirst [vɪrst] vb siehe **werden**

Wirt, in [vɪrt(ɪn)] (-(e)s, -e) m(f) landlord, landlady

Wirtschaft ['vɪrtʃaft] f (Gaststätte) pub; (Haushalt) housekeeping; (eines Landes) economy; (Geschäftsleben) industry and commerce; (umg: Durcheinander) mess; **wirtschaften** vi (sparsam sein): **gut wirtschaften können** to be economical; **Wirtschafter** m (Verwalter) manager; **Wirtschafterin** f (im Haushalt, Heim etc) housekeeper; **wirtschaftlich** adj economical; (Pol) economic; **Wirtschaftlichkeit** f economy; (von Betrieb) viability

Wirtschafts- zW: **Wirtschaftsgeld** nt housekeeping (money); **Wirtschaftsgeografie** f economic geography; **Wirtschaftshilfe** f economic aid; **Wirtschaftskrise** f economic crisis; **Wirtschaftsminister** m minister of economic affairs; **Wirtschaftsordnung** f economic system; **Wirtschaftspolitik** f economic policy; **Wirtschaftsprüfer** m chartered accountant (Brit), certified public accountant (US); **Wirtschaftsspionage** f industrial espionage; **Wirtschaftswachstum** nt economic growth; **Wirtschaftswissenschaft** f economics sing; **Wirtschaftswunder** nt economic miracle; **Wirtschaftszweig** m branch of industry

Wirtshaus nt inn

Wisch [vɪʃ] (-(e)s, -e) m scrap of paper

wischen vt to wipe

Wischer (-s, -) m (Aut) wiper

Wischiwaschi [vɪʃiˈvaʃiː] (-s) (pej: umg) nt drivel

Wisent ['viːzɛnt] (-s, -e) m bison

WiSo ['vɪzo] abk (= Wirtschafts- und Sozialwissenschaften) economics and social sciences

wispern ['vɪspərn] vt, vi to whisper

Wiss. abk = **Wissenschaft**

wiss. abk = **wissenschaftlich**

W

389

Wissbegier ['vɪsbəgiːr], **Wissbegierde** ['vɪsbəgiːrdə] f thirst for knowledge
wissbegierig adj eager for knowledge
wissen ['vɪsən] unreg vt, vi to know; **von jdm/ etw nichts ~ wollen** not to be interested in sb/sth; **sie hält sich für wer weiß wie klug** (umg) she doesn't half think she's clever; **gewusst wie/wo!** etc sheer brilliance!; **ich weiß seine Adresse nicht mehr** (sich erinnern) I can't remember his address; **Wissen (-s)** nt knowledge; **etw gegen (sein) besseres Wissen tun** to do sth against one's better judgement; **nach bestem Wissen und Gewissen** to the best of one's knowledge and belief
Wissenschaft ['vɪsənʃaft] f science
Wissenschaftler, in (-s, -) m(f) scientist; (Geisteswissenschaftler) academic
wissenschaftlich adj scientific; **W~er Assistent** assistant lecturer
wissenswert adj worth knowing
wissentlich adj knowing
wittern ['vɪtərn] vt to scent; (fig) to suspect
Witterung f weather; (Geruch) scent
Witwe ['vɪtvə] (-, -n) f widow
Witwer (-s, -) m widower
Witz [vɪts] (-es, -e) m joke; **der ~ an der Sache ist, dass ...** the great thing about it is that ...; **Witzbold** (-(e)s, -e) m joker
witzeln vi to joke
witzig adj funny
witzlos (umg) adj (unsinnig) pointless, futile
WM (-) f abk = **Weltmeisterschaft**
wo [voː] adv where; (umg: irgendwo) somewhere ▷ konj (wenn) if; **im Augenblick, wo ...** the moment (that) ...; **die Zeit, wo ...** the time when ...
woanders [voːˈandərs] adv elsewhere
wob etc [voːp] vb siehe **weben**
wobei [voːˈbaɪ] adv (rel) ... in/by/with which; (interrog) how; what ... in/by/with; **~ mir gerade einfällt ...** which reminds me ...
Woche ['vɔxə] (-, -n) f week
Wochenbett nt: **im ~ sterben** to die in childbirth
Wochen- zW: **Wochenende** nt weekend; **Wochenendhaus** nt weekend house; **Wochenkarte** f weekly ticket; **wochenlang** adj lasting weeks ▷ adv for weeks; **Wochenschau** f newsreel; **Wochentag** m weekday
wöchentlich ['vœçəntlɪç] adj, adv weekly
Wochenzeitung f weekly (paper)
Wöchnerin ['vœçnərɪn] f woman who has recently given birth
Wodka ['vɔtka] (-s, -s) m vodka
wodurch [voːˈdʊrç] adv (rel) through which; (interrog) what ... through
wofür [voːˈfyːr] adv (rel) for which; (interrog) what ... for
wog etc [voːk] vb siehe **wiegen²**
Woge ['voːgə] (-, -n) f wave
wogegen [voːˈgeːgən] adv (rel) against which; (interrog) what ... against

wogen vi to heave, surge
woher [voˈheːr] adv where ... from; **~ kommt es eigentlich, dass ...?** how is it that ...?
wohin [voˈhɪn] adv where ... to; **~ man auch schaut** wherever you look
wohingegen konj whereas, while
Wohl (-(e)s) nt welfare; **zum ~!** cheers!

⊙ SCHLÜSSELWORT

wohl [voːl] adv **1** well; (behaglich) at ease, comfortable; **sich wohl fühlen** siehe **wohlfühlen**; **wohl gemeint** = **wohlgemeint**; **bei den Gedanken ist mir nicht wohl** I'm not very happy at the thought; **wohl oder übel** whether one likes it or not; **er weiß das sehr wohl** he knows that perfectly well
2 (wahrscheinlich) probably; (vermutlich) I suppose; (gewiss) certainly; (vielleicht) perhaps; **sie ist wohl zu Hause** she's probably at home; **sie wird wohl das Haus verkaufen** I suppose od presumably she's going to sell the house; **das ist doch wohl nicht dein Ernst!** surely you're not serious!; **das mag wohl sein** that may well be; **ob das wohl stimmt?** I wonder if that's true; siehe auch **wohltun**

wohl- zW: **wohlauf** [voːlˈaʊf] adj well, in good health; **Wohlbefinden** nt well-being; **Wohlbehagen** nt comfort; **wohlbehalten** adj safe and sound; **Wohlergehen** nt welfare; **Wohlfahrt** f welfare; **Wohlfahrtsstaat** m welfare state; **wohlfühlen** vr (zufrieden) to feel happy; (gesundheitlich) to feel well; **Wohlgefallen** nt: **sich in Wohlgefallen auflösen** (hum: Gegenstände, Probleme) to vanish into thin air; (zerfallen) to fall apart; **wohlgemeint** adj well-intentioned; **wohlgemerkt** adv mark you; **wohlhabend** adj wealthy
wohlig adj contented; (gemütlich) comfortable
wohl- zW: **Wohlklang** m melodious sound; **wohlmeinend** adj well-meaning; **wohlschmeckend** adj delicious; **Wohlstand** m prosperity; **Wohlstandsgesellschaft** f affluent society; **Wohltat** f (Gefallen) favour (Brit), favor (US); (gute Tat) good deed; (Erleichterung) relief; **Wohltäter** m benefactor; **wohltätig** adj charitable; **Wohltätigkeit** f charity; **wohltuend** adj pleasant; **wohltun** unreg vi: **jdm wohltun** to do sb good; **wohlverdient** adj (Ruhe) well-earned; (Strafe) well-deserved; **wohlweislich** adv prudently; **Wohlwollen** (-s) nt good will; **wohlwollend** adj benevolent
Wohnblock ['voːnblɔk] (-s, -s) m block of flats (Brit), apartment house (US)
wohnen ['voːnən] vi to live
wohn- zW: **Wohnfläche** f living space; **Wohngeld** nt housing benefit; **Wohngemeinschaft** f people sharing a flat (Brit) od apartment (US); (von Hippies) commune; **wohnhaft** adj resident; **Wohnheim**

nt (*für Studenten*) hall (of residence), dormitory (US); (*für Senioren*) home; (*bes für Arbeiter*) hostel; **Wohnkomfort** *m*: **mit sämtlichem Wohnkomfort** with all mod cons (Brit); **wohnlich** *adj* comfortable; **Wohnmobil** *nt* motor caravan (Brit), motor home (US); **Wohnort** *m* domicile; **Wohnsilo** *nt* concrete block of flats (Brit) *od* apartment block (US); **Wohnsitz** *m* place of residence; **ohne festen Wohnsitz** of no fixed abode

Wohnung *f* house; (*Etagenwohnung*) flat (Brit), apartment (US)

Wohnungs- *zW*: **Wohnungsamt** *nt* housing office; **Wohnungsbau** *m* house-building; **Wohnungsmarkt** *m* housing market; **Wohnungsnot** *f* housing shortage

wohn- *zW*: **Wohnviertel** *nt* residential area; **Wohnwagen** *m* caravan (Brit), trailer (US); **Wohnzimmer** *nt* living room

wölben ['vœlbən] *vt, vr* to curve

Wölbung *f* curve

Wolf [vɔlf] (**-(e)s, -̈e**) *m* wolf; (*Tech*) shredder; (*Fleischwolf*) mincer (Brit), grinder (US)

Wölfin ['vœlfɪn] *f* she-wolf

Wolke ['vɔlkə] (**-, -n**) *f* cloud; **aus allen ~n fallen** (*fig*) to be flabbergasted (*umg*)

Wolken- *zW*: **Wolkenbruch** *m* cloudburst; **wolkenbruchartig** *adj* torrential; **Wolkenkratzer** *m* skyscraper; **Wolkenkuckucksheim** *nt* cloud-cuckoo-land (Brit), cloudland (US); **wolkenlos** *adj* cloudless

wolkig ['vɔlkɪç] *adj* cloudy

Wolle ['vɔlə] (**-, -n**) *f* wool; **sich mit jdm in die ~ kriegen** (*fig: umg*) to start squabbling with sb

SCHLÜSSELWORT

wollen[1] ['vɔlən] *unreg* (*pt* **wollte**, *pp* **gewollt** *od* (*als Hilfsverb*) **wollen**) *vt, vi* to want; **ich will nach Hause** I want to go home; **er will nicht** he doesn't want to; **sie wollte das nicht** she didn't want it; **wenn du willst** if you like; **ich will, dass du mir zuhörst** I want you to listen to me; **oh, das hab ich nicht gewollt** oh, I didn't mean to do that; **ich weiß nicht, was er will** (*verstehe ihn nicht*) I don't know what he's on about

▷ *Hilfsverb*: **er will ein Haus kaufen** he wants to buy a house; **ich wollte, ich wäre ...** I wish I were ...; **etw gerade tun wollen** to be just about to *od* going to do sth; **und so jemand** *od* **etwas will Lehrer sein!** (*umg*) and he calls himself a teacher!; **das will alles gut überlegt sein** that needs a lot of thought

wollen[2] *adj* woollen (Brit), woolen (US)

Wollsachen *pl* wool(l)ens *pl*

wollüstig ['vɔlʏstɪç] *adj* lusty, sensual

wo- *zW*: **womit** [vo'mɪt] *adv* (*rel*) with which; (*interrog*) what ... with; **womit kann ich dienen?** what can I do for you?; **womöglich** [vo'møːklɪç] *adv* probably, I suppose; **wonach** [vo'naːx] *adv* (*rel*) after/for which; (*interrog*)

what ... after

Wonne ['vɔnə] (**-, -n**) *f* joy, bliss

woran [vo'ran] *adv* (*rel*) on/at which; (*interrog*) what ... on/at; **~ liegt das?** what's the reason for it?

worauf [vo'rauf] *adv* (*rel*) on which; (*interrog*) what ... on; (*zeitlich*) whereupon; **~ du dich verlassen kannst** of that you can be sure

woraus [vo'raus] *adv* (*rel*) from/out of which; (*interrog*) what ... from/out of

worden ['vɔrdən] *vb siehe* **werden**

worin [vo'rɪn] *adv* (*rel*) in which; (*interrog*) what ... in

Wort [vɔrt] (**-(e)s, -̈er** *od* **-e**) *nt* word; **jdn beim ~ nehmen** to take sb at his word; **ein ernstes ~ mit jdm reden** to have a serious talk with sb; **man kann sein eigenes ~ nicht (mehr) verstehen** you can't hear yourself speak; **jdm aufs ~ gehorchen** to obey sb's every word; **zu ~ kommen** to get a chance to speak; **jdm das ~ erteilen** to allow sb to speak; **Wortart** *f* (*Gram*) part of speech; **wortbrüchig** *adj* not true to one's word

Wörtchen *nt*: **da habe ich wohl ein ~ mitzureden** (*umg*) I think I have some say in that

Wörterbuch ['vœrtərbuːx] *nt* dictionary

Wort- *zW*: **Wortfetzen** *pl* snatches *pl* of conversation; **Wortführer** *m* spokesman; **wortgetreu** *adj* true to one's word; (*Übersetzung*) literal; **wortgewaltig** *adj* eloquent; **wortkarg** *adj* taciturn; **Wortlaut** *m* wording; **im Wortlaut** verbatim

wörtlich ['vœrtlɪç] *adj* literal

Wort- *zW*: **wortlos** *adj* mute; **Wortmeldung** *f*: **wenn es keine weiteren Wortmeldungen gibt, ...** if nobody else wishes to speak ...; **wortreich** *adj* wordy, verbose; **Wortschatz** *m* vocabulary; **Wortspiel** *nt* play on words, pun; **Wortwechsel** *m* dispute; **wortwörtlich** *adj* word-for-word ▷ *adv* quite literally

worüber [vo'ryːbər] *adv* (*rel*) over/about which; (*interrog*) what ... over/about

worum [vo'rum] *adv* (*rel*) about/round which; (*interrog*) what ... about/round; **~ handelt es sich?** what's it about?

worunter [vo'runtər] *adv* (*rel*) under which; (*interrog*) what ... under

wo- *zW*: **wovon** [vo'fɔn] *adv* (*rel*) from which; (*interrog*) what ... from; **wovor** [vo'fɔr] *adv* (*rel*) in front of/before which; (*interrog*) in front of/before what; **wozu** [vo'tsu] *adv* (*rel*) to/for which; (*interrog*) what ... for/to; (*warum*) why; **wozu soll das gut sein?** what's the point of that?

Wrack [vrak] (**-(e)s, -s**) *nt* wreck

wrang *etc* [vraŋ] *vb siehe* **wringen**

wringen ['vrɪŋən] *unreg vt* to wring

WS *abk* = **Wintersemester**

WSV *abk* = **Winterschlussverkauf**

Wucher ['vuːxər] (**-s**) *m* profiteering; **Wucherer** (**-s, -**) *m*, **Wucherin** *f* profiteer; **wucherisch** *adj* profiteering

wuchern | Wz

wuchern vi (Pflanzen) to grow wild
Wucherpreis m exorbitant price
Wucherung f (Med) growth
Wuchs [vuːks] (-es) m (Wachstum) growth; (Statur) build
wuchs etc vb siehe **wachsen¹**
Wucht [vʊxt] (-) f force
wuchtig adj massive, solid
wühlen ['vyːlən] vi to scrabble; (Tier) to root; (Maulwurf) to burrow; (umg: arbeiten) to slave away ▷ vt to dig
Wühlmaus f vole
Wühltisch m (in Kaufhaus) bargain counter
Wulst [vʊlst] (-es, ¨e) m bulge; (an Wunde) swelling
wulstig adj bulging; (Rand, Lippen) thick
wund [vʊnt] adj sore; **sich** dat **die Füße ~ laufen** (lit) to get sore feet from walking; (fig) to walk one's legs off; **ein ~er Punkt** a sore point; **Wundbrand** m gangrene
Wunde ['vʊndə] (-, -n) f wound; **alte ~n wieder aufreißen** (fig) to open up old wounds
Wunder (-s, -) nt miracle; **es ist kein ~** it's no wonder; **meine Eltern denken ~ was passiert ist** my parents think goodness knows what has happened; **wunderbar** adj wonderful, marvellous (Brit), marvelous (US); **Wunderkerze** f sparkler; **Wunderkind** nt child prodigy; **wunderlich** adj odd, peculiar
wundern vt to surprise ▷ vr: **sich ~ über** +akk to be surprised at
Wunder- zW: **wunderschön** adj beautiful; **Wundertüte** f lucky bag; **wundervoll** adj wonderful
Wundfieber (-s) nt traumatic fever
Wundstarrkrampf ['vʊntʃtarkrampf] m tetanus, lockjaw
Wunsch [vʊnʃ] (-(e)s, ¨e) m wish; **haben Sie (sonst) noch einen ~?** (beim Einkauf etc) is there anything else you'd like?; **auf jds (besonderen/ausdrücklichen) ~ hin** at sb's (special/express) request; **Wunschdenken** nt wishful thinking
Wünschelrute ['vʏnʃəlruːtə] f divining rod
wünschen ['vʏnʃən] vt to wish ▷ vi: **zu wünschen/viel zu ~ übrig lassen** to leave something/a great deal to be desired; **sich** dat **etw ~** to want sth, wish for sth; **was ~ Sie?** (in Geschäft) what can I do for you?; (in Restaurant) what would you like?
wünschenswert adj desirable
Wunsch- zW: **Wunschkind** nt planned child; **Wunschkonzert** nt (Rundf) musical request programme (Brit) od program (US); **wunschlos** adj: **wunschlos glücklich** perfectly happy; **Wunschtraum** m dream; (unrealistisch) pipe dream; **Wunschzettel** m list of things one would like
wurde etc ['vʊrdə] vb siehe **werden**
Würde ['vʏrdə] (-, -n) f dignity; (Stellung)

honour (Brit), honor (US); **unter aller ~ sein** to be beneath contempt
Würdenträger m dignitary
würdevoll adj dignified
würdig ['vʏrdɪç] adj worthy; (würdevoll) dignified
würdigen ['vʏrdɪgən] vt to appreciate; **etw zu ~ wissen** to appreciate sth; **jdn keines Blickes ~** not to so much as look at sb
Wurf [vʊrf] (-(e)s, ¨e) m throw; (Junge) litter
Würfel ['vʏrfəl] (-s, -) m dice; (Math) cube; **die ~ sind gefallen** the die is cast; **Würfelbecher** m (dice) cup
würfeln vi to play dice ▷ vt to dice
Würfelspiel nt game of dice
Würfelzucker m lump sugar
Wurf- zW: **Wurfgeschoss** nt projectile; **Wurfsendung** f circular; **Wurfsendungen** pl (Reklame) junk mail
Würgegriff (-(e)s) m (lit, fig) stranglehold
würgen ['vʏrgən] vt, vi to choke; **mit Hängen und W~** by the skin of one's teeth
Wurm [vʊrm] (-(e)s, ¨er) m worm; **da steckt der ~ drin** (fig: umg) there's something wrong somewhere; (verdächtig) there's something fishy about it (umg)
wurmen (umg) vt to rile, nettle
Wurmfortsatz m (Med) appendix
wurmig adj worm-eaten
wurmstichig adj worm-ridden
Wurst [vʊrst] (-, ¨e) f sausage; **das ist mir ~** (umg) I don't care, I don't give a damn; **jetzt geht es um die ~** (fig: umg) the moment of truth has come
Würstchen ['vʏrstçən] nt frankfurter, hot dog sausage; **Würstchenbude** f, **Würstchenstand** m hot dog stall
Württemberg ['vʏrtəmberk] nt Württemberg
Würze ['vʏrtsə] (-, -n) f seasoning
Wurzel ['vʊrtsəl] (-, -n) f root; **~n schlagen** (lit) to root; (fig) to put down roots; **die ~ aus 4 ist 2** (Math) the square root of 4 is 2
würzen vt to season; (würzig machen) to spice
würzig adj spicy
wusch etc [vuːʃ] vb siehe **waschen**
wusste etc ['vʊstə] vb siehe **wissen**
Wust [vuːst] (-(e)s) (umg) m (Durcheinander) jumble; (Menge) pile
wüst [vyːst] adj untidy, messy; (ausschweifend) wild; (öde) waste; (umg: heftig) terrible; **jdn ~ beschimpfen** to use vile language to sb
Wüste (-, -n) f desert; **die ~ Gobi** the Gobi Desert; **jdn in die ~ schicken** (fig) to send sb packing
Wut [vuːt] (-) f rage, fury; **eine ~ (auf jdn/etw) haben** to be furious (with sb/sth); **Wutanfall** m fit of rage
wüten ['vyːtən] vi to rage
wütend adj furious, enraged
wutentbrannt adj furious, enraged
Wz abk (= Warenzeichen)®

Xx

X, x [ɪks] *nt* X, x; **X wie Xanthippe** ≈ X for Xmas; **jdm ein X für ein U vormachen** to put one over on sb (*umg*)

X-Beine ['ɪksbaɪnə] *pl* knock-knees *pl*

x-beliebig [ɪksbə'liːbiç] *adj* any (... whatever)

Xerografie [kserogra'fiː] *f* xerography

xerokopieren [kseroko'piːrən] *vt* to xerox, photocopy

x-fach ['ɪksfax] *adj*: **die ~e Menge** (*Math*) n times the amount

x-mal ['ɪksmaːl] *adv* any number of times, n times

XML *abk* (*Comput*: = *extensible markup language*) XML

x-te ['ɪkstə] *adj* (*Math*: *umg*) nth; **zum ~n Male** (*umg*) for the nth *od* umpteenth time

Xylofon, Xylophon [ksylo'foːn] (**-s, -e**) *nt* xylophone

X

Yy

Y, y ['ʏpsilɔn] *nt* Y, y; **Y wie Ypsilon** ≈ Y for Yellow, Y for Yoke (US)

Yen [jɛn] **(-(s), -(s))** *m* yen

Yoga ['joːga] **(-(s))** *m od nt* yoga

Ypsilon ['ʏpsilɔn] **(-(s), -s)** *nt* the letter Y

Zz

Z, z [tsɛt] nt Z, z; **Z wie Zacharias** ≈ Z for Zebra

Zack [tsak] m: **auf ~ sein** (umg) to be on the ball

Zacke ['tsakə] (-, -n) f point; (Bergzacke) jagged peak; (Gabelzacke) prong; (Kammzacke) tooth

zackig ['tsakıç] adj jagged; (umg) smart; (: Tempo) brisk

zaghaft ['tsa:khaft] adj timid

Zaghaftigkeit f timidity

Zagreb ['za:grɛp] (-s) nt Zagreb

zäh [tsɛ:] adj tough; (Mensch) tenacious; (Flüssigkeit) thick; (schleppend) sluggish; **zähflüssig** adj viscous; (Verkehr) slow-moving

Zähigkeit f toughness; tenacity

Zahl [tsa:l] (-, -en) f number

zahlbar adj payable

zahlen vt, vi to pay; **~ bitte!** the bill od check (US) please!

zählen ['tsɛ:lən] vt to count ▷ vi (sich verlassen): **~ auf** +akk to count on; **seine Tage sind gezählt** his days are numbered; **~ zu** to be numbered among

Zahlen- zW: **Zahlenangabe** f figure; **Zahlenkombination** f combination of figures; **zahlenmäßig** adj numerical; **Zahlenschloss** nt combination lock

Zahler (-s, -) m payer

Zähler (-s, -) m (Tech) meter; (Math) numerator; **Zählerstand** m meter reading

Zahl- zW: **Zahlgrenze** f fare stage; **Zahlkarte** f transfer form; **zahllos** adj countless; **Zahlmeister** m (Naut) purser; **zahlreich** adj numerous; **Zahltag** m payday

Zahlung f payment; **in ~ geben/nehmen** to give/take in part exchange

Zahlungs- zW: **Zahlungsanweisung** f transfer order; **Zahlungsaufforderung** f request for payment; **zahlungsfähig** adj solvent; **Zahlungsmittel** nt means sing of payment; (Münzen, Banknoten) currency; **Zahlungsrückstände** pl arrears pl; **zahlungsunfähig** adj insolvent; **Zahlungsverzug** m default

Zahlwort nt numeral

zahm [tsa:m] adj tame

zähmen ['tsɛ:mən] vt to tame; (fig) to curb

Zahn [tsa:n] (-(e)s, ¨e) m tooth; **die dritten Zähne** (umg) false teeth pl; **einen ~ draufhaben** (umg: Geschwindigkeit) to be going

like the clappers (Brit) od like crazy (US); **jdm auf den ~ fühlen** (fig) to sound sb out; **einen ~ zulegen** (fig) to get a move on; **Zahnarzt** m, **Zahnärztin** f dentist; **Zahnbelag** m plaque; **Zahnbürste** f toothbrush; **Zahncreme** f toothpaste; **zahnen** vi to teethe; **Zahnersatz** m denture; **Zahnfäule** (-) f tooth decay, caries sing; **Zahnfleisch** nt gums pl; **auf dem Zahnfleisch gehen** (fig: umg) to be all in, be at the end of one's tether; **zahnlos** adj toothless; **Zahnmedizin** f dentistry; **Zahnpasta** f, **Zahnpaste** f toothpaste; **Zahnrad** nt cog(wheel); **Zahnradbahn** f rack railway; **Zahnschmelz** m (tooth) enamel; **Zahnschmerzen** pl toothache sing; **Zahnseide** f dental floss; **Zahnspange** f brace; **Zahnstein** m tartar; **Zahnstocher** (-s, -) m toothpick; **Zahntechniker**, in m(f) dental technician; **Zahnweh** nt toothache

Zaire [za'i:r] (-s) nt Zaire

Zange ['tsaŋə] (-, -n) f pliers pl; (Zuckerzange etc) tongs pl; (Beißzange, Zool) pincers pl; (Med) forceps pl; **jdn in die ~ nehmen** (fig) to put the screws on sb (umg)

Zangengeburt f forceps delivery

Zankapfel m bone of contention

zanken ['tsaŋkən] vi, vr to quarrel

zänkisch ['tsɛŋkıʃ] adj quarrelsome

Zäpfchen ['tsɛpfçən] nt (Anat) uvula; (Med) suppository

Zapfen ['tsapfən] (-s, -) m plug; (Bot) cone; (Eiszapfen) icicle

zapfen vt to tap

Zapfenstreich m (Mil) tattoo

Zapfsäule f petrol (Brit) od gas (US) pump

zappelig ['tsapəlıç] adj wriggly; (unruhig) fidgety

zappeln ['tsapəln] vi to wriggle; to fidget; **jdn ~ lassen** (fig: umg) to keep sb in suspense

Zar [tsa:r] (-en, -en) m tzar, czar

zart [tsa:rt] adj (weich, leise) soft; (Braten etc) tender; (fein, schwächlich) delicate; **zartbesaitet** ['tsa:rtbəzaıtət] adj highly sensitive; **zartbitter** adj (Schokolade) plain (Brit), bittersweet (US); **Zartgefühl** nt tact; **Zartheit** f softness; tenderness; delicacy

zärtlich ['tsɛ:rtlıç] adj tender, affectionate; **Zärtlichkeit** f tenderness; **Zärtlichkeiten** pl

Z

caresses *pl*

Zäsium ['tsɛ:zɪʊm] *nt* = **Cäsium**

Zäsur [tsɛ'zu:r] *f* caesura; (*fig*) break

Zauber ['tsaʊbər] (-s, -) *m* magic; (*Zauberbann*) spell; **fauler ~** (*umg*) humbug

Zauberei [tsaʊbə'raɪ] *f* magic

Zauberer (-s, -) *m* magician; (*Zauberkünstler*) conjurer

Zauber- *zW*: **zauberhaft** *adj* magical, enchanting; **Zauberin** *f* magician; conjurer; **Zauberkünstler** *m* conjurer; **Zauberkunststück** *nt* conjuring trick; **Zaubermittel** *nt* magical cure; (*Trank*) magic potion

zaubern *vi* to conjure, do magic

Zauberspruch *m* (magic) spell

Zauberstab *m* magic wand

zaudern ['tsaʊdərn] *vi* to hesitate

Zaum [tsaʊm] (-(e)s, Zäume) *m* bridle; **etw im ~ halten** to keep sth in check

Zaun [tsaʊn] (-(e)s, Zäune) *m* fence; **vom ~(e) brechen** (*fig*) to start; **Zaungast** *m* (*Person*) mere onlooker; **Zaunkönig** *m* wren

z. B. *abk* (= *zum Beispiel*) e.g.

z. d. A. *abk* (= *zu den Akten*) to be filed

ZDF *nt see culture note*

Zebra ['tse:bra] (-s, -s) *nt* zebra; **Zebrastreifen** *m* pedestrian crossing (*Brit*), crosswalk (*US*)

Zeche ['tsɛçə] (-, -n) *f* (*Rechnung*) bill, check (*US*); (*Bergbau*) mine

zechen *vi* to booze (*umg*)

Zechprellerei [tsɛçprɛlə'raɪ] *f skipping payment in restaurants etc*

Zecke ['tsɛkə] (-, -n) *f* tick

Zeder ['tse:dər] (-, -n) *f* cedar

Zeh [tse:] (-s, -en) *m* toe

Zehe ['tse:ə] (-, -n) *f* toe; (*Knoblauchzehe*) clove

Zehenspitze *f*: **auf ~n** on tiptoe

zehn [tse:n] *num* ten

Zehnerpackung *f* packet of ten

Zehnfingersystem *nt* touch-typing method

Zehnkampf *m* (*Sport*) decathlon

zehnte, r, s *adj* tenth

Zehntel (-s, -) *nt* tenth (part)

zehren ['tse:rən] *vi*: **an jdm/etw ~** (*an Mensch, Kraft*) to wear sb/sth out

Zeichen ['tsaɪçən] (-s, -) *nt* sign; (*Comput*) character; **jdm ein ~ geben** to give sb a signal; **unser/Ihr ~** (*Comm*) our/your reference; **Zeichenblock** *m* sketch pad; **Zeichencode** *m* (*Comput*) character code; **Zeichenerklärung** *f* key; (*auf Karten*) legend; **Zeichenfolge** *f*

(*Comput*) string; **Zeichenkette** *f* (*Comput*) character string; **Zeichensatz** *m* (*Comput*) character set; **Zeichensetzung** *f* punctuation; **Zeichentrickfilm** *m* (animated) cartoon

zeichnen *vt* to draw; (*kennzeichnen*) to mark; (*unterzeichnen*) to sign ▷ *vi* to draw; to sign

Zeichner, in (-s, -) *m(f)* artist; **technischer ~** draughtsman (*Brit*), draftsman (*US*)

Zeichnung *f* drawing; (*Markierung*) markings *pl*

zeichnungsberechtigt *adj* authorized to sign

Zeigefinger *m* index finger

zeigen ['tsaɪgən] *vt* to show ▷ *vi* to point ▷ *vr* to show o.s.; **~ auf** +*akk* to point to; **es wird sich ~** time will tell; **es zeigte sich, dass ...** it turned out that ...

Zeiger (-s, -) *m* pointer; (*Uhrzeiger*) hand

Zeile ['tsaɪlə] (-, -n) *f* line; (*Häuserzeile*) row

Zeilen- *zW*: **Zeilenabstand** *m* line spacing; **Zeilenausrichtung** *f* justification; **Zeilendrucker** *m* line printer; **Zeilenumbruch** *m* (*Comput*) wraparound; **Zeilenvorschub** *m* (*Comput*) line feed

zeit [tsaɪt] *präp* +*gen*: **~ meines Lebens** in my lifetime

Zeit [tsaɪt] (-, -en) *f* time; (*Gram*) tense; **sich** *dat* **~ lassen** to take one's time; **eine Stunde ~ haben** to have an hour (to spare); **sich** *dat* **für jdn/etw ~ nehmen** to devote time to sb/sth; **eine ~ lang** a while, a time; **von ~ zu Zeit** from time to time; **~ raubend** = **zeitraubend**; **in letzter ~** recently; **nach ~ bezahlt werden** to be paid by the hour; **zu der ~, als ...** (at the time) when ...; *siehe auch* **zurzeit**

Zeit- *zW*: **Zeitalter** *nt* age; **Zeitansage** *f* (*Rundf*) time check; (*Tel*) speaking clock; **Zeitarbeit** *f* temporary work; **Zeitaufwand** *m* time (*needed for a task*); **Zeitbombe** *f* time bomb; **Zeitdruck** *m*: **unter Zeitdruck stehen** to be under pressure; **Zeitgeist** *m* spirit of the times; **zeitgemäß** *adj* in keeping with the times; **Zeitgenosse** *m* contemporary; **zeitgenössisch** ['tsaɪtgənœsɪʃ] *adj* contemporary

zeitig *adj, adv* early

Zeit- *zW*: **Zeitkarte** *f* season ticket; **zeitkritisch** *adj* (*Aufsatz*) commenting on contemporary issues; **zeitlebens** *adv* all one's life; **zeitlich** *adj* temporal ▷ *adv*: **das kann sie zeitlich nicht einrichten** she can't find (the) time for that; **das Zeitliche segnen** (*euph*) to depart this life; **zeitlos** *adj* timeless; **Zeitlupe** *f* slow motion; **Zeitlupentempo** *nt*: **im Zeitlupentempo** at a snail's pace; **Zeitnot** *f*: **in Zeitnot geraten** to run short of time; **Zeitplan** *m* schedule; **Zeitpunkt** *m* moment, point in time; **Zeitraffer** (-s) *m* time-lapse photography; **zeitraubend** *adj* time-consuming; **Zeitraum** *m* period; **Zeitrechnung** *f* time, era; **nach/vor unserer Zeitrechnung** A.D./B.C.; **Zeitschrift** *f* periodical; **Zeittafel** *f* chronological table

Zeitung *f* newspaper

Zeitungs- *zW*: **Zeitungsanzeige** *f* newspaper advertisement; **Zeitungsausschnitt** *m* press cutting; **Zeitungshändler** *m* newsagent

(Brit), newsdealer (US); **Zeitungspapier** nt newsprint; **Zeitungsstand** m newsstand

Zeit- zW: **Zeitverschwendung** f waste of time; **Zeitvertreib** m pastime, diversion; **zeitweilig** adj temporary; **zeitweise** adv for a time; **Zeitwort** nt verb; **Zeitzeichen** nt (Rundf) time signal; **Zeitzone** f time zone; **Zeitzünder** m time fuse

Zelle ['tsɛlə] (-, -n) f cell; (Telefonzelle) callbox (Brit), booth

Zellkern m cell, nucleus

Zellophan [tsɛlo'faːn] (-s) nt cellophane

Zellstoff m cellulose

Zelt [tsɛlt] (-(e)s, -e) nt tent; **seine ~e aufschlagen/abbrechen** to settle down/pack one's bags; **Zeltbahn** f groundsheet; **zelten** vi to camp; **Zeltlager** nt camp; **Zeltplatz** m camp site

Zement [tse'mɛnt] (-(e)s, -e) m cement

zementieren [tsemɛn'tiːrən] vt to cement

Zementmaschine f cement mixer

Zenit [tse'niːt] (-(e)s) m (lit, fig) zenith

zensieren [tsɛn'ziːrən] vt to censor; (Sch) to mark

Zensur [tsɛn'zuːr] f censorship; (Sch) mark

Zensus ['tsɛnzʊs] (-, -) m census

Zentimeter [tsɛnti'meːtər] m od nt centimetre (Brit), centimeter (US); **Zentimetermaß** nt (metric) tape measure

Zentner ['tsɛntnər] (-s, -) m hundredweight

zentral [tsɛn'traːl] adj central

Zentrale (-, -n) f central office; (Tel) exchange

Zentraleinheit f (Comput) central processing unit

Zentralheizung f central heating

zentralisieren [tsɛntrali'ziːrən] vt to centralize

Zentralverriegelung f (Aut) central locking

Zentrifugalkraft [tsɛntrifu'gaːlkraft] f centrifugal force

Zentrifuge [tsɛntri'fuːgə] (-, -n) f centrifuge; (für Wäsche) spin-dryer

Zentrum ['tsɛntrʊm] (-s, **Zentren**) nt centre (Brit), center (US)

Zepter ['tsɛptər] (-s, -) nt sceptre (Brit), scepter (US)

zerbrechen unreg vt, vi to break

zerbrechlich adj fragile

zerbröckeln [tsɛr'brœkəln] vt, vi to crumble (to pieces)

zerdeppern [tsɛr'dɛpərn] vt to smash

zerdrücken vt to squash; to crush; (Kartoffeln) to mash

Zeremonie [tseremo'niː] f ceremony

Zeremoniell [tseremoni'ɛl] (-s, -e) nt ceremonial

zerfahren adj scatterbrained, distracted

Zerfall m decay, disintegration; (von Kultur, Gesundheit) decline; **zerfallen** unreg vi to disintegrate, decay; (sich gliedern): **zerfallen in** +akk to fall into

zerfetzen [tsɛr'fɛtsən] vt to tear to pieces

zerfleischen [tsɛr'flaɪʃən] vt to tear to pieces

zerfließen unreg vi to dissolve, melt away

zerfressen unreg vt to eat away; (Motten, Mäuse etc) to eat

zergehen unreg vi to melt, dissolve

zerkleinern [tsɛr'klaɪnərn] vt to reduce to small pieces

zerklüftet [tsɛr'klʏftət] adj: **tief ~es Gestein** deeply fissured rock

zerknirscht [tsɛr'knɪrʃt] adj overcome with remorse

zerknüllen [tsɛr'knʏlən] vt to crumple up

zerlaufen unreg vi to melt

zerlegbar [tsɛr'leːkbaːr] adj able to be dismantled

zerlegen vt to take to pieces; (Fleisch) to carve; (Satz) to analyse

zerlumpt [tsɛr'lʊmpt] adj ragged

zermalmen [tsɛr'malmən] vt to crush

zermürben [tsɛr'mʏrbən] vt to wear down

zerpflücken vt (lit, fig) to pick to pieces

zerplatzen vi to burst

zerquetschen vt to squash

Zerrbild ['tsɛrbɪlt] nt (fig) caricature, distorted picture

zerreden vt (Problem) to flog to death

zerreiben unreg vt to grind down

zerreißen unreg vt to tear to pieces ▷ vi to tear, rip

Zerreißprobe f (lit) pull test; (fig) real test

zerren ['tsɛrən] vt to drag ▷ vi: **~ (an** +dat) to tug (at)

zerrinnen unreg vi to melt away; (Geld) to disappear

zerrissen [tsɛr'rɪsən] pp von **zerreißen** ▷ adj torn, tattered; **Zerrissenheit** f tattered state; (Pol) disunion, discord; (innere) disintegration

Zerrspiegel ['tsɛrʃpiːgəl] m (lit) distorting mirror; (fig) travesty

Zerrung f: **eine ~** a pulled ligament/muscle

zerrütten [tsɛr'rʏtən] vt to wreck, destroy

zerrüttet adj wrecked, shattered

Zerrüttungsprinzip nt (bei Ehescheidung) principle of irretrievable breakdown

zerschellen [tsɛr'ʃɛlən] vi (Schiff, Flugzeug) to be smashed to pieces

zerschießen unreg vt to shoot to pieces

zerschlagen unreg vt to shatter, smash; (fig: Opposition) to crush; (: Vereinigung) to break up ▷ vr to fall through

zerschleißen [tsɛr'ʃlaɪsən] unreg vt, vi to wear out

zerschmelzen unreg vi to melt

zerschmettern unreg vt to shatter; (Feind) to crush ▷ vi to shatter

zerschneiden unreg vt to cut up

zersetzen vt, vr to decompose, dissolve

zersetzend adj (fig) subversive

zersplittern [tsɛr'ʃplɪtərn] vt, vi to split (into pieces); (Glas) to shatter

zerspringen unreg vi to shatter ▷ vi (fig) to burst

zerstäuben [tsɛr'ʃtɔʏbən] vt to spray

Zerstäuber (-s, -) m atomizer

zerstören vt to destroy

Zerstörer (-s, -) m (Naut) destroyer

Z

397

Zerstörung f destruction
Zerstörungswut f destructive mania
zerstoßen unreg vt to pound, pulverize
zerstreiten unreg vr to fall out, break up
zerstreuen vt to disperse, scatter; (Zweifel etc) to dispel ▷ vr (sich verteilen) to scatter; (fig) to be dispelled; (sich ablenken) to take one's mind off things
zerstreut adj scattered; (Mensch) absent-minded; **Zerstreutheit** f absent-mindedness
Zerstreuung f dispersion; (Ablenkung) diversion
zerstritten adj: **mit jdm ~ sein** to be on very bad terms with sb
zerstückeln [tsɛrˈʃtʏkəln] vt to cut into pieces
zerteilen vt to divide into parts
Zertifikat [tsɛrtifiˈkaːt] (-(e)s, -e) nt certificate
zertreten unreg vt to crush underfoot
zertrümmern [tsɛrˈtrʏmərn] vt to shatter; (Gebäude etc) to demolish
zerwühlen vt to ruffle up, tousle; (Bett) to rumple (up)
Zerwürfnis [tsɛrˈvʏrfnɪs] (-ses, -se) nt dissension, quarrel
zerzausen [tsɛrˈtsauzən] vt (Haare) to ruffle up, tousle
zetern [ˈtseːtərn] (pej) vi to clamour (Brit), clamor (US); (keifen) to scold
Zettel [ˈtsɛtəl] (-s, -) m piece od slip of paper; (Notizzettel) note; (Formular) form; „~ **ankleben verboten“** "stick no bills"; **Zettelkasten** m card index (box); **Zettelwirtschaft** (pej) f: **eine Zettelwirtschaft haben** to have bits of paper everywhere
Zeug [tsɔʏk] (-(e)s, -e) (umg) nt stuff; (Ausrüstung) gear; **dummes ~** (stupid) nonsense; **das ~ haben zu** to have the makings of; **sich ins ~ legen** to put one's shoulder to the wheel; **was das ~ hält** for all one is worth; **jdm am ~ flicken** to find fault with sb
Zeuge [ˈtsɔʏgə] (-n, -n) m witness
zeugen vi to bear witness, testify ▷ vt (Kind) to father; **es zeugt von ...** it testifies to ...
Zeugenaussage f evidence
Zeugenstand m witness box (Brit) od stand (US)
Zeugin f witness
Zeugnis [ˈtsɔʏgnɪs] (-ses, -se) nt certificate; (Sch) report; (Referenz) reference; (Aussage) evidence, testimony; **~ geben von** to be evidence of, testify to; **Zeugniskonferenz** f (Sch) staff meeting to decide on marks etc
Zeugung [ˈtsɔʏgʊŋ] f procreation
zeugungsunfähig adj sterile
ZH abk = **Zentralheizung**
z. H., z. Hd. abk (= zu Händen) att., attn.
Zicken [ˈtsɪkən] (umg) pl: **~ machen** to make trouble
zickig adj (albern) silly; (prüde) prudish
Zickzack [ˈtsɪktsak] (-(e)s, -e) m zigzag
Ziege [ˈtsiːgə] (-, -n) f goat; (pej: umg: Frau) cow (!)
Ziegel [ˈtsiːgəl] (-s, -) m brick; (Dachziegel) tile

Ziegelei [tsiːgəˈlaɪ] f brickworks
Ziegelstein m brick
Ziegenbock m billy goat
Ziegenleder nt kid
Ziegenpeter m mumps sing
Ziehbrunnen m well
ziehen [ˈtsiːən] unreg vt to draw; (zerren) to pull; (Schach etc) to move; (züchten) to rear ▷ vi to draw; (umziehen, wandern) to move; (Rauch, Wolke etc) to drift; (reißen) to pull ▷ vb unpers: **es zieht** there is a draught (Brit) od draft (US), it's draughty (Brit) od drafty (US) ▷ vr (Gummi) to stretch; (Grenze etc) to run; (Gespräche) to be drawn out; **etw nach sich ~** to lead to sth, entail sth; **etw ins Lächerliche ~** to ridicule sth; **so was zieht bei mir nicht** I don't like that sort of thing; **zu jdm ~** to move in with sb; **mir ziehts im Rücken** my back hurts; **Ziehen** (-s, -) nt (Schmerz) ache; (im Unterleib) dragging pain
Ziehharmonika [ˈtsiːharmoːnika] f concertina
Ziehung [ˈtsiːʊŋ] f (Losziehung) drawing
Ziel [tsiːl] (-(e)s, -e) nt (einer Reise) destination; (Sport) finish; (Mil) target; (Absicht) goal, aim; **jdm/sich ein ~ stecken** to set sb/o.s. a goal; **am ~ sein** to be at one's destination; (fig) to have reached one's goal; **über das ~ hinausschießen** (fig) to overshoot the mark; **zielbewusst** adj purposeful; **zielen** vi: **zielen (auf** +akk) to aim (at); **Zielfernrohr** nt telescopic sight; **Zielfoto** nt (Sport) photo-finish, photograph; **Zielgruppe** f target group; **Ziellinie** f (Sport) finishing line; **ziellos** adj aimless; **Zielort** m destination; **Zielscheibe** f target; **zielstrebig** adj purposeful
ziemen [ˈtsiːmən] vr unpers (geh): **das ziemt sich nicht (für dich)** it is not proper (for you)
ziemlich [ˈtsiːmlɪç] adj attrib (Anzahl) fair ▷ adv quite, pretty (umg); (beinahe) almost, nearly; **eine ~e Anstrengung** quite an effort; **~ lange** quite a long time; **~ fertig** almost od nearly ready
Zierde [ˈtsiːrdə] (-, -n) f ornament, decoration; (Schmuckstück) adornment
zieren [ˈtsiːrən] vr to act coy
Zierleiste f border; (an Wand, Möbeln) moulding (Brit), molding (US); (an Auto) trim
zierlich adj dainty; **Zierlichkeit** f daintiness
Zierstrauch m flowering shrub
Ziffer [ˈtsɪfər] (-, -n) f figure, digit; **römische/arabische ~n** roman/arabic numerals; **Zifferblatt** nt dial, (clock od watch) face
zig [tsɪk] (umg) adj umpteen
Zigarette [tsigaˈrɛtə] f cigarette
Zigaretten- zW: **Zigarettenautomat** m cigarette machine; **Zigarettenpause** f break for a cigarette; **Zigarettenschachtel** f cigarette packet od pack (US); **Zigarettenspitze** f cigarette holder
Zigarillo [tsigaˈrɪlo] (-s, -s) nt od m cigarillo
Zigarre [tsiˈgarə] (-, -n) f cigar
Zigeuner, in [tsiˈgɔʏnər(ɪn)] (-s, -) m(f) gipsy; **Zigeunerschnitzel** nt (Koch) cutlet served in a spicy

sauce with green and red peppers; **Zigeunersprache** f Romany (language)

Zimmer ['tsɪmər] **(-s, -)** nt room; **Zimmerantenne** f indoor aerial; **Zimmerdecke** f ceiling; **Zimmerlautstärke** f reasonable volume; **Zimmermädchen** nt chambermaid; **Zimmermann (-(e)s,** pl **-leute)** m carpenter

zimmern vt to make from wood

Zimmer- zW: **Zimmernachweis** m accommodation service; **Zimmerpflanze** f indoor plant; **Zimmervermittlung** f accommodation (Brit) od accommodations (US) service

zimperlich ['tsɪmpərlɪç] adj squeamish; (pingelig) fussy, finicky

Zimt [tsɪmt] **(-(e)s, -e)** m cinnamon; **Zimtstange** f cinnamon stick

Zink [tsɪŋk] **(-(e)s)** nt zinc

Zinke (-, -n) f (Gabelzinke) prong; (Kammzinke) tooth

Zinken (-s, -) (umg) m (Nase) hooter

zinken vt (Karten) to mark

Zinksalbe f zinc ointment

Zinn [tsɪn] **(-(e)s)** nt (Element) tin; (in Zinnwaren) pewter; **Zinnbecher** m pewter tankard

zinnoberrot [tsɪ'no:bərrot] adj vermilion

Zinnsoldat m tin soldier

Zinnwaren pl pewter sing

Zins [tsɪns] **(-es, -en)** m interest

Zinseszins m compound interest

Zins- zW: **Zinsfuß** m rate of interest; **zinslos** adj interest-free; **Zinssatz** m rate of interest; **Zinssteuer** f tax on interest

Zionismus [tsio'nɪsmʊs] m Zionism

Zipfel ['tsɪpfəl] **(-s, -)** m corner; (von Land) tip; (Hemdzipfel) tail; (Wurstzipfel) end; **Zipfelmütze** f pointed cap

zirka ['tsɪrka] adv = **circa**

Zirkel ['tsɪrkəl] **(-s, -)** m circle; (Math) pair of compasses; **Zirkelkasten** m geometry set

zirkulieren [tsɪrku'li:rən] vi to circulate

Zirkus ['tsɪrkʊs] **(-, -se)** m circus; (umg: Getue) fuss, to-do

zirpen ['tsɪrpən] vi to chirp, cheep

Zirrhose [tsɪ'ro:zə] **(-, -n)** f cirrhosis

zischeln ['tsɪʃəln] vt, vi to whisper

zischen ['tsɪʃən] vi to hiss; (Limonade) to fizz; (Fett) to sizzle

Zitat [tsi'ta:t] **(-(e)s, -e)** nt quotation, quote

zitieren [tsi'ti:rən] vt to quote; (vorladen, rufen): **~ (vor** +akk) to summon (before)

Zitronat [tsitro'na:t] **(-(e)s, -e)** nt candied lemon peel

Zitrone [tsi'tro:nə] **(-, -n)** f lemon

Zitronen- zW: **Zitronenlimonade** f lemonade; **Zitronensaft** m lemon juice; **Zitronensäure** f citric acid; **Zitronenscheibe** f lemon slice

zitterig ['tsɪtərɪç], **zittrig** ['tsɪtrɪç] adj shaky

zittern ['tsɪtərn] vi to tremble; **vor jdm ~** to be terrified of sb

Zitze ['tsɪtsə] **(-, -n)** f teat, dug

Zivi ['tsivi] **(-s, -s)** m abk = **Zivildienstleistender**

zivil [tsi'vi:l] adj civilian; (anständig) civil; (Preis) moderate; **~er Ungehorsam** civil disobedience; **Zivil (-s)** nt plain clothes pl; (Mil) civilian clothing; **Zivilbevölkerung** f civilian population; **Zivilcourage** f courage of one's convictions

Zivildienst m alternative service (for conscientious objectors); see culture note

Zivildienstleistender m conscientious objector doing alternative community service

Zivilisation [tsivilizatsi'o:n] f civilization

Zivilisationserscheinung f phenomenon of civilization

Zivilisationskrankheit f disease of civilized man

zivilisieren [tsivili'zi:rən] vt to civilize

zivilisiert adj civilized

Zivilist [tsivi'lɪst] m civilian

Zivilrecht nt civil law

ZK (-s, -s) nt abk (= Zentralkomitee) central committee

Zobel ['tso:bəl] **(-s, -)** m (auch: **Zobelpelz**) sable (fur)

Zofe ['tso:fə] **(-, -n)** f lady's maid; (von Königin) lady-in-waiting

zog etc [tso:k] vb siehe **ziehen**

zögern ['tsø:gərn] vi to hesitate

Zölibat [tsøli'ba:t] **(-(e)s)** nt od m celibacy

Zoll¹ [tsɔl] **(-(e)s, -)** m (Maß) inch

Zoll² (-(e)s, ̈e) m customs pl; (Abgabe) duty; **Zollabfertigung** f customs clearance; **Zollamt** nt customs office; **Zollbeamte, r** m customs official; **Zollerklärung** f customs declaration; **zollfrei** adj duty-free; **Zollgutlager** nt bonded warehouse; **Zollkontrolle** f customs (check); **zollpflichtig** adj liable to duty, dutiable

Zollstock m inch rule

Zone ['tso:nə] **(-, -n)** f zone; (von Fahrkarte) fare stage

Zoo [tso:] **(-s, -s)** m zoo; **Zoohandlung** f pet shop

Zoologe [tsoo'lo:gə] **(-n, -n)** m zoologist

Zoologie f zoology

Zoologin f zoologist

zoologisch adj zoological

Zoom [zu:m] **(-s, -s)** nt zoom shot; (Objektiv) zoom lens

Zopf [tsɔpf] **(-(e)s, ̈e)** m plait; pigtail; **alter ~** antiquated custom

Zorn [tsɔrn] **(-(e)s)** m anger

zornig adj angry

Zote | zudrücken

Zote ['tso:tə] (-, -n) *f* smutty joke/remark
zottig ['tsɔtɪç] *adj* shaggy
ZPO *abk* (= *Zivilprozessordnung*) ≈ General Practice
Act (US)
z. T. *abk* = **zum Teil**

 SCHLÜSSELWORT

zu [tsu:] *präp+dat* **1** (*örtlich*) to; **zum Bahnhof/
Arzt gehen** to go to the station/doctor; **zur
Schule/Kirche gehen** to go to school/church;
sollen wir zu Euch gehen? shall we go to
your place?; **sie sah zu ihm hin** she looked
towards him; **zum Fenster herein** through
the window; **zu meiner Linken** to *od* on my
left
2 (*zeitlich*) at; **zu Ostern** at Easter; **bis zum 1.
Mai** until May 1st; (*nicht später als*) by May 1st;
zu meiner Zeit in my time
3 (*Zusatz*) with; **Wein zum Essen trinken**
to drink wine with one's meal; **sich zu
jdm setzen** to sit down beside sb; **setz
dich doch zu uns** (come and) sit with us;
Anmerkungen zu etw notes on sth
4 (*Zweck*) for; **Wasser zum Waschen** water
for washing; **Papier zum Schreiben** paper to
write on; **etw zum Geburtstag bekommen**
to get sth for one's birthday; **es ist zu seinem
Besten** it's for his own good
5 (*Veränderung*) into; **zu etw werden** to turn
into sth; **jdn zu etw machen** to make sb
(into) sth; **zu Asche verbrennen** to burn to
ashes
6 (*mit Zahlen*): **3 zu 2** (*Sport*) 3-2; **das Stück zu 5
Euro** at 5 euros each; **zum ersten Mal** for the
first time
7: **zu meiner Freude** *etc* to my joy *etc*; **zum
Glück** luckily; **zu Fuß** on foot; **es ist zum
Weinen** it's enough to make you cry
▷ *konj* to; **etw zu essen** sth to eat; **um besser
sehen zu können** in order to see better; **ohne
es zu wissen** without knowing it; **noch zu
bezahlende Rechnungen** outstanding bills
▷ *adv* **1** (*allzu*) too; **zu sehr** too much; **zu viel**
too much; (*umg: zu viele*) too many; **er kriegt
zu viel** (*umg*) he gets annoyed; **zu wenig** too
little; (*umg: zu wenige*) too few
2 (*örtlich*) toward(s); **er kam auf mich zu** he
came towards *od* up to me
3 (*geschlossen*) shut; closed; **die Geschäfte
haben zu** the shops are closed; **zu sein** to be
closed; **auf/zu** (*Wasserhahn etc*) on/off
4 (*umg: los*): **nur zu!** just keep at it!; **mach zu!**
hurry up!

zuallererst *adv* first of all
zuallerletzt *adv* last of all
zubauen ['tsu:bauən] *vt* (*Lücke*) to fill in; (*Platz,
Gebäude*) to build up
Zubehör ['tsu:bəhø:r] (**-(e)s, -e**) *nt* accessories
pl
Zuber ['tsu:bər] (**-s, -**) *m* tub
zubereiten ['tsu:bəraitən] *vt* to prepare

zubilligen ['tsu:bɪlɪgən] *vt* to grant
zubinden ['tsu:bɪndən] *unreg vt* to tie up; **jdm
die Augen ~** to blindfold sb
zubleiben ['tsu:blaibən] *unreg vi* to stay shut
zubringen ['tsu:brɪŋən] *unreg vt* to spend;
(*herbeibringen*) to bring, take; (*umg: Tür*) to get
shut
Zubringer (**-s, -**) *m* (*Tech*) feeder, conveyor;
(*Verkehrsmittel*) shuttle; (*zum Flughafen*)
airport bus; **Zubringerbus** *m* shuttle (bus);
Zubringerstraße *f* slip road (Brit), entrance
ramp (US)
Zucchini [tsʊ'ki:ni:] *pl* courgettes *pl* (Brit),
zucchini(s) *pl* (US)
Zucht [tsʊxt] (**-, -en**) *f* (*von Tieren*) breeding; (*von
Pflanzen*) cultivation; (*Rasse*) breed; (*Erziehung*)
raising; (*Disziplin*) discipline; **Zuchtbulle** *m*
breeding bull
züchten ['tsʏçtən] *vt* (*Tiere*) to breed; (*Pflanzen*)
to cultivate, grow
Züchter, in (**-s, -**) *m(f)* breeder; grower
Zuchthaus *nt* prison, penitentiary (US)
Zuchthengst *m* stallion, stud
züchtig ['tsʏçtɪç] *adj* modest, demure
züchtigen ['tsʏçtɪgən] *vt* to chastise
Züchtigung *f* chastisement; **körperliche ~**
corporal punishment
Zuchtperle *f* cultured pearl
Züchtung *f* (*von Tieren*) breeding; (*von Pflanzen*)
cultivation; (*Zuchtart: von Tier*) breed; (*: von
Pflanze*) strain
zucken ['tsʊkən] *vi* to jerk, twitch; (*Strahl etc*)
to flicker ▷ *vt* to shrug; **der Schmerz zuckte
(mir) durch den ganzen Körper** the pain
shot right through my body
zücken ['tsʏkən] *vt* (*Schwert*) to draw;
(*Geldbeutel*) to pull out
Zucker ['tsʊkər] (**-s, -**) *m* sugar; (*Med*) diabetes;
~ haben (*umg*) to be a diabetic; **Zuckerdose**
f sugar bowl; **Zuckererbse** *f* mangetout
(Brit), sugar pea (US); **Zuckerguss** *m* icing;
Zuckerhut *m* sugar loaf; **zuckerkrank** *adj*
diabetic; **Zuckerkrankheit** *f* diabetes *sing*;
Zuckerlecken *nt*: **das ist kein Zuckerlecken**
it's no picnic
zuckern *vt* to sugar
Zucker- *zW*: **Zuckerrohr** *nt* sugar cane;
Zuckerrübe *f* sugar beet; **Zuckerspiegel**
m (*Med*) (blood) sugar level; **zuckersüß** *adj*
sugary; **Zuckerwatte** *f* candy floss (Brit),
cotton candy (US)
Zuckung *f* convulsion, spasm; (*leicht*) twitch
zudecken ['tsu:dɛkən] *vt* to cover (up); (*im Bett*)
to tuck up *od* in
zudem [tsu'de:m] *adv* in addition (to this)
zudrehen ['tsu:dre:ən] *vt* to turn off
zudringlich ['tsu:drɪŋlɪç] *adj* forward, pushy;
(*Nachbar etc*) intrusive; **~ werden** to make
advances; **Zudringlichkeit** *f* forwardness;
intrusiveness
zudrücken ['tsu:drʏkən] *vt* to close; **jdm die
Kehle ~** to throttle sb; **ein Auge ~** to turn a
blind eye

zueinander [tsu|aɪˈnandər] *adv* to one other; (*in Verbverbindung*) together

zuerkennen [ˈtsuːˌʔɛrkɛnən] *unreg vt*: **jdm etw ~** to award sth to sb, award sb sth

zuerst [tsuˈʔeːrst] *adv* first; (*zu Anfang*) at first; **~ einmal** first of all

Zufahrt [ˈtsuːfaːrt] *f* approach; **„keine ~ zum Krankenhaus"** "no access to hospital"

Zufahrtsstraße *f* approach road; (*von Autobahn etc*) slip road (*Brit*), entrance ramp (*US*)

Zufall [ˈtsuːfal] *m* chance; (*Ereignis*) coincidence; **durch ~** by accident; **so ein ~!** what a coincidence!

zufallen *unreg vi* to close, shut; (*Anteil, Aufgabe*): **jdm ~** to fall to sb

zufällig [ˈtsuːfɛlɪç] *adj* chance ▷ *adv* by chance; (*in Frage*) by any chance

Zufallstreffer *m* fluke

zufassen [ˈtsuːfasən] *vi* (*zugreifen*) to take hold (*of it od them*); (*fig: schnell handeln*) to seize the opportunity; (*helfen*) to lend a hand

zufliegen [ˈtsuːfliːgən] *unreg vi*: **ihm fliegt alles nur so zu** (*fig*) everything comes so easily to him

Zuflucht [ˈtsuːflʊxt] *f* recourse; (*Ort*) refuge; **zu etw ~ nehmen** (*fig*) to resort to sth

Zufluchtsort *m*, **Zufluchtsstätte** *f* place of refuge

Zufluss [ˈtsuːflʊs] *m* (*Zufließen*) inflow, influx; (*Geog*) tributary; (*Comm*) supply

zufolge [tsuˈfɔlgə] *präp +dat od +gen* (*laut*) according to; (*aufgrund*) as a result of

zufrieden [tsuˈfriːdən] *adj* content(ed); **er ist mit nichts ~** nothing pleases him; **zufriedengeben** *unreg vr*: **sich mit etw zufriedengeben** to be satisfied with sth; **Zufriedenheit** *f* contentedness; (*Befriedigtsein*) satisfaction; **zufriedenlassen** *unreg vt*: **lass mich damit zufrieden!** (*umg*) shut up about it!; **zufriedenstellen** *vt* to satisfy; **zufriedenstellend** *adj* satisfactory

zufrieren [ˈtsuːfriːrən] *unreg vi* to freeze up *od* over

zufügen [ˈtsuːfyːgən] *vt* to add; (*Leid etc*): **jdm etw ~** to cause sb sth

Zufuhr [ˈtsuːfuːr] (**-, -en**) *f* (*Herbeibringen*) supplying; (*Met*) influx; (*Mil*) supplies *pl*

zuführen [ˈtsuːfyːrən] *vt* (*bringen*) to bring; (*transportieren*) to convey; (*versorgen*) to supply ▷ *vi*: **auf etw** *akk* **~** to lead to sth

Zug [tsuːk] (**-(e)s, ̈e**) *m* (*Eisenbahnzug*) train; (*Luftzug*) draught (*Brit*), draft (*US*); (*Ziehen*) pull(ing); (*Gesichtszug*) feature; (*Schach etc*) move; (*Klingelzug*) pull; (*Schriftzug, beim Schwimmen*) stroke; (*Atemzug*) breath; (*Charakterzug*) trait; (*an Zigarette*) puff, pull, drag; (*Schluck*) gulp; (*Menschengruppe*) procession; (*von Vögeln*) migration; (*Mil*) platoon; **etw in vollen Zügen genießen** to enjoy sth to the full; **in den letzten Zügen liegen** (*umg*) to be at one's last gasp; **im ~(e)** *+gen* (*im Verlauf*) in the course of; **~ um Zug** (*fig*) step by step; **zum ~(e) kommen** (*umg*) to get

a look-in; **etw in groben Zügen darstellen** *od* **umreißen** to outline sth; **das war kein schöner ~ von dir** that wasn't nice of you

Zugabe [ˈtsuːgaːbə] *f* extra; (*in Konzert etc*) encore

Zugabteil *nt* train compartment

Zugang [ˈtsuːgaŋ] *m* entrance; (*Zutritt, fig*) access

zugänglich [ˈtsuːgɛŋlɪç] *adj* accessible; (*öffentliche Einrichtungen*) open; (*Mensch*) approachable

Zugangscode *m* (*Comput*) access code

Zugbegleiter *m* (*Eisenb*) guard (*Brit*), conductor (*US*)

Zugbrücke *f* drawbridge

zugeben [ˈtsuːgeːbən] *unreg vt* (*beifügen*) to add, throw in; (*zugestehen*) to admit; (*erlauben*) to permit; **zugegeben ... granted ...

zugegebenermaßen [ˈtsuːgegəˌbənərˈmaːsən] *adv* admittedly

zugegen [tsuˈgeːgən] *adv* (*geh*): **~ sein** to be present

zugehen [ˈtsuːgeːən] *unreg vi* (*schließen*) to shut ▷ *vi unpers* (*sich ereignen*) to go on, happen; **auf jdn/etw ~** to walk towards sb/sth; **dem Ende ~** to be finishing; **er geht schon auf die siebzig zu** he's getting on for seventy; **hier geht es nicht mit rechten Dingen zu** there's something odd going on here; **dort geht es ... zu** things are ... there

Zugehörigkeit [ˈtsuːgəhøːrɪçkaɪt] *f*: **~ (zu)** membership (of), belonging (to)

Zugehörigkeitsgefühl *nt* feeling of belonging

zugeknöpft [ˈtsuːgəknœpft] (*umg*) *adj* reserved, stand-offish

Zügel [ˈtsyːgəl] (**-s, -**) *m* rein, reins *pl*; (*fig*) rein, curb; **die ~ locker lassen** to slacken one's hold on the reins; **die ~ locker lassen bei** (*fig*) to give free rein to

zugelassen [ˈtsuːgəlasən] *adj* authorized; (*Heilpraktiker*) registered; (*Kfz*) licensed

zügellos *adj* unrestrained; (*sexuell*) licentious

Zügellosigkeit *f* lack of restraint; licentiousness

zügeln *vt* to curb; (*Pferd*) to rein in

zugesellen *vr*: **sich jdm ~** to join sb, join up with sb

Zugeständnis [ˈtsuːgəʃtɛntnɪs] (**-ses, -se**) *nt* concession; **~se machen** to make allowances

zugestehen *unreg vt* to admit; (*Rechte*) to concede

zugetan [ˈtsuːgətaːn] *adj*: **jdm/etw ~ sein** to be fond of sb/sth

Zugewinn (**-(e)s**) *m* (*Jur*) *property acquired during marriage*

Zugezogene, r [ˈtsuːgətsoːgənə(r)] *f(m)* newcomer

Zugführer *m* (*Eisenb*) chief guard (*Brit*) *od* conductor (*US*); (*Mil*) platoon commander

zugig *adj* draughty (*Brit*), drafty (*US*)

zügig [ˈtsyːgɪç] *adj* speedy, swift

zugkräftig *adj* (*fig: Werbetext, Titel*) eye-catching; (*Schauspieler*) crowd-pulling *attr*, popular

zugleich [tsu'glaɪç] *adv* (*zur gleichen Zeit*) at the same time; (*ebenso*) both

Zugluft *f* draught (*Brit*), draft (*US*)

Zugmaschine *f* traction engine, tractor

zugreifen ['tsu:graɪfən] *unreg vi* to seize *od* grab it/them; (*helfen*) to help; (*beim Essen*) to help o.s.

Zugriff ['tsu:grɪf] *m* (*Comput*) access; **sich dem ~ der Polizei entziehen** (*fig*) to evade justice

zugrunde, zu Grunde [tsu'grʊndə] *adv*: **~ gehen** to collapse; (*Mensch*) to perish; **er wird daran nicht ~ gehen** he'll survive; (*finanziell*) it won't ruin him; **einer Sache** *dat* **etw ~ legen** to base sth on sth; **einer Sache** *dat* **~ liegen** to be based on sth; **~ richten** to ruin, destroy

zugunsten, zu Gunsten [tsu'gʊnstən] *präp* +*gen od* +*dat* in favour (*Brit*) *od* favor (*US*) of

zugutehalten [tsu'gu:təhaltən] *unreg vt*: **jdm etw ~** to concede sth to sb

zugutekommen [tsu'gu:təkɔmən] *unreg vt*: **jdm ~** to be of assistance to sb

Zug- *zW*: **Zugverbindung** *f* train connection; **Zugvogel** *m* migratory bird; **Zugzwang** *m* (*Schach*) zugzwang; **unter Zugzwang stehen** (*fig*) to be in a tight spot

zuhalten ['tsu:haltən] *unreg vt* to hold shut ▷ *vi*: **auf jdn/etw ~** to make for sb/sth; **sich** *dat* **die Nase ~** to hold one's nose

Zuhälter ['tsu:hɛltər] (**-s, -**) *m* pimp

zuhause [tsu'haʊzə] *adv* at home

Zuhause (**-s**) *nt* home

Zuhilfenahme [tsu'hɪlfəna:mə] *f*: **unter ~ von** with the help of

zuhören ['tsu:hø:rən] *vi* to listen

Zuhörer (**-s, -**) *m* listener; **Zuhörerschaft** *f* audience

zujubeln ['tsu:ju:bəln] *vi*: **jdm ~** to cheer sb

zukehren ['tsu:ke:rən] *vt* (*zuwenden*) to turn

zuklappen ['tsu:klapən] *vt* (*Buch, Deckel*) to close ▷ *vi* (*Hilfsverb sein: Tür etc*) to click shut

zukleben ['tsu:kle:bən] *vt* to paste up

zukneifen ['tsu:knaɪfən] *vt* (*Augen*) to screw up; (*Mund*) to shut tight(ly)

zuknöpfen ['tsu:knœpfən] *vt* to button (up), fasten (up)

zukommen ['tsu:kɔmən] *unreg vi* to come up; **auf jdn ~** to come up to sb; **jdm ~** (*sich gehören*) to be fitting for sb; **diesem Treffen kommt große Bedeutung zu** this meeting is of the utmost importance; **jdm etw ~ lassen** to give sb sth; **die Dinge auf sich** *akk* **~ lassen** to take things as they come

Zukunft ['tsu:kʊnft] (**-, no pl**) *f* future

zukünftig ['tsu:kʏnftɪç] *adj* future ▷ *adv* in future; **mein ~er Mann** my husband-to-be

Zukunfts- *zW*: **Zukunftsaussichten** *pl* future prospects *pl*; **Zukunftsmusik** (*umg*) *f* wishful thinking; **Zukunftsroman** *m* science-fiction novel; **zukunftsträchtig** *adj* promising for the future; **zukunftsweisend** *adj* trend-setting

Zulage ['tsu:la:gə] *f* bonus

zulande [tsu'landə] *adv*: **bei uns ~** in our country

zulangen ['tsu:laŋən] (*umg*) *vi* (*Dieb, beim Essen*) to help o.s.

zulassen ['tsu:lasən] *unreg vt* (*hereinlassen*) to admit; (*erlauben*) to permit; (*Auto*) to license; (*umg: nicht öffnen*) to keep shut

zulässig ['tsu:lɛsɪç] *adj* permissible, permitted; **~e Höchstgeschwindigkeit** (upper) speed limit

Zulassung *f* (*amtlich*) authorization; (*von Kfz*) licensing; (*als praktizierender Arzt*) registration

Zulauf *m*: **großen ~ haben** (*Geschäft*) to be very popular

zulaufen ['tsu:laʊfən] *unreg vi*: **~ auf** +*akk* to run towards; **jdm ~** (*Tier*) to adopt sb; **spitz ~** to come to a point

zulegen ['tsu:le:gən] *vt* to add; (*Geld*) to put in; (*Tempo*) to accelerate, quicken; (*schließen*) to cover over; **sich** *dat* **etw ~** (*umg*) to get oneself sth

zuleide [tsu'laɪdə] *adj*: **jdm etw ~ tun** to harm sb

zuleiten ['tsu:laɪtən] *vt* (*Wasser*) to supply; (*schicken*) to send

Zuleitung *f* (*Tech*) supply

zuletzt [tsu'lɛtst] *adv* finally, at last; **wir blieben bis ~** we stayed to the very end; **nicht ~ wegen** not least because of

zuliebe [tsu'li:bə] *adv*: **jdm ~** (in order) to please sb

Zulieferbetrieb ['tsu:li:fərbətri:p] *m* (*Comm*) supplier

zum [tsʊm] = **zu dem**; **~ dritten Mal** for the third time; **~ Scherz** as a joke; **~ Trinken** for drinking; **bis ~ 15. April** until 15th April; (*nicht später als*) by 15th April; **~ ersten Mal(e)** for the first time; **es ist ~ Weinen** it's enough to make you (want to) weep; **~ Glück** luckily

zumachen ['tsu:maxən] *vt* to shut; (*Kleidung*) to do up, fasten ▷ *vi* to shut; (*umg*) to hurry up

zumal [tsu'ma:l] *konj* especially (as)

zumeist [tsu'maɪst] *adv* mostly

zumessen ['tsu:mɛsən] *unreg vt* (+*dat*) (*Zeit*) to allocate (for); (*Bedeutung*) to attach (to)

zumindest [tsu'mɪndəst] *adv* at least

zumutbar ['tsu:mu:tba:r] *adj* reasonable

zumute [tsu'mu:tə] *adv*: **wie ist ihm ~?** how does he feel?

zumuten ['tsu:mu:tən] *vt*: **(jdm) etw ~** to expect *od* ask sth (of sb); **sich** *dat* **zu viel ~** to take on too much

Zumutung *f* unreasonable expectation *od* demand; (*Unverschämtheit*) impertinence; **das ist eine ~!** that's a bit much!

zunächst [tsu'nɛ:çst] *adv* first of all; **~ einmal** to start with

zunageln ['tsu:na:gəln] *vt* (*Fenster etc*) to nail up; (*Kiste etc*) to nail down

zunähen ['tsu:nɛ:ən] *vt* to sew up

Zunahme ['tsu:na:mə] (**-, -n**) *f* increase

Zuname ['tsu:na:mə] *m* surname

zünden ['tsʏndən] *vi* (*Feuer*) to light, ignite;

(*Motor*) to fire; (*fig*) to kindle enthusiasm ▷ *vt* to ignite; (*Rakete*) to fire

zündend *adj* fiery

Zünder (-s, -) *m* fuse; (*Mil*) detonator

Zünd- *zW*: **Zündholz** *nt* match; **Zündkabel** *nt* (*Aut*) plug lead; **Zündkerze** *f* (*Aut*) spark(ing) plug; **Zündplättchen** *nt* cap; **Zündschlüssel** *m* ignition key; **Zündschnur** *f* fuse wire; **Zündstoff** *m* fuel; (*fig*) dynamite

Zündung *f* ignition

zunehmen ['tsuːneːmən] *unreg vi* to increase, grow; (*Mensch*) to put on weight

zunehmend *adj*: **mit ~em Alter** with advancing age

zuneigen ['tsuːnaɪgən] *vi* to incline, lean; **sich dem Ende ~** to draw to a close; **einer Auffassung ~** to incline towards a view; **jdm zugeneigt sein** to be attracted to sb

Zuneigung *f* affection

Zunft [tsʊnft] **(-, ̈e)** *f* guild

zünftig ['tsʏnftɪç] *adj* (*Arbeit*) professional; (*umg: ordentlich*) proper, real

Zunge ['tsʊŋə] *f* tongue; (*Fisch*) sole; **böse ~n behaupten, ...** malicious gossip has it ...

züngeln ['tsʏŋəln] *vi* (*Flammen*) to lick

Zungenbrecher *m* tongue-twister

zungenfertig *adj* glib

Zünglein ['tsʏŋlaɪn] *nt*: **das ~ an der Waage sein** (*fig*) to tip the scales

zunichtemachen [tsuˈnɪçtəmaxən] *vt* to ruin, destroy

zunichtewerden [tsuˈnɪçtəveːrdən] *unreg vi* to come to nothing

zunutze [tsuˈnʊtsə] *adv*: **sich** *dat* **etw ~ machen** to make use of sth

zuoberst [tsuˈ|oːbərst] *adv* at the top

zuordnen ['tsuː|ɔrdnən] *vt* to assign

zupacken ['tsuːpakən] (*umg*) *vi* (*zugreifen*) to make a grab for it; (*bei der Arbeit*) to get down to it; **mit ~** (*helfen*) to give me/them *etc* a hand

zupfen ['tsʊpfən] *vt* to pull, pick, pluck; (*Gitarre*) to pluck

zur [tsuːr] = **zu der**

zurate, zu Rate [tsuˈraːtə] *adv*: **jdn ~ ziehen** to consult sb

zurechnungsfähig ['tsuːreçnʊŋsfeːɪç] *adj* (*Jur*) responsible, of sound mind; **Zurechnungsfähigkeit** *f* responsibility, accountability

zurecht- *zW*: **zurechtbiegen** *unreg vt* to bend into shape; (*fig*) to twist; **zurechtfinden** *unreg vr* to find one's way (about); **zurechtkommen** *unreg vi* (*rechtzeitig kommen*) to come in time; (*schaffen*) to cope; (*finanziell*) to manage; **zurechtlegen** *vt* to get ready; (*Ausrede etc*) to have ready; **zurechtmachen** *vt* to prepare ▷ *vr* to get ready; (*sich schminken*) to put on one's make-up; **zurechtweisen** *unreg vt* to reprimand; **Zurechtweisung** *f* reprimand, rebuff

zureden ['tsuːreːdən] *vi*: **jdm ~** to persuade sb, urge sb

zureiten ['tsuːraɪtən] *unreg vt* (*Pferd*) to break in

Zürich ['tsyːrɪç] **(-s)** *nt* Zurich

zurichten ['tsuːrɪçtən] *vt* (*Essen*) to prepare; (*beschädigen*) to batter, bash up

zürnen ['tsʏrnən] *vi*: **jdm ~** to be angry with sb

zurück [tsuˈrʏk] *adv* back; (*mit Zahlungen*) behind; (*fig: zurückgeblieben: von Kind*) backward; **~!** get back!; **zurückbehalten** *unreg vt* to keep back; **er hat Schäden zurückbehalten** he suffered lasting damage; **zurückbekommen** *unreg vt* to get back; **zurückbezahlen** *vt* to repay, pay back; **zurückbleiben** *unreg vi* (*Mensch*) to remain behind; (*nicht nachkommen*) to fall behind, lag; (*Schaden*) to remain; **zurückbringen** *unreg vt* to bring back; **zurückdatieren** *vt* to backdate; **zurückdrängen** *vt* (*Gefühle*) to repress; (*Feind*) to push back; **zurückdrehen** *vt* to turn back; **zurückerobern** *vt* to reconquer; **zurückerstatten** *vt* to refund; **zurückfahren** *unreg vi* to travel back; (*vor Schreck*) to recoil ▷ *vt* to drive back; **zurückfallen** *unreg vi* to fall back; (*in Laster*) to relapse; (*in Leistungen*) to fall behind; (*an Besitzer*): **zurückfallen an** +*akk* to revert to; **zurückfinden** *unreg vi* to find one's way back; **zurückfordern** *vt* to demand back; **zurückführen** *vt* to lead back; **etw auf etw** *akk* **zurückführen** to trace sth back to sth; **zurückgeben** *unreg vt* to give back; (*antworten*) to retort with; **zurückgeblieben** *adj* retarded; **zurückgehen** *unreg vi* to go back; (*fallen*) to go down, fall; (*zeitlich*): **zurückgehen (auf** +*akk***)** to date back (to); **Waren zurückgehen lassen** to send back goods; **zurückgezogen** *adj* retired, withdrawn; **zurückgreifen** *unreg vi*: **zurückgreifen (auf** +*akk***)** (*fig*) to fall back (upon); (*zeitlich*) to go back (to); **zurückhalten** *unreg vt* to hold back; (*Mensch*) to restrain; (*hindern*) to prevent ▷ *vr* (*reserviert sein*) to be reserved; (*im Essen*) to hold back; (*im Hintergrund bleiben*) to keep in the background; (*bei Verhandlung*) to keep a low profile; **zurückhaltend** *adj* reserved; **Zurückhaltung** *f* reserve; **zurückholen** *vt* (*Comput: Daten*) to retrieve; **zurückkehren** *vi* to return; **zurückkommen** *unreg vi* to come back; **auf etw** *akk* **zurückkommen** to return to sth; **zurücklassen** *unreg vt* to leave behind; **zurücklegen** *vt* to put back; (*Geld*) to put by; (*reservieren*) to keep back; (*Strecke*) to cover ▷ *vr* to lie back; **zurückliegen** *unreg vi*: **der Unfall liegt etwa eine Woche zurück** the accident was about a week ago; **zurücknehmen** *unreg vt* to take back; **zurückreichen** *vi* (*Tradition etc*): **zurückreichen (in** +*akk***)** to go back (to); **zurückrufen** *unreg vt, vi* to call back; **etw ins Gedächtnis zurückrufen** to recall sth; **zurückschrauben** *vt*: **seine Ansprüche zurückschrauben** to lower one's sights; **zurückschrecken** *vi*: **zurückschrecken vor** +*dat* to shrink from; **vor nichts zurückschrecken** to stop at nothing; **zurücksetzen** *vt* to put back; (*im Preis*) to reduce; (*benachteiligen*) to put at a disadvantage ▷ vi (mit Fahrzeug) to reverse, back; **zurückstecken** vt to put back ▷ vi (fig) to moderate one's wishes; **zurückstellen** vt to put back, replace; (aufschieben) to put off, postpone; (Mil) to turn down; (Interessen) to defer; (Ware) to keep; **persönliche Interessen hinter etw** dat **zurückstellen** to put sth before one's personal interests; **zurückstoßen** unreg vt to repulse; **zurückstufen** vt to downgrade; **zurücktreten** unreg vi to step back; (vom Amt) to retire; (von einem Vertrag etc): **zurücktreten (von)** to withdraw (from); **gegenüber** od **hinter etw** dat **zurücktreten** to diminish in importance in view of sth; **bitte zurücktreten!** stand back, please!; **zurückverfolgen** vt (fig) to trace back; **zurückversetzen** vt (in alten Zustand): **zurückversetzen (in** +akk) to restore (to) ▷ vr: **sich zurückversetzen (in** +akk) to think back (to); **zurückweichen** unreg vi: **zurückweichen (vor** +dat) to shrink back (from); **zurückweisen** unreg vt to turn down; (Mensch) to reject; **zurückwerfen** unreg vt (Ball, Kopf) to throw back; (Strahlen, Schall) to reflect; (fig: Feind) to repel; (: wirtschaftlich): **zurückwerfen (um)** to set back (by); **zurückzahlen** vt to pay back, repay; **Zurückzahlung** f repayment; **zurückziehen** unreg vt to pull back; (Angebot) to withdraw ▷ vr to retire

Zuruf ['tsu:ru:f] m shout, cry

zurzeit [tsʊr'tsaɪt] adv at the moment

zus. abk = **zusammen; zusätzlich**

Zusage ['tsu:za:gə] f promise; (Annahme) consent

zusagen vt to promise ▷ vi to accept; **jdm etw auf den Kopf** ~ (umg) to tell sb sth outright; **jdm** ~ (gefallen) to appeal to od please sb

zusammen [tsu'zamən] adv together; **Zusammenarbeit** f cooperation; **zusammenarbeiten** vi to cooperate; **Zusammenballung** f accumulation; **zusammenbauen** vt to assemble; **zusammenbeißen** unreg vt (Zähne) to clench; **zusammenbleiben** unreg vi to stay together; **zusammenbrauen** (umg) vt to concoct ▷ vr (Gewitter, Unheil etc) to be brewing; **zusammenbrechen** unreg vi (Hilfsverb sein) to collapse; (Mensch) to break down, collapse; (Verkehr etc) to come to a standstill; **zusammenbringen** unreg vt to bring od get together; (Geld) to get; (Sätze) to put together; **Zusammenbruch** m collapse; (Comput) crash; **zusammenfahren** unreg vi to collide; (erschrecken) to start; **zusammenfallen** unreg vi (einstürzen) to collapse; (Ereignisse) to coincide; **zusammenfassen** vt to summarize; (vereinigen) to unite; **zusammenfassend** adj summarizing ▷ adv to summarize; **Zusammenfassung** f summary, résumé; **zusammenfinden** unreg vi, vr to meet (together); **zusammenfließen** unreg vi to flow together, meet; **Zusammenfluss** m confluence;

zusammenfügen vt to join (together), unite; **zusammenführen** vt to bring together; (Familie) to reunite; **zusammengehören** vi to belong together; (Paar) to match; **Zusammengehörigkeitsgefühl** nt sense of belonging; **zusammengesetzt** adj compound, composite; **zusammengewürfelt** adj motley; **zusammenhalten** unreg vt to hold together ▷ vi to hold together; (Freunde, fig) to stick together; **Zusammenhang** m connection; **im/aus dem Zusammenhang** in/out of context; **etw aus dem Zusammenhang reißen** to take sth out of its context; **zusammenhängen** unreg vi to be connected od linked; **zusammenhängend** adj (Erzählung) coherent; **zusammenhanglos, zusammenhangslos** adj incoherent; **zusammenklappbar** adj folding, collapsible; **zusammenklappen** vt (Messer etc) to fold ▷ vi (umg: Mensch) to flake out; **zusammenknüllen** vt to crumple up; **zusammenkommen** unreg vi to meet, assemble; (sich ereignen) to occur at once od happen; **zusammenkramen** vt to gather (together); **Zusammenkunft (-, -künfte)** f meeting; **zusammenlaufen** unreg vi to run od come together; (Straßen, Flüsse etc) to converge, meet; (Farben) to run into one another; **zusammenlegen** vt to put together; (stapeln) to pile up; (falten) to fold; (verbinden) to combine, unite; (Termine, Feste) to combine; (Geld) to collect; **zusammennehmen** unreg vt to summon up ▷ vr to pull o.s. together; **alles zusammengenommen** all in all; **zusammenpassen** vi to go well together, match; **Zusammenprall** m (lit) collision; (fig) clash; **zusammenprallen** vi (Hilfsverb sein) to collide; **zusammenreimen** (umg) vt: **das kann ich mir nicht zusammenreimen** I can't make head nor tail of this; **zusammenreißen** unreg vr to pull o.s. together; **zusammenrotten** unreg (pej) vr to gang up; **zusammenschlagen** unreg vt (jdn) to beat up; (Dinge) to smash up; (falten) to fold; (Hände) to clap; (Hacken) to click; **zusammenschließen** unreg vt, vr to join (together); **Zusammenschluss** m amalgamation; **zusammenschmelzen** unreg vi (verschmelzen) to fuse; (zerschmelzen) to melt (away); (Anzahl) to dwindle; **zusammenschrecken** unreg vi to start; **zusammenschreiben** unreg vt to write together; (Bericht) to put together; **zusammenschrumpfen** vi (Hilfsverb sein) to shrink, shrivel up; **Zusammensein (-s)** nt get-together; **zusammensetzen** vt to put together ▷ vr: **sich zusammensetzen aus** to consist of; **Zusammensetzung** f composition; **Zusammenspiel** nt teamwork; (von Kräften etc) interaction; **zusammenstellen** vt to put together; **Zusammenstellung** f list; (Vorgang) compilation; **Zusammenstoß** m collision; **zusammenstoßen** unreg vi (Hilfsverb sein) to collide; **zusammenströmen** vi (Hilfsverb sein: Menschen) to flock together; **zusammentragen** unreg vt to collect;

Zusammentreffen nt meeting; (Zufall) coincidence; **zusammentreffen** unreg vi (Hilfsverb sein) to coincide; (Menschen) to meet; **zusammentreten** unreg vi (Verein etc) to meet; **zusammenwachsen** unreg vi to grow together; **zusammenwirken** vi to combine; **zusammenzählen** vt to add up; **zusammenziehen** unreg vt (verengern) to draw together; (vereinigen) to bring together; (addieren) to add up ▷ vr to shrink; (sich bilden) to form, develop; **zusammenzucken** vi (Hilfsverb sein) to start

Zusatz ['tsu:tsats] m addition; **Zusatzantrag** m (Pol) amendment; **Zusatzgerät** nt attachment

zusätzlich ['tsu:tsɛtslɪç] adj additional

Zusatzmittel nt additive

zuschauen ['tsu:ʃaʊən] vi to watch, look on

Zuschauer (-s, -) m spectator ▷ pl (Theat) audience sing

zuschicken ['tsu:ʃɪkən] vt: **jdm etw ~** to send od forward sth to sb

zuschießen ['tsu:ʃi:sən] unreg vt to fire; (Geld) to put in ▷ vi: **~ auf** +akk to rush towards

Zuschlag ['tsu:ʃla:k] m extra charge; (Erhöhung) surcharge; (Eisenb) supplement

zuschlagen ['tsu:ʃla:gən] unreg vt (Tür) to slam; (Ball) to hit; (bei Auktion) to knock down; (Steine etc) to knock into shape ▷ vi (Fenster, Tür) to shut; (Mensch) to hit, punch

zuschlagfrei adj (Eisenb) not subject to a supplement

zuschlagpflichtig adj subject to surcharge

Zuschlagskarte f (Eisenb) supplementary ticket

zuschließen ['tsu:ʃli:sən] unreg vt to lock (up)

zuschmeißen ['tsu:ʃmaɪsən] unreg (umg) vt to slam, bang shut

zuschmieren ['tsu:ʃmi:rən] vt to smear over; (Löcher) to fill in

zuschneiden ['tsu:ʃnaɪdən] unreg vt to cut to size; (Nähen) to cut out; **auf etw** akk **zugeschnitten sein** (fig) to be geared to sth

zuschnüren ['tsu:ʃny:rən] vt to tie up; **die Angst schnürte ihm die Kehle zu** (fig) he was choked with fear

zuschrauben ['tsu:ʃraʊbən] vt to screw shut

zuschreiben ['tsu:ʃraɪbən] unreg vt (fig) to ascribe, attribute; (Comm) to credit; **das hast du dir selbst zu~** you've only got yourself to blame

Zuschrift ['tsu:ʃrɪft] f letter, reply

zuschulden, zu Schulden [tsu:ʃʊldən] adv: **sich** dat **etw ~ kommen lassen** to make o.s. guilty of sth

Zuschuss ['tsu:ʃʊs] m subsidy

Zuschussbetrieb m loss-making concern

zuschütten ['tsu:ʃʏtən] vt to fill up

zusehen ['tsu:tse:ən] unreg vi to watch; (dafür sorgen) to take care; (etw dulden) to sit back (and watch); **jdm/etw ~** to watch sb/sth

zusehends adv visibly

zu sein ['tsu:zaɪn] siehe **zu**

zusenden ['tsu:zɛndən] unreg vt to forward, send on

zusetzen ['tsu:tsɛtsən] vt (beifügen) to add; (Geld) to lose ▷ vi: **jdm ~** to harass sb; (Krankheit) to take a lot out of sb; (unter Druck setzen) to lean on sb (umg); (schwer treffen) to hit sb hard

zusichern ['tsu:zɪçərn] vt: **jdm etw ~** to assure sb of sth

Zusicherung f assurance

zusperren ['tsu:ʃpɛrən] vt to bar

zuspielen ['tsu:ʃpi:lən] vt, vi to pass; **jdm etw ~** to pass sth to sb; (fig) to pass sth on to sb; **etw der Presse ~** to leak sth to the press

zuspitzen ['tsu:ʃpɪtsən] vt to sharpen ▷ vr (Lage) to become critical

zusprechen ['tsu:ʃprɛçən] unreg vt (zuerkennen): **jdm etw ~** to award sb sth, award sth to sb ▷ vi: **jdm ~** to speak to sb; **jdm Trost ~** to comfort sb; **dem Essen/Alkohol ~** to eat/drink a lot

Zuspruch ['tsu:ʃprʊx] m encouragement; (Anklang) popularity

Zustand ['tsu:ʃtant] m state, condition; **in gutem/schlechtem ~** in good/poor condition; (Haus) in good/bad repair; **Zustände bekommen** od **kriegen** (umg) to have a fit

zustande, zu Stande [tsu:ʃtandə] adv: **~ bringen** to bring about; **~ kommen** to come about

zuständig ['tsu:ʃtɛndɪç] adj competent, responsible; **Zuständigkeit** f competence, responsibility; **Zuständigkeitsbereich** m area of responsibility

zustattenkommen [tsu:ʃtatənkɔmən] unreg vi: **jdm ~** (geh) to come in useful for sb

zustehen ['tsu:ʃte:ən] unreg vi: **jdm ~** to be sb's right

zusteigen ['tsu:ʃtaɪgən] unreg vi: **noch jemand zugestiegen?** (in Zug) any more tickets?

zustellen ['tsu:ʃtɛlən] vt (verstellen) to block; (Post etc) to send

Zustellung f delivery

zusteuern ['tsu:ʃtɔʏərn] vi: **auf etw** akk **~** to head for sth; (beim Gespräch) to steer towards sth ▷ vt (beitragen) to contribute

zustimmen ['tsu:ʃtɪmən] vi to agree

Zustimmung f agreement; (Einwilligung) consent; **allgemeine ~ finden** to meet with general approval

zustoßen ['tsu:ʃto:sən] unreg vi (fig): **jdm ~** to happen to sb

Zustrom ['tsu:ʃtro:m] m (fig: Menschenmenge) stream (of visitors etc); (hineinströmend) influx; (Met) inflow

zustürzen ['tsu:ʃtʏrtsən] vi: **auf jdn/etw ~** to rush up to sb/sth

zutage, zu Tage [tsu:ta:gə] adv: **~ bringen** to bring to light; **~ treten** to come to light

Zutaten ['tsu:ta:tən] pl ingredients pl; (fig) accessories pl

zuteilen ['tsu:taɪlən] vt to allocate, assign

zuteilwerden [tsu:taɪlve:rdən] unreg vi (geh): **jdm wird etw zuteil** sb is granted sth,

405

z

sth is granted to sb

zutiefst [tsu'ti:fst] *adv* deeply

zutragen ['tsu:tra:gən] *unreg vt*: **jdm etw ~** to bring sb sth, bring sth to sb ▷ *vt* (*Klatsch*) to tell sb sth ▷ *vr* to happen

zuträglich ['tsu:trɛ:klıç] *adj* beneficial

zutrauen ['tsu:travən] *vt*: **jdm etw ~** to credit sb with sth; **sich** *dat* **nichts ~** to have no confidence in o.s.; **jdm viel ~** to think a lot of sb; **jdm wenig ~** not to think much of sb; **Zutrauen (-s)** *nt*: **Zutrauen (zu)** trust (in); **zu jdm Zutrauen fassen** to begin to trust sb

zutraulich *adj* trusting; (*Tier*) friendly; **Zutraulichkeit** *f* trust

zutreffen ['tsu:trɛfən] *unreg vi* to be correct; (*gelten*) to apply

zutreffend *adj* (*richtig*) accurate; **Z~es bitte unterstreichen** please underline where applicable

zutrinken ['tsu:trıŋkən] *unreg vi*: **jdm ~** to drink to sb

Zutritt ['tsu:trıt] *m* access; (*Einlass*) admittance; **kein ~, ~ verboten** no admittance

zutun ['tsu:tu:n] *unreg vt* to add; (*schließen*) to shut

Zutun (-s) *nt* assistance

zuunterst [tsu'|untərst] *adv* right at the bottom

zuverlässig ['tsu:fɛrlɛsıç] *adj* reliable; **Zuverlässigkeit** *f* reliability

Zuversicht ['tsu:fɛrzıçt] **(-)** *f* confidence; **zuversichtlich** *adj* confident; **Zuversichtlichkeit** *f* confidence

zu viel [tsu'fi:l] *siehe* **zu**

zuvor [tsu'fo:r] *adv* before, previously

zuvorderst [tsu'fɔrdərst] *adv* right at the front

zuvorkommen *unreg vi +dat* to anticipate; (*Gefahr etc*) to forestall; **jdm ~** to beat sb to it

zuvorkommend *adj* courteous; (*gefällig*) obliging

Zuwachs ['tsu:vaks] **(-es)** *m* increase, growth; (*umg*) addition

zuwachsen *unreg vi* to become overgrown; (*Wunde*) to heal (up)

Zuwachsrate *f* rate of increase

zuwandern ['tsu:vandərn] *vi* to immigrate

zuwege, zu Wege [tsu've:gə] *adv*: **etw ~ bringen** to accomplish sth; **mit etw ~ kommen** to manage sth; **gut ~ sein** to be (doing) well

zuweilen [tsu'vaılən] *adv* at times, now and then

zuweisen ['tsu:vaızən] *unreg vt* to assign, allocate

zuwenden ['tsu:vɛndən] *unreg vt +dat* to turn towards ▷ *vr +dat* to turn to; (*sich widmen*) to devote o.s. to; **jdm seine Aufmerksamkeit ~** to give sb one's attention

Zuwendung *f* (*Geld*) financial contribution; (*Liebe*) love and care

zu wenig [tsu've:nıç] *siehe* **zu**

zuwerfen ['tsu:vɛrfən] *unreg vt*: **jdm etw ~** to throw sth to sb, throw sb sth

zuwider [tsu'vi:dər] *adv*: **etw ist jdm ~** sb loathes sth, sb finds sth repugnant ▷ *präp +dat* contrary to; **zuwiderhandeln** *vi +dat* to act contrary to; **einem Gesetz zuwiderhandeln** to contravene a law; **Zuwiderhandlung** *f* contravention; **zuwiderlaufen** *unreg vi*: **einer Sache** *dat* **zuwiderlaufen** to run counter to sth

zuwinken *vi*: **jdm ~** to wave to sb

zuz. *abk* = **zuzüglich**

zuzahlen ['tsu:tsa:lən] *vt*: **10 Euro ~** to pay another 10 euros

zuziehen ['tsu:tsi:ən] *unreg vt* (*schließen*: *Vorhang*) to draw, close; (*herbeirufen*: *Experten*) to call in ▷ *vi* to move in, come; **sich** *dat* **etw ~** (*Krankheit*) to catch sth; (*Zorn*) to incur sth; **sich** *dat* **eine Verletzung ~** (*form*) to sustain an injury

Zuzug ['tsu:tsuk] **(-(e)s)** *m* (*Zustrom*) influx; (*von Familie etc*): **~ nach** move to

zuzüglich ['tsu:tsy:klıç] *präp +gen* plus, with the addition of

zuzwinkern ['tsu:tsvınkərn] *vi*: **jdm ~** to wink at sb

ZVS *f abk* (= *Zentralstelle für die Vergabe von Studienplätzen*) central body organizing the granting of places at university

Zwang (-(e)s, ⸚e) *m* compulsion; (*Gewalt*) coercion; **gesellschaftliche Zwänge** social constraints; **tu dir keinen ~ an** don't feel you have to be polite

zwang *etc* [tsvaŋ] *vb siehe* **zwingen**

zwängen ['tsvɛŋən] *vt, vr* to squeeze

Zwang- *zW*: **zwanghaft** *adj* compulsive; **zwanglos** *adj* informal; **Zwanglosigkeit** *f* informality

Zwangs- *zW*: **Zwangsabgabe** *f* (*Comm*) compulsory levy; **Zwangsarbeit** *f* forced labour (*Brit*) *od* labor (*US*); **Zwangsernährung** *f* force-feeding; **Zwangsjacke** *f* straitjacket; **Zwangslage** *f* predicament, tight corner; **zwangsläufig** *adj* inevitable; **Zwangsmaßnahme** *f* compulsory measure; (*Pol*) sanction; **Zwangsvollstreckung** *f* execution; **Zwangsvorstellung** *f* (*Psych*) obsession; **zwangsweise** *adv* compulsorily

zwanzig ['tsvantsıç] *num* twenty

zwanzigste, r, s *adj* twentieth

zwar [tsva:r] *adv* to be sure, indeed; **das ist ~ ..., aber ...** that may be ... but ...; **und ~** in fact, actually; **und ~ am Sonntag** on Sunday to be precise; **und ~ so schnell, dass ...** in fact so quickly that ...

Zweck [tsvɛk] **(-(e)s, -e)** *m* purpose, aim; **es hat keinen ~, darüber zu reden** there is no point (in) talking about it; **zweckdienlich** *adj* practical; (*nützlich*) useful; **zweckdienliche Hinweise** (any) relevant information

Zwecke (-, -n) *f* hobnail; (*Heftzwecke*) drawing pin (*Brit*), thumbtack (*US*)

Zweck- *zW*: **zweckentfremden** *vt untr* to use for another purpose; **Zweckentfremdung** *f* misuse; **zweckfrei** *adj* (*Forschung etc*) pure; **zwecklos** *adj* pointless; **zweckmäßig** *adj*

suitable, appropriate; **Zweckmäßigkeit** f
suitability

zwecks präp +gen (form) for (the purpose of)

zweckwidrig adj unsuitable

zwei [tsvaɪ] num two; **Zweibettzimmer**
nt twin-bedded room; **zweideutig** adj
ambiguous; (unanständig) suggestive;
Zweidrittelmehrheit f (Parl) two-thirds
majority; **zweieiig** adj (Zwillinge) non-identical

zweierlei ['tsvaɪər'laɪ] adj two kinds od sorts of;
~ **Stoff** two different kinds of material; ~ **zu
tun haben** to have two different things to do

zweifach adj double

Zweifel ['tsvaɪfəl] (-s, -) m doubt; **ich bin mir
darüber im** ~ I'm in two minds about it;
zweifelhaft adj doubtful, dubious; **zweifellos**
adj doubtless

zweifeln vi: **(an etw** dat) ~ to doubt (sth)

Zweifelsfall m: **im** ~ in case of doubt

Zweifrontenkrieg m war(fare) on two fronts

Zweig [tsvaɪk] (-(e)s, -e) m branch;
Zweiggeschäft nt (Comm) branch

zweigleisig ['tsvaɪɡlaɪzɪç] adj: ~
argumentieren to argue along two different
lines

Zweigstelle f branch (office)

zwei- zW: **zweihändig** adj two-handed;
(Mus) for two hands; **Zweiheit** f duality;
zweihundert num two hundred; **Zweikampf**
m duel; **zweimal** adv twice; **das lasse ich
mir nicht zweimal sagen** I don't have to be
told twice; **zweimotorig** adj twin-engined;
zweireihig adj (Anzug) double-breasted;
Zweisamkeit f togetherness; **zweischneidig**
adj (fig) double-edged; **Zweisitzer (-s, -)** m
two-seater; **zweisprachig** adj bilingual;
Zweispurgerät, Zweispurtonbandgerät nt
twin-track (tape) recorder; **zweispurig** adj
(Aut) two-lane; **zweistellig** adj (Zahl) two-digit
attrib, with two digits; **zweistimmig** adj for
two voices

zweit [tsvaɪt] adv: **zu** ~ (in Paaren) in twos

Zweitaktmotor m two-stroke engine

zweitbeste, r, s adj second best

zweite, r, s adj second; **Bürger ~r Klasse**
second-class citizen(s pl)

zweiteilig ['tsvaɪtaɪlɪç] adj (Buch, Film etc) in two
parts; (Kleidung) two-piece

zweitens adv secondly

zweit- zW: **zweitgrößte, r, s** adj second
largest; **zweitklassig** adj second-class;
zweitletzte, r, s adj last but one, penultimate;
zweitrangig adj second-rate; **Zweitschlüssel**
m duplicate key; **Zweitstimme** f second vote;
siehe auch **Erststimme**

zweitürig ['tsvaɪtyːrɪç] adj two-door

Zweitwagen m second car

Zweitwohnung f second home

zweizeilig adj two-lined; (Typ: Abstand) double-
spaced

Zweizimmerwohnung f two-room(ed) flat
(Brit) od apartment (US)

Zwerchfell ['tsvɛrçfɛl] nt diaphragm

Zwerg, in [tsvɛrk, 'tsvɛrgɪn] **(-(e)s, -e)** m(f)
dwarf; (fig: Knirps) midget; **Zwergschule** (umg)
f village school

Zwetsche ['tsvɛtʃə], **Zwetschge** ['tsvɛtʃɡə]
(-, -n) f plum

Zwickel ['tsvɪkəl] **(-s, -)** m gusset

zwicken ['tsvɪkən] vt to pinch, nip

Zwickmühle ['tsvɪkmyːlə] f: **in der ~ sitzen**
(fig) to be in a dilemma

Zwieback ['tsviːbak] **(-(e)s, -e** od **-bäcke)** m rusk

Zwiebel ['tsviːbəl] **(-, -n)** f onion; (Blumenzwiebel)
bulb; **zwiebelartig** adj bulbous; **Zwiebelturm**
m (tower with an) onion dome

Zwie- zW: **Zwiegespräch** nt dialogue (Brit),
dialog (US); **Zwielicht** nt twilight; **ins
Zwielicht geraten sein** (fig) to appear
in an unfavourable (Brit) od unfavorable
(US) light; **zwielichtig** adj shady, dubious;
Zwiespalt m conflict; (zwischen Menschen) rift,
gulf; **zwiespältig** adj (Gefühle) conflicting;
(Charakter) contradictory; **Zwietracht** f
discord, dissension

Zwilling ['tsvɪlɪŋ] **(-s, -e)** m twin; **Zwillinge** pl
(Astrol) Gemini

zwingen ['tsvɪŋən] unreg vt to force

zwingend adj (Grund etc) compelling; (logisch
notwendig) necessary; (Schluss, Beweis)
conclusive

Zwinger (-s, -) m (Käfig) cage; (Hundezwinger) run

zwinkern ['tsvɪŋkərn] vi to blink; (absichtlich)
to wink

Zwirn [tsvɪrn] **(-(e)s, -e)** m thread

zwischen ['tsvɪʃən] präp (+akk od dat) between;
(bei mehreren) among; **Zwischenaufenthalt** m
stopover; **Zwischenbemerkung** f (incidental)
remark; **zwischenblenden** vt (Film, Rundf,
TV) to insert; **Zwischending** nt cross;
Zwischendividende f interim dividend;
zwischendurch adv in between; (räumlich)
here and there; **Zwischenergebnis** nt
intermediate result; **Zwischenfall** m incident;
Zwischenfrage f question; **Zwischengröße**
f in-between size; **Zwischenhandel**
m wholesaling; **Zwischenhändler** m
middleman, agent; **Zwischenlagerung**
f temporary storage; **Zwischenlandung**
f (Aviat) stopover; **Zwischenlösung** f
temporary solution; **zwischenmahlzeit** f
snack (between meals); **zwischenmenschlich**
adj interpersonal; **Zwischenprüfung** f
intermediate examination; **Zwischenraum**
m gap, space; **Zwischenruf** m interjection,
interruption; **Zwischenrufe** pl heckling
sing; **Zwischensaison** f low season;
Zwischenspeicher m (Comput) buffer;
Zwischenspiel nt (Theat, fig) interlude; (Mus)
intermezzo; **zwischenstaatlich** adj interstate;
(international) international; **Zwischenstation**
f intermediate station; **Zwischenstecker** m
(Elek) adapter; **Zwischenstück** nt connecting
piece; **Zwischensumme** f subtotal;
Zwischenwand f partition; **Zwischenzeit** f
interval; **in der Zwischenzeit** in the interim,

Zwist | z. Z.

meanwhile; **Zwischenzeugnis** nt (Sch) interim report

Zwist [tsvɪst] (**-es, -e**) m dispute

zwitschern ['tsvɪtʃərn] vt, vi to twitter, chirp; **einen ~** (umg) to have a drink

Zwitter ['tsvɪtər] (**-s, -**) m hermaphrodite

zwo [tsvoː] num (Tel, Mil) two

zwölf [tsvœlf] num twelve; **fünf Minuten vor ~** (fig) at the eleventh hour

Zwölffingerdarm (**-(e)s**) m duodenum

Zyankali [tsyaːnˈkaːli] (**-s**) nt (Chem) potassium cyanide

Zyklon [tsyˈkloːn] (**-s, -e**) m cyclone

Zyklus ['tsyːklʊs] (**-, Zyklen**) m cycle

Zylinder [tsiˈlɪndər] (**-s, -**) m cylinder; (Hut) top hat; **zylinderförmig** adj cylindrical

Zyniker, in ['tsyːnikər(ɪn)] (**-s, -**) m(f) cynic

zynisch ['tsyːnɪʃ] adj cynical

Zynismus [tsyˈnɪsmʊs] m cynicism

Zypern ['tsyːpərn] (**-s**) nt Cyprus

Zypresse [tsyˈprɛsə] (**-, -n**) f (Bot) cypress

Zypriot, in [tsypriˈoːt(ɪn)] (**-en, -en**) m(f) Cypriot

zypriotisch adj Cypriot, Cyprian

zyprisch ['tsyːprɪʃ] adj Cypriot, Cyprian

Zyste ['tsʏstə] (**-, -n**) f cyst

zz., zzt. abk = zurzeit

z. Z., z. Zt. abk = zur Zeit

English–German

Englisch–Deutsch

Aa

A¹, a [eɪ] n (letter) A nt, a nt; (Scol) ≈ Eins f,
sehr gut nt; **A for Andrew, A for Able**
(US) ≈ A wie Anton; **A road** (Brit: Aut)
Hauptverkehrsstraße f; **A shares** (Brit: Stock
Exchange) stimmrechtslose Aktien pl
A² [eɪ] n (Mus) A nt, a nt

○ KEYWORD

a [ə] (before vowel and silent h: **an**) indef art **1** ein;
(before feminine noun) eine; **a book** ein Buch;
a lamp eine Lampe; **she's a doctor** sie ist
Ärztin; **I haven't got a car** ich habe kein
Auto; **a hundred/thousand etc pounds**
einhundert/eintausend etc Pfund
2 (in expressing ratios, prices etc) pro; **3 a day/week**
3 pro Tag/Woche, 3 am Tag/in der Woche; **10
km an hour** 10 km pro Stunde

A2 (Brit) n (Scol) Mit "A2" wird das zweite Jahr der
britischen Sekundarstufe II bezeichnet, in dem die
übrigen drei Wahlpflichtfächer unterrichtet und am
Ende des Schuljahres geprüft werden. Die Note für den
"A level" setzt sich aus den Noten der Jahre "AS" und
"A2" zusammen

AA n abbr (Brit: = Automobile Association)
Autofahrerorganisation, ≈ ADAC m; (US: = Associate
in Art) akademischer Grad für Geisteswissenschaftler;
(= Alcoholics Anonymous) Anonyme Alkoholiker
pl, AA pl
AAA n abbr (= American Automobile Association)
Autofahrerorganisation, ≈ ADAC m; (Brit: = Amateur
Athletics Association) Leichtathletikverband der
Amateure
A & E n abbr (= Accident and Emergency): ~
department Notfallstation f, Notaufnahme f
abaci ['æbəsaɪ] npl of **abacus**
aback [ə'bæk] adv: **to be taken** ~ verblüfft sein
abacus ['æbəkəs] (pl **abaci**) n Abakus m
abandon [ə'bændən] vt verlassen; (child)
aussetzen; (give up) aufgeben ▷ n (wild
behaviour): **with** ~ selbstvergessen; **to** ~ **ship**
das Schiff verlassen
abandoned [ə'bændənd] adj verlassen; (child)
ausgesetzt; (unrestrained) selbstvergessen
abase [ə'beɪs] vt: **to** ~ **o.s.** sich erniedrigen;
to ~ **o.s. so far as to do sth** sich dazu

erniedrigen, etw zu tun
abashed [ə'bæʃt] adj verlegen
abate [ə'beɪt] vi nachlassen, sich legen
abatement [ə'beɪtmənt] n: **noise** ~ **society**
Gesellschaft f zur Lärmbekämpfung
abattoir ['æbətwɑ:ʳ] (Brit) n Schlachthof m
abbey ['æbɪ] n Abtei f
abbot ['æbət] n Abt m
abbreviate [ə'bri:vɪeɪt] vt abkürzen; (essay etc)
kürzen
abbreviation [əbri:vɪ'eɪʃən] n Abkürzung f
ABC n abbr (= American Broadcasting Companies)
Fernsehsender
abdicate ['æbdɪkeɪt] vt verzichten auf +acc ▷ vi
(monarch) abdanken
abdication [æbdɪ'keɪʃən] n (see vb) Verzicht m;
Abdankung f
abdomen ['æbdəmɛn] n Unterleib m
abdominal [æb'dɔmɪnl] adj (pain etc)
Unterleibs-
abduct [æb'dʌkt] vt entführen
abduction [æb'dʌkʃən] n Entführung f
Aberdonian [æbə'dəʊnɪən] adj (Geog)
Aberdeener inv ▷ n Aberdeener(in) m(f)
aberration [æbə'reɪʃən] n Anomalie f; **in a
moment of mental** ~ in einem Augenblick
geistiger Verwirrung
abet [ə'bɛt] vt see **aid**
abeyance [ə'beɪəns] n: **in** ~ (law) außer Kraft;
(matter) ruhend
abhor [əb'hɔ:ʳ] vt verabscheuen
abhorrent [əb'hɔrənt] adj abscheulich
abide [ə'baɪd] vt: **I can't** ~ **it/him** ich kann es/
ihn nicht ausstehen
▷ **abide by** vt fus sich halten an +acc
abiding [ə'baɪdɪŋ] adj (memory, impression)
bleibend
ability [ə'bɪlɪtɪ] n Fähigkeit f; **to the best of
my** ~ so gut ich es kann
abject ['æbdʒɛkt] adj (poverty) bitter; (apology)
demütig; (coward) erbärmlich
ablaze [ə'bleɪz] adj in Flammen; ~ **with light**
hell erleuchtet
able ['eɪbl] adj fähig; **to be** ~ **to do sth** etw tun
können
able-bodied ['eɪbl'bɔdɪd] adj kräftig; ~ **seaman**
(Brit) Vollmatrose m

ablutions [əˈbluːʃənz] *npl* Waschungen *pl*
ably [ˈeɪblɪ] *adv* gekonnt
ABM *n abbr* (= *antiballistic missile*) Anti-Raketen-Rakete *f*
abnormal [æbˈnɔːməl] *adj* abnorm; (*child*) anormal
abnormality [æbnɔːˈmælɪtɪ] *n* Abnormität *f*
aboard [əˈbɔːd] *adv* (*Naut, Aviat*) an Bord ▷ *prep* an Bord +*gen*; **~ the train/bus** im Zug/Bus
abode [əˈbəud] *n* (*Law*): **of no fixed ~** ohne festen Wohnsitz
abolish [əˈbɔlɪʃ] *vt* abschaffen
abolition [æbəˈlɪʃən] *n* Abschaffung *f*
abominable [əˈbɔmɪnəbl] *adj* scheußlich
abominably [əˈbɔmɪnəblɪ] *adv* scheußlich
Aborigine [æbəˈrɪdʒɪnɪ] *n* Ureinwohner(in) *m(f)* Australiens
abort [əˈbɔːt] *vt* abtreiben; (*Med: miscarry*) fehlgebären; (*Comput*) abbrechen
abortion [əˈbɔːʃən] *n* Abtreibung *f*; (*miscarriage*) Fehlgeburt *f*; **to have an ~** abtreiben lassen
abortionist [əˈbɔːʃənɪst] *n* Abtreibungshelfer(in) *m(f)*
abortive [əˈbɔːtɪv] *adj* misslungen
abound [əˈbaund] *vi* im Überfluss vorhanden sein; **to ~ in** *or* **with** reich sein an +*dat*

○ KEYWORD

about [əˈbaut] *adv* **1** (*approximately*) etwa, ungefähr; **about a hundred/thousand** *etc* etwa hundert/tausend *etc*; **at about two o'clock** etwa um zwei Uhr; **I've just about finished** ich bin gerade fertig
2 (*referring to place*) herum; **to run/walk** *etc* **about** herumlaufen/-gehen *etc*; **is Paul about?** ist Paul da?
3: to be about to do sth im Begriff sein, etw zu tun; **he was about to cry** er fing fast an zu weinen; **she was about to leave/wash the dishes** sie wollte gerade gehen/das Geschirr spülen
▷ *prep* **1** (*relating to*) über +*acc*; **what is it about?** worum geht es?; (*book etc*) wovon handelt es?; **we talked about it** wir haben darüber geredet; **what** *or* **how about going to the cinema?** wollen wir ins Kino gehen?
2 (*referring to place*) um ... herum; **to walk about the town** durch die Stadt gehen; **her clothes were scattered about the room** ihre Kleider waren über das ganze Zimmer verstreut

about-face [əˈbautˈfeɪs] (*US*) *n* = **about-turn**
about-turn [əˈbautˈtəːn] (*Brit*) *n* Kehrtwendung *f*
above [əˈbʌv] *adv* oben; (*greater, more*) darüber ▷ *prep* über +*dat*; **to cost ~ £10** mehr als £10 kosten; **mentioned ~** oben genannt; **he's not ~ a bit of blackmail** er ist sich dat nicht zu gut für eine kleine Erpressung; **~ all** vor allem
above board *adj* korrekt
abrasion [əˈbreɪʒən] *n* Abschürfung *f*

abrasive [əˈbreɪzɪv] *adj* (*substance*) Scheuer-; (*person, manner*) aggressiv
abreast [əˈbrest] *adv* nebeneinander; **three ~** zu dritt nebeneinander; **to keep ~ of** (*fig*) auf dem Laufenden bleiben mit
abridge [əˈbrɪdʒ] *vt* kürzen
abroad [əˈbrɔːd] *adv* (*be*) im Ausland; (*go*) ins Ausland; **there is a rumour ~ that ...** (*fig*) ein Gerücht geht um *or* kursiert, dass ...
abrupt [əˈbrʌpt] *adj* abrupt; (*person, behaviour*) schroff
abruptly [əˈbrʌptlɪ] *adv* abrupt
abscess [ˈæbsɪs] *n* Abszess *m*
abscond [əbˈskɔnd] *vi*: **to ~ with** sich davonmachen mit; **to ~ (from)** fliehen (aus)
abseil [ˈæbseɪl] *vi* sich abseilen
absence [ˈæbsəns] *n* Abwesenheit *f*; **in the ~ of** (*person*) in Abwesenheit +*gen*; (*thing*) in Ermangelung +*gen*
absent [ˈæbsənt] *adj* abwesend, nicht da
▷ *vt*: **to ~ o.s. from** fernbleiben +*dat*; **to be ~** fehlen; **to be ~ without leave** (*Mil*) sich unerlaubt von der Truppe entfernen
absentee [æbsənˈtiː] *n* Abwesende(r) *f(m)*
absenteeism [æbsənˈtiːɪzəm] *n* (*from school*) Schwänzen *nt*; (*from work*) Nichterscheinen *nt* am Arbeitsplatz
absent-minded [ˈæbsəntˈmaɪndɪd] *adj* zerstreut
absent-mindedly [ˈæbsəntˈmaɪndɪdlɪ] *adv* zerstreut; (*look*) abwesend
absent-mindedness [ˈæbsəntˈmaɪndɪdnɪs] *n* Zerstreutheit *f*
absolute [ˈæbsəluːt] *adj* absolut; (*power*) uneingeschränkt
absolutely [æbsəˈluːtlɪ] *adv* absolut; (*agree*) vollkommen; **~! genau!**
absolution [æbsəˈluːʃən] *n* Lossprechung *f*
absolve [əbˈzɔlv] *vt*: **to ~ sb (from)** jdn lossprechen (von); (*responsibility*) jdn entbinden (von)
absorb [əbˈzɔːb] *vt* aufnehmen (*also fig*); (*light, heat*) absorbieren; (*group, business*) übernehmen; **to be ~ed in a book** in ein Buch vertieft sein
absorbent [əbˈzɔːbənt] *adj* saugfähig
absorbent cotton (*US*) *n* Watte *f*
absorbing [əbˈzɔːbɪŋ] *adj* saugfähig; (*book, film, work etc*) fesselnd
absorption [əbˈsɔːpʃən] *n* (*see vb*) Aufnahme *f*; Absorption *f*; Übernahme *f*; (*interest*) Faszination *f*
abstain [əbˈsteɪn] *vi* (*voting*) sich (der Stimme) enthalten; **to ~ (from)** (*eating, drinking etc*) sich enthalten (+*gen*)
abstemious [əbˈstiːmɪəs] *adj* enthaltsam
abstention [əbˈstenʃən] *n* (*Stimm*)enthaltung *f*
abstinence [ˈæbstɪnəns] *n* Enthaltsamkeit *f*
abstract [ˈæbstrækt] *adj* abstrakt ▷ *n* (*summary*) Zusammenfassung *f* ▷ *vt*: **to ~ sth (from)** (*summarize*) etw entnehmen (aus); (*remove*) etw entfernen (aus)

abstruse [æb'stru:s] *adj* abstrus

absurd [əb'sə:d] *adj* absurd

absurdity [əb'sə:dıtı] *n* Absurdität *f*

ABTA ['æbtə] *n abbr* (= *Association of British Travel Agents*) Verband der Reiseveranstalter

Abu Dhabi ['æbu:'da:bı] *n* (*Geog*) Abu Dhabi *nt*

abundance [ə'bʌndəns] *n* Reichtum *m*; **an ~ of** eine Fülle von; **in ~** in Hülle und Fülle

abundant [ə'bʌndənt] *adj* reichlich

abundantly [ə'bʌndəntlı] *adv* reichlich; **~ clear** völlig klar

abuse [ə'bju:s] *n* (*insults*) Beschimpfungen *pl*; (*ill-treatment*) Misshandlung *f*; (*misuse*) Missbrauch *m* ▷ *vt* (*see n*) beschimpfen; misshandeln; missbrauchen; **to be open to ~** sich leicht missbrauchen lassen

abuser [ə'bju:zər] *n* (*also*: **drug abuser**) *jd, der Drogen missbraucht*; (*also*: **child abuser**) *jd, der Kinder missbraucht oder misshandelt*

abusive [ə'bju:sıv] *adj* beleidigend

abysmal [ə'bızməl] *adj* entsetzlich; (*ignorance etc*) grenzenlos

abysmally [ə'bızməlı] *adv* (*see adj*) entsetzlich; grenzenlos

abyss [ə'bıs] *n* Abgrund *m*

AC *abbr* = **alternating current**; (*US*: = *athletic club*) ≈ SV *m*

a/c *abbr* (*Banking etc*) = **account**; (= *current account*) Girokonto *nt*

academic [ækə'dɛmık] *adj* akademisch (*also pej*); (*work*) wissenschaftlich; (*person*) intellektuell ▷ *n* Akademiker(in) *m(f)*

academic year *n* (*university year*) Universitätsjahr *nt*; (*school year*) Schuljahr *nt*

academy [ə'kædəmı] *n* Akademie *f*; (*school*) Hochschule *f*; **~ of music** Musikhochschule *f*; **military/naval ~** Militär-/Marineakademie *f*

ACAS ['eɪkæs] (*Brit*) *n abbr* (= *Advisory Conciliation and Arbitration Service*) Schlichtungsstelle für Arbeitskonflikte

accede [æk'si:d] *vi*: **to ~ to** zustimmen +*dat*

accelerate [æk'sɛləreɪt] *vt* beschleunigen ▷ *vi* (*Aut*) Gas geben

acceleration [æksɛlə'reɪʃən] *n* Beschleunigung *f*

accelerator [æk'sɛləreɪtər] *n* Gaspedal *nt*

accent ['æksɛnt] *n* Akzent *m*; (*fig: emphasis, stress*) Betonung *f*; **to speak with an Irish ~** mit einem irischen Akzent sprechen; **to have a strong ~** einen starken Akzent haben

accentuate [æk'sɛntjueɪt] *vt* betonen; (*need, difference etc*) hervorheben

accept [ək'sɛpt] *vt* annehmen; (*fact, situation*) sich abfinden mit; (*risk*) in Kauf nehmen; (*responsibility*) übernehmen; (*blame*) auf sich *acc* nehmen

acceptable [ək'sɛptəbl] *adj* annehmbar

acceptance [ək'sɛptəns] *n* Annahme *f*; **to meet with general ~** allgemeine Anerkennung finden

access ['æksɛs] *n* Zugang *m* ▷ *vt* (*Comput*) zugreifen auf +*dat*; **the burglars gained ~ through a window** die Einbrecher gelangten durch ein Fenster hinein

accessible [æk'sɛsəbl] *adj* erreichbar; (*knowledge, art etc*) zugänglich

accession [æk'sɛʃən] *n* Antritt *m*; (*of monarch*) Thronbesteigung *f*; (*to library*) Neuanschaffung *f*

accessory [æk'sɛsərı] *n* Zubehörteil *nt*; (*Dress*) Accessoire *nt*; (*Law*): **~ to** Mitschuldige(r) *f(m)* an +*dat*; **accessories** *npl* Zubehör *nt*; **toilet accessories** (*Brit*) Toilettenartikel *pl*

access road *n* Zufahrt(sstraße) *f*

access time *n* (*Comput*) Zugriffszeit *f*

accident ['æksıdənt] *n* Zufall *m*; (*mishap, disaster*) Unfall *m*; **to meet with** *or* **to have an ~** einen Unfall haben, verunglücken; **~s at work** Arbeitsunfälle *pl*; **by ~** zufällig

accidental [æksı'dɛntl] *adj* zufällig; (*death, damage*) Unfall-

accidentally [æksı'dɛntəlı] *adv* zufällig

accident insurance *n* Unfallversicherung *f*

accident-prone ['æksıdənt'prəun] *adj* vom Pech verfolgt

accident risk *n* Unfallrisiko *f*

acclaim [ə'kleɪm] *n* Beifall *m* ▷ *vt*: **to be ~ed for one's achievements** für seine Leistungen gefeiert werden

acclamation [æklə'meɪʃən] *n* Anerkennung *f*; (*applause*) Beifall *m*

acclimate [ə'klaɪmət] (*US*) *vt* = **acclimatize**

acclimatize [ə'klaɪmətaɪz], (*US*) **acclimate** *vt*: **to become ~d** sich akklimatisieren; **to become ~d to** sich gewöhnen an +*acc*

accolade ['ækəleɪd] *n* (*fig*) Auszeichnung *f*

accommodate [ə'kɔmədeɪt] *vt* unterbringen; (*subj: car, hotel etc*) Platz bieten +*dat*; (*oblige, help*) entgegenkommen +*dat*; **to ~ one's plans to** seine Pläne anpassen an +*acc*

accommodating [ə'kɔmədeɪtɪŋ] *adj* entgegenkommend

accommodation [əkɔmə'deɪʃən] *n* Unterkunft *f*; **accommodations** (*US*) *npl* Unterkunft *f*; **have you any ~?** haben Sie eine Unterkunft?; **"~ to let"** „Zimmer zu vermieten"; **they have ~ for 500** sie können 500 Personen unterbringen; **the hall has seating ~ for 600** (*Brit*) in dem Saal können 600 Personen sitzen

accompaniment [ə'kʌmpənɪmənt] *n* Begleitung *f*

accompanist [ə'kʌmpənɪst] *n* Begleiter(in) *m(f)*

accompany [ə'kʌmpənɪ] *vt* begleiten

accomplice [ə'kʌmplɪs] *n* Komplize *m*, Komplizin *f*

accomplish [ə'kʌmplɪʃ] *vt* vollenden; (*achieve*) erreichen

accomplished [ə'kʌmplɪʃt] *adj* ausgezeichnet

accomplishment [ə'kʌmplɪʃmənt] *n* Vollendung *f*; (*achievement*) Leistung *f*; (*skill: gen pl*) Fähigkeit *f*

accord [ə'kɔ:d] *n* Übereinstimmung *f*; (*treaty*) Vertrag *m* ▷ *vt* gewähren; **of his own ~** freiwillig; **with one ~** geschlossen; **to be in ~** übereinstimmen

accordance [ə'kɔːdəns] *n*: **in ~ with** in Übereinstimmung mit

according [ə'kɔːdɪŋ] *prep*: **~ to** zufolge +*dat*; **~ to plan** wie geplant

accordingly [ə'kɔːdɪŋlɪ] *adv* entsprechend; *(as a result)* folglich

accordion [ə'kɔːdɪən] *n* Akkordeon *nt*

accost [ə'kɔst] *vt* ansprechen

account [ə'kaunt] *n* (*Comm*: *bill*) Rechnung *f*; *(in bank, department store)* Konto *nt*; *(report)* Bericht *m*; **accounts** *npl* (*Comm*) Buchhaltung *f*; *(Bookkeeping)* (Geschäfts)bücher *pl*; **"~ payee only"** *(Brit)* „nur zur Verrechnung"; **to keep an ~ of** Buch führen über +*acc*; **to bring sb to ~ for sth/for having embezzled £50,000** jdn für etw/für die Unterschlagung von £50.000 zur Rechenschaft ziehen; **by all ~s** nach allem, was man hört; **of no ~** ohne Bedeutung; **on ~** auf Kredit; **to pay £5 on ~** eine Anzahlung von £5 leisten; **on no ~** auf keinen Fall; **on ~ of** wegen +*gen*; **to take into account, take ~ of** berücksichtigen
  ▸ **account for** *vt fus* erklären; *(expenditure)* Rechenschaft ablegen für; *(represent)* ausmachen; **all the children were ~ed for** man wusste, wo alle Kinder waren; **four people are still not ~ed for** vier Personen werden immer noch vermisst

accountability [ə'kauntə'bɪlɪtɪ] *n* Verantwortlichkeit *f*

accountable [ə'kauntəbl] *adj*: **~ (to)** verantwortlich (gegenüber +*dat*); **to be held ~ for sth** für etw verantwortlich gemacht werden

accountancy [ə'kauntənsɪ] *n* Buchhaltung *f*

accountant [ə'kauntənt] *n* Buchhalter(in) *m(f)*

accounting [ə'kauntɪŋ] *n* Buchhaltung *f*

accounting period *n* Abrechnungszeitraum *m*

account number *n* Kontonummer *f*

accounts payable *npl* Verbindlichkeiten *pl*

accounts receivable *npl* Forderungen *pl*

accredited [ə'kredɪtɪd] *adj* anerkannt

accretion [ə'kriːʃən] *n* Ablagerung *f*

accrue [ə'kruː] *vi* sich ansammeln; **to ~ to** zufließen +*dat*

accrued interest *n* aufgelaufene Zinsen *pl*

accumulate [ə'kjuːmjuleɪt] *vt* ansammeln ▷ *vi* sich ansammeln

accumulation [əkjuːmju'leɪʃən] *n* Ansammlung *f*

accuracy ['ækjurəsɪ] *n* Genauigkeit *f*

accurate ['ækjurɪt] *adj* genau

accurately ['ækjurɪtlɪ] *adv* genau; *(answer)* richtig

accusation [ækju'zeɪʃən] *n* Vorwurf *m*; *(instance)* Beschuldigung *f*; *(Law)* Anklage *f*

accusative [ə'kjuːzətɪv] *n* Akkusativ *m*

accuse [ə'kjuːz] *vt*: **to ~ sb (of sth)** jdn (einer Sache *gen*) beschuldigen; *(Law)* jdn (wegen etw *dat*) anklagen

accused [ə'kjuːzd] *n* (*Law*): **the ~** der/die Angeklagte

accuser [ə'kjuːzər] *n* Ankläger(in) *m(f)*

accusing [ə'kjuːzɪŋ] *adj* anklagend

accustom [ə'kʌstəm] *vt* gewöhnen; **to ~ o.s. to sth** sich an etw *acc* gewöhnen

accustomed [ə'kʌstəmd] *adj* gewohnt; *(in the habit)*: **~ to** gewohnt an +*acc*

AC/DC *abbr* (= *alternating current/direct current*) WS/GS

ACE [eɪs] *n abbr* (= *American Council on Education*) akademischer Verband für das Erziehungswesen

ace [eɪs] *n* As *nt*

acerbic [ə'səːbɪk] *adj* scharf

acetate ['æsɪteɪt] *n* Acetat *nt*

ache [eɪk] *n* Schmerz *m* ▷ *vi* schmerzen, wehtun; *(yearn)*: **to ~ to do sth** sich danach sehnen, etw zu tun; **I've got (a) stomach ~** ich habe Magenschmerzen; **I'm aching all over** mir tut alles weh; **my head ~s** mir tut der Kopf weh

achieve [ə'tʃiːv] *vt* (*aim, result*) erreichen; *(success)* erzielen; *(victory)* erringen

achievement [ə'tʃiːvmənt] *n* (*act of achieving*) Erreichen *nt*; *(success, feat)* Leistung *f*

Achilles heel [ə'kɪliːz-] *n* Achillesferse *f*

acid ['æsɪd] *adj* sauer ▷ *n* (*Chem*) Säure *f*; *(inf: LSD)* Acid *nt*

Acid House *n* Acid House *nt*, elektronische Funk-Diskomusik

acidic [ə'sɪdɪk] *adj* sauer

acidity [ə'sɪdɪtɪ] *n* Säure *f*

acid rain *n* saurer Regen *m*

acid test *n* (*fig*) Feuerprobe *f*

acknowledge [ək'nɔlɪdʒ] *vt* (*also*: **acknowledge receipt of**) den Empfang +*gen* bestätigen; *(fact)* zugeben; *(situation)* zur Kenntnis nehmen; *(person)* grüßen

acknowledgement [ək'nɔlɪdʒmənt] *n* Empfangsbestätigung *f*; **acknowledgements** *npl* (*in book*) ≈ Danksagung *f*

ACLU *n abbr* (= *American Civil Liberties Union*) Bürgerrechtsverband

acme ['ækmɪ] *n* Gipfel *m*, Höhepunkt *m*

acne ['æknɪ] *n* Akne *f*

acorn ['eɪkɔːn] *n* Eichel *f*

acoustic [ə'kuːstɪk] *adj* akustisch

acoustic coupler *n* (*Comput*) Akustikkoppler *m*

acoustics [ə'kuːstɪks] *n* Akustik *f*

acoustic screen *n* Trennwand *f* zur Schalldämpfung

acquaint [ə'kweɪnt] *vt*: **to ~ sb with sth** jdn mit etw vertraut machen; **to be ~ed with** *(person)* bekannt sein mit; *(fact)* vertraut sein mit

acquaintance [ə'kweɪntəns] *n* Bekannte(r) *f(m)*; *(with person)* Bekanntschaft *f*; *(with subject)* Kenntnis *f*; **to make sb's ~** jds Bekanntschaft machen

acquiesce [ækwɪ'ɛs] *vi* einwilligen; **to ~ (to)** *(demand, arrangement, request)* einwilligen (in +*acc*)

acquire [ə'kwaɪər] *vt* erwerben; *(interest)* entwickeln; *(habit)* annehmen

acquired [ə'kwaɪəd] *adj* erworben; **whisky is an ~ taste** man muss sich an Whisky erst gewöhnen

acquisition [ækwɪˈzɪʃən] n (*see vb*) Erwerb m, Entwicklung f, Annahme f; (*thing acquired*) Errungenschaft f

acquisitive [əˈkwɪzɪtɪv] adj habgierig; **the ~ society** die Erwerbsgesellschaft

acquit [əˈkwɪt] vt freisprechen; **to ~ o.s. well** seine Sache gut machen

acquittal [əˈkwɪtl] n Freispruch m

acre [ˈeɪkəʳ] n Morgen m

acreage [ˈeɪkərɪdʒ] n Fläche f

acrid [ˈækrɪd] adj bitter; (*smoke: fig*) beißend

acrimonious [ækrɪˈməʊnɪəs] adj bitter; (*dispute*) erbittert

acrimony [ˈækrɪmənɪ] n Erbitterung f

acrobat [ˈækrəbæt] n Akrobat(in) m(f)

acrobatic [ækrəˈbætɪk] adj akrobatisch

acrobatics [ækrəˈbætɪks] npl Akrobatik f

acronym [ˈækrənɪm] n Akronym nt

Acropolis [əˈkrɔpəlɪs] n: **the ~** (*Geog*) die Akropolis

across [əˈkrɔs] prep über +acc; (*on the other side of*) auf der anderen Seite +gen ▷ adv (*direction*) hinüber, herüber; (*measurement*) breit; **to take sb ~ the road** jdn über die Straße bringen; **a road ~ the wood** eine Straße durch den Wald; **the lake is 12 km ~** der See ist 12 km breit; **~ from** gegenüber +dat; **to get sth ~ (to sb)** (jdm) etw klarmachen

acrylic [əˈkrɪlɪk] adj (*acid, paint, blanket*) Acryl- ▷ n Acryl nt; **acrylics** npl: **he paints in ~s** er malt mit Acrylfarbe

ACT® n abbr (= *American College Test*) Eignungstest für Studienbewerber

act [ækt] n Tat f; (*of play*) Akt m; (*in a show etc*) Nummer f; (*Law*) Gesetz nt ▷ vi handeln; (*behave*) sich verhalten; (*have effect*) wirken; (*Theat*) spielen ▷ vt spielen; **it's only an ~** es ist nur Schau; **~ of God** (*Law*) höhere Gewalt f; **to be in the ~ of doing sth** dabei sein, etw zu tun; **to catch sb in the ~** jdn auf frischer Tat ertappen; **to ~ the fool** (*Brit*) herumalbern; **he is only ~ing** er tut (doch) nur so; **to ~ as** fungieren als; **it ~s as a deterrent** es dient zur Abschreckung

▶ **act on** vt: **to ~ on sth** (*take action*) auf etw +acc hin handeln

▶ **act out** vt (*event*) durchspielen; (*fantasies*) zum Ausdruck bringen

acting [ˈæktɪŋ] adj stellvertretend ▷ n (*profession*) Schauspielkunst f; (*activity*) Spielen nt; **~ in my capacity as chairman ...** in meiner Eigenschaft als Vorsitzender ...

action [ˈækʃən] n Tat f; (*motion*) Bewegung f; (*Mil*) Kampf m, Gefecht nt; (*Law*) Klage f ▷ vt (*Comm*) in die Tat umsetzen; **to bring an ~ against sb** (*Law*) eine Klage gegen jdn anstrengen; **killed in ~** (*Mil*) gefallen; **out of ~** (*person*) nicht einsatzfähig; (*thing*) außer Betrieb; **to take ~** etwas unternehmen; **to put a plan into ~** einen Plan in die Tat umsetzen

action replay n (*TV*) Wiederholung f

activate [ˈæktɪveɪt] vt in Betrieb setzen; (*Chem, Phys*) aktivieren

active [ˈæktɪv] adj aktiv; (*volcano*) tätig; **to play an ~ part in sth** sich aktiv an etw dat beteiligen

active duty (*US*) n (*Mil*) Einsatz m

actively [ˈæktɪvlɪ] adv aktiv; (*dislike*) offen

active partner n (*Comm*) aktiver Teilhaber m

active service (*Brit*) n (*Mil*) Einsatz m

active suspension n (*Aut*) aktives or computergesteuertes Fahrwerk nt

activist [ˈæktɪvɪst] n Aktivist(in) m(f)

activity [ækˈtɪvɪtɪ] n Aktivität f; (*pastime, pursuit*) Betätigung f

activity holiday n Aktivurlaub m

actor [ˈæktəʳ] n Schauspieler m

actress [ˈæktrɪs] n Schauspielerin f

actual [ˈæktjʊəl] adj wirklich; (*emphatic use*) eigentlich

actually [ˈæktjʊəlɪ] adv wirklich; (*in fact*) tatsächlich; (*even*) sogar

actuary [ˈæktjʊərɪ] n Aktuar m

actuate [ˈæktjʊeɪt] vt auslösen

acuity [əˈkjuːɪtɪ] n Schärfe f

acumen [ˈækjʊmən] n Scharfsinn m; **business ~** Geschäftssinn m

acupuncture [ˈækjʊpʌŋktʃəʳ] n Akupunktur f

acute [əˈkjuːt] adj akut; (*anxiety*) heftig; (*mind*) scharf; (*person*) scharfsinnig; (*Math: angle*) spitz; (*Ling*): **~ accent** Akut m

AD adv abbr (= *Anno Domini*) n. Chr. ▷ n abbr (*US: Mil*) = **active duty**

ad [æd] (*inf*) n = **advertisement**

adage [ˈædɪdʒ] n Sprichwort nt

adamant [ˈædəmənt] adj: **to be ~ that ...** darauf bestehen, dass ...; **to be ~ about sth** auf etw dat bestehen

Adam's apple [ˈædəmz-] n Adamsapfel m

adapt [əˈdæpt] vt anpassen; (*novel etc*) bearbeiten ▷ vi: **to ~ (to)** sich anpassen (an +acc)

adaptability [ədæptəˈbɪlɪtɪ] n Anpassungsfähigkeit f

adaptable [əˈdæptəbl] adj anpassungsfähig; (*device*) vielseitig

adaptation [ædæpˈteɪʃən] n (*of novel etc*) Bearbeitung f; (*of machine etc*) Umstellung f

adapter [əˈdæptəʳ] n (*Elec*) Adapter m; (*: for several plugs*) Mehrfachsteckdose f

adaptor [əˈdæptəʳ] n = **adapter**

ADC n abbr (*Mil*) = **aide-de-camp**; (*US* = *Aid to Dependent Children*) Beihilfe für sozialschwache Familien

add [æd] vt hinzufügen; (*figures: also:* **add up**) zusammenzählen ▷ vi: **to ~ to** (*increase*) beitragen zu

▶ **add on** vt (*amount*) dazurechnen; (*room*) anbauen

▶ **add up** vt (*figures*) zusammenzählen ▷ vi (*fig*): **it doesn't ~ up** es ergibt keinen Sinn; **it doesn't ~ up to much** (*fig*) das ist nicht berühmt (*inf*)

addenda [əˈdɛndə] npl of **addendum**

addendum [əˈdɛndəm] (*pl* **addenda**) n

Nachtrag *m*

adder ['ædə^r] *n* Kreuzotter *f*, Viper *f*

addict ['ædɪkt] *n* Süchtige(r) *f(m)*; *(enthusiast)* Anhänger(in) *m(f)*

addicted [ə'dɪktɪd] *adj*: **to be ~ to drugs/drink** drogensüchtig/alkoholsüchtig sein; **to be ~ to football** *(fig)* ohne Fußball nicht mehr leben können

addiction [ə'dɪkʃən] *n* Sucht *f*

addictive [ə'dɪktɪv] *adj*: **to be ~** *(drug)* süchtig machen; *(activity)* zur Sucht werden können

adding machine ['ædɪŋ-] *n* Addiermaschine *f*

Addis Ababa ['ædɪs'æbəbə] *n* *(Geog)* Addis Abeba *nt*

addition [ə'dɪʃən] *n* *(adding up)* Zusammenzählen *nt*; *(thing added)* Zusatz *m*; *(: to payment, bill)* Zuschlag *m*; *(: to building)* Anbau *m*; **in ~ (to)** zusätzlich (zu)

additional [ə'dɪʃənl] *adj* zusätzlich

additive ['ædɪtɪv] *n* Zusatz *m*

addled ['ædld] *adj* *(Brit: egg)* faul; *(brain)* verwirrt

address [ə'drɛs] *n* Adresse *f*; *(speech)* Ansprache *f* ▷ *vt* adressieren; *(speak to: person)* ansprechen; *(: audience)* sprechen zu; **form of ~** (Form *f* der) Anrede *f*; **what form of ~ do you use for ...?** wie redet man ... an?; **absolute/relative ~** *(Comput)* absolute/relative Adresse; **to ~ (o.s. to)** *(problem)* sich befassen mit

address book *n* Adressbuch *nt*

addressee [ædrɛ'si:] *n* Empfänger(in) *m(f)*

Aden ['eɪdən] *n* *(Geog)*: **Gulf of ~** Golf *m* von Aden

adenoids ['ædɪnɔɪdz] *npl* Rachenmandeln *pl*

adept ['ædɛpt] *adj*: **to be ~ at** gut sein in +*dat*

adequacy ['ædɪkwəsɪ] *n* *(of resources)* Adäquatheit *f*; *(of performance, proposals etc)* Angemessenheit *f*

adequate ['ædɪkwɪt] *adj* ausreichend, adäquat; *(satisfactory)* angemessen

adequately ['ædɪkwɪtlɪ] *adv* ausreichend; *(satisfactorily)* zufriedenstellend

adhere [əd'hɪə^r] *vi*: **to ~ to** haften an +*dat*; *(fig: abide by)* sich halten an +*acc*; *(: hold to)* festhalten an +*dat*

adhesion [əd'hi:ʒən] *n* Haften *nt*, Haftung *f*

adhesive [əd'hi:zɪv] *adj* klebend, Klebe- ▷ *n* Klebstoff *m*

adhesive tape *n* *(Brit)* Klebstreifen *m*; *(US: Med)* Heftpflaster *nt*

ad hoc [æd'hɔk] *adj* *(committee, decision)* Ad-hoc- ▷ *adv* ad hoc

ad infinitum ['ædɪnfɪ'naɪtəm] *adv* ad infinitum

adjacent [ə'dʒeɪsənt] *adj*: **~ to** neben +*dat*

adjective ['ædʒɛktɪv] *n* Adjektiv *nt*, Eigenschaftswort *nt*

adjoin [ə'dʒɔɪn] *vt*: **the hotel ~ing the station** das Hotel neben dem Bahnhof

adjoining [ə'dʒɔɪnɪŋ] *adj* benachbart, Neben-

adjourn [ə'dʒə:n] *vt* vertagen ▷ *vi* sich vertagen; **to ~ a meeting till the following week** eine Besprechung auf die nächste Woche vertagen; **they ~ed to the pub** *(Brit: inf)* sie begaben sich in die Kneipe

adjournment [ə'dʒə:nmənt] *n* Unterbrechung *f*

Adjt. *abbr* *(Mil)* = **adjutant**

adjudicate [ə'dʒu:dɪkeɪt] *vt* *(contest)* Preisrichter sein bei; *(claim)* entscheiden ▷ *vi* entscheiden; **to ~ on** urteilen bei +*dat*

adjudication [ədʒu:dɪ'keɪʃən] *n* Entscheidung *f*

adjudicator [ə'dʒu:dɪkeɪtə^r] *n* Schiedsrichter(in) *m(f)*; *(in contest)* Preisrichter(in) *m(f)*

adjust [ə'dʒʌst] *vt* anpassen; *(change)* ändern; *(clothing)* zurechtrücken; *(machine etc)* einstellen; *(Insurance)* regulieren ▷ *vi*: **to ~ (to)** sich anpassen (an +*acc*)

adjustable [ə'dʒʌstəbl] *adj* verstellbar

adjuster [ə'dʒʌstə^r] *n* *see* **loss**

adjustment [ə'dʒʌstmənt] *n* Anpassung *f*; *(to machine)* Einstellung *f*

adjutant ['ædʒətənt] *n* Adjutant *m*

ad-lib [æd'lɪb] *vi*, *vt* improvisieren ▷ *adv*: **ad lib** aus dem Stegreif

adman ['ædmæn] *(inf: irreg: like* **man***)* *n* Werbefachmann *m*

admin ['ædmɪn] *(inf)* *n* = **administration**

administer [əd'mɪnɪstə^r] *vt* *(country, department)* verwalten; *(justice)* sprechen; *(oath)* abnehmen; *(Med: drug)* verabreichen

administration [ədmɪnɪs'treɪʃən] *n* *(management)* Verwaltung *f*; *(government)* Regierung *f*; **the A~** *(US)* die Regierung

administrative [əd'mɪnɪstrətɪv] *adj* *(department, reform etc)* Verwaltungs-

administrator [əd'mɪnɪstreɪtə^r] *n* Verwaltungsbeamte(r) *f(m)*

admirable ['ædmərəbl] *adj* bewundernswert

admiral ['ædmərəl] *n* Admiral *m*

Admiralty ['ædmərəltɪ] *(Brit)* *n*: **the ~** *(also:* **the Admiralty Board***)* das Marineministerium

admiration [ædmə'reɪʃən] *n* Bewunderung *f*; **to have great ~ for sb/sth** jdn/etw sehr bewundern

admire [əd'maɪə^r] *vt* bewundern

admirer [əd'maɪərə^r] *n* *(suitor)* Verehrer *m*; *(fan)* Bewunderer *m*, Bewunderin *f*

admiring [əd'maɪərɪŋ] *adj* bewundernd

admissible [əd'mɪsəbl] *adj* *(evidence, as evidence)* zulässig

admission [əd'mɪʃən] *n* *(admittance)* Zutritt *m*; *(to exhibition, night club etc)* Einlass *m*; *(to club, hospital)* Aufnahme *f*; *(entry fee)* Eintritt(spreis) *m*; *(confession)* Geständnis *nt*; **"~ free", "free admission"** „Eintritt frei"; **by his own ~** nach eigenem Eingeständnis

admit [əd'mɪt] *vt* *(confess)* gestehen; *(permit to enter)* einlassen; *(to club, hospital)* aufnehmen; *(responsibility etc)* anerkennen; **"children not ~ted"** „kein Zutritt für Kinder"; **this ticket ~s two** diese Karte ist für zwei Personen; **I must ~ that ...** ich muss zugeben, dass ...; **to ~ defeat** sich geschlagen geben

▸ **admit of** *vt fus* *(interpretation etc)* erlauben

▸ **admit to** *vt fus (murder etc)* gestehen

admittance [əd'mɪtəns] *n* Zutritt *m*; **"no ~"** „kein Zutritt"

admittedly [əd'mɪtɪdlɪ] *adv* zugegebenermaßen

admonish [əd'mɔnɪʃ] *vt* ermahnen

ad nauseam [æd'nɔːsɪæm] *adv (talk)* endlos; *(repeat)* bis zum Gehtnichtmehr *(inf)*

ado [ə'duː] *n*: **without (any) more ~** ohne weitere Umstände

adolescence [ædəu'lɛsns] *n* Jugend *f*

adolescent [ædəu'lɛsnt] *adj* heranwachsend; *(remark, behaviour)* pubertär ▷ *n* Jugendliche(r) *f(m)*

adopt [ə'dɔpt] *vt* adoptieren; *(Pol: candidate)* aufstellen; *(policy, attitude, accent)* annehmen

adopted [ə'dɔptɪd] *adj (child)* adoptiert

adoption [ə'dɔpʃən] *n (see vb)* Adoption *f*; Aufstellung *f*; Annahme *f*

adoptive [ə'dɔptɪv] *adj (parents etc)* Adoptiv-; ~ **country** Wahlheimat *f*

adorable [ə'dɔːrəbl] *adj* entzückend

adoration [ædə'reɪʃən] *n* Verehrung *f*

adore [ə'dɔːʳ] *vt (person)* verehren; *(film, activity etc)* schwärmen für

adoring [ə'dɔːrɪŋ] *adj (fans etc)* ihn/sie bewundernd; *(husband/wife)* sie/ihn innig liebend

adoringly [ə'dɔːrɪŋlɪ] *adv* bewundernd

adorn [ə'dɔːn] *vt* schmücken

adornment [ə'dɔːnmənt] *n* Schmuck *m*

ADP *n abbr* = **automatic data processing**

adrenalin [ə'drɛnəlɪn] *n* Adrenalin *nt*; **it gets the ~ going** das bringt einen in Fahrt

Adriatic [eɪdrɪ'ætɪk] *n*: **the ~ (Sea)** *(Geog)* die Adria, das Adriatische Meer

adrift [ə'drɪft] *adv (Naut)* treibend; *(fig)* ziellos; **to be ~** *(Naut)* treiben; **to come ~** *(boat)* sich losmachen; *(fastening etc)* sich lösen

adroit [ə'drɔɪt] *adj* gewandt

ADSL *n abbr* (= *asymmetric digital subscriber line*) ADSL *nt*

ADT *(US) abbr* (= *Atlantic Daylight Time*) atlantische Sommerzeit

adulation [ædju'leɪʃən] *n* Verherrlichung *f*

adult ['ædʌlt] *n* Erwachsene(r) *f(m)* ▷ *adj* erwachsen; *(animal)* ausgewachsen; *(literature etc)* für Erwachsene

adult education *n* Erwachsenenbildung *f*

adulterate [ə'dʌltəreɪt] *vt* verunreinigen; *(with water)* panschen

adulterer [ə'dʌltərəʳ] *n* Ehebrecher *m*

adulteress [ə'dʌltərɪs] *n* Ehebrecherin *f*

adultery [ə'dʌltərɪ] *n* Ehebruch *m*

adulthood ['ædʌlthud] *n* Erwachsenenalter *nt*

advance [əd'vɑːns] *n (movement)* Vorrücken *nt*; *(progress)* Fortschritt *m*; *(money)* Vorschuss *m* ▷ *vt (money)* vorschießen; *(theory, idea)* vorbringen ▷ *vi (move forward)* vorrücken; *(make progress)* Fortschritte machen ▷ *adj*: ~ **booking** Vorverkauf *m*; **to make ~s (to sb)** Annäherungsversuche (bei jdm) machen; **in ~** im Voraus; **to give sb ~ notice** jdm frühzeitig Bescheid sagen; **to give sb ~ warning** jdn vorwarnen

advanced [əd'vɑːnst] *adj (Scol: studies)* für Fortgeschrittene; *(country)* fortgeschritten; *(child)* weit entwickelt; *(ideas)* fortschrittlich; ~ **in years** in fortgeschrittenem Alter

Advanced Higher *(Scot) n (Scol)* Mit "*Advanced Higher*" wird das Ausbildungsjahr nach "*Higher*" bezeichnet, dessen erfolgreicher Abschluss eine Hochschulzugangsberechtigung darstellt

advancement [əd'vɑːnsmənt] *n (improvement)* Förderung *f*; *(in job, rank)* Aufstieg *m*

advantage [əd'vɑːntɪdʒ] *n* Vorteil *m*; **to take ~ of** ausnutzen; *(opportunity)* nutzen; **it's to our ~ (to)** es ist für uns von Vorteil(, wenn wir)

advantageous [ædvən'teɪdʒəs] *adj*: ~ **(to)** vorteilhaft (für), von Vorteil (für)

advent ['ædvənt] *n (of innovation)* Aufkommen *nt*; *(Rel)*: **A~** Advent *m*

Advent calendar *n* Adventskalender *m*

adventure [əd'vɛntʃəʳ] *n* Abenteuer *nt*

adventure playground *n* Abenteuerspielplatz *m*

adventurous [əd'vɛntʃərəs] *adj* abenteuerlustig; *(bold)* mutig

adverb ['ædvəːb] *n* Adverb *nt*

adversarial [ædvə'sɛərɪəl] *adj* konfliktreich

adversary ['ædvəsərɪ] *n* Widersacher(in) *m(f)*

adverse ['ædvəːs] *adj* ungünstig; **in ~ circumstances** unter widrigen Umständen; ~ **to** ablehnend gegenüber +*dat*

adversity [əd'vəːsɪtɪ] *n* Widrigkeit *f*

advert ['ædvəːt] *(Brit) n* = **advertisement**

advertise ['ædvətaɪz] *vi (Comm)* werben; *(in newspaper)* annoncieren, inserieren ▷ *vt (product, event)* werben für; *(job)* ausschreiben; **to ~ for** *(staff etc)* (per Anzeige) suchen

advertisement [əd'vəːtɪsmənt] *n (Comm)* Werbung *f*, Reklame *f*; *(in classified ads)* Anzeige *f*, Inserat *nt*

advertiser ['ædvətaɪzəʳ] *n (in newspaper)* Inserent(in) *m(f)*; *(on television etc)* Firma, die im Fernsehen *etc* wirbt

advertising ['ædvətaɪzɪŋ] *n* Werbung *f*

advertising agency *n* Werbeagentur *f*

advertising campaign *n* Werbekampagne *f*

advice [əd'vaɪs] *n* Rat *m*; *(notification)* Benachrichtigung *f*, Avis *m* or *nt (Comm)*; **a piece of ~** ein Rat(schlag); **to ask sb for ~** jdn um Rat fragen; **to take legal ~** einen Rechtsanwalt zurate ziehen

advice note *(Brit) n (Comm)* Avis *m* or *nt*

advisable [əd'vaɪzəbl] *adj* ratsam

advise [əd'vaɪz] *vt (person)* raten +*dat*; *(company etc)* beraten; **to ~ sb of sth** jdn von etw in Kenntnis setzen; **to ~ against sth** von etw abraten; **to ~ against doing sth** davon abraten, etw zu tun; **you would be well-/ill-~d to go** Sie wären gut/schlecht beraten, wenn Sie gingen

advisedly [əd'vaɪzɪdlɪ] *adv* bewusst

adviser [əd'vaɪzəʳ] *n* Berater(in) *m(f)*

advisor [əd'vaɪzəʳ] *n* = **adviser**

advisory [əd'vaɪzərɪ] *adj* beratend, Beratungs-; **in an ~ capacity** in beratender Funktion

advocate ['ædvəkɪt] *vt* befürworten ▷ *n* (*Law*) (Rechts)anwalt *m*, (Rechts)anwältin *f*; (*supporter, upholder*): ~ **of** Befürworter(in) *m(f)* +*gen*; **to be an ~ of sth** etw befürworten

advt. *abbr* = **advertisement**

AEA (*Brit*) *n abbr* (= *Atomic Energy Authority*) britische Atomenergiebehörde; (*Brit: Scol*: = *Advanced Extension Award*) eine besondere Qualifikation für leistungsstarke Schüler des "A level"

AEC (*US*) *n abbr* (= *Atomic Energy Commission*) amerikanische Atomenergiebehörde

AEEU (*Brit*) *n abbr* (= *Amalgamated Engineering and Electrical Union*) Gewerkschaft der Ingenieure und Elektriker

Aegean [iːˈdʒiːən] *n*: **the ~ (Sea)** (*Geog*) die Ägäis, das Ägäische Meer

aegis ['iːdʒɪs] *n*: **under the ~ of** unter der Schirmherrschaft +*gen*

aeon ['iːən] *n* Äon *m*, Ewigkeit *f*

aerial ['ɛərɪəl] *n* Antenne *f* ▷ *adj* (*view, bombardment etc*) Luft-

aero ... ['ɛərə(u)] *pref* Luft-

aerobatics ['ɛərəuˈbætɪks] *npl* fliegerische Kunststücke *pl*

aerobics [ɛəˈrəubɪks] *n* Aerobic *nt*

aerodrome ['ɛərədrəum] (*Brit*) *n* Flugplatz *m*

aerodynamic ['ɛərəudaɪˈnæmɪk] *adj* aerodynamisch

aeronautics [ɛərəˈnɔːtɪks] *n* Luftfahrt *f*, Aeronautik *f*

aeroplane ['ɛərəpleɪn] (*Brit*) *n* Flugzeug *nt*

aerosol ['ɛərəsɔl] *n* Sprühdose *f*

aerospace industry ['ɛərəuspeɪs-] *n* Raumfahrtindustrie *f*

aesthetic [iːsˈθɛtɪk] *adj* ästhetisch

aesthetically [iːsˈθɛtɪklɪ] *adv* ästhetisch

afar [əˈfɑːʳ] *adv*: **from ~** aus der Ferne

AFB (*US*) *n abbr* (= *Air Force Base*) Luftwaffenstützpunkt *m*

affable ['æfəbl] *adj* umgänglich, freundlich

affair [əˈfɛəʳ] *n* Angelegenheit *f*; (*romance: also*: **love affair**) Verhältnis *nt*; **affairs** *npl* Geschäfte *pl*

affect [əˈfɛkt] *vt* (*influence*) sich auswirken auf +*acc*; (*subj: disease*) befallen; (*move deeply*) bewegen; (*concern*) betreffen; (*feign*) vortäuschen; **to be ~ed by sth** von etw beeinflusst werden

affectation [æfɛkˈteɪʃən] *n* Affektiertheit *f*

affected [əˈfɛktɪd] *adj* affektiert

affection [əˈfɛkʃən] *n* Zuneigung *f*

affectionate [əˈfɛkʃənɪt] *adj* liebevoll, zärtlich; (*animal*) anhänglich

affectionately [əˈfɛkʃənɪtlɪ] *adv* liebevoll, zärtlich

affidavit [æfɪˈdeɪvɪt] *n* (*Law*) eidesstattliche Erklärung *f*

affiliated [əˈfɪlieɪtɪd] *adj* angeschlossen

affinity [əˈfɪnɪtɪ] *n*: **to have an ~ with** *or* **for** sich verbunden fühlen mit; (*resemblance*): **to have an ~ with** verwandt sein mit

affirm [əˈfəːm] *vt* versichern; (*profess*) sich bekennen zu

affirmation [æfəˈmeɪʃən] *n* (*of facts*) Bestätigung *f*; (*of beliefs*) Bekenntnis *nt*

affirmative [əˈfəːmətɪv] *adj* bejahend ▷ *n*: **to reply in the ~** mit „Ja" antworten

affix [əˈfɪks] *vt* aufkleben

afflict [əˈflɪkt] *vt* quälen; (*misfortune*) heimsuchen

affliction [əˈflɪkʃən] *n* Leiden *nt*

affluence ['æfluəns] *n* Wohlstand *m*

affluent ['æfluənt] *adj* wohlhabend; **the ~ society** die Wohlstandsgesellschaft

afford [əˈfɔːd] *vt* sich *dat* leisten; (*time*) aufbringen; (*provide*) bieten; **can we ~ a car?** können wir uns ein Auto leisten?; **I can't ~ the time** ich habe einfach nicht die Zeit

affordable [əˈfɔːdəbl] *adj* erschwinglich

affray [əˈfreɪ] (*Brit*) *n* Schlägerei *f*

affront [əˈfrʌnt] *n* Beleidigung *f*

affronted [əˈfrʌntɪd] *adj* beleidigt

Afghan ['æfgæn] *adj* afghanisch ▷ *n* Afghane *m*, Afghanin *f*

Afghanistan [æfˈgænɪstæn] *n* Afghanistan *nt*

afield [əˈfiːld] *adv*: **far ~** weit fort; **from far ~** aus weiter Ferne

AFL-CIO *n abbr* (= *American Federation of Labor and Congress of Industrial Organizations*) amerikanischer Gewerkschafts-Dachverband

afloat [əˈfləut] *adv* auf dem Wasser ▷ *adj*: **to be ~** schwimmen; **to stay ~** sich über Wasser halten; **to keep/get a business ~** ein Geschäft über Wasser halten/auf die Beine stellen

afoot [əˈfut] *adv*: **there is something ~** da ist etwas im Gang

aforementioned [əˈfɔːmɛnʃənd] *adj* oben erwähnt

aforesaid [əˈfɔːsɛd] *adj* = **aforementioned**

afraid [əˈfreɪd] *adj* ängstlich; **to be ~ of** Angst haben vor +*dat*; **to be ~ of doing sth** *or* **to do sth** Angst davor haben, etw zu tun; **to be ~ to** sich scheuen, ...; **I am ~ that ...** leider ...; **I am ~ so/not** leider ja/nein

afresh [əˈfrɛʃ] *adv* von Neuem, neu

Africa ['æfrɪkə] *n* Afrika *nt*

African ['æfrɪkən] *adj* afrikanisch ▷ *n* Afrikaner(in) *m(f)*

Afrikaans [æfrɪˈkɑːns] *n* Afrikaans *nt*

Afrikaner [æfrɪˈkɑːnəʳ] *n* Afrika(a)nder(in) *m(f)*

Afro-American ['æfrəuəˈmɛrɪkən] *adj* afro-amerikanisch

AFT (*US*) *n abbr* (= *American Federation of Teachers*) Lehrergewerkschaft

aft [ɑːft] *adv* (*be*) achtern; (*go*) nach achtern

after [ɑːftəʳ] *prep* nach +*dat*; (*of place*) hinter +*dat* ▷ *adv* danach ▷ *conj* nachdem; ~ **dinner** nach dem Essen; **the day ~ tomorrow** übermorgen; **what are you ~?** was willst du; **who are you ~?** wen suchst du?; **the police are ~ him** die Polizei ist hinter ihm her; **to name sb ~ sb** jdn nach jdm nennen; **it's twenty ~ eight** (*US*) es ist zwanzig nach acht;

to ask ~ **sb** nach jdm fragen; ~ **all** schließlich; ~ **you!** nach Ihnen!; ~ **he left** nachdem er gegangen war; ~ **having shaved** nachdem er sich rasiert hatte

afterbirth ['ɑːftəbəːθ] *n* Nachgeburt *f*

aftercare ['ɑːftəkɛəʳ] (*Brit*) *n* Nachbehandlung *f*

aftereffects ['ɑːftərɪfɛkts] *npl* Nachwirkungen *pl*

afterlife ['ɑːftəlaɪf] *n* Leben *nt* nach dem Tod

aftermath ['ɑːftəmɑːθ] *n* Auswirkungen *pl*; **in the ~ of** nach +*dat*

afternoon ['ɑːftə'nuːn] *n* Nachmittag *m*

afternoon market *n* (*Econ*) Nachmittagsmarkt *m*

afters ['ɑːftəz] (*Brit: inf*) *n* Nachtisch *m*

after-sales service [ɑːftə'seɪlz-] (*Brit*) *n* Kundendienst *m*

aftershave ['ɑːftəʃeɪv], **aftershave lotion** *n* Rasierwasser *nt*

aftershock ['ɑːftəʃɔk] *n* Nachbeben *nt*

aftersun ['ɑːftəsʌn] *n* After-Sun-Lotion *f*

aftertaste ['ɑːftəteɪst] *n* Nachgeschmack *m*

afterthought ['ɑːftəθɔːt] *n*: **as an ~** nachträglich; **I had an ~** mir ist noch etwas eingefallen

afterwards, (*US*) **afterward** ['ɑːftəwəd(z)] *adv* danach

again [ə'gɛn] *adv* (*once more*) noch einmal; (*repeatedly*) wieder; **not him ~!** nicht schon wieder er!; **to do sth ~** etw noch einmal tun; **to begin ~** noch einmal anfangen; **to see ~** wiedersehen; **he's opened it ~** er hat er schon wieder geöffnet; **~ and again** immer wieder; **now and ~** ab und zu, hin und wieder

against [ə'gɛnst] *prep* gegen +*acc*; (*leaning on*) an +*acc*; (*compared to*) gegenüber +*dat*; **~ a blue background** vor einem blauen Hintergrund; **(as) ~** gegenüber +*dat*

age [eɪdʒ] *n* Alter *nt*; (*period*) Zeitalter *nt* ▷ *vi* altern, alt werden ▷ *vt* alt machen; **what ~ is he?** wie alt ist er?; **20 years of ~** 20 Jahre alt; **under ~** minderjährig; **to come of ~** mündig werden; **it's been ~s since ...** es ist ewig her, seit ...

aged¹ [eɪdʒd] *adj*: **~ ten** zehn Jahre alt, zehnjährig

aged² ['eɪdʒɪd] *npl*: **the ~** die Alten *pl*

age group *n* Altersgruppe *f*; **the 40 to 50 ~** die Gruppe der Vierzig- bis Fünfzigjährigen

ageing ['eɪdʒɪŋ] *adj* (*person, population*) alternd; (*thing*) älter werdend; (*system, technology*) veraltend

ageless ['eɪdʒlɪs] *adj* zeitlos

age limit *n* Altersgrenze *f*

agency ['eɪdʒənsɪ] *n* Agentur *f*; (*government body*) Behörde *f*; **through** *or* **by the ~ of** durch die Vermittlung von

agenda [ə'dʒɛndə] *n* Tagesordnung *f*

agent ['eɪdʒənt] *n* (*Comm*) Vertreter(in) *m(f)*; (*representative, spy*) Agent(in) *m(f)*; (*Chem*) Mittel *nt*; (*fig*) Kraft *f*

aggravate ['ægrəveɪt] *vt* verschlimmern; (*inf: annoy*) ärgern

aggravating ['ægrəveɪtɪŋ] (*inf*) *adj* ärgerlich

aggravation [ægrə'veɪʃən] (*inf*) *n* Ärger *m*

aggregate ['ægrɪgɪt] *n* Gesamtmenge *f* ▷ *vt* zusammenzählen; **on ~** (*Sport*) nach Toren

aggression [ə'grɛʃən] *n* Aggression *f*

aggressive [ə'grɛsɪv] *adj* aggressiv

aggressiveness [ə'grɛsɪvnɪs] *n* Aggressivität *f*

aggressor [ə'grɛsəʳ] *n* Aggressor(in) *m(f)*, Angreifer(in) *m(f)*

aggrieved [ə'griːvd] *adj* verärgert

aggro ['ægrəu] (*Brit: inf*) *n* (*hassle*) Ärger *m*, Theater *nt*; (*aggressive behaviour*) Aggressivität *f*

aghast [ə'gɑːst] *adj* entsetzt

agile ['ædʒaɪl] *adj* beweglich, wendig

agility [ə'dʒɪlɪtɪ] *n* Beweglichkeit *f*, Wendigkeit *f*; (*of mind*) (geistige) Beweglichkeit *f*

agitate ['ædʒɪteɪt] *vt* aufregen; (*liquid: stir*) aufrühren; (*: shake*) schütteln ▷ *vi*: **to ~ for/ against sth** für/gegen etw agitieren

agitated ['ædʒɪteɪtɪd] *adj* aufgeregt

agitator ['ædʒɪteɪtəʳ] *n* Agitator(in) *m(f)*

AGM *n abbr* (= *annual general meeting*) JHV *f*

agnostic [æg'nɔstɪk] *n* Agnostiker(in) *m(f)*

ago [ə'gəu] *adv*: **two days ~** vor zwei Tagen; **not long ~** vor Kurzem; **as long ~ as 1980** schon 1980; **how long ~?** wie lange ist das her?

agog [ə'gɔg] *adj* gespannt

agonize ['ægənaɪz] *vi*: **to ~ over sth** sich *dat* den Kopf über etw *acc* zermartern

agonizing ['ægənaɪzɪŋ] *adj* qualvoll; (*pain etc*) quälend

agony ['ægənɪ] *n* (*pain*) Schmerz *m*; (*torment*) Qual *f*; **to be in ~** Qualen leiden

agony aunt (*Brit: inf*) *n* Briefkastentante *f*

agony column *n* Kummerkasten *m*

agree [ə'griː] *vt* (*price, date*) vereinbaren ▷ *vi* übereinstimmen; (*consent*) zustimmen; **to ~ with sb** (*subj: person*) jdm zustimmen; (*: food*) jdm bekommen; **to ~ to sth** einer Sache *dat* zustimmen; **to ~ to do sth** sich bereit erklären, etw zu tun; **to ~ on sth** sich auf etw *acc* einigen; **to ~ that** (*admit*) zugeben, dass; **garlic doesn't ~ with me** Knoblauch vertrage ich nicht; **it was ~d that ...** es wurde beschlossen, dass ...; **they ~d on this** sie haben sich in diesem Punkt geeinigt; **they ~d on going** sie einigten sich darauf, zu gehen; **they ~d on a price** sie vereinbarten einen Preis

agreeable [ə'griːəbl] *adj* angenehm; (*willing*) einverstanden; **are you ~ to this?** sind Sie hiermit einverstanden?

agreed [ə'griːd] *adj* vereinbart; **to be ~** sich *dat* einig sein

agreement [ə'griːmənt] *n* (*concurrence*) Übereinstimmung *f*; (*consent*) Zustimmung *f*; (*arrangement*) Abmachung *f*; (*contract*) Vertrag *m*; **to be in ~ (with sb)** (mit jdm) einer Meinung sein; **by mutual ~** in gegenseitigem Einverständnis

agricultural [ægrɪ'kʌltʃərəl] *adj* landwirtschaftlich; (*show*) Landwirtschafts-

agriculture ['ægrɪkʌltʃəʳ] n Landwirtschaft f
aground [ə'graund] adv: **to run** ~ auf Grund laufen
ahead [ə'hɛd] adv vor uns/ihnen etc; ~ **of** (in advance of) vor +dat; **to be** ~ **of sb** (in progress, ranking) vor jdm liegen; **to be** ~ **of schedule** schneller als geplant vorankommen; ~ **of time** zeitlich voraus; **to arrive** ~ **of time** zu früh ankommen; **go right** or **straight** ~ gehen/fahren Sie geradeaus; **go** ~! (fig) machen Sie nur!, nur zu!; **they were (right)** ~ **of us** sie waren (genau) vor uns
AI n abbr (= Amnesty International) AI no art; (Comput) = **artificial intelligence**
AID n abbr (= artificial insemination by donor) künstliche Besamung durch Samenspender; (US: = Agency for International Development) Abteilung zur Koordination von Entwicklungshilfe und Außenpolitik
aid [eɪd] n Hilfe f; (to less developed country) Entwicklungshilfe f; (device) Hilfsmittel nt ▷ vt (help) helfen, unterstützen; **with the** ~ **of** mithilfe von; **in** ~ **of** zugunsten +gen; **to** ~ **and abet** Beihilfe leisten; see also **hearing aid**
aide [eɪd] n Berater(in) m(f); (Mil) Adjutant m
aide-de-camp ['eɪddə'kɒŋ] n (Mil) Adjutant m
AIDS [eɪdz] n abbr (= acquired immune deficiency syndrome) AIDS nt
AIH n abbr (= artificial insemination by husband) künstliche Besamung durch den Ehemann/Partner
ailing ['eɪlɪŋ] adj kränklich; (economy, industry etc) krank
ailment ['eɪlmənt] n Leiden nt
aim [eɪm] vt: **to** ~ **at** (gun, missile, camera) richten auf +acc; (blow) zielen auf +acc; (remark) richten an +acc ▷ vi (also: **take aim**) zielen ▷ n (objective) Ziel nt; (in shooting) Zielsicherheit f; **to** ~ **at** zielen auf +acc; (objective) anstreben +acc; **to** ~ **to do sth** vorhaben, etw zu tun
aimless ['eɪmlɪs] adj ziellos
aimlessly ['eɪmlɪslɪ] adv ziellos
ain't [eɪnt] (inf) = **am not; aren't; isn't**
air [ɛəʳ] n Luft f; (tune) Melodie f; (appearance) Auftreten nt; (demeanour) Haltung f; (of house etc) Atmosphäre f ▷ vt lüften; (grievances, views) Luft machen +dat; (knowledge) zur Schau stellen; (ideas) darlegen ▷ cpd Luft-; **into the** ~ in die Luft; **by** ~ mit dem Flugzeug; **to be on the** ~ (Radio, TV: programme) gesendet werden; (: station) senden; (: person) auf Sendung sein
air base n Luftwaffenstützpunkt m
air bed (Brit) n Luftmatratze f
airborne ['ɛəbɔːn] adj in der Luft; (plane, particles) in der Luft befindlich; (troops) Luftlande-
air cargo n Luftfracht f
air-conditioned ['ɛəkən'dɪʃənd] adj klimatisiert
air conditioning n Klimaanlage f
air-cooled ['ɛəkuːld] adj (engine) luftgekühlt
aircraft ['ɛəkrɑːft] n inv Flugzeug nt
aircraft carrier n Flugzeugträger m
air cushion n Luftkissen nt

airfield ['ɛəfiːld] n Flugplatz m
Air Force n Luftwaffe f
air freight n Luftfracht f
air freshener n Raumspray nt
air gun n Luftgewehr nt
air hostess (Brit) n Stewardess f
airily ['ɛərɪlɪ] adv leichtfertig
airing ['ɛərɪŋ] n: **to give an** ~ **to** (fig: ideas) darlegen; (: views) Luft machen +dat
air letter (Brit) n Luftpostbrief m
airlift ['ɛəlɪft] n Luftbrücke f
airline ['ɛəlaɪn] n Fluggesellschaft f
airliner ['ɛəlaɪnəʳ] n Verkehrsflugzeug nt
airlock ['ɛəlɔk] n (in pipe etc) Luftblase f; (compartment) Luftschleuse f
air mail n: **by** ~ per or mit Luftpost
air mattress n Luftmatratze f
airplane ['ɛəpleɪn] (US) n Flugzeug nt
air pocket n Luftloch nt
airport ['ɛəpɔːt] n Flughafen m
air raid n Luftangriff m
air rifle n Luftgewehr nt
airsick ['ɛəsɪk] adj luftkrank
airspace ['ɛəspeɪs] n Luftraum m
airspeed ['ɛəspiːd] n Fluggeschwindigkeit f
airstrip ['ɛəstrɪp] n Start-und-Lande-Bahn f
air terminal n Terminal m or nt
airtight ['ɛətaɪt] adj luftdicht
airtime ['ɛətaɪm] n (Radio, TV) Sendezeit f
air-traffic control ['ɛətræfɪk-] n Flugsicherung f
air-traffic controller ['ɛətræfɪk-] n Fluglotse m
air waybill n Luftfrachtbrief m
airy ['ɛərɪ] adj luftig; (casual) lässig
aisle [aɪl] n Gang m; (section of church) Seitenschiff nt
aisle seat n Sitz m am Gang
ajar [ə'dʒɑːʳ] adj angelehnt
AK (US) abbr (Post) = **Alaska**
a.k.a. abbr (= also known as) alias
akin [ə'kɪn] adj: ~ **to** ähnlich +dat
AL (US) abbr (Post) = **Alabama**
ALA n abbr (= American Library Association) akademischer Verband für das Bibliothekswesen
Ala. (US) abbr (Post) = Alabama
alabaster ['æləbɑːstəʳ] n Alabaster m
à la carte adv à la carte
alacrity [ə'lækrɪtɪ] n Bereitwilligkeit f; **with** ~ ohne zu zögern
alarm [ə'lɑːm] n (anxiety) Besorgnis f; (in shop, bank) Alarmanlage f ▷ vt (worry) beunruhigen; (frighten) erschrecken
alarm call n Weckruf m
alarm clock n Wecker m
alarmed [ə'lɑːmd] adj beunruhigt; **don't be** ~ erschrecken Sie nicht
alarming [ə'lɑːmɪŋ] adj (worrying) beunruhigend; (frightening) erschreckend
alarmingly [ə'lɑːmɪŋlɪ] adv erschreckend
alarmist [ə'lɑːmɪst] n Panikmacher(in) m(f)
alas [ə'læs] excl leider
Alaska [ə'læskə] n Alaska nt
Albania [æl'beɪnɪə] n Albanien nt

Albanian [æl'beɪnɪən] *adj* albanisch ▷ *n* (*Ling*) Albanisch *nt*

albatross ['ælbətrɔs] *n* Albatros *m*

albeit [ɔːl'biːɪt] *conj* wenn auch

album ['ælbəm] *n* Album *nt*

albumen ['ælbjumɪn] *n* Albumen *nt*

alchemy ['ælkɪmɪ] *n* Alchimie *f*, Alchemie *f*

alcohol ['ælkəhɔl] *n* Alkohol *m*

alcoholic [ælkə'hɔlɪk] *adj* alkoholisch ▷ *n* Alkoholiker(in) *m(f)*

alcoholism ['ælkəhɔlɪzəm] *n* Alkoholismus *m*

alcove ['ælkəʊv] *n* Alkoven *m*, Nische *f*

Ald. *abbr* = **alderman**

alderman ['ɔːldəmən] (*irreg: like* **man**) *n* ≈ Stadtrat *m*

ale [eɪl] *n* Ale *nt*

alert [ə'lɜːt] *adj* aufmerksam ▷ *n* Alarm *m* ▷ *vt* alarmieren; **to be ~ to** (*danger, opportunity*) sich *dat* bewusst sein +*gen*; **to be on the ~** wachsam sein; **to ~ sb (to sth)** jdn (vor etw *dat*) warnen

Aleutian Islands [ə'luːʃən-] *npl* Aleuten *pl*

A level (*Brit*) *n* ≈ Abschluss *m* der Sekundarstufe 2, ≈ Abitur *nt*

Alexandria [ælɪg'zɑːndrɪə] *n* Alexandria *nt*

alfresco [æl'frɛskəʊ] *adj, adv* im Freien

algebra ['ældʒɪbrə] *n* Algebra *f*

Algeria [æl'dʒɪərɪə] *n* Algerien *nt*

Algerian [æl'dʒɪərɪən] *adj* algerisch ▷ *n* Algerier(in) *m(f)*

Algiers [æl'dʒɪəz] *n* Algier *nt*

algorithm ['ælgərɪðəm] *n* Algorithmus *m*

alias ['eɪlɪəs] *adv* alias ▷ *n* Deckname *m*

alibi ['ælɪbaɪ] *n* Alibi *nt*

alien ['eɪlɪən] *n* Ausländer(in) *m(f)*; (*extraterrestrial*) außerirdisches Wesen *nt* ▷ *adj*: **~ (to)** fremd (+*dat*)

alienate ['eɪlɪəneɪt] *vt* entfremden; (*antagonize*) befremden

alienation [eɪlɪə'neɪʃən] *n* Entfremdung *f*

alight [ə'laɪt] *adj* brennend; (*eyes, expression*) leuchtend ▷ *vi* (*bird*) sich niederlassen; (*passenger*) aussteigen

align [ə'laɪn] *vt* ausrichten

alignment [ə'laɪnmənt] *n* Ausrichtung *f*; **it's out of ~ (with)** es ist nicht richtig ausgerichtet (nach)

alike [ə'laɪk] *adj* ähnlich ▷ *adv* (*similarly*) ähnlich; (*equally*) gleich; **to look ~** sich *dat* ähnlich sehen; **winter and summer ~** Sommer wie Winter

alimony ['ælɪmənɪ] *n* Unterhalt *m*

alive [ə'laɪv] *adj* (*living*) lebend; (*lively*) lebendig; (*active*) lebhaft; **~ with** erfüllt von; **to be ~ to sth** sich *dat* einer Sache *gen* bewusst sein

alkali ['ælkəlaɪ] *n* Base *f*, Lauge *f*

alkaline ['ælkəlaɪn] *adj* basisch, alkalisch

○ KEYWORD

all [ɔːl] *adj* alle(r, s); **all day/night** den ganzen Tag/die ganze Nacht (über); **all men are equal** alle Menschen sind gleich; **all five**
came alle fünf kamen; **all the books** die ganzen Bücher, alle Bücher; **all the food** das ganze Essen; **all the time** die ganze Zeit (über); **all his life** sein ganzes Leben (lang)
▷ *pron* **1** alles; **I ate it all, I ate all of it** ich habe alles gegessen; **all of us/the boys went** wir alle/alle Jungen gingen; **we all sat down** wir setzten uns alle; **is that all?** ist das alles?; (*in shop*) sonst noch etwas?

2 (*in phrases*): **above all** vor allem; **after all** schließlich; **all in all** alles in allem
▷ *adv* ganz; **all alone** ganz allein; **it's not as hard as all that** so schwer ist es nun auch wieder nicht; **all the more/the better** um so mehr/besser; **all but** (*all except for*) alle außer; (*almost*) fast; **the score is 2 all** der Spielstand ist 2 zu 2

allay [ə'leɪ] *vt* (*fears*) zerstreuen

all clear *n* Entwarnung *f*

allegation [ælɪ'geɪʃən] *n* Behauptung *f*

allege [ə'lɛdʒ] *vt* behaupten; **he is ~d to have said that ...** er soll angeblich gesagt haben, dass ...

alleged [ə'lɛdʒd] *adj* angeblich

allegedly [ə'lɛdʒɪdlɪ] *adv* angeblich

allegiance [ə'liːdʒəns] *n* Treue *f*

allegory ['ælɪgərɪ] *n* Allegorie *f*

all-embracing ['ɔːlɪm'breɪsɪŋ] *adj* (*all*) umfassend

allergic [ə'lɜːdʒɪk] *adj* (*rash, reaction*) allergisch; (*person*): **~ to** allergisch gegen

allergy ['ælədʒɪ] *n* Allergie *f*

alleviate [ə'liːvɪeɪt] *vt* lindern

alley ['ælɪ] *n* Gasse *f*

alleyway ['ælɪweɪ] *n* Durchgang *m*

alliance [ə'laɪəns] *n* Bündnis *nt*

allied ['ælaɪd] *adj* verbündet, alliiert; (*products, industries*) verwandt

alligator ['ælɪgeɪtər] *n* Alligator *m*

all-important ['ɔːlɪm'pɔːtənt] *adj* entscheidend, äußerst wichtig

all in (*Brit*) *adv* inklusive

all-in ['ɔːlɪn] (*Brit*) *adj* (*price*) Inklusiv-

all-in wrestling *n* (*esp Brit*) Freistilringen *nt*

alliteration [əlɪtə'reɪʃən] *n* Alliteration *f*

all-night ['ɔːl'naɪt] *adj* (*café, cinema*) die ganze Nacht geöffnet; (*party*) die ganze Nacht dauernd

allocate ['æləkeɪt] *vt* zuteilen

allocation [æləu'keɪʃən] *n* Verteilung *f*; (*of money, resources*) Zuteilung *f*

allot [ə'lɔt] *vt*: **to ~ (to)** zuteilen (+*dat*); **in the ~ted time** in der vorgesehenen Zeit

allotment [ə'lɔtmənt] *n* (*share*) Anteil *m*; (*garden*) Schrebergarten *m*

all-out ['ɔːlaut] *adj* (*effort, dedication etc*) äußerste(r, s); (*strike*) total ▷ *adv*: **all out** mit aller Kraft; **to go all out for** sein Letztes *or* Äußerstes geben für

allow [ə'lau] *vt* erlauben; (*behaviour*) zulassen; (*sum, time*) einplanen; (*claim, goal*) anerkennen; (*concede*): **to ~ that** annehmen, dass; **to ~ sb**

to do sth jdm erlauben, etw zu tun; **he is ~ed to …** er darf …; **smoking is not ~ed** Rauchen ist nicht gestattet; **we must ~ three days for the journey** wir müssen für die Reise drei Tage einplanen
▶ **allow for** vt fus einplanen, berücksichtigen

allowance [ə'lauəns] n finanzielle Unterstützung f; (welfare payment) Beihilfe f; (pocket money) Taschengeld nt; (tax allowance) Freibetrag m; **to make ~s for** (person) Zugeständnisse machen für; (thing) berücksichtigen

alloy ['ælɔɪ] n Legierung f

all right adv (well) gut; (correctly) richtig; (as answer) okay, in Ordnung

all-rounder [ɔːl'raundəʳ] n Allrounder m; (athlete etc) Allroundsportler(in) m(f)

allspice ['ɔːlspaɪs] n Piment m or nt

all-time ['ɔːl'taɪm] adj aller Zeiten

allude [ə'luːd] vi: **to ~ to** anspielen auf +acc

alluring [ə'ljuərɪŋ] adj verführerisch

allusion [ə'luːʒən] n Anspielung f

alluvium [ə'luːvɪəm] n Anschwemmung f

ally ['ælaɪ] n Verbündete(r) f(m); (during wars) Alliierte(r) f(m) ▷ vt: **to ~ o.s. with** sich verbünden mit

almighty [ɔːl'maɪtɪ] adj allmächtig; (tremendous) mächtig

almond ['ɑːmənd] n Mandel f; (tree) Mandelbaum m

almost ['ɔːlməust] adv fast, beinahe; **he ~ fell** er wäre beinahe gefallen

alms [ɑːmz] npl Almosen pl

aloft [ə'lɔft] adv (hold, carry) empor

alone [ə'ləun] adj, adv allein; **to leave sb ~** jdn in Ruhe lassen; **to leave sth ~** die Finger von etw lassen; **let ~ …** geschweige denn …

along [ə'lɔŋ] prep entlang +acc ▷ adv: **is he coming ~ with us?** kommt er mit?; **he was hopping/limping ~** er hüpfte/humpelte daher; **~ with** (together with) zusammen mit; **all ~** (all the time) die ganze Zeit

alongside [ə'lɔŋ'saɪd] prep neben +dat; (ship) längsseits +gen ▷ adv (come) nebendran; (be) daneben; **we brought our boat ~** wir brachten unser Boot heran; **a car drew up ~** ein Auto fuhr neben mich/ihn etc heran

aloof [ə'luːf] adj unnahbar ▷ adv: **to stand ~** abseitsstehen

aloofness [ə'luːfnɪs] n Unnahbarkeit f

aloud [ə'laud] adv laut

alphabet ['ælfəbet] n Alphabet nt

alphabetical [ælfə'betɪkl] adj alphabetisch; **in ~ order** in alphabetischer Reihenfolge

alphanumeric ['ælfənjuː'merɪk] adj alphanumerisch

alpine ['ælpaɪn] adj alpin, Alpen-

Alps [ælps] npl: **the ~** die Alpen

already [ɔːl'redɪ] adv schon

alright [ɔːl'raɪt] (Brit) adv = **all right**

Alsace ['ælsæs] n Elsass nt

Alsatian [æl'seɪʃən] (Brit) n (dog) Schäferhund m

also ['ɔːlsəu] adv (too) auch; (moreover) außerdem

altar ['ɔltəʳ] n Altar m

alter ['ɔltəʳ] vt ändern; (clothes) umändern ▷ vi sich (ver)ändern

alteration [ɔltə'reɪʃən] n Änderung f; (to clothes) Umänderung f; (to building) Umbau m; **alterations** npl (Sewing) Änderungen pl; (Archit) Umbau m

altercation [ɔltə'keɪʃən] n Auseinandersetzung f

alternate [adj ɔl'təːnɪt, vi 'ɔltəneɪt] adj abwechselnd; (US: alternative: plans etc) Alternativ- ▷ vi: **to ~ (with)** sich abwechseln (mit); **on ~ days** jeden zweiten Tag

alternately [ɔl'təːnɪtlɪ] adv abwechselnd

alternating current ['ɔltəːneɪtɪŋ-] n Wechselstrom m

alternative [ɔl'təːnətɪv] adj alternativ; (solution etc) Alternativ- ▷ n Alternative f

alternative energy n Alternativenergie f

alternatively [ɔl'təːnətɪvlɪ] adv: **~ one could …** oder man könnte …

alternative medicine n Alternativmedizin f

alternative society n Alternativgesellschaft f

alternator ['ɔltəːneɪtəʳ] n (Aut) Lichtmaschine f

although [ɔːl'ðəu] conj obwohl

altitude ['æltɪtjuːd] n Höhe f

alto ['æltəu] n Alt m

altogether [ɔːltə'geðəʳ] adv ganz; (on the whole, in all) im Ganzen, insgesamt; **how much is that ~?** was macht das zusammen?

altruism ['æltruɪzəm] n Altruismus m

altruistic [æltru'ɪstɪk] adj uneigennützig, altruistisch

aluminium [ælju'mɪnɪəm], (US) **aluminum** [ə'luːmɪnəm] n Aluminium nt

always ['ɔːlweɪz] adv immer; **we can ~ …** (if all else fails) wir können ja auch …

Alzheimer's ['æltshaɪməz], **Alzheimer's disease** n (Med) Alzheimerkrankheit f

AM abbr (= amplitude modulation) AM, ≈ MW ▷ n abbr (Brit: in Wales: Pol: = Assembly Member) Mitglied nt der walisischen Versammlung

am [æm] vb see **be**

a.m. adv abbr (= ante meridiem) morgens; (later) vormittags

AMA n abbr (= American Medical Association) Medizinerverband

amalgam [ə'mælgəm] n Amalgam nt; (fig) Mischung f

amalgamate [ə'mælgəmeɪt] vi, vt fusionieren

amalgamation [əmælgə'meɪʃən] n Fusion f

amass [ə'mæs] vt anhäufen; (evidence) zusammentragen

amateur ['æmətəʳ] n Amateur m ▷ adj (Sport) Amateur-; **~ dramatics** Laientheater nt

amateurish ['æmətərɪʃ] adj laienhaft; (pej) dilettantisch, stümperhaft

amaze [ə'meɪz] vt erstaunen; **to be ~d (at)** erstaunt sein (über +acc)

amazement [ə'meɪzmənt] n Erstaunen nt

amazing [ə'meɪzɪŋ] adj erstaunlich; (bargain,

offer) sensationell

amazingly [əˈmeɪzɪŋlɪ] *adv* erstaunlich

Amazon [ˈæməzən] *n* (*river*) Amazonas *m*; **the ~ basin** das Amazonastiefland; **the ~ jungle** der Amazonas-Regenwald

Amazonian [æməˈzəʊnɪən] *adj* amazonisch

ambassador [æmˈbæsədəʳ] *n* Botschafter(in) *m(f)*

amber [ˈæmbəʳ] *n* Bernstein *m*; **at ~** (*Brit: traffic lights*) auf Gelb; (: *move off*) bei Gelb

ambidextrous [æmbɪˈdɛkstrəs] *adj* beidhändig

ambience [ˈæmbɪəns] *n* Atmosphäre *f*

ambiguity [æmbɪˈgjuːtɪ] *n* Zweideutigkeit *f*; (*lack of clarity*) Unklarheit *f*

ambiguous [æmˈbɪgjuəs] *adj* zweideutig; (*not clear*) unklar

ambition [æmˈbɪʃən] *n* Ehrgeiz *m*; (*desire*) Ambition *f*; **to achieve one's ~** seine Ambitionen erfüllen

ambitious [æmˈbɪʃəs] *adj* ehrgeizig

ambivalence [æmˈbɪvələns] *n* Ambivalenz *f*

ambivalent [æmˈbɪvələnt] *adj* ambivalent

amble [ˈæmbl] *vi* schleudern

ambulance [ˈæmbjuləns] *n* Krankenwagen *m*

ambulanceman [ˈæmbjulənsmən] (*irreg: like man*) *n* Sanitäter *m*

ambush [ˈæmbʊʃ] *n* Hinterhalt *m*; (*attack*) Überfall *m* aus dem Hinterhalt ▷ *vt* (aus dem Hinterhalt) überfallen

ameba [əˈmiːbə] (*US*) *n* = **amoeba**

ameliorate [əˈmiːlɪəreɪt] *vt* verbessern

amen [ˈɑːˈmɛn] *excl* amen

amenable [əˈmiːnəbl] *adj*: **~ to** zugänglich +*dat*; (*to flattery etc*) empfänglich für; **~ to the law** dem Gesetz verantwortlich

amend [əˈmɛnd] *vt* ändern; (*habits, behaviour*) bessern

amendment [əˈmɛndmənt] *n* Änderung *f*; (*to law*) Amendement *nt*

amends [əˈmɛndz] *npl*: **to make ~** es wiedergutmachen; **to make ~ for sth** etw wiedergutmachen

amenities [əˈmiːnɪtɪz] *npl* Einkaufs-, Unterhaltungs- und Transportmöglichkeiten

amenity [əˈmiːnɪtɪ] *n* (*Freizeit*)einrichtung *f*

America [əˈmɛrɪkə] *n* Amerika *nt*

American [əˈmɛrɪkən] *adj* amerikanisch ▷ *n* Amerikaner(in) *m(f)*

Americanize [əˈmɛrɪkənaɪz] *vt* amerikanisieren

amethyst [ˈæmɪθɪst] *n* Amethyst *m*

Amex [ˈæmɛks] *n abbr* (= *American Stock Exchange*) US-Börse; (= *American Express®*) *Kreditkarte*

amiable [ˈeɪmɪəbl] *adj* liebenswürdig

amiably [ˈeɪmɪəblɪ] *adv* liebenswürdig

amicable [ˈæmɪkəbl] *adj* freundschaftlich; (*settlement*) gütlich

amicably [ˈæmɪkəblɪ] *adv* (*part, discuss*) in aller Freundschaft; (*settle*) gütlich

amid [əˈmɪd], **amidst** [əˈmɪdst] *prep* inmitten +*gen*

amiss [əˈmɪs] *adj, adv*: **to take sth ~** etw übel nehmen; **there's something ~** da stimmt

irgendetwas nicht

ammeter [ˈæmɪtəʳ] *n* Amperemeter *nt*

ammo [ˈæməʊ] (*inf*) *n* = **ammunition**

ammonia [əˈməʊnɪə] *n* Ammoniak *nt*

ammunition [æmjuˈnɪʃən] *n* Munition *f*

ammunition dump *n* Munitionslager *nt*

amnesia [æmˈniːzɪə] *n* Amnesie *f*, Gedächtnisschwund *m*

amnesty [ˈæmnɪstɪ] *n* Amnestie *f*; **to grant an ~ to** amnestieren

Amnesty International *n* Amnesty International *no art*

amoeba, (*US*) **ameba** [əˈmiːbə] *n* Amöbe *f*

amok [əˈmɒk] *adv*: **to run ~** Amok laufen

among [əˈmʌŋ], **amongst** [əˈmʌŋst] *prep* unter +*dat*

amoral [æˈmɒrəl] *adj* unmoralisch

amorous [ˈæmərəs] *adj* amourös

amorphous [əˈmɔːfəs] *adj* formlos, gestaltlos

amortization [əmɔːtaɪˈzeɪʃən] *n* Amortisation *f*

amount [əˈmaʊnt] *n* (*quantity*) Menge *f*; (*sum of money*) Betrag *m*; (*total*) Summe *f*; (*of bill etc*) Höhe *f* ▷ *vi*: **to ~ to** (*total*) sich belaufen auf +*acc*; (*be same as*) gleichkommen +*dat*; **the total ~** (*of money*) die Gesamtsumme

amp [æmp], **ampère** [ˈæmpɛəʳ] *n* Ampere *nt*; **a 3 ~(ère) fuse** eine Sicherung von 3 Ampere; **a 13 ~(ère) plug** ein Stecker mit einer Sicherung von 13 Ampere

ampersand [ˈæmpəsænd] *n* Et-Zeichen *nt*, Und-Zeichen *nt*

amphetamine [æmˈfɛtəmiːn] *n* Amphetamin *nt*

amphibian [æmˈfɪbɪən] *n* Amphibie *f*

amphibious [æmˈfɪbɪəs] *adj* amphibisch; (*vehicle*) Amphibien-

amphitheatre, (*US*) **amphitheater** [ˈæmfɪθɪətəʳ] *n* Amphitheater *nt*

ample [ˈæmpl] *adj* (*large*) üppig; (*abundant*) reichlich; (*enough*) genügend; **this is ~** das ist reichlich; **to have ~ time/room** genügend Zeit/Platz haben

amplifier [ˈæmplɪfaɪəʳ] *n* Verstärker *m*

amplify [ˈæmplɪfaɪ] *vt* verstärken; (*expand: idea etc*) genauer ausführen

amply [ˈæmplɪ] *adv* reichlich

ampoule, (*US*) **ampule** [ˈæmpuːl] *n* Ampulle *f*

amputate [ˈæmpjuteɪt] *vt* amputieren

amputation [æmpjuˈteɪʃən] *n* Amputation *f*

amputee [æmpjuˈtiː] *n* Amputierte(r) *f(m)*

Amsterdam [ˈæmstədæm] *n* Amsterdam *nt*

amt *abbr* = **amount**

amuck [əˈmʌk] *adv* = **amok**

amuse [əˈmjuːz] *vt* (*entertain*) unterhalten; (*make smile*) amüsieren, belustigen; **to ~ o.s. with sth/by doing sth** sich die Zeit mit etw vertreiben/damit vertreiben, etw zu tun; **to be ~d at** sich amüsieren über +*acc*; **he was not ~d** er fand das gar nicht komisch *or* zum Lachen

amusement [əˈmjuːzmənt] *n* (*mirth*) Vergnügen *nt*; (*pleasure*) Unterhaltung *f*;

423

(*pastime*) Zeitvertreib *m*; **much to my** ~ zu meiner großen Belustigung
amusement arcade *n* Spielhalle *f*
amusement park *n* Vergnügungspark *m*
amusing [ə'mjuːzɪŋ] *adj* amüsant, unterhaltsam
an [æn, ən] *indef art see* **a**
ANA *n abbr* (= *American Newspaper Association*) amerikanischer Zeitungsverband; (= *American Nurses Association*) Verband amerikanischer Krankenschwestern und Krankenpfleger
anachronism [ə'nækrənɪzəm] *n* Anachronismus *m*
anaemia, (US) **anemia** [ə'niːmɪə] *n* Anämie *f*
anaemic, (US) **anemic** [ə'niːmɪk] *adj* blutarm
anaesthetic, (US) **anesthetic** [ænɪs'θetɪk] *n* Betäubungsmittel *nt*; **under (the)** ~ unter Narkose; **local** ~ örtliche Betäubung *f*; **general** ~ Vollnarkose *f*
anaesthetist [æ'niːsθɪtɪst] *n* Anästhesist(in) *m(f)*
anagram ['ænəgræm] *n* Anagramm *nt*
anal ['eɪnl] *adj* anal, Anal-
analgesic [ænæl'dʒiːsɪk] *adj* schmerzstillend ▷ *n* Schmerzmittel *nt*, schmerzstillendes Mittel *nt*
analogous [ə'næləgəs] *adj*: ~ **(to** *or* **with)** analog (zu)
analogue, (US) **analog** ['ænəlɒg] *adj* (*watch, computer*) Analog-
analogy [ə'nælədʒɪ] *n* Analogie *f*; **to draw an** ~ **between** eine Analogie herstellen zwischen +*dat*; **by** ~ durch einen Analogieschluss
analyse, (US) **analyze** ['ænəlaɪz] *vt* analysieren; (*Chem, Med*) untersuchen; (*person*) psychoanalytisch behandeln
analyses [ə'næləsiːz] *npl of* **analysis**
analysis [ə'næləsɪs] (*pl* **analyses**) *n* (*see vb*) Analyse *f*; Untersuchung *f*; Psychoanalyse *f*; **in the last** ~ letzten Endes
analyst ['ænəlɪst] *n* Analytiker(in) *m(f)*; (US) Psychoanalytiker(in) *m(f)*
analytic [ænə'lɪtɪk], **analytical** [ænə'lɪtɪkəl] *adj* analytisch
analyze ['ænəlaɪz] (US) *vt* = **analyse**
anarchic [æ'nɑːkɪk] *adj* anarchisch
anarchist ['ænəkɪst] *adj* anarchistisch ▷ *n* Anarchist(in) *m(f)*
anarchy ['ænəkɪ] *n* Anarchie *f*
anathema [ə'næθɪmə] *n*: **that is** ~ **to him** das ist ihm ein Gräuel
anatomical [ænə'tɒmɪkl] *adj* anatomisch
anatomy [ə'nætəmɪ] *n* Anatomie *f*; (*body*) Körper *m*
ANC *n abbr* (= *African National Congress*) ANC *m*
ancestor ['ænsɪstə'] *n* Vorfahr(in) *m(f)*
ancestral [æn'sestrəl] *adj* angestammt; ~ **home** Stammsitz *m*
ancestry ['ænsɪstrɪ] *n* Abstammung *f*
anchor ['æŋkə'] *n* Anker *m* ▷ *vi* (*also*: **to drop anchor**) ankern, vor Anker gehen ▷ *vt* (*fig*) verankern; **to** ~ **sth to** etw verankern in +*dat*; **to weigh** ~ den Anker lichten

anchorage ['æŋkərɪdʒ] *n* Ankerplatz *m*
anchorman [æŋkəmæn] (*irreg: like* **man**) *n* (*TV, Radio*) = Moderator *m*
anchor store *n* (*attractive store*) = Magnetbetrieb *m*
anchorwoman [æŋkəwʊmən] (*irreg: like* **woman**) *n* (*TV, Radio*) = Moderatorin *f*
anchovy ['æntʃəvɪ] *n* Sardelle *f*, An(s)chovis *f*
ancient ['eɪnʃənt] *adj* alt; (*person, car*) uralt
ancient monument *n* historisches Denkmal *nt*
ancillary [æn'sɪlərɪ] *adj* Hilfs-
and [ænd] *conj* und; ~ **so on** und so weiter; **try** ~ **come please** bitte versuche zu kommen; **better** ~ **better** immer besser
Andes ['ændiːz] *npl*: **the** ~ die Anden *pl*
Andorra [æn'dɔːrə] *n* Andorra *nt*
anecdote ['ænɪkdəʊt] *n* Anekdote *f*
anemia *etc* [ə'niːmɪə] (US) = **anaemia** *etc*
anemone [ə'nemənɪ] *n* (*Bot*) Anemone *f*, Buschwindröschen *nt*
anesthetic *etc* [ænɪs'θetɪk] (US) = **anaesthetic** *etc*
anew [ə'njuː] *adv* von Neuem
angel ['eɪndʒəl] *n* Engel *m*
angel dust (*inf*) *n* als halluzinogene Droge missbrauchtes Medikament
angelic [æn'dʒelɪk] *adj* engelhaft
anger ['æŋgə'] *n* Zorn *m* ▷ *vt* ärgern; (*enrage*) erzürnen; **red with** ~ rot vor Wut
angina [æn'dʒaɪnə] *n* Angina pectoris *f*
angle ['æŋgl] *n* Winkel *m*; (*viewpoint*): **from their** ~ von ihrem Standpunkt aus ▷ *vi*: **to** ~ **for** (*invitation*) aus sein auf +*acc*; (*compliments*) fischen nach ▷ *vt*: **to** ~ **sth towards** *or* **to** etw ausrichten auf +*acc*
angler ['æŋglə'] *n* Angler(in) *m(f)*
Anglican ['æŋglɪkən] *adj* anglikanisch ▷ *n* Anglikaner(in) *m(f)*
anglicize ['æŋglɪsaɪz] *vt* anglisieren
angling ['æŋglɪŋ] *n* Angeln *nt*
Anglo- ['æŋgləʊ] *pref* Anglo-, anglo-
Anglo-German ['æŋgləʊ'dʒɜːmən] *adj* englisch-deutsch
Anglo-Saxon ['æŋgləʊ'sæksən] *adj* angelsächsisch ▷ *n* Angelsachse *m*, Angelsächsin *f*
Angola [æŋ'gəʊlə] *n* Angola *nt*
Angolan [æŋ'gəʊlən] *adj* angolanisch ▷ *n* Angolaner(in) *m(f)*
angrily ['æŋgrɪlɪ] *adv* verärgert
angry ['æŋgrɪ] *adj* verärgert; (*wound*) entzündet; **to be** ~ **with sb** auf jdn böse sein; **to be** ~ **at sth** über etw *acc* verärgert sein; **to get** ~ wütend werden; **to make sb** ~ jdn wütend machen
anguish ['æŋgwɪʃ] *n* Qual *f*
anguished ['æŋgwɪʃt] *adj* gequält
angular ['æŋgjʊlə'] *adj* eckig; (*features*) kantig
animal ['ænɪməl] *n* Tier *nt*; (*living creature*) Lebewesen *nt*; (*pej: person*) Bestie *f* ▷ *adj* tierhaft; (*attraction etc*) animalisch
animal spirits *npl* Vitalität *f*

animate [vt 'ænɪmeɪt, adj 'ænɪmɪt] vt beleben
▷ adj lebend

animated ['ænɪmeɪtɪd] adj lebhaft; (film)
Zeichentrick-

animation [ænɪ'meɪʃən] n (liveliness)
Lebhaftigkeit f; (film) Animation f

animosity [ænɪ'mɒsɪtɪ] n Feindseligkeit f

aniseed ['ænɪsiːd] n Anis m

Ankara ['æŋkərə] n Ankara nt

ankle ['æŋkl] n Knöchel m

ankle sock (Brit) n Söckchen nt

annex ['æneks] n (also: annexe: Brit) Anhang m;
(building) Nebengebäude nt; (extension) Anbau m
▷ vt (take over) annektieren

annexation [ænɛk'seɪʃən] n Annexion f

annihilate [ə'naɪəleɪt] vt (also fig) vernichten

annihilation [ənaɪə'leɪʃən] n Vernichtung f

anniversary [ænɪ'vɜːsərɪ] n Jahrestag m

anno Domini adv anno Domini, nach Christus

annotate ['ænəuteɪt] vt kommentieren

announce [ə'nauns] vt ankündigen; (birth,
death etc) anzeigen; he ~d that he wasn't
going er verkündete, dass er nicht gehen
würde

announcement [ə'naunsmənt] n
Ankündigung f; (official) Bekanntmachung f;
(of birth, death etc) Anzeige f; I'd like to make
an ~ ich möchte etwas bekannt geben

announcer [ə'naunsəʳ] n Ansager(in) m(f)

annoy [ə'nɔɪ] vt ärgern; to be ~ed (at sth/
with sb) sich (über etw/jdn) ärgern; don't
get ~ed! reg dich nicht auf!

annoyance [ə'nɔɪəns] n Ärger m

annoying [ə'nɔɪɪŋ] adj ärgerlich; (person, habit)
lästig

annual ['ænjuəl] adj jährlich; (income) Jahres-
▷ n (Bot) einjährige Pflanze f; (book) Jahresband
m

annual general meeting (Brit) n
Jahreshauptversammlung f

annually ['ænjuəlɪ] adv jährlich

annual report n Geschäftsbericht m

annuity [ə'njuːɪtɪ] n Rente f; life ~ Rente f auf
Lebenszeit

annul [ə'nʌl] vt annullieren; (law) aufheben

annulment [ə'nʌlmənt] n (see vb) Annullierung
f; Aufhebung f

annum ['ænəm] n see per

Annunciation [ənʌnsɪ'eɪʃən] n Mariä
Verkündigung f

anode ['ænəud] n Anode f

anodyne ['ænədaɪn] (fig) n Wohltat f ▷ adj
schmerzlos

anoint [ə'nɔɪnt] vt salben

anomalous [ə'nɒmələs] adj anomal

anomaly [ə'nɒməlɪ] n Anomalie f

anon. [ə'nɒn] abbr = anonymous

anonymity [ænə'nɪmɪtɪ] n Anonymität f

anonymous [ə'nɒnɪməs] adj anonym

anorak ['ænəræk] n Anorak m

anorexia [ænə'rɛksɪə] n Magersucht f,
Anorexie f

anorexic [ænə'rɛksɪk] adj magersüchtig

another [ə'nʌðəʳ] pron (additional) noch eine(r,
s); (different) ein(e) andere(r, s) ▷ adj: ~ book
(one more) noch ein Buch; (a different one)
ein anderes Buch; ~ drink? noch etwas zu
trinken?; in ~ five years in weiteren fünf
Jahren; see also one

ANSI [eɪɛnɛs'aɪ] n abbr (= American National
Standards Institution) amerikanischer
Normenausschuss

answer ['ɑːnsəʳ] n Antwort f; (to problem)
Lösung f ▷ vi antworten; (Tel) sich melden
▷ vt (reply to: person) antworten +dat; (: letter,
question) beantworten; (problem) lösen; (prayer)
erhören; in ~ to your letter in Beantwortung
Ihres Schreibens; to ~ the phone ans Telefon
gehen; to ~ the bell or the door die Tür
aufmachen

▶ answer back vi widersprechen; (child) frech
sein

▶ answer for vt fus (person) verantwortlich sein
für, sich verbürgen für

▶ answer to vt fus (description) entsprechen +dat

answerable ['ɑːnsərəbl] adj: to be ~ to sb for
sth jdm gegenüber für etw verantwortlich
sein; I am ~ to no-one ich brauche mich vor
niemandem zu verantworten

answering machine ['ɑːnsərɪŋ-] n
Anrufbeantworter m

ant [ænt] n Ameise f

antagonism [æn'tægənɪzəm] n Feindseligkeit
f, Antagonismus m

antagonist [æn'tægənɪst] n Gegner(in) m(f),
Antagonist(in) m(f)

antagonistic [æntægə'nɪstɪk] adj feindselig

antagonize [æn'tægənaɪz] vt gegen sich
aufbringen

Antarctic [ænt'ɑːktɪk] n: the ~ die Antarktis

Antarctica [ænt'ɑːktɪkə] n Antarktik f

Antarctic Circle n: the ~ der südliche
Polarkreis

Antarctic Ocean n: the ~ das Südpolarmeer

ante ['æntɪ] n: to up the ~ den Einsatz erhöhen

ante ... ['æntɪ] pref vor-

anteater ['æntiːtəʳ] n Ameisenbär m

antecedent [æntɪ'siːdənt] n Vorläufer m; (of
living creature) Vorfahr m; antecedents npl
Herkunft f

antechamber ['æntɪtʃeɪmbəʳ] n Vorzimmer nt

antelope ['æntɪləup] n Antilope f

antenatal ['æntɪ'neɪtl] adj vor der Geburt,
Schwangerschafts-

antenatal clinic n Sprechstunde f für
werdende Mütter

antenna [æn'tɛnə] (pl ~e) n (of insect) Fühler m;
(Radio, TV) Antenne f

antennae [æn'tɛniː] npl of antenna

anteroom ['æntɪrum] n Vorzimmer nt

anthem ['ænθəm] n: national ~
Nationalhymne f

ant hill n Ameisenhaufen m

anthology [æn'θɒlədʒɪ] n Anthologie f

anthropologist [ænθrə'pɒlədʒɪst] n
Anthropologe m, Anthropologin f

anthropology [ænθrə'pɔlədʒɪ] n
Anthropologie f
anti ... ['æntɪ] pref Anti-, anti-
anti-aircraft ['æntɪ'ɛəkrɑːft] adj (gun, rocket)
Flugabwehr-
anti-aircraft defence n Luftverteidigung f
antiballistic ['æntɪbə'lɪstɪk] adj (missile) Anti-
Raketen-
antibiotic ['æntɪbaɪ'ɔtɪk] n Antibiotikum nt
antibody ['æntɪbɔdɪ] n Antikörper m
anticipate [æn'tɪsɪpeɪt] vt erwarten; (foresee)
vorhersehen; (look forward to) sich freuen auf
+acc; (forestall) vorwegnehmen; **this is worse
than I ~d** es ist schlimmer, als ich erwartet
hatte; **as ~d** wie erwartet
anticipation [æntɪsɪ'peɪʃən] n Erwartung
f; (eagerness) Vorfreude f; **thanking you in ~**
vielen Dank im Voraus
anticlimax ['æntɪ'klaɪmæks] n Enttäuschung f
anticlockwise ['æntɪ'klɔkwaɪz] (Brit) adv gegen
den Uhrzeigersinn
antics ['æntɪks] npl Mätzchen pl; (of politicians
etc) Gehabe nt
anticyclone ['æntɪ'saɪkləun] n
Hoch(druckgebiet) nt
antidote ['æntɪdəut] n Gegenmittel nt
antifreeze ['æntɪfriːz] n Frostschutzmittel
nt
anti-globalist [æntɪ'gləubəlɪst] n, **anti-
globalization protester** [æntɪgləublaɪ'zeɪʃn-]
▷ n Globalisierungsgegner(in) m(f)
antihistamine ['æntɪ'hɪstəmɪn] n
Antihistamin n
Antilles [æn'tɪliːz] npl: **the ~** die Antillen pl
antipathy [æn'tɪpəθɪ] n Antipathie f,
Abneigung f
antiperspirant ['æntɪ'pəːspɪrənt] n
Antitranspirant nt
Antipodean [æntɪpə'diːən] adj antipodisch
Antipodes [æn'tɪpədiːz] npl: **the ~** Australien
und Neuseeland nt
antiquarian [æntɪ'kwɛərɪən] n (collector)
Antiquitätensammler(in) m(f); (seller)
Antiquitätenhändler(in) m(f) ▷ adj: **~
bookshop** Antiquariat nt
antiquated ['æntɪkweɪtɪd] adj antiquiert
antique [æn'tiːk] n Antiquität f ▷ adj antik
antique dealer n Antiquitätenhändler(in)
m(f)
antique shop n Antiquitätenladen m
antiquity [æn'tɪkwɪtɪ] n (period) Antike f;
antiquities npl (objects) Altertümer pl
anti-Semitic ['æntɪsɪ'mɪtɪk] adj antisemitisch
anti-Semitism ['æntɪ'semɪtɪzəm] n
Antisemitismus m
antiseptic [æntɪ'septɪk] n Antiseptikum nt
▷ adj antiseptisch
antisocial ['æntɪ'səuʃəl] adj unsozial; (person)
ungesellig
antitank ['æntɪ'tæŋk] adj (gun, fire)
Panzerabwehr-
antitheses [æn'tɪθɪsiːz] npl of **antithesis**
antithesis [æn'tɪθɪsɪs] (pl **antitheses**) n

Gegensatz m; **she's the ~ of a good cook**
sie ist das genaue Gegenteil einer guten
Köchin
antitrust ['æntɪ'trʌst] (US) adj: **~ legislation**
Kartellgesetzgebung f
antiviral ['æntɪ'vaɪərəl] adj (Med) antiviral
anti-virus [æntɪ'vaɪrəs] adj (Comput) Antiviren-
anti-virus software n Antivirensoftware f
antlers ['æntləz] npl Geweih nt
Antwerp ['æntwəːp] n Antwerpen nt
anus ['eɪnəs] n After m
anvil ['ænvɪl] n Amboss m
anxiety [æŋ'zaɪətɪ] n (worry) Sorge f; (Med)
Angstzustand m; (eagerness): **~ to do sth**
Verlangen (danach), etw zu tun
anxious ['æŋkʃəs] adj (worried) besorgt;
(situation) Angst einflößend; (question,
moments) bang(e); (keen): **to be ~ to do sth** etw
unbedingt tun wollen; **I'm very ~ about you**
ich mache mir große Sorgen um dich
anxiously ['æŋkʃəslɪ] adv besorgt

 KEYWORD

any ['enɪ] adj **1** (in questions etc): **have you any
butter/children?** haben Sie Butter/Kinder?;
if there are any tickets left falls noch
Karten da sind
2 (with negative) kein(e); **I haven't any money/
books** ich habe kein Geld/keine Bücher
3 (no matter which) irgendein(e); **choose any
book you like** nehmen Sie irgendein Buch or
ein beliebiges Buch
4 (in phrases): **in any case** in jedem Fall; **any
day now** jeden Tag; **at any moment** jeden
Moment; **at any rate** auf jeden Fall; **any
time** (at any moment) jeden Moment; (whenever)
jederzeit
▷ pron **1** (in questions etc): **have you got any?**
haben Sie welche?; **can any of you sing?**
kann (irgend)einer von euch singen?
2 (with negative): **I haven't any (of them)** ich
habe keine (davon)
3 (no matter which one(s)): **take
any of those books (you like)** nehmen Sie
irgendwelche von diesen Büchern
▷ adv **1** (in questions etc): **do you want any more
soup/sandwiches?** möchtest du noch Suppe/
Butterbrote?; **are you feeling any better?**
geht es Ihnen etwas besser?
2 (with negative): **I can't hear him any more**
ich kann ihn nicht mehr hören; **don't wait
any longer** warte nicht noch länger

anybody ['enɪbɔdɪ] pron = **anyone**

 KEYWORD

anyhow ['enɪhau] adv **1** (at any rate) sowieso,
ohnehin; **I shall go anyhow** ich gehe auf
jeden Fall
2 (haphazard): **do it anyhow you like** machen
Sie es, wie Sie wollen

○ KEYWORD

anyone ['ɛnɪwʌn] *pron* **1** (*in questions etc*) (irgend)
jemand; **can you see anyone?** siehst du
jemanden?
2 (*with negative*) keine(r); **I can't see anyone**
ich kann keinen *or* niemanden sehen
3 (*no matter who*) jede(r); **anyone could do it**
das kann jeder

anyplace ['ɛnɪpleɪs] (*US*) *adv* = **anywhere**

○ KEYWORD

anything ['ɛnɪθɪŋ] *pron* **1** (*in questions etc*)
(irgend)etwas; **can you see anything?**
kannst du etwas sehen?
2 (*with negative*) nichts; **I can't see anything**
ich kann nichts sehen
3 (*no matter what*) irgendetwas; **you can say
anything you like** du kannst sagen, was du
willst; **anything between 15 and 20 pounds**
(ungefähr) zwischen 15 und 20 Pfund

○ KEYWORD

anyway ['ɛnɪweɪ] *adv* **1** (*at any rate*) sowieso,
ohnehin; **I shall go anyway** ich gehe auf
jeden Fall
2 (*besides*): **anyway, I can't come** jedenfalls
kann ich nicht kommen; **why are you
phoning, anyway?** warum rufst du
überhaupt *or* eigentlich an?

○ KEYWORD

anywhere ['ɛnɪwɛə'] *adv* **1** (*in questions etc*)
irgendwo; **can you see him anywhere?**
kannst du ihn irgendwo sehen?
2 (*with negative*) nirgendwo, nirgends; **I can't
see him anywhere** ich kann ihn nirgendwo
or nirgends sehen
3 (*no matter where*) irgendwo; **put the books
down anywhere** legen Sie die Bücher
irgendwohin

Anzac ['ænzæk] *n abbr* (= *Australia-New
Zealand Army Corps*) (*soldier*) australischer/
neuseeländischer Soldat *m*; *siehe Info-Artikel*

⬤ ANZAC DAY

⬤ *Anzac Day*, der 25 April, ist in Australien und
⬤ Neuseeland ein Feiertag zum Gedenken
⬤ an die Landung der australischen und
⬤ neuseeländischen Truppen in Gallipoli im
⬤ Ersten Weltkrieg.

apace [ə'peɪs] *adv*: **to continue ~** (*negotiations,
preparations etc*) rasch vorangehen
apart [ə'pɑːt] *adv* (*be*) entfernt; (*move*)
auseinander; (*aside*) beiseite; (*separately*)

getrennt; **10 miles ~** 10 Meilen voneinander
entfernt; **a long way ~** weit auseinander;
they are living ~ sie leben getrennt; **with
one's legs ~** mit gespreizten Beinen; **to take
~** auseinandernehmen; **~ from** (*excepting*)
abgesehen von; (*in addition*) außerdem
apartheid [ə'pɑːteɪt] *n* Apartheid *f*
apartment [ə'pɑːtmənt] *n* (*US: flat*) Wohnung
f; (*room*) Raum *m*, Zimmer *nt*
apartment building (*US*) *n* Wohnblock *m*
apathetic [æpə'θɛtɪk] *adj* apathisch,
teilnahmslos
apathy ['æpəθɪ] *n* Apathie *f*,
Teilnahmslosigkeit *f*
APB (*US*) *n abbr* (= *all points bulletin*) *polizeiliche
Fahndung*
ape [eɪp] *n* (Menschen)affe *m* ▷ *vt* nachahmen
Apennines ['æpənaɪnz] *npl*: **the ~** die
Apenninen *pl*, der Apennin
apéritif *n* Aperitif *m*
aperture ['æpətʃjuə'] *n* Öffnung *f*; (*Phot*)
Blende *f*
APEX ['eɪpɛks] *n abbr* (*Aviat, Rail*: = *advance
purchase excursion*) APEX
apex ['eɪpɛks] *n* Spitze *f*
aphid ['æfɪd] *n* Blattlaus *f*
aphorism ['æfərɪzəm] *n* Aphorismus *m*
aphrodisiac [æfrəu'dɪzɪæk] *adj* aphrodisisch
▷ *n* Aphrodisiakum *nt*
apiece [ə'piːs] *adv* (*each person*) pro Person; (*each
thing*) pro Stück
aplomb [ə'plɒm] *n* Gelassenheit *f*
APO (*US*) *n abbr* (= *Army Post Office*) *Poststelle der
Armee*
apocalypse [ə'pɒkəlɪps] *n* Apokalypse *f*
apolitical [eɪpə'lɪtɪkl] *adj* apolitisch
apologetic [əpɒlə'dʒɛtɪk] *adj* entschuldigend;
to be very ~ (about sth) sich (wegen etw *gen*)
sehr entschuldigen
apologize [ə'pɒlədʒaɪz] *vi*: **to ~ (for sth to sb)**
sich (für etw bei jdm) entschuldigen
apology [ə'pɒlədʒɪ] *n* Entschuldigung *f*; **to
send one's apologies** sich entschuldigen
lassen; **please accept my apologies** ich bitte
um Verzeihung
apoplectic [æpə'plɛktɪk] *adj* (*Med*)
apoplektisch; (*fig*): **to be ~ with rage** vor Wut
fast platzen
apoplexy ['æpəplɛksɪ] *n* Schlaganfall *m*
apostle [ə'pɒsl] *n* Apostel *m*
apostrophe [ə'pɒstrəfɪ] *n* Apostroph *m*,
Auslassungszeichen *nt*
app [æp] *n abbr* (*Comput*) = **application**
appal [ə'pɔːl] *vt* entsetzen; **to be ~led by**
entsetzt sein über +*acc*
Appalachian Mountains [æpə'leɪʃən-] *npl*: **the
~** die Appalachen *pl*
appalling [ə'pɔːlɪŋ] *adj* entsetzlich; **she's an ~
cook** sie kann überhaupt nicht kochen
apparatus [æpə'reɪtəs] *n* Gerät *nt*; (*in
gymnasium*) Geräte *pl*; (*of organization*) Apparat *m*;
a piece of ~ ein Gerät *nt*
apparel [ə'pærəl] (*US*) *n* Kleidung *f*

apparent [ə'pærənt] *adj* (*seeming*) scheinbar; (*obvious*) offensichtlich; **it is ~ that ...** es ist klar, dass ...

apparently [ə'pærəntlɪ] *adv* anscheinend

apparition [æpə'rɪʃən] *n* Erscheinung *f*

appeal [ə'pi:l] *vi* (*Law*) Berufung einlegen ▷ *n* (*Law*) Berufung *f*; (*plea*) Aufruf *m*; (*charm*) Reiz *m*; **to ~ (to sb) for** (jdn) bitten um; **to ~ to** (*be attractive to*) gefallen +*dat*; **it doesn't ~ to me** es reizt mich nicht; **right of ~** (*Law*) Berufungsrecht *nt*; **on ~** (*Law*) in der Berufung

appealing [ə'pi:lɪŋ] *adj* ansprechend; (*touching*) rührend

appear [ə'pɪər] *vi* erscheinen; (*seem*) scheinen; **to ~ on TV/in "Hamlet"** im Fernsehen/in „Hamlet" auftreten; **it would ~ that ...** anscheinend ...

appearance [ə'pɪərəns] *n* Erscheinen *nt*; (*look*) Aussehen *nt*; (*in public, on TV*) Auftritt *m*; **to put in** *or* **make an ~** sich sehen lassen; **in** *or* **by order of ~** (*Theat etc*) in der Reihenfolge ihres Auftritts; **to keep up ~s** den (äußeren) Schein wahren; **to all ~s** allem Anschein nach

appease [ə'pi:z] *vt* beschwichtigen

appeasement [ə'pi:zmənt] *n* Beschwichtigung *f*

append [ə'pend] *vt* (*Comput*) anhängen

appendage [ə'pendɪdʒ] *n* Anhängsel *nt*

appendices [ə'pendɪsi:z] *npl of* **appendix**

appendicitis [əpendɪ'saɪtɪs] *n* Blinddarmentzündung *f*

appendix [ə'pendɪks] (*pl* **appendices**) *n* (*Anat*) Blinddarm *m*; (*to publication*) Anhang *m*; **to have one's ~ out** sich *dat* den Blinddarm herausnehmen lassen

appetite ['æpɪtaɪt] *n* Appetit *m*; (*fig*) Lust *f*; **that walk has given me an ~** von dem Spaziergang habe ich Appetit bekommen

appetizer ['æpɪtaɪzər] *n* (*food*) Appetithappen *m*; (*drink*) appetitanregendes Getränk *nt*

appetizing ['æpɪtaɪzɪŋ] *adj* appetitanregend

applaud [ə'plɔ:d] *vi* applaudieren, klatschen ▷ *vt* (*actor etc*) applaudieren +*dat*, Beifall spenden *or* klatschen +*dat*; (*action, attitude*) loben; (*decision*) begrüßen

applause [ə'plɔ:z] *n* Applaus *m*, Beifall *m*

apple ['æpl] *n* Apfel *m*; **he's the ~ of her eye** er ist ihr Ein und Alles

apple tree *n* Apfelbaum *m*

apple turnover *n* Apfeltasche *f*

appliance [ə'plaɪəns] *n* Gerät *nt*

applicable [ə'plɪkəbl] *adj*: **~ (to)** anwendbar (auf +*acc*); (*on official forms*) zutreffend (auf +*acc*); **the law is ~ from January** das Gesetz gilt ab Januar

applicant ['æplɪkənt] *n* Bewerber(in) *m(f)*

application [æplɪ'keɪʃən] *n* (*for job*) Bewerbung *f*; (*for grant etc*) Antrag *m*; (*hard work*) Fleiß *m*; (*applying: of paint etc*) Auftragen *nt*; (*Comput*) Anwendung *f*; **on ~** auf Antrag

application form *n* (*for a job*) Bewerbungsformular *nt*; (*for a grant etc*) Antragsformular *nt*

application program *n* (*Comput*) Anwendungsprogramm *nt*

applications package *n* (*Comput*) Anwendungspaket *nt*

applied [ə'plaɪd] *adj* angewandt

apply [ə'plaɪ] *vt* anwenden; (*paint etc*) auftragen ▷ *vi*: **to ~ (to)** (*be applicable*) gelten (für); **to ~ the brakes** die Bremse betätigen, bremsen; **to ~ o.s. to sth** sich bei etw anstrengen; **to ~ to** (*ask*) sich wenden an +*acc*; **to ~ for** (*permit, grant*) beantragen; (*job*) sich bewerben um

appoint [ə'pɔɪnt] *vt* ernennen; (*date, place*) festlegen, festsetzen

appointed [ə'pɔɪntɪd] *adj*: **at the ~ time** zur festgesetzten Zeit

appointee [əpɔɪn'ti:] *n* Ernannte(r) *f(m)*

appointment [ə'pɔɪntmənt] *n* Ernennung *f*; (*post*) Stelle *f*; (*arranged meeting*) Termin *m*; **to make an ~ (with sb)** einen Termin (mit jdm) vereinbaren; **by ~** nach Anmeldung, mit Voranmeldung

apportion [ə'pɔ:ʃən] *vt* aufteilen; (*blame*) zuweisen; **to ~ sth to sb** jdm etw zuteilen

apposition [æpə'zɪʃən] *n* Apposition *f*, Beifügung *f*; **A is in ~ to B** A ist eine Apposition zu B

appraisal [ə'preɪzl] *n* Beurteilung *f*

appraise [ə'preɪz] *vt* beurteilen

appreciable [ə'pri:ʃəbl] *adj* merklich, deutlich

appreciably [ə'pri:ʃəblɪ] *adv* merklich

appreciate [ə'pri:ʃɪeɪt] *vt* (*like*) schätzen; (*be grateful for*) zu schätzen wissen; (*understand*) verstehen; (*be aware of*) sich *dat* bewusst sein +*gen* ▷ *vi* (*Comm: currency, shares*) im Wert steigen; **I ~ your help** ich weiß Ihre Hilfe zu schätzen

appreciation [əpri:ʃɪ'eɪʃən] *n* (*enjoyment*) Wertschätzung *f*; (*understanding*) Verständnis *nt*; (*gratitude*) Dankbarkeit *f*; (*Comm: in value*) (Wert)steigerung *f*

appreciative [ə'pri:ʃɪətɪv] *adj* dankbar; (*comment*) anerkennend

apprehend [æprɪ'hend] *vt* (*arrest*) festnehmen; (*understand*) verstehen

apprehension [æprɪ'henʃən] *n* (*fear*) Besorgnis *f*; (*arrest*) Festnahme *f*

apprehensive [æprɪ'hensɪv] *adj* ängstlich; **to be ~ about sth** sich *dat* Gedanken *or* Sorgen um etw machen

apprentice [ə'prentɪs] *n* Lehrling *m*, Auszubildende(r) *f(m)* ▷ *vt*: **to be ~d to sb** bei jdm in der Lehre sein

apprenticeship [ə'prentɪsʃɪp] *n* Lehre *f*, Lehrzeit *f*; **to serve one's ~** seine Lehre machen

appro ['æprəu] (*Brit: inf*) *abbr* (*Comm: = approval*): **on ~** zur Ansicht

approach [ə'prəutʃ] *vi* sich nähern; (*event*) nahen ▷ *vt* (*come to*) sich nähern +*dat*; (*ask, apply to: person*) herantreten an +*acc*, ansprechen; (*situation, problem*) herangehen an +*acc*, angehen ▷ *n* (*advance*) (Heran)nahen *nt*;

(access) Zugang m; (: for vehicles) Zufahrt f; (to problem etc) Ansatz m; **to ~ sb about sth** jdn wegen etw ansprechen

approachable [ə'prəutʃəbl] adj (person) umgänglich; (place) zugänglich

approach road n Zufahrtsstraße f

approbation [æprə'beɪʃən] n Zustimmung f

appropriate [adj ə'prəuprɪɪt, vt ə'prəuprɪeɪt] adj (apt) angebracht; (relevant) entsprechend ▷ vt sich dat aneignen; **it would not be ~ for me to comment** es wäre nicht angebracht, wenn ich mich dazu äußern würde

appropriately [ə'prəuprɪɪtlɪ] adv entsprechend

appropriation [əprəuprɪ'eɪʃən] n Zuteilung f, Zuweisung f

approval [ə'pru:vəl] n (approbation) Zustimmung f, Billigung f; (permission) Einverständnis f; **to meet with sb's ~** jds Zustimmung or Beifall finden; **on ~** (Comm) zur Probe

approve [ə'pru:v] vt billigen; (motion, decision) annehmen
 ▶ **approve of** vt fus etwas halten von; **I don't ~ of it/him** ich halte nichts davon/von ihm

approved school [ə'pru:vd-] (Brit) n Erziehungsheim nt

approvingly [ə'pru:vɪŋlɪ] adv zustimmend

approx. abbr = **approximately**

approximate [adj ə'prɒksɪmɪt, vb ə'prɒksɪmeɪt] adj ungefähr ▷ vt, vi: **to ~ (to)** nahe kommen +dat

approximately [ə'prɒksɪmɪtlɪ] adv ungefähr

approximation [ə'prɒksɪ'meɪʃən] n Annäherung f

APR n abbr (= annual(ized) percentage rate) Jahreszinssatz m

Apr. abbr = **April**

apricot ['eɪprɪkɒt] n Aprikose f

April ['eɪprəl] n April m; **~ fool!** April, April!; see also **July**

apron ['eɪprən] n Schürze f; (Aviat) Vorfeld nt

apse [æps] n Apsis f

Apt. abbr = **apartment**

apt [æpt] adj (suitable) passend, treffend; (likely): **to be ~ to do sth** dazu neigen, etw zu tun

aptitude ['æptɪtju:d] n Begabung f

aptitude test n Eignungstest m

aptly ['æptlɪ] adv passend, treffend

aqualung ['ækwəlʌŋ] n Tauchgerät nt

aquarium [ə'kwɛərɪəm] n Aquarium nt

Aquarius [ə'kwɛərɪəs] n Wassermann m; **to be ~** (ein) Wassermann sein

aquatic [ə'kwætɪk] adj (plants etc) Wasser-; (life) im Wasser

aqueduct ['ækwɪdʌkt] n Aquädukt m or nt

AR (US) abbr (Post) = **Arkansas**

ARA (Brit) n abbr (= Associate of the Royal Academy) Qualifikationsnachweis im künstlerischen Bereich

Arab ['ærəb] adj arabisch ▷ n Araber(in) m(f)

Arabia [ə'reɪbɪə] n Arabien nt

Arabian [ə'reɪbɪən] adj arabisch

Arabian Desert n: **the ~** die Arabische Wüste

Arabian Sea n: **the ~** das Arabische Meer

Arabic ['ærəbɪk] adj arabisch ▷ n (Ling) Arabisch nt

arable ['ærəbl] adj (land) bebaubar; **~ farm** Bauernhof, der ausschließlich Ackerbau betreibt

ARAM (Brit) n abbr (= Associate of the Royal Academy of Music) Qualifikationsnachweis in Musik

arbiter ['ɑ:bɪtər] n Vermittler m

arbitrary ['ɑ:bɪtrərɪ] adj willkürlich

arbitrate ['ɑ:bɪtreɪt] vi vermitteln

arbitration [ɑ:bɪ'treɪʃən] n Schlichtung f; **the dispute went to ~** der Streit wurde vor eine Schlichtungskommission gebracht

arbitrator ['ɑ:bɪtreɪtər] n Vermittler(in) m(f); (Industry) Schlichter(in) m(f)

ARC n abbr (= American Red Cross) ≈ DRK nt

arc [ɑ:k] n Bogen m

arcade [ɑ:'keɪd] n Arkade f; (shopping mall) Passage f

arch [ɑ:tʃ] n Bogen m; (of foot) Gewölbe nt ▷ vt (back) krümmen ▷ adj schelmisch ▷ pref Erz-

archaeological [ɑ:kɪə'lɒdʒɪkl] adj archäologisch

archaeologist [ɑ:kɪ'ɔlədʒɪst] n Archäologe m, Archäologin f

archaeology, (US) **archeology** [ɑ:kɪ'ɔlədʒɪ] n Archäologie f

archaic [ɑ:'keɪɪk] adj altertümlich; (language) veraltet, archaisch

archangel ['ɑ:keɪndʒəl] n Erzengel m

archbishop [ɑ:tʃ'bɪʃəp] n Erzbischof m

archenemy ['ɑ:tʃ'enəmɪ] n Erzfeind(in) m(f)

archeology etc [ɑ:kɪ'ɔlədʒɪ] (US) = **archaeology** etc

archery ['ɑ:tʃərɪ] n Bogenschießen nt

archetypal ['ɑ:kɪtaɪpəl] adj (arche)typisch

archetype ['ɑ:kɪtaɪp] n Urbild nt, Urtyp m

archipelago [ɑ:kɪ'pelɪgəu] n Archipel m

architect ['ɑ:kɪtekt] n Architekt(in) m(f)

architectural [ɑ:kɪ'tektʃərəl] adj architektonisch

architecture ['ɑ:kɪtektʃər] n Architektur f

archive file n (Comput) Archivdatei f

archives ['ɑ:kaɪvz] npl Archiv nt

archivist ['ɑ:kɪvɪst] n Archivar(in) m(f)

archway ['ɑ:tʃweɪ] n Torbogen m

ARCM (Brit) n abbr (= Associate of the Royal College of Music) Qualifikationsnachweis in Musik

Arctic ['ɑ:ktɪk] adj arktisch ▷ n: **the ~** die Arktis

Arctic Circle n: **the ~** der nördliche Polarkreis

Arctic Ocean n: **the ~** das Nordpolarmeer

ardent ['ɑ:dənt] adj leidenschaftlich; (admirer) glühend

ardour, (US) **ardor** ['ɑ:dər] n Leidenschaft f

arduous ['ɑ:djuəs] adj mühsam

are [ɑ:r] vb see **be**

area ['ɛərɪə] n Gebiet nt; (Geom etc) Fläche f; (dining area etc) Bereich m; **in the London ~** im Raum London

area code (US) n Vorwahl(nummer) f

arena [ə'ri:nə] n Arena f

aren't [ɑ:nt] = **are not**

Argentina [ɑ:dʒən'ti:nə] n Argentinien nt

Argentinian [ɑːdʒənˈtɪnɪən] *adj* argentinisch ▷ *n* Argentinier(in) *m(f)*

arguable [ˈɑːgjuəbl] *adj*: **it is ~ whether** ... es ist (noch) die Frage, ob ...; **it is ~ that** ... man kann (wohl) sagen, dass ...

arguably [ˈɑːgjuəblɪ] *adv* wohl; **it is ~ ...** es dürfte wohl ... sein

argue [ˈɑːgjuː] *vi* (*quarrel*) sich streiten; (*reason*) diskutieren ▷ *vt* (*debate*) diskutieren, erörtern; **to ~ that ...** den Standpunkt vertreten, dass ...; **to ~ about sth** sich über etw *acc* streiten; **to ~ for/against sth** sich für/gegen etw aussprechen

argument [ˈɑːgjumənt] *n* (*reasons*) Argument *nt*; (*quarrel*) Streit *m*, Auseinandersetzung *f*; (*debate*) Diskussion *f*; **~ for/against** Argument für/gegen; **to have an ~** sich streiten

argumentative [ɑːgjuˈmɛntətɪv] *adj* streitlustig

aria [ˈɑːrɪə] *n* Arie *f*

ARIBA [əˈriːbə] (*Brit*) *n abbr* (= *Associate of the Royal Institute of British Architects*) Qualifikationsnachweis in Architektur

arid [ˈærɪd] *adj* (*land*) dürr; (*subject*) trocken

aridity [əˈrɪdɪtɪ] *n* Dürre *f*, Trockenheit *f*

Aries [ˈɛərɪz] *n* Widder *m*; **to be ~** (ein) Widder sein

arise [əˈraɪz] (*pt* **arose**, *pp* **~n**) *vi* (*difficulty etc*) sich ergeben; (*question*) sich stellen; **to ~ from** sich ergeben aus, herrühren von; **should the need ~** falls es nötig wird

arisen [əˈrɪzn] *pp of* **arise**

aristocracy [ærɪsˈtɔkrəsɪ] *n* Aristokratie *f*, Adel *m*

aristocrat [ˈærɪstəkræt] *n* Aristokrat(in) *m(f)*, Ad(e)lige(r) *f(m)*

aristocratic [ærɪstəˈkrætɪk] *adj* aristokratisch, ad(e)lig

arithmetic [əˈrɪθmətɪk] *n* Rechnen *nt*; (*calculation*) Rechnung *f*

arithmetical [ærɪθˈmɛtɪkl] *adj* rechnerisch, arithmetisch

Ariz. (*US*) *abbr* (*Post*) = *Arizona*

ark [ɑːk] *n*: **Noah's A~** die Arche Noah

arm [ɑːm] *n* Arm *m*; (*of clothing*) Ärmel *m*; (*of chair*) Armlehne *f*; (*of organization etc*) Zweig *m* ▷ *vt* bewaffnen; **arms** *npl* (*weapons*) Waffen *pl*; (*Heraldry*) Wappen *nt*

armaments [ˈɑːməmənts] *npl* (*weapons*) (Aus) rüstung *f*

armband [ˈɑːmbænd] *n* Armbinde *f*

armchair [ˈɑːmtʃɛəʳ] *n* Sessel *m*, Lehnstuhl *m*

armed [ɑːmd] *adj* bewaffnet; **the ~ forces** die Streitkräfte *pl*

armed robbery *n* bewaffneter Raubüberfall *m*

Armenia [ɑːˈmiːnɪə] *n* Armenien *nt*

Armenian [ɑːˈmiːnɪən] *adj* armenisch ▷ *n* Armenier(in) *m(f)*; (*Ling*) Armenisch *nt*

armful [ˈɑːmful] *n* Armvoll *m*

armistice [ˈɑːmɪstɪs] *n* Waffenstillstand *m*

armour, (*US*) **armor** [ˈɑːməʳ] *n* (*Hist*) Rüstung *f*; (*also*: **armour-plating**) Panzerplatte *f*; (*Mil*: *tanks*) Panzerfahrzeuge *pl*

armoured car [ˈɑːməd-] *n* Panzerwagen *m*

armoury [ˈɑːmərɪ] *n* (*storeroom*) Waffenlager *nt*

armpit [ˈɑːmpɪt] *n* Achselhöhle *f*

armrest [ˈɑːmrest] *n* Armlehne *f*

arms control [ɑːmz-] *n* Rüstungskontrolle *f*

arms race [ɑːmz-] *n*: **the ~** das Wettrüsten

army [ˈɑːmɪ] *n* Armee *f*, Heer *nt*; (*fig: host*) Heer

aroma [əˈrəumə] *n* Aroma *nt*, Duft *m*

aromatherapy [ərəuməˈθɛrəpɪ] *n* Aromatherapie *f*

aromatic [ærəˈmætɪk] *adj* aromatisch, duftend

arose [əˈrəuz] *pt of* **arise**

around [əˈraund] *adv* (*about*) herum; (*in the area*) in der Nähe ▷ *prep* (*encircling*) um ... herum; (*near*) in der Nähe von; (*fig: about: dimensions*) etwa; (: *time*) gegen; (: *date*) um; **is he ~?** ist er da?; **~ £5** um die £5, etwa £5; **~ 3 o'clock** gegen 3 Uhr

arousal [əˈrauzəl] *n* (*sexual*) Erregung *f*; (*of feelings, interest*) Weckung *f*

arouse [əˈrauz] *vt* (*feelings, interest*) wecken

arpeggio [ɑːˈpɛdʒɪəu] *n* Arpeggio *nt*

arrange [əˈreɪndʒ] *vt* (*meeting etc*) vereinbaren; (*tour etc*) planen; (*books etc*) anordnen; (*flowers*) arrangieren; (*Mus*) arrangieren, bearbeiten ▷ *vi*: **we have ~d for a car to pick you up** wir haben veranlasst, dass Sie mit dem Auto abgeholt werden; **it was ~d that ...** es wurde vereinbart, dass ...; **to ~ to do sth** vereinbaren *or* ausmachen, etw zu tun

arrangement [əˈreɪndʒmənt] *n* (*agreement*) Vereinbarung *f*; (*layout*) Anordnung *f*; (*Mus*) Arrangement *nt*, Bearbeitung *f*; **arrangements** *npl* Pläne *pl*; (*preparations*) Vorbereitungen *pl*; **to come to an ~ with sb** eine Regelung mit jdm treffen; **home deliveries by ~** nach Vereinbarung Lieferung ins Haus; **I'll make ~s for you to be met** ich werde veranlassen, dass Sie abgeholt werden

arrant [ˈærənt] *adj* (*coward, fool etc*) Erz-; (*nonsense*) total

array [əˈreɪ] *n*: **an ~ of** (*things*) eine Reihe von; (*people*) Aufgebot an +*dat*; (*Math, Comput*) (Daten)feld *nt*

arrears [əˈrɪəz] *npl* Rückstand *m*; **to be in ~ with one's rent** mit seiner Miete im Rückstand sein

arrest [əˈrest] *vt* (*person*) verhaften; (*sb's attention*) erregen ▷ *n* Verhaftung *f*; **under ~** verhaftet

arresting [əˈrestɪŋ] *adj* (*fig*) atemberaubend

arrival [əˈraɪvl] *n* Ankunft *f*; (*Comm: of goods*) Sendung *f*; **new ~** (*person*) Neuankömmling *m*; (*baby*) Neugeborene(s) *nt*

arrive [əˈraɪv] *vi* ankommen
▸ **arrive at** *vt fus* (*fig: conclusion*) kommen zu; (: *situation*) es bringen zu

arrogance [ˈærəgəns] *n* Arroganz *f*, Überheblichkeit *f*

arrogant [ˈærəgənt] *adj* arrogant, überheblich

arrow [ˈærəu] *n* Pfeil *m*

arse [ɑːs] (*Brit*: *inf!*) *n* Arsch *m* (!)

arsenal [ˈɑːsɪnl] *n* Waffenlager *nt*; (*stockpile*)

Arsenal *nt*
arsenic ['ɑːsnɪk] *n* Arsen *nt*
arson ['ɑːsn] *n* Brandstiftung *f*
art [ɑːt] *n* Kunst *f*; **Arts** *npl* (*Scol*)
Geisteswissenschaften *pl*; **work of ~**
Kunstwerk *nt*
art and design (*Brit*) *n* (*Scol*) ≈ Kunst und
Design
arterial [ɑːˈtɪərɪəl] *adj* arteriell; **~ road**
Fernverkehrsstraße *f*; **~ line** (*Rail*)
Hauptstrecke *f*
artery ['ɑːtərɪ] *n* Arterie *f*, Schlagader *f*; (*fig*)
Verkehrsader *f*
artful ['ɑːtful] *adj* raffiniert
art gallery *n* Kunstgalerie *f*
arthritic [ɑːˈθrɪtɪk] *adj* arthritisch
arthritis [ɑːˈθraɪtɪs] *n* Arthritis *f*
artichoke ['ɑːtɪtʃəuk] *n* (*also:* **globe artichoke**)
Artischocke *f*; (*also:* **Jerusalem artichoke**)
Topinambur *m*
article ['ɑːtɪkl] *n* Artikel *m*; (*object, item*)
Gegenstand *m*; **articles** (*Brit*) *npl* (*Law*)
(Rechts)referendarzeit *f*; **~ of clothing**
Kleidungsstück *nt*
articles of association *npl* (*Comm*)
Gesellschaftsvertrag *m*
articulate [*adj* ɑːˈtɪkjulɪt, *vt, vi* ɑːˈtɪkjuleɪt] *adj*
(*speech, writing*) klar; (*speaker*) redegewandt ▷ *vt*
darlegen ▷ *vi* artikulieren; **to be ~** (*person*) sich
gut ausdrücken können
articulated lorry (*Brit*) *n* Sattelschlepper *m*
artifice ['ɑːtɪfɪs] *n* List *f*
artificial [ɑːtɪˈfɪʃəl] *adj* künstlich; (*manner*)
gekünstelt; **to be ~** (*person*) gekünstelt *or*
unnatürlich wirken
artificial insemination [-ɪnsɛmɪˈneɪʃən] *n*
künstliche Besamung *f*
artificial intelligence *n* künstliche Intelligenz
f
artificial respiration *n* künstliche Beatmung *f*
artillery [ɑːˈtɪlərɪ] *n* Artillerie *f*
artisan ['ɑːtɪzæn] *n* Handwerker *m*
artist ['ɑːtɪst] *n* Künstler(in) *m(f)*
artistic [ɑːˈtɪstɪk] *adj* künstlerisch
artistry ['ɑːtɪstrɪ] *n* künstlerisches Geschick *nt*
artless ['ɑːtlɪs] *adj* arglos
art school *n* Kunstakademie *f*,
Kunsthochschule *f*
artwork ['ɑːtwəːk] *n* (*for advert etc, material for
printing*) Druckvorlage *f*; (*in book*) Bildmaterial
nt
ARV *n abbr* (*Bible:* = *American Revised Version*)
amerikanische revidierte Bibelübersetzung
AS (*US*) *n abbr* (= *Associate in Science*) akademischer
Grad in Naturwissenschaften ▷ *abbr* (*Post*) = *American
Samoa*

○ KEYWORD

as [æz] *conj* **1** (*referring to time*) als; **as the years
went by** mit den Jahren; **he came in as I was
leaving** als er hereinkam, ging ich gerade; **as
from tomorrow** ab morgen

2 (*in comparisons*): **as big as** so groß wie; **twice
as big as** zweimal so groß wie; **as much/
many as** so viel/so viele wie; **as soon as**
sobald; **much as I admire her …** sosehr ich
sie auch bewundere …
3 (*since, because*) da, weil; **as you can't come
I'll go without you** da du nicht mitkommen
kannst, gehe ich ohne dich
4 (*referring to manner, way*) wie; **do as you wish**
mach, was du willst; **as she said** wie sie
sagte; **he gave it to me as a present** er gab es
mir als Geschenk; **as it were** sozusagen
5 (*in the capacity of*) als; **he works as a driver** er
arbeitet als Fahrer
6 (*concerning*): **as for** *or* **to that** was das betrifft
or angeht
7: as if *or* **though** als ob; *see also* **long; such;
well**

ASA *n abbr* (= *American Standards Association*)
amerikanischer Normenausschuss; (*Brit*) = *Advertising
Standards Authority*
a.s.a.p. *adv abbr* (= *as soon as possible*)
baldmöglichst
asbestos [æzˈbɛstəs] *n* Asbest *m*
ascend [əˈsɛnd] *vt* hinaufsteigen; (*throne*)
besteigen
ascendancy [əˈsɛndənsɪ] *n* Vormachtstellung
f; **~ over sb** Vorherrschaft *f* über jdn
ascendant [əˈsɛndənt] *n*: **to be in the ~** im
Aufstieg begriffen sein
ascension [əˈsɛnʃən] *n*: **the A~** (*Rel*) die
Himmelfahrt *f* (Christi)
Ascension Island *n* Ascension *nt*
ascent [əˈsɛnt] *n* Aufstieg *m*
ascertain [æsəˈteɪn] *vt* feststellen
ascetic [əˈsɛtɪk] *adj* asketisch
asceticism [əˈsɛtɪsɪzəm] *n* Askese *f*
ASCII ['æskiː] *n abbr* (*Comput:* = *American Standard
Code for Information Interchange*) ASCII
ascribe [əˈskraɪb] *vt*: **to ~ sth to** etw
zuschreiben +*dat*; (*cause*) etw zurückführen
auf +*acc*
ASCU (*US*) *n abbr* (= *Association of State
Colleges and Universities*) Verband staatlicher
Bildungseinrichtungen
ASEAN ['æsɪæn] *n abbr* (= *Association of
Southeast Asian Nations*) ASEAN *f* (*Gemeinschaft
südostasiatischer Staaten*)
ASH [æʃ] (*Brit*) *n abbr* (= *Action on Smoking and
Health*) Antiraucherinitiative
ash [æʃ] *n* Asche *f*; (*wood, tree*) Esche *f*
ashamed [əˈʃeɪmd] *adj* beschämt; **to be ~ of**
sich schämen für; **to be ~ of o.s. for having
done sth** sich schämen, dass man etw getan
hat
A shares *npl* stimmrechtslose Aktien *pl*
ashen ['æʃən] *adj* (*face*) aschfahl
ashore [əˈʃɔːʳ] *adv* an Land
ashtray ['æʃtreɪ] *n* Aschenbecher *m*
Ash Wednesday *n* Aschermittwoch *m*
Asia ['eɪʃə] *n* Asien *nt*
Asia Minor *n* Kleinasien *nt*

Asian ['eɪʃən] *adj* asiatisch ▷ *n* Asiat(in) *m(f)*

Asiatic [eɪsɪ'ætɪk] *adj* asiatisch

aside [ə'saɪd] *adv* zur Seite; *(take)* beiseite ▷ *n* beiseite gesprochene Worte *pl*; **to brush objections ~** Einwände beiseiteschieben

aside from *prep* außer +*dat*

ask [ɑːsk] *vt* fragen; *(invite)* einladen; **to ~ sb to do sth** jdn bitten, etw zu tun; **to ~ (sb) sth** (jdn) etw fragen; **to ~ sb a question** jdm eine Frage stellen; **to ~ sb the time** jdn nach der Uhrzeit fragen; **to ~ sb about sth** jdn nach etw fragen; **to ~ sb out to dinner** jdn zum Essen einladen
  ▶ **ask after** *vt fus* fragen nach
  ▶ **ask for** *vt fus* bitten um; *(trouble)* haben wollen; **it's just ~ing for trouble/it** das kann ja nicht gut gehen

askance [ə'skɑːns] *adv*: **to look ~ at sb** jdn misstrauisch ansehen; **to look ~ at sth** etw mit Misstrauen betrachten

askew [ə'skjuː] *adv* schief

asking price ['ɑːskɪŋ-] *n*: **the ~** der geforderte Preis

asleep [ə'sliːp] *adj* schlafend; **to be ~** schlafen; **to fall ~** einschlafen

AS level *n abbr* (= *Advanced Subsidiary level*) Mit *"AS level" wird das erste Jahr der Sekundarstufe II bezeichnet, nach dessen Abschluss Prüfungen in drei der insgesamt sechs für den "A level" benötigten Wahlpflichtfächern abgehalten werden*

asp [æsp] *n* Natter *f*

asparagus [əs'pærəgəs] *n* Spargel *m*

asparagus tips *npl* Spargelspitzen *pl*

ASPCA *n abbr* (= *American Society for the Prevention of Cruelty to Animals*) Tierschutzverein

aspect ['æspɛkt] *n* (*of subject*) Aspekt *m*; (*of building etc*) Lage *f*; (*quality, air*) Erscheinung *f*; **to have a south-westerly ~** nach Südwesten liegen

aspersions [əs'pəːʃənz] *npl*: **to cast ~ on** sich abfällig äußern über +*acc*

asphalt ['æsfælt] *n* Asphalt *m*

asphyxiate [æs'fɪksɪeɪt] *vt* ersticken

asphyxiation [æsfɪksɪ'eɪʃən] *n* Erstickung *f*

aspirate ['æspəreɪt] *vt* aspirieren, behauchen

aspirations [æspə'reɪʃənz] *npl* Hoffnungen *pl*; **to have ~ to(wards) sth** etw anstreben

aspire [əs'paɪəʳ] *vi*: **to ~ to** streben nach

aspirin ['æsprɪn] *n* Kopfschmerztablette *f*, Aspirin® *nt*

aspiring [əs'paɪərɪŋ] *adj* aufstrebend

ass [æs] *n* (*also fig*) Esel *m*; (*US: inf!*) Arsch! *m*

assail [ə'seɪl] *vt* angreifen; (*fig*): **to be ~ed by doubts** von Zweifeln geplagt werden

assailant [ə'seɪlənt] *n* Angreifer(in) *m(f)*

assassin [ə'sæsɪn] *n* Attentäter(in) *m(f)*

assassinate [ə'sæsɪneɪt] *vt* ermorden, ein Attentat verüben auf +*acc*

assassination [əsæsɪ'neɪʃən] *n* Ermordung *f*, (geglücktes) Attentat *nt*

assault [ə'sɔːlt] *n* Angriff *m* ▷ *vt* angreifen; (*sexually*) vergewaltigen; **~ and battery** (*Law*) Körperverletzung *f*

assemble [ə'sɛmbl] *vt* versammeln; (*car, machine*) montieren; (*furniture etc*) zusammenbauen ▷ *vi* sich versammeln

assembly [ə'sɛmblɪ] *n* Versammlung *f*; (*of car, machine*) Montage *f*; (*of furniture*) Zusammenbau *m*

assembly language *n* (*Comput*) Assemblersprache *f*

assembly line *n* Fließband *nt*

assent [ə'sɛnt] *n* Zustimmung *f* ▷ *vi*: **to ~ (to)** zustimmen (+*dat*)

assert [ə'səːt] *vt* behaupten; (*innocence*) beteuern; (*authority*) geltend machen; **to ~ o.s.** sich durchsetzen

assertion [ə'səːʃən] *n* Behauptung *f*

assertive [ə'səːtɪv] *adj* (*person*) selbstbewusst; (*manner*) bestimmt

assess [ə'sɛs] *vt* (*situation*) einschätzen; (*abilities etc*) beurteilen; (*tax*) festsetzen; (*damages, property etc*) schätzen

assessment [ə'sɛsmənt] *n* (*see vt*) Einschätzung *f*; Beurteilung *f*; Festsetzung *f*; Schätzung *f*

assessor [ə'sɛsəʳ] *n* (*Law*) Gutachter(in) *m(f)*

asset ['æsɛt] *n* Vorteil *m*; (*person*) Stütze *f*; **assets** *npl* (*property, funds*) Vermögen *nt*; (*Comm*) Aktiva *pl*

asset-stripping ['æsɛt'strɪpɪŋ] *n* (*Comm*) Aufkauf *von finanziell gefährdeten Firmen und anschließender Verkauf ihrer Vermögenswerte*

assiduous [ə'sɪdjuəs] *adj* gewissenhaft

assign [ə'saɪn] *vt*: **to ~ (to)** (*date*) zuweisen (+*dat*); (*task*) übertragen (+*dat*); (*person*) einteilen (für); (*cause*) zuschreiben (+*dat*); (*meaning*) zuordnen (+*dat*); **to ~ sb to do sth** jdn damit beauftragen, etw zu tun

assignment [ə'saɪnmənt] *n* Aufgabe *f*

assimilate [ə'sɪmɪleɪt] *vt* aufnehmen; (*immigrants*) integrieren

assimilation [əsɪmɪ'leɪʃən] *n* (*see vt*) Aufnahme *f*; Integration *f*

assist [ə'sɪst] *vt* helfen; (*with money etc*) unterstützen

assistance [ə'sɪstəns] *n* Hilfe *f*; (*with money etc*) Unterstützung *f*

assistant [ə'sɪstənt] *n* Assistent(in) *m(f)*; (*Brit: also: **shop assistant***) Verkäufer(in) *m(f)*

assistant manager *n* stellvertretender Geschäftsführer *m*, stellvertretende Geschäftsführerin *f*

assisted living [əsɪstd'lɪvɪŋ] *n* (*US*) betreutes Wohnen *nt*

associate [*adj, n* ə'səuʃɪɪt, *vt, vi* ə'səuʃɪeɪt] *adj* (*director*) assoziiert; (*member, professor*) außerordentlich ▷ *n* (*at work*) Kollege *m*, Kollegin *f* ▷ *vt* in Verbindung bringen ▷ *vi*: **to ~ with sb** mit jdm verkehren

associated company [ə'səuʃɪeɪtɪd-] *n* Partnerfirma *f*

association [əsəusɪ'eɪʃən] *n* (*group*) Verband *m*; (*involvement*) Verbindung *f*; (*Psych*) Assoziation *f*; **in ~ with** in Zusammenarbeit mit

association football *n* Fußball *m*

assorted [əˈsɔːtɪd] *adj* gemischt; (*various*) diverse(r, s); **in ~ sizes** in verschiedenen Größen

assortment [əˈsɔːtmənt] *n* Mischung *f*; (*of books, people etc*) Ansammlung *f*

Asst *abbr* = **assistant**

assuage [əˈsweɪdʒ] *vt* (*grief, pain*) lindern; (*thirst, appetite*) stillen, befriedigen

assume [əˈsjuːm] *vt* annehmen; (*responsibilities etc*) übernehmen

assumed name [əˈsjuːmd-] *n* Deckname *m*

assumption [əˈsʌmpʃən] *n* Annahme *f*; (*of power etc*) Übernahme *f*; **on the ~ that ...** vorausgesetzt, dass ...

assurance [əˈʃuərəns] *n* Versicherung *f*; (*promise*) Zusicherung *f*; (*confidence*) Zuversicht *f*; **I can give you no ~s** ich kann Ihnen nichts versprechen

assure [əˈʃuər] *vt* versichern; (*guarantee*) sichern

assured [əˈʃuəd] *adj* sicher

AST (*US*) *abbr* (= *Atlantic Standard Time*) Ortszeit in Ostkanada

asterisk [ˈæstərɪsk] *n* Sternchen *nt*

astern [əˈstɜːn] *adv* achtern

asteroid [ˈæstərɔɪd] *n* Asteroid *m*

asthma [ˈæsmə] *n* Asthma *nt*

asthmatic [æsˈmætɪk] *adj* asthmatisch ▷ *n* Asthmatiker(in) *m(f)*

astigmatism [əˈstɪgmətɪzəm] *n* Astigmatismus *m*

astir [əˈstɜːʳ] *adv*: **to be ~** (*out of bed*) auf sein

astonish [əˈstɒnɪʃ] *vt* erstaunen

astonishing [əˈstɒnɪʃɪŋ] *adj* erstaunlich; **I find it ~ that ...** es überrascht mich, dass ...

astonishingly [əˈstɒnɪʃɪŋlɪ] *adv* erstaunlich; **~, ...** erstaunlicherweise ...

astonishment [əˈstɒnɪʃmənt] *n* Erstaunen *nt*

astound [əˈstaʊnd] *vt* verblüffen, sehr erstaunen

astounded [əˈstaʊndɪd] *adj* (höchst) erstaunt

astounding [əˈstaʊndɪŋ] *adj* erstaunlich

astray [əˈstreɪ] *adv*: **to go ~** (*letter*) verloren gehen; (*fig*) auf Abwege geraten; **to lead ~** auf Abwege bringen; **to go ~ in one's calculations** sich verrechnen

astride [əˈstraɪd] *adv* (*sit, ride*) rittlings; (*stand*) breitbeinig ▷ *prep* rittlings auf +*dat*; breitbeinig über +*dat*

astringent [əsˈtrɪndʒənt] *adj* adstringierend; (*fig: caustic*) ätzend, beißend ▷ *n* Adstringens *nt*

astrologer [əsˈtrɒlədʒəʳ] *n* Astrologe *m*, Astrologin *f*

astrology [əsˈtrɒlədʒɪ] *n* Astrologie *f*

astronaut [ˈæstrənɔːt] *n* Astronaut(in) *m(f)*

astronomer [əsˈtrɒnəməʳ] *n* Astronom(in) *m(f)*

astronomical [æstrəˈnɒmɪkl] *adj* (*also fig*) astronomisch

astronomy [əsˈtrɒnəmɪ] *n* Astronomie *f*

astrophysics [ˈæstrəʊfɪzɪks] *n* Astrophysik *f*

astute [əsˈtjuːt] *adj* scharfsinnig; (*operator, behaviour*) geschickt

asunder [əˈsʌndəʳ] *adv*: **to tear ~** auseinanderreißen

ASV *n abbr* (*Bible*: = *American Standard Version*) amerikanische Standard-Bibelübersetzung

asylum [əˈsaɪləm] *n* Asyl *nt*; (*mental hospital*) psychiatrische Klinik *f*; **to seek political ~** um (politisches) Asyl bitten

asymmetrical [eɪsɪˈmetrɪkl] *adj* asymmetrisch

○ KEYWORD

at [æt] *prep* **1** (*referring to position, direction*) an +*dat*, in +*dat*; **at the top** an der Spitze; **at home** zu Hause; **at school** in der Schule; **at the baker's** beim Bäcker; **to look at sth** auf etw *acc* blicken

2 (*referring to time*): **at four o'clock** um vier Uhr; **at night/dawn** bei Nacht/Tagesanbruch; **at Christmas** zu Weihnachten; **at times** zuweilen

3 (*referring to rates, speed etc*): **at £2 a kilo** zu £2 pro Kilo; **two at a time** zwei auf einmal; **at 50 km/h** mit 50 km/h

4 (*referring to activity*): **to be at work** (*in office etc*) auf der Arbeit sein; **to play at cowboys** Cowboy spielen; **to be good at sth** gut in etw *dat* sein

5 (*referring to cause*): **shocked/surprised/annoyed at sth** schockiert/überrascht/verärgert über etw *acc*; **I went at his suggestion** ich ging auf seinen Vorschlag hin

6: **not at all** (*in answer to question*) überhaupt nicht, ganz und gar nicht; (*in answer to thanks*) nichts zu danken, keine Ursache; **I'm not at all tired** ich bin überhaupt nicht müde; **anything at all** irgendetwas

7 (@ *symbol*) At-Zeichen *nt*

ate [eɪt] *pt of* **eat**

atheism [ˈeɪθɪɪzəm] *n* Atheismus *m*

atheist [ˈeɪθɪɪst] *n* Atheist(in) *m(f)*

Athenian [əˈθiːnɪən] *adj* Athener ▷ *n* Athener(in) *m(f)*

Athens [ˈæθɪnz] *n* Athen *nt*

athlete [ˈæθliːt] *n* Athlet(in) *m(f)*

athletic [æθˈletɪk] *adj* sportlich; (*muscular*) athletisch

athletics [æθˈletɪks] *n* Leichtathletik *f*

Atlantic [ətˈlæntɪk] *adj* atlantisch; (*coast etc*) Atlantik- ▷ *n*: **the ~ (Ocean)** der Atlantik

atlas [ˈætləs] *n* Atlas *m*

Atlas Mountains *npl*: **the ~** der Atlas, das Atlasgebirge

ATM *abbr* (= *automated teller machine*) Geldautomat *m*

atmosphere [ˈætməsfɪəʳ] *n* Atmosphäre *f*; (*air*) Luft *f*

atmospheric [ætməsˈferɪk] *adj* atmosphärisch

atmospherics [ætməsˈferɪks] *npl* atmosphärische Störungen *pl*

atoll [ˈætɒl] *n* Atoll *nt*

atom [ˈætəm] *n* Atom *nt*

atom bomb *n* Atombombe *f*

atomic [əˈtɒmɪk] *adj* atomar; (*energy, weapons*) Atom-

atomic bomb n Atombombe f
atomizer ['ætəmaɪzə'] n Zerstäuber m
atone [ə'təʊn] vi: **to ~ for** büßen für
atonement [ə'təʊnmənt] n Buße f
A to Z® n Stadtplan m
ATP n abbr (= Association of Tennis Professionals)
  Tennis-Profiverband
atrocious [ə'trəʊʃəs] adj grauenhaft
atrocity [ə'trɒsɪtɪ] n Gräueltat f
atrophy ['ætrəfɪ] n Schwund m, Atrophie
  f ▷ vt schwinden lassen ▷ vi schwinden,
  verkümmern
attach [ə'tætʃ] vt befestigen; (document, letter)
  anheften, beiheften; (employee, troops) zuteilen;
  (importance etc) beimessen; **to be ~ed to sb/sth**
  (like) an jdm/etw hängen; (be connected with)
  mit jdm/etw zu tun haben; **the ~ed letter** der
  beiliegende Brief; **to ~ a file to an email** eine
  Datei an eine E-Mail anhängen
attaché [ə'tæʃeɪ] n Attaché m
attaché case n Aktenkoffer m
attachment [ə'tætʃmənt] n (tool) Zubehörteil
  nt; (love): **~ (to sb)** Zuneigung f (zu jdm); (to
  email) Attachment nt, Anhang m
attack [ə'tæk] vt angreifen; (subj: criminal)
  überfallen; (task, problem etc) in Angriff
  nehmen ▷ n (also fig) Angriff m; (on sb's life)
  Anschlag m; (of illness) Anfall m; **heart ~**
  Herzanfall m, Herzinfarkt m
attacker [ə'tækə'] n Angreifer(in) m(f)
attain [ə'teɪn] vt (also: **attain to**) erreichen;
  (knowledge) erlangen
attainments [ə'teɪnmənts] npl Fähigkeiten pl
attempt [ə'tɛmpt] n Versuch m ▷ vt versuchen;
  to make an ~ on sb's life einen Anschlag auf
  jdn verüben
attempted [ə'tɛmptɪd] adj versucht; **~
  murder/suicide** Mord-/Selbstmordversuch
  m; **~ theft** versuchter Diebstahl
attend [ə'tɛnd] vt besuchen; (patient)
  behandeln
  ▶ **attend to** vt fus sich kümmern um; (needs)
  nachkommen +dat; (customer) bedienen
attendance [ə'tɛndəns] n Anwesenheit
  f; (people present) Besucherzahl f; (Sport)
  Zuschauerzahl f
attendant [ə'tɛndənt] n (helper) Begleiter(in)
  m(f); (in garage) Tankwart m; (in museum)
  Aufseher(in) m(f) ▷ adj damit verbunden
attention [ə'tɛnʃən] n Aufmerksamkeit f; (care)
  Fürsorge f ▷ excl (Mil) Achtung!; **attentions** npl
  (acts of courtesy) Aufmerksamkeiten pl; **for the
  ~ of** ... zu Händen von ...; **it has come to my ~
  that** ... ich bin darauf aufmerksam geworden,
  dass ...; **to stand to** or **at ~** (Mil) stillstehen
attentive [ə'tɛntɪv] adj aufmerksam
attentively [ə'tɛntɪvlɪ] adv aufmerksam
attenuate [ə'tɛnjʊeɪt] vt abschwächen ▷ vi
  schwächer werden
attest [ə'tɛst] vt, vi: **to ~ (to)** bezeugen
attic ['ætɪk] n Dachboden m
attire [ə'taɪə'] n Kleidung f
attitude ['ætɪtjuːd] n (posture, manner) Haltung

f; (mental): **~ to** or **towards** Einstellung f zu
attorney [ə'təːnɪ] n (US: lawyer) (Rechts)
  anwalt m, (Rechts)anwältin f; (having
  proxy) Bevollmächtigte(r) f(m); **power of ~**
  Vollmacht f
Attorney General n (Brit) ≈ Justizminister(in)
  m(f); (US) ≈ Generalbundesanwalt m, ≈
  Generalbundesanwältin f
attract [ə'trækt] vt (draw) anziehen; (interest)
  auf sich acc lenken; (attention) erregen
attraction [ə'trækʃən] n Anziehungskraft
  f; (of house, city) Reiz m; (gen pl: amusements)
  Attraktion f; (fig): **to feel an ~ towards sb/
  sth** sich von jdm/etw angezogen fühlen
attractive [ə'træktɪv] adj attraktiv; (price, idea,
  offer) verlockend, reizvoll
attribute [n 'ætrɪbjuːt, vt ə'trɪbjuːt] n
  Eigenschaft f ▷ vt: **to ~ sth to** (cause) etw
  zurückführen auf +acc; (poem, painting) etw
  zuschreiben +dat; (quality) etw beimessen +dat
attribution [ætrɪ'bjuːʃən] n (see vt)
  Zurückführung f; Zuschreibung f;
  Beimessung f
attrition [ə'trɪʃən] n: **war of ~**
  Zermürbungskrieg m
Atty. Gen. abbr = **Attorney General**
ATV n abbr (= all-terrain vehicle) Geländefahrzeug
  nt
atypical [eɪ'tɪpɪkl] adj atypisch
aubergine ['əʊbəʒiːn] n Aubergine f; (colour)
  Aubergine nt
auburn ['ɔːbən] adj rotbraun
auction ['ɔːkʃən] n (also: **sale by auction**)
  Versteigerung f, Auktion f ▷ vt versteigern
auctioneer [ɔːkʃə'nɪə'] n Versteigerer m
auction room n Auktionssaal m
audacious [ɔː'deɪʃəs] adj wagemutig, kühn
audacity [ɔː'dæsɪtɪ] n Kühnheit f,
  Verwegenheit f; (pej: impudence)
  Dreistigkeit f
audible ['ɔːdɪbl] adj hörbar
audience ['ɔːdɪəns] n Publikum nt; (Radio)
  Zuhörer pl; (TV) Zuschauer pl; (with queen etc)
  Audienz f
audiovisual ['ɔːdɪəʊ'vɪzjuəl] adj audiovisuell
audiovisual aid n audiovisuelles Lehrmittel nt
audit ['ɔːdɪt] vt (Comm) prüfen ▷ n
  Buchprüfung f, Rechnungsprüfung f
audition [ɔː'dɪʃən] n Vorsprechprobe f ▷ vi: **to ~
  (for)** vorsprechen (für)
auditor ['ɔːdɪtə'] n Buchprüfer(in) m(f),
  Rechnungsprüfer(in) m(f)
auditorium [ɔːdɪ'tɔːrɪəm] n (building)
  Auditorium nt; (audience area) Zuschauerraum
  m
AU n abbr = African Union
Aug. abbr = **August**
augment [ɔːg'mɛnt] vt vermehren; (income,
  diet) verbessern
augur ['ɔːgə'] vi: **it ~s well** das ist ein gutes
  Zeichen or Omen
August ['ɔːgəst] n August m; see also **July**
august [ɔː'gʌst] adj erhaben

aunt [ɑ:nt] n Tante f
auntie ['ɑ:ntɪ] n dimin of **aunt**
aunty ['ɑ:ntɪ] n dimin of **aunt**
au pair ['əʊ'peəʳ] n (also: **au pair girl**) Aupair(mädchen) nt, Au-pair(-Mädchen) nt
aura ['ɔ:rə] n Aura f
auspices ['ɔ:spɪsɪz] npl: **under the ~ of** unter der Schirmherrschaft +gen
auspicious [ɔ:s'pɪʃəs] adj verheißungsvoll; (opening, start) vielversprechend
austere [ɔs'tɪəʳ] adj streng; (room, decoration) schmucklos; (person, lifestyle) asketisch
austerity [ɔs'tɛrɪtɪ] n Strenge f; (of room etc) Schmucklosigkeit f; (hardship) Entbehrung f
Australasia [ɔ:strə'leɪzɪə] n Australien und Ozeanien nt
Australasian [ɔ:strə'leɪzɪən] adj ozeanisch, südwestpazifisch
Australia [ɔs'treɪlɪə] n Australien nt
Australian [ɔs'treɪlɪən] adj australisch ▷ n Australier(in) m(f)
Austria ['ɔstrɪə] n Österreich nt
Austrian ['ɔstrɪən] adj österreichisch ▷ n Österreicher(in) m(f)
AUT (Brit) n abbr (= Association of University Teachers) Gewerkschaft der Universitätsdozenten
authentic [ɔ:'θɛntɪk] adj authentisch
authenticate [ɔ:'θɛntɪkeɪt] vt beglaubigen
authenticity [ɔ:θɛn'tɪsɪtɪ] n Echtheit f
author ['ɔ:θəʳ] n (of text) Verfasser(in) m(f); (profession) Autor(in) m(f), Schriftsteller(in) m(f); (creator) Urheber(in) m(f); (: of plan) Initiator(in) m(f)
authoritarian [ɔ:θɔrɪ'tɛərɪən] adj autoritär
authoritative [ɔ:'θɔrɪtətɪv] adj (person, manner) bestimmt, entschieden; (source, account) zuverlässig; (study, treatise) maßgeblich, maßgebend
authority [ɔ:'θɔrɪtɪ] n Autorität f; (government body) Behörde f, Amt nt; (official permission) Genehmigung f; **the authorities** npl (ruling body) die Behörden pl; **to have the ~ to do sth** befugt sein, etw zu tun
authorization [ɔ:θəraɪ'zeɪʃən] n Genehmigung f
authorize ['ɔ:θəraɪz] vt genehmigen; **to ~ sb to do sth** jdn ermächtigen, etw zu tun
authorized capital ['ɔ:θəraɪzd-] n autorisiertes Aktienkapital nt
authorship ['ɔ:θəʃɪp] n Autorschaft f, Verfasserschaft f
autistic [ɔ:'tɪstɪk] adj autistisch
auto ['ɔ:təʊ] (US) n Auto nt, Wagen m
autobiographical ['ɔ:təbaɪə'græfɪkl] adj autobiografisch
autobiography [ɔ:təbaɪ'ɔgrəfɪ] n Autobiografie f
autocratic [ɔ:tə'krætɪk] adj autokratisch
Autocue® ['ɔ:təʊkju:] n Teleprompter m
autograph ['ɔ:təgrɑ:f] n Autogramm nt ▷ vt signieren
autoimmune [ɔ:təʊ'mju:n] adj (disease) Autoimmun-

automat ['ɔ:təmæt] n Automat m; (US) Automatenrestaurant nt
automata [ɔ:'tɔmətə] npl of **automaton**
automate ['ɔ:təmeɪt] vt automatisieren
automatic [ɔ:tə'mætɪk] adj automatisch ▷ n (gun) automatische Waffe; (washing machine) Waschautomat m; (car) Automatikwagen m
automatically [ɔ:tə'mætɪklɪ] adv automatisch
automatic data processing n automatische Datenverarbeitung f
automation [ɔ:tə'meɪʃən] n Automatisierung f
automaton [ɔ:'tɔmətən] (pl **automata**) n Roboter m
automobile ['ɔ:təməbi:l] (US) n Auto(mobil) nt
autonomous [ɔ:'tɔnəməs] adj autonom
autonomy [ɔ:'tɔnəmɪ] n Autonomie f
autopsy ['ɔ:tɔpsɪ] n Autopsie f
autumn ['ɔ:təm] n Herbst m; **in ~** im Herbst
autumnal [ɔ:'tʌmnəl] adj herbstlich
auxiliary [ɔ:g'zɪlɪərɪ] adj (tool, verb) Hilfs- ▷ n (assistant) Hilfskraft f
AV n abbr (Bible: = Authorized Version) englische Bibelübersetzung von 1611 ▷ abbr = **audiovisual**
avail [ə'veɪl] vt: **to ~ o.s. of** Gebrauch machen von ▷ n: **to no ~** vergeblich, erfolglos
availability [əveɪlə'bɪlɪtɪ] n Erhältlichkeit f; (of staff) Vorhandensein nt
available [ə'veɪləbl] adj erhältlich; (person: unoccupied) frei, abkömmlich; (: unattached) zu haben; (time) frei, verfügbar; **every ~ means** alle verfügbaren Mittel; **is the manager ~?** ist der Geschäftsführer zu sprechen?; **to make sth ~ to sb** jdm etw zur Verfügung stellen
avalanche ['ævəlɑ:nʃ] n (also fig) Lawine f
avant-garde ['ævɑ̃'gɑ:d] adj avantgardistisch
avarice ['ævərɪs] n Habsucht f
avaricious [ævə'rɪʃəs] adj habsüchtig
avdp. abbr (= avoirdupois) Handelsgewicht
Ave abbr = **avenue**
avenge [ə'vɛndʒ] vt rächen
avenue ['ævənju:] n Straße f; (drive) Auffahrt f; (means) Weg m
average ['ævərɪdʒ] n Durchschnitt m ▷ adj durchschnittlich, Durchschnitts- ▷ vt (reach an average of) einen Durchschnitt erreichen von; **on ~** im Durchschnitt, durchschnittlich; **above/below (the) ~** über/unter dem Durchschnitt
▷ **average out** vi: **to ~ out at** durchschnittlich ausmachen
averse [ə'və:s] adj: **to be ~ to sth/doing sth** eine Abneigung gegen etw haben/dagegen haben, etw zu tun; **I wouldn't be ~ to a drink** ich hätte nichts gegen einen Drink
aversion [ə'və:ʃən] n Abneigung f; **to have an ~ to sb/sth** eine Abneigung gegen jdn/etw haben
avert [ə'və:t] vt (prevent) verhindern; (ward off) abwehren; (turn away) abwenden
aviary ['eɪvɪərɪ] n Vogelhaus nt
aviation [eɪvɪ'eɪʃən] n Luftfahrt f
avid ['ævɪd] adj begeistert, eifrig

avidly ['ævɪdlɪ] *adv* begeistert, eifrig

avocado [ævə'kɑːdəʊ] (*Brit*) *n* (*also:* **avocado pear**) Avocado *f*

avoid [ə'vɔɪd] *vt* (*person, obstacle*) ausweichen +*dat*; (*trouble*) vermeiden; (*danger*) meiden

avoidable [ə'vɔɪdəbl] *adj* vermeidbar

avoidance [ə'vɔɪdəns] *n* (*of tax*) Umgehung *f*; (*of issue*) Vermeidung *f*

avowed [ə'vaʊd] *adj* erklärt

AVP (*US*) *n abbr* (= *assistant vice president*) stellvertretender Vizepräsident

avuncular [ə'vʌŋkjʊləʳ] *adj* onkelhaft

AWACS ['eɪwæks] *n abbr* (= *airborne warning and control system*) AWACS

await [ə'weɪt] *vt* warten auf +*acc*; **~ing attention/delivery** zur Bearbeitung/ Lieferung bestimmt; **long ~ed** lang ersehnt

awake [ə'weɪk] (*pt* **awoke**, *pp* **awoken** *or* **~d**) *adj* wach ▷ *vt* wecken ▷ *vi* erwachen, aufwachen; **~ to** sich *dat* bewusst werden +*gen*

awakening [ə'weɪknɪŋ] *n* (*also fig*) Erwachen *nt*

award [ə'wɔːd] *n* Preis *m*; (*for bravery*) Auszeichnung *f*; (*damages*) Entschädigung(ssumme) *f* ▷ *vt* (*prize*) verleihen; (*damages*) zusprechen

aware [ə'wɛəʳ] *adj*: **~ (of)** bewusst (+*gen*); **to become ~ of** sich *dat* bewusst werden +*gen*; **to become ~ that ...** sich *dat* bewusst werden, dass ...; **politically/socially ~** politik-/ sozialbewusst; **I am fully ~ that** es ist mir völlig klar *or* bewusst, dass

awareness [ə'wɛənɪs] *n* Bewusstsein *nt*; **to develop people's ~ of sth** den Menschen etw zu Bewusstsein bringen

awash [ə'wɔʃ] *adj* (*also fig*) überflutet

away [ə'weɪ] *adv* weg, fort; (*position*) entfernt; **two kilometres ~** zwei Kilometer entfernt; **two hours ~ by car** zwei Autostunden entfernt; **the holiday was two weeks ~** es war noch zwei Wochen bis zum Urlaub; **he's ~ for a week** er ist eine Woche nicht da; **he's ~ in Milan** er ist in Mailand; **to take ~ (from)** (*remove*) entfernen (von); (*subtract*) abziehen (von); **to work/pedal** *etc* **~** unablässig arbeiten/strampeln *etc*; **to fade ~** (*colour, light*) verblassen; (*sound*) verhallen; (*enthusiasm*) schwinden

away game *n* Auswärtsspiel *nt*

awe [ɔː] *n* Ehrfurcht *f*

awe-inspiring ['ɔːɪnspaɪərɪŋ] *adj* Ehrfurcht gebietend

awesome ['ɔːsəm] *adj* Ehrfurcht gebietend; (*fig*: *inf*) überwältigend

awe-struck ['ɔːstrʌk] *adj* von Ehrfurcht ergriffen

awful ['ɔːfəl] *adj* furchtbar, schrecklich; **an ~ lot (of)** furchtbar viel(e)

awfully ['ɔːfəlɪ] *adv* furchtbar, schrecklich

awhile [ə'waɪl] *adv* eine Weile

awkward ['ɔːkwəd] *adj* (*clumsy*) unbeholfen; (*inconvenient, difficult*) ungünstig; (*embarrassing*) peinlich

awkwardness ['ɔːkwədnɪs] *n* (*see adj*) Unbeholfenheit *f*; Ungünstigkeit *f*; Peinlichkeit *f*

awl [ɔːl] *n* Ahle *f*, Pfriem *m*

awning ['ɔːnɪŋ] *n* (*of tent, caravan*) Vordach *nt*; (*of shop etc*) Markise *f*

awoke [ə'wəʊk] *pt of* **awake**

awoken [ə'wəʊkən] *pp of* **awake**

AWOL ['eɪwɒl] *abbr* (*Mil*: = *absent without leave*) *see* **absent**

awry [ə'raɪ] *adv*: **to be ~** (*clothes*) schief sitzen; **to go ~** schiefgehen

axe, (*US*) **ax** [æks] *n* Axt *f*, Beil *nt* ▷ *vt* (*employee*) entlassen; (*project, jobs etc*) streichen; **to have an ~ to grind** (*fig*) ein persönliches Interesse haben

axes¹ ['æksɪz] *npl of* **axe**

axes² ['æksiːz] *npl of* **axis**

axiom ['æksɪəm] *n* Axiom *nt*, Grundsatz *m*

axiomatic [æksɪəʊ'mætɪk] *adj* axiomatisch

axis ['æksɪs] (*pl* **axes²**) *n* Achse *f*

axle ['æksl] *n* (*also:* **axletree**) Achse *f*

aye [aɪ] *excl* (*yes*) ja ▷ *n*: **the ~s** die Jastimmen *pl*

AYH *n abbr* (= *American Youth Hostels*) Jugendherbergsverband, ≈ DJHV *m*

AZ (*US*) *abbr* (*Post*) = **Arizona**

azalea [ə'zeɪlɪə] *n* Azalee *f*

Azerbaijan [æzəbaɪ'dʒɑːn] *n* Aserbaidschan *nt*

Azerbaijani [æzəbaɪ'dʒɑːnɪ], **Azeri** [ə'zeərɪ] *adj* aserbaidschanisch ▷ *n* Aserbaidschaner(in) *m(f)*

Azores [ə'zɔːz] *npl*: **the ~** die Azoren *pl*

AZT *n abbr* (= *azidothymidine*) AZT *nt*

Aztec ['æztɛk] *adj* aztekisch ▷ *n* Azteke *m*, Aztekin *f*

azure ['eɪʒəʳ] *adj* azurblau, tiefblau

Bb

B¹, b [biː] n (letter) B nt, b nt; (Scol) ≈ Zwei f, ≈ Gut nt; **B for Benjamin, B for Baker** (US) ≈ B wie Bertha; **B road** (Brit) Landstraße f
B² [biː] n (Mus) H nt, h nt
b. abbr = **born**
BA n abbr (= Bachelor of Arts) see **bachelor**; (= British Academy) Verband zur Förderung der Künste und Geisteswissenschaften
babble ['bæbl] vi schwatzen; (baby) plappern; (brook) plätschern ▷ n: **a ~ of voices** ein Stimmengewirr nt
babe [beɪb] n (liter) Kindlein nt; (esp US: address) Schätzchen nt; **~ in arms** Säugling m
baboon [bə'buːn] n Pavian m
baby ['beɪbɪ] n Baby nt; (US: inf: darling) Schatz m, Schätzchen nt
baby carriage (US) n Kinderwagen m
baby grand n (also: **baby grand piano**) Stutzflügel m
babyhood ['beɪbɪhʊd] n frühe Kindheit f
babyish ['beɪbɪɪʃ] adj kindlich
baby-minder ['beɪbɪ'maɪndə'] (Brit) n Tagesmutter f
baby-sit ['beɪbɪsɪt] vi babysitten
baby-sitter ['beɪbɪsɪtə'] n Babysitter(in) m(f)
baby wipe n Ölpflegetuch nt
bachelor ['bætʃələ'] n Junggeselle m; **B~ of Arts/Science (degree)** ≈ Magister m der philosophischen Fakultät/der Naturwissenschaften
bachelorhood ['bætʃələhʊd] n Junggesellentum nt
bachelor party (US) n Junggesellenparty f

- **BACHELOR'S DEGREE**
- *Bachelor's Degree* ist der akademische Grad,
- den man nach drei- oder vierjährigem,
- erfolgreich abgeschlossenem
- Universitätsstudium erhält. Die
- am häufigsten verliehenen Grade
- sind *BA* (Bachelor of Arts = Magister
- der Geisteswissenschaften), *BSc*
- (Bachelor of Science = Magister
- der Naturwissenschaften), *BEd*
- (Bachelor of Education = Magister
- der Erziehungswissenschaften) und

- LLB (Bachelor of Laws = Magister der
- Rechtswissenschaften). Siehe auch *master's*
- *degree, doctorate.*

back [bæk] n Rücken m; (of house, page) Rückseite f; (of chair) (Rücken)lehne f; (of train) Ende nt; (Football) Verteidiger m ▷ vt (candidate: also: **back up**) unterstützen; (horse) setzen or wetten auf +acc; (car) zurücksetzen, zurückfahren ▷ vi (also: **back up**: person) rückwärtsgehen; (car etc) zurücksetzen, zurückfahren ▷ cpd (payment, rent) ausstehend ▷ adv hinten; **in the ~ (of the car)** hinten (im Auto); **at the ~ of the book/crowd/audience** hinten im Buch/in der Menge/im Publikum; **~ to front** verkehrt herum; **to break the ~ of a job** (Brit) mit einer Arbeit über den Berg sein; **to have one's ~ to the wall** (fig) in die Enge getrieben sein; **~ room** Hinterzimmer nt; **~ garden** Garten m (hinter dem Haus); **~ seat** (Aut) Rücksitz m; **to take a ~ seat** (fig) sich zurückhalten; **~ wheels** Hinterräder pl; **he's ~** er ist zurück or wieder da; **throw the ball ~** wirf den Ball zurück; **he called ~** er rief zurück; **he ran ~** er rannte zurück; **when will you be ~?** wann kommen Sie wieder?; **can I have it ~?** kann ich es zurückhaben or wiederhaben?
  ▶ **back down** vi nachgeben
  ▶ **back on to** vt fus: **the house ~s on to the golf course** das Haus grenzt hinten an den Golfplatz an
  ▶ **back out** vi (of promise) einen Rückzieher machen
  ▶ **back up** vt (support) unterstützen; (Comput) sichern
backache ['bækeɪk] n Rückenschmerzen pl

- **BACK BENCH**
- *Back Bench* bezeichnet im britischen
- Unterhaus die am weitesten vom
- Mittelgang entfernten Bänke, im
- Gegensatz zur *front bench*. Auf diesen
- hinteren Bänken sitzen diejenigen
- Unterhausabgeordneten (auch
- backbenchers genannt), die kein

- Regierungsamt bzw. keine wichtige
- Stellung in der Opposition innehaben.

backbencher ['bæk'bɛntʃə^r] (*Brit*) *n*
Abgeordnete(r) *f(m)* (*in den hinteren Reihen im
britischen Parlament*), Hinterbänkler(in) *m(f)*
(*pej*); *see also* **back bench**
backbiting ['bækbaɪtɪŋ] *n* Lästern *nt*
backbone ['bækbəʊn] *n* (*also fig*) Rückgrat *nt*
backchat ['bæktʃæt] (*Brit: inf*) *n* Widerrede *f*
backcloth ['bækklɔθ] (*Brit*) *n* Hintergrund *m*
backcomb ['bækkəʊm] (*Brit*) *vt* toupieren
backdate [bæk'deɪt] *vt* (zu)rückdatieren;
~d **pay rise** rückwirkend geltende
Gehaltserhöhung *f*
backdrop ['bækdrɔp] *n* = **backcloth**
backer ['bækə^r] *n* (*Comm*) Geldgeber *m*
backfire [bæk'faɪə^r] *vi* (*Aut*) Fehlzündungen
haben; (*plans*) ins Auge gehen
backgammon ['bækgæmən] *n* Backgammon
nt
background ['bækgraʊnd] *n* Hintergrund
m; (*basic knowledge*) Grundkenntnisse
pl; (*experience*) Erfahrung *f* ▷ *cpd* (*music*)
Hintergrund-; **family ~** Herkunft *f*; **~ noise**
Geräuschkulisse *f*; **~ reading** vertiefende
Lektüre *f*
backhand ['bækhænd] *n* (*Tennis: also:*
backhand stroke) Rückhand *f*
backhanded ['bæk'hændɪd] *adj* (*fig: compliment*)
zweifelhaft
backhander ['bæk'hændə^r] (*Brit*) *n*
Schmiergeld *nt*
backing ['bækɪŋ] *n* (*Comm: fig*) Unterstützung *f*;
(*Mus*) Begleitung *f*
backlash ['bæklæʃ] *n* (*fig*) Gegenreaktion *f*
backlog ['bæklɔg] *n*: **to have a ~ of work** mit
der Arbeit im Rückstand sein
back number *n* alte Ausgabe *f or* Nummer *f*
backpack ['bækpæk] *n* Rucksack *m*
backpacker ['bækpækə^r] *n* Rucksacktourist(in)
m(f)
back pay *n* Nachzahlung *f*
back-pedal ['bækpɛdl] *vi* (*fig*) einen Rückzieher
machen
back-seat driver *n* Mitfahrer, der dem Fahrer
dazwischenredet
backside ['bæksaɪd] (*inf*) *n* Hintern *m*
backslash ['bækslæʃ] *n* Backslash *m*
backslide ['bækslaɪd] *vi* rückfällig werden
backspace ['bækspeɪs] *vi* (*in typing*) die
Rücktaste betätigen
backstage [bæk'steɪdʒ] *adv* (*Theat*) hinter
den Kulissen; (: *in dressing-room area*) in der
Garderobe
backstreet ['bækstri:t] *n* Seitenstraße *f* ▷ *cpd*: **~
abortionist** Engelmacher(in) *m(f)*
backstroke ['bækstrəʊk] *n*
Rückenschwimmen *nt*
backtrack ['bæktræk] *vi* (*fig*) einen Rückzieher
machen
backup ['bækʌp] *adj* (*train, plane*) Entlastungs-;
(*Comput: copy etc*) Sicherungs- ▷ *n* (*support*)

Unterstützung *f*; (*Comput: also:* **backup disk,
backup file**) Sicherungskopie *f*, Back-up *nt*
backward ['bækwəd] *adj* (*movement*)
Rückwärts-; (*person*) zurückgeblieben; (*country*)
rückständig; **~ and forward movement** Vor-
und Zurückbewegung *f*; **~ step/glance** Blick
m/Schritt *m* zurück
backwards ['bækwədz] *adv* rückwärts; (*read*)
von hinten nach vorne; (*fall*) nach hinten; (*in
time*) zurück; **to know sth ~, to know sth ~
and forwards** (*US*) etw in- und auswendig
kennen
backwater ['bækwɔ:tə^r] *n* (*fig*) Kaff *nt*
back yard *n* Hinterhof *m*
bacon ['beɪkən] *n* (Frühstücks)speck *m*,
(Schinken)speck *m*
bacteria [bæk'tɪərɪə] *npl* Bakterien *pl*
bacteriology [bæktɪərɪ'ɔlədʒɪ] *n* Bakteriologie
f
bad [bæd] *adj* schlecht; (*naughty*) unartig,
ungezogen; (*mistake, accident, injury*) schwer;
his ~ leg sein schlimmes Bein; **to go ~**
verderben, schlecht werden; **to have a ~ time
of it** es schwer haben; **I feel ~ about it** es tut
mir leid; **in ~ faith** mit böser Absicht
bad debt *n* uneinbringliche Forderung *f*
baddy ['bædɪ] (*inf*) *n* Bösewicht *m*
bade [bæd] *pt of* **bid**
badge [bædʒ] *n* Plakette *f*; (*stick-on*) Aufkleber
m; (*fig*) Merkmal *nt*
badger ['bædʒə^r] *n* Dachs *m* ▷ *vt* zusetzen +*dat*
bad hair day *n* (*inf*) Scheißtag *f*, Tag *m*, an dem
alles schiefgeht
badly ['bædlɪ] *adv* schlecht; **~ wounded** schwer
verletzt; **he needs it ~** er braucht es dringend;
things are going ~ es sieht schlecht *or* nicht
gut aus; **to be ~ off (for money)** wenig Geld
haben
bad-mannered ['bæd'mænəd] *adj* ungezogen,
unhöflich
badminton ['bædmɪntən] *n* Federball *m*
bad-tempered ['bæd'tɛmpəd] *adj* schlecht
gelaunt; (*by nature*) übellaunig
baffle ['bæfl] *vt* verblüffen
baffling ['bæflɪŋ] *adj* rätselhaft, verwirrend
bag [bæg] *n* Tasche *f*; (*made of paper, plastic*)
Tüte *f*; (*handbag*) (Hand)tasche *f*; (*satchel*)
Schultasche *f*; (*case*) Reisetasche *f*; (*of hunter*)
Jagdbeute *f*; (*pej: woman*) Schachtel *f*; **~s of**
(*inf: lots of*) jede Menge; **to pack one's ~s** die
Koffer packen; **~s under the eyes** Ringe *pl*
unter den Augen
bagful ['bægful] *n*: **a ~ of** eine Tasche/Tüte voll
baggage ['bægɪdʒ] *n* Gepäck *nt*
baggage allowance *n* Freigepäck *nt*
baggage car (*US*) *n* Gepäckwagen *m*
baggage claim *n* Gepäckausgabe *f*
baggy ['bægɪ] *adj* weit; (*out of shape*) ausgebeult
Baghdad [bæg'dæd] *n* Bagdad *nt*
bag lady (*esp US*) *n* Stadtstreicherin *f*
bagpipes ['bægpaɪps] *npl* Dudelsack *m*
bag-snatcher ['bægsnætʃə^r] (*Brit*) *n*
Handtaschendieb(in) *m(f)*

Bahamas [bə'hɑːməz] *npl*: **the** ~ die Bahamas *pl*, die Bahamainseln *pl*

Bahrain [bɑː'reɪn] *n* Bahrain *nt*

bail [beɪl] *n* (*Law: payment*) Kaution *f*; (: *release*) Freilassung *f* gegen Kaution ▷ *vt* (*prisoner*) gegen Kaution freilassen; (*boat: also:* **bail out**) ausschöpfen; **to be on** ~ gegen Kaution freigelassen sein; **to be released on** ~ gegen Kaution freigelassen werden; *see also* **bale**
▶ **bail out** *vt* (*prisoner*) gegen Kaution freibekommen; (*firm, friend*) aus der Patsche helfen +*dat*

bailiff ['beɪlɪf] *n* (*Law: Brit*) Gerichtsvollzieher(in) *m(f)*; (: *US*) Gerichtsdiener(in) *m(f)*; (*Brit: factor*) (Guts)verwalter(in) *m(f)*

bait [beɪt] *n* Köder *m* ▷ *vt* (*hook, trap*) mit einem Köder versehen; (*tease*) necken

baize [beɪz] *n* Flausch *m*; **green** ~ Billardtuch *nt*

bake [beɪk] *vt* backen; (*clay etc*) brennen ▷ *vi* backen

baked beans [beɪkt-] *npl* gebackene Bohnen *pl* (in Tomatensoße)

baked potato *n* in der Schale gebackene Kartoffel *f*

baker ['beɪkə'] *n* Bäcker(in) *m(f)*

baker's dozen *n* dreizehn (Stück)

bakery ['beɪkərɪ] *n* Bäckerei *f*

baking ['beɪkɪŋ] *n* Backen *nt*; (*batch*) Ofenladung *f* ▷ *adj* (*inf: hot*) wie im Backofen

baking powder *n* Backpulver *nt*

baking tin *n* Backform *f*

baking tray *n* Backblech *nt*

balaclava [bælə'klɑːvə] *n* (*also:* **balaclava helmet**) Kapuzenmütze *f*

balance ['bæləns] *n* (*equilibrium*) Gleichgewicht *nt*; (*Comm: sum*) Saldo *m*; (*remainder*) Restbetrag *m*; (*scales*) Waage *f* ▷ *vt* ausgleichen; (*Aut: wheels*) auswuchten; (*pros and cons*) (gegeneinander) abwägen; **on** ~ alles in allem; ~ **of trade/payments** Handels-/Zahlungsbilanz *f*; ~ **carried forward** or **brought forward** (*Comm*) Saldovortrag *m*, Saldoübertrag *m*; **to** ~ **the books** (*Comm*) die Bilanz ziehen or machen

balanced ['bælənst] *adj* ausgeglichen; (*report*) ausgewogen

balance sheet *n* Bilanz *f*

balance wheel *n* Unruh *f*

balcony ['bælkənɪ] *n* Balkon *m*; (*in theatre*) oberster Rang *m*

bald [bɔːld] *adj* kahl; (*tyre*) abgefahren; (*statement*) knapp

baldness ['bɔːldnɪs] *n* Kahlheit *f*

bale [beɪl] *n* (*Agr*) Bündel *nt*; (*of papers etc*) Packen *m*
▶ **bale out** *vi* (*of a plane*) abspringen ▷ *vt* (*water*) schöpfen; (*boat*) ausschöpfen

Balearic Islands [bælɪ'ærɪk-] *npl*: **the** ~ die Balearen *pl*

baleful ['beɪlful] *adj* böse

balk [bɔːk] *vi*: **to** ~ (**at**) (*subj: person*) zurückschrecken (vor +*dat*); (: *horse*) scheuen

(vor +*dat*)

Balkan ['bɔːlkən] *adj* (*countries etc*) Balkan-
▷ *n*: **the** ~**s** der Balkan, die Balkanländer *pl*

ball [bɔːl] *n* Ball *m*; (*of wool, string*) Knäuel *m* or *nt*; **to set the** ~ **rolling** (*fig*) den Stein ins Rollen bringen; **to play** ~ (**with sb**) (*fig*) (mit jdm) mitspielen; **to be on the** ~ (: *competent*) am Ball sein; (: *alert*) auf Draht or Zack sein; **the** ~ **is in their court** (*fig*) sie sind am Ball

ballad ['bæləd] *n* Ballade *f*

ballast ['bæləst] *n* Ballast *m*

ball bearing *npl* Kugellager *nt*; (*individual ball*) Kugellagerkugel *f*

ball cock *n* Schwimmerhahn *m*

ballerina [bælə'riːnə] *n* Ballerina *f*

ballet ['bæleɪ] *n* Ballett *nt*

ballet dancer *n* Balletttänzer(in) *m(f)*

ballistic [bə'lɪstɪk] *adj* ballistisch

ballistic missile *n* Raketengeschoss *nt*

ballistics [bə'lɪstɪks] *n* Ballistik *f*

balloon [bə'luːn] *n* (Luft)ballon *m*; (*hot air balloon*) Heißluftballon *m*; (*in comic strip*) Sprechblase *f*

balloonist [bə'luːnɪst] *n* Ballonfahrer(in) *m(f)*

ballot ['bælət] *n* (geheime) Abstimmung *f*

ballot box *n* Wahlurne *f*

ballot paper *n* Stimmzettel *m*

ballpark ['bɔːlpɑːk] (*US*) *n* (*Sport*) Baseballstadion *nt*

ballpark figure (*inf*) *n* Richtzahl *f*

ballpoint ['bɔːlpɔɪnt], **ballpoint pen** *n* Kugelschreiber *m*

ballroom ['bɔːlrʊm] *n* Tanzsaal *m*

balls [bɔːlz] (*inf!*) *npl* (*testicles*) Eier *pl* (!); (*courage*) Schneid *m*, Mumm *m* ▷ *excl* red keinen Scheiß! (!)

balm [bɑːm] *n* Balsam *m*

balmy ['bɑːmɪ] *adj* (*breeze*) sanft; (*air*) lau, lind; (*Brit: inf*) = **barmy**

BALPA ['bælpə] *n abbr* (= *British Airline Pilots' Association*) Flugpilotengewerkschaft

balsa ['bɔːlsə], **balsa wood** *n* Balsaholz *nt*

balsam ['bɔːlsəm] *n* Balsam *m*

Baltic ['bɔːltɪk] *n*: **the** ~ (**Sea**) die Ostsee

balustrade [bæləs'treɪd] *n* Balustrade *f*

bamboo [bæm'buː] *n* Bambus *m*

bamboozle [bæm'buːzl] (*inf*) *vt* hereinlegen; **to** ~ **sb into doing sth** jdn durch Tricks dazu bringen, etw zu tun

ban [bæn] *n* Verbot *nt* ▷ *vt* verbieten; **he was** ~**ned from driving** (*Brit*) ihm wurde Fahrverbot erteilt

banal [bə'nɑːl] *adj* banal

banana [bə'nɑːnə] *n* Banane *f*

band [bænd] *n* (*group*) Gruppe *f*, Schar *f*; (*Mus: jazz, rock etc*) Band *f*; (: *military etc*) (Musik)kapelle *f*; (*strip, range*) Band *nt*; (*stripe*) Streifen *m*
▶ **band together** *vi* sich zusammenschließen

bandage ['bændɪdʒ] *n* Verband *m* ▷ *vt* verbinden

Band-Aid® ['bændeɪd] (*US*) *n* Heftpflaster *nt*

B & B *n abbr* = **bed and breakfast**

bandit ['bændɪt] n Bandit m
bandstand ['bændstænd] n Musikpavillion m
bandwagon ['bændwægən] n: **to jump on the
~** (fig) auf den fahrenden Zug aufspringen
bandy ['bændɪ] vt (jokes) sich erzählen; (ideas)
diskutieren; (insults) sich an den Kopf werfen
▶ **bandy about** vt (word, expression) immer
wieder gebrauchen; (name) immer wieder
nennen
bandy-legged ['bændɪ'lɛgɪd] adj o-beinig
bane [beɪn] n: **it/he is the ~ of my life** das/er
ist noch mal mein Ende
bang [bæŋ] n (of door) Knallen nt; (of gun, exhaust)
Knall m; (blow) Schlag m ▷ excl peng ▷ vt (door)
zuschlagen, zuknallen; (one's head etc) sich dat
stoßen +acc ▷ vi knallen ▷ adv: **to be ~ on time**
(Brit: inf) auf die Sekunde pünktlich sein; **to
~ at the door** gegen die Tür hämmern; **to ~
into sth** sich an etw dat stoßen
banger ['bæŋə'] (Brit: inf) n (car: also: **old
banger**) Klapperkiste f; (sausage) Würstchen
nt; (firework) Knallkörper m
Bangkok [bæŋ'kɔk] n Bangkok nt
Bangladesh [bæŋglə'dɛʃ] n Bangladesch nt
bangle ['bæŋgl] n Armreif(en) m
bangs [bæŋz] (US) npl (fringe) Pony m
banish ['bænɪʃ] vt verbannen
banister ['bænɪstə'] n, **banisters** ['bænɪstəz]
▷ npl Geländer nt
banjo ['bændʒəu] (pl **banjoes** or **~s**) n Banjo nt
bank [bæŋk] n Bank f; (of river, lake) Ufer nt; (of
earth) Wall m; (of switches) Reihe f ▷ vi (Aviat)
sich in die Kurve legen; (Comm): **they ~ with
Pitt's** sie haben ihr Konto bei Pitt's
▶ **bank on** vt fus sich verlassen auf +acc
bank account n Bankkonto nt
bank balance n Kontostand m
bank card n Scheckkarte f
bank charges (Brit) npl
Kontoführungsgebühren pl
bank draft n Bankanweisung f
banker ['bæŋkə'] n Bankier m
banker's card (Brit) n = **bank card**
banker's order (Brit) n Dauerauftrag m
bank giro n Banküberweisung f
bank holiday (Brit) n (öffentlicher) Feiertag m;
siehe Info-Artikel

○ **BANK HOLIDAY**
○
○ Als bank holiday wird in Großbritannien
○ ein gesetzlicher Feiertag bezeichnet, an
○ dem die Banken geschlossen sind. Die
○ meisten dieser Feiertage, abgesehen von
○ Weihnachten und Ostern, fallen auf
○ Montage im Mai und August. An diesen
○ langen Wochenenden (bank holiday
○ weekends) fahren viele Briten in Urlaub,
○ sodass dann auf den Straßen, Flughäfen
○ und bei der Bahn sehr viel Betrieb ist.

banking ['bæŋkɪŋ] n Bankwesen nt
banking hours npl Schalterstunden pl

bank loan n Bankkredit m
bank manager n Filialleiter(in) m(f) (einer
Bank)
banknote ['bæŋknəut] n Geldschein m,
Banknote f
bank rate n Diskontsatz m
bankrupt ['bæŋkrʌpt] adj bankrott ▷ n
Bankrotteur(in) m(f); **to go ~** Bankrott
machen
bankruptcy ['bæŋkrʌptsɪ] n (Comm: fig)
Bankrott m
bank statement n Kontoauszug m
banner ['bænə'] n Banner nt; (in demonstration)
Spruchband nt
banner headline n Schlagzeile f
bannister ['bænɪstə'] n, **bannisters**
['bænɪstəz] ▷ n(pl) = **banister; banisters**
banns [bænz] npl Aufgebot nt
banquet ['bæŋkwɪt] n Bankett nt
bantamweight ['bæntəmweɪt] n
Bantamgewicht nt
banter ['bæntə'] n Geplänkel nt
BAOR n abbr (= British Army of the Rhine) britische
Rheinarmee
baptism ['bæptɪzəm] n Taufe f
Baptist ['bæptɪst] n Baptist(in) m(f)
baptize [bæp'taɪz] vt taufen
bar [bɑ:'] n (for drinking) Lokal nt; (counter)
Theke f; (rod) Stange f; (on window etc) (Gitter)
stab m; (slab: of chocolate) Tafel f; (fig: obstacle)
Hindernis nt; (prohibition) Verbot nt; (Mus)
Takt m ▷ vt (road) blockieren, versperren;
(window) verriegeln; (person) ausschließen;
(activity) verbieten; **~ of soap** Stück nt Seife;
behind ~s hinter Gittern; **the B~** (Law) die
Anwaltschaft; **~ none** ohne Ausnahme
Barbados [bɑ:'beɪdɔs] n Barbados nt
barbaric [bɑ:'bærɪk] adj barbarisch
barbarous ['bɑ:bərəs] adj barbarisch
barbecue ['bɑ:bɪkju:] n Grill m; (meal, party)
Barbecue nt
barbed wire ['bɑ:bd-] n Stacheldraht m
barber ['bɑ:bə'] n (Herren)friseur m
barbiturate [bɑ:'bɪtjurɪt] n Schlafmittel nt,
Barbiturat nt
Barcelona [bɑ:sə'ləunə] n Barcelona nt
bar chart n Balkendiagramm nt
bar code n Strichcode m
bare [bɛə'] adj nackt; (trees, countryside) kahl;
(minimum) absolut ▷ vt entblößen; (teeth)
blecken; **the ~ essentials, the ~ necessities**
das Allernotwendigste; **to ~ one's soul** sein
Innerstes entblößen
bareback ['bɛəbæk] adv ohne Sattel
barefaced ['bɛəfeɪst] adj (fig) unverfroren,
schamlos
barefoot ['bɛəfut] adj barfüßig ▷ adv barfuß
bareheaded [bɛə'hɛdɪd] adj barhäuptig ▷ adv
ohne Kopfbedeckung
barely ['bɛəlɪ] adv kaum
Barents Sea ['bærənts-] n: **the ~** die Barentssee
bargain ['bɑ:gɪn] n (deal) Geschäft
nt; (transaction) Handel m; (good offer)

Sonderangebot nt; (good buy) guter Kauf m
▷ vi: **to ~ (with sb)** (mit jdm) verhandeln;
(haggle) (mit jdm) handeln; **into the ~**
obendrein
▶ **bargain for** vt fus: **he got more than he ~ed
for** er bekam mehr, als er erwartet hatte
bargaining ['bɑːgənɪŋ] n Verhandeln nt
bargaining position n Verhandlungsposition
f

barge [bɑːdʒ] n Lastkahn m, Frachtkahn m
▶ **barge in** vi (enter) hereinplatzen; (interrupt)
unterbrechen
▶ **barge into** vt fus (place) hereinplatzen;
(person) anrempeln
bargepole ['bɑːdʒpəul] n: **I wouldn't touch it
with a ~** (fig) das würde ich nicht mal mit der
Kneifzange anfassen
baritone ['bærɪtəun] n Bariton m
barium meal ['bɛərɪəm-] n Kontrastbrei m
bark [bɑːk] n (of tree) Rinde f; (of dog) Bellen nt
▷ vi bellen; **she's ~ing up the wrong tree** (fig)
sie ist auf dem Holzweg
barley ['bɑːlɪ] n Gerste f
barley sugar n Malzbonbon nt or m
barmaid ['bɑːmeɪd] n Bardame f
barman ['bɑːmən] (irreg: like man) n Barmann m
barmy ['bɑːmɪ] (Brit: inf) adj bekloppt
barn [bɑːn] n Scheune f
barnacle ['bɑːnəkl] n Rankenfußkrebs m
barn owl n Schleiereule f
barometer [bə'rɒmɪtə'] n Barometer nt
baron ['bærən] n Baron m; **industrial ~**
Industriemagnat m; **press ~** Pressezar m
baroness ['bærənɪs] n (baron's wife) Baronin f;
(baron's daughter) Baroness f, Baronesse f
baronet ['bærənɪt] n Baronet m
barracking ['bærəkɪŋ] n Buhrufe pl
barracks ['bærəks] npl Kaserne f
barrage ['bærɑːʒ] n (Mil) Sperrfeuer nt; (dam)
Staustufe f; (fig: of criticism, questions etc) Hagel m
barrel ['bærəl] n Fass nt; (of oil) Barrel nt; (of gun)
Lauf m
barrel organ n Drehorgel f
barren ['bærən] adj unfruchtbar
barricade [bærɪ'keɪd] n Barrikade f ▷ vt (road,
entrance) verbarrikadieren; **to ~ o.s. (in)** sich
verbarrikadieren
barrier ['bærɪə'] n (at frontier, entrance) Schranke
f; (Brit: also: **crash barrier**) Leitplanke f; (fig)
Barriere f; (: to progress etc) Hindernis nt
barrier cream (Brit) n Hautschutzcreme f
barring ['bɑːrɪŋ] prep außer im Falle +gen
barrister ['bærɪstə'] n (Brit) n Rechtsanwalt m,
Rechtsanwältin f; siehe Info-Artikel

⊙ **BARRISTER**

⊙ Barrister oder barrister-at-law ist in England
⊙ die Bezeichnung für einen Rechtsanwalt,
⊙ der seine Klienten vor allem vor Gericht
⊙ vertritt; im Gegensatz zum solicitor, der
⊙ nicht vor Gericht auftritt, sondern einen
⊙ barrister mit dieser Aufgabe beauftragt.

barrow ['bærəu] n Schubkarre f, Schubkarren
m; (cart) Karren m
bar stool n Barhocker m
Bart. (Brit) abbr = **baronet**
bartender ['bɑːtɛndə'] (US) n Barmann m
barter ['bɑːtə'] n Tauschhandel m ▷ vt: **to ~ sth
for sth** etw gegen etw tauschen
barter exchange n Tauschbörse f
base [beɪs] n (of tree etc) Fuß m; (of cup, box etc)
Boden m; (foundation) Grundlage f; (centre)
Stützpunkt m, Standort m; (for organization) Sitz
m ▷ adj gemein, niederträchtig ▷ vt: **to ~ sth
on** etw gründen or basieren auf +acc; **to be ~d
at** (troops) stationiert sein in +dat; (employee)
arbeiten in +dat; **I'm ~d in London** ich wohne
in London; **a Paris-~d firm** eine Firma mit
Sitz in Paris; **coffee-~d** auf Kaffeebasis
baseball ['beɪsbɔːl] n Baseball m
baseboard ['beɪsbɔːd] (US) n Fußleiste f
base camp n Basislager nt, Versorgungslager
nt
Basel [bɑːl] n = **Basle**
baseline ['beɪslaɪn] n (Tennis) Grundlinie f;
(fig: standard) Ausgangspunkt m
basement ['beɪsmənt] n Keller m
base rate n Eckzins m, Leitzins m
bases¹ ['beɪsɪz] npl of **base**
bases² ['beɪsiːz] npl of **basis**
bash [bæʃ] (inf) vt schlagen, hauen ▷ n: **I'll
have a ~ (at it)** (Brit) ich probier's mal
▶ **bash up** vt (car) demolieren; (Brit: person)
vermöbeln
bashful ['bæʃful] adj schüchtern
bashing ['bæʃɪŋ] (inf) n Prügel pl; **Paki-/
queer-~** Überfälle pl auf Pakistaner/Schwule
BASIC ['beɪsɪk] n (Comput) BASIC nt
basic ['beɪsɪk] adj (method, needs etc)
Grund-; (principles) grundlegend; (problem)
grundsätzlich; (knowledge) elementar;
(facilities) primitiv
basically ['beɪsɪklɪ] adv im Grunde
basic rate n Eingangssteuersatz m
basics ['beɪsɪks] npl: **the ~** das Wesentliche
basil ['bæzl] n Basilikum nt
basin ['beɪsn] n Gefäß nt; (Brit: for food) Schüssel
f; (also: **wash basin**) (Wasch)becken nt; (of river,
lake) Becken nt
basis ['beɪsɪs] (pl **bases**) n Basis f, Grundlage f;
on a part-time ~ stundenweise; **on a trial
~** zur Probe; **on the ~ of what you've said**
aufgrund dessen, was Sie gesagt haben
bask [bɑːsk] vi: **to ~ in the sun** sich sonnen
basket ['bɑːskɪt] n Korb m; (smaller) Körbchen nt
basketball ['bɑːskɪtbɔːl] n Basketball m
basketball player n Basketballspieler(in) m(f)
Basle [bɑːl] n Basel nt
basmati rice [bəz'mætɪ-] n Basmatireis m
Basque [bæsk] adj baskisch ▷ n Baske m,
Baskin f
bass [beɪs] n Bass m
bass clef n Bassschlüssel m
bassoon [bə'suːn] n Fagott nt

441

bastard ['bɑːstəd] *n* uneheliches Kind *nt*; (*inf!*) Arschloch *nt* (*!*)

baste [beɪst] *vt* (*Culin*) (mit Fett und Bratensaft) begießen; (*Sewing*) heften, reihen

bastion ['bæstɪən] *n* Bastion *f*

bat [bæt] *n* (*Zool*) Fledermaus *f*; (*for cricket, baseball etc*) Schlagholz *nt*; (*Brit: for table tennis*) Schläger *m* ▷ *vt*: **he didn't ~ an eyelid** er hat nicht mit der Wimper gezuckt; **off one's own ~** auf eigene Faust

batch [bætʃ] *n* (*of bread*) Schub *m*; (*of letters, papers*) Stoß *m*, Stapel *m*; (*of applicants*) Gruppe *f*; (*of work*) Schwung *m*; (*of goods*) Ladung *f*, Sendung *f*

batch processing *n* (*Comput*) Stapelverarbeitung *f*

bated ['beɪtɪd] *adj*: **with ~ breath** mit angehaltenem Atem

bath [bɑːθ] *n* Bad *nt*; (*bathtub*) (Bade)wanne *f* ▷ *vt* baden; **to have a ~** baden, ein Bad nehmen; *see also* **baths**

bathe [beɪð] *vi, vt* (*also fig*) baden

bather ['beɪðə^r] *n* Badende(r) *f(m)*

bathing ['beɪðɪŋ] *n* Baden *nt*

bathing cap *n* Bademütze *f*, Badekappe *f*

bathing costume, (*US*) **bathing suit** *n* Badeanzug *m*

bath mat *n* Bademattte *f*, Badevorleger *m*

bathrobe ['bɑːrəub] *n* Bademantel *m*

bathroom ['bɑːθrum] *n* Bad(ezimmer) *nt*

baths [bɑːðz] *npl* (*also*: **swimming baths**) (Schwimm)bad *nt*

bath towel *n* Badetuch *nt*

bathtub ['bɑːθtʌb] *n* (Bade)wanne *f*

batman ['bætmən] (*irreg: like* **man**) (*Brit*) *n* (*Mil*) (Offiziers)bursche *m*

baton ['bætən] *n* (*Mus*) Taktstock *m*; (*Athletics*) Staffelholz *nt*; (*policeman's*) Schlagstock *m*

battalion [bə'tælɪən] *n* Bataillon *nt*

batten ['bætn] *n* Leiste *f*, Latte *f*; (*Naut: on sail*) Segellatte *f*
   ▶ **batten down** *vt* (*Naut*): **to ~ down the hatches** die Luken dicht machen

batter ['bætə^r] *vt* schlagen, misshandeln; (*subj: rain*) schlagen; (*wind*) rütteln ▷ *n* (*Culin*) Teig *m*; (*for frying*) (Ausback)teig *m*

battered ['bætəd] *adj* (*hat, pan*) verbeult; **~ wife** misshandelte Ehefrau; **~ child** misshandeltes Kind

battering ram ['bætərɪŋ-] *n* Rammbock *m*

battery ['bætərɪ] *n* Batterie *f*; (*of tests, reporters*) Reihe *f*

battery charger *n* (Batterie)ladegerät *nt*

battery farming *n* Batteriehaltung *f*

battle ['bætl] *n* (*Mil*) Schlacht *f*; (*fig*) Kampf *m* ▷ *vi* kämpfen; **that's half the ~** damit ist schon viel gewonnen; **it's a losing ~, we're fighting a losing ~** (*fig*) es ist ein aussichtsloser Kampf

battledress ['bætldres] *n* Kampfanzug *m*

battlefield ['bætlfiːld] *n* Schlachtfeld *nt*

battlements ['bætlmənts] *npl* Zinnen *pl*

battleship ['bætlʃɪp] *n* Schlachtschiff *nt*

batty ['bætɪ] (*inf*) *adj* verrückt

bauble ['bɔːbl] *n* Flitter *m*

baud [bɔːd] *n* (*Comput*) Baud *nt*

baud rate *n* (*Comput*) Baudrate *f*

baulk [bɔːlk] *vi* = **balk**

bauxite ['bɔːksaɪt] *n* Bauxit *m*

Bavaria [bə'veərɪə] *n* Bayern *nt*

Bavarian [bə'veərɪən] *adj* bay(e)risch ▷ *n* Bayer(in) *m(f)*

bawdy ['bɔːdɪ] *adj* derb, obszön

bawl [bɔːl] *vi* brüllen, schreien

bay [beɪ] *n* Bucht *f*; (*Brit: for parking*) Parkbucht *f*; (: *for loading*) Ladeplatz *m*; (*horse*) Braune(r) *m*; **to hold sb at ~** jdn in Schach halten

bay leaf *n* Lorbeerblatt *nt*

bayonet ['beɪənɪt] *n* Bajonett *nt*

bay tree *n* Lorbeerbaum *m*

bay window *n* Erkerfenster *nt*

bazaar [bə'zɑː^r] *n* Basar *m*

bazooka [bə'zuːkə] *n* Panzerfaust *f*

BB (*Brit*) *n abbr* (= *Boys' Brigade*) Jugendorganisation *für Jungen*

BBB (*US*) *n abbr* (= *Better Business Bureau*) *amerikanische Verbraucherbehörde*

BBC *n abbr* BBC *f*; *siehe Info-Artikel*

▨ **BBC**

▨
▨
▨ BBC (Abkürzung für British Broadcasting
▨ Corporation) ist die staatliche britische
▨ Rundfunk- und Fernsehanstalt.
▨ Die Fernsehsender BBC1 und BBC2
▨ bieten beide ein umfangsreiches
▨ Fernsehprogramm, wobei BBC1 mehr
▨ Sendungen von allgemeinem Interesse
▨ wie z.B. leichte Unterhaltung, Sport,
▨ Aktuelles, Kinderprogramme und
▨ Außenübertragungen zeigt. BBC2
▨ berücksichtigt Reisesendungen, Drama,
▨ Musik und internationale Filme. Die 5
▨ landesweiten Radiosender bieten von
▨ Popmusik bis Kricket etwas für jeden
▨ Geschmack; dazu gibt es noch 37 regionale
▨ Radiosender. Der BBC World Service ist auf
▨ der ganzen Welt auf Englisch oder in einer
▨ von 35 anderen Sprachen zu empfangen.
▨ Finanziert wird die BBC vor allem durch
▨ Fernsehgebühren und ins Ausland
▨ verkaufte Sendungen. Obwohl die BBC
▨ dem Parlament gegenüber verantwortlich
▨ ist, werden die Sendungen nicht vom Staat
▨ kontrolliert.

BC *adv abbr* (= *before Christ*) v. Chr. ▷ *abbr* (*Canada*: = *British Columbia*) Britisch-Kolumbien *nt*

BCG *n abbr* (= *bacille Calmette-Guérin*) BCG *m*

BD *n abbr* (= *Bachelor of Divinity*) *akademischer Grad in Theologie*

B/D *abbr* = **bank draft**

BDS *n abbr* (= *Bachelor of Dental Surgery*) *akademischer Grad in Zahnmedizin*

B/E *abbr* = **bill of exchange**

○ KEYWORD

be [bi:] (pt **was, were**, pp **been**) aux vb **1** (with present participle: forming continuous tenses): **what are you doing?** was machst du?; **it is raining** es regnet; **have you been to Rome?** waren Sie schon einmal in Rom?

2 (with pp: forming passives) werden; **to be killed** getötet werden; **the box had been opened** die Kiste war geöffnet worden

3 (in tag questions): **he's good-looking, isn't he?** er sieht gut aus, nicht (wahr)?; **she's back again, is she?** sie ist wieder da, oder?

4 (+ to + infinitive): **the house is to be sold** das Haus soll verkauft werden; **he's not to open it** er darf es nicht öffnen

▷ vb + complement **1** sein; **I'm tired/English** ich bin müde/Engländer(in); **I'm hot/cold** mir ist heiß/kalt; **2 and 2 are 4** 2 und 2 ist or macht 4; **she's tall/pretty** sie ist groß/hübsch; **be careful/quiet** sei vorsichtig/ruhig

2 (of health): **how are you?** wie geht es Ihnen?

3 (of age): **how old are you?** wie alt bist du?; **I'm sixteen (years old)** ich bin sechzehn (Jahre alt)

4 (cost) kosten; **how much was the meal?** was hat das Essen gekostet?; **that'll be 5 pounds please** das macht 5 Pfund, bitte

▷ vi **1** (exist, occur etc) sein; **there is/are** es gibt; **is there a God?** gibt es einen Gott?; **be that as it may** wie dem auch sei; **so be it** gut (und schön)

2 (referring to place) sein, liegen; **Edinburgh is in Scotland** Edinburgh liegt or ist in Schottland; **I won't be here tomorrow** morgen bin ich nicht da

3 (referring to movement) sein; **where have you been?** wo warst du?

▷ impers vb **1** (referring to time, distance, weather) sein; **it's 5 o'clock** es ist 5 Uhr; **it's 10 km to the village** es sind 10 km bis zum Dorf; **it's too hot/cold** es ist zu heiß/kalt

2 (emphatic): **it's only me** ich bins nur; **it's only the postman** es ist nur der Briefträger

beach [bi:tʃ] n Strand m ▷ vt (boat) auf (den) Strand setzen

beach buggy n Strandbuggy m

beachcomber ['bi:tʃkəumər] n Strandgutsammler m

beachwear ['bi:tʃwɛər] n Strandkleidung f

beacon ['bi:kən] n Leuchtfeuer nt; (marker) Bake f; (also: **radio beacon**) Funkfeuer nt

bead [bi:d] n Perle f; **beads** npl (necklace) Perlenkette f

beady ['bi:dɪ] adj: ~ **eyes** Knopfaugen pl

beagle ['bi:gl] n Beagle m

beak [bi:k] n Schnabel m

beaker ['bi:kər] n Becher m

beam [bi:m] n (Archit) Balken m; (of light) Strahl m; (Radio) Leitstrahl m ▷ vi (smile) strahlen ▷ vt ausstrahlen, senden; **to ~ at sb** jdn

anstrahlen; **to drive on full** or **main** or **high ~ mit Fernlicht fahren**

beaming ['bi:mɪŋ] adj strahlend

bean [bi:n] n Bohne f; **runner ~** Stangenbohne f; **broad ~** dicke Bohne; **coffee ~** Kaffeebohne f

beanpole ['bi:npəul] n (lit, fig) Bohnenstange f

beanshoots ['bi:nʃu:ts] npl Sojabohnensprossen pl

beansprouts ['bi:nsprauts] npl = **beanshoots**

bear [bɛər] (pt **bore**, pp **borne**) n Bär m; (Stock Exchange) Baissier m ▷ vt tragen; (tolerate, endure) ertragen; (examination) standhalten +dat; (traces, signs) aufweisen, zeigen; (Comm: interest) tragen, bringen; (produce: children) gebären; (: fruit) tragen ▷ vi: **to ~ right/left** (Aut) sich rechts/links halten; **to ~ the responsibility** die Verantwortung tragen für; **to ~ comparison with** einem Vergleich standhalten mit; **I can't ~ him** ich kann ihn nicht ausstehen; **to bring pressure to ~ on sb** Druck auf jdn ausüben

▶ **bear out** vt (person, suspicions etc) bestätigen

▶ **bear up** vi Haltung bewahren; **he bore up well** er hat sich gut gehalten

▶ **bear with** vt fus Nachsicht haben mit; **~ with me a minute** bitte gedulden Sie sich einen Moment

bearable ['bɛərəbl] adj erträglich

beard [bɪəd] n Bart m

bearded ['bɪədɪd] adj bärtig

bearer ['bɛərər] n (of letter, news) Überbringer(in) m(f); (of cheque, passport, title etc) Inhaber(in) m(f)

bearing ['bɛərɪŋ] n (posture) Haltung f; (air) Auftreten nt; (connection) Bezug m; (Tech) Lager nt; **bearings** npl (also: **ball bearings**) Kugellager nt; **to take a ~ with a compass** den Kompasskurs feststellen; **to get one's ~s** sich zurechtfinden

beast [bi:st] n (animal) Tier nt; (inf: person) Biest nt

beastly ['bi:stlɪ] adj scheußlich

beat [bi:t] (pt ~, pp ~**en**) n (of heart) Schlag m; (Mus) Takt m; (of policeman) Revier nt ▷ vt schlagen; (record) brechen ▷ vi (heart) schlagen; **to ~ time** den Takt schlagen; **to ~ it** (inf) abhauen, verschwinden; **that ~s everything** das ist doch wirklich der Gipfel or die Höhe; **to ~ about the bush** um den heißen Brei herumreden; **off the ~en track** abgelegen

▶ **beat down** vt (door) einschlagen; (price) herunterhandeln; (seller) einen niedrigeren Preis aushandeln mit ▷ vi (rain) herunterprasseln; (sun) herunterbrennen

▶ **beat off** vt (attack, attacker) abwehren

▶ **beat up** vt (person) zusammenschlagen; (mixture, eggs) schlagen

beater ['bi:tər] n (for eggs, cream) Schneebesen m

beating ['bi:tɪŋ] n Schläge pl, Prügel pl; **to take a ~** (fig) eine Schlappe einstecken

beat-up ['bi:t'ʌp] (inf) adj zerbeult, ramponiert

beautician [bju:'tɪʃən] n Kosmetiker(in) m(f)

beautiful ['bju:tɪful] adj schön

beautifully ['bjuːtɪflɪ] adv (play, sing, drive etc) hervorragend; (quiet, empty etc) schön
beautify ['bjuːtɪfaɪ] vt verschönern
beauty ['bjuːtɪ] n Schönheit f; (fig: attraction) Schöne nt; **the ~ of it is that ...** das Schöne daran ist, dass ...
beauty contest n Schönheitswettbewerb m
beauty queen n Schönheitskönigin f
beauty salon n Kosmetiksalon m
beauty sleep n (Schönheits)schlaf m
beauty spot (Brit) n besonders schöner Ort m
beaver ['biːvəʳ] n Biber m
becalmed [bɪ'kɑːmd] adj: **to be ~** (sailing ship) in eine Flaute geraten
became [bɪ'keɪm] pt of **become**
because [bɪ'kɒz] conj weil; **~ of** wegen +gen or (inf) +dat
beck [bɛk] n: **to be at sb's ~ and call** nach jds Pfeife tanzen
beckon ['bɛkən] vt (also: **beckon to**) winken ▷ vi locken
become [bɪ'kʌm] (irreg: like **come**) vi werden; **it became known that** es wurde bekannt, dass; **what has ~ of him?** was ist aus ihm geworden?
becoming [bɪ'kʌmɪŋ] adj (behaviour) schicklich; (clothes) kleidsam
BECTU ['bɛktu] (Brit) n abbr (= Broadcasting, Entertainment, Cinematographic and Theatre Union) Gewerkschaft für Beschäftigte in der Unterhaltungsindustrie
BEd n abbr (= Bachelor of Education) akademischer Grad im Erziehungswesen
bed [bɛd] n Bett nt; (of coal) Flöz nt; (of clay) Schicht f; (of river) (Fluss)bett nt; (of sea) (Meeres)boden m, (Meeres)grund m; (of flowers) Beet nt; **to go to ~** ins or zu Bett gehen
▶ **bed down** vi sein Lager aufschlagen
bed and breakfast n (place) (Frühstücks)pension f; (terms) Übernachtung f mit Frühstück; siehe Info-Artikel

⬤ **BED AND BREAKFAST**
⬤
⬤ Bed and breakfast bedeutet „Übernachtung
⬤ mit Frühstück", wobei sich dies in
⬤ Großbritannien nicht auf Hotels, sondern
⬤ auf kleinere Pensionen, Privathäuser
⬤ und Bauernhöfe bezieht, wo man
⬤ wesentlich preisgünstiger übernachten
⬤ kann als in Hotels. Oft wird für Bed and
⬤ Breakfast, auch B & B genannt, durch ein
⬤ entsprechendes Schild im Garten oder an
⬤ der Einfahrt geworben.

bedbug ['bɛdbʌg] n Wanze f
bedclothes ['bɛdkləʊðz] npl Bettzeug nt
bedding ['bɛdɪŋ] n Bettzeug nt
bedevil [bɪ'dɛvl] vt (person) heimsuchen; (plans) komplizieren; **to be ~led by misfortune/bad luck** vom Schicksal/Pech verfolgt sein
bedfellow ['bɛdfɛləʊ] n: **they are strange ~s** (fig) sie sind ein merkwürdiges Gespann

bedlam ['bɛdləm] n Chaos nt
bedpan ['bɛdpæn] n Bettpfanne f, Bettschüssel f
bedpost ['bɛdpəʊst] n Bettpfosten m
bedraggled [bɪ'drægld] adj (wet) triefnass, tropfnass; (dirty) verdreckt
bedridden ['bɛdrɪdn] adj bettlägerig
bedrock ['bɛdrɔk] n (fig) Fundament nt; (Geog) Grundgebirge nt, Grundgestein nt
bedroom ['bɛdrum] n Schlafzimmer nt
Beds [bɛdz] (Brit) abbr (Post) = Bedfordshire
bed settee n Sofabett nt
bedside ['bɛdsaɪd] n: **at sb's ~** an jds Bett; **~ lamp** Nachttischlampe f; **~ book** Bettlektüre f
bedsit ['bɛdsɪt], **bedsitter** ['bɛdsɪtəʳ] (Brit) n möbliertes Zimmer nt
bedspread ['bɛdsprɛd] n Tagesdecke f
bedtime ['bɛdtaɪm] n Schlafenszeit f; **it's ~** ist Zeit, ins Bett zu gehen
bee [biː] n Biene f; **to have a ~ in one's bonnet about cleanliness** einen Sauberkeitsfimmel or Sauberkeitstick haben
beech [biːtʃ] n Buche f
beef [biːf] n Rind(fleisch) nt; **roast ~** Rinderbraten m
▶ **beef up** (inf) vt aufmotzen; (essay) auswalzen
beefburger ['biːfbɜːgəʳ] n Hamburger m
beefeater ['biːfiːtəʳ] n Beefeater m
beehive ['biːhaɪv] n Bienenstock m
beekeeping ['biːkiːpɪŋ] n Bienenzucht f, Imkerei f
beeline ['biːlaɪn] n: **to make a ~ for** schnurstracks zugehen auf +acc
been [biːn] pp of **be**
beep [biːp] (inf) n Tut(tut) nt ▷ vi tuten ▷ vt: **to ~ one's horn** hupen
beer [bɪəʳ] n Bier nt
beer belly (inf) n Bierbauch m
beer can n Bierdose f
beet [biːt] n Rübe f; (US: also: **red beet**) Rote Bete f
beetle ['biːtl] n Käfer m
beetroot ['biːtruːt] (Brit) n Rote Bete f
befall [bɪ'fɔːl] (irreg: like **fall**) vi sich zutragen ▷ vt widerfahren +dat
befit [bɪ'fɪt] vt sich gehören für
before [bɪ'fɔːʳ] prep vor +dat; (with movement) vor +acc ▷ conj bevor ▷ adv (time) vorher; (space) davor; **~ going** bevor er/sie etc geht/ging; **~ she goes** bevor sie geht; **the week ~** die Woche davor; **I've never seen it ~** ich habe es noch nie gesehen
beforehand [bɪ'fɔːhænd] adv vorher
befriend [bɪ'frɛnd] vt sich annehmen +gen
befuddled [bɪ'fʌdld] adj: **to be ~** verwirrt sein
beg [bɛg] vi betteln ▷ vt (food, money) betteln um; (favour, forgiveness etc) bitten um; **to ~ for** (food etc) betteln um; (forgiveness, mercy etc) bitten um; **to ~ sb to do sth** jdn bitten, etw zu tun; **I ~ your pardon** (apologizing) entschuldigen Sie bitte; (: not hearing) (wie) bitte?; **to ~ the question** der Frage ausweichen; see also **pardon**

began [bɪˈgæn] pt of **begin**
beggar [ˈbɛgəʳ] n Bettler(in) m(f)
begin [bɪˈgɪn] (pt **began**, pp **begun**) vt, vi
beginnen, anfangen; **to ~ doing** or **to do sth**
anfangen, etw zu tun; **~ning (from) Monday**
ab Montag; **I can't ~ to thank you** ich kann
Ihnen gar nicht genug danken; **we'll have
soup to ~ with** als Vorspeise hätten wir
gern Suppe; **to ~ with, I'd like to know ...**
zunächst einmal möchte ich wissen, ...
beginner [bɪˈgɪnəʳ] n Anfänger(in) m(f)
beginning [bɪˈgɪnɪŋ] n Anfang m; **right from
the ~** von Anfang an
begrudge [bɪˈgrʌdʒ] vt: **to ~ sb sth** jdm etw
missgönnen or nicht gönnen
beguile [bɪˈgaɪl] vt betören
beguiling [bɪˈgaɪlɪŋ] adj (charming)
verführerisch; (deluding) betörend
begun [bɪˈgʌn] pp of **begin**
behalf [bɪˈhɑːf] n: **on ~ of, in ~ of** (US: as
representative of) im Namen von; (for benefit of)
zugunsten von; **on my/his ~** in meinem/
seinem Namen; zu meinen/seinen Gunsten
behave [bɪˈheɪv] vi (person) sich verhalten,
sich benehmen; (thing) funktionieren;
(also: **behave o.s.**) sich benehmen
behaviour, (US) **behavior** [bɪˈheɪvjəʳ] n
Verhalten nt; (manner) Benehmen nt
behead [bɪˈhɛd] vt enthaupten
beheld [bɪˈhɛld] pt, pp of **behold**
behind [bɪˈhaɪnd] prep hinter ▷ adv (at/towards
the back) hinten ▷ n (buttocks) Hintern m,
Hinterteil nt; (fig) hinter den
Kulissen; **we're ~ them in technology** auf
dem Gebiet der Technologie liegen wir hinter
ihnen zurück; **to be ~** (schedule) im Rückstand
or Verzug sein; **to leave/stay ~** zurücklassen/-
bleiben
behold [bɪˈhəʊld] (irreg: like **hold**) vt sehen,
erblicken
beige [beɪʒ] adj beige
Beijing [ˈbeɪˈdʒɪŋ] n Peking nt
being [ˈbiːɪŋ] n (creature) (Lebe)wesen nt;
(existence) Leben nt, (Da)sein nt; **to come into
~** entstehen
Beirut [beɪˈruːt] n Beirut nt
Belarus [bɛləˈrus] n Weißrussland nt
Belarussian adj belarussisch, weißrussisch
▷ n Weißrusse m, Weißrussin f; (Ling)
Weißrussisch nt
belated [bɪˈleɪtɪd] adj verspätet
belch [bɛltʃ] vi rülpsen ▷ vt (also: **belch
out**: smoke etc) ausstoßen
beleaguered [bɪˈliːgɪd] adj (city) belagert; (army)
eingekesselt; (fig) geplagt
Belfast [ˈbɛlfɑːst] n Belfast nt
belfry [ˈbɛlfrɪ] n Glockenstube f
Belgian [ˈbɛldʒən] adj belgisch ▷ n Belgier(in)
m(f)
Belgium [ˈbɛldʒəm] n Belgien nt
Belgrade [bɛlˈgreɪd] n Belgrad nt
belie [bɪˈlaɪ] vt (contradict) im Widerspruch
stehen zu; (give false impression of)

hinwegtäuschen über +acc; (disprove)
widerlegen, Lügen strafen
belief [bɪˈliːf] n Glaube m; (opinion)
Überzeugung f; **it's beyond ~** es ist
unglaublich or nicht zu glauben; **in the ~
that** im Glauben, dass
believable [bɪˈliːvəbl] adj glaubhaft
believe [bɪˈliːv] vt glauben ▷ vi (an Gott)
glauben; **he is ~d to be abroad** es heißt, dass
er im Ausland ist; **to ~ in** (God, ghosts) glauben
an +acc; (method etc) Vertrauen haben zu; **I
don't ~ in corporal punishment** ich halte
nicht viel von der Prügelstrafe
believer [bɪˈliːvəʳ] n (in idea, activity)
Anhänger(in) m(f); (Rel) Gläubige(r) f(m); **she's
a great ~ in healthy eating** sie ist sehr für
eine gesunde Ernährung
belittle [bɪˈlɪtl] vt herabsetzen
Belize [bɛˈliːz] n Belize nt
bell [bɛl] n Glocke f; (small) Glöckchen nt,
Schelle f; (on door) Klingel f; **that rings a ~** (fig)
das kommt mir bekannt vor
bell-bottoms [ˈbɛlbɔtəmz] npl Hose f mit
Schlag
bellboy [ˈbɛlbɔɪ] n Page m, Hoteljunge m
bellhop [ˈbɛlhɔp] (US) n = **bellboy**
belligerence [bɪˈlɪdʒərəns] n Angriffslust f
belligerent [bɪˈlɪdʒərənt] adj angriffslustig
bellow [ˈbɛləʊ] vi, vt brüllen
bellows [ˈbɛləʊz] npl Blasebalg m
bell push (Brit) n Klingel f
belly [ˈbɛlɪ] n Bauch m
bellyache [ˈbɛlɪeɪk] (inf) n Bauchschmerzen pl
▷ vi murren
bellybutton [ˈbɛlɪbʌtn] n Bauchnabel m
bellyful [ˈbɛlɪful] (inf) n: **I've had a ~ of that**
davon habe ich die Nase voll
belong [bɪˈlɔŋ] vi: **to ~ to** (person) gehören +dat;
(club etc) angehören +dat; **this book ~s here**
dieses Buch gehört hierher
belongings [bɪˈlɔŋɪŋz] npl Sachen pl,
Habe f; **personal ~** persönlicher Besitz m,
persönliches Eigentum nt
Belorussia [bɛleʊˈrʌʃə] n Weißrussland nt
Belorussian [bɛleʊˈrʌʃən] adj, n = **Belarussian**
beloved [bɪˈlʌvɪd] adj geliebt ▷ n Geliebte(r)
f(m)
below [bɪˈləʊ] prep (beneath) unterhalb +gen;
(less than) unter +dat ▷ adv (beneath) unten;
see ~ siehe unten; **temperatures ~ normal**
Temperaturen unter dem Durchschnitt
belt [bɛlt] n Gürtel m; (Tech) (Treib)riemen m
▷ vt schlagen ▷ vi (Brit: inf): **to ~ along** rasen;
to ~ down/into hinunter-/hineinrasen;
industrial ~ Industriegebiet nt
▶ **belt out** vt (song) schmettern
▶ **belt up** (Brit: inf) vi den Mund or die Klappe
halten
beltway [ˈbɛltweɪ] (US) n Umgehungsstraße
f, Ringstraße f; (motorway)
Umgehungsautobahn f
bemoan [bɪˈməʊn] vt beklagen
bemused [bɪˈmjuːzd] adj verwirrt

bench [bɛntʃ] n Bank f; (work bench) Werkbank f; **the B~** (Law: judges) die Richter pl, der Richterstand

benchmark ['bɛntʃmɑ:k] n (fig) Maßstab m

bend [bɛnd] (pt, pp **bent**) vt (leg, arm) beugen; (pipe) biegen ▷ vi (person) sich beugen ▷ n (Brit: in road) Kurve f; (in pipe, river) Biegung f; **bends** npl (Med): **the ~s** die Taucherkrankheit
▶ **bend down** vi sich bücken
▶ **bend over** vi sich bücken

beneath [bɪ'ni:θ] prep unter +dat ▷ adv darunter

benefactor ['bɛnɪfæktəʳ] n Wohltäter m

benefactress ['bɛnɪfæktrɪs] n Wohltäterin f

beneficial [bɛnɪ'fɪʃəl] adj (effect) nützlich; (influence) vorteilhaft; **~ (to)** gut (für)

beneficiary [bɛnɪ'fɪʃərɪ] n (Law) Nutznießer(in) m(f)

benefit ['bɛnɪfɪt] n (advantage) Vorteil m; (money) Beihilfe f; (also: **benefit concert, benefit match**) Benefizveranstaltung f ▷ vt nützen +dat, zugutekommen +dat ▷ vi: **he'll ~ from it** er wird davon profitieren

Benelux ['bɛnɪlʌks] n die Beneluxstaaten pl

benevolent [bɪ'nɛvələnt] adj wohlwollend; (organization) Wohltätigkeits-

BEng n abbr (= Bachelor of Engineering) akademischer Grad für Ingenieure

benign [bɪ'naɪn] adj gütig; (Med) gutartig

bent [bɛnt] pt, pp of **bend** ▷ n Neigung f ▷ adj (wire, pipe) gebogen; (inf: dishonest) korrupt; (: pej: homosexual) andersrum; **to be ~ on** entschlossen sein zu

bequeath [bɪ'kwi:ð] vt vermachen

bequest [bɪ'kwɛst] n Vermächtnis nt, Legat nt

bereaved [bɪ'ri:vd] adj leidtragend ▷ npl: **the ~** die Hinterbliebenen pl

bereavement [bɪ'ri:vmənt] n schmerzlicher Verlust m

bereft [bɪ'rɛft] adj: **~ of** beraubt +gen

beret ['bɛreɪ] n Baskenmütze f

Bering Sea ['bɛrɪŋ-] n: **the ~** das Beringmeer

berk [bə:k] n (inf) Dussel m

Berks [bɑ:ks] (Brit) abbr (Post) = Berkshire

Berlin [bə:'lɪn] n Berlin nt; **East/West ~** (formerly) Ost-/Westberlin nt

berm [bə:m] n (US) n Seitenstreifen m

Bermuda [bə:'mju:də] n Bermuda nt, die Bermudinseln pl

Bermuda shorts npl Bermudashorts pl

Bern [bə:n] n Bern nt

berry ['bɛrɪ] n Beere f

berserk [bə'sə:k] adj: **to go ~** wild werden

berth [bə:θ] n (bed) Bett nt; (on ship) Koje f; (on train) Schlafwagenbett nt; (for ship) Liegeplatz m ▷ vi anlegen; **to give sb a wide ~** (fig) einen großen Bogen um jdn machen

beseech [bɪ'si:tʃ] (pt, pp **besought**) vt anflehen

beset [bɪ'sɛt] (pt, pp **~**) vt (subj: difficulties) bedrängen; (: fears, doubts) befallen; **~ with** (problems, dangers etc) voller +dat

beside [bɪ'saɪd] prep neben +dat; (with movement) neben +acc; **to be ~ o.s.** außer sich sein; **that's ~ the point** das hat damit nichts zu

tun

besides [bɪ'saɪdz] adv außerdem ▷ prep außer +dat

besiege [bɪ'si:dʒ] vt belagern; (fig) belagern, bedrängen

besmirch [bɪ'smə:tʃ] vt besudeln

besotted [bɪ'sɔtɪd] (Brit) adj: **~ with** vernarrt in +acc

besought [bɪ'sɔ:t] pt, pp of **beseech**

bespectacled [bɪ'spɛktɪkld] adj bebrillt

bespoke [bɪ'spəuk] (Brit) adj (garment) maßgeschneidert; (suit) Maß-; **~ tailor** Maßschneider m

best [bɛst] adj beste(r, s) ▷ adv am besten ▷ n: **at ~** bestenfalls; **the ~ thing to do is ...** das Beste ist ...; **the ~ part of** der größte Teil +gen; **to make the ~ of sth** das Beste aus etw machen; **to do one's ~** sein Bestes tun; **to the ~ of my knowledge** meines Wissens; **to the ~ of my ability** so gut ich kann; **he's not exactly patient at the ~ of times** er ist schon normalerweise ziemlich ungeduldig

best-before date n Mindesthaltbarkeitsdatum nt

bestial ['bɛstɪəl] adj bestialisch

best man n Trauzeuge m (des Bräutigams)

bestow [bɪ'stəu] vt schenken; **to ~ sth on sb** (honour, praise) jdm etw zuteilwerden lassen; (title) jdm etw verleihen

best seller n Bestseller m

bet [bɛt] (pt, pp **~** or **betted**) n Wette f ▷ vi wetten ▷ vt: **to ~ sb sth** mit jdm um etw wetten; **it's a safe ~** (fig) es ist so gut wie sicher; **to ~ money on sth** Geld auf etw acc setzen

Bethlehem ['bɛθlɪhɛm] n Bethlehem nt

betray [bɪ'treɪ] vt verraten; (trust, confidence) missbrauchen

betrayal [bɪ'treɪəl] n Verrat m

better ['bɛtəʳ] adj, adv besser ▷ vt verbessern ▷ n: **to get the ~ of sb** jdn unterkriegen; (curiosity) über jdn siegen; **I had ~ go** ich gehe jetzt (wohl) besser; **you had ~ do it** tun Sie es lieber; **he thought ~ of it** er überlegte es sich dat anders; **to get ~** gesund werden; **that's ~!** so ist es besser!; **a change for the ~** eine Wendung zum Guten

better off adj (wealthier) bessergestellt; (more comfortable etc) besser dran; (fig): **you'd be ~ this way** so wäre es besser für Sie

betting ['bɛtɪŋ] n Wetten nt

betting shop (Brit) n Wettbüro nt

between [bɪ'twi:n] prep zwischen +dat; (with movement) zwischen +acc; (amongst) unter +acc or dat ▷ adv dazwischen; **the road ~ here and London** die Straße zwischen hier und London; **we only had £5 ~ us** wir hatten zusammen nur £5

bevel ['bɛvəl] n (also: **bevel edge**) abgeschrägte Kante f

bevelled ['bɛvəld] adj: **a ~ edge** eine Schrägkante, eine abgeschrägte Kante

beverage ['bɛvərɪdʒ] n Getränk nt

bevy ['bɛvɪ] n: **a ~ of** eine Schar +gen

b

bewail [bɪ'weɪl] vt beklagen
beware [bɪ'weəʳ] vi: **to ~ (of)** sich in Acht nehmen (vor +dat); **"~ of the dog"** „Vorsicht, bissiger Hund"
bewildered [bɪ'wɪldəd] adj verwirrt
bewildering [bɪ'wɪldrɪŋ] adj verwirrend
bewitching [bɪ'wɪtʃɪŋ] adj bezaubernd, hinreißend
beyond [bɪ'jɔnd] prep (in space) jenseits +gen; (exceeding) über +acc ... hinaus; (after) nach; (above) über +dat ▷ adv (in space) dahinter; (in time) darüber hinaus; **it is ~ doubt** es steht außer Zweifel; **~ repair** nicht mehr zu reparieren; **it is ~ my understanding** es übersteigt mein Begriffsvermögen; **it's ~ me** das geht über meinen Verstand
b/f abbr (Comm: = brought forward) Übertr.
BFPO n abbr (= British Forces Post Office) Postbehörde der britischen Armee
bhp n abbr (Aut: = brake horsepower) Bremsleistung f
bi ... [baɪ] pref Bi-, bi-
biannual [baɪ'ænjuəl] adj zweimal jährlich
bias ['baɪəs] n (prejudice) Vorurteil nt; (preference) Vorliebe f
biased, biassed ['baɪəst] adj voreingenommen; **to be bias(s)ed against** voreingenommen sein gegen
biathlon [baɪ'æθlən] n Biathlon nt
bib [bɪb] n Latz m
Bible ['baɪbl] n Bibel f
biblical ['bɪblɪkl] adj biblisch
bibliography [bɪblɪ'ɔgrəfɪ] n Bibliografie f
bicarbonate of soda [baɪ'kɑːbənɪt-] n Natron nt
bicentenary [baɪsen'tiːnərɪ] n Zweihundertjahrfeier f
bicentennial [baɪsen'tenɪəl] (US) n = **bicentenary**
biceps ['baɪseps] n Bizeps m
bicker ['bɪkəʳ] vi sich zanken
bickering ['bɪkərɪŋ] n Zankerei f
bicycle ['baɪsɪkl] n Fahrrad nt
bicycle path n (Fahr)radweg m
bicycle pump n Luftpumpe f
bicycle track n (Fahr)radweg m
bid [bɪd] (pt **bade** or **~**, pp **bidden** or **~**) n (at auction) Gebot nt; (in tender) Angebot nt; (attempt) Versuch m ▷ vi bieten; (Cards) bieten, reizen ▷ vt bieten; **to ~ sb good day** jdm einen Guten Tag wünschen
bidder ['bɪdəʳ] n: **the highest ~** der/die Höchstbietende or Meistbietende
bidding ['bɪdɪŋ] n Steigern nt, Bieten nt; (order, command): **to do sb's ~** tun, was jd einem sagt
bide [baɪd] vt: **to ~ one's time** den rechten Augenblick abwarten
bidet ['biːdeɪ] n Bidet nt
bidirectional ['baɪdɪ'rekʃənl] adj (Comput) bidirektional
biennial [baɪ'enɪəl] adj zweijährlich ▷ n zweijährige Pflanze f
bifocals [baɪ'fəuklz] npl Bifokalbrille f

big [bɪg] adj groß; **to do things in a ~ way** alles im großen Stil tun
bigamist ['bɪgəmɪst] n Bigamist(in) m(f)
bigamous ['bɪgəməs] adj bigamistisch
bigamy ['bɪgəmɪ] n Bigamie f
big dipper [-'dɪpəʳ] n Achterbahn f
big end n (Aut) Pleuelfuß m, Schubstangenkopf m
biggish ['bɪgɪʃ] adj ziemlich groß
bigheaded ['bɪg'hedɪd] adj eingebildet
big-hearted ['bɪg'hɑːtɪd] adj großherzig
bigot ['bɪgət] n Eiferer m; (about religion) bigotter Mensch m
bigoted ['bɪgətɪd] adj (see n) eifernd; bigott
bigotry ['bɪgətrɪ] n (see n) eifernde Borniertheit f; Bigotterie f
big toe n große Zehe f
big top n Zirkuszelt nt
big wheel n Riesenrad nt
bigwig ['bɪgwɪg] (inf) n hohes Tier nt
bike [baɪk] n (Fahr)rad nt; (motorcycle) Motorrad nt
bike lane n Fahrradspur f
bikini [bɪ'kiːnɪ] n Bikini m
bilateral [baɪ'lætərəl] adj bilateral
bile [baɪl] n Galle(nflüssigkeit) f; (fig: invective) Beschimpfungen pl
bilingual [baɪ'lɪŋgwəl] adj zweisprachig
bilious ['bɪlɪəs] adj unwohl; (fig: colour) widerlich; **he felt ~** ihm war schlecht or übel
bill [bɪl] n Rechnung f; (Pol) (Gesetz)entwurf m, (Gesetzes)vorlage f; (US: banknote) Banknote f, (Geld)schein m; (of bird) Schnabel m ▷ vt (item) in Rechnung stellen, berechnen; (customer) eine Rechnung ausstellen +dat; **"post no ~s"** „Plakate ankleben verboten"; **on the ~** (Theat) auf dem Programm; **to fit** or **fill the ~** (fig) der/die/das Richtige sein; **~ of exchange** Wechsel m, Tratte f; **~ of fare** Speisekarte f; **~ of lading** Seefrachtbrief m, Konnossement nt; **~ of sale** Verkaufsurkunde f
billboard ['bɪlbɔːd] n Reklametafel f
billet ['bɪlɪt] (Mil) n Quartier nt ▷ vt einquartieren
billfold ['bɪlfəuld] (US) n Brieftasche f
billiards ['bɪljədz] n Billard nt
billion ['bɪljən] n (Brit) Billion f; (US) Milliarde f
billionaire [bɪljə'neəʳ] n Milliardär(in) m(f)
billow ['bɪləu] n (of smoke) Schwaden m ▷ vi (smoke) in Schwaden aufsteigen; (sail) sich blähen
billy goat ['bɪlɪ-] n Ziegenbock m
bimbo ['bɪmbəu] (inf: pej) n (woman) Puppe f, Häschen nt
bin [bɪn] n (Brit) Mülleimer m; (container) Behälter m
binary ['baɪnərɪ] adj binär
bind [baɪnd] (pt, pp **bound**) vt binden; (tie together: hands and feet) fesseln; (constrain, oblige) verpflichten ▷ n (inf: nuisance) Last f
▶ **bind over** vt rechtlich verpflichten
▶ **bind up** vt (wound) verbinden; **to be bound up in** sehr beschäftigt sein mit; **to be bound**

447

up with verbunden or verknüpft sein mit

binder ['baɪndəʳ] n (file) Hefter m; (for magazines) Mappe f

binding ['baɪndɪŋ] adj bindend, verbindlich ▷ n (of book) Einband m

binge [bɪndʒ] (inf) n: **to go on a ~** auf eine Sauftour gehen

bingo ['bɪŋgəʊ] n Bingo nt

bin liner n Müllbeutel m

binoculars [bɪ'nɒkjʊləz] npl Fernglas nt

biochemistry [baɪə'kɛmɪstrɪ] n Biochemie f

biodegradable ['baɪəʊdɪ'greɪdəbl] adj biologisch abbaubar

biodiversity ['baɪəʊdaɪ'vɜːsɪtɪ] n biologische Vielfalt f

biofuel n Biotreibstoff m

biographer [baɪ'ɒgrəfəʳ] n Biograf(in) m(f)

biographic [baɪə'græfɪk], **biographical** [baɪə'græfɪkl] adj biografisch

biography [baɪ'ɒgrəfɪ] n Biografie f

biological [baɪə'lɒdʒɪkl] adj biologisch

biological clock n biologische Uhr f

biological waste n Bioabfall m

biologist [baɪ'ɒlədʒɪst] n Biologe m, Biologin f

biology [baɪ'ɒlədʒɪ] n Biologie f

biophysics ['baɪəʊ'fɪzɪks] n Biophysik f

biopic ['baɪəʊpɪk] n Filmbiografie f

biopsy ['baɪɒpsɪ] n Biopsie f

biosphere ['baɪəsfɪəʳ] n Biosphäre f

biotechnology ['baɪəʊtɛk'nɒlədʒɪ] n Biotechnik f

biped ['baɪpɛd] n Zweifüßer m

birch [bɜːtʃ] n Birke f

bird [bɜːd] n Vogel m; (Brit: inf: girl) Biene f

bird of prey n Raubvogel m

bird's-eye view ['bɜːdzaɪ-] n Vogelperspektive f; (overview) Überblick m

bird-watcher ['bɜːdwɒtʃəʳ] n Vogelbeobachter(in) m(f)

Biro® ['baɪərəʊ] n Kugelschreiber m, Kuli m (inf)

birth [bɜːθ] n Geburt f; **to give ~ to** (subj: woman) gebären, entbunden werden von; (: animal) werfen

birth certificate n Geburtsurkunde f

birth control n Geburtenkontrolle f, Geburtenregelung f

birthday ['bɜːθdeɪ] n Geburtstag m ▷ cpd Geburtstags-; see also **happy**

birthmark ['bɜːθmɑːk] n Muttermal nt

birthplace ['bɜːθpleɪs] n Geburtsort m; (house) Geburtshaus nt; (fig) Entstehungsort m

birth rate ['bɜːθreɪt] n Geburtenrate f, Geburtenziffer f

Biscay ['bɪskeɪ] n: **the Bay of ~** der Golf von Biskaya

biscuit ['bɪskɪt] n (Brit) Keks m or nt; (US) Brötchen nt

bisect [baɪ'sɛkt] vt halbieren

bisexual ['baɪ'sɛksjʊəl] adj bisexuell ▷ n Bisexuelle(r) f(m)

bishop ['bɪʃəp] n (Rel) Bischof m; (Chess) Läufer m

bistro ['biːstrəʊ] n Bistro nt

bit [bɪt] pt of **bite** ▷ n (piece) Stück nt; (of drill) (Bohr)einsatz m, Bohrer m; (of plane) (Hobel) messer nt; (Comput) Bit nt; (of horse) Gebiss nt; (US): **two/four/six ~s** 25/50/75 Cent(s); **a ~ of** ein bisschen; **a ~ mad** ein bisschen verrückt; **a ~ dangerous** etwas gefährlich; **~ by bit** nach und nach; **to come to ~s** kaputtgehen; **bring all your ~s and pieces** bringen Sie Ihre (Sieben)sachen mit; **to do one's ~** sein(en) Teil tun or beitragen

bitch [bɪtʃ] n (dog) Hündin f; (inf!: woman) Miststück nt

bite [baɪt] (pt bit, pp bitten) vt, vi beißen; (subj: insect etc) stechen ▷ n (insect bite) Stich m; (mouthful) Bissen m; **to ~ one's nails** an seinen Nägeln kauen; **let's have a ~ (to eat)** (inf) lasst uns eine Kleinigkeit essen

biting ['baɪtɪŋ] adj (wind) schneidend; (wit) scharf

bit part n kleine Nebenrolle f

bitten ['bɪtn] pp of **bite**

bitter ['bɪtəʳ] adj bitter; (person) verbittert; (wind, weather) bitterkalt, eisig; (criticism) scharf ▷ n (Brit: beer) halbdunkles obergäriges Bier; **to the ~ end** bis zum bitteren Ende

bitterly ['bɪtəlɪ] adv (complain, weep) bitterlich; (oppose) erbittert; (criticize) scharf; (disappointed) bitter; (jealous) sehr; **it's ~ cold** es ist bitterkalt

bitterness ['bɪtənɪs] n Bitterkeit f

bittersweet ['bɪtəswiːt] adj bittersüß

bitty ['bɪtɪ] (Brit: inf) adj zusammengestoppelt, zusammengestückelt

bitumen ['bɪtjumɪn] n Bitumen nt

bivouac ['bɪvuæk] n Biwak nt

bizarre [bɪ'zɑːʳ] adj bizarr

bk abbr = **bank; book**

BL n abbr (= Bachelor of Law) akademischer Grad für Juristen; (= Bachelor of Letters) akademischer Grad für Literaturwissenschaftler; (US: = Bachelor of Literature) akademischer Grad für Literaturwissenschaftler

B/L abbr = **bill of lading**

blab [blæb] (inf) vi quatschen

black [blæk] adj schwarz ▷ vt (Brit: Industry) boykottieren ▷ n Schwarz nt; (person): **B~** Schwarze(r) f(m); **to give sb a ~ eye** jdm ein blaues Auge schlagen; **~ and blue** grün und blau; **there it is in ~ and white** (fig) da steht es schwarz auf weiß; **to be in the ~** in den schwarzen Zahlen sein

▸ **black out** vi (faint) ohnmächtig werden

black belt n (US) Gebiet in den Südstaaten der USA, das vorwiegend von Schwarzen bewohnt wird; (Judo) schwarzer Gürtel m

blackberry ['blækbərɪ] n Brombeere f

blackbird ['blækbɜːd] n Amsel f

blackboard ['blækbɔːd] n Tafel f

black box n (Aviat) Flugschreiber m

black coffee n schwarzer Kaffee m

Black Country (Brit) n: **the ~** Industriegebiet in den englischen Midlands

blackcurrant ['blæk'kʌrənt] n Johannisbeere f

black economy n: **the ~** die

Schattenwirtschaft

blacken ['blækn] vt: **to ~ sb's name/
reputation** (fig) jdn verunglimpfen

Black Forest n: **the ~** der Schwarzwald

blackhead ['blækhɛd] n Mitesser m

black hole n schwarzes Loch nt

black ice n Glatteis nt

blackjack ['blækdʒæk] n (Cards)
Siebzehnundvier nt; (US: truncheon)
Schlagstock m

blackleg ['blæklɛg] (Brit) n Streikbrecher(in)
m(f)

blacklist ['blæklɪst] n schwarze Liste f ▷ vt auf
die schwarze Liste setzen

blackmail ['blækmeɪl] n Erpressung f ▷ vt
erpressen

blackmailer ['blækmeɪlər] n Erpresser(in) m(f)

black market n Schwarzmarkt m

blackout ['blækaut] n (in wartime)
Verdunkelung f; (power cut) Stromausfall m;
(TV, Radio) Ausfall m; (faint) Ohnmachtsanfall
m

black pepper n schwarzer Pfeffer m

Black Sea n: **the ~** das Schwarze Meer

black sheep n (fig) schwarzes Schaf nt

blacksmith ['blæksmɪθ] n Schmied m

black spot n (Aut) Gefahrenstelle f; (for
unemployment etc) Gebiet, in dem ein Problem
besonders ausgeprägt ist

bladder ['blædər] n Blase f

blade [bleɪd] n (of knife etc) Klinge f; (of oar,
propeller) Blatt nt; **a ~ of grass** ein Grashalm m

Blairite ['blɛəraɪt] (Pol) adj blairistisch ▷ n
Blair-Anhänger(in) m(f)

blame [bleɪm] n Schuld f ▷ vt: **to ~ sb for sth**
jdm die Schuld an etw dat geben; **to be to ~**
Schuld daran haben, schuld sein; **who's to ~?**
wer hat Schuld or ist schuld?; **I'm not to ~** es
ist nicht meine Schuld

blameless ['bleɪmlɪs] adj schuldlos

blanch [blɑːntʃ] vi blass werden ▷ vt (Culin)
blanchieren

blancmange [blə'mɒnʒ] n Pudding m

bland [blænd] adj (taste, food) fade

blank [blæŋk] adj (paper) leer, unbeschrieben;
(look) ausdruckslos ▷ n (on form) Lücke f;
(cartridge) Platzpatrone f; **my mind was a ~** ich
hatte ein Brett vor dem Kopf; **we drew a ~** (fig)
wir hatten kein Glück

blank cheque n Blankoscheck m; **to give sb
a ~ to do sth** (fig) jdm freie Hand geben, etw
zu tun

blanket ['blæŋkɪt] n Decke f ▷ adj (statement)
pauschal; (agreement) Pauschal-

blanket cover n umfassende Versicherung f

blare [blɛər] vi (brass band) schmettern; (horn)
tuten; (radio) plärren
  ▶ **blare out** vi (radio, stereo) plärren

blasé ['blɑːzeɪ] adj blasiert

blaspheme [blæs'fiːm] vi Gott lästern

blasphemous ['blæsfɪməs] adj lästerlich,
blasphemisch

blasphemy ['blæsfɪmɪ] n (Gottes)lästerung f,

Blasphemie f

blast [blɑːst] n (of wind) Windstoß m; (of whistle)
Trillern nt; (shock wave) Druckwelle f; (of air,
steam) Schwall m; (of explosive) Explosion f ▷ vt
(blow up) sprengen ▷ excl (Brit: inf) verdammt!,
so ein Mist!; **at full ~** (play music) mit voller
Lautstärke; (move, work) auf Hochtouren
  ▶ **blast off** vi (Space) abheben, starten

blast furnace n Hochofen m

blastoff ['blɑːstɒf] n (Space) Abschuss m

blatant ['bleɪtənt] adj offensichtlich

blatantly ['bleɪtəntlɪ] adv (lie) unverfroren; **it's
~ obvious** es ist überdeutlich

blaze [bleɪz] n (fire) Feuer nt, Brand m; (fig: of
colour) Farbenpracht f; (: of glory) Glanz m ▷ vi
(fire) lodern; (guns) feuern; (fig: eyes) glühen
  ▷ vt: **to ~ a trail** (fig) den Weg bahnen; **in a ~
of publicity** mit viel Publicity

blazer ['bleɪzər] n Blazer m

bleach [bliːtʃ] n (also: **household bleach**) ≈
Reinigungsmittel nt ▷ vt bleichen

bleached [bliːtʃt] adj gebleicht

bleachers ['bliːtʃəz] (US) npl unüberdachte
Zuschauertribüne f

bleak [bliːk] adj (countryside) öde; (weather,
situation) trostlos; (prospect) trüb; (expression,
voice) deprimiert

bleary-eyed ['blɪərɪ'aɪd] adj triefäugig

bleat [bliːt] vi (goat) meckern; (sheep) blöken ▷ n
Meckern nt; Blöken nt

bled [blɛd] pt, pp of **bleed**

bleed [bliːd] (pt, pp **bled**) vi bluten; (colour)
auslaufen ▷ vt (brakes, radiator) entlüften; **my
nose is ~ing** ich habe Nasenbluten

bleep [bliːp] n Piepton m ▷ vi piepen ▷ vt (doctor
etc) rufen, anpiepen (inf)

bleeper ['bliːpər] n Piepser m (inf),
Funkrufempfänger m

blemish ['blɛmɪʃ] n Makel m

blend [blɛnd] n Mischung f ▷ vt (Culin)
mischen, mixen; (colours, styles, flavours etc)
vermischen ▷ vi (colours etc: also: **blend in**)
harmonieren

blender ['blɛndər] n (Culin) Mixer m

bless [blɛs] (pt, pp **~ed** or **blest**) vt segnen; **to
be ~ed with** gesegnet sein mit; **~ you!** (after
sneeze) Gesundheit!

blessed ['blɛsɪd] adj heilig; (happy) selig; **it
rains every ~ day** (inf) es regnet aber auch
jeden Tag

blessing ['blɛsɪŋ] n (approval) Zustimmung f;
(Rel: fig) Segen m; **to count one's ~s** von Glück
sagen können; **it was a ~ in disguise** es war
schließlich doch ein Segen

blew [bluː] pt of **blow**

blight [blaɪt] vt zerstören; (hopes) vereiteln;
(life) verderben ▷ n (of plants) Brand m

blimey ['blaɪmɪ] (Brit: inf) excl Mensch!

blind [blaɪnd] adj blind ▷ n (for window) Rollo nt,
Rouleau nt; (also: **Venetian blind**) Jalousie f ▷ vt
blind machen; (dazzle) blenden; (deceive: with
facts etc) verblenden; **the blind** npl (blind people)
die Blinden pl; **to turn a ~ eye (on** or **to)** ein

449

Auge zudrücken (bei); **to be ~ to sth** (*fig*) blind für etw sein

blind alley *n* (*fig*) Sackgasse *f*

blind corner (*Brit*) *n* unübersichtliche Ecke *f*

blind date *n* Rendezvous *nt* mit einem/einer Unbekannten

blindfold ['blaɪndfəʊld] *n* Augenbinde *f* ▷ *adj*, *adv* mit verbundenen Augen ▷ *vt* die Augen verbinden +*dat*

blinding ['blaɪndɪŋ] *adj* (*dazzling*) blendend; (*remarkable*) bemerkenswert

blindly ['blaɪndlɪ] *adv* (*without seeing*) wie blind; (*without thinking*) blindlings

blindness ['blaɪndnɪs] *n* Blindheit *f*

blind spot *n* (*Aut*) toter Winkel *m*; (*fig: weak spot*) schwacher Punkt *m*

blink [blɪŋk] *vi* blinzeln; (*light*) blinken ▷ *n*: **the TV's on the ~** (*inf*) der Fernseher ist kaputt

blinkers ['blɪŋkəz] *npl* Scheuklappen *pl*

blinking ['blɪŋkɪŋ] (*Brit: inf*) *adj*: **this ~ ...** diese(r, s) verflixte ...

blip [blɪp] *n* (*on radar screen*) leuchtender Punkt *m*; (*in a straight line*) Ausschlag *m*; (*fig*) (zeitweilige) Abweichung *f*

bliss [blɪs] *n* Glück *nt*, Seligkeit *f*

blissful ['blɪsfʊl] *adj* (*event, day*) herrlich; (*smile*) selig; **a ~ sigh** ein wohliger Seufzer *m*; **in ~ ignorance** in herrlicher Ahnungslosigkeit

blissfully ['blɪsfəlɪ] *adv* selig; **~ happy** überglücklich; **~ unaware of ...** ohne auch nur zu ahnen, dass ...

blister ['blɪstəʳ] *n* Blase *f* ▷ *vi* (*paint*) Blasen werfen

BLit, BLitt *n abbr* (= *Bachelor of Literature; Bachelor of Letters*) akademischer Grad für Literaturwissenschaftler

blithely ['blaɪðlɪ] *adv* (*unconcernedly*) unbekümmert, munter; (*joyfully*) fröhlich

blithering ['blɪðərɪŋ] (*inf*) *adj*: **this ~ idiot** dieser Trottel

blitz [blɪts] *n* (*Mil*) Luftangriff *m*; **to have a ~ on sth** (*fig*) einen Großangriff auf etw *acc* starten

blizzard ['blɪzəd] *n* Schneesturm *m*

bloated ['bləʊtɪd] *adj* aufgedunsen; (*full*) (über) satt

blob [blɒb] *n* Tropfen *m*; (*sth indistinct*) verschwommener Fleck *m*

bloc [blɒk] *n* (*Pol*) Block *m*

block [blɒk] *n* Block *m*; (*toy*) Bauklotz *m*; (*in pipes*) Verstopfung *f* ▷ *vt* blockieren; (*progress*) aufhalten; (*Comput*) blocken; **~ of flats** (*Brit*) Wohnblock *m*; **3 ~s from here** 3 Blocks or Straßen weiter; **mental ~** geistige Sperre *f*, Mattscheibe *f* (*inf*); **~ and tackle** Flaschenzug *m* ▶ **block up** *vt*, *vi* verstopfen

blockade [blɒ'keɪd] *n* Blockade *f* ▷ *vt* blockieren

blockage ['blɒkɪdʒ] *n* Verstopfung *f*

block booking *n* Gruppenbuchung *f*

blockbuster ['blɒkbʌstəʳ] *n* Knüller *m*

block capitals *npl* Blockschrift *f*

blockhead ['blɒkhɛd] (*inf*) *n* Dummkopf *m*

block letters *npl* Blockschrift *f*

block release (*Brit*) *n* blockweise Freistellung von Auszubildenden zur Weiterbildung

block vote (*Brit*) *n* Stimmenblock *m*

blog [blɒg] *n* (*Comput*) Blog *m*, Weblog *m* ▷ *vi* bloggen

blogging ['blɒgɪŋ] *n* (*Comput*) Blogging *nt*

bloke [bləʊk] (*Brit: inf*) *n* Typ *m*

blond, blonde [blɒnd] *adj* blond ▷ *n*: **~(e)** (*woman*) Blondine *f*

blood [blʌd] *n* Blut *nt*; **new ~** (*fig*) frisches Blut *nt*

blood bank *n* Blutbank *f*

blood bath *n* Blutbad *nt*

blood count *n* Blutbild *nt*

bloodcurdling ['blʌdkə:dlɪŋ] *adj* grauenerregend

blood donor *n* Blutspender(in) *m(f)*

blood group *n* Blutgruppe *f*

bloodhound ['blʌdhaʊnd] *n* Bluthund *m*

bloodless ['blʌdlɪs] *adj* (*victory*) unblutig; (*pale*) blutleer

blood-letting ['blʌdlɛtɪŋ] *n* (*also fig*) Aderlass *m*

blood poisoning *n* Blutvergiftung *f*

blood pressure *n* Blutdruck *m*; **to have high/ low ~** hohen/niedrigen Blutdruck haben

bloodshed ['blʌdʃɛd] *n* Blutvergießen *nt*

bloodshot ['blʌdʃɒt] *adj* (*eyes*) blutunterlaufen

blood sport *n* Jagdsport *m* (*und andere Sportarten, bei denen Tiere getötet werden*)

bloodstained ['blʌdsteɪnd] *adj* blutbefleckt

bloodstream ['blʌdstri:m] *n* Blut *nt*, Blutkreislauf *m*

blood test *n* Blutprobe *f*

bloodthirsty ['blʌdθə:stɪ] *adj* blutrünstig

blood transfusion *n* Blutübertragung *f*, (Blut) transfusion *f*

blood type *n* Blutgruppe *f*

blood vessel *n* Blutgefäß *nt*

bloody ['blʌdɪ] *adj* blutig; (*Brit: inf!*): **this ~ ...** diese(r, s) verdammte ...; **~ strong** (*inf!*) verdammt stark; **~ good** (*inf!*) echt gut

bloody-minded ['blʌdɪ'maɪndɪd] (*Brit: inf*) *adj* stur

bloom [blu:m] *n* Blüte *f* ▷ *vi* blühen; **to be in ~** in Blüte stehen

blooming ['blu:mɪŋ] (*Brit: inf*) *adj*: **this ~ ...** diese(r, s) verflixte ...

blossom ['blɒsəm] *n* Blüte *f* ▷ *vi* blühen; (*fig*): **to ~ into** erblühen or aufblühen zu

blot [blɒt] *n* Klecks *m*; (*fig: on name etc*) Makel *m* ▷ *vt* (*liquid*) aufsaugen; (*make blot on*) beklecksen; **to be a ~ on the landscape** ein Schandfleck in der Landschaft sein; **to ~ one's copy book** (*fig*) sich unmöglich machen ▶ **blot out** *vt* (*view*) verdecken; (*memory*) auslöschen

blotchy ['blɒtʃɪ] *adj* fleckig

blotter ['blɒtəʳ] *n* (Tinten)löscher *m*

blotting paper ['blɒtɪŋ-] *n* Löschpapier *nt*

blotto ['blɒtəʊ] (*inf*) *adj* (*drunk*) sternhagelvoll

blouse [blaʊz] *n* Bluse *f*

blow [bləʊ] (*pt* **blew**, *pp* **~n**) *n* (*also fig*) Schlag *m* ▷ *vi* (*wind*) wehen; (*person*) blasen ▷ *vt*

(*subj*: *wind*) wehen; (*instrument, whistle*) blasen; (*fuse*) durchbrennen lassen; **to come to ~s** handgreiflich werden; **to ~ off course** (*ship*) vom Kurs abgetrieben werden; **to ~ one's nose** sich *dat* die Nase putzen; **to ~ a whistle** pfeifen
  ▶ **blow away** *vt* wegblasen ▷ *vi* wegfliegen
  ▶ **blow down** *vt* umwehen
  ▶ **blow off** *vt* wegwehen ▷ *vi* wegfliegen
  ▶ **blow out** *vi* ausgehen
  ▶ **blow over** *vi* sich legen
  ▶ **blow up** *vi* ausbrechen ▷ *vt* (*bridge*) in die Luft jagen; (*tyre*) aufblasen; (*Phot*) vergrößern

blow-dry ['bləʊdraɪ] *vt* föhnen ▷ *n*: **to have a ~** sich föhnen lassen
blowlamp ['bləʊlæmp] (*Brit*) *n* Lötlampe *f*
blown [bləʊn] *pp of* **blow**
blowout ['bləʊaʊt] *n* Reifenpanne *f*; (*inf: big meal*) Schlemmerei *f*; (*of oil-well*) Ölausbruch *m*
blowtorch ['bləʊtɔːtʃ] *n* = **blowlamp**
blow-up ['bləʊʌp] *n* Vergrößerung *f*
blowzy ['blaʊzɪ] (*Brit*) *adj* schlampig
BLS (*US*) *n abbr* (= *Bureau of Labor Statistics*) Amt für Arbeitsstatistik
blubber ['blʌbəʳ] *n* Walfischspeck *m* ▷ *vi* (*pej*) heulen
bludgeon ['blʌdʒən] *vt* niederknüppeln; (*fig*): **to ~ sb into doing sth** jdm so lange zusetzen, bis er etw tut
blue [bluː] *adj* blau; (*depressed*) deprimiert, niedergeschlagen ▷ *n*: **out of the ~** (*fig*) aus heiterem Himmel; **blues** *n* (*Mus*): **the ~s** der Blues; **~ film** Pornofilm *m*; **~ joke** schlüpfriger Witz *m*; **(only) once in a ~ moon** (nur) alle Jubeljahre einmal; **to have the ~s** deprimiert *or* niedergeschlagen sein
blue baby *n* Baby *nt* mit angeborenem Herzfehler
bluebell ['bluːbɛl] *n* Glockenblume *f*
bluebottle ['bluːbɒtl] *n* Schmeißfliege *f*
blue cheese *n* Blauschimmelkäse *m*
blue-chip ['bluːtʃɪp] *adj*: **~ investment** sichere Geldanlage *f*
blue-collar worker ['bluːkɔlə-] *n* Arbeiter(in) *m(f)*
blue jeans *npl* (Blue)jeans *pl*
blueprint ['bluːprɪnt] *n* (*fig*): **a ~ (for)** ein Plan *m* *or* Entwurf *m* (für)
bluff [blʌf] *vi* bluffen ▷ *n* Bluff *m*; (*cliff*) Klippe *f*; (*promontory*) Felsvorsprung *m*; **to call sb's ~** es darauf ankommen lassen
blunder ['blʌndəʳ] *n* (dummer) Fehler *m* ▷ *vi* einen (dummen) Fehler machen; **to ~ into sb** mit jdm zusammenstoßen; **to ~ into sth** in etw *acc* (hinein)tappen
blunt [blʌnt] *adj* stumpf; (*person*) direkt; (*talk*) unverblümt ▷ *vt* stumpf machen; **~ instrument** (*Law*) stumpfer Gegenstand *m*
bluntly ['blʌntlɪ] *adv* (*speak*) unverblümt
bluntness ['blʌntnɪs] *n* (*of person*) Direktheit *f*
blur [bləːʳ] *n* (*shape*) verschwommener Fleck *m*; (*scene etc*) verschwommenes Bild *nt*; (*memory*) verschwommene Erinnerung *f* ▷ *vt* (*vision*)

trüben; (*distinction*) verwischen
blurb [bləːb] *n* Informationsmaterial *nt*
blurred [bləːd] *adj* (*photograph, TV picture etc*) verschwommen; (*distinction*) verwischt
blurt out [bləːt-] *vt* herausplatzen mit
blush [blʌʃ] *vi* erröten ▷ *n* Röte *f*
blusher ['blʌʃəʳ] *n* Rouge *nt*
bluster ['blʌstəʳ] *n* Toben *nt*, Geschrei *nt* ▷ *vi* toben
blustering ['blʌstərɪŋ] *adj* polternd
blustery ['blʌstərɪ] *adj* stürmisch
Blvd *abbr* = **boulevard**
BM *n abbr* (= *British Museum*) Britisches Museum *nt*; (= *Bachelor of Medicine*) akademischer Grad für Mediziner
BMA *n abbr* (= *British Medical Association*) Dachverband der Ärzte
BMJ *n abbr* (= *British Medical Journal*) vom BMA herausgegebene Zeitschrift
BMus *n abbr* (= *Bachelor of Music*) akademischer Grad für Musikwissenschaftler
BMX *n abbr* (= *bicycle motocross*): **~ bike** BMX-Rad *nt*
bn *abbr* = **billion**
BO *n abbr* (*inf*: = *body odour*) Körpergeruch *m*; = **box office**
boar [bɔːʳ] *n* (*male pig*) Eber *m*; (*wild pig*) Keiler *m*
board [bɔːd] *n* Brett *nt*; (*cardboard*) Pappe *f*; (*committee*) Ausschuss *m*; (*in firm*) Vorstand *m* ▷ *vt* (*ship*) an Bord +*gen* gehen; (*train*) einsteigen in +*acc*; **on ~** (*Naut, Aviat*) an Bord; **full/half ~** (*Brit*) Voll-/Halbpension *f*; **~ and lodging** Unterkunft und Verpflegung *f*; **to go by the ~** (*fig*) unter den Tisch fallen; **above ~** (*fig*) korrekt; **across the ~** (*fig*) allgemein; (: *criticize, reject*) pauschal
  ▶ **board up** *vt* mit Brettern vernageln
boarder ['bɔːdəʳ] *n* Internatsschüler(in) *m(f)*
board game *n* Brettspiel *nt*
boarding card ['bɔːdɪŋ-] *n* (*Aviat, Naut*) = **boarding pass**
boarding house ['bɔːdɪŋ-] *n* Pension *f*
boarding party ['bɔːdɪŋ-] *n* (*Naut*) Enterkommando *nt*
boarding pass ['bɔːdɪŋ-] *n* Bordkarte *f*
boarding school ['bɔːdɪŋ-] *n* Internat *nt*
board meeting *n* Vorstandssitzung *f*
boardroom ['bɔːdruːm] *n* Sitzungssaal *m*
boardwalk ['bɔːdwɔːk] (*US*) *n* Holzsteg *m*
boast [bəʊst] *vi* prahlen ▷ *vt* (*fig: possess*) sich rühmen +*gen*, besitzen; **to ~ about** *or* **of** prahlen mit
boastful ['bəʊstful] *adj* prahlerisch
boastfulness ['bəʊstfulnɪs] *n* Prahlerei *f*
boat [bəʊt] *n* Boot *nt*; (*ship*) Schiff *nt*; **to go by ~** mit dem Schiff fahren; **to be in the same ~** (*fig*) in einem Boot *or* im gleichen Boot sitzen
boater ['bəʊtəʳ] *n* steifer Strohhut *m*, Kreissäge *f* (*inf*)
boating ['bəʊtɪŋ] *n* Bootfahren *nt*
boat people *npl* Bootsflüchtlinge *pl*
boatswain ['bəʊsn] *n* Bootsmann *m*
bob [bɔb] *vi* (*also*: **bob up and down**) sich auf

und ab bewegen ▷ *n* (*Brit: inf*) = **shilling**
▶ **bob up** *vi* auftauchen
bobbin ['bɔbɪn] *n* Spule *f*
bobby ['bɔbɪ] (*Brit: inf*) *n* Bobby *m*, Polizist *m*
bobsleigh ['bɔbsleɪ] *n* Bob *m*
bode [bəud] *vi*: **to ~ well/ill (for)** ein gutes/
schlechtes Zeichen sein (für)
bodice ['bɔdɪs] *n* (*of dress*) Oberteil *nt*
bodily ['bɔdɪlɪ] *adj* körperlich; (*needs*) leiblich
▷ *adv* (*lift, carry*) mit aller Kraft
body ['bɔdɪ] *n* Körper *m*; (*corpse*) Leiche *f*; (*main
part*) Hauptteil *m*; (*of car*) Karosserie *f*; (*of
plane*) Rumpf *m*; (*group*) Gruppe *f*; (*organization*)
Organ *nt*; **ruling ~** amtierendes Organ; **in a ~**
geschlossen
body blow *n* (*fig: setback*) schwerer Schlag *m*
body building *n* Bodybuilding *nt*
body double *n* (*Film, TV*) *Double für Szenen, in
denen Körperpartien in Nahaufnahme gezeigt werden*
bodyguard ['bɔdɪɡaːd] *n* (*group*) Leibwache *f*;
(*one person*) Leibwächter *m*
body language *n* Körpersprache *f*
body repairs *npl* Karosseriearbeiten *pl*
body search *n* Leibesvisitation *f*
body stocking *n* Body(stocking) *m*
bodywork ['bɔdɪwəːk] *n* Karosserie *f*
boffin ['bɔfɪn] (*Brit*) *n* Fachidiot *m*
bog [bɔɡ] *n* Sumpf *m* ▷ *vt*: **to get ~ged down**
(*fig*) sich verzetteln
bogey ['bəuɡɪ] *n* Schreckgespenst *nt*;
(*also*: **bogeyman**) Butzemann *m*, schwarzer
Mann *m*
boggle ['bɔɡl] *vi*: **the mind ~s** das ist nicht *or*
kaum auszumalen
bogie ['bəuɡɪ] *n* Drehgestell *nt*; (*trolley*)
Draisine *f*
Bogotá [bəuɡə'taː] *n* Bogotá *nt*
bogus ['bəuɡəs] *adj* (*workman etc*) falsch; (*claim*)
erfunden
Bohemia [bəu'hiːmɪə] *n* Böhmen *nt*
Bohemian [bəu'hiːmɪən] *adj* böhmisch
▷ *n* Böhme *m*, Böhmin *f*; (*also*: **bohemian**)
Bohemien *m*
boil [bɔɪl] *vt, vi* kochen ▷ *n* (*Med*) Furunkel *nt*
or m; **to come to the ~** (*Brit*), **to come to a ~**
(*US*) zu kochen anfangen
▶ **boil down to** *vt fus* (*fig*) hinauslaufen auf +*acc*
▶ **boil over** *vi* überkochen
boiled egg [bɔɪld-] *n* gekochtes Ei *nt*
boiled potatoes *npl* Salzkartoffeln *pl*
boiler ['bɔɪlə*r*] *n* Boiler *m*
boiler suit (*Brit*) *n* Overall *m*
boiling ['bɔɪlɪŋ] *adj*: **I'm ~ (hot)** (*inf*) mir ist
fürchterlich heiß; **it's ~** es ist eine Affenhitze
(*inf*)
boiling point *n* Siedepunkt *m*
boil-in-the-bag [bɔɪlɪnðə'bæɡ] *adj* (*meals*)
Kochbeutel-
boisterous ['bɔɪstərəs] *adj* ausgelassen
bold [bəuld] *adj* (*brave*) mutig; (*pej: cheeky*)
dreist; (*pattern, colours*) kräftig
boldly ['bəuldlɪ] *adv* (*see adj*) mutig; dreist;
kräftig

boldness ['bəuldnɪs] *n* Mut *m*; (*cheekiness*)
Dreistigkeit *f*
bold type *n* Fettdruck *m*
Bolivia [bə'lɪvɪə] *n* Bolivien *nt*
Bolivian [bə'lɪvɪən] *adj* bolivisch, bolivianisch
▷ *n* Bolivier(in) *m(f)*, Bolivianer(in) *m(f)*
bollard ['bɔləd] (*Brit*) *n* Poller *m*
Bollywood ['bɔlɪwud] *n* Bollywood *nt*
bolshy ['bɔlʃɪ] (*Brit: inf*) *adj* (*stroppy*) pampig
bolster ['bəulstə*r*] *n* Nackenrolle *f*
▶ **bolster up** *vt* stützen; (*case*) untermauern
bolt [bəult] *n* Riegel *m*; (*with nut*) Schraube *f*; (*of
lightning*) Blitz(strahl) *m* ▷ *vt* (*door*) verriegeln;
(*also*: **bolt together**) verschrauben; (*food*)
hinunterschlingen ▷ *vi* (*run away: person*)
weglaufen; (: *horse*) durchgehen ▷ *adv*: **~
upright** kerzengerade; **a ~ from the blue**
(*fig*) ein Blitz *m* aus heiterem Himmel
bomb [bɔm] *n* Bombe *f* ▷ *vt* bombardieren;
(*plant bomb in or near*) einen Bombenanschlag
verüben auf +*acc*
bombard [bɔm'baːd] *vt* (*also fig*) bombardieren
bombardment [bɔm'baːdmənt] *n*
Bombardierung *f*, Bombardement *nt*
bombastic [bɔm'bæstɪk] *adj* bombastisch
bomb disposal *n*: **~ unit**
Bombenräumkommando *nt*; **~
expert** Bombenräumexperte *m*,
Bombenräumexpertin *f*
bomber ['bɔmə*r*] *n* Bomber *m*; (*terrorist*)
Bombenattentäter(in) *m(f)*
bombing ['bɔmɪŋ] *n* Bombenangriff *m*
bomb scare *n* Bombenalarm *m*
bombshell ['bɔmʃel] *n* (*fig: revelation*) Bombe *f*
bomb site *n* Trümmergrundstück *nt*
bona fide ['bəunə'faɪdɪ] *adj* echt; **~ offer**
Angebot *nt* auf Treu und Glauben
bonanza [bə'nænzə] *n* (*Econ*) Boom *m*
bond [bɔnd] *n* Band *nt*, Bindung *f*; (*Fin*)
festverzinsliches Wertpapier *nt*, Bond *m*
bondage ['bɔndɪdʒ] *n* Sklaverei *f*
bonded warehouse ['bɔndɪd] *n* Zolllager *nt*
bone [bəun] *n* Knochen *m*; (*of fish*) Gräte *f* ▷ *vt*
(*meat*) die Knochen herauslösen aus; (*fish*)
entgräten; **I've got a ~ to pick with you**
ich habe mit Ihnen (noch) ein Hühnchen zu
rupfen
bone china *n* feines Porzellan *nt*
bone-dry ['bəun'draɪ] *adj* knochentrocken
bone idle *adj* stinkfaul
bone marrow *n* Knochenmark *nt*
boner ['bəunə*r*] (*US*) *n* Schnitzer *m*
bonfire ['bɔnfaɪə*r*] *n* Feuer *nt*
bonk [bɔŋk] (*inf*) *vt, vi* (*have sex (with)*) bumsen
bonkers ['bɔŋkəz] (*Brit: inf*) *adj* (*mad*) verrückt
Bonn [bɔn] *n* Bonn *nt*
bonnet ['bɔnɪt] *n* Haube *f*; (*for baby*) Häubchen
nt; (*Brit: of car*) Motorhaube *f*
bonny ['bɔnɪ] (*Scot, Northern English*) *adj* schön,
hübsch
bonus ['bəunəs] *n* Prämie *f*; (*on wages*) Zulage
f; (*at Christmas*) Gratifikation *f*; (*fig: additional
benefit*) Plus *nt*

bony ['bəʊnɪ] *adj* knochig; (*Med*) knöchern; (*tissue*) knochenartig; (*meat*) mit viel Knochen; (*fish*) mit viel Gräten

boo [buː] *excl* buh ▷ *vt* auspfeifen, ausbuhen

boob [buːb] (*inf*) *n* (*breast*) Brust *f*; (*Brit: mistake*) Schnitzer *m*

booby prize ['buːbɪ-] *n* Scherzpreis für den schlechtesten Teilnehmer

booby trap ['buːbɪ-] *n* versteckte Bombe *f*; (*fig: joke etc*) als Schabernack versteckt angebrachte Falle

booby-trapped ['buːbɪtræpt] *adj*: **a ~ car** ein Auto *nt*, in dem eine Bombe versteckt ist

book [buk] *n* Buch *nt*; (*of stamps, tickets*) Heftchen *nt* ▷ *vt* bestellen; (*seat, room*) buchen, reservieren lassen; (*subj: traffic warden, policeman*) aufschreiben; (: *referee*) verwarnen; **books** *npl* (*Comm: accounts*) Bücher *pl*; **to keep the ~s** die Bücher führen; **by the ~** nach Vorschrift; **to throw the ~ at sb** jdn nach allen Regeln der Kunst fertig machen
▶ **book in** (*Brit*) *vi* sich eintragen
▶ **book up** *vt*: **all seats are ~ed up** es ist bis auf den letzten Platz ausverkauft; **the hotel is ~ed up** das Hotel ist ausgebucht

bookable ['bukəbl] *adj*: **all seats are ~** Karten für alle Plätze können vorbestellt werden

bookcase ['bukkeɪs] *n* Bücherregal *nt*

book ends *npl* Bücherstützen *pl*

booking ['bukɪŋ] (*Brit*) *n* Bestellung *f*; (*of seat, room*) Buchung *f*, Reservierung *f*

booking office (*Brit*) *n* (*Rail*) Fahrkartenschalter *m*; (*Theat*) Vorverkaufsstelle *f*, Vorverkaufskasse *f*

book-keeping ['buk'kiːpɪŋ] *n* Buchhaltung *f*, Buchführung *f*

booklet ['buklɪt] *n* Broschüre *f*

bookmaker ['bukmeɪkəʳ] *n* Buchmacher *m*

bookmark ['bukmɑːk] *n* Lesezeichen *nt*; (*Comput*) Bookmark *nt* ▷ *vt* (*Comput*) ein Bookmark einrichten für, bookmarken

bookseller ['bukselə'] *n* Buchhändler(in) *m(f)*

bookshelf ['bukʃɛlf] *n* Bücherbord *nt*; **bookshelves** *npl* Bücherregal *nt*

bookshop ['bukʃɔp] *n* Buchhandlung *f*

bookstall ['bukstɔːl] *n* Bücher- und Zeitungskiosk *m*

book store *n* = **bookshop**

book token *n* Buchgutschein *m*

book value *n* Buchwert *m*, Bilanzwert *m*

bookworm ['bukwəːm] *n* (*fig*) Bücherwurm *m*

boom [buːm] *n* Donnern *nt*, Dröhnen *nt*; (*in prices, population etc*) rapider Anstieg *m*; (*Econ*) Hochkonjunktur *f*; (*busy period*) Boom *m* ▷ *vi* (*guns*) donnern; (*thunder*) hallen; (*voice*) dröhnen; (*business*) florieren

boomerang ['buːməræŋ] *n* Bumerang *m* ▷ *vi* (*fig*) einen Bumerangeffekt haben

boom town *n* Goldgräberstadt *f*

boon [buːn] *n* Segen *m*

boorish ['buərɪʃ] *adj* rüpelhaft

boost [buːst] *n* Auftrieb *m* ▷ *vt* (*confidence*) stärken; (*sales, economy etc*) ankurbeln; **to give**

a ~ to sb/sb's spirits jdm Auftrieb geben

booster ['buːstəʳ] *n* (*Med*) Wiederholungsimpfung *f*; (*TV*) Zusatzgleichrichter *m*; (*Elec*) Puffersatz *m*; (*also:* **booster rocket**) Booster *m*, Startrakete *f*

booster seat *n* (*Aut*) Sitzerhöhung *f*

boot [buːt] *n* Stiefel *m*; (*ankle boot*) hoher Schuh *m*; (*Brit: of car*) Kofferraum *m* ▷ *vt* (*Comput*) laden; ... **to ~** (*in addition*) obendrein ...; **to give sb the ~** (*inf*) jdn rauswerfen *or* rausschmeißen

booth [buːð] *n* (*at fair*) Bude *f*, Stand *m*; (*telephone booth*) Zelle *f*; (*voting booth*) Kabine *f*

bootleg ['buːtlɛg] *adj* (*alcohol*) schwarzgebrannt; (*fuel*) schwarz hergestellt; (*tape etc*) schwarz mitgeschnitten

bootlegger ['buːtlɛgəʳ] *n* Bootlegger *m*, Schwarzhändler *m*

booty ['buːtɪ] *n* Beute *f*

booze [buːz] (*inf*) *n* Alkohol *m* ▷ *vi* saufen

boozer ['buːzəʳ] (*inf*) *n* (*person*) Säufer(in) *m(f)*; (*Brit: pub*) Kneipe *f*

border ['bɔːdəʳ] *n* Grenze *f*; (*for flowers*) Rabatte *f*; (*on cloth etc*) Bordüre *f* ▷ *vt* (*road*) säumen; (*another country: also:* **border on**) grenzen an +*acc*; **Borders** *n*: **the B~s** das Grenzgebiet zwischen England und Schottland
▶ **border on** *vt fus* (*fig*) grenzen an +*acc*

borderline ['bɔːdəlaɪn] *n* (*fig*): **on the ~** an der Grenze

borderline case *n* Grenzfall *m*

bore [bɔːʳ] *pt of* **bear** ▷ *vt* bohren; (*person*) langweilen ▷ *n* Langweiler *m*; (*of gun*) Kaliber *nt*; **to be ~d** sich langweilen; **he's ~d to tears** *or* **~d to death** *or* **~d stiff** er langweilt sich zu Tode

boredom ['bɔːdəm] *n* Langeweile *f*; (*boring quality*) Langweiligkeit *f*

boring ['bɔːrɪŋ] *adj* langweilig

born [bɔːn] *adj*: **to be ~** geboren werden; **I was ~ in 1960** ich bin *or* wurde 1960 geboren; **~ blind** blind geboren, von Geburt (an) blind; **a ~ comedian** ein geborener Komiker

born-again [bɔːnə'gɛn] *adj* wiedergeboren

borne [bɔːn] *pp of* **bear**

Borneo ['bɔːnɪəu] *n* Borneo *nt*

borough ['bʌrə] *n* Bezirk *m*, Stadtgemeinde *f*

borrow ['bɔrəu] *vt*: **to ~ sth** etw borgen, sich *dat* etw leihen; (*from library*) sich *dat* etw ausleihen; **may I ~ your car?** kann ich mit deinem Wagen leihen?

borrower ['bɔrəuəʳ] *n* (*of loan etc*) Kreditnehmer(in) *m(f)*

borrowing ['bɔrəuɪŋ] *n* Kreditaufnahme *f*

borstal ['bɔːstl] (*Brit*) *n* (*formerly*) Besserungsanstalt *f*

Bosnia ['bɔznɪə] *n* Bosnien *nt*

Bosnia-Herzegovina *n* Bosnien-Herzegowina *nt*

Bosnian ['bɔznɪən] *adj* bosnisch ▷ *n* Bosnier(in) *m(f)*

bosom ['buzəm] *n* Busen *m*; (*fig: of family*) Schoß *m*

bosom friend n Busenfreund(in) m(f)

boss [bɔs] n Chef(in) m(f); (leader) Boss
m ▷ vt (also: **boss around**, **boss about**)
herumkommandieren; **stop ~ing everyone
about!** hör auf mit dem ständigen
Herumkommandieren!

bossy ['bɔsɪ] adj herrisch

bosun ['bəusn] n Bootsmann m

botanical [bə'tænɪkl] adj botanisch

botanist ['bɔtənɪst] n Botaniker(in) m(f)

botany ['bɔtənɪ] n Botanik f

botch [bɔtʃ] vt (also: **botch up**) verpfuschen

both [bəuθ] adj beide ▷ pron beide; (two different
things) beides ▷ adv: ~ **A and B** sowohl A als
auch B; ~ **(of them)** (alle) beide; ~ **of us
went, we ~ went** wir gingen beide; **they
sell ~ the fabric and the finished curtains**
sie verkaufen sowohl den Stoff als auch die
fertigen Vorhänge

bother ['bɔðər] vt Sorgen machen +dat; (disturb)
stören ▷ vi (also: **bother o.s.**) sich dat Sorgen
or Gedanken machen ▷ n (trouble) Mühe f;
(nuisance) Plage f ▷ excl Mist! (inf); **don't ~
phoning** du brauchst nicht anzurufen; **I'm
sorry to ~ you** es tut mir leid, dass ich Sie
belästigen muss; **I can't be ~ed** ich habe
keine Lust; **please don't ~** bitte machen Sie
sich keine Umstände; **don't ~!** lass es!; **it is
a ~ to have to shave every morning** es ist
wirklich lästig, sich jeden Morgen rasieren zu
müssen; **it's no ~** es ist kein Problem

Botswana [bɔt'swaːnə] n Botswana nt

bottle ['bɔtl] n Flasche f; (Brit: inf: courage)
Mumm m ▷ vt in Flaschen abfüllen;
(fruit) einmachen; **a ~ of wine/milk** eine
Flasche Wein/Milch; **wine/milk ~** Wein-/
Milchflasche f
▶ **bottle up** vt in sich dat aufstauen

bottle bank n Altglascontainer m

bottle-fed ['bɔtlfɛd] adj mit der Flasche
ernährt

bottleneck ['bɔtlnɛk] n (also fig) Engpass m

bottle-opener ['bɔtləupnər] n Flaschenöffner
m

bottom ['bɔtəm] n Boden m; (buttocks) Hintern
m; (of page, list) Ende nt; (of chair) Sitz m; (of
mountain, tree) Fuß m ▷ adj (lower) untere(r, s);
(last) unterste(r, s); **at the ~ of** unten an/in
+dat; **at the ~ of the page/list** unten auf der
Seite/Liste; **to be at the ~ of the class** der/
die Letzte in der Klasse sein; **to get to the
~ of sth** (fig) einer Sache dat auf den Grund
kommen

bottomless ['bɔtəmlɪs] adj (fig) unerschöpflich

bottom line n (of accounts) Saldo m; (fig): **that's
the ~ (of it)** (what it amounts to) darauf läuft es
im Endeffekt hinaus

botulism ['bɔtjulɪzəm] n Botulismus m,
Nahrungsmittelvergiftung f

bough [bau] n Ast m

bought [bɔːt] pt, pp of **buy**

boulder ['bəuldər] n Felsblock m

boulevard ['buːləvaːd] n Boulevard m

bounce [bauns] vi (auf)springen; (cheque)
platzen ▷ vt (ball) (auf)springen lassen; (signal)
reflektieren ▷ n Aufprall m; **he's got plenty
of ~** (fig) er hat viel Schwung

bouncer ['baunsər] (inf) n Rausschmeißer
m

bouncy castle ['baunsɪ-] n Hüpfburg f

bound [baund] pt, pp of **bind** ▷ n Sprung m; (gen
pl: limit) Grenze f ▷ vi springen ▷ vt begrenzen
▷ adj: ~ **by** gebunden durch; **to be ~ to do sth**
(obliged) verpflichtet sein, etw zu tun; (very
likely) etw bestimmt tun; **he's ~ to fail** es kann
ihm ja gar nicht gelingen; ~ **for** nach; **the
area is out of ~s** das Betreten des Gebiets ist
verboten

boundary ['baundrɪ] n Grenze f

boundless ['baundlɪs] adj grenzenlos

bountiful ['bauntɪful] adj großzügig; (God)
gütig; (supply) reichlich

bounty ['bauntɪ] n Freigebigkeit f; (reward)
Kopfgeld nt

bounty hunter n Kopfgeldjäger m

bouquet ['bukeɪ] n (Blumen)strauß m; (of wine)
Bukett nt, Blume f

bourbon ['buəbən] (US) n (also: **bourbon
whiskey**) Bourbon m

bourgeois ['buəʒwaː] adj bürgerlich, spießig
(pej) ▷ n Bürger(in) m(f), Bourgeois m

bout [baut] n Anfall m; (Boxing etc) Kampf m

boutique [buː'tiːk] n Boutique f

bow[1] [bəu] n Schleife f; (weapon, Mus) Bogen m

bow[2] [bau] n Verbeugung f; (Naut: also:
bows) Bug m ▷ vi sich verbeugen; (yield): **to
~ to** or **before** sich beugen +dat; **to ~ to the
inevitable** sich in das Unvermeidliche
fügen

bowels ['bauəlz] npl Darm m; (of the earth etc)
Innere nt

bowl [bəul] n Schüssel f; (shallower) Schale
f; (ball) Kugel f; (of pipe) Kopf m; (US: stadium)
Stadion nt ▷ vi werfen
▶ **bowl over** vt (fig) überwältigen

bow-legged ['bəu'lɛgɪd] adj o-beinig

bowler ['bəulər] n Werfer(in) m(f); (Brit: also:
bowler hat) Melone f

bowling ['bəulɪŋ] n Kegeln nt; (on grass)
Bowling nt

bowling alley n Kegelbahn f

bowling green n Bowlingrasen m

bowls [bəulz] n Bowling nt

bow tie [bəu-] n Fliege f

box [bɔks] n Schachtel f; (cardboard box) Karton
m; (crate) Kiste f; (Theat) Loge f; (Brit: Aut) gelb
schraffierter Kreuzungsbereich; (on form) Feld nt
▷ vt (in eine Schachtel etc) verpacken; (fighter)
boxen ▷ vi boxen; **to ~ sb's ears** jdm eine
Ohrfeige geben
▶ **box in** vt einkeilen
▶ **box off** vt abtrennen

boxer ['bɔksər] n (person, dog) Boxer m

box file n Sammelordner m

boxing ['bɔksɪŋ] n Boxen nt

Boxing Day (Brit) n zweiter Weihnachts(feier)

tag *m*; *siehe Info-Artikel*

● **BOXING DAY**

Boxing Day ist ein Feiertag in
Großbritannien. Wenn Weihnachten auf
ein Wochenende fällt, wird der Feiertag
am nächsten darauffolgenden Wochentag
nachgeholt. Der Name geht auf einen
alten Brauch zurück; früher erhielten
Händler und Lieferanten an diesem Tag
ein Geschenk, die sogenannte Christmas
Box.

boxing gloves *npl* Boxhandschuhe *pl*
boxing ring *n* Boxring *m*
box number *n* Chiffre *f*
box office *n* Kasse *f*
boxroom ['bɔksrum] *n* Abstellraum *m*
boy [bɔɪ] *n* Junge *m*
boycott ['bɔɪkɔt] *n* Boykott *m* ▷ *vt* boykottieren
boyfriend ['bɔɪfrɛnd] *n* Freund *m*
boyish ['bɔɪɪʃ] *adj* jungenhaft; (*woman*)
knabenhaft
boy scout *n* Pfadfinder *m*
bp *abbr* = **bishop**
bra [brɑː] *n* BH *m*
brace [breɪs] *n* (*on teeth*) (Zahn)klammer
f, (Zahn)spange *f*; (*tool*) (Hand)bohrer *m*;
(*also:* **brace bracket**) geschweifte Klammer *f*
▷ *vt* spannen; **braces** *npl* (*Brit*) Hosenträger *pl*;
to ~ o.s. (*for weight*) sich stützen; (*for shock*) sich
innerlich vorbereiten
bracelet ['breɪslɪt] *n* Armband *nt*
bracing ['breɪsɪŋ] *adj* belebend
bracken ['brækən] *n* Farn *m*
bracket ['brækɪt] *n* Träger *m*; (*group, range*)
Gruppe *f*; (*also:* **round bracket**) (runde)
Klammer *f*; (*also:* **brace bracket**) geschweifte
Klammer *f*; (*also:* **square bracket**) eckige
Klammer *f* ▷ *vt* (*also:* **bracket together**)
zusammenfassen; (*word, phrase*) einklammern;
income ~ Einkommensgruppe *f*; **in ~s** in
Klammern
brackish ['brækɪʃ] *adj* brackig
brag [bræg] *vi* prahlen
braid [breɪd] *n* Borte *f*; (*of hair*) Zopf *m*
Braille [breɪl] *n* Blindenschrift *f*, Brailleschrift *f*
brain [breɪn] *n* Gehirn *nt*; **brains** *npl* (Culin)
Hirn *nt*; (*intelligence*) Intelligenz *f*; **he's got ~s**
er hat Köpfchen *or* Grips
brainchild ['breɪntʃaɪld] *n* Geistesprodukt *nt*
braindead ['breɪndɛd] *adj* hirntot; (*inf*) hirnlos
brain drain *n* Abwanderung *f* von
Wissenschaftlern, Braindrain *m*
brainless ['breɪnlɪs] *adj* dumm
brainstorm ['breɪnstɔːm] *n* (*fig*) Anfall *m*
geistiger Umnachtung; (*US: brain wave*)
Geistesblitz *m*
brainwash ['breɪnwɔʃ] *vt* einer Gehirnwäsche
dat unterziehen
brain wave *n* Geistesblitz *m*
brainy ['breɪnɪ] *adj* intelligent

braise [breɪz] *vt* schmoren
brake [breɪk] *n* Bremse *f* ▷ *vi* bremsen
brake fluid *n* Bremsflüssigkeit *f*
brake light *n* Bremslicht *nt*
brake pedal *n* Bremspedal *nt*
bramble ['bræmbl] *n* Brombeerstrauch *m*;
(*fruit*) Brombeere *f*
bran [bræn] *n* Kleie *f*
branch [brɑːntʃ] *n* Ast *m*; (*of family, organization*)
Zweig *m*; (Comm) Filiale *f*, Zweigstelle *f*; (: *bank,
company etc*) Geschäftsstelle *f* ▷ *vi* sich gabeln
▶ **branch out** *vi* (*fig*): **to ~ out into** seinen
(Geschäfts)bereich erweitern auf +*acc*
branch line *n* (Rail) Zweiglinie *f*, Nebenlinie *f*
branch manager *n* Zweigstellenleiter(in) *m(f)*,
Filialleiter(in) *m(f)*
brand [brænd] *n* (*also:* **brand name**) Marke *f*;
(*fig: type*) Art *f* ▷ *vt* mit einem Brandzeichen
kennzeichnen; (*fig: pej*): **to ~ sb a communist**
jdn als Kommunist brandmarken
brandish ['brændɪʃ] *vt* schwingen
brand name *n* Markenname *m*
brand-new ['brænd'njuː] *adj* nagelneu,
brandneu
brandy ['brændɪ] *n* Weinbrand *m*
brash [bræʃ] *adj* dreist
Brasilia [brə'zɪlɪə] *n* Brasilia *nt*
brass [brɑːs] *n* Messing *nt*; **the ~** (*Mus*) die
Blechbläser *pl*
brass band *n* Blaskapelle *f*
brassière ['bræsɪəʳ] *n* Büstenhalter *m*
brass tacks *npl*: **to get down to ~** zur Sache
kommen
brassy ['brɑːsɪ] *adj* (*colour*) messingfarben;
(*sound*) blechern; (*appearance, behaviour*) auffällig
brat [bræt] (*pej*) *n* Balg *m or nt*, Gör *nt*
bravado [brə'vɑːdəʊ] *n* Draufgängertum *nt*
brave [breɪv] *adj* mutig; (*attempt, smile*) tapfer
▷ *n* (indianischer) Krieger *m* ▷ *vt* trotzen +*dat*
bravely ['breɪvlɪ] *adv* (*see adj*) mutig; tapfer
bravery ['breɪvərɪ] *n* (*see adj*) Mut *m*; Tapferkeit *f*
bravo [brɑː'vəʊ] *excl* bravo
brawl [brɔːl] *n* Schlägerei *f* ▷ *vi* sich schlagen
brawn [brɔːn] *n* Muskeln *pl*; (*meat*)
Schweinskopfsülze *f*
brawny ['brɔːnɪ] *adj* muskulös, kräftig
bray [breɪ] *vi* schreien ▷ *n* (Esels)schrei *m*
brazen ['breɪzn] *adj* unverschämt, dreist; (*lie*)
schamlos ▷ *vt*: **to ~ it out** durchhalten
brazier ['breɪzɪəʳ] *n* (*container*) Kohlenbecken *nt*
Brazil [brə'zɪl] *n* Brasilien *nt*
Brazilian [brə'zɪljən] *adj* brasilianisch ▷ *n*
Brasilianer(in) *m(f)*
Brazil nut *n* Paranuss *f*
breach [briːtʃ] *vt* (*defence*) durchbrechen;
(*wall*) eine Bresche schlagen in +*acc* ▷ *n* (*gap*)
Bresche *f*; (*estrangement*) Bruch *m*; (*breaking*): **~
of contract** Vertragsbruch *m*; **~ of the
peace** öffentliche Ruhestörung *f*; **~ of trust**
Vertrauensbruch *m*
bread [brɛd] *n* Brot *nt*; (*inf: money*) Moos *nt*, Kies
m; **to earn one's daily ~** sein Brot verdienen;
to know which side one's ~ is buttered (on)

wissen, wo etwas zu holen ist
bread and butter n Butterbrot nt; (fig)
Broterwerb m
bread bin (Brit) n Brotkasten m
breadboard ['brɛdbɔːd] n Brot(schneide)brett
nt; (Comput) Leiterplatte f
bread box (US) n Brotkasten m
breadcrumbs ['brɛdkrʌmz] npl Brotkrumen pl;
(Culin) Paniermehl nt
breadline ['brɛdlaɪn] n: **to be on the ~** nur das
Allernotwendigste zum Leben haben
breadth [brɛtθ] n (also fig) Breite f
breadwinner ['brɛdwɪnər] n Ernährer(in) m(f)
break [breɪk] (pt **broke**, pp **broken**) vt
zerbrechen; (leg, arm) sich dat brechen; (promise,
record) brechen; (law) verstoßen gegen ▷ vi
zerbrechen, kaputtgehen; (storm) losbrechen;
(weather) umschlagen; (dawn) anbrechen;
(story, news) bekannt werden ▷ n Pause f; (gap)
Lücke f; (fracture) Bruch m; (chance) Chance
f, Gelegenheit f; (holiday) Urlaub m; **to ~ the
news to sb** es jdm sagen; **to ~ even** seine (Un)
kosten decken; **to ~ with sb** mit jdm brechen,
sich von jdm trennen; **to ~ free** or **loose** sich
losreißen; **to take a ~** (eine) Pause machen;
(holiday) Urlaub machen; **without a ~** ohne
Unterbrechung or Pause, ununterbrochen; **a
lucky ~** ein Durchbruch m
▶ **break down** vt (figures, data) aufschlüsseln;
(door etc) einrennen ▷ vi (car) eine Panne
haben; (machine) kaputtgehen; (person,
resistance) zusammenbrechen; (talks) scheitern
▶ **break in** vt (horse) zureiten ▷ vi einbrechen;
(interrupt) unterbrechen
▶ **break into** vt fus einbrechen in +acc
▶ **break off** vi abbrechen ▷ vt (talks) abbrechen;
(engagement) lösen
▶ **break open** vt, vi aufbrechen
▶ **break out** vi ausbrechen; **to ~ out in
spots/a rash** Pickel/einen Ausschlag
bekommen
▶ **break through** vi: **the sun broke through**
die Sonne kam durch ▷ vt fus durchbrechen
▶ **break up** vi (ship) zerbersten; (crowd, meeting,
partnership) sich auflösen; (marriage) scheitern;
(friends) sich trennen; (Scol) in die Ferien
gehen ▷ vt zerbrechen; (journey, fight etc)
unterbrechen; (meeting) auflösen; (marriage)
zerstören
breakable ['breɪkəbl] adj zerbrechlich ▷ n: **~s**
zerbrechliche Ware f
breakage ['breɪkɪdʒ] n Bruch m; **to pay for ~s**
für zerbrochene Ware or für Bruch bezahlen
breakaway ['breɪkəweɪ] adj (group etc) Splitter-
break dancing n Breakdance m
breakdown ['breɪkdaʊn] n (Aut) Panne
f; (in communications) Zusammenbruch m;
(of marriage) Scheitern nt; (also: **nervous
breakdown**) (Nerven)zusammenbruch m; (of
statistics) Aufschlüsselung f
breakdown service (Brit) n Pannendienst m
breakdown van (Brit) n Abschleppwagen m
breaker ['breɪkər] n (wave) Brecher m

breakeven ['breɪk'iːvn] cpd: **~ chart**
Gewinnschwellendiagramm nt; **~ point**
Gewinnschwelle f
breakfast ['brɛkfəst] n Frühstück nt ▷ vi
frühstücken
breakfast cereal n Getreideflocken pl
break-in ['breɪkɪn] n Einbruch m
breaking and entering ['breɪkɪŋən'ɛntrɪŋ] n
(Law) Einbruch m
breaking point ['breɪkɪŋ-] n (fig): **to reach ~**
völlig am Ende sein
breakthrough ['breɪkθruː] n Durchbruch m
break-up ['breɪkʌp] n (of partnership) Auflösung
f; (of marriage) Scheitern nt
break-up value n (Comm) Liquidationswert m
breakwater ['breɪkwɔːtər] n Wellenbrecher m
breast [brɛst] n Brust f; (of meat) Brust f,
Bruststück nt
breast-feed ['brɛstfiːd] (irreg: like **feed**) vt, vi
stillen
breast pocket n Brusttasche f
breaststroke ['brɛststrəʊk] n
Brustschwimmen nt
breath [brɛθ] n Atem m; (a breath) Atemzug
m; **to go out for a ~ of air** an die frische Luft
gehen, frische Luft schnappen gehen; **out of
~** außer Atem, atemlos; **to get one's ~ back**
wieder zu Atem kommen
breathalyse ['brɛθəlaɪz] vt blasen lassen (inf)
Breathalyser® ['brɛθəlaɪzər] n Promillemesser
m
breathe [briːð] vt, vi atmen; **I won't ~ a word
about it** ich werde kein Sterbenswörtchen
darüber sagen
▶ **breathe in** vt, vi einatmen
▶ **breathe out** vt, vi ausatmen
breather ['briːðər] n Atempause f,
Verschnaufpause f
breathing ['briːðɪŋ] n Atmung f
breathing space n (fig) Atempause f,
Ruhepause f
breathless ['brɛθlɪs] adj atemlos, außer Atem;
(Med) an Atemnot leidend; **I was ~ with
excitement** die Aufregung verschlug mir den
Atem
breathtaking ['brɛθteɪkɪŋ] adj atemberaubend
breath test n Atemalkoholtest m
bred [brɛd] pt, pp of **breed**
-bred suff: **well/ill-~** gut/schlecht erzogen
breed [briːd] (pt, pp **bred**) vt züchten; (fig: give rise
to) erzeugen; (: hate, suspicion) hervorrufen ▷ vi
Junge pl haben ▷ n Rasse f; (type, class) Art f
breeder ['briːdər] n Züchter(in) m(f);
(also: **breeder reactor**) Brutreaktor m, Brüter m
breeding ['briːdɪŋ] n Erziehung f
breeding ground n (also fig) Brutstätte f
breeze [briːz] n Brise f
breeze block (Brit) n Ytong® m
breezy ['briːzɪ] adj (manner, tone) munter;
(weather) windig
Breton ['brɛtən] adj bretonisch ▷ n Bretone m,
Bretonin f
brevity ['brɛvɪtɪ] n Kürze f

brew [bru:] vt (tea) aufbrühen, kochen; (beer) brauen ▷ vi (tea) ziehen; (beer) gären; (storm: fig) sich zusammenbrauen

brewer ['bru:ə^r] n Brauer m

brewery ['bru:ərɪ] n Brauerei f

briar ['braɪə^r] n Dornbusch m; (wild rose) wilde Rose f

bribe [braɪb] n Bestechungsgeld nt ▷ vt bestechen; **to ~ sb to do sth** jdn bestechen, damit er etw tut

bribery ['braɪbərɪ] n Bestechung f

bric-a-brac ['brɪkəbræk] n Nippes pl, Nippsachen pl

brick [brɪk] n Ziegelstein m, Backstein m; (of ice cream) Block m

bricklayer ['brɪkleɪə^r] n Maurer(in) m(f)

brickwork ['brɪkwə:k] n Mauerwerk nt

bridal ['braɪdl] adj (gown, veil etc) Braut-

bride [braɪd] n Braut f

bridegroom ['braɪdgru:m] n Bräutigam m

bridesmaid ['braɪdzmeɪd] n Brautjungfer f

bridge [brɪdʒ] n Brücke f; (Naut) (Kommando) brücke f; (of nose) Sattel m; (Cards) Bridge nt ▷ vt (river) eine Brücke schlagen or bauen über +acc; (fig) überbrücken

bridging loan ['brɪdʒɪŋ-] (Brit) n Überbrückungskredit m

bridle ['braɪdl] n Zaum m ▷ vt aufzäumen ▷ vi: **to ~ (at)** sich entrüstet wehren (gegen)

bridle path n Reitweg m

brief [bri:f] adj kurz ▷ n (Law) Auftrag m; (task) Aufgabe f ▷ vt instruieren; (Mil etc): **to ~ sb (about)** jdn instruieren (über +acc); **briefs** npl Slip m; **in ~** ... kurz (gesagt) ...

briefcase ['bri:fkeɪs] n Aktentasche f

briefing ['bri:fɪŋ] n Briefing nt, Lagebesprechung f

briefly ['bri:flɪ] adv kurz; **to glimpse sth ~** einen flüchtigen Blick von etw erhaschen

Brig. abbr = **brigadier**

brigade [brɪ'geɪd] n Brigade f

brigadier [brɪgə'dɪə^r] n Brigadegeneral m

bright [braɪt] adj (light, room) hell; (weather) heiter; (clever) intelligent; (lively) heiter, fröhlich; (colour) leuchtend; (outlook, future) glänzend; **to look on the ~ side** die Dinge von der positiven Seite betrachten

brighten ['braɪtn] (also: **brighten up**) vt aufheitern; (event) beleben ▷ vi (weather, face) sich aufheitern; (person) fröhlicher werden; (prospects) sich verbessern

brightly ['braɪtlɪ] adv (shine) hell; (smile) fröhlich; (talk) heiter

brill [brɪl] (Brit: inf) adj toll

brilliance ['brɪljəns] n Strahlen nt; (of person) Genialität f, Brillanz f; (of talent, skill) Großartigkeit f

brilliant ['brɪljənt] adj strahlend; (person, idea) genial, brillant; (career) großartig; (inf: holiday etc) fantastisch

brilliantly ['brɪljəntlɪ] adv (see adj) strahlend; genial, brillant; großartig; fantastisch

brim [brɪm] n Rand m; (of hat) Krempe f

brimful ['brɪm'ful] adj: ~ **(of)** randvoll (mit); (fig) voll (von)

brine [braɪn] n Lake f

bring [brɪŋ] (pt, pp **brought**) vt bringen; (with you) mitbringen; **to ~ sth to an end** etw zu Ende bringen; **I can't ~ myself to fire him** ich kann es nicht über mich bringen, ihn zu entlassen

▶ **bring about** vt herbeiführen

▶ **bring back** vt (restore) wiedereinführen; (return) zurückbringen

▶ **bring down** vt (government) zu Fall bringen; (plane) herunterholen; (price) senken

▶ **bring forward** vt (meeting) vorverlegen; (proposal) vorbringen; (Bookkeeping) übertragen

▶ **bring in** vt (money) (ein)bringen; (include) einbeziehen; (person) einschalten; (legislation) einbringen; (verdict) fällen

▶ **bring off** vt (plan) durchführen; (deal) zustande bringen

▶ **bring out** vt herausholen; (meaning, book, album) herausbringen

▶ **bring round** vt (after faint) wieder zu Bewusstsein bringen

▶ **bring up** vt heraufbringen; (educate) erziehen; (question, subject) zur Sprache bringen; (food) erbrechen

bring-and-buy sale n Basar m (wo mitgebrachte Sachen verkauft werden)

brink [brɪŋk] n Rand m; **on the ~ of doing sth** nahe daran, etw zu tun; **she was on the ~ of tears** sie war den Tränen nahe

brisk [brɪsk] adj (abrupt: person, tone) forsch; (pace) flott; (trade) lebhaft, rege; **to go for a ~ walk** einen ordentlichen Spaziergang machen; **business is ~** das Geschäft ist rege

bristle ['brɪsl] n Borste f; (of beard) Stoppel f ▷ vi zornig werden; **bristling with** strotzend von

bristly ['brɪslɪ] adj borstig; (chin) stoppelig

Brit [brɪt] (inf) n (= British person) Brite m, Britin f

Britain ['brɪtən] n (also: **Great Britain**) Großbritannien nt

British ['brɪtɪʃ] adj britisch ▷ npl: **the ~** die Briten pl

British Isles npl: **the ~** die Britischen Inseln

British Rail n britische Eisenbahngesellschaft

British Summer Time n britische Sommerzeit f

Briton ['brɪtən] n Brite m, Britin f

Brittany ['brɪtənɪ] n die Bretagne

brittle ['brɪtl] adj spröde; (glass) zerbrechlich; (bones) schwach

broach [brəʊtʃ] vt (subject) anschneiden

broad [brɔ:d] adj breit; (general) allgemein; (accent) stark ▷ n (US: inf) Frau f; **in ~ daylight** am helllichten Tag; ~ **hint** deutlicher Wink m

broadband ['brɔ:dbænd] (Comput) adj Breitband- ▷ n Breitband nt

broad bean n dicke Bohne f, Saubohne f

broadcast ['brɔ:dka:st] (pt, pp ~) n Sendung f ▷ vt, vi senden

broadcaster ['brɔ:dka:stə^r] n (Radio, TV) Rundfunk-/Fernsehpersönlichkeit f

broadcasting ['brɔːdkɑːstɪŋ] n (Radio) Rundfunk m; (TV) Fernsehen nt
broadcasting station n (Radio) Rundfunkstation f; (TV) Fernsehstation f
broaden ['brɔːdn] vt erweitern ▷ vi breiter werden, sich verbreitern; **to ~ one's mind** seinen Horizont erweitern
broadly ['brɔːdlɪ] adv (in general terms) in großen Zügen; **~ speaking** allgemein or generell gesagt
broad-minded ['brɔːd'maɪndɪd] adj tolerant
broadsheet ['brɔːdʃiːt] n (newspaper) großformatige Zeitung
broccoli ['brɔkəlɪ] n Brokkoli pl, Spargelkohl m
brochure ['brəʊʃjuəʳ] n Broschüre f
brogue [brəʊg] n Akzent m; (shoe) fester Schuh m
broil [brɔɪl] (US) vt grillen
broiler ['brɔɪləʳ] n Brathähnchen nt
broke [brəʊk] pt of **break** ▷ adj (inf) pleite; **to go ~** pleitegehen
broken ['brəʊkn] pp of **break** ▷ adj zerbrochen; (machine: also: **broken down**) kaputt; (promise, vow) gebrochen; **a ~ leg** ein gebrochenes Bein; **a ~ marriage** eine gescheiterte Ehe; **a ~ home** zerrüttete Familienverhältnisse pl; **in ~ English/German** in gebrochenem Englisch/Deutsch
broken-down ['brəʊkn'daun] adj kaputt; (house) baufällig
brokenhearted [brəʊkn'hɑːtɪd] adj untröstlich
broker ['brəʊkəʳ] n Makler(in) m(f)
brokerage ['brəʊkrɪdʒ] n (commission) Maklergebühr f; (business) Maklergeschäft nt
brolly ['brɔlɪ] (Brit: inf) n (Regen)schirm m
bronchitis [brɔŋ'kaɪtɪs] n Bronchitis f
bronze [brɔnz] n Bronze f
bronzed [brɔnzd] adj braun, (sonnen)gebräunt
brooch [brəʊtʃ] n Brosche f
brood [bruːd] n Brut f ▷ vi (hen) brüten; (person) grübeln
▶ **brood on** vt fus nachgrübeln über +acc
▶ **brood over** vt fus = **brood on**
broody ['bruːdɪ] adj (person) grüblerisch; (hen) brütig
brook [bruk] n Bach m
broom [brum] n Besen m; (Bot) Ginster m
broomstick ['brumstɪk] n Besenstiel m
bros., Bros. abbr (Comm: = brothers) Gebr.
broth [brɔθ] n Suppe f, Fleischbrühe f
brothel ['brɔθl] n Bordell nt
brother ['brʌðəʳ] n Bruder m; (in trade union, society etc) Kollege m
brotherhood ['brʌðəhud] n Brüderlichkeit f
brother-in-law ['brʌðərɪn'lɔː] n Schwager m
brotherly ['brʌðəlɪ] adj brüderlich
brought [brɔːt] pt, pp of **bring**
brought forward adj (Comm) vorgetragen
brow [brau] n Stirn f; (eyebrow) (Augen)braue f; (of hill) (Berg)kuppe f
browbeat ['braubiːt] vt: **to ~ sb (into doing sth)** jdn (so) unter Druck setzen(, dass er etw tut)

brown [braun] adj braun ▷ n Braun nt ▷ vt (Culin) (an)bräunen; **to go ~** braun werden
brown bread n Graubrot nt, Mischbrot nt
Brownie ['braunɪ] n (also: **Brownie Guide**) Wichtel m
brownie ['braunɪ] (US) n kleiner Schokoladenkuchen
brown paper n Packpapier nt
brown rice n Naturreis m
brown sugar n brauner Zucker m
browse [brauz] vi (in shop) sich umsehen; (animal) weiden; (: deer) äsen ▷ vti (Comput) browsen ▷ n: **to have a ~ (around)** sich umsehen; **to ~ through a book** in einem Buch schmökern
browser ['brauzəʳ] n (Comput) Browser m
bruise [bruːz] n blauer Fleck m, Bluterguss m; (on fruit) Druckstelle f ▷ vt (arm, leg etc) sich dat stoßen; (person) einen blauen Fleck schlagen; (fruit) beschädigen ▷ vi (fruit) eine Druckstelle bekommen; **to ~ one's arm** sich dat den Arm stoßen, sich dat einen blauen Fleck am Arm holen
bruising ['bruːzɪŋ] adj (experience, encounter) schmerzhaft ▷ n Quetschung f
Brum [brʌm] (Brit: inf) n abbr (= Birmingham)
Brummie ['brʌmɪ] (inf) n aus Birmingham stammende oder dort wohnhafte Person, Birminghamer(in) m(f)
brunch [brʌntʃ] n Brunch m
brunette [bruː'net] n Brünette f
brunt [brʌnt] n: **to bear the ~ of** die volle Wucht +gen tragen
brush [brʌʃ] n Bürste f; (for painting, shaving etc) Pinsel m; (quarrel) Auseinandersetzung f ▷ vt fegen; (groom) bürsten; (teeth) putzen; (also: **brush against**) streifen; **to have a ~ with sb** (verbally) sich mit jdm streiten; (physically) mit jdm aneinandergeraten; **to have a ~ with the police** mit der Polizei aneinandergeraten
▶ **brush aside** vt abtun
▶ **brush past** vt streifen
▶ **brush up** vt auffrischen
brushed [brʌʃt] adj (steel, chrome etc) gebürstet; (denim etc) aufgeraut; **~ nylon** Nylonvelours m
brushoff ['brʌʃɔf] (inf) n: **to give sb the ~** jdm eine Abfuhr erteilen
brushwood ['brʌʃwud] n Reisig nt
brusque [bruːsk] adj brüsk; (tone) schroff
Brussels ['brʌslz] n Brüssel nt
Brussels sprouts npl Rosenkohl m
brutal ['bruːtl] adj brutal
brutality [bruː'tælɪtɪ] n Brutalität f
brutalize ['bruːtəlaɪz] vt brutalisieren; (ill-treat) brutal behandeln
brute [bruːt] n brutaler Kerl m; (animal) Tier nt ▷ adj: **by ~ force** mit roher Gewalt
brutish ['bruːtɪʃ] adj tierisch
BS (US) n abbr (= Bachelor of Science) akademischer Grad für Naturwissenschaftler
BSA n abbr (= Boy Scouts of America) amerikanische Pfadfinderorganisation

BSc abbr (= Bachelor of Science) akademischer Grad für Naturwissenschaftler

BSE n abbr (= bovine spongiform encephalopathy) BSE f

BSI n abbr (= British Standards Institution) britischer Normenausschuss

BST abbr = **British Summer Time**

Bt (Brit) abbr = **baronet**

btu n abbr (= British thermal unit) britische Wärmeeinheit

bubble ['bʌbl] n Blase f ▷ vi sprudeln; (sparkle) perlen; (fig: person) übersprudeln

bubble bath n Schaumbad nt

bubble gum n Bubblegum m

bubble-jet printer n Bubblejetdrucker m

bubble pack n (Klar)sichtpackung f

bubbly ['bʌblɪ] adj (person) lebendig; (liquid) sprudelnd ▷ n (inf: champagne) Schampus m

Bucharest [buːkəˈrest] n Bukarest nt

buck [bʌk] n (rabbit) Rammler m; (deer) Bock m; (US: inf) Dollar m ▷ vi bocken; **to pass the ~** die Verantwortung abschieben; **to pass the ~ to sb** jdm die Verantwortung zuschieben
▶ **buck up** vi (cheer up) aufleben ▷ vt: **to ~ one's ideas up** sich zusammenreißen

bucket ['bʌkɪt] n Eimer m ▷ vi (Brit: inf): **the rain is ~ing (down)** es gießt or schüttet (wie aus Kübeln)

○ **BUCKINGHAM PALACE**
○
○ Buckingham Palace ist die offizielle
○ Londoner Residenz der britischen
○ Monarchen und liegt am St James Park.
○ Der Palast wurde 1703 für den Herzog
○ von Buckingham erbaut, 1762 von Georg
○ III. gekauft, zwischen 1821 und 1836 von
○ John Nash umgebaut und Anfang des 20.
○ Jahrhunderts teilweise neu gestaltet. Teile
○ des Buckingham Palace sind heute der
○ Öffentlichkeit zugänglich.

buckle ['bʌkl] n Schnalle f ▷ vt zuschnallen; (wheel) verbiegen ▷ vi sich verbiegen
▶ **buckle down** vi sich dahinter klemmen; **to ~ down to sth** sich hinter etw acc klemmen

Bucks [bʌks] (Brit) abbr (Post) = Buckinghamshire

bud [bʌd] n Knospe f ▷ vi knospen, Knospen treiben

Budapest [bjuːdəˈpest] n Budapest nt

Buddha ['budə] n Buddha m

Buddhism ['budɪzəm] n Buddhismus m

Buddhist ['budɪst] adj buddhistisch ▷ n Buddhist(in) m(f)

budding ['bʌdɪŋ] adj angehend

buddy ['bʌdɪ] (US) n Kumpel m

budge [bʌdʒ] vt (von der Stelle) bewegen; (fig) zum Nachgeben bewegen ▷ vi sich von der Stelle rühren; (fig) nachgeben

budgerigar ['bʌdʒərɪɡɑːʳ] n Wellensittich m

budget ['bʌdʒɪt] n Budget nt, Etat m, Haushalt m ▷ vi Haus halten, haushalten, wirtschaften; **I'm on a tight ~** ich habe nicht viel Geld zur Verfügung; **she works out her ~ every**

month sie macht (sich dat) jeden Monat einen Haushaltsplan; **to ~ for sth** etw kostenmäßig einplanen

budgie ['bʌdʒɪ] n = **budgerigar**

Buenos Aires ['bweɪnɔsˈaɪrɪz] n Buenos Aires nt

buff [bʌf] adj gelbbraun ▷ n (inf) Fan m

buffalo ['bʌfələu] (pl ~ or **buffaloes**) n (Brit) Büffel m; (US) Bison m

buffer ['bʌfəʳ] n Puffer m, (Comput) Zwischenspeicher m, Pufferspeicher m; (Rail) Prellbock m; (fig) Polster nt ▷ vi (Comput) zwischenspeichern

buffering ['bʌfərɪŋ] n (Comput) Pufferung f

buffer state n Pufferstaat m

buffer zone n Pufferzone f

buffet¹ ['bufeɪ] (Brit) n Büfett nt, Bahnhofsrestaurant nt; (food) kaltes Buffet nt

buffet² ['bʌfɪt] vt (subj: sea) hin und her werfen; (: wind) schütteln

buffet car (Brit) n Speisewagen m

buffet lunch n Buffet nt

buffoon [bəˈfuːn] n Clown m

bug [bʌg] n (esp US) Insekt nt; (Comput: of program) Programmfehler m; (: of equipment) Fehler m; (fig: germ) Bazillus m; (hidden microphone) Wanze f ▷ vt (inf) nerven; (telephone etc) abhören; (room) verwanzen; **I've got the travel ~** (fig) mich hat die Reiselust gepackt

bugbear ['bʌgbɛəʳ] n Schreckgespenst nt

bugger ['bʌgəʳ] (inf!) n Scheißkerl m, Arschloch nt ▷ vb: **~ off!** hau ab!; **~ (it)!** Scheiße!

buggy ['bʌgɪ] n (for baby) Sportwagen m

bugle ['bjuːgl] n Bügelhorn nt

build [bɪld] n (pt, pp **built**) n Körperbau m ▷ vt bauen
▶ **build on** vt fus (fig) aufbauen auf +dat
▶ **build up** vt aufbauen; (production) steigern; (morale) stärken; (stocks) anlegen; **don't ~ your hopes up too soon** mach dir nicht zu früh Hoffnungen

builder ['bɪldəʳ] n Bauunternehmer m

building ['bɪldɪŋ] n (industry) Bauindustrie f; (construction) Bau m; (structure) Gebäude nt, Bau

building contractor n Bauunternehmer m

building industry n Bauindustrie f

building site n Baustelle f

building society (Brit) n Bausparkasse f

building trade n Baubranche f or -gewerbe nt

build-up ['bɪldʌp] n Ansammlung f; (publicity): **to give sb/sth a good ~** jdn/etw ganz groß herausbringen

built [bɪlt] pt, pp of **build** ▷ adj: **~-in** eingebaut, Einbau-; (safeguards) eingebaut; **well-~** gut gebaut

built-up area ['bɪltʌp-] n bebautes Gebiet nt

bulb [bʌlb] n (Blumen)zwiebel f; (Elec) (Glüh) birne f

bulbous ['bʌlbəs] adj knollig

Bulgaria [bʌlˈgeərɪə] n Bulgarien nt

Bulgarian [bʌlˈgeərɪən] adj bulgarisch ▷ n Bulgare m, Bulgarin f; (Ling) Bulgarisch nt

bulge [bʌldʒ] n Wölbung f; (in birth rate, sales) Zunahme f ▷ vi (pocket) prall gefüllt sein;

(cheeks) voll sein; *(file)* (zum Bersten) voll sein; **to be bulging with** prall gefüllt sein mit
bulimia [bə'lɪmɪə] n Bulimie f
bulk [bʌlk] n *(of thing)* massige Form f; *(of person)* massige Gestalt f; **in ~** im Großen, en gros; **the ~ of** der Großteil +gen
bulk buying [-'baɪɪŋ] n Mengeneinkauf m, Großeinkauf m
bulk carrier n Bulkcarrier m
bulkhead ['bʌlkhɛd] n Schott nt
bulky ['bʌlkɪ] adj sperrig
bull [bul] n Stier m; *(male elephant or whale)* Bulle m; *(Stock Exchange)* Haussier m, Haussespekulant m; *(Rel)* Bulle f
bulldog ['buldɔg] n Bulldogge f
bulldoze ['buldəuz] vt mit Bulldozern wegräumen; *(building)* mit Bulldozern abreißen; **I was ~d into it** *(fig: inf)* ich wurde gezwungen or unter Druck gesetzt, es zu tun
bulldozer ['buldəuzə'] n Bulldozer m, Planierraupe f
bullet ['bulɪt] n Kugel f
bulletin ['bulɪtɪn] n *(TV etc)* Kurznachrichten pl; *(journal)* Bulletin nt
bulletin board n *(Comput)* Schwarzes Brett nt
bulletproof ['bulɪtpruːf] adj kugelsicher
bullfight ['bulfaɪt] n Stierkampf m
bullfighter ['bulfaɪtə'] n Stierkämpfer m
bullfighting ['bulfaɪtɪŋ] n Stierkampf m
bullion ['buljən] n: **gold/silver ~** Barrengold nt/-silber nt
bullock ['bulək] n Ochse m
bullring ['bulrɪŋ] n Stierkampfarena f
bull's-eye ['bulzaɪ] n *(on a target)*: **the ~** der Scheibenmittelpunkt, das Schwarze
bullshit ['bulʃɪt] *(inf!)* n Scheiß m, Quatsch m ▷ vi Scheiß erzählen; **~!** Quatsch!
bully ['bulɪ] n Tyrann m ▷ vt tyrannisieren; *(frighten)* einschüchtern
bullying ['bulɪɪŋ] n Tyrannisieren nt
bum [bʌm] *(inf)* n Hintern m; *(esp US: good-for-nothing)* Rumtreiber m; *(tramp)* Penner m
▸ **bum around** *(inf)* vi herumgammeln
bumblebee ['bʌmblbiː] n Hummel f
bumf [bʌmf] *(inf)* n Papierkram m
bump [bʌmp] n Zusammenstoß m; *(jolt)* Erschütterung f; *(swelling)* Beule f; *(on road)* Unebenheit f ▷ vt stoßen; *(car)* eine Delle fahren in +acc
▸ **bump along** vi entlangholpern
▸ **bump into** vt fus *(obstacle)* stoßen gegen; *(inf: person)* treffen
bumper ['bʌmpə'] n Stoßstange f ▷ adj: **~ crop, ~ harvest** Rekordernte f
bumper cars npl Autoskooter pl
bumper sticker n Aufkleber m
bumph [bʌmf] n = **bumf**
bumptious ['bʌmpʃəs] adj wichtigtuerisch
bumpy ['bʌmpɪ] adj holperig; **it was a ~ flight/ride** während des Fluges/auf der Fahrt wurden wir tüchtig durchgerüttelt
bun [bʌn] n Brötchen nt; *(of hair)* Knoten m

bunch [bʌntʃ] n Strauß m; *(of keys)* Bund m; *(of bananas)* Büschel nt; *(of people)* Haufen m; **bunches** npl *(in hair)* Zöpfe pl; **~ of grapes** Weintraube f
bundle ['bʌndl] n Bündel nt ▷ vt *(also: **bundle up**)* bündeln; *(put)*: **to ~ sth into** etw stopfen or packen in +acc; **to ~ sb into** jdn schaffen in +acc
▸ **bundle off** vt schaffen
▸ **bundle out** vt herausschaffen
bun fight *(Brit: inf)* n Festivitäten pl; *(tea party)* Teegesellschaft f
bung [bʌŋ] n Spund m, Spundzapfen m ▷ vt *(Brit: inf: also: **bung in**)* schmeißen; *(also: **bung up**)* verstopfen; **my nose is ~ed up** meine Nase ist verstopft
bungalow ['bʌŋgələu] n Bungalow m
bungee jumping ['bʌndʒiː'dʒʌmpɪŋ] n Bungeespringen nt
bungle ['bʌŋgl] vt verpfuschen
bunion ['bʌnjən] n entzündeter Ballen m
bunk [bʌŋk] n Bett nt, Koje f; **to do a ~** *(inf)* abhauen
▸ **bunk off** *(inf)* vi abhauen
bunk beds npl Etagenbett nt
bunker ['bʌŋkə'] n Kohlenbunker m; *(Mil, Golf)* Bunker m
bunny ['bʌnɪ] n *(also: **bunny rabbit**)* Hase m, Häschen nt
bunny girl *(Brit)* n Häschen nt
bunny hill *(US)* n *(Ski)* Anfängerhügel m
bunting ['bʌntɪŋ] n *(flags)* Wimpel pl, Fähnchen pl
buoy [bɔɪ] n Boje f
▸ **buoy up** vt *(fig)* Auftrieb geben +dat
buoyancy ['bɔɪənsɪ] n *(of ship, object)* Schwimmfähigkeit f
buoyant ['bɔɪənt] adj *(ship, object)* schwimmfähig; *(market)* fest; *(economy)* stabil; *(prices, currency)* fest, stabil; *(person, nature)* heiter
burden ['bəːdn] n Belastung f; *(load)* Last f ▷ vt: **to ~ sb with sth** jdn mit etw belasten; **to be a ~ to sb** jdm zur Last fallen
bureau ['bjuərəu] (pl **-x**) n *(Brit: writing desk)* Sekretär m; *(US: chest of drawers)* Kommode f; *(office)* Büro nt
bureaucracy [bjuə'rɔkrəsɪ] n Bürokratie f
bureaucrat ['bjuərəkræt] n Bürokrat(in) m(f)
bureaucratic [bjuərə'krætɪk] adj bürokratisch
bureaux ['bjuərəuz] npl of **bureau**
burgeon ['bəːdʒən] vi hervorsprießen
burger ['bəːgə'] *(inf)* n Hamburger m
burglar ['bəːglə'] n Einbrecher(in) m(f)
burglar alarm n Alarmanlage f
burglarize ['bəːgləraɪz] *(US)* vt einbrechen in +acc
burglary ['bəːglərɪ] n Einbruch m
burgle ['bəːgl] vt einbrechen in +acc
Burgundy ['bəːgəndɪ] n Burgund nt
burial ['bɛrɪəl] n Beerdigung f
burial ground n Begräbnisstätte f

b

burlesque [bə:'lɛsk] n (parody) Persiflage f; (US: Theat) Burleske f

burly ['bə:lɪ] adj kräftig, stämmig

Burma ['bə:mə] n Birma nt, Burma nt

Burmese [bə:'mi:z] adj birmanisch, burmisch ▷ n inv Birmane m, Burmese m, Birmanin f, Burmesin f ▷ n (Ling) Birmanisch nt, Burmesisch nt

burn [bə:n] (pt, pp **burned** or **~t**) vt verbrennen; (fuel) als Brennstoff verwenden; (food) anbrennen lassen; (house etc) niederbrennen ▷ vi brennen; (food) anbrennen ▷ n Verbrennung f; **the cigarette ~t a hole in her dress** die Zigarette brannte ein Loch in ihr Kleid; **I've ~t myself!** ich habe mich verbrannt!
▶ **burn down** vt abbrennen
▶ **burn out** vt: **to ~ o.s. out** (writer etc) sich völlig verausgaben; **the fire ~t itself out** das Feuer brannte aus

burner ['bə:nə'] n Brenner m

burning ['bə:nɪŋ] adj brennend; (sand, desert) glühend heiß

burnish ['bə:nɪʃ] vt polieren

burnt [bə:nt] pt, pp of **burn**

burnt sugar (Brit) n Karamell m

burp [bə:p] (inf) n Rülpser m ▷ vt (baby) aufstoßen lassen ▷ vi rülpsen

burrow ['bʌrəu] n Bau m ▷ vi graben; (rummage) wühlen

bursar ['bə:sə'] n Schatzmeister m, Finanzverwalter m

bursary ['bə:sərɪ] (Brit) n Stipendium nt

burst [bə:st] (pt, pp **~**) vt zum Platzen bringen, platzen lassen ▷ vi platzen ▷ n Salve f; (also: **burst pipe**) (Rohr)bruch m; **the river has ~ its banks** der Fluss ist über die Ufer getreten; **to ~ into flames** in Flammen aufgehen; **to ~ into tears** in Tränen ausbrechen; **to ~ out laughing** in Lachen ausbrechen; **~ blood vessel** geplatzte Ader f; **to be ~ing with** zum Bersten voll sein mit; (pride) fast platzen vor +dat; **to ~ open** aufspringen; **a ~ of energy** ein Ausbruch m von Energie; **a ~ of enthusiasm** ein

Begeisterungsausbruch m; **a ~ of speed** ein Spurt m; **~ of laughter** Lachsalve f; **~ of applause** Beifallssturm m
▶ **burst in on** vt fus: **to ~ in on sb** bei jdm hereinplatzen
▶ **burst into** vt fus (into room) platzen in +acc
▶ **burst out of** vt fus (of room) stürmen or stürzen aus

bury ['bɛrɪ] vt begraben; (at funeral) beerdigen; **to ~ one's face in one's hands** das Gesicht in den Händen vergraben; **to ~ one's head in the sand** (fig) den Kopf in den Sand stecken; **to ~ the hatchet** (fig) das Kriegsbeil begraben

bus [bʌs] n (Auto)bus m, (Omni)bus m; (double decker) Doppeldecker m (inf)

bus boy (US) n Bedienungshilfe f

bush [buʃ] n Busch m, Strauch m; (scrubland) Busch; **to beat about the ~** um den heißen Brei herumreden

bushed [buʃt] (inf) adj (exhausted) groggy

bushel ['buʃl] n Scheffel m

bushfire n Buschfeuer nt

bushy ['buʃɪ] adj buschig

busily ['bɪzɪlɪ] adv eifrig; **to be ~ doing sth** eifrig etw tun

business ['bɪznɪs] n (matter) Angelegenheit f; (trading) Geschäft nt; (firm) Firma f, Betrieb m; (occupation) Beruf m; **to be away on ~** geschäftlich unterwegs sein; **I'm here on ~** ich bin geschäftlich hier; **he's in the insurance/transport ~** er arbeitet in der Versicherungs-/Transportbranche; **to do ~ with sb** Geschäfte pl mit jdm machen; **it's my ~ to ...** es ist meine Aufgabe, zu ...; **it's none of my ~** es geht mich nichts an; **he means ~** er meint es ernst

business address n Geschäftsadresse f

business card n (Visiten)karte f

businesslike ['bɪznɪslaɪk] adj geschäftsmäßig

businessman ['bɪznɪsmən] (irreg: like **man**) n Geschäftsmann m

business trip n Geschäftsreise f

businesswoman ['bɪznɪswumən] (irreg: like **woman**) n Geschäftsfrau f

busker ['bʌskə'] (Brit) n Straßenmusikant(in) m(f)

bus lane (Brit) n Busspur f

bus shelter n Wartehäuschen nt

bus station n Busbahnhof m

bus stop n Bushaltestelle f

bust [bʌst] n Busen m; (measurement) Oberweite f; (sculpture) Büste f ▷ adj (inf) kaputt ▷ vt (inf) verhaften; **to go ~** pleitegehen

bustle ['bʌsl] n Betrieb m ▷ vi eilig herumlaufen

bustling ['bʌslɪŋ] adj belebt

bust-up ['bʌstʌp] (Brit: inf) n Krach m

busty ['bʌstɪ] adj (woman) vollbusig

busy ['bɪzɪ] adj (person) beschäftigt; (shop, street) belebt; (Tel, esp US) besetzt ▷ vt: **to ~ o.s. with** sich beschäftigen mit; **he's a ~ man** er ist ein viel beschäftigter Mann; **he's ~** er hat (zurzeit) viel zu tun

busybody ['bɪzɪbɒdɪ] n: **to be a ~** sich ständig einmischen

busy signal (US) n (Tel) Besetztzeichen nt

 KEYWORD

but [bʌt] conj **1** (yet) aber; **not blue but red** nicht blau, sondern rot; **he's not very bright, but he's hard-working** er ist nicht sehr intelligent, aber er ist fleißig

2 (however): **I'd love to come, but I'm busy** ich würde gern kommen, bin aber beschäftigt

3 (showing disagreement, surprise etc): **but that's far too expensive!** aber das ist viel zu teuer!; **but that's fantastic!** das ist doch toll!

▷ prep (apart from, except) außer +dat; **nothing but trouble** nichts als Ärger; **no-one but him can do it** keiner außer ihm kann es machen; **but for you** wenn Sie nicht gewesen wären; **but for your help** ohne Ihre Hilfe; **I'll do anything but that** ich mache alles, nur nicht das; **the last house but one** das vorletzte Haus; **the next street but one** die übernächste Straße

▷ adv (just, only) nur; **she's but a child** sie ist doch noch ein Kind; **I can but try** ich kann es ja versuchen

butane ['bju:teɪn] n (also: **butane gas**) Butan(gas) nt

butch [butʃ] (inf) adj maskulin

butcher ['butʃəʳ] n Fleischer m, Metzger m; (pej: murderer) Schlächter m ▷ vt schlachten; (prisoners etc) abschlachten

butcher's ['butʃəz], **butcher's shop** n Fleischerei f, Metzgerei f

butler ['bʌtləʳ] n Butler m

butt [bʌt] n großes Fass nt, Tonne f; (thick end) dickes Ende nt; (of gun) Kolben m; (of cigarette) Kippe f; (Brit: fig: target) Zielscheibe f; (US: inf!) Arsch m ▷ vt (goat) mit den Hörnern stoßen; (person) mit dem Kopf stoßen
  ▶ **butt in** vi sich einmischen, dazwischenfunken (inf)

butter ['bʌtəʳ] n Butter f ▷ vt buttern

buttercup ['bʌtəkʌp] n Butterblume f

butter dish n Butterdose f

butterfingers ['bʌtəfɪŋgəz] (inf) n Schussel m

butterfly ['bʌtəflaɪ] n Schmetterling m; (Swimming: also: **butterfly stroke**) Schmetterlingsstil m, Butterfly m

buttocks ['bʌtəks] npl Gesäß nt

button ['bʌtn] n Knopf m; (US: badge) Plakette f ▷ vt (also: **button up**) zuknöpfen ▷ vi geknöpft werden

buttonhole ['bʌtnhəul] n Knopfloch nt; (flower) Blume f im Knopfloch ▷ vt zu fassen bekommen, sich dat schnappen (inf)

buttress ['bʌtrɪs] n Strebepfeiler m

buxom ['bʌksəm] adj drall

buy [baɪ] (pt, pp **bought**) vt kaufen; (company) aufkaufen ▷ n Kauf m; **that was a good/bad ~** das war ein guter/schlechter Kauf;

to ~ sb sth jdm etw kaufen; **to ~ sth from sb** etw bei jdm kaufen; (from individual) jdm etw abkaufen; **to ~ sb a drink** jdm einen ausgeben (inf)
  ▶ **buy back** vt zurückkaufen
  ▶ **buy in** (Brit) vt einkaufen
  ▶ **buy into** (Brit) vt fus sich einkaufen in +acc
  ▶ **buy off** vt kaufen
  ▶ **buy out** vt (partner) auszahlen; (business) aufkaufen
  ▶ **buy up** vt aufkaufen

buyer ['baɪəʳ] n Käufer(in) m(f); (Comm) Einkäufer(in) m(f)

buyer's market ['baɪəz-] n Käufermarkt m

buyout ['baɪaut] n (of firm: by workers, management) Aufkauf m

buzz [bʌz] vi summen, brummen; (saw) kreischen ▷ vt rufen; (with buzzer) (mit dem Summer) rufen; (Aviat: plane, building) dicht vorbeifliegen an +dat ▷ n Summen nt, Brummen nt; (inf): **to give sb a ~** jdn anrufen; **my head is ~ing** mir schwirrt der Kopf
  ▶ **buzz off** (inf) vi abhauen

buzzard ['bʌzəd] n Bussard m

buzzer ['bʌzəʳ] n Summer m

buzz word (inf) n Modewort nt

 KEYWORD

by [baɪ] prep **1** (referring to cause, agent) von +dat, durch +acc; **killed by lightning** vom Blitz or durch einen Blitz getötet; **a painting by Picasso** ein Bild von Picasso

2 (referring to method, manner, means): **by bus/car/train** mit dem Bus/Auto/Zug; **to pay by cheque** mit or per Scheck bezahlen; **by saving hard, he was able to ...** indem er eisern sparte, konnte er ...

3 (via, through) über +acc; **we came by Dover** wir sind über Dover gekommen

4 (close to) bei +dat, an +dat; **the house by the river** das Haus am Fluss

5 (past) an ... dat vorbei; **she rushed by me** sie eilte an mir vorbei

6 (not later than) bis +acc; **by 4 o'clock** bis 4 Uhr; **by this time tomorrow** morgen um diese Zeit

7 (amount): **by the kilo/metre** kilo-/meterweise; **to be paid by the hour** stundenweise bezahlt werden

8 (Math, measure): **to divide by 3** durch 3 teilen; **to multiply by 3** mit 3 malnehmen; **it missed me by inches** es hat mich um Zentimeter verfehlt

9 (according to): **to play by the rules** sich an die Regeln halten; **it's all right by me** von mir aus ist es in Ordnung

10: **(all) by myself/himself** etc (ganz) allein

11: **by the way** übrigens

▷ adv **1** see **go**, **pass** etc

2: **by and by** irgendwann

3: **by and large** im Großen und Ganzen

bye ['baɪ], **bye-bye** ['baɪ'baɪ] *excl* (auf)
Wiedersehen, tschüss (*inf*)
bye-law ['baɪlɔː] *n see* **by-law**
by-election ['baɪɪlekʃən] (*Brit*) *n* Nachwahl *f*
Byelorussia [bjɛləʊ'rʌʃə] *n* = **Belorussia**
Byelorussian [bjɛləʊ'rʌʃən] *adj, n* = **Belarussian**
bygone ['baɪɡɒn] *adj* (längst) vergangen
▷ *n*: **let ~s be ~s** wir sollten die Vergangenheit
ruhen lassen
by-law ['baɪlɔː] *n* Verordnung *f*
bypass ['baɪpɑːs] *n* Umgehungsstraße *f*; (*Med*)

Bypassoperation *f* ▷ *vt* (*also fig*) umgehen
by-product ['baɪprɒdʌkt] *n* Nebenprodukt *nt*
byre ['baɪə^r] (*Brit*) *n* Kuhstall *m*
bystander ['baɪstændə^r] *n* Zuschauer(in) *m(f)*
byte [baɪt] *n* (*Comput*) Byte *nt*
byway ['baɪweɪ] *n* Seitenweg *m*
byword ['baɪwəːd] *n*: **to be a ~ for** der Inbegriff
+*gen* sein, gleichbedeutend sein mit
by-your-leave ['baɪjɔː'liːv] *n*: **without so
much as a ~** ohne auch nur (um Erlaubnis)
zu fragen

b

Cc

C¹, c¹ [siː] n (letter) C nt, c nt; (Scol) ≈ Drei f, ≈
Befriedigend nt; **C for Charlie** ≈ C wie Cäsar
C² [siː] n (Mus) C nt, c nt
C³ [siː] abbr = **Celsius; centigrade**
c² abbr = **century**; (= circa) ca.; (US etc: = cent(s))
Cent
CA n abbr (Brit) = **chartered accountant** ▷ abbr =
Central America; (US: Post) = California
C/A abbr (Comm) = **capital account; credit
account; current account**
ca. abbr (= circa) ca.
CAA n abbr (Brit) = **Civil Aviation
Authority**; (US: = Civil Aeronautics Authority)
Zivilluftfahrtbehörde
CAB (Brit) n abbr = **Citizens' Advice Bureau**
cab [kæb] n Taxi nt; (of truck, train etc)
Führerhaus nt; (horse-drawn) Droschke f
cabaret ['kæbəreɪ] n Kabarett nt
cabbage ['kæbɪdʒ] n Kohl m
cabbie, cabby ['kæbɪ] n Taxifahrer(in) m(f)
cab driver n Taxifahrer(in) m(f)
cabin ['kæbɪn] n Kabine f; (house) Hütte f
cabin cruiser n Kajütboot nt
cabinet ['kæbɪnɪt] n kleiner Schrank m;
(also: **display cabinet**) Vitrine f; (Pol) Kabinett
nt
cabinet-maker ['kæbɪnɪt'meɪkə'] n
Möbeltischler m
cabinet minister n Mitglied nt des Kabinetts,
Minister(in) m(f)
cable ['keɪbl] n Kabel nt ▷ vt kabeln
cable car n (Draht)seilbahn f
cablegram ['keɪblgræm] n (Übersee)
telegramm nt, Kabel nt
cable railway n Seilbahn f
cable television n Kabelfernsehen nt
cable TV n = **cable television**
cache [kæʃ] n Versteck nt, geheimes Lager nt; **a
~ of food** ein geheimes Proviantlager
cackle ['kækl] vi (person: laugh) meckernd
lachen; (hen) gackern
cacti ['kæktaɪ] npl of **cactus**
cactus ['kæktəs] (pl **cacti**) n Kaktus m
CAD n abbr (= computer-aided design) CAD nt
caddie ['kædɪ] n (Golf) Caddie m
caddy ['kædɪ] n = **caddie**
cadence ['keɪdəns] n (of voice) Tonfall m
cadet [kə'dɛt] n Kadett m; **police ~**

Polizeianwärter(in) m(f)
cadge [kædʒ] (inf) vt: **to ~ (from** or **off)**
schnorren (bei or von +dat); **to ~ a lift with sb**
von jdm mitgenommen werden
cadger ['kædʒə'] (Brit: inf) n Schnorrer(in) m(f)
cadre ['kædrɪ] n Kader m
Caesarean [siː'zɛərɪən] n: **~ (section)**
Kaiserschnitt m
CAF (Brit) abbr (= cost and freight) cf
café ['kæfeɪ] n Café nt
cafeteria [kæfɪ'tɪərɪə] n Cafeteria f
caffeine, caffein ['kæfiːn] n Koffein nt
cage [keɪdʒ] n Käfig m; (of lift) Fahrkorb m ▷ vt
einsperren
cagey ['keɪdʒɪ] (inf) adj vorsichtig; (evasive)
ausweichend
cagoule [kə'guːl] n Regenjacke f
cahoots [kə'huːts] (inf) n: **to be in ~ with**
unter einer Decke stecken mit
CAI n abbr (= computer-aided instruction) CAI nt
Cairo ['kaɪərəu] n Kairo nt
cajole [kə'dʒəul] vt: **to ~ sb into doing sth** jdn
bereden, etw zu tun
cake [keɪk] n Kuchen m; (small) Gebäckstück
nt; (of soap) Stück nt; **it's a piece of ~** (inf) das
ist ein Kinderspiel or ein Klacks; **he wants
to have his ~ and eat it (too)** (fig) er will das
eine, ohne das andere zu lassen
caked [keɪkt] adj: **~ with** (mud, blood) verkrustet
mit
cake shop n Konditorei f
Cal. (US) abbr (Post) = California
calamine lotion ['kæləmaɪn-] n Galmeilotion f
calamitous [kə'læmɪtəs] adj katastrophal
calamity [kə'læmɪtɪ] n Katastrophe f
calcium ['kælsɪəm] n Kalzium nt
calculate ['kælkjuleɪt] vt (work out) berechnen;
(estimate) abschätzen
▶ **calculate on** vt fus: **to ~ on sth** mit etw
rechnen; **to ~ on doing sth** damit rechnen,
etw zu tun
calculated ['kælkjuleɪtɪd] adj (insult) bewusst;
(action) vorsätzlich; **a ~ risk** ein kalkuliertes
Risiko
calculating ['kælkjuleɪtɪŋ] adj (scheming)
berechnend
calculation [kælkju'leɪʃən] n (see vt)
Berechnung f; Abschätzung f; (sum) Rechnung

_f_
calculator ['kælkjuleɪtəʳ] _n_ Rechner _m_
calculus ['kælkjuləs] _n_ Infinitesimalrechnung
_f_; **integral/differential** ~ Integral-/
Differenzialrechnung _f_
calendar ['kæləndəʳ] _n_ Kalender _m_; _(timetable,_
schedule) (Termin)kalender _m_
calendar month _n_ Kalendermonat _m_
calendar year _n_ Kalenderjahr _nt_
calf [kɑːf] _(pl_ **calves**) _n_ Kalb _nt_; _(of elephant, seal_
etc) Junge(s) _nt_; _(also:_ **calfskin**) Kalb(s)leder _nt_;
(Anat) Wade _f_
caliber ['kælɪbəʳ] _(US) n_ = **calibre**
calibrate ['kælɪbreɪt] _vt (gun etc)_ kalibrieren;
(scale of measuring instrument) eichen
calibre, _(US)_ **caliber** ['kælɪbəʳ] _n_ Kaliber _nt_; _(of_
person) Format _nt_
calico ['kælɪkəu] _n (Brit)_ Kattun _m_, Kaliko _m_;
_(US)_ bedruckter Kattun
Calif. _(US) abbr (Post)_ = **California**
California [kælɪˈfɔːnɪə] _n_ Kalifornien _nt_
calipers ['kælɪpəz] _(US) npl_ = **callipers**
call [kɔːl] _vt (name, consider)_ nennen; _(shout_
out, summon) rufen; _(Tel)_ anrufen; _(witness,_
flight) aufrufen; _(meeting)_ einberufen;
(strike) ausrufen ▷ _vi_ rufen; _(Tel)_ anrufen;
(visit: also: **call in, call round**) vorbeigehen,
vorbeikommen ▷ _n_ Ruf _m_; _(Tel)_ Anruf _m_; _(visit)_
Besuch _m_; _(for a service etc)_ Nachfrage _f_; _(for_
flight etc) Aufruf _m_; _(fig: lure)_ Ruf _m_, Verlockung
_f_; **to be ~ed** _(named)_ heißen; **who is ~ing?**
(Tel) wer spricht da bitte?; **London ~ing**
(Radio) hier ist London; **please give me a ~**
at 7 rufen Sie mich bitte um 7 an; **to make**
a ~ ein (Telefon)gespräch führen; **to pay**
a ~ on sb jdn besuchen; **on ~** dienstbereit;
to be on ~ einsatzbereit sein; _(doctor etc)_
Bereitschaftsdienst haben; **there's not**
much ~ for these items es besteht keine
große Nachfrage nach diesen Dingen
▸ **call at** _vt fus (subj: ship)_ anlaufen; _(: train)_
halten in +_dat_
▸ **call back** _vi (return)_ wiederkommen; _(Tel)_
zurückrufen ▷ _vt (Tel)_ zurückrufen
▸ **call for** _vt fus (demand)_ fordern; _(fetch)_
abholen
▸ **call in** _vt (doctor, expert, police)_ zurate ziehen;
(books, cars, stock etc) aus dem Verkehr ziehen
▷ _vi_ vorbeigehen, vorbeikommen
▸ **call off** _vt_ absagen
▸ **call on** _vt fus_ besuchen; _(appeal to)_ appellieren
an +_acc_; **to ~ on sb to do sth** jdn bitten or
auffordern, etw zu tun
▸ **call out** _vi_ rufen ▷ _vt_ rufen; _(police, troops)_
alarmieren
▸ **call up** _vt (Mil)_ einberufen; _(Tel)_ anrufen
Callanetics® _n sing_ Callanetics _f_
call box _(Brit) n_ Telefonzelle _f_
call centre _n_ Telefoncenter _nt_, Callcenter _nt_
caller ['kɔːləʳ] _n_ Besucher(in) _m(f)_; _(Tel)_
Anrufer(in) _m(f)_; **hold the line, ~!** _(Tel)_ bitte
bleiben Sie am Apparat!
caller ID ['kɔːləʳaɪdiː] _n (Tel)_ Anruferkennung

_m_; _(of email, text message)_ Absenderkennung _m_
call girl _n_ Callgirl _nt_
call-in ['kɔːlɪn] _(US) n (Radio, TV)_ Phone-in _nt_
calling ['kɔːlɪŋ] _n (trade)_ Beruf _m_; _(vocation)_
Berufung _f_
calling card _(US) n_ Visitenkarte _f_
callipers, _(US)_ **calipers** ['kælɪpəz] _npl (Math)_
Tastzirkel _m_; _(Med)_ Schiene _f_
callous ['kæləs] _adj_ herzlos
callousness ['kæləsnɪs] _n_ Herzlosigkeit _f_
callow ['kæləu] _adj_ unreif
calm [kɑːm] _adj_ ruhig; _(unworried)_ gelassen ▷ _n_
Ruhe _f_ ▷ _vt_ beruhigen; _(fears)_ zerstreuen; _(grief)_
lindern
▸ **calm down** _vt_ beruhigen ▷ _vi_ sich beruhigen
calmly ['kɑːmlɪ] _adv (see adj)_ ruhig; gelassen
calmness ['kɑːmnɪs] _n (see adj)_ Ruhe _f_;
Gelassenheit _f_
Calor gas® ['kæləʳ-] _n_ Butangas _nt_
calorie ['kælərɪ] _n_ Kalorie _f_; **low-~ product**
kalorienarmes Produkt _nt_
calve [kɑːv] _vi_ kalben
calves [kɑːvz] _npl of_ **calf**
CAM _n abbr (= computer-aided manufacture)_ CAM _nt_
camber ['kæmbəʳ] _n_ Wölbung _f_
Cambodia [kæmˈbəudɪə] _n_ Kambodscha _nt_
Cambodian [kæmˈbəudɪən] _adj_
kambodschanisch ▷ _n_ Kambodschaner(in)
_m(f)_
Cambs _(Brit) abbr (Post)_ = _Cambridgeshire_
camcorder ['kæmkɔːdəʳ] _n_ Camcorder _m_,
Kamerarekorder _m_
came [keɪm] _pt of_ **come**
camel ['kæməl] _n_ Kamel _nt_
cameo ['kæmɪəu] _n_ Kamee _f_; _(Theat, Liter)_
Miniatur _f_
camera ['kæmərə] _n (Cine, Phot)_ Kamera
_f_; _(also:_ **cine camera, movie camera**)
Filmkamera _f_; **35 mm ~** Kleinbildkamera _f_; **in**
~ _(Law)_ unter Ausschluss der Öffentlichkeit
cameraman ['kæmərəmæn] _(irreg: like_ **man**) _n_
Kameramann _m_
camera phone _n_ Kameratelefon _nt_
Cameroon [kæməˈruːn] _n_ Kamerun _nt_
Cameroun [kæməˈruːn] _n_ = **Cameroon**
camomile ['kæməumaɪl] _n_ Kamille _f_
camouflage ['kæməflɑːʒ] _n_ Tarnung _f_ ▷ _vt_
tarnen
camp [kæmp] _n_ Lager _nt_; _(barracks)_ Kaserne _f_
▷ _vi_ zelten ▷ _adj (effeminate)_ tuntenhaft _(inf)_
campaign [kæmˈpeɪn] _n (Mil)_ Feldzug _m_; _(Pol_
etc) Kampagne _f_ ▷ _vi_ kämpfen; **to ~ for/**
against sich einsetzen für/gegen
campaigner [kæmˈpeɪnəʳ] _n_: **~ for**
Befürworter(in) _m(f)_ +_gen_; **~ against**
Gegner(in) _m(f)_ +_gen_
camp bed _(Brit) n_ Campingliege _f_
camper ['kæmpəʳ] _n (person)_ Camper _m_; _(vehicle)_
Wohnmobil _nt_
camping ['kæmpɪŋ] _n_ Camping _nt_; **to go ~**
zelten gehen, campen
camping site, camp site _n_ Campingplatz _m_
campus ['kæmpəs] _n (Univ)_

Universitätsgelände *nt*, Campus *m*
camshaft ['kæmʃɑːft] *n* Nockenwelle *f*
can¹ [kæn] *n* Büchse *f*, Dose *f*; (*for oil, water*)
Kanister *m* ▷ *vt* eindosen, in Büchsen *or* Dosen
einmachen; **a ~ of beer** eine Dose Bier; **he
had to carry the ~** (*Brit: inf*) er musste die
Sache ausbaden

 KEYWORD

can² (*negative* **cannot, can't**, *conditional and pt*
could) *aux vb* **1** (*be able to, know how to*) können;
you can do it if you try du kannst es, wenn
du es nur versuchst; **I can't see you** ich kann
dich nicht sehen; **I can swim/drive** ich kann
schwimmen/Auto fahren; **can you speak
English?** sprechen Sie Englisch?
2 (*may*) können, dürfen; **can I use your
phone?** kann *or* darf ich Ihr Telefon
benutzen?; **could I have a word with you?**
könnte ich Sie mal sprechen?
3 (*expressing disbelief, puzzlement*): **it can't be
true!** das darf doch nicht wahr sein!
4 (*expressing possibility, suggestion, etc*): **he could
be in the library** er könnte in der Bibliothek
sein

Canada ['kænədə] *n* Kanada *nt*
Canadian [kə'neɪdɪən] *adj* kanadisch ▷ *n*
Kanadier(in) *m(f)*
canal [kə'næl] *n* (*also Anat*) Kanal *m*
Canaries [kə'nɛərɪz] *npl* = **Canary Islands**
canary [kə'nɛərɪ] *n* Kanarienvogel *m*
Canary Islands [kə'nɛərɪ 'aɪləndz] *npl*: **the ~**
die Kanarischen Inseln *pl*
Canberra ['kænbərə] *n* Canberra *nt*
cancel ['kænsəl] *vt* absagen; (*reservation*)
abbestellen; (*train, flight*) ausfallen lassen;
(*contract*) annullieren; (*order*) stornieren;
(*cross out*) durchstreichen; (*stamp*) entwerten;
(*cheque*) ungültig machen
▶ **cancel out** *vt* aufheben; **they ~ each other
out** sie heben sich gegenseitig auf
cancellation [kænsə'leɪʃən] *n* Absage *f*; (*of
reservation*) Abbestellung *f*; (*of train, flight*)
Ausfall *m*; (*Tourism*) Rücktritt *m*
cancer ['kænsəʳ] *n* (*also*: **Cancer**: *Astrol*) Krebs *m*;
to be C~ (ein) Krebs sein
cancerous ['kænsrəs] *adj* krebsartig
cancer patient *n* Krebskranke(r) *f(m)*
cancer research *n* Krebsforschung *f*
c and f (*Brit*) *abbr* (*Comm*: = *cost and freight*) cf
candid ['kændɪd] *adj* offen, ehrlich
candidacy ['kændɪdəsɪ] *n* Kandidatur *f*
candidate ['kændɪdeɪt] *n* Kandidat(in) *m(f)*;
(*for job*) Bewerber(in) *m(f)*
candidature ['kændɪdətʃəʳ] (*Brit*) *n* =
candidacy
candied ['kændɪd] *adj* kandiert; **~ apple** (*US*)
kandierter Apfel *m*
candle ['kændl] *n* Kerze *f*; (*of tallow*) Talglicht *nt*
candleholder ['kændlhəʊldəʳ] *n* *see*
candlestick

candlelight ['kændllaɪt] *n*: **by ~** bei Kerzenlicht
candlestick ['kændlstɪk] *n* (*also*, *candleholder*)
Kerzenhalter *m*; (*bigger, ornate*) Kerzenleuchter
m
candour, (*US*) **candor** ['kændəʳ] *n* Offenheit *f*
C & W *n abbr* = **country and western**
candy ['kændɪ] *n* (*also*: **sugar-candy**)
Kandis(zucker) *m*; (*US*) Bonbon *nt or m*
candyfloss ['kændɪflɔs] (*Brit*) *n* Zuckerwatte *f*
candy store (*US*) *n* Süßwarenhandlung *f*
cane [keɪn] *n* Rohr *nt*; (*stick*) Stock *m*; (: *for
walking*) (Spazier)stock *m* ▷ *vt* (*Brit: Scol*) mit
dem Stock schlagen
canine ['keɪnaɪn] *adj* (*species*) Hunde-
canister ['kænɪstəʳ] *n* Dose *f*; (*pressurized
container*) Sprühdose *f*; (*of gas, chemicals etc*)
Kanister *m*
cannabis ['kænəbɪs] *n* Haschisch *nt*;
(*also*: **cannabis plant**) Hanf *m*, Cannabis *m*
canned [kænd] *adj* Dosen-; (*inf: music*) aus
der Konserve; (*US: inf: worker*) entlassen,
rausgeschmissen (*inf*)
cannibal ['kænɪbəl] *n* Kannibale *m*, Kannibalin
f
cannibalism ['kænɪbəlɪzəm] *n* Kannibalismus
m
cannibalization [kænɪbəlaɪ'zeɪʃn] *n* (*Econ*)
Kannibalisierung *f*
cannon ['kænən] (*pl* **~** *or* **cannons**) *n* Kanone *f*
cannonball ['kænənbɔːl] *n* Kanonenkugel *f*
cannon fodder *n* Kanonenfutter *nt*
cannot ['kænɔt] = **can not**
canny ['kænɪ] *adj* schlau
canoe [kə'nuː] *n* Kanu *nt*
canoeing [kə'nuːɪŋ] *n* Kanusport *m*
canon ['kænən] *n* Kanon *m*; (*clergyman*)
Kanoniker *m*, Kanonikus *m*
canonize ['kænənaɪz] *vt* kanonisieren,
heiligsprechen
can-opener ['kænəʊpnəʳ] *n* Dosenöffner *m*,
Büchsenöffner *m*
canopy ['kænəpɪ] *n* (*also fig*) Baldachin *m*
cant [kænt] *n* scheinheiliges Gerede *nt*
can't [kænt] = **can not**
Cantab. (*Brit*) *abbr* (*in degree
titles*: = *Cantabrigiensis*) der Universität Cambridge
cantankerous [kæn'tæŋkərəs] *adj* mürrisch
canteen [kæn'tiːn] *n* (*in school, workplace*)
Kantine *f*; (: *mobile*) Feldküche *f*; (*Brit: of cutlery*)
Besteckkasten *m*
canter ['kæntəʳ] *vi* leicht galoppieren, kantern
▷ *n* leichter Galopp *m*, Kanter *m*
cantilever ['kæntɪliːvəʳ] *n* Ausleger *m*
canvas ['kænvəs] *n* Leinwand *f*; (*painting*)
Gemälde *nt*; (*Naut*) Segeltuch *nt*; **under ~** im
Zelt
canvass ['kænvəs] *vt* (*opinions, views*)
erforschen; (*person*) für seine Partei zu
gewinnen suchen; (*place*) Wahlwerbung
machen in +*dat* ▷ *vi*: **to ~ for ...** (*Pol*) um
Stimmen für ... werben
canvasser ['kænvəsəʳ] *n* (*Pol*) Wahlhelfer(in)
m(f)

canvassing ['kænvəsɪŋ] n (Pol) Wahlwerbung f

canyon ['kænjən] n Cañon m

CAP n abbr (= Common Agricultural Policy) gemeinsame Agrarpolitik f der EG

cap [kæp] n Mütze f, Kappe f; (of pen) (Verschluss)kappe f; (of bottle) Verschluss m, Deckel m; (contraceptive: also: **Dutch cap**) Pessar nt; (for toy gun) Zündplättchen nt; (for swimming) Bademütze f, Badekappe f; (Sport) Ehrenkappe, die Nationalspielern verliehen wird ▷ vt (outdo) überbieten; (Sport) für die Nationalmannschaft aufstellen; **~ped with** ... mit ... obendrauf; **and to ~ it all,** ... und obendrein ...

capability [keɪpə'bɪlɪtɪ] n Fähigkeit f; (Mil) Potenzial nt

capable ['keɪpəbl] adj fähig; **to be ~ of doing sth** etw tun können, fähig sein, etw zu tun; **to be ~ of sth** (interpretation etc) etw zulassen

capacious [kə'peɪʃəs] adj geräumig

capacity [kə'pæsɪtɪ] n Fassungsvermögen nt; (of lift etc) Höchstlast f; (capability) Fähigkeit f; (position, role) Eigenschaft f; (of factory) Kapazität f; **filled to ~** randvoll; (stadium etc) bis auf den letzten Platz besetzt; **in his ~ as** ... in seiner Eigenschaft als ...; **this work is beyond my ~** zu dieser Arbeit bin ich nicht fähig; **in an advisory ~** in beratender Funktion; **to work at full ~** voll ausgelastet sein

cape [keɪp] n Kap nt; (cloak) Cape nt, Umhang m

Cape of Good Hope n: **the ~** das Kap der guten Hoffnung

caper ['keɪpəʳ] n (Culin: usu pl) Kaper f; (prank) Eskapade f, Kapriole f

Cape Town n Kapstadt nt

capita ['kæpɪtə] see **per capita**

capital ['kæpɪtl] n (also: **capital city**) Hauptstadt f; (money) Kapital nt; (also: **capital letter**) Großbuchstabe m

capital account n Kapitalverkehrsbilanz f; (of country) Kapitalkonto nt

capital allowance n (Anlage)abschreibung f

capital assets npl Kapitalvermögen nt

capital expenditure n Kapitalaufwendungen pl

capital gains tax n Kapitalertragssteuer f

capital goods npl Investitionsgüter pl

capital-intensive ['kæpɪtlɪn'tensɪv] adj kapitalintensiv

capitalism ['kæpɪtəlɪzəm] n Kapitalismus m

capitalist ['kæpɪtəlɪst] adj kapitalistisch ▷ n Kapitalist(in) m(f)

capitalize ['kæpɪtəlaɪz] vt (Comm) kapitalisieren ▷ vi: **to ~ on** Kapital schlagen aus

capital punishment n Todesstrafe f

capital transfer tax (Brit) n Erbschafts- und Schenkungssteuer f

Capitol ['kæpɪtl] n: **the ~** das Kapitol; siehe

Info-Artikel

capitulate [kə'pɪtjuleɪt] vi kapitulieren

capitulation [kəpɪtju'leɪʃən] n Kapitulation f

capricious [kə'prɪʃəs] adj launisch

Capricorn ['kæprɪkɔːn] n (Astrol) Steinbock m; **to be ~** (ein) Steinbock sein

caps. [kæps] abbr (= capital letters) Großbuchstaben pl

capsize [kæp'saɪz] vt zum Kentern bringen ▷ vi kentern

capstan ['kæpstən] n Poller m

capsule ['kæpsjuːl] n Kapsel f

Capt. abbr (Mil) = **captain**

captain ['kæptɪn] n Kapitän m; (of plane) (Flug)kapitän m; (in army) Hauptmann m ▷ vt (ship) befehligen; (team) anführen

caption ['kæpʃən] n Bildunterschrift f

captivate ['kæptɪveɪt] vt fesseln

captive ['kæptɪv] adj gefangen ▷ n Gefangene(r) f(m)

captivity [kæp'tɪvɪtɪ] n Gefangenschaft f

captor ['kæptəʳ] n: **his ~s** diejenigen, die ihn gefangen nahmen

capture ['kæptʃəʳ] vt (animal) (ein)fangen; (person) gefangen nehmen; (town, country, share of market) erobern; (attention) erregen; (Comput) erfassen ▷ n (of animal) Einfangen nt; (of person) Gefangennahme f; (of town etc) Eroberung f; (also: **data capture**) Erfassung f

car [kɑːʳ] n Auto nt, Wagen m; (Rail) Wagen m; **by ~** mit dem Auto or Wagen

carafe [kə'ræf] n Karaffe f

caramel ['kærəməl] n Karamelle f, Karamellbonbon m or nt; (burnt sugar) Karamell m

carat ['kærət] n Karat nt; **18 ~ gold** achtzehnkarätiges Gold

caravan ['kærəvæn] n (Brit) Wohnwagen m; (in desert) Karawane f

caravan site (Brit) n Campingplatz m für Wohnwagen

caraway seed n Kümmel m

carbohydrate [kɑːbəu'haɪdreɪt] n Kohle(n)hydrat nt

carbolic acid [kɑː'bɔlɪk-] n Karbolsäure f

car bomb n Autobombe f

carbon ['kɑːbən] n Kohlenstoff m

carbonated ['kɑːbəneɪtɪd] adj mit Kohlensäure (versetzt)

carbon copy n Durchschlag m

carbon dioxide n Kohlendioxid nt

carbon footprint n ökologischer Fußabdruck

carbon monoxide [mɔ'nɔksaɪd] n Kohlenmonoxid nt

carbon paper n Kohlepapier nt

carbon ribbon n Kohlefarbband nt

car-boot sale n auf einem Parkplatz stattfindender Flohmarkt mit dem Kofferraum als Auslage

carburettor, (US) **carburetor** [kɑ:bju'rɛtəʳ] n Vergaser m

carcass ['kɑ:kəs] n Kadaver m

carcinogenic [kɑ:sɪnə'dʒɛnɪk] adj krebserregend, karzinogen

card [kɑ:d] n Karte f; (material) (dünne) Pappe f, Karton m; (also: **record card, index card** etc) (Kartei)karte f; (also: **membership card**) (Mitglieds)ausweis m; (also: **playing card**) (Spiel)karte f; (also: **visiting card**) (Visiten) karte f; **to play ~s** Karten spielen

cardamom ['kɑ:dəməm] n Kardamom m

cardboard ['kɑ:dbɔ:d] n Pappe f

cardboard box n (Papp)karton m

card-carrying ['kɑ:d'kærɪɪŋ] adj: ~ **member** eingetragenes Mitglied nt

card game n Kartenspiel nt

cardiac ['kɑ:dɪæk] adj (failure, patient) Herz-

cardigan ['kɑ:dɪgən] n Strickjacke f

cardinal ['kɑ:dɪnl] adj (principle, importance) Haupt- ▷ n Kardinal m; ~ **number** Kardinalzahl f; ~ **sin** Todsünde f

card index n Kartei f

cardphone n Kartentelefon nt

cardsharp ['kɑ:dʃɑ:p] n Falschspieler m

card vote (Brit) n Abstimmung f durch Wahlmänner

CARE [kɛəʳ] n abbr (= Cooperative for American Relief Everywhere) karitative Organisation

care [kɛəʳ] n (attention) Versorgung f; (worry) Sorge f; (charge) Obhut f, Fürsorge f ▷ vi: **to ~ about** sich kümmern um; ~ **of** bei; "**handle with ~**" „Vorsicht, zerbrechlich"; **in sb's ~** in jds Obhut; **to take ~** aufpassen; **to take ~ to do sth** sich bemühen, etw zu tun; **to take ~ of** sich kümmern um; **the child has been taken into ~** das Kind ist in Pflege genommen worden; **would you ~ to/for ...?** möchten Sie gerne ...?; **I wouldn't ~ to do it** ich möchte es nicht gern tun; **I don't ~** es ist mir egal or gleichgültig; **I couldn't ~ less** es ist mir völlig egal or gleichgültig

▶ **care for** vt fus (look after) sich kümmern um; (like) mögen

career [kə'rɪəʳ] n Karriere f; (job, profession) Beruf m; (life) Laufbahn f ▷ vi (also: **career along**) rasen

career girl n Karrierefrau f

careers officer [kə'rɪəz-] n Berufsberater(in) m(f)

career woman n Karrierefrau f

carefree ['kɛəfri:] adj sorglos

careful ['kɛəful] adj vorsichtig; (thorough) sorgfältig; (**be**) ~**!** Vorsicht!, pass auf!; **to be ~ with one's money** sein Geld gut zusammenhalten

carefully ['kɛəfəlɪ] adv vorsichtig; (methodically) sorgfältig

careless ['kɛəlɪs] adj leichtsinnig; (negligent) nachlässig; (remark) gedankenlos

carelessly ['kɛəlɪslɪ] adv (see adj) leichtsinnig; nachlässig; gedankenlos

carelessness ['kɛəlɪsnɪs] n (see adj) Leichtsinn m; Nachlässigkeit f; Gedankenlosigkeit f

caress [kə'rɛs] n Streicheln nt ▷ vt streicheln

caretaker ['kɛəteɪkəʳ] n Hausmeister(in) m(f)

caretaker government (Brit) n geschäftsführende Regierung f

car ferry n Autofähre f

cargo ['kɑ:gəu] (pl ~**es**) n Fracht f, Ladung f

cargo boat n Frachter m, Frachtschiff nt

cargo plane n Transportflugzeug nt

car hire (Brit) n Autovermietung f

Caribbean [kærɪ'bi:ən] adj karibisch ▷ n: **the ~ (Sea)** die Karibik, das Karibische Meer

caricature ['kærɪkətjuəʳ] n Karikatur f

caring ['kɛərɪŋ] adj liebevoll; (society, organization) sozial; (behaviour) fürsorglich

carjacking n Angriff durch Banditen, die gewaltsam in PKWs eindringen und den Wagen samt Insassen entführen

carnage ['kɑ:nɪdʒ] n (Mil) Blutbad nt, Gemetzel nt

carnal ['kɑ:nl] adj fleischlich, sinnlich

carnation [kɑ:'neɪʃən] n Nelke f

carnival ['kɑ:nɪvl] n Karneval m; (US: funfair) Kirmes f

carnivorous [kɑ:'nɪvərəs] adj fleischfressend

carol ['kærəl] n: (**Christmas**) ~ Weihnachtslied nt

carouse [kə'rauz] vi zechen

carousel [kærə'sɛl] (US) n Karussell nt

carp [kɑ:p] n Karpfen m

▶ **carp at** vt fus herumnörgeln an +dat

car park n Parkplatz m; (building) Parkhaus nt

car-park ticket n Parkschein m

carpenter ['kɑ:pɪntəʳ] n Zimmermann m

carpentry ['kɑ:pɪntrɪ] n Zimmerhandwerk nt; (school subject, hobby) Tischlern nt

carpet ['kɑ:pɪt] n (also fig) Teppich m ▷ vt (mit Teppichen/Teppichboden) auslegen; **fitted ~** (Brit) Teppichboden m

carpet bombing n Flächenbombardierung f

carpet slippers npl Pantoffeln pl

carpet-sweeper ['kɑ:pɪtswi:pəʳ] n Teppichkehrer m

car phone n (Telec) Autotelefon nt

carport ['kɑ:pɔ:t] n Einstellplatz m

car rental n Autovermietung f

carriage ['kærɪdʒ] n (Rail, of typewriter) Wagen m; (horse-drawn vehicle) Kutsche f; (of goods) Beförderung f; (transport costs) Beförderungskosten pl; ~ **forward** Fracht zahlt Empfänger; ~ **free** frachtfrei; ~ **paid** frei Haus

carriage return n (on typewriter) Wagenrücklauf m; (Comput) Return nt

carriageway ['kærɪdʒweɪ] (Brit) n Fahrbahn f

carrier ['kærɪəʳ] n Spediteur m, Transportunternehmer m; (Med) Überträger m

carrier bag (Brit) n Tragetasche f, Tragetüte f
carrier pigeon n Brieftaube f
carrion ['kærɪən] n Aas nt
carrot ['kærət] n Möhre f, Mohrrübe f, Karotte
f; (fig) Köder m
carry ['kærɪ] vt tragen; (transport)
transportieren; (a motion, bill) annehmen;
(responsibilities etc) mit sich bringen; (disease,
virus) übertragen ▷ vi (sound) tragen; **to get
carried away** (fig) sich hinreißen lassen; **this
loan carries 10% interest** dieses Darlehen
wird mit 10% verzinst
▶ **carry forward** vt übertragen, vortragen
▶ **carry on** vi weitermachen; (inf: make a fuss)
(ein) Theater machen ▷ vt fortführen; **to ~
on with sth** mit etw weitermachen; **to ~ on
singing/eating** weitersingen/-essen
▶ **carry out** vt (orders) ausführen; (investigation)
durchführen; (idea) in die Tat umsetzen;
(threat) wahr machen
carrycot ['kærɪkɒt] (Brit) n Babytragetasche f
carry-on ['kærɪ'ɒn] (inf) n Theater nt
cart [kɑːt] n Wagen m, Karren m; (for passengers)
Wagen m; (handcart) (Hand)wagen m ▷ vt (inf)
mit sich herumschleppen
carte blanche ['kɑːt'blɒnʃ] n: **to give sb ~** jdm
Carte blanche or (eine) Blankovollmacht geben
cartel [kɑː'tɛl] n Kartell nt
cartilage ['kɑːtɪlɪdʒ] n Knorpel m
cartographer [kɑː'tɒɡrəfə'] n Kartograf(in)
m(f)
cartography [kɑː'tɒɡrəfɪ] n Kartografie f
carton ['kɑːtən] n (Papp)karton m; (of yogurt)
Becher m; (of milk) Tüte f; (of cigarettes) Stange f
cartoon [kɑː'tuːn] n (drawing) Karikatur
f; (Brit: comic strip) Cartoon m; (Cine)
Zeichentrickfilm m
cartoonist [kɑː'tuːnɪst] n Karikaturist(in) m(f)
cartridge ['kɑːtrɪdʒ] n (for gun, pen) Patrone f;
(music tape, for camera) Kassette f; (of record-player)
Tonabnehmer m
cartwheel ['kɑːtwiːl] n Rad nt; **to turn a ~** Rad
schlagen
carve [kɑːv] vt (meat) (ab)schneiden; (wood)
schnitzen; (stone) meißeln; (initials, design)
einritzen
▶ **carve up** vt (land etc) aufteilen; (meat)
aufschneiden
carving ['kɑːvɪŋ] n Skulptur f; (in wood etc)
Schnitzerei f
carving knife n Tran(s)chiermesser nt
car wash n Autowaschanlage f
Casablanca [kæsə'blæŋkə] n Casablanca nt
cascade [kæs'keɪd] n Wasserfall m, Kaskade f;
(of money) Regen m; (of hair) wallende Fülle f ▷ vi
(in Kaskaden) herabfallen; (hair etc) wallen;
(people) strömen
case [keɪs] n Fall m; (for spectacles etc) Etui nt;
(Brit: also: **suitcase**) Koffer m; (of wine, whisky
etc) Kiste f; (Typ): **lower/upper ~** klein-/
großgeschrieben; **to have a good ~** gute
Chancen haben, durchzukommen; **there's
a strong ~ for reform** es spricht viel für eine

Reform; **in ~ ... falls ...; in ~ of fire** bei Feuer;
in ~ of emergency im Notfall; **in ~ he comes**
falls er kommt; **in any ~** sowieso; **just in ~** für
alle Fälle
case-hardened ['keɪshɑːnd] adj (fig)
abgebrüht (inf)
case history n (Med) Krankengeschichte f
case study n Fallstudie f
cash [kæʃ] n (Bar)geld nt ▷ vt (cheque etc)
einlösen; **to pay (in) ~** bar bezahlen; **~ on
delivery** per Nachnahme; **~ with order**
zahlbar bei Bestellung
▶ **cash in** vt einlösen
▶ **cash in on** vt fus Kapital schlagen aus
cash account n Kassenbuch nt
cash-and-carry [kæʃən'kærɪ] n Abholmarkt m
cash-book ['kæʃbʊk] n Kassenkonto nt
cash box n (Geld)kassette f
cash card (Brit) n (Geld)automatenkarte f
cash crop n zum Verkauf bestimmte Ernte f
cash desk (Brit) n Kasse f
cash discount n Skonto m or nt
cash dispenser (Brit) n Geldautomat m
cashew [kæ'ʃuː] n (also: **cashew nut**)
Cashewnuss f
cash flow n Cashflow m
cashier [kæ'ʃɪə'] n Kassierer(in) m(f)
cashmere ['kæʃmɪə'] n Kaschmir m
cash point n Geldautomat m
cash price n Bar(zahlungs)preis m
cash register n Registrierkasse f
cash sale n Barverkauf m
casing ['keɪsɪŋ] n Gehäuse nt
casino [kə'siːnəu] n Kasino nt
cask [kɑːsk] n Fass nt
casket ['kɑːskɪt] n Schatulle f; (US: coffin) Sarg m
Caspian Sea ['kæspɪən-] n: **the ~** das Kaspische
Meer
casserole ['kæsərəul] n Auflauf m; (pot,
container) Kasserolle f
cassette [kæ'sɛt] n Kassette f
cassette deck n Kassettendeck nt
cassette player n Kassettenrekorder m
cassette recorder n Kassettenrekorder m
cast [kɑːst] (pt, pp ~) vt werfen; (net, fishing-
line) auswerfen; (metal, statue) gießen ▷ vi
die Angel auswerfen ▷ n (Theat) Besetzung
f; (mould) (Guss)form f; (also: **plaster cast**)
Gipsverband m; **to ~ sb as Hamlet** (Theat)
die Rolle des Hamlet mit jdm besetzen; **to
~ one's vote** seine Stimme abgeben; **to ~
one's eyes over sth** einen Blick auf etw acc
werfen; **to ~ aspersions on sb/sth** abfällige
Bemerkungen über jdn/etw machen; **to ~
doubts on sth** etw in Zweifel ziehen; **to ~ a
spell on sb/sth** jdn/etw verzaubern; **to ~ its
skin** sich häuten
▶ **cast aside** vt fallen lassen
▶ **cast off** vi (Naut) losmachen; (Knitting)
abketten ▷ vt abketten
▶ **cast on** vi, vt (Knitting) anschlagen,
aufschlagen
castaway ['kɑːstəweɪ] n Schiffbrüchige(r) f(m)

caste [kɑːst] n Kaste f; (system) Kastenwesen nt
caster sugar ['kɑːstə-] (Brit) n Raffinade f
casting vote ['kɑːstɪŋ-] (Brit) n
ausschlaggebende Stimme f
cast iron n Gusseisen nt ▷ adj: **cast-iron**
(fig: will) eisern; (: alibi, excuse etc) hieb- und
stichfest
castle ['kɑːsl] n Schloss nt; (manor) Herrenhaus
nt; (fortified) Burg f; (Chess) Turm m
cast off n abgelegtes Kleidungsstück nt
castor ['kɑːstəʳ] n Rolle f
castor oil n Rizinusöl nt
castrate [kæs'treɪt] vt kastrieren
casual ['kæʒjul] adj (by chance) zufällig;
(work etc) Gelegenheits-; (unconcerned)
lässig, gleichgültig; (clothes) leger; ~ **wear**
Freizeitkleidung f
casual labour n Gelegenheitsarbeit f
casually ['kæʒjulɪ] adv lässig; (glance) beiläufig;
(dress) leger; (by chance) zufällig
casualty ['kæʒjultɪ] n (of war etc) Opfer nt;
(someone injured) Verletzte(r) f(m); (someone killed)
Tote(r) f(m); (Med) Unfallstation f; **heavy**
casualties (Mil) schwere Verluste pl
casualty ward (Brit) n Unfallstation f
cat [kæt] n Katze f; (lion etc) (Raub)katze f
catacombs ['kætəkuːmz] npl Katakomben pl
catalogue, (US) **catalog** ['kætəlɔg] n Katalog m
▷ vt katalogisieren
catalyst ['kætəlɪst] n Katalysator m
catalytic converter [kætə'lɪtɪk kən'vɜːtəʳ] n
(Aut) Katalysator m
catapult ['kætəpʌlt] (Brit) n Schleuder
f; (Mil) Katapult nt or m ▷ vi geschleudert
or katapultiert werden ▷ vt schleudern,
katapultieren
cataract ['kætərækt] n (Med) grauer Star m
catarrh [kə'tɑːʳ] n Katarrh m
catastrophe [kə'tæstrəfɪ] n Katastrophe f
catastrophic [kætə'strofɪk] adj katastrophal
catcalls ['kætkɔːlz] npl Pfiffe und Buhrufe pl
catch [kætʃ] (pt, pp **caught**) vt fangen; (take: bus,
train etc) nehmen; (arrest) festnehmen; (surprise)
erwischen, ertappen; (breath) holen; (attention)
erregen; (hit) treffen; (hear) mitbekommen;
(illness) sich dat zuziehen or holen; (person: also:
catch up) einholen ▷ vi (fire) (anfangen zu)
brennen; (become trapped) hängen bleiben
▷ n Fang m; (trick, hidden problem) Haken m; (of
lock) Riegel m; (game) Fangen nt; **to ~ sb's**
attention/eye jdn auf sich acc aufmerksam
machen; **to ~ fire** Feuer fangen; **to ~ sight of**
erblicken
 ▶ **catch on** vi (grow popular) sich durchsetzen;
to ~ on (to sth) (etw) kapieren
 ▶ **catch out** (Brit) vt (fig) hereinlegen
 ▶ **catch up** vi (fig: with person) mitkommen; (: on
work) aufholen ▷ vt: **to ~ sb up, to ~ up with**
sb jdn einholen
catch-22 ['kætʃtwentɪ'tuː] n: **it's a ~ situation**
es ist eine Zwickmühle
catching ['kætʃɪŋ] adj ansteckend
catchment area ['kætʃmənt-] (Brit) n

Einzugsgebiet nt
catch phrase n Schlagwort nt, Slogan m
catchy ['kætʃɪ] adj (tune) eingängig
catechism ['kætɪkɪzəm] n Katechismus m
categoric [kætɪ'gɔrɪk], **categorical**
[kætɪ'gɔrɪkəl] adj kategorisch
categorize ['kætɪgəraɪz] vt kategorisieren
category ['kætɪgərɪ] n Kategorie f
cater ['keɪtəʳ] vi: **to ~ (for)** die Speisen und
Getränke liefern (für)
 ▶ **cater for** (Brit) vt fus (needs, tastes) gerecht
werden +dat; (readers, consumers) eingestellt or
ausgerichtet sein auf +acc
caterer ['keɪtərəʳ] n Lieferant(in) m(f) von
Speisen und Getränken; (company) Lieferfirma
f für Speisen und Getränke
catering ['keɪtərɪŋ] n Gastronomie f
caterpillar ['kætəpɪləʳ] n Raupe f ▷ cpd (vehicle)
Raupen-
caterpillar track n Raupenkette f, Gleiskette f
cat flap n Katzentür f
cathedral [kə'θiːdrəl] n Kathedrale f, Dom m
cathode ['kæθəud] n Kat(h)ode f
cathode-ray tube [kæθəud'reɪ-] n Kat(h)
odenstrahlröhre f
Catholic ['kæθəlɪk] adj katholisch ▷ n
Katholik(in) m(f)
catholic ['kæθəlɪk] adj vielseitig
CAT scanner n abbr (Med: = computerized axial
tomography scanner) CAT-Scanner m
Catseye® ['kætsaɪ] (Brit) n Katzenauge nt
catsup ['kætsəp] (US) n Ket(s)chup m or nt
cattle ['kætl] npl Vieh nt
catty ['kætɪ] adj gehässig
catwalk ['kætwɔːk] n Steg m; (for models)
Laufsteg m
Caucasian [kɔː'keɪzɪən] adj kaukasisch ▷ n
Kaukasier(in) m(f)
Caucasus ['kɔːkəsəs] n Kaukasus m
caucus ['kɔːkəs] n (group) Gremium nt,
Ausschuss m; (US) Parteiversammlung f; siehe
Info-Artikel

   ● **CAUCUS**

   Caucus bedeutet vor allem in den USA ein
   privates Treffen von Parteifunktionären,
   bei dem z. B. Kandidaten ausgewählt
   oder Grundsatzentscheidungen getroffen
   werden. Meist wird ein solches Treffen vor
   einer öffentlichen Parteiversammlung
   abgehalten. Der Begriff bezieht sich im
   weiteren Sinne auch auf den kleinen, aber
   mächtigen Kreis von Parteifunktionären,
   der beim caucus zusammentrifft.

caught [kɔːt] pt, pp of **catch**
cauliflower ['kɔlɪflauəʳ] n Blumenkohl m
cause [kɔːz] n Ursache f; (reason) Grund m; (aim)
Sache f ▷ vt verursachen; **there is no ~ for**
concern es besteht kein Grund zur Sorge; **to**
~ sth to be done veranlassen, dass etw getan
wird; **to ~ sb to do sth** jdn veranlassen, etw

zu tun

causeway ['kɔːzweɪ] n Damm m

caustic ['kɔːstɪk] adj ätzend, kaustisch; (remark) bissig

cauterize ['kɔːtəraɪz] vt kauterisieren

caution ['kɔːʃən] n Vorsicht f; (warning) Warnung f; (: Law) Verwarnung f ▷ vt warnen; (Law) verwarnen

cautious ['kɔːʃəs] adj vorsichtig

cautiously ['kɔːʃəslɪ] adv vorsichtig

cautiousness ['kɔːʃəsnɪs] n Vorsicht f

cavalier [kævə'lɪəʳ] adj unbekümmert

cavalry ['kævəlrɪ] n Kavallerie f

cave [keɪv] n Höhle f ▷ vi: **to go caving** auf Höhlenexpedition(en) gehen
  ▸ **cave in** vi einstürzen; (to demands) nachgeben

caveman ['keɪvmæn] (irreg: like **man**) n Höhlenmensch m

cavern ['kævən] n Höhle f

caviar, caviare ['kævɪɑːʳ] n Kaviar m

cavity ['kævɪtɪ] n Hohlraum m; (in tooth) Loch nt

cavity wall insulation n Schaumisolierung f

cavort [kə'vɔːt] vi tollen, toben

cayenne [keɪ'ɛn] n (also: **cayenne pepper**) Cayennepfeffer m

CB n abbr (= Citizens' Band (Radio)) CB-Funk m

CBC n abbr (= Canadian Broadcasting Corporation) kanadische Rundfunkgesellschaft

CBE (Brit) n abbr (= Commander of (the Order of) the British Empire) britischer Ordenstitel

CBI n abbr (= Confederation of British Industry) britischer Unternehmerverband, ≈ BDI m

CBS (US) n abbr (= Columbia Broadcasting System) Rundfunkgesellschaft

CC (Brit) abbr = **county council**

cc abbr (= cubic centimetre) ccm; = **carbon copy**

CCTV n abbr = **closed-circuit television**

CCU (US) n abbr (= cardiac or coronary care unit) Intensivstation für Herzpatienten

CD abbr (Brit: = Corps Diplomatique) CD ▷ n abbr (Mil: Brit: = Civil Defence (Corps)) Zivilschutz m; (: US: = Civil Defense) Zivilschutz m; (= compact disc) CD f; **CD player** CD-Spieler m

CDC (US) n abbr (= Center for Disease Control) Seuchenkontrollbehörde

Cdr abbr (Mil) = **commander**

CD-ROM n abbr (= compact disc read-only memory) CD-ROM f

CDT (US) abbr (= Central Daylight Time) mittelamerikanische Sommerzeit; (Brit: Scol: = Craft, Design and Technology) Arbeitslehre f

cease [siːs] vt beenden ▷ vi aufhören

ceasefire ['siːsfaɪəʳ] n Waffenruhe f

ceaseless ['siːslɪs] adj endlos, unaufhörlich

CED (US) n abbr (= Committee for Economic Development) Komitee für wirtschaftliche Entwicklung

cedar ['siːdəʳ] n Zeder f; (wood) Zedernholz nt

cede [siːd] vt abtreten

cedilla [sɪ'dɪlə] n Cedille f

CEEB (US) n abbr (= College Entry Examination Board) akademische Zulassungsstelle

ceilidh ['keɪlɪ] (Scott) n Fest mit Volksmusik, Gesang

und Tanz

ceiling ['siːlɪŋ] n Decke f; (upper limit) Obergrenze f, Höchstgrenze f

celebrate ['sɛlɪbreɪt] vt feiern; (mass) zelebrieren ▷ vi feiern

celebrated ['sɛlɪbreɪtɪd] adj gefeiert

celebration [sɛlɪ'breɪʃən] n Feier f

celebrity [sɪ'lɛbrɪtɪ] n berühmte Persönlichkeit f

celeriac [sə'lɛrɪæk] n (Knollen)sellerie f

celery ['sɛlərɪ] n (Stangen)sellerie f

celestial [sɪ'lɛstɪəl] adj himmlisch

celibacy ['sɛlɪbəsɪ] n Zölibat nt or m

cell [sɛl] n Zelle f

cellar ['sɛləʳ] n Keller m; (for wine) (Wein)keller m

cellist ['tʃɛlɪst] n Cellist(in) m(f)

cello ['tʃɛləu] n Cello nt

cellophane ['sɛləfeɪn] n Cellophan nt

cellphone n Handy nt, Mobiltelefon nt

cellular ['sɛljuləʳ] adj (Biol) zellular, Zell-; (fabrics) aus porösem Material

Celluloid® ['sɛljulɔɪd] n Zelluloid nt

cellulose ['sɛljuləus] n Zellulose f, Zellstoff m

Celsius ['sɛlsɪəs] adj (scale) Celsius-

Celt [kɛlt] n Kelte m, Keltin f

Celtic ['kɛltɪk] adj keltisch ▷ n (Ling) Keltisch nt

cement [sə'mɛnt] n Zement m; (concrete) Beton m; (glue) Klebstoff m ▷ vt zementieren; (stick, glue) kleben; (fig) festigen

cement mixer n Betonmischmaschine f

cemetery ['sɛmɪtrɪ] n Friedhof m

cenotaph ['sɛnətɑːf] n Ehrenmal nt

censor ['sɛnsəʳ] n Zensor(in) m(f) ▷ vt zensieren

censorship ['sɛnsəʃɪp] n Zensur f

censure ['sɛnʃəʳ] vt tadeln ▷ n Tadel m

census ['sɛnsəs] n Volkszählung f

cent [sɛnt] n Cent m; see also **per cent**

centenary [sɛn'tiːnərɪ] n hundertster Jahrestag m

centennial [sɛn'tɛnɪəl] (US) n = **centenary**

center etc ['sɛntəʳ] (US) = **centre** etc

centigrade ['sɛntɪɡreɪd] adj (scale) Celsius-

centilitre, (US) **centiliter** ['sɛntɪliːtəʳ] n Zentiliter m or nt

centimetre, (US) **centimeter** ['sɛntɪmiːtəʳ] n Zentimeter m or nt

centipede ['sɛntɪpiːd] n Tausendfüßler m

central ['sɛntrəl] adj zentral; (committee, government) Zentral-; (idea) wesentlich

Central African Republic n Zentralafrikanische Republik f

Central America n Mittelamerika nt

central heating n Zentralheizung f

centralize ['sɛntrəlaɪz] vt zentralisieren

central processing unit n (Comput) Zentraleinheit f

central reservation (Brit) n Mittelstreifen m

centre, (US) **center** ['sɛntəʳ] n Mitte f; (health centre etc, town centre) Zentrum nt; (of attention, interest) Mittelpunkt m; (of action, belief etc) Kern m ▷ vt zentrieren; (ball) zur Mitte spielen ▷ vi (*concentrate*): **to ~ on** sich konzentrieren auf +*acc*

centrefold, (US) **centerfold** ['sɛntəfəuld] *n* doppelseitiges Bild in der Mitte einer Zeitschrift

centre forward *n* Mittelstürmer(in) *m(f)*

centre half *n* Stopper(in) *m(f)*

centrepiece, (US) **centerpiece** ['sɛntəpi:s] *n* Tafelaufsatz *m*; (*fig*) Kernstück *nt*

centre spread (*Brit*) *n* Doppelseite in der Mitte einer Zeitschrift

centre-stage [sɛntə'steɪdʒ] (*fig*) *adv*: **to be ~ im** Mittelpunkt stehen ▷ *n*: **to take centre stage** in den Mittelpunkt rücken

centrifugal [sɛn'trɪfjugl] *adj* (*force*) Zentrifugal-

centrifuge ['sɛntrɪfju:ʒ] *n* Zentrifuge *f*, Schleuder *f*

century ['sɛntjʊrɪ] *n* Jahrhundert *nt*; (*Cricket*) Hundert *f*; **in the twentieth ~ im** zwanzigsten Jahrhundert

CEO *n abbr* = **chief executive officer**

ceramic [sɪ'ræmɪk] *adj* keramisch; (*tiles*) Keramik-

ceramics [sɪ'ræmɪks] *npl* Keramiken *pl*

cereal ['si:rɪəl] *n* Getreide *nt*; (*food*) Getreideflocken *pl* (*Cornflakes etc*)

cerebral ['sɛrɪbrəl] *adj* (*Med*) zerebral; (*intellectual*) geistig

ceremonial [sɛrɪ'məunɪəl] *n* Zeremoniell *nt* ▷ *adj* zeremoniell

ceremony ['sɛrɪmənɪ] *n* Zeremonie *f*; (*behaviour*) Förmlichkeit *f*; **to stand on ~** förmlich sein

cert [sə:t] (*Brit: inf*) *n*: **it's a dead ~** es ist todsicher

certain ['sə:tən] *adj* sicher; **a ~ Mr Smith** ein gewisser Herr Smith; **~ days/places** bestimmte Tage/Orte; **a ~ coldness** eine gewisse Kälte; **to make ~ of** sich vergewissern +*gen*; **for ~** ganz sicher, ganz genau

certainly ['sə:tənlɪ] *adv* bestimmt; (*of course*) sicherlich; **~!** (aber) sicher!

certainty ['sə:təntɪ] *n* Sicherheit *f*; (*inevitability*) Gewissheit *f*

certificate [sə'tɪfɪkɪt] *n* Urkunde *f*; (*diploma*) Zeugnis *nt*

certified letter ['sə:tɪfaɪd-] (US) *n* Einschreibebrief *m*

certified mail (US) *n* Einschreiben *nt*

certified public accountant ['sə:tɪfaɪd-] (US) *n* geprüfter Buchhalter *m*, geprüfte Buchhalterin *f*

certify ['sə:tɪfaɪ] *vt* bescheinigen; (*award a diploma to*) ein Zeugnis verleihen +*dat*; (*declare insane*) für unzurechnungsfähig erklären ▷ *vi*: **to ~ to** sich verbürgen für

cervical ['sə:vɪkl] *adj*: **~ cancer** Gebärmutterhalskrebs *m*; **~ smear** Abstrich *m*

cervix ['sə:vɪks] *n* Gebärmutterhals *m*

Cesarean [sɪ'zɛərɪən] (US) *n* = **Caesarean**

cessation [sə'seɪʃən] *n* (*of hostilities etc*) Einstellung *f*, Ende *nt*

cesspit ['sɛspɪt] *n* (*sewage tank*) Senkgrube *f*

CET *abbr* (= *Central European Time*) MEZ

Ceylon [sɪ'lɔn] *n* Ceylon *nt*

cf. *abbr* (= *compare*) vgl.

c/f *abbr* (*Comm*: = *carried forward*) Übertr.

CFC *n abbr* (= *chlorofluorocarbon*) FCKW *m*

CG (US) *n abbr* = **coastguard**

cg *abbr* (= *centigram*) cg

CH (*Brit*) *n abbr* (= *Companion of Honour*) britischer Ordenstitel

ch. *abbr* (= *chapter*) Kap.

Chad [tʃæd] *n* Tschad *m*

chafe [tʃeɪf] *vt* (*wund*) reiben ▷ *vi* (*fig*): **to ~ against** sich ärgern über +*acc*

chaffinch ['tʃæfɪntʃ] *n* Buchfink *m*

chagrin ['ʃægrɪn] *n* Ärger *m*

chain [tʃeɪn] *n* Kette *f* ▷ *vt* (*also*: **chain up**: *prisoner*) anketten; (: *dog*) an die Kette legen

chain reaction *n* Kettenreaktion *f*

chain-smoke ['tʃeɪnsməuk] *vi* eine Zigarette nach der anderen rauchen

chain store *n* Kettenladen *m*

chair [tʃɛəʳ] *n* Stuhl *m*; (*armchair*) Sessel *m*; (*of university*) Lehrstuhl *m*; (*of meeting, committee*) Vorsitz *m* ▷ *vt* den Vorsitz führen bei; **the ~** (US) der elektrische Stuhl

chair lift *n* Sessellift *m*

chairman ['tʃɛəmən] (*irreg: like* **man**) *n* Vorsitzende(r) *f(m)*; (*Brit: of company*) Präsident *m*

chairperson ['tʃɛəpə:sn] *n* Vorsitzende(r) *f(m)*

chairwoman ['tʃɛəwumən] (*irreg: like* **woman**) *n* Vorsitzende *f*

chalet ['ʃæleɪ] *n* Chalet *nt*

chalice ['tʃælɪs] *n* Kelch *m*

chalk [tʃɔ:k] *n* Kalkstein *m*, Kreide *f*; (*for writing*) Kreide *f*
▷ **chalk up** *vt* aufschreiben, notieren; (*fig: success etc*) verbuchen

challenge ['tʃælɪndʒ] *n* (*of new job*) Anforderungen *pl*; (*of unknown etc*) Reiz *m*; (*to authority etc*) Infragestellung *f*; (*dare*) Herausforderung *f* ▷ *vt* herausfordern; (*authority, right, idea etc*) infrage stellen; **to ~ sb to do sth** jdn dazu auffordern, etw zu tun; **to ~ sb to a fight/game** jdn zu einem Kampf/ Spiel herausfordern

challenger ['tʃælɪndʒəʳ] *n* Herausforderer *m*, Herausforderin *f*

challenging ['tʃælɪndʒɪŋ] *adj* (*career, task*) anspruchsvoll; (*tone, look etc*) herausfordernd

chamber ['tʃeɪmbəʳ] *n* Kammer *f*; (*Brit: Law: gen pl*: *of barristers*) Kanzlei *f*; (: *of judge*) Amtszimmer *nt*; **~ of commerce** Handelskammer *f*

chambermaid ['tʃeɪmbəmeɪd] *n* Zimmermädchen *nt*

chamber music *n* Kammermusik *f*

chamber pot *n* Nachttopf *m*

chameleon [kə'mi:lɪən] *n* Chamäleon *nt*

chamois ['ʃæmwɑ:] *n* Gämse *f*; (*cloth*) Ledertuch *nt*, Fensterleder *nt*

chamois leather ['ʃæmɪ-] *n* Ledertuch *nt*, Fensterleder *nt*

champagne [ʃæm'peɪn] *n* Champagner *m*

champers ['ʃæmpəz] (inf) n (champagne)
Schampus m
champion ['tʃæmpɪən] n Meister(in) m(f); (of
cause, principle) Verfechter(in) m(f); (of person)
Fürsprecher(in) m(f) ▷ vt eintreten für, sich
engagieren für
championship ['tʃæmpɪənʃɪp] n Meisterschaft
f; (title) Titel m
chance [tʃɑːns] n (hope) Aussicht
f; (likelihood, possibility) Möglichkeit f;
(opportunity) Gelegenheit f; (risk) Risiko nt
▷ vt riskieren ▷ adj zufällig; **the ~s are
that** ... aller Wahrscheinlichkeit nach ...,
wahrscheinlich ...; **there is little ~ of his
coming** es ist unwahrscheinlich, dass er
kommt; **to take a ~** es darauf ankommen
lassen; **by ~** durch Zufall, zufällig; **it's the ~
of a lifetime** es ist eine einmalige Chance;
to ~ to do sth zufällig etw tun; **to ~ it** es
riskieren
▶ **chance (up)on** vt fus (person) zufällig
begegnen +dat, zufällig treffen; (thing) zufällig
stoßen auf +acc
chancel ['tʃɑːnsəl] n Altarraum m
chancellor ['tʃɑːnsələr] n Kanzler m
Chancellor of the Exchequer (Brit) n
Schatzkanzler m, Finanzminister m
chancy ['tʃɑːnsɪ] adj riskant
chandelier [ʃændə'lɪər] n Kronleuchter m
change [tʃeɪndʒ] vt ändern; (wheel, job, money,
baby's nappy) wechseln; (bulb) auswechseln;
(baby) wickeln ▷ vi sich verändern; (traffic
lights) umspringen ▷ n Veränderung f;
(difference) Abwechslung f; (of government,
climate, job) Wechsel m; (coins) Kleingeld
nt; (money returned) Wechselgeld nt; **to ~ sb
into** jdn verwandeln in +acc; **to ~ gear** (Aut)
schalten; **to ~ one's mind** seine Meinung
ändern, es sich dat anders überlegen; **to ~
hands** den Besitzer wechseln; **to ~ (trains/
buses/planes** etc) umsteigen; **to ~ (one's
clothes)** sich umziehen; **to ~ into** (be
transformed) sich verwandeln in +acc; **she ~d
into an old skirt** sie zog einen alten Rock an;
a ~ of clothes Kleidung f zum Wechseln; **~
of government/climate/job** Regierungs-/
Klima-/Berufswechsel m; **small ~** Kleingeld
nt; **to give sb ~ for** or **of £10** jdm £10
wechseln; **keep the ~** das stimmt so, der Rest
ist für Sie; **for a ~** zur Abwechslung
changeable ['tʃeɪndʒəbl] adj (weather)
wechselhaft, veränderlich; (mood) wechselnd;
(person) unbeständig
change machine n (Geld)wechselautomat m
changeover ['tʃeɪndʒəʊvər] n Umstellung f
changing ['tʃeɪndʒɪŋ] adj sich verändernd
changing room (Brit) n (Umkleide)kabine f;
(Sport) Umkleideraum m
channel ['tʃænl] n (TV) Kanal m; (of river,
waterway) Fluss)bett nt; (for boats) Fahrrinne
f; (groove) Rille f; (fig: means) Weg m ▷ vt leiten;
(fig): **to ~ into** lenken auf +acc; **through the
usual ~s** auf dem üblichen Wege; **green ~**

(Customs) „nichts zu verzollen"; **red ~** (Customs)
„Waren zu verzollen"; **the (English) C~** der
Ärmelkanal; **the C~ Islands** die Kanalinseln
pl
channel-hopping ['tʃænlhɔpɪŋ] n (TV)
ständiges Umschalten
Channel Tunnel n: **the ~** der Kanaltunnel
chant [tʃɑːnt] n Sprechchor m; (Rel) Gesang m
▷ vt im (Sprech)chor rufen; (Rel) singen ▷ vi
Sprechchöre anstimmen; (Rel) singen; **the
demonstrators ~ed their disapproval** die
Demonstranten machten ihrem Unmut in
Sprechchören Luft
chaos ['keɪɔs] n Chaos nt, Durcheinander nt
chaos theory n Chaostheorie f
chaotic [keɪ'ɔtɪk] adj chaotisch
chap [tʃæp] (Brit: inf) n Kerl m, Typ m; **old ~** alter
Knabe or Junge
chapel ['tʃæpl] n Kapelle f; (Brit: non-conformist
chapel) Sektenkirche f; (: of union) Betriebsgruppe
innerhalb der Gewerkschaft der Drucker und
Journalisten
chaperone ['ʃæpərəʊn] n Anstandsdame f ▷ vt
begleiten
chaplain ['tʃæplɪn] n Pfarrer(in) m(f); (Roman
Catholic) Kaplan m
chapped [tʃæpt] adj aufgesprungen, rau
chapter ['tʃæptər] n Kapitel nt; **a ~ of
accidents** eine Serie von Unfällen
char [tʃɑːr] vt verkohlen ▷ vi (Brit) putzen gehen
▷ n (Brit) = **charlady**
character ['kærɪktər] n Charakter m;
(personality) Persönlichkeit f; (in novel, film) Figur
f, Gestalt f; (eccentric) Original nt; (letter: also
Comput) Zeichen nt; **a person of good ~** ein
guter Mensch
character code n (Comput) Zeichencode m
characteristic [kærɪktə'rɪstɪk] n Merkmal n
▷ adj: **~ (of)** charakteristisch (für), typisch (für)
characterize ['kærɪktəraɪz] vt kennzeichnen,
charakterisieren; (describe the character of): **to ~
(as)** beschreiben (als)
charade [ʃə'rɑːd] n Scharade f
charcoal ['tʃɑːkəʊl] n Holzkohle f; (for drawing)
Kohle f, Kohlestift m
charge [tʃɑːdʒ] n (fee) Gebühr f; (accusation)
Anklage f; (responsibility) Verantwortung f;
(attack) Angriff m ▷ vt (customer) berechnen
+dat; (sum) berechnen; (battery) (auf)laden;
(gun) laden; (enemy) angreifen; (sb with task)
beauftragen ▷ vi angreifen; (usu with: up,
along etc) stürmen; **charges** npl Gebühren
pl; **labour ~s** Arbeitskosten pl; **to reverse
the ~s** (Brit: Tel) ein R-Gespräch führen; **is
there a ~?** kostet das etwas?; **there's no
~** es ist umsonst, es kostet nichts; **at no
extra ~** ohne Aufpreis; **free of ~** kostenlos,
gratis; **to take ~ of** (child) sich kümmern
um; (company) übernehmen; **to be in ~ of**
die Verantwortung haben für; (business)
leiten; **they ~d us for the meal** das
Essen kostete £10; **how much do you ~?** was
verlangen Sie?; **to ~ an expense (up) to sb's**

account eine Ausgabe auf jds Rechnung *acc* setzen; **to ~ sb (with)** (*Law*) jdn anklagen (wegen)

charge account *n* Kunden(kredit)konto *nt*

charge card *n* Kundenkreditkarte *f*

chargé d'affaires *n* Chargé d'affaires *m*

charge hand (*Brit*) *n* Vorarbeiter(in) *m(f)*

charger ['tʃɑːdʒəʳ] *n* (*also*: **battery charger**) Ladegerät *nt*; (*warhorse*) (Schlacht)ross *nt*

chariot ['tʃærɪət] *n* (Streit)wagen *m*

charisma [kæ'rɪsmə] *n* Charisma *nt*

charitable ['tʃærɪtəbl] *adj* (*organization*) karitativ, Wohltätigkeits-; (*remark*) freundlich

charity ['tʃærɪtɪ] *n* (*organization*) karitative Organisation *f*, Wohltätigkeitsverein *m*; (*kindness, generosity*) Menschenfreundlichkeit *f*; (*money, gifts*) Almosen *nt*

charlady ['tʃɑːleɪdɪ] (*irreg*: *like* **lady**) (*Brit*) *n* Putzfrau *f*, Reinemachefrau *f*

charlatan ['ʃɑːlətən] *n* Scharlatan *m*

charm [tʃɑːm] *n* Charme *m*; (*to bring good luck*) Talisman *m*; (*on bracelet etc*) Anhänger *m* ▷ *vt* bezaubern

charm bracelet *n* Armband *nt* mit Anhängern

charming ['tʃɑːmɪŋ] *adj* reizend, charmant; (*place*) bezaubernd

chart [tʃɑːt] *n* Schaubild *nt*, Diagramm *nt*; (*map*) Karte *f*; (*also*: **weather chart**) Wetterkarte *f* ▷ *vt* (*course*) planen; (*progress*) aufzeichnen; **charts** *npl* (*hit parade*) Hitliste *f*

charter ['tʃɑːtəʳ] *vt* chartern ▷ *n* Charta *f*; (*of university, company*) Gründungsurkunde *f*; **on ~** gechartert

chartered accountant ['tʃɑːtəd-] (*Brit*) *n* Wirtschaftsprüfer(in) *m(f)*

charter flight *n* Charterflug *m*

charwoman ['tʃɑːwumən] (*irreg*: *like* **woman**) *n* Putzfrau *f*, Reinemachefrau *f*

chary ['tʃɛərɪ] *adj*: **to be ~ of doing sth** zögern, etw zu tun

chase [tʃeɪs] *vt* jagen, verfolgen; (*also*: **chase away**) wegjagen, vertreiben; (*business, job etc*) her sein hinter +*dat* (*inf*) ▷ *n* Verfolgungsjagd *f*
  ▶ **chase down** (*US*) *vt* = **chase up**
  ▶ **chase up** (*Brit*) *vt* (*person*) rankriegen (*inf*); (*information*) ranschaffen (*inf*)

chasm ['kæzəm] *n* Kluft *f*

chassis ['ʃæsɪ] *n* Fahrgestell *nt*

chaste [tʃeɪst] *adj* keusch

chastened ['tʃeɪsnd] *adj* zur Einsicht gebracht

chastening ['tʃeɪsnɪŋ] *adj* ernüchternd

chastise [tʃæs'taɪz] *vt* (*scold*) schelten

chastity ['tʃæstɪtɪ] *n* Keuschheit *f*

chat [tʃæt] *vi* (*also*: **have a chat**) plaudern, sich unterhalten; (*Comput*) chatten ▷ *n* Plauderei *f*, Unterhaltung *f*; (*Comput*) Chat
  ▶ **chat up** (*Brit*: *inf*) *vt* anmachen

chatline ['tʃætlaɪn] *n* Telefondienst, der Anrufern die Teilnahme an einer Gesprächsrunde ermöglicht

chatroom ['tʃætruːm] *n* (*Comput*) Chatroom *m*

chat show (*Brit*) *n* Talkshow *f*

chattel ['tʃætl] *n*: **goods and ~s** *see* **good**

chatter ['tʃætəʳ] *vi* schwatzen; (*monkey*) schnattern; (*teeth*) klappern ▷ *n* (*see vi*) Schwatzen *nt*; Schnattern *nt*; Klappern *nt*; **my teeth are ~ing** mir klappern die Zähne

chatterbox ['tʃætəbɔks] (*inf*) *n* Quasselstrippe *f*

chattering classes ['tʃætərɪŋ 'klɑːsɪz] *npl*: **the ~** die intellektuellen Schwätzer *pl*

chatty ['tʃætɪ] *adj* geschwätzig; (*letter*) im Plauderton

chauffeur ['ʃəufəʳ] *n* Chauffeur *m*, Fahrer *m*

chauvinism ['ʃəuvɪnɪzəm] *n* (*also*: **male chauvinism**) Chauvinismus *m*

chauvinist ['ʃəuvɪnɪst] *n* Chauvinist *m*

chauvinistic [ʃəuvɪ'nɪstɪk] *adj* chauvinistisch

ChE *abbr* (= *chemical engineer*) Titel für Chemotechniker

cheap [tʃiːp] *adj* billig; (*reduced*) ermäßigt; (*poor quality*) billig, minderwertig; (*behaviour, joke*) ordinär ▷ *adv*: **to buy/sell sth ~** etw billig kaufen/verkaufen

cheap day return *n* Tagesrückfahrkarte *f* (*zu einem günstigeren Tarif*)

cheapen ['tʃiːpn] *vt* entwürdigen

cheaper ['tʃiːpəʳ] *adj* billiger

cheaply ['tʃiːplɪ] *adv* billig

cheat [tʃiːt] *vi* mogeln (*inf*), schummeln (*inf*) ▷ *n* Betrüger(in) *m(f)* ▷ *vt*: **to ~ sb (out of sth)** jdn (um etw) betrügen; **to ~ on sb** (*inf*) jdn betrügen

cheating ['tʃiːtɪŋ] *n* Mogeln *nt* (*inf*), Schummeln *nt* (*inf*)

check [tʃɛk] *vt* überprüfen; (*passport, ticket*) kontrollieren; (*facts*) nachprüfen; (*enemy, disease*) aufhalten; (*impulse*) unterdrücken; (*person*) zurückhalten ▷ *vi* nachprüfen ▷ *n* Kontrolle *f*; (*curb*) Beschränkung *f*; (*US*) = **cheque**; (*: bill*) Rechnung *f*; (*pattern: gen pl*) Karo(muster) *nt* ▷ *adj* kariert; **to ~ o.s.** sich beherrschen; **to ~ with sb** bei jdm nachfragen; **to keep a ~ on sb/sth** jdn/etw kontrollieren
  ▶ **check in** *vi* (*at hotel*) sich anmelden; (*at airport*) einchecken ▷ *vt* (*luggage*) abfertigen lassen
  ▶ **check off** *vt* abhaken
  ▶ **check out** *vi* (*of hotel*) abreisen ▷ *vt* (*luggage*) abfertigen; (*investigate*) überprüfen
  ▶ **check up** *vi*: **to ~ up on sth** etw überprüfen; **to ~ up on sb** Nachforschungen über jdn anstellen

checkered ['tʃɛkəd] (*US*) *adj* = **chequered**

checkers ['tʃɛkəz] (*US*) *npl* Damespiel *nt*

check guarantee card (*US*) *n* Scheckkarte *f*

check-in ['tʃɛkɪn], **check-in desk** *n* (*at airport*) Abfertigung *f*, Abfertigungsschalter *m*

checking account ['tʃɛkɪŋ-] (*US*) *n* Girokonto *nt*

check list *n* Prüfliste *f*, Checkliste *f*

checkmate ['tʃɛkmeɪt] *n* Schachmatt *nt*

checkout ['tʃɛkaut] *n* Kasse *f*

checkpoint ['tʃɛkpɔɪnt] *n* Kontrollpunkt *m*

checkroom ['tʃɛkrum] (*US*) *n* (*left-luggage office*) Gepäckaufbewahrung *f*

checkup ['tʃɛkʌp] *n* Untersuchung *f*

cheek [tʃiːk] n Backe f; (impudence) Frechheit f; (nerve) Unverschämtheit f

cheekbone ['tʃiːkbəun] n Backenknochen m

cheeky ['tʃiːkɪ] adj frech

cheep [tʃiːp] vi (bird) piep(s)en ▷ n Piep(s) m, Piepser m

cheer [tʃɪər] vt zujubeln +dat; (gladden) aufmuntern, aufheitern ▷ vi jubeln, Hurra rufen ▷ n (gen pl) Hurraruf m, Beifallsruf m; **cheers** npl Hurrageschrei nt, Jubel m; ~s! prost!
  ▶ **cheer on** vt anspornen, anfeuern
  ▶ **cheer up** vi vergnügter or fröhlicher werden ▷ vt aufmuntern, aufheitern

cheerful ['tʃɪəful] adj fröhlich

cheerfulness ['tʃɪəfulnɪs] n Fröhlichkeit f

cheerio [tʃɪərɪ'əu] (Brit) excl tschüss (inf)

cheerleader ['tʃɪəliːdər] n jd, der bei Sportveranstaltungen etc die Zuschauer zu Beifallsrufen anfeuert

cheerless ['tʃɪəlɪs] adj freudlos, trüb; (room) trostlos

cheese [tʃiːz] n Käse m

cheeseboard ['tʃiːzbɔːd] n Käsebrett nt; (with cheese on it) Käseplatte f

cheeseburger ['tʃiːzbəːgər] n Cheeseburger m

cheesecake ['tʃiːzkeɪk] n Käsekuchen m

cheetah ['tʃiːtə] n Gepard m

chef [ʃɛf] n Küchenchef(in) m(f)

chemical ['kɛmɪkl] adj chemisch ▷ n Chemikalie f

chemical engineering n Chemotechnik f

chemist ['kɛmɪst] n (Brit: pharmacist) Apotheker(in) m(f); (scientist) Chemiker(in) m(f)

chemistry ['kɛmɪstrɪ] n Chemie f

chemist's ['kɛmɪsts]

chemist's shop (Brit) n Drogerie f; (also: **dispensing chemist's**) Apotheke f

chemotherapy [kiːməu'θɛrəpɪ] n Chemotherapie f

cheque [tʃɛk] (Brit) n Scheck m; **to pay by** ~ mit (einem) Scheck bezahlen

chequebook ['tʃɛkbuk] n Scheckbuch nt

cheque card (Brit) n Scheckkarte f

chequered, (US) **checkered** ['tʃɛkəd] adj (fig) bewegt

cherish ['tʃɛrɪʃ] vt (person) liebevoll sorgen für; (memory) in Ehren halten; (dream) sich hingeben +dat; (hope) hegen

cheroot [ʃə'ruːt] n Stumpen m

cherry ['tʃɛrɪ] n Kirsche f; (also: **cherry tree**) Kirschbaum m

chervil ['tʃəːvɪl] n Kerbel m

Ches. (Brit) abbr (Post) = Cheshire

chess [tʃɛs] n Schach(spiel) nt

chessboard ['tʃɛsbɔːd] n Schachbrett nt

chessman ['tʃɛsmən] (irreg: like **man**) n Schachfigur f

chess player n Schachspieler(in) m(f)

chest [tʃɛst] n Brust f, Brustkorb m; (box) Kiste f, Truhe f; **to get sth off one's** ~ (inf) sich dat etw von der Seele reden

chest measurement n Brustweite f, Brustumfang m

chestnut ['tʃɛsnʌt] n Kastanie f ▷ adj kastanienbraun

chest of drawers n Kommode f

chesty ['tʃɛstɪ] adj (cough) tief sitzend

chew [tʃuː] vt kauen

chewing gum ['tʃuːɪŋ-] n Kaugummi m

chic [ʃiːk] adj chic inv, schick

chick [tʃɪk] n Küken nt; (inf: girl) Mieze f

chicken ['tʃɪkɪn] n Huhn nt; (meat) Hähnchen nt; (inf: coward) Feigling m
  ▶ **chicken out** (inf) vi: **to ~ out of doing sth** davor kneifen, etw zu tun

chicken feed n (inf: money) ein paar Pfennige pl (Hist); (as salary) ein Hungerlohn m

chickenpox ['tʃɪkɪnpɔks] n Windpocken pl

chickpea ['tʃɪkpiː] n Kichererbse f

chicory ['tʃɪkərɪ] n (in coffee) Zichorie f; (salad vegetable) Chicorée f or m

chide [tʃaɪd] vt: **to ~ sb (for)** jdn schelten (wegen)

chief [tʃiːf] n Häuptling m; (of organization, department) Leiter(in) m(f), Chef(in) m(f) ▷ adj Haupt-, wichtigste(r, s)

chief constable (Brit) n Polizeipräsident m, Polizeichef m

chief executive, (US) **chief executive officer** n Generaldirektor(in) m(f)

chiefly ['tʃiːflɪ] adv hauptsächlich

Chief of Staff n Stabschef m

chiffon ['ʃɪfɔn] n Chiffon m

chilblain ['tʃɪlbleɪn] n Frostbeule f

child [tʃaɪld] (pl **children**) n Kind nt; **do you have any children?** haben Sie Kinder?

child benefit (Brit) n Kindergeld nt

childbirth ['tʃaɪldbəːθ] n Geburt f, Entbindung f

childhood ['tʃaɪldhud] n Kindheit f

childish ['tʃaɪldɪʃ] adj kindisch

childless ['tʃaɪldlɪs] adj kinderlos

childlike ['tʃaɪldlaɪk] adj kindlich

child minder (Brit) n Tagesmutter f

child prodigy n Wunderkind nt

children ['tʃɪldrən] npl of **child**

children's home ['tʃɪldrənz-] n Kinderheim nt

child's play ['tʃaɪldz-] n: **it was** ~ es war ein Kinderspiel

Chile ['tʃɪlɪ] n Chile nt

Chilean ['tʃɪlɪən] adj chilenisch ▷ n Chilene m, Chilenin f

chill [tʃɪl] n Kühle f; (illness) Erkältung f ▷ adj kühl; (fig: reminder) erschreckend ▷ vt kühlen; (person) frösteln or frieren lassen; **"serve ~ed"** „gekühlt servieren"

chilli, (US) **chili** ['tʃɪlɪ] n Peperoni pl

chilling ['tʃɪlɪn] adj (wind, morning) eisig; (fig: effect, prospect etc) beängstigend

chill out (inf) vi sich entspannen, relaxen

chilly ['tʃɪlɪ] adj kühl; (person, response, look) kühl, frostig; **to feel** ~ frösteln, frieren

chime [tʃaɪm] n Glockenspiel nt ▷ vi läuten

chimney ['tʃɪmnɪ] n Schornstein m

chimney sweep n Schornsteinfeger(in) m(f)

chimpanzee [tʃɪmpæn'ziː] n Schimpanse m

chin [tʃɪn] n Kinn nt
China ['tʃaɪnə] n China nt
china ['tʃaɪnə] n Porzellan nt
Chinese [tʃaɪ'niːz] adj chinesisch ▷ n inv
Chinese m, Chinesin f; (Ling) Chinesisch nt
chink [tʃɪŋk] n (in door, wall etc) Ritze f, Spalt m;
(of bottles etc) Klirren nt
chintz [tʃɪnts] n Chintz m
chinwag ['tʃɪnwæg] (Brit: inf) n Schwatz m
chip [tʃɪp] n (gen pl) Pommes frites pl; (US: also:
potato chip) Chip m; (of wood) Span m; (of glass,
stone) Splitter m; (in glass, cup etc) abgestoßene
Stelle f; (in gambling) Chip m, Spielmarke f;
(Comput: also: **microchip**) Chip m ▷ vt (cup, plate)
anschlagen; **when the ~s are down** (fig)
wenn es drauf ankommt
  ▶ **chip in** (inf) vi (contribute) etwas beisteuern;
(interrupt) sich einschalten
chip and PIN n: **~ machine** Chip-und-Pin-
Kartenlesegerät nt
chipboard ['tʃɪpbɔːd] n Spanplatte f
chipmunk ['tʃɪpmʌŋk] n Backenhörnchen nt
chippings ['tʃɪpɪŋz] npl: **loose ~** (on road)
Schotter m

● **CHIP SHOP**
●
● *Chip shop*, auch „fish-and-chip shop", ist
● die traditionelle britische Imbissbude,
● in der vor allem frittierte Fischfilets und
● Pommes frites, aber auch andere einfache
● Mahlzeiten angeboten werden. Früher
● wurde das Essen zum Mitnehmen in
● Zeitungspapier verpackt. Manche chip
● shops haben auch einen Essraum.

chiropodist [kɪ'rɒpədɪst] (Brit) n Fußpfleger(in)
m(f)
chirp [tʃəːp] vi (bird) zwitschern; (crickets) zirpen
chirpy ['tʃəːpɪ] (inf) adj munter
chisel ['tʃɪzl] n (for stone) Meißel m; (for wood)
Beitel m
chit [tʃɪt] n Zettel m
chitchat ['tʃɪttʃæt] n Plauderei f
chivalrous ['ʃɪvəlrəs] adj ritterlich
chivalry ['ʃɪvəlrɪ] n Ritterlichkeit f
chives [tʃaɪvz] npl Schnittlauch m
chloride ['klɔːraɪd] n Chlorid nt
chlorinate ['klɔrɪneɪt] vt chloren
chlorine ['klɔːriːn] n Chlor nt
chock [tʃɒk] n Bremskeil m, Bremsklotz m
chock-a-block ['tʃɒk'blɒk] adj gerammelt voll
chock-full [tʃɒk'fʊl] adj = **chock-a-block**
chocolate ['tʃɒklɪt] n Schokolade f; (drink)
Kakao m, Schokolade f; (sweet) Praline f
choice [tʃɔɪs] n Auswahl f; (option) Möglichkeit
f; (preference) Wahl f ▷ adj Qualitäts-,
erstklassig; **I did it by** or **from ~** ich habe
es mir so ausgesucht; **a wide ~** eine große
Auswahl
choir ['kwaɪər] n Chor m
choirboy ['kwaɪəbɔɪ] n Chorknabe m
choke [tʃəʊk] vi ersticken; (with smoke, dust,

anger etc) keine Luft mehr bekommen ▷ vt
erwürgen, erdrosseln ▷ n (Aut) Choke m,
Starterklappe f; **to be ~d (with)** verstopft sein
(mit)
cholera ['kɒlərə] n Cholera f
cholesterol [kə'lɛstərɒl] n Cholesterin nt
choose [tʃuːz] (pt **chose**, pp **chosen**) vt (aus)
wählen; (profession, friend) sich dat aussuchen
▷ vi: **to ~ between** wählen zwischen +dat,
eine Wahl treffen zwischen +dat; **to ~ from**
wählen aus or unter +dat, eine Wahl treffen
aus or unter +dat; **to ~ to do sth** beschließen,
etw zu tun
choosy ['tʃuːzɪ] adj wählerisch
chop [tʃɒp] vt (wood) hacken; (also: **chop
up**: vegetables, fruit, meat) klein schneiden ▷ n
Kotelett nt; **chops** (inf) npl (of animal) Maul nt;
(of person) Mund m; **to get the ~** (Brit: inf: project)
dem Rotstift zum Opfer fallen; (: be sacked)
rausgeschmissen werden
  ▶ **chop down** vt (tree) fällen
chopper ['tʃɒpər] (inf) n Hubschrauber m
choppy ['tʃɒpɪ] adj (sea) kabbelig, bewegt
chopsticks ['tʃɒpstɪks] npl Stäbchen pl
choral ['kɔːrəl] adj (singing) Chor-; (society)
Gesang-
chord [kɔːd] n Akkord m; (Math) Sehne f
chore [tʃɔːr] n Hausarbeit f; (routine task) lästige
Routinearbeit f; **household ~s** (inf) npl
choreographer [kɒrɪ'ɒgrəfər] n Choreograf(in)
m(f)
choreography [kɒrɪ'ɒgrəfɪ] n Choreografie f
chorister ['kɒrɪstər] n Chorsänger(in) m(f)
chortle ['tʃɔːtl] vi glucksen
chorus ['kɔːrəs] n Chor m; (refrain) Refrain m; (of
complaints) Flut f
chose [tʃəʊz] pt of **choose**
chosen ['tʃəʊzn] pp of **choose**
chow [tʃaʊ] n Chow-Chow m
chowder ['tʃaʊdər] n (sämige) Fischsuppe f
Christ [kraɪst] n Christus m
christen ['krɪsn] vt taufen
christening ['krɪsnɪŋ] n Taufe f
Christian ['krɪstɪən] adj christlich ▷ n
Christ(in) m(f)
Christianity [krɪstɪ'ænɪtɪ] n Christentum nt
Christian name n Vorname m
Christmas ['krɪsməs] n Weihnachten
nt; **Happy** or **Merry ~!** frohe or fröhliche
Weihnachten!
Christmas card n Weihnachtskarte f
Christmas Day n der erste Weihnachtstag
Christmas Eve n Heiligabend m
Christmas Island n Weihnachtsinsel f
Christmas tree n Weihnachtsbaum m,
Christbaum m
chrome [krəʊm] n = **chromium**
chromium ['krəʊmɪəm] n Chrom nt;
(also: **chromium plating**) Verchromung f
chromosome ['krəʊməsəʊm] n Chromosom nt
chronic ['krɒnɪk] adj (also fig) chronisch; (severe)
schlimm
chronicle ['krɒnɪkl] n Chronik f

chronological [krɔnə'lɔdʒɪkl] *adj*
chronologisch

chrysanthemum [krɪ'sænθəməm] *n*
Chrysantheme *f*

chubby ['tʃʌbɪ] *adj* pummelig; **~ cheeks**
Pausbacken *pl*

chuck [tʃʌk] *(inf) vt* werfen, schmeißen;
(Brit: also: **chuck up, chuck in:** *job)*
hinschmeißen; *(: person)* Schluss machen mit
► **chuck out** *vt (person)* rausschmeißen; *(rubbish etc)* wegschmeißen

chuckle ['tʃʌkl] *vi* leise in sich *acc* hineinlachen

chuffed [tʃʌft] *(Brit: inf) adj* vergnügt und
zufrieden; *(flattered)* gebauchpinselt

chug [tʃʌɡ] *vi (also:* **chug along)** tuckern

chum [tʃʌm] *n* Kumpel *m*

chump [tʃʌmp] *(inf) n* Trottel *m*

chunk [tʃʌŋk] *n* großes Stück *nt*

chunky ['tʃʌŋkɪ] *adj (furniture etc)* klobig; *(person)*
stämmig, untersetzt; *(knitwear)* dick

church [tʃə:tʃ] *n* Kirche *f*; **the C~ of England**
die anglikanische Kirche

churchyard ['tʃə:tʃjɑ:d] *n* Friedhof *m*

churlish ['tʃə:lɪʃ] *adj* griesgrämig; *(behaviour)*
ungehobelt

churn [tʃə:n] *n* Butterfass *nt*; *(also:* **milk churn)**
Milchkanne *f*
► **churn out** *vt* am laufenden Band
produzieren

chute [ʃu:t] *n (also:* **rubbish chute)**
Müllschlucker *m*; *(for coal, parcels etc)* Rutsche *f*;
(Brit: slide) Rutschbahn *f*, Rutsche *f*

chutney ['tʃʌtnɪ] *n* Chutney *nt*

CIA *(US) n abbr (= Central Intelligence Agency)* CIA
f or m

cicada [sɪ'kɑ:də] *n* Zikade *f*

CID *(Brit) n abbr =* **Criminal Investigation
Department**

cider ['saɪdəʳ] *n* Apfelwein *m*

c.i.f., CIF *abbr (Comm: = cost, insurance, and freight)*
cif

cigar [sɪ'ɡɑ:ʳ] *n* Zigarre *f*

cigarette [sɪɡə'rɛt] *n* Zigarette *f*

cigarette case *n* Zigarettenetui *nt*

cigarette end *n* Zigarettenstummel *m*

cigarette holder *n* Zigarettenspitze *f*

C in C *abbr (Mil) =* **commander in chief**

cinch [sɪntʃ] *(inf) n:* **it's a ~** das ist ein
Kinderspiel *or* ein Klacks

Cinderella [sɪndə'rɛlə] *n* Aschenputtel *nt*,
Aschenbrödel *nt*

cinders ['sɪndəz] *npl* Asche *f*

cine camera ['sɪnɪ-] *(Brit) n (Schmal)*
filmkamera *f*

cine film *(Brit) n* Schmalfilm *m*

cinema ['sɪnəmə] *n* Kino *nt*; *(film-making)* Film
m

cine projector *(Brit) n* Filmprojektor *m*

cinnamon ['sɪnəmən] *n* Zimt *m*

cipher ['saɪfəʳ] *n (code)* Chiffre *f*; *(fig)* Niemand
m; **in ~** chiffriert

circa ['sə:kə] *prep* circa

circle ['sə:kl] *n* Kreis *m*; *(in cinema, theatre)* Rang

m ► *vi* kreisen ► *vt* kreisen um; *(surround)*
umgeben

circuit ['sə:kɪt] *n* Runde *f*; *(Elec)* Stromkreis *m*;
(track) Rennbahn *f*

circuit board *n* Platine *f*, Leiterplatte *f*

circuitous [sə:'kjuɪtəs] *adj* umständlich

circular ['sə:kjuləʳ] *adj* rund; *(route)* Rund- ► *n*
(letter) Rundschreiben *nt*, Rundbrief *m*; *(as
advertisement)* Wurfsendung *f*; **~ argument**
Zirkelschluss *m*

circulate ['sə:kjuleɪt] *vi (traffic)* fließen; *(blood,
report)* zirkulieren; *(news, rumour)* kursieren, in
Umlauf sein; *(person)* die Runde machen ► *vt*
herumgehen *or* zirkulieren lassen

circulating capital [sə:kju'leɪtɪŋ-] *n (Comm)*
flüssiges Kapital *nt*, Umlaufkapital *nt*

circulation [sə:kju'leɪʃən] *n (of traffic)* Fluss *m*;
(of air etc) Zirkulation *f*; *(of newspaper)* Auflage *f*;
(Med: of blood) Kreislauf *m*

circumcise ['sə:kəmsaɪz] *vt* beschneiden

circumference [sə'kʌmfərəns] *n* Umfang *m*;
(edge) Rand *m*

circumflex ['sə:kəmflɛks] *n (also:* **circumflex
accent)** Zirkumflex *m*

circumscribe ['sə:kəmskraɪb] *vt (Math)* einen
Kreis umbeschreiben; *(fig)* eingrenzen

circumspect ['sə:kəmspɛkt] *adj* umsichtig

circumstances ['sə:kəmstənsɪz] *npl* Umstände
pl; *(financial condition)* (finanzielle) Verhältnisse
pl; **in the ~** unter diesen Umständen; **under
no ~** unter (gar) keinen Umständen, auf
keinen Fall

circumstantial [sə:kəm'stænʃl] *adj*
ausführlich; **~ evidence** Indizienbeweis *m*

circumvent [sə:kəm'vɛnt] *vt* umgehen

circus ['sə:kəs] *n* Zirkus *m*; *(also:* **Circus:** *in place
names)* Platz *m*

cirrhosis [sɪ'rəusɪs] *n (also:* **cirrhosis of the
liver)** Leberzirrhose *f*

CIS *n abbr (= Commonwealth of Independent States)*
GUS *f*

cissy ['sɪsɪ] *n, adj see* **sissy**

cistern ['sɪstən] *n* Zisterne *f*; *(of toilet)*
Spülkasten *m*

citation [saɪ'teɪʃən] *n* Zitat *nt*; *(US)* Belobigung
f; *(Law)* Vorladung *f* (vor Gericht)

cite [saɪt] *vt* zitieren; *(example)* anführen; *(Law)*
vorladen

citizen ['sɪtɪzn] *n* Staatsbürger(in) *m(f)*; *(of
town)* Bürger(in) *m(f)*

Citizens' Advice Bureau ['sɪtɪznz-] *n ≈*
Bürgerberatungsstelle *f*

citizenship ['sɪtɪznʃɪp] *n* Staatsbürgerschaft *f*;
(Brit: Scol) Gesellschaftskunde *f*

citric acid ['sɪtrɪk-] *n* Zitronensäure *f*

citrus fruit ['sɪtrəs-] *n* Zitrusfrucht *f*

city ['sɪtɪ] *n (Groß)stadt *f*; **the C~** *(Fin)* die City,
das Londoner Banken- und Börsenviertel

city centre *n* Stadtzentrum *nt*, Innenstadt *f*

City Hall *n* Rathaus *nt*; *(US: municipal government)*
Stadtverwaltung *f*

civic ['sɪvɪk] *adj (authorities etc)* Stadt-, städtisch;
(duties, pride) Bürger-, bürgerlich

civic centre (*Brit*) *n* Stadtverwaltung *f*

civil ['sɪvɪl] *adj* (*disturbances, rights*) Bürger-; (*liberties, law*) bürgerlich; (*polite*) höflich

Civil Aviation Authority (*Brit*) *n* Behörde *f* für Zivilluftfahrt

civil defence *n* Zivilschutz *m*

civil disobedience *n* ziviler Ungehorsam *m*

civil engineer *n* Bauingenieur(in) *m(f)*

civil engineering *n* Hoch- und Tiefbau *m*

civilian [sɪ'vɪlɪən] *adj* (*population*) Zivil- ▷ *n* Zivilist *m*; ~ **casualties** Verluste *pl* unter der Zivilbevölkerung

civilization [sɪvɪlaɪ'zeɪʃən] *n* Zivilisation *f*; (*a society*) Kultur *f*

civilized ['sɪvɪlaɪzd] *adj* zivilisiert; (*person*) kultiviert; (*place, experience*) gepflegt

civil law *n* Zivilrecht *nt*, bürgerliches Recht *nt*

civil liberties *n* (bürgerliche) Freiheitsrechte *pl*

civil rights *npl* Bürgerrechte *pl*

civil servant *n* (Staats)beamter *m*, (Staats) beamtin *f*

Civil Service *n* Beamtenschaft *f*

civil war *n* Bürgerkrieg *m*

civvies ['sɪvɪz] (*inf*) *npl* Zivilklamotten *pl*

cl *abbr* (= *centilitre*) cl

clad [klæd] *adj*: ~ **(in)** gekleidet (in +*acc*)

claim [kleɪm] *vt* (*assert*) behaupten; (*responsibility*) übernehmen; (*credit*) in Anspruch nehmen; (*rights, inheritance*) Anspruch erheben auf +*acc*; (*expenses*) sich *dat* zurückerstatten lassen; (*compensation, damages*) verlangen ▷ *vi* (*for insurance*) Ansprüche geltend machen ▷ *n* (*assertion*) Behauptung *f*; (*for pension, wage rise, compensation*) Forderung *f*; (*right: to inheritance, land*) Anspruch *m*; (*for expenses*) Spesenabrechnung *f*; (**insurance**) ~ (Versicherungs)anspruch *m*; **to put in a ~ for** beantragen

claimant ['kleɪmənt] *n* Antragsteller(in) *m(f)*

claim form *n* Antragsformular *nt*

clairvoyant [klɛə'vɔɪənt] *n* Hellseher(in) *m(f)*

clam [klæm] *n* Venusmuschel *f*
▶ **clam up** (*inf*) *vi* keinen Piep (mehr) sagen

clamber ['klæmbə'] *vi* klettern

clammy ['klæmɪ] *adj* feucht

clamour, (*US*) **clamor** ['klæmə'] *n* Lärm *m*; (*protest*) Protest *m*, Aufschrei *m* ▷ *vi*: **to ~ for** schreien nach

clamp [klæmp] *n* Schraubzwinge *f*, Klemme *f* ▷ *vt* (*two things*) zusammenklemmen; (*one thing on another*) klemmen; (*wheel*) krallen
▶ **clamp down on** *vt fus* rigoros vorgehen gegen

clampdown ['klæmpdaun] *n*: ~ **(on)** hartes Durchgreifen *nt* (gegen)

clan [klæn] *n* Clan *m*

clandestine [klæn'dɛstɪn] *adj* geheim, Geheim-

clang [klæŋ] *vi* klappern; (*bell*) läuten ▷ *n* (*see vi*) Klappern *nt*; Läuten *nt*

clanger ['klæŋə'] (*Brit: inf*) *n* Fauxpas *m*; **to drop a ~** ins Fettnäpfchen treten

clansman ['klænzmən] *n* (*irreg: like* **man**)

Clanmitglied *nt*

clap [klæp] *vi* (*Beifall*) klatschen ▷ *vt*: **to ~ (one's hands)** (in die Hände) klatschen ▷ *n*: **a ~ of thunder** ein Donnerschlag *m*

clapping ['klæpɪŋ] *n* Beifall *m*

claptrap ['klæptræp] (*inf*) *n* Geschwafel *nt*

claret ['klærət] *n* roter Bordeaux(wein) *m*

clarification [klærɪfɪ'keɪʃən] *n* Klärung *f*

clarify ['klærɪfaɪ] *vt* klären

clarinet [klærɪ'nɛt] *n* Klarinette *f*

clarity ['klærɪtɪ] *n* Klarheit *f*

clash [klæʃ] *n* (*fight*) Zusammenstoß *m*; (*disagreement*) Streit *m*, Auseinandersetzung *f*; (*of beliefs, ideas, views*) Konflikt *m*; (*of colours, styles, personalities*) Unverträglichkeit *f*; (*of events, dates, appointments*) Überschneidung *f*; (*noise*) Klirren *nt* ▷ *vi* (*fight*) zusammenstoßen; (*disagree*) sich streiten, eine Auseinandersetzung haben; (*beliefs, ideas, views*) aufeinanderprallen; (*colours*) sich beißen; (*styles, personalities*) nicht zusammenpassen; (*two events, dates, appointments*) sich überschneiden; (*make noise*) klirrend aneinanderschlagen

clasp [klɑːsp] *n* Griff *m*; (*embrace*) Umklammerung *f*; (*of necklace, bag*) Verschluss *m* ▷ *vt* (er)greifen; (*embrace*) umklammern

class [klɑːs] *n* Klasse *f*; (*lesson*) (Unterrichts) stunde *f* ▷ *adj* (*struggle, distinction*) Klassen- ▷ *vt* einordnen, einstufen

class-conscious ['klɑːs'kɔnʃəs] *adj* klassenbewusst, standesbewusst

class-consciousness ['klɑːs'kɔnʃəsnɪs] *n* Klassenbewusstsein *nt*, Standesbewusstsein *nt*

classic ['klæsɪk] *adj* klassisch ▷ *n* Klassiker *m*; (*race*) bedeutendes Pferderennen für dreijährige Pferde; **classics** *npl* (*Scol*) Altphilologie *f*

classical ['klæsɪkl] *adj* klassisch

classification [klæsɪfɪ'keɪʃən] *n* Klassifikation *f*; (*category*) Klasse *f*; (*system*) Einteilung *f*

classified ['klæsɪfaɪd] *adj* geheim

classified advertisement *n* Kleinanzeige *f*

classify ['klæsɪfaɪ] *vt* klassifizieren, (ein) ordnen

classless ['klɑːslɪs] *adj*: ~ **society** klassenlose Gesellschaft *f*

classmate ['klɑːsmeɪt] *n* Klassenkamerad(in) *m(f)*

classroom ['klɑːsrum] *n* Klassenzimmer *nt*

classroom assistant *n* Assistenzlehrkraft *f*

classy ['klɑːsɪ] (*inf*) *adj* nobel, exklusiv; (*person*) todschick

clatter ['klætə'] *n* Klappern *nt*; (*of hooves*) Trappeln *nt* ▷ *vi* (*see n*) klappern; trappeln

clause [klɔːz] *n* (*Law*) Klausel *f*; (*Ling*) Satz *m*

claustrophobia [klɔːstrə'fəubɪə] *n* Klaustrophobie *f*, Platzangst *f*

claustrophobic [klɔːstrə'fəubɪk] *adj* (*place, situation*) beengend; (*person*): **to be/feel ~** Platzangst haben/bekommen

claw [klɔː] *n* Kralle *f*; (*of lobster*) Schere *f*, Zange *f*
▶ **claw at** *vt fus* sich krallen an +*acc*

clay [kleɪ] n Ton m; (soil) Lehm m
clean [kli:n] adj sauber; (fight) fair; (record, reputation) einwandfrei; (joke, story) stubenrein, anständig; (edge, fracture) glatt ▷ vt sauber machen; (car, hands, face etc) waschen ▷ adv: **he ~ forgot** er hat es glatt(weg) vergessen; **to have a ~ driving licence, to have a ~ driving record** (US) keine Strafpunkte haben; **to ~ one's teeth** (Brit) sich dat die Zähne putzen; **the thief got ~ away** der Dieb konnte entkommen; **to come ~** (inf) auspacken
▶ **clean off** vt abwaschen, abwischen
▶ **clean out** vt gründlich sauber machen; (inf: person) ausnehmen
▶ **clean up** vt aufräumen; (child) sauber machen; (fig) für Ordnung sorgen in +dat ▷ vi aufräumen, sauber machen; (inf: make profit) absahnen
clean-cut ['kli:n'kʌt] adj gepflegt; (situation) klar
cleaner ['kli:nə'] n Raumpfleger(in) m(f); (woman) Putzfrau f; (substance) Reinigungsmittel nt, Putzmittel nt
cleaner's ['kli:nəz] n (also: **dry cleaner's**) Reinigung f
cleaning ['kli:nɪŋ] n Putzen nt
cleaning lady n Putzfrau f, Reinemachefrau f
cleanliness ['klɛnlɪnɪs] n Sauberkeit f, Reinlichkeit f
cleanly ['kli:nlɪ] adv sauber
cleanse [klɛnz] vt (purify) läutern; (face, cut) reinigen
cleanser ['klɛnzə'] n (for face) Reinigungscreme f, Reinigungsmilch f
clean-shaven ['kli:n'ʃeɪvn] adj glatt rasiert
cleansing department ['klɛnzɪŋ-] (Brit) n ≈ Stadtreinigung f
clean sweep n: **to make a ~** (Sport) alle Preise einstecken
clean-up ['kli:nʌp] n: **to give sth a ~** etw gründlich sauber machen
clear [klɪə'] adj klar; (footprint) deutlich; (photograph) scharf; (commitment) eindeutig; (glass, plastic) durchsichtig; (road, way, floor etc) frei; (conscience, skin) rein ▷ vt (room) ausräumen; (trees) abholzen; (weeds etc) entfernen; (slums etc, stock) räumen; (Law) freisprechen; (fence, wall) überspringen; (cheque) verrechnen ▷ vi (weather, sky) aufklaren; (fog, smoke) sich auflösen; (room etc) sich leeren ▷ adv: **to be ~ of the ground** den Boden nicht berühren ▷ n: **to be in the ~** (out of debt) schuldenfrei sein; (free of suspicion) von jedem Verdacht frei sein; (out of danger) außer Gefahr sein; **~ profit** Reingewinn m; **I have a ~ day tomorrow** (Brit) ich habe morgen nichts vor; **to make o.s. ~** sich klar ausdrücken; **to make it ~ to sb that ...** es jdm (unmissverständlich) klarmachen, dass ...; **to ~ the table** den Tisch abräumen; **to ~ a space (for sth)** (für etw) Platz schaffen; **to ~ one's throat** sich räuspern; **to ~ a profit** einen Gewinn machen; **to keep ~ of sb** jdm

aus dem Weg gehen; **to keep ~ of sth** etw meiden; **to keep ~ of trouble** allem Ärger aus dem Weg gehen
▶ **clear off** (inf) vi abhauen, verschwinden
▶ **clear up** vt aufräumen; (mystery) aufklären; (problem) lösen ▷ vi (bad weather) sich aufklären; (illness) sich bessern
clearance ['klɪərəns] n (of slums) Räumung f; (of trees) Abholzung f; (permission) Genehmigung f; (free space) lichte Höhe f
clearance sale n Räumungsverkauf m
clear-cut ['klɪə'kʌt] adj klar
clearing ['klɪərɪŋ] n Lichtung f; (Brit: Banking) Clearing nt
clearing bank (Brit) n Clearingbank f
clearing house n (Comm) Clearingstelle f
clearly ['klɪəlɪ] adv klar; (obviously) eindeutig
clearway ['klɪəweɪ] (Brit) n Straße f mit Halteverbot
cleavage ['kli:vɪdʒ] n (of woman's breasts) Dekolleté nt
cleaver ['kli:və'] n Hackbeil nt
clef [klɛf] n (Noten)schlüssel m
cleft [klɛft] n Spalte f
cleft palate n (Med) Gaumenspalte f
clemency ['klɛmənsɪ] n Milde f
clement ['klɛmənt] adj mild
clench [klɛntʃ] vt (fist) ballen; (teeth) zusammenbeißen
clergy ['klə:dʒɪ] n Klerus m, Geistlichkeit f
clergyman ['klə:dʒɪmən] (irreg: like **man**) n Geistliche(r) m
clerical ['klɛrɪkl] adj (job, worker) Büro-; (error) Schreib-; (Rel) geistlich
clerk [kla:k, (US) klə:rk] n (Brit) Büroangestellte(r) f(m); (US: sales person) Verkäufer(in) m(f)
Clerk of Court n Protokollführer(in) m(f)
clever ['klɛvə'] adj klug; (deft, crafty) schlau, clever (inf); (device, arrangement) raffiniert
cleverly ['klɛvəlɪ] adv geschickt
clew [klu:] (US) n = **clue**
cliché ['kli:ʃeɪ] n Klischee nt
click [klɪk] vi klicken ▷ vt: **to ~ one's tongue** mit der Zunge schnalzen; **to ~ one's heels** die Hacken zusammenschlagen
client ['klaɪənt] n Kunde m, Kundin f; (of bank, lawyer) Klient(in) m(f); (of restaurant) Gast m
clientele [kli:ɑ̃:'ntɛl] n Kundschaft f
cliff [klɪf] n Kliff nt
cliffhanger ['klɪfhæŋə'] n spannungsgeladene Szene am Ende einer Filmepisode, Cliffhanger m
climactic [klaɪ'mæktɪk] adj: **~ point** Höhepunkt m
climate ['klaɪmɪt] n Klima nt
climate conference n (Pol) Klimakonferenz f
climax ['klaɪmæks] n (sexual) Höhepunkt m
climb [klaɪm] vi klettern; (plane, sun, prices, shares) steigen ▷ vt (stairs, ladder) hochsteigen, hinaufsteigen; (tree) klettern auf +acc; (hill) steigen auf +acc ▷ n Aufstieg m; (of prices etc) Anstieg m; **to ~ over a wall/into a car** über eine Mauer/in ein Auto steigen or klettern

▶ **climb down** (Brit) vi (fig) nachgeben
climb-down ['klaɪmdaʊn] n Nachgeben nt, Rückzieher m (inf)
climber ['klaɪmə'] n Bergsteiger(in) m(f); (plant) Kletterpflanze f
climbing ['klaɪmɪŋ] n Bergsteigen nt
clinch [klɪntʃ] vt (deal) perfekt machen; (argument) zum Abschluss bringen
clincher ['klɪntʃə'] n ausschlaggebender Faktor m
cling [klɪŋ] (pt, pp **clung**) vi: **to ~ to** (mother, support) sich festklammern an +dat; (idea, belief) festhalten an +dat; (subj: clothes, dress) sich anschmiegen +dat
clingfilm ['klɪŋfɪlm] n, **clingwrap** ['klɪŋræp] n (US) Frischhaltefolie f
clinic ['klɪnɪk] n Klinik f; (session) Sprechstunde f; (: Sport) Trainingstunde f
clinical ['klɪnɪkl] adj klinisch; (fig) nüchtern, kühl; (: building, room) steril
clink [klɪŋk] vi klirren
clip [klɪp] n (also: **paper clip**) Büroklammer f; (Brit: also: **bulldog clip**) Klammer f; (holding wire, hose etc) Klemme f; (for hair) Spange f; (TV, Cine) Ausschnitt m ▷ vt festklemmen; (also: **clip together**) zusammenheften; (cut) schneiden
clippers ['klɪpəz] npl (for gardening) Schere f; (also: **nail clippers**) Nagelzange f
clipping ['klɪpɪŋ] n (from newspaper) Ausschnitt m
clique [kliːk] n Clique f, Gruppe f
clitoris ['klɪtərɪs] n Klitoris f
cloak [kləʊk] n Umhang m ▷ vt (fig) hüllen
cloakroom ['kləʊkrʊm] n Garderobe f; (Brit: WC) Toilette f
clobber ['klɔbə'] (inf) n Klamotten pl ▷ vt (hit) hauen, schlagen; (defeat) in die Pfanne hauen
clock [klɔk] n Uhr f; **round the ~** rund um die Uhr; **30,000 on the ~** (Brit: Aut) ein Tachostand von 30.000; **to work against the ~** gegen die Uhr arbeiten
▶ **clock in** (Brit) vi (den Arbeitsbeginn) stempeln or stechen
▶ **clock off** (Brit) vi (das Arbeitsende) stempeln or stechen
▶ **clock on** (Brit) vi = **clock in**
▶ **clock out** (Brit) vi = **clock off**
▶ **clock up** vt (miles) fahren; (hours) arbeiten
clockwise ['klɔkwaɪz] adv im Uhrzeigersinn
clockwork ['klɔkwə:k] n Uhrwerk nt ▷ adj aufziehbar, zum Aufziehen; **like ~** wie am Schnürchen
clog [klɔg] n Clog m; (wooden) Holzschuh m ▷ vt verstopfen ▷ vi (also: **clog up**) verstopfen
cloister ['klɔɪstə'] n Kreuzgang m
clone [kləʊn] n Klon m
close¹ [kləʊs] adj (writing, friend, contact) eng; (texture) dicht, fest; (relative) nahe; (examination) genau, gründlich; (watch) streng, scharf; (contest) knapp; (weather) schwül; (room) stickig ▷ adv nahe; **~ (to)** nahe (+gen); **~ to** in der Nähe +gen; **~ by, ~ at hand** in der Nähe; **how ~ is Edinburgh to Glasgow?** wie weit

ist Edinburgh von Glasgow entfernt?; **a ~ friend** ein guter or enger Freund; **to have a ~ shave** (fig) gerade noch davonkommen; **at ~ quarters** aus der Nähe
close² [kləʊz] vt schließen, zumachen; (sale, deal, case) abschließen; (speech) schließen, beenden ▷ vi schließen, zumachen; (door, lid) sich schließen, zugehen; (end) aufhören ▷ n Ende nt, Schlus m; **to bring sth to a ~** etw beenden
▶ **close down** vi (factory) stillgelegt werden; (magazine etc) eingestellt werden
▶ **close in** vi (night) hereinbrechen; (fog) sich verdichten; **to ~ in on sb/sth** jdm/etw auf den Leib rücken; **the days are closing in** die Tage werden kürzer
▶ **close off** vt (area) abriegeln; (road) sperren
closed [kləʊzd] adj geschlossen; (road) gesperrt
closed-circuit television n Fernsehüberwachungsanlage f
closed shop n Betrieb m mit Gewerkschaftszwang
close-knit ['kləʊs'nɪt] adj eng zusammengewachsen
closely ['kləʊslɪ] adv (examine, watch) genau; (connected) eng; (related) nah(e); (resemble) sehr; **we are ~ related** wir sind nah verwandt; **a ~ guarded secret** ein streng gehütetes Geheimnis
close season ['kləʊs-] n Schonzeit f; (Sport) Sommerpause f
closet ['klɔzɪt] n Wandschrank m
close-up ['kləʊsʌp] n Nahaufnahme f
closing ['kləʊzɪŋ] adj (stages) Schluss-; (remarks) abschließend
closing price n (Stock Exchange) Schlusskurs m, Schlussnotierung f
closing time (Brit) n (in pub) Polizeistunde f, Sperrstunde f
closure ['kləʊʒə'] n (of factory) Stilllegung f; (of magazine) Einstellung f; (of road) Sperrung f; (of border) Schließung f
clot [klɔt] n (blood clot) (Blut)gerinnsel nt; (inf: idiot) Trottel m ▷ vi gerinnen; (external bleeding) zum Stillstand kommen
cloth [klɔθ] n (material) Stoff m, Tuch nt; (rag) Lappen m; (Brit: also: **teacloth**) (Spül)tuch nt; (also: **tablecloth**) Tischtuch nt, Tischdecke f
clothe [kləʊð] vt anziehen, kleiden
clothes [kləʊðz] npl Kleidung f, Kleider pl; **to put one's ~ on** sich anziehen; **to take one's ~ off** sich ausziehen
clothes brush n Kleiderbürste f
clothesline ['kləʊðzlaɪn] n Wäscheleine f
clothes peg, (US) **clothes pin** n Wäscheklammer f
clothing ['kləʊðɪŋ] n = **clothes**
clotted cream ['klɔtɪd-] (Brit) n Sahne aus erhitzter Milch
cloud [klaʊd] n Wolke f ▷ vt trüben; **every ~ has a silver lining** (proverb) auf Regen folgt Sonnenschein; **to ~ the issue** es unnötig kompliziert machen; (deliberately) die

Angelegenheit verschleiern
▸ **cloud over** vi (sky) sich bewölken, sich
bedecken; (face, eyes) sich verfinstern

cloudburst ['klaʊdbəːst] n Wolkenbruch m

cloud-cuckoo-land [klaʊd'kuku:lænd] (Brit) n
Wolkenkuckucksheim nt

cloudy ['klaʊdɪ] adj wolkig, bewölkt; (liquid)
trüb

clout [klaʊt] vt schlagen, hauen ▸ n (fig)
Schlagkraft f

clove [kləʊv] n Gewürznelke f; ~ **of garlic**
Knoblauchzehe f

clover ['kləʊvəʳ] n Klee m

cloverleaf ['kləʊvəliːf] n Kleeblatt nt

clown [klaʊn] n Clown m ▸ vi (also: **clown
about, clown around**) herumblödeln,
herumkaspern

cloying ['klɔɪɪŋ] adj süßlich

club [klʌb] n Klub m, Verein m; (weapon) Keule f,
Knüppel m; (also: **golf club**: object) Golfschläger
m ▸ vt knüppeln ▸ vi: **to ~ together**
zusammenlegen; **clubs** npl (Cards) Kreuz nt

club car (US) n Speisewagen m

club class n Klubklasse f, Businessklasse f

clubhouse ['klʌbhaʊs] n Klubhaus nt

club soda (US) n (soda water) Sodawasser nt

cluck [klʌk] vi glucken

clue [kluː] n Hinweis m, Anhaltspunkt m; (in
crossword) Frage f; **I haven't a ~** ich habe keine
Ahnung

clued-up ['kluːdʌp], (US: inf) **clued in** adj: **to be
~ on sth** über etw acc im Bilde sein

clueless ['kluːlɪs] adj ahnungslos, unbedarft

clump [klʌmp] n Gruppe f

clumsy ['klʌmzɪ] adj ungeschickt; (object)
unförmig; (effort, attempt) plump

clung [klʌŋ] pt, pp of **cling**

cluster ['klʌstəʳ] n Gruppe f ▸ vi (people) sich
scharen; (houses) sich drängen

clutch [klʌtʃ] n Griff m; (Aut) Kupplung f
▸ vt (purse, hand) umklammern; (stick) sich
festklammern an +dat ▸ vi: **to ~ at** sich
klammern an +acc

clutter ['klʌtəʳ] vt (also: **clutter up**: room)
vollstopfen; (: table) vollstellen ▸ n Kram m (inf)

cm abbr (= centimetre) cm

CNAA (Brit) n abbr (= Council for National
Academic Awards) Zentralstelle zur Vergabe von
Qualifikationsnachweisen

CND (Brit) n abbr (= Campaign for Nuclear
Disarmament) Organisation für atomare Abrüstung

CO n abbr = **commanding officer;**
(Brit: = Commonwealth Office) Regierungsstelle für
Angelegenheiten des Commonwealth ▸ abbr (US:
Post) = Colorado

Co. abbr = **company; county**

c/o abbr (= care of) bei, c/o

coach [kəʊtʃ] n (Reise)bus m; (horse-drawn)
Kutsche f; (of train) Wagen m; (Sport) Trainer m;
(Scol) Nachhilfelehrer(in) m(f) ▸ vt trainieren;
(student) Nachhilfeunterricht geben +dat

coach trip n Busfahrt f

coagulate [kəʊ'ægjʊleɪt] vi (blood) gerinnen;

(paint etc) eindicken ▸ vt (blood) gerinnen
lassen; (paint) dick werden lassen

coal [kəʊl] n Kohle f

coalface ['kəʊlfeɪs] n Streb m

coalfield ['kəʊlfiːld] n Kohlenrevier nt

coalition [kəʊə'lɪʃən] n (Pol) Koalition f; (of
pressure groups etc) Zusammenschluss m

coalman ['kəʊlmən] (irreg: like **man**) n
Kohlenhändler m

coal merchant n = **coalman**

coal mine n Kohlenbergwerk nt, Zeche f

coal miner n Bergmann m, Kumpel m (inf)

coal mining n (Kohlen)bergbau m

coarse [kɔːs] adj (texture) grob; (vulgar)
gewöhnlich, derb; (salt, sand etc) grobkörnig

coast [kəʊst] n Küste f ▸ vi (im Leerlauf) fahren

coastal ['kəʊstl] adj Küsten-

coaster ['kəʊstəʳ] n (Naut) Küstenfahrzeug nt;
(for glass) Untersetzer m

coastguard ['kəʊstgɑːd] n (officer)
Küstenwächter m; (service) Küstenwacht f

coastline ['kəʊstlaɪn] n Küste f

coat [kəʊt] n Mantel m; (of animal) Fell nt;
(layer) Schicht f; (: of paint) Anstrich m ▸ vt
überziehen

coat hanger n Kleiderbügel m

coating ['kəʊtɪŋ] n (of chocolate etc) Überzug m;
(of dust etc) Schicht f

coat of arms n Wappen nt

coauthor [kəʊ'ɔːθəʳ] n Mitautor(in) m(f),
Mitverfasser(in) m(f)

coax [kəʊks] vt (person) überreden

cob [kɔb] n see **corn**

cobbler ['kɔbləʳ] n Schuster m

cobbles ['kɔblz] npl Kopfsteinpflaster nt

cobblestones ['kɔblstəʊnz] npl = **cobbles**

COBOL ['kəʊbɔl] n COBOL nt

cobra ['kəʊbrə] n Kobra f

cobweb ['kɔbwɛb] n Spinnennetz nt

cocaine [kə'keɪn] n Kokain nt

cock [kɔk] n Hahn m; (male bird) Männchen nt
▸ vt (gun) entsichern; **to ~ one's ears** (fig) die
Ohren spitzen

cock-a-hoop [kɔkə'huːp] adj ganz aus dem
Häuschen

cockerel ['kɔkərl] n junger Hahn m

cock-eyed ['kɔkaɪd] adj (fig) verrückt,
widersinnig

cockle ['kɔkl] n Herzmuschel f

cockney ['kɔknɪ] n Cockney m, echter Londoner
m; (Ling) Cockney nt

cockpit ['kɔkpɪt] n Cockpit nt

cockroach ['kɔkrəʊtʃ] n Küchenschabe f,
Kakerlak m

cocktail ['kɔkteɪl] n Cocktail m; **fruit ~**
Obstsalat m; **prawn ~** Krabbencocktail m

cocktail cabinet n Hausbar f

cocktail party n Cocktailparty f

cocktail shaker [-'ʃeɪkəʳ] n Mixbecher m

cock-up ['kɔkʌp] (inf!) n Schlamassel m

cocky ['kɔkɪ] adj großspurig

cocoa ['kəʊkəʊ] n Kakao m

coconut ['kəʊkənʌt] n Kokosnuss f

cocoon [kə'ku:n] *n* Puppe *f*, Kokon *m*; *(fig)* schützende Umgebung *f*

COD *abbr (Brit)* = **cash on delivery**; *(US)* = **collect on delivery**

cod [kɔd] *n* Kabeljau *m*

code [kəud] *n (cipher)* Chiffre *f*; *(also:* **dialling code**) Vorwahl *f*; *(also:* **post code**) Postleitzahl *f*; ~ **of behaviour** Sittenkodex *m*; ~ **of practice** Verfahrensregeln *pl*

codeine ['kəudi:n] *n* Codein *nt*

codger ['kɔdʒə^r] *(inf) n*: **old** ~ komischer Kauz *m*

codicil ['kɔdɪsɪl] *n (Law)* Kodizill *nt*

codify ['kəudɪfaɪ] *vt* kodifizieren

cod-liver oil ['kɔdlɪvə-] *n* Lebertran *m*

co-driver ['kəu'draɪvə^r] *n* Beifahrer(in) *m(f)*

co-ed ['kəu'ɛd] *(Scol) adj abbr* = **coeducational** ▷ *n abbr (US: female pupil/student)* Schülerin/Studentin an einer gemischten Schule/Universität; *(Brit: school)* gemischte Schule *f*

coeducational ['kəuɛdju'keɪʃənl] *adj (school)* Koedukations-, gemischt

coerce [kəu'ə:s] *vt* zwingen

coercion [kəu'ə:ʃən] *n* Zwang *m*

coexistence ['kəuɪg'zɪstəns] *n* Koexistenz *f*

C of C *n abbr* = **chamber of commerce**

C of E *abbr* = **Church of England**

coffee ['kɔfɪ] *n* Kaffee *m*; **black** ~ schwarzer Kaffee *m*; **white** ~ Kaffee mit Milch; ~ **with cream** Kaffee mit Sahne

coffee bar *(Brit) n* Café *nt*

coffee bean *n* Kaffeebohne *f*

coffee break *n* Kaffeepause *f*

coffee cake *(US) n* Kuchen *m* zum Kaffee

coffee cup *n* Kaffeetasse *f*

coffeepot ['kɔfɪpɔt] *n* Kaffeekanne *f*

coffee table *n* Couchtisch *m*

coffin ['kɔfɪn] *n* Sarg *m*

C of I *abbr* (= *Church of Ireland*) anglikanische Kirche Irlands

C of S *abbr* (= *Church of Scotland*) presbyterianische Kirche in Schottland

cog [kɔg] *n (wheel)* Zahnrad *nt*; *(tooth)* Zahn *m*

cogent ['kəudʒənt] *adj* stichhaltig, zwingend

cognac ['kɔnjæk] *n* Kognak *m*

cogwheel ['kɔgwi:l] *n* Zahnrad *m*

cohabit [kəu'hæbɪt] *vi (formal)* in eheähnlicher Gemeinschaft leben; **to** ~ **(with sb)** (mit jdm) zusammenleben

coherent [kəu'hɪərənt] *adj (speech)* zusammenhängend; *(answer, theory)* schlüssig; *(person)* bei klarem Verstand

cohesion [kəu'hi:ʒən] *n* Geschlossenheit *f*

cohesive [kə'hi:sɪv] *adj* geschlossen

coil [kɔɪl] *n* Rolle *f*; *(one loop)* Windung *f*; *(of smoke)* Kringel *m*; *(Aut, Elec)* Spule *f*; *(contraceptive)* Spirale *f* ▷ *vt* aufrollen, aufwickeln

coin [kɔɪn] *n* Münze *f* ▷ *vt* prägen

coinage ['kɔɪnɪdʒ] *n* Münzen *pl*; *(Ling)* Prägung *f*

coin box *(Brit) n* Münzfernsprecher *m*

coincide [kəuɪn'saɪd] *vi (events)* zusammenfallen; *(ideas, views)*

übereinstimmen

coincidence [kəu'ɪnsɪdəns] *n* Zufall *m*

coin-operated ['kɔɪn'ɔpəreɪtɪd] *adj* Münz-

Coke® [kəuk] *n* Coca-Cola® *nt or f*, Coke® *nt*

coke [kəuk] *n* Koks *m*

Col. *abbr* = **colonel**

COLA *(US) n abbr* (= *cost of living adjustment*) Anpassung der Löhne und Gehälter an steigende Lebenshaltungskosten

colander ['kɔləndə^r] *n* Durchschlag *m*

cold [kəuld] *adj* kalt; *(unemotional)* kalt, kühl ▷ *n* Kälte *f*; *(Med)* Erkältung *f*; **it's** ~ es ist kalt; **to be/feel** ~ *(person)* frieren; *(object)* kalt sein; **in** ~ **blood** kaltblütig; **to have** ~ **feet** *(fig)* kalte Füße bekommen; **to give sb the** ~ **shoulder** jdm die kalte Schulter zeigen; **to catch** ~, **to catch a** ~ sich erkälten

cold-blooded ['kəuld'blʌdɪd] *adj* kaltblütig

cold calling *n (Comm: on phone)* unaufgeforderte Telefonwerbung; *(: visit)* unaufgeforderter Vertreterbesuch

cold cream *n* (halbfette) Feuchtigkeitscreme *f*

coldly ['kəuldlɪ] *adv* kalt, kühl

cold-shoulder [kəuld'ʃəuldə^r] *vt* die kalte Schulter zeigen +*dat*

cold sore *n* Bläschenausschlag *m*

cold sweat *n*: **to come out in a** ~ **(about sth)** (wegen etw) in kalten Schweiß ausbrechen

cold turkey *n*: **to do** ~ Totalentzug machen

Cold War *n*: **the** ~ der Kalte Krieg

coleslaw ['kəulslɔ:] *n* Krautsalat *m*

colic ['kɔlɪk] *n* Kolik *f*

colicky ['kɔlɪkɪ] *adj*: **to be** ~ Kolik *f or* Leibschmerzen *pl* haben

collaborate [kə'læbəreɪt] *vi* zusammenarbeiten; *(with enemy)* kollaborieren

collaboration [kəlæbə'reɪʃən] *n* Zusammenarbeit *f*; Kollaboration *f*

collaborator [kə'læbəreɪtə^r] *n (see vb)* Mitarbeiter(in) *m(f)*; Kollaborateur(in) *m(f)*

collage [kɔ'lɑ:ʒ] *n* Collage *f*

collagen ['kɔlədʒən] *n* Kollagen *nt*

collapse [kə'læps] *vi* zusammenbrechen; *(building)* einstürzen; *(plans)* scheitern; *(government)* stürzen ▷ *n (see vb)* Zusammenbruch *m*; Einsturz *m*; Scheitern *nt*; Sturz *m*

collapsible [kə'læpsəbl] *adj* Klapp-, zusammenklappbar

collar ['kɔlə^r] *n* Kragen *m*; *(of dog, cat)* Halsband *nt*; *(Tech)* Bund *m* ▷ *vt (inf)* schnappen

collarbone ['kɔləbəun] *n* Schlüsselbein *nt*

collate [kɔ'leɪt] *vt* vergleichen

collateral [kə'lætərl] *n (Comm)* (zusätzliche) Sicherheit *f*

collateral damage *n (Mil)* Schäden *pl* in Wohngebieten; *(: casualties)* Opfer *pl* unter der Zivilbevölkerung

collation [kə'leɪʃən] *n* Vergleich *m*; *(Culin)*: **a cold** ~ ein kalter Imbiss *m*

colleague ['kɔli:g] *n* Kollege *m*, Kollegin *f*

collect [kə'lɛkt] *vt* sammeln; *(mail: Brit: fetch)* abholen; *(debts)* eintreiben; *(taxes)* einziehen

▷ *vi* sich ansammeln ▷ *adv* (*US: Tel*): **to call ~** ein R-Gespräch führen; **to ~ one's thoughts** seine Gedanken ordnen, sich sammeln; **~ on delivery** (*US: Comm*) per Nachnahme

collected [kə'lɛktɪd] *adj*: **~ works** gesammelte Werke *pl*

collection [kə'lɛkʃən] *n* Sammlung *f*; (*from place, person, of mail*) Abholung *f*; (*in church*) Kollekte *f*

collective [kə'lɛktɪv] *adj* kollektiv, gemeinsam ▷ *n* Kollektiv *nt*; **~ farm** landwirtschaftliche Produktionsgenossenschaft *f*

collective bargaining *n* Tarifverhandlungen *pl*

collector [kə'lɛktər] *n* Sammler(in) *m(f)*; (*of taxes etc*) Einnehmer(in) *m(f)*; (*of rent, cash*) Kassierer(in) *m(f)*; **~'s item** *or* **piece** Sammlerstück *nt*, Liebhaberstück *nt*

college ['kɔlɪdʒ] *n* College *nt*; (*of agriculture, technology*) Fachhochschule *f*; **to go to ~** studieren; **~ of education** pädagogische Hochschule *f*

collide [kə'laɪd] *vi*: **to ~ (with)** zusammenstoßen (mit); (*fig: clash*) eine heftige Auseinandersetzung haben (mit)

collie ['kɔlɪ] *n* Collie *m*

colliery ['kɔlɪərɪ] (*Brit*) *n* (Kohlen)bergwerk *nt*, Zeche *f*

collision [kə'lɪʒən] *n* Zusammenstoß *m*; **to be on a ~ course** (*also fig*) auf Kollisionskurs sein

collision damage waiver *n* (*Insurance*) *Verzicht auf Haftungsbeschränkung bei Unfällen mit Mietwagen*

colloquial [kə'ləukwɪəl] *adj* umgangssprachlich

collusion [kə'lu:ʒən] *n* (geheime) Absprache *f*; **to be in ~ with** gemeinsame Sache machen mit

Colo. (*US*) *abbr* (*Post*) = *Colorado*

Cologne [kə'ləun] *n* Köln *nt*

cologne [kə'ləun] *n* (*also*: **eau de cologne**) Kölnischwasser *nt*, Eau de Cologne *nt*

Colombia [kə'lɔmbɪə] *n* Kolumbien *nt*

Colombian [kə'lɔmbɪən] *adj* kolumbianisch ▷ *n* Kolumbianer(in) *m(f)*

colon ['kəulən] *n* Doppelpunkt *m*; (*Anat*) Dickdarm *m*

colonel ['kə:nl] *n* Oberst *m*

colonial [kə'ləunɪəl] *adj* Kolonial-

colonize ['kɔlənaɪz] *vt* kolonisieren

colony ['kɔlənɪ] *n* Kolonie *f*

color *etc* ['kʌlər] (*US*) = **colour** *etc*

Colorado beetle [kɔlə'rɑ:dəu-] *n* Kartoffelkäfer *m*

colossal [kə'lɔsl] *adj* riesig, kolossal

colour, (*US*) **color** ['kʌlər] *n* Farbe *f*; (*skin colour*) Hautfarbe *f*; (*of spectacle etc*) Atmosphäre *f* ▷ *vt* bemalen; (*with crayons*) ausmalen; (*dye*) färben; (*fig*) beeinflussen ▷ *vi* (*blush*) erröten, rot werden ▷ *cpd* Farb-; **colours** *npl* (*of party, club etc*) Farben *pl*; **in ~** (*film*) in Farbe; (*illustrations*) bunt

▶ **colour in** *vt* ausmalen

colour bar *n* Rassenschranke *f*

colour-blind ['kʌləblaɪnd] *adj* farbenblind

coloured ['kʌləd] *adj* farbig; (*photo*) Farb-; (*illustration etc*) bunt

colour film *n* Farbfilm *m*

colourful ['kʌləful] *adj* bunt; (*account, story*) farbig, anschaulich; (*personality*) schillernd

colouring ['kʌlərɪŋ] *n* Gesichtsfarbe *f*, Teint *m*; (*in food*) Farbstoff *m*

colour scheme *n* Farbzusammenstellung *f*

colour supplement (*Brit*) *n* Farbbeilage *f*, Magazin *nt*

colour television *n* Farbfernsehen *nt*; (*set*) Farbfernseher *m*

colt [kəult] *n* Hengstfohlen *nt*

column ['kɔləm] *n* Säule *f*; (*of people*) Kolonne *f*; (*of print*) Spalte *f*; (*gossip/sports column*) Kolumne *f*; **the editorial ~** der Leitartikel

columnist ['kɔləmnɪst] *n* Kolumnist(in) *m(f)*

coma ['kəumə] *n* Koma *nt*; **to be in a ~** im Koma liegen

comb [kəum] *n* Kamm *m* ▷ *vt* kämmen; (*area*) durchkämmen

combat ['kɔmbæt] *n* Kampf *m* ▷ *vt* bekämpfen

combination [kɔmbɪ'neɪʃən] *n* Kombination *f*

combination lock *n* Kombinationsschloss *nt*

combine [*vti* kəm'baɪn, *n* 'kɔmbaɪn] *vt* verbinden ▷ *vi* sich zusammenschließen; (*Chem*) sich verbinden ▷ *n* Konzern *m*; (*Agr*) = **combine harvester**; **~d effort** vereintes Unternehmen

combine harvester *n* Mähdrescher *m*

combo ['kɔmbəu] *n* Combo *f*

combustible [kəm'bʌstɪbl] *adj* brennbar

combustion [kəm'bʌstʃən] *n* Verbrennung *f*

 KEYWORD

come [kʌm] (*pt* **came**, *pp* **come**) *vi* **1** (*movement towards*) kommen; **come with me** kommen Sie mit mir; **to come running** angelaufen kommen; **coming!** ich komme!

2 (*arrive*) kommen; **they came to a river** sie kamen an einen Fluss; **to come home** nach Hause kommen

3 (*reach*): **to come to** kommen an +*acc*; **her hair came to her waist** ihr Haar reichte ihr bis zur Hüfte; **to come to a decision** zu einer Entscheidung kommen

4 (*occur*): **an idea came to me** mir kam eine Idee

5 (*be, become*) werden; **I've come to like him** mittlerweile mag ich ihn; **if it comes to it** wenn es darauf ankommt

▶ **come about** *vi* geschehen

▶ **come across** *vt fus* (*find: person, thing*) stoßen auf +*acc*

▷ *vi*: **to come across well/badly** (*idea etc*) gut/ schlecht ankommen; (*meaning*) gut/schlecht verstanden werden

▶ **come along** *vi* (*arrive*) daherkommen; (*make progress*) vorankommen; **come along!** komm schon!

▶ **come apart** vi (*break in pieces*) auseinandergehen

▶ **come away** vi (*leave*) weggehen; (*become detached*) abgehen

▶ **come back** vi (*return*) zurückkommen; **to come back into fashion** wieder in Mode kommen

▶ **come by** vt fus (*acquire*) kommen zu

▶ **come down** vi (*price*) sinken, fallen; (*building: be demolished*) abgerissen werden; (*tree: during storm*) umstürzen

▶ **come forward** vi (*volunteer*) sich melden

▶ **come from** vt fus kommen von, stammen aus; (*person*) kommen aus

▶ **come in** vi (*enter*) hereinkommen; (*report, news*) eintreffen; (*on deal etc*) sich beteiligen; **come in!** herein!

▶ **come in for** vt fus (*criticism etc*) einstecken müssen

▶ **come into** vt fus (*inherit: money*) erben; **to come into fashion** in Mode kommen; **money doesn't come into it** Geld hat nichts damit zu tun

▶ **come off** vi (*become detached: button, handle*) sich lösen; (*succeed: attempt, plan*) klappen ▷ vt fus (*inf*): **come off it!** mach mal halblang!

▶ **come on** vi (*pupil, work, project*) vorankommen; (*lights etc*) angehen; **come on!** (*hurry up*) mach schon!; (*encouragement*) los!

▶ **come out** vi herauskommen; (*stain*) herausgehen; **to come out (on strike)** in den Streik treten

▶ **come over** vt fus: **I don't know what's come over him!** ich weiß nicht, was in ihn gefahren ist

▶ **come round** vi (*after faint, operation*) wieder zu sich kommen; (*visit*) vorbeikommen; (*agree*) zustimmen

▶ **come through** vi (*survive*) durchkommen; (*telephone call*) (durch)kommen ▷ vt fus (*illness etc*) überstehen

▶ **come to** vi (*regain consciousness*) wieder zu sich kommen ▷ vt fus (*add up to*): **how much does it come to?** was macht das zusammen?

▶ **come under** vt fus (*heading*) kommen unter +*acc*; (*criticism, pressure, attack*) geraten unter +*acc*

▶ **come up** vi (*approach*) herankommen; (*sun*) aufgehen; (*problem*) auftauchen; (*event*) bevorstehen; (*in conversation*) genannt werden; **something's come up** etwas ist dazwischengekommen

▶ **come up against** vt fus (*resistance, difficulties*) stoßen auf +*acc*

▶ **come upon** vt fus (*find*) stoßen auf +*acc*

▶ **come up to** vt fus: **the film didn't come up to our expectations** der Film entsprach nicht unseren Erwartungen; **it's coming up to 10 o'clock** es ist gleich 10 Uhr

▶ **come up with** vt fus (*idea*) aufwarten mit; (*money*) aufbringen

comeback ['kʌmbæk] n (*of film star etc*) Comeback nt; (*reaction, response*) Reaktion f

comedian [kə'miːdɪən] n Komiker m

comedienne [kəmiːdɪ'ɛn] n Komikerin f

comedown ['kʌmdaun] (*inf*) n Enttäuschung f; (*professional*) Abstieg m

comedy ['kɔmɪdɪ] n Komödie f; (*humour*) Witz m

comet ['kɔmɪt] n Komet m

comeuppance [kʌm'ʌpəns] n: **to get one's ~** die Quittung bekommen

comfort ['kʌmfət] n (*physical*) Behaglichkeit f; (*material*) Komfort m; (*solace, relief*) Trost m ▷ vt trösten; **comforts** npl (*of home etc*) Komfort m, Annehmlichkeiten pl

comfortable ['kʌmfətəbl] adj bequem; (*room*) komfortabel; (*walk, climb etc*) geruhsam; (*income*) ausreichend; (*majority*) sicher; **to be ~** (*physically*) sich wohlfühlen; (*financially*) sehr angenehm leben; **the patient is ~** dem Patienten geht es den Umständen entsprechend gut; **I don't feel very ~ about it** mir ist nicht ganz wohl bei der Sache

comfortably ['kʌmfətəblɪ] adv (*sit*) bequem; (*live*) angenehm

comforter ['kʌmfətəʳ] (*US*) n Schnuller m

comfort shopping n Frustkauf m

comfort station (*US*) n öffentliche Toilette f

comic ['kɔmɪk] adj (*also:* **comical**) komisch ▷ n Komiker(in) m(f); (*Brit: magazine*) Comicheft nt

comical ['kɔmɪkl] adj komisch

comic strip n Comicstrip m

coming ['kʌmɪŋ] n Ankunft f, Kommen nt ▷ adj kommend; (*next*) nächste(r, s); **in the ~ weeks** in den nächsten Wochen

coming and going n, **comings and goings** ▷ npl Kommen und Gehen nt

Comintern ['kɔmɪntəːn] n (*Pol*) Komintern f

comma ['kɔmə] n Komma nt

command [kə'mɑːnd] n (*also Comput*) Befehl m; (*control, charge*) Führung f; (*Mil: authority*) Kommando nt, Befehlsgewalt f; (*mastery*) Beherrschung f ▷ vt (*troops*) befehligen, kommandieren; (*be able to get*) verfügen über +*acc*; (*deserve: respect, admiration etc*) verdient haben; **to be in ~ of** das Kommando or den (Ober)befehl haben über +*acc*; **to have ~ of** das Kommando haben über +*acc*; **to take ~ of** das Kommando übernehmen +*gen*; **to have at one's ~** verfügen über +*acc*; **to ~ sb to do sth** jdm befehlen, etw zu tun

commandant ['kɔməndænt] n Kommandant m

command economy n Kommandowirtschaft f

commandeer [kɔmən'dɪəʳ] vt requirieren, beschlagnahmen; (*fig*) sich aneignen

commander [kə'mɑːndəʳ] n Befehlshaber m, Kommandant m

commander in chief n Oberbefehlshaber m

commanding [kə'mɑːndɪŋ] adj (*appearance*) imposant; (*voice, tone*) gebieterisch; (*lead*) entscheidend; (*position*) vorherrschend

commanding officer n befehlshabender Offizier m

commandment [kə'mɑːndmənt] n Gebot nt

command module n Kommandokapsel f

commando [kə'mɑːndəu] n Kommando nt, Kommandotrupp m; (soldier) Angehörige(r) m eines Kommando(trupp)s

commemorate [kə'mɛməreɪt] vt gedenken +gen

commemoration [kəmɛmə'reɪʃən] n Gedenken nt

commemorative [kə'mɛmərətɪv] adj Gedenk-

commence [kə'mɛns] vt, vi beginnen

commend [kə'mɛnd] vt loben; **to ~ sth to sb** jdm etw empfehlen

commendable [kə'mɛndəbl] adj lobenswert

commendation [kɔmɛn'deɪʃən] n Auszeichnung f

commensurate [kə'mɛnʃərɪt] adj: **~ with** or **to** entsprechend +dat

comment ['kɔmɛnt] n Bemerkung f; (on situation etc) Kommentar m ▷ vi: **to ~ (on)** sich äußern (über +acc or zu); (on situation etc) einen Kommentar abgeben (zu); **"no ~"** „kein Kommentar!"; **to ~ that ...** bemerken, dass ...

commentary ['kɔməntərɪ] n Kommentar m; (Sport) Reportage f

commentator ['kɔmənteɪtə'] n Kommentator(in) m(f); (Sport) Reporter(in) m(f)

commerce ['kɔmɜːs] n Handel m

commercial [kə'mɜːʃəl] adj kommerziell; (organization) Wirtschafts- ▷ n (advertisement) Werbespot m

commercial bank n Handelsbank f

commercial break n Werbung f

commercial college n Fachschule f für kaufmännische Berufe

commercialism [kə'mɜːʃəlɪzəm] n Kommerzialisierung f

commercialize [kə'mɜːʃəlaɪz] vt kommerzialisieren

commercialized [kə'mɜːʃəlaɪzd] (pej) adj kommerzialisiert

commercial radio n kommerzielles Radio nt

commercial television n kommerzielles Fernsehen nt

commercial traveller n Handelsvertreter(in) m(f)

commercial vehicle n Lieferwagen m

commiserate [kə'mɪzəreɪt] vi: **to ~ with sb** jdm sein Mitgefühl zeigen

commission [kə'mɪʃən] n (order for work) Auftrag m; (Comm) Provision f; (committee) Kommission f; (Mil) Offizierspatent nt ▷ vt (work of art) in Auftrag geben; (Mil) (zum Offizier) ernennen; **out of ~** außer Betrieb; (Naut) nicht im Dienst; **I get 10% ~** ich bekomme 10% Provision; **~ of inquiry** Untersuchungsausschuss m, Untersuchungskommission f; **to ~ sb to do sth** jdn damit beauftragen, etw zu tun; **to ~ sth from sb** jdm etw in Auftrag geben

commissionaire [kəmɪʃə'nɛə'] (Brit) n Portier m

commissioner [kə'mɪʃənə'] n Polizeipräsident m

commit [kə'mɪt] vt (crime) begehen; (money, resources) einsetzen; (to sb's care) anvertrauen; **to ~ o.s.** sich festlegen; **to ~ o.s. to do sth** sich (dazu) verpflichten, etw zu tun; **to ~ suicide** Selbstmord begehen; **to ~ to writing** zu Papier bringen; **to ~ sb for trial** jdn einem Gericht überstellen

commitment [kə'mɪtmənt] n Verpflichtung f; (to ideology, system) Engagement nt

committed [kə'mɪtɪd] adj engagiert

committee [kə'mɪtɪ] n Ausschuss m, Komitee nt; **to be on a ~** in einem Ausschuss or Komitee sein or sitzen

committee meeting n Ausschusssitzung f

commodity [kə'mɔdɪtɪ] n Ware f; (food) Nahrungsmittel nt

common ['kɔmən] adj (shared by all) gemeinsam; (good) Gemein-; (property) Gemeinschafts-; (usual, ordinary) häufig; (vulgar) gewöhnlich ▷ n Gemeindeland nt; **the Commons** (Brit: Pol) npl das Unterhaus; **in ~ use** allgemein gebräuchlich; **it's ~ knowledge that** es ist allgemein bekannt, dass; **to the ~ good** für das Gemeinwohl; **to have sth in ~ (with sb)** etw (mit jdm) gemein haben

common cold n Schnupfen m

common denominator n (Math: fig) gemeinsamer Nenner m

commoner ['kɔmənə'] n Bürgerliche(r) f(m)

common ground n (fig) gemeinsame Basis f

common land n Gemeindeland nt

common-law n Gewohnheitsrecht nt

common-law ['kɔmənlɔː] adj: **she is his ~ wife** sie lebt mit ihm in eheähnlicher Gemeinschaft

commonly ['kɔmənlɪ] adv häufig

Common Market n: **the ~** der Gemeinsame Markt

commonplace ['kɔmənpleɪs] adj alltäglich

common room n Aufenthaltsraum m, Tagesraum m

common sense n gesunder Menschenverstand m

Commonwealth ['kɔmənwɛlθ] (Brit) n: **the ~** das Commonwealth; siehe Info-Artikel

COMMONWEALTH

Das Commonwealth, offiziell Commonwealth of Nations, ist ein lockerer Zusammenschluss aus souveränen Staaten, die früher unter britischer Regierung standen, und von Großbritannien abhängigen Gebieten. Die Mitgliedstaaten erkennen den britischen Monarchen als Oberhaupt des Commonwealth an. Bei der Commonwealth Conference, einem Treffen der Staatsoberhäupter

der Commonwealthländer, werden
Angelegenheiten von gemeinsamem
Interesse diskutiert.

commotion [kə'məʊʃən] *n* Tumult *m*

communal ['kɔmjuːnl] *adj* gemeinsam,
Gemeinschafts-; (*life*) Gemeinschafts-

commune [*n* 'kɔmjuːn, *vi* kə'mjuːn] *n*
Kommune *f* ▷ *vi*: **to ~ with** Zwiesprache
halten mit

communicate [kə'mjuːnɪkeɪt] *vt* mitteilen;
(*idea, feeling*) vermitteln ▷ *vi*: **to ~ (with)** (*by
speech, gesture*) sich verständigen (mit); (*in
writing*) in Verbindung *or* Kontakt stehen (mit)

communication [kɔmjuːnɪ'keɪʃən] *n*
Kommunikation *f*; (*letter, call*) Mitteilung *f*

communication cord (*Brit*) *n* Notbremse *f*

communications network
[kəmjuːnɪ'keɪʃənz-] *n* Kommunikationsnetz *nt*

communications satellite *n*
Kommunikationssatellit *m*,
Nachrichtensatellit *m*

communicative [kə'mjuːnɪkətɪv] *adj*
gesprächig, mitteilsam

communion [kə'mjuːnɪən] *n* (*also*: **Holy
Communion**: *Catholic*) Kommunion *f*;
(: *Protestant*) Abendmahl *nt*

communiqué [kə'mjuːnɪkeɪ] *n* Kommuniqué
nt, (amtliche) Verlautbarung *f*

communism ['kɔmjunɪzəm] *n* Kommunismus
m

communist ['kɔmjunɪst] *adj* kommunistisch
▷ *n* Kommunist(in) *m(f)*

community [kə'mjuːnɪtɪ] *n* Gemeinschaft *f*;
(*within larger group*) Bevölkerungsgruppe *f*

community centre *n* Gemeindezentrum *nt*

community charge (*Brit*) *n* (*formerly*)
Gemeindesteuer *f*

community chest (*US*) *n* Wohltätigkeitsfonds
m, Hilfsfonds *m*

community health centre *n* Gemeinde-
Ärztezentrum *nt*

community home (*Brit*) *n* Erziehungsheim *nt*

community service *n* Sozialdienst *m*

community spirit *n* Gemeinschaftssinn *m*

commutation ticket [kɔmjuː'teɪʃən-] (*US*) *n*
Zeitkarte *f*

commute [kə'mjuːt] *vi* pendeln ▷ *vt* (*Law,
Math*) umwandeln

commuter [kə'mjuːtəʳ] *n* Pendler(in) *m(f)*

compact [*adj* kəm'pækt, *n* 'kɔmpækt] *adj*
kompakt ▷ *n* (*also*: **powder compact**)
Puderdose *f*

compact disc *n* Compact Disc *f*, CD *f*

compact disc player *n* CD-Spieler *m*

companion [kəm'pænjən] *n* Begleiter(in) *m(f)*

companionship [kəm'pænjənʃɪp] *n*
Gesellschaft *f*

companionway [kəm'pænjənweɪ] *n* (*Naut*)
Niedergang *m*

company ['kʌmpənɪ] *n* Firma *f*; (*Theat*)
(Schauspiel)truppe *f*; (*Mil*) Kompanie *f*;
(*companionship*) Gesellschaft *f*; **he's good ~**

seine Gesellschaft ist angenehm; **to keep sb
~** jdm Gesellschaft leisten; **to part ~ with** sich
trennen von; **Smith and C~** Smith & Co

company car *n* Firmenwagen *m*

company director *n* Direktor(in) *m(f)*,
Firmenchef(in) *m(f)*

company secretary (*Brit*) *n* ≈ Prokurist(in)
m(f)

comparable ['kɔmpərəbl] *adj* vergleichbar

comparative [kəm'pærətɪv] *adj* relativ; (*study,
literature*) vergleichend; (*Ling*) komparativ

comparatively [kəm'pærətɪvlɪ] *adv* relativ

compare [kəm'pɛəʳ] *vt*: **to ~ (with** *or* **to)**
vergleichen (mit) ▷ *vi*: **to ~ (with)** sich
vergleichen lassen (mit); **how do the prices
~?** wie lassen sich die Preise vergleichen?; **~d
with** *or* **to** im Vergleich zu, verglichen mit

comparison [kəm'pærɪsn] *n* Vergleich *m*; **in ~
(with)** im Vergleich (zu)

compartment [kəm'pɑːtmənt] *n* (*Rail*) Abteil
nt; (*section*) Fach *nt*

compass ['kʌmpəs] *n* Kompass *m*; (*fig: scope*)
Bereich *m*; **compasses** *npl* (*also*: **pair of
compasses**) Zirkel *m*; **within the ~ of** im
Rahmen *or* Bereich +*gen*; **beyond the ~ of** über
den Rahmen *or* Bereich +*gen* hinaus

compassion [kəm'pæʃən] *n* Mitgefühl *nt*

compassionate [kəm'pæʃənɪt] *adj*
mitfühlend; **on ~ grounds** aus familiären
Gründen

compassionate leave *n* (*esp Mil*) Beurlaubung
wegen Krankheit oder Trauerfall in der Familie

compatibility [kəmpætɪ'bɪlɪtɪ] *n* (*see adj*)
Vereinbarkeit *f*; Zueinanderpassen *nt*;
Kompatibilität *f*

compatible [kəm'pætɪbl] *adj* (*ideas etc*)
vereinbar; (*people*) zueinanderpassend;
(*Comput*) kompatibel

compel [kəm'pɛl] *vt* zwingen

compelling [kəm'pɛlɪŋ] *adj* zwingend

compendium [kəm'pɛndɪəm] *n* Kompendium
nt

compensate ['kɔmpənseɪt] *vt* entschädigen
▷ *vi*: **to ~ for** (*loss*) ersetzen; (*disappointment,
change etc*) (wieder) ausgleichen

compensation [kɔmpən'seɪʃən] *n* (*see vb*)
Entschädigung *f*; Ersatz *m*; Ausgleich *m*;
(*money*) Schaden(s)ersatz *m*

compère ['kɔmpɛəʳ] *n* Conférencier *m*

compete [kəm'piːt] *vi* (*in contest, game*)
teilnehmen; (*two theories, statements*)
unvereinbar sein; **to ~ (with)** (*companies, rivals*)
konkurrieren (mit)

competence ['kɔmpɪtəns] *n* Fähigkeit *f*

competent ['kɔmpɪtənt] *adj* fähig

competing [kəm'piːtɪŋ] *adj* konkurrierend

competition [kɔmpɪ'tɪʃən] *n* Konkurrenz
f; (*contest*) Wettbewerb *m*; **in ~ with** im
Wettbewerb mit

competitive [kəm'pɛtɪtɪv] *adj* (*industry, society*)
wettbewerbsbetont, wettbewerbsorientiert;
(*person*) vom Konkurrenzdenken geprägt; (*price,
product*) wettbewerbsfähig, konkurrenzfähig;

(*sport*) (Wett)kampf-

competitive examination n (*for places*) Auswahlprüfung f; (*for prizes*) Wettbewerb m

competitor [kəm'pɛtɪtə^r] n Konkurrent(in) m(f); (*participant*) Teilnehmer(in) m(f)

compilation [kɔmpɪ'leɪʃən] n Zusammenstellung f

compile [kəm'paɪl] vt zusammenstellen; (*book*) verfassen

complacency [kəm'pleɪsnsɪ] n Selbstzufriedenheit f, Selbstgefälligkeit f

complacent [kəm'pleɪsnt] adj selbstzufrieden, selbstgefällig

complain [kəm'pleɪn] vi (*protest*) sich beschweren; **to ~ (about)** sich beklagen (über +acc); **to ~ of** (*headache etc*) klagen über +acc

complaint [kəm'pleɪnt] n Klage f; (*in shop etc*) Beschwerde f; (*illness*) Beschwerden pl

complement ['kɔmplɪmənt] n Ergänzung f; (*esp ship's crew*) Besatzung f ▷ vt ergänzen; **to have a full ~ of ...** (*people*) die volle Stärke an ... dat haben; (*items*) die volle Zahl an ... dat haben

complementary [kɔmplɪ'mɛntərɪ] adj komplementär, einander ergänzend

complete [kəm'pli:t] adj (*total: silence*) vollkommen; (: *change*) völlig; (: *success*) voll; (*whole*) ganz; (: *set*) vollständig; (: *edition*) Gesamt-; (*finished*) fertig ▷ vt fertigstellen; (*task*) beenden; (*set, group etc*) vervollständigen; (*fill in*) ausfüllen; **it's a ~ disaster** es ist eine totale Katastrophe

completely [kəm'pli:tlɪ] adv völlig, vollkommen

completion [kəm'pli:ʃən] n Fertigstellung f; (*of contract*) Abschluss m; **to be nearing ~** kurz vor dem Abschluss sein or stehen; **on ~ of the contract** bei Vertragsabschluss

complex ['kɔmplɛks] adj kompliziert ▷ n Komplex m

complexion [kəm'plɛkʃən] n Teint m, Gesichtsfarbe f; (*of event etc*) Charakter m; (*political, religious*) Anschauung f; **to put a different ~ on sth** etw in einem anderen Licht erscheinen lassen

complexity [kəm'plɛksɪtɪ] n Kompliziertheit f

compliance [kəm'plaɪəns] n Fügsamkeit f; (*agreement*) Einverständnis nt; **~ with** Einverständnis mit, Zustimmung f zu; **in ~ with** gemäß +dat

compliant [kəm'plaɪənt] adj gefällig, entgegenkommend

complicate ['kɔmplɪkeɪt] vt komplizieren

complicated ['kɔmplɪkeɪtɪd] adj kompliziert

complication [kɔmplɪ'keɪʃən] n Komplikation f

complicity [kəm'plɪsɪtɪ] n Mittäterschaft f

compliment [n 'kɔmplɪmənt, vt 'kɔmplɪment] n Kompliment nt ▷ vt ein Kompliment/Komplimente machen; **compliments** npl (*regards*) Grüße pl; **to pay sb a ~** jdm ein Kompliment machen; **to ~ sb (on sth)** jdm Komplimente (wegen etw) machen; **to ~ sb**

on doing sth jdm Komplimente machen, dass er/sie etw getan hat

complimentary [kɔmplɪ'mɛntərɪ] adj schmeichelhaft; (*ticket, copy of book etc*) Frei-

compliments slip n Empfehlungszettel m

comply [kəm'plaɪ] vi: **to ~ with** (*law*) einhalten +acc; (*ruling*) sich richten nach

component [kəm'pəunənt] adj einzeln ▷ n Bestandteil m

compose [kəm'pəuz] vt (*music*) komponieren; (*poem*) verfassen; (*letter*) abfassen; **to be ~d of** bestehen aus; **to ~ o.s.** sich sammeln

composed [kəm'pəuzd] adj ruhig, gelassen

composer [kəm'pəuzə^r] n Komponist(in) m(f)

composite ['kɔmpəzɪt] adj zusammengesetzt; (*Bot*) Korbblütler-; (*Math*) teilbar; (*Bot*): **~ plant** Korbblütler m

composition [kɔmpə'zɪʃən] n Zusammensetzung f; (*essay*) Aufsatz m; (*Mus*) Komposition f

compositor [kəm'pɔzɪtə^r] n (Schrift)setzer(in) m(f)

compos mentis ['kɔmpɔs 'mɛntɪs] adj zurechnungsfähig

compost ['kɔmpɔst] n Kompost m; (*also*: **potting compost**) Blumenerde f

composure [kəm'pəuʒə^r] n Fassung f, Beherrschung f

compound [n, adj 'kɔmpaund, vt kəm'paund] n (*Chem*) Verbindung f; (*enclosure*) umzäuntes Gebiet or Gelände nt; (*Ling*) Kompositum nt ▷ adj zusammengesetzt; (*eye*) Facetten- ▷ vt verschlimmern, vergrößern

compound fracture n komplizierter Bruch m

compound interest n Zinseszins m

comprehend [kɔmprɪ'hɛnd] vt begreifen, verstehen

comprehension [kɔmprɪ'hɛnʃən] n Verständnis nt

comprehensive [kɔmprɪ'hɛnsɪv] adj umfassend; (*insurance*) Vollkasko- ▷ n = **comprehensive school**

comprehensive school (*Brit*) n Gesamtschule f; *siehe Info-Artikel*

    COMPREHENSIVE SCHOOL

    Comprehensive school ist in Großbritannien eine nicht selektive, weiterführende Schule, an der alle Kinder aus einem Einzugsgebiet gemeinsam unterrichtet werden. An einer solchen Gesamtschule können alle Schulabschlüsse gemacht werden. Die meisten staatlichen Schulen in Großbritannien sind comprehensive schools.

compress [vt kəm'prɛs, n 'kɔmprɛs] vt (*information etc*) verdichten; (*air*) komprimieren; (*cotton, paper etc*) zusammenpressen ▷ n (*Med*) Kompresse f

compressed air [kəm'prɛst-] n Druckluft f, Pressluft f

compression [kəmˈprɛʃən] n (see vb) Verdichtung f; Kompression f; Zusammenpressen nt

comprise [kəmˈpraɪz] vt (also: **be comprised of**) bestehen aus; (constitute) bilden, ausmachen

compromise [ˈkɔmprəmaɪz] n Kompromiss m ⊳ vt (beliefs, principles) verraten; (person) kompromittieren ⊳ vi Kompromisse schließen ⊳ cpd (solution etc) Kompromiss-

compulsion [kəmˈpʌlʃən] n Zwang m; (force) Druck m, Zwang m; **under** ~ unter Druck or Zwang

compulsive [kəmˈpʌlsɪv] adj zwanghaft; **it makes** ~ **viewing/reading** das muss man einfach sehen/lesen; **he's a** ~ **smoker** das Rauchen ist bei ihm zur Sucht geworden

compulsory [kəmˈpʌlsərɪ] adj obligatorisch; (retirement) Zwangs-

compulsory purchase n Enteignung f

compunction [kəmˈpʌŋkʃən] n Schuldgefühle pl, Gewissensbisse pl; **to have no** ~ **about doing sth** etw tun, ohne sich schuldig zu fühlen

computer [kəmˈpjuːtəʳ] n Computer m, Rechner m ⊳ cpd Computer-; **the process is done by** ~ das Verfahren wird per Computer durchgeführt

computer game n Computerspiel nt

computerization [kəmpjuːtəraɪˈzeɪʃən] n Computerisierung f

computerize [kəmˈpjuːtəraɪz] vt auf Computer umstellen; (information) computerisieren

computer literate adj: **to be** ~ Computerkenntnisse haben

computer programmer n Programmierer(in) m(f)

computer programming n Programmieren nt

computer science n Informatik f

computer scientist n Informatiker(in) m(f)

computing [kəmˈpjuːtɪŋ] n Informatik f; (activity) Computerarbeit f

comrade [ˈkɔmrɪd] n Genosse m, Genossin f; (friend) Kamerad(in) m(f)

comradeship [ˈkɔmrɪdʃɪp] n Kameradschaft f

Comsat® [ˈkɔmsæt] n abbr = **communications satellite**

con [kɔn] vt betrügen; (cheat) hereinlegen ⊳ n Schwindel m; **to** ~ **sb into doing sth** jdn durch einen Trick dazu bringen, dass er/sie etw tut

concave [ˈkɔnkeɪv] adj konkav

conceal [kənˈsiːl] vt verbergen; (information) verheimlichen

concede [kənˈsiːd] vt zugeben ⊳ vi nachgeben; (admit defeat) sich geschlagen geben; **to** ~ **defeat** sich geschlagen geben; **to** ~ **a point to sb** jdm in einem Punkt recht geben

conceit [kənˈsiːt] n Einbildung f

conceited [kənˈsiːtɪd] adj eingebildet

conceivable [kənˈsiːvəbl] adj denkbar, vorstellbar; **it is** ~ **that** ... es ist denkbar, dass ...

conceivably [kənˈsiːvəblɪ] adv: **he may** ~ **be**

right es ist durchaus denkbar, dass er recht hat

conceive [kənˈsiːv] vt (child) empfangen; (plan) kommen auf +acc; (policy) konzipieren ⊳ vi empfangen; **to** ~ **of sth** sich dat etw vorstellen; **to** ~ **of doing sth** sich dat vorstellen, etw zu tun

concentrate [ˈkɔnsəntreɪt] vi sich konzentrieren ⊳ vt konzentrieren

concentration [kɔnsənˈtreɪʃən] n Konzentration f

concentration camp n Konzentrationslager nt, KZ nt

concentric [kɔnˈsɛntrɪk] adj konzentrisch

concept [ˈkɔnsɛpt] n Vorstellung f; (principle) Begriff m

conception [kənˈsɛpʃən] n Vorstellung f; (of child) Empfängnis f

concern [kənˈsəːn] n Angelegenheit f; (anxiety, worry) Sorge f; (Comm) Konzern m ⊳ vt Sorgen machen +dat; (involve) angehen; (relate to) betreffen; **to be ~ed (about)** sich dat Sorgen machen (um); **"to whom it may** ~" (on certificate) „Bestätigung"; (on reference) „Zeugnis"; **as far as I am ~ed** was mich betrifft; **to be ~ed with** sich interessieren für; **the department ~ed** (under discussion) die betreffende Abteilung; (involved) die zuständige Abteilung

concerning [kənˈsəːnɪŋ] prep bezüglich +gen, hinsichtlich +gen

concert [ˈkɔnsət] n Konzert nt; **in** ~ (Mus) live; (activities, actions etc) gemeinsam

concerted [kənˈsəːtɪd] adj gemeinsam

concert hall n Konzerthalle f, Konzertsaal m

concertina [kɔnsəˈtiːnə] n Konzertina f ⊳ vi sich wie eine Ziehharmonika zusammenschieben

concerto [kənˈtʃəːtəu] n Konzert nt

concession [kənˈsɛʃən] n Zugeständnis nt, Konzession f; (Comm) Konzession; **tax** ~ Steuervergünstigung f

concessionaire [kənsɛʃəˈnɛəʳ] n Konzessionär m

concessionary [kənˈsɛʃənrɪ] adj ermäßigt

conciliation [kənsɪlɪˈeɪʃən] n Schlichtung f

conciliatory [kənˈsɪlɪətrɪ] adj versöhnlich

concise [kənˈsaɪs] adj kurz gefasst, prägnant

conclave [ˈkɔnkleɪv] n Klausur f; (Rel) Konklave f

conclude [kənˈkluːd] vt beenden, schließen; (treaty, deal etc) abschließen; (decide) schließen, folgern ⊳ vi schließen; (events): **to** ~ **(with)** enden (mit); **"That," he ~d, "is why we did it"** „Darum", schloss er, „haben wir es getan"; **I** ~ **that** ... ich komme zu dem Schluss, dass ...

concluding [kənˈkluːdɪŋ] adj (remarks etc) abschließend, Schluss-

conclusion [kənˈkluːʒən] n (see vb) Ende nt; Schluss m; Abschluss m; Folgerung f; **to come to the** ~ **that** ... zu dem Schluss kommen, dass ...

conclusive [kənˈkluːsɪv] adj (evidence) schlüssig;

(*defeat*) endgültig

concoct [kən'kɔkt] *vt* (*excuse etc*) sich *dat* ausdenken; (*meal, sauce*) improvisieren

concoction [kən'kɔkʃən] *n* Zusammenstellung *f*; (*drink*) Gebräu *nt*

concord ['kɔŋkɔːd] *n* Eintracht *f*; (*treaty*) Vertrag *m*

concourse ['kɔŋkɔːs] *n* (Eingangs)halle *f*; (*crowd*) Menge *f*

concrete ['kɔŋkriːt] *n* Beton *m* ▷ *adj* (*ceiling, block*) Beton-; (*proposal, idea*) konkret

concrete mixer *n* Betonmischmaschine *f*

concur [kən'kəːʳ] *vi* übereinstimmen; **to ~ with** beipflichten +*dat*

concurrently [kən'kʌrntlɪ] *adv* gleichzeitig

concussion [kən'kʌʃən] *n* Gehirnerschütterung *f*

condemn [kən'dɛm] *vt* verurteilen; (*building*) für abbruchreif erklären

condemnation [kɔndɛm'neɪʃən] *n* Verurteilung *f*

condensation [kɔndɛn'seɪʃən] *n* Kondenswasser *nt*

condense [kən'dɛns] *vi* kondensieren, sich niederschlagen ▷ *vt* zusammenfassen

condensed milk [kən'dɛnst-] *n* Kondensmilch *f*, Büchsenmilch *f*

condescend [kɔndɪ'sɛnd] *vi* herablassend sein; **to ~ to do sth** sich dazu herablassen, etw zu tun

condescending [kɔndɪ'sɛndɪŋ] *adj* herablassend

condition [kən'dɪʃən] *n* Zustand *m*; (*requirement*) Bedingung *f*; (*illness*) Leiden *nt* ▷ *vt* konditionieren; (*hair*) in Form bringen; **conditions** *npl* (*circumstances*) Verhältnisse *pl*; **in good/poor ~** (*person*) in guter/schlechter Verfassung; (*thing*) in gutem/schlechtem Zustand; **a heart ~** ein Herzleiden *nt*; **weather ~s** die Wetterlage; **on ~ that ...** unter der Bedingung, dass ...

conditional [kən'dɪʃənl] *adj* bedingt; **to be ~ upon** abhängen von

conditioner [kən'dɪʃənəʳ] *n* (*for hair*) Pflegespülung *f*; (*for fabrics*) Weichspüler *m*

condo ['kɔndəu] (*US: inf*) *n abbr* = **condominium**

condolences [kən'dəulənsɪz] *npl* Beileid *nt*

condom ['kɔndəm] *n* Kondom *m or nt*

condominium [kɔndə'mɪnɪəm] (*US*) *n* Haus *nt* mit Eigentumswohnungen; (*rooms*) Eigentumswohnung *f*

condone [kən'dəun] *vt* gutheißen

conducive [kən'djuːsɪv] *adj*: **~ to** förderlich +*dat*

conduct [*n* 'kɔndʌkt, *vt* kən'dʌkt] *n* Verhalten *nt* ▷ *vt* (*investigation etc*) durchführen; (*manage*) führen; (*orchestra, choir etc*) dirigieren; (*heat, electricity*) leiten; **to ~ o.s.** sich verhalten

conducted tour [kən'dʌktɪd-] *n* Führung *f*

conductor [kən'dʌktəʳ] *n* (*of orchestra*) Dirigent(in) *m(f)*; (*on bus*) Schaffner *m*; (*US: on train*) Zugführer(in) *m(f)*; (*Elec*) Leiter *m*

conductress [kən'dʌktrɪs] *n* (*on bus*) Schaffnerin *f*

conduit ['kɔndjuɪt] *n* (*Tech*) Leitungsrohr *nt*; (*Elec*) Isolierrohr *nt*

cone [kəun] *n* Kegel *m*; (*on road*) Leitkegel *m*; (*Bot*) Zapfen *m*; (*ice cream cornet*) (Eis)tüte *f*

confectioner [kən'fɛkʃənəʳ] *n* (*maker*) Süßwarenhersteller(in) *m(f)*; (*seller*) Süßwarenhändler(in) *m(f)*; (*of cakes*) Konditor(in) *m(f)*

confectioner's [kən'fɛkʃənəz], **confectioner's shop** *n* Süßwarenladen *m*; (*cake shop*) Konditorei *f*

confectionery [kən'fɛkʃənrɪ] *n* Süßwaren *pl*, Süßigkeiten *pl*; (*cakes*) Konditorwaren *pl*

confederate [kən'fɛdrɪt] *adj* verbündet ▷ *n* (*pej*) Komplize *m*, Komplizin *f*; (*US: Hist*): **the C-s** die Konföderierten *pl*

confederation [kənfɛdə'reɪʃən] *n* Bund *m*; (*Pol*) Bündnis *nt*; (*Comm*) Verband *m*

confer [kən'fəːʳ] *vt*: **to ~ sth (on sb)** (jdm) etw verleihen ▷ *vi* sich beraten; **to ~ with sb about sth** sich mit jdm über etw *acc* beraten, etw mit jdm besprechen

conference ['kɔnfərəns] *n* Konferenz *f*; (*more informal*) Besprechung *f*; **to be in ~** in or bei einer Konferenz/Besprechung sein

conference room *n* Konferenzraum *m*; (*smaller*) Besprechungszimmer *nt*

confess [kən'fɛs] *vt* bekennen; (*sin*) beichten; (*crime*) zugeben, gestehen ▷ *vi* (*admit*) gestehen; **to ~ to sth** (*crime*) etw gestehen; (*weakness etc*) sich zu etw bekennen; **I must ~ that I didn't enjoy it at all** ich muss sagen, dass es mir überhaupt keinen Spaß gemacht hat

confession [kən'fɛʃən] *n* Geständnis *nt*; (*Rel*) Beichte *f*; **to make a ~** ein Geständnis ablegen

confessor [kən'fɛsəʳ] *n* Beichtvater *m*

confetti [kən'fɛtɪ] *n* Konfetti *nt*

confide [kən'faɪd] *vi*: **to ~ in** sich anvertrauen +*dat*

confidence ['kɔnfɪdns] *n* Vertrauen *nt*; (*self-assurance*) Selbstvertrauen *nt*; (*secret*) vertrauliche Mitteilung *f*, Geheimnis *nt*; **to have ~ in sb/sth** Vertrauen zu jdm/ etw haben; **to have (every) ~ that ...** ganz zuversichtlich sein, dass ...; **motion of no ~** Misstrauensantrag *m*; **to tell sb sth in strict ~** jdm etw ganz im Vertrauen sagen; **in ~** vertraulich

confidence trick *n* Schwindel *m*

confident ['kɔnfɪdənt] *adj* (selbst)sicher; (*positive*) zuversichtlich

confidential [kɔnfɪ'dɛnʃəl] *adj* vertraulich; (*secretary*) Privat-

confidentiality [kɔnfɪdɛnʃɪ'ælɪtɪ] *n* Vertraulichkeit *f*

configuration [kənfɪgju'reɪʃən] *n* Anordnung *f*; (*Comput*) Konfiguration *f*

confine [kən'faɪn] *vt* (*shut up*) einsperren; **to ~ (to)** beschränken (auf +*acc*); **to ~ o.s. to sth** sich auf etw *acc* beschränken; **to ~ o.s. to doing sth** sich darauf beschränken, etw zu tun

489

confined [kən'faɪnd] *adj* begrenzt

confinement [kən'faɪnmənt] *n* Haft *f*

confines ['kɔnfaɪnz] *npl* Grenzen *pl*; *(of situation)* Rahmen *m*

confirm [kən'fə:m] *vt* bestätigen; **to be ~ed** *(Rel)* konfirmiert werden

confirmation [kɔnfə'meɪʃən] *n* Bestätigung *f*; *(Rel)* Konfirmation *f*

confirmed [kən'fə:md] *adj (bachelor)* eingefleischt; *(teetotaller)* überzeugt

confiscate ['kɔnfɪskeɪt] *vt* beschlagnahmen, konfiszieren

confiscation [kɔnfɪs'keɪʃən] *n* Beschlagnahme *f*, Konfiszierung *f*

conflagration [kɔnflə'greɪʃən] *n* Feuersbrunst *f*

conflict ['kɔnflɪkt] *n* Konflikt *m*; *(fighting)* Zusammenstoß *m*, Kampf *m* ▷ *vi*: **to ~ (with)** im Widerspruch stehen (zu)

conflicting [kən'flɪktɪŋ] *adj* widersprüchlich

conform [kən'fɔ:m] *vi* sich anpassen; **to ~ to** entsprechen +*dat*

conformist [kən'fɔ:mɪst] *n* Konformist(in) *m(f)*

confound [kən'faʊnd] *vt* verwirren; *(amaze)* verblüffen

confounded [kən'faʊndɪd] *adj* verdammt, verflixt *(inf)*

confront [kən'frʌnt] *vt (problems, task)* sich stellen +*dat*; *(enemy, danger)* gegenübertreten +*dat*

confrontation [kɔnfrən'teɪʃən] *n* Konfrontation *f*

confuse [kən'fju:z] *vt* verwirren; *(mix up)* verwechseln; *(complicate)* durcheinanderbringen

confused [kən'fju:zd] *adj (person)* verwirrt; *(situation)* verworren, konfus; **to get ~** konfus werden

confusing [kən'fju:zɪŋ] *adj* verwirrend

confusion [kən'fju:ʒən] *n (mix-up)* Verwechslung *f*; *(perplexity)* Verwirrung *f*; *(disorder)* Durcheinander *nt*

congeal [kən'dʒi:l] *vi (blood)* gerinnen; *(sauce, oil)* erstarren

congenial [kən'dʒi:nɪəl] *adj* ansprechend, sympathisch; *(atmosphere, place, work, company)* angenehm

congenital [kən'dʒenɪtl] *adj* angeboren

conger eel ['kɔŋgər-] *n* Seeaal *m*

congested [kən'dʒestɪd] *adj (road)* verstopft; *(area)* überfüllt; *(nose)* verstopft; **his lungs are ~** in seiner Lunge hat sich Blut angestaut

congestion [kən'dʒestʃən] *n (Med)* Blutstau *m*; *(of road)* Verstopfung *f*; *(of area)* Überfüllung *f*

congestion charge *n* City-Maut *f*

conglomerate [kən'glɔmərɪt] *n (Comm)* Konglomerat *nt*

conglomeration [kənglɔmə'reɪʃən] *n* Ansammlung *f*

Congo ['kɔŋgəʊ] *n (state)* Kongo *m*

congratulate [kən'grætjuleɪt] *vt* gratulieren; **to ~ sb (on sth)** jdm (zu etw) gratulieren

congratulations [kəngrætju'leɪʃənz] *npl* Glückwunsch *m*, Glückwünsche *pl*; **~!** herzlichen Glückwunsch!; **~ on** Glückwünsche zu

congregate ['kɔŋgrɪgeɪt] *vi* sich versammeln

congregation [kɔŋgrɪ'geɪʃən] *n* Gemeinde *f*

congress ['kɔŋgres] *n* Kongress *m*; *(US)*: **C~** der Kongress; *siehe Info-Artikel*

> **CONGRESS**
>
> Der *Congress* ist die nationale gesetzgebende Versammlung der USA, die in Washington im *Capitol* zusammentritt. Der Kongress besteht aus dem Repräsentantenhaus (435 Abgeordnete, entsprechend den Bevölkerungszahlen auf die einzelnen Bundesstaaten verteilt und jeweils für 2 Jahre gewählt) und dem Senat (100 Senatoren, 2 für jeden Bundesstaat, für 6 Jahre gewählt, wobei ein Drittel alle zwei Jahre neu gewählt wird). Sowohl die Abgeordneten als auch die Senatoren werden in direkter Wahl vom Volk gewählt.

congressman ['kɔŋgresmən] *(US)* *n (irreg: like* **man***)* Kongressabgeordnete(r) *m*

congresswoman ['kɔŋgreswʊmən] *(US)* *n (irreg: like* **woman***)* *n* Kongressabgeordnete *f*

conical ['kɔnɪkl] *adj* kegelförmig, konisch

conifer ['kɔnɪfər] *n* Nadelbaum *m*

coniferous [kə'nɪfərəs] *adj* Nadel-

conjecture [kən'dʒektʃər] *n* Vermutung *f*, Mutmaßung *f* ▷ *vi* vermuten, mutmaßen

conjugal ['kɔndʒʊgl] *adj* ehelich

conjugate ['kɔndʒugeɪt] *vt* konjugieren

conjugation [kɔndʒə'geɪʃən] *n* Konjugation *f*

conjunction [kən'dʒʌŋkʃən] *n* Konjunktion *f*; **in ~ with** zusammen mit, in Verbindung mit

conjunctivitis [kəndʒʌŋktɪ'vaɪtɪs] *n* Bindehautentzündung *f*

conjure ['kʌndʒər] *vi* zaubern ▷ *vt (also fig)* hervorzaubern

▶ **conjure up** *vt (ghost, spirit)* beschwören; *(memories)* heraufbeschwören

conjurer ['kʌndʒərər] *n* Zauberer *m*, Zauberkünstler(in) *m(f)*

conjuring trick ['kʌndʒərɪŋ-] *n* Zaubertrick *m*, Zauberkunststück *nt*

conker ['kɔŋkər] *(Brit)* *n* (Ross)kastanie *f*

conk out [kɔŋk-] *(inf)* *vi* den Geist aufgeben

con man *n* Schwindler *m*

Conn. *(US)* *abbr (Post)* = Connecticut

connect [kə'nekt] *vt* verbinden; *(Elec)* anschließen; *(Tel: caller)* verbinden; *(: subscriber)* anschließen; *(fig: associate)* in Zusammenhang bringen ▷ *vi*: **to ~ with** *(train, plane etc)* Anschluss haben an +*acc*; **to ~ sth to sth** etw mit einer Sache verbinden; **to be ~ed with** *(associated)* in einer Beziehung or in Verbindung stehen zu; *(have dealings with)* zu tun haben mit; **I am trying to ~ you** *(Tel)* ich versuche, Sie zu verbinden

connection [kə'nɛkʃən] n Verbindung f; (Elec) Kontakt m; (train, plane etc, Tel: subscriber) Anschluss m; (fig: association) Beziehung f, Zusammenhang m; **in ~ with** in Zusammenhang mit; **what is the ~ between them?** welche Verbindung besteht zwischen ihnen?; **business ~s** Geschäftsbeziehungen pl; **to get/miss one's ~** seinen Anschluss erreichen/verpassen

connexion [kə'nɛkʃən] (Brit) n = **connection**

conning tower ['kɔnɪŋ-] n Kommandoturm m

connive [kə'naɪv] vi: **to ~ at** stillschweigend dulden

connoisseur [kɔnɪ'sɜːʳ] n Kenner(in) m(f)

connotation [kɔnə'teɪʃən] n Konnotation f

connubial [kə'njuːbɪəl] adj ehelich

conquer ['kɔŋkəʳ] vt erobern; (enemy, fear, feelings) besiegen

conqueror ['kɔŋkərəʳ] n Eroberer m

conquest ['kɔŋkwɛst] n Eroberung f

cons [kɔnz] npl see **convenience**, **pro**

conscience ['kɔnʃəns] n Gewissen nt; **to have a guilty/clear ~** ein schlechtes/gutes Gewissen haben; **in all ~** allen Ernstes

conscientious [kɔnʃɪ'ɛnʃəs] adj gewissenhaft

conscientious objector n Wehrdienst- or Kriegsdienstverweigerer m (aus Gewissensgründen)

conscious ['kɔnʃəs] adj bewusst; (awake) bei Bewusstsein; **to become ~ of sth** sich dat einer Sache gen bewusst werden; **to become ~ that ...** sich dat bewusst werden, dass ...

consciousness ['kɔnʃəsnɪs] n Bewusstsein nt; **to lose ~** bewusstlos werden; **to regain ~** wieder zu sich kommen

conscript ['kɔnskrɪpt] n Wehrpflichtige(r) m

conscription [kən'skrɪpʃən] n Wehrpflicht f

consecrate ['kɔnsɪkreɪt] vt weihen

consecutive [kən'sɛkjutɪv] adj aufeinanderfolgend; **on three ~ occasions** dreimal hintereinander

consensus [kən'sɛnsəs] n Übereinstimmung f; **the ~ (of opinion)** die allgemeine Meinung

consent [kən'sɛnt] n Zustimmung f ▷ vi: **to ~ to** zustimmen +dat; **age of ~** Ehemündigkeitsalter nt; **by common ~** auf allgemeinen Wunsch

consenting [kən'sɛntɪŋ] adj: **between ~ adults** ≈ zwischen Erwachsenen

consequence ['kɔnsɪkwəns] n Folge f; **of ~** bedeutend, wichtig; **it's of little ~** es spielt kaum eine Rolle; **in ~** folglich

consequently ['kɔnsɪkwəntlɪ] adv folglich

conservation [kɔnsə'veɪʃən] n Erhaltung f, Schutz m; (of energy) Sparen nt; (also: **nature conservation**) Umweltschutz m; (of paintings, books) Erhaltung f, Konservierung f; **energy ~** Energieeinsparung f

conservationist [kɔnsə'veɪʃnɪst] n Umweltschützer(in) m(f)

conservative [kən'sɜːvətɪv] adj konservativ; (cautious) vorsichtig; (Brit: Pol): **C~** konservativ ▷ n (Brit: Pol): **C~** Konservative(r) f(m)

Conservative Party n: **the ~** die Konservative Partei f

conservatory [kən'sɜːvətrɪ] n Wintergarten m; (Mus) Konservatorium nt

conserve [kən'sɜːv] vt erhalten; (supplies, energy) sparen ▷ n Konfitüre f

consider [kən'sɪdəʳ] vt (study) sich dat überlegen; (take into account) in Betracht ziehen; **to ~ that ...** der Meinung sein, dass ...; **to ~ sb/sth as ...** halten; **to ~ doing sth** in Erwägung ziehen, etw zu tun; **they ~ themselves to be superior** sie halten sich für etwas Besseres; **she ~ed it a disaster** sie betrachtete es als eine Katastrophe; **~ yourself lucky** Sie können sich glücklich schätzen; **all things ~ed** alles in allem

considerable [kən'sɪdərəbl] adj beträchtlich

considerably [kən'sɪdərəblɪ] adv beträchtlich; (bigger, smaller etc) um einiges

considerate [kən'sɪdərɪt] adj rücksichtsvoll

consideration [kənsɪdə'reɪʃən] n Überlegung f; (factor) Gesichtspunkt m, Faktor m; (thoughtfulness) Rücksicht f; (reward) Entgelt nt; **out of ~ for** aus Rücksicht auf +acc; **to be under ~** geprüft werden; **my first ~ is my family** ich denke zuerst an meine Familie

considered [kən'sɪdəd] adj: **~ opinion** ernsthafte Überzeugung f

considering [kən'sɪdərɪŋ] prep in Anbetracht +gen; **~ (that)** wenn man bedenkt(, dass)

consign [kən'saɪn] vt: **to ~ to** (object: to place) verbannen in +acc; (person: to sb's care) anvertrauen +dat; (: to poverty) verurteilen zu; (send) versenden an +acc

consignment [kən'saɪnmənt] n Sendung f, Lieferung f

consignment note n Frachtbrief m

consist [kən'sɪst] vi: **to ~ of** bestehen aus

consistency [kən'sɪstənsɪ] n (of actions etc) Konsequenz f; (of cream etc) Konsistenz f, Dicke f

consistent [kən'sɪstənt] adj konsequent; (argument, idea) logisch, folgerichtig; **to be ~ with** entsprechen +dat

consolation [kɔnsə'leɪʃən] n Trost m

console [kən'səul] vt trösten ▷ n (panel) Schalttafel f

consolidate [kən'sɔlɪdeɪt] vt festigen

consols ['kɔnsɔlz] (Brit) npl (Stock Exchange) Konsols pl, konsolidierte Staatsanleihen pl

consommé [kən'sɔmeɪ] n Kraftbrühe f, Consommé f

consonant ['kɔnsənənt] n Konsonant m, Mitlaut m

consort ['kɔnsɔːt] n Gemahl(in) m(f), Gatte m, Gattin f ▷ vi: **to ~ with sb** mit jdm verkehren; **prince ~** Prinzgemahl m

consortium [kən'sɔːtɪəm] n Konsortium nt

conspicuous [kən'spɪkjuəs] adj auffallend; **to make o.s. ~** auffallen

conspiracy [kən'spɪrəsɪ] n Verschwörung f, Komplott nt

conspiratorial [kənspɪrə'tɔːrɪəl] adj verschwörerisch

conspire [kən'spaɪəʳ] vi sich verschwören; (events) zusammenkommen

constable ['kʌnstəbl] (Brit) n Polizist m; **chief ~** Polizeipräsident m, Polizeichef m

constabulary [kən'stæbjulərɪ] (Brit) n Polizei f

constant ['kɔnstənt] adj dauernd, ständig; (fixed) konstant, gleichbleibend

constantly ['kɔnstəntlɪ] adv (an)dauernd, ständig

constellation [kɔnstə'leɪʃən] n Sternbild nt

consternation [kɔnstə'neɪʃən] n Bestürzung f

constipated ['kɔnstɪpeɪtɪd] adj: **to be ~** Verstopfung haben, verstopft sein

constipation [kɔnstɪ'peɪʃən] n Verstopfung f

constituency [kən'stɪtjuənsɪ] n (Pol) Wahlkreis m; (electors) Wähler pl (eines Wahlkreises)

constituency party n Parteiorganisation in einem Wahlkreis

constituent [kən'stɪtjuənt] n (Pol) Wähler(in) m(f); (component) Bestandteil m

constitute ['kɔnstɪtjuːt] vt (represent) darstellen; (make up) bilden, ausmachen

constitution [kɔnstɪ'tjuːʃən] n (Pol) Verfassung f; (of club etc) Satzung f; (health) Konstitution f, Gesundheit f; (make-up) Zusammensetzung f

constitutional [kɔnstɪ'tjuːʃənl] adj (government) verfassungsmäßig; (reform etc) Verfassungs-

constitutional monarchy n konstitutionelle Monarchie f

constrain [kən'streɪn] vt zwingen

constrained [kən'streɪnd] adj gezwungen

constraint [kən'streɪnt] n Beschränkung f, Einschränkung f; (compulsion) Zwang m; (embarrassment) Befangenheit f

constrict [kən'strɪkt] vt einschnüren; (blood vessel) verengen; (limit, restrict) einschränken

constriction [kən'strɪkʃən] n Einschränkung f; (tightness) Verengung f; (squeezing) Einschnürung f

construct [kən'strʌkt] vt bauen; (machine) konstruieren; (theory, argument) entwickeln

construction [kən'strʌkʃən] n Bau m; (structure) Konstruktion f; (fig: interpretation) Deutung f; **under ~** in or im Bau

construction industry n Bauindustrie f

constructive [kən'strʌktɪv] adj konstruktiv

construe [kən'struː] vt auslegen, deuten

consul ['kɔnsl] n Konsul(in) m(f)

consulate ['kɔnsjulɪt] n Konsulat nt

consult [kən'sʌlt] vt (doctor, lawyer) konsultieren; (friend) sich beraten or besprechen mit; (reference book) nachschlagen in+dat; **to ~ sb (about sth)** jdn (wegen etw) fragen

consultancy [kən'sʌltənsɪ] n Beratungsbüro nt or -firma f; (Med: job) Facharztstelle f

consultant [kən'sʌltənt] n (Med) Facharzt m, Fachärztin f; (other specialist) Berater(in) m(f) ▷ cpd: **~ engineer** beratender Ingenieur m; **~ paediatrician** Facharzt/-ärztin m/f für Pädiatrie or Kinderheilkunde; **legal/management ~** Rechts-/

Unternehmensberater(in) m(f); **consultants** npl Beratungsbüro nt or -firma f

consultation [kɔnsəl'teɪʃən] n (Med, Law) Konsultation f; (discussion) Beratung f, Besprechung f; **in ~ with** in gemeinsamer Beratung mit

consultative [kən'sʌltətɪv] adj beratend

consulting room [kən'sʌltɪŋ-] (Brit) n Sprechzimmer nt

consume [kən'sjuːm] vt (food, drink) zu sich nehmen, konsumieren; (fuel, energy) verbrauchen; (time) in Anspruch nehmen; (subj: emotion) verzehren; (: fire) vernichten

consumer [kən'sjuːməʳ] n Verbraucher(in) m(f)

consumer credit n Verbraucherkredit m

consumer durables npl (langlebige) Gebrauchsgüter pl

consumer goods npl Konsumgüter pl

consumerism [kən'sjuːmərɪzəm] n Verbraucherschutz m

consumer society n Konsumgesellschaft f

consumer watchdog n Verbraucherschutzorganisation f

consummate ['kɔnsʌmeɪt] vt (marriage) vollziehen; (ambition etc) erfüllen

consumption [kən'sʌmpʃən] n Verbrauch m; (of food) Verzehr m; (of drinks, buying) Konsum m; (Med) Schwindsucht f; **not fit for human ~** zum Verzehr ungeeignet

cont. abbr (= continued) Forts.

contact ['kɔntækt] n Kontakt m; (touch) Berührung f; (person) Kontaktperson f ▷ vt sich in Verbindung setzen mit; **to be in ~ with sb/sth** mit jdm/etw in Verbindung or Kontakt stehen; (touch) jdn/etw berühren; **business ~s** Geschäftsverbindungen pl

contact lenses npl Kontaktlinsen pl

contagious [kən'teɪdʒəs] adj ansteckend

contain [kən'teɪn] vt enthalten; (growth, spread) in Grenzen halten; (feeling) beherrschen; **to ~ o.s.** an sich acc halten

container [kən'teɪnəʳ] n Behälter m; (for shipping etc) Container m ▷ cpd Container-

containerize [kən'teɪnəraɪz] vt in Container verpacken; (port) auf Container umstellen

container ship n Containerschiff nt

contaminate [kən'tæmɪneɪt] vt (water, food) verunreinigen; (soil etc) verseuchen

contamination [kəntæmɪ'neɪʃən] n (see vb) Verunreinigung f; Verseuchung f

cont'd abbr (= continued) Forts.

contemplate ['kɔntəmpleɪt] vt nachdenken über +acc; (course of action) in Erwägung ziehen; (person, painting etc) betrachten

contemplation [kɔntəm'pleɪʃən] n Betrachtung f

contemporary [kən'tempərərɪ] adj zeitgenössisch; (present-day) modern ▷ n Altersgenosse m, Altersgenossin f; **Samuel Pepys and his contemporaries** Samuel Pepys und seine Zeitgenossen

contempt [kən'tempt] n Verachtung f; **~ of court** (Law) Missachtung f (der Würde) des

Gerichts, Ungebühr f vor Gericht; **to have ~ for sb/sth** jdn/etw verachten; **to hold sb in ~** jdn verachten

contemptible [kən'tɛmptəbl] *adj* verachtenswert

contemptuous [kən'tɛmptjuəs] *adj* verächtlich, geringschätzig

contend [kən'tɛnd] *vt*: **to ~ that ...** behaupten, dass ...; **to ~ with** fertig werden mit; **to ~ for** kämpfen um; **to have to ~ with** es zu tun haben mit; **he has a lot to ~ with** er hat viel um die Ohren

contender [kən'tɛndəʳ] *n* (*Sport*) Wettkämpfer(in) *m(f)*; (*for title*) Anwärter(in) *m(f)*; (*Pol*) Kandidat(in) *m(f)*

content [*adj, vt* kən'tɛnt, *n* 'kɔntɛnt] *adj* zufrieden ▷ *vt* zufriedenstellen ▷ *n* Inhalt *m*; (*fat content, moisture content etc*) Gehalt *m*; **contents** *npl* Inhalt; **(table of) ~s** Inhaltsverzeichnis *nt*; **to be ~ with** zufrieden sein mit; **to ~ o.s. with sth** sich mit etw zufriedengeben *or* begnügen; **to ~ o.s. with doing sth** sich damit zufriedengeben *or* begnügen, etw zu tun

contented [kən'tɛntɪd] *adj* zufrieden

contentedly [kən'tɛntɪdlɪ] *adv* zufrieden

contention [kən'tɛnʃən] *n* Behauptung *f*; (*disagreement, argument*) Streit *m*; **bone of ~** Zankapfel *m*

contentious [kən'tɛnʃəs] *adj* strittig, umstritten

contentment [kən'tɛntmənt] *n* Zufriedenheit *f*

contest [*n* 'kɔntɛst, *vt* kən'tɛst] *n* (*competition*) Wettkampf *m*; (*for control, power etc*) Kampf *m* ▷ *vt* (*election, competition*) teilnehmen an +*dat*; (*compete for*) kämpfen um; (*statement*) bestreiten; (*decision*) angreifen; (*Law*) anfechten

contestant [kən'tɛstənt] *n* (*in quiz*) Kandidat(in) *m(f)*; (*in competition*) Teilnehmer(in) *m(f)*; (*in fight*) Kämpfer(in) *m(f)*

context ['kɔntɛkst] *n* Zusammenhang *m*, Kontext *m*; **in ~** im Zusammenhang; **out of ~** aus dem Zusammenhang gerissen

continent ['kɔntɪnənt] *n* Kontinent *m*, Erdteil *m*; **the C~** (*Brit*) (Kontinental)europa *nt*; **on the C~** in (Kontinental)europa, auf dem Kontinent

continental [kɔntɪ'nɛntl] *adj* kontinental; (*European*) europäisch ▷ *n* (*Brit*) (Festlands) europäer(in) *m(f)*

continental breakfast *n* kleines Frühstück *nt*

continental quilt (*Brit*) *n* Steppdecke *f*

contingency [kən'tɪndʒənsɪ] *n* möglicher Fall *m*, Eventualität *f*

contingency plan *n* Plan *m* für den Eventualfall

contingent [kən'tɪndʒənt] *n* Kontingent *nt* ▷ *adj*: **to be ~ upon** abhängen von

continual [kən'tɪnjuəl] *adj* ständig; (*process*) ununterbrochen

continually [kən'tɪnjuəlɪ] *adv* (*see adj*) ständig;

ununterbrochen

continuation [kəntɪnju'eɪʃən] *n* Fortsetzung *f*; (*extension*) Weiterführung *f*

continue [kən'tɪnju:] *vi* weitermachen, andauern; (*performance, road*) weitergehen; (*person: talking*) fortfahren ▷ *vt* fortsetzen; **to ~ to do sth/doing sth** etw weiter tun; **"to be ~d"** „Fortsetzung folgt"; **"~d on page 10"** „Fortsetzung auf Seite 10"

continuing education [kən'tɪnjuɪŋ-] *n* Erwachsenenbildung *f*

continuity [kɔntɪ'nju:ɪtɪ] *n* Kontinuität *f*; (*TV, Cine*) Anschluß *m* ▷ *cpd* (*TV*): **~ announcer** Ansager(in) *m(f)*; **~ studio** Ansagestudio *nt*

continuous [kən'tɪnjuəs] *adj* ununterbrochen; (*growth etc*) kontinuierlich; **~ form** (*Ling*) Verlaufsform *f*; **~ performance** (*Cine*) durchgehende Vorstellung *f*

continuously [kən'tɪnjuəslɪ] *adv* dauernd, ständig; (*uninterruptedly*) ununterbrochen

continuous stationery *n* (*Comput*) Endlospapier *nt*

contort [kən'tɔ:t] *vt* (*body*) verrenken, verdrehen; (*face*) verziehen

contortion [kən'tɔ:ʃən] *n* Verrenkung *f*

contortionist [kən'tɔ:ʃənɪst] *n* Schlangenmensch *m*

contour ['kɔntuəʳ] *n* (*also*: **contour line**) Höhenlinie *f*; (*shape, outline: gen pl*) Kontur *f*, Umriss *m*

contraband ['kɔntrəbænd] *n* Schmuggelware *f* ▷ *adj* Schmuggel-

contraception [kɔntrə'sɛpʃən] *n* Empfängnisverhütung *f*

contraceptive [kɔntrə'sɛptɪv] *adj* empfängnisverhütend ▷ *n* Verhütungsmittel *nt*

contract [*n, cpd* 'kɔntrækt, *vb* kən'trækt] *n* Vertrag *m* ▷ *vi* schrumpfen; (*metal, muscle*) sich zusammenziehen ▷ *vt* (*illness*) erkranken an +*dat* ▷ *cpd* vertraglich festgelegt; (*work*) Auftrags-; **~ of employment/service** Arbeitsvertrag *m*; **to ~ to do sth** (*Comm*) sich vertraglich verpflichten, etw zu tun
▶ **contract in** (*Brit*) *vi* beitreten
▶ **contract out** (*Brit*) *vi* austreten

contraction [kən'trækʃən] *n* Zusammenziehen *nt*; (*Ling*) Kontraktion *f*; (*Med*) Wehe *f*

contractor [kən'træktəʳ] *n* Auftragnehmer *m*; (*also*: **building contractor**) Bauunternehmer *m*

contractual [kən'træktjuəl] *adj* vertraglich

contradict [kɔntrə'dɪkt] *vt* widersprechen +*dat*

contradiction [kɔntrə'dɪkʃən] *n* Widerspruch *m*; **to be in ~ with** im Widerspruch stehen zu; **a ~ in terms** ein Widerspruch in sich

contradictory [kɔntrə'dɪktərɪ] *adj* widersprüchlich

contralto [kən'træltəu] *n* (*Mus*) Altistin *f*; (: *voice*) Alt *m*

contraption [kən'træpʃən] (*pej*) *n* (*device*) Vorrichtung *f*; (*machine*) Gerät *nt*, Apparat *m*

contrary[1] ['kɔntrərɪ] *adj* entgegengesetzt;

(*ideas, opinions*) gegensätzlich; (*unfavourable*)
widrig ▷ *n* Gegenteil *nt*; ~ **to what we
thought** im Gegensatz zu dem, was wir
dachten; **on the ~** im Gegenteil; **unless you
hear to the ~** sofern Sie nichts Gegenteiliges
hören

contrary² [kən'treəri] *adj* widerspenstig

contrast ['kɔntrɑ:st] *n* Gegensatz *m*, Kontrast
m ▷ *vt* vergleichen, gegenüberstellen; **in ~ to**
or **with** im Gegensatz zu

contrasting [kən'trɑ:stɪŋ] *adj* (*colours*)
kontrastierend; (*attitudes*) gegensätzlich

contravene [kɔntrə'vi:n] *vt* verstoßen gegen

contravention [kɔntrə'vɛnʃən] *n* Verstoß *m*;
to be in ~ of sth gegen etw verstoßen

contribute [kən'trɪbju:t] *vi* beitragen ▷ *vt*: **to
~ £10/an article to** £10/einen Artikel
beisteuern zu; **to ~ to** (*charity*) spenden für;
(*newspaper*) schreiben für; (*discussion, problem etc*)
beitragen zu

contribution [kɔntrɪ'bju:ʃən] *n* Beitrag *m*;
(*donation*) Spende *f*

contributor [kən'trɪbjutə*ʳ*] *n* (*to appeal*)
Spender(in) *m(f)*; (*to newspaper*) Mitarbeiter(in)
m(f)

contributory [kən'trɪbjutəri] *adj*: **a ~ cause**
ein Faktor, der mit eine Rolle spielt; **it was a ~
factor in** ... es trug zu ... bei

contributory pension scheme (*Brit*) *n*
beitragspflichtige Rentenversicherung *f*

contrite ['kɔntraɪt] *adj* zerknirscht

contrivance [kən'traɪvəns] *n* (*scheme*) List *f*;
(*device*) Vorrichtung *f*

contrive [kən'traɪv] *vt* (*meeting*) arrangieren
▷ *vi*: **to ~ to do sth** es fertigbringen, etw zu
tun

control [kən'trəul] *vt* (*country*) regieren;
(*organization*) leiten; (*machinery, process*) steuern;
(*wages, prices*) kontrollieren; (*temper*) zügeln;
(*disease, fire*) unter Kontrolle bringen ▷ *n* (*of
country*) Kontrolle *f*; (*of organization*) Leitung *f*;
(*of oneself, emotions*) Beherrschung *f*; (*Sci: also:*
control group) Kontrollgruppe *f*; **controls** *npl*
(*of vehicle*) Steuerung *f*; (*on radio, television etc*)
Bedienungsfeld *nt*; (*governmental*) Kontrolle
f; **to ~ o.s.** sich beherrschen; **to take ~ of**
die Kontrolle übernehmen über +*acc*; (*Comm*)
übernehmen; **to be in ~ of** unter Kontrolle
haben; (*in charge of*) unter sich *dat* haben;
out of/under ~ außer/unter Kontrolle;
everything is under ~ ich habe/wir haben
etc die Sache im Griff (*inf*); **the car went
out of ~** der Fahrer verlor die Kontrolle über
den Wagen; **circumstances beyond our ~**
unvorhersehbare Umstände

control key *n* (*Comput*) Controltaste *f*,
Steuerungstaste *f*

controlled substance *n*
veschreibungspflichtiges Medikament

controller [kən'trəulə*ʳ*] *n* (*Radio, TV*)
Intendant(in) *m(f)*

controlling interest [kən'trəulɪŋ-] *n*
Mehrheitsanteil *m*

control panel *n* Schalttafel *f*; (*on television*)
Bedienungsfeld *nt*

control point *n* Kontrollpunkt *m*,
Kontrollstelle *f*

control room *n* (*Naut*) Kommandoraum
m; (*Mil*) (Operations)zentrale *f*; (*Radio, TV*)
Regieraum *m*

control tower *n* Kontrollturm *m*

control unit *n* (*Comput*) Steuereinheit *f*

controversial [kɔntrə'və:ʃl] *adj* umstritten,
kontrovers

controversy ['kɔntrəvə:si] *n* Streit *m*,
Kontroverse *f*

conurbation [kɔnə'beɪʃən] *n* Ballungsgebiet
nt, Ballungsraum *m*

convalesce [kɔnvə'lɛs] *vi* genesen

convalescence [kɔnvə'lɛsns] *n* Genesungszeit
f

convalescent [kɔnvə'lɛsnt] *adj* (*leave etc*)
Genesungs-, Kur- ▷ *n* Genesende(r) *f(m)*

convector [kən'vɛktə*ʳ*] *n* Heizlüfter *m*

convene [kən'vi:n] *vt* einberufen ▷ *vi*
zusammentreten

convener [kən'vi:nə*ʳ*] *n* (*organizer*)
Organisator(in) *m(f)*; (*chairperson*)
Vorsitzende(r) *f(m)*

convenience [kən'vi:nɪəns] *n* Annehmlichkeit
f; (*suitability*): **the ~ of this arrangement/
location** diese günstige Vereinbarung/Lage;
I like the ~ of having a shower mir gefällt,
wie angenehm es ist, eine Dusche zu haben;
I like the ~ of living in the city mir gefällt,
wie praktisch es ist, in der Stadt zu wohnen;
at your ~ wann es Ihnen passt; **at your
earliest ~** möglichst bald, baldmöglichst;
with all modern ~s, with all mod cons (*Brit*)
mit allem modernen Komfort; *see also* **public
convenience**

convenience foods *npl* Fertiggerichte *pl*

convenient [kən'vi:nɪənt] *adj* günstig; (*handy*)
praktisch; (*house etc*) günstig gelegen; **if it is
~ to you** wenn es Ihnen (so) passt, wenn es
Ihnen keine Umstände macht

conveniently [kən'vi:nɪəntlɪ] *adv* (*happen*)
günstigerweise; (*situated*) günstig

convenor [kən'vi:nə*ʳ*] *n* = **convener**

convent ['kɔnvənt] *n* Kloster *nt*

convention [kən'vɛnʃən] *n* Konvention *f*;
(*conference*) Tagung *f*, Konferenz *f*; (*agreement*)
Abkommen *nt*

conventional [kən'vɛnʃənl] *adj* konventionell

convent school *n* Klosterschule *f*

converge [kən'və:dʒ] *vi* (*roads*)
zusammenlaufen ▷ *vi* sich einander
annähern; **to ~ on sb/a place** (*people*) von
überallher zu jdm/an einen Ort strömen

conversant [kən'və:snt] *adj*: **to be ~ with**
vertraut sein mit

conversation [kɔnvə'seɪʃən] *n* Gespräch *nt*,
Unterhaltung *f*

conversational [kɔnvə'seɪʃənl] *adj* (*tone, style*)
Unterhaltungs-; (*language*) gesprochen; **~
mode** (*Comput*) Dialogbetrieb *m*

conversationalist [kɔnvə'seɪʃnəlɪst] *n*
Unterhalter(in) *m(f)*, Gesprächspartner(in)
m(f)

converse [*n* 'kɔnvəːs, *vi* kən'vəːs] *n* Gegenteil *nt*
▷ *vi*: **to ~ (with sb) (about sth)** sich (mit jdm)
(über etw) unterhalten

conversely [kɔn'vəːslɪ] *adv* umgekehrt

conversion [kən'vəːʃən] *n* Umwandlung *f*; (*of
weights etc*) Umrechnung *f*; (*Rel*) Bekehrung *f*;
(*Brit: of house*) Umbau *m*

conversion table *n* Umrechnungstabelle *f*

convert [*vt* kən'vəːt, *n* 'kɔnvəːt] *vt* umwandeln;
(*person*) bekehren; (*building*) umbauen; (*vehicle*)
umrüsten; (*Comm*) konvertieren; (*Rugby*)
verwandeln ▷ *n* Bekehrte(r) *f(m)*

convertible [kən'vəːtəbl] *adj* (*currency*)
konvertierbar ▷ *n* (*Aut*) Kabriolett *nt*

convex ['kɔnvɛks] *adj* konvex

convey [kən'veɪ] *vt* (*information etc*) vermitteln;
(*cargo, traveller*) befördern; (*thanks*) übermitteln

conveyance [kən'veɪəns] *n* Beförderung *f*,
Spedition *f*; (*vehicle*) Gefährt *nt*

conveyancing [kən'veɪənsɪŋ] *n* (Eigentums)
übertragung *f*

conveyor belt *n* Fließband *nt*

convict [*vt* kən'vɪkt, *n* 'kɔnvɪkt] *vt* verurteilen
▷ *n* Sträfling *m*

conviction [kən'vɪkʃən] *n* Überzeugung *f*;
(*Law*) Verurteilung *f*

convince [kən'vɪns] *vt* überzeugen; **to ~ sb (of
sth)** jdn (von etw) überzeugen; **to ~ sb that ...**
jdn davon überzeugen, dass ...

convinced [kən'vɪnst] *adj*: **~ (of)** überzeugt
(von); **~ that ...** überzeugt davon, dass ...

convincing [kən'vɪnsɪŋ] *adj* überzeugend

convincingly [kən'vɪnsɪŋlɪ] *adv* überzeugend

convivial [kən'vɪvɪəl] *adj* freundlich; (*event*)
gesellig

convoluted ['kɔnvəluːtɪd] *adj* verwickelt,
kompliziert; (*shape*) gewunden

convoy ['kɔnvɔɪ] *n* Konvoi *m*

convulse [kən'vʌls] *vt*: **to be ~d with
laughter/pain** sich vor Lachen schütteln/
Schmerzen krümmen

convulsion [kən'vʌlʃən] *n* Schüttelkrampf *m*

coo [kuː] *vi* gurren

cook [kuk] *vt* kochen, zubereiten ▷ *vi* (*person,
food*) kochen; (*fry, roast*) braten; (*pie*) backen ▷ *n*
Koch *m*, Köchin *f*

   ▶ **cook up** (*inf*) *vt* sich *dat* einfallen lassen,
zurechtbasteln

cookbook ['kukbuk] *n* Kochbuch *nt*

cook-chill ['kuktʃɪl] *adj* durch rasches Kühlen
haltbar gemacht

cooker ['kukə⁸] *n* Herd *m*

cookery ['kukərɪ] *n* Kochen *nt*, Kochkunst *f*

cookery book (*Brit*) *n* = **cookbook**

cookie ['kukɪ] (*US*) *n* Keks *m* or *nt*, Plätzchen *nt*;
(*Comput*) Cookie *n*

cooking ['kukɪŋ] *n* Kochen *nt*; (*food*) Essen *nt*
▷ *cpd* Koch-; (*chocolate*) Block-

cookout ['kukaut] (*US*) *n* ≈ Grillparty *f*

cool [kuːl] *adj* kühl; (*dress, clothes*) leicht,

luftig; (*person: calm*) besonnen; (: *unfriendly*)
kühl ▷ *vt* kühlen ▷ *vi* kühlen; **it's ~** es ist
kühl; **to keep sth ~** or **in a ~ place** etw kühl
aufbewahren

   ▶ **cool down** *vi* abkühlen; (*fig*) sich beruhigen

coolant ['kuːlənt] *n* Kühlflüssigkeit *f*

cool box *n* Kühlbox *f*

cooler ['kuːlə⁸] (*US*) *n* = **cool box**

cooling ['kuːlɪŋ] *adj* (*drink, shower*) kühlend;
(*feeling, emotion*) abkühlend

cooling tower ['kuːlɪŋ-] *n* Kühlturm *m*

coolly ['kuːlɪ] *adv* (*calmly*) besonnen, ruhig; (*in
unfriendly way*) kühl

coolness ['kuːlnɪs] *n* (*see adj*) Kühle *f*;
Leichtigkeit *f*, Luftigkeit *f*; Besonnenheit *f*

coop [kuːp] *n* (*for rabbits*) Kaninchenstall *m*;
(*for poultry*) Hühnerstall *m* ▷ *vt*: **to ~ up** (*fig*)
einsperren

co-op ['kəuɔp] *n abbr* (= *cooperative (society)*)
Genossenschaft *f*

cooperate [kəu'ɔpəreɪt] *vi* zusammenarbeiten;
(*assist*) mitmachen, kooperieren; **to ~ with sb**
mit jdm zusammenarbeiten

cooperation [kəuɔpə'reɪʃən] *n* (*see vb*)
Zusammenarbeit *f*; Mitarbeit *f*, Kooperation *f*

cooperative [kəu'ɔpərətɪv] *adj* (*farm, business*)
auf Genossenschaftsbasis; (*person*) kooperativ;
(: *helpful*) hilfsbereit ▷ *n* Genossenschaft *f*,
Kooperative *f*

coopt [kəu'ɔpt] *vt*: **to ~ sb onto a committee**
jdn in ein Komitee hinzuwählen or
kooptieren

coordinate [*vt* kəu'ɔːdɪneɪt, *n* kəu'ɔːdɪnət]
vt koordinieren ▷ *n* (*Math*) Koordinate *f*;
coordinates *npl* (*clothes*) Kleidung *f* zum
Kombinieren

coordination [kəuɔːdɪ'neɪʃən] *n*
Koordinierung *f*, Koordination *f*

coownership [kəu'əunəʃɪp] *n* Mitbesitz *m*

cop [kɔp] (*inf*) *n* Polizist(in) *m(f)*, Bulle *m* (*pej*)

cope [kəup] *vi* zurechtkommen; **to ~ with**
fertig werden mit

Copenhagen ['kəupn'heɪɡən] *n* Kopenhagen *nt*

copier ['kɔpɪə⁸] *n* (*also*: **photocopier**)
Kopiergerät *nt*, Kopierer *m*

copilot ['kəupaɪlɔt] *n* Kopilot(in) *m(f)*

copious ['kəupɪəs] *adj* reichlich

copper ['kɔpə⁸] *n* Kupfer *nt*; (*Brit: inf*)
Polizist(in) *m(f)*, Bulle *m* (*pej*); **coppers** *npl*
(*small change, coins*) Kleingeld *nt*

coppice ['kɔpɪs], **copse** [kɔps] *n* Wäldchen *nt*

copulate ['kɔpjuleɪt] *vi* kopulieren

copy ['kɔpɪ] *n* Kopie *f*; (*of book, record, newspaper*)
Exemplar *nt*; (*for printing*) Artikel *m* ▷ *vt* (*person*)
nachahmen; (*idea etc*) nachmachen; (*something
written*) abschreiben; **this murder story will
make good ~** (*Press*) aus diesem Mord kann
man etwas machen

   ▶ **copy out** *vt* abschreiben

copycat ['kɔpɪkæt] (*pej*) *n* Nachahmer(in) *m(f)*

copyright ['kɔpɪraɪt] *n* Copyright *nt*,
Urheberrecht *nt*; **~ reserved** urheberrechtlich
geschützt

C

copy typist n Schreibkraft f (die mit Textvorlagen arbeitet)

copywriter ['kɔpɪraɪtəʳ] n Werbetexter(in) m(f)

coral ['kɔrəl] n Koralle f

coral reef n Korallenriff nt

Coral Sea n: **the ~** das Korallenmeer

cord [kɔːd] n Schnur f; (string) Kordel f; (Elec) Kabel nt, Schnur f; (fabric) Cord(samt) m; **cords** npl (trousers) Cordhosen pl

cordial ['kɔːdɪəl] adj herzlich ▷ n (Brit) Fruchtsaftkonzentrat nt

cordless ['kɔːdlɪs] adj schnurlos

cordon ['kɔːdn] n Kordon m, Absperrkette f
► cordon off vt (area) absperren, abriegeln; (crowd) mit einer Absperrkette zurückhalten

corduroy ['kɔːdərɔɪ] n Cord(samt) m

CORE [kɔːʳ] (US) n abbr (= Congress of Racial Equality) Ausschuss für Rassengleichheit

core [kɔːʳ] n Kern m; (of fruit) Kerngehäuse nt ▷ vt das Kerngehäuse ausschneiden aus; **rotten to the ~** durch und durch schlecht

core (business) activity n (Econ) Kerngeschäft nt

Corfu [kɔːˈfuː] n Korfu nt

coriander [kɔrɪˈændəʳ] n Koriander m

cork [kɔːk] n (stopper) Korken m; (substance) Kork m

corkage ['kɔːkɪdʒ] n Korkengeld nt

corked [kɔːkt] adj: **the wine is ~** der Wein schmeckt nach Kork

corkscrew ['kɔːkskruː] n Korkenzieher m

corky ['kɔːkɪ] (US) adj = **corked**

corm [kɔːm] n Knolle f

cormorant ['kɔːmərnt] n Kormoran m

corn [kɔːn] n (Brit) Getreide nt, Korn nt; (US) Mais m; (on foot) Hühnerauge nt; **~ on the cob** Maiskolben m

cornea ['kɔːnɪə] n Hornhaut f

corned beef ['kɔːnd-] n Corned Beef nt

corner ['kɔːnəʳ] n Ecke f; (bend) Kurve f ▷ vt in die Enge treiben; (Comm: market) monopolisieren ▷ vi (in car) die Kurve nehmen; **to cut ~s** (fig) das Verfahren abkürzen

corner flag n Eckfahne f

corner kick n Eckball m

cornerstone ['kɔːnəstəun] n (fig) Grundstein m, Eckstein m

cornet ['kɔːnɪt] n (Mus) Kornett nt; (Brit: for ice cream) Eistüte f

cornflakes ['kɔːnfleɪks] npl Cornflakes pl

cornflour ['kɔːnflauəʳ] (Brit) n Stärkemehl nt

cornice ['kɔːnɪs] n (Ge)sims nt

Cornish ['kɔːnɪʃ] adj kornisch, aus Cornwall

corn oil n (Mais)keimöl nt

cornstarch ['kɔːnstaːtʃ] (US) n = **cornflour**

cornucopia [kɔːnjuˈkəupɪə] n Fülle f

Cornwall ['kɔːnwəl] n Cornwall nt

corny ['kɔːnɪ] (inf) adj (joke) blöd

corollary [kəˈrɔlərɪ] n (logische) Folge f

coronary ['kɔrənərɪ] n (also: **coronary thrombosis**) Herzinfarkt m

coronation [kɔrəˈneɪʃən] n Krönung f

coroner ['kɔrənəʳ] n Beamter, der Todesfälle untersucht, die nicht eindeutig eine natürliche Ursache haben

coronet ['kɔrənɪt] n Krone f

Corp. abbr = **corporation**; (Mil) = **corporal**

corporal ['kɔːpərl] n Stabsunteroffizier m

corporal punishment n Prügelstrafe f

corporate ['kɔːpərɪt] adj (organization) körperschaftlich; (action, effort, ownership) gemeinschaftlich; (finance) Unternehmens-; (image, identity) Firmen-

corporate hospitality n Empfänge, Diners etc auf Kosten der ausrichtenden Firma

corporation [kɔːpəˈreɪʃən] n (Comm) Körperschaft f; (of town) Gemeinde f, Stadt f

corporation tax n Körperschaftssteuer f

corps [kɔːʳ] (pl ~) n Korps nt; **the press ~** die Presse

corpse [kɔːps] n Leiche f

corpuscle ['kɔːpʌsl] n Blutkörperchen nt

corral [kəˈrɑːl] n Korral m

correct [kəˈrɛkt] adj richtig; (proper) korrekt ▷ vt korrigieren; (mistake) berichtigen, verbessern; **you are ~** Sie haben recht

correction [kəˈrɛkʃən] n (see vb) Korrektur f; Berichtigung f, Verbesserung f

correctly [kəˈrɛktlɪ] adv (see adj) richtig; korrekt

correlate ['kɔrɪleɪt] vt zueinander in Beziehung setzen ▷ vi: **to ~ with** in einer Beziehung stehen zu

correlation [kɔrɪˈleɪʃən] n Beziehung f, Zusammenhang m

correspond [kɔrɪsˈpɔnd] vi: **to ~ (with)** (write) korrespondieren (mit); (be in accordance) übereinstimmen (mit); **to ~ to** (be equivalent) entsprechen +dat

correspondence [kɔrɪsˈpɔndəns] n Korrespondenz f, Briefwechsel m; (relationship) Beziehung f

correspondence column n Leserbriefspalte f

correspondence course n Fernkurs m

correspondent [kɔrɪsˈpɔndənt] n Korrespondent(in) m(f)

corresponding [kɔrɪsˈpɔndɪŋ] adj entsprechend

corridor ['kɔrɪdɔːʳ] n Korridor m; (in train) Gang m

corroborate [kəˈrɔbəreɪt] vt bestätigen

corrode [kəˈrəud] vt zerfressen ▷ vi korrodieren

corrosion [kəˈrəuʒən] n Korrosion f

corrosive [kəˈrəuzɪv] adj korrosiv

corrugated ['kɔrəgeɪtɪd] adj (roof) gewellt; (cardboard) Well-

corrugated iron n Wellblech nt

corrupt [kəˈrʌpt] adj korrupt; (depraved) verdorben ▷ vt korrumpieren; (morally) verderben; **~ practices** Korruption f

corruption [kəˈrʌpʃən] n Korruption f

corset ['kɔːsɪt] n Korsett nt; (Med) Stützkorsett nt

Corsica ['kɔːsɪkə] n Korsika nt

Corsican ['kɔːsɪkən] adj korsisch ▷ n Korse m, Korsin f

cortège [kɔ:'teɪʒ] n (also: **funeral cortège**) Leichenzug m

cortisone ['kɔ:tɪzəun] n Kortison nt

coruscating ['kɒrəskeɪtɪŋ] adj sprühend

cosh [kɒʃ] (Brit) n Totschläger m

cosignatory ['kəu'sɪgnətərɪ] n Mitunterzeichner(in) m(f)

cosiness ['kəuzɪnɪs] n Gemütlichkeit f, Behaglichkeit f

cos lettuce ['kɒs-] n römischer Salat m

cosmetic [kɒz'metɪk] n Kosmetikum nt ▷ adj kosmetisch; ~ **surgery** (Med) kosmetische Chirurgie f

cosmic ['kɒzmɪk] adj kosmisch

cosmonaut ['kɒzmənɔ:t] n Kosmonaut(in) m(f)

cosmopolitan [kɒzmə'pɒlɪtn] adj kosmopolitisch

cosmos ['kɒzmɒs] n: **the** ~ der Kosmos

cosset ['kɒsɪt] vt verwöhnen

cost [kɒst] (pt, pp ~) n Kosten pl; (fig: loss, damage etc) Preis m ▷ vt kosten; (find out cost of) (pt, pp **-ed**) veranschlagen; **costs** npl (Comm, Law) Kosten pl; **the** ~ **of living** die Lebenshaltungskosten pl; **at all** ~s um jeden Preis; **how much does it** ~? wie viel or was kostet es?; **it** ~s £5/too much es kostet £5/ist zu teuer; **what will it** ~ **to have it repaired?** wie viel kostet die Reparatur?; **to** ~ **sb time/effort** jdn Zeit/Mühe kosten; **it** ~ **him his life/job** es kostete ihn das Leben/seine Stelle

cost accountant n Kostenbuchhalter(in) m(f)

co-star ['kəustɑ:ʳ] n einer der Hauptdarsteller m, eine der Hauptdarstellerinnen f; **she was Sean Connery's** ~ **in ...** sie spielte neben Sean Connery in ...

Costa Rica ['kɒstə'ri:kə] n Costa Rica nt

cost centre n Kostenstelle f

cost control n Kostenkontrolle f

cost-effective ['kɒstɪ'fektɪv] adj rentabel; (Comm) kostengünstig

cost-effectiveness ['kɒstɪ'fektɪvnɪs] n Rentabilität f

costing ['kɒstɪŋ] n Kalkulation f

costly ['kɒstlɪ] adj teuer, kostspielig; (in time, effort) aufwendig

cost-of-living ['kɒstəv'lɪvɪŋ] adj Lebenshaltungskosten-; (index) Lebenshaltungs-

cost price (Brit) n Selbstkostenpreis m; **to sell/buy at** ~ zum Selbstkostenpreis verkaufen/kaufen

costume ['kɒstju:m] n Kostüm nt; (Brit: also: **swimming costume**) Badeanzug m

costume jewellery n Modeschmuck m

cosy, (US) **cozy** ['kəuzɪ] adj gemütlich, behaglich; (chat, scarf, gloves) warm; (chat, evening) gemütlich; **I'm very** ~ **here** ich fühle mich hier sehr wohl, ich finde es hier sehr gemütlich

cot [kɒt] n (Brit) Kinderbett nt; (US: campbed) Feldbett nt

cot death n Krippentod m, plötzlicher Kindstod m

Cotswolds ['kɒtswəuldz] npl: **the** ~ die Cotswolds pl

cottage ['kɒtɪdʒ] n Cottage nt, Häuschen nt

cottage cheese n Hüttenkäse m

cottage industry n Heimindustrie f

cottage pie n Hackfleisch mit Kartoffelbrei überbacken

cotton ['kɒtn] n (fabric) Baumwollstoff m; (plant) Baumwollstrauch m; (thread) (Baumwoll)garn nt; (dress etc) Baumwoll-
▶ **cotton on** (inf) vi: **to** ~ **on** es kapieren or schnallen; **to** ~ **on to sth** etw kapieren or schnallen

cotton candy (US) n Zuckerwatte f

cotton wool (Brit) n Watte f

couch [kautʃ] n Couch f ▷ vt formulieren

couchette [ku:'ʃet] n Liegewagen(platz) m

couch potato (esp US: inf) n Dauerglotzer(in) m(f)

cough [kɒf] vi husten; (engine) stottern ▷ n Husten m

cough drop n Hustenpastille f

cough mixture n Hustensaft m

cough syrup n = **cough mixture**

could [kud] pt of **can²**

couldn't ['kudnt] = **could not**

council ['kaunsl] n Rat m; **city/town** ~ Stadtrat m; **C~ of Europe** Europarat m

council estate (Brit) n Siedlung f mit Sozialwohnungen

council house (Brit) n Sozialwohnung f

council housing n sozialer Wohnungsbau m; (accommodation) Sozialwohnungen pl

councillor ['kaunslə'] n Stadtrat m, Stadträtin f

council tax (Brit) n Gemeindesteuer f

counsel ['kaunsl] n Rat(schlag) m; (lawyer) Rechtsanwalt m, Rechtsanwältin f ▷ vt beraten; **to** ~ **sth** etw raten or empfehlen; **to** ~ **sb to do sth** jdm raten or empfehlen, etw zu tun; ~ **for the defence** Verteidiger(in) m(f); ~ **for the prosecution** Vertreter(in) m(f) der Anklage

counsellor ['kaunslə'] n Berater(in) m(f); (US: lawyer) Rechtsanwalt m, Rechtsanwältin f

count [kaunt] vt zählen; (include) mitrechnen, mitzählen ▷ vi zählen; (be considered) betrachtet or angesehen werden ▷ n Zählung f; (level) Zahl f; (nobleman) Graf m; **to** ~ **(up) to 10** bis 10 zählen; **not** ~**ing the children** die Kinder nicht mitgerechnet; **10** ~**ing him** 10, wenn man ihn mitrechnet; **to** ~ **the cost of sth** die Folgen von etw abschätzen; **it** ~**s for very little** es zählt nicht viel; ~ **yourself lucky** Sie können sich glücklich schätzen; **to keep** ~ **of sth** die Übersicht über etw acc behalten; **blood** ~ Blutbild nt; **cholesterol/alcohol** ~ Cholesterin-/Alkoholspiegel m
▶ **count on** vt fus rechnen mit; (depend on) sich verlassen auf +acc; **to** ~ **on doing sth** die feste Absicht haben, etw zu tun
▶ **count up** vt zusammenzählen, zusammenrechnen

countdown ['kauntdaun] n Countdown m

497

countenance ['kauntınəns] n Gesicht nt ▷ vt
gutheißen

counter ['kauntə'] n (in shop) Ladentisch m;
(in café) Theke f; (in bank, post office) Schalter
m; (in game) Spielmarke f; (Tech) Zähler m ▷ vt
(oppose: sth said, sth done) begegnen +dat; (blow)
kontern ▷ adv: ~ **to** gegen +acc; **to buy sth
under the ~** (fig) etw unter dem Ladentisch
bekommen; **to ~ sth with sth** auf etw acc mit
etw antworten; **to ~ sth by doing sth** einer
Sache damit begegnen, dass man etw tut

counteract ['kauntər'ækt] vt entgegenwirken
+dat; (effect) neutralisieren

counterattack ['kauntərə'tæk] n Gegenangriff
m ▷ vi einen Gegenangriff starten

counterbalance ['kauntə'bæləns] vt
Gegengewicht nt

counterclockwise ['kauntə'klɔkwaız] adv
gegen den Uhrzeigersinn

counterespionage ['kauntər'ɛspıɑnɑ:ʒ] n
Gegenspionage f, Spionageabwehr f

counterfeit ['kauntəfıt] n Fälschung f ▷ vt
fälschen ▷ adj (coin) Falsch-

counterfoil ['kauntəfɔıl] n Kontrollabschnitt
m

counterintelligence ['kauntərın'tɛlıdʒəns] n
Gegenspionage f, Spionageabwehr f

countermand ['kauntəmɑ:nd] vt aufheben,
widerrufen

countermeasure ['kauntəmɛʒə'] n
Gegenmaßnahme f

counteroffensive ['kauntərə'fɛnsıv] n
Gegenoffensive f

counterpane ['kauntəpeın] n Tagesdecke f

counterpart ['kauntəpɑ:t] n Gegenüber nt; (of
document etc) Gegenstück nt, Pendant nt

counterproductive ['kauntəprə'dʌktıv] adj
widersinnig

counterproposal ['kauntəprə'pəuzl] n
Gegenvorschlag m

countersign ['kauntəsaın] vt gegenzeichnen

countersink ['kauntəsıŋk] vt senken

countess ['kauntıs] n Gräfin f

countless ['kauntlıs] adj unzählig, zahllos

countrified ['kʌntrıfaıd] adj ländlich

country ['kʌntrı] n Land nt; (native land)
Heimatland nt; **in the ~** auf dem Land;
mountainous ~ gebirgige Landschaft f

**country and western, country and western
music** n Country-und-Western-Musik f

country dancing (Brit) n Volkstanz m

country house n Landhaus nt

countryman ['kʌntrımən] (irreg: like **man**) n
(compatriot) Landsmann m; (country dweller)
Landmann m

countryside ['kʌntrısaıd] n Land nt; (scenery)
Landschaft f, Gegend f

country-wide ['kʌntrı'waıd] adj, adv
landesweit

county ['kauntı] n (Brit) Grafschaft f; (US)
(Verwaltungs)bezirk m

county council (Brit) n Gemeinderat m (einer
Grafschaft)

county town (Brit) n Hauptstadt einer Grafschaft

coup [ku:] (pl **-s**) n (also: **coup d'état**)
Staatsstreich m, Coup d'Etat m; (achievement)
Coup m

coupé [ku:'peı] n Coupé nt

couple ['kʌpl] n Paar nt; (also: **married couple**)
Ehepaar nt ▷ vt verbinden; (vehicles) koppeln; **a
~ of** (two) zwei; (a few) ein paar

couplet ['kʌplıt] n Verspaar nt

coupling ['kʌplıŋ] n Kupplung f

coupon ['ku:pɔn] n Gutschein m; (detachable
form) Abschnitt m; (Comm) Coupon m

courage ['kʌrıdʒ] n Mut m

courageous [kə'reıdʒəs] adj mutig

courgette [kuə'ʒɛt] (Brit) n Zucchino m

courier ['kurıə'] n (messenger) Kurier(in) m(f);
(for tourists) Reiseleiter(in) m(f)

course [kɔ:s] n (Scol) Kurs(us) m; (of ship) Kurs
m; (of life, events, time etc, of river) Lauf m; (of
argument) Richtung f; (part of meal) Gang m; (of
golf) Platz m; **of ~** natürlich; **of ~!** (aber)
natürlich!, (aber) selbstverständlich!; **(no) of
~ not!** natürlich nicht!; **in the ~ of the next
few days** während or im Laufe der nächsten
paar Tage; **in due ~** zu gegebener Zeit; **~ (of
action)** Vorgehensweise f; **the best ~ would
be to ...** das Beste wäre es, zu ...; **we have no
other ~ but to ...** es bleibt uns nichts anderes
übrig, als zu ...; **~ of lectures** Vorlesungsreihe
f; **~ of treatment** (Med) Behandlung f; **first/
last ~** erster/letzter Gang, Vor-/Nachspeise f

court [kɔ:t] n (Royal) Hof m; (Law) Gericht nt; (for
tennis, badminton etc) Platz m ▷ vt den Hof
machen +dat; (favour, popularity) werben
um; (death, disaster) herausfordern; **out of ~**
(Law) außergerichtlich; **to take to ~** (Law)
verklagen, vor Gericht bringen

courteous ['kə:tıəs] adj höflich

courtesan [kɔ:tı'zæn] n Kurtisane f

courtesy ['kə:təsı] n Höflichkeit f; **(by) ~ of**
freundlicherweise zur Verfügung gestellt von

courtesy bus, courtesy coach n
gebührenfreier Bus m

courtesy light n Innenleuchte f

court fine n Ordnungsgeld nt; **to issue/face
a ~** ein Ordnungsgeld verhängen/zu zahlen
haben

courthouse ['kɔ:thaus] (US) n
Gerichtsgebäude nt

courtier ['kɔ:tıə'] n Höfling m

court martial (pl **courts martial**) n
Militärgericht nt

court of appeal (pl **courts of appeal**) n
Berufungsgericht nt

court of inquiry (pl **courts of inquiry**) n
Untersuchungskommission f

courtroom ['kɔ:trum] n Gerichtssaal m

court shoe n Pumps m

courtyard ['kɔ:tjɑ:d] n Hof m

cousin ['kʌzn] n (male) Cousin m, Vetter m;
(female) Cousine f; **first ~** Cousin(e) ersten
Grades

cove [kəuv] n (kleine) Bucht f

covenant ['kʌvənənt] n Schwur m ▷ vt: **to ~ £200 per year to a charity** sich vertraglich verpflichten, £200 im Jahr für wohltätige Zwecke zu spenden

Coventry ['kɔvəntrɪ] n: **to send sb to ~** (fig) jdn schneiden (inf)

cover ['kʌvər] vt bedecken; (distance) zurücklegen; (Insurance) versichern; (topic) behandeln; (include) erfassen; (Press: report on) berichten über +acc ▷ n (for furniture) Bezug m; (for typewriter, PC etc) Hülle f; (of book, magazine) Umschlag m; (shelter) Schutz m; (Insurance) Versicherung f; (fig: for illegal activities) Tarnung f; **to be ~ed in** or **with** bedeckt sein mit; **£10 will ~ my expenses** £10 decken meine Unkosten; **to take ~** (from rain) sich unterstellen; **under ~** geschützt; **under ~ of darkness** im Schutz(e) der Dunkelheit; **under separate ~** getrennt

▶ **cover up** vt zudecken; (fig: facts, feelings) verheimlichen; (: mistakes) vertuschen ▷ vi (fig): **to ~ up for sb** jdn decken

coverage ['kʌvərɪdʒ] n Berichterstattung f; **television ~ of the conference** Fernsehberichte pl über die Konferenz; **to give full ~ to** ausführlich berichten über +acc

coveralls ['kʌvərɔːlz] (US) npl Overall m

cover charge n Kosten pl für ein Gedeck

covering ['kʌvərɪŋ] n Schicht f; (of snow, dust etc) Decke f

covering letter, (US) **cover letter** n Begleitbrief m

cover note n (Insurance) Deckungszusage f

cover price n Einzel(exemplar)preis m

covert ['kʌvət] adj versteckt; (glance) verstohlen

cover-up ['kʌvərʌp] n Vertuschung f, Verschleierung f

covet ['kʌvɪt] vt begehren

cow [kau] n (animal, inf!: woman) Kuh f ▷ cpd Kuh- ▷ vt einschüchtern

coward ['kauəd] n Feigling m

cowardice ['kauədɪs] n Feigheit f

cowardly ['kauədlɪ] adj feige

cowboy ['kaubɔɪ] n (in US) Cowboy m; (pej: tradesman) Pfuscher m

cow elephant n Elefantenkuh f

cower ['kauər] vi sich ducken; (squatting) kauern

cowshed ['kauʃɛd] n Kuhstall m

cowslip ['kauslɪp] n Schlüsselblume f

cox [kɔks] n abbr = **coxswain**

coxswain ['kɔksn] n Steuermann m; (of ship) Boot(s)führer m

coy [kɔɪ] adj verschämt

coyote [kɔɪ'əutɪ] n Kojote m

cozy ['kəuzɪ] (US) adj = **cosy**

CP n abbr (= Communist Party) KP f

cp. abbr (= compare) vgl.

CPA (US) n abbr = **certified public accountant**

CPI n abbr (= Consumer Price Index) (Verbraucher) preisindex m

Cpl abbr (Mil) = **corporal**

CP/M n abbr (= Control Program for Microprocessors)

CP/M nt

cps abbr (Comput, Typ: = characters per second) cps, Zeichen pl pro Sekunde

CPSA (Brit) n abbr (= Civil and Public Services Association) Gewerkschaft im öffentlichen Dienst

CPU n abbr (Comput) = **central processing unit**

cr. abbr = **credit; creditor**

crab [kræb] n Krabbe f, Krebs m; (meat) Krabbe f

crab apple n Holzapfel m

crack [kræk] n (noise) Knall m; (of wood breaking) Knacks m; (gap) Spalte f; (in bone, dish, glass) Sprung m; (in wall) Riss m; (joke) Witz m; (Drugs) Crack nt ▷ vt (whip) knallen mit; (twig) knacken mit; (dish, glass) einen Sprung machen in +acc; (bone) anbrechen; (nut, code) knacken; (wall) rissig machen; (problem) lösen; (joke) reißen ▷ adj erstklassig; **to have a ~ at sth** (inf) etw mal probieren; **to ~ jokes** (inf) Witze reißen; **to get ~ing** (inf) loslegen

▶ **crack down on** vt fus hart durchgreifen gegen

▶ **crack up** vi durchdrehen, zusammenbrechen

crackdown ['krækdaun] n: **~ (on)** scharfes Durchgreifen nt (gegen)

cracked [krækt] (inf) adj übergeschnappt

cracker ['krækər] n (biscuit) Cracker m; (also: **Christmas cracker**) Knallbonbon nt; (firework) Knallkörper m, Kracher m; **a ~ of a ...** (Brit: inf) ein(e) tolle(r, s) ...; **he's ~s** (Brit: inf) er ist übergeschnappt

crackle ['krækl] vi (fire) knistern, prasseln; (twig) knacken

crackling ['kræklɪŋ] n (of fire) Knistern nt, Prasseln nt; (of twig, on radio, telephone) Knacken nt; (of pork) Kruste f (des Schweinebratens)

crackpot ['krækpɔt] (inf) n Spinner(in) m(f) ▷ adj verrückt

cradle ['kreɪdl] n Wiege f ▷ vt fest in den Armen halten

craft [krɑːft] n (skill) Geschicklichkeit f; (art) Kunsthandwerk nt; (trade) Handwerk nt; (pl inv: boat) Boot nt; (pl inv: plane) Flugzeug nt

craftsman ['krɑːftsmən] (irreg: like **man**) n Handwerker m

craftsmanship ['krɑːftsmənʃɪp] n handwerkliche Ausführung f

crafty ['krɑːftɪ] adj schlau, clever

crag [kræg] n Fels m

craggy ['krægɪ] adj (mountain) zerklüftet; (cliff) felsig; (face) kantig

cram [kræm] vt vollstopfen ▷ vi büffeln (inf); **to ~ with** vollstopfen mit; **to ~ sth into** etw hineinstopfen in +acc

cramming ['kræmɪŋ] n (for exams) Pauken nt, Büffeln nt

cramp [kræmp] n Krampf m ▷ vt hemmen

cramped [kræmpt] adj eng

crampon ['kræmpən] n Steigeisen nt

cranberry ['krænbərɪ] n Preiselbeere f

crane [kreɪn] n Kran m; (bird) Kranich m ▷ vt: **to ~ one's neck** den Hals recken ▷ vi: **to ~ forward** den Hals recken

cranium ['kreɪnɪəm] (pl **crania**) n Schädel m
crank [kræŋk] n Spinner(in) m(f); (handle)
Kurbel f
crankshaft ['kræŋkʃɑ:ft] n Kurbelwelle f
cranky ['kræŋkɪ] adj verrückt
cranny ['krænɪ] n see **nook**
crap [kræp] (inf!) n Scheiße f(!) ▷ vi scheißen
(!); **to have a** ~ scheißen (!)
crappy ['kræpɪ] (inf!) adj beschissen (!)
crash [kræʃ] n (noise) Krachen nt; (of car)
Unfall m; (of plane etc) Unglück nt; (collision)
Zusammenstoß m; (of stock market, business
etc) Zusammenbruch m ▷ vt (car) einen
Unfall haben mit; (plane etc) abstürzen mit
▷ vi (plane) abstürzen; (car) einen Unfall
haben; (two cars) zusammenstoßen; (market)
zusammenbrechen; (firm) Pleite machen; **to**
~ **into** krachen or knallen gegen; **he ~ed the
car into a wall** er fuhr mit dem Auto gegen
eine Mauer
crash barrier (Brit) n Leitplanke f
crash course n Schnellkurs m, Intensivkurs m
crash helmet n Sturzhelm m
crash-landing ['kræʃlændɪŋ] n Bruchlandung f
crass [kræs] adj krass; (behaviour) unfein, derb
crate [kreɪt] n (also inf) Kiste f; (for bottles)
Kasten m
crater ['kreɪtəʳ] n Krater m
cravat [krə'væt] n Halstuch nt
crave [kreɪv] vt, vi: **to** ~ **(for)** sich sehnen nach
craven ['kreɪvən] adj feige
craving ['kreɪvɪŋ] n: ~ **(for)** Verlangen nt (nach)
crawl [krɔ:l] vi kriechen; (child) krabbeln ▷ n
(Swimming) Kraulstil m, Kraul(en) nt; **to ~ to
sb** (inf) vor jdm kriechen; **to drive along
at a** ~ im Schneckentempo or Kriechtempo
vorankommen
crawler lane (Brit) n (Aut) Kriechspur f
crayfish ['kreɪfɪʃ] n inv (freshwater) Flusskrebs m;
(saltwater) Languste f
crayon ['kreɪən] n Buntstift m
craze [kreɪz] n Fimmel m; **to be all the** ~ große
Mode sein
crazed [kreɪzd] adj wahnsinnig; (pottery, glaze)
rissig
crazy ['kreɪzɪ] adj wahnsinnig, verrückt; ~
about sb/sth (inf) verrückt or wild auf jdn/
etw; **to go** ~ wahnsinnig or verrückt werden
crazy paving (Brit) n Mosaikpflaster nt
creak [kri:k] vi knarren
cream [kri:m] n Sahne f, Rahm m (Südd);
(artificial cream, cosmetic) Creme f; (élite) Creme
f, Elite f ▷ adj cremefarben; **whipped** ~
Schlagsahne f
▷ **cream off** vt absahnen (inf)
cream cake n Sahnetorte f; (small)
Sahnetörtchen nt
cream cheese n (Doppelrahm)frischkäse m
creamery ['kri:mərɪ] n (shop) Milchgeschäft nt;
(factory) Molkerei f
creamy ['kri:mɪ] adj (colour) cremefarben;
(taste) sahnig
crease [kri:s] n Falte f; (in trousers) Bügelfalte

f ▷ vt zerknittern; (forehead) runzeln ▷ vi
knittern; (forehead) sich runzeln
crease-resistant ['kri:srɪzɪstənt] adj
knitterfrei
create [kri:'eɪt] vt schaffen; (interest)
hervorrufen; (problems) verursachen; (produce)
herstellen; (design) entwerfen, kreieren;
(impression, fuss) machen
creation [kri:'eɪʃən] n (see vb) Schaffung f;
Hervorrufen nt; Verursachung f; Herstellung f;
Entwurf m, Kreation f; (Rel) Schöpfung f
creative [kri:'eɪtɪv] adj kreativ, schöpferisch
creativity [kri:eɪ'tɪvɪtɪ] n Kreativität f
creator [kri:'eɪtəʳ] n Schöpfer(in) m(f)
creature ['kri:tʃəʳ] n Geschöpf nt; (living animal)
Lebewesen nt
creature comforts [-'kʌmfəts] npl
Lebensgenüsse pl
crèche [krɛʃ] n (Kinder)krippe f; (all day)
(Kinder)tagesstätte f
credence ['kri:dns] n: **to lend** or **give** ~ **to sth**
etw glaubwürdig erscheinen lassen or machen
credentials [krɪ'dɛnʃlz] npl Referenzen pl,
Zeugnisse pl; (papers of identity) (Ausweis)
papiere pl
credibility [krɛdɪ'bɪlɪtɪ] n Glaubwürdigkeit f
credible ['krɛdɪbl] adj glaubwürdig
credit ['krɛdɪt] n (loan) Kredit m; (recognition)
Anerkennung f; (Scol) Schein m ▷ adj
(Comm: terms etc) Kredit- ▷ vt (Comm)
gutschreiben; (believe: also: **give credit to**)
glauben; **credits** npl (Cine, TV: at beginning)
Vorspann m; (: at end) Nachspann m; **to be in**
~ (person) Geld auf dem Konto haben; (bank
account) im Haben sein; **on** ~ auf Kredit; **it is
to his** ~ **that** ... es ehrt ihn, dass ...; **to take
the** ~ **for** das Verdienst in Anspruch nehmen
für; **it does him** ~ es spricht für ihn; **he's a** ~
to his family er macht seiner Familie Ehre;
to ~ **sb with sth** (fig) jdm etw zuschreiben; **to**
~ **£5 to sb** jdm £5 gutschreiben
creditable ['krɛdɪtəbl] adj lobenswert,
anerkennenswert
credit account n Kreditkonto nt
credit agency (Brit) n Kreditauskunftei f
credit balance n Kontostand m
credit bureau (US) n = **credit agency**
credit card n Kreditkarte f
credit control n Kreditüberwachung f
credit crunch n Kreditklemme f
credit facilities npl (Comm)
Kreditmöglichkeiten pl
credit limit n Kreditgrenze f
credit note (Brit) n Gutschrift f
creditor ['krɛdɪtəʳ] n Gläubiger m
credit transfer n Banküberweisung f
creditworthy ['krɛdɪt'wə:ðɪ] adj kreditwürdig
credulity [krɪ'dju:lɪtɪ] n Leichtgläubigkeit f
creed [kri:d] n Glaubensbekenntnis nt
creek [kri:k] n (kleine) Bucht f; (US: stream)
Bach m; **to be up the** ~ (inf) in der Tinte sitzen
creel [kri:l] n (also: **lobster creel**)
Hummer(fang)korb m

creep [kri:p] (pt, pp **crept**) vi schleichen; (plant: horizontally) kriechen; (: vertically) klettern ▷ n (inf) Kriecher m; **to ~ up on sb** sich an jdn heranschleichen; (time etc) langsam auf jdn zukommen; **he's a ~** er ist ein widerlicher or fieser Typ; **it gives me the ~s** davon kriege ich das kalte Grausen

creeper ['kri:pə'] n Kletterpflanze f

creepers ['kri:pəz] (US) npl Schuhe mit weichen Sohlen

creepy ['kri:pɪ] adj gruselig; (experience) unheimlich, gruselig

creepy-crawly ['kri:pɪ'krɔ:lɪ] (inf) n Krabbeltier nt

cremate [krɪ'meɪt] vt einäschern

cremation [krɪ'meɪʃən] n Einäscherung f, Kremation f

crematoria [krɛmə'tɔ:rɪə] npl of **crematorium**

crematorium [krɛmə'tɔ:rɪəm] (pl **crematoria**) n Krematorium nt

creosote ['krɪəsəʊt] n Kreosot nt

crepe [kreɪp] n Krepp m; (rubber) Krepp(gummi) m

crepe bandage (Brit) n elastische Binde f

crepe paper n Krepppapier nt

crepe sole n Kreppsohle f

crept [krɛpt] pt, pp of **creep**

crescendo [krɪ'ʃɛndəʊ] n Höhepunkt m; (Mus) Crescendo nt

crescent ['krɛsnt] n Halbmond m; (street) halbkreisförmig verlaufende Straße

cress [krɛs] n Kresse f

crest [krɛst] n (of hill) Kamm m; (of bird) Haube f; (coat of arms) Wappen nt

crestfallen ['krɛstfɔ:lən] adj niedergeschlagen

Crete [kri:t] n Kreta nt

crevasse [krɪ'væs] n Gletscherspalte f

crevice ['krɛvɪs] n Spalte f

crew [kru:] n Besatzung f; (TV, Cine) Crew f; (gang) Bande f

crew cut n Bürstenschnitt m

crew neck n runder (Hals)ausschnitt m

crib [krɪb] n Kinderbett nt; (Rel) Krippe f ▷ vt (inf: copy) abschreiben

cribbage ['krɪbɪdʒ] n Cribbage nt

crib death (US) n = **cot death**

crick [krɪk] n Krampf m

cricket ['krɪkɪt] n Kricket nt; (insect) Grille f

cricketer ['krɪkɪtə'] n Kricketspieler(in) m(f)

crime [kraɪm] n (no pl: illegal activities) Verbrechen pl; (illegal action: fig) Verbrechen nt; **minor ~** kleinere Vergehen pl

crime wave n Verbrechenswelle f

criminal ['krɪmɪnl] n Kriminelle(r) f(m), Verbrecher(in) m(f) ▷ adj kriminell; **C~ Investigation Department** Kriminalpolizei f

criminal code n Strafgesetzbuch nt

criminal profile n Täterprofil nt

crimp [krɪmp] vt kräuseln; (hair) wellen

crimson ['krɪmzn] adj purpurrot

cringe [krɪndʒ] vi (in fear) zurückweichen; (in embarrassment) zusammenzucken

crinkle ['krɪŋkl] vt (zer)knittern

cripple ['krɪpl] n Krüppel m ▷ vt zum Krüppel machen; (ship, plane) aktionsunfähig machen; (production, exports) lahmlegen, lähmen; **~d with rheumatism** von Rheuma praktisch gelähmt

crippling ['krɪplɪŋ] adj (disease) schwer; (taxation, debts) erdrückend

crises ['kraɪsi:z] npl of **crisis**

crisis ['kraɪsɪs] (pl **crises**) n Krise f

crisp [krɪsp] adj (vegetables etc) knackig; (bacon etc) knusprig; (weather) frisch; (manner, tone, reply) knapp

crisps [krɪsps] (Brit) npl Chips pl

crisscross ['krɪskrɔs] adj (pattern) Kreuz- ▷ vt kreuz und quer durchziehen

criteria [kraɪ'tɪərɪə] npl of **criterion**

criterion [kraɪ'tɪərɪən] (pl **criteria**) n Kriterium nt

critic ['krɪtɪk] n Kritiker(in) m(f)

critical ['krɪtɪkl] adj kritisch; **to be ~ of sb/sth** jdn/etw kritisieren; **he is in a ~ condition** sein Zustand ist kritisch

critically ['krɪtɪklɪ] adv kritisch; (ill) schwer

criticism ['krɪtɪsɪzəm] n Kritik f

criticize ['krɪtɪsaɪz] vt kritisieren

critique [krɪ'ti:k] n Kritik f

croak [krəʊk] vi (frog) quaken; (bird, person) krächzen

Croat n Kroate m, Kroatin f; (Ling) Kroatisch nt

Croatia [krəʊ'eɪʃə] n Kroatien nt

Croatian [krəʊ'eɪʃən] adj kroatisch

crochet ['krəʊʃeɪ] n (activity) Häkeln nt; (result) Häkelei f

crock [krɔk] n Topf m; (inf: also: **old crock**: vehicle) Kiste f; (: person) Wrack nt

crockery ['krɔkərɪ] n Geschirr nt

crocodile ['krɔkədaɪl] n Krokodil nt

crocus ['krəʊkəs] n Krokus m

croft [krɔft] (Brit) n kleines Pachtgut nt

crofter ['krɔftə'] (Brit) n Kleinpächter(in) m(f)

crone [krəʊn] n alte Hexe f

crony ['krəʊnɪ] (inf: pej) n Kumpan(in) m(f)

crook [kruk] n (criminal) Gauner m; (of shepherd) Hirtenstab m; (of arm) Beuge f

crooked ['krukɪd] adj krumm; (dishonest) unehrlich

crop [krɔp] n (Feld)frucht f; (amount produced) Ernte f; (riding crop) Reitpeitsche f; (of bird) Kropf m ▷ vt (hair) stutzen; (subj: animal: grass) abfressen

▶ **crop up** vi aufkommen

cropper ['krɔpə'] (inf) n: **to come a ~** hinfallen; (fig: fail) auf die Nase fallen

crop spraying [-'spreɪŋ] n Schädlingsbekämpfung f (durch Besprühen)

croquet ['krəʊkeɪ] (Brit) n Krocket nt

croquette [krə'kɛt] n Krokette f

cross [krɔs] n Kreuz nt; (Biol, Bot) Kreuzung f ▷ vt (street) überqueren; (room etc) durchqueren; (cheque) zur Verrechnung ausstellen; (arms) verschränken; (legs) übereinanderschlagen; (animal, plant) kreuzen; (thwart: person) verärgern; (: plan) durchkreuzen ▷ adj

ärgerlich, böse ▷ vi: **the boat ~es from ...
to ...** das Schiff fährt von ... nach ...; **to ~ o.s.**
sich bekreuzigen; **we have a ~ed line** (*Brit*) es
ist jemand in der Leitung; **they've got their
lines** *or* **wires ~ed** (*fig*) sie reden aneinander
vorbei; **to be/get ~ with sb (about sth)** mit
jdm *or* auf jdn (wegen etw) böse sein/werden
▶ **cross out** *vt* streichen
▶ **cross over** *vi* hinübergehen

crossbar ['krɔsbaːʳ] *n* (*Sport*) Querlatte *f*; (*of
bicycle*) Stange *f*
crossbow *n* Armbrust *f*
crossbreed ['krɔsbriːd] *n* Kreuzung *f*
cross-Channel ferry ['krɔs'tʃænl-] *n*
Kanalfähre *f*
crosscheck ['krɔstʃɛk] *n* Gegenprobe *f* ▷ *vt*
überprüfen
cross-country ['krɔs'kʌntrɪ], **cross-country
race** *n* Querfeldeinrennen *nt*
cross-dressing [krɔs'drɛsɪŋ] *n* (*transvestism*)
Transvestismus *m*
cross-examination ['krɔsɪgzæmɪ'neɪʃən] *n*
Kreuzverhör *nt*
cross-examine ['krɔsɪg'zæmɪn] *vt* ins
Kreuzverhör nehmen
cross-eyed ['krɔsaɪd] *adj* schielend; **to be ~**
schielen
crossfire ['krɔsfaɪəʳ] *n* Kreuzfeuer *nt*; **to get
caught in the ~** (*also fig*) ins Kreuzfeuer
geraten
crossing ['krɔsɪŋ] *n* Überfahrt *f*;
(*also*: **pedestrian crossing**) Fußgängerüberweg *m*
crossing guard (*US*) *n* ≈ Schülerlotse *m*
crossing point *n* Übergangsstelle *f*
cross-purposes ['krɔs'pə:pəsɪz] *npl*: **to be at ~
with sb** jdn missverstehen; **we're (talking)
at ~** wir reden aneinander vorbei
cross-question ['krɔs'kwɛstʃən] *vt* ins
Kreuzverhör nehmen
cross-reference ['krɔs'rɛfrəns] *n* (Quer)
verweis *m*
crossroads ['krɔsrəudz] *n* Kreuzung *f*
cross section *n* Querschnitt *m*
crosswalk ['krɔswɔːk] (*US*) *n*
Fußgängerüberweg *m*
crosswind ['krɔswɪnd] *n* Seitenwind *m*
crosswise ['krɔswaɪz] *adv* quer
crossword ['krɔswəːd] *n* (*also*: **crossword
puzzle**) Kreuzworträtsel *nt*
crotch [krɔtʃ] *n* Unterleib *m*; (*of garment*) Schritt
m
crotchet ['krɔtʃɪt] *n* Viertelnote *f*
crotchety ['krɔtʃɪtɪ] *adj* reizbar
crouch [krautʃ] *vi* kauern
croup [kruːp] *n* (*Med*) Krupp *m*
croupier ['kruːpɪəʳ] *n* Croupier *m*
crouton ['kruːtɔn] *n* Crouton *m*
crow [krəu] *n* (*bird*) Krähe *f*; (*of cock*) Krähen *nt*
▷ *vi* krähen; (*fig*) sich brüsten, angeben
crowbar ['krəubaːʳ] *n* Brechstange *f*
crowd [kraud] *n* (Menschen)menge *f* ▷ *vt*
(*room, stadium*) füllen ▷ *vi*: **to ~ round**

sich herumdrängen; **~s of people**
Menschenmassen *pl*; **the/our ~** (*of friends*)
die/unsere Clique *f*; **to ~ sb/sth in** jdn/
etw hineinstopfen; **to ~ sb/sth into** jdn
pferchen/etw stopfen in +*acc*; **to ~ in** sich
hineindrängen
crowded ['kraudɪd] *adj* überfüllt; (*densely
populated*) dicht besiedelt; **~ with** voll von
crowd scene *n* Massenszene *f*
crown [kraun] *n* (*also of tooth*) Krone *f*; (*of head*)
Wirbel *m*; (*of hill*) Kuppe *f*; (*of hat*) Kopf *m* ▷ *vt*
krönen; (*tooth*) überkronen; **the C~** die Krone;
and to ~ it all ... (*fig*) und zur Krönung des
Ganzen ...

crowning ['kraunɪŋ] *adj* krönend
crown jewels *npl* Kronjuwelen *pl*
crown prince *n* Kronprinz *m*
crow's-feet ['krəuzfiːt] *npl* Krähenfüße *pl*
crow's-nest ['krəuznɛst] *n* Krähennest *nt*,
Mastkorb *m*
crucial ['kruːʃl] *adj* (*decision*) äußerst wichtig;
(*vote*) entscheidend; **~ to** äußerst wichtig für
crucifix ['kruːsɪfɪks] *n* Kruzifix *nt*
crucifixion [kruːsɪ'fɪkʃən] *n* Kreuzigung *f*
crucify ['kruːsɪfaɪ] *vt* kreuzigen; (*fig*) in der Luft
zerreißen
crude [kruːd] *adj* (*oil, fibre*) Roh-; (*fig: basic*)
primitiv; (: *vulgar*) ordinär ▷ *n* = **crude oil**
crude oil *n* Rohöl *nt*
cruel ['kruəl] *adj* grausam
cruelty ['kruəltɪ] *n* Grausamkeit *f*
cruet ['kruːɪt] *n* Gewürzständer *m*
cruise [kruːz] *n* Kreuzfahrt *f* ▷ *vi* (*ship*) kreuzen;
(*car*) (mit Dauergeschwindigkeit) fahren;
(*aircraft*) (mit Reisegeschwindigkeit) fliegen;
(*taxi*) gemächlich fahren
cruise missile *n* Marschflugkörper *m*
cruiser ['kruːzəʳ] *n* Motorboot *nt*; (*warship*)
Kreuzer *m*
cruising speed *n* Reisegeschwindigkeit *f*
crumb [krʌm] *n* Krümel *m*; (*fig: of information*)
Brocken *m*; **a ~ of comfort** ein winziger Trost
crumble ['krʌmbl] *vt* (*bread*) zerbröckeln;
(*biscuit etc*) zerkrümeln ▷ *vi* (*building, earth
etc*) zerbröckeln; (*plaster*) abbröckeln;
(*fig: opposition*) sich auflösen; (: *belief*) ins
Wanken geraten
crumbly ['krʌmblɪ] *adj* krümelig
crummy ['krʌmɪ] (*inf*) *adj* mies
crumpet ['krʌmpɪt] *n* Teekuchen *m* (*zum
Toasten*)
crumple ['krʌmpl] *vt* zerknittern

crunch [krʌntʃ] vt (biscuit, apple etc) knabbern; (underfoot) zertreten ▷ n: **the ~** der große Krach; **if it comes to the ~** wenn es wirklich dahin kommt; **when the ~ comes** wenn es hart auf hart geht

crunchy ['krʌntʃɪ] adj knusprig; (apple etc) knackig; (gravel, snow etc) knirschend

crusade [kru:'seɪd] n Feldzug m ▷ vi: **to ~ for/against sth** für/gegen etw zu Felde ziehen

crusader [kru:'seɪdə'] n Kreuzritter m; (fig): **~ (for)** Apostel m (+gen)

crush [krʌʃ] n (crowd) Gedränge nt ▷ vt quetschen; (grapes) zerquetschen; (paper, clothes) zerknittern; (garlic, ice) (zer)stoßen; (defeat) niederschlagen; (devastate) vernichten; **to have a ~ on sb** (love) für jdn schwärmen; **lemon ~** Zitronensaftgetränk nt

crush barrier (Brit) n Absperrung f

crushing ['krʌʃɪŋ] adj vernichtend

crust [krʌst] n Kruste f

crustacean [krʌs'teɪʃən] n Schalentier nt, Krustazee f

crusty ['krʌstɪ] adj knusprig

crutch [krʌtʃ] n Krücke f; (support) Stütze f; see also **crotch**

crux [krʌks] n Kern m

cry [kraɪ] vi weinen; (also: **cry out**) aufschreien ▷ n Schrei m; (shout) Ruf m; **what are you ~ing about?** warum weinst du?; **to ~ for help** um Hilfe rufen; **she had a good ~** sie hat sich (mal richtig) ausgeweint; **it's a far ~ from ...** (fig) das ist etwas ganz anderes als ...
▶ **cry off** (inf) vi absagen

crying ['kraɪɪŋ] adj (fig: need) dringend; **it's a ~ shame** es ist ein Jammer

crypt [krɪpt] n Krypta f

cryptic ['krɪptɪk] adj hintergründig, rätselhaft; (clue) verschlüsselt

crystal ['krɪstl] n Kristall m; (glass) Kristall(glas) nt

crystal clear adj glasklar

crystallize ['krɪstəlaɪz] vt (opinion, thoughts) (feste) Form geben +dat ▷ vi (sugar etc) kristallisieren; **~d fruits** (Brit) kandierte Früchte pl

CSA n abbr (= Child Support Agency) Amt zur Regelung von Unterhaltszahlungen für Kinder

CSC n abbr (= Civil Service Commission) Einstellungsbehörde für den öffentlichen Dienst

CSE (Brit) n abbr (formerly: = Certificate of Secondary Education) Schulabschlusszeugnis, ≈ mittlere Reife f

CS gas (Brit) n ≈ Tränengas nt

CST (US) abbr (= Central Standard Time) mittelamerikanische Standardzeit

CT (US) abbr (Post) = Connecticut

ct abbr = **cent**; **court**

CTC (Brit) n abbr = **city technology college**

CT scanner n abbr (Med: = computerized tomography scanner) CT-Scanner m

cu ['si:ju:] abbr (= see you: in text messages) bis dann, bis später

cu. abbr = **cubic**

cub [kʌb] n Junge(s) nt; (also: **cub scout**)

Wölfling m

Cuba ['kju:bə] n Kuba nt

Cuban ['kju:bən] adj kubanisch ▷ n Kubaner(in) m(f)

cubbyhole ['kʌbɪhəul] n (room) Kabuff nt; (space) Eckchen nt

cube [kju:b] n Würfel m; (Math: of number) dritte Potenz f ▷ vt (Math) in die dritte Potenz erheben, hoch drei nehmen

cube farm n (inf) Großraumbüro nt (mit Trennwänden)

cube root n Kubikwurzel f

cubic ['kju:bɪk] adj (volume) Kubik-; **~ metre** etc Kubikmeter m etc

cubic capacity n Hubraum m

cubicle ['kju:bɪkl] n Kabine f; (in hospital) Bettnische f

cuckoo ['kuku:] n Kuckuck m

cuckoo clock n Kuckucksuhr f

cucumber ['kju:kʌmbə'] n Gurke f

cud [kʌd] n: **to chew the ~** (animal) wiederkäuen; (fig: person) vor sich acc hin grübeln

cuddle ['kʌdl] vt in den Arm nehmen, drücken ▷ vi schmusen

cuddly ['kʌdlɪ] adj (toy) zum Liebhaben or Drücken; (person) knuddelig (inf)

cudgel ['kʌdʒl] n Knüppel m ▷ vt: **to ~ one's brains** sich dat das (Ge)hirn zermartern

cue [kju:] n (Sport) Billardstock m, Queue nt; (Theat: word) Stichwort nt; (: action) (Einsatz)zeichen nt; (Mus) Einsatz m

cuff [kʌf] n (of sleeve) Manschette f; (US: of trousers) Aufschlag m; (blow) Klaps m ▷ vt einen Klaps geben +dat; **off the ~** aus dem Stegreif

cuff links npl Manschettenknöpfe pl

cu. in. abbr (= cubic inches) Kubikzoll

cuisine [kwɪ'zi:n] n Küche f

cul-de-sac ['kʌldəsæk] n Sackgasse f

culinary ['kʌlɪnərɪ] adj (skill) Koch-; (delight) kulinarisch

cull [kʌl] vt (zusammen)sammeln; (animals) ausmerzen ▷ n Erlegen überschüssiger Tierbestände

culminate ['kʌlmɪneɪt] vi: **to ~ in** gipfeln in +dat

culmination [kʌlmɪ'neɪʃən] n Höhepunkt m

culottes [kju:'lɔts] npl Hosenrock m

culpable ['kʌlpəbl] adj schuldig

culprit ['kʌlprɪt] n Täter(in) m(f)

cult [kʌlt] n Kult m

cult figure n Kultfigur f

cultivate ['kʌltɪveɪt] vt (land) bebauen, landwirtschaftlich nutzen; (crop) anbauen; (feeling) entwickeln; (person) sich dat warm halten (inf), die Beziehung pflegen zu

cultivation [kʌltɪ'veɪʃən] n (of land) Bebauung f, landwirtschaftliche Nutzung f; (of crop) Anbau m

cultural ['kʌltʃərəl] adj kulturell

culture ['kʌltʃə'] n Kultur f

cultured ['kʌltʃəd] adj kultiviert; (pearl) Zucht-

cumbersome ['kʌmbəsəm] adj (suitcase etc) sperrig, unhandlich; (piece of machinery) schwer zu handhaben; (*clothing*) hinderlich; (*process*) umständlich

cumin ['kʌmɪn] *n* Kreuzkümmel *m*

cumulative ['kju:mjulətɪv] *adj* (*effect, result*) Gesamt-

cunning ['kʌnɪŋ] *n* Gerissenheit *f* ▷ *adj* gerissen; (*device, idea*) schlau

cunt [kʌnt] (*inf!*) *n* (*vagina*) Fotze *f* (!); (*term of abuse*) Arsch *m* (!)

cup [kʌp] *n* Tasse *f*; (*as prize*) Pokal *m*; (*of bra*) Körbchen *nt*; **a ~ of tea** eine Tasse Tee

cupboard ['kʌbəd] *n* Schrank *m*

cup final (*Brit*) *n* Pokalendspiel *nt*

cupful ['kʌpful] *n* Tasse *f*

Cupid ['kju:pɪd] *n* Amor *m*; (*figurine*) Amorette *f*

cupidity [kju:'pɪdɪtɪ] *n* Begierde *f*, Gier *f*

cupola ['kju:pələ] *n* Kuppel *f*

cuppa ['kʌpə] (*Brit: inf*) *n* Tasse *f* Tee

cup tie (*Brit*) *n* Pokalspiel *nt*

curable ['kjuərəbl] *adj* heilbar

curate ['kjuərɪt] *n* Vikar *m*

curator [kjuə'reɪtər] *n* Kustos *m*

curb [kə:b] *vt* einschränken; (*person*) an die Kandare nehmen ▷ *n* Einschränkung *f*; (*US: kerb*) Bordstein *m*

curd cheese *n* Weißkäse *m*

curdle ['kə:dl] *vi* gerinnen

curds [kə:dz] *npl* ≈ Quark *m*

cure [kjuəʳ] *vt* heilen; (*Culin: salt*) pökeln; (*: smoke*) räuchern; (*: dry*) trocknen; (*problem*) abhelfen +*dat* ▷ *n* (*remedy*) (Heil)mittel *nt*; (*treatment*) Heilverfahren *nt*; (*solution*) Abhilfe *f*; **to be ~d of sth** von etw geheilt sein

cure-all ['kjuərɔ:l] *n* (*also fig*) Allheilmittel *nt*

curfew ['kə:fju:] *n* Ausgangssperre *f*; (*time*) Sperrstunde *f*

curio ['kjuərɪəu] *n* Kuriosität *f*

curiosity [kjuərɪ'ɒsɪtɪ] *n* (*see adj*) Wissbegier(de) *f*; Neugier *f*; Merkwürdigkeit *f*

curious ['kjuərɪəs] *adj* (*interested*) wissbegierig; (*nosy*) neugierig; (*strange, unusual*) sonderbar, merkwürdig; **I'm ~ about him** ich bin gespannt auf ihn

curiously ['kjuərɪəslɪ] *adv* neugierig; (*inquisitively*) wissbegierig; **~ enough, ...** merkwürdigerweise ...

curl [kə:l] *n* Locke *f*; (*of smoke etc*) Kringel *m* ▷ *vt* (*hair: loosely*) locken; (*: tightly*) kräuseln ▷ *vi* sich locken; sich kräuseln; (*smoke*) sich kringeln
▶ **curl up** *vi* sich zusammenrollen

curler ['kə:lər] *n* Lockenwickler *m*; (*Sport*) Curlingspieler(in) *m(f)*

curlew ['kə:lu:] *n* Brachvogel *m*

curling ['kə:lɪŋ] *n* (*Sport*) Curling *nt*

curling tongs, (*US*) **curling irons** *npl* Lockenschere *f*, Brennschere *f*

curly ['kə:lɪ] *adj* lockig; (*tightly curled*) kraus

currant ['kʌrnt] *n* Korinthe *f*; (*blackcurrant, redcurrant*) Johannisbeere *f*

currency ['kʌrnsɪ] *n* (*system*) Währung *f*; (*money*) Geld *nt*; **foreign ~** Devisen *pl*; **to gain ~** (*fig*) sich verbreiten, um sich greifen

current ['kʌrnt] *n* Strömung *f*; (*Elec*) Strom

m; (*of opinion*) Tendenz *f*, Trend *m* ▷ *adj* gegenwärtig; (*expression*) gebräuchlich; (*idea, custom*) verbreitet; **direct/alternating ~** (*Elec*) Gleich-/Wechselstrom *m*; **the ~ issue of a magazine** die neueste *or* letzte Nummer einer Zeitschrift; **in ~ use** allgemein gebräuchlich

current account (*Brit*) *n* Girokonto *nt*

current affairs *npl* Tagespolitik *f*

current assets *npl* (*Comm*) Umlaufvermögen *nt*

current liabilities *npl* (*Comm*) kurzfristige Verbindlichkeiten *pl*

currently ['kʌrntlɪ] *adv* zurzeit

curricula [kə'rɪkjulə] *npl of* **curriculum**

curriculum [kə'rɪkjuləm] (*pl* **~s** *or* **curricula**) *n* Lehrplan *m*

curriculum vitae [-'vi:taɪ] *n* Lebenslauf *m*

curry ['kʌrɪ] *n* (*dish*) Currygericht *nt* ▷ *vt*: **to ~ favour with** sich einschmeicheln bei

curry powder *n* Curry *m or nt*, Currypulver *nt*

curse [kə:s] *vi* fluchen ▷ *vt* verfluchen ▷ *n* Fluch *m*

cursor ['kə:sər] *n* (*Comput*) Cursor *m*

cursory ['kə:sərɪ] *adj* flüchtig; (*examination*) oberflächlich

curt [kə:t] *adj* knapp, kurz angebunden

curtail [kə:'teɪl] *vt* einschränken; (*visit etc*) abkürzen

curtain ['kə:tn] *n* Vorhang *m*; (*net*) Gardine *f*; **to draw the ~s** (*together*) die Vorhänge zuziehen; (*apart*) die Vorhänge aufmachen

curtain call *n* (*Theat*) Vorhang *m*

curtsey, curtsy ['kə:tsɪ] *vi* knicksen ▷ *n* Knicks *m*

curvature ['kə:vətfər] *n* Krümmung *f*

curve [kə:v] *n* Bogen *m*; (*in the road*) Kurve *f* ▷ *vi* einen Bogen machen; (*surface, arch*) sich wölben ▷ *vt* biegen

curved [kə:vd] *adj* (*line*) gebogen; (*table legs etc*) geschwungen; (*surface, arch, sides of ship*) gewölbt

cushion ['kuʃən] *n* Kissen *nt* ▷ *vt* dämpfen; (*seat*) polstern

cushy ['kuʃɪ] (*inf*) *adj*: **a ~ job** ein gemütlicher *or* ruhiger Job; **to have a ~ time** eine ruhige Kugel schieben

custard ['kʌstəd] *n* (*for pouring*) Vanillesoße *f*

custard powder (*Brit*) *n* Vanillesoßenpulver *nt*

custodial [kʌs'təudɪəl] *adj*: **~ sentence** Gefängnisstrafe *f*

custodian [kʌs'təudɪən] *n* Verwalter(in) *m(f)*; (*of museum etc*) Aufseher(in) *m(f)*, Wächter(in) *m(f)*

custody ['kʌstədɪ] *n* (*of child*) Vormundschaft *f*; (*for offenders*) (polizeilicher) Gewahrsam *m*, Haft *f*; **to take into ~** verhaften; **in the ~ of** unter der Obhut +*gen*; **the mother has ~ of the children** die Kinder sind der Mutter zugesprochen worden

custom ['kʌstəm] *n* Brauch *m*; (*habit*) (An)gewohnheit *f*; (*Law*) Gewohnheitsrecht *nt*; (*Comm*) Kundschaft *f*

customary ['kʌstəmərɪ] *adj* (*conventional*) üblich; (*habitual*) gewohnt; **it is ~ to do it** es

ist üblich, es zu tun
custom-built ['kʌstəm'bɪlt] *adj* speziell
angefertigt
customer ['kʌstəmə'] *n* Kunde *m*, Kundin *f*;
he's an awkward ~ (*inf*) er ist ein schwieriger
Typ
customer profile *n* Kundenprofil *nt*
customized ['kʌstəmaɪzd] *adj* individuell
aufgemacht
custom-made ['kʌstəm'meɪd] *adj* (*shirt etc*)
maßgefertigt, nach Maß; (*car etc*) speziell
angefertigt
customs ['kʌstəmz] *npl* Zoll *m*; **to go through
(the) ~** durch den Zoll gehen
Customs and Excise (*Brit*) *n* die Zollbehörde *f*
customs duty *n* Zoll *m*
customs officer *n* Zollbeamte(r) *m*,
Zollbeamtin *f*
cut [kʌt] (*pt, pp ~*) *vt* schneiden; (*text,
programme, spending*) kürzen; (*prices*) senken,
heruntersetzen, herabsetzen; (*supply*)
einschränken; (*cloth*) zuschneiden; (*road*)
schlagen, hauen; (*inf: lecture, appointment*)
schwänzen ▷ *vi* schneiden; (*lines*)
sich schneiden ▷ *n* Schnitt *m*; (*in skin*)
Schnittwunde *f*; (*in salary, spending etc*) Kürzung
f; (*of meat*) Stück *nt*; (*of jewel*) Schnitt *m*,
Schliff *m*; **to ~ a tooth** zahnen, einen Zahn
bekommen; **to ~ one's finger/hand/knee**
sich den Finger/in die Hand/am Knie
schneiden; **to get one's hair ~** sich *dat* die
Haare schneiden lassen; **to ~ sth short** etw
vorzeitig abbrechen; **to ~ sb dead** jdn wie Luft
behandeln; **cold ~s** (*US*) Aufschnitt *m*; **power
~** Stromausfall *m*
▶ **cut back** *vt* (*plants*) zurückschneiden;
(*production*) zurückschrauben; (*expenditure*)
einschränken
▶ **cut down** *vt* (*tree*) fällen; (*consumption*)
einschränken; **to ~ sb down to size** (*fig*) jdn
auf seinen Platz verweisen
▶ **cut down on** *vt fus* einschränken
▶ **cut in** *vi* (*Aut*) sich direkt vor ein anderes
Auto setzen; **to ~ in (on)** (*conversation*) sich
einschalten (in +*acc*)
▶ **cut off** *vt* abschneiden; (*supply*) sperren; (*Tel*)
unterbrechen; **we've been ~ off** (*Tel*) wir sind
unterbrochen worden
▶ **cut out** *vt* ausschneiden; (*an activity etc*)
aufhören mit; (*remove*) herausschneiden
▶ **cut up** *vt* klein schneiden; **it really ~ me up**
(*inf*) es hat mich ziemlich mitgenommen; **to
feel ~ up about sth** (*inf*) betroffen über etw
acc sein
cut and dried *adj* (*also: **cut-and-dry**: answer*)
eindeutig; (: *solution*) einfach
cutaway ['kʌtəweɪ] *n* (*coat*) Cut(away)
m; (*drawing*) Schnittdiagramm *nt*; (*model*)
Schnittmodell *nt*; (*Cine, TV*) Schnitt *m*
cutback ['kʌtbæk] *n* Kürzung *f*
cute [kjuːt] *adj* süß, niedlich; (*clever*) schlau
cut glass *n* geschliffenes Glas *nt*
cuticle ['kjuːtɪkl] *n* Nagelhaut *f*; **~ remover**

Nagelhautentferner *m*
cutlery ['kʌtlərɪ] *n* Besteck *nt*
cutlet ['kʌtlɪt] *n* Schnitzel *nt*; (*also: **vegetable
cutlet, nut cutlet**) Bratling *m*
cutoff ['kʌtɔf] *n* (*also: **cutoff point**) Trennlinie *f*
cutoff switch *n* Ausschaltmechanismus *m*
cutout ['kʌtaut] *n* (*switch*) Unterbrecher *m*;
(*shape*) Ausschneidemodell *nt*; (*paper figure*)
Ausschneidepuppe *f*
cut-price ['kʌt'praɪs] *adj* (*goods*)
heruntergesetzt; (*offer*) Billig-
cut-rate ['kʌt'reɪt] (*US*) *adj* = **cut-price**
cutthroat ['kʌtθrəut] *n* Mörder(in) *m(f)* ▷ *adj*
unbarmherzig, mörderisch
cutting ['kʌtɪŋ] *adj* (*edge, remark*) scharf ▷ *n*
(*Brit: from newspaper*) Ausschnitt *m*; (: *Rail*)
Durchstich *m*; (*from plant*) Ableger *m*
cutting edge *n* (*fig*) Spitzenstellung *f*; **on the ~
(of)** an der Spitze +*gen*
cuttlefish ['kʌtlfɪʃ] *n* Tintenfisch *m*
CV *n abbr* = **curriculum vitae**
c.w.o. *abbr* (*Comm*) = **cash with order**
cwt *abbr* = **hundredweight**
cyanide ['saɪənaɪd] *n* Zyanid *nt*
cybercafé ['saɪbəkæfeɪ] *n* Internetcafé *nt*
cybernetics [saɪbə'nɛtɪks] *n* Kybernetik *f*
cyclamen ['sɪkləmən] *n* Alpenveilchen *nt*
cycle ['saɪkl] *n* (*bicycle*) (Fahr)rad *nt*; (*series: of
seasons, songs etc*) Zyklus *m*; (: *of events*) Gang *m*;
(: *Tech*) Periode *f* ▷ *vi* Rad fahren
cycle lane, cycle path *n* (Fahr)radweg *m*
cycle race *n* Radrennen *nt*
cycle rack *n* Fahrradständer *m*
cycling ['saɪklɪŋ] *n* Radfahren *nt*; **to go on
a ~ holiday** (*Brit*) Urlaub mit dem Fahrrad
machen
cyclist ['saɪklɪst] *n* (Fahr)radfahrer(in) *m(f)*
cyclone ['saɪkləun] *n* Zyklon *m*
cygnet ['sɪgnɪt] *n* Schwanjunge(s) *nt*
cylinder ['sɪlɪndə'] *n* Zylinder *m*; (*of gas*)
Gasflasche *f*
cylinder block *n* Zylinderblock *m*
cylinder head *n* Zylinderkopf *m*
cylinder-head gasket ['sɪlɪndəhɛd-] *n*
Zylinderkopfdichtung *f*
cymbals ['sɪmblz] *npl* (*Mus*) Becken *nt*
cynic ['sɪnɪk] *n* Zyniker(in) *m(f)*
cynical ['sɪnɪkl] *adj* zynisch
cynicism ['sɪnɪsɪzəm] *n* Zynismus *m*
cypress ['saɪprɪs] *n* Zypresse *f*
Cypriot ['sɪprɪət] *adj* zypriotisch, zyprisch ▷ *n*
Zypriot(in) *m(f)*
Cyprus ['saɪprəs] *n* Zypern *nt*
cyst [sɪst] *n* Zyste *f*
cystitis [sɪs'taɪtɪs] *n* Blasenentzündung *f*,
Zystitis *f*
CZ (*US*) *n abbr* (= *Canal Zone*) Bereich des
Panamakanals
czar [zɑː'] *n* = **tsar**
Czech [tʃɛk] *adj* tschechisch ▷ *n* Tscheche *m*,
Tschechin *f*; (*language*) Tschechisch *nt*; **the ~
Republic** die Tschechische Republik *f*
Czechoslovak [tʃɛkə'sləuvæk] *adj, n* =

Czechoslovakian
Czechoslovakia [tʃɛkəslə'vækɪə] n (formerly) die
Tschechoslowakei f

Czechoslovakian [tʃɛkəslə'vækɪən] (formerly)
adj tschechoslowakisch ▷ n Tschechoslowake
m, Tschechoslowakin f

D¹, d¹ [di:] n (letter) D nt, d nt; **D for David, D for Dog** (US) ≈ D wie Dora

D² [di:] n (Mus) D nt, d nt

D³ [di:] (US) abbr (Pol) = **Democrat; Democratic**

d² (Brit: formerly) abbr = **penny**

d. abbr (= died): **Henry Jones, d. 1754** Henry Jones, gest. 1754

DA (US) n abbr = **district attorney**

dab [dæb] vt betupfen; (paint, cream) tupfen ▷ n Tupfer m; **to be a ~ hand at sth** gut in etw dat sein; **to be a ~ hand at doing sth** sich darauf verstehen, etw zu tun
▷ **dab at** vt betupfen

dabble ['dæbl] vi: **to ~ in** sich (nebenbei) beschäftigen mit

dachshund ['dækshund] n Dackel m

dad [dæd] (inf) n Papa m, Vati m

daddy ['dædɪ] (inf) n = **dad**

daddy-longlegs [dædɪ'lɒŋlɛgz] (inf) n Schnake f

daffodil ['dæfədɪl] n Osterglocke f, Narzisse f

daft [dɑ:ft] (inf) adj doof (inf), blöd (inf); **to be ~ about sb/sth** verrückt nach jdm/etw sein

dagger ['dægə^r] n Dolch m; **to be at ~s drawn with sb** mit jdm auf Kriegsfuß stehen; **to look ~s at sb** jdn mit Blicken durchbohren

dahlia ['deɪljə] n Dahlie f

daily ['deɪlɪ] adj täglich; (wages) Tages- ▷ n (paper) Tageszeitung f; (Brit: also: **daily help**) Putzfrau f ▷ adv täglich; **twice ~** zweimal täglich or am Tag

dainty ['deɪntɪ] adj zierlich

dairy ['dɛərɪ] n (Brit: shop) Milchgeschäft nt; (company) Molkerei f; (on farm) Milchkammer f ▷ cpd Milch-; (herd, industry, farming) Milchvieh-

dairy farm n auf Milchviehhaltung spezialisierter Bauernhof

dairy products npl Milchprodukte pl, Molkereiprodukte pl

dairy store (US) n Milchgeschäft nt

dais ['deɪɪs] n Podium nt

daisy ['deɪzɪ] n Gänseblümchen nt

daisywheel ['deɪzɪwi:l] n Typenrad nt

daisywheel printer n Typenraddrucker m

Dakar ['dækə^r] n Dakar nt

dale [deɪl] (Brit) n Tal nt

dally ['dælɪ] vi (herum)trödeln; **to ~ with** (plan, idea) spielen mit

dalmatian [dæl'meɪʃən] n Dalmatiner m

dam [dæm] n (Stau)damm m; (reservoir) Stausee m ▷ vt stauen

damage ['dæmɪdʒ] n Schaden m ▷ vt schaden +dat; (spoil, break) beschädigen; **damages** npl (Law) Schaden(s)ersatz m; **~ to property** Sachbeschädigung f; **to pay £5,000 in ~s** 5000 Pfund Schaden(s)ersatz (be)zahlen

damaging ['dæmɪdʒɪŋ] adj: **~ (to)** schädlich (für)

Damascus [də'mɑ:skəs] n Damaskus nt

dame [deɪm] n Dame f; (US: inf) Weib nt; (Theat) (komische) Alte f (von einem Mann gespielt)

damn [dæm] vt verfluchen; (condemn) verurteilen ▷ adj (inf: also: **damned**) verdammt ▷ n (inf): **I don't give a ~** das ist mir scheißegal (!); **~ (it)!** verdammt (noch mal)!

damnable ['dæmnəbl] adj grässlich

damnation [dæm'neɪʃən] n Verdammnis f ▷ excl (inf) verdammt

damning ['dæmɪŋ] adj belastend

damp [dæmp] adj feucht ▷ n Feuchtigkeit f ▷ vt (also: **dampen**) befeuchten, anfeuchten; (enthusiasm etc) dämpfen

dampcourse ['dæmpkɔ:s] n Dämmschicht f

damper ['dæmpə^r] n (Mus) Dämpfer m; (of fire) (Luft)klappe f; **to put a ~ on** (fig) einen Dämpfer aufsetzen +dat

dampness ['dæmpnɪs] n Feuchtigkeit f

damson ['dæmzən] n Damaszenerpflaume f

dance [dɑ:ns] n Tanz m; (social event) Tanz(abend) m ▷ vi tanzen; **to ~ about** (herum)tänzeln

dance hall n Tanzsaal m

dancer ['dɑ:nsə^r] n Tänzer(in) m(f)

dancing ['dɑ:nsɪŋ] n Tanzen nt ▷ cpd (teacher, school, class etc) Tanz-

D and C n abbr (Med: = dilation and curettage) Ausschabung f

dandelion ['dændɪlaɪən] n Löwenzahn m

dandruff ['dændrəf] n Schuppen pl

D and T (Brit) n abbr (Scol) = **Design and Technology**

dandy ['dændɪ] n Dandy m ▷ adj (US: inf) prima

Dane [deɪn] n Däne m, Dänin f

danger ['deɪndʒə^r] n Gefahr f; **there is ~ of fire/poisoning** es besteht Feuer-/Vergiftungsgefahr; **there is a ~ of sth**

happening es besteht die Gefahr, dass etw geschieht; **"~!"** „Achtung!"; **in ~** in Gefahr; **to be in ~ of doing sth** Gefahr laufen, etw zu tun; **out of ~** außer Gefahr

danger list *n*: **on the ~** in Lebensgefahr

dangerous ['deɪndʒrəs] *adj* gefährlich

dangerously ['deɪndʒrəslɪ] *adv* gefährlich; (*close*) bedenklich; **~ ill** schwer krank

danger zone *n* Gefahrenzone *f*

dangle ['dæŋgl] *vt* baumeln lassen ▷ *vi* baumeln

Danish ['deɪnɪʃ] *adj* dänisch ▷ *n* (*Ling*) Dänisch *nt*

Danish pastry *n* Plundergebäck *nt*

dank [dæŋk] *adj* (unangenehm) feucht

Danube ['dænju:b] *n*: **the ~** die Donau

dapper ['dæpəʳ] *adj* gepflegt

Dardanelles [dɑ:də'nɛlz] *npl*: **the ~** die Dardanellen *pl*

dare [dɛəʳ] *vt*: **to ~ sb to do sth** jdn dazu herausfordern, etw zu tun ▷ *vi*: **to ~ (to) do sth** es wagen, etw zu tun; **I ~n't tell him** (*Brit*) ich wage nicht, es ihm zu sagen; **I ~ say** ich nehme an

daredevil ['dɛədɛvl] *n* Draufgänger *m*

Dar-es-Salaam ['dɑ:rɛssə'lɑ:m] *n* Daressalam *nt*

daring ['dɛərɪŋ] *adj* kühn, verwegen; (*bold*) gewagt ▷ *n* Kühnheit *f*

dark [dɑ:k] *adj* dunkel; (*look*) finster ▷ *n*: **in the ~** im Dunkeln; **to be in the ~ about** (*fig*) keine Ahnung haben von; **after ~** nach Einbruch der Dunkelheit; **it is/is getting ~** es ist/wird dunkel; **~ chocolate** Zartbitterschokolade *f*

Dark Ages *npl*: **the ~** das finstere Mittelalter

darken [dɑ:kn] *vt* dunkel machen ▷ *vi* sich verdunkeln

dark glasses *npl* Sonnenbrille *f*

dark horse *n* (*in competition*) Unbekannte(r) *f(m)* (mit Außenseiterchancen); (*quiet person*) stilles Wasser *nt*

darkly ['dɑ:klɪ] *adv* finster

darkness ['dɑ:knɪs] *n* Dunkelheit *f*, Finsternis *f*

darkroom ['dɑ:krum] *n* Dunkelkammer *f*

darling ['dɑ:lɪŋ] *adj* lieb ▷ *n* Liebling *m*; **to be the ~ of** der Liebling +*gen* sein; **she is a ~** sie ist ein Schatz

darn [dɑ:n] *vt* stopfen

dart [dɑ:t] *n* (*in game*) (Wurf)pfeil *m*; (*in sewing*) Abnäher *m* ▷ *vi*: **to ~ towards** (*also*: **make a dart towards**) zustürzen auf +*acc*; **to ~ away/ along** davon-/entlangflitzen

dartboard ['dɑ:tbɔ:d] *n* Dartscheibe *f*

darts [dɑ:ts] *n* Darts *nt*, Pfeilwurfspiel *nt*

dash [dæʃ] *n* (*sign*) Gedankenstrich *m*; (*rush*) Jagd *f* ▷ *vt* (*throw*) schleudern; (*hopes*) zunichtemachen ▷ *vi*: **to ~ towards** zustürzen auf +*acc*; **a ~ of ...** (*small quantity*) etwas ..., ein Schuss *m* ...; **to make a ~ for sth** auf etw *acc* zustürzen; **we'll have to make a ~ for it** wir müssen rennen, so schnell wir können
 ▸ **dash away** *vi* losstürzen
 ▸ **dash off** *vi* = **dash away**

dashboard ['dæʃbɔ:d] *n* Armaturenbrett *nt*

dashing ['dæʃɪŋ] *adj* flott

dastardly ['dæstədlɪ] *adj* niederträchtig

DAT *n abbr* (= *digital audio tape*) DAT *nt*

data ['deɪtə] *npl* Daten *pl*

data analysis *n* Datenanalyse *f*

database ['deɪtəbeɪs] *n* Datenbank *f*

data capture *n* Datenerfassung *f*

data processing *n* Datenverarbeitung *f*

data projector *n* Beamer *m*

data transmission *n* Datenübertragung *f*

date [deɪt] *n* Datum *nt*; (*with friend*) Verabredung *f*; (*fruit*) Dattel *f* ▷ *vt* datieren; (*person*) ausgehen mit; **what's the ~ today?** der Wievielte ist heute?; **~ of birth** Geburtsdatum *nt*; **closing ~** Einsendeschluss *m*; **to ~** bis heute; **out of ~** altmodisch; (*expired*) abgelaufen; **up to ~** auf dem neuesten Stand; **to bring up to ~** auf den neuesten Stand bringen; (*person*) über den neuesten Stand der Dinge informieren; **a letter ~d 5 July** ein vom 5. Juli datierter Brief

dated ['deɪtɪd] *adj* altmodisch

dateline ['deɪtlaɪn] *n* (*Geog*) Datumsgrenze *f*; (*Press*) Datumszeile *f*

date rape *n* Vergewaltigung *f* einer Bekannten (mit der der Täter eine Verabredung hatte)

date stamp *n* Datumsstempel *m*

dative ['deɪtɪv] *n* Dativ *m*

daub [dɔ:b] *vt* schmieren; **to ~ with** beschmieren mit

daughter ['dɔ:təʳ] *n* Tochter *f*

daughter-in-law ['dɔ:tərɪnlɔ:] *n* Schwiegertochter *f*

daunt [dɔ:nt] *vt* entmutigen

daunting ['dɔ:ntɪŋ] *adj* entmutigend

dauntless ['dɔ:ntlɪs] *adj* unerschrocken, beherzt

dawdle ['dɔ:dl] *vi* trödeln; **to ~ over one's work** bei der Arbeit bummeln or trödeln

dawn [dɔ:n] *n* Tagesanbruch *m*, Morgengrauen *nt*; (*of period*) Anbruch *m* ▷ *vi* dämmern; (*fig*): **it ~ed on him that ...** es dämmerte ihm, dass ...; **from ~ to dusk** von morgens bis abends

dawn chorus (*Brit*) *n* Morgenkonzert *nt* der Vögel

day [deɪ] *n* Tag *m*; (*heyday*) Zeit *f*; **the ~ before/ after** am Tag zuvor/danach; **the ~ after tomorrow** übermorgen; **the ~ before yesterday** vorgestern; **(on) the following ~** am Tag danach; **the ~ that ...** (am Tag,) als ...; **~ by day** jeden Tag, täglich; **by ~** tagsüber; **paid by the ~** tageweise bezahlt; **to work an eight hour ~** einen Achtstundentag haben; **these ~s, in the present ~** heute, heutzutage

daybook ['deɪbʊk] (*Brit*) *n* Journal *nt*

dayboy ['deɪbɔɪ] *n* Externe(r) *m*

daybreak ['deɪbreɪk] *n* Tagesanbruch *m*

day-care centre ['deɪkɛə-] *n* (*for children*) (Kinder)tagesstätte *f*; (*for old people*) Altentagesstätte *f*

daydream ['deɪdri:m] *vi* (mit offenen Augen) träumen ▷ *n* Tagtraum *m*, Träumerei *f*

daygirl ['deɪgəːl] n Externe f
daylight ['deɪlaɪt] n Tageslicht nt
daylight robbery (inf) n Halsabschneiderei f
daylight-saving time (US) n Sommerzeit f
day release n: **to be on ~** tageweise (zur Weiterbildung) freigestellt sein
day return (Brit) n Tagesrückfahrkarte f
day shift n Tagschicht f
daytime ['deɪtaɪm] n Tag m; **in the ~** tagsüber, bei Tage
day-to-day ['deɪtə'deɪ] adj täglich, Alltags-; **on a ~ basis** tageweise
day trader n (Stock Exchange) Day-Trader(in) m(f), Tageshändler(in) m(f)
day trip n Tagesausflug m
day-tripper ['deɪ'trɪpəʳ] n Tagesausflügler(in) m(f)
daze [deɪz] vt benommen machen ▷ n: **in a ~** ganz benommen
dazed [deɪzd] adj benommen
dazzle ['dæzl] vt blenden
dazzling ['dæzlɪŋ] adj (light) blendend; (smile) strahlend; (career, achievements) glänzend
DC abbr = **direct current**
DCC n abbr (= digital compact cassette) DCC f
DD n abbr (= Doctor of Divinity) ≈ Dr. theol.
DD abbr = **direct debit**
D-day ['diːdeɪ] n der Tag X
DDS (US) n abbr (= Doctor of Dental Surgery) ≈ Dr. med. dent.
DDT n abbr (= dichlorodiphenyltrichloroethane) DDT nt
deacon ['diːkən] n Diakon m
dead [dɛd] adj tot; (flowers) verwelkt; (numb) abgestorben, taub; (battery) leer; (place) wie ausgestorben ▷ adv total, völlig; (directly, exactly) genau ▷ npl: **the ~** die Toten pl; **to shoot sb ~** jdn erschießen; **~ silence** Totenstille f; **in the ~ centre (of)** genau in der Mitte (+gen); **the line has gone ~** (Tel) die Leitung ist tot; **~ on time** auf die Minute pünktlich; **~ tired** todmüde; **to stop ~** abrupt stehen bleiben
dead beat (inf) adj (tired) völlig kaputt
deaden [dɛdn] vt (blow) abschwächen; (pain) mildern; (sound) dämpfen
dead end n Sackgasse f
dead-end ['dɛdɛnd] adj: **a ~ job** ein Job m ohne Aufstiegsmöglichkeiten
dead heat n: **to finish in a ~** unentschieden ausgehen
dead letter office n Amt nt für unzustellbare Briefe
deadline ['dɛdlaɪn] n (letzter) Termin m; **to work to a ~** auf einen Termin hinarbeiten
deadlock ['dɛdlɔk] n Stillstand m; **the meeting ended in ~** die Verhandlung war festgefahren
dead loss (inf) n: **to be a ~** ein hoffnungsloser Fall sein
deadly ['dɛdlɪ] adj tödlich ▷ adv: **~ dull** todlangweilig
deadpan ['dɛdpæn] adj (look) unbewegt; (tone) trocken

Dead Sea n: **the ~** das Tote Meer
dead season n tote Saison f
deaf [dɛf] adj taub; (partially) schwerhörig; **to turn a ~ ear to sth** sich einer Sache dat gegenüber taub stellen
deaf aid (Brit) n Hörgerät nt
deaf-and-dumb ['dɛfən'dʌm] adj taubstumm; **~ alphabet** Taubstummensprache f
deafen ['dɛfn] vt taub machen
deafening ['dɛfnɪŋ] adj ohrenbetäubend
deaf-mute ['dɛfmjuːt] n Taubstumme(r) f(m)
deafness ['dɛfnɪs] n Taubheit f
deal [diːl] n (pt, pp **~t**) n Geschäft nt, Handel m ▷ vt (blow) versetzen; (card) geben, austeilen; **to strike a ~ with sb** ein Geschäft mit jdm abschließen; **it's a ~!** (inf) abgemacht!; **he got a fair/bad ~ from them** er ist von ihnen anständig/schlecht behandelt worden; **a good ~** (a lot) ziemlich viel; **a great ~ (of)** ziemlich viel
  ▶ **deal in** vt fus handeln mit
  ▶ **deal with** vt fus (person) sich kümmern um; (problem) sich befassen mit; (successfully) fertig werden mit; (subject) behandeln
dealer ['diːləʳ] n Händler(in) m(f); (in drugs) Dealer m; (Cards) Kartengeber(in) m(f)
dealership ['diːləʃɪp] n (Vertrags)händler m
dealings ['diːlɪŋz] npl Geschäfte pl; (relations) Beziehungen pl
dealt [dɛlt] pt, pp of **deal**
dean [diːn] n Dekan m; (US: Scol: administrator) Schul- oder Collegeverwalter mit Beratungs- und Disziplinarfunktion
dear [dɪəʳ] adj lieb; (expensive) teuer ▷ n: **(my) ~** (mein) Liebling m ▷ excl: **~ me!** (ach) du liebe Zeit!; **D~ Sir/Madam** Sehr geehrte Damen und Herren; **D~ Mr/Mrs X** Sehr geehrter Herr/geehrte Frau X; (less formal) Lieber Herr/Liebe Frau X
dearly ['dɪəlɪ] adv (love) von ganzem Herzen; (pay) teuer
dear money n (Comm) teures Geld nt
dearth [dəːθ] n: **a ~ of** ein Mangel m an +dat
death [dɛθ] n Tod m; (fatality) Tote(r) f(m), Todesfall m
deathbed ['dɛθbɛd] n: **to be on one's ~** auf dem Sterbebett liegen
death certificate n Sterbeurkunde f, Totenschein m
deathly ['dɛθlɪ] adj (silence) eisig ▷ adv (pale etc) toten-
death penalty n Todesstrafe f
death rate n Sterbeziffer f
death row [-'rəu] (US) n Todestrakt m
death sentence n Todesurteil nt
death squad n Todeskommando nt
death toll n Zahl f der Todesopfer or Toten
deathtrap ['dɛθtræp] n Todesfalle f
deb [dɛb] (inf) n abbr = **debutante**
debacle [deɪ'baːkl] n Debakel nt
debar [dɪ'baːʳ] vt: **to ~ sb from doing sth** jdn davon ausschließen, etw zu tun; **to ~ sb from**

d

a club jdn aus einem Klub ausschließen

debase [dɪ'beɪs] vt (value, quality) mindern, herabsetzen; (person) erniedrigen, entwürdigen

debatable [dɪ'beɪtəbl] adj fraglich

debate [dɪ'beɪt] n Debatte f ▷ vt debattieren über +acc; (course of action) überlegen ▷ vi: **to ~ whether** hin und her überlegen, ob

debauchery [dɪ'bɔ:tʃərɪ] n Ausschweifungen pl

debenture [dɪ'bentʃər] n Schuldschein m

debilitate [dɪ'bɪlɪteɪt] vt schwächen

debilitating [dɪ'bɪlɪteɪtɪŋ] adj schwächend

debit ['dɛbɪt] n Schuldposten m ▷ vt: **to ~ a sum to sb/sb's account** jdn/jds Konto mit einer Summe belasten; see also **direct**

debit balance n Sollsaldo nt, Debetsaldo nt

debit note n Lastschriftanzeige f

debonair adj flott

debrief [di:'bri:f] vt befragen

debriefing [di:'bri:fɪŋ] n Befragung f

debris ['dɛbri:] n Trümmer pl, Schutt m

debt [dɛt] n Schuld f; (state of owing money) Schulden pl, Verschuldung f; **to be in ~** Schulden haben, verschuldet sein; **bad ~** uneinbringliche Forderung f

debt collector n Inkassobeauftragte(r) f(m), Schuldeneintreiber(in) m(f)

debtor ['dɛtər] n Schuldner(in) m(f)

debug [di:'bʌg] vt (Comput) Fehler beseitigen in +dat

debunk [di:'bʌŋk] vt (myths, ideas) bloßstellen; (claim) entlarven; (person, institution) vom Sockel stoßen

debut ['deɪbju:] n Debüt nt

debutante ['dɛbjutænt] n Debütantin f

Dec. abbr = **December**

decade ['dɛkeɪd] n Jahrzehnt nt

decadence ['dɛkədəns] n Dekadenz f

decadent ['dɛkədənt] adj dekadent

decaff ['di:kæf] n koffeinfreier Kaffee m

decaffeinated [dɪ'kæfɪneɪtɪd] adj koffeinfrei

decamp [dɪ'kæmp] (inf) vi verschwinden, sich aus dem Staub machen

decant [dɪ'kænt] vt umfüllen

decanter [dɪ'kæntər] n Karaffe f

decarbonize [di:'kɑ:bənaɪz] vt entkohlen

decathlon [dɪ'kæθlən] n Zehnkampf m

decay [dɪ'keɪ] n Verfall m; (of tooth) Fäule f ▷ vi (body) verwesen; (teeth) faulen; (leaves) verrotten; (fig: society etc) verfallen

decease [dɪ'si:s] n (Law): **upon your ~** bei Ihrem Ableben

deceased [dɪ'si:st] n: **the ~** der/die Tote or Verstorbene

deceit [dɪ'si:t] n Betrug m

deceitful [dɪ'si:tful] adj betrügerisch

deceive [dɪ'si:v] vt täuschen; (husband, wife etc) betrügen; **to ~ o.s.** sich dat etwas vormachen

decelerate [di:'sɛləreɪt] vi (car etc) langsamer werden; (driver) die Geschwindigkeit herabsetzen

December [dɪ'sɛmbər] n Dezember m; see also **July**

decency ['di:sənsɪ] n (propriety) Anstand m; (kindness) Anständigkeit f

decent ['di:sənt] adj anständig; **we expect you to do the ~ thing** wir erwarten, dass Sie die Konsequenzen ziehen; **they were very ~ about it** sie haben sich sehr anständig verhalten; **that was very ~ of him** das war sehr anständig von ihm; **are you ~?** (dressed) hast du etwas an?

decently ['di:səntlɪ] adv anständig

decentralization ['di:sɛntrəlaɪ'zeɪʃən] n Dezentralisierung f

decentralize [di:'sɛntrəlaɪz] vt dezentralisieren

deception [dɪ'sɛpʃən] n Täuschung f, Betrug m

deceptive [dɪ'sɛptɪv] adj irreführend, täuschend

decibel ['dɛsɪbɛl] n Dezibel nt

decide [dɪ'saɪd] vt entscheiden; (persuade) veranlassen ▷ vi sich entscheiden; **to ~ to do sth/that** beschließen, etw zu tun/dass; **to ~ on sth** sich für etw entscheiden; **to ~ on/against doing sth** sich dafür/dagegen entscheiden, etw zu tun

decided [dɪ'saɪdɪd] adj entschieden; (character) entschlossen; (difference) deutlich

decidedly [dɪ'saɪdɪdlɪ] adv entschieden; (emphatically) entschlossen

deciding [dɪ'saɪdɪŋ] adj entscheidend

deciduous [dɪ'sɪdjuəs] adj (tree, woods) Laub-

decimal ['dɛsɪməl] adj (system, number) Dezimal- ▷ n Dezimalzahl f; **to three ~ places** auf drei Dezimalstellen

decimalize ['dɛsɪməlaɪz] (Brit) vt auf das Dezimalsystem umstellen

decimal point n Komma nt

decimate ['dɛsɪmeɪt] vt dezimieren

decipher [dɪ'saɪfər] vt entziffern

decision [dɪ'sɪʒən] n Entscheidung f; (decisiveness) Bestimmtheit f, Entschlossenheit f; **to make a ~** eine Entscheidung treffen

decisive [dɪ'saɪsɪv] adj (action etc) entscheidend; (person) entschlussfreudig; (manner, reply) bestimmt, entschlossen

deck [dɛk] n Deck nt; (also: **record deck**) Plattenspieler m; (of cards) Spiel nt; **to go up on ~** an Deck gehen; **below ~** unter Deck; **top ~** (of bus) Oberdeck nt; **cassette ~** Tapedeck nt

deck chair n Liegestuhl m

deck hand n Deckshelfer(in) m(f)

declaration [dɛklə'reɪʃən] n Erklärung f

declare [dɪ'klɛər] vt erklären; (result) bekannt geben, veröffentlichen; (income etc) angeben; (goods at customs) verzollen

declassify [di:'klæsɪfaɪ] vt freigeben

decline [dɪ'klaɪn] n Rückgang m; (decay) Verfall m ▷ vt ablehnen ▷ vi (strength) nachlassen; (business) zurückgehen; (old person) abbauen; **~ in/of** Rückgang m +gen; **~ in living standards** Sinken nt des Lebensstandards

declutch ['di:'klʌtʃ] vi auskuppeln

decode ['di:'kəud] vt entschlüsseln

decoder [di:'kəudər] n Decoder m

decompose [di:kəm'pəuz] vi (*organic matter*) sich zersetzen; (*corpse*) verwesen

decomposition [di:kɒmpə'zɪʃən] n Zersetzung f

decompression [di:kəm'prɛʃən] n Dekompression f, Druckverminderung f

decompression chamber n Dekompressionskammer f

decongestant [di:kən'dʒɛstənt] n (*Med*) abschwellendes Mittel nt; (: *drops*) Nasentropfen pl

decontaminate [di:kən'tæmɪneɪt] vt entgiften

decontrol [di:kən'trəul] vt freigeben

décor ['deɪkɔːʳ] n Ausstattung f; (*Theat*) Dekor m or nt

decorate ['dɛkəreɪt] vt: **to ~ (with)** verzieren (mit); (*tree, building*) schmücken (mit) ▷ vt (*room, house: from bare walls*) anstreichen und tapezieren; (: *redecorate*) renovieren

decoration [dɛkə'reɪʃən] n Verzierung f; (*on tree, building*) Schmuck m; (*act: see verb*) Verzieren nt; Schmücken nt; (An)streichen nt; Tapezieren nt; (*medal*) Auszeichnung f

decorative ['dɛkərətɪv] adj dekorativ

decorator ['dɛkəreɪtəʳ] n Maler(in) m(f), Anstreicher(in) m(f)

decorum [dɪ'kɔːrəm] n Anstand m

decoy ['di:kɔɪ] n Lockvogel m; (*object*) Köder m; **they used him as a ~ for the enemy** sie benutzten ihn dazu, den Feind anzulocken

decrease ['di:kri:s] vt verringern, reduzieren ▷ vi abnehmen, zurückgehen ▷ n: **~ (in)** Abnahme f (+gen), Rückgang m (+gen); **to be on the ~** abnehmen, zurückgehen

decreasing [di:'kri:sɪŋ] adj abnehmend, zurückgehend

decree [dɪ'kri:] n (*Admin, Law*) Verfügung f; (*Pol*) Erlass m; (*Rel*) Dekret nt ▷ vt: **to ~ (that)** verfügen(, dass), verordnen(, dass)

decree absolute n endgültiges Scheidungsurteil nt

decree nisi [-'naɪsaɪ] n vorläufiges Scheidungsurteil nt

decrepit [dɪ'krɛpɪt] adj (*shack*) baufällig; (*person*) klapprig (*inf*)

decry [dɪ'kraɪ] vt schlechtmachen

dedicate ['dɛdɪkeɪt] vt: **to ~ to** widmen +dat

dedicated ['dɛdɪkeɪtɪd] adj hingebungsvoll, engagiert; (*Comput*) dediziert; **~ word processor** dediziertes Textverarbeitungssystem nt

dedication [dɛdɪ'keɪʃən] n Hingabe f; (*in book, on radio*) Widmung f

deduce [dɪ'dju:s] vt: **to ~ (that)** schließen(, dass), folgern(, dass)

deduct [dɪ'dʌkt] vt abziehen; **to ~ sth (from)** etw abziehen (von); (*esp from wage etc*) etw einbehalten (von)

deduction [dɪ'dʌkʃən] n (*act of deducting*) Abzug m; (*act of deducing*) Folgerung f

deed [di:d] n Tat f; (*Law*) Urkunde f; **~ of covenant** Vertragsurkunde f

deem [di:m] vt (*formal*) erachten für, halten für; **to ~ it wise/helpful to do sth** es für klug/hilfreich halten, etw zu tun

deep [di:p] adj tief ▷ adv: **the spectators stood 20 ~** die Zuschauer standen in 20 Reihen hintereinander; **to be 4 metres ~** 4 Meter tief sein; **knee-~ in water** bis zu den Knien im Wasser; **he took a ~ breath** er holte tief Luft

deepen ['di:pn] vt vertiefen ▷ vi (*crisis*) sich verschärfen; (*mystery*) größer werden

deepfreeze ['di:p'fri:z] n Tiefkühltruhe f

deep-fry ['di:p'fraɪ] vt frittieren

deeply ['di:plɪ] adv (*breathe*) tief; (*interested*) höchst; (*moved, grateful*) zutiefst

deep-rooted ['di:p'ru:tɪd] adj tief verwurzelt; (*habit*) fest eingefahren

deep-sea ['di:p'si:] cpd Tiefsee-; (*fishing*) Hochsee-

deep-seated ['di:p'si:tɪd] adj tief sitzend

deep-set ['di:p'sɛt] adj tief liegend

deer [dɪəʳ] n inv Reh nt; (*male*) Hirsch m; **(red) ~** Rotwild nt; **(roe) ~** Reh nt; **(fallow) ~** Damwild nt

deerskin ['dɪəskɪn] n Hirschleder nt, Rehleder nt

deerstalker ['dɪəstɔːkəʳ] n ≈ Sherlock-Holmes-Mütze f

deface [dɪ'feɪs] vt (*with paint etc*) beschmieren; (*slash, tear*) zerstören

defamation [dɛfə'meɪʃən] n Diffamierung f, Verleumdung f

defamatory [dɪ'fæmətrɪ] adj diffamierend, verleumderisch

default [dɪ'fɔːlt] n (*also:* **default value**) Voreinstellung f ▷ vi: **to ~ on a debt** einer Zahlungsverpflichtung nicht nachkommen; **to win by ~** kampflos gewinnen

defaulter [dɪ'fɔːltəʳ] n säumiger Zahler m, säumige Zahlerin f

default option n Voreinstellung f

defeat [dɪ'fi:t] vt besiegen, schlagen ▷ n (*failure*) Niederlage f; (*of enemy*): **~ (of)** Sieg m (über +acc)

defeatism [dɪ'fi:tɪzəm] n Defätismus m

defeatist [dɪ'fi:tɪst] adj defätistisch ▷ n Defätist(in) m(f)

defect [n 'di:fɛkt, vi dɪ'fɛkt] n Fehler m ▷ vi: **to ~ to the enemy** zum Feind überlaufen; **physical/mental ~** körperlicher/geistiger Schaden m or Defekt m; **to ~ to the West** sich in den Westen absetzen

defective [dɪ'fɛktɪv] adj fehlerhaft

defector [dɪ'fɛktəʳ] n Überläufer(in) m(f)

defence, (*US*) **defense** [dɪ'fɛns] n Verteidigung f; (*justification*) Rechtfertigung f; **in ~ of** zur Verteidigung +gen; **witness for the ~** Zeuge m/Zeugin f der Verteidigung; **the Ministry of D~, the Department of Defense** (*US*) das Verteidigungsministerium

defenceless [dɪ'fɛnslɪs] adj schutzlos

defend [dɪ'fɛnd] vt verteidigen

defendant [dɪ'fɛndənt] n Angeklagte(r) f(m); (*in civil case*) Beklagte(r) f(m)

defender [dɪ'fɛndə^r] n Verteidiger(in) m(f)
defending champion [dɪ'fɛndɪŋ-] n (Sport) Titelverteidiger(in) m(f)
defending counsel [dɪ'fɛndɪŋ-] n Verteidiger(in) m(f)
defense [dɪ'fɛns] (US) n = **defence**
defensive [dɪ'fɛnsɪv] adj defensiv ▷ n: **on the ~** in der Defensive
defer [dɪ'fɜː^r] vt verschieben
deference ['dɛfərəns] n Achtung f, Respekt m; **out of** or **in ~ to** aus Rücksicht auf +acc
deferential [dɛfə'rɛnʃəl] adj ehrerbietig, respektvoll
defiance [dɪ'faɪəns] n Trotz m; **in ~ of sth** einer Sache dat zum Trotz, unter Missachtung einer Sache gen
defiant [dɪ'faɪənt] adj trotzig; (challenging) herausfordernd
defiantly [dɪ'faɪəntlɪ] adv (see adj) trotzig; herausfordernd
deficiency [dɪ'fɪʃənsɪ] n Mangel m; (defect) Unzulänglichkeit f; (deficit) Defizit nt
deficiency disease n Mangelkrankheit f
deficient [dɪ'fɪʃənt] adj: **sb/sth is ~ in sth** jdm/etw fehlt es an etw dat
deficit ['dɛfɪsɪt] n Defizit nt
defile [dɪ'faɪl] vt (memory) beschmutzen; (statue etc) schänden ▷ n Hohlweg m
define [dɪ'faɪn] vt (limits, boundaries) bestimmen, festlegen; (word) definieren
definite ['dɛfɪnɪt] adj definitiv; (date etc) fest; (clear, obvious) klar, eindeutig; (certain) bestimmt; **he was ~ about it** er war sich dat sehr sicher
definite article n bestimmter Artikel m
definitely ['dɛfɪnɪtlɪ] adv bestimmt; (decide) fest, definitiv
definition [dɛfɪ'nɪʃən] n (of word) Definition f; (of photograph etc) Schärfe f
definitive [dɪ'fɪnɪtɪv] adj (account) definitiv; (version) maßgeblich
deflate [diː'fleɪt] vt (tyre, balloon) die Luft ablassen aus; (person) einen Dämpfer versetzen +dat; (Econ) deflationieren
deflation [diː'fleɪʃən] n Deflation f
deflationary [diː'fleɪʃənrɪ] adj deflationistisch
deflect [dɪ'flɛkt] vt (attention) ablenken; (criticism) abwehren; (shot) abfälschen; (light) brechen, beugen
defog ['diː'fɒg] (US) vt von Beschlag freimachen
defogger ['diː'fɒgə^r] (US) n Gebläse nt
deform [dɪ'fɔːm] vt deformieren, verunstalten
deformed [dɪ'fɔːmd] adj deformiert, missgebildet
deformity [dɪ'fɔːmɪtɪ] n Deformität f, Missbildung f
defraud [dɪ'frɔːd] vt: **to ~ sb (of sth)** jdn (um etw) betrügen
defray [dɪ'freɪ] vt: **to ~ sb's expenses** jds Unkosten tragen or übernehmen
defrost [diː'frɒst] vt (fridge) abtauen; (windscreen) entfrosten; (food) auftauen

defroster [diː'frɒstə^r] (US) n (Aut) Gebläse nt
deft [dɛft] adj geschickt
defunct [dɪ'fʌŋkt] adj (industry) stillgelegt; (organization) nicht mehr bestehend
defuse [diː'fjuːz] vt entschärfen
defy [dɪ'faɪ] vt sich widersetzen +dat; (challenge) auffordern; **it defies description** es spottet jeder Beschreibung
degenerate [dɪ'dʒɛnəreɪt] vi degenerieren ▷ adj degeneriert
degradation [dɛgrə'deɪʃən] n Erniedrigung f
degrade [dɪ'greɪd] vt erniedrigen; (reduce the quality of) degradieren
degrading [dɪ'greɪdɪŋ] adj erniedrigend
degree [dɪ'griː] n Grad m; (Scol) akademischer Grad m; **10 ~s below (zero)** 10 Grad unter null; **6 ~s of frost** 6 Grad Kälte or unter null; **a considerable ~ of risk** ein gewisses Risiko; **a ~ in maths** ein Hochschulabschluss m in Mathematik; **by ~s** nach und nach; **to some ~, to a certain ~** einigermaßen, in gewissem Maße
dehydrated [diːhaɪ'dreɪtɪd] adj ausgetrocknet, dehydriert; (milk, eggs) pulverisiert, Trocken-
dehydration [diːhaɪ'dreɪʃən] n Austrocknung f, Dehydration f
de-ice ['diː'aɪs] vt enteisen
de-icer ['diː'aɪsə^r] n Defroster m
deign [deɪn] vi: **to ~ to do sth** sich herablassen, etw zu tun
deity ['diːɪtɪ] n Gottheit f
dejected [dɪ'dʒɛktɪd] adj niedergeschlagen, deprimiert
dejection [dɪ'dʒɛkʃən] n Niedergeschlagenheit f, Depression f
Del. (US) abbr (Post) = Delaware
delay [dɪ'leɪ] vt (decision, ceremony) verschieben, aufschieben; (person, plane, train) aufhalten ▷ vi zögern ▷ n Verzögerung f; (postponement) Aufschub m; **to be ~ed** (person) sich verspäten; (departure etc) verspätet sein; (flight etc) Verspätung haben; **without ~** unverzüglich
delayed-action [dɪ'leɪd'ækʃən] adj (bomb, mine) mit Zeitzünder; (Phot): **~ shutter release** Selbstauslöser m
delectable [dɪ'lɛktəbl] adj (person) reizend; (food) köstlich
delegate ['dɛlɪgɪt] n Delegierte(r) f(m) ▷ vt delegieren; **to ~ sth to sb** jdm mit etw beauftragen; **to ~ sb to do sth** jdn damit beauftragen, etw zu tun
delegation [dɛlɪ'geɪʃən] n Delegation f; (group) Abordnung f, Delegation f
delete [dɪ'liːt] vt streichen; (Comput) löschen
Delhi ['dɛlɪ] n Delhi nt
deli ['dɛlɪ] n Feinkostgeschäft nt
deliberate [adj dɪ'lɪbərɪt, vi dɪ'lɪbəreɪt] adj absichtlich; (action, insult) bewusst; (slow) bedächtig ▷ vi überlegen
deliberately [dɪ'lɪbərɪtlɪ] adv absichtlich, bewusst; (slowly) bedächtig
deliberation [dɪlɪbə'reɪʃən] n Überlegung f; (usu pl: discussions) Beratungen pl

delicacy ['dɛlɪkəsɪ] n Feinheit f, Zartheit f; (of problem) Delikatheit f; (choice food) Delikatesse f

delicate ['dɛlɪkɪt] adj fein; (colour, health) zart; (approach) feinfühlig; (problem) delikat, heikel

delicately ['dɛlɪkɪtlɪ] adv zart, fein; (act, express) feinfühlig

delicatessen [dɛlɪkə'tɛsn] n Feinkostgeschäft nt

delicious [dɪ'lɪʃəs] adj köstlich; (feeling, person) herrlich

delight [dɪ'laɪt] n Freude f ▷ vt erfreuen; **sb takes (a) ~ in sth** etw bereitet jdm große Freude; **sb takes (a) ~ in doing sth** es bereitet jdm große Freude, etw zu tun; **to be the ~ of** die Freude +gen sein; **she was a ~ to interview** es war eine Freude, sie zu interviewen; **the ~s of country life** die Freuden des Landlebens

delighted [dɪ'laɪtɪd] adj: **~ (at** or **with)** erfreut (über +acc), entzückt (über +acc); **to be ~ to do sth** etw gern tun; **I'd be ~** ich würde mich sehr freuen

delightful [dɪ'laɪtful] adj reizend, wunderbar

delimit [di:'lɪmɪt] vt abgrenzen

delineate [dɪ'lɪnɪeɪt] vt (fig) beschreiben

delinquency [dɪ'lɪŋkwənsɪ] n Kriminalität f

delinquent [dɪ'lɪŋkwənt] adj straffällig ▷ n Delinquent(in) m(f)

delirious [dɪ'lɪrɪəs] adj: **to be ~** (with fever) im Delirium sein; (with excitement) im Taumel sein

delirium [dɪ'lɪrɪəm] n Delirium nt

deliver [dɪ'lɪvə'] vt liefern; (letters, papers) zustellen; (hand over) übergeben; (message) überbringen; (speech) halten; (blow) versetzen; (Med: baby) zur Welt bringen; (warning) geben; (ultimatum) stellen; (free): **to ~ (from)** befreien (von); **to ~ the goods** (fig) halten, was man versprochen hat

deliverance [dɪ'lɪvrəns] n Befreiung f

delivery [dɪ'lɪvərɪ] n Lieferung f; (of letters, papers) Zustellung f; (of speaker) Vortrag m; (Med) Entbindung f; **to take ~ of sth** etw in Empfang nehmen

delivery note n Lieferschein m

delivery van, (US) **delivery truck** n Lieferwagen m

delouse ['di:'laus] vt entlausen

delta ['dɛltə] n Delta nt

delude [dɪ'lu:d] vt täuschen; **to ~ o.s.** sich dat etwas vormachen

deluge ['dɛlju:dʒ] n (of rain) Guss m; (fig: of petitions, requests) Flut f

delusion [dɪ'lu:ʒən] n Irrglaube m; **to have ~s of grandeur** größenwahnsinnig sein

de luxe [də'lʌks] adj (hotel, model) Luxus-

delve [dɛlv] vi: **to ~ into** (subject) sich eingehend befassen mit; (cupboard, handbag) tief greifen in +acc

Dem. (US) abbr (Pol) = **Democrat; Democratic**

demagogue ['dɛməgɔg] n Demagoge m, Demagogin f

demand [dɪ'mɑ:nd] vt verlangen; (rights) fordern; (need) erfordern, verlangen ▷ n Verlangen nt; (claim) Forderung f; (Econ) Nachfrage f; **to ~ sth (from** or **of sb)** etw (von jdm) verlangen or fordern; **to be in ~** gefragt sein; **on ~** (available) auf Verlangen; (payable) bei Vorlage or Sicht

demand draft n Sichtwechsel m

demanding [dɪ'mɑ:ndɪŋ] adj anspruchsvoll; (work, child) anstrengend

demarcation [di:mɑ:'keɪʃən] n (of area, tasks) Abgrenzung f

demarcation dispute n Streit m um den Zuständigkeitsbereich

demean [dɪ'mi:n] vt: **to ~ o.s.** sich erniedrigen

demeanour, (US) **demeanor** [dɪ'mi:nə'] n Benehmen nt, Auftreten nt

demented [dɪ'mɛntɪd] adj wahnsinnig

demerger [di:'mɜ:dʒə'] n (Comm) Abspaltung f, Demerger m

demilitarized zone [di:'mɪlɪtəraɪzd-] n entmilitarisierte Zone f

demise [dɪ'maɪz] n Ende nt; (death) Tod m

demist [di:'mɪst] (Brit) vt (Aut: windscreen) von Beschlag freimachen

demister [di:'mɪstə'] (Brit) n (Aut) Gebläse nt

demo ['dɛməu] (inf) n abbr = **demonstration**

demob [di:'mɔb] (inf) vt = **demobilize**

demobilize [di:'məubɪlaɪz] vt aus dem Kriegsdienst entlassen, demobilisieren

democracy [dɪ'mɔkrəsɪ] n Demokratie f

democrat ['dɛməkræt] n Demokrat(in) m(f)

democratic [dɛmə'krætɪk] adj demokratisch

Democratic Party (US) n: **the ~** die Demokratische Partei

demography [dɪ'mɔgrəfɪ] n Demografie f

demolish [dɪ'mɔlɪʃ] vt abreißen, abbrechen; (fig: argument) widerlegen

demolition [dɛmə'lɪʃən] n Abriss m, Abbruch m; (of argument) Widerlegung f

demon ['di:mən] n Dämon m ▷ adj teuflisch gut

demonstrate ['dɛmənstreɪt] vt (theory) demonstrieren; (skill) zeigen, beweisen; (appliance) vorführen ▷ vi: **to ~ (for/against)** demonstrieren (für/gegen)

demonstration [dɛmən'streɪʃən] n Demonstration f; (of gadget, machine etc) Vorführung f; **to hold a ~** eine Demonstration veranstalten or durchführen

demonstrative [dɪ'mɔnstrətɪv] adj demonstrativ

demonstrator ['dɛmənstreɪtə'] n Demonstrant(in) m(f); (sales person) Vorführer(in) m(f); (car) Vorführwagen m; (computer etc) Vorführgerät nt

demoralize [dɪ'mɔrəlaɪz] vt entmutigen

demote [dɪ'məut] vt zurückstufen; (Mil) degradieren

demotion [dɪ'məuʃən] n Zurückstufung f; (Mil) Degradierung f

demur [dɪ'mə:'] (form) vi Einwände pl erheben ▷ n: without ~ widerspruchslos; **they ~red at the suggestion** sie erhoben Einwände gegen den Vorschlag

demure [dɪ'mjuə'] adj zurückhaltend; (smile)

höflich; (*dress*) schlicht

demurrage [dɪ'mʌrɪdʒ] n Liegegeld nt

den [dɛn] n Höhle f; (*of fox*) Bau m; (*room*) Bude f

denationalization ['di:næʃnəlaɪ'zeɪʃən] n Privatisierung f

denationalize [di:'næʃnəlaɪz] vt privatisieren

denatured alcohol [di:'neɪtʃəd-] (*US*) n vergällter Alkohol m

denial [dɪ'naɪəl] n Leugnen nt; (*of rights*) Verweigerung f

denier ['dɛnɪəʳ] n Denier nt

denigrate ['dɛnɪɡreɪt] vt verunglimpfen

denim ['dɛnɪm] n Jeansstoff m; **denims** npl (Blue) Jeans pl

denim jacket n Jeansjacke f

denizen ['dɛnɪzn] n Bewohner(in) m(f); (*person in town*) Einwohner(in) m(f); (*foreigner*) eingebürgerter Ausländer m, eingebürgerte Ausländerin f

Denmark ['dɛnmɑːk] n Dänemark nt

denomination [dɪnɒmɪ'neɪʃən] n (*of money*) Nennwert m; (*Rel*) Konfession f

denominator [dɪ'nɒmɪneɪtəʳ] n Nenner m

denote [dɪ'nəut] vt (*indicate*) hindeuten auf +acc; (*represent*) bezeichnen

denounce [dɪ'nauns] vt (*person*) anprangern; (*action*) verurteilen

dense [dɛns] adj dicht; (*inf: person*) beschränkt

densely ['dɛnslɪ] adv dicht

density ['dɛnsɪtɪ] n Dichte f; **single/double-~ disk** (*Comput*) Diskette f mit einfacher/ doppelter Dichte

dent [dɛnt] n Beule f; (*in pride, ego*) Knacks m ▷ vt (*also*: **make a dent in**) einbeulen; (*pride, ego*) anknacksen

dental ['dɛntl] adj (*filling, hygiene etc*) Zahn-; (*treatment*) zahnärztlich

dental floss [-flɔs] n Zahnseide f

dental surgeon n Zahnarzt m, Zahnärztin f

dentifrice ['dɛntɪfrɪs] n Zahnpasta f

dentist ['dɛntɪst] n Zahnarzt m, Zahnärztin f; (*also*: **dentist's (surgery)**) Zahnarzt m, Zahnarztpraxis f

dentistry ['dɛntɪstrɪ] n Zahnmedizin f

dentures ['dɛntʃəz] npl Zahnprothese f; (*full*) Gebiss nt

denuded [di:'nju:dɪd] adj: ~ **of** entblößt von

denunciation [dɪnʌnsɪ'eɪʃən] n (*of person*) Anprangerung f; (*of action*) Verurteilung f

deny [dɪ'naɪ] vt leugnen; (*involvement*) abstreiten; (*permission, chance*) verweigern; (*country, religion etc*) verleugnen; **he denies having said it** er leugnet or bestreitet, das gesagt zu haben

deodorant [di:'əudərənt] n Deodorant nt

depart [dɪ'pɑːt] vi (*visitor*) abreisen; (: *on foot*) weggehen; (*bus, train*) abfahren; (*plane*) abfliegen; **to ~ from** (*fig*) abweichen von

departed [dɪ'pɑːtɪd] adj: **the (dear) ~** der/ die (liebe) Verstorbene m/f, die (lieben) Verstorbenen pl

department [dɪ'pɑːtmənt] n Abteilung f; (*Scol*) Fachbereich m; (*Pol*) Ministerium nt; **that's**

not my ~ (*fig*) dafür bin ich nicht zuständig; **D~ of State** (*US*) Außenministerium nt

departmental [di:pɑ:t'mɛntl] adj (*budget, costs*) der Abteilung; (*level*) Abteilungs-; ~ **manager** Abteilungsleiter(in) m(f)

department store n Warenhaus nt

departure [dɪ'pɑːtʃəʳ] n (*of visitor*) Abreise f; (*on foot, of employee etc*) Weggang m; (*of bus, train*) Abfahrt f; (*of plane*) Abflug m; (*fig*): ~ **from** Abweichen nt von; **a new ~** ein neuer Weg m

departure lounge n Abflughalle f

depend [dɪ'pɛnd] vi: **to ~ on** abhängen von; (*rely on, trust*) sich verlassen auf +acc; (*financially*) abhängig sein von, angewiesen sein auf +acc; **it ~s** es kommt darauf an; **~ing on the result ...** je nachdem, wie das Ergebnis ausfällt, ...

dependable [dɪ'pɛndəbl] adj zuverlässig

dependant [dɪ'pɛndənt] n abhängige(r) (Familien)angehörige(r) f(m)

dependence [dɪ'pɛndəns] n Abhängigkeit f

dependent [dɪ'pɛndənt] adj: **to be ~ on** (*person*) abhängig sein von, angewiesen sein auf +acc; (*decision*) abhängen von ▷ n = **dependant**

depict [dɪ'pɪkt] vt (*in picture*) darstellen; (*describe*) beschreiben

depilatory [dɪ'pɪlətrɪ] n (*also*: **depilatory cream**) Enthaarungsmittel nt

depleted [dɪ'pli:tɪd] adj (*reserves*) aufgebraucht; (*stocks*) erschöpft

deplorable [dɪ'plɔːrəbl] adj bedauerlich

deplore [dɪ'plɔːʳ] vt verurteilen

deploy [dɪ'plɔɪ] vt einsetzen

depopulate [di:'pɒpjuleɪt] vt entvölkern

depopulation ['di:pɔpju'leɪʃən] n Entvölkerung f

deport [dɪ'pɔːt] vt (*criminal*) deportieren; (*illegal immigrant*) abschieben

deportation [di:pɔ:'teɪʃən] n (*see vb*) Deportation f; Abschiebung f

deportation order n Ausweisung f

deportee [di:pɔ:'ti:] n Deportierte(r) f(m)

deportment [dɪ'pɔːtmənt] n Benehmen nt

depose [dɪ'pəuz] vt absetzen

deposit [dɪ'pɔzɪt] n (*in account*) Guthaben nt; (*down payment*) Anzahlung f; (*for hired goods etc*) Sicherheit f, Kaution f; (*on bottle etc*) Pfand nt; (*Chem*) Ablagerung f; (*of ore, oil*) Lagerstätte f ▷ vt deponieren; (*subj: river: sand etc*) ablagern; **to put down a ~ of £50** eine Anzahlung von £50 machen

deposit account n Sparkonto nt

depositary [dɪ'pɔzɪtərɪ] n Treuhänder(in) m(f)

depositor [dɪ'pɔzɪtəʳ] n Deponent(in) m(f), Einzahler(in) m(f)

depository [dɪ'pɔzɪtərɪ] n (*person*) Treuhänder(in) m(f); (*place*) Lager(haus) nt

depot ['dɛpəu] n Lager(haus) nt; (*for vehicles*) Depot nt; (*US: station*) Bahnhof m; (: *bus station*) Busbahnhof m

depraved [dɪ'preɪvd] adj verworfen

depravity [dɪ'prævɪtɪ] n Verworfenheit f

deprecate ['dɛprɪkeɪt] vt missbilligen

deprecating ['dɛprɪkeɪtɪŋ] *adj (disapproving)* missbilligend; *(apologetic)* entschuldigend
depreciate [dɪ'priːʃɪeɪt] *vi* an Wert verlieren; *(currency)* an Kaufkraft verlieren; *(value)* sinken
depreciation [dɪpriːʃɪ'eɪʃən] *n (see vb)* Wertminderung *f*; Kaufkraftverlust *m*; Sinken *nt*
depress [dɪ'prɛs] *vt* deprimieren; *(price, wages)* drücken; *(press down)* herunterdrücken
depressant [dɪ'prɛsnt] *n* Beruhigungsmittel *nt*
depressed [dɪ'prɛst] *adj* deprimiert, niedergeschlagen; *(price)* gesunken; *(industry)* geschwächt; *(area)* Notstands-; **to get ~** deprimiert werden
depressing [dɪ'prɛsɪŋ] *adj* deprimierend
depression [dɪ'prɛʃən] *n (Psych)* Depressionen *pl*; *(Econ)* Wirtschaftskrise *f*; *(Met)* Tief(druckgebiet) *nt*; *(hollow)* Vertiefung *f*
deprivation [dɛprɪ'veɪʃən] *n* Entbehrung *f*, Not *f*; *(of freedom, rights etc)* Entzug *m*
deprive [dɪ'praɪv] *vt*: **to ~ sb of sth** *(liberty)* jdm etw entziehen; *(life)* jdm etw nehmen
deprived [dɪ'praɪvd] *adj* benachteiligt; *(area)* Not leidend
dept *abbr* = **department**
depth [dɛpθ] *n* Tiefe *f*; **in the ~s of** in den Tiefen *+gen*; **in the ~s of despair** in tiefster Verzweiflung; **in the ~s of winter** im tiefsten Winter; **at a ~ of 3 metres** in 3 Meter Tiefe; **to be out of one's ~** *(in water)* nicht mehr stehen können; *(fig)* überfordert sein; **to study sth in ~** etw gründlich *or* eingehend studieren
depth charge *n* Wasserbombe *f*
deputation [dɛpju'teɪʃən] *n* Abordnung *f*
deputize ['dɛpjutaɪz] *vi*: **to ~ for sb** jdn vertreten
deputy ['dɛpjutɪ] *cpd* stellvertretend ▷ *n* (Stell)vertreter(in) *m(f)*; *(Pol)* Abgeordnete(r) *f(m)*; *(US: also:* **deputy sheriff**) Hilfssheriff *m*; **~ head** *(Brit: Scol)* Konrektor(in) *m(f)*
derail [dɪ'reɪl] *vt*: **to be ~ed** entgleisen
derailment [dɪ'reɪlmənt] *n* Entgleisung *f*
deranged [dɪ'reɪndʒd] *adj*: **to be mentally ~** geistesgestört sein
derby ['dɜːrbɪ] *n* Derby *nt*; *(US: hat)* Melone *f*
deregulate [dɪ'rɛgjuleɪt] *vt* staatliche Kontrollen aufheben bei
deregulation [dɪ'rɛgju'leɪʃən] *n* Aufhebung *f* staatlicher Kontrollen
derelict ['dɛrɪlɪkt] *adj* verfallen
deride [dɪ'raɪd] *vt* sich lustig machen über *+acc*
derision [dɪ'rɪʒən] *n* Hohn *m*, Spott *m*
derisive [dɪ'raɪsɪv] *adj* spöttisch
derisory [dɪ'raɪsərɪ] *adj* spöttisch; *(sum)* lächerlich
derivation [dɛrɪ'veɪʃən] *n* Ableitung *f*
derivative [dɪ'rɪvətɪv] *n (Ling)* Ableitung *f*; *(Chem)* Derivat *nt* ▷ *adj* nachahmend
derive [dɪ'raɪv] *vt*: **to ~ (from)** gewinnen (aus); *(benefit)* ziehen (aus) ▷ *vi*: **to ~ from** *(originate in)* sich herleiten *or* ableiten von; **to ~ pleasure from** Freude haben an *+dat*
dermatitis [dɜːmə'taɪtɪs] *n* Hautentzündung

f, Dermatitis *f*
dermatology [dɜːmə'tɔlədʒɪ] *n* Dermatologie *f*
derogatory [dɪ'rɔgətərɪ] *adj* abfällig
derrick ['dɛrɪk] *n (on ship)* Derrickkran *m*; *(on well)* Bohrturm *m*
derv [dɜːv] *(Brit) n (Aut)* Diesel(kraftstoff) *m*
desalination [diːsælɪ'neɪʃən] *n* Entsalzung *f*
descend [dɪ'sɛnd] *vt* hinuntergehen, hinuntersteigen; *(lift, vehicle)* hinunterfahren; *(road)* hinunterführen ▷ *vi* hinuntergehen; *(lift)* nach unten fahren; **to ~ from** abstammen von; **to ~ to** sich erniedrigen zu; **in ~ing order of importance** nach Wichtigkeit geordnet
▸ **descend on** *vt fus* überfallen; *(subj: misfortune)* hereinbrechen über *+acc*; *(: gloom)* befallen; *(: silence)* sich senken auf *+acc*; **visitors ~ed (up)on us** der Besuch hat uns überfallen
descendant [dɪ'sɛndənt] *n* Nachkomme *m*
descent [dɪ'sɛnt] *n* Abstieg *m*; *(origin)* Abstammung *f*
describe [dɪs'kraɪb] *vt* beschreiben
description [dɪs'krɪpʃən] *n* Beschreibung *f*; *(sort)*: **of every ~** aller Art
descriptive [dɪs'krɪptɪv] *adj* deskriptiv
desecrate ['dɛsɪkreɪt] *vt* schänden
desegregate [diː'sɛgrɪgeɪt] *vt* die Rassentrennung aufheben in *+dat*
desert [*n* 'dɛzət, *vb* dɪ'zɜːt] *n* Wüste *f* ▷ *vt* verlassen ▷ *vi* desertieren; *see also* **deserts**
deserter [dɪ'zɜːtə^r] *n* Deserteur *m*
desertion [dɪ'zɜːʃən] *n* Desertion *f*, Fahnenflucht *f*; *(Law)* böswilliges Verlassen *nt*
desert island *n* einsame *or* verlassene Insel *f*
deserts [dɪ'zɜːts] *npl*: **to get one's just ~** bekommen, was man verdient
deserve [dɪ'zɜːv] *vt* verdienen
deservedly [dɪ'zɜːvɪdlɪ] *adv* verdientermaßen
deserving [dɪ'zɜːvɪŋ] *adj* verdienstvoll
desiccated ['dɛsɪkeɪtɪd] *adj* vertrocknet; *(coconut)* getrocknet
design [dɪ'zaɪn] *n* Design *nt*; *(process)* Entwurf *m*, Gestaltung *f*; *(sketch)* Entwurf *m*; *(layout, shape)* Form *f*; *(pattern)* Muster *nt*; *(of car)* Konstruktion *f*; *(intention)* Plan *m*, Absicht *f* ▷ *vt* entwerfen; **to have ~s on** es abgesehen haben auf *+acc*; **well-~ed** mit gutem Design
design and technology *(Brit) n (Scol)* = Design und Technologie
designate [*vt* 'dɛzɪgneɪt, *adj* 'dɛzɪgnɪt] *vt* bestimmen, ernennen ▷ *adj* designiert
designation [dɛzɪg'neɪʃən] *n* Bezeichnung *f*
designer [dɪ'zaɪnə^r] *n* Designer(in) *m(f)*; *(Tech)* Konstrukteur(in) *m(f)*; *(also:* **fashion designer**) Modeschöpfer(in) *m(f)* ▷ *adj (clothes etc)* Designer-
desirability [dɪzaɪərə'bɪlɪtɪ] *n*: **they discussed the ~ of the plan** sie besprachen, ob der Plan wünschenswert sei
desirable [dɪ'zaɪərəbl] *adj (proper)* wünschenswert; *(attractive)* reizvoll, attraktiv
desire [dɪ'zaɪə^r] *n* Wunsch *m*; *(sexual)* Verlangen *nt*, Begehren *nt* ▷ *vt* wünschen; *(lust after)*

begehren; **to ~ to do sth/that** wünschen, etw zu tun/dass

desirous [dɪˈzaɪərəs] *adj*: **to be ~ of doing sth** den Wunsch haben, etw zu tun

desist [dɪˈzɪst] *vi*: **to ~ (from)** absehen (von), Abstand nehmen (von)

desk [dɛsk] *n* Schreibtisch *m*; *(for pupil)* Pult *nt*; *(in hotel)* Empfang *m*; *(at airport)* Schalter *m*; *(Brit: in shop, restaurant)* Kasse *f*

desk job *n* Bürojob *m*

desktop [ˈdɛsktɔp] *n* Arbeitsfläche *f*

desktop publishing *n* Desktop-Publishing *nt*

desolate [ˈdɛsəlɪt] *adj* trostlos

desolation [dɛsəˈleɪʃən] *n* Trostlosigkeit *f*

despair [dɪsˈpɛər] *n* Verzweiflung *f* ▷ *vi*: **to ~ of** alle Hoffnung aufgeben auf +*acc*; **to be in ~** verzweifelt sein

despatch [dɪsˈpætʃ] *n, vt* = **dispatch**

desperate [ˈdɛspərɪt] *adj* verzweifelt; *(shortage)* akut; *(criminal)* zum Äußersten entschlossen; **to be ~ for sth/to do sth** etw dringend brauchen/unbedingt tun wollen

desperately [ˈdɛspərɪtlɪ] *adv* (shout, struggle etc) verzweifelt; *(ill)* schwer; *(unhappy etc)* äußerst

desperation [dɛspəˈreɪʃən] *n* Verzweiflung *f*; **in (sheer) ~** aus (reiner) Verzweiflung

despicable [dɪsˈpɪkəbl] *adj* (action) verabscheuungswürdig; *(person)* widerwärtig

despise [dɪsˈpaɪz] *vt* verachten

despite [dɪsˈpaɪt] *prep* trotz +*gen*

despondent [dɪsˈpɔndənt] *adj* niedergeschlagen, mutlos

despot [ˈdɛspɔt] *n* Despot *m*

dessert [dɪˈzəːt] *n* Nachtisch *m*, Dessert *nt*

dessertspoon [dɪˈzəːtspuːn] *n* Dessertlöffel *m*

destabilize [diːˈsteɪbɪlaɪz] *vt* destabilisieren

destination [dɛstɪˈneɪʃən] *n* (Reise)ziel *nt*; *(of mail)* Bestimmungsort *m*

destined [ˈdɛstɪnd] *adj*: **to be ~ to do sth** dazu bestimmt *or* ausersehen sein, etw zu tun; **to be ~ for** bestimmt *or* ausersehen sein für

destiny [ˈdɛstɪnɪ] *n* Schicksal *nt*

destitute [ˈdɛstɪtjuːt] *adj* mittellos

destroy [dɪsˈtrɔɪ] *vt* zerstören; *(animal)* töten

destroyer [dɪsˈtrɔɪər] *n* Zerstörer *m*

destruction [dɪsˈtrʌkʃən] *n* Zerstörung *f*

destructive [dɪsˈtrʌktɪv] *adj* zerstörerisch; *(child, criticism etc)* destruktiv

desultory [ˈdɛsəltərɪ] *adj* flüchtig; *(conversation)* zwanglos

detach [dɪˈtætʃ] *vt* (remove) entfernen; *(unclip)* abnehmen; *(unstick)* ablösen

detachable [dɪˈtætʃəbl] *adj* abnehmbar

detached [dɪˈtætʃt] *adj* distanziert; *(house)* frei stehend, Einzel-

detachment [dɪˈtætʃmənt] *n* Distanz *f*; *(Mil)* Sonderkommando *nt*

detail [ˈdiːteɪl] *n* Einzelheit *f*; *(no pl: in picture, one's work etc)* Detail *nt*; *(trifle)* unwichtige Einzelheit *f* ▷ *vt* (einzeln) aufführen; **in ~** in Einzelheiten; **to go into ~s** auf Einzelheiten eingehen, ins Detail gehen

detailed [ˈdiːteɪld] *adj* detailliert, genau

detain [dɪˈteɪn] *vt* aufhalten; *(in captivity)* in Haft halten; *(in hospital)* festhalten

detainee [diːteɪˈniː] *n* Häftling *m*

detect [dɪˈtɛkt] *vt* wahrnehmen; *(Med, Tech)* feststellen; *(Mil)* ausfindig machen

detection [dɪˈtɛkʃən] *n* Entdeckung *f*, Feststellung *f*; **crime ~** Ermittlungsarbeit *f*; **to escape ~** *(criminal)* nicht gefasst werden; *(mistake)* der Aufmerksamkeit *dat* entgehen

detective [dɪˈtɛktɪv] *n* Kriminalbeamte(r) *m*; **private ~** Privatdetektiv *m*

detective story *n* Kriminalgeschichte *f*, Detektivgeschichte *f*

detector [dɪˈtɛktər] *n* Detektor *m*

détente [deɪˈtɑːnt] *n* Entspannung *f*, Détente *f*

detention [dɪˈtɛnʃən] *n* (arrest) Festnahme *f*; *(captivity)* Haft *f*; *(Scol)* Nachsitzen *nt*

deter [dɪˈtəː] *vt* (discourage) abschrecken; *(dissuade)* abhalten

detergent [dɪˈtəːdʒənt] *n* Reinigungsmittel *nt*; *(for clothes)* Waschmittel *nt*; *(for dishes)* Spülmittel *nt*

deteriorate [dɪˈtɪərɪəreɪt] *vi* sich verschlechtern

deterioration [dɪtɪərɪəˈreɪʃən] *n* Verschlechterung *f*

determination [dɪtəːmɪˈneɪʃən] *n* Entschlossenheit *f*; *(establishment)* Festsetzung *f*

determine [dɪˈtəːmɪn] *vt* (facts) feststellen; *(limits etc)* festlegen; **to ~ that** beschließen, dass; **to ~ to do sth** sich entschließen, etw zu tun

determined [dɪˈtəːmɪnd] *adj* entschlossen; *(quantity)* bestimmt; **to be ~ to do sth** (fest) entschlossen sein, etw zu tun

deterrence [dɪˈtɛrəns] *n* Abschreckung *f*

deterrent [dɪˈtɛrənt] *n* Abschreckungsmittel *nt*; **to act as a ~** als Abschreckung(smittel) dienen

detest [dɪˈtɛst] *vt* verabscheuen

detestable [dɪˈtɛstəbl] *adj* abscheulich, widerwärtig

detonate [ˈdɛtəneɪt] *vi* detonieren ▷ *vt* zur Explosion bringen

detonator [ˈdɛtəneɪtər] *n* Sprengkapsel *f*

detour [ˈdiːtuər] *n* Umweg *m*; *(US: Aut)* Umleitung *f*

detract [dɪˈtrækt] *vi*: **to ~ from** schmälern; *(effect)* beeinträchtigen

detractor [dɪˈtræktər] *n* Kritiker(in) *m(f)*

detriment [ˈdɛtrɪmənt] *n*: **to the ~ of** zum Schaden +*gen*; **without ~ to** ohne Schaden für

detrimental [dɛtrɪˈmɛntl] *adj*: **to be ~ to** schaden +*dat*

deuce [djuːs] *n* (Tennis) Einstand *m*

devaluation [dɪvæljuˈeɪʃən] *n* Abwertung *f*

devalue [ˈdiːˈvæljuː] *vt* abwerten

devastate [ˈdɛvəsteɪt] *vt* verwüsten; *(fig: shock)*: **to be ~d by** niedergeschmettert sein von

devastating [ˈdɛvəsteɪtɪŋ] *adj* verheerend; *(announcement, news)* niederschmetternd

devastation [dɛvəs'teɪʃən] n Verwüstung f

develop [dɪ'vɛləp] vt entwickeln; (business) erweitern, ausbauen; (land, resource) erschließen; (disease) bekommen ▷ vi sich entwickeln; (facts) an den Tag kommen; (symptoms) auftreten; **to ~ a taste for sth** Geschmack an etw finden; **the machine/car ~ed a fault/engine trouble** an dem Gerät/ dem Wagen trat ein Defekt/ein Motorschaden auf; **to ~ into** sich entwickeln zu, werden

developer [dɪ'vɛləpəʳ] n (also: **property developer**) Bauunternehmer und Immobilienmakler

developing country [dɪ'vɛləpɪŋ-] n Entwicklungsland nt

development [dɪ'vɛləpmənt] n Entwicklung f; (of land) Erschließung f

development area n Entwicklungsgebiet nt

deviant ['di:vɪənt] adj abweichend

deviate ['di:vɪeɪt] vi: **to ~ (from)** abweichen (von)

deviation [di:vɪ'eɪʃən] n Abweichung f

device [dɪ'vaɪs] n Gerät nt; (ploy, stratagem) Trick m; **explosive ~** Sprengkörper m

devil ['dɛvl] n Teufel m; **go on, be a ~!** nur zu, riskier mal was!; **talk of the ~!** wenn man vom Teufel spricht!

devilish ['dɛvlɪʃ] adj teuflisch

devil's advocate ['dɛvlz-] n Advocatus Diaboli m

devious ['di:vɪəs] adj (person) verschlagen; (route, path) gewunden

devise [dɪ'vaɪz] vt sich dat ausdenken; (machine) entwerfen

devoid [dɪ'vɔɪd] adj: **~ of** bar +gen, ohne +acc

devolution [di:və'lu:ʃən] n Dezentralisierung f

devolve [dɪ'vɔlv] vt übertragen ▷ vi: **to ~ (up) on** übergehen auf +acc

devote [dɪ'vəut] vt: **to ~ sth/o.s. to** etw/sich widmen +dat

devoted [dɪ'vəutɪd] adj treu; (admirer) eifrig; **to be ~ to sb** jdn innig lieben; **the book is ~ to politics** das Buch widmet sich ganz der Politik dat

devotee [dɛvəu'ti:] n (fan) Liebhaber(in) m(f); (Rel) Anhänger(in) m(f)

devotion [dɪ'vəuʃən] n (affection) Ergebenheit f; (dedication) Hingabe f; (Rel) Andacht f

devour [dɪ'vauəʳ] vt verschlingen

devout [dɪ'vaut] adj fromm

dew [dju:] n Tau m

dexterity [dɛks'tɛrɪtɪ] n Geschicklichkeit f; (mental) Gewandtheit f

dexterous, dextrous ['dɛkstrəs] adj geschickt

DfEE (Brit) n abbr (= Department for Education and Employment) ≈ Ministerium nt für Bildung und Arbeit

dg abbr (= decigram) dg

DHSS (Brit) n abbr (formerly: = Department of Health and Social Security) Ministerium für Gesundheit und Sozialfürsorge

diabetes [daɪə'bi:ti:z] n Zuckerkrankheit f

diabetic [daɪə'bɛtɪk] adj zuckerkrank; (chocolate, jam) Diabetiker- ▷ n Diabetiker(in) m(f)

diabolical [daɪə'bɔlɪkl] (inf) adj schrecklich, fürchterlich

diaeresis [daɪ'ɛrɪsɪs] n Diärese f

diagnose [daɪəg'nəuz] vt diagnostizieren

diagnoses [-si:z] pl of **diagnosis**

diagnosis [daɪəg'nəusɪs] (pl **diagnoses**) n Diagnose f

diagonal [daɪ'ægənl] adj diagonal ▷ n Diagonale f

diagram ['daɪəgræm] n Diagramm nt, Schaubild nt

dial ['daɪəl] n Zifferblatt nt; (on radio set) Einstellskala f; (of phone) Wählscheibe f ▷ vt wählen; **to ~ a wrong number** sich verwählen; **can I ~ London direct?** kann ich nach London durchwählen?

dial. abbr = **dialect**

dial code (US) n = **dialling code**

dialect ['daɪəlɛkt] n Dialekt m

dialling code ['daɪəlɪŋ-], (US) **dial code** n Vorwahl f

dialling tone, (US) **dial tone** n Amtszeichen nt

dialogue, (US) **dialog** ['daɪəlɔg] n Dialog m; (conversation) Gespräch nt, Dialog m

dial tone (US) n = **dialling tone**

dialysis [daɪ'ælɪsɪs] n Dialyse f

diameter [daɪ'æmɪtəʳ] n Durchmesser m

diametrically [daɪə'mɛtrɪklɪ] adv: **~ opposed (to)** diametral entgegengesetzt (+dat)

diamond ['daɪəmənd] n Diamant m; (shape) Raute f; **diamonds** npl (Cards) Karo nt

diamond ring n Diamantring m

diaper ['daɪəpəʳ] (US) n Windel f

diaphragm ['daɪəfræm] n Zwerchfell nt; (contraceptive) Pessar nt

diarrhoea, (US) **diarrhea** [daɪə'ri:ə] n Durchfall m

diary ['daɪərɪ] n (Termin)kalender m; (daily account) Tagebuch nt; **to keep a ~** Tagebuch führen

diatribe ['daɪətraɪb] n Schmährede f; (written) Schmähschrift f

dice [daɪs] n inv Würfel m ▷ vt in Würfel schneiden

dicey ['daɪsɪ] (inf) adj riskant

dichotomy [daɪ'kɔtəmɪ] n Dichotomie f, Kluft f

dickhead ['dɪkhɛd] (inf) n Knallkopf m

Dictaphone® ['dɪktəfəun] n Diktafon nt, Diktiergerät nt

dictate [dɪk'teɪt] vt diktieren ▷ n Diktat nt; (principle): **the ~s of** die Gebote +gen ▷ vi: **to ~ to** diktieren +dat; **I won't be ~d to** ich lasse mir keine Vorschriften machen

dictation [dɪk'teɪʃən] n Diktat nt; **at ~ speed** im Diktiertempo

dictator [dɪk'teɪtəʳ] n Diktator m

dictatorship [dɪk'teɪtəʃɪp] n Diktatur f

diction ['dɪkʃən] n Diktion f

dictionary ['dɪkʃənrɪ] n Wörterbuch nt

did [dɪd] pt of **do**

didactic [daɪ'dæktɪk] adj didaktisch

diddle ['dɪdl] (inf) vt übers Ohr hauen

d

517

didn't ['dɪdnt] = **did not**

die [daɪ] n (pl: **dice**) Würfel m; (: dies) Gussform f ▷ vi sterben; (plant) eingehen; (fig: noise) aufhören; (: smile) vergehen; (engine) stehen bleiben; **to ~ of** or **from** sterben an +dat; **to be dying** im Sterben liegen; **to be dying for sth** etw unbedingt brauchen; **to be dying to do sth** darauf brennen, etw zu tun

▶ **die away** vi (sound) schwächer werden; (light) nachlassen

▶ **die down** vi (wind) sich legen; (fire) herunterbrennen; (excitement, noise) nachlassen

▶ **die out** vi aussterben

die-hard ['daɪhɑːd] n Ewiggestrige(r) f(m)

diesel ['diːzl] n (vehicle) Diesel m; (also: **diesel oil**) Diesel(kraftstoff) m

diesel engine n Dieselmotor m

diet ['daɪət] n Ernährung f; (Med) Diät f; (when slimming) Schlankheitskur f ▷ vi (also: **be on a diet**) eine Schlankheitskur machen; **to live on a ~ of** sich ernähren von, leben von

dietician [daɪə'tɪʃən] n Diätassistent(in) m(f)

differ ['dɪfəʳ] vi (be different): **to ~ (from)** sich unterscheiden (von); (disagree): (disagree): **to ~ (about)** anderer Meinung sein (über +acc); **to agree to ~** sich dat verschiedene Meinungen zugestehen

difference ['dɪfrəns] n Unterschied m; (disagreement) Differenz f, Auseinandersetzung f; **it makes no ~ to me** das ist mir egal or einerlei; **to settle one's ~s** die Differenzen or Meinungsverschiedenheiten beilegen

different ['dɪfrənt] adj (various people, things) verschieden, unterschiedlich; **to be ~ (from)** anders sein (als)

differential [dɪfə'rɛnʃəl] n (Math) Differenzial nt; (Brit: in wages) (Einkommens)unterschied m

differentiate [dɪfə'rɛnʃɪeɪt] vi: **to ~ (between)** unterscheiden (zwischen) ▷ vt: **to ~ A from B** A von B unterscheiden

differently ['dɪfrəntlɪ] adv anders; (shaped, designed) verschieden, unterschiedlich

difficult ['dɪfɪkəlt] adj schwierig; (task, problem) schwer, schwierig; **~ to understand** schwer zu verstehen

difficulty ['dɪfɪkəltɪ] n Schwierigkeit f; **to be in/get into difficulties** in Schwierigkeiten sein/geraten

diffidence ['dɪfɪdəns] n Bescheidenheit f, Zurückhaltung f

diffident ['dɪfɪdənt] adj bescheiden, zurückhaltend

diffuse [dɪ'fjuːs] adj diffus ▷ vt verbreiten

dig [dɪg] (pt, pp **dug**) vt graben; (garden) umgraben ▷ n (prod) Stoß m; (archaeological) (Aus)grabung f; (remark) Seitenhieb m, spitze Bemerkung f; **to ~ one's nails into sth** seine Nägel in etw acc krallen

▶ **dig in** vi (fig: inf: eat) reinhauen ▷ vt (compost) untergraben, eingraben; (knife) hineinstoßen; (claw) festkrallen; **to ~ one's heels in** (fig) sich auf die Hinterbeine stellen (inf)

▶ **dig into** vt fus (savings) angreifen; (snow, soil) ein Loch graben in +acc; **to ~ into one's pockets for sth** in seinen Taschen nach etw suchen or wühlen

▶ **dig out** vt ausgraben

▶ **dig up** vt ausgraben

digest [daɪ'dʒɛst] vt verdauen ▷ n Digest m or nt, Auswahl f

digestible [dɪ'dʒɛstəbl] adj verdaulich

digestion [dɪ'dʒɛstʃən] n Verdauung f

digestive [dɪ'dʒɛstɪv] adj (system, upsets) Verdauungs- ▷ n Keks aus Vollkornmehl

digit ['dɪdʒɪt] n (number) Ziffer f; (finger) Finger m

digital ['dɪdʒɪtl] adj (watch, display etc) Digital-

digital computer n Digitalrechner m

digital projector n Beamer m

digital TV n Digitalfernsehen nt

dignified ['dɪgnɪfaɪd] adj würdevoll

dignitary ['dɪgnɪtərɪ] n Würdenträger(in) m(f)

dignity ['dɪgnɪtɪ] n Würde f

digress [daɪ'grɛs] vi: **to ~ (from)** abschweifen (von)

digression [daɪ'grɛʃən] n Abschweifung f

digs [dɪgz] (Brit: inf) npl Bude f

dike [daɪk] n = **dyke**

dilapidated [dɪ'læpɪdeɪtɪd] adj verfallen

dilate [daɪ'leɪt] vi sich weiten ▷ vt weiten

dilatory ['dɪlətərɪ] adj langsam

dilemma [daɪ'lɛmə] n Dilemma nt; **to be in a ~** sich in einem Dilemma befinden, in der Klemme sitzen (inf)

diligence ['dɪlɪdʒəns] n Fleiß m

diligent ['dɪlɪdʒənt] adj fleißig; (research) sorgfältig, genau

dill [dɪl] n Dill m

dilly-dally ['dɪlɪ'dælɪ] vi trödeln

dilute [daɪ'luːt] vt verdünnen; (belief, principle) schwächen ▷ adj verdünnt

dim [dɪm] adj schwach; (outline, figure) undeutlich, verschwommen; (room) dämmerig; (future) düster; (prospects) schlecht; (inf: person) schwer von Begriff ▷ vt (light) dämpfen; (US: Aut) abblenden; **to take a ~ view of sth** wenig or nicht viel von etw halten

dime [daɪm] (US) n Zehncentstück nt

dimension [daɪ'mɛnʃən] n (aspect) Dimension f; (measurement) Abmessung f, Maß nt; (also pl: scale, size) Ausmaß nt

-dimensional [dɪ'mɛnʃənl] adj suff -dimensional

diminish [dɪ'mɪnɪʃ] vi sich verringern ▷ vt verringern

diminished responsibility n verminderte Zurechnungsfähigkeit f

diminutive [dɪ'mɪnjutɪv] adj winzig ▷ n Verkleinerungsform f

dimly ['dɪmlɪ] adv schwach; (see) undeutlich, verschwommen

dimmer ['dɪmə] n (also: **dimmer switch**) Dimmer m; (US: Aut) Abblendschalter m

dimmer ['dɪmə]

dimmer switch n (Elec) Dimmer m; (US: Aut) Abblendschalter m

dimmers ['dɪməz] (US) npl (Aut: dipped headlights) Abblendlicht nt; (: parking lights) Parklicht nt

dimple ['dɪmpl] n Grübchen nt

dim-witted ['dɪm'wɪtɪd] (inf) adj dämlich

din [dɪn] n Lärm m, Getöse nt ▷ vt (inf): **to ~ sth into sb** jdm etw einbläuen

dine [daɪn] vi speisen

diner ['daɪnər] n Gast m; (US: restaurant) Esslokal nt

dinghy ['dɪŋgɪ] n (also: **rubber dinghy**) Schlauchboot nt; (also: **sailing dinghy**) Dingi nt

dingy ['dɪndʒɪ] adj schäbig; (clothes, curtains etc) schmuddelig

dining car ['daɪnɪŋ-] (Brit) n Speisewagen m

dining room n Esszimmer nt; (in hotel) Speiseraum m

dinner ['dɪnər] n (evening meal) Abendessen nt; (lunch) Mittagessen nt; (banquet) (Fest)essen nt

dinner jacket n Smokingjackett nt

dinner party n Abendgesellschaft f (mit Essen)

dinner service n Tafelservice nt

dinner time n Essenszeit f

dinosaur ['daɪnəsɔːr] n Dinosaurier m

dint [dɪnt] n: **by ~ of** durch +acc

diocese ['daɪəsɪs] n Diözese f

dioxide [daɪ'ɔksaɪd] n Dioxid nt

Dip. (Brit) abbr = **diploma**

dip [dɪp] n Senke f; (in sea) kurzes Bad nt; (Culin) Dip m; (for sheep) Desinfektionslösung f ▷ vt eintauchen; (Brit: Aut) abblenden ▷ vi abfallen

diphtheria [dɪf'θɪərɪə] n Diphtherie f

diphthong ['dɪfθɒŋ] n Diphthong m

diploma [dɪ'pləumə] n Diplom nt

diplomacy [dɪ'pləuməsɪ] n Diplomatie f

diplomat ['dɪpləmæt] n Diplomat(in) m(f)

diplomatic [dɪplə'mætɪk] adj diplomatisch; **to break off ~ relations (with)** die diplomatischen Beziehungen abbrechen (mit)

diplomatic corps n diplomatisches Korps nt

diplomatic immunity n Immunität f

dip rod ['dɪprɒd] (US) n Ölmessstab m

dipstick ['dɪpstɪk] (Brit) n Ölmessstab m

dip switch (Brit) n Abblendschalter m

dire [daɪər] adj schrecklich

direct [daɪ'rɛkt] adj, adv direkt ▷ vt (company, project, programme etc) leiten; (play, film) Regie führen bei; **to ~ sb to do sth** jdn anweisen, etw zu tun; **can you ~ me to ...?** können Sie mir den Weg nach ... sagen?

direct access n (Comput) Direktzugriff m

direct cost n direkte Kosten pl

direct current n Gleichstrom m

direct debit (Brit) n Einzugsauftrag m; (transaction) automatische Abbuchung f

direct dialling n Selbstwahl f

direct hit n Volltreffer m

direction [dɪ'rɛkʃən] n Richtung f; (TV, Radio) Leitung f; (Cine) Regie f; **directions** npl (instructions) Anweisungen pl; **sense of ~** Orientierungssinn m; **~s for use** Gebrauchsanweisung f, Gebrauchsanleitung f; **to ask for ~s** nach dem Weg fragen; **in the ~ of** in Richtung

directional [dɪ'rɛkʃənl] adj (aerial) Richt-

directive [dɪ'rɛktɪv] n Direktive f, Weisung f; **government ~** Regierungserlass m

direct labour n (Comm) Produktionsarbeit f; (Brit) eigene Arbeitskräfte pl

directly [dɪ'rɛktlɪ] adv direkt; (at once) sofort, gleich

direct mail n Werbebriefe pl

direct mailshot (Brit) n Direktwerbung f per Post

directness [daɪ'rɛktnɪs] n Direktheit f

director [dɪ'rɛktər] n Direktor(in) m(f); (of project, TV, Radio) Leiter(in) m(f); (Cine) Regisseur(in) m(f)

Director of Public Prosecutions (Brit) n ≈ Generalstaatsanwalt m, ≈ Generalstaatsanwältin f

directory [dɪ'rɛktərɪ] n (also: **telephone directory**) Telefonbuch nt; (also: **street directory**) Einwohnerverzeichnis nt; (Comput) Verzeichnis nt; (Comm) Branchenverzeichnis nt

directory enquiries, (US) **directory assistance** n (Fernsprech)auskunft f

dirt [dəːt] n Schmutz m; (earth) Erde f; **to treat sb like ~** jdn wie (den letzten) Dreck behandeln

dirt-cheap ['dəːt'tʃiːp] adj spottbillig

dirt road n unbefestigte Straße f

dirty ['dəːtɪ] adj schmutzig; (story) unanständig ▷ vt beschmutzen

dirty bomb n schmutzige Bombe f

dirty trick n gemeiner Trick m

disability [dɪsə'bɪlɪtɪ] n Behinderung f

disability allowance n Behindertenbeihilfe f

disable [dɪs'eɪbl] vt zum Invaliden machen; (tank, gun) unbrauchbar machen

disabled [dɪs'eɪbld] adj behindert ▷ npl: **the ~** die Behinderten pl

disabuse [dɪsə'bjuːz] vt: **to ~ sb (of)** jdn befreien (von)

disadvantage [dɪsəd'vɑːntɪdʒ] n Nachteil m; (detriment) Schaden m; **to be at a ~** benachteiligt or im Nachteil sein

disadvantaged [dɪsəd'vɑːntɪdʒd] adj benachteiligt

disadvantageous [dɪsædvɑːn'teɪdʒəs] adj ungünstig

disaffected [dɪsə'fɛktɪd] adj entfremdet

disaffection [dɪsə'fɛkʃən] n Entfremdung f

disagree [dɪsə'griː] vi nicht übereinstimmen; (to be against, think differently): **to ~ (with)** nicht einverstanden sein (mit); **I ~ with you** ich bin anderer Meinung; **garlic ~s with me** ich vertrage keinen Knoblauch, Knoblauch bekommt mir nicht

disagreeable [dɪsə'griːəbl] adj unangenehm; (person) unsympathisch

disagreement [dɪsə'griːmənt] n Uneinigkeit f; (argument) Meinungsverschiedenheit f; **to have a ~ with sb** sich mit jdm nicht einig sein

disallow ['dɪsə'lau] vt (appeal) abweisen; (goal) nicht anerkennen, nicht geben

519

disappear [dɪsə'pɪəʳ] vi verschwinden; (custom etc) aussterben

disappearance [dɪsə'pɪərəns] n (see vi) Verschwinden nt; Aussterben nt

disappoint [dɪsə'pɔɪnt] vt enttäuschen

disappointed [dɪsə'pɔɪntɪd] adj enttäuscht

disappointing [dɪsə'pɔɪntɪŋ] adj enttäuschend

disappointment [dɪsə'pɔɪntmənt] n Enttäuschung f

disapproval [dɪsə'pruːvəl] n Missbilligung f

disapprove [dɪsə'pruːv] vi dagegen sein; **to ~ of** missbilligen +acc

disapproving [dɪsə'pruːvɪŋ] adj missbilligend

disarm [dɪs'ɑːm] vt entwaffnen; (criticism) zum Verstummen bringen ▷ vi abrüsten

disarmament [dɪs'ɑːməmənt] n Abrüstung f

disarming [dɪs'ɑːmɪŋ] adj entwaffnend

disarray [dɪsə'reɪ] n: **in ~** (army, organization) in Auflösung (begriffen); (hair, clothes) unordentlich; (thoughts) durcheinander; **to throw into ~** durcheinanderbringen

disaster [dɪ'zɑːstəʳ] n Katastrophe f; (Aviat etc) Unglück nt; (fig: mess) Fiasko nt

disaster area n Katastrophengebiet nt; (fig: person) Katastrophe f; **my office is a ~ in** meinem Büro sieht es katastrophal aus

disastrous [dɪ'zɑːstrəs] adj katastrophal

disband [dɪs'bænd] vt auflösen ▷ vi sich auflösen

disbelief ['dɪsbə'liːf] n Ungläubigkeit f; **in ~** ungläubig

disbelieve ['dɪsbə'liːv] vt (person) nicht glauben +dat; (story) nicht glauben; **I don't ~ you** ich bezweifle nicht, was Sie sagen

disc [dɪsk] n (Anat) Bandscheibe f; (record) Platte f; (Comput) = **disk**

disc. abbr (Comm) = **discount**

discard [dɪs'kɑːd] vt ausrangieren; (fig: idea, plan) verwerfen

disc brake n Scheibenbremse f

discern [dɪ'sɜːn] vt wahrnehmen; (identify) erkennen

discernible [dɪ'sɜːnəbl] adj erkennbar; (object) wahrnehmbar

discerning [dɪ'sɜːnɪŋ] adj (judgement) scharfsinnig; (look) kritisch; (listeners etc) anspruchsvoll

discharge [dɪs'tʃɑːdʒ] vt (duties) nachkommen +dat; (debt) begleichen; (waste) ablassen; (Elec) entladen; (Med) ausscheiden, absondern; (patient, employee, soldier) entlassen; (defendant) freisprechen ▷ n (of gas) Ausströmen nt; (of liquid) Ausfließen nt; (Elec) Entladung f; (Med) Ausfluss m; (of patient, employee, soldier) Entlassung f; (of defendant) Freispruch m; **to ~ a gun** ein Gewehr abfeuern

discharged bankrupt [dɪs'tʃɑːdʒd-] n (Law) entlasteter Konkursschuldner m, entlastete Konkursschuldnerin f

disciple [dɪ'saɪpl] n Jünger m; (fig: follower) Schüler(in) m(f)

disciplinary ['dɪsɪplɪnərɪ] adj (powers etc) Disziplinar-; **to take ~ action against sb** ein Disziplinarverfahren gegen jdn einleiten

discipline ['dɪsɪplɪn] n Disziplin f ▷ vt disziplinieren; (punish) bestrafen; **to ~ o.s. to do sth** sich dazu anhalten or zwingen, etw zu tun

disc jockey n Discjockey m

disclaim [dɪs'kleɪm] vt (knowledge) abstreiten; (responsibility) von sich weisen

disclaimer [dɪs'kleɪməʳ] n Dementi nt; **to issue a ~** eine Gegenerklärung abgeben

disclose [dɪs'kləuz] vt enthüllen, bekannt geben

disclosure [dɪs'kləuʒəʳ] n Enthüllung f

disco ['dɪskəu] n = **discotheque**

discolor etc [dɪs'kʌləʳ] (US) = **discolour** etc

discolour [dɪs'kʌləʳ] vt verfärben ▷ vi sich verfärben

discolouration [dɪskʌlə'reɪʃən] n Verfärbung f

discoloured [dɪs'kʌləd] adj verfärbt

discomfort [dɪs'kʌmfət] n (unease) Unbehagen nt; (physical) Beschwerden pl

disconcert [dɪskən'sɜːt] vt beunruhigen, irritieren

disconcerting [dɪskən'sɜːtɪŋ] adj beunruhigend, irritierend

disconnect [dɪskə'nɛkt] vt abtrennen; (Elec, Radio) abstellen; **I've been ~ed** (Tel) das Gespräch ist unterbrochen worden; (supply, connection) man hat mir das Telefon/den Strom/das Gas etc abgestellt

disconnected [dɪskə'nɛktɪd] adj unzusammenhängend

disconsolate [dɪs'kɔnsəlɪt] adj niedergeschlagen

discontent [dɪskən'tɛnt] n Unzufriedenheit f

discontented [dɪskən'tɛntɪd] adj unzufrieden

discontinue [dɪskən'tɪnjuː] vt einstellen; **"~d"** (Comm) „ausgelaufene Serie"

discord ['dɪskɔːd] n Zwietracht f; (Mus) Dissonanz f

discordant [dɪs'kɔːdənt] adj unharmonisch

discotheque ['dɪskəutɛk] n Diskothek f

discount [n 'dɪskaunt, vt dɪs'kaunt] n Rabatt m ▷ vt nachlassen; (idea, fact) unberücksichtigt lassen; **to give sb a ~ on sth** jdm auf etw acc Rabatt geben; **~ for cash** Skonto nt or m (bei Barzahlung); **at a ~** mit Rabatt

discount house n Diskontbank f; (also: **discount store**) Diskontgeschäft nt

discount rate n Diskontsatz m

discourage [dɪs'kʌrɪdʒ] vt entmutigen; **to ~ sb from doing sth** jdm davon abraten, etw zu tun

discouragement [dɪs'kʌrɪdʒmənt] n Mutlosigkeit f; **to act as a ~ to sb** entmutigend für jdn sein

discouraging [dɪs'kʌrɪdʒɪŋ] adj entmutigend

discourteous [dɪs'kɜːtɪəs] adj unhöflich

discover [dɪs'kʌvəʳ] vt entdecken; (missing person) finden; **to ~ that ...** herausfinden, dass ...

discovery [dɪs'kʌvərɪ] n Entdeckung f

discredit [dɪs'krɛdɪt] vt in Misskredit bringen

▷ *n*: **to sb's** ~ zu jds Schande
discreet [dɪsˈkriːt] *adj* diskret; *(unremarkable)*
dezent
discreetly [dɪsˈkriːtlɪ] *adv* diskret;
(unremarkably) dezent
discrepancy [dɪsˈkrepənsɪ] *n* Diskrepanz *f*
discretion [dɪsˈkreʃən] *n* Diskretion *f*; **at the**
~ **of** im Ermessen +*gen*; **use your own** ~ Sie
müssen nach eigenem Ermessen handeln
discretionary [dɪsˈkreʃənrɪ] *adj*: ~ **powers**
Ermessensspielraum *m*; ~ **payments**
Ermessenszahlungen *pl*
discriminate [dɪsˈkrɪmɪneɪt] *vi*: **to** ~ **between**
unterscheiden zwischen +*dat*; **to** ~ **against**
diskriminieren +*acc*
discriminating [dɪsˈkrɪmɪneɪtɪŋ] *adj*
anspruchsvoll, kritisch; *(tax, duty)*
Differenzial-
discrimination [dɪskrɪmɪˈneɪʃən]
n Diskriminierung *f*; *(discernment)*
Urteilsvermögen *nt*; **racial** ~
Rassendiskriminierung *f*; **sexual** ~
Diskriminierung aufgrund des Geschlechts
discus [ˈdɪskəs] *n* Diskus *m*; *(event)*
Diskuswerfen *nt*
discuss [dɪsˈkʌs] *vt* besprechen; *(debate)*
diskutieren; *(analyse)* erörtern, behandeln
discussion [dɪsˈkʌʃən] *n* Besprechung *f*; *(debate)*
Diskussion *f*; **under** ~ in der Diskussion
disdain [dɪsˈdeɪn] *n* Verachtung *f* ▷ *vt*
verachten ▷ *vi*: **to** ~ **to do sth** es für unter
seiner Würde halten, etw zu tun
disease [dɪˈziːz] *n* Krankheit *f*
diseased [dɪˈziːzd] *adj* krank; *(tree)* befallen
disembark [dɪsɪmˈbɑːk] *vt* ausschiffen ▷ *vi*
(passengers) von Bord gehen
disembarkation [dɪsɛmbɑːˈkeɪʃən] *n*
Ausschiffung *f*
disembodied [ˈdɪsɪmˈbɔdɪd] *adj (voice)*
geisterhaft; *(hand)* körperlos
disembowel [ˈdɪsɪmˈbauəl] *vt* die Eingeweide
herausnehmen +*dat*
disenchanted [ˈdɪsɪnˈtʃɑːntɪd] *adj*: ~ **(with)**
enttäuscht (von)
disenfranchise [ˈdɪsɪnˈfræntʃaɪz] *vt (Pol)*
das Wahlrecht entziehen +*dat*; *(Comm)* die
Konzession entziehen +*dat*
disengage [dɪsɪnˈɡeɪdʒ] *vt (Tech)* ausrasten; **to**
~ **the clutch** auskuppeln
disengagement [dɪsɪnˈɡeɪdʒmənt] *n (Pol)*
Disengagement *nt*
disentangle [dɪsɪnˈtæŋɡl] *vt* befreien; *(wool,
wire)* entwirren
disfavour, *(US)* **disfavor** [dɪsˈfeɪvəʳ] *n*
Missfallen *nt*; **to fall into** ~ **(with sb)** (bei
jdm) in Ungnade fallen
disfigure [dɪsˈfɪɡəʳ] *vt* entstellen; *(object, place)*
verunstalten
disgorge [dɪsˈɡɔːdʒ] *vt (liquid)* ergießen; *(people)*
ausspeien
disgrace [dɪsˈɡreɪs] *n* Schande *f*; *(scandal)*
Skandal *m* ▷ *vt* Schande bringen über +*acc*
disgraceful [dɪsˈɡreɪsful] *adj* skandalös

disgruntled [dɪsˈɡrʌntld] *adj* verärgert
disguise [dɪsˈɡaɪz] *n* Verkleidung *f* ▷ *vt*: **to** ~
(as) *(person)* verkleiden (als); *(object)* tarnen
(als); **in** ~ *(person)* verkleidet; **there's no**
disguising the fact that ... es kann nicht
geleugnet werden, dass ...; **to** ~ **o.s. as** sich
verkleiden als
disgust [dɪsˈɡʌst] *n* Abscheu *m* ▷ *vt* anwidern;
she walked off in ~ sie ging voller Empörung
weg
disgusting [dɪsˈɡʌstɪŋ] *adj* widerlich
dish [dɪʃ] *n* Schüssel *f*; *(flat)* Schale *f*; *(recipe,
food)* Gericht *nt*; *(also:* **satellite dish**)
Parabolantenne *f*, Schüssel *(inf)*; **to do** *or* **wash
the** ~**es** Geschirr spülen, abwaschen
▶ **dish out** *vt* verteilen; *(food, money)* austeilen;
(advice) erteilen
▶ **dish up** *vt (food)* auftragen, servieren; *(facts,
statistics)* auftischen *(inf)*
dishcloth [ˈdɪʃklɔθ] *n* Spültuch *nt*,
Spüllappen *m*
dishearten [dɪsˈhɑːtn] *vt* entmutigen
dishevelled, *(US)* **disheveled** [dɪˈʃevəld] *adj*
unordentlich; *(hair)* zerzaust
dishonest [dɪsˈɔnɪst] *adj* unehrlich; *(means)*
unlauter
dishonesty [dɪsˈɔnɪstɪ] *n* Unehrlichkeit *f*
dishonor *etc* [dɪsˈɔnəʳ] *(US)* = **dishonour** *etc*
dishonour [dɪsˈɔnəʳ] *n* Schande *f*
dishonourable [dɪsˈɔnərəbl] *adj* unehrenhaft
dish soap *(US)* *n* Spülmittel *nt*
dishtowel [ˈdɪʃtauəl] *(US)* *n* Geschirrtuch *nt*
dishwasher [ˈdɪʃwɔʃəʳ] *n (machine)* (Geschirr)
spülmaschine *f*
dishy [ˈdɪʃɪ] *(inf: Brit)* *adj* attraktiv
disillusion [dɪsɪˈluːʒən] *vt* desillusionieren
▷ *n* = **disillusionment**; **to become** ~**ed (with)**
seine Illusionen (über +*acc*) verlieren
disillusionment [dɪsɪˈluːʒənmənt] *n*
Desillusionierung *f*
disincentive [dɪsɪnˈsentɪv] *n* Entmutigung
f; **it's a** ~ es hält die Leute ab; **to be a** ~ **to sb**
jdm keinen Anreiz bieten
disinclined [dɪsɪnˈklaɪnd] *adj*: **to be** ~ **to do
sth** abgeneigt sein, etw zu tun
disinfect [dɪsɪnˈfekt] *vt* desinfizieren
disinfectant [dɪsɪnˈfektənt] *n*
Desinfektionsmittel *nt*
disinflation [dɪsɪnˈfleɪʃən] *n (Econ)* Rückgang *m*
einer inflationären Entwicklung
disinformation [dɪsɪnfəˈmeɪʃən] *n*
Desinformation *f*
disingenuous [dɪsɪnˈdʒenjuəs] *adj*
unaufrichtig
disinherit [dɪsɪnˈherɪt] *vt* enterben
disintegrate [dɪsˈɪntɪɡreɪt] *vi* zerfallen;
(marriage, partnership) scheitern; *(organization)*
sich auflösen
disinterested [dɪsˈɪntrəstɪd] *adj (advice)*
unparteiisch, unvoreingenommen; *(help)*
uneigennützig
disjointed [dɪsˈdʒɔɪntɪd] *adj*
unzusammenhängend

d

disk [dɪsk] n Diskette f; **single-/double-sided** ~ einseitige/zweiseitige Diskette

disk drive n Diskettenlaufwerk nt

diskette [dɪs'kɛt] (US) n = **disk**

disk operating system n Betriebssystem nt

dislike [dɪs'laɪk] n Abneigung f ▷ vt nicht mögen; **to take a ~ to sb/sth** eine Abneigung gegen jdn/etw entwickeln; **I ~ the idea** die Idee gefällt mir nicht; **he ~s it** er kann es nicht leiden, er mag es nicht

dislocate ['dɪsləkeɪt] vt verrenken, ausrenken; **he has ~d his shoulder** er hat sich dat den Arm ausgekugelt

dislodge [dɪs'lɒdʒ] vt verschieben

disloyal [dɪs'lɔɪəl] adj illoyal

dismal ['dɪzml] adj trübe, trostlos; (song, person, mood) trübsinnig; (failure) kläglich

dismantle [dɪs'mæntl] vt (machine) demontieren

dismast [dɪs'mɑːst] vt (Naut) entmasten

dismay [dɪs'meɪ] n Bestürzung f ▷ vt bestürzen; **much to my ~** zu meiner Bestürzung; **in ~** bestürzt

dismiss [dɪs'mɪs] vt entlassen; (case) abweisen; (possibility, idea) abtun

dismissal [dɪs'mɪsl] n Entlassung f

dismount [dɪs'maunt] vi absteigen

disobedience [dɪsə'biːdɪəns] n Ungehorsam m

disobedient [dɪsə'biːdɪənt] adj ungehorsam

disobey [dɪsə'beɪ] vt nicht gehorchen +dat; (order) nicht befolgen

disorder [dɪs'ɔːdər] n Unordnung f; (rioting) Unruhen pl; (Med) (Funktions)störung f; **civil** ~ öffentliche Unruhen pl

disorderly [dɪs'ɔːdəlɪ] adj unordentlich; (meeting) undiszipliniert; (behaviour) ungehörig

disorderly conduct n (Law) ungebührliches Benehmen nt

disorganize [dɪs'ɔːɡənaɪz] vt durcheinanderbringen

disorganized [dɪs'ɔːɡənaɪzd] adj chaotisch

disorientated [dɪs'ɔːrɪenteɪtd] adj desorientiert, verwirrt

disown [dɪs'əun] vt (action) verleugnen; (child) verstoßen

disparaging [dɪs'pærɪdʒɪŋ] adj (remarks) abschätzig, geringschätzig; **to be ~ about sb/sth** (person) abschätzig or geringschätzig über jdn/etw urteilen

disparate ['dɪspərɪt] adj völlig verschieden

disparity [dɪs'pærɪtɪ] n Unterschied m

dispassionate [dɪs'pæʃənət] adj nüchtern

dispatch [dɪs'pætʃ] vt senden, schicken; (deal with) erledigen; (kill) töten ▷ n Senden nt, Schicken nt; (Press) Bericht m; (Mil) Depesche f

dispatch department n Versandabteilung f

dispatch rider n (Mil) Meldefahrer m

dispel [dɪs'pɛl] vt (myths) zerstören; (fears) zerstreuen

dispensary [dɪs'pɛnsərɪ] n Apotheke f; (in chemist's) Raum in einer Apotheke, wo Arzneimittel abgefüllt werden

dispensation [dɪspən'seɪʃən] n (of treatment) Vergabe f; (special permission) Dispens m; ~ **of justice** Rechtsprechung f

dispense [dɪs'pɛns] vt (medicines) abgeben; (charity) austeilen; (advice) erteilen
▶ **dispense with** vt fus verzichten auf +acc

dispenser [dɪs'pɛnsər] n (machine) Automat m

dispensing chemist [dɪs'pɛnsɪŋ-] (Brit) n (shop) Apotheke f

dispersal [dɪs'pəːsl] n (of objects) Verstreuen nt; (of group, crowd) Auflösung f, Zerstreuen nt

disperse [dɪs'pəːs] vt (objects) verstreuen; (crowd etc) auflösen, zerstreuen; (knowledge, information) verbreiten ▷ vi (crowd) sich auflösen or zerstreuen

dispirited [dɪs'pɪrɪtɪd] adj entmutigt

displace [dɪs'pleɪs] vt ablösen

displaced person [dɪs'pleɪst-] n Verschleppte(r) f(m)

displacement [dɪs'pleɪsmənt] n Ablösung f; (of people) Vertreibung f; (Phys) Verdrängung f

display [dɪs'pleɪ] n (in shop) Auslage f; (exhibition) Ausstellung f; (of feeling) Zeigen nt; (pej) Zurschaustellung f; (Comput, Tech) Anzeige f ▷ vt zeigen; (ostentatiously) zur Schau stellen; (results, departure times) aushängen; **on ~** ausgestellt

display advertising n Displaywerbung f

displease [dɪs'pliːz] vt verstimmen, verärgern

displeased [dɪs'pliːzd] adj: **I am very ~ with you** ich bin sehr enttäuscht von dir

displeasure [dɪs'plɛʒər] n Missfallen nt

disposable [dɪs'pəuzəbl] adj (lighter) Wegwerf-; (bottle) Einweg-; (income) verfügbar

disposable nappy (Brit) n Papierwindel f

disposal [dɪs'pəuzl] n (of goods for sale) Loswerden nt; (of property, belongings: by selling) Verkauf m; (: by giving away) Abgeben nt; (of rubbish) Beseitigung f; **at one's ~** zur Verfügung; **to put sth at sb's ~** jdm etw zur Verfügung stellen

dispose [dɪs'pəuz]: ~ **of** vt fus (body) aus dem Weg schaffen; (unwanted goods) loswerden; (problem, task) erledigen; (stock) verkaufen

disposed [dɪs'pəuzd] adj: **to be ~ to do sth** (inclined) geneigt sein, etw zu tun; (willing) bereit sein, etw zu tun; **to be well ~ towards sb** jdm wohlwollen

disposition [dɪspə'zɪʃən] n (nature) Veranlagung f; (inclination) Neigung f

dispossess ['dɪspə'zɛs] vt enteignen; **to ~ sb of his/her land** jds Land enteignen

disproportion [dɪsprə'pɔːʃən] n Missverhältnis nt

disproportionate [dɪsprə'pɔːʃənət] adj unverhältnismäßig; (amount) unverhältnismäßig hoch/niedrig

disprove [dɪs'pruːv] vt widerlegen

dispute [dɪs'pjuːt] n Streit m; (also: **industrial dispute**) Auseinandersetzung f zwischen Arbeitgebern und Arbeitnehmern; (Pol, Mil) Streitigkeiten pl ▷ vt bestreiten; (ownership etc) anfechten; **to be in** or **under ~** umstritten sein

disqualification [dɪskwɔlɪfɪ'keɪʃən]
n: ~ **(from)** Ausschluss *m* (von);
Disqualifizierung *f* (von); ~ **(from driving)**
(*Brit*) Führerscheinentzug *m*

disqualify [dɪs'kwɔlɪfaɪ] *vt* disqualifizieren; **to**
~ **sb for sth** jdn für etw ungeeignet machen;
to ~ **sb from doing sth** jdn ungeeignet
machen, etw zu tun; **to** ~ **sb from driving**
(*Brit*) jdm den Führerschein entziehen

disquiet [dɪs'kwaɪət] *n* Unruhe *f*

disquieting [dɪs'kwaɪətɪŋ] *adj* beunruhigend

disregard [dɪsrɪ'gɑːd] *vt* nicht beachten,
ignorieren ▷ *n*: ~ **(for)** Missachtung *f* (+gen);
(*for danger, money*) Geringschätzung *f* (+gen)

disrepair ['dɪsrɪ'pɛəʳ] *n*: **to fall into** ~ (*machine*)
vernachlässigt werden; (*building*) verfallen

disreputable [dɪs'rɛpjutəbl] *adj* (*person*)
unehrenhaft; (*behaviour*) unfein

disrepute ['dɪsrɪ'pjuːt] *n* schlechter Ruf *m*; **to**
bring/fall into ~ in Verruf bringen/kommen

disrespectful [dɪsrɪ'spɛktful] *adj* respektlos

disrupt [dɪs'rʌpt] *vt* (*plans*)
durcheinanderbringen; (*conversation,*
proceedings) unterbrechen

disruption [dɪs'rʌpʃən] *n* Unterbrechung *f*;
(*disturbance*) Störung *f*

disruptive [dɪs'rʌptɪv] *adj* störend; (*action*) Stör-

dissatisfaction [dɪssætɪs'fækʃən] *n*
Unzufriedenheit *f*

dissatisfied [dɪs'sætɪsfaɪd] *adj*: ~ **(with)**
unzufrieden (mit)

dissect [dɪ'sɛkt] *vt* sezieren

disseminate [dɪ'sɛmɪneɪt] *vt* verbreiten

dissent [dɪ'sɛnt] *n* abweichende Meinungen *pl*

dissenter [dɪ'sɛntəʳ] *n* Abweichler(in) *m(f)*

dissertation [dɪsə'teɪʃən] *n* (*speech*) Vortrag
m; (*piece of writing*) Abhandlung *f*; (*for PhD*)
Dissertation *f*

disservice [dɪs'sə:vɪs] *n*: **to do sb a** ~ jdm einen
schlechten Dienst erweisen

dissident ['dɪsɪdnt] *adj* andersdenkend; (*voice*)
kritisch ▷ *n* Dissident(in) *m(f)*

dissimilar [dɪ'sɪmɪləʳ] *adj*: ~ **(to)** anders (als)

dissipate ['dɪsɪpeɪt] *vt* (*heat*) neutralisieren;
(*clouds*) auflösen; (*money, effort*) verschwenden

dissipated ['dɪsɪpeɪtɪd] *adj* zügellos,
ausschweifend

dissociate [dɪ'səuʃɪeɪt] *vt* trennen; **to** ~ **o.s.**
from sich distanzieren von

dissolute ['dɪsəluːt] *adj* zügellos,
ausschweifend

dissolution [dɪsə'luːʃən] *n* Auflösung *f*

dissolve [dɪ'zɔlv] *vt* auflösen ▷ *vi* sich auflösen;
to ~ **in(to) tears** in Tränen zerfließen

dissuade [dɪ'sweɪd] *vt*: **to** ~ **sb (from sth)** jdn
(von etw) abbringen

distaff ['dɪstɑːf] *n*: **the** ~ **side** die mütterliche
Seite

distance ['dɪstns] *n* Entfernung *f*; (*in time*)
Abstand *m*; (*reserve*) Abstand, Distanz *f* ▷ *vt*: **to**
~ **o.s. (from)** sich distanzieren (von); **in the**
~ in der Ferne; **what's the** ~ **to London?** wie
weit ist es nach London?; **it's within walking**

~ **es ist zu Fuß erreichbar**; **at a** ~ **of 2 metres**
in 2 Meter(n) Entfernung; **keep your** ~!
halten Sie Abstand!

distant ['dɪstnt] *adj* (*place*) weit entfernt, fern;
(*time*) weit zurückliegend; (*relative*) entfernt;
(*manner*) distanziert, kühl

distaste [dɪs'teɪst] *n* Widerwille *m*

distasteful [dɪs'teɪstful] *adj* widerlich; **to be** ~
to sb jdm zuwider sein

Dist. Atty. (*US*) *abbr* = **district attorney**

distemper [dɪs'tɛmpəʳ] *n* (*paint*) Temperafarbe
f; (*disease of dogs*) Staupe *f*

distend [dɪs'tɛnd] *vt* blähen ▷ *vi* sich blähen

distended [dɪs'tɛndɪd] *adj* aufgebläht

distil, (*US*) **distill** [dɪs'tɪl] *vt* destillieren; (*fig*)
(heraus)destillieren

distillery [dɪs'tɪlərɪ] *n* Brennerei *f*

distinct [dɪs'tɪŋkt] *adj* deutlich, klar; (*possibility*)
eindeutig; (*different*) verschieden; **as** ~ **from**
im Unterschied zu

distinction [dɪs'tɪŋkʃən] *n* Unterschied *m*;
(*honour*) Ehre *f*; (*in exam*) Auszeichnung *f*; **to**
draw a ~ **between** einen Unterschied machen
zwischen +*dat*; **a writer of** ~ ein Schriftsteller
von Rang

distinctive [dɪs'tɪŋktɪv] *adj* unverwechselbar

distinctly [dɪs'tɪŋktlɪ] *adv* deutlich, klar; (*tell*)
ausdrücklich; (*unhappy*) ausgeprochen; (*better*)
entschieden

distinguish [dɪs'tɪŋgwɪʃ] *vt* unterscheiden;
(*details etc*) erkennen, ausmachen; **to** ~
(between) unterscheiden (zwischen +*dat*); **to**
~ **o.s.** sich hervortun

distinguished [dɪs'tɪŋgwɪʃt] *adj* von hohem
Rang; (*career*) hervorragend; (*in appearance*)
distinguiert

distinguishing [dɪs'tɪŋgwɪʃɪŋ] *adj*
charakteristisch

distort [dɪs'tɔːt] *vt* verzerren; (*argument*)
verdrehen

distortion [dɪs'tɔːʃən] *n* (*see vb*) Verzerrung *f*;
Verdrehung *f*

distract [dɪs'trækt] *vt* ablenken

distracted [dɪs'træktɪd] *adj* unaufmerksam;
(*anxious*) besorgt, beunruhigt

distraction [dɪs'trækʃən] *n*
Unaufmerksamkeit *f*; (*confusion*) Verstörtheit
f; (*sth which distracts*) Ablenkung *f*; (*amusement*)
Zerstreuung *f*; **to drive sb to** ~ jdn zur
Verzweiflung treiben

distraught [dɪs'trɔːt] *adj* verzweifelt

distress [dɪs'trɛs] *n* Verzweiflung *f* ▷ *vt*
Kummer machen +*dat*; **in** ~ (*ship*) in
Seenot; (*person*) verzweifelt; **~ed area** (*Brit*)
Notstandsgebiet *nt*

distressing [dɪs'trɛsɪŋ] *adj* beunruhigend

distress signal *n* Notsignal *nt*

distribute [dɪs'trɪbjuːt] *vt* verteilen; (*profits*)
aufteilen

distribution [dɪstrɪ'bjuːʃən] *n* Vertrieb *m*; (*of*
profits) Aufteilung *f*

distribution costs *npl* Vertriebskosten *pl*

distribution management *n* (*Comm*)

d

Vertriebscontrolling nt
distributor [dɪs'trɪbjutə^r] n (Comm)
Vertreiber(in) m(f); (Aut, Tech) Verteiler m
district ['dɪstrɪkt] n Gebiet nt; (of town) Stadtteil
m; (Admin) (Verwaltungs)bezirk m
district attorney (US) n Bezirksstaatsanwalt
m, Bezirksstaatsanwältin f

⬤ **DISTRICT COUNCIL**

⬤ District Council heißt der in jedem
⬤ der britischen districts (Bezirke)
⬤ alle vier Jahre neu gewählte
⬤ Bezirksrat, der für bestimmte
⬤ Bereiche der Kommunalverwaltung
⬤ (Gesundheitswesen, Wohnungs-
⬤ beschaffung, Baugenehmigungen,
⬤ Müllabfuhr) zuständig ist. Die
⬤ district councils werden durch
⬤ Kommunalabgaben und durch einen
⬤ Zuschuss von der Regierung finanziert.
⬤ Ihre Ausgaben werden von einer
⬤ unabhängigen Prüfungskommission
⬤ kontrolliert, und bei zu hohen Ausgaben
⬤ wird der Regierungszuschuss gekürzt.

district nurse (Brit) n Gemeindeschwester f
distrust [dɪs'trʌst] n Misstrauen nt ▷ vt
misstrauen +dat
distrustful [dɪs'trʌstful] adj: ~ **(of)**
misstrauisch (gegenüber +dat)
disturb [dɪs'təːb] vt stören; (upset)
beunruhigen; (disorganize)
durcheinanderbringen; **sorry to ~ you**
entschuldigen Sie bitte die Störung
disturbance [dɪs'təːbəns] n Störung f; (political
etc) Unruhe f; (violent event) Unruhen pl; (by
drunks etc) (Ruhe)störung f; **to cause a ~**
Unruhe/eine Ruhestörung verursachen; **~ of
the peace** Ruhestörung f
disturbed [dɪs'təːbd] adj beunruhigt; (childhood)
unglücklich; **mentally/emotionally ~**
geistig/seelisch gestört
disturbing [dɪs'təːbɪŋ] adj beunruhigend
disuse [dɪs'juːs] n: **to fall into ~** nicht mehr
benutzt werden
disused [dɪs'juːzd] adj (building) leer stehend;
(airfield) stillgelegt
ditch [dɪtʃ] n Graben m ▷ vt (inf: partner)
sitzen lassen; (: plan) sausen lassen; (: car etc)
loswerden
dither ['dɪðə^r] (pej) vi zaudern
ditto ['dɪtəu] adv dito, ebenfalls
divan [dɪ'væn] n (also: **divan bed**) Polsterbett nt
dive [daɪv] n Sprung m; (underwater) Tauchen
nt; (of submarine) Untertauchen nt; (pej: place)
Spelunke f (inf) ▷ vi springen; (under water)
tauchen; (bird) einen Sturzflug machen;
(submarine) untertauchen; **to ~ into** (bag, drawer
etc) greifen in +acc; (shop, car etc) sich stürzen
in +acc
diver ['daɪvə^r] n Taucher(in) m(f); (also: **deep-
sea diver**) Tiefseetaucher(in) m(f)

diverge [daɪ'vəːdʒ] vi auseinandergehen
divergent [daɪ'vəːdʒənt] adj unterschiedlich;
(views) voneinander abweichend; (interests)
auseinandergehend
diverse [daɪ'vəːs] adj verschiedenartig
diversification [daɪvəːsɪfɪ'keɪʃən] n
Diversifikation f
diversify [daɪ'vəːsɪfaɪ] vi diversifizieren
diversion [daɪ'vəːʃən] n (Brit: Aut) Umleitung f;
(distraction) Ablenkung f; (of funds) Umlenkung f
diversionary [daɪ'vəːʃənrɪ] adj: ~ **tactics**
Ablenkungsmanöver pl
diversity [daɪ'vəːsɪtɪ] n Vielfalt f
divert [daɪ'vəːt] vt (sb's attention) ablenken;
(funds) umlenken; (re-route) umleiten
divest [daɪ'vɛst] vt: **to ~ sb of office/his
authority** jdn seines Amtes entkleiden/
seiner Macht entheben
divide [dɪ'vaɪd] vt trennen; (Math) dividieren,
teilen; (share out) verteilen ▷ vi sich teilen;
(road) sich gabeln; (people, groups) sich aufteilen
▷ n Kluft f; **to ~ (between** or **among)** aufteilen
(unter +dat); **40 ~d by 5** 40 geteilt or dividiert
durch 5
  ▶ **divide out** vt: **to ~ out (between** or **among)**
aufteilen (unter +dat)
divided [dɪ'vaɪdɪd] adj geteilt; **to be ~ about** or
over sth geteilter Meinung über etw acc sein
divided highway (US) n ≈ Schnellstraße f
dividend ['dɪvɪdɛnd] n Dividende f; (fig): **to pay
~s** sich bezahlt machen
dividend cover n (Comm) Dividendendeckung f
dividers [dɪ'vaɪdəz] npl (Math, Tech) Stechzirkel
m; (between pages) Register nt
divine [dɪ'vaɪn] adj göttlich ▷ vt (future)
weissagen, prophezeien; (truth) erahnen;
(water, metal) aufspüren
diving ['daɪvɪŋ] n Tauchen nt; (Sport)
Kunstspringen nt
diving board n Sprungbrett nt
diving suit n Taucheranzug m
divinity [dɪ'vɪnɪtɪ] n Göttlichkeit f; (god or
goddess) Gottheit f; (Scol) Theologie f
divisible [dɪ'vɪzəbl] adj: ~ **(by)** teilbar (durch);
to be ~ into teilbar sein in +acc
division [dɪ'vɪʒən] n Teilung f; (Math)
Teilen nt, Division f; (sharing out) Verteilung
f; (disagreement) Uneinigkeit f; (Brit: Pol)
Abstimmung f durch Hammelsprung; (Comm)
Abteilung f; (Mil) Division f; (esp Football) Liga
f; **~ of labour** Arbeitsteilung f
divisive [dɪ'vaɪsɪv] adj: **to be ~** (tactics) auf
Spaltung abzielen; (system) zu Feindseligkeit
führen
divorce [dɪ'vɔːs] n Scheidung f ▷ vt sich
scheiden lassen von; (dissociate) trennen
divorced [dɪ'vɔːst] adj geschieden
divorcee [dɪvɔː'siː] n Geschiedene(r) f(m)
divot ['dɪvət] n vom Golfschläger etc ausgehacktes
Rasenstück
divulge [daɪ'vʌldʒ] vt preisgeben
DIY (Brit) n abbr = **do-it-yourself**
dizziness ['dɪzɪnɪs] n Schwindel m

dizzy ['dɪzɪ] *adj* schwind(e)lig; (*turn, spell*) Schwindel-; (*height*) schwindelerregend; **I feel ~** mir ist *or* ich bin schwind(e)lig

DJ *n abbr* = **disc jockey**

dj *n abbr* = **dinner jacket**

Djakarta [dʒə'kɑːtə] *n* Jakarta *nt*

DJIA (US) *n abbr* (= *Dow-Jones Industrial Average*) Dow-Jones-Index *m*

dl *abbr* (= *decilitre*) dl

DLit, DLitt *n abbr* (= *Doctor of Literature, Doctor of Letters*) akademischer Grad in Literaturwissenschaft

dm *abbr* (= *decimetre*) dm

DMus *n abbr* (= *Doctor of Music*) Doktor der Musikwissenschaft

DMZ *n abbr* = **demilitarized zone**

DNA *n abbr* (= *deoxyribonucleic acid*) DNS *f*

DNA test *n* DNS-Test *m*

⭕ **KEYWORD**

do [duː] (*pt* **did**, *pp* **done**) *aux vb* **1** (*in negative constructions*): **I don't understand** ich verstehe nicht

2 (*to form questions*): **didn't you know?** wusstest du das nicht?; **what do you think?** was meinst du?

3 (*for emphasis*): **she does seem rather upset** sie scheint wirklich recht aufgeregt zu sein; **do sit down/help yourself** bitte nehmen Sie Platz/bedienen Sie sich; **oh do shut up!** halte endlich den Mund!

4 (*to avoid repeating vb*): **she swims better than I do** sie schwimmt besser als ich; **she lives in Glasgow — so do I** sie wohnt in Glasgow — ich auch; **who made this mess? — I did** wer hat dieses Durcheinander gemacht? — ich

5 (*in question tags*): **you like him, don't you?** du magst ihn, nicht wahr?; **I don't know him, do I?** ich kenne ihn nicht, oder?

▷ *vt* **1** (*carry out, perform*) tun, machen; **what are you doing tonight?** was machen Sie heute Abend?; **what do you do (for a living)?** was machen Sie beruflich?; **to do one's teeth/nails** sich *dat* die Zähne putzen/die Nägel schneiden

2 (*Aut etc*) fahren; **the car was doing 100** das Auto fuhr 100

▷ *vi* **1** (*act, behave*): **do as I do** mach es wie ich

2 (*get on, fare*): **he's doing well/badly at school** er ist gut/schlecht in der Schule; **the company is doing well** der Firma geht es gut; **how do you do?** guten Tag/Morgen/Abend!

3 (*suit, be sufficient*) reichen; **will that do?** reicht das?; **will this dress do for the party?** ist dieses Kleid gut genug für die Party?; **will £10 do?** reichen £10?; **that'll do** das reicht; (*in annoyance*) jetzt reichts aber!; **to make do with** auskommen mit

▷ *n* (*inf: party etc*) Party *f*, Fete *f*; **it was quite a do** es war ganz schön was los

▶ **do away with** *vt fus* (*get rid of*) abschaffen

▶ **do for** (*inf*) *vt fus*: **to be done for** erledigt sein

▶ **do in** (*inf*) *vt* (*kill*) umbringen

▶ **do out of** (*inf*) *vt* (*deprive*) bringen um

▶ **do up** *vt fus* (*laces, dress, buttons*) zumachen; (*renovate: room, house*) renovieren

▶ **do with** *vt fus* **1** (*need*) brauchen; **I could do with some help/a drink** ich könnte Hilfe/einen Drink gebrauchen

2: it has to do with money es hat mit Geld zu tun

▶ **do without** *vt fus* auskommen ohne

do. *abbr* = **ditto**

DOA *abbr* (= *dead on arrival*) bei Einlieferung ins Krankenhaus bereits tot

d.o.b. *abbr* = **date of birth**

doc [dɔk] (*inf*) *n* Doktor *m*

docile ['dəʊsaɪl] *adj* sanft(mütig)

dock [dɔk] *n* Dock *nt*; (*Law*) Anklagebank *f*; (*Bot*) Ampfer *m* ▷ *vi* anlegen; (*Space*) docken ▷ *vt*: **they ~ed a third of his wages** sie kürzten seinen Lohn um ein Drittel; **docks** *npl* (*Naut*) Hafen *m*

dock dues [-djuːz] *npl* Hafengebühr *f*

docker ['dɔkə^r] *n* Hafenarbeiter *m*, Docker *m*

docket ['dɔkɪt] *n* Inhaltserklärung *f*; (*on parcel etc*) Warenbegleitschein *m*, Laufzettel *m*

dockyard ['dɔkjɑːd] *n* Werft *f*

doctor ['dɔktə^r] *n* Arzt *m*, Ärztin *f*; (*PhD etc*) Doktor *m* ▷ *vt*: **to ~ a drink** *etc* einem Getränk *etc* etwas beimischen; **~'s office** (US) Sprechzimmer *nt*

doctorate ['dɔktərɪt] *n* Doktorwürde *f*; *siehe Info-Artikel*

○ **DOCTORATE**

Doctorate ist der höchste akademische Grad auf jedem Wissensgebiet und wird nach erfolgreicher Vorlage einer Doktorarbeit verliehen. Die Studienzeit (meist mindestens 3 Jahre) und Länge der Doktorarbeit ist je nach Hochschule verschieden. Am häufigsten wird der Titel PhD (Doctor of Philosophy) auf dem Gebiet der Geisteswissenschaften, Naturwissenschaften und des Ingenieurwesens verliehen, obwohl es auch andere Doktortitel (in Musik, Jura usw.) gibt. Siehe auch *Bachelor's degree*, *Master's degree*.

Doctor of Philosophy *n* Doktor *m* der Philosophie

doctrine ['dɔktrɪn] *n* Doktrin *f*

docudrama ['dɔkjudrɑːmə] *n* Dokumentarspiel *nt*

document ['dɔkjumənt] *n* Dokument *nt* ▷ *vt* dokumentieren

documentary [dɔkju'mentərɪ] *adj* dokumentarisch ▷ *n* Dokumentarfilm *m*

documentation [dɔkjumən'teɪʃən] *n* Dokumentation *f*

DOD (US) *n abbr* (= *Department of Defense*)

Verteidigungsministerium *nt*
doddering ['dɒdərɪŋ] *adj* (*shaky, unsteady*) zittrig
doddery ['dɒdərɪ] *adj* = **doddering**
doddle ['dɒdl] (*inf*) *n*: **a** ~ ein Kinderspiel *nt*
Dodecanese [dəʊdɪkə'niːz], **Dodecanese Islands** *npl*: **the** ~ **(Islands)** der Dodekanes
dodge [dɒdʒ] *n* Trick *m* ▷ *vt* ausweichen +*dat*; (*tax*) umgehen ▷ *vi* ausweichen; **to** ~ **out of the way** zur Seite springen; **to** ~ **through the traffic** sich durch den Verkehr schlängeln
dodgems ['dɒdʒəmz] (*Brit*) *npl* Autoskooter *pl*
dodgy ['dɒdʒɪ] (*inf*) *adj* (*person*) zweifelhaft; (*plan etc*) gewagt
DOE *n abbr* (*Brit*: = *Department of the Environment*) *Umweltministerium*; (*US*: = *Department of Energy*) *Energieministerium*
doe [dəʊ] *n* Reh *nt*, Ricke *f*; (*rabbit*) (Kaninchen) weibchen *nt*
does [dʌz] *vb see* **do**
doesn't ['dʌznt] = **does not**
dog [dɒg] *n* Hund *m* ▷ *vt* (*subj*: *person*) auf den Fersen bleiben +*dat*; (: *bad luck, memory etc*) verfolgen; **to go to the ~s** (*inf*) vor die Hunde gehen
dog biscuits *npl* Hundekuchen *pl*
dog collar *n* Hundehalsband *nt*; (*Rel*) Kragen *m* des Geistlichen
dog-eared ['dɒgɪəd] *adj* mit Eselsohren
dog food *n* Hundefutter *nt*
dogged ['dɒgɪd] *adj* beharrlich
doggy ['dɒgɪ] *n* Hündchen *nt*
doggy bag *n* Tüte für Essensreste, die man nach Hause mitnehmen möchte
dogma ['dɒgmə] *n* Dogma *nt*
dogmatic [dɒg'mætɪk] *adj* dogmatisch
do-gooder [duː'gʊdəʳ] (*pej*) *n* Weltverbesserer(in) *m(f)*
dogsbody ['dɒgzbɒdɪ] (*Brit*: *inf*) *n* Mädchen *nt* für alles
doily ['dɔɪlɪ] *n* Deckchen *nt*
doing ['duːɪŋ] *n*: **this is your** ~ das ist dein Werk
doings ['duːɪŋz] *npl* Treiben *nt*
do-it-yourself ['duːɪtjɔː'sɛlf] *n* Heimwerken *nt*, Do-it-yourself *nt*
doldrums ['dɒldrəmz] *npl*: **to be in the** ~ (*person*) niedergeschlagen sein; (*business*) in einer Flaute stecken
dole [dəʊl] (*Brit*) *n* Arbeitslosenunterstützung *f*; **on the** ~ arbeitslos
▶ **dole out** *vt* austeilen, verteilen
doleful ['dəʊlful] *adj* traurig
doll [dɒl] *n* (*toy, also US*: *inf*: *woman*) Puppe *f*
dollar ['dɒləʳ] (*US etc*) *n* Dollar *m*
dollar area *n* Dollarblock *m*
dolled up (*inf*) *adj* aufgedonnert
dollop ['dɒləp] (*inf*) *n* Schlag *m*
dolly ['dɒlɪ] (*inf*) *n* (*doll, woman*) Puppe *f*
Dolomites ['dɒləmaɪts] *npl*: **the** ~ die Dolomiten *pl*
dolphin ['dɒlfɪn] *n* Delfin *m*
domain [də'meɪn] *n* Bereich *m*; (*empire*) Reich *nt*
dome [dəʊm] *n* Kuppel *f*

domestic [də'mɛstɪk] *adj* (*trade*) Innen-; (*situation*) innenpolitisch; (*news*) Inland-, aus dem Inland; (*tasks, appliances*) Haushalts-; (*animal*) Haus-; (*duty, happiness*) häuslich
domesticated [də'mɛstɪkeɪtɪd] *adj* (*animal*) zahm; (*person*) häuslich
domesticity [dəʊmɛs'tɪsɪtɪ] *n* häusliches Leben *nt*
domestic servant *n* Hausangestellte(r) *f(m)*
domicile ['dɒmɪsaɪl] *n* Wohnsitz *m*
dominant ['dɒmɪnənt] *adj* dominierend; (*share*) größte(r, s)
dominate ['dɒmɪneɪt] *vt* dominieren, beherrschen
domination [dɒmɪ'neɪʃən] *n* (Vor)herrschaft *f*
domineering [dɒmɪ'nɪərɪŋ] *adj* herrschsüchtig
Dominican Republic [də'mɪnɪkən-] *n*: **the** ~ die Dominikanische Republik
dominion [də'mɪnɪən] *n* (*territory*) Herrschaftsgebiet *nt*; (*authority*): **to have** ~ **over** Macht haben über +*acc*
domino ['dɒmɪnəʊ] (*pl* **~es**) *n* (*block*) Domino(stein) *m*
domino effect *n* Dominoeffekt *m*
dominoes ['dɒmɪnəʊz] *n* (*game*) Domino(spiel) *nt*
don [dɒn] *n* (*Brit*) (Universitäts)dozent *m* (*besonders in Oxford und Cambridge*) ▷ *vt* anziehen
donate [də'neɪt] *vt*: **to** ~ **(to)** (*organization, cause*) spenden (für)
donation [də'neɪʃən] *n* (*act of donating*) Spenden *nt*; (*contribution*) Spende *f*
done [dʌn] *pp of* **do**
donkey ['dɒŋkɪ] *n* Esel *m*
donkey-work ['dɒŋkɪwəːk] (*Brit*: *inf*) *n* Dreckarbeit *f*
donor ['dəʊnəʳ] *n* Spender(in) *m(f)*
donor card *n* Organspenderausweis *m*
donor conference *n* (*Pol, Econ*) Geberkonferenz *f*
donor fatigue *n* Spendenmüdigkeit *f*
don't [dəʊnt] = **do not**
donut ['dəʊnʌt] (*US*) *n* = **doughnut**
doodle ['duːdl] *vi* Männchen malen ▷ *n* Kritzelei *f*
doom [duːm] *n* Unheil *nt* ▷ *vt*: **to be ~ed to failure** zum Scheitern verurteilt sein
doomsday ['duːmzdeɪ] *n* der Jüngste Tag
door [dɔːʳ] *n* Tür *f*; **to go from** ~ **to door** von Tür zu Tür gehen
door bell *n* Türklingel *f*
door handle *n* Türklinke *f*; (*of car*) Türgriff *m*
doorman ['dɔːmən] (*irreg: like* **man**) *n* Portier *m*
doormat ['dɔːmæt] *n* Fußmatte *f*; (*fig*) Fußabtreter *m*
doorpost ['dɔːpəʊst] *n* Türpfosten *m*
doorstep ['dɔːstɛp] *n* Eingangsstufe *f*, Türstufe *f*; **on the** ~ vor der Haustür
door-to-door ['dɔːtə'dɔːʳ] *adj* (*selling*) von Haus zu Haus; ~ **salesman** Vertreter *m*
doorway ['dɔːweɪ] *n* Eingang *m*
dope [dəʊp] *n* (*inf*) Stoff *m*, Drogen *pl*; (: *person*) Esel *m*, Trottel *m*; (: *information*) Informationen

pl ▷ vt dopen

dopey ['dəupɪ] (inf) adj (groggy) benebelt; (stupid) blöd, bekloppt

dormant ['dɔːmənt] adj (plant) ruhend; (volcano) untätig; (idea, report etc): **to lie ~** schlummern

dormer ['dɔːmə^r] n (also: **dormer window**) Mansardenfenster nt

dormice ['dɔːmaɪs] npl of **dormouse**

dormitory ['dɔːmɪtrɪ] n Schlafsaal m; (US: building) Wohnheim nt

dormouse ['dɔːmaus] (pl **dormice**) n Haselmaus f

DOS [dɔs] n abbr (Comput: = disk operating system) DOS

dosage ['dəusɪdʒ] n Dosis f; (on label) Dosierung f

dose [dəus] n Dosis f; (Brit: bout) Ration f
▷ vt: **to ~ o.s.** Medikamente nehmen; **a ~ of flu** eine Grippe

dosser ['dɔsə^r] (Brit: inf) n Penner(in) m(f)

dosshouse ['dɔshaus] (Brit: inf) n Obdachlosenheim nt

dossier ['dɔsɪeɪ] n Dossier nt

DOT (US) n abbr (= Department of Transportation) ≈ Verkehrsministerium nt

dot [dɔt] n Punkt m ▷ vt: **~ted with** übersät mit; **on the ~** (auf die Minute) pünktlich

dote [dəut]: **~ on** vt fus abgöttisch lieben

dot-matrix printer [dɔt'meɪtrɪks-] n Nadeldrucker m

dotted line ['dɔtɪd-] n punktierte Linie f; **to sign on the ~** (fig) seine formelle Zustimmung geben

dotty ['dɔtɪ] (inf) adj schrullig

double ['dʌbl] adj doppelt; (chin) Doppel- ▷ adv (cost) doppelt so viel ▷ n Doppelgänger(in) m(f) ▷ vt verdoppeln; (paper, blanket) (einmal) falten ▷ vi sich verdoppeln; **~ five two six (5526)** (Brit: Tel) fünfundfünfzig sechsundzwanzig; **it's spelt with a ~ "l"** es wird mit zwei l geschrieben; **an egg with a ~ yolk** ein Ei mit zwei Dottern; **on the ~, at the ~** (Brit: quickly) schnell; (immediately) unverzüglich; **to ~ as ...** (person) auch als ... fungieren; (thing) auch als ... dienen

▶ **double back** vi kehrtmachen, zurückgehen/-fahren

▶ **double up** vi sich krümmen; (share room) sich ein Zimmer teilen

double bass n Kontrabass m

double bed n Doppelbett nt

double bend (Brit) n S-Kurve f

double-blind adj: **~ experiment** Doppelblindversuch m

double-breasted ['dʌbl'brɛstɪd] adj (jacket, coat) zweireihig

double-check ['dʌbl'tʃɛk] vt noch einmal (über)prüfen ▷ vi es noch einmal (über)prüfen

double-clutch ['dʌbl'klʌtʃ] (US) vi mit Zwischengas schalten

double cream (Brit) n Sahne f mit hohem Fettgehalt, ≈ Schlagsahne f

double-cross [dʌbl'krɔs] vt ein Doppelspiel

treiben mit

double-decker [dʌbl'dɛkə^r] n Doppeldecker m

double-declutch ['dʌbldiː'klʌtʃ] (Brit) vi mit Zwischengas schalten

double exposure n doppelt belichtetes Foto nt

double glazing [-'gleɪzɪŋ] (Brit) n Doppelverglasung f

double-page spread ['dʌblpeɪdʒ-] n Doppelseite f

double-parking [dʌbl'pɑːkɪŋ] n Parken nt in der zweiten Reihe

double room n Doppelzimmer nt

doubles ['dʌblz] n (Tennis) Doppel nt

double time n doppelter Lohn m

double whammy [-'wæmɪ] (inf) n Doppelschlag m

doubly ['dʌblɪ] adv (ganz) besonders

doubt [daut] n Zweifel m ▷ vt bezweifeln; **without (a) ~** ohne Zweifel; **to ~ sb** jdm nicht glauben; **I ~ it (very much)** das bezweifle ich (sehr), das möchte ich (stark) bezweifeln; **to ~ if or whether ...** bezweifeln, dass ...; **I don't ~ that ...** ich bezweifle nicht, dass ...

doubtful ['dautful] adj zweifelhaft; **to be ~ about sth** an etw dat zweifeln; **to be ~ about doing sth** Bedenken haben, ob man etw tun soll; **I'm a bit ~** ich bin nicht ganz sicher

doubtless ['dautlɪs] adv ohne Zweifel, sicherlich

dough [dəu] n Teig m; (inf: money) Kohle f, Knete f

doughnut, (US) **donut** ['dəunʌt] n ≈ Berliner (Pfannkuchen) m

dour [duə^r] adj mürrisch, verdrießlich

douse [dauz] vt Wasser schütten über +acc; (extinguish) löschen; **to ~ with** übergießen mit

dove [dʌv] n Taube f

Dover ['dəuvə^r] n Dover nt

dovetail ['dʌvteɪl] vi übereinstimmen ▷ n (also: **dovetail joint**) Schwalbenschwanzverbindung f

dowager ['dauədʒə^r] n (adlige) Witwe f

dowdy ['daudɪ] adj ohne jeden Schick; (clothes) unmodern

Dow-Jones average ['dau'dʒəunz-] (US) n Dow-Jones-Index m

down [daun] n Daunen pl ▷ adv hinunter, herunter; (on the ground) unten ▷ prep hinunter, herunter; (movement along) entlang ▷ vt (inf: drink) runterkippen; **~ there/here** da/hier unten; **the price of meat is ~** die Fleischpreise sind gefallen; **I've got it ~ in my diary** ich habe es in meinem Kalender notiert; **to pay £2 ~** £2 anzahlen; **England is two goals ~** England liegt mit zwei Toren zurück; **to ~ tools** (Brit) die Arbeit niederlegen; **~ with ...!** nieder mit ...!

down-and-out ['daunəndaut] n Penner(in) m(f) (inf)

down-at-heel ['daunət'hiːl] adj (appearance, person) schäbig, heruntergekommen; (shoes) abgetreten

downbeat ['daunbiːt] n (Mus) erster betonter

Taktteil *m* ▷ *adj* zurückhaltend
downcast ['daunka:st] *adj* niedergeschlagen
downer ['daunə'] (*inf*) *n* (*drug*)
Beruhigungsmittel *nt*; **to be on a ~**
deprimiert sein
downfall ['daunfɔ:l] *n* Ruin *m*; (*of dictator etc*)
Sturz *m*, Fall *m*
downgrade ['daungreid] *vt* herunterstufen
downhearted ['daun'hɑ:tid] *adj*
niedergeschlagen, entmutigt
downhill ['daun'hil] *adv* bergab ▷ *n* (*Ski: also:*
downhill race) Abfahrtslauf *m*; **to go ~** (*road*)
bergab führen; (*person*) hinuntergehen,
heruntergehen; (*car*) hinunterfahren,
herunterfahren; (*fig*) auf dem absteigenden
Ast sein

● **DOWNING STREET**

Downing Street ist die Straße in London, die
von Whitehall zum St James Park führt
und in der sich der offizielle Wohnsitz
des Premierministers (Nr. 10) und des
Finanzministers (Nr. 11) befindet. Im
weiteren Sinne bezieht sich der Begriff
Downing Street auf die britische
Regierung.

download ['daunləud] *vt* (*Comput*)
herunterladen, downloaden ▷ *n* Download *m*
downloadable ['daunləudəbl] *adj* (*Comput*)
herunterladbar
down-market ['daun'mɑ:kit] *adj* (*product*) für
den Massenmarkt
down payment *n* Anzahlung *f*
downplay ['daunplei] (*US*) *vt* herunterspielen
downpour ['daunpɔ:'] *n* Wolkenbruch *m*
downright ['daunrait] *adj* (*liar etc*)
ausgesprochen; (*refusal, lie*) glatt
Downs [daunz] (*Brit*) *npl*: **the ~** die Downs *pl*,
Hügellandschaft in Südengland
downscale ['daunskeil] *adj* (*US*) wenig
anspruchsvoll; (*goods, products*) minderwertig;
(*service*) mangelhaft; (*restaurant, hotel*) der
unteren Preisklasse
downsize ['daun'saiz] *vi* (*Econ: company*) sich
verkleinern
Down's syndrome *n* (*Med*) Downsyndrom *nt*
downstairs ['daun'stɛəz] *adv* unten;
(*downwards*) nach unten
downstream ['daunstri:m] *adv* flussabwärts,
stromabwärts
downtime ['dauntaim] *n* Ausfallzeit *f*
down-to-earth ['dauntu'ə:θ] *adj* (*person*)
nüchtern; (*solution*) praktisch
downtown ['daun'taun] (*esp US*) *adv* im
Zentrum, in der (Innen)stadt; (*go*) ins
Zentrum, in die (Innen)stadt ▷ *adj*: **~ Chicago**
das Zentrum von Chicago
downtrodden ['dauntrɔdn] *adj* unterdrückt,
geknechtet
down under *adv* (*be*) in Australien/
Neuseeland; (*go*) nach Australien/Neuseeland

downward ['daunwəd] *adj, adv* nach unten; **a ~**
trend ein Abwärtstrend *m*
downwards ['daunwədz] *adv* = **downward**
dowry ['dauri] *n* Mitgift *f*
doz. *abbr* = **dozen**
doze [dəuz] *vi* ein Nickerchen *nt* machen
▶ **doze off** *vi* einschlafen, einnicken
dozen ['dʌzn] *n* Dutzend *nt*; **a ~ books** ein
Dutzend Bücher; **8op a ~** 8o Pence das
Dutzend; **~s of** Dutzende von
DPh, DPhil *n abbr* (= *Doctor of Philosophy*) ≈ Dr. phil.
DPP (*Brit*) *n abbr* (= *Director of Public Prosecutions*)
DPT *n abbr* (= *diphtheria, pertussis, tetanus*)
Diphtherie, Keuchhusten und Tetanus
Dr *abbr* = **doctor**; (*in street names*: = *Drive*) ≈ Str.
dr *abbr* (*Comm*) = **debtor**
drab [dræb] *adj* trist
draft [drɑ:ft] *n* Entwurf *m*; (*also*: **bank draft**)
Tratte *f*; (*US: call-up*) Einberufung *f* ▷ *vt*
entwerfen; *see also* **draught**
draftsman *etc* ['drɑ:ftsmən] (*US*) *n* =
draughtsman *etc*
drag [dræg] *vt* schleifen, schleppen; (*river*)
absuchen ▷ *vi* sich hinziehen ▷ *n* (*Aviat*)
Luftwiderstand *m*; (*Naut*) Wasserwiderstand
m; (*inf*): **to be a ~** (*boring*) langweilig sein; (*a*
nuisance) lästig sein; (*women's clothing*): **in ~** in
Frauenkleidung
▶ **drag away** *vt*: **to ~ away (from)**
wegschleppen *or* wegziehen (von)
▶ **drag on** *vi* sich hinziehen
dragnet ['drægnet] *n* Schleppnetz *nt*; (*fig*) groß
angelegte Polizeiaktion *f*
dragon ['drægn] *n* Drache *m*
dragonfly ['drægənflai] *n* Libelle *f*
dragoon [drə'gu:n] *n* Dragoner *m* ▷ *vt*: **to ~ sb**
into doing sth (*Brit*) jdn zwingen, etw zu tun
drain [drein] *n* Belastung *f*; (*in street*) Gully
m ▷ *vt* entwässern; (*pond*) trockenlegen;
(*vegetables*) abgießen; (*glass, cup*) leeren ▷ *vi*
ablaufen; **to feel ~ed** (*of energy/emotion*)
sich ausgelaugt fühlen
drainage ['dreinidʒ] *n* Entwässerungssystem
nt; (*process*) Entwässerung *f*
draining board ['dreiniŋ-], (*US*) **drainboard**
['dreinbɔ:d] *n* Ablaufbrett *nt*
drainpipe ['dreinpaip] *n* Abflussrohr *nt*
drake [dreik] *n* Erpel *m*, Enterich *m*
dram [dræm] (*Scot*) *n* (*drink*) Schluck *m*
drama ['drɑ:mə] *n* Drama *nt*
dramatic [drə'mætik] *adj* dramatisch;
(*theatrical*) theatralisch
dramatically [drə'mætikli] *adv* dramatisch;
(*say, announce, pause*) theatralisch
dramatist ['dræmətist] *n* Dramatiker(in) *m(f)*
dramatize ['dræmətaiz] *vt* dramatisieren;
(*for TV/cinema*) für das Fernsehen/den Film
bearbeiten
drank [dræŋk] *pt of* **drink**
drape [dreip] *vt* drapieren
drapes [dreips] (*US*) *npl* Vorhänge *pl*
drastic ['dræstik] *adj* drastisch
drastically ['dræstikli] *adv* drastisch

draught, (US) **draft** [drɑːft] n (Luft)zug m; (Naut) Tiefgang m; (of chimney) Zug m; **on ~** vom Fass

draught beer n Bier nt vom Fass

draughtboard ['drɑːftbɔːd] (Brit) n Damebrett nt

draughts [drɑːfts] (Brit) n Damespiel nt

draughtsman, (US) **draftsman** ['drɑːftsmən] (irreg: like **man**) n Zeichner(in) m(f); (as job) technischer Zeichner m, technische Zeichnerin f

draughtsmanship, (US) **draftsmanship** ['drɑːftsmənʃɪp] n zeichnerisches Können nt; (art) Zeichenkunst f

draw [drɔː] (pt **drew**, pp **~n**) vt zeichnen; (cart, gun, tooth, conclusion) ziehen; (curtain: open) aufziehen; (: close) zuziehen; (admiration, attention) erregen; (money) abheben; (wages) bekommen ▷ vi (Sport) unentschieden spielen ▷ n (Sport) Unentschieden nt; (lottery) Lotterie f; (: picking of ticket) Ziehung f; **to ~ a comparison/distinction (between)** einen Vergleich ziehen/Unterschied machen (zwischen +dat); **to ~ near** näher kommen; (event) nahen; **to ~ to a close** zu Ende gehen
  ▶ **draw back** vi: **to ~ back (from)** zurückweichen (von)
  ▶ **draw in** vi (Brit: car) anhalten; (: train) einfahren; (nights) länger werden
  ▶ **draw on** vt (resources) zurückgreifen auf +acc; (imagination) zu Hilfe nehmen; (person) einsetzen
  ▶ **draw out** vi länger werden ▷ vt (money) abheben
  ▶ **draw up** vi (an)halten ▷ vt (chair etc) heranziehen; (document) aufsetzen

drawback ['drɔːbæk] n Nachteil m

drawbridge ['drɔːbrɪdʒ] n Zugbrücke f

drawee [drɔːˈiː] n Bezogene(r) f(m)

drawer [drɔːʳ] n Schublade f

drawing ['drɔːɪŋ] n Zeichnung f; (skill, discipline) Zeichnen nt

drawing board n Reißbrett nt; **back to the ~** (fig) das muss noch einmal neu überdacht werden

drawing pin (Brit) n Reißzwecke f

drawing room n Salon m

drawl [drɔːl] n schleppende Sprechweise f ▷ vi schleppend sprechen

drawn [drɔːn] pp of **draw** ▷ adj abgespannt

drawstring ['drɔːstrɪŋ] n Kordel f zum Zuziehen

dread [drɛd] n Angst f, Furcht f ▷ vt große Angst haben vor +dat

dreadful ['drɛdful] adj schrecklich, furchtbar; **I feel ~!** (ill) ich fühle mich schrecklich; (ashamed) es ist mir schrecklich peinlich

dream [driːm] (pt, pp **dreamed** or **~t**) n Traum m ▷ vt, vi träumen; **to have a ~ about sb/sth** von jdm/etw träumen; **sweet ~s!** träume süß!
  ▶ **dream up** vt sich dat einfallen lassen, sich dat ausdenken

dreamer ['driːməʳ] n Träumer(in) m(f)

dreamt [drɛmt] pt, pp of **dream**

dream world n Traumwelt f

dreamy ['driːmɪ] adj verträumt; (music) zum Träumen

dreary ['drɪərɪ] adj langweilig; (weather) trüb

dredge [drɛdʒ] vt ausbaggern
  ▶ **dredge up** vt ausbaggern; (fig: unpleasant facts) ausgraben

dredger ['drɛdʒəʳ] n (ship) Schwimmbagger m; (machine) Bagger m; (Brit: also: **sugar dredger**) Zuckerstreuer m

dregs [drɛgz] npl Bodensatz m; (of humanity) Abschaum m

drench [drɛntʃ] vt durchnässen; **~ed to the skin** nass bis auf die Haut

dress [drɛs] n Kleid nt; (no pl: clothing) Kleidung f ▷ vt anziehen; (wound) verbinden ▷ vi sich anziehen; **she ~es very well** sie kleidet sich sehr gut; **to ~ a shop window** ein Schaufenster dekorieren; **to get ~ed** sich anziehen
  ▶ **dress up** vi sich fein machen; (in fancy dress) sich verkleiden

dress circle (Brit) n (Theat) erster Rang m

dress designer n Modezeichner(in) m(f)

dresser ['drɛsəʳ] n (Brit) Anrichte f; (US) Kommode f; (also: **window dresser**) Dekorateur(in) m(f)

dressing ['drɛsɪŋ] n Verband m; (Culin) (Salat)soße f

dressing gown (Brit) n Morgenrock m

dressing room n Umkleidekabine f; (Theat) (Künstler)garderobe f

dressing table n Frisierkommode f

dressmaker ['drɛsmeɪkəʳ] n (Damen)schneider(in) m(f)

dressmaking ['drɛsmeɪkɪŋ] n Schneidern nt

dress rehearsal n Generalprobe f

dressy ['drɛsɪ] (inf) adj elegant

drew [druː] pt of **draw**

dribble ['drɪbl] vi tropfen; (baby) sabbern; (Football) dribbeln ▷ vt (ball) dribbeln mit

dried [draɪd] adj (fruit) getrocknet, Dörr-; **~ egg** Trockenei nt, Eipulver nt; **~ milk** Trockenmilch f, Milchpulver nt

drier ['draɪəʳ] n = **dryer**

drift [drɪft] n Strömung f; (of snow) Schneewehe f; (of questions) Richtung f ▷ vi treiben; (sand) wehen; **to let things ~** die Dinge treiben lassen; **to ~ apart** sich auseinanderleben; **I get or catch your ~** ich verstehe, worauf Sie hinauswollen

drifter ['drɪftəʳ] n: **to be a ~** sich treiben lassen

driftwood ['drɪftwud] n Treibholz nt

drill [drɪl] n Bohrer m; (machine) Bohrmaschine f; (Mil) Drill m ▷ vt bohren; (troops) drillen ▷ vi: **to ~ (for)** bohren (nach); **to ~ pupils in grammar** mit den Schülern Grammatik pauken

drilling ['drɪlɪŋ] n Bohrung f

drilling rig n Bohrturm m; (at sea) Bohrinsel f

drily ['draɪlɪ] adv = **dryly**

drink [drɪŋk] (pt **drank**, pp **drunk**) n Getränk nt;

(alcoholic) Glas nt, Drink m; *(sip)* Schluck m ▷ vt, vi trinken; **to have a ~ etwas trinken; a ~ of water** etwas Wasser; **we had ~s before lunch** vor dem Mittagessen gab es einen Drink; **would you like something to ~?** möchten Sie etwas trinken?

▶ **drink in** vt *(fresh air)* einatmen, einsaugen; *(story, sight)* (begierig) in sich aufnehmen

drinkable ['drɪŋkəbl] adj trinkbar

drink-driving ['drɪŋk'draɪvɪŋ] n Trunkenheit f am Steuer

drinker ['drɪŋkəʳ] n Trinker(in) m(f)

drinking ['drɪŋkɪŋ] n Trinken nt

drinking fountain n Trinkwasserbrunnen m

drinking water n Trinkwasser nt

drip [drɪp] n Tropfen nt; *(one drip)* Tropfen m; *(Med)* Tropf m ▷ vi tropfen; *(wall)* triefnass sein

drip-dry ['drɪp'draɪ] adj bügelfrei

drip-feed ['drɪpfiːd] vt künstlich ernähren ▷ n: **to be on a ~** künstlich ernährt werden

dripping ['drɪpɪŋ] n Bratenfett nt ▷ adj triefend; **I'm ~** ich bin klatschnass *(inf)*; **~ wet** triefnass

drive [draɪv] *(pt* **drove**, *pp* **~n**) n Fahrt f; *(also:* **driveway**) Einfahrt f; *(: longer)* Auffahrt f; *(energy)* Schwung m, Elan m; *(campaign)* Aktion f; *(Sport)* Treibschlag m; *(Comput: also:* **disk drive**) Laufwerk nt ▷ vt fahren; *(Tech)* antreiben ▷ vi fahren; **to go for a ~** ein bisschen (raus)fahren; **it's 3 hours' ~ from London** es ist drei Stunden Fahrt von London (entfernt); **left-/right-hand ~** Links-/ Rechtssteuerung f; **front-/rear-wheel ~** Vorderrad-/Hinterradantrieb m; **he ~s a taxi** er ist Taxifahrer; **to ~ sth into sth** *(nail, stake etc)* etw in etw schlagen *acc; (animal)* treiben; *(ball)* weit schlagen; *(incite, encourage: also:* **drive on**) antreiben; **to ~ sb home/to the airport** jdn nach Hause/zum Flughafen fahren; **to ~ sb mad** jdn verrückt machen; **to ~ sb to (do) sth** jdn dazu treiben, etw zu tun; **to ~ at 50 km an hour** mit (einer Geschwindigkeit von) 50 Stundenkilometern fahren; **what are you driving at?** worauf wollen Sie hinaus?

▶ **drive off** vt vertreiben

▶ **drive out** vt *(evil spirit)* austreiben; *(person)* verdrängen

drive-by shooting ['draɪvbaɪ-] n Schusswaffenangriff aus einem vorbeifahrenden Wagen

drive-in ['draɪvɪn] *(esp US)* adj, n: **~ (cinema)** Autokino nt; **~ (restaurant)** Autorestaurant nt

drive-in window *(US)* n Autoschalter m

drivel ['drɪvl] *(inf)* n Blödsinn m

driven ['drɪvn] pp of **drive**

driver ['draɪvəʳ] n Fahrer(in) m(f); *(Rail)* Führer(in) m(f)

driver's license ['draɪvəz-] *(US)* n Führerschein m

driveway ['draɪvweɪ] n Einfahrt f; *(longer)* Auffahrt f

driving ['draɪvɪŋ] n Fahren nt ▷ adj: **~ rain** strömender Regen m; **~ snow** Schneetreiben nt

driving belt n Treibriemen m

driving force n treibende Kraft f

driving instructor n Fahrlehrer(in) m(f)

driving lesson n Fahrstunde f

driving licence *(Brit)* n Führerschein m

driving mirror n Rückspiegel m

driving school n Fahrschule f

driving test n Fahrprüfung f

drizzle ['drɪzl] n Nieselregen m ▷ vi nieseln

droll [drəul] adj drollig

dromedary ['drɔmədərɪ] n Dromedar nt

drone [drəun] n Brummen nt; *(male bee)* Drohne f ▷ vi brummen; *(bee)* summen; *(also:* **drone on**) eintönig sprechen

drool [druːl] vi sabbern; **to ~ over sth/sb** etw/ jdn sehnsüchtig anstarren

droop [druːp] vi *(flower)* den Kopf hängen lassen; **his shoulders/head ~ed** er ließ die Schultern/den Kopf herabhängen

drop [drɔp] n Tropfen m; *(lessening)* Rückgang m; *(distance)* Höhenunterschied m; *(in salary)* Verschlechterung f; *(also:* **parachute drop**) (Ab)sprung m ▷ vt fallen lassen; *(voice, eyes, price)* senken; *(set down from car)* absetzen; *(omit)* weglassen ▷ vi (herunter)fallen; *(wind)* sich legen; **drops** npl Tropfen pl; **a 300 ft ~** ein Höhenunterschied von 300 Fuß; **a ~ of 10%** ein Rückgang um 10%; **cough ~s** Hustentropfen pl; **to ~ anchor** ankern, vor Anker gehen; **to ~ sb a line** jdm ein paar Zeilen schreiben

▶ **drop in** *(inf)* vi: **to ~ in (on sb)** (bei jdm) vorbeikommen

▶ **drop off** vi einschlafen ▷ vt *(passenger)* absetzen

▶ **drop out** vi *(withdraw)* ausscheiden; *(student)* sein Studium abbrechen

droplet ['drɔplɪt] n Tröpfchen nt

dropout ['drɔpaʊt] n Aussteiger(in) m(f); *(Scol)* Studienabbrecher(in) m(f)

dropper ['drɔpəʳ] n Pipette f

droppings ['drɔpɪŋz] npl Kot m

dross [drɔs] n Schlacke f; *(fig)* Schund m

drought [draut] n Dürre f

drove [drəuv] pt of **drive** ▷ n: **~s of people** Scharen pl von Menschen

drown [draun] vt ertränken; *(fig: also:* **drown out**) übertönen ▷ vi ertrinken

drowse [drauz] vi (vor sich acc hin) dösen or dämmern

drowsy ['drauzɪ] adj schläfrig

drudge [drʌdʒ] n Arbeitstier nt

drudgery ['drʌdʒərɪ] n (stumpfsinnige) Plackerei f *(inf)*; **housework is sheer ~** Hausarbeit ist eine einzige Plackerei

drug [drʌg] n Medikament nt, Arzneimittel nt; *(narcotic)* Droge f, Rauschgift nt ▷ vt betäuben; **to be on ~s** drogensüchtig sein; **hard/soft ~s** harte/weiche Drogen pl

drug abuse n Drogenmissbrauch m; **~ prevention** Drogenprävention f

drug addict n Drogensüchtige(r) f(m), Rauschgiftsüchtige(r) f(m)

druggist ['drʌgɪst] *(US)* n Drogist(in) m(f)

drug peddler n Drogenhändler(in) m(f), Dealer m (inf)

drugstore ['drʌgstɔ:ʳ] (US) n Drogerie f

drum [drʌm] n Trommel f; (for oil, petrol) Fass nt ▷ vi trommeln; **drums** npl (kit) Schlagzeug nt ▶ **drum up** vt (enthusiasm) erwecken; (support) auftreiben

drummer ['drʌməʳ] n Trommler(in) m(f); (in band, pop group) Schlagzeuger(in) m(f)

drum roll n Trommelwirbel m

drumstick ['drʌmstɪk] n Trommelstock m; (of chicken) Keule f

drunk [drʌŋk] pp of **drink** ▷ adj betrunken ▷ n (also: **drunkard**) Trinker(in) m(f); **to get** ~ sich betrinken; **a ~ driving offence** Trunkenheit f am Steuer

drunken ['drʌŋkən] adj betrunken; (party) feucht-fröhlich; **~ driving** Trunkenheit f am Steuer

drunkenness ['drʌŋkənnɪs] n (state) Betrunkenheit f; (habit) Trunksucht f

dry [draɪ] adj trocken ▷ vt, vi trocknen; **on ~ land** auf festem Boden; **to ~ one's hands/ hair/eyes** sich dat die Hände (ab)trocknen/die Haare trocknen/die Tränen abwischen; **to ~ the dishes** (das Geschirr) abtrocknen ▶ **dry up** vi austrocknen; (in speech) den Faden verlieren

dry-clean ['draɪ'kli:n] vt chemisch reinigen

dry-cleaner ['draɪ'kli:nəʳ] n (job) Inhaber(in) m(f) einer chemischen Reinigung; (shop: also: **dry-cleaner's**) chemische Reinigung f

dry-cleaning ['draɪ'kli:nɪŋ] n (process) chemische Reinigung f

dry dock n Trockendock nt

dryer ['draɪəʳ] n Wäschetrockner m; (US: spin-dryer) Wäscheschleuder f

dry goods npl Kurzwaren pl

dry ice n Trockeneis nt

dryly ['draɪlɪ] adv (say, remark) trocken

dryness ['draɪnɪs] n Trockenheit f

dry rot n (Haus)schwamm m, (Holz)schwamm m

dry run n (fig) Probe f

dry ski slope n Trockenskipiste f

DSc n abbr (= Doctor of Science) ≈ Dr. rer. nat.

DSL n abbr (Comput: = digital subscriber line) DSL

DSL connection n (Comput) DSL-Anschluss m

DSS n abbr (= Department of Social Security) Ministerium für Sozialfürsorge

DST abbr = **daylight-saving time**

DTI (Brit) n abbr (= Department of Trade and Industry) ≈ Wirtschaftsministerium nt

DTP n abbr (= desktop publishing) DTP nt; see also **desktop publishing**; (= diphtheria, tetanus, pertussis) Diphtherie, Tetanus und Keuchhusten

DT's (inf) npl abbr (= delirium tremens) Delirium tremens nt; **to have the** ~ vom Trinken den Tatterich haben (inf)

dual ['djuəl] adj doppelt; (personality) gespalten

dual carriageway (Brit) n ≈ Schnellstraße f

dual nationality n doppelte

Staatsangehörigkeit f

dual-purpose ['djuəl'pə:pəs] adj zweifach verwendbar

dubbed [dʌbd] adj synchronisiert; (nicknamed) getauft

dubious ['dju:bɪəs] adj zweifelhaft; **I'm very ~ about it** ich habe da (doch) starke Zweifel

Dublin ['dʌblɪn] n Dublin nt

Dubliner ['dʌblɪnəʳ] n Dubliner(in) m(f)

duchess ['dʌtʃɪs] n Herzogin f

duck [dʌk] n Ente f ▷ vi (also: **duck down**) sich ducken ▷ vt (blow) ausweichen +dat; (duty, responsibility) aus dem Weg gehen +dat

duckling ['dʌklɪŋ] n Entenküken nt; (Culin) (junge) Ente f

duct [dʌkt] n Rohr nt; (Anat) Röhre f; **tear ~** Tränenkanal m

dud [dʌd] n Niete f (inf); (note) Blüte f (inf) ▷ adj: ~ **cheque** (Brit) ungedeckter Scheck m

due [dju:] adj fällig; (attention etc) gebührend; (consideration) reiflich ▷ n: **to give sb his/her ~** jdn gerecht behandeln ▷ adv: ~ **north** direkt nach Norden; **dues** npl Beitrag m; (in harbour) Gebühren pl; **in ~ course** zu gegebener Zeit; (eventually) im Laufe der Zeit; ~ **to** (owing to) wegen +gen, aufgrund +gen; **to be ~ to do sth** etw tun sollen; **the rent is ~ on the 30th** die Miete ist am 30. fällig; **the train is ~ at 8** der Zug soll (laut Fahrplan) um 8 ankommen; **she is ~ back tomorrow** sie müsste morgen zurück sein; **I am ~ 6 days' leave** mir stehen 6 Tage Urlaub zu

due date n Fälligkeitsdatum nt

duel ['djuəl] n Duell nt

duet [dju:'ɛt] n Duett nt

duff [dʌf] (Brit: inf) adj kaputt ▶ **duff up** vt vermöbeln

duffel bag ['dʌfl-] n Matchbeutel m

duffel coat n Dufflecoat m

duffer ['dʌfəʳ] (inf) n Versager m, Flasche f

dug [dʌg] pt, pp of **dig**

dugout ['dʌgaut] n (canoe) Einbaum m; (shelter) Unterstand m

duke [dju:k] n Herzog m

dull [dʌl] adj trüb; (intelligence, wit) schwerfällig, langsam; (event) langweilig; (sound, pain) dumpf ▷ vt (pain, grief) betäuben; (mind, senses) abstumpfen

duly ['dju:lɪ] adv (properly) gebührend; (on time) pünktlich

dumb [dʌm] adj stumm; (pej: stupid) dumm, doof (inf); **he was struck** ~ es verschlug ihm die Sprache ▶ **dumb down** vi an Niveau or Qualität verlieren, verflachen ▷ vt fus verdummen, dumm machen

dumbbell ['dʌmbɛl] n Hantel f

dumbfounded [dʌm'faundɪd] adj verblüfft

dumbing down [dʌmɪŋ'daun] n Verdummung f, Qualitätsverlust m

dummy ['dʌmɪ] n (Schneider)puppe f; (mock-up) Attrappe f; (Sport) Finte f; (Brit: for baby) Schnuller m ▷ adj (firm) fiktiv; ~ **bullets**

d

Übungsmunition f

dummy run n Probe f

dump [dʌmp] n (also: **rubbish dump**) Abfallhaufen m; (inf: place) Müllkippe f; (Mil) Depot nt ▷ vt fallen lassen; (get rid of) abladen; (car) abstellen; (Comput: data) ausgeben; **to be down in the ~s** (inf) deprimiert or down sein; **"no ~ing"** „Schuttabladen verboten"

dumpling ['dʌmplɪŋ] n Kloß m, Knödel m

dumpy ['dʌmpɪ] adj pummelig

dunce [dʌns] n Niete f

dune [djuːn] n Düne f

dung [dʌŋ] n (Agr) Dünger m, Mist m; (Zool) Dung m

dungarees [dʌŋɡə'riːz] npl Latzhose f

dungeon ['dʌndʒən] n Kerker m, Verlies nt

dunk [dʌŋk] vt (ein)tunken

Dunkirk [dʌn'kɜːk] n Dünkirchen nt

duo ['djuːəʊ] n Duo nt

duodenal [djuːəʊ'diːnl] adj Duodenal-; **~ ulcer** Zwölffingerdarmgeschwür nt

duodenum [djuːəʊ'diːnəm] n Zwölffingerdarm m

dupe [djuːp] n Betrogene(r) f(m) ▷ vt betrügen

duplex ['djuːplɛks] (US) n Zweifamilienhaus nt; (apartment) zweistöckige Wohnung f

duplicate [n, adj 'djuːplɪkət, vt 'djuːplɪkeɪt] n (also: **duplicate copy**) Duplikat nt, Kopie f; (also: **duplicate key**) Zweitschlüssel m ▷ adj doppelt ▷ vt kopieren; (repeat) wiederholen; **in ~** in doppelter Ausfertigung

duplicating machine ['djuːplɪkeɪtɪŋ-] n Vervielfältigungsapparat m

duplicator ['djuːplɪkeɪtəʳ] n Vervielfältigungsapparat m

duplicity [djuː'plɪsɪtɪ] n Doppelspiel nt

Dur. (Brit) abbr (Post) = Durham

durability [djʊərə'bɪlɪtɪ] n Haltbarkeit f

durable ['djʊərəbl] adj haltbar

duration [djʊə'reɪʃən] n Dauer f

duress [djʊə'rɛs] n: **under ~** unter Zwang

Durex® ['djʊərɛks] (Brit) n Gummi m (inf)

during ['djʊərɪŋ] prep während +gen

dusk [dʌsk] n (Abend)dämmerung f

dusky ['dʌskɪ] adj (room) dunkel; (light) Dämmer-

dust [dʌst] n Staub m ▷ vt abstauben; (cake etc): **to ~ with** bestäuben mit
▶ **dust off** vt abwischen, wegwischen; (fig) hervorkramen

dustbin ['dʌstbɪn] (Brit) n Mülltonne f

dustbin liner (Brit) n Müllsack m

duster ['dʌstəʳ] n Staubtuch nt

dust jacket n (Schutz)umschlag m

dustman ['dʌstmən] (Brit: irreg: like **man**) n Müllmann m

dustpan ['dʌstpæn] n Kehrschaufel f, Müllschaufel f

dusty ['dʌstɪ] adj staubig

Dutch [dʌtʃ] adj holländisch, niederländisch ▷ n Holländisch nt, Niederländisch nt ▷ adv: **to go ~** (inf) getrennte Kasse machen; **the Dutch** npl die Holländer pl, die Niederländer pl

Dutch auction n Versteigerung mit stufenweise erniedrigtem Ausbietungspreis

Dutchman ['dʌtʃmən] (irreg: like **man**) n Holländer m, Niederländer m

Dutchwoman ['dʌtʃwumən] (irreg: like **woman**) n Holländerin f, Niederländerin f

dutiable ['djuːtɪəbl] adj zollpflichtig

dutiful ['djuːtɪful] adj pflichtbewusst; (son, daughter) gehorsam

duty ['djuːtɪ] n Pflicht f; (tax) Zoll m; **duties** npl (functions) Aufgaben pl; **to make it one's ~ to do sth** es sich dat zur Pflicht machen, etw zu tun; **to pay ~ on sth** Zoll auf etw acc zahlen; **on/off ~** im/nicht im Dienst

duty-free ['djuːtɪ'friː] adj zollfrei; **~ shop** Dutyfreeshop m, Duty-free-Shop m

duty officer n Offizier m vom Dienst

duvet ['duːveɪ] (Brit) n Federbett nt

DV abbr (= Deo volente) so Gott will

DVD n abbr (= digital versatile or video disc) DVD f

DVLA (Brit) n abbr (= Driver and Vehicle Licensing Authority) Zulassungsbehörde für Kraftfahrzeuge

DVM (US) n abbr (= Doctor of Veterinary Medicine) = Dr. med. vet.

dwarf [dwɔːf] (pl **dwarves**) n Zwerg(in) m(f) ▷ vt: **to be ~ed by sth** neben etw dat klein erscheinen

dwarves [dwɔːvz] npl of **dwarf**

dwell [dwɛl] (pt, pp **dwelt**) vi wohnen, leben
▶ **dwell on** vt fus (in Gedanken) verweilen bei

dweller ['dwɛləʳ] n Bewohner(in) m(f); **city ~** Stadtbewohner(in) m(f)

dwelling ['dwɛlɪŋ] n Wohnhaus nt

dwelt [dwɛlt] pt, pp of **dwell**

dwindle ['dwɪndl] vi abnehmen; (interest) schwinden; (attendance) zurückgehen

dwindling ['dwɪndlɪŋ] adj (strength, interest) schwindend; (resources, supplies) versiegend

dye [daɪ] n Farbstoff m; (for hair) Färbemittel n ▷ vt färben

dyestuffs ['daɪstʌfs] npl Farbstoffe pl

dying ['daɪɪŋ] adj sterbend; (moments, words) letzte(r, s)

dyke [daɪk] n (Brit: wall) Deich m, Damm m; (channel) (Entwässerungs)graben m; (causeway) Fahrdamm m

dynamic [daɪ'næmɪk] adj dynamisch

dynamics [daɪ'næmɪks] n or npl Dynamik f

dynamite ['daɪnəmaɪt] n Dynamit nt ▷ vt sprengen

dynamo ['daɪnəməʊ] n Dynamo m; (Aut) Lichtmaschine f

dynasty ['dɪnəstɪ] n Dynastie f

dysentery ['dɪsntrɪ] n (Med) Ruhr f

dyslexia [dɪs'lɛksɪə] n Legasthenie f

dyslexic [dɪs'lɛksɪk] adj legasthenisch ▷ n Legastheniker(in) m(f)

dyspepsia [dɪs'pɛpsɪə] n Dyspepsie f, Verdauungsstörung f

dystrophy ['dɪstrəfɪ] n Dystrophie f, Ernährungsstörung f; **muscular ~** Muskelschwund m

Ee

E¹, e [i:] *n* (*letter*) E *nt*, e *nt*; **E for Edward, E for Easy** (*US*) E wie Emil

E² [i:] *n* (*Mus*) E *nt*, e *nt*

E³ [i:] *abbr* (= *east*) O ▷ *n abbr* (*drug*: = *Ecstasy*) Ecstasy *nt*

e- *pref* E-, elektronisch

E111 *n abbr* (*also*: **form E111**) E111-Formular *nt*

ea. *abbr* = **each**

each [i:tʃ] *adj, pron* jede(r, s); ~ **other** sich, einander; **they hate ~ other** sie hassen sich *or* einander; **you are jealous of ~ other** ihr seid eifersüchtig aufeinander; ~ **day** jeden Tag; **they have 2 books ~** sie haben je 2 Bücher; **they cost £5 ~** sie kosten 5 Pfund das Stück; ~ **of us** jede(r, s) von uns

eager ['i:gəʳ] *adj* eifrig; **to be ~ to do sth** etw unbedingt tun wollen; **to be ~ for sth** auf etw *acc* erpicht *or* aus (*inf*) sein

eagerly ['i:gəlɪ] *adv* eifrig; (*awaited*) gespannt, ungeduldig

eagle ['i:gl] *n* Adler *m*

ear [ɪəʳ] *n* Ohr *nt*; (*of corn*) Ähre *f*; **to be up to one's ~s in debt/work** bis über beide Ohren in Schulden/Arbeit stecken; **to be up to one's ~s in paint/baking** mitten im Anstreichen/Backen stecken; **to give sb a thick ~** jdm ein paar hinter die Ohren geben; **we'll play it by ~** (*fig*) wir werden es auf uns zukommen lassen

earache ['ɪəreɪk] *n* Ohrenschmerzen *pl*

eardrum ['ɪədrʌm] *n* Trommelfell *nt*

earful ['ɪəful] (*inf*) *n*: **to give sb an ~** jdm was erzählen; **to get an ~** was zu hören bekommen

earl [ə:l] (*Brit*) *n* Graf *m*

earlier ['ə:lɪəʳ] *adj, adv* früher; **I can't come any ~** ich kann nicht früher *or* eher kommen

early ['ə:lɪ] *adv* früh; (*ahead of time*) zu früh ▷ *adj* früh; (*Christians*) Ur-; (*death, departure*) vorzeitig; (*reply*) baldig; ~ **in the morning** früh am Morgen; **to have an ~ night** früh ins Bett gehen; **in the ~ hours** in den frühen Morgenstunden; **in the ~** *or* ~ **in the spring/19th century** Anfang des Frühjahrs/des 19. Jahrhunderts; **take the ~ train** nimm den früheren Zug; **you're ~!** Sie sind früh dran!; **she's in her ~ forties** sie ist Anfang Vierzig; **at your earliest convenience** so

bald wie möglich

early retirement *n*: **to take ~** vorzeitig in den Ruhestand gehen

early retirement benefits *npl* Vorruhestandsleistungen *pl*

early warning system *n* Frühwarnsystem *nt*

earmark ['ɪəmɑ:k] *vt*: **to ~ (for)** bestimmen (für), vorsehen (für)

earn [ə:n] *vt* verdienen; (*interest*) bringen; **to ~ one's living** seinen Lebensunterhalt verdienen; **this ~ed him much praise, he ~ed much praise for this** das trug ihm viel Lob ein; **he's ~ed his rest/reward** er hat sich seine Pause/Belohnung verdient

earned income [ə:nd-] *n* Arbeitseinkommen *nt*

earnest ['ə:nɪst] *adj* ernsthaft; (*wish, desire*) innig ▷ *n* (*also*: **earnest money**) Angeld *nt*; **in ~** (*adv*) richtig; (*adj*): **to be in ~** es ernst meinen; **work on the tunnel soon began in ~** die Tunnelarbeiten begannen bald richtig; **is the Minister in ~ about these proposals?** meint der Minister diese Vorschläge ernst?

earnings ['ə:nɪŋz] *npl* Verdienst *m*; (*of company etc*) Ertrag *m*

ear, nose and throat specialist *n* Hals-Nasen-Ohren-Arzt *m*, Hals-Nasen-Ohren-Ärztin *f*

earphones ['ɪəfəunz] *npl* Kopfhörer *pl*

earplugs ['ɪəplʌgz] *npl* Ohropax® *nt*

earring ['ɪərɪŋ] *n* Ohrring *m*

earset ['ɪəset] *n* (*Tel*) Earset *nt*, Ohrhörer *m*

earshot ['ɪəʃɔt] *n*: **within/out of ~** in/außer Hörweite

earth [ə:θ] *n* Erde *f*; (*of fox*) Bau *m* ▷ *vt* (*Brit*: *Elec*) erden

earthenware ['ə:θnwɛəʳ] *n* Tongeschirr *nt* ▷ *adj* Ton-

earthly ['ə:θlɪ] *adj* irdisch; ~ **paradise** Paradies *nt* auf Erden; **there is no ~ reason to think ...** es besteht nicht der geringste Grund für die Annahme ...

earthquake ['ə:θkweɪk] *n* Erdbeben *nt*

earthshattering ['ə:θʃætərɪŋ] *adj* (*fig*) weltbewegend

earth tremor *n* Erdstoß *m*

earthworks ['ə:θwə:ks] *npl* Erdarbeiten *pl*

earthworm ['ə:θwə:m] *n* Regenwurm *m*

earthy ['ə:θɪ] *adj* (*humour*) derb

earwig ['ɪəwɪg] *n* Ohrwurm *m*

ease [i:z] *n* Leichtigkeit *f*; (*comfort*) Behagen *nt* ▷ *vt* (*problem*) vereinfachen; (*pain*) lindern; (*tension*) verringern; (*loosen*) lockern ▷ *vi* nachlassen; (*situation*) sich entspannen; **to ~ sth in/out** (*push/pull*) etw behutsam hineinschieben/herausziehen; **at ~!** (*Mil*) rührt euch!; **with ~** mit Leichtigkeit; **life of ~** Leben *nt* der Muße; **to ~ in the clutch** die Kupplung behutsam kommen lassen
  ▶ **ease off** *vi* nachlassen; (*slow down*) langsamer werden
  ▶ **ease up** *vi* = **ease off**

easel ['i:zl] *n* Staffelei *f*

easily ['i:zɪlɪ] *adv* (*see adj*) leicht; ungezwungen; bequem

easiness ['i:zɪnɪs] *n* Leichtigkeit *f*; (*of manner*) Ungezwungenheit *f*

east [i:st] *n* Osten *m* ▷ *adj* (*coast, Asia etc*) Ost- ▷ *adv* ostwärts, nach Osten; **the E~** der Osten

Easter ['i:stə'] *n* Ostern *nt* ▷ *adj* (*holidays etc*) Oster-

Easter egg *n* Osterei *nt*

Easter Island *n* Osterinsel *f*

easterly ['i:stəlɪ] *adj* östlich; (*wind*) Ost-

Easter Monday *n* Ostermontag *m*

eastern ['i:stən] *adj* östlich; **E~ Europe** Osteuropa *nt*; **the E~ bloc** (*formerly*) der Ostblock

Easter Sunday *n* Ostersonntag *m*

East Germany *n* (*formerly*) die DDR *f*

eastward ['i:stwəd], **eastwards** ['i:stwədz] *adv* ostwärts, nach Osten

easy ['i:zɪ] *adj* leicht; (*relaxed*) ungezwungen; (*comfortable*) bequem ▷ *adv*: **to take it/things ~** (*go slowly*) sich *dat* Zeit lassen; (*not worry*) es nicht so schwernehmen; (*rest*) sich schonen; **payment on ~ terms** Zahlung zu günstigen Bedingungen; **that's easier said than done** das ist leichter gesagt als getan; **I'm ~** (*inf*) mir ist alles recht

easy chair *n* Sessel *m*

easy-going ['i:zɪ'gəʊɪŋ] *adj* gelassen

easy touch (*inf*) *n*: **to be an ~** (*for money etc*) leicht anzuzapfen sein

eat [i:t] (*pt* **ate**, *pp* **~en**) *vt, vi* essen; (*animal*) fressen
  ▶ **eat away** *vt* (*subj: sea*) auswaschen; (*: acid*) zerfressen
  ▶ **eat away at** *vt fus* (*metal*) anfressen; (*savings*) angreifen
  ▶ **eat into** *vt fus* = **eat away at**
  ▶ **eat out** *vi* essen gehen
  ▶ **eat up** *vt* aufessen; **it ~s up electricity** es verbraucht viel Strom

eatable ['i:təbl] *adj* genießbar

eau de Cologne ['əʊdəkə'ləʊn] *n* Kölnischwasser *nt*, Eau de Cologne *nt*

eaves [i:vz] *npl* Dachvorsprung *m*

eavesdrop ['i:vzdrɔp] *vi* lauschen; **to ~ on** belauschen +*acc*

ebb [ɛb] *n* Ebbe *f* ▷ *vi* ebben; (*fig: also*: **ebb away**) dahinschwinden; (*: feeling*) abebben; **the ~ and flow** (*fig*) das Auf und Ab; **to be at a low ~** (*fig*) auf einem Tiefpunkt angelangt sein

ebb tide *n* Ebbe *f*

ebony ['ɛbənɪ] *n* Ebenholz *nt*

ebullient [ɪ'bʌlɪənt] *adj* überschäumend, übersprudelnd

EC *n abbr* (= *European Community*) EG *f*

e-card ['i:kɑ:d] *n abbr* (= *electronic card*) E-Card *nt*, *elektronische Grußkarte*

ECB *n abbr* (= *European Central Bank*) EZB *f*

eccentric [ɪk'sɛntrɪk] *adj* exzentrisch ▷ *n* Exzentriker(in) *m(f)*

ecclesiastic [ɪkli:zɪ'æstɪk], **ecclesiastical** [ɪkli:zɪ'æstɪkl] *adj* kirchlich

ECG *n abbr* (= *electrocardiogram*) EKG *nt*

echo ['ɛkəʊ] (*pl* **~es**) *n* Echo *nt* ▷ *vt* wiederholen ▷ *vi* widerhallen; (*place*) hallen

éclair [eɪ'klɛə'] *n* Eclair *nt*

eclipse [ɪ'klɪps] *n* Finsternis *f* ▷ *vt* in den Schatten stellen

eco- ['i:kəʊ] *pref* Öko-, öko-

ecofriendly *adj* umweltfreundlich

ecological [i:kə'lɔdʒɪkəl] *adj* ökologisch; (*damage, disaster*) Umwelt-

ecologist [ɪ'kɔlədʒɪst] *n* Ökologe *m*, Ökologin *f*

ecology [ɪ'kɔlədʒɪ] *n* Ökologie *f*

e-commerce [i:'kɔmə:s] *n* E-Commerce *nt*, elektronischer Handel

economic [i:kə'nɔmɪk] *adj* (*system, policy etc*) Wirtschafts-; (*profitable*) wirtschaftlich

economical [i:kə'nɔmɪkl] *adj* wirtschaftlich; (*person*) sparsam

economically [i:kə'nɔmɪklɪ] *adv* wirtschaftlich; (*thriftily*) sparsam

economics [i:kə'nɔmɪks] *n* Wirtschaftswissenschaften *pl* ▷ *npl* Wirtschaftlichkeit *f*; (*of situation*) wirtschaftliche Seite *f*

economist [ɪ'kɔnəmɪst] *n* Wirtschaftswissenschaftler(in) *m(f)*

economize [ɪ'kɔnəmaɪz] *vi* sparen

economy [ɪ'kɔnəmɪ] *n* Wirtschaft *f*; (*financial prudence*) Sparsamkeit *f*; **economies of scale** (*Comm*) Einsparungen *pl* durch erhöhte Produktion

economy class *n* Touristenklasse *f*

economy size *n* Sparpackung *f*

ecosystem ['i:kəʊsɪstəm] *n* Ökosystem *nt*

ecotourism ['i:kəʊ'tʊərɪzm] *n* Ökotourismus *m*

ECSC *n abbr* (= *European Coal and Steel Community*) *Europäische Gemeinschaft für Kohle und Stahl*

ecstasy ['ɛkstəsɪ] *n* Ekstase *f*; (*drug*) Ecstasy *nt*; **to go into ecstasies over** in Verzückung geraten über +*acc*; **in ~** verzückt

ecstatic [ɛks'tætɪk] *adj* ekstatisch

ECT *n abbr* = **electroconvulsive therapy**

Ecuador ['ɛkwədɔ:'] *n* Ecuador *nt*, Ekuador *nt*

ecumenical [i:kju'mɛnɪkl] *adj* ökumenisch

eczema ['ɛksɪmə] *n* Ekzem *nt*

eddy ['ɛdɪ] *n* Strudel *m*

edge [ɛdʒ] *n* Rand *m*; (*of table, chair*) Kante *f*; (*of lake*) Ufer *nt*; (*of knife etc*) Schneide *f* ▷ *vt*

einfassen ▷ vi: **to ~ forward** sich nach vorne
schieben; **on ~** (fig) = **edgy**; **to have the ~
on** überlegen sein +dat; **to ~ away from** sich
allmählich entfernen von; **to ~ past** sich
vorbeischieben, sich vorbeidrücken
edgeways ['ɛdʒweɪz] adv: **he couldn't get a
word in ~** er kam überhaupt nicht zu Wort
edging ['ɛdʒɪŋ] n Einfassung f
edgy ['ɛdʒɪ] adj nervös
edible ['ɛdɪbl] adj essbar, genießbar
edict ['iːdɪkt] n Erlass m
edifice ['ɛdɪfɪs] n Gebäude nt
edifying ['ɛdɪfaɪɪŋ] adj erbaulich
Edinburgh ['ɛdɪnbərə] n Edinburg(h) nt
edit ['ɛdɪt] vt (text) redigieren; (book)
lektorieren; (film, broadcast) schneiden, cutten;
(newspaper, magazine) herausgeben; (Comput)
editieren
edition [ɪ'dɪʃən] n Ausgabe f
editor ['ɛdɪtə'] n Redakteur(in) m(f); (of
newspaper, magazine) Herausgeber(in) m(f); (of
book) Lektor(in) m(f); (Cine, Radio, TV) Cutter(in)
m(f)
editorial [ɛdɪ'tɔːrɪəl] adj redaktionell; (staff)
Redaktions- ▷ n Leitartikel m
EDP n abbr (Comput: = electronic data processing)
EDV f
EDT (US) abbr (= Eastern Daylight Time)
ostamerikanische Sommerzeit
educate ['ɛdjukeɪt] vt erziehen; **~d at ...** zur
Schule/Universität gegangen in ...
educated ['ɛdjukeɪtɪd] adj gebildet
educated guess ['ɛdjukeɪtɪd-] n wohl
begründete Vermutung f
education [ɛdju'keɪʃən] n Erziehung f;
(schooling) Ausbildung f; (knowledge, culture)
Bildung f; **primary ~, elementary ~** (US)
Grundschul(aus)bildung f; **secondary ~**
höhere Schul(aus)bildung f
educational [ɛdju'keɪʃənl] adj
pädagogisch; (experience) lehrreich; (toy)
pädagogisch wertvoll; **~ technology**
Unterrichtstechnologie f
Edwardian [ɛd'wɔːdɪən] adj aus der Zeit
Edwards VII
EE abbr = **electrical engineer**
EEG n abbr (= electroencephalogram) EEG nt
eel [iːl] n Aal m
EEOC (US) n abbr (= Equal Employment Opportunity
Commission) Kommission für Gleichberechtigung am
Arbeitsplatz
eerie ['ɪərɪ] adj unheimlich
EET abbr (= Eastern European Time) OEZ f
efface [ɪ'feɪs] vt auslöschen; **to ~ o.s.** sich im
Hintergrund halten
effect [ɪ'fɛkt] n Wirkung f, Effekt m ▷ vt
bewirken; (repairs) durchführen; **effects** npl
Effekten pl; (Theat, Cine etc) Effekte pl; **to take
~** (law) in Kraft treten; (drug) wirken; **to put
into ~** in Kraft setzen; **to have an ~ on sb/
sth** eine Wirkung auf jdn/etw haben; **in ~**
eigentlich, praktisch; **his letter is to the ~
that ...** sein Brief hat zum Inhalt, dass ...

effective [ɪ'fɛktɪv] adj effektiv, wirksam;
(actual) eigentlich, wirklich; **to become
~ in Kraft treten; ~ date** Zeitpunkt m des
Inkrafttretens
effectively [ɪ'fɛktɪvlɪ] adv effektiv
effectiveness [ɪ'fɛktɪvnɪs] n Wirksamkeit f,
Effektivität f
effeminate [ɪ'fɛmɪnɪt] adj feminin,
effeminiert
effervescent [ɛfə'vɛsnt] adj sprudelnd
efficacy ['ɛfɪkəsɪ] n Wirksamkeit f
efficiency [ɪ'fɪʃənsɪ] n (see adj) Fähigkeit
f, Tüchtigkeit f; Rationalität f;
Leistungsfähigkeit f
efficiency apartment (US) n
Einzimmerwohnung f
efficient [ɪ'fɪʃənt] adj fähig, tüchtig;
(organization) rationell; (machine) leistungsfähig
efficiently [ɪ'fɪʃəntlɪ] adv gut, effizient
effigy ['ɛfɪdʒɪ] n Bildnis nt
effluent ['ɛfluənt] n Abwasser nt
effort ['ɛfət] n Anstrengung f; (attempt)
Versuch m; **to make an ~ to do sth** sich
bemühen, etw zu tun
effortless ['ɛfətlɪs] adj mühelos; (style) flüssig
effrontery [ɪ'frʌntərɪ] n Unverschämtheit f; **to
have the ~ to do sth** die Frechheit besitzen,
etw zu tun
effusive [ɪ'fjuːsɪv] adj überschwänglich
EFL n abbr (Scol: = English as a Foreign Language)
Englisch nt als Fremdsprache
EFTA ['ɛftə] n abbr (= European Free Trade
Association) EFTA f
e.g. adv abbr (= exempli gratia) z. B.
egalitarian [ɪgælɪ'tɛərɪən] adj egalitär;
(principles) Gleichheits- ▷ n Verfechter(in) m(f)
des Egalitarismus
egg [ɛg] n Ei nt; **hard-boiled/soft-boiled ~**
hart/weich gekochtes Ei nt
  ▶ **egg on** vt anstacheln
egg cup n Eierbecher m
eggplant ['ɛgplɑːnt] n (esp US) Aubergine f
eggshell ['ɛgʃel] n Eierschale f ▷ adj
eierschalenfarben
egg timer n Eieruhr f
egg white n Eiweiß nt
egg yolk n Eigelb nt
ego ['iːgəu] n (self-esteem) Selbstbewusstsein nt
egoism ['ɛgəuɪzəm] n Egoismus m
egoist ['ɛgəuɪst] n Egoist(in) m(f)
egotism ['ɛgəutɪzəm] n Ichbezogenheit f,
Egotismus m
egotist ['ɛgəutɪst] n ichbezogener Mensch m,
Egotist(in) m(f)
ego trip (inf) n Egotrip m
Egypt ['iːdʒɪpt] n Ägypten nt
Egyptian [ɪ'dʒɪpʃən] adj ägyptisch ▷ n
Ägypter(in) m(f)
eiderdown ['aɪdədaun] n Federbett nt,
Daunendecke f
eight [eɪt] num acht
eighteen [eɪ'tiːn] num achtzehn
eighteenth [eɪ'tiːnθ] num achtzehnte(r, s)

535

eighth [eɪtθ] num achte(r, s) ▷ n Achtel nt
eighty ['eɪtɪ] num achtzig
Eire ['ɛərə] n (Republik f) Irland nt
EIS n abbr (= Educational Institute of Scotland) schottische Lehrergewerkschaft
either ['aɪðəʳ] adj (one or other) eine(r, s) (von beiden); (both, each) beide pl, jede(r, s) ▷ pron: ~ **(of them)** eine(r, s) (davon) ▷ adv auch nicht ▷ conj: ~ **yes or no** entweder ja oder nein; **on** ~ **side** (on both sides) auf beiden Seiten; (on one or other side) auf einer der beiden Seiten; **I don't like** ~ ich mag beide nicht or keinen von beiden; **no, I don't** ~ nein, ich auch nicht; **I haven't seen** ~ **one or the other** ich habe weder den einen noch den anderen gesehen
ejaculation [ɪdʒækju'leɪʃən] n Ejakulation f, Samenerguss m
eject [ɪ'dʒɛkt] vt ausstoßen; (tenant, gatecrasher) hinauswerfen ▷ vi den Schleudersitz betätigen
ejector seat [ɪ'dʒɛktə-] n Schleudersitz m
eke out vt (make last) strecken
EKG (US) n abbr = **electrocardiogram**
el [ɛl] (US: inf) n abbr = **elevated railroad**
elaborate [adj ɪ'læbərɪt, vb ɪ'læbəreɪt] adj kompliziert; (plan) ausgefeilt ▷ vt näher ausführen; (refine) ausarbeiten ▷ vi mehr ins Detail gehen; **to ~ on** näher ausführen
elapse [ɪ'læps] vi vergehen, verstreichen
elastic [ɪ'læstɪk] n Gummi nt ▷ adj elastisch
elastic band (Brit) n Gummiband nt
elasticity [ɪlæs'tɪsɪtɪ] n Elastizität f
elated [ɪ'leɪtɪd] adj: **to be** ~ hocherfreut or in Hochstimmung sein
elation [ɪ'leɪʃən] n große Freude f, Hochstimmung f
elbow ['ɛlbəu] n Ell(en)bogen m ▷ vt: **to ~ one's way through the crowd** sich durch die Menge boxen
elbow grease (inf) n Muskelkraft f
elbowroom ['ɛlbəurum] n Ellbogenfreiheit f
elder ['ɛldəʳ] adj älter ▷ n (Bot) Holunder m; (older person: gen pl) Ältere(r) f(m)
elderly ['ɛldəlɪ] adj ältere(r, s) ▷ npl: **the** ~ ältere Leute pl
elder statesman n erfahrener Staatsmann m
eldest ['ɛldɪst] adj älteste(r, s) ▷ n Älteste(r) f(m)
elect [ɪ'lɛkt] vt wählen ▷ adj: **the president** ~ der designierte or künftige Präsident; **to ~ to do sth** sich dafür entscheiden, etw zu tun
election [ɪ'lɛkʃən] n Wahl f; **to hold an** ~ eine Wahl abhalten
election campaign n Wahlkampf m
election débâcle n Wahldebakel nt
electioneering [ɪlɛkʃə'nɪərɪŋ] n Wahlkampf m
elector [ɪ'lɛktəʳ] n Wähler(in) m(f)
electoral [ɪ'lɛktərəl] adj Wähler-
electoral college n Wahlmännergremium nt
electorate [ɪ'lɛktərɪt] n Wähler pl, Wählerschaft f
electric [ɪ'lɛktrɪk] adj elektrisch
electrical [ɪ'lɛktrɪkl] adj elektrisch; (appliance) Elektro-; (failure) Strom-

electrical engineer n Elektrotechniker m
electric blanket n Heizdecke f
electric chair (US) n elektrischer Stuhl m
electric cooker n Elektroherd m
electric current n elektrischer Strom m
electric fire (Brit) n elektrisches Heizgerät nt
electrician [ɪlɛk'trɪʃən] n Elektriker(in) m(f)
electricity [ɪlɛk'trɪsɪtɪ] n Elektrizität f; (supply) (elektrischer) Strom m ▷ cpd Strom-; **to switch on/off the** ~ den Strom an-/abschalten
electricity board (Brit) n Elektrizitätswerk nt
electricity price n Strompreis m
electricity rate n Stromtarif m
electric light n elektrisches Licht nt
electric shock n elektrischer Schlag m, Stromschlag m
electrify [ɪ'lɛktrɪfaɪ] vt (fence) unter Strom setzen; (rail network) elektrifizieren; (audience) elektrisieren
electro... [ɪ'lɛktrəu] pref Elektro-
electrocardiogram [ɪ'lɛktrə'kɑːdɪəgræm] n Elektrokardiogramm nt
electroconvulsive therapy [ɪ'lɛktrəkən'vʌlsɪv-] n Elektroschocktherapie f
electrocute [ɪ'lɛktrəkjuːt] vt durch einen Stromschlag töten; (US: criminal) auf dem elektrischen Stuhl hinrichten
electrode [ɪ'lɛktrəud] n Elektrode f
electroencephalogram [ɪ'lɛktrəuɛn'sɛfələgræm] n Elektroenzephalogramm nt
electrolysis [ɪlɛk'trɔlɪsɪs] n Elektrolyse f
electromagnetic [ɪ'lɛktrəmæg'nɛtɪk] adj elektromagnetisch
electron [ɪ'lɛktrɔn] n Elektron nt
electronic [ɪlɛk'trɔnɪk] adj elektronisch
electronic data processing n elektronische Datenverarbeitung f
electronic mail n elektronische Post f
electronics [ɪlɛk'trɔnɪks] n Elektronik f
electronic tag n elektronische Fußfessel f
electron microscope n Elektronenmikroskop nt
electroplated [ɪ'lɛktrə'pleɪtɪd] adj galvanisiert
electrotherapy [ɪ'lɛktrə'θɛrəpɪ] n Elektrotherapie f
elegance ['ɛlɪgəns] n Eleganz f
elegant ['ɛlɪgənt] adj elegant
element ['ɛlɪmənt] n Element nt; (of heater, kettle etc) Heizelement nt
elementary [ɛlɪ'mɛntərɪ] adj grundlegend; ~ **school** Grundschule f; siehe Info-Artikel; ~ **education** Elementarunterricht m; ~ **maths/ French** Grundbegriffe pl der Mathematik/des Französischen

---

⬤ **ELEMENTARY SCHOOL**

⬤ *Elementary school* ist in den USA und Kanada
⬤ eine Grundschule, an der ein Kind die
⬤ ersten sechs bis acht Schuljahre verbringt.

In den USA heißt diese Schule auch „grade school" oder „grammar school". Siehe auch *high school*.

elephant ['ɛlɪfənt] *n* Elefant *m*

elevate ['ɛlɪveɪt] *vt* erheben; *(physically)* heben

elevated railroad ['ɛlɪveɪtɪd-] *(US)* *n* Hochbahn *f*

elevation [ɛlɪ'veɪʃən] *n* Erhebung *f*; *(height)* Höhe *f* über dem Meeresspiegel; *(Archit)* Aufriss *m*

elevator ['ɛlɪveɪtər] *n* *(US)* Aufzug *m*, Fahrstuhl *m*; *(in warehouse etc)* Lastenaufzug *m*

eleven [ɪ'lɛvn] *num* elf

elevenses [ɪ'lɛvnzɪz] *(Brit)* *npl* zweites Frühstück *nt*

eleventh [ɪ'lɛvnθ] *num* elfte(r, s); **at the ~ hour** *(fig)* in letzter Minute

elf [ɛlf] *(pl* **elves**) *n* Elf *m*, Elfe *f*; *(mischievous)* Kobold *m*

elicit [ɪ'lɪsɪt] *vt:* **to ~ from sb** *(information)* (aus jdm) herausbekommen; *(reaction, response)* (von jdm) bekommen

eligible ['ɛlɪdʒəbl] *adj* *(marriage partner)* begehrt; **to be ~ for sth** für etw infrage kommen; **to be ~ for a pension** pensionsberechtigt sein

eliminate [ɪ'lɪmɪneɪt] *vt* beseitigen; *(candidate etc)* ausschließen; *(team, contestant)* aus dem Wettbewerb werfen

elimination [ɪlɪmɪ'neɪʃən] *n* *(see vb)* Beseitigung *f*; Ausschluss *m*; Ausscheiden *nt*; **by process of ~** durch negative Auslese

élite [eɪ'li:t] *n* Elite *f*

élitist [eɪ'li:tɪst] *(pej)* *adj* elitär

elixir [ɪ'lɪksər] *n* Elixier *nt*

Elizabethan [ɪlɪzə'bi:θən] *adj* elisabethanisch

ellipse [ɪ'lɪps] *n* Ellipse *f*

elliptical [ɪ'lɪptɪkl] *adj* elliptisch

elm [ɛlm] *n* Ulme *f*

elocution [ɛlə'kju:ʃən] *n* Sprechtechnik *f*

elongated ['i:lɔŋgeɪtɪd] *adj* lang gestreckt; *(shadow)* verlängert

elope [ɪ'ləup] *vi* weglaufen

elopement [ɪ'ləupmənt] *n* Weglaufen *nt*

eloquence ['ɛləkwəns] *n* *(see adj)* Beredtheit *f*, Wortgewandtheit *f*; Ausdrucksfülle *f*

eloquent ['ɛləkwənt] *adj* beredt, wortgewandt; *(speech, description)* ausdrucksvoll

else [ɛls] *adv* andere(r, s); **something ~** etwas anderes; **somewhere ~** woanders, anderswo; **everywhere ~** sonst überall; **where ~?** wo sonst?; **is there anything ~ I can do?** kann ich sonst noch etwas tun?; **there was little ~ to do** es gab nicht viel anderes zu tun; **everyone ~** alle anderen; **nobody ~ spoke** niemand anders sagte etwas, sonst sagte niemand etwas

elsewhere [ɛls'wɛər] *adv* woanders, anderswo; *(go)* woandershin, anderswohin

ELT *n abbr* *(Scol:* = *English Language Teaching)* Englisch als Unterrichtsfach

elucidate [ɪ'lu:sɪdeɪt] *vt* erläutern

elude [ɪ'lu:d] *vt (captor)* entkommen +*dat*;

(capture) sich entziehen +*dat*; **this fact/idea ~d him** diese Tatsache/Idee entging ihm

elusive [ɪ'lu:sɪv] *adj* schwer zu fangen; *(quality)* unerreichbar; **he's very ~** er ist sehr schwer zu erreichen

elves [ɛlvz] *npl of* **elf**

emaciated [ɪ'meɪsɪeɪtɪd] *adj* abgezehrt, ausgezehrt

email ['i:meɪl] *n abbr* (= *electronic mail)* E-Mail *f* ▷ *vt* eine E-Mail schicken +*dat*

emanate ['ɛməneɪt] *vi:* **to ~ from** stammen von; *(sound, light etc)* ausgehen von

emancipate [ɪ'mænsɪpeɪt] *vt* *(women)* emanzipieren; *(poor)* befreien; *(slave)* freilassen

emancipation [ɪmænsɪ'peɪʃən] *n* *(see vb)* Emanzipation *f*; Befreiung *f*; Freilassung *f*

emasculate [ɪ'mæskjuleɪt] *vt* schwächen

embalm [ɪm'ba:m] *vt* einbalsamieren

embankment [ɪm'bæŋkmənt] *n* Böschung *f*; *(of railway)* Bahndamm *m*; *(of river)* Damm *m*

embargo [ɪm'ba:gəu] *(pl* **~es**) *n* Embargo *nt* ▷ *vt* mit einem Embargo belegen; **to put** *or* **impose** *or* **place an ~ on sth** ein Embargo über etw *acc* verhängen; **to lift an ~** ein Embargo aufheben

embark [ɪm'ba:k] *vt* einschiffen ▷ *vi:* **to ~ (on)** sich einschiffen (auf); **to ~ on** *(journey)* beginnen; *(task)* in Angriff nehmen; *(course of action)* einschlagen

embarkation [ɛmba:'keɪʃən] *n* Einschiffung *f*

embarkation card *n* Bordkarte *f*

embarrass [ɪm'bærəs] *vt* in Verlegenheit bringen

embarrassed [ɪm'bærəst] *adj* verlegen

embarrassing [ɪm'bærəsɪŋ] *adj* peinlich

embarrassment [ɪm'bærəsmənt] *n* Verlegenheit *f*; *(embarrassing problem)* Peinlichkeit *f*

embassy ['ɛmbəsɪ] *n* Botschaft *f*; **the Swiss E~** die Schweizer Botschaft

embedded [ɪm'bɛdɪd] *adj* eingebettet; *(attitude, belief, feeling)* verwurzelt

embellish [ɪm'bɛlɪʃ] *vt (account)* ausschmücken; **to be ~ed with** geschmückt sein mit

embers ['ɛmbəz] *npl* Glut *f*

embezzle [ɪm'bɛzl] *vt* unterschlagen

embezzlement [ɪm'bɛzlmənt] *n* Unterschlagung *f*

embezzler [ɪm'bɛzlər] *n jd, der eine Unterschlagung begangen hat*

embitter [ɪm'bɪtər] *vt* verbittern

embittered [ɪm'bɪtəd] *adj* verbittert

emblem ['ɛmbləm] *n* Emblem *nt*; *(symbol)* Wahrzeichen *nt*

embodiment [ɪm'bɔdɪmənt] *n* Verkörperung *f*; **to be the ~ of ...** *(subj: thing)* ... verkörpern; *(: person)* ... in Person sein

embody [ɪm'bɔdɪ] *vt* verkörpern; *(include, contain)* enthalten

embolden [ɪm'bəuldn] *vt* ermutigen

embolism ['ɛmbəlɪzəm] *n* Embolie *f*

embossed [ɪm'bɔst] *adj* geprägt; **~ with a logo**

e

mit geprägtem Logo

embrace [ɪm'breɪs] vt umarmen; (include) umfassen ▷ vi sich umarmen ▷ n Umarmung f

embroider [ɪm'brɔɪdəʳ] vt (cloth) besticken; (fig: story) ausschmücken

embroidery [ɪm'brɔɪdərɪ] n Stickerei f; (activity) Sticken nt

embroil [ɪm'brɔɪl] vt: **to become ~ed (in sth)** (in etw acc) verwickelt or hineingezogen werden

embryo ['ɛmbrɪəu] n Embryo m; (fig) Keim m

emcee [ɛm'si:] n Conférencier m

emend [ɪ'mɛnd] vt verbessern, korrigieren

emerald ['ɛmərəld] n Smaragd m

emerge [ɪ'mɜ:dʒ] vi: **to ~ (from)** auftauchen (aus); (from sleep) erwachen (aus); (from imprisonment) entlassen werden (aus); (from discussion etc) sich herausstellen (bei); (new idea, industry, society) entstehen (aus); **it ~s that** (Brit) es stellt sich heraus, dass

emergence [ɪ'mɜ:dʒəns] n Entstehung f

emergency [ɪ'mɜ:dʒənsɪ] n Notfall m ▷ cpd Not-; (repair) notdürftig; **in an ~** im Notfall; **state of ~** Notstand m

emergency cord (US) n Notbremse f

emergency exit n Notausgang m

emergency landing n Notlandung f

emergency lane (US) n Seitenstreifen m

emergency road service (US) n Pannendienst m

emergency services npl: **the ~** der Notdienst

emergency stop (Brit) n Vollbremsung f

emergent [ɪ'mɜ:dʒənt] adj jung, aufstrebend

emeritus [ɪ'mɛrɪtəs] adj emeritiert

emery board ['ɛmərɪ-] n Papiernagelfeile f

emery paper ['ɛmərɪ-] n Schmirgelpapier nt

emetic [ɪ'mɛtɪk] n Brechmittel nt

emigrant ['ɛmɪɡrənt] n Auswanderer m, Auswanderin f, Emigrant(in) m(f)

emigrate ['ɛmɪɡreɪt] vi auswandern, emigrieren

emigration [ɛmɪ'ɡreɪʃən] n Auswanderung f, Emigration f

émigré ['ɛmɪɡreɪ] n Emigrant(in) m(f)

eminence ['ɛmɪnəns] n Bedeutung f

eminent ['ɛmɪnənt] adj bedeutend

eminently ['ɛmɪnəntlɪ] adv ausgesprochen

emirate ['ɛmɪrɪt] n Emirat nt

emission [ɪ'mɪʃən] n Emission f

emissions [ɪ'mɪʃənz] npl Emissionen pl

emit [ɪ'mɪt] vt abgeben; (smell) ausströmen; (light, heat) ausstrahlen

emolument [ɪ'mɔljumənt] n (often pl) Vergütung f; (fee) Honorar nt; (salary) Bezüge pl

emoticon [ɪ'məutɪkən] n (Comput) Emoticon nt

emotion [ɪ'məuʃən] n Gefühl nt

emotional [ɪ'məuʃənl] adj emotional; (exhaustion) seelisch; (scene) ergreifend; (speech) gefühlsbetont

emotionally [ɪ'məuʃnəlɪ] adv emotional; (be involved) gefühlsmäßig; (speak) gefühlvoll; **~ disturbed** seelisch gestört

emotive [ɪ'məutɪv] adj emotional

empathy ['ɛmpəθɪ] n Einfühlungsvermögen nt; **to feel ~ with sb** sich in jdn einfühlen

emperor ['ɛmpərəʳ] n Kaiser m

emphasis ['ɛmfəsɪs] (pl **emphases**) n Betonung f; (importance) (Schwer)gewicht nt; **to lay** or **place ~ on sth** etw betonen; **the ~ is on reading** das Schwergewicht liegt auf dem Lesen

emphasize ['ɛmfəsaɪz] vt betonen; (feature) hervorheben; **I must ~ that ...** ich möchte betonen, dass ...

emphatic [ɛm'fætɪk] adj nachdrücklich; (denial) energisch; (person, manner) bestimmt, entschieden

emphatically [ɛm'fætɪklɪ] adv nachdrücklich; (certainly) eindeutig

emphysema [ɛmfɪ'si:mə] n Emphysem nt

empire ['ɛmpaɪəʳ] n Reich nt

empirical [ɛm'pɪrɪkl] adj empirisch

employ [ɪm'plɔɪ] vt beschäftigen; (tool, weapon) verwenden; **he's ~ed in a bank** er ist bei einer Bank angestellt

employee [ɪmplɔɪ'i:] n Angestellte(r) f(m)

employer [ɪm'plɔɪəʳ] n Arbeitgeber(in) m(f)

employment [ɪm'plɔɪmənt] n Arbeit f; **to find ~** Arbeit or eine (An)stellung finden; **without ~** stellungslos; **your place of ~** Ihre Arbeitsstätte f

employment agency n Stellenvermittlung f

employment exchange (Brit) n Arbeitsamt nt

empower [ɪm'pauəʳ] vt: **to ~ sb to do sth** jdn ermächtigen, etw zu tun

empress ['ɛmprɪs] n Kaiserin f

empties ['ɛmptɪz] npl Leergut nt

emptiness ['ɛmptɪnɪs] n Leere f

empty ['ɛmptɪ] adj leer; (house, room) leer stehend; (space) frei ▷ vt leeren; (place, house etc) räumen ▷ vi sich leeren; (liquid) abfließen; (river) münden; **on an ~ stomach** auf nüchternen Magen; **to ~ into** (river) münden or sich ergießen in +acc

empty-handed ['ɛmptɪ'hændɪd] adj mit leeren Händen; **he returned ~** er kehrte unverrichteter Dinge zurück

empty-headed ['ɛmptɪ'hɛdɪd] adj strohdumm

EMS n abbr (= European Monetary System) EWS nt

EMT (US) n abbr (= emergency medical technician) = Sanitäter(in) m(f)

EMU n abbr (= Economic and Monetary Union) EWU f

emu ['i:mju:] n Emu m

emulate ['ɛmjuleɪt] vt nacheifern +dat

emulsion [ɪ'mʌlʃən] n Emulsion f; (also: **emulsion paint**) Emulsionsfarbe f

enable [ɪ'neɪbl] vt: **to ~ sb to do sth** (permit) es jdm erlauben, etw zu tun; (make possible) es jdm ermöglichen, etw zu tun

enact [ɪ'nækt] vt (law) erlassen; (play) aufführen; (role) darstellen, spielen

enamel [ɪ'næməl] n Email nt, Emaille f; (also: **enamel paint**) Email(le)lack m; (of tooth) Zahnschmelz m

enamoured [ɪ'næməd] adj: **to be ~ of** (person) verliebt sein in +acc; (pastime, idea, belief) angetan sein von

encampment [ɪnˈkæmpmənt] n Lager nt

encased [ɪnˈkeɪst] adj: ~ **in** (shell) umgeben von; **to be ~ in** (limb) in Gips liegen or sein

encash [ɪnˈkæʃ] (Brit) vt einlösen

enchant [ɪnˈtʃɑːnt] vt bezaubern

enchanted [ɪnˈtʃɑːntɪd] adj verzaubert

enchanting [ɪnˈtʃɑːntɪŋ] adj bezaubernd

encircle [ɪnˈsəːkl] vt umgeben; (person) umringen; (building: police etc) umstellen

encl. abbr (on letters etc: = enclosed, enclosure) Anl.

enclave [ˈenkleɪv] n: **an ~ (of)** eine Enklave (+gen)

enclose [ɪnˈkləuz] vt umgeben; (land, space) begrenzen; (with fence) einzäunen; (letter etc): **to ~ (with)** beilegen (+dat); **please find ~d** als Anlage übersenden wir Ihnen

enclosure [ɪnˈkləuʒər] n eingefriedeter Bereich m; (in letter etc) Anlage f

encoder [ɪnˈkəudər] n Codierer m

encompass [ɪnˈkʌmpəs] vt umfassen

encore [ɔŋˈkɔːr] excl Zugabe! ▷ n Zugabe f

encounter [ɪnˈkauntər] n Begegnung f ▷ vt begegnen +dat; (problem) stoßen auf +acc

encourage [ɪnˈkʌrɪdʒ] vt (activity, attitude) unterstützen; (growth, industry) fördern; **to ~ sb (to do sth)** jdn ermutigen(, etw zu tun)

encouragement [ɪnˈkʌrɪdʒmənt] n (see vb) Unterstützung f; Förderung f; Ermutigung f

encouraging [ɪnˈkʌrɪdʒɪŋ] adj ermutigend

encroach [ɪnˈkrəutʃ] vi: **to ~ (up)on** (rights) eingreifen in +acc; (property) eindringen in +acc; (time) in Anspruch nehmen

encrusted [ɪnˈkrʌstɪd] adj: ~ **with** (gems) besetzt mit; (snow, dirt) verkrustet mit

encumber [ɪnˈkʌmbər] vt: **to be ~ed with** beladen sein mit; (debts) belastet sein mit

encyclopaedia, encyclopedia [ɛnsaɪkləuˈpiːdɪə] n Lexikon nt, Enzyklopädie f

end [end] n Ende nt; (of film, book) Schluss m, Ende nt; (of table) Schmalseite f; (of pointed object) Spitze f; (aim) Zweck m, Ziel nt ▷ vt (also: **bring to an end, put an end to**) beenden ▷ vi enden; **from ~ to end** von einem Ende zum anderen; **to come to an ~** zu Ende gehen; **to be at an ~** zu Ende sein; **in the ~** schließlich; **on ~** hochkant; **to stand on ~** (hair) zu Berge stehen; **for hours on ~** stundenlang ununterbrochen; **for 5 hours on ~** 5 Stunden ununterbrochen; **at the ~ of the street** am Ende der Straße; **at the ~ of the day** (Brit: fig) letztlich; **to this end, with this ~ in view** mit diesem Ziel vor Augen
 ▶ **end up** vi: **to ~ up in** (place) landen in +dat; **to ~ up in trouble** Ärger bekommen; **to ~ up doing sth** etw schließlich tun

endanger [ɪnˈdeɪndʒər] vt gefährden; **an ~ed species** eine vom Aussterben bedrohte Art

endear [ɪnˈdɪər] vt: **to ~ o.s. to sb** sich bei jdm beliebt machen

endearing [ɪnˈdɪərɪŋ] adj gewinnend

endearment [ɪnˈdɪəmənt] n: **to whisper ~s** zärtliche Worte flüstern; **term of ~** Kosewort

nt, Kosename m

endeavour, (US) endeavor [ɪnˈdɛvər] n Anstrengung f, Bemühung f; (effort) Bestrebung f ▷ vi: **to ~ to do sth** (attempt) sich anstrengen or bemühen, etw zu tun; (strive) bestrebt sein, etw zu tun

endemic [ɛnˈdɛmɪk] adj endemisch, verbreitet

ending [ˈendɪŋ] n Ende nt, Schluss m; (Ling) Endung f

endive [ˈendaɪv] n Endivie f; (chicory) Chicorée f or m

endless [ˈendlɪs] adj endlos; (patience, resources, possibilities) unbegrenzt

endorse [ɪnˈdɔːs] vt (cheque) indossieren, auf der Rückseite unterzeichnen; (proposal, plan) billigen; (candidate) unterstützen

endorsee [ɪndɔːˈsiː] n Indossat m

endorsement [ɪnˈdɔːsmənt] n Billigung f; (of candidate) Unterstützung f; (Brit: on driving licence) Strafvermerk m

endow [ɪnˈdau] vt (institution) eine Stiftung machen an +acc; **to be ~ed with** besitzen

endowment [ɪnˈdaumənt] n Stiftung f; (quality) Begabung f

endowment assurance n Versicherung f auf den Erlebensfall, Erlebensversicherung f

endowment mortgage n Hypothek f mit Lebensversicherung

end product n Endprodukt nt; (fig) Produkt nt

end result n Endergebnis nt

endurable [ɪnˈdjuərəbl] adj erträglich

endurance [ɪnˈdjuərəns] n Durchhaltevermögen nt; (patience) Geduld f

endurance test n Belastungsprobe f

endure [ɪnˈdjuər] vt ertragen ▷ vi Bestand haben

enduring [ɪnˈdjuərɪŋ] adj dauerhaft

end user n (Comput) Endbenutzer m

enema [ˈenɪmə] n Klistier nt, Einlauf m

enemy [ˈenəmɪ] adj feindlich; (strategy) des Feindes ▷ n Feind(in) m(f); **to make an ~ of sb** sich dat jdn zum Feind machen

energetic [enəˈdʒetɪk] adj aktiv

energy [ˈenədʒɪ] n Energie f; **Department of E~** Energieministerium nt

energy crisis n Energiekrise f

energy-saving [ˈenədʒɪˈseɪvɪŋ] adj energiesparend; (policy) energiebewusst

enervating [ˈenəveɪtɪŋ] adj strapazierend

enforce [ɪnˈfɔːs] vt (law, rule, decision) Geltung verschaffen +dat

enforced [ɪnˈfɔːst] adj erzwungen

enfranchise [ɪnˈfræntʃaɪz] vt das Wahlrecht geben or erteilen +dat

engage [ɪnˈgeɪdʒ] vt in Anspruch nehmen; (employ) einstellen; (lawyer) sich dat nehmen; (Mil) angreifen ▷ vi (Tech) einrasten; **to ~ the clutch** einkuppeln; **to ~ sb in conversation** jdn in ein Gespräch verwickeln; **to ~ in** sich beteiligen an +dat; **to ~ in commerce** kaufmännisch tätig sein; **to ~ in study** studieren

engaged [ɪnˈgeɪdʒd] adj verlobt; (Brit: busy,

in use) besetzt; **to get ~** sich verloben;
he is ~ in research/a survey er ist mit
Forschungsarbeit/einer Umfrage beschäftigt

engaged tone (*Brit*) *n* Besetztzeichen *nt*

engagement [ɪn'geɪdʒmənt] *n* Verabredung *f*;
(*booking*) Engagement *nt*; (*to marry*) Verlobung *f*;
(*Mil*) Gefecht *nt*, Kampf *m*; **I have a previous ~**
ich habe schon eine Verabredung

engagement ring *n* Verlobungsring *m*

engaging [ɪn'geɪdʒɪŋ] *adj* einnehmend

engender [ɪn'dʒendə*ʳ*] *vt* erzeugen

engine ['endʒɪn] *n* Motor *m*; (*Rail*) Lok(omotive)
f

engine driver *n* (*Rail*) Lok(omotiv)führer(in)
m(f)

engineer [endʒɪ'nɪə*ʳ*] *n* Ingenieur(in) *m(f)*;
(*Brit: for repairs*) Techniker(in) *m(f)*; (*US: Rail*)
Lok(omotiv)führer(in) *m(f)*; (*on ship*)
Maschinist(in) *m(f)*; **civil/mechanical ~**
Bau-/Maschinenbauingenieur(in) *m(f)*

engineering [endʒɪ'nɪərɪŋ] *n* Technik *f*; (*design,
construction*) Konstruktion *f* ▷ *cpd*: **~ works** *or*
factory Maschinenfabrik *f*

engine failure *n* Maschinenschaden *m*; (*Aut*)
Motorschaden *m*

engine trouble *n* Maschinenschaden *m*; (*Aut*)
Motorschaden *m*

England ['ɪŋglənd] *n* England *nt*

English ['ɪŋglɪʃ] *adj* englisch ▷ *n* Englisch *nt*;
the English *npl* die Engländer *pl*; **an ~ speaker**
jd, der Englisch spricht

English Channel *n*: **the ~** der Ärmelkanal

Englishman ['ɪŋglɪʃmən] (*irreg: like* **man**) *n*
Engländer *m*

English-speaking ['ɪŋglɪʃ'spi:kɪŋ] *adj* (*country*)
englischsprachig

Englishwoman ['ɪŋglɪʃwumən] (*irreg: like*
woman) *n* Engländerin *f*

engrave [ɪn'greɪv] *vt* gravieren; (*name etc*)
eingravieren; (*fig*) einprägen

engraving [ɪn'greɪvɪŋ] *n* Stich *m*

engrossed [ɪn'grəust] *adj*: **~ in** vertieft in +*acc*

engulf [ɪn'gʌlf] *vt* verschlingen; (*subj: panic, fear*)
überkommen

enhance [ɪn'hɑːns] *vt* verbessern; (*enjoyment,
beauty*) erhöhen

enigma [ɪ'nɪgmə] *n* Rätsel *nt*

enigmatic [enɪg'mætɪk] *adj* rätselhaft

enjoy [ɪn'dʒɔɪ] *vt* genießen; (*health, fortune*) sich
erfreuen +*gen*; (*success*) haben; **to ~ o.s.** sich
amüsieren; **I ~ dancing** ich tanze gerne

enjoyable [ɪn'dʒɔɪəbl] *adj* nett, angenehm

enjoyment [ɪn'dʒɔɪmənt] *n* Vergnügen *nt*;
(*activity*) Freude *f*

enlarge [ɪn'lɑːdʒ] *vt* vergrößern; (*scope*)
erweitern ▷ *vi*: **to ~ on** weiter ausführen

enlarged [ɪn'lɑːdʒd] *adj* erweitert; (*Med*)
vergrößert

enlargement [ɪn'lɑːdʒmənt] *n* Vergrößerung *f*

enlighten [ɪn'laɪtn] *vt* aufklären

enlightened [ɪn'laɪtnd] *adj* aufgeklärt

enlightening [ɪn'laɪtnɪŋ] *adj* aufschlussreich

enlightenment [ɪn'laɪtnmənt] *n* (*also*

Hist: *Enlightenment*) Aufklärung *f*

enlist [ɪn'lɪst] *vt* anwerben; (*support, help*)
gewinnen ▷ *vi*: **to ~ in** eintreten in +*acc*; **~ed
man** (*US: Mil*) gemeiner Soldat *m*; (*US: in navy*)
Matrose *m*

enliven [ɪn'laɪvn] *vt* beleben

enmity ['enmɪtɪ] *n* Feindschaft *f*

ennoble [ɪ'nəubl] *vt* adeln; (*fig: dignify*) erheben

enormity [ɪ'nɔːmɪtɪ] *n* ungeheure Größe *f*

enormous [ɪ'nɔːməs] *adj* gewaltig, ungeheuer;
(*pleasure, success etc*) riesig

enormously [ɪ'nɔːməslɪ] *adv* enorm; (*rich*)
ungeheuer

enough [ɪ'nʌf] *adj* genug, genügend ▷ *pron*
genug ▷ *adv*: **big ~** groß genug; **he has not
worked ~** er hat nicht genug *or* genügend
gearbeitet; **have you got ~?** haben Sie genug?;
~ to eat genug zu essen; **will 5 be ~?** reichen
5?; **I've had ~!** jetzt reichts mir aber!; **it's hot
~ (as it is)** es ist heiß genug; **he was kind ~
to lend me the money** er war so gut und hat
mir das Geld geliehen; **~!** es reicht!; **that's
~, thanks** danke, das reicht *or* ist genug;
I've had ~ of him ich habe genug von ihm;
funnily/oddly ~ ... komischerweise ...

enquire [ɪn'kwaɪə*ʳ*] *vt, vi* = **inquire**

enrage [ɪn'reɪdʒ] *vt* wütend machen

enrich [ɪn'rɪtʃ] *vt* bereichern

enrol, (*US*) **enroll** [ɪn'rəul] *vt* anmelden; (*at
university*) einschreiben, immatrikulieren ▷ *vi*
(*see vt*) sich anmelden; sich einschreiben, sich
immatrikulieren

enrolment, (*US*) **enrollment** [ɪn'rəulmənt]
n (*see vb*) Anmeldung *f*; Einschreibung *f*,
Immatrikulation *f*

en route [ɔn'ruːt] *adv* unterwegs; **~ for** auf
dem Weg nach; **~ from London to Berlin** auf
dem Weg von London nach Berlin

ensconced [ɪn'skɔnst] *adj*: **she is ~ in ...** sie
hat es sich *dat* in ... gut *or* gemütlich gemacht

ensemble [ɔn'sɔmbl] *n* Ensemble *nt*

enshrine [ɪn'ʃraɪn] *vt* bewahren; **to be ~d in**
verankert sein in +*dat*

ensue [ɪn'sjuː] *vi* folgen

ensuing [ɪn'sjuːɪŋ] *adj* folgend

ensure [ɪn'ʃuə*ʳ*] *vt* garantieren; **to ~ that**
sicherstellen, dass

ENT *n abbr* (*Med*: = *ear, nose, and throat*) HNO

entail [ɪn'teɪl] *vt* mit sich bringen

entangled [ɪn'tæŋgld] *adj*: **to become ~ (in)**
sich verfangen (in +*dat*)

enter ['entə*ʳ*] *vt* betreten; (*club*) beitreten
+*dat*; (*army*) gehen zu; (*profession*) ergreifen;
(*race, contest*) sich beteiligen an +*dat*; (*sb for a
competition*) anmelden; (*write down*) eintragen;
(*Comput: data*) eingeben ▷ *vi* (*come in*)
hereinkommen; (*go in*) hineingehen
▶ **enter for** *vt fus* anmelden für
▶ **enter into** *vt fus* (*discussion, negotiations*)
aufnehmen; (*correspondence*) treten in +*acc*;
(*agreement*) schließen
▶ **enter up** *vt* eintragen
▶ **enter (up)on** *vt fus* (*career, policy*) einschlagen

enteritis [ɛntəˈraɪtɪs] n
Dünndarmentzündung f
enterprise [ˈɛntəpraɪz] n Unternehmen
nt; (initiative) Initiative f; **free** ~ freies
Unternehmertum nt; **private** ~
Privatunternehmertum nt
enterprising [ˈɛntəpraɪzɪŋ] adj einfallsreich
entertain [ɛntəˈteɪn] vt unterhalten; (invite)
einladen; (idea, plan) erwägen
entertainer [ɛntəˈteɪnəʳ] n Unterhalter(in)
m(f), Entertainer(in) m(f)
entertaining [ɛntəˈteɪnɪŋ] adj amüsant ▷ n: **to
do a lot of** ~ sehr oft Gäste haben
entertainment [ɛntəˈteɪnmənt] n
Unterhaltung f; (show) Darbietung f
entertainment allowance n
Aufwandspauschale f
enthral [ɪnˈθrɔːl] vt begeistern; (story) fesseln
enthralled [ɪnˈθrɔːld] adj gefesselt; **he was** ~
by or **with the book** das Buch fesselte ihn
enthralling [ɪnˈθrɔːlɪŋ] adj fesselnd; (details)
spannend
enthuse [ɪnˈθuːz] vi: **to** ~ **about** or **over**
schwärmen von
enthusiasm [ɪnˈθuːzɪæzəm] n Begeisterung f
enthusiast [ɪnˈθuːzɪæst] n Enthusiast(in) m(f);
he's a jazz/sports ~ er begeistert sich für
Jazz/Sport
enthusiastic [ɪnθuːzɪˈæstɪk] adj begeistert;
(response, reception) enthusiastisch; **to be** ~
about begeistert sein von
entice [ɪnˈtaɪs] vt locken; (tempt) verleiten
enticing [ɪnˈtaɪsɪŋ] adj verlockend
entire [ɪnˈtaɪəʳ] adj ganz
entirely [ɪnˈtaɪəlɪ] adv völlig
entirety [ɪnˈtaɪərətɪ] n: **in its** ~ in seiner
Gesamtheit
entitle [ɪnˈtaɪtl] vt: **to** ~ **sb to sth** jdn zu etw
berechtigen; **to** ~ **sb to do sth** jdn dazu
berechtigen, etw zu tun
entitled [ɪnˈtaɪtld] adj: **a book/film** etc ~ ... ein
Buch/Film etc mit dem Titel ...; **to be** ~ **to do**
sth das Recht haben, etw zu tun
entity [ˈɛntɪtɪ] n Wesen nt
entourage [ɔntuˈrɑːʒ] n Gefolge nt
entrails [ˈɛntreɪlz] npl Eingeweide pl
entrance [n ˈɛntrns, vt ɪnˈtrɑːns] n Eingang
m; (arrival) Ankunft f; (on stage) Auftritt m ▷ vt
bezaubern; **to gain** ~ **to** (building etc) sich
dat Zutritt verschaffen zu; (university) die
Zulassung erhalten zu; (profession etc) Zugang
erhalten zu
entrance examination n Aufnahmeprüfung f
entrance fee n Eintrittsgeld nt
entrance ramp (US) n Auffahrt f
entrancing [ɪnˈtrɑːnsɪŋ] adj bezaubernd
entrant [ˈɛntrnt] n Teilnehmer(in) m(f); (Brit: in
exam) Prüfling m
entreat [ɛnˈtriːt] vt: **to** ~ **sb to do sth** jdn
anflehen, etw zu tun
entreaty [ɛnˈtriːtɪ] n (flehentliche) Bitte f
entrée [ˈɔntreɪ] n Hauptgericht nt
entrenched [ɛnˈtrɛntʃt] adj verankert; (ideas)

festgesetzt
entrepreneur [ˈɔntrəprəˈnəːʳ] n
Unternehmer(in) m(f)
entrepreneurial [ˈɔntrəprəˈnəːrɪəl] adj
unternehmerisch
entrust [ɪnˈtrʌst] vt: **to** ~ **sth to sb** jdm etw
anvertrauen; **to** ~ **sb with sth** (task) jdn
mit etw betrauen; (secret, valuables) jdm etw
anvertrauen
entry [ˈɛntrɪ] n Eingang m; (in competition)
Meldung f; (in register, account book, reference
book) Eintrag m; (arrival) Eintritt m; (to country)
Einreise f; **"no** ~" „Zutritt verboten"; (Aut)
„Einfahrt verboten"; **single/double** ~ **book-
keeping** einfache/doppelte Buchführung f
entry form n Anmeldeformular nt
entry phone (Brit) n Türsprechanlage f
entwine [ɪnˈtwaɪn] vt verflechten
enumerate [ɪˈnjuːməreɪt] vt aufzählen
enunciate [ɪˈnʌnsɪeɪt] vt artikulieren;
(principle, plan etc) formulieren
envelop [ɪnˈvɛləp] vt einhüllen
envelope [ˈɛnvələup] n Umschlag m
enviable [ˈɛnvɪəbl] adj beneidenswert
envious [ˈɛnvɪəs] adj neidisch; **to be** ~ **of sth/
sb** auf etw/jdn neidisch sein
environment [ɪnˈvaɪərnmənt] n
Umwelt f; **Department of the E~** (Brit)
Umweltministerium nt
environmental [ɪnvaɪərnˈmɛntl] adj
(problems, pollution etc) Umwelt-; ~ **expert**
Umweltexperte m, Umweltexpertin f; ~
studies Umweltkunde f
environmentalist [ɪnvaɪərnˈmɛntlɪst] n
Umweltschützer(in) m(f)
Environmental Protection Agency (US) n
staatliche Umweltbehörde der USA
environment-friendly adj umweltfreundlich
envisage [ɪnˈvɪzɪdʒ] vt sich dat vorstellen; **I** ~
that ... ich stelle mir vor, dass ...
envision [ɪnˈvɪʒən] (US) vt = **envisage**
envoy [ˈɛnvɔɪ] n Gesandte(r) f(m)
envy [ˈɛnvɪ] n Neid m ▷ vt beneiden; **to** ~ **sb
sth** jdn um etw beneiden
enzyme [ˈɛnzaɪm] n Enzym nt
eon [ˈiːən] n Äon m, Ewigkeit f
EPA (US) n abbr = **Environmental Protection
Agency**
ephemeral [ɪˈfɛmərl] adj kurzlebig
epic [ˈɛpɪk] n Epos nt ▷ adj (journey) lang und
abenteuerlich
epicentre, (US) epicenter [ˈɛpɪsɛntəʳ] n
Epizentrum nt
epidemic [ɛpɪˈdɛmɪk] n Epidemie f
epigram [ˈɛpɪgræm] n Epigramm nt
epilepsy [ˈɛpɪlɛpsɪ] n Epilepsie f
epileptic [ɛpɪˈlɛptɪk] adj epileptisch ▷ n
Epileptiker(in) m(f)
epilogue [ˈɛpɪlɔg] n Epilog m, Nachwort nt
Epiphany [ɪˈpɪfənɪ] n Dreikönigsfest nt
episcopal [ɪˈpɪskəpl] adj bischöflich; **the E~
Church** die Episkopalkirche
episode [ˈɛpɪsəud] n Episode f; (TV, Radio)

541

Folge f

epistle [ɪ'pɪsl] n Epistel f; (Rel) Brief m

epitaph ['ɛpɪtɑ:f] n Epitaph nt; (on gravestone etc) Grab(in)schrift f

epithet ['ɛpɪθɛt] n Beiname m

epitome [ɪ'pɪtəmɪ] n Inbegriff m

epitomize [ɪ'pɪtəmaɪz] vt verkörpern

epoch ['i:pɔk] n Epoche f

epoch-making ['i:pɔkmeɪkɪŋ] adj epochal; (discovery) epochemachend

eponymous [ɪ'pɒnɪməs] adj namengebend

equable ['ɛkwəbl] adj ausgeglichen; (reply) sachlich

equal ['i:kwl] adj gleich ▷ n Gleichgestellte(r) f(m) ▷ vt gleichkommen +dat; (number) gleich sein +dat; **they are roughly ~ in size** sie sind ungefähr gleich groß; **the number of exports should be ~ to imports** Export- und Importzahlen sollten gleich sein; **~ opportunities** Chancengleichheit f; **to be ~ to** (task) gewachsen sein +dat; **two times two ~s four** zwei mal zwei ist (gleich) vier

equality [i:'kwɒlɪtɪ] n Gleichheit f; **~ of opportunity** Chancengleichheit f

equalize ['i:kwəlaɪz] vt angleichen ▷ vi (Sport) ausgleichen

equally ['i:kwəlɪ] adv gleichmäßig; (good, bad etc) gleich; **they are ~ clever** sie sind beide gleich klug

Equal Opportunities Commission, (US) **Equal Employment Opportunity Commission** n Ausschuss m für Chancengleichheit am Arbeitsplatz

equal sign, equals sign n Gleichheitszeichen nt

equanimity [ɛkwə'nɪmɪtɪ] n Gleichmut m, Gelassenheit f

equate [ɪ'kweɪt] vt: **to ~ sth with** etw gleichsetzen mit ▷ vt (compare) auf die gleiche Stufe stellen; **to ~ A to B** A und B auf die gleiche Stufe stellen

equation [ɪ'kweɪʃən] n Gleichung f

equator [ɪ'kweɪtər] n Äquator m

equatorial [ɛkwə'tɔ:rɪəl] adj äquatorial

Equatorial Guinea n Äquatorial-Guinea nt

equestrian [ɪ'kwɛstrɪən] adj (sport, dress etc) Reit-; (statue) Reiter- ▷ n Reiter(in) m(f)

equilibrium [i:kwɪ'lɪbrɪəm] n Gleichgewicht nt

equinox ['i:kwɪnɔks] n Tagundnachtgleiche f; **the spring/autumn ~** die Frühjahrs-/die Herbst-Tagundnachtgleiche f

equip [ɪ'kwɪp] vt: **to ~ (with)** (person, army) ausrüsten (mit); (room, car etc) ausstatten (mit); **to ~ sb for** jdn vorbereiten auf +acc; **to be well ~ped** gut ausgerüstet sein

equipment [ɪ'kwɪpmənt] n Ausrüstung f

equitable ['ɛkwɪtəbl] adj gerecht

equities ['ɛkwɪtɪz] (Brit) npl Stammaktien pl

equity ['ɛkwɪtɪ] n Gerechtigkeit f

equity capital n Eigenkapital nt

equivalent [ɪ'kwɪvələnt] adj gleich, gleichwertig ▷ n Gegenstück nt; **to be ~ to** or **the ~ of** entsprechen +dat

equivocal [ɪ'kwɪvəkl] adj vieldeutig; (open to suspicion) zweifelhaft

equivocate [ɪ'kwɪvəkeɪt] vi ausweichen, ausweichend antworten

equivocation [ɪkwɪvə'keɪʃən] n Ausflucht f, ausweichende Antwort f

ER (Brit) abbr (= Elizabeth Regina) offizieller Namenszug der Königin

ERA (US) n abbr (Pol: = Equal Rights Amendment) Artikel der amerikanischen Verfassung zur Gleichberechtigung; (Baseball: = earned run average) durch Eigenleistung erzielte Läufe

era ['ɪərə] n Ära f, Epoche f

eradicate [ɪ'rædɪkeɪt] vt ausrotten

erase [ɪ'reɪz] vt (tape: Comput) löschen; (writing) ausradieren; (thought, feeling) auslöschen

eraser [ɪ'reɪzər] n Radiergummi m

erect [ɪ'rɛkt] adj aufrecht; (tail) hoch erhoben; (ears) gespitzt ▷ vt bauen; (assemble) aufstellen

erection [ɪ'rɛkʃən] n Bauen nt; (of statue) Errichten nt; (of tent, machinery etc) Aufstellen nt; (Physiol) Erektion f

ergonomics [ə:gə'nɒmɪks] n sing Ergonomie f, Ergonomik f

ERISA (US) n abbr (= Employee Retirement Income Security Act) Gesetz zur Regelung der Rentenversicherung

Eritrea n Eritrea nt

ERM n abbr (= Exchange Rate Mechanism) Wechselkursmechanismus m

ermine ['ə:mɪn] n (fur) Hermelin m

Ernie, Ernie ['ə:nɪ] (Brit) n abbr (= Electronic Random Number Indicator Equipment) Gerät zur Ermittlung von Gewinnnummern für Prämiensparer

erode [ɪ'rəud] vt erodieren, auswaschen; (metal) zerfressen; (confidence, power) untergraben

erogenous [ɪ'rɒdʒənəs] adj erogen

erosion [ɪ'rəuʒən] n (see vb) Erosion f, Auswaschen nt; Zerfressen nt; Untergraben nt

erotic [ɪ'rɒtɪk] adj erotisch

eroticism [ɪ'rɒtɪsɪzəm] n Erotik f

err [ə:r] vi sich irren; **to ~ on the side of caution/simplicity** (im Zweifelsfall) zur Vorsicht/Vereinfachung neigen

errand ['ɛrənd] n Besorgung f; (to give a message etc) Botengang m; **to run ~s** Besorgungen/ Botengänge machen; **~ of mercy** Rettungsaktion f

erratic [ɪ'rætɪk] adj unberechenbar; (attempts) unkoordiniert; (noise) unregelmäßig

erroneous [ɪ'rəunɪəs] adj irrig

error ['ɛrər] n Fehler m; **typing/spelling ~** Tipp-/Rechtschreibfehler m; **in ~** irrtümlicherweise; **~s and omissions excepted** Irrtum vorbehalten

error message n Fehlermeldung f

erstwhile ['ə:stwaɪl] adj einstig, vormalig

erudite ['ɛrjudaɪt] adj gelehrt

erupt [ɪ'rʌpt] vi ausbrechen

eruption [ɪ'rʌpʃən] n Ausbruch m

ESA n abbr (= European Space Agency) Europäische Weltraumbehörde f

escalate ['ɛskəleɪt] vi eskalieren, sich
ausweiten

escalation [ɛskə'leɪʃən] n Eskalation f

escalator ['ɛskəleɪtəʳ] n Rolltreppe f

escalator clause n Gleitklausel f

escapade [ɛskə'peɪd] n Eskapade f

escape [ɪs'keɪp] n Flucht f; (Tech: of liquid)
Ausfließen nt; (of gas) Ausströmen nt; (of
air, heat) Entweichen nt ▷ vi entkommen;
(from prison) ausbrechen; (liquid) ausfließen;
(gas) ausströmen; (air, heat) entweichen ▷ vt
(pursuers etc) entkommen +dat; (punishment etc)
entgehen +dat; **his name ~s me** sein Name
ist mir entfallen; **to ~ from** flüchten aus;
(prison) ausbrechen aus; (person) entkommen
+dat; **to ~ to Peru** nach Peru fliehen; **to ~ to
safety** sich in Sicherheit bringen; **to ~ notice**
unbemerkt bleiben

escape artist n Entfesselungskünstler(in) m(f)

escape clause n (in contract) Befreiungsklausel
f

escapee [ɪskeɪ'piː] n entwichener Häftling m

escape hatch n Notluke f

escape key n (Comput) Escape-Taste f

escape route n Fluchtweg m

escapism [ɪs'keɪpɪzəm] n Wirklichkeitsflucht
f, Eskapismus m

escapist [ɪs'keɪpɪst] adj eskapistisch

escapologist [ɛskə'pɔlədʒɪst] (Brit) n = **escape
artist**

escarpment [ɪs'kɑːpmənt] n Steilhang m

eschew [ɪs'tʃuː] vt meiden

escort [n 'ɛskɔːt, vt ɪs'kɔːt] n Eskorte f;
(companion) Begleiter(in) m(f) ▷ vt begleiten;
his ~ seine Begleiterin; **her ~** ihr Begleiter

escort agency n Agentur f für Begleiter(innen)

Eskimo ['ɛskɪməu] n Eskimo(frau) m(f)

ESL n abbr (Scol: = English as a Second Language)
Englisch nt als Zweitsprache

esophagus [iː'sɔfəgəs] (US) n = **oesophagus**

esoteric [ɛsə'tɛrɪk] adj esoterisch

ESP n abbr = **extrasensory perception**;
(Scol: = English for Specific (or Special) Purposes)
Englischunterricht für spezielle Fachbereiche

esp. abbr = **especially**

especially [ɪs'pɛʃlɪ] adv besonders

espionage ['ɛspɪənɑːʒ] n Spionage f

esplanade [ɛsplə'neɪd] n Promenade f

espouse [ɪs'pauz] vt eintreten für

Esquire [ɪs'kwaɪəʳ] n (abbr Esq.): **J. Brown, ~**
Herrn J. Brown

essay ['ɛseɪ] n Aufsatz m; (Liter) Essay m or nt

essence ['ɛsns] n Wesen nt; (Culin) Essenz
f; **in ~** im Wesentlichen; **speed is of the ~**
Geschwindigkeit ist von entscheidender
Bedeutung

essential [ɪ'sɛnʃl] adj notwendig; (basic)
wesentlich ▷ n (see adj) Notwendigste(s) nt;
Wesentliche(s) nt; **it is ~ that** es ist unbedingt
or absolut erforderlich, dass

essentially [ɪ'sɛnʃəlɪ] adv im Grunde
genommen

EST (US) abbr (= Eastern Standard Time)

ostamerikanische Standardzeit

est. abbr = **established; estimate; estimated**

establish [ɪs'tæblɪʃ] vt gründen; (facts)
feststellen; (proof) erstellen; (relations, contact)
aufnehmen; (reputation) sich dat verschaffen

established [ɪs'tæblɪʃt] adj üblich; (business)
eingeführt

establishment [ɪs'tæblɪʃmənt] n (see vb)
Gründung f; Feststellung f; Erstellung f;
Aufnahme f; (of reputation) Begründung
f; (shop etc) Unternehmen nt; **the E~** das
Establishment

estate [ɪs'teɪt] n Gut nt; (Brit: also: **housing
estate**) Siedlung f; (Law) Nachlass m

estate agency (Brit) n Maklerbüro nt

estate agent (Brit) n Immobilienmakler(in)
m(f)

estate car (Brit) n Kombiwagen m

esteem [ɪs'tiːm] n: **to hold sb in high ~** eine
hohe Meinung von jdm haben

esthetic [ɪs'θɛtɪk] (US) adj = **aesthetic**

estimate ['ɛstɪmət] n Schätzung f; (assessment)
Einschätzung f; (Comm) (Kosten)voranschlag
m ▷ vt schätzen ▷ vi (Brit: Comm): **to ~ for** einen
Kostenvoranschlag machen für; **to give sb an
~ of sth** jdm eine Vorstellung von etw geben;
to ~ for einen Kostenvoranschlag machen
für; **at a rough ~** grob geschätzt, über den
Daumen gepeilt (inf); **I ~ that** ich schätze, dass

estimation [ɛstɪ'meɪʃən] n Schätzung f;
(opinion) Einschätzung f; **in my ~** meiner
Einschätzung nach

estimator ['ɛstɪmeɪtəʳ] n Schätzer(in) m(f)

Estonia [ɛs'təunɪə] n Estland nt

Estonian [ɛs'təunɪən] adj estnisch ▷ n Este m,
Estin f; (Ling) Estnisch nt

estranged [ɪs'treɪndʒd] adj entfremdet; (from
spouse) getrennt; (couple) getrennt lebend

estrangement [ɪs'treɪndʒmənt] n
Entfremdung f; (from spouse) Trennung f

estrogen ['iːstrəudʒən] (US) n = **oestrogen**

estuary ['ɛstjuərɪ] n Mündung f

ET (Brit) n abbr (= Employment Training)
Ausbildungsmaßnahmen für Arbeitslose

ETA n abbr (= estimated time of arrival)
voraussichtliche Ankunftszeit f

et al. abbr (= et alii) u. a.

etc. abbr (= et cetera) etc.

etch [ɛtʃ] vt (design, surface: with needle) radieren;
(: with acid) ätzen; (: with chisel) meißeln; **it will
be ~ed on my memory** es wird sich tief in
mein Gedächtnis eingraben

etching ['ɛtʃɪŋ] n Radierung f

ETD n abbr (= estimated time of departure)
voraussichtliche Abflugzeit f

eternal [ɪ'təːnl] adj ewig

eternity [ɪ'təːnɪtɪ] n Ewigkeit f

ether ['iːθəʳ] n Äther m

ethereal [ɪ'θɪərɪəl] adj ätherisch

ethical ['ɛθɪkl] adj ethisch

ethics ['ɛθɪks] n Ethik f ▷ npl (morality) Moral f

Ethiopia [iːθɪ'əupɪə] n Äthiopien nt

Ethiopian [iːθɪ'əupɪən] adj äthiopisch ▷ n

e

Äthiopier(in) *m(f)*
ethnic ['εθnɪk] *adj* ethnisch; *(music)* folkloristisch; *(culture etc)* urwüchsig
ethnic cleansing [-'klɛnzɪŋ] *n* ethnische Säuberung *f*
ethnic minority *n* ethnische Minderheit *f*
ethnology [εθ'nɔlədʒɪ] *n* Ethnologie *f*, Völkerkunde *f*
ethos ['i:θɔs] *n* Ethos *nt*
e-ticket ['i:tɪkɪt] *n abbr* (= *electronic ticket*) E-Ticket *nt*, *elektronische Eintrittskarte/Fahrkarte etc*
etiquette ['εtɪkεt] *n* Etikette *f*
ETV (*US*) *n abbr* (= *educational television*) *Fernsehsender, der Bildungs- und Kulturprogramme ausstrahlt*
etymology [εtɪ'mɔlədʒɪ] *n* Etymologie *f*; (*of word*) Herkunft *f*
EU *n abbr* (= *European Union*) EU *f*
eucalyptus [ju:kə'lɪptəs] *n* Eukalyptus *m*
Eucharist ['ju:kərɪst] *n*: **the ~** die Eucharistie, das (heilige) Abendmahl
eulogy ['ju:lədʒɪ] *n* Lobrede *f*
euphemism ['ju:fəmɪzəm] *n* Euphemismus *m*
euphemistic [ju:fə'mɪstɪk] *adj* euphemistisch, verhüllend
euphoria [ju:'fɔ:rɪə] *n* Euphorie *f*
Eurasia [juə'reɪʒə] *n* Eurasien *nt*
Eurasian [juə'reɪʃən] *adj* eurasisch ▷ *n* Eurasier(in) *m(f)*
Euratom [juə'rætəm] *n abbr* (= *European Atomic Energy Community*) Euratom *f*
euro ['juərəu] *n* (*Fin*) Euro *m*
Euro- ['juərəu] *pref* Euro-
euro cent ['juərəu-] *n* Eurocent *m*
Eurocrat ['juərəukræt] *n* Eurokrat(in) *m(f)*
Eurodollar ['juərəudɔlər] *n* Eurodollar *m*
Euroland ['juərəulænd] *n* (*Fin*) Eurozone *f*
Europe ['juərəp] *n* Europa *nt*
European [juərə'pi:ən] *adj* europäisch ▷ *n* Europäer(in) *m(f)*
European Central Bank *n*: **the ~** die Europäische Zentralbank
European Community *n*: **the ~** die Europäische Gemeinschaft
European Convention *n* Europäische(r) Konvent *m*, EU-Konvent *m*
European Court of Justice *n*: **the ~** der Europäische Gerichtshof
European Economic Community *n* (*formerly*): **the ~** die Europäische Wirtschaftsgemeinschaft
Euro-sceptic ['juərəuskεptɪk] *n* Euroskeptiker(in) *m(f)*
euthanasia [ju:θə'neɪzɪə] *n* Euthanasie *f*
evacuate [ɪ'vækjueɪt] *vt* evakuieren; (*place*) räumen
evacuation [ɪvækju'eɪʃən] *n* (*see verb*) Evakuierung *f*; Räumung *f*
evacuee [ɪvækju'i:] *n* Evakuierte(r) *f(m)*
evade [ɪ'veɪd] *vt* (*person, question*) ausweichen +*dat*; (*tax*) hinterziehen; (*duty, responsibility*) sich entziehen +*dat*

evaluate [ɪ'væljueɪt] *vt* bewerten; (*situation*) einschätzen
evangelical [i:væn'dʒεlɪkl] *adj* evangelisch
evangelist [ɪ'vændʒəlɪst] *n* Evangelist(in) *m(f)*
evangelize [ɪ'vændʒəlaɪz] *vi* evangelisieren
evaporate [ɪ'væpəreɪt] *vi* verdampfen; (*feeling, attitude*) dahinschwinden
evaporated milk [ɪ'væpəreɪtɪd-] *n* Kondensmilch *f*, Büchsenmilch *f*
evaporation [ɪvæpə'reɪʃən] *n* Verdampfung *f*
evasion [ɪ'veɪʒən] *n* Ausweichen *nt*; (*of tax*) Hinterziehung *f*
evasive [ɪ'veɪsɪv] *adj* ausweichend; **to take ~ action** ein Ausweichmanöver machen
eve [i:v] *n*: **on the ~ of** am Tag vor +*dat*; **Christmas E~** Heiligabend *m*; **New Year's E~** Silvester *m or nt*
even ['i:vn] *adj* (*level*) eben; (*smooth*) glatt; (*equal*) gleich; (*number*) gerade ▷ *adv* sogar, selbst; (*introducing a comparison*) sogar noch; **~ if, ~ though** selbst wenn; **~ more** sogar noch mehr; **he loves her ~ more** er liebt sie umso mehr; **it's going ~ faster now** es fährt jetzt sogar noch schneller; **~ so** (*aber*) trotzdem; **not ~** nicht einmal; **~ he was there** sogar er war da; **to break ~** die Kosten decken; **to get ~ with sb** es jdm heimzahlen
▶ **even out** *vi* sich ausgleichen ▷ *vt* ausgleichen
even-handed ['i:vnhændɪd] *adj* gerecht
evening ['i:vnɪŋ] *n* Abend *m*; **in the ~** abends, am Abend; **this ~** heute Abend; **tomorrow/ yesterday ~** morgen/gestern Abend
evening class *n* Abendkurs *m*
evening dress *n* (*no pl*) Abendkleidung *f*; (*woman's*) Abendkleid *nt*
evenly ['i:vnlɪ] *adv* gleichmäßig
evensong ['i:vnsɔŋ] *n* Abendandacht *f*
event [ɪ'vεnt] *n* Ereignis *nt*; (*Sport*) Wettkampf *m*; **in the normal course of ~s** normalerweise; **in the ~ of** im Falle +*gen*; **in the ~** schließlich; **at all ~s** (*Brit*), **in any ~** auf jeden Fall
eventful [ɪ'vεntful] *adj* ereignisreich
eventing [ɪ'vεntɪŋ] *n* (*Horseriding*) Military *f*
eventual [ɪ'vεntʃuəl] *adj* schließlich; (*goal*) letztlich
eventuality [ɪvεntʃu'ælɪtɪ] *n* Eventualität *f*
eventually [ɪ'vεntʃuəlɪ] *adv* endlich; (*in time*) schließlich
ever ['εvər] *adv* immer; (*at any time*) je(mals); **why ~ not?** warum denn bloß nicht?; **the best ~** der/die/das Allerbeste; **have you ~ seen it?** haben Sie es schon einmal gesehen?; **for ~** für immer; **hardly ~** kaum je(mals); **better than ~** besser als je zuvor; **~ since** *adv* seitdem ▷ *conj* seit, seitdem; **~ so pretty** unheimlich hübsch (*inf*); **thank you ~ so much** ganz herzlichen Dank; **yours ~** (*Brit*: *in letters*) alles Liebe
Everest ['εvərɪst] *n* (*also*: **Mount Everest**) Mount Everest *m*

evergreen ['ɛvəgriːn] n (tree/bush)
immergrüner Baum/Strauch m
everlasting [ɛvə'lɑːstɪŋ] adj ewig

🔵 KEYWORD

every ['ɛvrɪ] adj 1 jede(r, s); **every one of them**
(persons) jede(r) (Einzelne) von ihnen; (objects)
jedes einzelne Stück; **every day** jeden Tag;
every week jede Woche; **every other car**
jedes zweite Auto; **every other/third day**
alle zwei/drei Tage; **every shop in the town
was closed** alle Geschäfte der Stadt waren
geschlossen; **every now and then** ab und zu,
hin und wieder
2 (all possible): **I have every confidence in him**
ich habe volles Vertrauen in ihn; **we wish you
every success** wir wünschen Ihnen alles Gute

everybody ['ɛvrɪbɔdɪ] pron jeder, alle pl; ~
knows about it alle wissen es; ~ **else** alle
anderen pl
everyday ['ɛvrɪdeɪ] adj täglich; (usual, common)
alltäglich; (life, language) Alltags-
everyone ['ɛvrɪwʌn] pron = **everybody**
everything ['ɛvrɪθɪŋ] pron alles; **he did ~
possible** er hat sein Möglichstes getan
everywhere ['ɛvrɪwɛəʳ] adv überall; (wherever)
wo auch or immer; ~ **you go you meet …** wo
man auch or wo immer man hingeht, trifft
man …
evict [ɪ'vɪkt] vt zur Räumung zwingen
eviction [ɪ'vɪkʃən] n Ausweisung f
eviction notice n Räumungskündigung f
eviction order n Räumungsbefehl m
evidence ['ɛvɪdns] n Beweis m; (of witness)
Aussage f; (sign, indication) Zeichen nt, Spur f;
to give ~ (als Zeuge) aussagen; **to show ~ of**
zeigen; **in ~** sichtbar
evident ['ɛvɪdnt] adj offensichtlich
evidently ['ɛvɪdntlɪ] adv offensichtlich
evil ['iːvl] adj böse; (influence) schlecht ▷ n
Böse(s) nt; (unpleasant situation or activity) Übel nt
evocative [ɪ'vɔkətɪv] adj evokativ
evoke [ɪ'vəuk] vt hervorrufen; (memory) wecken
evolution [iːvə'luːʃən] n Evolution f;
(development) Entwicklung f
evolve [ɪ'vɔlv] vt entwickeln ▷ vi sich
entwickeln
ewe [juː] n Mutterschaf nt
ewer ['juːəʳ] n (Wasser)krug m
ex- [ɛks] pref Ex-, frühere(r, s); **the price ex
works** der Preis ab Werk
exacerbate [ɛks'æsəbeɪt] vt verschärfen; (pain)
verschlimmern
exact [ɪg'zækt] adj genau; (word) richtig ▷ vt: **to
~ sth (from)** etw verlangen (von); (payment)
etw eintreiben (von)
exacting [ɪg'zæktɪŋ] adj anspruchsvoll
exactly [ɪg'zæktlɪ] adv genau; ~! (ganz) genau!;
not ~ (hardly) nicht gerade
exaggerate [ɪg'zædʒəreɪt] vt, vi übertreiben
exaggerated [ɪg'zædʒəreɪtɪd] adj übertrieben

exaggeration [ɪgzædʒə'reɪʃən] n Übertreibung
f
exalt [ɪg'zɔːlt] vt preisen
exalted [ɪg'zɔːltɪd] adj hoch; (elated) exaltiert
exam [ɪg'zæm] n abbr = **examination**
examination [ɪgzæmɪ'neɪʃən] n (see vb)
Untersuchung f; Prüfung f; Verhör nt; **to take
an ~, to sit an ~** (Brit) eine Prüfung machen;
the matter is under ~ die Angelegenheit
wird geprüft or untersucht
examine [ɪg'zæmɪn] vt untersuchen; (accounts,
candidate) prüfen; (witness) verhören
examiner [ɪg'zæmɪnəʳ] n Prüfer(in) m(f)
example [ɪg'zɑːmpl] n Beispiel nt; **for ~** zum
Beispiel; **to set a good/bad ~** ein gutes/
schlechtes Beispiel geben
exasperate [ɪg'zɑːspəreɪt] vt (annoy) verärgern;
(frustrate) zur Verzweiflung bringen; **~d by** or
with verärgert/verzweifelt über +acc
exasperating [ɪg'zɑːspəreɪtɪŋ] adj ärgerlich;
(job) leidig
exasperation [ɪgzɑːspə'reɪʃən] n Verzweiflung
f; **in ~** verzweifelt
excavate ['ɛkskəveɪt] vt ausgraben; (hole)
graben ▷ vi Ausgrabungen machen
excavation [ɛkskə'veɪʃən] n Ausgrabung f
excavator ['ɛkskəveɪtəʳ] n Bagger m
exceed [ɪk'siːd] vt übersteigen; (hopes)
übertreffen; (limit, budget, powers) überschreiten
exceedingly [ɪk'siːdɪŋlɪ] adv äußerst
excel [ɪk'sɛl] vt übertreffen ▷ vi: **to ~ (in or at)**
sich auszeichnen (in +dat); **to ~ o.s.** (Brit) sich
selbst übertreffen
excellence ['ɛksələns] n hervorragende
Leistung f
Excellency ['ɛksələnsɪ] n: **His ~** Seine Exzellenz
excellent ['ɛksələnt] adj ausgezeichnet,
hervorragend
except [ɪk'sɛpt] prep (also: **except for**) außer
+dat ▷ vt: **to ~ sb (from)** jdn ausnehmen (bei);
~ if, ~ when außer wenn; **~ that** nur dass
excepting [ɪk'sɛptɪŋ] prep außer +dat, mit
Ausnahme +gen
exception [ɪk'sɛpʃən] n Ausnahme f; **to take ~
to** Anstoß nehmen an +dat; **with the ~ of** mit
Ausnahme von
exceptional [ɪk'sɛpʃnl] adj außergewöhnlich
excerpt ['ɛksəːpt] n Auszug m
excess [ɪk'sɛs] n Übermaß nt; (Insurance)
Selbstbeteiligung f; **excesses** npl Exzesse
pl; **an ~ of £15, a £15 excess** eine
Selbstbeteiligung von £15; **in ~ of** über +dat
excess baggage n Übergepäck nt
excess fare (Brit) n Nachlösegebühr f
excessive [ɪk'sɛsɪv] adj übermäßig
excess supply n Überangebot nt
exchange [ɪks'tʃeɪndʒ] n Austausch m;
(conversation) Wortwechsel m; (also: **telephone
exchange**) Fernsprechamt nt ▷ vt: **to ~ (for)**
tauschen (gegen); (in shop) umtauschen
(gegen); **in ~ for** für; **foreign ~**
Devisenhandel m; (money) Devisen pl
exchange control n Devisenkontrolle f

545

exchange market n Devisenmarkt m

exchange rate n Wechselkurs m

Exchequer [ɪksˈtʃɛkəʳ] (Brit) n: **the ~** das Finanzministerium

excisable [ɪkˈsaɪzəbl] adj steuerpflichtig

excise [ˈɛksaɪz] n Verbrauchssteuer f ▷ vt entfernen

excise duties npl Verbrauchssteuern pl

excitable [ɪkˈsaɪtəbl] adj (leicht) erregbar

excite [ɪkˈsaɪt] vt aufregen; (arouse) erregen; **to get ~d** sich aufregen

excitement [ɪkˈsaɪtmənt] n Aufregung f; (exhilaration) Hochgefühl nt

exciting [ɪkˈsaɪtɪŋ] adj aufregend

excl. abbr = **excluding; exclusive (of)**

exclaim [ɪksˈkleɪm] vi aufschreien

exclamation [ɛkskləˈmeɪʃən] n Ausruf m; **~ of joy** Freudenschrei m

exclamation mark n Ausrufezeichen nt

exclude [ɪksˈkluːd] vt ausschließen

excluding [ɪksˈkluːdɪŋ] prep: **~ VAT** ohne Mehrwertsteuer

exclusion [ɪksˈkluːʒən] n Ausschluss m; **to concentrate on sth to the ~ of everything else** sich ausschließlich auf etw dat konzentrieren

exclusion clause n Freizeichnungsklausel f

exclusion zone n Sperrzone f

exclusive [ɪksˈkluːsɪv] adj exklusiv; (story, interview) Exklusiv-; (use) ausschließlich ▷ n Exklusivbericht m ▷ adv: **from 1st to 15th March ~** vom 1. bis zum 15. März ausschließlich; **~ of postage** ohne or exklusive Porto; **~ of tax** ausschließlich or exklusive Steuern; **to be mutually ~** sich or einander ausschließen

exclusively [ɪksˈkluːsɪvlɪ] adv ausschließlich

exclusive rights npl Exklusivrechte pl

excommunicate [ɛkskəˈmjuːnɪkeɪt] vt exkommunizieren

excrement [ˈɛkskrəmənt] n Kot m, Exkremente pl

excruciating [ɪksˈkruːʃɪeɪtɪŋ] adj grässlich, fürchterlich; (noise, embarrassment) unerträglich

excursion [ɪksˈkəːʃən] n Ausflug m

excursion ticket n verbilligte Fahrkarte f

excusable [ɪksˈkjuːzəbl] adj verzeihlich, entschuldbar

excuse [n ɪksˈkjuːs, vb ɪksˈkjuːz] n Entschuldigung f ▷ vt entschuldigen; (forgive) verzeihen; **to ~ sb from sth** jdm etw erlassen; **to ~ sb from doing sth** jdn davon befreien, etw zu tun; **~ me!** entschuldigen Sie!, Entschuldigung!; **if you will ~ me ...** entschuldigen Sie mich bitte ...; **to ~ o.s. for sth** sich für or wegen etw entschuldigen; **to ~ o.s. for doing sth** sich entschuldigen, dass man etw tut; **to make ~s for sb** jdn entschuldigen; **that's no ~!** das ist keine Ausrede!

ex-directory [ˈɛksdɪˈrɛktərɪ] (Brit) adj (number) geheim; **she's ~** sie steht nicht im Telefonbuch

execrable [ˈɛksɪkrəbl] adj scheußlich; (manners) abscheulich

execute [ˈɛksɪkjuːt] vt ausführen; (person) hinrichten

execution [ɛksɪˈkjuːʃən] n (see vb) Ausführung f; Hinrichtung f

executioner [ɛksɪˈkjuːʃnəʳ] n Scharfrichter m

executive [ɪgˈzɛkjutɪv] n leitende(r) Angestellte(r) f(m); (committee) Vorstand m ▷ adj geschäftsführend; (role) führend; (secretary) Chef-; (car, chair) für gehobene Ansprüche; (toys) Manager-; (plane) ≈ Privat-

executive director n leitender Direktor m, leitende Direktorin f

executor [ɪgˈzɛkjutəʳ] n Testamentsvollstrecker(in) m(f)

exemplary [ɪgˈzɛmplərɪ] adj vorbildlich, beispielhaft; (punishment) exemplarisch

exemplify [ɪgˈzɛmplɪfaɪ] vt verkörpern; (illustrate) veranschaulichen

exempt [ɪgˈzɛmpt] adj: **~ from** befreit von ▷ vt: **to ~ sb from** jdn befreien von

exemption [ɪgˈzɛmpʃən] n Befreiung f

exercise [ˈɛksəsaɪz] n Übung f; (no pl: keep-fit) Gymnastik f; (: energetic movement) Bewegung f; (: of authority etc) Ausübung f ▷ vt (patience) üben; (right) ausüben; (dog) ausführen; (mind) beschäftigen ▷ vi (also: **to take exercise**) Sport treiben

exercise book n (Schul)heft nt

exert [ɪgˈzəːt] vt (influence) ausüben; (authority) einsetzen; **to ~ o.s.** sich anstrengen

exertion [ɪgˈzəːʃən] n Anstrengung f

ex gratia [ˈɛksˈgreɪʃə] adj: **~ payment** freiwillige Zahlung f

exhale [ɛksˈheɪl] vt, vi ausatmen

exhaust [ɪgˈzɔːst] n (also: **exhaust pipe**) Auspuff m; (fumes) Auspuffgase pl ▷ vt erschöpfen; (money) aufbrauchen; (topic) erschöpfend behandeln; **to ~ o.s.** sich verausgaben

exhausted [ɪgˈzɔːstɪd] adj erschöpft

exhausting [ɪgˈzɔːstɪŋ] adj anstrengend

exhaustion [ɪgˈzɔːstʃən] n Erschöpfung f; **nervous ~** nervöse Erschöpfung

exhaustive [ɪgˈzɔːstɪv] adj erschöpfend

exhibit [ɪgˈzɪbɪt] n Ausstellungsstück nt; (Law) Beweisstück nt ▷ vt zeigen, an den Tag legen; (paintings) ausstellen

exhibition [ɛksɪˈbɪʃən] n Ausstellung f; **to make an ~ of o.s.** sich unmöglich aufführen; **an ~ of bad manners** schlechte Manieren pl; **an ~ of draughtsmanship** zeichnerisches Können n

exhibitionist [ɛksɪˈbɪʃənɪst] n Exhibitionist(in) m(f)

exhibitor [ɪgˈzɪbɪtəʳ] n Aussteller(in) m(f)

exhilarating [ɪgˈzɪləreɪtɪŋ] adj erregend, berauschend; (news) aufregend

exhilaration [ɪgzɪləˈreɪʃən] n Hochgefühl nt

exhort [ɪgˈzɔːt] vt: **to ~ sb to do sth** jdn ermahnen, etw zu tun

exile ['ɛksaɪl] n Exil nt; (person) Verbannte(r) f(m) ▷ vt verbannen; **in ~** im Exil
exist [ɪg'zɪst] vi existieren
existence [ɪg'zɪstəns] n Existenz f; **to be in ~** existieren
existentialism [ɛgzɪs'tɛnʃlɪzəm] n Existenzialismus m
existing [ɪg'zɪstɪŋ] adj bestehend
exit ['ɛksɪt] n Ausgang m; (from motorway) Ausfahrt f; (departure) Abgang m ▷ vi (Theat) abgehen; (Comput: from program/file etc) das Programm/die Datei etc verlassen; **to ~ from** hinausgehen aus; (motorway etc) abfahren von
exit poll n bei Wählern unmittelbar nach Verlassen der Wahllokale durchgeführte Umfrage
exit ramp (US) n Ausfahrt f
exit visa n Ausreisevisum nt
exodus ['ɛksədəs] n Auszug m; **the ~ to the cities** die Abwanderung in die Städte
ex officio ['ɛksə'fɪʃɪəu] adj von Amts wegen ▷ adv kraft seines Amtes
exonerate [ɪg'zɔnəreɪt] vt: **to ~ from** entlasten von
exorbitant [ɪg'zɔːbɪtnt] adj (prices, rents) astronomisch, unverschämt; (demands) maßlos, übertrieben
exorcize ['ɛksɔːsaɪz] vt exorzieren; (spirit) austreiben
exotic [ɪg'zɔtɪk] adj exotisch
expand [ɪks'pænd] vt erweitern; (staff, numbers etc) vergrößern; (influence) ausdehnen ▷ vi expandieren; (population) wachsen; (gas, metal) sich ausdehnen; **to ~ on** weiter ausführen
expanse [ɪks'pæns] n Weite f
expansion [ɪks'pænʃən] n Expansion f; (of population) Wachstum nt; (of gas, metal) Ausdehnung f
expansionism [ɪks'pænʃənɪzəm] n Expansionspolitik f
expansionist [ɪks'pænʃənɪst] adj Expansions-, expansionistisch
expatriate [ɛks'pætrɪət] n im Ausland Lebende(r) f(m)
expect [ɪks'pɛkt] vt erwarten; (suppose) denken, glauben; (count on) rechnen mit ▷ vi: **to be ~ing** ein Kind erwarten; **to ~ sb to do sth** erwarten, dass jd etw tut; **to ~ to do sth** vorhaben, etw zu tun; **as ~ed** wie erwartet; **I ~ so** ich glaube schon
expectancy [ɪks'pɛktənsɪ] n Erwartung f; **life ~** Lebenserwartung f
expectant [ɪks'pɛktənt] adj erwartungsvoll
expectantly [ɪks'pɛktəntlɪ] adv erwartungsvoll
expectant mother n werdende Mutter f
expectation [ɛkspɛk'teɪʃən] n Erwartung f; (hope) Hoffnung f; **in ~ of** in Erwartung +gen; **against** or **contrary to all ~(s)** wider Erwarten; **to come** or **live up to sb's ~s** jds Erwartungen dat entsprechen
expedience [ɪks'piːdɪəns] n = **expediency**
expediency [ɪks'piːdɪənsɪ] n Zweckmäßigkeit f; **for the sake of ~** aus Gründen der Zweckmäßigkeit
expedient [ɪks'piːdɪənt] adj zweckmäßig ▷ n Hilfsmittel nt
expedite ['ɛkspədaɪt] vt beschleunigen
expedition [ɛkspə'dɪʃən] n Expedition f; (for shopping etc) Tour f
expeditionary force [ɛkspə'dɪʃənrɪ-] n Expeditionskorps nt
expeditious [ɛkspə'dɪʃəs] adj schnell
expel [ɪks'pɛl] vt (from school) verweisen; (from organization) ausschließen; (from place) vertreiben; (gas, liquid) ausstoßen
expend [ɪks'pɛnd] vt ausgeben; (time, energy) aufwenden
expendable [ɪks'pɛndəbl] adj entbehrlich
expenditure [ɪks'pɛndɪtʃəʳ] n Ausgaben pl; (of energy, time) Aufwand m
expense [ɪks'pɛns] n Kosten pl; (expenditure) Ausgabe f; **expenses** npl Spesen pl; **at the ~ of** auf Kosten +gen; **to go to the ~ of buying a new car** (viel) Geld für ein neues Auto anlegen; **at great/little ~** mit hohen/ geringen Kosten
expense account n Spesenkonto nt
expensive [ɪks'pɛnsɪv] adj teuer; **to have ~ tastes** einen teuren Geschmack haben
experience [ɪks'pɪərɪəns] n Erfahrung f; (event, activity) Erlebnis nt ▷ vt erleben; **by** or **from ~** aus Erfahrung; **to learn by ~** durch eigene Erfahrung lernen
experienced [ɪks'pɪərɪənst] adj erfahren
experiment [ɪks'pɛrɪmənt] n Experiment nt, Versuch m ▷ vi: **to ~ (with/on)** experimentieren (mit/an +dat); **to perform** or **carry out an ~** einen Versuch or ein Experiment durchführen; **as an ~** versuchsweise
experimental [ɪkspɛrɪ'mɛntl] adj experimentell; **at the ~ stage** im Versuchsstadium
expert ['ɛkspəːt] adj ausgezeichnet, geschickt; (opinion, help etc) eines Fachmanns ▷ n Fachmann m, Fachfrau f, Experte m, Expertin f; **to be ~ in** or **at doing sth** etw ausgezeichnet können; **an ~ on sth/on the subject of sth** ein Experte für etw/auf dem Gebiet einer Sache gen; **~ witness** (Law) sachverständiger Zeuge m
expertise [ɛkspəː'tiːz] n Sachkenntnis f
expire [ɪks'paɪəʳ] vi ablaufen
expiry [ɪks'paɪərɪ] n Ablauf m
expiry date n Ablauftermin m; (of voucher, special offer etc) Verfallsdatum nt
explain [ɪks'pleɪn] vt erklären
▶ **explain away** vt eine Erklärung finden für
explanation [ɛksplə'neɪʃən] n Erklärung f; **to find an ~ for sth** eine Erklärung für etw finden
explanatory [ɪks'plænətrɪ] adj erklärend
expletive [ɪks'pliːtɪv] n Kraftausdruck m
explicable [ɪks'plɪkəbl] adj erklärbar; **for no ~ reason** aus unerfindlichen Gründen
explicit [ɪks'plɪsɪt] adj ausdrücklich; (sex,

e

547

violence) deutlich, unverhüllt; **to be ~** *(frank)* sich deutlich ausdrücken

explode [ɪks'pləud] *vi* explodieren; *(population)* sprunghaft ansteigen ▷ *vt* zur Explosion bringen; *(myth, theory)* zu Fall bringen

exploit ['eksplɔɪt] *n* Heldentat *f* ▷ *vt* ausnutzen; *(workers etc)* ausbeuten; *(resources)* nutzen

exploitation [eksplɔɪ'teɪʃən] *n (see vb)* Ausnutzung *f*; Ausbeutung *f*; Nutzung *f*

exploration [eksplə'reɪʃən] *n (see vb)* Erforschung *f*; Erkundung *f*; Untersuchung *f*

exploratory [ɪks'plɔrətrɪ] *adj* exploratorisch; *(expedition)* Forschungs-; **~ operation** *(Med)* Explorationsoperation *f*; **~ talks** Sondierungsgespräche *pl*

explore [ɪks'plɔːʳ] *vt* erforschen; *(with hands etc, idea)* untersuchen

explorer [ɪks'plɔːrəʳ] *n* Forschungsreisende(r) *f(m)*; *(of place)* Erforscher(in) *m(f)*

explosion [ɪks'pləuʒən] *n* Explosion *f*; *(outburst)* Ausbruch *m*

explosive [ɪks'pləusɪv] *adj* explosiv; *(device)* Spreng-; *(temper)* aufbrausend ▷ *n* Sprengstoff *m*; *(device)* Sprengkörper *m*

exponent [ɪks'pəunənt] *n* Vertreter(in) *m(f)*, Exponent(in) *m(f)*; *(Math)* Exponent *m*

exponential [ekspəu'nenʃl] *adj* exponentiell; *(Math: function etc)* Exponential-

export [eks'pɔːt] *vt* exportieren, ausführen; *(ideas, values)* verbreiten ▷ *n* Export *m*, Ausfuhr *f*; *(product)* Exportgut *nt* ▷ *cpd* Export-, Ausfuhr-

exportation [ekspɔː'teɪʃən] *n* Export *m*, Ausfuhr *f*

exporter [eks'pɔːtəʳ] *n* Exporteur *m*

expose [ɪks'pəuz] *vt* freilegen; *(to heat, radiation)* aussetzen; *(unmask)* entlarven; **to ~ o.s.** sich entblößen

exposé [ɪk'spəuzeɪ] *n* Enthüllung *f*

exposed [ɪks'pəuzd] *adj* ungeschützt; *(wire)* bloßliegend; **to be ~ to** *(radiation, heat etc)* ausgesetzt sein +*dat*

exposition [ekspə'zɪʃn] *n* Erläuterung *f*; *(exhibition)* Ausstellung *f*

exposure [ɪks'pəuʒəʳ] *n (to heat, radiation)* Aussetzung *f*; *(publicity)* Publicity *f*; *(of person)* Entlarvung *f*; *(Phot)* Belichtung *f*; *(: shot)* Aufnahme *f*; **to be suffering from ~** an Unterkühlung leiden; **to die from ~** erfrieren

exposure meter *n* Belichtungsmesser *m*

expound [ɪks'paund] *vt* darlegen, erläutern

express [ɪks'pres] *adj* ausdrücklich; *(intention)* bestimmt; *(Brit: letter etc)* Express-, Eil- ▷ *n* *(train)* Schnellzug *m*; *(bus)* Schnellbus *m* ▷ *adv* *(send)* per Express ▷ *vt* ausdrücken; *(view, emotion)* zum Ausdruck bringen; **to ~ o.s.** sich ausdrücken

expression [ɪks'preʃən] *n* Ausdruck *m*; *(on face)* (Gesichts)ausdruck *m*

expressionism [ɪks'preʃənɪzəm] *n* Expressionismus *m*

expressive [ɪks'presɪv] *adj* ausdrucksvoll; **~ ability** Ausdrucksfähigkeit *f*

expressly [ɪks'preslɪ] *adv* ausdrücklich; *(intentionally)* absichtlich

expressway [ɪks'presweɪ] *(US)* *n* Schnellstraße *f*

expropriate [eks'prəuprɪeɪt] *vt* enteignen

expulsion [ɪks'pʌlʃən] *n (Scol)* Verweisung *f*; *(Pol)* Ausweisung *f*; *(of gas, liquid etc)* Ausstoßen *nt*

expurgate ['ekspə:geɪt] *vt* zensieren; **the ~d version** die zensierte *or* bereinigte Fassung

exquisite [eks'kwɪzɪt] *adj* exquisit, erlesen; *(keenly felt)* köstlich

exquisitely [eks'kwɪzɪtlɪ] *adv* exquisit; *(carved)* kunstvoll; *(polite, sensitive)* äußerst

ex-serviceman ['eks'sə:vɪsmən] *(irreg: like* **man**) *n* ehemaliger Soldat *m*

ext. *abbr (Tel) =* **extension**

extemporize [ɪks'tempəraɪz] *vi* improvisieren

extend [ɪks'tend] *vt* verlängern; *(building)* anbauen an +*acc*; *(offer, invitation)* aussprechen; *(arm, hand)* ausstrecken; *(deadline)* verschieben ▷ *vi* sich erstrecken; *(period)* dauern

extension [ɪks'tenʃən] *n* Verlängerung *f*; *(of building)* Anbau *m*; *(of time)* Aufschub *m*; *(of campaign, rights)* Erweiterung *f*; *(Tel)* (Neben)anschluss *m*; **~ 3718** *(Tel)* Apparat 3718

extension cable *n* Verlängerungskabel *nt*

extension lead *n* Verlängerungsschnur *f*

extensive [ɪks'tensɪv] *adj* ausgedehnt; *(effect)* weitreichend; *(damage)* beträchtlich; *(coverage, discussion)* ausführlich; *(inquiries)* umfangreich; *(use)* häufig

extensively [ɪks'tensɪvlɪ] *adv:* **he's travelled ~** er ist viel gereist

extent [ɪks'tent] *n* Ausdehnung *f*; *(of problem, damage, loss etc)* Ausmaß *nt*; **to some ~** bis zu einem gewissen Grade; **to a certain ~** in gewissem Maße; **to a large ~** in hohem Maße; **to the ~ of ...** *(debts)* in Höhe von ...; **to go to the ~ of doing sth** so weit gehen, etw zu tun; **to such an ~ that ...** dermaßen, dass ...; **to what ~?** inwieweit?

extenuating [ɪks'tenjueɪtɪŋ] *adj:* **~ circumstances** mildernde Umstände *pl*

exterior [eks'tɪərɪəʳ] *adj (surface, angle, world)* Außen- ▷ *n* Außenseite *f*; *(appearance)* Äußere(s) *nt*

exterminate [ɪks'tə:mɪneɪt] *vt* ausrotten

extermination [ɪkstə:mɪ'neɪʃən] *n* Ausrottung *f*

external [eks'tə:nl] *adj (wall etc)* Außen-; *(use)* äußerlich; *(evidence)* unabhängig; *(examiner, auditor)* extern ▷ *n:* **the ~s** die Äußerlichkeiten *pl*; **for ~ use only** nur äußerlich (anzuwenden); **~ affairs** *(Pol)* auswärtige Angelegenheiten *pl*

externally [eks'tə:nəlɪ] *adv* äußerlich

extinct [ɪks'tɪŋkt] *adj* ausgestorben; *(volcano)* erloschen

extinction [ɪks'tɪŋkʃən] *n* Aussterben *nt*

extinguish [ɪks'tɪŋgwɪʃ] *vt* löschen; *(hope)* zerstören

extinguisher [ɪks'tɪŋgwɪʃəʳ] *n (also:* **fire**

extinguisher) Feuerlöscher *m*

extol, *(US)* **extoll** [ɪks'təul] *vt* preisen, rühmen

extort [ɪks'tɔːt] *vt* erpressen; *(confession)* erzwingen

extortion [ɪks'tɔːʃən] *n* *(see vb)* Erpressung *f*; Erzwingung *f*

extortionate [ɪks'tɔːʃnɪt] *adj* überhöht; *(price)* Wucher-

extra ['ɛkstrə] *adj* zusätzlich ▷ *adv* extra ▷ *n* Extra *nt*; *(surcharge)* zusätzliche Kosten *pl*; *(Cine, Theat)* Statist(in) *m(f)*; **wine will cost ~** Wein wird extra berechnet

extra ... ['ɛkstrə] *pref* außer-, extra-

extract [*vt* ɪks'trækt, *n* 'ɛkstrækt] *vt* *(tooth)* ziehen; *(mineral)* gewinnen ▷ *n* Auszug *m*; *(also:* **malt extract, vanilla extract** *etc)* Extrakt *m*; **to ~ (from)** *(object)* herausziehen (aus); *(money)* herausholen (aus); *(promise)* abringen +*dat*

extraction [ɪks'trækʃən] *n* *(see vb)* Ziehen *nt*; Gewinnung *f*; Herausziehen *nt*; Herausholen *nt*; Abringen *nt*; *(Dentistry)* Extraktion *f*; *(descent)* Herkunft *f*, Abstammung *f*; **to be of Scottish ~, to be Scottish by ~** schottischer Herkunft *or* Abstammung sein

extractor fan [ɪks'træktə-] *n* Sauglüfter *m*

extracurricular ['ɛkstrəkə'rɪkjuləʳ] *adj* außerhalb des Lehrplans

extradite ['ɛkstrədaɪt] *vt* ausliefern

extradition [ɛkstrə'dɪʃən] *n* Auslieferung *f* ▷ *cpd* Auslieferungs-

extramarital ['ɛkstrə'mærɪtl] *adj* außerehelich

extramural ['ɛkstrə'mjuərl] *adj* außerhalb der Universität; **~ classes** von der Universität veranstaltete Teilzeitkurse *pl*

extraneous [ɛks'treɪnɪəs] *adj* unwesentlich

extraordinary [ɪks'trɔːdnrɪ] *adj* ungewöhnlich; *(special)* außerordentlich; **the ~ thing is that ...** das Merkwürdige ist, dass ...

extraordinary general meeting *n* außerordentliche Hauptversammlung *f*

extrapolation [ɛkstræpə'leɪʃən] *n* Extrapolation *f*

extrasensory perception ['ɛkstrə'sɛnsərɪ-] *n* außersinnliche Wahrnehmung *f*

extra time *n* *(Football)* Verlängerung *f*

extravagance [ɪks'trævəgəns] *n* *(no pl)* Verschwendungssucht *f*; *(example of spending)* Luxus *m*

extravagant [ɪks'trævəgənt] *adj* extravagant; *(tastes, gift)* teuer; *(wasteful)* verschwenderisch; *(praise)* übertrieben; *(ideas)* ausgefallen

extreme [ɪks'triːm] *adj* extrem; *(point, edge, poverty)* äußerste(r, s) ▷ *n* Extrem *nt*; **the ~ right/left** *(Pol)* die äußerste *or* extreme Rechte/Linke; **~s of temperature** extreme Temperaturen *pl*

extremely [ɪks'triːmlɪ] *adv* äußerst, extrem

extremist [ɪks'triːmɪst] *n* Extremist(in) *m(f)* ▷ *adj* extremistisch

extremities [ɪks'trɛmɪtɪz] *npl* Extremitäten *pl*

extremity [ɪks'trɛmɪtɪ] *n* Rand *m*; *(end)* äußerstes Ende *nt*; *(of situation)* Ausmaß *nt*

extricate ['ɛkstrɪkeɪt] *vt*: **to ~ sb/sth (from)** jdn/etw befreien (aus)

extrovert ['ɛkstrəvəːt] *n* extravertierter Mensch *m*

exuberance [ɪg'zjuːbərns] *n* Überschwänglichkeit *f*

exuberant [ɪg'zjuːbərnt] *adj* überschwänglich; *(imagination etc)* lebhaft

exude [ɪg'zjuːd] *vt* ausstrahlen; *(liquid)* absondern; *(smell)* ausströmen

exult [ɪg'zʌlt] *vi*: **to ~ (in)** jubeln (über +*acc*)

exultant [ɪg'zʌltənt] *adj* jubelnd; *(shout)* Jubel-; **to be ~** jubeln

exultation [ɛgzʌl'teɪʃən] *n* Jubel *m*

eye [aɪ] *n* Auge *nt*; *(of needle)* Öhr *nt* ▷ *vt* betrachten; **to keep an ~ on** aufpassen auf +*acc*; **as far as the ~ can see** so weit das Auge reicht; **in the public ~** im Blickpunkt der Öffentlichkeit; **to have an ~ for sth** einen Blick für etw haben; **with an ~ to doing sth** *(Brit)* mit der Absicht, etw zu tun; **there's more to this than meets the ~** da steckt mehr dahinter(, als man auf den ersten Blick meint)

eyeball ['aɪbɔːl] *n* Augapfel *m*

eyebath ['aɪbɑːθ] *(Brit)* *n* Augenbadewanne *f*

eyebrow ['aɪbrau] *n* Augenbraue *f*

eyebrow pencil *n* Augenbrauenstift *m*

eye-catching ['aɪkætʃɪŋ] *adj* auffallend

eyecup ['aɪkʌp] *(US)* *n* = **eyebath**

eye drops *npl* Augentropfen *pl*

eyeful ['aɪful] *n*: **to get an ~ of sth** *(lit)* etw ins Auge bekommen; *(fig: have a good look)* einiges von etw zu sehen bekommen; **she's quite an ~** sie hat allerhand zu bieten

eyeglass ['aɪglɑːs] *n* Augenglas *nt*

eyelash ['aɪlæʃ] *n* Augenwimper *f*

eyelet ['aɪlɪt] *n* Öse *f*

eye level *n*: **at ~** in Augenhöhe

eyelevel ['aɪlɛvl] *adj* in Augenhöhe

eyelid ['aɪlɪd] *n* Augenlid *nt*

eyeliner ['aɪlaɪnəʳ] *n* Eyeliner *m*

eye-opener ['aɪəupnəʳ] *n* Überraschung *f*; **to be an ~ to sb** jdm die Augen öffnen

eye shadow *n* Lidschatten *m*

eyesight ['aɪsaɪt] *n* Sehvermögen *nt*

eyesore ['aɪsɔːʳ] *n* Schandfleck *m*

eyestrain ['aɪstreɪn] *n*: **to get ~** seine Augen überanstrengen

eyetooth ['aɪtuːθ] *(pl* **eyeteeth** *)* *n* Eckzahn *m*, Augenzahn *m*; **to give one's eyeteeth for sth** alles für etw geben; **to give one's eyeteeth to do sth** alles darum geben, etw zu tun

eyewash ['aɪwɔʃ] *n* Augenwasser *nt*; *(fig)* Gewäsch *nt*

eyewitness ['aɪwɪtnɪs] *n* Augenzeuge *m*, Augenzeugin *f*

eyrie ['ɪərɪ] *n* Horst *m*

e

Ff

F¹, f [ɛf] n (letter) F nt, f nt; **F for Frederick, F for Fox** (US) ≈ F wie Friedrich

F² [ɛf] n (Mus) F nt, f nt

F³ [ɛf] abbr (= Fahrenheit) F

FA (Brit) n abbr (= Football Association) englischer Fußball-Dachverband, ≈ DFB m

FAA (US) n abbr (= Federal Aviation Administration) amerikanische Luftfahrtbehörde

fable ['feɪbl] n Fabel f

fabric ['fæbrɪk] n Stoff m; (of society) Gefüge nt; (of building) Bausubstanz f

fabricate ['fæbrɪkeɪt] vt herstellen; (story) erfinden; (evidence) fälschen

fabrication [fæbrɪ'keɪʃən] n Herstellung f; (lie) Erfindung f

fabric ribbon n (for typewriter) Gewebefarbband nt

fabulous ['fæbjuləs] adj fabelhaft, toll (inf); (extraordinary) sagenhaft; (mythical) legendär

façade [fə'sɑːd] n Fassade f

face [feɪs] n Gesicht nt; (expression) Gesichtsausdruck m; (grimace) Grimasse f; (of clock) Zifferblatt nt; (of mountain, cliff) (Steil) wand f; (of building) Fassade f; (side, surface) Seite f ▷ vt (subj: person) gegenübersitzen/-stehen +dat etc; (: building, street etc) liegen zu; (: north, south etc) liegen nach; (unpleasant situation) sich gegenübersehen +dat; (facts) ins Auge sehen +dat; **~ down** mit dem Gesicht nach unten; (card) mit der Bildseite nach unten; (object) mit der Vorderseite nach unten; **to lose/save ~** das Gesicht verlieren/wahren; **to make** or **pull a ~** das Gesicht verziehen; **in the ~ of** trotz +gen; **on the ~ of it** so, wie es aussieht; **to come ~ to ~ with sb** jdn treffen; **to come ~ to ~ with a problem** einem Problem gegenüberstehen; **to ~ each other** einander gegenüberstehen/-liegen/-sitzen etc; **to ~ the fact that ...** der Tatsache ins Auge sehen, dass ...; **the man facing me** der Mann mir gegenüber

▶ **face up to** vt fus (obligations, difficulty) auf sich acc nehmen; (situation, possibility) sich abfinden mit; (danger, fact) ins Auge sehen +dat

face cloth n (Brit) Waschlappen m

face cream n Gesichtscreme f

faceless ['feɪslɪs] adj (fig) anonym

face-lift ['feɪslɪft] n Facelifting nt; (of building etc) Verschönerung f

face powder n Gesichtspuder m

face-saving ['feɪs'seɪvɪŋ] adj: **a ~ excuse/tactic** eine Entschuldigung/Taktik, um das Gesicht zu wahren

facet ['fæsɪt] n Seite f, Aspekt m; (of gem) Facette f

face time n (US) Zeit, die man mit jemandem im direkten persönlichen Gespräch verbringt

facetious [fə'siːʃəs] adj witzelnd

face-to-face [feɪstə'feɪs] adj persönlich; (confrontation) direkt

face value n Nennwert m; **to take sth at ~** (fig) etw für bare Münze nehmen

facia ['feɪʃə] n = **fascia**

facial ['feɪʃl] adj (expression, massage etc) Gesichts- ▷ n kosmetische Gesichtsbehandlung f

facile ['fæsaɪl] adj oberflächlich; (comment) nichtssagend

facilitate [fə'sɪlɪteɪt] vt erleichtern

facilities [fə'sɪlɪtɪz] npl Einrichtungen pl; **cooking ~** Kochgelegenheit f; **credit ~** Kreditmöglichkeiten pl

facility [fə'sɪlɪtɪ] n Einrichtung f; **to have a ~ for** (skill, aptitude) eine Begabung haben für

facing ['feɪsɪŋ] prep gegenüber +dat ▷ n (Sewing) Besatz m

facsimile [fæk'sɪmɪlɪ] n Faksimile nt; (also: **facsimile machine**) Fernkopierer m, (Tele)faxgerät nt; (transmitted document) Fernkopie f, (Tele)fax nt

fact [fækt] n Tatsache f; (truth) Wirklichkeit f; **in ~** eigentlich; (in reality) tatsächlich, in Wirklichkeit; **to know for a ~ that ...** ganz genau wissen, dass ...; **the ~ (of the matter) is that ...** die Sache ist die, dass ...; **it's a ~ of life that ...** es ist eine Tatsache, dass ...; **to tell sb the ~s of life** (sex) jdn aufklären

fact-finding ['fæktfaɪndɪŋ] adj: **a ~ tour** or **mission** eine Informationstour f

faction ['fækʃən] n Fraktion f

factional ['fækʃənl] adj (dispute, system) Fraktions-

factor ['fæktər] n Faktor m; (Comm) Kommissionär m; (: agent) Makler m; **safety ~** Sicherheitsfaktor m; **human ~** menschlicher Faktor

factory ['fæktərɪ] n Fabrik f
factory farming (Brit) n industriell betriebene Viehzucht f
factory floor n: **the ~** (workers) die Fabrikarbeiter pl; **on the ~** bei or unter den Fabrikarbeitern
factory ship n Fabrikschiff nt
factual ['fæktjuəl] adj sachlich; (information) Sach-
faculty ['fækəltɪ] n Vermögen nt, Kraft f; (ability) Talent nt; (of university) Fakultät f; (US: teaching staff) Lehrkörper m
fad [fæd] n Fimmel m, Tick m
fade [feɪd] vi verblassen; (light) nachlassen; (sound) schwächer werden; (flower) verblühen; (hope) zerrinnen; (smile) verschwinden
  ▸ **fade in** vt sep allmählich einblenden
  ▸ **fade out** vt sep ausblenden
faeces, (US) **feces** ['fiːsiːz] npl Kot m
fag [fæg] n (Brit: inf: cigarette) Glimmstängel m; (: chore) Schinderei f (inf), Plackerei f (inf); (US: inf: homosexual) Schwule(r) m
fail [feɪl] vt (exam) nicht bestehen; (candidate) durchfallen lassen; (subj: courage) verlassen; (: leader, memory) im Stich lassen ▸ vi (candidate) durchfallen; (attempt) fehlschlagen; (brakes) versagen; (also: **be failing**: health) sich verschlechtern; (: eyesight, light) nachlassen; **to ~ to do sth** etw nicht tun; (neglect) (es) versäumen, etw zu tun; **without ~** ganz bestimmt
failing ['feɪlɪŋ] n Schwäche f, Fehler m ▸ prep in Ermangelung +gen; **~ that** (oder) sonst, und wenn das nicht möglich ist
fail-safe ['feɪlseɪf] adj (ab)gesichert
failure ['feɪljər] n Misserfolg m; (person) Versager(in) m(f); (of brakes, heart) Versagen nt; (of engine, power) Ausfall m; (of crops) Missernte f; (in exam) Durchfall m; **his ~ to turn up meant that we had to ...** weil er nicht kam, mussten wir ...; **it was a complete ~** es war ein totaler Fehlschlag
faint [feɪnt] adj schwach; (breeze, trace) leicht ▸ n Ohnmacht f ▸ vi ohnmächtig werden, in Ohnmacht fallen; **she felt ~** ihr wurde schwach
faintest ['feɪntɪst] adj, n: **I haven't the ~ (idea)** ich habe keinen blassen Schimmer
faint-hearted ['feɪnt'hɑːtɪd] adj zaghaft
faintly ['feɪntlɪ] adv schwach
fair [fɛər] adj gerecht, fair; (size, number) ansehnlich; (chance, guess) recht gut; (hair) blond; (skin, complexion) hell; (weather) schön ▸ adv: **to play ~** fair spielen ▸ n (also: **trade fair**) Messe f; (Brit: funfair) Jahrmarkt m, Rummel m; **it's not ~!** das ist nicht fair!; **a ~ amount of** ziemlich viel
fair copy n Reinschrift f
fair game n: **to be ~ (for)** (for attack, criticism) Freiwild nt sein (für)
fairground ['fɛəgraund] n Rummelplatz m
fair-haired [fɛə'hɛəd] adj blond
fairly ['fɛəlɪ] adv gerecht; (quite) ziemlich; **I'm ~**

sure ich bin (mir) ziemlich sicher
fairness ['fɛənɪs] n Gerechtigkeit f; **in all ~** gerechterweise, fairerweise
fair play n faires Verhalten nt, Fair Play nt
fairway ['fɛəweɪ] n (Golf): **the ~** das Fairway
fairy ['fɛərɪ] n Fee f
fairy godmother n gute Fee f
fairy lights (Brit) npl bunte Lichter pl
fairy tale n Märchen nt
faith [feɪθ] n Glaube m; (trust) Vertrauen nt; **to have ~ in sb** jdm vertrauen; **to have ~ in sth** Vertrauen in etw acc haben
faithful ['feɪθful] adj (account) genau; **~ (to)** (person) treu +dat
faithfully ['feɪθfəlɪ] adv (see adj) genau; treu
faith healer n Gesundbeter(in) m(f)
fake [feɪk] n Fälschung f; (person) Schwindler(in) m(f) ▸ adj gefälscht ▸ vt fälschen; (illness, emotion) vortäuschen; **his illness is a ~** er simuliert seine Krankheit nur
falcon ['fɔːlkən] n Falke m
Falkland Islands ['fɔːlklənd-] npl: **the ~** die Falklandinseln pl
fall [fɔːl] (pt **fell**, pp **~en**) n Fall m; (of price, temperature) Sinken nt; (: sudden) Sturz m; (US: autumn) Herbst m ▸ vi fallen; (night, darkness) hereinbrechen; (silence) eintreten; **falls** npl (waterfall) Wasserfall m; **a ~ of snow** ein Schneefall m; **a ~ of earth** ein Erdrutsch m; **to ~ flat** auf die Nase fallen; (plan) ins Wasser fallen; (joke) nicht ankommen; **to ~ in love (with sb/sth)** sich (in jdn/etw) verlieben; **to ~ short of sb's expectations** jds Erwartungen nicht erfüllen
  ▸ **fall apart** vi auseinanderfallen, kaputtgehen; (inf: emotionally) durchdrehen
  ▸ **fall back** vi zurückweichen
  ▸ **fall back on** vi zurückgreifen auf +acc; **to have sth to ~ back on** auf etw acc zurückgreifen können
  ▸ **fall behind** vi zurückbleiben; (fig: with payment) in Rückstand geraten
  ▸ **fall down** vi hinfallen; (building) einstürzen
  ▸ **fall for** vt fus (trick, story) hereinfallen auf +acc; (person) sich verlieben in +acc
  ▸ **fall in** vi einstürzen; (Mil) antreten
  ▸ **fall in with** vt fus eingehen auf +acc
  ▸ **fall off** vi herunterfallen; (takings, attendance) zurückgehen
  ▸ **fall out** vi (hair, teeth) ausfallen; **to ~ out with sb** sich mit jdm zerstreiten
  ▸ **fall over** vi hinfallen; (object) umfallen ▸ vt: **to ~ over o.s. to do sth** sich dat die größte Mühe geben, etw zu tun
  ▸ **fall through** vi (plan, project) ins Wasser fallen
fallacy ['fæləsɪ] n Irrtum m
fall-back ['fɔːlbæk] adj: **~ position** Rückzugsbasis f
fallen ['fɔːlən] pp of **fall**
fallible ['fæləbl] adj fehlbar
falling ['fɔːlɪŋ] adj: **~ market** (Comm) Baissemarkt m
falling off n Rückgang m

falling-out ['fɔːlɪŋ'aut] n (break-up) Bruch m
Fallopian tube [fə'ləupɪən-] n Eileiter m
fallout ['fɔːlaut] n radioaktiver Niederschlag m
fallout shelter n Atombunker m
fallow ['fæləu] adj brach(liegend)
false [fɔːls] adj falsch; (imprisonment) widerrechtlich
false alarm n falscher or blinder Alarm m
falsehood ['fɔːlshud] n Unwahrheit f
falsely ['fɔːlslɪ] adv (accuse) zu Unrecht
false pretences npl: **under ~** unter Vorspiegelung falscher Tatsachen
false teeth (Brit) npl Gebiss nt
falsify ['fɔːlsɪfaɪ] vt fälschen
falter ['fɔːltər] vi stocken; (hesitate) zögern
fame [feɪm] n Ruhm m
familiar [fə'mɪlɪər] adj vertraut; (intimate) vertraulich; **to be ~ with** vertraut sein mit; **to make o.s. ~ with sth** sich mit etw vertraut machen; **to be on ~ terms with sb** mit jdm auf vertrautem Fuß stehen
familiarity [fəmɪlɪ'ærɪtɪ] n (see adj) Vertrautheit f; Vertraulichkeit f
familiarize [fə'mɪlɪəraɪz] vt: **to ~ o.s. with sth** sich mit etw vertraut machen
family ['fæmɪlɪ] n Familie f; (relations) Verwandtschaft f
family business, family company n Familienunternehmen nt or -betrieb m
family credit n Beihilfe für einkommensschwache Familien
family doctor n Hausarzt m, Hausärztin f
family life n Familienleben nt
family man n (home-loving) häuslich veranlagter Mann m; (with a family) Familienvater m
family planning n Familienplanung f; **~ clinic** ≈ Familienberatungsstelle f
family tree n Stammbaum m
famine ['fæmɪn] n Hungersnot f
famished ['fæmɪʃt] (inf) adj ausgehungert; **I'm ~** ich sterbe vor Hunger
famous ['feɪməs] adj berühmt
famously ['feɪməslɪ] adv (get on) prächtig
fan [fæn] n (person) Fan m; (object: folding) Fächer m; (: Elec) Ventilator m ▷ vt fächeln; (fire) anfachen; (quarrel) schüren
  ▶ **fan out** vi ausschwärmen; (unfurl) sich fächerförmig ausbreiten
fanatic [fə'nætɪk] n Fanatiker(in) m(f); (enthusiast) Fan m
fanatical [fə'nætɪkl] adj fanatisch
fan belt n (Aut) Keilriemen m
fanciful ['fænsɪful] adj (idea) abstrus, seltsam; (design, name) fantasievoll; (object) reich verziert
fan club n Fanklub m
fancy ['fænsɪ] n Laune f; (imagination) Fantasie f; (fantasy) Fantasievorstellung f ▷ adj (clothes, hat) toll, chic inv; (hotel) fein, vornehm; (food) ausgefallen ▷ vt mögen; (imagine) sich dat einbilden; (think) glauben; **to take a ~ to sth** Lust auf etw acc bekommen; **when the ~ takes him** wenn ihm gerade danach ist;

it took or **caught my ~** es gefiel mir; **to ~ that ...** meinen, dass ...; **~ that!** (nein) so was!; **he fancies her** (inf) sie gefällt ihm
fancy dress n Verkleidung f, (Masken)kostüm nt
fancy-dress ball ['fænsɪdrɛs-] n Maskenball m
fancy goods npl Geschenkartikel pl
fanfare ['fænfɛər] n Fanfare f
fanfold paper ['fænfəuld-] n Endlospapier nt
fang [fæŋ] n (tooth) Fang m; (: of snake) Giftzahn m
fan heater (Brit) n Heizlüfter m
fanlight ['fænlaɪt] n Oberlicht nt
fanny ['fænɪ] n (US: inf: bottom) Po m; (Brit: inf!: genitals) Möse f (!)
fantasize ['fæntəsaɪz] vi fantasieren
fantastic [fæn'tæstɪk] adj fantastisch
fantasy ['fæntəsɪ] n Fantasie f; (dream) Traum m
fanzine ['fænziːn] n Fanmagazin nt
FAO n abbr (= Food and Agriculture Organization) FAO f
FAQ abbr (Comput: = frequently-asked questions) FAQ pl
far [fɑːr] adj: **at the ~ side** auf der anderen Seite ▷ adv weit; **at the ~ end** am anderen Ende; **the ~ left/right** die extreme Linke/Rechte; **~ away, ~ off** weit entfernt or weg; **her thoughts were ~ away** sie war mit ihren Gedanken weit weg; **~ from** (fig) alles andere als; **by ~** bei Weitem; **is it ~ to London?** ist es weit bis nach London?; **it's not ~ from here** es ist nicht weit von hier; **go as ~ as the church** gehen/fahren Sie bis zur Kirche; **as ~ back as the 13th century** schon im 13. Jahrhundert; **as ~ as I know** soweit ich weiß; **as ~ as possible** so weit wie möglich; **how ~?** wie weit?; **how ~ have you got with your work?** wie weit sind Sie mit Ihrer Arbeit (gekommen)?
faraway ['fɑːrəweɪ] adj weit entfernt; (look, voice) abwesend
farce [fɑːs] n Farce f
farcical ['fɑːsɪkl] adj absurd, grotesk
fare [fɛər] n Fahrpreis m; (money) Fahrgeld nt; (passenger) Fahrgast m; (food) Kost f ▷ vi: **he ~d well/badly** es ging ihm gut/schlecht; **half/full ~** halber/voller Fahrpreis; **how did you ~?** wie ist es Ihnen ergangen?; **they ~d badly in the recent elections** sie haben bei den letzten Wahlen schlecht abgeschnitten
Far East n: **the ~** der Ferne Osten
farewell [fɛə'wɛl] excl lebe/lebt etc wohl! ▷ n Abschied m ▷ cpd Abschieds-
far-fetched ['fɑː'fɛtʃt] adj weit hergeholt
farm [fɑːm] n Bauernhof m ▷ vt bebauen
  ▶ **farm out** vt (work etc) vergeben
farmer ['fɑːmər] n Bauer m, Bäu(e)rin f, Landwirt(in) m(f)
farm hand n Landarbeiter(in) m(f)
farmhouse ['fɑːmhaus] n Bauernhaus nt
farming ['fɑːmɪŋ] n Landwirtschaft f; (of crops) Ackerbau m; (of animals) Viehzucht f;

sheep ~ Schafzucht f; **intensive ~** (of crops) Intensivanbau m; (of animals) Intensivhaltung f

farm labourer n = **farm hand**

farmland ['fɑːmlænd] n Ackerland nt

farm produce n landwirtschaftliche Produkte pl

farm worker n = **farm hand**

farmyard ['fɑːmjɑːd] n Hof m

Faroe Islands ['fɛərəu-] npl: **the ~** die Färöer pl

Faroes ['fɛərəuz] npl = **Faroe Islands**

far-reaching ['fɑːˈriːtʃɪŋ] adj weitreichend

far-sighted ['fɑːˈsaɪtɪd] adj weitsichtig; (fig) weitblickend

fart [fɑːt] vi furzen (inf!) ▷ n Furz m (inf!)

farther ['fɑːðər] adv weiter ▷ adj weiter entfernt

farthest ['fɑːðɪst] superl of **far**

FAS, f.a.s. (Brit) abbr (= free alongside ship) frei Kai

fascia ['feɪʃə] n (Aut) Armaturenbrett nt

fascinate ['fæsɪneɪt] vt faszinieren

fascinating ['fæsɪneɪtɪŋ] adj faszinierend

fascination [fæsɪˈneɪʃən] n Faszination f

fascism ['fæʃɪzəm] n Faschismus m

fascist ['fæʃɪst] adj faschistisch ▷ n Faschist(in) m(f)

fashion ['fæʃən] n Mode f; (manner) Art f ▷ vt formen; **in ~** modern; **out of ~** unmodern; **after a ~** recht und schlecht; **in the Greek ~** im griechischen Stil

fashionable ['fæʃnəbl] adj modisch, modern; (subject) Mode-; (club, writer) in Mode

fashion designer n Modezeichner(in) m(f)

fashion show n Modenschau f

fashion victim n Modefreak m

fast [fɑːst] adj schnell; (dye, colour) farbecht ▷ adv schnell; (stuck, held) fest ▷ n Fasten nt; (period of fasting) Fastenzeit f ▷ vi fasten; **my watch is (5 minutes) ~** meine Uhr geht (5 Minuten) vor; **to be ~ asleep** tief or fest schlafen; **as ~ as I can** so schnell ich kann; **to make a boat ~** (Brit) ein Boot festmachen

fasten ['fɑːsn] vt festmachen; (coat, belt etc) zumachen ▷ vi (see vt) festgemacht werden; zugemacht werden
▶ **fasten (up)on** vt fus sich dat in den Kopf setzen

fastener ['fɑːsnər] n Verschluss m

fastening ['fɑːsnɪŋ] n = **fastener**

fast food n Fast Food nt, Schnellgerichte pl

fast-food ['fɑːstfuːd] cpd (industry, chain) Fast-Food-; **~ restaurant** Schnellimbiss m

fastidious [fæsˈtɪdɪəs] adj penibel

fast lane n (Aut): **the ~** die Überholspur

fat [fæt] adj dick; (person) dick, fett (pej); (animal) fett; (profit) üppig ▷ n Fett nt; **that's a ~ lot of use** (inf) das hilft herzlich wenig; **to live off the ~ of the land** wie Gott in Frankreich or wie die Made im Speck leben

fatal ['feɪtl] adj tödlich; (mistake) verhängnisvoll

fatalistic [feɪtəˈlɪstɪk] adj fatalistisch

fatality [fəˈtælɪtɪ] n Todesopfer nt

fatally ['feɪtəlɪ] adv (see adj) tödlich; verhängnisvoll

fate [feɪt] n Schicksal nt; **to meet one's ~** vom Schicksal ereilt werden

fated ['feɪtɪd] adj (person) unglückselig; (project) zum Scheitern verurteilt; (governed by fate) vorherbestimmt

fateful ['feɪtful] adj schicksalhaft

fat-free ['fætˈfriː] adj fettfrei

father ['fɑːðər] n Vater m

Father Christmas n der Weihnachtsmann

fatherhood ['fɑːðəhud] n Vaterschaft f

father-in-law ['fɑːðərənlɔː] n Schwiegervater m

fatherland ['fɑːðəlænd] n Vaterland nt

fatherly ['fɑːðəlɪ] adj väterlich

fathom ['fæðəm] n (Naut) Faden m ▷ vt (also: **fathom out**) verstehen

fatigue [fəˈtiːg] n Erschöpfung f; **fatigues** npl (Mil) Arbeitsanzug m; **metal ~** Metallermüdung f

fatness ['fætnɪs] n Dicke f

fatten ['fætn] vt mästen ▷ vi (person) dick werden; (animal) fett werden; **chocolate is ~ing** Schokolade macht dick

fatty ['fætɪ] adj fett ▷ n (inf) Dickerchen nt

fatuous ['fætjuəs] adj albern, töricht

faucet ['fɔːsɪt] (US) n (Wasser)hahn m

fault [fɔːlt] n Fehler m; (blame) Schuld f; (in machine) Defekt m; (Geog) Verwerfung f ▷ vt (also: **find fault with**) etwas auszusetzen haben an +dat; **it's my ~** es ist meine Schuld; **at ~** im Unrecht; **generous to a ~** übermäßig großzügig

faultless ['fɔːltlɪs] adj fehlerlos

faulty ['fɔːltɪ] adj defekt

fauna ['fɔːnə] n Fauna f

faux pas ['fəuˈpɑː] n inv Fauxpas m

favor etc (US) = **favour** etc

favour, (US) **favor** ['feɪvər] n (approval) Wohlwollen nt; (help) Gefallen m ▷ vt bevorzugen; (be favourable for) begünstigen; **to ask a ~ of sb** jdn um einen Gefallen bitten; **to do sb a ~** jdm einen Gefallen tun; **to find ~ with sb** bei jdm Anklang finden; **in ~ of** (biased) zugunsten von; (rejected) zugunsten +gen; **to be in ~ of sth** für etw sein; **to be in ~ of doing sth** dafür sein, etw zu tun

favourable ['feɪvrəbl] adj günstig; (reaction) positiv; (comparison) vorteilhaft

favourably ['feɪvrəblɪ] adv (react) positiv; (compare) vorteilhaft

favourite ['feɪvrɪt] adj Lieblings- ▷ n Liebling m; (in race) Favorit(in) m(f)

favouritism ['feɪvrɪtɪzəm] n Günstlingswirtschaft f

fawn [fɔːn] n Rehkitz nt ▷ adj (also: **fawn-coloured**) hellbraun ▷ vi: **to ~ (up)on** sich einschmeicheln bei

fax [fæks] n Fax nt; (machine) Fax(gerät) nt ▷ vt faxen

FBI (US) n abbr (= Federal Bureau of Investigation) FBI nt

553

FCC (US) n abbr (= Federal Communications Commission) Aufsichtsbehörde im Medienbereich

FCO (Brit) n abbr (= Foreign and Commonwealth Office) ≈ Auswärtiges Amt nt

FD (US) n abbr = **fire department**

FDA (US) n abbr (= Food and Drug Administration) Nahrungs- und Arzneimittelbehörde

fear [fɪər] n Furcht f, Angst f ▷ vt fürchten, Angst haben vor +dat; (be worried about) befürchten ▷ vi sich fürchten; **~ of heights** Höhenangst f; **for ~ of doing sth** aus Angst, etw zu tun; **to ~ for** fürchten um; **to ~ that ...** befürchten, dass ...

fearful ['fɪəful] adj (frightening) furchtbar, schrecklich; (apprehensive) ängstlich; **to be ~ of** Angst haben vor +dat

fearfully ['fɪəfəlɪ] adv ängstlich; (inf: very) furchtbar, schrecklich

fearless ['fɪəlɪs] adj furchtlos

fearsome ['fɪəsəm] adj furchterregend

feasibility [fiːzə'bɪlɪtɪ] n Durchführbarkeit f

feasibility study n Machbarkeits- or Durchführbarkeitsstudie f

feasible ['fiːzəbl] adj machbar; (proposal, plan) durchführbar

feast [fiːst] n Festmahl nt; (Rel: also: **feast day**) Festtag m, Feiertag m ▷ vi schlemmen; **to ~ on** sich gütlich tun an +dat

feat [fiːt] n Leistung f

feather ['feðər] n Feder f ▷ cpd Feder-; (mattress) Federkern- ▷ vt: **to ~ one's nest** (fig) sein Schäfchen ins Trockene bringen

featherweight ['feðəweɪt] n Leichtgewicht nt; (Boxing) Federgewicht nt

feature ['fiːtʃər] n Merkmal nt; (Press, TV) Feature nt ▷ vt: **the film ~s Marlon Brando** Marlon Brando spielt in dem Film mit ▷ vi: **to ~ in** vorkommen in +dat; (film) mitspielen in +dat; **features** npl (of face) (Gesichts)züge pl; **it ~d prominently in** es spielte eine große Rolle in +dat; **a special ~ on sth/sb** ein Sonderbeitrag m über etw/jdn

feature film n Spielfilm m

featureless ['fiːtʃəlɪs] adj (landscape) eintönig

Feb. abbr (= February) Feb.

February ['fɛbruərɪ] n Februar m; see also **July**

feces ['fiːsiːz] (US) npl = **faeces**

feckless ['fɛklɪs] adj nutzlos

Fed [fɛd] (US: inf) n abbr: **the ~ = Federal Reserve Board**

Fed. (US) abbr = **federal; federation**

fed [fɛd] pt, pp of **feed**

federal ['fɛdərəl] adj föderalistisch

Federal Republic of Germany n Bundesrepublik f Deutschland

Federal Reserve Board (US) n Kontrollorgan der US-Zentralbank

Federal Trade Commission (US) n Handelskontrollbehörde

federation [fɛdə'reɪʃən] n Föderation f, Bund m

fed up adj: **to be ~ with** die Nase vollhaben von

fee [fiː] n Gebühr f; (of doctor, lawyer) Honorar nt; **school ~s** Schulgeld nt; **entrance**

~ Eintrittsgebühr f; **membership ~** Mitgliedsbeitrag m; **for a small ~** gegen eine geringe Gebühr

feeble ['fiːbl] adj schwach; (joke) lahm

feeble-minded ['fiːbl'maɪndɪd] adj dümmlich

feed [fiːd] (pt, pp **fed**) n Mahlzeit f; (of animal) Fütterung f; (on printer) Papiervorschub m ▷ vt füttern; (family etc) ernähren; (machine) versorgen; **to ~ sth into sth** etw in etw acc einfüllen or eingeben; (data, information) etw in etw acc eingeben; **to ~ material into sth** Material in etw acc eingeben

▶ **feed back** vt zurückleiten

▶ **feed on** vt fus sich nähren von

feedback ['fiːdbæk] n Feedback nt, Rückmeldung f; (from person) Reaktion f

feeder ['fiːdər] n (road) Zubringer m; (railway line, air route) Zubringerlinie f; (baby's bottle) Flasche f

feeding bottle ['fiːdɪŋ-] (Brit) n Flasche f

feel [fiːl] (pt, pp **felt**) n (sensation, touch) Gefühl nt; (impression) Atmosphäre f ▷ vt (object) fühlen; (desire, anger, grief) empfinden; (pain) spüren; (cold) leiden unter +dat; (think, believe): **I ~ that you ought to do it** ich meine or ich bin der Meinung, dass Sie es tun sollten; **it has a soft ~** es fühlt sich weich an; **I ~ hungry** ich habe Hunger; **I ~ cold** mir ist kalt; **to ~ lonely/better** sich einsam/besser fühlen; **I don't ~ well** mir geht es nicht gut; **I ~ sorry for him** er tut mir leid; **it ~s soft** es fühlt sich weich an; **it ~s colder here** es kommt mir hier kälter vor; **it ~s like velvet** es fühlt sich wie Samt an; **to ~ like** (desire) Lust haben auf +acc; **to ~ like doing sth** Lust haben, etw zu tun; **to get the ~ of sth** ein Gefühl für etw bekommen; **I'm still ~ing my way** ich versuche noch, mich zu orientieren

▶ **feel about** vi umhertasten; **to ~ about or around in one's pocket for** in seiner Tasche herumsuchen nach

▶ **feel around** vi = **feel about**

feelbad factor ['fiːlbæd-] n (inf) Frustfaktor m

feeler ['fiːlər] n Fühler m; **to put out a ~ or feelers** (fig) seine Fühler ausstrecken

feelgood ['fiːlgʊd] adj (film, song) Feelgood-

feeling ['fiːlɪŋ] n Gefühl nt; (impression) Eindruck m; **~s ran high about it** man ereiferte sich sehr darüber; **what are your ~s about the matter?** was meinen Sie dazu?; **I have a ~ that ...** ich habe das Gefühl, dass ...; **my ~ is that ...** meine Meinung ist, dass ...; **to hurt sb's ~s** jdn verletzen

fee-paying ['fiːpeɪɪŋ] adj (school) Privat-; **~ pupils** Schüler, deren Eltern Schulgeld zahlen

feet [fiːt] npl of **foot**

feign [feɪn] vt vortäuschen

feigned [feɪnd] adj vorgetäuscht

feint [feɪnt] n fein liniertes Papier nt

felicitous [fɪ'lɪsɪtəs] adj glücklich

feline ['fiːlaɪn] adj (eyes etc) Katzen-; (features, grace) katzenartig

fell [fɛl] pt of **fall** ▷ vt fällen; (opponent) niederstrecken ▷ n (Brit: mountain) Berg m;

(: *moorland*): **the ~s** das Moor(land) ▷ *adj*: **in one ~ swoop** auf einen Schlag

fellow ['fɛləu] *n* Mann *m*, Typ *m* (*inf*); (*comrade*) Kamerad *m*; (*of learned society*) Mitglied *nt*; (*of university*) Fellow *m*; **their ~ prisoners/ students** ihre Mitgefangenen/Kommilitonen (und Kommilitoninnen); **his ~ workers** seine Kollegen (und Kolleginnen)

fellow citizen *n* Mitbürger(in) *m(f)*

fellow countryman (*irreg*: *like* **man**) *n* Landsmann *m*, Landsmännin *f*

fellow men *npl* Mitmenschen *pl*

fellowship ['fɛləuʃɪp] *n* Kameradschaft *f*; (*society*) Gemeinschaft *f*; (*Scol*) Forschungsstipendium *nt*

fell-walking ['fɛlwɔːkɪŋ] (*Brit*) *n* Bergwandern *nt*

felon ['fɛlən] *n* (*Law*) (Schwer)verbrecher *m*

felony ['fɛlənɪ] *n* (*Law*) (schweres) Verbrechen *nt*

felt [fɛlt] *pt*, *pp of* **feel** ▷ *n* Filz *m*

felt-tip pen ['fɛlttɪp-] *n* Filzstift *m*

female ['fiːmeɪl] *n* Weibchen *nt*; (*pej*: *woman*) Frau *f*, Weib *nt* (*pej*) ▷ *adj* weiblich; (*vote etc*) Frauen-; (*Elec*: *connector, plug*) Mutter-, Innen-; **male and ~ students** Studenten und Studentinnen

Femidom® ['fɛmɪdɔm] *n* Kondom *nt* für die Frau, Femidom® *nt*

feminine ['fɛmɪnɪn] *adj* weiblich, feminin ▷ *n* Femininum *nt*

femininity [fɛmɪ'nɪnɪtɪ] *n* Weiblichkeit *f*

feminism ['fɛmɪnɪzəm] *n* Feminismus *m*

feminist ['fɛmɪnɪst] *n* Feminist(in) *m(f)*

fen [fɛn] (*Brit*) *n*: **the F~s** *die Niederungen in East Anglia*

fence [fɛns] *n* Zaun *m*; (*Sport*) Hindernis *nt* ▷ *vt* (*also*: **fence in**) einzäunen ▷ *vi* (*Sport*) fechten; **to sit on the ~** (*fig*) neutral bleiben, nicht Partei ergreifen

fencing ['fɛnsɪŋ] *n* (*Sport*) Fechten *nt*

fend [fɛnd] *vi*: **to ~ for o.s.** für sich (selbst) sorgen, sich allein durchbringen
▶ **fend off** *vt* abwehren

fender ['fɛndəʳ] *n* Kamingitter *nt*; (*on boat*) Fender *m*; (*US*: *of car*) Kotflügel *m*

fennel ['fɛnl] *n* Fenchel *m*

ferment [vi fə'mɛnt, *n* 'fəːmɛnt] *vi* gären ▷ *n* (*fig*: *unrest*) Unruhe *f*

fermentation [fəːmɛn'teɪʃən] *n* Gärung *f*

fern [fəːn] *n* Farn *m*

ferocious [fə'rəuʃəs] *adj* wild; (*behaviour*) heftig; (*competition*) scharf

ferocity [fə'rɔsɪtɪ] *n* (*see adj*) Wildheit *f*; Heftigkeit *f*; Schärfe *f*

ferret ['fɛrɪt] *n* Frettchen *nt*
▶ **ferret about** *vi* herumstöbern
▶ **ferret around** *vi* = **ferret about**
▶ **ferret out** *vt* aufspüren

ferry ['fɛrɪ] *n* (*also*: **ferryboat**) Fähre *f* ▷ *vt* transportieren; **to ~ sth/sb across** *or* **over** jdn/etw übersetzen

ferryman ['fɛrɪmən] (*irreg*: *like* **man**) *n*

Fährmann *m*

fertile ['fəːtaɪl] *adj* fruchtbar; **~ period** fruchtbare Tage *pl*

fertility [fə'tɪlɪtɪ] *n* Fruchtbarkeit *f*

fertility drug *n* Fruchtbarkeitsmedikament *nt*

fertilization [fəːtɪlaɪ'zeɪʃən] *n* (*Biol*) Befruchtung *f*

fertilize ['fəːtɪlaɪz] *vt* düngen; (*Biol*) befruchten

fertilizer ['fəːtɪlaɪzəʳ] *n* Dünger *m*

fervent ['fəːvənt] *adj* leidenschaftlich; (*admirer*) glühend

fervour, (US) fervor ['fəːvəʳ] *n* Leidenschaft *f*

fester ['fɛstəʳ] *vi* (*wound*) eitern; (*insult*) nagen; (*row*) sich verschlimmern

festival ['fɛstɪvəl] *n* Fest *nt*; (*Art, Mus*) Festival *nt*, Festspiele *pl*

festive ['fɛstɪv] *adj* festlich; **the ~ season** (*Brit*: *Christmas and New Year*) die Festzeit *f*

festivities [fɛs'tɪvɪtɪz] *npl* Feierlichkeiten *pl*

festoon [fɛs'tuːn] *vt*: **to ~ with** schmücken mit

fetch [fɛtʃ] *vt* holen; (*sell for*) (ein)bringen; **would you ~ me a glass of water please?** kannst du mir bitte ein Glas Wasser bringen?; **how much did it ~?** wie viel hat es eingebracht?
▶ **fetch up** (*inf*) *vi* landen (*inf*)

fetching ['fɛtʃɪŋ] *adj* bezaubernd, reizend

fête [feɪt] *n* Fest *nt*

fetid ['fɛtɪd] *adj* übel riechend

fetish ['fɛtɪʃ] *n* Fetisch *m*

fetter ['fɛtəʳ] *vt* fesseln; (*horse*) anpflocken; (*fig*) in Fesseln legen

fetters ['fɛtəz] *npl* Fesseln *pl*

fettle ['fɛtl] (*Brit*) *n*: **in fine ~** in bester Form

fetus ['fiːtəs] (*US*) *n* = **foetus**

feud [fjuːd] *n* Streit *m* ▷ *vi* im Streit liegen; **a family ~** ein Familienstreit *m*

feudal ['fjuːdl] *adj* (*society etc*) Feudal-

feudalism ['fjuːdlɪzəm] *n* Feudalismus *m*

fever ['fiːvəʳ] *n* Fieber *nt*; **he has a ~** er hat Fieber

feverish ['fiːvərɪʃ] *adj* fiebrig; (*activity, emotion*) fieberhaft

few [fjuː] *adj* wenige; **a ~** (*adj*) ein paar, einige; (*pron*) ein paar; **a ~ more (days)** noch ein paar (Tage); **they were ~** sie waren nur wenige; **~ succeed** nur wenigen gelingt es; **very ~ survive** nur sehr wenige überleben; **I know a ~** ich kenne einige; **a good ~, quite a ~** ziemlich viele; **in the next/past ~ days** in den nächsten/letzten paar Tagen; **every ~ days/months** alle paar Tage/Monate

fewer ['fjuːəʳ] *adj* weniger; **there are ~ buses on Sundays** Sonntags fahren weniger Busse

fewest ['fjuːɪst] *adj* die wenigsten

FHA (*US*) *n abbr* (= *Federal Housing Administration*): **~ loan** Baudarlehen *nt*

fiancé [fɪ'ãːŋseɪ] *n* Verlobte(r) *m*

fiancée [fɪ'ãːŋseɪ] *n* Verlobte *f*

fiasco [fɪ'æskəu] *n* Fiasko *nt*

fib [fɪb] *n* Flunkerei *f* (*inf*)

fibre, (US) fiber ['faɪbəʳ] *n* Faser *f*; (*cloth*) (Faser)stoff *m*; (*roughage*) Ballaststoffe *pl*; (*Anat*: *tissue*)

Gewebe nt

fibreboard, (US) fiberboard ['faɪbəbɔːd] n
Faserplatte f

fibreglass, (US) fiberglass ['faɪbəglɑːs] n
Fiberglas nt

fibrositis [faɪbrə'saɪtɪs] n
Bindegewebsentzündung f

FICA (US) n abbr (= Federal Insurance Contributions
Act) Abgabe zur Sozialversicherung

fickle ['fɪkl] adj unbeständig; (weather)
wechselhaft

fiction ['fɪkʃən] n Erfindung f; (Liter)
Erzähllitteratur f, Prosaliteratur f

fictional ['fɪkʃənl] adj erfunden

fictionalize ['fɪkʃnəlaɪz] vt fiktionalisieren

fictitious [fɪk'tɪʃəs] adj (false) falsch; (invented)
fiktiv, frei erfunden

fiddle ['fɪdl] n Fiedel f (inf), Geige f; (fraud,
swindle) Schwindelei f ▷ vt (Brit: accounts)
frisieren (inf); **tax ~** Steuermanipulation f; **to
work a ~** ein krummes Ding drehen (inf)
▶ **fiddle with** vt fus herumspielen mit

fiddler ['fɪdlə^r] n Geiger(in) m(f)

fiddly ['fɪdlɪ] adj knifflig (inf); (object) fummelig

fidelity [fɪ'delɪtɪ] n Treue f; (accuracy)
Genauigkeit f

fidget ['fɪdʒɪt] vi zappeln

fidgety ['fɪdʒɪtɪ] adj zappelig

fiduciary [fɪ'djuːʃɪərɪ] n (Law) Treuhänder m

field [fiːld] n Feld nt; (Sport: ground) Platz m;
(subject, area of interest) Gebiet nt; (Comput)
Datenfeld nt ▷ cpd Feld-; **to lead the ~** das Feld
anführen; **~ trip** Exkursion f

field day n: **to have a ~** einen herrlichen Tag
haben

field glasses npl Feldstecher m

field hospital n Feldlazarett nt

field marshal n Feldmarschall m

field work n Feldforschung f; (Archaeology, Geog)
Arbeit f im Gelände

fiend [fiːnd] n Teufel m

fiendish ['fiːndɪʃ] adj teuflisch; (problem)
verzwickt

fierce [fɪəs] adj wild; (look) böse; (fighting, wind)
heftig; (loyalty) leidenschaftlich; (enemy)
erbittert; (heat) glühend

fiery ['faɪərɪ] adj glühend; (temperament) feurig,
hitzig

FIFA ['fiːfə] n abbr (= Fédération Internationale de
Football Association) FIFA f

fifteen [fɪf'tiːn] num fünfzehn

fifteenth [fɪf'tiːnθ] num fünfzehnte(r, s)

fifth [fɪfθ] num fünfte(r, s) ▷ n Fünftel nt

fiftieth ['fɪftɪɪθ] num fünfzigste(r, s)

fifty ['fɪftɪ] num fünfzig

fifty-fifty ['fɪftɪ'fɪftɪ] adj, adv halbe-halbe,
fifty-fifty; **to go/share ~ with sb** mit jdm
halbe-halbe or fifty-fifty machen; **we have a
~ chance (of success)** unsere Chancen stehen
fifty-fifty

fig [fɪg] n Feige f

fight [faɪt] (pt, pp **fought**) n Kampf m; (quarrel)
Streit m; (punch-up) Schlägerei f ▷ vt kämpfen

mit or gegen; (prejudice etc) bekämpfen; (election)
kandidieren bei; (emotion) ankämpfen gegen;
(Law: case) durchkämpfen, durchfechten ▷ vi
kämpfen; (quarrel) sich streiten; (punch-up)
sich schlagen; **to put up a ~** sich zur Wehr
setzen; **to ~ one's way through a crowd/the
undergrowth** sich dat einen Weg durch die
Menge/das Unterholz bahnen; **to ~ against**
bekämpfen; **to ~ for one's rights** für seine
Rechte kämpfen
▶ **fight back** vi zurückschlagen; (Sport)
zurückkämpfen; (after illness) zu Kräften
kommen ▷ vt fus unterdrücken
▶ **fight down** vt unterdrücken
▶ **fight off** vt abwehren; (sleep, urge)
ankämpfen gegen
▶ **fight out** vt: **to ~ it out** es untereinander
ausfechten

fighter ['faɪtə^r] n Kämpfer(in) m(f); (plane)
Jagdflugzeug nt; (fig) Kämpfernatur f

fighter pilot n Jagdflieger m

fighting ['faɪtɪŋ] n Kämpfe pl; (brawl)
Schlägereien pl

figment ['fɪgmənt] n: **a ~ of the imagination**
ein Hirngespinst nt, pure Einbildung f

figurative ['fɪgjʊrətɪv] adj bildlich,
übertragen; (style) gegenständlich

figure ['fɪgə^r] n Figur f; (illustration) Abbildung
f; (number, statistic, cipher) Zahl f; (person) Gestalt
f; (personality) Persönlichkeit f ▷ vt (esp US)
glauben, schätzen ▷ vi eine Rolle spielen; **to
put a ~ on sth** eine Zahl für etw angeben;
public ~ Persönlichkeit f des öffentlichen
Lebens
▶ **figure out** vt ausrechnen

figurehead ['fɪgəhed] n Galionsfigur f

figure of speech n Redensart f, Redewendung f

figure skating n Eiskunstlaufen nt

Fiji ['fiːdʒiː] n, **Fiji Islands** npl Fidschi-Inseln
pl

filament ['fɪləmənt] n Glühfaden m; (Bot)
Staubfaden m

filch [fɪltʃ] (inf) vt filzen

file [faɪl] n Akte f; (folder) (Akten)ordner m;
(for loose leaf) (Akten)mappe f; (Comput) Datei
f; (row) Reihe f; (tool) Feile f ▷ vt ablegen,
abheften; (claim) einreichen; (wood,
metal, fingernails) feilen ▷ vi: **to ~ in/out**
nacheinander hereinkommen/hinausgehen;
to ~ a suit against sb eine Klage gegen
jdn erheben; **to ~ past** in einer Reihe
vorbeigehen; **to ~ for divorce** die Scheidung
einreichen

filename ['faɪlneɪm] n (Comput) Dateiname m

filibuster ['fɪlɪbʌstə^r] (esp US: Pol) n
(also: **filibusterer**) Dauerredner(in) m(f) ▷ vi
filibustern, Obstruktion betreiben

filing ['faɪlɪŋ] n Ablegen nt, Abheften nt

filing cabinet n Aktenschrank m

filing clerk n Angestellte(r) f(m) in der
Registratur

Filipino [fɪlɪ'piːnəʊ] n Filipino m, Filipina f;
(Ling) Philippinisch nt

fill [fɪl] vt füllen; (space, area) ausfüllen; (tooth) plombieren; (need) erfüllen ▷ vi sich füllen ▷ n: **to eat one's ~** sich satt essen; **we've already ~ed that vacancy** wir haben diese Stelle schon besetzt
▸ **fill in** vt füllen; (time) überbrücken; (form) ausfüllen ▷ vi: **to ~ in for sb** für jdn einspringen; **to ~ sb in on sth** (inf) jdn über etw acc ins Bild setzen
▸ **fill out** vt ausfüllen
▸ **fill up** vt füllen ▷ vi (Aut) tanken; **~ it up, please** (Aut) bitte volltanken

fillet ['fɪlɪt] n Filet nt ▷ vt filetieren
fillet steak n Filetsteak nt
filling ['fɪlɪŋ] n Füllung f; (for tooth) Plombe f
filling station n Tankstelle f
fillip ['fɪlɪp] n (stimulus) Ansporn m
filly ['fɪlɪ] n Stutfohlen nt
film [fɪlm] n Film m; (of powder etc) Schicht f; (for wrapping) Plastikfolie f ▷ vt, vi filmen
film star n Filmstar m
film strip n Filmstreifen m
film studio n Filmstudio nt
Filofax® ['faɪləʊfæks] n Filofax® nt, Terminplaner m
filter ['fɪltər] n Filter m ▷ vt filtern
▸ **filter in** vi durchsickern
▸ **filter through** vi = **filter in**
filter coffee n Filterkaffee m
filter lane (Brit) n Abbiegespur f
filter tip n Filter m
filter-tipped ['fɪltə'tɪpt] adj (cigarette) Filter-
filth [fɪlθ] n Dreck m, Schmutz m
filthy ['fɪlθɪ] adj dreckig, schmutzig; (language) unflätig
fin [fɪn] n Flosse f; (Tech) Seitenflosse f
final ['faɪnl] adj letzte(r, s); (ultimate) letztendlich; (definitive) endgültig ▷ n Finale nt, Endspiel nt; **finals** npl (Univ) Abschlussprüfung f
final demand n letzte Zahlungsaufforderung f
finale [fɪ'nɑːlɪ] n Finale nt; (Theat) Schlussszene f
finalist ['faɪnəlɪst] n Endrundenteilnehmer(in) m(f), Finalist(in) m(f)
finality [faɪ'nælɪtɪ] n Endgültigkeit f; **with an air of ~** mit Bestimmtheit
finalize ['faɪnəlaɪz] vt endgültig festlegen
finally ['faɪnəlɪ] adv endlich, schließlich; (lastly) schließlich, zum Schluss; (irrevocably) endgültig
finance [faɪ'næns] n Geldmittel pl; (money management) Finanzwesen nt ▷ vt finanzieren; **finances** npl (personal) Finanzen pl, Finanzlage f
financial [faɪ'nænʃəl] adj finanziell; **~ statement** Bilanz f
financially [faɪ'nænʃəlɪ] adv finanziell
financial year n Geschäftsjahr nt
financier [faɪ'nænsɪər] n Finanzier m
find [faɪnd] (pt, pp **found**) vt finden; (discover) entdecken ▷ n Fund m; **to ~ sb guilty** jdn für schuldig befinden; **to ~ (some) difficulty in doing sth** (einige) Schwierigkeiten haben,

etw zu tun
▸ **find out** vt herausfinden; (person) erwischen
▷ vi: **to ~ out about** etwas herausfinden über +acc; (by chance) etwas erfahren über +acc
findings ['faɪndɪŋz] npl (Law) Urteil nt; (of report) Ergebnis nt
fine [faɪn] adj fein; (excellent) gut; (thin) dünn ▷ adv gut; (small) fein ▷ n Geldstrafe f ▷ vt mit einer Geldstrafe belegen; **he's ~** es geht ihm gut; **the weather is ~** das Wetter ist schön; **that's cutting it (a bit) ~** das ist aber (ein bisschen) knapp; **you're doing ~** das machen Sie gut
fine arts npl schöne Künste pl
finely ['faɪnlɪ] adv schön; (chop) klein; (slice) dünn; (adjust) fein
fine print n: **the ~** das Kleingedruckte
finery ['faɪnərɪ] n (of dress) Staat m
finesse [fɪ'nɛs] n Geschick nt
fine-tooth comb ['faɪntuː:θ-] n: **to go through sth with a ~** (fig) etw genau unter die Lupe nehmen
finger ['fɪŋgər] n Finger m ▷ vt befühlen; **little ~** kleiner Finger; **index ~** Zeigefinger m
fingernail ['fɪŋgəneɪl] n Fingernagel m
fingerprint ['fɪŋgəprɪnt] n Fingerabdruck m
▷ vt Fingerabdrücke abnehmen +dat
fingerstall ['fɪŋgəstɔ:l] n Fingerling m
fingertip ['fɪŋgətɪp] n Fingerspitze f; **to have sth at one's ~s** (to hand) etw parat haben; (know well) etw aus dem Effeff kennen (inf)
finicky ['fɪnɪkɪ] adj pingelig
finish ['fɪnɪʃ] n Schluss m, Ende nt; (Sport) Finish nt; (polish etc) Verarbeitung f ▷ vt fertig sein mit; (work) erledigen; (book) auslesen; (use up) aufbrauchen ▷ vi enden; (person) fertig sein; **to ~ doing sth** mit etw fertig werden; **to ~ third** als Dritter durchs Ziel gehen; **to have ~ed with sth** mit etw fertig sein; **she's ~ed with him** sie hat mit ihm Schluss gemacht
▸ **finish off** vt fertig machen; (kill) den Gnadenstoß geben
▸ **finish up** vt (food) aufessen; (drink) austrinken ▷ vi (end up) landen
finished ['fɪnɪʃt] adj fertig; (performance) ausgereift; (inf: tired) erledigt
finishing line ['fɪnɪʃɪŋ-] n Ziellinie f
finishing school n höhere Mädchenschule f (in der auch Etikette und gesellschaftliches Verhalten gelehrt wird)
finishing touches npl: **the ~** der letzte Schliff
finite ['faɪnaɪt] adj begrenzt; (verb) finit
Finland ['fɪnlənd] n Finnland nt
Finn [fɪn] n Finne m, Finnin f
Finnish ['fɪnɪʃ] adj finnisch ▷ n (Ling) Finnisch nt
fiord [fjɔːd] n = **fjord**
fir [fəːr] n Tanne f
fire ['faɪər] n Feuer nt; (in hearth) (Kamin)feuer nt; (accidental fire) Brand m ▷ vt abschießen; (imagination) beflügeln; (enthusiasm) befeuern; (inf: dismiss) feuern ▷ vi feuern, schießen; **to ~ a gun** ein Gewehr abschießen; **to be**

on ~ brennen; **to set ~ to sth, set sth
on ~** etw anzünden; **insured against ~**
feuerversichert; **electric/gas ~** Elektro-/
Gasofen m; **to come/be under ~ (from)** unter
Beschuss (von) geraten/stehen
fire alarm n Feuermelder m
firearm ['faɪɑːm] n Feuerwaffe f,
Schusswaffe f
fire brigade n Feuerwehr f
fire chief n Branddirektor m
fire department (US) n Feuerwehr f
fire door n Feuertür f
fire drill n Probealarm m
fire engine n Feuerwehrauto nt
fire escape n Feuertreppe f
fire-extinguisher ['faɪərɪk'stɪŋgwɪʃəʳ] n
Feuerlöscher m
fireguard ['faɪəgɑːd] (Brit) n (Schutz)gitter nt
(vor dem Kamin)
fire hazard n: **that's a ~** das ist
feuergefährlich
fire hydrant n Hydrant m
fire insurance n Feuerversicherung f
fireman ['faɪəmən] (irreg: like **man**) n
Feuerwehrmann m
fireplace ['faɪəpleɪs] n Kamin m
fireplug ['faɪəplʌg] (US) n = **fire hydrant**
fire practice n = **fire drill**
fireproof ['faɪəpruːf] adj feuerfest
fire regulations npl Brand-
schutzbestimmungen pl
fire screen n Ofenschirm m
fireside ['faɪəsaɪd] n: **by the ~** am Kamin
fire station n Feuerwache f
firewood ['faɪəwud] n Brennholz nt
fireworks ['faɪəwɜːks] npl Feuerwerkskörper pl;
(display) Feuerwerk nt
firing line ['faɪərɪŋ-] n Feuerlinie f, Schusslinie
f; **to be in the ~** (fig) in der Schusslinie sein
firing squad n Exekutionskommando nt
firm [fɜːm] adj fest; (mattress) hart; (measures)
durchgreifend ▷ n Firma f; **to be a ~ believer
in sth** fest von etw überzeugt sein
firmly ['fɜːmlɪ] adv (see adj) fest; hart; (definitely)
entschlossen
firmness ['fɜːmnɪs] n (see adj) Festigkeit f; Härte
f; (definiteness) Entschlossenheit f
first [fɜːst] adj erste(r, s) ▷ adv als Erste(r, s);
(before other things) zuerst; (when listing reasons
etc) erstens; (for the first time) zum ersten Mal
▷ n Erste(r, s); (Aut: also: **first gear**) der erste
Gang; (Brit: Scol) ≈ Eins f; **the ~ of January** der
erste Januar; **at ~** zuerst, zunächst; **~ of all** vor
allem; **in the ~ instance** zuerst or zunächst
einmal; **I'll do it ~ thing (tomorrow)** ich
werde es (morgen) als Erstes tun; **from the
very ~** gleich von Anfang an
first aid n erste Hilfe f
first-aid kit [fɜːst'eɪd-] n Erste-Hilfe-
Ausrüstung f
first-class ['fɜːst'klɑːs] adj erstklassig; (carriage,
ticket) Erste(r)-Klasse-; (post) bevorzugt
befördert ▷ adv (travel, send) erster Klasse

first-hand ['fɜːst'hænd] adj aus erster Hand
first lady (US) n First Lady f; **the ~ of jazz** die
Königin des Jazz
firstly ['fɜːstlɪ] adv erstens, zunächst einmal
first name n Vorname m
first night n Premiere f
first-rate ['fɜːst'reɪt] adj erstklassig
first-time buyer ['fɜːsttaɪm-] n jd, der zum ersten
Mal ein Haus/eine Wohnung kauft
fir tree n Tannenbaum m
fiscal ['fɪskl] adj (year) Steuer-; (policies) Finanz-
fish [fɪʃ] n inv Fisch m ▷ vt (area) fischen in +dat;
(river) angeln in +dat ▷ vi fischen; (as sport,
hobby) angeln; **to go ~ing** fischen/angeln
gehen
▶ **fish out** vt herausfischen
fish bone n (Fisch)gräte f
fish cake n Fischfrikadelle f
fisherman ['fɪʃəmən] (irreg: like **man**) n Fischer
m
fishery ['fɪʃərɪ] n Fischereigebiet nt
fish factory (Brit) n Fischfabrik f
fish farm n Fischzucht(anlage) f
fishfingers [fɪʃ'fɪŋgəz] (Brit) npl Fischstäbchen
pl
fish-hook ['fɪʃhuk] n Angelhaken m
fishing boat ['fɪʃɪŋ-] n Fischerboot nt
fishing line n Angelschnur f
fishing net n Fischnetz nt
fishing rod n Angelrute f
fishing tackle n Angelgeräte pl
fish market n Fischmarkt m
fishmonger ['fɪʃmʌŋgəʳ] (esp Brit) n
Fischhändler(in) m(f)
fishmonger's ['fɪʃmʌŋgəz], **fishmonger's
shop** (esp Brit) n Fischgeschäft nt
fish slice (Brit) n Fischvorlegemesser nt
fish sticks (US) npl = **fishfingers**
fishy ['fɪʃɪ] (inf) adj verdächtig, faul
fission ['fɪʃən] n Spaltung f; **atomic** or **nuclear
~** Atomspaltung f, Kernspaltung f
fissure ['fɪʃəʳ] n Riss m, Spalte f
fist [fɪst] n Faust f
fist fight n Faustkampf m
fit [fɪt] adj geeignet; (healthy) gesund; (Sport)
fit ▷ vt passen +dat; (adjust) anpassen; (match)
entsprechen +dat; (be suitable for) passen auf
+acc; (put in) einbauen; (attach) anbringen;
(equip) ausstatten ▷ vi passen; (parts)
zusammenpassen; (in space, gap) hineinpassen
▷ n (Med) Anfall m; **to ~ the description** der
Beschreibung entsprechen; **~ to** bereit zu; **~
to eat** essbar; **~ to drink** trinkbar; **to be ~
to keep** es wert sein, aufbewahrt zu werden;
~ for geeignet für; **~ for work** arbeitsfähig;
to keep ~ sich fit halten; **do as you think** or
see ~ tun Sie, was Sie für richtig halten; **a ~
of anger** ein Wutanfall m; **a ~ of pride** eine
Anwandlung von Stolz; **to have a ~** einen
Anfall haben; (inf, fig) einen Anfall kriegen;
this dress is a good ~ dieses Kleid sitzt or
passt gut; **by ~s and starts** unregelmäßig
▶ **fit in** vi (person) sich einfügen; (object)

hineinpassen ▷ vt (fig: appointment)
unterbringen, einschieben; (visitor) Zeit
finden für; **to ~ in with sb's plans** sich mit
jds Plänen vereinbaren lassen

fitful ['fɪtful] adj unruhig

fitment ['fɪtmənt] n Einrichtungsgegenstand
m

fitness ['fɪtnɪs] n Gesundheit f; (Sport) Fitness f

fitness instructor n Fitnesstrainer(in) m(f)

fitted carpet ['fɪtɪd-] n Teppichboden m

fitted cupboards npl Einbauschränke pl

fitted kitchen (Brit) n Einbauküche f

fitter ['fɪtə^r] n Monteur m; (for machines)
(Maschinen)schlosser m

fitting ['fɪtɪŋ] adj passend; (thanks) gebührend
▷ n (of dress) Anprobe f; (of piece of equipment)
Installation f; **fittings** npl Ausstattung f

fitting room n Anprobe(kabine) f

five [faɪv] num fünf

five-day week ['faɪvdeɪ-] n Fünftagewoche f

fiver ['faɪvə^r] (inf) n (Brit) Fünfpfundschein m;
(US) Fünfdollarschein m

fix [fɪks] vt (attach) befestigen; (arrange)
festsetzen, festlegen; (mend) reparieren; (meal,
drink) machen; (inf) manipulieren ▷ n: **to be
in a ~** in der Patsche or Klemme sitzen; **to ~
sth to/on sth** etw an/auf etw dat befestigen;
to ~ one's eyes/attention on seinen Blick/
seine Aufmerksamkeit richten auf +acc;
the fight was a ~ (inf) der Kampf war eine
abgekartete Sache
 ▶ **fix up** vt arrangieren; **to ~ sb up with sth**
jdm etw besorgen

fixation [fɪk'seɪʃən] n Fixierung f

fixative ['fɪksətɪv] n Fixativ nt

fixed [fɪkst] adj fest; (ideas) fix; (smile) starr;
~ charge Pauschale f; **how are you ~ for
money?** wie sieht es bei dir mit dem Geld aus?

fixed assets npl Anlagevermögen nt

fixture ['fɪkstʃə^r] n Ausstattungsgegenstand
m; (Football etc) Spiel nt; (Athletics etc)
Veranstaltung f

fizz [fɪz] vi sprudeln; (firework) zischen

fizzle out ['fɪzl-] vi (plan) im Sande verlaufen;
(interest) sich verlieren

fizzy ['fɪzɪ] adj sprudelnd

fjord [fjɔːd] n Fjord m

FL, Fla. [fl] abbr (Post) = Florida

flabbergasted ['flæbəgɑːstɪd] adj verblüfft

flabby ['flæbɪ] adj schwammig, wabbelig (inf)

flag [flæg] n Fahne f; (of country) Flagge f; (for
signalling) Signalflagge f; (also: **flagstone**)
(Stein)platte f ▷ vi erlahmen; **~ of
convenience** Billigflagge f; **to ~ down**
anhalten

flagon ['flægən] n Flasche f; (jug) Krug m

flagpole ['flægpəʊl] n Fahnenstange f

flagrant ['fleɪgrənt] adj flagrant; (injustice)
himmelschreiend

flagship ['flægʃɪp] n Flaggschiff nt

flagstone ['flægstəʊn] n (Stein)platte f

flag stop (US) n Bedarfshaltestelle f

flair [fleə^r] n Talent nt; (style) Flair nt

flak [flæk] n Flakfeuer nt; **to get a lot of ~ (for
sth)** (inf: criticism) (wegen etw) unter Beschuss
geraten

flake [fleɪk] n Splitter m; (of snow, soap powder)
Flocke f ▷ vi (also: **flake off**) abblättern,
absplittern
 ▶ **flake out** (inf) vi aus den Latschen kippen;
(go to sleep) einschlafen

flaky ['fleɪkɪ] adj brüchig; (skin) schuppig

flaky pastry n Blätterteig m

flamboyant [flæm'bɔɪənt] adj extravagant

flame [fleɪm] n Flamme f; **to burst into ~s** in
Flammen aufgehen; **an old ~** (inf) eine alte
Flamme

flaming ['fleɪmɪŋ] (inf!) adj verdammt

flamingo [flə'mɪŋgəʊ] n Flamingo m

flammable ['flæməbl] adj leicht entzündbar

flan [flæn] n Kuchen m; **~ case** Tortenboden m

Flanders ['flɑːndəz] n Flandern nt

flange [flændʒ] n Flansch m

flank [flæŋk] n Flanke f ▷ vt flankieren

flannel ['flænl] n Flanell m; (Brit: also: **face
flannel**) Waschlappen m; (: inf) Geschwafel nt;
flannels npl (trousers) Flanellhose f

flannelette [flænə'lɛt] n Baumwollflanell m,
Biber m or nt

flap [flæp] n Klappe f; (of envelope) Lasche f ▷ vt
schlagen mit ▷ vi flattern; (inf: also: **be in a
flap**) in heller Aufregung sein

flapjack ['flæpdʒæk] n (US: pancake)
Pfannkuchen m; (Brit: biscuit) Haferkeks m

flare [fleə^r] n Leuchtsignal nt; (in skirt etc) Weite
f
 ▶ **flare up** vi auflodern; (person) aufbrausen;
(fighting, violence, trouble) ausbrechen; see also
flared

flared ['flɛəd] adj (trousers) mit Schlag; (skirt)
ausgestellt

flash [flæʃ] n Aufblinken nt; (also: **newsflash**)
Eilmeldung f; (Phot) Blitz m, Blitzlicht nt;
(US: torch) Taschenlampe f ▷ vt aufleuchten
lassen; (news, message) durchgeben; (look, smile)
zuwerfen ▷ vi aufblinken; (light on ambulance)
blinken; (eyes) blitzen; **in a ~** im Nu; **quick as
a ~** blitzschnell; **~ of inspiration** Geistesblitz
m; **to ~ one's headlights** die Lichthupe
betätigen; **the thought ~ed through his
mind** der Gedanke schoss ihm durch den
Kopf; **to ~ by** or **past** vorbeiflitzen (inf)

flashback ['flæʃbæk] n Rückblende f

flashbulb ['flæʃbʌlb] n Blitzbirne f

flash card n Leselernkarte f

flashcube ['flæʃkjuːb] n Blitzwürfel m

flasher ['flæʃə^r] n (Aut) Lichthupe f; (inf!: man)
Exhibitionist m

flashlight ['flæʃlaɪt] n Blitzlicht nt

flash point n (fig): **to be at ~** auf dem
Siedepunkt sein

flashy ['flæʃɪ] (pej) adj auffällig, protzig

flask [flɑːsk] n Flakon m; (Chem) Glaskolben m;
(also: **vacuum flask**) Thermosflasche® f

flat [flæt] adj flach; (surface) eben; (tyre) platt;
(battery) leer; (beer) schal; (refusal, denial) glatt;

(note, voice) zu tief; (rate, fee) Pauschal- ▷ n
(Brit: apartment) Wohnung f; (Aut) (Reifen)
panne f; (Mus) Erniedrigungszeichen nt; **to
work ~ out** auf Hochtouren arbeiten; **~ rate
of pay** Pauschallohn m

flat-footed ['flæt'futɪd] adj: **to be ~** Plattfüße
pl haben

flatly ['flætlɪ] adv (refuse, deny) glatt, kategorisch

flatmate ['flætmeɪt] (Brit) n Mitbewohner(in)
m(f)

flatness ['flætnɪs] n Flachheit f

flat screen n Flachbildschirm m

flat-screen monitor n Flachbildschirm m

flatten ['flætn] vt (also: **flatten out**) (ein)
ebnen; (paper, fabric etc) glätten; (building, city)
dem Erdboden gleichmachen; (crop) zu Boden
drücken; (inf: person) umhauen; **to ~ o.s.
against a wall/door** etc sich platt gegen or an
eine Wand/Tür etc drücken

flatter ['flætər] vt schmeicheln +dat

flatterer ['flætərər] n Schmeichler(in) m(f)

flattering ['flætərɪŋ] adj schmeichelhaft; (dress
etc) vorteilhaft

flattery ['flætərɪ] n Schmeichelei f

flatulence ['flætjuləns] n Blähungen pl

flaunt [flɔ:nt] vt zur Schau stellen, protzen mit

flavour, (US) flavor ['fleɪvər] n Geschmack
m; (of ice-cream etc) Geschmacksrichtung f ▷ vt
Geschmack verleihen +dat; **to give or add ~
to** Geschmack verleihen +dat; **music with an
African ~** (fig) Musik mit einer afrikanischen
Note; **strawberry--ed** mit Erdbeergeschmack

flavouring ['fleɪvərɪŋ] n Aroma nt

flaw [flɔ:] n Fehler m

flawless ['flɔ:lɪs] adj (performance) fehlerlos;
(complexion) makellos

flax [flæks] n Flachs m

flaxen ['flæksən] adj (hair) flachsblond

flea [fli:] n Floh m

flea market n Flohmarkt m

fleck [flɛk] n Tupfen m, Punkt m; (of dust)
Flöckchen nt; (of mud, paint, colour) Fleck(en) m
▷ vt bespritzen; **brown ~ed with white** braun
mit weißen Punkten

fled [flɛd] pt, pp of **flee**

fledgeling, fledgling ['flɛdʒlɪŋ] n Jungvogel m
▷ adj (inexperienced: actor etc) Nachwuchs-; (newly
started: business etc) jung

flee [fli:] (pt, pp **fled**) vt fliehen or flüchten
vor +dat; (country) fliehen or flüchten aus ▷ vi
fliehen, flüchten

fleece [fli:s] n Schafwolle f; (sheep's coat)
Schaffell nt, Vlies nt ▷ vt (inf: cheat) schröpfen

fleecy ['fli:sɪ] adj flauschig; (cloud) Schäfchen-

fleet [fli:t] n Flotte f; (of lorries, cars) Fuhrpark m

fleeting ['fli:tɪŋ] adj flüchtig

Flemish ['flɛmɪʃ] adj flämisch ▷ n (Ling)
Flämisch nt; **the Flemish** npl die Flamen

flesh [flɛʃ] n Fleisch nt; (of fruit) Fruchtfleisch nt
▶ **flesh out** vt ausgestalten

flesh wound [-wu:nd] n Fleischwunde f

flew [flu:] pt of **fly**

flex [flɛks] n Kabel nt ▷ vt beugen; (muscles)
spielen lassen

flexibility [flɛksɪ'bɪlɪtɪ] n (see adj) Flexibilität f;
Biegsamkeit f

flexible ['flɛksəbl] adj flexibel; (material)
biegsam

flexitime ['flɛksɪtaɪm] n gleitende Arbeitszeit
f, Gleitzeit f

flick [flɪk] n (of finger) Schnipsen nt; (of hand)
Wischen nt; (of whip) Schnalzen nt; (of towel
etc) Schlagen nt; (of switch) Knipsen nt ▷ vt
schnipsen; (with hand) wischen; (whip) knallen
mit; (switch) knipsen; **flicks** (inf) npl Kino nt;
to ~ a towel at sb mit einem Handtuch nach
jdm schlagen
▶ **flick through** vt fus durchblättern

flicker ['flɪkər] vi flackern; (eyelids) zucken ▷ n
Flackern nt; (of pain, fear) Aufflackern nt; (of
smile) Anflug m; (of eyelid) Zucken nt

flick knife (Brit) n Klappmesser nt

flier ['flaɪər] n Flieger(in) m(f)

flight [flaɪt] n Flug m; (escape) Flucht f;
(also: **flight of steps**) Treppe f; **to take ~** die
Flucht ergreifen; **to put to ~** in die Flucht
schlagen

flight attendant (US) n Flugbegleiter(in) m(f)

flight crew n Flugbesatzung f

flight deck n (Aviat) Cockpit nt; (Naut) Flugdeck
nt

flight path n Flugbahn f

flight recorder n Flugschreiber m

flimsy ['flɪmzɪ] adj leicht, dünn; (building) leicht
gebaut; (excuse) fadenscheinig; (evidence) nicht
stichhaltig

flinch [flɪntʃ] vi zusammenzucken; **to ~ from**
zurückschrecken vor +dat

fling [flɪŋ] (pt, pp **flung**) vt schleudern; (arms)
werfen; (oneself) stürzen ▷ n (flüchtige) Affäre
f

flint [flɪnt] n Feuerstein m

flip [flɪp] vt (switch) knipsen; (coin) werfen;
(US: pancake) umdrehen ▷ vi: **to ~ for sth** (US)
um etw mit einer Münze knobeln
▶ **flip through** vt fus durchblättern; (records etc)
durchgehen

flippant ['flɪpənt] adj leichtfertig

flipper ['flɪpər] n Flosse f; (for swimming)
(Schwimm)flosse f

flip side n (of record) B-Seite f

flirt [flə:t] vi flirten; (with idea) liebäugeln
▷ n: **he/she is a ~** er/sie flirtet gern

flirtation [flə:'teɪʃən] n Flirt m

flit [flɪt] vi flitzen; (expression, smile) huschen

float [fləut] n Schwimmkork m; (for fishing)
Schwimmer m; (lorry) Festwagen m; (money)
Wechselgeld nt ▷ vi schwimmen; (swimmer)
treiben; (through air) schweben; (currency)
floaten ▷ vt (currency) freigeben, floaten lassen;
(company) gründen; (idea, plan) in den Raum
stellen
▶ **float around** vi im Umlauf sein; (person)
herumschweben (inf); (object) herumfliegen
(inf)

flock [flɔk] n Herde f; (of birds) Schwarm m

▷ vi: **to ~ to** (place) strömen nach; (event) in Scharen kommen zu

floe [fləu] n (also: **ice floe**) Eisscholle f

flog [flɔg] vt auspeitschen; (inf: sell) verscherbeln

flood [flʌd] n Überschwemmung f; (of letters, imports etc) Flut f ▷ vt überschwemmen; (Aut) absaufen lassen (inf) ▷ vi überschwemmt werden; **to be in ~** Hochwasser führen; **to ~ the market** den Markt überschwemmen; **to ~ into Hungary/the square/the palace** nach Ungarn/auf den Platz/in den Palast strömen

flooding ['flʌdɪŋ] n Überschwemmung f

floodlight ['flʌdlaɪt] n Flutlicht nt ▷ vt (mit Flutlicht) beleuchten; (building) anstrahlen

floodlit ['flʌdlɪt] pt, pp of **floodlight** ▷ adj (mit Flutlicht) beleuchtet; (building) angestrahlt

flood tide n Flut f

floodwater ['flʌdwɔːtəʳ] n Hochwasser nt

floor [flɔːʳ] n (Fuß)boden m; (storey) Stock nt; (of sea, valley) Boden m ▷ vt (subj: blow) zu Boden werfen; (: question, remark) die Sprache verschlagen +dat; **on the ~** auf dem Boden; **ground ~** (Brit), **first ~** (US) Erdgeschoss nt, Erdgeschoß nt (Österr); **first ~** (Brit), **second ~** (US) erster Stock m; **top ~** oberstes Stockwerk nt; **to have the ~** (speaker: at meeting) das Wort haben

floorboard ['flɔːbɔːd] n Diele f

flooring ['flɔːrɪŋ] n (Fuß)boden m; (covering) Fußbodenbelag m

floor lamp (US) n Stehlampe f

floor show n Show f, Vorstellung f

floorwalker ['flɔːwɔːkəʳ] (esp US) n Ladenaufsicht f

floozy ['fluːzɪ] (inf) n Flittchen nt

flop [flɔp] n Reinfall m ▷ vi (play, book) durchfallen; (fall) sich fallen lassen; (scheme) ein Reinfall sein

floppy ['flɔpɪ] adj schlaff, schlapp ▷ n (also: **floppy disk**) Diskette f, Floppy Disk f; **~ hat** Schlapphut m

floppy disk n Diskette f, Floppy Disk f

flora ['flɔːrə] n Flora f

floral ['flɔːrl] adj geblümt

Florence ['flɔrəns] n Florenz nt

Florentine ['flɔrəntaɪn] adj florentinisch

florid ['flɔrɪd] adj (style) blumig; (complexion) kräftig

florist ['flɔrɪst] n Blumenhändler(in) m(f)

florist's ['flɔrɪsts], **florist's shop** n Blumengeschäft nt

flotation [fləuˈteɪʃən] n (of shares) Auflegung f; (of company) Umwandlung f in eine Aktiengesellschaft

flotsam ['flɔtsəm] n (also: **flotsam and jetsam**) Strandgut nt; (floating) Treibgut nt

flounce [flauns] n Volant m

▶ **flounce out** vi hinausstolzieren

flounder ['flaundəʳ] vi sich abstrampeln; (fig: speaker) ins Schwimmen kommen; (economy) in Schwierigkeiten geraten ▷ n

Flunder f

flour ['flauəʳ] n Mehl nt

flourish ['flʌrɪʃ] vi gedeihen; (business) blühen, florieren ▷ vt schwenken ▷ n (in writing) Schnörkel m; (bold gesture): **with a ~** mit einer schwungvollen Bewegung

flourishing ['flʌrɪʃɪŋ] adj gut gehend, florierend

flout [flaut] vt sich hinwegsetzen über +acc

flow [fləu] n Fluss m; (of sea) Flut f ▷ vi fließen; (clothes, hair) wallen

flow chart n Flussdiagramm nt

flow diagram n = **flow chart**

flower ['flauəʳ] n Blume f; (blossom) Blüte f ▷ vi blühen; **to be in ~** blühen

flowerbed ['flauəbɛd] n Blumenbeet nt

flowerpot ['flauəpɔt] n Blumentopf m

flowery ['flauərɪ] adj blumig; (pattern) Blumen-

flown [fləun] pp of **fly**

flu [fluː] n Grippe f

fluctuate ['flʌktjueɪt] vi schwanken; (opinions, attitudes) sich ändern

fluctuation [flʌktjuˈeɪʃən] n: **~ (in)** Schwankung f (+gen)

flue [fluː] n Rauchfang m, Rauchabzug m

fluency ['fluːənsɪ] n Flüssigkeit f; **his ~ in German** sein flüssiges Deutsch

fluent ['fluːənt] adj flüssig; **he speaks ~ German, he's ~ in German** er spricht fließend Deutsch

fluently ['fluːəntlɪ] adv flüssig; (speak a language) fließend

fluff [flʌf] n Fussel m; (fur) Flaum m ▷ vt (inf: do badly) verpatzen; (also: **fluff out**) aufplustern

fluffy ['flʌfɪ] adj flaumig; (jacket etc) weich, kuschelig; **~ toy** Kuscheltier nt

fluid ['fluːɪd] adj fließend; (situation, arrangement) unklar ▷ n Flüssigkeit f

fluid ounce (Brit) n flüssige Unze f (= 28 ml)

fluke [fluːk] (inf) n Glücksfall m; **by a ~** durch einen glücklichen Zufall

flummox ['flʌməks] vt verwirren, durcheinanderbringen

flung [flʌŋ] pt, pp of **fling**

flunky ['flʌŋkɪ] n Lakai m

fluorescent [fluəˈrɛsnt] adj fluoreszierend; (paint) Leucht-; (light) Neon-

fluoride ['fluəraɪd] n Fluorid nt

fluorine ['fluəriːn] n Fluor nt

flurry ['flʌrɪ] n (of snow) Gestöber nt; **a ~ of activity/excitement** hektische Aktivität/ Aufregung

flush [flʌʃ] n Röte f; (fig: of beauty etc) Blüte f ▷ vt (durch)spülen, (aus)spülen ▷ vi erröten ▷ adj: **~ with** auf gleicher Ebene mit; **~ against** direkt an +dat; **in the first ~ of youth** in der ersten Jugendblüte; **in the first ~ of freedom** im ersten Freiheitstaumel; **hot ~es** (Brit) Hitzewallungen pl; **to ~ the toilet** spülen, die Wasserspülung betätigen

▶ **flush out** vt aufstöbern

flushed [flʌʃt] adj rot

fluster ['flʌstəʳ] n: **in a ~** nervös; (confused)

f

durcheinander ▷ vt nervös machen; (confuse) durcheinanderbringen

flustered ['flʌstəd] adj nervös; (confused) durcheinander

flute [fluːt] n Querflöte f

fluted ['fluːtɪd] adj gerillt; (column) kanneliert

flutter ['flʌtəʳ] n Flattern nt; (of panic, nerves) kurzer Anfall m; (of excitement) Beben nt ▷ vi flattern; (person) tänzeln; **to have a ~** (Brit: inf: gamble) sein Glück (beim Wetten) versuchen

flux [flʌks] n: **in a state of ~** im Fluss

fly [flaɪ] (pt flew, pp flown) n Fliege f; (on trousers: also: **flies**) (Hosen)schlitz m ▷ vt fliegen; (kite) steigen lassen ▷ vi fliegen; (escape) fliehen; (flag) wehen; **to ~ open** auffliegen; **to ~ off the handle** an die Decke gehen (inf); **pieces of metal went ~ing everywhere** überall flogen Metallteile herum; **she came ~ing into the room** sie kam ins Zimmer gesaust; **her glasses flew off** die Brille flog ihr aus dem Gesicht

▸ **fly away** vi wegfliegen

▸ **fly in** vi einfliegen; **he flew in yesterday** er ist gestern mit dem Flugzeug gekommen

▸ **fly off** vi = **fly away**

▸ **fly out** vi ausfliegen; **he flew out yesterday** er ist gestern hingeflogen

fly-fishing ['flaɪfɪʃɪŋ] n Fliegenfischen nt

flying ['flaɪɪŋ] n Fliegen nt ▷ adj: **a ~ visit** ein Blitzbesuch m; **he doesn't like ~** er fliegt nicht gerne; **with ~ colours** mit fliegenden Fahnen

flying buttress n Strebebogen m

flying picket n mobiler Streikposten m

flying saucer n fliegende Untertasse f

flying squad n mobiles Einsatzkommando nt

flying start n: **to get off to a ~** (Sport) hervorragend wegkommen; (fig) einen glänzenden Start haben

flyleaf ['flaɪliːf] n Vorsatzblatt nt

flyover ['flaɪəuvəʳ] n (Brit) Überführung f; (US) Luftparade f

fly-past ['flaɪpɑːst] n Luftparade f

flysheet ['flaɪʃiːt] n (for tent) Überzelt nt

flyweight ['flaɪweɪt] n Fliegengewicht nt

flywheel ['flaɪwiːl] n Schwungrad nt

FM abbr (Brit: Mil) = **field marshal**; (Radio: = frequency modulation) FM, ≈ UKW

FMB (US) n abbr (= Federal Maritime Board) Dachausschuss der Handelsmarine

FMCS (US) n abbr (= Federal Mediation and Conciliation Service) Schlichtungsstelle für Arbeitskonflikte

FO (Brit) n abbr = **Foreign Office**

foal [fəul] n Fohlen nt

foam [fəum] n Schaum m; (also: **foam rubber**) Schaumgummi m ▷ vi schäumen

fob [fɔb] vt: **to ~ sb off** jdn abspeisen ▷ n (also: **watch fob**) Uhrkette f

f.o.b. abbr (Comm: = free on board) frei Schiff

foc (Brit) abbr (Comm: = free of charge) gratis

focal point ['fəukl-] n Mittelpunkt m; (of

camera, telescope etc) Brennpunkt m

focus ['fəukəs] (pl **~es**) n Brennpunkt m; (of storm) Zentrum nt ▷ vt einstellen; (light rays) bündeln ▷ vi: **to ~ (on)** (with camera) klar or scharf einstellen +acc; (person) sich konzentrieren (auf +acc); **in/out of ~** (camera etc) scharf/unscharf eingestellt; (photograph) scharf/unscharf

focus group n (Pol) Fokusgruppe f

fodder ['fɔdəʳ] n Futter nt

FoE n abbr (= Friends of the Earth) Umweltschutzorganisation

foe [fəu] n Feind(in) m(f)

foetus, (US)**fetus** ['fiːtəs] n Fötus m, Fetus m

fog [fɔg] n Nebel m

fogbound ['fɔgbaund] adj (airport) wegen Nebel geschlossen

foggy ['fɔgɪ] adj neb(e)lig

fog lamp, (US)**fog light** n (Aut) Nebelscheinwerfer m

foible ['fɔɪbl] n Eigenheit f

foil [fɔɪl] vt vereiteln ▷ n Folie f; (complement) Kontrast m; (Fencing) Florett nt; **to act as a ~ to** einen Kontrast darstellen zu

foist [fɔɪst] vt: **to ~ sth on sb** (goods) jdm etw andrehen; (task) etw an jdn abschieben; (ideas, views) jdm etw aufzwingen

fold [fəuld] n Falte f; (Agr) Pferch m; (fig) Schoß m ▷ vt (zusammen)falten; (arms) verschränken ▷ vi (business) eingehen (inf)

▸ **fold up** vi sich zusammenfalten lassen; (bed, table) sich zusammenklappen lassen; (business) eingehen (inf) ▷ vt zusammenfalten

folder ['fəuldəʳ] n Aktenmappe f; (binder) Hefter m; (brochure) Informationsblatt nt

folding ['fəuldɪŋ] adj (chair, bed) Klapp-

foliage ['fəulɪɪdʒ] n Laubwerk nt

folk [fəuk] npl Leute pl ▷ cpd Volks-; **my ~s** (parents) meine alten Herrschaften

folklore ['fəuklɔːʳ] n Folklore f

folk music n Volksmusik f; (contemporary) Folk m

folk song n Volkslied nt; (contemporary) Folksong m

follow ['fɔləu] vt folgen +dat; (with eyes) verfolgen; (advice, instructions) befolgen ▷ vi folgen; **to ~ in sb's footsteps** in jds Fußstapfen acc treten; **I don't quite ~ you** ich kann Ihnen nicht ganz folgen; **it ~s that** daraus folgt, dass; **to ~ suit** (fig) jds Beispiel dat folgen

▸ **follow on** vi (continue): **to ~ on from** aufbauen auf +dat

▸ **follow out** vt (idea, plan) zu Ende verfolgen

▸ **follow through** vt = **follow out**

▸ **follow up** vt nachgehen +dat; (offer) aufgreifen; (case) weiterverfolgen

follower ['fɔləuəʳ] n Anhänger(in) m(f)

following ['fɔləuɪŋ] adj folgend ▷ n Anhängerschaft f

follow-up ['fɔləuʌp] n Weiterführung f ▷ adj: **~ treatment** Nachbehandlung f

folly ['fɔlɪ] n Torheit f; (building) exzentrisches Bauwerk nt

fond [fɔnd] *adj* liebevoll; (*memory*) lieb; (*hopes, dreams*) töricht; **to be ~ of** mögen; **she's ~ of swimming** sie schwimmt gerne

fondle ['fɔndl] *vt* streicheln

fondly ['fɔndlɪ] *adv* liebevoll; (*naïvely*) törichterweise; **he ~ believed that ...** er war so naiv zu glauben, dass ...

fondness ['fɔndnɪs] *n* (*for things*) Vorliebe *f*; (*for people*) Zuneigung *f*; **a special ~ for** eine besondere Vorliebe für/Zuneigung zu

font [fɔnt] *n* Taufbecken *nt*; (*Typ*) Schrift *f*

food [fuːd] *n* Essen *nt*; (*for animals*) Futter *nt*; (*nourishment*) Nahrung *f*; (*groceries*) Lebensmittel *pl*

food chain *n* Nahrungskette *f*

food combining *n* Trennkost *f*

food mixer *n* Küchenmixer *m*

food poisoning *n* Lebensmittelvergiftung *f*

food processor *n* Küchenmaschine *f*

food stamp *n* Lebensmittelmarke *f*

foodstuffs ['fuːdstʌfs] *npl* Lebensmittel *pl*

fool [fuːl] *n* Dummkopf *m*; (*Culin*) Sahnespeise aus Obstpüree ▷ *vt* hereinlegen, täuschen ▷ *vi* herumalbern; **to make a ~ of sb** jdn lächerlich machen; (*trick*) jdn hereinlegen; **to make a ~ of o.s.** sich blamieren; **you can't ~ me** du kannst mich nicht zum Narren halten
▸ **fool about** (*pej*) *vi* herumtrödeln; (*behave foolishly*) herumalbern
▸ **fool around** *vi* = **fool about**

foolhardy ['fuːlhɑːdɪ] *adj* tollkühn

foolish ['fuːlɪʃ] *adj* dumm

foolishly ['fuːlɪʃlɪ] *adv* dumm; **~, I forgot ...** dummerweise habe ich ... vergessen

foolishness ['fuːlɪʃnɪs] *n* Dummheit *f*

foolproof ['fuːlpruːf] *adj* idiotensicher

foolscap ['fuːlskæp] *n* = Kanzleipapier *nt*

foot [fut] (*pl* **feet**) *n* Fuß *m*; (*of animal*) Pfote *f* ▷ *vt* (*bill*) bezahlen; **on ~** zu Fuß; **to find one's feet** sich eingewöhnen; **to put one's ~ down** (*Aut*) Gas geben; (*say no*) ein Machtwort sprechen

footage ['futɪdʒ] *n* Filmmaterial *nt*

foot-and-mouth [futənd'mauθ], **foot-and-mouth disease** *n* Maul- und Klauenseuche *f*

football ['futbɔːl] *n* Fußball *m*; (*US*) Football *m*, amerikanischer Fußball *m*

footballer ['futbɔːlər] (*Brit*) *n* Fußballspieler(in) *m(f)*

football ground *n* Fußballplatz *m*

football match (*Brit*) *n* Fußballspiel *nt*

football player *n* (*Brit*) Fußballspieler(in) *m(f)*; (*US*) Footballspieler(in) *m(f)*

foot brake *n* Fußbremse *f*

footbridge ['futbrɪdʒ] *n* Fußgängerbrücke *f*

foothills ['futhɪlz] *npl* (Gebirgs)ausläufer *pl*

foothold ['futhəuld] *n* Halt *m*; **to get a ~** Fuß fassen

footing ['futɪŋ] *n* Stellung *f*; (*relationship*) Verhältnis *nt*; **to lose one's ~** den Halt verlieren; **on an equal ~** auf gleicher Basis

footlights ['futlaɪts] *npl* Rampenlicht *nt*

footman ['futmən] (*irreg: like* **man**) *n* Lakai *m*

footnote ['futnəut] *n* Fußnote *f*

footpath ['futpɑːθ] *n* Fußweg *m*; (*in street*) Bürgersteig *m*

footprint ['futprɪnt] *n* Fußabdruck *m*; (*of animal*) Spur *f*

footrest ['futrɛst] *n* Fußstütze *f*

Footsie ['futsɪ] (*inf*) *n* = **FTSE 100 Index**

footsie ['futsɪ] (*inf*) *n*: **to play ~ with sb** mit jdm füßeln

footsore ['futsɔːr] *adj*: **to be ~** wunde Füße haben

footstep ['futstɛp] *n* Schritt *m*; (*footprint*) Fußabdruck *m*; **to follow in sb's ~s** in jds Fußstapfen *acc* treten

footwear ['futwɛər] *n* Schuhe *pl*, Schuhwerk *nt*

 KEYWORD

for [fɔːr] *prep* **1** für +*acc*; **is this for me?** ist das für mich?; **the train for London** der Zug nach London; **it's time for lunch** es ist Zeit zum Mittagessen; **what's it for?** wofür ist das?; **he works for the government/a local firm** er arbeitet für die Regierung/eine Firma am Ort; **he's mature for his age** er ist reif für sein Alter; **I sold it for £20** ich habe es für £20 verkauft; **I'm all for it** ich bin ganz dafür; **G for George** ≈ G wie Gustav

2 (*because of*): **for this reason** aus diesem Grund; **for fear of being criticised** aus Angst, kritisiert zu werden

3 (*referring to distance*): **there are roadworks for 5 km** die Straßenbauarbeiten erstrecken sich über 5 km; **we walked for miles** wir sind meilenweit gelaufen

4 (*referring to time*): **he was away for 2 years** er war 2 Jahre lang weg; **I have known her for years** ich kenne sie bereits seit Jahren

5 (*with infinitive clause*): **it is not for me to decide** es liegt nicht an mir, das zu entscheiden; **for this to be possible ...** um dies möglich zu machen, ...

6 (*in spite of*) trotz +*gen or dat*; **for all his complaints, he is very fond of her** trotz seiner vielen Klagen mag er sie sehr ▷ *conj* (*form: since, as*) denn; **she was very angry, for he was late again** sie war sehr böse, denn er kam wieder zu spät

f.o.r. *abbr* (*Comm*: = *free on rail*) frei Bahn

forage ['fɔrɪdʒ] *n* Futter *nt* ▷ *vi* herumstöbern; **to ~ (for food)** nach Futter suchen

forage cap *n* Schiffchen *nt*

foray ['fɔreɪ] n (Raub)überfall m
forbad, forbade [fə'bæd] pt of **forbid**
forbearing [fɔː'bɛərɪŋ] adj geduldig
forbid [fə'bɪd] (pt **forbade**, pp **~den**) vt
verbieten; **to ~ sb to do sth** jdm verbieten,
etw zu tun
forbidden [fə'bɪdn] pp of **forbid** ▷ adj verboten
forbidding [fə'bɪdɪŋ] adj (look) streng; (prospect)
grauenhaft
force [fɔːs] n Kraft f; (violence) Gewalt f; (of
blow, impact) Wucht f; (influence) Macht f ▷ vt
zwingen; (push) drücken; (: person) drängen;
(lock, door) aufbrechen; **the Forces** (Brit) npl
die Streitkräfte pl; **in ~** (law etc) geltend;
(people: arrive etc) zahlreich; **to come into ~** in
Kraft treten; **to join ~s** sich zusammentun;
a ~ 5 wind Windstärke 5; **the sales ~** das
Verkaufspersonal; **to ~ o.s./sb to do sth**
sich/jdn zwingen, etw zu tun
▶ **force back** vt zurückdrängen; (tears)
unterdrücken
▶ **force down** vt (food) hinunterwürgen (inf)
forced [fɔːst] adj gezwungen; **~ labour**
Zwangsarbeit f; **~ landing** Notlandung f
force-feed ['fɔːsfiːd] vt zwangsernähren;
(animal) stopfen
forceful ['fɔːsful] adj energisch; (attack)
wirkungsvoll; (point) überzeugend
forceps ['fɔːseps] npl Zange f
forcible ['fɔːsəbl] adj gewaltsam; (reminder,
lesson) eindringlich
forcibly ['fɔːsəblɪ] adv mit Gewalt; (express)
eindringlich
ford [fɔːd] n Furt f ▷ vt durchqueren; (on foot)
durchwaten
fore [fɔːʳ] n: **to come to the ~** ins Blickfeld
geraten
forearm ['fɔːrɑːm] n Unterarm m
forebear ['fɔːbɛəʳ] n Vorfahr(in) m(f), Ahn(e)
m(f)
foreboding [fɔː'bəudɪŋ] n Vorahnung f
forecast ['fɔːkɑːst] (irreg: like **cast**) n Prognose
f; (of weather) (Wetter)vorhersage f ▷ vt
voraussagen
foreclose [fɔː'kləuz] vt (Law: also: **foreclose
on**) kündigen; **to ~ sb** (on loan/mortgage) jds
Darlehen/Hypothek kündigen
foreclosure [fɔː'kləuʒəʳ] n
Zwangsvollstreckung f
forecourt ['fɔːkɔːt] n Vorplatz m
forefathers ['fɔːfɑːðəz] npl Vorfahren pl
forefinger ['fɔːfɪŋgəʳ] n Zeigefinger m
forefront ['fɔːfrʌnt] n: **in the ~ of** an der Spitze
+gen
forego [fɔː'gəu] (irreg: like **go**) vt verzichten auf
+acc
foregoing ['fɔːgəuɪŋ] adj vorhergehend
▷ n: **the ~** das Vorhergehende
foregone ['fɔːgɔn] pp of **forego** ▷ adj: **it's a ~
conclusion** es steht von vornherein fest
foreground ['fɔːgraund] n Vordergrund m
forehand ['fɔːhænd] n (Tennis) Vorhand f
forehead ['fɔrɪd] n Stirn f

foreign ['fɔrɪn] adj ausländisch; (holiday) im
Ausland; (customs, appearance) fremdartig;
(trade, policy) Außen-; (correspondent) Auslands-;
(object, matter) fremd; **goods from ~
countries/a ~ country** Waren aus dem
Ausland
foreign body n Fremdkörper m
foreign currency n Devisen pl
foreigner ['fɔrɪnəʳ] n Ausländer(in) m(f)
foreign exchange n Devisenhandel m; (money)
Devisen pl
foreign exchange market n Devisenmarkt m
foreign exchange rate n Devisenkurs m
foreign investment n Auslandsinvestition f
foreign minister n Außenminister(in) m(f)
Foreign Office (Brit) n Außenministerium nt
Foreign Secretary (Brit) n Außenminister(in)
m(f)
foreleg ['fɔːlɛg] n Vorderbein nt
foreman ['fɔːmən] (irreg: like **man**) n Vorarbeiter
m; (of jury) Obmann m
foremost ['fɔːməust] adj führend ▷ adv: **first
and ~** zunächst, vor allem
forename ['fɔːneɪm] n Vorname m
forensic [fə'rɛnsɪk] adj (test) forensisch;
(medicine) Gerichts-; (expert) Spurensicherungs-
foreplay ['fɔːpleɪ] n Vorspiel nt
forerunner ['fɔːrʌnəʳ] n Vorläufer m
foresee [fɔː'siː] (irreg: like **see**) vt vorhersehen
foreseeable [fɔː'siːəbl] adj vorhersehbar; **in
the ~ future** in absehbarer Zeit
foreseen [fɔː'siːn] pp of **foresee**
foreshadow [fɔː'ʃædəu] vt andeuten
foreshore ['fɔːʃɔː] n Strand m
foreshorten [fɔː'ʃɔːtn] vt perspektivisch
verkürzen
foresight ['fɔːsaɪt] n Voraussicht f, Weitblick m
foreskin ['fɔːskɪn] n (Anat) Vorhaut f
forest ['fɔrɪst] n Wald m
forestall [fɔː'stɔːl] vt zuvorkommen +dat;
(discussion) im Keim ersticken
forestry ['fɔrɪstrɪ] n Forstwirtschaft f
foretaste ['fɔːteɪst] n: **a ~ of** ein Vorgeschmack
von
foretell [fɔː'tɛl] (irreg: like **tell**) vt vorhersagen
forethought ['fɔːθɔːt] n Vorbedacht m
foretold [fɔː'təuld] pt, pp of **foretell**
forever [fə'rɛvəʳ] adv für immer; (endlessly)
ewig; (consistently) dauernd, ständig; **you're
~ finding difficulties** du findest ständig or
dauernd neue Schwierigkeiten
forewarn [fɔː'wɔːn] vt vorwarnen
forewent [fɔː'wɛnt] pt of **forego**
forewoman ['fɔːwumən] (irreg: like **woman**) n
Vorarbeiterin f; (of jury) Obmännin f
foreword ['fɔːwəːd] n Vorwort nt
forfeit ['fɔːfɪt] n Strafe f, Buße f ▷ vt (right)
verwirken; (friendship etc) verlieren; (one's
happiness, health) einbüßen
forgave [fə'geɪv] pt of **forgive**
forge [fɔːdʒ] n Schmiede f ▷ vt fälschen;
(wrought iron) schmieden
▶ **forge ahead** vi große or schnelle Fortschritte

machen

forger ['fɔːdʒər] n Fälscher(in) m(f)

forgery ['fɔːdʒərɪ] n Fälschung f

forget [fə'gɛt] (pt **forgot**, pp **forgotten**) vt
vergessen ▷ vi es vergessen; **to ~ o.s.** sich
vergessen

forgetful [fə'gɛtful] adj vergesslich; **~ of sth**
(of duties etc) nachlässig gegenüber etw

forgetfulness [fə'gɛtfulnɪs] n Vergesslichkeit
f; (oblivion) Vergessenheit f

forget-me-not [fə'gɛtmɪnɔt] n
Vergissmeinnicht nt

forgive [fə'gɪv] (pt **forgave**, pp **~n**) vt verzeihen
+dat, vergeben +dat; **to ~ sb for sth** jdm etw
verzeihen or vergeben; **to ~ sb for doing sth**
jdm verzeihen or vergeben, dass er etw getan
hat; **~ me, but ...** entschuldigen Sie, aber ...;
they could be ~n for thinking that ... es ist
verständlich, wenn sie denken, dass ...

forgiveness [fə'gɪvnɪs] n Verzeihung f

forgiving [fə'gɪvɪŋ] adj versöhnlich

forgo [fɔː'gəu] (pt **forwent**, pp **~ne**) vt = **forego**

forgot [fə'gɒt] pt of **forget**

forgotten [fə'gɔtn] pp of **forget**

fork [fɔːk] n Gabel f; (in road, river, railway)
Gabelung f ▷ vi (road) sich gabeln
▶ **fork out** (inf) vt, vi (pay) blechen

forked [fɔːkt] adj (lightning) zickzackförmig

fork-lift truck ['fɔːklɪft-] n Gabelstapler m

forlorn [fə'lɔːn] adj verlassen; (person) einsam
und verlassen; (attempt) verzweifelt; (hope)
schwach

form [fɔːm] n Form f; (Scol) Klasse f;
(questionnaire) Formular nt ▷ vt formen,
gestalten; (queue, organization, group) bilden;
(idea, habit) entwickeln; **in the ~ of** in Form
von or +gen; **in the ~ of Peter** in Gestalt von
Peter; **to be in good ~** gut in Form sein; **in
top ~** in Hochform; **on ~** in Form; **to ~ part of
sth** Teil von etw sein

formal ['fɔːməl] adj offiziell; (person, behaviour)
förmlich, formell; (occasion, dinner) feierlich;
(clothes) Gesellschafts-; (garden) formell
angelegt; (Art, Philosophy) formal; **~ dress**
Gesellschaftskleidung f

formalities [fɔː'mælɪtɪz] npl Formalitäten pl

formality [fɔː'mælɪtɪ] n Förmlichkeit f;
(procedure) Formalität f

formalize ['fɔːməlaɪz] vt formell machen

formally ['fɔːməlɪ] adv (see adj) offiziell;
förmlich, formell; feierlich; **to be ~ invited**
ausdrücklich eingeladen sein

format ['fɔːmæt] n Format nt; (form, style)
Aufmachung f ▷ vt (Comput) formatieren

formation [fɔː'meɪʃən] n Bildung f; (of theory)
Entstehung f; (of business) Gründung f;
(pattern: of rocks, clouds) Formation f

formative ['fɔːmətɪv] adj (influence) prägend;
(years) entscheidend

former ['fɔːmər] adj früher; **the ~ ... the
latter ...** Erstere(r, s) ... Letztere(r, s); **the ~
president** der ehemalige Präsident; **the ~
East Germany** die ehemalige DDR

formerly ['fɔːməlɪ] adv früher

form feed n (on printer) Papiervorschub m

Formica® [fɔː'maɪkə] n Resopal® nt

formidable ['fɔːmɪdəbl] adj (task) gewaltig,
enorm; (opponent) furchterregend

formula ['fɔːmjulə] (pl **formulae** or **~s**) n Formel
f; **F~ One** (Aut) Formel Eins

formulate ['fɔːmjuleɪt] vt formulieren

fornicate ['fɔːnɪkeɪt] vi Unzucht treiben

forsake [fə'seɪk] (pt **forsook**, pp **~n**) vt im Stich
lassen; (belief) aufgeben

forsook [fə'suk] pt of **forsake**

fort [fɔːt] n Fort nt; **to hold the ~** die Stellung
halten

forte ['fɔːtɪ] n Stärke f, starke Seite f

forth [fɔːθ] adv aus; **back and ~** hin und her;
to go back and ~ auf und ab gehen; **to bring
~** hervorbringen; **and so ~** und so weiter

forthcoming [fɔːθ'kʌmɪŋ] adj (event)
bevorstehend; (person) mitteilsam; **to be ~**
(help) erfolgen; (evidence) geliefert werden

forthright ['fɔːθraɪt] adj offen

forthwith ['fɔːθ'wɪθ] adv umgehend

fortieth ['fɔːtɪɪθ] num vierzigste(r, s)

fortification [fɔːtɪfɪ'keɪʃən] n Befestigung f,
Festungsanlage f

fortified wine ['fɔːtɪfaɪd-] n weinhaltiges
Getränk nt (Sherry, Portwein etc)

fortify ['fɔːtɪfaɪ] vt (city) befestigen; (person)
bestärken; (: subj: food, drink) stärken

fortitude ['fɔːtɪtjuːd] n innere Kraft or Stärke f

fortnight ['fɔːtnaɪt] (Brit) n vierzehn Tage
pl, zwei Wochen pl; **it's a ~ since ...** es ist
vierzehn Tage or zwei Wochen her, dass ...

fortnightly ['fɔːtnaɪtlɪ] adj vierzehntägig,
zweiwöchentlich ▷ adv alle vierzehn Tage,
alle zwei Wochen

FORTRAN ['fɔːtræn] n FORTRAN nt

fortress ['fɔːtrɪs] n Festung f

fortuitous [fɔː'tjuːɪtəs] adj zufällig

fortunate ['fɔːtʃənɪt] adj glücklich; **to be ~**
Glück haben; **he is ~ to have ...** er kann sich
glücklich schätzen, ... zu haben; **it is ~ that ...**
es ist ein Glück, dass ...

fortunately ['fɔːtʃənɪtlɪ] adv glücklicherweise,
zum Glück

fortune ['fɔːtʃən] n Glück nt; (wealth) Vermögen
nt; **to make a ~** ein Vermögen machen; **to
tell sb's ~** jdm wahrsagen

fortune-teller ['fɔːtʃəntɛlər] n Wahrsager(in)
m(f)

forty ['fɔːtɪ] num vierzig

forum ['fɔːrəm] n Forum nt

forward ['fɔːwəd] adj vordere(r, s); (movement)
Vorwärts-; (not shy) dreist; (Comm: buying,
price) Termin- ▷ adv nach vorn; (movement)
vorwärts; (in time) voraus ▷ n (Sport) Stürmer
m ▷ vt (letter etc) nachsenden; (career, plans)
voranbringen; **~ planning** Vorausplanung
f; **to move ~** vorwärtskommen; **"please ~"**
„bitte nachsenden"

forwards ['fɔːwədz] adv nach vorn; (movement)
vorwärts; (in time) voraus

fossil [ˈfɒsl] n Fossil nt

fossil fuel n fossiler Brennstoff m

foster [ˈfɒstəʳ] vt (child) in Pflege nehmen; (idea, activity) fördern

foster child n Pflegekind nt

foster mother n Pflegemutter f

fought [fɔːt] pt, pp of **fight**

foul [faul] adj abscheulich; (taste, smell, temper) übel; (water) faulig; (air) schlecht; (language) unflätig ▷ n (Sport) Foul nt ▷ vt beschmutzen; (Sport) foulen; (entangle) sich verheddern in +dat

foul play n unnatürlicher or gewaltsamer Tod m; ~ **is not suspected** es besteht kein Verdacht auf ein Verbrechen

found [faund] pt, pp of **find** ▷ vt gründen

foundation [faunˈdeɪʃən] n Gründung f; (base: also: fig) Grundlage f; (organization) Stiftung f; (also: **foundation cream**) Grundierungscreme f; **foundations** npl (of building) Fundament nt; **the rumours are without** ~ die Gerüchte entbehren jeder Grundlage; **to lay the ~s** (fig) die Grundlagen schaffen

foundation stone n Grundstein m

founder [ˈfaundəʳ] n Gründer(in) m(f) ▷ vi (ship) sinken

founder member n Gründungsmitglied nt

founding [ˈfaundɪŋ] adj: ~ **fathers** (esp US) Väter pl

foundry [ˈfaundrɪ] n Gießerei f

fount [faunt] n Quelle f; (Typ) Schrift f

fountain [ˈfauntɪn] n Brunnen m

fountain pen n Füllfederhalter m, Füller m

four [fɔːʳ] num vier; **on all ~s** auf allen vieren

four-letter word [ˈfɔːlɛtə-] n Vulgärausdruck m

four-poster [ˈfɔːˈpəustəʳ] n (also: **four-poster bed**) Himmelbett nt

foursome [ˈfɔːsəm] n Quartett nt; **in** or **as a ~** zu viert

fourteen [ˈfɔːˈtiːn] num vierzehn

fourteenth [ˈfɔːˈtiːnθ] num vierzehnte(r, s)

fourth [fɔːθ] num vierte(r, s) ▷ n (Aut: also: **fourth gear**) der vierte (Gang)

four-wheel drive [ˈfɔːwiːl-] n (Aut): **with ~** mit Vierradantrieb m

fowl [faul] n Vogel m (besonders Huhn, Gans, Ente etc)

fox [fɒks] n Fuchs m ▷ vt verblüffen

foxglove [ˈfɒksglʌv] n (Bot) Fingerhut m

fox-hunting [ˈfɒkshʌntɪŋ] n Fuchsjagd f

foxtrot [ˈfɒkstrɒt] n Foxtrott m

foyer [ˈfɔɪeɪ] n Foyer nt

FPA (Brit) n abbr (= Family Planning Association) Organisation für Familienplanung

Fr. abbr (Rel) = **father; friar**

fr. abbr (= franc) Fr.

fracas [ˈfrækɑː] n Aufruhr m, Tumult m

fraction [ˈfrækʃən] n Bruchteil m; (Math) Bruch m

fractionally [ˈfrækʃnəlɪ] adv geringfügig

fractious [ˈfrækʃəs] adj verdrießlich

fracture [ˈfræktʃəʳ] n Bruch m ▷ vt brechen

fragile [ˈfrædʒaɪl] adj zerbrechlich; (economy) schwach; (health) zart; (person) angeschlagen

fragment [n ˈfrægmənt, vb frægˈmɛnt] n Stück nt ▷ vt aufsplittern ▷ vi sich aufsplittern

fragmentary [ˈfrægməntərɪ] adj fragmentarisch, bruchstückhaft

fragrance [ˈfreɪɡrəns] n Duft m

fragrant [ˈfreɪɡrənt] adj duftend

frail [freɪl] adj schwach, gebrechlich; (structure) zerbrechlich

frame [freɪm] n Rahmen m; (of building) (Grund)gerippe nt; (of human, animal) Gestalt f; (of spectacles: also: **frames**) Gestell nt ▷ vt (of picture) rahmen; (reply) formulieren; (law, theory) entwerfen; ~ **of mind** Stimmung f, Laune f; **to ~ sb** (inf) jdm etwas anhängen

framework [ˈfreɪmwəːk] n Rahmen m

France [frɑːns] n Frankreich nt

franchise [ˈfræntʃaɪz] n Wahlrecht nt; (Comm) Konzession f, Franchise f

franchisee [fræntʃaɪˈziː] n Franchisenehmer(in) m(f)

franchiser [ˈfræntʃaɪzəʳ] n Franchisegeber(in) m(f)

frank [fræŋk] adj offen ▷ vt (letter) frankieren

Frankfurt [ˈfræŋkfəːt] n Frankfurt nt

frankfurter [ˈfræŋkfəːtəʳ] n (Frankfurter) Würstchen nt

franking machine [ˈfræŋkɪŋ-] n Frankiermaschine f

frankly [ˈfræŋklɪ] adv ehrlich gesagt; (candidly) offen

frankness [ˈfræŋknɪs] n Offenheit f

frantic [ˈfræntɪk] adj verzweifelt; (hectic) hektisch; (desperate) übersteigert

frantically [ˈfræntɪklɪ] adv verzweifelt; (hectically) hektisch

fraternal [frəˈtəːnl] adj brüderlich

fraternity [frəˈtəːnɪtɪ] n Brüderlichkeit f; (US: Univ) Verbindung f; **the legal/medical/golfing ~** die Juristen/Mediziner/Golfer pl

fraternize [ˈfrætənaɪz] vi Umgang haben

fraud [frɔːd] n Betrug m; (person) Betrüger(in) m(f)

fraudulent [ˈfrɔːdjulənt] adj betrügerisch

fraught [frɔːt] adj (person) nervös; **to be ~ with danger/problems** voller Gefahren/Probleme sein

fray [freɪ] n: **the ~** der Kampf m ▷ vi (cloth) ausfransen; (rope) sich durchscheuern; **to return to the ~** sich wieder ins Getümmel stürzen; **tempers were ~ed** die Gemüter erhitzten sich; **her nerves were ~ed** sie war mit den Nerven am Ende

FRB (US) n abbr = **Federal Reserve Board**

FRCM (Brit) n abbr (= Fellow of the Royal College of Music) Qualifikationsnachweis in Musik

FRCO (Brit) n abbr (= Fellow of the Royal College of Organists) Qualifikationsnachweis für Organisten

FRCP (Brit) n abbr (= Fellow of the Royal College of Physicians) Qualifikationsnachweis für Ärzte

FRCS (Brit) n abbr (= Fellow of the Royal College of

Surgeons) Qualifikationsnachweis für Chirurgen
freak [friːk] n Irre(r) f(m); (in
appearance) Missgeburt f; (event,
accident) außergewöhnlicher Zufall m;
(pej: fanatic): **health** ~ Gesundheitsapostel m
▶ **freak out** (inf) vi aussteigen; (on drugs)
ausflippen
freakish ['friːkɪʃ] adj verrückt
freckle ['frɛkl] n Sommersprosse f
freckled ['frɛkld] adj sommersprossig
free [friː] adj frei; (costing nothing) kostenlos,
gratis ▷ vt freilassen, frei lassen; (jammed
object) lösen; **to give sb a ~ hand** jdm freie
Hand lassen; **~ and easy** ungezwungen;
admission ~ Eintritt frei; **~ (of charge), for
free** umsonst, gratis
free agent n: **to be a ~** sein eigener Herr sein
freebie ['friːbɪ] (inf) n (promotional gift)
Werbegeschenk nt
freedom ['friːdəm] n Freiheit f
freedom fighter n Freiheitskämpfer(in) m(f)
free enterprise n freies Unternehmertum nt
Freefone® ['friːfəʊn] n: **call ~ 0800** rufen Sie
gebührenfrei 0800 an
free-for-all ['friːfərɔːl] n Gerangel nt; **the fight
turned into a ~** schließlich beteiligten sich
alle an der Schlägerei
free gift n Werbegeschenk nt
freehold ['friːhəʊld] n (of property) Besitzrecht nt
free kick n Freistoß m
freelance ['friːlɑːns] adj (journalist etc)
frei(schaffend), freiberuflich tätig
freelance work n freiberufliche Arbeit f
freeloader ['friːləʊdər] (pej) n Schmarotzer(in)
m(f)
freely ['friːlɪ] adv frei; (spend) mit vollen
Händen; (liberally) großzügig; **drugs are ~
available in the city** Drogen sind in der Stadt
frei erhältlich
free-market economy ['friːmɑːkɪt-] n freie
Marktwirtschaft f
Freemason ['friːmeɪsn] n Freimaurer m
Freemasonry ['friːmeɪsnrɪ] n Freimaurerei f
Freepost® ['friːpəʊst] n ≈ „Gebühr zahlt
Empfänger"
free-range ['friːˈreɪndʒ] adj (eggs) von frei
laufenden Hühnern
free sample n Gratisprobe f
freesia ['friːzɪə] n Freesie f
free speech n Redefreiheit f
freestyle ['friːstaɪl] n Freistil m
free trade n Freihandel m
freeway ['friːweɪ] (US) n Autobahn f
freewheel [friːˈwiːl] vi im Freilauf fahren
free will n freier Wille m; **of one's own ~** aus
freien Stücken
freeze [friːz] (pt **froze**, pp **frozen**) vi frieren;
(liquid) gefrieren; (pipe) einfrieren; (person: stop
moving) erstarren ▷ vt einfrieren; (water, lake)
gefrieren ▷ n Frost m; (on arms, wages) Stopp m
▶ **freeze over** vi (river) überfrieren; (windscreen,
windows) vereisen
▶ **freeze up** vi zufrieren

freeze-dried ['friːzdraɪd] adj gefriergetrocknet
freezer ['friːzər] n Tiefkühltruhe f; (upright)
Gefrierschrank m; (in fridge: also: **freezer
compartment**) Gefrierfach nt
freezing ['friːzɪŋ] adj: **~ (cold)** eiskalt ▷ n: **3
degrees below ~** 3 Grad unter null; **I'm ~** mir
ist eiskalt
freezing point n Gefrierpunkt m
freight [freɪt] n Fracht f; (money charged)
Frachtkosten pl; **~ forward** Fracht gegen
Nachnahme; **~ inward** Eingangsfracht f
freight car (US) n Güterwagen m
freighter ['freɪtər] n (Naut) Frachter m,
Frachtschiff nt; (Aviat) Frachtflugzeug nt
freight forwarder [-ˈfɔːwədər] n Spediteur m
freight train (US) n Güterzug m
French [frɛntʃ] adj französisch ▷ n (Ling)
Französisch nt; **the French** npl die Franzosen
pl
French bean (Brit) n grüne Bohne f
French Canadian adj frankokanadisch ▷ n
Frankokanadier(in) m(f)
French dressing n Vinaigrette f
French fried potatoes npl Pommes frites pl
French fries [-fraɪz] (US) npl = **French fried
potatoes**
French Guiana [-ɡaɪˈænə] n Französisch-
Guyana nt
Frenchman ['frɛntʃmən] (irreg: like **man**) n
Franzose m
French Riviera n: **the ~** die französische
Riviera
French stick n Stangenbrot nt
French window n Verandatür f
Frenchwoman ['frɛntʃwʊmən] (irreg: like
woman) n Französin f
frenetic [frəˈnɛtɪk] adj frenetisch, rasend
frenzied ['frɛnzɪd] adj rasend
frenzy ['frɛnzɪ] n Raserei f; (of joy, excitement)
Taumel m; **to drive sb into a ~** jdn zum Rasen
bringen; **to be in a ~** in wilder Aufregung
sein
frequency ['friːkwənsɪ] n Häufigkeit f; (Radio)
Frequenz f
frequency modulation n
Frequenzmodulation f
frequent [adj 'friːkwənt, vt frɪˈkwɛnt] adj
häufig ▷ vt (pub, restaurant) oft or häufig
besuchen
frequently ['friːkwəntlɪ] adv oft, häufig
fresco ['frɛskəʊ] n Fresko nt
fresh [frɛʃ] adj frisch; (instructions, approach, start)
neu; (cheeky) frech; **to make a ~ start** einen
neuen Anfang machen
freshen ['frɛʃən] vi (wind) auffrischen; (air)
frisch werden
▶ **freshen up** vi sich frisch machen
freshener ['frɛʃnər] n: **skin ~** Gesichtswasser
nt; **air ~** Raumspray m or nt
fresher ['frɛʃər] (Brit: inf) n Erstsemester(in) m(f)
freshly ['frɛʃlɪ] adv frisch
freshman ['frɛʃmən] (US: irreg: like **man**) n =
fresher

f

freshness ['frɛʃnɪs] n Frische f

freshwater ['frɛʃwɔːtəʳ] adj (fish etc) Süßwasser-

fret [frɛt] vi sich dat Sorgen machen

fretful ['frɛtful] adj (child) quengelig

Freudian ['frɔɪdɪən] adj freudianisch, freudsch; **~ slip** freudscher Versprecher m

FRG n abbr (Hist: = Federal Republic of Germany) BRD f

Fri. abbr (= Friday) Fr.

friar ['fraɪəʳ] n Mönch m, (Ordens)bruder m

friction ['frɪkʃən] n Reibung f; (between people) Reibereien pl

friction feed n (on printer) Friktionsvorschub m

Friday ['fraɪdɪ] n Freitag m; see also **Tuesday**

fridge [frɪdʒ] (Brit) n Kühlschrank m

fridge-freezer ['frɪdʒ'friːzəʳ] n Kühl- und Gefrierkombination f

fried [fraɪd] pt, pp of **fry** ▷ adj gebraten; **~ egg** Spiegelei nt; **~ fish** Bratfisch m

friend [frɛnd] n Freund(in) m(f); (less intimate) Bekannte(r) f(m) ▷ vt (Internet): **to ~ sb** einen Freund/eine Freundin hinzufügen; **to make ~s with** sich anfreunden mit

friendliness ['frɛndlɪnɪs] n Freundlichkeit f

friendly ['frɛndlɪ] adj freundlich; (government) befreundet; (game, match) Freundschafts- ▷ n (also: **friendly match**) Freundschaftsspiel nt; **to be ~ with** befreundet sein mit; **to be ~ to** freundlich or nett sein zu

friendly fire n Beschuss m durch die eigene Seite

friendly society n Versicherungsverein m auf Gegenseitigkeit

friendship ['frɛndʃɪp] n Freundschaft f

frieze [friːz] n Fries m

frigate ['frɪgɪt] n Fregatte f

fright [fraɪt] n Schreck(en) m; **to take ~** es mit der Angst zu tun bekommen; **she looks a ~** sie sieht verboten or zum Fürchten aus (inf)

frighten ['fraɪtn] vt erschrecken
▶ **frighten away** or **off** vt verscheuchen

frightened ['fraɪtnd] adj ängstlich; **to be ~ (of)** Angst haben (vor +dat)

frightening ['fraɪtnɪŋ] adj furchterregend

frightful ['fraɪtful] adj schrecklich, furchtbar

frightfully ['fraɪtfəlɪ] adv schrecklich, furchtbar; **I'm ~ sorry** es tut mir schrecklich leid

frigid ['frɪdʒɪd] adj frigide

frigidity [frɪ'dʒɪdɪtɪ] n Frigidität f

frill [frɪl] n Rüsche f; **without ~s** (fig) schlicht

fringe [frɪndʒ] n (Brit: of hair) Pony m; (decoration) Fransen pl; (edge, also fig) Rand m

fringe benefits npl zusätzliche Leistungen pl

fringe theatre n avantgardistisches Theater nt

Frisbee® ['frɪzbɪ] n Frisbee® nt

frisk [frɪsk] vt durchsuchen, filzen (inf) ▷ vi umhertollen

frisky ['frɪskɪ] adj lebendig, ausgelassen

fritter ['frɪtəʳ] n Schmalzgebackenes nt no pl mit Füllung
▶ **fritter away** vt vergeuden

frivolity [frɪ'vɔlɪtɪ] n Frivolität f

frivolous ['frɪvələs] adj frivol; (activity)

leichtfertig

frizzy ['frɪzɪ] adj kraus

fro [frəu] adv: **to and ~** hin und her; (walk) auf und ab

frock [frɔk] n Kleid nt

frog [frɔg] n Frosch m; **to have a ~ in one's throat** einen Frosch im Hals haben

frogman ['frɔgmən] (irreg: like **man**) n Froschmann m

frogmarch ['frɔgmɑːtʃ] (Brit) vt: **to ~ sb in/out** jdn herein-/herausschleppen

frolic ['frɔlɪk] vi umhertollen ▷ n Ausgelassenheit f; (fun) Spaß m

 KEYWORD

from [frɔm] prep **1** (indicating starting place, origin) von +dat; **where do you come from?** woher kommen Sie?; **from London to Glasgow** von London nach Glasgow; **a letter/telephone call from my sister** ein Brief/Anruf von meiner Schwester; **to drink from the bottle** aus der Flasche trinken
2 (indicating time) from (... an); **from one o'clock to** or **until** or **till now** von ein Uhr bis jetzt; **from January (on)** von Januar an, ab Januar
3 (indicating distance) von ... entfernt; **the hotel is 1 km from the beach** das Hotel ist 1 km vom Strand entfernt
4 (indicating price, number etc): **trousers from £20** Hosen ab £20; **prices range from £10 to £50** die Preise liegen zwischen £10 und £50
5 (indicating difference): **he can't tell red from green** er kann Rot und Grün nicht unterscheiden; **to be different from sb/sth** anders sein als jd/etw
6 (because of, on the basis of): **from what he says** nach dem, was er sagt; **to act from conviction** aus Überzeugung handeln; **weak from hunger** schwach vor Hunger

frond [frɔnd] n Wedel m

front [frʌnt] n Vorderseite f; (of dress) Vorderteil nt; (promenade: also: **sea front**) Strandpromenade f; (Mil, Met) Front f; (fig: appearances) Fassade f ▷ adj vorderste(r, s); (wheel, tooth, view) Vorder- ▷ vi: **to ~ onto sth** (house) auf etw acc hinausliegen; (window) auf etw acc hinausgehen; **in ~** vorne; **in ~ of** vor; **at the ~ of the coach/train/car** vorne im Bus/Zug/Auto; **on the political ~, little progress has been made** an der politischen Front sind kaum Fortschritte gemacht worden

frontage ['frʌntɪdʒ] n Vorderseite f, Front f; (of shop) Front

frontal ['frʌntl] adj (attack etc) Frontal-

front bench (Brit) n (Pol) vorderste or erste Reihe f

Regierungs- und Oppositionsseite zur Rechten und Linken des Sprechers. Im weiteren Sinne bezieht sich front bench auf die Spitzenpolitiker der verschiedenen Parteien, die auf dieser Bank sitzen (auch „frontbenchers" genannt), d. h. die Minister auf der einen Seite und die Mitglieder des Schattenkabinetts auf der anderen.

front desk (US) n Rezeption f

front door n Haustür f

frontier ['frʌntɪəʳ] n Grenze f

frontispiece ['frʌntɪspiːs] n Frontispiz nt

front page n erste Seite f, Titelseite f

front room (Brit) n Wohnzimmer nt

frontrunner ['frʌntrʌnəʳ] n Spitzenreiter m

front-wheel drive ['frʌntwiːl-] n (Aut) Vorderradantrieb m

frost [frɒst] n Frost m; (also: **hoarfrost**) Raureif m

frostbite ['frɒstbaɪt] n Erfrierungen pl

frosted ['frɒstɪd] adj (glass) Milch-; (esp US) glasiert, mit Zuckerguss überzogen

frosting ['frɒstɪŋ] (esp US) n Zuckerguss m

frosty ['frɒstɪ] adj frostig; (look) eisig; (window) bereift

froth [frɒθ] n Schaum m

frothy ['frɒθɪ] adj schäumend

frown [fraʊn] n Stirnrunzeln nt ▷ vi die Stirn runzeln
  ▶ **frown on** vt fus missbilligen

froze [frəʊz] pt of **freeze**

frozen ['frəʊzn] pp of **freeze** ▷ adj tiefgekühlt; (food) Tiefkühl-; (Comm) eingefroren

FRS n abbr (Brit: = Fellow of the Royal Society) Auszeichnung für Naturwissenschaftler; (US: = Federal Reserve System) amerikanische Zentralbank

frugal ['fruːgl] adj genügsam; (meal) einfach

fruit [fruːt] n inv Frucht f; (collectively) Obst nt; (fig: results) Früchte pl

fruiterer ['fruːtərəʳ] (esp Brit) n Obsthändler(in) m(f)

fruit fly n Fruchtfliege f

fruitful ['fruːtful] adj fruchtbar

fruition [fruːˈɪʃən] n: **to come to ~** (plan) Wirklichkeit werden; (efforts) Früchte tragen; (hope) in Erfüllung gehen

fruit juice n Fruchtsaft m

fruitless ['fruːtlɪs] adj fruchtlos, ergebnislos

fruit machine (Brit) n Spielautomat m

fruit salad n Obstsalat m

fruity ['fruːtɪ] adj (taste, smell etc) Frucht-, Obst-; (wine) fruchtig; (voice, laugh) volltönend

frump [frʌmp] n: **to feel a ~** sich dat wie eine Vogelscheuche vorkommen

frustrate [frʌsˈtreɪt] vt frustrieren; (attempt) vereiteln; (plan) durchkreuzen

frustrated [frʌsˈtreɪtɪd] adj frustriert

frustrating [frʌsˈtreɪtɪŋ] adj frustrierend

frustration [frʌsˈtreɪʃən] n Frustration f; (of attempt) Vereitelung f; (of plan) Zerschlagung f

fry [fraɪ] (pt, pp **fried**) vt braten; see also **small**

frying pan ['fraɪɪŋ-] n Bratpfanne f

FT (Brit) n abbr (= Financial Times) Wirtschaftszeitung; **the FT index** der Aktienindex der „Financial Times"

ft. abbr = **foot; feet**

FTC (US) n abbr = **Federal Trade Commission**

FTSE 100 Index n Aktienindex der "Financial Times"

fuchsia ['fjuːʃə] n Fuchsie f

fuck [fʌk] (inf!) vt, vi ficken (!); ~ **off!** (inf!) verpiss dich! (!)

fuddled ['fʌdld] adj verwirrt

fuddy-duddy ['fʌdɪdʌdɪ] (pej) n Langweiler m

fudge [fʌdʒ] n Fondant m ▷ vt (issue, problem) ausweichen +dat, aus dem Weg gehen +dat

fuel ['fjʊəl] n Brennstoff m; (for vehicle) Kraftstoff m; (: petrol) Benzin nt; (for aircraft, rocket) Treibstoff m ▷ vt (furnace etc) betreiben; (aircraft, ship etc) antreiben

fuel oil n Gasöl nt

fuel poverty n durch hohe Energiekosten verursachte Armut

fuel pump n (Aut) Benzinpumpe f

fuel tank n Öltank m; (in vehicle) (Benzin)tank m

fug [fʌg] (Brit: inf) n Mief m (inf)

fugitive ['fjuːdʒɪtɪv] n Flüchtling m

fulfil, (US) **fulfill** [ful'fɪl] vt erfüllen; (order) ausführen

fulfilled [ful'fɪld] adj ausgefüllt

fulfilment, (US) **fulfillment** [ful'fɪlmənt] n Erfüllung f

full [ful] adj voll; (complete) vollständig; (skirt) weit; (life) ausgefüllt ▷ adv: **to know ~ well that ...** sehr wohl wissen, dass ...; ~ **up** (hotel etc) ausgebucht; **I'm ~ (up)** ich bin satt; **a ~ two hours** volle zwei Stunden; ~ **marks** die beste Note, ≈ eine Eins; (fig) höchstes Lob nt; **at ~ speed** in voller Fahrt; **in ~** ganz, vollständig; **to pay in ~** den vollen Betrag bezahlen; **to write one's name** etc **in ~** seinen Namen etc ausschreiben

fullback ['fulbæk] n (Rugby, Football) Verteidiger m

full-blooded ['ful'blʌdɪd] adj (vigorous) kräftig; (virile) vollblütig

full board n Vollpension f

full-cream ['ful'kriːm] adj: ~ **milk** (Brit) Vollmilch f

full employment n Vollbeschäftigung f

full grown adj ausgewachsen

full-length ['ful'leŋθ] adj (film) abendfüllend; (coat) lang; (portrait) lebensgroß; (mirror) groß

full moon n Vollmond m

fullness ['fulnɪs] n: **in the ~ of time** zu gegebener Zeit

full-page ['fulpeɪdʒ] adj ganzseitig

full-scale ['fulskeɪl] adj (war) richtig; (attack) Groß-; (model) in Originalgröße; (search) groß angelegt

full-sized ['ful'saɪzd] adj lebensgroß

full stop n Punkt m

full-time ['ful'taɪm] adj (work) Ganztags-; (study) Voll- ▷ adv ganztags

fully ['fulɪ] adv völlig; ~ **as big as** mindestens

so groß wie

fully fledged [-'flɛdʒd] *adj* richtiggehend; (*doctor etc*) voll qualifiziert; (*member*) Voll-; (*bird*) flügge

fulsome ['fulsəm] (*pej*) *adj* übertrieben

fumble ['fʌmbl] *vi*: **to ~ with** herumfummeln an +*dat* ▷ *vt* (*ball*) nicht sicher fangen

fume [fju:m] *vi* wütend sein, kochen (*inf*)

fumes [fju:mz] *npl* (*of fire*) Rauch *m*; (*of fuel*) Dämpfe *pl*; (*of car*) Abgase *pl*

fumigate ['fju:mɪgeɪt] *vt* ausräuchern

fun [fʌn] *n* Spaß *m*; **he's good ~ (to be with)** es macht viel Spaß, mit ihm zusammen zu sein; **for ~** aus *or* zum Spaß; **it's not much ~** es macht keinen Spaß; **to make ~ of, to poke ~ at** sich lustig machen über +*acc*

function ['fʌŋkʃən] *n* Funktion *f*; (*social occasion*) Veranstaltung *f*, Feier *f* ▷ *vi* funktionieren; **to ~ as** (*thing*) dienen als; (*person*) fungieren als

functional ['fʌŋkʃənl] *adj* (*operational*) funktionsfähig; (*practical*) funktionell, zweckmäßig

functional food *adj* Functional Food *nt*, Funktionsnahrung *f*

function key *n* (*Comput*) Funktionstaste *f*

fund [fʌnd] *n* (*of money*) Fonds *m*; (*source, store*) Schatz *m*, Vorrat *m*; **funds** *npl* (*money*) Mittel *pl*, Gelder *pl*

fundamental [fʌndə'mentl] *adj* fundamental, grundlegend

fundamentalism [fʌndə'mentəlɪzəm] *n* Fundamentalismus *m*

fundamentalist [fʌndə'mentəlɪst] *n* Fundamentalist(in) *m(f)*

fundamentally [fʌndə'mentəlɪ] *adv* im Grunde; (*radically*) von Grund auf

fundamentals [fʌndə'mentlz] *npl* Grundbegriffe *pl*

funding ['fʌndɪŋ] *n* Finanzierung *f*

fund-raising ['fʌndreɪzɪŋ] *n* Geldbeschaffung *f*

funeral ['fju:nərəl] *n* Beerdigung *f*

funeral director *n* Beerdigungsunternehmer(in) *m(f)*

funeral parlour *n* Leichenhalle *f*

funeral service *n* Trauergottesdienst *m*

funereal [fju:'nɪərɪəl] *adj* traurig, trübselig

funfair ['fʌnfɛər] (*Brit*) *n* Jahrmarkt *m*

fungi ['fʌŋgaɪ] *npl of* **fungus**

fungus ['fʌŋgəs] (*pl* **fungi**) *n* Pilz *m*; (*mould*) Schimmel(pilz) *m*

funicular [fju:'nɪkjulər] *n* (*also:* **funicular railway**) Seilbahn *f*

funky ['fʌŋkɪ] *adj* (*music*) Funk-

funnel ['fʌnl] *n* Trichter *m*; (*of ship*) Schornstein *m*

funnily ['fʌnɪlɪ] *adv* komisch; **~ enough** komischerweise

funny ['fʌnɪ] *adj* komisch; (*strange*) seltsam, komisch

funny bone *n* Musikantenknochen *m*

fun run *n* ≈ Volkslauf *m*

fur [fə:ʳ] *n* Fell *nt*, Pelz *m*; (*Brit: in kettle etc*) Kesselstein *m*

fur coat *n* Pelzmantel *m*

furious ['fjuərɪəs] *adj* wütend; (*exchange, argument*) heftig; (*effort*) riesig; (*speed*) rasend; **to be ~ with sb** wütend auf jdn sein

furiously ['fjuərɪəslɪ] *adv* (*see adj*) wütend; (*struggle etc*) heftig; (*run*) schnell

furl [fə:l] *vt* (*Naut*) einrollen

furlong ['fə:lɔŋ] *n* Achtelmeile *f* (= 201,17 m)

furlough ['fə:ləu] *n* (*Mil*) Urlaub *m*

furnace ['fə:nɪs] *n* (*in foundry*) Schmelzofen *m*; (*in power plant*) Hochofen *m*

furnish ['fə:nɪʃ] *vt* einrichten; (*room*) möblieren; **to ~ sb with sth** jdm etw liefern; **~ed flat, ~ed apartment** (*US*) möblierte Wohnung *f*

furnishings ['fə:nɪʃɪŋz] *npl* Einrichtung *f*

furniture ['fə:nɪtʃər] *n* Möbel *pl*; **piece of ~** Möbelstück *nt*

furniture polish *n* Möbelpolitur *f*

furore [fjuə'rɔ:rɪ] *n* (*protests*) Proteste *pl*; (*enthusiasm*) Furore *f or nt*

furrier ['fʌrɪəʳ] *n* Kürschner(in) *m(f)*

furrow ['fʌrəu] *n* Furche *f*; (*in skin*) Runzel *f* ▷ *vt* (*brow*) runzeln

furry ['fə:rɪ] *adj* (*coat, tail*) flauschig; (*animal*) Pelz-; (*toy*) Plüsch-

further ['fə:ðəʳ] *adj* weitere(r, s) ▷ *adv* weiter; (*moreover*) darüber hinaus ▷ *vt* fördern; **until ~ notice** bis auf Weiteres; **how much ~ is it?** wie weit ist es noch?; **~ to your letter of ...** (*Comm*) Bezug nehmend auf Ihr Schreiben vom ...

further education (*Brit*) *n* Weiterbildung *f*, Fortbildung *f*

furthermore [fə:ðə'mɔ:ʳ] *adv* außerdem

furthermost ['fə:ðəməust] *adj* äußerste(r, s)

furthest ['fə:ðɪst] *superl of* **far**

furtive ['fə:tɪv] *adj* verstohlen

furtively ['fə:tɪvlɪ] *adv* verstohlen

fury ['fjuərɪ] *n* Wut *f*; **to be in a ~** in Rage sein

fuse, (*US*) **fuze** [fju:z] *n* (*Elec*) Sicherung *f*; (*for bomb etc*) Zündschnur *f* ▷ *vt* (*pieces of metal*) verschmelzen; (*fig*) vereinigen ▷ *vi* (*pieces of metal*) sich verbinden; (*fig*) sich vereinigen; **to ~ the lights** (*Brit*) die Sicherung durchbrennen lassen; **a ~ has blown** eine Sicherung ist durchgebrannt

fuse box *n* Sicherungskasten *m*

fuselage ['fju:zəla:ʒ] *n* Rumpf *m*

fuse wire *n* Schmelzdraht *m*

fusillade [fju:zɪ'leɪd] *n* Salve *f*

fusion ['fju:ʒən] *n* Verschmelzung *f*; (*also:* **nuclear fusion**) Kernfusion *f*

fuss [fʌs] *n* Theater *nt* (*inf*) ▷ *vi* sich (unnötig) aufregen ▷ *vt* keine Ruhe lassen +*dat*; **to make a ~** Krach schlagen (*inf*); **to make a ~ of sb** viel Getue um jdn machen (*inf*)
▷ **fuss over** *vt fus* bemuttern

fusspot ['fʌspɔt] *n* Nörgler(in) *m(f)*

fussy ['fʌsɪ] *adj* kleinlich, pingelig (*inf*); (*clothes, room etc*) verspielt; **I'm not ~** es ist mir egal

fusty ['fʌstɪ] *adj* muffig

futile ['fju:taɪl] *adj* vergeblich; (*existence*)

sinnlos; *(comment)* zwecklos
futility [fjuːˈtɪlɪtɪ] *n (see adj)* Vergeblichkeit *f*;
Sinnlosigkeit *f*; Zwecklosigkeit *f*
futon [ˈfuːtɒn] *n* Futon *m*
future [ˈfjuːtʃə] *adj* zukünftig ▷ *n* Zukunft
f; *(Ling)* Futur *nt*; **futures** *npl (Comm)*
Termingeschäfte *pl*; **in (the) ~** in Zukunft;
in the near ~ in der nahen Zukunft; **in the
immediate ~** sehr bald

futuristic [fjuːtʃəˈrɪstɪk] *adj* futuristisch
fuze [fjuːz] *(US) n, vt, vi* = **fuse**
fuzz [fʌz] *(inf) n (police)*: **the ~** die Bullen *pl*
fuzzy [ˈfʌzɪ] *adj* verschwommen; *(hair)* kraus;
(thoughts) verworren
fwd. *abbr* = **forward**
fwy *(US) abbr* = **freeway**
FYI *abbr* (= *for your information*) zu Ihrer
Information

Gg

G¹, g¹ [dʒiː] n (letter) G nt, g nt; **G for George** = G wie Gustav

G² [dʒiː] n (Mus) G nt, g nt

G³ [dʒiː] n abbr (Brit: Scol) = **good**; (US: Cine: = general (audience)) Klassifikation für jugendfreie Filme; (Phys): **G-force** g-Druck m

g² abbr (= gram(me)) g; (Phys) = **gravity**

G8 n abbr (Pol: = Group of Eight) G8 f

G20 n abbr (Pol: = Group of Twenty) G20 f

GA (US) n abbr (Post) = Georgia

gab [gæb] (inf) n: **to have the gift of the ~** reden können, nicht auf den Mund gefallen sein

gabble ['gæbl] vi brabbeln (inf)

gaberdine [gæbə'diːn] n Gabardine m

gable ['geɪbl] n Giebel m

Gabon [gə'bɔn] n Gabun nt

gad about [gæd-] (inf) vi herumziehen

gadget ['gædʒɪt] n Gerät nt

gadgetry ['gædʒɪtrɪ] n Geräte pl

Gaelic ['geɪlɪk] adj gälisch ▷ n (Ling) Gälisch nt

gaffe [gæf] n Fauxpas m

gaffer ['gæfər] (Brit: inf) n (boss) Chef m; (foreman) Vorarbeiter m; (old man) Alte(r) m

gag [gæg] n Knebel m; (joke) Gag m ▷ vt knebeln ▷ vi würgen

gaga ['gɑːgɑː] (inf) adj: **to go ~** verkalken

gage [geɪdʒ] (US) n, vt = **gauge**

gaiety ['geɪtɪ] n Fröhlichkeit f

gaily ['geɪlɪ] adv fröhlich; **~ coloured** farbenfroh, farbenprächtig

gain [geɪn] n Gewinn m ▷ vt gewinnen ▷ vi (clock, watch) vorgehen; **to do sth for ~** etw aus Berechnung tun; (for money) etw des Geldes wegen tun; **~ (in)** (increase) Zunahme f (an +dat); (in rights, conditions) Verbesserung f +gen; **to ~ ground** (an) Boden gewinnen; **to ~ speed** schneller werden; **to ~ weight** zunehmen; **to ~ 3lbs (in weight)** 3 Pfund zunehmen; **to ~ (in) confidence** sicherer werden; **to ~ from sth** von etw profitieren; **to ~ in strength** stärker werden; **to ~ by doing sth** davon profitieren, etw zu tun; **to ~ on sb** jdn einholen

gainful ['geɪnful] adj: **~ employment** Erwerbstätigkeit f

gainfully ['geɪnfəlɪ] adv: **~ employed** erwerbstätig

gainsay [geɪn'seɪ] (irreg: like **say**) vt widersprechen +dat; (fact) leugnen

gait [geɪt] n Gang m; **to walk with a slow/confident ~** mit langsamen Schritten/selbstbewusst gehen

gal. abbr = **gallon**

gala ['gɑːlə] n Galaveranstaltung f; **swimming ~** großes Schwimmfest nt

Galapagos [gə'læpəgəs] n die Galapagosinseln pl

Galapagos Islands npl: **(the) ~** = **Galapagos**

galaxy ['gæləksɪ] n Galaxis f, Sternsystem nt

gale [geɪl] n Sturm m; **~ force 10** Sturmstärke 10

gall [gɔːl] n Galle f; (fig: impudence) Frechheit f ▷ vt maßlos ärgern

gall. abbr = **gallon**

gallant ['gælənt] adj tapfer; (polite) galant

gallantry ['gæləntrɪ] n (see adj) Tapferkeit f; Galanterie f

gall bladder n Gallenblase f

galleon ['gæliən] n Galeone f

gallery ['gælərɪ] n (also: **art gallery**) Galerie f, Museum nt; (private) (Privat)galerie f; (in hall, church) Galerie f; (in theatre) oberster Rang m, Balkon m

galley ['gælɪ] n Kombüse f; (ship) Galeere f; (also: **galley proof**) Fahne f, Fahnenabzug m

Gallic ['gælɪk] adj gallisch; (French) französisch

galling ['gɔːlɪŋ] adj äußerst ärgerlich

gallon ['gæln] n Gallone f (Brit = 4,5 l, US = 3,8 l)

gallop ['gæləp] n Galopp m ▷ vi galoppieren; **~ing inflation** galoppierende Inflation f

gallows ['gæləuz] n Galgen m

gallstone ['gɔːlstəun] n Gallenstein m

Gallup poll ['gæləp-] n Meinungsumfrage f

galore [gə'lɔːr] adv in Hülle und Fülle

galvanize ['gælvənaɪz] vt (fig) mobilisieren; **to ~ sb into action** jdn plötzlich aktiv werden lassen

galvanized ['gælvənaɪzd] adj (metal) galvanisiert

Gambia ['gæmbɪə] n Gambia nt

gambit ['gæmbɪt] n: **(opening) ~** (einleitender) Schachzug m; (in conversation) (einleitende) Bemerkung f

gamble ['gæmbl] n Risiko nt ▷ vt einsetzen ▷ vi ein Risiko eingehen; (bet) spielen; (on horses etc) wetten; **to ~ on the Stock Exchange** an der Börse spekulieren; **to ~ on sth** (horses, race) auf etw acc wetten; (success, outcome etc) sich auf etw acc verlassen

gambler ['gæmblə'] n Spieler(in) m(f)

gambling ['gæmblɪŋ] n Spielen nt; (on horses etc) Wetten nt

gambol ['gæmbl] vi herumtollen

game [geɪm] n Spiel nt; (sport) Sport m; (strategy, scheme) Vorhaben nt; (Culin, Hunting) Wild nt ▷ adj: **to be ~ (for)** mitmachen (bei); **games** npl (Scol) Sport m; **to play a ~ of football/ tennis** Fußball/(eine Partie) Tennis spielen; **big ~** Großwild nt

game bird n Federwild nt no pl

gamekeeper ['geɪmkiːpə'] n Wildhüter(in) m(f)

gamely ['geɪmlɪ] adv mutig

gamer ['geɪmə'] n Gamer(in) m(f), Computerspieler(in) m(f)

game reserve n Wildschutzreservat nt

games console ['geɪmz-] n (Comput) Gameboy® m, Konsole f

game show n (TV) Spielshow f

gamesmanship ['geɪmzmənʃɪp] n Gerissenheit f beim Spiel

gaming ['geɪmɪŋ] n (gambling) Spielen nt; (Comput) Computerspielen nt

gammon ['gæmən] n Schinken m

gamut ['gæmət] n Skala f; **to run the ~ of** die ganze Skala +gen durchlaufen

gander ['gændə'] n Gänserich m

gang [gæŋ] n Bande f; (of friends) Haufen m; (of workmen) Kolonne f
▶ **gang up** vi: **to ~ up on sb** sich gegen jdn zusammentun

Ganges ['gændʒiːz] n: **the ~** der Ganges

gangland ['gæŋlænd] adj (killer, boss) Unterwelt-

gangling ['gæŋglɪŋ], **gangly** ['gæŋglɪ] adj schlaksig, hoch aufgeschossen

gangplank ['gæŋplæŋk] n Laufplanke f

gangrene ['gæŋgriːn] n (Med) Brand m

gangster ['gæŋstə'] n Gangster m

gangway ['gæŋweɪ] n Laufplanke f, Gangway f; (in cinema, bus, plane etc) Gang m

gantry ['gæntrɪ] n (for crane) Portal nt; (for railway signal) Signalbrücke f; (for rocket) Abschussrampe f

GAO (US) n abbr (= General Accounting Office) Rechnungshof der USA

gaol [dʒeɪl] (Brit) n, vt = **jail**

gap [gæp] n Lücke f; (in time) Pause f; (difference): **~ (between)** Kluft f (zwischen +dat)

gape [geɪp] vi starren, gaffen; (hole) gähnen; (shirt) offen stehen

gaping ['geɪpɪŋ] adj (hole) gähnend; (shirt) offen

garage ['gærɑːʒ] n Garage f; (for car repairs) (Reparatur)werkstatt f; (petrol station) Tankstelle f

garb [gɑːb] n Gewand nt, Kluft f

garbage ['gɑːbɪdʒ] n (US: rubbish) Abfall m, Müll m; (inf: nonsense) Blödsinn m, Quatsch m; (fig: film, book) Schund m

garbage can (US) n Mülleimer m, Abfalleimer m

garbage collector (US) n Müllmann m

garbage disposal, **garbage disposal unit** n Müllschlucker m

garbage truck (US) n Müllwagen m

garbled ['gɑːbld] adj (account) wirr; (message) unverständlich

garden ['gɑːdn] n Garten m ▷ vi gärtnern; **gardens** npl (public park) Park m; (private) Gartenanlagen pl; **she was ~ing** sie arbeitete im Garten

garden centre n Gartencenter nt

garden city n Gartenstadt f

gardener ['gɑːdnə'] n Gärtner(in) m(f)

gardening ['gɑːdnɪŋ] n Gartenarbeit f

gargle ['gɑːgl] vi gurgeln ▷ n Gurgelwasser nt

gargoyle ['gɑːgɔɪl] n Wasserspeier m

garish ['gɛərɪʃ] adj grell

garland ['gɑːlənd] n Kranz m

garlic ['gɑːlɪk] n Knoblauch m

garment ['gɑːmənt] n Kleidungsstück nt

garner ['gɑːnə'] vt sammeln

garnish ['gɑːnɪʃ] vt garnieren

garret ['gærɪt] n Dachkammer f, Mansarde f

garrison ['gærɪsn] n Garnison f

garrulous ['gærʊləs] adj geschwätzig

garter ['gɑːtə'] n Strumpfband nt; (US: suspender) Strumpfhalter m

garter belt (US) n Strumpfgürtel m

gas [gæs] n Gas nt; (US: gasoline) Benzin nt ▷ vt mit Gas vergiften; (Mil) vergasen; **to be given ~** (as anaesthetic) Lachgas bekommen

gas cooker (Brit) n Gasherd m

gas cylinder n Gasflasche f

gaseous ['gæsɪəs] adj gasförmig

gas fire (Brit) n Gasofen m

gas-fired ['gæsfaɪəd] adj (heater etc) Gas-

gash [gæʃ] n klaffende Wunde f; (tear) tiefer Schlitz m ▷ vt aufschlitzen

gasket ['gæskɪt] n Dichtung f

gas mask n Gasmaske f

gas meter n Gaszähler m

gasoline ['gæsəliːn] (US) n Benzin nt

gasp [gɑːsp] n tiefer Atemzug m ▷ vi keuchen; (in surprise) nach Luft schnappen; **to give a ~ (of shock)** (vor Schreck) die Luft anhalten; **to be ~ing for** sich sehnen nach +dat
▶ **gasp out** vt hervorstoßen

gas permeable adj (lenses) luftdurchlässig

gas ring n Gasbrenner m

gas station (US) n Tankstelle f

gas stove n (cooker) Gasherd m; (for camping) Gaskocher m

gassy ['gæsɪ] adj (drink) kohlensäurehaltig

gas tank n Benzintank m

gastric ['gæstrɪk] adj (upset, ulcer etc) Magen-

gastric flu n Darmgrippe f

gastroenteritis ['gæstrəʊɛntə'raɪtɪs] n Magen-Darm-Katarrh m

gastronomy [gæs'trɔnəmɪ] n Gastronomie f

gasworks ['gæswəːks] n Gaswerk nt

gate [geɪt] n (of garden) Pforte f; (of field) Gatter

g

nt; (of building) Tor nt; (at airport) Flugsteig m; (of level crossing) Schranke f; (of lock) Tor nt

gateau ['gætəu] (pl **-x**) n Torte f

gate-crash ['geɪtkræʃ] (Brit) vt (party) ohne Einladung besuchen; (concert) eindringen in +acc ▷ vi ohne Einladung hingehen; eindringen

gate-crasher ['geɪtkræʃəʳ] n ungeladener Gast m

gatehouse ['geɪthaus] n Pförtnerhaus nt

gateway ['geɪtweɪ] n (also fig) Tor nt

gather ['gæðəʳ] vt sammeln; (flowers, fruit) pflücken; (understand) schließen; (Sewing) kräuseln ▷ vi (assemble) sich versammeln; (dust) sich ansammeln; (clouds) sich zusammenziehen; **to ~ (from)** schließen (aus); **to ~ (that)** annehmen(, dass); **as far as I can ~** so wie ich es sehe; **to ~ speed** schneller werden

gathering ['gæðərɪŋ] n Versammlung f

GATT [gæt] n abbr (= General Agreement on Tariffs and Trade) GATT nt

gauche [gəuʃ] adj linkisch

gaudy ['gɔːdɪ] adj knallig

gauge, (US) **gage** [geɪdʒ] n Messgerät nt, Messinstrument nt; (Rail) Spurweite f ▷ vt messen; (fig) beurteilen; **petrol ~, fuel ~, gas gage** (US) Benzinuhr f; **to ~ the right moment** den richtigen Moment abwägen

Gaul [gɔːl] n Gallien nt; (person) Gallier(in) m(f)

gaunt [gɔːnt] adj (haggard) hager; (bare, stark) öde

gauntlet ['gɔːntlɪt] n (Stulpen)handschuh m; (fig): **to run the ~** Spießruten laufen; **to throw down the ~** den Fehdehandschuh hinwerfen

gauze [gɔːz] n Gaze f

gave [geɪv] pt of **give**

gavel ['gævl] n Hammer m

gawk [gɔːk] (inf) vi gaffen, glotzen

gawky ['gɔːkɪ] adj schlaksig

gawp [gɔːp] vi: **to ~ at** angaffen, anglotzen (inf)

gay [geɪ] adj (homosexual) schwul; (cheerful) fröhlich; (dress) bunt

gay marriage adj gleichgeschlechtliche Ehe f, Homoehe f (inf)

gaze [geɪz] n Blick m ▷ vi: **to ~ at sth** etw anstarren

gazelle [gə'zɛl] n Gazelle f

gazette [gə'zɛt] n Zeitung f; (official) Amtsblatt nt

gazetteer [gæzə'tɪəʳ] n alphabetisches Ortsverzeichnis nt

gazump [gə'zʌmp] (Brit) vt: **to be ~ed** ein mündlich zugesagtes Haus an einen Höherbietenden verlieren

GB abbr (= Great Britain) GB

GBH (Brit) n abbr (Law) = **grievous bodily harm**

GC (Brit) n abbr (= George Cross) britische Tapferkeitsmedaille

GCE (Brit) n abbr (= General Certificate of Education) Schulabschlusszeugnis, ≈ Abitur nt

GCHQ (Brit) n abbr (= Government Communications

Headquarters) Zentralstelle des britischen Nachrichtendienstes

GCSE (Brit) n abbr (= General Certificate of Secondary Education) Schulabschlusszeugnis, ≈ mittlere Reife f

Gdns abbr (in street names: = Gardens) ≈ Str.

GDP n abbr = **gross domestic product**

GDR n abbr (Hist: = German Democratic Republic) DDR f

gear [gɪəʳ] n (equipment) Ausrüstung f; (belongings) Sachen pl; (Tech) Getriebe nt; (Aut) Gang m; (on bicycle) Gangschaltung f ▷ vt (fig: adapt): **to ~ sth to** etw ausrichten auf +acc; **top/low/bottom ~, high/low/bottom ~** (US) hoher/niedriger/erster Gang; **to put a car into ~** einen Gang einlegen; **to leave the car in ~** den Gang eingelegt lassen; **to leave out of ~** im Leerlauf lassen; **our service is ~ed to meet the needs of the disabled** unser Betrieb ist auf die Bedürfnisse von Behinderten eingerichtet

▶ **gear up** vt, vi: **to ~ (o.s.) up (to)** sich vorbereiten (auf +acc) ▷ vt: **to ~ o.s. up to do sth** sich darauf vorbereiten, etw zu tun

gearbox ['gɪəbɒks] n Getriebe nt

gear lever, (US) **gear shift** n Schalthebel m

GED (US) n abbr (Scol: = general educational development) allgemeine Lernentwicklung

geek-speak ['giːkspiːk] n (US: inf) Fachchinesisch nt

geese [giːs] npl of **goose**

geezer ['giːzəʳ] (inf) n Kerl m, Typ m

Geiger counter ['gaɪgə-] n Geigerzähler m

gel [dʒɛl] n Gel nt

gelatin, gelatine ['dʒɛlətiːn] n Gelatine f

gelignite ['dʒɛlɪgnaɪt] n Plastiksprengstoff m

gem [dʒɛm] n Edelstein m; **she/the house is a ~** (fig) sie/das Haus ist ein Juwel; **a ~ of an idea** eine ausgezeichnete Idee

Gemini ['dʒɛmɪnaɪ] n (Astrol) Zwillinge pl; **to be ~** (ein) Zwilling sein

gen [dʒɛn] (Brit: inf) n: **to give sb the ~ on sth** jdn über etw acc informieren

Gen. abbr (Mil: = General) Gen.

gen. abbr = **general, generally**

gender ['dʒɛndəʳ] n Geschlecht nt

gene [dʒiːn] n Gen nt

genealogy [dʒiːnɪ'ælədʒɪ] n Genealogie f, Stammbaumforschung f; (family history) Stammbaum m

general ['dʒɛnərl] n General m ▷ adj allgemein; (widespread) weitverbreitet; (non-specific) generell; **in ~** im Allgemeinen; **the ~ public** die Öffentlichkeit, die Allgemeinheit; **~ audit** (Comm) Jahresabschlussprüfung f

general anaesthetic n Vollnarkose f

general delivery (US) n: **to send sth ~** etw postlagernd schicken

general election n Parlamentswahlen pl

generalization ['dʒɛnrəlaɪ'zeɪʃən] n Verallgemeinerung f

generalize ['dʒɛnrəlaɪz] vi verallgemeinern

generally ['dʒɛnrəlɪ] adv im Allgemeinen

general manager n Hauptgeschäftsführer(in)

m(f)

general practitioner n praktischer Arzt m, praktische Ärztin f

general strike n Generalstreik m

generate ['dʒɛnəreɪt] vt erzeugen; (jobs) schaffen; (profits) einbringen

generation [dʒɛnə'reɪʃən] n Generation f; (of electricity etc) Erzeugung f

generator ['dʒɛnəreɪtəʳ] n Generator m

generic [dʒɪ'nɛrɪk] adj allgemein; **~ term** Oberbegriff m

generosity [dʒɛnə'rɒsɪtɪ] n Großzügigkeit f

generous ['dʒɛnərəs] adj großzügig; (measure, remuneration) reichlich

genesis ['dʒɛnɪsɪs] n Entstehung f

genetic [dʒɪ'nɛtɪk] adj genetisch

genetically adv genetisch; **~ modified** genmanipuliert

genetic engineering n Gentechnologie f

genetic fingerprint n genetischer Fingerabdruck m

genetics [dʒɪ'nɛtɪks] n Genetik f

Geneva [dʒɪ'niːvə] n Genf nt

genial ['dʒiːnɪəl] adj freundlich; (climate) angenehm

genitals ['dʒɛnɪtlz] npl Genitalien pl, Geschlechtsteile pl

genitive ['dʒɛnɪtɪv] n Genitiv m

genius ['dʒiːnɪəs] n Talent nt; (person) Genie nt

Genoa ['dʒɛnəuə] n Genua nt

genocide ['dʒɛnəusaɪd] n Völkermord m

Genoese [dʒɛnəu'iːz] adj genuesisch ▷ n inv Genuese m, Genuesin f

gent [dʒɛnt] (Brit: inf) n abbr = **gentleman**

genteel [dʒɛn'tiːl] adj vornehm, fein

gentle ['dʒɛntl] adj sanft; (movement, breeze) leicht; **a ~ hint** ein zarter Hinweis

gentleman ['dʒɛntlmən] (irreg: like **man**) n Herr m; (referring to social position or good manners) Gentleman m; **~'s agreement** Vereinbarung f auf Treu und Glauben

gentlemanly ['dʒɛntlmənlɪ] adj zuvorkommend

gentleness ['dʒɛntlnɪs] n (see adj) Sanftheit f; Leichtheit f; Zartheit f

gently ['dʒɛntlɪ] adv (see adj) sanft; leicht; zart

gentry ['dʒɛntrɪ] n inv: **the ~** die Gentry, der niedere Adel

gents [dʒɛnts] n: **the ~** die Herrentoilette

genuine ['dʒɛnjuɪn] adj echt; (person) natürlich, aufrichtig

genuinely ['dʒɛnjuɪnlɪ] adv wirklich

geographer [dʒɪ'ɒgrəfəʳ] n Geograf(in) m(f)

geographic [dʒɪə'græfɪk], **geographical** [dʒɪə'græfɪkl] adj geografisch

geography [dʒɪ'ɒgrəfɪ] n Geografie f; (Scol) Erdkunde f

geological [dʒɪə'lɒdʒɪkl] adj geologisch

geologist [dʒɪ'ɒlədʒɪst] n Geologe m, Geologin f

geology [dʒɪ'ɒlədʒɪ] n Geologie f

geometric [dʒɪə'mɛtrɪk], **geometrical** [dʒɪə'mɛtrɪkl] adj geometrisch

geometry [dʒɪ'ɒmətrɪ] n Geometrie f

Geordie ['dʒɔːdɪ] (inf) n aus dem Gebiet von Newcastle stammende oder dort wohnhafte Person

Georgia ['dʒɔːdʒə] n (in Eastern Europe) Georgien nt

Georgian ['dʒɔːdʒən] adj georgisch ▷ n Georgier(in) m(f); (Ling) Georgisch nt

geranium [dʒɪ'reɪnɪəm] n Geranie f

geriatric [dʒɛrɪ'ætrɪk] adj geriatrisch ▷ n Greis(in) m(f)

germ [dʒəːm] n Bazillus m; (Biol: fig) Keim m

German ['dʒəːmən] adj deutsch ▷ n Deutsche(r) f(m); (Ling) Deutsch nt

German Democratic Republic n (formerly) Deutsche Demokratische Republik f

germane [dʒəː'meɪn] adj: **~ (to)** von Belang (für)

German measles (Brit) n Röteln pl

German Shepherd, German Shepherd dog (esp US) n Schäferhund m

Germany ['dʒəːmənɪ] n Deutschland nt

germinate ['dʒəːmɪneɪt] vi keimen; (fig) aufkeimen

germination [dʒəːmɪ'neɪʃən] n Keimung f

germ warfare n biologische Kriegsführung f, Bakterienkrieg m

gerrymandering ['dʒɛrɪmændərɪŋ] n Wahlkreisschiebungen pl

gestation [dʒɛs'teɪʃən] n (of animals) Trächtigkeit f; (of humans) Schwangerschaft f

gesticulate [dʒɛs'tɪkjuleɪt] vi gestikulieren

gesture ['dʒɛstjəʳ] n Geste f; **as a ~ of friendship** als Zeichen der Freundschaft

○ KEYWORD

get [gɛt] (pt, pp **got**, US pp **gotten**) vi **1** (become, be) werden; **to get old/tired/cold** alt/müde/ kalt werden; **to get dirty** sich schmutzig machen; **to get killed** getötet werden; **to get married** heiraten

2 (go): **to get (from …) to …** (von …) nach … kommen; **how did you get here?** wie sind Sie hierhin gekommen?

3 (begin): **to get to know sb** jdn kennenlernen; **let's get going** or **started** fangen wir an!

▷ modal aux vb: **you've got to do it** du musst es tun

▷ vt **1**: **to get sth done** (do oneself) etw gemacht bekommen; (have done) etw machen lassen; **to get one's hair cut** sich dat die Haare schneiden lassen; **to get the car going** or **to go** das Auto in Gang bringen; **to get sb to do sth** etw von jdm machen lassen; (persuade) jdn dazu bringen, etw zu tun

2 (obtain: money, permission, results) erhalten; (find: job, flat) finden; (fetch: person, doctor, object) holen; **to get sth for sb** jdm etw besorgen; **can I get you a drink?** kann ich Ihnen etwas zu trinken anbieten?

3 (receive, acquire: present, prize) bekommen; **how much did you get for the painting?** wie viel haben Sie für das Bild bekommen?

4 (catch) bekommen, kriegen (inf); (hit: target

575

etc) treffen; **to get sb by the arm/throat** jdn am Arm/Hals packen; **the bullet got him in the leg** die Kugel traf ihn ins Bein

5 (*take, move*) bringen; **to get sth to sb** jdm etw zukommen lassen

6 (*plane, bus etc: take*) nehmen; (: *catch*) bekommen

7 (*understand: joke etc*) verstehen; **I get it** ich verstehe

8 (*have, possess*): **to have got** haben; **how many have you got?** wie viele hast du?

▶ **get about** *vi* (*person*) herumkommen; (*news, rumour*) sich verbreiten

▶ **get across** *vt* (*message, meaning*) klarmachen

▶ **get along** *vi* (*be friends*) (*miteinander*) auskommen; (*depart*) sich auf den Weg machen

▶ **get around** *vt fus* = **get round**

▶ **get at** *vt fus* (*attack, criticize*) angreifen; (*reach*) herankommen an +*acc*; **what are you getting at?** worauf willst du hinaus?

▶ **get away** *vi* (*leave*) wegkommen; (*on holiday*) verreisen; (*escape*) entkommen

▶ **get away with** *vt fus* (*stolen goods*) entkommen mit; **he'll never get away with it!** damit kommt er nicht durch

▶ **get back** *vi* (*return*) zurückkommen

▷ *vt* (*regain*) zurückbekommen; **get back!** zurück!

▶ **get back at** (*inf*) *vt fus*: **to get back at sb for sth** jdm etw heimzahlen

▶ **get back to** *vt fus* (*return to*) zurückkehren zu; (*contact again*) zurückkommen auf +*acc*; **to get back to sleep** wieder einschlafen

▶ **get by** *vi* (*pass*) vorbeikommen; (*manage*) zurechtkommen; **I can get by in German** ich kann mich auf Deutsch verständlich machen

▶ **get down** *vi* (*from tree, ladder etc*) heruntersteigen; (*from horse*) absteigen; (*leave table*) aufstehen; (*bend down*) sich bücken; (*duck*) sich ducken

▷ *vt* (*depress: person*) fertigmachen; (*write*) aufschreiben

▶ **get down to** *vt fus*: **to get down to sth** (*work*) etw in Angriff nehmen; (*find time*) zu etw kommen; **to get down to business** (*fig*) zur Sache kommen

▶ **get in** *vi* (*be elected: candidate, party*) gewählt werden; (*arrive*) ankommen

▷ *vt* (*bring in: harvest*) einbringen; (: *shopping, supplies*) (herein)holen

▶ **get into** *vt fus* (*conversation, argument, fight*) geraten in +*acc*; (*vehicle*) einsteigen in +*acc*; (*clothes*) hineinkommen in +*acc*; **to get into bed** ins Bett gehen; **to get into the habit of doing sth** sich *dat* angewöhnen, etw zu tun

▶ **get off** *vi* (*from train etc*) aussteigen; (*escape punishment*) davonkommen

▷ *vt* (*remove: clothes*) ausziehen; (: *stain*) herausbekommen

▷ *vt fus* (*leave: train, bus*) aussteigen aus; **we get 3 days off at Christmas** zu Weihnachten bekommen wir 3 Tage frei; **to get off to a**

good start (*fig*) einen guten Anfang machen

▶ **get on** *vi* (*be friends*) (*miteinander*) auskommen

▷ *vt fus* (*bus, train*) einsteigen in +*acc*; **how are you getting on?** wie kommst du zurecht?; **time is getting on** es wird langsam spät

▶ **get on to** (*Brit*) *vt fus* (*subject, topic*) übergehen zu; (*contact: person*) sich in Verbindung setzen mit

▶ **get on with** *vt fus* (*person*) auskommen mit; (*meeting, work etc*) weitermachen mit

▶ **get out** *vi* (*leave: on foot*) hinausgehen; (*of vehicle*) aussteigen; (*news etc*) herauskommen

▷ *vt* (*take out: book etc*) herausholen; (*remove: stain*) herausbekommen

▶ **get out of** *vt fus* (*money: bank etc*) abheben von; (*avoid: duty etc*) herumkommen um

▷ *vt* (*extract: confession etc*) herausbekommen aus; (*derive: pleasure*) haben an +*dat*; (: *benefit*) haben von

▶ **get over** *vt fus* (*overcome*) überwinden; (: *illness*) sich erholen von; (*communicate: idea etc*) verständlich machen

▷ *vt*: **to get it over with** (*finish*) es hinter sich *acc* bringen

▶ **get round** *vt fus* (*law, rule*) umgehen; (*person*) herumkriegen

▶ **get round to** *vt fus*: **to get round to doing sth** dazu kommen, etw zu tun

▶ **get through** *vi* (*Tel*) durchkommen

▷ *vt fus* (*finish: work*) schaffen; (: *book*) lesen

▶ **get through to** *vt fus* (*Tel*) durchkommen zu; (*make o.s. understood*) durchdringen zu

▶ **get together** *vi* (*people*) zusammenkommen

▷ *vt* (*people*) zusammenbringen; (*project, plan etc*) zusammenstellen

▶ **get up** *vi* (*rise*) aufstehen

▷ *vt*: **to get up enthusiasm for sth** Begeisterung für etw aufbringen

▶ **get up to** *vt fus* (*prank etc*) anstellen

getaway ['gɛtəweɪ] *n*: **to make a/one's ~** sich davonmachen

getaway car *n* Fluchtauto *nt*

get-together ['gɛttəgɛðəʳ] *n* Treffen *nt*; (*party*) Party *f*

get-up ['gɛtʌp] (*inf*) *n* Aufmachung *f*

get-well card [gɛt'wɛl-] *n* Karte *f* mit Genesungswünschen

geyser ['giːzəʳ] *n* Geiser *m*; (*Brit: water heater*) Durchlauferhitzer *m*

Ghana ['gɑːnə] *n* Ghana *nt*

Ghanaian [gɑːˈneɪən] *adj* ghanaisch ▷ *n* Ghanaer(in) *m(f)*

ghastly ['gɑːstlɪ] *adj* grässlich; (*complexion*) totenblass; **you look ~!** (*ill*) du siehst grässlich aus!

gherkin ['gəːkɪn] *n* Gewürzgurke *f*

ghetto ['gɛtəu] *n* G(h)etto *nt*

ghetto blaster [-ˈblɑːstəʳ] (*inf*) *n* Gettoblaster *m*

ghost [gəust] *n* Geist *m*, Gespenst *nt* ▷ *vt* für jdn (als Ghostwriter) schreiben; **to give up the ~**

den Geist aufgeben

ghost town n Geisterstadt f

ghostwriter ['gəʊstraɪtə'] n Ghostwriter(in) m(f)

ghoul [gu:l] n böser Geist m

ghoulish ['gu:lɪʃ] adj makaber

GHQ n abbr (Mil: = General Headquarters) Hauptquartier nt

GHz abbr (= gigahertz) GHz

GI (US: inf) n abbr (= government issue) GI m

giant ['dʒaɪənt] n (also fig) Riese m ▷ adj riesig, riesenhaft; **~ (size) packet** Riesenpackung f

giant killer n (fig) Goliathbezwinger(in) m(f)

gibber ['dʒɪbə'] vi brabbeln

gibberish ['dʒɪbərɪʃ] n Quatsch m

gibe [dʒaɪb] n spöttische Bemerkung f ▷ vi: **to ~ at** spöttische Bemerkungen machen über +acc

giblets ['dʒɪblɪts] npl Geflügelinnereien pl

Gibraltar [dʒɪ'brɔ:ltə'] n Gibraltar nt

giddiness ['gɪdɪnɪs] n Schwindelgefühl nt

giddy ['gɪdɪ] adj: **I am/feel ~** mir ist schwind(e)lig; (height) schwindelerregend; **~ with excitement** vor Aufregung ganz ausgelassen

gift [gɪft] n Geschenk nt; (donation) Spende f; (Comm: also: **free gift**) (Werbe)geschenk nt; (ability) Gabe f; **to have a ~ for sth** ein Talent für etw haben

gift card n (US) elektronische Guthabenkarte f, Gift Card f (häufig in Form eines Gutscheins)

gifted ['gɪftɪd] adj begabt

gift token n Geschenkgutschein m

gift voucher n = **gift token**

gig [gɪg] (inf) n Konzert nt

gigabyte ['dʒɪgəbaɪt] n Gigabyte nt

gigantic [dʒaɪ'gæntɪk] adj riesig, riesengroß

giggle ['gɪgl] vi kichern ▷ n Spaß m; **to do sth for a ~** etw aus Spaß tun

GIGO ['gaɪgəʊ] (inf) abbr (Comput: = garbage in, garbage out) GIGO

gild [gɪld] vt vergolden

gill [dʒɪl] n Gill nt (Brit = 15 cl, US = 12 cl)

gills [gɪlz] npl Kiemen pl

gilt [gɪlt] adj vergoldet ▷ n Vergoldung f; **gilts** npl (Comm) mündelsichere Wertpapiere pl

gilt-edged ['gɪltɛdʒd] adj (stocks, securities) mündelsicher

gimlet ['gɪmlɪt] n Handbohrer m

gimmick ['gɪmɪk] n Gag m; **sales ~** Verkaufsmasche f, Verkaufstrick m

gin [dʒɪn] n Gin m

ginger ['dʒɪndʒə'] n Ingwer m ▷ adj (hair) rötlich; (cat) rötlich gelb

ginger ale n Gingerale nt

ginger beer n Ingwerbier nt

gingerbread ['dʒɪndʒəbrɛd] n (cake) Ingwerkuchen m; (biscuit) ≈ Pfefferkuchen m

ginger group (Brit) n Aktionsgruppe f

gingerly ['dʒɪndʒəlɪ] adv vorsichtig

gingham ['gɪŋəm] n Cingan m, Gingham m

ginseng ['dʒɪnsɛŋ] n Ginseng m

gipsy ['dʒɪpsɪ] n Zigeuner(in) m(f)

gipsy caravan n Zigeunerwagen m

giraffe [dʒɪ'rɑ:f] n Giraffe f

girder ['gə:də'] n Träger m

girdle ['gə:dl] n Hüftgürtel m, Hüfthalter m ▷ vt (fig) umgeben

girl [gə:l] n Mädchen nt; (young unmarried woman) (junges) Mädchen nt; (daughter) Tochter f; **this is my little ~** das ist mein Töchterchen; **an English ~** eine Engländerin

girlfriend ['gə:lfrɛnd] n Freundin f

Girl Guide n Pfadfinderin f

girlish ['gə:lɪʃ] adj mädchenhaft

Girl Scout (US) n Pfadfinderin f

Giro ['dʒaɪrəʊ] n: **the National ~** (Brit) der Postscheckdienst

giro ['dʒaɪrəʊ] n Giro nt, Giroverkehr m; (post office giro) Postscheckverkehr m; (Brit: welfare cheque) Sozialhilfescheck m

girth [gə:θ] n Umfang m; (of horse) Sattelgurt m

gist [dʒɪst] n Wesentliche(s) nt

 KEYWORD

give [gɪv] (pt **gave**, pp **given**) vt **1** (hand over): **to give sb sth, give sth to sb** jdm etw geben; **I'll give you £5 for it** ich gebe dir £5 dafür

2 (used with noun to replace a verb): **to give a sigh/cry/laugh** etc seufzen/schreien/lachen etc; **to give a speech/a lecture** eine Rede/einen Vortrag halten; **to give three cheers** ein dreifaches Hoch ausbringen

3 (tell, deliver: news, message etc) mitteilen; (: advice, answer) geben

4 (supply, provide: opportunity, job etc) geben; (: surprise) bereiten; (bestow: title, honour, right) geben, verleihen; **that's given me an idea** dabei kommt mir eine Idee

5 (devote: time, one's life) geben; (: attention) schenken

6 (organize: party, dinner etc) geben

▷ vi **1** (also: **give way**: break, collapse) nachgeben

2 (stretch: fabric) sich dehnen

▶ **give away** vt (money, opportunity) verschenken; (secret, information) verraten; (bride) zum Altar führen; **that immediately gave him away** dadurch verriet er sich sofort

▶ **give back** vt (money, book etc) zurückgeben

▶ **give in** vi (yield) nachgeben

▷ vt (essay etc) abgeben

▶ **give off** vt (heat, smoke) abgeben

▶ **give out** vt (prizes, books, drinks etc) austeilen

▷ vi (be exhausted: supplies) zu Ende gehen; (fail) versagen

▶ **give up** vt, vi aufgeben; **to give up smoking** das Rauchen aufgeben; **to give o.s. up** sich stellen; (after siege etc) sich ergeben

▶ **give way** vi (yield, collapse) nachgeben; (Brit: Aut) die Vorfahrt achten

give-and-take ['gɪvənd'teɪk] n (gegenseitiges) Geben und Nehmen nt

giveaway ['gɪvəweɪ] (inf) n: **her expression was a ~** ihr Gesichtsausdruck verriet alles; **the exam was a ~!** die Prüfung war geschenkt!; **~ prices** Schleuderpreise pl

g

given ['gɪvn] *pp of* **give** ▷ *adj* (*time, amount*) bestimmt ▷ *conj*: ~ **the circumstances ...** unter den Umständen ...; ~ **that ...** angesichts der Tatsache, dass ...

glacial ['gleɪsɪəl] *adj* (*landscape etc*) Gletscher-; (*fig*) eisig

glacier ['glæsɪəʳ] *n* Gletscher *m*

glad [glæd] *adj* froh; **to be ~ about sth** sich über etw *acc* freuen; **to be ~ that** sich freuen, dass; **I was ~ of his help** ich war froh über seine Hilfe

gladden ['glædn] *vt* erfreuen

glade [gleɪd] *n* Lichtung *f*

gladioli [glædɪ'əʊlaɪ] *npl* Gladiolen *pl*

gladly ['glædlɪ] *adv* gern(e)

glamorous ['glæmərəs] *adj* reizvoll; (*model etc*) glamourös

glamour ['glæməʳ] *n* Glanz *m*, Reiz *m*

glance [glɑːns] *n* Blick *m* ▷ *vi*: **to ~ at** einen Blick werfen auf +*acc*
  ▸ **glance off** *vt fus* abprallen von

glancing ['glɑːnsɪŋ] *adj*: **to strike sth a ~ blow** etw streifen

gland [glænd] *n* Drüse *f*

glandular fever ['glændjulə-] (*Brit*) *n* Drüsenfieber *nt*

glare [glɛəʳ] *n* wütender Blick *m*; (*of light*) greller Schein *m*; (*of publicity*) grelles Licht *nt* ▷ *vi* (*light*) grell scheinen; **to ~ at** (wütend) anstarren

glaring ['glɛərɪŋ] *adj* eklatant

glasnost ['glæznɔst] *n* Glasnost *f*

glass [glɑːs] *n* Glas *nt*; **glasses** *npl* (*spectacles*) Brille *f*

glass-blowing ['glɑːsbləʊɪŋ] *n* Glasbläserei *f*

glass ceiling *n* (*fig*) gläserne Decke *f*

glass fibre *n* Glasfaser *f*

glasshouse ['glɑːshaʊs] *n* Gewächshaus *nt*

glassware ['glɑːswɛəʳ] *n* Glaswaren *pl*

glassy ['glɑːsɪ] *adj* glasig

Glaswegian [glæs'wiːdʒən] *adj* Glasgower ▷ *n* Glasgower(in) *m(f)*

glaze [gleɪz] *vt* (*door, window*) verglasen; (*pottery*) glasieren ▷ *n* Glasur *f*

glazed [gleɪzd] *adj* (*eyes*) glasig; (*pottery, tiles*) glasiert

glazier ['gleɪzɪəʳ] *n* Glaser(in) *m(f)*

gleam [gliːm] *vi* (*light*) schimmern; (*polished surface, eyes*) glänzen ▷ *n*: **a ~ of hope** ein Hoffnungsschimmer *m*

gleaming ['gliːmɪŋ] *adj* schimmernd, glänzend

glean [gliːn] *vt* (*information*) herausbekommen, ausfindig machen

glee [gliː] *n* Freude *f*

gleeful ['gliːful] *adj* fröhlich

glen [glɛn] *n* Tal *nt*

glib [glɪb] *adj* (*person*) glatt; (*promise, response*) leichthin gemacht

glibly ['glɪblɪ] *adv* (*talk*) gewandt; (*answer*) leichthin

glide [glaɪd] *vi* gleiten ▷ *n* Gleiten *nt*

glider ['glaɪdəʳ] *n* Segelflugzeug *nt*

gliding ['glaɪdɪŋ] *n* Segelfliegen *nt*

glimmer ['glɪməʳ] *n* Schimmer *m*; (*of interest, hope*) Funke *m* ▷ *vi* schimmern

glimpse [glɪmps] *n* Blick *m* ▷ *vt* einen Blick werfen auf +*acc*; **to catch a ~ (of)** einen flüchtigen Blick erhaschen (von +*dat*)

glint [glɪnt] *vi* glitzern; (*eyes*) funkeln ▷ *n* (*see vb*) Glitzern *nt*; Funkeln *nt*

glisten ['glɪsn] *vi* glänzen

glitter ['glɪtəʳ] *vi* glitzern; (*eyes*) funkeln ▷ *n* (*see vb*) Glitzern *nt*; Funkeln *nt*

glittering ['glɪtərɪŋ] *adj* glitzernd; (*eyes*) funkelnd; (*career*) glänzend

glitz [glɪts] (*inf*) *n* Glanz *m*

gloat [gləʊt] *vi*: **to ~ (over)** (*own success*) sich brüsten (mit); (*sb's failure*) sich hämisch freuen (über +*acc*)

global ['gləʊbl] *adj* global

globalization [gləʊblaɪ'zeɪʃn] *n* (*Pol, Econ*) Globalisierung *f*

global player *n* (*Econ*) Weltfirma *f*, Global Player *m*

global warming [-'wɔːmɪŋ] *n* Erwärmung *f* der Erdatmosphäre

globe [gləʊb] *n* Erdball *m*; (*model*) Globus *m*; (*shape*) Kugel *f*

globetrotter ['gləʊbtrɔtəʳ] *n* Globetrotter(in) *m(f)*, Weltenbummler(in) *m(f)*

globule ['glɔbjuːl] *n* Tröpfchen *nt*

gloom [gluːm] *n* Düsterkeit *f*; (*sadness*) düstere *or* gedrückte Stimmung *f*

gloomily ['gluːmɪlɪ] *adv* düster

gloomy ['gluːmɪ] *adj* düster; (*person*) bedrückt; (*situation*) bedrückend

glorification [glɔːrɪfɪ'keɪʃən] *n* Verherrlichung *f*

glorify ['glɔːrɪfaɪ] *vt* verherrlichen

glorious ['glɔːrɪəs] *adj* herrlich; (*victory*) ruhmreich; (*future*) glanzvoll

glory ['glɔːrɪ] *n* Ruhm *m*; (*splendour*) Herrlichkeit *f* ▷ *vi*: **to ~ in** sich sonnen in +*dat*

glory hole (*inf*) *n* Rumpelkammer *f*

Glos (*Brit*) *abbr* (*Post*) = Gloucestershire

gloss [glɔs] *n* Glanz *m*; (*also*: **gloss paint**) Lack *m*, Lackfarbe *f*
  ▸ **gloss over** *vt fus* vom Tisch wischen

glossary ['glɔsərɪ] *n* Glossar *nt*

glossy ['glɔsɪ] *adj* glänzend; (*photograph, magazine*) Hochglanz- ▷ *n* (*also*: **glossy magazine**) (Hochglanz)magazin *nt*

glove [glʌv] *n* Handschuh *m*

glove compartment *n* Handschuhfach *nt*

glow [gləʊ] *vi* glühen; (*stars, eyes*) leuchten ▷ *n* (*see vb*) Glühen *nt*; Leuchten *nt*

glower ['glaʊəʳ] *vi*: **to ~ at sb** jdn finster ansehen

glowing ['gləʊɪŋ] *adj* glühend; (*complexion*) blühend; (*fig: report, description etc*) begeistert

glow-worm ['gləʊwəːm] *n* Glühwürmchen *nt*

glucose ['gluːkəʊs] *n* Traubenzucker *m*

glue [gluː] *n* Klebstoff *m* ▷ *vt*: **to ~ sth onto sth** etw an etw *acc* kleben; **to ~ sth into place** etw festkleben

glue-sniffing ['gluːsnɪfɪŋ] *n* (Klebstoff-)

Schnüffeln *nt*

glum [glʌm] *adj* bedrückt, niedergeschlagen

glut [glʌt] *n*: ~ **(of)** Überangebot *nt* (an +*dat*)
  ▷ *vt*: **to be ~ted (with)** überschwemmt sein
  (mit); **a ~ of pears** eine Birnenschwemme

glutinous ['glu:tɪnəs] *adj* klebrig

glutton ['glʌtn] *n* Vielfraß *m*; **a ~ for work**
  ein Arbeitstier *nt*; **a ~ for punishment** ein
  Masochist *m*

gluttonous ['glʌtənəs] *adj* gefräßig

gluttony ['glʌtənɪ] *n* Völlerei *f*

glycerin, glycerine ['glɪsəri:n] *n* Glyzerin *nt*

GM *abbr* = **genetically modified**

gm *abbr* (= *gram(me)*) g

GMAT (*US*) *n abbr* (= *Graduate Management
  Admissions Test*) Zulassungsprüfung für
  Handelsschulen

GMT *abbr* (= *Greenwich Mean Time*) WEZ *f*

gnarled [nɑ:ld] *adj* (*tree*) knorrig; (*hand*) knotig

gnash [næʃ] *vt*: **to ~ one's teeth** mit den
  Zähnen knirschen

gnat [næt] *n* (Stech)mücke *f*

gnaw [nɔ:] *vt* nagen an +*dat* ▷ *vi* (*fig*): **to ~ at**
  quälen

gnome [nəum] *n* Gnom *m*; (*in garden*)
  Gartenzwerg *m*

GNP *n abbr* (= *gross national product*) BSP *nt*

GNVQ (*Brit*) *n abbr* (= *General National Vocational
  Qualification*) allgemeine, auf die Arbeitswelt bezogene
  Qualifikation

go [gəu] (*pt* **went**, *pp* **gone**) *vi* **1** gehen; (*travel*)
  fahren; **a car went by** ein Auto fuhr vorbei
  2 (*depart*) gehen; **"I must go," she said** „ich
  muss gehen", sagte sie; **she has gone to
  Sheffield/Australia** (*permanently*) sie ist nach
  Sheffield/Australien gegangen
  3 (*attend, take part in activity*) gehen; **she went
  to university in Oxford** sie ist in Oxford
  zur Universität gegangen; **to go for a walk**
  spazieren gehen; **to go dancing** tanzen gehen
  4 (*work*) funktionieren; **the tape recorder
  was still going** das Tonband lief noch
  5 (*become*): **to go pale/mouldy** blass/
  schimmelig werden
  6 (*be sold*): **to go for £100** für £100 weggehen *or*
  verkauft werden
  7 (*be about to, intend to*): **we're going to stop in
  an hour** wir hören in einer Stunde auf; **are
  you going to come?** kommst du?, wirst du
  kommen?
  8 (*time*) vergehen
  9 (*event, activity*) ablaufen; **how did it go?** wie
  wars?
  10 (*be given*): **the job is to go to someone else**
  die Stelle geht an jemand anders
  11 (*break etc*) kaputtgehen; **the fuse went** die
  Sicherung ist durchgebrannt
  12 (*be placed*) hingehören; **the milk goes
  in the fridge** die Milch kommt in den
  Kühlschrank
  ▷ *n* **1** (*try*): **to have a go at sth** etw versuchen;
  I'll have a go at mending it ich will

versuchen, es zu reparieren; **to have a go** es
versuchen
  2 (*turn*): **whose go is it?** wer ist dran *or* an der
  Reihe?
  3 (*move*): **to be on the go** auf Trab sein
  ▸ **go about** *vi* (*also*: **go around**: *rumour*)
  herumgehen
  ▷ *vt fus*: **how do I go about this?** wie soll
  ich vorgehen?; **to go about one's business**
  seinen eigenen Geschäften nachgehen
  ▸ **go after** *vt fus* (*pursue: person*) nachgehen +*dat*;
  (: *job etc*) sich bemühen um; (: *record*) erreichen
  wollen
  ▸ **go against** *vt fus* (*be unfavourable to*) ungünstig
  verlaufen für; (*disregard: advice, wishes etc*)
  handeln gegen
  ▸ **go ahead** *vi* (*proceed*) weitergehen; **to go
  ahead with** weitermachen mit
  ▸ **go along** *vi* gehen
  ▸ **go along with** *vt fus* (*agree with*) zustimmen
  +*dat*; (*accompany*) mitgehen mit
  ▸ **go away** *vi* (*leave*) weggehen
  ▸ **go back** *vi* zurückgehen
  ▸ **go back on** *vt fus* (*promise*) zurücknehmen
  ▸ **go by** *vi* (*years, time*) vergehen
  ▷ *vt fus* (*rule etc*) sich richten nach
  ▸ **go down** *vi* (*descend*) hinuntergehen; (*ship,
  sun*) untergehen; (*price, level*) sinken
  ▷ *vt fus* (*stairs, ladder*) hinuntergehen; **his
  speech went down well** seine Rede kam gut
  an
  ▸ **go for** *vt fus* (*fetch*) holen (gehen); (*like*)
  mögen; (*attack*) losgehen auf +*acc*; (*apply to*)
  gelten für
  ▸ **go in** *vi* (*enter*) hineingehen
  ▸ **go in for** *vt fus* (*competition*) teilnehmen an
  +*dat*; (*favour*) stehen auf +*acc*
  ▸ **go into** *vt fus* (*enter*) hineingehen in +*acc*;
  (*investigate*) sich befassen mit; (*career*) gehen
  in +*acc*
  ▸ **go off** *vi* (*leave*) weggehen; (*food*) schlecht
  werden; (*bomb, gun*) losgehen; (*event*)
  verlaufen; (*lights etc*) ausgehen
  ▷ *vt fus* (*inf*): **I've gone off it/him** ich mache
  mir nichts mehr daraus/aus ihm; **the gun
  went off** das Gewehr ging los; **to go off to
  sleep** einschlafen; **the party went off well**
  die Party verlief gut
  ▸ **go on** *vi* (*continue*) weitergehen; (*happen*) vor
  sich gehen; (*lights*) angehen
  ▷ *vt fus* (*be guided by*) sich stützen auf +*acc*; **to go
  on doing sth** mit etw weitermachen; **what's
  going on here?** was geht hier vor?, was ist
  hier los?
  ▸ **go on at** (*inf*) *vt fus* (*nag*) herumnörgeln an
  +*dat*
  ▸ **go on with** *vt fus* weitermachen mit
  ▸ **go out** *vt fus* (*leave*) hinausgehen
  ▷ *vi* (*for entertainment*) ausgehen; (*fire, light*)
  ausgehen; (*couple*): **they went out for 3 years**
  sie gingen 3 Jahre lang miteinander
  ▸ **go over** *vi* hinübergehen
  ▷ *vt* (*check*) durchgehen; **to go over sth in**

one's mind etw überdenken

▶ **go round** vi (circulate: news, rumour) umgehen; (revolve) sich drehen; (suffice) ausreichen; (visit): **to go round (to sb's)** (bei jdm) vorbeigehen; **there's not enough to go round** es reicht nicht (für alle)

▶ **go through** vt fus (place) gehen durch; (by car) fahren durch; (undergo) durchmachen; (search through: files, papers) durchsuchen; (describe: list, book, story) durchgehen; (perform) durchgehen

▶ **go through with** vt fus (plan, crime) durchziehen; **I couldn't go through with it** ich brachte es nicht fertig

▶ **go under** vi (sink: person) untergehen; (fig: business, project) scheitern

▶ **go up** vi (ascend) hinaufgehen; (price, level) steigen; **to go up in flames** in Flammen aufgehen

▶ **go with** vt fus (suit) passen zu

▶ **go without** vt fus (food, treats) verzichten auf +acc

goad [gəud] vt aufreizen
▶ **goad on** vt anstacheln

go-ahead ['gəuəhɛd] adj zielstrebig; (firm) fortschrittlich ▷ n grünes Licht nt; **to give sb the ~** jdm grünes Licht geben

goal [gəul] n Tor nt; (aim) Ziel nt; **to score a ~** ein Tor schießen or erzielen

goal difference n Tordifferenz f

goalie ['gəulɪ] (inf) n Tormann m

goalkeeper ['gəulkiːpəʳ] n Torwart m

goal post n Torpfosten m

goat [gəut] n Ziege f

gobble ['gɔbl] vt (also: **gobble down, gobble up**) verschlingen

go-between ['gəubɪtwiːn] n Vermittler(in) m(f)

Gobi Desert ['gəubɪ-] n: **the ~** die Wüste Gobi

goblet ['gɔblɪt] n Pokal m

goblin ['gɔblɪn] n Kobold m

go-cart ['gəukɑːt] n Gokart m

God [gɔd] n Gott m ▷ excl o Gott!

god [gɔd] n Gott m

god-awful [gɔd'ɔːfəl] (inf) adj beschissen (!)

godchild ['gɔdtʃaɪld] n Patenkind nt

goddamn ['gɔdæm], **goddamned** ['gɔdæmd] (US: inf) adj gottverdammt

goddaughter ['gɔdɔːtəʳ] n Patentochter f

goddess ['gɔdɪs] n Göttin f

godfather ['gɔdfɑːðəʳ] n Pate m

God-fearing ['gɔdfɪərɪŋ] adj gottesfürchtig

godforsaken ['gɔdfəseɪkən] adj gottverlassen

godmother ['gɔdmʌðəʳ] n Patin f

godparent ['gɔdpɛərənt] n Pate m, Patin f

godsend ['gɔdsɛnd] n Geschenk nt des Himmels

godson ['gɔdsʌn] n Patensohn m

goes [gəuz] vb see **go**

gofer ['gəufəʳ] (inf) n Mädchen nt für alles

go-getter ['gəugɛtəʳ] (inf) n Ellbogentyp (pej, inf) m

goggle ['gɔgl] (inf) vi: **to ~ at** anstarren, anglotzen

goggles ['gɔglz] npl Schutzbrille f

going ['gəuɪŋ] n: **it was slow/hard ~** (fig) es ging nur langsam/schwer voran ▷ adj: **the ~ rate** der gängige Preis; **when the ~ gets tough** wenn es schwierig wird; **a ~ concern** ein gut gehendes Unternehmen

going-over [gəuɪŋ'əuvəʳ] (inf) n (check) Untersuchung f; (beating-up) Abreibung f; **to give sb a good ~** jdm eine tüchtige Abreibung verpassen

goings-on ['gəuɪŋz'ɔn] (inf) npl Vorgänge pl, Dinge pl

go-kart ['gəukɑːt] n = **go-cart**

gold [gəuld] n Gold nt; (also: **gold medal**) Gold nt, Goldmedaille f ▷ adj golden; (reserves, jewellery, tooth) Gold-

golden ['gəuldən] adj (also fig) golden

golden age n Blütezeit f

golden handshake (Brit) n Abstandssumme f

golden rule n goldene Regel f

goldfish ['gəuldfɪʃ] n Goldfisch m

gold leaf n Blattgold nt

gold medal n Goldmedaille f

gold mine n (also fig) Goldgrube f

gold-plated ['gəuld'pleɪtɪd] adj vergoldet

goldsmith ['gəuldsmɪθ] n Goldschmied(in) m(f)

gold standard n Goldstandard m

golf [gɔlf] n Golf nt

golf ball n (for game) Golfball m; (on typewriter) Kugelkopf m

golf club n Golfklub m; (stick) Golfschläger m

golf course n Golfplatz m

golfer ['gɔlfəʳ] n Golfspieler(in) m(f), Golfer(in) m(f)

golfing ['gɔlfɪŋ] n Golf(spielen) nt; **he does a lot of ~** er spielt viel Golf ▷ cpd Golf-

gondola ['gɔndələ] n Gondel f

gondolier [gɔndə'lɪəʳ] n Gondoliere m

gone [gɔn] pp of **go** ▷ adj weg; (days) vorbei

goner ['gɔnəʳ] (inf) n: **to be a ~** hinüber sein

gong [gɔŋ] n Gong m

good [gud] adj gut; (well-behaved) brav, lieb ▷ n (virtue, morality) Gute(s) nt; (benefit) Wohl nt; **goods** npl (Comm) Güter pl; **to have a ~ time** sich (gut) amüsieren; **to be ~ at sth** (swimming, talking etc) etw gut können; (science, sports etc) gut in etw dat sein; **to be ~ for sb/ sth** gut für jdn/zu etw dat sein; **it's ~ for you** das tut dir gut; **it's a ~ thing you were there** gut, dass Sie da waren; **she is ~ with children** sie kann gut mit Kindern umgehen; **she is ~ with her hands** sie ist geschickt; **to feel ~** sich wohlfühlen; **it's ~ to see you** (es ist) schön, Sie zu sehen; **would you be ~ enough to ...?** könnten Sie bitte ...?; **that's very ~ of you** das ist wirklich nett von Ihnen; **a ~ deal (of)** ziemlich viel; **a ~ many** ziemlich viele; **take a ~ look** sieh dir das genau or gut an; **a ~ while ago** vor einiger Zeit; **to make ~** (damage) wiedergutmachen; (loss) ersetzen; **it's no ~ complaining** es ist sinnlos or es nützt nichts, sich zu beklagen; **~ morning/ afternoon/evening!** guten Morgen/Tag/ Abend!; **~ night!** gute Nacht!; **he's up to no ~** er führt nichts Gutes im Schilde; **for the common ~** zum Wohle aller; **is this any ~?** (*will it help you?*) können Sie das gebrauchen?; (*is it good enough?*) reicht das?; **is the book/ film any ~?** was halten Sie von dem Buch/ Film?; **for ~** für immer; **~s and chattels** Hab und Gut *nt*

goodbye [gud'baɪ] *excl* auf Wiedersehen!; **to say ~** sich verabschieden

good-for-nothing ['gudfənʌθɪŋ] *adj* nichtsnutzig

Good Friday *n* Karfreitag *m*

good-humoured ['gud'hju:məd] *adj* gut gelaunt; (*good-natured*) gutmütig; (*remark, joke*) harmlos

good-looking ['gud'lukɪŋ] *adj* gut aussehend

good-natured ['gud'neɪtʃəd] *adj* gutmütig; (*discussion*) freundlich

goodness ['gudnɪs] *n* Güte *f*; **for ~ sake!** um Himmels willen!; **~ gracious!** ach du liebe *or* meine Güte!

goods train (*Brit*) *n* Güterzug *m*

goodwill [gud'wɪl] *n* Wohlwollen *nt*; (*Comm*) Goodwill *m*

goody ['gudɪ] (*inf*) *n* Gute(r) *m*, Held *m*

goody-goody ['gudɪgudɪ] (*pej*) *n* Tugendlamm *nt*, Musterkind (*inf*) *nt*

gooey ['gu:ɪ] (*inf*) *adj* (*sticky*) klebrig; (*cake*) üppig; (*fig: sentimental*) rührselig

goose [gu:s] (*pl* **geese**) *n* Gans *f*

gooseberry ['guzbərɪ] *n* Stachelbeere *f*; **to play ~** (*Brit*) das fünfte Rad am Wagen sein

goose flesh *n* = **goose pimples**

goose pimples *npl* Gänsehaut *f*

goose step *n* Stechschritt *m*

GOP (*US: inf*) *n abbr* (*Pol:* = *Grand Old Party*) Republikanische Partei

gopher ['gəufər] *n* (*Zool*) Taschenratte *f*

gore [gɔ:r] *vt* aufspießen ▷ *n* Blut *nt*

gorge [gɔ:dʒ] *n* Schlucht *f* ▷ *vt*: **to ~ o.s. (on)** sich vollstopfen (mit)

gorgeous ['gɔ:dʒəs] *adj* herrlich; (*person*) hinreißend

gorilla [gə'rɪlə] *n* Gorilla *m*

gormless ['gɔ:mlɪs] (*Brit: inf*) *adj* doof

gorse [gɔ:s] *n* Stechginster *m*

gory ['gɔ:rɪ] *adj* blutig

go-slow ['gəu'sləu] (*Brit*) *n* Bummelstreik *m*

gospel ['gɔspl] *n* Evangelium *nt*; (*doctrine*) Lehre *f*

gossamer ['gɔsəmər] *n* Spinnfäden *pl*; (*light fabric*) hauchdünne Gaze *f*

gossip ['gɔsɪp] *n* (*rumours*) Klatsch *m*, Tratsch *m*; (*chat*) Schwatz *m*; (*person*) Klatschbase *f* ▷ *vi* schwatzen; **a piece of ~** eine Neuigkeit

gossip column *n* Klatschkolumne *f*, Klatschspalte *f*

got [gɔt] *pt, pp of* **get**

Gothic ['gɔθɪk] *adj* gotisch

gotten ['gɔtn] (*US*) *pp of* **get**

gouge [gaudʒ] *vt* (*also:* **gouge out**: *hole etc*) bohren; (: *initials*) eingravieren; **to ~ sb's eyes out** jdm die Augen ausstechen

gourd [guəd] *n* (*container*) Kürbisflasche *f*

gourmet ['guəmeɪ] *n* Feinschmecker(in) *m(f)*, Gourmet *m*

gout [gaut] *n* Gicht *f*

govern ['gʌvən] *vt* (*also Ling*) regieren; (*event, conduct*) bestimmen

governess ['gʌvənɪs] *n* Gouvernante *f*

governing ['gʌvənɪŋ] *adj* (*Pol*) regierend

governing body *n* Vorstand *m*

government ['gʌvnmənt] *n* Regierung *f* ▷ *cpd* Regierungs-; **local ~** Kommunalverwaltung *f*, Gemeindeverwaltung *f*

governmental [gʌvn'mentl] *adj* Regierungs-

government stocks *npl* Staatspapiere *pl*, Staatsanleihen *pl*

governor ['gʌvənər] *n* Gouverneur(in) *m(f)*; (*of bank, hospital, Brit: of prison*) Direktor(in) *m(f)*; (*of school*) ≈ Mitglied *nt* des Schulbeirats

Govt *abbr* = **government**

gown [gaun] *n* (Abend)kleid *nt*; (*of teacher, Brit: of judge*) Robe *f*

GP *n abbr* = **general practitioner**

GPMU (*Brit*) *n abbr* (= *Graphical Paper and Media Union*) Mediengewerkschaft

GPO *n abbr* (*Brit: formerly:* = *general post office*) Postbehörde *f*; (*US:* = *Government Printing Office*) regierungsamtliche Druckanstalt

gr. *abbr* (*Comm*) = **gross**; (= *gram(me)*) g

grab [græb] *vt* packen; (*chance, opportunity*) (beim Schopf) ergreifen ▷ *vi*: **to ~ at** greifen *or* grapschen nach +*dat*; **to ~ some food** schnell etwas essen; **to ~ a few hours sleep** ein paar Stunden schlafen

grace [greɪs] *n* Gnade *f*; (*gracefulness*) Anmut *f* ▷ *vt* (*honour*) beehren; (*adorn*) zieren; **5 days' ~** 5 Tage Aufschub; **with (a) good ~** anstandslos; **with (a) bad ~** widerwillig; **his sense of humour is his saving ~** was einen mit ihm versöhnt, ist sein Sinn für Humor; **to say ~** das Tischgebet sprechen

graceful ['greɪsful] *adj* anmutig; (*style, shape*) gefällig; (*refusal, behaviour*) charmant

gracious ['greɪʃəs] *adj* (*kind, courteous*) liebenswürdig; (*compassionate*) gnädig; (*smile*) freundlich; (*house, mansion etc*) stilvoll; (*living etc*) kultiviert ▷ *excl*: **(good) ~!** (ach) du meine Güte!, (ach du) lieber Himmel!

gradation [grə'deɪʃən] *n* Abstufung *f*

grade [greɪd] *n* (*Comm*) (Güte)klasse *f*; (*in hierarchy*) Rang *m*; (*Scol: mark*) Note *f*; (*US: school class*) Klasse *f*; (: *gradient: upward*) Neigung *f*, Steigung *f*; (: *downward*) Neigung *f*, Gefälle *nt* ▷ *vt* klassifizieren; (*work, student*) einstufen; **to make the ~** (*fig*) es schaffen

grade crossing (*US*) *n* Bahnübergang *m*

grade school (*US*) *n* Grundschule *f*

gradient ['greɪdɪənt] *n* (*upward*) Neigung *f*, Steigung *f*; (*downward*) Neigung, Gefälle *nt*; (*Geom*) Gradient *m*

gradual ['grædjuəl] *adj* allmählich

g

gradually ['grædjʊəlɪ] *adv* allmählich

graduate [*n* 'grædjʊɪt, *vi* 'grædjʊeɪt] *n* (*of university*) Hochschulabsolvent(in) *m(f)*; (*US: of high school*) Schulabgänger(in) *m(f)* ▷ *vi* (*from university*) graduieren; (*US*) die (Schul)abschlussprüfung bestehen

graduated pension ['grædjʊeɪtɪd-] *n* gestaffelte Rente *f*

graduation [grædjʊ'eɪʃən] *n* (Ab)schlussfeier *f*

graffiti [grə'fi:tɪ] *n, npl* Graffiti *pl*

graft [grɑ:ft] *n* (*Agr*) (Pfropf)reis *nt*; (*Med*) Transplantat *nt*; (*Brit: inf: hard work*) Schufterei *f*; (*bribery*) Schiebung *f* ▷ *vt*: **to ~ (onto)** (*Agr*) (auf)pfropfen (auf *+acc*); (*Med*) übertragen (auf *+acc*), einpflanzen (in *+acc*); (*fig*) aufpfropfen *+dat*

grain [greɪn] *n* Korn *nt*; (*no pl: cereals*) Getreide *nt*; (*US: corn*) Getreide *nt*, Korn; (*of wood*) Maserung *f*; **it goes against the ~** (*fig*) es geht einem gegen den Strich

gram [græm] *n* Gramm *nt*

grammar ['græmər] *n* Grammatik *f*, Sprachlehre *f*

grammar school (*Brit*) *n* ≈ Gymnasium *nt*

grammatical [grə'mætɪkl] *adj* grammat(ikal)isch

gramme [græm] *n* = **gram**

gramophone ['græməfəʊn] (*Brit*) *n* Grammofon *nt*

granary ['grænərɪ] *n* Kornspeicher *m*; **G-®** **bread/loaf** Körnerbrot *nt*

grand [grænd] *adj* großartig; (*inf: wonderful*) fantastisch ▷ *n* (*inf*) ≈ Riese *m* (1000 *Pfund/Dollar*)

grandchild ['græntʃaɪld] (*irreg: like* **child**) *n* Enkelkind *nt*, Enkel(in) *m(f)*

granddad ['grændæd] (*inf*) *n* Opa *m*

granddaughter ['grændɔːtər] *n* Enkelin *f*

grandeur ['grændjər] *n* (*of scenery etc*) Erhabenheit *f*; (*of building*) Vornehmheit *f*

grandfather ['grændfɑːðər] *n* Großvater *m*

grandiose ['grændɪəʊs] (*also pej*) *adj* grandios

grand jury (*US*) *n* Großes Geschworenengericht *nt*

grandma ['grænmɑː] (*inf*) *n* Oma *f*

grandmother ['grænmʌðər] *n* Großmutter *f*

grandpa ['grænpɑː] (*inf*) *n* Opa *m*

grandparents ['grændpɛərənts] *npl* Großeltern *pl*

grand piano *n* Flügel *m*

Grand Prix ['grɑ̃:'priː] *n* (*Aut*) Grand Prix *m*

grandson ['grænsʌn] *n* Enkel *m*

grandstand ['grændstænd] *n* Haupttribüne *f*

grand total *n* Gesamtsumme *f*, Endsumme *f*

granite ['grænɪt] *n* Granit *m*

granny ['grænɪ] (*inf*) *n* Oma *f*

grant [grɑːnt] *vt* (*money*) bewilligen; (*request etc*) gewähren; (*visa*) erteilen; (*admit*) zugeben ▷ *n* Stipendium *nt*; (*subsidy*) Subvention *f*; **to take sth for ~ed** etw für selbstverständlich halten; **to take sb for ~ed** jdn als selbstverständlich hinnehmen; **to ~ that** zugeben, dass

granulated sugar ['grænjʊleɪtɪd-] *n* (Zucker)raffinade *f*

granule ['grænjuːl] *n* Körnchen *nt*

grape [greɪp] *n* (Wein)traube *f*; **a bunch of ~s** eine (ganze) Weintraube

grapefruit ['greɪpfruːt] (*pl* **~** *or* **grapefruits**) *n* Pampelmuse *f*, Grapefruit *f*

grapevine ['greɪpvaɪn] *n* Weinstock *m*; **I heard it on the ~** (*fig*) es ist mir zu Ohren gekommen

graph [grɑːf] *n* (*diagram*) grafische Darstellung *f*, Schaubild *nt*

graphic ['græfɪk] *adj* plastisch, anschaulich; (*art, design*) grafisch; *see also* **graphics**

graphic designer *n* Grafiker(in) *m(f)*

graphic equalizer [-iːkwəlaɪzər] *n* (Graphic) Equalizer *m*

graphics ['græfɪks] *n* Grafik *f* ▷ *npl* (*drawings*) Zeichnungen *pl*, grafische Darstellungen *pl*

graphite ['græfaɪt] *n* Grafit *m*

graph paper *n* Millimeterpapier *nt*

grapple ['græpl] *vi*: **to ~ with sb/sth** mit jdm/etw kämpfen; **to ~ with a problem** sich mit einem Problem herumschlagen

grasp [grɑːsp] *vt* (*seize*) ergreifen; (*hold*) festhalten; (*understand*) begreifen ▷ *n* Griff *m*; (*understanding*) Verständnis *nt*; **it slipped from my ~** es entglitt mir; **to have sth within one's ~** etw in greifbarer Nähe haben; **to have a good ~ of sth** (*fig*) etw gut beherrschen ▷ **grasp at** *vt fus* greifen nach; (*fig: opportunity*) ergreifen

grasping ['grɑːspɪŋ] *adj* habgierig

grass [grɑːs] *n* Gras *nt*; (*lawn*) Rasen *m*; (*Brit: inf: informer*) (Polizei)spitzel *m*

grasshopper ['grɑːshɔpər] *n* Grashüpfer *m*, Heuschrecke *f*

grass-roots ['grɑːsruːts] *npl* (*of party etc*) Basis *f* ▷ *adj* (*opinion*) des kleinen Mannes; **at ~ level** an der Basis

grass snake *n* Ringelnatter *f*

grassy ['grɑːsɪ] *adj* Gras-, grasig

grate [greɪt] *n* (Feuer)rost *m* ▷ *vt* reiben; (*carrots etc*) raspeln ▷ *vi*: **to ~ (on)** kratzen (auf *+dat*)

grateful ['greɪtful] *adj* dankbar; (*thanks*) aufrichtig

gratefully ['greɪtfəlɪ] *adv* dankbar

grater ['greɪtər] *n* Reibe *f*

gratification [grætɪfɪ'keɪʃən] *n* (*pleasure*) Genugtuung *f*; (*satisfaction*) Befriedigung *f*

gratify ['grætɪfaɪ] *vt* (*please*) erfreuen; (*satisfy*) befriedigen

gratifying ['grætɪfaɪɪŋ] *adj* (*see vt*) erfreulich; befriedigend

grating ['greɪtɪŋ] *n* Gitter *nt* ▷ *adj* (*noise*) knirschend; (*voice*) schrill

gratitude ['grætɪtjuːd] *n* Dankbarkeit *f*

gratuitous [grə'tjuːɪtəs] *adj* unnötig

gratuity [grə'tjuːɪtɪ] *n* Trinkgeld *nt*

grave [greɪv] *n* Grab *nt* ▷ *adj* (*decision, mistake*) schwer (wiegend), schwerwiegend; (*expression, person*) ernst

grave digger *n* Totengräber *m*

gravel ['grævl] *n* Kies *m*

gravely ['greɪvlɪ] *adv* (*see adj*) schwer, ernst; **~ ill** schwer krank

gravestone ['greɪvstəʊn] n Grabstein m

graveyard ['greɪvjɑːd] n Friedhof m

gravitas ['grævɪtæs] n Seriosität f

gravitate ['grævɪteɪt] vi: **to ~ towards** angezogen werden von

gravity ['grævɪtɪ] n Schwerkraft f; (seriousness) Ernst m, Schwere f

gravy ['greɪvɪ] n (juice) (Braten)saft m; (sauce) (Braten)soße f

gravy boat n Sauciere f, Soßenschüssel f

gravy train (inf) n: **to ride the ~** leichtes Geld machen

gray [greɪ] (US) adj = **grey**

graze [greɪz] vi grasen, weiden ▷vt streifen; (scrape) aufschürfen ▷ n (Med) Abschürfung f

grazing ['greɪzɪŋ] n Weideland nt

grease [griːs] n (lubricant) Schmiere f; (fat) Fett nt ▷vt (see n) schmieren; fetten; **to ~ the skids** (US: fig) die Maschinerie in Gang halten

grease gun n Fettspritze f, Fettpresse f

greasepaint ['griːspeɪnt] n (Fett)schminke f

greaseproof paper ['griːspruː-f-] (Brit) n Pergamentpapier nt

greasy ['griːsɪ] adj fettig; (food: containing grease) fett; (tools) schmierig, ölig; (clothes) speckig; (Brit: road, surface) glitschig, schlüpfrig

great [greɪt] adj groß; (city) bedeutend; (inf: terrific) prima, toll; **they're ~ friends** sie sind gute Freunde; **we had a ~ time** wir haben uns glänzend amüsiert; **it was ~!** es war toll!; **the ~ thing is that …** das Wichtigste ist, dass …

Great Barrier Reef n: **the ~** das Große Barriereriff

Great Britain n Großbritannien nt

greater ['greɪtər] adj (see great) größer; bedeutender; **people in G~ Calcutta** die Leute in Kalkutta und Umgebung; **G~ Manchester** Groß-Manchester nt

great-grandchild [greɪt'græntʃaɪld] (irreg: like **child**) n Urenkel(in) m(f)

great-grandfather [greɪt'grænfɑːðər] n Urgroßvater m

great-grandmother [greɪt'grænmʌðər] n Urgroßmutter f

Great Lakes npl: **the ~** die Großen Seen pl

greatly ['greɪtlɪ] adv sehr; (influenced) stark

greatness ['greɪtnɪs] n Bedeutung f

Grecian ['griːʃən] adj griechisch

Greece [griːs] n Griechenland nt

greed [griːd] n (also: **greediness**): **~ for** Gier f nach; **~ for power** Machtgier f; **~ for money** Geldgier f

greedily ['griːdɪlɪ] adv gierig

greedy ['griːdɪ] adj gierig

Greek [griːk] adj griechisch ▷n Grieche m, Griechin f; (Ling) Griechisch nt; **ancient/ modern ~** Alt-/Neugriechisch nt

green [griːn] adj (also ecological) grün ▷ n (also Golf) Grün nt; (stretch of grass) Rasen m, Grünfläche f; (also: **village green**) Dorfwiese f, Anger m; **greens** npl (vegetables) Grüngemüse nt; (Pol): **the G~s** die Grünen pl; **to have ~**

fingers, to have a ~ thumb (US) eine Hand für Pflanzen haben; **to give sb the ~ light** jdm grünes Licht geben

green belt n Grüngürtel m

green card n (Aut) grüne (Versicherungs)karte f; (US) ≈ Aufenthaltserlaubnis f

greenery ['griːnərɪ] n Grün nt

greenfly ['griːnflaɪ] (Brit) n Blattlaus f

greengage ['griːngeɪdʒ] n Reneklode f

greengrocer ['griːnɡrəʊsər] (Brit) n Obst- und Gemüsehändler(in) m(f)

greenhouse ['griːnhaʊs] n Gewächshaus nt, Treibhaus nt; **~ effect** Treibhauseffekt m; **~ gas** Treibhausgas nt

greenish ['griːnɪʃ] adj grünlich

Greenland ['griːnlənd] n Grönland nt

Greenlander ['griːnləndər] n Grönländer(in) m(f)

green light n grünes Licht nt; **to give sb the ~** jdm grünes Licht or freie Fahrt geben

Green Party n (Pol): **the ~** die Grünen pl

green pepper n grüne Paprikaschote f

green pound n grünes Pfund nt

greet [griːt] vt begrüßen; (news) aufnehmen

greeting ['griːtɪŋ] n Gruß m; (welcome) Begrüßung f; **Christmas ~s** Weihnachtsgrüße pl; **birthday ~s** Geburtstagsglückwünsche pl; **Season's ~s** frohe Weihnachten und ein glückliches neues Jahr

greeting card, greetings card n Grußkarte f; (congratulating) Glückwunschkarte f

gregarious [grəˈgɛərɪəs] adj gesellig

grenade [grəˈneɪd] n (also: **hand grenade**) (Hand)granate f

grew [gruː] pt of **grow**

grey, (US) **gray** [greɪ] adj grau; (dismal) trüb, grau; **to go ~** grau werden

grey-haired [greɪˈhɛəd] adj grauhaarig

greyhound ['greɪhaʊnd] n Windhund m

grid [grɪd] n Gitter nt; (Elec) (Verteiler)netz nt; (US: Aut: intersection) Kreuzung f

griddle ['grɪdl] n gusseiserne Pfanne zum Braten und Pfannkuchenbacken

gridiron ['grɪdaɪən] n Bratrost m

gridlock ['grɪdlɒk] n (esp US: on road) totaler Stau m; (stalemate) Patt nt ▷ vt: **to be ~ed** (roads) total verstopft sein; (talks etc) festgefahren sein

grief [griːf] n Kummer m, Trauer f; **to come to ~** (plan) scheitern; (person) zu Schaden kommen; **good ~!** ach du liebe Güte!

grievance ['griːvəns] n Beschwerde f; (feeling of resentment) Groll m

grieve [griːv] vi trauern ▷vt Kummer bereiten +dat, betrüben; **to ~ for** trauern um

grievous ['griːvəs] adj (mistake) schwer; (situation) beträblich; **~ bodily harm** (Law) schwere Körperverletzung f

grill [grɪl] n Grill m; (grilled food: also: **mixed grill**) Grillgericht nt; (restaurant) = **grillroom** ▷ vt (Brit) grillen; (inf: question) in die Zange nehmen, ausquetschen

g

grille [grɪl] n (screen) Gitter nt; (Aut) Kühlergrill m

grillroom ['grɪlrum] n Grillrestaurant nt

grim [grɪm] adj trostlos; (serious, stern) grimmig

grimace [grɪ'meɪs] n Grimasse f ▷ vi Grimassen schneiden

grime [graɪm] n Dreck m, Schmutz m

grimy ['graɪmɪ] adj dreckig, schmutzig

grin [grɪn] n Grinsen nt ▷ vi grinsen; **to ~ at sb** jdn angrinsen

grind [graɪnd] (pt, pp **ground**) vt zerkleinern; (coffee, pepper etc) mahlen; (US: meat) hacken, durch den Fleischwolf drehen; (knife) schleifen, wetzen; (gem, lens) schleifen ▷ vi (car gears) knirschen ▷ n (work) Schufterei f; **to ~ one's teeth** mit den Zähnen knirschen; **to ~ to a halt** (vehicle) quietschend zum Stehen kommen; (fig: talks, scheme) sich festfahren; (work) stocken; (production) zum Erliegen kommen; **the daily ~** (inf) der tägliche Trott

grinder ['graɪndə'] n (for coffee) Kaffeemühle f; (for waste disposal etc) Müllzerkleinerungsanlage f

grindstone ['graɪndstəun] n: **to keep one's nose to the ~** hart arbeiten

grip [grɪp] n Griff m; (of tyre, shoe) Halt m; (holdall) Reisetasche f ▷ vt packen; (audience, attention) fesseln; **to come to ~s with sth** etw in den Griff bekommen; **to lose one's ~** den Halt verlieren; (fig) nachlassen; **to ~ the road** (car) gut auf der Straße liegen

gripe [graɪp] (inf) n (complaint) Meckerei f ▷ vi meckern; **the ~s** (Med) Kolik f, Bauchschmerzen pl

gripping ['grɪpɪŋ] adj fesselnd, packend

grisly ['grɪzlɪ] adj grässlich, grausig

grist [grɪst] n (fig): **it's all ~ to the mill** das kann man alles verwerten

gristle ['grɪsl] n Knorpel m

grit [grɪt] n (for icy roads: sand) Sand m; (crushed stone) Splitt m; (determination, courage) Mut m ▷ vt (road) streuen; **grits** npl (US) Grütze f; **I've got a piece of ~ in my eye** ich habe ein Staubkorn im Auge; **to ~ one's teeth** die Zähne zusammenbeißen

grizzle ['grɪzl] (Brit) vi quengeln

grizzly ['grɪzlɪ] n (also: **grizzly bear**) Grizzlybär m

groan [grəun] n Stöhnen nt ▷ vi stöhnen; (tree, floorboard etc) ächzen, knarren

grocer ['grəusə'] n Lebensmittelhändler(in) m(f)

groceries ['grəusərɪz] npl Lebensmittel pl

grocer's, grocer's shop n Lebensmittelgeschäft nt

grog [grɔg] n Grog m

groggy ['grɔgɪ] adj angeschlagen

groin [grɔɪn] n Leistengegend f

groom [gru:m] n Stallbursche m; (also: **bridegroom**) Bräutigam m ▷ vt (horse) striegeln; (fig): **to ~ sb for** (job) jdn aufbauen für; **well-~ed** gepflegt

groove [gru:v] n Rille f

grope [grəup] vi: **to ~ for** tasten nach; (fig: try to think of) suchen nach

grosgrain ['grəugreɪn] n grob gerippter Stoff m

gross [grəus] adj (neglect) grob; (injustice) krass; (behaviour, speech) grob, derb; (Comm: income, weight) Brutto- ▷ n inv Gros nt ▷ vt: **to ~ £500,000** £500 000 brutto einnehmen

gross domestic product n Bruttoinlandsprodukt nt

grossly ['grəuslɪ] adv äußerst; (exaggerated) grob

gross national product n Bruttosozialprodukt nt

grotesque [grə'tɛsk] adj grotesk

grotto ['grɔtəu] n Grotte f

grotty ['grɔtɪ] (inf) adj mies

grouch [grautʃ] (inf) vi schimpfen ▷ n (person) Miesepeter m, Muffel m

ground [graund] pt, pp of **grind** ▷ n Boden m, Erde f; (land) Land nt; (Sport) Platz m, Feld nt; (US: Elec: also **ground wire**) Erde f; (reason: gen pl) Grund m ▷ vt (plane) aus dem Verkehr ziehen; (US: Elec) erden ▷ adj (coffee etc) gemahlen ▷ vi (ship) auflaufen; **grounds** npl (of coffee etc) Satz m; (gardens etc) Anlagen pl; **below ~** unter der Erde; **to gain/lose ~** Boden gewinnen/verlieren; **common ~** Gemeinsame(s) nt; **on the ~s that** mit der Begründung, dass

ground cloth (US) n = **groundsheet**

ground control n (Aviat, Space) Bodenkontrolle f

ground floor n Erdgeschoss nt, Erdgeschoß nt (Österr)

grounding ['graundɪŋ] n (in education) Grundwissen nt

groundless ['graundlɪs] adj grundlos, unbegründet

groundnut ['graundnʌt] n Erdnuss f

ground rent (Brit) n Erbbauzins m

ground rule n Grundregel f

groundsheet ['graundʃiːt] (Brit) n Zeltboden m

groundskeeper ['graundzkiːpə'] (US) n = **groundsman**

groundsman ['graundzmən] (irreg: like **man**) n (Sport) Platzwart m

ground staff n (Aviat) Bodenpersonal nt

groundswell n: **there was a ~ of public opinion against him** die Öffentlichkeit wandte sich gegen ihn

ground-to-air missile ['graundtə'ɛə'-] n Boden-Luft-Rakete f

ground-to-ground missile ['graundtə'graund-] n Boden-Boden-Rakete f

groundwork ['graundwəːk] n Vorarbeit f

group [gruːp] n Gruppe f; (Comm) Konzern m ▷ vt (also: **group together**: in one group) zusammentun; (: in several groups) in Gruppen einteilen ▷ vi (also: **group together**) sich zusammentun

groupie ['gruːpɪ] (inf) n Groupie nt

group therapy n Gruppentherapie f

grouse [graus] n inv schottisches Moorhuhn nt ▷ vi (complain) schimpfen

grove [grəuv] n Hain m, Wäldchen nt

grovel ['grɒvl] vi (*crawl*) kriechen; (*fig*): **to ~ (before)** kriechen (vor +*dat*)

grow [grəu] (*pt* **grew**, *pp* **~n**) vi wachsen; (*increase*) zunehmen; (*become*) werden ▷ vt (*roses*) züchten; (*vegetables*) anbauen, ziehen; (*beard*) sich *dat* wachsen lassen; **to ~ tired of waiting** das Warten leid sein; **to ~ (out of** or **from)** (*develop*) entstehen (aus)

▶ **grow apart** vi (*fig*) sich auseinander-entwickeln

▶ **grow away from** vt fus (*fig*) sich entfremden +*dat*

▶ **grow on** vt fus: **that painting is ~ing on me** allmählich finde ich Gefallen an dem Bild

▶ **grow out of** vt fus (*clothes*) herauswachsen aus; (*habit*) ablegen; **he'll ~ out of it** diese Phase geht auch vorbei

▶ **grow up** vi aufwachsen; (*mature*) erwachsen werden; (*idea, friendship*) entstehen

grower ['grəuə^r] n (*Bot*) Züchter(in) *m(f)*; (*Agr*) Pflanzer(in) *m(f)*

growing ['grəuɪŋ] adj wachsend; (*number*) zunehmend; **~ pains** Wachstumsschmerzen pl; (*fig*) Kinderkrankheiten pl, Anfangsschwierigkeiten pl

growl [graul] vi knurren

grown [grəun] pp of **grow**

grown-up [grəun'ʌp] n Erwachsene(r) *f(m)*

growth [grəuθ] n Wachstum *nt*; (*what has grown: of weeds, beard etc*) Wuchs *m*; (*of person, character*) Entwicklung *f*; (*Med*) Gewächs *nt*, Wucherung *f*

growth rate n Wachstumsrate *f*, Zuwachsrate *f*

grub [grʌb] n (*larva*) Larve *f*; (*inf: food*) Fressalien pl, Futter *nt* ▷ vi: **to ~ about** or **around (for)** (herum)wühlen (nach)

grubby ['grʌbɪ] adj (*dirty*) schmuddelig; (*fig*) schmutzig

grudge [grʌdʒ] n Groll *m* ▷ vt: **to ~ sb sth** jdm etw nicht gönnen; **to bear sb a ~** jdm böse sein, einen Groll gegen jdn hegen

grudging ['grʌdʒɪŋ] adj widerwillig

grudgingly ['grʌdʒɪŋlɪ] adv widerwillig

gruelling, (*US*) **grueling** ['gruəlɪŋ] adj (*encounter*) aufreibend; (*trip, journey*) äußerst strapaziös

gruesome ['gru:səm] adj grauenhaft

gruff [grʌf] adj barsch, schroff

grumble ['grʌmbl] vi murren, schimpfen

grumpy ['grʌmpɪ] adj mürrisch, brummig

grunge [grʌndʒ] n (*inf*) Grunge *nt*

grunt [grʌnt] vi grunzen ▷ n Grunzen *nt*

G-string ['dʒi:strɪŋ] n Minislip *m*, Tangaslip *m*

GT abbr (*Aut*: = *gran turismo*) GT

GU (*US*) abbr (*Post*) = *Guam*

guarantee [gærən'ti:] n Garantie *f* ▷ vt garantieren; **he can't ~ (that) he'll come** er kann nicht dafür garantieren, dass er kommt

guarantor [gærən'tɔ:^r] n (*Comm*) Bürge *m*

guard [gɑ:d] n Wache *f*; (*Boxing, Fencing*) Deckung *f*; (*Brit: Rail*) Schaffner(in) *m(f)*; (*on machine*) Schutz *m*, Schutzvorrichtung *f*; (*also*: **fireguard**) (Schutz)gitter *nt* ▷ vt (*prisoner*) bewachen; (*protect*): **to ~ (against)** (be)schützen (vor +*dat*); (*secret*) hüten (vor +*dat*); **to be on one's ~** auf der Hut sein

▶ **guard against** vt fus (*disease*) vorbeugen +*dat*; (*damage, accident*) verhüten

guard dog n Wachhund *m*

guarded ['gɑ:dɪd] adj vorsichtig, zurückhaltend

guardian ['gɑ:dɪən] n Vormund *m*; (*defender*) Hüter *m*

guardrail ['gɑ:dreɪl] n (Schutz)geländer *nt*

guard's van (*Brit*) n (*Rail*) Schaffnerabteil *nt*, Dienstwagen *m*

Guatemala [gwɑ:tɪ'mɑ:lə] n Guatemala *nt*

Guatemalan [gwɑ:tɪ'mɑ:lən] adj guatemaltekisch, aus Guatemala

Guernsey ['gə:nzɪ] n Guernsey *nt*

guerrilla [gə'rɪlə] n Guerilla *m*, Guerillakämpfer(in) *m(f)*

guerrilla warfare n Guerillakrieg *m*

guess [ges] vt schätzen; (*answer*) (er)raten; (*US: think*) schätzen (*inf*) ▷ vi (*see vt*) schätzen; raten ▷ n Vermutung *f*; **I ~ you're right** da haben Sie wohl recht; **to keep sb ~ing** jdn im Ungewissen lassen; **to take** or **have a ~** raten; (*estimate*) schätzen; **my ~ is that ...** ich schätze or vermute, dass ...

guesstimate ['gestɪmɪt] (*inf*) n grobe Schätzung *f*

guesswork ['geswə:k] n Vermutungen pl; **I got the answer by ~** ich habe die Antwort nur geraten

guest [gest] n Gast *m*; **be my ~** (*inf*) nur zu!

guesthouse ['gesthaus] n Pension *f*

guest room n Gästezimmer *nt*

guff [gʌf] (*inf*) n Quatsch *m*, Käse *m*

guffaw [gʌ'fɔ:] vi schallend lachen ▷ n schallendes Lachen *nt*

guidance ['gaɪdəns] n Rat *m*, Beratung *f*; **under the ~ of** unter der Leitung von; **vocational ~** Berufsberatung *f*; **marriage ~** Eheberatung *f*

guide [gaɪd] n (*person*) Führer(in) *m(f)*; (*book*) Führer *m*; (*Brit: also* **girl guide**) Pfadfinderin *f* ▷ vt führen; (*direct*) lenken; **to be ~d by sb/sth** sich von jdm/etw leiten lassen

guidebook ['gaɪdbuk] n Führer *m*

guided missile n Lenkwaffe *f*

guide dog n Blindenhund *m*

guidelines ['gaɪdlaɪnz] npl Richtlinien pl

guild [gɪld] n Verein *m*

guildhall ['gɪldhɔ:l] (*Brit*) n Gildehaus *nt*

guile [gaɪl] n Arglist *f*

guileless ['gaɪllɪs] adj arglos

guillotine ['gɪləti:n] n Guillotine *f*, Fallbeil *nt*; (*for paper*) (Papier)schneidemaschine *f*

guilt [gɪlt] n Schuld *f*; (*remorse*) Schuldgefühl *nt*

guilty ['gɪltɪ] adj schuldig; (*expression*) schuldbewusst; (*secret*) dunkel; **to plead ~/ not ~** sich schuldig/nicht schuldig bekennen; **to feel ~ about doing sth** ein schlechtes Gewissen haben, etw zu tun

Guinea [ˈgɪnɪ] *n*: **Republic of** ~ Guinea *nt*
guinea [ˈgɪnɪ] (*Brit*) *n* (*old*) Guinee *f*
guinea pig *n* Meerschweinchen *nt*; (*fig: person*) Versuchskaninchen *nt*
guise [gaɪz] *n*: **in** *or* **under the** ~ **of** in der Form +*gen*, in Gestalt +*gen*
guitar [gɪˈtɑːʳ] *n* Gitarre *f*
guitarist [gɪˈtɑːrɪst] *n* Gitarrist(in) *m(f)*
gulch [gʌltʃ] (*US*) *n* Schlucht *f*
gulf [gʌlf] *n* Golf *m*; (*abyss*) Abgrund *m*; (*fig: difference*) Kluft *f*; **the (Persian) G**~ der (Persische) Golf
Gulf States *npl*: **the** ~ die Golfstaaten *pl*
Gulf Stream *n*: **the** ~ der Golfstrom
Gulf War *n*: **the** ~ der Golfkrieg
gull [gʌl] *n* Möwe *f*
gullet [ˈgʌlɪt] *n* Speiseröhre *f*
gullibility [gʌlɪˈbɪlɪtɪ] *n* Leichtgläubigkeit *f*
gullible [ˈgʌlɪbl] *adj* leichtgläubig
gully [ˈgʌlɪ] *n* Schlucht *f*
gulp [gʌlp] *vi* schlucken ▷ *vt* (*also*: **gulp down**) hinunterschlucken ▷ *n*: **at one** ~ mit einem Schluck
gum [gʌm] *n* (*Anat*) Zahnfleisch *nt*; (*glue*) Klebstoff *m*; (*also*: **gumdrop**) Weingummi *nt*; (*also*: **chewing-gum**) Kaugummi *m* ▷ *vt*: **to** ~ **(together)** (zusammen)kleben
  ▶ **gum up** *vt*: **to** ~ **up the works** (*inf*) alles vermasseln
gumboots [ˈgʌmbuːts] (*Brit*) *npl* Gummistiefel *pl*
gumption [ˈgʌmpʃən] *n* Grips *m* (*inf*)
gumtree [ˈgʌmtriː] *n*: **to be up a** ~ (*fig: inf*) aufgeschmissen sein
gun [gʌn] *n* (*small*) Pistole *f*; (*medium-sized*) Gewehr *nt*; (*large*) Kanone *f* ▷ *vt* (*also*: **gun down**) erschießen; **to stick to one's** ~**s** (*fig*) nicht nachgeben, festbleiben
gunboat [ˈgʌnbəut] *n* Kanonenboot *nt*
gun dog *n* Jagdhund *m*
gunfire [ˈgʌnfaɪəʳ] *n* Geschützfeuer *nt*
gunge [gʌndʒ] (*inf*) *n* Schmiere *f*
gung ho [ˈgʌŋˈhəu] (*inf*) *adj* übereifrig
gunman [ˈgʌnmən] (*irreg: like* **man**) *n* bewaffneter Verbrecher *m*
gunner [ˈgʌnəʳ] *n* Kanonier *m*, Artillerist *m*
gunpoint [ˈgʌnpɔɪnt] *n*: **at** ~ mit vorgehaltener Pistole; mit vorgehaltenem Gewehr
gunpowder [ˈgʌnpaudəʳ] *n* Schießpulver *nt*
gunrunner [ˈgʌnrʌnəʳ] *n* Waffen-schmuggler(in) *m(f)*, Waffenschieber(in) *m(f)*
gunrunning [ˈgʌnrʌnɪŋ] *n* Waffenschmuggel *m*, Waffenschieberei *f*
gunshot [ˈgʌnʃɔt] *n* Schuss *m*
gunsmith [ˈgʌnsmɪθ] *n* Büchsenmacher *m*
gurgle [ˈgəːgl] *vi* (*baby*) glucksen; (*water*) gluckern
guru [ˈguruː] *n* Guru *m*
gush [gʌʃ] *vi* hervorquellen, hervorströmen; (*person*) schwärmen ▷ *vt* Strahl *m*
gushing [ˈgʌʃɪŋ] *adj* (*fig*) überschwänglich

gusset [ˈgʌsɪt] *n* Keil *m*, Zwickel *m*
gust [gʌst] *n* Windstoß *m*, Bö(e) *f*; (*of smoke*) Wolke *f*
gusto [ˈgʌstəu] *n*: **with** ~ mit Genuss, mit Schwung
gusty [ˈgʌstɪ] *adj* (*wind*) böig; (*day*) stürmisch
gut [gʌt] *n* (*Anat*) Darm *m*; (*for violin, racket*) Darmsaiten *pl* ▷ *vt* (*poultry, fish*) ausnehmen; (*building*) ausräumen; (*by fire*) ausbrennen; **guts** *npl* (*Anat*) Eingeweide *pl*; (*inf: courage*) Mumm *m*; **to hate sb's** ~**s** jdn auf den Tod nicht ausstehen können
gut reaction *n* rein gefühlsmäßige Reaktion *f*
gutsy [ˈgʌtsɪ] (*inf*) *adj* (*vivid*) rasant; (*courageous*) mutig
gutter [ˈgʌtəʳ] *n* (*in street*) Gosse *f*, Rinnstein *m*; (*of roof*) Dachrinne *f*
gutter press *n* Boulevardpresse *f*
guttural [ˈgʌtərl] *adj* guttural
guy [gaɪ] *n* (*inf: man*) Typ *m*, Kerl *m*; (*also*: **guyrope**) Haltetau *nt*, Halteseil *nt*; (*for Guy Fawkes' night*) (Guy-Fawkes-)Puppe *f*

● **GUY FAWKES' NIGHT**

● Guy Fawkes' Night, auch „bonfire night"
● genannt, erinnert an den „Gunpowder
● Plot", einen Attentatsversuch auf James
● I. und sein Parlament am 5. November
● 1605. Einer der Verschwörer, Guy Fawkes,
● wurde auf frischer Tat ertappt, als er das
● Parlamentsgebäude in die Luft sprengen
● wollte. Vor der Guy Fawkes' Night
● basteln Kinder in Großbritannien eine
● Puppe des Guy Fawkes, mit der sie Geld
● für Feuerwerkskörper von Passanten
● erbetteln, und die dann am 5. November
● auf einem Lagerfeuer mit Feuerwerk
● verbrannt wird.

Guyana [gaɪˈænə] *n* Guyana *nt*
guzzle [ˈgʌzl] *vt* (*food*) futtern; (*drink*) saufen (*inf*)
gym [dʒɪm] *n* (*also*: **gymnasium**) Turnhalle *f*; (*also*: **gymnastics**) Gymnastik *f*, Turnen *nt*
gymkhana [dʒɪmˈkɑːnə] *n* Reiterfest *nt*
gymnasium [dʒɪmˈneɪzɪəm] *n* Turnhalle *f*
gymnast [ˈdʒɪmnæst] *n* Turner(in) *m(f)*
gymnastics [dʒɪmˈnæstɪks] *n* Gymnastik *f*, Turnen *nt*
gym shoes *npl* Turnschuhe *pl*
gymslip [ˈdʒɪmslɪp] (*Brit*) *n* (Schul)trägerrock *m*
gynaecologist, (*US*) **gynecologist** [gaɪnɪˈkɔlədʒɪst] *n* Gynäkologe *m*, Gynäkologin *f*, Frauenarzt *m*, Frauenärztin *f*
gynaecology, (*US*) **gynecology** [gaɪnɪˈkɔlədʒɪ] *n* Gynäkologie *f*, Frauenheilkunde *f*
gypsy [ˈdʒɪpsɪ] *n* = **gipsy**
gyrate [dʒaɪˈreɪt] *vi* kreisen, sich drehen
gyroscope [ˈdʒaɪərəskəup] *n* Gyroskop *nt*

Hh

H, h [eɪtʃ] n (letter) H, h nt; **H for Harry, H for How** (US) ≈ H wie Heinrich

habeas corpus ['heɪbɪəs'kɔ:pəs] n Habeaskorpusakte f

haberdashery [hæbə'dæʃərɪ] (Brit) n Kurzwaren pl

habit ['hæbɪt] n Gewohnheit f; (esp undesirable) Angewohnheit f; (addiction) Sucht f; (Rel) Habit m or nt; **to get out of/into the ~ of doing sth** sich abgewöhnen/angewöhnen, etw zu tun; **to be in the ~ of doing sth** die (An)gewohnheit haben, etw zu tun

habitable ['hæbɪtəbl] adj bewohnbar

habitat ['hæbɪtæt] n Heimat f; (of animals) Lebensraum m, Heimat f

habitation [hæbɪ'teɪʃən] n Wohnstätte f; **fit for human ~** für Wohnzwecke geeignet, bewohnbar

habitual [hə'bɪtjuəl] adj (action) gewohnt; (drinker) Gewohnheits-; (liar) gewohnheitsmäßig

habitually [hə'bɪtjuəlɪ] adv ständig

hack [hæk] vt, vi (also Comput) hacken ▷ n (pej: writer) Schreiberling m; (horse) Mietpferd nt

hacker ['hækəʳ] n (Comput) Hacker m

hackles ['hæklz] npl: **to make sb's ~ rise** (fig) jdn auf die Palme bringen (inf)

hackney cab ['hæknɪ-] n Taxi nt

hackneyed ['hæknɪd] adj abgedroschen

hacksaw ['hæksɔ:] n Metallsäge f

had [hæd] pt, pp of **have**

haddock ['hædək] (pl ~ or **haddocks**) n Schellfisch m

hadn't ['hædnt] = **had not**

haematology, (US) **hematology** ['hi:mə'tɔlədʒɪ] n Hämatologie f

haemoglobin, (US) **hemoglobin** ['hi:mə'gləubɪn] n Hämoglobin nt

haemophilia, (US) **hemophilia** ['hi:mə'fɪlɪə] n Bluterkrankheit f

haemorrhage, (US) **hemorrhage** ['hɛmərɪdʒ] n Blutung f

haemorrhoids, (US) **hemorrhoids** ['hɛmərɔɪdz] npl Hämorr(ho)iden pl

hag [hæg] n alte Hexe f; (witch) Hexe f

haggard ['hægəd] adj ausgezehrt; (from worry) abgehärmt; (from tiredness) abgespannt

haggis ['hægɪs] (Scot) n Gericht aus gehackten Schafsinnereien und Haferschrot, im Schafsmagen gekocht

haggle ['hægl] vi: **to ~ (over)** feilschen (um)

haggling ['hæglɪŋ] n Feilschen nt

Hague [heɪg] n: **The ~** Den Haag m

hail [heɪl] n Hagel m ▷ vt (person) zurufen +dat; (taxi) herbeiwinken, anhalten; (acclaim: person) zujubeln +dat; (: event etc) bejubeln ▷ vi hageln; **he ~s from Scotland** er kommt or stammt aus Schottland

hailstone ['heɪlstəun] n Hagelkorn nt

hailstorm ['heɪlstɔ:m] n Hagelschauer m

hair [hɛəʳ] n (collectively: of person) Haar nt, Haare pl; (: of animal) Fell nt; (single hair) Haar nt; **to do one's ~** sich frisieren; **by a ~'s breadth** um Haaresbreite

hairbrush ['hɛəbrʌʃ] n Haarbürste f

haircut ['hɛəkʌt] n Haarschnitt m; (style) Frisur f

hairdo ['hɛədu:] n Frisur f

hairdresser ['hɛədrɛsəʳ] n Friseur m, Friseuse f

hairdresser's ['hɛədrɛsəz] n Friseursalon m

hair dryer n Haartrockner m, Föhn f, Fön® m

-haired [hɛəd] suff: **fair-~** blond; **long-~** langhaarig

hairgrip ['hɛəgrɪp] n Haarklemme f

hairline ['hɛəlaɪn] n Haaransatz m

hairline fracture n Haarriss m

hairnet ['hɛənɛt] n Haarnetz nt

hair oil n Haaröl nt

hairpiece ['hɛəpi:s] n Haarteil nt; (for men) Toupet nt

hairpin ['hɛəpɪn] n Haarnadel f

hairpin bend, (US) **hairpin curve** n Haarnadelkurve f

hair-raising ['hɛəreɪzɪŋ] adj haarsträubend

hair remover n Enthaarungscreme f

hair slide n Haarspange f

hair spray n Haarspray nt

hairstyle ['hɛəstaɪl] n Frisur f

hairy ['hɛərɪ] adj behaart; (inf: situation) brenzlig, haarig

Haiti ['heɪtɪ] n Haiti nt

hake [heɪk] (pl ~ or **hakes**) n Seehecht m

halcyon ['hælsɪən] adj glücklich

hale [heɪl] adj: **~ and hearty** gesund und munter

half [hɑ:f] (pl **halves**) n Hälfte f; (of beer etc)

kleines Bier *nt etc*; (*Rail, bus*) Fahrkarte *f* zum halben Preis ▷ *adj, adv* halb; **first/second ~** (*Sport*) erste/zweite Halbzeit *f*; **two and a ~** zweieinhalb; **--an-hour** eine halbe Stunde; **~ a dozen/pound** ein halbes Dutzend/Pfund; **a week and a ~** eineinhalb *or* anderthalb Wochen; **~ (of it)** die Hälfte; **~ (of)** die Hälfte (von *or* +*gen*); **~ the amount of** die halbe Menge an +*dat*; **to cut sth in ~** etw halbieren; **~ past three** halb vier; **to go halves (with sb)** (mit jdm) halbe-halbe machen; **she never does things by halves** sie macht keine halben Sachen; **he's too clever by ~** er ist ein richtiger Schlaumeier; **~ empty** halb leer; **~ closed** halb geschlossen

half-baked ['hɑːf'beɪkt] *adj* blödsinnig (*inf*)
half board *n* Halbpension *f*
half-breed ['hɑːfbriːd] *n* (*pej*) = **half-caste**
half-brother ['hɑːfbrʌðəʳ] *n* Halbbruder *m*
half-caste ['hɑːfkɑːst] *n* (*pej*) Mischling *m*
half-day [hɑːf'deɪ] *n* halber freier Tag *m*
half-hearted ['hɑːf'hɑːtɪd] *adj* halbherzig, lustlos
half-hour [hɑːf'auəʳ] *n* halbe Stunde *f*
half-life ['hɑːflaɪf] *n* (*Tech*) Halbwertszeit *f*
half-mast ['hɑːf'mɑːst]: **at ~** *adv* (auf) halbmast
halfpenny ['heɪpnɪ] (*Brit*) *n* halber Penny *m*
half-price ['hɑːf'praɪs] *adj, adv* zum halben Preis
half-sister ['hɑːfsɪstəʳ] *n* Halbschwester *f*
half term (*Brit*) *n* kleine Ferien *pl* (*in der Mitte des Trimesters*)
half-timbered [hɑːf'tɪmbəd] *adj* (*house*) Fachwerk-
half-time [hɑːf'taɪm] *n* (*Sport*) Halbzeit *f*
halfway ['hɑːf'weɪ] *adv*: **~ to** auf halbem Wege nach; **~ through** mitten in +*dat*; **to meet sb ~** (*fig*) jdm auf halbem Wege entgegenkommen
halfway house *n* (*hostel*) offene Anstalt *f*; (*fig*) Zwischending *nt*; (: *compromise*) Kompromiss *m*
halfwit ['hɑːfwɪt] *n* Schwachsinnige(r) *f(m)*; (*fig: inf*) Schwachkopf *m*
half-yearly [hɑːf'jɪəlɪ] *adv* halbjährlich, jedes halbe Jahr ▷ *adj* halbjährlich
halibut ['hælɪbət] *n inv* Heilbutt *m*
halitosis [hælɪ'təusɪs] *n* schlechter Atem *m*, Mundgeruch *m*
hall [hɔːl] *n* Diele *f*, (*Haus*)flur *m*; (*corridor*) Korridor *m*, Flur *m*; (*mansion*) Herrensitz *m*, Herrenhaus *nt*; (*for concerts etc*) Halle *f*; **to live in ~** (*Brit*) im Wohnheim wohnen
hallmark ['hɔːlmɑːk] *n* (*on gold, silver*) (Feingehalts)stempel *m*; (*of writer, artist etc*) Kennzeichen *nt*
hallo [hə'ləu] *excl* = **hello**
hall of residence (*pl* **halls of residence**) (*Brit*) *n* Studentenwohnheim *nt*
hallowed ['hæləud] *adj* (*ground*) heilig; (*fig: respected, revered*) geheiligt
Hallowe'en ['hæləu'iːn] *n* der Tag vor Allerheiligen

Hallowe'en ist der 31. Oktober, der Vorabend von Allerheiligen und nach altem Glauben der Abend, an dem man Geister und Hexen sehen kann. In Großbritannien und vor allem in den USA feiern die Kinder Hallowe'en, indem sie sich verkleiden und mit selbst gemachten Laternen aus Kürbissen von Tür zu Tür ziehen.

hallucination [həluːsɪ'neɪʃən] *n* Halluzination *f*
hallucinogenic [həluːsɪnəu'dʒɛnɪk] *adj* (*drug*) halluzinogen ▷ *n* Halluzinogen *nt*
hallway ['hɔːlweɪ] *n* Diele *f*, (*Haus*)flur *m*
halo ['heɪləu] *n* Heiligenschein *m*; (*circle of light*) Hof *m*
halt [hɔːlt] *vt* anhalten; (*progress etc*) zum Stillstand bringen ▷ *vi* anhalten, zum Stillstand kommen ▷ *n*: **to come to a ~** zum Stillstand kommen; **to call a ~ to sth** (*fig*) einer Sache *dat* ein Ende machen
halter ['hɔːltəʳ] *n* Halfter *nt*
halter-neck ['hɔːltənɛk] *adj* (*dress*) rückenfrei mit Nackenverschluss
halve [hɑːv] *vt* halbieren
halves [hɑːvz] *pl of* **half**
ham [hæm] *n* Schinken *m*; (*inf: also*: **radio ham**) Funkamateur *m*; (: *actor*) Schmierenkomödiant(in) *m(f)*
Hamburg ['hæmbəːg] *n* Hamburg *nt*
hamburger ['hæmbəːgəʳ] *n* Hamburger *m*
ham-fisted ['hæm'fɪstɪd], (*US*) **ham-handed** ['hæm'hændɪd] *adj* ungeschickt
hamlet ['hæmlɪt] *n* Weiler *m*, kleines Dorf *nt*
hammer ['hæməʳ] *n* Hammer *m* ▷ *vt* hämmern; (*fig: criticize*) vernichtend kritisieren; (: *defeat*) vernichtend schlagen ▷ *vi* hämmern; **to ~ sth into sb, to ~ sth across to sb** jdm etw einhämmern *or* einbläuen ► **hammer out** *vt* hämmern; (*solution, agreement*) ausarbeiten
hammock ['hæmək] *n* Hängematte *f*
hamper ['hæmpəʳ] *vt* behindern ▷ *n* Korb *m*
hamster ['hæmstəʳ] *n* Hamster *m*
hamstring ['hæmstrɪŋ] *n* Kniesehne *f* ▷ *vt* einengen
hand [hænd] *n* Hand *f*; (*of clock*) Zeiger *m*; (*handwriting*) Hand(schrift) *f*; (*worker*) Arbeiter(in) *m(f)*; (*of cards*) Blatt *nt*; (*measurement: of horse*) ≈ 10 cm ▷ *vt* geben, reichen; **to give** *or* **lend sb a ~** jdm helfen; **at ~** (*place*) in der Nähe; (*time*) unmittelbar bevorstehend; **by ~** von Hand; **in ~** (*time*) zur Verfügung; (*job*) anstehend; (*situation*) unter Kontrolle; **we have the matter in ~** wir haben die Sache im Griff; **on ~** zur Verfügung; **out of ~** *adj* außer Kontrolle ▷ *adv* (*reject etc*) rundweg; **to ~** zur Hand; **on the one ~ ...**, **on the other ~ ...** einerseits ... andererseits ...;

to force sb's ~ jdn zwingen; **to have a free ~** freie Hand haben; **to change ~s** den Besitzer wechseln; **to have in one's ~** (also fig) in der Hand halten; **"~s off!"** „Hände weg!"
▶ **hand down** vt (knowledge) weitergeben; (possessions) vererben; (Law: judgement, sentence) fällen
▶ **hand in** vt abgeben, einreichen
▶ **hand out** vt verteilen; (information) austeilen; (punishment) verhängen
▶ **hand over** vt übergeben
▶ **hand round** vt (Brit) verteilen; (chocolates etc) herumreichen
handbag ['hændbæg] n Handtasche f
hand baggage n Handgepäck nt
handball ['hændbɔ:l] n Handball m
hand basin n Handwaschbecken nt
handbook ['hændbuk] n Handbuch nt
handbrake ['hændbreɪk] n Handbremse f
h & c (Brit) abbr (= hot and cold (water)) h. u. k.
hand cream n Handcreme f
handcuff ['hændkʌf] vt Handschellen anlegen +dat
handcuffs ['hændkʌfs] npl Handschellen pl
handful ['hændful] n Handvoll f
hand-held ['hænd'held] adj (camera) Hand-
handicap ['hændɪkæp] n Behinderung f; (disadvantage) Nachteil m; (Sport) Handicap nt ▷ vt benachteiligen; **mentally/physically ~ped** geistig/körperlich behindert
handicraft ['hændɪkrɑ:ft] n Kunsthandwerk nt; (object) Kunsthandwerksarbeit f
handiwork ['hændɪwə:k] n Arbeit f; **this looks like his ~** (pej) das sieht nach seiner Arbeit aus
handkerchief ['hæŋkətʃɪf] n Taschentuch nt
handle ['hændl] n Griff m; (of door) Klinke f; (of cup) Henkel m; (of broom, brush etc) Stiel m; (for winding) Kurbel f; (CB Radio: name) Sendezeichen nt ▷ vt anfassen, berühren; (problem etc) sich befassen mit; (: successfully) fertig werden mit; (people) umgehen mit; **"~ with care"** „Vorsicht – zerbrechlich"; **to fly off the ~** an die Decke gehen; **to get a ~ on a problem** (inf) ein Problem in den Griff bekommen
handlebar ['hændlbɑ:ʳ] n, **handlebars** ['hændlbɑ:z] ▷ npl Lenkstange f
handling ['hændlɪŋ] n: **~ (of)** (of plant, animal, issue etc) Behandlung f +gen; (of person, tool, machine etc) Umgang m (mit); (Admin) Bearbeitung f +gen
handling charges npl Bearbeitungsgebühr f; (Banking) Kontoführungsgebühr f
hand luggage n Handgepäck nt
handmade ['hænd'meɪd] adj handgearbeitet
hand-out ['hændaut] n (money, food etc) Unterstützung f; (publicity leaflet) Flugblatt nt; (summary) Informationsblatt nt
hand-picked ['hænd'pɪkt] adj von Hand geerntet; (staff etc) handverlesen
handrail ['hændreɪl] n Geländer nt
handset ['hændset] n (Tel) Hörer m
hands-free ['hændzfri:] adj (telephone, microphone) Freisprech-

handshake ['hændʃeɪk] n Händedruck m
handsome ['hænsəm] adj gut aussehend; (building) schön; (gift) großzügig; (profit, return) ansehnlich
hands-on ['hændz'ɔn] adj (training) praktisch; (approach etc) aktiv; **~ experience** praktische Erfahrung
handstand ['hændstænd] n: **to do a ~** einen Handstand machen
hand-to-mouth ['hændtə'mauθ] adj: **to lead a ~ existence** von der Hand in den Mund leben
handwriting ['hændraɪtɪŋ] n Handschrift f
handwritten ['hændrɪtn] adj handgeschrieben
handy ['hændɪ] adj praktisch; (skilful) geschickt; (close at hand) in der Nähe; **to come in ~** sich als nützlich erweisen
handyman ['hændɪmæn] (irreg: like **man**) n (at home) Heimwerker m; (in hotel etc) Faktotum nt
hang [hæŋ] (pt, pp **hung**) vt aufhängen; (criminal: pt, pp **~ed**) hängen; (head) hängen lassen ▷ vi hängen; (hair, drapery) fallen ▷ n: **to get the ~ of sth** (inf) den richtigen Dreh (bei etw) herauskriegen
▶ **hang about** vi herumlungern
▶ **hang around** vi = **hang about**
▶ **hang back** vi: **to ~ back (from doing sth)** zögern(, etw zu tun)
▶ **hang on** vi warten ▷ vt fus (depend on) abhängen von; **to ~ on to** festhalten; (for protection, support) sich festhalten an +dat; (hope, position) sich klammern an +acc; (ideas) festhalten an +dat; (keep) behalten
▶ **hang out** vt draußen aufhängen ▷ vi heraushängen; (inf: live) wohnen
▶ **hang together** vi (argument) folgerichtig or zusammenhängend sein; (story, explanation) zusammenhängend sein; (statements) zusammenpassen
▶ **hang up** vt aufhängen ▷ vi (Tel): **to ~ up (on sb)** einfach auflegen
hangar ['hæŋəʳ] n Hangar m, Flugzeughalle f
hangdog ['hæŋdɔg] adj zerknirscht
hanger ['hæŋəʳ] n Bügel m
hanger-on [hæŋəʳ'ɔn] n (parasite) Trabant m (inf); **the hangers-on** der Anhang
hang-glide ['hæŋglaɪd] vi drachenfliegen
hang-glider ['hæŋglaɪdəʳ] n (Flug)drachen m
hang-gliding ['hæŋglaɪdɪŋ] n Drachenfliegen nt
hanging ['hæŋɪŋ] n (execution) Hinrichtung f durch den Strang; (for wall) Wandbehang m
hangman ['hæŋmən] (irreg: like **man**) n Henker m
hangover ['hæŋəuvəʳ] n Kater m; (from past) Überbleibsel nt
hang-up ['hæŋʌp] n Komplex m
hank [hæŋk] n Strang m
hanker ['hæŋkəʳ] vi: **to ~ after** sich sehnen nach
hankering ['hæŋkərɪŋ] n: **~ (for)** Verlangen nt (nach)
hankie, hanky ['hæŋkɪ] (pl **~s**) n = **handkerchief**

589

haphazard [hæp'hæzəd] *adj* planlos, wahllos

hapless ['hæplɪs] *adj* glücklos

happen ['hæpən] *vi* geschehen; **to ~ to do sth** zufällig(erweise) etw tun; **as it ~s** zufälligerweise; **what's ~ing?** was ist los?; **she ~ed to be free** sie hatte zufällig(erweise) gerade Zeit; **if anything ~ed to him** wenn ihm etwas zustoßen *or* passieren sollte
▶ **happen (up)on** *vt fus* zufällig stoßen auf +*acc*; *(person)* zufällig treffen

happening ['hæpnɪŋ] *n* Ereignis *nt*, Vorfall *m*

happily ['hæpɪlɪ] *adv (luckily)* glücklicherweise; *(cheerfully)* fröhlich

happiness ['hæpɪnɪs] *n* Glück *nt*

happy ['hæpɪ] *adj* glücklich; *(cheerful)* fröhlich; **to be ~ (with)** zufrieden sein (mit); **to be ~ to do sth** etw gerne tun; **~ birthday!** herzlichen Glückwunsch zum Geburtstag!

happy-go-lucky ['hæpɪgəʊ'lʌkɪ] *adj* unbekümmert

happy hour *n* Zeit, in der Bars, Pubs usw Getränke zu ermäßigten Preisen anbieten

harangue [hə'ræŋ] *vt* predigen +*dat* (*inf*)

harass ['hærəs] *vt* schikanieren

harassed ['hærəst] *adj* geplagt

harassment ['hærəsmənt] *n* Schikanierung *f*; **sexual ~** sexuelle Belästigung *f*

harbour, *(US)* **harbor** ['hɑːbəʳ] *n* Hafen *m* ▷ *vt (hope, fear, grudge etc)* hegen; *(criminal, fugitive)* Unterschlupf gewähren +*dat*

harbour dues *npl* Hafengebühren *pl*

harbour master *n* Hafenmeister *m*

hard [hɑːd] *adj* hart; *(question, problem)* schwierig; *(evidence)* gesichert ▷ *adv (work)* hart, schwer; *(think)* scharf; *(try)* sehr; **~ luck!** Pech!; **no ~ feelings!** ich nehme es dir nicht übel; **to be ~ of hearing** schwerhörig sein; **to be ~ done by** ungerecht behandelt werden; **I find it ~ to believe that ...** ich kann es kaum glauben, dass ...; **to look ~ at sth** *(object)* sich +*dat* etw genau ansehen; *(idea)* etw gründlich prüfen

hard-and-fast ['hɑːdən'fɑːst] *adj* fest

hardback ['hɑːdbæk] *n* gebundene Ausgabe *f*

hardboard ['hɑːdbɔːd] *n* Hartfaserplatte *f*

hard-boiled egg ['hɑːd'bɔɪld-] *n* hart gekochtes Ei *nt*

hard cash *n* Bargeld *nt*

hard copy *n (Comput)* Ausdruck *m*

hard core *n* harter Kern *m*

hard-core ['hɑːd'kɔːʳ] *adj (pornography)* hart; *(supporters)* zum harten Kern gehörend

hard court *n (Tennis)* Hartplatz *m*

hard disk *n (Comput)* Festplatte *f*

harden ['hɑːdn] *vt* härten; *(attitude, person)* verhärten ▷ *vi* hart werden, sich verhärten

hardened ['hɑːdnd] *adj (criminal)* Gewohnheits-; **to be ~ to sth** gegen etw abgehärtet sein

hardening ['hɑːdnɪŋ] *n* Verhärtung *f*

hard graft *n*: **by sheer ~** durch harte Arbeit

hard-headed ['hɑːd'hedɪd] *adj* nüchtern

hardhearted ['hɑːd'hɑːtɪd] *adj* hartherzig

hard-hitting ['hɑːd'hɪtɪŋ] *adj (fig: speech,*

journalist etc) knallhart

hard labour *n* Zwangsarbeit *f*

hardliner [hɑːd'laɪnəʳ] *n* Vertreter(in) *m(f)* der harten Linie

hard-luck story ['hɑːdlʌk-] *n* Leidensgeschichte *f*

hardly ['hɑːdlɪ] *adv* kaum; *(harshly)* hart, streng; **it's ~ the case** *(ironic)* das ist wohl kaum der Fall; **I can ~ believe it** ich kann es kaum glauben

hard-nosed [hɑːd'nəʊzd] *adj* abgebrüht

hard-pressed [hɑːd'prest] *adj*: **to be ~** unter Druck sein; **~ for money** in Geldnot

hard sell *n* aggressive Verkaufstaktik *f*

hardship ['hɑːdʃɪp] *n* Not *f*

hard shoulder *(Brit)* *n (Aut)* Seitenstreifen *m*

hard up *(inf)* *adj* knapp bei Kasse

hardware ['hɑːdwɛəʳ] *n* Eisenwaren *pl*; *(household goods)* Haushaltswaren *pl*; *(Comput)* Hardware *f*; *(Mil)* Waffen *pl*

hardware shop *n* Eisenwarenhandlung *f*

hard-wearing [hɑːd'wɛərɪŋ] *adj* strapazierfähig

hard-won [hɑːd'wʌn] *adj* schwer erkämpft

hard-working [hɑːd'wəːkɪŋ] *adj* fleißig

hardy ['hɑːdɪ] *adj (animals)* zäh; *(people)* abgehärtet; *(plant)* winterhart

hare [hɛəʳ] *n* Hase *m*

harebrained ['hɛəbreɪnd] *adj* verrückt

harelip ['hɛəlɪp] *n* Hasenscharte *f*

harem [hɑː'riːm] *n* Harem *m*

hark back [hɑːk-] *vi*: **to ~ to** zurückkommen auf +*acc*

harm [hɑːm] *n* Schaden *m*; *(injury)* Verletzung *f* ▷ *vt* schaden +*dat*; *(person: physically)* verletzen; **to mean no ~** es nicht böse meinen; **out of ~'s way** in Sicherheit; **there's no ~ in trying** es kann nicht schaden, es zu versuchen

harmful ['hɑːmful] *adj* schädlich

harmless ['hɑːmlɪs] *adj* harmlos

harmonic [hɑː'mɔnɪk] *adj* harmonisch

harmonica [hɑː'mɔnɪkə] *n* Harmonika *f*

harmonics [hɑː'mɔnɪks] *npl* Harmonik *f*

harmonious [hɑː'məʊnɪəs] *adj* harmonisch

harmonium [hɑː'məʊnɪəm] *n* Harmonium *nt*

harmonize ['hɑːmənaɪz] *vi (Mus)* mehrstimmig singen/spielen; *(: one person)* die zweite Stimme singen/spielen; *(colours, ideas)* harmonieren

harmony ['hɑːmənɪ] *n* Einklang *m*; *(Mus)* Harmonie *f*

harness ['hɑːnɪs] *n (for horse)* Geschirr *nt*; *(for child)* Laufgurt *m*; *(also:* **safety harness***)* Sicherheitsgurt *m* ▷ *vt (resources, energy etc)* nutzbar machen; *(horse, dog)* anschirren

harp [hɑːp] *n* Harfe *f* ▷ *vi*: **to ~ on about** *(pej)* herumreiten auf +*dat*

harpist ['hɑːpɪst] *n* Harfenspieler(in) *m(f)*

harpoon [hɑː'puːn] *n* Harpune *f*

harpsichord ['hɑːpsɪkɔːd] *n* Cembalo *nt*

harried ['hærɪd] *adj* bedrängt

harrow ['hærəʊ] *n* Egge *f*

harrowing ['hærəʊɪŋ] *adj (film)* erschütternd;

(experience) grauenhaft

harry ['hærɪ] vt bedrängen, zusetzen +dat

harsh [hɑːʃ] adj *(sound, light)* grell; *(judge, winter)* streng; *(criticism, life)* hart

harshly ['hɑːʃlɪ] adv *(judge)* streng; *(say)* barsch; *(criticize)* hart

harshness ['hɑːʃnɪs] n *(see adj)* Grelle f; Strenge f; Härte f

harvest ['hɑːvɪst] n Ernte f ▷ vt ernten

harvester ['hɑːvɪstə^r] n *(also:* **combine harvester***)* Mähdrescher m

has [hæz] vb *see* **have**

has-been ['hæzbiːn] *(inf)* n: **he's/she's a ~** er/sie ist eine vergangene or vergessene Größe

hash [hæʃ] n *(Culin)* Haschee nt; *(fig)*: **to make a ~ of sth** etw verpfuschen *(inf)* ▷ n abbr *(inf)* *(= hashish)* Hasch nt

hashish ['hæʃɪʃ] n Haschisch nt

hasn't ['hæznt] = **has not**

hassle ['hæsl] *(inf)* n *(bother)* Theater nt ▷ vt schikanieren

haste [heɪst] n Hast f; *(speed)* Eile f; **in ~** in Eile

hasten ['heɪsn] vt beschleunigen ▷ vi: **to ~ to do sth** sich beeilen, etw zu tun; **I ~ to add …** ich muss allerdings hinzufügen, …; **she ~ed back to the house** sie eilte zum Haus zurück

hastily ['heɪstɪlɪ] adv *(see adj)* hastig, eilig; vorschnell

hasty ['heɪstɪ] adj hastig, eilig; *(rash)* vorschnell

hat [hæt] n Hut m; **to keep sth under one's ~** etw für sich behalten

hatbox ['hætbɒks] n Hutschachtel f

hatch [hætʃ] n *(Naut: also:* **hatchway***)* Luke f; *(also:* **service hatch***)* Durchreiche f ▷ vi *(bird)* ausschlüpfen ▷ vt ausbrüten; **the eggs ~ed after 10 days** nach 10 Tagen schlüpften die Jungen aus

hatchback ['hætʃbæk] n *(Aut: car)* Heckklappenmodell nt

hatchet ['hætʃɪt] n Beil nt; **to bury the ~** das Kriegsbeil begraben

hatchet job *(inf)* adj: **to do a ~ on sb** jdn fertigmachen

hatchet man *(inf)* n *(fig)* Vollstrecker m

hate [heɪt] vt hassen ▷ n Hass m; **I ~ him/milk** ich kann ihn/ Milch nicht ausstehen; **to ~ to do/doing sth** es hassen, etw zu tun; *(weaker)* etw ungern tun; **I ~ to trouble you, but …** es ist mir sehr unangenehm, dass ich Sie belästigen muss, aber …

hateful ['heɪtful] adj abscheulich

hater ['heɪtə^r] n Hasser(in) m(f); **cop-~** Bullenhasser(in) m(f); **woman-~** Frauenhasser m

hatred ['heɪtrɪd] n Hass m; *(dislike)* Abneigung f

hat trick n Hattrick m

haughty ['hɔːtɪ] adj überheblich

haul [hɔːl] vt ziehen; *(by lorry)* transportieren; *(Naut)* den Kurs ändern +gen ▷ n Beute f; *(of fish)* Fang m; **he ~ed himself out of the pool** er stemmte sich aus dem Schwimmbecken

haulage ['hɔːlɪdʒ] n *(cost)* Transportkosten pl; *(business)* Transport m

haulage contractor *(Brit)* n Transportunternehmen nt, Spedition f; *(person)* Transportunternehmer(in) m(f), Spediteur m

hauler ['hɔːlə^r] *(US)* n Transportunternehmer(in) m(f), Spediteur m

haulier ['hɔːlɪə^r] *(Brit)* n Transportunternehmer(in) m(f), Spediteur m

haunch [hɔːntʃ] n Hüftpartie f; *(of meat)* Keule f

haunt [hɔːnt] vt *(place)* spuken in +dat, umgehen in +dat; *(person, fig)* verfolgen ▷ n Lieblingsplatz m; *(of crooks etc)* Treffpunkt m

haunted ['hɔːntɪd] adj *(expression)* gehetzt, gequält; **this building/room is ~ in** diesem Gebäude/Zimmer spukt es

haunting ['hɔːntɪŋ] adj *(music)* eindringlich; **a ~ sight** ein Anblick, der einen nicht loslässt

Havana [hə'vænə] n Havanna nt

 KEYWORD

have [hæv] *(pt, pp* **had***)* aux vb **1** haben; *(with verbs of motion)* sein; **to have arrived/gone** angekommen/gegangen sein; **to have eaten/slept** gegessen/geschlafen haben; **he has been promoted** er ist befördert worden; **having eaten** or **when he had eaten, he left** nachdem er gegessen hatte, ging er

2 *(in tag questions)*: **you've done it, haven't you?** du hast es gemacht, nicht wahr?; **he hasn't done it, has he?** er hat es nicht gemacht, oder?

3 *(in short answers and questions)*: **you've made a mistake — no I haven't/so I have** du hast einen Fehler gemacht — nein(, das habe ich nicht)/ja, stimmt; **we haven't paid — yes we have!** wir haben nicht bezahlt — doch!; **I've been there before — have you?** ich war schon einmal da — wirklich or tatsächlich? ▷ modal aux vb *(be obliged)*: **to have (got) to do sth** etw tun müssen; **this has (got) to be a mistake** das muss ein Fehler sein ▷ vt **1** *(possess)* haben; **she has (got) blue eyes/ dark hair** sie hat blaue Augen/dunkle Haare; **I have (got) an idea** ich habe eine Idee

2 *(referring to meals etc)*: **to have breakfast** frühstücken; **to have lunch/dinner** zu Mittag/Abend essen; **to have a drink** etwas trinken; **to have a cigarette** eine Zigarette rauchen

3 *(receive, obtain etc)* haben; **may I have your address?** kann ich Ihre Adresse haben or bekommen?; **to have a baby** ein Kind bekommen

4 *(allow)*: **I won't have this nonsense** dieser Unsinn kommt nicht infrage!; **we can't have that** das kommt nicht infrage

5: **to have sth done** etw machen lassen; **to have one's hair cut** sich dat die Haare schneiden lassen; **to have sb do sth** *(order)* jdn etw tun lassen; **he soon had them all laughing/working** bald hatte er alle zum Lachen/Arbeiten gebracht

591

6 (*experience, suffer*): **to have a cold/flu** eine Erkältung/die Grippe haben; **she had her bag stolen** ihr *dat* wurde die Tasche gestohlen
7 (*+ noun: take, hold etc*): **to have a swim** schwimmen gehen; **to have a walk** spazieren gehen; **to have a rest** sich ausruhen; **to have a meeting** eine Besprechung haben; **to have a party** eine Party geben
8 (*inf: dupe*): **you've been had** man hat dich hereingelegt
▸ **have in** (*inf*) *vt*: **to have it in for sb** jdn auf dem Kieker haben
▸ **have on** *vt* (*wear*) anhaben; (*Brit: inf: tease*) auf den Arm nehmen; **I don't have any money on me** ich habe kein Geld bei mir; **do you have** *or* **have you anything on tomorrow?** haben Sie morgen etwas vor?
▸ **have out** *vt*: **to have it out with sb** (*settle a problem etc*) ein Wort mit jdm reden

haven ['heɪvn] *n* Hafen *m*; (*safe place*) Zufluchtsort *m*
haven't ['hævnt] = **have not**
haversack ['hævəsæk] *n* Rucksack *m*
haves [hævz] (*inf*) *npl*: **the ~ and the have-nots** die Betuchten und die Habenichtse
havoc ['hævək] *n* Verwüstung *f*; (*confusion*) Chaos *nt*; **to play ~ with sth** (*disrupt*) etw völlig durcheinanderbringen
Hawaii [hə'waiː] *n* Hawaii *nt*
Hawaiian [hə'waɪjən] *adj* hawaiisch ▷ *n* Hawaiianer(in) *m(f)*; (*Ling*) Hawaiisch *nt*
hawk [hɔ:k] *n* Habicht *m*
hawker ['hɔ:kə'] *n* Hausierer(in) *m(f)*
hawkish ['hɔ:kɪʃ] *adj* (*person, approach*) knallhart
hawthorn ['hɔ:θɔ:n] *n* Weißdorn *m*, Rotdorn *m*
hay [heɪ] *n* Heu *nt*
hay fever *n* Heuschnupfen *m*
haystack ['heɪstæk] *n* Heuhaufen *m*
haywire ['heɪwaɪə'] (*inf*) *adj*: **to go ~** (*machine*) verrücktspielen; (*plans etc*) über den Haufen geworfen werden
hazard ['hæzəd] *n* Gefahr *f* ▷ *vt* riskieren; **to be a health/fire ~** eine Gefahr für die Gesundheit/feuergefährlich sein; **to ~ a guess** (*es*) wagen, eine Vermutung anzustellen
hazard lights (*Aut*) Warnblinkanlage *f*
hazardous ['hæzədəs] *adj* gefährlich
hazard pay (*US*) *n* Gefahrenzulage *f*
hazard warning lights *npl* = **hazard lights**
haze [heɪz] *n* Dunst *m*
hazel ['heɪzl] *n* Hasel(nuss)strauch *m*, Haselbusch *m* ▷ *adj* haselnussbraun
hazelnut ['heɪzlnʌt] *n* Haselnuss *f*
hazy ['heɪzi] *adj* dunstig, diesig; (*idea, memory*) unklar, verschwommen; **I'm rather ~ about the details** an die Einzelheiten kann ich mich nur vage *or* verschwommen erinnern; (*ignorant*) die genauen Einzelheiten sind mir nicht bekannt
H-bomb ['eɪtʃbɔm] *n* H-Bombe *f*
HD *n abbr* (= *high definition*) hochauflösend

HDTV *n abbr* (= *high definition television*) hochauflösendes Fernsehen
HE *abbr* (*Rel, Diplomacy*: = *His/Her Excellency*) Seine/Ihre Exzellenz; (= *high explosive*) hochexplosiver Sprengstoff *m*
he [hi:] *pron* er ▷ *pref* männlich; **he who ...** wer ...
head [hɛd] *n* Kopf *m*; (*of table*) Kopfende *nt*; (*of queue*) Spitze *f*; (*of company, organization*) Leiter(in) *m(f)*; (*of school*) Schulleiter(in) *m(f)*; (*on coin*) Kopfseite *f*; (*on tape recorder*) Tonkopf *m* ▷ *vt* anführen, an der Spitze stehen von; (*group, company*) leiten; (*Football: ball*) köpfen; **~s (or tails)** Kopf (oder Zahl); **~ over heels** Hals über Kopf; (*in love*) bis über beide Ohren; **£10 a** *or* **per ~** 10 Pfund pro Kopf; **at the ~ of the list** oben auf der Liste; **to have a ~ for business** einen guten Geschäftssinn haben; **to have no ~ for heights** nicht schwindelfrei sein; **to come to a ~** sich zuspitzen; **they put their ~s together** sie haben sich zusammengesetzt; **off the top of my** *etc* **~** ohne lange zu überlegen; **on your own ~ be it!** auf Ihre eigene Verantwortung *or* Kappe (*inf*)!; **to bite** *or* **snap sb's ~ off** jdn grob anfahren; **he won't bite your ~ off** er wird dir schon nicht den Kopf abreißen; **it went to my ~** es ist mir in den Kopf *or* zu Kopf gestiegen; **to lose/keep one's ~** den Kopf verlieren/nicht verlieren; **I can't make ~ nor tail of this** hieraus werde ich nicht schlau; **he's off his ~!** (*inf*) er ist nicht (ganz) bei Trost!
▸ **head for** *vt fus* (*on foot*) zusteuern auf +*acc*; (*by car*) in Richtung ... fahren; (*plane, ship*) Kurs nehmen auf +*acc*; **you are ~ing for trouble** du wirst Ärger bekommen
▸ **head off** *vt* abwenden
headache ['hɛdeɪk] *n* Kopfschmerzen *pl*, Kopfweh *nt*; (*fig*) Problem *nt*; **to have a ~** Kopfschmerzen *or* Kopfweh haben
headband ['hɛdbænd] *n* Stirnband *nt*
headboard ['hɛdbɔ:d] *n* Kopfteil *nt*
head cold *n* Kopfgrippe *f*
headdress ['hɛddrɛs] (*Brit*) *n* Kopfschmuck *m*
headed notepaper ['hɛdɪd-] *n* Schreibpapier *nt* mit Briefkopf
header ['hɛdə'] (*Brit: inf*) *n* (*Football*) Kopfball *m*
headfirst ['hɛd'fə:st] *adv* (*lit*) kopfüber; (*fig*) Hals über Kopf
head-hunt ['hɛdhʌnt] *vt* abwerben
head-hunter ['hɛdhʌntə'] *n* (*Comm*) Kopfjäger(in) *m(f)*
heading ['hɛdɪŋ] *n* Überschrift *f*
headlamp ['hɛdlæmp] (*Brit*) *n* = **headlight**
headland ['hɛdlənd] *n* Landspitze *f*
headlight ['hɛdlaɪt] *n* Scheinwerfer *m*
headline ['hɛdlaɪn] *n* Schlagzeile *f*; (*Radio, TV*): **(news) ~s** Nachrichtenüberblick *m*
headlong ['hɛdlɔŋ] *adv* kopfüber; (*rush*) Hals über Kopf
headmaster [hɛd'mɑ:stə'] *n* Schulleiter *m*
headmistress [hɛd'mɪstrɪs] *n* Schulleiterin *f*
head office *n* Zentrale *f*

head of state (*pl* **heads of state**) *n* Staatsoberhaupt *nt*

head-on ['hɛd'ɔn] *adj* (*collision*) frontal; (*confrontation*) direkt

headphones ['hɛdfəunz] *npl* Kopfhörer *pl*

headquarters ['hɛdkwɔːtəz] *npl* Zentrale *f*; (*Mil*) Hauptquartier *nt*

headrest ['hɛdrɛst] *n* (*Aut*) Kopfstütze *f*

headroom ['hɛdrum] *n* (*in car*) Kopfraum *m*; (*under bridge*) lichte Höhe *f*

headscarf ['hɛdskaːf] *n* Kopftuch *nt*

headset ['hɛdsɛt] *n* = **headphones**

head start *n* Vorsprung *m*

headstone ['hɛdstəun] *n* Grabstein *m*

headstrong ['hɛdstrɔŋ] *adj* eigensinnig

head waiter *n* Oberkellner *m*

headway ['hɛdweɪ] *n*: **to make ~** vorankommen

headwind ['hɛdwɪnd] *n* Gegenwind *m*

heady ['hɛdɪ] *adj* (*experience etc*) aufregend; (*drink, atmosphere*) berauschend

heal [hiːl] *vt, vi* heilen

health [hɛlθ] *n* Gesundheit *f*

health care *n* Gesundheitsfürsorge *f*

health centre (*Brit*) *n* Ärztezentrum *nt*

health food *n* Reformkost *f*, Naturkost *f*

health food shop *n* Reformhaus *nt*, Naturkostladen *m*

health hazard *n* Gefahr *f* für die Gesundheit

health service (*Brit*) *n*: **the Health Service** das Gesundheitswesen

healthy ['hɛlθɪ] *adj* gesund; (*profit*) ansehnlich

heap [hiːp] *n* Haufen *m* ▷ *vt*: **to ~ (up)** (auf) häufen; **~s of** (*inf*) jede Menge; **to ~ sth with** etw beladen mit; **to ~ sth on** etw häufen auf +*acc*; **to ~ favours/gifts etc on sb** jdn mit Gefälligkeiten/Geschenken *etc* überhäufen; **to ~ praises on sb** jdn mit Lob überschütten

hear [hɪəʳ] (*pt, pp* **~d**) *vt* hören; (*Law: case*) verhandeln; (: *witness*) vernehmen; **to ~ about** hören von; **to ~ from sb** von jdm hören; **I've never ~d of that book** von dem Buch habe ich noch nie etwas gehört; **I wouldn't ~ of it!** davon will ich nichts hören

▶ **hear out** *vt* ausreden lassen

heard [həːd] *pt, pp of* **hear**

hearing ['hɪərɪŋ] *n* Gehör *nt*; (*of facts, by committee*) Anhörung *f*; (*of witnesses*) Vernehmung *f*; (*of a case*) Verhandlung *f*; **to give sb a ~** (*Brit*) jdn anhören

hearing aid *n* Hörgerät *nt*

hearsay ['hɪəseɪ] *n* Gerüchte *pl*; **by ~** vom Hörensagen

hearse [həːs] *n* Leichenwagen *m*

heart [haːt] *n* Herz *nt*; (*of problem*) Kern *m*; **hearts** *npl* (*Cards*) Herz *nt*; **to lose ~** den Mut verlieren; **to take ~** Mut fassen; **at ~** im Grunde; **by ~** auswendig; **to set one's ~ on sth** sein Herz an etw *acc* hängen; **to set one's ~ on doing sth** alles daransetzen, etw zu tun; **the ~ of the matter** der Kern der Sache

heartache ['haːteɪk] *n* Kummer *m*

heart attack *n* Herzanfall *m*

heartbeat ['haːtbiːt] *n* Herzschlag *m*

heartbreak ['haːtbreɪk] *n* großer Kummer *m*, Leid *nt*

heartbreaking ['haːtbreɪkɪŋ] *adj* herzzerreißend

heartbroken ['haːtbrəukən] *adj*: **to be ~** todunglücklich sein

heartburn ['haːtbəːn] *n* Sodbrennen *nt*

-hearted ['haːtɪd] *suff*: **kind-~** gutherzig

heartening ['haːtnɪŋ] *adj* ermutigend

heart failure *n* Herzversagen *nt*

heartfelt ['haːtfɛlt] *adj* tief empfunden

hearth [haːθ] *n* ≈ Kamin *m*

heartily ['haːtɪlɪ] *adv* (*see adj*) (laut und) herzlich; herzhaft; tief; ungeteilt

heartland ['haːtlænd] *n* Herz *nt*; **Britain's industrial ~** Großbritanniens Industriezentrum *nt*

heartless ['haːtlɪs] *adj* herzlos

heartstrings ['haːtstrɪŋz] *npl*: **to tug at sb's ~** bei jdm auf die Tränendrüsen drücken

heart-throb ['haːtθrɔb] (*inf*) *n* Schwarm *m*

heart-to-heart ['haːt'tə'haːt] *adj, adv* ganz im Vertrauen

heart transplant *n* Herztransplantation *f*, Herzverpflanzung *f*

heart-warming ['haːtwɔːmɪŋ] *adj* herzerfreuend

hearty ['haːtɪ] *adj* (*person*) laut und herzlich; (*laugh, appetite*) herzhaft; (*welcome*) herzlich; (*dislike*) tief; (*support*) ungeteilt

heat [hiːt] *n* Hitze *f*; (*warmth*) Wärme *f*; (*temperature*) Temperatur *f*; (*Sport: also*: **qualifying heat**) Vorrunde *f* ▷ *vt* erhitzen, heiß machen; (*room, house*) heizen; **in ~, on ~** (*Brit: Zool*) brünstig, läufig

▶ **heat up** *vi* sich erwärmen, warm werden ▷ *vt* aufwärmen; (*water, room*) erwärmen

heated ['hiːtɪd] *adj* geheizt; (*pool*) beheizt; (*argument*) hitzig

heater ['hiːtəʳ] *n* (Heiz)ofen *m*; (*in car*) Heizung *f*

heath [hiːθ] (*Brit*) *n* Heide *f*

heathen ['hiːðn] *n* Heide *m*, Heidin *f*

heather ['hɛðəʳ] *n* Heidekraut *nt*, Erika *f*

heating ['hiːtɪŋ] *n* Heizung *f*

heat-resistant ['hiːtrɪzɪstənt] *adj* hitzebeständig

heat-seeking ['hiːtsiːkɪŋ] *adj* Wärme suchend

heatstroke ['hiːtstrəuk] *n* Hitzschlag *m*

heat wave *n* Hitzewelle *f*

heave [hiːv] *vt* (*pull*) ziehen; (*push*) schieben; (*lift*) (hoch)heben ▷ *vi* sich heben und senken; (*retch*) sich übergeben ▷ *n* (*see vt*) Zug *m*; Stoß *m*; Heben *nt*; **to ~ a sigh** einen Seufzer ausstoßen

▶ **heave to** (*pt, pp* **hove**) *vi* (*Naut*) beidrehen

heaven ['hɛvn] *n* Himmel *m*; **thank ~!** Gott sei Dank!; **~ forbid!** bloß nicht!; **for ~'s sake!** um Himmels *or* Gottes willen!

heavenly ['hɛvnlɪ] *adj* himmlisch

heaven-sent [hɛvn'sɛnt] *adj* ideal

heavily ['hɛvɪlɪ] *adv* schwer; (*drink, smoke, depend, rely*) stark; (*sleep, sigh*) tief; (*say*) mit schwerer Stimme

heavy ['hɛvɪ] *adj* schwer; (*clothes*) dick; (*rain, snow, drinker, smoker*) stark; (*build, frame*) kräftig; (*breathing, sleep*) tief; (*schedule, week*) anstrengend; (*weather*) drückend, schwül; **the conversation was ~ going** die Unterhaltung war mühsam; **the book was ~ going** das Buch las sich schwer

heavy cream (*US*) *n* Sahne mit hohem Fettgehalt, ≈ Schlagsahne *f*

heavy-duty ['hɛvɪ'dju:tɪ] *adj* strapazierfähig

heavy goods vehicle *n* Lastkraftwagen *m*

heavy-handed ['hɛvɪ'hændɪd] *adj* schwerfällig, ungeschickt

heavy industry *n* Schwerindustrie *f*

heavy metal *n* (*Mus*) Heavymetal *nt*

heavyset ['hɛvɪ'sɛt] (*esp US*) *adj* kräftig gebaut

heavyweight ['hɛvɪweɪt] *n* (*Sport*) Schwergewicht *nt*

Hebrew ['hi:bru:] *adj* hebräisch ▷ *n* (*Ling*) Hebräisch *nt*

Hebrides ['hɛbrɪdi:z] *npl*: **the ~** die Hebriden *pl*

heck [hɛk] (*inf*) *interj*: **oh ~!** zum Kuckuck!
▷ *n*: **a ~ of a lot** irrsinnig viel

heckle ['hɛkl] *vt* durch Zwischenrufe stören

heckler ['hɛklə'] *n* Zwischenrufer(in) *m(f)*, Störer(in) *m(f)*

hectare ['hɛktɑ:'] (*Brit*) *n* Hektar *nt* or *m*

hectic ['hɛktɪk] *adj* hektisch

hector ['hɛktə'] *vt* tyrannisieren

he'd [hi:d] = **he would; he had**

hedge [hɛdʒ] *n* Hecke *f* ▷ *vi* ausweichen, sich nicht festlegen ▷ *vt*: **to ~ one's bets** (*fig*) sich absichern; **as a ~ against inflation** als Absicherung *or* Schutz gegen die Inflation
▶ **hedge in** *vt* (*person*) (in seiner Freiheit) einschränken; (*proposals etc*) behindern

hedgehog ['hɛdʒhɒg] *n* Igel *m*

hedgerow ['hɛdʒrəu] *n* Hecke *f*

hedonism ['hi:dənɪzəm] *n* Hedonismus *m*

heed [hi:d] *vt* (*also*: **take heed of**) beachten
▷ *n*: **to pay (no) ~ to, take (no) ~ of** (nicht) beachten

heedless ['hi:dlɪs] *adj* achtlos; **~ of sb/sth** ohne auf jdn/etw zu achten

heel [hi:l] *n* Ferse *f*; (*of shoe*) Absatz *m* ▷ *vt* (*shoe*) mit einem neuen Absatz versehen; **to bring to ~** (*dog*) bei Fuß gehen lassen; (*fig: person*) an die Kandare nehmen; **to take to one's ~s** (*inf*) sich aus dem Staub machen

hefty ['hɛftɪ] *adj* kräftig; (*parcel etc*) schwer; (*profit*) ansehnlich

heifer ['hɛfə'] *n* Färse *f*

height [haɪt] *n* Höhe *f*; (*of person*) Größe *f*; (*fig: of luxury, good taste etc*) Gipfel *m*; **what ~ are you?** wie groß bist du?; **of average ~** durchschnittlich groß; **to be afraid of ~s** nicht schwindelfrei sein; **it's the ~ of fashion** das ist die neueste Mode; **at the ~ of the tourist season** in der Hauptsaison

heighten ['haɪtn] *vt* erhöhen

heinous ['heɪnəs] *adj* abscheulich, verabscheuungswürdig

heir [ɛə'] *n* Erbe *m*; **the ~ to the throne** der Thronfolger

heir apparent *n* gesetzlicher Erbe *m*

heiress ['ɛərɛs] *n* Erbin *f*

heirloom ['ɛəlu:m] *n* Erbstück *nt*

heist [haɪst] (*US: inf*) *n* Raubüberfall *m*

held [hɛld] *pt, pp of* **hold**

helicopter ['hɛlɪkɒptə'] *n* Hubschrauber *m*

heliport ['hɛlɪpɔ:t] *n* Hubschrauberflugplatz *m*, Heliport *m*

helium ['hi:lɪəm] *n* Helium *nt*

hell [hɛl] *n* Hölle *f*; **~!** (*inf!*) verdammt! (*inf!*); **a ~ of a lot** (*inf*) verdammt viel (*inf*); **a ~ of a mess** (*inf*) ein wahnsinniges Chaos (*inf*); **a ~ of a noise** (*inf*) ein Höllenlärm *m*; **a ~ of a nice guy** ein wahnsinnig netter Typ

he'll [hi:l] = **he will; he shall**

hellbent [hɛl'bɛnt] *adj*: **~ (on)** versessen (auf +*acc*)

hellish ['hɛlɪʃ] (*inf*) *adj* höllisch

hello [hə'ləu] *excl* hallo; (*expressing surprise*) nanu, he

Hell's Angels *npl* Hell's Angels *pl*

helm [hɛlm] *n* Ruder *nt*, Steuer *nt*; **at the ~** am Ruder

helmet ['hɛlmɪt] *n* Helm *m*

helmsman ['hɛlmzmən] (*irreg: like* **man**) *n* Steuermann *m*

help [hɛlp] *n* Hilfe *f*; (*charwoman*) (Haushalts)hilfe *f* ▷ *vt* helfen +*dat*; **with the ~ of** (*person*) mit (der) Hilfe +*gen*; (*tool etc*) mithilfe +*gen*; **to be of ~ to sb** jdm behilflich sein, jdm helfen; **can I ~ you?** (*in shop*) womit kann ich Ihnen dienen?; **~ yourself** bedienen Sie sich; **he can't ~ it** er kann nichts dafür; **I can't ~ thinking that ...** ich kann mir nicht helfen, ich glaube, dass ...

helper ['hɛlpə'] *n* Helfer(in) *m(f)*

helpful ['hɛlpful] *adj* hilfsbereit; (*advice, suggestion*) nützlich, hilfreich

helping ['hɛlpɪŋ] *n* Portion *f*

helping hand *n*: **to give** *or* **lend sb a ~** jdm behilflich sein

helpless ['hɛlplɪs] *adj* hilflos

helplessly ['hɛlplɪslɪ] *adv* hilflos

helpline ['hɛlplaɪn] *n* (*for emergencies*) Notruf *m*; (*for information*) Informationsdienst *m*

Helsinki ['hɛlsɪŋkɪ] *n* Helsinki *nt*

helter-skelter ['hɛltə'skɛltə'] (*Brit*) *n* Rutschbahn *f*

hem [hɛm] *n* Saum *m* ▷ *vt* säumen
▶ **hem in** *vt* einschließen, umgeben; **to feel ~med in** (*fig*) sich eingeengt fühlen

hematology ['hi:mə'tɔlədʒɪ] (*US*) *n* = **haematology**

hemisphere ['hɛmɪsfɪə'] *n* Hemisphäre *f*; (*of sphere*) Halbkugel *f*

hemlock ['hɛmlɔk] *n* Schierling *m*

hemoglobin ['hi:mə'gləubɪn] (*US*) *n* = **haemoglobin**

hemophilia ['hi:mə'fɪlɪə] (*US*) *n* = **haemophilia**

hemorrhage ['hɛmərɪdʒ] (*US*) *n* = **haemorrhage**

hemorrhoids ['hɛmərɔɪdz] (*US*) *npl* =

haemorrhoids

hemp [hɛmp] *n* Hanf *m*

hen [hɛn] *n* Henne *f*, Huhn *nt*; *(female bird)* Weibchen *nt*

hence [hɛns] *adv* daher; **2 years ~** in zwei Jahren

henceforth [hɛns'fɔ:θ] *adv* von nun an; *(from that time on)* von da an

henchman ['hɛntʃmən] *(irreg: like* **man***) (pej) n* Spießgeselle *m*

henna ['hɛnə] *n* Henna *nt*

hen night, hen party *(inf) n* Damenkränzchen *nt; siehe Info-Artikel*

● **HEN NIGHT**

Als *hen night* bezeichnet man eine feuchtfröhliche Frauenparty, die kurz vor einer Hochzeit von der Braut und ihren Freundinnen meist in einem Gasthaus oder Nachtklub abgehalten wird und bei der die Freundinnen dafür sorgen, dass vor allem die Braut große Mengen an Alkohol konsumiert. Siehe auch *stag night*.

henpecked ['hɛnpɛkt] *adj:* **to be ~** unter dem Pantoffel stehen; **~ husband** Pantoffelheld *m*

hepatitis [hɛpə'taɪtɪs] *n* Hepatitis *f*

her [hə:ʳ] *pron* sie; *(indirect)* ihr ▷ *adj* ihr; **I see ~** ich sehe sie; **give ~ a book** gib ihr ein Buch; **after ~** nach ihr; *see also* **me; my**

herald ['hɛrəld] *n* (Vor)bote *m* ▷ *vt* ankündigen

heraldic [hɛ'rældɪk] *adj* heraldisch, Wappen-

heraldry ['hɛrəldrɪ] *n* Wappenkunde *f*, Heraldik *f*; *(coats of arms)* Wappen *pl*

herb [hə:b] *n* Kraut *nt*

herbaceous [hə:'beɪʃəs] *adj:* **~ border** Staudenrabatte *f*; **~ plant** Staude *f*

herbal ['hə:bl] *adj (tea, medicine)* Kräuter-

herbicide ['hə:bɪsaɪd] *n* Unkrautvertilgungsmittel *nt*, Herbizid *nt*

herd [hə:d] *n* Herde *f*; *(of wild animals)* Rudel *nt* ▷ *vt* treiben; *(gather)* zusammentreiben; **~ed together** zusammengetrieben

here [hɪəʳ] *adv* hier; **she left ~ yesterday** sie ist gestern von hier abgereist; **~ is/are ...** hier ist/sind ...; **~ you are** *(giving)* (hier,) bitte; **~ we are!** *(finding sth)* da ist es ja!; **~ she is!** da ist sie ja!; **~ she comes** da kommt sie ja; **come ~!** komm hierher *or* hierhin!; **~ and there** hier und da; **"~'s to ..."** „auf ... *acc*"

hereabouts ['hɪərə'bauts] *adv* hier

hereafter [hɪər'ɑ:ftəʳ] *adv* künftig

hereby [hɪə'baɪ] *adv* hiermit

hereditary [hɪ'rɛdɪtrɪ] *adj* erblich, Erb-

heredity [hɪ'rɛdɪtɪ] *n* Vererbung *f*

heresy ['hɛrəsɪ] *n* Ketzerei *f*

heretic ['hɛrətɪk] *n* Ketzer(in) *m(f)*

heretical [hɪ'rɛtɪkl] *adj* ketzerisch

herewith [hɪə'wɪð] *adv* hiermit

heritage ['hɛrɪtɪdʒ] *n* Erbe *nt*; **our national ~** unser nationales Erbe

hermetically [hə:'mɛtɪklɪ] *adv:* **~ sealed** hermetisch verschlossen

hermit ['hə:mɪt] *n* Einsiedler(in) *m(f)*

hernia ['hə:nɪə] *n* Bruch *m*

hero ['hɪərəu] *(pl* **~es***) n* Held *m*; *(idol)* Idol *nt*

heroic [hɪ'rəuɪk] *adj* heroisch; *(figure, person)* heldenhaft

heroin ['hɛrəuɪn] *n* Heroin *nt*

heroin addict *n* Heroinsüchtige(r) *f(m)*

heroine ['hɛrəuɪn] *n* Heldin *f*; *(idol)* Idol *nt*

heroism ['hɛrəuɪzəm] *n* Heldentum *nt*

heron ['hɛrən] *n* Reiher *m*

hero worship *n* Heldenverehrung *f*

herring ['hɛrɪŋ] *n* Hering *m*

hers [hə:z] *pron* ihre(r, s); **a friend of ~** ein Freund von ihr; **this is ~** das gehört ihr; *see also* **mine**

herself [hə:'sɛlf] *pron* sich; *(emphatic)* (sie) selbst; *see also* **oneself**

Herts [hɑ:ts] *(Brit) abbr (Post)* = Hertfordshire

he's [hi:z] = **he is; he has**

hesitant ['hɛzɪtənt] *adj* zögernd; **to be ~ about doing sth** zögern, etw zu tun

hesitate ['hɛzɪteɪt] *vi* zögern; *(be unwilling)* Bedenken haben; **to ~ about** Bedenken haben wegen; **don't ~ to see a doctor if you are worried** gehen Sie ruhig zum Arzt, wenn Sie sich Sorgen machen

hesitation [hɛzɪ'teɪʃən] *n* Zögern *nt*; Bedenken *pl*; **to have no ~ in saying sth** etw ohne Weiteres sagen können

hessian ['hɛsɪən] *n* Sackleinwand *f*, Rupfen *m*

heterogenous [hɛtə'rɔdʒɪnəs] *adj* heterogen

heterosexual ['hɛtərəu'sɛksjuəl] *adj* heterosexuell ▷ *n* Heterosexuelle(r) *f(m)*

het up [hɛt-] *(inf) adj:* **to get ~ (about)** sich aufregen (über *+acc*)

HEW *(US) n abbr (= Department of Health, Education and Welfare) Ministerium für Gesundheit, Erziehung und Sozialfürsorge*

hew [hju:] *(pt, pp* **hewed** *or* **~n***) vt (stone)* behauen; *(wood)* hacken

hex [hɛks] *(US) n* Fluch *m* ▷ *vt* verhexen

hexagon ['hɛksəgən] *n* Sechseck *nt*

hexagonal [hɛk'sægənl] *adj* sechseckig

hey [heɪ] *excl* he; *(to attract attention)* he du/Sie

heyday ['heɪdeɪ] *n:* **the ~ of** *(person)* die Glanzzeit *+gen*; *(nation, group etc)* die Blütezeit *+gen*

HF *n abbr (= high frequency)* HF

HGV *(Brit) n abbr (Hist: = heavy goods vehicle)* Lkw *m*

HI *(US) abbr (Post)* = Hawaii

hi [haɪ] *excl* hallo

hiatus [haɪ'eɪtəs] *n* Unterbrechung *f*

hibernate ['haɪbəneɪt] *vi* Winterschlaf halten *or* machen

hibernation [haɪbə'neɪʃən] *n* Winterschlaf *m*

hiccough ['hɪkʌp] *vi* hicksen

hiccoughs ['hɪkʌps] *npl* Schluckauf *m*; **to have (the) ~** den Schluckauf haben

hiccup ['hɪkʌp] *vi* = **hiccough**

hiccups ['hɪkʌps] *npl* = **hiccoughs**

hick [hɪk] *(US: inf) n* Hinterwäldler *m*

hid [hɪd] *pt of* **hide**

hidden ['hɪdn] *pp of* **hide** ▷ *adj* (*advantage, danger*) unsichtbar; (*place*) versteckt; **there are no ~ extras** es gibt keine versteckten Extrakosten
hide [haɪd] (*pt* **hid**, *pp* **hidden**) *n* Haut *f*, Fell *nt*; (*of birdwatcher etc*) Versteck *nt* ▷ *vt* verstecken; (*feeling, information*) verbergen; (*obscure*) verdecken ▷ *vi*: **to ~ (from sb)** sich (vor jdm) verstecken; **to ~ sth (from sb)** etw (vor jdm) verstecken
hide-and-seek ['haɪdən'si:k] *n* Versteckspiel *nt*; **to play ~** Verstecken spielen
hideaway ['haɪdəweɪ] *n* Zufluchtsort *m*
hideous ['hɪdɪəs] *adj* scheußlich; (*conditions*) furchtbar
hideously ['hɪdɪəslɪ] *adv* furchtbar
hide-out ['haɪdaut] *n* Versteck *nt*
hiding ['haɪdɪŋ] *n* Tracht *f* Prügel; **to be in ~** (*concealed*) sich versteckt halten
hiding place *n* Versteck *nt*
hierarchy ['haɪərɑ:kɪ] *n* Hierarchie *f*
hieroglyphics [haɪərə'glɪfɪks] *npl* Hieroglyphen *pl*
hi-fi ['haɪfaɪ] *n abbr* (= **high fidelity**) Hi-Fi *nt* ▷ *adj* (*equipment etc*) Hi-Fi-
higgledy-piggledy ['hɪgldɪ'pɪgldɪ] *adj* durcheinander
high [haɪ] *adj* hoch; (*wind*) stark; (*risk*) groß; (*quality*) gut; (*inf: on drugs*) high; (*: on drink*) blau; (*Brit: food*) schlecht; (*: game*) anbrüchig ▷ *adv* hoch ▷ *n*: **exports have reached a new ~** der Export hat einen neuen Höchststand erreicht; **to pay a ~ price for sth** etw teuer bezahlen; **it's ~ time you did it** es ist *or* wird höchste Zeit, dass du es machst; **~ in the air** hoch oben in der Luft
highball ['haɪbɔ:l] (*US*) *n* Highball *m*
highboy ['haɪbɔɪ] (*US*) *n* hohe Kommode *f*
highbrow ['haɪbrau] *adj* intellektuell; (*book, discussion etc*) anspruchsvoll
highchair ['haɪtʃeə'] *n* Hochstuhl *m*
high-class ['haɪ'klɑ:s] *adj* erstklassig; (*neighbourhood*) vornehm

higher ['haɪə'] *adj* (*form of study, life etc*) höher (entwickelt) ▷ *adv* höher ▷ *n* (*Scot: Scol*): **H~** mit

„Higher" wird die vorgeschrittenenstufe des „Scottish certificate of education" und auch der Abschluss dieses Ausbildungsjahr bezeichnet
higher education *n* Hochschulbildung *f*
highfalutin [haɪfə'lu:tɪn] (*inf*) *adj* hochtrabend
high finance *n* Hochfinanz *f*
high-flier, high-flyer [haɪ'flaɪə'] *n* Senkrechtstarter(in) *m(f)*
high-flying [haɪ'flaɪɪŋ] *adj* (*person*) erfolgreich; (*lifestyle*) exklusiv
high-handed [haɪ'hændɪd] *adj* eigenmächtig
high-heeled [haɪ'hi:ld] *adj* hochhackig
high heels *npl* hochhackige Schuhe *pl*
high jump *n* Hochsprung *m*
Highlands ['haɪləndz] *npl*: **the ~** das Hochland
high-level ['haɪlɛvl] *adj* (*talks etc*) auf höchster Ebene; **~ language** (*Comput*) höhere Programmiersprache *f*
highlight ['haɪlaɪt] *n* (*of event*) Höhepunkt *m*; (*in hair*) Strähnchen *nt* ▷ *vt* (*problem, need*) ein Schlaglicht werfen auf +*acc*
highlighter ['haɪlaɪtə'] *n* Textmarker *m*
highly ['haɪlɪ] *adv* hoch-; **to speak ~ of** sich sehr positiv äußern über +*acc*; **to think ~ of** eine hohe Meinung haben von
highly strung *adj* nervös
High Mass *n* Hochamt *nt*
highness ['haɪnɪs] *n*: **Her/His/Your H~** Ihre/ Seine/Eure Hoheit *f*
high-pitched [haɪ'pɪtʃt] *adj* hoch
high point *n* Höhepunkt *m*
high-powered ['haɪ'pauəd] *adj* (*engine*) Hochleistungs-; (*job*) Spitzen-; (*businessman*) dynamisch; (*person*) äußerst fähig; (*course*) anspruchsvoll
high-pressure ['haɪprɛʃə'] *adj* (*area, system*) Hochdruck-; (*inf: sales technique*) aggressiv
high-rise ['haɪraɪz] *adj* (*apartment, block*) Hochhaus-; **~ building/flats** Hochhaus *nt*
high school *n* ≈ Oberschule *f*

high season (*Brit*) *n* Hochsaison *f*
high spirits *npl* Hochstimmung *f*
high street (*Brit*) *n* Hauptstraße *f*
high strung (*US*) *adj* = **highly strung**
high tide *n* Flut *f*
highway ['haɪweɪ] (*US*) *n* Straße *f*; (*between towns, states*) Landstraße *f*; **information ~** Datenautobahn *f*

Highway Code (Brit) n
Straßenverkehrsordnung f

highwayman ['haɪweɪmən] (irreg: like **man**) n
Räuber m, Wegelagerer m

hijack ['haɪdʒæk] vt entführen ▷ n
(also: **hijacking**) Entführung f

hijacker ['haɪdʒækə'] n Entführer(in) m(f)

hike [haɪk] vi wandern ▷ n Wanderung f; (inf: in
prices etc) Erhöhung f ▷ vt (inf) erhöhen

hiker ['haɪkə'] n Wanderer m, Wanderin f

hiking ['haɪkɪŋ] n Wandern nt

hilarious [hɪ'lɛərɪəs] adj urkomisch

hilarity [hɪ'lærɪtɪ] n übermütige
Ausgelassenheit f

hill [hɪl] n Hügel m; (fairly high) Berg m; (slope)
Hang m; (on road) Steigung f

hillbilly ['hɪlbɪlɪ] (US) n Hillbilly m; (pej)
Hinterwäldler(in) m(f), Landpomeranze f

hillock ['hɪlək] n Hügel m, Anhöhe f

hillside ['hɪlsaɪd] n Hang m

hill start n (Aut) Anfahren nt am Berg

hilltop ['hɪltɔp] n Gipfel m

hill walking n Bergwandern nt

hilly ['hɪlɪ] adj hügelig

hilt [hɪlt] n (of sword, knife) Heft nt; **to the ~** voll
und ganz

him [hɪm] pron ihn; (indirect) ihm; see also **me**

Himalayas [hɪmə'leɪəz] npl: **the ~** der
Himalaja

himself [hɪm'sɛlf] pron sich; (emphatic) (er)
selbst; see also **oneself**

hind [haɪnd] adj (legs) Hinter- ▷ n (female deer)
Hirschkuh f

hinder ['hɪndə'] vt behindern; **to ~ sb from
doing sth** jdn daran hindern, etw zu tun

hindquarters ['haɪnd'kwɔːtəz] npl Hinterteil nt

hindrance ['hɪndrəns] n Behinderung f

hindsight ['haɪndsaɪt] n: **with ~** im
Nachhinein

Hindu ['hɪndu:] adj hinduistisch, Hindu-

hinge [hɪndʒ] n (on door) Angel f ▷ vi: **to ~ on**
anhängen von

hint [hɪnt] n Andeutung f; (advice) Tipp m;
(sign, glimmer) Spur f ▷ vt: **to ~ that** andeuten,
dass ▷ vi: **to ~ at** andeuten; **to drop a ~** eine
Andeutung machen; **give me a ~** geben Sie
mir einen Hinweis; **white with a ~ of pink**
weiß mit einem Hauch von Rosa

hip [hɪp] n Hüfte f

hip flask n Taschenflasche f, Flachmann m (inf)

hip-hop ['hɪphɔp] n Hip-Hop nt

hippie ['hɪpɪ] n Hippie m

hippo ['hɪpəu] n Nilpferd nt

hip pocket n Gesäßtasche f

hippopotamus [hɪpə'pɔtəməs] (pl **-es** or
hippopotami) n Nilpferd nt

hippy ['hɪpɪ] n = **hippie**

hire ['haɪə'] vt (Brit) mieten; (worker) einstellen
▷ n (Brit) Mieten nt; **for ~** (taxi) frei; (boat) zu
vermieten; **on ~** gemietet
▶ **hire out** vt vermieten

hire car, hired car (Brit) n Mietwagen m,
Leihwagen m

hire-purchase [haɪə'pəːtʃɪs] (Brit) n Ratenkauf
m; **to buy sth on ~** etw auf Raten kaufen

his [hɪz] pron seine(r, s) ▷ adj sein; see also **my;
mine²**

hiss [hɪs] vi zischen; (cat) fauchen ▷ n Zischen
nt; (of cat) Fauchen nt

histogram ['hɪstəgræm] n Histogramm nt

historian [hɪ'stɔːrɪən] n Historiker(in) m(f)

historic [hɪ'stɔrɪk] adj historisch

historical [hɪ'stɔrɪkl] adj historisch

history ['hɪstərɪ] n Geschichte f; **there's a ~
of heart disease in his family** Herzleiden
liegen bei ihm in der Familie; **medical ~**
Krankengeschichte f

hit [hɪt] (pt, pp **~**) vt schlagen; (reach,
affect) treffen; (vehicle: another vehicle)
zusammenstoßen mit; (: wall, tree) fahren
gegen; (: more violently) prallen gegen; (: person)
anfahren ▷ n Schlag m; (success) Erfolg m; (song)
Hit m; **to ~ it off with sb** sich gut mit jdm
verstehen; **to ~ the headlines** Schlagzeilen
machen; **to ~ the road** (inf) sich auf den Weg
or die Socken (inf) machen; **to ~ the roof** (inf)
an die Decke or in die Luft gehen
▶ **hit back** vi: **to ~ back at sb** jdm
zurückschlagen; (fig) jdm Kontra geben
▶ **hit out at** vt fus auf jdn losschlagen; (fig) jdn
scharf angreifen
▶ **hit (up)on** vt fus stoßen auf +acc, finden

hit-and-miss ['hɪtən'mɪs] adj = **hit-or-miss**

hit-and-run driver ['hɪtən'rʌn-] n
unfallflüchtiger Fahrer m, unfallflüchtige
Fahrerin f

hitch [hɪtʃ] vt festmachen, anbinden;
(also: **hitch up**: trousers, skirt) hochziehen
▷ n Schwierigkeit f, Problem nt; **to ~ a lift**
trampen, per Anhalter fahren; **technical ~**
technische Panne f
▶ **hitch up** vt anspannen; see also **hitch**

hitchhike ['hɪtʃhaɪk] vi trampen, per Anhalter
fahren

hitchhiker ['hɪtʃhaɪkə'] n Tramper(in) m(f),
Anhalter(in) m(f)

hi-tech ['haɪ'tɛk] adj Hightech-, hoch
technisiert ▷ n Hightech nt, Hochtechnologie f

hitherto [hɪðə'tu:] adv bisher, bis jetzt

hit list n Abschussliste f

hit man (inf) n Killer m

hit-or-miss ['hɪtə'mɪs] adj ungeplant; **to be
a ~ affair** eine unsichere Sache sein; **it's ~
whether …** es ist nicht zu sagen, ob …

hit parade n Hitparade f

hits counter n (on website) Zugriffs- or
Besucherzähler m, Counter m

HIV n abbr (= human immunodeficiency virus) HIV;
~-negative HIV-negativ; **~-positive** HIV-
positiv

hive [haɪv] n Bienenkorb m; **to be a ~ of
activity** einem Bienenhaus gleichen
▶ **hive off** (inf) vt ausgliedern, abspalten

hl abbr (= hectolitre) hl

HM abbr (= His/Her Majesty) S./I.M.

HMG (Brit) abbr (= His/Her Majesty's Government)

h

die Regierung Seiner/Ihrer Majestät

HMI (Brit) n abbr (Scol: = His/Her Majesty's Inspector) regierungsamtlicher Schulaufsichtsbeauftragter

HMO (US) n abbr (= Health Maintenance Organization) Organisation zur Gesundheitsfürsorge

HMS (Brit) abbr (= His (or Her) Majesty's Ship) Namensteil von Schiffen der Kriegsmarine

HNC (Brit) n abbr (= Higher National Certificate) Berufsschulabschluss

HND (Brit) n abbr (= Higher National Diploma) Qualifikationsnachweis in technischen Fächern

hoard [hɔːd] n (of food) Vorrat m; (of money etc) Schatz m ▷ vt (food) hamstern; (money) horten

hoarding ['hɔːdɪŋ] (Brit) n Plakatwand f

hoarfrost ['hɔːfrɔst] n (Rau)reif m

hoarse [hɔːs] adj heiser

hoax [həʊks] n (false alarm) blinder Alarm m

hob [hɔb] n Kochmulde f

hobble ['hɔbl] vi humpeln

hobby ['hɔbɪ] n Hobby nt, Steckenpferd nt

hobbyhorse ['hɔbɪhɔːs] n (fig) Lieblingsthema nt

hobnail boot ['hɔbneɪl-] n Nagelschuh m

hobnob ['hɔbnɔb] vi: **to ~ with** auf Du und Du stehen mit

hobo ['həʊbəʊ] (US) n Penner m (inf)

hock [hɔk] n (Brit) weißer Rheinwein m; (of animal) Sprunggelenk nt; (US: Culin) Gelenkstück nt; (inf): **to be in ~** (person: in debt) in Schulden stecken; (object) verpfändet or im Leihhaus sein

hockey ['hɔkɪ] n Hockey nt

hocus-pocus ['həʊkəs'pəʊkəs] n Hokuspokus m; (trickery) faule Tricks pl; (jargon) Jargon m

hod [hɔd] n (for bricks etc) Tragemulde f

hodgepodge ['hɔdʒpɔdʒ] (US) n = **hotchpotch**

hoe [həʊ] n Hacke f ▷ vt hacken

hog [hɔg] n (Mast)schwein nt ▷ vt (road) für sich beanspruchen; (telephone etc) in Beschlag nehmen; **to go the whole ~** Nägel mit Köpfen machen

Hogmanay [hɔgmə'neɪ] (Scot) n Silvester nt

hogwash ['hɔgwɔʃ] (inf) n (nonsense) Quatsch m

ho hum ['həʊ'hʌm] interj na gut

hoist [hɔɪst] n Hebevorrichtung f ▷ vt hochheben; (flag, sail) hissen

hoity-toity [hɔɪtɪ'tɔɪtɪ] (inf: pej) adj hochnäsig

hold [həʊld] (pt, pp **held**) vt halten; (contain) enthalten; (power, qualification) haben; (opinion) vertreten; (meeting) abhalten; (conversation) führen; (prisoner, hostage) festhalten ▷ vi halten; (be valid) gelten; (weather) sich halten ▷ n (grasp) Griff m; (of ship, plane) Laderaum m; **to ~ one's head up** den Kopf hochhalten; **to ~ sb responsible/liable** etc jdn verantwortlich/haftbar etc machen; **~ the line!** (Tel) bleiben Sie am Apparat!; **~ it!** Moment mal!; **to ~ one's own** sich behaupten; **he ~s the view that ...** er ist der Meinung or er vertritt die Ansicht, dass ...; **to ~ firm** or **fast** halten; **~ still!, ~ steady!** stillhalten!; **his luck held** das Glück blieb ihm treu; **I don't ~ with ...** ich bin gegen ...; **to catch** or **get (a) ~ of** sich

festhalten an +dat; **to get ~ of** (fig) finden, auftreiben; **to get ~ of o.s.** sich in den Griff bekommen; **to have a ~ over** in der Hand haben

▶ **hold back** vt zurückhalten; (tears, laughter) unterdrücken; (secret) verbergen; (information) geheim halten

▶ **hold down** vt niederhalten; (job) sich halten in +dat

▶ **hold forth** vi: **to ~ forth (about)** sich ergehen or sich auslassen (über +acc)

▶ **hold off** vt abwehren ▷ vi: **if the rain ~s off** wenn es nicht regnet

▶ **hold on** vi sich festhalten; (wait) warten; **~ on!** (Tel) einen Moment bitte!

▶ **hold on to** vt fus sich festhalten an; (keep) behalten

▶ **hold out** vt (hand) ausstrecken; (hope) haben; (prospect) bieten ▷ vi nicht nachgeben

▶ **hold over** vt vertagen

▶ **hold up** vt hochheben; (support) stützen; (delay) aufhalten; (rob) überfallen

holdall ['həʊldɔːl] (Brit) n Tasche f; (for clothes) Reisetasche f

holder ['həʊldə^r] n Halter m; (of ticket, record, office, title etc) Inhaber(in) m(f)

holding ['həʊldɪŋ] n (share) Anteil m; (small farm) Gut m ▷ adj (operation, tactic) zur Schadensbegrenzung

holding company n Dachgesellschaft f, Holdinggesellschaft f

hold-up ['həʊldʌp] n bewaffneter Raubüberfall m; (delay) Verzögerung f; (Brit: in traffic) Stockung f

hole [həʊl] n Loch nt; (unpleasant town) Kaff nt (inf) ▷ vt (ship) leckschlagen; (building etc) durchlöchern; **~ in the heart** Loch im Herz(en); **to pick ~s** (fig) (über)kritisch sein; **to pick ~s in sth** (fig) an etw dat herumkritisieren

▶ **hole up** vi sich verkriechen

holiday ['hɔlɪdeɪ] n (Brit) Urlaub m; (Scol) Ferien pl; (day off) freier Tag m; (also: **public holiday**) Feiertag m; **on ~** im Urlaub, in den Ferien

holiday camp (Brit) n (also: **holiday centre**) Feriendorf nt

holiday home n Ferienhaus nt

holiday-maker ['hɔlɪdɪmeɪkə^r] (Brit) n Urlauber(in) m(f)

holiday pay n Lohn-/Gehaltsfortzahlung während des Urlaubs

holiday resort n Ferienort m

holiday season n Urlaubszeit f

holiness ['həʊlɪnɪs] n Heiligkeit f

holistic [həʊ'lɪstɪk] adj holistisch

Holland ['hɔlənd] n Holland nt

holler ['hɔlə^r] (inf) vi brüllen ▷ n Schrei m

hollow ['hɔləʊ] adj hohl; (eyes) tief liegend; (laugh) unecht; (sound) dumpf; (fig) leer; (: victory, opinion) wertlos ▷ n Vertiefung f ▷ vt: **to ~ out** aushöhlen

holly ['hɔlɪ] n Stechpalme f, Ilex m; (leaves) Stechpalmenzweige pl

hollyhock ['hɔlɪhɔk] n Malve f
Hollywood ['hɔlɪwud] n Hollywood nt
holocaust ['hɔləkɔ:st] n Inferno nt; (in Third Reich) Holocaust m
hologram ['hɔləgræm] n Hologramm nt
hols [hɔlz] (inf) npl Ferien pl
holster ['həulstə^r] n Pistolenhalfter m or nt
holy ['həulɪ] adj heilig
Holy Communion n heilige Kommunion f
Holy Father n Heiliger Vater m
Holy Ghost n Heiliger Geist m
Holy Land n: **the ~** das Heilige Land
holy orders npl Priesterweihe f
Holy Spirit n Heiliger Geist m
homage ['hɔmɪdʒ] n Huldigung f; **to pay ~ to** huldigen +dat
home [həum] n Heim nt; (house, flat) Zuhause nt; (area, country) Heimat f; (institution) Anstalt f ▷ cpd Heim-; (Econ, Pol) Innen- ▷ adv (go etc) nach Hause, heim; **at ~** zu Hause (Österr, Schweiz); (in country) im Inland; **to be or feel at ~** (fig) sich wohlfühlen; **make yourself at ~** machen Sie es sich dat gemütlich or bequem; **to make one's ~ somewhere** sich irgendwo niederlassen; **the ~ of free enterprise/jazz etc** die Heimat des freien Unternehmertums/ Jazz etc; **when will you be ~?** wann bist du wieder zu Hause?; **a ~ from home** ein zweites Zuhause nt; **~ and dry** aus dem Schneider; **to drive a nail ~** einen Nagel einschlagen; **to bring sth ~ to sb** jdm etw klarmachen
▸ **home in on** vt fus (missiles) sich ausrichten auf +acc
home address n Heimatanschrift f
home-brew [həum'bru:] n selbst gebrautes Bier nt
homecoming ['həumkʌmɪŋ] n Heimkehr f
home computer n Heimcomputer m
Home Counties (Brit) npl: **the ~** die Grafschaften, die an London angrenzen
home economics n Hauswirtschaft(slehre) f
home ground n (Sport) eigener Platz m; **to be on ~** (fig) sich auf vertrautem Terrain bewegen
home-grown ['həumgrəun] adj (not foreign) einheimisch; (from garden) selbst gezogen
home help n Haushaltshilfe f
homeland ['həumlænd] n Heimat f, Heimatland nt
homeless ['həumlɪs] adj obdachlos; (refugee) heimatlos
home loan n Hypothek f
homely ['həumlɪ] adj einfach; (US: plain) unscheinbar
home-made [həum'meɪd] adj selbst gemacht
Home Office (Brit) n Innenministerium nt
homeopath ['həumɪəupæθ] (US) n = **homoeopath**
homeopathy [həumɪ'ɔpəθɪ] (US) n = **homoeopathy**
home page n (Comput) Homepage f
home rule n Selbstbestimmung f, Selbstverwaltung f

Home Secretary (Brit) n Innenminister(in) m(f)
homesick ['həumsɪk] adj heimwehkrank; **to be ~** Heimweh haben
homestead ['həumstɛd] n Heimstätte f; (farm) Gehöft nt
home town n Heimatstadt f
home truth n bittere Wahrheit f; **to tell sb some ~s** jdm deutlich die Meinung sagen
homeward ['həumwəd] adj (journey) Heim- ▷ adv = **homewards**
homewards ['həumwədz] adv nach Hause, heim
homework ['həumwə:k] n Hausaufgaben pl
homicidal [hɔmɪ'saɪdl] adj gemeingefährlich
homicide ['hɔmɪsaɪd] (US) n Mord m
homily ['hɔmɪlɪ] n Predigt f
homing ['həumɪŋ] adj (device, missile) mit Zielsucheinrichtung; **~ pigeon** Brieftaube f
homoeopath, (US) **homeopath** ['həumɪəupæθ] n Homöopath(in) m(f)
homoeopathy, (US) **homeopathy** [həumɪ'ɔpəθɪ] n Homöopathie f
homogeneous [hɔməu'dʒi:nɪəs] adj homogen
homogenize [hə'mɔdʒənaɪz] vt homogenisieren
homosexual [hɔməu'seksjuəl] adj homosexuell ▷ n Homosexuelle(r) f(m)
Hon. abbr = **honourable; honorary**
Honduras [hɔn'djuərəs] n Honduras nt
hone [həun] n Schleifstein m ▷ vt schleifen; (fig: groom) erziehen
honest ['ɔnɪst] adj ehrlich; (trustworthy) redlich; (sincere) aufrichtig; **to be quite ~ with you ...** um ehrlich zu sein, ...
honestly ['ɔnɪstlɪ] adv (see adj) ehrlich; redlich; aufrichtig
honesty ['ɔnɪstɪ] n (see adj) Ehrlichkeit f; Redlichkeit f; Aufrichtigkeit f
honey ['hʌnɪ] n Honig m; (US: inf) Schätzchen nt
honeycomb ['hʌnɪkəum] n Bienenwabe f; (pattern) Wabe f ▷ vt: **to ~ with** durchlöchern mit
honeymoon ['hʌnɪmu:n] n Flitterwochen pl; (trip) Hochzeitsreise f
honeysuckle ['hʌnɪsʌkl] n Geißblatt nt
Hong Kong ['hɔŋ'kɔŋ] n Hongkong nt
honk [hɔŋk] vi (Aut) hupen
Honolulu [hɔnə'lu:lu:] n Honolulu nt
honor etc ['ɔnə^r] (US) = **honour** etc
honorary ['ɔnərərɪ] adj ehrenamtlich; (title, degree) Ehren-
honour, (US) **honor** ['ɔnə^r] vt ehren; (commitment, promise) stehen zu ▷ n Ehre f; (tribute) Auszeichnung f; **in ~ of** zu Ehren von or +gen
honourable ['ɔnərəbl] adj (person) ehrenwert; (action, defeat) ehrenvoll
honour-bound ['ɔnə'baund] adj: **to be ~ to do sth** moralisch verpflichtet sein, etw zu tun
honours degree ['ɔnəz-] n akademischer Grad mit

599

Prüfung im Spezialfach; *siehe Info-Artikel*

● **HONOURS DEGREE**
●
● *Honours degree* ist ein Universitätsabschluss
● mit einer guten Note, also der Note I (first
● class), II:1 (upper second class), II:2 (lower
● second class), oder III (third class). Wer
● ein honours degree erhalten hat, darf die
● Abkürzung *Hons* nach seinem Namen und
● Titel führen, z. B. Mary Smith MA Hons.
● Heute sind fast alle Universitätsabschlusse
● in Großbritannien honours degrees. Siehe
● auch *ordinary degree*.

honours list *n* Liste verliehener/zu verleihender
  Ehrentitel; *siehe Info-Artikel*

● **HONOURS LIST**
●
● *Honours list* ist eine Liste von Adelstiteln
● und Orden, die der britische Monarch
● zweimal jährlich (zu Neujahr und am
● offiziellen Geburtstag des Monarchen)
● an Bürger Großbritanniens und im
● Commonwealth verleiht. Die Liste wird
● vom Premierminister zusammengestellt,
● aber drei Orden (der Hosenbandorden, der
● Verdienstorden und der Victoria-Orden)
● werden vom Monarchen persönlich
● vergeben. Erfolgreiche Geschäftsleute,
● Militärangehörige, Sportler und andere
● Prominente, aber auch im sozialen Bereich
● besonders aktive Bürger werden auf diese
● Weise geehrt.

Hons. *abbr* (*Univ*) = **Honours degree**
hood [hʊd] *n* (*of coat etc*) Kapuze *f*; (*of cooker*)
  Abzugshaube *f*; (*Aut: Brit: folding roof*) Verdeck
  nt; (*: US: bonnet*) (Motor)haube *f*
hooded ['hʊdɪd] *adj* maskiert; (*jacket etc*) mit
  Kapuze
hoodlum ['huːdləm] *n* Gangster *m*
hoodwink ['hʊdwɪŋk] *vt* (he)reinlegen
hoof [huːf] (*pl* **hooves**) *n* Huf *m*
hook [hʊk] *n* Haken *m* ▷ *vt* festhaken; (*fish*) an
  die Angel bekommen; **by ~ or by crook** auf
  Biegen und Brechen; **to be ~ed on** (*inf: film,
  exhibition, etc*) fasziniert sein von; (*: drugs*)
  abhängig sein von; (*: person*) stehen auf +*acc*
  ▶ **hook up** *vt* (*Radio, TV etc*) anschließen
hook and eye (*pl* **hooks and eyes**) *n* Haken und
  Öse *pl*
hooligan ['huːlɪgən] *n* Rowdy *m*
hooliganism ['huːlɪgənɪzəm] *n* Rowdytum *nt*
hoop [huːp] *n* Reifen *m*; (*for croquet: arch*) Tor *nt*
hooray [huːˈreɪ] *excl* = **hurrah**
hoot [huːt] *vi* hupen; (*siren*) heulen; (*owl*)
  schreien, rufen; (*person*) johlen ▷ *vt* (*horn*)
  drücken auf +*acc* ▷ *n* (*see vi*) Hupen *nt*; Heulen
  nt; Schreien *nt*, Rufen *nt*; Johlen *nt*; **to ~ with
  laughter** in johlendes Gelächter ausbrechen
hooter ['huːtə'] *n* (*Brit: Aut*) Hupe *f*; (*Naut, of*

factory) Sirene *f*
Hoover® ['huːvə'] (*Brit*) *n* Staubsauger *m*
  ▷ *vt*: **hoover** (*carpet*) saugen
hooves [huːvz] *npl of* **hoof**
hop [hɒp] *vi* hüpfen ▷ *n* Hüpfer *m*; *see also* **hops**
hope [həʊp] *vi* hoffen ▷ *n* Hoffnung *f*
  ▷ *vt*: **to ~ that** hoffen, dass; **I ~ so** ich hoffe
  es, hoffentlich; **I ~ not** ich hoffe nicht,
  hoffentlich nicht; **to ~ for the best** das Beste
  hoffen; **to have no ~ of sth/doing sth** keine
  Hoffnung auf etw +*acc* haben/darauf haben,
  etw zu tun; **in the ~ of/that** in der Hoffnung
  auf/, dass; **to ~ to do sth** hoffen, etw zu tun
hopeful ['həʊpfʊl] *adj* hoffnungsvoll;
  (*situation*) vielversprechend; **I'm ~ that she'll
  manage** ich hoffe, dass sie es schafft
hopefully ['həʊpfʊlɪ] *adv* hoffnungsvoll;
  (*one hopes*) hoffentlich; **~, he'll come back**
  hoffentlich kommt er wieder
hopeless ['həʊplɪs] *adj* hoffnungslos; (*situation*)
  aussichtslos; (*useless*): **to be ~ at sth** etw
  überhaupt nicht können
hopper ['hɒpə'] *n* Einfülltrichter *m*
hops [hɒps] *npl* Hopfen *m*
horde [hɔːd] *n* Horde *f*
horizon [həˈraɪzn] *n* Horizont *m*
horizontal [hɒrɪˈzɒntl] *adj* horizontal
hormone ['hɔːməʊn] *n* Hormon *nt*
hormone replacement therapy *n*
  Hormonersatztherapie *f*
horn [hɔːn] *n* Horn *nt*; (*Aut*) Hupe *f*
horned [hɔːnd] *adj* (*animal*) mit Hörnern
hornet ['hɔːnɪt] *n* Hornisse *f*
horn-rimmed ['hɔːnˈrɪmd] *adj* (*spectacles*) Horn-
horny ['hɔːnɪ] (*inf*) *adj* (*aroused*) scharf, geil
horoscope ['hɒrəskəʊp] *n* Horoskop *nt*
horrendous [həˈrendəs] *adj* abscheulich,
  entsetzlich
horrible ['hɒrɪbl] *adj* fürchterlich, schrecklich;
  (*scream, dream*) furchtbar
horrid ['hɒrɪd] *adj* entsetzlich, schrecklich
horrific [həˈrɪfɪk] *adj* entsetzlich, schrecklich
horrify ['hɒrɪfaɪ] *vt* entsetzen
horrifying ['hɒrɪfaɪɪŋ] *adj* schrecklich,
  fürchterlich, entsetzlich
horror ['hɒrə'] *n* Entsetzen *nt*, Grauen *nt*; **~ (of
  sth)** (*abhorrence*) Abscheu *m* (vor etw *dat*); **the
  ~s of war** die Schrecken *pl* des Krieges
horror film *n* Horrorfilm *m*
horror-stricken ['hɒrəstrɪkn] *adj* = **horror-
  struck**
horror-struck ['hɒrəstrʌk] *adj* von Entsetzen *or*
  Grauen gepackt
hors d'œuvre [ɔːˈdəːvrə] *n* Hors d'œuvre *nt*,
  Vorspeise *f*
horse [hɔːs] *n* Pferd *nt*
horseback ['hɔːsbæk]: **on ~** *adj*, *adv* zu Pferd
horsebox ['hɔːsbɒks] *n* Pferdetransporter *m*
horse chestnut *n* Rosskastanie *f*
horse-drawn ['hɔːsdrɔːn] *adj* von Pferden
  gezogen
horsefly ['hɔːsflaɪ] *n* (Pferde)bremse *f*
horseman ['hɔːsmən] (*irreg: like* **man**) *n*

Reiter m

horsemanship ['hɔːsmənʃɪp] n Reitkunst f

horseplay ['hɔːspleɪ] n Alberei f, Balgerei f

horsepower ['hɔːspauəʳ] n Pferdestärke f

horse racing n Pferderennen nt

horseradish ['hɔːsrædɪʃ] n Meerrettich m

horseshoe ['hɔːsʃuː] n Hufeisen nt

horse show n Reitturnier nt

horse trading n Kuhhandel m

horse trials npl = **horse show**

horsewhip ['hɔːswɪp] n Reitpeitsche f ▷ vt
auspeitschen

horsewoman ['hɔːswumən] (irreg: like **woman**)
n Reiterin f

horsey ['hɔːsɪ] adj pferdenärrisch; (appearance)
pferdeähnlich

horticulture ['hɔːtɪkʌltʃəʳ] n Gartenbau m

hose [həuz] n (also: **hose pipe**) Schlauch m
▶ **hose down** vt abspritzen

hosiery ['həuzɪərɪ] n Strumpfwaren pl

hospice ['hɒspɪs] n Pflegeheim nt (für unheilbar
Kranke)

hospitable ['hɒspɪtəbl] adj gastfreundlich;
(climate) freundlich

hospital ['hɒspɪtl] n Krankenhaus nt; **in ~, in
the ~** (US) im Krankenhaus

hospitality [hɒspɪ'tælɪtɪ] n Gastfreundschaft
f

hospitalize ['hɒspɪtəlaɪz] vt ins Krankenhaus
einweisen

host [həust] n Gastgeber m; (Rel) Hostie f ▷ adj
Gast- ▷ vt Gastgeber sein bei; **a ~ of** eine
Menge

hostage ['hɒstɪdʒ] n Geisel f; **to be taken/
held ~** als Geisel genommen/festgehalten
werden

hostel ['hɒstl] n (Wohn)heim nt; (also: **youth
hostel**) Jugendherberge f

hostelling ['hɒstlɪŋ] n: **to go (youth) ~** in
Jugendherbergen übernachten

hostess ['həustɪs] n Gastgeberin f; (Brit: also: **air
hostess**) Stewardess f; (in night-club) Hostess f

hostile ['hɒstaɪl] adj (conditions) ungünstig;
(environment) unwirtlich; (**to** or
towards) feindselig (gegenüber +dat)

hostility [hɒ'stɪlɪtɪ] n Feindseligkeit f;
hostilities npl (fighting) Feindseligkeiten pl

hot [hɒt] adj heiß; (moderately hot) warm; (spicy)
scharf; (temper) hitzig; **I am** or **feel ~** mir ist
heiß; **to be ~ on sth** (knowledgeable etc) sich
gut mit etw auskennen; (strict) sehr auf etw
acc achten
▶ **hot up** (Brit: inf) vi (situation) sich verschärfen
or zuspitzen; (party) in Schwung kommen ▷ vt
(pace) steigern; (engine) frisieren

hot air n leeres Gerede nt

hot-air balloon [hɒt'ɛəʳ-] n Heißluftballon m

hotbed ['hɒtbɛd] n (fig) Brutstätte f

hot-blooded [hɒt'blʌdɪd] adj heißblütig

hotchpotch ['hɒtʃpɒtʃ] (Brit) n Durcheinander
nt, Mischmasch m

hot dog n Hotdog m or nt

hotel [həu'tɛl] n Hotel nt

hotelier [həu'tɛlɪəʳ] n Hotelier(in) m(f)

hotel industry n Hotelgewerbe nt

hotel room n Hotelzimmer nt

hot flash (US) n = **hot flush**

hot flush n (Med) Hitzewallung f

hotfoot ['hɒtfut] adv eilends

hothead ['hɒthɛd] n Hitzkopf m

hot-headed [hɒt'hɛdɪd] adj hitzköpfig

hothouse ['hɒthaus] n Treibhaus nt

hot line n (Pol) heißer Draht m

hotly ['hɒtlɪ] adv (contest) heiß; (speak, deny)
heftig

hotplate ['hɒtpleɪt] n Kochplatte f

hotpot ['hɒtpɒt] (Brit) n Fleischeintopf m

hot potato (fig: inf) n heißes Eisen nt; **to drop
sb like a ~** jdn wie eine heiße Kartoffel fallen
lassen

hot seat n: **to be in the ~** auf dem
Schleudersitz sitzen

hotspot ['hɒtspɒt] n (Comput) Hotspot m

hot spot n (fig) Krisenherd m

hot spring n heiße Quelle f, Thermalquelle f

hot stuff n große Klasse f

hot-tempered ['hɒt'tɛmpəd] adj leicht
aufbrausend, jähzornig

hot-water bottle [hɒt'wɔːtəʳ-] n Wärmflasche
f

hot-wire (inf) vt (car) kurzschließen

hound [haund] vt hetzen, jagen ▷ n Jagdhund
m; **the ~s** die Meute

hour ['auəʳ] n Stunde f; (time) Zeit f; **at 60
miles an ~** mit 60 Meilen in der Stunde;
lunch ~ Mittagspause f; **to pay sb by the ~**
jdn stundenweise bezahlen

hourly ['auəlɪ] adj stündlich; (rate) Stunden-
▷ adv stündlich, jede Stunde; (soon) jederzeit

house [haus] n Haus nt; (household)
Haushalt m; (dynasty) Geschlecht nt, Haus
nt; (Theat: performance) Vorstellung f ▷ vt
unterbringen; **at my ~** bei mir (zu Hause); **to
my ~** zu mir (nach Hause); **on the ~** (fig) auf
Kosten des Hauses; **the H~ (of Commons)**
(Brit) das Unterhaus; **the H~ (of Lords)** (Brit)
das Oberhaus; **the H~ (of Representatives)**
(US) das Repräsentantenhaus; siehe Info-Artikel

house arrest n Hausarrest m

houseboat ['hausbəut] n Hausboot nt

housebound ['hausbaund] adj ans Haus
gefesselt

housebreaking ['hausbreɪkɪŋ] n Einbruch m

house-broken ['hausbrəukn] (US) adj = **house-
trained**

housecoat ['hauskəut] n Morgenrock m

household ['haushəuld] n Haushalt m; **to be a
~ name** ein Begriff sein

householder ['haushəuldəʳ] n Hausinhaber(in)
m(f); (of flat) Wohnungsinhaber(in) m(f)

house-hunting ['haushʌntɪŋ] n: **to go ~** nach
einem Haus suchen

housekeeper ['hauski:pəʳ] n Haushälterin f

housekeeping ['hauski:pɪŋ] n Hauswirtschaft
f; (money) Haushaltsgeld nt, Wirtschaftsgeld nt

houseman ['hausmən] (Brit: irreg: like **man**) n

h

(*Med*) Assistenzarzt *m*, Assistenzärztin *f*

HOUSE OF COMMONS

Das *House of Commons* ist das Unterhaus des britischen Parlaments, mit 651 Abgeordneten, die in Wahlkreisen in allgemeiner Wahl gewählt werden. Das Unterhaus hat die Regierungsgewalt inne und tagt etwa 175 Tage im Jahr unter Vorsitz des Sprechers. Als *House of Lords* wird das Oberhaus des britischen Parlaments bezeichnet. Die Mitglieder sind nicht gewählt, sondern werden auf Lebenszeit ernannt („life peers") oder sie haben ihren Oberhaussitz geerbt („hereditary peers"). Das *House of Lords* setzt sich aus Kirchenmännern und Adeligen zusammen („Lords Spiritual/Temporal"). Es hat im Grunde keine Regierungsgewalt, kann aber vom Unterhaus erlassene Gesetze abändern und ist das oberste Berufungsgericht in Großbritannien (außer Schottland).

HOUSE OF REPRESENTATIVES

Das *House of Representatives* bildet zusammen mit dem Senat die amerikanische gesetzgebende Versammlung (den Kongress). Es besteht aus 435 Abgeordneten, die entsprechend den Bevölkerungszahlen auf die einzelnen Bundesstaaten verteilt sind und jeweils für 2 Jahre direkt vom Volk gewählt werden. Es tritt im „Capitol" in Washington zusammen. Siehe auch „Congress".

house owner *n* Hausbesitzer(in) *m(f)*
house party *n* mehrtägige Einladung *f*; (*people*) Gesellschaft *f*
house plant *n* Zimmerpflanze *f*
house-proud ['hauspraud] *adj* auf Ordnung und Sauberkeit im Haushalt bedacht
house-to-house ['haustə'haus] *adj* von Haus zu Haus
house-trained ['haustreind] (*Brit*) *adj* (*animal*) stubenrein
house-warming ['hauswɔ:mɪŋ], **house-warming party** *n* Einzugsparty *f*
housewife ['hauswaɪf] (*irreg: like* **wife**) *n* Hausfrau *f*
housework ['hauswə:k] *n* Hausarbeit *f*
housing ['hauzɪŋ] *n* Wohnungen *pl*; (*provision*) Wohnungsbeschaffung *f* ▷ *cpd* Wohnungs-
housing association *n* Wohnungsbaugesellschaft *f*
housing benefit *n* ≈ Wohngeld *nt*
housing conditions *npl* Wohnbedingungen *pl*, Wohnverhältnisse *pl*
housing development *n* (Wohn)siedlung *f*

housing estate *n* (Wohn)siedlung *f*
hovel ['hɒvl] *n* (armselige) Hütte *f*
hover ['hɒvəʳ] *vi* schweben; (*person*) herumstehen; **to ~ round sb** jdm nicht von der Seite weichen
hovercraft ['hɒvəkrɑ:ft] *n* Hovercraft *nt*, Luftkissenfahrzeug *nt*
hoverport ['hɒvəpɔ:t] *n* Anlegestelle *f* für Hovercrafts

Ⓞ KEYWORD

how [hau] *adv* **1** (*in what way*) wie; **how was the film?** wie war der Film?; **how is school?** was macht die Schule?; **how are you?** wie geht es Ihnen?

2 (*to what degree*): **how much milk?** wie viel Milch?; **how many people?** wie viele Leute?; **how long have you been here?** wie lange sind Sie schon hier?; **how old are you?** wie alt bist du?; **how lovely/awful!** wie schön/furchtbar!

however [hau'ɛvəʳ] *conj* jedoch, aber ▷ *adv* wie ... auch; (*in questions*) wie ... bloß or nur
howl [haul] *vi* heulen; (*animal*) jaulen; (*baby, person*) schreien ▷ *n* (*see vb*) Heulen *nt*; Jaulen *nt*; Schreien *nt*
howler ['haulaʳ] (*inf*) *n* (*mistake*) Schnitzer *m*
howling ['haulɪŋ] *adj* (*wind, gale*) heulend
HP (*Brit*) *n abbr* = **hire-purchase**
h.p. *abbr* (*Aut*: = *horsepower*) PS
HQ *abbr* = **headquarters**
HR (*US*) *n abbr* (*Pol*: = *House of Representatives*) Repräsentantenhaus *nt*; = *Human Resources*
hr *abbr* (= *hour*) Std.
HRH (*Brit*) *abbr* (= *His/Her Royal Highness*) Seine/Ihre Königliche Hoheit
hrs *abbr* (= *hours*) Std.
HST (*US*) *abbr* (= *Hawaiian Standard Time*) Normalzeit in Hawaii
HTML (*Comput*) *abbr* (= *hypertext markup language*) HTML *f*
hub [hʌb] *n* (*Rad*)nabe *f*; (*fig: centre*) Mittelpunkt *m*, Zentrum *nt*
hubbub ['hʌbʌb] *n* Lärm *m*; (*commotion*) Tumult *m*
hubcap ['hʌbkæp] *n* Radkappe *f*
HUD (*US*) *n abbr* (= *Department of Housing and Urban Development*) Ministerium für Wohnungsbau und Stadtentwicklung
huddle ['hʌdl] *vi*: **to ~ together** sich zusammendrängen ▷ *n*: **in a ~** dicht zusammengedrängt
hue [hju:] *n* Farbton *m*
hue and cry *n* großes Geschrei *nt*
huff [hʌf] *n*: **in a ~** beleidigt, eingeschnappt ▷ *vi*: **to ~ and puff** sich aufregen
huffy ['hʌfɪ] (*inf*) *adj* beleidigt
hug [hʌg] *vt* umarmen; (*thing*) umklammern ▷ *n* Umarmung *f*; **to give sb a ~** jdn umarmen
huge [hju:dʒ] *adj* riesig
hugely ['hju:dʒlɪ] *adv* ungeheuer

hulk [hʌlk] n (wrecked ship) Wrack nt; (person, building etc) Klotz m

hulking ['hʌlkɪŋ] adj: ~ **great** massig

hull [hʌl] n Schiffsrumpf m; (of nuts) Schale f; (of fruit) Blättchen nt ▷ vt (fruit) entstielen

hullaballoo [hʌləbə'lu:] (inf) n Spektakel m

hullo [hə'ləu] excl = **hello**

hum [hʌm] vt summen ▷ vi summen; (machine) brummen ▷ n Summen nt; (of traffic) Brausen nt; (of machines) Brummen nt; (of voices) Gemurmel nt

human ['hju:mən] adj menschlich ▷ n (also: **human being**) Mensch m

humane [hju:'meɪn] adj human

humanism ['hju:mənɪzəm] n Humanismus m

humanitarian [hju:mænɪ'tɛərɪən] adj humanitär

humanity [hju:'mænɪtɪ] n Menschlichkeit f; (mankind) Menschheit f; (humaneness) Humanität f; **humanities** npl (Scol): **the humanities** die Geisteswissenschaften pl

humanly ['hju:mənlɪ] adv menschlich; **if (at all)** ~ **possible** wenn es irgend möglich ist

humanoid ['hju:mənɔɪd] adj menschenähnlich ▷ n menschenähnliches Wesen nt

human rights npl Menschenrechte pl

humble ['hʌmbl] adj bescheiden ▷ vt demütigen

humbly ['hʌmblɪ] adv bescheiden

humbug ['hʌmbʌg] n Humbug m, Mumpitz m; (Brit: sweet) Pfefferminzbonbon m or nt

humdrum ['hʌmdrʌm] adj eintönig, langweilig

humid ['hju:mɪd] adj feucht

humidifier [hju:'mɪdɪfaɪər] n Luftbefeuchter m

humidity [hju:'mɪdɪtɪ] n Feuchtigkeit f

humiliate [hju:'mɪlɪeɪt] vt demütigen

humiliating [hju:'mɪlɪeɪtɪŋ] adj demütigend

humiliation [hju:mɪlɪ'eɪʃən] n Demütigung f

humility [hju:'mɪlɪtɪ] n Bescheidenheit f

humor etc (US) = **humour** etc

humorist ['hju:mərɪst] n Humorist(in) m(f)

humorous ['hju:mərəs] adj (remark) witzig; (book) lustig; (person) humorvoll

humour, (US) **humor** ['hju:mər] n Humor m; (mood) Stimmung f ▷ vt seinen Willen lassen +dat; **sense of** ~ (Sinn m für) Humor; **to be in good/bad** ~ gute/schlechte Laune haben

humourless ['hju:məlɪs] adj humorlos

hump [hʌmp] n Hügel m; (of camel) Höcker m; (deformity) Buckel m

humpbacked ['hʌmpbækt] adj: ~ **bridge** gewölbte Brücke f

humus ['hju:məs] n Humus m

hunch [hʌntʃ] n Gefühl nt, Ahnung f; **I have a** ~ **that** ... ich habe den (leisen) Verdacht, dass ...

hunchback ['hʌntʃbæk] n Bucklige(r) f(m)

hunched [hʌntʃt] adj gebeugt; (shoulders) hochgezogen; (back) krumm

hundred ['hʌndrəd] num hundert; **a** or **one** ~ **books/people/dollars** (ein)hundert Bücher/

Personen/Dollar; ~**s of** Hunderte von; **I'm a** ~ **per cent sure** ich bin absolut sicher

hundredth ['hʌndrədθ] num hundertste(r, s)

hundredweight ['hʌndrɪdweɪt] n Gewichtseinheit (Brit = 50,8 kg; US = 45,3 kg) ≈ Zentner m

hung [hʌŋ] pt, pp of **hang**

Hungarian [hʌŋ'gɛərɪən] adj ungarisch ▷ n Ungar(in) m(f); (Ling) Ungarisch nt

Hungary ['hʌŋgərɪ] n Ungarn nt

hunger ['hʌŋgər] n Hunger m ▷ vi: **to** ~ **for** hungern nach

hunger strike n Hungerstreik m

hung over (inf) adj verkatert

hungrily ['hʌŋgrəlɪ] adv hungrig

hungry ['hʌŋgrɪ] adj hungrig; **to be** ~ Hunger haben; **to be** ~ **for** hungern nach; (news) sehnsüchtig warten auf; **to go** ~ hungern

hung up (inf) adj: **to be** ~ **on** (person) ein gestörtes Verhältnis haben zu; **to be** ~ **about** nervös sein wegen

hunk [hʌŋk] n großes Stück nt; (inf: man) (großer, gut aussehender) Mann m

hunt [hʌnt] vt jagen; (criminal, fugitive) fahnden nach ▷ vi (Sport) jagen ▷ n (see vb) Jagd f; Fahndung f; (search) Suche f; **to** ~ **for** (search) suchen (nach)

► **hunt down** vt Jagd machen auf +acc

hunter ['hʌntər] n Jäger(in) m(f)

hunting ['hʌntɪŋ] n Jagd f, Jagen nt

hurdle ['hə:dl] n Hürde f

hurl [hə:l] vt schleudern; **to** ~ **sth at sb** (also fig) jdm etw entgegenschleudern

hurling ['hə:lɪŋ] n (Sport) Hurling nt, irische Hockeyart

hurly-burly ['hə:lɪ'bə:lɪ] n Rummel m

hurrah [hu'rɑ:] n Hurra nt ▷ excl hurra

hurray [hu'reɪ] n = **hurrah**

hurricane ['hʌrɪkən] n Orkan m

hurried ['hʌrɪd] adj eilig; (departure) überstürzt

hurriedly ['hʌrɪdlɪ] adv eilig

hurry ['hʌrɪ] n Eile f ▷ vi eilen; (to do sth) sich beeilen ▷ vt (zur Eile) antreiben; (work) beschleunigen; **to be in a** ~ es eilig haben; **to do sth in a** ~ etw schnell tun; **there's no** ~ es eilt nicht; **what's the** ~? warum so eilig?; **they hurried to help him** sie eilten ihm zu Hilfe; **to** ~ **home** nach Hause eilen

► **hurry along** vi sich beeilen

► **hurry away** vi schnell weggehen, forteilen

► **hurry off** vi = **hurry away**

► **hurry up** vt (zur Eile) antreiben ▷ vi sich beeilen

hurt [hə:t] (pt, pp ~) vt wehtun +dat; (injure, fig) verletzen ▷ vi wehtun ▷ adj verletzt; **I've** ~ **my arm** ich habe mir am Arm wehgetan; (injured) ich habe mir den Arm verletzt; **where does it** ~? wo tut es weh?

hurtful ['hə:tful] adj verletzend

hurtle ['hə:tl] vi: **to** ~ **past** vorbeisausen; **to** ~ **down** (fall) hinunterfallen

husband ['hʌzbənd] n (Ehe)mann m

hush [hʌʃ] n Stille f ▷ vt zum Schweigen

bringing; ~! pst!

▶ **hush up** vt vertuschen

hushed [hʌʃt] adj still; (voice) gedämpft

hush-hush [hʌʃ'hʌʃ] (inf) adj streng geheim

husk [hʌsk] n Schale f; (of wheat) Spelze f; (of maize) Hüllblatt nt

husky ['hʌskɪ] adj (voice) rau ▷ n Schlittenhund m

hustings ['hʌstɪŋz] (Brit) npl (Pol) Wahlkampf m

hustle ['hʌsl] vt drängen ▷ n: ~ **and bustle** Geschäftigkeit f

hut [hʌt] n Hütte f

hutch [hʌtʃ] n (Kaninchen)stall m

hyacinth ['haɪəsɪnθ] n Hyazinthe f

hybrid ['haɪbrɪd] n (plant, animal) Kreuzung f; (mixture) Mischung f ▷ adj Misch-

hybrid car, **hybrid vehicle** n Hybridfahrzeug nt or -auto nt

hydrant ['haɪdrənt] n (also: **fire hydrant**) Hydrant m

hydraulic [haɪ'drɔ:lɪk] adj hydraulisch

hydraulics [haɪ'drɔ:lɪks] n Hydraulik f

hydrochloric acid ['haɪdrəu'klɔrɪk-] n Salzsäure f

hydroelectric ['haɪdrəu'lɛktrɪk] adj hydroelektrisch

hydrofoil ['haɪdrəfɔɪl] n Tragflächenboot nt, Tragflügelboot nt

hydrogen ['haɪdrədʒən] n Wasserstoff m

hydrogen bomb n Wasserstoffbombe f

hydrophobia ['haɪdrə'fəubɪə] n Hydrophobie f, Wasserscheu f

hydroplane ['haɪdrəpleɪn] n Gleitboot nt; (plane) Wasserflugzeug nt ▷ vi (boat) abheben

hyena [haɪ'i:nə] n Hyäne f

hygiene ['haɪdʒi:n] n Hygiene f

hygienic [haɪ'dʒi:nɪk] adj hygienisch

hymn [hɪm] n Kirchenlied nt

hype [haɪp] (inf) n Rummel m

hyperactive ['haɪpər'æktɪv] adj überaktiv

hyperinflation ['haɪpərɪn'fleɪʃən] n galoppierende Inflation f

hypermarket ['haɪpəmɑ:kɪt] (Brit) n Verbrauchermarkt m

hypertension ['haɪpə'tɛnʃən] n Hypertonie f, Bluthochdruck m

hypertext ['haɪpətɛkst] n (Comput) Hypertext m

hyphen ['haɪfn] n Bindestrich m; (at end of line) Trennungsstrich m

hyphenated ['haɪfəneɪtɪd] adj mit Bindestrich (geschrieben)

hypnosis [hɪp'nəusɪs] n Hypnose f

hypnotic [hɪp'nɒtɪk] adj hypnotisierend; (trance) hypnotisch

hypnotism ['hɪpnətɪzəm] n Hypnotismus m

hypnotist ['hɪpnətɪst] n Hypnotiseur m, Hypnotiseuse f

hypnotize ['hɪpnətaɪz] vt hypnotisieren

hypoallergenic ['haɪpəuælə'dʒɛnɪk] adj für äußerst empfindliche Haut

hypochondriac [haɪpə'kɒndrɪæk] n Hypochonder m

hypocrisy [hɪ'pɒkrɪsɪ] n Heuchelei f

hypocrite ['hɪpəkrɪt] n Heuchler(in) m(f)

hypocritical [hɪpə'krɪtɪkl] adj heuchlerisch

hypodermic [haɪpə'də:mɪk] adj (injection) subkutan ▷ n (Injektions)spritze f

hypotenuse [haɪ'pɒtɪnju:z] n Hypotenuse f

hypothermia [haɪpə'θə:mɪə] n Unterkühlung f

hypothesis [haɪ'pɒθɪsɪs] (pl **hypotheses**) n Hypothese f

hypothesize [haɪ'pɒθɪsaɪz] vi Hypothesen aufstellen ▷ vt annehmen

hypothetic [haɪpəu'θetɪk], **hypothetical** [haɪpəu'θetɪkl] adj hypothetisch

hysterectomy [hɪstə'rɛktəmɪ] n Hysterektomie f

hysteria [hɪ'stɪərɪə] n Hysterie f

hysterical [hɪ'stɛrɪkl] adj hysterisch; (situation) wahnsinnig komisch; **to become ~** hysterisch werden

hysterically [hɪ'stɛrɪklɪ] adv hysterisch; ~ **funny** wahnsinnig komisch

hysterics [hɪ'stɛrɪks] npl: **to be in** or **to have ~** einen hysterischen Anfall haben; (laughter) einen Lachanfall haben

Hz abbr (= hertz) Hz.

I i

I¹, i [aɪ] n (letter) I nt, i nt; **I for Isaac, I for Item** (US) ≈ I wie Ida

I² [aɪ] pron ich

I. abbr = **island; isle**

IA (US) abbr (Post) = Iowa

IAEA n abbr = **International Atomic Energy Agency**

ib abbr (= ibidem) ib(id).

Iberian [aɪˈbɪərɪən] adj: **the ~ Peninsula** die Iberische Halbinsel

ibid abbr (= ibidem) ib(id).

i/c (Brit) abbr (= in charge (of)) see **charge**

ICBM n abbr (= intercontinental ballistic missile) Interkontinentalrakete f

ICC n abbr = **International Chamber of Commerce**; (US: = Interstate Commerce Commission) Kommission zur Regelung des Warenverkehrs zwischen den US-Bundesstaaten

ice [aɪs] n Eis nt; (on road) Glatteis nt ▷ vt (cake) mit Zuckerguss überziehen, glasieren ▷ vi (also: **ice over, ice up**) vereisen; (puddle etc) zufrieren; **to put sth on ~** (fig) etw auf Eis legen

Ice Age n Eiszeit f

ice axe n Eispickel m

iceberg [ˈaɪsbəːɡ] n Eisberg m; **the tip of the ~** (fig) die Spitze des Eisbergs

icebox [ˈaɪsbɔks] n (US: fridge) Kühlschrank m; (Brit: compartment) Eisfach nt; (insulated box) Kühltasche f

icebreaker [ˈaɪsbreɪkəʳ] n Eisbrecher m

ice bucket n Eiskühler m

icecap [ˈaɪskæp] n Eisdecke f; (polar) Eiskappe f

ice-cold [ˈaɪsˈkəʊld] adj eiskalt

ice cream n Eis nt

ice-cream soda [ˈaɪskriː-m-] n Eisbecher mit Sirup und Sodawasser

ice cube n Eiswürfel m

iced [aɪst] adj (cake) mit Zuckerguss überzogen, glasiert; (beer etc) eisgekühlt; (tea, coffee) Eis-

ice hockey n Eishockey nt

Iceland [ˈaɪslənd] n Island nt

Icelander [ˈaɪsləndəʳ] n Isländer(in) m(f)

Icelandic [aɪsˈlændɪk] adj isländisch ▷ n (Ling) Isländisch nt

ice lolly (Brit) n Eis nt am Stiel

ice pick n Eispickel m

ice rink n (Kunst)eisbahn f, Schlittschuhbahn f

ice skate n Schlittschuh m

ice-skate [ˈaɪsskeɪt] vi Schlittschuh laufen

ice-skating [ˈaɪsskeɪtɪŋ] n Eislauf m, Schlittschuhlaufen nt

icicle [ˈaɪsɪkl] n Eiszapfen m

icing [ˈaɪsɪŋ] n (Culin) Zuckerguss m; (Aviat etc) Vereisung f

icing sugar (Brit) n Puderzucker m

ICJ n abbr = **International Court of Justice**

icon [ˈaɪkɔn] n Ikone f; (Comput) Ikon nt

ICR (US) n abbr (= Institute for Cancer Research) Krebsforschungsinstitut

ICT (Brit) n abbr (Scol) = **information and communication technology**

ICU n abbr (Med) = **intensive care unit**

icy [ˈaɪsɪ] adj eisig; (road) vereist

ID, Ida. (US) abbr (Post) = Idaho; = identification (document)

I'd [aɪd] = **I would; I had**

ID card n = **identity card**

IDD (Brit) n abbr (Tel: = international direct dialling) Selbstwählferndienst ins Ausland

idea [aɪˈdɪə] n Idee f; (opinion) Ansicht f; (notion) Vorstellung f; (objective) Ziel nt; **good ~!** gute Idee!; **to have a good ~ that** sich dat ziemlich sicher sein, dass; **I haven't the least ~** ich habe nicht die leiseste Ahnung

ideal [aɪˈdɪəl] n Ideal nt ▷ adj ideal

idealist [aɪˈdɪəlɪst] n Idealist(in) m(f)

ideally [aɪˈdɪəlɪ] adv ideal; **~ the book should ...** idealerweise or im Idealfall sollte das Buch ...; **she's ~ suited for ...** sie eignet sich hervorragend für ...

identical [aɪˈdɛntɪkl] adj identisch; (twins) eineiig

identification [aɪdɛntɪfɪˈkeɪʃən] n Identifizierung f; **(means of) ~** Ausweispapiere pl

identify [aɪˈdɛntɪfaɪ] vt (recognize) erkennen; (distinguish) identifizieren; **to ~ sb/sth with** jdn/etw identifizieren mit

Identikit® [aɪˈdɛntɪkɪt] n: **~ (picture)** Phantombild nt

identity [aɪˈdɛntɪtɪ] n Identität f

identity card n (Personal)ausweis m

identity papers npl Ausweispapiere pl

identity parade (Brit) n Gegenüberstellung f

ideological [aɪdɪəˈlɔdʒɪkl] adj ideologisch,

weltanschaulich

ideology [aɪdɪ'ɔlədʒɪ] n Ideologie f, Weltanschauung f

idiocy ['ɪdɪəsɪ] n Idiotie f, Dummheit f

idiom ['ɪdɪəm] n (style) Ausdrucksweise f; (phrase) Redewendung f

idiomatic [ɪdɪə'mætɪk] adj idiomatisch

idiosyncrasy [ɪdɪəʊ'sɪŋkrəsɪ] n Eigenheit f, Eigenart f

idiosyncratic [ɪdɪəʊsɪŋ'krætɪk] adj eigenartig; (way, method, style) eigen

idiot ['ɪdɪət] n Idiot(in) m(f), Dummkopf m

idiotic [ɪdɪ'ɔtɪk] adj idiotisch, blöd(sinnig)

idle ['aɪdl] adj untätig; (lazy) faul; (unemployed) unbeschäftigt; (machinery, factory) stillstehend; (question) müßig; (conversation, pleasure) leer ▷ vi leerlaufen, im Leerlauf sein; **to lie ~** (machinery) außer Betrieb sein; (factory) die Arbeit eingestellt haben
   ▸ **idle away** vt (time) vertrödeln, verbummeln

idleness ['aɪdlnɪs] n Untätigkeit f; (laziness) Faulheit f

idler ['aɪdləʳ] n Faulenzer(in) m(f)

idle time n (Comm) Leerlaufzeit f

idly ['aɪdlɪ] adv untätig; (glance) abwesend

idol ['aɪdl] n Idol nt; (Rel) Götzenbild nt

idolize ['aɪdəlaɪz] vt vergöttern

idyllic [ɪ'dɪlɪk] adj idyllisch

i.e. abbr (= id est) d. h.

○ KEYWORD

if [ɪf] conj **1** (given that, providing that etc) wenn, falls; **if anyone comes in** wenn or falls jemand hereinkommt; **if necessary** wenn or falls nötig; **if I were you** wenn ich Sie wäre, an Ihrer Stelle
   2 (whenever) wenn
   3 (although): **(even) if** auch or selbst wenn; **I like it, (even) if you don't** mir gefällt es, auch wenn du es nicht magst
   4 (whether) ob; **ask him if he can come** frag ihn, ob er kommen kann
   5: **if so/not** falls ja/nein; **if only** wenn nur; see also **as**

iffy ['ɪfɪ] (inf) adj (uncertain) unsicher; (plan, proposal) fragwürdig; **he was a bit ~ about it** er hat sich sehr vage ausgedrückt

igloo ['ɪɡluː] n Iglu m or nt

ignite [ɪɡ'naɪt] vt entzünden ▷ vi sich entzünden

ignition [ɪɡ'nɪʃən] n (Aut) Zündung f

ignition key n (Aut) Zündschlüssel m

ignoble [ɪɡ'nəʊbl] adj schändlich, unehrenhaft

ignominious [ɪɡnə'mɪnɪəs] adj schmachvoll

ignoramus [ɪɡnə'reɪməs] n Ignorant(in) m(f)

ignorance ['ɪɡnərəns] n Unwissenheit f, Ignoranz f; **to keep sb in ~ of sth** jdn in Unkenntnis über etw acc lassen

ignorant ['ɪɡnərənt] adj unwissend, ignorant; **to be ~ of** (subject) sich nicht auskennen in +dat; (events) nicht informiert sein über +acc

ignore [ɪɡ'nɔːʳ] vt ignorieren; (fact) außer Acht lassen

ikon ['aɪkɔn] n = **icon**

IL (US) abbr (Post) = Illinois

I'll [aɪl] = **I will; I shall**

ill [ɪl] adj krank; (effects) schädlich ▷ n Übel nt; (trouble) Schlechte(s) nt ▷ adv: **to speak ~ of sb** Schlechtes über jdn sagen; **to be taken ~** krank werden; **to think ~ of sb** schlecht von jdm denken

ill-advised [ɪləd'vaɪzd] adj unklug; (person) schlecht beraten

ill at ease adj unbehaglich

ill-considered [ɪlkən'sɪdəd] adj unüberlegt

ill-disposed [ɪldɪs'pəʊzd] adj: **to be ~ toward sb/sth** jdm/etw nicht wohlgesinnt sein

illegal [ɪ'liːɡl] adj illegal

illegally [ɪ'liːɡəlɪ] adv illegal

illegible [ɪ'lɛdʒɪbl] adj unleserlich

illegitimate [ɪlɪ'dʒɪtɪmət] adj (child) unehelich; (activity, treaty) unzulässig

ill-fated [ɪl'feɪtɪd] adj unglückselig

ill-favoured, (US) **ill-favored** [ɪl'feɪvəd] adj ungestalt (liter), hässlich

ill feeling n Verstimmung f

ill-gotten ['ɪlɡɔtn] adj: **~ gains** unrechtmäßig erworbener Gewinn m

ill health n schlechter Gesundheitszustand m

illicit [ɪ'lɪsɪt] adj verboten

ill-informed [ɪlɪn'fɔːmd] adj (judgement) wenig sachkundig; (person) schlecht informiert or unterrichtet

illiterate [ɪ'lɪtərət] adj (person) des Lesens und Schreibens unkundig; (letter) voller Fehler

ill-mannered [ɪl'mænəd] adj unhöflich

illness ['ɪlnɪs] n Krankheit f

illogical [ɪ'lɔdʒɪkl] adj unlogisch

ill-suited [ɪl'suːtɪd] adj nicht zusammenpassend; **he is ~ to the job** er ist für die Stelle ungeeignet

ill-timed [ɪl'taɪmd] adj ungelegen, unpassend

ill-treat [ɪl'triːt] vt misshandeln

ill-treatment [ɪl'triːtmənt] n Misshandlung f

illuminate [ɪ'luːmɪneɪt] vt beleuchten

illuminated sign [ɪ'luːmɪneɪtɪd-] n Leuchtzeichen nt

illuminating [ɪ'luːmɪneɪtɪŋ] adj aufschlussreich

illumination [ɪluːmɪ'neɪʃən] n Beleuchtung f; **illuminations** npl (decorative lights) festliche Beleuchtung f, Illumination f

illusion [ɪ'luːʒən] n Illusion f; (trick) (Zauber) trick m; **to be under the ~ that ...** sich dat einbilden, dass ...

illusive [ɪ'luːsɪv] adj = **illusory**

illusory [ɪ'luːsərɪ] adj illusorisch, trügerisch

illustrate ['ɪləstreɪt] vt veranschaulichen; (book) illustrieren

illustration [ɪlə'streɪʃən] n Illustration f; (example) Veranschaulichung f

illustrator ['ɪləstreɪtəʳ] n Illustrator(in) m(f)

illustrious [ɪ'lʌstrɪəs] adj (career) glanzvoll; (predecessor) berühmt

ill will n böses Blut nt

ILO n abbr = **International Labour Organization**

IM n abbr (= instant messaging) IM nt

I'm [aɪm] = **I am**

image ['ɪmɪdʒ] n Bild nt; (public face) Image nt; (reflection) Abbild nt

image-building campaign ['ɪmɪdʒbɪldɪŋ-] n Imagekampagne f

imagery ['ɪmɪdʒərɪ] n (in writing) Metaphorik f; (in painting etc) Symbolik f

imaginable [ɪ'mædʒɪnəbl] adj vorstellbar, denkbar; **we've tried every ~ solution** wir haben jede denkbare Lösung ausprobiert; **she had the prettiest hair ~** sie hatte das schönste Haar, das man sich vorstellen kann

imaginary [ɪ'mædʒɪnərɪ] adj erfunden; (being) Fantasie-; (danger) eingebildet

imagination [ɪmædʒɪ'neɪʃən] n Fantasie f; (illusion) Einbildung f; **it's just your ~** das bildest du dir nur ein

imaginative [ɪ'mædʒɪnətɪv] adj fantasievoll; (solution) einfallsreich

imagine [ɪ'mædʒɪn] vt sich dat vorstellen; (dream) sich dat träumen lassen; (suppose) vermuten

imbalance [ɪm'bæləns] n Unausgeglichenheit f

imbecile ['ɪmbəsiːl] n Schwachkopf m, Idiot m

imbue [ɪm'bjuː] vt: **to ~ sb/sth with** jdn/etw durchdringen mit

IMF n abbr (= International Monetary Fund) IWF m

imitate ['ɪmɪteɪt] vt imitieren; (mimic) nachahmen

imitation [ɪmɪ'teɪʃən] n Imitation f, Nachahmung f

imitator ['ɪmɪteɪtər] n Imitator(in) m(f), Nachahmer(in) m(f)

immaculate [ɪ'mækjulət] adj makellos; (appearance, piece of work) tadellos; (Rel) unbefleckt

immaterial [ɪmə'tɪərɪəl] adj unwichtig, unwesentlich

immature [ɪmə'tjuər] adj unreif; (organism) noch nicht voll entwickelt

immaturity [ɪmə'tjuərɪtɪ] n Unreife f

immeasurable [ɪ'mɛʒrəbl] adj unermesslich groß

immediacy [ɪ'miːdɪəsɪ] n Unmittelbarkeit f, Direktheit f; (of needs) Dringlichkeit f

immediate [ɪ'miːdɪət] adj sofortig; (need) dringend; (neighbourhood, family) nächste(r, s)

immediately [ɪ'miːdɪətlɪ] adv sofort; (directly) unmittelbar; **~ next to** direkt neben

immense [ɪ'mɛns] adj riesig, enorm

immensely [ɪ'mɛnslɪ] adv unheimlich; (grateful, complex etc) äußerst

immensity [ɪ'mɛnsɪtɪ] n ungeheure Größe f, Unermesslichkeit f; (of problems etc) gewaltiges Ausmaß nt

immerse [ɪ'məːs] vt eintauchen; **to ~ sth in** etw tauchen in +acc; **to be ~d in** (fig) vertieft sein in +acc

immersion heater [ɪ'məːʃən-] (Brit) n elektrischer Heißwasserboiler m

immigrant ['ɪmɪgrənt] n Einwanderer m, Einwanderin f

immigration [ɪmɪ'greɪʃən] n Einwanderung f; (at airport etc) Einwanderungsstelle f

imminent ['ɪmɪnənt] adj bevorstehend

immobile [ɪ'məubaɪl] adj unbeweglich

immobilize [ɪ'məubɪlaɪz] vt (person) handlungsunfähig machen; (machine) zum Stillstand bringen

immobilizer [ɪ'məubɪlaɪzər] n (Aut) Wegfahrsperre f

immoderate [ɪ'mɔdərət] adj unmäßig; (opinion, reaction) extrem; (demand) maßlos

immodest [ɪ'mɔdɪst] adj unanständig; (boasting) unbescheiden

immoral [ɪ'mɔrl] adj unmoralisch; (behaviour) unsittlich

immorality [ɪmə'rælɪtɪ] n (see adj) Unmoral f; Unsittlichkeit f

immortal [ɪ'mɔːtl] adj unsterblich

immortality [ɪmɔː'tælɪtɪ] n Unsterblichkeit f

immortalize [ɪ'mɔːtlaɪz] vt unsterblich machen

immovable [ɪ'muːvəbl] adj unbeweglich; (person, opinion) fest

immune [ɪ'mjuːn] adj: **~ (to)** (disease) immun (gegen); (flattery) unempfänglich (für); (criticism) unempfindlich (gegen); (attack) sicher (vor +dat)

immune system n Immunsystem nt

immunity [ɪ'mjuːnɪtɪ] n (see adj) Immunität f; Unempfänglichkeit f; Unempfindlichkeit f; Sicherheit f; (of diplomat, from prosecution) Immunität f

immunization [ɪmjunaɪ'zeɪʃən] n Immunisierung f

immunize ['ɪmjunaɪz] vt: **to ~ (against)** immunisieren (gegen)

imp [ɪmp] n Kobold m; (child) Racker m (inf)

impact ['ɪmpækt] n Aufprall m; (of crash) Wucht f; (of law, measure) (Aus)wirkung f

impair [ɪm'pɛər] vt beeinträchtigen

impaired [ɪm'pɛəd] adj beeinträchtigt; (hearing) schlecht; **~ vision** schlechte Augen pl

impale [ɪm'peɪl] vt: **to ~ sth (on)** etw aufspießen (auf +dat)

impart [ɪm'paːt] vt: **to ~ (to)** (information) mitteilen +dat; (flavour) verleihen +dat

impartial [ɪm'paːʃl] adj unparteiisch

impartiality [ɪmpaːʃɪ'ælɪtɪ] n Unparteilichkeit f

impassable [ɪm'paːsəbl] adj unpassierbar

impasse [æm'paːs] n Sackgasse f

impassive [ɪm'pæsɪv] adj gelassen

impatience [ɪm'peɪʃəns] n Ungeduld f

impatient [ɪm'peɪʃənt] adj ungeduldig; **to get** or **grow ~** ungeduldig werden; **to be ~ to do sth** es nicht erwarten können, etw zu tun

impatiently [ɪm'peɪʃəntlɪ] adv ungeduldig

impeach [ɪm'piːtʃ] vt anklagen; (public official) eines Amtsvergehens anklagen

impeachment [ɪm'piːtʃmənt] n Anklage f

wegen eines Amtsvergehens, Impeachment *nt*

impeccable [ɪm'pekəbl] *adj (dress)* untadelig; *(manners)* tadellos

impecunious [ɪmpɪ'kjuːnɪəs] *adj* mittellos

impede [ɪm'piːd] *vt* behindern

impediment [ɪm'pedɪmənt] *n* Hindernis *nt*; *(also: speech impediment)* Sprachfehler *m*

impel [ɪm'pel] *vt*: **to ~ sb to do sth** jdn (dazu) nötigen, etw zu tun

impending [ɪm'pendɪŋ] *adj* bevorstehend; *(catastrophe)* drohend

impenetrable [ɪm'penɪtrəbl] *adj* undurchdringlich; *(fig)* unergründlich

imperative [ɪm'perətɪv] *adj* dringend; *(tone)* Befehls- ▷ *n (Ling)* Imperativ *m*, Befehlsform *f*

imperceptible [ɪmpə'septɪbl] *adj* nicht wahrnehmbar, unmerklich

imperfect [ɪm'pəːfɪkt] *adj* mangelhaft; *(goods)* fehlerhaft ▷ *n (Ling: also: imperfect tense)* Imperfekt *nt*, Vergangenheit *f*

imperfection [ɪmpə'fekʃən] *n* Fehler *m*

imperial [ɪm'pɪərɪəl] *adj* kaiserlich; *(Brit: measure)* britisch

imperialism [ɪm'pɪərɪəlɪzəm] *n* Imperialismus *m*

imperil [ɪm'perɪl] *vt* gefährden

imperious [ɪm'pɪərɪəs] *adj* herrisch, gebieterisch

impersonal [ɪm'pəːsənl] *adj* unpersönlich

impersonate [ɪm'pəːsəneɪt] *vt* sich ausgeben als; *(Theat)* imitieren

impersonation [ɪmpəːsə'neɪʃən] *n (Theat)* Imitation *f*; **~ of** *(Law)* Auftreten *nt* als

impertinent [ɪm'pəːtɪnənt] *adj* unverschämt

imperturbable [ɪmpə'təːbəbl] *adj* unerschütterlich

impervious [ɪm'pəːvɪəs] *adj*: **~ to** *(criticism, pressure)* unberührt von; *(charm, influence)* unempfänglich für

impetuous [ɪm'petjuəs] *adj* ungestüm, stürmisch; *(act)* impulsiv

impetus ['ɪmpətəs] *n* Schwung *m*; *(fig: driving force)* treibende Kraft *f*

impinge [ɪm'pɪndʒ]: **to ~ on** *vt fus* sich auswirken auf +acc; *(rights)* einschränken

impish ['ɪmpɪʃ] *adj* schelmisch

implacable [ɪm'plækəbl] *adj* unerbittlich, erbittert

implant [ɪm'plɑːnt] *vt (Med)* einpflanzen; *(fig: idea, principle)* einimpfen

implausible [ɪm'plɔːzɪbl] *adj* unglaubwürdig

implement [*n* 'ɪmplɪmənt, *vt* 'ɪmplɪment] *n* Gerät *nt*, Werkzeug *nt* ▷ *vt* durchführen

implicate ['ɪmplɪkeɪt] *vt* verwickeln

implication [ɪmplɪ'keɪʃən] *n* Auswirkung *f*; *(involvement)* Verwicklung *f*; **by ~** implizit

implicit [ɪm'plɪsɪt] *adj (inferred)* implizit, unausgesprochen; *(unquestioning)* absolut

implicitly [ɪm'plɪsɪtlɪ] *adv (see adj)* implizit; absolut

implore [ɪm'plɔːʳ] *vt* anflehen

imply [ɪm'plaɪ] *vt* andeuten; *(mean)* bedeuten

impolite [ɪmpə'laɪt] *adj* unhöflich

imponderable [ɪm'pɒndərəbl] *adj* unberechenbar ▷ *n* unberechenbare Größe *f*

import [*vt* ɪm'pɔːt, *n* 'ɪmpɔːt] *vt* importieren, einführen ▷ *n* Import *m*, Einfuhr *f*; *(article)* Importgut *nt* ▷ *cpd* Import-, Einfuhr-

importance [ɪm'pɔːtns] *n (see adj)* Wichtigkeit *f*; Bedeutung *f*; **to be of little/great ~** nicht besonders wichtig/sehr wichtig sein

important [ɪm'pɔːtənt] *adj* wichtig; *(influential)* bedeutend; **it's not ~** es ist unwichtig

importantly [ɪm'pɔːtəntlɪ] *adv* wichtigtuerisch; **but more ~ ...** aber was noch wichtiger ist, ...

importation [ɪmpɔː'teɪʃən] *n* Import *m*, Einfuhr *f*

imported [ɪm'pɔːtɪd] *adj* importiert, eingeführt

importer [ɪm'pɔːtəʳ] *n* Importeur *m*

impose [ɪm'pəuz] *vt* auferlegen; *(sanctions)* verhängen ▷ *vi*: **to ~ on sb** jdm zur Last fallen

imposing [ɪm'pəuzɪŋ] *adj* eindrucksvoll

imposition [ɪmpə'zɪʃən] *n (of tax etc)* Auferlegung *f*; **to be an ~ on** eine Zumutung sein für

impossibility [ɪmpɒsə'bɪlɪtɪ] *n* Unmöglichkeit *f*

impossible [ɪm'pɒsɪbl] *adj* unmöglich; **it's ~ for me to leave now** ich kann jetzt unmöglich gehen

impossibly [ɪm'pɒsɪblɪ] *adv* unmöglich

imposter [ɪm'pɒstəʳ] *n* = **impostor**

impostor [ɪm'pɒstəʳ] *n* Hochstapler(in) *m(f)*

impotence ['ɪmpətns] *n (see adj)* Machtlosigkeit *f*; Impotenz *f*

impotent ['ɪmpətnt] *adj* machtlos; *(Med)* impotent

impound [ɪm'paund] *vt* beschlagnahmen

impoverished [ɪm'pɒvərɪʃt] *adj* verarmt

impracticable [ɪm'præktɪkəbl] *adj (idea)* undurchführbar; *(solution)* unbrauchbar

impractical [ɪm'præktɪkl] *adj (plan)* undurchführbar; *(person)* unpraktisch

imprecise [ɪmprɪ'saɪs] *adj* ungenau

impregnable [ɪm'pregnəbl] *adj* uneinnehmbar; *(fig)* unerschütterlich

impregnate ['ɪmpregneɪt] *vt* tränken

impresario [ɪmprɪ'sɑːrɪəu] *n (Theat)* Impresario *m*

impress [ɪm'pres] *vt* beeindrucken; *(mark)* aufdrücken; **to ~ sth on sb** jdm etw einschärfen

impression [ɪm'preʃən] *n* Eindruck *m*; *(of stamp, seal)* Abdruck *m*; *(imitation)* Nachahmung *f*, Imitation *f*; **to make a good/bad ~ on sb** einen guten/schlechten Eindruck auf jdn machen; **to be under the ~ that ...** den Eindruck haben, dass ...

impressionable [ɪm'preʃnəbl] *adj* leicht zu beeindrucken

impressionist [ɪm'preʃənɪst] *n* Impressionist(in) *m(f)*; *(entertainer)* Imitator(in) *m(f)*

impressive [ɪm'presɪv] *adj* beeindruckend

imprint ['ɪmprɪnt] *n (of hand etc)* Abdruck *m*;

(*Publishing*) Impressum *nt*

imprinted [ɪmˈprɪntɪd] *adj*: **it is ~ on my memory/mind** es hat sich mir eingeprägt

imprison [ɪmˈprɪzn] *vt* inhaftieren, einsperren

imprisonment [ɪmˈprɪznmənt] *n* Gefangenschaft *f*; **three years' ~** drei Jahre Gefängnis *or* Freiheitsstrafe

improbable [ɪmˈprɔbəbl] *adj* unwahrscheinlich

impromptu [ɪmˈprɔmptju:] *adj* improvisiert

improper [ɪmˈprɔpəʳ] *adj* ungehörig; (*procedure*) unrichtig; (*dishonest*) unlauter

impropriety [ɪmprəˈpraɪətɪ] *n* (*see adj*) Ungehörigkeit *f*; Unrichtigkeit *f*; Unlauterkeit *f*

improve [ɪmˈpru:v] *vt* verbessern ▷ *vi* sich bessern; **the patient is improving** dem Patienten geht es besser
  ▶ **improve (up)on** *vt fus* verbessern

improvement [ɪmˈpru:vmənt] *n*: **~ (in)** Verbesserung *f* (*+gen*); **to make ~s to** Verbesserungen durchführen an *+dat*

improvisation [ɪmprəvaɪˈzeɪʃən] *n* Improvisation *f*

improvise [ˈɪmprəvaɪz] *vt*, *vi* improvisieren

imprudence [ɪmˈpru:dns] *n* Unklugheit *f*

imprudent [ɪmˈpru:dnt] *adj* unklug

impudent [ˈɪmpjudnt] *adj* unverschämt

impugn [ɪmˈpju:n] *vt* angreifen; (*sincerity, motives, reputation*) in Zweifel ziehen

impulse [ˈɪmpʌls] *n* Impuls *m*; (*urge*) Drang *m*; **to act on ~** aus einem Impuls heraus handeln

impulse buy *n* Impulsivkauf *m*

impulsive [ɪmˈpʌlsɪv] *adj* impulsiv, spontan; (*purchase*) Impulsiv-

impunity [ɪmˈpju:nɪtɪ] *n*: **with ~** ungestraft

impure [ɪmˈpjuəʳ] *adj* unrein; (*adulterated*) verunreinigt

impurity [ɪmˈpjuərɪtɪ] *n* Verunreinigung *f*

IN (*US*) *abbr* (*Post*) = *Indiana*

◯ KEYWORD

in [ɪn] *prep* **1** (*indicating place, position*) in *+dat*; (*with motion*) in *+acc*; **in the house/garden** im Haus/Garten; **in town** in der Stadt; **in the country** auf dem Land; **in here** hierin; **in there** darin

2 (*with place names: of town, region, country*) in *+dat*; **in London/Bavaria** in London/Bayern

3 (*indicating time*) in *+dat*; **in spring/summer/ May** im Frühling/Sommer/Mai; **in 1994** 1994; **in the afternoon** am Nachmittag; **at 4 o'clock in the afternoon** um 4 Uhr nachmittags; **I did it in 3 hours/days** ich habe es in 3 Stunden/Tagen gemacht; **in 2 weeks** *or* **2 weeks' time** in 2 Wochen

4 (*indicating manner, circumstances, state*) in *+dat*; **in a loud/soft voice** mit lauter/weicher Stimme; **in English/German** auf Englisch/ Deutsch; **in the sun** in der Sonne; **in the rain** im Regen; **in good condition** in guter Verfassung

5 (*with ratios, numbers*): **1 in 10** eine(r, s) von 10; **20 pence in the pound** 20 Pence pro Pfund; **they lined up in twos** sie stellten sich in Zweierreihen auf

6 (*referring to people, works*): **the disease is common in children** die Krankheit ist bei Kindern verbreitet; **in (the works of) Dickens** bei Dickens; **they have a good leader in him** in ihm haben sie einen guten Führer

7 (*indicating profession etc*): **to be in teaching/ the army** Lehrer(in)/beim Militär sein

8 (*with present participle*): **in saying this, I ...** wenn ich das sage, ...
  ▷ *adv*: **to be in** (*person: at home, work*) da sein; (*train, ship, plane*) angekommen sein; (*in fashion*) in sein; **to ask sb in** jdn hereinbitten; **to run/limp etc in** hereinlaufen/-humpeln *etc*
  ▷ *n*: **the ins and outs** (*of proposal, situation etc*) die Einzelheiten *pl*

in. *abbr* = **inch**

inability [ɪnəˈbɪlɪtɪ] *n* Unfähigkeit *f*

inaccessible [ɪnəkˈsɛsɪbl] *adj* unzugänglich

inaccuracy [ɪnˈækjurəsɪ] *n* (*see adj*) Ungenauigkeit *f*; Unrichtigkeit *f*; (*mistake*) Fehler *m*

inaccurate [ɪnˈækjurət] *adj* ungenau; (*not correct*) unrichtig

inaction [ɪnˈækʃən] *n* Untätigkeit *f*

inactive [ɪnˈæktɪv] *adj* untätig

inactivity [ɪnækˈtɪvɪtɪ] *n* Untätigkeit *f*

inadequacy [ɪnˈædɪkwəsɪ] *n* Unzulänglichkeit *f*

inadequate [ɪnˈædɪkwət] *adj* unzulänglich

inadmissible [ɪnədˈmɪsəbl] *adj* unzulässig

inadvertently [ɪnədˈvə:tntlɪ] *adv* ungewollt

inadvisable [ɪnədˈvaɪzəbl] *adj* unratsam; **it is ~ to ...** es ist nicht ratsam, zu ...

inane [ɪˈneɪn] *adj* dumm

inanimate [ɪnˈænɪmət] *adj* unbelebt

inapplicable [ɪnˈæplɪkəbl] *adj* unzutreffend

inappropriate [ɪnəˈprəuprɪət] *adj* unpassend; (*word, expression*) unangebracht

inapt [ɪnˈæpt] *adj* unpassend

inarticulate [ɪnɑ:ˈtɪkjulət] *adj* (*speech*) unverständlich; **he is ~** er kann sich nur schlecht ausdrücken

inasmuch as [ɪnəzˈmʌtʃ-] *adv* da, weil; (*in so far as*) insofern als

inattention [ɪnəˈtɛnʃən] *n* Unaufmerksamkeit *f*

inattentive [ɪnəˈtɛntɪv] *adj* unaufmerksam

inaudible [ɪnˈɔ:dɪbl] *adj* unhörbar

inaugural [ɪˈnɔ:gjurəl] *adj* (*speech, meeting*) Eröffnungs-

inaugurate [ɪˈnɔ:gjureɪt] *vt* einführen; (*president, official*) (feierlich) in sein/ihr Amt einführen

inauguration [ɪnɔ:gjuˈreɪʃən] *n* (*see vb*) Einführung *f*; (feierliche) Amtseinführung *f*

inauspicious [ɪnɔ:sˈpɪʃəs] *adj* Unheil verheißend

i

in-between [ɪnbɪ'twiːn] *adj* Mittel-, Zwischen-
inborn [ɪn'bɔːn] *adj* angeboren
inbred [ɪn'bred] *adj* angeboren; **an ~ family**
eine Familie, in der Inzucht herrscht
inbreeding [ɪn'briːdɪŋ] *n* Inzucht *f*
in-built ['ɪnbɪlt] *adj* (*quality*) ihm/ihr *etc* eigen;
(*feeling etc*) angeboren
Inc. *abbr* = **incorporated company**
Inca ['ɪŋkə] *adj* (*also*: **Incan**) Inka-, inkaisch ▷ *n*
Inka *mf*
incalculable [ɪn'kælkjuləbl] *adj* (*effect*)
unabsehbar; (*loss*) unermesslich
incapable [ɪn'keɪpəbl] *adj* hilflos; **to be ~ of**
sth unfähig zu etw sein; **to be ~ of doing sth**
unfähig sein, etw zu tun
incapacitate [ɪnkə'pæsɪteɪt] *vt*: **to ~ sb** jdn
unfähig machen
incapacitated [ɪnkə'pæsɪteɪtɪd] *adj* (*Law*)
entmündigt
incapacity [ɪnkə'pæsɪtɪ] *n* Hilflosigkeit *f*;
(*inability*) Unfähigkeit *f*
incarcerate [ɪn'kɑːsəreɪt] *vt* einkerkern
incarnate [ɪn'kɑːnɪt] *adj* leibhaftig, in Person;
evil ~ das leibhaftige Böse
incarnation [ɪnkɑː'neɪʃən] *n* Inbegriff *m*; (*Rel*)
Menschwerdung *f*
incendiary [ɪn'sɛndɪərɪ] *adj* (*bomb*) Brand-; **~**
device Brandsatz *m*
incense [*n* 'ɪnsɛns, *vt* ɪn'sɛns] *n* Weihrauch *m*;
(*perfume*) Duft *m* ▷ *vt* wütend machen
incense burner *n* Weihrauchschwenker *m*
incentive [ɪn'sɛntɪv] *n* Anreiz *m*
inception [ɪn'sɛpʃən] *n* Beginn *m*, Anfang *m*
incessant [ɪn'sɛsnt] *adj* unablässig
incessantly [ɪn'sɛsntlɪ] *adv* unablässig
incest ['ɪnsɛst] *n* Inzest *m*
inch [ɪntʃ] *n* Zoll *m*; **to be within an ~ of sth**
kurz vor etw *dat* stehen; **he didn't give an ~**
(*fig*) er gab keinen Fingerbreit nach
▶ **inch forward** *vi* sich millimeterweise
vorwärtsschieben
incidence ['ɪnsɪdns] *n* Häufigkeit *f*
incident ['ɪnsɪdnt] *n* Vorfall *m*; (*diplomatic etc*)
Zwischenfall *m*
incidental [ɪnsɪ'dɛntl] *adj* zusätzlich;
(*unimportant*) nebensächlich; **~ to** verbunden
mit; **~ expenses** Nebenkosten *pl*
incidentally [ɪnsɪ'dɛntəlɪ] *adv* übrigens
incidental music *n* Begleitmusik *f*
incident room *n* Einsatzzentrale *f*
incinerate [ɪn'sɪnəreɪt] *vt* verbrennen
incinerator [ɪn'sɪnəreɪtəʳ] *n* (*for waste, refuse*)
(Müll)verbrennungsanlage *f*
incipient [ɪn'sɪpɪənt] *adj* einsetzend
incision [ɪn'sɪʒən] *n* Einschnitt *m*
incisive [ɪn'saɪsɪv] *adj* treffend
incisor [ɪn'saɪzəʳ] *n* Schneidezahn *m*
incite [ɪn'saɪt] *vt* (*rioters*) aufhetzen; (*violence,*
hatred) schüren
incl. *abbr* = **including; inclusive (of)**
inclement [ɪn'klɛmənt] *adj* (*weather*) rau,
unfreundlich
inclination [ɪnklɪ'neɪʃən] *n* Neigung *f*

incline [*n* 'ɪnklaɪn, *vb* ɪn'klaɪn] *n* Abhang *m* ▷ *vt*
neigen ▷ *vi* sich neigen; **to be ~d to** neigen
zu; **to be well ~d towards sb** jdm geneigt *or*
gewogen sein
include [ɪn'kluːd] *vt* einbeziehen; (*in price*)
einschließen; **the tip is not ~d in the price**
Trinkgeld ist im Preis nicht inbegriffen
including [ɪn'kluːdɪŋ] *prep* einschließlich; **~**
service charge inklusive Bedienung
inclusion [ɪn'kluːʒən] *n* (*see vb*) Einbeziehung *f*;
Einschluss *m*
inclusive [ɪn'kluːsɪv] *adj* (*terms*) inklusive;
(*price*) Inklusiv-, Pauschal-; **~ of** einschließlich
+*gen*
incognito [ɪnkɒg'niːtəu] *adv* inkognito
incoherent [ɪnkəu'hɪərənt] *adj*
zusammenhanglos; (*speech*) wirr; (*person*) sich
unklar *or* undeutlich ausdrückend
income ['ɪnkʌm] *n* Einkommen *nt*; (*from*
property, investment, pension) Einkünfte *pl*;
gross/net ~ Brutto-/Nettoeinkommen
nt; **~ and expenditure account** Gewinn-
und Verlustrechnung *f*; **~ bracket**
Einkommensklasse *f*
income support *n* ≈ Sozialhilfe *f*
income tax *n* Einkommensteuer *f* ▷ *cpd*
Steuer-
incoming ['ɪnkʌmɪŋ] *adj* (*passenger*)
ankommend; (*flight*) landend; (*call, mail*)
eingehend; (*government, official*) neu; (*wave*)
hereinbrechend; **~ tide** Flut *f*
incommunicado ['ɪnkəmjunɪ'kɑːdəu] *adj*: **to**
hold sb ~ jdn ohne jede Verbindung zur
Außenwelt halten
incomparable [ɪn'kɒmpərəbl] *adj*
unvergleichlich
incompatible [ɪnkəm'pætɪbl] *adj* unvereinbar
incompetence [ɪn'kɒmpɪtns] *n* Unfähigkeit *f*
incompetent [ɪn'kɒmpɪtnt] *adj* unfähig; (*job*)
unzulänglich
incomplete [ɪnkəm'pliːt] *adj* unfertig; (*partial*)
unvollständig
incomprehensible [ɪnkɒmprɪ'hɛnsɪbl] *adj*
unverständlich
inconceivable [ɪnkən'siːvəbl] *adj*: **it is ~**
(that ...) es ist unvorstellbar *or* undenkbar(,
dass ...)
inconclusive [ɪnkən'kluːsɪv] *adj* (*experiment,*
discussion) ergebnislos; (*evidence, argument*) nicht
überzeugend; (*result*) unbestimmt
incongruous [ɪn'kɒŋgruəs] *adj* (*strange*) absurd;
(*inappropriate*) unpassend
inconsequential [ɪnkɒnsɪ'kwɛnʃl] *adj*
unbedeutend, unwichtig
inconsiderable [ɪnkən'sɪdərəbl] *adj*: **not ~**
beachtlich; (*sum*) nicht unerheblich
inconsiderate [ɪnkən'sɪdərət] *adj*
rücksichtslos
inconsistency [ɪnkən'sɪstənsɪ] *n* (*see adj*)
Widersprüchlichkeit *f*; Inkonsequenz *f*;
Unbeständigkeit *f*
inconsistent [ɪnkən'sɪstnt] *adj*
widersprüchlich; (*person*) inkonsequent; (*work*)

unbeständig; **to be ~ with** im Widerspruch stehen zu
inconsolable [ɪnkən'səʊləbl] adj untröstlich
inconspicuous [ɪnkən'spɪkjuəs] adj unauffällig; **to make o.s. ~** sich unauffällig benehmen
incontinence [ɪn'kɒntɪnəns] n (Med) Unfähigkeit f, Stuhl und/oder Harn zurückzuhalten, Inkontinenz f
incontinent [ɪn'kɒntɪnənt] adj (Med) unfähig, Stuhl und/oder Harn zurückzuhalten, inkontinent
inconvenience [ɪnkən'viːnjəns] n Unannehmlichkeit f; (trouble) Umstände pl ▷ vt Umstände bereiten +dat; **don't ~ yourself** machen Sie sich keine Umstände
inconvenient [ɪnkən'viːnjənt] adj (time, place) ungünstig; (house) unbequem, unpraktisch; (visitor) ungelegen
incorporate [ɪn'kɔːpəreɪt] vt aufnehmen; (contain) enthalten; **safety features have been ~d in the design** in der Konstruktion sind auch Sicherheitsvorkehrungen enthalten
incorporated company [ɪn'kɔːpəreɪtɪd-] (US) n eingetragene Gesellschaft f
incorrect [ɪnkə'rɛkt] adj falsch
incorrigible [ɪn'kɒrɪdʒɪbl] adj unverbesserlich
incorruptible [ɪnkə'rʌptɪbl] adj unbestechlich
increase [vb ɪn'kriːs, n 'ɪnkriːs] vi (level etc) zunehmen; (price) steigen; (in size) sich vergrößern; (in number, quantity) sich vermehren ▷ vt vergrößern; (price) erhöhen ▷ n: ~ **(in)** Zunahme f (+gen); (in wages, spending etc) Erhöhung f (+gen); **an ~ of 5%** eine Erhöhung von 5%, eine Zunahme um 5%; **to be on the ~** zunehmen
increasing [ɪn'kriːsɪŋ] adj zunehmend
increasingly [ɪn'kriːsɪŋlɪ] adv zunehmend
incredible [ɪn'krɛdɪbl] adj unglaublich; (amazing, wonderful) unwahrscheinlich (inf), sagenhaft (inf)
incredulity [ɪnkrɪ'djuːlɪtɪ] n Ungläubigkeit f
incredulous [ɪn'krɛdjuləs] adj ungläubig
increment ['ɪnkrɪmənt] n (in salary) Erhöhung f, Zulage f
incriminate [ɪn'krɪmɪneɪt] vt belasten
incriminating [ɪn'krɪmɪneɪtɪŋ] adj belastend
incrusted [ɪn'krʌstɪd] adj = **encrusted**
incubate ['ɪnkjubeɪt] vt ausbrüten ▷ vi ausgebrütet werden; (disease) zum Ausbruch kommen
incubation [ɪnkju'beɪʃən] n Ausbrüten nt; (of illness) Inkubation f
incubation period n Inkubationszeit f
incubator ['ɪnkjubeɪtəʳ] n (for babies) Brutkasten m, Inkubator m
inculcate ['ɪnkʌlkeɪt] vt: **to ~ sth in(to) sb** jdm etw einprägen
incumbent [ɪn'kʌmbənt] n Amtsinhaber(in) m(f) ▷ adj: **it is ~ on him to ...** es obliegt ihm or es ist seine Pflicht, zu ...
incur [ɪn'kəːʳ] vt (expenses, debt) machen; (loss)

erleiden; (disapproval, anger) sich dat zuziehen
incurable [ɪn'kjuərəbl] adj unheilbar
incursion [ɪn'kəːʃən] n (Mil) Einfall m
Ind. (US) abbr (Post) = Indiana
indebted [ɪn'dɛtɪd] adj: **to be ~ to sb** jdm (zu Dank) verpflichtet sein
indecency [ɪn'diːsnsɪ] n Unanständigkeit f, Anstößigkeit f
indecent [ɪn'diːsnt] adj unanständig, anstößig; (haste) ungebührlich
indecent assault (Brit) n Sexualverbrechen nt
indecent exposure n Erregung f öffentlichen Ärgernisses
indecipherable [ɪndɪ'saɪfərəbl] adj unleserlich; (expression, glance etc) unergründlich
indecision [ɪndɪ'sɪʒən] n Unentschlossenheit f
indecisive [ɪndɪ'saɪsɪv] adj unentschlossen
indeed [ɪn'diːd] adv aber sicher; (in fact) tatsächlich, in der Tat; (furthermore) sogar; **yes ~!** oh ja!, das kann man wohl sagen!
indefatigable [ɪndɪ'fætɪgəbl] adj unermüdlich
indefensible [ɪndɪ'fɛnsɪbl] adj (conduct) unentschuldbar
indefinable [ɪndɪ'faɪnəbl] adj undefinierbar
indefinite [ɪn'dɛfɪnɪt] adj unklar, vage; (period, number) unbestimmt
indefinite article n (Ling) unbestimmter Artikel m
indefinitely [ɪn'dɛfɪnɪtlɪ] adv (continue) endlos; (wait) unbegrenzt (lange); (postpone) auf unbestimmte Zeit
indelible [ɪn'dɛlɪbl] adj (mark, stain) nicht zu entfernen; **~ pen** Tintenstift m; **~ ink** Wäschetinte f
indelicate [ɪn'dɛlɪkɪt] adj taktlos; (not polite) ungehörig
indemnify [ɪn'dɛmnɪfaɪ] vt entschädigen
indemnity [ɪn'dɛmnɪtɪ] n (insurance) Versicherung f; (compensation) Entschädigung f
indent [ɪn'dɛnt] vt (text) einrücken, einziehen
indentation [ɪndɛn'teɪʃən] n Einkerbung f; (Typ) Einrückung f, Einzug m; (on metal) Delle f
indenture [ɪn'dɛntʃəʳ] n Ausbildungsvertrag m, Lehrvertrag m
independence [ɪndɪ'pɛndns] n Unabhängigkeit f

⬤ **INDEPENDENCE DAY**

⬤ Independence Day (der 4. Juli) ist in den USA
⬤ ein gesetzlicher Feiertag zum Gedenken
⬤ an die Unabhängigkeitserklärung
⬤ vom 4. Juli 1776, mit der die 13
⬤ amerikanischen Kolonien ihre Freiheit
⬤ und Unabhängigkeit von Großbritannien
⬤ erklärten.

independent [ɪndɪ'pɛndnt] adj unabhängig
independently [ɪndɪ'pɛndntlɪ] adv unabhängig
in-depth ['ɪndɛpθ] adj eingehend
indescribable [ɪndɪs'kraɪbəbl] adj unbeschreiblich

indestructible [ɪndɪs'trʌktəbl] *adj* unzerstörbar

indeterminate [ɪndɪ'tə:mɪnɪt] *adj* unbestimmt

index ['ɪndɛks] (*pl* **~es**) *n* (*in book*) Register *nt*; (*in library etc*) Katalog *m*; (*also*: **card index**) Kartei *f* (*pl* **indices**: *ratio*) Index *m*; (: *sign*) (An)zeichen *nt*

index card *n* Karteikarte *f*

indexed ['ɪndɛkst] (US) *adj* = **index-linked**

index finger *n* Zeigefinger *m*

index-linked ['ɪndɛks'lɪŋkt] *adj* der Inflationsrate *dat* angeglichen

India ['ɪndɪə] *n* Indien *nt*

Indian ['ɪndɪən] *adj* indisch; (*American Indian*) indianisch ▷ *n* Inder(in) *m(f)*; **American ~** Indianer(in) *m(f)*

Indian Ocean *n*: **the ~** der Indische Ozean

Indian summer *n* Altweibersommer *m*

India paper *n* Dünndruckpapier *nt*

India rubber *n* Gummi *m*, Kautschuk *m*

indicate ['ɪndɪkeɪt] *vt* (an)zeigen; (*point to*) deuten auf +*acc*; (*mention*) andeuten ▷ *vi* (*Brit*: *Aut*): **to ~ left/right** links/rechts blinken

indication [ɪndɪ'keɪʃən] *n* (An)zeichen *nt*

indicative [ɪn'dɪkətɪv] *n* (*Ling*) Indikativ *m*, Wirklichkeitsform *f* ▷ *adj*: **to be ~ of sth** auf etw *acc* schließen lassen

indicator ['ɪndɪkeɪtəʳ] *n* (*instrument, gauge*) Anzeiger *m*; (*fig*) (An)zeichen *nt*; (*Aut*) Richtungsanzeiger *m*, Blinker *m*

indices ['ɪndɪsi:z] *npl of* **index**

indict [ɪn'daɪt] *vt* anklagen

indictable [ɪn'daɪtəbl] *adj* (*person*) strafrechtlich verfolgbar; **~ offence** strafbare Handlung *f*

indictment [ɪn'daɪtmənt] *n* Anklage *f*; **to be an ~ of sth** (*fig*) ein Armutszeugnis *nt* für etw sein

indifference [ɪn'dɪfrəns] *n* Gleichgültigkeit *f*

indifferent [ɪn'dɪfrənt] *adj* gleichgültig; (*mediocre*) mittelmäßig

indigenous [ɪn'dɪdʒɪnəs] *adj* einheimisch

indigestible [ɪndɪ'dʒɛstɪbl] *adj* unverdaulich

indigestion [ɪndɪ'dʒɛstʃən] *n* Magenverstimmung *f*

indignant [ɪn'dɪgnənt] *adj*: **to be ~ at sth/ with sb** entrüstet über etw/jdn sein

indignation [ɪndɪg'neɪʃən] *n* Entrüstung *f*

indignity [ɪn'dɪgnɪtɪ] *n* Demütigung *f*

indigo ['ɪndɪgəu] *n* Indigo *m* or *m*

indirect [ɪndɪ'rɛkt] *adj* indirekt; **~ way** or **route** Umweg *m*

indirectly [ɪndɪ'rɛktlɪ] *adv* indirekt

indiscreet [ɪndɪs'kri:t] *adj* indiskret

indiscretion [ɪndɪs'krɛʃən] *n* Indiskretion *f*

indiscriminate [ɪndɪs'krɪmɪnət] *adj* wahllos; (*taste*) unkritisch

indispensable [ɪndɪs'pɛnsəbl] *adj* unentbehrlich

indisposed [ɪndɪs'pəuzd] *adj* unpässlich

indisputable [ɪndɪs'pju:təbl] *adj* unbestreitbar

indistinct [ɪndɪs'tɪŋkt] *adj* undeutlich; (*image*) verschwommen; (*noise*) schwach

indistinguishable [ɪndɪs'tɪŋgwɪʃəbl] *adj*: **~**

from nicht zu unterscheiden von

individual [ɪndɪ'vɪdjuəl] *n* Individuum *nt*, Einzelne(r) *f(m)* ▷ *adj* eigen; (*single*) einzeln; (*case, portion*) Einzel-; (*particular*) individuell

individualist [ɪndɪ'vɪdjuəlɪst] *n* Individualist(in) *m(f)*

individuality [ɪndɪvɪdju'ælɪtɪ] *n* Individualität *f*

individually [ɪndɪ'vɪdjuəlɪ] *adv* einzeln, individuell

indivisible [ɪndɪ'vɪzɪbl] *adj* unteilbar

Indochina [ɪndəu'tʃaɪnə] *n* Indochina *nt*

indoctrinate [ɪn'dɔktrɪneɪt] *vt* indoktrinieren

indoctrination [ɪndɔktrɪ'neɪʃən] *n* Indoktrination *f*

indolence ['ɪndələns] *n* Trägheit *f*

indolent ['ɪndələnt] *adj* träge

Indonesia [ɪndə'ni:zɪə] *n* Indonesien *nt*

Indonesian [ɪndə'ni:zɪən] *adj* indonesisch ▷ *n* Indonesier(in) *m(f)*; (*Ling*) Indonesisch *nt*

indoor ['ɪndɔ:ʳ] *adj* (*plant, aerial*) Zimmer-; (*clothes, shoes*) Haus-; (*swimming pool, sport*) Hallen-; (*games*) im Haus

indoors [ɪn'dɔ:z] *adv* drinnen; **to go ~** hineingehen

indubitable [ɪn'dju:bɪtəbl] *adj* unzweifelhaft

indubitably [ɪn'dju:bɪtəblɪ] *adv* zweifellos

induce [ɪn'dju:s] *vt* herbeiführen; (*persuade*) dazu bringen; (*Med*: *birth*) einleiten; **to ~ sb to do sth** jdn dazu bewegen *or* bringen, etw zu tun

inducement [ɪn'dju:smənt] *n* Anreiz *m*; (*pej*: *bribe*) Bestechung *f*

induct [ɪn'dʌkt] *vt* (in sein/ihr *etc* Amt) einführen

induction [ɪn'dʌkʃən] *n* (*Med*: *of birth*) Einleitung *f*

induction course (*Brit*) *n* Einführungskurs *m*

indulge [ɪn'dʌldʒ] *vt* nachgeben +*dat*; (*person, child*) verwöhnen ▷ *vi*: **to ~ in** sich hingeben +*dat*

indulgence [ɪn'dʌldʒəns] *n* (*pleasure*) Luxus *m*; (*leniency*) Nachgiebigkeit *f*

indulgent [ɪn'dʌldʒənt] *adj* nachsichtig

industrial [ɪn'dʌstrɪəl] *adj* industriell; (*accident*) Arbeits-; (*city*) Industrie-

industrial action *n* Arbeitskampfmaßnahmen *pl*

industrial design *n* Industriedesign *nt*

industrial estate (*Brit*) *n* Industriegebiet *nt*

industrialist [ɪn'dʌstrɪəlɪst] *n* Industrielle(r) *f(m)*

industrialize [ɪn'dʌstrɪəlaɪz] *vt* industrialisieren

industrial park (US) *n* = **industrial estate**

industrial relations *npl* Beziehungen zwischen Arbeitgebern, Arbeitnehmern und Gewerkschaften

industrial tribunal (*Brit*) *n* Arbeitsgericht *nt*

industrial unrest (*Brit*) *n* Arbeitsunruhen *pl*

industrious [ɪn'dʌstrɪəs] *adj* fleißig

industry ['ɪndəstrɪ] *n* Industrie *f*; (*diligence*) Fleiß *m*

inebriated [ɪ'ni:brɪeɪtɪd] *adj* betrunken

inedible [ɪnˈɛdɪbl] *adj* ungenießbar
ineffective [ɪnɪˈfɛktɪv] *adj* wirkungslos; (*government*) unfähig
ineffectual [ɪnɪˈfɛktʃuəl] *adj* = **ineffective**
inefficiency [ɪnɪˈfɪʃənsɪ] *n* (*see adj*) Ineffizienz *f*; Leistungsunfähigkeit *f*
inefficient [ɪnɪˈfɪʃənt] *adj* ineffizient; (*machine*) leistungsunfähig
inelegant [ɪnˈɛlɪgənt] *adj* unelegant
ineligible [ɪnˈɛlɪdʒɪbl] *adj* (*candidate*) nicht wählbar; **to be ~ for sth** zu etw nicht berechtigt sein
inept [ɪˈnɛpt] *adj* (*politician*) unfähig; (*management*) stümperhaft
ineptitude [ɪˈnɛptɪtjuːd] *n* (*see adj*) Unfähigkeit *f*; Stümperhaftigkeit *f*
inequality [ɪnɪˈkwɔlɪtɪ] *n* Ungleichheit *f*
inequitable [ɪnˈɛkwɪtəbl] *adj* ungerecht
inert [ɪˈnɜːt] *adj* unbeweglich; **~ gas** Edelgas *nt*
inertia [ɪˈnɜːʃə] *n* Trägheit *f*
inertia-reel seat belt [ɪˈnɜːʃəˈriːl-] *n* Automatikgurt *m*
inescapable [ɪnɪˈskeɪpəbl] *adj* unvermeidlich; (*conclusion*) zwangsläufig
inessential [ɪnɪˈsɛnʃl] *adj* unwesentlich; (*furniture etc*) entbehrlich
inessentials [ɪnɪˈsɛnʃlz] *npl* Nebensächlichkeiten *pl*
inestimable [ɪnˈɛstɪməbl] *adj* unschätzbar
inevitability [ɪnɛvɪtəˈbɪlɪtɪ] *n* Unvermeidlichkeit *f*; **it is an ~** es ist nicht zu vermeiden
inevitable [ɪnˈɛvɪtəbl] *adj* unvermeidlich; (*result*) zwangsläufig
inevitably [ɪnˈɛvɪtəblɪ] *adv* zwangsläufig; **~, he was late** es konnte ja nicht ausbleiben, dass er zu spät kam; **as ~ happens ...** wie es immer so ist ...
inexact [ɪnɪgˈzækt] *adj* ungenau
inexcusable [ɪnɪksˈkjuːzəbl] *adj* unentschuldbar, unverzeihlich
inexhaustible [ɪnɪgˈzɔːstɪbl] *adj* unerschöpflich
inexorable [ɪnˈɛksərəbl] *adj* unaufhaltsam
inexpensive [ɪnɪkˈspɛnsɪv] *adj* preisgünstig
inexperience [ɪnɪkˈspɪərɪəns] *n* Unerfahrenheit *f*
inexperienced [ɪnɪkˈspɪərɪənst] *adj* unerfahren; (*swimmer etc*) ungeübt; **to be ~ in sth** wenig Erfahrung mit etw haben
inexplicable [ɪnɪkˈsplɪkəbl] *adj* unerklärlich
inexpressible [ɪnɪkˈspresɪbl] *adj* unbeschreiblich
inextricable [ɪnɪkˈstrɪkəbl] *adj* unentwirrbar; (*dilemma*) unlösbar
inextricably [ɪnɪkˈstrɪkəblɪ] *adv* unentwirrbar; (*linked*) untrennbar
infallibility [ɪnfæləˈbɪlɪtɪ] *n* Unfehlbarkeit *f*
infallible [ɪnˈfælɪbl] *adj* unfehlbar
infamous [ˈɪnfəməs] *adj* niederträchtig
infamy [ˈɪnfəmɪ] *n* Verrufenheit *f*
infancy [ˈɪnfənsɪ] *n* frühe Kindheit *f*; (*of movement, firm*) Anfangsstadium *nt*

infant [ˈɪnfənt] *n* Säugling *m*; (*young child*) Kleinkind *nt* ▷ *cpd* Säuglings-
infantile [ˈɪnfəntaɪl] *adj* kindisch, infantil; (*disease*) Kinder-
infantry [ˈɪnfəntrɪ] *n* Infanterie *f*
infantryman [ˈɪnfəntrɪmən] (*irreg: like* **man**) *n* Infanterist *m*
infant school (*Brit*) *n* Grundschule *f* (*für die ersten beiden Jahrgänge*)
infatuated [ɪnˈfætjueɪtɪd] *adj*: **~ with** vernarrt in +*acc*; **to become ~ with** sich vernarren in +*acc*
infatuation [ɪnfætjuˈeɪʃən] *n* Vernarrtheit *f*
infect [ɪnˈfɛkt] *vt* anstecken (*also fig*), infizieren; (*food*) verseuchen; **to become ~ed** (*wound*) sich entzünden
infection [ɪnˈfɛkʃən] *n* Infektion *f*, Entzündung *f*; (*contagion*) Ansteckung *f*
infectious [ɪnˈfɛkʃəs] *adj* ansteckend
infer [ɪnˈfɜːʳ] *vt* schließen; (*imply*) andeuten
inference [ˈɪnfərəns] *n* (*see vb*) Schluss *m*; Andeutung *f*
inferior [ɪnˈfɪərɪəʳ] *adj* (*in rank*) untergeordnet, niedriger; (*in quality*) minderwertig; (*in quantity, number*) geringer ▷ *n* Untergebene(r) *f(m)*; **to feel ~ (to sb)** sich (jdm) unterlegen fühlen
inferiority [ɪnfɪərɪˈɔrətɪ] *n* (*see adj*) untergeordnete Stellung *f*, niedriger Rang *m*; Minderwertigkeit *f*; geringere Zahl *f*
inferiority complex *n* Minderwertigkeitskomplex *m*
infernal [ɪnˈfɜːnl] *adj* höllisch; (*temper*) schrecklich
inferno [ɪnˈfɜːnəu] *n* (*blaze*) Flammenmeer *nt*
infertile [ɪnˈfɜːtaɪl] *adj* unfruchtbar
infertility [ɪnfɜːˈtɪlɪtɪ] *n* Unfruchtbarkeit *f*
infested [ɪnˈfɛstɪd] *adj*: **~ (with)** verseucht (mit)
infidelity [ɪnfɪˈdɛlɪtɪ] *n* Untreue *f*
infighting [ˈɪnfaɪtɪŋ] *n* interne Machtkämpfe *pl*
infiltrate [ˈɪnfɪltreɪt] *vt* (*organization etc*) infiltrieren, unterwandern; (: *to spy*) einschleusen
infinite [ˈɪnfɪnɪt] *adj* unendlich; (*time, money*) unendlich viel
infinitely [ˈɪnfɪnɪtlɪ] *adv* unendlich viel
infinitesimal [ɪnfɪnɪˈtɛsɪməl] *adj* unendlich klein, winzig
infinitive [ɪnˈfɪnɪtɪv] *n* (*Ling*) Infinitiv *m*, Grundform *f*
infinity [ɪnˈfɪnɪtɪ] *n* Unendlichkeit *f*; (*Math, Phot*) Unendliche *nt*; **an ~ of ...** unendlich viel(e) ...
infirm [ɪnˈfɜːm] *adj* schwach, gebrechlich
infirmary [ɪnˈfɜːmərɪ] *n* Krankenhaus *nt*
infirmity [ɪnˈfɜːmɪtɪ] *n* Schwäche *f*, Gebrechlichkeit *f*
inflame [ɪnˈfleɪm] *vt* aufbringen
inflamed [ɪnˈfleɪmd] *adj* entzündet
inflammable [ɪnˈflæməbl] *adj* feuergefährlich
inflammation [ɪnfləˈmeɪʃən] *n* Entzündung *f*

i

inflammatory [ɪnˈflæmətərɪ] *adj* (*speech*) aufrührerisch, Hetz-

inflatable [ɪnˈfleɪtəbl] *adj* aufblasbar; (*dinghy*) Schlauch-

inflate [ɪnˈfleɪt] *vt* aufpumpen; (*balloon*) aufblasen; (*price*) hochtreiben; (*expectation*) steigern; (*position, ideas etc*) hochspielen

inflated [ɪnˈfleɪtɪd] *adj* (*value, price*) überhöht

inflation [ɪnˈfleɪʃən] *n* Inflation *f*

inflationary [ɪnˈfleɪʃənərɪ] *adj* inflationär; (*spiral*) Inflations-

inflexible [ɪnˈfleksɪbl] *adj* inflexibel; (*rule*) starr

inflict [ɪnˈflɪkt] *vt*: **to ~ sth on sb** (*damage, suffering, wound*) jdm etw zufügen; (*punishment*) jdm etw auferlegen; (*fig: problems*) jdn mit etw belasten

infliction [ɪnˈflɪkʃən] *n* (*see vb*) Zufügen *nt*; Auferlegung *f*; Belastung *f*

in-flight [ˈɪnflaɪt] *adj* während des Fluges

inflow [ˈɪnfləʊ] *n* Zustrom *m*

influence [ˈɪnfluəns] *n* Einfluss *m* ▷ *vt* beeinflussen; **under the ~ of alcohol** unter Alkoholeinfluss

influential [ɪnfluˈenʃl] *adj* einflussreich

influenza [ɪnfluˈenzə] *n* (*Med*) Grippe *f*

influx [ˈɪnflʌks] *n* (*of refugees*) Zustrom *m*; (*of funds*) Zufuhr *f*

inform [ɪnˈfɔːm] *vt*: **to ~ sb of sth** jdn von etw unterrichten, jdn über etw *acc* informieren ▷ *vi*: **to ~ on sb** jdn denunzieren

informal [ɪnˈfɔːml] *adj* ungezwungen; (*manner, clothes*) leger; (*unofficial*) inoffiziell; (*announcement, invitation*) informell

informality [ɪnfɔːˈmælɪtɪ] *n* (*see adj*) Ungezwungenheit *f*; legere Art *f*; inoffizieller Charakter *m*; informeller Charakter *m*

informally [ɪnˈfɔːməlɪ] *adv* (*see adj*) ungezwungen; leger; inoffiziell; informell

informant [ɪnˈfɔːmənt] *n* Informant(in) *m(f)*

information [ɪnfəˈmeɪʃən] *n* Informationen *pl*, Auskunft *f*; (*knowledge*) Wissen *nt*; **to get ~ on** sich informieren über +*acc*; **a piece of ~** eine Auskunft *or* Information; **for your ~** zu Ihrer Information

information and communication technology (*Brit*) *n* (*Scol*) = Informations- und Kommunikationstechnologie

information bureau *n* Auskunftsbüro *nt*

information desk *n* Auskunftsschalter *m*

information office *n* Auskunftsbüro *nt*

information processing *n* Informationsverarbeitung *f*

information retrieval *n* Informationsabruf *m*, Datenabruf *m*

information science *n* Informatik *f*

information superhighway *n* (*Comput*) Datenautobahn *f*

information technology *n* Informationstechnik *f*

informative [ɪnˈfɔːmətɪv] *adj* aufschlussreich

informed [ɪnˈfɔːmd] *adj* informiert; (*guess, opinion*) wohlbegründet; **to be well/better ~** gut/besser informiert sein

informer [ɪnˈfɔːməʳ] *n* Informant(in) *m(f)*; (*also*: **police informer**) Polizeispitzel *m*

infra dig [ˈɪnfrəˈdɪg] (*inf*) *adj abbr* (= *infra dignitatem*) unter meiner/seiner *etc* Würde

infrared [ɪnfrəˈred] *adj* infrarot

infrastructure [ˈɪnfrəstrʌktʃəʳ] *n* Infrastruktur *f*

infrequent [ɪnˈfriːkwənt] *adj* selten

infringe [ɪnˈfrɪndʒ] *vt* (*law*) verstoßen gegen, übertreten ▷ *vi*: **to ~ on** (*rights*) verletzen

infringement [ɪnˈfrɪndʒmənt] *n* (*see vb*) Verstoß *m*, Übertretung *f*; Verletzung *f*

infuriate [ɪnˈfjʊərɪeɪt] *vt* wütend machen

infuriating [ɪnˈfjʊərɪeɪtɪŋ] *adj* äußerst ärgerlich

infuse [ɪnˈfjuːz] *vt* (*tea etc*) aufgießen; **to ~ sb with sth** (*fig*) jdm etw einflößen

infusion [ɪnˈfjuːʒən] *n* (*tea etc*) Aufguss *m*

ingenious [ɪnˈdʒiːnjəs] *adj* genial

ingenuity [ɪndʒɪˈnjuːɪtɪ] *n* Einfallsreichtum *m*; (*skill*) Geschicklichkeit *f*

ingenuous [ɪnˈdʒenjuəs] *adj* offen, aufrichtig; (*innocent*) naiv

ingot [ˈɪŋgət] *n* Barren *m*

ingrained [ɪnˈgreɪnd] *adj* (*habit*) fest; (*belief*) unerschütterlich

ingratiate [ɪnˈgreɪʃɪeɪt] *vt*: **to ~ o.s. with sb** sich bei jdm einschmeicheln

ingratiating [ɪnˈgreɪʃɪeɪtɪŋ] *adj* schmeichlerisch

ingratitude [ɪnˈgrætɪtjuːd] *n* Undank *m*

ingredient [ɪnˈgriːdɪənt] *n* (*of cake etc*) Zutat *f*; (*of situation*) Bestandteil *m*

ingrowing [ˈɪngrəʊɪŋ] *adj*: **~ toenail** eingewachsener Zehennagel *m*

inhabit [ɪnˈhæbɪt] *vt* bewohnen, wohnen in +*dat*

inhabitant [ɪnˈhæbɪtnt] *n* Einwohner(in) *m(f)*; (*of street, house*) Bewohner(in) *m(f)*

inhale [ɪnˈheɪl] *vt* einatmen ▷ *vi* einatmen; (*when smoking*) inhalieren

inhaler [ɪnˈheɪləʳ] *n* Inhalationsapparat *m*

inherent [ɪnˈhɪərənt] *adj*: **~ in** *or* **to** eigen +*dat*

inherently [ɪnˈhɪərəntlɪ] *adv* von Natur aus

inherit [ɪnˈherɪt] *vt* erben

inheritance [ɪnˈherɪtəns] *n* Erbe *nt*

inhibit [ɪnˈhɪbɪt] *vt* hemmen

inhibited [ɪnˈhɪbɪtɪd] *adj* gehemmt

inhibiting [ɪnˈhɪbɪtɪŋ] *adj* hemmend; **~ factor** Hemmnis *nt*

inhibition [ɪnhɪˈbɪʃən] *n* Hemmung *f*

inhospitable [ɪnhɔsˈpɪtəbl] *adj* ungastlich; (*place, climate*) unwirtlich

in-house [ˈɪnˈhaʊs] *adj, adv* hausintern

inhuman [ɪnˈhjuːmən] *adj* (*behaviour*) unmenschlich; (*appearance*) nicht menschlich

inhumane [ɪnhjuːˈmeɪn] *adj* inhuman; (*treatment*) menschenunwürdig

inimitable [ɪˈnɪmɪtəbl] *adj* unnachahmlich

iniquitous [ɪˈnɪkwɪtəs] *adj* (*unfair*) ungerecht

iniquity [ɪˈnɪkwɪtɪ] *n* Ungerechtigkeit *f*; (*wickedness*) Ungeheuerlichkeit *f*

initial [ɪˈnɪʃl] *adj* anfänglich; (*stage*) Anfangs-

▷ *n* Initiale *f*, Anfangsbuchstabe *m* ▷ *vt*
(*document*) abzeichnen; **initials** *npl* Initialen *pl*;
(*as signature*) Namenszeichen *nt*
initialize [ɪ'nɪʃəlaɪz] *vt* initialisieren
initially [ɪ'nɪʃəlɪ] *adv* zu Anfang; (*first*) zuerst
initiate [ɪ'nɪʃɪeɪt] *vt* (*talks*) eröffnen; (*process*)
einleiten; (*new member*) feierlich aufnehmen;
to ~ sb into a secret jdn in ein Geheimnis
einweihen; **to ~ proceedings against sb**
(*Law*) einen Prozess gegen jdn anstrengen
initiation [ɪnɪʃɪ'eɪʃən] *n* (*beginning*) Einführung
f; (*into secret etc*) Einweihung *f*
initiative [ɪ'nɪʃətɪv] *n* Initiative *f*; **to take the**
~ die Initiative ergreifen
inject [ɪn'dʒɛkt] *vt* (ein)spritzen; (*fig: funds*)
hineinpumpen; **to ~ sb with sth** jdm etw
spritzen *or* injizieren; **to ~ money into sth**
(*fig*) Geld in etw *acc* pumpen
injection [ɪn'dʒɛkʃən] *n* Spritze *f*, Injektion *f*;
to give/have an ~ eine Spritze *or* Injektion
geben/bekommen; **an ~ of money/funds**
(*fig*) eine Finanzspritze
injudicious [ɪndʒu'dɪʃəs] *adj* unklug
injunction [ɪn'dʒʌŋkʃən] *n* (*Law*) gerichtliche
Verfügung *f*
injure ['ɪndʒəʳ] *vt* verletzen; (*reputation*) schaden
+*dat*; **to ~ o.s.** sich verletzen
injured ['ɪndʒəd] *adj* verletzt; (*tone*) gekränkt; **~**
party (*Law*) Geschädigte(r) *f(m)*
injurious [ɪn'dʒuərɪəs] *adj*: **to be ~ to** schaden
+*dat*, schädlich sein +*dat*
injury ['ɪndʒərɪ] *n* Verletzung *f*; **to escape**
without ~ unverletzt davonkommen
injury time *n* (*Sport*) Nachspielzeit *f*; **to play ~**
nachspielen
injustice [ɪn'dʒʌstɪs] *n* Ungerechtigkeit *f*; **you**
do me an ~ Sie tun mir unrecht
ink [ɪŋk] *n* Tinte *f*; (*in printing*) Druckfarbe *f*
ink-jet printer ['ɪŋkdʒɛt-] *n*
Tintenstrahldrucker *m*
inkling ['ɪŋklɪŋ] *n* (dunkle) Ahnung *f*; **to have**
an ~ of ahnen
ink pad *n* Stempelkissen *nt*
inky ['ɪŋkɪ] *adj* tintenschwarz; (*fingers*)
tintenbeschmiert
inlaid ['ɪnleɪd] *adj* eingelegt
inland ['ɪnlənd] *adj* (*port, sea, waterway*) Binnen-
▷ *adv* (*travel*) landeinwärts
Inland Revenue (*Brit*) *n* ≈ Finanzamt *nt*
in-laws ['ɪnlɔːz] *npl* (*parents-in-law*)
Schwiegereltern *pl*; (*other relatives*)
angeheiratete Verwandte *pl*
inlet ['ɪnlɛt] *n* (schmale) Bucht *f*
inlet pipe *n* Zuleitung *f*, Zuleitungsrohr *nt*
inmate ['ɪnmeɪt] *n* Insasse *m*, Insassin *f*
inmost ['ɪnməust] *adj* innerst
inn [ɪn] *n* Gasthaus *nt*
innards ['ɪnədz] (*inf*) *npl* Innereien *pl*
innate [ɪ'neɪt] *adj* angeboren
inner ['ɪnəʳ] *adj* innere(r, s); (*courtyard*) Innen-
inner city *n* Innenstadt *f*
innermost ['ɪnəməust] *adj* = **inmost**
inner tube *n* (*of tyre*) Schlauch *m*

innings ['ɪnɪŋz] *n* (*Cricket*) Innenrunde *f*; **he's**
had a good ~ (*fig*) er kann auf ein langes,
ausgefülltes Leben zurückblicken
innocence ['ɪnəsns] *n* Unschuld *f*
innocent ['ɪnəsnt] *adj* unschuldig
innocuous [ɪ'nɔkjuəs] *adj* harmlos
innovation [ɪnəu'veɪʃən] *n* Neuerung *f*
innuendo [ɪnju'ɛndəu] (*pl* **~es**) *n* versteckte
Andeutung *f*
innumerable [ɪ'njuːmrəbl] *adj* unzählig
inoculate [ɪ'nɔkjuleɪt] *vt*: **to ~ sb against sth**
jdn gegen etw impfen; **to ~ sb with sth** jdm
etw einimpfen
inoculation [ɪnɔkju'leɪʃən] *n* Impfung *f*
inoffensive [ɪnə'fɛnsɪv] *adj* harmlos
inopportune [ɪn'ɔpətjuːn] *adj* unangebracht;
(*moment*) ungelegen
inordinate [ɪ'nɔːdɪnət] *adj* (*thirst etc*) unmäßig;
(*amount, pleasure*) ungeheuer
inordinately [ɪ'nɔːdɪnətlɪ] *adv* (*proud*)
unmäßig; (*long, large etc*) ungeheuer
inorganic [ɪnɔː'gænɪk] *adj* anorganisch
inpatient ['ɪnpeɪʃənt] *n* stationär behandelter
Patient *m*, stationär behandelte Patientin *f*
input ['ɪnput] *n* (*of capital, manpower*) Investition
f; (*of energy*) Zufuhr *f*; (*Comput*) Eingabe *f*, Input
m or nt ▷ *vt* (*Comput*) eingeben
inquest ['ɪnkwɛst] *n* gerichtliche
Untersuchung *f* der Todesursache
inquire [ɪn'kwaɪəʳ] *vi*: **to ~ about** sich
erkundigen nach, fragen nach ▷ *vt* sich
erkundigen nach, fragen nach; **to ~ when/**
where/whether fragen *or* sich erkundigen,
wann/wo/ob
  ▸ **inquire after** *vt fus* sich erkundigen nach
  ▸ **inquire into** *vt fus* untersuchen
inquiring [ɪn'kwaɪərɪŋ] *adj* wissensdurstig
inquiry [ɪn'kwaɪərɪ] *n* Untersuchung *f*;
(*question*) Anfrage *f*; **to hold an ~ into sth** eine
Untersuchung +*gen* durchführen
inquiry desk (*Brit*) *n* Auskunft *f*,
Auskunftsschalter *m*
inquiry office (*Brit*) *n* Auskunft *f*,
Auskunftsbüro *nt*
inquisition [ɪnkwɪ'zɪʃən] *n* Untersuchung *f*;
(*Rel*): **the I~** die Inquisition
inquisitive [ɪn'kwɪzɪtɪv] *adj* neugierig
inroads ['ɪnrəudz] *npl*: **to make ~ into** (*savings,*
supplies) angreifen
ins *abbr* (= *inches*) *see* **inch**
insane [ɪn'seɪn] *adj* wahnsinnig; (*Med*)
geisteskrank
insanitary [ɪn'sænɪtərɪ] *adj* unhygienisch
insanity [ɪn'sænɪtɪ] *n* Wahnsinn *m*; (*Med*)
Geisteskrankheit *f*
insatiable [ɪn'seɪʃəbl] *adj* unersättlich
inscribe [ɪn'skraɪb] *vt* (*on ring*) eingravieren;
(*on stone*) einmeißeln; (*on banner*) schreiben;
to ~ a ring/stone/banner with sth etw
in einen Ring eingravieren/in einen Stein
einmeißeln/auf ein Spruchband schreiben;
to ~ a book eine Widmung in ein Buch
schreiben

inscription [ɪnˈskrɪpʃən] n Inschrift f; (in book) Widmung f

inscrutable [ɪnˈskruːtəbl] adj (comment) unergründlich; (expression) undurchdringlich

inseam measurement [ˈɪnsiːmˌ] (US) n innere Beinlänge f

insect [ˈɪnsɛkt] n Insekt nt

insect bite n Insektenstich m

insecticide [ɪnˈsɛktɪsaɪd] n Insektizid nt, Insektengift nt

insect repellent n Insektenbekämpfungsmittel nt

insecure [ɪnsɪˈkjʊəʳ] adj unsicher

insecurity [ɪnsɪˈkjʊərɪtɪ] n Unsicherheit f

insemination [ɪnsɛmɪˈneɪʃən] n: **artificial ~** künstliche Besamung f

insensible [ɪnˈsɛnsɪbl] adj bewusstlos; **~ to** unempfindlich gegen; **~ of** nicht bewusst +gen

insensitive [ɪnˈsɛnsɪtɪv] adj gefühllos

insensitivity [ɪnsɛnsɪˈtɪvɪtɪ] n Gefühllosigkeit f

inseparable [ɪnˈsɛprəbl] adj untrennbar; (friends) unzertrennlich

insert [vt ɪnˈsəːt, n ˈɪnsəːt] vt einfügen; (into sth) hineinstecken ▷ n (in newspaper etc) Beilage f; (in shoe) Einlage f

insertion [ɪnˈsəːʃən] n Hineinstecken nt; (of needle) Einstechen nt; (of comment) Einfügen nt

in-service [ˈɪnˈsəːvɪs] adj: **~ training** (berufsbegleitende) Fortbildung f; **~ course** Fortbildungslehrgang m

inshore [ˈɪnˈʃɔːʳ] adj (fishing, waters) Küsten- ▷ adv in Küstennähe; (move) auf die Küste zu

inside [ˈɪnˈsaɪd] n Innere(s) nt, Innenseite f; (of road: in Britain) linke Spur f; (: in US, Europe etc) rechte Spur f ▷ adj innere(r, s); (pocket, cabin, light) Innen- ▷ adv (go) nach innen, hinein; (be) drinnen ▷ prep (location) in +dat; (motion) in +acc; **~ 10 minutes** innerhalb von 10 Minuten; **insides** npl (inf) Bauch m; (innards) Eingeweide pl

inside forward n (Sport) Halbstürmer m

inside information n Insiderinformation f

inside knowledge n Insiderwissen nt

inside lane n (Brit) linke Spur f; (in US, Europe etc) rechte Spur f

inside leg measurement (Brit) n innere Beinlänge f

inside out adv (know) in- und auswendig; (piece of clothing: be) links or verkehrt herum; (: turn) nach links

insider [ɪnˈsaɪdəʳ] n Insider m, Eingeweihte(r) f(m)

insider dealing, insider trading n (Stock Exchange) Insiderhandel m or -geschäfte pl

inside story n Insidestory f, Inside Story f

insidious [ɪnˈsɪdɪəs] adj heimtückisch

insight [ˈɪnsaɪt] n Verständnis nt; **to gain (an) ~ into** einen Einblick gewinnen in +acc

insignia [ɪnˈsɪgnɪə] npl Insignien pl

insignificant [ɪnsɪgˈnɪfɪknt] adj belanglos

insincere [ɪnsɪnˈsɪəʳ] adj unaufrichtig, falsch

insincerity [ɪnsɪnˈsɛrɪtɪ] n Unaufrichtigkeit f,

Falschheit f

insinuate [ɪnˈsɪnjʊeɪt] vt anspielen auf +acc

insinuation [ɪnsɪnjuˈeɪʃən] n Anspielung f

insipid [ɪnˈsɪpɪd] adj fad(e); (person) geistlos; (colour) langweilig

insist [ɪnˈsɪst] vi bestehen; **to ~ on** bestehen auf +dat; **to ~ that** darauf bestehen, dass; (claim) behaupten, dass

insistence [ɪnˈsɪstəns] n (determination) Bestehen nt

insistent [ɪnˈsɪstənt] adj (determined) hartnäckig; (continual) andauernd, penetrant (pej)

in so far as adv insofern als

insole [ˈɪnsəʊl] n Einlegesohle f

insolence [ˈɪnsələns] n Frechheit f, Unverschämtheit f

insolent [ˈɪnsələnt] adj frech, unverschämt

insoluble [ɪnˈsɔljubl] adj unlösbar

insolvency [ɪnˈsɔlvənsɪ] n Zahlungsunfähigkeit f

insolvent [ɪnˈsɔlvənt] adj zahlungsunfähig

insomnia [ɪnˈsɔmnɪə] n Schlaflosigkeit f

insomniac [ɪnˈsɔmnɪæk] n: **to be an ~** an Schlaflosigkeit leiden

inspect [ɪnˈspɛkt] vt kontrollieren; (examine) prüfen; (troops) inspizieren

inspection [ɪnˈspɛkʃən] n (see vb) Kontrolle f; Prüfung f; Inspektion f

inspector [ɪnˈspɛktəʳ] n Inspektor(in) m(f); (Brit: on buses, trains) Kontrolleur(in) m(f); (: Police) Kommissar(in) m(f)

inspiration [ɪnspəˈreɪʃən] n Inspiration f; (idea) Eingebung f

inspire [ɪnˈspaɪəʳ] vt inspirieren; (confidence, hope etc) (er)wecken

inspired [ɪnˈspaɪəd] adj genial; **in an ~ moment** in einem Augenblick der Inspiration

inspiring [ɪnˈspaɪərɪŋ] adj inspirierend

inst. (Brit) abbr (Comm: = instant): **of the 16th ~** vom 16. d. M.

instability [ɪnstəˈbɪlɪtɪ] n Instabilität f; (of person) Labilität f

install [ɪnˈstɔːl] vt installieren; (telephone) anschließen; (official) einsetzen; **to ~ o.s.** sich niederlassen

installation [ɪnstəˈleɪʃən] n Installation f; (of telephone) Anschluss m; (Industry, Mil: plant) Anlage f

installment plan (US) n Ratenzahlung f

instalment, (US) **installment** [ɪnˈstɔːlmənt] n Rate f; (of story) Fortsetzung f; (of TV serial etc) (Sende)folge f; **in ~s** in Raten

instance [ˈɪnstəns] n Beispiel nt; **for ~** zum Beispiel; **in that ~** in diesem Fall; **in many ~s** in vielen Fällen; **in the first ~** zuerst or zunächst (einmal)

instant [ˈɪnstənt] n Augenblick m ▷ adj (reaction) unmittelbar; (success) sofortig; **~ food** Schnellgerichte pl; **~ coffee** Instantkaffee m; **the 10th ~** (Comm, Admin) der 10. dieses Monats

instantaneous [ɪnstənˈteɪnɪəs] adj

unmittelbar

instantly ['ɪnstəntlɪ] *adv* sofort

instant messaging [-'mɛsɪdʒɪŋ] *n* Instant Messaging *nt*

instant replay *n* (TV) Wiederholung *f*

instead [ɪn'stɛd] *adv* stattdessen; **~ of** statt +*gen*; **~ of sb** an jds Stelle *dat*; **~ of doing sth** anstatt *or* anstelle etw zu tun

instep ['ɪnstɛp] *n* Spann *m*; (*of shoe*) Blatt *nt*

instigate ['ɪnstɪgeɪt] *vt* anstiften, anzetteln; (*talks etc*) initiieren

instigation [ɪnstɪ'geɪʃən] *n* (*see vb*) Anstiftung *f*, Anzettelung *f*; Initiierung *f*; **at sb's ~** auf jds Betreiben *acc*

instil [ɪn'stɪl] *vt*: **to ~ sth into sb** (*confidence, fear etc*) jdm etw einflößen

instinct ['ɪnstɪŋkt] *n* Instinkt *m*; (*reaction, inclination*) instinktive Reaktion *f*

instinctive [ɪn'stɪŋktɪv] *adj* instinktiv

institute ['ɪnstɪtjuːt] *n* Institut *nt*; (*for teaching*) Hochschule *f*; (*professional body*) Bund *m*, Verband *m* ▷ *vt* einführen; (*inquiry, course of action*) einleiten; (*proceedings*) anstrengen

institution [ɪnstɪ'tjuːʃən] *n* Einführung *f*; (*organization*) Institution *f*, Einrichtung *f*; (*hospital, mental home*) Anstalt *f*, Heim *nt*

institutional [ɪnstɪ'tjuːʃənl] *adj* (*education*) institutionell; (*value, quality etc*) institutionalisiert; **~ care** Unterbringung *f* in einem Heim *or* einer Anstalt; **to be in ~ care** in einem Heim *or* einer Anstalt sein

instruct [ɪn'strʌkt] *vt*: **to ~ sb in sth** jdn in etw *dat* unterrichten; **to ~ sb to do sth** jdn anweisen, etw zu tun

instruction [ɪn'strʌkʃən] *n* Unterricht *m*; **instructions** *npl* (*orders*) Anweisungen *pl*; **~s (for use)** Gebrauchsanweisung *f*, Gebrauchsanleitung *f*; **~ book/manual/ leaflet** *etc* Bedienungsanleitung *f*

instructive [ɪn'strʌktɪv] *adj* lehrreich; (*response*) aufschlussreich

instructor [ɪn'strʌktər] *n* Lehrer(in) *m(f)*

instrument ['ɪnstrumənt] *n* Instrument *nt*; (*Mus*) (Musik)instrument *nt*

instrumental [ɪnstru'mɛntl] *adj* (*Mus: music, accompaniment*) Instrumental-; **to be ~ in** eine bedeutende Rolle spielen bei

instrumentalist [ɪnstru'mɛntəlɪst] *n* Instrumentalist(in) *m(f)*

instrument panel *n* Armaturenbrett *nt*

insubordination [ɪnsəbɔːdɪ'neɪʃən] *n* Gehorsamsverweigerung *f*

insufferable [ɪn'sʌfrəbl] *adj* unerträglich

insufficient [ɪnsə'fɪʃənt] *adj* unzureichend

insufficiently [ɪnsə'fɪʃəntlɪ] *adv* unzureichend

insular ['ɪnsjulər] *adj* engstirnig

insulate ['ɪnsjuleɪt] *vt* isolieren; (*person, group*) abschirmen

insulating tape ['ɪnsjuleɪtɪŋ-] *n* Isolierband *nt*

insulation [ɪnsju'leɪʃən] *n* (*see vb*) Isolierung *f*; Abschirmung *f*

insulator ['ɪnsjuleɪtər] *n* Isolierstoff *m*

insulin ['ɪnsjulɪn] *n* Insulin *nt*

insult [*n* 'ɪnsʌlt, *vt* ɪn'sʌlt] *n* Beleidigung *f* ▷ *vt* beleidigen

insulting [ɪn'sʌltɪŋ] *adj* beleidigend

insuperable [ɪn'sjuːprəbl] *adj* unüberwindlich

insurance [ɪn'ʃuərəns] *n* Versicherung *f*; **fire/life ~** Brand-/Lebensversicherung *f*; **to take out ~ (against)** eine Versicherung abschließen (gegen)

insurance agent *n* Versicherungsvertreter(in) *m(f)*

insurance broker *n* Versicherungsmakler(in) *m(f)*

insurance policy *n* Versicherungspolice *f*

insurance premium *n* Versicherungsprämie *f*

insure [ɪn'ʃuər] *vt* versichern; **to ~ o.s./ sth against sth** sich/etw gegen etw versichern; **to ~ o.s.** *or* **one's life** eine Lebensversicherung abschließen; **to ~ (o.s.) against sth** (*fig*) sich gegen etw absichern; **to be ~d for £5,000** für £5000 versichert sein

insured [ɪn'ʃuəd] *n*: **the ~** der/die Versicherte

insurer [ɪn'ʃuərər] *n* Versicherer *m*

insurgent [ɪn'sɜːdʒənt] *adj* aufständisch ▷ *n* Aufständische(r) *f(m)*

insurmountable [ɪnsə'mauntəbl] *adj* unüberwindlich

insurrection [ɪnsə'rɛkʃən] *n* Aufstand *m*

intact [ɪn'tækt] *adj* intakt; (*whole*) ganz; (*unharmed*) unversehrt

intake ['ɪnteɪk] *n* (*of food*) Aufnahme *f*; (*of air*) Zufuhr *f*; (*Brit: Scol*): **an ~ of 200 a year** 200 neue Schüler pro Jahr

intangible [ɪn'tændʒɪbl] *adj* unbestimmbar; (*idea*) vage; (*benefit*) immateriell

integer ['ɪntɪdʒər] *n* (*Math*) ganze Zahl *f*

integral ['ɪntɪgrəl] *adj* wesentlich

integrate ['ɪntɪgreɪt] *vt* integrieren ▷ *vi* sich integrieren

integrated circuit ['ɪntɪgreɪtɪd-] *n* (*Comput*) integrierter Schaltkreis *m*

integration [ɪntɪ'greɪʃən] *n* Integration *f*; **racial ~** Rassenintegration *f*

integrity [ɪn'tɛgrɪtɪ] *n* Integrität *f*; (*of group*) Einheit *f*; (*of culture, text*) Unversehrtheit *f*

intellect ['ɪntəlɛkt] *n* Intellekt *m*

intellectual [ɪntə'lɛktjuəl] *adj* intellektuell, geistig ▷ *n* Intellektuelle(r) *f(m)*

intelligence [ɪn'tɛlɪdʒəns] *n* Intelligenz *f*; (*information*) Informationen *pl*

intelligence quotient *n* Intelligenzquotient *m*

intelligence service *n* Nachrichtendienst *m*, Geheimdienst *m*

intelligence test *n* Intelligenztest *m*

intelligent [ɪn'tɛlɪdʒənt] *adj* intelligent; (*decision*) klug

intelligently [ɪn'tɛlɪdʒəntlɪ] *adv* intelligent

intelligentsia [ɪntɛlɪ'dʒɛntsɪə] *n*: **the ~** die Intelligenz

intelligible [ɪn'tɛlɪdʒɪbl] *adj* verständlich

intemperate [ɪn'tɛmpərət] *adj* unmäßig; (*remark*) überzogen

intend [ɪn'tɛnd] *vt*: **to be ~ed for sb** für jdn gedacht sein; **to ~ to do sth** beabsichtigen, etw zu tun

intended [ɪn'tɛndɪd] *adj (effect, victim)* beabsichtigt; *(journey)* geplant; *(insult)* absichtlich

intense [ɪn'tɛns] *adj* intensiv; *(anger, joy)* äußerst groß; *(person)* ernsthaft

intensely [ɪn'tɛnslɪ] *adv* äußerst; **I dislike him ~** ich verabscheue ihn

intensify [ɪn'tɛnsɪfaɪ] *vt* intensivieren, verstärken

intensity [ɪn'tɛnsɪtɪ] *n* Intensität *f*; *(of anger)* Heftigkeit *f*

intensive [ɪn'tɛnsɪv] *adj* intensiv

intensive care *n*: **to be in ~** auf der Intensivstation sein

intensive care unit *n* Intensivstation *f*

intent [ɪn'tɛnt] *n* Absicht *f* ▷ *adj (attentive)* aufmerksam; *(absorbed)*: **~ (on)** versunken (in +*acc*); **to all ~s and purposes** im Grunde; **to be ~ on doing sth** entschlossen sein, etw zu tun

intention [ɪn'tɛnʃən] *n* Absicht *f*

intentional [ɪn'tɛnʃənl] *adj* absichtlich

intentionally [ɪn'tɛnʃnəlɪ] *adv* absichtlich

intently [ɪn'tɛntlɪ] *adv* konzentriert

inter [ɪn'tə:ʳ] *vt* bestatten

interact [ɪntər'ækt] *vi (people)* interagieren; *(things)* aufeinander einwirken; *(ideas)* sich gegenseitig beeinflussen; **to ~ with** interagieren mit; einwirken auf +*acc*; beeinflussen

interaction [ɪntər'ækʃən] *n (see vb)* Interaktion *f*; gegenseitige Einwirkung *f*; gegenseitige Beeinflussung *f*

interactive [ɪntər'æktɪv] *adj (also Comput)* interaktiv

intercede [ɪntə'si:d] *vi*: **to ~ (with sb/on behalf of sb)** sich (bei jdm/für jdn) einsetzen

intercept [ɪntə'sɛpt] *vt* abfangen

interception [ɪntə'sɛpʃən] *n* Abfangen *nt*

interchange ['ɪntətʃeɪndʒ] *n* Austausch *m*; *(on motorway)* (Autobahn)kreuz *nt*

interchangeable [ɪntə'tʃeɪndʒəbl] *adj* austauschbar

intercity [ɪntə'sɪtɪ] *adj*: **~ train** Intercityzug *m*

intercom ['ɪntəkɔm] *n* (Gegen)sprechanlage *f*

interconnect [ɪntəkə'nɛkt] *vi (rooms)* miteinander verbunden sein

intercontinental ['ɪntəkɔntɪ'nɛntl] *adj (flight, missile)* Interkontinental-

intercourse ['ɪntəkɔ:s] *n (sexual)* (Geschlechts)verkehr *m*; *(social, verbal)* Verkehr *m*

intercultural [ɪntə'kʌltʃərəl] *adj* interkulturell

interdependence [ɪntədɪ'pɛndəns] *n* gegenseitige Abhängigkeit *f*

interdependent [ɪntədɪ'pɛndənt] *adj* voneinander abhängig

interest ['ɪntrɪst] *n* Interesse *nt*; *(Comm: in company)* Anteil *m*; (: *sum of money)* Zinsen *pl* ▷ *vt* interessieren; **compound ~** Zinseszins *m*; **simple ~** einfache Zinsen; **British ~s in the Middle East** britische Interessen im Nahen Osten; **his main ~ is ...** er interessiert sich

hauptsächlich für ...

interested ['ɪntrɪstɪd] *adj* interessiert; *(party, body etc)* beteiligt; **to be ~ in sth** sich für etw interessieren; **to be ~ in doing sth** daran interessiert sein, etw zu tun

interest-free ['ɪntrɪst'fri:] *adj, adv* zinslos

interesting ['ɪntrɪstɪŋ] *adj* interessant

interest rate *n* Zinssatz *m*

interface ['ɪntəfeɪs] *n* Verbindung *f*; *(Comput)* Schnittstelle *f*

interfere [ɪntə'fɪəʳ] *vi*: **to ~ in** sich einmischen in +*acc*; **to ~ with** *(object)* sich zu schaffen machen an +*dat*; *(plans)* durchkreuzen; *(career, duty, decision)* beeinträchtigen; **don't ~** misch dich nicht ein

interference [ɪntə'fɪərəns] *n* Einmischung *f*; *(Radio, TV)* Störung *f*

interfering [ɪntə'fɪərɪŋ] *adj (person)* sich ständig einmischend

interim ['ɪntərɪm] *adj (agreement, government etc)* Übergangs- ▷ *n*: **in the ~** in der Zwischenzeit

interim dividend *n (Comm)* Abschlagsdividende *f*

interior [ɪn'tɪərɪəʳ] *n* Innere(s) *nt*; *(decor etc)* Innenausstattung *f* ▷ *adj* Innen-

interior decorator *n* Innenausstatter(in) *m(f)*

interior designer *n* Innenarchitekt(in) *m(f)*

interjection [ɪntə'dʒɛkʃən] *n* Einwurf *m*; *(Ling)* Interjektion *f*

interlock [ɪntə'lɔk] *vi* ineinandergreifen

interloper ['ɪntələupəʳ] *n* Eindringling *m*

interlude ['ɪntəlu:d] *n* Unterbrechung *f*, Pause *f*; *(Theat)* Zwischenspiel *nt*

intermarry [ɪntə'mærɪ] *vi* untereinander heiraten

intermediary [ɪntə'mi:dɪərɪ] *n* Vermittler(in) *m(f)*

intermediate [ɪntə'mi:dɪət] *adj (stage)* Zwischen-; **an ~ student** ein fortgeschrittener Anfänger

interment [ɪn'tə:mənt] *n* Bestattung *f*

interminable [ɪn'tə:mɪnəbl] *adj* endlos

intermission [ɪntə'mɪʃən] *n* Pause *f*

intermittent [ɪntə'mɪtnt] *adj (noise)* periodisch auftretend; *(publication)* in unregelmäßigen Abständen veröffentlicht

intermittently [ɪntə'mɪtntlɪ] *adv (see adj)* periodisch; in unregelmäßigen Abständen

intern [*vt* ɪn'tə:n, *n* 'ɪntə:n] *vt* internieren ▷ *n* *(US)* Assistenzarzt *m*, Assistenzärztin *f*

internal [ɪn'tə:nl] *adj* innere(r, s); *(pipes)* im Haus; *(politics)* Innen-; *(dispute, reform, memo, structure etc)* intern

internally [ɪn'tə:nəlɪ] *adv*: **"not to be taken ~"** „nicht zum Einnehmen"

Internal Revenue Service *(US) n* ≈ Finanzamt *nt*

international [ɪntə'næʃənl] *adj* international ▷ *n (Brit: Sport)* Länderspiel *nt*

International Atomic Energy Agency *n* Internationale Atomenergiebehörde

International Chamber of Commerce *n* Internationale Handelskammer *f*

International Court of Justice n
Internationaler Gerichtshof m
international date line n Datumsgrenze f
International Labour Organization n
Internationale Arbeitsorganisation f
internationally [ɪntəˈnæʃnəlɪ] adv
international
International Monetary Fund n
Internationaler Währungsfonds m
international relations npl
zwischenstaatliche Beziehungen pl
internecine [ɪntəˈniːsaɪn] adj mörderisch;
(war) Vernichtungs-
internee [ɪntəːˈniː] n Internierte(r) f(m)
Internet [ˈɪntənɛt] n Internet nt
Internet café n Internetcafé nt
internment [ɪnˈtəːnmənt] n Internierung f
interplay [ˈɪntəpleɪ] n: ~ **(of** or **between)**
Zusammenspiel nt (von)
Interpol [ˈɪntəpɔl] n Interpol f
interpret [ɪnˈtəːprɪt] vt auslegen,
interpretieren; (translate) dolmetschen ▷ vi
dolmetschen
interpretation [ɪntəːprɪˈteɪʃən] n (see vb)
Auslegung f, Interpretation f; Dolmetschen nt
interpreter [ɪnˈtəːprɪtər] n Dolmetscher(in)
m(f)
interpreting [ɪnˈtəːprɪtɪŋ] n Dolmetschen nt
interrelated [ɪntərɪˈleɪtɪd] adj
zusammenhängend
interrogate [ɪnˈtɛrəʊgeɪt] vt verhören;
(witness) vernehmen
interrogation [ɪntɛrəʊˈgeɪʃən] n (see vb) Verhör
nt; Vernehmung f
interrogative [ɪntəˈrɔgətɪv] adj (Ling: pronoun)
Interrogativ-, Frage-
interrogator [ɪnˈtɛrəgeɪtər] n (Police)
Vernehmungsbeamte(r) m; **the hostage's ~**
derjenige, der die Geisel verhörte
interrupt [ɪntəˈrʌpt] vt, vi unterbrechen
interruption [ɪntəˈrʌpʃən] n Unterbrechung
f
intersect [ɪntəˈsɛkt] vi sich kreuzen ▷ vt
durchziehen; (Math) schneiden
intersection [ɪntəˈsɛkʃən] n Kreuzung f; (Math)
Schnittpunkt m
intersperse [ɪntəˈspəːs] vt: **to be ~d with**
durchsetzt sein mit; **he ~d his lecture
with ...** er spickte seine Rede mit ...
intertwine [ɪntəˈtwaɪn] vi sich ineinander
verschlingen
interval [ˈɪntəvl] n Pause f; (Mus) Intervall nt;
bright ~s (in weather) Aufheiterungen pl; **at ~s**
in Abständen
intervene [ɪntəˈviːn] vi eingreifen; (event)
dazwischenkommen; (time) dazwischenliegen
intervening [ɪntəˈviːnɪŋ] adj (period, years)
dazwischenliegend
intervention [ɪntəˈvɛnʃən] n Eingreifen nt
interview [ˈɪntəvjuː] n (for job)
Vorstellungsgespräch nt; (for place at college etc)
Auswahlgespräch nt; (Radio, TV etc) Interview
nt ▷ vt (see n) ein Vorstellungsgespräch/

Auswahlgespräch führen mit; interviewen
interviewee [ɪntəvjuˈiː] n (for job)
Stellenbewerber(in) m(f); (TV etc)
Interviewgast m
interviewer [ˈɪntəvjuər] n Leiter(in) m(f) des
Vorstellungsgesprächs/Auswahlgesprächs;
(Radio, TV etc) Interviewer(in) m(f)
intestate [ɪnˈtɛsteɪt] adv: **to die ~** ohne
Testament sterben
intestinal [ɪnˈtɛstɪnl] adj (infection etc) Darm-
intestine [ɪnˈtɛstɪn] n Darm m
intimacy [ˈɪntɪməsɪ] n Vertrautheit f
intimate [adj ˈɪntɪmət, vt ˈɪntɪmeɪt] adj eng;
(sexual, also restaurant, dinner, atmosphere)
intim; (conversation, matter, detail) vertraulich;
(knowledge) gründlich ▷ vt andeuten; (make
known) zu verstehen geben
intimately [ˈɪntɪmətlɪ] adv (see adj) eng; intim;
vertraulich; gründlich
intimation [ɪntɪˈmeɪʃən] n Andeutung f
intimidate [ɪnˈtɪmɪdeɪt] vt einschüchtern
intimidation [ɪntɪmɪˈdeɪʃən] n
Einschüchterung f

○ KEYWORD

into [ˈɪntu] prep **1** (indicating motion or direction) in
+acc; **to go into town** in die Stadt gehen; **he
worked late into the night** er arbeitete bis
spät in die Nacht; **the car bumped into the
wall** der Wagen fuhr gegen die Mauer
2 (indicating change of condition, result): **it broke
into pieces** es zerbrach in Stücke; **she
translated into English** sie übersetzte ins
Englische; **to change pounds into dollars**
Pfund in Dollar wechseln; **5 into 25** 25 durch 5

intolerable [ɪnˈtɔlərəbl] adj unerträglich
intolerance [ɪnˈtɔlərns] n Intoleranz f
intolerant [ɪnˈtɔlərnt] adj: ~ **(of)** intolerant
(gegenüber)
intonation [ɪntəʊˈneɪʃən] n Intonation f
intoxicated [ɪnˈtɔksɪkeɪtɪd] adj betrunken;
(fig) berauscht
intoxication [ɪntɔksɪˈkeɪʃən] n (Be)
trunkenheit f; (fig) Rausch m
intractable [ɪnˈtræktəbl] adj hartnäckig; (child)
widerspenstig; (temper) unbeugsam
intranet [ˈɪntrənɛt] n (Comput) Intranet nt
intransigence [ɪnˈtrænsɪdʒəns] n
Unnachgiebigkeit f
intransigent [ɪnˈtrænsɪdʒənt] adj
unnachgiebig
intransitive [ɪnˈtrænsɪtɪv] adj (Ling) intransitiv
intrauterine device [ˈɪntrəˈjuːtəraɪn-] n (Med)
Intrauterinpessar nt, Spirale f (inf)
intravenous [ɪntrəˈviːnəs] adj intravenös
in-tray [ˈɪntreɪ] n Ablage f für Eingänge
intrepid [ɪnˈtrɛpɪd] adj unerschrocken
intricacy [ˈɪntrɪkəsɪ] n Kompliziertheit
f
intricate [ˈɪntrɪkət] adj kompliziert
intrigue [ɪnˈtriːg] n Intrigen pl ▷ vt faszinieren

intriguing [ɪn'triːgɪŋ] *adj* faszinierend

intrinsic [ɪn'trɪnsɪk] *adj* wesentlich

introduce [ɪntrə'djuːs] *vt* (*sth new*) einführen; (*speaker, TV show etc*) ankündigen; **to ~ sb (to sb)** jdn (jdm) vorstellen; **to ~ sb to** (*pastime, technique*) jdn einführen in +*acc*; **may I ~ ...?** darf ich ... vorstellen?

introduction [ɪntrə'dʌkʃən] *n* Einführung *f*; (*of person*) Vorstellung *f*; (*to book*) Einleitung *f*; **a letter of ~** ein Einführungsschreiben *nt*

introductory [ɪntrə'dʌktəri] *adj* Einführungs-; **~ remarks** einführende Bemerkungen *pl*; **~ offer** Einführungsangebot *nt*

introspection [ɪntrəu'spekʃən] *n* Selbstbeobachtung *f*, Introspektion *f*

introspective [ɪntrəu'spektɪv] *adj* in sich gekehrt

introvert ['ɪntrəuvəːt] *n* Introvertierte(r) *f(m)* ▷ *adj* (*also:* **introverted**) introvertiert

intrude [ɪn'truːd] *vi* eindringen; **to ~ on** stören; (*conversation*) sich einmischen in +*acc*; **am I intruding?** störe ich?

intruder [ɪn'truːdəʳ] *n* Eindringling *m*

intrusion [ɪn'truːʒən] *n* Eindringen *nt*

intrusive [ɪn'truːsɪv] *adj* aufdringlich

intuition [ɪntjuː'ɪʃən] *n* Intuition *f*

intuitive [ɪn'tjuːɪtɪv] *adj* intuitiv; (*feeling*) instinktiv

inundate ['ɪnʌndeɪt] *vt*: **to ~ with** überschwemmen mit

inure [ɪn'juəʳ] *vt*: **to ~ o.s. to** sich gewöhnen an +*acc*

invade [ɪn'veɪd] *vt* einfallen in +*acc*; (*fig*) heimsuchen

invader [ɪn'veɪdəʳ] *n* Invasor *m*

invalid [*n* 'ɪnvəlɪd, *adj* ɪn'vælɪd] *n* Kranke(r) *f(m)*; (*disabled*) Invalide *m* ▷ *adj* ungültig

invalidate [ɪn'vælɪdeɪt] *vt* entkräften; (*law, marriage, election*) ungültig machen

invaluable [ɪn'væljuəbl] *adj* unschätzbar

invariable [ɪn'vɛərɪəbl] *adj* unveränderlich

invariably [ɪn'vɛərɪəbli] *adv* ständig, unweigerlich; **she is ~ late** sie kommt immer zu spät

invasion [ɪn'veɪʒən] *n* Invasion *f*; **an ~ of privacy** ein Eingriff *m* in die Privatsphäre

invective [ɪn'vɛktɪv] *n* Beschimpfungen *pl*

inveigle [ɪn'viːgl] *vt*: **to ~ sb into sth/doing sth** jdn zu etw verleiten/dazu verleiten, etw zu tun

invent [ɪn'vɛnt] *vt* erfinden

invention [ɪn'vɛnʃən] *n* Erfindung *f*

inventive [ɪn'vɛntɪv] *adj* erfinderisch

inventiveness [ɪn'vɛntɪvnɪs] *n* Einfallsreichtum *m*

inventor [ɪn'vɛntəʳ] *n* Erfinder(in) *m(f)*

inventory ['ɪnvəntri] *n* Inventar *nt*

inventory control *n* (*Comm*) Bestandskontrolle *f*

inverse [ɪn'vəːs] *adj* umgekehrt; **in ~ proportion (to)** im umgekehrten Verhältnis (zu)

invert [ɪn'vəːt] *vt* umdrehen

invertebrate [ɪn'vəːtɪbrət] *n* wirbelloses Tier *nt*

inverted commas [ɪn'vəːtɪd-] (*Brit*) *npl* Anführungszeichen *pl*

invest [ɪn'vɛst] *vt* investieren ▷ *vi*: **~ in** investieren in +*acc*; (*fig*) sich *dat* anschaffen; **to ~ sb with sth** jdm etw verleihen

investigate [ɪn'vɛstɪgeɪt] *vt* untersuchen

investigation [ɪnvɛstɪ'geɪʃən] *n* Untersuchung *f*

investigative [ɪn'vɛstɪgeɪtɪv] *adj*: **~ journalism** Enthüllungsjournalismus *m*

investigator [ɪn'vɛstɪgeɪtəʳ] *n* Ermittler(in) *m(f)*; **private ~** Privatdetektiv(in) *m(f)*

investiture [ɪn'vɛstɪtʃəʳ] *n* (*of chancellor*) Amtseinführung *f*; (*of prince*) Investitur *f*

investment [ɪn'vɛstmənt] *n* Investition *f*

investment income *n* Kapitalerträge *pl*

investment trust *n* Investmenttrust *m*

investor [ɪn'vɛstəʳ] *n* (Kapital)anleger(in) *m(f)*

inveterate [ɪn'vɛtərət] *adj* unverbesserlich

invidious [ɪn'vɪdɪəs] *adj* (*task, job*) unangenehm; (*comparison, decision*) ungerecht

invigilator [ɪn'vɪdʒɪleɪtəʳ] *n* Aufsicht *f*

invigorating [ɪn'vɪgəreɪtɪŋ] *adj* belebend; (*experience etc*) anregend

invincible [ɪn'vɪnsɪbl] *adj* unbesiegbar; (*belief, conviction*) unerschütterlich

inviolate [ɪn'vaɪələt] *adj* sicher; (*truth*) unantastbar

invisible [ɪn'vɪzɪbl] *adj* unsichtbar

invisible mending *n* Kunststopfen *nt*

invitation [ɪnvɪ'teɪʃən] *n* Einladung *f*; **by ~ only** nur auf Einladung; **at sb's ~** auf jds Aufforderung *acc* (hin)

invite [ɪn'vaɪt] *vt* einladen; (*discussion*) auffordern zu; (*criticism*) herausfordern; **to ~ sb to do sth** jdn auffordern, etw zu tun; **to ~ sb to dinner** jdn zum Abendessen einladen ▷ **invite out** *vt* einladen

inviting [ɪn'vaɪtɪŋ] *adj* einladend; (*desirable*) verlockend

invoice ['ɪnvɔɪs] *n* Rechnung *f* ▷ *vt* in Rechnung stellen; **to ~ sb for goods** jdm für Waren eine Rechnung ausstellen

invoke [ɪn'vəuk] *vt* anrufen; (*feelings, memories etc*) heraufbeschwören

involuntary [ɪn'vɔləntri] *adj* unbeabsichtigt; (*reflex*) unwillkürlich

involve [ɪn'vɔlv] *vt* (*person*) beteiligen; (*thing*) verbunden sein mit; (*concern, affect*) betreffen; **to ~ sb in sth** jdn in etw *acc* verwickeln

involved [ɪn'vɔlvd] *adj* kompliziert; **the work/problems ~** die damit verbundene Arbeit/verbundenen Schwierigkeiten; **to be ~ in** beteiligt sein an +*dat*; (*be engrossed*) engagiert sein in +*dat*; **to become ~ with sb** Umgang mit jdm haben; (*emotionally*) mit jdm eine Beziehung anfangen

involvement [ɪn'vɔlvmənt] *n* Engagement *nt*; (*participation*) Beteiligung *f*

invulnerable [ɪn'vʌlnərəbl] *adj* unverwundbar; (*ship, building etc*) uneinnehmbar

inward ['ɪnwəd] *adj* innerste(r, s); (*movement*)

nach innen ▷ *adv* nach innen
inwardly ['ɪnwədlɪ] *adv* innerlich
inwards ['ɪnwədz] *adv* nach innen
I/O *abbr* (Comput: = *input/output*) E/A
IOC *n abbr* (= *International Olympic Committee*) IOC *nt*, IOK *nt*
iodine ['aɪəudiːn] *n* Jod *nt*
IOM (*Brit*) *abbr* (Post) = *Isle of Man*
ion ['aɪən] *n* Ion *nt*
Ionian Sea [aɪ'əunɪən-] *n*: **the ~** das Ionische Meer
ionizer ['aɪənaɪzər] *n* Ionisator *m*
iota [aɪ'əutə] *n* Jota *nt*
IOU *n abbr* (= *I owe you*) Schuldschein *m*
IOW (*Brit*) *abbr* (Post) = *Isle of Wight*
IP *abbr* (Comput: = *Internet Protocol*) IP
IPA *n abbr* (= *International Phonetic Alphabet*) internationale Lautschrift *f*
iPod® ['aɪpɔd] *n* iPod® *m*
IQ *n abbr* (= *intelligence quotient*) IQ *m*
IRA *n abbr* (= *Irish Republican Army*) IRA *f*; (*US*: = *individual retirement account*) *privates Rentensparkonto*
Iran [ɪ'rɑːn] *n* (der) Iran
Iranian [ɪ'reɪnɪən] *adj* iranisch ▷ *n* Iraner(in) *m(f)*; (*Ling*) Iranisch *nt*
Iraq [ɪ'rɑːk] *n* (der) Irak
Iraqi [ɪ'rɑːkɪ] *adj* irakisch ▷ *n* Iraker(in) *m(f)*
irascible [ɪ'ræsɪbl] *adj* jähzornig
irate [aɪ'reɪt] *adj* zornig
Ireland ['aɪələnd] *n* Irland *nt*; **the Republic of ~** die Republik Irland
iris ['aɪrɪs] (*pl* **-es**) *n* (*Anat*) Iris *f*, Regenbogenhaut *f*; (*Bot*) Iris, Schwertlilie *f*
Irish ['aɪrɪʃ] *adj* irisch ▷ *npl*: **the ~** die Iren *pl*, die Irländer *pl*
Irishman ['aɪrɪʃmən] (*irreg: like* **man**) *n* Ire *m*, Irländer *m*
Irish Sea *n*: **the ~** die Irische See
Irishwoman ['aɪrɪʃwumən] (*irreg: like* **woman**) *n* Irin *f*, Irländerin *f*
irk [əːk] *vt* ärgern
irksome ['əːksəm] *adj* lästig
IRN *n abbr* (= *Independent Radio News*) *Nachrichtendienst des kommerziellen Rundfunks*
iron ['aɪən] *n* Eisen *nt*; (*for clothes*) Bügeleisen *nt* ▷ *cpd* Eisen-; (*will, discipline etc*) eisern ▷ *vt* bügeln
▶ **iron out** *vt* (*fig*) aus dem Weg räumen
Iron Curtain *n*: **the ~** der Eiserne Vorhang
ironic [aɪ'rɔnɪk], **ironical** [aɪ'rɔnɪkl] *adj* ironisch; (*situation*) paradox, witzig
ironically [aɪ'rɔnɪklɪ] *adv* ironisch; **~, the intelligence chief was the last to find out** witzigerweise war der Geheimdienstchef der Letzte, der es erfuhr
ironing ['aɪənɪŋ] *n* Bügeln *nt*; (*clothes*) Bügelwäsche *f*
ironing board *n* Bügelbrett *nt*
iron lung *n* (*Med*) eiserne Lunge *f*
ironmonger ['aɪənmʌŋgər] (*Brit*) *n* Eisen- und Haushaltswarenhändler(in) *m(f)*;
ironmonger's (shop) (*Brit*) Eisen- und

Haushaltswarenhandlung *f*
iron ore *n* Eisenerz *nt*
irons ['aɪəns] *npl* Hand- und Fußschellen *pl*; **to clap sb in ~** jdn in Eisen legen
irony ['aɪrənɪ] *n* Ironie *f*; **the ~ of it is that …** das Ironische daran ist, dass …
irrational [ɪ'ræʃənl] *adj* irrational
irreconcilable [ɪrekən'saɪləbl] *adj* unvereinbar
irredeemable [ɪrɪ'diːməbl] *adj* (*Comm*) nicht einlösbar; (*loan*) unkündbar; (*fault, character*) unverbesserlich
irrefutable [ɪrɪ'fjuːtəbl] *adj* unwiderlegbar
irregular [ɪ'regjulər] *adj* unregelmäßig; (*surface*) uneben; (*behaviour*) ungehörig
irregularity [ɪregju'lærɪtɪ] *n* (*see adj*) Unregelmäßigkeit *f*; Unebenheit *f*; Ungehörigkeit *f*
irrelevance [ɪ'reləvəns] *n* Irrelevanz *f*
irrelevant [ɪ'reləvənt] *adj* unwesentlich, irrelevant
irreligious [ɪrɪ'lɪdʒəs] *adj* unreligiös
irreparable [ɪ'reprəbl] *adj* nicht wiedergutzumachen
irreplaceable [ɪrɪ'pleɪsəbl] *adj* unersetzlich
irrepressible [ɪrɪ'presəbl] *adj* (*good humour*) unerschütterlich; (*enthusiasm etc*) unbändig; (*person*) nicht unterzukriegen
irreproachable [ɪrɪ'prəutʃəbl] *adj* untadelig
irresistible [ɪrɪ'zɪstɪbl] *adj* unwiderstehlich
irresolute [ɪ'rezəluːt] *adj* unentschlossen
irrespective [ɪrɪ'spektɪv] *adj*: **~ of** *prep* ungeachtet +*gen*
irresponsible [ɪrɪ'spɔnsɪbl] *adj* verantwortungslos; (*action*) unverantwortlich
irretrievable [ɪrɪ'triːvəbl] *adj* (*object*) nicht mehr wiederzubekommen; (*loss*) unersetzlich; (*damage*) nicht wiedergutzumachen
irreverent [ɪ'revərnt] *adj* respektlos
irrevocable [ɪ'revəkəbl] *adj* unwiderruflich
irrigate ['ɪrɪgeɪt] *vt* bewässern
irrigation [ɪrɪ'geɪʃən] *n* Bewässerung *f*
irritable ['ɪrɪtəbl] *adj* reizbar
irritant ['ɪrɪtənt] *n* Reizerreger *m*; (*situation etc*) Ärgernis *nt*
irritate ['ɪrɪteɪt] *vt* ärgern, irritieren; (*Med*) reizen
irritating ['ɪrɪteɪtɪŋ] *adj* ärgerlich, irritierend; **he is ~** er kann einem auf die Nerven gehen
irritation [ɪrɪ'teɪʃən] *n* Ärger *m*; (*Med*) Reizung *f*; (*annoying thing*) Ärgernis *nt*
IRS (*US*) *n abbr* (= *Internal Revenue Service*) *Steuereinzugsbehörde*
is [ɪz] *vb see* **be**
ISA ['aɪsə] *n abbr* (= *individual savings account*) *steuerfreies Sparsystem mit begrenzter Einlagenhöhe*
ISBN *n abbr* (= *International Standard Book Number*) ISBN *f*
ISDN *n abbr* (= *Integrated Services Digital Network*) ISDN *nt*
Islam ['ɪzlɑːm] *n* der Islam; (*Islamic countries*) die islamischen Länder *pl*
Islamic [ɪz'læmɪk] *adj* islamisch
island ['aɪlənd] *n* Insel *f*; (*also*: **traffic island**)

Verkehrsinsel f

islander ['aɪləndəʳ] n Inselbewohner(in) m(f)

isle [aɪl] n Insel f

isn't ['ɪznt] = **is not**

isobar ['aɪsəubɑ:ʳ] n Isobare f

isolate ['aɪsəleɪt] vt isolieren

isolated ['aɪsəleɪtɪd] adj isoliert; (place) abgelegen; ~ **incident** Einzelfall m

isolation [aɪsə'leɪʃən] n Isolierung f

isolationism [aɪsə'leɪʃənɪzəm] n Isolationismus m

isotope ['aɪsəutəup] n Isotop nt

ISP (Comput) n abbr (= Internet Service Provider) Provider m

Israel ['ɪzreɪl] n Israel nt

Israeli [ɪz'reɪlɪ] adj israelisch ▷ n Israeli mf

issue ['ɪʃju:] n Frage f; (subject) Thema nt; (problem) Problem nt; (of book, stamps etc) Ausgabe f; (offspring) Nachkommenschaft f ▷ vt ausgeben; (statement) herausgeben; (documents) ausstellen ▷ vi: **to ~ (from)** dringen (aus); (liquid) austreten (aus); **the point at ~** der Punkt, um den es geht; **to avoid the ~** ausweichen; **to confuse** or **obscure the ~** es unnötig kompliziert machen; **to ~ sth to sb** or **~ sb with sth** jdm etw geben; (documents) jdm etw ausstellen; (gun etc) jdn mit etw ausstatten; **to take ~ with sb (over)** jdm widersprechen (in +dat); **to make an ~ of sth** etw aufbauschen

isthmus ['ɪsməs] n Landenge f, Isthmus m

IT n abbr = **information technology**

🅞 KEYWORD

it [ɪt] pron **1** (specific: subject) er/sie/es; (: direct object) ihn/sie/es; (: indirect object) ihm/ihr/ihm; **it's on the table** es ist auf dem Tisch; **I can't find it** ich kann es nicht finden; **give it to me** gib es mir; **about it** darüber; **from it** davon; **in it** darin; **of it** davon; **what did you learn from it?** was hast du daraus gelernt?; **I'm proud of it** ich bin stolz darauf

2 (impersonal) es; **it's raining** es regnet; **it's Friday tomorrow** morgen ist Freitag; **who is it? — it's me** wer ist da? — ich bins

---

ITA, (Brit) **i.t.a.** n abbr (= initial teaching alphabet) Alphabet zum Lesenlernen

Italian [ɪ'tæljən] adj italienisch ▷ n Italiener(in) m(f); (Ling) Italienisch nt; **the ~s** die Italiener pl

italics [ɪ'tælɪks] npl Kursivschrift f

Italy ['ɪtəlɪ] n Italien nt

ITC (Brit) n abbr (= Independent Television Commission) Fernseh-Aufsichtsgremium

itch [ɪtʃ] n Juckreiz m ▷ vi jucken; **I am ~ing all over** mich juckt es überall; **to ~ to do sth** darauf brennen, etw zu tun

itchy ['ɪtʃɪ] adj juckend; **my back is ~** mein Rücken juckt

it'd ['ɪtd] = **it would; it had**

item ['aɪtəm] n Punkt m; (of collection) Stück nt; (also: **news item**) Meldung f; (: in newspaper) Zeitungsnotiz f; **~s of clothing** Kleidungsstücke pl

itemize ['aɪtəmaɪz] vt einzeln aufführen

itemized bill ['aɪtəmaɪzd-] n Rechnung, auf der die Posten einzeln aufgeführt sind

itinerant [ɪ'tɪnərənt] adj (labourer, priest etc) Wander-; (salesman) reisend

itinerary [aɪ'tɪnərərɪ] n Reiseroute f

it'll ['ɪtl] = **it will; it shall**

ITN (Brit) n abbr (TV: = Independent Television News) Nachrichtendienst des kommerziellen Fernsehens

its [ɪts] adj sein(e), ihr(e) ▷ pron seine(r, s), ihre(r, s)

it's [ɪts] = **it is; it has**

itself [ɪt'sɛlf] pron sich; (emphatic) selbst

ITV (Brit) n abbr (TV: = Independent Television) kommerzieller Fernsehsender; siehe Info-Artikel

---

◉ ITV

◉ ITV steht für „Independent Television"
◉ und ist ein landesweiter privater
◉ Fernsehsender in Großbritannien. Unter
◉ der Oberaufsicht einer unabhängigen
◉ Rundfunkbehörde produzieren
◉ Privatfirmen die Programme für die
◉ verschiedenen Sendegebiete. ITV, das seit
◉ 1955 Programme ausstrahlt, wird ganz
◉ durch Werbung finanziert und bietet
◉ etwa ein Drittel Informationssendungen
◉ (Nachrichten, Dokumentarfilme,
◉ Aktuelles) und ansonsten Unterhaltung
◉ (Sport, Komödien, Drama, Spielshows,
◉ Filme).

IUD n abbr = **intrauterine device**

I've [aɪv] = **I have**

ivory ['aɪvərɪ] n Elfenbein nt

Ivory Coast n Elfenbeinküste f

ivory tower n (fig) Elfenbeinturm m

ivy ['aɪvɪ] n Efeu m

Ivy League (US) n Eliteuniversitäten der USA

◉ IVY LEAGUE

◉ Als Ivy League bezeichnet man die acht
◉ renommiertesten Universitäten im
◉ Nordosten der Vereinigten Staaten
◉ (Brown, Columbia, Cornell, Dartmouth
◉ College, Harvard, Princeton, University
◉ of Pennsylvania, Yale), die untereinander
◉ Sportwettkämpfe austragen. Der Name
◉ bezieht sich auf die efeubewachsenen
◉ Mauern der Universitätsgebäude.

Jj

J, j [dʒeɪ] n (letter) J nt, j nt; **J for Jack, J for Jig**
(US) = J wie Julius
JA n abbr = **judge advocate; joint account**
J/A abbr = **joint account**
jab [dʒæb] vt stoßen; (with finger, needle) stechen
▷ n (inf) Spritze f ▷ vi: **to ~ at** einstechen auf
+acc; **to ~ sth into sth** etw in etw acc stoßen/
stechen
jack [dʒæk] n (Aut) Wagenheber m; (Bowls)
Zielkugel f; (Cards) Bube m
▶ **jack in** (inf) vt aufgeben
▶ **jack up** vt (Aut) aufbocken
jackal ['dʒækl] n Schakal m
jackass ['dʒækæs] (inf) n (person) Esel m
jackdaw ['dʒækdɔ:] n Dohle f
jacket ['dʒækɪt] n Jackett nt; (of book)
Schutzumschlag m; **potatoes in their ~s, ~
potatoes** in der Schale gebackene Kartoffeln
pl
jack-in-the-box ['dʒækɪnðəbɔks] n
Schachtelteufel m, Kastenteufel m
jack-knife ['dʒæknaɪf] n Klappmesser
nt ▷ vi: **the lorry ~d** der Anhänger (des
Lastwagens) hat sich quer gestellt
jack-of-all-trades ['dʒækəv'ɔːltreɪdz] n
Alleskönner m
jack plug n Bananenstecker m
jackpot ['dʒækpɔt] n Hauptgewinn m; **to hit
the ~** (fig) das große Los ziehen
Jacuzzi® [dʒə'ku:zɪ] n Whirlpool m
jade [dʒeɪd] n Jade m or f
jaded ['dʒeɪdɪd] adj abgespannt; **to get ~** die
Nase vollhaben
JAG n abbr = **Judge Advocate General**
jagged ['dʒægɪd] adj gezackt
jaguar ['dʒægjuər] n Jaguar m
jail [dʒeɪl] n Gefängnis nt ▷ vt einsperren
jailbird ['dʒeɪlbə:d] n Knastbruder m (inf)
jailbreak ['dʒeɪlbreɪk] n (Gefängnis)ausbruch
m
jalopy [dʒə'lɔpɪ] (inf) n alte (Klapper)kiste f or
Mühle f
jam [dʒæm] n Marmelade f, Konfitüre f;
(also: **traffic jam**) Stau m; (inf: difficulty) Klemme
f ▷ vt blockieren; (mechanism, drawer etc)
verklemmen; (Radio) stören ▷ vi klemmen;
(gun) Ladehemmung haben; **I'm in a real ~**
(inf) ich stecke wirklich in der Klemme; **to get**

sb out of a ~ (inf) jdm aus der Klemme helfen;
to ~ sth into sth etw in etw acc stopfen; **the
telephone lines are ~med** die Leitungen
sind belegt
Jamaica [dʒə'meɪkə] n Jamaika nt
Jamaican [dʒə'meɪkən] adj jamaikanisch ▷ n
Jamaikaner(in) m(f)
jamb [dʒæm] n (of door) (Tür)pfosten m; (of
window) (Fenster)pfosten m
jamboree [dʒæmbə'ri:] n Fest nt
jam-packed [dʒæm'pækt] adj: **~ (with)**
vollgestopft (mit)
jam session n (Mus) Jamsession f
Jan. abbr (= January) Jan.
jangle ['dʒæŋgl] vi klimpern
janitor ['dʒænɪtər] n Hausmeister(in) m(f)
January ['dʒænjuərɪ] n Januar m; see also **July**
Japan [dʒə'pæn] n Japan nt
Japanese [dʒæpə'ni:z] adj japanisch ▷ n inv
Japaner(in) m(f); (Ling) Japanisch nt
jar [dʒɑ:r] n Topf m, Gefäß nt; (glass) Glas nt ▷ vi
(sound) gellen; (colours) nicht harmonieren,
sich beißen ▷ vt erschüttern; **to ~ on sb** jdm
auf die Nerven gehen
jargon ['dʒɑ:gən] n Jargon m
jarring ['dʒɑ:rɪŋ] adj (sound) gellend, schrill;
(colour) schreiend
jasmine ['dʒæzmɪn] n Jasmin m
jaundice ['dʒɔ:ndɪs] n Gelbsucht f
jaundiced ['dʒɔ:ndɪst] adj (view, attitude) zynisch
jaunt [dʒɔ:nt] n Spritztour f
jaunty ['dʒɔ:ntɪ] adj munter; (step)
schwungvoll
Java ['dʒɑ:və] n Java nt
javelin ['dʒævlɪn] n Speer m
jaw [dʒɔ:] n Kiefer m
jawbone ['dʒɔ:bəun] n Kieferknochen m
jay [dʒeɪ] n Eichelhäher m
jaywalker ['dʒeɪwɔ:kər] n unachtsamer
Fußgänger m, unachtsame Fußgängerin f
jazz [dʒæz] n Jazz m
▶ **jazz up** vt aufpeppen (inf)
jazz band n Jazzband f
JCB® n Erdräummaschine f
JCS (US) n abbr (= Joint Chiefs of Staff) Stabschefs pl
JD (US) n abbr (= Doctor of Laws) ≈ Dr. jur.; (= Justice
Department), ≈ Justizministerium nt
jealous ['dʒɛləs] adj eifersüchtig; (envious)

neidisch

jealously ['dʒɛləslɪ] adv eifersüchtig; (enviously) neidisch; (watchfully) sorgsam

jealousy ['dʒɛləsɪ] n Eifersucht f; (envy) Neid m

jeans [dʒiːnz] npl Jeans pl

Jeep® [dʒiːp] n Jeep® m

jeer [dʒɪəʳ] vi höhnische Bemerkungen machen; **to ~ at** verhöhnen

jeering ['dʒɪərɪŋ] adj höhnisch; (crowd) johlend ▷ n Johlen nt

jeers ['dʒɪəz] npl Buhrufe pl

jelly ['dʒɛlɪ] n Götterspeise f; (jam) Gelee m or nt

jelly baby (Brit) n Gummibärchen nt

jellyfish ['dʒɛlɪfɪʃ] n Qualle f

jeopardize ['dʒɛpədaɪz] vt gefährden

jeopardy ['dʒɛpədɪ] n: **to be in ~** gefährdet sein

jerk [dʒəːk] n Ruck m; (inf: idiot) Trottel m ▷ vt reißen ▷ vi (vehicle) ruckeln

jerkin ['dʒəːkɪn] n Wams nt

jerky ['dʒəːkɪ] adj ruckartig

jerry-built ['dʒɛrɪbɪlt] adj schlampig gebaut

jerry can ['dʒɛrɪ-] n großer Blechkanister m

Jersey ['dʒəːzɪ] n Jersey nt

jersey ['dʒəːzɪ] n Pullover m; (fabric) Jersey m

Jerusalem [dʒəˈruːsləm] n Jerusalem nt

jest [dʒɛst] n Scherz m

jester ['dʒɛstəʳ] n Narr m

Jesus ['dʒiːzəs] n Jesus m; **~ Christ** Jesus Christus m

jet [dʒɛt] n Strahl m; (Aviat) Düsenflugzeug nt; (Mineralogy, Jewellery) Jett m or nt, Gagat m

jet-black ['dʒɛt'blæk] adj pechschwarz

jet engine n Düsentriebwerk nt

jet lag n Jetlag nt

jet-propelled ['dʒɛtprəˈpɛld] adj Düsen-, mit Düsenantrieb

jetsam ['dʒɛtsəm] n Strandgut nt; (floating) Treibgut nt

jet-setter ['dʒɛtsɛtəʳ] n: **to be a ~** zum Jetset gehören

jettison ['dʒɛtɪsn] vt abwerfen; (from ship) über Bord werfen

jetty ['dʒɛtɪ] n Landesteg m, Pier m

Jew [dʒuː] n Jude m, Jüdin f

jewel ['dʒuːəl] n Edelstein m, Juwel nt (also fig); (in watch) Stein m

jeweller, (US) **jeweler** ['dʒuːələʳ] n Juwelier m

jeweller's, **jeweller's shop** n Juwelier m, Juweliergeschäft nt

jewellery, (US) **jewelry** ['dʒuːəlrɪ] n Schmuck m

Jewess ['dʒuːɪs] n Jüdin f

Jewish ['dʒuːɪʃ] adj jüdisch

JFK (US) n abbr (= John Fitzgerald Kennedy International Airport) John-F.-Kennedy-Flughafen m

jib [dʒɪb] n (Naut) Klüver m; (of crane) Ausleger m ▷ vi (horse) scheuen, bocken; **to ~ at doing sth** sich dagegen sträuben, etw zu tun

jibe [dʒaɪb] n = **gibe**

jiffy ['dʒɪfɪ] (inf) n: **in a ~** sofort

jig [dʒɪg] n lebhafter Volkstanz

jigsaw ['dʒɪgsɔː] n (also: **jigsaw puzzle**)

Puzzle(spiel) nt; (tool) Stichsäge f

jilt [dʒɪlt] vt sitzen lassen

jingle ['dʒɪŋgl] n (tune) Jingle m ▷ vi (bracelets) klimpern; (bells) bimmeln

jingoism ['dʒɪŋgəʊɪzəm] n Hurrapatriotismus m

jinx [dʒɪŋks] (inf) n Fluch m; **there's a ~ on it** es ist verhext

jitters ['dʒɪtəz] (inf) npl: **to get the ~** das große Zittern bekommen

jittery ['dʒɪtərɪ] (inf) adj nervös, rappelig

jiujitsu [dʒuː'dʒɪtsuː] n Jiu-Jitsu nt

job [dʒɔb] n Arbeit f; (post, employment) Stelle f, Job m; **it's not my ~** es ist nicht meine Aufgabe; **a part-time ~** eine Teilzeitbeschäftigung; **a full-time ~** eine Ganztagsstelle; **he's only doing his ~** er tut nur seine Pflicht; **it's a good ~ that ...** nur gut, dass ...; **just the ~!** genau das Richtige!

jobber ['dʒɔbəʳ] (Brit) n Börsenhändler m

jobbing ['dʒɔbɪŋ] (Brit) adj Gelegenheits-

job centre (Brit) n Arbeitsamt nt

job creation scheme n Arbeits-beschaffungsmaßnahmen pl

job description n Tätigkeitsbeschreibung f

job interview n Vorstellungs- or Bewerbungsgespräch nt

jobless ['dʒɔblɪs] adj arbeitslos ▷ npl: **the ~** die Arbeitslosen pl

job lot n (Waren)posten m

job satisfaction n Zufriedenheit f am Arbeitsplatz

job security n Sicherheit f des Arbeitsplatzes

job sharing n Jobsharing nt, Arbeitsplatzteilung f

job specification n Tätigkeitsbeschreibung f

Jock [dʒɔk] (inf) n Schotte m

jockey ['dʒɔkɪ] n Jockey m ▷ vi: **to ~ for position** um eine gute Position rangeln

jockey box (US) n (Aut) Handschuhfach nt

jocular ['dʒɔkjʊləʳ] adj spaßig, witzig

jog [dʒɔg] vt (an)stoßen ▷ vi joggen, Dauerlauf machen; **to ~ sb's memory** jds Gedächtnis dat nachhelfen

▶ **jog along** vi entlangzuckeln (inf)

jogger ['dʒɔgəʳ] n Jogger(in) m(f)

jogging ['dʒɔgɪŋ] n Jogging nt, Joggen nt

john [dʒɔn] (US: inf) n (toilet) Klo nt

join [dʒɔɪn] vt (club, party) beitreten +dat; (queue) sich stellen in +acc; (things, places) verbinden; (group of people) sich anschließen +dat ▷ vi (roads) sich treffen; (rivers) zusammenfließen ▷ n Verbindungsstelle f; **to ~ forces (with)** (fig) sich zusammentun (mit); **will you ~ us for dinner?** wollen Sie mit uns zu Abend essen?; **I'll ~ you later** ich komme später

▶ **join in** vi mitmachen ▷ vt fus sich beteiligen an +dat

▶ **join up** vi sich treffen; (Mil) zum Militär gehen

joiner ['dʒɔɪnəʳ] (Brit) n Schreiner(in) m(f)

joinery ['dʒɔɪnərɪ] (Brit) n Schreinerei f

joint [dʒɔɪnt] n (in woodwork) Fuge f; (in pipe

etc) Verbindungsstelle *f*; (*Anat*) Gelenk *nt*; (*Brit: Culin*) Braten *m*; (*inf: place*) Laden *m*; (*: of cannabis*) Joint *m* ▷ *adj* gemeinsam; (*combined*) vereint

joint account *n* gemeinsames Konto *nt*

jointly ['dʒɔɪntlɪ] *adv* gemeinsam

joint ownership *n* Miteigentum *nt*

joint-stock company ['dʒɔɪnt'stɔk-] *n* Aktiengesellschaft *f*

joint venture *n* Gemeinschaftsunternehmen *nt*, Joint Venture *nt*

joist [dʒɔɪst] *n* Balken *m*, Träger *m*

joke [dʒəʊk] *n* Witz *m*; (*also*: **practical joke**) Streich *m* ▷ *vi* Witze machen; **to play a ~ on sb** jdm einen Streich spielen

joker ['dʒəʊkəʳ] *n* (*Cards*) Joker *m*

joking ['dʒəʊkɪŋ] *adj* scherzhaft

jokingly ['dʒəʊkɪŋlɪ] *adv* scherzhaft, im Spaß

jollity ['dʒɒlɪtɪ] *n* Fröhlichkeit *f*

jolly ['dʒɒlɪ] *adj* fröhlich; (*enjoyable*) lustig ▷ *adv* (*Brit: inf: very*) ganz (schön) ▷ *vt* (*Brit*): **to ~ sb along** jdm aufmunternd zureden; **~ good!** prima!

jolt [dʒəʊlt] *n* Ruck *m*; (*shock*) Schock *m* ▷ *vt* schütteln; (*subj: bus etc*) durchschütteln; (*emotionally*) aufrütteln

Jordan ['dʒɔ:dən] *n* Jordanien *nt*; (*river*) Jordan *m*

Jordanian [dʒɔ:'deɪnɪən] *adj* jordanisch ▷ *n* Jordanier(in) *m(f)*

joss stick [dʒɒs-] *n* Räucherstäbchen *nt*

jostle ['dʒɒsl] *vt* anrempeln ▷ *vi* drängeln

jot [dʒɒt] *n*: **not one ~** kein bisschen
▸ **jot down** *vt* notieren

jotter ['dʒɒtəʳ] (*Brit*) *n* Notizbuch *nt*; (*pad*) Notizblock *m*

journal ['dʒə:nl] *n* Zeitschrift *f*; (*diary*) Tagebuch *nt*

journalese [dʒə:nə'li:z] (*pej*) *n* Pressejargon *m*

journalism ['dʒə:nəlɪzəm] *n* Journalismus *m*

journalist ['dʒə:nəlɪst] *n* Journalist(in) *m(f)*

journey ['dʒə:nɪ] *n* Reise *f* ▷ *vi* reisen; **a 5-hour ~** eine Fahrt von 5 Stunden; **return ~** Rückreise *f*; (*both ways*) Hin- und Rückreise *f*

jovial ['dʒəʊvɪəl] *adj* fröhlich; (*atmosphere*) freundlich, herzlich

jowl [dʒaʊl] *n* Backe *f*

joy [dʒɔɪ] *n* Freude *f*

joyful ['dʒɔɪful] *adj* freudig

joyride ['dʒɔɪraɪd] *n* Spritztour in einem gestohlenen Auto

joyrider ['dʒɔɪraɪdəʳ] *n* Autodieb, der den Wagen nur für eine Spritztour benutzt

joystick ['dʒɔɪstɪk] *n* (*Aviat*) Steuerknüppel *m*; (*Comput*) Joystick *m*

JP *n abbr* = **Justice of the Peace**

Jr *abbr* (*in names*: = *junior*) jun.

JTPA (*US*) *n abbr* (= *Job Training Partnership Act*) Arbeitsbeschaffungsprogramm für benachteiligte Bevölkerungsteile und Minderheiten

jubilant ['dʒu:bɪlnt] *adj* überglücklich

jubilation [dʒu:bɪ'leɪʃən] *n* Jubel *m*

jubilee ['dʒu:bɪli:] *n* Jubiläum *nt*; **silver ~** 25-jähriges Jubiläum; **golden ~** 50-jähriges Jubiläum

judge [dʒʌdʒ] *n* Richter(in) *m(f)*; (*in competition*) Preisrichter(in) *m(f)*; (*fig: expert*) Kenner(in) *m(f)* ▷ *vt* (*Law: person*) die Verhandlung führen über +*acc*; (*: case*) verhandeln; (*competition*) Preisrichter(in) sein bei; (*person etc*) beurteilen; (*consider*) halten für; (*estimate*) einschätzen ▷ *vi*: **judging by** *or* **to ~ by his expression** seinem Gesichtsausdruck nach zu urteilen; **she's a good ~ of character** sie ist ein guter Menschenkenner; **I'll be the ~ of that** das müssen Sie mich schon selbst beurteilen lassen; **as far as I can ~** soweit ich es beurteilen kann; **I ~d it necessary to inform him** ich hielt es für nötig, ihn zu informieren

judge advocate *n* (*Mil*) Beisitzer(in) *m(f)* bei einem Kriegsgericht

Judge Advocate General *n* (*Mil*) Vorsitzender des obersten Militärgerichts

judgment, judgement ['dʒʌdʒmənt] *n* Urteil *nt*; (*Rel*) Gericht *nt*; (*view, opinion*) Meinung *f*; (*discernment*) Urteilsvermögen *nt*; **in my ~** meiner Meinung nach; **to pass ~ (on)** (*Law*) das Urteil sprechen (über +*acc*); (*fig*) ein Urteil fällen (über +*acc*)

judicial [dʒu:'dɪʃl] *adj* gerichtlich, Justiz-; (*fig*) kritisch; **~ review** gerichtliche Überprüfung *f*

judiciary [dʒu:'dɪʃɪərɪ] *n*: **the ~** die Gerichtsbehörden *pl*

judicious [dʒu:'dɪʃəs] *adj* klug

judo ['dʒu:dəu] *n* Judo *nt*

jug [dʒʌg] *n* Krug *m*

jugged hare ['dʒʌgd-] (*Brit*) *n* ≈ Hasenpfeffer *m*

juggernaut ['dʒʌgənɔ:t] (*Brit*) *n* Fernlastwagen *m*

juggle ['dʒʌgl] *vi* jonglieren

juggler ['dʒʌgləʳ] *n* Jongleur *m*

Jugoslav *etc* ['ju:gəu'sla:v] = **Yugoslav** *etc*

jugular ['dʒʌgjuləʳ] *adj*: **~ (vein)** Drosselvene *f*

juice [dʒu:s] *n* Saft *m*; (*inf: petrol*): **we've run out of ~** wir haben keinen Sprit mehr

juicy ['dʒu:sɪ] *adj* saftig

jukebox ['dʒu:kbɔks] *n* Musikbox *f*

Jul. *abbr* = **July**

July [dʒu:'laɪ] *n* Juli *m*; **the first of ~** der erste Juli; **on the eleventh of ~** am elften Juli; **in the month of ~** im (Monat) Juli; **at the beginning/end of ~** Anfang/Ende Juli; **in the middle of ~** Mitte Juli; **during ~** im Juli; **in ~ of next year** im Juli nächsten Jahres; **each** *or* **every ~** jedes Jahr im Juli; **~ was wet this year** der Juli war dieses Jahr ein nasser Monat

jumble ['dʒʌmbl] *n* Durcheinander *nt*; (*items for sale*) gebrauchte Sachen *pl*; *siehe Info-Artikel* ▷ *vt* (*also*: **jumble up**) durcheinanderbringen

JUMBLE SALE

Jumble sale ist ein Wohltätigkeitsbasar, meist in einer Aula oder einem Gemeindehaus abgehalten, bei dem alle möglichen Gebrauchtwaren (vor allem Kleidung, Spielzeug, Bücher,

Geschirr und Möbel) verkauft werden. Der Erlös fließt entweder einer Wohltätigkeitsorganisation zu oder wird für örtliche Zwecke verwendet, z. B. die Pfadfinder, die Grundschule, Reparatur der Kirche usw.

jumbo ['dʒʌmbəʊ]

jumbo jet n Jumbo(jet) m

jumbo-size ['dʒʌmbəʊsaɪz] adj (packet etc) Riesen-

jump [dʒʌmp] vi springen; (with fear, surprise) zusammenzucken; (increase) sprunghaft ansteigen ▷vt springen über +acc ▷n (see vb) Sprung m; Zusammenzucken nt; sprunghafter Anstieg m; **to ~ the queue** (Brit) sich vordrängeln

▸**jump about** vi herumspringen

▸**jump at** vt fus (idea) sofort aufgreifen; (chance) sofort ergreifen; **he ~ed at the offer** er griff bei dem Angebot sofort zu

▸**jump down** vi herunterspringen

▸**jump up** vi hochspringen; (from seat) aufspringen

jumped-up ['dʒʌmptʌp] (Brit: pej) adj eingebildet

jumper ['dʒʌmpəʳ] n (Brit) Pullover m; (US: dress) Trägerkleid nt; (Sport) Springer(in) m(f)

jumper cables (US) npl = **jump leads**

jumping jack n Knallfrosch m

jump jet n Senkrechtstarter m

jump leads (Brit) npl Starthilfekabel nt

jump-start ['dʒʌmpstɑːt] vt (Aut: engine) durch Anschieben des Wagens in Gang bringen

jump suit n Overall m

jumpy ['dʒʌmpɪ] adj nervös

Jun. abbr = **June**

junction ['dʒʌŋkʃən] (Brit) n Kreuzung f; (Rail) Gleisanschluss m

juncture ['dʒʌŋktʃəʳ] n: **at this ~** zu diesem Zeitpunkt

June [dʒuːn] n Juni m; see also **July**

jungle ['dʒʌŋgl] n Urwald m, Dschungel m (also fig)

junior ['dʒuːnɪəʳ] adj jünger; (subordinate) untergeordnet ▷n Jüngere(r) f(m); (young person) Junior m; **he's ~ to me (by 2 years), he's ~y ~ (by 2 years)** (younger) er ist (2 Jahre) jünger als ich; **he's ~ to me** (subordinate) er steht unter mir

junior executive n Zweiter Geschäftsführer m, Zweite Geschäftsführerin f

junior high school (US) n ≈ Mittelschule f

junior minister (Brit) n Staatssekretär(in) m(f)

junior partner n Juniorpartner(in) m(f)

junior school (Brit) n ≈ Grundschule f

junior sizes npl (Comm) Kindergrößen pl

juniper ['dʒuːnɪpəʳ] n: **~ berry** Wacholderbeere f

junk [dʒʌŋk] n (rubbish) Gerümpel nt; (cheap goods) Ramsch m; (ship) Dschunke f ▷vt (inf) ausrangieren

junk bond n (Fin) niedrig eingestuftes Wertpapier mit hohen Ertragschancen bei erhöhtem Risiko

junket ['dʒʌŋkɪt] n Dickmilch f; (inf: pej: free trip): **to go on a ~** eine Reise auf Kosten des Steuerzahlers machen

junk food n ungesundes Essen nt

junkie ['dʒʌŋkɪ] (inf) n Fixer(in) m(f)

junk mail n (Post)wurfsendungen pl

junk room n Rumpelkammer f

junk shop n Trödelladen m

Junr abbr (in names: = junior) jun.

junta ['dʒʌntə] n Junta f

Jupiter ['dʒuːpɪtəʳ] n Jupiter m

jurisdiction [dʒuərɪs'dɪkʃən] n Gerichtsbarkeit f; (Admin) Zuständigkeit f, Zuständigkeitsbereich m; **it falls** or **comes within/outside my ~** dafür bin ich zuständig/nicht zuständig

jurisprudence [dʒuərɪs'pruːdəns] n Jura no art, Rechtswissenschaft f

juror ['dʒuərəʳ] n Schöffe m, Schöffin f; (for capital crimes) Geschworene(r) f(m); (in competition) Preisrichter(in) m(f)

jury ['dʒuərɪ] n: **the ~** die Schöffen pl; (for capital crimes) die Geschworenen pl; (for competition) die Jury, das Preisgericht

jury box n Schöffenbank f; Geschworenenbank f

juryman ['dʒuərɪmən] (irreg: like **man**) n = **juror**

just [dʒʌst] adj gerecht ▷adv (exactly) genau; (only) nur; **he's ~ done it/left** er hat es gerade getan/ist gerade gegangen; **~ as I expected** genau wie ich erwartet habe; **~ right** genau richtig; **~ two o'clock** erst zwei Uhr; **we were ~ going** wir wollten gerade gehen; **I was ~ about to phone** ich wollte gerade anrufen; **she's ~ as clever as you** sie ist genauso klug wie du; **it's ~ as well (that ...)** nur gut, dass ...; **~ as he was leaving** gerade als er gehen wollte; **~ before** gerade noch; **~ enough** gerade genug; **~ here** genau hier, genau an dieser Stelle; **he ~ missed** er hat genau danebengetroffen; **it's ~ me** ich bins nur; **it's ~ a mistake** es ist nur ein Fehler; **~ listen** hör mal; **~ ask someone the way** frage doch einfach jemanden nach dem Weg; **not ~ now** nicht gerade jetzt; **~ a minute!, ~ one moment!** einen Moment, bitte!

justice ['dʒʌstɪs] n Justiz f; (of cause, complaint) Berechtigung f; (fairness) Gerechtigkeit f; (US: judge) Richter(in) m(f); **Lord Chief J~** (Brit) oberster Richter in Großbritannien; **to do ~ to** (fig) gerecht werden +dat

Justice of the Peace n Friedensrichter(in) m(f)

justifiable [dʒʌstɪ'faɪəbl] adj gerechtfertigt, berechtigt

justifiably [dʒʌstɪ'faɪəblɪ] adv zu Recht, berechtigterweise

justification [dʒʌstɪfɪ'keɪʃən] n Rechtfertigung f; (Typ) Justierung f

justify ['dʒʌstɪfaɪ] vt rechtfertigen; (text) justieren; **to be justified in doing sth** etw zu or mit Recht tun

justly ['dʒʌstlɪ] adv zu or mit Recht; (deservedly) gerecht
jut [dʒʌt] vi (also: **jut out**) vorstehen
jute [dʒuːt] n Jute f
juvenile ['dʒuːvənaɪl] adj (crime, offenders) Jugend-; (humour, mentality) kindisch, unreif
▷ n Jugendliche(r) f(m)

juvenile delinquency n Jugendkriminalität f
juvenile delinquent n jugendlicher Straftäter m, jugendliche Straftäterin f
juxtapose ['dʒʌkstəpəʊz] vt nebeneinanderstellen
juxtaposition ['dʒʌkstəpə'zɪʃən] n Nebeneinanderstellung f

j

Kk

K¹, k [keɪ] *n* (*letter*) K *nt*, k *nt*; **K for King** = K wie Kaufmann

K² [keɪ] *abbr* (= *one thousand*) K; (*Comput*: = *kilobyte*) KB; (*Brit*: *in titles*) = **knight**

kaftan ['kæftæn] *n* Kaftan *m*

Kalahari Desert [kælə'hɑːrɪ-] *n*: **the ~** die Kalahari

kale [keɪl] *n* Grünkohl *m*

kaleidoscope [kə'laɪdəskəup] *n* Kaleidoskop *nt*

kamikaze ['kæmɪ'kɑːzɪ] *adj* (*mission etc*) Kamikaze-, Selbstmord-

Kampala [kæm'pɑːlə] *n* Kampala *nt*

Kampuchea [kæmpu'tʃɪə] *n* Kampuchea *nt*

Kampuchean [kæmpu'tʃɪən] *adj* kampucheanisch

kangaroo [kæŋgə'ruː] *n* Känguru *nt*

Kans. (*US*) *abbr* (*Post*) = *Kansas*

kaput [kə'put] (*inf*) *adj*: **to be ~** kaputt sein

karaoke [kɑːrə'əukɪ] *n* Karaoke *nt*

karate [kə'rɑːtɪ] *n* Karate *nt*

Kashmir [kæʃ'mɪər] *n* Kaschmir *nt*

kayak ['kaɪæk] *n* Kajak *m or nt*

Kazakhstan [kæzæk'stɑːn] *n* Kasachstan *nt*

KC (*Brit*) *n abbr* (*Law*: = *King's Counsel*) Kronanwalt *m*

kebab [kə'bæb] *n* Kebab *m*

keel [kiːl] *n* Kiel *m*; **on an even ~** (*fig*) stabil

▶ **keel over** *vi* kentern; (*person*) umkippen

keen [kiːn] *adj* begeistert, eifrig; (*interest*) groß; (*desire*) heftig; (*eye, intelligence, competition, edge*) scharf; **to be ~ to do** *or* **on doing sth** scharf darauf sein, etw zu tun (*inf*); **to be ~ on sth** an etw *dat* sehr interessiert sein; **to be ~ on sb** von jdm sehr angetan sein; **I'm not ~ on going** ich brenne nicht gerade darauf, zu gehen

keenly ['kiːnlɪ] *adv* (*enthusiastically*) begeistert; (*feel*) leidenschaftlich; (*look*) aufmerksam

keenness ['kiːnnɪs] *n* Begeisterung *f*, Eifer *m*; **his ~ to go is suspicious** dass er so unbedingt gehen will, ist verdächtig

keep [kiːp] (*pt, pp* **kept**) *vt* behalten; (*preserve, store*) aufbewahren; (*house, shop, accounts, diary*) führen; (*garden etc*) pflegen; (*chickens, bees, promise*) halten; (*family etc*) versorgen, unterhalten; (*detain*) aufhalten; (*prevent*) abhalten ▷ *vi* (*remain*) bleiben; (*food*) sich halten ▷ *n* (*food etc*) Unterhalt *m*; (*of castle*) Bergfried *m*; **to ~ doing sth** etw immer wieder tun; **to ~ sb happy** jdn zufriedenstellen; **to ~ a room tidy** ein Zimmer in Ordnung halten; **to ~ sb waiting** jdn warten lassen; **to ~ an appointment** eine Verabredung einhalten; **to ~ a record of sth** über etw *acc* Buch führen; **to ~ sth to o.s.** etw für sich behalten; **to ~ sth (back) from sb** etw vor jdm geheim halten; **to ~ sb from doing sth** jdn davon abhalten, etw zu tun; **to ~ sth from happening** etw verhindern; **to ~ time** (*clock*) genau gehen; **enough for his ~** genug für seinen Unterhalt

▶ **keep away** *vt* fernhalten ▷ *vi*: **to ~ away (from)** wegbleiben (von)

▶ **keep back** *vt* zurückhalten; (*tears*) unterdrücken; (*money*) einbehalten ▷ *vi* zurückbleiben

▶ **keep down** *vt* (*prices*) niedrig halten; (*spending*) einschränken; (*food*) bei sich behalten ▷ *vi* unten bleiben

▶ **keep in** *vt* im Haus behalten; (*at school*) nachsitzen lassen ▷ *vi* (*inf*): **to ~ in with sb** sich mit jdm gut stellen

▶ **keep off** *vt* fernhalten ▷ *vi* wegbleiben; **"~ off the grass"** „Betreten des Rasens verboten"; **~ your hands off** Hände weg

▶ **keep on** *vi*: **to ~ on doing sth** (*continue*) etw weiter tun; **to ~ on (about sth)** unaufhörlich (von etw) reden

▶ **keep out** *vt* fernhalten; **"~ out"** „Zutritt verboten"

▶ **keep up** *vt* (*payments*) weiterbezahlen; (*standards etc*) aufrechterhalten ▷ *vi*: **to ~ up (with)** mithalten können (mit)

keeper ['kiːpər] *n* Wärter(in) *m(f)*

keep fit *n* Fitnesstraining *nt*

keeping ['kiːpɪŋ] *n* (*care*) Obhut *f*; **in ~ with** in Übereinstimmung mit; **out of ~ with** nicht im Einklang mit; **I'll leave this in your ~** ich vertraue dies deiner Obhut an

keeps [kiːps] *n*: **for ~** (*inf*) für immer

keepsake ['kiːpseɪk] *n* Andenken *nt*

keg [keg] *n* Fässchen *nt*; **~ beer** Bier *nt* vom Fass

Ken. (*US*) *abbr* (*Post*) = *Kentucky*

kennel ['kenl] *n* Hundehütte *f*

kennels ['kenlz] *n* Hundeheim *nt*; **we had to leave our dog in ~ over Christmas** wir mussten unseren Hund über Weihnachten in

ein Heim geben
Kenya ['kɛnjə] n Kenia nt
Kenyan ['kɛnjən] adj kenianisch ▷ n
Kenianer(in) m(f)
kept [kɛpt] pt, pp of **keep**
kerb [kə:b] (Brit) n Bordstein m
kerb crawler [-'krɔ:lə'] (inf) n Freier m im
Autostrich
kernel ['kə:nl] n Kern m
kerosene ['kɛrəsi:n] n Kerosin nt
kestrel ['kɛstrəl] n Turmfalke m
ketchup ['kɛtʃəp] n Ket(s)chup m or nt
kettle ['kɛtl] n Kessel m
kettledrum ['kɛtldrʌm] n (Kessel)pauke f
key [ki:] n Schlüssel m; (Mus) Tonart f; (of
piano, computer, typewriter) Taste f ▷ cpd (issue etc)
Schlüssel- ▷ vt (also: **key in**) eingeben
keyboard ['ki:bɔ:d] n Tastatur f
keyboarder ['ki:bɔ:də'] n Datentypist(in) m(f)
keyed up [ki:d-] adj: **to be (all)** ~ (ganz)
aufgedreht sein (inf)
keyhole ['ki:həul] n Schlüsselloch nt
keyhole surgery n Schlüssellochchirurgie f,
minimal invasive Chirurgie f
keynote ['ki:nəut] n Grundton m; (of speech)
Leitgedanke m
keypad ['ki:pæd] n Tastenfeld nt
key ring n Schlüsselring m
keystroke ['ki:strəuk] n Anschlag m
kg abbr (= kilogram) kg
KGB n abbr (Pol: formerly) KGB m
khaki ['kɑ:ki] n K(h)aki nt
kHz abbr (= kilohertz) kHz
kibbutz [kɪ'buts] n Kibbuz m
kick [kɪk] vt treten; (table, ball) treten
gegen +acc; (inf: habit) ablegen; (: addiction)
wegkommen von ▷ vi (horse) ausschlagen ▷ n
Tritt m; (to ball) Schuss m; (of rifle) Rückstoß m;
(thrill): **he does it for ~s** er macht es zum Spaß
▶ **kick around** (inf) vi (person) rumhängen;
(thing) rumliegen
▶ **kick off** vi (Sport) anstoßen
kickoff ['kɪkɔf] n (Sport) Anstoß m
kick start n (Aut: also: **kick starter**) Kickstarter
m
kid [kɪd] n (inf: child) Kind nt; (animal) Kitz nt;
(leather) Ziegenleder nt, Glacéleder nt ▷ vi (inf)
Witze machen; ~ **brother** kleiner Bruder m; ~
sister kleine Schwester f
kid gloves npl: **to treat sb with** ~ (fig) jdn mit
Samthandschuhen anfassen
kidnap ['kɪdnæp] vt entführen, kidnappen
kidnapper ['kɪdnæpə'] n Entführer(in) m(f),
Kidnapper(in) m(f)
kidnapping ['kɪdnæpɪŋ] n Entführung f,
Kidnapping nt
kidney ['kɪdnɪ] n Niere f
kidney bean n Gartenbohne f
kidney machine n (Med) künstliche Niere f
Kilimanjaro [kɪlɪmən'dʒɑːrəu] n: **Mount** ~ der
Kilimandscharo
kill [kɪl] vt töten; (murder) ermorden,
umbringen; (plant) eingehen lassen; (proposal)

zu Fall bringen; (rumour) ein Ende machen
+dat ▷ n Abschuss m; **to** ~ **time** die Zeit
totschlagen; **to** ~ **o.s. to do sth** (fig) sich
fast umbringen, um etw zu tun; **to** ~ **o.s.**
(laughing) (fig) sich totlachen
▶ **kill off** vt abtöten; (fig: romance) beenden
killer ['kɪlə'] n Mörder(in) m(f)
killer instinct n (fig) Tötungsinstinkt m
killing ['kɪlɪŋ] n Töten nt; (instance) Mord m; **to**
make a ~ (inf) einen Riesengewinn machen
killjoy ['kɪldʒɔɪ] n Spielverderber(in) m(f)
kiln [kɪln] n Brennofen m
kilo ['ki:ləu] n Kilo nt
kilobyte ['ki:ləubaɪt] n Kilobyte nt
kilogram, kilogramme ['kɪləugræm] n
Kilogramm nt
kilohertz ['kɪləuhə:ts] n inv Kilohertz nt
kilometre, (US) kilometer ['kɪləmi:tə'] n
Kilometer m
kilowatt ['kɪləuwɔt] n Kilowatt nt
kilt [kɪlt] n Kilt m, Schottenrock m
kilter ['kɪltə'] n: **out of** ~ nicht in Ordnung
kimono [kɪ'məunəu] n Kimono m
kin [kɪn] n see **kith; next**
kind [kaɪnd] adj freundlich ▷ n Art f; (sort) Sorte
f; **would you be** ~ **enough to ...?, would**
you be so ~ **as to ...?** wären Sie (vielleicht)
so nett und ...?; **it's very** ~ **of you (to do ...)**
es ist wirklich nett von Ihnen(, ... zu tun); **in**
~ (Comm) in Naturalien; **a** ~ **of ...** eine Art ...;
they are two of a ~ sie sind beide von der
gleichen Art; (people) sie sind vom gleichen
Schlag
kindergarten ['kɪndəgɑ:tn] n Kindergarten m
kind-hearted [kaɪnd'hɑ:tɪd] adj gutherzig
kindle ['kɪndl] vt anzünden; (emotion) wecken
kindling ['kɪndlɪŋ] n Anzündholz nt
kindly ['kaɪndlɪ] adj, adv freundlich, nett; **will**
you ~ ... würden Sie bitte ...; **he didn't take it**
~ er konnte sich damit nicht anfreunden
kindness ['kaɪndnɪs] n Freundlichkeit f
kindred ['kɪndrɪd] adj: ~ **spirit**
Gleichgesinnte(r) f(m)
kinetic [kɪ'nɛtɪk] adj kinetisch
king [kɪŋ] n (also fig) König m
kingdom ['kɪŋdəm] n Königreich nt
kingfisher ['kɪŋfɪʃə'] n Eisvogel m
kingpin ['kɪŋpɪn] n (Tech) Bolzen m; (Aut)
Achsschenkelbolzen m; (fig) wichtigste Stütze
f
king-size ['kɪŋsaɪz], **king-sized** ['kɪŋsaɪzd] adj
extragroß; (cigarette) Kingsize-
kink [kɪŋk] n Knick m; (in hair) Welle f; (fig)
Schrulle f
kinky ['kɪŋkɪ] (pej) adj schrullig; (sexually)
abartig
kinship ['kɪnʃɪp] n Verwandtschaft f
kinsman ['kɪnzmən] (irreg: like **man**) n
Verwandte(r) m
kinswoman ['kɪnzwumən] (irreg: like **woman**) n
Verwandte f
kiosk ['ki:ɔsk] n Kiosk m; (Brit) (Telefon)zelle f;
(also: **newspaper kiosk**) (Zeitungs)kiosk m

kipper ['kɪpəʳ] n Räucherhering m
Kirghizia [kəːˈgɪzɪə] n Kirgistan nt
kiss [kɪs] n Kuß m ▷ vt küssen ▷ vi sich küssen;
  to ~ (each other) sich küssen; **to ~ sb
  goodbye** jdm einen Abschiedskuss geben
kissagram ['kɪsəgræm] n durch eine(n)
  Angestellte(n) einer Agentur persönlich übermittelter
  Kuss
kiss of life (Brit) n: **the ~** Mund-zu-Mund-
  Beatmung f
kit [kɪt] n Zeug nt, Sachen pl; (equipment, also Mil)
  Ausrüstung f; (set of tools) Werkzeug nt; (for
  assembly) Bausatz m
  ▶ **kit out** (Brit) vt ausrüsten, ausstatten
kitbag ['kɪtbæg] n Seesack m
kitchen ['kɪtʃɪn] n Küche f
kitchen garden n Küchengarten m
kitchen sink n Spüle f
kitchen unit (Brit) n Küchenschrank m
kitchenware ['kɪtʃɪnwɛəʳ] n Küchengeräte pl
kite [kaɪt] n Drachen m; (Zool) Milan m
kith [kɪθ] n: **~ and kin** Freunde und Verwandte
  pl
kitten ['kɪtn] n Kätzchen nt
kitty ['kɪtɪ] n (gemeinsame) Kasse f
kiwi ['kiːwiː], **kiwi fruit** n Kiwi(frucht) f
KKK (US) n abbr (= Ku Klux Klan) Ku-Klux-Klan m
Kleenex® ['kliːnɛks] n Tempo(taschentuch)®
  nt
kleptomaniac [klɛptəuˈmeɪnɪæk] n
  Kleptomane m, Kleptomanin f
km abbr (= kilometre) km
km/h abbr (= kilometres per hour) km/h
knack [næk] n: **to have the ~ of doing sth** es
  heraushaben, wie man etw macht; **there's a
  ~ to doing this** da ist ein Trick or Kniff dabei
knackered ['nækəd] (Brit: inf) adj kaputt
knapsack ['næpsæk] n Rucksack m
knead [niːd] vt kneten
knee [niː] n Knie nt
kneecap ['niːkæp] n Kniescheibe f
kneecapping ['niːkæpɪŋ] n Durchschießen nt
  der Kniescheibe
knee-deep ['niːˈdiːp] adj, adv: **the water was
  ~** das Wasser ging mir etc bis zum Knie; **~ in
  mud** knietief or bis zu den Knien im Schlamm
kneejerk reaction ['niːdʒəːk-] n (fig)
  instinktive Reaktion f
kneel [niːl] (pt, pp **knelt**) vi knien; (also: **kneel
  down**) niederknien
kneepad ['niːpæd] n Knieschützer m
knell [nɛl] n Totengeläut(e) nt; (fig) Ende nt
knelt [nɛlt] pt, pp of **kneel**
knew [njuː] pt of **know**
knickers ['nɪkəz] (Brit) npl Schlüpfer m
knick-knacks ['nɪknæks] npl Nippsachen pl
knife [naɪf] (pl **knives**) n Messer nt ▷ vt (injure,
  attack) einstechen auf +acc; **~, fork and spoon**
  Messer, Gabel und Löffel
knife edge n: **to be balanced on a ~** (fig) auf
  Messers Schneide stehen
knight [naɪt] n (Brit) Ritter m; (Chess) Springer
  m, Pferd nt

knighthood ['naɪthud] (Brit) n: **to get a ~** in
  den Adelsstand erhoben werden
knit [nɪt] vt stricken ▷ vi stricken; (bones)
  zusammenwachsen; **to ~ one's brows** die
  Stirn runzeln
knitted ['nɪtɪd] adj gestrickt, Strick-
knitting ['nɪtɪŋ] n Stricken nt; (garment being
  made) Strickzeug nt
knitting machine n Strickmaschine f
knitting needle n Stricknadel f
knitting pattern n Strickmuster nt
knitwear ['nɪtwɛəʳ] n Strickwaren pl
knives [naɪvz] npl of **knife**
knob [nɔb] n Griff m; (of stick) Knauf m; (on
  radio, TV etc) Knopf m; **a ~ of butter** (Brit) ein
  Stückchen nt Butter
knobbly ['nɔblɪ], (US) **knobby** adj (wood)
  knorrig; (surface) uneben; **~ knees**
  Knubbelknie pl (inf)
knock [nɔk] vt schlagen; (bump into) stoßen
  gegen +acc; (inf: criticize) runtermachen ▷ vi
  klopfen ▷ n Schlag m; (bump) Stoß m; (on door)
  Klopfen nt; **to ~ a nail into sth** einen Nagel
  in etw acc schlagen; **to ~ some sense into sb**
  jdn zur Vernunft bringen; **to ~ at/on** klopfen
  an/auf +acc; **he ~ed at the door** er klopfte an,
  er klopfte an die Tür
  ▶ **knock about** (inf) vt schlagen, verprügeln
  ▷ vi rumziehen; **~ about with** sich
  rumtreiben mit
  ▶ **knock around** vt, vi = **knock about**
  ▶ **knock back** (inf) vt (drink) sich dat hinter die
  Binde kippen
  ▶ **knock down** vt anfahren; (fatally)
  überfahren; (building etc) abreißen; (price: buyer)
  herunterhandeln; (: seller) heruntergehen mit
  ▶ **knock off** vi (inf) Feierabend machen ▷ vt
  (from price) nachlassen; (inf: steal) klauen; **to ~
  off £10** £10 nachlassen
  ▶ **knock out** vt bewusstlos schlagen;
  (subj: drug) bewusstlos werden lassen; (Boxing)
  k. o. schlagen; (in game, competition) besiegen
  ▶ **knock over** vt umstoßen; (with car) anfahren
knockdown ['nɔkdaun] adj: **~ price**
  Schleuderpreis m
knocker ['nɔkəʳ] n Türklopfer m
knock-for-knock ['nɔkfəˈnɔk] (Brit)
  adj: **~ agreement** Vereinbarung, bei der jede
  Versicherungsgesellschaft den Schaden am von ihr
  versicherten Fahrzeug übernimmt
knocking ['nɔkɪŋ] n Klopfen nt
knock-kneed [nɔkˈniːd] adj x-beinig; **to be ~**
  X-Beine haben
knockout ['nɔkaut] n (Boxing) K.-o.-Schlag
  m, Ko.-Schlag m ▷ cpd (competition etc)
  Ausscheidungs-
knock-up ['nɔkʌp] n (Tennis): **to have a ~** ein
  paar Bälle schlagen
knot [nɔt] n Knoten m; (in wood) Ast m ▷ vt
  einen Knoten machen in +acc; (knot together)
  verknoten; **to tie a ~** einen Knoten machen
knotty ['nɔtɪ] adj (fig: problem) verwickelt
know [nəu] (pt **knew**, pp **~n**) vt kennen; (facts)

wissen; (*language*) können ▷ *vi*: **to ~ about** or **of sth/sb** von etw/jdm gehört haben; **to ~ how to swim** schwimmen können; **to get to ~ sth** etw erfahren; (*place*) etw kennenlernen; **I don't ~ him** ich kenne ihn nicht; **to ~ right from wrong** Gut und Böse unterscheiden können; **as far as I ~** soviel ich weiß; **yes, I ~** ja, ich weiß; **I don't ~** ich weiß (es) nicht

know-all ['nəʊɔːl] (*Brit: pej*) *n* Alleswisser *m*

know-how ['nəʊhaʊ] *n* Know-how *nt*, Sachkenntnis *f*

knowing ['nəʊɪŋ] *adj* wissend

knowingly ['nəʊɪŋlɪ] *adv* (*purposely*) bewusst; (*smile, look*) wissend

know-it-all ['nəʊɪtɔːl] (*US*) *n* = **know-all**

knowledge ['nɒlɪdʒ] *n* Wissen *nt*, Kenntnis *f*; (*learning, things learnt*) Kenntnisse *pl*; **to have no ~ of** nichts wissen von; **not to my ~** nicht, dass ich wüsste; **without my ~** ohne mein Wissen; **it is common ~ that ...** es ist allgemein bekannt, dass ...; **it has come to my ~ that ...** ich habe erfahren, dass ...; **to have a working ~ of French** Grundkenntnisse in Französisch haben

knowledgeable ['nɒlɪdʒəbl] *adj* informiert

known [nəʊn] *pp of* **know** ▷ *adj* bekannt; (*expert*) anerkannt

knuckle ['nʌkl] *n* (Finger)knöchel *m*

▶ **knuckle down** (*inf*) *vi* sich dahinter klemmen; **to ~ down to work** sich an die Arbeit machen

▶ **knuckle under** (*inf*) *vi* sich fügen, spuren

knuckle-duster ['nʌkl'dʌstəʳ] *n* Schlagring *m*

KO *n abbr* (= *knockout*) K. o. *m* ▷ *vt* k. o. schlagen

koala [kəʊ'ɑːlə] *n* (*also*: **koala bear**) Koala(bär) *m*

kook [kuːk] (*US: inf*) *n* Spinner *m*

Koran [kɔ'rɑːn] *n*: **the ~** der Koran

Korea [kə'rɪə] *n* Korea *nt*; **North ~** Nordkorea *nt*; **South ~** Südkorea *nt*

Korean [kə'rɪən] *adj* koreanisch ▷ *n* Koreaner(in) *m(f)*

kosher ['kəʊʃəʳ] *adj* koscher

kowtow ['kaʊ'taʊ] *vi*: **to ~ to sb** vor jdm dienern or einen Kotau machen

Kremlin ['krɛmlɪn] *n*: **the ~** der Kreml

KS (*US*) *abbr* (*Post*) = Kansas

Kt (*Brit*) *abbr* (*in titles*) = **knight**

Kuala Lumpur ['kwɑːlə'lumpuəʳ] *n* Kuala Lumpur *nt*

kudos ['kjuːdɒs] *n* Ansehen *nt*, Ehre *f*

Kurd [kəːd] *n* Kurde *m*, Kurdin *f*

Kuwait [ku'weɪt] *n* Kuwait *nt*

Kuwaiti [ku'weɪtɪ] *adj* kuwaitisch ▷ *n* Kuwaiter(in) *m(f)*

kW *abbr* (= *kilowatt*) kW

KY (*US*) *abbr* (*Post*) = Kentucky

k

L l

L¹, l¹ [ɛl] n (letter) L nt, l nt; **L for Lucy, L for Love** (US) ≈ L wie Ludwig

L² [ɛl] abbr (Brit: Aut: = learner) am Auto angebrachtes Kennzeichen für Fahrschüler; = **lake**; (= large) gr.; (= left) l.

l² abbr (= litre) l

LA (US) n abbr = Los Angeles ▷ abbr (Post) = Louisiana

La. (US) abbr (Post) = Louisiana

lab [læb] n abbr = laboratory

label ['leɪbl] n Etikett nt; (brand: of record) Label nt ▷ vt etikettieren; (fig: person) abstempeln

labor etc ['leɪbə'] (US) n = **labour** etc

laboratory [lə'bɔrətərɪ] n Labor nt

laborious [lə'bɔːrɪəs] adj mühsam

labor union (US) n Gewerkschaft f

labour, (US) labor ['leɪbə'] n Arbeit f; (work force) Arbeitskräfte pl; (Med): **to be in ~** in den Wehen liegen ▷ vi: **to ~ (at sth)** sich (mit etw) abmühen ▷ vt: **to ~ a point** auf einem Thema herumreiten; **L~, the ~ Party** (Brit) die Labour Party; **hard ~** Zwangsarbeit f

labour camp n Arbeitslager nt

labour cost n Lohnkosten pl

labour dispute n Arbeitskampf m

laboured ['leɪbəd] adj (breathing) schwer; (movement, style) schwerfällig

labourer ['leɪbərə'] n Arbeiter(in) m(f); **farm ~** Landarbeiter(in) m(f)

labour force n Arbeiterschaft f

labour intensive adj arbeitsintensiv

labour market n Arbeitsmarkt m

labour pains npl Wehen pl

labour relations npl Beziehungen pl zwischen Arbeitnehmern, Arbeitgebern und Gewerkschaften

labour-saving ['leɪbəseɪvɪŋ] adj arbeitsparend

laburnum [lə'bɜːnəm] n (Bot) Goldregen m

labyrinth ['læbɪrɪnθ] n Labyrinth nt

lace [leɪs] n (fabric) Spitze f; (of shoe etc) (Schuh)band nt, Schnürsenkel m ▷ vt (also: **lace up**) (zu)

schnüren; **to ~ a drink** einen Schuss Alkohol in ein Getränk geben

lacemaking ['leɪsmeɪkɪŋ] n Klöppelei f

lacerate ['læsəreɪt] vt zerschneiden

laceration [læsə'reɪʃən] n Schnittwunde f

lace-up ['leɪsʌp] adj (shoes etc) Schnür-

lack [læk] n Mangel m ▷ vt, vi: **sb ~s sth, sb is ~ing in sth** jdm fehlt es an etw dat; **through** or **for ~ of** aus Mangel an +dat; **to be ~ing** fehlen

lackadaisical [lækə'deɪzɪkl] adj lustlos

lackey ['lækɪ] (pej) n Lakai m

lacklustre, (US) lackluster ['læklʌstə'] adj farblos, langweilig

laconic [lə'kɔnɪk] adj lakonisch

lacquer ['lækə'] n Lack m; (also: **hair lacquer**) Haarspray nt

lacrosse [lə'krɔs] n Lacrosse nt

lacy ['leɪsɪ] adj Spitzen-; (like lace) spitzenartig

lad [læd] n Junge m

ladder ['lædə'] n (also fig) Leiter f; (Brit: in tights) Laufmasche f ▷ vt (Brit) Laufmaschen bekommen in +dat ▷ vi (Brit) Laufmaschen bekommen

laden ['leɪdn] adj: **~ (with)** beladen (mit); **fully ~** vollbeladen

ladle ['leɪdl] n Schöpflöffel m, (Schöpf)kelle f ▷ vt schöpfen
▶ **ladle out** vt (fig) austeilen

lady ['leɪdɪ] n (woman) Frau f; (: dignified, graceful etc) Dame f; (Brit: title) Lady f; **ladies and gentlemen ...** meine Damen und Herren ...; **young ~** junge Dame; **the ladies' (room)** die Damentoilette

ladybird ['leɪdɪbɜːd], (US) **ladybug** n Marienkäfer m

lady-in-waiting ['leɪdɪɪn'weɪtɪŋ] n Hofdame f

lady-killer ['leɪdɪkɪlə'] n Herzensbrecher m

ladylike ['leɪdɪlaɪk] adj damenhaft

ladyship ['leɪdɪʃɪp] n: **your L~** Ihre Ladyschaft

lag [læg] n (period of time) Zeitabstand m ▷ vi (also: **lag behind**) zurückbleiben; (trade, investment etc) zurückgehen ▷ vt (pipes etc) isolieren; **old ~** (inf: prisoner) (ehemaliger) Knacki m

lager ['lɑːgə'] n helles Bier nt

lager lout (Brit: inf) n betrunkener Rowdy m

lagging ['lægɪŋ] n Isoliermaterial nt

lagoon [lə'gu:n] n Lagune f
Lagos ['leɪgɔs] n Lagos nt
laid [leɪd] pt, pp of **lay**
laid-back [leɪd'bæk] (inf) adj locker
laid up adj: **to be ~ (with)** im Bett liegen (mit)
lain [leɪn] pp of **lie**
lair [lɛə^r] n Lager nt; (cave) Höhle f; (den) Bau m
laissez faire [lɛseɪ'fɛə^r] n Laisser-faire nt
laity ['leɪətɪ] n or npl Laien pl
lake [leɪk] n See m
Lake District (Brit) n: **the ~** der Lake Distrikt, Seengebiet im NW Englands
lamb [læm] n Lamm nt; (meat) Lammfleisch nt
lamb chop n Lammkotelett nt
lambskin ['læmskɪn] n Lammfell nt
lamb's wool n Lammwolle f
lame [leɪm] adj lahm; (argument, answer) schwach
lame duck n (person) Niete f; (business) unwirtschaftliche Firma f
lamely ['leɪmlɪ] adv lahm
lament [lə'mɛnt] n Klage f ▷ vt beklagen
lamentable ['læməntəbl] adj beklagenswert
laminated ['læmɪneɪtɪd] adj laminiert; (metal) geschichtet; **~ glass** Verbundglas nt; **~ wood** Sperrholz nt
lamp [læmp] n Lampe f
lamplight ['læmplaɪt] n: **by ~** bei Lampenlicht
lampoon [læm'pu:n] n Schmähschrift f ▷ vt verspotten
lamppost ['læmppəust] (Brit) n Laternenpfahl m
lampshade ['læmpʃeɪd] n Lampenschirm m
lance [lɑ:ns] n Lanze f ▷ vt (Med) aufschneiden
lance corporal (Brit) n Obergefreite(r) m
lancet ['lɑ:nsɪt] n (Med) Lanzette f
Lancs [læŋks] (Brit) abbr (Post) = Lancashire
land [lænd] n Land nt; (as property) Grund und Boden m ▷ vi (Aviat, fig) landen; (from ship) an Land gehen ▷ vt (passengers) absetzen; (goods) an Land bringen; **to own ~** Land besitzen; **to go** or **travel by ~** auf dem Landweg reisen; **to ~ on one's feet** (fig) auf die Füße fallen; **to ~ sb with sth** (inf) jdm etw aufhalsen
▶ **land up** vi: **to ~ up in/at** landen in +dat
landed gentry ['lændɪd-] n Landadel m
landfill site ['lændfɪl-] n ≈ Mülldeponie f
landing ['lændɪŋ] n (of house) Flur m; (outside flat door) Treppenabsatz m; (Aviat) Landung f
landing card n Einreisekarte f
landing craft n inv Landungsboot nt
landing gear n (Aviat) Fahrgestell nt
landing stage n Landesteg m
landing strip n Landebahn f
landlady ['lændleɪdɪ] n Vermieterin f; (of pub) Wirtin f
landlocked ['lændlɔkt] adj von Land eingeschlossen; **~ country** Binnenstaat m
landlord ['lændlɔ:d] n Vermieter m; (of pub) Wirt m
landlubber ['lændlʌbə^r] (old) n Landratte f
landmark ['lændmɑ:k] n Orientierungspunkt m; (famous building) Wahrzeichen nt; (fig)

Meilenstein m
landowner ['lændəunə^r] n Grundbesitzer(in) m(f)
landscape ['lændskeɪp] n Landschaft f ▷ vt landschaftlich or gärtnerisch gestalten
landscape architect n Landschaftsarchitekt(in) m(f)
landscape gardener n Landschaftsgärtner(in) m(f)
landscape painting n Landschaftsmalerei f
landslide ['lændslaɪd] n Erdrutsch m; (fig: electoral) Erdrutschsieg m
lane [leɪn] n (in country) Weg m; (in town) Gasse f; (of carriageway) Spur f; (of race course, swimming pool) Bahn f; **shipping ~** Schifffahrtsweg m
language ['læŋgwɪdʒ] n Sprache f; **bad ~** Kraftausdrücke pl
language laboratory n Sprachlabor nt
languid ['læŋgwɪd] adj träge, matt
languish ['læŋgwɪʃ] vi schmachten; (project, case) erfolglos bleiben
lank [læŋk] adj (hair) strähnig
lanky ['læŋkɪ] adj schlaksig
lanolin, lanoline ['lænəlɪn] n Lanolin nt
lantern ['læntən] n Laterne f
Laos [laus] n Laos nt
lap [læp] n Schoß m; (in race) Runde f ▷ vt (also: **lap up**) aufschlecken ▷ vi (water) plätschern
▶ **lap up** vt (fig) genießen
lapdog ['læpdɔg] (pej) n (fig) Schoßhund m
lapel [lə'pɛl] n Aufschlag m, Revers nt or m
Lapland ['læplænd] n Lappland nt
Lapp [læp] adj lappländisch ▷ n Lappe m, Lappin f; (Ling) Lappländisch nt
lapse [læps] n (bad behaviour) Fehltritt m; (of memory etc) Schwäche f; (of time) Zeitspanne f ▷ vi ablaufen; (law) ungültig werden; **to ~ into bad habits** in schlechte Gewohnheiten verfallen
laptop ['læptɔp] (Comput) n Laptop m ▷ cpd Laptop-
larceny ['lɑ:sənɪ] n Diebstahl m
larch [lɑ:tʃ] n Lärche f
lard [lɑ:d] n Schweineschmalz nt
larder ['lɑ:də^r] n Speisekammer f; (cupboard) Speiseschrank m
large [lɑ:dʒ] adj groß; (person) korpulent; **to make ~r** vergrößern; **a ~ number of people** eine große Anzahl von Menschen; **on a ~ scale** im großen Rahmen; (extensive) weitreichend; **at ~** (as a whole) im Allgemeinen; (at liberty) auf freiem Fuß; **by and ~** im Großen und Ganzen
large goods vehicle n Lastkraftwagen m
largely ['lɑ:dʒlɪ] adv (mostly) zum größten Teil; (mainly) hauptsächlich
large-scale ['lɑ:dʒ'skeɪl] adj im großen Rahmen; (extensive) weitreichend; (map, diagram) in einem großen Maßstab
largesse [lɑ:'ʒɛs] n Großzügigkeit f
lark [lɑ:k] n (bird) Lerche f; (joke) Spaß m, Jux m
▶ **lark about** vi herumalbern

larva ['lɑ:və] (pl **~e**) n Larve f
larvae ['lɑ:vi:] npl of **larva**
laryngitis [lærɪn'dʒaɪtɪs] n Kehlkopfentzündung f
larynx ['lærɪŋks] n Kehlkopf m
lasagne [lə'zænjə] n Lasagne pl
lascivious [lə'sɪvɪəs] adj lüstern
laser ['leɪzəʳ] n Laser m
laser beam n Laserstrahl m
laser printer n Laserdrucker m
lash [læʃ] n (also: **eyelash**) Wimper f; (blow with whip) Peitschenhieb m ▷ vt peitschen; (rain, wind) peitschen gegen; (tie): **to ~ to** festbinden an +dat; **to ~ together** zusammenbinden
  ▸ **lash down** vt festbinden ▷ vi (rain) niederprasseln
  ▸ **lash out** vi um sich schlagen; **to ~ out at sb** auf jdn losschlagen; **to ~ out at** or **against sb** (criticize) gegen jdn wettern
lashing ['læʃɪŋ] n: **~s of** (Brit: inf) massenhaft
lass [læs] (Brit) n Mädchen nt
lasso [læ'su:] n Lasso nt ▷ vt mit dem Lasso einfangen
last [lɑ:st] adj letzte(r, s) ▷ adv (most recently) zuletzt, das letzte Mal; (finally) als Letztes ▷ vi (continue) dauern; (: in good condition) sich halten; (money, commodity) reichen; **~ week** letzte Woche; **~ night** gestern Abend; **~ but one** vorletzte(r, s); **the ~ time** das letzte Mal; **at ~** endlich; **it ~s (for) 2 hours** es dauert 2 Stunden
last-ditch ['lɑ:st'dɪtʃ] adj (attempt) allerletzte(r, s)
lasting ['lɑ:stɪŋ] adj dauerhaft
lastly ['lɑ:stlɪ] adv (finally) schließlich; (last of all) zum Schluss
last-minute ['lɑ:stmɪnɪt] adj in letzter Minute
latch [lætʃ] n Riegel m; **to be on the ~** nur eingeklinkt sein
  ▸ **latch on to** vt fus (person) sich anschließen +dat; (idea) abfahren auf +acc (inf)
latchkey ['lætʃki:] n Hausschlüssel m
latchkey child n Schlüsselkind nt
late [leɪt] adj spät; (not on time) verspätet ▷ adv spät; (behind time) zu spät; (recently): **~ of Glasgow** bis vor Kurzem in Glasgow wohnhaft; **the ~ Mr X** (deceased) der verstorbene Herr X; **in ~ May** Ende Mai; **to be (10 minutes) ~** (10 Minuten) zu spät kommen; (train etc) (10 Minuten) Verspätung haben; **to work ~** länger arbeiten; **~ in life** relativ spät (im Leben); **of ~** in letzter Zeit
latecomer ['leɪtkʌməʳ] n Nachzügler(in) m(f)
lately ['leɪtlɪ] adv in letzter Zeit
lateness ['leɪtnɪs] n (of person) Zuspätkommen nt; (of train, event) Verspätung f
latent ['leɪtnt] adj (energy) ungenutzt; (skill, ability) verborgen
later ['leɪtəʳ] adj, adv später; **~ on** nachher
lateral ['lætərəl] adj seitlich; **~ thinking** kreatives Denken nt
latest ['leɪtɪst] adj neueste(r, s) ▷ n: **at the ~** spätestens

latex ['leɪtæks] n Latex m
lathe [leɪð] n Drehbank f
lather ['lɑ:ðəʳ] n (Seifen)schaum m ▷ vt einschäumen
Latin ['lætɪn] n Latein nt; (person) Südländer(in) m(f) ▷ adj lateinisch; (temperament etc) südländisch
Latin America n Lateinamerika nt
Latin American adj lateinamerikanisch ▷ n Lateinamerikaner(in) m(f)
Latino [læ'ti:nəu] (US) adj aus Lateinamerika stammend ▷ n Latino mf, in den USA lebende(r) Lateinamerikaner(in)
latitude ['lætɪtju:d] n (Geog) Breite f; (fig: freedom) Freiheit f
latrine [lə'tri:n] n Latrine f
latter ['lætəʳ] adj (of two) letztere(r, s); (later) spätere(r, s); (second part of period) zweite(r, s); (recent) letzte(r, s) ▷ n: **the ~** der/die/das Letztere, die Letzteren
latter-day ['lætədeɪ] adj modern
latterly ['lætəlɪ] adv in letzter Zeit
lattice ['lætɪs] n Gitter nt
lattice window n Gitterfenster nt
Latvia ['lætvɪə] n Lettland nt
Latvian ['lætvɪən] adj lettisch ▷ n Lette m, Lettin f; (Ling) Lettisch nt
laudable ['lɔ:dəbl] adj lobenswert
laudatory ['lɔ:dətrɪ] adj (comments) lobend; (speech) Lob-
laugh [lɑ:f] n Lachen nt ▷ vi lachen; **(to do sth) for a ~** (etw) aus Spaß (tun)
  ▸ **laugh at** vt fus lachen über +acc
  ▸ **laugh off** vt mit einem Lachen abtun
laughable ['lɑ:fəbl] adj lächerlich, lachhaft
laughing gas ['lɑ:fɪŋ-] n Lachgas nt
laughing matter n: **this is no ~** das ist nicht zum Lachen
laughing stock n: **to be the ~ of** zum Gespött +gen werden
laughter ['lɑ:ftəʳ] n Lachen nt, Gelächter nt
launch [lɔ:ntʃ] n (of rocket, missile) Abschuss m; (of satellite) Start m; (Comm: of product) Einführung f; (: with publicity) Lancierung f; (motorboat) Barkasse f ▷ vt (ship) vom Stapel lassen; (rocket, missile) abschießen; (satellite) starten; (fig: start) beginnen mit; (Comm) auf den Markt bringen; (: with publicity) lancieren
  ▸ **launch into** vt fus (speech) vom Stapel lassen; (activity) in Angriff nehmen
  ▸ **launch out** vi: **to ~ out (into)** beginnen (mit)
launching ['lɔ:ntʃɪŋ] n (of ship) Stapellauf m; (of rocket, missile) Abschuss m; (of satellite) Start m; (fig: start) Beginn m; (Comm: of product) Einführung f; (: with publicity) Lancierung f
launching pad, launch pad n Startrampe f, Abschussrampe f
launder ['lɔ:ndəʳ] vt waschen und bügeln; (pej: money) waschen
laundrette [lɔ:n'drɛt] (Brit) n Waschsalon m
Laundromat® ['lɔ:ndrəmæt] (US) n Waschsalon m

laundry ['lɔ:ndrɪ] n Wäsche f; (dirty) (schmutzige) Wäsche; (business) Wäscherei f; (room) Waschküche f; **to do the ~** (Wäsche) waschen

laureate ['lɔ:rɪət] adj see **poet laureate**

laurel ['lɔrl] n (tree) Lorbeer(baum) m; **to rest on one's ~s** sich auf seinen Lorbeeren ausruhen

Lausanne [ləu'zæn] n Lausanne nt

lava ['lɑ:və] n Lava f

lavatory ['lævətərɪ] n Toilette f

lavatory paper n Toilettenpapier nt

lavender ['lævəndə^r] n Lavendel m

lavish ['lævɪʃ] adj großzügig; (meal) üppig; (surroundings) feudal; (wasteful) verschwenderisch ▷ vt: **to ~ sth on sb** jdn mit etw überhäufen

lavishly ['lævɪʃlɪ] adv (generously) großzügig; (sumptuously) aufwendig

law [lɔ:] n Recht nt; (a rule: also of nature, science) Gesetz nt; (professions connected with law) Rechtswesen nt; (Scol) Jura no art; **against the ~** rechtswidrig; **to study ~** Jura or Recht(swissenschaft) studieren; **to go to ~** vor Gericht gehen; **to break the ~** gegen das Gesetz verstoßen

law-abiding ['lɔ:əbaɪdɪŋ] adj gesetzestreu

law and order n Ruhe und Ordnung f

lawbreaker ['lɔ:breɪkə^r] n Rechtsbrecher(in) m(f)

law court n Gerichtshof m, Gericht nt

lawful ['lɔ:ful] adj rechtmäßig

lawfully ['lɔ:fəlɪ] adv rechtmäßig

lawless ['lɔ:lɪs] adj gesetzwidrig

Law Lord (Brit) n Mitglied des Oberhauses mit besonderem Verantwortungsbereich in Rechtsfragen

lawn [lɔ:n] n Rasen m

lawn mower n Rasenmäher m

lawn tennis n Rasentennis nt

law school (US) n juristische Hochschule f

law student n Jurastudent(in) m(f)

lawsuit ['lɔ:su:t] n Prozess m

lawyer ['lɔ:jə^r] n (Rechts)anwalt m, (Rechts)anwältin f

lax [læks] adj lax

laxative ['læksətɪv] n Abführmittel nt

laxity ['læksɪtɪ] n Laxheit f; **moral ~** lockere or laxe Moral f

lay [leɪ] (pt, pp **laid**) pt of **lie** ▷ adj (Rel: preacher etc) Laien- ▷ vt legen; (table) decken; (carpet, cable etc) verlegen; (plans) schmieden; (trap) stellen; **the ~ person** (not expert) der Laie; **to ~ facts/proposals before sb** jdm Tatsachen vorlegen/Vorschläge unterbreiten; **to ~ one's hands on sth** (fig) etw in die Finger bekommen; **to get laid** (inf!) bumsen (!)

▶ **lay aside** vt weglegen, zur Seite legen

▶ **lay by** vt beiseitelegen, auf die Seite legen

▶ **lay down** vt hinlegen; (rules, laws etc) festlegen; **to ~ down the law** Vorschriften machen; **to ~ down one's life** sein Leben geben

▶ **lay in** vt (supply) anlegen

▶ **lay into** vt fus losgehen auf +acc; (criticize) herunterputzen

▶ **lay off** vt (workers) entlassen

▶ **lay on** vt (meal) auftischen; (entertainment etc) sorgen für; (water, gas) anschließen; (paint) auftragen

▶ **lay out** vt ausbreiten; (inf: spend) ausgeben

▶ **lay up** vt (illness) außer Gefecht setzen; see also **lay by**

layabout ['leɪəbaut] (inf: pej) n Faulenzer m

lay-by ['leɪbaɪ] (Brit) n Parkbucht f

lay days npl Liegezeit f

layer ['leɪə^r] n Schicht f

layette ['leɪ'ɛt] n Babyausstattung f

layman ['leɪmən] (irreg: like **man**) n Laie m

lay-off ['leɪɔf] n Entlassung f

layout ['leɪaut] n (of garden) Anlage f; (of building) Aufteilung f; (Typ) Layout nt

laze [leɪz] vi (also: **laze about**) (herum)faulenzen

laziness ['leɪzɪnɪs] n Faulheit f

lazy ['leɪzɪ] adj faul; (movement, action) langsam, träge

LB (Canada) abbr = **Labrador**

lb abbr (= pound (weight)) britisches Pfund (0,45 kg), ≈ Pfd.

lbw abbr (Cricket: = leg before wicket) Regelverletzung beim Kricket

LC (US) n abbr (= Library of Congress) Bibliothek des US-Parlaments

L/C abbr = **letter of credit**

lc abbr (Typ: = lower case) see **case**

lcd, LCD n abbr (= liquid-crystal display) LCD nt

Ld (Brit) abbr (in titles) = **lord**

LDS n abbr (Brit: = Licentiate in Dental Surgery) ≈ Dr. med. dent. ▷ n abbr (= Latter-day Saints) Heilige pl der Letzten Tage

LEA (Brit) n abbr (= Local Education Authority) örtliche Schulbehörde

lead¹ [li:d] (pt, pp **led**) n (Sport, fig) Führung f; (clue) Spur f; (in play, film) Hauptrolle f; (for dog) Leine f; (Elec) Kabel nt ▷ vt anführen; (guide) führen; (organization, orchestra) leiten ▷ vi führen; **to be in the ~** (Sport, fig) in Führung liegen; **to take the ~** (Sport) in Führung gehen; **to ~ the way** vorangehen; **to ~ sb astray** jdn vom rechten Weg abführen; (mislead) jdn irreführen; **to ~ sb to believe that ...** jdm den Eindruck vermitteln, dass ...; **to ~ sb to do sth** jdn dazu bringen, etw zu tun

▶ **lead away** vt wegführen; (prisoner etc) abführen

▶ **lead back** vt zurückführen

▶ **lead off** vi (in conversation etc) den Anfang machen; (room, road) abgehen ▷ vt fus abgehen von

▶ **lead on** vt (tease) aufziehen

▶ **lead to** vt fus führen zu

▶ **lead up to** vt fus (events) vorangehen +dat; (in conversation) hinauswollen auf +acc

lead² [lɛd] n Blei nt; (in pencil) Mine f

leaded ['lɛdɪd] adj (window) bleiverglast; (petrol) verbleit

635

leaden ['lɛdn] *adj* (*sky, sea*) bleiern; (*movements*) bleischwer

leader ['li:də^r] *n* Führer(in) *m(f)*; (*Sport*) Erste(r) *f(m)*; (*in newspaper*) Leitartikel *m*; **the L~ of the House (of Commons/of Lords)** (*Brit*) der Führer des Unterhauses/des Oberhauses

leadership ['li:dəʃɪp] *n* Führung *f*; (*position*) Vorsitz *m*; (*quality*) Führungsqualitäten *pl*

lead-free ['lɛdfri:] (*old*) *adj* bleifrei

leading ['li:dɪŋ] *adj* führend; (*role*) Haupt-; (*first, front*) vorderste(r, s)

leading lady *n* (*Theat*) Hauptdarstellerin *f*

leading light *n* führende Persönlichkeit *f*

leading man *n* (*Theat*) Hauptdarsteller *m*

leading question *n* Suggestivfrage *f*

lead pencil [lɛd-] *n* Bleistift *m*

lead poisoning [lɛd-] *n* Bleivergiftung *f*

lead singer [li:d-] *n* Leadsänger(in) *m(f)*

lead time [li:d-] *n* (*Comm: for production*) Produktionszeit *f*; (*: for delivery*) Lieferzeit *f*

lead-up ['li:dʌp] *n*: **the ~ to sth** die Zeit vor etw *dat*

leaf [li:f] (*pl* **leaves**) *n* Blatt *nt*; (*of table*) Ausziehplatte *f*; **to turn over a new ~** einen neuen Anfang machen; **to take a ~ out of sb's book** sich *dat* von jdm eine Scheibe abschneiden

▶ **leaf through** *vt fus* durchblättern

leaflet ['li:flɪt] *n* Informationsblatt *nt*

leafy ['li:fɪ] *adj* (*tree, branch*) belaubt; (*lane, suburb*) grün

league [li:g] *n* (*of people, clubs*) Verband *m*; (*of countries*) Bund *m*; (*Football*) Liga *f*; **to be in ~ with sb** mit jdm gemeinsame Sache machen

league table *n* Tabelle *f*

leak [li:k] *n* Leck *nt*; (*in roof, pipe etc*) undichte Stelle *f*; (*piece of information*) zugespielte Information *f* ▷ *vi* (*shoes, roof, pipe*) undicht sein; (*ship*) lecken; (*liquid*) auslaufen; (*gas*) ausströmen ▷ *vt* (*information*) durchsickern lassen; **to ~ sth to sb** jdm etw zuspielen

▶ **leak out** *vi* (*liquid*) auslaufen; (*news, information*) durchsickern

leakage ['li:kɪdʒ] *n* (*of liquid*) Auslaufen *nt*; (*of gas*) Ausströmen *nt*

leaky ['li:kɪ] *adj* (*roof, container*) undicht

lean [li:n] (*pt, pp* **leaned** or **~t**) *adj* (*person*) schlank; (*meat, time*) mager ▷ *vt*: **to ~ sth on sth** etw an etw *acc* lehnen; (*rest*) etw auf etw *acc* stützen ▷ *vi* (*slope*) sich neigen; **to ~ against** sich lehnen gegen; **to ~ on sich** stützen auf +*acc*; **to ~ forward/back** sich vorbeugen/zurücklehnen; **to ~ towards** tendieren zu

▶ **lean out** *vi* sich hinauslehnen

▶ **lean over** *vi* sich vorbeugen

leaning ['li:nɪŋ] *n* Hang *m*, Neigung *f*

leant [lɛnt] *pt, pp of* **lean**

lean-to ['li:ntu:] *n* Anbau *m*

leap [li:p] (*pt, pp* **leaped** or **~t**) *n* Sprung *m*; (*in price, number etc*) sprunghafter Anstieg *m* ▷ *vi* springen; (*price, number etc*) sprunghaft (an)steigen

▶ **leap at** *vt fus* (*offer*) sich stürzen auf +*acc*; (*opportunity*) beim Schopf ergreifen

▶ **leap up** *vi* aufspringen

leapfrog ['li:pfrɔg] *n* Bockspringen *nt*

leapt [lɛpt] *pt, pp of* **leap**

leap year *n* Schaltjahr *nt*

learn [lə:n] (*pt, pp* **learned** or **~t**) *vt* lernen; (*facts*) erfahren ▷ *vi* lernen; **to ~ about** or **of sth** von etw erfahren; **to ~ about sth** (*study*) etw lernen; **to ~ that** ... (*hear, read*) erfahren, dass ...; **to ~ to do sth** etw lernen

learned ['lə:nɪd] *adj* gelehrt; (*book, paper*) wissenschaftlich

learner ['lə:nə^r] (*Brit*) *n* (*also*: **learner driver**) Fahrschüler(in) *m(f)*

learning ['lə:nɪŋ] *n* Gelehrsamkeit *f*

learnt [lə:nt] *pt, pp of* **learn**

lease [li:s] *n* Pachtvertrag *m* ▷ *vt*: **to ~ sth (to sb)** etw (an jdn) verpachten; **on ~ (to)** verpachtet (an +*acc*); **to ~ sth (from sb)** etw (von jdm) pachten

▶ **lease back** *vt* rückmieten

leaseback ['li:sbæk] *n* Verkauf und Rückmiete *pl*

leasehold ['li:shəuld] *n* Pachtbesitz *m* ▷ *adj* gepachtet

leash [li:ʃ] *n* Leine *f*

least [li:st] *adv* am wenigsten ▷ *adj*: **the ~** (+*noun*) der/die/das wenigste; (*: slightest*) der/die/das geringste; **the ~ expensive car** das billigste Auto; **at ~** mindestens; (*still, rather*) wenigstens; **you could at ~ have written** du hättest wenigstens schreiben können; **not in the ~** nicht im Geringsten; **it was the ~ I could do** das war das wenigste, was ich tun konnte

leather ['lɛðə^r] *n* Leder *nt*

leave [li:v] (*pt, pp* **left**) *vt* verlassen; (*leave behind*) zurücklassen; (*mark, stain*) hinterlassen; (*object: accidentally*) liegen lassen, stehen lassen; (*food*) übrig lassen; (*space, time etc*) lassen ▷ *vi* (*go away*) (weg)gehen; (*bus, train*) abfahren ▷ *n* Urlaub *m*; **to ~ sth to sb** (*money etc*) jdm etw hinterlassen; **to ~ sb with sth** (*impose*) jdm etw aufhalsen; (*possession*) jdm etw lassen; **they were left with nothing** ihnen blieb nichts; **to be left** übrig sein; **to be left over** (*remain*) übrig (geblieben) sein; **to ~ for** gehen/fahren nach; **to take one's ~ of sb** sich von jdm verabschieden; **on ~** auf Urlaub

▶ **leave behind** *vt* zurücklassen; (*object: accidentally*) liegen lassen, stehen lassen

▶ **leave off** *vt* (*cover, lid*) ablassen; (*heating, light*) auslassen ▷ *vi* (*inf: stop*) aufhören

▶ **leave on** *vt* (*light, heating*) anlassen

▶ **leave out** *vt* auslassen

leave of absence *n* Beurlaubung *f*

leaves [li:vz] *npl of* **leaf**

Lebanese [lɛbə'ni:z] *adj* libanesisch ▷ *n inv* Libanese *m*, Libanesin *f*

Lebanon ['lɛbənən] *n* Libanon *m*

lecherous ['lɛtʃərəs] (*pej*) *adj* lüstern

lectern ['lɛktə:n] n Rednerpult nt
lecture ['lɛktʃəʳ] n Vortrag m; (Univ) Vorlesung f ▷ vi Vorträge/Vorlesungen halten ▷ vt (scold): **to ~ sb on** or **about sth** jdm wegen etw eine Strafpredigt halten; **to give a ~ on** einen Vortrag/eine Vorlesung halten über +acc
lecture hall n Hörsaal m
lecturer ['lɛktʃərəʳ] (Brit) n Dozent(in) m(f); (speaker) Redner(in) m(f)
LED n abbr (Elec: = light-emitting diode) LED f
led [lɛd] pt, pp of **lead¹**
ledge [lɛdʒ] n (of mountain) (Fels)vorsprung m; (of window) Fensterbrett nt; (on wall) Leiste f
ledger ['lɛdʒəʳ] n (Comm) Hauptbuch nt
lee [li:] n Windschatten m; (Naut) Lee f
leech [li:tʃ] n Blutegel m; (fig) Blutsauger m
leek [li:k] n Porree m, Lauch m
leer [lɪəʳ] vi: **to ~ at sb** jdm lüsterne Blicke zuwerfen
leeward ['li:wəd] (Naut) adj (side etc) Lee- ▷ adv leewärts ▷ n: **to ~** an der Leeseite; (direction) nach der Leeseite
leeway ['li:weɪ] n (fig): **to have some ~** etwas Spielraum haben; **there's a lot of ~ to make up** ein großer Rückstand muss aufgeholt werden
left [lɛft] pt, pp of **leave** ▷ adj (remaining) übrig; (of position) links; (of direction) nach links ▷ n linke Seite f ▷ adv links; nach links; **on the ~, to the ~** links; **the L~** (Pol) die Linke
left-click ['lɛftklɪk] (Comput) vt links klicken ▷ vi links klicken auf +acc
left-hand drive ['lɛfthænd-] adj mit Linkssteuerung
left-handed [lɛft'hændɪd] adj linkshändig
left-hand side ['lɛfthænd-] n linke Seite f
leftie ['lɛftɪ] (inf) n Linke(r) f(m)
leftist ['lɛftɪst] (Pol) n Linke(r) f(m) ▷ adj linke(r, s)
left-luggage [lɛft'lʌgɪdʒ], **left-luggage office** (Brit) n Gepäckaufbewahrung f
leftovers ['lɛftəuvəz] npl Reste pl
left-wing ['lɛft'wɪŋ] adj (Pol) linke(r, s)
left-winger ['lɛft'wɪŋgəʳ] n (Pol) Linke(r) f(m)
lefty ['lɛftɪ] n = **leftie**
leg [lɛg] n Bein nt; (Culin) Keule f; (Sport) Runde f; (: of relay race) Teilstrecke f; (of journey etc) Etappe f; **to stretch one's ~s** sich dat die Beine vertreten; **to get one's ~ over** (inf) bumsen
legacy ['lɛgəsɪ] n Erbschaft f; (fig) Erbe nt
legal ['li:gl] adj (requirement) rechtlich, gesetzlich; (system) Rechts-; (allowed by law) legal, rechtlich zulässig; **to take ~ action** or **proceedings against sb** jdn verklagen
legal adviser n juristischer Berater m
legal holiday (US) n gesetzlicher Feiertag m
legality [lɪ'gælɪtɪ] n Legalität f
legalize ['li:gəlaɪz] vt legalisieren
legally ['li:gəlɪ] adv rechtlich, gesetzlich; (in accordance with the law) rechtmäßig; **~ binding** rechtsverbindlich
legal tender n gesetzliches Zahlungsmittel nt

legation [lɪ'geɪʃən] n Gesandtschaft f
legend ['lɛdʒənd] n Legende f, Sage f; (fig: person) Legende f
legendary ['lɛdʒəndərɪ] adj legendär; (very famous) berühmt
-legged [lɛgd] suff -beinig
leggings ['lɛgɪŋz] npl Leggings pl, Leggins pl
leggy ['lɛgɪ] adj langbeinig
legibility [lɛdʒɪ'bɪlɪtɪ] n Lesbarkeit f
legible ['lɛdʒəbl] adj leserlich
legibly ['lɛdʒəblɪ] adv leserlich
legion ['li:dʒən] n Legion f ▷ adj zahlreich
legionnaire [li:dʒə'nɛəʳ] n Legionär m
legionnaire's disease n Legionärskrankheit f
legislate ['lɛdʒɪsleɪt] vi Gesetze/ein Gesetz erlassen
legislation [lɛdʒɪs'leɪʃən] n Gesetzgebung f; (laws) Gesetze pl
legislative ['lɛdʒɪslətɪv] adj gesetzgebend; **~ reforms** Gesetzesreformen pl
legislator ['lɛdʒɪsleɪtəʳ] n Gesetzgeber m
legislature ['lɛdʒɪslətʃəʳ] n Legislative f
legitimacy [lɪ'dʒɪtɪməsɪ] n (validity) Berechtigung f; (legality) Rechtmäßigkeit f
legitimate [lɪ'dʒɪtɪmət] adj (reasonable) berechtigt; (excuse) begründet; (legal) rechtmäßig
legitimize [lɪ'dʒɪtɪmaɪz] vt legitimieren
legless ['lɛglɪs] (inf) adj (drunk) sternhagelvoll
legroom ['lɛgru:m] n Beinfreiheit f
Leics (Brit) abbr (Post) = Leicestershire
leisure ['lɛʒəʳ] n Freizeit f; **at ~** in Ruhe
leisure centre n Freizeitzentrum nt
leisurely ['lɛʒəlɪ] adj geruhsam
leisure suit n Freizeitanzug m
lemon ['lɛmən] n Zitrone f; (colour) Zitronengelb nt
lemonade [lɛmə'neɪd] n Limonade f
lemon cheese n = **lemon curd**
lemon curd n zähflüssiger Brotaufstrich mit Zitronengeschmack
lemon juice n Zitronensaft m
lemon squeezer n Zitronenpresse f
lemon tea n Zitronentee m
lend [lɛnd] (pt, pp lent) vt: **to ~ sth to sb** jdm etw leihen; **to ~ sb a hand (with sth)** jdm (bei etw) helfen; **it ~s itself to ...** es eignet sich für ...
lender ['lɛndəʳ] n Verleiher(in) m(f)
lending library ['lɛndɪŋ-] n Leihbücherei f
length [lɛŋθ] n Länge f; (piece) Stück nt; (amount of time) Dauer f; **the ~ of the island** (all along) die ganze Insel entlang; **2 metres in ~** 2 Meter lang; **at ~** (at last) schließlich; (for a long time) lange; **to go to great ~s to do sth** sich dat sehr viel Mühe geben, etw zu tun; **to fall full-~** lang hinfallen; **to lie full-~** in voller Länge daliegen
lengthen ['lɛŋθən] vt verlängern ▷ vi länger werden
lengthways ['lɛŋθweɪz] adv der Länge nach
lengthy ['lɛŋθɪ] adj lang
leniency ['li:nɪənsɪ] n Nachsicht f

637

lenient ['li:nɪənt] *adj* nachsichtig
leniently ['li:nɪəntlɪ] *adv* nachsichtig
lens [lɛnz] *n* (*of spectacles*) Glas *nt*; (*of camera*) Objektiv *nt*; (*of telescope*) Linse *f*
Lent [lɛnt] *n* Fastenzeit *f*
lent [lɛnt] *pt, pp of* **lend**
lentil ['lɛntɪl] *n* Linse *f*
Leo ['li:əu] *n* Löwe *m*; **to be** ~ Löwe sein
leopard ['lɛpəd] *n* Leopard *m*
leotard ['li:əta:d] *n* Gymnastikanzug *m*
leper ['lɛpəʳ] *n* Leprakranke(r) *f(m)*
leper colony *n* Leprasiedlung *f*
leprosy ['lɛprəsɪ] *n* Lepra *f*
lesbian ['lɛzbɪən] *adj* lesbisch ▷ *n* Lesbierin *f*
lesion ['li:ʒən] *n* Verletzung *f*
Lesotho [lɪ'su:tu:] *n* Lesotho *nt*
less [lɛs] *adj, pron, adv* weniger ▷ *prep:* ~ **tax/10% discount** abzüglich Steuer/10% Rabatt; ~ **than half** weniger als die Hälfte; ~ **than ever** weniger denn je; ~ **and less** immer weniger; **the** ~ **he works ...** je weniger er arbeitet ...; **the Prime Minister, no** ~ kein Geringerer als der Premierminister
lessee [lɛ'si:] *n* Pächter(in) *m(f)*
lessen ['lɛsn] *vi* nachlassen, abnehmen ▷ *vt* verringern
lesser ['lɛsəʳ] *adj* geringer; **to a** ~ **extent** in geringerem Maße
lesson ['lɛsn] *n* (*class*) Stunde *f*; (*example, warning*) Lehre *f*; **to teach sb a** ~ (*fig*) jdm eine Lektion erteilen
lessor ['lɛsɔːʳ] *n* Verpächter(in) *m(f)*
lest [lɛst] *conj* damit ... nicht
let [lɛt] (*pt, pp* ~) *vt* (*allow*) lassen; (*Brit: lease*) vermieten; **to** ~ **sb do sth** jdn etw tun lassen, jdm erlauben, etw zu tun; **to** ~ **sb know sth** jdn etw wissen lassen; ~**'s go** gehen wir!; ~ **him come** lassen Sie ihn kommen; **"to** ~**"** „zu vermieten"
▶ **let down** *vt* (*tyre etc*) die Luft herauslassen aus; (*person*) im Stich lassen; (*dress etc*) länger machen; (*hem*) auslassen; **to** ~ **one's hair down** (*fig*) aus sich herausgehen
▶ **let go** *vi* loslassen ▷ *vt* (*release*) freilassen; **to** ~ **go of** loslassen; **to** ~ **o.s. go** aus sich herausgehen; (*neglect o.s.*) sich gehen lassen
▶ **let in** *vt* hereinlassen; (*water*) durchlassen
▶ **let off** *vt* (*culprit*) laufen lassen; (*firework, bomb*) hochgehen lassen; (*gun*) abfeuern; **to** ~ **sb off sth** (*excuse*) jdm etw erlassen; **to** ~ **off steam** (*inf: fig*) sich abreagieren
▶ **let on** *vi* verraten
▶ **let out** *vt* herauslassen; (*sound*) ausstoßen; (*house, room*) vermieten
▶ **let up** *vi* (*cease*) aufhören; (*diminish*) nachlassen
letdown ['lɛtdaun] *n* Enttäuschung *f*
lethal ['li:θl] *adj* tödlich
lethargic [lɛ'θa:dʒɪk] *adj* träge, lethargisch
lethargy ['lɛθədʒɪ] *n* Trägheit *f*, Lethargie *f*
letter ['lɛtəʳ] *n* Brief *m*; (*of alphabet*) Buchstabe *m*; **small/capital** ~ Klein-/Großbuchstabe *m*
letter bomb *n* Briefbombe *f*

letter box (*Brit*) *n* Briefkasten *m*
letterhead ['lɛtəhɛd] *n* Briefkopf *m*
lettering ['lɛtərɪŋ] *n* Beschriftung *f*
letter of credit *n* Akkreditiv *nt*
letter opener *n* Brieföffner *m*
letterpress ['lɛtəprɛs] *n* Hochdruck *m*
letter-quality printer ['lɛtəkwɔlɪtɪ-] *n* Schönschreibdrucker *m*
letters patent *npl* Patent *nt*, Patenturkunde *f*
lettuce ['lɛtɪs] *n* Kopfsalat *m*
let-up ['lɛtʌp] *n* Nachlassen *nt*; **there was no** ~ es ließ nicht nach
leukaemia, (*US*) **leukemia** [lu:'ki:mɪə] *n* Leukämie *f*
level ['lɛvl] *adj* eben ▷ *n* (*on scale, of liquid*) Stand *m*; (*of lake, river*) Wasserstand *m*; (*height*) Höhe *f*; (*fig: standard*) Niveau *nt*; (*also:* **spirit level**) Wasserwaage *f* ▷ *vt* (*building*) abreißen; (*forest etc*) einebnen ▷ *vi:* **to** ~ **with sb** (*inf*) ehrlich mit jdm sein ▷ *adv:* **to draw** ~ **with** einholen; **to be** ~ **with** auf gleicher Höhe sein mit; **to do one's** ~ **best** sein Möglichstes tun; **"A"** ~**s** (*Brit*) ≈ Abitur *nt*; **"O"** ~**s** (*Brit*) ≈ mittlere Reife *f*; **on the** ~ (*fig: honest*) ehrlich, reell; **to** ~ **a gun at sb** ein Gewehr auf jdn richten; **to** ~ **an accusation at** *or* **against sb** eine Anschuldigung gegen jdn erheben; **to** ~ **a criticism at** *or* **against sb** Kritik an jdm üben
▶ **level off** *vi* (*prices etc*) sich beruhigen
▶ **level out** *vi* = **level off**
level crossing (*Brit*) *n* (beschrankter) Bahnübergang *m*
level-headed [lɛvl'hɛdɪd] *adj* (*calm*) ausgeglichen
levelling ['lɛvlɪŋ] *n* Nivellierung *f*
level playing field *n* Chancengleichheit *f*; **to compete on a** ~ unter gleichen Bedingungen antreten
lever ['li:vəʳ] *n* Hebel *m*; (*bar*) Brechstange *f*; (*fig*) Druckmittel *nt* ▷ *vt:* **to** ~ **up** hochhieven; **to** ~ **out** heraushieven
leverage ['li:vərɪdʒ] *n* Hebelkraft *f*; (*fig: influence*) Einfluss *m*
levity ['lɛvɪtɪ] *n* Leichtfertigkeit *f*
levy ['lɛvɪ] *n* (*tax*) Steuer *f*; (*charge*) Gebühr *f* ▷ *vt* erheben
lewd [lu:d] *adj* (*look etc*) lüstern; (*remark*) anzüglich
lexicographer [lɛksɪ'kɔgrəfəʳ] *n* Lexikograf(in) *m(f)*
lexicography [lɛksɪ'kɔgrəfɪ] *n* Lexikografie *f*
LGV (*Brit*) *n abbr* (= *large goods vehicle*) Lkw *m*
LI (*US*) *abbr* = **Long Island**
liability [laɪə'bɪlətɪ] *n* Belastung *f*; (*Law*) Haftung *f*; **liabilities** *npl* (*Comm*) Verbindlichkeiten *pl*
liable ['laɪəbl] *adj:* **to be** ~ **to** (*subject to*) unterliegen +*dat*; (*prone to*) anfällig sein für; ~ **for** (*responsible*) haftbar für; **to be** ~ **to do sth** dazu neigen, etw zu tun
liaise [li:'eɪz] *vi:* **to** ~ **(with)** sich in Verbindung setzen (mit)
liaison [li:'eɪzɔn] *n* Zusammenarbeit *f*; (*sexual*

relationship) Liaison *f*
liar ['laɪə^r] *n* Lügner(in) *m(f)*
libel ['laɪbl] *n* Verleumdung *f* ▷ *vt* verleumden
libellous, (US) **libelous** ['laɪbləs] *adj* verleumderisch
liberal ['lɪbərl] *adj* (Pol) liberal; (*tolerant*) aufgeschlossen; (*generous: offer*) großzügig; (*: amount etc*) reichlich ▷ *n* (*tolerant person*) liberal eingestellter Mensch *m*; (Pol): **L~** Liberale(r) *f(m)*; **~ with** großzügig mit
Liberal Democrat *n* Liberaldemokrat(in) *m(f)*
liberalize ['lɪbərəlaɪz] *vt* liberalisieren
liberally ['lɪbrəlɪ] *adv* großzügig
liberal-minded ['lɪbərl'maɪndɪd] *adj* liberal (eingestellt)
liberate ['lɪbəreɪt] *vt* befreien
liberation [lɪbə'reɪʃən] *n* Befreiung *f*
liberation theology *n* Befreiungstheologie *f*
Liberia [laɪ'bɪərɪə] *n* Liberia *nt*
Liberian [laɪ'bɪərɪən] *adj* liberianisch ▷ *n* Liberianer(in) *m(f)*
liberty ['lɪbətɪ] *n* Freiheit *f*; **to be at ~** (*criminal*) auf freiem Fuß sein; **to be at ~ to do sth** etw tun dürfen; **to take the ~ of doing sth** sich *dat* erlauben, etw zu tun
libido [lɪ'biːdəʊ] *n* Libido *f*
Libra ['liːbrə] *n* Waage *f*; **to be ~** Waage sein
librarian [laɪ'brɛərɪən] *n* Bibliothekar(in) *m(f)*
library ['laɪbrərɪ] *n* Bibliothek *f*; (*institution*) Bücherei *f*
library book *n* Buch *nt* aus der Bücherei
libretto [lɪ'brɛtəʊ] *n* Libretto *nt*
Libya ['lɪbɪə] *n* Libyen *nt*
Libyan ['lɪbɪən] *adj* libysch ▷ *n* Libyer(in) *m(f)*
lice [laɪs] *npl of* **louse**
licence, (US) **license** ['laɪsns] *n* (*document*) Genehmigung *f*; (*also*: **driving licence**) Führerschein *m*; (Comm) Lizenz *f*; (*excessive freedom*) Zügellosigkeit *f*; **to get a TV ~** ≈ Fernsehgebühren bezahlen; **under ~** (Comm) in Lizenz
license ['laɪsns] *n* (US) = **licence** ▷ *vt* (*person, organization*) eine Lizenz vergeben an +*acc*; (*activity*) eine Genehmigung erteilen für
licensed ['laɪsnst] *adj*: **the car is ~** die Kfz-Steuer für das Auto ist bezahlt; **~ hotel/restaurant** Hotel/Restaurant mit Schankerlaubnis
licensee [laɪsən'siː] *n* (*of bar*) Inhaber(in) *m(f)* einer Schankerlaubnis
license plate (US) *n* Nummernschild *nt*
licensing hours ['laɪsnsɪŋ-] (Brit) *npl* Ausschankzeiten *pl*
licentious [laɪ'sɛnʃəs] *adj* ausschweifend, zügellos
lichen ['laɪkən] *n* Flechte *f*
lick [lɪk] *vt* lecken; (*stamp etc*) lecken an +*dat*; (*inf: defeat*) in die Pfanne hauen ▷ *n* Lecken *nt*; **to ~ one's lips** sich *dat* die Lippen lecken; (*fig*) sich *dat* die Finger lecken; **a ~ of paint** ein Anstrich *m*
licorice ['lɪkərɪs] (US) *n* = **liquorice**
lid [lɪd] *n* Deckel *m*; (*eyelid*) Lid *nt*; **to take the ~**

off sth (*fig*) etw enthüllen *or* aufdecken
lido ['laɪdəʊ] (Brit) *n* Freibad *nt*
lie¹ [laɪ] (*pt, pp* **~d**) *vi* lügen ▷ *n* Lüge *f*; **to tell ~s** lügen
lie² [laɪ] (*pt* **lay**, *pp* **lain**) *vi* (*lit, fig*) liegen; **to ~ low** (*fig*) untertauchen
  ▶ **lie about** *vi* herumliegen
  ▶ **lie around** *vi* = **lie about**
  ▶ **lie back** *vi* sich zurücklehnen; (*fig: accept the inevitable*) sich fügen
  ▶ **lie down** *vi* sich hinlegen
  ▶ **lie up** *vi* (*hide*) untertauchen; (*rest*) im Bett bleiben
Liechtenstein ['lɪktənstaɪn] *n* Liechtenstein *nt*
lie detector *n* Lügendetektor *m*
lie-down ['laɪdaʊn] (Brit) *n*: **to have a ~** ein Schläfchen machen
lie-in ['laɪɪn] (Brit) *n*: **to have a ~** (sich) ausschlafen
lieu [luː]: **in ~ of** *prep* anstelle von, anstatt +*gen*
Lieut. *abbr* (Mil: = *lieutenant*) Lt.
lieutenant [lɛf'tɛnənt, (US) luː'tɛnənt] *n* Leutnant *m*
lieutenant colonel *n* Oberstleutnant *m*
life [laɪf] (*pl* **lives**) *n* Leben *nt*; (*of machine etc*) Lebensdauer *f*; **true to ~** lebensecht; **painted from ~** aus dem Leben gegriffen; **to be sent to prison for ~** zu einer lebenslänglichen Freiheitsstrafe verurteilt werden; **such is ~** so ist das Leben; **to come to ~** (*fig: person*) munter werden; (*: party etc*) in Schwung kommen
life annuity *n* Leibrente *f*
life assurance (Brit) *n* = **life insurance**
life belt (Brit) *n* Rettungsgürtel *m*
lifeblood ['laɪfblʌd] *n* (*fig*) Lebensnerv *m*
lifeboat ['laɪfbəʊt] *n* Rettungsboot *nt*
life buoy *n* Rettungsring *m*
life expectancy *n* Lebenserwartung *f*
lifeguard ['laɪfɡɑːd] *n* (*at beach*) Rettungsschwimmer(in) *m(f)*; (*at swimming pool*) Bademeister(in) *m(f)*
life imprisonment *n* lebenslängliche Freiheitsstrafe *f*
life insurance *n* Lebensversicherung *f*
life jacket *n* Schwimmweste *f*
lifeless ['laɪflɪs] *adj* leblos; (*fig: person, party etc*) langweilig
lifelike ['laɪflaɪk] *adj* lebensecht; (*painting*) naturgetreu
lifeline ['laɪflaɪn] *n* (*fig*) Rettungsanker *m*; (*rope*) Rettungsleine *f*
lifelong ['laɪflɒŋ] *adj* lebenslang
life preserver (US) *n* = **life belt**; **life jacket**
lifer ['laɪfə^r] (*inf*) *n* Lebenslängliche(r) *f(m)*
life raft *n* Rettungsfloß *nt*
life-saver ['laɪfseɪvə^r] *n* Lebensretter(in) *m(f)*
life sciences *npl* Biowissenschaften *pl*
life sentence *n* lebenslängliche Freiheitsstrafe *f*
life-size ['laɪfsaɪz], **life-sized** ['laɪfsaɪzd] *adj* in Lebensgröße
life span *n* Lebensdauer *f*; (*of person*) Lebenszeit *f*

life style ['laɪfstaɪl] n Lebensstil m
life-support system ['laɪfsəpɔːt-] n (Med) Lebenserhaltungssystem nt
lifetime ['laɪftaɪm] n Lebenszeit f; (of thing) Lebensdauer f; (of parliament) Legislaturperiode f; **in my** ~ während meines Lebens; **the chance of a** ~ eine einmalige Chance
lift [lɪft] vt (raise) heben; (end: ban etc) aufheben; (plagiarize) abschreiben; (inf: steal) mitgehen lassen, klauen ▷ vi (fog) sich auflösen ▷ n (Brit) Aufzug m, Fahrstuhl m; **to take the** ~ mit dem Aufzug or Fahrstuhl fahren; **to give sb a** ~ (Brit) jdn (im Auto) mitnehmen
▶ **lift off** vi abheben
▶ **lift up** vt hochheben
liftoff ['lɪftɔf] n Abheben nt
ligament ['lɪgəmənt] n (Anat) Band nt
light [laɪt] (pt, pp **lit**) n Licht nt ▷ vt (candle, cigarette, fire) anzünden; (room) beleuchten ▷ adj leicht; (pale, bright) hell; (traffic etc) gering; (music) Unterhaltungs- ▷ adv: **to travel** ~ mit leichtem Gepäck reisen; **lights** npl (Aut: also: **traffic lights**) Ampel f; **the** ~**s** (of car) die Beleuchtung; **have you got a** ~? haben Sie Feuer?; **to turn the** ~ **on/off** das Licht an-/ ausmachen; **to come to** ~ ans Tageslicht kommen; **to cast** or **shed** or **throw** ~ **on** (fig) Licht bringen in +acc; **in the** ~ **of** angesichts +gen; **to make** ~ **of sth** (fig) etw auf die leichte Schulter nehmen; ~ **blue/green** etc hellblau/-grün etc
▶ **light up** vi (face) sich erhellen ▷ vt (illuminate) beleuchten, erhellen
light bulb n Glühbirne f
lighten ['laɪtn] vt (make less heavy) leichter machen ▷ vi (become less dark) sich aufhellen
lighter ['laɪtəʳ] n (also: **cigarette lighter**) Feuerzeug nt
light-fingered [laɪt'fɪŋgəd] (inf) adj langfingerig
light-headed [laɪt'hɛdɪd] adj (dizzy) benommen; (excited) ausgelassen
light-hearted [laɪt'hɑːtɪd] adj unbeschwert; (question, remark etc) scherzhaft
lighthouse ['laɪthaus] n Leuchtturm m
lighting ['laɪtɪŋ] n Beleuchtung f
lighting-up time [laɪtɪŋ'ʌp-] n Zeitpunkt, zu dem die Fahrzeugbeleuchtung eingeschaltet werden muss
lightly ['laɪtlɪ] adv leicht; (not seriously) leichthin; **to get off** ~ glimpflich davonkommen
light meter n Belichtungsmesser m
lightness ['laɪtnɪs] n (in weight) Leichtigkeit f
lightning ['laɪtnɪŋ] n Blitz m ▷ adj (attack etc) Blitz-; **with** ~ **speed** blitzschnell
lightning conductor n Blitzableiter m
lightning rod (US) n = **lightning conductor**
light pen n Lichtstift m, Lichtgriffel m
lightship ['laɪtʃɪp] n Feuerschiff nt
lightweight ['laɪtweɪt] adj leicht ▷ n (Boxing) Leichtgewichtler m
light year n Lichtjahr nt
like [laɪk] vt mögen ▷ prep wie; (such as)

wie (zum Beispiel) ▷ n: **and the** ~ und dergleichen; **I would** ~, **I'd** ~ ich hätte or möchte gern; **would you** ~ **a coffee?** möchten Sie einen Kaffee?; **if you** ~ wenn Sie wollen; **to be/look** ~ **sb/sth** jdm/etw ähnlich sein/ sehen; **something** ~ **that** so etwas Ähnliches; **what does it look/taste/sound** ~? wie sieht es aus/schmeckt es/hört es sich an?; **what's he/the weather** ~? wie ist er/das Wetter?; **I feel** ~ **a drink** ich möchte gerne etwas trinken; **there's nothing** ~ ... es geht nichts über +acc; **that's just** ~ **him** das sieht ihm ähnlich; **do it** ~ **this** mach es so; **it is nothing** ~ (+noun) es ist ganz anders als; (+adj) es ist alles andere als; **it is nothing** ~ **as** ... es ist bei Weitem nicht so ...; **his** ~**s and dislikes** seine Vorlieben und Abneigungen
likeable ['laɪkəbl] adj sympathisch
likelihood ['laɪklɪhud] n Wahrscheinlichkeit f; **there is every** ~ **that** ... es ist sehr wahrscheinlich, dass ...; **in all** ~ aller Wahrscheinlichkeit nach
likely ['laɪklɪ] adj wahrscheinlich; **to be** ~ **to do sth** wahrscheinlich etw tun; **not** ~! (inf) wohl kaum!
like-minded ['laɪk'maɪndɪd] adj gleich gesinnt
liken ['laɪkən] vt: **to** ~ **sth to sth** etw mit etw vergleichen
likeness ['laɪknɪs] n Ähnlichkeit f; **that's a good** ~ (photo, portrait) das ist ein gutes Bild von ihm/ihr etc
likewise ['laɪkwaɪz] adv ebenso; **to do** ~ das Gleiche tun
liking ['laɪkɪŋ] n: ~ **(for)** (person) Zuneigung f (zu); (thing) Vorliebe f (für); **to be to sb's** ~ nach jds Geschmack sein; **to take a** ~ **to sb** an jdm Gefallen finden
lilac ['laɪlək] n (Bot) Flieder m ▷ adj fliederfarben, (zart)lila
Lilo® ['laɪləu] n Luftmatratze f
lilt [lɪlt] n singender Tonfall m
lilting ['lɪltɪŋ] adj singend
lily ['lɪlɪ] n Lilie f
lily of the valley n Maiglöckchen nt
Lima ['liːmə] n Lima nt
limb [lɪm] n Glied nt; (of tree) Ast m; **to be out on a** ~ (fig) (ganz) allein (da)stehen
limber up ['lɪmbəʳ-] vi Lockerungsübungen machen
limbo ['lɪmbəu] n: **to be in** ~ (fig: plans etc) in der Schwebe sein; (: person) in der Luft hängen (inf)
lime [laɪm] n (fruit) Limone f; (tree) Linde f; (also: **lime juice**) Limonensaft m; (for soil) Kalk m; (rock) Kalkstein m
limelight ['laɪmlaɪt] n: **to be in the** ~ im Rampenlicht stehen
limerick ['lɪmərɪk] n Limerick m
limestone ['laɪmstəun] n Kalkstein m
limit ['lɪmɪt] n Grenze f; (restriction) Beschränkung f ▷ vt begrenzen, einschränken; **within** ~**s** innerhalb gewisser Grenzen

limitation [lɪmɪ'teɪʃən] n Einschränkung f;
limitations npl (shortcomings) Grenzen pl
limited ['lɪmɪtɪd] adj begrenzt, beschränkt; **to
be ~ to** beschränkt sein auf +acc
limited edition n beschränkte Ausgabe f
limited company, limited liability company
(Brit) n ≈ Gesellschaft f mit beschränkter
Haftung
limitless ['lɪmɪtlɪs] adj grenzenlos
limousine ['lɪməziːn] n Limousine f
limp [lɪmp] adj schlaff; (material etc) weich ▷ vi
hinken ▷ n: **to have a ~** hinken
limpet ['lɪmpɪt] n Napfschnecke f
limpid ['lɪmpɪd] adj klar
limply ['lɪmplɪ] adv schlaff
linchpin ['lɪntʃpɪn] n (fig) wichtigste Stütze f
Lincs [lɪŋks] (Brit) abbr (Post) = Lincolnshire
line [laɪn] n Linie f; (written, printed) Zeile f;
(wrinkle) Falte f; (row: of people) Schlange f;
(: of things) Reihe f; (for fishing, washing) Leine
f; (wire, Tel) Leitung f; (railway track) Gleise pl;
(fig: attitude) Standpunkt m; (: business) Branche
f; (Comm: of product(s)) Art f ▷ vt (road) säumen;
(container) auskleiden; (clothing) füttern; **hold
the ~ please!** (Tel) bleiben Sie am Apparat!;
to cut in ~ (US) sich vordrängeln; **in ~** in
einer Reihe; **in ~ with** im Einklang mit, in
Übereinstimmung mit; **to be in ~ for sth** mit
etw an der Reihe sein; **to bring sth into ~
with sth** etw auf die gleiche Linie wie etw acc
bringen; **on the right ~s** auf dem richtigen
Weg; **I draw the ~ at that** da mache ich nicht
mehr mit; **to ~ sth with sth** etw mit etw
auskleiden; (drawers etc) etw mit etw auslegen;
to ~ the streets die Straßen säumen
▶ **line up** vi sich aufstellen ▷ vt (in a row)
aufstellen; (engage) verpflichten; (prepare)
arrangieren; **to have sb ~d up** jdn
verpflichtet haben; **to have sth ~d up** etw
geplant haben
linear ['lɪnɪəʳ] adj linear; (shape, form) gerade
lined [laɪnd] adj (face) faltig; (paper) liniert;
(skirt, jacket) gefüttert
line editing n (Comput) zeilenweise
Aufbereitung f
line feed n (Comput) Zeilenvorschub m
lineman ['laɪnmən] (US: irreg: like **man**) n
(Football) Stürmer m
linen ['lɪnɪn] n (cloth) Leinen nt; (tablecloths,
sheets etc) Wäsche f
line printer n (Comput) Zeilendrucker m
liner ['laɪnəʳ] n (ship) Passagierschiff nt;
(also: **bin liner**) Müllbeutel m
linesman ['laɪnzmən] (irreg: like **man**) n (Sport)
Linienrichter m
line-up ['laɪnʌp] n (US: queue) Schlange f; (Sport)
Aufstellung f; (at concert etc) Künstleraufgebot
nt; (identity parade) Gegenüberstellung f
linger ['lɪŋgəʳ] vi (smell) sich halten; (tradition
etc) fortbestehen; (person) sich aufhalten
lingerie ['lænʒəriː] n (Damen)unterwäsche f
lingering ['lɪŋgərɪŋ] adj bleibend
lingo ['lɪŋgəʊ] (pl **~es**) (inf) n Sprache f

linguist ['lɪŋgwɪst] n (person who speaks several
languages) Sprachkundige(r) f(m)
linguistic [lɪŋ'gwɪstɪk] adj sprachlich
linguistics [lɪŋ'gwɪstɪks] n
Sprachwissenschaft f
liniment ['lɪnɪmənt] n Einreibemittel nt
lining ['laɪnɪŋ] n (cloth) Futter nt; (Anat: of
stomach) Magenschleimhaut f; (Tech)
Auskleidung f; (of brakes) (Brems)belag m
link [lɪŋk] n Verbindung f, Beziehung f;
(communications link) Verbindung; (of a chain)
Glied nt; (Comput) Link m ▷ vi (Comput): **to
~ to a site** einen Link zu einer Website
haben ▷ vt (join) verbinden; (Comput) per Link
verbinden; **links** npl (Golf) Golfplatz m; **rail ~**
Bahnverbindung f
▶ **link up** vt verbinden ▷ vi verbunden werden
linkup ['lɪŋkʌp] n Verbindung f; (of spaceships)
Koppelung f
lino ['laɪnəʊ] n = **linoleum**
linoleum [lɪ'nəʊlɪəm] n Linoleum nt
linseed oil ['lɪnsiːd-] n Leinöl nt
lint [lɪnt] n Mull m
lintel ['lɪntl] n (Archit) Sturz m
lion ['laɪən] n Löwe m
lion cub n Löwenjunge(s) nt
lioness ['laɪənɪs] n Löwin f
lip [lɪp] n (Anat) Lippe f; (of cup etc) Rand m;
(inf: insolence) Frechheiten pl
liposuction ['lɪpəʊsʌkʃən] n Liposuktion f
lip-read ['lɪpriːd] vi von den Lippen ablesen
lip salve n Fettstift m
lip service (pej) n: **to pay ~ to sth** ein
Lippenbekenntnis nt zu etw ablegen
lipstick ['lɪpstɪk] n Lippenstift m
liquefy ['lɪkwɪfaɪ] vt verflüssigen ▷ vi sich
verflüssigen
liqueur [lɪ'kjʊəʳ] n Likör m
liquid ['lɪkwɪd] adj flüssig ▷ n Flüssigkeit f
liquid assets npl flüssige Vermögenswerte pl
liquidate ['lɪkwɪdeɪt] vt liquidieren
liquidation [lɪkwɪ'deɪʃən] n Liquidation f
liquidation sale (US) n Verkauf m wegen
Geschäftsaufgabe
liquidator ['lɪkwɪdeɪtəʳ] n Liquidator m
liquid-crystal display ['lɪkwɪd'krɪstl-] n
Flüssigkristallanzeige f
liquidity [lɪ'kwɪdɪtɪ] n Liquidität f
liquidize ['lɪkwɪdaɪz] vt (im Mixer) pürieren
liquidizer ['lɪkwɪdaɪzəʳ] n Mixer m
liquor ['lɪkəʳ] n Spirituosen pl, Alkohol m; **hard
~** harte Drinks pl
liquorice ['lɪkərɪs] (Brit) n Lakritze f
liquor store (US) n Spirituosengeschäft nt
Lisbon ['lɪzbən] n Lissabon nt
lisp [lɪsp] n Lispeln nt ▷ vi lispeln
list [lɪst] n Liste f ▷ vt aufführen; (Comput)
auflisten; (write down) aufschreiben ▷ vi (ship)
Schlagseite haben
listed building ['lɪstɪd-] (Brit) n unter
Denkmalschutz stehendes Gebäude nt
listed company n börsennotierte Firma f
listen ['lɪsn] vi hören; **to ~ (out) for** horchen

I

auf +*acc*; **to ~ to sb** jdm zuhören; **to ~ to sth** etw hören; **~! hör zu!**

listener ['lɪsnə^r] *n* Zuhörer(in) *m(f)*; (*Radio*) Hörer(in) *m(f)*

listeria [lɪs'tɪərɪə] *n* Listeriose *f*

listing ['lɪstɪŋ] *n* Auflistung *f*; (*entry*) Eintrag *m*

listless ['lɪstlɪs] *adj* lustlos

listlessly ['lɪstlɪslɪ] *adv* lustlos

list price *n* Listenpreis *m*

lit [lɪt] *pt, pp of* **light**

litany ['lɪtənɪ] *n* Litanei *f*

liter ['liːtə^r] (*US*) *n* = **litre**

literacy ['lɪtərəsɪ] *n* die Fähigkeit, lesen und schreiben zu können

literacy campaign *n* Kampagne *f* gegen das Analphabetentum

literal ['lɪtərəl] *adj* wörtlich, eigentlich; (*translation*) (wort)wörtlich

literally ['lɪtrəlɪ] *adv* buchstäblich

literary ['lɪtərərɪ] *adj* literarisch

literate ['lɪtərət] *adj* (*educated*) gebildet; **to be ~** lesen und schreiben können

literature ['lɪtrɪtʃə^r] *n* Literatur *f*; (*printed information*) Informationsmaterial *nt*

lithe [laɪð] *adj* gelenkig; (*animal*) geschmeidig

lithography [lɪ'θɒgrəfɪ] *n* Lithografie *f*

Lithuania [lɪθ ju'eɪnɪə] *n* Litauen *nt*

Lithuanian [lɪθ ju'eɪnɪən] *adj* litauisch ▷ *n* Litauer(in) *m(f)*; (*Ling*) Litauisch *nt*

litigation [lɪtɪ'geɪʃən] *n* Prozess *m*

litmus paper ['lɪtməs-] *n* Lackmuspapier *nt*

litre, (US) liter ['liːtə^r] *n* Liter *m or nt*

litter ['lɪtə^r] *n* (*rubbish*) Abfall *m*; (*young animals*) Wurf *m*

litter bin (*Brit*) *n* Abfalleimer *m*

litterbug ['lɪtəbʌg] *n* Dreckspatz *m*

littered ['lɪtəd] *adj*: **~ with** (*scattered*) übersät mit

litter lout *n* Dreckspatz *m*

little ['lɪtl] *adj* klein; (*short*) kurz ▷ *adv* wenig; **a ~** ein wenig, ein bisschen; **a ~ bit** ein kleines bisschen; **to have ~ time/money** wenig Zeit/Geld haben; **~ by little** nach und nach

little finger *n* kleiner Finger *m*

little-known ['lɪtl'nəun] *adj* wenig bekannt

liturgy ['lɪtədʒɪ] *n* Liturgie *f*

live [*vi* lɪv, *adj* laɪv] *vi* leben; (*in house, town*) wohnen ▷ *adj* lebend; (*TV, Radio*) live; (*performance, pictures etc*) Live-; (*Elec*) Strom führend; (*bullet, bomb etc*) scharf; **to ~ with sb** mit jdm zusammenleben

▶ **live down** *vt* hinwegkommen über +*acc*

▶ **live for** *vt* leben für

▶ **live in** *vi* (*student/servant*) im Wohnheim/Haus wohnen

▶ **live off** *vt fus* leben von; (*parents etc*) auf Kosten +*gen* leben

▶ **live on** *vt fus* leben von

▶ **live out** *vi* (*Brit: student/servant*) außerhalb (des Wohnheims/Hauses) wohnen ▷ *vt*: **to ~ out one's days** *or* **life** sein Leben verbringen

▶ **live together** *vi* zusammenleben

▶ **live up** *vt*: **to ~ it up** einen draufmachen (*inf*)

▶ **live up to** *vt fus* erfüllen, entsprechen +*dat*

live-in ['lɪvɪn] *adj* (*cook, maid*) im Haus wohnend; **her ~ lover** ihr Freund, der bei ihr wohnt

livelihood ['laɪvlɪhud] *n* Lebensunterhalt *m*

liveliness ['laɪvlɪnɪs] *n* (*see adj*) Lebhaftigkeit *f*; Lebendigkeit *f*

lively ['laɪvlɪ] *adj* lebhaft; (*place, event, book etc*) lebendig

liven up ['laɪvn-] *vt* beleben, Leben bringen in +*acc*; (*person*) aufmuntern ▷ *vi* (*person*) aufleben; (*discussion, evening etc*) in Schwung kommen

liver ['lɪvə^r] *n* (*Anat, Culin*) Leber *f*

liverish ['lɪvərɪʃ] *adj*: **to be ~** sich unwohl fühlen

Liverpudlian [lɪvə'pʌdliən] *adj* Liverpooler ▷ *n* Liverpooler(in) *m(f)*

livery ['lɪvərɪ] *n* Livree *f*

lives [laɪvz] *npl of* **life**

livestock ['laɪvstɒk] *n* Vieh *nt*

live wire (*inf*) *n* (*person*) Energiebündel *nt*

livid ['lɪvɪd] *adj* (*colour*) bleifarben; (*inf: furious*) fuchsteufelswild

living ['lɪvɪŋ] *adj* lebend ▷ *n*: **to earn** *or* **make a ~** sich *dat* seinen Lebensunterhalt verdienen; **within ~ memory** seit Menschengedenken; **the cost of ~** die Lebenshaltungskosten *pl*

living conditions *npl* Wohnverhältnisse *pl*

living expenses *npl* Lebenshaltungskosten *pl*

living room *n* Wohnzimmer *nt*

living standards *npl* Lebensstandard *m*

living wage *n* ausreichender Lohn *m*

lizard ['lɪzəd] *n* Eidechse *f*

llama ['lɑːmə] *n* Lama *nt*

LLB *n abbr* (= *Bachelor of Laws*) akademischer Grad für Juristen

LLD *n abbr* (= *Doctor of Laws*) ≈ Dr. jur.

LMT (*US*) *abbr* (= *Local Mean Time*) Ortszeit

load [ləud] *n* Last *f*; (*of vehicle*) Ladung *f*; (*weight, Elec*) Belastung *f* ▷ *vt* (*also*: **load up**) beladen; (*gun, program, data*) laden; **that's a ~ of rubbish** (*inf*) das ist alles Blödsinn; **~s of, a ~ of** (*fig*) jede Menge; **to ~ a camera** einen Film einlegen

loaded ['ləudɪd] *adj* (*inf: rich*) steinreich; (*dice*) präpariert; (*vehicle*): **to be ~ with** beladen sein mit; **a ~ question** eine Fangfrage

loading bay ['ləudɪŋ-] *n* Ladeplatz *m*

loaf [ləuf] (*pl* **loaves**) *n* Brot *nt*, Laib *m* ▷ *vi* (*also*: **loaf about, loaf around**) faulenzen; **use your ~!** (*inf*) streng deinen Grips an!

loam [ləum] *n* Lehmerde *f*

loan [ləun] *n* Darlehen *nt* ▷ *vt*: **to ~ sth to sb** jdm etw leihen; **on ~** geliehen

loan account *n* Darlehenskonto *nt*

loan capital *n* Anleihekapital *nt*

loan shark (*inf*) *n* Kredithai *m*

loath [ləuθ] *adj*: **to be ~ to do sth** etw ungern tun

loathe [ləuð] *vt* verabscheuen

loathing ['ləuðɪŋ] *n* Abscheu *m*

loathsome ['ləuðsəm] *adj* abscheulich

loaves [ləuvz] *npl of* **loaf**
lob [lɔb] *vt* (*ball*) lobben
lobby ['lɔbɪ] *n* (*of building*) Eingangshalle *f*;
(*Pol: pressure group*) Interessenverband *m* ▷ *vt*
Einfluss nehmen auf +*acc*
lobbyist ['lɔbɪɪst] *n* Lobbyist(in) *m(f)*
lobe [ləub] *n* Ohrläppchen *nt*
lobster ['lɔbstər] *n* Hummer *m*
lobster pot *n* Hummer(fang)korb *m*
local ['ləukl] *adj* örtlich; (*council*) Stadt-,
Gemeinde-; (*paper*) Lokal- ▷ *n* (*pub*)
Stammkneipe *f*; **the locals** *npl* (*local inhabitants*)
die Einheimischen *pl*
local anaesthetic *n* örtliche Betäubung *f*
local authority *n* Gemeindeverwaltung *f*,
Stadtverwaltung *f*
local call *n* Ortsgespräch *nt*
local government *n* Kommunalverwaltung *f*
locality [ləu'kælɪtɪ] *n* Gegend *f*
localize ['ləukəlaɪz] *vt* lokalisieren
locally ['ləukəlɪ] *adv* am Ort
locate [ləu'keɪt] *vt* (*find*) ausfindig machen; **to
be ~d in** sich befinden in +*dat*
location [ləu'keɪʃən] *n* Ort *m*; (*position*) Lage *f*;
(*Cine*) Drehort *m*; **he's on ~ in Mexico** er ist bei
Außenaufnahmen in Mexiko; **to be filmed
on ~** als Außenaufnahme gedreht werden
loch [lɔx] (*Scot*) *n* See *m*
lock [lɔk] *n* (*of door etc*) Schloss *nt*; (*on canal*)
Schleuse *f*; (*also:* **lock of hair**) Locke *f* ▷ *vt* (*door
etc*) abschließen; (*steering wheel*) sperren;
(*Comput: keyboard*) verriegeln ▷ *vi* (*door etc*) sich
abschließen lassen; (*wheels, mechanism etc*)
blockieren; **on full ~** (*Aut*) voll eingeschlagen;
~, stock and barrel mit allem Drum und
Dran; **his jaw ~ed** er hatte Mundsperre
▶ **lock away** *vt* wegschließen; (*criminal*)
einsperren
▶ **lock in** *vt* einschließen
▶ **lock out** *vt* aussperren
▶ **lock up** *vt* (*criminal etc*) einsperren; (*house*)
abschließen ▷ *vi* abschließen
locker ['lɔkər] *n* Schließfach *nt*
locker room *n* Umkleideraum *m*
locket ['lɔkɪt] *n* Medaillon *nt*
lockjaw ['lɔkdʒɔ:] *n* Wundstarrkrampf *m*
lockout ['lɔkaut] *n* Aussperrung *f*
locksmith ['lɔksmɪθ] *n* Schlosser *m*
lockup ['lɔkʌp] *n* (*US: inf: jail*) Gefängnis *nt*;
(*also:* **lock-up garage**) Garage *f*
locomotive [ləukə'məutɪv] *n* Lokomotive *f*
locum ['ləukəm] *n* (*Med*) Vertreter(in) *m(f)*
locust ['ləukəst] *n* Heuschrecke *f*
lodge [lɔdʒ] *n* Pförtnerhaus *nt*; (*also:* **hunting
lodge**) Hütte *f*; (*Freemasonry*) Loge *f* ▷ *vt*
(*complaint, protest etc*) einlegen ▷ *vi* (*bullet*)
stecken bleiben; (*person*): **to ~ (with)** zur
Untermiete wohnen (bei)
lodger ['lɔdʒər] *n* Untermieter(in) *m(f)*
lodging ['lɔdʒɪŋ] *n* Unterkunft *f*
lodging house *n* Pension *f*
lodgings ['lɔdʒɪŋz] *npl* möbliertes Zimmer *nt*;
(*several rooms*) Wohnung *f*

loft [lɔft] *n* Boden *m*, Speicher *m*
lofty ['lɔftɪ] *adj* (*noble*) hoch(fliegend); (*self-
important*) hochmütig; (*high*) hoch
log [lɔg] *n* (*of wood*) Holzblock *m*, Holzklotz *m*;
(*written account*) Log *nt* ▷ *n abbr* (*Math*: = *logarithm*)
log ▷ *vt* (ins Logbuch) eintragen
▶ **log in** *vi* (*Comput*) sich anmelden
▶ **log off** *vi* (*Comput*) sich abmelden
▶ **log on** *vi* (*Comput*) = **log in**
▶ **log out** *vi* (*Comput*) = **log off**
logarithm ['lɔgərɪðm] *n* Logarithmus *m*
logbook ['lɔgbuk] *n* (*Naut*) Logbuch *nt*; (*Aviat*)
Bordbuch *nt*; (*of car*) Kraftfahrzeugbrief *m*; (*of
lorry driver*) Fahrtenbuch *nt*; (*of events*) Tagebuch
nt; (*of movement of goods etc*) Dienstbuch *nt*
log fire *n* Holzfeuer *nt*
logger ['lɔgər] *n* (*lumberjack*) Holzfäller *m*
loggerheads ['lɔgəhɛdz] *npl*: **to be at ~** Streit
haben
logic ['lɔdʒɪk] *n* Logik *f*
logical ['lɔdʒɪkl] *adj* logisch
logically ['lɔdʒɪkəlɪ] *adv* logisch; (*reasonably*)
logischerweise
login ['lɔgɪn] *n* (*Comput*) Log-in *nt*, Ammeldung *f*
logistics [lɔ'dʒɪstɪks] *n* Logistik *f*
log jam *n* (*fig*) Blockierung *f*; **to break the ~**
freie Bahn schaffen
logo ['ləugəu] *n* Logo *nt*
loin [lɔɪn] *n* Lende *f*
loincloth ['lɔɪnklɔθ] *n* Lendenschurz *m*
loiter ['lɔɪtər] *vi* sich aufhalten
lol *abbr* (*Internet, Tel*: = *laugh out load*) lol (*lautes
Lachen*)
loll [lɔl] *vi* (*also:* **loll about**: *person*)
herumhängen; (*head*) herunterhängen;
(*tongue*) heraushängen
lollipop ['lɔlɪpɔp] *n* Lutscher *m*
lollipop lady (*Brit*) *n* ≈ Schülerlotsin *f*
lollipop man (*Brit*) *n* ≈ Schülerlotse *m*; *siehe
Info-Artikel*

LOLLIPOP MAN/LADY

Lollipop man/lady heißen in Großbritannien
die Männer bzw. Frauen, die mithilfe
eines runden Stoppschildes den Verkehr
anhalten, damit Schulkinder die Straße
gefahrlos überqueren können. Der Name
bezieht sich auf die Form des Schildes, die
an einen Lutscher erinnert.

lollop ['lɔləp] *vi* zockeln
lolly ['lɔlɪ] (*inf*) *n* (*lollipop*) Lutscher *m*; (*money*)
Mäuse *pl*
London ['lʌndən] *n* London *nt*
Londoner ['lʌndənər] *n* Londoner(in) *m(f)*
lone [ləun] *adj* einzeln, einsam; (*only*) einzig
loneliness ['ləunlɪnɪs] *n* Einsamkeit *f*
lonely ['ləunlɪ] *adj* einsam
lonely hearts *adj*: **~ ad** Kontaktanzeige *f*; **the ~
column** die Kontaktanzeigen *pl*
lone parent *n* Alleinerziehende(r) *f(m)*
loner ['ləunər] *n* Einzelgänger(in) *m(f)*

643

long [lɔŋ] *adj* lang ▷ *adv* lang(e) ▷ *vi*: **to ~ for sth** sich nach etw sehnen; **in the ~ run** auf die Dauer; **how ~ is the lesson?** wie lange dauert die Stunde?; **6 metres/months ~** 6 Meter/Monate lang; **so** *or* **as ~ as** *(on condition that)* solange; *(while)* während; **don't be ~!** bleib nicht so lange!; **all night ~** die ganze Nacht; **he no ~er comes** er kommt nicht mehr; **~ ago** vor langer Zeit; **~ before/after** lange vorher/danach; **before ~** bald; **at ~ last** schließlich und endlich; **the ~ and the short of it is that** ... kurz gesagt, ...

long-distance [lɔŋ'dɪstəns] *adj* *(travel, phone call)* Fern-; *(race)* Langstrecken-

longevity [lɒn'dʒɛvɪtɪ] *n* Langlebigkeit *f*

long-haired ['lɔŋ'hɛəd] *adj* langhaarig; *(animal)* Langhaar-

longhand ['lɔŋhænd] *n* Langschrift *f*

longing ['lɔŋɪŋ] *n* Sehnsucht *f*

longingly ['lɔŋɪŋlɪ] *adv* sehnsüchtig

longitude ['lɔŋgɪtjuːd] *n* Länge *f*

long johns [-dʒɒnz] *npl* lange Unterhose *f*

long jump *n* Weitsprung *m*

long-life ['lɔŋlaɪf] *adj* *(batteries etc)* mit langer Lebensdauer; **~ milk** H-Milch *f*

long-lost ['lɔŋlɒst] *adj* verloren geglaubt

long-playing record ['lɔŋpleɪŋ-] *n* Langspielplatte *f*

long-range ['lɔŋ'reɪndʒ] *adj* *(plan, forecast)* langfristig; *(missile, plane etc)* Langstrecken-

longshoreman ['lɔŋʃɔːmən] *(US: irreg: like* **man***)* *n* Hafenarbeiter *m*

long-sighted ['lɔŋ'saɪtɪd] *adj* weitsichtig

long-standing ['lɔŋ'stændɪŋ] *adj* langjährig

long-suffering [lɔŋ'sʌfərɪŋ] *adj* schwer geprüft

long-term ['lɔŋtəːm] *adj* langfristig

long wave *n* Langwelle *f*

long-winded [lɔŋ'wɪndɪd] *adj* umständlich, langatmig

loo [luː] *(Brit: inf)* *n* Klo *nt*

loofah ['luːfə] *n* Luffa(schwamm) *m*

look [luk] *vi* sehen, schauen, gucken *(inf)*; *(seem, appear)* aussehen ▷ *n* *(glance)* Blick *m*; *(appearance)* Aussehen *nt*; *(expression)* Miene *f*; *(Fashion)* Look *m*; **looks** *npl* *(good looks)* (gutes) Aussehen; **to ~ (out) onto the sea/south** *(building etc)* Blick aufs Meer/nach Süden haben; **~ (here)!** *(expressing annoyance)* hör (mal) zu!; **~!** *(expressing surprise)* sieh mal!; **to ~ like sb/sth** wie jd/etw aussehen; **it ~s like him** es sieht ihm ähnlich; **it ~s about 4 metres long** es scheint etwa 4 Meter lang zu sein; **it ~s all right to me** es scheint mir in Ordnung zu sein; **to ~ ahead** vorausschauen; **to have a ~ at sth** sich etw ansehen; **let me have a ~** lass mich mal sehen; **to have a ~ for sth** nach etw suchen

▶ **look after** *vt fus* sich kümmern um

▶ **look at** *vt fus* ansehen; *(read quickly)* durchsehen; *(study, consider)* betrachten

▶ **look back** *vi*: **to ~ back (on)** zurückblicken (auf +*acc*); **to ~ back at sth/sb** sich nach jdm/etw umsehen

▶ **look down on** *vt fus* *(fig)* herabsehen auf +*acc*

▶ **look for** *vt fus* suchen

▶ **look forward to** *vt fus* sich freuen auf +*acc*; **we ~ forward to hearing from you** *(in letters)* wir hoffen, bald von Ihnen zu hören

▶ **look in** *vi*: **to ~ in on sb** bei jdm vorbeikommen

▶ **look into** *vt fus* *(investigate)* untersuchen

▶ **look on** *vi* *(watch)* zusehen

▶ **look out** *vi* *(beware)* aufpassen

▶ **look out for** *vt fus* Ausschau halten nach

▶ **look over** *vt* *(essay etc)* durchsehen; *(house, town etc)* sich dat ansehen; *(person)* mustern

▶ **look round** *vi* sich umsehen

▶ **look through** *vt fus* durchsehen

▶ **look to** *vt fus* *(rely on)* sich verlassen auf +*acc*

▶ **look up** *vi* aufsehen; *(situation)* sich bessern ▷ *vt* *(word etc)* nachschlagen; **things are ~ing up** es geht bergauf

▶ **look up to** *vt fus* aufsehen zu

lookalike ['lukəlaɪk] *n* Doppelgänger(in) *m(f)*

look-in ['lukɪn] *n*: **to get a ~** *(inf)* eine Chance haben

lookout ['lukaut] *n* *(tower etc)* Ausguck *m*; *(person)* Wachtposten *m*; **to be on the ~ for sth** nach etw Ausschau halten

loom [luːm] *vi* *(also:* **loom up**: *object, shape)* sich abzeichnen; *(event)* näher rücken ▷ *n* Webstuhl *m*

loony ['luːnɪ] *(inf)* *adj* verrückt ▷ *n* Verrückte(r) *f(m)*

loop [luːp] *n* Schlaufe *f*; *(Comput)* Schleife *f* ▷ *vt*: **to ~ sth around sth** etw um etw schlingen

loophole ['luːphəul] *n* Hintertürchen *nt*; **a ~ in the law** eine Lücke im Gesetz

loose [luːs] *adj* lose, locker; *(clothes etc)* weit; *(long hair)* offen; *(not strictly controlled, promiscuous)* locker; *(definition)* ungenau; *(translation)* frei ▷ *vt* *(animal)* loslassen; *(prisoner)* freilassen; *(set off, unleash)* entfesseln ▷ *n*: **to be on the ~** frei herumlaufen

loose change *n* Kleingeld *nt*

loose chippings *npl* Schotter *m*

loose end *n*: **to be at a ~**, **to be at ~s** *(US)* nichts mit sich *dat* anzufangen wissen; **to tie up ~s** die offenstehenden Probleme lösen

loose-fitting ['luːsfɪtɪŋ] *adj* weit

loose-leaf ['luːsliːf] *adj* Loseblatt-; **~ binder** Ringbuch *nt*

loose-limbed [luːs'lɪmd] *adj* gelenkig, beweglich

loosely ['luːslɪ] *adv* lose, locker

loosely-knit ['luːslɪ'nɪt] *adj* *(fig)* locker

loosen ['luːsn] *vt* lösen, losmachen; *(clothing, belt etc)* lockern

▶ **loosen up** *vi* *(before game)* sich auflockern; *(relax)* auftauen

loot [luːt] *n* *(inf)* Beute *f* ▷ *vt* plündern

looter ['luːtər] *n* Plünderer *m*

looting ['luːtɪŋ] *n* Plünderung *f*

lop off [lɒp-] *vt* abhacken

lopsided ['lɒp'saɪdɪd] *adj* schief

lord [lɔːd] n (Brit) Lord m; **L~ Smith** Lord Smith; **the L~** (Rel) der Herr; **my ~** (to bishop) Exzellenz; (to noble) Mylord; (to judge) Euer Ehren; **good L~!** ach, du lieber Himmel!; **the (House of) L~s** (Brit) das Oberhaus

lordly ['lɔːdlɪ] adj hochmütig

lordship ['lɔːdʃɪp] n: **your L~** Eure Lordschaft

lore [lɔːʳ] n Überlieferungen pl

lorry ['lɒrɪ] (Brit) n Lastwagen m, Lkw m

lorry driver (Brit) n Lastwagenfahrer m

lose [luːz] (pt, pp **lost**) vt verlieren; (opportunity) verpassen; (pursuers) abschütteln ▷ vi verlieren; **to ~ (time)** (clock) nachgehen; **to ~ weight** abnehmen; **to ~ 5 pounds** 5 Pfund abnehmen; **to ~ sight of sth** (also fig) etw aus den Augen verlieren

loser ['luːzəʳ] n Verlierer(in) m(f); (inf: failure) Versager m; **to be a good/bad ~** ein guter/schlechter Verlierer sein

loss [lɒs] n Verlust m; **to make a ~ (of £1,000)** (1000 Pfund) Verlust machen; **to sell sth at a ~** etw mit Verlust verkaufen; **heavy ~es** schwere Verluste pl; **to cut one's ~es** aufgeben, bevor es noch schlimmer wird; **to be at a ~** nicht mehr weiterwissen

loss adjuster n Schadenssachverständige(r) f(m)

loss leader n (Comm) Lockvogelangebot nt

lost [lɒst] pt, pp of **lose** ▷ adj (person, animal) vermisst; (object) verloren; **to be ~** sich verlaufen/verfahren haben; **to get ~** sich verlaufen/verfahren; **get ~!** (inf) verschwinde!; **~ in thought** in Gedanken verloren

lost and found (US) n = **lost property**

lost cause n aussichtslose Sache f

lost property (Brit) n Fundsachen pl; (also: **lost property office**) Fundbüro nt

lot [lɒt] n (kind) Art f; (group) Gruppe f; (at auctions, destiny) Los nt; **to draw ~s** losen, Lose ziehen; **the ~** alles; **a ~ (of)** (a large number (of)) viele; (a great deal (of)) viel; **~s of** viele; **I read a ~** ich lese viel; **this happens a ~** das kommt oft vor

loth [ləʊθ] adj = **loath**

lotion ['ləʊʃən] n Lotion f

lottery ['lɒtərɪ] n Lotterie f

loud [laud] adj laut; (clothes) schreiend ▷ adv laut; **to be ~ in one's support of sb/sth** jdn/etw lautstark unterstützen; **out ~** (read, laugh etc) laut

loud-hailer [laud'heɪləʳ] (Brit) n Megafon nt

loudly ['laudlɪ] adv laut

loudmouthed ['laudmauθd] adj großmäulig

loudspeaker [laud'spiːkəʳ] n Lautsprecher m

lounge [laundʒ] n (in house) Wohnzimmer nt; (in hotel) Lounge f; (at airport, station) Wartehalle f; (Brit: also: **lounge bar**) Salon m ▷ vi faulenzen
  ▶ **lounge about** vi herumliegen, herumsitzen, herumstehen
  ▶ **lounge around** vi = **lounge about**

lounge suit (Brit) n Straßenanzug m

louse [laus] (pl **lice**) n Laus f

▶ **louse up** (inf) vt vermasseln

lousy ['lauzɪ] (inf) adj (bad-quality) lausig, mies; (despicable) fies, gemein; (ill): **to feel ~** sich miserabel or elend fühlen

lout [laut] n Lümmel m, Flegel m

louvre, (US) **louver** ['luːvəʳ] adj (door, window) Lamellen-

lovable ['lʌvəbl] adj liebenswert

love [lʌv] n Liebe f ▷ vt lieben; (thing, activity etc) gern mögen; **"~ (from) Anne"** (on letter) „mit herzlichen Grüßen, Anne"; **to be in ~ with** verliebt sein in +acc; **to fall in ~ with** sich verlieben in +acc; **to make ~** sich lieben; **~ at first sight** Liebe auf den ersten Blick; **to send one's ~ to sb** jdn grüßen lassen; **"fifteen ~"** (Tennis) „fünfzehn null"; **to ~ doing sth** etw gern tun; **I'd ~ to come** ich würde sehr gerne kommen; **I ~ chocolate** ich esse Schokolade liebend gern

love affair n Verhältnis nt, Liebschaft f

love child n uneheliches Kind nt, Kind nt der Liebe

loved ones ['lʌvdwʌnz] npl enge Freunde und Verwandte pl

love-hate relationship ['lʌvheɪt-] n Hassliebe f

love letter n Liebesbrief m

love life n Liebesleben nt

lovely ['lʌvlɪ] adj (beautiful) schön; (delightful) herrlich; (person) sehr nett

lover ['lʌvəʳ] n Geliebte(r) f(m); (person in love) Liebende(r) f(m); **~ of art/music** Kunst-/Musikliebhaber(in) m(f); **to be ~s** ein Liebespaar sein

lovesick ['lʌvsɪk] adj liebeskrank

love song n Liebeslied nt

loving ['lʌvɪŋ] adj liebend; (actions) liebevoll

low [ləʊ] adj niedrig; (bow, curtsey) tief; (quality) schlecht; (sound: deep) tief; (: quiet) leise; (depressed) niedergeschlagen, bedrückt ▷ adv (sing) leise; (fly) tief ▷ n (Met) Tief nt; **to be/run ~** knapp sein/werden; **sb is running ~ on sth** jdm wird etw knapp; **to reach a new** or **an all-time ~** einen neuen Tiefstand erreichen

low-alcohol ['ləʊ'ælkəhɒl] adj alkoholarm

lowbrow ['ləʊbrau] adj (geistig) anspruchslos

low-calorie ['ləʊ'kælərɪ] adj kalorienarm

low-carb ['ləʊ'kɑːb] adj low-carb, kohlenhydratarm; **~ bread** kohlenhydratarmes Brot

low-cut ['ləʊkʌt] adj (dress) tief ausgeschnitten

lowdown ['ləʊdaun] (inf) n: **he gave me the ~ on it** er hat mich darüber informiert

lower ['ləʊəʳ] adj untere(r, s); (lip, jaw, arm) Unter- ▷ vt senken

low-fat ['ləʊ'fæt] adj fettarm

low-key ['ləʊ'kiː] adj zurückhaltend; (not obvious) unaufdringlich

lowlands ['ləʊləndz] npl Flachland nt

low-level language ['ləʊlɛvl-] n (Comput) niedere Programmiersprache f

low-loader ['ləʊ'ləʊdəʳ] n Tieflader m

lowly ['ləʊlɪ] adj (position) niedrig; (origin)

bescheiden

low-lying [ləu'laɪɪŋ] *adj* tief gelegen

low-paid [ləu'peɪd] *adj* schlecht bezahlt

low-rise ['ləuraɪz] *adj* niedrig (gebaut)

low-tech ['ləutɛk] *adj* nicht mit Hightech ausgestattet

loyal ['lɔɪəl] *adj* treu; (support) loyal

loyalist ['lɔɪəlɪst] *n* Loyalist(in) *m(f)*

loyalty ['lɔɪəltɪ] *n* (see adj) Treue *f*; Loyalität *f*

loyalty card (Brit) *n* (Comm) Paybackkarte *f*

lozenge ['lɔzɪndʒ] *n* Pastille *f*; (shape) Raute *f*

LP *n abbr* (= long player) LP *f*; see also **long-playing record**

LPG *n abbr* (= liquefied petroleum gas) Flüssiggas *nt*

● **L-PLATES**

Als *L-plates* werden in Großbritannien die weißen Schilder mit einem roten „L" bezeichnet, die vorne und hinten an jedem von einem Fahrschüler geführten Fahrzeug befestigt werden müssen. Fahrschüler müssen einen vorläufigen Führerschein beantragen und dürfen damit unter der Aufsicht eines erfahrenen Autofahrers auf allen Straßen außer Autobahnen fahren.

LPN (US) *n abbr* (= Licensed Practical Nurse) staatlich anerkannte Krankenschwester *f*, staatlich anerkannter Krankenpfleger *m*

LRAM (Brit) *n abbr* (= Licentiate of the Royal Academy of Music) Qualifikationsnachweis in Musik

LSAT (US) *n abbr* (= Law School Admissions Test) Zulassungsprüfung für juristische Hochschulen

LSD *n abbr* (= lysergic acid diethylamide) LSD *nt*; (Brit: also: **L.S.D.**: = pounds, shillings and pence) früheres britisches Währungssystem

LSE (Brit) *n abbr* (= London School of Economics) Londoner Wirtschaftshochschule

Lt *abbr* (Mil: = lieutenant) Lt.

Ltd *abbr* (Comm: = limited (liability)) ≈ GmbH *f*

lubricant ['lu:brɪkənt] *n* Schmiermittel *nt*

lubricate ['lu:brɪkeɪt] *vt* schmieren, ölen

lucid ['lu:sɪd] *adj* klar; (person) bei klarem Verstand

lucidity [lu:'sɪdɪtɪ] *n* Klarheit *f*

luck [lʌk] *n* (esp good luck) Glück *nt*; **bad ~** Unglück *nt*; **good ~!** viel Glück!; **bad** or **hard** or **tough ~!** so ein Pech!; **hard** or **tough ~!** (showing no sympathy) Pech gehabt!; **to be in ~** Glück haben; **to be out of ~** kein Glück haben

luckily ['lʌkɪlɪ] *adv* glücklicherweise

luckless ['lʌklɪs] *adj* glücklos

lucky ['lʌkɪ] *adj* (situation, event) glücklich; (object) Glück bringend; (person): **to be ~** Glück haben; **to have a ~ escape** noch einmal davonkommen; **~ charm** Glücksbringer *m*

lucrative ['lu:krətɪv] *adj* einträglich

ludicrous ['lu:dɪkrəs] *adj* grotesk

ludo ['lu:dəu] *n* Mensch, ärgere dich nicht *nt*

lug [lʌg] (inf) *vt* schleppen

luggage ['lʌgɪdʒ] *n* Gepäck *nt*

luggage car (US) *n* = **luggage van**

luggage rack *n* Gepäckträger *m*; (in train) Gepäckablage *f*

luggage van (Brit) *n* (Rail) Gepäckwagen *m*

lugubrious [lu'gu:brɪəs] *adj* schwermütig

lukewarm ['lu:kwɔ:m] *adj* lauwarm; (fig: person, reaction etc) lau

lull [lʌl] *n* Pause *f* ▷ *vt*: **to ~ sb to sleep** jdn einlullen or einschläfern; **to be ~ed into a false sense of security** in trügerische Sicherheit gewiegt werden

lullaby ['lʌləbaɪ] *n* Schlaflied *nt*

lumbago [lʌm'beɪgəu] *n* Hexenschuss *m*

lumber ['lʌmbəʳ] *n* (wood) Holz *nt*; (junk) Gerümpel *nt* ▷ *vi*: **to ~ about/along** herum-/entlangtapsen

▶ **lumber with** *vt*: **to be/get ~ed with sth** etw am Hals haben/aufgehalst bekommen

lumberjack ['lʌmbədʒæk] *n* Holzfäller *m*

lumber room (Brit) *n* Rumpelkammer *f*

lumberyard ['lʌmbəjɑ:d] (US) *n* Holzlager *nt*

luminous ['lu:mɪnəs] *adj* leuchtend, Leucht-

lump [lʌmp] *n* Klumpen *m*; (on body) Beule *f*; (in breast) Knoten *m*; (also: **sugar lump**) Stück *nt* (Zucker) ▷ *vt*: **to ~ together** in einen Topf werfen; **a ~ sum** eine Pauschalsumme

lumpy ['lʌmpɪ] *adj* klumpig

lunacy ['lu:nəsɪ] *n* Wahnsinn *m*

lunar ['lu:nəʳ] *adj* Mond-

lunatic ['lu:nətɪk] *adj* wahnsinnig ▷ *n* Wahnsinnige(r) *f(m)*, Irre(r) *f(m)*

lunatic asylum *n* Irrenanstalt *f*

lunatic fringe *n*: **the ~** die Extremisten *pl*

lunch [lʌntʃ] *n* Mittagessen *nt*; (time) Mittagszeit *f* ▷ *vi* zu Mittag essen

lunch break *n* Mittagspause *f*

luncheon ['lʌntʃən] *n* Mittagessen *nt*

luncheon meat *n* Frühstücksfleisch *nt*

luncheon voucher (Brit) *n* Essensmarke *f*

lunch hour *n* Mittagspause *f*

lunch time *n* Mittagszeit *f*

lung [lʌŋ] *n* Lunge *f*

lunge [lʌndʒ] *vi* (also: **lunge forward**) sich nach vorne stürzen; **to ~ at** sich stürzen auf +acc

lupin ['lu:pɪn] *n* Lupine *f*

lurch [lə:tʃ] *vi* ruckeln; (person) taumeln ▷ *n* Ruck *m*; (of person) Taumeln *nt*; **to leave sb in the ~** jdn im Stich lassen

lure [luəʳ] *n* Verlockung *f* ▷ *vt* locken

lurid ['luərɪd] *adj* (story etc) reißerisch; (pej: brightly coloured) grell, in grellen Farben

lurk [lə:k] *vi* (also fig) lauern

luscious ['lʌʃəs] *adj* (attractive) fantastisch; (food) köstlich, lecker

lush [lʌʃ] *adj* (fields) saftig; (gardens) üppig; (luxurious) luxuriös

lust [lʌst] (pej) *n* (sexual) (sinnliche) Begierde *f*; (for money, power etc) Gier *f*

▶ **lust after** *vt fus* (sexually) begehren; (crave) gieren nach

▶ **lust for** *vt fus* = **lust after**

lustful ['lʌstful] *adj* lüstern

lustre, (US) **luster** ['lʌstəʳ] *n* Schimmer *m*,

Glanz *m*
lusty ['lʌstɪ] *adj* gesund und munter
lute [luːt] *n* Laute *f*
luvvie, luvvy ['lʌvɪ] (*inf*) *n* Schätzchen *nt*
Luxembourg ['lʌksəmbəːg] *n* Luxemburg *nt*
luxuriant [lʌg'zjuərɪənt] *adj* üppig
luxuriate [lʌg'zjuərɪeɪt] *vi*: **to ~ in sth** sich in
etw *dat* aalen
luxurious [lʌg'zjuərɪəs] *adj* luxuriös
luxury ['lʌkʃərɪ] *n* Luxus *m* (*no pl*) ▷ *cpd* (*hotel, car etc*) Luxus-; **little luxuries** kleine Genüsse

LV (Brit) *n abbr* = **luncheon voucher**
LW *abbr* (Radio: = *long wave*) LW
Lycra® ['laɪkrə] *n* Lycra *nt*
lying ['laɪɪŋ] *n* Lügen *nt* ▷ *adj* verlogen
lynch [lɪntʃ] *vt* lynchen
lynx [lɪŋks] *n* Luchs *m*
lyric ['lɪrɪk] *adj* lyrisch
lyrical ['lɪrɪkl] *adj* lyrisch; (*fig: praise etc*) schwärmerisch
lyricism ['lɪrɪsɪzəm] *n* Lyrik *f*
lyrics ['lɪrɪks] *npl* (*of song*) Text *m*

Mm

M¹, m¹ [ɛm] *n* (*letter*) M *nt*, m *nt*; **M for Mary, M for Mike** (*US*) ≈ M wie Martha
M² [ɛm] *n abbr* (*Brit:* = *motorway*): **the M8** ≈ die A8 ▷ *abbr* = **medium**
m² *abbr* (= *metre*) m; = **mile**; (= *million*) Mio.
MA *n abbr* (= *Master of Arts*) akademischer Grad für Geisteswissenschaftler; (= *military academy*) Militärakademie *f* ▷ *abbr* (*US: Post*) = Massachusetts
mac [mæk] (*Brit*) *n* Regenmantel *m*
macabre [məˈkɑːbrə] *adj* makaber
macaroni [mækəˈrəʊnɪ] *n* Makkaroni *pl*
macaroon [mækəˈruːn] *n* Makrone *f*
mace [meɪs] *n* (*weapon*) Keule *f*; (*ceremonial*) Amtsstab *m*; (*spice*) Muskatblüte *f*
Macedonia [mæsɪˈdəʊnɪə] *n* Makedonien *nt*
Macedonian [mæsɪˈdəʊnɪən] *adj* makedonisch ▷ *n* Makedonier(in) *m(f)*; (*Ling*) Makedonisch *nt*
machinations [mækɪˈneɪʃənz] *npl* Machenschaften *pl*
machine [məˈʃiːn] *n* Maschine *f*; (*fig: party machine etc*) Apparat *m* ▷ *vt* (*Tech*) maschinell herstellen *or* bearbeiten; (*dress etc*) mit der Maschine nähen
machine code *n* Maschinencode *m*
machine gun *n* Maschinengewehr *nt*
machine language *n* Maschinensprache *f*
machine-readable [məˈʃiːnriːdəbl] *adj* maschinenlesbar
machinery [məˈʃiːnərɪ] *n* Maschinen *pl*; (*fig: of government*) Apparat *m*
machine shop *n* Maschinensaal *m*
machine tool *n* Werkzeugmaschine *f*
machine washable *adj* waschmaschinenfest
machinist [məˈʃiːnɪst] *n* Maschinist(in) *m(f)*
macho [ˈmætʃəʊ] *adj* Macho-; **a ~ man** ein Macho *m*
mackerel [ˈmækrl] *n inv* Makrele *f*
mackintosh [ˈmækɪntɒʃ] (*Brit*) *n* Regenmantel *m*
macro ... [ˈmækrəʊ] *pref* Makro-, makro-
macroeconomics [ˈmækrəʊiːkəˈnɒmɪks] *npl* Makroökonomie *f*
mad [mæd] *adj* wahnsinnig, verrückt; (*angry*) böse, sauer (*inf*); **to be ~ about** verrückt sein auf +*acc*; **to be ~ at sb** böse *or* sauer auf jdn sein; **to go ~** (*insane*) verrückt *or* wahnsinnig werden; (*angry*) böse *or* sauer werden

madam [ˈmædəm] *n* gnädige Frau *f*; **yes, ~** ja(wohl); **M~ Chairman** Frau Vorsitzende
madcap [ˈmædkæp] *adj* (*idea*) versponnen; (*tricks*) toll
mad cow disease *n* Rinderwahn *m*
madden [ˈmædn] *vt* ärgern, fuchsen (*inf*)
maddening [ˈmædnɪŋ] *adj* unerträglich
made [meɪd] *pt, pp of* **make**
Madeira [məˈdɪərə] *n* Madeira *nt*; (*wine*) Madeira *m*
made-to-measure [ˈmeɪdtəˈmɛʒəʳ] (*Brit*) *adj* maßgeschneidert
madhouse [ˈmædhaʊs] *n* (*also fig*) Irrenhaus *nt*
madly [ˈmædlɪ] *adv* wie verrückt; **~ in love** bis über beide Ohren verliebt
madman [ˈmædmən] (*irreg: like* **man**) *n* Verrückte(r) *m*, Irre(r) *m*
madness [ˈmædnɪs] *n* Wahnsinn *m*
Madrid [məˈdrɪd] *n* Madrid *nt*
Mafia [ˈmæfɪə] *n* Mafia *f*
mag [mæg] (*Brit: inf*) *n* = **magazine**
magazine [mægəˈziːn] *n* Zeitschrift *f*; (*Radio, TV*) Magazin *nt*; (*Radio, TV, of firearm*) Magazin *nt*; (*Mil: store*) Depot *nt*
maggot [ˈmægət] *n* Made *f*
magic [ˈmædʒɪk] *n* Magie *f*; (*conjuring*) Zauberei *f* ▷ *adj* magisch; (*formula*) Zauber-; (*fig: place, moment etc*) zauberhaft
magical [ˈmædʒɪkl] *adj* magisch; (*experience, evening*) zauberhaft
magician [məˈdʒɪʃən] *n* (*wizard*) Magier *m*; (*conjurer*) Zauberer *m*
magistrate [ˈmædʒɪstreɪt] *n* Friedensrichter(in) *m(f)*
magnanimous [mægˈnænɪməs] *adj* großmütig
magnate [ˈmægneɪt] *n* Magnat *m*
magnesium [mægˈniːzɪəm] *n* Magnesium *nt*
magnet [ˈmægnɪt] *n* Magnet *m*
magnetic [mægˈnɛtɪk] *adj* magnetisch; (*field, compass, pole etc*) Magnet-; (*personality*) anziehend
magnetic disk *n* (*Comput*) Magnetplatte *f*
magnetic tape *n* Magnetband *nt*
magnetism [ˈmægnɪtɪzəm] *n* Magnetismus *m*; (*of person*) Anziehungskraft *f*
magnetize [ˈmægnɪtaɪz] *vt* magnetisieren
magnification [mægnɪfɪˈkeɪʃən] *n*

Vergrößerung f

magnificence [mæg'nɪfɪsns] n Großartigkeit f; (of robes) Pracht f

magnificent [mæg'nɪfɪsnt] adj großartig; (robes) prachtvoll

magnify ['mægnɪfaɪ] vt vergrößern; (sound) verstärken; (fig: exaggerate) aufbauschen

magnifying glass ['mægnɪfaɪɪŋ-] n Vergrößerungsglas nt, Lupe f

magnitude ['mægnɪtjuːd] n (size) Ausmaß nt, Größe f; (importance) Bedeutung f

magnolia [mæg'nəʊlɪə] n Magnolie f

magpie ['mægpaɪ] n Elster f

mahogany [mə'hɔgənɪ] n Mahagoni nt ▷ cpd Mahagoni-

maid [meɪd] n Dienstmädchen nt; **old ~** (pej) alte Jungfer

maiden ['meɪdn] n (liter) Mädchen nt ▷ adj unverheiratet; (speech, voyage) Jungfern-

maiden name n Mädchenname m

mail [meɪl] n Post f ▷ vt aufgeben; **by ~** mit der Post

mailbox ['meɪlbɔks] n (US) Briefkasten m; (Comput) Mailbox f, elektronischer Briefkasten m

mailing list ['meɪlɪŋ-] n Anschriftenliste f

mailman ['meɪlmæn] (US: irreg: like **man**) n Briefträger m, Postbote m

mail order n (system) Versand m ▷ cpd: **mail-order firm** or **business** Versandhaus nt; **by ~** durch Bestellung per Post

mailshot ['meɪlʃɔt] (Brit) n Werbebrief m

mail train n Postzug m

mail truck (US) n Postauto nt

mail van (Brit) n (Aut) Postauto nt; (Rail) Postwagen m

maim [meɪm] vt verstümmeln

main [meɪn] adj Haupt-, wichtigste(r, s); (door, entrance, meal) Haupt- ▷ n Hauptleitung f; **the mains** npl (Elec) das Stromnetz; (gas, water) die Hauptleitung; **in the ~** im Großen und Ganzen

main course n (Culin) Hauptgericht nt

mainframe ['meɪnfreɪm] n (Comput) Großrechner m

mainland ['meɪnlənd] n Festland nt

mainline ['meɪnlaɪn] adj: **~ station** Fernbahnhof m ▷ vt (drugs slang) spritzen ▷ vi (drugs slang) fixen

main line n Hauptstrecke f

mainly ['meɪnlɪ] adv hauptsächlich

main road n Hauptstraße f

mainstay ['meɪnsteɪ] n (foundation) (wichtigste) Stütze f; (chief constituent) Hauptbestandteil m

mainstream ['meɪnstriːm] n Hauptrichtung f ▷ adj (cinema etc) populär; (politics) der Mitte

maintain [meɪn'teɪn] vt (preserve) aufrechterhalten; (keep up) beibehalten; (provide for) unterhalten; (look after: building) instand halten; (: equipment) warten; (affirm: opinion) vertreten; (: innocence) beteuern; **to ~ that ...** behaupten, dass ...

maintenance ['meɪntənəns] n (of building)

Instandhaltung f; (of equipment) Wartung f; (preservation) Aufrechterhaltung f; (Law: alimony) Unterhalt m

maintenance contract n Wartungsvertrag m

maintenance order n (Law) Unterhaltsurteil nt

maisonette [meɪzə'nɛt] (Brit) n Maisonettewohnung f

maize [meɪz] n Mais m

Maj. abbr (Mil) = **major**

majestic [mə'dʒɛstɪk] adj erhaben

majesty ['mædʒɪstɪ] n (title): **Your M~** Eure Majestät; (splendour) Erhabenheit f

major ['meɪdʒəʳ] n Major m ▷ adj bedeutend; (Mus) Dur ▷ vi (US): **to ~ in French** Französisch als Hauptfach belegen; **a ~ operation** eine größere Operation

Majorca [mə'jɔːkə] n Mallorca nt

major general n Generalmajor m

majority [mə'dʒɔrɪtɪ] n Mehrheit f ▷ cpd (verdict, holding) Mehrheits-

make [meɪk] (pt, pp **made**) vt machen; (clothes) nähen; (cake) backen; (speech) halten; (manufacture) herstellen; (earn) verdienen; (cause to be): **to ~ sb sad** jdn traurig machen; (force): **to ~ sb do sth** jdn zwingen, etw zu tun; (cause) jdn dazu bringen, etw zu tun; (equal): **2 and 2 ~ 4** 2 und 2 ist or macht 4 ▷ n Marke f, Fabrikat nt; **to ~ a fool of sb** jdn lächerlich machen; **to ~ a profit/loss** Gewinn/Verlust machen; **to ~ it** (arrive) es schaffen; (succeed) Erfolg haben; **what time do you ~ it?** wie spät hast du?; **to ~ good** erfolgreich sein; (threat) wahr machen; (promise) einlösen; (damage) wiedergutmachen; (loss) ersetzen; **to ~ do with** auskommen mit

▶ **make for** vt fus (place) zuhalten auf +acc

▶ **make off** vi sich davonmachen

▶ **make out** vt (decipher) entziffern; (understand) verstehen; (see) ausmachen; (write: cheque) ausstellen; (claim, imply) behaupten; (pretend) so tun, als ob; **to ~ out a case for sth** für etw argumentieren

▶ **make over** vt: **to ~ over (to)** überschreiben (+dat)

▶ **make up** vt (constitute) bilden; (invent) erfinden; (prepare: bed) zurechtmachen; (: parcel) zusammenpacken ▷ vi (after quarrel) sich versöhnen; (with cosmetics) sich schminken; **to be made up of** bestehen aus

▶ **make up for** vt fus (loss) ersetzen; (disappointment etc) ausgleichen

make-believe ['meɪkbɪliːv] n Fantasie f; **a world of ~** eine Fantasiewelt; **it's just ~** es ist nicht wirklich

makeover ['meɪkəʊvəʳ] n grundlegende Veränderung des Aussehens; **to give sb a ~** jdm ein neues Aussehen verpassen

maker ['meɪkəʳ] n Hersteller m; **film ~** Filmemacher(in) m(f)

makeshift ['meɪkʃɪft] adj behelfsmäßig

make-up ['meɪkʌp] n Make-up nt, Schminke f

make-up bag n Kosmetiktasche f

make-up remover n Make-up-Entferner m

m

making ['meɪkɪŋ] n (fig): **in the ~** im
Entstehen; **to have the ~s of** das Zeug haben
zu

maladjusted [mælə'dʒʌstɪd] adj
verhaltensgestört

maladroit [mælə'drɔɪt] adj ungeschickt

malaise [mæ'leɪz] n Unbehagen nt

malaria [mə'leərɪə] n Malaria f

Malawi [mə'lɑːwɪ] n Malawi nt

Malay [mə'leɪ] adj malaiisch ▷ n Malaie m,
Malaiin f; (Ling) Malaiisch nt

Malaya [mə'leɪə] n Malaya nt

Malayan [mə'leɪən] adj, n = **Malay**

Malaysia [mə'leɪzɪə] n Malaysia nt

Malaysian [mə'leɪzɪən] adj malaysisch ▷ n
Malaysier(in) m(f)

Maldives ['mɔːldɪvz] npl Malediven pl

male [meɪl] n (animal) Männchen nt; (man)
Mann m ▷ adj männlich; (Elec): **~ plug** Stecker
m; **because he is ~** weil er ein Mann/Junge
ist; **~ and female students** Studenten und
Studentinnen; **a ~ child** ein Junge

male chauvinist n Chauvinist m

male nurse n Krankenpfleger m

malevolence [mə'levələns] n Boshaftigkeit f;
(of action) Böswilligkeit f

malevolent [mə'levələnt] adj boshaft;
(intention) böswillig

malfunction [mæl'fʌŋkʃən] n (of computer)
Funktionsstörung f; (of machine) Defekt m
▷ vi (computer) eine Funktionsstörung haben;
(machine) defekt sein

malice ['mælɪs] n Bosheit f

malicious [mə'lɪʃəs] adj boshaft; (Law)
böswillig

malign [mə'laɪn] vt verleumden ▷ adj (influence)
schlecht; (interpretation) böswillig

malignant [mə'lɪgnənt] adj bösartig; (intention)
böswillig

malingerer [mə'lɪŋgərəʳ] n Simulant(in) m(f)

mall [mɔːl] n (also: **shopping mall**)
Einkaufszentrum nt

malleable ['mælɪəbl] adj (lit, fig) formbar

mallet ['mælɪt] n Holzhammer m

malnutrition [mælnjuː'trɪʃən] n
Unterernährung f

malpractice [mæl'præktɪs] n Berufsvergehen
nt

malt [mɔːlt] n Malz nt; (also: **malt whisky**) Malt
Whisky m

Malta ['mɔːltə] n Malta nt

Maltese [mɔːl'tiːz] adj maltesisch ▷ n inv
Malteser(in) m(f); (Ling) Maltesisch nt

maltreat [mæl'triːt] vt schlecht behandeln;
(violently) misshandeln

mammal ['mæml] n Säugetier nt

mammoth ['mæməθ] n Mammut nt ▷ adj (task)
Mammut-

man [mæn] (pl **men**) n Mann m; (mankind) der
Mensch, die Menschen pl; (Chess) Figur f ▷ vt
(ship) bemannen; (gun, machine) bedienen; (post)
besetzen; **~ and wife** Mann und Frau

manage ['mænɪdʒ] vi: **to ~ to do sth** es

schaffen, etw zu tun; (get by financially)
zurechtkommen ▷ vt (business, organization)
leiten; (control) zurechtkommen mit; **to ~
without sb/sth** ohne jdn/etw auskommen;
well ~d (business, shop etc) gut geführt

manageable ['mænɪdʒəbl] adj (task) zu
bewältigen; (number) überschaubar

management ['mænɪdʒmənt] n Leitung f,
Führung f; (persons) Unternehmensleitung f;
"under new ~" „unter neuer Leitung"

management accounting n Kosten- und
Leistungsrechnung f

management consultant n
Unternehmensberater(in) m(f)

manager ['mænɪdʒəʳ] n (of business)
Geschäftsführer(in) m(f); (of institution etc)
Direktor(in) m(f); (of department) Leiter(in) m(f);
(of pop star) Manager(in) m(f); (Sport) Trainer(in)
m(f); **sales ~** Verkaufsleiter(in) m(f)

manageress [mænɪdʒə'res] n (of shop, business)
Geschäftsführerin f; (of office, department etc)
Leiterin f

managerial [mænɪ'dʒɪərɪəl] adj (role, post)
leitend; (decisions) geschäftlich; **~ staff/skills**
Führungskräfte pl/-qualitäten pl

managing director ['mænɪdʒɪŋ-] n
Geschäftsführer(in) m(f)

Mancunian [mæŋ'kjuːnɪən] n Bewohner(in)
m(f) Manchesters

mandarin ['mændərɪn] n (also: **mandarin
orange**) Mandarine f; (official: Chinese)
Mandarin m; (: gen) Funktionär m

mandate ['mændeɪt] n Mandat nt; (task)
Auftrag m

mandatory ['mændətərɪ] adj obligatorisch

mandolin, mandoline ['mændəlɪn] n
Mandoline f

mane [meɪn] n Mähne f

maneuver etc [mə'nuːvəʳ] (US) = **manoeuvre** etc

manfully ['mænfəlɪ] adv mannhaft, beherzt

manganese [mæŋgə'niːz] n Mangan nt

mangetout ['mɔnʒ'tuː] (Brit) n Zuckererbse f

mangle ['mæŋgl] vt (übel) zurichten ▷ n
Mangel f

mango ['mæŋgəʊ] (pl **~es**) n Mango f

mangrove ['mæŋgrəʊv] n Mangrove(n)baum
m

mangy ['meɪndʒɪ] adj (animal) räudig

manhandle ['mænhændl] vt (mistreat)
grob behandeln; (move by hand) (von Hand)
befördern

manhole ['mænhəʊl] n Kanalschacht m

manhood ['mænhud] n Mannesalter nt

man-hour ['mænaʊəʳ] n Arbeitsstunde f

manhunt ['mænhʌnt] n Fahndung f

mania ['meɪnɪə] n Manie f; (craze) Sucht f;
persecution ~ Verfolgungswahn m

maniac ['meɪnɪæk] n Wahnsinnige(r) f(m),
Verrückte(r) f(m); (fig) Fanatiker(in) m(f)

manic ['mænɪk] adj (behaviour) manisch;
(activity) rasend

manic-depressive ['mænɪkdɪ'presɪv] n
Manisch-Depressive(r) f(m) ▷ adj manisch-

depressiv

manicure ['mænɪkjuəʳ] n Maniküre f ▷ vt manikürien

manicure set n Nageletui nt, Maniküreetui nt

manifest ['mænɪfɛst] vt zeigen, bekunden ▷ adj offenkundig ▷ n Manifest nt

manifestation [mænɪfɛs'teɪʃən] n Anzeichen nt

manifesto [mænɪ'fɛstəu] n Manifest nt

manifold ['mænɪfəuld] adj vielfältig ▷ n: **exhaust ~** Auspuffkrümmer m

Manila [mə'nɪlə] n Manila nt

manila [mə'nɪlə] adj: **~ envelope** brauner Briefumschlag m

manipulate [mə'nɪpjuleɪt] vt manipulieren

manipulation [mənɪpju'leɪʃən] n Manipulation f

mankind [mæn'kaɪnd] n Menschheit f

manliness ['mænlɪnɪs] n Männlichkeit f

manly ['mænlɪ] adj männlich

man-made ['mæn'meɪd] adj künstlich; (fibre) synthetisch

manna ['mænə] n Manna nt

mannequin ['mænɪkɪn] n (dummy) Schaufensterpuppe f; (fashion model) Mannequin nt

manner ['mænəʳ] n (way) Art f, Weise f; (behaviour) Art f; (type, sort): **all ~ of things** die verschiedensten Dinge; **manners** npl (conduct) Manieren pl, Umgangsformen pl; **bad ~s** schlechte Manieren; **that's bad ~s** das gehört sich nicht

mannerism ['mænərɪzəm] n Eigenheit f

mannerly ['mænəlɪ] adj wohlerzogen

manning ['mænɪŋ] n Besatzung f

manoeuvrable, (US) **maneuverable** [mə'nu:vrəbl] adj manövrierfähig

manoeuvre, (US) **maneuver** [mə'nu:vəʳ] vt manövrieren; (situation) manipulieren ▷ vi manövrieren ▷ n (skilful move) Manöver nt; **manoeuvres** npl (Mil) Manöver nt, Truppenübungen pl; **to ~ sb into doing sth** jdn dazu bringen, etw zu tun

manor ['mænəʳ] n (also: **manor house**) Herrenhaus nt

manpower ['mænpauəʳ] n Personal nt, Arbeitskräfte pl

Manpower Services Commission (Brit) n Behörde für Arbeitsbeschaffung, Arbeitsvermittlung und Berufsausbildung

manservant ['mænsə:vənt] (pl **menservants**) n Diener m

mansion ['mænʃən] n Villa f

manslaughter ['mænslɔ:təʳ] n Totschlag m

mantelpiece ['mæntlpi:s] n Kaminsims nt or m

mantle ['mæntl] n Decke f; (fig) Deckmantel m

man-to-man ['mæntə'mæn] adj, adv von Mann zu Mann

manual ['mænjuəl] adj manuell, Hand-; (controls) von Hand ▷ n Handbuch nt

manufacture [mænju'fæktʃəʳ] vt herstellen ▷ n Herstellung f

manufactured goods npl Fertigerzeugnisse pl

manufacturer [mænju'fæktʃərəʳ] n Hersteller m

manufacturing [mænju'fæktʃərɪŋ] n Herstellung f

manure [mə'njuəʳ] n Dung m

manuscript ['mænjuskrɪpt] n Manuskript nt; (old document) Handschrift f

many ['mɛnɪ] adj, pron viele; **a great ~** eine ganze Reihe; **how ~?** wie viele?; **too ~ difficulties** zu viele Schwierigkeiten; **twice as ~** doppelt so viele; **~ a time** so manches Mal

Maori ['maurɪ] adj maorisch ▷ n Maori mf

map [mæp] n (Land)karte f; (of town) Stadtplan m ▷ vt eine Karte anfertigen von
▶ **map out** vt planen; (plan) entwerfen; (essay) anlegen

maple ['meɪpl] n (tree, wood) Ahorn m

Mar. abbr = **March**

mar [ma:ʳ] vt (appearance) verunstalten; (day) verderben; (event) stören

marathon ['mærəθən] n Marathon m ▷ adj: **a ~ session** eine Marathonsitzung

marathon runner n Marathonläufer(in) m(f)

marauder [mə'rɔ:dəʳ] n (robber) Plünderer m; (killer) Mörder m

marble ['ma:bl] n Marmor m; (toy) Murmel f

marbles ['ma:blz] n (game) Murmeln pl

March [ma:tʃ] n März m; see also **July**

march [ma:tʃ] vi marschieren; (protesters) ziehen ▷ n Marsch m; (demonstration) Demonstration f; **to ~ out of/into** (heraus) marschieren aus +dat/(herein)marschieren in +acc

marcher ['ma:tʃəʳ] n Demonstrant(in) m(f)

marching orders ['ma:tʃɪŋ-] npl: **to give sb his/her ~** (employee) jdn entlassen; (lover) jdm den Laufpass geben

march past n Vorbeimarsch m

mare [mɛəʳ] n Stute f

margarine [ma:dʒə'ri:n] n Margarine f

marge [ma:dʒ] (Brit: inf) n = **margarine**

margin ['ma:dʒɪn] n Rand m; (of votes) Mehrheit f; (for safety, error etc) Spielraum m; (Comm) Gewinnspanne f

marginal ['ma:dʒɪnl] adj geringfügig; (note) Rand-

marginally ['ma:dʒɪnəlɪ] adv nur wenig, geringfügig

marginal (seat) n (Pol) mit knapper Mehrheit gewonnener Wahlkreis

marigold ['mærɪgəuld] n Ringelblume f

marijuana [mærɪ'wɑ:nə] n Marihuana nt

marina [mə'ri:nə] n Jachthafen m

marinade [mærɪ'neɪd] n Marinade f ▷ vt = **marinate**

marinate ['mærɪneɪt] vt marinieren

marine [mə'ri:n] adj (plant, biology) Meeres- ▷ n (Brit: soldier) Marineinfanterist m; (US: sailor) Marinesoldat m; **~ engineer** Schiff(s)bauingenieur m; **~ engineering** Schiff(s)bau m

marine insurance n Seeversicherung f

marital ['mærɪtl] adj ehelich; (problem) Ehe-;

~ status Familienstand *m*
maritime ['mærɪtaɪm] *adj* (*nation*) Seefahrer-; (*museum*) Seefahrts-; (*law*) See-
marjoram ['mɑːdʒərəm] *n* Majoran *m*
mark [mɑːk] *n* Zeichen *nt*; (*stain*) Fleck *m*; (*in snow, mud etc*) Spur *f*; (*Brit: Scol*) Note *f*; (*level, point*): **the halfway ~** die Hälfte *f*; (*currency*) Mark *f*; (*Brit: Tech*): **M~ 2/3** Version *f* 2/3 ▷ *vt* (*with pen*) beschriften; (*with shoes etc*) schmutzig machen; (*with tyres etc*) Spuren hinterlassen auf +*dat*; (*damage*) beschädigen; (*stain*) Flecken machen auf +*dat*; (*indicate*) markieren; (: *price*) auszeichnen; (*commemorate*) begehen; (*characterize*) kennzeichnen; (*Brit: Scol*) korrigieren (und benoten); (*Sport: player*) decken; **punctuation ~s** Satzzeichen *pl*; **to be quick off the ~ (in doing sth)** (*fig*) blitzschnell reagieren (und etw tun); **to be up to the ~** den Anforderungen entsprechen; **to ~ time** auf der Stelle treten
▶ **mark down** *vt* (*prices, goods*) herabsetzen, heruntersetzen
▶ **mark off** *vt* (*tick off*) abhaken
▶ **mark out** *vt* markieren; (*person*) auszeichnen
▶ **mark up** *vt* (*price*) heraufsetzen
marked [mɑːkt] *adj* deutlich
markedly ['mɑːkɪdlɪ] *adv* deutlich
marker ['mɑːkəʳ] *n* Markierung *f*; (*bookmark*) Lesezeichen *nt*
market ['mɑːkɪt] *n* Markt *m* ▷ *vt* (*sell*) vertreiben; (*new product*) auf den Markt bringen; **to be on the ~** auf dem Markt sein; **on the open ~** auf dem freien Markt; **to play the ~** (*Stock Exchange*) an der Börse spekulieren
marketable ['mɑːkɪtəbl] *adj* marktfähig
market analysis *n* Marktanalyse *f*
market day *n* Markttag *m*
market demand *n* Marktbedarf *m*
market economy *n* Marktwirtschaft *f*
market expert *n* Marktexperte *m*, Marktexpertin *f*
market forces *npl* Marktkräfte *pl*
market garden (*Brit*) *n* Gemüseanbaubetrieb *m*
marketing ['mɑːkɪtɪŋ] *n* Marketing *nt*
marketing manager *n* Marketingmanager(in) *m(f)*
marketplace ['mɑːkɪtpleɪs] *n* Marktplatz *m*; (*Comm*) Markt *m*
market price *n* Marktpreis *m*
market research *n* Marktforschung *f*
market sector *n* Marktsegment *nt or* -sektor *m*
market value *n* Marktwert *m*
marking ['mɑːkɪŋ] *n* (*on animal*) Zeichnung *f*; (*on road*) Markierung *f*
marksman ['mɑːksmən] (*irreg: like* **man**) *n* Scharfschütze *m*
marksmanship ['mɑːksmənʃɪp] *n* Treffsicherheit *f*
mark-up ['mɑːkʌp] *n* (*Comm: margin*) Handelsspanne *f*; (: *increase*) (Preis)aufschlag *m*
marmalade ['mɑːməleɪd] *n* Orangenmarmelade *f*

maroon [mə'ruːn] *vt*: **to be ~ed** festsitzen ▷ *adj* kastanienbraun
marquee [mɑː'kiː] *n* Festzelt *nt*
marquess, marquis ['mɑːkwɪs] *n* Marquis *m*
Marrakech, Marrakesh [mærə'kɛʃ] *n* Marrakesch *nt*
marriage ['mærɪdʒ] *n* Ehe *f*; (*institution*) die Ehe; (*wedding*) Hochzeit *f*; **~ of convenience** Vernunftehe *f*
marriage bureau *n* Ehevermittlung *f*
marriage certificate *n* Heiratsurkunde *f*
marriage guidance, (*US*) **marriage counseling** *n* Eheberatung *f*
married ['mærɪd] *adj* verheiratet; (*life*) Ehe-; (*love*) ehelich; **to get ~** heiraten
marrow ['mærəʊ] *n* (*vegetable*) Kürbis *m*; (*also:* **bone marrow**) (Knochen)mark *nt*
marry ['mærɪ] *vt* heiraten; (*father*) verheiraten; (*priest*) trauen ▷ *vi* heiraten
Mars [mɑːz] *n* Mars *m*
Marseilles [mɑː'seɪlz] *n* Marseilles *nt*
marsh [mɑːʃ] *n* Sumpf *m*; (*also:* **salt marsh**) Salzsumpf *m*
marshal ['mɑːʃl] *n* (*Mil: also:* **field marshal**) (Feld)marschall *m*; (*official*) Ordner *m*; (*US: of police*) Bezirkspolizeichef *m* ▷ *vt* (*thoughts*) ordnen; (*support*) auftreiben; (*soldiers*) aufstellen
marshalling yard ['mɑːʃlɪŋ-] *n* (*Rail*) Rangierbahnhof *m*
marshmallow [mɑːʃ'mæləʊ] *n* (*Bot*) Eibisch *m*; (*sweet*) Marshmallow *nt*
marshy ['mɑːʃɪ] *adj* sumpfig
marsupial [mɑː'suːpɪəl] *n* Beuteltier *nt*
martial ['mɑːʃl] *adj* kriegerisch
martial arts *npl* Kampfsport *m*; **the ~** die Kampfkunst *sing*
martial law *n* Kriegsrecht *nt*
Martian ['mɑːʃən] *n* Marsmensch *m*
martin ['mɑːtɪn] *n* (*also:* **house martin**) Schwalbe *f*
martyr ['mɑːtəʳ] *n* Märtyrer(in) *m(f)* ▷ *vt* martern
martyrdom ['mɑːtədəm] *n* Martyrium *nt*
marvel ['mɑːvl] *n* Wunder *nt* ▷ *vi*: **to ~ (at)** staunen (über +*acc*)
marvellous, (*US*) **marvelous** ['mɑːvləs] *adj* wunderbar
Marxism ['mɑːksɪzəm] *n* Marxismus *m*
Marxist ['mɑːksɪst] *adj* marxistisch ▷ *n* Marxist(in) *m(f)*
marzipan ['mɑːzɪpæn] *n* Marzipan *nt*
mascara [mæs'kɑːrə] *n* Wimperntusche *f*
mascot ['mæskət] *n* Maskottchen *nt*
masculine ['mæskjulɪn] *adj* männlich; (*atmosphere, woman*) maskulin; (*Ling*) männlich, maskulin
masculinity [mæskju'lɪnɪtɪ] *n* Männlichkeit *f*
MASH [mæʃ] (*US*) *n abbr* (= *mobile army surgical hospital*) mobiles Lazarett *nt*
mash [mæʃ] *vt* zerstampfen
mashed potatoes [mæʃt-] *npl* Kartoffelpüree

nt, Kartoffelbrei *m*

mask [mɑ:sk] *n* Maske *f* ▷ *vt* (*cover*) verdecken; (*hide*) verbergen; **surgical ~** Mundschutz *m*

masking tape ['mɑ:skɪŋ-] *n* Abdeckband *nt*

masochism ['mæsəʊkɪzəm] *n* Masochismus *m*

masochist ['mæsəʊkɪst] *n* Masochist(in) *m(f)*

mason ['meɪsn] *n* (*also:* **stone mason**) Steinmetz *m*; (*also:* **freemason**) Freimaurer *m*

masonic [mə'sɒnɪk] *adj* (*lodge etc*) Freimaurer-

masonry ['meɪsnrɪ] *n* Mauerwerk *nt*

masquerade [mæskə'reɪd] *vi:* **to ~ as** sich ausgeben als ▷ *n* Maskerade *f*

Mass. (*US*) *abbr* (*Post*) = *Massachusetts*

mass [mæs] *n* Masse *f*; (*of people*) Menge *f*; (*large amount*) Fülle *f*; (*Rel*): **M~** Messe *f* ▷ *cpd* Massen- ▷ *vi* (*troops*) sich massieren; (*protesters*) sich versammeln; **the masses** *npl* (*ordinary people*) die Masse, die Massen *pl*; **to go to M~** zur Messe gehen; **~es of** (*inf*) massenhaft, jede Menge

massacre ['mæsəkə'] *n* Massaker *nt* ▷ *vt* massakrieren

massage ['mæsɑ:ʒ] *n* Massage *f* ▷ *vt* massieren

masseur [mæ'sə:'] *n* Masseur *m*

masseuse [mæ'sə:z] *n* Masseurin *f*

massive ['mæsɪv] *adj* (*furniture, person*) wuchtig; (*support*) massiv; (*changes, increase*) enorm

mass market *n* Massenmarkt *m*

mass media *npl* Massenmedien *pl*

mass meeting *n* Massenveranstaltung *f*; (*of everyone concerned*) Vollversammlung *f*; (*Pol*) Massenkundgebung *f*

mass-produce ['mæsprə'dju:s] *vt* in Massenproduktion herstellen

mass-production ['mæsprə'dʌkʃən] *n* Massenproduktion *f*

mast [mɑ:st] *n* (*Naut*) Mast *m*; (*Radio etc*) Sendeturm *m*

mastectomy [mæs'tɛktəmɪ] *n* Brustamputation *f*

master ['mɑ:stə'] *n* Herr *m*; (*teacher*) Lehrer *m*; (*title*): **M~ X** (der junge) Herr X; (*Art, Mus, of craft etc*) Meister *m* ▷ *cpd:* **~ baker/plumber** *etc* Bäcker-/Klempnermeister *etc m* ▷ *vt* meistern; (*feeling*) unter Kontrolle bringen; (*skill, language*) beherrschen

master disk *n* (*Comput*) Stammdiskette *f*

masterful ['mɑ:stəful] *adj* gebieterisch; (*skilful*) meisterhaft

master key *n* Hauptschlüssel *m*

masterly ['mɑ:stəlɪ] *adj* meisterhaft

mastermind ['mɑ:stəmaɪnd] *n* (führender) Kopf *m* ▷ *vt* planen und ausführen

Master of Arts *n* Magister *m* der philosophischen Fakultät

Master of Ceremonies *n* Zeremonienmeister *m*; (*for variety show etc*) Conférencier *m*

Master of Science *n* Magister *m* der naturwissenschaftlichen Fakultät

masterpiece ['mɑ:stəpi:s] *n* Meisterwerk *nt*

master plan *n* kluger Plan *m*

masterstroke ['mɑ:stəstrəʊk] *n* Meisterstück *nt*

mastery ['mɑ:stərɪ] *n* (*of language etc*) Beherrschung *f*; (*skill*) (meisterhaftes) Können *nt*

mastiff ['mæstɪf] *n* Dogge *f*

masturbate ['mæstəbeɪt] *vi* masturbieren, onanieren

masturbation [mæstə'beɪʃən] *n* Masturbation *f*, Onanie *f*

mat [mæt] *n* Matte *f*; (*also:* **doormat**) Fußmatte *f*; (*also:* **table mat**) Untersetzer *m*; (: *of cloth*) Deckchen *nt* ▷ *adj* = **matt**

match [mætʃ] *n* Wettkampf *m*; (*team game*) Spiel *nt*; (*Tennis*) Match *nt*; (*for lighting fire etc*) Streichholz *nt*; (*equivalent*): **to be a good/ perfect ~** gut/perfekt zusammenpassen ▷ *vt* (*go well with*) passen zu; (*equal*) gleichkommen +*dat*; (*correspond to*) entsprechen +*dat*; (*suit*) sich anpassen +*dat*; (*also:* **match up**: *pair*) passend zusammenbringen ▷ *vi* zusammenpassen; **to be no ~ for** sich nicht messen können mit; **with shoes to ~** mit (dazu) passenden Schuhen

▶ **match up** *vi* zusammenpassen

matchbox ['mætʃbɒks] *n* Streichholzschachtel *f*

matching ['mætʃɪŋ] *adj* (dazu) passend

matchless ['mætʃlɪs] *adj* unvergleichlich

mate [meɪt] *n* (*inf: friend*) Freund(in) *m(f)*, Kumpel *m*; (*animal*) Männchen *nt*, Weibchen *nt*; (*assistant*) Gehilfe *m*, Gehilfin *f*; (*in merchant navy*) Maat *m* ▷ *vi* (*animals*) sich paaren

material [mə'tɪərɪəl] *n* Material *nt*; (*cloth*) Stoff *m* ▷ *adj* (*possessions, existence*) materiell; (*relevant*) wesentlich; **materials** *npl* (*equipment*) Material *nt*

materialistic [mətɪərɪə'lɪstɪk] *adj* materialistisch

materialize [mə'tɪərɪəlaɪz] *vi* (*event*) zustande kommen; (*plan*) verwirklicht werden; (*hope*) sich verwirklichen; (*problem*) auftreten; (*crisis, difficulty*) eintreten

maternal [mə'tə:nl] *adj* mütterlich, Mutter-

maternity [məˈtəːnɪtɪ] n Mutterschaft f ▷ cpd
(ward etc) Entbindungs-; (care) für werdende
und junge Mütter

maternity benefit n Mutterschaftsgeld nt

maternity dress n Umstandskleid nt

maternity hospital n Entbindungsheim nt

maternity leave n Mutterschaftsurlaub m

matey [ˈmeɪtɪ] (Brit: inf) adj kumpelhaft

math [mæθ] (US) n = **maths**

mathematical [mæθəˈmætɪkl] adj
mathematisch

mathematician [mæθəməˈtɪʃən] n
Mathematiker(in) m(f)

mathematics [mæθəˈmætɪks] n Mathematik f

maths [mæθs], (US) **math** [mæθ] n Mathe f

matinée [ˈmætɪneɪ] n Nachmittagsvorstellung
f

mating [ˈmeɪtɪŋ] n Paarung f

mating call n Lockruf m

mating season n Paarungszeit f

matriarchal [meɪtrɪˈɑːkl] adj matriarchalisch

matrices [ˈmeɪtrɪsiːz] npl of **matrix**

matriculation [mətrɪkjuˈleɪʃən] n
Immatrikulation f

matrimonial [mætrɪˈməʊnɪəl] adj Ehe-

matrimony [ˈmætrɪmənɪ] n Ehe f

matrix [ˈmeɪtrɪks] (pl **matrices**) n (Math) Matrix
f; (framework) Gefüge nt

matron [ˈmeɪtrən] n (in hospital) Oberschwester
f; (in school) Schwester f

matronly [ˈmeɪtrənlɪ] adj matronenhaft

matt [mæt] adj matt; (paint) Matt-

matted [ˈmætɪd] adj verfilzt

matter [ˈmætər] n (event, situation) Sache f,
Angelegenheit f; (Phys) Materie f; (substance,
material) Stoff m; (Med: pus) Eiter m ▷ vi (be
important) wichtig sein; **matters** npl (affairs)
Angelegenheiten pl, Dinge pl; (situation) Lage
f; **what's the ~?** was ist los?; **no ~ what** egal
was (passiert); **that's another ~** das ist etwas
anderes; **as a ~ of course** selbstverständlich;
as a ~ of fact eigentlich; **it's a ~ of habit**
es ist eine Gewohnheitssache; **vegetable ~**
pflanzliche Stoffe pl; **printed ~** Drucksachen
pl; **reading ~** (Brit) Lesestoff m; **it doesn't ~** es
macht nichts

matter-of-fact [ˈmætərəvˈfækt] adj sachlich

matting [ˈmætɪŋ] n Matten pl; **rush ~**
Binsenmatten pl

mattress [ˈmætrɪs] n Matratze f

mature [məˈtjʊər] adj reif; (wine) ausgereift ▷ vi
reifen; (Comm) fällig werden

mature student n älterer Student m, ältere
Studentin f

maturity [məˈtjʊərɪtɪ] n Reife f; **to have
reached ~** (person) erwachsen sein; (animal)
ausgewachsen sein

maudlin [ˈmɔːdlɪn] adj gefühlsselig

maul [mɔːl] vt (anfallen und) übel zurichten

Mauritania [mɔːrɪˈteɪnɪə] n Mauritanien nt

Mauritius [məˈrɪʃəs] n Mauritius nt

mausoleum [mɔːsəˈlɪəm] n Mausoleum nt

mauve [məʊv] adj mauve

maverick [ˈmævrɪk] n (dissenter) Abtrünnige(r)
m; (independent thinker) Querdenker m

mawkish [ˈmɔːkɪʃ] adj rührselig

max. abbr = **maximum**

maxim [ˈmæksɪm] n Maxime f

maxima [ˈmæksɪmə] npl of **maximum**

maximize [ˈmæksɪmaɪz] vt maximieren

maximum [ˈmæksɪməm] (pl **maxima** or **~s**) adj
(amount, speed etc) Höchst-; (efficiency) maximal
▷ n Maximum nt

May [meɪ] n Mai m; see also **July**

may [meɪ] (conditional **might**) vi (be possible)
können; (have permission) dürfen; **he ~ come**
vielleicht kommt er; **~ I smoke?** darf ich
rauchen?; **~ God bless you!** (wish) Gott
segne dich!; **~ I sit here?** kann ich mich hier
hinsetzen?; **he might be there** er könnte
da sein; **you might like to try** vielleicht
möchten Sie es mal versuchen; **you ~ as well
go** Sie können ruhig gehen

maybe [ˈmeɪbiː] adv vielleicht; **~ he'll ...**
es kann sein, dass er ...; **~ not** vielleicht
nicht

Mayday [ˈmeɪdeɪ] n Maydaysignal nt, ≈ SOS-
Ruf m

May Day n der 1. Mai

mayhem [ˈmeɪhɛm] n Chaos nt

mayonnaise [meɪəˈneɪz] n Mayonnaise f

mayor [mɛər] n Bürgermeister m

mayoress [ˈmɛərɛs] n Bürgermeisterin f;
(partner) Frau f des Bürgermeisters

maypole [ˈmeɪpəʊl] n Maibaum m

maze [meɪz] n Irrgarten m; (fig) Wirrwarr m

MB abbr (Comput: = megabyte) MB;
(Canada) = Manitoba

MBA n abbr (= Master of Business Administration)
akademischer Grad in Betriebswirtschaft

MBE (Brit) n abbr (= Member of (the Order of) the
British Empire) britischer Ordenstitel

MC n abbr = **Master of Ceremonies**

MCAT (US) n abbr (= Medical College Admissions
Test) Zulassungsprüfung für medizinische Fachschulen

m-commerce [ˈɛmˈkɔməːs] n (Comm)
M-Commerce m, mobiler Handel m

MD n abbr (= Doctor of Medicine) ≈ Dr. med.;
(Comm) = **managing director** ▷ abbr
(US: Post) = Maryland

MDT (US) abbr (= Mountain Daylight Time)
amerikanische Sommerzeitzone

ME n abbr (US) = **medical examiner**;
(Med: = myalgic encephalomyelitis) krankhafter
Energiemangel (oft nach Viruserkrankungen) ▷ abbr
(US: Post) = Maine

○ **KEYWORD**

me [miː] pron **1** (direct) mich; **can you hear me?**
können Sie mich hören?; **it's me** ich bins
2 (indirect) mir; **he gave me the money, he
gave the money to me** er gab mir das Geld
3 (after prep): **it's for me** es ist für mich; **with
me** mit mir; **give them to me** gib sie mir;
without me ohne mich

meadow ['mɛdəu] n Wiese f

meagre, (US) **meager** ['mi:gəʳ] adj (amount) kläglich; (meal) dürftig

meal [mi:l] n Mahlzeit f; (food) Essen nt; (flour) Schrotmehl nt; **to go out for a ~** essen gehen; **to make a ~ of sth** (fig) etw auf sehr umständliche Art machen

meals on wheels n sing Essen nt auf Rädern

mealtime ['mi:ltaɪm] n Essenszeit f

mealy-mouthed ['mi:lɪmauðd] adj unaufrichtig; (politician) schönfärberisch

mean [mi:n] (pt, pp **~t**) adj (with money) geizig; (unkind) gemein; (US: inf: animal) bösartig; (shabby) schäbig; (average) Durchschnitts-, mittlere(r, s) ▷ vt (signify) bedeuten; (refer to) meinen; (intend) beabsichtigen ▷ n (average) Durchschnitt m; **means** npl (way) Möglichkeit f; (money) Mittel pl; **by ~s of** durch; **by all ~s!** aber natürlich or selbstverständlich!; **do you ~ it?** meinst du das ernst?; **what do you ~?** was willst du damit sagen?; **to be ~t for sb/sth** für jdn/etw bestimmt sein; **to ~ to do sth** etw tun wollen

meander [mɪ'ændəʳ] vi (river) sich schlängeln; (person: walking) schlendern; (: talking) abschweifen

meaning ['mi:nɪŋ] n Sinn m; (of word, gesture) Bedeutung f

meaningful ['mi:nɪŋful] adj sinnvoll; (glance, remark) vielsagend, bedeutsam; (relationship) tiefer gehend

meaningless ['mi:nɪŋlɪs] adj sinnlos; (word, song) bedeutungslos

meanness ['mi:nnɪs] n (with money) Geiz m; (unkindness) Gemeinheit f; (shabbiness) Schäbigkeit f

means test [mi:nz-] n Überprüfung f der Einkommens- und Vermögensverhältnisse

means-tested ['mi:nztɛstɪd] adj von den Einkommens- und Vermögensverhältnissen abhängig

meant [mɛnt] pt, pp of **mean**

meantime ['mi:ntaɪm] adv (also: **in the meantime**) inzwischen

meanwhile ['mi:nwaɪl] adv = **meantime**

measles ['mi:zlz] n Masern pl

measly ['mi:zlɪ] (inf) adj mick(e)rig

measurable ['mɛʒərəbl] adj messbar

measure ['mɛʒəʳ] vt, vi messen ▷ n (amount) Menge f; (ruler) Messstab m; (of achievement) Maßstab m; (action) Maßnahme f; **a litre ~** ein Messbecher m, der einen Liter fasst; **a/some ~ of** ein gewisses Maß an +dat; **to take ~s to do sth** Maßnahmen ergreifen, um etw zu tun
▶ **measure up** vi: **to ~ up to** herankommen an +acc

measured ['mɛʒəd] adj (tone) bedächtig; (step) gemessen

measurement ['mɛʒəmənt] n (measure) Maß nt; (act) Messung f; **chest/hip ~** Brust-/Hüftumfang m

measurements ['mɛʒəmənts] npl Maße pl; **to take sb's ~** bei jdm Maß nehmen

meat [mi:t] n Fleisch nt; **cold ~s** (Brit) Aufschnitt m; **crab ~** Krabbenfleisch nt

meatball ['mi:tbɔ:l] n Fleischkloß m

meat pie n Fleischpastete f

meaty ['mi:tɪ] adj (meal, dish) mit viel Fleisch; (fig: satisfying: book etc) gehaltvoll; (: brawny: person) kräftig (gebaut)

Mecca ['mɛkə] n (Geog, fig) Mekka nt

mechanic [mɪ'kænɪk] n Mechaniker(in) m(f)

mechanical [mɪ'kænɪkl] adj mechanisch

mechanical engineering n Maschinenbau m

mechanics [mɪ'kænɪks] n (Phys) Mechanik f
▷ npl (of reading etc) Technik f; (of government etc) Mechanismus m

mechanism ['mɛkənɪzəm] n Mechanismus m

mechanization [mɛkənaɪ'zeɪʃən] n Mechanisierung f

mechanize ['mɛkənaɪz] vt, vi mechanisieren

MEd n abbr (= Master of Education) akademischer Grad für Lehrer

medal ['mɛdl] n Medaille f; (decoration) Orden m

medallion [mɪ'dælɪən] n Medaillon nt

medallist, (US) **medalist** ['mɛdlɪst] n Medaillengewinner(in) m(f)

meddle ['mɛdl] vi: **to ~ (in)** sich einmischen (in +acc); **to ~ with sb** sich mit jdm einlassen; **to ~ with sth** (tamper) sich dat an etw dat zu schaffen machen

meddlesome ['mɛdlsəm], **meddling** ['mɛdlɪŋ] adj sich ständig einmischend

media ['mi:dɪə] npl Medien pl

media bashing (inf) n Medienschelte f

media circus n Medienrummel m

mediaeval [mɛdɪ'i:vl] adj = **medieval**

median ['mi:dɪən] (US) n (also: **median strip**) Mittelstreifen m

mediate ['mi:dɪeɪt] vi vermitteln

mediation [mi:dɪ'eɪʃən] n Vermittlung f

mediator ['mi:dɪeɪtəʳ] n Vermittler(in) m(f)

Medicaid ['mɛdɪkeɪd] (US) n staatliche Krankenversicherung und Gesundheitsfürsorge für Einkommensschwache

medical ['mɛdɪkl] adj (care) medizinisch; (treatment) ärztlich ▷ n (ärztliche) Untersuchung f

medical certificate n (confirming health) ärztliches Gesundheitszeugnis nt; (confirming illness) ärztliches Attest nt

medical examiner (US) n ≈ Gerichtsmediziner(in) m(f); (performing autopsy) Leichenbeschauer m

medical student n Medizinstudent(in) m(f)

Medicare ['mɛdɪkɛəʳ] (US) n staatliche Krankenversicherung und Gesundheitsfürsorge für ältere Bürger

medicated ['mɛdɪkeɪtɪd] adj medizinisch

medication [mɛdɪ'keɪʃən] n Medikamente pl

medicinal [mɛ'dɪsɪnl] adj (substance) Heil-; (qualities) heilend; (purposes) medizinisch

medicine ['mɛdsɪn] n Medizin f; (drug) Arznei f

medicine ball n Medizinball m

medicine chest n Hausapotheke f

medicine man n Medizinmann m

m

medieval [mɛdɪˈiːvl] adj mittelalterlich
mediocre [miːdɪˈəukəʳ] adj mittelmäßig
mediocrity [miːdɪˈɔkrɪtɪ] n Mittelmäßigkeit f
meditate [ˈmɛdɪteɪt] vi nachdenken; (Rel) meditieren
meditation [mɛdɪˈteɪʃən] n Nachdenken nt; (Rel) Meditation f
Mediterranean [mɛdɪtəˈreɪnɪən] adj (country, climate etc) Mittelmeer-; **the ~ (Sea)** das Mittelmeer
medium [ˈmiːdɪəm] (pl **media** or **~s**) adj mittlere(r, s) ▷ n (means) Mittel nt; (substance, material) Medium nt (pl **~s**) (person) Medium nt; **of ~ height** mittelgroß; **to strike a happy ~** den goldenen Mittelweg finden
medium-dry [ˈmiːdɪəmˈdraɪ] adj (wine, sherry) halbtrocken
medium-sized [ˈmiːdɪəmˈsaɪzd] adj mittelgroß
medium wave n (Radio) Mittelwelle f
medley [ˈmɛdlɪ] n Gemisch nt; (Mus) Medley nt
meek [miːk] adj sanft(mütig), duldsam
meet [miːt] (pt, pp **met**) vt (encounter) treffen; (by arrangement) sich treffen mit; (for the first time) kennenlernen; (go and fetch) abholen; (opponent) treffen auf +acc; (condition, standard) erfüllen; (need, expenses) decken; (problem) stoßen auf +acc; (challenge) begegnen +dat; (bill) begleichen; (join: line) sich schneiden mit; (: road etc) treffen auf +acc ▷ vi (encounter) sich begegnen; (by arrangement) sich treffen; (for the first time) sich kennenlernen; (for talks etc) zusammenkommen; (committee) tagen; (join: lines) sich schneiden; (: roads etc) aufeinandertreffen ▷ n (Brit: Hunting) Jagd f; (US: Sport) Sportfest nt; **pleased to ~ you!** (sehr) angenehm!
▸ **meet up** vi: **to ~ up with sb** sich mit jdm treffen
▸ **meet with** vt fus (difficulty, success) haben
meeting [ˈmiːtɪŋ] n (assembly, people assembling) Versammlung f; (Comm, of committee etc) Sitzung f; (also: **business meeting**) Besprechung f; (encounter) Begegnung f; (: arranged) Treffen nt; (Pol) Gespräch nt; (Sport) Veranstaltung f; **she's at** or **in a ~** (Comm) sie ist bei einer Besprechung; **to call a ~** eine Sitzung/Versammlung einberufen
meeting-place [ˈmiːtɪŋpleɪs] n Treffpunkt m
megabyte [ˈmɛgəbaɪt] n Megabyte nt
megalomaniac [mɛgələˈmeɪnɪæk] n Größenwahnsinnige(r) f(m)
megaphone [ˈmɛgəfəun] n Megafon nt
megawatt [ˈmɛgəwɔt] n Megawatt nt
melancholy [ˈmɛlənkəlɪ] n Melancholie f, Schwermut f ▷ adj melancholisch, schwermütig
mellow [ˈmɛləu] adj (sound) voll, weich; (light, colour, stone) warm; (weathered) verwittert; (person) gesetzt; (wine) ausgereift ▷ vi (person) gesetzter werden
melodious [mɪˈləudɪəs] adj melodisch
melodrama [ˈmɛləudrɑːmə] n Melodrama nt
melodramatic [mɛlədrəˈmætɪk] adj

melodramatisch
melody [ˈmɛlədɪ] n Melodie f
melon [ˈmɛlən] n Melone f
melt [mɛlt] vi (lit, fig) schmelzen ▷ vt schmelzen; (butter) zerlassen
▸ **melt down** vt einschmelzen
meltdown [ˈmɛltdaun] n (in nuclear reactor) Kernschmelze f
melting point [ˈmɛltɪŋ-] n Schmelzpunkt m
melting pot n (lit, fig) Schmelztiegel m; **to be in the ~** in der Schwebe sein
member [ˈmɛmbəʳ] n Mitglied nt; (Anat) Glied nt ▷ cpd: **~ country** Mitgliedsland nt; **~ state** Mitgliedsstaat m; **M~ of Parliament** (Brit) Abgeordnete(r) f(m) (des Unterhauses); **M~ of the European Parliament** (Brit) Abgeordnete(r) f(m) des Europaparlaments
membership [ˈmɛmbəʃɪp] n Mitgliedschaft f; (members) Mitglieder pl; (number of members) Mitgliederzahl f
membership card n Mitgliedsausweis m
membrane [ˈmɛmbreɪn] n Membran(e) f
memento [məˈmɛntəu] n Andenken nt
memo [ˈmɛməu] n Memo nt, Mitteilung f
memoir [ˈmɛmwɑːʳ] n Kurzbiografie f
memoirs [ˈmɛmwɑːz] npl Memoiren pl
memo pad n Notizblock m
memorable [ˈmɛmərəbl] adj denkwürdig; (unforgettable) unvergesslich
memorandum [mɛməˈrændəm] (pl **memoranda**) n Mitteilung f
memorial [mɪˈmɔːrɪəl] n Denkmal nt ▷ adj (service, prize) Gedenk-
Memorial Day (US) n ≈ Volkstrauertag m; siehe Info-Artikel

memorize [ˈmɛməraɪz] vt sich dat einprägen
memory [ˈmɛmərɪ] n Gedächtnis nt; (sth remembered) Erinnerung f; (Comput) Speicher m; **in ~ of** zur Erinnerung an +acc; **to have a good/bad ~** ein gutes/schlechtes Gedächtnis haben; **loss of ~** Gedächtnisschwund m
memory stick n (Comput) Memorystick® nt
men [mɛn] npl of **man**
menace [ˈmɛnɪs] n Bedrohung f; (nuisance) (Land)plage f ▷ vt bedrohen; **a public ~** eine Gefahr für die Öffentlichkeit
menacing [ˈmɛnɪsɪŋ] adj drohend
mend [mɛnd] vt reparieren; (darn) flicken ▷ n: **to be on the ~** auf dem Wege der Besserung sein; **to ~ one's ways** sich bessern
mending [ˈmɛndɪŋ] n Reparaturen pl; (clothes) Flickarbeiten pl
menial [ˈmiːnɪəl] (often pej) adj niedrig, untergeordnet

meningitis [mɛnɪn'dʒaɪtɪs] n
Hirnhautentzündung f

menopause ['mɛnəupɔːz] n: **the ~** die
Wechseljahre pl

menservants ['mɛnsəːvənts] npl of
manservant

men's room (US) n Herrentoilette f

menstrual ['mɛnstruəl] adj (Biol: cycle etc)
Menstruations-; **~ period** Monatsblutung f

menstruate ['mɛnstrueɪt] vi die Menstruation
haben

menstruation [mɛnstru'eɪʃən] n
Menstruation f

menswear ['mɛnzwɛəʳ] n Herren(be)kleidung f

mental ['mɛntl] adj geistig; (illness) Geistes-; **~
arithmetic** Kopfrechnen nt

mental hospital n psychiatrische Klinik f

mentality [mɛn'tælɪtɪ] n Mentalität f

mentally ['mɛntlɪ] adv: **to be ~ handicapped**
geistig behindert sein

menthol ['mɛnθɒl] n Menthol nt

mention ['mɛnʃən] n Erwähnung f ▷ vt
erwähnen; **don't ~ it!** (bitte,) gern
geschehen!; **not to ~ ...** von ... ganz zu
schweigen

mentor ['mɛntɔːʳ] n Mentor m

menu ['mɛnjuː] n Menü nt; (printed) Speisekarte
f

menu-driven ['mɛnjuːdrɪvn] adj (Comput)
menügesteuert

MEP (Brit) n abbr (= Member of the European
Parliament) Abgeordnete(r) f(m) des
Europaparlaments

mercantile ['məːkəntaɪl] adj (class, society)
Handel treibend; (law) Handels-

mercenary ['məːsɪnərɪ] adj (person) geldgierig
▷ n Söldner m

merchandise ['məːtʃəndaɪz] n Ware f

merchandiser ['məːtʃəndaɪzəʳ] n
Verkaufsförderungsexperte m

merchant ['məːtʃənt] n Kaufmann m; **timber/
wine ~** Holz-/Weinhändler m

merchant bank (Brit) n Handelsbank f

merchantman ['məːtʃəntmən] (irreg: like man)
n Handelsschiff nt

merchant navy, (US) **merchant marine** n
Handelsmarine f

merciful ['məːsɪful] adj gnädig; **a ~ release**
eine Erlösung

mercifully ['məːsɪflɪ] adv glücklicherweise

merciless ['məːsɪlɪs] adj erbarmungslos

mercurial [məːˈkjuərɪəl] adj (unpredictable)
sprunghaft, wechselhaft; (lively) quecksilbrig

mercury ['məːkjurɪ] n Quecksilber nt

mercy ['məːsɪ] n Gnade f; **to have ~ on sb**
Erbarmen mit jdm haben; **at the ~ of**
ausgeliefert +dat

mercy killing n Euthanasie f

mere [mɪəʳ] adj bloß; **his ~ presence irritates
her** schon or allein seine Anwesenheit ärgert
sie; **she is a ~ child** sie ist noch ein Kind; **it's
a ~ trifle** es ist eine Lappalie; **by ~ chance**
rein durch Zufall

merely ['mɪəlɪ] adv lediglich, bloß

merge [məːdʒ] vt (combine) vereinen;
(Comput: files) mischen ▷ vi (Comm) fusionieren;
(colours, sounds, shapes) ineinander übergehen;
(roads) zusammenlaufen

merger ['məːdʒəʳ] n (Comm) Fusion f

meridian [mə'rɪdɪən] n Meridian m

meringue [mə'ræŋ] n Baiser nt

merit ['mɛrɪt] n (worth, value) Wert m; (advantage)
Vorzug m; (achievement) Verdienst nt ▷ vt
verdienen

meritocracy [mɛrɪ'tɔkrəsɪ] n
Leistungsgesellschaft f

mermaid ['məːmeɪd] n Seejungfrau f,
Meerjungfrau f

merrily ['mɛrɪlɪ] adv vergnügt

merriment ['mɛrɪmənt] n Heiterkeit f

merry ['mɛrɪ] adj vergnügt; (music)
fröhlich; **M~ Christmas!** fröhliche or frohe
Weihnachten!

merry-go-round ['mɛrɪgəuraund] n Karussell
nt

mesh [mɛʃ] n Geflecht nt; **wire ~**
Maschendraht m

mesmerize ['mɛzməraɪz] vt (fig) faszinieren

mess [mɛs] n Durcheinander nt; (dirt)
Dreck m; (Mil) Kasino nt; **to be in a ~**
(untidy) unordentlich sein; (in difficulty)
in Schwierigkeiten stecken; **to be a ~**
(fig: life) verkorkst sein; **to get o.s. in a ~** in
Schwierigkeiten geraten

▸ **mess about** (inf) vi (fool around) herumalbern

▸ **mess about with** (inf) vt fus (play around with)
herumfummeln an +dat

▸ **mess around** (inf) vi = **mess about**

▸ **mess around with** (inf) vt fus = **mess about
with**

▸ **mess up** vt durcheinanderbringen; (dirty)
verdrecken

message ['mɛsɪdʒ] n Mitteilung f, Nachricht
f; (meaning) Aussage f; **to get the ~** (inf: fig)
kapieren

message switching [-'swɪtʃɪŋ] n (Comput)
Speichervermittlung f

messenger ['mɛsɪndʒəʳ] n Bote m

Messiah [mɪ'saɪə] n Messias m

Messrs ['mɛsəz] abbr (on letters: = messieurs) An
(die Herren)

messy ['mɛsɪ] adj (dirty) dreckig; (untidy)
unordentlich

Met [mɛt] (US) n abbr (= Metropolitan Opera) Met f

met [mɛt] pt, pp of **meet**

met. adj abbr (= meteorological): **the M~ Office**
das Wetteramt

metabolism [mɛ'tæbəlɪzəm] n Stoffwechsel m

metal ['mɛtl] n Metall nt

metal fatigue n Metallermüdung f

metalled ['mɛtld] adj (road) asphaltiert

metallic [mɪ'tælɪk] adj metallisch; (made of
metal) aus Metall

metallurgy [mɛ'tælədʒɪ] n Metallurgie f

metalwork ['mɛtlwəːk] n Metallarbeit f

metamorphosis [mɛtə'mɔːfəsɪs] (pl

m

657

metamorphoses) n Verwandlung f
metaphor ['mɛtəfəʳ] n Metapher f
metaphorical [mɛtə'fɔrɪkl] adj metaphorisch
metaphysics [mɛtə'fɪzɪks] n Metaphysik f
meteor ['miːtɪəʳ] n Meteor m
meteoric [miːtɪ'ɔrɪk] adj (fig) kometenhaft
meteorite ['miːtɪəraɪt] n Meteorit m
meteorological [miːtɪərə'lɒdʒɪkl] adj
  (conditions, office etc) Wetter-
meteorology [miːtɪə'rɔlədʒɪ] n Wetterkunde f,
  Meteorologie f
mete out [miːt-] vt austeilen; **to ~ justice**
  Recht sprechen
meter ['miːtəʳ] n Zähler m; (also: **water meter**)
  Wasseruhr f; (also: **parking meter**) Parkuhr f;
  (US: unit) = **metre**
methane ['miːθeɪn] n Methan nt
method ['mɛθəd] n Methode f; **~ of payment**
  Zahlungsweise f
methodical [mɪ'θɒdɪkl] adj methodisch
Methodist ['mɛθədɪst] n Methodist(in) m(f)
methodology [mɛθə'dɔlədʒɪ] n Methodik f
meths [mɛθs] (Brit) n = **methylated spirit**
methylated spirit ['mɛθɪleɪtɪd-] (Brit) n
  (Brenn)spiritus m
meticulous [mɪ'tɪkjuləs] adj sorgfältig; (detail)
  genau
metre, (US) **meter** ['miːtəʳ] n Meter m or nt
metric ['mɛtrɪk] adj metrisch; **to go ~** auf das
  metrische Maßsystem umstellen
metrical ['mɛtrɪkl] adj metrisch
metrication [mɛtrɪ'keɪʃən] n Umstellung f auf
  das metrische Maßsystem
metric system n metrisches Maßsystem nt
metric ton n Metertonne f
metronome ['mɛtrənəum] n Metronom nt
metropolis [mɪ'trɔpəlɪs] n Metropole f
metropolitan [mɛtrə'pɔlɪtn] adj großstädtisch
Metropolitan Police (Brit) n: **the ~** die
  Londoner Polizei
mettle ['mɛtl] n: **to be on one's ~** auf dem
  Posten sein
mew [mjuː] vi miauen
mews [mjuːz] (Brit) n Gasse f mit ehemaligen
  Kutscherhäuschen
Mexican ['mɛksɪkən] adj mexikanisch ▷ n
  Mexikaner(in) m(f)
Mexico ['mɛksɪkəu] n Mexiko nt
Mexico City n Mexico City f
mezzanine ['mɛtsəniːn] n Mezzanin nt
MFA (US) n abbr (= Master of Fine Arts) akademischer
  Grad in Kunst
mfr abbr = **manufacture; manufacturer**
mg abbr (= milligram(me)) mg
Mgr abbr (= Monseigneur, Monsignor) Mgr.; (Comm)
  = **manager**
MHR (US, Australia) n abbr (= Member of the House
  of Representatives) Abgeordnete(r) f(m) des
  Repräsentantenhauses
MHz abbr (= megahertz) MHz
MI (US) abbr (Post) = Michigan
MI5 (Brit) n abbr (= Military Intelligence, section five)
  britischer Spionageabwehrdienst

MI6 (Brit) n abbr (= Military Intelligence, section six)
  britischer Geheimdienst
MIA abbr (Mil: = missing in action) vermisst
miaow [miː'au] vi miauen
mice [maɪs] npl of **mouse**
Mich. (US) abbr (Post) = Michigan
micro ['maɪkrəu] n = **microcomputer**
micro ... ['maɪkrəu] pref mikro-, Mikro-
microbe ['maɪkrəub] n Mikrobe f
microbiology [maɪkrəubaɪ'ɔlədʒɪ] n
  Mikrobiologie f
microchip ['maɪkrəutʃɪp] n Mikrochip m
microcomputer ['maɪkrəukəm'pjuːtəʳ] n
  Mikrocomputer m
microcosm ['maɪkrəukɔzəm] n Mikrokosmos
  m
microeconomics ['maɪkrəuiːkə'nɔmɪks] n
  Mikroökonomie f
microelectronics ['maɪkrəuɪlɛk'trɔnɪks] n
  Mikroelektronik f
microfiche ['maɪkrəufiːʃ] n Mikrofiche m or nt
microfilm ['maɪkrəufɪlm] n Mikrofilm m
microlight ['maɪkrəulaɪt] n
  Ultraleichtflugzeug nt
micrometer [maɪ'krɔmɪtəʳ] n Messschraube f
microphone ['maɪkrəfəun] n Mikrofon nt
microprocessor ['maɪkrəu'prəusɛsəʳ] n
  Mikroprozessor m
microscope ['maɪkrəskəup] n Mikroskop nt;
  under the ~ unter dem Mikroskop
microscopic [maɪkrə'skɔpɪk] adj
  mikroskopisch; (creature) mikroskopisch klein
microwave ['maɪkrəuweɪv] n Mikrowelle f;
  (also: **microwave oven**) Mikrowellenherd m
mid [mɪd] adj: **in ~May** Mitte Mai; **in
  ~afternoon** (mitten) am Nachmittag; **in ~air**
  (mitten) in der Luft; **he's in his ~thirties** er
  ist Mitte dreißig
midday [mɪd'deɪ] n Mittag m
middle ['mɪdl] n Mitte f ▷ adj mittlere(r, s); **in
  the ~ of the night** mitten in der Nacht; **I'm
  in the ~ of reading it** ich bin mittendrin; **a ~
  course** ein Mittelweg m
middle age n mittleres Lebensalter nt
middle-aged [mɪdl'eɪdʒd] adj mittleren Alters
Middle Ages npl Mittelalter nt
middle-class [mɪdl'klɑːs] adj mittelständisch
middle class(es) n(pl) Mittelstand m
Middle East n Naher Osten m
middleman ['mɪdlmæn] (irreg: like **man**) n
  Zwischenhändler m
middle management n mittleres
  Management nt
middle name n zweiter Vorname m
middle-of-the-road ['mɪdləvðə'rəud] adj
  gemäßigt; (politician) der Mitte; (Mus) leicht
middleweight ['mɪdlweɪt] n (Boxing)
  Mittelgewicht nt
middling ['mɪdlɪŋ] adj mittelmäßig
Middx (Brit) abbr (Post) = Middlesex
midge [mɪdʒ] n Mücke f
midget ['mɪdʒɪt] n Liliputaner(in) m(f)
midi system ['mɪdɪ-] n Midi-System nt

Midlands ['mɪdləndz] (*Brit*) *npl*: **the ~** Mittelengland *nt*

midnight ['mɪdnaɪt] *n* Mitternacht *f* ▷ *cpd* Mitternachts-; **at ~** um Mitternacht

midriff ['mɪdrɪf] *n* Taille *f*

midst [mɪdst] *n*: **in the ~ of** mitten in +*dat*; **to be in the ~ of doing sth** mitten dabei sein, etw zu tun

midsummer [mɪd'sʌmər] *n* Hochsommer *m*; **M~('s) Day** Sommersonnenwende *f*

midway [mɪd'weɪ] *adj*: **we have reached the ~ point** wir haben die Hälfte hinter uns *dat* ▷ *adv* auf halbem Weg; **~ between** (*in space*) auf halbem Weg zwischen; **~ through** (*in time*) mitten in +*dat*

midweek [mɪd'wiːk] *adv* mitten in der Woche ▷ *adj* Mitte der Woche

midwife ['mɪdwaɪf] (*pl* **midwives**) *n* Hebamme *f*

midwifery ['mɪdwɪfərɪ] *n* Geburtshilfe *f*

midwinter [mɪd'wɪntər] *n*: **in ~** im tiefsten Winter

miffed [mɪft] (*inf*) *adj*: **to be ~** eingeschnappt sein

might [maɪt] *vb see* **may** ▷ *n* Macht *f*; **with all one's ~** mit aller Kraft

mighty ['maɪtɪ] *adj* mächtig

migraine ['miːgreɪn] *n* Migräne *f*

migrant ['maɪgrənt] *adj* (*bird*) Zug-; (*worker*) Wander- ▷ *n* (*bird*) Zugvogel *m*; (*worker*) Wanderarbeiter(in) *m(f)*

migrate [maɪ'greɪt] *vi* (*bird*) ziehen; (*person*) abwandern

migration [maɪ'greɪʃən] *n* Wanderung *f*; (*to cities*) Abwanderung *f*; (*of birds*) (Vogel)zug *m*

mike [maɪk] *n* = **microphone**

Milan [mɪ'læn] *n* Mailand *nt*

mild [maɪld] *adj* mild; (*gentle*) sanft; (*slight: infection etc*) leicht; (: *interest*) gering

mildew ['mɪldjuː] *n* Schimmel *m*

mildly ['maɪldlɪ] *adv* (*say*) sanft; (*slight*) leicht; **to put it ~** gelinde gesagt

mildness ['maɪldnɪs] *n* Milde *f*; (*gentleness*) Sanftheit *f*; (*of infection etc*) Leichtigkeit *f*

mile [maɪl] *n* Meile *f*; **to do 30 ~s per gallon** ≈ 9 Liter auf 100 km verbrauchen

mileage ['maɪlɪdʒ] *n* Meilenzahl *f*; (*fig*) Nutzen *m*; **to get a lot of ~ out of sth** etw gründlich ausnutzen; **there is a lot of ~ in the idea** aus der Idee lässt sich viel machen

mileage allowance *n* ≈ Kilometergeld *nt*

mileometer [maɪ'lɒmɪtər] *n* ≈ Kilometerzähler *m*

milestone ['maɪlstəun] *n* (*lit, fig*) Meilenstein *m*

milieu ['miːljə:] *n* Milieu *nt*

militant ['mɪlɪtnt] *adj* militant ▷ *n* Militante(r) *f(m)*

militarism ['mɪlɪtərɪzəm] *n* Militarismus *m*

militaristic [mɪlɪtə'rɪstɪk] *adj* militaristisch

military ['mɪlɪtərɪ] *adj* (*history, leader etc*) Militär- ▷ *n*: **the ~** das Militär

military police *n* Militärpolizei *f*

military service *n* Militärdienst *m*

militate ['mɪlɪteɪt] *vi*: **to ~ against** negative Auswirkungen haben auf +*acc*

militia [mɪ'lɪʃə] *n* Miliz *f*

milk [mɪlk] *n* Milch *f* ▷ *vt* (*lit, fig*) melken

milk chocolate *n* Vollmilchschokolade *f*

milk float (*Brit*) *n* Milchwagen *m*

milking ['mɪlkɪŋ] *n* Melken *nt*

milkman ['mɪlkmən] (*irreg: like* **man**) *n* Milchmann *m*

milk shake *n* Milchmixgetränk *nt*

milk tooth *n* Milchzahn *m*

milk truck (*US*) *n* = **milk float**

milky ['mɪlkɪ] *adj* milchig; (*drink*) mit viel Milch; **~ coffee** Milchkaffee *m*

Milky Way *n* Milchstraße *f*

mill [mɪl] *n* Mühle *f*; (*factory*) Fabrik *f*; (*woollen mill*) Spinnerei *f* ▷ *vt* mahlen ▷ *vi* (*also*: **mill about**) umherlaufen

millennium [mɪ'lɛnɪəm] (*pl* **~s** *or* **millennia**) *n* Jahrtausend *nt*

millennium bug *n* (*Comput*) Jahrtausendfehler *m*

miller ['mɪlər] *n* Müller *m*

millet ['mɪlɪt] *n* Hirse *f*

milli... ['mɪlɪ] *pref* Milli-

milligram, milligramme ['mɪlɪgræm] *n* Milligramm *nt*

millilitre, (US) milliliter ['mɪlɪliːtər] *n* Milliliter *m or nt*

millimetre, (US) millimeter ['mɪlɪmiːtər] *n* Millimeter *m or nt*

millinery ['mɪlɪnərɪ] *n* Hüte *pl*

million ['mɪljən] *n* Million *f*; **a ~ times** (*fig*) tausend Mal, x-mal

millionaire [mɪljə'nɛər] *n* Millionär *m*

millipede ['mɪlɪpiːd] *n* Tausendfüßler *m*

millstone ['mɪlstəun] *n* (*fig*): **it's a ~ round his neck** es ist für ihn ein Klotz am Bein

millwheel ['mɪlwiːl] *n* Mühlrad *nt*

milometer [maɪ'lɒmɪtər] *n* = **mileometer**

mime [maɪm] *n* Pantomime *f*; (*actor*) Pantomime *m* ▷ *vt* pantomimisch darstellen

mimic ['mɪmɪk] *n* Imitator *m* ▷ *vt* (*for amusement*) parodieren; (*animal, person*) imitieren, nachahmen

mimicry ['mɪmɪkrɪ] *n* Nachahmung *f*

Min. (*Brit*) *abbr* (*Pol*) = **ministry**

min. *abbr* (= *minute*) Min. = **minimum**

minaret [mɪnə'rɛt] *n* Minarett *nt*

mince [mɪns] *vt* (*meat*) durch den Fleischwolf drehen ▷ *vi* (*in walking*) trippeln ▷ *n* (*Brit: meat*) Hackfleisch *nt*; **he does not ~ (his) words** er nimmt kein Blatt vor den Mund

mincemeat ['mɪnsmiːt] *n* *süße Gebäckfüllung aus Dörrobst und Sirup*; (*US: meat*) Hackfleisch *nt*; **to make ~ of sb** (*inf*) Hackfleisch aus jdm machen

mince pie *n* *mit Mincemeat gefülltes Gebäck*

mincer ['mɪnsər] *n* Fleischwolf *m*

mincing ['mɪnsɪŋ] *adj* (*walk*) trippelnd; (*voice*) geziert

mind [maɪnd] *n* Geist *m*, Verstand *m*; (*thoughts*) Gedanken *pl*; (*memory*) Gedächtnis *nt* ▷ *vt*

m

aufpassen auf +acc; (office etc) nach dem
Rechten sehen in +dat; (object to) etwas haben
gegen; **to my ~** meiner Meinung nach; **to be
out of one's ~** verrückt sein; **it is on my ~** es
beschäftigt mich; **to keep** or **bear sth in ~**
etw nicht vergessen, an etw denken; **to make
up one's ~** sich entscheiden; **to change
one's ~** es sich dat anders überlegen; **to be in
two ~s about sth** sich dat über etw acc nicht
im Klaren sein; **to have it in ~ to do sth**
die Absicht haben, etw zu tun; **to have sb/
sth in ~** an jdn/etw denken; **it slipped my
~** ich habe es vergessen; **to bring** or **call sth
to ~** etw in Erinnerung rufen; **I can't get it
out of my ~** es geht mir nicht aus dem Kopf;
his ~ was on other things er war mit den
Gedanken woanders; **"~ the step"** „Vorsicht
Stufe"; **do you ~ if ...?** macht es Ihnen etwas
aus, wenn ...?; **I don't ~** es ist mir egal; **~
you, ...** allerdings ...; **never ~!** (it makes no odds)
ist doch egal!; (don't worry) macht nichts!

mind-boggling ['maɪndbɒglɪŋ] (inf) adj
atemberaubend

-minded ['maɪndɪd] adj: **fair~** gerecht; **an
industrially~ nation** ein auf Industrie
ausgerichtetes Land

minder ['maɪndəʳ] n Betreuer(in) m(f);
(inf: bodyguard) Aufpasser(in) m(f)

mindful ['maɪndful] adj: **~ of** unter
Berücksichtigung +gen

mindless ['maɪndlɪs] adj (violence) sinnlos;
(work) geistlos

mine¹ [maɪn] n (also: **coal mine, gold mine**)
Bergwerk nt; (bomb) Mine f ▷ vt (coal) abbauen;
(beach etc) verminen; (ship) eine Mine
befestigen an +dat

mine² [maɪn] pron meine(r, s); **that book
is ~** das Buch ist mein(e)s, das Buch gehört
mir; **this is ~** das ist meins; **a friend of ~** ein
Freund/eine Freundin von mir

mine detector n Minensuchgerät nt

minefield ['maɪnfiːld] n Minenfeld nt; (fig)
brisante Situation f

miner ['maɪnəʳ] n Bergmann m, Bergarbeiter m

mineral ['mɪnərəl] adj (deposit, resources)
Mineral- ▷ n Mineral nt; **minerals** npl (Brit: soft
drinks) Erfrischungsgetränke pl

mineralogy [mɪnə'rælədʒɪ] n Mineralogie f

mineral water n Mineralwasser nt

minesweeper ['maɪnswiːpəʳ] n
Minensuchboot nt

mingle ['mɪŋgl] vi: **to ~ (with)** sich vermischen
(mit); **to ~ with** (people) Umgang haben
mit; (at party etc) sich unterhalten mit; **you
should ~ a bit** du solltest dich unter die Leute
mischen

mingy ['mɪndʒɪ] (inf) adj knick(e)rig; (amount)
mick(e)rig

mini... ['mɪnɪ] pref Mini-

miniature ['mɪnətʃəʳ] adj winzig; (version etc)
Miniatur- ▷ n Miniatur f; **in ~** im Kleinen, im
Kleinformat

minibus ['mɪnɪbʌs] n Kleinbus m

minicab ['mɪnɪkæb] n Kleintaxi nt

minicomputer ['mɪnɪkəm'pjuːtəʳ] n
Minicomputer m

minim ['mɪnɪm] n (Mus) halbe Note f

minima ['mɪnɪmə] npl of **minimum**

minimal ['mɪnɪml] adj minimal

minimalist ['mɪnɪməlɪst] adj minimalistisch

minimize ['mɪnɪmaɪz] vt auf ein Minimum
reduzieren; (play down) herunterspielen

minimum ['mɪnɪməm] (pl **minima**) n
Minimum nt ▷ adj (income, speed) Mindest-;
to reduce to a ~ auf ein Mindestmaß
reduzieren; **~ wage** Mindestlohn m

minimum lending rate n Diskontsatz m

mining ['maɪnɪŋ] n Bergbau m ▷ cpd Bergbau-

minion ['mɪnjən] (pej) n Untergebene(r) f(m)

miniseries ['mɪnɪsɪəriːz] n Miniserie f

miniskirt ['mɪnɪskəːt] n Minirock m

minister ['mɪnɪstəʳ] n (Brit: Pol) Minister(in)
m(f); (Rel) Pfarrer m ▷ vi: **to ~ to** sich kümmern
um; (needs) befriedigen

ministerial [mɪnɪs'tɪərɪəl] (Brit) adj (Pol)
ministeriell

ministry ['mɪnɪstrɪ] n (Brit: Pol) Ministerium nt;
to join the ~ (Rel) Geistliche(r) werden

Ministry of Defence (Brit) n
Verteidigungsministerium nt

mink [mɪŋk] (pl **minks** or **~**) n Nerz m

mink coat n Nerzmantel m

Minn. (US) abbr (Post) = **Minnesota**

minnow ['mɪnəu] n Elritze f

minor ['maɪnəʳ] adj kleinere(r, s); (poet)
unbedeutend; (planet) klein; (Mus) Moll ▷ n
Minderjährige(r) f(m)

Minorca [mɪ'nɔːkə] n Menorca nt

minority [maɪ'nɔrɪtɪ] n Minderheit f; **to be in
a ~** in der Minderheit sein

minster ['mɪnstəʳ] n Münster nt

minstrel ['mɪnstrəl] n Spielmann m

mint [mɪnt] n Minze f; (sweet)
Pfefferminz(bonbon) nt; (place): **the M~**
die Münzanstalt ▷ vt (coins) prägen; **in ~
condition** neuwertig

mint sauce n Minzsoße f

minuet [mɪnjʊ'et] n Menuett nt

minus ['maɪnəs] n (also: **minus sign**)
Minuszeichen nt ▷ prep minus, weniger; **~
24°C** 24 Grad unter null

minuscule ['mɪnəskjuːl] adj winzig

minute¹ [maɪ'njuːt] adj winzig; (search)
peinlich genau; (detail) kleinste(r, s); **in ~
detail** in allen Einzelheiten

minute² ['mɪnɪt] n Minute f; (fig) Augenblick
m, Moment m; **minutes** npl (of meeting)
Protokoll nt; **it is 5 ~s past 3** es ist 5 Minuten
nach 3; **wait a ~!** einen Augenblick or
Moment!; **up-to-the-~** (news) hochaktuell;
(technology) allerneueste(r, s); **at the last ~** in
letzter Minute

minute book n Protokollbuch nt

minute hand n Minutenzeiger m

minutely [maɪ'njuːtlɪ] adv (in detail)
genauestens; (by a small amount) ganz

geringfügig

minutiae [mɪˈnjuːʃiː] npl Einzelheiten pl

miracle [ˈmɪrəkl] n (Rel, fig) Wunder nt

miraculous [mɪˈrækjuləs] adj wunderbar; (powers, effect, cure) Wunder-; (success, change) unglaublich; **to have a ~ escape** wie durch ein Wunder entkommen

mirage [ˈmɪrɑːʒ] n Fata Morgana f; (fig) Trugbild nt

mire [ˈmaɪəʳ] n Morast m

mirror [ˈmɪrəʳ] n Spiegel m ▷ vt (lit, fig) widerspiegeln

mirror image n Spiegelbild nt

mirth [mɜːθ] n Heiterkeit f

misadventure [mɪsədˈvɛntʃəʳ] n Missgeschick nt; **death by ~** (Brit) Tod m durch Unfall

misanthropist [mɪˈzænθrəpɪst] n Misanthrop m, Menschenfeind m

misapply [mɪsəˈplaɪ] vt (term) falsch verwenden; (rule) falsch anwenden

misapprehension [ˈmɪsæprɪˈhɛnʃən] n Missverständnis nt; **you are under a ~** Sie befinden sich im Irrtum

misappropriate [mɪsəˈprəuprɪeɪt] vt veruntreuen

misappropriation [ˈmɪsəprəuprɪˈeɪʃən] n Veruntreuung f

misbehave [mɪsbɪˈheɪv] vi sich schlecht benehmen

misbehaviour, (US) **misbehavior** [mɪsbɪˈheɪvjəʳ] n schlechtes Benehmen nt

misc. abbr = **miscellaneous**

miscalculate [mɪsˈkælkjuleɪt] vt falsch berechnen; (misjudge) falsch einschätzen

miscalculation [ˈmɪskælkjuˈleɪʃən] n Rechenfehler m; (misjudgement) Fehleinschätzung f

miscarriage [ˈmɪskærɪdʒ] n (Med) Fehlgeburt f; **~ of justice** (Law) Justizirrtum m

miscarry [mɪsˈkærɪ] vi (Med) eine Fehlgeburt haben; (fail: plans) fehlschlagen

miscellaneous [mɪsɪˈleɪnɪəs] adj verschieden; (subjects, items) divers; **~ expenses** sonstige Unkosten pl

mischance [mɪsˈtʃɑːns] n unglücklicher Zufall m

mischief [ˈmɪstʃɪf] n (bad behaviour) Unfug m; (playfulness) Verschmitztheit f; (harm) Schaden m; (pranks) Streiche pl; **to get into ~** etwas anstellen; **to do sb a ~** jdm etwas antun

mischievous [ˈmɪstʃɪvəs] adj (naughty) ungezogen; (playful) verschmitzt

misconception [ˈmɪskənˈsɛpʃən] n fälschliche Annahme f

misconduct [mɪsˈkɔndʌkt] n Fehlverhalten nt; **professional ~** Berufsvergehen nt

misconstrue [mɪskənˈstruː] vt missverstehen

miscount [mɪsˈkaunt] vt falsch zählen ▷ vi sich verzählen

misdemeanour, (US) **misdemeanor** [mɪsdɪˈmiːnəʳ] n Vergehen nt

misdirect [mɪsdɪˈrɛkt] vt (person) in die falsche Richtung schicken; (talent) vergeuden

miser [ˈmaɪzəʳ] n Geizhals m

miserable [ˈmɪzərəbl] adj (unhappy) unglücklich; (wretched) erbärmlich, elend; (unpleasant: weather) trostlos; (: person) gemein; (contemptible: offer, donation) armselig; (: failure) kläglich; **to feel ~** sich elend fühlen

miserably [ˈmɪzərəblɪ] adv (fail) kläglich; (live) elend; (smile, speak) unglücklich; (small) jämmerlich

miserly [ˈmaɪzəlɪ] adj geizig; (amount) armselig

misery [ˈmɪzərɪ] n (unhappiness) Kummer m; (wretchedness) Elend nt; (inf: person) Miesepeter m

misfire [mɪsˈfaɪəʳ] vi (plan) fehlschlagen; (car engine) fehlzünden

misfit [ˈmɪsfɪt] n Außenseiter(in) m(f)

misfortune [mɪsˈfɔːtʃən] n Pech nt, Unglück nt

misgiving [mɪsˈgɪvɪŋ] n Bedenken pl; **to have ~s about sth** sich bei etw nicht wohlfühlen

misguided [mɪsˈgaɪdɪd] adj töricht; (opinion, view) irrig; (misplaced) unangebracht

mishandle [mɪsˈhændl] vt falsch handhaben

mishap [ˈmɪshæp] n Missgeschick nt

mishear [mɪsˈhɪəʳ] (irreg: like **hear**) vt falsch hören ▷ vi sich verhören

misheard [mɪsˈhɜːd] pt, pp of **mishear**

mishmash [ˈmɪʃmæʃ] (inf) n Mischmasch m

misinform [mɪsɪnˈfɔːm] vt falsch informieren

misinterpret [mɪsɪnˈtəːprɪt] vt (gesture, situation) falsch auslegen; (comment) falsch auffassen

misinterpretation [ˈmɪsɪntəːprɪˈteɪʃən] n falsche Auslegung f

misjudge [mɪsˈdʒʌdʒ] vt falsch einschätzen

mislay [mɪsˈleɪ] (irreg: like **lay**) vt verlegen

mislead [mɪsˈliːd] (irreg: like **lead**) vt irreführen

misleading [mɪsˈliːdɪŋ] adj irreführend

misled [mɪsˈlɛd] pt, pp of **mislead**

mismanage [mɪsˈmænɪdʒ] vt (business) herunterwirtschaften; (institution) schlecht führen

mismanagement [mɪsˈmænɪdʒmənt] n Misswirtschaft f

misnomer [mɪsˈnəuməʳ] n unzutreffende Bezeichnung f

misogynist [mɪˈsɔdʒɪnɪst] n Frauenfeind m

misplaced [mɪsˈpleɪst] adj (misguided) unangebracht; (wrongly positioned) an der falschen Stelle

misprint [ˈmɪsprɪnt] n Druckfehler m

mispronounce [mɪsprəˈnauns] vt falsch aussprechen

misquote [ˈmɪsˈkwəut] vt falsch zitieren

misread [mɪsˈriːd] (irreg: like **read**) vt falsch lesen; (misinterpret) falsch verstehen

misrepresent [mɪsrɛprɪˈzɛnt] vt falsch darstellen; **he was ~ed** seine Worte wurden verfälscht wiedergegeben

Miss [mɪs] n Fräulein nt; **Dear ~ Smith** Liebe Frau Smith

miss [mɪs] vt (train etc, chance, opportunity) verpassen; (target) verfehlen; (notice loss of, regret absence of) vermissen; (class, meeting) fehlen bei ▷ vi danebentreffen; (missile, object) danebengehen ▷ n Fehltreffer m; **you can't ~**

m

it du kannst es nicht verfehlen; **the bus just ~ed the wall** der Bus wäre um ein Haar gegen die Mauer gefahren; **you're ~ing the point** das geht an der Sache vorbei
▶ **miss out** (Brit) vt auslassen
▶ **miss out on** vt fus (party) verpassen; (fun) zu kurz kommen bei

missal ['mɪsl] n Messbuch nt

misshapen [mɪs'ʃeɪpən] adj missgebildet

missile ['mɪsaɪl] n (Mil) Rakete f; (object thrown) (Wurf)geschoss nt, (Wurf)geschoß nt (Österr)

missile base n Raketenbasis f

missile launcher [-'lɔ:ntʃəʳ] n Startrampe f

missing ['mɪsɪŋ] adj (lost: person) vermisst; (: object) verschwunden; (absent, removed) fehlend; **to be ~** fehlen; **to go ~** verschwinden; **~ person** Vermisste(r) f(m)

mission ['mɪʃən] n (task) Mission f, Auftrag m; (representatives) Gesandtschaft f; (Mil) Einsatz m; (Rel) Mission f; **on a ~ to ...** (to place/people) im Einsatz in +dat/bei ...

missionary ['mɪʃənrɪ] n Missionar(in) m(f)

missive ['mɪsɪv] (form) n Schreiben nt

misspell ['mɪs'spel] (irreg: like **spell**) vt falsch schreiben

misspent ['mɪs'spent] adj (youth) vergeudet

mist [mɪst] n Nebel m; (light) Dunst m ▷ vi (also: **mist over**: eyes) sich verschleiern; (Brit: also: **mist over**, **mist up**: windows) beschlagen

mistake [mɪs'teɪk] (irreg: like **take**) n Fehler m ▷ vt sich irren in +dat; (intentions) falsch verstehen; **by ~** aus Versehen; **to make a ~** (in writing, calculation) sich vertun; **to make a ~ (about sb/sth)** sich (in jdm/etw) irren; **to ~ A for B** A mit B verwechseln

mistaken [mɪs'teɪkən] pp of **mistake** ▷ adj falsch; **to be ~** sich irren

mistaken identity n Verwechslung f

mistakenly [mɪs'teɪkənlɪ] adv irrtümlicherweise

mister ['mɪstəʳ] (inf) n (sir) not translated; see **Mr**

mistletoe ['mɪsltəʊ] n Mistel f

mistook [mɪs'tʊk] pt of **mistake**

mistranslation [mɪstræns'leɪʃən] n falsche Übersetzung f

mistreat [mɪs'tri:t] vt schlecht behandeln

mistress ['mɪstrɪs] n (lover) Geliebte f; (of house, servant, situation) Herrin f; (Brit: teacher) Lehrerin f

mistrust [mɪs'trʌst] vt misstrauen +dat ▷ n: **~ (of)** Misstrauen nt (gegenüber)

mistrustful [mɪs'trʌstful] adj: **~ (of)** misstrauisch (gegenüber)

misty ['mɪstɪ] adj (day etc) neblig; (glasses, windows) beschlagen

misty-eyed ['mɪstɪ'aɪd] adj mit verschleiertem Blick

misunderstand [mɪsʌndə'stænd] (irreg: like **understand**) vt missverstehen, falsch verstehen ▷ vi es falsch verstehen

misunderstanding ['mɪsʌndə'stændɪŋ] n Missverständnis nt; (disagreement)

Meinungsverschiedenheit f

misunderstood [mɪsʌndə'stud] pt, pp of **misunderstand**

misuse [n mɪs'ju:s, vt mɪs'ju:z] n Missbrauch m ▷ vt missbrauchen; (word) falsch gebrauchen

MIT (US) n abbr (= Massachusetts Institute of Technology) private technische Fachhochschule

mite [maɪt] n (small quantity) bisschen nt; (Brit: small child) Würmchen nt

miter ['maɪtəʳ] (US) n = **mitre**

mitigate ['mɪtɪgeɪt] vt mildern; **mitigating circumstances** mildernde Umstände pl

mitigation [mɪtɪ'geɪʃən] n Milderung f

mitre, (US) **miter** ['maɪtəʳ] n (of bishop) Mitra f; (Carpentry) Gehrung f

mitt ['mɪt], **mitten** ['mɪtn] n Fausthandschuh m

mix [mɪks] vt mischen; (drink) mixen; (sauce, cake) zubereiten; (ingredients) verrühren ▷ vi: **to ~ (with)** verkehren (mit) ▷ n Mischung f; **to ~ sth with sth** etw mit etw vermischen; **to ~ business with pleasure** das Angenehme mit dem Nützlichen verbinden; **cake ~** Backmischung f
▶ **mix in** vt (eggs etc) unterrühren
▶ **mix up** vt (people) verwechseln; (things) durcheinanderbringen; **to be ~ed up in sth** in etw acc verwickelt sein

mixed [mɪkst] adj gemischt; **~ marriage** Mischehe f

mixed-ability ['mɪkstə'bɪlɪtɪ] adj (group etc) mit unterschiedlichen Fähigkeiten

mixed bag n (of things, problems) Sammelsurium nt; (of people) gemischter Haufen m

mixed blessing n: **it's a ~** das ist ein zweischneidiges Schwert

mixed doubles npl gemischtes Doppel nt

mixed economy n gemischte Wirtschaftsform f

mixed grill (Brit) n Grillteller m

mixed-up [mɪkst'ʌp] adj durcheinander

mixer ['mɪksəʳ] n (for food) Mixer m; (drink) Tonic etc zum Auffüllen von alkoholischen Mixgetränken; **to be a good ~** (sociable person) kontaktfreudig sein

mixer tap n Mischbatterie f

mixture ['mɪkstʃəʳ] n Mischung f; (Culin) Gemisch nt; (: for cake) Teig m; (Med) Mixtur f

mix-up ['mɪksʌp] n Durcheinander nt

MK (Brit) abbr (Tech) = **mark**

mkt abbr = **market**

MLA (Brit) n abbr (Pol: = Member of the Legislative Assembly (of Northern Ireland)) Abgeordnete(r) f(m) der gesetzgebenden Versammlung

MLitt n abbr (= Master of Literature, Master of Letters) akademischer Grad in Literaturwissenschaft

MLR (Brit) n abbr = **minimum lending rate**

mm abbr (= millimetre) mm

MMS n abbr (= Multimedia Messaging Service) MMS® m

MN abbr (Brit) = **merchant navy**; (US: Post) = Minnesota

MO n abbr (= medical officer) Sanitätsoffizier m;

(US: *inf*) = **modus operandi**

moan [məʊn] *n* Stöhnen *nt* ▷ *vi* stöhnen; (*inf: complain*): **to ~ (about)** meckern (über +*acc*)

moaner ['məʊnə'] (*inf*) *n* Miesmacher(in) *m(f)*

moat [məʊt] *n* Wassergraben *m*

mob [mɔb] *n* Mob *m*; (*organized*) Bande *f* ▷ *vt* herfallen über +*acc*

mobile ['məʊbaɪl] *adj* beweglich; (*workforce, society*) mobil ▷ *n* (*decoration*) Mobile *nt*; **applicants must be ~** Bewerber müssen motorisiert sein

mobile home *n* Wohnwagen *m*

mobile (phone) *n* Funktelefon *nt*, Handy *nt*

mobility [məʊ'bɪlɪtɪ] *n* Beweglichkeit *f*; (*of workforce etc*) Mobilität *f*

mobility allowance *n* Beihilfe für Gehbehinderte

mobilize ['məʊbɪlaɪz] *vt* mobilisieren; (*Mil*) mobil machen ▷ *vi* (*Mil*) mobil machen

moccasin ['mɔkəsɪn] *n* Mokassin *m*

mock [mɔk] *vt* sich lustig machen über +*acc* ▷ *adj* (*fake: Elizabethan etc*) Pseudo-; (*exam*) Probe-; (*battle*) Schein-

mockery ['mɔkərɪ] *n* Spott *m*; **to make a ~ of sb** jdn zum Gespött machen; **to make a ~ of sth** etw zur Farce machen

mocking ['mɔkɪŋ] *adj* spöttisch

mockingbird ['mɔkɪŋbəːd] *n* Spottdrossel *f*

mock-up ['mɔkʌp] *n* Modell *nt*

MOD (*Brit*) *n abbr* = **Ministry of Defence**

mod cons ['mɔd'kɔnz] (*Brit*) *npl* (= *modern conveniences*) Komfort *m*

mode [məʊd] *n* Form *f*; (*Comput, Tech*) Betriebsart *f*; **~ of life** Lebensweise *f*; **~ of transport** Transportmittel *nt*

model ['mɔdl] *n* Modell *nt*; (*also:* **fashion model**) Mannequin *nt*; (*example*) Muster *nt* ▷ *adj* (*excellent*) vorbildlich; (*small scale: railway etc*) Modell- ▷ *vt* (*clothes*) vorführen; (*with clay etc*) modellieren, formen ▷ *vi* (*for designer, photographer etc*) als Modell arbeiten; **to ~ o.s. on sb** sich *dat* jdn zum Vorbild nehmen

modeller, (US) **modeler** ['mɔdlə'] *n* Modellbauer *m*

model railway *n* Modelleisenbahn *f*

modem ['məʊdɛm] *n* Modem *nt*

moderate [*adj* 'mɔdərət, *vb* 'mɔdəreɪt] *adj* gemäßigt; (*amount*) nicht allzu groß; (*change*) leicht ▷ *n* Gemäßigte(r) *f(m)* ▷ *vi* (*storm, wind etc*) nachlassen ▷ *vt* (*tone, demands*) mäßigen

moderately ['mɔdərətlɪ] *adv* mäßig; (*expensive, difficult*) nicht allzu; (*pleased, happy*) einigermaßen; **~ priced** nicht allzu teuer

moderation [mɔdə'reɪʃən] *n* Mäßigung *f*; **in ~** in or mit Maßen

moderator ['mɔdəreɪtə'] *n* (*Eccl*) Synodalpräsident *m*

modern ['mɔdən] *adj* modern; **~ languages** moderne Fremdsprachen *pl*

modernization [mɔdənaɪ'zeɪʃən] *n* Modernisierung *f*

modernize ['mɔdənaɪz] *vt* modernisieren

modest ['mɔdɪst] *adj* bescheiden; (*chaste*) schamhaft

modestly ['mɔdɪstlɪ] *adv* bescheiden; (*behave*) schamhaft; (*to a moderate extent*) mäßig

modesty ['mɔdɪstɪ] *n* Bescheidenheit *f*; (*chastity*) Schamgefühl *nt*

modicum ['mɔdɪkəm] *n*: **a ~ of** ein wenig or bisschen

modification [mɔdɪfɪ'keɪʃən] *n* Änderung *f*; (*to policy etc*) Modifizierung *f*; **to make ~s to** (Ver)änderungen vornehmen an +*dat*, modifizieren

modify ['mɔdɪfaɪ] *vt* (ver)ändern; (*policy etc*) modifizieren

modish ['məʊdɪʃ] *adj* (*fashionable*) modisch

Mods [mɔdz] (*Brit*) *n abbr* (*Scol*: = (*Honour*) *Moderations*) akademische Prüfung an der Universität Oxford

modular ['mɔdjulə'] *adj* (*unit, furniture*) aus Bauelementen (zusammengesetzt); (*Comput*) modular

modulate ['mɔdjuleɪt] *vt* modulieren; (*process, activity*) umwandeln

modulation [mɔdju'leɪʃən] *n* Modulation *f*; (*modification*) Veränderung *f*

module ['mɔdjuːl] *n* (Bau)element *nt*; (*Space*) Raumkapsel *f*; (*Scol*) Kurs *m*

modus operandi ['məʊdəsɔpə'rændiː] *n* Modus Operandi *m*

Mogadishu [mɔgə'dɪʃuː] *n* Mogadischu *nt*

mogul ['məʊgl] *n* (*fig*) Mogul *m*

MOH (*Brit*) *n abbr* (= *Medical Officer of Health*) Amtsarzt *m*, Amtsärztin *f*

mohair ['məʊhɛə'] *n* Mohair *m*

Mohammed [mə'hæmɛd] *n* Mohammed *m*

moist [mɔɪst] *adj* feucht

moisten ['mɔɪsn] *vt* anfeuchten

moisture ['mɔɪstʃə'] *n* Feuchtigkeit *f*

moisturize ['mɔɪstʃəraɪz] *vt* (*skin*) mit einer Feuchtigkeitscreme behandeln

moisturizer ['mɔɪstʃəraɪzə'] *n* Feuchtigkeitscreme *f*

molar ['məʊlə'] *n* Backenzahn *m*

molasses [mə'læsɪz] *n* Melasse *f*

mold *etc* [məʊld] (US) *n, vt* = **mould** *etc*

Moldavia [mɔl'deɪvɪə] *n* Moldawien *nt*

Moldavian [mɔl'deɪvɪən] *adj* moldawisch

Moldova [mɔl'dəʊvə] *n* Moldawien *nt*

Moldovan *adj* moldawisch

mole [məʊl] *n* (*on skin*) Leberfleck *m*; (*Zool*) Maulwurf *m*; (*fig: spy*) Spion(in) *m(f)*

molecular [məʊ'lɛkjulə'] *adj* molekular; (*biology*) Molekular-

molecule ['mɔlɪkjuːl] *n* Molekül *nt*

molehill ['məʊlhɪl] *n* Maulwurfshaufen *m*

molest [mə'lɛst] *vt* (*assault sexually*) sich vergehen an +*dat*; (*harass*) belästigen

mollusc ['mɔləsk] *n* Weichtier *nt*

mollycoddle ['mɔlɪkɔdl] *vt* verhätscheln

Molotov cocktail ['mɔlətɔf-] *n* Molotowcocktail *m*

molt [məʊlt] (US) *vi* = **moult**

molten ['məʊltən] *adj* geschmolzen, flüssig

mom [mɔm] (US) *n* = **mum**

moment ['məʊmənt] *n* Moment *m*, Augenblick *m*; (*importance*) Bedeutung *f*; **for a**

m

~ (für) einen Moment or Augenblick; **at that**
~ in diesem Moment or Augenblick; **at the ~**
momentan; **for the ~** vorläufig; **in a ~** gleich;
"one ~ please" (Tel) „bleiben Sie am Apparat"

momentarily ['məʊməntrɪlɪ] adv für einen
Augenblick or Moment; (US: very soon) jeden
Augenblick or Moment

momentary ['məʊməntərɪ] adj (brief) kurz

momentous [məʊ'mɛntəs] adj (occasion)
bedeutsam; (decision) von großer Tragweite

momentum [məʊ'mɛntəm] n (Phys) Impuls m;
(fig: of movement) Schwung m; (: of events, change)
Dynamik f; **to gather ~** schneller werden; (fig)
richtig in Gang kommen

mommy ['mɒmɪ] (US) n = **mummy**

Mon. abbr (= Monday) Mo.

Monaco ['mɒnəkəʊ] n Monaco nt

monarch ['mɒnək] n Monarch(in) m(f)

monarchist ['mɒnəkɪst] n Monarchist(in) m(f)

monarchy ['mɒnəkɪ] n Monarchie f; **the M~**
(royal family) die königliche Familie

monastery ['mɒnəstərɪ] n Kloster nt

monastic [mə'næstɪk] adj Kloster-, klösterlich;
(fig) mönchisch, klösterlich einfach

Monday ['mʌndɪ] n Montag m; see also **Tuesday**

Monegasque [mɒnə'gæsk] adj monegassisch
▷ n Monegasse m, Monegassin f

monetarist ['mʌnɪtərɪst] n Monetarist(in) m(f)
▷ adj monetaristisch

monetary ['mʌnɪtərɪ] adj (system, union)
Währungs-

money ['mʌnɪ] n Geld nt; **to make ~** (person)
Geld verdienen; (business) etwas einbringen;
danger ~ (Brit) Gefahrenzulage f; **I've got no
~ left** ich habe kein Geld mehr

moneyed ['mʌnɪd] (form) adj begütert

moneylender ['mʌnɪlɛndəʳ] n
Geldverleiher(in) m(f)

moneymaker ['mʌnɪmeɪkəʳ] n (person)
Finanzgenie nt; (idea) einträgliche Sache f;
(product) Verkaufserfolg m

moneymaking ['mʌnɪmeɪkɪŋ] adj einträglich

money market n Geldmarkt m

money order n Zahlungsanweisung f

money-spinner ['mʌnɪspɪnəʳ] (inf) n
Verkaufsschlager m; (person, business)
Goldgrube f

money supply n Geldvolumen nt

Mongol ['mɒŋgəl] n Mongole m, Mongolin f;
(Ling) Mongolisch nt

mongol ['mɒŋgəl] (offensive) n Mongoloide(r)
f(m)

Mongolia [mɒŋ'gəʊlɪə] n die Mongolei

Mongolian [mɒŋ'gəʊlɪən] adj mongolisch ▷ n
Mongole m, Mongolin f; (Ling) Mongolisch nt

mongoose ['mɒŋguːs] n Mungo m

mongrel ['mʌŋgrəl] n Promenadenmischung f

monitor ['mɒnɪtəʳ] n Monitor m ▷ vt
überwachen; (broadcasts) mithören

monk [mʌŋk] n Mönch m

monkey ['mʌŋkɪ] n Affe m

monkey business (inf) n faule Sachen pl

monkey nut (Brit) n Erdnuss f

monkey tricks npl = **monkey business**

monkey wrench n verstellbarer
Schraubenschlüssel m

mono ['mɒnəʊ] adj (recording etc) Mono-

monochrome ['mɒnəkrəʊm] adj (photograph,
television) Schwarzweiß-; (Comput: screen)
Monochrom-

monogamous [mə'nɒgəməs] adj monogam

monogamy [mə'nɒgəmɪ] n Monogamie f

monogram ['mɒnəgræm] n Monogramm nt

monolith ['mɒnəlɪθ] n Monolith m

monolithic [mɒnə'lɪθɪk] adj monolithisch

monologue ['mɒnəlɒg] n Monolog m

monoplane ['mɒnəpleɪn] n Eindecker m

monopolize [mə'nɒpəlaɪz] vt beherrschen;
(person) mit Beschlag belegen; (conversation) an
sich acc reißen

monopoly [mə'nɒpəlɪ] n Monopol nt; **to have
a ~ on** or **of sth** (fig: domination) etw für sich
gepachtet haben; **Monopolies and Mergers
Commission** (Brit) ≈ Kartellamt nt

monorail ['mɒnəʊreɪl] n Einschienenbahn f

monosodium glutamate [mɒnə'səʊdɪəm-
'gluːtəmeɪt] n Glutamat nt

monosyllabic [mɒnəsɪ'læbɪk] adj einsilbig

monosyllable ['mɒnəsɪləbl] n einsilbiges
Wort nt

monotone ['mɒnətəʊn] n: **in a ~** monoton

monotonous [mə'nɒtənəs] adj monoton,
eintönig

monotony [mə'nɒtənɪ] n Monotonie f,
Eintönigkeit f

monsoon [mɒn'suːn] n Monsun m

monster ['mɒnstəʳ] n Ungetüm nt, Monstrum
nt; (imaginary creature) Ungeheuer nt, Monster
nt; (person) Unmensch m

monstrosity [mɒn'strɒsɪtɪ] n Ungetüm nt,
Monstrum nt

monstrous ['mɒnstrəs] adj (huge) riesig; (ugly)
abscheulich; (atrocious) ungeheuerlich

Mont. (US) abbr (Post) = Montana

montage [mɒn'tɑːʒ] n Montage f

Mont Blanc [mɔ̃'blɑ̃] n Montblanc m

month [mʌnθ] n Monat m; **every ~** jeden
Monat; **300 dollars a ~** 300 Dollar im Monat

monthly ['mʌnθlɪ] adj monatlich; (ticket,
magazine) Monats- ▷ adv monatlich; **twice ~**
zweimal im Monat

Montreal [mɒntrɪ'ɔːl] n Montreal nt

monument ['mɒnjumənt] n Denkmal nt

monumental [mɒnju'mɛntl] adj (building,
statue) gewaltig, monumental; (book, piece of
work) unsterblich; (storm, row) ungeheuer

moo [muː] vi muhen

mood [muːd] n Stimmung f; (of person) Laune
f, Stimmung f; **to be in a good/bad ~** gut/
schlecht gelaunt sein; **to be in the ~ for**
aufgelegt sein zu

moodily ['muːdɪlɪ] adv launisch; (sullenly)
schlecht gelaunt

moody ['muːdɪ] adj launisch; (sullen) schlecht
gelaunt

moon [muːn] n Mond m

moonlight ['muːnlaɪt] n Mondschein m ▷ vi (inf) schwarzarbeiten

moonlighting ['muːnlaɪtɪŋ] (inf) n Schwarzarbeit f

moonlit ['muːnlɪt] adj (night) mondhell

moonshot ['muːnʃɒt] n Mondflug m

moor [muər] n (Hoch)moor nt, Heide f ▷ vt vertäuen ▷ vi anlegen

mooring ['muərɪŋ] n Anlegeplatz m; **moorings** npl (chains) Verankerung f

Moorish ['muərɪʃ] adj maurisch

moorland ['muələnd] n Moorlandschaft f, Heidelandschaft f

moose [muːs] n inv Elch m

moot [muːt] vt: **to be ~ed** vorgeschlagen werden ▷ adj: **it's a ~ point** das ist fraglich

mop [mɒp] n (for floor) Mop m; (for dishes) Spülbürste f; (of hair) Mähne f ▷ vt (floor) wischen; (face) abwischen; (eyes) sich dat wischen; **to ~ the sweat from one's brow** sich dat den Schweiß von der Stirn wischen
▶ **mop up** vt aufwischen

mope [məup] vi Trübsal blasen
▶ **mope about** vi mit einer Jammermiene herumlaufen
▶ **mope around** vi = **mope about**

moped ['məupɛd] n Moped nt

moquette [mɒ'kɛt] n Mokett m

MOR adj abbr (Mus) = **middle-of-the-road**

moral ['mɒrl] adj moralisch; (welfare, values) sittlich; (behaviour) moralisch einwandfrei ▷ n Moral f; **morals** npl (principles, values) Moralvorstellungen pl; **~ support** moralische Unterstützung f

morale [mɒ'rɑːl] n Moral f

morality [mə'rælɪtɪ] n Sittlichkeit f; (system of morals) Moral f, Ethik f; (correctness) moralische Richtigkeit f

moralize ['mɒrəlaɪz] vi moralisieren; **to ~ about** sich moralisch entrüsten über +acc

morally ['mɒrəlɪ] adv moralisch; (live, behave) moralisch einwandfrei

moral victory n moralischer Sieg m

morass [mə'ræs] n Morast m, Sumpf f, Sumpf m (also fig)

moratorium [mɒrə'tɔːrɪəm] n Stopp m; Moratorium nt

morbid ['mɔːbɪd] adj (imagination) krankhaft; (interest) unnatürlich; (comments, behaviour) makaber

Ⓞ KEYWORD

more [mɔːʳ] adj 1 (greater in number etc) mehr; **more people/work/letters than we expected** mehr Leute/Arbeit/Briefe, als wir erwarteten; **I have more wine/money than you** ich habe mehr Wein/Geld als du
2 (additional): **do you want (some) more tea?** möchten Sie noch mehr Tee?; **is there any more wine?** ist noch Wein da?; **I have no more money, I don't have any more money** ich habe kein Geld mehr
▷ pron 1 (greater amount) mehr; **more than 10** mehr als 10; **it cost more than we expected** es kostete mehr, als wir erwarteten
2 (further or additional amount): **is there any more?** gibt es noch mehr?; **there's no more** es ist nichts mehr da; **many/much more** viel mehr
▷ adv mehr; **more dangerous/difficult/easily** etc (than) gefährlicher/schwerer/leichter etc (als); **more and more** immer mehr; **more and more excited/expensive** immer aufgeregter/teurer; **more or less** mehr oder weniger; **more than ever** mehr denn je, mehr als jemals zuvor; **more beautiful than ever** schöner denn je; **no more, not any more** nicht mehr

moreover [mɔː'rəuvəʳ] adv außerdem, zudem

morgue [mɔːg] n Leichenschauhaus nt

MORI ['mɔːrɪ] (Brit) n abbr (= Market and Opinion Research Institute) Markt- und Meinungsforschungsinstitut

moribund ['mɒrɪbʌnd] adj dem Untergang geweiht

Mormon ['mɔːmən] n Mormone m, Mormonin f

morning ['mɔːnɪŋ] n Morgen m; (as opposed to afternoon) Vormittag m ▷ cpd Morgen-; **in the ~** morgens; vormittags; (tomorrow) morgen früh; **7 o'clock in the ~** 7 Uhr morgens; **this ~** heute Morgen

morning-after pill ['mɔːnɪŋ'ɑːftə-] n Pille f danach

morning market n (Econ) Vormittagsmarkt m

morning sickness n (Schwangerschafts) übelkeit f

Moroccan [mə'rɒkən] adj marokkanisch ▷ n Marokkaner(in) m(f)

Morocco [mə'rɒkəu] n Marokko nt

moron ['mɔːrɒn] (inf) n Schwachkopf m

moronic [mə'rɒnɪk] (inf) adj schwachsinnig

morose [mə'rəus] adj missmutig

morphine ['mɔːfiːn] n Morphium nt

morris dancing ['mɒrɪs-] n Moriskentanz m, alter englischer Volkstanz

Morse [mɔːs] n (also: **Morse code**) Morsealphabet nt

morsel ['mɔːsl] n Stückchen nt

mortal ['mɔːtl] adj sterblich; (wound, combat) tödlich; (danger) Todes-; (sin, enemy) Tod- ▷ n (human being) Sterbliche(r) f(m)

mortality [mɔː'tælɪtɪ] n Sterblichkeit f; (number of deaths) Todesfälle pl

mortality rate n Sterblichkeitsziffer f

mortar ['mɔːtəʳ] n (Mil) Minenwerfer m; (Constr) Mörtel m; (Culin) Mörser m

mortgage ['mɔːgɪdʒ] n Hypothek f ▷ vt mit einer Hypothek belasten; **to take out a ~** eine Hypothek aufnehmen

mortgage company (US) n Hypothekenbank f

mortgagee [mɔːgə'dʒiː] n Hypothekengläubiger m

m

mortgagor ['mɔːgədʒəˈ] n Hypotheken-
schuldner m
mortician [mɔːˈtɪʃən] (US) n Bestattungs-
unternehmer m
mortified ['mɔːtɪfaɪd] adj: **he was ~** er empfand
das als beschämend; (embarrassed) es war ihm
schrecklich peinlich
mortify ['mɔːtɪfaɪ] vt beschämen
mortise lock ['mɔːtɪs-] n Einsteckschloss nt
mortuary ['mɔːtjuərɪ] n Leichenhalle f
mosaic [məʊˈzeɪɪk] n Mosaik nt
Moscow ['mɔskəʊ] n Moskau nt
Moslem ['mɔzləm] adj, n = **Muslim**
mosque [mɔsk] n Moschee f
mosquito [mɔsˈkiːtəʊ] (pl **~es**) n Stechmücke f;
(in tropics) Moskito m
mosquito net n Moskitonetz nt
moss [mɔs] n Moos nt
mossy ['mɔsɪ] adj bemoost

 KEYWORD

most [məʊst] adj **1** (almost all: people, things etc)
meiste(r, s); **most people** die meisten Leute
2 (largest, greatest: interest, money etc) meiste(r,
s); **who has (the) most money?** wer hat das
meiste Geld?
▷ pron (greatest quantity, number) der/die/das
meiste; **most of it** das meiste (davon); **most
of them** die meisten von ihnen; **most of the
time/work** die meiste Zeit/Arbeit; **most of
the time he's very helpful** er ist meistens
sehr hilfsbereit; **to make the most of sth**
das Beste aus etw machen; **at the (very)
most** (aller)höchstens
▷ adv (+ vb: spend, eat, work etc) am meisten;
(+ adv: carefully, easily etc) äußerst; (very: polite,
interesting etc) höchst; (+ adj): **the most
intelligent/expensive** etc der/die/
das intelligenteste/teuerste etc; **a most
interesting book** ein höchst interessantes
Buch

mostly ['məʊstlɪ] adv (chiefly) hauptsächlich;
(usually) meistens
MOT (Brit) n abbr (= Ministry of Transport): **~ (test)**
≈ TÜV m; **the car failed its ~** das Auto ist
nicht durch den TÜV gekommen
motel [məʊˈtɛl] n Motel nt
moth [mɔθ] n Nachtfalter m; (also: **clothes
moth**) Motte f
mothball ['mɔθbɔːl] n Mottenkugel f
moth-eaten ['mɔθiːtn] (pej) adj
mottenzerfressen
mother ['mʌðəˈ] n Mutter f ▷ adj (country)
Heimat-; (company) Mutter- ▷ vt großziehen;
(pamper, protect) bemuttern
motherboard ['mʌðəbɔːd] n (Comput)
Hauptplatine f
motherhood ['mʌðəhʊd] n Mutterschaft f
mother-in-law ['mʌðərɪnlɔː] n
Schwiegermutter f
motherly ['mʌðəlɪ] adj mütterlich

mother-of-pearl ['mʌðərəvˈpəːl] n Perlmutt nt
mother's help n Haushaltshilfe f
mother-to-be ['mʌðətəˈbiː] n werdende
Mutter f
mother tongue n Muttersprache f
mothproof ['mɔθpruːf] adj mottenfest
motif [məʊˈtiːf] n Motiv nt
motion ['məʊʃən] n Bewegung f; (proposal)
Antrag m; (Brit: also: **bowel motion**) Stuhlgang
m ▷ vt, vi: **to ~ (to) sb to do sth** jdm ein
Zeichen geben, dass er/sie etw tun solle; **to
be in ~** (vehicle) fahren; **to set in ~** in Gang
bringen; **to go through the ~s (of doing sth)**
(fig) etw der Form halber tun; (pretend) so tun,
als ob (man etw täte)
motionless ['məʊʃənlɪs] adj reg(ungs)los
motion picture n Film m
motivate ['məʊtɪveɪt] vt motivieren
motivated ['məʊtɪveɪtɪd] adj motiviert; **~ by**
getrieben von
motivation [məʊtɪˈveɪʃən] n Motivation f
motive ['məʊtɪv] n Motiv nt, Beweggrund m
▷ adj (power, force) Antriebs-; **from the best
(of) ~s** mit den besten Absichten
motley ['mɔtlɪ] adj bunt (gemischt)
motor ['məʊtəˈ] n Motor m; (Brit: inf: car) Auto nt
▷ cpd (industry, trade) Auto(mobil)-
motorbike ['məʊtəbaɪk] n Motorrad nt
motorboat ['məʊtəbəʊt] n Motorboot nt
motorcade ['məʊtəkeɪd] n Fahrzeugkolonne f
motorcar ['məʊtəkaː] n (Brit) (Personenkraft)
wagen m
motorcoach ['məʊtəkəʊtʃ] (Brit) n Reisebus m
motorcycle ['məʊtəsaɪkl] n Motorrad nt
motorcycle racing n Motorradrennen nt
motorcyclist ['məʊtəsaɪklɪst] n
Motorradfahrer(in) m(f)
motoring ['məʊtərɪŋ] (Brit) n Autofahren nt
▷ cpd Auto-; (offence, accident) Verkehrs-
motorist ['məʊtərɪst] n Autofahrer(in) m(f)
motorized ['məʊtəraɪzd] adj motorisiert
motor oil n Motorenöl nt
motor racing (Brit) n Autorennen nt
motor scooter n Motorroller m
motor vehicle n Kraftfahrzeug nt
motorway ['məʊtəweɪ] (Brit) n Autobahn f
mottled ['mɔtld] adj gesprenkelt
motto ['mɔtəʊ] (pl **~es**) n Motto nt
mould, (US) **mold** [məʊld] n (cast) Form f; (: for
metal) Gussform f; (mildew) Schimmel m ▷ vt
(lit, fig) formen
moulder, (US) **molder** ['məʊldəˈ] vi (decay)
vermodern
moulding, (US) **molding** ['məʊldɪŋ] n (Archit)
Zierleiste f
mouldy, (US) **moldy** ['məʊldɪ] adj schimmelig;
(smell) moderig
moult, (US) **molt** [məʊlt] vi (animal) sich
haaren; (bird) sich mausern
mound [maʊnd] n (of earth) Hügel m; (heap)
Haufen m
mount [maʊnt] n (in proper names): **M~ Carmel**
der Berg Karmel; (horse) Pferd nt; (for picture)

Passepartout nt ▷ vt (horse) besteigen; (exhibition etc) vorbereiten; (jewel) (ein)fassen; (picture) mit einem Passepartout versehen; (staircase) hochgehen; (stamp) aufkleben; (attack, campaign) organisieren ▷ vi (increase) steigen; (: problems) sich häufen; (on horse) aufsitzen
▶ **mount up** vi (costs, savings) sich summieren, sich zusammenläppern (inf)
mountain ['mauntɪn] n Berg m ▷ cpd (road, stream) Gebirgs-; **to make a ~ out of a molehill** aus einer Mücke einen Elefanten machen
mountain bike n Mountainbike nt
mountaineer [mauntɪ'nɪəʳ] n Bergsteiger(in) m(f)
mountaineering [mauntɪ'nɪərɪŋ] n Bergsteigen nt; **to go ~** bergsteigen gehen
mountainous ['mauntɪnəs] adj gebirgig
mountain range n Gebirgskette f
mountain rescue team n Bergwacht f
mountainside ['mauntɪnsaɪd] n (Berg)hang m
mounted ['mauntɪd] adj (police) beritten
Mount Everest n Mount Everest m
mourn [mɔːn] vt betrauern ▷ vi: **to ~ (for)** trauern (um)
mourner ['mɔːnəʳ] n Trauernde(r) f(m)
mournful ['mɔːnful] adj traurig
mourning ['mɔːnɪŋ] n Trauer f; **to be in ~** trauern; (wear special clothes) Trauer tragen
mouse [maus] (pl **mice**) n (Zool, Comput) Maus f; (fig: person) schüchternes Mäuschen nt
mouse potato n (inf) Computerjunkie m, Mouse Potato f
mousetrap ['maustræp] n Mausefalle f
moussaka [muː'sɑːkə] n Moussaka f
mousse [muːs] n (Culin) Mousse f; (cosmetic) Schaumfestiger m
moustache, (US) **mustache** [məs'tɑːʃ] n Schnurrbart m
mousy ['mausɪ] adj (hair) mausgrau
mouth [mauθ] (pl **~s**) n Mund m; (of cave, hole, bottle) Öffnung f; (of river) Mündung f
mouthful ['mauθful] n (of food) Bissen m; (of drink) Schluck m
mouth organ n Mundharmonika f
mouthpiece ['mauθpiːs] n Mundstück nt; (spokesman) Sprachrohr nt
mouth-to-mouth ['mauθtə'mauθ] adj: **~ resuscitation** Mund-zu-Mund-Beatmung f
mouthwash ['mauθwɒʃ] n Mundwasser nt
mouth-watering ['mauθwɔː'tərɪŋ] adj appetitlich
movable ['muːvəbl] adj beweglich; **~ feast** beweglicher Feiertag m
move [muːv] n (movement) Bewegung f; (in game) Zug m; (change: of house) Umzug m; (: of job) Stellenwechsel m ▷ vt bewegen; (furniture) (ver)rücken; (car) umstellen; (in game) ziehen mit; (emotionally) bewegen, ergreifen; (Pol: resolution etc) beantragen ▷ vi sich bewegen; (traffic) vorankommen; (in game) ziehen; (also: **move house**) umziehen; (develop) sich entwickeln;

it's my ~ ich bin am Zug; **to get a ~ on** sich beeilen; **to ~ sb to do sth** jdn (dazu) veranlassen, etw zu tun; **to ~ towards** sich nähern +dat
▶ **move about** vi sich (hin- und her) bewegen; (travel) unterwegs sein; (from place to place) umherziehen; (change residence) umziehen; (change job) die Stelle wechseln; **I can hear him moving about** ich höre ihn herumlaufen
▶ **move along** vi weitergehen
▶ **move around** vi = **move about**
▶ **move away** vi (from town, area) wegziehen
▶ **move back** vi (return) zurückkommen
▶ **move forward** vi (advance) vorrücken
▶ **move in** vi (to house) einziehen; (police, soldiers) anrücken
▶ **move off** vi (car) abfahren
▶ **move on** vi (leave) weitergehen; (travel) weiterfahren ▷ vt (onlookers) zum Weitergehen auffordern
▶ **move out** vi (of house) ausziehen
▶ **move over** vi (to make room) (zur Seite) rücken
▶ **move up** vi (employee) befördert werden; (pupil) versetzt werden; (deputy) aufrücken
moveable ['muːvəbl] adj = **movable**
movement ['muːvmənt] n (action, group) Bewegung f; (freedom to move) Bewegungsfreiheit f; (transportation) Beförderung f; (shift) Trend m; (Mus) Satz m; (Med: also: **bowel movement**) Stuhlgang m
mover ['muːvəʳ] n (of proposal) Antragsteller(in) m(f)
movie ['muːvɪ] n Film m; **to go to the ~s** ins Kino gehen
movie camera n Filmkamera f
moviegoer ['muːvɪɡəuəʳ] (US) n Kinogänger(in) m(f)
moving ['muːvɪŋ] adj beweglich; (emotional) ergreifend; (instigating): **the ~ spirit/force** die treibende Kraft
mow [məu] (pt **~ed**, pp **mowed** or **~n**) vt mähen
▶ **mow down** vt (kill) niedermähen
mower ['məuəʳ] n (also: **lawnmower**) Rasenmäher m
Mozambique [məuzəm'biːk] n Mosambik nt
MP n abbr (= Member of Parliament) ≈ MdB; = **military police**; (Canada: = Mounted Police) berittene Polizei f
MP3 abbr (Comput) MP3
MP3 player n (Comput) MP3-Spieler m
mpg n abbr (= miles per gallon) see **mile**
mph abbr (= miles per hour) Meilen pro Stunde
MPhil n abbr (= Master of Philosophy) ≈ M.A.
MPS (Brit) n abbr (= Member of the Pharmaceutical Society) Qualifikationsnachweis für Pharmazeuten
Mr, (US) **Mr.** ['mɪstəʳ] n: **Mr Smith** Herr Smith
MRC (Brit) n abbr (= Medical Research Council) medizinischer Forschungsausschuss
MRCP (Brit) n abbr (= Member of the Royal College of Physicians) höchster akademischer Grad in Medizin
MRCS (Brit) n abbr (= Member of the Royal College of Surgeons) höchster akademischer Grad für Chirurgen

MRCVS (Brit) n abbr (= Member of the Royal College of Veterinary Surgeons) höchster akademischer Grad für Tiermediziner

Mrs, (US) **Mrs.** ['mɪsɪz] n: ~ **Smith** Frau Smith

MS n abbr (= multiple sclerosis) MS f; (US: = Master of Science) akademischer Grad in Naturwissenschaften ▷ abbr (US: Post) = Mississippi

MS. (pl **MSS.**) n abbr (= manuscript) Ms.

Ms, (US) **Ms.** [mɪz] n (= Miss or Mrs): **Ms Smith** Frau Smith

MSA (US) n abbr (= Master of Science in Agriculture) akademischer Grad in Agronomie

MSc n abbr (= Master of Science) akademischer Grad in Naturwissenschaften

MSG n abbr = **monosodium glutamate**

MSP (Brit) n abbr (Pol: = Member of the Scottish Parliament) Abgeordnete(r) f(m) des schottischen Parlaments

MST (US) abbr (= Mountain Standard Time) amerikanische Standardzeitzone

MSW (US) n abbr (= Master of Social Work) akademischer Grad in Sozialwissenschaft

MT n abbr (Comput, Ling: = machine translation) maschinelle Übersetzung f

Mt abbr (Geog) = **mount**

MTV (esp US) n abbr (= music television) MTV nt

◯ KEYWORD

much [mʌtʃ] adj (time, money, effort) viel; **how much money/time do you need?** wie viel Geld/Zeit brauchen Sie?; **he's done so much work for us** er hat so viel für uns gearbeitet; **as much as** so viel wie; **I have as much money/intelligence as you** ich besitze genauso viel Geld/Intelligenz wie du ▷ pron viel; **how much is it?** was kostet es? ▷ adv **1** (greatly, a great deal) sehr; **thank you very much** vielen Dank, danke sehr; **I read as much as I can** ich lese so viel wie ich kann **2** (by far) viel; **I'm much better now** mir geht es jetzt viel besser **3** (almost) fast; **how are you feeling? — much the same** wie fühlst du dich? — fast genauso; **the two books are much the same** die zwei Bücher sind sich sehr ähnlich

muck [mʌk] n (dirt) Dreck m
▶ **muck about** (inf) vi (fool about) herumalbern ▷ vt: **to ~ sb about** mit jdm beliebig umspringen
▶ **muck around** vi, vt = **muck about**
▶ **muck in** (Brit: inf) vi mit anpacken
▶ **muck out** vt (stable) ausmisten
▶ **muck up** (inf) vt (exam etc) verpfuschen

muckraking ['mʌkreɪkɪŋ] (fig: inf) n Sensationsmache f ▷ adj sensationslüstern

mucky ['mʌkɪ] adj (dirty) dreckig; (field) matschig

mucus ['mjuːkəs] n Schleim m

mud [mʌd] n Schlamm m

muddle ['mʌdl] n (mess) Durcheinander nt;

(confusion) Verwirrung f ▷ vt (person) verwirren; (also: **muddle up**) durcheinanderbringen; **to be in a ~** völlig durcheinander sein; **to get in a ~** (person) konfus werden; (things) durcheinandergeraten
▶ **muddle along** vi vor sich acc hin wursteln
▶ **muddle through** vi (get by) sich durchschlagen

muddle-headed [mʌdl'hɛdɪd] adj zerstreut

muddy ['mʌdɪ] adj (floor) schmutzig; (field) schlammig

mud flats npl Watt(enmeer) nt

mudguard ['mʌdɡɑːd] (Brit) n Schutzblech nt

mudpack ['mʌdpæk] n Schlammpackung f

mud-slinging ['mʌdslɪŋɪŋ] n (fig) Schlechtmacherei f

muesli ['mjuːzlɪ] n Müsli nt

muffin ['mʌfɪn] n (Brit) weiches, flaches Milchbrötchen, meist warm gegessen; (US) kleiner runder Rührkuchen

muffle ['mʌfl] vt (sound) dämpfen; (against cold) einmummeln

muffled ['mʌfld] adj (see vt) gedämpft; eingemummelt

muffler ['mʌflər] n (US: Aut) Auspufftopf m; (scarf) dicker Schal m

mufti ['mʌftɪ] n: **in ~** in Zivil

mug [mʌɡ] n (cup) Becher m; (for beer) Krug m; (inf: face) Visage f; (: fool) Trottel m ▷ vt (auf der Straße) überfallen; **it's a ~'s game** (Brit) das ist doch Schwachsinn
▶ **mug up** (Brit: inf) vt (also: **mug up on**) pauken

mugger ['mʌɡər] n Straßenräuber m

mugging ['mʌɡɪŋ] n Straßenraub m

muggins ['mʌɡɪnz] (Brit: inf) n Dummkopf m; **... and ~ does all the work** ... und ich bin mal wieder der/die Dumme und mache die ganze Arbeit

muggy ['mʌɡɪ] adj (weather, day) schwül

mug shot (inf) n (of criminal) Verbrecherfoto nt; (for passport) Passbild nt

mulatto [mjuː'lætəʊ] (pl **-es**) n Mulatte m, Mulattin f

mulberry ['mʌlbrɪ] n (fruit) Maulbeere f; (tree) Maulbeerbaum m

mule [mjuːl] n Maultier nt

mulled [mʌld] adj: **~ wine** Glühwein m

mullioned ['mʌlɪənd] adj (windows) längs unterteilt

mull over [mʌl-] vt sich dat durch den Kopf gehen lassen

multi... ['mʌltɪ] pref multi-, Multi-

multi-access ['mʌltɪ'æksɛs] adj (Comput: system etc) Mehrplatz-

multicoloured, (US) **multicolored** ['mʌltɪkʌləd] adj mehrfarbig

multifarious [mʌltɪ'fɛərɪəs] adj vielfältig

multifocals ['mʌltɪfəʊklz] npl Gleitsichtgläser pl

multilateral [mʌltɪ'lætərl] adj multilateral

multi-level ['mʌltɪlɛvl] (US) adj = **multistorey**

multimillionaire [mʌltɪmɪljə'nɛəʳ] n Multimillionär m

multinational [mʌltɪ'næʃənl] adj multinational ▷ n multinationaler Konzern m, Multi m (inf)

multiple ['mʌltɪpl] adj (injuries) mehrfach; (interests, causes) vielfältig ▷ n Vielfache(s) nt; ~ **collision** Massenkarambolage f

multiple-choice ['mʌltɪpltʃɔɪs] adj (question etc) Multiple-Choice-

multiple sclerosis n multiple Sklerose f

multiplex ['mʌltɪplɛks] n: ~ **transmitter** Multiplexsender m; ~ **(cinema)** Multiplexkino nt ▷ adj (Tech) Mehrfach- ▷ vt (Tel) gleichzeitig senden

multiplication [mʌltɪplɪ'keɪʃən] n Multiplikation f; (increase) Vervielfachung f

multiplication table n Multiplikationstabelle f

multiplicity [mʌltɪ'plɪsɪtɪ] n: **a ~ of** eine Vielzahl von

multiply ['mʌltɪplaɪ] vt multiplizieren ▷ vi (increase: problems) stark zunehmen; (: number) sich vervielfachen; (breed) sich vermehren

multiracial [mʌltɪ'reɪʃl] adj gemischtrassig; (school) ohne Rassentrennung; ~ **policy** Politik f der Rassenintegration

multistorey [mʌltɪ'stɔ:rɪ] (Brit) adj (building, car park) mehrstöckig

multitude ['mʌltɪtju:d] n Menge f; **a ~ of** eine Vielzahl von, eine Menge

mum [mʌm] (Brit: inf) n Mutti f, Mama f ▷ adj: **to keep ~** den Mund halten; **~'s the word** nichts verraten!

mumble ['mʌmbl] vt, vi (indistinctly) nuscheln; (quietly) murmeln

mumbo jumbo ['mʌmbəu-] n (nonsense) Geschwafel nt

mummify ['mʌmɪfaɪ] vt mumifizieren

mummy ['mʌmɪ] n (Brit: mother) Mami f; (embalmed body) Mumie f

mumps [mʌmps] n Mumps m or f

munch [mʌntʃ] vt, vi mampfen

mundane [mʌn'deɪn] adj (life) banal; (task) stumpfsinnig

Munich ['mju:nɪk] n München nt

municipal [mju:'nɪsɪpl] adj städtisch, Stadt-; (elections, administration) Kommunal-

municipality [mju:nɪsɪ'pælɪtɪ] n Gemeinde f, Stadt f

munitions [mju:'nɪʃənz] npl Munition f

mural ['mjuərl] n Wandgemälde nt

murder ['mə:dəʳ] n Mord m ▷ vt ermorden; (spoil: piece of music, language) verhunzen; **to commit ~** einen Mord begehen

murderer ['mə:dərəʳ] n Mörder m

murderess ['mə:dərɪs] n Mörderin f

murderous ['mə:dərəs] adj blutrünstig; (attack) Mord-; (fig: look, attack) vernichtend; (: pace, heat) mörderisch

murk [mə:k] n Düsternis f

murky ['mə:kɪ] adj düster; (water) trübe

murmur ['mə:məʳ] n (of voices) Murmeln nt; (of wind, waves) Rauschen nt ▷ vt, vi murmeln; **heart ~** Herzgeräusche pl

MusB, MusBac n abbr (= Bachelor of Music) akademischer Grad in Musikwissenschaft

muscle ['mʌsl] n Muskel m; (fig: strength) Macht f
  ▶ **muscle in** vi: **to ~ in (on sth)** (bei etw) mitmischen

muscular ['mʌskjuləʳ] adj (pain, dystrophy) Muskel-; (person, build) muskulös

muscular dystrophy n Muskeldystrophie f

MusD, MusDoc n abbr (= Doctor of Music) Doktorat in Musikwissenschaft

muse [mju:z] vi nachgrübeln ▷ n Muse f

museum [mju:'zɪəm] n Museum nt

mush [mʌʃ] n Brei m; (pej) Schmalz m

mushroom ['mʌʃrum] n (edible) (essbarer) Pilz m; (poisonous) Giftpilz m; (button mushroom) Champignon m ▷ vi (fig: buildings etc) aus dem Boden schießen; (: town, organization) explosionsartig wachsen

mushroom cloud n Atompilz m

mushy ['mʌʃɪ] adj matschig; (consistency) breiig; (inf: sentimental) rührselig; ~ **peas** Erbsenbrei m

music ['mju:zɪk] n Musik f; (written music, score) Noten pl

musical ['mju:zɪkl] adj musikalisch; (sound, tune) melodisch ▷ n Musical nt

musical box n = **music box**

musical chairs n die Reise f nach Jerusalem

musical instrument n Musikinstrument nt

music box n Spieldose f

music centre n Musikcenter nt

music hall n Varieté nt

musician [mju:'zɪʃən] n Musiker(in) m(f)

music stand n Notenständer m

musk [mʌsk] n Moschus m

musket ['mʌskɪt] n Muskete f

muskrat ['mʌskræt] n Bisamratte f

musk rose n Moschusrose f

Muslim ['mʌzlɪm] adj moslemisch ▷ n Moslem m, Moslime f

muslin ['mʌzlɪn] n Musselin m

musquash ['mʌskwɒʃ] n Bisamratte f; (fur) Bisam m

mussel ['mʌsl] n (Mies)muschel f

must [mʌst] aux vb müssen; (in negative) dürfen ▷ n Muss nt; **I ~ do it** ich muss es tun; **you ~ not do that** das darfst du nicht tun; **he ~ be there by now** jetzt müsste er schon dort sein; **you ~ come and see me soon** Sie müssen mich bald besuchen; **why ~ he behave so badly?** warum muss er sich so schlecht benehmen?; **I ~ have made a mistake** ich muss mich geirrt haben; **the film is a ~** den Film muss man unbedingt gesehen haben

mustache ['mʌstæʃ] (US) n = **moustache**

mustard ['mʌstəd] n Senf m

mustard gas n (Mil) Senfgas nt

muster ['mʌstəʳ] vt (support) zusammenbekommen; (also: **muster**

m

669

up: *energy, strength, courage)* aufbringen; *(troops, members)* antreten lassen ▷ *n:* **to pass ~** den Anforderungen genügen

mustiness ['mʌstɪnɪs] *n* Muffigkeit *f*

mustn't ['mʌsnt] = **must not**

musty ['mʌstɪ] *adj* muffig; *(building)* moderig

mutant ['mju:tənt] *n* Mutante *f*

mutate [mju:'teɪt] *vi (Biol)* mutieren

mutation [mju:'teɪʃən] *n (Biol)* Mutation *f*; *(alteration)* Veränderung *f*

mute [mju:t] *adj* stumm

muted ['mju:tɪd] *adj (colour)* gedeckt; *(reaction, criticism)* verhalten; *(sound, trumpet, Mus)* gedämpft

mutilate ['mju:tɪleɪt] *vt* verstümmeln

mutilation [mju:tɪ'leɪʃən] *n* Verstümmelung *f*

mutinous ['mju:tɪnəs] *adj* meuterisch; *(attitude)* rebellisch

mutiny ['mju:tɪnɪ] *n* Meuterei *f* ▷ *vi* meutern

mutter ['mʌtər] *vt, vi* murmeln

mutton ['mʌtn] *n* Hammelfleisch *nt*

mutual ['mju:tʃuəl] *adj (feeling, attraction)* gegenseitig; *(benefit)* beiderseitig; *(interest, friend)* gemeinsam; **the feeling was ~** das beruhte auf Gegenseitigkeit

mutually ['mju:tʃuəlɪ] *adv (beneficial, satisfactory)* für beide Seiten; *(accepted)* von beiden Seiten; **to be ~ exclusive** einander ausschließen; **~ incompatible** nicht miteinander vereinbar

Muzak® ['mju:zæk] *n* Berieselungsmusik *f (inf)*

muzzle ['mʌzl] *n (of dog)* Maul *nt*; *(of gun)* Mündung *f*; *(guard: for dog)* Maulkorb *m* ▷ *vt (dog)* einen Maulkorb anlegen +*dat*; *(fig: press, person)* mundtot machen

MV *abbr (= motor vessel)* MS

MVP *(US) n abbr (Sport: = most valuable player)* wertvollster Spieler *m*, wertvollste Spielerin *f*

MW *abbr (Radio: = medium wave)* MW

○ **KEYWORD**

my [maɪ] *adj* mein(e); **this is my brother/ sister/house** das ist mein Bruder/meine Schwester/mein Haus; **I've washed my hair/cut my finger** ich habe mir die Haare gewaschen/mir *or* mich in den Finger geschnitten; **is this my pen or yours?** ist das mein Stift oder deiner?

Myanmar ['maɪænma:ʳ] *n* Myanmar *nt*

myopic [maɪ'ɒpɪk] *adj (Med, fig)* kurzsichtig

myriad ['mɪrɪəd] *n* Unzahl *f*

myrrh [mɜ:ʳ] *n* Myrr(h)e *f*

myself [maɪ'sɛlf] *pron (acc)* mich; *(dat)* mir; *(emphatic)* selbst; *see also* **oneself**

mysterious [mɪs'tɪərɪəs] *adj* geheimnisvoll, mysteriös

mysteriously [mɪs'tɪərɪəslɪ] *adv* auf mysteriöse Weise; *(smile)* geheimnisvoll

mystery ['mɪstərɪ] *n (puzzle)* Rätsel *nt*; *(strangeness)* Rätselhaftigkeit *f* ▷ *cpd (guest, voice)* mysteriös; **~ tour** Fahrt *f* ins Blaue

mystery caller *n* Testanrufer(in) *m(f)*

mystery calling *n* Testanruf *m*

mystery shopper *n* Testkäufer(in) *m(f)*

mystery story *n* Kriminalgeschichte *f*

mystery visitor *n* Testbesucher(in) *m(f)*

mystic ['mɪstɪk] *n* Mystiker(in) *m(f)* ▷ *adj* mystisch

mystical ['mɪstɪkl] *adj* mystisch

mystify ['mɪstɪfaɪ] *vt* vor ein Rätsel stellen

mystique [mɪs'ti:k] *n* geheimnisvoller Nimbus *m*

myth [mɪθ] *n* Mythos *m*; *(fallacy)* Märchen *nt*

mythical ['mɪθɪkl] *adj* mythisch; *(jobs, opportunities etc)* fiktiv

mythological [mɪθə'lɒdʒɪkl] *adj* mythologisch

mythology [mɪ'θɒlədʒɪ] *n* Mythologie *f*

N n

N¹, n [ɛn] *n* (*letter*) N *nt*, n *nt*; **N for Nellie, N for Nan** (*US*) = N wie Nordpol

N² [ɛn] *abbr* (= *north*) N

NA (*US*) *n abbr* (= *Narcotics Anonymous*) Hilfsorganisation für Drogensüchtige; (= *National Academy*) Dachverband verschiedener Forschungsunternehmen

n/a *abbr* (= *not applicable*) entf.

NAACP (*US*) *n abbr* (= *National Association for the Advancement of Colored People*) Vereinigung zur Förderung Farbiger

NAAFI ['næfɪ] (*Brit*) *n abbr* (= *Navy, Army, & Air Force Institutes*) Laden für britische Armeeangehörige

NACU (*US*) *n abbr* (= *National Association of Colleges and Universities*) Fachhochschul- und Universitätsverband

nadir ['neɪdɪəʳ] *n* (*fig*) Tiefstpunkt *m*; (*Astron*) Nadir *m*

NAFTA *n abbr* (= *North Atlantic Free Trade Agreement*) amerikanische Freihandelszone

nag [næg] *vt* herumnörgeln an +*dat* ▷ *vi* nörgeln ▷ *n* (*pej: horse*) Gaul *m*; (: *person*) Nörgler(in) *m(f)*; **to ~ at sb** jdn plagen, jdm keine Ruhe lassen

nagging ['nægɪŋ] *adj* (*doubt, suspicion*) quälend; (*pain*) dumpf

nail [neɪl] *n* Nagel *m* ▷ *vt* (*inf: thief etc*) drankriegen; (: *fraud*) aufdecken; **to ~ sth to sth** etw an etw *acc* nageln; **to ~ sb down (to sth)** jdn (auf etw *acc*) festnageln

nailbrush ['neɪlbrʌʃ] *n* Nagelbürste *f*

nailfile ['neɪlfaɪl] *n* Nagelfeile *f*

nail polish *n* Nagellack *m*

nail polish remover *n* Nagellackentferner *m*

nail scissors *npl* Nagelschere *f*

nail varnish (*Brit*) *n* = **nail polish**

Nairobi [naɪˈrəʊbɪ] *n* Nairobi *nt*

naive [naːˈiːv] *adj* naiv

naïveté [naːˈiːvˈteɪ] *n* = **naivety**

naivety [naɪˈiːvtɪ] *n* Naivität *f*

naked ['neɪkɪd] *adj* nackt; (*flame, light*) offen; **with the ~ eye** mit bloßem Auge; **to the ~ eye** für das bloße Auge

nakedness ['neɪkɪdnɪs] *n* Nacktheit *f*

NAM (*US*) *n abbr* (= *National Association of Manufacturers*) nationaler Verband der verarbeitenden Industrie

name [neɪm] *n* Name *m* ▷ *vt* nennen; (*ship*) taufen; (*identify*) (beim Namen) nennen; (*date etc*) bestimmen, festlegen; **what's your ~?** wie heißen Sie?; **my ~ is Peter** ich heiße Peter; **by ~** mit Namen; **in the ~ of** im Namen +*gen*; **to give one's ~ and address** Namen und Adresse angeben; **to make a ~ for o.s.** sich *dat* einen Namen machen; **to give sb a bad ~** jdn in Verruf bringen; **to call sb ~s** jdn beschimpfen; **to be ~d after sb/sth** nach jdm/etw benannt werden

name-dropping ['neɪmdrɔpɪŋ] *n* Angeberei *f* mit berühmten Namen

nameless ['neɪmlɪs] *adj* namenlos; **who/ which shall remain ~** der/die/das ungenannt bleiben soll

namely ['neɪmlɪ] *adv* nämlich

nameplate ['neɪmpleɪt] *n* Namensschild *nt*

namesake ['neɪmseɪk] *n* Namensvetter(in) *m(f)*

nan bread [naːn-] *n* Nan-Brot *nt, fladenförmiges Weißbrot als Beilage zu indischen Gerichten*

nanny ['nænɪ] *n* Kindermädchen *nt*

nanny-goat ['nænɪgəʊt] *n* Geiß *f*

nap [næp] *n* Schläfchen *nt*; (*of fabric*) Strich *m* ▷ *vi*: **to be caught ~ping** (*fig*) überrumpelt werden; **to have a ~** ein Schläfchen *or* ein Nickerchen (*inf*) machen

NAPA (*US*) *n abbr* (= *National Association of Performing Artists*) Künstlergewerkschaft

napalm ['neɪpaːm] *n* Napalm *nt*

nape [neɪp] *n*: **the ~ of the neck** der Nacken

napkin ['næpkɪn] *n* (*also:* **table napkin**) Serviette *f*

Naples ['neɪplz] *n* Neapel *nt*

Napoleonic [nəpəʊlɪˈɔnɪk] *adj* napoleonisch

nappy ['næpɪ] (*Brit*) *n* Windel *f*

nappy liner (*Brit*) *n* Windeleinlage *f*

nappy rash *n* Wundsein *nt*

narcissistic [naːsɪˈsɪstɪk] *adj* narzisstisch

narcissus [naːˈsɪsəs] (*pl* **narcissi**) *n* Narzisse *f*

narcotic [naːˈkɔtɪk] *adj* narkotisch ▷ *n* Narkotikum *nt*; **narcotics** *npl* (*drugs*) Drogen *pl*; **~ drug** Rauschgift *nt*

nark [naːk] (*Brit: inf*) *vt*: **to be ~ed at sth** sauer über etw *acc* sein

narrate [nəˈreɪt] *vt* erzählen; (*film, programme*) kommentieren

narration [nəˈreɪʃən] *n* Kommentar *m*

narrative ['nærətɪv] n Erzählung f; (of journey etc) Schilderung f

narrator [nə'reɪtə^r] n Erzähler(in) m(f); (in film etc) Kommentator(in) m(f)

narrow ['nærəu] adj eng; (ledge etc) schmal; (majority, advantage, victory, defeat) knapp; (ideas, view) engstirnig ▷ vi sich verengen; (gap, difference) sich verringern ▷ vt (gap, difference) verringern; (eyes) zusammenkneifen; **to have a ~ escape** mit knapper Not davonkommen; **to ~ sth down (to sth)** etw (auf etw acc) beschränken

narrow gauge ['nærəugeɪdʒ] adj (Rail) Schmalspur-

narrowly ['nærəulɪ] adv knapp; (escape) mit knapper Not

narrow-minded [nærəu'maɪndɪd] adj engstirnig

NAS (US) n abbr (= National Academy of Sciences) Akademie der Wissenschaften

NASA ['næsə] (US) n abbr (= National Aeronautics and Space Administration) NASA f

nasal ['neɪzl] adj Nasen-; (voice) näselnd

Nassau ['næsɔ:] n Nassau nt

nastily ['nɑ:stɪlɪ] adv gemein; (say) gehässig

nastiness ['nɑ:stɪnɪs] n Gemeinheit f; (of remark) Gehässigkeit f; (of smell, taste etc) Ekelhaftigkeit f

nasturtium [nəs'tə:ʃəm] n Kapuzinerkresse f

nasty ['nɑ:stɪ] adj (remark) gehässig; (person) gemein; (taste, smell) ekelhaft; (wound, disease, accident, shock) schlimm; (problem, question) schwierig; (weather, temper) abscheulich; **to turn ~** unangenehm werden; **it's a ~ business** es ist schrecklich; **he's got a ~ temper** mit ihm ist nicht gut Kirschen essen

NAS/UWT (Brit) n abbr (= National Association of Schoolmasters/Union of Women Teachers) Lehrergewerkschaft

nation ['neɪʃən] n Nation f; (people) Volk nt

national ['næʃənl] adj (character, flag) National-; (interests) Staats-; (newspaper) überregional ▷ n Staatsbürger(in) m(f); **foreign ~** Ausländer(in) m(f)

national anthem n Nationalhymne f

National Curriculum n zentraler Lehrplan für Schulen in England und Wales

national debt n Staatsverschuldung f

national dress n Nationaltracht f

National Guard (US) n Nationalgarde f

National Health Service (Brit) n Staatlicher Gesundheitsdienst m

National Insurance (Brit) n Sozial-versicherung f

nationalism ['næʃnəlɪzəm] n Nationalismus m

nationalist ['næʃnəlɪst] adj nationalistisch ▷ n Nationalist(in) m(f)

nationality [næʃə'nælɪtɪ] n Staats-angehörigkeit f, Nationalität f

nationalization [næʃnəlaɪ'zeɪʃən] n Verstaatlichung f

nationalize ['næʃnəlaɪz] vt verstaatlichen

National Lottery n ≈ Lotto nt

nationally ['næʃnəlɪ] adv landesweit

national park n Nationalpark m

national press n überregionale Presse f

National Security Council (US) n Nationaler Sicherheitsrat m

national service n Wehrdienst m

National Trust (Brit) n Organisation zum Schutz historischer Bauten und Denkmäler sowie zum Landschaftsschutz; siehe Info-Artikel

> **NATIONAL TRUST**
>
> Der National Trust ist ein 1895 gegründeter Natur- und Denkmalschutzverband in Großbritannien, der Gebäude und Gelände von besonderem historischem oder ästhetischem Interesse erhält und der Öffentlichkeit zugänglich macht. Viele Gebäude im Besitz des National Trust sind (z. T. gegen ein Eintrittsgeld) zu besichtigen.

nationwide ['neɪʃənwaɪd] adj, adv landesweit

native ['neɪtɪv] n Einheimische(r) f(m) ▷ adj einheimisch; (country) Heimat-; (language) Mutter-; (innate) angeboren; **a ~ of Germany, a ~ German** ein gebürtiger Deutscher, eine gebürtige Deutsche; **~ to** beheimatet in +dat

Native American adj indianisch, der Ureinwohner Amerikas ▷ n Ureinwohner(in) m(f) Amerikas

native speaker n Muttersprachler(in) m(f)

Nativity [nə'tɪvɪtɪ] n: **the ~** Christi Geburt f

nativity play n Krippenspiel nt

NATO ['neɪtəu] n abbr (= North Atlantic Treaty Organization) NATO f

natter ['nætə^r] (Brit) vi quatschen (inf) ▷ n: **to have a ~** einen Schwatz halten

natural ['nætʃrəl] adj natürlich; (disaster) Natur-; (innate) angeboren; (born) geboren; (Mus) ohne Vorzeichen; **to die of ~ causes** eines natürlichen Todes sterben; **~ foods** Naturkost f; **she played F ~ not F sharp** sie spielte f statt fis

natural childbirth n natürliche Geburt f

natural gas n Erdgas nt

natural history n Naturkunde f; **the ~ of England** die Naturgeschichte Englands

naturalist ['nætʃrəlɪst] n Naturforscher(in) m(f)

naturalize ['nætʃrəlaɪz] vt: **to become ~d** eingebürgert werden

naturally ['nætʃrəlɪ] adv natürlich; (happen) auf natürlichem Wege; (die) eines natürlichen Todes; (cheerful, talented, blonde) von Natur aus

naturalness ['nætʃrəlnɪs] n Natürlichkeit f

natural resources npl Naturschätze pl

natural selection n natürliche Auslese f

natural wastage n natürliche Personalreduzierung f

nature ['neɪtʃə^r] n (Nature) Natur f; (kind, sort) Art f; (character) Wesen nt; **by ~** von Natur aus; **by its (very) ~** naturgemäß; **documents of a**

confidential ~ Unterlagen vertraulicher Art
-natured ['neɪtʃəd] *suff*: **good--** gutmütig; **ill--**
  bösartig
nature reserve (*Brit*) *n* Naturschutzgebiet
  nt
nature trail *n* Naturlehrpfad *m*
naturist ['neɪtʃərɪst] *n* Anhänger(in) *m(f)* der
  Freikörperkultur
naught [nɔːt] *n* = **nought**
naughtiness ['nɔːtɪnɪs] *n* (*see adj*) Unartigkeit *f*,
  Ungezogenheit *f*; Unanständigkeit *f*
naughty ['nɔːtɪ] *adj* (*child*) unartig, ungezogen;
  (*story, film, words*) unanständig
nausea ['nɔːsɪə] *n* Übelkeit *f*
nauseate ['nɔːsɪeɪt] *vt* Übelkeit verursachen
  +*dat*; (*fig*) anwidern
nauseating ['nɔːsɪeɪtɪŋ] *adj* ekelerregend; (*fig*)
  widerlich
nauseous ['nɔːsɪəs] *adj* ekelhaft; **I feel** ~ mir
  ist übel
nautical ['nɔːtɪkl] *adj* (*chart*) See-; (*uniform*)
  Seemanns-
nautical mile *n* Seemeile *f*
naval ['neɪvl] *adj* Marine-; (*battle, forces*) See-
naval officer *n* Marineoffizier *m*
nave [neɪv] *n* Hauptschiff *nt*, Mittelschiff *nt*
navel ['neɪvl] *n* Nabel *m*
navel piercing ['neɪvl] *n* Nabelpiercing *nt*
navigable ['nævɪgəbl] *adj* schiffbar
navigate ['nævɪgeɪt] *vt* (*river*) befahren; (*path*)
  begehen ▷ *vi* navigieren; (*Aut*) den Fahrer
  dirigieren
navigation [nævɪ'geɪʃən] *n* Navigation *f*
navigator ['nævɪgeɪtə'] *n* (*Naut*) Steuermann
  m; (*Aviat*) Navigator(in) *m(f)*; (*Aut*)
  Beifahrer(in) *m(f)*
navvy ['nævɪ] (*Brit*) *n* Straßenarbeiter *m*
navy ['neɪvɪ] *n* (Kriegs)marine *f*; (*ships*) (Kriegs)
  flotte *f* ▷ *adj* marineblau; **Department of the
  N~** (*US*) Marineministerium *nt*
navy-blue ['neɪvɪ'bluː] *adj* marineblau
Nazareth ['næzərɪθ] *n* Nazareth *nt*
Nazi ['nɑːtsɪ] *n* Nazi *m*
NB *abbr* (= *nota bene*) NB; (*Canada*) = *New
  Brunswick*
NBA (*US*) *n abbr* (= *National Basketball Association*)
  Basketball-Dachverband; (= *National Boxing
  Association*) Boxsport-Dachverband
NBC (*US*) *n abbr* (= *National Broadcasting Company*)
  Fernsehsender
NBS (*US*) *n abbr* (= *National Bureau of Standards*)
  amerikanischer Normenausschuss
NC *abbr* (*Comm etc*: = *no charge*) frei;
  (*US: Post*) = *North Carolina*
NCC (*US*) *n abbr* (= *National Council of Churches*)
  Zusammenschluss protestantischer und orthodoxer
  Kirchen
NCCL (*Brit*) *n abbr* (= *National Council for Civil
  Liberties*) Organisation zum Schutz von Freiheitsrechten
NCO *n abbr* (*Mil*: = *noncommissioned officer*) Uffz.
ND (*US*) *abbr* (*Post*) = *North Dakota*
N.Dak. (*US*) *abbr* (*Post*) = *North Dakota*
NE *abbr* = **north-east**; (*US: Post*) = *New*

England; Nebraska
NEA (*US*) *n abbr* (= *National Education Association*)
  Verband für das Erziehungswesen
neap [niːp] *n* (*also*: **neap tide**) Nippflut *f*
Neapolitan [nɪə'pɒlɪtən] *adj* neapolitanisch
  ▷ *n* Neapolitaner(in) *m(f)*
near [nɪə'] *adj* nahe ▷ *adv* nahe; (*almost*) fast,
  beinahe ▷ *prep* (*also*: **near to**: *in space*) nahe an
  +*dat*; (: *in time*) um *acc* ... herum; (: *in situation, in
  intimacy*) nahe +*dat* ▷ *vt* sich nähern +*dat*; (*state,
  situation*) kurz vor +*dat* stehen; **Christmas is** ~
  bald ist Weihnachten; **£25,000 or ~est offer**
  (*Brit*) £25.000 oder das nächstbeste Angebot;
  in the ~ future in naher Zukunft, bald; **in
  ~ darkness** fast im Dunkeln; **a ~ tragedy**
  beinahe eine Tragödie; **~ here/there** hier/
  dort in der Nähe; **to be ~ (to) doing sth**
  nahe daran sein, etw zu tun; **the building is
  ~ing completion** der Bau steht kurz vor dem
  Abschluss
nearby [nɪə'baɪ] *adj* nahe gelegen ▷ *adv* in der
  Nähe
Near East *n*: **the** ~ der Nahe Osten
nearer ['nɪərə'] *adj comp, adv comp of* **near**
nearest ['nɪərəst] *adj superl, adv superl of* **near**
nearly ['nɪəlɪ] *adv* fast; **I ~ fell** ich wäre
  beinahe gefallen; **it's not ~ big enough** es
  ist bei Weitem nicht groß genug; **she was ~
  crying** sie war den Tränen nahe
near miss *n* Beinahezusammenstoß *m*; **that
  was a ~** (*shot*) das war knapp daneben
nearness ['nɪənɪs] *n* Nähe *f*
nearside ['nɪəsaɪd] (*Aut*) *adj* (*when driving on left*)
  linksseitig; (*when driving on right*) rechtsseitig
  ▷ *n*: **the** ~ (*when driving on left*) die linke Seite;
  (*when driving on right*) die rechte Seite
near-sighted [nɪə'saɪtɪd] *adj* kurzsichtig
neat [niːt] *adj* ordentlich; (*handwriting*) sauber;
  (*plan, solution*) elegant; (*description*) prägnant;
  (*spirits*) pur; **I drink it ~** ich trinke es pur
neatly ['niːtlɪ] *adv* ordentlich; (*conveniently*)
  sauber
neatness ['niːtnɪs] *n* Ordentlichkeit *f*; (*of
  solution, plan*) Sauberkeit *f*
Nebr. (*US*) *abbr* (*Post*) = *Nebraska*
nebulous ['nɛbjuləs] *adj* vage, unklar
necessarily ['nɛsɪsrɪlɪ] *adv* notwendigerweise;
  not ~ nicht unbedingt
necessary ['nɛsɪsrɪ] *adj* notwendig, nötig;
  (*inevitable*) unausweichlich; **if ~** wenn nötig,
  nötigenfalls; **it is ~ to** ... man muss ...
necessitate [nɪ'sɛsɪteɪt] *vt* erforderlich
  machen
necessity [nɪ'sɛsɪtɪ] *n* Notwendigkeit *f*; **of
  ~** notgedrungen; **out of ~** aus Not; **the
  necessities (of life)** das Notwendigste (zum
  Leben)
neck [nɛk] *n* Hals *m*; (*of shirt, dress, jumper*)
  Ausschnitt *m* ▷ *vi* (*inf*) knutschen; **~ and neck**
  Kopf an Kopf; **to stick one's ~ out** (*inf*) seinen
  Kopf riskieren
necklace ['nɛklɪs] *n* (Hals)kette *f*
neckline ['nɛklaɪn] *n* Ausschnitt *m*

n

673

necktie ['nɛktaɪ] (esp US) n Krawatte f

nectar ['nɛktə^r] n Nektar m

nectarine ['nɛktərɪn] n Nektarine f

née [neɪ] prep: ~ **Scott** geborene Scott

need [niːd] n Bedarf m; (necessity) Notwendigkeit f; (requirement) Bedürfnis nt; (poverty) Not f ▷ vt brauchen; (could do with) nötig haben; **in ~** bedürftig; **to be in ~ of sth** etw nötig haben; **£10 will meet my immediate ~s** mit £ 10 komme ich erst einmal aus; **(there's) no ~** (das ist) nicht nötig; **there's no ~ to get so worked up about it** du brauchst dich darüber nicht so aufzuregen; **he had no ~ to work** er hatte es nicht nötig zu arbeiten; **I ~ to do it** ich muss es tun; **you don't ~ to go, you needn't go** du brauchst nicht zu gehen; **a signature is ~ed** das bedarf einer Unterschrift gen

needle ['niːdl] n Nadel f ▷ vt (fig: inf: goad) ärgern, piesacken

needless ['niːdlɪs] adj unnötig; **~ to say** natürlich

needlessly ['niːdlɪslɪ] adv unnötig

needlework ['niːdlwəːk] n Handarbeit f

needn't ['niːdnt] = **need not**

needy ['niːdɪ] adj bedürftig ▷ npl: **the ~** die Bedürftigen pl

negation [nɪ'geɪʃən] n Verweigerung f

negative ['nɛgətɪv] adj negativ; (answer) abschlägig ▷ n (Phot) Negativ nt; (Ling) Verneinungswort nt, Negation f; **to answer in the ~** eine verneinende Antwort geben

negative equity n Differenz zwischen gefallenem Wert und hypothekarischer Belastung eines Wohnungseigentums

neglect [nɪ'glɛkt] vt vernachlässigen; (writer, artist) unterschätzen ▷ n Vernachlässigung f

neglected [nɪ'glɛktɪd] adj vernachlässigt; (writer, artist) unterschätzt

neglectful [nɪ'glɛktful] adj nachlässig; (father) pflichtvergessen; **to be ~ of sth** etw vernachlässigen

negligee ['nɛglɪʒeɪ] n Negligee nt, Negligé nt

negligence ['nɛglɪdʒəns] n Nachlässigkeit f; (Law) Fahrlässigkeit f

negligent ['nɛglɪdʒənt] adj nachlässig; (Law) fahrlässig; (casual) lässig

negligently ['nɛglɪdʒəntlɪ] adv (see adj) nachlässig; fahrlässig; lässig

negligible ['nɛglɪdʒɪbl] adj geringfügig

negotiable [nɪ'gəuʃɪəbl] adj verhandlungsfähig; (path, river) passierbar; **not ~** (on cheque etc) nicht übertragbar

negotiate [nɪ'gəuʃɪeɪt] vi verhandeln ▷ vt aushandeln; (obstacle, hill) überwinden; (bend) nehmen; **to ~ with sb (for sth)** mit jdm (über etw acc) verhandeln

negotiating table [nɪ'gəuʃɪeɪtɪŋ-] n Verhandlungstisch m

negotiation [nɪgəuʃɪ'eɪʃən] n Verhandlung f; **the matter is still under ~** über die Sache wird noch verhandelt

negotiator [nɪ'gəuʃɪeɪtə^r] n Unterhändler(in) m(f)

Negress ['niːgrɪs] n Negerin f

Negro ['niːgrəu] (pl **N~es**) adj (boy, slave) Neger- ▷ n Neger m

neigh [neɪ] vi wiehern

neighbour, (US) **neighbor** ['neɪbə^r] n Nachbar(in) m(f)

neighbourhood ['neɪbəhud] n (place) Gegend f; (people) Nachbarschaft f; **in the ~ of ...** in der Nähe von ...; (sum of money) so um die ...

neighbourhood watch n Vereinigung von Bürgern, die Straßenwachen etc zur Unterstützung der Polizei bei der Verbrechensbekämpfung organisiert

neighbouring ['neɪbərɪŋ] adj benachbart, Nachbar-

neighbourly ['neɪbəlɪ] adj nachbarlich

neither ['naɪðə^r] conj: **I didn't move and ~ did John** ich bewegte mich nicht und John auch nicht ▷ pron keine(r, s) (von beiden) ▷ adv: **~ ... nor ...** weder ... noch ...; **~ story is true** keine der beiden Geschichten stimmt; **~ is true** beides stimmt nicht; **~ do I/have I** ich auch nicht

neo- ['niːəu] pref neo-, Neo-

neolithic [nɪə'lɪθɪk] adv jungsteinzeitlich, neolithisch

neologism [nɪ'ɔlədʒɪzəm] n (Wort)neubildung f, Neologismus m

neon ['niːɔn] n Neon nt

neon light n Neonlampe f

neon sign n Neonreklame f

Nepal [nɪ'pɔːl] n Nepal nt

nephew ['nɛvjuː] n Neffe m

nepotism ['nɛpətɪzəm] n Vetternwirtschaft f

nerd [nəːd] (inf) n Schwachkopf m

nerve [nəːv] n (Anat) Nerv m; (courage) Mut m; (impudence) Frechheit f; **nerves** npl (anxiety) Nervosität f; (emotional strength) Nerven pl; **he gets on my ~s** er geht mir auf die Nerven; **to lose one's ~** die Nerven verlieren

nerve-centre, (US) **nerve-center** ['nəːvsɛntə^r] n (fig) Schaltzentrale f

nerve gas n Nervengas nt

nerve-racking ['nəːvrækɪŋ] adj nervenaufreibend

nervous ['nəːvəs] adj Nerven-, nervlich; (anxious) nervös; **to be ~ of/about** Angst haben vor +dat

nervous breakdown n Nervenzusammenbruch m

nervously ['nəːvəslɪ] adv nervös

nervousness ['nəːvəsnɪs] n Nervosität f

nervous system n Nervensystem nt

nervous wreck (inf) n Nervenbündel nt; **to be a ~** mit den Nerven völlig am Ende sein

nervy ['nəːvɪ] (inf) adj (Brit: tense) nervös; (US: cheeky) dreist

nest [nɛst] n Nest nt ▷ vi nisten; **a ~ of tables** ein Satz Tische or von Tischen

nest egg n Notgroschen m

nestle ['nɛsl] vi sich kuscheln; (house) eingebettet sein

nestling ['nɛstlɪŋ] n Nestling m

Net [nɛt] n: **the ~** (Comput) das Internet
net [nɛt] n Netz nt; (fabric) Tüll m ▷ adj (Comm)
Netto-; (final: result, effect) End- ▷ vt (mit einem
Netz) fangen; (profit) einbringen; (deal, sale,
fortune) an Land ziehen; ~ **of tax** steuerfrei; **he
earns £10,000 ~ per year** er verdient £ 10.000
netto im Jahr; **it weighs 250g ~** es wiegt 250
g netto
netball ['nɛtbɔːl] n Netzball m
net curtains npl Gardinen pl, Stores pl
Netherlands ['nɛðələndz] npl: **the ~** die
Niederlande pl
netiquette ['nɛtɪkɛt] n Netiquette f
nett [nɛt] adj = **net**
netting ['nɛtɪŋ] n (for fence etc) Maschendraht
m; (fabric) Netzgewebe nt, Tüll m
nettle ['nɛtl] n Nessel f
network ['nɛtwəːk] n Netz nt; (TV, Radio)
Sendenetz nt ▷ vt (Radio, TV) im ganzen
Netzbereich ausstrahlen; (computers) in einem
Netzwerk zusammenschließen
neuralgia [njuəˈrældʒə] n Neuralgie f,
Nervenschmerzen pl
neurological [njuərəˈlɒdʒɪkl] adj neurologisch
neurotic [njuəˈrɒtɪk] adj neurotisch ▷ n
Neurotiker(in) m(f)
neuter ['njuːtəʳ] adj (Ling) sächlich ▷ vt
kastrieren; (female) sterilisieren
neutral ['njuːtrəl] adj neutral ▷ n (Aut) Leerlauf
m
neutrality [njuːˈtrælɪtɪ] n Neutralität f
neutralize ['njuːtrəlaɪz] vt neutralisieren,
aufheben
neutron bomb n Neutronenbombe f
Nev. (US) abbr (Post) = Nevada
never ['nɛvəʳ] adv nie; (not) nicht; ~ **in my life**
noch nie; ~ **again** nie wieder; **well I ~!** nein, so
was!; see also **mind**
never-ending [nɛvərˈɛndɪŋ] adj endlos
nevertheless [nɛvəðəˈlɛs] adv trotzdem,
dennoch
new [njuː] adj neu; (mother) jung; **as good as ~**
so gut wie neu; **to be ~ to sb** jdm neu sein
New Age n New Age nt
newbie ['njuːbɪ] (inf) n Neuling m
newborn ['njuːbɔːn] adj neugeboren
newcomer ['njuːkʌməʳ] n Neuankömmling m;
(in job) Neuling m
new-fangled ['njuːˈfæŋgld] (pej) adj
neumodisch
new-found ['njuːfaund] adj neu entdeckt;
(confidence) neu geschöpft
Newfoundland ['njuːfənlənd] n Neufundland
nt
New Guinea n Neuguinea nt
newly ['njuːlɪ] adv neu
newly-weds ['njuːlɪwɛdz] npl Neuvermählte
pl, Frischvermählte pl
new moon n Neumond m
newness ['njuːnɪs] n Neuheit f; (of cheese, bread
etc) Frische f
New Orleans [-ˈɔːliːənz] n New Orleans nt
news [njuːz] n Nachricht f; **a piece of ~** eine

Neuigkeit; **the ~** (Radio, TV) die Nachrichten
pl; **good/bad ~** gute/schlechte Nachrichten
news agency n Nachrichtenagentur f
newsagent ['njuːzeɪdʒənt] (Brit) n
Zeitungshändler(in) m(f)
news bulletin n Bulletin nt
newscaster ['njuːzkɑːstəʳ] n
Nachrichtensprecher(in) m(f)
newsdealer ['njuːzdiːləʳ] (US) n = **newsagent**
newsflash ['njuːzflæʃ] n Kurzmeldung f
newsletter ['njuːzlɛtəʳ] n Rundschreiben nt,
Mitteilungsblatt nt
newspaper ['njuːzpeɪpəʳ] n Zeitung f; **daily/
weekly ~** Tages-/Wochenzeitung f
newsprint ['njuːzprɪnt] n Zeitungspapier nt
newsreader ['njuːzriːdəʳ] n = **newscaster**
newsreel ['njuːzriːl] n Wochenschau f
newsroom ['njuːzruːm] n
Nachrichtenredaktion f; (Radio, TV)
Nachrichtenstudio nt
newsstand ['njuːzstænd] n Zeitungsstand m
newsworthy ['njuːzwəːðɪ] adj: **to be ~**
Neuigkeitswert haben
newt [njuːt] n Wassermolch m
new town (Brit) n neue, teilweise mit
Regierungsgeldern errichtete städtische Siedlung
New Year n neues Jahr nt; (New Year's Day)
Neujahr nt; **Happy ~!** (ein) glückliches or
frohes neues Jahr!
New Year's Day n Neujahr nt, Neujahrstag m
New Year's Eve n Silvester nt
New York [-ˈjɔːk] n New York nt; (also: **New
York State**) der Staat New York
New Zealand [-ˈziːlənd] n Neuseeland nt ▷ adj
neuseeländisch
New Zealander [-ˈziːləndəʳ] n
Neuseeländer(in) m(f)
next [nɛkst] adj nächste(r, s); (room) Neben-
▷ adv dann; (do, happen) als Nächstes;
(afterwards) danach; **the ~ day** am nächsten
or folgenden Tag; ~ **time** das nächste Mal;
~ **year** nächstes Jahr; ~ **please!** der Nächste
bitte!; **who's ~?** wer ist der Nächste?; **"turn
to the ~ page"** „bitte umblättern"; **the week
after ~** übernächste Woche; **the ~ on the
right/left** der/die/das Nächste rechts/links;
the ~ thing I knew das Nächste, woran ich
mich erinnern konnte; ~ **to** neben +dat; ~ **to
nothing** so gut wie nichts; **when do we meet
~?** wann treffen wir uns wieder or das nächste
Mal?; **the ~ best** der/die/das Nächstbeste
next door adv nebenan ▷ adj: **next-door**
nebenan; **the house ~** das Nebenhaus; **to
go ~** nach nebenan gehen; **my next-door
neighbour** mein direkter Nachbar
next-of-kin ['nɛkstəvˈkɪn] n nächster
Verwandter m, nächste Verwandte f
NF n abbr (Brit: Pol: = National Front) rechtsradikale
Partei ▷ abbr (Canada) = Newfoundland
NFL (US) n abbr (= National Football League) Fußball-
Nationalliga
NG (US) abbr = **National Guard**
NGO n abbr (= nongovernmental organization)

n

675

nichtstaatliche Organisation

NH (US) *n abbr* (Post) = New Hampshire

NHL (US) *n abbr* (= National Hockey League) Hockey-Nationalliga

NHS (Brit) *n abbr* = **National Health Service**

NI *abbr* = **Northern Ireland**; (Brit) = **National Insurance**

Niagara Falls [naɪˈægərə-] *npl* Niagarafälle *pl*

nib [nɪb] *n* Feder *f*

nibble [ˈnɪbl] *vt* knabbern; (*bite*) knabbern an +*dat* ▷ *vi*: **to ~ at** knabbern an +*dat*

Nicaragua [nɪkəˈrægjuə] *n* Nicaragua *nt*

Nicaraguan [nɪkəˈrægjuən] *adj* nicaraguanisch ▷ *n* Nicaraguaner(in) *m(f)*

Nice [niːs] *n* Nizza *nt*

nice [naɪs] *adj* nett; (*holiday, weather, picture etc*) schön; (*taste*) gut; (*person, clothes etc*) hübsch

nicely [ˈnaɪslɪ] *adv* (*attractively*) hübsch; (*politely*) nett; (*satisfactorily*) gut; **that will do ~** das reicht (vollauf)

niceties [ˈnaɪsɪtɪz] *npl*: **the ~** die Feinheiten *pl*

niche [niːʃ] *n* Nische *f*; (*job, position*) Plätzchen *nt*

nick [nɪk] *n* Kratzer *m*; (*in metal, wood etc*) Kerbe *f* ▷ *vt* (Brit: *inf: steal*) klauen; (: *arrest*) einsperren, einlochen; (*cut*): **to ~ o.s.** sich schneiden; **in good ~** (Brit: *inf*) gut in Schuss; **in the ~** (Brit: *inf: in prison*) im Knast; **in the ~ of time** gerade noch rechtzeitig

nickel [ˈnɪkl] *n* Nickel *nt*; (US) Fünfcentstück *nt*

nickname [ˈnɪkneɪm] *n* Spitzname *m* ▷ *vt* betiteln, taufen (*inf*)

Nicosia [nɪkəˈsiːə] *n* Nikosia *nt*

nicotine [ˈnɪkətiːn] *n* Nikotin *nt*

nicotine patch *n* Nikotinpflaster *nt*

niece [niːs] *n* Nichte *f*

nifty [ˈnɪftɪ] (*inf*) *adj* flott; (*gadget, tool*) schlau

Niger [ˈnaɪdʒəʳ] *n* Niger *m*

Nigeria [naɪˈdʒɪərɪə] *n* Nigeria *nt*

Nigerian [naɪˈdʒɪərɪən] *adj* nigerianisch ▷ *n* Nigerianer(in) *m(f)*

niggardly [ˈnɪgədlɪ] *adj* knauserig; (*allowance, amount*) armselig

nigger [ˈnɪgəʳ] (*offensive*) *n* Nigger *m* (*inf!*)

niggle [ˈnɪgl] *vt* plagen, zu schaffen machen +*dat* ▷ *vi* herumkritisieren

niggling [ˈnɪglɪŋ] *adj* quälend; (*pain, ache*) bohrend

night [naɪt] *n* Nacht *f*; (*evening*) Abend *m*; **the ~ before last** vorletzte Nacht, vorgestern Abend; **at ~, by ~** nachts, abends; **nine o'clock at ~** neun Uhr abends; **in the ~, during the ~** in der Nacht; **~ and day** Tag und Nacht

nightcap [ˈnaɪtkæp] *n* Schlaftrunk *m*

nightclub [ˈnaɪtklʌb] *n* Nachtlokal *nt*

nightdress [ˈnaɪtdrɛs] *n* Nachthemd *nt*

nightfall [ˈnaɪtfɔːl] *n* Einbruch *m* der Dunkelheit

nightgown [ˈnaɪtgaun] *n* = **nightdress**

nightie [ˈnaɪtɪ] *n* = **nightdress**

nightingale [ˈnaɪtɪŋgeɪl] *n* Nachtigall *f*

nightlife [ˈnaɪtlaɪf] *n* Nachtleben *nt*

nightly [ˈnaɪtlɪ] *adj* (all)nächtlich, Nacht-;

(*every evening*) (all)abendlich, Abend- ▷ *adv* jede Nacht; (*every evening*) jeden Abend

nightmare [ˈnaɪtmɛəʳ] *n* Albtraum *m*

night porter *n* Nachtportier *m*

night safe *n* Nachtsafe *m*

night school *n* Abendschule *f*

nightshade [ˈnaɪtʃeɪd] *n*: **deadly ~** Tollkirsche *f*

night shift *n* Nachtschicht *f*

night-time [ˈnaɪttaɪm] *n* Nacht *f*

night watchman *n* Nachtwächter *m*

nihilism [ˈnaɪɪlɪzəm] *n* Nihilismus *m*

nil [nɪl] *n* Nichts *nt*; (Brit: *Sport*) Null *f*

Nile [naɪl] *n*: **the ~** der Nil

nimble [ˈnɪmbl] *adj* flink; (*mind*) beweglich

nine [naɪn] *num* neun

nineteen [ˈnaɪnˈtiːn] *num* neunzehn

nineteenth [naɪnˈtiːnθ] *num* neunzehnte(r, s)

ninety [ˈnaɪntɪ] *num* neunzig

ninth [naɪnθ] *num* neunte(r, s) ▷ *n* Neuntel *nt*

nip [nɪp] *vt* zwicken ▷ *n* Biss *m*; (*drink*) Schlückchen *nt* ▷ *vi* (Brit: *inf*): **to ~ out/down/up** kurz raus-/runter-/raufgehen; **to ~ into a shop** (Brit: *inf*) kurz in einen Laden gehen

nipple [ˈnɪpl] *n* (*Anat*) Brustwarze *f*

nippy [ˈnɪpɪ] (Brit) *adj* (*quick: person*) flott; (: *car*) spritzig; (*cold*) frisch

nit [nɪt] *n* Nisse *f*; (*inf: idiot*) Dummkopf *m*

nitpicking [ˈnɪtpɪkɪŋ] (*inf*) *n* Kleinigkeitskrämerei *f*

nitrogen [ˈnaɪtrədʒən] *n* Stickstoff *m*

nitroglycerin, nitroglycerine [ˈnaɪtrəuˈglɪsəriːn] *n* Nitroglyzerin *nt*

nitty-gritty [ˈnɪtɪˈgrɪtɪ] (*inf*) *n*: **to get down to the ~** zur Sache kommen

nitwit [ˈnɪtwɪt] (*inf*) *n* Dummkopf *m*

NJ (US) *abbr* (Post) = New Jersey

NLF *n abbr* (= National Liberation Front) *vietnamesische Befreiungsbewegung während des Vietnamkrieges*

NLRB (US) *n abbr* (= National Labor Relations Board) *Ausschuss zur Regelung der Beziehungen zwischen Arbeitgebern und Arbeitnehmern*

NM, N.Mex. (US) *abbr* (Post) = New Mexico

 KEYWORD

no [nəu] (*pl* **noes**) *adv* (*opposite of "yes"*) nein; **no thank you** nein danke
▷ *adj* (*not any*) kein(e); **I have no money/time/books** ich habe kein Geld/keine Zeit/keine Bücher; **"no entry"** „kein Zutritt"; **"no smoking"** „Rauchen verboten"
▷ *n* Nein *nt*; **there were 20 noes and one abstention** es gab 20 Neinstimmen und eine Enthaltung; **I won't take no for an answer** ich bestehe darauf

no. *abbr* (= *number*) Nr.

nobble [ˈnɔbl] (Brit: *inf*) *vt* (*bribe*) (sich *dat*) kaufen; (*grab*) sich *dat* schnappen; (*Racing: horse, dog*) lahmlegen

Nobel Prize [nəuˈbɛl-] *n* Nobelpreis *m*

nobility [nəuˈbɪlɪtɪ] *n* Adel *m*; (*quality*) Edelmut

m

noble ['nəubl] *adj* edel, nobel; *(aristocratic)* ad(e)lig; *(impressive)* prächtig

nobleman ['nəublmən] *(irreg: like* **man***) n* Ad(e)lige(r) *f(m)*

nobly ['nəublɪ] *adv* edel

nobody ['nəubədɪ] *pron* niemand, keiner
▷ *n:* **he's a ~** er ist ein Niemand *m*

no-claims bonus [nəu'kleɪmz-] *n* Schadenfreiheitsrabatt *m*

nocturnal [nɒk'tə:nl] *adj* nächtlich; *(animal)* Nacht-

nod [nɒd] *vi* nicken; *(fig: flowers etc)* wippen
▷ *vt:* **to ~ one's head** mit dem Kopf nicken ▷ *n* Nicken *nt;* **they ~ded their agreement** sie nickten zustimmend
▸ **nod off** *vi* einnicken

no-fly zone [nəu'flaɪ-] *n* Sperrzone *f* für den Flugverkehr

noise [nɔɪz] *n* Geräusch *nt;* *(din)* Lärm *m*

noiseless ['nɔɪzlɪs] *adj* geräuschlos

noisily ['nɔɪzɪlɪ] *adv* laut

noisy ['nɔɪzɪ] *adj* laut

nomad ['nəumæd] *n* Nomade *m*, Nomadin *f*

nomadic [nəu'mædɪk] *adj* Nomaden-, nomadisch

no-man's-land ['nəumænzlænd] *n* Niemandsland *nt*

nominal ['nɒmɪnl] *adj* nominell

nominate ['nɒmɪneɪt] *vt* nominieren; *(appoint)* ernennen

nomination [nɒmɪ'neɪʃən] *n* Nominierung *f;* *(appointment)* Ernennung *f*

nominee [nɒmɪ'niː] *n* Kandidat(in) *m(f)*

non- [nɒn] *pref* nicht-, Nicht-

non-alcoholic [nɒnælkə'hɒlɪk] *adj* alkoholfrei

non-aligned [nɒnə'laɪnd] *adj* blockfrei

non-breakable [nɒn'breɪkəbl] *adj* unzerbrechlich

nonce word ['nɒns-] *n* Ad-hoc-Bildung *f*

nonchalant ['nɒnʃələnt] *adj* lässig, nonchalant

noncommissioned officer [nɒnkə'mɪʃənd-] *n* Unteroffizier *m*

non-committal [nɒnkə'mɪtl] *adj* zurückhaltend; *(answer)* unverbindlich

nonconformist [nɒnkən'fɔ:mɪst]
n Nonkonformist(in) *m(f)* ▷ *adj* nonkonformistisch

non-cooperation ['nɒnkəuɒpə'reɪʃən] *n* unkooperative Haltung *f*

nondescript ['nɒndɪskrɪpt] *adj* unauffällig; *(colour)* unbestimmbar

none [nʌn] *pron (not one)* kein(e, er, es); *(not any)* nichts; **~ of us** keiner von uns; **I've ~ left** *(not any)* ich habe nichts übrig; *(not one)* ich habe kein(e, en, es) übrig; **~ at all** *(not any)* überhaupt nicht; *(not one)* überhaupt kein(e, er, es); **I was ~ the wiser** ich war auch nicht klüger; **she would have ~ of it** sie wollte nichts davon hören; **it was ~ other than X** es war kein anderer als X

nonentity [nɒ'nɛntɪtɪ] *n (person)* Nichts *nt*, unbedeutende Figur *f*

non-essential [nɒnɪ'sɛnʃl] *adj* unnötig ▷ *n:* **~s** nicht (lebens)notwendige Dinge *pl*

nonetheless ['nʌnðə'lɛs] *adv* nichtsdestoweniger, trotzdem

nonevent [nɒnɪ'vɛnt] *n* Reinfall *m*

non-existent [nɒnɪg'zɪstənt] *adj* nicht vorhanden

non-fiction [nɒn'fɪkʃən] *n* Sachbücher *pl* ▷ *adj (book)* Sach-; *(prize)* Sachbuch-

non-flammable [nɒn'flæməbl] *adj* nicht entzündbar

non-intervention ['nɒnɪntə'vɛnʃən] *n* Nichteinmischung *f*, Nichteingreifen *nt*

no-no ['nəunəu] *n:* **it's a ~** *(inf)* das kommt nicht infrage

non obst. *abbr* (= *non obstante*) dennoch

no-nonsense [nəu'nɒnsəns] *adj (approach, look)* nüchtern

non-payment [nɒn'peɪmənt] *n* Nichtzahlung *f*, Zahlungsverweigerung *f*

nonplussed [nɒn'plʌst] *adj* verdutzt, verblüfft

non-profit making ['nɒn'prɒfɪt-] *adj (organization)* gemeinnützig

nonreturnable [nɒnrə'tə:nəbl] *adj:* **~ bottle** Einwegflasche *f*

nonsense ['nɒnsəns] *n* Unsinn *m;* **~!** Unsinn!, Quatsch!; **it is ~ to say that ...** es ist dummes Gerede zu sagen, dass ...; **to make (a) ~ of sth** etw ad absurdum führen

nonsensical [nɒn'sɛnsɪkl] *adj (idea, action etc)* unsinnig

non-shrink [nɒn'ʃrɪŋk] *(Brit) adj* nicht einlaufend

non-smoker ['nɒn'sməukəʳ] *n* Nichtraucher(in) *m(f)*

nonstarter [nɒn'stɑːtəʳ] *n (fig):* **it's a ~** *(idea etc)* es hat keine Erfolgschance

non-stick ['nɒn'stɪk] *adj* kunststoffbeschichtet, Teflon-®

non-stop ['nɒn'stɒp] *adj* ununterbrochen; *(flight)* Nonstop-, Non-Stop- ▷ *adv* ununterbrochen; *(fly)* nonstop

non-taxable [nɒn'tæksəbl] *adj* nicht steuerpflichtig

non-U [nɒn'juː] *(Brit: inf) adj abbr* (= *non-upper class)* nicht vornehm

non-white ['nɒn'waɪt] *adj* farbig ▷ *n* Farbige(r) *f(m)*

noodles ['nuːdlz] *npl* Nudeln *pl*

nook [nuk] *n:* **every ~ and cranny** jeder Winkel

noon [nuːn] *n* Mittag *m*

no-one ['nəuwʌn] *pron* = **nobody**

noose [nuːs] *n* Schlinge *f*

nor [nɔːʳ] *conj, adv* = **neither**

Norf *(Brit) abbr (Post)* = Norfolk

norm [nɔːm] *n* Norm *f*

normal ['nɔːməl] *adj* normal ▷ *n:* **to return to ~** sich wieder normalisieren

normality [nɔː'mælɪtɪ] *n* Normalität *f*

normally ['nɔːməlɪ] *adv* normalerweise; *(act, behave)* normal

Normandy ['nɔːməndɪ] *n* Normandie *f*

north [nɔːθ] n Norden m ▷ adj nördlich, Nord-
▷ adv nach Norden; ~ **of** nördlich von

North Africa n Nordafrika nt

North African adj nordafrikanisch ▷ n
Nordafrikaner(in) m(f)

North America n Nordamerika nt

North American adj nordamerikanisch ▷ n
Nordamerikaner(in) m(f)

Northants [nɔːˈθænts] (Brit) abbr
(Post) = Northamptonshire

northbound [ˈnɔːθbaund] adj in Richtung
Norden; (carriageway) nach Norden (führend)

Northd (Brit) abbr (Post) = Northumberland

north-east [nɔːθˈiːst] n Nordosten m ▷ adj
nordöstlich, Nordost- ▷ adv nach Nordosten; ~
of nordöstlich von

northerly [ˈnɔːðəlɪ] adj nördlich

northern [ˈnɔːðən] adj nördlich, Nord-

Northern Ireland n Nordirland nt

North Korea n Nordkorea nt

North Pole n: **the** ~ der Nordpol

North Sea n: **the** ~ die Nordsee f

North Sea oil n Nordseeöl nt

northward [ˈnɔːθwəd], **northwards**
[ˈnɔːθwədz] adv nach Norden, nordwärts

north-west [nɔːθˈwest] n Nordwesten m
▷ adj nordwestlich, Nordwest- ▷ adv nach
Nordwesten; ~ **of** nordwestlich von

Norway [ˈnɔːweɪ] n Norwegen nt

Norwegian [nɔːˈwiːdʒən] adj norwegisch ▷ n
Norweger(in) m(f); (Ling) Norwegisch nt

nos. abbr (= numbers) Nrn.

nose [nəuz] n Nase f; (of car) Schnauze f ▷ vi
(also: **nose one's way**) sich schieben; **to follow
one's** ~ immer der Nase nach gehen; **to get
up one's** ~ (inf) auf die Nerven gehen +dat; **to
have a (good)** ~ **for sth** eine (gute) Nase für
etw haben; **to keep one's** ~ **clean** (inf) eine
saubere Weste behalten; **to look down one's**
~ **at sb/sth** (inf) auf jdn/etw herabsehen; **to
pay through the** ~ **(for sth)** (inf) (für etw)
viel blechen; **to rub sb's** ~ **in sth** (inf) jdm
etw unter die Nase reiben; **to turn one's** ~
up at sth (inf) die Nase über etw acc rümpfen;
under sb's ~ vor jds Augen
▶ **nose about** vi herumschnüffeln
▶ **nose around** vi = **nose about**

nosebleed [ˈnəuzbliːd] n Nasenbluten nt

nose-dive [ˈnəuzdaɪv] n (of plane) Sturzflug m
▷ vi (plane) im Sturzflug herabgehen

nose drops npl Nasentropfen pl

nosey [ˈnəuzɪ] (inf) adj = **nosy**

nostalgia [nɔsˈtældʒɪə] n Nostalgie f

nostalgic [nɔsˈtældʒɪk] adj nostalgisch

nostril [ˈnɔstrɪl] n Nasenloch nt; (of animal)
Nüster f

nosy [ˈnəuzɪ] (inf) adj neugierig

KEYWORD

not [nɔt] adv nicht; **he is not** or **isn't here** er
ist nicht hier; **you must not** or **you mustn't
do that** das darfst du nicht tun; **it's too late,**
isn't it? es ist zu spät, nicht wahr?; **not that I
don't like him** nicht, dass ich ihn nicht mag;
not yet noch nicht; **not now** nicht jetzt; see
also **all; only**

notable [ˈnəutəbl] adj bemerkenswert

notably [ˈnəutəblɪ] adv hauptsächlich;
(markedly) bemerkenswert

notary [ˈnəutərɪ] n (also: **notary public**)
Notar(in) m(f)

notation [nəuˈteɪʃən] n Notation f; (Mus)
Notenschrift f

notch [nɔtʃ] n Kerbe f; (in blade, saw) Scharte f;
(fig) Klasse f
▶ **notch up** vt erzielen; (victory) erringen

note [nəut] n Notiz f; (of lecturer) Manuskript
nt; (of student etc) Aufzeichnung f; (in book etc)
Anmerkung f; (letter) paar Zeilen pl; (banknote)
Note f, Schein m; (Mus: sound) Ton m; (: symbol)
Note f; (tone) Ton m, Klang m ▷ vt beachten;
(point out) anmerken; (also: **note down**)
notieren; **of** ~ bedeutend; **to make a** ~ **of
sth** sich dat etw notieren; **to take** ~**s** Notizen
machen, mitschreiben; **to take** ~ **of sth** etw
zur Kenntnis nehmen

notebook [ˈnəutbuk] n Notizbuch nt; (for
shorthand) Stenoblock m

notecase [ˈnəutkeɪs] (Brit) n Brieftasche f

noted [ˈnəutɪd] adj bekannt

notepad [ˈnəutpæd] n Notizblock m

notepaper [ˈnəutpeɪpəʳ] n Briefpapier nt

noteworthy [ˈnəutwɜːðɪ] adj beachtenswert

nothing [ˈnʌθɪŋ] n nichts; ~ **new/worse** etc
nichts Neues/Schlimmeres etc; ~ **much** nicht
viel; ~ **else** sonst nichts; **for** ~ umsonst; ~ **at
all** überhaupt nichts

notice [ˈnəutɪs] n Bekanntmachung f; (sign)
Schild nt; (warning) Ankündigung f; (dismissal)
Kündigung f; (Brit: review) Kritik f, Rezension f
▷ vt bemerken; **to bring sth to sb's** ~ jdn auf
etw acc aufmerksam machen; **to take no** ~ **of**
ignorieren, nicht beachten; **to escape sb's** ~
jdm entgehen; **it has come to my** ~ **that ...**
es ist mir zu Ohren gekommen, dass ...; **to
give sb** ~ **of sth** jdm von etw Bescheid geben;
without ~ ohne Ankündigung; **advance** ~
Vorankündigung f; **at short/a moment's** ~
kurzfristig/innerhalb kürzester Zeit; **until
further** ~ bis auf Weiteres; **to hand in one's**
~ kündigen; **to be given one's** ~ gekündigt
werden +dat

noticeable [ˈnəutɪsəbl] adj deutlich

noticeboard [ˈnəutɪsbɔːd] (Brit) n
Anschlagbrett nt

notification [nəutɪfɪˈkeɪʃən] n
Benachrichtigung f

notify [ˈnəutɪfaɪ] vt: **to** ~ **sb (of sth)** jdn (von
etw) benachrichtigen

notion [ˈnəuʃən] n Vorstellung f; **notions** (US)
npl (haberdashery) Kurzwaren pl

notoriety [nəutəˈraɪətɪ] n traurige
Berühmtheit f

notorious [nəuˈtɔːrɪəs] adj berüchtigt

notoriously [nəʊˈtɔːrɪəslɪ] adv notorisch
Notts [nɒts] (Brit) abbr (Post) = Nottinghamshire
notwithstanding [nɒtwɪθˈstændɪŋ] adv
  trotzdem ▷ prep trotz +dat
nougat [ˈnuːgɑː] n Nugat m
nought [nɔːt] n Null f
noughties [ˈnɔːtɪz] npl (inf) das erste Jahrzehnt des
  dritten Jahrtausends, Nullerjahre pl
noun [naʊn] n Hauptwort nt, Substantiv nt
nourish [ˈnʌrɪʃ] vt nähren
nourishing [ˈnʌrɪʃɪŋ] adj nahrhaft
nourishment [ˈnʌrɪʃmənt] n Nahrung f
Nov. abbr (= November) Nov.
Nova Scotia [ˈnəʊvəˈskəʊʃə] n Neuschottland
  nt
novel [ˈnɒvl] n Roman m ▷ adj neu(artig)
novelist [ˈnɒvəlɪst] n Romanschriftsteller(in)
  m(f)
novelty [ˈnɒvəltɪ] n Neuheit f; (object)
  Kleinigkeit f
November [nəʊˈvɛmbər] n November m; see
  also **July**
novice [ˈnɒvɪs] n Neuling m, Anfänger(in) m(f);
  (Rel) Novize m, Novizin f
NOW [naʊ] (US) n abbr (= National Organization for
  Women) Frauenvereinigung
now [naʊ] adv jetzt; (these days) heute ▷ conj: ~
  (that) jetzt, wo; **right ~** gleich, sofort; **by ~**
  inzwischen, mittlerweile; **that's the fashion
  just ~** das ist gerade modern; **I saw her
  just ~** ich habe sie gerade gesehen; **(every)
  ~ and then, (every) ~ and again** ab und zu,
  gelegentlich; **from ~ on** von nun an; **in 3
  days from ~** (heute) in 3 Tagen; **between ~
  and Monday** bis Montag; **that's all for ~** das
  ist erst einmal alles; **any day ~** jederzeit; **~
  then** also
nowadays [ˈnaʊədeɪz] adv heute
nowhere [ˈnəʊwɛər] adv (be) nirgends,
  nirgendwo; (go) nirgendwohin; **~ else**
  nirgendwo anders
no-win situation [nəʊˈwɪn-] n aussichtslose
  Lage f
noxious [ˈnɒkʃəs] adj (gas, fumes) schädlich;
  (smell) übel
nozzle [ˈnɒzl] n Düse f
NP n abbr (Law) = **notary public**
NS (Canada) abbr = Nova Scotia
NSC (US) n abbr = **National Security Council**
NSF (US) n abbr (= National Science Foundation)
  Organisation zur Förderung der Wissenschaft
NSPCC (Brit) n abbr (= National Society
  for the Prevention of Cruelty to Children)
  Kinderschutzbund m
NSW (Australia) abbr (Post) = New South Wales
NT n abbr (Bible: = New Testament) NT
nth [ɛnθ] (inf) adj: **to the ~ degree** in der n-ten
  Potenz
nuance [ˈnjuːɑ̃ːns] n Nuance f
nubile [ˈnjuːbaɪl] adj gut entwickelt
nuclear [ˈnjuːklɪər] adj (bomb, industry etc) Atom-;
  ~ physics Kernphysik f; **~ war** Atomkrieg m
nuclear disarmament n nukleare or atomare
  Abrüstung f
nuclear family n Kleinfamilie f, Kernfamilie f
nuclear-free zone [ˈnjuːklɪəˈfriː-] n
  atomwaffenfreie Zone f
nuclei [ˈnjuːklɪaɪ] npl of **nucleus**
nucleus [ˈnjuːklɪəs] (pl **nuclei**) n Kern m
NUCPS (Brit) n abbr (= National Union of Civil and
  Public Servants) Gewerkschaft für Beschäftigte im
  öffentlichen Dienst
nude [njuːd] adj nackt ▷ n (Art) Akt m; **in the
  ~** nackt
nudge [nʌdʒ] vt anstoßen
nudist [ˈnjuːdɪst] n Nudist(in) m(f)
nudist colony n FKK-Kolonie f
nudity [ˈnjuːdɪtɪ] n Nacktheit f
nugget [ˈnʌgɪt] n (of gold) Klumpen m; (fig: of
  information) Brocken m
nuisance [ˈnjuːsns] n: **to be a ~** lästig
  sein; (situation) ärgerlich sein; **he's a ~** er
  geht einem auf die Nerven; **what a ~!** wie
  ärgerlich/lästig!
NUJ (Brit) n abbr (= National Union of Journalists)
  Journalistengewerkschaft
null [nʌl] adj: **~ and void** null und nichtig
nullify [ˈnʌlɪfaɪ] vt zunichtemachen; (claim,
  law) für null und nichtig erklären
NUM (Brit) n abbr (= National Union of Mineworkers)
  Bergarbeitergewerkschaft
numb [nʌm] adj taub, gefühllos; (fig: with fear
  etc) wie betäubt ▷ vt taub or gefühllos machen;
  (pain, mind) betäuben
number [ˈnʌmbər] n Zahl f; (quantity) (An)
  zahl f; (of house, bank account, bus etc) Nummer
  f ▷ vt (pages etc) nummerieren; (amount to)
  zählen; **a ~ of** einige; **any ~ of** beliebig viele;
  (reasons) alle möglichen; **wrong ~** (Tel) falsch
  verbunden; **to be ~ed among** zählen zu
number plate (Brit) n (Aut) Nummernschild nt
Number Ten (Brit) n (Pol: = 10 Downing Street)
  Nummer zehn f (Downing Street)
numbness [ˈnʌmnɪs] n Taubheit f, Starre f; (fig)
  Benommenheit f, Betäubung f
numbskull [ˈnʌmskʌl] n = **numskull**
numeral [ˈnjuːmərəl] n Ziffer f
numerate [ˈnjuːmərɪt] (Brit) adj: **to be ~**
  rechnen können
numerical [njuːˈmɛrɪkl] adj numerisch
numerous [ˈnjuːmərəs] adj zahlreich
numskull [ˈnʌmskʌl] n (inf) Holzkopf m
nun [nʌn] n Nonne f
nunnery [ˈnʌnərɪ] n (Nonnen)kloster nt
nuptial [ˈnʌpʃəl] adj (feast, celebration)
  Hochzeits-; **~ bliss** Eheglück nt
nurse [nɜːs] n Krankenschwester f;
  (also: **nursemaid**) Kindermädchen nt ▷ vt
  pflegen; (cold, toothache etc) auskurieren; (baby)
  stillen; (fig: desire, grudge) hegen
nursery [ˈnɜːsərɪ] n Kindergarten m; (room)
  Kinderzimmer nt; (for plants) Gärtnerei f
nursery rhyme n Kinderreim m
nursery school n Kindergarten m
nursery slope (Brit) n (Ski) Anfängerhügel m
nursing [ˈnɜːsɪŋ] n Krankenpflege f; (care)

n

Pflege f
nursing home n Pflegeheim nt
nursing mother n stillende Mutter f
nurture ['nɔːtʃəʳ] vt hegen und pflegen;
(fig: ideas, creativity) fördern
NUS (Brit) n abbr (= National Union of Students)
Studentengewerkschaft
NUT (Brit) n abbr (= National Union of Teachers)
Lehrergewerkschaft
nut [nʌt] n (Tech) (Schrauben)mutter f; (Bot)
Nuss f; (inf: lunatic) Spinner(in) m(f)
nutcase ['nʌtkeɪs] (inf) n Spinner(in) m(f)
nutcrackers ['nʌtkrækəz] npl Nussknacker m
nutmeg ['nʌtmeg] n Muskat m, Muskatnuss f
nutrient ['njuːtrɪənt] n Nährstoff m
nutrition [njuːˈtrɪʃən] n Ernährung f;
(nourishment) Nahrung f
nutritionist [njuːˈtrɪʃənɪst] n
Ernährungswissenschaftler(in) m(f)
nutritious [njuːˈtrɪʃəs] adj nahrhaft

nuts [nʌts] (inf) adj verrückt; **he's ~ er spinnt**
nutshell ['nʌtʃɛl] n Nussschale f; **in a ~** (fig)
kurz gesagt
nutty ['nʌtɪ] adj (flavour) Nuss-; (inf: idea etc)
bekloppt
nuzzle ['nʌzl] vi: **to ~ up to** sich drücken or
schmiegen an +acc
NV (US) abbr (Post) = Nevada
NVQ n abbr (= National Vocational Qualification)
Qualifikation für berufsbegleitende Ausbildungsinhalte
NW abbr = **north-west**
NY (US) abbr (Post) = New York
nylon ['naɪlɒn] n Nylon nt ▷ adj Nylon-; **nylons**
npl (stockings) Nylonstrümpfe pl
nymph [nɪmf] n Nymphe f
nymphomaniac ['nɪmfəʊˈmeɪnɪæk] n
Nymphomanin f
NYSE (US) n abbr (= New York Stock Exchange) New
Yorker Börse
NZ abbr = **New Zealand**

Oo

O, **o** [əʊ] n (letter) O nt, o nt; (US: Scol: outstanding) ≈ Eins f; (Tel etc) Null f; **O for Olive**, **O for Oboe** (US) ≈ O wie Otto

oaf [əʊf] n Trottel m

oak [əʊk] n (tree, wood) Eiche f ▷ adj (furniture, door) Eichen-

O & M n abbr (= organization and method) Organisation und Arbeitsweise pl

OAP (Brit) n abbr = **old age pensioner**

oar [ɔːʳ] n Ruder nt; **to put** or **shove one's ~ in** (inf: fig) mitmischen, sich einmischen

oarsman ['ɔːzmən] (irreg: like **man**) n Ruderer m

oarswoman ['ɔːzwʊmən] (irreg: like **woman**) n Ruderin f

OAS n abbr (= Organization of American States) OAS f

oasis [əʊ'eɪsɪs] (pl **oases**) n (lit, fig) Oase f

oath [əʊθ] n (promise) Eid m, Schwur m; (swear word) Fluch m; **on ~** (Brit): **under ~** unter Eid; **to take the ~** (Law) vereidigt werden

oatmeal ['əʊtmiːl] n Haferschrot m; (colour) Hellbeige nt

oats [əʊts] npl Hafer m; **he's getting his ~** (Brit: inf: fig) er kommt im Bett auf seine Kosten

obdurate ['ɒbdjʊrɪt] adj unnachgiebig

OBE (Brit) n abbr (= Officer of (the order of) the British Empire) britischer Ordenstitel

obedience [ə'biːdɪəns] n Gehorsam m; **in ~ to** gemäß +dat

obedient [ə'biːdɪənt] adj gehorsam; **to be ~ to sb** jdm gehorchen

obelisk ['ɒbɪlɪsk] n Obelisk m

obese [əʊ'biːs] adj fettleibig

obesity [əʊ'biːsɪtɪ] n Fettleibigkeit f

obey [ə'beɪ] vt (person) gehorchen +dat, folgen +dat; (orders, law) befolgen ▷ vi gehorchen

obituary [ə'bɪtjʊərɪ] n Nachruf m

object [n 'ɒbdʒɪkt, vi əb'dʒɛkt] n (also Ling) Objekt nt; (aim, purpose) Ziel nt, Zweck m ▷ vi dagegen sein; **to be an ~ of ridicule** (person) sich lächerlich machen; (thing) lächerlich wirken; **money is no ~** Geld spielt keine Rolle; **he ~ed that ...** er wandte ein, dass ...; **I ~!** ich protestiere!; **do you ~ to my smoking?** haben Sie etwas dagegen, wenn ich rauche?

objection [əb'dʒɛkʃən] n (argument) Einwand m; **I have no ~ to ...** ich habe nichts dagegen, dass ...; **if you have no ~** wenn Sie nichts dagegen haben; **to raise** or **voice an ~** einen Einwand erheben or vorbringen

objectionable [əb'dʒɛkʃənəbl] adj (language, conduct) anstößig; (person) unausstehlich

objective [əb'dʒɛktɪv] adj objektiv ▷ n Ziel nt

objectively [əb'dʒɛktɪvlɪ] adv objektiv

objectivity [ɒbdʒɪk'tɪvɪtɪ] n Objektivität f

object lesson n: **an ~ in** ein Paradebeispiel nt für

objector [əb'dʒɛktəʳ] n Gegner(in) m(f)

obligation [ɒblɪ'geɪʃən] n Pflicht f; **to be under an ~ to do sth** verpflichtet sein, etw zu tun; **to be under an ~ to sb** jdm verpflichtet sein; **"no ~ to buy"** (Comm) „kein Kaufzwang"

obligatory [ə'blɪgətərɪ] adj obligatorisch

oblige [ə'blaɪdʒ] vt (compel) zwingen; (do a favour for) einen Gefallen tun +dat; **I felt ~d to invite him in** ich fühlte mich verpflichtet, ihn hereinzubitten; **to be ~d to sb for sth** (grateful) jdm für etw dankbar sein; **anything to ~!** (inf) stets zu Diensten!

obliging [ə'blaɪdʒɪŋ] adj entgegenkommend

oblique [ə'bliːk] adj (line, angle) schief; (reference, compliment) indirekt, versteckt ▷ n (Brit: also: **oblique stroke**) Schrägstrich m

obliterate [ə'blɪtəreɪt] vt (village etc) vernichten; (fig: memory, error) auslöschen

oblivion [ə'blɪvɪən] n (unconsciousness) Bewusstlosigkeit f; (being forgotten) Vergessenheit f; **to sink into ~** (event etc) in Vergessenheit geraten

oblivious [ə'blɪvɪəs] adj: **he was ~ of** or **to it** er war sich dessen nicht bewusst

oblong ['ɒblɒŋ] adj rechteckig ▷ n Rechteck nt

obnoxious [əb'nɒkʃəs] adj widerwärtig, widerlich

o.b.o. (US) abbr (in classified ads: = or best offer) bzw. Höchstgebot

oboe ['əʊbəʊ] n Oboe f

obscene [əb'siːn] adj obszön; (fig: wealth) unanständig; (income etc) unverschämt

obscenity [əb'sɛnɪtɪ] n Obszönität f

obscure [əb'skjʊəʳ] adj (little known) unbekannt, obskur; (difficult to understand) unklar ▷ vt (obstruct, conceal) verdecken

obscurity [əb'skjʊərɪtɪ] n (of person, book) Unbekanntheit f; (of remark etc) Unklarheit f

obsequious [əb'siːkwɪəs] adj unterwürfig

o

observable [əbˈzɜːvəbl] *adj* wahrnehmbar; (*noticeable*) erkennbar

observance [əbˈzɜːvəns] *n* (*of law etc*) Befolgung *f*; **religious ~s** religiöse Feste *pl*

observant [əbˈzɜːvənt] *adj* aufmerksam

observation [ɔbzəˈveɪʃən] *n* (*remark*) Bemerkung *f*; (*act of observing, Med*) Beobachtung *f*; **she's in hospital under ~** sie ist zur Beobachtung im Krankenhaus

observation post *n* Beobachtungsposten *m*

observatory [əbˈzɜːvətrɪ] *n* Observatorium *nt*

observe [əbˈzɜːv] *vt* (*watch*) beobachten; (*notice, comment*) bemerken; (*abide by: rule etc*) einhalten

observer [əbˈzɜːvəʳ] *n* Beobachter(in) *m(f)*

obsess [əbˈsɛs] *vt* verfolgen; **to be ~ed by** *or* **with sb/sth** von jdm/etw besessen sein

obsession [əbˈsɛʃən] *n* Besessenheit *f*

obsessive [əbˈsɛsɪv] *adj* (*person*) zwanghaft; (*interest, hatred, tidiness*) krankhaft; **to be ~ about cleaning/tidying up** einen Putz-/Ordnungsfimmel haben (*inf*)

obsolescence [ɔbsəˈlɛsns] *n* Veralten *nt*; **built-in** *or* **planned ~** (*Comm*) geplanter Verschleiß *m*

obsolete [ˈɔbsəliːt] *adj* veraltet

obstacle [ˈɔbstəkl] *n* (*lit, fig*) Hindernis *nt*

obstacle race *n* Hindernisrennen *nt*

obstetrician [ɔbstəˈtrɪʃən] *n* Geburtshelfer(in) *m(f)*

obstetrics [ɔbˈstɛtrɪks] *n* Geburtshilfe *f*

obstinacy [ˈɔbstɪnəsɪ] *n* (*of person*) Starrsinn *m*

obstinate [ˈɔbstɪnɪt] *adj* (*person*) starrsinnig, stur; (*refusal, cough etc*) hartnäckig

obstruct [əbˈstrʌkt] *vt* (*road, path*) blockieren; (*traffic, fig*) behindern

obstruction [əbˈstrʌkʃən] *n* (*object*) Hindernis *nt*; (*of plan, law*) Behinderung *f*

obstructive [əbˈstrʌktɪv] *adj* hinderlich, obstruktiv (*esp Pol*); **she's being ~** sie macht Schwierigkeiten

obtain [əbˈteɪn] *vt* erhalten, bekommen ▷ *vi* (*form: exist, be the case*) gelten

obtainable [əbˈteɪnəbl] *adj* erhältlich

obtrusive [əbˈtruːsɪv] *adj* aufdringlich; (*conspicuous*) auffällig

obtuse [əbˈtjuːs] *adj* (*person, remark*) einfältig; (*Math*) stumpf

obverse [ˈɔbvəːs] *n* (*of situation, argument*) Kehrseite *f*

obviate [ˈɔbvɪeɪt] *vt* (*need, problem etc*) vorbeugen +*dat*

obvious [ˈɔbvɪəs] *adj* offensichtlich; (*lie*) klar; (*predictable*) naheliegend

obviously [ˈɔbvɪəslɪ] *adv* (*clearly*) offensichtlich; (*of course*) natürlich; **~!** selbstverständlich!; **~ not** offensichtlich nicht; **he was ~ not drunk** er war natürlich nicht betrunken; **he was not ~ drunk** offenbar war er nicht betrunken

OCAS *n abbr* (= *Organization of Central American States*) mittelamerikanischer Staatenbund

occasion [əˈkeɪʒən] *n* Gelegenheit *f*; (*celebration etc*) Ereignis *nt* ▷ *vt* (*form: cause*) verursachen; **on ~** (*sometimes*) gelegentlich; **on that ~** bei

der Gelegenheit; **to rise to the ~** sich der Lage gewachsen zeigen

occasional [əˈkeɪʒənl] *adj* gelegentlich; **he likes the ~ cigar** er raucht gelegentlich gern eine Zigarre

occasionally [əˈkeɪʒənəlɪ] *adv* gelegentlich; **very ~** sehr selten

occasional table *n* Beistelltisch *m*

occult [ɔˈkʌlt] *n*: **the ~** der Okkultismus ▷ *adj* okkult

occupancy [ˈɔkjupənsɪ] *n* (*of room etc*) Bewohnen *nt*

occupant [ˈɔkjupənt] *n* (*of house etc*) Bewohner(in) *m(f)*; (*temporary: of car*) Insasse *m*, Insassin *f*; **the ~ of this table/office** derjenige, der an diesem Tisch sitzt/in diesem Büro arbeitet

occupation [ɔkjuˈpeɪʃən] *n* (*job*) Beruf *m*; (*pastime*) Beschäftigung *f*; (*of building, country etc*) Besetzung *f*

occupational guidance [ɔkjuˈpeɪʃənl-] (*Brit*) *n* Berufsberatung *f*

occupational hazard *n* Berufsrisiko *nt*

occupational pension scheme *n* betriebliche Altersversorgung *f*

occupational therapy *n* Beschäftigungstherapie *f*

occupier [ˈɔkjupaɪəʳ] *n* Bewohner(in) *m(f)*

occupy [ˈɔkjupaɪ] *vt* (*house, office*) bewohnen; (*place etc*) belegen; (*building, country etc*) besetzen; (*time, attention*) beanspruchen; (*position, space*) einnehmen; **to ~ o.s. (in** *or* **with sth)** sich (mit etw) beschäftigen; **to ~ o.s. in** *or* **with doing sth** sich damit beschäftigen, etw zu tun; **to be occupied in** *or* **with sth** mit etw beschäftigt sein; **to be occupied in** *or* **with doing sth** damit beschäftigt sein, etw zu tun

occur [əˈkəːʳ] *vi* (*take place*) geschehen, sich ereignen; (*exist*) vorkommen; **to ~ to sb** jdm einfallen

occurrence [əˈkʌrəns] *n* (*event*) Ereignis *nt*; (*incidence*) Auftreten *nt*

ocean [ˈəuʃən] *n* Ozean *m*, Meer *nt*; **~s of** (*inf*) jede Menge

ocean bed *n* Meeresgrund *m*

ocean-going [ˈəuʃəngəuɪŋ] *adj* (*ship, vessel*) Hochsee-

Oceania [əuʃɪˈeɪnɪə] *n* Ozeanien *nt*

ocean liner *n* Ozeandampfer *m*

ochre, (*US*) **ocher** [ˈəukəʳ] *adj* ockerfarben

o'clock [əˈklɔk] *adv*: **it is 5 ~** es ist 5 Uhr

OCR *n abbr* (*Comput*) = **optical character reader; optical character recogniton**

Oct. *abbr* (= *October*) Okt.

octagonal [ɔkˈtægənl] *adj* achteckig

octane [ˈɔkteɪn] *n* Oktan *nt*; **high-~ petrol, high-~ gas** (*US*) Benzin *nt* mit hoher Oktanzahl

octave [ˈɔktɪv] *n* Oktave *f*

October [ɔkˈtəubəʳ] *n* Oktober *m*; *see also* **July**

octogenarian [ˈɔktəudʒɪˈnɛərɪən] *n* Achtzigjährige(r) *f(m)*

octopus ['ɔktəpəs] n Tintenfisch m

odd [ɔd] adj (person) sonderbar, komisch; (behaviour, shape) seltsam; (number) ungerade; (sock, shoe etc) einzeln; (occasional) gelegentlich; **60-~** etwa 60; **at ~ times** ab und zu; **to be the ~ one out** der Außenseiter/die Außenseiterin sein; **add meat or the ~ vegetable to the soup** fügen Sie der Suppe Fleisch oder auch etwas Gemüse bei

oddball ['ɔdbɔːl] (inf) n komischer Kauz m

oddity ['ɔdɪtɪ] n (person) Sonderling m; (thing) Merkwürdigkeit f

odd-job man [ɔd'dʒɔb-] n Mädchen nt für alles

odd jobs npl Gelegenheitsarbeiten pl

oddly ['ɔdlɪ] adv (behave, dress) seltsam; see also **enough**

oddments ['ɔdmənts] npl (Comm) Restposten m

odds [ɔdz] npl (in betting) Gewinnquote f; (fig) Chancen pl; **the ~ are in favour of/against his coming** es sieht so aus, als ob er kommt/nicht kommt; **to succeed against all the ~** allen Erwartungen zum Trotz erfolgreich sein; **it makes no ~** es spielt keine Rolle; **to be at ~ (with)** (in disagreement) uneinig sein (mit); (at variance) sich nicht vertragen (mit)

odds and ends npl Kleinigkeiten pl

odds-on [ɔdz'ɔn] adj: **the ~ favourite** der klare Favorit ▷ adv: **it's ~ that she'll win** es ist so gut wie sicher, dass sie gewinnt

ode [əud] n Ode f

odious ['əudɪəs] adj widerwärtig

odometer [ɔ'dɔmɪtəʳ] (US) n Tacho(meter) m

odor etc (US) = **odour** etc

odour, (US) **odor** ['əudəʳ] n Geruch m

odourless ['əudəlɪs] adj geruchlos

OECD n abbr (= Organization for Economic Cooperation and Development) OECD f

oesophagus, (US) **esophagus** [iːˈsɔfəgəs] n Speiseröhre f

oestrogen, (US) **estrogen** ['iːstrəudʒən] n Östrogen nt

 KEYWORD

of [ɔv] prep **1** von; **the history of Germany** die Geschichte Deutschlands; **a friend of ours** ein Freund von uns; **a boy of ten** ein Junge von zehn Jahren, ein zehnjähriger Junge; **that was kind of you** das war nett von Ihnen; **the city of New York** die Stadt New York
2 (expressing quantity, amount, dates etc): **a kilo of flour** ein Kilo Mehl; **how much of this do you need?** wie viel brauchen Sie davon?; **3 of them** (people) 3 von ihnen; (objects) 3 davon; **a cup of tea** eine Tasse Tee; **a vase of flowers** eine Vase mit Blumen; **the 5th of July** der 5. Juli
3 (from, out of) aus; **a bracelet of solid gold** ein Armband aus massivem Gold; **made of wood** aus Holz (gemacht)

Ofcom ['ɔfkɔm] (Brit) n abbr (= Office of Communications Regulation) Regulierungsbehörde für die Kommunikationsindustrie

 KEYWORD

off [ɔf] adv **1** (referring to distance, time): **it's a long way off** es ist sehr weit weg; **the game is 3 days off** es sind noch 3 Tage bis zum Spiel
2 (departure): **to go off to Paris/Italy** nach Paris/Italien fahren; **I must be off** ich muss gehen
3 (removal): **to take off one's coat/clothes** seinen Mantel/sich ausziehen; **the button came off** der Knopf ging ab; **10 % off** (Comm) 10% Nachlass
4: **to be off** (on holiday) im Urlaub sein; (due to sickness) krank sein; **I'm off on Fridays** freitags habe ich frei; **he was off on Friday** Freitag war er nicht da; **to have a day off** (from work) einen Tag freihaben; **to be off sick** wegen Krankheit fehlen
▷ adj **1** (not turned on: machine, light, engine etc) aus; (: water, gas) abgedreht; (: tap) zu
2: **to be off** (meeting, match) ausfallen; (agreement) nicht mehr gelten
3 (Brit: not fresh) verdorben, schlecht
4: **on the off chance that ...** für den Fall, dass ...; **to have an off day** (not as good as usual) nicht in Form sein; **to be badly off** sich schlecht stehen
▷ prep **1** (indicating motion, removal etc) von +dat; **to fall off a cliff** von einer Klippe fallen; **to take a picture off the wall** ein Bild von der Wand nehmen
2 (distant from): **5 km off the main road** 5 km von der Hauptstraße entfernt; **an island off the coast** eine Insel vor der Küste
3: **I'm off meat/beer** (no longer eat/drink it) ich esse kein Fleisch/trinke kein Bier mehr; (no longer like it) ich kann kein Fleisch/Bier etc mehr sehen

offal ['ɔfl] n (Culin) Innereien pl

off-beat ['ɔfbiːt] adj (clothes, ideas) ausgefallen

off-centre, (US) **off-center** [ɔfˈsɛntəʳ] adj nicht genau in der Mitte, links/rechts von der Mitte ▷ adv asymmetrisch

off-colour ['ɔfˈkʌləʳ] (Brit) adj (ill) unpässlich; **to feel ~** sich unwohl fühlen

offence, (US) **offense** [əˈfɛns] n (crime) Vergehen nt; (insult) Beleidigung f, Kränkung f; **to commit an ~** eine Straftat begehen; **to take ~ (at)** Anstoß nehmen (an +dat); **to give ~ (to)** Anstoß erregen (bei); **"no ~"** „nichts für ungut"

offend [əˈfɛnd] vt (upset) kränken; **to ~ against** (law, rule) verstoßen gegen

offender [əˈfɛndəʳ] n Straftäter(in) m(f)

offending [əˈfɛndɪŋ] adj (item etc) anstoßerregend

offense [əˈfɛns] (US) n = **offence**

offensive [əˈfɛnsɪv] adj (remark, behaviour) verletzend; (smell etc) übel; (weapon) Angriffs- ▷ n (Mil) Offensive f

offer ['ɒfə^r] n Angebot nt ▷ vt anbieten; (money, opportunity, service) bieten; (reward) aussetzen; **to make an ~ for sth** ein Angebot für etw machen; **on ~** (Comm: available) erhältlich; (: cheaper) im Angebot; **to ~ sth to sb** jdm etw anbieten; **to ~ to do sth** anbieten, etw zu tun
offering ['ɒfərɪŋ] n Darbietung f; (Rel) Opfergabe f
off-hand [ɒf'hænd] adj (casual) lässig; (impolite) kurz angebunden ▷ adv auf Anhieb; **I can't tell you ~** das ich Ihnen auf Anhieb nicht sagen
office ['ɒfɪs] n Büro nt; (position) Amt nt; **doctor's ~** (US) Praxis f; **to take ~** das Amt antreten; **in ~** (minister etc) im Amt; **through his good ~s** durch seine guten Dienste; **O~ of Fair Trading** (Brit) Behörde f gegen unlauteren Wettbewerb
office block, (US) **office building** n Bürogebäude nt
office boy n Bürogehilfe m
office holder n Amtsinhaber(in) m(f)
office hours npl (Comm) Bürostunden pl; (US: Med) Sprechstunde f
office manager n Büroleiter(in) m(f)
officer ['ɒfɪsə^r] n (Mil etc) Offizier m; (also: **police officer**) Polizeibeamte(r) m, Polizeibeamtin f; (of organization) Funktionär m
office work n Büroarbeit f
office worker n Büroangestellte(r) f(m)
official [ə'fɪʃl] adj offiziell ▷ n (in government) Beamte(r) m, Beamtin f; (in trade union etc) Funktionär m
officialdom [ə'fɪʃldəm] (pej) n Bürokratie f
officially [ə'fɪʃəlɪ] adv offiziell
official receiver n (Comm) Konkursverwalter m
officiate [ə'fɪʃɪeɪt] vi amtieren; **to ~ at a marriage** eine Trauung vornehmen
officious [ə'fɪʃəs] adj übereifrig
offing ['ɒfɪŋ] n: **in the ~** in Sicht
off-key [ɒf'kiː] adj (Mus: sing, play) falsch; (instrument) verstimmt
off-licence ['ɒflaɪsns] (Brit) n = Wein- und Spirituosenhandlung f; siehe Info-Artikel

● **OFF-LICENCE**

● Off-licence ist ein Geschäft (oder eine Theke
● in einer Gaststätte), wo man alkoholische
● Getränke kaufen kann, die aber anderswo
● konsumiert werden müssen. In solchen
● Geschäften, die oft von landesweiten
● Ketten betrieben werden, kann man auch
● andere Getränke, Süßigkeiten, Zigaretten
● und Knabbereien kaufen.

off-limits [ɒf'lɪmɪts] adj verboten
off-line [ɒf'laɪn] (Comput) adj Offline- ▷ adv offline; (switched off) abgetrennt
off-load ['ɒfləud] vt abladen
off-peak ['ɒf'piːk] adj (heating) Nachtspeicher-; (electricity) Nacht-; (train) außerhalb der Stoßzeit; **~ ticket** Fahrkarte f zur Fahrt außerhalb der Stoßzeit

off-putting ['ɒfputɪŋ] (Brit) adj (remark, behaviour) abstoßend
off-season ['ɒf'siːzn] adj, adv außerhalb der Saison
offset ['ɒfsɛt] (irreg: like **set**) vt (counteract) ausgleichen
offshoot ['ɒfʃuːt] n (Bot, fig) Ableger m
offshore [ɒf'ʃɔː^r] adj (breeze) ablandig; (oil rig, fishing) küstennah
offside ['ɒf'saɪd] adj (Sport) im Abseits; (Aut: when driving on left) rechtsseitig; (: when driving on right) linksseitig ▷ n: **the ~** (Aut: when driving on left) die rechte Seite; (: when driving on right) die linke Seite
offspring ['ɒfsprɪŋ] n inv Nachwuchs m
offstage [ɒf'steɪdʒ] adv hinter den Kulissen
off-the-cuff [ɒfðə'kʌf] adj (remark) aus dem Stegreif
off-the-job ['ɒfðə'dʒɒb] adj: **~ training** außerbetriebliche Weiterbildung f
off-the-peg ['ɒfðə'pɛg], (US) **off-the-rack** ['ɒfðə'ræk] adv von der Stange
off-the-record ['ɒfðə'rɛkɔːd] adj (conversation, briefing) inoffiziell; **that's strictly ~** das ist ganz im Vertrauen
off-white ['ɒfwaɪt] adj gebrochen weiß
Ofgem ['ɒfgɛm] n Überwachungsgremium zum Verbraucherschutz nach Privatisierung der Stromindustrie
often ['ɒfn] adv oft; **how ~?** wie oft?; **more ~ than not** meistens; **as ~ as not** ziemlich oft; **every so ~** ab und zu
Ofwat ['ɒfwɒt] n Überwachungsgremium zum Verbraucherschutz nach Privatisierung der Wasserindustrie
ogle ['əugl] vt schielen nach, begaffen (pej)
ogre ['əugə^r] n (monster) Menschenfresser m
OH (US) abbr (Post) = Ohio
oh [əu] excl oh
ohm [əum] n Ohm nt
OHMS (Brit) abbr (= On His/Her Majesty's Service) Aufdruck auf amtlichen Postsendungen
oil [ɔɪl] n Öl nt; (petroleum) (Erd)öl nt ▷ vt ölen
oilcan ['ɔɪlkæn] n Ölkanne f
oil change n Ölwechsel m
oilcloth ['ɔɪlklɒθ] n Wachstuch nt
oilfield ['ɔɪfiːld] n Ölfeld nt
oil filter n Ölfilter m
oil-fired ['ɔɪfaɪəd] adj (boiler, central heating) Öl-
oil gauge n Ölstandsmesser m
oil painting n Ölgemälde nt
oil refinery n Ölraffinerie f
oil rig n Ölförderturm m; (at sea) Bohrinsel f
oilskins ['ɔɪlskɪnz] npl Ölzeug nt
oil slick n Ölteppich m
oil tanker n (ship) (Öl)tanker m; (truck) Tankwagen m
oil well n Ölquelle f
oily ['ɔɪlɪ] adj (substance) ölig; (rag) öldurchtränkt; (food) fettig
ointment ['ɔɪntmənt] n Salbe f
OK (US) abbr (Post) = Oklahoma

O.K. ['əu'keɪ] (inf) excl okay; (granted) gut
▷ adj (average) einigermaßen; (acceptable) in
Ordnung ▷ vt genehmigen ▷ n: **to give sb/
sth the ~** jdm/etw seine Zustimmung geben;
is it ~? ist es in Ordnung?; **are you ~?** bist du
in Ordnung?; **are you ~ for money?** hast du
(noch) genug Geld?; **it's ~ with** or **by me** mir
ist es recht

okay ['əu'keɪ] excl = **O.K.**

Okla. (US) abbr (Post) = Oklahoma

old [əuld] adj alt; **how ~ are you?** wie alt bist
du?; **he's 10 years ~** er ist 10 Jahre alt; **~er
brother** ältere(r) Bruder; **any ~ thing will do
for him** ihm ist alles recht

old age n Alter nt

old age pension n Rente f

old age pensioner (Brit) n Rentner(in) m(f)

old-fashioned ['əuld'fæʃnd] adj altmodisch

old hand n alter Hase m

old hat adj: **to be ~** ein alter Hut sein

old maid n alte Jungfer f

old people's home n Altersheim nt

old-style ['əuldstaɪl] adj im alten Stil

old-time dancing ['əuldtaɪm-] n Tänze pl im
alten Stil

old-timer [əuld'taɪmər] (esp US) n Veteran m

old wives' tale n Ammenmärchen nt

oleander [əulɪ'ændər] n Oleander m

O level (Brit) n (formerly) ≈ Abschluss m der
Sekundarstufe 1 ≈ mittlere Reife f

olive ['ɒlɪv] n Olive f; (tree) Olivenbaum m ▷ adj
(also: **olive-green**) olivgrün; **to offer an ~
branch to sb** (fig) jdm ein Friedensangebot
machen

olive oil n Olivenöl nt

Olympic [əu'lɪmpɪk] adj olympisch

Olympic Games npl: **the ~** (also: **the Olympics**)
die Olympischen Spiele pl

OM (Brit) n abbr (= Order of Merit) britischer
Verdienstorden

Oman [əu'mɑːn] n Oman nt

OMB (US) n abbr (= Office of Management and
Budget) Regierungsbehörde für Verwaltung und Etat

ombudsman ['ɒmbudzmən] n Ombudsmann m

omelette, (US) **omelet** ['ɒmlɪt] n Omelett
nt; **ham/cheese omelet(te)** Schinken-/
Käseomelett nt

omen ['əumən] n Omen nt

ominous ['ɒmɪnəs] adj (silence, warning) ominös;
(clouds, smoke) bedrohlich

omission [əu'mɪʃən] n (thing omitted)
Auslassung f; (act of omitting) Auslassen nt

omit [əu'mɪt] vt (deliberately) unterlassen;
(by mistake) auslassen ▷ vi: **to ~ to do sth** es
unterlassen, etw zu tun

omnivorous [ɒm'nɪvrəs] adj: **to be ~**
Allesfresser sein

ON (Canada) abbr = Ontario

 KEYWORD

on [ɒn] prep **1** (indicating position) auf +dat; (with
vb of motion) auf +acc; **it's on the table** es ist

auf dem Tisch; **she put the book on the
table** sie legte das Buch auf den Tisch; **on the
left** links; **on the right** rechts; **the house
is on the main road** das Haus liegt an der
Hauptstraße

2 (indicating means, method, condition etc): **on
foot** (go, be) zu Fuß; **to be on the train/plane**
im Zug/Flugzeug sein; **to go on the train/
plane** mit dem Zug/Flugzeug reisen; **(to
be wanted) on the telephone** am Telefon
(verlangt werden); **on the radio/television**
im Radio/Fernsehen; **to be on drugs** Drogen
nehmen; **to be on holiday** im Urlaub sein;
I'm here on business ich bin geschäftlich
hier

3 (referring to time): **on Friday** am Freitag; **on
Fridays** freitags; **on June 20th** am 20. Juni;
on Friday, June 20th am Freitag, dem 20.
Juni; **a week on Friday** Freitag in einer
Woche; **on (his) arrival he went straight
to his hotel** bei seiner Ankunft ging er direkt
in sein Hotel; **on seeing this he ...** als er das
sah, ... er ...

4 (about, concerning) über +acc; **a book on
physics** ein Buch über Physik

▷ adv **1** (referring to dress): **to have one's coat on**
seinen Mantel anhaben; **what's she got on?**
was hat sie an?

2 (referring to covering): **screw the lid on tightly**
dreh den Deckel fest zu

3 (further, continuously): **to walk/drive/read on**
weitergehen/-fahren/-lesen

▷ adj **1** (functioning, in operation: machine, radio, TV,
light) an; (: tap) auf; (: handbrake) angezogen;
there's a good film on at the cinema im
Kino läuft ein guter Film

2: **that's not on!** (inf: of behaviour) das ist nicht
drin!

once [wʌns] adv (on one occasion) einmal;
(formerly) früher; (a long time ago) früher einmal
▷ conj (as soon as) sobald; **at ~** (immediately)
sofort; (simultaneously) gleichzeitig; **~ a week**
einmal pro Woche; **~ more** or **again** noch
einmal; **~ and for all** ein für alle Mal; **~
upon a time** es war einmal; **~ in a while**
ab und zu; **all at ~** (suddenly) plötzlich; **for
~** ausnahmsweise (einmal); **~ or twice** ein
paarmal; **~ he had left** sobald er gegangen
war; **~ it was done** nachdem es getan war

oncoming ['ɒnkʌmɪŋ] adj (traffic etc)
entgegenkommend

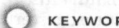 KEYWORD

one [wʌn] num ein(e); (counting) eins; **one
hundred and fifty** (ein)hundert(und)fünfzig;
**one day there was a sudden knock at the
door** eines Tages klopfte es plötzlich an der
Tür; **one by one** einzeln
▷ adj **1** (sole) einzige(r, s); **the one book
which ...** das einzige Buch, das ...
2 (same): **they came in the one car** sie kamen

O

685

in demselben Wagen; **they all belong to the one family** sie alle gehören zu ein und derselben Familie

▷ *pron* **1: this one** diese(r, s); **that one** der/die/das (da); **which one?** welcher/welche/welches; **he is one of us** er ist einer von uns; **I've already got one/a red one** ich habe schon eins/ein rotes

2: one another einander; **do you two ever see one another?** seht ihr zwei euch jemals?

3 (*impersonal*) man; **one never knows** man weiß nie; **to cut one's finger** sich *dat* in den Finger schneiden

one-day excursion ['wʌndeɪ-] (*US*) *n* (*day return*) Tagesrückfahrkarte *f*
one-man ['wʌn'mæn] *adj* (*business, show*) Einmann-
one-man band *n* Einmannkapelle *f*
one-off [wʌn'ɔf] (*Brit: inf*) *n* einmaliges Ereignis *nt*
one-parent family ['wʌnpɛərənt-] *n* Familie *f* mit nur einem Elternteil
one-piece ['wʌnpiːs] *adj*: ~ **swimsuit** einteiliger Badeanzug *m*
onerous ['ɔnərəs] *adj* (*duty etc*) schwer

 KEYWORD

oneself [wʌn'sɛlf] *pron* (*reflexive: after prep*) sich; (*emphatic*) selbst; **to hurt oneself** sich *dat* wehtun; **to keep sth for oneself** etw für sich behalten; **to talk to oneself** Selbstgespräche führen

one-shot ['wʌnʃɔt] (*US*) *n* = **one-off**
one-sided [wʌn'saɪdɪd] *adj* einseitig
one-time ['wʌntaɪm] *adj* ehemalig
one-to-one ['wʌntəwʌn] *adj* (*relationship, tuition*) Einzel-
one-upmanship [wʌn'ʌpmənʃɪp] *n*: **the art of** ~ die Kunst, anderen um einen Schritt voraus zu sein
one-way ['wʌnweɪ] *adj* (*street, traffic*) Einbahn-; (*ticket*) Einzel-
ongoing ['ɔngəʊɪŋ] *adj* (*project*) laufend; (*situation etc*) andauernd
onion ['ʌnjən] *n* Zwiebel *f*
on-line ['ɔnlaɪn] (*Comput*) *adj* (*printer, database*) Online-; (*switched on*) gekoppelt ▷ *adv* online
onlooker ['ɔnlʊkə^r] *n* Zuschauer(in) *m(f)*
only ['əʊnlɪ] *adv* nur ▷ *adj* einzige(r, s) ▷ *conj* nur, bloß; **I ~ took one** ich nahm nur eins; **I saw her ~ yesterday** ich habe sie erst gestern gesehen; **I'd be ~ too pleased to help** ich würde allzu gern helfen; **not ~ ... but (also) ...** nicht nur ..., sondern auch ...; **an ~ child** ein Einzelkind *nt*; **I would come, ~ I'm too busy** ich würde kommen, wenn ich nicht so viel zu tun hätte
ono (*Brit*) *abbr* (*in classified ads*: = or near(est) offer) *see* **near**
onset ['ɔnsɛt] *n* Beginn *m*

onshore ['ɔnʃɔː^r] *adj* (*wind*) auflandig, See-
onslaught ['ɔnslɔːt] *n* Attacke *f*
on-the-job ['ɔnðə'dʒɔb] *adj*: ~ **training** Ausbildung *f* am Arbeitsplatz
onto ['ɔntu] *prep* = **on to**
onus ['əʊnəs] *n* Last *f*, Pflicht *f*; **the ~ is on him to prove it** er trägt die Beweislast
onward ['ɔnwəd], **onwards** ['ɔnwədz] *adv* weiter; **from that time ~(s)** von der Zeit an ▷ *adj* fortschreitend
onyx ['ɔnɪks] *n* Onyx *m*
ooze [uːz] *vi* (*mud, water etc*) triefen
opacity [əu'pæsɪtɪ] *n* (*of substance*) Undurchsichtigkeit *f*
opal ['əupl] *n* Opal *m*
opaque [əu'peɪk] *adj* (*substance*) undurchsichtig, trüb
OPEC ['əupɛk] *n abbr* (= *Organization of Petroleum-Exporting Countries*) OPEC *f*
open ['əupn] *adj* offen; (*packet, shop, museum*) geöffnet; (*view*) frei; (*meeting, debate*) öffentlich; (*ticket, return*) unbeschränkt; (*vacancy*) verfügbar ▷ *vt* öffnen, aufmachen; (*book, paper etc*) aufschlagen; (*account*) eröffnen; (*blocked road*) frei machen ▷ *vi* (*door, eyes, mouth*) sich öffnen; (*shop, bank etc*) aufmachen; (*commence*) beginnen; (*film, play*) Premiere haben; (*flower*) aufgehen; **in the ~ (air)** im Freien; **the ~ sea** das offene Meer; **to have an ~ mind on sth** etw *dat* aufgeschlossen gegenüberstehen; **to be ~ to** (*ideas etc*) offen sein für; **to be ~ to criticism** der Kritik *dat* ausgesetzt sein; **to be ~ to the public** für die Öffentlichkeit zugänglich sein; **to ~ one's mouth** (*speak*) den Mund aufmachen

▶ **open on to** *vt fus* (*room, door*) führen auf +*acc*
▶ **open up** *vi* (*unlock*) aufmachen; (*confide*) sich äußern

open-air [əupn'ɛə^r] *adj* im Freien; ~ **concert** Open-Air-Konzert *nt*; ~ **swimming pool** Freibad *nt*
open-and-shut ['əupnən'ʃʌt] *adj*: ~ **case** klarer Fall *m*
open day *n* Tag *m* der offenen Tür
open-ended [əupn'ɛndɪd] *adj* (*question etc*) mit offenem Ausgang; (*contract*) unbefristet
opener ['əupnə^r] *n* (*also*: **tin opener, can opener**) Dosenöffner *m*
open-heart [əupn'hɑːt] *adj*: ~ **surgery** Eingriff *m* am offenen Herzen
opening ['əupnɪŋ] *adj* (*commencing: stages, scene*) erste(r, s); (*remarks, ceremony etc*) Eröffnungs- ▷ *n* (*gap, hole*) Öffnung *f*; (*of play etc*) Anfang *m*; (*of new building etc*) Eröffnung *f*; (*opportunity*) Gelegenheit *f*
opening hours *npl* Öffnungszeiten *pl*
opening night *n* (*Theat*) Eröffnungsabend *m*
open learning *n* Weiterbildungssystem auf Teilzeitbasis
openly ['əupnlɪ] *adv* offen
open-minded [əupn'maɪndɪd] *adj* aufgeschlossen
open-necked ['əupnnɛkt] *adj* (*shirt*) mit

offenem Kragen
openness ['əupnnɪs] n (frankness) Offenheit f
open-plan ['əupn'plæn] adj (office) Großraum-
open prison n offenes Gefängnis nt
open sandwich n belegtes Brot nt
open shop n Unternehmen ohne Gewerkschaftszwang
Open University (Brit) n ≈ Fernuniversität f; siehe Info-Artikel

○ **OPEN UNIVERSITY**
○
○ Open University ist eine 1969 in
○ Großbritannien gegründete
○ Fernuniversität für Spätstudierende.
○ Der Unterricht findet durch
○ Fernseh- und Radiosendungen statt,
○ schriftliche Arbeiten werden mit der
○ Post verschickt, und der Besuch von
○ Sommerkursen ist Pflicht. Die Studenten
○ müssen eine bestimmte Anzahl
○ von Unterrichtseinheiten in einem
○ bestimmten Zeitraum absolvieren und für
○ die Verleihung eines akademischen Grades
○ eine Mindestzahl von Scheinen machen.

open verdict n (Law) Todesfeststellung ohne Angabe der Todesursache
opera ['ɔpərə] n Oper f
opera glasses npl Opernglas nt
opera house n Opernhaus nt
opera singer n Opernsänger(in) m(f)
operate ['ɔpəreɪt] vt (machine etc) bedienen
▷ vi (machine etc) funktionieren; (company) arbeiten; (laws, forces) wirken; (Med) operieren; **to ~ on sb** jdn operieren
operatic [ɔpə'rætɪk] adj (singer etc) Opern-
operating room ['ɔpəreɪtɪŋ-] (US) n Operationssaal m
operating system n (Comput) Betriebssystem nt
operating table n (Med) Operationstisch m
operating theatre n (Med) Operationssaal m
operation [ɔpə'reɪʃən] n (activity) Unternehmung f; (of machine etc) Betrieb m; (Mil, Med) Operation f; (Comm) Geschäft nt; **to be in ~** (law, scheme) in Kraft sein; **to have an ~** (Med) operiert werden; **to perform an ~** (Med) eine Operation vornehmen
operational [ɔpə'reɪʃənl] adj (machine etc) einsatzfähig
operative ['ɔpərətɪv] adj (measure, system) wirksam; (law) gültig ▷ n (in factory) Maschinenarbeiter(in) m(f); **the ~ word** das entscheidende Wort
operator ['ɔpəreɪtəʳ] n (Tel) Vermittlung f; (of machine) Bediener(in) m(f)
operetta [ɔpə'rɛtə] n Operette f
ophthalmic [ɔf'θælmɪk] adj (department) Augen-
ophthalmic optician n Augenoptiker(in) m(f)
ophthalmologist [ɔfθæl'mɔlədʒɪst] n Augenarzt m, Augenärztin f

opinion [ə'pɪnjən] n Meinung f; **in my ~** meiner Meinung nach; **to have a good/high ~ of sb/o.s.** eine gute/hohe Meinung von jdm/sich haben; **to be of the ~ that ...** der Ansicht or Meinung sein, dass ...; **to get a second ~** (Med etc) ein zweites Gutachten einholen
opinionated [ə'pɪnjəneɪtɪd] (pej) adj rechthaberisch
opinion poll n Meinungsumfrage f
opium ['əupɪəm] n Opium nt
opponent [ə'pəunənt] n Gegner(in) m(f)
opportune ['ɔpətjuːn] adj (moment) günstig
opportunism [ɔpə'tjuːnɪsəm] (pej) n Opportunismus m
opportunist [ɔpə'tjuːnɪst] (pej) n Opportunist(in) m(f)
opportunity [ɔpə'tjuːnɪtɪ] n Gelegenheit f, Möglichkeit f; (prospects) Chance f; **to take the ~ of doing sth** die Gelegenheit ergreifen, etw zu tun
oppose [ə'pəuz] vt (opinion, plan) ablehnen; **to be ~d to sth** gegen etw sein; **as ~d to** im Gegensatz zu
opposing [ə'pəuzɪŋ] adj (side, team) gegnerisch; (ideas, tendencies) entgegengesetzt
opposite ['ɔpəzɪt] adj (house, door) gegenüberliegend; (end, direction) entgegengesetzt; (point of view, effect) gegenteilig ▷ adv gegenüber ▷ prep (in front of) gegenüber; (next to: on list, form etc) neben ▷ n: **the ~** das Gegenteil; **the ~ sex** das andere Geschlecht; **"see ~ page"** „siehe gegenüber"
opposite number n (person) Gegenspieler(in) m(f)
opposition [ɔpə'zɪʃən] n (resistance) Widerstand m; (Sport) Gegner pl; **the O~** (Pol) die Opposition
oppress [ə'prɛs] vt unterdrücken
oppressed [ə'prɛst] adj unterdrückt
oppression [ə'prɛʃən] n Unterdrückung f
oppressive [ə'prɛsɪv] adj (weather, heat) bedrückend; (political regime) repressiv
opprobrium [ə'prəubrɪəm] n (form) Schande f, Schmach f
opt [ɔpt] vi: **to ~ for** sich entscheiden für; **to ~ to do sth** sich entscheiden, etw zu tun
▶ **opt out (of)** vi (not participate) sich nicht beteiligen (an +dat); (of insurance scheme etc) kündigen; **to ~ out (of local authority control)** (Pol: hospital, school) aus der Kontrolle der Gemeindeverwaltung austreten
optical ['ɔptɪkl] adj optisch
optical character reader n optischer Klarschriftleser m
optical character recognition n optische Zeichenerkennung f
optical illusion n optische Täuschung f
optician [ɔp'tɪʃən] n Optiker(in) m(f)
optics ['ɔptɪks] n Optik f
optimism ['ɔptɪmɪzəm] n Optimismus m
optimist ['ɔptɪmɪst] n Optimist(in) m(f)
optimistic [ɔptɪ'mɪstɪk] adj optimistisch

o

optimum ['ɔptɪməm] *adj* optimal
option ['ɔpʃən] *n* (*choice*) Möglichkeit *f*; (*Scol*) Wahlfach *nt*; (*Comm*) Option *f*; **to keep one's ~s open** sich *dat* alle Möglichkeiten offenhalten; **to have no ~** keine (andere) Wahl haben
optional ['ɔpʃənl] *adj* freiwillig; **~ extras** (*Comm*) Extras *pl*
opulence ['ɔpjuləns] *n* Reichtum *m*
opulent ['ɔpjulənt] *adj* (*very wealthy*) reich, wohlhabend
OR (*US*) *abbr* (*Post*) = *Oregon*
or [ɔːʳ] *conj* oder; **he hasn't seen or heard anything** er hat weder etwas gesehen noch gehört; **or else** (*otherwise*) sonst; **fifty or sixty people** fünfzig bis sechzig Leute
oracle ['ɔrəkl] *n* Orakel *nt*
oral ['ɔːrəl] *adj* (*test, report*) mündlich; (*Med: vaccine, contraceptive*) zum Einnehmen ▷ *n* (*exam*) mündliche Prüfung *f*
orange ['ɔrɪndʒ] *n* Orange *f*, Apfelsine *f* ▷ *adj* (*colour*) orange
orangeade [ɔrɪndʒ'eɪd] *n* Orangenlimonade *f*
oration [ɔː'reɪʃən] *n* Ansprache *f*
orator ['ɔrətəʳ] *n* Redner(in) *m(f)*
orb [ɔːb] *n* Kugel *f*
orbit ['ɔːbɪt] *n* (*of planet etc*) Umlaufbahn *f* ▷ *vt* umkreisen
orbital motorway ['ɔːbɪtəl-] *n* Ringautobahn *f*
orchard ['ɔːtʃəd] *n* Obstgarten *m*; **apple ~** Obstgarten mit Apfelbäumen
orchestra ['ɔːkɪstrə] *n* Orchester *nt*; (*US: stalls*) Parkett *nt*
orchestral [ɔː'kɛstrəl] *adj* (*piece, musicians*) Orchester-
orchestrate ['ɔːkɪstreɪt] *vt* orchestrieren
orchid ['ɔːkɪd] *n* Orchidee *f*
ordain [ɔː'deɪn] *vt* (*Rel*) ordinieren; (*decree*) verfügen
ordeal [ɔː'diːl] *n* Qual *f*
order ['ɔːdəʳ] *n* (*command*) Befehl *m*; (*Comm, in restaurant*) Bestellung *f*; (*sequence*) Reihenfolge *f*; (*discipline, organization*) Ordnung *f*; (*Rel*) Orden *m* ▷ *vt* (*command*) befehlen; (*Comm, in restaurant*) bestellen; (*also: put in order*) ordnen; **in ~** (*permitted*) in Ordnung; **in (working) ~** betriebsfähig; **in ~ to do sth** um etw zu tun; **in ~ of size** nach Größe (geordnet); **on ~** (*Comm*) bestellt; **out of ~** (*not working*) außer Betrieb; (*in the wrong sequence*) durcheinander; (*motion, proposal*) nicht zulässig; **to place an ~ for sth with sb** eine Bestellung für etw bei jdm aufgeben; **made to ~** (*Comm*) auf Bestellung (gemacht); **to be under ~s to do sth** die Anweisung haben, etw zu tun; **to take ~s** Befehle entgegennehmen; **a point of ~** (*in debate etc*) eine Verfahrensfrage; **"pay to the ~ of ..."** „zahlbar an *+dat* ..."; **of** *or* **in the ~ of** in der Größenordnung von; **to ~ sb to do sth** jdn anweisen, etw zu tun
▶ **order around** *vt* (*also:* **order about**) herumkommandieren

order book *n* (*Comm*) Auftragsbuch *nt*
order form *n* Bestellschein *m*
orderly ['ɔːdəlɪ] *n* (*Mil*) Offiziersbursche *m*; (*Med*) Pfleger(in) *m(f)* ▷ *adj* (*manner*) ordentlich; (*sequence, system*) geordnet
order number *n* (*Comm*) Bestellnummer *f*
ordinal ['ɔːdɪnl] *adj*: **~ number** Ordinalzahl *f*
ordinarily ['ɔːdnrɪlɪ] *adv* normalerweise
ordinary ['ɔːdnrɪ] *adj* (*everyday*) gewöhnlich, normal; (*pej: mediocre*) mittelmäßig; **out of the ~** außergewöhnlich

ordinary seaman (*Brit*) *n* Leichtmatrose *m*
ordinary shares *npl* Stammaktien *pl*
ordination [ɔːdɪ'neɪʃən] *n* (*Rel*) Ordination *f*
ordnance ['ɔːdnəns] *n* (*unit*) Technische Truppe *f* ▷ *adj* (*factory, supplies*) Munitions-
Ordnance Survey (*Brit*) *n* Landesvermessung *f*
ore [ɔːʳ] *n* Erz *nt*
Ore. (*US*) *abbr* (*Post*) = *Oregon*
organ ['ɔːgən] *n* (*Anat*) Organ *nt*; (*Mus*) Orgel *f*
organic [ɔː'gænɪk] *adj* organisch; (*farming, vegetables*) Bio-, Öko-; **~ food** Biokost *f*
organism ['ɔːgənɪzəm] *n* Organismus *m*
organist ['ɔːgənɪst] *n* Organist(in) *m(f)*
organization [ɔːgənaɪ'zeɪʃən] *n* Organisation *f*
organization chart *n* Organisationsplan *m*
organize ['ɔːgənaɪz] *vt* organisieren; **to get ~d** sich fertig machen
organized crime *n* organisiertes Verbrechen *nt*
organized labour *n* organisierte Arbeiterschaft *f*
organizer ['ɔːgənaɪzəʳ] *n* (*of conference etc*) Organisator *m*, Veranstalter *m*
orgasm ['ɔːgæzəm] *n* Orgasmus *m*
orgy ['ɔːdʒɪ] *n* Orgie *f*; **an ~ of destruction** eine Zerstörungsorgie
Orient ['ɔːrɪənt] *n*: **the ~** der Orient
orient ['ɔːrɪənt] *vt*: **to ~ o.s. (to)** sich orientieren (in *+dat*); **to be ~ed towards** ausgerichtet sein auf *+acc*
oriental [ɔːrɪ'ɛntl] *adj* orientalisch
orientate ['ɔːrɪənteɪt] *vt*: **to ~ o.s.** sich orientieren; (*fig*) sich zurechtfinden; **to be ~d towards** ausgerichtet sein auf *+acc*
orifice ['ɔrɪfɪs] *n* (*Anat*) Öffnung *f*
origin ['ɔrɪdʒɪn] *n* Ursprung *m*; (*of person*) Herkunft *f*; **country of ~** Herkunftsland *nt*
original [ə'rɪdʒɪnl] *adj* (*first*) ursprünglich; (*genuine*) original; (*imaginative*) originell ▷ *n* Original *nt*

originality [ərɪdʒɪ'nælɪtɪ] n Originalität f

originally [ə'rɪdʒɪnəlɪ] adv (at first) ursprünglich

originate [ə'rɪdʒɪneɪt] vi: **to ~ in** (idea, custom etc) entstanden sein in +dat; **to ~ with** or **from** stammen von

originator [ə'rɪdʒɪneɪtə'] n (of idea, custom) Urheber(in) m(f)

Orkneys ['ɔːknɪz] npl: **the ~** (also: **the Orkney Islands**) die Orkneyinseln pl

ornament ['ɔːnəmənt] n (object) Ziergegenstand m; (decoration) Verzierungen pl

ornamental [ɔːnə'mɛntl] adj (garden, pond) Zier-

ornamentation [ɔːnəmɛn'teɪʃən] n Verzierungen pl

ornate [ɔː'neɪt] adj (necklace, design) kunstvoll

ornithologist [ɔːnɪ'θɒlədʒɪst] n Ornithologe m, Ornithologin f

ornithology [ɔːnɪ'θɒlədʒɪ] n Ornithologie f, Vogelkunde f

orphan ['ɔːfn] n Waise f, Waisenkind nt ▷ vt: **to be ~ed** zur Waise werden

orphanage ['ɔːfənɪdʒ] n Waisenhaus nt

orthodox ['ɔːθədɒks] adj orthodox; **~ medicine** die konventionelle Medizin

orthodoxy ['ɔːθədɒksɪ] n Orthodoxie f

orthopaedic, (US) **orthopedic** [ɔːθə'piːdɪk] adj orthopädisch

OS abbr (Brit) = **Ordnance Survey**; (Naut) = **ordinary seaman**; (Dress) = **outsize**

o.s. abbr (Comm: = out of stock) nicht auf Lager

Oscar ['ɒskə'] n Oscar m

oscillate ['ɒsɪleɪt] vi (Elec, Phys) schwingen, oszillieren; (fig) schwanken

OSHA (US) n abbr (= Occupational Safety and Health Administration) Regierungsstelle für Arbeitsschutzvorschriften

Oslo ['ɒzləʊ] n Oslo nt

OST n abbr (= Office of Science and Technology) Ministerium für Wissenschaft und Technologie

ostensible [ɒs'tɛnsɪbl] adj vorgeblich, angeblich

ostensibly [ɒs'tɛnsɪblɪ] adv angeblich

ostentation [ɒstɛn'teɪʃən] n Pomp m, Protz m

ostentatious [ɒstɛn'teɪʃəs] adj (building, car etc) pompös; (person) protzig

osteopath ['ɒstɪəpæθ] n Osteopath(in) m(f)

ostracize ['ɒstrəsaɪz] vt ächten

ostrich ['ɒstrɪtʃ] n Strauß m

OT abbr (Bible: = Old Testament) AT

OTB (US) n abbr (= offtrack betting) Wetten außerhalb des Rennbahngeländes

OTE abbr (Comm: = on-target earnings) Einkommensziel nt

other ['ʌðə'] adj andere(r, s) ▷ pron: **the ~ (one)** der/die/das andere; **~s** andere pl; **the ~s** die anderen pl; **~ than** (apart from) außer; **the ~ day** (recently) neulich; **some actor or ~** irgendein Schauspieler; **somebody or ~** irgendjemand; **the car was none ~ than Robert's** das Auto gehörte keinem anderen als Robert

otherwise ['ʌðəwaɪz] adv (differently) anders; (apart from that, if not) sonst, ansonsten; **an ~**

good piece of work eine im Übrigen gute Arbeit

OTT (inf) abbr (= over the top) see **top**

otter ['ɒtə'] n Otter m

OU (Brit) n abbr = **Open University**

ouch [aʊtʃ] excl autsch

ought [ɔːt] (pt ~) aux vb: **I ~ to do it** ich sollte es tun; **this ~ to have been corrected** das hätte korrigiert werden müssen; **he ~ to win** (he probably will win) er dürfte wohl gewinnen; **you ~ to go and see it** das solltest du dir ansehen

ounce [aʊns] n Unze f; (fig: small amount) bisschen nt

our ['aʊə'] adj unsere(r, s); see also **my**

ours [aʊəz] pron unsere(r, s); see also **mine¹**

ourselves [aʊə'sɛlvz] pron pl uns (selbst); (emphatic) selbst; **we did it (all) by ~** wir haben alles selbst gemacht; see also **oneself**

oust [aʊst] vt (forcibly remove) verdrängen

 KEYWORD

out¹ [aʊt] adv **1** (not in) draußen; **out in the rain/snow** draußen im Regen/Schnee; **out here** hier; **out there** dort; **to go/come etc out** hinausgehen/-kommen etc; **to speak out loud** laut sprechen

2 (not at home, absent) nicht da

3 (indicating distance): **the boat was 10 km out** das Schiff war 10 km weit draußen; **3 days out from Plymouth** 3 Tage nach dem Auslaufen von Plymouth

4 (Sport) aus; **the ball is out/has gone out** der Ball ist aus

▷ adj **1: to be out** (person: unconscious) bewusstlos sein; (: out of game) ausgeschieden sein; (: out of fashion: style, singer) out sein

2 (have appeared: flowers) da; (: news, secret) heraus

3 (extinguished, finished: fire, light, gas) aus; **before the week was out** ehe die Woche zu Ende war

4: to be out to do sth (intend) etw tun wollen

5 (wrong): **to be out in one's calculations** sich in seinen Berechnungen irren

out² [aʊt] vt (inf: expose as homosexual) outen

outage ['aʊtɪdʒ] (esp US) n (power failure) Stromausfall m

out-and-out ['aʊtəndaʊt] adj (liar, thief etc) ausgemacht

outback ['aʊtbæk] n (in Australia): **the ~** das Hinterland

outbid [aʊt'bɪd] vt überbieten

outboard ['aʊtbɔːd] n (also: **outboard motor**) Außenbordmotor m

outbound ['aʊtbaʊnd] adj (ship) auslaufend

outbreak ['aʊtbreɪk] n (of war, disease etc) Ausbruch m

outbuilding ['aʊtbɪldɪŋ] n Nebengebäude nt

outburst ['aʊtbəːst] n (of anger etc) Gefühlsausbruch m

outcast ['aʊtkɑːst] n Ausgestoßene(r) f(m)

outclass [aʊt'klɑːs] vt deklassieren

outcome ['aʊtkʌm] n Ergebnis nt, Resultat nt

o

outcrop ['autkrɔp] n (of rock) Block m

outcry ['autkraɪ] n Aufschrei m

outdated [aut'deɪtɪd] adj (custom, idea) veraltet

outdo [aut'duː] (irreg: like **do**) vt übertreffen

outdoor [aut'dɔːʳ] adj (activities) im Freien; (clothes) für draußen; ~ **swimming pool** Freibad nt; **she's an ~ person** sie liebt die freie Natur

outdoors [aut'dɔːz] adv (play, sleep) draußen, im Freien

outer ['autəʳ] adj äußere(r, s); ~ **suburbs** (äußere) Vorstädte pl; **the ~ office** das Vorzimmer

outer space n der Weltraum

outfit ['autfɪt] n (clothes) Kleidung f; (inf: team) Verein m

outfitter's ['autfɪtəz] (Brit) n (shop) Herrenausstatter m

outgoing ['autgəʊɪŋ] adj (extrovert) kontaktfreudig; (retiring: president etc) scheidend; (mail etc) ausgehend

outgoings ['autgəʊɪŋz] (Brit) npl Ausgaben pl

outgrow [aut'grəʊ] (irreg: like **grow**) vt (clothes) herauswachsen aus; (habits etc) ablegen

outhouse ['authaʊs] n Nebengebäude nt

outing ['autɪŋ] n Ausflug m

outlandish [aut'lændɪʃ] adj eigenartig, seltsam

outlast [aut'lɑːst] vt überleben

outlaw ['autlɔː] n Geächtete(r) f(m) ▷ vt verbieten

outlay ['autleɪ] n Auslagen pl

outlet ['autlet] n (hole, pipe) Abfluss m; (US: Elec) Steckdose f; (Comm: also: **retail outlet**) Verkaufsstelle f; (fig: for grief, anger etc) Ventil nt

outline ['autlaɪn] n (shape) Umriss m; (brief explanation) Abriss m; (rough sketch) Skizze f ▷ vt (fig: theory, plan etc) umreißen, skizzieren

outlive [aut'lɪv] vt (survive) überleben

outlook ['autluk] n (attitude) Einstellung f; (prospects) Aussichten pl; (for weather) Vorhersage f

outlying ['autlaɪɪŋ] adj (area, town etc) entlegen

outmanoeuvre, (US) **outmaneuver** [autmə'nuːvəʳ] vt ausmanövrieren

outmoded [aut'məʊdɪd] adj veraltet

outnumber [aut'nʌmbəʳ] vt zahlenmäßig überlegen sein +dat; **to be ~ed (by) 5 to 1** im Verhältnis 5 zu 1 in der Minderheit sein

◯ KEYWORD

out of prep **1** (outside, beyond: position) nicht in +dat; (: motion) aus +dat; **to look out of the window** aus dem Fenster blicken; **to be out of danger** außer Gefahr sein
2 (cause, origin) aus +dat; **out of curiosity/fear/greed** aus Neugier/Angst/Habgier; **to drink sth out of a cup** etw aus einer Tasse trinken
3 (from among) von +dat; **one out of every three smokers** einer von drei Rauchern
4 (without): **to be out of sugar/milk/petrol** etc keinen Zucker/keine Milch/kein Benzin etc mehr haben

out of bounds adj: **to be ~** verboten sein

out-of-court [autəv'kɔːt] adj (settlement) außergerichtlich; see also **court**

out-of-date [autəv'deɪt] adj (passport, ticket etc) abgelaufen; (clothes, idea) veraltet

out-of-doors [autəv'dɔːz] adv (play, stay etc) im Freien

out-of-the-way ['autəvðə'weɪ] adj (place) entlegen; (pub, restaurant etc) kaum bekannt

out-of-work ['autəvwəːk] adj arbeitslos

outpatient ['autpeɪʃənt] n ambulanter Patient m, ambulante Patientin f

outpost ['autpəʊst] n (Mil, Comm) Vorposten m

outpouring ['autpɔːrɪŋ] n (of emotion etc) Erguss m

output ['autput] n (production: of factory, writer etc) Produktion f; (Comput) Output m, Ausgabe f ▷ vt (Comput) ausgeben

outrage ['autreɪdʒ] n (scandal) Skandal m; (atrocity) Verbrechen nt, Ausschreitung f; (anger) Empörung f ▷ vt (shock, anger) empören

outrageous [aut'reɪdʒəs] adj (remark etc) empörend; (clothes) unmöglich; (scandalous) skandalös

outrider ['autraɪdəʳ] n (on motorcycle) Kradbegleiter m

outright [aut'raɪt] adv (kill) auf der Stelle; (win) überlegen; (buy) auf einen Schlag; (ask, refuse) ohne Umschweife ▷ adj (winner, victory) unbestritten; (refusal, hostility) total

outrun [aut'rʌn] (irreg: like **run**) vt schneller laufen als

outset ['autset] n Anfang m, Beginn m; **from the ~** von Anfang an; **at the ~** am Anfang

outshine [aut'ʃaɪn] (irreg: like **shine**) vt (fig) in den Schatten stellen

outside [aut'saɪd] n (of building etc) Außenseite f ▷ adj (wall, lavatory) Außen- ▷ adv (be, wait) draußen; (go) nach draußen ▷ prep außerhalb +gen; (door etc) vor +dat; **at the ~** (at the most) höchstens; (at the latest) spätestens; **an ~ chance** eine geringe Chance

outside broadcast n außerhalb des Studios produzierte Sendung f

outside lane n Überholspur f

outside line n (Tel) Amtsanschluss m

outsider [aut'saɪdəʳ] n (stranger) Außenstehende(r) f(m); (odd one out, in race etc) Außenseiter(in) m(f)

outsize ['autsaɪz] adj (clothes) übergroß

outskirts ['autskəːts] npl (of town) Stadtrand m

outsmart [aut'smɑːt] vt austricksen (inf)

outspoken [aut'spəʊkən] adj offen

outspread [aut'spred] adj (wings, arms etc) ausgebreitet

outstanding [aut'stændɪŋ] adj (exceptional) hervorragend; (remaining) ausstehend; **your account is still ~** Ihr Konto weist noch Außenstände auf

outstay [aut'steɪ] vt: **to ~ one's welcome** länger bleiben als erwünscht

outstretched [aut'stretʃt] adj ausgestreckt

outstrip [aut'strɪp] vt (competitors, supply): **to ~ (in)** übertreffen (an +dat)
out tray n Ablage f für Ausgänge
outvote [aut'vəut] vt überstimmen
outward ['autwəd] adj (sign, appearances) äußere(r, s) ▷ adv (move, face) nach außen; **~ journey** Hinreise f
outwardly ['autwədlɪ] adv (on the surface) äußerlich
outwards ['autwədz] adv (move, face) nach außen
outweigh [aut'weɪ] vt schwerer wiegen als
outwit [aut'wɪt] vt überlisten
ova ['əuvə] npl of **ovum**
oval ['əuvl] adj oval ▷ n Oval nt

● OVAL OFFICE

● Oval Office, ein großer ovaler Raum im
● Weißen Haus, ist das private Büro des
● amerikanischen Präsidenten. Im weiteren
● Sinne bezieht sich dieser Begriff oft auf die
● Präsidentschaft selbst.

ovarian [əu'vɛərɪən] adj (Anat) des Eierstocks/ der Eierstöcke; **~ cyst** Zyste f im Eierstock
ovary ['əuvərɪ] n (Anat, Med) Eierstock m
ovation [əu'veɪʃən] n Ovation f
oven ['ʌvn] n (Culin) Backofen m
ovenproof ['ʌvnpru:f] adj (dish etc) feuerfest
oven-ready ['ʌvnrɛdɪ] adj backfertig
ovenware ['ʌvnwɛər] n feuerfestes Geschirr nt

◯ KEYWORD

over ['əuvər] adv 1 (across: walk, jump, fly etc) hinüber; **over here** hier; **over there** dort (drüben); **to ask sb over** (to one's house) jdn zu sich einladen
2 (indicating movement): **to fall over** (person) hinfallen; (object) umfallen; **to knock sth over** etw umstoßen; **to turn over** (in bed) sich umdrehen; **to bend over** sich bücken
3 (finished): **to be over** (game, life, relationship etc) vorbei sein, zu Ende sein
4 (excessively: clever, rich, fat etc) übermäßig
5 (remaining: money, food etc) übrig; **is there any cake (left) over?** ist noch Kuchen übrig?
6: **all over** (everywhere) überall
7 (repeatedly): **over and over (again)** immer (und immer) wieder; **five times over** fünfmal
▷ prep 1 (on top of, above) über +dat; (with vb of motion) über +acc; **to spread a sheet over sth** ein Laken über etw acc breiten
2 (on the other side of): **the pub over the road** die Kneipe gegenüber; **he jumped over the wall** er sprang über die Mauer
3 (more than) über +acc; **over 200 people** über 200 Leute; **over and above my normal duties** über meine normalen Pflichten hinaus; **over and above that** darüber hinaus

4 (during) während; **let's discuss it over dinner** wir sollten es beim Abendessen besprechen

over ... ['əuvər] pref über-
overact [əuvər'ækt] vi übertreiben
overall ['əuvərɔ:l] adj (length, cost etc) Gesamt-; (impression, view) allgemein ▷ adv (measure, cost) insgesamt; (generally) im Allgemeinen ▷ n (Brit) Kittel m; **overalls** npl Overall m
overall majority n absolute Mehrheit f
overanxious [əuvər'æŋkʃəs] adj überängstlich
overawe [əuvər'ɔ:] vt: **to be ~d (by)** überwältigt sein (von)
overbalance [əuvə'bæləns] vi das Gleichgewicht verlieren
overbearing [əuvə'bɛərɪŋ] adj (person, manner) aufdringlich
overboard ['əuvəbɔ:d] adv (Naut) über Bord; **to go ~** (fig) es übertreiben, zu weit gehen
overbook [əuvə'buk] vt überbuchen
overcame [əuvə'keɪm] pt of **overcome**
overcapitalize [əuvə'kæpɪtəlaɪz] vt überkapitalisieren
overcast ['əuvəka:st] adj (day, sky) bedeckt
overcharge [əuvə'tʃa:dʒ] vt zu viel berechnen +dat
overcoat ['əuvəkəut] n Mantel m
overcome [əuvə'kʌm] (irreg: like **come**) vt (problem, fear) überwinden ▷ adj überwältigt; **she was ~ with grief** der Schmerz übermannte sie
overconfident [əuvə'kɒnfɪdənt] adj zu selbstsicher
overcrowded [əuvə'kraudɪd] adj überfüllt
overcrowding [əuvə'kraudɪŋ] n Überfüllung f
overdo [əuvə'du:] (irreg: like **do**) vt übertreiben; **to ~ it** es übertreiben
overdose ['əuvədəus] n Überdosis f
overdraft ['əuvədra:ft] n Kontoüberziehung f; **to have an ~** sein Konto überziehen
overdrawn [əuvə'drɔ:n] adj (account) überzogen; **I am ~** ich habe mein Konto überzogen
overdrive ['əuvədraɪv] n (Aut) Schongang m
overdue [əuvə'dju:] adj überfällig; **that change was long ~** diese Änderung war schon lange fällig
overemphasis [əuvər'ɛmfəsɪs] n: **~ on** Überbetonung +gen
overestimate [əuvər'ɛstɪmeɪt] vt überschätzen
overexcited [əuvərɪk'saɪtɪd] adj ganz aufgeregt
overexertion [əuvərɪg'zə:ʃən] n Überanstrengung f
overexpose [əuvərɪk'spəuz] vt (Phot) überbelichten
overflow [əuvə'fləu] vi (river) über die Ufer treten; (bath, jar etc) überlaufen ▷ n (also: **overflow pipe**) Überlaufrohr nt
overgenerous [əuvə'dʒenərəs] adj allzu großzügig

overgrown [əuvə'grəun] *adj* (*garden*)
verwildert; **he's just an ~ schoolboy** er ist
nur ein großes Kind

overhang ['əuvə'hæŋ] (*irreg: like* **hang**) *vt*
herausragen über +*acc* ▷ *vi* überhängen ▷ *n*
Überhang *m*

overhaul [əuvə'hɔ:l] *vt* (*equipment, car etc*)
überholen ▷ *n* Überholung *f*

overhead [əuvə'hɛd] *adv* (*above*) oben; (*in
the sky*) in der Luft ▷ *adj* (*lighting*) Decken-;
(*cables, wires*) Überland- ▷ *n* (*US*) = **overheads**

overheads *npl* allgemeine Unkosten *pl*

overhear [əuvə'hɪə'] (*irreg: like* **hear**) *vt*
(*zufällig*) mit anhören

overheat [əuvə'hi:t] *vi* (*engine*) heißlaufen

overjoyed [əuvə'dʒɔɪd] *adj* überglücklich; **to
be ~ (at)** überglücklich sein (über +*acc*)

overkill ['əuvəkɪl] *n* (*fig*): **it would be ~** das
wäre zu viel des Guten

overland ['əuvəlænd] *adj* (*journey*) Überland-
▷ *adv* (*travel*) über Land

overlap [əuvə'læp] *vi* (*figures, ideas etc*) sich
überschneiden

overleaf [əuvə'li:f] *adv* umseitig, auf der
Rückseite

overload [əuvə'ləud] *vt* (*vehicle*) überladen;
(*Elec*) überbelasten; (*fig: with work etc*)
überlasten

overlook [əuvə'luk] *vt* (*have view over*)
überblicken; (*fail to notice*) übersehen; (*excuse,
forgive*) hinwegsehen über +*acc*

overlord ['əuvəlɔ:d] *n* oberster Herr *m*

overmanning [əuvə'mænɪŋ] *n* Überbesetzung
f

overnight [əuvə'naɪt] *adv* über Nacht ▷ *adj*
(*bag, clothes*) Reise-; (*accommodation, stop*) für
die Nacht; **to travel ~** nachts reisen; **he'll
be away ~** (*tonight*) er kommt erst morgen
zurück; **to stay ~** über Nacht bleiben; **~ stay**
Übernachtung *f*

overpass ['əuvəpɑ:s] (*esp US*) *n* Überführung *f*

overpay [əuvə'peɪ] *vt*: **to ~ sb by £50** jdm £ 50
zu viel bezahlen

overplay [əuvə'pleɪ] *vt* (*overact*) übertrieben
darstellen; **to ~ one's hand** den Bogen
überspannen

overpower [əuvə'pauə'] *vt* überwältigen

overpowering [əuvə'pauərɪŋ] *adj* (*heat*)
unerträglich; (*stench*) durchdringend; (*feeling,
desire*) überwältigend

overproduction ['əuvəprə'dʌkʃən] *n*
Überproduktion *f*

overrate [əuvə'reɪt] *vt* überschätzen

overreach [əuvə'ri:tʃ] *vt*: **to ~ o.s.** sich
übernehmen

overreact [əuvəri:'ækt] *vi* übertrieben
reagieren

override [əuvə'raɪd] (*irreg: like* **ride**) *vt* (*order etc*)
sich hinwegsetzen über +*acc*

overriding [əuvə'raɪdɪŋ] *adj* vorrangig

overrule [əuvə'ru:l] *vt* (*claim, person*)
zurückweisen; (*decision*) aufheben

overrun [əuvə'rʌn] (*irreg: like* **run**) *vt* (*country,*

continent) einfallen in +*acc* ▷ *vi* (*meeting etc*) zu
lange dauern; **the town is ~ with tourists**
die Stadt ist von Touristen überlaufen

overseas [əuvə'si:z] *adv* (*live, work*) im Ausland;
(*travel*) ins Ausland ▷ *adj* (*market, trade*)
Übersee-; (*student, visitor*) aus dem Ausland

oversee [əuvə'si:] *vt* (*supervise*) beaufsichtigen,
überwachen

overseer ['əuvəsɪə'] *n* Aufseher(in) *m(f)*

overshadow [əuvə'ʃædəu] *vt* (*place, building etc*)
überschatten; (*fig*) in den Schatten stellen

overshoot [əuvə'ʃu:t] (*irreg: like* **shoot**) *vt* (*target,
runway*) hinausschießen über +*acc*

oversight ['əuvəsaɪt] *n* Versehen *nt*; **due to an
~** aus Versehen

oversimplify [əuvə'sɪmplɪfaɪ] *vt* zu stark
vereinfachen

oversleep [əuvə'sli:p] (*irreg: like* **sleep**) *vi*
verschlafen

overspend [əuvə'spɛnd] (*irreg: like* **spend**) *vi*
zu viel ausgeben; **we have overspent by
5,000 dollars** wir haben 5000 Dollar zu viel
ausgegeben

overspill ['əuvəspɪl] *n* (*excess population*)
Bevölkerungsüberschuss *m*

overstaffed [əuvə'stɑ:ft] *adj*: **to be ~**
überbesetzt sein

overstate [əuvə'steɪt] *vt* (*exaggerate*) zu sehr
betonen

overstatement [əuvə'steɪtmənt] *n*
Übertreibung *f*

overstay [əuvə'steɪ] *vt see* **outstay**

overstep [əuvə'stɛp] *vt*: **to ~ the mark** zu weit
gehen

overstock [əuvə'stɔk] *vt* zu große Bestände
anlegen in +*dat*

overstretched [əuvə'stretʃt] *adj* (*person,
resources*) überfordert

overstrike ['əuvəstraɪk] (*irreg: like* **strike**)
n (*on printer*) Mehrfachdruck *m* ▷ *vt*
mehrfachdrucken

oversubscribed [əuvəsəb'skraɪbd] *adj* (*Comm
etc*) überzeichnet

overt [əu'vɜ:t] *adj* offen

overtake [əuvə'teɪk] (*irreg: like* **take**) *vt* (*Aut*)
überholen; (*event, change*) hereinbrechen über
+*acc*; (*emotion*) befallen ▷ *vi* (*Aut*) überholen

overtaking [əuvə'teɪkɪŋ] *n* (*Aut*) Überholen *nt*

overtax [əuvə'tæks] *vt* (*Econ*) zu hoch
besteuern; (*strength, patience*) überfordern; **to ~
o.s.** sich übernehmen

overthrow [əuvə'θrəu] (*irreg: like* **throw**) *vt*
(*government etc*) stürzen

overtime ['əuvətaɪm] *n* Überstunden *pl*; **to do**
or **work ~** Überstunden machen

overtime ban *n* Überstundenverbot *nt*

overtone ['əuvətəun] *n* (*fig: also:* **overtones**): **~s
of** Untertöne *pl* von

overture ['əuvətʃuə'] *n* (*Mus*) Ouvertüre *f*; (*fig*)
Annäherungsversuch *m*

overturn [əuvə'tə:n] *vt* (*car, chair*) umkippen;
(*fig: decision*) aufheben; (*: government*)
stürzen ▷ *vi* (*train etc*) umkippen; (*car*) sich

überschlagen; (*boat*) kentern

overview ['əuvəvju:] *n* Überblick *m*

overweight [əuvə'weɪt] *adj* (*person*)
übergewichtig

overwhelm [əuvə'wɛlm] *vt* überwältigen

overwhelming [əuvə'wɛlmɪŋ] *adj*
überwältigend; **one's ~ impression is of
heat/noise** man bemerkt vor allem die Hitze/
den Lärm

overwhelmingly [əuvə'wɛlmɪŋlɪ] *adv* (*vote,
reject*) mit überwältigender Mehrheit;
(*appreciative, generous etc*) über alle Maßen;
(*opposed etc*) überwiegend

overwork [əuvə'wə:k] *n* Überarbeitung *f* ▷ *vt*
(*person*) (mit Arbeit) überlasten; (*cliché etc*)
überstrapazieren ▷ *vi* sich überarbeiten

overwrite [əuvə'raɪt] *vt* (*Comput*) überschreiben

overwrought [əuvə'rɔ:t] *adj* (*person*) überreizt

ovulate ['ɔvjuleɪt] *vi* ovulieren

ovulation [ɔvju'leɪʃən] *n* Eisprung *m*,
Ovulation *f*

ovum ['əuvəm] (*pl* **ova**) *n* Eizelle *f*

owe [əu] *vt*: **to ~ sb sth, to ~ sth to sb** (*lit, fig*)
jdm etw schulden; (*life, talent, good looks etc*)
jdm etw verdanken

owing to ['əuɪŋ-] *prep* (*because of*) wegen +*gen*,
aufgrund +*gen*

owl [aul] *n* Eule *f*

own [əun] *vt* (*possess*) besitzen ▷ *vi* (*Brit: form*): **to
~ up to sth** etw zugeben ▷ *adj* eigen; **a room
of my ~** mein eigenes Zimmer; **to get one's
~ back** (*take revenge*) sich rächen; **on one's ~**
allein; **to come into one's ~** sich entfalten
▶ **own up** *vi* gestehen, es zugeben

own brand *n* (*Comm*) Hausmarke *f*

owner ['əunə'] *n* Besitzer(in) *m(f)*,
Eigentümer(in) *m(f)*

owner-occupier ['əunər'ɔkjupaɪə'] *n* (*Admin,*
Law) Bewohner(in) *m(f)* im eigenen Haus

ownership ['əunəʃɪp] *n* Besitz *m*; **under new ~**
(*shop etc*) unter neuer Leitung

own goal *n* (*also fig*) Eigentor *nt*

ox [ɔks] (*pl* **oxen**) *n* Ochse *m*

○ **OXBRIDGE**
○
○ *Oxbridge*, eine Mischung aus Ox(ford)
○ und (Cam)bridge, bezieht sich auf die
○ traditionsreichen Universitäten von
○ Oxford und Cambridge. Dieser Begriff
○ ist oft wertend und bringt das Prestige
○ und die Privilegien zum Ausdruck,
○ die traditionellerweise mit diesen
○ Universitäten in Verbindung gebracht
○ werden.

OXFAM (*Brit*) *n abbr* (= *Oxford Committee for Famine*
Relief) *karitative Vereinigung zur Hungerhilfe*

oxide ['ɔksaɪd] *n* Oxid *nt*

oxidize ['ɔksɪdaɪz] *vi* oxidieren

Oxon. ['ɔksn] (*Brit*) *abbr* (*Post*) = *Oxfordshire*; (*in*
degree titles: = *Oxoniensis*) *der Universität Oxford*

oxtail ['ɔksteɪl] *n*: **~ soup**
Ochsenschwanzsuppe *f*

oxyacetylene ['ɔksɪə'sɛtɪliːn] *adj*
(*flame*) Azetylensauerstoff-; **~ burner**
Schweißbrenner *m*; **~ welding**
Autogenschweißen *nt*

oxygen ['ɔksɪdʒən] *n* Sauerstoff *m*

oxygen mask *n* Sauerstoffmaske *f*

oxygen tent *n* Sauerstoffzelt *nt*

oyster ['ɔɪstə'] *n* Auster *f*

oz *abbr* = **ounce**

ozone ['əuzəun] *n* Ozon *nt*

ozone hole *n* Ozonloch *nt*

ozone layer *n*: **the ~** die Ozonschicht

Pp

P, p¹ [piː] n (letter) P nt, p nt; **P for Peter** ≈ P wie Paula

P. abbr = **president; prince**

p² (Brit) abbr = **penny; pence**

p. abbr (= page) S.

PA n abbr = **personal assistant; public-address system** ▷ abbr (US: Post) = Pennsylvania

pa [pɑː] (inf) n Papa m

p.a. abbr (= per annum) p.a.

PAC (US) n abbr (= political action committee) politisches Aktionskomitee

pace [peɪs] n (step) Schritt m; (speed) Tempo nt ▷ vi: **to ~ up and down** auf und ab gehen; **to keep ~ with** Schritt halten mit; **to set the ~** das Tempo angeben; **to put sb through his/ her ~s** (fig) jdn auf Herz und Nieren prüfen

pacemaker ['peɪsmeɪkəʳ] n (Med) (Herz) schrittmacher m; (Sport: pacesetter) Schrittmacher m

pacesetter ['peɪssɛtəʳ] n (Sport) = **pacemaker**

Pacific [pə'sɪfɪk] n (Geog): **the ~ (Ocean)** der Pazifik, der Pazifische Ozean

pacific [pə'sɪfɪk] adj (intentions etc) friedlich

pacifier ['pæsɪfaɪəʳ] (US) n (dummy) Schnuller m

pacifist ['pæsɪfɪst] n Pazifist(in) m(f)

pacify ['pæsɪfaɪ] vt (person, fears) beruhigen

pack [pæk] n (packet) Packung f; (US: of cigarettes) Schachtel f; (of people, hounds) Meute f; (also: **back pack**) Rucksack m; (of cards) (Karten)spiel nt ▷ vt (clothes etc) einpacken; (suitcase etc, Comput) packen; (press down) pressen ▷ vi packen; **to ~ one's bags** (fig) die Koffer packen; **to ~ into** (cram: people, objects) hineinstopfen in +acc; **to send sb ~ing** (inf) jdn kurz abfertigen

▶ **pack in** (Brit: inf) vt (job) hinschmeißen; **~ it in!** hör auf!

▶ **pack off** vt schicken

▶ **pack up** vi (Brit: inf: machine) den Geist aufgeben; (: person) Feierabend machen ▷ vt (belongings) zusammenpacken

package ['pækɪdʒ] n (parcel, Comput) Paket nt; (also: **package deal**) Pauschalangebot nt ▷ vt verpacken

package holiday (Brit), **package tour** (US) n Pauschalreise f

packaging ['pækɪdʒɪŋ] n Verpackung f

packaging industry n Verpackungsindustrie f

packed [pækt] adj (crowded) randvoll

packed lunch (Brit) n Lunchpaket nt

packer ['pækəʳ] n Packer(in) m(f)

packet ['pækɪt] n Packung f; (of cigarettes) Schachtel m; **to make a ~** (Brit: inf) einen Haufen Geld verdienen

packet switching n (Comput) Paketvermittlung f

pack ice ['pækaɪs] n Packeis nt

packing ['pækɪŋ] n (act) Packen nt; (material) Verpackung f

packing case n Kiste f

pact [pækt] n Pakt m

pad [pæd] n (paper) Block m; (to prevent damage) Polster nt; (inf: home) Bude f ▷ vt (upholstery etc) polstern ▷ vi: **to ~ about/in** herum-/ hereintrotten

padded cell ['pædɪd-] n Gummizelle f

padding ['pædɪŋ] n (material) Polsterung f; (fig) Füllwerk nt

paddle ['pædl] n (oar) Paddel nt; (US: for table tennis) Schläger m ▷ vt paddeln ▷ vi (at seaside) plan(t)schen

paddle steamer n Raddampfer m

paddling pool ['pædlɪŋ-] (Brit) n Plan(t) schbecken nt

paddock ['pædək] n (small field) Koppel f; (at race course) Sattelplatz m

paddy field ['pædɪ-] n Reisfeld nt

padlock ['pædlɔk] n Vorhängeschloss nt ▷ vt (mit einem Vorhängeschloss) verschließen

padre ['pɑːdrɪ] n (Rel) Feldgeistliche(r) m

paediatrician [piːdɪə'trɪʃən] n Kinderarzt m, Kinderärztin f

paediatrics, (US) **pediatrics** [piːdɪ'ætrɪks] n Kinderheilkunde f, Pädiatrie f

paedophile ['piːdəufaɪl] n Pädophile(r) f(m) ▷ adj pädophil

paedophilia [piːdəu'fɪlɪə] n Pädophilie f

pagan ['peɪgən] adj heidnisch ▷ n Heide m, Heidin f

page [peɪdʒ] n (of book etc) Seite f; (also: **pageboy**: in hotel) Page m ▷ vt (in hotel etc) ausrufen lassen

pageant ['pædʒənt] n (historical procession) Festzug m; (show) Historienspiel nt

pageantry ['pædʒəntrɪ] n Prunk m

pageboy ['peɪdʒbɔɪ] n see **page**

pager ['peɪdʒə^r] n Funkrufempfänger m,
Piepser m (inf)
paginate ['pædʒɪneɪt] vt paginieren
pagination [pædʒɪ'neɪʃən] n Paginierung f
pagoda [pə'gəudə] n Pagode f
paid [peɪd] pt, pp of **pay** ▷ adj bezahlt; **to put ~
to** (Brit) zunichtemachen
paid-up ['peɪdʌp], (US) **paid-in** adj (member)
zahlend; (Comm: shares) eingezahlt; **~ capital**
eingezahltes Kapital nt
pail [peɪl] n Eimer m
pain [peɪn] n Schmerz m; (also: **pain in the
neck**: inf: nuisance) Plage f; **to have a ~ in
the chest/arm** Schmerzen in der Brust/im
Arm haben; **to be in ~** Schmerzen haben;
to take ~s to do sth (make an effort) sich dat
Mühe geben, etw zu tun; **on ~ of death** bei
Todesstrafe; **he is/it is a right ~ (in the
neck)** (inf) er/das geht einem auf den Wecker
pained [peɪnd] adj (expression) gequält
painful ['peɪnful] adj (back, injury etc)
schmerzhaft; (sight, decision etc) schmerzlich;
(laborious) mühsam; (embarrassing) peinlich
painfully ['peɪnfəlɪ] adv (fig: extremely) furchtbar
painkiller ['peɪnkɪlə^r] n schmerzstillendes
Mittel nt
painless ['peɪnlɪs] adj schmerzlos
painstaking ['peɪnzteɪkɪŋ] adj (work, person)
gewissenhaft
paint [peɪnt] n Farbe f ▷ vt (door, house etc)
anstreichen; (person, picture) malen; (fig)
zeichnen; **a tin of ~** eine Dose Farbe; **to ~ the
door blue** die Tür blau streichen; **to ~ in oils**
in Öl malen
paintbox ['peɪntbɒks] n Farbkasten m,
Malkasten m
paintbrush ['peɪntbrʌʃ] n Pinsel m
painter ['peɪntə^r] n (artist) Maler(in) m(f);
(decorator) Anstreicher(in) m(f)
painting ['peɪntɪŋ] n (activity: of artist) Malerei
f; (: of decorator) Anstreichen nt; (picture) Bild nt,
Gemälde nt
paint stripper n Abbeizmittel nt
paintwork ['peɪntwə:k] n (of wall etc) Anstrich
m; (of car) Lack m
pair [pɛə^r] n Paar nt; **a ~ of scissors** eine
Schere; **a ~ of trousers** eine Hose
▶ **pair off** vi: **to ~ off with sb** sich jdm
anschließen
pajamas [pə'dʒɑːməz] (US) npl Schlafanzug m,
Pyjama m
Pakistan [pɑːkɪ'stɑːn] n Pakistan nt
Pakistani [pɑːkɪ'stɑːnɪ] adj pakistanisch ▷ n
Pakistani m, Pakistaner(in) m(f)
PAL n abbr (TV: = phase alternation line) PAL nt
pal [pæl] (inf) n (friend) Kumpel m, Freund(in)
m(f)
palace ['pæləs] n Palast m
palaeontology [pælɪɔn'tɔlədʒɪ] n
Paläontologie f
palatable ['pælɪtəbl] adj (food, drink) genießbar;
(fig: idea, fact etc) angenehm
palate ['pælɪt] n (Anat) Gaumen m; (sense of

taste) Geschmackssinn m
palatial [pə'leɪʃəl] adj (residence etc) prunkvoll
palaver [pə'lɑːvə^r] (inf) n (fuss) Theater nt
pale [peɪl] adj blass; (light) fahl ▷ vi erblassen
▷ n: **beyond the ~** (unacceptable: behaviour)
indiskutabel; **to grow** or **turn ~**
erblassen, blass werden; **~ blue** zartblau;
to ~ into insignificance (beside) zur
Bedeutungslosigkeit herabsinken (gegenüber
+dat)
paleness ['peɪlnɪs] n Blässe f
Palestine ['pælɪstaɪn] n Palästina nt
Palestinian [pælɪs'tɪnɪən] adj palästinensisch
▷ n Palästinenser(in) m(f)
palette ['pælɪt] n Palette f
palings ['peɪlɪŋz] npl (fence) Lattenzaun m
palisade [pælɪ'seɪd] n Palisade f
pall [pɔːl] n (cloud of smoke) (Rauch)wolke f ▷ vi
an Reiz verlieren
pallet ['pælɪt] n (for goods) Palette f
palliative ['pælɪətɪv] n (Med) Linderungsmittel
nt; (fig) Beschönigung f
pallid ['pælɪd] adj bleich
pallor ['pælə^r] n Bleichheit f
pally ['pælɪ] (inf) adj: **they're very ~** sie sind
dicke Freunde
palm [pɑːm] n (also: **palm tree**) Palme f; (of
hand) Handteller m ▷ vt: **to ~ sth off on sb**
(inf) jdm etw andrehen
palmistry ['pɑːmɪstrɪ] n Handlesekunst f
Palm Sunday n Palmsonntag m
palpable ['pælpəbl] adj (obvious) offensichtlich
palpitations [pælpɪ'teɪʃənz] npl (Med)
Herzklopfen nt
paltry ['pɔːltrɪ] adj (amount, wage) armselig
pamper ['pæmpə^r] vt verwöhnen
pamphlet ['pæmflət] n Broschüre f; (political)
Flugschrift f
pan [pæn] n (also: **saucepan**) Topf m;
(also: **frying pan**) Pfanne f ▷ vi (Cine, TV)
schwenken ▷ vt (inf: book, film) verreißen; **to ~
for gold** Gold waschen
panacea [pænə'sɪə] n Allheilmittel nt
panache [pə'næʃ] n Elan m, Schwung m
Panama ['pænəmɑː] n Panama nt
panama [pænə'mɑː] n (also: **panama hat**)
Panamahut m
Panama Canal n: **the ~** der Panamakanal
Panamanian [pænə'meɪnɪən] adj panamaisch
▷ n Panamaer(in) m(f)
pancake ['pænkeɪk] n Pfannkuchen m
Pancake Day (Brit) n Fastnachtsdienstag m
pancake roll n gefüllte Pfannkuchenrolle
pancreas ['pæŋkrɪəs] n Bauchspeicheldrüse f
panda ['pændə] n Panda m
panda car (Brit) n Streifenwagen m
pandemic [pæn'dɛmɪk] n Pandemie f
pandemonium [pændɪ'məunɪəm] n Chaos nt
pander ['pændə^r] vi: **to ~ to** (person, desire etc)
sich richten nach, entgegenkommen +dat
p & h (US) abbr (= postage and handling) Porto und
Bearbeitungsgebühr
P & L abbr (= profit and loss) Gewinn und Verlust;

P

695

see also **profit**

p & p (*Brit*) *abbr* (= *postage and packing*) Porto und Verpackung

pane [peɪn] *n* (*of glass*) Scheibe *f*

panel ['pænl] *n* (*wood, metal, glass etc*) Platte *f*, Tafel *f*; (*group of experts etc*) Diskussionsrunde *f*; ~ **of judges** Jury *f*

panel game (*Brit*) *n* Ratespiel *nt*

panelling, (*US*) **paneling** ['pænəlɪŋ] *n* Täfelung *f*

panellist, (*US*) **panelist** ['pænəlɪst] *n* Diskussionsteilnehmer(in) *m(f)*

pang [pæŋ] *n*: **to have** *or* **feel a ~ of regret** Reue empfinden; **hunger ~s** quälender Hunger *m*; ~**s of conscience** Gewissensbisse *pl*

panhandler ['pænhændlər] (*US: inf*) *n* Bettler(in) *m(f)*

panic ['pænɪk] *n* Panik *f* ⊳ *vi* in Panik geraten

panic buying [-baɪɪŋ] *n* Panikkäufe *pl*

panicky ['pænɪkɪ] *adj* (*person*) überängstlich; (*feeling*) Angst-; (*reaction*) Kurzschluss-

panic-stricken ['pænɪkstrɪkən] *adj* (*person, face*) von Panik erfasst

pannier ['pænɪər] *n* (*on bicycle*) Satteltasche *f*; (*on animal*) (Trage)korb *m*

panorama [pænə'rɑːmə] *n* (*view*) Panorama *nt*

panoramic [pænə'ræmɪk] *adj* (*view*) Panorama-

pansy ['pænzɪ] *n* (*Bot*) Stiefmütterchen *nt*; (*inf: pej: sissy*) Tunte *f*

pant [pænt] *vi* (*person*) keuchen; (*animal*) hecheln

pantechnicon [pæn'tɛknɪkən] (*Brit*) *n* Möbelwagen *m*

panther ['pænθər] *n* Pant(h)er *m*

panties ['pæntɪz] *npl* Höschen *nt*

panto ['pæntəʊ] *n*, **pantomime** ['pæntəʊmaɪm] *n* siehe Info-Artikel

---

⊙ PANTOMIME

⊙

⊙ *Pantomime* oder umgangssprächlich
⊙ *panto* ist in Großbritannien ein
⊙ zur Weihnachtszeit aufgeführtes
⊙ Märchenspiel mit possenhaften
⊙ Elementen, Musik, Standardrollen (ein
⊙ als Frau verkleideter Mann, ein Junge,
⊙ ein Bösewicht) und aktuellen Witzen.
⊙ Publikumsbeteiligung wird gern gesehen
⊙ (z. B. warnen die Kinder den Helden mit
⊙ dem Ruf „He's behind you" vor einer
⊙ drohenden Gefahr), und viele der Witze
⊙ sprechen vor allem Erwachsene an, sodass
⊙ pantomimes Unterhaltung für die ganze
⊙ Familie bieten.

---

pantry ['pæntrɪ] *n* (*cupboard*) Vorratsschrank *m*; (*room*) Speisekammer *f*

pants [pænts] *npl* (*Brit: woman's*) Höschen *nt*; (: *man's*) Unterhose *f*; (*US: trousers*) Hose *f*

panty hose (*US*) *npl* Strumpfhose *f*

papacy ['peɪpəsɪ] *n* Papsttum *nt*; **during the** ~ **of Paul VI** während der Amtszeit von Papst Paul VI

papal ['peɪpəl] *adj* päpstlich

paparazzi [pæpə'rætsiː] *npl* Pressefotografen *pl*, Paparazzi *pl*

paper ['peɪpər] *n* Papier *nt*; (*also:* **newspaper**) Zeitung *f*; (*exam*) Arbeit *f*; (*academic essay*) Referat *nt*; (*document*) Dokument *nt*, Papier; (*wallpaper*) Tapete *f* ⊳ *adj* (*made from paper: hat, plane etc*) Papier-, aus Papier ⊳ *vt* (*room*) tapezieren; **papers** *npl* (*also:* **identity papers**) Papiere *pl*; **a piece of** ~ (*odd bit*) ein Stück *nt* Papier, ein Zettel *m*; (*sheet*) ein Blatt *nt* Papier; **to put sth down on** ~ etw schriftlich festhalten

paper advance *n* (*on printer*) Papiervorschub *m*

paperback ['peɪpəbæk] *n* Taschenbuch *nt*, Paperback *nt* ⊳ *adj*: ~ **edition** Taschenbuchausgabe *f*

paper bag *n* Tüte *f*

paperboy ['peɪpəbɔɪ] *n* Zeitungsjunge *m*

paperclip ['peɪpəklɪp] *n* Büroklammer *f*

paper hankie *n* Tempotaschentuch® *nt*

paper mill *n* Papierfabrik *f*

paper money *n* Papiergeld *nt*

paper shop *n* Zeitungsladen *m*

paperweight ['peɪpəweɪt] *n* Briefbeschwerer *m*

paperwork ['peɪpəwɑːk] *n* Schreibarbeit *f*

papier-mâché [pæpjeɪ'mæʃeɪ] *n* Papiermaschee *nt*

paprika ['pæprɪkə] *n* Paprika *m*

Pap Smear, Pap Test *n* (*Med*) Abstrich *m*

par [pɑːr] *n* (*Golf*) Par *nt*; **to be on a ~ with** sich messen können mit; **at** ~ (*Comm*) zum Nennwert; **above/below** ~ (*Comm*) über/ unter dem Nennwert; **above** *or* **over** ~ (*Golf*) über dem Par; **below** *or* **under** ~ (*Golf*) unter dem Par; **to feel below** *or* **under** ~ sich nicht auf der Höhe fühlen; **to be** ~ **for the course** (*fig*) zu erwarten sein

parable ['pærəbl] *n* Gleichnis *nt*

parabola [pə'ræbələ] *n* (*Math*) Parabel *f*

parachute ['pærəʃuːt] *n* Fallschirm *m*

parachute jump *n* Fallschirmabsprung *m*

parachutist ['pærəʃuːtɪst] *n* Fallschirmspringer(in) *m(f)*

parade [pə'reɪd] *n* (*procession*) Parade *f*; (*ceremony*) Zeremonie *f* ⊳ *vt* (*people*) aufmarschieren lassen; (*wealth, knowledge etc*) zur Schau stellen ⊳ *vi* (*Mil*) aufmarschieren; **fashion** ~ Modenschau *f*

parade ground *n* Truppenübungsplatz *m*, Exerzierplatz *m*

paradise ['pærədaɪs] *n* (*also fig*) Paradies *nt*

paradox ['pærədɒks] *n* Paradox *nt*

paradoxical [pærə'dɒksɪkl] *adj* (*situation*) paradox

paradoxically [pærə'dɒksɪklɪ] *adv* paradoxerweise

paraffin ['pærəfɪn] (*Brit*) *n* (*also:* **paraffin oil**) Petroleum *nt*; **liquid** ~ Paraffinöl *nt*

paraffin heater (*Brit*) *n* Petroleumofen *m*

paraffin lamp (*Brit*) *n* Petroleumlampe *f*

paragon ['pærəgən] *n*: **a** ~ **of** (*honesty, virtue etc*) ein Muster *nt* an +*dat*

paragraph ['pærəgrɑːf] n Absatz m, Paragraf m; **to begin a new** ~ einen neuen Absatz beginnen

parallel ['pærəlɛl] adj (also Comput) parallel; (fig: similar) vergleichbar ▷ n Parallele f; (Geog) Breitenkreis m; **to run** ~ **(with** or **to)** (lit, fig) parallel verlaufen (zu); **to draw** ~**s between/ with** Parallelen ziehen zwischen/mit; **in** ~ (Elec) parallel

paralyse ['pærəlaɪz] (Brit) vt (also fig) lähmen

paralysis [pəˈrælɪsɪs] (pl **paralyses**) n Lähmung f

paralytic [pærəˈlɪtɪk] adj paralytisch, Lähmungs-; (Brit: inf: drunk) sternhagelvoll

paralyze ['pærəlaɪz] (US) vt = **paralyse**

paramedic [pærəˈmɛdɪk] n Sanitäter(in) m(f); (in hospital) medizinisch-technischer Assistent m, medizinisch-technische Assistentin f

parameter [pəˈræmɪtər] n (Math) Parameter m; (fig: factor) Faktor m; (: limit) Rahmen m

paramilitary [pærəˈmɪlɪtərɪ] adj paramilitärisch

paramount ['pærəmaunt] adj vorherrschend; **of** ~ **importance** von höchster or größter Wichtigkeit

paranoia [pærəˈnɔɪə] n Paranoia f

paranoid ['pærənɔɪd] adj paranoid

paranormal [pærəˈnɔːml] adj übersinnlich, paranormal ▷ n: **the** ~ das Übersinnliche

parapet ['pærəpɪt] n Brüstung f

paraphernalia [pærəfəˈneɪlɪə] n Utensilien pl

paraphrase ['pærəfreɪz] vt umschreiben

paraplegic [pærəˈpliːdʒɪk] n Paraplegiker(in) m(f), doppelseitig Gelähmte(r) f(m)

parapsychology [pærəsaɪˈkɔlədʒɪ] n Parapsychologie f

parasite ['pærəsaɪt] n (also fig) Parasit m

parasol ['pærəsɔl] n Sonnenschirm m

paratrooper ['pærətruːpər] n Fallschirmjäger m

parcel ['pɑːsl] n Paket nt ▷ vt (also: **parcel up**) verpacken
▶ **parcel out** vt aufteilen

parcel bomb (Brit) n Paketbombe f

parcel post n Paketpost f

parch [pɑːtʃ] vt ausdörren, austrocknen

parched [pɑːtʃt] adj ausgetrocknet; **I'm** ~ (inf: thirsty) ich bin am Verdursten

parchment ['pɑːtʃmənt] n Pergament nt

pardon ['pɑːdn] n (Law) Begnadigung f ▷ vt (forgive) verzeihen +dat, vergeben +dat; (Law) begnadigen; ~ **me!, I beg your pardon!** (I'm sorry!) verzeihen Sie bitte!; **(I beg your)** ~?, ~ **me?** (US: what did you say?) bitte?

pare [pɛər] vt (Brit: nails) schneiden; (fruit etc) schälen; (fig: costs etc) reduzieren

parent ['pɛərənt] n (mother) Mutter f; (father) Vater m; **parents** npl (mother and father) Eltern pl

parentage ['pɛərəntɪdʒ] n Herkunft f; **of unknown** ~ unbekannter Herkunft

parental [pəˈrɛntl] adj (love, control etc) elterlich

parent company n Mutterunternehmen nt

parentheses [pəˈrɛnθɪsiːz] npl of **parenthesis**

parenthesis [pəˈrɛnθɪsɪs] (pl **parentheses**) n Klammer f; **in** ~ in Klammern

parenthood ['pɛərənthʊd] n Elternschaft f

parenting ['pɛərəntɪŋ] n elterliche Pflege f

Paris ['pærɪs] n Paris nt

parish ['pærɪʃ] n Gemeinde f

parish council (Brit) n Gemeinderat m

parishioner [pəˈrɪʃənər] n Gemeindemitglied nt

Parisian [pəˈrɪzɪən] adj Pariser inv, paris(er)isch ▷ n Pariser(in) m(f)

parity ['pærɪtɪ] n (equality) Gleichstellung f

park [pɑːk] n Park m ▷ vt, vi (Aut) parken

parka ['pɑːkə] n Parka m

parking ['pɑːkɪŋ] n Parken nt; **"no** ~**"** „Parken verboten"

parking lights npl Parklicht nt

parking lot (US) n Parkplatz m

parking meter n Parkuhr f

parking offence (Brit) n Parkvergehen nt

parking place n Parkplatz m

parking ticket n Strafzettel m

parking violation (US) n = **parking offence**

Parkinson's ['pɑːkɪnsənz], **Parkinson's disease** n parkinsonsche Krankheit f

parkway ['pɑːkweɪ] (US) n Allee f

parlance ['pɑːləns] n: **in common/modern** ~ im allgemeinen/modernen Sprachgebrauch

parliament ['pɑːləmənt] n Parlament nt

○ **PARLIAMENT**
○
○ Parliament ist die höchste gesetzgebende
○ Versammlung in Großbritannien und
○ tritt im Parlamentsgebäude in London
○ zusammen. Die Legislaturperiode beträgt
○ normalerweise 5 Jahre von einer Wahl zur
○ nächsten. Das Parlament besteht aus zwei
○ Kammern, dem Oberhaus (siehe House of
○ Lords und dem Unterhaus (siehe House of
○ Commons).

parliamentary [pɑːləˈmɛntərɪ] adj parlamentarisch

parlour, (US) **parlor** ['pɑːlər] n Salon m

parlous ['pɑːləs] adj (state) prekär

Parmesan [pɑːmɪˈzæn] n (also: **Parmesan cheese**) Parmesan(käse) m

parochial [pəˈrəukɪəl] (pej) adj (person, attitude) engstirnig

parody ['pærədɪ] n Parodie f ▷ vt parodieren

parole [pəˈrəul] n (Law) Bewährung f; **on** ~ auf Bewährung

paroxysm ['pærəksɪzəm] n (also Med) Anfall m

parquet ['pɑːkeɪ] n (also: **parquet floor(ing)**) Parkettboden m

parrot ['pærət] n Papagei m

parrot-fashion ['pærətfæʃən] adv (say, learn) mechanisch; (repeat) wie ein Papagei

parry ['pærɪ] vt (blow, argument) parieren, abwehren

parsimonious [pɑːsɪˈməunɪəs] adj geizig

parsley ['pɑːslɪ] n Petersilie f

parsnip ['pɑːsnɪp] n Pastinake f

P

parson ['pɑːsn] n Pfarrer m
part [pɑːt] n Teil m; (Tech) Teil nt; (Theat, Cine etc: role) Rolle f; (US: in hair) Scheitel m; (Mus) Stimme f ▷ adv = **partly** ▷ vt (separate) trennen; (hair) scheiteln ▷ vi (roads, people) sich trennen; (crowd) sich teilen; **to take ~ in** teilnehmen an +dat; **to take sth in good ~** etw nicht übel nehmen; **to take sb's ~** (support) sich auf jds Seite acc stellen; **on his ~** seinerseits; **for my ~** für meinen Teil; **for the most ~** (generally) zumeist; **for the better** or **best ~ of the day** die meiste Zeit des Tages; **to be ~ and parcel of** dazugehören zu; **~ of speech** (Ling) Wortart f
▶ **part with** vt fus sich trennen von
partake [pɑːˈteɪk] (irreg: like **take**) vi (form): **to ~ of sth** etw zu sich nehmen
part exchange (Brit) n: **to give/take sth in ~** etw in Zahlung geben/nehmen
partial ['pɑːʃl] adj (victory, solution) Teil-; (support) teilweise; (biassed) parteiisch; **to be ~ to** (person, drink etc) eine Vorliebe haben für
partially ['pɑːʃəlɪ] adv (to some extent) teilweise, zum Teil
participant [pɑːˈtɪsɪpənt] n Teilnehmer(in) m(f)
participate [pɑːˈtɪsɪpeɪt] vi sich beteiligen; **to ~ in** teilnehmen an +dat
participation [pɑːtɪsɪˈpeɪʃən] n Teilnahme f
participle ['pɑːtɪsɪpl] n Partizip nt
particle ['pɑːtɪkl] n Teilchen nt, Partikel f
particular [pəˈtɪkjʊləʳ] adj (distinct: person, time, place etc) bestimmt, speziell; (special) speziell, besondere(r, s) ▷ n: **in ~** im Besonderen, besonders; **particulars** npl Einzelheiten pl; (name, address etc) Personalien pl; **to be very ~ about sth** (fussy) in Bezug auf etw acc sehr eigen sein
particularly [pəˈtɪkjʊləlɪ] adv besonders
parting ['pɑːtɪŋ] n (action) Teilung f; (farewell) Abschied m; (Brit: in hair) Scheitel m ▷ adj (words, gift etc) Abschieds-; **his ~ shot was ...** (fig) seine Bemerkung zum Abschied war ...
partisan [pɑːtɪˈzæn] adj (politics, views) voreingenommen ▷ n (supporter) Anhänger(in) m(f); (fighter) Partisan m
partition [pɑːˈtɪʃən] n (wall, screen) Trennwand f; (of country) Teilung f ▷ vt (room, office) aufteilen; (country) teilen
partly ['pɑːtlɪ] adv teilweise, zum Teil
partner ['pɑːtnəʳ] n Partner(in) m(f); (Comm) Partner(in), Teilhaber(in) m(f) ▷ vt (at dance, cards etc) als Partner(in) haben
partnership ['pɑːtnəʃɪp] n (Pol etc) Partnerschaft f; (Comm) Teilhaberschaft f; **to go into ~ (with sb), form a ~ (with sb)** (mit jdm) eine Partnerschaft eingehen
part payment n Anzahlung f
partridge ['pɑːtrɪdʒ] n Rebhuhn nt
part-time ['pɑːt'taɪm] adj (work, staff) Teilzeit-, Halbtags- ▷ adv: **to work ~** Teilzeit arbeiten; **to study ~** Teilzeitstudent(in) m(f) sein
part-timer [pɑːt'taɪməʳ] n (also: **part-time**

worker) Teilzeitbeschäftigte(r) f(m)
party ['pɑːtɪ] n (Pol, Law) Partei f; (celebration, social event) Party f, Fete f; (group of people) Gruppe f, Gesellschaft f ▷ cpd (Pol) Partei-; **dinner ~** Abendgesellschaft f; **to give** or **throw a ~** eine Party geben, eine Fete machen; **we're having a ~ next Saturday** bei uns ist nächsten Samstag eine Party; **our son's birthday ~** die Geburtstagsfeier unseres Sohnes; **to be a ~ to a crime** an einem Verbrechen beteiligt sein
party dress n Partykleid nt
party line n (Tel) Gemeinschaftsanschluss m; (Pol) Parteilinie f
party piece (inf) n: **to do one's ~** auf einer Party etwas zum Besten geben
party political adj parteipolitisch
party political broadcast n parteipolitische Sendung f
par value n (Comm: of share, bond) Nennwert m
pass [pɑːs] vt (spend: time) verbringen; (hand over) reichen, geben; (go past) vorbeikommen an +dat; (: in car) vorbeifahren an +dat; (overtake) überholen; (fig: exceed) übersteigen; (exam) bestehen; (law, proposal) genehmigen ▷ vi (go past) vorbeigehen; (: in car) vorbeifahren; (in exam) bestehen ▷ n (permit) Ausweis m; (in mountains, Sport) Pass m; **to ~ sth through sth** etw durch etw führen; **to ~ the ball to** den Ball zuspielen +dat; **could you ~ the vegetables round?** könnten Sie das Gemüse herumreichen?; **to get a ~ in ...** (Scol) die Prüfung in ... bestehen; **things have come to a pretty ~ when ...** (Brit: inf) so weit ist es schon gekommen, dass ...; **to make a ~ at sb** (inf) jdn anmachen
▶ **pass away** vi (die) dahinscheiden
▶ **pass by** vi (go past) vorbeigehen; (: in car) vorbeifahren ▷ vt (ignore) vorbeigehen an +dat
▶ **pass down** vt (customs, inheritance) weitergeben
▶ **pass for** vt: **she could ~ for 25** sie könnte für 25 durchgehen
▶ **pass on** vi (die) verscheiden ▷ vt: **to ~ on (to)** weitergeben (an +acc)
▶ **pass out** vi (faint) ohnmächtig werden; (Brit: Mil) die Ausbildung beenden
▶ **pass over** vt (ignore) übergehen ▷ vi (die) entschlafen
▶ **pass up** vt (opportunity) sich dat entgehen lassen
passable ['pɑːsəbl] adj (road) passierbar; (acceptable) passabel
passage ['pæsɪdʒ] n Gang m; (in book) Passage f; (way through crowd etc, Anat) Weg m; (act of passing: of train etc) Durchfahrt f; (journey: on boat) Überfahrt f
passageway ['pæsɪdʒweɪ] n Gang m
passenger ['pæsɪndʒəʳ] n (in boat, plane) Passagier m; (in car) Fahrgast m
passer-by [pɑːsəˈbaɪ] (pl **passers-by**) n Passant(in) m(f)
passing ['pɑːsɪŋ] adj (moment, thought etc)

flüchtig; **in ~** (*incidentally*) beiläufig, nebenbei; **to mention sth in ~** etw beiläufig *or* nebenbei erwähnen

passing place *n* (*Aut*) Ausweichstelle *f*

passion ['pæʃən] *n* Leidenschaft *f*; **to have a ~ for sth** eine Leidenschaft für etw haben

passionate ['pæʃənɪt] *adj* leidenschaftlich

passion fruit *n* Passionsfrucht *f*, Maracuja *f*

Passion play *n* Passionsspiel *nt*

passive ['pæsɪv] *adj* passiv; (*Ling*) Passiv- ▷ *n* (*Ling*) Passiv *nt*

passive smoking *n* passives Rauchen, Passivrauchen *nt*

passkey ['pɑ:ski:] *n* Hauptschlüssel *m*

Passover ['pɑ:səʊvəʳ] *n* Passah(fest) *nt*

passport ['pɑ:spɔ:t] *n* Pass *m*; (*fig: to success etc*) Schlüssel *m*

passport control *n* Passkontrolle *f*

passport office *n* Passamt *nt*

password ['pɑ:swɜ:d] *n* Kennwort *nt*; (*Comput*) Passwort *nt*

past [pɑ:st] *prep* (*in front of*) vorbei an +*dat*; (*beyond*) hinter +*dat*; (*later than*) nach ▷ *adj* (*government etc*) früher, ehemalig; (*week, month etc*) vergangen ▷ *n* Vergangenheit *f*; *adv*: **to run ~** vorbeilaufen; **he's ~ 40** er ist über 40; **it's ~ midnight** es ist nach Mitternacht; **ten/quarter ~ eight** zehn/Viertel nach acht; **he ran ~ me** er lief an mir vorbei; **I'm ~ caring** es kümmert mich nicht mehr; **to be ~ it** (*Brit: inf: person*) es nicht mehr bringen; **for the ~ few/3 days** während der letzten Tage/3 Tage; **in the ~** (*also Ling*) in der Vergangenheit

pasta ['pæstə] *n* Nudeln *pl*

paste [peɪst] *n* (*wet mixture*) Teig *m*; (*glue*) Kleister *m*; (*jewellery*) Strass *m*; (*fish, tomato paste*) Paste *f* ▷ *vt* (*stick*) kleben

pastel ['pæstl] *adj* (*colour*) Pastell-

pasteurized ['pæstʃəraɪzd] *adj* pasteurisiert

pastille ['pæstɪl] *n* Pastille *f*

pastime ['pɑ:staɪm] *n* Zeitvertreib *m*, Hobby *nt*

past master (*Brit*) *n*: **to be a ~ at sth** ein Experte *m* in etw *dat* sein

pastor ['pɑ:stəʳ] *n* Pastor(in) *m(f)*

pastoral ['pɑ:stərl] *adj* (*Rel: duties etc*) als Pastor

pastry ['peɪstrɪ] *n* (*dough*) Teig *m*; (*cake*) Gebäckstück *nt*

pasture ['pɑ:stʃəʳ] *n* Weide *f*

pasty [*n* 'pæstɪ, *adj* 'peɪstɪ] *n* (*pie*) Pastete *f* ▷ *adj* (*complexion*) bläßlich

pat [pæt] *vt* (*with hand*) tätscheln ▷ *adj* (*answer, remark*) glatt ▷ *n*: **to give sb/o.s. a ~ on the back** (*fig*) jdm/sich auf die Schulter klopfen; **he knows it off ~, he has it down ~** (*US*) er kennt das in- und auswendig

patch [pætʃ] *n* (*piece of material*) Flicken *m*; (*also*: **eye patch**) Augenklappe *f*; (*damp, bald etc*) Fleck *m*; (*of land*) Stück *nt*; (: *for growing vegetables etc*) Beet *nt* ▷ *vt* (*clothes*) flicken; **(to go through) a bad ~** eine schwierige Zeit (durchmachen)

▶ **patch up** *vt* (*clothes etc*) flicken; (*quarrel*) beilegen

patchwork ['pætʃwə:k] *n* (*Sewing*) Patchwork *nt*

patchy ['pætʃɪ] *adj* (*colour*) ungleichmäßig; (*information, knowledge etc*) lückenhaft

pate [peɪt] *n*: **a bald ~** eine Glatze

pâté ['pæteɪ] *n* Pastete *f*

patent ['peɪtnt] *n* Patent *nt* ▷ *vt* patentieren lassen ▷ *adj* (*obvious*) offensichtlich

patent leather *n* Lackleder *nt*

patently ['peɪtntlɪ] *adv* (*obvious, wrong*) vollkommen

patent medicine *n* patentrechtlich geschütztes Arzneimittel *nt*

Patent Office *n* Patentamt *nt*

paternal [pə'tə:nl] *adj* väterlich; **my ~ grandmother** meine Großmutter väterlicherseits

paternalistic [pətə:nə'lɪstɪk] *adj* patriarchalisch

paternity [pə'tə:nɪtɪ] *n* Vaterschaft *f*

paternity leave *n* Vaterschaftsurlaub *m*

paternity suit *n* Vaterschaftsprozess *m*

path [pɑ:θ] *n* (*also fig*) Weg *m*; (*trail, track*) Pfad *m*; (*trajectory: of bullet, aircraft, planet*) Bahn *f*

pathetic [pə'θetɪk] *adj* (*pitiful*) mitleiderregend; (*very bad*) erbärmlich

pathological [pæθə'lɔdʒɪkl] *adj* (*liar, hatred*) krankhaft; (*Med*) pathologisch

pathologist [pə'θɔlədʒɪst] *n* Pathologe *m*, Pathologin *f*

pathology [pə'θɔlədʒɪ] *n* Pathologie *f*

pathos ['peɪθɔs] *n* Pathos *nt*

pathway ['pɑ:θweɪ] *n* Pfad *m*, Weg *m*; (*fig*) Weg

patience ['peɪʃns] *n* Geduld *f*; (*Brit: Cards*) Patience *f*; **to lose (one's) ~** die Geduld verlieren

patient ['peɪʃnt] *n* Patient(in) *m(f)* ▷ *adj* geduldig; **to be ~ with sb** Geduld mit jdm haben

patiently ['peɪʃntlɪ] *adv* geduldig

patio ['pætɪəʊ] *n* Terrasse *f*

patriot ['peɪtrɪət] *n* Patriot(in) *m(f)*

patriotic [pætrɪ'ɔtɪk] *adj* patriotisch

patriotism ['pætrɪətɪzəm] *n* Patriotismus *m*

patrol [pə'trəʊl] *n* (*Mil*) Patrouille *f*; (*Police*) Streife *f* ▷ *vt* (*Mil, Police: city, streets etc*) patrouillieren; **to be on ~** (*Mil*) auf Patrouille sein; (*Police*) auf Streife sein

patrol boat *n* Patrouillenboot *nt*

patrol car *n* Streifenwagen *m*

patrolman [pə'trəʊlmən] (*US: irreg: like* **man**) *n* (*Police*) (Streifen)polizist *m*

patron ['peɪtrən] *n* (*customer*) Kunde *m*, Kundin *f*; (*benefactor*) Förderer *m*; **~ of the arts** Kunstmäzen *m*

patronage ['pætrənɪdʒ] *n* (*of artist, charity etc*) Förderung *f*

patronize ['pætrənaɪz] *vt* (*pej: look down on*) von oben herab behandeln; (*artist etc*) fördern; (*shop, club*) besuchen

patronizing ['pætrənaɪzɪŋ] *adj* herablassend

patron saint *n* Schutzheilige(r) *f(m)*

patter ['pætəʳ] *n* (*of feet*) Trappeln *nt*; (*of rain*) Prasseln *nt*; (*sales talk etc*) Sprüche *pl* ▷ *vi*

P

(*footsteps*) trappeln; (*rain*) prasseln

pattern ['pætən] *n* Muster *nt*; (*Sewing*)
Schnittmuster *nt*; **behaviour -s**
Verhaltensmuster *pl*

patterned ['pætənd] *adj* gemustert; **~ with
flowers** mit Blumenmuster

paucity ['pɔːsɪtɪ] *n*: **a ~ of** ein Mangel *m* an +*dat*

paunch [pɔːntʃ] *n* Bauch *m*, Wanst *m*

pauper ['pɔːpəʳ] *n* Arme(r) *f(m)*; **~'s grave**
Armengrab *nt*

pause [pɔːz] *n* Pause *f* ▷ *vi* eine Pause machen;
(*hesitate*) innehalten; **to ~ for breath** eine
Verschnaufpause einlegen

pave [peɪv] *vt* (*street, yard etc*) pflastern; **to ~
the way for** (*fig*) den Weg bereiten *or* bahnen
für

pavement ['peɪvmənt] *n* (*Brit*) Bürgersteig *m*;
(*US: roadway*) Straße *f*

pavilion [pə'vɪlɪən] *n* (*Sport*) Klubhaus *nt*

paving ['peɪvɪŋ] *n* (*material*) Straßenbelag *m*

paving stone *n* Pflasterstein *m*

paw [pɔː] *n* (*of cat, dog etc*) Pfote *f*; (*of lion, bear etc*)
Tatze *f*, Pranke *f* ▷ *vt* (*pej: touch*) betatschen; **to
~ the ground** (*animal*) scharren

pawn [pɔːn] *n* (*Chess*) Bauer *m*; (*fig*) Schachfigur
f ▷ *vt* versetzen

pawnbroker ['pɔːnbrəukəʳ] *n* Pfandleiher *m*

pawnshop ['pɔːnʃɔp] *n* Pfandhaus *nt*

pay [peɪ] (*pt, pp* **paid**) *n* (*wage*) Lohn *m*; (*salary*)
Gehalt *nt* ▷ *vt* (*sum of money, wage*) zahlen;
(*bill, person*) bezahlen ▷ *vi* (*be profitable*) sich
bezahlt machen; (*fig*) sich lohnen; **how
much did you ~ for it?** wie viel hast du dafür
bezahlt?; **I paid 10 pounds for that book**
ich habe 10 Pfund für das Buch bezahlt, das
Buch hat mich 10 Pfund gekostet; **to ~ one's
way** seinen Beitrag leisten; **to ~ dividends**
(*fig*) sich bezahlt machen; **to ~ the price/
penalty for sth** (*fig*) den Preis/die Strafe
für etw zahlen; **to ~ sb a compliment** jdm
ein Kompliment machen; **to ~ attention
(to)** achtgeben (auf +*acc*); **to ~ sb a visit** jdn
besuchen; **to ~ one's respects to sb** jdm
seine Aufwartung machen
▶ **pay back** *vt* zurückzahlen; **I'll ~ you back
next week** ich gebe dir das Geld nächste
Woche zurück
▶ **pay for** *vt fus* (*also fig*) (be)zahlen für
▶ **pay in** *vt* einzahlen
▶ **pay off** *vt* (*debt*) abbezahlen; (*person*)
auszahlen; (*creditor*) befriedigen; (*mortgage*)
tilgen ▷ *vi* sich auszahlen; **to ~ sth off in
instalments** etw in Raten (ab)zahlen
▶ **pay out** *vt* (*money*) ausgeben; (*rope*) ablaufen
lassen
▶ **pay up** *vi* zahlen

payable ['peɪəbl] *adj* zahlbar; **to make
a cheque ~ to sb** einen Scheck auf jdn
ausstellen

pay award *n* Lohn-/Gehaltserhöhung *f*

payday ['peɪdeɪ] *n* Zahltag *m*

PAYE (*Brit*) *n abbr* (= *pay as you earn*)
Lohnsteuerabzugsverfahren

payee [peɪ'iː] *n* Zahlungsempfänger *m*

pay envelope (*US*) *n* = **pay packet**

paying guest ['peɪɪŋ-] *n* zahlender Gast *m*

payload ['peɪləud] *n* Nutzlast *f*

payment ['peɪmənt] *n* (*act*) Zahlung *f*,
Bezahlung *f*; (*of bill*) Begleichung *f*; (*sum
of money*) Zahlung *f*; **advance ~** (*part sum*)
Anzahlung *f*; (*total sum*) Vorauszahlung
f; **deferred payment, ~ by instalments**
Ratenzahlung *f*; **monthly ~** (*sum of money*)
Monatsrate *f*; **on ~ of** gegen Zahlung von

pay packet (*Brit*) *n* Lohntüte *f*

pay-per-click ['peɪpəːˈklɪk] *n* (*Comput*) Pay-per-
Click *nt*

payphone ['peɪfəun] *n* Münztelefon *nt*; (*card
phone*) Kartentelefon *nt*

payroll ['peɪrəul] *n* Lohnliste *f*; **to be on a
firm's ~** bei einer Firma beschäftigt sein

pay slip (*Brit*) *n see* **pay** Lohnstreifen *m*;
Gehaltsstreifen *m*

pay station (*US*) *n* = **payphone**

PBS (*US*) *n abbr* (= *Public Broadcasting Service*)
öffentliche Rundfunkanstalt

PC *n abbr* (= *personal computer*) PC *m*; (*Brit*) = **police
constable** ▷ *adj abbr* = **politically correct** ▷ *abbr*
(*Brit*) = **Privy Councillor**

pc *abbr* = **per cent; postcard**

p/c *abbr* = **petty cash**

PCB *n abbr* (*Elec, Comput*) = **printed circuit board**;
(= *polychlorinated biphenyl*) PCB *nt*

pcm *abbr* (= *per calendar month*) pro Monat

PD (*US*) *n abbr* = **police department**

pd *abbr* (= *paid*) bez.

PDA *abbr* (*Comput*) *of* **personal digital assistant**
PDA *m*

pdq (*inf*) *adv abbr* (= *pretty damn quick*) verdammt
schnell

PDSA (*Brit*) *n abbr* (= *People's Dispensary for Sick
Animals*) *kostenloses Behandlungszentrum für
Haustiere*

PDT (*US*) *abbr* (= *Pacific Daylight Time*) *pazifische
Sommerzeit*

PE *n abbr* (*Scol*) = **physical education**

pea [piː] *n* Erbse *f*

peace [piːs] *n* Frieden *m*; **to be at ~ with sb/
sth** mit jdm/etw in Frieden leben; **to keep
the ~** (*policeman*) die öffentliche Ordnung
aufrechterhalten; (*citizen*) den Frieden wahren

peaceable ['piːsəbl] *adj* friedlich

peaceful ['piːsful] *adj* friedlich

peacekeeper ['piːskiːpəʳ] *n*
Friedenswächter(in) *m(f)*

peacekeeping force ['piːskiːpɪŋ-] *n*
Friedenstruppen *pl*

peace offering *n* Friedensangebot *nt*

peach [piːtʃ] *n* Pfirsich *m*

peacock ['piːkɔk] *n* Pfau *m*

peak [piːk] *n* (*of mountain*) Spitze *f*, Gipfel *m*; (*of
cap*) Schirm *m*; (*fig*) Höhepunkt *m*

peak hours *npl* Stoßzeit *f*

peak period *n* Spitzenzeit *f*, Stoßzeit *f*

peak rate *n* Höchstrate *f*

peaky ['piːkɪ] (*Brit: inf*) *adj* blass

peal [pi:l] n (of bells) Läuten nt; **~s of laughter** schallendes Gelächter nt
peanut ['pi:nʌt] n Erdnuss f
peanut butter n Erdnussbutter f
pear [pɛəʳ] n Birne f
pearl [pɜ:l] n Perle f
peasant ['pɛznt] n Bauer m
peat [pi:t] n Torf m
pebble ['pɛbl] n Kieselstein m
peck [pɛk] vt (bird) picken; (also: **peck at**) picken an +dat ▷ n (of bird) Schnabelhieb m; (kiss) Küsschen nt
pecking order ['pɛkɪŋ-] n (fig) Hackordnung f
peckish ['pɛkɪʃ] (Brit: inf) adj (hungry) leicht hungrig; **I'm feeling ~** ich könnte was zu essen gebrauchen
peculiar [pɪ'kju:lɪəʳ] adj (strange) seltsam; **~ to** (exclusive to) charakteristisch für
peculiarity [pɪkju:lɪ'ærɪtɪ] n (strange habit) Eigenart f; (distinctive feature) Besonderheit f, Eigentümlichkeit f
peculiarly [pɪ'kju:lɪəlɪ] adv (oddly) seltsam; (distinctively) unverkennbar
pecuniary [pɪ'kju:nɪərɪ] adj finanziell
pedal ['pɛdl] n Pedal nt ▷ vi in die Pedale treten
pedal bin (Brit) n Treteimer m
pedant ['pɛdənt] n Pedant(in) m(f)
pedantic [pɪ'dæntɪk] adj pedantisch
peddle ['pɛdl] vt (goods) feilbieten, verkaufen; (drugs) handeln mit; (gossip) verbreiten
peddler ['pɛdləʳ] n (also: **drug peddler**) Pusher m
pedestal ['pɛdəstl] n Sockel m
pedestrian [pɪ'dɛstrɪən] n Fußgänger(in) m(f) ▷ adj Fußgänger-; (fig) langweilig
pedestrian crossing (Brit) n Fußgängerüberweg m
pedestrian mall (US) n Fußgängerzone f
pedestrian precinct (Brit) n Fußgängerzone f
pediatrics [pi:dɪ'ætrɪks] (US) n = **paediatrics**
pedigree ['pɛdɪgri:] n (of animal) Stammbaum m; (fig: background) Vorgeschichte f ▷ cpd (dog) Rasse-, reinrassig
pee [pi:] (inf) vi pinkeln
peek [pi:k] vi: **to ~ at/over/into** etc gucken nach/über +acc/in +acc etc ▷ n: **to have** or **take a ~ (at)** einen (kurzen) Blick werfen (auf +acc)
peel [pi:l] n Schale f ▷ vt schälen ▷ vi (paint) abblättern; (wallpaper) sich lösen; (skin, back etc) sich schälen
▸ **peel back** vt abziehen
peeler ['pi:ləʳ] n (potato peeler etc) Schälmesser nt
peelings ['pi:lɪŋz] npl Schalen pl
peep [pi:p] n (look) kurzer Blick m; (sound) Pieps m ▷ vi (look) gucken; **to have** or **take a ~ (at)** einen kurzen Blick werfen (auf +acc)
▸ **peep out** vi hervorgucken
peephole ['pi:phəul] n Guckloch nt
peer [pɪəʳ] n (noble) Peer m; (equal) Gleichrangige(r) f(m); (contemporary) Gleichaltrige(r) f(m) ▷ vi: **to ~ at** starren auf +acc
peerage ['pɪərɪdʒ] n (title) Adelswürde f; (position) Adelsstand m; **the ~** (all the peers) der

Adel
peerless ['pɪəlɪs] adj unvergleichlich
peeved [pi:vd] adj verärgert, sauer (inf)
peevish ['pi:vɪʃ] adj (bad-tempered) mürrisch
peg [pɛg] n (hook, knob) Haken m; (Brit: also: **clothes peg**) Wäscheklammer f; (also: **tent peg**) Zeltpflock m, Hering m ▷ vt (washing) festklammern; (prices) festsetzen; **off the ~** von der Stange
pejorative [pɪ'dʒɔrətɪv] adj abwertend
Pekin [pi:'kɪn] n = **Peking**
Pekinese [pi:kɪ'ni:z] n = **Pekingese**
Peking [pi:'kɪŋ] n Peking nt
Pekingese [pi:kɪ'ni:z] n (dog) Pekinese m
pelican ['pɛlɪkən] n Pelikan m
pelican crossing (Brit) n (Aut) Fußgängerüberweg m mit Ampel
pellet ['pɛlɪt] n (of paper etc) Kügelchen nt; (of mud etc) Klümpchen nt; (for shotgun) Schrotkugel f
pell-mell ['pɛl'mɛl] adv in heillosem Durcheinander
pelmet ['pɛlmɪt] n (wooden) Blende f; (fabric) Querbehang m
pelt [pɛlt] vi (rain: also: **pelt down**) niederprasseln; (inf: run) rasen ▷ n (animal skin) Pelz m, Fell nt ▷ vt: **to ~ sb with sth** jdn mit etw bewerfen
pelvis ['pɛlvɪs] n Becken nt
pen [pɛn] n (also: **fountain pen**) Füller m; (also: **ballpoint pen**) Kugelschreiber m; (also: **felt-tip pen**) Filzstift m; (enclosure: for sheep, pigs etc) Pferch m; (US: inf: prison) Knast m; **to put ~ to paper** zur Feder greifen
penal ['pi:nl] adj (Law: colony, institution) Straf-; (: system, reform) Strafrechts-; **~ code** Strafgesetzbuch nt
penalize ['pi:nəlaɪz] vt (punish) bestrafen; (fig) benachteiligen
penal servitude [-'sə:vɪtju:d] n Zwangsarbeit f
penalty ['pɛnltɪ] n Strafe f; (Sport) Strafstoß m; (: Football) Elfmeter m
penalty area (Brit) n (Sport) Strafraum m
penalty clause n Strafklausel f
penalty kick n (Rugby) Strafstoß m; (Football) Elfmeter m
penalty shoot-out [-'ʃu:taut] n (Football) Elfmeterschießen nt
penance ['pɛnəns] n (Rel): **to do ~ for one's sins** für seine Sünden Buße tun
pence [pɛns] npl of **penny**
penchant ['pā:ʃã:ŋ] n Vorliebe f, Schwäche f; **to have a ~ for** eine Schwäche haben für
pencil ['pɛnsl] n Bleistift m ▷ vt: **to ~ sb/sth in** jdn/etw vormerken
pencil case n Federmäppchen nt
pencil sharpener n Bleistiftspitzer m
pendant ['pɛndnt] n Anhänger m
pending ['pɛndɪŋ] adj anstehend ▷ prep: **~ his return** bis zu seiner Rückkehr; **~ a decision** bis eine Entscheidung getroffen ist
pendulum ['pɛndjuləm] n Pendel nt
penetrate ['pɛnɪtreɪt] vt (person: territory etc)

P

durchdringen; (*light, water, sound*) eindringen in +acc

penetrating ['pɛnɪtreɪtɪŋ] *adj* (*sound, gaze*) durchdringend; (*mind, observation*) scharf

penetration [pɛnɪ'treɪʃən] *n* Durchdringen *nt*

pen friend (*Brit*) *n* Brieffreund(in) *m(f)*

penguin ['pɛŋgwɪn] *n* Pinguin *m*

penicillin [pɛnɪ'sɪlɪn] *n* Penizillin *nt*

peninsula [pə'nɪnsjulə] *n* Halbinsel *f*

penis ['piːnɪs] *n* Penis *m*

penitence ['pɛnɪtns] *n* Reue *f*

penitent ['pɛnɪtnt] *adj* reuig

penitentiary [pɛnɪ'tɛnʃərɪ] (*US*) *n* Gefängnis *nt*

penknife ['pɛnnaɪf] *n* Taschenmesser *nt*

Penn. (*US*) *abbr* (*Post*) = *Pennsylvania*

pen name *n* Pseudonym *nt*

pennant ['pɛnənt] *n* (*Naut*) Wimpel *m*

penniless ['pɛnɪlɪs] *adj* mittellos

Pennines ['pɛnaɪnz] *npl*: **the ~** die Pennines *pl*

penny ['pɛnɪ] (*Brit*) (*pl* **pence**) *n* Penny *m*; (*US*) Cent *m*; **it was worth every ~** es war jeden Pfennig wert; **it won't cost you a ~** es kostet dich keinen Pfennig

pen pal *n* Brieffreund(in) *m(f)*

penpusher ['pɛnpuʃəʳ] *n* Schreiberling *m*

pension ['pɛnʃən] *n* Rente *f*

▸ **pension off** *vt* (vorzeitig) pensionieren

pensionable ['pɛnʃnəbl] *adj* (*age*) Pensions-; (*job*) mit Pensionsberechtigung

pensioner ['pɛnʃənəʳ] (*Brit*) *n* Rentner(in) *m(f)*

pension scheme *n* Rentenversicherung *f*

pensive ['pɛnsɪv] *adj* nachdenklich

pentagon ['pɛntəgən] (*US*) *n*: **the P~** das Pentagon; *siehe Info-Artikel*

● **PENTAGON**

● Pentagon heißt das fünfeckige Gebäude
● in Arlington, Virginia, in dem das
● amerikanische Verteidigungsministerium
● untergebracht ist. Im weiteren Sinne
● bezieht sich dieses Wort auf die
● amerikanische Militärführung.

Pentecost ['pɛntɪkɔst] *n* (*in Judaism*) Erntefest *nt*; (*in Christianity*) Pfingsten *nt*

penthouse ['pɛnthaus] *n* Penthouse *nt*

pent-up ['pɛntʌp] *adj* (*feelings*) aufgestaut

penultimate [pɛ'nʌltɪmət] *adj* vorletzte(r, s)

penury ['pɛnjurɪ] *n* Armut *f*, Not *f*

people ['piːpl] *npl* (*persons*) Leute *pl*; (*inhabitants*) Bevölkerung *f* ▸ *n* (*nation, race*) Volk *nt*; **old ~** alte Menschen *or* Leute; **young ~** junge Leute; **the room was full of ~** das Zimmer war voller Leute *or* Menschen; **several ~ came** mehrere (Leute) kamen; **~ say that ...** man sagt, dass ...; **the ~** (*Pol*) das Volk; **a man of the ~** ein Mann des Volkes

PEP *n abbr* (= *personal equity plan*) *steuerbegünstigte Kapitalinvestition*

pep [pɛp] (*inf*) *n* Schwung *m*, Pep *m*

▸ **pep up** *vt* (*person*) aufmöbeln; (*food*) pikanter machen

pepper ['pɛpəʳ] *n* (*spice*) Pfeffer *m*; (*vegetable*) Paprika *m* ▸ *vt*: **~ with** (*fig*) übersäen mit; **two ~s** zwei Paprikaschoten

peppercorn ['pɛpəkɔːn] *n* Pfefferkorn *nt*

pepper mill *n* Pfeffermühle *f*

peppermint ['pɛpəmɪnt] *n* (*sweet*) Pfefferminz *nt*; (*plant*) Pfefferminze *f*

pepperoni [pɛpə'rəunɪ] *n* ≈ Pfeffersalami *f*

pepper pot *n* Pfefferstreuer *m*

pep talk (*inf*) *n* aufmunternde Worte *pl*

per [pɜːʳ] *prep* (*for each*) pro; **~ day/person/ kilo** pro Tag/Person/Kilo; **~ annum** pro Jahr; **as ~ your instructions** gemäß Ihren Anweisungen

per capita [-'kæpɪtə] *adj* (*income*) Pro-Kopf- ▸ *adv* pro Kopf

perceive [pə'siːv] *vt* (*see*) wahrnehmen; (*view, understand*) verstehen

per cent *n* Prozent *nt*; **a 20 ~ discount** 20 Prozent Rabatt

percentage [pə'sɛntɪdʒ] *n* Prozentsatz *m*; **on a ~ basis** auf Prozentbasis

percentage point *n* Prozent *nt*

perceptible [pə'sɛptɪbl] *adj* (*difference, change*) wahrnehmbar, merklich

perception [pə'sɛpʃən] *n* (*insight*) Einsicht *f*; (*opinion, understanding*) Erkenntnis *f*; (*faculty*) Wahrnehmung *f*

perceptive [pə'sɛptɪv] *adj* (*person*) aufmerksam; (*analysis etc*) erkenntnisreich

perch [pɜːtʃ] *n* (*for bird*) Stange *f*; (*fish*) Flussbarsch *m* ▸ *vi*: **to ~ (on)** (*bird*) sitzen (auf +*dat*); (*person*) hocken (auf +*dat*)

percolate ['pɜːkəleɪt] *vt* (*coffee*) (mit einer Kaffeemaschine) zubereiten ▸ *vi* (*coffee*) durchlaufen; **to ~ through/into** (*idea, light etc*) durchsickern durch/in +*acc*

percolator ['pɜːkəleɪtəʳ] *n* (*also:* **coffee percolator**) Kaffeemaschine *f*

percussion [pə'kʌʃən] *n* (*Mus*) Schlagzeug *nt*

peremptory [pə'rɛmptərɪ] (*pej*) *adj* (*person*) herrisch; (*order*) kategorisch

perennial [pə'rɛnɪəl] *adj* (*plant*) mehrjährig; (*fig: problem, feature etc*) immer wiederkehrend ▸ *n* (*Bot*) mehrjährige Pflanze *f*

perfect [*adj, n* 'pɜːfɪkt, *vt* pə'fɛkt] *adj* perfekt; (*nonsense, idiot etc*) ausgemacht ▸ *vt* (*technique*) perfektionieren ▸ *n*: **the ~** (*also:* **the perfect tense**) das Perfekt; **he's a ~ stranger to me** er ist mir vollkommen fremd

perfection [pə'fɛkʃən] *n* Perfektion *f*, Vollkommenheit *f*

perfectionist [pə'fɛkʃənɪst] *n* Perfektionist(in) *m(f)*

perfectly ['pɜːfɪktlɪ] *adv* vollkommen; (*faultlessly*) perfekt; **I'm ~ happy with the situation** ich bin mit der Lage vollkommen zufrieden; **you know ~ well that ...** Sie wissen ganz genau, dass ...

perforate ['pɜːfəreɪt] *vt* perforieren

perforated ulcer ['pɜːfəreɪtəd-] *n* durchgebrochenes Geschwür *nt*

perforation [pɜːfə'reɪʃən] *n* (*small hole*) Loch *nt*;

(line of holes) Perforation f

perform [pə'fɔ:m] vt (operation, ceremony etc) durchführen; (task) erfüllen; (piece of music, play etc) aufführen ▷ vi auftreten; **to ~ well/ badly** eine gute/schlechte Leistung zeigen

performance [pə'fɔ:məns] n Leistung f; (of play, show) Vorstellung f; **the team put up a good ~** die Mannschaft zeigte eine gute Leistung

performer [pə'fɔ:mə^r] n Künstler(in) m(f)

performing [pə'fɔ:mɪŋ] adj (animal) dressiert

performing arts npl: **the ~** die darstellenden Künste pl

perfume ['pə:fju:m] n Parfüm nt; (fragrance) Duft m ▷ vt parfümieren

perfunctory [pə'fʌŋktərɪ] adj flüchtig

perhaps [pə'hæps] adv vielleicht; **he'll come** er kommt vielleicht; **~ not** vielleicht nicht

peril ['perɪl] n Gefahr f

perilous ['perɪləs] adj gefährlich

perilously ['perɪləslɪ] adv: **they came ~ close to being caught** sie wären um ein Haar gefangen worden

perimeter [pə'rɪmɪtə^r] n Umfang m

perimeter fence n Umzäunung f

period ['pɪərɪəd] n (length of time) Zeitraum m, Periode f; (era) Zeitalter nt; (Scol) Stunde f; (esp US: full stop) Punkt m; (Med: also: **menstrual period**) Periode ▷ adj (costume etc) zeitgenössisch; **for a ~ of 3 weeks** für eine Dauer or einen Zeitraum von 3 Wochen; **the holiday ~** (Brit) die Urlaubszeit; **I won't do it. P~**. ich mache das nicht, und damit basta!

periodic [pɪərɪ'ɔdɪk] adj periodisch

periodical [pɪərɪ'ɔdɪkl] n Zeitschrift f ▷ adj periodisch

periodically [pɪərɪ'ɔdɪklɪ] adv periodisch

period pains (Brit) npl Menstruationsschmerzen pl

peripatetic [perɪpə'tetɪk] adj (Brit: teacher) an mehreren Schulen tätig; **~ life** Wanderleben nt

peripheral [pə'rɪfərəl] adj (feature, issue) Rand-, nebensächlich; (vision) peripher ▷ n (Comput) Peripheriegerät nt

periphery [pə'rɪfərɪ] n Peripherie f

periscope ['perɪskəup] n Periskop nt

perish ['perɪʃ] vi (die) umkommen; (rubber, leather etc) verschleißen

perishable ['perɪʃəbl] adj (food) leicht verderblich

perishables ['perɪʃəblz] npl leicht verderbliche Waren pl

perishing ['perɪʃɪŋ] (Brit: inf) adj: **it's ~ (cold)** es ist eisig kalt

peritonitis [perɪtə'naɪtɪs] n Bauchfellentzündung f

perjure ['pə:dʒə^r] vt: **to ~ o.s.** einen Meineid leisten

perjury ['pə:dʒərɪ] n (in court) Meineid m; (breach of oath) Eidesverletzung f

perks [pə:ks] (inf) npl (extras) Vergünstigungen pl

perk up vi (cheer up) munter werden

perky ['pə:kɪ] adj (cheerful) munter

perm [pə:m] n Dauerwelle f ▷ vt: **to have one's hair ~ed** sich dat eine Dauerwelle machen lassen

permanence ['pə:mənəns] n Dauerhaftigkeit f

permanent ['pə:mənənt] adj dauerhaft; (job, position) fest; **~ address** ständiger Wohnsitz m; **I'm not ~ here** ich bin hier nicht fest angestellt

permanently ['pə:mənəntlɪ] adv (damage) dauerhaft; (stay, live) ständig; (locked, open, frozen etc) dauernd

permeable ['pə:mɪəbl] adj durchlässig

permeate ['pə:mɪeɪt] vt durchdringen ▷ vi: **to ~ through** dringen durch

permissible [pə'mɪsɪbl] adj zulässig

permission [pə'mɪʃən] n Erlaubnis f, Genehmigung f; **to give sb ~ to do sth** jdm die Erlaubnis geben, etw zu tun

permissive [pə'mɪsɪv] adj permissiv

permit [n 'pə:mɪt, vt pə'mɪt] n Genehmigung f ▷ vt (allow) erlauben; (make possible) gestatten; **fishing ~** Angelschein m; **to ~ sb to do sth** jdm erlauben, etw zu tun; **weather ~ting** wenn das Wetter es zulässt

permutation [pə:mju'teɪʃən] n Permutation f; (fig) Variation f

pernicious [pə'nɪʃəs] adj (lie, nonsense) bösartig; (effect) schädlich

pernickety [pə'nɪkɪtɪ] (inf) adj pingelig

perpendicular [pə:pən'dɪkjulə^r] adj senkrecht ▷ n: **the ~** die Senkrechte; **~ to** senkrecht zu

perpetrate ['pə:pɪtreɪt] vt (crime) begehen

perpetual [pə'petjuəl] adj ständig, dauernd

perpetuate [pə'petjueɪt] vt (custom, belief etc) bewahren; (situation) aufrechterhalten

perpetuity [pə:pɪ'tju:ɪtɪ] n: **in ~** auf ewig

perplex [pə'pleks] vt verblüffen

perplexing [pə'pleksɪŋ] adj verblüffend

perquisites ['pə:kwɪzɪts] (form) npl Vergünstigungen pl

per se [-seɪ] adv an sich

persecute ['pə:sɪkju:t] vt verfolgen

persecution [pə:sɪ'kju:ʃən] n Verfolgung f

perseverance [pə:sɪ'vɪərns] n Beharrlichkeit f, Ausdauer f

persevere [pə:sɪ'vɪə^r] vi durchhalten, beharren

Persia ['pə:ʃə] n Persien nt

Persian ['pə:ʃən] adj persisch ▷ n (Ling) Persisch nt; **the (persian) Gulf** der (Persische) Golf

Persian cat n Perserkatze f

persist [pə'sɪst] vi: **to ~ (with or in)** beharren (auf +dat), festhalten (an +dat); **to ~ in doing sth** darauf beharren, etw zu tun

persistence [pə'sɪstəns] n Beharrlichkeit f

persistent [pə'sɪstənt] adj (person, noise) beharrlich; (smell, cough etc) hartnäckig; (lateness, rain) andauernd; **~ offender** Wiederholungstäter(in) m(f)

persnickety [pə'snɪkɪtɪ] (US: inf) adj = **pernickety**

person ['pə:sn] n Person f, Mensch m; **in ~**

P

703

persönlich; **on** or **about one's** ~ bei sich; ~ **to** ~ **call** (*Tel*) Gespräch *nt* mit Voranmeldung

personable ['pɜːsnəbl] *adj* von angenehmer Erscheinung

personal ['pɜːsnl] *adj* persönlich; (*life*) Privat-; **nothing** ~! nehmen Sie es nicht persönlich!

personal allowance *n* (*Tax*) persönlicher Steuerfreibetrag *m*

personal assistant *n* persönlicher Referent *m*, persönliche Referentin *f*

personal column *n* private Kleinanzeigen *pl*

personal computer *n* Personal Computer *m*

personal details *npl* Personalien *pl*

personal hygiene *n* Körperhygiene *f*

personal identification number *n* Geheimnummer *f*, PIN-Nummer *f*

personality [pɜːsə'nælɪtɪ] *n* (*character, person*) Persönlichkeit *f*

personal loan *n* Personaldarlehen *nt*

personally ['pɜːsnəlɪ] *adv* persönlich; **to take sth** ~ etw persönlich nehmen

personal organizer *n* Terminplaner *m*

personal, social and health education (*Brit*) *n* (*Scol*) ≈ persönlichkeits-, gesellschafts- und gesundheitsbezogene Erziehung

personal stereo *n* Walkman® *m*

personal trainer *n* (persönlicher) Fitnesstrainer *m*, (persönliche) Fitnesstrainerin *f*

personify [pə'sɒnɪfaɪ] *vt* personifizieren; (*embody*) verkörpern

personnel [pɜːsə'nel] *n* Personal *nt*

personnel department *n* Personalabteilung *f*

personnel manager *n* Personalleiter(in) *m(f)*

perspective [pə'spektɪv] *n* (*also fig*) Perspektive *f*; **to get sth into** ~ (*fig*) etw in Relation zu anderen Dingen sehen

Perspex® ['pɜːspeks] *n* Acrylglas *nt*

perspicacity [pɜːspɪ'kæsɪtɪ] *n* Scharfsinn *m*

perspiration [pɜːspɪ'reɪʃən] *n* Transpiration *f*

perspire [pə'spaɪə'] *vi* transpirieren

persuade [pə'sweɪd] *vt*: **to** ~ **sb to do sth** jdn dazu überreden, etw zu tun; **to** ~ **sb that** jdn davon überzeugen, dass; **to be** ~**d of sth** von etw überzeugt sein

persuasion [pə'sweɪʒən] *n* (*act*) Überredung *f*; (*creed*) Überzeugung *f*

persuasive [pə'sweɪsɪv] *adj* (*person, argument*) überzeugend

pert [pɜːt] *adj* (*person*) frech; (*nose, buttocks*) keck; (*hat*) kess

pertaining [pɜː'teɪnɪŋ]: ~ **to** *prep* betreffend +*acc*

pertinent ['pɜːtɪnənt] *adj* relevant

perturb [pə'tɜːb] *vt* beunruhigen

Peru [pə'ruː] *n* Peru *nt*

perusal [pə'ruːzl] *n* Durchsicht *f*

peruse [pə'ruːz] *vt* durchsehen

Peruvian [pə'ruːvjən] *adj* peruanisch ▷ *n* Peruaner(in) *m(f)*

pervade [pə'veɪd] *vt* (*smell, feeling*) erfüllen

pervasive [pə'veɪzɪv] *adj* (*smell*) durchdringend; (*influence*) weitreichend; (*mood, atmosphere*) allumfassend

perverse [pə'vɜːs] *adj* (*person*) borniert; (*behaviour*) widernatürlich, pervers

perversion [pə'vɜːʃən] *n* (*sexual*) Perversion *f*; (*of truth, justice*) Verzerrung *f*, Pervertierung *f*

perversity [pə'vɜːsɪtɪ] *n* Widernatürlichkeit *f*

pervert [*n* 'pɜːvɜːt, *vt* pə'vɜːt] *n* (*sexual deviant*) perverser Mensch *m* ▷ *vt* (*person, mind*) verderben; (*distort: truth, custom*) verfälschen

pessimism ['pesɪmɪzəm] *n* Pessimismus *m*

pessimist ['pesɪmɪst] *n* Pessimist(in) *m(f)*

pessimistic [pesɪ'mɪstɪk] *adj* pessimistisch

pest [pest] *n* (*insect*) Schädling *m*; (*fig: nuisance*) Plage *f*

pest control *n* Schädlingsbekämpfung *f*

pester ['pestə'] *vt* belästigen

pesticide ['pestɪsaɪd] *n* Schädlingsbekämpfungsmittel *nt*, Pestizid *nt*

pestilence ['pestɪləns] *n* Pest *f*

pestle ['pesl] *n* Stößel *m*

pet [pet] *n* (*animal*) Haustier *nt* ▷ *adj* (*theory etc*) Lieblings- ▷ *vt* (*stroke*) streicheln ▷ *vi* (*inf: sexually*) herumknutschen; **teacher's** ~ (*favourite*) Lehrers Liebling *m*; **a** ~ **rabbit/ snake** *etc* ein Kaninchen/eine Schlange *etc* (als Haustier); **that's my** ~ **hate** das hasse ich besonders

petal ['petl] *n* Blütenblatt *nt*

peter out ['piːtə-] *vi* (*road etc*) allmählich aufhören, zu Ende gehen; (*conversation, meeting*) sich totlaufen

petite [pə'tiːt] *adj* (*woman*) zierlich

petition [pə'tɪʃən] *n* (*signed document*) Petition *f*; (*Law*) Klage *f* ▷ *vt* ersuchen ▷ *vi*: **to** ~ **for divorce** die Scheidung einreichen

pet name (*Brit*) *n* Kosename *m*

petrified ['petrɪfaɪd] *adj* (*fig: terrified*) starr vor Angst

petrify ['petrɪfaɪ] *vt* (*fig: terrify*) vor Angst erstarren lassen

petrochemical [petrə'kemɪkl] *adj* petrochemisch

petrodollars ['petrəʊdɒləz] *npl* Petrodollar *pl*

petrol ['petrəl] (*Brit*) *n* Benzin *nt*; **two-star** ~ Normalbenzin *nt*; **four-star** ~ Super(benzin) *nt*; **unleaded** ~ bleifreies or unverbleites Benzin

petrol bomb *n* Benzinbombe *f*

petrol can (*Brit*) *n* Benzinkanister *m*

petrol engine (*Brit*) *n* Benzinmotor *m*

petroleum [pə'trəʊlɪəm] *n* Petroleum *nt*

petroleum jelly *n* Vaseline *f*

petrol pump (*Brit*) *n* (*in garage*) Zapfsäule *f*; (*in engine*) Benzinpumpe *f*

petrol station (*Brit*) *n* Tankstelle *f*

petrol tank (*Brit*) *n* Benzintank *m*

petticoat ['petɪkəʊt] *n* (*underskirt: full-length*) Unterkleid *nt*; (: *waist*) Unterrock *m*

pettifogging ['petɪfɒgɪŋ] *adj* kleinlich

pettiness ['petɪnɪs] *n* Kleinlichkeit *f*

petty ['petɪ] *adj* (*trivial*) unbedeutend; (*small-minded*) kleinlich; (*crime*) geringfügig; (*official*) untergeordnet; (*excuse*) billig; (*remark*) spitz

petty cash n (in office) Portokasse f
petty officer n Maat m
petulant ['pɛtjulənt] adj (person, expression) gereizt
pew [pju:] n (in church) Kirchenbank f
pewter ['pju:təʳ] n Zinn nt
PG n abbr (Cine: = parental guidance) Klassifikation für Filme, die Kinder nur in Begleitung Erwachsener sehen dürfen
PGA n abbr (= Professional Golfers' Association) Golf-Profiverband
PGA 13 (US) abbr (Cine: = Parental Guidance 13) Klassifikation für Kinofilme, welche Kinder unter 13 Jahren nur in Begleitung Erwachsener sehen dürfen
pH n abbr (= potential of hydrogen) pH
PHA (US) n abbr (= Public Housing Administration) Regierungsbehörde für sozialen Wohnungsbau
phallic ['fælɪk] adj phallisch; (symbol) Phallus-
phantom ['fæntəm] n Phantom nt ▷ adj (fig) Phantom-
Pharaoh ['fɛərəu] n Pharao m
pharmaceutical [fɑ:məˈsju:tɪkl] adj pharmazeutisch
pharmaceuticals [fɑ:məˈsju:tɪklz] npl Arzneimittel pl, Pharmaka pl
pharmacist ['fɑ:məsɪst] n Apotheker(in) m(f)
pharmacy ['fɑ:məsɪ] n (shop) Apotheke f; (science) Pharmazie f
phase [feɪz] n Phase f ▷ vt: **to ~ sth in/out** etw stufenweise einführen/abschaffen
phat [fæt] adj (inf) abgefahren, geil
PhD n abbr (= Doctor of Philosophy) ≈ Dr. phil.
pheasant ['fɛznt] n Fasan m
phenomena [fəˈnɒmɪnə] npl of **phenomenon**
phenomenal [fəˈnɒmɪnl] adj phänomenal
phenomenon [fəˈnɒmɪnən] (pl **phenomena**) n Phänomen nt
phew [fju:] excl puh!
phial ['faɪəl] n Fläschchen nt
philanderer [fɪˈlændərəʳ] n Schwerenöter m
philanthropic [fɪlənˈθrɒpɪk] adj philanthropisch
philanthropist [fɪˈlænθrəpɪst] n Philanthrop(in) m(f)
philatelist [fɪˈlætəlɪst] n Philatelist(in) m(f)
philately [fɪˈlætəlɪ] n Philatelie f
Philippines ['fɪlɪpi:nz] npl: **the ~** die Philippinen pl
Philistine ['fɪlɪstaɪn] n (boor) Banause m
philosopher [fɪˈlɒsəfəʳ] n Philosoph(in) m(f)
philosophical [fɪləˈsɒfɪkl] adj philosophisch; (fig: calm, resigned) gelassen
philosophize [fɪˈlɒsəfaɪz] vi philosophieren
philosophy [fɪˈlɒsəfɪ] n Philosophie f
phlegm [flɛm] n (Med) Schleim m
phlegmatic [flɛgˈmætɪk] adj phlegmatisch
phobia ['fəubjə] n Phobie f
phone [fəun] n Telefon nt ▷ vt anrufen ▷ vi anrufen, telefonieren; **to be on the ~** (possess a phone) Telefon haben; (be calling) telefonieren
▶ **phone back** vt, vi zurückrufen
▶ **phone up** vt, vi anrufen
phone book n Telefonbuch nt

phone booth n Telefonzelle f
phone box (Brit) n Telefonzelle f
phone call n Anruf m
phonecard ['fəunkɑ:d] n Telefonkarte f
phone-in ['fəunɪn] (Brit) n (Radio, TV) Radio-/Fernsehsendung mit Hörer-/Zuschauerbeteiligung per Telefon, Phone-in nt ▷ adj mit Hörer-/Zuschaueranrufen
phone tapping [-tæpɪŋ] n Abhören nt von Telefonleitungen
phonetics [fəˈnɛtɪks] n Phonetik f
phoney ['fəunɪ] adj (address) falsch; (accent) unecht; (person) unaufrichtig
phonograph ['fəunəgrɑ:f] (US) n Grammofon nt
phony ['fəunɪ] adj = **phoney**
phosphate ['fɒsfeɪt] n Phosphat nt
phosphorus ['fɒsfərəs] n Phosphor m
photo ['fəutəu] n Foto nt
photo... ['fəutəu] pref Foto-
photocopier ['fəutəukɒpɪəʳ] n Fotokopierer m
photocopy ['fəutəukɒpɪ] n Fotokopie f ▷ vt fotokopieren
photoelectric [fəutəuɪˈlɛktrɪk] adj (effect) fotoelektrisch; (cell) Photo-
photo finish n Fotofinish nt
Photofit® ['fəutəufɪt] n, **Photofit® picture** ▷ n Phantombild nt
photogenic [fəutəuˈdʒɛnɪk] adj fotogen
photograph ['fəutəgrɑ:f] n Fotografie f ▷ vt fotografieren; **to take a ~ of sb** jdn fotografieren
photographer [fəˈtɒgrəfəʳ] n Fotograf(in) m(f)
photographic [fəutəˈgræfɪk] adj (equipment etc) fotografisch, Foto-
photography [fəˈtɒgrəfɪ] n Fotografie f
photo opportunity n Fototermin m; (accidental) Fotogelegenheit f
photostat ['fəutəustæt] n Fotokopie f
photosynthesis [fəutəuˈsɪnθəsɪs] n Fotosynthese f
phrase [freɪz] n Satz m; (Ling) Redewendung f; (Mus) Phrase f ▷ vt ausdrücken; (letter) formulieren
phrase book n Sprachführer m
physical ['fɪzɪkl] adj (bodily) körperlich; (geography, properties) physikalisch; (law, explanation) natürlich; **~ examination** ärztliche Untersuchung f; **the ~ sciences** die Naturwissenschaften
physical education n Sportunterricht m
physically ['fɪzɪklɪ] adv (fit, attractive) körperlich
physician [fɪˈzɪʃən] n Arzt m, Ärztin f
physicist ['fɪzɪsɪst] n Physiker(in) m(f)
physics ['fɪzɪks] n Physik f
physiological ['fɪzɪəˈlɒdʒɪkl] adj physiologisch
physiology [fɪzɪˈɒlədʒɪ] n Physiologie f
physiotherapist [fɪzɪəuˈθɛrəpɪst] n Physiotherapeut(in) m(f)
physiotherapy [fɪzɪəuˈθɛrəpɪ] n Physiotherapie f
physique [fɪˈzi:k] n Körperbau m

pianist ['piːənɪst] n Pianist(in) m(f)
piano [pɪ'ænəu] n Klavier nt, Piano nt
piano accordion (Brit) n Akkordeon nt
piccolo ['pɪkələu] n Piccoloflöte f
pick [pɪk] n (also: **pickaxe**) Spitzhacke f ▷ vt (select) aussuchen; (gather: fruit, mushrooms) sammeln; (: flowers) pflücken; (remove, take out) herausnehmen; (lock) knacken; (scab, spot) kratzen an +dat; **take your ~** (choose) Sie haben die Wahl; **the ~ of** (best) das Beste +gen; **to ~ one's nose** in der Nase bohren; **to ~ one's teeth** in den Zähnen stochern; **to ~ sb's brains** jdn als Informationsquelle nutzen; **to ~ sb's pocket** jdn bestehlen; **to ~ a quarrel (with sb)** einen Streit (mit jdm) anfangen
▶ **pick at** vt fus (food) herumstochern in +dat
▶ **pick off** vt (shoot) abschießen
▶ **pick on** vt fus (criticize) herumhacken auf +dat
▶ **pick out** vt (distinguish) ausmachen; (select) aussuchen
▶ **pick up** vi (health) sich verbessern; (economy) sich erholen ▷ vt (from floor etc) aufheben; (arrest) festnehmen; (collect: person, parcel etc) abholen; (hitchhiker) mitnehmen; (for sexual encounter) aufreißen; (learn: skill etc) mitbekommen; (Radio) empfangen; **to ~ up where one left off** da weitermachen, wo man aufgehört hat; **to ~ up speed** schneller werden; **to ~ o.s. up** (after falling etc) sich aufrappeln
pickaxe, (US) **pickax** ['pɪkæks] n Spitzhacke f
picket ['pɪkɪt] n (in strike) Streikposten m ▷ vt (factory etc) Streikposten aufstellen vor +dat
picketing ['pɪkɪtɪŋ] n Aufstellen nt von Streikposten
picket line n Streikpostenkette f
pickings ['pɪkɪŋz] npl: **there are rich ~ to be had here** hier ist die Ausbeute gut
pickle ['pɪkl] n (also: **pickles**: as condiment) Pickles pl ▷ vt einlegen; **to be in a ~** in der Klemme sitzen; **to get in a ~** in eine Klemme geraten
pick-me-up ['pɪkmiːʌp] n Muntermacher m
pickpocket ['pɪkpɔkɪt] n Taschendieb(in) m(f)
pick-up ['pɪkʌp] n (also: **pick-up truck**) offener Kleintransporter m; (Brit: on record player) Tonabnehmer m
picnic ['pɪknɪk] n Picknick nt ▷ vi picknicken
picnicker ['pɪknɪkə'] n Picknicker(in) m(f)
pictorial [pɪk'tɔːrɪəl] adj (record, coverage etc) bildlich
picture ['pɪktʃə'] n Bild nt; (film) Film m ▷ vt (imagine) sich dat vorstellen; **the ~s** (Brit: inf: the cinema) das Kino; **to take a ~ of sb** ein Bild von jdm machen; **to put sb in the ~** jdn ins Bild setzen
picture book n Bilderbuch nt
picture messaging n Picture Messaging nt
picturesque [pɪktʃə'resk] adj malerisch
picture window n Aussichtsfenster nt
piddling ['pɪdlɪŋ] (inf) adj lächerlich
pidgin ['pɪdʒɪn] adj: **~ English** Pidginenglisch nt
pie [paɪ] n (vegetable, meat) Pastete f; (fruit) Torte f

piebald ['paɪbɔːld] adj (horse) scheckig
piece [piːs] n Stück nt; (Draughts etc) Stein m; (Chess) Figur f; **in ~s** (broken) kaputt; (taken apart) auseinandergenommen, in Einzelteilen; **a ~ of clothing/furniture/music** ein Kleidungs-/Möbel-/Musikstück nt; **a ~ of machinery** eine Maschine; **a ~ of research** eine Forschungsarbeit; **a ~ of advice** ein Rat m; **to take sth to ~s** etw auseinandernehmen; **in one ~** (object) unbeschädigt; (person) wohlbehalten; **a 10p ~** (Brit) ein 10-Pence-Stück nt; **~ by piece** Stück für Stück; **a six-~ band** eine sechsköpfige Band; **let her say her ~** lass sie ausreden
▶ **piece together** vt zusammenfügen
piecemeal ['piːsmiːl] adv stückweise, Stück für Stück
piecework ['piːswəːk] n Akkordarbeit f
pie chart n Tortendiagramm nt
pier [pɪə'] n Pier m
pierce [pɪəs] vt durchstechen; **to have one's ears ~d** sich dat die Ohrläppchen durchstechen lassen
piercing ['pɪəsɪŋ] adj (fig: cry, eyes, stare) durchdringend; (wind) schneidend
piety ['paɪətɪ] n Frömmigkeit f
piffling ['pɪflɪŋ] (inf) adj lächerlich
pig [pɪg] n (also pej) Schwein nt; (greedy person) Vielfraß m
pigeon ['pɪdʒən] n Taube f
pigeonhole ['pɪdʒənhəul] n (for letters etc) Fach nt; (fig) Schublade f ▷ vt (fig: person) in eine Schublade stecken
pigeon-toed ['pɪdʒəntəud] adj mit einwärtsgerichteten Zehen
piggy bank ['pɪgɪ-] n Sparschwein nt
pig-headed ['pɪg'hedɪd] (pej) adj dickköpfig
piglet ['pɪglɪt] n Schweinchen nt, Ferkel nt
pigment ['pɪgmənt] n Pigment nt
pigmentation [pɪgmən'teɪʃən] n Pigmentierung f, Färbung f
pigmy ['pɪgmɪ] n = **pygmy**
pigskin ['pɪgskɪn] n Schweinsleder nt
pigsty ['pɪgstaɪ] n (also fig) Schweinestall m
pigtail ['pɪgteɪl] n Zopf m
pike [paɪk] n (fish) Hecht m; (spear) Spieß m
pilchard ['pɪltʃəd] n Sardine f
pile [paɪl] n (heap) Haufen m; (stack) Stapel m; (of carpet, velvet) Flor m; (pillar) Pfahl m ▷ vt (also: **pile up**) (auf)stapeln; **in a ~** in einem Haufen; **to ~ into/out of** (vehicle) sich drängen in +acc/aus
▶ **pile on** vt: **to ~ it on** (inf) zu dick auftragen
▶ **pile up** vi sich stapeln
piles [paɪlz] npl (Med) Hämorr(ho)iden pl
pile-up ['paɪlʌp] n (Aut) Massenkarambolage f
pilfer ['pɪlfə'] vt, vi stehlen
pilfering ['pɪlfərɪŋ] n Diebstahl m
pilgrim ['pɪlgrɪm] n Pilger(in) m(f)
pilgrimage ['pɪlgrɪmɪdʒ] n Pilgerfahrt f, Wallfahrt f
pill [pɪl] n Tablette f, Pille f; **the ~** (contraceptive) die Pille; **to be on the ~** die Pille nehmen

pillage ['pɪlɪdʒ] n Plünderung f ▷ vt plündern

pillar ['pɪlər] n Säule f; **a ~ of society** (fig) eine Säule or Stütze der Gesellschaft

pillar box (Brit) n Briefkasten m

pillion ['pɪljən] n: **to ride ~** (on motorcycle) auf dem Soziussitz mitfahren; (on horse) hinten auf dem Pferd mitreiten

pillory ['pɪlərɪ] vt (criticize) anprangern ▷ n Pranger m

pillow ['pɪləu] n (Kopf)kissen nt

pillowcase ['pɪləukeɪs] n (Kopf)kissenbezug m

pillowslip ['pɪləuslɪp] n = **pillowcase**

pilot ['paɪlət] n (Aviat) Pilot(in) m(f); (Naut) Lotse m ▷ adj (scheme, study etc) Pilot- ▷ vt (aircraft) steuern; (fig: new law, scheme) sich zum Fürsprecher machen +gen

pilot boat n Lotsenboot nt

pilot light n (on cooker, boiler) Zündflamme f

pilot test n (Test) Pilot- od Modellversuch m

pimento [pɪ'mɛntəu] n (spice) Piment nt

pimp [pɪmp] n Zuhälter m

pimple ['pɪmpl] n Pickel m

pimply ['pɪmplɪ] adj pick(e)lig

PIN n abbr (= personal identification number) PIN; **~ number** PIN-Nummer f

pin [pɪn] n (metal: for clothes, papers) Stecknadel f; (Tech) Stift m; (Brit: also: **drawing pin**) Heftzwecke f; (in grenade) Sicherungsstift m; (Brit: Elec) Pol m ▷ vt (fasten with pin) feststecken; **~s and needles** (in arms, legs etc) Kribbeln nt; **to ~ sb against/to sth** jdn gegen/an etw acc pressen; **to ~ sth on sb** (fig) jdm etw anhängen

▶ **pin down** vt (fig: person) festnageln; **there's something strange here but I can't quite ~ it down** hier stimmt etwas nicht, aber ich weiß nicht genau was

pinafore ['pɪnəfɔːr] (Brit) n (also: **pinafore dress**) Trägerkleid nt

pinball ['pɪnbɔːl] n (game) Flippern nt; (machine) Flipper m

pincers ['pɪnsəz] npl (tool) Kneifzange f; (of crab, lobster etc) Schere f

pinch [pɪntʃ] n (of salt etc) Prise f ▷ vt (with finger and thumb) zwicken, kneifen; (inf: steal) klauen ▷ vi (shoe) drücken; **at a ~** zur Not; **to feel the ~** (fig) die schlechte Lage zu spüren bekommen

pinched [pɪntʃt] adj (face) erschöpft; **~ with cold** verfroren

pincushion ['pɪnkuʃən] n Nadelkissen nt

pine [paɪn] n (also: **pine tree**) Kiefer f; (wood) Kiefernholz nt ▷ vi: **to ~ for** sich sehnen nach

▶ **pine away** vi sich (vor Kummer) verzehren

pineapple ['paɪnæpl] n Ananas f

pine cone n Kiefernzapfen m

pine needles npl Kiefernnadeln pl

ping [pɪŋ] n (noise) Klingeln nt

Ping-Pong® ['pɪŋpɔŋ] n Pingpong nt

pink [pɪŋk] adj rosa inv ▷ n (colour) Rosa nt; (Bot) Gartennelke f

pinking shears npl Zickzackschere f

pin money (Brit: inf) n Nadelgeld nt

pinnacle ['pɪnəkl] n (of building, mountain) Spitze f; (fig) Gipfel m

pinpoint ['pɪnpɔɪnt] vt (identify) genau festlegen, identifizieren; (position of sth) genau aufzeigen

pinstripe ['pɪnstraɪp] adj: **~ suit** Nadelstreifenanzug m

pint [paɪnt] n (Brit: = 568 cc) (britisches) Pint nt; (US: = 473 cc) (amerikanisches) Pint; **a ~** (Brit: inf: of beer) ≈ eine Halbe

pin-up ['pɪnʌp] n (picture) Pin-up-Foto nt

pioneer [paɪə'nɪər] n (lit, fig) Pionier m ▷ vt (invention etc) Pionierarbeit leisten für

pious ['paɪəs] adj fromm

pip [pɪp] n (of apple, orange) Kern m ▷ vt: **to be ~ped at the post** (Brit: fig) um Haaresbreite geschlagen werden; **the pips** npl (Brit: Radio) das Zeitzeichen

pipe [paɪp] n (for water, gas) Rohr nt; (for smoking) Pfeife f; (Mus) Flöte f ▷ vt (water, gas, oil) (durch Rohre) leiten; **pipes** npl (also: **bagpipes**) Dudelsack m

▶ **pipe down** vi (inf) (be quiet) ruhig sein

pipe cleaner n Pfeifenreiniger m

piped music [paɪpt-] n Berieselungsmusik f

pipe dream n Hirngespinst nt

pipeline ['paɪplaɪn] n Pipeline f; **it's in the ~** (fig) es ist in Vorbereitung

piper ['paɪpər] n (bagpipe player) Dudelsackspieler(in) m(f)

pipe tobacco n Pfeifentabak m

piping ['paɪpɪŋ] adv: **~ hot** kochend heiß

piquant ['piːkənt] adj (also fig) pikant

pique ['piːk] n: **in a fit of ~** eingeschnappt, pikiert

piracy ['paɪərəsɪ] n Piraterie f, Seeräuberei f; (Comm): **to commit ~** ein Plagiat nt begehen

pirate ['paɪərət] n Pirat m, Seeräuber m ▷ vt (Comm: video tape, cassette etc) illegal herstellen

pirate radio station (Brit) n Piratensender m

pirouette [pɪru'ɛt] n Pirouette f ▷ vi Pirouetten drehen

Pisces ['paɪsiːz] n Fische pl; **to be ~** Fische or (ein) Fisch sein

piss [pɪs] (inf!) vi pissen ▷ n Pisse f; **~ off!** verpiss dich!; **to be ~ed off (with sb/sth)** (von jdm/etw) die Schnauze vollhaben; **it's ~ing down** (Brit: raining) es schifft; **to take the ~ out of sb** (Brit) jdn verarschen

pissed [pɪst] (inf!) adj (drunk) besoffen

pistol ['pɪstl] n Pistole f

piston ['pɪstən] n Kolben m

pit [pɪt] n Grube f; (in surface of road) Schlagloch nt; (coal mine) Zeche f; (also: **orchestra pit**) Orchestergraben m ▷ vt: **to ~ one's wits against sb** seinen Verstand mit jdm messen; **the pits** npl (Aut) die Box; **to ~ o.s. against sth** den Kampf gegen etw aufnehmen; **to ~ sb against sb** jdn gegen jdn antreten lassen; **the ~ of one's stomach** die Magengrube

pitapat ['pɪtə'pæt] (Brit) adv: **to go ~** (heart) pochen, klopfen; (rain) prasseln

pitch [pɪtʃ] n (Brit: Sport: field) Spielfeld nt; (Mus) Tonhöhe f; (fig: level, degree) Grad m; (tar) Pech

P

nt; (also: **sales pitch**) Verkaufsmasche f; (Naut) Stampfen nt ▷ vt (throw) werfen, schleudern; (set: price, message) ansetzen ▷ vi (fall forwards) hinschlagen; (Naut) stampfen; **to ~ a tent** ein Zelt aufschlagen; **to be ~ed forward** vornüber geworfen werden

pitch-black ['pɪtʃ'blæk] adj pechschwarz

pitched battle [pɪtʃt-] n offene Schlacht f

pitcher ['pɪtʃəʳ] n (jug) Krug m; (US: Baseball) Werfer m

pitchfork ['pɪtʃfɔːk] n Heugabel f

piteous ['pɪtɪəs] adj kläglich, erbärmlich

pitfall ['pɪtfɔːl] n Falle f

pith [pɪθ] n (of orange etc) weiße Haut f; (of plant) Mark nt; (fig) Kern m

pithead ['pɪthɛd] n Schachtanlagen pl über Tage

pithy ['pɪθɪ] adj (comment etc) prägnant

pitiable ['pɪtɪəbl] adj mitleiderregend

pitiful ['pɪtɪful] adj (sight etc) mitleiderregend; (excuse, attempt) jämmerlich, kläglich

pitifully ['pɪtɪfəlɪ] adv (thin, frail) jämmerlich; (inadequate, ill-equipped) fürchterlich

pitiless ['pɪtɪlɪs] adj mitleidlos

pittance ['pɪtns] n Hungerlohn m

pitted ['pɪtɪd] adj: ~ **with** übersät mit; ~ **with rust** voller Rost

pity ['pɪtɪ] n Mitleid nt ▷ vt bemitleiden, bedauern; **what a ~!** wie schade!; **it is a ~ that you can't come** schade, dass du nicht kommen kannst; **to take ~ on sb** Mitleid mit jdm haben

pitying ['pɪtɪɪŋ] adj mitleidig

pivot ['pɪvət] n (Tech) Drehpunkt m; (fig) Dreh- und Angelpunkt m ▷ vi sich drehen
▶ **pivot on** (depend on) abhängen von

pixel ['pɪksl] n (Comput) Pixel nt

pixie ['pɪksɪ] n Elf m, Elfe f

pizza ['piːtsə] n Pizza f

placard ['plækɑːd] n Plakat nt, Aushang m; (in march etc) Transparent nt

placate [plə'keɪt] vt beschwichtigen, besänftigen

placatory [plə'keɪtərɪ] adj beschwichtigend, besänftigend

place [pleɪs] n Platz m; (position) Stelle f, Ort m; (seat: on committee etc) Sitz m; (home) Wohnung f; (in street names) ≈ Straße f ▷ vt (put: object) stellen, legen; (identify: person) unterbringen; ~ **of birth** Geburtsort m; **to take ~** (happen) geschehen, passieren; **at/to his ~** (home) bei/zu ihm; **from ~ to place** von Ort zu Ort; **all over the ~** überall; **in ~s** stellenweise; **in sb's/sth's ~** anstelle von jdm/etw; **to take sb's/sth's ~** an die Stelle von jdm/etw treten, jdn/etw ersetzen; **out of ~** (inappropriate) unangebracht; **I feel out of ~ here** ich fühle mich hier fehl am Platze; **in the first ~** (first of all) erstens; **to change ~s with sb** mit jdm den Platz tauschen; **to put sb in his ~** (fig) jdn in seine Schranken weisen; **he's going ~s** er bringt es noch mal weit; **it's not my ~ to do it** es ist nicht an mir, das zu tun; **to be**

~d (in race, exam) platziert sein; **to be ~d third** den dritten Platz belegen; **to ~ an order with sb (for sth)** eine Bestellung bei jdm (für etw) aufgeben; **how are you ~d next week?** wie sieht es bei Ihnen nächste Woche aus?

placebo [plə'siːbəu] n Placebo nt; (fig) Beruhigungsmittel nt

place mat n Set nt or m

placement ['pleɪsmənt] n Platzierung f

place name n Ortsname m

placenta [plə'sɛntə] n Plazenta f

place setting n Gedeck nt

placid ['plæsɪd] adj (person) ruhig, gelassen; (place, river etc) friedvoll

plagiarism ['pleɪdʒərɪzəm] n Plagiat nt

plagiarist ['pleɪdʒərɪst] n Plagiator(in) m(f)

plagiarize ['pleɪdʒəraɪz] vt (idea, work) kopieren, plagiieren

plague [pleɪg] n (Med) Seuche f; (fig: of locusts etc) Plage f ▷ vt (fig: problems etc) plagen; **to ~ sb with questions** jdn mit Fragen quälen

plaice [pleɪs] n inv Scholle f

plaid [plæd] n Plaid nt

plain [pleɪn] adj (unpatterned) einfarbig; (simple) einfach, schlicht; (clear, easily understood) klar; (not beautiful) unattraktiv; (frank) offen ▷ adv (wrong, stupid etc) einfach ▷ n (area of land) Ebene f; (Knitting) rechte Masche f; **to make sth ~ to sb** jdm etw klarmachen

plain chocolate n Bitterschokolade f

plain-clothes ['pleɪnkləuðz] adj (police officer) in Zivil

plainly ['pleɪnlɪ] adv (obviously) eindeutig; (clearly) deutlich, klar

plainness ['pleɪnnɪs] n (of person) Reizlosigkeit f

plain speaking n Offenheit f; **a bit of ~** ein paar offene Worte

plain-spoken ['pleɪn'spəukn] adj offen

plaintiff ['pleɪntɪf] n Kläger(in) m(f)

plaintive ['pleɪntɪv] adj (cry, voice) klagend; (song) schwermütig; (look) traurig

plait [plæt] n (of hair) Zopf m; (of rope, leather) Geflecht nt ▷ vt flechten

plan [plæn] n Plan m ▷ vt planen; (building, schedule) entwerfen ▷ vi planen; **to ~ to do sth** planen or vorhaben, etw zu tun; **how long do you ~ to stay?** wie lange haben Sie vor, zu bleiben?; **to ~ for or on** (expect) sich einstellen auf +acc; **to ~ on doing sth** vorhaben, etw zu tun

plane [pleɪn] n (Aviat) Flugzeug nt; (Math) Ebene f; (fig: level) Niveau nt; (tool) Hobel m; (also: **plane tree**) Platane f ▷ vt (wood) hobeln ▷ vi (Naut, Aut) gleiten

planet ['plænɪt] n Planet m

planetarium [plænɪ'tɛərɪəm] n Planetarium nt

plank [plæŋk] n (of wood) Brett nt; (fig: of policy etc) Schwerpunkt m

plankton ['plæŋktən] n Plankton nt

planned economy ['plænd-] n Planwirtschaft f

planner ['plænəʳ] n Planer(in) m(f)

planning ['plænɪŋ] n Planung f

planning permission (Brit) n
Baugenehmigung f

plant [plɑ:nt] n (Bot) Pflanze f; (machinery)
Maschinen pl; (factory) Anlage f ▷ vt (seed,
plant, crops) pflanzen; (field, garden) bepflanzen;
(microphone, bomb etc) anbringen; (incriminating
evidence) schleusen; (fig: object) stellen; (: kiss)
drücken

plantation [plæn'teɪʃən] n Plantage f; (wood)
Anpflanzung f

plant pot (Brit) n Blumentopf m

plaque [plæk] n (on building etc) Tafel f, Plakette
f; (on teeth) Zahnbelag m

plasma ['plæzmə] n Plasma nt

plaster ['plɑ:stə^r] n (for walls) Putz m;
(also: **plaster of Paris**) Gips m; (Brit: also:
sticking plaster) Pflaster nt ▷ vt (wall, ceiling)
verputzen; **in ~** (Brit) in Gips; **to ~ with** (cover)
bepflastern mit

plasterboard ['plɑ:stəbɔ:d] n Gipskarton m

plaster cast n (Med) Gipsverband m; (model,
statue) Gipsform f

plastered ['plɑ:stəd] (inf) adj (drunk)
sturzbesoffen

plasterer ['plɑ:stərə^r] n Gipser m

plastic ['plæstɪk] n Plastik nt ▷ adj (bucket, cup
etc) Plastik-; (flexible) formbar; **the ~ arts** die
bildende Kunst

plastic bag n Plastiktüte f

plastic bullet n Plastikgeschoss nt

plastic explosive n Plastiksprengstoff m

Plasticine® ['plæstɪsi:n] n Plastilin nt

plastic surgery n plastische Chirurgie f

plate [pleɪt] n Teller m; (metal cover) Platte f;
(Typ) Druckplatte f; (Aut) Nummernschild
nt; (in book: picture) Tafel f; (also: **dental plate**)
Gaumenplatte f; (on door) Schild nt; **gold/
silver ~** vergoldeter/versilberter Artikel m;
that necklace is just ~ die Halskette ist nur
vergoldet/versilbert

plateau ['plætəʊ] (pl **plateaus** or **~x**) n (Geog)
Plateau nt, Hochebene f; (fig) stabiler Zustand
m

plateful ['pleɪtful] n Teller m

plate glass n Tafelglas nt

platen ['plætən] n (on typewriter, printer) (Schreib)
walze f

plate rack n Geschirrständer m

platform ['plætfɔ:m] n (stage) Podium nt; (for
landing, loading on etc, Brit: of bus) Plattform f;
(Rail) Bahnsteig m; (Pol) Programm nt; **the
train leaves from ~ 7** der Zug fährt von Gleis
7 ab

platform ticket (Brit) n (Rail) Bahnsteigkarte f

platinum ['plætɪnəm] n Platin nt

platitude ['plætɪtju:d] n Plattitüde f,
Gemeinplatz m

platonic [plə'tɔnɪk] adj (relationship) platonisch

platoon [plə'tu:n] n Zug m

platter ['plætə^r] n Platte f

plaudits ['plɔ:dɪts] npl Ovationen pl

plausible ['plɔ:zɪbl] adj (theory, excuse) plausibel;
(liar etc) glaubwürdig

play [pleɪ] n (Theat) (Theater)stück nt; (TV)
Fernsehspiel nt; (Radio) Hörspiel nt; (activity)
Spiel nt ▷ vt spielen; (team, opponent) spielen
gegen ▷ vi spielen; **to bring into ~** ins Spiel
bringen; **a ~ on words** ein Wortspiel nt; **to ~
a trick on sb** jdn hereinlegen; **to ~ a part** or
role in sth (fig) eine Rolle bei etw spielen; **to
~ for time** (fig) auf Zeit spielen, Zeit gewinnen
wollen; **to ~ safe** auf Nummer sicher gehen;
to ~ into sb's hands jdm in die Hände spielen
▶ **play about with** vt fus = **play around with**
▶ **play along with** vt fus (person) sich richten
nach; (plan, idea) eingehen auf +acc
▶ **play around with** vt fus (fiddle with)
herumspielen mit
▶ **play at** vt fus (do casually) spielen mit; **to ~ at
being sb/sth** jdn/etw spielen
▶ **play back** vt (recording) abspielen
▶ **play down** vt herunterspielen
▶ **play on** vt fus (sb's feelings etc) ausnutzen; **to ~
on sb's mind** jdm im Kopf herumgehen
▶ **play up** vi (machine, knee etc) Schwierigkeiten
machen; (children) frech werden

play-act ['pleɪækt] vi Theater spielen

playboy ['pleɪbɔɪ] n Playboy m

player ['pleɪə^r] n (Sport, Mus) Spieler(in) m(f);
(Theat) Schauspieler(in) m(f)

playful ['pleɪful] adj (person, gesture) spielerisch;
(animal) verspielt

playgoer ['pleɪgəʊə^r] n Theaterbesucher(in)
m(f)

playground ['pleɪgraund] n (in park) Spielplatz
m; (in school) Schulhof m

playgroup ['pleɪgru:p] n Spielgruppe f

playing card ['pleɪɪŋ-] n Spielkarte f

playing field n Sportplatz m

playmaker ['pleɪmeɪkə^r] n (Sport)
Spielmacher(in) m(f)

playmate ['pleɪmeɪt] n Spielkamerad(in) m(f)

play-off ['pleɪɔf] n Ausscheidungsspiel nt,
Play-off nt

playpen ['pleɪpɛn] n Laufstall m

playroom ['pleɪru:m] n Spielzimmer nt

playschool ['pleɪsku:l] n = **playgroup**

plaything ['pleɪθɪŋ] n (also fig) Spielzeug nt

playtime ['pleɪtaɪm] n (kleine) Pause f

playwright ['pleɪraɪt] n Dramatiker(in) m(f)

plc (Brit) n abbr (= public limited company) ≈ AG f

plea [pli:] n (request) Bitte f; (Law): **to enter
a ~ of guilty/not guilty** sich schuldig/
unschuldig erklären; (excuse) Vorwand m

plea bargaining n Verhandlungen zwischen
Anklage und Verteidigung mit dem Ziel, bestimmte
Anklagepunkte fallen zu lassen, wenn der Angeklagte
sich in anderen Punkten schuldig bekennt

plead [pli:d] vi (Law) vor Gericht eine Schuld-/
Unschuldserklärung abgeben ▷ vt (Law): **to ~ sb's
case** jdn vertreten; (give as excuse: ignorance, ill
health etc) vorgeben, sich berufen auf +acc; **to
~ with sb** jdn inständig bitten; **to ~ for
sth** um etw nachsuchen; **to ~ guilty/not
guilty** sich schuldig/nicht schuldig bekennen

pleasant ['plɛznt] adj angenehm; (smile)

P

709

freundlich

pleasantly ['plɛzntlɪ] adv (surprised) angenehm; (say, behave) freundlich

pleasantries ['plɛzntrɪz] npl Höflichkeiten pl, Nettigkeiten pl

please [pli:z] excl bitte ▷ vt (satisfy) zufriedenstellen ▷ vi (give pleasure) gefällig sein; ~ **Miss/Sir!** (to attract teacher's attention) = Frau/Herr X!; **yes**, ~ ja, bitte; **my bill**, ~ die Rechnung, bitte; ~ **don't cry!** bitte wein doch nicht!; ~ **yourself!** (inf) wie du willst!; **do as you** ~ machen Sie, was Sie für richtig halten

pleased [pli:zd] adj (happy) erfreut; (satisfied) zufrieden; ~ **to meet you** freut mich(, Sie kennenzulernen); ~ **with** zufrieden mit; **we are** ~ **to inform you that ...** wir freuen uns, Ihnen mitzuteilen, dass ...

pleasing ['pli:zɪŋ] adj (remark, picture etc) erfreulich; (person) sympathisch

pleasurable ['plɛʒərəbl] adj angenehm

pleasure ['plɛʒə'] n (happiness, satisfaction) Freude f; (fun, enjoyable experience) Vergnügen nt; **it's a** ~, **my** ~ gern geschehen; **with** ~ gern, mit Vergnügen; **is this trip for business or** ~? ist diese Reise geschäftlich oder zum Vergnügen?

pleasure boat n Vergnügungsschiff nt

pleasure cruise n Vergnügungsfahrt f

pleat [pli:t] n Falte f

pleb [plɛb] (inf: pej) n Prolet m

plebiscite ['plɛbɪsɪt] n Volksentscheid m, Plebiszit nt

plectrum ['plɛktrəm] n Plektron nt, Plektrum nt

pledge [plɛdʒ] n (promise) Versprechen nt ▷ vt (promise) versprechen; **to** ~ **sb to secrecy** jdn zum Schweigen verpflichten

plenary ['pli:nərɪ] adj (powers) unbeschränkt; ~ **session** Plenarsitzung f; ~ **meeting** Vollversammlung f

plentiful ['plɛntɪful] adj reichlich

plenty ['plɛntɪ] n (lots) eine Menge; (sufficient) reichlich; ~ **of** eine Menge; **we've got** ~ **of time to get there** wir haben jede Menge Zeit, dorthin zu kommen

plethora ['plɛθərə] n: **a** ~ **of** eine Fülle von, eine Unmenge an +dat

pleurisy ['pluərɪsɪ] n Rippenfellentzündung f

Plexiglas® ['plɛksɪglɑ:s] (US) n Plexiglas® nt

pliable ['plaɪəbl] adj (material) biegsam; (fig: person) leicht beeinflussbar

pliant ['plaɪənt] adj = **pliable**

pliers ['plaɪəz] npl Zange f

plight [plaɪt] n (of person, country) Not f

plimsolls ['plɪmsəlz] (Brit) npl Turnschuhe pl

plinth [plɪnθ] n Sockel m

PLO n abbr (= Palestine Liberation Organization) PLO f

plod [plɒd] vi (walk) trotten; (fig) sich abplagen

plodder ['plɒdə'] (pej) n (slow worker) zäher Arbeiter m, zähe Arbeiterin f

plonk [plɒŋk] (inf) n (Brit: wine) (billiger) Wein m ▷ vt: **to** ~ **sth down** etw hinknallen

plot [plɒt] n (secret plan) Komplott nt, Verschwörung f; (of story, play, film) Handlung f ▷ vt (sb's downfall etc) planen; (on chart, graph) markieren ▷ vi (conspire) sich verschwören; **a** ~ **of land** ein Grundstück nt; **a vegetable** ~ (Brit) ein Gemüsebeet nt

plotter ['plɒtə'] n (instrument, Comput) Plotter m

plough, (US) **plow** [plau] n Pflug m ▷ vt pflügen; **to** ~ **money into sth** (project etc) Geld in etw acc stecken
▸ **plough back** vt (Comm) reinvestieren
▸ **plough into** vt fus (crowd) rasen in +acc

ploughman, (US) **plowman** ['plaumən] (irreg: like **man**) n Pflüger m

ploughman's lunch ['plaumənz-] (Brit) n Imbiss aus Brot, Käse und Pickles

plow etc (US) = **plough** etc

ploy [plɔɪ] n Trick m

pls abbr (= please) b.

pluck [plʌk] vt (fruit, flower, leaf) pflücken; (musical instrument, eyebrows) zupfen; (bird) rupfen ▷ n (courage) Mut m; **to** ~ **up courage** allen Mut zusammennehmen

plucky ['plʌkɪ] (inf) adj (person) tapfer

plug [plʌg] n (Elec) Stecker m; (stopper) Stöpsel m; (Aut: also: **spark(ing) plug**) Zündkerze f ▷ vt (hole) zustopfen; (inf: advertise) Reklame machen für; **to give sb/sth a** ~ für jdn/etw Reklame machen
▸ **plug in** vt (Elec) einstöpseln, anschließen ▷ vi angeschlossen werden

plughole ['plʌghəul] (Brit) n Abfluss m

plum [plʌm] n (fruit) Pflaume f ▷ adj (inf): **a** ~ **job** ein Traumjob m

plumage ['plu:mɪdʒ] n Gefieder nt

plumb [plʌm] vt: **to** ~ **the depths of despair/ humiliation** die tiefste Verzweiflung/ Erniedrigung erleben
▸ **plumb in** vt anschließen, installieren

plumber ['plʌmə'] n Installateur m, Klempner m

plumbing ['plʌmɪŋ] n (piping) Installationen pl, Rohrleitungen pl; (trade) Klempnerei f; (work) Installationsarbeiten pl

plumb line n Lot nt, Senkblei nt

plume [plu:m] n (of bird) Feder f; (on helmet, horse's head) Federbusch m; ~ **of smoke** Rauchfahne f

plummet ['plʌmɪt] vi (bird, aircraft) (hinunter) stürzen; (price, rate) rapide absacken

plump [plʌmp] adj (person) füllig, mollig
▸ **plump for** (inf) vt fus sich entscheiden für
▸ **plump up** vt (cushion) aufschütteln

plunder ['plʌndə'] n (activity) Plünderung f; (stolen things) Beute f ▷ vt (city, tomb) plündern

plunge [plʌndʒ] n (of bird, person) Sprung m; (fig: of prices, rates etc) Sturz m ▷ vt (hand, knife) stoßen ▷ vi (thing) stürzen; (bird, person) sich stürzen; (fig: prices, rates etc) abfallen, stürzen; **to take the** ~ (fig) den Sprung wagen; **the room was** ~**d into darkness** das Zimmer war in Dunkelheit getaucht

plunger ['plʌndʒə'] n (for sink) Sauger m

plunging ['plʌndʒɪŋ] adj: ~ **neckline** tiefer

Ausschnitt m

pluperfect [plu:'pə:fɪkt] n: **the ~** das Plusquamperfekt

plural ['pluərl] adj Plural- ▷ n Plural m, Mehrzahl f

plus [plʌs] n (also: **plus sign**) Pluszeichen nt ▷ prep, adj plus; **it's a ~** (fig) es ist ein Vorteil or ein Pluspunkt; **ten/twenty ~** (more than) über zehn/zwanzig; **B ~** (Scol) = Zwei plus

plus fours npl Überfallhose f

plush [plʌʃ] adj (car, hotel etc) feudal ▷ n (fabric) Plüsch m

plutonium [plu:'təunɪəm] n Plutonium nt

ply [plaɪ] vt (a trade) ausüben, nachgehen +dat; (tool) gebrauchen, anwenden ▷ vi (ship) verkehren ▷ n (of wool, rope) Stärke f; (also: **plywood**) Sperrholz nt; **to ~ sb with drink** jdn ausgiebig bewirten; **two-/three-~ wool** zwei-/dreifädige Wolle

plywood ['plaɪwud] n Sperrholz nt

PM (Brit) abbr = **Prime Minister**

p.m. adv abbr (= post meridiem) nachmittags; (later) abends

PMT abbr = **premenstrual tension**

pneumatic [nju:'mætɪk] adj pneumatisch

pneumatic drill n Pressluftbohrer m

pneumonia [nju:'məunɪə] n Lungenentzündung f

PO n abbr = **Post Office**; (Mil) = **petty officer**

p.o. abbr = **postal order**

POA (Brit) n abbr (= Prison Officers' Association) Gewerkschaft der Gefängnisbeamten

poach [pəutʃ] vt (steal: fish, animals, birds) illegal erbeuten, wildern; (Culin: egg) pochieren; (: fish) dünsten ▷ vi (steal) wildern

poached [pəutʃt] adj: **~ eggs** verlorene Eier

poacher ['pəutʃəʳ] n Wilderer m

PO Box n abbr = Post Office Box) Postf.

pocket ['pɔkɪt] n Tasche f; (fig: small area) vereinzelter Bereich m ▷ vt (put in one's pocket, steal) einstecken; **to be out of ~** (Brit) Verlust machen; **~ of resistance** Widerstandsnest nt

pocketbook ['pɔkɪtbuk] n (notebook) Notizbuch nt; (US: wallet) Brieftasche f; (: handbag) Handtasche f

pocket calculator n Taschenrechner m

pocketknife ['pɔkɪtnaɪf] n Taschenmesser nt

pocket money n Taschengeld nt

pocket-sized ['pɔkɪtsaɪzd] adj im Taschenformat

pockmarked ['pɔkmɑ:kt] adj (face) pockennarbig

pod [pɔd] n Hülse f

podcast ['pɔdkɑ:st] n Podcast m

podgy ['pɔdʒɪ] (inf) adj rundlich, pummelig

podiatrist [pɔ'di:ətrɪst] (US) n Fußspezialist(in) m(f)

podiatry [pɔ'di:ətrɪ] (US) n Fußpflege f

podium ['pəudɪəm] n Podium nt

POE n abbr (= port of embarkation) Ausgangshafen m; (= port of entry) Eingangshafen m

poem ['pəuɪm] n Gedicht nt

poet ['pəuɪt] n Dichter(in) m(f)

poetic [pəu'ɛtɪk] adj poetisch, dichterisch; (fig) malerisch

poetic justice n ausgleichende Gerechtigkeit f

poetic licence n dichterische Freiheit f

poet laureate n Hofdichter m; siehe Info-Artikel

- **POET LAUREATE**

  Poet laureate ist in Großbritannien ein Dichter, der ein Gehalt als Hofdichter bezieht und kraft seines Amtes ein lebenslanges Mitglied des britischen Königshofes ist. Der Poet Laureate schrieb traditionellerweise ausführliche Gedichte zu Staatsanlässen; ein Brauch, der heute kaum noch befolgt wird. Der erste Poet Laureate 1616 war Ben Jonson.

poetry ['pəuɪtrɪ] n (poems) Gedichte pl; (writing) Poesie f

poignant ['pɔɪnjənt] adj ergreifend; (situation) herzzerreißend

point [pɔɪnt] n Punkt m; (of needle, knife etc) Spitze f; (purpose) Sinn m, Zweck m; (significant part) Entscheidende(s) nt; (moment) Zeitpunkt m; (Elec: also: **power point**) Steckdose f; (also: **decimal point**) = Komma nt ▷ vt (show, mark) deuten auf +acc ▷ vi (with finger, stick etc) zeigen, deuten; **points** npl (Aut) (Unterbrecher)kontakte pl; (Rail) Weichen pl; **two ~ five** (= 2.5) zwei Komma fünf; **good/ bad ~s** (of person) gute/schlechte Seiten or Eigenschaften; **the train stops at Carlisle and all ~s south** der Zug hält in Carlisle und allen Orten weiter südlich; **to be on the ~ of doing sth** im Begriff sein, etw zu tun; **to make a ~ of doing sth** besonders darauf achten, etw zu tun; (make a habit of) Wert darauf legen, etw zu tun; **to get/miss the ~** verstehen/nicht verstehen, worum es geht; **to come** or **get to the ~** zur Sache kommen; **to make one's ~** seinen Standpunkt klarmachen; **that's the whole ~!** darum geht es ja gerade!; **what's the ~?** was solls?; **to be beside the ~** unwichtig or irrelevant sein; **there's no ~ talking to you** es ist sinnlos, mit dir zu reden; **you've got a ~ there!** da könnten Sie recht haben!; **in ~ of fact** in Wirklichkeit; **~ of sale** (Comm) Verkaufsstelle f; **to ~ sth at sb** (gun etc) etw auf jdn richten; (finger) mit etw auf jdn acc zeigen; **to ~ at** zeigen auf +acc; **to ~ to** zeigen auf +acc; (fig) hinweisen auf +acc

▶ **point out** vt hinweisen auf +acc

▶ **point to** vt fus hindeuten auf +acc

point-blank ['pɔɪnt'blæŋk] adv (say, ask) direkt; (refuse) glatt; (also: **at point-blank range**) aus unmittelbarer Entfernung

point duty (Brit) n: **to be on ~** Verkehrsdienst haben

pointed ['pɔɪntɪd] adj spitz; (fig: remark) spitz, scharf

pointedly ['pɔɪntɪdlɪ] adv (ask, reply etc) spitz,

P

scharf

pointer ['pɔɪntə^r] n (on chart, machine) Zeiger m; (fig: piece of information or advice) Hinweis m; (stick) Zeigestock m; (dog) Pointer m

pointing ['pɔɪntɪŋ] n (Constr) Ausfugung f

pointless ['pɔɪntlɪs] adj sinnlos, zwecklos

point of view n Ansicht f, Standpunkt m; **from a practical ~** von einem praktischen Standpunkt aus

poise [pɔɪz] n (composure) Selbstsicherheit f; (balance) Haltung f ▷ vt: **to ~d for sth** (fig) bereit zu etw sein

poison ['pɔɪzn] n Gift nt ▷ vt vergiften

poisoning ['pɔɪznɪŋ] n Vergiftung f

poisonous ['pɔɪznəs] adj (animal, plant) Gift-; (fumes, chemicals etc) giftig; (fig: rumours etc) zersetzend

poison-pen letter [pɔɪzn'pɛn] n anonymer Brief m (mit Indiskretionen)

poke [pəʊk] vt (with finger, stick etc) stoßen; (fire) schüren ▷ n (jab) Stoß m, Schubs m (inf); **to ~ sth in(to)** (put) etw stecken in +acc; **to ~ one's head out of the window** seinen Kopf aus dem Fenster strecken; **to ~ fun at sb** sich über jdn lustig machen

▶ **poke about** vi (search) herumstochern

▶ **poke out** vi (stick out) vorstehen

poker ['pəʊkə^r] n (metal bar) Schürhaken m; (Cards) Poker nt

poker-faced ['pəʊkə'feɪst] adj mit unbewegter Miene, mit Pokergesicht

poky ['pəʊkɪ] (pej) adj (room, house) winzig

Poland ['pəʊlənd] n Polen nt

polar ['pəʊlə^r] adj (icecap) polar; (region) Polar-

polar bear n Eisbär m

polarize ['pəʊləraɪz] vt polarisieren

Pole [pəʊl] n Pole m, Polin f

pole [pəʊl] n (post, stick) Stange f; (flag pole, telegraph pole etc) Mast m; (Geog, Elec) Pol m; **to be ~s apart** (fig) durch Welten (voneinander) getrennt sein

poleaxe, (US) **poleax** ['pəʊlæks] vt (fig) umhauen

pole bean (US) n (runner bean) Stangenbohne f

polecat ['pəʊlkæt] n Iltis m

Pol. Econ. ['pɒlɪkɒn] n abbr (= political economy) Volkswirtschaft f

polemic [pɒ'lɛmɪk] n Polemik f

Pole Star n Polarstern m

pole vault ['pəʊlvɔːlt] n Stabhochsprung m

police [pə'liːs] npl (organization) Polizei f; (members) Polizisten pl, Polizeikräfte pl ▷ vt (street, area, town) kontrollieren; **a large number of ~ were hurt** viele Polizeikräfte wurden verletzt

police car n Polizeiauto nt

police constable (Brit) n Polizist(in) m(f), Polizeibeamte(r) m, Polizeibeamtin f

police department (US) n Polizei f

police force n Polizei f

policeman [pə'liːsmən] (irreg: like **man**) n Polizist m

police officer n = **police constable**

police record n: **to have a ~** vorbestraft sein

police state n (Pol) Polizeistaat m

police station n Polizeiwache f

policewoman [pə'liːswʊmən] (irreg: like **woman**) n Polizistin f

policy ['pɒlɪsɪ] n (Pol, Econ) Politik f; (also: **insurance policy**) (Versicherungs)police f; (of newspaper) Grundsatz m; **to take out a ~** (Insurance) eine Versicherung abschließen

policyholder ['pɒlɪsɪ'həʊldə^r] n (Insurance) Versicherungsnehmer(in) m(f)

policy making n Strategieplanung f

polio ['pəʊlɪəʊ] n Kinderlähmung f, Polio f

Polish ['pəʊlɪʃ] adj polnisch ▷ n (Ling) Polnisch nt

polish ['pɒlɪʃ] n (for shoes) Creme f; (for furniture) Politur f; (for floors) Bohnerwachs nt; (shine: on shoes, floor etc) Glanz m; (fig: refinement) Schliff m ▷ vt (shoes) putzen; (floor, furniture etc) polieren

▶ **polish off** vt (work) erledigen; (food) verputzen

polished ['pɒlɪʃt] adj (fig: person) mit Schliff; (: style) geschliffen

polite [pə'laɪt] adj höflich; (company, society) fein; **it's not ~ to do that** es gehört sich nicht, das zu tun

politely [pə'laɪtlɪ] adv höflich

politeness [pə'laɪtnɪs] n Höflichkeit f

politic ['pɒlɪtɪk] adj klug, vernünftig

political [pə'lɪtɪkl] adj politisch

political asylum n politisches Asyl nt

politically [pə'lɪtɪklɪ] adv politisch; **~ correct** politisch korrekt

politician [pɒlɪ'tɪʃən] n Politiker(in) m(f)

politics ['pɒlɪtɪks] n Politik f ▷ npl (beliefs, opinions) politische Ansichten pl

polka ['pɒlkə] n Polka f

poll [pəʊl] n (also: **opinion poll**) (Meinungs) umfrage f; (election) Wahl f ▷ vt (in opinion poll) befragen; (number of votes) erhalten; **to go to the ~s** (voters) zur Wahl gehen; (government) sich den Wählern stellen

pollen ['pɒlən] n Pollen m, Blütenstaub m

pollen count n Pollenkonzentration f

pollinate ['pɒlɪneɪt] vt bestäuben

polling booth ['pəʊlɪŋ-] (Brit) n Wahlkabine f

polling day (Brit) n Wahltag m

polling station (Brit) n Wahllokal nt

pollster ['pəʊlstə^r] n Meinungsforscher(in) m(f)

poll tax n Kopfsteuer f

pollutant [pə'luːtənt] n Schadstoff m

pollute [pə'luːt] vt verschmutzen

pollution [pə'luːʃən] n (process) Verschmutzung f; (substances) Schmutz m

polo ['pəʊləʊ] n Polo nt

polo neck n (jumper) Rollkragenpullover m

polo-necked ['pəʊləʊnɛkt] adj (jumper, sweater) Rollkragen-

poltergeist ['pɔːltəgaɪst] n Poltergeist m

poly ['pɒlɪ] (Brit) n = **polytechnic**

poly bag (inf) n Plastiktüte f

polyester [pɒlɪ'ɛstə^r] n Polyester m

polygamy [pə'lɪgəmɪ] n Polygamie f
polygraph ['pɒlɪgrɑːf] (US) n (lie detector)
Lügendetektor m
Polynesia [pɒlɪ'niːzɪə] n Polynesien nt
Polynesian [pɒlɪ'niːzɪən] adj polynesisch ▷ n
Polynesier(in) m(f)
polyp ['pɒlɪp] n Polyp m
polystyrene [pɒlɪ'staɪriːn] n ≈ Styropor® nt
polytechnic [pɒlɪ'tɛknɪk] n technische
Hochschule f
polythene ['pɒlɪθiːn] n Polyäthylen nt
polythene bag n Plastiktüte f
polyurethane [pɒlɪ'juərɪθeɪn] n Polyurethan
nt
pomegranate ['pɒmɪgrænɪt] n Granatapfel m
pommel ['pɒml] n (on saddle) Sattelknopf m ▷ vt
(US) = **pummel**
po-mo ['pəʊməʊ] abbr (= postmodern)
postmodern; (= postmodernism) Postmoderne f
pomp [pɒmp] n Pomp m, Prunk m
pompom ['pɒmpɒm] n Troddel f
pompous ['pɒmpəs] (pej) adj (person)
aufgeblasen; (piece of writing) geschwollen
pond [pɒnd] n Teich m
ponder ['pɒndəʳ] vt nachdenken über +acc ▷ vi
nachdenken
ponderous ['pɒndərəs] adj (style, language)
schwerfällig
pong [pɒŋ] (Brit: inf) n Gestank m ▷ vi stinken
pontiff ['pɒntɪf] n Papst m
pontificate [pɒn'tɪfɪkeɪt] vi dozieren
pontoon [pɒn'tuːn] n (floating platform) Ponton
m; (Cards) Siebzehnundvier nt
pony ['pəʊnɪ] n Pony nt
ponytail ['pəʊnɪteɪl] n Pferdeschwanz m; **to
have one's hair in a** ~ einen Pferdeschwanz
tragen
pony trekking (Brit) n Ponytrecken nt
poodle ['puːdl] n Pudel m
pooh-pooh ['puː'puː] vt verächtlich abtun
pool [puːl] n (pond) Teich m; (also: **swimming
pool**) Schwimmbad nt; (of blood) Lache f;
(Sport) Poolbillard nt; (of cash, workers) Bestand
m; (Cards: kitty) Kasse f; (Comm: consortium)
Interessengemeinschaft f ▷ vt (money)
zusammenlegen; (knowledge, resources)
vereinigen; **pools** npl (also: **football pools**)
≈ Fußballtoto nt; **a ~ of sunlight/shade**
eine sonnige/schattige Stelle; **car ~**
Fahrgemeinschaft f; **typing ~, secretary ~**
(US) Schreibzentrale f; **to do the (football) ~s**
≈ im Fußballtoto spielen
poor [puəʳ] adj arm; (bad) schlecht ▷ npl: **the ~**
die Armen pl; ~ **in** (resources etc) arm an +dat; ~
Bob der arme Bob
poorly ['puəlɪ] adj (ill) elend, krank ▷ adv
(badly: designed, paid, furnished) schlecht
pop [pɒp] n (Mus) Pop m; (fizzy drink) Limonade
f; (US: inf: father) Papa m; (sound) Knall m ▷ vi
(balloon) platzen; (cork) knallen ▷ vt: **to ~ sth
into/onto sth** etw schnell in etw acc stecken/
auf etw acc legen; **his eyes ~ped out of his
head** (inf) ihm fielen fast die Augen aus dem

Kopf; **she ~ped her head out of the window**
sie streckte den Kopf aus dem Fenster
▶ **pop in** vi vorbeikommen
▶ **pop out** vi kurz weggehen
▶ **pop up** vi auftauchen; (Comput: window)
aufpoppen
popcorn ['pɒpkɔːn] n Popcorn nt
pope [pəʊp] n Papst m
poplar ['pɒpləʳ] n Pappel f
poplin ['pɒplɪn] n Popeline f
popper ['pɒpəʳ] (Brit: inf) n (for fastening)
Druckknopf m
poppy ['pɒpɪ] n Mohn m
poppycock ['pɒpɪkɒk] (inf) n Humbug m,
dummes Zeug nt
Popsicle® ['pɒpsɪkl] (US) n Eis nt am Stiel
pop star n Popstar m
populace ['pɒpjʊləs] n: **the** ~ die Bevölkerung,
das Volk
popular ['pɒpjʊləʳ] adj (well-liked, fashionable)
beliebt, populär; (general, non-specialist)
allgemein; (idea) weitverbreitet;
(Pol: movement) Volks-; (: cause) des Volkes; **to
be ~ with** beliebt sein bei; **the ~ press** die
Boulevardpresse
popularity [pɒpjʊ'lærɪtɪ] n Beliebtheit f,
Popularität f
popularize ['pɒpjʊləraɪz] vt (sport, music, fashion)
populär machen; (science, ideas) popularisieren
popularly ['pɒpjʊləlɪ] adv (commonly) allgemein
population [pɒpjʊ'leɪʃən] n Bevölkerung
f; (of a species) Zahl f, Population f; **a
prison ~ of 44,000** (eine Zahl von) 44.000
Gefängnisinsassen; **the civilian ~** die
Zivilbevölkerung
population explosion n
Bevölkerungsexplosion f
populous ['pɒpjʊləs] adj dicht besiedelt
pop-up window ['pɒpʌp-] n (Comput) Popup-
Fenster nt
porcelain ['pɔːslɪn] n Porzellan nt
porch [pɔːtʃ] n (entrance) Vorbau m; (US)
Veranda f
porcupine ['pɔːkjʊpaɪn] n Stachelschwein nt
pore [pɔːʳ] n Pore f ▷ vi: **to ~ over** (book etc)
gründlich studieren
pork [pɔːk] n Schweinefleisch nt
pork chop n Schweinekotelett nt
porn [pɔːn] (inf) n Porno m; ~ **channel/
magazine/shop** Pornokanal m/-magazin
nt/-laden m
pornographic [pɔːnə'græfɪk] adj
pornografisch
pornography [pɔː'nɒgrəfɪ] n Pornografie f
porous ['pɔːrəs] adj porös
porpoise ['pɔːpəs] n Tümmler m
porridge ['pɒrɪdʒ] n Haferbrei m, Porridge nt
port [pɔːt] n (harbour) Hafen m; (Naut: left side)
Backbord nt; (wine) Portwein m; (Comput)
Port m ▷ adj (Naut) Backbord-; ~ (Naut) an
Backbord; ~ **of call** (Naut) Anlaufhafen m
portable ['pɔːtəbl] adj (television, typewriter etc)
tragbar, portabel

P

713

portal ['pɔ:tl] n Portal nt
portaloo ['pɔ:təlu:] n Mobiltoilette f
portcullis [pɔ:'kʌlɪs] n Fallgitter nt
portent ['pɔ:tent] n Vorzeichen nt
porter ['pɔ:təʳ] n (for luggage) Gepäckträger m; (doorkeeper) Pförtner m; (US: Rail) Schlafwagenschaffner(in) m(f)
portfolio [pɔ:t'fəulɪəu] n (case) Aktenmappe f; (Pol) Geschäftsbereich m; (Fin) Portefeuille nt; (of artist) Kollektion f
porthole ['pɔ:thəul] n Bullauge nt
portico ['pɔ:tɪkəu] n Säulenhalle f
portion ['pɔ:ʃən] n (part) Teil m; (helping of food) Portion f
portly ['pɔ:tlɪ] adj beleibt, korpulent
portrait ['pɔ:treɪt] n Porträt nt
portray [pɔ:'treɪ] vt darstellen
portrayal [pɔ:'treɪəl] n Darstellung f
Portugal ['pɔ:tjugl] n Portugal nt
Portuguese [pɔ:tju'gi:z] adj portugiesisch ▷ n inv (person) Portugiese m, Portugiesin f; (Ling) Portugiesisch nt
Portuguese man-of-war [-mænəv'wɔ:ʳ] n (Zool) Röhrenqualle f, Portugiesische Galeere f
pose [pəuz] n Pose f ▷ vt (question, problem) aufwerfen; (danger) mit sich bringen ▷ vi: to ~ as (pretend) sich ausgeben als; to ~ for (painting etc) Modell sitzen für, posieren für
poser ['pəuzəʳ] n (problem, puzzle) harte Nuss f (inf); (person) = **poseur**
poseur [pəu'zə:ʳ] (pej) n Angeber(in) m(f)
posh [pɔʃ] (inf) adj vornehm; to talk ~ vornehm daherreden
position [pə'zɪʃən] n (place: of thing, person) Position f, Lage f; (of person's body) Stellung f; (job) Stelle f; (in race etc) Platz m; (attitude) Haltung f, Standpunkt m; (situation) Lage ▷ vt (person, thing) stellen; to be in a ~ to do sth in der Lage sein, etw zu tun
positive ['pɔzɪtɪv] adj positiv; (certain) sicher; (decisive: action, policy) konstruktiv
positively ['pɔzɪtɪvlɪ] adv (emphatic: rude, stupid etc) eindeutig; (encouragingly, Elec) positiv; the body has been ~ identified die Leiche ist eindeutig identifiziert worden
posse ['pɔsɪ] (US) n (Polizei)truppe f
possess [pə'zɛs] vt besitzen; (subj: feeling, belief) Besitz ergreifen von; like a man ~ed wie besessen; whatever ~ed you to do it? was ist in dich gefahren, das zu tun?
possession [pə'zɛʃən] n Besitz m; **possessions** npl (belongings) Besitz m; to take ~ of Besitz ergreifen von
possessive [pə'zɛsɪv] adj (nature etc) besitzergreifend; (Ling: pronoun) Possessiv-; (: adjective) besitzanzeigend; to be ~ about sb/sth Besitzansprüche an jdn/etw acc stellen
possessiveness [pə'zɛsɪvnɪs] n besitzergreifende Art f
possessor [pə'zɛsəʳ] n Besitzer(in) m(f)
possibility [pɔsɪ'bɪlɪtɪ] n Möglichkeit f
possible ['pɔsɪbl] adj möglich; it's ~ (may be

true) es ist möglich, es kann sein; it's ~ to do it es ist machbar or zu machen; as far as ~ so weit wie möglich; if ~ falls or wenn möglich; as soon as ~ so bald wie möglich
possibly ['pɔsɪblɪ] adv (perhaps) möglicherweise, vielleicht; (conceivably) überhaupt; if you ~ can falls überhaupt möglich; what could they ~ want? was um alles in der Welt wollen sie?; I cannot ~ come ich kann auf keinen Fall kommen
post [pəust] n (Brit) Post f; (pole, goal post) Pfosten m; (job) Stelle f; (Mil) Posten m; (also: trading post) Handelsniederlassung f; (on internet forum) Posting nt ▷ vt (Brit: letter) aufgeben; (Mil) aufstellen; (to internet) posten; by ~ (Brit) per Post; by return of ~ (Brit) postwendend, umgehend; to keep sb ~ed (informed) jdn auf dem Laufenden halten; to ~ sb to (town, country) jdn versetzen nach; (embassy, office) jdn versetzen zu; (Mil) jdn abkommandieren nach
  ▶ **post up** vt anschlagen
post ... [pəust] pref Post-, post-; **~-1990** nach 1990
postage ['pəustɪdʒ] n Porto nt
postage stamp n Briefmarke f
postal ['pəustl] adj (charges, service) Post-
postal order (Brit) n Postanweisung f
postbag ['pəustbæg] (Brit) n Postsack m; (letters) Posteingang m
postbox ['pəustbɔks] n Briefkasten m
postcard ['pəustkɑ:d] n Postkarte f
postcode ['pəustkəud] (Brit) n Postleitzahl f
postdate ['pəust'deɪt] vt (cheque) vordatieren
poster ['pəustəʳ] n Poster nt, Plakat nt
poste restante [pəust'restã:nt] (Brit) n Stelle f für postlagernde Sendungen ▷ adv postlagernd
posterior [pɔs'tɪərɪəʳ] (hum) n Allerwerteste(r) m
posterity [pɔs'tɛrɪtɪ] n die Nachwelt
poster paint n Plakatfarbe f
post exchange (US) n (Mil) Laden für US-Militärpersonal
post-free [pəust'fri:] (Brit) adj, adv portofrei
postgraduate ['pəust'grædjuət] n Graduierte(r) f(m) (im Weiterstudium)
posthumous ['pɔstjuməs] adj posthum
posthumously ['pɔstjuməslɪ] adv posthum
posting ['pəustɪŋ] n (job) Stelle f
postman ['pəustmən] (irreg: like **man**) n Briefträger m, Postbote m
postmark ['pəustmɑ:k] n Poststempel m
postmaster ['pəustmɑ:stəʳ] n Postmeister m
Postmaster General n = Postminister(in) m(f)
postmistress ['pəustmɪstrɪs] n Postmeisterin f
postmortem [pəust'mɔ:təm] n (Med) Obduktion f; (fig) nachträgliche Erörterung f
postnatal ['pəust'neɪtl] adj nach der Geburt, postnatal
post office n (building) Post f, Postamt nt; **the Post Office** (organization) die Post
Post Office Box n Postfach nt

post-paid ['pəust'peɪd] adj, adv = **post-free**

postpone [pəus'pəun] vt verschieben

postponement [pəus'pəunmənt] n Aufschub m

postscript ['pəustskrɪpt] n (to letter) Nachschrift f, PS nt

postulate ['pɒstjuleɪt] vt ausgehen von, postulieren

posture ['pɒstʃəʳ] n (also fig) Haltung f ▷ vi (pej) posieren

postwar [pəust'wɔːʳ] adj Nachkriegs-

posy ['pəuzɪ] n Blumensträußchen nt

pot [pɒt] n Topf m; (teapot, coffee pot, potful) Kanne f; (inf: marijuana) Pot nt ▷ vt (plant) eintopfen; **to go to ~** (inf) auf den Hund kommen; **~s of** (Brit: inf) jede Menge

potash ['pɒtæʃ] n Pottasche f

potassium [pə'tæsɪəm] n Kalium nt

potato [pə'teɪtəu] (pl **~es**) n Kartoffel f

potato chips (US) npl = **potato crisps**

potato crisps npl Kartoffelchips pl

potato flour n Kartoffelmehl nt

potato peeler n Kartoffelschäler m

potbellied ['pɒtbelɪd] adj (from overeating) dickbäuchig; (from malnutrition) blähbäuchig

potency ['pəutnsɪ] n (sexual) Potenz f; (of drink, drug) Stärke f

potent ['pəutnt] adj (powerful) stark; (sexually) potent

potentate ['pəutnteɪt] n Machthaber m, Potentat m

potential [pə'tenʃl] adj potenziell ▷ n Potenzial nt; **to have ~** (person, machine) Fähigkeiten or Potenzial haben; (idea, plan) ausbaufähig sein

potentially [pə'tenʃəlɪ] adv potentziell; **it's ~ dangerous** es könnte gefährlich sein

pothole ['pɒthəul] n (in road) Schlagloch nt; (cave) Höhle f

potholing ['pɒthəulɪŋ] (Brit) n: **to go ~** Höhlenforschung betreiben

potion ['pəuʃən] n Elixier nt

potluck [pɒt'lʌk] n: **to take ~** sich überraschen lassen

potpourri [pəu'puriː] n (dried petals) Duftsträußchen nt; (fig) Sammelsurium nt

pot roast n Schmorbraten m

pot shot n: **to take a ~ at** aufs Geratewohl schießen auf +acc

potted ['pɒtɪd] adj (food) eingemacht; (plant) Topf-; (abbreviated: history etc) Kurz-, kurz gefasst

potter ['pɒtəʳ] n Töpfer(in) m(f) ▷ vi: **to ~ around, ~ about** (Brit) herumhantieren; **to ~ around the house** im Haus herumwerkeln

potter's wheel n Töpferscheibe f

pottery ['pɒtərɪ] n (pots, dishes etc) Keramik f, Töpferwaren pl; (work, hobby) Töpfern nt; (factory, workshop) Töpferei f; **a piece of ~** ein Töpferstück nt

potty ['pɒtɪ] adj (inf: mad) verrückt ▷ n (for child) Töpfchen nt

potty-training ['pɒtɪtreɪnɪŋ] n Entwöhnung f vom Windeltragen

pouch [pautʃ] n Beutel m (also Zool)

pouf, pouffe [puːf] n (stool) gepolsterter Hocker m

poultice ['pəultɪs] n Umschlag m

poultry ['pəultrɪ] n Geflügel nt

poultry farm n Geflügelfarm f

poultry farmer n Geflügelzüchter(in) m(f)

pounce [pauns] vi: **to ~ on** (also fig) sich stürzen auf +acc

pound [paund] n (unit of money) Pfund nt; (unit of weight) (britisches) Pfund (= 453,6g); (for dogs) Zwinger m; (for cars) Abholstelle f (für abgeschleppte Fahrzeuge) ▷ vt (beat: table, wall etc) herumhämmern auf +dat; (crush: grain, spice etc) zerstoßen; (bombard) beschießen ▷ vi (heart) klopfen, pochen; (head) dröhnen; **half a ~ of butter** ein halbes Pfund Butter; **a five-~ note** ein Fünfpfundschein m

pounding ['paundɪŋ] n: **to take a ~** (fig) schwer angegriffen werden; (team) eine Schlappe einstecken müssen

pound sterling n Pfund nt Sterling

pour [pɔːʳ] vt (tea, wine etc) gießen; (cereal etc) schütten ▷ vi strömen; **to ~ sb a glass of wine/a cup of tea** jdm ein Glas Wein/eine Tasse Tee einschenken; **to ~ with rain** in Strömen gießen

▶ **pour away** vt wegschütten

▶ **pour in** vi (people) hereinströmen; (letters etc) massenweise eintreffen

▶ **pour out** vi (people) herausströmen ▷ vt (tea, wine etc) eingießen; (fig: thoughts, feelings, etc) freien Lauf lassen +dat

pouring ['pɔːrɪŋ] adj: **~ rain** strömender Regen m

pout [paut] vi einen Schmollmund ziehen

poverty ['pɒvətɪ] n Armut f

poverty line n Armutsgrenze f

poverty risk n Armutsrisiko f

poverty-stricken ['pɒvətɪstrɪkn] adj verarmt, Not leidend

poverty trap (Brit) n gleichbleibend schlechte wirtschaftliche Situation aufgrund des Wegfalls von Sozialleistungen bei verbessertem Einkommen, Armutsfalle f

POW n abbr = **prisoner of war**

powder ['paudəʳ] n Pulver nt ▷ vt: **to ~ one's face** sich dat das Gesicht pudern; **to ~ one's nose** (euph) kurz mal verschwinden

powder compact n Puderdose f

powdered milk ['paudəd-] n Milchpulver nt

powder keg n (also fig) Pulverfass nt

powder puff n Puderquaste f

powder room (euph) n Damentoilette f

power ['pauəʳ] n (control, legal right) Macht f; (ability) Fähigkeit f; (of muscles, ideas, words) Kraft f; (of explosion, engine) Gewalt f; (electricity) Strom m; **2 to the ~ (of) 3** (Math) 2 hoch 3; **to do everything in one's ~ to help** alles in seiner Macht Stehende tun, um zu helfen; **a world ~** eine Weltmacht; **the ~s that be** (authority) diejenigen, die das Sagen haben; **~ of attorney** Vollmacht f; **to be in ~** (Pol etc) an

p

715

der Macht sein

powerboat ['pauəbəut] *n* schnelles Motorboot *nt*, Rennboot *nt*

power cut *n* Stromausfall *m*

powered ['pauəd] *adj*: ~ **by** angetrieben von; **nuclear-~ submarine** atomgetriebenes U-Boot

power failure *n* Stromausfall *m*

powerful ['pauəful] *adj* (*person, organization*) mächtig; (*body, voice, blow etc*) kräftig; (*engine*) stark; (*unpleasant: smell*) streng; (*emotion*) überwältigend; (*argument, evidence*) massiv

powerhouse ['pauəhaus] *n*: **he is a ~ of ideas** er hat ständig neue Ideen

powerless ['pauəlɪs] *adj* machtlos; **to be ~ to do sth** nicht die Macht haben, etw zu tun

power line *n* Stromkabel *nt*

power point (*Brit*) *n* Steckdose *f*

power station *n* Kraftwerk *nt*

power steering *n* (*Aut*) Servolenkung *f*

powwow ['pauwau] *n* Besprechung *f*

pp *abbr* (= *per procurationem*) ppa.

pp. *abbr* (= *pages*) S.

PPE (*Brit*) *n abbr* (*Univ:* = *philosophy, politics, and economics*) Studiengang bestehend aus Philosophie, Politologie und Volkswirtschaft

PPS *n abbr* (= *post postscriptum*) PPS; (*Brit:* = *parliamentary private secretary*) Privatsekretär eines Ministers

PQ (*Canada*) *abbr* (= *Province of Quebec*)

PR *n abbr* = **public relations**; (*Pol*) = **proportional representation** ▷ *abbr* (*US: Post*) = *Puerto Rico*

Pr. *abbr* = **prince**

practicability [præktɪkə'bɪlɪtɪ] *n* Durchführbarkeit *f*

practicable ['præktɪkəbl] *adj* (*scheme, idea*) durchführbar

practical ['præktɪkl] *adj* praktisch; (*person: good with hands*) praktisch veranlagt; (*ideas, methods*) praktikabel

practicality [præktɪ'kælɪtɪ] *n* (*of person*) praktische Veranlagung *f*; **practicalities** *npl* (*of situation etc*) praktische Einzelheiten *pl*

practical joke *n* Streich *m*

practically ['præktɪklɪ] *adv* praktisch

practice ['præktɪs] *n* (*also Med, Law*) Praxis *f*; (*custom*) Brauch *m*; (*exercise*) Übung *f* ▷ *vt, vi* (*US*) = **practise**; **in** ~ in der Praxis; **out of** ~ aus der Übung; **2 hours' piano** ~ 2 Stunden Klavierübungen; **it's common** *or* **standard** ~ es ist allgemein üblich; **to put sth into** ~ etw in die Praxis umsetzen; **target** ~ Zielschießen *nt*

practice match *n* Übungsspiel *nt*

practise, (*US*) **practice** ['præktɪs] *vt* (*train at*) üben; (*carry out: custom*) pflegen; (*: activity etc*) ausüben; (*profession*) praktizieren ▷ *vi* (*train*) üben; (*lawyer, doctor etc*) praktizieren

practised ['præktɪst] (*Brit*) *adj* (*person, liar*) geübt; (*performance*) gekonnt; **with a ~ eye** mit geschultem Auge

practising ['præktɪsɪŋ] *adj* praktizierend

practitioner [præk'tɪʃənəʳ] *n*: **medical ~**

praktischer Arzt *m*, praktische Ärztin *f*; **legal ~** Rechtsanwalt *m*, Rechtsanwältin *f*

pragmatic [præg'mætɪk] *adj* pragmatisch

pragmatism ['prægmətɪzəm] *n* Pragmatismus *m*

Prague [prɑːg] *n* Prag *nt*

prairie ['prɛərɪ] *n* (*Gras*)steppe *f*; **the ~s** (*US*) die Prärien

praise [preɪz] *n* Lob *nt* ▷ *vt* loben; (*Rel*) loben, preisen

praiseworthy ['preɪzwə:ðɪ] *adj* lobenswert

pram [præm] (*Brit*) *n* Kinderwagen *m*

prance [prɑːns] *vi* (*horse*) tänzeln; **to ~ about/in/out** (*person*) herum-/hinein-/hinausstolzieren

prank [præŋk] *n* Streich *m*

prat [præt] (*Brit: inf*) *n* (*idiot*) Trottel *m*

prattle ['prætl] *vi*: **to ~ on (about)** pausenlos plappern (über +*acc*)

prawn [prɔːn] *n* (*Culin, Zool*) Garnele *f*, Krabbe *f*; **~ cocktail** Krabbencocktail *m*

pray [preɪ] *vi* beten; **to ~ for sb/sth** (*Rel, fig*) für jdn/um etw beten

prayer [prɛəʳ] *n* Gebet *nt*; **to say one's ~s** beten

prayer book *n* Gebetbuch *nt*

pre ... [priː] *pref* Prä-, prä-; **~-1970** vor 1970

preach [priːtʃ] *vi* (*Rel*) predigen; (*pej: moralize*) Predigten halten ▷ *vt* (*sermon*) direkt halten; (*fig: advocate*) predigen, verkünden; **to ~ at sb** (*fig*) jdm Moralpredigten halten; **to ~ to the converted** (*fig*) offene Türen einrennen

preacher ['priːtʃəʳ] *n* Prediger(in) *m(f)*

preamble [prɪ'æmbl] *n* Vorbemerkung *f*

prearranged [priːə'reɪndʒd] *adj* (*vorher*) vereinbart

precarious [prɪ'kɛərɪəs] *adj* prekär

precaution [prɪ'kɔːʃən] *n* Vorsichtsmaßnahme *f*; **to take ~s** Vorsichtsmaßnahmen treffen

precautionary [prɪ'kɔːʃənrɪ] *adj* (*measure*) vorbeugend, Vorsichts-

precede [prɪ'siːd] *vt* (*event*) vorausgehen +*dat*; (*person*) vorangehen +*dat*; (*words, sentences*) vorangestellt sein +*dat*

precedence ['presɪdəns] *n* (*priority*) Vorrang *m*; **to take ~ over** Vorrang haben vor +*dat*

precedent ['presɪdənt] *n* (*Law*) Präzedenzfall *m*; **without ~** noch nie da gewesen; **to establish** *or* **set a ~** einen Präzedenzfall schaffen

preceding [prɪ'siːdɪŋ] *adj* vorhergehend

precept ['priːsept] *n* Grundsatz *m*, Regel *f*

precinct ['priːsɪŋkt] *n* (*US: part of city*) Bezirk *m*; **precincts** *npl* (*of cathedral, palace*) Gelände *nt*; **shopping ~** (*Brit*) Einkaufsviertel *nt*; (*under cover*) Einkaufscenter *nt*

precious ['preʃəs] *adj* wertvoll, kostbar; (*pej: person, writing*) geziert; (*ironic: damned*) heiß geliebt, wundervoll ▷ *adv* (*inf*): **~ little/few** herzlich wenig/wenige

precious stone *n* Edelstein *m*

precipice ['presɪpɪs] *n* (*also fig*) Abgrund *m*

precipitate [*vt* prɪ'sɪpɪteɪt, *adj* prɪ'sɪpɪtɪt] *vt* (*event*) heraufbeschwören ▷ *adj* (*hasty*) überstürzt, übereilt

precipitation [prɪsɪpɪ'teɪʃən] n (rain) Niederschlag m

precipitous [prɪ'sɪpɪtəs] adj (steep) steil; (hasty) übereilt

précis ['preɪsi:] n inv Zusammenfassung f

precise [prɪ'saɪs] adj genau, präzise; **at 4 o'clock to be ~** um 4 Uhr, um genau zu sein

precisely [prɪ'saɪslɪ] adv genau, exakt; (emphatic) ganz genau; **~!** genau!

precision [prɪ'sɪʒən] n Genauigkeit f, Präzision f

preclude [prɪ'klu:d] vt ausschließen; **to ~ sb from doing sth** jdn daran hindern, etw zu tun

precocious [prɪ'kəuʃəs] adj (child, behaviour) frühreif

preconceived [pri:kən'si:vd] adj (idea) vorgefasst

preconception ['pri:kən'sɛpʃən] n vorgefasste Meinung f

precondition ['pri:kən'dɪʃən] n Vorbedingung f

precursor [pri:'kə:sər] n Vorläufer m

predate ['pri:'deɪt] vt (precede) vorausgehen +dat

predator ['predətər] n (Zool) Raubtier nt; (fig) Eindringling m

predatory ['predətərɪ] adj (animal) Raub-; (person, organization) auf Beute lauernd

predecessor ['pri:dɪsɛsər] n Vorgänger(in) m(f)

predestination [pri:dɛstɪ'neɪʃən] n Vorherbestimmung f

predetermine [pri:dɪ'tə:mɪn] vt vorherbestimmen

predicament [prɪ'dɪkəmənt] n Notlage f, Dilemma nt; **to be in a ~** in einer Notlage or einem Dilemma stecken

predicate ['predɪkɪt] n (Ling) Prädikat nt

predict [prɪ'dɪkt] vt vorhersagen

predictable [prɪ'dɪktəbl] adj vorhersagbar

predictably [prɪ'dɪktəblɪ] adv (behave, react) wie vorherzusehen; **~ she didn't come** wie vorherzusehen war, kam sie nicht

prediction [prɪ'dɪkʃən] n Voraussage f

predispose ['pri:dɪs'pəuz] vt: **to ~ sb to sth** jdn zu etw veranlassen; **to be ~d to do sth** geneigt sein, etw zu tun

predominance [prɪ'dɔmɪnəns] n Vorherrschaft f

predominant [prɪ'dɔmɪnənt] adj vorherrschend; **to become ~** vorherrschend werden

predominantly [prɪ'dɔmɪnəntlɪ] adv überwiegend

predominate [prɪ'dɔmɪneɪt] vi (in number, size) vorherrschen; (in strength, influence) überwiegen

pre-eminent [pri:'ɛmɪnənt] adj herausragend

pre-empt [pri:'ɛmt] vt zuvorkommen +dat

pre-emptive [pri:'ɛmtɪv] adj: **~ strike** Präventivschlag m

preen [pri:n] vt: **to ~ itself** (bird) sich putzen; **to ~ o.s.** sich herausputzen

prefab ['pri:fæb] n Fertighaus nt

prefabricated [pri:'fæbrɪkeɪtɪd] adj vorgefertigt

preface ['prefəs] n Vorwort nt ▷ vt: **to ~ with/by** (speech, action) einleiten mit/durch

prefect ['pri:fɛkt] (Brit) n (in school) Aufsichtsschüler(in) m(f)

prefer [prɪ'fə:r] vt (like better) vorziehen; **to ~ charges** (Law) Anklage erheben; **to ~ doing** or **to do sth** (es) vorziehen, etw zu tun; **I ~ tea to coffee** ich mag lieber Tee als Kaffee

preferable ['prefrəbl] adj: **to be ~ (to)** vorzuziehen sein (+dat)

preferably ['prefrəblɪ] adv vorzugsweise, am besten

preference ['prefrəns] n: **to have a ~ for** (liking) eine Vorliebe haben für; **I drink beer in ~ to wine** ich trinke lieber Bier als Wein; **to give ~ to** (priority) vorziehen, Vorrang einräumen +dat

preference shares (Brit) npl (Comm) Vorzugsaktien pl

preferential [prefə'rɛnʃəl] adj: **~ treatment** bevorzugte Behandlung f; **to give sb ~ treatment** jdn bevorzugt behandeln

preferred stock [prɪ'fəd-] (US) npl = **preference shares**

prefix ['pri:fɪks] n (Ling) Präfix nt

pregnancy ['pregnənsɪ] n (of woman) Schwangerschaft f; (of female animal) Trächtigkeit f

pregnancy test n Schwangerschaftstest m

pregnant ['pregnənt] adj (woman) schwanger; (female animal) trächtig; (fig: pause, remark) bedeutungsschwer; **3 months ~** im vierten Monat (schwanger)

prehistoric ['pri:hɪs'tɔrɪk] adj prähistorisch, vorgeschichtlich

prehistory [pri:'hɪstərɪ] n Vorgeschichte f

prejudge [pri:'dʒʌdʒ] vt vorschnell beurteilen

prejudice ['predʒʊdɪs] n (bias against) Vorurteil nt; (bias in favour) Voreingenommenheit f ▷ vt beeinträchtigen; **without ~ to** (form) unbeschadet +gen, ohne Beeinträchtigung +gen; **to ~ sb in favour of/against sth** jdn für/gegen etw einnehmen

prejudiced ['predʒʊdɪst] adj (person, view) voreingenommen

prelate ['prelət] n Prälat m

preliminaries [prɪ'lɪmɪnərɪz] npl Vorbereitungen pl; (of competition) Vorrunde f

preliminary [prɪ'lɪmɪnərɪ] adj (step, arrangements) vorbereitend; (remarks) einleitend

pre-loaded [prɪ'ləudɪd] adj (Comput: program etc) vorinstalliert

prelude ['prelju:d] n (Mus) Präludium nt; (: as introduction) Vorspiel nt; **a ~ to** (fig) ein Vorspiel or ein Auftakt zu

premarital ['pri:'mærɪtl] adj vorehelich

premature ['premətʃuər] adj (earlier than expected) vorzeitig; (too early) verfrüht; **you are being a little ~** Sie sind etwas voreilig; **~ baby** Frühgeburt f

premeditated [pri:'mɛdɪteɪtɪd] adj vorsätzlich

premeditation [pri:mɛdɪ'teɪʃən] n Vorsatz m

P

717

premenstrual tension [priː'mɛnstruəl-] n prämenstruelles Syndrom nt

premier ['prɛmɪəʳ] adj (best) beste(r, s), bedeutendste(r, s) ▷ n (Pol) Premierminister(in) m(f)

premiere ['prɛmɪɛəʳ] n Premiere f

premise ['prɛmɪs] n (of argument) Voraussetzung f; **premises** npl (of business etc) Räumlichkeiten pl; **on the ~s** im Hause

premium ['priːmɪəm] n (Comm, Insurance) Prämie f; **to be at a ~** (expensive) zum Höchstpreis gehandelt werden; (hard to get) Mangelware sein

premium bond (Brit) n Prämienanleihe f; siehe Info-Artikel

◉ **PREMIUM BONDS**

◉
◉ *Premium bonds*, eigentlich *premium savings*
◉ *bonds*, sind Lotterieaktien, die seit 1956
◉ vom britischen Finanzministerium
◉ ausgegeben werden und keine Zinsen
◉ bringen, sondern stattdessen an einer
◉ monatlichen Auslosung teilnehmen. Die
◉ Gewinnnummern für die verschiedenen
◉ Geldpreise werden in Blackpool von einem
◉ Computer namens „ERNIE" (Electronic
◉ Random Number Indicator Equipment)
◉ ermittelt.

---

premium gasoline (US) n Super(benzin) nt

premonition [prɛmə'nɪʃən] n Vorahnung f

preoccupation [priːɔkju'peɪʃən] n: **~ with** (vorrangige) Beschäftigung mit

preoccupied [priː'ɔkjupaɪd] adj (thoughtful) gedankenverloren; (with work, family) beschäftigt

prep [prɛp] (Scol) adj (= preparatory) see **prep school** ▷ n (= preparation) Hausaufgaben pl

prepaid [priː'peɪd] adj (paid in advance) im Voraus bezahlt; (envelope) frankiert

preparation [prɛpə'reɪʃən] n Vorbereitung f; (food, medicine, cosmetic) Zubereitung f; **preparations** npl Vorbereitungen pl; **in ~ for sth** als Vorbereitung für etw

preparatory [prɪ'pærətərɪ] adj vorbereitend; **~ to sth/to doing sth** als Vorbereitung für etw/, um etw zu tun

prepare [prɪ'pɛəʳ] vt vorbereiten; (food, meal) zubereiten ▷ vi: **to ~ for** sich vorbereiten auf +acc

prepared [prɪ'pɛəd] adj: **to be ~ to do sth** (willing) bereit sein, etw zu tun; **to be ~ for sth** (ready) auf etw acc vorbereitet sein

preponderance [prɪ'pɔndərns] n Übergewicht nt

preposition [prɛpə'zɪʃən] n Präposition f

prepossessing [priːpə'zɛsɪŋ] adj von angenehmer Erscheinung

preposterous [prɪ'pɔstərəs] adj grotesk, widersinnig

prep school n = **prep(aratory) school**; siehe Info-Artikel

◉ **PREP(ARATORY) SCHOOL**

◉
◉ Prep(aratory) school ist in Großbritannien
◉ eine meist private Schule für Kinder
◉ im Alter von 7 bis 13 Jahren, die auf eine
◉ weiterführende Privatschule vorbereiten
◉ soll.

---

prerecorded ['priːrɪ'kɔːdɪd] adj (broadcast) aufgezeichnet; (cassette, video) bespielt

prerequisite [priː'rɛkwɪzɪt] n Vorbedingung f, Grundvoraussetzung f

prerogative [prɪ'rɔgətɪv] n Vorrecht nt, Privileg nt

Presbyterian [prɛzbɪ'tɪərɪən] adj presbyterianisch ▷ n Presbyterianer(in) m(f)

presbytery ['prɛzbɪtərɪ] n Pfarrhaus nt

preschool ['priː'skuːl] adj (age, child, education) Vorschul-

prescribe [prɪ'skraɪb] vt (Med) verschreiben; (demand) anordnen, vorschreiben

prescribed adj (duties, period) vorgeschrieben

prescription [prɪ'skrɪpʃən] n (Med: slip of paper) Rezept nt; (: medicine) Medikament nt; **to make up a ~, to fill a ~** (US) ein Medikament zubereiten; **"only available on ~"** „rezeptpflichtig"

prescription charges (Brit) npl Rezeptgebühr f

prescriptive [prɪ'skrɪptɪv] adj normativ

presence ['prɛzns] n Gegenwart f, Anwesenheit f; (fig: personality) Ausstrahlung f; (spirit, invisible influence) Erscheinung f; **in sb's ~** in jds dat Gegenwart or Beisein; **~ of mind** Geistesgegenwart f

present [adj, n 'prɛznt, vt prɪ'zɛnt] adj (current) gegenwärtig, derzeitig; (in attendance) anwesend ▷ n (gift) Geschenk nt; (Ling: also: **present tense**) Präsens nt, Gegenwart f ▷ vt (give: prize) überreichen; (plan, report) vorlegen; (cause, provide, portray) darstellen; (information, view) darlegen; (Radio, TV) leiten; **to be ~ at** anwesend or zugegen sein bei; **those ~** die Anwesenden; **to give sb a ~** jdm ein Geschenk geben; **the ~** (actuality) die Gegenwart; **at ~** gegenwärtig, im Augenblick; **to ~ sth to sb, ~ sb with sth** jdm etw übergeben or überreichen; **to ~ sb (to)** (formally: introduce) jdn vorstellen +dat; **to ~ itself** (opportunity) sich bieten

presentable [prɪ'zɛntəbl] adj (person) präsentabel, ansehnlich

presentation [prɛzn'teɪʃən] n (of prize) Überreichung f; (of plan, report etc) Vorlage f; (appearance) Erscheinungsbild nt; (talk) Vortrag m; **on ~ of** (voucher etc) gegen Vorlage +gen

present-day ['prɛzntdeɪ] adj heutig, gegenwärtig

presenter [prɪ'zɛntəʳ] n (on radio, TV) Moderator(in) m(f)

presently ['prɛzntlɪ] adv (soon after) gleich darauf; (soon) bald, in Kürze; (currently) derzeit, gegenwärtig

present participle n Partizip nt Präsens

preservation [prɛzə'veɪʃən] n (of peace, standards etc) Erhaltung f; (of furniture, building) Konservierung f

preservative [prɪ'zə:vətɪv] n Konservierungsmittel nt

preserve [prɪ'zə:v] vt erhalten; (peace) wahren; (wood) schützen; (food) konservieren ▷ n (often pl: jam, chutney etc) Eingemachte(s) nt; (for game, fish) Revier nt; **a male ~** (fig) eine männliche Domäne; **a working class ~** (fig) eine Domäne der Arbeiterklasse

preshrunk ['pri:'ʃrʌŋk] adj (jeans etc) vorgewaschen

preside [prɪ'zaɪd] vi: **to ~ over** (meeting etc) vorsitzen +dat, den Vorsitz haben bei

presidency ['prezɪdənsɪ] n (Pol) Präsidentschaft f; (US: of company) Vorsitz m

president ['prezɪdənt] n (Pol) Präsident(in) m(f); (of organization) Vorsitzende(r) f(m)

presidential [prezɪ'dɛnʃl] adj (election, campaign etc) Präsidentschafts-; (adviser, representative etc) des Präsidenten

press [prɛs] n (also: **printing press**) Presse f; (of switch, bell) Druck m; (for wine) Kelter f ▷ vt drücken, pressen; (button, sb's hand etc) drücken; (iron: clothes) bügeln; (put pressure on: person) drängen; (pursue: idea, claim) vertreten ▷ vi (squeeze) drücken, pressen; **the P~** (newspaper, journalists) die Presse; **to go to ~** (newspaper) in Druck gehen; **to be in ~** (at the printer's) im Druck sein; **to be in the ~** (in the newspapers) in der Zeitung stehen; **at the ~ of a button** auf Knopfdruck; **to ~ sth (up) on sb** (force) jdm etw aufdrängen; **we are ~ed for time/money** wir sind in Geldnot/Zeitnot; **to ~ sb for an answer** auf jds acc Antwort drängen; **to ~ sb to do** or **into doing sth** jdn drängen, etw zu tun; **to ~ charges (against sb)** (Law) Klage (gegen jdn) erheben; **to ~ for** (changes etc) drängen auf +acc
▸ **press ahead** vi weitermachen; **to ~ ahead with sth** etw durchziehen
▸ **press on** vi weitermachen

press agency n Presseagentur f

press clipping n Zeitungsausschnitt m

press conference n Pressekonferenz f

press cutting n = **press clipping**

press-gang ['prɛsgæn] vt: **to ~ sb into doing sth** jdn bedrängen, etw zu tun

pressing ['prɛsɪn] adj (urgent) dringend

press officer n Pressesprecher(in) m(f)

press release n Pressemitteilung f

press stud (Brit) n Druckknopf m

press-up ['prɛsʌp] (Brit) n Liegestütz m

pressure ['prɛʃəʳ] n (also fig) Druck m ▷ vt: **to ~ sb to do sth** jdn dazu drängen, etw zu tun; **to put ~ on sb (to do sth)** Druck auf jdn ausüben(, etw zu tun); **high/low ~** (Tech, Met) Hoch-/Tiefdruck m

pressure cooker n Schnellkochtopf m

pressure gauge n Druckmesser m, Manometer

nt

pressure group n Interessenverband m, Pressuregroup f

pressurize ['prɛʃəraɪz] vt: **to ~ sb (to do sth** or **into doing sth)** jdn unter Druck setzen(, etw zu tun)

pressurized ['prɛʃəraɪzd] adj (cabin, container etc) Druck-

Prestel® ['prɛstɛl] n ≈ Bildschirmtext m, Btx nt

prestige [prɛs'ti:ʒ] n Prestige nt

prestigious [prɛs'tɪdʒəs] adj (institution, appointment) mit hohem Prestigewert

presumably [prɪ'zju:məblɪ] adv vermutlich; **~ he did it** vermutlich or wahrscheinlich hat er es getan

presume [prɪ'zju:m] vt: **to ~ (that)** (assume) annehmen(, dass); **to ~ to do sth** (dare) sich anmaßen, etw zu tun; **I ~ so** das nehme ich an

presumption [prɪ'zʌmpʃən] n (supposition) Annahme f; (audacity) Anmaßung f

presumptuous [prɪ'zʌmpʃəs] adj anmaßend

presuppose [pri:sə'pəuz] vt voraussetzen

presupposition [pri:sʌpə'zɪʃən] n Voraussetzung f

pretax [pri:'tæks] adj (profit) vor (Abzug der) Steuern

pretence, (US) **pretense** [prɪ'tɛns] n (false appearance) Vortäuschung f; **under false ~s** unter Vorspiegelung falscher Tatsachen; **she is devoid of all ~** sie ist völlig natürlich; **to make a ~ of doing sth** vortäuschen, etw zu tun

pretend [prɪ'tɛnd] vt (feign) vorgeben ▷ vi (feign) sich verstellen, so tun, als ob; **I don't ~ to understand it** (claim) ich erhebe nicht den Anspruch, es zu verstehen

pretense [prɪ'tɛns] (US) n = **pretence**

pretentious [prɪ'tɛnʃəs] adj anmaßend

preterite ['prɛtərɪt] n Imperfekt nt, Präteritum nt

pretext ['pri:tɛkst] n Vorwand m; **on** or **under the ~ of doing sth** unter dem Vorwand, etw zu tun

pretty ['prɪtɪ] adj hübsch, nett ▷ adv: **~ clever** ganz schön schlau; **~ good** ganz gut

prevail [prɪ'veɪl] vi (be current) vorherrschen; (triumph) siegen; **to ~ (up)on sb to do sth** (persuade) jdn dazu bewegen or überreden, etw zu tun

prevailing [prɪ'veɪlɪn] adj (wind, fashion etc) vorherrschend

prevalent ['prɛvələnt] adj (belief, custom) vorherrschend

prevaricate [prɪ'værɪkeɪt] vi (by saying sth) Ausflüchte machen; (by doing sth) Ausweichmanöver machen

prevarication [prɪværɪ'keɪʃən] n (see vi) Ausflucht f; Ausweichmanöver nt

prevent [prɪ'vɛnt] vt verhindern; **to ~ sb from doing sth** jdn daran hindern, etw zu tun; **to ~ sth from happening** verhindern, dass etw geschieht

preventable [prɪ'vɛntəbl] adj verhütbar,

P

vermeidbar

preventative [prɪ'vɛntətɪv] adj = **preventive**

prevention [prɪ'vɛnʃən] n Verhütung f

preventive [prɪ'vɛntɪv] adj (measures, medicine) vorbeugend

preview ['pri:vju:] n (of film) Vorpremiere f; (of exhibition) Vernissage f

previous ['pri:vɪəs] adj (earlier) früher; (preceding) vorhergehend; ~ **to** vor +dat

previously ['pri:vɪəslɪ] adv (before) zuvor; (formerly) früher

prewar [pri:'wɔ:ʳ] adj (period) Vorkriegs-

prey [preɪ] n Beute f; **to fall ~ to** (fig) zum Opfer fallen +dat

▶ **prey on** vt fus (animal) Jagd machen auf +acc; **it was ~ing on his mind** es ließ ihn nicht los

price [praɪs] n (also fig) Preis m ▷ vt (goods) auszeichnen; **what is the ~ of ...?** was kostet ...?; **to go up** or **rise in ~** im Preis steigen, teurer werden; **to put a ~ on sth** (also fig) einen Preis für etw festsetzen; **what ~ his promises now?** wie steht es jetzt mit seinen Versprechungen?; **he regained his freedom, but at a ~** er hat seine Freiheit wieder, aber zu welchem Preis!; **to be ~d at £30** £30 kosten; **to ~ o.s. out of the market** durch zu hohe Preise konkurrenzunfähig werden

price control n Preiskontrolle f

price-cutting ['praɪskʌtɪŋ] n Preissenkungen pl

priceless ['praɪslɪs] adj (diamond, painting) von unschätzbarem Wert; (inf: amusing) unbezahlbar, köstlich

price list n Preisliste f

price range n Preisklasse f; **it's within my ~** ich kann es mir leisten

price tag n Preisschild nt; (fig) Preis m

price war n Preiskrieg m

pricey ['praɪsɪ] (inf) adj kostspielig

prick [prɪk] n (sting) Stich m; (inf!: penis) Schwanz m; (: idiot) Arsch m ▷ vt stechen; (sausage, balloon) einstechen; **to ~ up one's ears** die Ohren spitzen

prickle ['prɪkl] n (of plant) Dorn m, Stachel m; (sensation) Prickeln nt

prickly ['prɪklɪ] adj (plant) stachelig; (fabric) kratzig

prickly heat n Hitzebläschen pl

prickly pear n Feigenkaktus m

pride [praɪd] n Stolz m; (pej: arrogance) Hochmut m ▷ vt: **to ~ o.s. on sth** sich rühmen +gen; **to take (a) ~ in** stolz sein auf +acc; **to take a ~ in doing sth** etw mit Stolz tun; **to have** or **take ~ of place** (Brit) die Krönung sein

priest [pri:st] n Priester m

priestess ['pri:stɪs] n Priesterin f

priesthood ['pri:sthud] n Priestertum nt

prig [prɪg] n: **he's a ~** er hält sich für ein Tugendbold

prim [prɪm] (pej) adj (person) etepetete

primacy ['praɪməsɪ] n (supremacy) Vorrang m; (position) Vorrangstellung f

prima-facie ['praɪmə'feɪʃɪ] adj: **to have a ~**

case (Law) eine gute Beweisgrundlage haben

primal ['praɪməl] adj ursprünglich; ~ **scream** Urschrei m

primarily ['praɪmərɪlɪ] adv in erster Linie, hauptsächlich

primary ['praɪmərɪ] adj (principal) Haupt-, hauptsächlich; (education, teacher) Grundschul- ▷ n (US: election) Vorwahl f; siehe Info-Artikel

◉ **PRIMARY**
◉
◉
◉ Als primary wird im amerikanischen
◉ Präsidentschaftswahlkampf eine
◉ Vorwahl bezeichnet, die mitentscheidet,
◉ welche Präsidentschaftskandidaten
◉ die beiden großen Parteien aufstellen.
◉ Vorwahlen werden nach komplizierten
◉ Regeln von Februar (New Hampshire) bis
◉ Juni in etwa 35 Staaten abgehalten. Der
◉ von den Kandidaten in den primaries
◉ erzielte Stimmenanteil bestimmt, wie
◉ viele Abgeordnete bei der endgültigen
◉ Auswahl der demokratischen bzw.
◉ republikanischen Kandidaten auf den
◉ nationalen Parteitagen im Juli/August für
◉ sie stimmen.

primary colour n Primärfarbe f

primary school (Brit) n Grundschule f; siehe Info-Artikel

◉ **PRIMARY SCHOOL**
◉
◉ Primary school ist in Großbritannien eine
◉ Grundschule für Kinder im Alter von 5 bis
◉ 11 Jahren. Oft wird sie aufgeteilt in „infant
◉ school" (5 bis 7 Jahre) und „junior school"
◉ (7 bis 11 Jahre). Siehe auch secondary school.

primate ['praɪmɪt] n (Zool) Primat m; (Rel) Primas m

prime [praɪm] adj (most important) oberste(r, s); (best quality) erstklassig ▷ n (of person's life) die besten Jahre pl ▷ vt (wood) grundieren; (fig: person) informieren; (gun) schussbereit machen; (pump) auffüllen; ~ **example** erstklassiges Beispiel; **in the ~ of life** im besten Alter

Prime Minister n Premierminister(in) m(f)

primer ['praɪməʳ] n (paint) Grundierung f; (book) Einführung f

prime time n (Radio, TV) Hauptsendezeit f

primeval [praɪ'mi:vl] adj (beast) urzeitlich; (fig: feelings) instinktiv; ~ **forest** Urwald m

primitive ['prɪmɪtɪv] adj (tribe, tool, conditions etc) primitiv; (life form, machine etc) frühzeitlich; (man) der Urzeit

primrose ['prɪmrəuz] n Primel f, gelbe Schlüsselblume f

primula ['prɪmjulə] n Primel f

Primus® ['praɪməs], **Primus stove** (Brit) n Primuskocher m

prince [prɪns] n Prinz m

Prince Charming (*hum*) *n* Märchenprinz *m*
princess [prɪnˈsɛs] *n* Prinzessin *f*
principal [ˈprɪnsɪpl] *adj* (*most important*) Haupt-, wichtigste(r, s) ▷ *n* (*of school, college*) Rektor(in) *m(f)*; (*Theat*) Hauptdarsteller(in) *m(f)*; (*Fin*) Kapitalsumme *f*
principality [prɪnsɪˈpælɪtɪ] *n* Fürstentum *nt*
principally [ˈprɪnsɪplɪ] *adv* vornehmlich
principle [ˈprɪnsɪpl] *n* Prinzip *nt*; **in ~** im Prinzip, prinzipiell; **on ~** aus Prinzip
print [prɪnt] *n* (*Art*) Druck *m*; (*Phot*) Abzug *m*; (*fabric*) bedruckter Stoff *m* ▷ *vt* (*produce*) drucken; (*publish*) veröffentlichen; (*cloth, pattern*) bedrucken; (*write in capitals*) in Druckschrift schreiben; **prints** *npl* (*fingerprints etc*) Abdrücke *pl*; **out of ~** vergriffen; **in ~** erhältlich; **the fine** *or* **small ~** das Kleingedruckte
  ▶ **print out** *vt* (*Comput*) ausdrucken
printed circuit [ˈprɪntɪd-] *n* gedruckte Schaltung *f*
printed circuit board *n* Leiterplatte *f*
printed matter *n* Drucksache *f*
printer [ˈprɪntər] *n* (*person*) Drucker(in) *m(f)*; (*firm*) Druckerei *f*; (*machine*) Drucker *m*
printhead [ˈprɪnthɛd] *n* Druckkopf *m*
printing [ˈprɪntɪŋ] *n* (*activity*) Drucken *nt*
printing press *n* Druckerpresse *f*
print-out [ˈprɪntaut] *n* (*Comput*) *n* Ausdruck *m*
print run *n* Auflage *f*
printwheel [ˈprɪntwiːl] *n* (*Comput*) Typenrad *nt*
prior [ˈpraɪər] *adj* (*previous: knowledge, warning*) vorherig; (: *engagement*) früher; (*more important: claim, duty*) vorrangig ▷ *n* (*Rel*) Prior *m*; **without ~ notice** ohne vorherige Ankündigung; **to have a ~ claim on sth** ein Vorrecht auf etw *acc* haben; **~ to** vor +*dat*
priority [praɪˈɒrɪtɪ] *n* vorrangige Angelegenheit *f*; **priorities** *npl* Prioritäten *pl*; **to take** *or* **have ~ (over sth)** Vorrang (vor etw *dat*) haben; **to give ~ to sb/sth** jdm/etw Vorrang einräumen
priory [ˈpraɪərɪ] *n* Kloster *nt*
prise [praɪz] (*Brit*) *vt*: **to ~ open** aufbrechen
prism [ˈprɪzəm] *n* Prisma *nt*
prison [ˈprɪzn] *n* Gefängnis *nt* ▷ *cpd* (*officer, food, cell etc*) Gefängnis-
prison camp *n* Gefangenenlager *nt*
prisoner [ˈprɪznər] *n* Gefangene(r) *f(m)*; **the ~ at the bar** (*Law*) der/die Angeklagte; **to take sb ~** jdn gefangen nehmen
prisoner of war *n* Kriegsgefangene(r) *f(m)*
prissy [ˈprɪsɪ] (*pej*) *adj* zimperlich
pristine [ˈprɪstiːn] *adj* makellos; **in ~ condition** in makellosem Zustand
privacy [ˈprɪvəsɪ] *n* Privatsphäre *f*
private [ˈpraɪvɪt] *adj* privat; (*life*) Privat-; (*thoughts, plans etc*) persönlich; (*place*) abgelegen; (*secretive: person*) verschlossen ▷ *n* (*Mil*) Gefreite(r) *m*; **"~"** (*on envelope*) „vertraulich"; (*on door*) „privat"; **in ~** privat; **in (his) ~ life** in seinem Privatleben; **to be in ~ practice** (*Med*) Privatpatienten haben; **~**

hearing (*Law*) nicht öffentliche Verhandlung *f*
private enterprise *n* Privatunternehmen *nt*
private eye *n* Privatdetektiv *m*
private limited company (*Brit*) *n* (*Comm*) = Aktiengesellschaft *f*
privately [ˈpraɪvɪtlɪ] *adv* privat; (*secretly*) insgeheim; **a ~ owned company** eine Firma im Privatbesitz
private parts *npl* (*Anat*) Geschlechtsteile *pl*
private property *n* Privatbesitz *m*
private school *n* (*fee-paying*) Privatschule *f*
privation [praɪˈveɪʃən] *n* Not *f*
privatize [ˈpraɪvɪtaɪz] *vt* privatisieren
privet [ˈprɪvɪt] *n* Liguster *m*
privilege [ˈprɪvɪlɪdʒ] *n* (*advantage*) Privileg *nt*; (*honour*) Ehre *f*
privileged [ˈprɪvɪlɪdʒd] *adj* privilegiert; **to be ~ to do sth** das Privileg *or* die Ehre haben, etw zu tun
privy [ˈprɪvɪ] *adj*: **to be ~ to** eingeweiht sein in +*acc*

Privy Councillor (*Brit*) *n* Geheimer Rat *m*
prize [praɪz] *n* Preis *m* ▷ *adj* (*prize-winning*) preisgekrönt; (*classic: example*) erstklassig ▷ *vt* schätzen; **~ idiot** (*inf*) Vollidiot *m*
prizefighter [ˈpraɪzfaɪtər] *n* Preisboxer *m*
prizegiving [ˈpraɪzɡɪvɪŋ] *n* Preisverleihung *f*
prize money *n* Geldpreis *m*
prizewinner [ˈpraɪzwɪnər] *n* Preisträger(in) *m(f)*
prizewinning [ˈpraɪzwɪnɪŋ] *adj* preisgekrönt
PRO *n abbr* = **public relations officer**
pro [prəu] *n* (*Sport*) Profi *m* ▷ *prep* (*in favour of*) pro +*acc*, für +*acc*; **the ~s and cons** das Für und Wider
pro- [prəu] *pref* (*in favour of*) Pro-, pro-; **~disarmament campaign** Kampagne *f* für Abrüstung
proactive [prəuˈæktɪv] *adj* proaktiv
probability [prɒbəˈbɪlɪtɪ] *n* Wahrscheinlichkeit *f*; **in all ~** aller Wahrscheinlichkeit nach
probable [ˈprɒbəbl] *adj* wahrscheinlich; **it seems ~ that ...** es ist wahrscheinlich, dass ...
probably [ˈprɒbəblɪ] *adv* wahrscheinlich
probate [ˈprəubɪt] *n* gerichtliche Testamentsbestätigung *f*
probation [prəˈbeɪʃən] *n*: **on ~** (*lawbreaker*) auf Bewährung; (*employee*) auf Probe
probationary [prəˈbeɪʃənrɪ] *adj* (*period*) Probe-

P

probationer [prəˈbeɪʃənəʳ] n (nurse: female) Lernschwester f; (: male) Lernpfleger m
probation officer n Bewährungshelfer(in) m(f)
probe [prəub] n (Med, Space) Sonde f; (enquiry) Untersuchung f ▷ vt (investigate) untersuchen; (poke) bohren in +dat
probity [ˈprəubɪtɪ] n Rechtschaffenheit f
problem [ˈprɒbləm] n Problem nt; **to have ~s with the car** Probleme or Schwierigkeiten mit dem Auto haben; **what's the ~?** wo fehlts?; **I had no ~ finding her** ich habe sie ohne Schwierigkeiten gefunden; **no ~!** kein Problem!
problematic [prɒbləˈmætɪk], **problematical** [prɒbləˈmætɪkl] adj problematisch
problem-solving [ˈprɒbləmsɒlvɪŋ] adj (skills, ability) zur Problemlösung ▷ n Problemlösung f
procedural [prəˈsiːdjurəl] adj (agreement, problem) verfahrensmäßig
procedure [prəˈsiːdʒəʳ] n Verfahren nt
proceed [prəˈsiːd] vi (carry on) fortfahren; (person: go) sich bewegen; **to ~ to do sth** etw tun; **to ~ with** fortfahren mit; **I am not sure how to ~** ich bin nicht sicher über die weitere Vorgehensweise; **to ~ against sb** (Law) gegen jdn gerichtlich vorgehen
proceedings [prəˈsiːdɪŋz] npl (organized events) Vorgänge pl; (Law) Verfahren nt; (records) Protokoll nt
proceeds [ˈprəusiːdz] npl Erlös m
process [ˈprəuses] n (series of actions) Verfahren nt; (Biol, Chem) Prozess m ▷ vt (raw materials, food, Comput: data) verarbeiten; (application) bearbeiten; (Phot) entwickeln; **in the ~** dabei; **to be in the ~ of doing sth** (gerade) dabei sein, etw zu tun
processed cheese [ˈprəusest-], (US) **process cheese** n Schmelzkäse m
processing [ˈprəusesɪŋ] n (Phot) Entwickeln nt
procession [prəˈseʃən] n Umzug m, Prozession f; **wedding/funeral ~** Hochzeits-/Trauerzug m
proclaim [prəˈkleɪm] vt verkünden, proklamieren
proclamation [prɒkləˈmeɪʃən] n Proklamation f
proclivity [prəˈklɪvɪtɪ] (form) n Vorliebe f
procrastinate [prəuˈkræstɪneɪt] vi zögern, zaudern
procrastination [prəukræstɪˈneɪʃən] n Zögern nt, Zaudern nt
procreation [prəukrɪˈeɪʃən] n Fortpflanzung f
procurator fiscal [ˈprɒkjureɪtə-] n (pl **procurators fiscal**) (Scot) ≈ Staatsanwalt m, ≈ Staatsanwältin f
procure [prəˈkjuəʳ] vt (obtain) beschaffen
procurement [prəˈkjuəmənt] n (Comm) Beschaffung f
prod [prɒd] vt (push: with finger, stick etc) stoßen, stupsen (inf); (fig: urge) anspornen ▷ n (with finger, stick etc) Stoß m, Stups m (inf); (fig: reminder) mahnender Hinweis m

prodigal [ˈprɒdɪgl] adj: **~ son** verlorener Sohn m
prodigious [prəˈdɪdʒəs] adj (cost, memory) ungeheuer
prodigy [ˈprɒdɪdʒɪ] n (person) Naturtalent nt; **child ~** Wunderkind nt
produce [n ˈprɒdjuːs, vt prəˈdjuːs] n (Agr) (Boden)produkte pl ▷ vt (result etc) hervorbringen; (goods, commodity) produzieren, herstellen; (Biol, Chem) erzeugen; (fig: evidence etc) liefern; (: passport etc) vorlegen; (play, film, programme) produzieren
producer [prəˈdjuːsəʳ] n (person) Produzent(in) m(f); (country, company) Produzent m, Hersteller m
product [ˈprɒdʌkt] n Produkt nt
production [prəˈdʌkʃən] n Produktion f; (Theat) Inszenierung f; **to go into ~** (goods) in Produktion gehen; **on ~ of** gegen Vorlage +gen
production agreement (US) n Produktivitätsabkommen nt
production line n Fließband nt, Fertigungsstraße f
production manager n Produktionsleiter(in) m(f)
productive [prəˈdʌktɪv] adj produktiv
productivity [prɒdʌkˈtɪvɪtɪ] n Produktivität f
productivity agreement (Brit) n Produktivitätsabkommen nt
productivity bonus n Leistungszulage f
Prof. n abbr (= professor) Prof.
profane [prəˈfeɪn] adj (language etc) profan; (secular) weltlich
profess [prəˈfes] vt (claim) vorgeben; (express: feeling, opinion) zeigen, bekunden; **I do not ~ to be an expert** ich behaupte nicht, ein Experte zu sein
professed [prəˈfest] adj (self-declared) erklärt
profession [prəˈfeʃən] n Beruf m; (people) Berufsstand m; **the ~s** die gehobenen Berufe
professional [prəˈfeʃənl] adj (organization, musician etc) Berufs-; (misconduct, advice) beruflich; (skilful) professionell ▷ n (doctor, lawyer, teacher etc) Fachmann m, Fachfrau f; (Sport) Profi m; (skilled person) Experte m, Expertin f; **to seek ~ advice** fachmännischen Rat einholen
professionalism [prəˈfeʃnəlɪzəm] n fachliches Können nt
professionally [prəˈfeʃnəlɪ] adv beruflich; (for a living) berufsmäßig; **I only know him ~** ich kenne ihn nur beruflich
professor [prəˈfesəʳ] n (Brit) Professor(in) m(f); (US, Canada) Dozent(in) m(f)
professorship [prəˈfesəʃɪp] n Professur f
proffer [ˈprɒfəʳ] vt (advice, drink, one's hand) anbieten; (apologies) aussprechen; (plate etc) hinhalten
proficiency [prəˈfɪʃənsɪ] n Können nt, Fertigkeiten pl
proficient [prəˈfɪʃənt] adj fähig; **to be ~ at** or **in** gut sein in +dat
profile [ˈprəufaɪl] n (of person's face) Profil nt; (fig: biography) Porträt nt; **to keep a low ~** (fig)

sich zurückhalten; **to have a high ~** (fig) eine
große Rolle spielen

profit ['prɔfɪt] n (Comm) Gewinn m, Profit m
▷ vi: **to ~ by** or **from** (fig) profitieren von; **~
and loss account** Gewinn-und-Verlust-
Rechnung; **to make a ~** einen Gewinn
machen; **to sell (sth) at a ~** (etw) mit Gewinn
verkaufen

profitability [prɔfɪtə'bɪlɪtɪ] n Rentabilität f

profitable ['prɔfɪtəbl] adj (business, deal)
rentabel, einträglich; (fig: useful) nützlich

profit centre n Bilanzabteilung f

profiteering [prɔfɪ'tɪərɪŋ] (pej) n
Profitmacherei f

profit-making ['prɔfɪtmeɪkɪŋ] adj (organization)
gewinnorientiert

profit margin n Gewinnspanne f

profit-sharing ['prɔfɪtʃɛərɪŋ] n
Gewinnbeteiligung f

profits tax (Brit) n Ertragssteuer f

profligate ['prɔflɪgɪt] adj (person, spending)
verschwenderisch; (waste) sinnlos; **~ with**
(extravagant) verschwenderisch mit

pro forma ['prəu'fɔ:mə] adj: **~ invoice** Pro-
forma-Rechnung f

profound [prə'faund] adj (shock) schwer, tief;
(effect, differences) weitreichend; (idea, book) tief
schürfend

profuse [prə'fju:s] adj (apologies)
überschwänglich

profusely [prə'fju:slɪ] adv (apologise, thank)
vielmals; (sweat, bleed) stark

profusion [prə'fju:ʒən] n Überfülle f

progeny ['prɔdʒɪnɪ] n Nachkommenschaft f

prognoses [prɔg'nəusi:z] npl of **prognosis**

prognosis [prɔg'nəusɪs] (pl **prognoses**) n
(Med, fig) Prognose f

program ['prəugræm] (Comput) n Programm nt
▷ vt programmieren

programme, (US) **program** ['prəugræm]
n Programm nt ▷ vt (machine, system)
programmieren

programmer ['prəugræmər] n
Programmierer(in) m(f)

programming, (US) **programing**
['prəugræmɪŋ] n Programmierung f

programming language n
Programmiersprache f

progress [n 'prəugrɛs, vi prə'grɛs] n Fortschritt
m; (improvement) Fortschritte pl ▷ vi (advance)
vorankommen; (become higher in rank)
aufsteigen; (continue) sich fortsetzen; **in ~**
(meeting, battle, match) im Gange; **to make ~**
Fortschritte machen

progression [prə'grɛʃən] n (development)
Fortschritt m, Entwicklung f; (series) Folge f

progressive [prə'grɛsɪv] adj (enlightened)
progressiv, fortschrittlich; (gradual)
fortschreitend

progressively [prə'grɛsɪvlɪ] adv (gradually)
zunehmend

progress report n (Med) Fortschrittsbericht m;
(Admin) Tätigkeitsbericht m

prohibit [prə'hɪbɪt] vt (ban) verbieten; **to ~ sb
from doing sth** jdm verbieten or untersagen,
etw zu tun; **"smoking ~ed"** „Rauchen
verboten"

prohibition [prəuɪ'bɪʃən] n Verbot nt; **P~** (US)
Prohibition f

prohibitive [prə'hɪbɪtɪv] adj (cost etc) untragbar

project [n 'prɔdʒɛkt, vt, vi prə'dʒɛkt] n (plan,
scheme) Projekt nt; (Scol) Referat nt ▷ vt (plan)
planen; (estimate) schätzen, voraussagen;
(light, film, picture) projizieren ▷ vi (stick out)
hervorragen

projectile [prə'dʒɛktaɪl] n Projektil nt,
Geschoss nt, Geschoß nt (Österr)

projection [prə'dʒɛkʃən] n (estimate) Schätzung
f, Voraussage f; (overhang) Vorsprung m; (Cine)
Projektion f

projectionist [prə'dʒɛkʃənɪst] n
Filmvorführer(in) m(f)

projection room n Vorführraum m

projector [prə'dʒɛktər] n Projektor m

proletarian [prəulɪ'tɛərɪən] adj proletarisch

proletariat [prəulɪ'tɛərɪət] n: **the ~** das
Proletariat

proliferate [prə'lɪfəreɪt] vi sich vermehren

proliferation [prəlɪfə'reɪʃən] n Vermehrung f,
Verbreitung f

prolific [prə'lɪfɪk] adj (artist, writer) produktiv

prologue, (US) **prolog** ['prəulɔg] n (of play, book)
Prolog m

prolong [prə'lɔŋ] vt verlängern

prom [prɔm] n abbr = **promenade**; (Mus)
= **promenade concert**; (US: college ball)
Studentenball m; siehe Info-Artikel

● **PROM**

● *Prom* (promenade concert) ist in
● Großbritannien ein Konzert, bei dem
● ein Teil der Zuhörer steht (ursprünglich
● spazieren ging). Die seit 1895 alljährlich
● stattfindenden Proms (seit 1941 immer in
● der Londoner Royal Albert Hall) zählen zu
● den bedeutendsten Musikereignissen in
● England. Der letzte Abend der Proms steht
● ganz im Zeichen des Patriotismus und
● gipfelt im Singen des Lieds „Land of Hope
● and Glory". In den USA und Kanada steht
● das Wort für *promenade*, ein Ball an einer
● *high school* oder einem *college*.

promenade [prɔmə'nɑ:d] n Promenade f

promenade concert (Brit) n
Promenadenkonzert nt

promenade deck n Promenadendeck nt

prominence ['prɔmɪnəns] n (importance)
Bedeutung f; **to rise to ~** bekannt werden

prominent ['prɔmɪnənt] adj (person)
prominent; (thing) bedeutend; (very noticeable)
herausragend; **he is ~ in the field of science**
er ist eine führende Persönlichkeit im
naturwissenschaftlichen Bereich

prominently ['prɔmɪnəntlɪ] adv (display, set)

p

723

deutlich sichtbar; **he figured ~ in the case** er spielte in dem Fall eine bedeutende Rolle

promiscuity [prɔmɪs'kjuːɪtɪ] n Promiskuität f

promiscuous [prə'mɪskjuəs] adj promisk

promise ['prɔmɪs] n (vow) Versprechen nt; (potential, hope) Hoffnung f ▷ vi versprechen ▷ vt: **to ~ sb sth, ~ sth to sb** jdm etw versprechen; **to make/break/keep a ~** ein Versprechen geben/brechen/halten; **a young man of ~** ein vielversprechender junger Mann; **she shows ~** sie gibt zu Hoffnungen Anlass; **it ~s to be lively** es verspricht lebhaft zu werden; **to ~ (sb) to do sth** (jdm) versprechen, etw zu tun

promising ['prɔmɪsɪŋ] adj vielversprechend

promissory note ['prɔmɪsərɪ-] n Schuldschein m

promontory ['prɔməntrɪ] n Felsvorsprung m

promote [prə'məut] vt (employee) befördern; (advertise) werben für; (encourage: peace etc) fördern; **the team was ~d to the first division** (Brit: Football) die Mannschaft stieg in die erste Division auf

promoter [prə'məutər] n (of concert, event) Veranstalter(in) m(f); (of cause, idea) Förderer m, Förderin f

promotion [prə'məuʃən] n (at work) Beförderung f; (of product, event) Werbung f; (of idea) Förderung f; (publicity campaign) Werbekampagne f

prompt [prɔmpt] adj prompt, sofortig ▷ adv (exactly) pünktlich ▷ n (Comput) Prompt m ▷ vt (cause) veranlassen; (when talking) auf die Sprünge helfen +dat; (Theat) soufflieren +dat; **they're very ~** (punctual) sie sind sehr pünktlich; **he was ~ to accept** er nahm unverzüglich an; **at 8 o'clock ~** (um) Punkt 8 Uhr; **to ~ sb to do sth** jdn dazu veranlassen, etw zu tun

prompter ['prɔmptər] n (Theat) Souffleur m, Souffleuse f

promptly ['prɔmptlɪ] adv (immediately) sofort; (exactly) pünktlich

promptness ['prɔmptnɪs] n Promptheit f

promulgate ['prɔməlgeɪt] vt (policy) bekannt machen, verkünden; (idea) verbreiten

prone [prəun] adj (face down) in Bauchlage; **to be ~ to sth** zu etw neigen; **she is ~ to burst into tears if ...** sie neigt dazu, in Tränen auszubrechen, wenn ...

prong [prɔŋ] n (of fork) Zinke f

pronoun ['prəunaun] n Pronomen nt, Fürwort nt

pronounce [prə'nauns] vt (word) aussprechen; (give verdict, opinion) erklären ▷ vi: **to ~ (up)on** sich äußern zu; **they ~d him dead/unfit to drive** sie erklärten ihn für tot/fahruntüchtig

pronounced [prə'naunst] adj (noticeable) ausgeprägt, deutlich

pronouncement [prə'naunsmənt] n Erklärung f

pronto ['prɔntəu] (inf) adv fix

pronunciation [prənʌnsɪ'eɪʃən] n Aussprache f

proof [pruːf] n (evidence) Beweis m; (Typ) (Korrektur)fahne f ▷ adj: **~ against** sicher vor +dat; **to be 70 % ~** (alcohol) ≈ einen Alkoholgehalt von 40% haben

proofreader ['pruːfriːdər] n Korrektor(in) m(f)

Prop. abbr (Comm: = proprietor) Inh.

prop [prɔp] n (support) Stütze f ▷ vt (lean): **to ~ sth against sth** etw an etw acc lehnen
  ▶ **prop up** vt sep (thing) (ab)stützen; (fig: government, industry) unterstützen

propaganda [prɔpə'gændə] n Propaganda f

propagate ['prɔpəgeɪt] vt (plants) züchten; (ideas etc) propagieren ▷ vi (plants, animals) sich fortpflanzen

propagation [prɔpə'geɪʃən] n (of ideas etc) Propagierung f; (of plants, animals) Fortpflanzung f

propel [prə'pɛl] vt (vehicle, machine) antreiben; (person) schubsen; (fig: person) treiben

propeller [prə'pɛlər] n Propeller m

propelling pencil [prə'pɛlɪŋ-] (Brit) n Drehbleistift m

propensity [prə'pɛnsɪtɪ] n: **a ~ for** or **to sth** ein Hang m or eine Neigung zu etw; **to have a ~ to do sth** dazu neigen, etw zu tun

proper ['prɔpər] adj (genuine, correct) richtig; (socially acceptable) schicklich; (inf: real) echt; **the town/city ~** die Stadt selbst; **to go through the ~ channels** den Dienstweg einhalten

properly ['prɔpəlɪ] adv (eat, work) richtig; (behave) anständig

proper noun n Eigenname m

property ['prɔpətɪ] n (possessions) Eigentum nt; (building and its land) Grundstück nt; (quality) Eigenschaft f; **it's their ~** es gehört ihnen

property developer n ≈ Grundstücksmakler(in) m(f)

property market n Immobilienmarkt m

property owner n Grundbesitzer(in) m(f)

property tax n Vermögenssteuer f

prophecy ['prɔfɪsɪ] n Prophezeiung f

prophesy ['prɔfɪsaɪ] vt prophezeien ▷ vi Prophezeiungen machen

prophet ['prɔfɪt] n Prophet m; **~ of doom** Unheilsprophet(in) m(f)

prophetic [prə'fɛtɪk] adj prophetisch

proportion [prə'pɔːʃən] n (part) Teil m; (number: of people, things) Anteil m; (ratio) Verhältnis nt; **in ~ to** im Verhältnis zu; **to be out of all ~ to sth** in keinem Verhältnis zu etw stehen; **to get sth in/out of ~** etw im richtigen/falschen Verhältnis sehen; **a sense of ~** (fig) ein Sinn für das Wesentliche

proportional [prə'pɔːʃənl] adj: **~ to** proportional zu

proportional representation n Verhältniswahlrecht nt

proportionate [prə'pɔːʃənɪt] adj = **proportional**

proposal [prə'pəuzl] n (plan) Vorschlag m; **~ (of marriage)** Heiratsantrag m

propose [prə'pəuz] vt (plan, idea) vorschlagen; (motion) einbringen; (toast) ausbringen ▷ vi (offer marriage) einen Heiratsantrag machen; **to ~ to do sth** or **doing sth** (intend) die Absicht haben, etw zu tun

proposer [prə'pəʊzə^r] n (of motion etc) Antragsteller(in) m(f)

proposition [prɔpə'zɪʃən] n (statement) These f; (offer) Angebot nt; **to make sb a ~** jdm ein Angebot machen

propound [prə'paʊnd] vt (idea etc) darlegen

proprietary [prə'praɪətərɪ] adj (brand, medicine) Marken-; (tone, manner) besitzergreifend

proprietor [prə'praɪətə^r] n (of hotel, shop etc) Inhaber(in) m(f); (of newspaper) Besitzer(in) m(f)

propriety [prə'praɪətɪ] n (seemliness) Schicklichkeit f

props [prɔps] npl (Theat) Requisiten pl

propulsion [prə'pʌlʃən] n Antrieb m

pro rata [prəʊ'rɑːtə] adj, adv anteilmäßig; **on a ~ basis** anteilmäßig

prosaic [prəʊ'zeɪɪk] adj prosaisch, nüchtern

Pros. Atty. (US) abbr = **prosecuting attorney**

proscribe [prə'skraɪb] (form) vt verbieten, untersagen

prose [prəʊz] n (not poetry) Prosa f; (Brit: Scol: translation) Übersetzung f in die Fremdsprache

prosecute ['prɔsɪkjuːt] vt (Law: person) strafrechtlich verfolgen; (: case) die Anklage vertreten in +dat

prosecuting attorney ['prɔsɪkjuːtɪŋ-] (US) n Staatsanwalt m, Staatsanwältin f

prosecution [prɔsɪ'kjuːʃən] n (Law: action) strafrechtliche Verfolgung f; (: accusing side) Anklage(vertretung) f

prosecutor ['prɔsɪkjuːtə^r] n Anklagevertreter(in) m(f); (also: **public prosecutor**) Staatsanwalt m, Staatsanwältin f

prospect [n 'prɔspekt, vi prə'spekt] n Aussicht f ⊳ vi: **to ~ (for)** suchen (nach); **prospects** npl (for work etc) Aussichten pl, Chancen pl; **we are faced with the ~ of higher unemployment** wir müssen mit der Möglichkeit rechnen, dass die Arbeitslosigkeit steigt

prospecting ['prɔspektɪŋ] n (for gold, oil etc) Suche f

prospective [prə'spektɪv] adj (son-in-law) zukünftig; (customer, candidate) voraussichtlich

prospectus [prə'spektəs] n (of college, company) Prospekt m

prosper ['prɔspə^r] vi (person) Erfolg haben; (business, city etc) gedeihen, florieren

prosperity [prɔ'sperɪtɪ] n Wohlstand m

prosperous ['prɔspərəs] adj (person) wohlhabend; (business, city etc) blühend

prostate ['prɔsteɪt] n (also: **prostate gland**) Prostata f

prostitute ['prɔstɪtjuːt] n (female) Prostituierte f; (male) männliche(r) Prostituierte(r) m, Strichjunge m (inf) ⊳ vt: **to ~ o.s.** (fig) sich prostituieren, sich unter Wert verkaufen

prostitution [prɔstɪ'tjuːʃən] n Prostitution f

prostrate ['prɔstreɪt] adj (face down) ausgestreckt (liegend); (fig)

niedergeschmettert ⊳ vt: **to ~ o.s. before** sich zu Boden werfen vor +dat

protagonist [prə'tægənɪst] n (of idea, movement) Verfechter(in) m(f); (Theat, Liter) Protagonist(in) m(f)

protect [prə'tekt] vt schützen

protection [prə'tekʃən] n Schutz m; **police ~** Polizeischutz m

protectionism [prə'tekʃənɪzəm] n Protektionismus m

protection racket n Organisation f zur Erpressung von Schutzgeld

protective [prə'tektɪv] adj (clothing, layer etc) Schutz-; (person) fürsorglich; **~ custody** Schutzhaft f

protector [prə'tektə^r] n (person) Beschützer(in) m(f); (device) Schutz m

protégé, protégée ['prəʊtɪʒeɪ] n Schützling m

protein ['prəʊtiːn] n Protein nt, Eiweiß nt

pro tem [prəʊ'tem] adv abbr (= pro tempore) vorläufig

protest [n 'prəʊtest, vi, vt prə'test] n Protest m ⊳ vi: **to ~ about** or **against** or **at sth** gegen etw protestieren ⊳ vt: **to ~ (that)** (insist) beteuern(, dass)

Protestant ['prɔtɪstənt] adj protestantisch ⊳ n Protestant(in) m(f)

protester [prə'testə^r] n (in demonstration) Demonstrant(in) m(f)

protest march n Protestmarsch m

protestor [prə'testə^r] n = **protester**

protocol ['prəʊtəkɔl] n Protokoll nt

prototype ['prəʊtətaɪp] n Prototyp m

protracted [prə'træktɪd] adj (meeting etc) langwierig, sich hinziehend; (absence) länger

protractor [prə'træktə^r] n (Geom) Winkelmesser m

protrude [prə'truːd] vi (rock, ledge, teeth) vorstehen

protuberance [prə'tjuːbərəns] n Auswuchs m

proud [praud] adj stolz; (arrogant) hochmütig; **~ of sb/sth** stolz auf jdn/etw; **to be ~ to do sth** stolz (darauf) sein, etw zu tun; **to do sb/o.s. ~** (inf) jdn/sich verwöhnen

proudly ['praudlɪ] adv stolz

prove [pruːv] vt beweisen ⊳ vi: **to ~ (to be) correct** sich als richtig herausstellen or erweisen; **to ~ o.s./itself) (to be) useful** sich als nützlich erweisen; **he was ~d right in the end** er hat schließlich recht behalten

proverb ['prɔvəːb] n Sprichwort nt

proverbial [prə'vəːbɪəl] adj sprichwörtlich

provide [prə'vaɪd] vt (food, money, shelter etc) zur Verfügung stellen; (answer, example etc) liefern; **to ~ sb with sth** jdm etw zur Verfügung stellen

▸ **provide for** vt fus (person) sorgen für; (future event) vorsorgen für

provided [prə'vaɪdɪd] conj: **~ (that)** vorausgesetzt(, dass)

Providence ['prɔvɪdəns] n die Vorsehung

providing [prə'vaɪdɪŋ] conj: **~ (that)** vorausgesetzt(, dass)

P

province ['prɔvɪns] n (of country) Provinz f; (responsibility etc) Bereich m, Gebiet nt; **provinces** npl: **the ~s** außerhalb der Hauptstadt liegende Landesteile, Provinz f

provincial [prə'vɪnʃəl] adj (town, newspaper etc) Provinz-; (pej: parochial) provinziell

provision [prə'vɪʒən] n (supplying) Bereitstellung f; (preparation) Vorsorge f, Vorkehrungen pl; (stipulation, clause) Bestimmung f; **provisions** npl (food) Proviant m; **to make ~ for** vorsorgen für; (for people) sorgen für; **there's no ~ for this in the contract** dies ist im Vertrag nicht vorgesehen

provisional [prə'vɪʒənl] adj vorläufig, provisorisch ▷ n: **P~** (Irish: Pol) Mitglied der provisorischen Irisch-Republikanischen Armee

provisional licence (Brit) n (Aut) vorläufige Fahrerlaubnis f

provisionally [prə'vɪʒnəlɪ] adv vorläufig

proviso [prə'vaɪzəu] n Vorbehalt m; **with the ~ that ...** unter dem Vorbehalt, dass ...

Provo ['prɔvəu] (Irish: inf) n abbr (Pol) = **Provisional**

provocation [prɔvə'keɪʃən] n Provokation f, Herausforderung f; **to be under ~** provoziert werden

provocative [prə'vɔkətɪv] adj provozierend, herausfordernd; (sexually stimulating) aufreizend

provoke [prə'vəuk] vt (person) provozieren, herausfordern; (fight) herbeiführen; (reaction etc) hervorrufen; **to ~ sb to do** or **into doing sth** jdn dazu provozieren, etw zu tun

provost ['prɔvəst] n (Brit: of university) Dekan m; (Scot) Bürgermeister(in) m(f)

prow [prau] n (of boat) Bug m

prowess ['prauɪs] n Können nt, Fähigkeiten pl; **his ~ as a footballer** sein fußballerisches Können

prowl [praul] vi (also: **prowl about, prowl around**) schleichen ▷ n: **on the ~** auf Streifzug

prowler ['praulə'] n Herumtreiber m

proximity [prɔk'sɪmɪtɪ] n Nähe f

proxy ['prɔksɪ] n: **by ~** durch einen Stellvertreter

prude [pru:d] n: **to be a ~** prüde sein

prudence ['pru:dns] n Klugheit f, Umsicht f

prudent ['pru:dnt] adj (sensible) klug

prudish ['pru:dɪʃ] adj prüde

prune [pru:n] n Backpflaume f ▷ vt (plant) stutzen, beschneiden

pry [praɪ] vi: **to ~ (into)** seine Nase hineinstecken (in +acc), herumschnüffeln (in +dat)

PS abbr (= postscript) PS

psalm [sɑ:m] n Psalm m

PSAT® (US) n abbr (= Preliminary Scholastic Aptitude Test) Schuleignungstest

PSBR (Brit) n abbr (Econ: = public sector borrowing requirement) staatlicher Kreditbedarf m

pseud [sju:d] (Brit: inf: pej) n Angeber(in) m(f)

pseudo- ['sju:dəu] pref Pseudo-

pseudonym ['sju:dənɪm] n Pseudonym nt

PSHE (Brit) n abbr (Scol) = **personal, social and health education**

PST (US) abbr (= Pacific Standard Time) pazifische Standardzeit

psyche ['saɪkɪ] n Psyche f

psychedelic [saɪkə'delɪk] adj (drug) psychedelisch; (clothes, colours) in psychedelischen Farben

psychiatric [saɪkɪ'ætrɪk] adj psychiatrisch

psychiatrist [saɪ'kaɪətrɪst] n Psychiater(in) m(f)

psychiatry [saɪ'kaɪətrɪ] n Psychiatrie f

psychic ['saɪkɪk] adj (person) übersinnlich begabt; (damage, disorder) psychisch ▷ n Mensch m mit übersinnlichen Fähigkeiten

psycho ['saɪkəu] (US: inf) n Verrückte(r) f(m)

psychoanalyse [saɪkəu'ænəlaɪz] vt psychoanalytisch behandeln, psychoanalysieren

psychoanalysis [saɪkəuə'nælɪsɪs] n Psychoanalyse f

psychoanalyst [saɪkəu'ænəlɪst] n Psychoanalytiker(in) m(f)

psychological [saɪkə'lɔdʒɪkl] adj psychologisch

psychologist [saɪ'kɔlədʒɪst] n Psychologe m, Psychologin f

psychology [saɪ'kɔlədʒɪ] n (science) Psychologie f; (character) Psyche f

psychopath ['saɪkəupæθ] n Psychopath(in) m(f)

psychoses [saɪ'kəusi:z] npl of **psychosis**

psychosis [saɪ'kəusɪs] (pl **psychoses**) n Psychose f

psychosomatic ['saɪkəusə'mætɪk] adj psychosomatisch

psychotherapy [saɪkəu'θɛrəpɪ] n Psychotherapie f

psychotic [saɪ'kɔtɪk] adj psychotisch

PT (Brit) n abbr (Scol: = physical training) Turnen nt

Pt abbr (in place names: = Point) Pt.

pt abbr = **pint; point**

PTA n abbr (= Parent-Teacher Association) Lehrer- und Elternverband

Pte (Brit) abbr (Mil) = **private**

PTO abbr (= please turn over) b. w.

PTV (US) n abbr (= pay television) Pay-TV nt; (= public television) öffentliches Fernsehen nt

pub [pʌb] n = **public house**; siehe Info-Artikel

PUB

Pub ist ein Gasthaus mit einer Lizenz zum Ausschank von alkoholischen Getränken. Ein Pub besteht meist aus verschiedenen gemütlichen (lounge, snug) oder einfacheren Räumen (public bar), in der oft auch Spiele wie Darts, Domino und Poolbillard zur Verfügung stehen. In Pubs werden vor allem mittags oft auch Mahlzeiten angeboten. Pubs sind normalerweise von 11 bis 23 Uhr geöffnet, aber manchmal nachmittags geschlossen.

pub-crawl ['pʌbkrɔ:l] (inf) n: **to go on a** ~ eine Kneipentour machen

puberty ['pju:bətɪ] n Pubertät f

pubic ['pju:bɪk] adj (hair) Scham-; ~ **bone** Schambein nt

public ['pʌblɪk] adj öffentlich ▷ n: **the** ~ (in general) die Öffentlichkeit; (particular set of people) das Publikum; **to be** ~ **knowledge** allgemein bekannt sein; **to make sth** ~ etw bekannt machen; **to go** ~ (Comm) in eine Aktiengesellschaft umgewandelt werden; **in** ~ in aller Öffentlichkeit; **the general** ~ die Allgemeinheit

public-address system [pʌblɪkə'dres-] n Lautsprecheranlage f

publican ['pʌblɪkən] n Gastwirt(in) m(f)

publication [pʌblɪ'keɪʃən] n Veröffentlichung f

public company n Aktiengesellschaft f

public convenience (Brit) n öffentliche Toilette f

public holiday n gesetzlicher Feiertag m

public house (Brit) n Gaststätte f

publicity [pʌb'lɪsɪtɪ] n (information) Werbung f; (attention) Publicity f

publicity tour n Werbetour f; **to be on a** ~ auf Werbetour sein

publicize ['pʌblɪsaɪz] vt (fact) bekannt machen; (event) Publicity machen für

public limited company n = Aktiengesellschaft f

publicly ['pʌblɪklɪ] adv öffentlich; **to be** ~ **owned** (Comm) in Staatsbesitz sein

public opinion n die öffentliche Meinung

public ownership n: **to be taken into** ~ verstaatlicht werden

Public Prosecutor n Staatsanwalt m, Staatsanwältin f

public relations n Public Relations pl, Öffentlichkeitsarbeit f

public relations officer n Beauftragte(r) f(m) für Öffentlichkeitsarbeit

public school n (Brit) Privatschule f; (US) staatliche Schule f; siehe Info-Artikel

○ **PUBLIC SCHOOL**
○
○ Public school bezeichnet vor allem
○ in England eine weiterführende
○ Privatschule, meist eine Internatsschule
○ mit hohem Prestige, an die oft auch
○ eine preparatory school angeschlossen
○ ist. Public schools werden von einem
○ Schulbeirat verwaltet und durch
○ Stiftungen und Schulgelder, die an den
○ bekanntesten Schulen wie Eton, Harrow
○ und Westminster sehr hoch sein können,
○ finanziert. Die meisten Schüler einer
○ public school gehen zur Universität,
○ oft nach Oxford oder Cambridge. Viele
○ Industrielle, Abgeordnete und hohe
○ Beamte haben eine public school besucht.

○ In Schottland und den USA bedeutet public
○ school eine öffentliche, vom Steuerzahler
○ finanzierte Schule.

public sector n: **the** ~ der öffentliche Sektor

public-service vehicle [pʌblɪk'sə:vɪs-] (Brit) n öffentliches Verkehrsmittel nt

public-spirited [pʌblɪk'spɪrɪtɪd] adj gemeinsinnig

public transport n öffentliche Verkehrsmittel pl

public utility n öffentlicher Versorgungsbetrieb m

public works npl öffentliche Bauprojekte pl

publish ['pʌblɪʃ] vt veröffentlichen

publisher ['pʌblɪʃəʳ] n (person) Verleger(in) m(f); (company) Verlag m

publishing ['pʌblɪʃɪŋ] n (profession) das Verlagswesen

publishing company n Verlag m, Verlagshaus nt

pub lunch n in Pubs servierter Imbiss

puce [pju:s] adj (face) hochrot

puck [pʌk] n (Ice Hockey) Puck m

pucker ['pʌkəʳ] vi (lips, face) sich verziehen; (fabric etc) Falten werfen ▷ vt (lips, face) verziehen; (fabric etc) Falten machen in +acc

pudding ['pudɪŋ] n (cooked sweet food) Süßspeise f; (Brit: dessert) Nachtisch m; **rice** ~ Milchreis m; **black** ~, **blood** ~ (US) = Blutwurst f

puddle ['pʌdl] n (of rain) Pfütze f; (of blood) Lache f

puerile ['pjuəraɪl] adj kindisch

Puerto Rico ['pwə:təu'ri:kəu] n Puerto Rico nt

puff [pʌf] n (of cigarette, pipe) Zug m; (gasp) Schnaufer m; (of air) Stoß m; (of smoke) Wolke f ▷ vt (also: **puff on**, **puff at**: cigarette, pipe) ziehen an +dat ▷ vi (gasp) keuchen, schnaufen

▶ **puff out** vt (one's chest) herausdrücken; (one's cheeks) aufblasen

puffed [pʌft] (inf) adj außer Puste

puffin ['pʌfɪn] n Papageientaucher m

puff pastry, (US) **puff paste** n Blätterteig m

puffy ['pʌfɪ] adj (eye) geschwollen; (face) aufgedunsen

pugnacious [pʌg'neɪʃəs] adj (person) streitsüchtig

pull [pul] vt (rope, handle etc) ziehen an +dat; (cart etc) ziehen; (close: curtain) zuziehen; (: blind) herunterlassen; (inf: attract: people) anlocken; (: sexual partner) aufreißen; (pint of beer) zapfen ▷ vi ziehen ▷ n (also fig: attraction) Anziehungskraft f; **to** ~ **the trigger** abdrücken; **to** ~ **a face** ein Gesicht schneiden; **to** ~ **a muscle** sich dat einen Muskel zerren; **not to** ~ **one's** or **any punches** (fig) sich dat keine Zurückhaltung auferlegen; **to** ~ **to pieces** (fig) zerreißen; **to** ~ **one's weight** (fig) sich ins Zeug legen; **to** ~ **o.s. together** sich zusammenreißen; **to** ~ **sb's leg** (fig) jdn auf den Arm nehmen; **to** ~ **strings (for sb)** seine Beziehungen (für jdn) spielen lassen; **to give sth a** ~ an etw dat ziehen

▶ **pull apart** vt (separate) trennen
▶ **pull away** vi (Aut) losfahren
▶ **pull back** vi (retreat) sich zurückziehen; (fig) einen Rückzieher machen (inf)
▶ **pull down** vt (building) abreißen
▶ **pull in** vi (Aut: at kerb) anhalten; (Rail) einfahren ▷ vt (inf: money) einsacken; (crowds, people) anlocken; (police: suspect) sich dat schnappen (inf)
▶ **pull off** vt (clothes etc) ausziehen; (fig: difficult thing) schaffen, bringen (inf)
▶ **pull out** vi (Aut: from kerb) losfahren; (: when overtaking) ausscheren; (Rail) ausfahren; (withdraw) sich zurückziehen ▷ vt (extract) herausziehen
▶ **pull over** vi (Aut) an den Straßenrand fahren
▶ **pull through** vi (Med) durchkommen
▶ **pull up** vi (Aut, Rail: stop) anhalten ▷ vt (raise) hochziehen; (uproot) herausreißen; (chair) heranrücken

pullback ['pulbæk] n (retreat) Rückzug m
pulley ['pulɪ] n Flaschenzug m
pull-out ['pulaut] n (in magazine) Beilage f (zum Heraustrennen)
pullover ['puləuvəʳ] n Pullover m
pulp [pʌlp] n (of fruit) Fruchtfleisch nt; (for paper) (Papier)brei m; (Liter: pej) Schund m ▷ adj (pej: magazine, novel) Schund-; **to reduce sth to a ~** etw zu Brei machen
pulpit ['pulpɪt] n Kanzel f
pulsate [pʌl'seɪt] vi (heart) klopfen; (music) pulsieren
pulse [pʌls] n (Anat) Puls m; (rhythm) Rhythmus m; **pulses** npl (Bot) Hülsenfrüchte pl; (Tech) Impuls m ▷ vi pulsieren; **to take** or **feel sb's ~** jdm den Puls fühlen; **to have one's finger on the ~ (of sth)** (fig) den Finger am Puls (einer Sache gen) haben
pulverize ['pʌlvəraɪz] vt pulverisieren; (fig: destroy) vernichten
puma ['pju:mə] n Puma m
pumice ['pʌmɪs] n (also: **pumice stone**) Bimsstein m
pummel ['pʌml] vt mit Faustschlägen bearbeiten
pump [pʌmp] n Pumpe f; (also: **petrol pump**) Zapfsäule f; (shoe) Turnschuh m ▷ vt pumpen; **to ~ sb for information** jdn aushorchen; **she had her stomach ~ed** ihr wurde der Magen ausgepumpt
▶ **pump up** vt (inflate) aufpumpen
pumpkin ['pʌmpkɪn] n Kürbis m
pun [pʌn] n Wortspiel nt
punch [pʌntʃ] n (blow) Schlag m; (fig: force) Schlagkraft f; (tool) Locher m; (drink) Bowle f, Punsch m ▷ vt (hit) schlagen; (make a hole in) lochen; **to ~ a hole in sth** ein Loch in etw acc stanzen
▶ **punch in** (US) vi (bei Arbeitsbeginn) stempeln
▶ **punch out** (US) vi (bei Arbeitsende) stempeln
Punch and Judy show n ≈ Kasper(le)theater nt

punch card, (US) **punched card** [pʌntʃt-] n Lochkarte f
punch-drunk ['pʌntʃdrʌŋk] (Brit) adj (boxer) angeschlagen
punch line n Pointe f
punch-up ['pʌntʃʌp] (Brit: inf) n Schlägerei f
punctual ['pʌŋktjuəl] adj pünktlich
punctuality [pʌŋktju'ælɪtɪ] n Pünktlichkeit f
punctually ['pʌŋktjuəlɪ] adv pünktlich; **it will start ~ at 6** es beginnt um Punkt 6 or pünktlich um 6
punctuation [pʌŋktju'eɪʃən] n Zeichensetzung f
punctuation mark n Satzzeichen nt
puncture ['pʌŋktʃəʳ] n (Aut) Reifenpanne f ▷ vt durchbohren; **I have a ~** ich habe eine Reifenpanne
pundit ['pʌndɪt] n Experte m, Expertin f
pungent ['pʌndʒənt] adj (smell, taste) scharf; (fig: speech, article etc) spitz, scharf
punish ['pʌnɪʃ] vt bestrafen; **to ~ sb for sth** jdn für etw bestrafen; **to ~ sb for doing sth** jdn dafür bestrafen, dass er etw getan hat
punishable ['pʌnɪʃəbl] adj strafbar
punishing ['pʌnɪʃɪŋ] adj (fig: exercise, ordeal) hart
punishment ['pʌnɪʃmənt] n (act) Bestrafung f; (way of punishing) Strafe f; **to take a lot of ~** (fig: car, person etc) viel abbekommen
punitive ['pju:nɪtɪv] adj (action) Straf-, zur Strafe; (measure) (extrem) hart
punk [pʌŋk] n (also: **punk rocker**) Punker(in) m(f); (also: **punk rock**) Punk m; (US: inf: hoodlum) Gangster m
punnet ['pʌnɪt] n (of raspberries etc) Körbchen nt
punt¹ [pʌnt] n (boat) Stechkahn m ▷ vi mit dem Stechkahn fahren
punt² [pʌnt] (Irish) n (currency) irisches Pfund nt
punter ['pʌntəʳ] (Brit) n (gambler) Wetter(in) m(f); **the ~s** (inf: customers) die Leute; **the average ~** (inf) Otto Normalverbraucher
puny ['pju:nɪ] adj (person, arms etc) schwächlich; (efforts) kläglich, kümmerlich
pup [pʌp] n (young dog) Welpe m, junger Hund m; **seal ~** Welpenjunge(s) nt
pupil ['pju:pl] n (Scol) Schüler(in) m(f); (of eye) Pupille f
puppet ['pʌpɪt] n Handpuppe f; (with strings, fig: person) Marionette f
puppet government n Marionettenregierung f
puppy ['pʌpɪ] n (young dog) Welpe m, junger Hund m
purchase ['pə:tʃɪs] n Kauf m; (grip) Halt m ▷ vt kaufen; **to get** or **gain (a) ~ on** (grip) Halt finden an +dat
purchase order n Bestellung f
purchase price n Kaufpreis m
purchaser ['pə:tʃɪsəʳ] n Käufer(in) m(f)
purchase tax n Kaufsteuer f
purchasing power ['pə:tʃɪsɪŋ-] n Kaufkraft f
pure [pjuəʳ] adj rein; **a ~ wool jumper** ein Pullover aus reiner Wolle; **it's laziness ~ and simple** es ist nichts als reine Faulheit

purebred ['pjuəbrɛd] *adj* reinrassig
puree ['pjʊəreɪ] *n* Püree *nt*
purely ['pjuəlɪ] *adv* rein
purgatory ['pə:gətərɪ] *n* (*Rel*) das Fegefeuer; (*fig*) die Hölle
purge [pə:dʒ] *n* (*Pol*) Säuberung *f* ▷ *vt* (*Pol: organization*) säubern; (: *extremists etc*) entfernen; (*fig: thoughts, mind etc*) befreien
purification [pjuərɪfɪ'keɪʃən] *n* Reinigung *f*
purify ['pjuərɪfaɪ] *vt* reinigen
purist ['pjuərɪst] *n* Purist(in) *m(f)*
puritan ['pjuərɪtən] *n* Puritaner(in) *m(f)*
puritanical [pjuərɪ'tænɪkl] *adj* puritanisch
purity ['pjuərɪtɪ] *n* Reinheit *f*
purl [pə:l] (*Knitting*) *n* linke Masche *f* ▷ *vt* links stricken
purloin [pə:'lɔɪn] (*form*) *vt* entwenden
purple ['pə:pl] *adj* violett
purport [pə:'pɔ:t] *vi*: **to ~ to be/do sth** vorgeben, etw zu sein/tun
purpose ['pə:pəs] *n* (*reason*) Zweck *m*; (*aim*) Ziel *nt*, Absicht *f*; **on ~** absichtlich; **for illustrative ~s** zu Illustrationszwecken; **for all practical ~s** praktisch (gesehen); **for the ~s of this meeting** zum Zweck dieses Treffens; **to little ~** mit wenig Erfolg; **to no ~** ohne Erfolg; **a sense of ~** ein Zielbewusstsein *nt*
purpose-built ['pə:pəs'bɪlt] (*Brit*) *adj* speziell angefertigt, Spezial-
purposeful ['pə:pəsful] *adj* entschlossen
purposely ['pə:pəslɪ] *adv* absichtlich, bewusst
purr [pə:ʳ] *vi* (*cat*) schnurren
purse [pə:s] *n* (*Brit: for money*) Geldbörse *f*, Portemonnaie *nt*; (*US: handbag*) Handtasche *f* ▷ *vt* (*lips*) kräuseln
purser ['pə:səʳ] *n* (*Naut*) Zahlmeister *m*
purse-snatcher ['pə:ssnætʃəʳ] (*US*) *n* Handtaschendieb *m*
pursue [pə'sju:] *vt* (*person, vehicle, plan, aim*) verfolgen; (*fig: interest etc*) nachgehen +*dat*
pursuer [pə'sju:əʳ] *n* Verfolger(in) *m(f)*
pursuit [pə'sju:t] *n* (*chase*) Verfolgung *f*; (*pastime*) Beschäftigung *f*; (*fig*): **~ of** (*of happiness etc*) Streben *nt* nach; **in ~ of** (*person, car etc*) auf der Jagd nach; (*fig: happiness etc*) im Streben nach
purveyor [pə'veɪəʳ] (*form*) *n* (*of goods etc*) Lieferant *m*
pus [pʌs] *n* Eiter *m*
push [puʃ] *n* Stoß *m*, Schub *m* ▷ *vt* (*press*) drücken; (*shove*) schieben; (*fig: put pressure on: person*) bedrängen; (: *promote: product*) werben für; (*inf: sell: drugs*) pushen ▷ *vi* (*press*) drücken; (*shove*) schieben; **at the ~ of a button** auf Knopfdruck; **at a ~** (*Brit: inf*) notfalls; **to ~ a door open/shut** eine Tür auf-/zudrücken; **"~"** (*on door*) „drücken"; (*on bell*) „klingeln"; **to be ~ed for time/money** (*inf*) in Zeitnot/Geldnot sein; **she is ~ing fifty** (*inf*) sie geht auf die fünfzig zu; **to ~ for** (*demand*) drängen auf +*acc*
▶ **push around** *vt* (*bully*) herumschubsen

▶ **push aside** *vt* beiseiteschieben
▶ **push in** *vi* sich dazwischendrängeln
▶ **push off** (*inf*) *vi* abhauen
▶ **push on** *vi* (*continue*) weitermachen
▶ **push over** *vt* umstoßen
▶ **push through** *vt* (*measure etc*) durchdrücken
▶ **push up** *vt* (*total, prices*) hochtreiben
push-bike ['puʃbaɪk] (*Brit*) *n* Fahrrad *nt*
push-button ['puʃbʌtn] *adj* (*machine, calculator*) Drucktasten-
pushchair ['puʃtʃeəʳ] (*Brit*) *n* Sportwagen *m*
pusher ['puʃəʳ] *n* (*drug dealer*) Pusher *m*
pushover ['puʃəuvəʳ] (*inf*) *n*: **it's a ~** das ist ein Kinderspiel
push-up ['puʃʌp] (*US*) *n* Liegestütz *m*
pushy ['puʃɪ] (*pej*) *adj* aufdringlich
puss [pus] (*inf*) *n* Mieze *f*
pussy ['pusɪ], **pussycat** ['pusɪkæt] (*inf*) *n* Mieze(katze) *f*
put [put] (*pt, pp* ~) *vt* (*thing*) tun; (: *upright*) stellen; (: *flat*) legen; (*person: in room, institution etc*) stecken; (: *in state, situation*) versetzen; (*express: idea etc*) ausdrücken; (*present: case, view*) vorbringen; (*ask: question*) stellen; (*classify*) einschätzen; (*write, type*) schreiben; **to ~ sb in a good/bad mood** jdn gut/schlecht stimmen; **to ~ sb to bed** jdn ins Bett bringen; **to ~ sb to a lot of trouble** jdm viele Umstände machen; **how shall I ~ it?** wie soll ich es sagen *or* ausdrücken?; **to ~ a lot of time into sth** viel Zeit auf etw *acc* verwenden; **to ~ money on a horse** Geld auf ein Pferd setzen; **the cost is now ~ at 2 million pounds** die Kosten werden jetzt auf 2 Millionen Pfund geschätzt; **I ~ it to you that ...** (*Brit*) ich behaupte, dass ...; **to stay ~** (an Ort und Stelle) bleiben
▶ **put about** *vi* (*Naut*) den Kurs ändern ▷ *vt* (*rumour*) verbreiten
▶ **put across** *vt* (*ideas etc*) verständlich machen
▶ **put around** *vt* = **put about**
▶ **put aside** *vt* (*work*) zur Seite legen; (*idea, problem*) unbeachtet lassen; (*sum of money*) zurücklegen
▶ **put away** *vt* (*store*) wegräumen; (*inf: consume*) verdrücken; (*save: money*) zurücklegen; (*imprison*) einsperren
▶ **put back** *vt* (*replace*) zurücktun; (: *upright*) zurückstellen; (: *flat*) zurücklegen; (*postpone*) verschieben; (*delay*) zurückwerfen
▶ **put by** *vt* (*money, supplies etc*) zurücklegen
▶ **put down** *vt* (*upright*) hinstellen; (*flat*) hinlegen; (*cup, glass*) absetzen; (*in writing*) aufschreiben; (*riot, rebellion*) niederschlagen; (*humiliate*) demütigen; (*kill*) töten
▶ **put down to** *vt* (*attribute*) zurückführen auf +*acc*
▶ **put forward** *vt* (*ideas etc*) vorbringen; (*watch, clock*) vorstellen; (*date, meeting*) vorverlegen
▶ **put in** *vt* (*application, complaint*) einreichen; (*time, effort*) investieren; (*gas, electricity etc*) installieren ▷ *vi* (*Naut*) einlaufen
▶ **put in for** *vt fus* (*promotion*) sich bewerben um; (*leave*) beantragen

▶ **put off** vt (delay) verschieben; (distract) ablenken; **to ~ sb off sth** (discourage) jdn von etw abbringen

▶ **put on** vt (clothes, brake) anziehen; (glasses, kettle) aufsetzen; (make-up, ointment etc) auftragen; (light, TV) anmachen; (play etc) aufführen; (record, tape, video) auflegen; (dinner etc) aufsetzen; (assume: look, behaviour etc) annehmen; (inf: tease) auf den Arm nehmen; (extra bus, train etc) einsetzen; **to ~ on airs** sich zieren; **to ~ on weight** zunehmen

▶ **put on to** vt (tell about) vermitteln

▶ **put out** vt (fire, light) ausmachen; (take out: rubbish) herausbringen; (: cat etc) vor die Tür setzen; (one's hand) ausstrecken; (story, announcement) verbreiten; (Brit: dislocate: shoulder etc) verrenken; (inf: inconvenience) Umstände machen +dat ▷ vi (Naut): **to ~ out to sea** in See stechen; **to ~ out from Plymouth** von Plymouth auslaufen

▶ **put through** vt (Tel: person) verbinden; (: call) durchstellen; (plan, agreement) durchbringen; **~ me through to Ms Blair** verbinden Sie mich mit Frau Blair

▶ **put together** vt (furniture etc) zusammenbauen; (plan, campaign) ausarbeiten; **more than the rest of them ~ together** mehr als alle anderen zusammen

▶ **put up** vt (fence, building) errichten; (tent) aufstellen; (umbrella) aufspannen; (hood) hochschlagen; (poster, sign etc) anbringen; (price, cost) erhöhen; (accommodate) unterbringen; **to ~ up resistance** Widerstand leisten; **to ~ up a fight** sich zur Wehr setzen; **to ~ sb up to sth** jdn zu etw anstiften; **to ~ sb up to doing sth** jdn dazu

anstiften, etw zu tun; **to ~ sth up for sale** etw zum Verkauf anbieten

▶ **put upon** vt fus: **to be ~ upon** (imposed on) ausgenutzt werden

▶ **put up with** vt fus sich abfinden mit

putative ['pju:tətɪv] adj mutmaßlich

putrid ['pju:trɪd] adj (mess, meat) faul

putt [pʌt] n Putt m

putter ['pʌtər] n (Golf) Putter m ▷ vi (US) = **potter**

putting green ['pʌtɪŋ-] n kleiner Golfplatz m zum Putten

putty ['pʌtɪ] n Kitt m

put-up ['pʊtʌp] adj: **a ~ job** ein abgekartetes Spiel nt

puzzle ['pʌzl] n (game, toy) Geschicklichkeitsspiel nt; (mystery) Rätsel nt ▷ vt verwirren ▷ vi: **to ~ over sth** sich dat über etw acc den Kopf zerbrechen; **to be ~d as to why ...** vor einem Rätsel stehen, warum ...

puzzling ['pʌzlɪŋ] adj verwirrend; (mysterious) rätselhaft

PVC n abbr (= polyvinyl chloride) PVC nt

Pvt. (US) abbr (Mil) = **private**

p.w. abbr (= per week) pro Woche

pygmy ['pɪgmɪ] n Pygmäe m

pyjamas, (US) **pajamas** [pə'dʒɑːməz] npl Pyjama m, Schlafanzug m; **a pair of ~** ein Schlafanzug

pylon ['paɪlən] n Mast m

pyramid ['pɪrəmɪd] n Pyramide f

Pyrenean [pɪrə'niːən] adj pyrenäisch

Pyrenees [pɪrə'niːz] npl: **the ~** die Pyrenäen pl

Pyrex® ['paɪrɛks] n ≈ Jenaer Glas® nt ▷ adj (dish, bowl) aus Jenaer Glas®

python ['paɪθən] n Pythonschlange f

Qq

Q, q [kjuː] *n* (*letter*) Q *nt*, q *nt*; **Q for Queen** ≈ Q wie Quelle
Qatar [kæˈtɑːʳ] *n* Katar *nt*
QC (*Brit*) *n abbr* (*Law*: = *Queen's Counsel*) Kronanwalt *m*; *siehe Info-Artikel*

QCA (*Brit*) *n abbr* (= *Qualifications and Curriculum Authority*) Behörde, die in England für die Entwicklung von Lehrplänen und deren Beachtung zuständig ist
QED *abbr* (= *quod erat demonstrandum*) q. e. d.
QM *n abbr* (*Mil*) = **quartermaster**
q.t. (*inf*) *n abbr* (= *quiet*): **on the ~** heimlich
quack [kwæk] *n* (*of duck*) Schnattern *nt*, Quaken *nt*; (*inf: pej: doctor*) Quacksalber *m* ▷ *vi* schnattern, quaken
quad [kwɔd] *abbr* = **quadrangle**; (= *quadruplet*) Vierling *m*
quadrangle [ˈkwɔdræŋgl] *n* (*courtyard*) Innenhof *m*
quadrilateral [kwɔdrɪˈlætərəl] *n* Viereck *nt*
quadruped [ˈkwɔdruped] *n* Vierfüßer *m*
quadruple [kwɔˈdruːpl] *vt* vervierfachen ▷ *vi* sich vervierfachen
quadruplets [kwɔˈdruːplɪts] *npl* Vierlinge *pl*
quagmire [ˈkwægmaɪəʳ] *n* (*also fig*) Sumpf *m*
quail [kweɪl] *n* Wachtel *f* ▷ *vi*: **he ~ed at the thought/before her anger** ihm schauderte bei dem Gedanken/vor ihrem Zorn
quaint [kweɪnt] *adj* (*house, village*) malerisch; (*ideas, customs*) urig, kurios
quake [kweɪk] *vi* beben, zittern ▷ *n* = **earthquake**
Quaker [ˈkweɪkəʳ] *n* Quäker(in) *m(f)*
qualification [kwɔlɪfɪˈkeɪʃən] *n* (*often pl: degree etc*) Qualifikation *f*; (*attribute*) Voraussetzung *f*; (*reservation*) Vorbehalt *m*; **what are your ~s?**

welche Qualifikationen haben Sie?
qualified [ˈkwɔlɪfaɪd] *adj* (*trained: doctor etc*) qualifiziert, ausgebildet; (*limited: agreement, praise*) bedingt; **to be/feel ~ to do sth** (*fit, competent*) qualifiziert sein/sich qualifiziert fühlen, etw zu tun; **it was a ~ success** es war kein voller Erfolg; **he's not ~ for the job** ihm fehlen die Qualifikationen für die Stelle
qualify [ˈkwɔlɪfaɪ] *vt* (*entitle*) qualifizieren; (*modify: statement*) einschränken ▷ *vi* (*pass examination*) sich qualifizieren; **to ~ for** (*be eligible*) die Berechtigung erlangen für; (*in competition*) sich qualifizieren für; **to ~ as an engineer** die Ausbildung zum Ingenieur abschließen
qualifying [ˈkwɔlɪfaɪɪŋ] *adj*: **~ exam** Auswahlprüfung *f*; **~ game** Vorrunden- *or* Qualifikationsspiel *f*; **~ group** Vorrunden- *or* Qualifikationsgruppe *f*; **~ round** Qualifikationsrunde *f*
qualitative [ˈkwɔlɪtətɪv] *adj* qualitativ
quality [ˈkwɔlɪtɪ] *n* Qualität *f*; (*characteristic*) Eigenschaft *f* ▷ *cpd* Qualitäts-; **of good/poor ~** von guter/schlechter Qualität; **~ of life** Lebensqualität *f*
quality control *n* Qualitätskontrolle *f*
quality papers (*Brit*) *npl*: **the ~** die seriösen Zeitungen *pl*; *siehe Info-Artikel*

qualm [kwɑːm] *n* Bedenken *pl*; **to have ~s about sth** Bedenken wegen etw haben
quandary [ˈkwɔndrɪ] *n*: **to be in a ~** in einem Dilemma sein
quango [ˈkwæŋgəu] (*Brit*) *n abbr* (= *quasi-autonomous nongovernmental organization*) ≈ (regierungsunabhängige) Kommission *f*
quantifiable [ˈkwɔntɪfaɪəbl] *adj*

q

quantifizierbar

quantitative ['kwɒntɪtətɪv] *adj* quantitativ

quantity ['kwɒntɪtɪ] *n* (*amount*) Menge *f*; **in large/small quantities** in großen/kleinen Mengen; **in ~** (*in bulk*) in großen Mengen; **an unknown ~** (*fig*) eine unbekannte Größe

quantity surveyor *n* Baukostenkalkulator(in) *m(f)*

quantum leap ['kwɒntəm-] *n* (*Phys*) Quantensprung *m*; (*fig*) Riesenschritt *m*

quarantine ['kwɒrntiːn] *n* Quarantäne *f*; **in ~** in Quarantäne

quark [kwɑːk] *n* (*cheese*) Quark *m*; (*Phys*) Quark *nt*

quarrel ['kwɒrl] *n* (*argument*) Streit *m* ▷ *vi* sich streiten; **to have a ~ with sb** sich mit jdm streiten; **I've no ~ with him** ich habe nichts gegen ihn; **I can't ~ with that** dagegen kann ich nichts einwenden

quarrelsome ['kwɒrəlsəm] *adj* streitsüchtig

quarry ['kwɒrɪ] *n* (*for stone*) Steinbruch *m*; (*prey*) Beute *f* ▷ *vt* (*marble etc*) brechen

quart [kwɔːt] *n* Quart *nt*

quarter ['kwɔːtər] *n* Viertel *nt*; (*US: coin*) 25-Cent-Stück *nt*; (*of year*) Quartal *nt*; (*district*) Viertel *nt* ▷ *vt* (*divide*) vierteln; (*Mil: lodge*) einquartieren; **quarters** *npl* (*Mil*) Quartier *nt*; (*also:* **living quarters**) Unterkünfte *pl*; **a ~ of an hour** eine viertel Stunde; **it's a ~ to three**, **it's a ~ of three** (*US*) es ist Viertel vor drei; **it's a ~ past three, it's a ~ after three** (*US*) es ist Viertel nach drei; **from all ~s** aus allen Richtungen; **at close ~s** aus unmittelbarer Nähe

quarterback ['kwɔːtəbæk] *n* (*American Football*) Quarterback *m*

quarterdeck ['kwɔːtədɛk] *n* (*Naut*) Quarterdeck *nt*

quarterfinal ['kwɔːtəˈfaɪnl] *n* Viertelfinale *nt*

quarterly ['kwɔːtəlɪ] *adj, adv* vierteljährlich ▷ *n* Vierteljahresschrift *f*

quartermaster ['kwɔːtəmɑːstər] *n* (*Mil*) Quartiermeister *m*

quartet [kwɔːˈtɛt] *n* (*Mus*) Quartett *nt*

quarto ['kwɔːtəu] *n* (*size of paper*) Quartformat *nt*; (*book*) im Quartformat

quartz [kwɔːts] *n* Quarz *m* ▷ *cpd* (*watch, clock*) Quarz-

quash [kwɒʃ] *vt* (*verdict*) aufheben

quasi- ['kweɪzaɪ] *pref* quasi-

quaver ['kweɪvər] *n* (*Brit: Mus*) Achtelnote *f* ▷ *vi* (*voice*) beben, zittern

quay [kiː] *n* Kai *m*

quayside ['kiːsaɪd] *n* Kai *m*

queasiness ['kwiːzɪnɪs] *n* Übelkeit *f*

queasy ['kwiːzɪ] *adj* (*nauseous*) übel; **I feel ~** mir ist übel *or* schlecht

Quebec [kwɪˈbɛk] *n* Quebec *nt*

queen [kwiːn] *n* (*also* Zool) Königin *f*; (*Cards, Chess*) Dame *f*

queen mother *n* Königinmutter *f*

Queen's speech (*Brit*) *n* ≈ Regierungserklärung *f*; *siehe Info-Artikel*

queer [kwɪər] *adj* (*odd*) sonderbar, seltsam ▷ *n* (*inf!: pej: male homosexual*) Schwule(r) *m*; **I feel ~** (*Brit: unwell*) mir ist ganz komisch

quell [kwɛl] *vt* (*riot*) niederschlagen; (*fears*) überwinden

quench [kwɛntʃ] *vt*: **to ~ one's thirst** seinen Durst stillen

querulous ['kwɛrʊləs] *adj* nörglerisch

query ['kwɪərɪ] *n* Anfrage *f* ▷ *vt* (*check*) nachfragen bezüglich +*gen*; (*express doubt about*) bezweifeln

quest [kwɛst] *n* Suche *f*

question ['kwɛstʃən] *n* Frage *f* ▷ *vt* (*interrogate*) befragen; (*doubt*) bezweifeln; **to ask sb a question, put a ~ to sb** jdm eine Frage stellen; **to bring** *or* **call sth into ~** etw infrage stellen; **the ~ is …** die Frage ist …; **there's no ~ of him playing for England** es ist ausgeschlossen, dass er für England spielt; **the person/night in ~** die fragliche Person/ Nacht; **to be beyond ~** außer Frage stehen; **to be out of the ~** nicht infrage kommen

questionable ['kwɛstʃənəbl] *adj* fraglich

questioner ['kwɛstʃənər] *n* Fragesteller(in) *m(f)*

questioning ['kwɛstʃənɪŋ] *adj* (*look*) fragend; (*mind*) forschend ▷ *n* (*Police*) Vernehmung *f*

question mark *n* Fragezeichen *nt*

questionnaire [kwɛstʃəˈnɛər] *n* Fragebogen *m*

queue [kjuː] (*Brit*) *n* Schlange *f* ▷ *vi* (*also:* **queue up**) Schlange stehen

quibble ['kwɪbl] *vi*: **to ~ about** *or* **over** sich streiten über +*acc*; **to ~ with** herumnörgeln an +*dat* ▷ *n* Krittelei *f*

quiche [kiːʃ] *n* Quiche *f*

quick [kwɪk] *adj* schnell; (*mind, wit*) wach; (*look, visit*) flüchtig ▷ *adv* schnell ▷ *n*: **to cut sb to the ~** (*fig*) jdn tief verletzen; **be ~!** mach schnell!; **to be ~ to act** schnell handeln; **she was ~ to see that …** sie begriff schnell, dass …; **she has a ~ temper** sie wird leicht hitzig

quicken ['kwɪkən] *vt* beschleunigen ▷ *vi* schneller werden, sich beschleunigen

quick-fire ['kwɪkfaɪər] *adj* (*questions*) wie aus der Pistole

quick fix *n* Sofortlösung *f*

quicklime ['kwɪklaɪm] *n* ungelöschter Kalk *m*

quickly ['kwɪklɪ] *adv* schnell

quickness ['kwɪknɪs] *n* Schnelligkeit *f*; **~ of mind** Scharfsinn *m*

quicksand ['kwɪksænd] n Treibsand m
quickstep ['kwɪkstɛp] n Quickstepp m
quick-tempered [kwɪk'tɛmpəd] adj hitzig, leicht erregbar
quick-witted [kwɪk'wɪtɪd] adj schlagfertig
quid [kwɪd] (Brit: inf) n inv Pfund nt
quid pro quo ['kwɪdprəu'kwəu] n Gegenleistung f
quiet ['kwaɪət] adj leise; (place) ruhig, still; (silent, reserved) still; (business, day) ruhig; (without fuss etc: wedding) in kleinem Rahmen ▷ n (peacefulness) Stille f, Ruhe f; (silence) Ruhe f ▷ vt, vi (US) = **quieten**; **keep** or **be ~!** sei still!; **I'll have a ~ word with him** ich werde mal unter vier Augen mit ihm reden; **on the ~** (in secret) heimlich
quieten ['kwaɪətn] (Brit: also: **quieten down**) vi ruhiger werden ▷ vt (person, animal) beruhigen
quietly ['kwaɪətlɪ] adv leise; (silently) still; (calmly) ruhig; **~ confident** insgeheim sicher
quietness ['kwaɪətnɪs] n (peacefulness) Ruhe f; (silence) Stille f
quill [kwɪl] n (pen) Feder f; (of porcupine) Stachel m
quilt [kwɪlt] n Decke f; (also: **continental quilt**) Federbett nt
quin [kwɪn] (Brit) n abbr (= quintuplet) Fünfling m
quince [kwɪns] n Quitte f
quinine [kwɪ'niːn] n Chinin nt
quintet [kwɪn'tɛt] n (Mus) Quintett nt
quintuplets [kwɪn'tjuːplɪts] npl Fünflinge pl
quip [kwɪp] n witzige or geistreiche Bemerkung f ▷ vt witzeln
quire ['kwaɪə'] n (of paper) 24 Bogen Papier
quirk [kwəːk] n Marotte f; **a ~ of fate** eine Laune des Schicksals
quit [kwɪt] (pt, pp ~ or **quitted**) vt (smoking) aufgeben; (job) kündigen; (premises) verlassen ▷ vi (give up) aufgeben; (resign) kündigen; **to ~**

doing sth aufhören, etw zu tun; **~ stalling!** (US: inf) weichen Sie nicht ständig aus!;
notice to ~ (Brit) Kündigung f
quite [kwaɪt] adv (rather) ziemlich; (entirely) ganz; **not ~** nicht ganz; **I ~ like it** ich mag es ganz gern; **I ~ understand** ich verstehe; **I don't ~ remember** ich erinnere mich nicht genau; **not ~ as many as the last time** nicht ganz so viele wie das letzte Mal; **that meal was ~ something!** das Essen konnte sich sehen lassen!; **it was ~ a sight** das war vielleicht ein Anblick; **~ a few of them** eine ganze Reihe von Ihnen; **~ (so)!** ganz recht!
quits [kwɪts] adj: **we're ~** wir sind quitt; **let's call it ~** lassen wirs dabei
quiver ['kwɪvə'] vi zittern
quiz [kwɪz] n (game) Quiz nt ▷ vt (question) befragen
quizzical ['kwɪzɪkl] adj (look, smile) wissend
quoits [kwɔɪts] npl (game) Wurfspiel mit Ringen
quorum ['kwɔːrəm] n Quorum nt
quota ['kwəutə] n (allowance) Quote f
quotation [kwəu'teɪʃən] n (from book etc) Zitat nt; (estimate) Preisangabe f; (Comm) Kostenvoranschlag m
quotation marks npl Anführungszeichen pl
quote [kwəut] n (from book etc) Zitat nt; (estimate) Kostenvoranschlag m ▷ vt zitieren; (fact, example) anführen; (price) nennen; **quotes** npl (quotation marks) Anführungszeichen pl; **in ~s** in Anführungszeichen; **the figure ~d for the repairs** die für die Reparatur genannte Summe; **~ ... unquote** Zitat Anfang ... Zitat Ende
quotient ['kwəuʃənt] n Quotient m
qv abbr (= quod vide) s.d.
qwerty keyboard ['kwəːtɪ-] n Qwerty-Tastatur f

q

Rr

R¹, r [ɑːʳ] *n* (*letter*) R *nt*, r *nt*; **R for Robert, R for Roger** (*US*) ≈ R wie Richard

R² [ɑːʳ] *abbr* (= *Réaumur* (*scale*)) R; (*US: Cine*: = *restricted*) *Klassifikation für nicht jugendfreie Filme*

R. *abbr* (= *right*) r. = *river*; (*US: Pol*) = **republican**; (*Brit*: = *Rex*) *König*; (= *Regina*) *Königin*

RA *abbr* (*Mil*) = **rear admiral** ▷ *n abbr* (*Brit*: = *Royal Academy*) *Gesellschaft zur Förderung der Künste*; (= *Royal Academician*) *Mitglied der Royal Academy*

RAAF *n abbr* (*Mil*: = *Royal Australian Air Force*) *australische Luftwaffe f*

Rabat [rəˈbɑːt] *n* Rabat *nt*

rabbi [ˈræbaɪ] *n* Rabbi *m*

rabbit [ˈræbɪt] *n* Kaninchen *nt* ▷ *vi* (*Brit: inf: also:* **to rabbit on**) quatschen, schwafeln

rabbit hole *n* Kaninchenbau *m*

rabbit hutch *n* Kaninchenstall *m*

rabble [ˈræbl] (*pej*) *n* Pöbel *m*

rabid [ˈræbɪd] *adj* (*animal*) tollwütig; (*fig: fanatical*) fanatisch

rabies [ˈreɪbiːz] *n* Tollwut *f*

RAC (*Brit*) *n abbr* (= *Royal Automobile Club*) *Autofahrerorganisation*, ≈ ADAC *m*

raccoon [rəˈkuːn] *n* Waschbär *m*

race [reɪs] *n* (*species*) Rasse *f*; (*competition*) Rennen *nt*; (*for power, control*) Wettlauf *m* ▷ *vt* (*horse, pigeon*) an Wettbewerben teilnehmen lassen; (*car etc*) ins Rennen schicken; (*person*) um die Wette laufen mit ▷ *vi* (*compete*) antreten; (*hurry*) rennen; (*pulse, heart*) rasen; (*engine*) durchdrehen; **the human ~** die Menschheit; **a ~ against time** ein Wettlauf mit der Zeit; **he ~d across the road** er raste über die Straße; **to ~ in/out** hinein-/hinausstürzen

race car (*US*) *n* = **racing car**

race car driver (*US*) *n* = **racing driver**

racecourse [ˈreɪskɔːs] *n* Rennbahn *f*

racehorse [ˈreɪshɔːs] *n* Rennpferd *nt*

race meeting *n* Rennveranstaltung *f*

race relations *npl* Beziehungen *pl* zwischen den Rassen

racetrack [ˈreɪstræk] *n* Rennbahn *f*; (*US*) = **racecourse**

racial [ˈreɪʃl] *adj* Rassen-

racialism [ˈreɪʃlɪzəm] *n* Rassismus *m*

racialist [ˈreɪʃlɪst] *adj* rassistisch ▷ *n* (*pej*) Rassist(in) *m(f)*

racing [ˈreɪsɪŋ] *n* (*also*: **horse racing**) Pferderennen *nt*; (*also*: **motor racing**) Rennsport *m*

racing car (*Brit*) *n* Rennwagen *m*

racing driver (*Brit*) *n* Rennfahrer(in) *m(f)*

racism [ˈreɪsɪzəm] *n* Rassismus *m*

racist [ˈreɪsɪst] *adj* rassistisch ▷ *n* (*pej*) Rassist(in) *m(f)*

rack [ræk] *n* (*also*: **luggage rack**) Gepäckablage *f*; (*also*: **roof rack**) Dachgepäckträger *m*; (*for dresses etc*) Ständer *m*; (*for dishes*) Gestell *nt* ▷ *vt*: **~ed by** (*pain etc*) gemartert von; **magazine/toast ~** Zeitungs-/Toastständer *m*; **to ~ one's brains** sich *dat* den Kopf zerbrechen; **to go to ~ and ruin** (*building*) zerfallen; (*business, country*) herunterkommen

racket [ˈrækɪt] *n* (*for tennis etc*) Schläger *m*; (*noise*) Krach *m*, Radau *m*; (*swindle*) Schwindel *m*

racketeer [rækɪˈtɪəʳ] (*esp US*) *n* Gangster *m*

racoon [rəˈkuːn] *n* = **raccoon**

racquet [ˈrækɪt] *n* (*for tennis etc*) Schläger *m*

racy [ˈreɪsɪ] *adj* (*book, story*) rasant

RADA [rɑːdə] (*Brit*) *n abbr* (= *Royal Academy of Dramatic Art*) *Schauspielschule*

radar [ˈreɪdɑːʳ] *n* Radar *m or nt* ▷ *cpd* Radar-

radar trap *n* Radarfalle *f*

radial [ˈreɪdɪəl] *adj* (*roads*) strahlenförmig verlaufend; (*pattern*) strahlenförmig ▷ *n* (*also*: **radial tyre**) Gürtelreifen *m*

radiance [ˈreɪdɪəns] *n* Glanz *m*

radiant [ˈreɪdɪənt] *adj* strahlend; (*Phys: heat*) Strahlungs-

radiate [ˈreɪdɪeɪt] *vt* (*lit, fig*) ausstrahlen ▷ *vi* (*lines, roads*) strahlenförmig verlaufen

radiation [reɪdɪˈeɪʃən] *n* (*radioactivity*) radioaktive Strahlung *f*; (*from sun etc*) Strahlung *f*

radiation sickness *n* Strahlenkrankheit *f*

radiator [ˈreɪdɪeɪtəʳ] *n* (*heater*) Heizkörper *m*; (*Aut*) Kühler *m*

radiator cap *n* (*Aut*) Kühlerdeckel *m*

radiator grill *n* (*Aut*) Kühlergrill *m*

radical [ˈrædɪkl] *adj* radikal ▷ *n* (*person*) Radikale(r) *f(m)*

radii [ˈreɪdɪaɪ] *npl of* **radius**

radio [ˈreɪdɪəu] *n* (*broadcasting*) Radio *nt*, Rundfunk *m*; (*device: for receiving broadcasts*)

Radio nt; (: for transmitting and receiving) Funkgerät nt ▷ vi: **to ~ sb** mit jdm per Funk sprechen ▷ vt (person) per Funk verständigen; (message, position) per Funk durchgeben; **on the ~** im Radio

radio ... ['reɪdɪəu] pref Radio ..., radio ...

radioactive ['reɪdɪəu'æktɪv] adj radioaktiv

radioactivity ['reɪdɪəuæk'tɪvɪtɪ] n Radioaktivität f

radio announcer n Rundfunksprecher(in) m(f)

radio-controlled ['reɪdɪəukən'trəuld] adj ferngesteuert

radiographer [reɪdɪ'ɒɡrəfər] n Röntgenologe m, Röntgenologin f

radiography [reɪdɪ'ɒɡrəfɪ] n Röntgenografie f

radiologist [reɪdɪ'ɒlədʒɪst] n Radiologe m, Radiologin f

radiology [reɪdɪ'ɒlədʒɪ] n Radiologie f

radio station n Radiosender m

radio taxi n Funktaxi nt

radiotelephone ['reɪdɪəu'tɛlɪfəun] n Funksprechgerät nt

radio telescope n Radioteleskop nt

radiotherapist ['reɪdɪəu'θɛrəpɪst] n Strahlentherapeut(in) m(f)

radiotherapy ['reɪdɪəu'θɛrəpɪ] n Strahlentherapie f

radish ['rædɪʃ] n Radieschen nt; (long white variety) Rettich m

radium ['reɪdɪəm] n Radium nt

radius ['reɪdɪəs] (pl **radii**) n Radius m; (area) Umkreis m; **within a ~ of 50 miles** in einem Umkreis von 50 Meilen

RAF (Brit) n abbr = **Royal Air Force**

raffia ['ræfɪə] n Bast m

raffish ['ræfɪʃ] adj (person) verwegen; (place) verkommen

raffle ['ræfl] n Verlosung f, Tombola f ▷ vt (prize) verlosen; **~ ticket** Los nt

raft [rɑːft] n Floß nt; (also: **life raft**) Rettungsfloß nt

rafter ['rɑːftər] n Dachsparren m

rag [ræɡ] n (piece of cloth) Lappen m; (torn cloth) Fetzen m; (pej: newspaper) Käseblatt nt; (Brit: Univ) studentische Wohltätigkeitsveranstaltung ▷ vt (Brit: tease) aufziehen; **rags** npl (torn clothes) Lumpen pl; **in ~s** (person) zerlumpt; **his was a ~s-to-riches story** er brachte es vom Tellerwäscher zum Millionär

rag-and-bone man [rægən'bəun-] (Brit) n Lumpensammler m

ragbag ['ræɡbæɡ] n (assortment) Sammelsurium nt

Studentenzeitschriften mit schlüpfrigen Witzen werden auf der Straße verkauft, und fast alle Universitäten und Colleges halten einen Ball ab. Der Erlös aller Veranstaltungen fließt Wohltätigkeitsorganisationen zu.

rag doll n Stoffpuppe f

rage [reɪdʒ] n (fury) Wut f, Zorn m ▷ vi toben, wüten; **it's all the ~** (fashionable) es ist der letzte Schrei; **to fly into a ~** einen Wutanfall bekommen

ragged ['ræɡɪd] adj (jagged) zackig; (clothes, person) zerlumpt; (beard) ausgefranst

raging ['reɪdʒɪŋ] adj (sea, storm, torrent) tobend, tosend; (fever) heftig; (thirst) brennend; (toothache) rasend

rag trade (inf) n: **the ~** die Modebranche f

raid [reɪd] n (Mil) Angriff m, Überfall m; (by police) Razzia f; (by criminal: forcefully) Überfall m; (: secretly) Einbruch m ▷ vt (Mil) angreifen, überfallen; (police) stürmen; (criminal: forcefully) überfallen; (: secretly) einbrechen in +acc

rail [reɪl] n Geländer nt; (on deck of ship) Reling f; **rails** npl (for train) Schienen pl; **by ~** mit der Bahn

railcard ['reɪlkɑːd] (Brit) n (for young people) ≈ Juniorenpass m; (for pensioners) ≈ Seniorenpass m

railing ['reɪlɪŋ] n, **railings** ['reɪlɪŋz] ▷ npl (fence) Zaun m

railroad ['reɪlrəud] (US) n = **railway**

railway ['reɪlweɪ] (Brit) n Eisenbahn f; (track) Gleis nt; (company) Bahn f

railway engine (Brit) n Lokomotive f

railway line (Brit) n Bahnlinie f; (track) Gleis nt

railwayman ['reɪlweɪmən] (irreg: like **man**); (Brit) n Eisenbahner m

railway station (Brit) n Bahnhof m

rain [reɪn] n Regen m ▷ vi regnen; **in the ~** im Regen; **as right as ~** voll auf der Höhe; **it's ~ing** es regnet; **it's ~ing cats and dogs** es regnet in Strömen

rainbow ['reɪnbəu] n Regenbogen m

rainbow family n gleichgeschlechtliches Paar mit Kind/Kindern, Regenbogenfamilie f

rainbow flag n Regenbogenfahne f or -flagge f

rain check (US) n: **to take a ~ on sth** sich dat etw noch einmal überlegen

raincoat ['reɪnkəut] n Regenmantel m

raindrop ['reɪndrɒp] n Regentropfen m

rainfall ['reɪnfɔːl] n Niederschlag m

rainforest ['reɪnfɒrɪst] n Regenwald m

rainproof ['reɪnpruːf] adj wasserfest

rainstorm ['reɪnstɔːm] n schwere Regenfälle pl

rainwater ['reɪnwɔːtər] n Regenwasser nt

rainy ['reɪnɪ] adj (day) regnerisch, verregnet; (area) regenreich; **~ season** Regenzeit f; **to save sth for a ~ day** etw für schlechte Zeiten aufheben

raise [reɪz] n (pay rise) Gehaltserhöhung f ▷ vt (lift: hand) hochheben; (: window) hochziehen; (siege) beenden; (embargo) aufheben; (increase)

r

erhöhen; (*improve*) verbessern; (*question etc*)
zur Sprache bringen; (*doubts etc*) vorbringen;
(*child, cattle*) aufziehen; (*crop*) anbauen;
(*army*) aufstellen; (*funds*) aufbringen; (*loan*)
aufnehmen; **to ~ a glass to sb/sth** das
Glas auf jdn/etw erheben; **to ~ one's voice**
die Stimme erheben; **to ~ sb's hopes** jdm
Hoffnungen machen; **to ~ a laugh/smile**
Gelächter/ein Lächeln hervorrufen; **this ~s
the question** ... das wirft die Frage auf ...
raisin ['reɪzn] n Rosine f
Raj [rɑːdʒ] n: **the ~** britische Regierung in Indien vor
1947
rajah ['rɑːdʒə] n Radscha m
rake [reɪk] n Harke f; (*old: person*) Schwerenöter
m ▷ vt harken; (*light, gun: area*) bestreichen;
he's raking it in (*inf*) er scheffelt das Geld
nur so
rake-off ['reɪkɔf] (*inf*) n Anteil m
rally ['rælɪ] n (*Pol etc*) Kundgebung f; (*Aut*)
Rallye f; (*Tennis etc*) Ballwechsel m ▷ vt (*support*)
sammeln ▷ vi (*sick person, Stock Exchange*) sich
erholen
▶ **rally round** vi sich zusammentun ▷ vt *fus* zu
Hilfe kommen +*dat*
rallying point ['rælɪɪŋ-] n Sammelstelle f
RAM [ræm] n abbr (*Comput: = random access
memory*) RAM
ram [ræm] n Widder m ▷ vt rammen
ramble ['ræmbl] n Wanderung f ▷ vi wandern;
(*also*: **ramble on**: *talk*) schwafeln
rambler ['ræmblər] n Wanderer m, Wanderin f;
(*Bot*) Kletterrose f
rambling ['ræmblɪŋ] adj (*speech, letter*)
weitschweifig; (*house*) weitläufig; (*Bot*)
rankend, Kletter-
rambunctious [ræm'bʌŋkʃəs] (*US*) adj =
rumbustious
RAMC (*Brit*) n abbr (= *Royal Army Medical Corps*)
*Verband zur Versorgung der Armee mit Stabsärzten und
Sanitätern*
ramifications [ræmɪfɪ'keɪʃənz] npl
Auswirkungen pl
ramp [ræmp] n Rampe f; (*in garage*) Hebebühne
f; **on ~** (*US: Aut*) Auffahrt f; **off ~** (*US: Aut*)
Ausfahrt f
rampage [ræm'peɪdʒ] n: **to be/go on the ~**
randalieren ▷ vi: **they went rampaging
through the town** sie zogen randalierend
durch die Stadt
rampant ['ræmpənt] adj: **to be ~** (*crime, disease
etc*) wild wuchern
rampart ['ræmpɑːt] n Schutzwall m
ram raiding [-reɪdɪŋ] n Einbruchdiebstahl, wobei
die Diebe mit einem Wagen in die Schaufensterfront
eines Ladens eindringen
ramshackle ['ræmʃækl] adj (*house*) baufällig;
(*cart*) klapprig; (*table*) altersschwach
RAN n abbr (= *Royal Australian Navy*) australische
Marine f
ran [ræn] pt of **run**
ranch [rɑːntʃ] n Ranch f
rancher ['rɑːntʃər] n Rancher(in) m(f); (*worker*)

Farmhelfer(in) m(f)
rancid ['rænsɪd] adj ranzig
rancour, (*US*) **rancor** ['ræŋkər] n Verbitterung f
R & B n abbr (= *rhythm and blues*) R & B
R & D n abbr = **research and development**
random ['rændəm] adj (*arrangement*)
willkürlich; (*selection*) zufällig; (*Comput*)
wahlfrei; (*Math*) Zufalls- ▷ n: **at ~** aufs
Geratewohl
random access n (*Comput*) wahlfreier Zugriff m
random access memory n (*Comput*) Schreib-
Lese-Speicher m
R & R (*US*) n abbr (*Mil*: = *rest and recreation*) Urlaub
m
randy ['rændɪ] (*Brit: inf*) adj geil, scharf
rang [ræŋ] pt of **ring**
range [reɪndʒ] n (*of mountains*) Kette f; (*of missile*)
Reichweite f; (*of voice*) Umfang m; (*series*)
Reihe f; (*of products*) Auswahl f; (*Mil: also*: **rifle
range**) Schießstand m; (*also*: **kitchen range**)
Herd m ▷ vt (*place in a line*) anordnen ▷ vi: **to ~
over** (*extend*) sich erstrecken über +*acc*; **price
~** Preisspanne f; **do you have anything else
in this price ~?** haben Sie noch etwas anderes
in dieser Preisklasse?; **within** (*firing*) **~** in
Schussweite; **at close ~** aus unmittelbarer
Entfernung; **~d left/right** (*text*) links-/
rechtsbündig; **to ~ from ... to ...** sich
zwischen ... und ... bewegen
ranger ['reɪndʒər] n Förster(in) m(f)
Rangoon [ræŋ'guːn] n Rangun nt
rank [ræŋk] n (*row*) Reihe f; (*Mil*) Rang m; (*social
class*) Schicht f; (*Brit: also*: **taxi rank**) Taxistand
m ▷ vi: **to ~ as/among** zählen zu ▷ vt: **he is
~ed third in the world** er steht weltweit
an dritter Stelle ▷ adj (*stinking*) stinkend;
(*sheer: hypocrisy etc*) rein; **the ranks** npl (*Mil*)
die Mannschaften pl; **the ~ and file** (*ordinary
members*) die Basis f; **to close ~s** (*Mil, fig*) die
Reihen schließen
rankle ['ræŋkl] vi (*insult*) nachwirken; **to ~
with sb** jdn wurmen
rank outsider n totaler Außenseiter m, totale
Außenseiterin f
ransack ['rænsæk] vt (*search*) durchwühlen;
(*plunder*) plündern
ransom ['rænsəm] n (*money*) Lösegeld nt; **to
hold sb to ~** (*hostage*) jdn als Geisel halten;
(*fig*) jdn erpressen
rant [rænt] vi schimpfen, wettern; **to ~ and
rave** herumwettern
ranting ['ræntɪŋ] n Geschimpfe nt
rap [ræp] vi klopfen ▷ vt: **to ~ sb's knuckles**
jdm auf die Finger klopfen ▷ n (*at door*) Klopfen
nt; (*also*: **rap music**) Rap m
rape [reɪp] n (*Jur*) Vergewaltigung f; (*Bot*) Raps m
▷ vt vergewaltigen
rape oil, **rapeseed oil** ['reɪpsiː-d-] n Rapsöl m
rapid ['ræpɪd] adj schnell; (*growth, change*)
schnell, rapide
rapidity [rə'pɪdɪtɪ] n Schnelligkeit f
rapidly ['ræpɪdlɪ] adv schnell; (*grow, change*)
schnell, rapide

rapids ['ræpɪdz] *npl* Stromschnellen *pl*

rapist ['reɪpɪst] *n* Vergewaltiger *m*

rapport [ræ'pɔːʳ] *n* enges Verhältnis *nt*

rapprochement [ræ'prɔʃmɑ̃:ŋ] *n* Annäherung *f*

rapt [ræpt] *adj* (*attention*) gespannt; **to be ~ in thought** in Gedanken versunken sein

rapture ['ræptʃəʳ] *n* Entzücken *nt*; **to go into ~s over** ins Schwärmen geraten über +*acc*

rapturous ['ræptʃərəs] *adj* (*applause, welcome*) stürmisch

rare [rɛəʳ] *adj* selten; (*steak*) nur angebraten, englisch (gebraten); **it is ~ to find that ...** es kommt nur selten vor, dass ...

rarebit ['rɛəbɪt] *n see* **Welsh rarebit**

rarefied ['rɛərɪfaɪd] *adj* (*air, atmosphere*) dünn; (*fig*) exklusiv

rarely ['rɛəlɪ] *adv* selten

raring ['rɛərɪŋ] *adj*: **~ to go** (*inf*) in den Startlöchern

rarity ['rɛərɪtɪ] *n* Seltenheit *f*

rascal ['rɑːskl] *n* (*child*) Frechdachs *m*; (*rogue*) Schurke *m*

rash [ræʃ] *adj* (*person*) unbesonnen; (*promise, act*) übereilt ▷ *n* (*Med*) Ausschlag *m*; (*of events etc*) Flut *f*; **to come out in a ~** einen Ausschlag bekommen

rasher ['ræʃəʳ] *n* (*of bacon*) Scheibe *f*

rashly ['ræʃlɪ] *adv* (*promise etc*) voreilig

rasp [rɑːsp] *n* (*tool*) Raspel *f*; (*sound*) Kratzen *nt* ▷ *vt, vi* krächzen

raspberry ['rɑːzbərɪ] *n* Himbeere *f*; **~ bush** Himbeerstrauch *m*; **to blow a ~** (*inf*) verächtlich schnauben

rasping ['rɑːspɪŋ] *adj*: **a ~ noise** ein kratzendes Geräusch

Rastafarian *n* Rastafarier *m*

rat [ræt] *n* Ratte *f*

ratable ['reɪtəbl] *adj* = **rateable**

ratchet ['rætʃɪt] *n* Sperrklinke *f*; **~ wheel** Sperrad *nt*

rate [reɪt] *n* (*speed: of change etc*) Tempo *nt*; (*of inflation, unemployment etc*) Rate *f*; (*of interest, taxation*) Satz *m*; (*price*) Preis *m* ▷ *vt* einschätzen; **rates** *npl* (*Brit: property tax*) Kommunalabgaben *pl*; **at a ~ of 60 kph** mit einem Tempo von 60 km/h; **~ of growth** (*Econ*) Wachstumsrate *f*; **~ of return** (*Fin*) Rendite *f*; **pulse ~** Pulszahl *f*; **at this/that ~** wenn es so weitergeht; **at any ~** auf jeden Fall; **to ~ sb/sth as** jdn/etw einschätzen als; **to ~ sb/sth among** jdn/etw zählen zu; **to ~ sb/sth highly** jdn/etw hoch einschätzen

rateable ['reɪtəbl] *adj*: **~ value** (*Brit*) ▷ *n* steuerbarer Wert *m*

ratepayer ['reɪtpeɪəʳ] (*Brit*) *n* Steuerzahler(in) *m(f)*

rather ['rɑːðəʳ] *adv* (*somewhat*) etwas; (*very*) ziemlich; **~ a lot** ziemlich *or* recht viel; **I would ~ go** ich würde lieber gehen; **~ than** (*instead of*) anstelle von; **or ~** (*more accurately*) oder vielmehr; **I'd ~ not say** das möchte ich lieber nicht sagen; **I ~ think he won't come**

ich glaube eher, dass er nicht kommt

ratification [rætɪfɪ'keɪʃən] *n* Ratifikation *f*

ratify ['rætɪfaɪ] *vt* (*treaty etc*) ratifizieren

rating ['reɪtɪŋ] *n* (*score*) Rate *f*; (*assessment*) Beurteilung *f*; (*Naut: Brit: sailor*) Matrose *m*; **ratings** *npl* (*Radio, TV*) Einschaltquote *f*; **~s hit** Quotenhit *m*

ratio ['reɪʃɪəu] *n* Verhältnis *nt*; **a ~ of 5 to 1** ein Verhältnis von 5 zu 1

ration ['ræʃən] *n* Ration *f* ▷ *vt* rationieren; **rations** *npl* (*Mil*) Rationen *pl*

rational ['ræʃənl] *adj* rational, vernünftig

rationale [ræʃə'nɑːl] *n* Grundlage *f*

rationalization [ræʃnəlaɪ'zeɪʃən] *n* (*justification*) Rechtfertigung *f*; (*of company, system*) Rationalisierung *f*

rationalize ['ræʃnəlaɪz] *vt* (*see n*) rechtfertigen, rationalisieren

rationally ['ræʃnəlɪ] *adv* vernünftig, rational

rationing ['ræʃnɪŋ] *n* Rationierung *f*

ratpack (*Brit: inf*) *n* (*reporters*) Pressemeute *f*

rat poison *n* Rattengift *nt*

rat race *n*: **the ~** der ständige *or* tägliche Konkurrenzkampf *m*

rattan [ræ'tæn] *n* Rattan *nt*, Peddigrohr *nt*

rattle ['rætl] *n* (*of door, window, snake*) Klappern *nt*; (*of train, car etc*) Rattern *nt*; (*of chain*) Rasseln *nt*; (*toy*) Rassel *f* ▷ *vi* (*chains*) rasseln; (*windows*) klappern; (*bottles*) klirren ▷ *vt* (*shake noisily*) rütteln an +*dat*; (*fig: unsettle*) nervös machen; **to ~ along** (*car, bus*) dahinrattern

rattlesnake ['rætlsneɪk] *n* Klapperschlange *f*

ratty ['rætɪ] (*inf*) *adj* gereizt

raucous ['rɔːkəs] *adj* (*voice etc*) rau

raucously ['rɔːkəslɪ] *adv* rau

raunchy ['rɔːntʃɪ] *adj* (*voice, song*) lüstern, geil

ravage ['rævɪdʒ] *vt* verwüsten

ravages ['rævɪdʒɪz] *npl* (*of war*) Verwüstungen *pl*; (*of weather*) zerstörende Auswirkungen *pl*; (*of time*) Spuren *pl*

rave [reɪv] *vi* (*in anger*) toben ▷ *adj* (*inf: review*) glänzend; (*scene, culture*) Rave- ▷ *n* (*Brit: inf: party*) Rave *m*, Fete *f*
▶ **rave about** schwärmen von

raven ['reɪvən] *n* Rabe *m*

ravenous ['rævənəs] *adj* (*person*) ausgehungert; (*appetite*) unersättlich

ravine [rə'viːn] *n* Schlucht *f*

raving ['reɪvɪŋ] *adj*: **a ~ lunatic** ein total verrückter Typ

ravings ['reɪvɪŋz] *npl* Fantastereien *pl*

ravioli [rævɪ'əulɪ] *n* Ravioli *pl*

ravishing ['rævɪʃɪŋ] *adj* hinreißend

raw [rɔː] *adj* roh; (*sore*) wund; (*inexperienced*) unerfahren; (*weather, day*) rau; **to get a ~ deal** ungerecht behandelt werden

Rawalpindi [rɔːl'pɪndɪ] *n* Rawalpindi *nt*

raw material *n* Rohmaterial *nt*

ray [reɪ] *n* Strahl *m*; **~ of hope** Hoffnungsschimmer *m*

rayon ['reɪɔn] *n* Reyon *nt*

raze [reɪz] *vt* (*also:* **to raze to the ground**) dem Erdboden gleichmachen

r

razor ['reɪzəʳ] n Rasierapparat m; (open razor) Rasiermesser nt

razor blade n Rasierklinge f

razzle ['ræzl] (Brit: inf) n: **to be/go on the ~** einen draufmachen

razzmatazz ['ræzmə'tæz] (inf) n Trubel m

RC abbr (= Roman Catholic) r.-k.

RCAF n abbr (= Royal Canadian Air Force) kanadische Luftwaffe f

RCMP n abbr (= Royal Canadian Mounted Police) kanadische berittene Polizei

RCN n abbr (= Royal Canadian Navy) kanadische Marine

RD (US) abbr (Post) = rural delivery Landpostzustellung f

Rd abbr (= road) Str.

RDC (Brit) n abbr = rural district council

RE (Brit) n abbr (Scol) = **religious education** (Mil: = Royal Engineers) Königliches Pionierkorps

re [riː] prep (with regard to) bezüglich +gen

reach [riːtʃ] n (range) Reichweite f ▷ vt erreichen; (conclusion, decision) kommen zu; (be able to touch) kommen an +acc ▷ vi (stretch out one's arm) langen; **reaches** npl (of river) Gebiete pl; **within/out of ~** in/außer Reichweite; **within easy ~ of the supermarket/station** ganz in der Nähe des Supermarkts/Bahnhofs; **beyond the ~ of sb/sth** außerhalb der Reichweite von jdm/etw; **"keep out of the ~ of children"** „von Kindern fernhalten"; **can I ~ you at your hotel?** kann ich Sie in Ihrem Hotel erreichen?

▶ **reach out** vt (hand) ausstrecken ▷ vi die Hand ausstrecken; **to ~ out for sth** nach etw greifen

react [riː'ækt] vi: **to ~ (to)** (also Med) reagieren (auf +acc); (Chem): **to ~ (with)** reagieren (mit); **to ~ (against)** (rebel) sich wehren (gegen)

reaction [riː'ækʃən] n Reaktion f; **reactions** npl (reflexes) Reaktionen pl; **a ~ against sth** Widerstand gegen etw

reactionary [riː'ækʃənrɪ] adj reaktionär ▷ n Reaktionär(in) m(f)

reactor [riː'æktəʳ] n (also: **nuclear reactor**) Kernreaktor m

read [riːd] (pt, pp ~) [rɛd] vi lesen; (piece of writing etc) sich lesen ▷ vt lesen; (meter, thermometer etc) ablesen; (understand: mood, thoughts) sich versetzen in +acc; (meter, thermometer etc: measurement) anzeigen; (study) studieren; **to ~ sb's lips** jdm von den Lippen ablesen; **to ~ sb's mind** jds Gedanken lesen; **to ~ between the lines** zwischen den Zeilen lesen; **to take sth as ~** (self-evident) etw für selbstverständlich halten; **you can take it as ~ that ...** Sie können davon ausgehen, dass ...; **do you ~ me?** (Tel) verstehen Sie mich?; **to ~ sth into sb's remarks** etw in jds Bemerkungen hineininterpretieren

▶ **read out** vt vorlesen

▶ **read over** vt durchlesen

▶ **read through** vt durchlesen

▶ **read up on** vt fus sich informieren über +acc

readable ['riːdəbl] adj (legible) lesbar; (book, author etc) lesenswert

reader ['riːdəʳ] n (person) Leser(in) m(f); (book) Lesebuch nt; (Brit: at university) ≈ Dozent(in) m(f); **to be an avid/slow ~** eifrig/langsam lesen

readership ['riːdəʃɪp] n (of newspaper etc) Leserschaft f

readily ['rɛdɪlɪ] adv (without hesitation) bereitwillig; (easily) ohne Weiteres

readiness ['rɛdɪnɪs] n Bereitschaft f; **in ~ for** bereit für

reading ['riːdɪŋ] n Lesen nt; (understanding) Verständnis nt; (from bible, of poetry etc) Lesung f; (on meter, thermometer etc) Anzeige f

reading lamp n Leselampe f

reading matter n Lesestoff m

reading room n Lesesaal m

readjust [riːə'dʒʌst] vt (position, knob, instrument etc) neu einstellen ▷ vi: **to ~ (to)** sich anpassen (an +acc)

readjustment [riːə'dʒʌstmənt] n (fig) Neuorientierung f

ready ['rɛdɪ] adj (prepared) bereit, fertig; (willing) bereit; (easy) leicht; (available) fertig ▷ n: **at the ~** (Mil) einsatzbereit; (fig) griffbereit; **~ for use** gebrauchsfertig; **to be ~ to do sth** bereit sein, etw zu tun; **to get ~** sich fertig machen; **to get sth ~** etw bereitmachen

ready cash n Bargeld nt

ready-cooked ['rɛdɪkukt] adj vorgekocht

ready-made ['rɛdɪ'meɪd] adj (clothes) von der Stange, Konfektions-; **~ meal** Fertiggericht nt

ready-mix ['rɛdɪmɪks] n (for cakes etc) Backmischung f; (concrete) Fertigbeton m

ready money n = **ready cash**

ready reckoner [-'rɛkənəʳ] (Brit) n Rechentabelle f

ready-to-wear ['rɛdɪtə'wɛəʳ] adj (clothes) von der Stange, Konfektions-

reaffirm [riːə'fəːm] vt bestätigen

reagent [riː'eɪdʒənt] n: **chemical ~** Reagens nt, Reagenz nt

real [rɪəl] adj (reason, result etc) wirklich; (leather, gold etc) echt; (life, feeling) wahr; (for emphasis) echt ▷ adv (US: inf: very) echt; **in ~ life** im wahren or wirklichen Leben; **in ~ terms** effektiv

real ale n Real Ale nt

real estate n Immobilien pl ▷ cpd (US: agent, business etc) Immobilien-

realign vt neu ausrichten

realism ['rɪəlɪzəm] n (also Art) Realismus m

realist ['rɪəlɪst] n Realist(in) m(f)

realistic [rɪə'lɪstɪk] adj realistisch

reality [riː'ælɪtɪ] n Wirklichkeit f, Realität f; **in ~** in Wirklichkeit

realization [rɪəlaɪ'zeɪʃən] n (understanding) Erkenntnis f; (fulfilment) Verwirklichung f, Realisierung f; (Fin: of asset) Realisation f

realize ['rɪəlaɪz] vt (understand) verstehen; (fulfil) verwirklichen, realisieren; (Fin: amount, profit) realisieren; **I ~ that ...** es ist mir klar, dass ...

really ['rɪəlɪ] *adv* wirklich; **what ~ happened**
was wirklich geschah; **~? wirklich?; ~!**
(*indicating annoyance*) also wirklich!

realm [rɛlm] *n* (*fig: field*) Bereich *m*; (*kingdom*)
Reich *nt*

real-time ['ri:ltaɪm] *adj* (*Comput: processing etc*)
Echtzeit-

Realtor® ['rɪəltɔːʳ] (*US*) *n*
Immobilienmakler(in) *m(f)*

ream [ri:m] *n* (*of paper*) Ries *nt*; **reams** (*inf: fig*)
Bände *pl*

reap [ri:p] *vt* (*crop*) einbringen, ernten;
(*fig: benefits*) ernten; (*: rewards*) bekommen

reaper ['ri:pəʳ] *n* (*machine*) Mähdrescher *m*

reappear [ri:ə'pɪəʳ] *vi* wieder auftauchen

reappearance [ri:ə'pɪərəns] *n*
Wiederauftauchen *nt*

reapply [ri:ə'plaɪ] *vi*: **to ~ for** sich erneut
bewerben um

reappoint [ri:ə'pɔɪnt] *vt* (*to job*)
wiedereinstellen

reappraisal [ri:ə'preɪzl] *n* (*of idea etc*)
Neubeurteilung *f*

rear [rɪəʳ] *adj* hintere(r, s); (*wheel etc*) Hinter- ▷ *n*
Rückseite *f*; (*buttocks*) Hinterteil *nt* ▷ *vt* (*family,
animals*) aufziehen ▷ *vi* (*also:* **rear up**: *horse*) sich
aufbäumen

rear admiral *n* Konteradmiral *m*

rear-engined ['rɪər'ɛndʒɪnd] *adj* mit
Heckmotor

rearguard ['rɪəgɑːd] *n* (*Mil*) Nachhut *f*; **to fight
a ~ action** (*fig*) sich erbittert wehren

rearm [ri:'ɑːm] *vi* (*country*) wiederaufrüsten ▷ *vt*
wiederbewaffnen

rearmament [ri:'ɑːməmənt] *n*
Wiederaufrüstung *f*

rearrange [ri:ə'reɪndʒ] *vt* (*furniture*) umstellen;
(*meeting*) den Termin ändern +*gen*

rear-view mirror ['rɪəvju:-] *n* Rückspiegel *m*

reason ['ri:zn] *n* (*cause*) Grund *m*; (*rationality*)
Verstand *m*; (*common sense*) Vernunft *f* ▷ *vi*: **to
~ with sb** vernünftig mit jdm reden; **the ~
for/why** der Grund für/, warum; **we have ~
to believe that ...** wir haben Grund zu der
Annahme, dass ...; **it stands to ~ that ...**
es ist zu erwarten, dass ...; **she claims with
good ~ that ...** sie behauptet mit gutem
Grund or mit Recht, dass ...; **all the more ~
why ...** ein Grund mehr, warum ...; **yes, but
within ~** ja, solange es sich im Rahmen hält

reasonable ['ri:znəbl] *adj* vernünftig; (*number,
amount*) angemessen; (*not bad*) ganz ordentlich;
be ~! sei doch vernünftig!

reasonably ['ri:znəblɪ] *adv* (*fairly*) ziemlich;
(*sensibly*) vernünftig; **one could ~ assume
that ...** man könnte durchaus annehmen,
dass ...

reasoned ['ri:znd] *adj* (*argument*) durchdacht

reasoning ['ri:znɪŋ] *n* Argumentation *f*

reassemble [ri:ə'sɛmbl] *vt* (*machine*)
wieder zusammensetzen ▷ *vi* sich wieder
versammeln

reassert [ri:ə'sə:t] *vt*: **to ~ oneself/one's**

authority seine Autorität wieder geltend
machen

reassurance [ri:ə'ʃuərəns] *n* (*comfort*)
Beruhigung *f*; (*guarantee*) Bestätigung *f*

reassure [ri:ə'ʃuəʳ] *vt* beruhigen

reassuring [ri:ə'ʃuərɪŋ] *adj* beruhigend

reawakening [ri:ə'weɪknɪŋ] *n*
Wiedererwachen *nt*

rebate ['ri:beɪt] *n* (*on tax etc*) Rückerstattung *f*;
(*discount*) Ermäßigung *f*

rebel ['rɛbl] *n* Rebell(in) *m(f)* ▷ *vi* rebellieren

rebellion [rɪ'bɛljən] *n* Rebellion *f*

rebellious [rɪ'bɛljəs] *adj* rebellisch

rebirth [ri:'bə:θ] *n* Wiedergeburt *f*

rebound [rɪ'baund] *vi* (*ball*) zurückprallen
▷ *n*: **on the ~** (*fig*) als Tröstung

rebuff [rɪ'bʌf] *n* Abfuhr *f* ▷ *vt* zurückweisen

rebuild [ri:'bɪld] (*irreg: like* **build**) *vt*
wiederaufbauen; (*confidence*) wiederherstellen

rebuke [rɪ'bju:k] *vt* zurechtweisen, tadeln ▷ *n*
Zurechtweisung *f*, Tadel *m*

rebut [rɪ'bʌt] (*form*) *vt* widerlegen

rebuttal [rɪ'bʌtl] (*form*) *n* Widerlegung *f*

recalcitrant [rɪ'kælsɪtrənt] *adj* aufsässig

recall [rɪ'kɔːl] *vt* (*remember*) sich erinnern
an +*acc*; (*ambassador*) abberufen; (*product*)
zurückrufen ▷ *n* (*of memories*) Erinnerung *f*; (*of
ambassador*) Abberufung *f*; (*of product*) Rückruf
m; **beyond ~** unwiederbringlich

recant [rɪ'kænt] *vi* widerrufen

recap ['ri:kæp] *vt*, *vi* zusammenfassen ▷ *n*
Zusammenfassung *f*

recapitulate [ri:kə'pɪtjuleɪt] *vt*, *vi* = **recap**

recapture [ri:'kæptʃəʳ] *vt* (*town*)
wiedereinnehmen; (*prisoner*) wiederergreifen;
(*atmosphere etc*) heraufbeschwören

rec'd *abbr* (*Comm*: = *received*) erh.

recede [rɪ'si:d] *vi* (*tide*) zurückgehen; (*lights
etc*) verschwinden; (*memory, hope*) schwinden;
his hair is beginning to ~ er bekommt eine
Stirnglatze

receding [rɪ'si:dɪŋ] *adj* (*hairline*)
zurückweichend; (*chin*) fliehend

receipt [rɪ'si:t] *n* (*document*) Quittung *f*; (*act
of receiving*) Erhalt *m*; **receipts** *npl* (*Comm*)
Einnahmen *pl*; **on ~ of** bei Erhalt +*gen*; **to be
in ~ of sth** etw erhalten

receivable [rɪ'si:vəbl] *adj* (*Comm*) zulässig;
(*owing*) ausstehend

receive [rɪ'si:v] *vt* erhalten, bekommen; (*injury*)
erleiden; (*treatment*) erhalten; (*visitor, guest*)
empfangen; **to be on the receiving end of
sth** der/die Leidtragende von etw sein; **"~d
with thanks"** (*Comm*) „dankend erhalten"

● **RECEIVED PRONUNCIATION**
○
○
● *Received Pronunciation* oder *RP* ist die
● hochsprachliche Standardaussprache des
● britischen Englisch, die bis vor Kurzem in
● der Ober- und Mittelschicht vorherrschte
● und auch noch großes Ansehen unter
● höheren Beamten genießt.

r

receiver [rɪ'siːvə^r] n (Tel) Hörer m; (Radio, TV) Empfänger m; (of stolen goods) Hehler(in) m(f); (Comm) Empfänger(in) m(f)
receivership [rɪ'siːvəʃɪp] n: **to go into** ~ in Konkurs gehen
recent ['riːsnt] adj (event) kürzlich; (times) letzte(r, s); **in** ~ **years** in den letzten Jahren
recently ['riːsntlɪ] adv (not long ago) kürzlich; (lately) in letzter Zeit; **as** ~ **as** erst; **until** ~ bis vor Kurzem
receptacle [rɪ'sɛptɪkl] n Behälter m
reception [rɪ'sɛpʃən] n (in hotel, office etc) Rezeption f; (party, Radio, TV) Empfang m; (welcome) Aufnahme f
reception centre (Brit) n Aufnahmelager nt
reception desk n Rezeption f
receptionist [rɪ'sɛpʃənɪst] n (in hotel) Empfangschef m, Empfangsdame f; (in doctor's surgery) Sprechstundenhilfe f
receptive [rɪ'sɛptɪv] adj aufnahmebereit
recess [rɪ'sɛs] n (in room) Nische f; (secret place) Winkel m; (Pol etc: holiday) Ferien pl; (US: Law: short break) Pause f; (esp US: Scol) Pause f
recession [rɪ'sɛʃən] n (Econ) Rezession f
recessionista [rɪsɛʃə'nɪstə] n modebewusste Person, die in Zeiten der Rezession auf die Kosten ihres Lebensstils achtet
recharge [riː'tʃɑːdʒ] vt (battery) aufladen
rechargeable [riː'tʃɑːdʒəbl] adj aufladbar
recipe ['rɛsɪpɪ] n Rezept nt; **a** ~ **for success** ein Erfolgsrezept nt; **to be a** ~ **for disaster** in die Katastrophe führen
recipient [rɪ'sɪpɪənt] n Empfänger(in) m(f)
reciprocal [rɪ'sɪprəkl] adj gegenseitig
reciprocate [rɪ'sɪprəkeɪt] vt (invitation, feeling) erwidern ▷ vi sich revanchieren
recital [rɪ'saɪtl] n (concert) Konzert nt
recite [rɪ'saɪt] vt (poem) vortragen; (complaints etc) aufzählen
reckless ['rɛkləs] adj (driving, driver) rücksichtslos; (spending) leichtsinnig
recklessly ['rɛkləslɪ] adv (drive) rücksichtslos; (spend, gamble) leichtsinnig
reckon ['rɛkən] vt (consider) halten für; (calculate) berechnen ▷ vi: **he is somebody to be ~ed with** mit ihm muss man rechnen; **I** ~ **that ...** (think) ich schätze, dass ...; **to** ~ **without sb/sth** nicht mit jdm/etw rechnen ▶ **reckon on** vt fus rechnen mit
reckoning ['rɛknɪŋ] n (calculation) Berechnung f; **the day of** ~ der Tag der Abrechnung
reclaim [rɪ'kleɪm] vt (luggage) abholen; (tax etc) zurückfordern; (land) gewinnen; (waste materials) zur Wiederverwertung sammeln
reclamation [rɛklə'meɪʃən] n (of land) Gewinnung f
recline [rɪ'klaɪn] vi (sit or lie back) zurückgelehnt sitzen
reclining [rɪ'klaɪnɪŋ] adj (seat) Liege-
recluse [rɪ'kluːs] n Einsiedler(in) m(f)
recognition [rɛkəg'nɪʃən] n (of person, place) Erkennen nt; (of problem, fact) Erkenntnis f; (of achievement) Anerkennung f; **in** ~ **of** in

Anerkennung +gen; **to gain** ~ Anerkennung finden; **she had changed beyond** ~ sie war nicht wieder zu erkennen
recognizable ['rɛkəgnaɪzəbl] adj erkennbar
recognize ['rɛkəgnaɪz] vt (person, place, voice) wiedererkennen; (sign, problem) erkennen; (qualifications, government, achievement) anerkennen; **to** ~ **sb by/as** jdn erkennen an +dat/als
recoil [rɪ'kɔɪl] vi (person): **to** ~ **from** zurückweichen vor +dat; (fig) zurückschrecken vor +dat ▷ n (of gun) Rückstoß m
recollect [rɛkə'lɛkt] vt (remember) sich erinnern an +acc
recollection [rɛkə'lɛkʃən] n Erinnerung f; **to the best of my** ~ soweit ich mich erinnern or entsinnen kann
recommend [rɛkə'mɛnd] vt empfehlen; **she has a lot to** ~ **her** es spricht sehr viel für sie
recommendation [rɛkəmɛn'deɪʃən] n Empfehlung f
recommended retail price (Brit) n (Comm) unverbindlicher Richtpreis m
recompense ['rɛkəmpɛns] n (reward) Belohnung f; (compensation) Entschädigung f
reconcilable ['rɛkənsaɪləbl] adj (ideas) (miteinander) vereinbar
reconcile ['rɛkənsaɪl] vt (people) versöhnen; (facts, beliefs) (miteinander) vereinbaren, in Einklang bringen; **to** ~ **o.s. to sth** sich mit etw abfinden
reconciliation [rɛkənsɪlɪ'eɪʃən] n (of people) Versöhnung f; (of facts, beliefs) Vereinbarung f
recondite [rɪ'kɔndaɪt] adj obskur
recondition [riːkən'dɪʃən] vt (machine) überholen
reconditioned [riːkən'dɪʃənd] adj (engine, TV) generalüberholt
reconnaissance [rɪ'kɔnɪsns] n (Mil) Aufklärung f
reconnoitre, (US) **reconnoiter** [rɛkə'nɔɪtə^r] vt (Mil) erkunden
reconsider [riːkən'sɪdə^r] vt (noch einmal) überdenken ▷ vi es sich dat noch einmal überlegen
reconstitute [riː'kɔnstɪtjuːt] vt (organization) neu bilden; (food) wiederherstellen
reconstruct [riːkən'strʌkt] vt (building) wiederaufbauen; (policy, system) neu organisieren; (event, crime) rekonstruieren
reconstruction [riːkən'strʌkʃən] n Wiederaufbau m; (of crime) Rekonstruktion f
reconvene [riːkən'viːn] vi (meet again) wieder zusammenkommen ▷ vt (meeting etc) wiedereinberufen
record ['rɛkɔːd] n (written account) Aufzeichnung f; (of meeting) Protokoll nt; (of decision) Beleg m; (Comput) Datensatz m; (file) Akte f; (Mus: disc) Schallplatte f; (history) Vorgeschichte f; (also: **criminal record**) Vorstrafen pl; (Sport) Rekord m ▷ vt aufzeichnen; (song etc) aufnehmen; (temperature, speed etc) registrieren ▷ adj (sales, profits) Rekord-; ~ **of attendance**

Anwesenheitsliste f; **public ~s** Urkunden pl des Nationalarchivs; **to keep a ~ of sth** etw schriftlich festhalten; **to have a good/poor ~** gute/schlechte Leistungen vorzuweisen haben; **to have a (criminal) ~** vorbestraft sein; **to set** or **put the ~ straight** (fig) Klarheit schaffen; **he is on ~ as saying that ...** er hat nachweislich gesagt, dass ...; **off the ~** (remark) inoffiziell ▷ adv (speak) im Vertrauen; **in ~ time** in Rekordzeit

recorded delivery [rɪ'kɔːdɪd-] (Brit) n (Post) Einschreiben nt; **to send sth (by) ~** etw per Einschreiben senden

recorder [rɪ'kɔːdəʳ] n (Mus) Blockflöte f; (Law) nebenamtlich als Richter tätiger Rechtsanwalt

record holder n (Sport) Rekordinhaber(in) m(f)

recording [rɪ'kɔːdɪŋ] n Aufnahme f

recording studio n Aufnahmestudio nt

record library n Schallplattenverleih m

record player n Plattenspieler m

recount [rɪ'kaunt] vt (story etc) erzählen

re-count ['riːkaunt] n (of votes) Nachzählung f ▷ vt (votes) nachzählen

recoup [rɪ'kuːp] vt: **to ~ one's losses** seine Verluste ausgleichen

recourse [rɪ'kɔːs] n: **to have ~ to sth** Zuflucht zu etw nehmen

recover [rɪ'kʌvəʳ] vt (get back) zurückbekommen; (stolen goods) sicherstellen; (wreck, body) bergen; (financial loss) ausgleichen ▷ vi sich erholen

re-cover [riː'kʌvəʳ] vt (chair etc) neu beziehen

recovery [rɪ'kʌvərɪ] n (from illness etc) Erholung f; (in economy) Aufschwung m; (of lost items) Wiederfinden nt; (of stolen goods) Sicherstellung f; (of wreck, body) Bergung f; (of financial loss) Ausgleich m

re-create [riːkrɪ'eɪt] vt (atmosphere, situation) wiederherstellen

recreation [rɛkrɪ'eɪʃən] n (leisure) Erholung f, Entspannung f

recreational [rɛkrɪ'eɪʃənl] adj (facilities etc) Freizeit-

recreational drug n Freizeitdroge f

recreational vehicle (US) n Caravan m

recrimination [rɪkrɪmɪ'neɪʃən] n gegenseitige Anschuldigungen pl

recruit [rɪ'kruːt] n (Mil) Rekrut m; (in company) neuer Mitarbeiter m, neue Mitarbeiterin f ▷ vt (Mil) rekrutieren; (staff, new members) anwerben

recruiting office [rɪ'kruːtɪŋ-] n (Mil) Rekrutierungsbüro nt

recruitment [rɪ'kruːtmənt] n (of staff) Anwerbung f

rectangle ['rɛktæŋgl] n Rechteck nt

rectangular [rɛk'tæŋgjuləʳ] adj (shape) rechteckig

rectify ['rɛktɪfaɪ] vt (mistake etc) korrigieren

rector ['rɛktəʳ] n (Rel) Pfarrer(in) m(f)

rectory ['rɛktərɪ] n Pfarrhaus nt

rectum ['rɛktəm] n Rektum nt, Mastdarm m

recuperate [rɪ'kjuːpəreɪt] vi (recover) sich erholen

recur [rɪ'kəːʳ] vi (error, event) sich wiederholen; (pain etc) wiederholt auftreten

recurrence [rɪ'kərns] n (see vi) Wiederholung f; wiederholtes Auftreten nt

recurrent [rɪ'kərnt] adj (see vi) sich wiederholend; wiederholt auftretend

recurring [rɪ'kərɪŋ] adj (problem, dream) sich wiederholend; (Math): **six point five four ~** sechs Komma fünf Periode vier

recycle [riː'saɪkl] vt (waste, paper etc) recyceln, wiederverwerten

recycling [riː'saɪklɪŋ] n Recycling nt; **~ site** Recycling- or Wertstoffhof m

red [rɛd] n Rot nt; (pej, Pol) Rote(r) f(m) ▷ adj rot; **to be in the ~** (business etc) in den roten Zahlen sein

red alert n: **to be on ~** in höchster Alarmbereitschaft sein

red-blooded ['rɛd'blʌdɪd] adj heißblütig

● **REDBRICK UNIVERSITY**
●
● Als redbrick university werden die jüngeren
● britischen Universitäten bezeichnet,
● die im späten 19. und Anfang des 20. Jh.
● in Städten wie Manchester, Liverpool
● und Bristol gegründet wurden. Der
● Name steht im Gegensatz zu Oxford
● und Cambridge und bezieht sich
● auf die roten Backsteinmauern der
● Universitätsgebäude.

---

red carpet treatment n: **to give sb the ~** den roten Teppich für jdn ausrollen

Red Cross n Rotes Kreuz nt

redcurrant ['rɛdkʌrənt] n Rote Johannisbeere f

redden ['rɛdn] vt röten ▷ vi (blush) erröten

reddish ['rɛdɪʃ] adj rötlich

redecorate [riː'dɛkəreɪt] vt, vi renovieren

redecoration [riː'dɛkə'reɪʃən] n Renovierung f

redeem [rɪ'diːm] vt (situation etc) retten; (voucher, sth in pawn) einlösen; (loan) abzahlen; (Rel) erlösen; **to ~ oneself for sth** etw wiedergutmachen

redeemable [rɪ'diːməbl] adj (voucher etc) einlösbar

redeeming [rɪ'diːmɪŋ] adj (feature, quality) versöhnend

redefine [riːdɪ'faɪn] vt neu definieren

redemption [rɪ'dɛmʃən] n (Rel) Erlösung f; **past** or **beyond ~** nicht mehr zu retten

redeploy [riːdɪ'plɔɪ] vt (resources, staff) umverteilen; (Mil) verlegen

redeployment [riːdɪ'plɔɪmənt] n (see vt) Umverteilung f; Verlegung f

redevelop [riːdɪ'vɛləp] vt (area) sanieren

redevelopment [riːdɪ'vɛləpmənt] n Sanierung f

red-handed [rɛd'hændɪd] adj: **to be caught ~** auf frischer Tat ertappt werden

redhead ['rɛdhɛd] n Rotschopf m

red herring n (fig) falsche Spur f

red-hot [rɛd'hɔt] adj (metal) rot glühend

r

redirect [riːdaɪˈrɛkt] vt (mail) nachsenden; (traffic) umleiten

rediscover [riːdɪsˈkʌvəʳ] vt wiederentdecken

redistribute [riːdɪsˈtrɪbjuːt] vt umverteilen

red-letter day [ˈrɛdlɛtə-] n besonderer Tag m

red light n (Aut): **to go through a ~** eine Ampel bei Rot überfahren

red-light district [ˈrɛdlaɪt-] n Rotlichtviertel nt

red meat n Rind- und Lammfleisch

redness [ˈrɛdnɪs] n Röte f

redo [riːˈduː] (irreg: like do) vt noch einmal machen

redolent [ˈrɛdələnt] adj: **to be ~ of sth** nach etw riechen; (fig) an etw erinnern

redouble [riːˈdʌbl] vt: **to ~ one's efforts** seine Anstrengungen verdoppeln

redraft [riːˈdrɑːft] vt (agreement) neu abfassen

redraw [riːˈdrɔː] vt neu zeichnen

redress [rɪˈdrɛs] n (compensation) Wiedergutmachung f ▷ vt (error etc) wiedergutmachen; **to ~ the balance** das Gleichgewicht wiederherstellen

Red Sea n: **the ~** das Rote Meer

redskin [ˈrɛdskɪn] (old: offensive) n Rothaut f

red tape n (fig) Bürokratie f

reduce [rɪˈdjuːs] vt (spending, numbers, risk etc) vermindern, reduzieren; **to ~ sth by/to 5%** etw um/auf 5% acc reduzieren; **to ~ sb to tears/silence** jdn zum Weinen/Schweigen bringen; **to ~ sb to begging/stealing** jdn zur Bettelei/zum Diebstahl zwingen; **"~ speed now"** (Aut) „langsam fahren"

reduced [rɪˈdjuːst] adj (goods, ticket etc) ermäßigt; **"greatly ~ prices"** „Preise stark reduziert"

reduction [rɪˈdʌkʃən] n (in price etc) Ermäßigung, Reduzierung f; (in numbers) Verminderung f

redundancy [rɪˈdʌndənsɪ] (Brit) n (dismissal) Entlassung f; (unemployment) Arbeitslosigkeit f; **compulsory ~** Entlassung f; **voluntary ~** freiwilliger Verzicht m auf den Arbeitsplatz

redundancy payment (Brit) n Abfindung f

redundant [rɪˈdʌndnt] adj (Brit: worker) arbeitslos; (word, object) überflüssig; **to be made ~** (worker) den Arbeitsplatz verlieren

reed [riːd] n (Bot) Schilf nt; (Mus: of clarinet etc) Rohrblatt nt

re-educate [riːˈɛdjukeɪt] vt umerziehen

reedy [ˈriːdɪ] adj (voice) Fistel-

reef [riːf] n (at sea) Riff nt

reek [riːk] vi: **to ~ (of)** (lit, fig) stinken (nach)

reel [riːl] n (of thread etc, on fishing-rod) Rolle f; (Cine: scene) Szene f; (of film, tape) Spule f; (dance) Reel m ▷ vi (sway) taumeln; **my head is ~ing** mir dreht sich der Kopf
  ▸ **reel in** vt (fish, line) einholen
  ▸ **reel off** vt (say) herunterrasseln

re-election [riːɪˈlɛkʃən] n Wiederwahl f

re-enter [riːˈɛntəʳ] vt (country) wieder einreisen in +acc; (Space) wieder eintreten in +acc

re-entry [riːˈɛntrɪ] n Wiedereinreise f; (Space) Wiedereintritt m

re-examine [riːɪgˈzæmɪn] vt (proposal etc) nochmals prüfen; (witness) nochmals vernehmen

re-export [ˈriːɪksˈpɔːt] vt wiederausführen ▷ n Wiederausfuhr f; (commodity) wiederausgeführte Ware f

ref [rɛf] (inf) n abbr (Sport) = **referee**

ref. abbr (Comm: = with reference to) betr.; **your ~** Ihr Zeichen:

refectory [rɪˈfɛktərɪ] n (in university) Mensa f

refer [rɪˈfəːʳ] vt: **to ~ sb to** (book etc) jdn verweisen auf +acc; (doctor, hospital) jdn überweisen zu; **to ~ sth to** (task, problem) etw übergeben an +acc; **he ~red me to the manager** er verwies mich an den Geschäftsführer
  ▸ **refer to** vt fus (mention) erwähnen; (relate to) sich beziehen auf +acc; (consult) hinzuziehen

referee [rɛfəˈriː] n (Sport) Schiedsrichter(in) m(f); (Brit: for job application) Referenz f ▷ vt als Schiedsrichter(in) leiten

reference [ˈrɛfrəns] n (mention) Hinweis m; (in book, article) Quellenangabe f; (for job application, person) Referenz f; **with ~ to** mit Bezug auf +acc; **"please quote this ~"** (Comm) „bitte dieses Zeichen angeben"

reference book n Nachschlagewerk nt

reference library n Präsenzbibliothek f

reference number n Aktenzeichen nt

referenda [rɛfəˈrɛndə] npl of **referendum**

referendum [rɛfəˈrɛndəm] (pl **referenda**) n Referendum nt, Volksentscheid m

referral [rɪˈfəːrəl] n (of matter, problem) Weiterleitung f; (to doctor, specialist) Überweisung f

refill [riːˈfɪl] vt nachfüllen ▷ n (for pen etc) Nachfüllmine f; (drink) Nachfüllung f

refine [rɪˈfaɪn] vt (sugar, oil) raffinieren; (theory, idea) verfeinern

refined [rɪˈfaɪnd] adj (person) kultiviert; (taste) fein, vornehm; (sugar, oil) raffiniert

refinement [rɪˈfaɪnmənt] n (of person) Kultiviertheit f; (of system, ideas) Verfeinerung f

refinery [rɪˈfaɪnərɪ] n (for oil etc) Raffinerie f

refit [riːˈfɪt] (Naut) n Überholung f ▷ vt (ship) überholen

reflate [riːˈfleɪt] vt (economy) ankurbeln

reflation [riːˈfleɪʃən] n (Econ) Reflation f

reflationary [riːˈfleɪʃənrɪ] adj (Econ) reflationär

reflect [rɪˈflɛkt] vt reflektieren; (fig) widerspiegeln ▷ vi (think) nachdenken
  ▸ **reflect on** vt fus (discredit) ein schlechtes Licht werfen auf +acc

reflection [rɪˈflɛkʃən] n (image) Spiegelbild nt; (of light, heat) Reflexion f; (fig) Widerspiegelung f; (: thought) Gedanke m; **on ~** nach genauerer Überlegung; **this is a ~ on ...** (criticism) das sagt einiges über ...

reflector [rɪˈflɛktəʳ] n (Aut etc) Rückstrahler m; (for light, heat) Reflektor m

reflex [ˈriːflɛks] adj Reflex-; **reflexes** npl (Physiol, Psych) Reflexe pl

reflexive [rɪˈflɛksɪv] adj (Ling) reflexiv

reform [rɪˈfɔ:m] n Reform f ▷ vt reformieren ▷ vi (criminal etc) sich bessern

reformat [ri:ˈfɔ:mæt] vt (Comput) neu formatieren

Reformation [rɛfəˈmeɪʃən] n: **the ~** die Reformation

reformatory [rɪˈfɔ:mətərɪ] (US) n Besserungsanstalt f

reformed [rɪˈfɔ:md] adj (character, alcoholic) gewandelt

refrain [rɪˈfreɪn] vi: **to ~ from doing sth** etw unterlassen ▷ n (of song) Refrain m

refresh [rɪˈfrɛʃ] vt erfrischen; **to ~ one's memory** sein Gedächtnis auffrischen

refresher course [rɪˈfrɛʃə-] n Auffrischungskurs m

refreshing [rɪˈfrɛʃɪŋ] adj erfrischend; (sleep) wohltuend; (idea etc) angenehm

refreshment [rɪˈfrɛʃmənt] n Erfrischung f

refreshments [rɪˈfrɛʃmənts] npl (food and drink) Erfrischungen pl

refrigeration [rɪfrɪdʒəˈreɪʃən] n Kühlung f

refrigerator [rɪˈfrɪdʒəreɪtəʳ] n Kühlschrank m

refuel [ri:ˈfjuəl] vt, vi auftanken

refuelling [ri:ˈfjuəlɪŋ] n Auftanken nt

refuge [ˈrɛfju:dʒ] n Zuflucht f; **to seek/take ~ in** Zuflucht suchen/nehmen in +dat

refugee [rɛfjuˈdʒi:] n Flüchtling m; **a political ~** ein politischer Flüchtling

refugee camp n Flüchtlingslager nt

refund [ˈri:fʌnd] n Rückerstattung f ▷ vt (money) zurückerstatten

refurbish [ri:ˈfə:bɪʃ] vt (shop etc) renovieren

refurbishment [ri:ˈfə:bɪʃmənt] n (of shop etc) Renovierung f

refurnish [ri:ˈfə:nɪʃ] vt neu möblieren

refusal [rɪˈfju:zəl] n Ablehnung f; **a ~ to do sth** eine Weigerung, etw zu tun; **to give sb first ~ on sth** jdm etw zuerst anbieten

refuse¹ [rɪˈfju:z] vt (request, offer etc) ablehnen; (gift) zurückweisen; (permission) verweigern ▷ vi ablehnen; (horse) verweigern; **to ~ to do sth** sich weigern, etw zu tun

refuse² [ˈrɛfju:s] n (rubbish) Abfall m, Müll m

refuse collection n Müllabfuhr f

refuse disposal n Müllbeseitigung f

refusenik [rɪˈfju:znɪk] n (inf) Verweigerer(in) m(f); (in former USSR) sowjetischer Jude, dem die Emigration nach Israel verweigert wurde

refute [rɪˈfju:t] vt (argument) widerlegen

regain [rɪˈgeɪn] vt wiedererlangen

regal [ˈri:gl] adj königlich

regale [rɪˈgeɪl] vt: **to ~ sb with sth** jdn mit etw verwöhnen

regalia [rɪˈgeɪlɪə] n (costume) Amtstracht f

regard [rɪˈgɑ:d] n (esteem) Achtung f ▷ vt (consider) ansehen, betrachten; (view) betrachten; **to give one's ~s to sb** jdm Grüße bestellen; **"with kindest ~s"** „mit freundlichen Grüßen"; **as regards, with ~ to** bezüglich +gen

regarding [rɪˈgɑ:dɪŋ] prep bezüglich +gen

regardless [rɪˈgɑ:dlɪs] adv trotzdem ▷ adj: **~ of** ohne Rücksicht auf +acc

regatta [rɪˈgætə] n Regatta f

regency [ˈri:dʒənsɪ] n Regentschaft f ▷ adj: **R~** (furniture etc) Regency-

regenerate [rɪˈdʒɛnəreɪt] vt (inner cities, arts) erneuern; (person, feelings) beleben ▷ vi (Biol) sich regenerieren

regent [ˈri:dʒənt] n Regent(in) m(f)

reggae [ˈrɛgeɪ] n Reggae m

regime [reɪˈʒi:m] n (government) Regime nt; (diet etc) Kur f

regiment [ˈrɛdʒɪmənt] n (Mil) Regiment nt ▷ vt reglementieren

regimental [rɛdʒɪˈmɛntl] adj Regiments-

regimentation [rɛdʒɪmɛnˈteɪʃən] n Reglementierung f

region [ˈri:dʒən] n (of land) Gebiet nt; (of body) Bereich m; (administrative division of country) Region f; **in the ~ of** (approximately) im Bereich von

regional [ˈri:dʒənl] adj regional

regional development n regionale Entwicklung f

regionalize [ˈri:dʒənəlaɪz] vt regionalisieren

register [ˈrɛdʒɪstəʳ] n (list, Mus) Register nt; (also: **electoral register**) Wählerverzeichnis nt; (Scol) Klassenbuch nt ▷ vt registrieren; (car) anmelden; (letter) als Einschreiben senden; (amount, measurement) verzeichnen ▷ vi (person) sich anmelden; (: at doctor's) sich (als Patient) eintragen; (amount etc) registriert werden; (make impression) (einen) Eindruck machen; **to ~ a protest** Protest anmelden

registered [ˈrɛdʒɪstəd] adj (letter, parcel) eingeschrieben; (drug addict, childminder etc) (offiziell) eingetragen

registered company n eingetragene Gesellschaft f

registered nurse (US) n staatlich geprüfte Krankenschwester f, staatlich geprüfter Krankenpfleger m

registered trademark n eingetragenes Warenzeichen nt

register office n = **registry office**

registrar [ˈrɛdʒɪstrɑ:ʳ] n (in registry office) Standesbeamte(r) m, Standesbeamtin f; (in college etc) Kanzler m; (Brit: in hospital) Krankenhausarzt m, Krankenhausärztin f

registration [rɛdʒɪsˈtreɪʃən] n Registrierung f; (of students, unemployed etc) Anmeldung f

registration number (Brit) n (Aut) polizeiliches Kennzeichen nt

registry [ˈrɛdʒɪstrɪ] n Registratur f

registry office (Brit) n Standesamt nt; **to get married in a ~** standesamtlich heiraten

regret [rɪˈgrɛt] n Bedauern nt ▷ vt bedauern; **with ~** mit Bedauern; **to have no ~s** nichts bereuen; **we ~ to inform you that ...** wir müssen Ihnen leider mitteilen, dass ...

regretfully [rɪˈgrɛtfəlɪ] adv mit Bedauern

regrettable [rɪˈgrɛtəbl] adj bedauerlich

regrettably [rɪˈgrɛtəblɪ] adv bedauerlicherweise; **~, he said ...**

r

743

bedauerlicherweise sagte er ...

Regt *abbr* (*Mil:* = *regiment*) Rgt.

regular ['rɛgjulə^r] *adj* (*also Ling*) regelmäßig; (*usual: time, doctor*) üblich; (: *customer*) Stamm-; (*soldier*) Berufs-; (*Comm: size*) normal ▷ *n* (*client*) Stammkunde *m*, Stammkundin *f*

regularity [rɛgju'lærɪtɪ] *n* Regelmäßigkeit *f*

regularly ['rɛgjuləlɪ] *adv* regelmäßig; (*breathe, beat: evenly*) gleichmäßig

regulate ['rɛgjuleɪt] *vt* regulieren

regulation [rɛgju'leɪʃən] *n* Regulierung *f*; (*rule*) Vorschrift *f*

regulatory [rɛgju'leɪtrɪ] *adj* (*system*) Regulierungs-; (*body, agency*) Überwachungs-

rehabilitate [riːə'bɪlɪteɪt] *vt* (*criminal, drug addict*) (in die Gesellschaft) wiedereingliedern; (*invalid*) rehabilitieren

rehabilitation ['riːəbɪlɪ'teɪʃən] *n* (*see vt*) Wiedereingliederung *f* (in die Gesellschaft); Rehabilitation *f*

rehash [riː'hæʃ] (*inf*) *vt* (*idea etc*) aufwärmen

rehearsal [rɪ'həːsəl] *n* (*Theat*) Probe *f*; **dress ~** Generalprobe *f*

rehearse [rɪ'həːs] *vt* (*play, speech etc*) proben

rehouse [riː'hauz] *vt* neu unterbringen

reign [reɪn] *n* (*lit, fig*) Herrschaft *f* ▷ *vi* (*lit, fig*) herrschen

reigning ['reɪnɪŋ] *adj* regierend; (*champion*) amtierend

reimburse [riːɪm'bəːs] *vt* die Kosten erstatten +*dat*

rein [reɪn] *n* Zügel *m*; **to give sb free ~** (*fig*) jdm freie Hand lassen; **to keep a tight ~ on sth** (*fig*) bei etw die Zügel kurz halten

reincarnation [riːɪnkɑː'neɪʃən] *n* (*belief*) die Wiedergeburt *f*; (*person*) Reinkarnation *f*

reindeer ['reɪndɪə^r] *n inv* Ren(tier) *nt*

reinforce [riːɪn'fɔːs] *vt* (*strengthen*) verstärken; (*support: idea etc*) stützen; (: *prejudice*) stärken

reinforced concrete *n* Stahlbeton *m*

reinforcement [riːɪn'fɔːsmənt] *n* (*strengthening*) Verstärkung *f*; (*of attitude etc*) Stärkung *f*; **reinforcements** *npl* (*Mil*) Verstärkung *f*

reinstate [riːɪn'steɪt] *vt* (*employee*) wiedereinstellen; (*tax, law*) wiedereinführen; (*text*) wiedereinfügen

reinstatement [riːɪn'steɪtmənt] *n* (*of employee*) Wiedereinstellung *f*

reissue [riː'ɪʃjuː] *vt* neu herausgeben

reiterate [riː'ɪtəreɪt] *vt* wiederholen

reject ['riːdʒɛkt] *n* (*Comm*) Ausschuss *m* *no pl* ▷ *vt* ablehnen; (*admirer*) abweisen; (*goods*) zurückweisen; (*machine: coin*) nicht annehmen; (*Med: heart, kidney*) abstoßen

rejection [rɪ'dʒɛkʃən] *n* Ablehnung *f*; (*of admirer*) Abweisung *f*; (*Med*) Abstoßung *f*

rejoice [rɪ'dʒɔɪs] *vi:* **to ~ at** *or* **over** jubeln über +*acc*

rejoinder [rɪ'dʒɔɪndə^r] *n* Erwiderung *f*

rejuvenate [rɪ'dʒuːvəneɪt] *vt* (*person*) verjüngen; (*organization etc*) beleben

rekindle [riː'kɪndl] *vt* (*interest, emotion etc*) wiedererwecken

relapse [rɪ'læps] *n* (*Med*) Rückfall *m* ▷ *vi:* **to ~ into** zurückfallen in +*acc*

relate [rɪ'leɪt] *vt* (*tell*) berichten; (*connect*) in Verbindung bringen ▷ *vi:* **to ~ to** (*empathize with: person, subject*) eine Beziehung finden zu; (*connect with*) zusammenhängen mit

related [rɪ'leɪtɪd] *adj:* **to be ~** (miteinander) verwandt sein; (*issues etc*) zusammenhängen

relating to [rɪ'leɪtɪŋ-] *prep* bezüglich +*gen*, mit Bezug auf +*acc*

relation [rɪ'leɪʃən] *n* (*member of family*) Verwandte(r) *f(m)*; (*connection*) Beziehung *f*; **relations** *npl* (*contact*) Beziehungen *pl*; **diplomatic/international ~s** diplomatische/ internationale Beziehungen; **in ~ to** im Verhältnis zu; **to bear no ~ to** in keinem Verhältnis stehen zu

relationship [rɪ'leɪʃənʃɪp] *n* Beziehung *f*; (*between countries*) Beziehungen *pl*; (*affair*) Verhältnis *nt*; **they have a good ~** sie haben ein gutes Verhältnis zueinander

relative ['rɛlətɪv] *n* Verwandte(r) *f(m)* ▷ *adj* relativ; **all her ~s** ihre ganze Verwandtschaft; **~ to** im Vergleich zu; **it's all ~** es ist alles relativ

relatively ['rɛlətɪvlɪ] *adv* relativ

relative pronoun *n* Relativpronomen *nt*

relax [rɪ'læks] *vi* (*person, muscle*) sich entspannen; (*calm down*) sich beruhigen ▷ *vt* (*one's grip*) lockern; (*mind, person*) entspannen; (*control etc*) lockern

relaxation [riːlæk'seɪʃən] *n* Entspannung *f*; (*of control etc*) Lockern *nt*

relaxed [rɪ'lækst] *adj* (*person, atmosphere*) entspannt; (*discussion*) locker

relaxing [rɪ'læksɪŋ] *adj* entspannend

relay ['riːleɪ] *n* (*race*) Staffel *f*, Staffellauf *m* ▷ *vt* (*message etc*) übermitteln; (*broadcast*) übertragen

release [rɪ'liːs] *n* (*from prison*) Entlassung *f*; (*from obligation, situation*) Befreiung *f*; (*of documents, funds etc*) Freigabe *f*; (*of gas etc*) Freisetzung *f*; (*of film, book, record*) Herausgabe *f*; (*record, film*) Veröffentlichung *f*; (*Tech: device*) Auslöser *m* ▷ *vt* (*from prison*) entlassen; (*person: from obligation, from wreckage*) befreien; (*gas etc*) freisetzen; (*Tech, Aut: catch, brake etc*) lösen; (*record, film*) herausbringen; (*news, figures*) bekannt geben; **on general ~** (*film*) überall in den Kinos; *see also* **press release**

relegate ['rɛləgeɪt] *vt* (*downgrade*) herunterstufen; (*Brit: Sport*): **to be ~d** absteigen

relent [rɪ'lɛnt] *vi* (*give in*) nachgeben

relentless [rɪ'lɛntlɪs] *adj* (*heat, noise*) erbarmungslos; (*enemy etc*) unerbittlich

relevance ['rɛləvəns] *n* Relevanz *f*, Bedeutung *f*; **the ~ of religion to society** die Relevanz *or* Bedeutung der Religion für die Gesellschaft

relevant ['rɛləvənt] *adj* relevant; (*chapter, area*) entsprechend; **~ to** relevant für

reliability [rɪlaɪə'bɪlɪtɪ] *n* Zuverlässigkeit *f*

reliable [rɪ'laɪəbl] *adj* zuverlässig

reliably [rɪ'laɪəblɪ] *adv*: **to be ~ informed that ...** zuverlässige Informationen darüber haben, dass ...

reliance [rɪ'laɪəns] *n*: **~ (on)** *(person)* Angewiesenheit *f* (auf +*acc*); *(drugs, financial support)* Abhängigkeit *f* (von)

reliant [rɪ'laɪənt] *adj*: **to be ~ on sth/sb** auf etw/jdn angewiesen sein

relic ['relɪk] *n* *(Rel)* Reliquie *f*; *(of the past)* Relikt *nt*

relief [rɪ'liːf] *n* *(from pain etc)* Erleichterung *f*; *(aid)* Hilfe *f*; *(Art, Geog)* Relief *nt* ▷ *cpd* *(bus)* Entlastungs-; *(driver)* zur Ablösung; **light ~** leichte Abwechslung *f*

relief map *n* Reliefkarte *f*

relief road *(Brit)* *n* Entlastungsstraße *f*

relieve [rɪ'liːv] *vt* *(pain)* lindern; *(fear, worry)* mildern; *(take over from)* ablösen; **to ~ sb of sth** *(load)* jdm etw abnehmen; *(duties, post)* jdn einer Sache *gen* entheben; **to ~ o.s.** *(euphemism)* sich erleichtern

relieved [rɪ'liːvd] *adj* erleichtert; **I'm ~ to hear it** es erleichtert mich, das zu hören

religion [rɪ'lɪdʒən] *n* Religion *f*

religious [rɪ'lɪdʒəs] *adj* religiös

religious education *n* Religionsunterricht *m*

religiously [rɪ'lɪdʒəslɪ] *adv* *(regularly, thoroughly)* gewissenhaft

relinquish [rɪ'lɪŋkwɪʃ] *vt* *(control etc)* aufgeben; *(claim)* verzichten auf +*acc*

relish ['relɪʃ] *n* *(Culin)* würzige Soße *f*, Relish *nt*; *(enjoyment)* Genuss *m* ▷ *vt* *(enjoy)* genießen; **to ~ doing sth** etw mit Genuss tun

relive [riː'lɪv] *vt* noch einmal durchleben

reload [riː'ləʊd] *vt* *(gun)* neu laden

relocate [riːləʊ'keɪt] *vt* verlegen ▷ *vi* den Standort wechseln; **to ~ in** seinen Standort verlegen nach

reluctance [rɪ'lʌktəns] *n* Widerwille *m*

reluctant [rɪ'lʌktənt] *adj* unwillig, widerwillig; **I'm ~ to do that** es widerstrebt mir, das zu tun

reluctantly [rɪ'lʌktəntlɪ] *adv* widerwillig, nur ungern

rely on [rɪ'laɪ-] *vt fus* *(be dependent on)* abhängen von; *(trust)* sich verlassen auf +*acc*

remain [rɪ'meɪn] *vi* bleiben; *(survive)* übrig bleiben; **to ~ silent** weiterhin schweigen; **to ~ in control** die Kontrolle behalten; **much ~s to be done** es ist noch viel zu tun; **the fact ~s that ...** Tatsache ist und bleibt, dass ...; **it ~s to be seen whether ...** es bleibt abzuwarten, ob ...

remainder [rɪ'meɪndəʳ] *n* Rest *m* ▷ *vt* *(Comm)* zu ermäßigtem Preis anbieten

remaining [rɪ'meɪnɪŋ] *adj* übrig

remains [rɪ'meɪnz] *npl* *(of meal)* Überreste *pl*; *(of building etc)* Ruinen *pl*; *(of body)* sterbliche Überreste *pl*

remand [rɪ'mɑːnd] *n*: **to be on ~** in Untersuchungshaft sein ▷ *vt*: **to be ~ed in custody** in Untersuchungshaft bleiben müssen

remand home *(formerly: Brit)* *n* Untersuchungsgefängnis *nt* für Jugendliche

remark [rɪ'mɑːk] *n* Bemerkung *f* ▷ *vt* bemerken ▷ *vi*: **to ~ on sth** Bemerkungen über etw *acc* machen; **to ~ that** die Bemerkung machen, dass

remarkable [rɪ'mɑːkəbl] *adj* bemerkenswert

remarry [riː'mærɪ] *vi* wieder heiraten

remedial [rɪ'miːdɪəl] *adj* *(tuition, classes)* Förder-; **~ exercise** Heilgymnastik *f*

remedy ['remədɪ] *n* *(lit, fig)* (Heil)mittel *nt* ▷ *vt* *(mistake, situation)* abhelfen +*dat*

remember [rɪ'membəʳ] *vt* *(call back to mind)* sich erinnern an +*acc*; *(bear in mind)* denken an +*acc*; **~ me to him** *(send greetings)* grüße ihn von mir; **I ~ seeing it, I ~ having seen it** ich erinnere mich (daran), es gesehen zu haben; **she ~ed to do it** sie hat daran gedacht, es zu tun

remembrance [rɪ'membrəns] *n* Erinnerung *f*; **in ~ of sb/sth** im Gedenken an +*acc*

Remembrance Sunday *(Brit)* *n* ≈ Volkstrauertag *m*; *siehe Info-Artikel*

○ **REMEMBRANCE SUNDAY**

○ *Remembrance Sunday* oder *Remembrance*
○ *Day* ist der britische Gedenktag für
○ die Gefallenen der beiden Weltkriege
○ und anderer Konflikte. Er fällt auf
○ einen Sonntag vor oder nach dem 11.
○ November (am 11. November 1918 endete
○ der Erste Weltkrieg) und wird mit einer
○ Schweigeminute, Kranzniederlegungen
○ an Kriegerdenkmälern und dem Tragen
○ von Anstecknadeln in Form einer
○ Mohnblume begangen.

remind [rɪ'maɪnd] *vt*: **to ~ sb to do sth** jdn daran erinnern, etw zu tun; **to ~ sb of sth** jdn an etw *acc* erinnern; **to ~ sb that ...** jdn daran erinnern, dass ...; **she ~s me of her mother** sie erinnert mich an ihre Mutter; **that ~s me!** dabei fällt mir etwas ein!

reminder [rɪ'maɪndəʳ] *n* *(of person, place etc)* Erinnerung *f*; *(letter)* Mahnung *f*

reminisce [remɪ'nɪs] *vi*: **to ~ (about)** sich in Erinnerungen ergehen (über +*acc*)

reminiscences [remɪ'nɪsnsɪz] *npl* Erinnerungen *pl*

reminiscent [remɪ'nɪsnt] *adj*: **to be ~ of sth** an etw *acc* erinnern

remiss [rɪ'mɪs] *adj* nachlässig; **it was ~ of him** es war nachlässig von ihm

remission [rɪ'mɪʃən] *n* *(of sentence)* Straferlass *m*; *(Med)* Remission *f*; *(Rel)* Erlass *m*

remit [rɪ'mɪt] *vt* *(money)* überweisen ▷ *n* *(of official etc)* Aufgabenbereich *m*

remittance [rɪ'mɪtns] *n* Überweisung *f*

remnant ['remnənt] *n* Überrest *m*; *(Comm: of cloth)* Rest *m*

remonstrate ['remənstreɪt] *vi*: **to ~ (with sb about sth)** sich beschweren (bei jdm wegen etw)

r

remorse [rɪ'mɔːs] n Reue f
remorseful [rɪ'mɔːsful] adj reumütig
remorseless [rɪ'mɔːslɪs] adj (noise, pain)
unbarmherzig
remote [rɪ'məut] adj (distant: place, time) weit
entfernt; (aloof) distanziert; (slight: chance etc)
entfernt; **there is a ~ possibility that ...** es
besteht eventuell die Möglichkeit, dass ...
remote control n Fernsteuerung f; (TV etc)
Fernbedienung f
remote-controlled [rɪ'məutkən'trəuld] adj
ferngesteuert
remotely [rɪ'məutlɪ] adv (slightly) entfernt
remoteness [rɪ'məutnɪs] n (of place)
Entlegenheit f; (of person) Distanziertheit f
remould ['riːməuld] (Brit) n (Aut)
runderneuerter Reifen m
removable [rɪ'muːvəbl] adj (detachable)
abnehmbar
removal [rɪ'muːvəl] n (of object etc) Entfernung
f; (of threat etc) Beseitigung f; (Brit: from house)
Umzug m; (dismissal) Entlassung f; (Med: of
kidney etc) Entfernung f
removal man (Brit) n Möbelpacker m
removal van (Brit) n Möbelwagen m
remove [rɪ'muːv] vt entfernen; (clothing)
ausziehen; (bandage etc) abnehmen; (employee)
entlassen; (name: from list) streichen; (doubt,
threat, obstacle) beseitigen; **my first cousin
once ~d** mein Vetter ersten Grades
remover [rɪ'muːvər] n (for paint, varnish)
Entferner m; **stain ~** Fleckentferner m; **make-
up ~** Make-up-Entferner m
remunerate [rɪ'mjuːnəreɪt] vt vergüten
remuneration [rɪmjuːnə'reɪʃən] n Vergütung f
Renaissance [rɪ'neɪsɑːs] n: **the ~** die
Renaissance
renal ['riːnl] adj (Med) Nieren-
renal failure n Nierenversagen nt
rename [riː'neɪm] vt umbenennen
rend [rɛnd] (pt, pp **rent**) vt (air, silence) zerreißen
render ['rɛndər] vt (give: assistance, aid) leisten;
(cause to become: unconscious, harmless, useless)
machen; (submit) vorlegen
rendering ['rɛndərɪŋ] (Brit) n = **rendition**
rendezvous ['rɒndɪvuː] n (meeting) Rendezvous
nt; (place) Treffpunkt m ▷ vi (people) sich
treffen; (spacecraft) ein Rendezvousmanöver
durchführen; **to ~ with sb** sich mit jdm
treffen
rendition [rɛn'dɪʃən] n (of song etc) Vortrag m
renegade ['rɛnɪɡeɪd] n Renegat(in) m(f),
Überläufer(in) m(f)
renew [rɪ'njuː] vt erneuern; (attack, negotiations)
wiederaufnehmen; (loan, contract etc)
verlängern; (relationship etc) wiederaufleben
lassen
renewable [rɪ'njuːəbl] vt (energy) erneuerbar
renewables npl erneuerbare Energien pl
renewal [rɪ'njuːəl] n Erneuerung f; (of
conflict) Wiederaufnahme f; (of contract etc)
Verlängerung f
renounce [rɪ'nauns] vt verzichten auf +acc;

(belief) aufgeben
renovate ['rɛnəveɪt] vt (building) restaurieren;
(machine) überholen
renovation [rɛnə'veɪʃən] n (see vb)
Restaurierung f; Überholung f
renown [rɪ'naun] n Ruf m
renowned [rɪ'naund] adj berühmt
rent [rɛnt] pt, pp of **rend** ▷ n (for house) Miete f
▷ vt mieten; (also: **rent out**) vermieten
rental ['rɛntl] n (for television, car) Mietgebühr f
rent boy (inf) n Strichjunge m
rent strike n Mietstreik m
renunciation [rɪnʌnsɪ'eɪʃən] n Verzicht m; (of
belief) Aufgabe f; (self-denial) Selbstverleugnung
f
reopen [riː'əupən] vt (shop etc) wiedereröffnen;
(negotiations, legal case etc) wiederaufnehmen
reopening [riː'əupnɪŋ] n (see vt)
Wiedereröffnung f; Wiederaufnahme f
reorder [riː'ɔːdər] vt (rearrange) umordnen
reorganization ['riːɔːɡənaɪ'zeɪʃən] n
Umorganisation f
reorganize [riː'ɔːɡənaɪz] vt umorganisieren
Rep. (US) abbr (Pol) = **representative;
Republican**
rep [rɛp] n abbr (Comm) = **representative**; (Theat)
= **repertory**
repair [rɪ'pɛər] n Reparatur f ▷ vt reparieren;
(clothes, road) ausbessern; **in good/bad ~** in
gutem/schlechtem Zustand; **beyond ~** nicht
mehr zu reparieren; **to be under ~** (road)
ausgebessert werden
repair kit n (for bicycle) Flickzeug nt
repair man n Handwerker m
repair shop n Reparaturwerkstatt f
repartee [rɛpɑː'tiː] n (exchange) Schlagabtausch
m; (reply) schlagfertige Bemerkung f
repast [rɪ'pɑːst] n (form) Mahl nt
repatriate [riː'pætrɪeɪt] vt repatriieren
repay [riː'peɪ] (irreg: like **pay**) vt zurückzahlen;
(sb's efforts, attention) belohnen; (favour)
erwidern
repayment [riː'peɪmənt] n Rückzahlung f
repeal [rɪ'piːl] n (of law) Aufhebung f ▷ vt (law)
aufheben
repeat [rɪ'piːt] n (Radio, TV) Wiederholung
f ▷ vt, vi wiederholen ▷ cpd (performance)
Wiederholungs-; (order) Nach-; **to ~ o.s./
itself** sich wiederholen; **to ~ an order for
sth** etw nachbestellen
repeatedly [rɪ'piːtɪdlɪ] adv wiederholt
repel [rɪ'pɛl] vt (drive away) zurückschlagen;
(disgust) abstoßen
repellent [rɪ'pɛlənt] adj abstoßend ▷ n: **insect
~** Insekten(schutz)mittel nt
repent [rɪ'pɛnt] vi: **to ~ of sth** etw bereuen
repentance [rɪ'pɛntəns] n Reue f
repercussions [riːpə'kʌʃənz] npl
Auswirkungen pl
repertoire ['rɛpətwɑːr] n (Mus, Theat) Repertoire
nt; (fig) Spektrum nt
repertory ['rɛpətərɪ] n (also: **repertory theatre**)
Repertoiretheater nt

repertory company n Repertoire-Ensemble nt
repetition [rɛpɪˈtɪʃən] n (repeat) Wiederholung f
repetitious [rɛpɪˈtɪʃəs] adj (speech etc) voller
  Wiederholungen
repetitive [rɪˈpɛtɪtɪv] adj eintönig, monoton
replace [rɪˈpleɪs] vt (put back: upright)
  zurückstellen; (: flat) zurücklegen; (take
  the place of) ersetzen; **to ~ X with Y** X durch
  Y ersetzen; **"~ the receiver"** (Tel) „Hörer
  auflegen"
replacement [rɪˈpleɪsmənt] n Ersatz m
replacement part n Ersatzteil nt
replay [ˈriːpleɪ] n (of match) Wiederholungsspiel
  nt ▷ vt (match) wiederholen; (track, song: on tape)
  nochmals abspielen
replenish [rɪˈplɛnɪʃ] vt (glass, stock etc) auffüllen
replete [rɪˈpliːt] adj (after meal) gesättigt; **~ with**
  reichlich ausgestattet mit
replica [ˈrɛplɪkə] n (of object) Nachbildung f
reply [rɪˈplaɪ] n Antwort f ▷ vi: **to ~ (to sb/
  sth)** (jdm/auf etw acc) antworten; **in ~ to** als
  Antwort auf +acc; **there's no ~** (Tel) es meldet
  sich niemand
reply coupon n Antwortschein m
report [rɪˈpɔːt] n Bericht m; (Brit: also:
  school report) Zeugnis nt; (of gun) Knall m
  ▷ vt berichten; (casualties, damage, theft etc)
  melden; (person: to police) anzeigen ▷ vi (make
  a report) Bericht erstatten; **to ~ to sb** (present
  o.s. to) sich bei jdm melden; (be responsible
  to) jdm unterstellt sein; **to ~ on sth** über
  etw acc Bericht erstatten; **to ~ sick** sich
  krankmelden; **it is ~ed that** es wird berichtet
  or gemeldet, dass ...
report card (US, Scot) n Zeugnis nt
reportedly [rɪˈpɔːtɪdlɪ] adv: **she is ~ living in
  Spain** sie lebt angeblich in Spanien
reported speech n (Ling) indirekte Rede f
reporter [rɪˈpɔːtəʳ] n Reporter(in) m(f)
repose [rɪˈpəʊz] n: **in ~** in Ruhestellung
repository [rɪˈpɒzɪtərɪ] n (person: of knowledge)
  Quelle f; (place: of collection etc) Lager nt
repossess [ˈriːpəˈzɛs] vt (wieder) in Besitz
  nehmen
repossession order [riːpəˈzɛʃən-] n
  Beschlagnahmungsverfügung f
reprehensible [rɛprɪˈhɛnsɪbl] adj verwerflich
represent [rɛprɪˈzɛnt] vt (person, nation)
  vertreten; (show: view, opinion) darstellen;
  (symbolize: idea) symbolisieren, verkörpern; **to ~
  sth as** (describe) etw darstellen als
representation [rɛprɪzɛnˈteɪʃən] n (state
  of being represented) Vertretung f; (picture etc)
  Darstellung f; **representations** npl (protest)
  Proteste pl
representative [rɛprɪˈzɛntətɪv] n (also Comm)
  Vertreter(in) m(f); (US: Pol) Abgeordnete(r)
  f(m) des Repräsentantenhauses ▷ adj
  repräsentativ; **~ of** repräsentativ für
repress [rɪˈprɛs] vt unterdrücken
repression [rɪˈprɛʃən] n Unterdrückung f
repressive [rɪˈprɛsɪv] adj repressiv
reprieve [rɪˈpriːv] n (cancellation) Begnadigung

f; (postponement) Strafaufschub m; (fig)
  Gnadenfrist f ▷ vt: **he was ~d** (see n) er wurde
  begnadigt; ihm wurde Strafaufschub gewährt
reprimand [ˈrɛprɪmɑːnd] n Tadel m ▷ vt tadeln
reprint [ˈriːprɪnt] n Nachdruck m ▷ vt
  nachdrucken
reprisal [rɪˈpraɪzl] n Vergeltung f; **reprisals** npl
  Repressalien pl; (in war) Vergeltungsaktionen
  pl; **to take ~s** zu Repressalien greifen; (in war)
  Vergeltungsaktionen durchführen
reproach [rɪˈprəʊtʃ] n (rebuke) Vorwurf m
  ▷ vt: **to ~ sb for sth** jdm etw zum Vorwurf
  machen; **beyond ~** über jeden Vorwurf
  erhaben; **to ~ sb with sth** jdm etw vorwerfen
reproachful [rɪˈprəʊtʃful] adj vorwurfsvoll
reproduce [riːprəˈdjuːs] vt reproduzieren ▷ vi
  (Biol) sich vermehren
reproduction [riːprəˈdʌkʃən] n Reproduktion f;
  (Biol) Fortpflanzung f
reproductive [riːprəˈdʌktɪv] adj (system, organs)
  Fortpflanzungs-
reproof [rɪˈpruːf] n (rebuke) Tadel m; **with ~**
  tadelnd
reprove [rɪˈpruːv] vt tadeln; **to ~ sb for sth** jdn
  wegen etw tadeln
reproving [rɪˈpruːvɪŋ] adj tadelnd
reptile [ˈrɛptaɪl] n Reptil nt
Repub. (US) abbr (Pol) = **Republican**
republic [rɪˈpʌblɪk] n Republik f
republican [rɪˈpʌblɪkən] adj republikanisch ▷ n
  Republikaner(in) m(f); **the R~s** (US: Pol) die
  Republikaner
repudiate [rɪˈpjuːdɪeɪt] vt (accusation)
  zurückweisen; (violence) ablehnen; (old: friend,
  wife etc) verstoßen
repugnance [rɪˈpʌgnəns] n Abscheu m
repugnant [rɪˈpʌgnənt] adj abstoßend
repulse [rɪˈpʌls] vt (attack etc) zurückschlagen;
  (sight, picture etc) abstoßen
repulsion [rɪˈpʌlʃən] n Abscheu m
repulsive [rɪˈpʌlsɪv] adj widerwärtig,
  abstoßend
reputable [ˈrɛpjutəbl] adj (make, company etc)
  angesehen
reputation [rɛpjuˈteɪʃən] n Ruf m; **to have a ~
  for** einen Ruf haben für; **he has a ~ for being
  awkward** er gilt als schwierig
repute [rɪˈpjuːt] n: **of ~** angesehen; **to be held
  in high ~** in hohem Ansehen stehen
reputed [rɪˈpjuːtɪd] adj angeblich; **he is ~ to
  be rich** er ist angeblich reich
reputedly [rɪˈpjuːtɪdlɪ] adv angeblich
request [rɪˈkwɛst] n (polite) Bitte f; (formal)
  Ersuchen nt; (Radio) Musikwunsch m ▷ vt
  (politely) bitten um; (formally) ersuchen; **at the
  ~ of** auf Wunsch von; **"you are ~ed not to
  smoke"** „bitte nicht rauchen"
request stop (Brit) n Bedarfshaltestelle f
requiem [ˈrɛkwɪəm] n (Rel: also: **requiem mass**)
  Totenmesse f; (Mus) Requiem nt
require [rɪˈkwaɪəʳ] vt (need) benötigen;
  (: situation) erfordern; (demand) verlangen; **to ~
  sb to do sth** von jdm verlangen, etw zu tun;

r

if ~d falls nötig; **what qualifications are ~d?** welche Qualifikationen werden verlangt?; **~d by law** gesetzlich vorgeschrieben

required [rɪˈkwaɪəd] *adj* erforderlich

requirement [rɪˈkwaɪəmənt] *n* (*need*) Bedarf *m*; (*condition*) Anforderung *f*; **to meet sb's ~s** jds Anforderungen erfüllen

requisite [ˈrɛkwɪzɪt] *adj* erforderlich; **requisites** *npl*: **toilet/travel ~s** Toiletten-/Reiseartikel *pl*

requisition [rɛkwɪˈzɪʃən] *n*: **~ (for)** (*demand*) Anforderung *f* (von) ▷ *vt* (*Mil*) beschlagnahmen

reroute [riːˈruːt] *vt* (*train etc*) umleiten

resale [riːˈseɪl] *n* Weiterverkauf *m*; **"not for ~"** „nicht zum Weiterverkauf bestimmt"

resale price maintenance *n* Preisbindung *f*

rescind [rɪˈsɪnd] *vt* (*law, order*) aufheben; (*decision*) rückgängig machen; (*agreement*) widerrufen

rescue [ˈrɛskjuː] *n* Rettung *f* ▷ *vt* retten; **to come to sb's ~** jdm zu Hilfe kommen

rescue party *n* Rettungsmannschaft *f*

rescuer [ˈrɛskjuəʳ] *n* Retter(in) *m(f)*

research [rɪˈsəːtʃ] *n* Forschung *f* ▷ *vt* erforschen ▷ *vi*: **to ~ into sth** etw erforschen; **to do ~** Forschung betreiben; **a piece of ~** eine Forschungsarbeit; **~ and development** Forschung und Entwicklung

researcher [rɪˈsəːtʃəʳ] *n* Forscher(in) *m(f)*

research work *n* Forschungsarbeit *f*

research worker *n* = **researcher**

resell [riːˈsɛl] (*irreg: like* **sell**) *vt* weiterverkaufen

resemblance [rɪˈzɛmbləns] *n* Ähnlichkeit *f*; **to bear a strong ~ to** starke Ähnlichkeit haben mit; **it bears no ~ to ...** es hat keine Ähnlichkeit mit ...

resemble [rɪˈzɛmbl] *vt* ähneln +*dat*, gleichen +*dat*

resent [rɪˈzɛnt] *vt* (*attitude, treatment*) missbilligen; (*person*) ablehnen

resentful [rɪˈzɛntful] *adj* (*person*) gekränkt; (*attitude*) missbilligend

resentment [rɪˈzɛntmənt] *n* Verbitterung *f*

reservation [rɛzəˈveɪʃən] *n* (*booking*) Reservierung *f*; (*doubt*) Vorbehalt *m*; (*land*) Reservat *nt*; **to make a ~** (*in hotel etc*) eine Reservierung vornehmen; **with ~(s)** (*doubts*) unter Vorbehalt

reservation desk *n* Reservierungsschalter *m*

reserve [rɪˈzəːv] *n* Reserve *f*, Vorrat *m*; (*fig: of talent etc*) Reserve *f*; (*Sport*) Reservespieler(in) *m(f)*; (*also:* **nature reserve**) Naturschutzgebiet *nt*; (*restraint*) Zurückhaltung *f* ▷ *vt* reservieren; (*table, ticket*) reservieren lassen; **reserves** *npl* (*Mil*) Reserve *f*; **in ~** in Reserve

reserve currency *n* Reservewährung *f*

reserved [rɪˈzəːvd] *adj* (*restrained*) zurückhaltend; (*seat*) reserviert

reserve price (*Brit*) *n* Mindestpreis *m*

reserve team (*Brit*) *n* Reservemannschaft *f*

reservist [rɪˈzəːvɪst] *n* (*Mil*) Reservist *m*

reservoir [ˈrɛzəvwɑːʳ] *n* (*lit, fig*) Reservoir *nt*

reset [riːˈsɛt] (*irreg: like* **set**) *vt* (*watch*) neu stellen; (*broken bone*) wieder einrichten; (*Comput*) zurückstellen

reshape [riːˈʃeɪp] *vt* (*policy, view*) umgestalten

reshuffle [riːˈʃʌfl] *n*: **cabinet ~** Kabinettsumbildung *f*

reside [rɪˈzaɪd] *vi* (*live: person*) seinen/ihren Wohnsitz haben

▶ **reside in** *vt fus* (*exist*) liegen in +*dat*

residence [ˈrɛzɪdəns] *n* (*form: home*) Wohnsitz *m*; (*length of stay*) Aufenthalt *m*; **to take up ~** sich niederlassen; **in ~** (*queen etc*) anwesend; **writer/artist in ~** Schriftsteller/Künstler, der in einer Ausbildungsstätte bei freier Unterkunft lehrt und arbeitet

residence permit (*Brit*) *n* Aufenthaltserlaubnis *f*

resident [ˈrɛzɪdənt] *n* (*of country, town*) Einwohner(in) *m(f)*; (*in hotel*) Gast *m* ▷ *adj* (*in country, town*) wohnhaft; (*population*) ansässig; (*doctor*) hauseigen; (*landlord*) im Hause wohnend

residential [rɛzɪˈdɛnʃəl] *adj* (*area*) Wohn-; (*course*) mit Wohnung am Ort; (*staff*) im Hause wohnend

residue [ˈrɛzɪdjuː] *n* (*Chem*) Rückstand *m*; (*fig*) Überrest *m*

resign [rɪˈzaɪn] *vt* (*one's post*) zurücktreten von ▷ *vi* (*from post*) zurücktreten; **to ~ o.s. to** (*situation etc*) sich abfinden mit

resignation [rɛzɪɡˈneɪʃən] *n* (*from post*) Rücktritt *m*; (*state of mind*) Resignation *f*; **to tender one's ~** seine Kündigung einreichen

resigned [rɪˈzaɪnd] *adj*: **to be ~ to sth** sich mit etw abgefunden haben

resilience [rɪˈzɪliəns] *n* (*of material*) Widerstandsfähigkeit *f*; (*of person*) Unverwüstlichkeit *f*

resilient [rɪˈzɪliənt] *adj* (*see n*) widerstandsfähig; unverwüstlich

resin [ˈrɛzɪn] *n* Harz *nt*

resist [rɪˈzɪst] *vt* (*change, demand*) sich widersetzen +*dat*; (*attack etc*) Widerstand leisten +*dat*; (*urge etc*) widerstehen +*dat*; **I couldn't ~ (doing) it** ich konnte nicht widerstehen(, es zu tun)

resistance [rɪˈzɪstəns] *n* (*also Elec*) Widerstand *m*; (*to illness*) Widerstandsfähigkeit *f*

resistant [rɪˈzɪstənt] *adj*: **~ (to)** (*to change etc*) widerstandsfähig (gegenüber); (*to antibiotics etc*) resistent (gegen)

resolute [ˈrɛzəluːt] *adj* (*person*) entschlossen, resolut; (*refusal*) entschieden

resolution [rɛzəˈluːʃən] *n* (*decision*) Beschluss *m*; (*determination*) Entschlossenheit *f*; (*of problem*) Lösung *f*; **to make a ~** einen Entschluss fassen

resolve [rɪˈzɔlv] *n* (*determination*) Entschlossenheit *f* ▷ *vt* (*problem*) lösen; (*difficulty*) beseitigen ▷ *vi*: **to ~ to do sth** beschließen, etw zu tun

resolved [rɪˈzɔlvd] *adj* (*determined*) entschlossen

resonance [ˈrɛzənəns] *n* Resonanz *f*

resonant ['rɛzənənt] adj (sound, voice)
volltönend; (place) widerhallend
resort [rɪ'zɔːt] n (town) Urlaubsort m; (recourse)
Zuflucht f ▷ vi: **to ~ to** Zuflucht nehmen
zu; **seaside ~** Seebad nt; **winter sports ~**
Wintersportort m; **as a last ~** als letzter
Ausweg; **in the last ~** schlimmstenfalls
resound [rɪ'zaund] vi: **to ~ (with)** widerhallen
(von)
resounding [rɪ'zaundɪŋ] adj (noise)
widerhallend; (voice) schallend; (fig: success)
durchschlagend; (: victory) überlegen
resource [rɪ'sɔːs] n (raw material) Bodenschatz
m; **resources** npl (coal, oil etc) Energiequellen
pl; (money) Mittel pl, Ressourcen pl; **natural ~s**
Naturschätze pl
resourceful [rɪ'sɔːsful] adj einfallsreich
resourcefulness [rɪ'sɔːsfulnɪs] n
Einfallsreichtum m
respect [rɪs'pɛkt] n (consideration, esteem)
Respekt m ▷ vt respektieren; **respects** npl
(greetings) Grüße pl; **to have ~ for sb/sth**
Respekt vor jdm/etw haben; **to show sb/sth**
~ Respekt vor jdm/etw zeigen; **out of ~ for**
aus Rücksicht auf +acc; **with ~ to, in ~ of** in
Bezug auf +acc; **in this ~** in dieser Hinsicht;
in some/many ~s in gewisser/vielfacher
Hinsicht; **with (all due) ~** bei allem Respekt
respectability [rɪspɛktə'bɪlɪtɪ] n
Anständigkeit f
respectable [rɪs'pɛktəbl] adj anständig;
(amount, income) ansehnlich; (standard, mark etc)
ordentlich
respected [rɪs'pɛktɪd] adj angesehen
respectful [rɪs'pɛktful] adj respektvoll
respectfully [rɪs'pɛktfəlɪ] adv (behave)
respektvoll
respective [rɪs'pɛktɪv] adj jeweilig
respectively [rɪs'pɛktɪvlɪ] adv
beziehungsweise; **Germany and**
Britain were 3rd and 4th ~ Deutschland
und Großbritannien belegten den 3.
beziehungsweise 4. Platz
respiration [rɛspɪ'reɪʃən] n see **artificial**
respirator ['rɛspɪreɪtəʳ] n Respirator m,
Beatmungsgerät nt
respiratory ['rɛspərətərɪ] adj (system, failure)
Atmungs-
respite ['rɛspaɪt] n (rest) Ruhepause f
resplendent [rɪs'plɛndənt] adj (clothes)
prächtig
respond [rɪs'pɔnd] vi (answer) antworten; (react)
reagieren
respondent [rɪs'pɔndənt] n (Law) Beklagte(r)
f(m)
response [rɪs'pɔns] n (to question) Antwort f;
(to event etc) Reaktion f; **in ~ to** als Antwort/
Reaktion auf +acc
responsibility [rɪspɔnsɪ'bɪlɪtɪ] n
Verantwortung f; **to take ~ for sth/sb** die
Verantwortung für etw/jdn übernehmen
responsible [rɪs'pɔnsɪbl] adj verantwortlich;
(reliable, important) verantwortungsvoll; **to be**

~ for sth für etw verantwortlich sein; **to be**
~ for doing sth dafür verantwortlich sein,
etw zu tun; **to be ~ to sb** jdm gegenüber
verantwortlich sein
responsibly [rɪs'pɔnsɪblɪ] adv
verantwortungsvoll
responsive [rɪs'pɔnsɪv] adj (person) ansprechbar
rest [rɛst] n (relaxation) Ruhe f; (pause)
Ruhepause f; (remainder) Rest m; (support)
Stütze f; (Mus) Pause f ▷ vi (relax) sich ausruhen
▷ vt (eyes, legs etc) ausruhen; **the ~ of them**
die Übrigen; **to put** or **set sb's mind at ~**
jdn beruhigen; **to come to ~** (object) zum
Stillstand kommen; **to lay sb to ~** jdn zur
letzten Ruhe betten; **to ~ on sth** (lit, fig) sich
auf etw acc stützen; **to let the matter ~** die
Sache auf sich beruhen lassen; **~ assured**
that ... seien Sie versichert, dass ...; **I won't**
~ until ... ich werde nicht ruhen, bis ...; **may**
he/she ~ in peace möge er/sie in Frieden
ruhen; **to ~ sth on/against sth** (lean) etw an
acc/gegen etw lehnen; **to ~ one's eyes** or **gaze**
on sth den Blick auf etw heften; **I ~ my case**
mehr brauche ich dazu wohl nicht zu sagen
restart [riː'stɑːt] vt (engine) wieder anlassen;
(work) wiederaufnehmen
restaurant ['rɛstərɔŋ] n Restaurant nt
restaurant car (Brit) n (Rail) Speisewagen m
rest cure n Erholung f
restful ['rɛstful] adj (music) ruhig; (lighting)
beruhigend; (atmosphere) friedlich
rest home n Pflegeheim nt
restitution [rɛstɪ'tjuːʃən] n: **to make ~ to**
sb of sth jdm etw zurückerstatten; (as
compensation) jdn für etw entschädigen
restive ['rɛstɪv] adj (person, crew) unruhig; (horse)
störrisch
restless ['rɛstlɪs] adj rastlos; (audience) unruhig;
to get ~ unruhig werden
restlessly ['rɛstlɪslɪ] adv (walk around) rastlos;
(turn over) unruhig
restock [riː'stɔk] vt (shop, freezer) wieder
auffüllen; (lake, river: with fish) wieder besetzen
restoration [rɛstə'reɪʃən] n (of painting etc)
Restauration f; (of law and order, health, sight etc)
Wiederherstellung f; (of land, rights) Rückgabe
f; (Hist): **the R~** die Restauration
restorative [rɪ'stɔrətɪv] adj (power, treatment)
stärkend ▷ n (old: drink) Stärkungsmittel nt
restore [rɪ'stɔːʳ] vt (painting etc) restaurieren;
(law and order, faith, health etc) wiederherstellen;
(property) zurückgeben; **to ~ sth to** (to former
state) etw zurückverwandeln in +acc; **to ~ sb**
to power jdn wieder an die Macht bringen
restorer [rɪ'stɔːrəʳ] n (Art etc) Restaurator(in)
m(f)
restrain [rɪs'treɪn] vt (person) zurückhalten;
(feeling) unterdrücken; (growth, inflation)
dämpfen; **to ~ sb from doing sth** jdn davon
abhalten, etw zu tun; **to ~ o.s. from doing**
sth sich beherrschen, etw nicht zu tun
restrained [rɪs'treɪnd] adj (person) beherrscht;
(style etc) zurückhaltend

r

restraint [rɪs'treɪnt] n (*restriction*)
Einschränkung f; (*moderation*) Zurückhaltung
f; **wage ~** Zurückhaltung f bei
Lohnforderungen
restrict [rɪs'trɪkt] vt beschränken
restricted area (*Brit*) n (*Aut*) Bereich m mit
Geschwindigkeitsbeschränkung
restriction [rɪs'trɪkʃən] n Beschränkung f
restrictive [rɪs'trɪktɪv] adj (*law, measure*)
restriktiv; (*clothing*) beengend
restrictive practices (*Brit*) npl (*Industry*)
wettbewerbshemmende Geschäftspraktiken
pl
rest room (*US*) n Toilette f
restructure [riː'strʌktʃəʳ] vt umstrukturieren
result [rɪ'zʌlt] n Resultat nt; (*of match, election,
exam etc*) Ergebnis nt ▷ vi: **to ~ in** führen zu;
as a ~ of the accident als Folge des Unfalls;
he missed the train as a ~ of sleeping in er
verpasste den Zug, weil er verschlafen hatte;
to ~ from resultieren or sich ergeben aus; **as a
~ it is too expensive** folglich ist es zu teuer
resultant [rɪ'zʌltənt] adj resultierend, sich
ergebend
resume [rɪ'zjuːm] vt (*work, journey*)
wiederaufnehmen; (*seat*) wieder einnehmen
▷ vi (*start again*) von Neuem beginnen
résumé ['reɪzjuːmeɪ] n Zusammenfassung f;
(*US: curriculum vitae*) Lebenslauf m
resumption [rɪ'zʌmpʃən] n (*of work etc*)
Wiederaufnahme f
resurgence [rɪ'səːdʒəns] n Wiederaufleben nt
resurrection [rezə'rekʃən] n (*of hopes,
fears*) Wiederaufleben nt; (*of custom etc*)
Wiederbelebung f; (*Rel*): **the R~** die
Auferstehung f
resuscitate [rɪ'sʌsɪteɪt] vt (*Med, fig*)
wiederbeleben
resuscitation [rɪsʌsɪ'teɪʃən] n Wiederbelebung
f
retail ['riːteɪl] adj (*trade, department*) Verkaufs-;
(*shop, goods*) Einzelhandels- ▷ adv im
Einzelhandel ▷ vt (*sell*) (im Einzelhandel)
verkaufen ▷ vi: **to ~ at** (im Einzelhandel)
kosten; **this product ~s at £25** dieses Produkt
kostet im Laden £25
retailer ['riːteɪləʳ] n Einzelhändler(in) m(f)
retail outlet n Einzelhandelsverkaufsstelle f
retail price n Einzelhandelspreis m
retail price index n Einzelhandelspreisindex
m
retain [rɪ'teɪn] vt (*keep*) behalten; (: *heat,
moisture*) zurückhalten
retainer [rɪ'teɪnəʳ] n (*fee*) Vorauszahlung f
retaliate [rɪ'tælɪeɪt] vi Vergeltung üben
retaliation [rɪtælɪ'eɪʃən] n Vergeltung f; **in ~
for** als Vergeltung für
retaliatory [rɪ'tælɪətərɪ] adj (*move, attack*)
Vergeltungs-
retarded [rɪ'tɑːdɪd] adj zurückgeblieben;
mentally ~ geistig zurückgeblieben
retch [retʃ] vi würgen
retention [rɪ'tenʃən] n (*of tradition etc*)

Beibehaltung f; (*of land, memories*) Behalten nt;
(*of heat, fluid etc*) Zurückhalten nt
retentive [rɪ'tentɪv] adj (*memory*) merkfähig
rethink [riː'θɪŋk] vt noch einmal überdenken
reticence ['retɪsns] n Zurückhaltung f
reticent ['retɪsnt] adj zurückhaltend
retina ['retɪnə] n Netzhaut f
retinue ['retɪnjuː] n Gefolge nt
retire [rɪ'taɪəʳ] vi (*give up work*) in den Ruhestand
treten; (*withdraw, go to bed*) sich zurückziehen
retired [rɪ'taɪəd] adj (*person*) im Ruhestand
retirement [rɪ'taɪəmənt] n (*state*) Ruhestand
m; (*act*) Pensionierung f
retirement age n Rentenalter nt
retiring [rɪ'taɪərɪŋ] adj (*leaving*) ausscheidend;
(*shy*) zurückhaltend
retort [rɪ'tɔːt] vi erwidern ▷ n (*reply*)
Erwiderung f
retrace [riː'treɪs] vt: **to ~ one's steps** (*lit, fig*)
seine Schritte zurückverfolgen
retract [rɪ'trækt] vt (*promise*) zurücknehmen;
(*confession*) zurückziehen; (*claws, undercarriage*)
einziehen
retractable [rɪ'træktəbl] adj (*undercarriage,
aerial*) einziehbar
retrain [riː'treɪn] vt umschulen ▷ vi
umgeschult werden
retraining [riː'treɪnɪŋ] n Umschulung f
retread ['riːtred] n (*tyre*) runderneuerter Reifen
m
retreat [rɪ'triːt] n (*place*) Zufluchtsort m;
(*withdrawal, also Mil*) Rückzug m ▷ vi sich
zurückziehen; **to beat a hasty ~** schleunigst
den Rückzug antreten
retrial [riː'traɪəl] n erneute Verhandlung f
retribution [retrɪ'bjuːʃən] n Strafe f
retrieval [rɪ'triːvəl] n (*of object*) Zurückholen nt;
(*Comput*) Abruf m
retrieve [rɪ'triːv] vt (*object*) zurückholen;
(*situation*) retten; (*error*) wiedergutmachen;
(*dog*) apportieren; (*Comput*) abrufen
retriever [rɪ'triːvəʳ] n (*dog*) Apportierhund m
retroactive [retrəu'æktɪv] adj rückwirkend
retrograde ['retrəgreɪd] adj (*step*) Rück-
retrospect ['retrəspekt] n: **in ~** rückblickend,
im Rückblick
retrospective [retrə'spektɪv] adj (*opinion etc*) im
Nachhinein; (*law, tax*) rückwirkend ▷ n (*Art*)
Retrospektive f
return [rɪ'təːn] n (*going or coming back*) Rückkehr
f; (*of sth stolen etc*) Rückgabe f; (*also:* **return
ticket**: *Brit*) Rückfahrkarte f; (*Fin: from
investment etc*) Ertrag m; (*of merchandise*)
Rücksendung f; (*official report*) Erklärung
f ▷ cpd (*journey*) Rück- ▷ vi (*person etc: come or
go back*) zurückkehren; (*feelings, symptoms
etc*) wiederkehren ▷ vt (*favour, greetings
etc*) erwidern; (*sth stolen etc*) zurückgeben;
(*Law: verdict*) fällen; (*Pol: candidate*) wählen;
(*ball*) zurückspielen; **returns** npl (*Comm*)
Gewinne pl; **in ~ (for)** als Gegenleistung (für);
by ~ of post postwendend; **many happy ~s
(of the day)!** herzlichen Glückwunsch zum

Geburtstag!; ~ **match** Rückspiel nt
▶ **return to** vt fus (regain: consciousness, power)
wiedererlangen

returnable [rɪ'tə:nəbl] adj (bottle etc) Mehrweg-

returner n jd, der nach längerer Abwesenheit wieder in die Arbeitswelt zurückkehrt

returning officer [rɪ'tə:nɪŋ-] (Brit) n
Wahlleiter(in) m(f)

return key n (Comput) Return-Taste f

reunion [ri:'ju:nɪən] n Treffen nt; (after long separation) Wiedervereinigung f

reunite [ri:ju:'naɪt] vt wiedervereinigen

Rev. abbr (Rel) = **Reverend**

rev [rɛv] n abbr (Aut: = revolution per minute)
Umdrehung f pro Minute, U/min. ▷ vt
(also: **rev up**: engine) aufheulen lassen

revaluation [ri:vælju'eɪʃən] n (of property)
Neuschätzung f; (of currency) Aufwertung f; (of attitudes) Neubewertung f

revamp [ri:'væmp] vt (company, system) auf
Vordermann bringen

rev counter (Brit) n (Aut) Drehzahlmesser m

Revd. abbr (Rel) = **Reverend**

reveal [rɪ'vi:l] vt (make known) enthüllen; (make visible) zum Vorschein bringen

revealing [rɪ'vi:lɪŋ] adj (comment, action)
aufschlussreich; (dress) tief ausgeschnitten

reveille [rɪ'vælɪ] n (Mil) Wecksignal nt

revel ['rɛvl] vi: **to ~ in sth** in etw schwelgen; **to ~ in doing sth** es genießen, etw zu tun

revelation [rɛvə'leɪʃən] n (disclosure)
Enthüllung f

reveller ['rɛvlə'] n Zecher(in) m(f)

revelry ['rɛvlrɪ] n Gelage nt

revenge [rɪ'vɛndʒ] n (for insult etc) Rache f ▷ vt
rächen; **to get one's ~ (for sth)** seine Rache
(für etw) bekommen; **to ~ o.s.** or **take one's ~
(on sb)** sich (an jdm) rächen

revengeful [rɪ'vɛndʒful] adj rachsüchtig

revenue ['rɛvənju:] n (of person, company)
Einnahmen pl; (of government) Staatseinkünfte pl

reverberate [rɪ'və:bəreɪt] vi (sound etc)
widerhallen; (fig: shock etc) Nachwirkungen
haben

reverberation [rɪvə:bə'reɪʃən] n (of sound)
Widerhall m; (fig: of event etc) Nachwirkungen pl

revere [rɪ'vɪə'] vt verehren

reverence ['rɛvərəns] n Ehrfurcht f

Reverend ['rɛvərənd] adj (in titles) Pfarrer; **the
~ John Smith** Pfarrer John Smith

reverent ['rɛvərənt] adj ehrfürchtig

reverie ['rɛvərɪ] n Träumerei f

reversal [rɪ'və:sl] n (of policy, trend) Umkehr f; **a
~ of roles** ein Rollentausch m

reverse [rɪ'və:s] n (opposite) Gegenteil
nt; (back: of cloth) linke Seite f; (: of coin,
paper) Rückseite f; (Aut: also: **reverse gear**)
Rückwärtsgang m; (setback) Rückschlag m ▷ adj
(side) Rück-; (process) umgekehrt ▷ vt (position,
trend etc) umkehren; (Law: verdict) revidieren;
(roles) vertauschen; (car) zurücksetzen ▷ vi

(Brit: Aut) zurücksetzen; **in ~** umgekehrt; **to
go into ~** den Rückwärtsgang einlegen; **in
~ order** in umgekehrter Reihenfolge; **to ~
direction** sich um 180 Grad drehen

reverse-charge call [rɪ'və:stʃɑ:dʒ-] (Brit) n
R-Gespräch nt

reverse video n (Comput) invertierte
Darstellung f

reversible [rɪ'və:səbl] adj (garment) auf beiden
Seiten tragbar; (decision, operation) umkehrbar

reversing lights [rɪ'və:sɪŋ-] (Brit) npl
Rückfahrscheinwerfer m

reversion [rɪ'və:ʃən] n: ~ **to** Rückfall in +acc;
(Zool) Rückentwicklung f

revert [rɪ'və:t] vi: **to ~ to** (former state)
zurückkehren zu, zurückfallen in +acc;
(Law: money, property) zurückfallen an +acc

review [rɪ'vju:] n (magazine) Zeitschrift f;
(Mil) Inspektion f; (of book, film etc) Kritik f,
Besprechung f, Rezension f; (of policy etc)
Überprüfung f ▷ vt (Mil: troops) inspizieren;
(book, film etc) besprechen, rezensieren;
(policy etc) überprüfen; **to be/come under ~**
überprüft werden

reviewer [rɪ'vju:ə'] n Kritiker(in) m(f),
Rezensent(in) m(f)

revile [rɪ'vaɪl] vt schmähen

revise [rɪ'vaɪz] vt (manuscript) überarbeiten,
revidieren; (opinion etc) ändern; (price, procedure)
revidieren ▷ vi (study) wiederholen; **~d edition**
überarbeitete Ausgabe

revision [rɪ'vɪʒən] n (of manuscript, law etc)
Überarbeitung f, Revision f; (for exam)
Wiederholung f

revitalize [ri:'vaɪtəlaɪz] vt neu beleben

revival [rɪ'vaɪvl] n (recovery) Aufschwung m;
(of interest, faith) Wiederaufleben nt; (Theat)
Wiederaufnahme f

revive [rɪ'vaɪv] vt (person) wiederbeleben;
(economy etc) Auftrieb geben +dat; (custom)
wiederaufleben lassen; (hope, interest etc) neu
beleben; (play) wiederaufnehmen ▷ vi (person)
wieder zu sich kommen; (activity, economy
etc) wieder aufblühen; (hope, interest etc)
wiedererweckt werden

revoke [rɪ'vəuk] vt (law etc) aufheben; (title,
licence) entziehen +dat; (promise, decision)
widerrufen

revolt [rɪ'vəult] n Revolte f, Aufstand m ▷ vi
rebellieren ▷ vt abstoßen; **to ~ against sb/
sth** gegen jdn/etw rebellieren

revolting [rɪ'vəultɪŋ] adj (disgusting)
abscheulich, ekelhaft

revolution [rɛvə'lu:ʃən] n (Pol etc) Revolution f;
(rotation) Umdrehung f

revolutionary [rɛvə'lu:ʃənrɪ] adj revolutionär;
(leader, army) Revolutions- ▷ n Revolutionär(in)
m(f)

revolutionize [rɛvə'lu:ʃənaɪz] vt
revolutionieren

revolve [rɪ'vɔlv] vi sich drehen; **to ~ (a)round**
sich drehen um

revolver [rɪ'vɔlvə'] n Revolver m

r

751

revolving [rɪ'vɒlvɪŋ] *adj* (*chair*) Dreh-; (*sprinkler etc*) drehbar

revolving door *n* Drehtür *f*

revue [rɪ'vju:] *n* (*Theat*) Revue *f*

revulsion [rɪ'vʌlʃən] *n* Abscheu *m*, Ekel *m*

reward [rɪ'wɔ:d] *n* Belohnung *f*; (*satisfaction*) Befriedigung *f* ▷ *vt* belohnen

reward card *n* Kundenkarte *f*, Pay-back-Karte® *f*

rewarding [rɪ'wɔ:dɪŋ] *adj* lohnend; **financially ~** einträglich

rewind [ri:'waɪnd] (*irreg: like* **wind**) *vt* (*tape etc*) zurückspulen

rewire [ri:'waɪər] *vt* neu verkabeln

reword [ri:'wə:d] *vt* (*message, note*) umformulieren

rework [ri:'wə:k] *vt* (*use again: theme etc*) wiederverarbeiten; (*revise*) neu fassen

rewritable [ri:'raɪtəbl] *adj* (*CD, DVD*) wiederbeschreibbar

rewrite [ri:'raɪt] (*irreg: like* **write**) *vt* neu schreiben

Reykjavik ['reɪkjəvi:k] *n* Reykjavik *nt*

RFD (*US*) *abbr* (*Post: = rural free delivery*) freie Landpostzustellung

RGN (*Brit*) *n abbr* (*= Registered General Nurse*) staatlich geprüfte Krankenschwester *f*, staatlich geprüfter Krankenpfleger *m*

Rh *abbr* (*Med: = rhesus*) Rh.

rhapsody ['ræpsədɪ] *n* (*Mus*) Rhapsodie *f*

rhesus negative *adj* Rhesus negativ

rhesus positive *adj* Rhesus positiv

rhetoric ['rɛtərɪk] *n* Rhetorik *f*

rhetorical [rɪ'tɒrɪkl] *adj* rhetorisch

rheumatic [ru:'mætɪk] *adj* rheumatisch

rheumatism ['ru:mətɪzəm] *n* Rheuma *nt*, Rheumatismus *m*

rheumatoid arthritis ['ru:mətɔɪd-] *n* Gelenkrheumatismus *m*

Rhine [raɪn] *n*: **the ~** der Rhein

rhinestone ['raɪnstəun] *n* Rheinkiesel *m*

rhinoceros [raɪ'nɒsərəs] *n* Rhinozeros *nt*

Rhodes [rəudz] *n* Rhodos *nt*

Rhodesia [rəu'di:ʒə] (*formerly*) *n* (*Geog*) Rhodesien *nt*

rhododendron [rəudə'dɛndrən] *n* Rhododendron *m or nt*

rhubarb ['ru:bɑ:b] *n* Rhabarber *m*

rhyme [raɪm] *n* Reim *m*; (*verse*) Verse *pl* ▷ *vi*: **to ~ (with)** sich reimen (mit); **without ~ or reason** ohne Sinn und Verstand

rhythm ['rɪðm] *n* Rhythmus *m*

rhythmic ['rɪðmɪk], **rhythmical** ['rɪðmɪkl] *adj* rhythmisch

rhythmically ['rɪðmɪklɪ] *adv* (*move, beat*) rhythmisch, im Rhythmus

rhythm method *n* Knaus-Ogino-Methode *f*

RI *n abbr* (*Brit: Scol: = religious instruction*) Religionsunterricht *m* ▷ *abbr* (*US: Post*) = Rhode Island

rib [rɪb] *n* Rippe *f* ▷ *vt* (*mock*) aufziehen

ribald ['rɪbəld] *adj* (*laughter, joke*) rüde; (*person*) anzüglich

ribbed [rɪbd] *adj* (*socks, sweater*) gerippt

ribbon ['rɪbən] *n* (*for hair, decoration*) Band *nt*; (*of typewriter*) Farbband *nt*; **in ~s** (*torn*) in Fetzen

rice [raɪs] *n* Reis *m*

ricefield ['raɪsfi:ld] *n* Reisfeld *nt*

rice pudding *n* Milchreis *m*

rich [rɪtʃ] *adj* reich; (*soil*) fruchtbar; (*food*) schwer; (*diet*) reichhaltig; (*colour*) satt; (*voice*) volltönend; (*tapestries, silks*) prächtig ▷ *npl*: **the ~** die Reichen; **~ in** reich an +*dat*

riches ['rɪtʃɪz] *npl* Reichtum *m*

richly ['rɪtʃlɪ] *adv* (*decorated, carved*) reich; (*reward, benefit*) reichlich; **~ deserved/earned** wohlverdient

richness ['rɪtʃnɪs] *n* (*wealth*) Reichtum *m*; (*of life, culture, food*) Reichhaltigkeit *f*; (*of soil*) Fruchtbarkeit *f*; (*of costumes, furnishings*) Pracht *f*

rickets ['rɪkɪts] *n* Rachitis *f*

rickety ['rɪkɪtɪ] *adj* (*chair etc*) wackelig

rickshaw ['rɪkʃɔ:] *n* Rikscha *f*

ricochet ['rɪkəʃeɪ] *vi* abprallen ▷ *n* Abpraller *m*

rid [rɪd] (*pt, pp* **~**) *vt*: **to ~ sb/sth of** jdn/etw befreien von; **to get ~ of** loswerden; (*inhibitions, illusions etc*) sich befreien von

riddance ['rɪdns] *n*: **good ~!** gut, dass wir den/die/das los sind!

ridden ['rɪdn] *pp of* **ride**

riddle ['rɪdl] *n* Rätsel *nt* ▷ *vt*: **to be ~d with** (*guilt, doubts*) geplagt sein von; (*holes, corruption*) durchsetzt sein von

ride [raɪd] (*pt* **rode**, *pp* **ridden**) *n* (*in car, on bicycle*) Fahrt *f*; (*on horse*) Ritt *m*; (*path*) Reitweg *m* ▷ *vi* (*on horse*) reiten; (*on bicycle, bus etc*) fahren ▷ *vt* (*see vi*) reiten; fahren; **car ~** Autofahrt *f*; **to go for a ~** eine Fahrt/einen Ausritt machen; **to take sb for a ~** (*fig*) jdn hereinlegen; **we rode all day/all the way** wir sind den ganzen Tag/den ganzen Weg geritten/gefahren; **to ~ at anchor** (*Naut*) vor Anker liegen; **can you ~ a bike?** kannst du Fahrrad fahren?

  ▶ **ride out** *vt*: **to ~ out the storm** (*fig*) den Sturm überstehen

rider ['raɪdər] *n* (*on horse*) Reiter(in) *m(f)*; (*on bicycle etc*) Fahrer(in) *m(f)*; (*in document etc*) Zusatz *m*

ridge [rɪdʒ] *n* (*of hill*) Grat *m*; (*of roof*) First *m*; (*in sand etc*) Rippelmarke *f*

ridicule ['rɪdɪkju:l] *n* Spott *m* ▷ *vt* (*person*) verspotten; (*proposal, system etc*) lächerlich machen; **she was the object of ~** alle machten sich über sie lustig

ridiculous [rɪ'dɪkjuləs] *adj* lächerlich

riding ['raɪdɪŋ] *n* Reiten *nt*

riding school *n* Reitschule *f*

rife [raɪf] *adj*: **to be ~** (*corruption, disease etc*) grassieren; **to be ~ with** (*rumours etc*) durchsetzt sein von

riffraff ['rɪfræf] *n* Gesindel *nt*

rifle ['raɪfl] *n* (*gun*) Gewehr *nt* ▷ *vt* (*wallet etc*) plündern

  ▶ **rifle through** *vt fus* (*papers etc*) durchwühlen

rifle range *n* Schießstand *m*

rift [rɪft] *n* Spalt *m*; (*fig*) Kluft *f*

rig [rɪg] n (also: **oil rig**: at sea) Bohrinsel f; (: on land) Bohrturm m ▷ vt (election, game etc) manipulieren
▶ **rig out** (Brit) vt: **to ~ sb out as/in** jdn ausstaffieren als/in +dat
▶ **rig up** vt (device) montieren

rigging ['rɪgɪŋ] n (Naut) Takelage f

right [raɪt] adj (correct) richtig; (not left) rechte(r, s) ▷ n Recht nt ▷ adv (correctly, properly) richtig; (directly, exactly) genau; (not on the left) rechts ▷ vt (ship, car etc) aufrichten; (fault, situation) korrigieren, berichtigen ▷ excl okay; **the ~ time** (exact) die genaue Zeit; (most suitable) die richtige Zeit; **to be ~** (person) recht haben; (answer, fact) richtig sein; (clock) genau gehen; (reading etc) korrekt sein; **to get sth ~** etw richtig machen; **let's get it ~ this time!** diesmal machen wir es richtig!; **you did the ~ thing** du hast das Richtige getan; **to put sth ~** (mistake etc) etw berichtigen; **on/to the ~** rechts; **the R~** (Pol) die Rechte; **by ~s** richtig genommen; **to be in the ~** im Recht sein; **you're within your ~s (to do that)** es ist dein gutes Recht(, das zu tun); **he is a well-known author in his own ~** er ist selbst auch ein bekannter Autor; **film ~s** Filmrechte pl; **~ now** im Moment; **~ before/after the party** gleich vor/nach der Party; **~ against the wall** unmittelbar an der Wand; **~ ahead** geradeaus; **~ away** (immediately) sofort; **~ in the middle** genau in der Mitte; **he went ~ to the end of the road** er ging bis ganz ans Ende der Straße

right angle n rechter Winkel m
right-click ['raɪtklɪk] (Comput) vi rechts klicken ▷ vt rechts klicken auf +acc
righteous ['raɪtʃəs] adj (person) rechtschaffen; (indignation) gerecht
righteousness ['raɪtʃəsnɪs] n Rechtschaffenheit f
rightful ['raɪtful] adj rechtmäßig
rightfully ['raɪtfəlɪ] adv von Rechts wegen
right-hand drive adj (vehicle) mit Rechtssteuerung
right-handed [raɪt'hændɪd] adj rechtshändig
right-hand man n rechte Hand f
right-hand side n rechte Seite f
rightly ['raɪtlɪ] adv (with reason) zu Recht; **if I remember ~** (Brit) wenn ich mich recht entsinne
right-minded [raɪt'maɪndɪd] adj vernünftig
right of way n (on path etc) Durchgangsrecht f; (Aut) Vorfahrt f
rights issue n (Stock Exchange) Bezugsrechtsemission f
right wing n (Pol, Sport) rechter Flügel m
right-wing [raɪt'wɪŋ] adj (Pol) rechtsgerichtet
right-winger [raɪt'wɪŋər] n (Pol) Rechte(r) f(m); (Sport) Rechtsaußen m
rigid ['rɪdʒɪd] adj (structure, views) starr; (principle, control etc) streng
rigidity [rɪ'dʒɪdɪtɪ] n (of structure etc) Starrheit f; (of attitude, views etc) Strenge f

rigidly ['rɪdʒɪdlɪ] adv (hold, fix etc) starr; (control, interpret) streng
rigmarole ['rɪgmərəʊl] n Gedöns nt (inf)
rigor ['rɪgər] (US) n = **rigour**
rigor mortis ['rɪgə'mɔ:tɪs] n Totenstarre f
rigorous ['rɪgərəs] adj (control etc) streng; (training) gründlich
rigorously ['rɪgərəslɪ] adv (test, assess etc) streng
rigour, (US) **rigor** ['rɪgər] n (of argument, law) Strenge f; (of research) Gründlichkeit; **the ~s of life/winter** die Härten des Lebens/des Winters
rig-out ['rɪgaʊt] (Brit: inf) n Aufzug m
rile [raɪl] vt ärgern
rim [rɪm] n (of glass, spectacles) Rand m; (of wheel) Felge f, Radkranz m
rimless ['rɪmlɪs] adj (spectacles) randlos
rimmed [rɪmd] adj: **~ with** umrandet von; **gold-~ spectacles** Brille f mit Goldfassung or Goldrand
rind [raɪnd] n (of bacon) Schwarte f; (of lemon, melon) Schale f; (of cheese) Rinde f
ring [rɪŋ] (pt **rang**, pp **rung**) n Ring m; (of people, objects) Kreis m; (of circus) Manege f; (bullring) Arena f; (sound of telephone) Klingeln nt; (sound of bell) Läuten nt; (on cooker) Kochstelle m ▷ vi (Tel: person) anrufen; (telephone, doorbell) klingeln; (bell) läuten; (also: **ring out**) ertönen ▷ vt (Brit: Tel) anrufen; (bell etc) läuten; (encircle) einen Kreis machen um; **to give sb a ~** (Brit: Tel) jdn anrufen; **that has a ~ of truth about it** das könnte stimmen; **to run ~s round sb** (inf: fig) jdn in die Tasche stecken; **to ~ true/false** wahr/falsch klingen; **my ears are ~ing** mir klingen die Ohren; **to ~ the doorbell** klingeln; **the name doesn't ~ a bell (with me)** der Name sagt mir nichts
▶ **ring back** (Brit) vt, vi (Tel) zurückrufen
▶ **ring off** (Brit) vi (Tel) (den Hörer) auflegen
▶ **ring up** (Brit) vt (Tel) anrufen
ring binder n Ringbuch nt
ring finger n Ringfinger m
ringing ['rɪŋɪŋ] n (of telephone) Klingeln nt; (of bell) Läuten nt; (in ears) Läuten nt
ringing tone (Brit) n (Tel) Rufzeichen nt
ringleader ['rɪŋli:dər] n Rädelsführer(in) m(f)
ringlets ['rɪŋlɪts] npl Ringellocken pl; **in ~** in Ringellocken
ring road (Brit) n Ringstraße f
ringtone ['rɪŋtəʊn] n (of mobile phone) Klingelton m
rink [rɪŋk] n (also: **ice rink**) Eisbahn f; (also: **roller skating rink**) Rollschuhbahn f
rinse [rɪns] n Spülen nt; (of hands) Abspülen nt; (hair dye) Tönung f ▷ vt spülen; (hands) abspülen; (also: **rinse out**: clothes) auswaschen; (: mouth) ausspülen; **to give sth a ~** etw spülen; (dishes) etw abspülen
Rio ['ri:əʊ], **Rio de Janeiro** ['ri:əʊdədʒə'nɪərəʊ] n Rio (de Janeiro) nt
riot ['raɪət] n (disturbance) Aufruhr m ▷ vi randalieren; **a ~ of colours** ein Farbenmeer nt; **to run ~** randalieren

r

rioter ['raɪətəʳ] n Randalierer m

riot gear n Schutzausrüstung f

riotous ['raɪətəs] adj (crowd) randalierend; (nights, party) ausschweifend; (welcome etc) tumultartig

riotously ['raɪətəslɪ] adv: ~ **funny** or **comic** urkomisch

riot police n Bereitschaftspolizei f; **hundreds of** ~ Hunderte von Bereitschaftspolizisten

RIP abbr (= requiescat or requiescant in pace) R.I.P.

rip [rɪp] n (tear) Riss m ▷ vt zerreißen ▷ vi reißen
  ▶ **rip off** vt (clothes) herunterreißen; (inf: swindle) übers Ohr hauen
  ▶ **rip up** vt zerreißen

ripcord ['rɪpkɔ:d] n Reißleine f

ripe [raɪp] adj reif; **to be ~ for sth** (fig) reif für etw sein; **he lived to a ~ old age** er erreichte ein stolzes Alter

ripen ['raɪpn] vt reifen lassen ▷ vi reifen

ripeness ['raɪpnɪs] n Reife f

rip-off ['rɪpɔf] (inf) n: **it's a ~!** das ist Wucher!

riposte [rɪ'pɔst] n scharfe Entgegnung f

ripple ['rɪpl] n (wave) kleine Welle f; (of laughter, applause) Welle f ▷ vi (water) sich kräuseln; (muscles) spielen ▷ vt (surface) kräuseln

rise [raɪz] (pt **rose**, pp **~n**) n (incline) Steigung f; (Brit: salary increase) Gehaltserhöhung f; (in prices, temperature etc) Anstieg m; (fig: to fame etc) Aufstieg m ▷ vi (prices, water) steigen; (sun, moon) aufgehen; (wind) aufkommen; (from bed, chair) aufstehen; (sound, voice) ansteigen; (also: **rise up**: tower, rebel) sich erheben; (in rank) aufsteigen; **to give ~ to** Anlass geben zu; **to ~ to power** an die Macht kommen

risen [rɪzn] pp of **rise**

rising ['raɪzɪŋ] adj (increasing) steigend; (up-and-coming) aufstrebend

rising damp n aufsteigende Feuchtigkeit f

rising star n (fig: person) Aufsteiger(in) m(f)

risk [rɪsk] n (danger, chance) Gefahr f; (deliberate) Risiko nt ▷ vt riskieren; **to take a ~** ein Risiko eingehen; **to run the ~ of sth** etw zu fürchten haben; **to run the ~ of doing sth** Gefahr laufen, etw zu tun; **at ~** in Gefahr; **at one's own ~** auf eigene Gefahr; **at the ~ of sounding rude** ... auf die Gefahr hin, unhöflich zu klingen, ...; **it's a fire/health ~** es ist ein Feuer-/Gesundheitsrisiko; **I'll ~ it** ich riskiere es

risk capital n Risikokapital nt

risky ['rɪskɪ] adj riskant

risqué ['ri:skeɪ] adj (joke) gewagt

rissole ['rɪsəul] n (of meat, fish etc) Frikadelle f

rite [raɪt] n Ritus m; **last ~s** (Rel) Letzte Ölung f

ritual ['rɪtjuəl] adj (law, murder) Ritual-; (dance) rituell ▷ n Ritual nt

rival ['raɪvl] n Rivale m, Rivalin f ▷ adj (firm, newspaper etc) Konkurrenz-; (teams, groups etc) rivalisierend ▷ vt (match) sich messen können mit; **to ~ sth/sb in sth** sich mit etw/jdm in Bezug auf etw messen können

rivalry ['raɪvlrɪ] n Rivalität f

river ['rɪvəʳ] n Fluss m; (fig: of blood etc) Strom m ▷ cpd (port, traffic) Fluss-; **up/down** ~ flussaufwärts/-abwärts

river bank n Flussufer nt

river bed n Flussbett nt

riverside ['rɪvəsaɪd] n = **river bank**

rivet ['rɪvɪt] n Niete f ▷ vt (fig: attention) fesseln; (: eyes) heften

riveting ['rɪvɪtɪŋ] adj (fig) fesselnd

Riviera [rɪvɪ'ɛərə] n: **the (French)** ~ die (französische) Riviera; **the Italian** ~ die italienische Riviera

Riyadh [rɪ'jɑ:d] n Riad nt

RMT n abbr (= National Union of Rail, Maritime and Transport Workers) Gewerkschaft der Eisenbahner, Seeleute und Transportarbeiter

RN n abbr (Brit) = **Royal Navy**; (US) = **registered nurse**

RNA n abbr (= ribonucleic acid) RNS f

RNLI (Brit) n abbr (= Royal National Lifeboat Institution) durch Spenden finanzierter Seenot-Rettungsdienst, = DLRG f

RNZAF n abbr (= Royal New Zealand Air Force) neuseeländische Luftwaffe f

RNZN n abbr (= Royal New Zealand Navy) neuseeländische Marine f

road [rəud] n Straße f; (fig) Weg m ▷ cpd (accident, sense) Verkehrs-; **main** ~ Hauptstraße f; **it takes four hours by** ~ man braucht vier Stunden mit dem Auto; **let's hit the** ~ machen wir uns auf den Weg!; **to be on the** ~ (salesman etc) unterwegs sein; (pop group etc) auf Tournee sein; **on the ~ to success** auf dem Weg zum Erfolg; **major/minor** ~ Haupt-/Nebenstraße f

road accident n Verkehrsunfall m

roadblock ['rəudblɔk] n Straßensperre f

road haulage n Spedition f

roadhog ['rəudhɔg] n Verkehrsrowdy m

road map n Straßenkarte f

road rage n Aggressivität f im Straßenverkehr

road safety n Verkehrssicherheit f

roadside ['rəudsaɪd] n Straßenrand m ▷ cpd (building, sign etc) am Straßenrand; **by the** ~ am Straßenrand

road sign n Verkehrszeichen nt

roadsweeper ['rəudswi:pəʳ] (Brit) n (person) Straßenkehrer(in) m(f); (vehicle) Straßenkehrmaschine f

road user n Verkehrsteilnehmer(in) m(f)

roadway ['rəudweɪ] n Fahrbahn f

road works npl Straßenbauarbeiten pl

roadworthy ['rəudwə:ðɪ] adj verkehrstüchtig

roam [rəum] vi wandern, streifen ▷ vt (streets, countryside) durchstreifen

roar [rɔ:ʳ] n (of animal, crowd) Brüllen nt; (of vehicle) Getöse nt; (of storm) Heulen nt ▷ vi (animal, person) brüllen; (engine, wind etc) heulen; **~s of laughter** brüllendes Gelächter; **to ~ with laughter** vor Lachen brüllen

roaring ['rɔ:rɪŋ] adj: **a ~ fire** ein prasselndes Feuer; **a ~ success** ein Bombenerfolg m; **to do a ~ trade (in sth)** ein Riesengeschäft (mit etw) machen

roast [rəʊst] n Braten m ▷ vt (meat, potatoes) braten; (coffee) rösten

roast beef n Roastbeef nt

roasting ['rəʊstɪŋ] (inf) adj (hot) knallheiß ▷ n (criticism) Verriss m; (telling-off) Standpauke f; **to give sb a ~** (criticize) jdn verreißen; (scold) jdm eine Standpauke halten

rob [rɒb] vt (person) bestehlen; (house, bank) ausrauben; **to ~ sb of sth** jdm etw rauben; (fig: deprive) jdm etw vorenthalten

robber ['rɒbəʳ] n Räuber(in) m(f)

robbery ['rɒbərɪ] n Raub m

robe [rəʊb] n (for ceremony etc) Gewand nt; (also: **bath robe**) Bademantel m; (US) Morgenrock m ▷ vt: **to be ~d in** (form) (festlich) in etw acc gekleidet sein

robin ['rɒbɪn] n Rotkehlchen nt

robot ['rəʊbɒt] n Roboter m

robotics [rə'bɒtɪks] n Robotik f

robust [rəʊ'bʌst] adj robust; (appetite) gesund

rock [rɒk] n (substance) Stein m; (boulder) Felsen m; (US: small stone) Stein m; (Brit: sweet) ≈ Zuckerstange f; (Mus: also: **rock music**) Rock m, Rockmusik f ▷ vt (swing gently: cradle) schaukeln; (: child) wiegen; (shake: also fig) erschüttern ▷ vi (object) schwanken; (person) schaukeln; **on the ~s** (drink) mit Eis; (ship) (auf Felsen) aufgelaufen; (marriage etc) gescheitert; **to ~ the boat** (fig) Unruhe stiften

rock and roll n Rock and Roll m

rock bottom ['rɒk'bɒtəm] adj (prices) Tiefst- ▷ n: **to reach** or **touch** or **hit ~** (person, prices) den Tiefpunkt erreichen

rock cake n ≈ Rosinenbrötchen nt

rock climber n Felsenkletterer(in) m(f)

rock climbing n Felsenklettern nt

rockery ['rɒkərɪ] n Steingarten m

rocket ['rɒkɪt] n Rakete f ▷ vi (prices) in die Höhe schießen

rocket launcher n Raketenwerfer m

rock face n Felswand f

rock fall n Steinschlag m

rocking chair ['rɒkɪŋ-] n Schaukelstuhl m

rocking horse n Schaukelpferd nt

rocky ['rɒkɪ] adj (path, ground) felsig; (fig: business, marriage) wackelig

Rocky Mountains npl: **the ~** die Rocky Mountains pl

rod [rɒd] n (also Tech) Stange f; (also: **fishing rod**) Angelrute f

rode [rəʊd] pt of **ride**

rodent ['rəʊdnt] n Nagetier nt

rodeo ['rəʊdɪəʊ] (US) n Rodeo nt

roe [rəʊ] n (Culin): **hard ~** Rogen m; **soft ~** Milch f

roe deer n inv Reh nt

rogue [rəʊg] n Gauner m

roguish ['rəʊgɪʃ] adj schelmisch

role [rəʊl] n Rolle f

role model n Rollenmodell nt

role play n Rollenspiel nt

roll [rəʊl] n (of paper) Rolle f; (of cloth) Ballen m; (of banknotes) Bündel nt; (also: **bread roll**)

Brötchen nt; (register, list) Verzeichnis nt; (of drums etc) Wirbel m ▷ vt rollen; (also: **roll up**: string) aufrollen; (: sleeves) aufkrempeln; (cigarette) drehen; (also: **roll out**: pastry) ausrollen; (flatten: lawn, road) walzen ▷ vi rollen; (drum) wirbeln; (thunder) grollen; (ship) schlingern; (tears, sweat) fließen; (camera, printing press) laufen; **cheese/ham ~** Käse-/ Schinkenbrötchen nt; **he's ~ing in it** (inf: rich) er schwimmt im Geld

▶ **roll about** vi sich wälzen

▶ **roll around** vi = **roll about**

▶ **roll in** vi (money, invitations) hereinströmen

▶ **roll over** vi sich umdrehen

▶ **roll up** vi (inf: arrive) aufkreuzen ▷ vt (carpet, umbrella etc) aufrollen; **to ~ o.s. up into a ball** sich zusammenrollen

roll call n namentlicher Aufruf m

rolled gold [rəʊld-] n Doublégold nt

roller ['rəʊləʳ] n Rolle f; (for lawn, road) Walze f; (for hair) Lockenwickler m

Rollerblades® npl Rollerblades pl

roller blind n Rollo nt

roller coaster n Achterbahn f

roller skates npl Rollschuhe pl

rollicking ['rɒlɪkɪŋ] adj toll, Mords-; **to have a ~ time** sich ganz toll amüsieren

rolling ['rəʊlɪŋ] adj (hills) wellig

rolling mill n Walzwerk nt

rolling pin n Nudelholz nt

rolling stock n (Rail) Fahrzeuge pl

roll-on-roll-off ['rəʊlɒn'rəʊlɒf] (Brit) adj (ferry) Roll-on-roll-off-

roly-poly ['rəʊlɪ'pəʊlɪ] (Brit) n ≈ Strudel m

ROM [rɒm] n abbr (Comput: = read only memory) ROM

Roman ['rəʊmən] adj römisch ▷ n (person) Römer(in) m(f)

Roman Catholic adj römisch-katholisch ▷ n Katholik(in) m(f)

romance [rə'mæns] n (love affair) Romanze f; (romanticism) Romantik f; (novel) fantastische Erzählung f

Romanesque [rəʊmə'nɛsk] adj romanisch

Romania [rəʊ'meɪnɪə] n Rumänien nt

Romanian [rəʊ'meɪnɪən] adj rumänisch ▷ n (person) Rumäne m, Rumänin f; (Ling) Rumänisch nt

Roman numeral n römische Ziffer f

romantic [rə'mæntɪk] adj romantisch

romanticism [rə'mæntɪsɪzəm] n (also Art, Liter) Romantik f

Romany ['rɒmənɪ] adj Roma- ▷ n (person) Roma mf; (Ling) Romani nt

Rome [rəʊm] n Rom nt

romp [rɒmp] n Klamauk m ▷ vi (also: **romp about**) herumtollen; **to ~ home** (horse) spielend gewinnen

rompers ['rɒmpəz] npl (clothing) einteiliger Spielanzug für Babys

rondo ['rɒndəʊ] n (Mus) Rondo nt

roof [ruːf] (pl **~s**) n Dach nt ▷ vt (house etc) überdachen; **the ~ of the mouth** der Gaumen

r

roof garden n Dachgarten m
roofing ['ru:fɪŋ] n Deckung f; ~ **felt** Dachpappe f
roof rack n Dachgepäckträger m
rook [ruk] n (bird) Saatkrähe f; (Chess) Turm m
rookie ['ruki:] (inf) n (esp Mil) Grünschnabel m
room [ru:m] n (in house, hotel) Zimmer nt; (space) Raum m, Platz m; (scope: for change etc) Raum m ▷ vi: **to ~ with sb** (esp US) ein Zimmer mit jdm teilen; **rooms** npl (lodging) Zimmer pl; **"~s to let", "~s for rent"** (US) „Zimmer zu vermieten"; **single/double ~** Einzel-/Doppelzimmer nt; **is there ~ for this?** ist dafür Platz vorhanden?; **to make ~ for sb** für jdn Platz machen; **there is ~ for improvement** es gibt Möglichkeiten zur Verbesserung
rooming house ['ru:mɪŋ-] (US) n Mietshaus nt
roommate ['ru:mmeɪt] n Zimmergenosse m, Zimmergenossin f
room service n Zimmerservice m
room temperature n Zimmertemperatur f
roomy ['ru:mɪ] adj (building, car) geräumig
roost [ru:st] vi (birds) sich niederlassen
rooster ['ru:stə'] (esp US) n Hahn m
root [ru:t] n (also Math) Wurzel f ▷ vi (plant) Wurzeln schlagen ▷ vt: **to be ~ed in** verwurzelt sein in +dat; **roots** npl (family origins) Wurzeln pl; **to take ~** (plant, idea) Wurzeln schlagen; **the ~ cause of the problem** die Wurzel des Problems
▶ **root about** vi (search) herumwühlen
▶ **root for** vt fus (support) anfeuern
▶ **root out** vt ausrotten
root beer (US) n kohlensäurehaltiges Getränk aus Wurzel- und Kräuterextrakten
rope [rəup] n Seil nt; (Naut) Tau nt ▷ vt (tie) festbinden; (also: **rope together**) zusammenbinden; **to know the ~s** (fig) sich auskennen
▶ **rope in** vt (fig: person) einspannen
▶ **rope off** vt (area) mit einem Seil absperren
rope ladder n Strickleiter f
ropey, ropy ['rəupɪ] (inf) adj (ill, poor quality) miserabel
rosary ['rəuzərɪ] n Rosenkranz m
rose [rəuz] pt of **rise** ▷ n (flower) Rose f; (also: **rosebush**) Rosenstrauch m; (on watering can) Brause f ▷ adj rosarot
rosé ['rəuzeɪ] n (wine) Rosé m
rosebed ['rəuzbɛd] n Rosenbeet nt
rosebud ['rəuzbʌd] n Rosenknospe f
rosebush ['rəuzbuʃ] n Rosenstrauch m
rosemary ['rəuzmərɪ] n Rosmarin m
rosette [rəu'zɛt] n Rosette f
ROSPA ['rɒspə] (Brit) n abbr (= Royal Society for the Prevention of Accidents) Verband, der Maßnahmen zur Unfallverhütung propagiert
roster ['rɒstə'] n: **duty ~** Dienstplan m
rostrum ['rɒstrəm] n Rednerpult nt
rosy ['rəuzɪ] adj (colour) rosarot; (face, situation) rosig; **a ~ future** eine rosige Zukunft
rot [rɒt] n (decay) Fäulnis f; (fig: rubbish) Quatsch

m ▷ vt verfaulen lassen ▷ vi (teeth, wood, fruit etc) verfaulen; **to stop the ~** (Brit: fig) den Verfall stoppen; **dry ~** Holzschwamm m; **wet ~** Nassfäule f
rota ['rəutə] n Dienstplan m; **on a ~ basis** reihum nach Plan
rotary ['rəutərɪ] adj (cutter) rotierend; (motion) Dreh-
rotate [rəu'teɪt] vt (spin) drehen, rotieren lassen; (crops) im Wechsel anbauen; (jobs) turnusmäßig wechseln ▷ vi (revolve) rotieren, sich drehen
rotating [rəu'teɪtɪŋ] adj (revolving) rotierend; (drum, mirror) Dreh-
rotation [rəu'teɪʃən] n (of planet, drum etc) Rotation f, Drehung f; (of crops) Wechsel m; (of jobs) turnusmäßiger Wechsel m; **in ~** der Reihe nach
rote [rəut] n: **by ~** auswendig
rotor ['rəutə'] n (also: **rotor blade**) Rotor m
rotten ['rɒtn] adj (decayed) faul, verfault; (inf: person, situation) gemein; (: film, weather, driver etc) mies; **to feel ~** sich elend fühlen
rotund [rəu'tʌnd] adj (person) rundlich
rouble, ruble ['ru:bl] n Rubel m
rouge [ru:ʒ] n Rouge nt
rough [rʌf] adj rau; (terrain, road) uneben; (person, plan, drawing, guess) grob; (life, conditions, journey) hart; (sea, crossing) stürmisch ▷ n (Golf): **in the ~** im Rough ▷ vt: **to ~ it** primitiv or ohne Komfort leben; **the sea is ~ today** die See ist heute stürmisch; **to have a ~ time** eine harte Zeit durchmachen; **can you give me a ~ idea of the cost?** können Sie mir eine ungefähre Vorstellung von den Kosten geben?; **to feel ~** (Brit) sich elend fühlen; **to sleep ~** (Brit) im Freien übernachten; **to play ~** (fig) auf die grobe Tour kommen
▶ **rough out** vt (drawing, idea etc) skizzieren
roughage ['rʌfɪdʒ] n Ballaststoffe pl
rough-and-ready ['rʌfən'rɛdɪ] adj provisorisch
rough-and-tumble ['rʌfən'tʌmbl] n (fighting) Balgerei f; (fig) Schlachtfeld nt
roughcast ['rʌfkɑ:st] n Rauputz m
rough copy n Entwurf m
rough draft n = **rough copy**
rough justice n Justizwillkür f
roughly ['rʌflɪ] adv grob; (approximately) ungefähr; **~ speaking** grob gesagt
roughness ['rʌfnɪs] n Rauheit f; (of manner) Grobheit f
roughshod ['rʌfʃɒd] adv: **to ride ~ over** sich rücksichtslos hinwegsetzen über +acc
roulette [ru:'lɛt] n Roulette nt
Roumania etc [ru:'meɪnɪə] n = **Romania** etc
round [raund] adj rund ▷ n Runde f; (of ammunition) Ladung f ▷ vt (corner) biegen um; (cape) umrunden ▷ prep um ▷ adv: **all ~** rundherum; **in ~ figures** rund gerechnet; **the daily ~** (fig) der tägliche Trott; **a ~ of applause** Beifall m; **a ~ (of drinks)** eine Runde; **a ~ of sandwiches** ein Butterbrot; **a ~ of toast** (Brit) eine Scheibe Toast; **it's just ~ the corner** (fig)

es steht vor der Tür; **to go ~ the back** hinten herum gehen; **to go ~ (an obstacle)** (um ein Hindernis) herumgehen; **~ the clock** rund um die Uhr; **~ his neck/the table** um seinen Hals/den Tisch; **to sail ~ the world** die Welt umsegeln; **to walk ~ the room/park** im Zimmer/Park herumgehen; **~ about 300** (*approximately*) ungefähr 300; **the long way ~** auf Umwegen; **all (the) year ~** das ganze Jahr über; **the wrong way ~** falsch herum; **to ask sb ~** jdn zu sich einladen; **I'll be ~ at 6 o'clock** ich komme um 6 Uhr; **to go ~** (*rotate*) sich drehen; **to go ~ to sb's (house)** jdn (zu Hause) besuchen; **enough to go ~** genug für alle

▶ **round off** *vt* abrunden

▶ **round up** *vt* (*cattle etc*) zusammentreiben; (*people*) versammeln; (*figure*) aufrunden

roundabout ['raundəbaut] (*Brit*) *n* (*Aut*) Kreisverkehr *m*; (*at fair*) Karussell *nt* ▷ *adj*: **by a ~ route** auf Umwegen; **in a ~ way** auf Umwegen

rounded ['raundɪd] *adj* (*hill, figure etc*) rundlich

rounders ['raundəz] *n* ≈ Schlagball *m*

roundly ['raundlɪ] *adv* (*fig: criticize etc*) nachdrücklich

round robin (*esp US*) *n* (*Sport*) Wettkampf, *bei dem jeder gegen jeden spielt*

round-shouldered ['raund'ʃəuldəd] *adj* mit runden Schultern

round trip *n* Rundreise *f*

roundup ['raundʌp] *n* (*of news etc*) Zusammenfassung *f*; (*of animals*) Zusammentreiben *nt*; (*of criminals*) Aufgreifen *nt*; **a ~ of the latest news** ein Nachrichtenüberblick *m*

rouse [rauz] *vt* (*wake up*) aufwecken; (*stir up*) reizen

rousing ['rauzɪŋ] *adj* (*speech*) mitreißend; (*welcome*) stürmisch

rout [raut] (*Mil*) *n* totale Niederlage *f* ▷ *vt* (*defeat*) vernichtend schlagen

route [ru:t] *n* Strecke *f*; (*of bus, train, shipping*) Linie *f*; (*of procession, fig*) Weg *m*; **"all ~s"** (*Aut*) „alle Richtungen"; **the best ~ to London** der beste Weg nach London

route map (*Brit*) *n* Streckenkarte *f*

routine [ru:'ti:n] *adj* (*work, check etc*) Routine- ▷ *n* (*habits*) Routine *f*; (*drudgery*) Stumpfsinn *m*; (*Theat*) Nummer *f*; **~ procedure** Routinesache *f*

rove [rəuv] *vt* (*area, streets*) ziehen durch

roving reporter ['rəuvɪŋ-] *n* Reporter(in) *m(f)* im Außendienst

row¹ [rəu] *n* (*line*) Reihe *f* ▷ *vi* (*in boat*) rudern ▷ *vt* (*boat*) rudern; **three times in a ~** dreimal hintereinander

row² [rau] *n* (*din*) Krach *m*, Lärm *m*; (*dispute*) Streit *m* ▷ *vi* (*argue*) sich streiten; **to have a ~** sich streiten

rowboat ['rəubəut] (*US*) *n* = **rowing boat**

rowdiness ['raudɪnɪs] *n* Rowdytum *nt*

rowdy ['raudɪ] *adj* (*person*) rüpelhaft; (*party etc*) lärmend

rowdyism ['raudɪɪzəm] *n* = **rowdiness**

rowing ['rəuɪŋ] *n* (*sport*) Rudern *nt*

rowing boat (*Brit*) *n* Ruderboot *nt*

rowlock ['rɔlək] (*Brit*) *n* Dolle *f*

royal ['rɔɪəl] *adj* königlich; **the ~ family** die königliche Familie

⬤ **ROYAL ACADEMY**

⬤ Die *Royal Academy* oder *Royal Academy of Arts*,
⬤ eine Akademie zur Förderung der Malerei,
⬤ Bildhauerei und Architektur, wurde 1768
⬤ unter der Schirmherrschaft von George
⬤ II. gegründet und befindet sich seit 1869
⬤ in Burlington House, Piccadilly, London.
⬤ Jeden Sommer findet dort eine Ausstellung
⬤ mit Werken zeitgenössischer Künstler
⬤ statt. Die Royal Academy unterhält auch
⬤ Schulen, an denen Malerei, Bildhauerei
⬤ und Architektur unterrichtet wird.

Royal Air Force (*Brit*) *n*: **the ~** die Königliche Luftwaffe

royal blue *adj* königsblau

royalist ['rɔɪəlɪst] *n* Royalist(in) *m(f)* ▷ *adj* royalistisch

Royal Navy (*Brit*) *n*: **the ~** die Königliche Marine

royalty ['rɔɪəltɪ] *n* (*royal persons*) die königliche Familie; **royalties** *npl* (*to author*) Tantiemen *pl*; (*to inventor*) Honorar *nt*

RP (*Brit*) *n abbr* (= *received pronunciation*) Standardaussprache des Englischen; *see also* **receive**

rpm *abbr* (= *revolutions per minute*) U/min.

RR (*US*) *abbr* = **railroad**

RRP (*Brit*) *n abbr* = **recommended retail price**

RSA (*Brit*) *n abbr* (= *Royal Society of Arts*) akademischer Verband zur Vergabe von Diplomen; (= *Royal Scottish Academy*) Kunstakademie

RSI *n abbr* (*Med*: = *repetitive strain injury*) RSI *nt*, Schmerzempfindung durch ständige Wiederholung bestimmter Bewegungen

RSPB (*Brit*) *n abbr* (= *Royal Society for the Protection of Birds*) Vogelschutzorganisation

RSPCA (*Brit*) *n abbr* (= *Royal Society for the Prevention of Cruelty to Animals*) Tierschutzverein *m*

RSVP *abbr* (= *répondez s'il vous plaît*) u. A. w. g.

RTA *n abbr* (= *road traffic accident*) Verkehrsunfall *m*

Rt Hon. (*Brit*) *abbr* (= *Right Honourable*) Titel für Abgeordnete des Unterhauses

Rt Rev. *abbr* (*Rel*: = *Right Reverend*) Titel für Bischöfe

rub [rʌb] *vt* reiben ▷ *n*: **to give sth a ~** (*polish*) etw polieren; **he ~bed his hands together** er rieb sich auf die Hände; **to ~ sb up the wrong way, to ~ sb the wrong way** (*US*) bei jdm anecken

▶ **rub down** *vt* (*body, horse*) abreiben

▶ **rub in** *vt* (*ointment*) einreiben; **don't ~ it in!** (*fig*) reite nicht so darauf herum!

▶ **rub off** *vi* (*paint*) abfärben

▶ **rub off on** *vt fus* abfärben auf +*acc*

r

757

▸ **rub out** vt (with eraser) ausradieren

rubber ['rʌbəʳ] n (also inf: condom) Gummi nt or m; (Brit: eraser) Radiergummi m

rubber band n Gummiband nt

rubber bullet n Gummigeschoss nt

rubber plant n Gummibaum m

rubber ring n (for swimming) Schwimmreifen m

rubber stamp n Stempel m

rubber-stamp [rʌbə'stæmp] vt (fig: decision) genehmigen

rubbery ['rʌbərɪ] adj (material) gummiartig; (meat, food) wie Gummi

rubbish ['rʌbɪʃ] (Brit) n (waste) Abfall m; (fig: junk) Schrott m; (: pej: nonsense) Quatsch m ▷ vt (inf) heruntermachen; ~! Quatsch!

rubbish bin (Brit) n Abfalleimer m

rubbish dump (Brit) n Müllabladeplatz m

rubbishy ['rʌbɪʃɪ] (Brit: inf) adj miserabel, mies

rubble ['rʌbl] n (debris) Trümmer pl; (Constr) Schutt m

ruble ['ru:bl] (US) n = **rouble**

ruby ['ru:bɪ] n (gem) Rubin m ▷ adj (red) rubinrot

RUC (Brit) n abbr (= Royal Ulster Constabulary) nordirische Polizeibehörde

rucksack ['rʌksæk] n Rucksack m

ructions ['rʌkʃənz] (inf) npl Krach m, Ärger m

rudder ['rʌdəʳ] n (of ship, plane) Ruder nt

ruddy ['rʌdɪ] adj (complexion etc) rötlich; (inf: damned) verdammt

rude [ru:d] adj (impolite) unhöflich; (naughty) unanständig; (unexpected: shock etc) böse; (crude: table, shelter etc) primitiv; **to be ~ to sb** unhöflich zu jdm sein; **a ~ awakening** ein böses Erwachen

rudely ['ru:dlɪ] adv (interrupt) unhöflich; (say, push) grob

rudeness ['ru:dnɪs] n (impoliteness) Unhöflichkeit f

rudimentary [ru:dɪ'mɛntərɪ] adj (equipment) primitiv; (knowledge) Grund-

rudiments ['ru:dɪmənts] npl Grundlagen pl

rue [ru:] vt bereuen

rueful ['ru:ful] adj (expression, person) reuevoll

ruff [rʌf] n (collar) Halskrause f

ruffian ['rʌfɪən] n Rüpel m

ruffle ['rʌfl] vt (hair, feathers) zerzausen; (water) kräuseln; (fig: person) aus der Fassung bringen

rug [rʌg] n (on floor) Läufer m; (Brit: blanket) Decke f

rugby ['rʌgbɪ] n (also: **rugby football**) Rugby nt

rugged ['rʌgɪd] adj (landscape) rau; (man) robust; (features, face) markig; (determination, independence) wild

rugger ['rʌgəʳ] (Brit: inf) n Rugby nt

ruin ['ru:ɪn] n (destruction, downfall) Ruin m; (remains) Ruine f ▷ vt ruinieren; (building) zerstören; (clothes, carpet etc) verderben; **ruins** npl (of castle) Ruinen pl; (of building) Trümmer pl; **in ~s** (lit, fig) in Trümmern

ruination [ru:ɪ'neɪʃən] n (of building etc) Zerstörung f; (of person, life) Ruinierung f

ruinous ['ru:ɪnəs] adj (expense, interest) ruinös

rule [ru:l] n (norm) Regel f; (regulation) Vorschrift

f; (government) Herrschaft f; (ruler) Lineal nt ▷ vt (country, people) herrschen über+acc ▷ vi (monarch etc) herrschen; **it's against the ~s** das ist nicht gestattet; **as a ~ of thumb** als Faustregel; **under British ~** unter britischer Herrschaft; **as a ~** in der Regel; **to ~ in favour of/against/on sth** (Law) für/gegen/über etw acc entscheiden; **to ~ that ...** (umpire, judge etc) entscheiden, dass ...

▸ **rule out** vt (possibility etc) ausschließen; **murder cannot be ~d out** Mord ist nicht auszuschließen

ruled [ru:ld] adj (paper) liniert

ruler ['ru:ləʳ] n (sovereign) Herrscher(in) m(f); (for measuring) Lineal nt

ruling ['ru:lɪŋ] adj (party) Regierungs-; (body) maßgebend ▷ n (Law) Entscheidung f; **the ~ class** die herrschende Klasse

rum [rʌm] n Rum m ▷ adj (Brit: inf: peculiar) komisch

Rumania etc n = **Romania** etc

rumble ['rʌmbl] n (of thunder) Grollen nt; (of traffic) Rumpeln nt; (of guns) Donnern nt; (of voices) Gemurmel nt ▷ vi (stomach) knurren; (thunder) grollen; (traffic) rumpeln; (guns) donnern

rumbustious [rʌm'bʌstʃəs] adj (person) ungebärdig

ruminate ['ru:mɪneɪt] vi (person) grübeln; (cow, sheep etc) wiederkäuen

rummage ['rʌmɪdʒ] vi herumstöbern

rummage sale (US) n Trödelmarkt m

rumour, (US) **rumor** ['ru:məʳ] n Gerücht nt ▷ vt: **it is ~ed that ...** man sagt, dass ...

rump [rʌmp] n (of animal) Hinterteil nt; (of group etc) Rumpf m

rumple ['rʌmpl] vt (clothes etc) zerknittern; (hair) zerzausen

rump steak n Rumpsteak nt

rumpus ['rʌmpəs] n Krach m; **to kick up a ~** Krach schlagen

run [rʌn] (pt **ran**, pp ~) n (as exercise, sport) Lauf m; (in car, train etc) Fahrt f; (series) Serie f; (Ski) Abfahrt f; (Cricket, Baseball) Run m; (Theat) Spielzeit f; (in tights etc) Laufmasche f ▷ vt (race, distance) laufen, rennen; (operate: business) leiten; (: hotel, shop) führen; (: competition, course) durchführen; (Comput: program) laufen lassen; (hand, fingers) streichen mit; (water, bath) einlaufen lassen; (Press: feature, article) bringen ▷ vi laufen, rennen; (flee) weglaufen; (bus, train) fahren; (river, tears) fließen; (colours) auslaufen; (jumper) färben; (in election) antreten; (road, railway etc) verlaufen; **to go for a ~** (as exercise) einen Dauerlauf machen; **to break into a ~** zu laufen or rennen beginnen; **a ~ of good/bad luck** eine Glücks-/Pechsträhne; **to have the ~ of sb's house** jds Haus zur freien Verfügung haben; **there was a ~ on ...** (meat, tickets) es gab einen Ansturm auf+acc; **in the long ~** langfristig; **in the short ~** kurzfristig; **to make a ~ for it** die Beine in die Hand nehmen; **on the ~** (fugitive) auf der Flucht; **I'll ~ you to the station** ich fahre dich zum Bahnhof; **to ~ the risk of doing sth** Gefahr laufen, etw zu tun; **she ran her finger down the list** sie ging die Liste mit dem Finger durch; **it's very cheap to ~** (*car, machine*) es ist sehr billig im Verbrauch; **to ~ a bath** das Badewasser einlaufen lassen; **to be ~ off one's feet** (*Brit*) ständig auf Trab sein; **the baby's nose was ~ning** dem Baby lief die Nase; **the train ~s between Gatwick and Victoria** der Zug verkehrt zwischen Gatwick und Victoria; **the bus ~s every 20 minutes** der Bus fährt alle 20 Minuten; **to ~ on petrol/off batteries** mit Benzin/auf Batterie laufen; **to ~ for president** für das Amt des Präsidenten kandidieren; **to ~ dry** (*well etc*) austrocknen; **tempers were ~ning high** alle waren sehr erregt; **unemployment is ~ning at 20 per cent** die Arbeitslosigkeit beträgt 20 Prozent; **blonde hair ~s in the family** blonde Haare liegen in der Familie

▸ **run across** *vt fus* (*find*) stoßen auf +*acc*

▸ **run after** *vt fus* nachlaufen +*dat*

▸ **run away** *vi* weglaufen

▸ **run down** *vt* (*production*) verringern; (*factory*) allmählich stilllegen; (*Aut: person*) überfahren; (*criticize*) schlechtmachen ▷ *vi* (*battery*) leer werden

▸ **run in** (*Brit*) *vt* (*car*) einfahren

▸ **run into** *vt fus* (*meet: person*) begegnen +*dat*; (: *trouble etc*) bekommen; (*collide with*) laufen/fahren gegen; **to ~ into debt** in Schulden geraten; **their losses ran into millions** ihre Schulden gingen in die Millionen

▸ **run off** *vt* (*liquid*) ablassen; (*copies*) machen ▷ *vi* weglaufen

▸ **run out** *vi* (*time, passport*) ablaufen; (*money*) ausgehen; (*luck*) zu Ende gehen

▸ **run out of** *vt fus*: **we're ~ning out of money/petrol** uns geht das Geld/das Benzin aus; **we're ~ning out of time** wir haben keine Zeit mehr

▸ **run over** *vt* (*Aut*) überfahren ▷ *vt fus* (*repeat*) durchgehen ▷ *vi* (*bath, water*) überlaufen

▸ **run through** *vt fus* (*instructions, lines*) durchgehen

▸ **run up** *vt* (*debt*) anhäufen

▸ **run up against** *vt fus* (*difficulties*) stoßen auf +*acc*

runabout ['rʌnəbaut] *n* (*Aut*) Flitzer *m*

run-around ['rʌnəraund] (*inf*) *n*: **to give sb the ~** jdn an der Nase herumführen

runaway ['rʌnəweɪ] *adj* (*horse*) ausgerissen; (*truck, train*) außer Kontrolle geraten; (*child, slave*) entlaufen; (*fig: inflation*) unkontrollierbar; (: *success*) überwältigend

rundown ['rʌndaun] *n* (*of industry etc*) allmähliche Stillegung *f* ▷ *adj*: **to be run-down** (*person*) total erschöpft sein; (*building, area*) heruntergekommen

rung [rʌŋ] *pp of* **ring** ▷ *n* (*also fig*) Sprosse *f*

run-in ['rʌnɪn] (*inf*) *n* Auseinandersetzung *f*

runner ['rʌnəʳ] *n* Läufer(in) *m(f)*; (*horse*)

Rennpferd *nt*; (*on sledge, drawer etc*) Kufe *f*

runner bean (*Brit*) *n* Stangenbohne *f*

runner-up [rʌnər'ʌp] *n* Zweitplatzierte(r) *f(m)*

running ['rʌnɪŋ] *n* (*sport*) Laufen *nt*; (*of business etc*) Leitung *f*; (*of machine etc*) Betrieb *m* ▷ *adj* (*water, stream*) laufend; **to be in/out of the ~ for sth** bei etw im Rennen liegen/aus dem Rennen sein; **to make the ~** (*in race, fig*) das Rennen machen; **6 days ~** 6 Tage hintereinander; **to have a ~ battle with sb** ständig im Streit mit jdm liegen; **to give a ~ commentary on sth** etw fortlaufend kommentieren; **a ~ sore** eine nässende Wunde

running costs *npl* (*of car, machine*) Unterhaltskosten *pl*

running head *n* (*Typ, Comput*) Kolumnentitel *m*

running mate (*US*) *n* (*Pol*) Vizepräsidentschaftskandidat *m*

runny ['rʌnɪ] *adj* (*egg, butter*) dünnflüssig; (*nose, eyes*) triefend

run-off ['rʌnɔf] *n* (*in contest, election*) Entscheidungsrunde *f*; (*extra race*) Entscheidungsrennen *nt*

run-of-the-mill ['rʌnəvðə'mɪl] *adj* gewöhnlich

runt [rʌnt] *n* (*animal*) kleinstes und schwächstes Tier eines Wurfs; (*pej: person*) Zwerg *m*

run-through ['rʌnθruː] *n* (*rehearsal*) Probe *f*

run-up ['rʌnʌp] *n*: **the ~ to** (*election etc*) die Zeit vor +*dat*

runway ['rʌnweɪ] *n* (*Aviat*) Start- und Landebahn *f*

rupee [ruː'piː] *n* Rupie *f*

rupture ['rʌptʃəʳ] *n* (*Med*) Bruch *m*; (*conflict*) Spaltung *f* ▷ *vt*: **to ~ o.s.** (*Med*) sich *dat* einen Bruch zuziehen

rural ['ruərl] *adj* ländlich; (*crime*) auf dem Lande

rural district council (*Brit*) *n* Landbezirksverwaltung *f*

ruse [ruːz] *n* List *f*

rush [rʌʃ] *n* (*hurry*) Eile *f*, Hetze *f*; (*Comm: sudden demand*) starke Nachfrage *f*; (*of water, air*) Stoß *m*; (*of feeling*) Woge *f* ▷ *vt* (*lunch, job etc*) sich beeilen bei; (*person, supplies etc*) schnellstens bringen ▷ *vi* (*person*) sich beeilen; (*air, water*) strömen; **rushes** *npl* (*Bot*) Schilf *nt*; (*for chair, basket etc*) Binsen *pl*; **is there any ~ for this?** eilt das?; **we've had a ~ of orders** wir hatten einen Zustrom von Bestellungen; **I'm in a ~ (to do sth)** ich habe es eilig (, etw zu tun); **gold ~** Goldrausch *m*; **don't ~ me!** drängen Sie mich nicht!; **to ~ sth off** (*send*) etw schnellstens abschicken; **to ~ sb into doing sth** jdn dazu drängen, etw zu tun

▸ **rush through** *vt* (*order, application*) schnellstens erledigen

rush hour *n* Hauptverkehrszeit *f*, Rushhour *f*

rush job *n* Eilauftrag *m*

rush matting *n* Binsenmatte *f*

rusk [rʌsk] *n* Zwieback *m*

Russia ['rʌʃə] *n* Russland *nt*

Russian ['rʌʃən] *adj* russisch ▷ *n* (*person*) Russe

r

759

m, Russin *f*; (*Ling*) Russisch *nt*

rust [rʌst] *n* Rost *m* ▷ *vi* rosten

rustic ['rʌstɪk] *adj* (*style, furniture*) rustikal ▷ *n* (*pej: person*) Bauer *m*

rustle ['rʌsl] *vi* (*paper, leaves*) rascheln ▷ *vt* (*paper*) rascheln mit; (*US: cattle*) stehlen

rustproof ['rʌstpru:f] *adj* nicht rostend

rustproofing ['rʌstpru:fɪŋ] *n* Rostschutz *m*

rusty ['rʌstɪ] *adj* (*car*) rostig; (*fig: skill etc*) eingerostet

rut [rʌt] *n* (*in path etc*) Furche *f*; (*Zool: season*) Brunft *f*, Brunst *f*; **to be in a ~** (*fig*) im Trott

stecken

rutabaga [ru:tə'beɪgə] (*US*) *n* Steckrübe *f*

ruthless ['ru:θlɪs] *adj* rücksichtslos

ruthlessness ['ru:θlɪsnɪs] *n* Rücksichtslosigkeit *f*

RV *abbr* (*Bible: = revised version*) *englische Bibelübersetzung von 1885* ▷ *n abbr* (*US*) = **recreational vehicle**

Rwanda [ru'ændə] *n* Ruanda *nt*

Rwandan [ru'ændən] *adj* ruandisch

rye [raɪ] *n* (*cereal*) Roggen *m*

rye bread *n* Roggenbrot *nt*

Ss

S¹, s [ɛs] n (letter) S nt, s nt; (US: Scol: satisfactory) ≈ 3; **S for sugar** ≈ S wie Samuel

S² [ɛs] abbr (= saint) St.; (= small) kl.; (= south) S

SA abbr = **South Africa; South America;** (= South Australia) Südaustralien nt

Sabbath ['sæbəθ] n (Jewish) Sabbat m; (Christian) Sonntag m

sabbatical [sə'bætɪkl] n (also: **sabbatical year**) Forschungsjahr nt

sabotage ['sæbətɑːʒ] n Sabotage f ▷ vt einen Sabotageakt verüben auf +acc; (plan, meeting) sabotieren

sabre ['seɪbəʳ] n Säbel m

sabre-rattling ['seɪbərætlɪŋ] n Säbelrasseln nt

saccharin, saccharine ['sækərɪn] n Sa(c)charin n ▷ adj (fig) zuckersüß

sachet ['sæʃeɪ] n (of shampoo) Beutel m; (of sugar etc) Tütchen nt

sack [sæk] n Sack m ▷ vt (dismiss) entlassen; (plunder) plündern; **to get the ~** rausfliegen (inf); **to give sb the ~** jdn rausschmeißen (inf)

sackful ['sækful] n: **a ~ of** ein Sack

sacking ['sækɪŋ] n (dismissal) Entlassung f; (material) Sackleinen nt

sacrament ['sækrəmənt] n Sakrament nt

sacred ['seɪkrɪd] adj heilig; (music, history) geistlich; (memory) geheiligt; (building) sakral

sacred cow n (lit, fig) heilige Kuh f

sacrifice ['sækrɪfaɪs] n Opfer nt ▷ vt opfern; **to make ~s (for sb)** (für jdn) Opfer bringen

sacrilege ['sækrɪlɪdʒ] n Sakrileg nt; **that would be ~** das wäre ein Sakrileg

sacrosanct ['sækrəʊsæŋkt] adj (lit, fig) sakrosankt

sad [sæd] adj traurig; **he was ~ to see her go** er war traurig (darüber), dass sie wegging

sadden ['sædn] vt betrüben

saddle ['sædl] n Sattel m ▷ vt (horse) satteln; **to be ~d with sb/sth** (inf) jdn/etw am Hals haben

saddlebag ['sædlbæg] n Satteltasche f

sadism ['seɪdɪzəm] n Sadismus m

sadist ['seɪdɪst] n Sadist(in) m(f)

sadistic [sə'dɪstɪk] adj sadistisch

sadly ['sædlɪ] adv traurig, betrübt; (unfortunately) leider, bedauerlicherweise; (seriously) schwer; **he is ~ lacking in humour** ihm fehlt leider jeglicher Humor

sadness ['sædnɪs] n Traurigkeit f

sadomasochism [seɪdəʊ'mæsəkɪzəm] n Sadomasochismus m

s.a.e. (Brit) abbr (= stamped addressed envelope) see **stamp**

safari [sə'fɑːrɪ] n Safari f; **to go on ~** auf Safari gehen

safari park n Safaripark m

safe [seɪf] adj sicher; (out of danger) in Sicherheit ▷ n Safe m or nt, Tresor m; **~ from** sicher vor +dat; **~ and sound** gesund und wohlbehalten; **(just) to be on the ~ side** (nur) um sicherzugehen; **to play ~** auf Nummer sicher gehen (inf); **it is ~ to say that ...** man kann wohl sagen, dass ...; **~ journey!** gute Fahrt or Reise!

safe bet n: **it's a ~ that ...** es ist sicher, dass ...

safe-breaker ['seɪfbreɪkəʳ] (Brit) n Safeknacker m (inf)

safe-conduct [seɪf'kɒndʌkt] n freies or sicheres Geleit nt

safe-cracker ['seɪfkrækəʳ] n = **safe-breaker**

safe-deposit ['seɪfdɪpɒzɪt] n (vault) Tresorraum m; (also: **safe-deposit box**) Banksafe m

safeguard ['seɪfgɑːd] n Schutz m ▷ vt schützen; (interests) wahren; (future) sichern; **as a ~ against** zum Schutz gegen

safe haven n Zufluchtsort m

safe house n geheimer Unterschlupf m

safekeeping ['seɪf'kiːpɪŋ] n sichere Aufbewahrung f

safely ['seɪflɪ] adv sicher; (assume, say) wohl, ruhig; (arrive) wohlbehalten; **I can ~ say ...** ich kann wohl sagen ...

safe passage n sichere Durchreise f

safe sex n Safer Sex m

safety ['seɪftɪ] n Sicherheit f; **~ first!** Sicherheit geht vor!

safety belt n Sicherheitsgurt m

safety catch n (on gun) Sicherung f; (on window, door) Sperre f

safety net n Sprungnetz nt, Sicherheitsnetz nt; (fig) Sicherheitsvorkehrung f

safety pin n Sicherheitsnadel f

safety valve n Sicherheitsventil nt

saffron ['sæfrən] n Safran m

sag [sæg] vi durchhängen; (breasts) hängen; (fig: spirits, demand) sinken

saga ['sɑ:gə] n Saga f; (fig) Geschichte f

sage [seɪdʒ] n (herb) Salbei m; (wise man) Weise(r) m

Sagittarius [sædʒɪ'tɛərɪəs] n Schütze m; **to be ~ Schütze** sein

sago ['seɪɡəʊ] n Sago m

Sahara [sə'hɑ:rə] n: **the ~ (Desert)** die (Wüste) Sahara

Sahel [sæ'hɛl] n Sahel m, Sahelzone f

said [sɛd] pt, pp of **say**

Saigon [saɪ'ɡɔn] n Saigon nt

sail [seɪl] n Segel nt ⊳ vt segeln ⊳ vi fahren; (Sport) segeln; (begin voyage: ship) auslaufen; (: passenger) abfahren; (fig: ball etc) fliegen, segeln; **to go for a ~** segeln gehen; **to set ~** losfahren, abfahren
▶ **sail through** vt fus (fig: exam etc) spielend schaffen

sailboat ['seɪlbəʊt] (US) n = **sailing boat**

sailing ['seɪlɪŋ] n (Sport) Segeln nt; (voyage) Überfahrt f; **to go ~** segeln gehen

sailing boat n Segelboot nt

sailing ship n Segelschiff nt

sailor ['seɪlər] n Seemann m, Matrose m

saint [seɪnt] n (lit, fig) Heilige(r) f(m)

saintly ['seɪntlɪ] adj heiligmäßig; (expression) fromm

sake [seɪk] n: **for the ~ of sb/sth, for sb's/ sth's sake** um jds/einer Sache gen willen; (out of consideration for) jdm/etw zuliebe; **he enjoys talking for talking's ~** er redet gerne, nur damit etwas gesagt wird; **for the ~ of argument** rein theoretisch; **art for art's ~** Kunst um der Kunst willen; **for heaven's ~!** um Gottes willen!

salad ['sæləd] n Salat m; **tomato ~** Tomatensalat m; **green ~** grüner Salat m

salad bowl n Salatschüssel f

salad cream (Brit) n ≈ Mayonnaise f

salad dressing n Salatsoße f

salami [sə'lɑ:mɪ] n Salami f

salaried ['sælərɪd] adj: **~ staff** Gehaltsempfänger pl

salary ['sælərɪ] n Gehalt nt

salary scale n Gehaltsskala f

sale [seɪl] n Verkauf m; (at reduced prices) Ausverkauf m; (auction) Auktion f; **sales** npl (total amount sold) Absatz m ⊳ cpd (campaign) Verkaufs-; (conference) Vertreter-; (figures) Absatz-; **"for ~"** „zu verkaufen"; **on ~** im Handel; **on ~ or return** auf Kommissionsbasis; **closing-down ~, liquidation ~** (US) Räumungsverkauf m

sale and lease back n (Comm) Verkauf m mit Rückmiete

saleroom ['seɪlru:m] n Auktionsraum m

sales assistant, (US) **sales clerk** [seɪlz-] n Verkäufer(in) m(f)

sales force n Vertreterstab m

salesman ['seɪlzmən] (irreg: like **man**) n Verkäufer m; (representative) Vertreter m

sales manager n Verkaufsleiter m

salesmanship ['seɪlzmənʃɪp] n

Verkaufstechnik f

sales tax (US) n Verkaufssteuer f

saleswoman ['seɪlzwʊmən] (irreg: like **woman**) n Verkäuferin f; (representative) Vertreterin f

salient ['seɪlɪənt] adj (features) hervorstechend; (points) Haupt-

saline ['seɪlaɪn] adj (solution etc) Salz-

saliva [sə'laɪvə] n Speichel m

sallow ['sæləʊ] adj (complexion) fahl

sally forth ['sælɪ-] (old) vi sich aufmachen

sally out vi = **sally forth**

salmon ['sæmən] n inv Lachs m

salmon trout n Lachsforelle f

salon ['sælɔn] n Salon m

saloon [sə'lu:n] n (US: bar) Saloon m; (Brit: Aut) Limousine f; (ship's lounge) Salon m

SALT [sɔ:lt] n abbr (= Strategic Arms Limitation Talks/Treaty) SALT

salt [sɔ:lt] n Salz nt ⊳ vt (preserve) einsalzen; (put salt on) salzen; (road) mit Salz streuen ⊳ cpd Salz-; (pork, beef) gepökelt; **the ~ of the earth** (fig) das Salz der Erde; **to take sth with a pinch** or **grain of ~** (fig) etw nicht ganz so ernst nehmen

salt cellar n Salzstreuer m

salt-free ['sɔ:lt'fri:] adj salzlos

salt mine n Salzbergwerk nt

saltwater ['sɔ:lt'wɔ:tər] adj (fish, plant) Meeres-

salty ['sɔ:ltɪ] adj salzig

salubrious [sə'lu:brɪəs] adj (district etc) fein; (air, living conditions) gesund

salutary ['sæljutərɪ] adj heilsam

salute [sə'lu:t] n (Mil, greeting) Gruß m; (Mil: with guns) Salut m ⊳ vt (Mil) grüßen, salutieren vor +dat; (fig) begrüßen

salvage ['sælvɪdʒ] n Bergung f; (things saved) Bergungsgut nt ⊳ vt bergen; (fig) retten

salvage vessel n Bergungsschiff nt

salvation [sæl'veɪʃən] n (Rel) Heil nt; (economic etc) Rettung f

Salvation Army n Heilsarmee f

salver ['sælvər] n Tablett nt

salvo ['sælvəʊ] (pl **~es**) n Salve f

Samaritan [sə'mærɪtən] n: **the ~s** ≈ die Telefonseelsorge

same [seɪm] adj (similar) gleiche(r, s); (identical) selbe(r, s) ⊳ pron: **the ~** (similar) der/die/das Gleiche; (identical) derselbe/dieselbe/dasselbe; **the ~ book as** das gleiche Buch wie; **they are the ~ age** sie sind gleichaltrig; **they are exactly the ~** sie sind genau gleich; **on the ~ day** am gleichen or selben Tag; **at the ~ time** (simultaneously) gleichzeitig, zur gleichen Zeit; (yet) doch; **they're one and the ~** (person) das ist doch ein und derselbe/dieselbe; (thing) das ist doch dasselbe; **~ again** (in bar etc) das Gleiche noch mal; **all** or **just the ~** trotzdem; **to do the ~ (as sb)** das Gleiche (wie jd) tun; **the ~ to you!** (danke) gleichfalls!; **~ here!** ich/wir etc auch!; **thanks all the ~** trotzdem vielen Dank; **it's all the ~ to me** es ist mir egal

same-sex marriage ['seɪmsɛks-] n

gleichgeschlechtliche Ehe f, Homoehe f (inf)
same-sex relationship ['seɪmsɛks-] n
gleichgeschlechtliche Beziehung f
sample ['sɑːmpl] n Probe f; (of merchandise)
Probe f, Muster nt ▷ vt probieren; **to take a ~**
eine Stichprobe machen; **free** ~ kostenlose
Probe
sanatorium [sænə'tɔːrɪəm] (pl **sanatoria**) n
Sanatorium nt
sanctify ['sæŋktɪfaɪ] vt heiligen
sanctimonious [sæŋktɪ'məʊnɪəs] adj
scheinheilig
sanction ['sæŋkʃən] n Zustimmung f ▷ vt
sanktionieren; **sanctions** npl (Pol) Sanktionen
pl; **to impose economic ~s on** or **against**
Wirtschaftssanktionen verhängen gegen
sanctity ['sæŋktɪtɪ] n (holiness) Heiligkeit f;
(inviolability) Unantastbarkeit f
sanctuary ['sæŋktjʊərɪ] n (for birds/animals)
Schutzgebiet nt; (place of refuge) Zuflucht f;
(Rel: in church) Altarraum m
sand [sænd] n Sand m ▷ vt (also: **sand down**)
abschmirgeln; see also **sands**
sandal ['sændl] n Sandale f
sandbag ['sændbæg] n Sandsack m
sandblast ['sændblɑːst] vt sandstrahlen
sandbox ['sændbɒks] (US) n Sandkasten m;
(Comput: antivirus software) Sandbox f
sandcastle ['sændkɑːsl] n Sandburg f
sand dune n Sanddüne f
sander ['sændər] n (tool) Schleifmaschine f
S & M (US) n abbr (= sadomasochism) S/M
sandpaper ['sændpeɪpər] n Schmirgelpapier nt
sandpit ['sændpɪt] n Sandkasten m;
(Comput: antivirus software) Sandbox f
sands [sændz] npl (beach) Sandstrand m
sandstone ['sændstəʊn] n Sandstein m
sandstorm ['sændstɔːm] n Sandsturm m
sandwich ['sændwɪtʃ] n Sandwich nt ▷ vt: **~ed**
between eingequetscht zwischen; **cheese/**
ham ~ Käse-/Schinkenbrot nt
sandwich board n Reklametafel f
sandwich course (Brit) n Ausbildungsgang, bei
dem sich Theorie und Praxis abwechseln
sandwich man n Sandwichmann m,
Plakatträger m
sandy ['sændɪ] adj sandig; (beach) Sand-; (hair)
rotblond
sane [seɪn] adj geistig gesund; (sensible)
vernünftig
sang [sæŋ] pt of **sing**
sanguine ['sæŋgwɪn] adj zuversichtlich
sanitarium [sænɪ'tɛərɪəm] (US) (pl **sanitaria**) n
= **sanatorium**
sanitary ['sænɪtərɪ] adj hygienisch; (facilities)
sanitär; (inspector) Gesundheits-
sanitary towel, (US) **sanitary napkin** n
Damenbinde f
sanitation [sænɪ'teɪʃən] n Hygiene f; (toilets etc)
sanitäre Anlagen pl; (drainage) Kanalisation f
sanitation department (US) n
Stadtreinigung f
sanity ['sænɪtɪ] n geistige Gesundheit f;

(common sense) Vernunft f
sank [sæŋk] pt of **sink**
Santa Claus [sæntə'klɔːz] n ≈ der
Weihnachtsmann
Santiago [sæntɪ'ɑːgəʊ] n (also: **Santiago de**
Chile) Santiago (de Chile) nt
sap [sæp] n Saft m ▷ vt (strength) zehren an +dat;
(confidence) untergraben
sapling ['sæplɪŋ] n junger Baum m
sapphire ['sæfaɪər] n Saphir m
sarcasm ['sɑːkæzm] n Sarkasmus m
sarcastic [sɑː'kæstɪk] adj sarkastisch
sarcophagus [sɑː'kɒfəgəs] (pl **sarcophagi**) n
Sarkophag m
sardine [sɑː'diːn] n Sardine f
Sardinia [sɑː'dɪnɪə] n Sardinien nt
Sardinian [sɑː'dɪnɪən] adj sardinisch, sardisch
▷ n (person) Sardinier(in) m(f); (Ling) Sardinisch
nt
sardonic [sɑː'dɒnɪk] adj (smile) süffisant
sari ['sɑːrɪ] n Sari m
SARS [sɑːz] n abbr (= severe acute respiratory
syndrome) SARS nt
sartorial [sɑː'tɔːrɪəl] adj: **his ~ elegance** seine
elegante Art, sich zu kleiden
SAS (Brit) n abbr (Mil: = Special Air Service)
Spezialeinheit der britischen Armee
SASE (US) n abbr (= self-addressed stamped envelope)
frankierter Rückumschlag m
sash [sæʃ] n Schärpe f; (of window)
Fensterrahmen m
sash window n Schiebefenster nt
SAT (US) n abbr (= Scholastic Aptitude Test)
Hochschulaufnahmeprüfung
sat [sæt] pt, pp of **sit**
Sat. abbr (= Saturday) Sa.
Satan ['seɪtn] n Satan m
satanic [sə'tænɪk] adj satanisch
satanism ['seɪtnɪzəm] n Satanismus m
satchel ['sætʃl] n (child's) Schultasche f
sated ['seɪtɪd] adj gesättigt; **to be ~ with sth**
(fig) von etw übersättigt sein
satellite ['sætəlaɪt] n Satellit m; (also: **satellite**
state) Satellitenstaat m
satellite dish n Satellitenantenne f,
Parabolantenne f
satellite receiver n Satellitenempfänger m
satellite television n Satellitenfernsehen nt
satiate ['seɪʃɪeɪt] vt (food) sättigen; (fig: pleasure
etc) übersättigen
satin ['sætɪn] n Satin m ▷ adj (dress etc) Satin-;
with a ~ finish mit Seidenglanz
satire ['sætaɪər] n Satire f
satirical [sə'tɪrɪkl] adj satirisch
satirist ['sætɪrɪst] n Satiriker(in) m(f)
satirize ['sætɪraɪz] vt satirisch darstellen
satisfaction [sætɪs'fækʃən] n Befriedigung
f; **to get ~ from sb** (refund, apology etc)
Genugtuung von jdm erhalten; **has it been**
done to your ~? sind Sie damit zufrieden?
satisfactorily [sætɪs'fæktərɪlɪ] adv
zufriedenstellend
satisfactory [sætɪs'fæktərɪ] adj

S

763

zufriedenstellend

satisfied ['sætisfaid] *adj* zufrieden

satisfy ['sætisfai] *vt* zufriedenstellen; (*needs, demand*) befriedigen; (*requirements, conditions*) erfüllen; **to ~ sb/o.s. that ...** jdn/sich davon überzeugen, dass ...

satisfying ['sætisfaiiŋ] *adj* befriedigend; (*meal*) sättigend

satsuma [sæt'su:mə] *n* Satsuma *f*

saturate ['sætʃəreit] *vt:* **to ~ (with)** durchnässen (mit); (*Chem: market*) sättigen; (*fig: area etc*) überschwemmen

saturated fat ['sætʃəreitid-] *n* gesättigtes Fett *nt*

saturation [sætʃə'reiʃən] *n* (*Chem*) Sättigung *f*; **~ advertising** flächendeckende Werbung *f*; **~ bombing** Flächenbombardierung *f*

Saturday ['sætədi] *n* Samstag *m*; *see also* **Tuesday**

sauce [sɔ:s] *n* Soße *f*

saucepan ['sɔ:spən] *n* Kochtopf *m*

saucer ['sɔ:sə^r] *n* Untertasse *f*

saucy ['sɔ:si] *adj* frech

Saudi ['saudi-] *adj* (*also:* **Saudi Arabian**) saudisch, saudi-arabisch

Saudi Arabia ['saudi-] *n* Saudi-Arabien *nt*

sauna ['sɔ:nə] *n* Sauna *f*

saunter ['sɔ:ntə^r] *vi* schlendern

sausage ['sɔsidʒ] *n* Wurst *f*

sausage roll *n* Wurst *f* im Schlafrock

sauté ['səutei] *vt* kurz anbraten ▷ *adj:* **~ed potatoes** Bratkartoffeln *pl*

savage ['sævidʒ] *adj* (*attack etc*) brutal; (*dog*) gefährlich; (*criticism*) schonungslos ▷ *n* (*old: pej*) Wilde(r) *f(m)* ▷ *vt* (*maul*) zerfleischen; (*fig: criticize*) verreißen

savagely ['sævidʒli] *adv* (*attack etc*) brutal; (*criticize*) schonungslos

savagery ['sævidʒri] *n* (*of attack*) Brutalität *f*

save [seiv] *vt* (*rescue*) retten; (*money, time*) sparen; (*food etc*) aufheben; (*work, trouble*) (er)sparen; (*keep: receipts etc*) aufbewahren; (*: seat etc*) frei halten; (*Comput: file*) abspeichern; (*Sport: shot, ball*) halten ▷ *vi* (*also:* **save up**) sparen ▷ *n* (*Sport*) (Ball)abwehr *f* ▷ *prep* (*form*) außer +*dat*; **it will ~ me an hour** dadurch spare ich eine Stunde; **to ~ face** das Gesicht wahren; **God ~ the Queen!** Gott schütze die Königin!

saving ['seiviŋ] *n* (*on price etc*) Ersparnis *f* ▷ *adj:* **the ~ grace of sth** das einzig Gute an etw *dat*; **savings** *npl* (*money*) Ersparnisse *pl*; **to make ~s** sparen

savings account *n* Sparkonto *nt*

savings bank *n* Sparkasse *f*

saviour, (*US*) **savior** ['seivjə^r] *n* Retter(in) *m(f)*; (*Rel*) Erlöser *m*

savoir-faire ['sævwɑ:fɛə^r] *n* Gewandtheit *f*

savour, (*US*) **savor** ['seivə^r] *vt* genießen ▷ *n* (*of food*) Geschmack *m*

savoury, (*US*) **savory** ['seivəri] *adj* pikant

savvy ['sævi] (*inf*) *n* Grips *m*; **he hasn't got much ~** er hat keine Ahnung

saw [sɔ:] (*pt* **~ed**, *pp* **sawed** *or* **~n**) *vt* sägen ▷ *n* Säge *f* ▷ *pt of* **see**; **to ~ sth up** etw zersägen

sawdust ['sɔ:dʌst] *n* Sägemehl *nt*

sawmill ['sɔ:mil] *n* Sägewerk *nt*

sawn [sɔ:n] *pp of* **saw**

sawn-off ['sɔ:nɔf], (*US*) **sawed-off** ['sɔ:dɔf] *adj:* **~ shotgun** Gewehr *nt* mit abgesägtem Lauf

saxophone ['sæksəfəun] *n* Saxofon *nt*

say [sei] (*pt, pp* **said**) *vt* sagen ▷ *n:* **to have one's ~** seine Meinung äußern; **could you ~ that again?** können Sie das wiederholen?; **my watch ~s 3 o'clock** auf meiner Uhr ist es 3 Uhr; **it ~s on the sign "No Smoking"** auf dem Schild steht „Rauchen verboten"; **shall we ~ Tuesday?** sagen wir Dienstag?; **come for dinner at, ~, 8 o'clock** kommt um, sagen wir mal 8 Uhr, zum Essen; **that doesn't ~ much for him** das spricht nicht gerade für ihn; **when all is said and done** letzten Endes; **there is something/a lot to be said for it** es spricht einiges/vieles dafür; **you can ~ that again!** das kann man wohl sagen!; **that is to ~** das heißt; **that goes without ~ing** das versteht sich von selbst; **to ~ nothing of ...** von ... ganz zu schweigen; **~ (that) ...** angenommen, (dass) ...; **to have a** *or* **some ~ in sth** ein Mitspracherecht bei etw haben

saying ['seiiŋ] *n* Redensart *f*

say-so ['seisəu] *n* Zustimmung *f*; **to do sth on sb's ~** etw auf jds Anweisung *acc* hin tun

SBA (*US*) *n abbr* (= *Small Business Administration*) *Regierungsstelle zur Unterstützung kleiner und mittelständischer Betriebe*

SC (*US*) *n abbr* = **Supreme Court** ▷ *abbr* (*Post*) = *South Carolina*

s/c *abbr* = **self-contained**

scab [skæb] *n* (*on wound*) Schorf *m*; (*pej*) Streikbrecher(in) *m(f)*

scabby ['skæbi] (*pej*) *adj* (*hands, skin*) schorfig

scaffold ['skæfəld] *n* (*for execution*) Schafott *nt*

scaffolding ['skæfəldiŋ] *n* Gerüst *nt*

scald [skɔ:ld] *n* Verbrühung *f* ▷ *vt* (*burn*) verbrühen

scalding ['skɔ:ldiŋ] *adj* (*also:* **scalding hot**) siedend heiß

scale [skeil] *n* Skala *f*; (*of fish*) Schuppe *f*; (*Mus*) Tonleiter *f*; (*size, extent*) Ausmaß *nt*, Umfang *m*; (*of map, model*) Maßstab *m* ▷ *vt* (*cliff, tree*) erklettern; (**pair of) scales** *npl* (*for weighing*) Waage *f*; **pay ~** Lohnskala *f*; **to draw sth to ~** etw maßstabgetreu zeichnen; **a small-~ model** ein Modell in verkleinertem Maßstab; **on a large ~** im großen Rahmen; **~ of charges** Gebührenordnung *f*
▶ **scale down** *vt* verkleinern; (*fig*) verringern

scaled-down [skeild'daun] *adj* verkleinert; (*project, forecast*) eingeschränkt

scale drawing *n* maßstabgetreue Zeichnung *f*

scallion ['skæljən] *n* Frühlingszwiebel *f*; (*US: shallot*) Schalotte *f*; (*: leek*) Lauch *m*

scallop ['skɔləp] *n* (*Zool*) Kammmuschel *f*;

(Sewing) Bogenkante f
scalp [skælp] n Kopfhaut f ▷ vt skalpieren
scalpel ['skælpl] n Skalpell nt
scalper ['skælpə^r] *(US: inf)* n *(ticket tout)* (Karten)schwarzhändler(in) m(f)
scam [skæm] *(inf)* n Betrug m
scamp [skæmp] *(inf)* n Frechdachs m
scamper ['skæmpə^r] vi: **to ~ away** *or* **off** verschwinden
scampi ['skæmpɪ] *(Brit)* npl Scampi pl
scan [skæn] vt *(horizon)* absuchen; *(newspaper etc)* überfliegen; *(TV, Radar)* abtasten ▷ vi *(poetry)* das richtige Versmaß haben ▷ n *(Med)* Scan m
scandal ['skændl] n Skandal m; *(gossip)* Skandalgeschichten pl
scandalize ['skændəlaɪz] vt schockieren
scandalous ['skændələs] adj skandalös
Scandinavia [skændɪ'neɪvɪə] n Skandinavien nt
Scandinavian [skændɪ'neɪvɪən] adj skandinavisch ▷ n Skandinavier(in) m(f)
scanner ['skænə^r] n *(Med)* Scanner m; *(Radar)* Richtantenne f
scant [skænt] adj wenig
scantily ['skæntɪlɪ] adv: **~ clad** *or* **dressed** spärlich bekleidet
scanty ['skæntɪ] adj *(information)* dürftig; *(meal)* kärglich; *(bikini)* knapp
scapegoat ['skeɪpgəut] n Sündenbock m
scar [skɑ:] n Narbe f; *(fig)* Wunde f ▷ vt eine Narbe hinterlassen auf +dat; *(fig)* zeichnen
scarce [skɛəs] adj knapp; **to make o.s. ~** *(inf)* verschwinden
scarcely ['skɛəslɪ] adv kaum; *(certainly not)* wohl kaum; **~ anybody** kaum jemand; **I can ~ believe it** ich kann es kaum glauben
scarcity ['skɛəsɪtɪ] n Knappheit f; **~ value** Seltenheitswert m
scare [skɛə^r] n *(fright)* Schreck(en) m; *(public fear)* Panik f ▷ vt *(frighten)* erschrecken; *(worry)* Angst machen +dat; **to give sb a ~** jdm einen Schrecken einjagen; **bomb ~** Bombendrohung f
▶ **scare away** vt *(animal)* verscheuchen; *(investor, buyer)* abschrecken
▶ **scare off** vt = **scare away**
scarecrow ['skɛəkrəu] n Vogelscheuche f
scared ['skɛəd] adj: **to be ~** Angst haben; **to be ~ stiff** fürchterliche Angst haben
scaremonger ['skɛəmʌŋgə^r] n Panikmacher m
scarf [skɑ:f] *(pl* **~s** *or* **scarves**) n Schal m; *(headscarf)* Kopftuch nt
scarlet ['skɑ:lɪt] adj (scharlach)rot
scarlet fever n Scharlach m
scarper ['skɑ:pə^r] *(Brit: inf)* vi abhauen
scarred [skɑ:d] adj narbig; *(fig)* gezeichnet
SCART socket ['skɑ:tsɔkɪt] n *(Comput)* SCART-Büchse f
scarves [skɑ:vz] npl of **scarf**
scary ['skɛərɪ] *(inf)* adj unheimlich; *(film)* gruselig
scathing ['skeɪðɪŋ] adj *(comments)* bissig;

(attack) scharf; **to be ~ about sth** bissige Bemerkungen über etw acc machen
scatter ['skætə^r] vt verstreuen; *(flock of birds)* aufscheuchen; *(crowd)* zerstreuen ▷ vi *(crowd)* sich zerstreuen
scatterbrained ['skætəbreɪnd] *(inf)* adj schusselig
scattered ['skætəd] adj verstreut; **~ showers** vereinzelte Regenschauer pl
scatty ['skætɪ] *(Brit: inf)* adj schusselig
scavenge ['skævəndʒ] vi: **to ~ for sth** nach etw suchen
scavenger ['skævəndʒə^r] n *(person)* Aasgeier m *(inf)*; *(animal, bird)* Aasfresser m
SCE n abbr *(= Scottish Certificate of Education)* Schulabschlusszeugnis in Schottland
scenario [sɪ'nɑ:rɪəu] n *(Theat, Cine)* Szenarium nt; *(fig)* Szenario nt
scene [si:n] n *(lit, fig)* Szene f; *(of crime)* Schauplatz m; *(of accident)* Ort m; *(sight)* Anblick m; **behind the ~s** *(fig)* hinter den Kulissen; **to make a ~** *(inf: fuss)* eine Szene machen; **to appear on the ~** *(fig)* auftauchen, auf der Bildfläche erscheinen; **the political ~** die politische Landschaft
scenery ['si:nərɪ] n *(Theat)* Bühnenbild nt; *(landscape)* Landschaft f
scenic ['si:nɪk] adj malerisch, landschaftlich schön
scent [sɛnt] n *(fragrance)* Duft m; *(track)* Fährte f; *(fig)* Spur f; *(liquid perfume)* Parfüm nt; **to put** *or* **throw sb off the ~** *(fig)* jdn von der Spur abbringen
sceptic, *(US)* **skeptic** ['skɛptɪk] n Skeptiker(in) m(f)
sceptical, *(US)* **skeptical** ['skɛptɪkl] adj skeptisch
scepticism, *(US)* **skepticism** ['skɛptɪsɪzəm] n Skepsis f
sceptre, *(US)* **scepter** ['sɛptə^r] n Zepter nt
schedule ['ʃɛdju:l, *(US)* 'skɛdju:l] n *(of trains, buses)* Fahrplan m; *(of events)* Programm nt; *(of prices, details etc)* Liste f ▷ vt planen; *(visit, meeting etc)* ansetzen; **on ~** wie geplant, pünktlich; **we are working to a very tight ~** wir arbeiten nach einem sehr knappen Zeitplan; **everything went according to ~** alles ist planmäßig verlaufen; **to be ahead of/behind ~** dem Zeitplan voraus sein/im Rückstand sein; **he was ~d to leave yesterday** laut Zeitplan hätte er gestern abfahren sollen
scheduled ['ʃɛdju:ld, *(US)* 'skɛdju:ld] adj *(date, time)* vorgesehen; *(visit, event)* geplant; *(train, bus, stop)* planmäßig
scheduled flight n Linienflug m
schematic [skɪ'mætɪk] adj schematisch
scheme [ski:m] n *(personal plan)* Plan m; *(plot)* raffinierter Plan m, Komplott nt; *(formal plan)* Programm nt ▷ vi Pläne schmieden, intrigieren; **colour ~** Farbzusammenstellung f; **pension ~** Rentenversicherung f
scheming ['ski:mɪŋ] adj intrigierend ▷ n

S

765

Machenschaften *pl*

schism ['skɪzəm] *n* Spaltung *f*

schizophrenia [skɪtsə'fri:nɪə] *n* Schizophrenie *f*

schizophrenic [skɪtsə'frenɪk] *adj* schizophren
▷ *n* Schizophrene(r) *f(m)*

scholar ['skɒlə'] *n* Gelehrte(r) *f(m)*; *(pupil)* Student(in) *m(f)*, Schüler(in) *m(f)*; *(scholarship holder)* Stipendiat(in) *m(f)*

scholarly ['skɒləlɪ] *adj* gelehrt; *(text, approach)* wissenschaftlich

scholarship ['skɒləʃɪp] *n* Gelehrsamkeit *f*; *(grant)* Stipendium *nt*

school [sku:l] *n* Schule *f*; *(US: inf: university)* Universität *f*; *(of whales, porpoises etc)* Schule *f*, Schwarm *m* ▷ *cpd* Schul-

school age *n* Schulalter *nt*

schoolbook ['sku:lbuk] *n* Schulbuch *nt*

schoolboy ['sku:lbɔɪ] *n* Schuljunge *m*, Schüler *m*

schoolchildren ['sku:ltʃɪldrən] *npl* Schulkinder *pl*, Schüler *pl*

schooldays ['sku:ldeɪz] *npl* Schulzeit *f*

schooled [sku:ld] *adj* geschult; **to be ~ in sth** über etw *acc* gut Bescheid wissen

schoolgirl ['sku:lgɜ:l] *n* Schulmädchen *nt*, Schülerin *f*

schooling ['sku:lɪŋ] *n* Schulbildung *f*

school-leaver [sku:l'li:və'] *(Brit)* *n* Schulabgänger(in) *m(f)*

schoolmaster ['sku:lmɑ:stə'] *n* Lehrer *m*

schoolmistress ['sku:lmɪstrɪs] *n* Lehrerin *f*

school report *(Brit)* *n* Zeugnis *nt*

schoolroom ['sku:lru:m] *n* Klassenzimmer *nt*

schoolteacher ['sku:lti:tʃə'] *n* Lehrer(in) *m(f)*

schoolyard ['sku:lja:d] *n* Schulhof *m*

schooner ['sku:nə'] *n* *(ship)* Schoner *m*; (Brit: *for sherry*) großes Sherryglas *nt*; *(US etc: for beer)* großes Bierglas *nt*

sciatica [saɪ'ætɪkə] *n* Ischias *m* or *nt*

science ['saɪəns] *n* Naturwissenschaft *f*; *(branch of knowledge)* Wissenschaft *f*; **the ~s** Naturwissenschaften *pl*

science fiction *n* Science-Fiction *f*

scientific [saɪən'tɪfɪk] *adj* wissenschaftlich

scientist ['saɪəntɪst] *n* Wissenschaftler(in) *m(f)*

sci-fi ['saɪfaɪ] *(inf)* *n abbr* (= *science fiction*) SF

Scillies ['sɪlɪz] *npl* = **Scilly Isles**

Scilly Isles ['sɪlɪ'aɪlz] *npl*: **the ~** die Scillyinseln *pl*

scintillating ['sɪntɪleɪtɪŋ] *adj* *(fig: conversation)* faszinierend; *(wit)* sprühend

scissors ['sɪzəz] *npl* Schere *f*; **a pair of ~** eine Schere

sclerosis [sklɪ'rəusɪs] *n* Sklerose *f*

scoff [skɒf] *vt* (Brit: *inf: eat*) futtern, verputzen ▷ *vi*: **to ~ (at)** *(mock)* spotten (über +*acc*), sich lustig machen (über +*acc*)

scold [skəuld] *vt* ausschimpfen

scolding ['skəuldɪŋ] *n* Schelte *f*; **to get a ~** ausgeschimpft werden

scone [skɒn] *n* brötchenartiges Teegebäck

scoop [sku:p] *n* *(for flour etc)* Schaufel *f*; *(for ice*

cream etc) Portionierer *m*; *(amount)* Kugel *f*; *(Press)* Knüller *m*
  ▶ **scoop out** *vt* aushöhlen
  ▶ **scoop up** *vt* aufschaufeln; *(liquid)* aufschöpfen

scooter ['sku:tə'] *n* (also: **motor scooter**) Motorroller *m*; *(toy)* (Tret)roller *m*

scope [skəup] *n* *(opportunity)* Möglichkeiten *pl*; *(range)* Ausmaß *nt*, Umfang *m*; *(freedom)* Freiheit *f*; **within the ~ of** im Rahmen +*gen*; **there is plenty of ~ for improvement** *(Brit)* es könnte noch viel verbessert werden

scorch [skɔ:tʃ] *vt* versengen; *(earth, grass)* verbrennen

scorched earth policy *n* (Mil) Politik *f* der verbrannten Erde

scorcher ['skɔ:tʃə'] *(inf)* *n* heißer Tag *m*

scorching ['skɔ:tʃɪŋ] *adj* *(day, weather)* brütend heiß

score [skɔ:'] *n* *(number of points)* (Punkte)stand *m*; *(of game)* Spielstand *m*; *(Mus)* Partitur *f*; *(twenty)* zwanzig ▷ *vt* *(goal)* schießen; *(point, success)* erzielen; *(mark)* einkerben; *(cut)* einritzen ▷ *vi* *(in game)* einen Punkt/Punkte erzielen; *(Football etc)* ein Tor schießen; *(keep score)* (Punkte) zählen; **to settle an old ~ with sb** *(fig)* eine alte Rechnung mit jdm begleichen; **what's the ~?** *(Sport)* wie stehts?; **~s of** Hunderte von; **on that ~** in dieser Hinsicht; **to ~ well** gut abschneiden; **to ~ 6 out of 10** 6 von 10 Punkten erzielen; **to ~ (a point) over sb** *(fig)* jdn ausstechen
  ▶ **score out** *vt* ausstreichen

scoreboard ['skɔ:bɔ:d] *n* Anzeigetafel *f*

scorecard ['skɔ:ka:d] *n* (Sport) Spielprotokoll *nt*

score line *n* (Sport) Spielstand *m*; (: *final score*) Endergebnis *nt*

scorer ['skɔ:rə'] *n* *(Football etc)* Torschütze *m*, Torschützin *f*; *(person keeping score)* Anschreiber(in) *m(f)*

scorn [skɔ:n] *n* Verachtung *f* ▷ *vt* verachten; *(reject)* verschmähen

scornful ['skɔ:nful] *adj* verächtlich, höhnisch

Scorpio ['skɔ:pɪəu] *n* Skorpion *m*; **to be ~** Skorpion sein

scorpion ['skɔ:pɪən] *n* Skorpion *m*

Scot [skɒt] *n* Schotte *m*, Schottin *f*

Scotch [skɒtʃ] *n* Scotch *m*

scotch [skɒtʃ] *vt* *(rumour)* aus der Welt schaffen; *(plan, idea)* unterbinden

Scotch tape® *n* ≈ Tesafilm® *m*

scot-free ['skɒt'fri:] *adv*: **to get off ~** ungeschoren davonkommen

Scotland ['skɒtlənd] *n* Schottland *nt*

Scots [skɒts] *adj* schottisch

Scotsman ['skɒtsmən] *(irreg: like* **man**) *n* Schotte *m*

Scotswoman ['skɒtswumən] *(irreg: like* **woman**) *n* Schottin *f*

Scottish ['skɒtɪʃ] *adj* schottisch

Scottish National Party *n* Partei, *die für die Unabhängigkeit Schottlands eintritt*

scoundrel ['skaundrl] *n* Schurke *m*

scour ['skaʊəʳ] vt (search) absuchen; (clean) scheuern

scourer ['skaʊərəʳ] n Topfkratzer m

scourge [skɜːdʒ] n (lit, fig) Geißel f

scout [skaʊt] n (Mil) Kundschafter m, Späher m; (also: **boy scout**) Pfadfinder m; **girl ~** (US) Pfadfinderin f
▶ **scout around** vi sich umsehen

scowl [skaʊl] vi ein böses Gesicht machen ▷ n böses Gesicht nt; **to ~ at sb** jdn böse ansehen

scrabble ['skræbl] vi (also: **scrabble around**) herumtasten ▷ n: **S-®** Scrabble® nt; **to ~ at sth** nach etw krallen; **to ~ about** or **around for sth** nach etw herumsuchen

scraggy ['skrægɪ] adj (animal) mager; (body, neck etc) dürr

scram [skræm] (inf) vi abhauen, verschwinden

scramble ['skræmbl] n (climb) Kletterpartie f; (rush) Hetze f; (struggle) Gerangel nt ▷ vi: **to ~ up/over** klettern auf/über +acc; **to ~ for** sich drängeln um; **to go scrambling** (Sport) Querfeldeinrennen fahren

scrambled eggs ['skræmbld-] n Rührei nt

scrap [skræp] n (bit) Stückchen nt; (fig: of truth, evidence) Spur f; (fight) Balgerei f; (also: **scrap metal**) Altmetall nt, Schrott m ▷ vt (machines etc) verschrotten; (fig: plans etc) fallen lassen ▷ vi (fight) sich balgen; **scraps** npl (leftovers) Reste pl; **to sell sth for ~** etw als Schrott or zum Verschrotten verkaufen

scrapbook ['skræpbuk] n Sammelalbum nt

scrap dealer n Schrotthändler(in) m(f)

scrape [skreɪp] vt abkratzen; (hand etc) abschürfen; (car) verschrammen ▷ n: **to get into a ~** (difficult situation) in Schwulitäten pl kommen (inf)
▶ **scrape through** vt (exam etc) durchrutschen durch (inf)
▶ **scrape together** vt (money) zusammenkratzen

scraper ['skreɪpəʳ] n Kratzer m

scrap heap n: **to be on the ~** (fig) zum alten Eisen gehören

scrap merchant (Brit) n Schrotthändler(in) m(f)

scrap metal n Altmetall nt, Schrott m

scrap paper n Schmierpapier nt

scrappy ['skræpɪ] adj zusammengestoppelt (inf)

scrap yard n Schrottplatz m

scratch [skrætʃ] n Kratzer m ▷ vt kratzen; (one's nose etc) sich kratzen an +dat; (paint, car, record) verkratzen; (Comput) löschen ▷ vi sich kratzen ▷ cpd (team, side) zusammengewürfelt; **to start from ~** ganz von vorne anfangen; **to be up to ~** den Anforderungen ansprechen; **to ~ the surface** (fig) an der Oberfläche bleiben

scratch pad (US) n Notizblock m

scrawl [skrɔːl] n Gekritzel nt; (handwriting) Klaue f (inf) ▷ vt hinkritzeln

scrawny ['skrɔːnɪ] adj dürr

scream [skriːm] n Schrei m ▷ vi schreien; **to be a ~** (inf) zum Schreien sein; **to ~ at sb (to do sth)** jdn anschreien(, etw zu tun)

scree [skriː] n Geröll nt

screech [skriːtʃ] vi kreischen; (tyres, brakes) quietschen ▷ n Kreischen nt; (of tyres, brakes) Quietschen nt

screen [skriːn] n (Cine) Leinwand f; (TV, Comput) Bildschirm m; (movable barrier) Wandschirm m; (fig: cover) Tarnung f; (also: **windscreen**) Windschutzscheibe f ▷ vt (protect) abschirmen; (from the wind etc) schützen; (conceal) verdecken; (film) zeigen, vorführen; (programme) senden; (candidates etc) überprüfen; (for illness): **to ~ sb for sth** jdn auf etw acc (hin) untersuchen

screen editing n (Comput) Bildschirmaufbereitung f

screening ['skriːnɪŋ] n (Med) Untersuchung f; (of film) Vorführung f; (TV) Sendung f; (for security) Überprüfung f

screen memory n (Comput) Bildschirmspeicher m

screenplay ['skriːnpleɪ] n Drehbuch nt

screen saver n (Comput) Bildschirmschoner m

screen test n Probeaufnahmen pl

screw [skruː] n Schraube f ▷ vt schrauben; (inf!) bumsen (!); **to ~ sth in** etw einschrauben; **to ~ sth to the wall** etw an der Wand festschrauben; **to have one's head ~ed on** (fig) ein vernünftiger Mensch sein
▶ **screw up** vt (paper etc) zusammenknüllen; (inf: ruin) vermasseln; **to ~ up one's eyes** die Augen zusammenkneifen

screwdriver ['skruːdraɪvəʳ] n Schraubenzieher m

screwed-up ['skruːd'ʌp] (inf) adj: **to be/get ~ about sth** sich wegen etw ganz verrückt machen

screwy ['skruːɪ] (inf) adj verrückt

scribble ['skrɪbl] n Gekritzel nt ▷ vt, vi kritzeln; **to ~ sth down** etw hinkritzeln

scribe [skraɪb] n Schreiber m

script [skrɪpt] n (Cine) Drehbuch nt; (of speech, play etc) Text m; (alphabet) Schrift f; (in exam) schriftliche Arbeit f

scripted ['skrɪptɪd] adj vorbereitet

scripture ['skrɪptʃəʳ] n, **scriptures** ['skrɪptʃəz] ▷ npl (heilige) Schrift f; **the S~(s)** (the Bible) die Heilige Schrift

scriptwriter ['skrɪptraɪtəʳ] n (Radio, TV) Autor(in) m(f); (Cine) Drehbuchautor(in) m(f)

scroll [skrəʊl] n Schriftrolle f ▷ vi (Comput) scrollen

scroll bar n (Comput) Bildlaufleiste f

scrotum ['skrəʊtəm] n Hodensack m

scrounge [skraʊndʒ] (inf) vt: **to ~ sth off sb** etw bei jdm schnorren ▷ vi schnorren ▷ n: **on the ~** am Schnorren

scrounger ['skraʊndʒəʳ] (inf) n Schnorrer(in) m(f)

scrub [skrʌb] n Gestrüpp nt ▷ vt (floor etc) schrubben; (inf: idea, plan) fallen lassen

scrubbing brush ['skrʌbɪŋ-] n Scheuerbürste f

scruff [skrʌf] n: **by the ~ of the neck** am Genick

scruffy ['skrʌfɪ] *adj* gammelig, verwahrlost

scrum ['skrʌm], **scrummage** ['skrʌmɪdʒ] *n* (*Rugby*) Gedränge *nt*

scruple ['skru:pl] *n* (*gen pl*) Skrupel *m*, Bedenken *nt*; **to have no ~s about doing sth** keine Skrupel *or* Bedenken haben, etw zu tun

scrupulous ['skru:pjuləs] *adj* gewissenhaft; (*honesty*) unbedingt

scrupulously ['skru:pjuləslɪ] *adv* gewissenhaft; (*honest, fair*) äußerst; (*clean*) peinlich

scrutinize ['skru:tɪnaɪz] *vt* prüfend ansehen; (*data, records etc*) genau prüfen *or* untersuchen

scrutiny ['skru:tɪnɪ] *n* genaue Untersuchung *f*; **under the ~ of sb** unter jds prüfendem Blick

scuba ['sku:bə] *n* (Schwimm)tauchgerät *nt*

scuba diving *n* Sporttauchen *nt*

scuff [skʌf] *vt* (*shoes, floor*) abwetzen

scuffle ['skʌfl] *n* Handgemenge *nt*

scull [skʌl] *n* Skull *nt*

scullery ['skʌlərɪ] *n* (*old*) Spülküche *f*

sculptor ['skʌlptəʳ] *n* Bildhauer(in) *m(f)*

sculpture ['skʌlptʃəʳ] *n* (*art*) Bildhauerei *f*; (*object*) Skulptur *f*

scum [skʌm] *n* (*on liquid*) Schmutzschicht *f*; (*pej*) Abschaum *m*

scupper ['skʌpəʳ] (*Brit: inf*) *vt* (*plan, idea*) zerschlagen

scurrilous ['skʌrɪləs] *adj* verleumderisch

scurry ['skʌrɪ] *vi* huschen
▶ **scurry off** *vi* forthasten

scurvy ['skə:vɪ] *n* Skorbut *m*

scuttle ['skʌtl] *n* (*also:* **coal scuttle**) Kohleneimer *m* ▷ *vt* (*ship*) versenken ▷ *vi*: **to ~ away** *or* **off** verschwinden

scythe [saɪð] *n* Sense *f*

SD, S.Dak. (*US*) *abbr* (*Post*) = *South Dakota*

SDI (*US*) *n abbr* (*Mil*: = *Strategic Defense Initiative*) SDI *f*

SDLP (*Brit*) *n abbr* (*Pol*: = *Social Democratic and Labour Party*) *sozialdemokratische Partei in Nordirland*

SE *abbr* (= *south-east*) SO

sea [si:] *n* Meer *nt*, See *f*; (*fig*) Meer *nt* ▷ *cpd* See-; **by ~** (*travel*) mit dem Schiff; **beside** *or* **by the ~** (*holiday*) am Meer, an der See; (*village*) am Meer; **on the ~** (*boat*) auf See; **at ~** auf See; **to be all at ~** (*fig*) nicht durchblicken (*inf*); **out to ~** aufs Meer (hinaus); **to look out to ~** aufs Meer hinausblicken; **heavy/rough ~(s)** schwere/raue See *f*

sea anemone *n* Seeanemone *f*

sea bed *n* Meeresboden *m*

seaboard ['si:bɔ:d] *n* Küste *f*

seafarer ['si:fɛərəʳ] *n* Seefahrer *m*

seafaring ['si:fɛərɪŋ] *adj* (*life, nation*) Seefahrer-

seafood ['si:fu:d] *n* Meeresfrüchte *pl*

seafront ['si:frʌnt] *n* Strandpromenade *f*

seagoing ['si:gəʊɪŋ] *adj* hochseetüchtig

seagull ['si:gʌl] *n* Möwe *f*

seal [si:l] *n* (*animal*) Seehund *m*; (*official stamp*) Siegel *nt*; (*in machine etc*) Dichtung *f*; (*on bottle etc*) Verschluss *m* ▷ *vt* (*envelope*) zukleben; (*crack, opening*) abdichten; (*with seal*) versiegeln;

(*agreement, sb's fate*) besiegeln; **to give sth one's ~ of approval** einer Sache *dat* seine offizielle Zustimmung geben
▶ **seal off** *vt* (*place*) abriegeln

sea level *n* Meeresspiegel *m*; **2,000 ft above/below ~** 2000 Fuß über/unter dem Meeresspiegel

sealing wax ['si:lɪŋ-] *n* Siegelwachs *nt*

sea lion *n* Seelöwe *m*

sealskin ['si:lskɪn] *n* Seehundfell *nt*

seam [si:m] *n* Naht *f*; (*lit, fig: where edges join*) Übergang *m*; (*of coal etc*) Flöz *nt*; **the hall was bursting at the ~s** der Saal platzte aus allen Nähten

seaman ['si:mən] (*irreg: like* **man**) *n* Seemann *m*

seamanship ['si:mənʃɪp] *n* Seemannschaft *f*

seamless ['si:mlɪs] *adj* (*lit, fig*) nahtlos

seamy ['si:mɪ] *adj* zwielichtig; **the ~ side of life** die Schattenseite des Lebens

séance ['seɪɔns] *n* spiritistische Sitzung *f*

seaplane ['si:pleɪn] *n* Wasserflugzeug *nt*

seaport ['si:pɔ:t] *n* Seehafen *m*

search [sə:tʃ] *n* Suche *f*; (*inspection*) Durchsuchung *f*; (*Comput*) Suchlauf *m* ▷ *vt* durchsuchen; (*mind, memory*) durchforschen ▷ *vi*: **to ~ for** suchen nach; **"~ and replace"** (*Comput*) „suchen und ersetzen"; **in ~ of** auf der Suche nach
▶ **search through** *vt fus* durchsuchen

searcher ['sə:tʃəʳ] *n* Suchende(r) *f(m)*

searching ['sə:tʃɪŋ] *adj* (*question*) bohrend; (*look*) prüfend; (*examination*) eingehend

searchlight ['sə:tʃlaɪt] *n* Suchscheinwerfer *m*

search party *n* Suchtrupp *m*; **to send out a ~** einen Suchtrupp ausschicken

search warrant *n* Durchsuchungsbefehl *m*

searing ['sɪərɪŋ] *adj* (*heat*) glühend; (*pain*) scharf

seashore ['si:ʃɔ:ʳ] *n* Strand *m*; **on the ~** am Strand

seasick ['si:sɪk] *adj* seekrank

seasickness ['si:sɪknɪs] *n* Seekrankheit *f*

seaside ['si:saɪd] *n* Meer *nt*, See *f*; **to go to the ~** ans Meer *or* an die See fahren; **at the ~** am Meer, an der See

seaside resort *n* Badeort *m*

season ['si:zn] *n* Jahreszeit *f*; (*Agr*) Zeit *f*; (*Sport, of films etc*) Saison *f*; (*Theat*) Spielzeit *f* ▷ *vt* (*food*) würzen; **strawberries are in ~/out of ~** für Erdbeeren ist jetzt die richtige Zeit/nicht die richtige Zeit; **the busy ~** die Hochsaison *f*; **the open ~** (*Hunting*) die Jagdzeit *f*

seasonal ['si:znl] *adj* (*work*) Saison-

seasoned ['si:znd] *adj* (*fig: traveller*) erfahren; (*wood*) abgelagert; **she's a ~ campaigner** sie ist eine alte Kämpferin

seasoning ['si:znɪŋ] *n* Gewürz *nt*

season ticket *n* (*Rail*) Zeitkarte *f*; (*Sport*) Dauerkarte *f*; (*Theat*) Abonnement *nt*

seat [si:t] *n* (*chair, of government, Pol*) Sitz *m*; (*place*) Platz *m*; (*buttocks*) Gesäß *nt*; (*of trousers*) Hosenboden *m*; (*of learning*) Stätte *f* ▷ *vt* setzen; (*have room for*) Sitzplätze bieten für; **are there**

any ~s left? sind noch Plätze frei?; **to take one's ~** sich setzen; **please be ~ed** bitte nehmen Sie Platz; **to be ~ed** sitzen

seat belt n Sicherheitsgurt m

seating arrangements ['si:tɪŋ-] npl Sitzordnung f

seating capacity n Sitzplätze pl

SEATO ['si:təu] n abbr (= Southeast Asia Treaty Organization) SEATO f

sea urchin n Seeigel m

sea water n Meerwasser nt

seaweed ['si:wi:d] n Seetang m

seaworthy ['si:wə:ðɪ] adj seetüchtig

SEC (US) n abbr (= Securities and Exchange Commission) amerikanische Börsenaufsichtsbehörde

sec. abbr (= second) Sek.

secateurs [sɛkə'tə:z] npl Gartenschere f

secede [sɪ'si:d] vi (Pol): **to ~ (from)** sich abspalten (von)

secluded [sɪ'klu:dɪd] adj (place) abgelegen; (life) zurückgezogen

seclusion [sɪ'klu:ʒən] n Abgeschiedenheit f; **in ~** zurückgezogen

second¹ [sɪ'kɔnd] (Brit) vt (employee) abordnen

second² ['sɛkənd] adj zweite(r, s) ▷ adv (come, be placed) Zweite(r, s); (when listing) zweitens ▷ n (time) Sekunde f; (Aut: also: **second gear**) der zweite Gang; (person) Zweite(r) f(m); (Comm: imperfect) zweite Wahl f ▷ vt (motion) unterstützen; **upper/lower ~** (Brit: Univ) ≈ Zwei plus/minus; **Charles the S~** Karl der Zweite; **just a ~!** einen Augenblick!; **~ floor** (Brit) zweiter Stock m; (US) erster Stock m; **to ask for a ~ opinion** ein zweites Gutachten einholen

secondary ['sɛkəndərɪ] adj weniger wichtig

secondary education n höhere Schulbildung f

secondary picketing n Aufstellung von Streikposten bei nur indirekt beteiligten Firmen

secondary school n höhere Schule f; siehe Info-Artikel

○ **SECONDARY SCHOOL**
○
○ *Secondary school* ist in Großbritannien eine
○ weiterführende Schule für Kinder von
○ 11 bis 18 Jahren. Manche Schüler gehen
○ schon mit 16 Jahren, wenn die allgemeine
○ Schulpflicht endet, von der Schule ab.
○ Die meisten secondary schools sind
○ heute Gesamtschulen, obwohl es auch
○ noch selektive Schulen gibt. Siehe auch
○ *comprehensive school, primary school.*

second-best [sɛkənd'bɛst] adj zweitbeste(r, s) ▷ n: **as a ~** als Ausweichlösung; **don't settle for ~** gib dich nur mit dem Besten zufrieden

second-class ['sɛkənd'klɑ:s] adj zweitklassig; (citizen) zweiter Klasse; (Rail, Post) Zweite-Klasse- ▷ adv (Rail, Post) zweiter Klasse; **to send sth ~** etw zweiter Klasse schicken; **to travel ~** zweiter Klasse reisen

second cousin n Cousin m/Cousine f zweiten Grades f

seconder ['sɛkəndəʳ] n Befürworter(in) m(f)

second-guess ['sɛkənd'gɛs] vt vorhersagen; **to ~ sb** vorhersagen, was jd machen wird

second-hand ['sɛkənd'hænd] adj gebraucht; (clothing) getragen ▷ adv (buy) gebraucht; **to hear sth secondhand** etw aus zweiter Hand haben; **~ car** Gebrauchtwagen m; **~ smoking** (US) Passivrauchen nt

second hand n (on clock) Sekundenzeiger m

second-in-command ['sɛkəndɪnkə'mɑ:nd] n (Mil) stellvertretender Kommandeur m; (Admin) stellvertretender Leiter m

secondly ['sɛkəndlɪ] adv zweitens

secondment [sɪ'kɔndmənt] (Brit) n Abordnung f; **to be on ~** abgeordnet sein

second-rate ['sɛkənd'reɪt] adj zweitklassig

second thoughts npl: **on ~, on second thought** (US) wenn ich es mir (recht) überlege; **to have ~ (about doing sth)** es sich dat anders überlegen (und etw doch nicht tun)

Second World War n: **the ~** der Zweite Weltkrieg

secrecy ['si:krəsɪ] n Geheimhaltung f; (of person) Verschwiegenheit f; **in ~** heimlich

secret ['si:krɪt] adj geheim; (admirer) heimlich ▷ n Geheimnis nt; **in ~** heimlich; **~ passage** Geheimgang m; **to keep sth ~ from sb** etw vor jdm geheim halten; **can you keep a ~?** kannst du schweigen?; **to make no ~ of sth** kein Geheimnis or keinen Hehl aus etw machen

secret agent n Geheimagent(in) m(f)

secretarial [sɛkrɪ'tɛərɪəl] adj (work) Büro-; (course) Sekretärinnen-; (staff) Sekretariats-

secretariat [sɛkrɪ'tɛərɪət] n (Pol, Admin) Sekretariat nt

secretary ['sɛkrətərɪ] n (Comm) Sekretär(in) m(f); (of club) Schriftführer(in) m(f); **S~ of State (for)** (Brit: Pol) Minister(in) m(f) (für); **S~ of State** (US: Pol) Außenminister(in) m(f)

secretary-general ['sɛkrətərɪ'dʒɛnərl] (pl **secretaries-general**) n Generalsekretär(in) m(f)

secrete [sɪ'kri:t] vt (Anat, Biol, Med) absondern; (hide) verbergen

secretion [sɪ'kri:ʃən] n (substance) Sekret nt

secretive ['si:krətɪv] adj verschlossen; (pej) geheimnistuerisch

secretly ['si:krɪtlɪ] adv heimlich; (hope) insgeheim

secret police n Geheimpolizei f

secret service n Geheimdienst m

sect [sɛkt] n Sekte f

sectarian [sɛk'tɛərɪən] adj (killing etc) konfessionell motiviert; **~ violence** gewalttätige Konfessionsstreitigkeiten pl

section ['sɛkʃən] n (part) Teil m; (department) Abteilung f; (of document) Absatz m; (cross-section) Schnitt m ▷ vt (divide) teilen; **the business/sport ~** (Press) der Wirtschafts-/Sportteil

S

sectional ['sɛkʃənl] *adj*: ~ **drawing** Darstellung *f* im Schnitt

sector ['sɛktə^r] *n* Sektor *m*

secular ['sɛkjulə^r] *adj* weltlich

secure [sɪ'kjuə^r] *adj* sicher; (*firmly fixed*) fest ▷ *vt* (*fix*) festmachen; (*votes etc*) erhalten; (*contract etc*) (sich *dat*) sichern; (*Comm: loan*) (ab)sichern; **to make sth** ~ etw sichern; **to ~ sth for sb** jdm etw sichern

secured creditor [sɪ'kjuəd-] *n* (*Comm*) abgesicherter Gläubiger *m*

securely [sɪ'kjuəlɪ] *adv* (*firmly*) fest; (*safely*) sicher

security [sɪ'kjuərɪtɪ] *n* Sicherheit *f*; (*freedom from anxiety*) Geborgenheit *f*; **securities** *npl* (*Stock Exchange*) Effekten *pl*, Wertpapiere *pl*; **securities market** Wertpapiermarkt *m*; **to increase/tighten** ~ die Sicherheitsvorkehrungen verschärfen; ~ **of tenure** Kündigungsschutz *m*

Security Council *n* Sicherheitsrat *m*

security forces *npl* Sicherheitskräfte *pl*

security guard *n* Sicherheitsbeamte(r) *m*; (*transporting money*) Wachmann *m*

security risk *n* Sicherheitsrisiko *nt*

secy. *abbr* = **secretary**

sedan [sə'dæn] (*US*) *n* (*Aut*) Limousine *f*

sedate [sɪ'deɪt] *adj* (*person*) ruhig, gesetzt; (*life*) geruhsam; (*pace*) gemächlich ▷ *vt* (*Med*) Beruhigungsmittel geben +*dat*

sedation [sɪ'deɪʃən] *n* (*Med*) Beruhigungsmittel *pl*; **to be under** ~ unter dem Einfluss von Beruhigungsmitteln stehen

sedative ['sɛdɪtɪv] *n* (*Med*) Beruhigungsmittel *nt*

sedentary ['sɛdntrɪ] *adj* (*occupation, work*) sitzend

sediment ['sɛdɪmənt] *n* (*in bottle*) (Boden)satz *m*; (*in lake etc*) Ablagerung *f*

sedimentary [sɛdɪ'mɛntərɪ] *adj* (*Geog*) sedimentär; ~ **rock** Sedimentgestein *nt*

sedition [sɪ'dɪʃən] *n* Aufwiegelung *f*

seduce [sɪ'djuːs] *vt* verführen; **to ~ sb into doing sth** jdn dazu verleiten, etw zu tun

seduction [sɪ'dʌkʃən] *n* (*attraction*) Verlockung *f*; (*act of seducing*) Verführung *f*

seductive [sɪ'dʌktɪv] *adj* verführerisch; (*fig: offer*) verlockend

see [siː] (*pt* **saw**, *pp* ~**n**) *vt* sehen; (*look at*) sich *dat* ansehen; (*understand*) verstehen, (ein) sehen; (*doctor etc*) aufsuchen ▷ *vi* sehen ▷ *n* (*Rel*) Bistum *nt*; **to ~ that** (*ensure*) dafür sorgen, dass; **to ~ sb to the door** jdn zur Tür bringen; **there was nobody to be ~n** es war niemand zu sehen; **to go and ~ sb** jdn besuchen (gehen); **to ~ a doctor** zum Arzt gehen; ~ **you!** tschüss! (*inf*); ~ **you soon!** bis bald!; **let me** ~ (*show me*) lass mich mal sehen; (*let me think*) lass mich mal überlegen; **I** ~ ich verstehe, aha; (*annoyed*) ach so; **you** ~ weißt du, siehst du; ~ **for yourself** überzeug dich doch selbst; **I don't know what she ~s in him** ich weiß nicht, was sie an ihm findet; **as far as I can** ~

▶ **see about** *vt fus* sich kümmern um +*acc*

▶ **see off** *vt* verabschieden

▶ **see through** *vt fus* durchschauen ▷ *vt*: **to ~ sb through sth** jdm in etw *dat* beistehen; **to ~ sth through to the end** etw zu Ende bringen; **this should ~ you through** das müsste dir reichen

▶ **see to** *vt fus* sich kümmern um +*acc*

seed [siːd] *n* Samen *m*; (*of fruit*) Kern *m*; (*fig: usu pl*) Keim *m*; (*Tennis*) gesetzter Spieler *m*, gesetzte Spielerin *f*; **to go to** ~ (*plant*) Samen bilden; (*lettuce etc*) schießen; (*fig: person*) herunterkommen

seedless ['siːdlɪs] *adj* kernlos

seedling ['siːdlɪŋ] *n* (*Bot*) Sämling *m*

seedy ['siːdɪ] *adj* (*person, place*) zwielichtig, zweifelhaft

seeing ['siːɪŋ] *conj*: ~ **as** *or* **that** da

seek [siːk] (*pt*, *pp* **sought**) *vt* suchen; **to ~ advice from sb** jdn um Rat fragen; **to ~ help from sb** jdn um Hilfe bitten

▶ **seek out** *vt* ausfindig machen

seem [siːm] *vi* scheinen; **there ~s to be a mistake** da scheint ein Fehler zu sein; **it ~s (that)** es scheint(, dass); **it ~s to me that ...** mir scheint, dass ...; **what ~s to be the trouble?** worum geht es denn?; (*doctor*) was fehlt Ihnen denn?

seemingly ['siːmɪŋlɪ] *adv* anscheinend

seemly ['siːmlɪ] *adj* schicklich

seen [siːn] *pp of* **see**

seep [siːp] *vi* sickern

seersucker ['sɪəsʌkə^r] *n* Krepp *m*, Seersucker *m*

seesaw ['siːsɔː] *n* (*Med*) Wippe *f*

seethe [siːð] *vi*: **to ~ with** (*place*) wimmeln von; **to ~ with anger** vor Wut kochen

see-through ['siːθruː] *adj* durchsichtig

segment ['sɛgmənt] *n* Teil *m*; (*of orange*) Stück *nt*

segregate ['sɛgrɪgeɪt] *vt* trennen, absondern

segregation [sɛgrɪ'geɪʃən] *n* Trennung *f*

Seine [seɪn] *n*: **the** ~ die Seine *f*

seismic shock *n* Erdstoß *m*

seize [siːz] *vt* packen, ergreifen; (*fig: opportunity*) ergreifen; (*power, control*) an sich *acc* reißen; (*territory, airfield*) besetzen; (*hostage*) nehmen; (*Law*) beschlagnahmen

▶ **seize up** *vi* (*engine*) sich festfressen

▶ **seize (up)on** *vt fus* sich stürzen auf +*acc*

seizure ['siːʒə^r] *n* (*Med*) Anfall *m*; (*of power*) Ergreifung *f*; (*Law*) Beschlagnahmung *f*

seldom ['sɛldəm] *adv* selten

select [sɪ'lɛkt] *adj* exklusiv ▷ *vt* (aus)wählen; (*Sport*) aufstellen; **a ~ few** wenige Auserwählte *pl*

selection [sɪ'lɛkʃən] *n* (*being chosen*) Wahl *f*; (*range*) Auswahl *f*

selection committee *n* Auswahlkomitee *nt*

selective [sɪ'lɛktɪv] *adj* wählerisch; (*not general*) selektiv

selector [sɪ'lɛktə^r] *n* (*Sport*) Mannschaftsaufsteller(in) *m(f)*; (*Tech*) Wählschalter *m*;

(: *button*) Taste f

self [sɛlf] (*pl* **selves**) *n* Selbst *nt*, Ich *nt*; **she was her normal ~ again** sie war wieder ganz die Alte

self ... [sɛlf] *pref* selbst-, Selbst-

self-addressed ['sɛlfə'drɛst] *adj*: **~ envelope** addressierter Rückumschlag m

self-adhesive [sɛlfəd'hiːzɪv] *adj* selbstklebend

self-appointed [sɛlfə'pɔɪntɪd] *adj* selbst ernannt

self-assertive [sɛlfə'sɜːtɪv] *adj* selbstbewusst

self-assurance [sɛlfə'ʃʊərəns] *n* Selbstsicherheit f

self-assured [sɛlfə'ʃʊəd] *adj* selbstsicher

self-catering [sɛlf'keɪtərɪŋ] (*Brit*) *adj* (*holiday, flat*) für Selbstversorger

self-centred, (*US*) **self-centered** [sɛlf'sɛntəd] *adj* egozentrisch, ichbezogen

self-cleaning [sɛlf'kliːnɪŋ] *adj* selbstreinigend

self-confessed [sɛlfkən'fɛst] *adj* erklärt

self-confidence [sɛlf'kɒnfɪdns] *n* Selbstbewusstsein *nt*, Selbstvertrauen *nt*

self-confident [sɛlf'kɒnfɪdənt] *adj* selbstbewusst, selbstsicher

self-conscious [sɛlf'kɒnʃəs] *adj* befangen, gehemmt

self-contained [sɛlfkən'teɪnd] (*Brit*) *adj* (*flat*) abgeschlossen; (*person*) selb(st)ständig

self-control [sɛlfkən'trəʊl] *n* Selbstbeherrschung f

self-defeating [sɛlfdɪ'fiːtɪŋ] *adj* unsinnig

self-defence, (*US*) **self-defense** [sɛlfdɪ'fɛns] *n* Selbstverteidigung f; (*Law*) Notwehr f; **in ~** zu seiner/ihrer *etc* Verteidigung; (*Law*) in Notwehr

self-discipline [sɛlf'dɪsɪplɪn] *n* Selbstdisziplin f

self-employed [sɛlfɪm'plɔɪd] *adj* selbstständig

self-esteem [sɛlfɪs'tiːm] *n* Selbstachtung f

self-evident [sɛlf'ɛvɪdnt] *adj* offensichtlich

self-explanatory [sɛlfɪks'plænətrɪ] *adj* unmittelbar verständlich

self-financing [sɛlffaɪ'nænsɪŋ] *adj* selbstfinanzierend

self-governing [sɛlf'ɡʌvənɪŋ] *adj* selbst verwaltet

self-help ['sɛlf'hɛlp] *n* Selbsthilfe f

self-importance [sɛlfɪm'pɔːtns] *n* Aufgeblasenheit f

self-indulgent [sɛlfɪn'dʌldʒənt] *adj* genießerisch; **to be ~** sich verwöhnen

self-inflicted [sɛlfɪn'flɪktɪd] *adj* selbst zugefügt

self-interest [sɛlf'ɪntrɪst] *n* Eigennutz m

selfish ['sɛlfɪʃ] *adj* egoistisch, selbstsüchtig

selfishly ['sɛlfɪʃlɪ] *adv* egoistisch, selbstsüchtig

selfishness ['sɛlfɪʃnɪs] *n* Egoismus m, Selbstsucht f

selfless ['sɛlflɪs] *adj* selbstlos

selflessly ['sɛlflɪslɪ] *adv* selbstlos

selflessness ['sɛlflɪsnɪs] *n* Selbstlosigkeit f

self-made ['sɛlfmeɪd] *adj*: **~ man** Selfmademan m

self-pity [sɛlf'pɪtɪ] *n* Selbstmitleid *nt*

self-portrait [sɛlf'pɔːtreɪt] *n* Selbstporträt *nt*,

Selbstbildnis *nt*

self-possessed [sɛlfpə'zɛst] *adj* selbstbeherrscht

self-preservation ['sɛlfprɛzə'veɪʃən] *n* Selbsterhaltung f

self-raising ['sɛlf'reɪzɪŋ], (*US*) **self-rising** ['sɛlf'raɪzɪŋ] *adj*: **~ flour** Mehl *mit bereits beigemischtem Backpulver*

self-reliant [sɛlfrɪ'laɪənt] *adj* selb(st)ständig

self-respect [sɛlfrɪs'pɛkt] *n* Selbstachtung f

self-respecting [sɛlfrɪs'pɛktɪŋ] *adj* mit Selbstachtung; (*genuine*) der/die/das etwas auf sich hält

self-righteous [sɛlf'raɪtʃəs] *adj* selbstgerecht

self-rising [sɛlf'raɪzɪŋ] (*US*) *adj* = **self-raising**

self-sacrifice [sɛlf'sækrɪfaɪs] *n* Selbstaufopferung f

self-same ['sɛlfseɪm] *adj*: **the ~** genau derselbe/dieselbe/dasselbe

self-satisfied [sɛlf'sætɪsfaɪd] *adj* selbstzufrieden

self-sealing [sɛlf'siːlɪŋ] *adj* selbstklebend

self-service [sɛlf'sɜːvɪs] *adj* (*shop, restaurant etc*) Selbstbedienungs-

self-styled ['sɛlfstaɪld] *adj* selbst ernannt

self-sufficient [sɛlfsə'fɪʃənt] *adj* (*country*) autark; (*person*) selb(st)ständig, unabhängig; **to be ~ in coal** seinen Kohlebedarf selbst decken können

self-supporting [sɛlfsə'pɔːtɪŋ] *adj* (*business*) sich selbst tragend

self-taught [sɛlf'tɔːt] *adj*: **to be ~** Autodidakt sein; **he is a ~ pianist** er hat sich das Klavierspielen selbst beigebracht

self-test ['sɛlftɛst] *n* (*Comput*) Selbsttest m

sell [sɛl] (*pt, pp* **sold**) *vt* verkaufen; (*shop: goods*) führen, haben (*inf*); (*fig: idea*) schmackhaft machen +*dat*, verkaufen (*inf*) ▷ *vi* sich verkaufen (lassen); **to ~ at** *or* **for 10 pounds** für 10 Pfund verkauft werden; **to ~ sb sth** jdm etw verkaufen; **to ~ o.s.** sich verkaufen

▶ **sell off** *vt* verkaufen

▶ **sell out** *vi*: **we/the tickets are sold out** wir/die Karten sind ausverkauft; **we have sold out of ...** wir haben kein ... mehr, ... ist ausverkauft

▶ **sell up** *vi* sein Haus/seine Firma *etc* verkaufen

sell-by date ['sɛlbaɪ-] *n* ≈ Haltbarkeitsdatum *nt*

seller ['sɛlər] *n* Verkäufer(in) m(f); **~'s market** Verkäufermarkt m

selling point ['sɛlɪŋ-] *n* Verkaufsanreiz m *or* -argument *nt*

selling price ['sɛlɪŋ-] *n* Verkaufspreis m

sellotape® ['sɛləʊteɪp] (*Brit*) *n* Klebeband *nt* ≈ Tesafilm® m

sellout ['sɛlaʊt] *n* (*inf: betrayal*) Verrat m; **the match was a ~** das Spiel war ausverkauft

selves [sɛlvz] *pl of* **self**

semantic [sɪ'mæntɪk] *adj* semantisch

semantics [sɪ'mæntɪks] *n* (*Ling*) Semantik f

semaphore ['sɛməfɔːr] *n* Flaggenalphabet *nt*

semblance ['sɛmblns] *n* Anschein m

S

semen ['si:mən] n Samenflüssigkeit f, Sperma nt

semester [sɪ'mɛstər] (esp US) n Semester nt

semi ['sɛmɪ] n = **semidetached house**

semi ... ['sɛmɪ] pref halb-, Halb-

semibreve ['sɛmɪbri:v] (Brit) n (Mus) ganze Note f

semicircle ['sɛmɪsə:kl] n Halbkreis m

semicircular ['sɛmɪ'sə:kjulər] adj halbkreisförmig

semicolon [sɛmɪ'kəulən] n Strichpunkt m, Semikolon nt

semiconductor [semɪkən'dʌktər] n Halbleiter m

semiconscious [sɛmɪ'kɔnʃəs] adj halb bewusstlos

semidetached

semidetached house (Brit) n Doppelhaushälfte f

semifinal [sɛmɪ'faɪnl] n Halbfinale nt

seminar ['sɛmɪna:ʳ] n Seminar nt

seminary ['sɛmɪnərɪ] n (Rel) Priesterseminar nt

semi-precious stone n Halbedelstein m

semiquaver ['sɛmɪkweɪvəʳ] (Brit) n (Mus) Sechzehntelnote f

semiskilled [sɛmɪ'skɪld] adj (work) Anlern-; (worker) angelernt

semi-skimmed [sɛmɪ'skɪmd] adj (milk) teilentrahmt, Halbfett-

semitone ['sɛmɪtəun] n (Mus) Halbton m

semolina [sɛmə'li:nə] n Grieß m

Sen., sen. abbr (US) = **senator**; (in names: = senior) sen.

senate ['sɛnɪt] n Senat m; siehe Info-Artikel

SENATE

Senate ist das Oberhaus des amerikanischen Kongresses (das Unterhaus ist das House of Representatives. Der Senat besteht aus 100 Senatoren, zwei für jeden Bundesstaat, die für sechs Jahre gewählt werden, wobei ein Drittel alle zwei Jahre neu gewählt wird. Die Senatoren werden in direkter Wahl vom Volk gewählt. Siehe auch congress.

senator ['sɛnɪtəʳ] n Senator(in) m(f)

send [sɛnd] (pt, pp **sent**) vt schicken; (transmit) senden; **to ~ sth by post, to ~ sth by mail** (US) etw mit der Post schicken; **to ~ sb for sth** (for check-up etc) jdn zu etw schicken; **to ~ word that ...** Nachricht geben, dass ...; **she ~s (you) her love** sie lässt dich grüßen; **to ~ sb to Coventry** (Brit) jdn schneiden (inf); **to ~ sb to sleep** jdn einschläfern; **to ~ sth flying** etw umwerfen

▸ **send away** vt wegschicken

▸ **send away for** vt fus (per Post) anfordern

▸ **send back** vt zurückschicken

▸ **send for** vt fus (per Post) anfordern; (doctor, police) rufen

▸ **send in** vt einsenden, einschicken

▸ **send off** vt abschicken; (Brit: player) vom Platz weisen

▸ **send on** vt (Brit: letter) nachsenden; (luggage etc) vorausschicken

▸ **send out** vt verschicken; (light, heat) abgeben; (signal) aussenden

▸ **send round** vt schicken; (circulate) zirkulieren lassen

▸ **send up** vt (astronaut) hochschießen; (price, blood pressure) hochtreiben; (Brit: parody) verulken (inf)

sender ['sɛndəʳ] n Absender(in) m(f)

sending-off ['sɛndɪŋɔf] n (Sport) Platzverweis m

send-off ['sɛndɔf] n: **a good ~** eine große Verabschiedung

send-up ['sɛndʌp] n Verulkung f (inf)

Senegal [sɛnɪ'gɔ:l] n Senegal nt

Senegalese [sɛnɪgə'li:z] adj senegalesisch ▷ n inv Senegalese m, Senegalesin f

senile ['si:naɪl] adj senil

senility [sɪ'nɪlɪtɪ] n Senilität f

senior ['si:nɪəʳ] adj (staff, manager) leitend; (officer) höher; (post, position) leitend ▷ n (Scol): **the ~s** die Oberstufenschüler pl; **to be ~ to sb** jdm übergeordnet sein; **she is 15 years his ~** sie ist 15 Jahre älter als er; **P. Jones ~** P. Jones senior

senior citizen n Senior(in) m(f)

senior high school (US) n Oberstufe f

seniority [si:nɪ'ɔrɪtɪ] n (in service) (längere) Betriebszugehörigkeit f; (in rank) (höhere) Position f

sensation [sɛn'seɪʃən] n (feeling) Gefühl nt; (great success) Sensation f; **to cause a ~** großes Aufsehen erregen

sensational [sɛn'seɪʃənl] adj (wonderful) wunderbar; (result) sensationell; (headlines etc) reißerisch

sense [sɛns] n Sinn m; (feeling) Gefühl nt; (good sense) Verstand m, gesunder Menschenverstand m; (meaning) Bedeutung f, Sinn m ▷ vt spüren; **~ of smell** Geruchssinn m; **it makes ~** (can be understood) es ergibt einen Sinn; (is sensible) es ist vernünftig or sinnvoll; **there's no ~ in that** das hat keinen Sinn; **there is no ~ in doing that** es hat keinen Sinn, das zu tun; **to come to one's ~s** Vernunft annehmen; **to take leave of one's ~s** den Verstand verlieren

senseless ['sɛnslɪs] adj (pointless) sinnlos; (unconscious) besinnungslos, bewusstlos

sense of humour n Sinn m für Humor

sensibility [sɛnsɪ'bɪlɪtɪ] n Empfindsamkeit f; (sensitivity) Empfindlichkeit f; **to offend sb's sensibilities** jds Zartgefühl verletzen

sensible ['sɛnsɪbl] adj vernünftig; (shoes, clothes) praktisch

sensitive ['sɛnsɪtɪv] adj empfindlich; (understanding) einfühlsam; (touchy: person) sensibel; (: issue) heikel; **to be ~ to sth** in Bezug auf etw acc empfindlich sein; **he is very ~ about it/to criticism** er reagiert sehr empfindlich darauf/auf Kritik

sensitivity [sɛnsɪ'tɪvɪtɪ] n Empfindlichkeit f; (understanding) Einfühlungsvermögen nt; (of issue etc) heikle Natur f; **an issue of great ~** ein sehr heikles Thema

sensual ['sɛnsjuəl] adj sinnlich; (person, life) sinnenfroh

sensuous ['sɛnsjuəs] adj sinnlich

sent [sɛnt] pt, pp of **send**

sentence ['sɛntns] n (Ling) Satz m; (Law: judgement) Urteil nt; (: punishment) Strafe f ▷ vt: **to ~ sb to death/to 5 years in prison** jdn zum Tode/zu 5 Jahren Haft verurteilen; **to pass ~ on sb** das Urteil über jdn verkünden; (fig) jdn verurteilen; **to serve a life ~** eine lebenslängliche Freiheitsstrafe verbüßen

sentiment ['sɛntɪmənt] n Sentimentalität f; (also pl: opinion) Ansicht f

sentimental [sɛntɪ'mɛntl] adj sentimental

sentimentality [sɛntɪmɛn'tælɪtɪ] n Sentimentalität f

sentry ['sɛntrɪ] n Wachtposten m

sentry duty n: **to be on ~** auf Wache sein

Seoul [səul] n Seoul nt

separable ['sɛprəbl] adj: **to be ~ from** trennbar sein von

separate ['sɛprɪt] adj getrennt; (occasions) verschieden; (rooms) separat ▷ vt trennen ▷ vi sich trennen; **~ from** getrennt von; **to go ~ ways** getrennte Wege gehen; **under ~ cover** (Comm) mit getrennter Post; **to ~ into** aufteilen in +acc; see also **separates**

separately ['sɛprɪtlɪ] adv getrennt

separates ['sɛprɪts] npl (clothes) kombinierbare Einzelteile pl

separation [sɛpə'reɪʃən] n Trennung f

sepia ['si:pjə] adj sepiafarben

Sept. abbr (= September) Sept.

September [sɛp'tɛmbər] n September m; see also **July**

septic ['sɛptɪk] adj vereitert, septisch; **to go ~** eitern

septicaemia, (US) **septicemia** [sɛptɪ'si:mɪə] n Blutvergiftung f

septic tank n Faulbehälter m

sequel ['si:kwl] n (follow-up) Nachspiel nt; (of film, story) Fortsetzung f

sequence ['si:kwəns] n Folge f; (dance/film sequence) Sequenz f; **in ~** der Reihe nach

sequential [sɪ'kwɛnʃəl] adj aufeinanderfolgend; **~ access** (Comput) sequenzieller Zugriff m

sequestrate [sɪ'kwɛstreɪt] vt (Law, Comm) sequestrieren, beschlagnahmen

sequin ['si:kwɪn] n Paillette f

Serbia ['sə:bɪə] n Serbien nt

Serbian ['sə:bɪən] adj serbisch ▷ n Serbier(in) m(f); (Ling) Serbisch nt

Serbo-Croat ['sə:bəu'krəuæt] n (Ling) Serbokroatisch nt

serenade [sɛrə'neɪd] n Serenade f ▷ vt ein Ständchen nt bringen +dat

serene [sɪ'ri:n] adj (landscape etc) friedlich; (expression) heiter; (person) gelassen

serenity [sə'rɛnɪtɪ] n (of landscape) Friedlichkeit f; (of expression) Gelassenheit f

sergeant ['sɑːdʒənt] n (Mil etc) Feldwebel m; (Police) Polizeimeister m

sergeant-major ['sɑːdʒənt'meɪdʒər] n Oberfeldwebel m

serial ['sɪərɪəl] n (TV) Serie f; (Radio) Sendereihe f; (in magazine) Fortsetzungsroman m ▷ adj (Comput) seriell

serialize ['sɪərɪəlaɪz] vt in Fortsetzungen veröffentlichen; (TV, Radio) in Fortsetzungen senden

serial killer n Serienmörder(in) m(f)

serial number n Seriennummer f

series ['sɪərɪz] n inv (group) Serie f, Reihe f; (of books) Reihe f; (TV) Serie f

serious ['sɪərɪəs] adj ernst; (important) wichtig; (: illness) schwer; (: condition) bedenklich; **are you ~ (about it)?** meinst du das ernst?

seriously ['sɪərɪəslɪ] adv ernst; (talk, interested) ernsthaft; (ill, hurt, damaged) schwer; (not jokingly) im Ernst; **to take sb/sth ~** jdn/etw ernst nehmen; **do you ~ believe that ...** glauben Sie ernsthaft or im Ernst, dass ...

seriousness ['sɪərɪəsnɪs] n Ernst m, Ernsthaftigkeit f; (of problem) Bedenklichkeit f

sermon ['sə:mən] n Predigt f; (fig) Moralpredigt f

serrated [sɪ'reɪtɪd] adj gezackt; **~ knife** Sägemesser nt

serum ['sɪərəm] n Serum nt

servant ['sə:vənt] n (lit, fig) Diener(in) m(f); (domestic) Hausangestellte(r) f(m)

serve [sə:v] vt dienen +dat; (in shop, with food/drink) bedienen; (food, meal) servieren; (purpose) haben; (apprenticeship) durchmachen; (prison term) verbüßen ▷ vi (at table) auftragen, servieren; (Tennis) aufschlagen; (soldier) dienen; (be useful): **to ~ as/for** dienen als ▷ n (Tennis) Aufschlag m; **are you being ~d?** werden Sie schon bedient?; **to ~ its purpose** seinen Zweck erfüllen; **to ~ sb's purpose** jds Zwecken dienen; **it ~s him right** das geschieht ihm recht; **to ~ on a committee** einem Ausschuss angehören; **to ~ on a jury** Geschworene(r) f(m) sein; **it's my turn to ~** (Tennis) ich habe Aufschlag; **it ~s to show/explain ...** das zeigt/erklärt ...

▶ **serve out** vt (food) auftragen, servieren

▶ **serve up** vt = **serve out**

service ['sə:vɪs] n Dienst m; (commercial) Dienstleistung f; (in hotel, restaurant) Bedienung f, Service m; (also: **train service**) Bahnverbindung f; (: generally) Zugverkehr m; (Rel) Gottesdienst m; (Aut) Inspektion f; (Tennis) Aufschlag m; (plates etc) Service nt ▷ vt (car, machine) warten; **the Services** npl (army, navy etc) die Streitkräfte pl; **military/national ~** Militärdienst m; **to be of ~ to sb** jdm nützen; **to do sb a ~** jdm einen Dienst erweisen; **to put one's car in for a ~** sein Auto zur Inspektion geben; **dinner ~** Essservice nt

serviceable ['sə:vɪsəbl] adj zweckmäßig

service area n (on motorway) Raststätte f
service charge (Brit) n Bedienungsgeld nt
service contract n Wartungsvertrag m
service industry n Dienstleistungsbranche f
serviceman ['sɜːvɪsmən] (irreg: like **man**) n
Militärangehörige(r) m
service station n Tankstelle f
serviette [sə:vɪ'ɛt] (Brit) n Serviette f
servile ['sɜːvaɪl] adj unterwürfig
session ['sɛʃən] n Sitzung f; (US, Scot: Scol)
Studienjahr nt; (: term) Semester nt; **recording**
~ Aufnahme f; **to be in ~** tagen
session musician n Session-Musiker(in) m(f)
set [sɛt] (pt, pp ~) n (of saucepans, books, keys etc)
Satz m; (group) Reihe f; (of cutlery) Garnitur
f; (also: **radio set**) Radio(gerät) nt; (also: **TV
set**) Fernsehgerät nt; (Tennis) Satz m; (group of
people) Kreis m; (Math) Menge f; (Theat: stage)
Bühne f; (: scenery) Bühnenbild nt; (Cine)
Drehort m; (Hairdressing) (Ein)legen nt ▷ adj
(fixed) fest; (ready) fertig, bereit ▷ vt (table)
decken; (place) auflegen; (time, price, rules etc)
festsetzen; (record) aufstellen; (alarm, watch,
task) stellen; (exam) zusammenstellen; (Typ)
setzen ▷ vi (sun) untergehen; (jam, jelly, concrete)
fest werden; (bone) zusammenwachsen; **a ~ of
false teeth** ein Gebiss nt; **a ~ of dining-room
furniture** eine Esszimmergarnitur; **a chess ~**
ein Schachspiel nt; **to be ~ on doing sth** etw
unbedingt tun wollen; **to be all ~ to do sth**
bereit sein, etw zu tun; **he's ~ in his ways** er
ist in seinen Gewohnheiten festgefahren; **a ~
phrase** eine feste Redewendung; **a novel ~ in
Rome** ein Roman, der in Rom spielt; **to ~ to
music** vertonen; **to ~ on fire** anstecken; **to ~
free** freilassen; **to ~ sail** losfahren
‣ **set about** vt fus (task) anpacken; **to ~ about
doing sth** sich daranmachen, etw zu tun
‣ **set aside** vt (money etc) beiseitelegen; (time)
einplanen
‣ **set back** vt: **to ~ sb back 5 pounds** jdn 5
Pfund kosten; **to ~ sb back (by)** (in time) jdn
zurückwerfen (um); **a house ~ back from
the road** ein Haus, das etwas von der Straße
abliegt
‣ **set in** vi (bad weather) einsetzen; (infection)
sich einstellen; **the rain has ~ in for the day**
es hat sich für heute eingeregnet
‣ **set off** vi (depart) aufbrechen ▷ vt (bomb)
losgehen lassen; (alarm, chain of events)
auslösen; (show up well) hervorheben
‣ **set out** vi (depart) aufbrechen ▷ vt (goods etc)
ausbreiten; (chairs etc) aufstellen; (arguments)
darlegen; **to ~ out to do sth** sich dat
vornehmen, etw zu tun; **to ~ out from home**
zu Hause aufbrechen
‣ **set up** vt (organization) gründen; (monument)
errichten; **to ~ up shop** ein Geschäft
eröffnen; (fig) sich selb(st)ständig machen
setback ['sɛtbæk] n Rückschlag m
set menu n Menü nt
set square n Zeichendreieck nt
settee [sɛ'tiː] n Sofa nt

setting ['sɛtɪŋ] n (background) Rahmen m;
(position) Einstellung f; (of jewel) Fassung f
setting lotion n (Haar)festiger m
settle ['sɛtl] vt (matter) regeln; (argument)
beilegen; (accounts) begleichen; (affairs, business)
in Ordnung bringen; (colonize: land) besiedeln
▷ vi (also: **settle down**) sich niederlassen; (sand,
dust etc) sich legen; (sediment) sich setzen; (calm
down) sich beruhigen; **to ~ one's stomach**
den Magen beruhigen; **that's ~d then!** das ist
also abgemacht!; **to ~ down to work** sich an
die Arbeit setzen; **to ~ down to watch TV** es
sich dat vor dem Fernseher gemütlich machen
‣ **settle for** vt fus sich zufriedengeben mit
‣ **settle in** vi sich einleben; (in job etc) sich
eingewöhnen
‣ **settle on** vt fus sich entscheiden für
‣ **settle up** vi: **to ~ up with sb** mit jdm
abrechnen
settlement ['sɛtlmənt] n (payment)
Begleichung f; (Law) Vergleich m; (agreement)
Übereinkunft f; (of conflict) Beilegung f; (village
etc) Siedlung f, Niederlassung f; (colonization)
Besiedelung f; **in ~ of our account** (Comm)
zum Ausgleich unseres Kontos
settler ['sɛtlə'] n Siedler(in) m(f)
setup, set-up ['sɛtʌp] n (organization)
Organisation f; (system) System nt; (Comput)
Setup nt
seven ['sɛvn] num sieben
seventeen [sɛvn'tiːn] num siebzehn
seventh ['sɛvnθ] num siebte(r, s)
seventy ['sɛvntɪ] num siebzig
sever ['sɛvə'] vt durchtrennen; (fig: relations)
abbrechen; (: ties) lösen
several ['sɛvərl] adj einige, mehrere ▷ pron
einige; **~ of us** einige von uns; **~ times** einige
Male, mehrmals
severance ['sɛvərəns] n (of relations) Abbruch m
severance pay n Abfindung f
severe [sɪ'vɪə'] adj (damage, shortage) schwer;
(pain) stark; (person, expression, dress, winter)
streng; (punishment) hart; (climate) rau
severely [sɪ'vɪəlɪ] adv (damage) stark; (punish)
hart; (wounded, ill) schwer
severity [sɪ'vɛrɪtɪ] n (gravity: of punishment) Härte
f; (: of manner, voice, winter) Strenge f; (: of weather)
Rauheit f; (austerity) Strenge f
sew [səu] (pt **~ed**, pp **~n**) vt, vi nähen
‣ **sew up** vt (zusammen)nähen; **it is all ~n
up** (fig) es ist unter Dach und Fach
sewage ['suːɪdʒ] n Abwasser nt
sewage works n Kläranlage f
sewer ['suːə'] n Abwasserkanal m
sewing ['səuɪŋ] n Nähen nt; (items) Näharbeit f
sewing machine n Nähmaschine f
sewn [səun] pp of **sew**
sex [sɛks] n (gender) Geschlecht nt; (lovemaking)
Sex m; **to have ~ with sb** (Geschlechts)
verkehr mit jdm haben
sex act n Geschlechtsakt m
sex appeal n Sex-Appeal m
sex education n Sexualerziehung f

sexism ['sɛksɪzəm] n Sexismus m

sexist ['sɛksɪst] adj sexistisch

sex life n Sexualleben nt

sex object n Sexualobjekt nt

sextet [sɛks'tɛt] n Sextett nt

sexual ['sɛksjuəl] adj sexuell; (reproduction) geschlechtlich; (equality) der Geschlechter

sexual assault n Vergewaltigung f

sexual harassment n sexuelle Belästigung f

sexual intercourse n Geschlechtsverkehr m

sexually ['sɛksjuəlɪ] adv sexuell; (segregate) nach Geschlechtern; (discriminate) aufgrund des Geschlechts; (reproduce) geschlechtlich

sexual orientation n sexuelle Orientierung f

sexy ['sɛksɪ] adj sexy; (pictures, underwear) sexy, aufreizend

Seychelles [seɪ'ʃɛl(z)] npl: **the ~** die Seychellen pl

SF n abbr (= science fiction) SF

SG (US) n abbr (Mil, Med) = **Surgeon General**

Sgt abbr (Police, Mil) = **sergeant**

shabbiness ['ʃæbɪnɪs] n Schäbigkeit f

shabby ['ʃæbɪ] adj schäbig

shack [ʃæk] n Hütte f
  ▶ **shack up** (inf) vi: **to ~ up (with sb)** (mit jdm) zusammenziehen

shackles ['ʃæklz] npl Ketten pl; (fig) Fesseln pl

shade [ʃeɪd] n Schatten m; (for lamp) (Lampen)schirm m; (of colour) (Farb)ton m; (US: also: **window shade**) Jalousie f, Rollo nt ▷ vt beschatten; (eyes) abschirmen; **shades** npl (inf: sunglasses) Sonnenbrille f; **in the ~** im Schatten; **a ~ of blue** ein Blauton; **a ~ (more/too large)** (small quantity) etwas or eine Spur (mehr/zu groß)

shadow ['ʃædəʊ] n Schatten m ▷ vt (follow) beschatten; **without** or **beyond a ~ of a doubt** ohne den geringsten Zweifel

shadow cabinet (Brit) n Schattenkabinett nt

shadow economy n (Econ) Schattenwirtschaft f

shadowy ['ʃædəʊɪ] adj schattig; (figure, shape) schattenhaft

shady ['ʃeɪdɪ] adj schattig; (fig: dishonest) zwielichtig; **~ deals** dunkle Geschäfte

shaft [ʃɑːft] n (of arrow, spear) Schaft m; (Aut, Tech) Welle f; (of mine, lift) Schacht m; (of light) Strahl m; **ventilation ~** Luftschacht m

shaggy ['ʃægɪ] adj zottelig; (dog, sheep) struppig

shake [ʃeɪk] (pt **shook**, pp **~n**) vt schütteln; (weaken, upset, surprise) erschüttern; (weaken: resolve) ins Wanken bringen ▷ vi zittern, beben; (building, table) wackeln; (earth) beben ▷ n Schütteln nt; **to ~ one's head** den Kopf schütteln; **to ~ hands with sb** jdm die Hand schütteln; **to ~ one's fist (at sb)** (jdm) mit der Faust drohen; **give it a good ~** schütteln Sie es gut durch; **a ~ of the head** ein Kopfschütteln
  ▶ **shake off** vt (lit, fig) abschütteln
  ▶ **shake up** vt schütteln; (fig: upset) erschüttern

shake-out ['ʃeɪkaut] n Freisetzung f von Arbeitskräften

shake-up ['ʃeɪkʌp] n (radikale) Veränderung f

shakily ['ʃeɪkɪlɪ] adv (reply) mit zittriger Stimme; (walk, stand) unsicher, wackelig

shaky ['ʃeɪkɪ] adj (hand, voice) zittrig; (memory) schwach; (knowledge, prospects, future, start) unsicher

shale [ʃeɪl] n Schiefer m

shall [ʃæl] aux vb: **I ~ go** ich werde gehen; **~ I open the door?** soll ich die Tür öffnen?; **I'll go, ~ I?** soll ich gehen?

shallot [ʃə'lɒt] (Brit) n Schalotte f

shallow ['ʃæləʊ] adj flach; (fig) oberflächlich; **the shallows** npl die Untiefen pl

sham [ʃæm] n Heuchelei f; (person) Heuchler(in) m(f); (object) Attrappe f ▷ adj unecht; (fight) Schein- ▷ vt vortäuschen

shambles ['ʃæmblz] n heilloses Durcheinander nt; **the economy is (in) a complete ~** die Wirtschaft befindet sich in einem totalen Chaos

shambolic [ʃæm'bɒlɪk] (inf) adj chaotisch

shame [ʃeɪm] n Scham f; (disgrace) Schande f ▷ vt beschämen; **it is a ~ that ...** es ist eine Schande, dass ...; **what a ~!** wie schade!; **to bring ~ on** in Schande bringen über +acc; **to put sb/sth to ~** jdn/etw in den Schatten stellen

shamefaced ['ʃeɪmfeɪst] adj betreten

shameful ['ʃeɪmful] adj schändlich

shameless ['ʃeɪmlɪs] adj schamlos

shampoo [ʃæm'puː] n Shampoo(n) nt ▷ vt waschen

shampoo and set n Waschen und Legen nt

shamrock ['ʃæmrɒk] n (plant) Klee m; (leaf) Kleeblatt nt

shandy ['ʃændɪ] n Bier nt mit Limonade, Radler m

shan't [ʃɑːnt] = **shall not**

shantytown ['ʃæntɪtaun] n Elendsviertel nt

SHAPE [ʃeɪp] n abbr (Mil: = Supreme Headquarters Allied Powers, Europe) Hauptquartier der alliierten Streitkräfte in Europa während des 2. Weltkriegs

shape [ʃeɪp] n Form f ▷ vt gestalten; (form) formen; (sb's ideas) prägen; (sb's life) bestimmen; **to take ~** Gestalt annehmen; **in the ~ of a heart** in Herzform; **I can't bear gardening in any ~ or form** ich kann Gartenarbeit absolut nicht ausstehen; **to get (o.s.) into ~** in Form kommen
  ▶ **shape up** vi sich entwickeln

-shaped [ʃeɪpt] suff: **heart-~** herzförmig

shapeless ['ʃeɪplɪs] adj formlos

shapely ['ʃeɪplɪ] adj (woman) wohlproportioniert; (legs) wohlgeformt

share [ʃɛəʳ] n (part) Anteil m; (contribution) Teil m; (Comm) Aktie f ▷ vt teilen; (room, bed, taxi) sich dat teilen; (have in common) gemeinsam haben; **to ~ in** (joy, sorrow) teilen; (profits) beteiligt sein an +dat; (work) sich beteiligen an +dat
  ▶ **share out** vt aufteilen

share capital n Aktienkapital nt

share certificate n Aktienurkunde f

shareholder ['ʃɛəhəʊldəʳ] n Aktionär(in) m(f)

share index n Aktienindex m; **the 100 Share**

S

Index *Aktienindex der Financial Times*
share issue n Aktienemission f
shark [ʃɑːk] n Hai(fisch) m
sharp [ʃɑːp] adj scharf; (point, nose, chin) spitz;
(pain) heftig; (cold) schneidend; (Mus) zu hoch;
(increase) stark; (person: quick-witted) clever;
(: dishonest) gerissen ▷ n (Mus) Kreuz nt ▷ adv: **at
2 o'clock ~** um Punkt 2 Uhr; **turn ~ left**
biegen Sie scharf nach links ab; **to be ~ with
sb** schroff mit jdm sein; **~ practices** (Comm)
unsaubere Geschäfte pl; **C ~** (Mus) Cis nt; **look
~!** (ein bisschen) dalli! (inf)
sharpen [ʃɑːpn] vt schleifen, schärfen; (pencil,
stick etc) (an)spitzen; (fig: appetite) anregen
sharpener [ʃɑːpnər] n (also: **pencil sharpener**)
(Bleistift)spitzer m; (also: **knife sharpener**)
Schleifgerät nt
sharp-eyed [ʃɑːpˈaɪd] adj scharfsichtig
sharpish [ʃɑːpɪʃ] (inf) adj (instantly) auf der
Stelle
sharply [ʃɑːplɪ] adv scharf; (stop) plötzlich;
(retort) schroff
sharp-tempered [ʃɑːpˈtɛmpəd] adj jähzornig
sharp-witted [ʃɑːpˈwɪtɪd] adj scharfsinnig
shatter [ʃætər] vt zertrümmern; (fig: hopes,
dreams) zunichtemachen; (: confidence)
zerstören ▷ vi zerbrechen, zerspringen
shattered [ʃætəd] adj erschüttert;
(inf: exhausted) fertig, kaputt
shattering [ʃætərɪŋ] adj erschütternd,
niederschmetternd; (exhausting) äußerst
anstrengend
shatterproof [ʃætəpruːf] adj splitterfest,
splitterfrei
shave [ʃeɪv] vt rasieren ▷ vi sich rasieren
▷ n: **to have a ~** sich rasieren
shaven [ʃeɪvn] adj (head) kahl geschoren
shaver [ʃeɪvər] n (also: **electric shaver**)
Rasierapparat m
shaving [ʃeɪvɪŋ] n Rasieren nt; **shavings** npl (of
wood etc) Späne pl
shaving brush n Rasierpinsel m
shaving cream n Rasiercreme f
shaving foam n Rasierschaum m
shaving point n Steckdose f für Rasierapparate
shaving soap n Rasierseife f
shawl [ʃɔːl] n (Woll)tuch nt
she [ʃiː] pron sie ▷ pref weiblich; **~-bear** Bärin f;
there ~ is da ist sie
sheaf [ʃiːf] (pl **sheaves**) n (of corn) Garbe f; (of
papers) Bündel nt
shear [ʃɪər] (pt **~ed**, pp **shorn**) vt scheren
▷ **shear off** vi abbrechen
shears [ʃɪəz] npl (for hedge) Heckenschere f
sheath [ʃiːθ] n (of knife) Scheide f; (contraceptive)
Kondom nt
sheathe [ʃiːð] vt ummanteln; (sword) in die
Scheide stecken
sheath knife n Fahrtenmesser nt
sheaves [ʃiːvz] npl of **sheaf**
shed [ʃɛd] (pt, pp **~**) n Schuppen m; (Industry,
Rail) Halle f ▷ vt (tears, blood) vergießen; (load)
verlieren; (workers) entlassen; **to ~ its skin**

sich häuten; **to ~ light on** (problem) erhellen
she'd [ʃiːd] = **she had; she would**
sheen [ʃiːn] n Glanz m
sheep [ʃiːp] n inv Schaf nt
sheepdog [ʃiːpdɔg] n Hütehund m
sheep farmer n Schaffarmer m
sheepish [ʃiːpɪʃ] adj verlegen
sheepskin [ʃiːpskɪn] n Schaffell nt ▷ cpd
Schaffell-
sheer [ʃɪər] adj (utter) rein; (steep) steil; (almost
transparent) (hauch)dünn ▷ adv (straight up)
senkrecht; **by ~ chance** rein zufällig
sheet [ʃiːt] n (on bed) (Bett)laken nt; (of paper)
Blatt nt; (of glass, metal) Platte f; (of ice) Fläche f
sheet feed n (on printer) Papiereinzug m
sheet lightning n Wetterleuchten nt
sheet metal n Walzblech nt
sheet music n Notenblätter pl
sheik, sheikh [ʃeɪk] n Scheich m
shelf [ʃɛlf] (pl **shelves**) n Brett nt, Bord nt; **set of
shelves** Regal nt
shelf life n Lagerfähigkeit f
shell [ʃɛl] n (on beach) Muschel f; (of egg, nut
etc) Schale f; (explosive) Granate f; (of building)
Mauern pl ▷ vt (peas) enthülsen; (Mil: fire on)
(mit Granaten) beschießen
▷ **shell out** (inf) vt: **to ~ out (for)** blechen (für)
she'll [ʃiːl] = **she will; she shall**
shellfish [ʃɛlfɪʃ] n inv Schalentier nt; (scallop etc)
Muschel f; (as food) Meeresfrüchte pl
shelter [ʃɛltər] n (building) Unterstand m; (refuge)
Schutz m; (also: **bus shelter**) Wartehäuschen
nt; (also: **night shelter**) Obdachlosenasyl
nt ▷ vt (protect) schützen; (homeless, refugees)
aufnehmen; (wanted man) Unterschlupf
gewähren +dat ▷ vi sich unterstellen; (from
storm) Schutz suchen; **to take ~ (from)** (from
danger) sich in Sicherheit bringen (vor +dat);
(from storm etc) Schutz suchen (vor +dat)
sheltered [ʃɛltəd] adj (life) behütet; (spot)
geschützt; **~ housing** (for old people)
Altenwohnungen pl; (for handicapped people)
Behindertenwohnungen pl
shelve [ʃɛlv] vt (fig: plan) ad acta legen
shelves [ʃɛlvz] npl of **shelf**
shelving [ʃɛlvɪŋ] n Regale pl
shepherd [ʃɛpəd] n Schäfer m ▷ vt (guide)
führen
shepherdess [ʃɛpədɪs] n Schäferin f
shepherd's pie (Brit) n Auflauf aus Hackfleisch und
Kartoffelbrei
sherbet [ʃɜːbət] n (Brit: powder) Brausepulver nt;
(US: water ice) Fruchteis nt
sheriff [ʃɛrɪf] (US) n Sheriff m
sherry [ʃɛrɪ] n Sherry m
she's [ʃiːz] = **she is; she has**
Shetland [ʃɛtlənd] n (also: **the Shetland
Islands**) die Shetlandinseln pl
Shetland pony n Shetlandpony nt
shield [ʃiːld] n (Mil) Schild m; (trophy) Trophäe
f; (fig: protection) Schutz m ▷ vt: **to ~ (from)**
schützen (vor +dat)
shift [ʃɪft] n (change) Änderung f; (work-

period, workers) Schicht *f* ▷ *vt* (*move*)
bewegen; (*furniture*) (ver)rücken; (*stain*)
herausbekommen ▷ *vi* (*move*) sich bewegen;
(*wind*) drehen; **a ~ in demand** (*Comm*) eine
Nachfrageverschiebung
shift key *n* Umschalttaste *f*
shiftless ['ʃɪftlɪs] *adj* träge
shift work *n* Schichtarbeit *f*; **to do ~** Schicht
arbeiten
shifty ['ʃɪftɪ] *adj* verschlagen
Shiite ['ʃiːaɪt] *adj* schiitisch ▷ *n* Schiit(in)
m(f)
shilling ['ʃɪlɪŋ] (*Brit: old*) *n* Shilling *m*
shilly-shally ['ʃɪlɪʃælɪ] *vi* unschlüssig sein
shimmer ['ʃɪmə*ʳ*] *vi* schimmern
shimmering ['ʃɪmərɪŋ] *adj* schimmernd
shin [ʃɪn] *n* Schienbein *nt* ▷ *vi*: **to ~ up a tree**
einen Baum hinaufklettern
shindig ['ʃɪndɪg] (*inf*) *n* Remmidemmi *nt*
shine [ʃaɪn] (*pt, pp* **shone**) *n* Glanz *m* ▷ *vi* (*sun,*
light) scheinen; (*eyes*) leuchten; (*hair: fig: person*)
glänzen ▷ *vt* (*polish: pt, pp* shined) polieren; **to ~**
a torch on sth etw mit einer Taschenlampe
anleuchten
shingle ['ʃɪŋgl] *n* (*on beach*) Kiesel(steine) *pl*; (*on*
roof) Schindel *f*
shingles ['ʃɪŋglz] *npl* (*Med*) Gürtelrose *f*
shining ['ʃaɪnɪŋ] *adj* glänzend; (*example*)
leuchtend
shiny ['ʃaɪnɪ] *adj* glänzend
ship [ʃɪp] *n* Schiff *nt* ▷ *vt* verschiffen; (*send*)
versenden; (*water*) übernehmen; **on board ~**
an Bord
shipbuilder ['ʃɪpbɪldə*ʳ*] *n* Schiffbauer *m*
shipbuilding ['ʃɪpbɪldɪŋ] *n* Schiffbau *m*
ship canal *n* Seekanal *m*
ship chandler [-'tʃɑːndlə*ʳ*] *n* Schiffsausrüster *m*
shipment ['ʃɪpmənt] *n* (*of goods*) Versand *m*;
(*amount*) Sendung *f*
shipowner ['ʃɪpəʊnə*ʳ*] *n* Schiffseigner *m*; (*of*
many ships) Reeder *m*
shipper ['ʃɪpə*ʳ*] *n* (*person*) Spediteur *m*; (*company*)
Spedition *f*
shipping ['ʃɪpɪŋ] *n* (*transport*) Versand *m*; (*ships*)
Schiffe *pl*
shipping agent *n* Reeder *m*
shipping company *n* Schifffahrtslinie *f*,
Reederei *f*
shipping lane *n* Schifffahrtsstraße *f*
shipping line *n* = **shipping company**
shipshape ['ʃɪpʃeɪp] *adj* tipptopp (*inf*)
shipwreck ['ʃɪprɛk] *n* Schiffbruch *m*; (*ship*)
Wrack *nt* ▷ *vt*: **to be ~ed** schiffbrüchig sein
shipyard ['ʃɪpjɑːd] *n* Werft *f*
shire ['ʃaɪə*ʳ*] (*Brit*) *n* Grafschaft *f*
shirk [ʃəːk] *vt* sich drücken vor +*dat*
shirt [ʃəːt] *n* (Ober)hemd *nt*; (*woman's*) (Hemd)
bluse *f*; **in (one's) ~ sleeves** in Hemdsärmeln
shirty ['ʃəːtɪ] (*Brit: inf*) *adj* sauer (*inf*)
shit [ʃɪt] (*inf!*) *excl* Scheiße (!)
shiver ['ʃɪvə*ʳ*] *n* Schauer *m* ▷ *vi* zittern; **to ~**
with cold vor Kälte zittern
shoal [ʃəʊl] *n* (*of fish*) Schwarm *m*;

(*also*: **shoals**: *fig*) Scharen *pl*
shock [ʃɔk] *n* Schock *m*; (*impact*) Erschütterung
f; (*also*: **electric shock**) Schlag *m* ▷ *vt* (*upset*)
erschüttern; (*offend*) schockieren; **to be**
suffering from ~ (*Med*) einen Schock haben;
to be in ~ unter Schock stehen; **it gave us a ~**
es hat uns erschreckt; **it came as a ~ to hear**
that ... wir hörten mit Bestürzung, dass ...
shock absorber *n* (*Aut*) Stoßdämpfer *m*
shocker ['ʃɔkə*ʳ*] (*inf*) *n* (*film etc*) Schocker *m*,
Reißer *m*; **that's a real ~** (*event etc*) das haut
einen echt um
shocking ['ʃɔkɪŋ] *adj* schrecklich, fürchterlich;
(*outrageous*) schockierend
shockproof ['ʃɔkpruːf] *adj* stoßfest
shock therapy *n* Schocktherapie *f*
shock treatment *n* = **shock therapy**
shock wave *n* (*lit*) Druckwelle *f*; (*fig*)
Schockwelle *f*
shod [ʃɔd] *pt, pp of* **shoe**
shoddy ['ʃɔdɪ] *adj* minderwertig
shoe [ʃuː] (*pt, pp* **shod**) *n* Schuh *m*; (*for horse*)
Hufeisen *nt*; (*also*: **brake shoe**) Bremsbacke *f*
▷ *vt* (*horse*) beschlagen
shoebrush ['ʃuːbrʌʃ] *n* Schuhbürste *f*
shoehorn ['ʃuːhɔːn] *n* Schuhanzieher *m*
shoelace ['ʃuːleɪs] *n* Schnürsenkel *m*
shoemaker ['ʃuːmeɪkə*ʳ*] *n* Schuhmacher *m*,
Schuster *m*
shoe polish *n* Schuhcreme *f*
shoe shop *n* Schuhgeschäft *nt*
shoestring ['ʃuːstrɪŋ] *n* (*fig*): **on a ~** mit ganz
wenig Geld
shoetree ['ʃuːtriː] *n* Schuhspanner *m*
shone [ʃɔn] *pt, pp of* **shine**
shoo [ʃuː] *excl* (*to dog etc*) pfui ▷ *vt* (*also*: **shoo**
away, shoo off, *etc*) verscheuchen; (*somewhere*)
scheuchen
shook [ʃʊk] *pt of* **shake**
shoot [ʃuːt] (*pt, pp* **shot**) *n* (*on branch*) Trieb *m*;
(*seedling*) Sämling *m*; (*Sport*) Jagd *f* ▷ *vt* (*gun*)
abfeuern; (*arrow, goal*) schießen; (*kill, execute*)
erschießen; (*wound*) anschießen; (*Brit: game*
birds) schießen; (*film*) drehen ▷ *vi*: **to ~ (at)**
schießen (auf +*acc*); **to ~ past (sb/sth)** (an
jdm/etw) vorbeischießen
▶ **shoot down** *vt* abschießen
▶ **shoot in** *vi* hereingeschossen kommen
▶ **shoot out (of)** *vi* herausgeschossen
kommen (aus +*dat*)
▶ **shoot up** *vi* (*fig: increase*) in die Höhe
schnellen
shooting ['ʃuːtɪŋ] *n* Schießen *nt*, Schüsse *pl*;
(*attack*) Schießerei *f*; (*murder*) Erschießung *f*;
(*Cine*) Drehen *nt*; (*Hunting*) Jagen *nt*
shooting range *n* Schießplatz *m*
shooting star *n* Sternschnuppe *f*
shop [ʃɔp] *n* Geschäft *nt*, Laden *m*; (*workshop*)
Werkstatt *f* ▷ *vi* (*also*: **go shopping**) einkaufen
(gehen); **repair ~** Reparaturwerkstatt *f*; **to**
talk ~ (*fig*) über die Arbeit reden
▶ **shop around** *vi* Preise vergleichen; (*fig*) sich
umsehen

S

shopaholic ['ʃɔpə'hɔlɪk] (inf) n: **to be a** ~ einen Einkaufsfimmel haben

shop assistant (Brit) n Verkäufer(in) m(f)

shop floor (Brit) n (workers) Arbeiter pl; **on the** ~ bei or unter den Arbeitern

shopkeeper ['ʃɔpkiːpəʳ] n Geschäftsinhaber(in) m(f), Ladenbesitzer(in) m(f)

shoplifter ['ʃɔplɪftəʳ] n Ladendieb(in) m(f)

shoplifting ['ʃɔplɪftɪŋ] n Ladendiebstahl m

shopper ['ʃɔpəʳ] n Käufer(in) m(f)

shopping ['ʃɔpɪŋ] n (goods) Einkäufe pl

shopping bag n Einkaufstasche f

shopping centre, (US) **shopping center** n Einkaufszentrum nt

shopping mall n Shoppingcenter nt

shop-soiled ['ʃɔpsɔɪld] adj angeschmutzt

shop steward (Brit) n gewerkschaftlicher Vertrauensmann m

shop window n Schaufenster nt

shore [ʃɔːʳ] n Ufer nt; (beach) Strand m ▷ vt: **to** ~ **(up)** abstützen; **on** ~ an Land

shore leave n (Naut) Landurlaub m

shorn [ʃɔːn] pp of **shear**; **to be** ~ **of** (power etc) entkleidet sein +gen

short [ʃɔːt] adj kurz; (person) klein; (curt) schroff, kurz angebunden (inf); (scarce) knapp ▷ n (also: **short film**) Kurzfilm m; **to be** ~ **of** ... zu wenig ... haben; **I'm 3** ~ ich habe 3 zu wenig, mir fehlen 3; **in** ~ kurz gesagt; **to be in** ~ **supply** knapp sein; **it is** ~ **for** ... es ist die Kurzform von ...; **a** ~ **time ago** vor Kurzem; **in the** ~ **term** auf kurze Sicht; ~ **of doing sth** außer etw zu tun; **to cut** ~ abbrechen; **everything** ~ **of** ... alles außer ... +dat; **to fall** ~ **of sth** etw nicht erreichen; (expectations) etw nicht erfüllen; **to run** ~ **of** ... nicht mehr viel ... haben; **to stop** ~ plötzlich innehalten; **to stop** ~ **of** haltmachen vor +dat; see also **shorts**

shortage ['ʃɔːtɪdʒ] n: **a** ~ **of** ein Mangel m an +dat

shortbread ['ʃɔːtbrɛd] n Mürbegebäck nt

short-change [ʃɔːt'tʃeɪndʒ] vt: **to** ~ **sb** jdm zu wenig Wechselgeld geben

short circuit n Kurzschluss m

shortcoming ['ʃɔːtkʌmɪŋ] n Fehler m, Mangel m

shortcrust pastry (Brit) n Mürbeteig m

short cut n Abkürzung f; (fig) Schnellverfahren nt

shorten ['ʃɔːtn] vt verkürzen

shortening ['ʃɔːtnɪŋ] n (Back)fett nt

shortfall ['ʃɔːtfɔːl] n Defizit nt

shorthand ['ʃɔːthænd] n Kurzschrift f, Stenografie f; (fig) Kurzform f; **to take sth down in** ~ etw stenografieren

shorthand notebook (Brit) n Stenoblock m

shorthand typist (Brit) n Stenotypist(in) m(f)

short list (Brit) n Auswahlliste f; **to be on the** ~ in der engeren Wahl sein

short-list ['ʃɔːtlɪst] (Brit) vt in die engere Wahl ziehen; **to be ~ed** in die engere Wahl kommen

short-lived ['ʃɔːt'lɪvd] adj kurzlebig; **to be** ~ nicht von Dauer sein

shortly ['ʃɔːtlɪ] adv bald

shorts [ʃɔːts] npl: **(a pair of)** ~ Shorts pl

short-sighted [ʃɔːt'saɪtɪd] (Brit) adj (lit, fig) kurzsichtig

short-sightedness [ʃɔːt'saɪtɪdnɪs] n Kurzsichtigkeit f

short-staffed [ʃɔːt'stɑːft] adj: **to be** ~ zu wenig Personal haben

short story n Kurzgeschichte f

short-tempered [ʃɔːt'tɛmpəd] adj gereizt

short-term ['ʃɔːttəːm] adj kurzfristig

short time n: **to work** ~, **to be on** ~ kurzarbeiten, Kurzarbeit haben

short-wave ['ʃɔːtweɪv] (Radio) adj auf Kurzwelle ▷ n Kurzwelle f

shot [ʃɔt] pt, pp of **shoot** ▷ n Schuss m; (shotgun pellets) Schrot m; (injection) Spritze f; (Phot) Aufnahme f; **to fire a** ~ **at sb/sth** einen Schuss auf jdn/etw abgeben; **to have a** ~ **at (doing) sth** etw mal versuchen; **to get** ~ **of sb/sth** (inf) jdn/etw loswerden; **a big** ~ (inf) ein hohes Tier; **a good/poor** ~ (person) ein guter/schlechter Schütze; **like a** ~ sofort

shotgun ['ʃɔtgʌn] n Schrotflinte f

should [ʃud] aux vb: **I** ~ **go now** ich sollte jetzt gehen; **he** ~ **be there now** er müsste eigentlich schon da sein; **I** ~ **go if I were you** an deiner Stelle würde ich gehen; **I** ~ **like to** ich möchte gerne, ich würde gerne; ~ **he phone** ... falls er anruft ...

shoulder ['ʃəuldəʳ] n Schulter f ▷ vt (fig) auf sich acc nehmen; **to rub** ~**s with sb** (fig) mit jdm in Berührung kommen; **to give sb the cold** ~ (fig) jdm die kalte Schulter zeigen

shoulder bag n Umhängetasche f

shoulder blade n Schulterblatt nt

shoulder strap n (on clothing) Träger m; (on bag) Schulterriemen m

shouldn't ['ʃudnt] = **should not**

shout [ʃaut] n Schrei m, Ruf m ▷ vt schreien, rufen ▷ vi (also: **shout out**) aufschreien; **to give sb a** ~ jdn rufen
  ▶ **shout down** vt niederbrüllen

shouting ['ʃautɪŋ] n Geschrei nt

shouting match (inf) n: **to have a** ~ sich gegenseitig anschreien

shove [ʃʌv] vt schieben; (with one push) stoßen, schubsen (inf) ▷ n: **to give sb a** ~ jdn stoßen or schubsen (inf); **to give sth a** ~ etw verrücken; (door) gegen etw stoßen; **to** ~ **sth in sth** (inf: put) etw in etw acc stecken; **he ~d me out of the way** er stieß mich zur Seite
  ▶ **shove off** vi abschieben

shovel ['ʃʌvl] n Schaufel f; (mechanical) Bagger m ▷ vt schaufeln

show [ʃəu] (pt ~**ed**, pp ~**n**) n (exhibition) Ausstellung f, Schau f; (Theat) Aufführung f; (TV) Show f; (Cine) Vorstellung f ▷ vt zeigen; (exhibit) ausstellen ▷ vi: **it** ~**s** man sieht es; (is evident) man merkt es; **to ask for a** ~ **of hands** um Handzeichen bitten; **without any** ~ **of**

emotion ohne jede Gefühlsregung; **it's just for** ~ es ist nur zur Schau; **on** ~ ausgestellt, zu sehen; **who's running the** ~ **here?** (*inf*) wer ist hier verantwortlich?; **to** ~ **sb to his seat/to the door** jdn an seinen Platz/zur Tür bringen; **to** ~ **a profit/loss** Gewinn/Verlust aufweisen; **it just goes to** ~ **that …** da sieht mans mal wieder, dass

▶ **show in** *vt* hereinführen

▶ **show off** (*pej*) *vi* angeben ▷ *vt* vorführen

▶ **show out** *vt* hinausbegleiten

▶ **show up** *vi* (*stand out*) sich abheben; (*inf: turn up*) auftauchen ▷ *vt* (*uncover*) deutlich erkennen lassen; (*shame*) blamieren

showbiz *n* = **show business**

show business *n* Showgeschäft *nt*

showcase ['ʃəʊkeɪs] *n* Schaukasten *m*; (*fig*) Werbung *f*

showdown ['ʃəʊdaʊn] *n* Kraftprobe *f*

shower ['ʃaʊəʳ] *n* (*of rain*) Schauer *m*; (*of stones etc*) Hagel *m*; (*for bathing in*) Dusche *f*; (*US: party*) Party, bei der jeder ein Geschenk für den Ehrengast mitbringt ▷ *vi* duschen ▷ *vt*: **to** ~ **sb with** (*gifts etc*) jdn überschütten mit; (*missiles, abuse etc*) auf jdn niederhageln lassen; **to have** *or* **take a** ~ duschen; **a** ~ **of sparks** ein Funkenregen *m*

showercap ['ʃaʊəkæp] *n* Duschhaube *f*

showergel *n* Duschgel *nt*

showerproof ['ʃaʊəpruːf] *adj* regenfest

showery ['ʃaʊərɪ] *adj* regnerisch

showground ['ʃəʊɡraʊnd] *n* Ausstellungsgelände *nt*

showing ['ʃəʊɪŋ] *n* (*of film*) Vorführung *f*

show jumping *n* Springreiten *nt*

showman ['ʃəʊmən] (*irreg: like* **man**) *n* (*at fair*) Schausteller *m*; (*at circus*) Artist *m*; (*fig*) Schauspieler *m*

showmanship ['ʃəʊmənʃɪp] *n* Talent *nt* für effektvolle Darbietung

shown [ʃəʊn] *pp of* **show**

show-off ['ʃəʊɒf] (*inf*) *n* Angeber(in) *m(f)*

showpiece ['ʃəʊpiːs] *n* (*of exhibition etc*) Schaustück *nt*; (*best example*) Paradestück *nt*; (*prime example*) Musterbeispiel *nt*

showroom ['ʃəʊrʊm] *n* Ausstellungsraum *m*

show trial *n* Schauprozess *m*

showy ['ʃəʊɪ] *adj* auffallend

shrank [ʃræŋk] *pt of* **shrink**

shrapnel ['ʃræpnl] *n* Schrapnell *nt*

shred [ʃred] *n* (*gen pl*) Fetzen *m*; (*fig*): **not a** ~ **of truth** kein Fünkchen Wahrheit; **not a** ~ **of evidence** keine Spur eines Beweises ▷ *vt* zerfetzen; (*Culin*) raspeln

shredder ['ʃredəʳ] *n* (*also:* **vegetable shredder**) Raspel *f*; (*also:* **document shredder**) Reißwolf *m*; (*also:* **garden shredder**) Häcksler *m*

shrew [ʃruː] *n* (*Zool*) Spitzmaus *f*; (*pej: woman*) Xanthippe *f*

shrewd [ʃruːd] *adj* klug

shrewdness ['ʃruːdnɪs] *n* Klugheit *f*

shriek [ʃriːk] *n* schriller Schrei *m* ▷ *vi* schreien; **to** ~ **with laughter** vor Lachen quietschen

shrift [ʃrɪft] *n*: **to give sb short** ~ jdn kurz abfertigen

shrill [ʃrɪl] *adj* schrill

shrimp [ʃrɪmp] *n* Garnele *f*

shrine [ʃraɪn] *n* Schrein *m*; (*fig*) Gedenkstätte *f*

shrink [ʃrɪŋk] (*pt* **shrank**, *pp* **shrunk**) *vi* (*cloth*) einlaufen; (*profits, audiences*) schrumpfen; (*forests*) schwinden; (*also:* **shrink away**) zurückweichen ▷ *vt* (*cloth*) einlaufen lassen ▷ *n* (*inf: pej*) Klapsdoktor *m*; **to** ~ **from sth** vor etw *dat* zurückschrecken; **to** ~ **from doing sth** davor zurückschrecken, etw zu tun

shrinkage ['ʃrɪŋkɪdʒ] *n* (*of clothes*) Einlaufen *nt*

shrink-wrap ['ʃrɪŋkræp] *vt* einschweißen

shrivel ['ʃrɪvl] (*also:* **shrivel up**) *vt* austrocknen ▷ *vi* austrocknen, verschrumpeln

shroud [ʃraʊd] *n* Leichentuch *nt* ▷ *vt*: ~**ed in mystery** von einem Geheimnis umgeben

Shrove Tuesday ['ʃrəʊv-] *n* Fastnachtsdienstag *m*

shrub [ʃrʌb] *n* Strauch *m*, Busch *m*

shrubbery ['ʃrʌbərɪ] *n* Gebüsch *nt*

shrug [ʃrʌɡ] *n* Achselzucken *nt* ▷ *vi, vt*: **to** ~ **(one's shoulders)** mit den Achseln zucken

▶ **shrug off** *vt* (*criticism*) auf die leichte Schulter nehmen; (*illness*) abschütteln

shrunk [ʃrʌŋk] *pp of* **shrink**

shrunken ['ʃrʌŋkn] *adj* (*ein*)geschrumpft

shudder ['ʃʌdəʳ] *n* Schauer *m* ▷ *vi* schaudern; **I** ~ **to think of it** (*fig*) mir graut, wenn ich nur daran denke

shuffle ['ʃʌfl] *vt* (*cards*) mischen ▷ *vi* schlurfen; **to** ~ **(one's feet)** mit den Füßen scharren

shun [ʃʌn] *vt* meiden; (*publicity*) scheuen

shunt [ʃʌnt] *vt* rangieren

shunting yard ['ʃʌntɪŋ-] *n* Rangierbahnhof *m*

shush [ʃʊʃ] *excl* pst!, sch!

shut [ʃʌt] (*pt, pp* ~) *vt* schließen, zumachen (*inf*) ▷ *vi* sich schließen, zugehen; (*shop*) schließen, zumachen (*inf*)

▶ **shut down** *vt* (*factory etc*) schließen; (*machine*) abschalten ▷ *vi* schließen, zumachen (*inf*)

▶ **shut off** *vt* (*gas, electricity*) abstellen; (*oil supplies etc*) abschneiden

▶ **shut out** *vt* (*person*) aussperren; (*cold, noise*) nicht hereinlassen; (*view*) versperren; (*memory, thought*) verdrängen

▶ **shut up** *vi* (*inf: keep quiet*) den Mund halten ▷ *vt* (*silence*) zum Schweigen bringen

shutdown ['ʃʌtdaʊn] *n* Schließung *f*

shutter ['ʃʌtəʳ] *n* Fensterladen *m*; (*Phot*) Verschluss *m*

shuttle ['ʃʌtl] *n* (*plane*) Pendelflugzeug *nt*; (*train*) Pendelzug *m*; (*also:* **space shuttle**) Raumtransporter *m*; (*also:* **shuttle service**) Pendelverkehr *m*; (*for weaving*) Schiffchen *nt* ▷ *vi*: **to** ~ **to and fro** pendeln; **to** ~ **between** pendeln zwischen ▷ *vt* (*passengers*) transportieren

shuttlecock ['ʃʌtlkɒk] *n* Federball *m*

shuttle diplomacy *n* Reisediplomatie *f*

shy [ʃaɪ] *adj* schüchtern; (*animal*) scheu ▷ *vi*: **to** ~ **away from doing sth** (*fig*) davor zurückschrecken, etw zu tun; **to fight** ~ **of**

S

779

aus dem Weg gehen +*dat*; **to be ~ of doing sth** Hemmungen haben, etw zu tun

shyly ['ʃaɪlɪ] *adv* schüchtern, scheu

shyness ['ʃaɪnɪs] *n* Schüchternheit *f*, Scheu *f*

Siam [saɪ'æm] *n* Siam *nt*

Siamese [saɪə'miːz] *adj*: **~ cat** Siamkatze *f*; **~ twins** siamesische Zwillinge *pl*

Siberia [saɪ'bɪərɪə] *n* Sibirien *nt*

sibling ['sɪblɪŋ] *n* Geschwister *nt*

Sicilian [sɪ'sɪlɪən] *adj* sizilianisch ▷ *n* Sizilianer(in) *m(f)*

Sicily ['sɪsɪlɪ] *n* Sizilien *nt*

sick [sɪk] *adj* krank; (*humour*, *joke*) makaber; **to be ~** (*vomit*) brechen, sich übergeben; **I feel ~** mir ist schlecht; **to fall ~** krank werden; **to be (off) ~** wegen Krankheit fehlen; **a ~ person** ein Kranker, eine Kranke; **to be ~ of** (*fig*) satthaben +*acc*

sickbag ['sɪkbæg] *n* Spucktüte *f*

sickbay ['sɪkbeɪ] *n* Krankenrevier *nt*

sickbed ['sɪkbed] *n* Krankenbett *nt*

sick building syndrome *n* Kopfschmerzen, Allergien etc, die in modernen, vollklimatisierten Bürogebäuden entstehen

sicken ['sɪkn] *vt* (*disgust*) anwidern ▷ *vi*: **to be ~ing for a cold/flu** eine Erkältung/Grippe bekommen

sickening ['sɪknɪŋ] *adj* (*fig*) widerlich, ekelhaft

sickle ['sɪkl] *n* Sichel *f*

sick leave *n*: **to be on ~** krankgeschrieben sein

sickle-cell anaemia *n* Sichelzellenanämie *f*

sick list *n*: **to be on the ~** auf der Krankenliste stehen

sickly ['sɪklɪ] *adj* kränklich; (*causing nausea*) widerlich, ekelhaft

sickness ['sɪknɪs] *n* Krankheit *f*; (*vomiting*) Erbrechen *nt*

sickness benefit *n* Krankengeld *nt*

sick note *n* Krankmeldung *f*

sick pay *n* Lohnfortzahlung *f* im Krankheitsfall; (*paid by insurance*) Krankengeld *nt*

sickroom ['sɪkruːm] *n* Krankenzimmer *nt*

side [saɪd] *n* Seite *f*; (*team*) Mannschaft *f*; (*in conflict etc*) Partei *f*, Seite *f*; (*of hill*) Hang *m* ▷ *adj* (*door, entrance*) Seiten-, Neben- ▷ *vi*: **to ~ with sb** jds Partei ergreifen; **by the ~ of** +*dat*; **~ by side** Seite an Seite; **the right/wrong ~** (*of cloth*) die rechte/linke Seite; **they are on our ~** sie stehen auf unserer Seite; **she never left my ~** sie wich mir nicht von der Seite; **to put sth to one ~** etw beiseitelegen; **from ~ to side** von einer Seite zur anderen; **to take ~s (with)** Partei ergreifen (für); **a ~ of beef** ein halbes Rind; **~ of bacon** eine Speckseite

sideboard ['saɪdbɔːd] *n* Sideboard *nt*; **sideboards** (*Brit*) *npl* = **sideburns**

sideburns ['saɪdbɜːnz] *npl* Koteletten *pl*

sidecar ['saɪdkɑːʳ] *n* Beiwagen *m*

side dish *n* Beilage *f*

side drum *n* kleine Trommel *f*

side effect *n* (*Med*, *fig*) Nebenwirkung *f*

sidekick ['saɪdkɪk] (*inf*) *n* Handlanger *m*

sidelight ['saɪdlaɪt] *n* (*Aut*) Begrenzungsleuchte *f*

sideline ['saɪdlaɪn] *n* (*Sport*) Seitenlinie *f*; (*fig: job*) Nebenerwerb *m*; **to stand on the ~s** (*fig*) unbeteiligter Zuschauer sein; **to wait on the ~s** (*fig*) in den Kulissen warten

sidelong ['saɪdlɒŋ] *adj* (*glance*) Seiten-; (*: surreptitious*) verstohlen; **to give sb a ~ glance** jdn kurz aus den Augenwinkeln ansehen

side plate *n* kleiner Teller *m*

side road *n* Nebenstraße *f*

side-saddle ['saɪdsædl] *adv* (*ride*) im Damensitz

sideshow ['saɪdʃəʊ] *n* Nebenattraktion *f*

sidestep ['saɪdstep] *vt* (*problem*) umgehen; (*question*) ausweichen +*dat* ▷ *vi* (*Boxing etc*) seitwärts ausweichen

side street *n* Seitenstraße *f*

sidetrack ['saɪdtræk] *vt* (*fig*) ablenken

sidewalk ['saɪdwɔːk] (*US*) *n* Bürgersteig *m*

sideways ['saɪdweɪz] *adv* seitwärts; (*lean, look*) zur Seite

siding ['saɪdɪŋ] *n* Abstellgleis *nt*

sidle ['saɪdl] *vi*: **to ~ up (to)** sich heranschleichen (an +*acc*)

SIDS *n abbr* (*Med*: = *sudden infant death syndrome*) plötzlicher Kindstod *m*

siege [siːdʒ] *n* Belagerung *f*; **to be under ~** belagert sein; **to lay ~** belagern

siege economy *n* Belagerungswirtschaft *f*

siege mentality *n* Belagerungsmentalität *f*

Sierra Leone [sɪ'ɛrəlɪ'əʊn] *n* Sierra Leone *f*

siesta [sɪ'ɛstə] *n* Siesta *f*

sieve [sɪv] *n* Sieb *nt* ▷ *vt* sieben

sift [sɪft] *vt* sieben; (*also*: **sift through**) durchgehen

sigh [saɪ] *n* Seufzer *m* ▷ *vi* seufzen; **to breathe a ~ of relief** erleichtert aufseufzen

sight [saɪt] *n* (*faculty*) Sehvermögen *nt*, Augenlicht *nt*; (*spectacle*) Anblick *m*; (*on gun*) Visier *nt* ▷ *vt* sichten; **in ~** in Sicht; **on ~** (*shoot*) sofort; **out of ~** außer Sicht; **at ~** (*Comm*) bei Sicht; **at first ~** auf den ersten Blick; **I know her by ~** ich kenne sie vom Sehen; **to catch ~ of sb/sth** jdn/etw sehen; **to lose ~ of sth** (*fig*) etw aus den Augen verlieren; **to set one's ~s on sth** ein Auge auf etw werfen

sighted ['saɪtɪd] *adj* sehend; **partially ~** sehbehindert

sightseeing ['saɪtsiːɪŋ] *n* Besichtigungen *pl*; **to go ~** auf Besichtigungstour gehen

sightseer ['saɪtsiːəʳ] *n* Tourist(in) *m(f)*

sign [saɪn] *n* Zeichen *nt*; (*notice*) Schild *nt*; (*evidence*) Anzeichen *nt*; (*also*: **road sign**) Verkehrsschild *nt* ▷ *vt* unterschreiben; (*player*) verpflichten; **a ~ of the times** ein Zeichen unserer Zeit; **it's a good/bad ~** es ist ein gutes/schlechtes Zeichen; **plus/minus ~** Plus-/Minuszeichen *nt*; **there's no ~ of her changing her mind** nichts deutet darauf hin, dass sie es sich anders überlegen wird; **he was showing ~s of improvement** er ließ Anzeichen einer Verbesserung erkennen; **to ~**

one's name unterschreiben; **to ~ sth over to
sb** jdm etw überschreiben
▶ **sign away** vt *(rights etc)* verzichten auf +acc
▶ **sign in** vi sich eintragen
▶ **sign off** vi *(Radio, TV)* sich verabschieden; *(in
letter)* Schluss machen
▶ **sign on** vi *(Mil)* sich verpflichten; *(Brit: as
unemployed)* sich arbeitslos melden; *(for course)*
sich einschreiben ▷ vt *(Mil)* verpflichten;
(employee) anstellen
▶ **sign out** vi *(from hotel etc)* sich (aus dem
Hotelgästebuch etc) austragen
▶ **sign up** vi *(Mil)* sich verpflichten; *(for
course)* sich einschreiben ▷ vt *(player, recruit)*
verpflichten
signal ['sɪgnl] n Zeichen nt; *(Rail)* Signal nt
▷ vi *(Aut)* ein Zeichen geben ▷ vt ein
Zeichen geben +dat; **to ~ a right/left turn**
(Aut) rechts/links blinken
signal box n Stellwerk nt
signalman ['sɪgnlmən] *(irreg: like **man**)* n
Stellwerkswärter m
signatory ['sɪgnətərɪ] n Unterzeichner m;
(state) Signatarstaat m
signature ['sɪgnətʃəʳ] n Unterschrift f; *(Zool,
Biol)* Kennzeichen nt
signature tune n Erkennungsmelodie f
signet ring ['sɪgnət-] n Siegelring m
significance [sɪg'nɪfɪkəns] n Bedeutung f; **that
is of no ~** das ist belanglos or bedeutungslos
significant [sɪg'nɪfɪkənt] adj bedeutend,
wichtig; *(look, smile)* vielsagend, bedeutsam; **it
is ~ that ...** es ist bezeichnend, dass ...
significantly [sɪg'nɪfɪkəntlɪ] adv bedeutend;
(smile) vielsagend, bedeutsam
signify ['sɪgnɪfaɪ] vt bedeuten; *(person)* zu
erkennen geben
sign language n Zeichensprache f
signpost ['saɪnpəust] n *(lit, fig)* Wegweiser m
Sikh [siːk] n Sikh mf ▷ adj *(province etc)* Sikh-
silage ['saɪlɪdʒ] n Silage f, Silofutter nt
silence ['saɪləns] n Stille f; *(of person)* Schweigen
nt ▷ vt zum Schweigen bringen; **in ~** still; *(not
talking)* schweigend
silencer ['saɪlənsəʳ] n *(on gun)* Schalldämpfer m;
(Brit: Aut) Auspufftopf m
silent ['saɪlənt] adj still; *(machine)* ruhig; **~ film**
Stummfilm m; **to remain ~** still bleiben;
(about sth) sich nicht äußern
silently ['saɪləntlɪ] adv lautlos; *(not talking)*
schweigend
silent partner n stiller Teilhaber m
silhouette [sɪluːˈɛt] n Silhouette f, Umriss m
▷ vt: **to be ~d against sth** sich als Silhouette
gegen etw abheben
silicon ['sɪlɪkən] n Silizium nt
silicon chip n Silikonchip m
silicone ['sɪlɪkəun] n Silikon nt
silk [sɪlk] n Seide f ▷ adj *(dress etc)* Seiden-
silky ['sɪlkɪ] adj seidig
sill [sɪl] n *(also: **window sill**)* (Fenster)sims m or
nt; *(of door)* Schwelle f; *(Aut)* Türleiste f
silly ['sɪlɪ] adj *(person)* dumm; **to do something**

~ etwas Dummes tun
silo ['saɪləu] n Silo nt; *(for missile)* Raketensilo nt
silt [sɪlt] n Schlamm m, Schlick m
▶ **silt up** vi verschlammen ▷ vt verschlämmen
silver ['sɪlvəʳ] n Silber nt; *(coins)* Silbergeld nt
▷ adj silbern
silver foil *(Brit)* n Alufolie f
silver paper *(Brit)* n Silberpapier nt
silver-plated [sɪlvəˈpleɪtɪd] adj versilbert
silversmith ['sɪlvəsmɪθ] n Silberschmied(in)
m(f)
silverware ['sɪlvəwɛəʳ] n Silber nt
silver wedding, silver wedding anniversary
n Silberhochzeit f
silvery ['sɪlvrɪ] adj silbern; *(sound)* silberhell
SIM card ['sɪmkɑːd] n *(Tel: = Subscriber Identity
Module card)* SIM-Karte f
similar ['sɪmɪləʳ] adj: **~ (to)** ähnlich (wie or +dat)
similarity [sɪmɪˈlærɪtɪ] n Ähnlichkeit f
similarly ['sɪmɪləlɪ] adv ähnlich; *(likewise)*
genauso
simile ['sɪmɪlɪ] n *(Ling)* Vergleich m
simmer ['sɪməʳ] vi auf kleiner Flamme kochen
▶ **simmer down** *(inf)* vi *(fig)* sich abregen
simper ['sɪmpəʳ] vi geziert lächeln
simpering ['sɪmpərɪŋ] adj geziert
simple ['sɪmpl] adj einfach; *(dress)* einfach,
schlicht; *(foolish)* einfältig; **the ~ truth is
that ...** es ist einfach so, dass ...
simple interest n Kapitalzinsen pl
simple-minded [sɪmplˈmaɪndɪd] *(pej)* adj
einfältig
simpleton ['sɪmpltən] *(pej)* n Einfaltspinsel m
simplicity [sɪmˈplɪsɪtɪ] n Einfachheit f; *(of dress)*
Schlichtheit f
simplification [sɪmplɪfɪˈkeɪʃən] n
Vereinfachung f
simplify ['sɪmplɪfaɪ] vt vereinfachen
simply ['sɪmplɪ] adv *(just, merely)* nur, bloß; *(in a
simple way)* einfach
simulate ['sɪmjuleɪt] vt vortäuschen, spielen;
(illness) simulieren
simulated ['sɪmjuleɪtɪd] adj *(hair, fur)* imitiert;
(Tech) simuliert
simulation [sɪmjuˈleɪʃən] n Vortäuschung f;
(simulated object) Imitation f; *(Tech)* Simulation f
simultaneous [sɪməlˈteɪnɪəs] adj gleichzeitig;
(translation, interpreting) Simultan-
simultaneously [sɪməlˈteɪnɪəslɪ] adv
gleichzeitig
sin [sɪn] n Sünde f ▷ vi sündigen
since [sɪns] adv inzwischen, seitdem ▷ prep seit
▷ conj *(time)* seit(dem); *(because)* da; **~ then,
ever since** seitdem
sincere [sɪnˈsɪəʳ] adj aufrichtig, offen; *(apology,
belief)* aufrichtig
sincerely [sɪnˈsɪəlɪ] adv aufrichtig, offen;
yours ~ *(in letter)* mit freundlichen Grüßen
sincerity [sɪnˈsɛrɪtɪ] n Aufrichtigkeit f
sine [saɪn] n Sinus m
sine qua non [sɪnɪkwɑːˈnɔn] n unerlässliche
Voraussetzung f
sinew ['sɪnjuː] n Sehne f

S

sinful ['sɪnfʊl] *adj* sündig, sündhaft

sing [sɪŋ] (*pt* **sang**, *pp* **sung**) *vt, vi* singen

Singapore [sɪŋgə'pɔːʳ] *n* Singapur *nt*

singe [sɪndʒ] *vt* versengen; (*lightly*) ansengen

singer ['sɪŋəʳ] *n* Sänger(in) *m(f)*

Singhalese [sɪŋə'liːz] *adj* = **Sinhalese**

singing ['sɪŋɪŋ] *n* Singen *nt*, Gesang *m*; **a ~ in the ears** ein Dröhnen in den Ohren

single ['sɪŋgl] *adj* (*solitary*) einzige(r, s); (*individual*) einzeln; (*unmarried*) ledig, unverheiratet; (*not double*) einfach ▷ *n* (*Brit: also:* **single ticket**) Einzelfahrschein *m*; (*record*) Single *f*; **not a ~ one was left** es war kein Einziges mehr übrig; **every ~ day** jeden Tag; **~ spacing** einfacher Zeilenabstand *m*
  ▶ **single out** *vt* auswählen; **to ~ out for praise** lobend erwähnen

single bed *n* Einzelbett *nt*

single-breasted ['sɪŋglbrestɪd] *adj* einreihig

Single European Market *n*: **the ~** der Europäische Binnenmarkt

single file *n*: **in ~** im Gänsemarsch

single-handed [sɪŋgl'hændɪd] *adv* ganz allein

single-minded [sɪŋgl'maɪndɪd] *adj* zielstrebig

single parent *n* Alleinerziehende(r) *f(m)*

single parent family *n* Einelternfamilie *f*

single room *n* Einzelzimmer *nt*

singles ['sɪŋglz] *npl* (*Tennis*) Einzel *nt*

singles bar *n* Singles-Bar *f*

single-sex school *n* reine Jungen-/ Mädchenschule *f*; **education in ~s** nach Geschlechtern getrennte Schulerziehung

singly ['sɪŋglɪ] *adv* einzeln

singsong ['sɪŋsɔŋ] *adj* (*tone*) singend ▷ *n*: **to have a ~** zusammen singen

singular ['sɪŋgjʊləʳ] *adj* (*odd*) eigenartig; (*outstanding*) einzigartig; (*Ling: form etc*) Singular- ▷ *n* (*Ling*) Singular *m*, Einzahl *f*; **in the ~** im Singular

singularly ['sɪŋgjʊlərlɪ] *adv* außerordentlich

Sinhalese [sɪnhə'liːz] *adj* singhalesisch

sinister ['sɪnɪstəʳ] *adj* unheimlich

sink [sɪŋk] (*pt* **sank**, *pp* **sunk**) *n* Spülbecken *nt* ▷ *vt* (*ship*) versenken; (*well*) bohren; (*foundations*) absenken ▷ *vi* (*ship*) sinken, untergehen; (*ground*) sich senken; (*person*) sinken; **to ~ one's teeth/claws into sth** die Zähne/seine Klauen in etw *acc* schlagen; **his heart/spirits sank at the thought** bei dem Gedanken verließ ihn der Mut; **he sank into the mud/a chair** er sank in den Schlamm ein/in einen Sessel
  ▶ **sink back** *vi* (zurück)sinken
  ▶ **sink down** *vi* (nieder)sinken
  ▶ **sink in** *vi* (*fig*) verstanden werden; **it's only just sunk in** ich begreife es erst jetzt

sinking ['sɪŋkɪŋ] *n* (*of ship*) Untergang *m*; (: *deliberate*) Versenkung *f* ▷ *adj*: **~ feeling** flaues Gefühl *nt* (im Magen)

sinking fund *n* Tilgungsfonds *m*

sink unit *n* Spüle *f*

sinner ['sɪnəʳ] *n* Sünder(in) *m(f)*

Sinn Féin [ʃɪn'feɪn] *n* republikanisch-nationalistische irische Partei

Sino- ['saɪnəʊ] *pref* chinesisch-

sinuous ['sɪnjʊəs] *adj* (*snake*) gewunden; (*dance*) geschmeidig

sinus ['saɪnəs] *n* (Nasen)nebenhöhle *f*

sip [sɪp] *n* Schlückchen *nt* ▷ *vt* nippen an +*dat*

siphon ['saɪfən] *n* Heber *m*; (*also:* **soda siphon**) Siphon *m*
  ▶ **siphon off** *vt* absaugen; (*petrol*) abzapfen

SIPS *n abbr* (= *side impact protection system*) Seitenaufprallschutz *m*

sir [səʳ] *n* mein Herr, Herr X; **S~ John Smith** Sir John Smith; **yes, ~** ja(, Herr X); **Dear S~ (or Madam)** (*in letter*) Sehr geehrte (Damen und) Herren!

siren ['saɪərn] *n* Sirene *f*

sirloin ['səːlɔɪn] *n* (*also:* **sirloin steak**) Filetsteak *nt*

sirocco [sɪ'rɔkəʊ] *n* Schirokko *m*

sisal ['saɪsəl] *n* Sisal *m*

sissy ['sɪsɪ] (*inf: pej*) *n* Waschlappen *m* ▷ *adj* weichlich

sister ['sɪstəʳ] *n* Schwester *f*; (*nun*) (Ordens)schwester *f*; (*Brit: nurse*) Oberschwester *f* ▷ *cpd*: **~ organization** Schwesterorganisation *f*; **~ ship** Schwesterschiff *nt*

sister-in-law ['sɪstərɪnlɔː] *n* Schwägerin *f*

sit [sɪt] (*pt, pp* **sat**) *vi* (*sit down*) sich setzen; (*be sitting*) sitzen; (*assembly*) tagen; (*for painter*) Modell sitzen ▷ *vt* (*exam*) machen; **to ~ on a committee** in einem Ausschuss sitzen; **to ~ tight** abwarten
  ▶ **sit about** *vi* herumsitzen
  ▶ **sit around** *vi* = **sit about**
  ▶ **sit back** *vi* sich zurücklehnen
  ▶ **sit down** *vi* sich (hin)setzen; **to be ~ting down** sitzen
  ▶ **sit in on** *vt fus* dabei sein bei
  ▶ **sit up** *vi* sich aufsetzen; (*straight*) sich gerade hinsetzen; (*not go to bed*) aufbleiben

sitcom ['sɪtkɔm] *n abbr* (*TV*) = **situation comedy**

sit-down ['sɪtdaʊn] *adj*: **a ~ strike** ein Sitzstreik *m*; **a ~ meal** eine richtige Mahlzeit

site [saɪt] *n* (*place*) Platz *m*; (*of crime*) Ort *m*; (*also:* **building site**) Baustelle *f*; (*Comput*) Site *f* ▷ *vt* (*factory*) legen; (*missiles*) stationieren

sit-in ['sɪtɪn] *n* Sit-in *nt*

siting ['saɪtɪŋ] *n* (*location*) Lage *f*

sits vac *abbr* (= *situations vacant*) Stellenangebote *pl*

sitter ['sɪtəʳ] *n* (*for painter*) Modell *nt*; (*also:* **babysitter**) Babysitter *m*

sitting ['sɪtɪŋ] *n* Sitzung *f*; **we have two ~s for lunch** bei uns wird das Mittagessen in zwei Schüben serviert; **at a single ~** auf einmal

sitting member *n* (*Pol*) (derzeitiger) Abgeordnete(r) *m*, (derzeitige) Abgeordnete *f*

sitting room *n* Wohnzimmer *nt*

sitting tenant (*Brit*) *n* (derzeitiger) Mieter *m*

situate ['sɪtjʊeɪt] *vt* legen

situated ['sɪtjʊeɪtɪd] *adj* gelegen; **to be ~** liegen

situation [sɪtjuˈeɪʃən] n Situation f, Lage f; (job) Stelle f; (location) Lage f; **"~s vacant** or **wanted"** „Stellenangebote"
situation comedy n (TV) Situationskomödie f
six [sɪks] num sechs
six-pack ['sɪkspæk] n Sechserpack m
sixteen [sɪks'tiːn] num sechzehn
sixth [sɪksθ] num sechste(r, s); **the upper/lower ~** (Brit: Scol) ≈ die Ober-/Unterprima
sixty ['sɪkstɪ] num sechzig
size [saɪz] n Größe f; (extent) Ausmaß nt; **I take ~ 14** ich habe Größe 14; **the small/large ~** (of soap powder etc) die kleine/große Packung; **it's the ~ of** ... es ist so groß wie ...; **cut to ~** auf die richtige Größe zurechtgeschnitten
  ▸ **size up** vt einschätzen
sizeable ['saɪzəbl] adj ziemlich groß; (income etc) ansehnlich
sizzle ['sɪzl] vi brutzeln
SK (Canada) abbr (= Saskatchewan)
skate [skeɪt] n (also: **ice skate**) Schlittschuh m; (also: **roller skate**) Rollschuh m; (fish: pl inv) Rochen m ▸ vi Schlittschuh laufen
  ▸ **skate around** vt fus (problem, issue) einfach übergehen
  ▸ **skate over** vt fus = **skate around**
skateboard ['skeɪtbɔːd] n Skateboard nt
skater ['skeɪtər] n Schlittschuhläufer(in) m(f)
skating ['skeɪtɪŋ] n Eislauf m
skating rink n Eisbahn f
skeleton ['skɛlɪtn] n Skelett nt ▸ attrib (plan, outline) skizzenhaft
skeleton key n Dietrich m; Nachschlüssel m
skeleton staff n Minimalbesetzung f
skeptic etc ['skɛptɪk] (US) = **sceptic** etc
sketch [skɛtʃ] n Skizze f; (Theat, TV) Sketch m ▸ vt skizzieren; (also: **sketch out**: ideas) umreißen
sketchbook ['skɛtʃbuk] n Skizzenbuch nt
sketchpad ['skɛtʃpæd] n Skizzenblock m
sketchy ['skɛtʃɪ] adj (coverage) oberflächlich; (notes etc) bruchstückhaft
skew [skjuː] adj schief
skewed [skjuːd] adj (distorted) verzerrt
skewer ['skjuːər] n Spieß m
ski [skiː] n Ski m ▸ vi Ski laufen or fahren
ski boot n Skistiefel m
skid [skɪd] n (Aut) Schleudern nt ▸ vi rutschen; (Aut) schleudern; **to go into a ~** ins Schleudern geraten or kommen
skid marks npl Reifenspuren pl; (from braking) Bremsspuren pl
skier ['skiːər] n Skiläufer(in) m(f), Skifahrer(in) m(f)
skiing ['skiːɪŋ] n Skilaufen nt, Skifahren nt; **to go ~** Ski laufen or Ski fahren gehen
ski instructor n Skilehrer(in) m(f)
ski jump n (event) Skispringen nt; (ramp) Sprungschanze f
skilful, (US) **skillful** ['skɪlful] adj geschickt
skilfully adv geschickt
ski lift n Skilift m
skill [skɪl] n (ability) Können nt; (dexterity) Geschicklichkeit f; **skills** (acquired abilities) Fähigkeiten pl; **computer/language ~s** Computer-/Sprachkenntnisse pl; **to learn a new ~** etwas Neues lernen
skilled [skɪld] adj (skilful) geschickt; (trained) ausgebildet; (work) qualifiziert
skillet ['skɪlɪt] n Bratpfanne f
skillful etc ['skɪlful] (US) = **skilful** etc
skim [skɪm] vt (also: **skim off**: cream, fat) abschöpfen; (glide over) gleiten über +acc ▸ vi: **to ~ through** (book etc) überfliegen
skimmed milk [skɪmd-] n Magermilch f
skimp [skɪmp] (also: **skimp on**) vt (work etc) nachlässig machen; (cloth etc) sparen an +dat
skimpy ['skɪmpɪ] adj (meagre) dürftig; (too small) knapp
skin [skɪn] n Haut f; (fur) Fell nt; (of fruit) Schale f ▸ vt (animal) häuten; **wet** or **soaked to the ~** nass bis auf die Haut
skin cancer n Hautkrebs m
skin-deep ['skɪn'diːp] adj oberflächlich
skin diver n Sporttaucher(in) m(f)
skin diving n Sporttauchen nt
skinflint ['skɪnflɪnt] n Geizkragen m
skin graft n Hautverpflanzung f
skinhead ['skɪnhɛd] n Skinhead m
skinny ['skɪnɪ] adj dünn
skin test n Hauttest m
skintight ['skɪntaɪt] adj hauteng
skip [skɪp] n Sprung m, Hüpfer m; (Brit: container) (Müll)container m ▸ vi springen, hüpfen; (with rope) seilspringen ▸ vt überspringen; (miss: lunch, lecture) ausfallen lassen; **to ~ school** (esp US) die Schule schwänzen
ski pants npl Skihose f
ski pass n Skipass nt
ski pole n Skistock m
skipper ['skɪpər] n (Naut) Kapitän m; (inf, Sport) Mannschaftskapitän m ▸ vt: **to ~ a boat/team** Kapitän eines Schiffes/einer Mannschaft sein
skipping rope ['skɪpɪŋ-] (Brit) n Sprungseil nt
ski resort n Wintersportort m
skirmish ['skəːmɪʃ] n (Mil) Geplänkel nt; (political etc) Zusammenstoß m
skirt [skəːt] n Rock m ▸ vt (fig) umgehen
skirting board ['skəːtɪŋ-] (Brit) n Fußleiste f
ski run n Skipiste f
ski slope n Skipiste f
ski suit n Skianzug m
skit [skɪt] n Parodie f
ski tow n Schlepplift m
skittle ['skɪtl] n Kegel m
skittles ['skɪtlz] n (game) Kegeln nt
skive [skaɪv] (Brit: inf) vi blaumachen; (from school) schwänzen
skulk [skʌlk] vi sich herumdrücken
skull [skʌl] n Schädel m
skullcap ['skʌlkæp] n Scheitelkäppchen nt
skunk [skʌŋk] n Skunk m, Stinktier nt; (fur) Skunk m
sky [skaɪ] n Himmel m; **to praise sb to the skies** jdn in den Himmel heben

S

783

sky-blue [skaɪ'bluː] adj himmelblau

skydiving ['skaɪdaɪvɪŋ] n Fallschirmspringen nt

sky-high ['skaɪ'haɪ] adj (prices, confidence) himmelhoch ▷ adv: to blow a bridge ~ eine Brücke in die Luft sprengen

skylark ['skaɪlɑːk] n Feldlerche f

skylight ['skaɪlaɪt] n Dachfenster nt

skyline ['skaɪlaɪn] n (horizon) Horizont m; (of city) Skyline f, Silhouette f

Skype® [skaɪp] n (Internet, Tel) Skype nt ▷ vt skypen

skyscraper ['skaɪskreɪpəʳ] n Wolkenkratzer m

slab [slæb] n (stone) Platte f; (of wood) Tafel f; (of cake, cheese) großes Stück nt

slack [slæk] adj (loose) locker; (rope) durchhängend; (skin) schlaff; (careless) nachlässig; (Comm: market) flau; (: demand) schwach; (period) ruhig ▷ n (in rope etc) durchhängendes Teil nt; slacks npl (trousers) Hose f; business is ~ das Geschäft geht schlecht

slacken ['slækn] vi (also: slacken off: speed, rain) nachlassen; (: pace) langsamer werden; (: demand) zurückgehen ▷ vt (grip) lockern; (speed) verringern; (pace) verlangsamen

slag heap [slæg-] n Schlackenhalde f

slag off (Brit: inf) vt (criticize) (he)runtermachen

slain [sleɪn] pp of slay

slake [sleɪk] vt (thirst) stillen

slam [slæm] vt (door) zuschlagen, zuknallen (inf); (throw) knallen (inf); (criticize) verreißen ▷ vi (door) zuschlagen, zuknallen (inf)

slammer ['slæməʳ] (inf) n (prison) Knast m

slander ['slɑːndəʳ] n (Law) Verleumdung f; (insult) Beleidigung f ▷ vt verleumden

slanderous ['slɑːndrəs] adj verleumderisch

slang [slæŋ] n Slang m; (jargon) Jargon m

slanging match ['slæŋɪŋ-] n gegenseitige Beschimpfungen pl

slant [slɑːnt] n Neigung f, Schräge f; (fig: approach) Perspektive f ▷ vi (floor) sich neigen; (ceiling) schräg sein

slanted ['slɑːntɪd] adj (roof) schräg; (eyes) schräg gestellt

slanting ['slɑːntɪŋ] adj = slanted

slap [slæp] n Schlag m, Klaps m ▷ vt schlagen ▷ adv (inf: directly) direkt; to ~ sth on sth etw auf etw acc klatschen

slapdash ['slæpdæʃ] adj nachlässig, schludrig (inf)

slapstick ['slæpstɪk] n Klamauk m

slap-up ['slæpʌp] adj: a ~ meal (Brit) ein Essen mit allem Drum und Dran

slash [slæʃ] vt aufschlitzen; (fig: prices) radikal senken; to ~ one's wrists sich dat die Pulsadern aufschneiden

slat [slæt] n Leiste f, Latte f

slate [sleɪt] n Schiefer m; (piece) Schieferplatte f ▷ vt (criticize) verreißen

slaughter ['slɔːtəʳ] n (of animals) Schlachten nt; (of people) Gemetzel nt ▷ vt (animals) schlachten; (people) abschlachten

slaughterhouse ['slɔːtəhaus] n Schlachthof m

Slav [slɑːv] adj slawisch ▷ n Slawe m, Slawin f

slave [sleɪv] n Sklave m, Sklavin f ▷ vi (also: slave away) sich abplagen, schuften (inf); to ~ (away) at sth sich mit etw herumschlagen

slave-driver ['sleɪvdraɪvəʳ] n Sklaventreiber(in) m(f)

slave labour n Sklavenarbeit f; it's just ~ (fig) es ist die reinste Sklavenarbeit

slaver ['slævəʳ] vi (dribble) geifern

slavery ['sleɪvərɪ] n Sklaverei f

Slavic ['slævɪk] adj slawisch

slavish ['sleɪvɪʃ] adj sklavisch

slavishly ['sleɪvɪʃlɪ] adv sklavisch

Slavonic [slə'vɒnɪk] adj slawisch

slay [sleɪ] (pt slew, pp slain) vt (liter) erschlagen

sleazy ['sliːzɪ] adj schäbig

sledge [slɛdʒ] n Schlitten m

sledgehammer ['slɛdʒhæməʳ] n Vorschlaghammer m

sleek [sliːk] adj glatt, glänzend; (car, boat etc) schnittig

sleep [sliːp] (pt, pp slept) n Schlaf m ▷ vi schlafen ▷ vt: we can ~ 4 bei uns können 4 Leute schlafen; to go to ~ einschlafen; to have a good night's ~ sich richtig ausschlafen; to put to ~ (euph: kill) einschläfern; to ~ lightly einen leichten Schlaf haben; to ~ with sb (euph: have sex) mit jdm schlafen

▶ sleep around vi mit jedem/jeder schlafen

▶ sleep in vi (oversleep) verschlafen; (rise late) lange schlafen

sleeper ['sliːpəʳ] n (train) Schlafwagenzug m; (berth) Platz m im Schlafwagen; (Brit: on track) Schwelle f; (person) Schläfer(in) m(f)

sleepily ['sliːpɪlɪ] adv müde, schläfrig

sleeping accommodation n (beds etc) Schlafgelegenheiten pl

sleeping arrangements npl Bettenverteilung f

sleeping bag n Schlafsack m

sleeping car n Schlafwagen m

sleeping partner (Brit) = silent partner

sleeping pill n Schlaftablette f

sleeping sickness n Schlafkrankheit f

sleepless ['sliːplɪs] adj (night) schlaflos

sleeplessness ['sliːplɪsnɪs] n Schlaflosigkeit f

sleepover ['sliːpəuvəʳ] n Übernachtung f (bei Freunden etc)

sleepwalk ['sliːpwɔːk] vi schlafwandeln

sleepwalker ['sliːpwɔːkəʳ] n Schlafwandler(in) m(f)

sleepy ['sliːpɪ] adj müde, schläfrig; (fig: village etc) verschlafen; to be or feel ~ müde sein

sleet [sliːt] n Schneeregen m

sleeve [sliːv] n Ärmel m; (of record) Hülle f; to have sth up one's ~ (fig) etw in petto haben

sleeveless ['sliːvlɪs] adj (garment) ärmellos

sleigh [sleɪ] n (Pferde)schlitten m

sleight [slaɪt] n: ~ of hand Fingerfertigkeit f

slender ['slɛndəʳ] adj schlank, schmal; (small) knapp

slept [slɛpt] *pt, pp of* **sleep**

sleuth [slu:θ] *n* Detektiv *m*

slew [slu:] *vi* (*Brit: also:* **slew round**) herumschwenken; **the bus ~ed across the road** der Bus rutschte über die Straße ▷ *pt of* **slay**

slice [slaɪs] *n* Scheibe *f*; (*utensil*) Wender *m* ▷ *vt* (in Scheiben) schneiden; **~d bread** aufgeschnittenes Brot *nt*; **the best thing since ~d bread** der/die/das Allerbeste

slick [slɪk] *adj* professionell; (*pej*) glatt ▷ *n* (*also:* **oil slick**) Ölteppich *m*

slid [slɪd] *pt, pp of* **slide**

slide [slaɪd] (*pt, pp* **slid**) *n* (*on ice etc*) Rutschen *nt*; (*fig: to ruin etc*) Abgleiten *nt*; (*in playground*) Rutschbahn *f*; (*Phot*) Dia *nt*; (*Brit: also:* **hair slide**) Spange *f*; (*microscope slide*) Objektträger *m*; (*in prices*) Preisrutsch *m* ▷ *vt* schieben ▷ *vi* (*slip*) rutschen; (*glide*) gleiten; **to let things ~** (*fig*) die Dinge schleifen lassen

slide projector *n* Diaprojektor *m*

slide rule *n* Rechenschieber *m*

sliding ['slaɪdɪŋ] *adj* (*door, window etc*) Schiebe-

sliding roof *n* (*Aut*) Schiebedach *nt*

sliding scale *n* gleitende Skala *f*

slight [slaɪt] *adj* zierlich; (*small*) gering; (*error, accent, pain etc*) leicht; (*trivial*) leicht ▷ *n*: **a ~ (on sb/sth)** ein Affront *m* (gegen jdn/etw); **the ~est noise** der geringste Lärm; **the ~est problem** das kleinste Problem; **I haven't the ~est idea** ich habe nicht die geringste Ahnung; **not in the ~est** nicht im Geringsten

slightly ['slaɪtlɪ] *adv* etwas, ein bisschen; **~ built** zierlich

slim [slɪm] *adj* schlank; (*chance*) gering ▷ *vi* eine Schlankheitskur machen, abnehmen

slime [slaɪm] *n* Schleim *m*

slimming ['slɪmɪŋ] *n* Abnehmen *nt*

slimy ['slaɪmɪ] *adj* (*lit, fig*) schleimig

sling [slɪŋ] (*pt, pp* **slung**) *n* Schlinge *f*; (*for baby*) Tragetuch *nt*; (*weapon*) Schleuder *f* ▷ *vt* schleudern; **to have one's arm in a ~** den Arm in der Schlinge tragen

slingshot ['slɪŋʃɒt] *n* Steinschleuder *f*

slink [slɪŋk] (*pt, pp* **slunk**) *vi*: **to ~ away** *or* **off** sich davonschleichen

slinky ['slɪŋkɪ] *adj* (*dress*) eng anliegend

slip [slɪp] *n* (*fall*) Ausrutschen *nt*; (*mistake*) Fehler *m*, Schnitzer *m*; (*underskirt*) Unterrock *m*; (*also:* **slip of paper**) Zettel *m* ▷ *vt* (*slide*) stecken ▷ *vi* ausrutschen; (*decline*) fallen; **he had a nasty ~** er ist ausgerutscht und böse gefallen; **to give sb the ~** jdm entwischen; **a ~ of the tongue** ein Versprecher *m*; **to ~ into/out of sth, to ~ sth on/off** in etw *acc*/ aus etw schlüpfen; **to let a chance ~ by** eine Gelegenheit ungenutzt lassen; **it ~ped from her hand** es rutschte ihr aus der Hand

▶ **slip away** *vi* sich davonschleichen

▶ **slip in** *vt* stecken in +*acc*

▶ **slip out** *vi* kurz weggehen

▶ **slip up** *vi* sich vertun (*inf*)

slip-on ['slɪpɒn] *adj* zum Überziehen; **~ shoes**

Slipper *pl*

slipped disc [slɪpt-] *n* Bandscheibenschaden *m*

slipper ['slɪpə^r] *n* Pantoffel *m*, Hausschuh *m*

slippery ['slɪpərɪ] *adj* (*lit, fig*) glatt; (*fish etc*) schlüpfrig

slippy ['slɪpɪ] *adj* (*slippery*) glatt

slip road (*Brit*) *n* (*to motorway etc*) Auffahrt *f*; (*from motorway etc*) Ausfahrt *f*

slipshod ['slɪpʃɒd] *adj* schludrig (*inf*)

slipstream ['slɪpstri:m] *n* (*Tech*) Sog *m*; (*Aut*) Windschatten *m*

slip-up ['slɪpʌp] *n* Fehler *m*, Schnitzer *m*

slipway ['slɪpweɪ] *n* (*Naut*) Ablaufbahn *f*

slit [slɪt] (*pt, pp* **~**) *n* Schlitz *m*; (*tear*) Riss *m* ▷ *vt* aufschlitzen; **to ~ sb's throat** jdm die Kehle aufschlitzen

slither ['slɪðə^r] *vi* rutschen; (*snake etc*) gleiten

sliver ['slɪvə^r] *n* (*of glass, wood*) Splitter *m*; (*of cheese etc*) Scheibchen *nt*

slob [slɒb] (*inf*) *n* Drecksau *f* (!)

slog [slɒg] (*Brit*) *vi* (*work hard*) schuften ▷ *n*: **it was a hard ~** es war eine ganz schöne Schufterei; **to ~ away at sth** sich mit etw abrackern

slogan ['sləugən] *n* Slogan *m*

slop [slɒp] *vi* schwappen ▷ *vt* verschütten

▶ **slop out** *vi* (*in prison etc*) den Toiletteneimer ausleeren

slope [sləup] *n* Hügel *m*; (*side of mountain*) Hang *m*; (*ski slope*) Piste *f*; (*slant*) Neigung *f* ▷ *vi*: **to ~ down** abfallen; **to ~ up** ansteigen

sloping ['sləupɪŋ] *adj* (*upwards*) ansteigend; (*downwards*) abfallend; (*roof, handwriting*) schräg

sloppy ['slɒpɪ] *adj* (*work*) nachlässig; (*appearance*) schlampig; (*sentimental*) rührselig

slops [slɒps] *npl* Abfallbrühe *f*

slosh [slɒʃ] (*inf*) *vi*: **to ~ around** *or* **about** (*person*) herumplan(t)schen; (*liquid*) herumschwappen

sloshed [slɒʃt] (*inf*) *adj* (*drunk*) blau

slot [slɒt] *n* Schlitz *m*; (*fig: in timetable*) Termin *m*; (*:, Radio, TV*) Sendezeit *f* ▷ *vt*: **to ~ sth in** etw hineinstecken ▷ *vi*: **to ~ into** sich einfügen lassen in +*acc*

sloth [sləuθ] *n* (*laziness*) Trägheit *f*, Faulheit *f*; (*Zool*) Faultier *nt*

slot machine *n* (*Brit*) Münzautomat *m*; (*for gambling*) Spielautomat *m*

slot meter (*Brit*) *n* Münzzähler *m*

slouch [slautʃ] *vi* eine krumme Haltung haben; (*when walking*) krumm gehen ▷ *vi*: **he's no ~** er hat etwas los (*inf*); **she was ~ed in a chair** sie hing auf einem Stuhl

Slovak ['sləuvæk] *adj* slowakisch ▷ *n* Slowake *m*, Slowakin *f*; (*Ling*) Slowakisch *nt*; **the ~ Republic** die Slowakische Republik

Slovakia [sləu'vækɪə] *n* die Slowakei

Slovakian [sləu'vækɪən] *adj, n* = **Slovak**

Slovene ['sləuvi:n] *n* Slowene *m*, Slowenin *f*; (*Ling*) Slowenisch *nt* ▷ *adj* slowenisch

Slovenia [sləu'vi:nɪə] *n* Slowenien *nt*

Slovenian [sləu'vi:nɪən] *adj, n* = **Slovene**

slovenly ['slʌvənlɪ] *adj* schlampig; (*careless*)

S

nachlässig, schludrig (*inf*)
slow [sləʊ] *adj* langsam; (*not clever*) langsam, begriffsstutzig ▷ *adv* langsam ▷ *vt* (*also*: **slow down, slow up**) verlangsamen; (*business*) verschlechtern ▷ *vi* (*also*: **slow down, slow up**) sich verlangsamen; (*business*) schlechter gehen; **to be ~** (*watch, clock*) nachgehen; "**~**" „langsam fahren"; **at a ~ speed** langsam; **to be ~ to act** sich *dat* Zeit lassen; **to be ~ to decide** lange brauchen, um sich zu entscheiden; **my watch is 20 minutes ~** meine Uhr geht 20 Minuten nach; **business is ~** das Geschäft geht schlecht; **to go ~** (*driver*) langsam fahren; (*Brit*: *in industrial dispute*) einen Bummelstreik machen
slow-acting [sləʊˈæktɪŋ] *adj* mit Langzeitwirkung
slow food *n* Slow Food *nt*
slowly [ˈsləʊlɪ] *adv* langsam
slow motion *n*: **in ~** in Zeitlupe
slow-moving [sləʊˈmuːvɪŋ] *adj* langsam; (*traffic*) kriechend
slowness [ˈsləʊnɪs] *n* Langsamkeit *f*
sludge [slʌdʒ] *n* Schlamm *m*
slue [sluː] (*US*) *vi* = **slew**
slug [slʌg] *n* Nacktschnecke *f*; (*US*: *inf*: *bullet*) Kugel *f*
sluggish [ˈslʌgɪʃ] *adj* träge; (*engine*) lahm; (*Comm*) flau
sluice [sluːs] *n* Schleuse *f*; (*channel*) (Wasch)rinne *f* ▷ *vt*: **to ~ down** *or* **out** abspritzen
slum [slʌm] *n* Slum *m*, Elendsviertel *nt*
slumber [ˈslʌmbə‌ᵊ] *n* Schlaf *m*
slump [slʌmp] *n* Rezession *f* ▷ *vi* fallen; **~ in sales** Absatzflaute *f*; **~ in prices** Preissturz *m*; **he was ~ed over the wheel** er war über dem Steuer zusammengesackt
slung [slʌŋ] *pt*, *pp of* **sling**
slunk [slʌŋk] *pt*, *pp of* **slink**
slur [slɜː‌ʳ] *n* (*fig*): **~ (on)** Beleidigung *f* (für) ▷ *vt* (*words*) undeutlich aussprechen; **to cast a ~ on** verunglimpfen
slurp [sləːp] (*inf*) *vt*, *vi* schlürfen
slurred [sləːd] *adj* (*speech, voice*) undeutlich
slush [slʌʃ] *n* (*melted snow*) Schneematsch *m*
slush fund *n* Schmiergelder *pl*, Schmiergeldfonds *m*
slushy [ˈslʌʃɪ] *adj* matschig; (*Brit*: *fig*) schmalzig
slut [slʌt] (*pej*) *n* Schlampe *f*
sly [slaɪ] *adj* (*smile, expression*) wissend; (*remark*) vielsagend; (*person*) schlau, gerissen; **on the ~** heimlich
S/M *n abbr* (= *sadomasochism*) S/M
smack [smæk] *n* Klaps *m*; (*on face*) Ohrfeige *f* ▷ *vt* (*hit*) schlagen; (: *child*) einen Klaps geben +*dat*; (: *on face*) ohrfeigen ▷ *vi*: **to ~ of** riechen nach ▷ *adv*: **it fell ~ in the middle** (*inf*) es fiel genau in die Mitte; **to ~ one's lips** schmatzen
smacker [ˈsmækə‌ʳ] (*inf*) *n* (*kiss*) Schmatzer *m*
small [smɔːl] *adj* klein ▷ *n*: **the ~ of the back** das Kreuz; **to get** *or* **grow ~er** (*thing*) kleiner werden; (*numbers*) zurückgehen; **to make ~er** (*amount, income*) kürzen; (*object, garment*)

kleiner machen; **a ~ shopkeeper** der Inhaber eines kleinen Geschäfts; **a ~ business** ein Kleinunternehmen *nt*
small ads (*Brit*) *npl* Kleinanzeigen *pl*
small arms *n* Handfeuerwaffen *pl*
small business *n* Kleinunternehmen *nt*
small change *n* Kleingeld *nt*
small fry *npl* (*unimportant people*) kleine Fische *pl*
smallholder [ˈsmɔːlhəʊldə‌ʳ] (*Brit*) *n* Kleinbauer *m*
smallholding [ˈsmɔːlhəʊldɪŋ] (*Brit*) *n* kleiner Landbesitz *m*
small hours *npl*: **in the ~** in den frühen Morgenstunden
smallish [ˈsmɔːlɪʃ] *adj* ziemlich klein
small-minded [smɔːlˈmaɪndɪd] *adj* engstirnig
smallpox [ˈsmɔːlpɒks] *n* Pocken *pl*
small print *n*: **the ~** das Kleingedruckte
small-scale [ˈsmɔːlskeɪl] *adj* (*map, model*) in verkleinertem Maßstab; (*business, farming*) klein angelegt
small talk *n* (oberflächliche) Konversation *f*
small-time [ˈsmɔːltaɪm] *adj* (*farmer etc*) klein; **a ~ thief** ein kleiner Ganove
small-town [ˈsmɔːltaʊn] *adj* kleinstädtisch
smarmy [ˈsmɑːmɪ] (*Brit*: *pej*) *adj* schmierig
smart [smɑːt] *adj* (*neat*) ordentlich, gepflegt; (*fashionable*) chic *inv*, elegant; (*clever*) intelligent, clever (*inf*); (*quick*) schnell ▷ *vi* (*sting*) brennen; (*suffer*) leiden; **the ~ set** die Schickeria (*inf*); **and look ~ (about it)!** und zwar ein bisschen plötzlich! (*inf*)
smart card *n* Chipkarte *f*
smarten up [ˈsmɑːtn-] *vi* sich fein machen ▷ *vt* verschönern
smartphone [ˈsmɑːtfəʊn] *n* (*Tel*) Smartphone *nt*, Internethandy *nt*
smash [smæʃ] *n* (*also*: **smash-up**) Unfall *m*; (*sound*) Krachen *nt*; (*song, play, film*) Superhit *m*; (*Tennis*) Schmetterball *m* ▷ *vt* (*break*) zerbrechen; (*car etc*) kaputt fahren; (*hopes*) zerschlagen; (*Sport*: *record*) haushoch schlagen ▷ *vi* (*break*) zerbrechen; (*against wall, into sth etc*) krachen
▶ **smash up** *vt* (*car*) kaputt fahren; (*room*) kurz und klein schlagen (*inf*)
smash hit *n* Superhit *m*
smashing [ˈsmæʃɪŋ] (*inf*) *adj* super, toll
smattering [ˈsmætərɪŋ] *n*: **a ~ of Greek** *etc* ein paar Brocken Griechisch *etc*
smear [smɪə‌ʳ] *n* (*trace*) verschmierter Fleck *m*; (*insult*) Verleumdung *f*; (*Med*) Abstrich *m* ▷ *vt* (*spread*) verschmieren; (*make dirty*) beschmieren; **his hands were ~ed with oil** seine Hände waren mit Öl beschmiert
smear campaign *n* Verleumdungskampagne *f*
smear test *n* Abstrich *m*
smell [smel] (*pt*, *pp* **smelt** *or* **~ed**) *n* Geruch *m*; (*sense*) Geruchssinn *m* ▷ *vt* riechen ▷ *vi* riechen; (*pej*) stinken; (*pleasantly*) duften; **to ~ of** riechen nach
smelly [ˈsmelɪ] (*pej*) *adj* stinkend
smelt [smelt] *pt*, *pp of* **smell** ▷ *vt* schmelzen

smile [smaɪl] n Lächeln nt ▷ vi lächeln
smiling ['smaɪlɪŋ] adj lächelnd
smirk [smɜ:k] (pej) n Grinsen nt
smithy ['smɪðɪ] n Schmiede f
smitten ['smɪtn] adj: ~ **with** vernarrt in +acc
smock [smɔk] n Kittel m; (US: overall) Overall m
smog [smɔg] n Smog m
smoke [sməuk] n Rauch m ▷ vi, vt rauchen; **to have a ~** eine rauchen; **to go up in ~** in Rauch (und Flammen) aufgehen; (fig) sich in Rauch auflösen; **do you ~?** rauchen Sie?
smoked [sməukt] adj geräuchert, Räucher-; ~ **glass** Rauchglas nt
smokeless fuel ['sməuklɪs-] n rauchlose Kohle f
smokeless zone (Brit) n rauchfreie Zone f
smoker ['sməukə^r] n Raucher(in) m(f); (Rail) Raucherabteil nt
smoke screen n Rauchvorhang m; (fig) Deckmantel m
smoke shop (US) n Tabakladen m
smoking ['sməukɪŋ] n Rauchen nt; **"no ~"** „Rauchen verboten"
smoking compartment, (US) **smoking car** n Raucherabteil nt
smoking room n Raucherzimmer nt
smoky ['sməukɪ] adj verraucht; (taste) rauchig
smolder ['sməuldə^r] (US) vi = **smoulder**
smoochy ['smu:tʃɪ] adj (music, tape) zum Schmusen
smooth [smu:ð] adj (lit, fig: pej) glatt; (flavour, whisky) weich; (movement) geschmeidig; (flight) ruhig
  ▶ **smooth out** vt glätten; (fig: difficulties) aus dem Weg räumen
  ▶ **smooth over** vt: **to ~ things over** (fig) die Sache bereinigen
smoothly ['smu:ðlɪ] adv reibungslos, glatt; **everything went ~** alles ging glatt über die Bühne
smoothness ['smu:ðnɪs] n Glätte f; (of flight) Ruhe f
smother ['smʌðə^r] vt (fire, person) ersticken; (repress) unterdrücken
smoulder, (US) **smolder** ['sməuldə^r] vi (lit, fig) glimmen, schwelen
SMS n abbr (= Short Message Service) SMS m
smudge [smʌdʒ] n Schmutzfleck m ▷ vt verwischen
smug [smʌg] (pej) adj selbstgefällig
smuggle ['smʌgl] vt schmuggeln; **to ~ in/out** einschmuggeln/herausschmuggeln
smuggler ['smʌglə^r] n Schmuggler(in) m(f)
smuggling ['smʌglɪŋ] n Schmuggel m
smut [smʌt] n (grain of soot) Rußflocke f; (in conversation etc) Schmutz m
smutty ['smʌtɪ] adj (fig: joke, book) schmutzig
snack [snæk] n Kleinigkeit f (zu essen); **to have a ~** eine Kleinigkeit essen
snack bar n Imbissstube f
snag [snæg] n Haken m, Schwierigkeit f
snail [sneɪl] n Schnecke f
snake [sneɪk] n Schlange f

snap [snæp] n Knacken nt; (photograph) Schnappschuss m; (card game) ≈ Schnippschnapp nt ▷ adj (decision) plötzlich, spontan ▷ vt (break) (zer)brechen ▷ vi (break) (zer)brechen; (rope, thread etc) reißen; **a cold ~** ein Kälteeinbruch m; **his patience ~ped** ihm riss der Geduldsfaden; **his temper ~ped** er verlor die Beherrschung; **to ~ one's fingers** mit den Fingern schnipsen or schnalzen; **to ~ open/shut** auf-/zuschnappen
  ▶ **snap at** vt fus (dog) schnappen nach; (fig: person) anschnauzen (inf)
  ▶ **snap off** vt (break) abbrechen
  ▶ **snap up** vt (bargains) wegschnappen
snap fastener n Druckknopf m
snappy ['snæpɪ] (inf) adj (answer) kurz und treffend; (slogan) zündend; **make it ~** ein bisschen dalli!; **he is a ~ dresser** er zieht sich flott an
snapshot ['snæpʃɔt] n Schnappschuss m
snare [snεə^r] n Falle f ▷ vt (lit, fig) fangen
snarl [snɑ:l] vi knurren ▷ vt: **to get ~ed up** (plans) durcheinanderkommen; (traffic) stocken
snarl-up ['snɑ:lʌp] n Verkehrschaos nt
snatch [snætʃ] n (of conversation) Fetzen m; (of song) paar Takte pl ▷ vt (grab) greifen; (steal) stehlen, klauen (inf); (child) entführen; (fig: opportunity) ergreifen; (: look) werfen ▷ vi: **don't ~!** nicht grapschen!; **to ~ a sandwich** schnell ein Butterbrot essen; **to ~ some sleep** etwas Schlaf ergattern
  ▶ **snatch up** vt schnappen
snazzy ['snæzɪ] (inf) adj flott
sneak [sni:k] (pt **snuck**) (US) vi: **to ~ in/out** sich einschleichen/sich hinausschleichen ▷ vt: **to ~ a look at sth** heimlich auf etw acc schielen ▷ n (inf: pej) Petze f
  ▶ **sneak up** vi: **to ~ up on sb** sich an jdn heranschleichen
sneakers ['sni:kəz] npl Freizeitschuhe pl
sneaking ['sni:kɪŋ] adj: **to have a ~ feeling/suspicion that …** das ungute Gefühl/den leisen Verdacht haben, dass …
sneaky ['sni:kɪ] (pej) adj raffiniert
sneer [snɪə^r] vi (smile nastily) spöttisch lächeln; (mock): **to ~ at** verspotten ▷ n (smile) spöttisches Lächeln nt; (remark) spöttische Bemerkung f
sneeze [sni:z] n Niesen nt ▷ vi niesen
  ▶ **sneeze at** vt fus: **it's not to be ~d at** es ist nicht zu verachten
snicker ['snɪkə^r] vi see **snigger**
snide [snaɪd] (pej) adj abfällig
sniff [snɪf] n Schniefen nt; (smell) Schnüffeln nt ▷ vi schniefen ▷ vt riechen, schnuppern an +dat; (glue) schnüffeln
sniffer dog ['snɪfə-] n Spürhund m
snigger ['snɪgə^r] vi kichern
snip [snɪp] n Schnitt m; (Brit: inf: bargain) Schnäppchen nt ▷ vt schnippeln; **to ~ sth off/through sth** etw abschnippeln/durchschnippeln

S

sniper ['snaɪpə'] *n* Heckenschütze *m*

snippet ['snɪpɪt] *n* (*of information*) Bruchstück *nt*; (*of conversation*) Fetzen *m*

snivelling, (US) **sniveling** ['snɪvlɪn] *adj* heulend

snob [snɒb] *n* Snob *m*

snobbery ['snɒbərɪ] *n* Snobismus *m*

snobbish ['snɒbɪʃ] *adj* snobistisch, versnobt (*inf*)

snog [snɒg] (*Brit: inf*) *n* Knutscherei *f*; **to have a ~ with sb** mit jdm (rum)knutschen ▷ *vi* (rum)knutschen

snooker ['snuːkə'] *n* Snooker *nt* ▷ *vt* (*Brit: inf*): **to be ~ed** festsitzen

snoop [snuːp] *vi*: **to ~ about** herumschnüffeln; **to ~ on sb** jdm nachschnüffeln

snooper ['snuːpə'] *n* Schnüffler(in) *m(f)*

snooty ['snuːtɪ] *adj* hochnäsig

snooze [snuːz] *n* Schläfchen *nt* ▷ *vi* ein Schläfchen machen

snore [snɔː'] *n* Schnarchen *nt* ▷ *vi* schnarchen

snoring ['snɔːrɪn] *n* Schnarchen *nt*

snorkel ['snɔːkl] *n* Schnorchel *m*

snort [snɔːt] *n* Schnauben *nt* ▷ *vi* (*animal*) schnauben; (*person*) prusten ▷ *vt* (*inf: cocaine*) schnüffeln

snotty ['snɒtɪ] (*inf*) *adj* (*handkerchief, nose*) Rotz-; (*pej: snobbish*) hochnäsig

snout [snaut] *n* Schnauze *f*

snow [snəu] *n* Schnee *m* ▷ *vi* schneien ▷ *vt*: **to be ~ed under with work** mit Arbeit reichlich eingedeckt sein; **it's ~ing** es schneit

snowball ['snəubɔːl] *n* Schneeball *m* ▷ *vi* (*fig: problem*) eskalieren; (: *campaign*) ins Rollen kommen

snowbound ['snəubaund] *adj* eingeschneit

snow-capped ['snəukæpt] *adj* schneebedeckt

snowdrift ['snəudrɪft] *n* Schneewehe *f*

snowdrop ['snəudrɒp] *n* Schneeglöckchen *nt*

snowfall ['snəufɔːl] *n* Schneefall *m*

snowflake ['snəufleɪk] *n* Schneeflocke *f*

snowline ['snəulaɪn] *n* Schneegrenze *f*

snowman ['snəumæn] (*irreg: like* **man**) *n* Schneemann *m*

snowplough, (US) **snowplow** ['snəuplau] *n* Schneepflug *m*

snowshoe ['snəuʃuː] *n* Schneeschuh *m*

snowstorm ['snəustɔːm] *n* Schneesturm *m*

snowy ['snəuɪ] *adj* schneeweiß; (*covered with snow*) verschneit

SNP (*Brit*) *n abbr* (*Pol*) = **Scottish National Party**

snub [snʌb] *vt* (*person*) vor den Kopf stoßen ▷ *n* Abfuhr *f*

snub-nosed [snʌb'nəuzd] *adj* stupsnasig

snuff [snʌf] *n* Schnupftabak *m* ▷ *vt* (*also:* **snuff out**: *candle*) auslöschen

snuff movie *n* Pornofilm, in dem jemand tatsächlich stirbt

snug [snʌg] *adj* behaglich, gemütlich; (*well-fitting*) gut sitzend; **it's a ~ fit** es passt genau

snuggle ['snʌgl] *vi*: **to ~ up to sb** sich an jdn kuscheln; **to ~ down in bed** sich ins Bett kuscheln

snugly ['snʌglɪ] *adv* behaglich; **it fits ~** (*object in pocket etc*) es passt genau hinein; (*garment*) es passt wie angegossen

SO *n abbr* (*Banking*) = **standing order**

 KEYWORD

so [səu] *adv* **1** (*thus, likewise*) so; **so saying he walked away** mit diesen Worten ging er weg; **if so** falls ja; **I didn't do it — you did so!** ich hab es nicht getan — hast du wohl!; **so do I, so am I** *etc* ich auch; **it's 5 o'clock — so it is!** es ist 5 Uhr — tatsächlich!; **I hope/think so** ich hoffe/glaube ja; **so far** bis jetzt

2 (*in comparisons etc: to such a degree*) so; **so big/ quickly (that)** so groß/schnell(, dass); **I'm so glad to see you** ich bin ja so froh, dich zu sehen

3: **so much** so viel; **I've got so much work** ich habe so viel Arbeit; **I love you so much** ich liebe dich so sehr; **so many** so viele

4 (*phrases*): **10 or so** 10 oder so; **so long!** (*inf: goodbye*) tschüss!

▷ *conj* **1** (*expressing purpose*): **so as to do sth** um etw zu tun; **so (that)** damit

2 (*expressing result*) also; **so I was right after all** ich hatte also doch Recht; **so you see, I could have gone** wie Sie sehen, hätte ich gehen können; **so (what)?** na und?

soak [səuk] *vt* (*drench*) durchnässen; (*steep*) einweichen ▷ *vi* einweichen; **to be ~ed through** völlig durchnässt sein
 ▶ **soak in** *vi* einziehen
 ▶ **soak up** *vt* aufsaugen

soaking ['səukɪn] *adj* (*also:* **soaking wet**) patschnass

so-and-so ['səuənsəu] *n* (*somebody*) Soundso *no art*; **Mr/Mrs ~** Herr/Frau Soundso; **the little ~!** (*pej*) das Biest!

soap [səup] *n* Seife *f*; (*TV: also:* **soap opera**) Fernsehserie *f*, Seifenoper *f* (*inf*)

soapbox ['səupbɒks] *n* (*lit*) Seifenkiste *f*; (*fig: platform*) Apfelsinenkiste *f*

soapflakes ['səupfleɪks] *npl* Seifenflocken *pl*

soap opera *n* (*TV*) Fernsehserie *f*, Seifenoper *f* (*inf*)

soap powder *n* Seifenpulver *nt*

soapsuds ['səupsʌdz] *npl* Seifenschaum *m*

soapy ['səupɪ] *adj* seifig; **~ water** Seifenwasser *nt*

soar [sɔː'] *vi* aufsteigen; (*price, temperature*) hochschnellen; (*building etc*) aufragen

soaring ['sɔːrɪn] *adj* (*prices*) in die Höhe schnellend; (*inflation*) unaufhaltsam

sob [sɒb] *n* Schluchzer *m* ▷ *vi* schluchzen

s.o.b. (US: *inf!*) *n abbr* (= *son of a bitch*) Scheißkerl *m*

sober ['səubə'] *adj* nüchtern; (*serious*) ernst; (*colour*) gedeckt; (*style*) schlicht
 ▶ **sober up** *vt* nüchtern machen ▷ *vi* nüchtern werden

sobriety [sə'braɪətɪ] *n* Nüchternheit *f*;

(seriousness) Ernst *m*
sobriquet ['səʊbrɪkeɪ] *n* Spitzname *m*
sob story *n* rührselige Geschichte *f*
Soc. *abbr* (= *society*) Ges.
so-called ['səʊ'kɔ:ld] *adj* sogenannt
soccer ['sɔkə^r] *n* Fußball *m*
soccer pitch *n* Fußballplatz *m*
soccer player *n* Fußballspieler(in) *m(f)*
sociable ['səʊʃəbl] *adj* gesellig
social ['səʊʃl] *adj* sozial; *(history)* Sozial-;
(structure) Gesellschafts-; *(event, contact)*
gesellschaftlich; *(person)* gesellig; *(animal)*
gesellig lebend ▷ *n* (party) geselliger Abend
m; ~ **life** gesellschaftliches Leben *nt*; **to**
have no ~ life nicht mit anderen Leuten
zusammenkommen
social climber *(pej)* *n* Emporkömmling *m*,
sozialer Aufsteiger *m*
social club *n* Klub *m* für geselliges
Beisammensein
Social Democrat *n* Sozialdemokrat(in) *m(f)*
social insurance (US) *n* Sozialversicherung *f*
socialism ['səʊʃəlɪzəm] *n* Sozialismus *m*
socialist ['səʊʃəlɪst] *adj* sozialistisch ▷ *n*
Sozialist(in) *m(f)*
socialite ['səʊʃəlaɪt] *n* Angehörige(r) *f(m)* der
Schickeria
socialize ['səʊʃəlaɪz] *vi* unter die Leute
kommen; **to ~ with** *(meet socially)*
gesellschaftlich verkehren mit; *(chat to)* sich
unterhalten mit
socially ['səʊʃəlɪ] *adv* *(visit)* privat; *(acceptable)*
in Gesellschaft
social networking [-'nɛtwə:kɪŋ] *n*
Netzwerken *nt*
social science *n* Sozialwissenschaft *f*
social security (Brit) *n* Sozialhilfe *f*;
Department of Social Security Ministerium
nt für Soziales
social services *npl* soziale Einrichtungen *pl*
social welfare *n* soziales Wohl *nt*
social work *n* Sozialarbeit *f*
social worker *n* Sozialarbeiter(in) *m(f)*
society [sə'saɪətɪ] *n* Gesellschaft *f*; *(people,*
their lifestyle) die Gesellschaft; *(club)* Verein *m*;
(also: **high society**) High Society *f* ▷ *cpd* (party,
lady) Gesellschafts-
socioeconomic ['səʊsɪəʊi:kə'nɒmɪk] *adj*
sozioökonomisch
sociological [səʊsɪə'lɒdʒɪkl] *adj* soziologisch
sociologist [səʊsɪ'ɒlədʒɪst] *n* Soziologe *m*,
Soziologin *f*
sociology [səʊsɪ'ɒlədʒɪ] *n* Soziologie *f*
sock [sɔk] *n* Socke *f* ▷ *vt* (inf: hit) hauen; **to pull**
one's ~s up (fig) sich am Riemen reißen
socket ['sɔkɪt] *n* *(of eye)* Augenhöhle *f*; *(of joint)*
Gelenkpfanne *f*; *(Brit: Elec: also:* **wall socket**)
Steckdose *f*; *(: for light bulb)* Fassung *f*
sod [sɔd] *n* *(earth)* Sode *f*; *(Brit: inf!)* Sau *f* (!); **the**
poor ~ das arme Schwein
▷ **sod off** *(Brit: inf!)* *vi*: **~ off!** verpiss dich!
soda ['səʊdə] *n* Soda *nt*; *(also:* **soda water**)
Soda(wasser) *nt*; *(US: also:* **soda pop**) Brause *f*

sodden ['sɔdn] *adj* durchnässt
sodium ['səʊdɪəm] *n* Natrium *nt*
sodium chloride *n* Natriumchlorid *nt*,
Kochsalz *nt*
sofa ['səʊfə] *n* Sofa *nt*
Sofia ['səʊfɪə] *n* Sofia *nt*
soft [sɔft] *adj* weich; *(not rough)* zart; *(voice,*
music, light, colour) gedämpft; *(lenient)*
nachsichtig; ~ **in the head** *(inf)* nicht ganz
richtig im Kopf
soft benefits *npl* ▷ *econ* nicht monetäre
(betriebliche) Leistungen *pl*
soft-boiled ['sɔftbɔɪld] *adj (egg)* weich (gekocht)
soft drink *n* alkoholfreies Getränk *nt*
soft drugs *npl* weiche Drogen *pl*
soften ['sɔfn] *vt* weich machen; *(effect, blow)*
mildern ▷ *vi* weich werden; *(voice, expression)*
sanfter werden
softener ['sɔfnə^r] *n* *(also:* **water softener**)
Enthärtungsmittel *nt*; *(also:* **fabric softener**)
Weichspüler *m*
soft fruit *(Brit)* *n* Beerenobst *nt*
soft furnishings *npl* Raumtextilien *pl*
soft-hearted [sɔft'ha:tɪd] *adj* weichherzig
softly ['sɔftlɪ] *adv (gently)* sanft; *(quietly)* leise
softness ['sɔftnɪs] *n* Weichheit *f*; *(gentleness)*
Sanftheit *f*
soft option *n* Weg *m* des geringsten
Widerstandes
soft sell *n* weiche Verkaufstaktik *f*
soft spot *n*: **to have a ~ for sb** eine Schwäche
für jdn haben
soft target *n* leicht verwundbares Ziel *nt*
soft toy *n* Stofftier *nt*
software ['sɔftwɛə^r] *n* *(Comput)* Software *f*
software package *n* *(Comput)* Softwarepaket *nt*
soft water *n* weiches Wasser *nt*
soggy ['sɔgɪ] *adj (ground)* durchweicht;
(sandwiches etc) matschig
soil [sɔɪl] *n* Erde *f*, Boden *m* ▷ *vt* beschmutzen
soiled [sɔɪld] *adj* schmutzig
sojourn ['sɔdʒə:n] *(form)* *n* Aufenthalt *m*
solace ['sɔlɪs] *n* Trost *m*
solar ['səʊlə^r] *adj (eclipse, power station etc)*
Sonnen-
solarium [sə'lɛərɪəm] *(pl* **solaria**) *n* Solarium *nt*
solar panel *n* Sonnenkollektor *m*
solar plexus [-'plɛksəs] *n* *(Anat)* Solarplexus *m*,
Magengrube *f*
solar power *n* Sonnenenergie *f*
solar system *n* Sonnensystem *nt*
solar wind *n* Sonnenwind *m*
sold [səʊld] *pt, pp of* **sell**
solder ['səʊldə^r] *vt* löten ▷ *n* Lötmittel *nt*
soldier ['səʊldʒə^r] *n* Soldat *m* ▷ *vi*: **to ~**
on unermüdlich weitermachen; **toy ~**
Spielzeugsoldat *m*
sold out *adj* ausverkauft
sole [səʊl] *n* Sohle *f*; *(fish: pl inv)* Seezunge *f*
▷ *adj* einzig, Allein-; *(exclusive)* alleinig; **the ~**
reason der einzige Grund
solely ['səʊllɪ] *adv* nur, ausschließlich; **I will**
hold you ~ responsible ich mache Sie allein

S

dafür verantwortlich

solemn ['soləm] *adj* feierlich; *(person)* ernst

sole trader *n* *(Comm)* Einzelunternehmer *m*

solicit [sə'lɪsɪt] *vt* *(request)* erbitten, bitten um ▷ *vi* *(prostitute)* Kunden anwerben

solicitor [sə'lɪsɪtə^r] *(Brit)* *n* Rechtsanwalt *m*, Rechtsanwältin *f*

solid ['sɒlɪd] *adj* *(not hollow, pure)* massiv; *(not liquid)* fest; *(reliable)* zuverlässig; *(strong: structure)* stabil; *(: foundations)* solide; *(substantial: advice)* gut; *(: experience)* solide; *(unbroken)* ununterbrochen ▷ *n* *(solid object)* Festkörper *m*; **solids** *npl* *(food)* feste Nahrung *f*; **to be on ~ ground** *(fig)* sich auf festem Boden befinden; **I read for 2 hours ~** ich habe 2 Stunden ununterbrochen gelesen

solidarity [sɒlɪ'dærɪtɪ] *n* Solidarität *f*

solid fuel *n* fester Brennstoff *m*

solidify [sə'lɪdɪfaɪ] *vi* fest werden ▷ *vt* fest werden lassen

solidity [sə'lɪdɪtɪ] *n* *(of structure)* Stabilität *f*; *(of foundations)* Solidität *f*

solidly ['sɒlɪdlɪ] *adv* *(built)* solide; *(in favour)* geschlossen, einmütig; **a ~ respectable family** eine durch und durch respektable Familie

solid-state ['sɒlɪdsteɪt] *adj* *(Elec: equipment)* Halbleiter-

soliloquy [sə'lɪləkwɪ] *n* Monolog *m*

solitaire [sɒlɪ'teə^r] *n* *(gem)* Solitär *m*; *(game)* Patience *f*

solitary ['sɒlɪtərɪ] *adj* einsam; *(single)* einzeln

solitary confinement *n* Einzelhaft *f*

solitude ['sɒlɪtjuːd] *n* Einsamkeit *f*; **to live in ~** einsam leben

solo ['səʊləʊ] *n* Solo *nt* ▷ *adv* *(fly)* allein; *(play, perform)* solo; **~ flight** Alleinflug *m*

soloist ['səʊləʊɪst] *n* Solist(in) *m(f)*

Solomon Islands ['sɒləmən-] *npl*: **the ~** die Salomoninseln *pl*

solstice ['sɒlstɪs] *n* Sonnenwende *f*

soluble ['sɒljʊbl] *adj* löslich

solution [sə'luːʃən] *n* *(answer, liquid)* Lösung *f*; *(to crossword)* Auflösung *f*

solve [sɒlv] *vt* lösen; *(mystery)* enträtseln

solvency ['sɒlvənsɪ] *n* *(Comm)* Zahlungsfähigkeit *f*

solvent ['sɒlvənt] *adj* *(Comm)* zahlungsfähig ▷ *n* *(Chem)* Lösungsmittel *nt*

solvent abuse *n* Lösungsmittelmissbrauch *m*

Som. *(Brit)* *abbr* *(Post)* = **Somerset**

Somali [sə'mɑːlɪ] *adj* somalisch ▷ *n* Somalier(in) *m(f)*

Somalia [sə'mɑːlɪə] *n* Somalia *nt*

Somaliland *n* *(formerly)* Somaliland *nt*

sombre, *(US)* **somber** ['sɒmbə^r] *adj* *(dark)* dunkel, düster; *(serious)* finster

 KEYWORD

some [sʌm] *adj* **1** *(a certain amount or number of)* einige; **some tea/water/money** etwas Tee/Wasser/Geld; **some biscuits** ein

paar Plätzchen; **some children came** einige Kinder kamen; **he asked me some questions** er stellte mir ein paar Fragen

2 *(certain: in contrasts)* manche(r, s); **some people say that ...** manche Leute sagen, dass ...; **some films were excellent** einige *or* manche Filme waren ausgezeichnet

3 *(unspecified)* irgendein(e); **some woman was asking for you** eine Frau hat nach Ihnen gefragt; **some day** eines Tages; **some day next week** irgendwann nächste Woche; **that's some house!** das ist vielleicht ein Haus!

▷ *pron* **1** *(a certain number)* einige; **I've got some** *(books etc)* ich habe welche

2 *(a certain amount)* etwas; **I've got some** *(money, milk)* ich habe welche(n); **I've read some of the book** ich habe das Buch teilweise gelesen

▷ *adv*: **some 10 people** etwa 10 Leute

somebody ['sʌmbədɪ] *pron* = **someone**

someday ['sʌmdeɪ] *adv* irgendwann

somehow ['sʌmhaʊ] *adv* irgendwie

someone ['sʌmwʌn] *pron* (irgend)jemand; **there's ~ coming** es kommt jemand; **I saw ~ in the garden** ich habe jemanden im Garten gesehen

someplace ['sʌmpleɪs] *(US)* *adv* = **somewhere**

somersault ['sʌməsɔːlt] *n* Salto *m* ▷ *vi* einen Salto machen; *(vehicle)* sich überschlagen

something ['sʌmθɪŋ] *pron* etwas; **~ nice** etwas Schönes; **there's ~ wrong** da stimmt etwas nicht; **would you like ~ to eat/drink?** möchten Sie was zu essen/trinken?

sometime ['sʌmtaɪm] *adv* irgendwann; **~ last month** irgendwann letzten Monat; **I'll finish it ~** ich werde es irgendwann fertig machen

sometimes ['sʌmtaɪmz] *adv* manchmal

somewhat ['sʌmwɒt] *adv* etwas, ein wenig; **~ to my surprise** ziemlich zu meiner Überraschung

somewhere ['sʌmweə^r] *adv* (be) irgendwo; *(go)* irgendwohin; **~ (or other) in Scotland** irgendwo in Schottland; **~ else** (be) woanders; *(go)* woandershin

son [sʌn] *n* Sohn *m*

sonar ['səʊnɑː^r] *n* Sonar(gerät) *nt*, Echolot *nt*

sonata [sə'nɑːtə] *n* Sonate *f*

song [sɒŋ] *n* Lied *nt*; *(of bird)* Gesang *m*

songbook ['sɒŋbʊk] *n* Liederbuch *nt*

songwriter ['sɒŋraɪtə^r] *n* Liedermacher *m*

sonic ['sɒnɪk] *adj* *(speed)* Schall-; **~ boom** Überschallknall *m*

son-in-law ['sʌnɪnlɔː] *n* Schwiegersohn *m*

sonnet ['sɒnɪt] *n* Sonett *nt*

sonny ['sʌnɪ] *(inf)* *n* Junge *m*

soon [suːn] *adv* bald; *(a short time after)* bald, schnell; *(early)* früh; **~ afterwards** kurz *or* bald danach; **quite ~** ziemlich bald; **how ~ can you finish it?** bis wann haben Sie es fertig?; **how ~ can you come back?** wann können Sie frühestens wiederkommen?; **see you ~!** bis bald!; *see also* **as**

sooner ['su:nə^r] *adv (time)* früher, eher; *(preference)* lieber; **I would ~ do that** das würde ich lieber tun; **~ or later** früher oder später; **the ~ the better** je eher, desto besser; **no ~ said than done** gesagt, getan; **no ~ had we left than …** wir waren gerade gegangen, da …

soot [sut] *n* Ruß *m*

soothe [su:ð] *vt* beruhigen; *(pain)* lindern

soothing ['su:ðɪŋ] *adj* beruhigend; *(ointment etc)* schmerzlindernd; *(drink)* wohltuend; *(bath)* entspannend

SOP *n abbr* (= *standard operating procedure*) normale Vorgehensweise *f*

sop [sɔp] *n*: **that's only a ~** das soll nur zur Beschwichtigung dienen

sophisticated [sə'fɪstɪkeɪtɪd] *adj (woman, lifestyle)* kultiviert; *(audience)* anspruchsvoll; *(machinery)* hoch entwickelt; *(arguments)* differenziert

sophistication [səfɪstɪ'keɪʃən] *n (of person)* Kultiviertheit *f*; *(of machine)* hoher Entwicklungsstand *m*; *(of argument etc)* Differenziertheit *f*

sophomore ['sɔfəmɔ:^r] *(US) n* Student(in) im 2. Studienjahr

soporific [sɔpə'rɪfɪk] *adj* einschläfernd ▷ *n* Schlafmittel *nt*

sopping ['sɔpɪŋ] *adj*: **~ (wet)** völlig durchnässt

soppy ['sɔpɪ] *(pej) adj (person)* sentimental; *(film)* schmalzig

soprano [sə'prɑ:nəu] *n* Sopranist(in) *m(f)*

sorbet ['sɔ:beɪ] *n* Sorbet *nt or m*, Fruchteis *nt*

sorcerer ['sɔ:sərə^r] *n* Hexenmeister *m*

sordid ['sɔ:dɪd] *adj (dirty)* verkommen; *(wretched)* elend

sore [sɔ:^r] *adj* wund; *(esp US: offended)* verärgert, sauer *(inf)* ▷ *n* wunde Stelle *f*; **to have a ~ throat** Halsschmerzen haben; **it's a ~ point** *(fig)* es ist ein wunder Punkt

sorely ['sɔ:lɪ] *adv*: **I am ~ tempted (to)** ich bin sehr in Versuchung(, zu)

soreness ['sɔ:nɪs] *n (pain)* Schmerz *m*

sorrel ['sɔrəl] *n (Bot)* (großer) Sauerampfer *m*

sorrow ['sɔrəu] *n* Trauer *f*; **sorrows** *npl (troubles)* Sorgen und Nöte *pl*

sorrowful ['sɔrəuful] *adj* traurig

sorry ['sɔrɪ] *adj* traurig; *(excuse)* faul; *(sight)* jämmerlich; **~!** Entschuldigung!, Verzeihung!; **~?** wie bitte?; **I feel ~ for him** er tut mir leid; **I'm ~ to hear that …** es tut mir leid, dass …; **I'm ~ about …** es tut mir leid wegen …

sort [sɔ:t] *n* Sorte *f*; *(make: of car etc)* Marke *f* ▷ *vt (also:* **sort out**) sortieren; *(: problems)* ins Reine bringen; *(Comput)* sortieren; **all ~s of reasons** alle möglichen Gründe; **what ~ do you want?** welche Sorte möchten Sie?; **what ~ of car?** was für ein Auto?; **I'll do nothing of the ~!** das kommt überhaupt nicht infrage!; **it's ~ of awkward** *(inf)* es ist irgendwie schwierig; **to ~ sth out** etw in Ordnung bringen

sort code *n* Bankleitzahl *f*

sortie ['sɔ:tɪ] *n (Mil)* Ausfall *m*; *(fig)* Ausflug *m*

sorting office ['sɔ:tɪŋ-] *n* Postverteilstelle *f*

SOS *n abbr* (= *save our souls*) SOS *nt*

so-so ['səusəu] *adv, adj* so lala

soufflé ['su:fleɪ] *n* Soufflé *nt*

sought [sɔ:t] *pt, pp of* **seek**

sought-after ['sɔ:tɑ:ftə^r] *adj* begehrt, gesucht; **a much ~ item** ein viel begehrtes Stück

soul [səul] *n* Seele *f*; *(Mus)* Soul *m*; **the poor ~ had nowhere to sleep** der Ärmste hatte keine Unterkunft; **I didn't see a ~** ich habe keine Menschenseele gesehen

soul-destroying ['səuldɪstrɔɪɪŋ] *adj* geisttötend

soulful ['səulful] *adj (eyes)* seelenvoll; *(music)* gefühlvoll

soulless ['səullɪs] *adj (place)* seelenlos; *(job)* eintönig

soul mate *n* Seelenfreund(in) *m(f)*

soul-searching ['səulsə:tʃɪŋ] *n*: **after much ~** nach reiflicher Überlegung

sound [saund] *adj (healthy)* gesund; *(safe, secure)* sicher; *(not damaged)* einwandfrei; *(reliable)* solide; *(thorough)* gründlich; *(sensible, valid)* vernünftig ▷ *adv*: **to be ~ asleep** tief und fest schlafen ▷ *n* Geräusch *nt*; *(Mus)* Klang *m*; *(on TV etc)* Ton *m*; *(Geog)* Meerenge *f*, Sund *m* ▷ *vt*: **to ~ the alarm** Alarm schlagen ▷ *vi (alarm, horn)* ertönen; *(fig: seem)* sich anhören, klingen; **to be of ~ mind** bei klarem Verstand sein; **I don't like the ~ of it** das klingt gar nicht gut; **to ~ one's horn** *(Aut)* hupen; **to ~ like** sich anhören wie; **that ~s like them arriving** das hört sich so an, als ob sie ankommen; **it ~s as if …** es klingt *or* es hört sich so an, als ob …

▸ **sound off** *(inf) vi*: **to ~ off (about)** sich auslassen (über +*acc*)

▸ **sound out** *vt (person)* aushorchen; *(opinion)* herausbekommen

sound barrier *n* Schallmauer *f*

sound bite *n* prägnantes Zitat *nt*

sound effects *npl* Toneffekte *pl*

sound engineer *n* Toningenieur(in) *m(f)*

sounding ['saundɪŋ] *n (Naut)* Loten *nt*, Peilung *f*

sounding board *n (Mus)* Resonanzboden *m*; *(fig)*: **to use sb as a ~ for one's ideas** seine Ideen an jdm testen

soundly ['saundlɪ] *adv (sleep)* tief und fest; *(beat)* tüchtig

soundproof ['saundpru:f] *adj* schalldicht ▷ *vt* schalldicht machen

sound system *n* Verstärkersystem *nt*

soundtrack ['saundtræk] *n* Filmmusik *f*

sound wave *n* Schallwelle *f*

soup [su:p] *n* Suppe *f*; **to be in the ~** *(fig)* in der Tinte sitzen

soup kitchen *n* Suppenküche *f*

soup plate *n* Suppenteller *m*

soupspoon ['su:pspu:n] *n* Suppenlöffel *m*

sour ['sauə^r] *adj* sauer; *(fig: bad-tempered)* säuerlich; **to go** *or* **turn ~** *(milk, wine)* sauer

S

werden; (fig: relationship) sich trüben; **it's ~ grapes** (fig) die Trauben hängen zu hoch

source [sɔːs] n Quelle f; (fig: of problem, anxiety) Ursache f; **I have it from a reliable ~ that ...** ich habe es aus sicherer Quelle, dass ...

south [sauθ] n Süden m ▷ adj südlich, Süd- ▷ adv nach Süden; **(to the) ~ of** im Süden or südlich von; **to travel ~** nach Süden fahren; **the S~ of France** Südfrankreich nt

South Africa n Südafrika nt

South African adj südafrikanisch ▷ n Südafrikaner(in) m(f)

South America n Südamerika nt

South American adj südamerikanisch ▷ n Südamerikaner(in) m(f)

southbound ['sauθbaund] adj in Richtung Süden; (carriageway) Richtung Süden

south-east [sauθ'iːst] n Südosten m

South-East Asia n Südostasien nt

southerly ['sʌðəlɪ] adj südlich; (wind) aus südlicher Richtung

southern ['sʌðən] adj südlich, Süd-; **the ~ hemisphere** die südliche Halbkugel or Hemisphäre

South Korea n Südkorea nt

South Pole n Südpol m

South Sea Islands npl Südseeinseln pl

South Seas npl Südsee f

southward ['sauθwəd], **southwards** ['sauθwədz] adv nach Süden, in Richtung Süden

south-west [sauθ'wɛst] n Südwesten m

souvenir [suːvə'nɪəʳ] n Andenken nt, Souvenir nt

sovereign ['sɒvrɪn] n Herrscher(in) m(f)

sovereignty ['sɒvrɪntɪ] n Oberhoheit f, Souveränität f

soviet ['səuvɪət] (formerly) adj sowjetisch ▷ n Sowjetbürger(in) m(f); **the S~ Union** die Sowjetunion f

sow[1] [sau] n Sau f

sow[2] [səu] (pt **~ed**, pp **~n**) vt (lit, fig) säen

soya ['sɔɪə], **soy** [sɔɪ] (US) n: **~ bean** Sojabohne f; **~ sauce** Sojasoße f

sozzled ['sɒzld] (Brit: inf) adj besoffen

spa [spɑː] n (town) Heilbad nt; (US: also: **health spa**) Fitnesszentrum nt

space [speɪs] n Platz m, Raum m; (gap) Lücke f; (beyond Earth) der Weltraum; (interval, period) Zeitraum m ▷ cpd Raum- ▷ vt (also: **space out**) verteilen; **to clear a ~ for sth** für etw Platz schaffen; **in a confined ~** auf engem Raum; **in a short ~ of time** in kurzer Zeit; **(with)in the ~ of an hour** innerhalb einer Stunde

space bar n (on keyboard) Leertaste f

spacecraft ['speɪskrɑːft] n Raumfahrzeug nt

spaceman ['speɪsmæn] (irreg: like **man**) n Raumfahrer m

spaceship ['speɪsʃɪp] n Raumschiff nt

space shuttle n Raumtransporter m

spacesuit ['speɪssuːt] n Raumanzug m

spacewoman ['speɪswumən] (irreg: like **woman**) n Raumfahrerin f

spacing ['speɪsɪŋ] n Abstand m; **single/double ~** einfacher/doppelter Zeilenabstand

spacious ['speɪʃəs] adj geräumig

spade [speɪd] n Spaten m; (child's) Schaufel f; **spades** npl (Cards) Pik nt

spadework ['speɪdwəːk] n (fig) Vorarbeit f

spaghetti [spə'gɛtɪ] n Spag(h)etti pl

Spain [speɪn] n Spanien nt

spam [spæm] (Comput) n Spam m ▷ vt wit Werbung bombardieren

span [spæn] n (of bird, plane, arch) Spannweite f; (in time) Zeitspanne f ▷ vt überspannen; (fig: time) sich erstrecken über +acc

Spaniard ['spænjəd] n Spanier(in) m(f)

spaniel ['spænjəl] n Spaniel m

Spanish ['spænɪʃ] adj spanisch ▷ n (Ling) Spanisch nt; **the Spanish** npl die Spanier pl; **~ omelette** Omelett mit Paprikaschoten, Zwiebeln, Tomaten etc

spank [spæŋk] vt: **to ~ sb's bottom** jdm den Hintern versohlen (inf)

spanner ['spænəʳ] (Brit) n Schraubenschlüssel m

spar [spɑːʳ] n (Naut) Sparren m ▷ vi (Boxing) ein Sparring nt machen

spare [spɛəʳ] adj (free) frei; (extra: part, fuse etc) Ersatz- ▷ n = **spare part** ▷ vt (save: trouble etc) (er)sparen; (make available) erübrigen; (afford to give) (übrig) haben; (refrain from hurting) verschonen; **these 2 are going ~** diese beiden sind noch übrig; **to ~** (surplus) übrig; **to ~ no expense** keine Kosten scheuen, an nichts sparen; **can you ~ the time?** haben Sie Zeit?; **I've a few minutes to ~** ich habe ein paar Minuten Zeit; **there is no time to ~** es ist keine Zeit; **~ me the details** verschone mich mit den Einzelheiten

spare part n Ersatzteil nt

spare room n Gästezimmer nt

spare time n Freizeit f

spare tyre n Reservereifen m

spare wheel n Reserverad nt

sparing ['spɛərɪŋ] adj: **to be ~ with** sparsam umgehen mit

sparingly ['spɛərɪŋlɪ] adv sparsam

spark [spɑːk] n (lit, fig) Funke m

sparking plug ['spɑːkɪŋ-] n = **spark plug**

sparkle ['spɑːkl] n Funkeln nt, Glitzern nt ▷ vi funkeln, glitzern

sparkler ['spɑːkləʳ] n (firework) Wunderkerze f

sparkling ['spɑːklɪŋ] adj (water) mit Kohlensäure; (conversation) vor Geist sprühend; (performance) glänzend; **~ wine** Schaumwein m

spark plug n Zündkerze f

sparring partner ['spɑːrɪŋ-] n (also fig) Sparringspartner m

sparrow ['spærəu] n Spatz m

sparse [spɑːs] adj spärlich; (population) dünn

spartan ['spɑːtən] adj (fig) spartanisch

spasm ['spæzəm] n (Med) Krampf m; (fig: of anger etc) Anfall m

spasmodic [spæz'mɔdɪk] adj (fig) sporadisch

spastic ['spæstɪk] (old) n Spastiker(in) m(f) ▷ adj

spastisch

spat [spæt] *pt, pp of* **spit** ▷ *n* (*US: quarrel*) Krach *m*

spate [speɪt] *n* (*fig*): **a ~ of** eine Flut von; **to be in full ~** (*river*) Hochwasser führen

spatial ['speɪʃl] *adj* räumlich

spatter ['spætə'] *vt* (*liquid*) verspritzen; (*surface*) bespritzen ▷ *vi* spritzen

spatula ['spætjulə] *n* (*Culin*) Spachtel *m*; (*Med*) Spatel *m*

spawn [spɔːn] *vi* laichen ▷ *vt* hervorbringen, erzeugen ▷ *n* Laich *m*

SPCA (*US*) *n abbr* (= *Society for the Prevention of Cruelty to Animals*) Tierschutzverein *m*

SPCC (*US*) *n abbr* (= *Society for the Prevention of Cruelty to Children*) Kinderschutzbund *m*

speak [spiːk] (*pt* **spoke**, *pp* **spoken**) *vt* (*say*) sagen; (*language*) sprechen ▷ *vi* (*make a speech*) sprechen; **to ~ one's mind** seine Meinung sagen; **to ~ to sb/of** *or* **about sth** mit jdm/über etw *acc* sprechen *or* reden; **~ up!** sprich lauter!; **to ~ at a conference** bei einer Tagung einen Vortrag halten; **to ~ in a debate** in einer Debatte sprechen; **he has no money to ~ of** er hat so gut wie kein Geld; **so to ~** sozusagen ▷ **speak for** *vt fus*: **to ~ for sb** (*on behalf of*) in jds Namen *dat or* für jdn sprechen; **that picture is already spoken for** (*in shop*) das Bild ist schon verkauft *or* vergeben; **~ for yourself!** das meinst auch nur du!

speaker ['spiːkə'] *n* (*in public*) Redner(in) *m(f)*; (*also*: **loudspeaker**) Lautsprecher *m*; (*Pol*): **the S~** (*Brit, US*) der Sprecher, die Sprecherin; **are you a Welsh ~?** sprechen Sie Walisisch?

speaking ['spiːkɪŋ] *adj* sprechend; **Italian-~people** Italienischsprechende *pl*; **to be on ~terms** miteinander reden *or* sprechen; **~ clock** telefonische Zeitansage

spear [spɪə'] *n* Speer *m* ▷ *vt* aufspießen

spearhead ['spɪəhɛd] *vt* (*Mil, fig*) anführen

spearmint ['spɪəmɪnt] *n* Grüne Minze *f*

spec [spɛk] (*inf*) *n*: **on ~** auf Verdacht, auf gut Glück; **to buy/go on ~** auf gut Glück kaufen/hingehen

spec. *n abbr* (*Tech*) = **specification**

special ['spɛʃl] *adj* besondere(r, s); (*service, performance, adviser, permission, school*) Sonder- ▷ *n* (*train*) Sonderzug *m*; **take ~ care** pass besonders gut auf; **nothing ~** nichts Besonderes; **today's ~** (*at restaurant*) Tagesgericht *nt*

special agent *n* Agent(in) *m(f)*

special correspondent *n* Sonderberichterstatter(in) *m(f)*

special delivery *n* (*Post*): **by ~** durch Eilzustellung

special effects *npl* Spezialeffekte *pl*

specialist ['spɛʃəlɪst] *n* Spezialist(in) *m(f)*; (*Med*) Facharzt *m*, Fachärztin *f*; **heart ~** Facharzt *m*/Fachärztin *f* für Herzkrankheiten

speciality [spɛʃɪ'ælɪtɪ] *n* Spezialität *f*; (*study*) Spezialgebiet *nt*

specialize ['spɛʃəlaɪz] *vi*: **to ~ (in)** sich

spezialisieren (auf +*acc*)

specially ['spɛʃlɪ] *adv* besonders, extra

special offer *n* Sonderangebot *nt*

specialty ['spɛʃəltɪ] (*esp US*) = **speciality**

species ['spiːʃiːz] *n inv* Art *f*

specific [spə'sɪfɪk] *adj* (*fixed*) bestimmt; (*exact*) genau; **to be ~** eigentümlich sein für

specifically [spə'sɪfɪklɪ] *adv* (*specially*) speziell; (*exactly*) genau; **more ~** und zwar

specification [spɛsɪfɪ'keɪʃən] *n* genaue Angabe *f*; (*requirement*) Bedingung *f*; **specifications** *npl* (*Tech*) technische Daten *pl*

specify ['spɛsɪfaɪ] *vt* angeben; **unless otherwise specified** wenn nicht anders angegeben

specimen ['spɛsɪmən] *n* Exemplar *nt*; (*Med*) Probe *f*

specimen copy *n* Belegexemplar *nt*, Probeexemplar *nt*

specimen signature *n* Unterschriftsprobe *f*

speck [spɛk] *n* Fleckchen *nt*; (*of dust*) Körnchen *nt*

speckled ['spɛkld] *adj* gesprenkelt

specs [spɛks] (*inf*) *npl* Brille *f*

spectacle ['spɛktəkl] *n* (*scene*) Schauspiel *nt*; (*sight*) Anblick *m*; (*grand event*) Spektakel *nt*; **spectacles** *npl* (*glasses*) Brille *f*

spectacle case (*Brit*) *n* Brillenetui *nt*

spectacular [spɛk'tækjulə'] *adj* sensationell; (*success*) spektakulär ▷ *n* (*Theat etc*) Show *f*

spectator [spɛk'teɪtə'] *n* Zuschauer(in) *m(f)*; **~ sport** Publikumssport *m*

spectra ['spɛktrə] *npl of* **spectrum**

spectre, (*US*) **specter** ['spɛktə'] *n* Gespenst *nt*; (*fig*) (Schreck)gespenst *nt*

spectrum ['spɛktrəm] (*pl* **spectra**) *n* (*lit, fig*) Spektrum *nt*

speculate ['spɛkjuleɪt] *vi* (*Fin*) spekulieren; **to ~ about** spekulieren *or* Vermutungen anstellen über +*acc*

speculation [spɛkju'leɪʃən] *n* Spekulation *f*

speculative ['spɛkjulətɪv] *adj* spekulativ

speculator ['spɛkjuleɪtə'] *n* Spekulant(in) *m(f)*

sped [spɛd] *pt, pp of* **speed**

speech [spiːtʃ] *n* Sprache *f*; (*manner of speaking*) Sprechweise *f*; (*enunciation*) (Aus)sprache *f*; (*formal talk, Theat*) Rede *f*

speech day (*Brit*) *n* (*Scol*) = Schulfeier *f*

speech impediment *n* Sprachfehler *m*

speechless ['spiːtʃlɪs] *adj* sprachlos

speech recognition software *n* (*Comput*) Spracherkennungssoftware *f*

speech therapist *n* Logopäde *m*, Logopädin *f*, Sprachtherapeut(in) *m(f)*

speech therapy *n* Logopädie *f*, Sprachtherapie *f*

speed [spiːd] (*pt, pp* **sped**) *n* Geschwindigkeit *f*, Schnelligkeit *f* ▷ *vi* (*exceed speed limit*) zu schnell fahren; **to ~ along** dahinsausen; **to ~ by** (*car etc*) vorbeisausen; (*years*) verfliegen; **at ~** (*Brit*) mit hoher Geschwindigkeit; **at full** *or* **top ~** mit Höchstgeschwindigkeit; **at a ~ of 70km/h** mit (einer Geschwindigkeit *or* einem

Tempo von) 70 km/h; **shorthand/typing**
~s Silben/Anschläge pro Minute; **a five--**
gearbox ein Fünfganggetriebe nt
▶ **speed up** (pt, pp **~ed up**) vi beschleunigen;
(fig) sich beschleunigen ▷ vt beschleunigen
speedboat ['spi:dbəut] n Rennboot nt
speed dial (Tel) n Kurzwahl f ▷ adj Kurzwahl-;
~ **button** Kurzwahltaste f
speedily ['spi:dɪlɪ] adv schnell
speeding ['spi:dɪŋ] n
Geschwindigkeitsüberschreitung f
speed limit n Tempolimit nt,
Geschwindigkeitsbegrenzung f
speedometer [spɪ'dɔmɪtə'] n Tachometer m
speed trap n Radarfalle f
speedway ['spi:dweɪ] n (also: **speedway**
racing) Speedway-Rennen nt
speedy ['spi:dɪ] adj schnell; (reply, settlement)
prompt
speleologist [spɛlɪ'ɔlədʒɪst] n
Höhlenkundler(in) m(f)
spell [spɛl] (Brit) (pt, pp **~ed**) n (also: **magic spell**)
Zauber m; (incantation) Zauberspruch m; (period
of time) Zeit f, Weile f ▷ vt schreiben; (also: **spell**
out: aloud) buchstabieren; (signify) bedeuten;
to cast a ~ on sb jdn verzaubern; **cold ~**
Kältewelle f; **how do you ~ your name?** wie
schreibt sich Ihr Name?; **can you ~ it for me?**
können Sie das bitte buchstabieren?; **he can't**
~ er kann keine Rechtschreibung
spellbound ['spɛlbaund] adj gebannt
spelling ['spɛlɪŋ] n Schreibweise f;
(ability) Rechtschreibung f; ~ **mistake**
Rechtschreibfehler m
spelt [spɛlt] pt, pp of **spell**
spend [spɛnd] (pt, pp **spent**) vt (money)
ausgeben; (time, life) verbringen; **to ~ time/**
money/effort on sth Zeit/Geld/Mühe für
etw aufbringen
spending ['spɛndɪŋ] n Ausgaben pl;
government ~ öffentliche Ausgaben pl
spending money n Taschengeld nt
spending power n Kaufkraft f
spendthrift ['spɛndθrɪft] n Verschwender(in)
m(f)
spent [spɛnt] pt, pp of **spend** ▷ adj (patience)
erschöpft; (cartridge, bullets) verbraucht; (match)
abgebrannt
sperm [spə:m] n Samenzelle f, Spermium nt
sperm bank n Samenbank f
sperm whale n Pottwal m
spew [spju:] vt (also: **spew up**) erbrechen; (fig)
ausspucken
sphere [sfɪə'] n Kugel f; (area) Gebiet nt, Bereich
m
spherical ['sfɛrɪkl] adj kugelförmig
sphinx [sfɪŋks] n Sphinx f
spice [spaɪs] n Gewürz nt ▷ vt würzen
spick-and-span ['spɪkən'spæn] adj blitzsauber
spicy ['spaɪsɪ] adj stark gewürzt
spider ['spaɪdə'] n Spinne f; ~'**s web**
Spinnengewebe nt, Spinnennetz nt
spidery ['spaɪdərɪ] adj (handwriting) krakelig

spiel [spi:l] (inf) n Sermon m
spike [spaɪk] n (point) Spitze f; (Bot) Ähre f; (Elec)
Spannungsspitze f; **spikes** npl (Sport) Spikes pl
spike heel (US) n Pfennigabsatz m
spiky ['spaɪkɪ] adj stachelig; (branch) dornig
spill [spɪl] (pt, pp **spilt** or **~ed**) vt verschütten ▷ vi
verschüttet werden; **to ~ the beans** (inf: fig)
alles ausplaudern
▶ **spill out** vi (people) herausströmen
▶ **spill over** vi überlaufen; (fig: spread) sich
ausbreiten; **to ~ over into** sich auswirken
auf +acc
spillage ['spɪlɪdʒ] n (act) Verschütten nt;
(quantity) verschüttete Menge f
spin [spɪn] (pt **spun, span**, pp **spun**) n (trip)
Spritztour f; (revolution) Drehung f; (Aviat)
Trudeln nt; (on ball) Drall m ▷ vt (wool etc)
spinnen; (ball, coin) (hoch)werfen; (wheel)
drehen; (Brit: also: **spin-dry**) schleudern ▷ vi
(make thread) spinnen; (person) sich drehen; (car
etc) schleudern; **to ~ a yarn** Seemannsgarn
spinnen; **to ~ a coin** (Brit) eine Münze werfen;
my head is ~ning mir dreht sich alles
▶ **spin out** vt (talk) ausspinnen; (job, holiday) in
die Länge ziehen; (money) strecken
spina bifida ['spaɪnə'bɪfɪdə] n offene
Wirbelsäule f, Spina bifida f
spinach ['spɪnɪtʃ] n Spinat m
spinal ['spaɪnl] adj (injury etc) Rückgrat-
spinal column n Wirbelsäule f
spinal cord n Rückenmark nt
spindly ['spɪndlɪ] adj spindeldürr
spin doctor n PR-Fachmann m, PR-Fachfrau f
spin-dry ['spɪn'draɪ] vt schleudern
spin-dryer [spɪn'draɪə'] (Brit) n (Wäsche)
schleuder f
spine [spaɪn] n (Anat) Rückgrat nt; (thorn)
Stachel m
spine-chilling ['spaɪntʃɪlɪŋ] adj schaurig,
gruselig
spineless ['spaɪnlɪs] adj (fig) rückgratlos
spinner ['spɪnə'] n (of thread) Spinner(in) m(f)
spinning ['spɪnɪŋ] n (art) Spinnen nt
spinning top n Kreisel m
spinning wheel n Spinnrad nt
spin-off ['spɪnɔf] n (fig) Nebenprodukt nt
spinster ['spɪnstə'] n unverheiratete Frau; (pej)
alte Jungfer
spiral ['spaɪərl] n Spirale f ▷ vi (fig: prices etc) in
die Höhe klettern; **the inflationary ~** die
Inflationsspirale
spiral staircase n Wendeltreppe f
spire ['spaɪə'] n Turmspitze f
spirit ['spɪrɪt] n Geist m; (soul) Seele f;
(energy) Elan m, Schwung m; (courage) Mut
m; (sense) Geist m, Sinn m; (frame of mind)
Stimmung f; **spirits** npl (drink) Spirituosen
pl; **in good ~s** guter Laune; **community ~**
Gemeinschaftssinn m
spirited ['spɪrɪtɪd] adj (resistance, defence) mutig;
(performance) lebendig
spirit level n Wasserwaage f
spiritual ['spɪrɪtjuəl] adj geistig, seelisch;

(*religious*) geistlich ⊳ *n* (*also*: **Negro spiritual**) Spiritual *nt*

spiritualism ['spɪrɪtjuəlɪzəm] *n* Spiritismus *m*

spit [spɪt] (*pt, pp* **spat**) *n* (*for roasting*) Spieß *m*; (*saliva*) Spucke *f* ⊳ *vi* spucken; (*fire*) Funken sprühen; (*cooking*) spritzen; (*inf: rain*) tröpfeln

spite [spaɪt] *n* Boshaftigkeit *f* ⊳ *vt* ärgern; **in ~ of** trotz +*gen*

spiteful ['spaɪtful] *adj* boshaft, gemein

spitroast ['spɪtrəʊst] *n* Spießbraten *m*

spitting ['spɪtɪŋ] *n*: **"~ prohibited"** „Spucken verboten" ⊳ *adj*: **to be the ~ image of sb** jdm wie aus dem Gesicht geschnitten sein

spittle ['spɪtl] *n* Speichel *m*, Spucke *f*

spiv [spɪv] (*Brit: inf: pej*) *n* schmieriger Typ *m*

splash [splæʃ] *n* (*sound*) Platschen *nt*; (*of colour*) Tupfer *m* ⊳ *excl* platsch! ⊳ *vi* bespritzen ⊳ *vi* (*also*: **splash about**) herumplan(t)schen; (*water, rain*) spritzen; **to ~ paint on the floor** den Fußboden mit Farbe bespritzen

splashdown ['splæʃdaʊn] *n* (*Space*) Wasserung *f*

splayfooted ['spleɪfʊtɪd] *adj* mit nach außen gestellten Füßen

spleen [spli:n] *n* Milz *f*

splendid ['splɛndɪd] *adj* hervorragend, ausgezeichnet; (*impressive*) prächtig

splendour, (*US*) **splendor** ['splɛndəʳ] *n* Pracht *f*; **splendours** *npl* Pracht *f*

splice [splaɪs] *vt* spleißen, kleben

splint [splɪnt] *n* Schiene *f*

splinter ['splɪntəʳ] *n* Splitter *m* ⊳ *vi* (zer)splittern

splinter group *n* Splittergruppe *f*

split [splɪt] (*pt, pp* **~**) *n* (*tear*) Riss *m*; (*fig: division*) Aufteilung *f*; (*: difference*) Kluft *f*; (*Pol*) Spaltung *f* ⊳ *vt* (*divide*) aufteilen; (*party*) spalten; (*share equally*) teilen ⊳ *vi* (*divide*) sich aufteilen; (*tear*) reißen; **to do the ~s** (einen) Spagat machen; **let's ~ the difference** teilen wir uns die Differenz

▸ **split up** *vi* sich trennen; (*meeting*) sich auflösen

split-level ['splɪtlɛvl] *adj* mit versetzten Geschossen

split peas *npl* getrocknete (halbe) Erbsen *pl*

split personality *n* gespaltene Persönlichkeit *f*

split second *n* Bruchteil *m* einer Sekunde

splitting ['splɪtɪŋ] *adj*: **a ~ headache** rasende Kopfschmerzen *pl*

splutter ['splʌtəʳ] *vi* (*engine etc*) stottern; (*person*) prusten

spoil [spɔɪl] (*pt, pp* **spoilt** *or* **~ed**) *vt* verderben; (*child*) verwöhnen; (*ballot paper, vote*) ungültig machen ⊳ *vi*: **to be ~ing for a fight** Streit suchen

spoils [spɔɪlz] *npl* Beute *f*; (*fig*) Gewinn *m*

spoilsport ['spɔɪlspɔːt] (*pej*) *n* Spielverderber *m*

spoilt [spɔɪlt] *pt, pp of* **spoil** ⊳ *adj* (*child*) verwöhnt; (*ballot paper*) ungültig

spoke [spəʊk] *pt of* **speak** ⊳ *n* Speiche *f*

spoken ['spəʊkn] *pp of* **speak**

spokesman ['spəʊksmən] (*irreg: like* **man**) *n*

Sprecher *m*

spokesperson ['spəʊkspɜːsn] *n* Sprecher(in) *m(f)*

spokeswoman ['spəʊkswumən] (*irreg: like* **woman**) *n* Sprecherin *f*

sponge [spʌndʒ] *n* Schwamm *m*; (*also*: **sponge cake**) Biskuit(kuchen) *m* ⊳ *vt* mit einem Schwamm waschen ⊳ *vi*: **to ~ off** *or* **on sb** jdm auf der Tasche liegen

sponge bag (*Brit*) *n* Waschbeutel *m*, Kulturbeutel *m*

sponger ['spʌndʒəʳ] (*pej*) *n* Schmarotzer *m*

spongy ['spʌndʒɪ] *adj* schwammig

sponsor ['spɒnsəʳ] *n* Sponsor(in) *m(f)*, Geldgeber(in) *m(f)*; (*Brit: for charitable event*) Sponsor(in) *m(f)*; (*for application, bill etc*) Befürworter(in) *m(f)* ⊳ *vt* sponsern, finanziell unterstützen; (*fund-raiser*) sponsern; (*applicant*) unterstützen; (*proposal, bill etc*) befürworten; **I ~ed him at 3p a mile** (*in fund-raising race*) ich habe mich verpflichtet, ihm 3 Pence pro Meile zu geben

sponsorship ['spɒnsəʃɪp] *n* finanzielle Unterstützung *f*

spontaneity [spɒntə'neɪɪtɪ] *n* Spontaneität *f*

spontaneous [spɒn'teɪnɪəs] *adj* spontan; **~ combustion** Selbstentzündung *f*

spoof [spu:f] *n* (*parody*) Parodie *f*; (*hoax*) Ulk *m*

spooky ['spu:kɪ] (*inf*) *adj* gruselig

spool [spu:l] *n* Spule *f*

spoon [spu:n] *n* Löffel *m*

spoon-feed ['spu:nfi:d] *vt* (mit dem Löffel) füttern; (*fig*) gängeln

spoonful ['spu:nful] *n* Löffel *m*

sporadic [spə'rædɪk] *adj* sporadisch, vereinzelt

sport [spɔːt] *n* Sport *m*; (*type*) Sportart *f*; (*also*: **good sport**: *person*) feiner Kerl *m* ⊳ *vt* (*wear*) tragen; **indoor ~s** Hallensport *m*; **outdoor ~s** Sport *m* im Freien

sporting ['spɔːtɪŋ] *adj* (*event etc*) Sport-; (*generous*) großzügig; **to give sb a ~ chance** jdm eine faire Chance geben

sport jacket (*US*) *n* = **sports jacket**

sports car *n* Sportwagen *m*

sports centre *n* Sportzentrum *nt*

sports ground *n* Sportplatz *m*

sports jacket (*Brit*) *n* Sakko *m*

sportsman ['spɔːtsmən] (*irreg: like* **man**) *n* Sportler *m*

sportsmanship ['spɔːtsmənʃɪp] *n* Sportlichkeit *f*

sports page *n* Sportseite *f*

sportswear ['spɔːtswɛəʳ] *n* Sportkleidung *f*

sportswoman ['spɔːtswumən] (*irreg: like* **woman**) *n* Sportlerin *f*

sporty ['spɔːtɪ] *adj* sportlich

spot [spɒt] *n* (*mark*) Fleck *m*; (*dot*) Punkt *m*; (*on skin*) Pickel *m*; (*place*) Stelle *f*, Platz *m*; (*Radio, TV*) Nummer *f*, Auftritt *m*; (*also*: **spot advertisement**) Werbespot *m*; (*small amount*): **a ~ of** ein bisschen ⊳ *vt* entdecken; **on the ~** (*in that place*) an Ort und Stelle; (*immediately*) auf der Stelle; **to be in a ~** in der Klemme

S

sitzen; **to put sb on the ~** jdn in Verlegenheit bringen; **to come out in ~s** Pickel bekommen
spot check n Stichprobe f
spotless ['spɒtlɪs] adj makellos sauber
spotlight ['spɒtlaɪt] n Scheinwerfer m; (in room) Strahler m
spot-on [spɒt'ɒn] (Brit: inf) adj genau richtig
spot price n Kassapreis m
spotted ['spɒtɪd] adj gepunktet
spotty ['spɒtɪ] adj pickelig
spouse [spaʊs] n (male) Gatte m; (female) Gattin f
spout [spaʊt] n (of jug, teapot) Tülle f; (of pipe) Ausfluss m; (of liquid) Strahl m ▷ vi spritzen; (flames) sprühen
sprain [spreɪn] n Verstauchung f ▷ vt: **to ~ one's ankle/wrist** sich dat den Knöchel/das Handgelenk verstauchen
sprang [spræŋ] pt of **spring**
sprawl [sprɔːl] vi (person) sich ausstrecken; (place) wild wuchern ▷ n: **urban ~** wild wuchernde Ausbreitung des Stadtgebietes; **to send sb ~ing** jdn zu Boden werfen
spray [spreɪ] n (small drops) Sprühnebel m; (sea spray) Gischt m or f; (container) Sprühdose f; (garden spray) Sprühgerät nt; (of flowers) Strauß m ▷ vt sprühen, spritzen; (crops) spritzen ▷ cpd (deodorant) Sprüh-; **~ can** Sprühdose f
spread [sprɛd] (pt, pp **~**) n (range) Spektrum nt; (selection) Auswahl f; (distribution) Verteilung f; (for bread) (Brot)aufstrich m; (inf: food) Festessen nt; (Press, Typ: two pages) Doppelseite f ▷ vt ausbreiten; (butter) streichen; (workload, wealth, repayments etc) verteilen; (scatter) verstreuen; (rumour, disease) verbreiten ▷ vi (disease, news) sich verbreiten; (also: **spread out**: stain) sich ausbreiten; **to get a middle-age ~** in den mittleren Jahren Speck ansetzen
  ▶ **spread out** vi (move apart) sich verteilen
spread-eagled ['sprɛdiːɡld] adj mit ausgestreckten Armen und Beinen; **to be** or **lie ~** mit ausgestreckten Armen und Beinen daliegen
spreadsheet ['sprɛdʃiːt] n (Comput) Tabellenkalkulation f
spree [spriː] n: **to go on a ~** (drinking) eine Zechtour machen; (spending) groß einkaufen gehen
sprig [sprɪɡ] n Zweig m
sprightly ['spraɪtlɪ] adj rüstig
spring [sprɪŋ] (pt **sprang**, pp **sprung**) n (coiled metal) Sprungfeder f; (season) Frühling m, Frühjahr nt; (of water) Quelle f ▷ vi (leap) springen ▷ vt: **to ~ a leak** (pipe etc) undicht werden; **in ~** im Frühling or Frühjahr; **to walk with a ~ in one's step** mit federnden Schritten gehen; **to ~ from** (result) herrühren von; **to ~ into action** aktiv werden; **he sprang the news on me** er hat mich mit der Nachricht überrascht
  ▶ **spring up** vi (building, plant) aus dem Boden schießen
springboard ['sprɪŋbɔːd] n (Sport, fig)

Sprungbrett nt
spring-clean [sprɪŋ'kliːn], **spring-cleaning** [sprɪŋ'kliːnɪŋ] n Frühjahrsputz m
spring onion (Brit) n Frühlingszwiebel f
spring roll n Frühlingsrolle f
springtime ['sprɪŋtaɪm] n Frühling m
springy ['sprɪŋɪ] adj federnd; (mattress) weich gefedert
sprinkle ['sprɪŋkl] vt (liquid) sprenkeln; (salt, sugar) streuen; **to ~ water on, ~ with water** mit Wasser besprengen; **to ~ sugar** etc **on, ~ with sugar** etc mit Zucker etc bestreuen
sprinkler ['sprɪŋklər] n (for lawn) Rasensprenger m; (to put out fire) Sprinkler m
sprinkling ['sprɪŋklɪŋ] n: **a ~ of** (water) ein paar Tropfen; (salt, sugar) eine Prise; (fig) ein paar ...
sprint [sprɪnt] n Sprint m ▷ vi rennen; (Sport) sprinten; **the 200 metres ~** der 200-Meter-Lauf
sprinter ['sprɪntər] n Sprinter(in) m(f)
sprite [spraɪt] n Kobold m
spritzer ['sprɪtsər] n Schorle f
sprocket ['sprɒkɪt] n Kettenzahnrad nt
sprout [spraʊt] vi sprießen; (vegetable) keimen
sprouts [spraʊts] npl (also: **Brussels sprouts**) Rosenkohl m
spruce [spruːs] n inv Fichte f ▷ adj gepflegt, adrett
  ▶ **spruce up** vt auf Vordermann bringen (inf); **to ~ o.s. up** sein Äußeres pflegen
sprung [sprʌŋ] pp of **spring**
spry [spraɪ] adj rüstig
SPUC n abbr (= Society for the Protection of the Unborn Child) Gesellschaft zum Schutz des ungeborenen Lebens
spud [spʌd] (inf) n Kartoffel f
spun [spʌn] pt, pp of **spin**
spur [spəːr] n Sporn m; (fig) Ansporn m ▷ vt (also: **spur on**: fig) anspornen; **on the ~ of the moment** ganz spontan
spurious ['spjʊərɪəs] adj falsch
spurn [spəːn] vt verschmähen
spurt [spəːt] n (of blood etc) Strahl m; (of energy) Anwandlung f ▷ vi (blood) (heraus)spritzen; **to put on a ~** (lit, fig) einen Spurt einlegen
sputter ['spʌtər] vi = **splutter**
spy [spaɪ] n Spion(in) m(f) ▷ vi: **to ~ on** nachspionieren +dat ▷ vt sehen ▷ cpd (film, story) Spionage-
spying ['spaɪɪŋ] n Spionage f
Sq. abbr (in address: = square) ≈ Pl.
sq. abbr = **square**
squabble ['skwɒbl] vi (sich) zanken ▷ n Streit m
squad [skwɒd] n (Mil) Trupp m; (Police) Kommando nt; (: drug/fraud squad) Dezernat nt; (Sport) Mannschaft f; **flying ~** (Police) Überfallkommando nt
squad car (Brit) n (Police) Streifenwagen m
squaddie ['skwɒdɪ] (Brit) n (private soldier) Gefreite(r) m
squadron ['skwɒdrn] n (Mil) Schwadron f; (Aviat) Staffel f; (Naut) Geschwader nt
squalid ['skwɒlɪd] adj verkommen; (conditions) elend; (sordid) erbärmlich

squall [skwɔ:l] n Bö(e) f

squalor ['skwɔlər] n Elend nt

squander ['skwɔndər] vt verschwenden; (chances) vertun

square [skwɛər] n Quadrat nt; (in town) Platz m; (US: block of houses) Block m; (also: **set square**) Zeichendreieck nt; (inf: person) Spießer m ▷ adj quadratisch; (inf: ideas, person) spießig ▷ vt (arrange) ausrichten; (Math) quadrieren; (reconcile) in Einklang bringen ▷ vi (accord) übereinstimmen; **we're back to ~ one** jetzt sind wir wieder da, wo wir angefangen haben; **all ~** (Sport) unentschieden; (fig) quitt; **a ~ meal** eine ordentliche Mahlzeit; **2 metres ~** 2 Meter im Quadrat; **2 ~ metres** 2 Quadratmeter; **I'll ~ it with him** (inf) ich mache das mit ihm ab; **can you ~ it with your conscience?** können Sie das mit Ihrem Gewissen vereinbaren?

▶ **square up** (Brit) vi abrechnen

square bracket n eckige Klammer f

squarely ['skwɛəlɪ] adv (directly) direkt, genau; (firmly) fest; (honestly) ehrlich; (fairly) gerecht, fair

square root n Quadratwurzel f

squash [skwɔʃ] n (Brit): **lemon/orange ~** Zitronen-/Orangensaftgetränk nt; (US: marrow etc) Kürbis m; (Sport) Squash nt ▷ vt zerquetschen

quat [skwɔt] adj gedrungen ▷ vi (also: **squat down**) sich (hin)hocken; (on property): **to ~ (in a house)** ein Haus besetzen

quatter ['skwɔtər] n Hausbesetzer(in) m(f)

quawk [skwɔ:k] vi kreischen

queak [skwi:k] vi quietschen; (mouse etc) piepsen ▷ n Quietschen nt; (of mouse etc) Piepsen nt

queaky-clean [skwi:kɪ'kli:n] (inf) adj blitzsauber

queal [skwi:l] vi quietschen

queamish ['skwi:mɪʃ] adj empfindlich

queeze [skwi:z] n Drücken nt; (Econ) Beschränkung f; (also: **credit squeeze**) Kreditbeschränkung f ▷ vt drücken; (lemon etc) auspressen ▷ vi: **to ~ past sth** sich an etw dat vorbeidrücken; **to ~ under sth** sich unter etw dat durchzwängen; **to give sth a ~** etw drücken; **a ~ of lemon** ein Spritzer m Zitronensaft

▶ **squeeze out** vt (juice etc) (her)auspressen; (fig: exclude) hinausdrängen

quelch [skwɛltʃ] vi (mud etc) quatschen

quib [skwɪb] n Knallfrosch m

quid [skwɪd] n Tintenfisch m

quiggle ['skwɪgl] n Schnörkel m

quint [skwɪnt] vi (in the sunlight) blinzeln ▷ n (Med) Schielen nt; **he has a ~** er schielt

quire ['skwaɪər] (Brit) n Gutsherr m; (inf) Chef m

quirm [skwə:m] vi (lit, fig) sich winden

quirrel ['skwɪrəl] n Eichhörnchen nt

quirt [skwə:t] vi, vt spritzen

r abbr (in names: = senior) sen.; (Rel) = **sister**

SRC (Brit) n abbr (= Students' Representative Council) studentische Vertretung

Sri Lanka [srɪ'læŋkə] n Sri Lanka nt

SRO (US) abbr (= standing room only) nur Stehplätze

SS abbr = **steamship**

SSA (US) n abbr (= Social Security Administration) Sozialversicherungsbehörde

SST (US) n abbr (= supersonic transport) Überschallverkehr m

ST (US) abbr = **standard time**

St abbr (= saint) St.; (= street) Str.

stab [stæb] n Stich m, Stoß m; (inf: try): **to have a ~ at sth** etw probieren ▷ vt (person) niederstechen; (body) einstechen auf +acc; **a ~ of pain** ein stechender Schmerz; **to ~ sb to death** jdn erstechen

stabbing ['stæbɪŋ] n Messerstecherei f ▷ adj (pain) stechend

stability [stə'bɪlɪtɪ] n Stabilität f

stabilization [steɪbəlaɪ'zeɪʃən] n Stabilisierung f

stabilize ['steɪbəlaɪz] vt stabilisieren ▷ vi sich stabilisieren

stabilizer ['steɪbəlaɪzər] n (Aviat) Stabilisierungsfläche f; (Naut, food additive) Stabilisator m

stable ['steɪbl] adj stabil; (marriage) dauerhaft ▷ n Stall m; **riding ~s** Reitstall m

staccato [stə'kɑ:təu] adv (Mus) stakkato ▷ adj abgehackt

stack [stæk] n Stapel m; (of books etc) Stoß m ▷ vt (also: **stack up**) aufstapeln; **~s of time** (Brit: inf) jede Menge Zeit; **to ~ with** vollstapeln mit

stadia ['steɪdɪə] npl of **stadium**

stadium ['steɪdɪəm] (pl **stadia** or **~s**) n Stadion nt

staff [stɑ:f] n (workforce, servants) Personal nt; (Brit: also: **teaching staff**) (Lehrer)kollegium nt; (stick, Mil) Stab m ▷ vt (mit Personal) besetzen; **one of his ~** einer seiner Mitarbeiter; **a member of ~** ein(e) Mitarbeiter(in) m(f); (Scol) ein(e) Lehrer(in) m(f)

staffroom ['stɑ:fru:m] n (Scol) Lehrerzimmer nt

Staffs (Brit) abbr (Post) = **Staffordshire**

stag [stæg] n Hirsch m; (Brit: Stock Exchange) Spekulant m (der junge Aktien aufkauft); **~ market** (Brit: Stock Exchange) Spekulantenmarkt m

stage [steɪdʒ] n Bühne f; (platform) Podium nt; (point, period) Stadium nt ▷ vt (play) aufführen; (demonstration) organisieren; (perform: recovery etc) schaffen; **the ~** das Theater, die Bühne; **in ~s** etappenweise; **to go through a difficult ~** eine schwierige Phase durchmachen; **in the early/final ~s** im Anfangs-/Endstadium

stagecoach ['steɪdʒkəutʃ] n Postkutsche f

stage door n Bühneneingang m

stage fright n Lampenfieber nt

stagehand ['steɪdʒhænd] n Bühnenarbeiter(in) m(f)

stage-manage ['steɪdʒmænɪdʒ] vt (fig) inszenieren

S

stage manager n Inspizient(in) m(f)
stagger ['stægə'] vi schwanken, taumeln ▷ vt (amaze) die Sprache verschlagen +dat; (hours, holidays) staffeln
staggering ['stægərɪŋ] adj (amazing) atemberaubend
staging post ['steɪdʒɪŋ-] n Zwischenstation f
stagnant ['stægnənt] adj (water) stehend; (economy etc) stagnierend
stagnate [stæg'neɪt] vi (economy etc) stagnieren; (person) verdummen
stagnation [stæg'neɪʃən] n Stagnation f
stag night, stag party n Herrenabend m; siehe Info-Artikel

⊙ **STAG NIGHT**
⊙
⊙ Als stag night bezeichnet man eine
⊙ feuchtfröhliche Männerparty, die kurz vor
⊙ einer Hochzeit vom Bräutigam und seinen
⊙ Freunden meist in einem Gasthaus oder
⊙ Nachtklub abgehalten wird. Diese Feiern
⊙ sind oft sehr ausgelassen und können
⊙ manchmal auch zu weit gehen (wenn
⊙ dem betrunkenen Bräutigam ein Streich
⊙ gespielt wird). Siehe auch hen night.

staid [steɪd] adj gesetzt
stain [steɪn] n Fleck m; (colouring) Beize f ▷ vt beflecken; (wood) beizen
stained glass window [steɪnd-] n buntes Glasfenster nt
stainless steel ['steɪnlɪs-] n (rostfreier) Edelstahl m
stain remover n Fleckentferner m
stair [steə'] n (step) Stufe f; **stairs** npl (flight of steps) Treppe f; **on the ~s** auf der Treppe
staircase ['steəkeɪs] n Treppe f
stairway ['steəweɪ] n = staircase
stairwell ['steəwel] n Treppenhaus nt
stake [steɪk] n (post) Pfahl m, Pfosten m; (Comm) Anteil m; (Betting: gen pl) Einsatz m ▷ vt (money) setzen; (also: **stake out**: area) abstecken; **to be at ~** auf dem Spiel stehen; **to have a ~ in sth** einen Anteil an etw dat haben; **to ~ a claim (to sth)** sich dat ein Anrecht (auf etw acc) sichern; **to ~ one's life on sth** seinen Kopf auf etw acc wetten; **to ~ one's reputation on sth** sich für etw verbürgen
stakeout ['steɪkaut] n (surveillance) Überwachung f
stalactite ['stæləktaɪt] n Stalaktit m
stalagmite ['stæləgmaɪt] n Stalagmit m
stale [steɪl] adj (bread) altbacken; (food) alt; (smell) muffig; (air) verbraucht; (beer) schal
stalemate ['steɪlmeɪt] n (Chess) Patt nt; (fig) Sackgasse f
stalk [stɔːk] n Stiel m ▷ vt sich heranpirschen an +acc ▷ vi: **to ~ out/off** hinaus-/davonstolzieren
stall [stɔːl] n (Brit: in market etc) Stand m; (in stable) Box f ▷ vt (engine, car) abwürgen; (fig: person) hinhalten; (: decision etc)

hinauszögern ▷ vi (engine) absterben; (car) stehen bleiben; (fig: person) ausweichen; **stalls** npl (Brit: in cinema, theatre) Parkett nt; **a seat in the ~s** ein Platz im Parkett; **a clothes/flower ~** ein Kleidungs-/Blumenstand; **to ~ for time** versuchen, Zeit zu gewinnen
stallholder ['stɔːlhəʊldə'] (Brit) n Standbesitzer(in) m(f)
stallion ['stæljən] n Hengst m
stalwart ['stɔːlwət] adj treu
stamen ['steɪmɛn] n Staubgefäß nt
stamina ['stæmɪnə] n Ausdauer f
stammer ['stæmə'] n Stottern nt ▷ vi stottern; **to have a ~** stottern
stamp [stæmp] n (lit, fig) Stempel m; (also: **postage stamp**) Briefmarke f ▷ vi stampfen; (also: **stamp one's foot**) (mit dem Fuß) aufstampfen ▷ vt stempeln; (with postage stamp) frankieren; **~ed addressed envelope** frankierter Rückumschlag
  ▶ **stamp out** vt (fire) austreten; (fig: crime) ausrotten; (: opposition) unterdrücken
stamp album n Briefmarkenalbum nt
stamp collecting n Briefmarkensammeln nt
stamp duty (Brit) n (Stempel)gebühr f
stampede [stæm'piːd] n (of animals) wilde Flucht f; (fig) Massenandrang m
stamp machine n Briefmarkenautomat m
stance [stæns] n Haltung f; (fig) Einstellung f
stand [stænd] (pt, pp **stood**) n (Comm) Stand m; (Sport) Tribüne f; (piece of furniture) Ständer m ▷ vi stehen; (rise) aufstehen; (remain) bestehen bleiben; (in election etc) kandidieren ▷ vt stellen; (tolerate, withstand) ertragen; **to make a ~ against sth** Widerstand gegen etw leisten; **to take a ~ on sth** einen Standpunkt zu etw vertreten; **to take the ~** (US: Law) in den Zeugenstand treten; **to ~ at** (value, score etc) betragen; (level) liegen bei; **to ~ for parliament** (Brit) in den Parlamentswahlen kandidieren; **to ~ to gain/lose sth** etw gewinnen/verlieren können; **it ~s to reason** es ist einleuchtend; **as things ~** nach Lage der Dinge; **to ~ sb a drink/meal** jdm einen Drink/ein Essen spendieren; **I can't ~ him** ich kann ihn nicht leiden or ausstehen; **we don't ~ a chance** wir haben keine Chance; **to ~ trial** vor Gericht stehen
  ▶ **stand by** vi (be ready) sich bereithalten; (fail to help) (unbeteiligt) danebenstehen ▷ vt fus (opinion, decision) stehen zu; (person) halten zu
  ▶ **stand down** vi sich zurückziehen
  ▶ **stand for** vt fus (signify) bedeuten; (represent) stehen für; (tolerate) sich dat gefallen lassen
  ▶ **stand in for** vt fus vertreten
  ▶ **stand out** vi hervorstechen
  ▶ **stand up** vi aufstehen
  ▶ **stand up for** vt fus eintreten für
  ▶ **stand up to** vt fus standhalten +dat; (person) sich behaupten gegenüber +dat
stand-alone ['stændələun] adj (Comput) selb(st)ständig
standard ['stændəd] n (level) Niveau nt; (norm)

Norm f; (criterion) Maßstab m; (flag) Standarte f ▷ adj (size, model, value etc) Standard-; (normal) normal; **standards** npl (morals) (sittliche) Maßstäbe pl; **to be** or **to come up to** ~ den Anforderungen genügen; **to apply a double** ~ mit zweierlei Maß messen

Standard Grade (Scot) n (Scol) Schulabschlusszeugnis, ≈ mittlere Reife f

standardization [stændədaɪ'zeɪʃən] n Vereinheitlichung f

standardize ['stændədaɪz] vt vereinheitlichen

standard lamp (Brit) n Stehlampe f

standard of living n Lebensstandard m

standard time n Normalzeit f

stand-by, standby ['stændbaɪ] n Reserve f; (also: **standby ticket**) Stand-by-Ticket nt ▷ adj (generator) Reserve-, Ersatz-; **to be on** ~ (doctor) Bereitschaftsdienst haben; (crew, firemen etc) in Bereitschaft sein, einsatzbereit sein

stand-by ticket n Stand-by-Ticket nt

stand-in ['stændɪn] n Ersatz m

standing ['stændɪŋ] adj (permanent) ständig; (army) stehend ▷ n (status) Rang m, Stellung f; **a ~ ovation** stürmischer Beifall; **of many years'** ~ von langjähriger Dauer; **a relationship of 6 months'** ~ eine seit 6 Monaten bestehende Beziehung; **a man of some** ~ ein angesehener Mann

standing joke n Standardwitz m

standing order (Brit) n (at bank) Dauerauftrag m

standing room n Stehplätze pl

standoff n (situation) ausweglose or verfahrene Situation f

stand-offish [stænd'ɔfɪʃ] adj distanziert

standpat ['stændpæt] (US) adj konservativ

standpipe ['stændpaɪp] n Steigrohr nt

standpoint ['stændpɔɪnt] n Standpunkt m

standstill ['stændstɪl] n: **to be at a** ~ stillstehen; (fig: negotiations) in eine Sackgasse geraten sein; **to come to a** ~ (traffic) zum Stillstand kommen

stank [stæŋk] pt of **stink**

stanza ['stænzə] n Strophe f

staple ['steɪpl] n (for papers) Heftklammer f; (chief product) Hauptartikel m ▷ adj (food, diet) Grund-, Haupt- ▷ vt heften

stapler ['steɪpləʳ] n Hefter m

star [stɑ:ʳ] n Stern m; (celebrity) Star m ▷ vt (Theat, Cine) in der Hauptrolle zeigen ▷ vi: **to** ~ **in** die Hauptrolle haben in; **the stars** npl (horoscope) das Horoskop; **4-~ hotel** 4-Sterne-Hotel nt; **2-~ petrol** (Brit) Normal(benzin) nt; **4-~ petrol** (Brit) Super(benzin) nt

star attraction n Hauptattraktion f

starboard ['stɑ:bɔ:d] adj (side) Steuerbord-; **to** ~ (nach) Steuerbord

starch [stɑ:tʃ] n Stärke f

starched [stɑ:tʃt] adj gestärkt

starchy ['stɑ:tʃɪ] adj (food) stärkehaltig; (pej: person) steif

stardom ['stɑ:dəm] n Berühmtheit f

stare [stɛəʳ] n starrer Blick m ▷ vi: **to** ~ **at**

anstarren

starfish ['stɑ:fɪʃ] n Seestern m

stark [stɑ:k] adj (bleak) kahl; (simplicity) schlicht; (colour) eintönig; (reality, poverty) nackt ▷ adv: ~ **naked** splitternackt

starkers ['stɑ:kəz] (inf) adj splitter(faser)nackt

starlet ['stɑ:lɪt] n (Film)sternchen nt, Starlet nt

starlight ['stɑ:laɪt] n Sternenlicht nt

starling ['stɑ:lɪŋ] n Star m

starlit ['stɑ:lɪt] adj sternklar

starry ['stɑ:rɪ] adj sternklar; ~ **sky** Sternenhimmel m

starry-eyed [stɑ:rɪ'aɪd] adj (innocent) arglos, blauäugig; (from wonder) verzückt

Stars and Stripes n sing Sternenbanner nt

star sign n Sternzeichen nt

star-studded ['stɑ:stʌdɪd] adj: **a ~ cast** eine Starbesetzung f

START n abbr (Mil: = Strategic Arms Reduction Talks) START

start [stɑ:t] n Beginn m, Anfang m; (departure) Aufbruch m; (advantage) Vorsprung m ▷ vt anfangen mit; (panic) auslösen; (fire) anzünden; (found) gründen; (: restaurant etc) eröffnen; (engine) anlassen; (car) starten ▷ vi anfangen; (with fright) zusammenfahren; (engine etc) anspringen; **at the** ~ am Anfang, zu Beginn; **for a** ~ erstens; **to make an early** ~ frühzeitig aufbrechen; **to give a** ~ zusammenfahren; **to wake up with a** ~ aus dem Schlaf hochschrecken; **to ~ doing** or **to do sth** anfangen, etw zu tun; **to ~ (off) with ...** (firstly) erstens; (at the beginning) zunächst

▶ **start off** vi (begin) anfangen; (begin moving) losgehen/-fahren

▶ **start out** vi (leave) sich aufmachen

▶ **start over** (US) vi noch einmal von vorn anfangen

▶ **start up** vt (business) gründen; (restaurant etc) eröffnen; (car) starten; (engine) anlassen

starter ['stɑ:təʳ] n (Aut) Anlasser m; (Sport): official, runner, horse) Starter m; (Brit: Culin) Vorspeise f; **for ~s** (inf) für den Anfang

starting point ['stɑ:tɪŋ-] n (lit, fig) Ausgangspunkt m

starting price n (at auction) Ausgangsangebot nt

startle ['stɑ:tl] vt erschrecken

startling ['stɑ:tlɪŋ] adj (news etc) überraschend

star turn (Brit) n Sensation f, Hauptattraktion f

starvation [stɑ:'veɪʃən] n Hunger m; **to die of/ from** ~ verhungern

starve [stɑ:v] vi hungern; (to death) verhungern ▷ vt hungern lassen; (fig: deprive): **to ~ sb of sth** jdm etw vorenthalten; **I'm starving** ich sterbe vor Hunger

Star Wars n Krieg m der Sterne

stash [stæʃ] vi (also: **stash away**) beiseiteschaffen ▷ n (secret store) geheimes Lager nt

state [steɪt] n (condition) Zustand m; (Pol) Staat m ▷ vt (say) feststellen; (declare) erklären; **the**

States npl (Geog) die (Vereinigten) Staaten pl; **to be in a ~** aufgeregt sein; (on edge) nervös sein; (in a mess) in einem schrecklichen Zustand sein; **to get into a ~** durchdrehen (inf); **in ~** feierlich; **to lie in ~** (feierlich) aufgebahrt sein; **~ of emergency** Notstand m; **~ of mind** Verfassung f

state control n staatliche Kontrolle f

stated ['steɪtɪd] adj erklärt

State Department (US) n Außenministerium nt

state education (Brit) n staatliche Erziehung f; (system) staatliches Bildungswesen nt

stateless ['steɪtlɪs] adj staatenlos

stately ['steɪtlɪ] adj würdevoll; (walk) gemessen; **~ home** Schloss nt

statement ['steɪtmənt] n (thing said) Feststellung f; (declaration) Erklärung f; (Fin) (Konto)auszug m; **official ~** (amtliche) Erklärung f; **bank ~** Kontoauszug m

state of the art n: **the ~** der neueste Stand der Technik ▷ adj: **state-of-the-art** auf dem neuesten Stand der Technik; (technology) Spitzen-

state-owned ['steɪtəʊnd] adj staatseigen

state school n öffentliche Schule f

state secret n Staatsgeheimnis nt

statesman ['steɪtsmən] (irreg: like **man**) n Staatsmann m

statesmanship ['steɪtsmənʃɪp] n Staatskunst f

static ['stætɪk] n (Radio, TV) atmosphärische Störungen pl ▷ adj (not moving) konstant

static electricity n Reibungselektrizität f

station ['steɪʃən] n (Rail) Bahnhof m; (also: **bus station**) Busbahnhof m; (also: **police station**) (Polizei)wache f; (Radio) Sender m ▷ vt (guards etc) postieren; (soldiers etc) stationieren; **action ~s** (Mil) Stellung f; **above one's ~** über seinem Stand

stationary ['steɪʃnərɪ] adj (vehicle) haltend; **to be ~** stehen

stationer ['steɪʃənə^r] n Schreibwarenhändler(in) m(f)

stationer's, stationer's shop n Schreibwarenhandlung f

stationery ['steɪʃnərɪ] n Schreibwaren pl; (writing paper) Briefpapier nt

stationmaster ['steɪʃənmɑːstə^r] n Bahnhofsvorsteher m

station wagon (US) n Kombi(wagen) m

statistic [stə'tɪstɪk] n Statistik f

statistical [stə'tɪstɪkl] adj statistisch

statistics [stə'tɪstɪks] n (science) Statistik f

statue ['stætjuː] n Statue f

statuesque [stætju'ɛsk] adj stattlich

statuette [stætju'ɛt] n Statuette f

stature ['stætʃə^r] n Wuchs m, Statur f; (fig: reputation) Format nt

status ['steɪtəs] n Status m; (position) Stellung f; **the ~ quo** der Status quo

status line n (Comput) Statuszeile f

status symbol n Statussymbol nt

statute ['stætjuːt] n Gesetz nt; **statutes** npl (of club etc) Satzung f

statute book n: **to be on the ~** geltendes Recht sein

statutory ['stætjutrɪ] adj gesetzlich; **~ declaration** eidesstattliche Erklärung f

staunch [stɔːntʃ] adj treu ▷ vt (flow) stauen; (blood) stillen

stave [steɪv] n (Mus) Notensystem nt

▶ **stave off** vt (attack) abwehren; (threat) abwenden

stay [steɪ] n Aufenthalt m ▷ vi bleiben; (with sb, as guest) wohnen; (in hotel) übernachten; **~ of execution** (Law) Aussetzung f; **to ~ put** bleiben; **to ~ with friends** bei Freunden untergebracht sein; **to ~ the night** übernachten

▶ **stay behind** vi zurückbleiben

▶ **stay in** vi (at home) zu Hause bleiben

▶ **stay on** vi bleiben

▶ **stay out** vi (of house) wegbleiben; (remain on strike) weiterstreiken

▶ **stay up** vi (at night) aufbleiben

staying power ['steɪɪŋ-] n Stehvermögen nt, Durchhaltevermögen nt

STD n abbr (Brit: Tel: = subscriber trunk dialling) Selbstwählferndienst m; (Med: = sexually transmitted disease) durch Geschlechtsverkehr übertragene Krankheit f

stead [stɛd] n: **in sb's ~** an jds Stelle; **to stand sb in good ~** jdm zugute- or zustattenkommen

steadfast ['stɛdfɑːst] adj standhaft

steadily ['stɛdɪlɪ] adv (regularly) regelmäßig; (constantly) stetig; (fixedly) fest, unverwandt

steady ['stɛdɪ] adj (job, boyfriend, girlfriend, look) fest; (income) regelmäßig; (speed) gleichmäßig; (rise) stetig; (person, character) zuverlässig, solide; (voice, hand etc) ruhig ▷ vt (stabilize) ruhig halten; (nerves) beruhigen; **to ~ o.s. on sth** sich auf etw acc stützen; **to ~ o.s. against sth** sich an etw dat abstützen

steak [steɪk] n Steak nt; (fish) Filet nt

steakhouse ['steɪkhaus] n Steakrestaurant nt

steal [stiːl] (pt **stole**, pp **stolen**) vt stehlen ▷ vi stehlen; (move secretly) sich stehlen, schleichen

▶ **steal away** vi sich davonschleichen

stealth [stɛlθ] n: **by ~** heimlich

stealthy ['stɛlθɪ] adj heimlich, verstohlen

steam [stiːm] n Dampf m ▷ vt (Culin) dämpfen, dünsten ▷ vi dampfen; **covered with ~** (window etc) beschlagen; **under one's own ~** (fig) allein, ohne Hilfe; **to run out of ~** (fig) den Schwung verlieren; **to let off ~** (inf: fig) Dampf ablassen

▶ **steam up** vi (window) beschlagen; **to get ~ed up about sth** (inf: fig) sich über etw acc aufregen

steam engine n (Rail) Dampflok(omotive) f

steamer ['stiːmə^r] n Dampfer m; (Culin) Dämpfer m

steam iron n Dampfbügeleisen nt

steamroller ['stiːmrəulə^r] n Dampfwalze f

steamship ['stiːmʃɪp] n = **steamer**

steamy ['sti:mɪ] adj (room) dampfig; (window) beschlagen; (book, film) heiß
steed [sti:d] (liter) n Ross nt
steel [sti:l] n Stahl m ▷ adj (girder, wool etc) Stahl-
steel band n (Mus) Steelband f
steel industry n Stahlindustrie f
steel mill n Stahlwalzwerk nt
steelworks ['sti:lwə:ks] n Stahlwerk nt
steely ['sti:lɪ] adj (determination) eisern; (eyes, gaze) hart, stählern
steep [sti:p] adj steil; (increase, rise) stark; (price, fees) gepfeffert ▷ vt einweichen; **to be ~ed in history** geschichtsträchtig sein
steeple ['sti:pl] n Kirchturm m
steeplechase ['sti:pltʃeɪs] n (for horses) Hindernisrennen nt; (for runners) Hindernislauf m
steeplejack ['sti:pldʒæk] n Turmarbeiter m
steeply ['sti:plɪ] adv steil
steer [stɪər] vt steuern; (car etc) lenken; (person) lotsen ▷ vi steuern; (in car etc) lenken; **to ~ for** zusteuern auf +acc; **to ~ clear of sb** (fig) jdm aus dem Weg gehen; **to ~ clear of sth** (fig) etw meiden
steering ['stɪərɪŋ] n (Aut) Lenkung f
steering column n (Aut) Lenksäule f
steering committee n Lenkungsausschuss m
steering wheel n (Aut) Lenkrad nt, Steuer nt
stellar ['stɛlər] adj stellar
stem [stɛm] n Stiel m; (of pipe) Hals m ▷ vt aufhalten; (flow) eindämmen; (bleeding) zum Stillstand bringen
▶ **stem from** vt fus zurückgehen auf +acc
stench [stɛntʃ] (pej) n Gestank m
stencil ['stɛnsl] n Schablone f ▷ vt mit Schablone zeichnen
stenographer [stɛ'nɔɡrəfər] (US) n Stenograf(in) m(f)
stenography [stɛ'nɔɡrəfɪ] (US) n Stenografie f
step [stɛp] n (lit, fig) Schritt m; (of stairs) Stufe f ▷ vi: **to ~ forward/back** vor-/zurücktreten; **steps** npl (Brit) = **stepladder**; **~ by step** (fig) Schritt für Schritt; **in/out of ~ (with)** im/nicht im Tritt (mit); (fig) im/nicht im Gleichklang (mit)
▶ **step down** vi (fig: resign) zurücktreten
▶ **step in** vi (fig) eingreifen
▶ **step off** vt fus aussteigen aus +dat
▶ **step on** vt fus treten auf +acc
▶ **step over** vt fus steigen über +acc
▶ **step up** vt (efforts) steigern; (pace etc) beschleunigen
stepbrother ['stɛpbrʌðər] n Stiefbruder m
stepchild ['stɛptʃaɪld] n Stiefkind nt
stepdaughter ['stɛpdɔ:tər] n Stieftochter f
stepfather ['stɛpfɑ:ðər] n Stiefvater m
stepladder ['stɛplædər] (Brit) n Trittleiter f
stepmother ['stɛpmʌðər] n Stiefmutter f
stepping stone ['stɛpɪŋ-] n Trittstein m; (fig) Sprungbrett nt
stepsister ['stɛpsɪstər] n Stiefschwester f
stepson ['stɛpsʌn] n Stiefsohn m
stereo ['stɛrɪəu] n (system) Stereoanlage f ▷ adj

(sound etc) Stereo-; **in ~** in Stereo
stereotype ['stɪərɪətaɪp] n Klischee nt, Klischeevorstellung f ▷ vt in ein Klischee zwängen; **~d** stereotyp
sterile ['stɛraɪl] adj steril, keimfrei; (barren) unfruchtbar; (fig: debate) fruchtlos
sterility [stɛ'rɪlɪtɪ] n Unfruchtbarkeit f
sterilization [stɛrɪlaɪ'zeɪʃən] n Sterilisation f, Sterilisierung f
sterilize ['stɛrɪlaɪz] vt sterilisieren
sterling ['stə:lɪŋ] adj (silver) Sterling-; (fig) gediegen ▷ n (Econ) das Pfund Sterling, das englische Pfund; **one pound ~** ein Pfund Sterling
sterling area n (Econ) Sterlingländer pl
stern [stə:n] adj streng ▷ n Heck nt
sternum ['stə:nəm] n Brustbein nt
steroid ['stɪərɔɪd] n Steroid nt
stethoscope ['stɛθəskəup] n Stethoskop nt
stevedore ['sti:vədɔ:ʳ] n Stauer m, Schauermann m
stew [stju:] n Eintopf m ▷ vt schmoren; (fruit, vegetables) dünsten ▷ vi schmoren; **~ed tea** bitterer Tee m; **~ed fruit** (Obst)kompott nt
steward ['stju:əd] n Steward m; (at public event) Ordner(in) m(f); (also: **shop steward**) gewerkschaftliche Vertrauensperson f
stewardess ['stjuədɛs] n Stewardess f
stewardship ['stjuədʃɪp] n Verwaltung f
stewing steak, (US) **stew meat** ['stju:ɪŋ-] n (Rinder)schmorfleisch nt
St. Ex. abbr = **stock exchange**
stg abbr = **sterling**
stick [stɪk] (pt, pp **stuck**) n Zweig m; (of dynamite) Stange f; (of chalk etc) Stück nt; (as weapon) Stock m; (also: **walking stick**) (Spazier)stock m ▷ vt (with glue etc) kleben; (inf: put) tun, stecken; (: tolerate) aushalten; (thrust) stoßen ▷ vi: **to ~ (to)** kleben (an +dat); (remain) (hängen) bleiben; (door etc) klemmen; (lift) stecken bleiben; **to get hold of the wrong end of the ~** (Brit: fig) es falsch verstehen; **to ~ in sb's mind** jdm im Gedächtnis (haften) bleiben
▶ **stick around** vi (inf) hier-/dableiben
▶ **stick out** vi (ears etc) abstehen ▷ vt: **to ~ it out** (inf) durchhalten
▶ **stick to** vt fus (one's word, promise) halten; (agreement, rules) sich halten an +acc; (the truth, facts) bleiben bei
▶ **stick up** vi hochstehen
▶ **stick up for** vt fus eintreten für
sticker ['stɪkər] n Aufkleber m
sticking plaster ['stɪkɪŋ-] n Heftpflaster nt
sticking point n Hindernis nt; (in discussion etc) strittiger Punkt m
stickleback ['stɪklbæk] n Stichling m
stickler ['stɪklər] n: **to be a ~ for sth** es mit etw peinlich genau nehmen
stick shift (US) n Schaltknüppel m; (car) Wagen m mit Handschaltung
stick-up ['stɪkʌp] (inf) n Überfall m
sticky ['stɪkɪ] adj klebrig; (label, tape) Klebe-; (weather, day) schwül

S

stiff [stɪf] adj steif; (hard, firm) hart; (paste, egg-white) fest; (door, zip etc) schwer gehend; (competition) hart; (sentence) schwer; (drink) stark ▷ adv (bored, worried, scared) zu Tode; **to be** or **feel ~** steif sein; **to have a ~ neck** einen steifen Hals haben; **to keep a ~ upper lip** (Brit: fig) die Haltung bewahren

stiffen ['stɪfn] vi steif werden; (body) erstarren

stiffness ['stɪfnɪs] n Steifheit f

stifle ['staɪfl] vt unterdrücken; (heat) erdrücken

stifling ['staɪflɪŋ] adj (heat) drückend

stigma ['stɪgmə] n Stigma nt; (Bot) Narbe f, Stigma nt; **stigmata** npl (Med) Wundmal nt

stile [staɪl] n Zaunübertritt m

stiletto [stɪ'letəu] (Brit) n (also: **stiletto heel**) Bleistiftabsatz m

still [stɪl] adj (motionless) bewegungslos; (tranquil) ruhig; (air, water) still; (Brit: drink) ohne Kohlensäure ▷ adv (immer) noch; (yet, even) noch; (nonetheless) trotzdem ▷ n (Cine) Standfoto nt; **to stand ~** (machine, motor) stillstehen; (motionless) still stehen; **keep ~!** halte still!; **he ~ hasn't arrived** er ist immer noch nicht angekommen

stillborn ['stɪlbɔːn] adj tot geboren

still life n Stillleben nt

stilt [stɪlt] n (pile) Pfahl m; (for walking on) Stelze f

stilted ['stɪltɪd] adj gestelzt

stimulant ['stɪmjulənt] n Anregungsmittel nt

stimulate ['stɪmjuleɪt] vt anregen, stimulieren; (demand) ankurbeln

stimulating ['stɪmjuleɪtɪŋ] adj anregend, stimulierend

stimulation [stɪmju'leɪʃən] n Anregung f, Stimulation f

stimuli ['stɪmjulaɪ] npl of **stimulus**

stimulus ['stɪmjuləs] (pl **stimuli**) n (incentive) Anreiz m; (Biol) Reiz m; (Psych) Stimulus m

sting [stɪŋ] (pt, pp **stung**) n Stich m; (pain) Stechen nt; (organ: of insect) Stachel m; (inf: confidence trick) Ding nt ▷ vt stechen; (fig) treffen, verletzen ▷ vi stechen; (eyes, ointment, plant etc) brennen; **my eyes are ~ing** mir brennen die Augen

stingy ['stɪndʒɪ] (pej) adj geizig, knauserig

stink [stɪŋk] (pt **stank**, pp **stunk**) n Gestank m ▷ vi stinken

stinker ['stɪŋkə'] (inf) n (problem) harter Brocken m; (person) Ekel nt

stinking ['stɪŋkɪŋ] (inf) adj (fig) beschissen (!); **a ~ cold** eine scheußliche Erkältung; **~ rich** stinkreich

stint [stɪnt] n (period) Zeit f; (batch of work) Pensum nt; (share) Teil m ▷ vi: **to ~ on** sparen mit

stipend ['staɪpend] n Gehalt nt

stipendiary [staɪ'pendɪərɪ] adj: **~ magistrate** bezahlter Friedensrichter m

stipulate ['stɪpjuleɪt] vt festsetzen; (condition) stellen

stipulation [stɪpju'leɪʃən] n Bedingung f, Auflage f

stir [stəː'] n (fig) Aufsehen nt ▷ vt umrühren; (fig: emotions) aufwühlen; (: person) bewegen ▷ vi sich bewegen; **to give sth a ~** etw umrühren; **to cause a ~** Aufsehen erregen
  ▶ **stir up** vt: **to ~ up trouble** Unruhe stiften; **to ~ things up** stänkern

stir-fry ['stəː'fraɪ] vt unter Rühren kurz anbraten ▷ n Pfannengericht nt (das unter Rühren kurz angebraten wurde)

stirring ['stəːrɪŋ] adj bewegend

stirrup ['stɪrəp] n Steigbügel m

stitch [stɪtʃ] n (Sewing) Stich m; (Knitting) Masche f; (Med) Faden m; (pain) Seitenstiche pl ▷ vt nähen; **he had to have ~es** er musste genäht werden

stoat [stəut] n Wiesel nt

stock [stɔk] n Vorrat m; (Comm) Bestand m; (Agr) Vieh nt; (Culin) Brühe f; (descent, origin) Abstammung f, Herkunft f; (Fin) Wertpapiere pl; (Rail: also: **rolling stock**) rollendes Material nt ▷ adj (reply, excuse etc) Standard- ▷ vt (in shop) führen; **in/out of ~** vorrätig/nicht vorrätig; **~s and shares** (Aktien und) Wertpapiere pl; **government ~** Staatsanleihe f; **to take ~ of** (fig) Bilanz ziehen über +acc; **well-~ed** (shop) mit gutem Sortiment
  ▶ **stock up** vi: **to ~ up (with)** sich eindecken (mit)

stockade [stɔ'keɪd] n Palisade f

stockbroker ['stɔkbrəukə'] n Börsenmakler m

stock control n Bestandsüberwachung f

stock cube (Brit) n Brühwürfel m

stock exchange n Börse f

stockholder ['stɔkhəuldə'] (esp US) n Aktionär(in) m(f)

Stockholm ['stɔkhəum] n Stockholm nt

stocking ['stɔkɪŋ] n Strumpf m

stock-in-trade ['stɔkɪn'treɪd] n (fig): **it's his ~** es gehört zu seinem festen Repertoire

stockist ['stɔkɪst] (Brit) n Händler m

stock market (Brit) n Börse f

stock phrase n Standardsatz m

stockpile ['stɔkpaɪl] n Vorrat m; (of weapons) Lager nt ▷ vt horten

stockroom ['stɔkruːm] n Lager nt, Lagerraum m

stocktaking ['stɔkteɪkɪŋ] (Brit) n Inventur f

stocky ['stɔkɪ] adj stämmig

stodgy ['stɔdʒɪ] adj (food) pampig (inf), schwer

stoic ['stəuɪk] n Stoiker(in) m(f) ▷ adj stoisch

stoical ['stəuɪkl] adj stoisch

stoke [stəuk] vt (fire) schüren; (furnace, boiler) heizen

stoker ['stəukə'] n Heizer m

stole [stəul] pt of **steal** ▷ n Stola f

stolen ['stəuln] pp of **steal**

stolid ['stɔlɪd] adj phlegmatisch, stur (inf)

stomach ['stʌmək] n Magen m; (belly) Bauch m ▷ vt (fig) vertragen

stomach ache n Magenschmerzen pl

stomach pump n Magenpumpe f

stomach ulcer n Magengeschwür nt

stomp [stɔmp] vi stapfen

stone [stəun] n Stein m; (Brit: weight) Gewichtseinheit f (= 6,35 kg) ▷ adj (wall, jar etc)

Stein-, steinern ▷ vt (person) mit Steinen bewerfen; (fruit) entkernen, entsteinen; **within a ~'s throw of the station** nur einen Katzensprung vom Bahnhof entfernt

Stone Age n Steinzeit f

stone-cold ['stəun'kəuld] adj eiskalt

stoned [stəund] (inf) adj (on drugs) stoned; (drunk) total zu

stone-deaf ['stəun'def] adj stocktaub

stonemason ['stəunmeisn] n Steinmetz m

stonewall [stəun'wɔ:l] vi mauern; (in answering questions) ausweichen

stonework ['stəunwə:k] n Mauerwerk nt

stony ['stəuni] adj steinig; (fig: silence etc) steinern

stood [stud] pt, pp of **stand**

stooge [stu:dʒ] n (inf) Handlanger(in) m(f); (Theat) Stichwortgeber(in) m(f)

stool [stu:l] n Hocker m

stoop [stu:p] vi (also: **stoop down**) sich bücken; (walk) gebeugt gehen; **to ~ to sth** (fig) sich zu etw herablassen; **to ~ to doing sth** sich dazu herablassen, etw zu tun

stop [stɔp] n Halt m; (short stay) Aufenthalt m; (in punctuation: also: **full stop**) Punkt m; (bus stop etc) Haltestelle f ▷ vt stoppen; (car etc) anhalten; (block) sperren; (prevent) verhindern ▷ vi (car etc) anhalten; (train) halten; (pedestrian, watch, clock) stehen bleiben; (end) aufhören; **to come to a ~** anhalten; **to put a ~ to** einen Riegel vorschieben +dat; **to ~ doing sth** aufhören, etw zu tun; **to ~ sb (from) doing sth** jdn davon abhalten, etw zu tun; **~ it!** lass das!, hör auf!

▶ **stop by** vi kurz vorbeikommen

▶ **stop off** vi kurz haltmachen, Zwischenstation machen

▶ **stop up** vt (hole) zustopfen

stopcock ['stɔpkɔk] n Absperrhahn m

stopgap ['stɔpgæp] n (person) Lückenbüßer m; (thing) Notbehelf m; **~ measure** Überbrückungsmaßnahme f

stop-go [stɔp'gəu] adj (economic cycle etc) mit ständigem Auf und Ab

stoplights ['stɔplaits] npl (Aut) Bremslichter pl

stopover ['stɔpəuvə'] n Zwischenaufenthalt m; (Aviat) Zwischenlandung f

stoppage ['stɔpidʒ] n (strike) Streik m; (blockage) Unterbrechung f; (of pay, cheque) Sperrung f; (deduction) Abzug m

stopper ['stɔpə'] n Stöpsel m

stop press n letzte Meldungen pl

stopwatch ['stɔpwɔtʃ] n Stoppuhr f

storage ['stɔ:ridʒ] n Lagerung f; (also: **storage space**) Stauraum m; (Comput) Speicherung f

storage capacity n (Comput) Speicherkapazität f

storage heater (Brit) n (Nacht)speicherofen m

store [stɔ:'] n Vorrat m; (depot) Lager nt; (Brit: large shop) Geschäft nt, Kaufhaus nt; (US: shop) Laden m; (fig): **a ~ of** eine Fülle an +dat ▷ vt lagern; (information etc, Comput) speichern; (food, medicines etc) aufbewahren;

(in filing system) ablegen; **stores** npl (provisions) Vorräte pl; **in ~** eingelagert; **who knows what's in ~ for us?** wer weiß, was uns bevorsteht?; **to set great/little ~ by sth** viel/wenig von etw halten

▶ **store up** vt einen Vorrat anlegen von; (memories) im Gedächtnis bewahren

storehouse ['stɔ:haus] n (US: Comm) Lager(haus) nt; (fig) Fundgrube f

storekeeper ['stɔ:ki:pə'] (US) n Ladenbesitzer(in) m(f)

storeroom ['stɔ:ru:m] n Lagerraum m

storey, (US) **story** ['stɔ:ri] n Stock m, Stockwerk nt

stork [stɔ:k] n Storch m

storm [stɔ:m] n (lit, fig) Sturm m; (bad weather) Unwetter nt; (also: **electrical storm**) Gewitter nt ▷ vi (fig) toben ▷ vt (attack) stürmen

storm cloud n Gewitterwolke f

storm door n äußere Windfangtür f

stormy ['stɔ:mi] adj (lit, fig) stürmisch

story ['stɔ:ri] n Geschichte f; (Press) Artikel m; (lie) Märchen nt; (US) = **storey**

storybook ['stɔ:ribuk] n Geschichtenbuch nt

storyteller ['stɔ:ritelə'] n Geschichtenerzähler(in) m(f)

stout [staut] adj (strong) stark; (fat) untersetzt; (resolute) energisch ▷ n Starkbier nt

stove [stəuv] n Herd m; (small) Kocher m; (for heating) (Heiz)ofen m; **gas ~** Gasherd m

stow [stəu] vt (also: **stow away**) verstauen

stowaway ['stəuəwei] n blinder Passagier m

straddle ['strædl] vt (sitting) rittlings sitzen auf +dat; (standing) breitbeinig stehen über +dat; (jumping) grätschen über +acc; (fig) überspannen

strafe [stra:f] vt beschießen

straggle ['strægl] vi (houses etc) verstreut liegen; (people etc) zurückbleiben

straggler ['stræglə'] n Nachzügler m

straggly ['strægli] adj (hair) unordentlich

straight [streit] adj gerade; (hair) glatt; (honest) offen, direkt; (simple) einfach; (: fight) direkt; (Theat) ernst; (inf: heterosexual) hetero; (whisky etc) pur ▷ adv (in time) sofort; (in direction) direkt; (drink) pur ▷ n (Sport) Gerade f; **to put** or **get sth ~** (make clear) etw klären; (make tidy) etw in Ordnung bringen; **let's get this ~** das wollen wir mal klarstellen; **10 ~ wins** 10 Siege hintereinander; **to go ~ home** direkt nach Hause gehen; **~ out** rundheraus; **~ away, ~ off** sofort, gleich

straighten ['streitn] vt (skirt, sheet etc) gerade ziehen

▶ **straighten out** vt (fig) klären

straighteners ['streitnəz] npl (for hair) Haarglätter m

straight-faced [streit'feist] adj: **to be/remain ~** ernst bleiben ▷ adv ohne zu lachen

straightforward [streit'fɔ:wəd] adj (simple) einfach; (honest) offen

straight sets npl (Tennis): **to win in ~** ohne Satzverlust gewinnen

strain [streɪn] n Belastung f; (Med: also: **back strain**) überanstrengter Rücken m; (: tension) Überlastung f; (of virus) Art f; (breed) Sorte f ▷ vt (back etc) überanstrengen; (resources) belasten; (Culin) abgießen ▷ vi: **to ~ to do sth** sich anstrengen, etw zu tun; **strains** npl (Mus) Klänge pl; **he's been under a lot of ~** er hat unter großem Stress gestanden

strained [streɪnd] adj (back) überanstrengt; (muscle) gezerrt; (forced) gezwungen; (relations) gespannt

strainer ['streɪnəʳ] n Sieb nt

strait [streɪt] n Meerenge f, Straße f; **straits** npl (fig): **to be in dire ~s** in großen Nöten sein

straitjacket ['streɪtdʒækɪt] n Zwangsjacke f

strait-laced [streɪt'leɪst] adj prüde, puritanisch

strand [strænd] n (lit, fig) Faden m; (of wire) Litze f; (of hair) Strähne f

stranded ['strændɪd] adj: **to be ~** (traveller) festsitzen; (ship, sea creature) gestrandet

strange [streɪndʒ] adj fremd; (odd) seltsam, merkwürdig

strangely ['streɪndʒlɪ] adv seltsam, merkwürdig; see also **enough**

stranger ['streɪndʒəʳ] n Fremde(r) f(m); **I'm a ~ here** ich bin hier fremd

strangle ['stræŋgl] vt erwürgen, erdrosseln; (fig: economy etc) ersticken

stranglehold ['stræŋglhəʊld] n (fig) absolute Machtposition f

strangulation [stræŋgju'leɪʃən] n Erwürgen nt, Erdrosseln nt

strap [stræp] n Riemen m; (of dress etc) Träger m ▷ vt (also: **strap in**) anschnallen; (also: **strap on**) umschnallen

straphanging ['stræphæŋɪŋ] n Pendeln nt (als stehender Fahrgast)

strapless ['stræplɪs] adj trägerlos, schulterfrei

strapped [stræpt] (inf) adj: **~ (for cash)** pleite

strapping ['stræpɪŋ] adj stramm

Strasbourg ['stræzbəːg] n Straßburg nt

strata ['strɑːtə] npl of **stratum**

stratagem ['strætɪdʒəm] n List f

strategic [strə'tiːdʒɪk] adj strategisch; (error) taktisch

strategist ['strætɪdʒɪst] n Stratege m, Strategin f

strategy ['strætɪdʒɪ] n Strategie f

stratosphere ['strætəsfɪəʳ] n Stratosphäre f

stratum ['strɑːtəm] (pl **strata**) n Schicht f

straw [strɔː] n Stroh nt; (also: **drinking straw**) Strohhalm m; **that's the last ~!** das ist der Gipfel!

strawberry ['strɔːbərɪ] n Erdbeere f

stray [streɪ] adj (animal) streunend; (bullet) verirrt; (scattered) einzeln, vereinzelt ▷ vi (children) sich verirren; (animals) streunen; (thoughts) abschweifen

streak [striːk] n Streifen m; (in hair) Strähne f; (fig: of madness etc) Zug m ▷ vt streifen ▷ vi: **to ~ past** vorbeiflitzen; **a winning/losing ~** eine Glücks-/Pechsträhne

streaker ['striːkəʳ] (inf) n Blitzer(in) m(f)

streaky ['striːkɪ] adj (bacon) durchwachsen

stream [striːm] n (small river) Bach m; (current) Strömung f; (of people, vehicles) Strom m; (of questions, insults etc) Flut f, Schwall m; (of smoke) Schwaden m; (Scol) Leistungsgruppe f ▷ vt (Scol) in Leistungsgruppen einteilen ▷ vi strömen; **against the ~** gegen den Strom; **to come on ~** (new power plant etc) in Betrieb genommen werden

streamer ['striːməʳ] n Luftschlange f

stream feed n automatischer Papiereinzug m

streamline ['striːmlaɪn] vt Stromlinienform geben +dat; (fig) rationalisieren

streamlined ['striːmlaɪnd] adj stromlinienförmig; (Aviat, Aut) windschlüpfrig; (fig) rationalisiert

street [striːt] n Straße f; **the back ~s** die Seitensträßchen pl; **to be on the ~s** (homeless) obdachlos sein; (as prostitute) auf den Strich gehen

streetcar ['striːtkɑːʳ] (US) n Straßenbahn f

street cred [-kred] (inf) n Glaubwürdigkeit f

street lamp n Straßenlaterne f

street lighting n Straßenbeleuchtung f

street map n Stadtplan m

street market n Straßenmarkt m

street plan n Stadtplan m

streetwise ['striːtwaɪz] (inf) adj: **to be ~** wissen, wos langgeht

strength [streŋθ] n (lit, fig) Stärke f; (physical) Kraft f, Stärke f; (of girder etc) Stabilität f; (of knot etc) Festigkeit f; (of chemical solution) Konzentration f; (of wine) Schwere f; **on the ~ of** aufgrund +gen; **at full ~** vollzählig; **to be below ~** nicht die volle Stärke haben

strengthen ['streŋθn] vt (lit, fig) verstärken; (muscle) kräftigen; (economy, currency, relationship) festigen

strenuous ['strenjuəs] adj anstrengend; (determined) unermüdlich

strenuously ['strenjuəslɪ] adv energisch; **she denied the rumour** sie leugnete das Gerücht hartnäckig

stress [stres] n Druck m; (mental) Belastung f, Stress m; (Ling) Betonung f; (emphasis) Akzent m, Gewicht nt ▷ vt betonen; **to lay great ~ on sth** großen Wert auf etw acc legen; **to be under ~** großen Belastungen ausgesetzt sein, unter Stress stehen

stressful ['stresful] adj anstrengend, stressig; (situation) angespannt

stretch [stretʃ] n (of sand, water etc) Stück nt; (of time) Zeit f ▷ vi (person, animal) sich strecken; (land, area) sich erstrecken ▷ vt (pull) spannen; (fig: job, task) fordern; **at a ~** an einem Stück, ohne Unterbrechung; **by no ~ of the imagination** beim besten Willen nicht; **to ~ to** or **as far as the frontier** (extend) sich bis zur Grenze erstrecken; **to ~ one's legs** sich dat die Beine vertreten

▶ **stretch out** vi sich ausstrecken ▷ vt ausstrecken

▶ **stretch to** vt fus (be enough) reichen für

stretcher ['strɛtʃəʳ] n (Trag)bahre f

stretcher-bearer ['strɛtʃəbɛərəʳ] n Krankenträger m

stretch marks npl Dehnungsstreifen pl; (through pregnancy) Schwangerschaftsstreifen pl

strewn [struːn] adj: ~ **with** übersät mit

stricken ['strɪkən] adj (person) leidend; (city, industry etc) Not leidend; ~ **with** (disease) geschlagen mit; (fear etc) erfüllt von

strict [strɪkt] adj streng; (precise) genau; **in the ~est confidence** streng vertraulich; **in the ~ sense of the word** streng genommen

strictly ['strɪktlɪ] adv streng; (exactly) genau; (solely) ausschließlich; ~ **confidential** streng vertraulich; ~ **speaking** genau genommen; **not ~ true** nicht ganz richtig; ~ **between ourselves** ganz unter uns

strictness ['strɪktnɪs] n Strenge f

stridden ['strɪdn] pp of **stride**

stride [straɪd] (pt **strode**, pp **stridden**) n Schritt m ▷ vi schreiten; **to take sth in one's ~** (fig) mit etw spielend fertig werden

strident ['straɪdnt] adj schrill, durchdringend; (demands) lautstark

strife [straɪf] n Streit m, Zwietracht f

strike [straɪk] (pt, pp **struck**) n Streik m, Ausstand m; (Mil) Angriff m ▷ vt (hit) schlagen; (fig: idea, thought) in den Sinn kommen +dat; (oil etc) finden, stoßen auf +acc; (bargain, deal) aushandeln; (coin, medal) prägen ▷ vi streiken; (illness, killer) zuschlagen; (disaster) hereinbrechen; (clock) schlagen; **on ~** streikend; **to be on ~** streiken; **to ~ a balance** einen Mittelweg finden; **to be struck by lightning** vom Blitz getroffen werden; **to ~ a match** ein Streichholz anzünden

▶ **strike back** vi (Mil) zurückschlagen; (fig) sich wehren

▶ **strike down** vt niederschlagen

▶ **strike off** vt (from list) (aus)streichen; (doctor etc) die Zulassung entziehen +dat

▶ **strike out** vi losziehen, sich aufmachen ▷ vt (word, sentence) (aus)streichen

▶ **strike up** vt (Mus) anstimmen; (conversation) anknüpfen; (friendship) schließen

strikebreaker ['straɪkbreɪkəʳ] n Streikbrecher m

strike pay n Streikgeld nt

striker ['straɪkəʳ] n Streikende(r) f(m); (Sport) Stürmer m

striking ['straɪkɪŋ] adj auffallend; (attractive) attraktiv

strimmer ['strɪməʳ] n Rasentrimmer m

string [strɪŋ] (pt, pp **strung**) n Schnur f; (of islands) Kette f; (of people, cars) Schlange f; (series) Serie f; (Comput) Zeichenfolge f; (Mus) Saite f ▷ vt: **to ~ together** aneinanderreihen; **the strings** npl (Mus) die Streichinstrumente pl; **to pull ~s** (fig) Beziehungen spielen lassen; **with no ~s attached** (fig) ohne Bedingungen; **to ~ sth out** etw verteilen

string bean n grüne Bohne f

stringed instrument n Saiteninstrument nt

stringent ['strɪndʒənt] adj streng; (measures) drastisch

string quartet n Streichquartett nt

strip [strɪp] n Streifen m; (of metal) Band nt; (Sport) Trikot nt, Dress m ▷ vt (undress) ausziehen; (paint) abbeizen; (also: **strip down**: machine etc) auseinandernehmen ▷ vi (undress) sich ausziehen

strip cartoon n Comic(strip) m

stripe [straɪp] n Streifen m; **stripes** npl (Mil, Police) (Ärmel)streifen pl

striped [straɪpt] adj gestreift

strip lighting (Brit) n Neonlicht nt

strip mall n Einkaufsmeile nt

stripper ['strɪpəʳ] n Stripper(in) m(f), Stripteasetänzer(in) m(f)

strip-search ['strɪpsɛtʃ] n Leibesvisitation f (bei der man sich ausziehen muss) ▷ vt: **to be ~ed** sich ausziehen müssen und durchsucht werden

striptease ['strɪptiːz] n Striptease m or nt

strive [straɪv] (pt **strove**, pp ~**n**) vi: **to ~ for sth** nach etw streben; **to ~ to do sth** danach streben, etw zu tun

striven ['strɪvn] pp of **strive**

strobe [strəʊb] n (also: **strobe lights**) Stroboskoplicht nt

strode [strəʊd] pt of **stride**

stroke [strəʊk] n Schlag m, Hieb m; (Swimming: style) Stil m; (Med) Schlaganfall m; (of clock) Schlag m; (of paintbrush) Strich m ▷ vt (caress) streicheln; **at a ~** mit einem Schlag; **on the ~ of** 5 Punkt 5 (Uhr); **a ~ of luck** ein Glücksfall m; **a 2-~ engine** ein Zweitaktmotor m

stroll [strəʊl] n Spaziergang m ▷ vi spazieren; **to go for a ~, have** or **take a ~** einen Spaziergang machen

stroller ['strəʊləʳ] (US) n (pushchair) Sportwagen m

strong [strɒŋ] adj stark; (person, arms, grip) stark, kräftig; (healthy) kräftig; (object, material) solide, stabil; (letter) geharnischt; (measure) drastisch; (language) derb; (nerves) gut; (taste, smell) streng ▷ adv: **to be going ~** (company) sehr erfolgreich sein; (person) gut in Schuss sein; **I have no ~ feelings about it** es ist mir ziemlich egal; **they are 50 ~** sie sind insgesamt 50

strong-arm ['strɒŋɑːm] adj brutal

strongbox ['strɒŋbɒks] n (Geld)kassette f

stronghold ['strɒŋhəʊld] n Festung f; (fig) Hochburg f

strongly ['strɒŋlɪ] adv (solidly) stabil; (forcefully) entschieden; (deeply) fest; **to feel ~ that ...** fest davon überzeugt sein, dass ...; **I feel ~ about** it mir liegt sehr viel daran; (negatively) ich bin sehr dagegen

strongman ['strɒŋmæn] (irreg: like **man**) n (lit, fig) starker Mann m

strongroom ['strɒŋruːm] n Tresorraum m

stroppy ['strɒpɪ] (Brit: inf) adj pampig; (obstinate) stur

805

strove [strəuv] *pt of* **strive**

struck [strʌk] *pt, pp of* **strike**

structural ['strʌktʃrəl] *adj* strukturell; *(damage)* baulich; *(defect)* Konstruktions-

structurally ['strʌktʃrəlɪ] *adv:* ~ **sound** mit guter Bausubstanz

structure ['strʌktʃəʳ] *n* Struktur *f*, Aufbau *m*; *(building)* Gebäude *nt*

struggle ['strʌgl] *n* Kampf *m*; *(difficulty)* Anstrengung *f* ▷ *vi (try hard)* sich abmühen; *(fight)* kämpfen; *(in self-defence)* sich wehren; **to have a ~ to do sth** Mühe haben, etw zu tun; **to be a ~ for sb** jdm große Schwierigkeiten bereiten

strum [strʌm] *vt (guitar)* klimpern auf +dat

strung [strʌŋ] *pt, pp of* **string**

strut [strʌt] *n* Strebe *f*, Stütze *f* ▷ *vi* stolzieren

strychnine ['strɪkniːn] *n* Strychnin *nt*

stub [stʌb] *n (of cheque, ticket etc)* Abschnitt *m*; *(of cigarette)* Kippe *f* ▷ *vt:* **to ~ one's toe** sich *dat* den Zeh stoßen

▷ **stub out** *vt (cigarette)* ausdrücken

stubble ['stʌbl] *n* Stoppeln *pl*

stubborn ['stʌbən] *adj* hartnäckig; *(child)* störrisch

stubby ['stʌbɪ] *adj* kurz und dick

stucco ['stʌkəu] *n* Stuck *m*

stuck [stʌk] *pt, pp of* **stick** ▷ *adj:* **to be ~** *(jammed)* klemmen; *(unable to answer)* nicht klarkommen; **to get ~** stecken bleiben; *(fig)* nicht weiterkommen

stuck-up [stʌk'ʌp] *(inf) adj* hochnäsig

stud [stʌd] *n (on clothing etc)* Niete *f*; *(on collar)* Kragenknopf *m*; *(earring)* Ohrstecker *m*; *(on boot)* Stollen *m*; *(also:* **stud farm)** Gestüt *nt*; *(also:* **stud horse)** Zuchthengst *m* ▷ *vt (fig):* ~**ded with** übersät mit; *(with jewels)* dicht besetzt mit

student ['stjuːdənt] *n* Student(in) *m(f)*; *(at school)* Schüler(in) *m(f)* ▷ *cpd* Studenten-; **law/ medical** ~ Jura-/Medizinstudent(in) *m(f)*; ~ **nurse** Krankenpflegeschüler(in) *m(f)*; ~ **teacher** Referendar(in) *m(f)*

student driver *(US) n* Fahrschüler(in) *m(f)*

students' union ['stjuːdənts-] *(Brit) n* Studentenvereinigung *f* ≈ AStA *m*; *(building)* Gebäude *nt* der Studentenvereinigung

studied ['stʌdɪd] *adj (expression)* einstudiert; *(attitude)* berechnet

studio ['stjuːdɪəu] *n* Studio *nt*; *(sculptor's etc)* Atelier *nt*

studio flat, *(US)* **studio apartment** *n* Einzimmerwohnung *f*

studious ['stjuːdɪəs] *adj* lernbegierig

studiously ['stjuːdɪəslɪ] *adv (carefully)* sorgsam

study ['stʌdɪ] *n* Studium *nt*, Lernen *nt*; *(room)* Arbeitszimmer *nt* ▷ *vt* studieren; *(face)* prüfend ansehen; *(evidence)* prüfen ▷ *vi* studieren, lernen; **studies** *npl (studying)* Studien *pl*; **to make a ~ of sth** etw untersuchen; *(academic)* etw studieren; **to ~ for an exam** sich auf eine Prüfung vorbereiten

stuff [stʌf] *n* Zeug *nt* ▷ *vt* ausstopfen; *(Culin)* füllen; *(inf: push)* stopfen; **my nose is ~ed up** ich habe eine verstopfte Nase; **get ~ed!** *(inf!)* du kannst mich mal!

stuffed toy [stʌft-] *n* Stofftier *nt*

stuffing ['stʌfɪŋ] *n* Füllung *f*; *(in sofa etc)* Polstermaterial *nt*

stuffy ['stʌfɪ] *adj (room)* stickig; *(person, ideas)* spießig

stumble ['stʌmbl] *vi* stolpern; **to ~ across** or **on** *(fig)* (zufällig) stoßen auf +*acc*

stumbling block ['stʌmblɪŋ-] *n* Hürde *f*, Hindernis *nt*

stump [stʌmp] *n* Stumpf *m* ▷ *vt:* **to be ~ed** überfragt sein

stun [stʌn] *vt* betäuben; *(news)* fassungslos machen

stung [stʌŋ] *pt, pp of* **sting**

stunk [stʌŋk] *pp of* **stink**

stunning ['stʌnɪŋ] *adj (news, event)* sensationell; *(girl, dress)* hinreißend

stunt [stʌnt] *n (in film)* Stunt *m*; *(publicity stunt)* (Werbe)gag *m*

stunted ['stʌntɪd] *adj* verkümmert

stuntman ['stʌntmæn] *(irreg: like* **man)** *n* Stuntman *m*

stupefaction [stjuːpɪ'fækʃən] *n* Verblüffung *f*

stupefy ['stjuːpɪfaɪ] *vt* benommen machen; *(fig)* verblüffen

stupendous [stjuː'pendəs] *adj* enorm

stupid ['stjuːpɪd] *adj* dumm

stupidity [stjuː'pɪdɪtɪ] *n* Dummheit *f*

stupidly ['stjuːpɪdlɪ] *adv* dumm

stupor ['stjuːpəʳ] *n* Benommenheit *f*; **in a ~** benommen

sturdily ['stəːdɪlɪ] *adv:* ~ **built** *(person)* kräftig gebaut; *(thing)* stabil gebaut

sturdy ['stəːdɪ] *adj (person)* kräftig; *(thing)* stabil

sturgeon ['stəːdʒən] *n* Stör *m*

stutter ['stʌtəʳ] *n* Stottern *nt* ▷ *vi* stottern; **to have a ~** stottern

Stuttgart ['stutgɑːt] *n* Stuttgart *nt*

sty [staɪ] *n* Schweinestall *m*

stye [staɪ] *n* Gerstenkorn *nt*

style [staɪl] *n* Stil *m*; *(design)* Modell *nt*; **in the latest ~** nach der neuesten Mode; **hair ~** Frisur *f*

styli ['staɪlaɪ] *npl of* **stylus**

stylish ['staɪlɪʃ] *adj* elegant

stylist ['staɪlɪst] *n (hair stylist)* Friseur *m*, Friseuse *f*; *(literary stylist)* Stilist(in) *m(f)*

stylized ['staɪlaɪzd] *adj* stilisiert

stylus ['staɪləs] *(pl* **styli** *or* **-es)** *n* Nadel *f*

Styrofoam® ['staɪrəfəum] *n* ≈ Styropor® *nt*

suave [swɑːv] *adj* zuvorkommend

sub [sʌb] *n abbr (Naut)* = **submarine**; *(Admin)* = **subscription**; *(Brit: Press)* = **subeditor**

sub ... [sʌb] *pref* Unter-, unter-

subcommittee ['sʌbkəmɪtɪ] *n* Unterausschuss *m*

subconscious [sʌb'kɔnʃəs] *adj* unterbewusst

subcontinent [sʌb'kɔntɪnənt] *n:* **the (Indian)** ~ der (indische) Subkontinent

subcontract [vt 'sʌbkən'trækt, n 'sʌb'kɔntrækt] vt (vertraglich) weitervergeben ▷ n Nebenvertrag m

subcontractor ['sʌbkən'træktə'] n Subunternehmer m

subdivide [sʌbdɪ'vaɪd] vt unterteilen

subdivision ['sʌbdɪvɪʒən] n Unterteilung f

subdue [səb'dju:] vt unterwerfen; (emotions) dämpfen

subdued [səb'dju:d] adj (light) gedämpft; (person) bedrückt

subeditor [sʌb'ɛdɪtə'] (Brit) n Redakteur(in) m(f)

subject [n 'sʌbdʒɪkt, vt səb'dʒɛkt] n (matter) Thema nt; (Scol) Fach nt; (of country) Staatsbürger(in) m(f); (Gram) Subjekt nt ▷ vt: **to ~ sb to sth** jdn einer Sache dat unterziehen; (expose) jdn einer Sache dat aussetzen; **to change the ~** das Thema wechseln; **to be ~ to** (law, tax) unterworfen sein +dat; (heart attacks etc) anfällig sein für; **~ to confirmation in writing** vorausgesetzt, es wird schriftlich bestätigt

subjection [səb'dʒɛkʃən] n Unterwerfung f

subjective [səb'dʒɛktɪv] adj subjektiv

subject matter n Stoff m; (content) Inhalt m

sub judice [sʌb'dju:dɪsɪ] adj (Law): **to be ~** verhandelt werden

subjugate ['sʌbdʒugeɪt] vt unterwerfen

subjunctive [səb'dʒʌŋktɪv] n Konjunktiv m; **in the ~** im Konjunktiv

sublet [sʌb'lɛt] vt untervermieten

sublime [sə'blaɪm] adj erhaben, vollendet; **that's going from the ~ to the ridiculous** das ist ein Abstieg ins Profane

subliminal [sʌb'lɪmɪnl] adj unterschwellig

submachine gun ['sʌbmə'ʃi:n-] n Maschinenpistole f

submarine [sʌbmə'ri:n] n Unterseeboot nt, U-Boot nt

submerge [səb'mə:dʒ] vt untertauchen; (flood) überschwemmen ▷ vi tauchen; **~d** unter Wasser

submersion [səb'mə:ʃən] n Untertauchen nt; (of submarine) Tauchen nt; (by flood) Überschwemmung f

submission [səb'mɪʃən] n (subjection) Unterwerfung f; (of plan, application etc) Einreichung f; (proposal) Vorlage f

submissive [səb'mɪsɪv] adj gehorsam; (gesture) demütig

submit [səb'mɪt] vt (proposal) vorlegen; (application etc) einreichen ▷ vi: **to ~ to sth** sich einer Sache dat unterwerfen

subnormal [sʌb'nɔ:ml] adj (below average) unterdurchschnittlich; (old: child etc) minderbegabt; **educationally ~** lernbehindert

subordinate [sə'bɔ:dɪnət] n Untergebene(r) f(m); (Ling): **~ clause** Nebensatz m ▷ adj untergeordnet; **to be ~ to sb** jdm untergeordnet sein

subpoena [səb'pi:nə] n (Law) Vorladung f ▷ vt vorladen

subroutine [sʌbru:'ti:n] n (Comput) Unterprogramm nt

subscribe [səb'skraɪb] vi spenden; **to ~ to** (opinion, theory) sich anschließen +dat; (fund, charity) regelmäßig spenden an +acc; (magazine etc) abonnieren

subscriber [səb'skraɪbə'] n (to magazine) Abonnent(in) m(f); (Tel) Teilnehmer(in) m(f)

subscript ['sʌbskrɪpt] n tiefgestelltes Zeichen nt

subscription [səb'skrɪpʃən] n (to magazine etc) Abonnement nt; (membership dues) (Mitglieds) beitrag m; **to take out a ~ to** (magazine etc) abonnieren

subsequent ['sʌbsɪkwənt] adj später, nachfolgend; (further) weiter; **~ to** im Anschluss an +acc

subsequently ['sʌbsɪkwəntlɪ] adv später

subservient [səb'sə:vɪənt] adj unterwürfig; (less important) untergeordnet; **to be ~ to** untergeordnet sein +dat

subside [səb'saɪd] vi (feeling, pain) nachlassen; (flood) sinken; (earth) sich senken

subsidence [səb'saɪdns] n Senkung f

subsidiarity [səbsɪdɪ'ærɪtɪ] n Subsidiarität f

subsidiary [səb'sɪdɪərɪ] adj (question, role, Brit, Scol: subject) Neben- ▷ n (also: **subsidiary company**) Tochtergesellschaft f

subsidize ['sʌbsɪdaɪz] vt subventionieren

subsidy ['sʌbsɪdɪ] n Subvention f

subsist [səb'sɪst] vi: **to ~ on sth** sich von etw ernähren

subsistence [səb'sɪstəns] n Existenz f; **enough for ~** genug zum (Über)leben

subsistence allowance n Unterhaltszuschuss m

subsistence level n Existenzminimum nt

substance ['sʌbstəns] n Substanz f, Stoff m; (fig: essence) Kern m; **a man of ~** ein vermögender Mann; **to lack ~** (book) keine Substanz haben; (argument) keine Durchschlagskraft haben

substance abuse n Missbrauch von Alkohol, Drogen, Arzneimitteln etc

substandard [sʌb'stændəd] adj minderwertig; (housing) unzulänglich

substantial [səb'stænʃl] adj (solid) solide; (considerable) beträchtlich, größere(r, s); (meal) kräftig

substantially [səb'stænʃəlɪ] adv erheblich; (in essence) im Wesentlichen

substantiate [səb'stænʃɪeɪt] vt erhärten, untermauern

substitute ['sʌbstɪtju:t] n Ersatz m ▷ vt: **to ~ A for B** durch A ersetzen

substitute teacher (US) n Vertretung f

substitution [sʌbstɪ'tju:ʃən] n Ersetzen nt; (Football) Auswechseln nt

subterfuge ['sʌbtəfju:dʒ] n Tricks pl; (trickery) Täuschung f

subterranean [sʌbtə'reɪnɪən] adj unterirdisch

subtitle ['sʌbtaɪtl] n Untertitel m

subtle ['sʌtl] *adj* fein; *(indirect)* raffiniert

subtlety ['sʌtltɪ] *n* Feinheit *f*; *(art of being subtle)* Finesse *f*

subtly ['sʌtlɪ] *adv (change, vary)* leicht; *(different)* auf subtile Weise; *(persuade)* raffiniert

subtotal [sʌb'təʊtl] *n* Zwischensumme *f*

subtract [səb'trækt] *vt* abziehen, subtrahieren

subtraction [səb'trækʃən] *n* Abziehen *nt*, Subtraktion *f*

subtropical [sʌb'trɒpɪkl] *adj* subtropisch

suburb ['sʌbɜːb] *n* Vorort *m*

suburban [sə'bɜːbən] *adj (train etc)* Vorort-; *(lifestyle etc)* spießig, kleinbürgerlich

suburbia [sə'bɜːbɪə] *n* die Vororte *pl*

subvention [səb'vɛnʃən] *n* Subvention *f*

subversion [səb'vɜːʃən] *n* Subversion *f*

subversive [səb'vɜːsɪv] *adj* subversiv

subway ['sʌbweɪ] *n* (US) Untergrundbahn *f*, U-Bahn *f*; *(Brit: underpass)* Unterführung *f*

sub-zero [sʌb'zɪərəʊ] *adj*: **~ temperatures** Temperaturen unter null

succeed [sək'siːd] *vi (plan etc)* gelingen, erfolgreich sein; *(person)* erfolgreich sein, Erfolg haben ▷ *vt (in job)* Nachfolger werden +*gen*; *(in order)* folgen +*dat*; **sb ~s in doing sth** es gelingt jdm, etw zu tun

succeeding [sək'siːdɪŋ] *adj* folgend; **~ generations** spätere *or* nachfolgende Generationen *pl*

success [sək'sɛs] *n* Erfolg *m*; **without ~** ohne Erfolg, erfolglos

successful [sək'sɛsful] *adj* erfolgreich; **to be ~** erfolgreich sein, Erfolg haben; **sb is ~ in doing sth** es gelingt jdm, etw zu tun

successfully [sək'sɛsfəlɪ] *adv* erfolgreich, mit Erfolg

succession [sək'sɛʃən] *n* Folge *f*, Serie *f*; *(to throne etc)* Nachfolge *f*; **3 years in ~** 3 Jahre nacheinander *or* hintereinander

successive [sək'sɛsɪv] *adj* aufeinanderfolgend; **on 3 ~ days** 3 Tage nacheinander *or* hintereinander

successor [sək'sɛsər] *n* Nachfolger(in) *m(f)*

succinct [sək'sɪŋkt] *adj* knapp, prägnant

succulent ['sʌkjulənt] *adj* saftig ▷ *n* Fettpflanze *f*, Sukkulente *f*

succumb [sə'kʌm] *vi*: **to ~ to** *(temptation)* erliegen +*dat*; *(illness: become affected by)* bekommen; (: *die of)* erliegen +*dat*

such [sʌtʃ] *adj (of that kind)*: **~ a book** so ein Buch; *(so much)*: **~ courage** so viel Mut; *(emphasizing similarity)*: **or some ~ place/name** *etc* oder so ähnlich ▷ *adv* so; **~ books** solche Bücher; **~ a lot of** so viel; **she made ~ a noise that ...** sie machte so einen Lärm, dass ...; **~ books as I have** was ich an Büchern habe; **I said no ~ thing** das habe ich nie gesagt; **~ a long trip** so eine lange Reise; **~ as** wie (zum Beispiel); **as ~** an sich

such-and-such ['sʌtʃənsʌtʃ] *adj* die und die, der und der, das und das

suchlike ['sʌtʃlaɪk] *(inf)* *pron*: **and ~** und dergleichen

suck [sʌk] *vt (sweet etc)* lutschen; *(ice-lolly)* lutschen an +*dat*; *(baby)* saugen an +*dat*; *(pump, machine)* saugen

sucker ['sʌkər] *n* (Zool) Saugnapf *m*; (Tech) Saugfuß *m*; (Bot) unterirdischer Ausläufer *m*; *(inf)* Dummkopf *m*

suckle ['sʌkl] *vt (baby)* stillen; *(animal)* säugen

sucrose ['suːkrəʊz] *n* (pflanzlicher) Zucker *m*

suction ['sʌkʃən] *n* Saugwirkung *f*

suction pump *n* Saugpumpe *f*

Sudan [su'dɑːn] *n* der Sudan

Sudanese [suːdə'niːz] *adj* sudanesisch ▷ *n* Sudanese *m*, Sudanesin *f*

sudden ['sʌdn] *adj* plötzlich; **all of a ~** ganz plötzlich

sudden death *n (also:* **sudden-death play-off)** Stichkampf *m*

suddenly ['sʌdnlɪ] *adv* plötzlich

sudoku [su'dəʊkuː] *n* Sudoku *nt*

suds [sʌdz] *npl* Seifenschaum *m*

sue [suː] *vt* verklagen ▷ *vi* klagen, vor Gericht gehen; **to ~ sb for damages** jdn auf Schadenersatz verklagen; **to ~ for divorce** die Scheidung einreichen

suede [sweɪd] *n* Wildleder *nt* ▷ *cpd* Wildleder-

suet ['suːt] *n* Nierenfett *nt*

Suez ['suːɪz] *n*: **the ~ Canal** der Suezkanal

Suff. (Brit) *abbr* (Post) = Suffolk

suffer ['sʌfər] *vt* erleiden; *(rudeness etc)* ertragen ▷ *vi* leiden; **to ~ from** leiden an +*dat*; **to ~ the effects of sth** an den Folgen von etw leiden

sufferance ['sʌfərns] *n*: **he was only there on ~** er wurde dort nur geduldet

sufferer ['sʌfərər] *n* Leidende(r) *f(m)*

suffering ['sʌfərɪŋ] *n* Leid *nt*

suffice [sə'faɪs] *vi* genügen

sufficient [sə'fɪʃənt] *adj* ausreichend; **~ money** genug Geld

sufficiently [sə'fɪʃəntlɪ] *adv* genug, ausreichend; **~ powerful** mächtig genug

suffix ['sʌfɪks] *n* Suffix *nt*, Nachsilbe *f*

suffocate ['sʌfəkeɪt] *vi (lit, fig)* ersticken

suffocation [sʌfə'keɪʃən] *n* Ersticken *nt*

suffrage ['sʌfrɪdʒ] *n* Wahlrecht *nt*

suffragette [sʌfrə'dʒɛt] *n* Suffragette *f*

suffused [sə'fjuːzd] *adj*: **~ with** erfüllt von; **~ with light** lichtdurchflutet

sugar ['ʃugər] *n* Zucker *m* ▷ *vt* zuckern

sugar beet *n* Zuckerrübe *f*

sugar bowl *n* Zuckerdose *f*

sugar cane *n* Zuckerrohr *nt*

sugar-coated ['ʃugə'kəʊtɪd] *adj* mit Zucker überzogen

sugar lump *n* Zuckerstück *nt*

sugar refinery *n* Zuckerraffinerie *f*

sugary ['ʃugərɪ] *adj* süß; *(fig: smile, phrase)* süßlich

suggest [sə'dʒɛst] *vt* vorschlagen; *(indicate)* andeuten, hindeuten auf +*acc*; **what do you ~ I do?** was schlagen Sie vor?

suggestion [sə'dʒɛstʃən] *n* Vorschlag *m*; *(indication)* Anflug *m*; *(trace)* Spur *f*

suggestive [sə'dʒɛstɪv] *(pej)* *adj* anzüglich

suicidal [suɪˈsaɪdl] *adj* selbstmörderisch; *(person)* selbstmordgefährdet; **to be** *or* **feel ~** Selbstmordgedanken haben
suicide [ˈsuɪsaɪd] *n (lit, fig)* Selbstmord *m*; *(person)* Selbstmörder(in) *m(f); see also* **commit**
suicide attack *n* Selbstmordanschlag *m*
suicide attacker *n* Selbstmordattentäter(in) *m(f)*
suicide attempt, suicide bid *n* Selbstmordversuch *m*
suicide bomber *n* Selbstmordattentäter(in) *m(f)*
suit [suːt] *n (man's)* Anzug *m; (woman's)* Kostüm *nt; (Law)* Prozess *m,* Verfahren *nt; (Cards)* Farbe *f* ▷ *vt* passen +*dat; (colour, clothes)* stehen +*dat;* **to bring a ~ against sb** *(Law)* gegen jdn Klage erheben *or* einen Prozess anstrengen; **to follow ~** *(fig)* das Gleiche tun; **to ~ sth to** etw anpassen an +*acc;* **to be ~ed to do sth** sich dafür eignen, etw zu tun; **~ yourself!** wie du willst!; **well ~ed** *(couple)* gut zusammenpassend
suitability [suːtəˈbɪlɪtɪ] *n* Eignung *f*
suitable [ˈsuːtəbl] *adj (convenient)* passend; *(appropriate)* geeignet; **would tomorrow be ~?** würde Ihnen morgen passen?; **Monday isn't ~** Montag passt nicht; **we found somebody ~** wir haben jemand Passenden gefunden
suitably [ˈsuːtəblɪ] *adv* passend; *(impressed)* gebührend
suitcase [ˈsuːtkeɪs] *n* Koffer *m*
suite [swiːt] *n (of rooms)* Suite *f,* Zimmerflucht *f; (Mus)* Suite *f;* **bedroom/dining room ~** Schlafzimmer-/Esszimmereinrichtung *f;* **a three-piece ~** eine dreiteilige Polstergarnitur
suitor [ˈsuːtəʳ] *n* Kläger(in) *m(f)*
sulfate [ˈsʌlfeɪt] *(US) n* = **sulphate**
sulfur [ˈsʌlfəʳ] *(US) n* = **sulphur**
sulfuric [sʌlˈfjuərɪk] *(US) adj* = **sulphuric**
sulk [sʌlk] *vi* schmollen
sulky [ˈsʌlkɪ] *adj* schmollend
sullen [ˈsʌlən] *adj* mürrisch, verdrossen
sulphate, *(US)* **sulfate** [ˈsʌlfeɪt] *n* Sulfat *nt,* schwefelsaures Salz *nt*
sulphur, *(US)* **sulfur** [ˈsʌlfəʳ] *n* Schwefel *m*
sulphur dioxide *n* Schwefeldioxid *nt*
sulphuric, *(US)* **sulfuric** [sʌlˈfjuərɪk] *adj:* **~ acid** Schwefelsäure *f*
sultan [ˈsʌltən] *n* Sultan *m*
sultana [sʌlˈtɑːnə] *n* Sultanine *f*
sultry [ˈsʌltrɪ] *adj* schwül
sum [sʌm] *n (calculation)* Rechenaufgabe *f; (amount)* Summe *f,* Betrag *m*
▶ **sum up** *vt* zusammenfassen; *(evaluate rapidly)* einschätzen ▷ *vi* zusammenfassen
Sumatra [suˈmɑːtrə] *n* Sumatra *nt*
summarize [ˈsʌməraɪz] *vt* zusammenfassen
summary [ˈsʌmərɪ] *n* Zusammenfassung *f* ▷ *adj (justice, executions)* im Schnellverfahren
summer [ˈsʌməʳ] *n* Sommer *m* ▷ *cpd* Sommer-; **in ~** im Sommer
summer camp *(US) n* Ferienlager *nt*
summer holidays *npl* Sommerferien *pl*

summerhouse [ˈsʌməhaus] *n (in garden)* Gartenhaus *nt,* Gartenlaube *f*
summertime [ˈsʌmətaɪm] *n* Sommer *m,* Sommerszeit *f*
summer time *n* Sommerzeit *f*
summery [ˈsʌmərɪ] *adj* sommerlich
summing-up [sʌmɪŋˈʌp] *n (Law)* Resümee *nt*
summit [ˈsʌmɪt] *n* Gipfel *m; (also:* **summit conference/meeting)** Gipfelkonferenz *f/*-treffen *nt*
summon [ˈsʌmən] *vt* rufen, kommen lassen; *(help)* holen; *(meeting)* einberufen; *(Law: witness)* vorladen
▶ **summon up** *vt* aufbringen
summons [ˈsʌmənz] *n (Law)* Vorladung *f; (fig)* Aufruf *m* ▷ *vt (Law)* vorladen; **to serve a ~ on sb** jdn vor Gericht laden
sumo [ˈsuːməu], **sumo wrestling** *n* Sumo(-Ringen) *nt*
sump [sʌmp] *(Brit) n* Ölwanne *f*
sumptuous [ˈsʌmptjuəs] *adj (meal)* üppig; *(costume)* aufwendig
Sun. *abbr* (= *Sunday*) So.
sun [sʌn] *n* Sonne *f;* **to catch the ~** einen Sonnenbrand bekommen; **everything under the ~** alles Mögliche
sunbathe [ˈsʌnbeɪð] *vi* sich sonnen
sunbeam [ˈsʌnbiːm] *n* Sonnenstrahl *m*
sunbed [ˈsʌnbed] *n (with sun lamp)* Sonnenbank *f*
sunblock *n* Sonnenschutzcreme *f*
sunburn [ˈsʌnbəːn] *n* Sonnenbrand *m*
sunburned [ˈsʌnbəːnd] *adj* = **sunburnt**
sunburnt [ˈsʌnbəːnt] *adj* sonnenverbrannt, sonnengebräunt; **to be ~** *(painfully)* einen Sonnenbrand haben
sun-cream [ˈsʌnkriːm] *n* Sonnencreme *f*
sundae [ˈsʌndeɪ] *n* Eisbecher *m*
Sunday [ˈsʌndɪ] *n* Sonntag *m; see also* **Tuesday**
Sunday paper *n* Sonntagszeitung *f; siehe Info-Artikel*

SUNDAY PAPERS

Die *Sunday papers* umfassen sowohl Massenblätter als auch seriöse Zeitungen. „The Observer" ist die älteste überregionale Sonntagszeitung der Welt. Die Sonntagszeitungen sind alle sehr umfangreich mit vielen Farb- und Sonderbeilagen. Zu den meisten Tageszeitungen gibt es parallele Sonntagsblätter, die aber separate Redaktionen haben.

Sunday school *n* Sonntagsschule *f*
sundial [ˈsʌndaɪəl] *n* Sonnenuhr *f*
sundown [ˈsʌndaun] *(esp US) n* Sonnenuntergang *m*
sundries [ˈsʌndrɪz] *npl* Verschiedenes *nt*
sundry [ˈsʌndrɪ] *adj* verschiedene; **all and ~** jedermann
sunflower [ˈsʌnflauəʳ] *n* Sonnenblume *f*
sunflower oil *n* Sonnenblumenöl *nt*

S

sung [sʌŋ] pp of **sing**

sunglasses ['sʌnglɑːsɪz] npl Sonnenbrille f

sunk [sʌŋk] pp of **sink**

sunken ['sʌŋkn] adj versunken; (eyes) tief liegend; (cheeks) eingefallen; (bath) eingelassen

sunlamp ['sʌnlæmp] n Höhensonne f

sunlight ['sʌnlaɪt] n Sonnenlicht nt

sunlit ['sʌnlɪt] adj sonnig, sonnenbeschienen

sunny ['sʌnɪ] adj sonnig; (fig) heiter

sunrise ['sʌnraɪz] n Sonnenaufgang m

sun roof n (Aut) Schiebedach nt; (on building) Sonnenterrasse f

sun screen n Sonnenschutzmittel nt

sunset ['sʌnsɛt] n Sonnenuntergang m

sunshade ['sʌnʃeɪd] n Sonnenschirm m

sunshine ['sʌnʃaɪn] n Sonnenschein m

sunspot ['sʌnspɒt] n Sonnenfleck m

sunstroke ['sʌnstrəʊk] n Sonnenstich m

suntan ['sʌntæn] n (Sonnen)bräune f; **to get a ~** braun werden

suntan lotion n Sonnenmilch f

suntanned ['sʌntænd] adj braun (gebrannt)

suntan oil n Sonnenöl nt

suntrap ['sʌntræp] n sonniges Eckchen nt

super ['suːpər] (inf) adj fantastisch, toll

superannuation [suːpərænjuˈeɪʃən] n Beitrag m zur Rentenversicherung

superb [suːˈpəːb] adj ausgezeichnet, großartig; (meal) vorzüglich

Super Bowl n Superbowl m, Super Bowl m, American-Football-Turnier zwischen den Spitzenreitern der Nationalligen

supercilious [suːpəˈsɪlɪəs] adj herablassend

superconductor [suːpəkənˈdʌktər] n (Phys) Superleiter m

superficial [suːpəˈfɪʃəl] adj oberflächlich

superficially [suːpəˈfɪʃəlɪ] adv oberflächlich; (from a superficial point of view) oberflächlich gesehen

superfluous [suːˈpəːfluəs] adj überflüssig

superglue ['suːpəgluː] n Sekundenkleber m

superhighway (US) n ≈ Autobahn f; **information ~** Datenautobahn f

superhuman [suːpəˈhjuːmən] adj übermenschlich

superimpose ['suːpərɪmˈpəʊz] vt (two things) übereinanderlegen; **to ~ on** legen auf +acc; **to ~ with** überlagern mit

superintend [suːpərɪnˈtɛnd] vt beaufsichtigen, überwachen

superintendent [suːpərɪnˈtɛndənt] n Aufseher(in) m(f); (Police) Kommissar(in) m(f)

superior [suːˈpɪərɪər] adj besser, überlegen +dat; (more senior) höhergestellt; (smug) überheblich; (: smile) überlegen ▷ n Vorgesetzte(r) f(m); **Mother S~** (Rel) Mutter Oberin

superiority [suːpɪərɪˈɒrɪtɪ] n Überlegenheit f

superlative [suːˈpəːlətɪv] n Superlativ m ▷ adj überragend

superman ['suːpəmæn] (irreg: like **man**) n Übermensch m

supermarket ['suːpəmɑːkɪt] n Supermarkt m

supermodel ['suːpəmɒdl] n Supermodell nt

supernatural [suːpəˈnætʃərəl] adj übernatürlich ▷ n: **the ~** das Übernatürliche

supernova [suːpəˈnəʊvə] n Supernova f

superpower ['suːpəpaʊər] n Supermacht f

superscript ['suːpəskrɪpt] n hochgestelltes Zeichen nt

supersede [suːpəˈsiːd] vt ablösen, ersetzen

supersonic ['suːpəˈsɒnɪk] adj (aircraft etc) Überschall-

superstar ['suːpəstɑːr] n Superstar m

superstition [suːpəˈstɪʃən] n Aberglaube m

superstitious [suːpəˈstɪʃəs] adj abergläubisch

superstore ['suːpəstɔːr] (Brit) n Großmarkt m

supertanker ['suːpətæŋkər] n Supertanker m

supertax ['suːpətæks] n Höchststeuer f

supervise ['suːpəvaɪz] vt beaufsichtigen

supervision [suːpəˈvɪʒən] n Beaufsichtigung f; **under medical ~** unter ärztlicher Aufsicht

supervisor ['suːpəvaɪzər] n Aufseher(in) m(f); (of students) Tutor(in) m(f)

supervisory ['suːpəvaɪzərɪ] adj beaufsichtigend, Aufsichts-

supine ['suːpaɪn] adj: **to be ~** auf dem Rücken liegen ▷ adv auf dem Rücken

supper ['sʌpər] n Abendessen nt; **to have ~** zu Abend essen

supplant [səˈplɑːnt] vt ablösen, ersetzen

supple ['sʌpl] adj geschmeidig; (person) gelenkig

supplement ['sʌplɪmənt] n Zusatz m; (of book) Ergänzungsband m; (of newspaper etc) Beilage f ▷ vt ergänzen

supplementary [sʌplɪˈmɛntərɪ] adj zusätzlich, ergänzend

supplementary benefit (Brit: old) n ≈ Sozialhilfe f

supplementary budget n (Pol) ≈ Nachtragshaushalt m or -etat m

supplier [səˈplaɪər] n Lieferant(in) m(f)

supply [səˈplaɪ] vt liefern; (provide) sorgen für; (a need) befriedigen ▷ n Vorrat m; (supplying) Lieferung f; **supplies** npl (food) Vorräte pl; (Mil) Nachschub m; **to ~ sth to sb** jdm etw liefern; **to ~ sth with sth** etw mit etw versorgen; **it comes supplied with an adaptor** es wird mit einem Adapter geliefert; **office supplies** Bürobedarf m; **to be in short ~** knapp sein; **the electricity/water/gas** die Strom-/Wasser-/Gasversorgung f; **~ and demand** Angebot nt und Nachfrage

supply teacher (Brit) n Vertretung f

support [səˈpɔːt] n Unterstützung f; (Tech) Stütze f ▷ vt unterstützen, eintreten für; (financially: family etc) unterhalten; (: party etc) finanziell unterstützen; (Tech) (ab)stützen; (theory etc) untermauern; **they stopped work in ~ of ...** sie sind in den Streik getreten, um für ... einzutreten; **to ~ o.s.** (financially) finanziell unabhängig sein; **to ~ Arsenal** Arsenal-Fan sein

supporter [səˈpɔːtər] n (Pol etc) Anhänger(in) m(f); (Sport) Fan m

supporting [sə'pɔːtɪŋ] adj: ~ **role** Nebenrolle f; ~ **actor** Schauspieler m in einer Nebenrolle; ~ **film** Vorfilm m

supportive [sə'pɔːtɪv] adj hilfreich; **to be ~ of sb/sth** jdn/etw unterstützen

suppose [sə'pəuz] vt annehmen, glauben; (imagine) sich dat vorstellen; **to be ~d to do sth** etw tun sollen; **it was worse than she'd ~d** es war schlimmer, als sie es sich vorgestellt hatte; **I don't ~ she'll come** ich glaube kaum, dass sie kommt; **he's about sixty, I ~** er muss wohl so um die Sechzig sein; **he's ~d to be an expert** er ist angeblich ein Experte; **I ~ so/not** ich glaube schon/nicht

supposedly [sə'pəuzɪdlɪ] adv angeblich

supposing [sə'pəuzɪŋ] conj angenommen

supposition [sʌpə'zɪʃən] n Annahme f

suppository [sə'pɒzɪtrɪ] n Zäpfchen nt

suppress [sə'pres] vt unterdrücken; (publication) verbieten

suppression [sə'preʃən] n Unterdrückung f

suppressor [sə'presər] n (Elec etc) Entstörungselement nt

supremacy [su'preməsɪ] n Vormachtstellung f

supreme [su'priːm] adj Ober-, oberste(r, s); (effort) äußerste(r, s); (achievement) höchste(r, s)

Supreme Court (US) n Oberster Gerichtshof m

supremo [su'priːməu] (Brit: inf) n Boss m

Supt abbr (Police) = **superintendent**

surcharge ['sɜːtʃɑːdʒ] n Zuschlag m

sure [ʃuər] adj sicher; (reliable) zuverlässig, sicher ▷ adv (inf: esp US): **that ~ is pretty, that's ~ pretty** das ist aber schön; **to make ~ of sth** sich einer Sache gen vergewissern; **to make ~ that** sich vergewissern, dass; **I'm ~ of it** ich bin mir da sicher; **I'm not ~ how/why/when** ich bin mir nicht sicher or ich weiß nicht genau, wie/warum/wann; **to be ~ of o.s.** selbstsicher sein; **~!** klar!; **~ enough** tatsächlich

sure-fire ['ʃuəfaɪər] (inf) adj todsicher

sure-footed [ʃuə'futɪd] adj trittsicher

surely ['ʃuəlɪ] adv sicherlich, bestimmt; **~ you don't mean that!** das meinen Sie doch bestimmt or sicher nicht (so)!

surety ['ʃuərətɪ] n Bürgschaft f, Sicherheit f; **to go** or **stand ~ for sb** für jdn bürgen

surf [sɜːf] n Brandung f

surface ['sɜːfɪs] n Oberfläche f ▷ vt (road) mit einem Belag versehen ▷ vi (lit, fig) auftauchen; (feeling) hochkommen; (rise from bed) hochkommen; **on the ~** (fig) oberflächlich betrachtet

surface area n Fläche f

surface mail n Post f auf dem Land-/Seeweg

surface-to-surface ['sɜːfɪstə'sɜːfɪs] adj (missile) Boden-Boden-

surfboard ['sɜːfbɔːd] n Surfbrett nt

surfeit ['sɜːfɪt] n: **a ~ of** ein Übermaß an +dat

surfer ['sɜːfər] n Surfer(in) m(f)

surfing ['sɜːfɪŋ] n Surfen nt; **to go ~** surfen gehen

surge [sɜːdʒ] n Anstieg m; (fig: of emotion) Woge f; (Elec) Spannungsstoß m ▷ vi (water) branden; (people) sich drängen; (vehicles) sich wälzen; (emotion) aufwallen; (Elec: power) ansteigen; **to ~ forward** nach vorne drängen

surgeon ['sɜːdʒən] n Chirurg(in) m(f)

Surgeon General (US) n (Med) ≈ Gesundheitsminister(in) m(f); (Mil) Sanitätsinspekteur(in) m(f)

surgery ['sɜːdʒərɪ] n Chirurgie f; (Brit: room) Sprechzimmer nt; (: building) Praxis f; (also: **surgery hours**): of doctor, MP etc) Sprechstunde f; **to have ~** operiert werden; **to need ~** operiert werden müssen

surgical ['sɜːdʒɪkl] adj chirurgisch; (treatment) operativ

surgical spirit (Brit) n Wundbenzin nt

surly ['sɜːlɪ] adj verdrießlich, mürrisch

surmise [sɜː'maɪz] vt vermuten, mutmaßen

surmount [sɜː'maunt] vt (fig) überwinden

surname ['sɜːneɪm] n Nachname m

surpass [sɜː'pɑːs] vt übertreffen

surplus ['sɜːpləs] n Überschuss m ▷ adj überschüssig; **it is ~ to our requirements** das benötigen wir nicht

surprise [sə'praɪz] n Überraschung f ▷ vt überraschen; (astonish) erstaunen; (army) überrumpeln; (thief) ertappen; **to take sb by ~** jdn überraschen

surprising [sə'praɪzɪŋ] adj überraschend; (situation) erstaunlich; **it is ~ how/that** es ist erstaunlich, wie/dass

surprisingly [sə'praɪzɪŋlɪ] adv überraschend, erstaunlich; **(somewhat) ~, he agreed** erstaunlicherweise war er damit einverstanden

surrealism [sə'rɪəlɪzəm] n Surrealismus m

surrealist [sə'rɪəlɪst] adj surrealistisch

surrender [sə'rendər] n Kapitulation f ▷ vi sich ergeben ▷ vt aufgeben

surrender value n Rückkaufswert m

surreptitious [sʌrəp'tɪʃəs] adj heimlich, verstohlen

surrogate ['sʌrəgɪt] n Ersatz m ▷ adj (parents) Ersatz-

surrogate mother n Leihmutter f

surround [sə'raund] vt umgeben; (Mil, Police etc) umstellen

surrounding [sə'raundɪŋ] adj umliegend; **the ~ area** die Umgebung

surroundings [sə'raundɪŋz] npl Umgebung f

surtax ['sɜːtæks] n Steuerzuschlag m

surveillance [sɜː'veɪləns] n Überwachung f; **to be under ~** überwacht werden

survey ['sɜːveɪ] n (of land) Vermessung f; (of house) Begutachtung f; (investigation) Untersuchung f; (report) Gutachten nt; (comprehensive view) Überblick m ▷ vt (land) vermessen; (house) inspizieren; (look at) betrachten

surveying [sə'veɪɪŋ] n (of land) Vermessung f

surveyor [sə'veɪər] n (of land) Landvermesser(in) m(f); (of house) Baugutachter(in) m(f)

S

811

survival [sə'vaɪvl] n Überleben nt; (relic) Überbleibsel nt; **~ course/kit** Überlebenstraining nt/-ausrüstung f; **~ bag** Expeditionsschlafsack m

survive [sə'vaɪv] vi überleben; (custom etc) weiter bestehen ▷ vt überleben

survivor [sə'vaɪvə^r] n Überlebende(r) f(m)

susceptible [sə'sɛptəbl] adj: **~ (to)** anfällig (für); (influenced by) empfänglich (für)

suspect ['sʌspɛkt] adj verdächtig ▷ n Verdächtige(r) f(m) ▷ vt: **to ~ sb of** jdn verdächtigen +gen; (think) vermuten; (doubt) bezweifeln

suspected [səs'pɛktɪd] adj (terrorist etc) mutmaßlich; **he is a ~ member of this organization** er steht im Verdacht, Mitglied dieser Organisation zu sein

suspend [səs'pɛnd] vt (hang) (auf)hängen; (delay, stop) einstellen; (from employment) suspendieren; **to be ~ed (from)** (hang) hängen (an +dat)

suspended animation [səs'pɛndɪd-] n vorübergehender Stillstand aller Körperfunktionen

suspended sentence n (Law) zur Bewährung ausgesetzte Strafe f

suspender belt [səs'pɛndə^r-] n Strumpfgürtel m

suspenders [səs'pɛndəz] npl (Brit) Strumpfhalter pl; (US) Hosenträger pl

suspense [səs'pɛns] n Spannung f; (uncertainty) Ungewissheit f; **to keep sb in ~** jdn auf die Folter spannen

suspension [səs'pɛnʃən] n (from job) Suspendierung f; (from team) Sperrung f; (Aut) Federung f; (of driving licence) zeitweiliger Entzug m; (of payment) zeitweilige Einstellung f

suspension bridge n Hängebrücke f

suspicion [səs'pɪʃən] n Verdacht m; (distrust) Misstrauen nt; (trace) Spur f; **to be under ~** unter Verdacht stehen; **arrested on ~ of murder** wegen Mordverdacht(s) festgenommen

suspicious [səs'pɪʃəs] adj (suspecting) misstrauisch; (causing suspicion) verdächtig; **to be ~ of** or **about sb/sth** jdn/etw mit Misstrauen betrachten

suss out [sʌs-] (Brit: inf) vt (discover) rauskriegen; (understand) durchschauen

sustain [səs'teɪn] vt (continue) aufrechterhalten; (food, drink) bei Kräften halten; (suffer: injury) erleiden

sustainable [səs'teɪnəbl] adj: **to be ~** aufrechtzuerhalten sein; **~ growth** stetiges Wachstum nt

sustained [səs'teɪnd] adj (effort) ausdauernd; (attack) anhaltend

sustenance ['sʌstɪnəns] n Nahrung f

suture ['suːtʃə^r] n Naht f

SUV n abbr (= sport utility vehicle) SUV m, Geländewagen m

SVQ n abbr (= Scottish Vocational Qualification) Qualifikation für berufsbegleitende Ausbildungsinhalte in Schottland

SW abbr (= south-west) SW; (Radio: = short-wave) KW

swab [swɔb] n (Med) Tupfer m ▷ vt (Naut: also: **swab down**) wischen

swagger ['swægə^r] vi stolzieren

swallow ['swɔləu] n (bird) Schwalbe f; (of food, drink etc) Schluck m ▷ vt (herunter)schlucken; (fig: story, insult, one's pride) schlucken
▶ **swallow up** vt verschlingen

swam [swæm] pt of **swim**

swamp [swɔmp] n Sumpf m ▷ vt (lit, fig) überschwemmen

swampy ['swɔmpɪ] adj sumpfig

swan [swɔn] n Schwan m

swank [swæŋk] (inf) vi angeben

swan song n (fig) Schwanengesang m

swap [swɔp] n Tausch m ▷ vt: **to ~ (for)** (ein)tauschen (gegen)

SWAPO ['swɑːpəu] n abbr (= South-West Africa People's Organization) SWAPO f

swarm [swɔːm] n Schwarm m; (of people) Schar f ▷ vi (bees, people) schwärmen; **to be ~ing with** wimmeln von

swarthy ['swɔːðɪ] adj (person, face) dunkelhäutig; (complexion) dunkel

swastika ['swɔstɪkə] n Hakenkreuz nt

SWAT (US) n abbr (= Special Weapons and Tactics): **~ team** ≈ schnelle Eingreiftruppe f

swat [swɔt] vt totschlagen ▷ n (Brit: also: **fly swat**) Fliegenklatsche f

swathe [sweɪð] vt: **to ~ in** wickeln in +acc

swatter ['swɔtə^r] n (also: **fly swatter**) Fliegenklatsche f

sway [sweɪ] vi schwanken ▷ vt (influence) beeinflussen ▷ n: **to hold ~** herrschen; **to hold ~ over sb** jdn beherrschen or in seiner Macht haben

swear [swɛə^r] (pt **swore**, pp **sworn**) vi (curse) fluchen ▷ vt (promise) schwören; **to ~ an oath** einen Eid ablegen
▶ **swear in** vt vereidigen

swearword ['swɛəwəːd] n Fluch m, Kraftausdruck m

sweat [swɛt] n Schweiß m ▷ vi schwitzen; **to be in a ~** schwitzen

sweatband ['swɛtbænd] n Schweißband nt

sweater ['swɛtə^r] n Pullover m

sweatshirt ['swɛtʃəːt] n Sweatshirt nt

sweatshop ['swɛtʃɔp] (pej) n Ausbeuterbetrieb m

sweaty ['swɛtɪ] adj verschwitzt; (hands) schweißig

Swede [swiːd] n Schwede m, Schwedin f

swede [swiːd] (Brit) n Steckrübe f

Sweden ['swiːdn] n Schweden nt

Swedish ['swiːdɪʃ] adj schwedisch ▷ n Schwedisch nt

sweep [swiːp] (pt, pp **swept**) n (curve) Bogen m; (range) Bereich m; (also: **chimney sweep**) Kaminkehrer m, Schornsteinfeger m ▷ vt fegen, kehren; (current) reißen ▷ vi (through air) gleiten; (wind) fegen; **to give sth a ~** etw fegen or kehren

▶**sweep away** vt hinwegfegen

▶**sweep past** vi vorbeirauschen

▶**sweep up** vi zusammenfegen, zusammenkehren

sweeper ['swi:pə^r] n (Football) Ausputzer m

sweeping ['swi:pɪŋ] adj (gesture) weit ausholend; (changes, reforms) weitreichend; (statement) verallgemeinernd

sweepstake ['swi:psteɪk] n Pferdewette, bei der der Preis aus der Summe der Einsätze besteht

sweet [swi:t] n (candy) Bonbon nt or m; (Brit: Culin) Nachtisch m ▷ adj süß; (air, water) frisch; (kind) lieb ▷ adv: **to smell/taste ~** süß duften/schmecken; **~ and sour** süß-sauer

sweetbread ['swi:tbred] n Bries nt

sweetcorn ['swi:tkɔ:n] n Mais m

sweeten ['swi:tn] vt süßen; (temper) bessern; (person) gnädig stimmen

sweetener ['swi:tnə^r] n Süßstoff m

sweetheart ['swi:thɑ:t] n Freund(in) m(f); (in speech, writing) Schatz m, Liebling m

sweetness ['swi:tnɪs] n Süße f; (kindness) Liebenswürdigkeit f

sweet pea n (Garten)wicke f

sweet potato n Süßkartoffel f, Batate f

sweet shop (Brit) n Süßwarengeschäft nt

sweet tooth n: **to have a ~** gern Süßes essen

swell [swel] (pt **~ed**, pp **swollen** or **~ed**) n Seegang m ▷ adj (US: inf) toll, prima ▷ vi (increase) anwachsen; (sound) anschwellen; (feeling) stärker werden; (also: **swell up**) anschwellen

swelling ['swelɪŋ] n Schwellung f

sweltering ['sweltərɪŋ] adj (heat) glühend; (weather, day) glühend heiß

swept [swept] pt, pp of **sweep**

swerve [swə:v] vi (animal) ausbrechen; (driver, vehicle) ausschwenken; **to ~ off the road** ausschwenken und von der Straße abkommen

swift [swɪft] n Mauersegler m ▷ adj schnell

swiftly ['swɪftlɪ] adv schnell

swiftness ['swɪftnɪs] n Schnelligkeit f

swig [swɪg] (inf) n Schluck m ▷ vt herunterkippen

swill [swɪl] vt (also: **swill out**) ausspülen; (also: **swill down**) abspülen ▷ n (for pigs) Schweinefutter nt

swim [swɪm] (pt **swam**, pp **swum**) vi schwimmen; (before one's eyes) verschwimmen; ▷ vt (the Channel etc) durchschwimmen; (a length) schwimmen ▷ n: **to go for a ~** schwimmen gehen; **to go ~ming** schwimmen gehen; **my head is ~ming** mir dreht sich der Kopf

swimmer ['swɪmə^r] n Schwimmer(in) m(f)

swimming ['swɪmɪŋ] n Schwimmen nt

swimming baths (Brit) npl Schwimmbad nt

swimming cap n Badekappe f, Bademütze f

swimming costume (Brit) n Badeanzug m

swimmingly ['swɪmɪŋlɪ] (inf) adv glänzend

swimming pool n Schwimmbad nt

swimming trunks npl Badehose f

swimsuit ['swɪmsu:t] n Badeanzug m

swindle ['swɪndl] n Schwindel m, Betrug m ▷ vt: **to ~ sb (out of sth)** jdn (um etw) betrügen or beschwindeln

swindler ['swɪndlə^r] n Schwindler(in) m(f)

swine [swaɪn] (inf!) n Schwein nt

swine flu n Schweinegrippe f

swing [swɪŋ] (pt, pp **swung**) n (in playground) Schaukel f; (movement) Schwung m; (change) Umschwung m; (Mus) Swing m ▷ vt (arms, legs) schwingen (mit); (also: **swing round**) herumschwenken ▷ vi schwingen; (also: **swing round**) sich umdrehen; (vehicle) herumschwenken; **a ~ to the left** (Pol) ein Linksruck m; **to get into the ~ of things** richtig reinkommen; **to be in full ~** (party etc) in vollem Gang sein

swing bridge n Drehbrücke f

swing door, (US) **swinging door** n Pendeltür f

swingeing ['swɪndʒɪŋ] (Brit) adj (blow) hart; (attack) scharf; (cuts, increases) extrem

swinging ['swɪŋɪŋ] adj (music) schwungvoll; (movement) schaukelnd

swipe [swaɪp] vt (also: **swipe at**) schlagen nach; (inf: steal) klauen ▷ n Schlag m

swirl [swə:l] vi wirbeln ▷ n Wirbeln nt

swish [swɪʃ] vi rauschen; (tail) schlagen ▷ n Rauschen nt; (of tail) Schlagen nt ▷ adj (inf) chic inv, schick

Swiss [swɪs] adj schweizerisch, Schweizer ▷ n inv Schweizer(in) m(f)

Swiss French adj französischschweizerisch

Swiss German adj deutsch-schweizerisch

Swiss roll n Biskuitrolle f

switch [swɪtʃ] n Schalter m; (change) Änderung f ▷ vt (change) ändern; (exchange) tauschen, wechseln; **to ~ (round** or **over)** vertauschen

▶**switch off** vt abschalten; (light) ausschalten ▷ vi (fig) abschalten

▶**switch on** vt einschalten; (radio) anstellen; (engine) anlassen

switchback ['swɪtʃbæk] (Brit) n (road) auf und ab führende Straße f; (roller-coaster) Achterbahn f

switchblade ['swɪtʃbleɪd] n Schnappmesser nt

switchboard ['swɪtʃbɔ:d] n Vermittlung f, Zentrale f

switchboard operator n Telefonist(in) m(f)

Switzerland ['swɪtsələnd] n die Schweiz f

swivel ['swɪvl] vi (also: **swivel round**) sich (herum)drehen

swollen ['swəulən] pp of **swell** ▷ adj geschwollen; (lake etc) angeschwollen

swoon [swu:n] vi beinahe ohnmächtig werden ▷ n Ohnmacht f

swoop [swu:p] n (by police etc) Razzia f; (of bird etc) Sturzflug m ▷ vi (also: **swoop down**: bird) herabstoßen; (plane) einen Sturzflug machen

swop [swɔp] = **swap**

sword [sɔ:d] n Schwert nt

swordfish ['sɔ:dfɪʃ] n Schwertfisch m

swore [swɔ:^r] pt of **swear**

sworn [swɔ:n] pp of **swear** ▷ adj (statement) eidlich; (evidence) unter Eid; (enemy)

S

geschworen

swot [swɔt] vi pauken ▷ n (pej) Streber(in) m(f)
  ▶ **swot up** vt: **to ~ up (on)** pauken (+acc)

swum [swʌm] pp of **swim**

swung [swʌŋ] pt, pp of **swing**

sycamore ['sɪkəmɔ:ʳ] n Bergahorn m

sycophant ['sɪkəfænt] n Kriecher m,
  Speichellecker m

sycophantic [sɪkə'fæntɪk] adj kriecherisch

Sydney ['sɪdnɪ] n Sydney nt

syllable ['sɪləbl] n Silbe f

syllabus ['sɪləbəs] n Lehrplan m; **on the ~** im
  Lehrplan

symbol ['sɪmbl] n Symbol nt

symbolic [sɪm'bɔlɪk], **symbolical** [sɪm'bɔlɪkl]
  adj symbolisch; **to be ~(al) of sth** etw
  symbolisieren, ein Symbol für etw sein

symbolism ['sɪmbəlɪzəm] n Symbolismus m

symbolize ['sɪmbəlaɪz] vt symbolisieren

symmetrical [sɪ'mɛtrɪkl] adj symmetrisch

symmetry ['sɪmɪtrɪ] n Symmetrie f

sympathetic [sɪmpə'θɛtɪk] adj (understanding)
  verständnisvoll; (showing pity) mitfühlend;
  (likeable) sympathisch; (supportive)
  wohlwollend; **to be ~ to a cause** (well-
  disposed) einer Sache wohlwollend
  gegenüberstehen

sympathetically [sɪmpə'θɛtɪklɪ] adv (showing
  understanding) verständnisvoll; (showing support)
  wohlwollend

sympathize ['sɪmpəθaɪz] vi: **to ~ with** (person)
  Mitleid haben mit; (feelings) Verständnis
  haben für; (cause) sympathisieren mit

sympathizer ['sɪmpəθaɪzəʳ] n (Pol)
  Sympathisant(in) m(f)

sympathy ['sɪmpəθɪ] n Mitgefühl nt;
  sympathies npl (support, tendencies) Sympathien
  pl; **with our deepest ~** mit aufrichtigem or
  herzlichem Beileid; **to come out in ~** (workers)
  in einen Sympathiestreik treten

symphonic [sɪm'fɔnɪk] adj sinfonisch

symphony ['sɪmfənɪ] n Sinfonie f

symphony orchestra n Sinfonieorchester nt

symposia [sɪm'pəuzɪə] npl of **symposium**

symposium [sɪm'pəuzɪəm] (pl **~s** or **symposia**)
  n Symposium nt

symptom ['sɪmptəm] n (Med, fig) Symptom nt,
  Anzeichen nt

symptomatic [sɪmptə'mætɪk] adj: **~ of**
  symptomatisch für

synagogue ['sɪnəgɔg] n Synagoge f

sync [sɪŋk] n abbr (= synchronization): **in ~**

synchron; **out of ~** nicht synchron

synchromesh [sɪŋkrəu'mɛʃ] n
  Synchrongetriebe nt

synchronize ['sɪŋkrənaɪz] vt (watches)
  gleichstellen; (movements) aufeinander
  abstimmen; (sound) synchronisieren ▷ vi: **to ~
  with** (sound) synchron sein mit

synchronized swimming ['sɪŋkrənaɪzd-] n
  Synchronschwimmen nt

syncopated ['sɪŋkəpeɪtɪd] adj synkopiert

syndicate ['sɪndɪkɪt] n
  Interessengemeinschaft f; (of businesses)
  Verband m; (of newspapers) Pressezentrale f

syndrome ['sɪndrəum] n Syndrom nt; (fig)
  Phänomen nt

synonym ['sɪnənɪm] n Synonym nt

synonymous [sɪ'nɔnɪməs] adj (fig): **~ (with)**
  gleichbedeutend (mit)

synopses [sɪ'nɔpsi:z] npl of **synopsis**

synopsis [sɪ'nɔpsɪs] (pl **synopses**) n Abriss m,
  Zusammenfassung f

syntactic [sɪn'tæktɪk] adj syntaktisch

syntax ['sɪntæks] n Syntax f

syntax error n (Comput) Syntaxfehler m

syntheses ['sɪnθəsi:z] npl of **synthesis**

synthesis ['sɪnθəsɪs] (pl **syntheses**) n Synthese
  f

synthesizer ['sɪnθəsaɪzəʳ] n Synthesizer m

synthetic [sɪn'θɛtɪk] adj synthetisch; (speech)
  künstlich; **synthetics** npl (man-made fabrics)
  Synthetik f

syphilis ['sɪfɪlɪs] n Syphilis f

syphon ['saɪfən] = **siphon**

Syria ['sɪrɪə] n Syrien nt

Syrian ['sɪrɪən] adj syrisch ▷ n Syrer(in)
  m(f)

syringe [sɪ'rɪndʒ] n Spritze f

syrup ['sɪrəp] n Sirup m; (also: **golden syrup**)
  (gelber) Sirup m

syrupy ['sɪrəpɪ] adj sirupartig;
  (pej: fig: sentimental) schmalzig

system ['sɪstəm] n System nt; (body) Körper m;
  (Anat) Apparat m, System nt; **it was a shock to
  his ~** er hatte schwer damit zu schaffen

systematic [sɪstə'mætɪk] adj systematisch

system disk n (Comput) Systemdiskette f

systems administrator ['sɪstəmz-] n (Comput)
  Systembetreuer(in) m(f)

systems analyst ['sɪstəmz-] n (Comput)
  Systemanalytiker(in) m(f)

systems engineer ['sɪstəmz-] n (Comput)
  Systemtechniker(in) m(f)

Tt

T, t [tiː] *n* (*letter*) T *nt*, t *nt*; **T for Tommy** ≈ T wie Theodor

TA (*Brit*) *n abbr* = **Territorial Army**

ta [taː] (*Brit: inf*) *interj* danke

tab [tæb] *n* (*on drinks can*) Ring *m*; (*on garment*) Etikett *nt*; **to keep ~s on sb/sth** (*fig*) jdn/etw im Auge behalten

tab [tæb] *n abbr* = **tabulator** ▷ *n* (*on drinks can*) Ring *m*; (*on garment*) Etikett *nt*; **to keep ~s on sb/sth** (*fig*) jdn/etw im Auge behalten

tabby ['tæbɪ] *n* (*also:* **tabby cat**) getigerte Katze *f*

tabernacle ['tæbənækl] *n* Tabernakel *nt*

table ['teɪbl] *n* Tisch *m*; (*Math, Chem etc*) Tabelle *f* ▷ *vt* (*Brit: Parl: motion etc*) einbringen; **to lay** *or* **set the ~** den Tisch decken; **to clear the ~** den Tisch abräumen; **league ~** (*Brit: Sport*) Tabelle *f*

tablecloth ['teɪblklɔθ] *n* Tischdecke *f*

table d'hôte [taːbl'dəut] *adj* (*menu, meal*) Tagesmenü *nt*

table lamp *n* Tischlampe *f*

tablemat ['teɪblmæt] *n* (*of cloth*) Set *nt or m*; (*for hot dish*) Untersatz *m*

table of contents *n* Inhaltsverzeichnis *nt*

table salt *n* Tafelsalz *nt*

tablespoon ['teɪblspuːn] *n* Esslöffel *m*; (*also:* **tablespoonful**) Esslöffel(voll) *m*

tablet ['tæblɪt] *n* (*Med*) Tablette *f*; (*Hist: for writing*) Tafel *f*; (*plaque*) Plakette *f*; **~ of soap** (*Brit*) Stück *nt* Seife

table tennis *n* Tischtennis *nt*

table wine *n* Tafelwein *m*

tabloid ['tæblɔɪd] *n* (*newspaper*) Boulevardzeitung *f*; **the ~s** die Boulevardpresse

taboo [tə'buː] *n* Tabu *nt* ▷ *adj* tabu; **a ~ subject/word** ein Tabuthema/Tabuwort

tabulate ['tæbjuleɪt] *vt* tabellarisieren

tabulator ['tæbjuleɪtə^r] *n* (*on typewriter*) Tabulator *m*

tachograph ['tækəɡrɑːf] *n* Fahrtenschreiber *m*

tachometer [tæ'kɔmɪtə^r] *n* Tachometer *m*

tacit ['tæsɪt] *adj* stillschweigend

taciturn ['tæsɪtəːn] *adj* schweigsam

tack [tæk] *n* (*nail*) Stift *m* + *vt* (*nail*) anheften; (*stitch*) heften ▷ *vi* (*Naut*) kreuzen; **to change ~** (*fig*) den Kurs ändern; **to ~ sth on to (the end of) sth** etw (hinten) an etw *acc* anheften

tackle ['tækl] *n* (*for fishing*) Ausrüstung *f*; (*for lifting*) Flaschenzug *m*; (*Football, Rugby*) Angriff *m* ▷ *vt* (*deal with: difficulty*) in Angriff nehmen; (*challenge: person*) zur Rede stellen; (*physically, also Sport*) angreifen

tacky ['tækɪ] *adj* (*sticky*) klebrig; (*pej: cheap-looking*) schäbig

tact [tækt] *n* Takt *m*

tactful ['tæktful] *adj* taktvoll; **to be ~** taktvoll sein

tactfully ['tæktfəlɪ] *adv* taktvoll

tactical ['tæktɪkl] *adj* taktisch; **~ error** taktischer Fehler; **~ voting** taktische Stimmabgabe

tactician [tæk'tɪʃən] *n* Taktiker(in) *m(f)*

tactics ['tæktɪks] *npl* Taktik *f*

tactless ['tæktlɪs] *adj* taktlos

tactlessly ['tæktlɪslɪ] *adv* taktlos

tadpole ['tædpəul] *n* Kaulquappe *f*

taffy ['tæfɪ] (*US*) *n* (*toffee*) Toffee *nt*, Sahnebonbon *nt*

tag [tæɡ] *n* (*label*) Anhänger *m*; **price/name ~** Preis-/Namensschild *nt*; (*electronic*) ~ (elektronische) Fußfessel *f*
▶ **tag along** *vi* sich anschließen

Tahiti [taː'hiːtɪ] *n* Tahiti *nt*

tail [teɪl] *n* (*of animal*) Schwanz *m*; (*of plane*) Heck *nt*; (*of shirt, coat*) Schoß *m* + *dat*; **tails** *npl* (*formal suit*) Frack *m*; **to turn ~** die Flucht ergreifen; *see also* **head**
▶ **tail off** *vi* (*in size etc*) abnehmen; (*voice*) schwächer werden

tailback ['teɪlbæk] (*Brit*) *n* (*Aut*) Stau *m*

tail coat *n* = **tails**

tail end *n* Ende *nt*

t

tailgate ['teɪlgeɪt] n (Aut) Heckklappe f

taillight ['teɪllaɪt] n (Aut) Rücklicht nt

tailor ['teɪlə'] n Schneider(in) m(f) ▷ vt: **to ~ sth (to)** etw abstimmen (auf +acc); **~'s shop** Schneiderei f

tailoring ['teɪlərɪŋ] n (craft) Schneiderei f; (cut) Verarbeitung f

tailor-made ['teɪlə'meɪd] adj (also fig) maßgeschneidert

tailwind ['teɪlwɪnd] n Rückenwind m

taint [teɪnt] vt (meat, food) verderben; (fig: reputation etc) beschmutzen

tainted ['teɪntɪd] adj (food, water, air) verdorben; (fig: profits, reputation etc): **~ with** behaftet mit

Taiwan ['taɪ'wɑːn] n Taiwan nt

Tajikistan [tɑːdʒɪkɪ'stɑːn] n Tadschikistan nt

take [teɪk] (pt **took**, pp **~n**) vt nehmen; (photo, notes) machen; (decision) fällen; (require: courage, time) erfordern; (tolerate: pain etc) ertragen; (hold: passengers etc) fassen; (accompany: person) begleiten; (carry, bring) mitnehmen; (exam, test) machen; (conduct: meeting) leiten; (: class) unterrichten ▷ vi (have effect: drug) wirken; (: dye) angenommen werden ▷ n (Cine) Aufnahme f; **to ~ sth from** (drawer etc) etw nehmen aus +dat; **I ~ it (that)** ich nehme an(, dass); **I took him for a doctor** (mistake) ich hielt ihn für einen Arzt; **to ~ sb's hand** jds Hand nehmen; **to ~ sb for a walk** mit jdm spazieren gehen; **to be ~n ill** krank werden; **to ~ it upon o.s. to do sth** es auf sich nehmen, etw zu tun; **~ the first (street) on the left** nehmen Sie die erste Straße links; **to ~ Russian at university** Russisch studieren; **it won't ~ long** es dauert nicht lange; **I was quite ~n with her/it** (attracted to) ich war von ihr/davon recht angetan

▶ **take after** vt fus (resemble) ähneln +dat, ähnlich sein +dat

▶ **take apart** vt auseinandernehmen

▶ **take away** vt wegnehmen; (carry off) wegbringen; (Math) abziehen ▷ vi: **to ~ away from** (detract from) schmälern, beeinträchtigen

▶ **take back** vt (return) zurückbringen; (one's words) zurücknehmen

▶ **take down** vt (write down) aufschreiben; (dismantle) abreißen

▶ **take in** vt (deceive: person) hereinlegen, täuschen; (understand) begreifen; (include) einschließen; (lodger) aufnehmen; (orphan, stray dog) zu sich nehmen; (dress, waistband) enger machen

▶ **take off** vi (Aviat) starten; (go away) sich absetzen ▷ vt (clothes) ausziehen; (glasses) abnehmen; (make-up) entfernen; (time) freinehmen; (imitate: person) nachmachen

▶ **take on** vt (work, responsibility) übernehmen; (employee) einstellen; (compete against) antreten gegen

▶ **take out** vt (invite) ausgehen mit; (remove: tooth) herausnehmen; (licence) erwerben; **to ~ sth out of sth** (drawer, pocket etc) etw aus etw nehmen; **don't ~ it out on me!** lass es nicht an mir aus!

▶ **take over** vt (business) übernehmen; (country) Besitz ergreifen von ▷ vi (replace): **to ~ over from sb** jdn ablösen

▶ **take to** vt fus (person, thing) mögen; (activity) Gefallen finden an +dat; (form habit of): **to ~ to doing sth** sich dat angewöhnen, etw zu tun

▶ **take up** vt (hobby, sport) anfangen mit; (job) antreten; (idea etc) annehmen; (time, space) beanspruchen; (continue: task, story) fortfahren mit; (shorten: hem, garment) kürzer machen ▷ vi (befriend): **to ~ up with sb** sich mit jdm anfreunden; **to ~ sb up on an offer/a suggestion** auf jds Angebot/Vorschlag eingehen

takeaway ['teɪkəweɪ] (Brit) n (shop, restaurant) ≈ Schnellimbiss m; (food) Imbiss m (zum Mitnehmen)

take-home pay ['teɪkhəum-] n Nettolohn m

taken ['teɪkən] pp of **take**

takeoff ['teɪkɔf] n (Aviat) Start m

takeout ['teɪkaut] (US) n = **takeaway**

takeover ['teɪkəuvə'] n (Comm) Übernahme f; (of country) Inbesitznahme f

takeover bid n Übernahmeangebot nt

takings ['teɪkɪŋz] npl Einnahmen pl

talc [tælk] n (also: **talcum powder**) Talkumpuder m

tale [teɪl] n Geschichte f; **to tell ~s (to sb)** (child) (jdm) Geschichten erzählen

talent ['tælnt] n Talent nt

talented ['tæləntɪd] adj talentiert, begabt

talent scout n Talentsucher(in) m(f)

talisman ['tælɪzmən] n Talisman m

talk [tɔːk] n (speech) Vortrag m; (conversation, discussion) Gespräch nt; (gossip) Gerede nt ▷ vi (speak) sprechen; (chat) reden; (gossip) klatschen; **talks** npl (Pol etc) Gespräche pl; **to give a ~** einen Vortrag halten; **to ~ about** (discuss) sprechen or reden über; **~ing of films, have you seen ...?** da wir gerade von Filmen sprechen: hast du ... gesehen?; **to ~ sb into doing sth** jdn zu etw überreden; **to ~ sb out of doing sth** jdm etw ausreden

▶ **talk over** vt (problem etc) besprechen, bereden

talkative ['tɔːkətɪv] adj gesprächig

talker ['tɔːkə'] n: **to be a good/entertaining/ fast** etc **~** gut/amüsant/schnell etc reden können

talking point ['tɔːkɪŋ-] n Gesprächsthema nt

talking-to ['tɔːkɪŋtu] n: **to give sb a (good) ~** jdm eine (ordentliche) Standpauke halten (inf)

talk show n Talkshow f

tall [tɔːl] adj (person) groß; (glass, bookcase, tree, building) hoch; (ladder) lang; **to be 6 feet ~** (person) ≈ 1,80m groß sein; **how ~ are you?** wie groß bist du?

tallboy ['tɔːlbɔɪ] (Brit) n Kommode f

tallness ['tɔːlnɪs] n (of person) Größe f; (of tree, building etc) Höhe f

tall story n unglaubliche Geschichte f

tally ['tælɪ] n (of marks, amounts etc) aktueller Stand m ▷ vi: **to ~ (with)** (figures, stories etc) übereinstimmen mit; **to keep a ~ of sth** über etw acc Buch führen

talon ['tælən] n Kralle f

tambourine [tæmbə'riːn] n Tamburin nt

tame [teɪm] adj (animal, bird) zahm; (fig: story, party, performance) lustlos, lahm (inf)

Tamil ['tæmɪl] adj tamilisch ▷ n Tamile m, Tamilin f; (Ling) Tamil nt

tamper ['tæmpəʳ] vi: **to ~ with sth** an etw dat herumpfuschen (inf)

tampon ['tæmpɔn] n Tampon m

tan [tæn] n (also: **suntan**) (Sonnen)bräune f ▷ vi (person, skin) braun werden ▷ vt (hide) gerben; (skin) bräunen ▷ adj (colour) hellbraun; **to get a ~** braun werden

tandem ['tændəm] n Tandem nt; (together): **in ~** (fig) zusammen

tandoori [tæn'duərɪ] n: **~ oven** Tandoori-Ofen m; **~ chicken** im Tandoori-Ofen gebratenes Huhn

tang [tæŋ] n (smell) Geruch m; (taste) Geschmack m

tangent ['tændʒənt] n (Math) Tangente f; **to go off at a ~** (fig) vom Thema abschweifen

tangerine [tændʒə'riːn] n (fruit) Mandarine f; (colour) Orangerot nt

tangible ['tændʒəbl] adj greifbar; **~ assets** (Comm) Sachanlagevermögen nt

Tangier [tæn'dʒɪəʳ] n Tanger nt

tangle ['tæŋgl] n (of branches, wire etc) Gewirr nt; **to be in a ~** verheddert sein; (fig) durcheinander sein; **to get in a ~** sich verheddern; (fig) durcheinandergeraten

tango ['tæŋgəu] n Tango m

tank [tæŋk] n Tank m; (for photographic processing) Wanne f; (also: **fish tank**) Aquarium nt; (Mil) Panzer m

tankard ['tæŋkəd] n Bierkrug m

tanker ['tæŋkəʳ] n (ship) Tanker m; (truck) Tankwagen m

tankini [tæŋ'kiːnɪ] n Tankini m

tanned [tænd] adj (person) braun gebrannt; (hide) gegerbt

tannin ['tænɪn] n Tannin nt

tanning ['tænɪŋ] n (of leather) Gerben nt

Tannoy® ['tænɔɪ] (Brit) n Lautsprechersystem nt; **over the ~** über Lautsprecher

tantalizing ['tæntəlaɪzɪŋ] adj (smell) verführerisch; (possibility) verlockend

tantamount ['tæntəmaunt] adj: **~ to** gleichbedeutend mit

tantrum ['tæntrəm] n Wutanfall m; **to throw a ~** einen Wutanfall bekommen

Tanzania [tænzə'nɪə] n Tansania nt

Tanzanian [tænzə'nɪən] adj tansanisch ▷ n (person) Tansanier(in) m(f)

tap [tæp] n (on sink, gas tap) Hahn m; (gentle blow) leichter Schlag m, Klaps m ▷ vt (hit gently) klopfen; (exploit: resources, energy) nutzen; (telephone) abhören, anzapfen; **on ~** (fig: resources) zur Verfügung; (beer) vom Fass

tap-dancing ['tæpdɑːnsɪŋ] n Stepptanz m

tape [teɪp] n (also: **magnetic tape**) Tonband nt; (cassette) Kassette f; (also: **sticky tape**) Klebeband nt; (for tying) Band nt ▷ vt (record, conversation) aufnehmen, aufzeichnen; (stick with tape) mit Klebeband befestigen; **on ~** (song etc) auf Band

tape deck n Tapedeck nt

tape measure n Bandmaß nt

taper ['teɪpəʳ] n (candle) lange, dünne Kerze ▷ vi sich verjüngen

tape recorder n Tonband(gerät) nt

tape recording n Tonbandaufnahme f

tapered ['teɪpəd] adj (skirt, jacket) nach unten enger werdend

tapering ['teɪpərɪŋ] adj spitz zulaufend

tapestry ['tæpɪstrɪ] n (on wall) Wandteppich m; (fig) Kaleidoskop nt

tapeworm ['teɪpwəːm] n Bandwurm m

tapioca [tæpɪ'əukə] n Tapioka f

tappet ['tæpɪt] n (Aut) Stößel m

tar [tɑː] n Teer m; **low/middle ~ cigarettes** Zigaretten mit niedrigem/mittlerem Teergehalt

tarantula [tə'ræntjulə] n Tarantel f

tardy ['tɑːdɪ] adj (reply, letter) verspätet; (progress) langsam

target ['tɑːgɪt] n Ziel nt; (fig: of joke, criticism etc) Zielscheibe f; **to be on ~** (project, work) nach Plan verlaufen

target practice n Zielschießen nt

tariff ['tærɪf] n (tax on goods) Zoll m; (Brit: in hotels etc) Preisliste f

tariff barrier n Zollschranke f

tarmac® ['tɑːmæk] n (Brit: on road) Asphalt m; (Aviat): **on the ~** auf dem Rollfeld ▷ vt (Brit: road etc) asphaltieren

tarn [tɑːn] n Bergsee m

tarnish ['tɑːnɪʃ] vt (silver, brass etc) stumpf werden lassen; (fig: reputation etc) beflecken, in Mitleidenschaft ziehen

tarot ['tærəu] n Tarot nt or m

tarpaulin [tɑː'pɔːlɪn] n Plane f

tarragon ['tærəgən] n Estragon m

tart [tɑːt] n (Culin) Torte f; (: small) Törtchen nt; (Brit: inf: prostitute) Nutte f ▷ adj (apple, grapefruit etc) säuerlich

 ▶ **tart up** (Brit: inf) vt (room, building) aufmotzen; **to ~ o.s. up** sich fein machen; (pej) sich auftakeln

tartan ['tɑːtn] n Tartan m, Schottenstoff m ▷ adj (scarf etc) mit Schottenmuster

tartar ['tɑːtəʳ] n (on teeth) Zahnstein m; (pej: person) Tyrann(in) m(f)

tartar sauce, tartare sauce ['tɑːtə-] n Remouladensoße f

task [tɑːsk] n Aufgabe f; **to take sb to ~** jdn ins Gebet nehmen

task force n (Mil) Sonderkommando nt; (Police) Spezialeinheit f

taskmaster ['tɑːskmɑːstəʳ] n: **a hard ~** ein strenger Lehrmeister

Tasmania [tæz'meɪnɪə] n Tasmanien nt

tassel ['tæsl] n Quaste f

taste [teɪst] n Geschmack m; (sample) Kostprobe f; (fig: of suffering, freedom etc) Vorgeschmack m ▷ vt (get flavour of) schmecken; (test) probieren, versuchen ▷ vi: **to ~ of/like sth** nach/wie etw schmecken; **sense of ~** Geschmackssinn m; **to have a ~ of sth** (sample) etw probieren; **to acquire a ~ for sth** (liking) Geschmack an etw dat finden; **to be in good/bad ~** (joke etc) geschmackvoll/geschmacklos sein; **you can ~ the garlic (in it)** (detect) man schmeckt den Knoblauch durch; **what does it ~ like?** wie schmeckt es?

taste buds npl Geschmacksknospen pl

tasteful ['teɪstful] adj geschmackvoll

tastefully ['teɪstfəlɪ] adv geschmackvoll

tasteless ['teɪstlɪs] adj geschmacklos

tasty ['teɪstɪ] adj schmackhaft

tattered ['tætəd] adj (clothes, paper etc) zerrissen; (fig: hopes etc) angeschlagen

tatters ['tætəz] npl: **to be in ~** (clothes) in Fetzen sein

tattoo [tə'tuː] n (on skin) Tätowierung f; (spectacle) Zapfenstreich m ▷ vt: **to ~ sth on sth** etw auf etw acc tätowieren

tatty ['tætɪ] (Brit: inf) adj schäbig

taught [tɔːt] pt, pp of **teach**

taunt [tɔːnt] n höhnische Bemerkung f ▷ vt (person) verhöhnen

Taurus ['tɔːrəs] n Stier m; **to be ~** (ein) Stier sein

taut [tɔːt] adj (skin, thread etc) straff

tavern ['tævən] n Taverne f

tawdry ['tɔːdrɪ] adj billig

tawny ['tɔːnɪ] adj gelbbraun

tawny owl n Waldkauz m

tax [tæks] n Steuer f ▷ vt (earnings, goods etc) besteuern; (fig: memory, knowledge) strapazieren; (: patience etc) auf die Probe stellen; **before/after ~** vor/nach Abzug der Steuern; **free of ~** steuerfrei

taxable ['tæksəbl] adj steuerpflichtig; (income) steuerbar

tax allowance n Steuerfreibetrag m

taxation [tæk'seɪʃən] n (system) Besteuerung f; (money paid) Steuern pl

tax avoidance n Steuerumgehung f

tax collector n Steuerbeamte(r) m, Steuerbeamtin f

tax disc (Brit) n (Aut) Steuerplakette f

tax evasion n Steuerhinterziehung f

tax exemption n Steuerbefreiung f

tax exile (person) n Steuerflüchtling m

tax-free ['tæksfriː] adj steuerfrei

tax haven n Steuerparadies nt

taxi ['tæksɪ] n Taxi nt ▷ vi (Aviat: plane) rollen

taxidermist ['tæksɪdəːmɪst] n Taxidermist(in) m(f), Tierpräparator(in) m(f)

taxi driver n Taxifahrer(in) m(f)

tax inspector (Brit) n Steuerinspektor(in) m(f)

taxi rank (Brit) n Taxistand m

taxi stand n = **taxi rank**

taxpayer ['tækspeɪər] n Steuerzahler(in) m(f)

tax rebate n Steuerrückvergütung f

tax relief n Steuernachlass m

tax return n Steuererklärung f

tax shelter n (Comm) System zur Verhinderung von Steuerbelastung

tax year n Steuerjahr nt

TB n abbr (= tuberculosis) Tb f, Tbc f

tbc abbr (= to be confirmed) noch zu bestätigen

TD (US) n abbr = **Treasury Department**; (Football) = **touchdown**

tea [tiː] n (drink) Tee m; (Brit: evening meal) Abendessen nt; **afternoon ~** (Brit) Nachmittagstee m

tea bag n Teebeutel m

tea break (Brit) n Teepause f

teacake ['tiːkeɪk] (Brit) n Rosinenbrötchen nt

teach [tiːtʃ] (pt, pp **taught**) vt: **to ~ sb sth, ~ sth to sb** (instruct) jdm etw beibringen; (in school) jdn in etw dat unterrichten ▷ vi unterrichten; **it taught him a lesson** (fig) er hat seine Lektion gelernt

teacher ['tiːtʃər] n Lehrer(in) m(f); **German ~** Deutschlehrer(in) m(f)

teacher training college n (for primary schools) ≈ pädagogische Hochschule f; (for secondary schools) ≈ Studienseminar nt

teaching ['tiːtʃɪŋ] n (work of teacher) Unterricht m

teaching aids npl Lehrmittel pl

teaching hospital (Brit) n Ausbildungskrankenhaus nt

teaching staff (Brit) n Lehrerkollegium nt

tea cosy n Teewärmer m

teacup ['tiːkʌp] n Teetasse f

teak [tiːk] n Teak nt

tea leaves npl Teeblätter pl

team [tiːm] n (of experts etc) Team nt; (Sport) Mannschaft f, Team nt; (of horses, oxen) Gespann nt
  ▶ **team up** vi: **to ~ up (with)** sich zusammentun (mit)

team game n Mannschaftsspiel nt

team spirit n Teamgeist m

teamwork ['tiːmwəːk] n Teamwork nt, Teamarbeit f

tea party n Teegesellschaft f

teapot ['tiːpɔt] n Teekanne f

tear¹ [tɛər] (pt **tore**, pp **torn**) n (hole) Riss m ▷ vt (rip) zerreißen ▷ vi (become torn) reißen; **to ~ sth to pieces** or **bits** or **shreds** (lit, fig) etw in Stücke reißen; **to ~ sb to pieces** jdn fertigmachen
  ▶ **tear along** vi (rush: driver, car) entlanggrasen
  ▶ **tear apart** vt (book, clothes, people) auseinanderreißen; (upset: person) hin- und herreißen
  ▶ **tear away** vt: **to ~ o.s. away (from sth)** (fig) sich (von etw) losreißen
  ▶ **tear out** vt (sheet of paper etc) herausreißen
  ▶ **tear up** vt (sheet of paper etc) zerreißen

tear² [tɪər] n (in eye) Träne f; **in ~s** in Tränen; **to burst into ~s** in Tränen ausbrechen

tearaway ['tɛərəweɪ] (Brit: inf) n Rabauke m

teardrop ['tɪədrɔp] n Träne f

tearful ['tɪəfʊl] *adj* (*person*) weinend; (*face*) tränenüberströmt

tear gas *n* Tränengas *nt*

tearing ['tɛərɪŋ] *adj*: **to be in a ~ hurry** es unheimlich eilig haben

tearoom ['tiːruːm] *n* = **teashop**

tease [tiːz] *vt* necken; (*unkindly*) aufziehen ▷ *n*: **she's a real ~** sie zieht einen ständig auf

tea set *n* Teeservice *nt*

teashop ['tiːʃɒp] (*Brit*) *n* Teestube *f*

Teasmade® ['tiːzmeɪd] *n* Teemaschine *f* (*mit Zeiteinstellung*)

teaspoon ['tiːspuːn] *n* Teelöffel *m*; (*also*: **teaspoonful**: *measure*) Teelöffel(voll) *m*

tea strainer *n* Teesieb *nt*

teat [tiːt] *n* (*on bottle*) Sauger *m*

teatime ['tiːtaɪm] *n* Teestunde *f*

tea towel (*Brit*) *n* Geschirrtuch *nt*

tea urn *n* Teespender *m*

tech [tɛk] (*inf*) *n abbr* = **technical college; technology**

technical ['tɛknɪkl] *adj* technisch; (*terms, language*) Fach-

technical college (*Brit*) *n* technische Fachschule *f*

technicality [tɛknɪ'kælɪtɪ] *n* (*point of law*) Formalität *f*; (*detail*) technische Einzelheit *f*; **on a (legal) ~** aufgrund einer (juristischen) Formalität

technically ['tɛknɪklɪ] *adv* (*strictly speaking*) genau genommen; (*regarding technique*) technisch (gesehen)

technician [tɛk'nɪʃən] *n* Techniker(in) *m(f)*

technique [tɛk'niːk] *n* Technik *f*

techno ['tɛknəʊ] *n* (*Mus*) Techno *nt*

technocrat ['tɛknəkræt] *n* Technokrat(in) *m(f)*

technological [tɛknə'lɒdʒɪkl] *adj* technologisch

technologist [tɛk'nɒlədʒɪst] *n* Technologe *m*, Technologin *f*

technology [tɛk'nɒlədʒɪ] *n* Technologie *f*

technology college *n* Oberstufenkolleg *mit technischem Schwerpunkt*

teddy ['tɛdɪ], **teddy bear** *n* Teddy(bär) *m*

tedious ['tiːdɪəs] *adj* langweilig

tedium ['tiːdɪəm] *n* Langeweile *f*

tee [tiː] *n* (*Golf*) Tee *nt*
▷ **tee off** *vi* (vom Tee) abschlagen

teem [tiːm] *vi*: **to ~ with** (*tourists etc*) wimmeln von; **it is ~ing down** es gießt in Strömen

teenage ['tiːneɪdʒ] *adj* (*fashions etc*) Jugend-; (*children*) im Teenageralter

teenager ['tiːneɪdʒəʳ] *n* Teenager *m*, Jugendliche(r) *f(m)*

teens [tiːnz] *npl*: **to be in one's ~** im Teenageralter sein

tee shirt *n* = **T-shirt**

teeter ['tiːtəʳ] *vi* (*also fig*) schwanken, taumeln

teeth [tiːθ] *npl of* **tooth**

teethe [tiːð] *vi* Zähne bekommen, zahnen

teething ring ['tiːðɪŋ-] *n* Beißring *m*

teething troubles *npl* (*fig*) Kinderkrankheiten *pl*

teetotal ['tiː'təʊtl] *adj* (*person*) abstinent

teetotaller, (*US*) **teetotaler** ['tiː'təʊtləʳ] *n* Abstinenzler(in) *m(f)*, Antialkoholiker(in) *m(f)*

TEFL ['tɛfl] *n abbr* (= *Teaching of English as a Foreign Language*) Unterricht in Englisch als Fremdsprache

Teflon® ['tɛflɒn] *n* Teflon® *nt*

Teheran [tɛə'rɑːn] *n* Teheran *nt*

tel. *abbr* (= *telephone*) Tel.

Tel Aviv ['tɛlə'viːv] *n* Tel Aviv *nt*

telecast ['tɛlɪkɑːst] *n* Fernsehsendung *f*

telecommunications ['tɛlɪkəmjuːnɪ'keɪʃənz] *n* Nachrichtentechnik *f*

teleconferencing ['tɛlɪ'kɒnfərənsɪŋ] *n* Telekonferenzen *pl*

telegram ['tɛlɪgræm] *n* Telegramm *nt*

telegraph ['tɛlɪgrɑːf] *n* (*system*) Telegraf *m*

telegraphic [tɛlɪ'græfɪk] *adj* (*equipment*) telegrafisch

telegraph pole *n* Telegrafenmast *m*

telegraph wire *n* Telegrafenleitung *f*

telepathic [tɛlɪ'pæθɪk] *adj* telepathisch

telepathy [tə'lɛpəθɪ] *n* Telepathie *f*

telephone ['tɛlɪfəʊn] *n* Telefon *nt* ▷ *vt* (*person*) anrufen ▷ *vi* anrufen, telefonieren; **to be on the ~** (*talking*) telefonieren; (*possessing phone*) ein Telefon haben

telephone box, (*US*) **telephone booth** *n* Telefonzelle *f*

telephone call *n* Anruf *m*

telephone directory *n* Telefonbuch *nt*

telephone exchange *n* Telefonzentrale *f*

telephone number *n* Telefonnummer *f*

telephone operator *n* Telefonist(in) *m(f)*

telephone tapping *n* Abhören *nt* von Telefonleitungen

telephonist [tə'lɛfənɪst] (*Brit*) *n* Telefonist(in) *m(f)*

telephoto ['tɛlɪ'fəʊtəʊ] *adj*: **~ lens** Teleobjektiv *nt*

teleprinter ['tɛlɪprɪntəʳ] *n* Fernschreiber *m*

Teleprompter® ['tɛlɪprɒmptəʳ] (*US*) *n* Teleprompter *m*

telesales ['tɛlɪseɪlz] *n* Verkauf *m* per Telefon

telescope ['tɛlɪskəʊp] *n* Teleskop *nt* ▷ *vi* (*fig*: *bus, lorry*) sich ineinanderschieben ▷ *vt* (*make shorter*) zusammenschieben

telescopic [tɛlɪ'skɒpɪk] *adj* (*legs, aerial*) ausziehbar; **~ lens** Fernrohrlinse *f*

Teletext® ['tɛlɪtɛkst] *n* Videotext *m*

telethon ['tɛlɪθɒn] *n* Spendenaktion *für wohltätige Zwecke in Form einer vielstündigen Fernsehsendung*

televise ['tɛlɪvaɪz] *vt* (im Fernsehen) übertragen

television ['tɛlɪvɪʒən] *n* Fernsehen *nt*; (*set*) Fernseher *m*, Fernsehapparat *m*; **to be on ~** im Fernsehen sein

television licence (*Brit*) *n* Fernsehgenehmigung *f*

television programme *n* Fernsehprogramm *nt*

television set *n* Fernseher *m*, Fernsehapparat *m*

teleworking ['tɛlɪwɜːkɪŋ] *n* Telearbeit *f*

t

telex ['tɛlɛks] n (system, machine, message) Telex nt ▷ vt (message) telexen; (person) ein Telex schicken +dat ▷ vi telexen

tell [tɛl] (pt, pp **told**) vt (say) sagen; (relate: story) erzählen; (distinguish): **to ~ sth from** etw unterscheiden von; (be sure) wissen ▷ vi (have an effect) sich auswirken; **to ~ sb to do sth** jdm sagen, etw zu tun; **to ~ sb of** or **about sth** jdm von etw erzählen; **to be able to ~ the time** (know how to) die Uhr kennen; **can you ~ me the time?** können Sie mir sagen, wie spät es ist?; **(I) ~ you what, let's go to the cinema** weißt du was? Lass uns ins Kino gehen!; **I can't ~ them apart** ich kann sie nicht unterscheiden
▸ **tell off** vt: **to ~ sb off** jdn ausschimpfen
▸ **tell on** vt fus (inform against) verpetzen

teller ['tɛləʳ] n (in bank) Kassierer(in) m(f)

telling ['tɛlɪŋ] adj (remark etc) verräterisch

telltale ['tɛlteɪl] adj verräterisch ▷ n (pej) Petzer m, Petze f

telly ['tɛlɪ] (Brit: inf) n abbr = **television**

temerity [tə'mɛrɪtɪ] n Unverschämtheit f

temp [tɛmp] (Brit: inf) n abbr (= temporary office worker) Zeitarbeitskraft f ▷ vi als Zeitarbeitskraft arbeiten

temper ['tɛmpəʳ] n (nature) Naturell nt; (mood) Laune f ▷ vt (moderate) mildern; **a (fit of) ~** ein Wutanfall m; **to be in a ~** gereizt sein; **to lose one's ~** die Beherrschung verlieren

temperament ['tɛmprəmənt] n Temperament nt

temperamental [tɛmprə'mɛntl] adj (person, car) launisch

temperate ['tɛmprət] adj gemäßigt

temperature ['tɛmprətʃəʳ] n Temperatur f; **to have** or **run a ~** Fieber haben; **to take sb's ~** bei jdm Fieber messen

temperature chart n (Med) Fiebertabelle f

tempered ['tɛmpəd] adj (steel) gehärtet

tempest ['tɛmpɪst] n Sturm m

tempestuous [tɛm'pɛstjuəs] adj (also fig) stürmisch; (person) leidenschaftlich

tempi ['tɛmpiː] npl of **tempo**

template ['tɛmplɪt] n Schablone f

temple ['tɛmpl] n (building) Tempel m; (Anat) Schläfe f

tempo ['tɛmpəu] (pl **~s** or **tempi**) n (Mus, fig) Tempo nt

temporal ['tɛmpərl] adj (non-religious) weltlich; (relating to time) zeitlich

temporarily ['tɛmpərərɪlɪ] adv vorübergehend; (unavailable, alone etc) zeitweilig

temporary ['tɛmpərərɪ] adj (arrangement) provisorisch; (worker, job) Aushilfs-; **~ refugee** Flüchtling m mit zeitlich begrenzter Aufenthaltserlaubnis; **~ secretary** Sekretärin zur Aushilfe; **~ teacher** Aushilfslehrer(in) m(f)

temporize ['tɛmpəraɪz] vi ausweichen

tempt [tɛmpt] vt in Versuchung führen; **to ~ sb into doing sth** jdn dazu verleiten, etw zu tun; **to be ~ed to do sth** versucht sein, etw

zu tun

temptation [tɛmp'teɪʃən] n Versuchung f

tempting ['tɛmptɪŋ] adj (offer) verlockend; (food) verführerisch

ten [tɛn] num zehn ▷ n: **~s of thousands** Zehntausende pl

tenable ['tɛnəbl] adj (argument, position) haltbar

tenacious [tə'neɪʃəs] adj zäh, hartnäckig

tenacity [tə'næsɪtɪ] n Zähigkeit f, Hartnäckigkeit f

tenancy ['tɛnənsɪ] n (of room) Mietverhältnis nt; (of land) Pachtverhältnis nt

tenant ['tɛnənt] n (of room) Mieter(in) m(f); (of land) Pächter(in) m(f)

tend [tɛnd] vt (crops, sick person) sich kümmern um ▷ vi: **to ~ to do sth** dazu neigen or tendieren, etw zu tun

tendency ['tɛndənsɪ] n (of person) Neigung f; (of thing) Tendenz f

tender ['tɛndəʳ] adj (person, care) zärtlich; (heart) gut; (sore) empfindlich; (meat, age) zart ▷ n (Comm) Angebot nt; (money): **legal ~** gesetzliches Zahlungsmittel nt ▷ vt (offer) vorlegen; (resignation) einreichen; (apology) anbieten; **to put in a ~ (for)** ein Angebot vorlegen (für); **to put work out to ~** (Brit) Arbeiten ausschreiben

tenderize ['tɛndəraɪz] vt (meat) zart machen

tenderly ['tɛndəlɪ] adv zärtlich, liebevoll

tenderness ['tɛndənɪs] n (affection) Zärtlichkeit f; (of meat) Zartheit f

tendon ['tɛndən] n Sehne f

tendril ['tɛndrɪl] n (Bot) Ranke f; (of hair etc) Strähne f

tenement ['tɛnəmənt] n Mietshaus nt

Tenerife [tɛnə'riːf] n Teneriffa nt

tenet ['tɛnət] n Prinzip nt

Tenn. (US) abbr (Post) = **Tennessee**

tenner ['tɛnəʳ] (Brit: inf) n Zehner m

tennis ['tɛnɪs] n Tennis nt

tennis ball n Tennisball m

tennis club n Tennisklub m

tennis court n Tennisplatz m

tennis elbow n (Med) Tennisell(en)bogen m

tennis match n Tennismatch nt

tennis player n Tennisspieler(in) m(f)

tennis racket n Tennisschläger m

tennis shoes npl Tennisschuhe pl

tenor ['tɛnəʳ] n (Mus) Tenor m; (of speech etc) wesentlicher Gehalt m

tenpin bowling ['tɛnpɪn-] (Brit) n Bowling nt

tense [tɛns] adj (person, muscle) angespannt; (smile) verkrampft; (period, situation) gespannt ▷ n (Ling) Zeit f, Tempus nt ▷ vt (muscles) anspannen

tenseness ['tɛnsnɪs] n Gespanntheit f

tension ['tɛnʃən] n (nervousness) Angespanntheit f; (between ropes etc) Spannung f

tent [tɛnt] n Zelt nt

tentacle ['tɛntəkl] n (Zool) Fangarm m; (fig) Klaue f

tentative ['tɛntətɪv] adj (person, smile) zögernd;

(step) unsicher; *(conclusion, plans)* vorläufig

tentatively ['tɛntətɪvlɪ] *adv (suggest)* versuchsweise; *(wave etc)* zögernd

tenterhooks ['tɛntəhuks] *npl*: **to be on ~** wie auf glühenden Kohlen sitzen

tenth [tɛnθ] *num* zehnte(r, s) ▷ *n* Zehntel *nt*

tent peg *n* Hering *m*

tent pole *n* Zeltstange *f*

tenuous ['tɛnjuəs] *adj (hold, links etc)* schwach

tenure ['tɛnjuə'] *n (of land etc)* Nutzungsrecht *nt; (of office)* Amtszeit *f; (Univ)*: **to have ~** eine Dauerstellung haben

tepid ['tɛpɪd] *adj (also fig)* lauwarm

Ter. *abbr (in street names:* = *terrace)* ≈ Str.

term [tɜːm] *n (word)* Ausdruck *m; (period in power etc)* Amtszeit *f; (Scol: three per year)* Trimester *nt* ▷ *vt (call)* nennen; **terms** *npl (also Comm)* Bedingungen *pl*; **in economic/political ~s** wirtschaftlich/politisch gesehen; **in ~s of business** was das Geschäft angeht *or* betrifft; **~ of imprisonment** Gefängnisstrafe *f;* **"easy ~s"** *(Comm)* „günstige Bedingungen"; **in the short/long ~** auf kurze/lange Sicht; **to be on good ~s with sb** sich mit jdm gut verstehen; **to come to ~s with** *(problem)* sich abfinden mit

terminal ['tɜːmɪnl] *adj (disease, patient)* unheilbar ▷ *n (Aviat, Comm, Comput)* Terminal *nt; (Elec)* Anschluss *m; (Brit: also: **bus terminal**)* Endstation *f*

terminate ['tɜːmɪneɪt] *vt* beenden ▷ *vi*: **to ~ in** enden in +*dat*

termination [tɜːmɪ'neɪʃən] *n* Beendigung *f; (expiry: of contract)* Ablauf *m; (Med: of pregnancy)* Abbruch *m*

termini ['tɜːmɪnaɪ] *npl of* **terminus**

terminology [tɜːmɪ'nɔlədʒɪ] *n* Terminologie *f*

terminus ['tɜːmɪnəs] *(pl* **termini***) n (for buses, trains)* Endstation *f*

termite ['tɜːmaɪt] *n* Termite *f*

term paper *(US) n (Univ)* ≈ Semesterarbeit *f*

Terr. *abbr (in street names:* = *terrace)* ≈ Str.

terrace ['tɛrəs] *n (Brit: row of houses)* Häuserreihe *f; (Agr, patio)* Terrasse *f;* **the terraces** *npl (Brit: Sport)* die Ränge *pl*

terraced ['tɛrəst] *adj (house)* Reihen-; *(garden)* terrassenförmig angelegt

terracotta ['tɛrə'kɔtə] *n (clay)* Terrakotta *f; (colour)* Braunrot *nt* ▷ *adj (pot, roof etc)* Terrakotta-

terrain [tɛ'reɪn] *n* Gelände *nt,* Terrain *nt*

terrible ['tɛrɪbl] *adj* schrecklich, furchtbar

terribly ['tɛrɪblɪ] *adv (very)* furchtbar; *(very badly)* entsetzlich

terrier ['tɛrɪə'] *n* Terrier *m*

terrific [tə'rɪfɪk] *adj (very great: thunderstorm, speed)* unheimlich; *(time, party)* sagenhaft

terrify ['tɛrɪfaɪ] *vt* erschrecken; **to be terrified** schreckliche Angst haben

terrifying ['tɛrɪfaɪɪŋ] *adj* entsetzlich, grauenvoll

territorial [tɛrɪ'tɔːrɪəl] *adj (boundaries, dispute)* territorial, Gebiets-; *(waters)* Hoheits- ▷ *n (Mil)*

Soldat *m* der Territorialarmee

Territorial Army *(Brit) n (Mil)*: **the ~** die Territorialarmee

territorial waters *npl* Hoheitsgewässer *pl*

territory ['tɛrɪtərɪ] *n (also fig)* Gebiet *nt*

terror ['tɛrə'] *n (great fear)* panische Angst *f*

terrorism ['tɛrərɪzəm] *n* Terrorismus *m*

terrorist ['tɛrərɪst] *n* Terrorist(in) *m(f)*

terrorize ['tɛrəraɪz] *vt* terrorisieren

terse [tɜːs] *adj* knapp

tertiary ['tɜːʃərɪ] *adj* tertiär; **~ education** *(Brit)* Universitätsausbildung *f*

Terylene® ['tɛrɪliːn] *n* Terylen® *nt* ▷ *adj* Terylen-

TESL ['tɛsl] *n abbr (= Teaching of English as a Second Language)* Unterricht in Englisch als Zweitsprache

TESSA ['tɛsə] *(Brit) n abbr (= Tax Exempt Special Savings Account)* steuerfreies Sparsystem mit begrenzter Einlagehöhe

test [tɛst] *n* Test *m; (of courage etc)* Probe *f; (Scol)* Prüfung *f; (also:* **driving test***)* Fahrprüfung *f* ▷ *vt* testen; *(check:„ Scol)* prüfen; **to put sth to the ~** etw auf die Probe stellen; **to ~ sth for sth** etw auf etw *acc* prüfen

testament ['tɛstəmənt] *n* Zeugnis *nt;* **the Old/New T~** das Alte/Neue Testament; **last will and ~** Testament *nt*

test ban *n (also:* **nuclear test ban***)* Teststopp *m*

test card *n (TV)* Testbild *nt*

test case *n (Law)* Musterfall *m; (fig)* Musterbeispiel *nt*

testes ['tɛstiːz] *npl* Testikel *pl,* Hoden *pl*

test flight *n* Testflug *m*

testicle ['tɛstɪkl] *n* Hoden *m*

testify ['tɛstɪfaɪ] *vi (Law)* aussagen; **to ~ to sth** *(Law, fig)* etw bezeugen

testimonial [tɛstɪ'məunɪəl] *n (Brit: reference)* Referenz *f; (Sport: also:* **testimonial match***)* Benefizspiel, dessen Erlös einem verdienten Spieler zugutekommt

testimony ['tɛstɪmənɪ] *n (statement)* Aussage *f; (clear proof)*: **to be (a) ~ to** ein Zeugnis *nt* sein für

testing ['tɛstɪŋ] *adj* schwierig

test match *n (Cricket, Rugby)* Testmatch *nt,* Test Match *nt,* Länderspiel *nt*

testosterone [tɛs'tɔstərəun] *n* Testosteron *nt*

test paper *n (Scol)* Klassenarbeit *f*

test pilot *n* Testpilot(in) *m(f)*

test tube *n* Reagenzglas *nt*

test-tube baby ['tɛsttjuːb-] *n* Retortenbaby *nt*

testy ['tɛstɪ] *adj* gereizt

tetanus ['tɛtənəs] *n* Tetanus *m*

tetchy ['tɛtʃɪ] *adj* gereizt

tether ['tɛðə'] *vt (animal)* festbinden ▷ *n*: **to be at the end of one's ~** völlig am Ende sein

text [tɛkst] *n* Text *m; (sent by mobile phone)* SMS *f* ▷ *vt (on mobile phone)* **to ~ sb** jdm eine SMS schreiben

textbook ['tɛkstbuk] *n* Lehrbuch *nt*

textiles ['tɛkstaɪlz] *npl* Textilien *pl*

text message *n (Tel)* SMS *f*

t

text messaging n (Tel) Textnachrichten pl

textual ['tɛkstjuəl] adj (analysis etc) Text-

texture ['tɛkstʃəʳ] n Beschaffenheit f, Struktur f

TGWU (Brit) n abbr (= Transport and General Workers' Union) Transportarbeitergewerkschaft

Thai [taɪ] adj thailändisch ▷ n Thailänder(in) m(f)

Thailand ['taɪlænd] n Thailand nt

thalidomide® [θə'lɪdəmaɪd] n Contergan® nt

Thames [tɛmz] n: the ~ die Themse

than [ðæn] conj (in comparisons) als; **more ~ 10** mehr als 10; **she is older ~ you think** sie ist älter, als Sie denken; **more ~ once** mehr als einmal

thank [θæŋk] vt danken +dat; ~ **you** danke; ~ **you very much** vielen Dank; ~ **God!** Gott sei Dank!

thankful ['θæŋkful] adj: ~ **(for/that)** dankbar (für/, dass)

thankfully ['θæŋkfəlɪ] adv dankbar; ~ **there were few victims** zum Glück gab es nur wenige Opfer

thankless ['θæŋklɪs] adj undankbar

thanks [θæŋks] npl Dank m ▷ excl (also: **many thanks, thanks a lot**) danke, vielen Dank; ~ **to** dank +gen

Thanksgiving ['θæŋksgɪvɪŋ], **Thanksgiving Day** (US) n Thanksgiving Day m

Thanksgiving (Day) ist ein Feiertag in den USA, der auf den vierten Donnerstag im November fällt. Er soll daran erinnern, wie die Pilgerväter die gute Ernte im Jahre 1621 feierten. In Kanada gibt es einen ähnlichen Erntedanktag (der aber nichts mit den Pilgervätern zu tun hat) am zweiten Montag im Oktober.

○ KEYWORD

that [ðæt, ðət] (pl **those**) adj (demonstrative) der/die/das; **that man** der Mann; **that woman** die Frau; **that book** das Buch; **that one** der/die/das da; **I want this one, not that one** ich will dieses (hier), nicht das (da)
▷ pron 1 (demonstrative) das; **who's/what's that?** wer/was ist das?; **is that you?** bist du das?; **will you eat all that?** isst du das alles?; **that's what he said** das hat er gesagt; **what happened after that?** was geschah danach?; **that is (to say)** das heißt; **and that's that!** und damit Schluss!
2 (relative: subject) der/die/das; (: (: pl)) die; (: direct object) den/die/das; (: (: pl)) die; (: indirect object) dem/der/dem; (: (: pl)) denen; **the man that I saw** den ich gesehen habe; **all that I have** alles was ich habe; **the people that I spoke to** die Leute, mit denen ich geredet habe
3 (relative: of time): **the day that he came** der

Tag, an dem er kam; **the winter that he came to see us** der Winter, in dem er uns besuchte
▷ conj dass; **he thought that I was ill** er dachte, dass ich krank sei, er dachte, ich sei krank
▷ adv (demonstrative) so; **I can't work that much** ich kann nicht so viel arbeiten; **that high** so hoch

thatched [θætʃt] adj strohgedeckt

Thatcherism ['θætʃərɪzəm] n Thatcherismus m

Thatcherite ['θætʃəraɪt] adj thatcheristisch ▷ n Thatcher-Anhänger(in) m(f)

thaw [θɔ:] n Tauwetter nt ▷ vi (ice) tauen; (food) auftauen ▷ vt (also: **thaw out**) auftauen; **it's ~ing** es taut

○ KEYWORD

the [ði:, ðə] def art 1 (before masculine noun) der; (before feminine noun) die; (before neuter noun) das; (before plural noun) die; **to play the piano/violin** Klavier/Geige spielen; **I'm going to the butcher's/the cinema** ich gehe zum Metzger/ins Kino
2 (+ adj to form noun): **the rich and the poor** die Reichen und die Armen; **to attempt the impossible** das Unmögliche versuchen
3 (in titles): **Elizabeth the First** Elisabeth die Erste; **Peter the Great** Peter der Große
4 (in comparisons): **the more he works the more he earns** je mehr er arbeitet, desto mehr verdient er; **the sooner the better** je eher, desto besser

theatre, (US) **theater** ['θɪətəʳ] n Theater nt; (also: **lecture theatre**) Hörsaal m; (also: **operating theatre**) Operationsaal m

theatre-goer ['θɪətəgəuəʳ] n Theaterbesucher(in) m(f)

theatrical [θɪ'ætrɪkl] adj (event, production) Theater-; (gestures etc) theatralisch

theft [θɛft] n Diebstahl m

their [ðɛəʳ] adj ihr

theirs [ðɛəz] pron ihre(r, s); **it is ~** es gehört ihnen; **a friend of ~** ein Freund/eine Freundin von ihnen; see also **my; mine¹**

them [ðɛm] pron (direct) sie; (indirect) ihnen; **I see ~** ich sehe sie; **give ~ the book** gib ihnen das Buch; **give me a few of ~** geben Sie mir ein paar davon; **with ~** mit ihnen; **without ~** ohne sie; see also **me**

theme [θi:m] n (also Mus) Thema nt

theme park n Themenpark m

theme song n Titelmusik f

theme tune n Titelmelodie f

themselves [ðəm'sɛlvz] pl pron (reflexive, after prep) sich; (emphatic, alone) selbst; **between ~** unter sich

then [ðɛn] adv (at that time) damals; (next, later) dann ▷ conj (therefore) also ▷ adj: **the ~ president** der damalige Präsident; **by ~** (past) bis dahin; (*future*) bis dann; **from ~ on** von da an; **before ~** davor; **until ~** bis dann; **and ~ what?** und was dann?; **what do you want me to do ~?** was soll ich dann machen?; **... but ~ (again) he's the boss** ... aber er ist ja der Chef

theologian [θɪəˈləʊdʒən] *n* Theologe *m*, Theologin *f*

theological [θɪəˈlɒdʒɪkl] *adj* theologisch

theology [θɪˈɒlədʒɪ] *n* Theologie *f*

theorem [ˈθɪərəm] *n* Lehrsatz *m*

theoretical [θɪəˈrɛtɪkl] *adj* theoretisch

theorize [ˈθɪəraɪz] *vi* theoretisieren

theory [ˈθɪərɪ] *n* Theorie *f*; **in ~** theoretisch

therapeutic [θɛrəˈpjuːtɪk] *adj* therapeutisch

therapist [ˈθɛrəpɪst] *n* Therapeut(in) *m(f)*

therapy [ˈθɛrəpɪ] *n* Therapie *f*

O KEYWORD

there [ðɛəʳ] *adv* **1: there is/are** da ist/sind; (*there exist(s)*) es gibt; **there are 3 of them** es gibt 3 davon; **there has been an accident** da war ein Unfall; **there will be a meeting tomorrow** morgen findet ein Treffen statt **2** (*referring to place*) da, dort; **down/over there** da unten/drüben; **put it in/on there** leg es dorthinein/-hinauf; **I want that book there** ich möchte das Buch da; **there he is!** da ist er ja!

3: there, there (*esp to child*) ist ja gut

thereabouts [ˈðɛərəˈbaʊts] *adv:* **or ~** (*place*) oder dortherum; (*amount, time*) oder so

thereafter [ðɛərˈɑːftəʳ] *adv* danach

thereby [ˈðɛəbaɪ] *adv* dadurch

therefore [ˈðɛəfɔːʳ] *adv* daher, deshalb

there's [ˈðɛəz] = **there is; there has**

thereupon [ðɛərəˈpɒn] *adv* (*at that point*) darauf(hin)

thermal [ˈθəːml] *adj* (*springs*) Thermal-; (*underwear, paper, printer*) Thermo-

thermodynamics [ˈθəːmədaɪˈnæmɪks] *n* Thermodynamik *f*

thermometer [θəˈmɒmɪtəʳ] *n* Thermometer *nt*

thermonuclear [ˈθəːməʊˈnjuːklɪəʳ] *adj* thermonuklear

Thermos® [ˈθəːməs] *n* (*also:* **Thermos flask**) Thermosflasche® *f*

thermostat [ˈθəːməʊstæt] *n* Thermostat *m*

thesaurus [θɪˈsɔːrəs] *n* Synonymwörterbuch *nt*

these [ðiːz] *pl adj, pl pron* diese

theses [ˈθiːsiːz] *npl of* **thesis**

thesis [ˈθiːsɪs] (*pl* **theses**) *n* These *f*; (*for doctorate etc*) Dissertation *f*, Doktorarbeit *f*

they [ðeɪ] *pl pron* sie; **~ say that ...** (*it is said that*) man sagt, dass ...

they'd [ðeɪd] = **they had;** = **they would**

they'll [ðeɪl] = **they shall; they will**

they're [ðɛəʳ] = **they are**

they've [ðeɪv] = **they have**

thick [θɪk] *adj* dick; (*sauce etc*) dickflüssig; (*fog, forest, hair etc*) dicht; (*inf: stupid*) blöd ▷ *n*: **in the ~ of the battle** mitten im Gefecht; **it's 20 cm**

~ es ist 20 cm dick

thicken [ˈθɪkn] *vi* (*fog etc*) sich verdichten ▷ *vt* (*sauce etc*) eindicken; **the plot ~s** die Sache wird immer verwickelter

thicket [ˈθɪkɪt] *n* Dickicht *nt*

thickly [ˈθɪklɪ] *adv* (*spread, cut*) dick; **~ populated** dicht bevölkert

thickness [ˈθɪknɪs] *n* (*of rope, wire*) Dicke *f*; (*layer*) Lage *f*

thickset [θɪkˈsɛt] *adj* (*person, body*) gedrungen

thick-skinned [θɪkˈskɪnd] *adj* (*also fig*) dickhäutig

thief [θiːf] (*pl* **thieves**) *n* Dieb(in) *m(f)*

thieves [θiːvz] *npl of* **thief**

thieving [ˈθiːvɪŋ] *n* Stehlen *nt*

thigh [θaɪ] *n* Oberschenkel *m*

thighbone [ˈθaɪbəʊn] *n* Oberschenkelknochen *m*

thimble [ˈθɪmbl] *n* Fingerhut *m*

thin [θɪn] *adj* dünn; (*fog*) leicht; (*hair, crowd*) spärlich ▷ *vt*: **to ~ (down)** (*sauce, paint*) verdünnen ▷ *vi* (*fog, crowd*) sich lichten; **his hair is ~ning** sein Haar lichtet sich

thing [θɪŋ] *n* Ding *nt*; (*matter*) Sache *f*; (*inf*): **to have a ~ about sth** (*be fascinated by*) wie besessen sein von etw; (*hate*) etw nicht ausstehen können; **things** *npl* (*belongings*) Sachen *pl*; **to do sth first ~ (every morning/ tomorrow morning)** etw (morgens/morgen früh) als Erstes tun; **I look awful first ~ in the morning** ich sehe frühmorgens immer furchtbar aus; **to do sth last ~ (at night)** etw als Letztes (am Abend) tun; **the ~ is ...** die Sache ist die: ...; **for one ~** zunächst mal; **don't worry about a ~** du brauchst dir überhaupt keine Sorgen zu machen; **you'll do no such ~!** das lässt du schön bleiben!; **poor ~** armes Ding; **the best ~ would be to ...** das Beste wäre, zu ...; **how are ~s?** wie gehts?

think [θɪŋk] (*pt, pp* **thought**) *vi* (*reflect*) nachdenken; (*reason*) denken ▷ *vt* (*be of the opinion*) denken; (*believe*) glauben; **to ~ of** denken an +*acc*; (*recall*) sich erinnern an +*acc*; **what did you ~ of them?** was hielten Sie von ihnen?; **to ~ about sth/sb** (*ponder*) über etw/ jdn nachdenken; **I'll ~ about it** ich werde es mir überlegen; **to ~ of doing sth** daran denken, etw zu tun; **to ~ highly of sb** viel von jdm halten; **to ~ aloud** laut nachdenken; **~ again!** denk noch mal nach!; **I ~ so/not** ich glaube ja/nein

▸ **think over** *vt* (*offer, suggestion*) überdenken; **I'd like to ~ things over** ich möchte mir die Sache noch einmal überlegen

▸ **think through** *vt* durchdenken

▸ **think up** *vt* sich *dat* ausdenken

thinking [ˈθɪŋkɪŋ] *n* Denken *nt*; **to my (way of) ~** meiner Meinung *or* Ansicht nach

think-tank [ˈθɪŋktæŋk] *n* Expertengremium *nt*

thinly [ˈθɪnlɪ] *adv* dünn; (*disguised, veiled*) kaum

thinness [ˈθɪnnɪs] *n* Dünne *f*

third [θəːd] *num* dritte(r, s) ▷ *n* (*fraction*) Drittel *nt*; (*Aut: also:* **third gear**) dritter Gang *m*;

t

(Brit: Scol: degree) ≈ Ausreichend nt; **a ~ of** ein Drittel +gen

third-degree burns ['θəːddɪgriː-] npl Verbrennungen pl dritten Grades

thirdly ['θəːdlɪ] adv drittens

third party insurance (Brit) n ≈ Haftpflichtversicherung f

third-rate ['θəːd'reɪt] (pej) adj drittklassig

Third World n: **the ~** die Dritte Welt ▷ adj der Dritten Welt

thirst [θəːst] n Durst m

thirsty ['θəːstɪ] adj durstig; **to be ~** Durst haben; **gardening is ~ work** Gartenarbeit macht durstig

thirteen [θəː'tiːn] num dreizehn

thirteenth ['θəː'tiːnθ] num dreizehnte(r, s)

thirtieth ['θəːtɪɪθ] num dreißigste(r, s)

thirty ['θəːtɪ] num dreißig

 KEYWORD

this [ðɪs] (pl **these**) adj (demonstrative) diese(r, s); **this man** dieser Mann; **this woman** diese Frau; **this book** dieses Buch; **this one** diese(r, s) (hier)
▷ pron (demonstrative) dies, das; **who/what is this?** wer/was ist das?; **this is where I live** hier wohne ich; **this is what he said** das hat er gesagt; **this is Mr Brown** (in introductions, photo) das ist Herr Brown; (on telephone) hier ist Herr Brown
▷ adv (demonstrative): **this high/long** etc so hoch/lang etc

thistle ['θɪsl] n Distel f

thong [θɒŋ] n Riemen m

thorn [θɔːn] n Dorn m

thorny ['θɔːnɪ] adj dornig; (fig: problem) heikel

thorough ['θʌrə] adj gründlich

thoroughbred ['θʌrəbred] n (horse) Vollblüter m

thoroughfare ['θʌrəfɛəʳ] n (road) Durchgangsstraße f; **"no ~"** (Brit) „Durchfahrt verboten"

thoroughgoing ['θʌrəgəʊɪŋ] adj (changes, reform) grundlegend; (investigation) gründlich

thoroughly ['θʌrəlɪ] adv gründlich; (very) äußerst; **I ~ agree** ich stimme vollkommen zu

thoroughness ['θʌrənɪs] n Gründlichkeit f

those [ðəʊz] pl adj, pl pron die (da); **~ (of you) who ...** diejenigen (von Ihnen), die ...

though [ðəʊ] conj obwohl ▷ adv aber; **even ~** obwohl; **it's not easy, ~** es ist aber nicht einfach

thought [θɔːt] pt, pp of **think** ▷ n Gedanke m; **thoughts** npl (opinion) Gedanken pl; **after much ~** nach langer Überlegung; **I've just had a ~** mir ist gerade etwas eingefallen; **to give sth some ~** sich dat Gedanken über etw acc machen

thoughtful ['θɔːtful] adj (deep in thought) nachdenklich; (considerate) aufmerksam

thoughtfully ['θɔːtfəlɪ] adv (look etc)

nachdenklich; (behave etc) rücksichtsvoll; (provide) rücksichtsvollerweise

thoughtless ['θɔːtlɪs] adj gedankenlos

thoughtlessly ['θɔːtlɪslɪ] adv gedankenlos

thoughtlessness ['θɔːtlɪsnɪs] n Gedankenlosigkeit f

thought-out [θɔːt'aut] adj durchdacht

thought-provoking ['θɔːtprəvəʊkɪŋ] adj: **to be ~** Denkanstöße geben

thousand ['θauzənd] num (ein)tausend; **two ~** zweitausend; **~s of** Tausende von

thousandth ['θauzəntθ] num tausendste(r, s)

thrash [θræʃ] vt (beat) verprügeln; (defeat) (vernichtend) schlagen
▸ **thrash about** vi um sich schlagen
▸ **thrash around** vi = **thrash about**
▸ **thrash out** vt (problem) ausdiskutieren

thrashing ['θræʃɪŋ] n: **to give sb a ~** jdn verprügeln

thread [θred] n (yarn) Faden m; (of screw) Gewinde nt ▷ vt (needle) einfädeln; **to ~ one's way between** sich hindurchschlängeln zwischen

threadbare ['θredbɛəʳ] adj (clothes) abgetragen; (carpet) abgelaufen

threat [θret] n Drohung f; (fig): **~ (to)** Gefahr f (für); **to be under ~ of** (closure etc) bedroht sein von

threaten ['θretn] vi bedrohen ▷ vt: **to ~ sb with sth** jdm mit etw drohen; **to ~ to do sth** (damit) drohen, etw zu tun

threatening ['θretnɪŋ] adj drohend, bedrohlich

three [θriː] num drei

three-dimensional [θriːdɪ'mɛnʃənl] adj dreidimensional

threefold ['θriːfəʊld] adv: **to increase ~** dreifach or um das Dreifache ansteigen

three-piece suit ['θriːpiːs-] n dreiteiliger Anzug m

three-piece suite n dreiteilige Polstergarnitur f

three-ply [θriː'plaɪ] adj (wool) dreifädig; (wood) dreilagig

three-quarters [θriː'kwɔːtəz] npl drei Viertel pl; **~ full** drei viertel voll

three-wheeler ['θriː'wiːləʳ] n (car) Dreiradwagen m

thresh [θreʃ] vt dreschen

threshing machine ['θreʃɪŋ-] n Dreschmaschine f

threshold ['θreʃhəʊld] n Schwelle f; **to be on the ~ of sth** (fig) an der Schwelle zu etw sein or stehen

threshold agreement n (Econ) Tarifvereinbarung über der Inflationsrate angeglichene Lohnerhöhungen

threw [θruː] pt of **throw**

thrift [θrɪft] n Sparsamkeit f

thrifty ['θrɪftɪ] adj sparsam

thrill [θrɪl] n (excitement) Aufregung f; (shudder) Erregung f ▷ vi zittern ▷ vt (person, audience) erregen; **to be ~ed** (with gift etc) sich riesig freuen

thriller ['θrɪlə'] n Thriller m
thrilling ['θrɪlɪŋ] adj (ride, performance etc) erregend; (news) aufregend
thrive [θraɪv] (pt **~d** or **throve**, pp **~d**) vi gedeihen; **to ~ on sth** von etw leben
thriving ['θraɪvɪŋ] adj (business, community) blühend, florierend
throat [θrəʊt] n Kehle f; **to have a sore ~** Halsschmerzen haben
throb [θrɒb] n (of heart) Klopfen nt; (pain) Pochen nt; (of engine) Dröhnen nt ▷ vi (heart) klopfen; (pain) pochen; (machine) dröhnen; **my head is ~bing** ich habe rasende Kopfschmerzen
throes [θrəʊz] npl: **in the ~ of** (war, moving house etc) mitten in +dat; **death ~** Todeskampf m
thrombosis [θrɒm'bəʊsɪs] n Thrombose f
throne [θrəʊn] n Thron m; **on the ~** auf dem Thron
throng ['θrɒŋ] n Masse f ▷ vt (streets etc) sich drängen in +dat ▷ vi: **to ~ to** strömen zu; **a ~ of people** eine Menschenmenge; **to be ~ed with** wimmeln von
throttle ['θrɒtl] n (in car) Gaspedal nt; (on motorcycle) Gashebel m ▷ vt (strangle) erdrosseln
through [θru:] prep durch; (time) während; (owing to) infolge +gen ▷ adj (ticket, train) durchgehend ▷ adv durch; **(from) Monday ~ Friday** (US) von Montag bis Freitag; **to be ~** (Tel) verbunden sein; **to be ~ with sb/sth** mit jdm/etw fertig sein; **we're ~!** es ist aus zwischen uns!; **"no ~ road", "no ~ traffic"** (US) „keine Durchfahrt"; **to let sb ~** jdn durchlassen; **to put sb ~ to sb** (Tel) jdn mit jdm verbinden
throughout [θru:'aʊt] adv (everywhere) überall; (the whole time) die ganze Zeit über ▷ prep (place) überall in +dat; (time): **~ the morning/afternoon** während des ganzen Morgens/Nachmittags; **~ her life** ihr ganzes Leben lang
throughput ['θru:pʊt] n (also Comput) Durchsatz m
throve [θrəʊv] pt of **thrive**
throw [θrəʊ] (pt **threw**, pp **~n**) n Wurf m ▷ vt werfen; (rider) abwerfen; (fig: confuse) aus der Fassung bringen; (pottery) töpfern; **to ~ a party** eine Party geben; **to ~ open** (doors, windows) aufreißen; (debate) öffnen
▸ **throw about** vt (money) herumwerfen mit
▸ **throw around** vt = **throw about**
▸ **throw away** vt wegwerfen; (waste) verschwenden
▸ **throw off** vt (get rid of: burden) abwerfen
▸ **throw out** vt (rubbish) wegwerfen; (idea) verwerfen; (person) hinauswerfen
▸ **throw together** vt (meal) hinhauen; (clothes) zusammenpacken
▸ **throw up** vi (vomit) sich übergeben
throwaway ['θrəʊəweɪ] adj (cutlery etc) Einweg-; (line, remark) beiläufig
throwback ['θrəʊbæk] n: **it's a ~ to** (reminder) es erinnert an +acc
throw-in ['θrəʊɪn] n (Football) Einwurf m

thrown [θrəʊn] pp of **throw**
thru [θru:] (US) prep, adj, adv = **through**
thrush [θrʌʃ] n (bird) Drossel f; (Med: esp in children) Soor m; (: Brit: in women) vaginale Pilzerkrankung f
thrust [θrʌst] (pt, pp **~**) n (Tech) Schubkraft f; (push) Stoß m; (fig: impetus) Stoßkraft f ▷ vt stoßen
thud [θʌd] n dumpfes Geräusch nt
thug [θʌg] n Schlägertyp m
thumb [θʌm] n Daumen m ▷ vt: **to ~ a lift** per Anhalter fahren; **to give sb/sth the ~s up** (approve) jdm/etw dat grünes Licht geben; **to give sb/sth the ~s down** (disapprove) jdn/etw ablehnen
▸ **thumb through** vt fus (book) durchblättern
thumb index n Daumenregister nt
thumbnail ['θʌmneɪl] n Daumennagel m
thumbnail sketch n kurze Darstellung f
thumbtack ['θʌmtæk] (US) n Heftzwecke f
thump [θʌmp] n (blow) Schlag m; (sound) dumpfer Schlag m ▷ vt schlagen auf +acc ▷ vi (heart etc) heftig pochen
thumping ['θʌmpɪŋ] adj (majority, victory etc) Riesen-; (headache, cold) fürchterlich
thunder ['θʌndə'] n Donner m ▷ vi donnern; (shout angrily) brüllen; **to ~ past** (train etc) vorbeidonnern
thunderbolt ['θʌndəbəʊlt] n Blitzschlag m
thunderclap ['θʌndəklæp] n Donnerschlag m
thunderous ['θʌndrəs] adj donnernd
thunderstorm ['θʌndəstɔ:m] n Gewitter nt
thunderstruck ['θʌndəstrʌk] adj: **to be ~** (shocked) wie von Donner gerührt sein
thundery ['θʌndərɪ] adj (weather) gewitterig
Thur., Thurs. abbr (= Thursday) Do.
Thursday ['θə:zdɪ] n Donnerstag m; see also **Tuesday**
thus [ðʌs] adv (in this way) so; (consequently) somit
thwart [θwɔ:t] vt (person) einen Strich durch die Rechnung machen +dat; (plans) vereiteln
thyme [taɪm] n Thymian m
thyroid ['θaɪrɔɪd] n (also: **thyroid gland**) Schilddrüse f
tiara [tɪ'ɑ:rə] n Diadem nt
Tiber ['taɪbə'] n: **the ~** der Tiber
Tibet [tɪ'bɛt] n Tibet nt
Tibetan [tɪ'bɛtən] adj tibetanisch ▷ n (person) Tibetaner(in) m(f); (Ling) Tibetisch nt
tibia ['tɪbɪə] n Schienbein nt
tic [tɪk] n nervöse Zuckung f, Tic m, Tick m
tick [tɪk] n (sound) Ticken nt; (mark) Häkchen nt; (Zool) Zecke f; (Brit: inf: moment) Augenblick m; (: credit): **to buy sth on ~** etw auf Pump kaufen ▷ vi (clock, watch) ticken ▷ vt (item on list) abhaken; **to put a ~ against sth** etw abhaken; **what makes him ~?** was ist er für ein Mensch?
▸ **tick off** vt (item on list) abhaken; (person) rüffeln
▸ **tick over** vi (engine) im Leerlauf sein; (fig: business etc) sich über Wasser halten
ticker tape ['tɪkəteɪp] n Lochstreifen m; (US: in

t

825

celebrations) ≈ Luftschlangen *pl*
ticket ['tɪkɪt] *n* (*for public transport*) Fahrkarte *f*;
(*for theatre etc*) Eintrittskarte *f*; (*in shop: on goods*)
Preisschild *nt*; (: *from cash register*) Kassenbon
m; (*for raffle*) Los *nt*; (*for library*) Ausweis *m*;
(*also:* **parking ticket:** *fine*) Strafzettel *m*;
(*US: Pol*) Wahlliste *f*; **to get a (parking) ~** (*Aut*)
einen Strafzettel bekommen
ticket agency *n* (*Theat*) Vorverkaufsstelle *f*
ticket collector *n* (*Rail: at station*)
Fahrkartenkontrolleur(in) *m(f)*; (*on train*)
Schaffner(in) *m(f)*
ticket holder *n* Karteninhaber(in) *m(f)*
ticket inspector *n* Fahrkartenkontrolleur(in)
m(f)
ticket office *n* (*Rail*) Fahrkartenschalter *m*;
(*Theat*) Theaterkasse *f*
tickle ['tɪkl] *vt* kitzeln; (*fig: amuse*) amüsieren
▷ *vi* kitzeln; **it ~s!** das kitzelt!
ticklish ['tɪklɪʃ] *adj* (*person, situation*) kitzlig
tidal ['taɪdl] *adj* (*force*) Gezeiten-, der Gezeiten;
(*river*) Tide-
tidal wave *n* Flutwelle *f*
tidbit ['tɪdbɪt] (*US*) *n* = **titbit**
tiddlywinks ['tɪdlɪwɪŋks] *n* Flohhüpfen *nt*
tide [taɪd] *n* (*in sea*) Gezeiten *pl*; (*fig: of events,
opinion etc*) Trend *m*; **high ~** Flut *f*; **low ~** Ebbe
f; **the ~ is in/out** es ist Flut/Ebbe; **the ~ is
coming in** die Flut kommt
▶ **tide over** *vt* über die Runden helfen +*dat*
tidily ['taɪdɪlɪ] *adv* ordentlich
tidiness ['taɪdɪnɪs] *n* Ordentlichkeit *f*
tidy ['taɪdɪ] *adj* (*room, desk*) ordentlich,
aufgeräumt; (*person*) ordnungsliebend;
(*sum, income*) ordentlich ▷ *vt* (*also:* **tidy up**)
aufräumen
tie [taɪ] *n* (*Brit: also:* **necktie**) Krawatte *f*;
(*string etc*) Band *nt*; (*fig: link*) Verbindung *f*;
(*Sport: match*) Spiel *nt*; (*in competition: draw*)
Unentschieden *nt* ▷ *vt* (*parcel*) verschnüren;
(*shoelaces*) zubinden; (*ribbon*) binden ▷ *vi*
(*Sport etc*): **to ~ with sb for first place** sich
mit jdm den ersten Platz teilen; **"black ~"**
„Abendanzug"; **"white ~"** „Frackzwang";
family ~s familiäre Bindungen; **to ~ sth in a
bow** etw zu einer Schleife binden; **to ~ a knot
in sth** einen Knoten in etw *acc* machen
▶ **tie down** *vt* (*fig: restrict*) binden; (: *to date, price
etc*) festlegen
▶ **tie in** *vi*: **to ~ in with** zusammenpassen mit
▶ **tie on** *vt* (*Brit*) anbinden
▶ **tie up** *vt* (*parcel*) verschnüren; (*dog*)
anbinden; (*boat*) festmachen; (*person*) fesseln;
(*arrangements*) unter Dach und Fach bringen;
to be ~d up (*busy*) zu tun haben, beschäftigt
sein
tie-break ['taɪbreɪk], **tie-breaker**
['taɪbreɪkə'] *n* (*Tennis*) Tiebreak *m*; (*in quiz*)
Entscheidungsfrage *f*
tie-on ['taɪɒn] (*Brit*) *adj* (*label*) Anhänge-
tiepin ['taɪpɪn] (*Brit*) *n* Krawattennadel *f*
tier [tɪə'] *n* (*of stadium etc*) Rang *m*; (*of cake*) Lage *f*
tie-tack ['taɪtæk] (*US*) *n* = **tiepin**

tiff [tɪf] *n* Krach *m*
tiger ['taɪgə'] *n* Tiger *m*
tiger economy *n* (*Econ*) Tigerstaat *m*
tight [taɪt] *adj* (*screw, knot, grip*) fest; (*shoes,
clothes, bend*) eng; (*security*) streng; (*budget,
money*) knapp; (*schedule*) gedrängt; (*inf: drunk*)
voll; (: *stingy*) knickerig ▷ *adv* fest; **to be
packed ~** (*suitcase*) prallvoll sein; (*room*)
gerammelt voll sein; **everybody hold ~!** stell
festhalten!
tighten ['taɪtn] *vt* (*rope, strap*) straffen; (*screw,
bolt*) anziehen; (*grip*) festigen; (*security*)
verschärfen ▷ *vi* (*grip*) sich festigen; (*rope etc*)
sich spannen
tightfisted [taɪt'fɪstɪd] *adj* knickerig (*inf*)
tight-lipped ['taɪt'lɪpt] *adj* (*fig: silence*) eisern; **to
be ~ about sth** über etw *acc* schweigen
tightly ['taɪtlɪ] *adv* fest
tightrope ['taɪtrəʊp] *n* Seil *nt*; **to be on** *or*
walking a ~ (*fig*) einen Balanceakt vollführen
tightrope walker *n* Seiltänzer(in) *m(f)*
tights [taɪts] (*Brit*) *npl* Strumpfhose *f*
tigress ['taɪgrɪs] *n* Tigerin *f*
tilde ['tɪldə'] *n* Tilde *f*
tile [taɪl] *n* (*on roof*) Ziegel *m*; (*on floor*) Fliese *f*; (*on
wall*) Kachel *f* ▷ *vt* (*floor*) mit Fliesen auslegen;
(*bathroom*) kacheln
tiled [taɪld] *adj* (*floor*) mit Fliesen ausgelegt;
(*wall*) gekachelt
till [tɪl] *n* (*in shop etc*) Kasse *f* ▷ *vt* (*land*) bestellen
▷ *prep, conj* = **until**
tiller ['tɪlə'] *n* (*Naut*) Ruderpinne *f*
tilt [tɪlt] *vt* neigen ▷ *vi* sich neigen ▷ *n* (*slope*)
Neigung *f*; **to wear one's hat at a ~** den Hut
schief aufhaben; **(at) full ~** mit Volldampf
timber ['tɪmbə'] *n* (*material*) Holz *nt*; (*trees*)
Nutzholz *nt*
time [taɪm] *n* Zeit *f*; (*occasion*) Gelegenheit
f, Mal *nt*; (*Mus*) Takt *m* ▷ *vt* (*measure time of*)
die Zeit messen bei; (*runner*) stoppen; (*fix
moment for: visit etc*) den Zeitpunkt festlegen
für; **a long ~** eine lange Zeit; **for the ~ being**
vorläufig; **4 at a ~** 4 auf einmal; **from ~ to
time** von Zeit zu Zeit; **~ after time, ~ and
again** immer (und immer) wieder; **at ~s**
manchmal, zuweilen; **in ~** (*soon enough*)
rechtzeitig; (*eventually*) mit der Zeit; (*Mus*) im
Takt; **in a week's ~** in einer Woche; **in no
~** im Handumdrehen; **any ~** jederzeit; **on ~**
rechtzeitig; **to be 30 minutes behind/ahead
of ~** 30 Minuten zurück/voraus sein; **by the ~
he arrived** als er ankam; **5 ~s 5** 5 mal 5; **what
~ is it?** wie spät ist es?; **to have a good ~** sich
amüsieren; **we/they** *etc* **had a hard ~** wir/sie
etc hatten es schwer; **~'s up!** die Zeit ist um!;
I've no ~ for it (*fig*) dafür habe ich nichts
übrig; **he'll do it in his own (good) ~** (*without
being hurried*) er macht es, ohne sich hetzen zu
lassen; **he'll do it in his own ~**, **he'll do it
on his own ~** (*US: out of working hours*) er macht
es in seiner Freizeit; **to be behind the ~s**
rückständig sein; **to ~ sth well/badly** den
richtigen/falschen Zeitpunkt für etw wählen;

the bomb was ~d to go off 5 minutes later die Bombe war so eingestellt, dass sie 5 Minuten später explodieren sollte

time-and-motion study ['taɪmənd'məʊʃən-] n Arbeitsstudie f

time bomb n (also fig) Zeitbombe f

time card n Stechkarte f

time clock n (in factory etc) Stechuhr f

time-consuming ['taɪmkənsjuːmɪŋ] adj zeitraubend

time difference n Zeitunterschied m

time frame n zeitlicher Rahmen m

time-honoured, (US) **time-honored** ['taɪmɔnəd] adj althergebracht

timekeeper ['taɪmkiːpər] n: **she's a good ~** sie erfüllt ihr Zeitsoll

time-lag ['taɪmlæg] n Verzögerung f

timeless ['taɪmlɪs] adj zeitlos

time limit n zeitliche Grenze f

timely ['taɪmlɪ] adj (arrival) rechtzeitig; (reminder) zur rechten Zeit

time management n Zeitmanagement nt

time off n: **to take ~** sich dat freinehmen

timer ['taɪmər] n (time switch) Schaltuhr f; (on cooker) Zeitmesser m; (on video) Timer m

time-saving ['taɪmseɪvɪŋ] adj zeitsparend

timescale ['taɪmskeɪl] (Brit) n Zeitspanne f

time-share ['taɪmʃɛər] n Ferienwohnung f auf Timesharingbasis

time-sharing ['taɪmʃɛərɪŋ] n (of property, Comput) Timesharing nt

time sheet n = **time card**

time signal n (Radio) Zeitzeichen nt

time switch n Zeitschalter m

timetable ['taɪmteɪbl] n (Rail etc) Fahrplan m; (Scol) Stundenplan m; (programme of events) Programm nt

time zone n Zeitzone f

timid ['tɪmɪd] adj (person) schüchtern; (animal) scheu

timidity [tɪ'mɪdɪtɪ] n (shyness) Schüchternheit f

timing ['taɪmɪŋ] n (Sport) Timing nt; **the ~ of his resignation** der Zeitpunkt seines Rücktritts

timing device n (on bomb) Zeitzünder m

timpani ['tɪmpənɪ] npl Kesselpauken pl

tin [tɪn] n (metal) Blech nt; (container) Dose f; (: for baking) Form f; (: Brit: can) Büchse f, Dose f; **two ~s of paint** zwei Dosen Farbe

tinfoil ['tɪnfɔɪl] n Alufolie f

tinge [tɪndʒ] n (of colour) Färbung f; (fig: of emotion etc) Anflug m, Anstrich m ▷ vt: **~d with blue/red** leicht blau/rot gefärbt; **to be ~d with sth** (fig: emotion etc) einen Anstrich von etw haben

tingle ['tɪŋgl] vi prickeln; (from cold) kribbeln; **I was tingling with excitement** ich zitterte vor Aufregung

tinker ['tɪŋkər] n (gipsy) Kesselflicker m
▶ **tinker with** vt fus herumbasteln an +dat

tinkle ['tɪŋkl] vi klingeln ▷ n (inf): **to give sb a ~** (Tel) bei jdm anklingeln

tin mine n Zinnbergwerk nt

tinned [tɪnd] (Brit) adj (food, peas) Dosen-, in Dosen

tinnitus ['tɪnɪtəs] n Tinnitus m, Ohrensummen nt

tinny ['tɪnɪ] (pej) adj (sound) blechern; (car etc) Schrott-

tin-opener ['tɪnəʊpnər] (Brit) n Dosenöffner m

tinsel ['tɪnsl] n Rauschgoldgirlanden pl

tint [tɪnt] n (colour) Ton m; (for hair) Tönung f
▷ vt (hair) tönen

tinted ['tɪntɪd] adj getönt

tiny ['taɪnɪ] adj winzig

tip [tɪp] n (end) Spitze f; (gratuity) Trinkgeld nt; (Brit: for rubbish) Müllkippe f; (: for coal) Halde f; (advice) Tipp m, Hinweis m ▷ vt (waiter) ein Trinkgeld geben +dat; (tilt) kippen; (also: **tip over**: overturn) umkippen; (also: **tip out**: empty) leeren; (predict: winner etc) tippen or setzen auf +acc; **he ~ped out the contents of the box** er kippte den Inhalt der Kiste aus
▶ **tip off** vt einen Tipp or Hinweis geben +dat

tip-off ['tɪpɔf] n Hinweis m

tipped [tɪpt] adj (Brit: cigarette) Filter-; **steel-~** mit Stahlspitze

Tipp-Ex® ['tɪpɛks] n Tipp-Ex® nt

tipple ['tɪpl] (Brit) vi picheln ▷ n: **to have a ~** einen trinken

tipster ['tɪpstər] n jd, der bei Pferderennen, Börsengeschäften etc Tipps gegen Bezahlung weitergibt

tipsy ['tɪpsɪ] (inf) adj beschwipst

tiptoe ['tɪptəʊ] n: **on ~** auf Zehenspitzen

tip-top ['tɪp'tɔp] adj: **in ~ condition** tipptopp

tirade ['taɪreɪd] n Tirade f

tire ['taɪər] n (US) = **tyre** ▷ vt müde machen, ermüden ▷ vi (become tired) müde werden; **to ~ of sth** genug von etw haben
▶ **tire out** vt erschöpfen

tired ['taɪəd] adj müde; **to be/look ~** müde sein/aussehen; **to feel ~** sich müde fühlen; **to be ~ of sth** etw satthaben; **to be ~ of doing sth** es satthaben, etw zu tun

tiredness ['taɪədnɪs] n Müdigkeit f

tireless ['taɪəlɪs] adj unermüdlich

tiresome ['taɪəsəm] adj lästig

tiring ['taɪərɪŋ] adj ermüdend, anstrengend

tissue ['tɪʃuː] n (Anat, Biol) Gewebe nt; (paper handkerchief) Papiertaschentuch nt

tissue paper n Seidenpapier nt

tit [tɪt] n (bird) Meise f; (inf: breast) Titte f; **~ for tat** wie du mir, so ich dir

titanium [tɪ'teɪnɪəm] n Titan nt

titbit, (US) **tidbit** ['tɪtbɪt] n (food, news) Leckerbissen m

titillate ['tɪtɪleɪt] vt erregen, reizen

titivate ['tɪtɪveɪt] vt fein machen

title ['taɪtl] n Titel m; (Law): **~ to** Anspruch auf +acc

title deed n Eigentumsurkunde f

title page n Titelseite f

title role n Titelrolle f

title track n Titelstück nt

titter ['tɪtər] vi kichern

tittle-tattle ['tɪtltætl] (inf) n Klatsch m, Gerede nt

t

827

tizzy ['tızı] *n*: **to be in a ~** aufgeregt sein; **to get in a ~** sich aufregen

T-junction ['ti:'dʒʌŋkʃən] *n* T-Kreuzung *f*

TM *abbr* (= *trademark*) Wz = **transcendental meditation**

TN (*US*) *abbr* (*Post*) = *Tennessee*

TNT *n abbr* (= *trinitrotoluene*) TNT *nt*

 KEYWORD

to [tu:] *prep* **1** (*direction*) nach +*dat*, zu +*dat*; **to go to France/London/school/the station** nach Frankreich/nach London/zur Schule/zum Bahnhof gehen; **to the left/right** nach links/rechts; **I have never been to Germany** ich war noch nie in Deutschland

2 (*as far as*) bis; **to count to 10** bis 10 zählen

3 (*with expressions of time*) vor +*dat*; **a quarter to 5** (*Brit*) Viertel vor 5

4 (*for, of*): **the key to the front door** der Schlüssel für die Haustür; **a letter to his wife** ein Brief an seine Frau

5 (*expressing indirect object*): **to give sth to sb** jdm etw geben; **to talk to sb** mit jdm sprechen; **I sold it to a friend** ich habe es an einen Freund verkauft; **you've done something to your hair** du hast etwas mit deinem Haar gemacht

6 (*in relation to*) zu; **A is to B as C is to D** A verhält sich zu B wie C zu D; **3 goals to 2** 3 zu 2 Tore; **40 miles to the gallon** 40 Meilen pro Gallone

7 (*purpose, result*) zu; **to sentence sb to death** jdn zum Tode verurteilen; **to my surprise** zu meiner Überraschung

▷ *with vb* **1** (*simple infinitive*): **to go** gehen; **to eat** essen

2 (*following another vb*): **to want to do sth** etw tun wollen; **to try/start to do sth** versuchen/anfangen, etw zu tun

3 (*with vb omitted*): **I don't want to** ich will nicht; **you ought to** du solltest es tun

4 (*purpose, result*) (um ...) zu; **I did it to help you** ich habe es getan, um dir zu helfen

5 (*equivalent to relative clause*) zu; **he has a lot to lose** er hat viel zu verlieren; **the main thing is to try** die Hauptsache ist, es zu versuchen

6 (*after adjective etc*): **ready to use** gebrauchsfertig; **too old/young to ...** zu alt/jung, um zu ...; **it's too heavy to lift** es ist zu schwer zu heben

▷ *adv*: **to push/pull the door** die Tür zudrücken/zuziehen; **to and fro** hin und her

toad [təud] *n* Kröte *f*

toadstool ['təudstu:l] *n* Giftpilz *m*

toady ['təudı] (*pej*) *vi*: **to ~ to sb** vor jdm kriechen

toast [təust] *n* (*bread, drink*) Toast *m* ▷ *vt* (*bread etc*) toasten; (*drink to*) einen Toast or Trinkspruch ausbringen auf +*acc*; **a piece** or **slice of ~** eine Scheibe Toast

toaster ['təustə'] *n* Toaster *m*

toastmaster ['təustmɑ:stə'] *n* Zeremonienmeister *m*

toast rack *n* Toastständer *m*

tobacco [tə'bækəu] *n* Tabak *m*; **pipe ~** Pfeifentabak *m*

tobacconist [tə'bækənıst] *n* Tabakhändler(in) *m(f)*

tobacconist's [tə'bækənısts], **tobacconist's shop** *n* Tabakwarenladen *m*

Tobago [tə'beıgəu] *n see* **Trinidad**

toboggan [tə'bɔgən] *n* Schlitten *m*

today [tə'deı] *adv, n* heute; **what day is it ~?** welcher Tag ist heute?; **what date is it ~?** der Wievielte ist heute?; **~ is the 4th of March** heute ist der 4. März; **a week ago ~** heute vor einer Woche; **~'s paper** die Zeitung von heute

toddle ['tɔdl] (*inf*) *vi*: **to ~ in/off/along** herein-/davon-/entlangwatscheln

toddler ['tɔdlə'] *n* Kleinkind *nt*

to-do [tə'du:] *n* Aufregung *f*, Theater *nt*

toe [təu] *n* Zehe *f*, Zeh *m*; (*of shoe, sock*) Spitze *f*; **to ~ the line** (*fig*) auf Linie bleiben; **big/little ~** großer/kleiner Zeh

toehold ['təuhəuld] *n* (*in climbing*) Halt *m* für die Fußspitzen; (*fig*): **to get/gain a ~ (in)** einen Einstieg bekommen/sich *dat* einen Einstieg verschaffen (in +*dat*)

toenail ['təuneıl] *n* Zehennagel *m*

toffee ['tɔfı] *n* Toffee *m*

toffee apple (*Brit*) *n* ≈ kandierter Apfel *m*

tofu ['təufu:] *n* Tofu *m*

toga ['təugə] *n* Toga *f*

together [tə'geðə'] *adv* zusammen; (*at the same time*) gleichzeitig; **~ with** gemeinsam mit

togetherness [tə'geðənıs] *n* Beisammensein *nt*

toggle switch ['tɔgl-] *n* (*Comput*) Toggle-Schalter *m*

Togo ['təugəu] *n* Togo *nt*

togs [tɔgz] (*inf*) *npl* Klamotten *pl*

toil [tɔıl] *n* Mühe *f* ▷ *vi* sich abmühen

toilet ['tɔılət] *n* Toilette *f* ▷ *cpd* (*kit, accessories etc*) Toiletten-; **to go to the ~** auf die Toilette gehen

toilet bag (*Brit*) *n* Kulturbeutel *m*

toilet bowl *n* Toilettenbecken *nt*

toilet paper *n* Toilettenpapier *nt*

toiletries ['tɔılətrız] *npl* Toilettenartikel *pl*

toilet roll *n* Rolle *f* Toilettenpapier

toilet soap *n* Toilettenseife *f*

toilet water *n* Toilettenwasser *nt*

to-ing and fro-ing ['tu:ıŋən'frəuıŋ] (*Brit*) *n* Hin und Her *nt*

token ['təukən] *n* (*sign, souvenir*) Zeichen *nt*; (*substitute coin*) Wertmarke *f* ▷ *adj* (*strike, payment etc*) symbolisch; **by the same ~** (*fig*) in gleicher Weise; **book/record/gift ~** (*Brit*) Bücher-/Platten-/Geschenkgutschein *m*

tokenism ['təukənızəm] *n*: **to be (pure) ~** (nur) eine Alibifunktion haben

Tokyo ['təukjəu] *n* Tokio *nt*

told [təuld] *pt, pp of* **tell**

tolerable ['tɔlərəbl] *adj* (*bearable*) erträglich;

(*fairly good*) passabel

tolerably ['tɒlərəblɪ] *adv*: ~ **good** ganz annehmbar *or* passabel

tolerance ['tɒlərns] *n* Toleranz *f*

tolerant ['tɒlərnt] *adj* tolerant; **to be ~ of sth** tolerant gegenüber etw sein

tolerate ['tɒləreɪt] *vt* (*pain, noise*) erdulden, ertragen; (*injustice*) tolerieren

toleration [tɒlə'reɪʃən] *n* (*of person, pain etc*) Duldung *f*; (*Rel, Pol*) Toleranz *f*

toll [təʊl] *n* (*of casualties, deaths*) (Gesamt)zahl *f*; (*tax, charge*) Gebühr *f* ▷ *vi* (*bell*) läuten; **the work took its ~ on us** die Arbeit blieb nicht ohne Auswirkungen auf uns

tollbridge ['təʊlbrɪdʒ] *n* gebührenpflichtige Brücke *f*, Mautbrücke *f*

toll call (*US*) *n* Ferngespräch *nt*

toll-free ['təʊlfriː] (*US*) *adj* gebührenfrei

toll road *n* gebührenpflichtige Straße *f*, Mautstraße *f*

tomato [tə'mɑːtəʊ] (*pl* ~**es**) *n* Tomate *f*

tomato purée *n* Tomatenmark *nt*

tomb [tuːm] *n* Grab *nt*

tombola [tɒm'bəʊlə] *n* Tombola *f*

tomboy ['tɒmbɔɪ] *n* Wildfang *m*

tombstone ['tuːmstəʊn] *n* Grabstein *m*

tomcat ['tɒmkæt] *n* Kater *m*

tome [təʊm] (*form*) *n* Band *m*

tomorrow [tə'mɒrəʊ] *adv* morgen ▷ *n* morgen; (*future*) Zukunft *f*; **the day after ~** übermorgen; **a week ~** morgen in einer Woche; **~ morning** morgen früh

ton [tʌn] *n* (*Brit*) (britische) Tonne *f*; (*US: also*: **short ton**) (US-)Tonne *f* (*ca. 907 kg*); (*also*: **metric ton**) (metrische) Tonne *f*; ~**s of** (*inf*) Unmengen von

tonal ['təʊnl] *adj* (*Mus*) klanglich, tonal

tone [təʊn] *n* Ton *m* ▷ *vi* (*also*: **tone in**: *colours*) (farblich) passen
  ▶ **tone down** *vt* (*also fig*) abschwächen
  ▶ **tone up** *vt* (*muscles*) kräftigen

tone-deaf [təʊn'dɛf] *adj* ohne Gefühl für Tonhöhen

toner ['təʊnər] *n* (*for photocopier*) Toner *m*

Tonga [tɒŋə] *n* Tonga *nt*

tongs [tɒŋz] *npl* Zange *f*; (*also*: **curling tongs**) Lockenstab *m*

tongue [tʌŋ] *n* Zunge *f*; (*form*: *language*) Sprache *f*; ~**-in-cheek** (*speak, say*) ironisch

tongue-tied ['tʌŋtaɪd] *adj* (*fig*) sprachlos

tongue-twister ['tʌŋtwɪstər] *n* Zungenbrecher *m*

tonic ['tɒnɪk] *n* (*Med*) Tonikum *nt*; (*fig*) Wohltat *f*; (*also*: **tonic water**) Tonic *nt*; (*Mus*) Tonika *f*, Grundton *m*

tonight [tə'naɪt] *adv* (*this evening*) heute Abend; (*this night*) heute Nacht ▷ *n* (*this evening*) der heutige Abend; (*this night*) die kommende Nacht; **(I'll) see you ~!** bis heute Abend!

tonnage ['tʌnɪdʒ] *n* Tonnage *f*

tonne [tʌn] (*Brit*) *n* (*metric ton*) Tonne *f*

tonsil ['tɒnsl] *n* Mandel *f*; **to have one's ~s out** sich *dat* die Mandeln herausnehmen lassen

tonsillitis [tɒnsɪ'laɪtɪs] *n* Mandelentzündung *f*

too [tuː] *adv* (*excessively*) zu; (*also*) auch; **it's ~ sweet** es ist zu süß; **I went ~** ich bin auch mitgegangen; **~ much** (*adj*) zu viel; (*adv*) zu sehr; **~ many** zu viele; **~ bad!** das ist eben Pech!

took [tʊk] *pt* of **take**

tool [tuːl] *n* (*also fig*) Werkzeug *nt*

tool box *n* Werkzeugkasten *m*

tool kit *n* Werkzeugsatz *m*

toot [tuːt] *n* (*of horn*) Hupton *m*; (*of whistle*) Pfeifton *m* ▷ *vi* (*with car-horn*) hupen

tooth [tuːθ] (*pl* **teeth**) *n* (*also Tech*) Zahn *m*; **to have a ~ out**, **to have a ~ pulled** (*US*) sich *dat* einen Zahn ziehen lassen; **to brush one's teeth** sich *dat* die Zähne putzen; **by the skin of one's teeth** (*fig*) mit knapper Not

toothache ['tuːθeɪk] *n* Zahnschmerzen *pl*; **to have ~** Zahnschmerzen haben

toothbrush ['tuːθbrʌʃ] *n* Zahnbürste *f*

toothpaste ['tuːθpeɪst] *n* Zahnpasta *f*

toothpick ['tuːθpɪk] *n* Zahnstocher *m*

tooth powder *n* Zahnpulver *nt*

top [tɒp] *n* (*of mountain, tree, ladder*) Spitze *f*; (*of cupboard, table, box*) Oberseite *f*; (*of street*) Ende *nt*; (*lid*) Verschluss *m*; (*Aut: also*: **top gear**) höchster Gang *m*; (*also*: **spinning top**: *toy*) Kreisel *m*; (*blouse etc*) Oberteil *nt*; (*of pyjamas*) Jacke *f* ▷ *adj* höchste(r, s); (*highest in rank*) oberste(r, s); (: *golfer etc*) Top- ▷ *vt* (*poll, vote, list*) anführen; (*estimate etc*) übersteigen; **at the ~ of the stairs/page** oben auf der Treppe/ Seite; **at the ~ of the street** am Ende der Straße; **on ~ of** (*above*) auf +*dat*; (*in addition to*) zusätzlich zu; **from ~ to bottom** von oben bis unten; **from ~ to toe** (*Brit*) von Kopf bis Fuß; **at the ~ of the list** oben auf der Liste; **at the ~ of his voice** so laut er konnte; **over the ~** (*inf: behaviour etc*) übertrieben; **to go over the ~** (*inf*) übertreiben; **at ~ speed** bei Höchstgeschwindigkeit
  ▶ **top up**, (*US*) **top off** *vt* (*drink*) nachfüllen; (*salary*) aufbessern

topaz ['təʊpæz] *n* Topas *m*

top-class ['tɒp'klɑːs] *adj* erstklassig; (*hotel, player etc*) Spitzen-

topcoat ['tɒpkəʊt] *n* (*overcoat*) Mantel *m*; (*of paint*) Deckanstrich *m*

top floor *n* oberster Stock *m*

top hat *n* Zylinder *m*

top-heavy [tɒp'hɛvɪ] *adj* (*also fig*) kopflastig

topic ['tɒpɪk] *n* Thema *nt*

topical ['tɒpɪkl] *adj* (*issue etc*) aktuell

topless ['tɒplɪs] *adj* (*waitress*) Oben-ohne-; (*bather*) barbusig ▷ *adv* oben ohne

top-level ['tɒplɛvl] *adj* auf höchster Ebene

topmost ['tɒpməʊst] *adj* oberste(r, s)

top-notch ['tɒp'nɒtʃ] *adj* erstklassig

topography [tə'pɒgrəfɪ] *n* Topografie *f*

topping ['tɒpɪŋ] *n* (*Culin*) Überzug *m*

topple ['tɒpl] *vt* (*government etc*) stürzen ▷ *vi* (*person*) stürzen; (*object*) fallen

top-ranking ['tɒpræŋkɪŋ] *adj* (*official*)

t

hochgestellt

top-secret ['tɒp'si:krɪt] *adj* streng geheim

top-security ['tɒpsə'kjʊərɪtɪ] (*Brit*) *adj* (*prison, wing*) Hochsicherheits-

topsy-turvy ['tɒpsɪ'tɜ:vɪ] *adj* auf den Kopf gestellt ▷ *adv* durcheinander; (*fall, land*) verkehrt herum

top-up ['tɒpʌp] *n*: **would you like a ~?** darf ich Ihnen nachschenken?

top-up loan *n* Ergänzungsdarlehen *nt*

torch [tɔ:tʃ] *n* Fackel *f*; (*Brit: electric*) Taschenlampe *f*

tore [tɔ:ʳ] *pt of* **tear**

torment [*n* 'tɔ:ment, *vt* tɔ:'ment] *n* Qual *f* ▷ *vt* quälen; (*annoy*) ärgern

torn [tɔ:n] *pp of* **tear**[1] ▷ *adj*: **~ between** (*fig*) hin- und hergerissen zwischen

tornado [tɔ:'neɪdəʊ] (*pl* **~es**) *n* (*storm*) Tornado *m*

torpedo [tɔ:'pi:dəʊ] (*pl* **~es**) *n* Torpedo *m*

torpedo boat *n* Torpedoboot *nt*

torpor ['tɔ:pəʳ] *n* Trägheit *f*

torrent ['tɒrnt] *n* (*flood*) Strom *m*; (*fig*) Flut *f*

torrential [tɒ'renʃl] *adj* (*rain*) wolkenbruchartig

torrid ['tɒrɪd] *adj* (*weather, love affair*) heiß

torso ['tɔ:səʊ] *n* Torso *m*

tortoise ['tɔ:təs] *n* Schildkröte *f*

tortoiseshell ['tɔ:təʃɛl] *adj* (*jewellery, ornaments*) aus Schildpatt; (*cat*) braungelbschwarz, braun-gelb-schwarz

tortuous ['tɔ:tjʊəs] *adj* (*path*) gewunden; (*argument, mind*) umständlich

torture ['tɔ:tʃəʳ] *n* Folter *f*; (*fig*) Qual *f* ▷ *vt* foltern; (*fig: torment*) quälen

torturer ['tɔ:tʃərəʳ] *n* Folterer *m*

Tory ['tɔ:rɪ] (*Brit: Pol*) *adj* konservativ ▷ *n* Tory *m*, Konservative(r) *f(m)*

toss [tɒs] *vt* (*throw*) werfen; (*one's head*) zurückwerfen; (*salad*) anmachen; (*pancake*) wenden ▷ *n*: **with a ~ of her head** mit einer Kopfbewegung; **to ~ a coin** eine Münze werfen; **to win/lose the ~** die Entscheidung per Münzwurf gewinnen/verlieren; **to ~ up for sth** etw per Münzwurf entscheiden; **to ~ and turn** (*in bed*) sich hin und her wälzen

tot [tɒt] *n* (*Brit: drink*) Schluck *m*; (*child*) Knirps *m*
▶ **tot up** (*Brit*) *vt* (*figures*) zusammenzählen

total ['təʊtl] *adj* (*number etc*) gesamt; (*failure, wreck etc*) völlig, total ▷ *n* Gesamtzahl *f* ▷ *vt* (*add up*) zusammenzählen; (*add up to*) sich belaufen auf; **in ~** insgesamt

totalitarian [təʊtælɪ'teərɪən] *adj* totalitär

totality [təʊ'tælɪtɪ] *n* Gesamtheit *f*

totally ['təʊtəlɪ] *adv* völlig

totem pole ['təʊtəm-] *n* Totempfahl *m*

totter ['tɒtəʳ] *vi* (*person*) wanken, taumeln; (*fig: government*) im Wanken sein

touch [tʌtʃ] *n* (*sense of touch*) Gefühl *nt*; (*contact*) Berührung *f*; (*skill: of pianist etc*) Hand *f* ▷ *vt* berühren; (*tamper with*) anrühren; (*emotionally*) rühren ▷ *vi* (*make contact*) sich berühren; **the personal ~** die persönliche Note; **to put the finishing ~es to sth** letzte Hand an etw *acc* legen; **a ~ of** (*fig: frost etc*) etwas,

ein Hauch von; **in ~ with** (*person, group*) in Verbindung mit; **to get in ~ with sb** mit jdm in Verbindung treten; **I'll be in ~** ich melde mich; **to lose ~** (*friends*) den Kontakt verlieren; **to be out of ~ with events** nicht auf dem Laufenden sein
▶ **touch on** *vt fus* (*topic*) berühren
▶ **touch up** *vt* (*car etc*) ausbessern

touch-and-go ['tʌtʃən'gəʊ] *adj* (*situation*) auf der Kippe; **it was ~ whether we'd succeed** es war völlig offen, ob wir Erfolg haben würden

touchdown ['tʌtʃdaʊn] *n* (*of rocket, plane*) Landung *f*; (*US: Football*) Touchdown *m*

touched [tʌtʃt] *adj* (*moved*) gerührt; (*inf: mad*) plemplem

touching ['tʌtʃɪŋ] *adj* rührend

touchline ['tʌtʃlaɪn] *n* (*Sport*) Seitenlinie *f*

touch screen *n* (*Tech*) Berührungsbildschirm *m*, Touchscreen *m*

touch screen mobile *n* Touchscreen-Handy *nt*

touch screen technology *n* Touchscreen-technologie *f*

touch-sensitive ['tʌtʃ'sɛnsɪtɪv] *adj* berührungsempfindlich; (*switch*) Kontakt-

touch-type ['tʌtʃtaɪp] *vi* blindschreiben

touchy ['tʌtʃɪ] *adj* (*person, subject*) empfindlich

tough [tʌf] *adj* (*strong, firm, difficult*) hart; (*resistant*) widerstandsfähig; (*meat, animal, person*) zäh; (*rough*) rau; **~ luck!** Pech!

toughen ['tʌfn] *vt* (*sb's character*) hart machen; (*glass etc*) härten

toughness ['tʌfnɪs] *n* Härte *f*

toupee ['tu:peɪ] *n* Toupet *nt*

tour ['tʊəʳ] *n* (*journey*) Reise *f*, Tour *f*; (*of factory, museum etc*) Rundgang *m*; (: *also*: **guided tour**) Führung *f*; (*by pop group etc*) Tournee *f* ▷ *vt* (*country, factory etc: on foot*) ziehen durch; (: *in car*) fahren durch; **to go on a ~ of a museum/ castle** an einer Museums-/Schlossführung teilnehmen; **to go on a ~ of the Highlands** die Highlands bereisen; **to go on ~** (*pop group, theatre company etc*) auf Tournee gehen

tour guide *n* Reiseleiter(in) *m(f)*

touring ['tʊərɪŋ] *n* Umherreisen *nt*

tourism ['tʊərɪzm] *n* Tourismus *m*

tourist ['tʊərɪst] *n* Tourist(in) *m(f)* ▷ *cpd* (*attractions, season*) Touristen-; **the ~ trade** die Tourismusbranche

tourist class *n* Touristenklasse *f*

tourist information centre (*Brit*) *n* Touristen-Informationszentrum *nt*

tourist office *n* Verkehrsamt *nt*

tournament ['tʊənəmənt] *n* Turnier *nt*

tourniquet ['tʊənɪkeɪ] *n* Aderpresse *f*

tour operator (*Brit*) *n* Reiseveranstalter *m*

tousled ['taʊzld] *adj* (*hair*) zerzaust

tout [taʊt] *vi*: **to ~ for business** die Reklametrommel schlagen; **to ~ for custom** auf Kundenfang gehen ▷ *n* (*also*: **ticket tout**) Schwarzhändler, *der Eintrittskarten zu überhöhten Preisen verkauft*

tow [təʊ] *vt* (*vehicle*) abschleppen; (*caravan, trailer*) ziehen ▷ *n*: **to give sb a ~** (*Aut*) jdn

abschleppen; **"on ~", "in ~"** (US) „Fahrzeug wird abgeschleppt"
▶ **tow away** vt (vehicle) abschleppen
toward [tə'wɔːd], **towards** [tə'wɔːdz] prep (direction) zu; (attitude) gegenüber +dat; (purpose) für; (in time) gegen; **~(s) noon/the end of the year** gegen Mittag/Ende des Jahres; **to feel friendly ~(s) sb** jdm freundlich gesinnt sein
towel ['tauəl] n Handtuch nt; **to throw in the ~** (fig) das Handtuch werfen
towelling ['tauəlɪŋ] n Frottee nt or m
towel rail, (US) **towel rack** n Handtuchstange f
tower ['tauəʳ] n Turm m ▷ vi aufragen; **to ~ above** or **over sb/sth** über jdm/etw aufragen
tower block (Brit) n Hochhaus nt
towering ['tauərɪŋ] adj hoch aufragend
towline ['təulaɪn] n Abschleppseil nt
town [taun] n Stadt f; **to go (in)to ~** in die Stadt gehen; **to go to ~ on sth** (fig) sich bei etw ins Zeug legen; **in ~** in der Stadt; **to be out of ~** (person) nicht in der Stadt sein
town centre n Stadtzentrum nt
town clerk n Stadtdirektor(in) m(f)
town council n Stadtrat m
town crier [-'kraɪəʳ] n Ausrufer m
town hall n Rathaus nt
townie ['tauni] (inf) n (town-dweller) Städter(in) m(f)
town plan n Stadtplan m
town planner n Stadtplaner(in) m(f)
town planning n Stadtplanung f
township ['taunʃɪp] n Stadt(gemeinde) f; (formerly: in South Africa) Township f
townspeople ['taunzpiːpl] npl Stadtbewohner pl
towpath ['təupɑːθ] n Leinpfad m
towrope ['təurəup] n Abschleppseil nt
tow truck (US) n Abschleppwagen m
toxic ['tɔksɪk] adj giftig, toxisch
toxic asset n (Econ) faule Wertpapiere pl
toxic bank n (Econ) Bad Bank f
toxin ['tɔksɪn] n Gift nt, Giftstoff m
toy [tɔɪ] n Spielzeug nt
▶ **toy with** vt fus (object, idea) spielen mit
toyshop ['tɔɪʃɔp] n Spielzeugladen m
trace [treɪs] n (sign, small amount) Spur f ▷ vt (draw) nachzeichnen; (follow) verfolgen; (locate) aufspüren; **without ~** (disappear) spurlos; **there was no ~ of it** es war spurlos verschwunden
trace element n Spurenelement nt
tracer ['treɪsəʳ] n (Mil: also: **tracer bullet**) Leuchtspurgeschoss nt; (Med) Indikator m
trachea [trə'kɪə] n Luftröhre f
tracing paper ['treɪsɪŋ-] n Pauspapier nt
track [træk] n Weg m; (of comet, Sport) Bahn f; (of suspect, animal) Spur f; (Rail) Gleis nt; (on tape, record) Stück nt, Track m ▷ vt (follow) verfolgen; **to keep ~ of sb/sth** (fig) jdn/etw im Auge behalten; **to be on the right ~** (fig) auf der richtigen Spur sein
▶ **track down** vt aufspüren

tracker dog ['trækə-] (Brit) n Spürhund m
track events npl Laufwettbewerbe f
tracking station ['trækɪŋ-] n Bodenstation f
track meet (US) n (Sport) Leichtathletikwettkampf m
track record n: **to have a good ~** (fig) gute Leistungen vorzuweisen haben
tracksuit ['træksuːt] n Trainingsanzug m
tract [trækt] n (Geog) Gebiet nt; (pamphlet) Traktat m or nt; **respiratory ~** Atemwege pl
traction ['trækʃən] n (power) Zugkraft f; (Aut: grip) Bodenhaftung f; (Med): **in ~** im Streckverband
traction engine n Zugmaschine f
tractor ['træktəʳ] n Traktor m
trade [treɪd] n (activity) Handel m; (skill, job) Handwerk nt ▷ vi (do business) handeln ▷ vt: **to ~ sth (for sth)** etw (gegen etw) eintauschen; **foreign ~** Außenhandel m; **Department of T~ and Industry** (Brit) ≈ Wirtschaftsministerium nt; **to ~ with** Handel treiben mit; **to ~ in** (merchandise) handeln in +dat
▶ **trade in** vt in Zahlung geben
trade barrier n Handelsschranke f
trade deficit n Handelsdefizit nt
Trade Descriptions Act (Brit) n Gesetz über korrekte Warenbeschreibungen
trade discount n Händlerrabatt m
trade fair n Handelsmesse f
trade figures npl Handelsziffern pl
trade-in ['treɪdɪn] n: **to take sth as a ~** etw in Zahlung nehmen
trade-in value n Gebrauchtwert m
trademark ['treɪdmɑːk] n Warenzeichen nt
trade mission n Handelsmission f
trade name n Handelsname m
trade-off ['treɪdɔf] n Handel m; **there's bound to be a ~ between speed and quality** es gibt entweder Einbußen bei der Schnelligkeit oder bei der Qualität
trader ['treɪdəʳ] n Händler(in) m(f)
trade secret n (also fig) Betriebsgeheimnis nt
tradesman ['treɪdzmən] n (irreg: like **man**) n (shopkeeper) Händler m
trade union n Gewerkschaft f
trade unionist [-'juːnjənɪst] n Gewerkschaftler(in) m(f)
trade wind n Passat m
trading ['treɪdɪŋ] n Handel m
trading estate (Brit) n Industriegelände nt
trading stamp n Rabattmarke f
tradition [trə'dɪʃən] n Tradition f
traditional [trə'dɪʃənl] adj traditionell
traditionally [trə'dɪʃnəli] adv traditionell
traffic ['træfɪk] n Verkehr m; (in drugs etc) Handel m ▷ vi: **to ~ in** handeln mit
traffic calming n Verkehrsberuhigung f
traffic circle (US) n Kreisverkehr m
traffic island n Verkehrsinsel f
traffic jam n Verkehrsstauung f, Stau m
trafficker ['træfɪkəʳ] n Händler(in) m(f)
traffic lights npl Ampel f

t

traffic offence (Brit) n Verkehrsdelikt nt
traffic sign n Verkehrszeichen nt
traffic violation (US) n = **traffic offence**
traffic warden n Verkehrspolizist für Parkvergehen;
(woman) = Politesse f
tragedy ['trædʒədɪ] n Tragödie f
tragic ['trædʒɪk] adj tragisch
trail [treɪl] n (path) Weg m; (track) Spur f; (of
smoke, dust) Wolke f ▷ vt (drag) schleifen;
(follow) folgen +dat ▷ vi (hang loosely) schleifen;
(in game, contest) zurückliegen; **to be on sb's ~**
jdm auf der Spur sein
▶ **trail away** vi (sound, voice) sich verlieren
▶ **trail behind** vi hinterhertrotten
▶ **trail off** vi = **trail away**
trailer ['treɪlə'] n (Aut) Anhänger m;
(US: caravan) Caravan m, Wohnwagen m; (Cine,
TV) Trailer m
trailer truck (US) n Sattelschlepper m
train [treɪn] n (Rail) Zug m; (of dress) Schleppe f
▷ vt (apprentice etc) ausbilden; (dog) abrichten;
(athlete) trainieren; (mind) schulen; (plant)
ziehen; (point: camera, gun etc): **to ~ on**
richten auf +acc ▷ vi (learn a skill) ausgebildet
werden; (Sport) trainieren; **~ of thought**
Gedankengang m; **to go by ~** mit dem Zug
fahren; **~ of events** Ereignisfolge f; **to ~ sb to
do sth** jdn dazu ausbilden, etw zu tun
train attendant (US) n Schlafwagenschaffner
m
trained [treɪnd] adj (worker) gelernt; (teacher)
ausgebildet; (animal) dressiert; (eye) geschult
trainee [treɪ'ni:] n Auszubildende(r) f(m)
trainer ['treɪnə'] n (Sport: coach) Trainer(in)
m(f); (: shoe) Trainingsschuh m; (of animals)
Dresseur(in) m(f)
training ['treɪnɪŋ] n (for occupation) Ausbildung
f; (Sport) Training nt; **in ~** (Sport) im Training
training college n (for teachers) = pädagogische
Hochschule f
training course n Ausbildungskurs m
train wreck n (fig) unabwendbare Katastrophe;
he's a complete ~ er ist ein Wrack
traipse [treɪps] vi: **to ~ in/out** hinein-/
herauslatschen
trait [treɪt] n Zug m, Eigenschaft f
traitor ['treɪtə'] n Verräter(in) m(f)
trajectory [trə'dʒɛktərɪ] n Flugbahn f
tram [træm] (Brit) n (also: **tramcar**)
Straßenbahn f
tramline ['træmlaɪn] n Straßenbahnschiene f
tramp [træmp] n Landstreicher m;
(pej: woman) Flittchen nt ▷ vi stapfen ▷ vt (walk
through: town, streets) latschen durch
trample ['træmpl] vt: **to ~ (underfoot)**
niedertrampeln ▷ vi (also fig): **to ~ on**
herumtrampeln auf +dat
trampoline ['træmpəli:n] n Trampolin nt
trance [trɑ:ns] n Trance f; **to go into a ~** in
Trance verfallen
tranquil ['træŋkwɪl] adj ruhig, friedlich
tranquillity, (US) **tranquility** [træŋ'kwɪlɪtɪ] n
Ruhe f

tranquillizer, (US) **tranquilizer**
['træŋkwɪlaɪzə'] n Beruhigungsmittel nt
transact [træn'zækt] vt (business) abwickeln
transaction [træn'zækʃən] n Geschäft nt; **cash
~** Bargeldtransaktion f
transatlantic ['trænzət'læntɪk] adj
transatlantisch; (phone-call) über den Atlantik
transcend [træn'sɛnd] vt überschreiten
transcendental [trænsɛn'dɛntl] adj: **~
meditation** transzendentale Meditation f
transcribe [træn'skraɪb] vt transkribieren
transcript ['trænskrɪpt] n Niederschrift f,
Transkription f
transcription [træn'skrɪpʃən] n Transkription
f
transept ['trænsɛpt] n Querschiff nt
transfer ['trænsfə'] n (of employees) Versetzung
f; (of money) Überweisung f; (of power)
Übertragung f; (Sport) Transfer m; (picture,
design) Abziehbild nt ▷ vt (employees) versetzen;
(money) überweisen; (power, ownership)
übertragen; **by bank ~** per Banküberweisung;
to ~ the charges (Brit: Tel) ein R-Gespräch
führen
transferable [træns'fə:rəbl] adj übertragbar;
"not ~" „nicht übertragbar"
transfix [træns'fɪks] vt aufspießen; **~ed with
fear** (fig) starr vor Angst
transform [træns'fɔ:m] vt umwandeln
transformation [trænsfə'meɪʃən] n
Umwandlung f
transformer [træns'fɔ:mə'] n (Elec)
Transformator m
transfusion [træns'fju:ʒən] n (also: **blood
transfusion**) Bluttransfusion f
transgress [træns'grɛs] vt (go beyond)
überschreiten; (violate: rules, law) verletzen
transient ['trænzɪənt] adj vorübergehend
transistor [træn'zɪstə'] n (Elec) Transistor m;
(also: **transistor radio**) Transistorradio nt
transit ['trænzɪt] n: **in ~** unterwegs
transit camp n Durchgangslager nt
transition [træn'zɪʃən] n Übergang m
transitional [træn'zɪʃənl] adj Übergangs-
transitive ['trænzɪtɪv] adj (verb) transitiv
transit lounge n Transithalle f
transitory ['trænzɪtərɪ] adj (emotion, arrangement
etc) vorübergehend
transit visa n Transitvisum nt
translate [trænz'leɪt] vt übersetzen; **to ~
(from/into)** übersetzen (aus/in +acc)
translation [trænz'leɪʃən] n Übersetzung f; **in
~** als Übersetzung
translator [trænz'leɪtə'] n Übersetzer(in) m(f)
translucent [trænz'lu:snt] adj (object)
lichtdurchlässig
transmission [trænz'mɪʃən] n (also TV)
Übertragung f; (of information) Übermittlung f;
(Aut) Getriebe nt
transmission rate n (Tel, Comput)
Übertragungsrate f
transmit [trænz'mɪt] vt (also TV) übertragen;
(message, signal) übermitteln

transmitter [trænz'mɪtəʳ] n (TV, Radio) Sender m

transparency [træns'pɛərnsɪ] n (of glass etc) Durchsichtigkeit f; (Brit: Phot) Dia nt

transparent [træns'pærnt] adj durchsichtig; (fig: obvious) offensichtlich

transpire [træns'paɪəʳ] vi (turn out) bekannt werden; (happen) passieren; **it finally ~d that ...** schließlich sickerte durch, dass ...

transplant [vt træns'plɑːnt, n 'trɑːnsplɑːnt] vt (organ, seedlings) verpflanzen ▷ n (Med) Transplantation f; **to have a heart ~** sich einer Herztransplantation unterziehen

transport ['trænspɔːt] n Transport m, Beförderung f ▷ vt transportieren; **do you have your own ~?** haben Sie ein Auto?; **public ~** öffentliche Verkehrsmittel pl; **Department of T~** (Brit) Verkehrsministerium nt

transportation ['trænspɔː'teɪʃən] n Transport m, Beförderung f; (means of transport) Beförderungsmittel nt; **Department of T~** (US) Verkehrsministerium nt

transport café (Brit) n Fernfahrerlokal nt

transpose [træns'pəuz] vt versetzen

transsexual [trænz'sɛksuəl] adj transsexuell ▷ n Transsexuelle(r) f(m)

transverse ['trænzvəːs] adj (beam etc) Quer-

transvestite [trænz'vestaɪt] n Transvestit m

trap [træp] n (also fig) Falle f; (carriage) zweirädriger Pferdewagen m ▷ vt (animal) (mit einer Falle) fangen; (person: trick) in die Falle locken; (: confine) gefangen halten; (immobilize) festsetzen; (capture: energy) stauen; **to set** or **lay a ~ (for sb)** (jdm) eine Falle stellen; **to shut one's ~** (inf) die Klappe halten; **to ~ one's finger in the door** sich dat den Finger in der Tür einklemmen

trap door n Falltür f

trapeze [trə'piːz] n Trapez nt

trapper ['træpəʳ] n Fallensteller m, Trapper m

trappings ['træpɪŋz] npl äußere Zeichen pl; (of power) Insignien pl

trash [træʃ] n (rubbish) Abfall m, Müll m; (pej: nonsense) Schund m, Mist m

trash can (US) n Mülleimer m

trashy ['træʃɪ] adj (goods) minderwertig, wertlos; (novel etc) Schund-

trauma ['trɔːmə] n Trauma nt

traumatic [trɔː'mætɪk] adj traumatisch

traumatize ['trɔːmətaɪz] vt traumatisieren

travel ['trævl] n (travelling) Reisen nt ▷ vi reisen; (short distance) fahren; (move: car, aeroplane) sich bewegen; (sound etc) sich fortpflanzen; (news) sich verbreiten ▷ vt (distance) zurücklegen; **travels** npl (journeys) Reisen pl; **this wine doesn't ~ well** dieser Wein verträgt den Transport nicht

travel agency n Reisebüro nt

travel agent n Reisebürokaufmann m, Reisebürokauffrau f

travel brochure n Reiseprospekt m

traveling etc (US) = **travelling** etc

traveller, (US) **traveler** ['trævləʳ] n Reisende(r)

f(m); (Comm) Vertreter(in) m(f)

traveller's cheque, (US) **traveler's check** n Reisescheck m

travelling, (US) **traveling** ['trævlɪŋ] n Reisen nt ▷ cpd (circus, exhibition) Wander-; (bag, clock) Reise-; **~ expenses** Reisespesen pl

travelling salesman n Vertreter m

travelogue ['trævəlɔg] n Reisebericht m

travel sickness n Reisekrankheit f

traverse ['trævəs] vt durchqueren

travesty ['trævəstɪ] n Travestie f

trawler ['trɔːləʳ] n Fischdampfer m

tray [treɪ] n (for carrying) Tablett nt; (also: **in-tray/out-tray**: on desk) Ablage f für Eingänge/ Ausgänge

treacherous ['trɛtʃərəs] adj (person, look) verräterisch; (ground, tide) tückisch; **road conditions are ~** die Straßen sind in gefährlichem Zustand

treachery ['trɛtʃərɪ] n Verrat m

treacle ['triːkl] n Sirup m

tread [trɛd] (pt **trod**, pp **trodden**) n (of tyre) Profil nt; (footstep) Schritt m; (of stair) Stufe f ▷ vi gehen

▶ **tread on** vt fus treten auf +acc

treadle ['trɛdl] n Pedal nt

treas. abbr = **treasurer**

treason ['triːzn] n Verrat m

treasure ['trɛʒəʳ] n (also fig) Schatz m ▷ vt schätzen; **treasures** npl (art treasures etc) Schätze pl, Kostbarkeiten pl

treasure hunt n Schatzsuche f

treasurer ['trɛʒərəʳ] n Schatzmeister(in) m(f)

treasury ['trɛʒərɪ] n: **the T~, the T~ Department** (US) das Finanzministerium

treasury bill n kurzfristiger Schatzwechsel m

treat [triːt] n (present) (besonderes) Vergnügen nt ▷ vt (also Med, Tech) behandeln; **it came as a ~** es war eine besondere Freude; **to ~ sth as a joke** etw als Witz ansehen; **to ~ sb to sth** jdm etw spendieren

treatment ['triːtmənt] n Behandlung f; **to have ~ for sth** wegen etw in Behandlung sein

treaty ['triːtɪ] n Vertrag m

treble ['trɛbl] adj (triple) dreifach; (Mus: voice, part) (Knaben)sopran-; (instrument) Diskant- ▷ n (singer) (Knaben)sopran m; (on hi-fi, radio etc) Höhen pl ▷ vt verdreifachen ▷ vi sich verdreifachen; **to be ~ the amount/size of sth** dreimal so viel/so groß wie etw sein

treble clef n Violinschlüssel m

tree [triː] n Baum m

tree-lined ['triːlaɪnd] adj baumbestanden

treetop ['triːtɔp] n Baumkrone f

tree trunk n Baumstamm m

trek [trɛk] n Treck m; (tiring walk) Marsch m ▷ vi trecken

trellis ['trɛlɪs] n Gitter nt

tremble ['trɛmbl] vi (voice, body, trees) zittern; (ground) beben

trembling ['trɛmblɪŋ] n (of ground) Beben nt, Erschütterung f; (of trees) Zittern nt ▷ adj (hand, voice etc) zitternd

833

tremendous [trɪ'mɛndəs] *adj* (*amount, success etc*) gewaltig, enorm; (*holiday, view etc*) fantastisch

tremendously [trɪ'mɛndəslɪ] *adv* (*difficult, exciting*) ungeheuer; **he enjoyed it ~** es hat ihm ausgezeichnet gefallen

tremor ['trɛməʳ] *n* Zittern *nt*; (*also:* **earth tremor**) Beben *nt*, Erschütterung *f*

trench [trɛntʃ] *n* Graben *m*

trench coat *n* Trenchcoat *m*

trench warfare *n* Stellungskrieg *m*

trend [trɛnd] *n* Tendenz *f*; (*fashion*) Trend *m*; **a ~ towards/away from sth** eine Tendenz zu/weg von etw; **to set a/the ~** richtungsweisend sein

trendy ['trɛndɪ] *adj* modisch

trepidation [trɛpɪ'deɪʃən] *n* (*apprehension*) Beklommenheit *f*; **in ~** beklommen

trespass ['trɛspəs] *vi*: **to ~ on** (*private property*) unbefugt betreten; **"no ~ing"** „Betreten verboten"

trespasser ['trɛspəsəʳ] *n* Unbefugte(r) *f(m)*; **"~s will be prosecuted"** „widerrechtliches Betreten wird strafrechtlich verfolgt"

tress [trɛs] *n* (*of hair*) Locke *f*

trestle ['trɛsl] *n* Bock *m*

trestle table *n* Klapptisch *m*

trial ['traɪəl] *n* (*Law*) Prozess *m*; (*test: of machine, drug etc*) Versuch *m*; (*worry*) Plage *f*; **trials** *npl* (*unpleasant experiences*) Schwierigkeiten *pl*; **~ by jury** Schwurgerichtsverfahren *nt*; **to be sent for ~** vor Gericht gestellt werden; **to be/go on ~** (*Law*) angeklagt sein/werden; **by ~ and error** durch Ausprobieren

trial balance *n* Probebilanz *f*

trial basis *n*: **on a ~** probeweise

trial period *n* Probezeit *f*

trial run *n* Versuch *m*

triangle ['traɪæŋgl] *n* Dreieck *nt*; (*US: set square*) (Zeichen)dreieck *nt*; (*Mus*) Triangel *f*

triangular [traɪ'æŋgjuləʳ] *adj* dreieckig

triathlon [traɪ'æθlən] *n* Triathlon *nt*

tribal ['traɪbl] *adj* (*warrior, warfare, dance*) Stammes-

tribe [traɪb] *n* Stamm *m*

tribesman ['traɪbzmən] (*irreg: like* **man**) *n* Stammesangehörige(r) *m*

tribulations [trɪbju'leɪʃənz] *npl* Kümmernisse *pl*

tribunal [traɪ'bjuːnl] *n* Gericht *nt*

tributary ['trɪbjutərɪ] *n* (*of river*) Nebenfluss *m*

tribute ['trɪbjuːt] *n* Tribut *m*; **to pay ~ to** Tribut zollen +*dat*

trice [traɪs] *n*: **in a ~** im Handumdrehen

trick [trɪk] *n* Trick *m*; (*Cards*) Stich *m* ▷ *vt* hereinlegen; **to play a ~ on sb** jdm einen Streich spielen; **it's a ~ of the light** das Licht täuscht; **that should do the ~** das müsste hinhauen; **to ~ sb into doing sth** jdn (mit einem Trick) dazu bringen, etw zu tun; **to ~ sb out of sth** jdn um etw prellen

trickery ['trɪkərɪ] *n* Tricks *pl*, Betrügerei *f*

trickle ['trɪkl] *n* (*of water etc*) Rinnsal *nt* ▷ *vi* (*water, rain etc*) rinnen; (*people*) sich langsam bewegen

trick photography *n* Trickfotografie *f*

trick question *n* Fangfrage *f*

trickster ['trɪkstəʳ] *n* Betrüger(in) *m(f)*

tricky ['trɪkɪ] *adj* (*job, problem*) schwierig

tricycle ['traɪsɪkl] *n* Dreirad *nt*

trifle ['traɪfl] *n* (*detail*) Kleinigkeit *f*; (*Culin*) Trifle *nt* ▷ *adv*: **a ~ long** ein bisschen lang ▷ *vi*: **to ~ with sb/sth** jdn/etw nicht ernst nehmen; **he is not (someone) to be ~d with** mit ihm ist nicht zu spaßen

trifling ['traɪflɪŋ] *adj* (*detail*) unbedeutend

trigger ['trɪgəʳ] *n* Abzug *m*
  ▶ **trigger off** *vt fus* auslösen

trigonometry [trɪgə'nɔmətrɪ] *n* Trigonometrie *f*

trilby ['trɪlbɪ] (*Brit*) *n* (*also:* **trilby hat**) Filzhut *m*

trill [trɪl] *n* (*Mus*) Triller *m*; (*of birds*) Trillern *nt*

trilogy ['trɪlədʒɪ] *n* Trilogie *f*

trim [trɪm] *adj* (*house, garden*) gepflegt; (*figure, person*) schlank ▷ *n* (*haircut etc*): **to have a ~** sich *dat* die Haare nachschneiden lassen; (*on clothes, car*) Besatz *m* ▷ *vt* (*hair, beard*) nachschneiden; (*decorate*): **to ~ (with)** besetzen (mit); (*Naut: a sail*) trimmen mit; **to keep o.s. in (good) ~** (gut) in Form bleiben

trimmings ['trɪmɪŋz] *npl* (*Culin*): **with all the ~** mit allem Drum und Dran; (*cuttings: of pastry etc*) Reste *pl*

Trinidad and Tobago ['trɪnɪdæd-] *n* Trinidad und Tobago *nt*

trinity ['trɪnɪtɪ] *n* (*Rel*) Dreieinigkeit *f*

trinket ['trɪŋkɪt] *n* (*ornament*) Schmuckgegenstand *m*; (*piece of jewellery*) Schmuckstück *nt*

trio ['triːəu] *n* Trio *nt*

trip [trɪp] *n* (*journey*) Reise *f*; (*outing*) Ausflug *m* ▷ *vi* (*stumble*) stolpern; (*go lightly*) trippeln; **on a ~** auf Reisen
  ▶ **trip over** *vt fus* stolpern über +*acc*
  ▶ **trip up** *vi* stolpern ▷ *vt* (*person*) zu Fall bringen

tripartite [traɪ'pɑːtaɪt] *adj* (*agreement, talks*) dreiseitig

tripe [traɪp] *n* (*Culin*) Kaldaunen *pl*; (*pej: rubbish*) Stuss *m*

triple ['trɪpl] *adj* dreifach ▷ *adv*: **~ the distance/the speed** dreimal so weit/schnell; **~ the amount** dreimal so viel

triple jump *n* Dreisprung *m*

triplets ['trɪplɪts] *npl* Drillinge *pl*

triplicate ['trɪplɪkət] *n*: **in ~** in dreifacher Ausfertigung

tripod ['traɪpɔd] *n* (*Phot*) Stativ *nt*

Tripoli ['trɪpəlɪ] *n* Tripolis *nt*

tripper ['trɪpəʳ] (*Brit*) *n* Ausflügler(in) *m(f)*

tripwire ['trɪpwaɪəʳ] *n* Stolperdraht *m*

trite [traɪt] (*pej*) *adj* (*comment, idea etc*) banal

triumph ['traɪʌmf] *n* Triumph *m* ▷ *vi*: **to ~ (over)** triumphieren (über +*acc*)

triumphal [traɪ'ʌmfl] *adj* (*return*) triumphal

triumphant [traɪ'ʌmfənt] *adj* triumphal;

(*victorious*) siegreich

triumphantly [traɪˈʌmfəntlɪ] *adv* triumphierend

trivia [ˈtrɪvɪə] (*pej*) *npl* Trivialitäten *pl*

trivial [ˈtrɪvɪəl] *adj* trivial

triviality [trɪvɪˈælɪtɪ] *n* Trivialität *f*

trivialize [ˈtrɪvɪəlaɪz] *vt* trivialisieren

trod [trɒd] *pt of* **tread**

trodden [ˈtrɒdn] *pp of* **tread**

trolley [ˈtrɒlɪ] *n* (*for luggage*) Kofferkuli *m*; (*for shopping*) Einkaufswagen *m*; (*table on wheels*) Teewagen *m*; (*also:* **trolley bus**) Oberleitungsomnibus *m*, Obus *m*

trollop [ˈtrɒləp] (*pej*) *n* (*woman*) Schlampe *f*

trombone [trɒmˈbəun] *n* Posaune *f*

troop [tru:p] *n* (*of people, monkeys etc*) Gruppe *f* ▷ *vi*: **to ~ in/out** hinein-/hinausströmen; **troops** *npl* (*Mil*) Truppen *pl*

troop carrier *n* Truppentransporter *m*; (*Naut: also:* **troopship**) Truppentransportschiff *nt*

trooper [ˈtru:pər] *n* (*Mil*) Kavallerist *m*; (*US: policeman*) Polizist *m*

trooping the colour [ˈtru:pɪŋ-] (*Brit*) *n* (*ceremony*) Fahnenparade *f*

troopship [ˈtru:pʃɪp] *n* Truppentransportschiff *nt*

trophy [ˈtrəufɪ] *n* Trophäe *f*

tropic [ˈtrɒpɪk] *n* Wendekreis *m*; **the tropics** *npl* die Tropen *pl*; **T~ of Cancer/Capricorn** Wendekreis des Krebses/Steinbocks

tropical [ˈtrɒpɪkl] *adj* tropisch

trot [trɒt] *n* (*fast pace*) Trott *m*; (*of horse*) Trab *m* ▷ *vi* (*horse*) traben; (*person*) trotten; **on the ~** (*Brit: fig*) hintereinander

▶ **trot out** *vt* (*facts, excuse etc*) vorbringen

trouble [ˈtrʌbl] *n* Schwierigkeiten *pl*; (*bother, effort*) Umstände *pl*; (*unrest*) Unruhen *pl* ▷ *vt* (*worry*) beunruhigen; (*disturb: person*) belästigen ▷ *vi*: **to ~ to do sth** sich *dat* die Mühe machen, etw zu tun; **troubles** *npl* (*personal*) Probleme *pl*; (*Pol etc*) Unruhen *pl*; **to be in ~** in Schwierigkeiten sein; **to have ~ doing sth** Schwierigkeiten *or* Probleme haben, etw zu tun; **to go to the ~ of doing sth** sich *dat* die Mühe machen, etw zu tun; **it's no ~!** das macht mir nichts aus!; **the ~ is ...** das Problem ist ...; **what's the ~?** wo fehlts?; **stomach** *etc* **~** Probleme mit dem Magen *etc*; **please don't ~ yourself** bitte bemühen Sie sich nicht

troubled [ˈtrʌbld] *adj* (*person*) besorgt; (*country, life, era*) von Problemen geschüttelt

trouble-free [ˈtrʌblfri:] *adj* problemlos

troublemaker [ˈtrʌblmeɪkər] *n* Unruhestifter(in) *m(f)*

troubleshooter [ˈtrʌblʃu:tər] *n* Vermittler(in) *m(f)*

troublesome [ˈtrʌbləsm] *adj* (*child*) schwierig; (*cough etc*) lästig

trouble spot *n* (*Mil*) Unruheherd *m*

troubling [ˈtrʌblɪŋ] *adj* (*question etc*) beunruhigend

trough [trɒf] *n* (*also:* **drinking trough**) Wassertrog *m*; (*also:* **feeding trough**) Futtertrog *m*; (*channel*) Rinne *f*; (*low point*) Tief *nt*; **a ~ of low pressure** ein Tiefdruckkeil *m*

trounce [trauns] *vt* (*defeat*) vernichtend schlagen

troupe [tru:p] *n* Truppe *f*

trouser press [ˈtrauzə-] *n* Hosenpresse *f*

trousers [ˈtrauzəz] *npl* Hose *f*; **short ~** kurze Hose; **a pair of ~** eine Hose

trouser suit (*Brit*) *n* Hosenanzug *m*

trousseau [ˈtru:səu] (*pl* **trousseaux** *or* **~s**) *n* Aussteuer *f*

trout [traut] *n inv* Forelle *f*

trowel [ˈtrauəl] *n* (*garden tool*) Pflanzkelle *f*; (*builder's tool*) (Maurer)kelle *f*

truant [ˈtruənt] (*Brit*) *n*: **to play ~** die Schule schwänzen

truce [tru:s] *n* Waffenstillstand *m*

truck [trʌk] *n* (*lorry*) Lastwagen *m*; (*Rail*) Güterwagen *m*; (*for luggage*) Gepäckwagen *m*; **to have no ~ with sb** nichts mit jdm zu tun haben

truck driver *n* Lkw-Fahrer(in) *m(f)*

trucker [ˈtrʌkər] (*US*) *n* Lkw-Fahrer(in) *m(f)*

truck farm (*US*) *n* Gemüsefarm *f*

trucking [ˈtrʌkɪŋ] (*US*) *n* Transport *m*

trucking company (*US*) *n* Spedition *f*

truculent [ˈtrʌkjulənt] *adj* aufsässig

trudge [trʌdʒ] *vi* (*also:* **trudge along**) sich dahinschleppen

true [tru:] *adj* wahr; (*accurate*) genau; (*genuine*) echt; (*faithful: friend*) treu; (*wall, beam*) gerade; (*circle*) rund; **to come ~** wahr werden; **~ to life** lebensecht

truffle [ˈtrʌfl] *n* (*fungus, sweet*) Trüffel *f*

truly [ˈtru:lɪ] *adv* wahrhaft, wirklich; (*truthfully*) wirklich; **yours ~** (*in letter*) mit freundlichen Grüßen

trump [trʌmp] *n* (*also:* **trump card**: *also: fig*) Trumpf *m*; **to turn up ~s** (*fig*) sich als Retter in der Not erweisen

trumped-up *adj*: **a ~ charge** eine erfundene Anschuldigung

trumpet [ˈtrʌmpɪt] *n* Trompete *f*

truncated [trʌŋˈkeɪtɪd] *adj* (*message, object*) verstümmelt

truncheon [ˈtrʌntʃən] (*Brit*) *n* Gummiknüppel *m*

trundle [ˈtrʌndl] *vt* (*trolley etc*) rollen ▷ *vi*: **to ~ along** (*person*) dahinschlendern; (*vehicle*) dahinrollen

trunk [trʌŋk] *n* (*of tree*) Stamm *m*; (*of person*) Rumpf *m*; (*of elephant*) Rüssel *m*; (*case*) Schrankkoffer *m*; (*US: Aut*) Kofferraum *m*; **trunks** *npl* (*also:* **swimming trunks**) Badehose *f*

trunk call (*Brit*) *n* Ferngespräch *nt*

trunk road (*Brit*) *n* Fernstraße *f*

truss [trʌs] *n* (*Med*) Bruchband *nt*

▶ **truss (up)** *vt* (*Culin*) dressieren; (*person*) fesseln

trust [trʌst] *n* Vertrauen *nt*; (*Comm: for charity etc*) Stiftung *f* ▷ *vt* vertrauen +*dat*; **to take sth**

on ~ (*advice etc*) etw einfach glauben; **to be in ~** (*Law*) treuhänderisch verwaltet werden; **to ~ (that)** (*hope*) hoffen(, dass)

trust company *n* Trust *m*

trusted ['trʌstɪd] *adj* (*friend, servant*) treu

trustee [trʌs'tiː] *n* (*Law*) Treuhänder(in) *m(f)*; (*of school etc*) Aufsichtsratsmitglied *nt*

trustful ['trʌstful] *adj* vertrauensvoll

trust fund *n* Treuhandvermögen *nt*

trusting ['trʌstɪŋ] *adj* vertrauensvoll

trustworthy ['trʌstwəːðɪ] *adj* (*person*) vertrauenswürdig

trusty ['trʌstɪ] *adj* getreu

truth [truːθ] (*pl* **~s**) *n*: **the ~** die Wahrheit *f*

truthful ['truːθful] *adj* (*person*) ehrlich; (*answer etc*) wahrheitsgemäß

truthfully ['truːθfəlɪ] *adv* (*answer*) wahrheitsgemäß

truthfulness ['truːθfəlnɪs] *n* Ehrlichkeit *f*

try [traɪ] *n* (*also Rugby*) Versuch *m* ▷ *vt* (*attempt*) versuchen; (*test*) probieren; (*Law*) vor Gericht stellen; (*strain: patience*) auf die Probe stellen ▷ *vi* es versuchen; **to have a ~** es versuchen, einen Versuch machen; **to ~ to do sth** versuchen, etw zu tun; **to ~ one's (very) best** *or* **hardest** sein Bestes versuchen *or* tun
▶ **try on** *vt* (*clothes*) anprobieren; **she's ~ing it on** (*fig*) sie probiert, wie weit sie gehen kann
▶ **try out** *vt* ausprobieren

trying ['traɪɪŋ] *adj* (*person*) schwierig; (*experience*) schwer

tsar [zɑːʳ] *n* Zar *m*

T-shirt ['tiːʃəːt] *n* T-Shirt *nt*

T-square ['tiːskwɛəʳ] *n* (*Tech*) Reißschiene *f*

TT *adj abbr* (*Brit: inf*) = **teetotal** ▷ *abbr* (*US: Post*: = *Trust Territories*) *der US-Verwaltungshoheit unterstellte Gebiete*

tub [tʌb] *n* (*container*) Kübel *m*; (*bath*) Wanne *f*

tuba ['tjuːbə] *n* Tuba *f*

tubby ['tʌbɪ] *adj* rundlich

tube [tjuːb] *n* (*pipe*) Rohr *nt*; (*container*) Tube *f*; (*Brit: underground*) U-Bahn *f*; (*US: inf*): **the ~** (*television*) die Röhre

tubeless ['tjuːblɪs] *adj* (*tyre*) schlauchlos

tuber ['tjuːbəʳ] *n* (*Bot*) Knolle *f*

tuberculosis [tjubəːkjuˈləusɪs] *n* Tuberkulose *f*

tube station (*Brit*) *n* U-Bahn-Station *f*

tubing ['tjuːbɪŋ] *n* Schlauch *m*; **a piece of ~** ein Schlauch

tubular ['tjuːbjuləʳ] *adj* röhrenförmig

TUC (*Brit*) *n abbr* (= *Trades Union Congress*) *britischer Gewerkschafts-Dachverband*

tuck [tʌk] *vt* (*put*) stecken ▷ *n* (*Sewing*) Biese *f*
▶ **tuck away** *vt* (*money*) wegstecken; **to be ~ed away** (*building*) versteckt liegen
▶ **tuck in** *vt* (*clothing*) feststecken; (*child*) zudecken ▷ *vi* (*eat*) zulangen
▶ **tuck up** *vt* (*invalid, child*) zudecken

tuck shop *n* Süßwarenladen *m*

Tue., Tues. *abbr* (= *Tuesday*) Di.

Tuesday ['tjuːzdɪ] *n* Dienstag *m*; **it is ~ 23rd March** heute ist Dienstag, der 23. März; **on ~** am Dienstag; **on ~s** dienstags; **every ~**

jeden Dienstag; **every other ~** jeden zweiten Dienstag; **last/next ~** letzten/nächsten Dienstag; **the following ~** am Dienstag darauf; **~'s newspaper** die Zeitung von Dienstag; **a week/fortnight on ~** Dienstag in einer Woche/in vierzehn Tagen; **the ~ before last** der vorletzte Dienstag; **the ~ after next** der übernächste Dienstag; **~ morning/lunchtime/afternoon/evening** Dienstag Morgen/Mittag/Nachmittag/Abend; **~ night** (*overnight*) Dienstag Nacht

tuft [tʌft] *n* Büschel *nt*

tug [tʌg] *n* (*ship*) Schlepper *m* ▷ *vt* zerren

tug of love *n* Tauziehen *nt* (*um das Sorgerecht für Kinder*)

tug-of-war [tʌgəvˈwɔːʳ] *n* (*also fig*) Tauziehen *nt*

tuition [tjuːˈɪʃən] *n* (*Brit*) Unterricht *m*; (*US: school fees*) Schulgeld *nt*

tulip ['tjuːlɪp] *n* Tulpe *f*

tumble ['tʌmbl] *n* (*fall*) Sturz *m* ▷ *vi* (*fall*) stürzen
▶ **tumble to** (*inf*) *vt fus* kapieren

tumbledown ['tʌmbldaun] *adj* (*building*) baufällig

tumble dryer (*Brit*) *n* Wäschetrockner *m*

tumbler ['tʌmbləʳ] *n* (*glass*) Trinkglas *nt*

tummy ['tʌmɪ] (*inf*) *n* Bauch *m*

tumour, (*US*) **tumor** ['tjuːməʳ] *n* (*Med*) Tumor *m*, Geschwulst *f*

tumult ['tjuːmʌlt] *n* Tumult *m*

tumultuous [tjuːˈmʌltjuəs] *adj* (*welcome, applause etc*) stürmisch

tuna ['tjuːnə] *n inv* (*also*: **tuna fish**) T(h)unfisch *m*

tune [tjuːn] *n* (*melody*) Melodie *f* ▷ *vt* (*Mus*) stimmen; (*Radio, TV, Aut*) einstellen; **to be in/out of ~** (*instrument*) richtig gestimmt/verstimmt sein; (*singer*) richtig/falsch singen; **to be in/out of ~ with** (*fig*) in Einklang/nicht in Einklang stehen mit; **she was robbed to the ~ of 10,000 pounds** sie wurde um einen Betrag in Höhe von 10.000 Pfund beraubt
▶ **tune in** *vi* (*Radio, TV*) einschalten; **to ~ in to BBC1** BBC1 einschalten
▶ **tune up** *vi* (*Mus*) (das Instrument/die Instrumente) stimmen

tuneful ['tjuːnful] *adj* melodisch

tuner ['tjuːnəʳ] *n*: **piano ~** Klavierstimmer(in) *m(f)*; (*radio set*) Tuner *m*

tuner amplifier *n* Steuergerät *nt*

tungsten ['tʌŋstən] *n* Wolfram *nt*

tunic ['tjuːnɪk] *n* Hemdbluse *f*

tuning fork ['tjuːnɪŋ-] *n* Stimmgabel *f*

Tunis ['tjuːnɪs] *n* Tunis *nt*

Tunisia [tjuːˈnɪzɪə] *n* Tunesien *nt*

Tunisian [tjuːˈnɪzɪən] *adj* tunesisch ▷ *n* (*person*) Tunesier(in) *m(f)*

tunnel ['tʌnl] *n* Tunnel *m*; (*in mine*) Stollen *m* ▷ *vi* einen Tunnel bauen

tunnel vision *n* (*Med*) Gesichtsfeldeinengung *f*; (*fig*) Engstirnigkeit *f*

tunny ['tʌnɪ] *n* T(h)unfisch *m*

turban ['təːbən] *n* Turban *m*

turbid ['tə:bɪd] *adj* (*water*) trüb; (*air*) schmutzig

turbine ['tə:baɪn] *n* Turbine *f*

turbo ['tə:bəu] *n* Turbo *m*; **~ engine** Turbomotor *m*

turbojet [tə:bəu'dʒɛt] *n* Düsenflugzeug *nt*

turboprop [tə:bəu'prɔp] *n* (*engine*) Turbo-Prop-Turbine *f*

turbot ['tə:bət] *n inv* Steinbutt *m*

turbulence ['tə:bjuləns] *n* (*Aviat*) Turbulenz *f*

turbulent ['tə:bjulənt] *adj* (*water, seas*) stürmisch; (*fig: career, period*) turbulent

tureen [tə'ri:n] *n* Terrine *f*

turf [tə:f] *n* (*grass*) Rasen *m*; (*clod*) Sode *f* ⊳ *vt* (*area*) mit Grassoden bedecken; **the T~** (*horse-racing*) der Pferderennsport

▶ **turf out** (*inf*) *vt* (*person*) rausschmeißen

turf accountant (*Brit*) *n* Buchmacher *m*

turgid ['tə:dʒɪd] *adj* geschwollen

Turin ['tjuə'rɪn] *n* Turin *nt*

Turk [tə:k] *n* Türke *m*, Türkin *f*

Turkey ['tə:kɪ] *n* die Türkei *f*

turkey ['tə:kɪ] *n* (*bird*) Truthahn *m*, Truthenne *f*; (*meat*) Puter *m*

Turkish ['tə:kɪʃ] *adj* türkisch ⊳ *n* (*Ling*) Türkisch *nt*

Turkish bath *n* türkisches Bad *nt*

Turkish delight *n* geleeartige Süßigkeit, mit Puderzucker oder Schokolade überzogen

turmeric ['tə:mərɪk] *n* Kurkuma *f*

turmoil ['tə:mɔɪl] *n* Aufruhr *m*; **in ~** in Aufruhr

turn [tə:n] *n* (*change*) Wende *f*; (*in road*) Kurve *f*; (*rotation*) Drehung *f*; (*performance*) Nummer *f*; (*inf, Med*) Anfall *m* ⊳ *vt* (*handle, key*) drehen; (*collar, steak*) wenden; (*page*) umblättern; (*shape: wood*) drechseln; (: *metal*) drehen ⊳ *vi* (*object*) sich drehen; (*person*) sich umdrehen; (*change direction*) abbiegen; (*milk*) sauer werden; **to do sb a good ~** jdm einen guten Dienst erweisen; **a ~ of events** eine Wendung der Dinge; **it gave me quite a ~** (*inf*) das hat mir einen schönen Schrecken eingejagt; **"no left ~"** (*Aut*) „Linksabbiegen verboten"; **it's your ~** du bist dran; **in ~** der Reihe nach; **to take ~s (at)** sich abwechseln (bei); **at the ~ of the century/year** zur Jahrhundertwende/ Jahreswende; **to take a ~ for the worse** (*events*) sich zum Schlechten wenden; **his health** *or* **he has taken a ~ for the worse** sein Befinden hat sich verschlechtert; **to ~ nasty/forty/grey** unangenehm/vierzig/grau werden

▶ **turn against** *vt fus* sich wenden gegen

▶ **turn around** *vi* sich umdrehen; (*in car*) wenden

▶ **turn away** *vi* sich abwenden ⊳ *vt* (*applicants*) abweisen; (*business*) zurückweisen

▶ **turn back** *vi* umkehren ⊳ *vt* (*person, vehicle*) zurückweisen

▶ **turn down** *vt* (*request*) ablehnen; (*heating*) kleiner stellen; (*radio etc*) leiser stellen; (*bedclothes*) aufschlagen

▶ **turn in** *vi* (*inf: go to bed*) sich hinhauen ⊳ *vt* (*to police*) anzeigen; **to ~ o.s. in** sich stellen

▶ **turn into** *vt fus* (*change*) sich verwandeln in +*acc* ⊳ *vt* machen zu

▶ **turn off** *vi* (*from road*) abbiegen ⊳ *vt* (*light, radio etc*) ausmachen; (*tap*) zudrehen; (*engine*) abstellen

▶ **turn on** *vt* (*light, radio etc*) anmachen; (*tap*) aufdrehen; (*engine*) anstellen

▶ **turn out** *vt* (*light*) ausmachen; (*gas*) abstellen ⊳ *vi* (*appear, attend*) erscheinen; **to ~ out to be** (*prove to be*) sich erweisen als; **to ~ out well/badly** (*situation*) gut/schlecht enden

▶ **turn over** *vi* (*person*) sich umdrehen ⊳ *vt* (*object*) umdrehen, wenden; (*page*) umblättern; **to ~ sth over to** (*to sb*) etw übertragen +*dat*; (*to sth*) etw verlagern zu

▶ **turn round** *vi* sich umdrehen; (*vehicle*) wenden

▶ **turn up** *vi* (*person*) erscheinen; (*lost object*) wieder auftauchen ⊳ *vt* (*collar*) hochklappen; (*heater*) höher stellen; (*radio etc*) lauter stellen

turnabout ['tə:nəbaut] *n* (*fig*) Kehrtwendung *f*

turnaround ['tə:nəraund] *n* = **turnabout**

turncoat ['tə:nkəut] *n* Überläufer(in) *m(f)*

turned-up ['tə:ndʌp] *adj*: **~ nose** Stupsnase *f*

turning ['tə:nɪŋ] *n* (*in road*) Abzweigung *f*; **the first ~ on the right** die erste Straße rechts

turning circle (*Brit*) *n* (*Aut*) Wendekreis *m*

turning point *n* (*fig*) Wendepunkt *m*

turning radius (*US*) *n* = **turning circle**

turnip ['tə:nɪp] *n* Rübe *f*

turnout ['tə:naut] *n* (*of voters etc*) Beteiligung *f*

turnover ['tə:nəuvə'] *n* (*Comm: amount of money*) Umsatz *m*; (: *of staff*) Fluktuation *f*; (*Culin*): **apple ~** Apfeltasche *f*; **there is a rapid ~ in staff** der Personalbestand wechselt ständig

turnpike ['tə:npaɪk] (*US*) *n* gebührenpflichtige Autobahn *f*

turnstile ['tə:nstaɪl] *n* Drehkreuz *nt*

turntable ['tə:nteɪbl] *n* (*on record player*) Plattenteller *m*

turn-up ['tə:nʌp] (*Brit*) *n* (*on trousers*) Aufschlag *m*; **that's a ~ for the books!** (*inf*) das ist eine echte Überraschung!

turpentine ['tə:pəntaɪn] *n* (*also:* **turps**) Terpentin *nt*

turquoise ['tə:kwɔɪz] *n* (*stone*) Türkis *m* ⊳ *adj* (*colour*) türkis

turret ['tʌrɪt] *n* Turm *m*

turtle ['tə:tl] *n* Schildkröte *f*

turtleneck ['tə:tlnɛk], **turtleneck sweater** *n* Pullover *m* mit rundem Kragen

Tuscan ['tʌskən] *adj* toskanisch ⊳ *n* (*person*) Toskaner(in) *m(f)*

Tuscany ['tʌskənɪ] *n* die Toskana

tusk [tʌsk] *n* (*of elephant*) Stoßzahn *m*

tussle ['tʌsl] *n* Gerangel *nt*

tutor ['tju:tə'] *n* Tutor(in) *m(f)*; (*private tutor*) Privatlehrer(in) *m(f)*

tutorial [tju:'tɔ:rɪəl] *n* Kolloquium *nt*

tuxedo [tʌk'si:dəu] (*US*) *n* Smoking *m*

TV [ti:'vi:] *n abbr* (= *television*) TV *nt*

TV dinner *n* Fertiggericht *nt*

t

twaddle ['twɔdl] (inf) n dummes Zeug nt

twang [twæŋ] n (of instrument) singender Ton m; (of voice) näselnder Ton m ▷ vi einen singenden Ton von sich geben ▷ vt (guitar) zupfen

tweak [twi:k] vt kneifen

tweed [twi:d] n Tweed m

tweezers ['twi:zəz] npl Pinzette f

twelfth [twɛlfθ] num zwölfte(r, s) ▷ n Zwölftel nt

Twelfth Night n ≈ Dreikönige nt

twelve [twɛlv] num zwölf; **at ~ (o'clock)** (midday) um zwölf Uhr (mittags); (midnight) um zwölf Uhr nachts

twentieth ['twɛntɪɪθ] num zwanzigste(r, s)

twenty ['twɛntɪ] num zwanzig

twenty-four seven ['twɛntɪfɔː'sɛvn] n (store) Geschäft, das an sieben Tagen die Woche und 24 Stunden am Tag geöffnet hat ▷ adj rund um die Uhr; **~ service** Service, der rund um die Uhr zur Verfügung steht

twerp [twəːp] (inf) n Schwachkopf m

twice [twaɪs] adv zweimal; **~ as much** zweimal so viel; **~ a week** zweimal die Woche; **she is ~ your age** sie ist doppelt so alt wie du

twiddle ['twɪdl] vt drehen an+dat ▷ vi: **to ~ (with)** herumdrehen (an+dat); **to ~ one's thumbs** (fig) Däumchen drehen

twig [twɪg] n Zweig m ▷ vi, vt (Brit: inf: realize) kapieren

twilight ['twaɪlaɪt] n Dämmerung f; **in the ~** in der Dämmerung

twill [twɪl] n (cloth) Köper m

twin [twɪn] adj (sister, brother) Zwillings-; (towers) Doppel- ▷ n Zwilling m; (room in hotel etc) Zweibettzimmer nt ▷ vt (towns etc): **to be ~ned with ... ...** als Partnerstadt haben

twin-bedded room ['twɪn'bɛdɪd-] n Zweibettzimmer nt

twin beds npl zwei (gleiche) Einzelbetten pl

twin-carburettor ['twɪnka:bju'retəʳ] adj Doppelvergaser-

twine [twaɪn] n Bindfaden m ▷ vi sich winden

twin-engined [twɪn'ɛndʒɪnd] adj zweimotorig

twinge [twɪndʒ] n (of pain) Stechen nt; **a ~ of conscience** Gewissensbisse pl; **a ~ of fear/guilt** ein Angst-/Schuldgefühl nt

twinkle ['twɪŋkl] vi funkeln ▷ n Funkeln nt

twin town n Partnerstadt f

twirl [twəːl] vt herumwirbeln ▷ vi wirbeln ▷ n Wirbel m

twist [twɪst] n (action) Drehung f; (in road) Kurve; (in coil, flex) Biegung f; (in story) Wendung f ▷ vt (turn) drehen; (injure: ankle etc) verrenken; (twine) wickeln; (fig: meaning etc) verdrehen ▷ vi (road, river) sich winden; **~ my arm!** (inf) überreden Sie mich einfach!

twisted ['twɪstɪd] adj (wire, rope) gedreht; (ankle) verrenkt; (fig: logic, mind) verdreht

twit [twɪt] (inf) n Trottel m

twitch [twɪtʃ] n (jerky movement) Zucken nt ▷ vi zucken

Twitter® ['twɪtəʳ] n Twitter nt ▷ vi twittern

two [tu:] num zwei; **~ by ~, in ~s** zu zweit; **to put ~ and ~ together** (fig) zwei und zwei zusammenzählen

two-bit [tu:'bɪt] (inf) adj (worthless) mies

two-door [tu:'dɔːʳ] adj zweitürig

two-faced [tu:'feɪst] (pej) adj scheinheilig

twofold ['tu:fəʊld] adv: **to increase ~** um das Doppelte ansteigen ▷ adj (increase) um das Doppelte; (aim, value etc) zweifach

two-piece ['tu:pi:s] n (also: **two-piece suit**) Zweiteiler m; (also: **two-piece swimsuit**) zweiteiliger Badeanzug m

two-ply ['tu:plaɪ] adj (wool) zweifädig; (tissues) zweilagig

two-seater ['tu:'si:təʳ] n (car) Zweisitzer m

twosome ['tu:səm] n (people) Paar nt

two-stroke ['tu:strəʊk] n (also: **two-stroke engine**) Zweitakter m ▷ adj (engine) Zweitakt-

two-tone ['tu:'təʊn] adj (in colour) zweifarbig

two-way ['tu:weɪ] adj: **~ traffic** Verkehr m in beiden Richtungen; **~ radio** Funksprechgerät nt

TX (US) abbr (Post) = Texas

tycoon [taɪ'ku:n] n Magnat m

type [taɪp] n (category, model, example) Typ m; (Typ) Schrift f ▷ vt (letter etc) tippen, (mit der) Maschine schreiben; **a ~ of** eine Art von; **what ~ do you want?** welche Sorte möchten Sie?; **in bold/italic ~** in Fett-/Kursivdruck

typecast ['taɪpka:st] (irreg: like cast) vt (actor) (auf eine Rolle) festlegen

typeface ['taɪpfeɪs] n Schrift f, Schriftbild nt

typescript ['taɪpskrɪpt] n (maschinengeschriebenes) Manuskript nt

typeset ['taɪpset] (irreg: like set) vt setzen

typesetter ['taɪpsetəʳ] n Setzer(in) m(f)

typewriter ['taɪpraɪtəʳ] n Schreibmaschine f

typewritten ['taɪprɪtn] adj maschine(n) geschrieben

typhoid ['taɪfɔɪd] n Typhus m

typhoon [taɪ'fu:n] n Taifun m

typhus ['taɪfəs] n Fleckfieber nt

typical ['tɪpɪkl] adj typisch; **~ (of)** typisch (für); **that's ~!** das ist typisch!

typify ['tɪpɪfaɪ] vt typisch sein für

typing ['taɪpɪŋ] n Maschine(n)schreiben nt

typing error n Tippfehler m

typing pool n Schreibzentrale f

typist ['taɪpɪst] n Schreibkraft f

typo ['taɪpəʊ] (inf) n abbr (= typographical error) Druckfehler m

typography [tɪ'pɔgrəfɪ] n Typografie f

tyranny ['tɪrənɪ] n Tyrannei f

tyrant ['taɪərnt] n Tyrann(in) m(f)

tyre, (US) tire ['taɪəʳ] n Reifen m

tyre pressure n Reifendruck m

Tyrol [tɪ'rəʊl] n Tirol nt

Tyrolean [tɪrə'li:ən] adj Tiroler ▷ n (person) Tiroler(in) m(f)

Tyrolese [tɪrə'li:z] = **Tyrolean**

Tyrrhenian Sea [tɪ'ri:nɪən-] n: **the ~** das Tyrrhenische Meer

tzar [za:ʳ] n = **tsar**

Uu

U¹, u [juː] n (letter) U nt, u nt; **U for Uncle** ≈ U
wie Ulrich

U² [juː] (Brit) n abbr (Cine: = universal) Klassifikation
für jugendfreie Filme

UAW (US) n abbr (= United Automobile Workers)
Automobilarbeitergewerkschaft

UB40 (Brit) n abbr (= unemployment benefit form 40)
Arbeitslosenausweis m

U-bend ['juːbend] n (in pipe) U-Krümmung f

ubiquitous [juːˈbɪkwɪtəs] adj allgegenwärtig

UCCA ['ʌkə] (Brit) n abbr (= Universities Central
Council on Admissions) akademische Zulassungsstelle,
≈ ZVS f

UDA (Brit) n abbr (= Ulster Defence Association)
paramilitärische protestantische Organisation in
Nordirland

UDC (Brit) n abbr (= Urban District Council)
Stadtverwaltung f

udder ['ʌdər] n Euter nt

UDI (Brit) n abbr (Pol: = unilateral
declaration of independence) einseitige
Unabhängigkeitserklärung f

UDR (Brit) n abbr (= Ulster Defence Regiment)
Regiment aus Teilzeitsoldaten zur Unterstützung der
britischen Armee und Polizei in Nordirland

UEFA [juːˈeɪfə] n abbr (= Union of European Football
Associations) UEFA f

UFO ['juːfəʊ] n abbr (= unidentified flying object)
UFO nt

Uganda [juːˈgændə] n Uganda nt

Ugandan [juːˈgændən] adj ugandisch ▷ n
Ugander(in) m(f)

UGC (Brit) n abbr (= University Grants Committee)
Ausschuss zur Verteilung von Geldern an Universitäten

ugh [əːh] excl igitt

ugliness ['ʌglɪnɪs] n Hässlichkeit f

ugly ['ʌglɪ] adj hässlich; (nasty) schlimm

UHF abbr (= ultrahigh frequency) UHF

UHT abbr (= ultra heat treated): **~ milk** H-Milch f

UK n abbr = **United Kingdom**

Ukraine [juːˈkreɪn] n Ukraine f

Ukrainian [juːˈkreɪnɪən] adj ukrainisch ▷ n
Ukrainer(in) m(f); (Ling) Ukrainisch nt

ulcer ['ʌlsər] n (stomach ulcer etc) Geschwür nt;
(also: **mouth ulcer**) Abszess m im Mund

Ulster ['ʌlstər] n Ulster nt

ulterior [ʌlˈtɪərɪər] adj: **~ motive**
Hintergedanke m

ultimata [ʌltɪˈmeɪtə] npl of **ultimatum**

ultimate ['ʌltɪmət] adj (final) letztendlich;
(greatest) größte(r, s); (: deterrent) äußerste(r, s);
(: authority) höchste(r, s) ▷ n: **the ~ in luxury**
das Äußerste or Höchste an Luxus

ultimately ['ʌltɪmətlɪ] adv (in the end)
schließlich, letzten Endes; (basically) im
Grunde (genommen)

ultimatum [ʌltɪˈmeɪtəm] (pl **~s** or **ultimata**) n
Ultimatum nt

ultrasonic [ʌltrəˈsɒnɪk] adj (sound) Ultraschall-

ultrasound ['ʌltrəsaʊnd] n Ultraschall m

ultraviolet ['ʌltrəˈvaɪəlɪt] adj ultraviolett

umbilical cord [ʌmˈbɪlɪkl-] n Nabelschnur f

umbrage ['ʌmbrɪdʒ] n: **to take ~ at** Anstoß
nehmen an +dat

umbrella [ʌmˈbrɛlə] n (for rain) (Regen)schirm
m; (for sun) Sonnenschirm m; (fig): **under the ~
of** unter der Leitung von

umlaut ['umlaut] n Umlaut m; (mark)
Umlautzeichen nt

umpire ['ʌmpaɪər] n Schiedsrichter(in) m(f) ▷ vt
(game) als Schiedsrichter leiten

umpteen [ʌmpˈtiːn] adj zig

umpteenth [ʌmpˈtiːnθ] adj: **for the ~ time**
zum x-ten Mal

UMWA n abbr (= United Mineworkers of America)
amerikanische Bergarbeitergewerkschaft

UN n abbr (= United Nations) UNO f

unabashed [ʌnəˈbæʃt] adj: **to be/seem ~**
unbeeindruckt sein/scheinen

unabated [ʌnəˈbeɪtɪd] adj unvermindert
▷ adv: **to continue ~** nicht nachlassen

unable [ʌnˈeɪbl] adj: **to be ~ to do sth** etw
nicht tun können

unabridged [ʌnəˈbrɪdʒd] adj ungekürzt

unacceptable [ʌnəkˈsɛptəbl] adj
unannehmbar, nicht akzeptabel

unaccompanied [ʌnəˈkʌmpənɪd] adj (child,
song) ohne Begleitung; (luggage) unbegleitet

unaccountably [ʌnəˈkaʊntəblɪ] adv
unerklärlich

unaccounted [ʌnəˈkaʊntɪd] adj: **to be ~ for**
(passengers, money etc) (noch) fehlen

unaccustomed [ʌnəˈkʌstəmd] adj: **to be ~ to**
nicht gewöhnt sein an +acc

unacquainted [ʌnəˈkweɪntɪd] adj: **to be ~
with** nicht vertraut sein mit

u

unadulterated [ʌnə'dʌltəreɪtɪd] *adj* rein
unaffected [ʌnə'fɛktɪd] *adj* (*person, behaviour*) natürlich, ungekünstelt; **to be ~ by sth** von etw nicht berührt werden
unafraid [ʌnə'freɪd] *adj*: **to be ~** keine Angst haben
unaided [ʌn'eɪdɪd] *adv* ohne fremde Hilfe
unanimity [juːnə'nɪmɪtɪ] *n* Einstimmigkeit *f*
unanimous [juː'nænɪməs] *adj* einstimmig
unanimously [juː'nænɪməslɪ] *adv* einstimmig
unanswered [ʌn'ɑːnsəd] *adj* unbeantwortet
unappetizing [ʌn'æpɪtaɪzɪŋ] *adj* (*food*) unappetitlich
unappreciative [ʌnə'priːʃɪətɪv] *adj* (*person*) undankbar; (*audience*) verständnislos
unarmed [ʌn'ɑːmd] *adj* unbewaffnet; **~ combat** Nahkampf *m* ohne Waffen
unashamed [ʌnə'ʃeɪmd] *adj* (*pleasure, greed etc*) unverhohlen
unassisted [ʌnə'sɪstɪd] *adv* ohne fremde Hilfe
unassuming [ʌnə'sjuːmɪŋ] *adj* bescheiden
unattached [ʌnə'tætʃt] *adj* (*single: person*) ungebunden; (*unconnected*) ohne Verbindung
unattended [ʌnə'tɛndɪd] *adj* (*car, luggage, child*) unbeaufsichtigt
unattractive [ʌnə'træktɪv] *adj* unattraktiv
unauthorized [ʌn'ɔːθəraɪzd] *adj* (*visit, use*) unbefugt; (*version*) nicht unautorisiert
unavailable [ʌnə'veɪləbl] *adj* (*article, room*) nicht verfügbar; (*person*) nicht zu erreichen; **~ for comment** nicht zu sprechen
unavoidable [ʌnə'vɔɪdəbl] *adj* unvermeidlich
unavoidably [ʌnə'vɔɪdəblɪ] *adv* (*delayed etc*) auf unvermeidliche Weise
unaware [ʌnə'wɛəʳ] *adj*: **he was ~ of it** er war sich *dat* dessen nicht bewusst
unawares [ʌnə'wɛəz] *adv* (*catch, take*) unerwartet
unbalanced [ʌn'bælənst] *adj* (*report*) unausgewogen; **(mentally) ~** geistig gestört
unbearable [ʌn'bɛərəbl] *adj* unerträglich
unbeatable [ʌn'biːtəbl] *adj* unschlagbar
unbeaten [ʌn'biːtn] *adj* ungeschlagen
unbecoming [ʌnbɪ'kʌmɪŋ] *adj* (*language, behaviour*) unpassend; (*garment*) unvorteilhaft
unbeknown [ʌnbɪ'nəʊn], **unbeknownst** [ʌnbɪ'nəʊnst] *adv*: **~(st) to me/Peter** ohne mein/Peters Wissen
unbelief [ʌnbɪ'liːf] *n* Ungläubigkeit *f*
unbelievable [ʌnbɪ'liːvəbl] *adj* unglaublich
unbelievably [ʌnbɪ'liːvəblɪ] *adv* unglaublich
unbend [ʌn'bɛnd] (*irreg: like* **bend**) *vi* (*relax*) aus sich herausgehen ▷ *vt* (*wire etc*) gerade biegen
unbending [ʌn'bɛndɪŋ] *adj* (*person, attitude*) unnachgiebig
unbiased, unbiassed [ʌn'baɪəst] *adj* unvoreingenommen
unblemished [ʌn'blɛmɪʃt] *adj* (*also fig*) makellos
unblock [ʌn'blɔk] *vt* (*pipe*) frei machen
unborn [ʌn'bɔːn] *adj* ungeboren
unbounded [ʌn'baʊndɪd] *adj* grenzenlos
unbreakable [ʌn'breɪkəbl] *adj* (*object*) unzerbrechlich

unbridled [ʌn'braɪdld] *adj* ungezügelt
unbroken [ʌn'brəʊkən] *adj* (*seal*) unversehrt; (*silence*) ununterbrochen; (*record, series*) ungebrochen
unbuckle [ʌn'bʌkl] *vt* aufschnallen
unburden [ʌn'bəːdn] *vt*: **to ~ o.s. (to sb)** (jdm) sein Herz ausschütten
unbusinesslike [ʌn'bɪznɪslaɪk] *adj* ungeschäftsmäßig
unbutton [ʌn'bʌtn] *vt* aufknöpfen
uncalled-for [ʌn'kɔːldfɔːʳ] *adj* (*remark etc*) unnötig
uncanny [ʌn'kænɪ] *adj* unheimlich
unceasing [ʌn'siːsɪŋ] *adj* (*search, flow etc*) unaufhörlich; (*loyalty*) unermüdlich
unceremonious [ʌnsɛrɪ'məʊnɪəs] *adj* (*abrupt, rude*) brüsk, barsch
uncertain [ʌn'səːtn] *adj* (*person*) unsicher; (*future, outcome*) ungewiss; **to be ~ about sth** unsicher über etw *acc* sein; **in no ~ terms** unzweideutig
uncertainty [ʌn'səːtntɪ] *n* Ungewissheit *f*; **uncertainties** *npl* (*doubts*) Unsicherheiten *pl*
unchallenged [ʌn'tʃælɪndʒd] *adj* unbestritten ▷ *adv* (*walk, enter*) ungehindert; **to go ~** unangefochten bleiben
unchanged [ʌn'tʃeɪndʒd] *adj* unverändert
uncharitable [ʌn'tʃærɪtəbl] *adj* (*remark, behaviour etc*) unfreundlich
uncharted [ʌn'tʃɑːtɪd] *adj* (*land, sea*) unverzeichnet
unchecked [ʌn'tʃɛkt] *adv* (*grow, continue*) ungehindert
uncivil [ʌn'sɪvɪl] *adj* (*person*) grob
uncivilized [ʌn'sɪvɪlaɪzd] *adj* unzivilisiert
uncle [ʌŋkl] *n* Onkel *m*
unclear [ʌn'klɪəʳ] *adj* unklar; **I'm still ~ about what I'm supposed to do** mir ist immer noch nicht klar, was ich tun soll
uncoil [ʌn'kɔɪl] *vt* (*rope, wire*) abwickeln ▷ *vi* (*snake*) sich strecken
uncomfortable [ʌn'kʌmfətəbl] *adj* (*person, chair*) unbequem; (*room*) ungemütlich; (*nervous*) unbehaglich; (*unpleasant: situation, fact*) unerfreulich
uncomfortably [ʌn'kʌmfətəblɪ] *adv* (*sit*) unbequem; (*smile*) unbehaglich
uncommitted [ʌnkə'mɪtɪd] *adj* nicht engagiert; **~ to** nicht festgelegt auf +*acc*
uncommon [ʌn'kɔmən] *adj* ungewöhnlich
uncommunicative [ʌnkə'mjuːnɪkətɪv] *adj* (*person*) schweigsam
uncomplicated [ʌn'kɔmplɪkeɪtɪd] *adj* unkompliziert
uncompromising [ʌn'kɔmprəmaɪzɪŋ] *adj* (*person, belief*) kompromisslos
unconcerned [ʌnkən'səːnd] *adj* (*person*) unbekümmert; **to be ~ about sth** sich nicht um etw kümmern
unconditional [ʌnkən'dɪʃənl] *adj* bedingungslos; (*acceptance*) vorbehaltlos
uncongenial [ʌnkən'dʒiːnɪəl] *adj* (*surroundings*) unangenehm

unconnected [ʌnkə'nɛktɪd] *adj* (*unrelated*) ohne Verbindung; **to be ~ with sth** nicht mit etw in Beziehung stehen

unconscious [ʌn'kɔnʃəs] *adj* (*in faint*) bewusstlos; (*unaware*): **~ of** nicht bewusst +*gen* ▷ *n*: **the ~** das Unbewusste; **to knock sb ~** jdn bewusstlos schlagen

unconsciously [ʌn'kɔnʃəslɪ] *adv* unbewusst

unconsciousness [ʌn'kɔnʃəsnɪs] *n* Bewusstlosigkeit *f*

unconstitutional ['ʌnkɔnstɪ'tjuːʃənl] *adj* verfassungswidrig

uncontested [ʌnkən'tɛstɪd] *adj* (Pol: *seat, election*) ohne Gegenkandidat; (*divorce*) ohne Einwände der Gegenseite

uncontrollable [ʌnkən'trəʊləbl] *adj* unkontrollierbar; (*laughter*) unbändig

uncontrolled [ʌnkən'trəʊld] *adj* (*behaviour*) ungezähmt; (*price rises etc*) ungehindert

unconventional [ʌnkən'vɛnʃənl] *adj* unkonventionell

unconvinced [ʌnkən'vɪnst] *adj*: **to be/remain ~** nicht überzeugt sein/bleiben

unconvincing [ʌnkən'vɪnsɪŋ] *adj* nicht überzeugend

uncork [ʌn'kɔːk] *vt* (*bottle*) entkorken

uncorroborated [ʌnkə'rɔbəreɪtɪd] *adj* (*evidence*) unbestätigt

uncouth [ʌn'kuːθ] *adj* (*person, behaviour*) ungehobelt

uncover [ʌn'kʌvər] *vt* aufdecken

unctuous ['ʌŋktjuəs] (*form*) *adj* (*person, behaviour*) salbungsvoll

undamaged [ʌn'dæmɪdʒd] *adj* unbeschädigt

undaunted [ʌn'dɔːntɪd] *adj* (*person*) unverzagt; **~, she struggled on** sie kämpfte unverzagt weiter

undecided [ʌndɪ'saɪdɪd] *adj* (*person*) unentschlossen; (*question*) unentschieden

undelivered [ʌndɪ'lɪvəd] *adj* (*goods*) nicht geliefert; (*letters*) nicht zugestellt; **if ~ return to sender** (*on envelope*) falls unzustellbar, zurück an Absender

undeniable [ʌndɪ'naɪəbl] *adj* unbestreitbar

undeniably [ʌndɪ'naɪəblɪ] *adv* (*true*) zweifellos; (*handsome*) unbestreitbar

under ['ʌndər] *prep* (*position*) unter +*dat*; (*motion*) unter +*acc*; (*according to: law etc*) nach, gemäß +*dat* ▷ *adv* (*go, fly etc*) darunter; **to come from ~ sth** unter etw *dat* hervorkommen; **~ there** darunter; **in ~ 2 hours** in weniger als 2 Stunden; **~ anaesthetic** unter Narkose; **to be ~ discussion** diskutiert werden; **~ repair** in Reparatur; **~ the circumstances** unter den Umständen

under ... ['ʌndər] *pref* Unter-, unter-

underage [ʌndər'eɪdʒ] *adj* (*person*) minderjährig; **~ drinking** Alkoholgenuss *m* von Minderjährigen

underarm ['ʌndərɑːm] *adv* (*bowl, throw*) von unten ▷ *adj* (*throw, shot*) von unten; (*deodorant*) Achselhöhlen-

undercapitalized ['ʌndə'kæpɪtəlaɪzd] *adj* unterkapitalisiert

undercarriage ['ʌndəkærɪdʒ] *n* (*Aviat*) Fahrgestell *nt*

undercharge [ʌndə'tʃɑːdʒ] *vt* zu wenig berechnen +*dat*

underclass ['ʌndəklɑːs] *n* Unterklasse *f*

underclothes ['ʌndəkləʊðz] *npl* Unterwäsche *f*

undercoat ['ʌndəkəʊt] *n* (*paint*) Grundierung *f*

undercover [ʌndə'kʌvər] *adj* (*duty, agent*) Geheim- ▷ *adv* (*work*) insgeheim

undercurrent ['ʌndəkʌrnt] *n* (*also fig*) Unterströmung *f*

undercut [ʌndə'kʌt] (*irreg: like* **cut**) *vt* (*person, prices*) unterbieten

underdeveloped ['ʌndədɪ'vɛləpt] *adj* unterentwickelt

underdog ['ʌndədɔg] *n*: **the ~** der/die Benachteiligte

underdone [ʌndə'dʌn] *adj* (*food*) nicht gar; (: *meat*) nicht durchgebraten

underemployment ['ʌndərɪm'plɔɪmənt] *n* Unterbeschäftigung *f*

underestimate ['ʌndər'ɛstɪmeɪt] *vt* unterschätzen

underexposed ['ʌndərɪks'pəʊzd] *adj* (*Phot*) unterbelichtet

underfed [ʌndə'fɛd] *adj* unterernährt

underfoot [ʌndə'fut] *adv*: **to crush sth ~** etw am Boden zerdrücken; **to trample sth ~** auf etw *dat* herumtrampeln

underfunded ['ʌndə'fʌndɪd] *adj* unterfinanziert

undergo [ʌndə'gəʊ] (*irreg: like* **go**) *vt* (*change*) durchmachen; (*test, operation*) sich unterziehen; **the car is ~ing repairs** das Auto wird gerade repariert

undergraduate [ʌndə'grædjuɪt] *n* Student(in) *m(f)* ▷ *cpd*: **~ courses** Kurse *pl* für nicht graduierte Studenten

underground ['ʌndəgraund] *adj* unterirdisch; (Pol: *newspaper, activities*) Untergrund- ▷ *adv* (*work*) unterirdisch; (: *miners*) unter Tage; (Pol): **to go ~** untertauchen ▷ *n*: **the ~** (*Brit*) die U-Bahn; (Pol) die Untergrundbewegung; **~ car park** Tiefgarage *f*

undergrowth ['ʌndəgrəʊθ] *n* Unterholz *nt*

underhand [ʌndə'hænd], **underhanded** [ʌndə'hændɪd] *adj* (fig: *behaviour, person*) hinterhältig

underinsured [ʌndərɪn'ʃuəd] *adj* unterversichert

underlay [ʌndə'leɪ] *n* Unterlage *f*

underlie [ʌndə'laɪ] (*irreg: like* **lie**) *vt* (fig: *be basis of*) zugrunde liegen +*dat*; **the underlying cause** der eigentliche Grund

underline [ʌndə'laɪn] *vt* unterstreichen; (fig: *emphasize*) betonen

underling ['ʌndəlɪŋ] (*pej*) *n* Befehlsempfänger(in) *m(f)*

undermanning [ʌndə'mænɪŋ] *n* Personalmangel *m*

undermentioned [ʌndə'mɛnʃənd] *adj* unten genannt

u

841

undermine [ʌndə'maɪn] vt unterminieren, unterhöhlen

underneath [ʌndə'niːθ] adv darunter ▷ prep (position) unter +dat; (motion) unter +acc

undernourished [ʌndə'nʌrɪʃt] adj unterernährt

underpaid [ʌndə'peɪd] adj unterbezahlt

underpants ['ʌndəpænts] npl Unterhose f

underpass ['ʌndəpɑːs] (Brit) n Unterführung f

underpin [ʌndə'pɪn] vt (argument) untermauern

underplay [ʌndə'pleɪ] (Brit) vt herunterspielen

underpopulated [ʌndə'pɒpjuleɪtɪd] adj unterbevölkert

underprice [ʌndə'praɪs] vt (goods) zu billig anbieten

underprivileged [ʌndə'prɪvɪlɪdʒd] adj unterprivilegiert

underrate [ʌndə'reɪt] vt unterschätzen

underscore [ʌndə'skɔːʳ] vt unterstreichen

underseal [ʌndə'siːl] (Brit) vt (car) mit Unterbodenschutz versehen ▷ n (of car) Unterbodenschutz m

undersecretary ['ʌndə'sɛkrətərɪ] n (Pol) Staatssekretär(in) m(f)

undersell [ʌndə'sɛl] (irreg: like sell) vt (competitors) unterbieten

undershirt ['ʌndəʃəːt] (US) n Unterhemd nt

undershorts ['ʌndəʃɔːts] (US) npl Unterhose f

underside ['ʌndəsaɪd] n Unterseite f

undersigned ['ʌndə'saɪnd] adj unterzeichnet ▷ n: **the ~** der/die Unterzeichnete; **we the ~ agree that ...** wir, die Unterzeichneten, kommen überein, dass ...

underskirt ['ʌndəskəːt] (Brit) n Unterrock m

understaffed [ʌndə'stɑːft] adj unterbesetzt

understand [ʌndə'stænd] (irreg: like stand) vt, vi verstehen; **I ~ (that) you have ...** (believe) soweit ich weiß, haben Sie ...; **to make o.s. understood** sich verständlich machen

understandable [ʌndə'stændəbl] adj verständlich

understanding [ʌndə'stændɪŋ] adj verständnisvoll ▷ n Verständnis nt; **to come to an ~ with sb** mit jdm übereinkommen; **on the ~ that ...** unter der Voraussetzung, dass ...

understate [ʌndə'steɪt] vt herunterspielen

understatement ['ʌndəsteɪtmənt] n Understatement nt, Untertreibung f; **that's an ~!** das ist untertrieben!

understood [ʌndə'stud] pt, pp of **understand** ▷ adj (agreed) abgemacht; (implied) impliziert

understudy ['ʌndəstʌdɪ] n zweite Besetzung f

undertake [ʌndə'teɪk] (irreg: like take) vt (task) übernehmen ▷ vi: **to ~ to do sth** es übernehmen, etw zu tun

undertaker ['ʌndəteɪkəʳ] n (Leichen)bestatter m

undertaking ['ʌndəteɪkɪŋ] n (job) Unternehmen nt; (promise) Zusicherung f

undertone ['ʌndətəun] n (of criticism etc) Unterton m; **in an ~** mit gedämpfter Stimme

undervalue [ʌndə'væljuː] vt (person, work etc) unterbewerten

underwater ['ʌndə'wɔːtəʳ] adv (swim etc) unter Wasser ▷ adj (exploration, camera etc) Unterwasser-

underwear ['ʌndəwɛəʳ] n Unterwäsche f

underweight [ʌndə'weɪt] adj: **to be ~** Untergewicht haben

underworld ['ʌndəwəːld] n Unterwelt f

underwrite [ʌndə'raɪt] vt (Fin) garantieren; (Insurance) versichern

underwriter ['ʌndəraɪtəʳ] n (Insurance) Versicherer(in) m(f)

undeserved [ʌndɪ'zəːvd] adj unverdient

undesirable [ʌndɪ'zaɪərəbl] adj unerwünscht

undeveloped [ʌndɪ'vɛləpt] adj (land) unentwickelt; (resources) ungenutzt

undies ['ʌndɪz] (inf) npl Unterwäsche f

undiluted ['ʌndaɪ'luːtɪd] adj (substance) unverdünnt; (emotion) unverfälscht

undiplomatic ['ʌndɪplə'mætɪk] adj undiplomatisch

undischarged ['ʌndɪs'tʃɑːdʒd] adj: **~ bankrupt** nicht entlasteter Konkursschuldner m, nicht entlastete Konkursschuldnerin f

undisciplined [ʌn'dɪsɪplɪnd] adj undiszipliniert

undiscovered ['ʌndɪs'kʌvəd] adj unentdeckt

undisguised ['ʌndɪs'gaɪzd] adj (dislike, amusement etc) unverhohlen

undisputed ['ʌndɪs'pjuːtɪd] adj unbestritten

undistinguished ['ʌndɪs'tɪŋgwɪʃt] adj (career, person) mittelmäßig; (appearance) durchschnittlich

undisturbed [ʌndɪs'təːbd] adj ungestört; **to leave sth ~** etw unberührt lassen

undivided [ʌndɪ'vaɪdɪd] adj: **you have my ~ attention** Sie haben meine ungeteilte Aufmerksamkeit

undo [ʌn'duː] (irreg: like do) vt (unfasten) aufmachen; (spoil) zunichtemachen

undoing [ʌn'duːɪŋ] n Verderben nt

undone [ʌn'dʌn] pp of **undo** ▷ adj: **to come ~** (shoelaces etc) aufgehen

undoubted [ʌn'dautɪd] adj unzweifelhaft

undoubtedly [ʌn'dautɪdlɪ] adv zweifellos

undress [ʌn'drɛs] vi sich ausziehen ▷ vt ausziehen

undrinkable [ʌn'drɪŋkəbl] adj (unpalatable) ungenießbar; (poisonous) nicht trinkbar

undue [ʌn'djuː] adj (excessive) übertrieben

undulating ['ʌndjuleɪtɪŋ] adj (movement) Wellen-; (hills) sanft

unduly [ʌn'djuːlɪ] adv (excessively) übermäßig

undying [ʌn'daɪɪŋ] adj (love, loyalty etc) ewig

unearned [ʌn'əːnd] adj (praise) unverdient; **~ income** Kapitaleinkommen nt

unearth [ʌn'əːθ] vt (skeleton etc) ausgraben; (fig: secrets etc) ausfindig machen

unearthly [ʌn'əːθlɪ] adj (eerie) unheimlich; **at some ~ hour** zu nachtschlafender Zeit

unease [ʌn'iːz] n Unbehagen nt

uneasy [ʌn'iːzɪ] adj (person) unruhig; (feeling) unbehaglich; (peace, truce) unsicher; **to feel ~ about doing sth** ein ungutes Gefühl dabei haben, etw zu tun

uneconomic ['ʌniːkə'nɔmɪk] *adj*
unwirtschaftlich

uneconomical ['ʌniːkə'nɔmɪkl] *adj*
unwirtschaftlich

uneducated [ʌn'edjukeɪtɪd] *adj* ungebildet

unemployed [ʌnɪm'plɔɪd] *adj* arbeitslos
▷ *npl*: **the ~** die Arbeitslosen *pl*

unemployment [ʌnɪm'plɔɪmənt] *n*
Arbeitslosigkeit *f*

unemployment benefit (*Brit*) *n*
Arbeitslosenunterstützung *f*

unemployment compensation (*US*) *n* =
unemployment benefit

unending [ʌn'endɪŋ] *adj* endlos

unenviable [ʌn'enviəbl] *adj* (*task, conditions etc*)
wenig beneidenswert

unequal [ʌn'iːkwəl] *adj* ungleich; **to feel ~ to**
sich nicht gewachsen fühlen +*dat*

unequalled, (*US*) **unequaled** [ʌn'iːkwəld] *adj*
unübertroffen

unequivocal [ʌnɪ'kwɪvəkl] *adj* (*answer*)
unzweideutig; **to be ~ about sth** eine klare
Haltung zu etw haben

unerring [ʌn'əːrɪŋ] *adj* unfehlbar

UNESCO [juː'neskəu] *n abbr* (= *United Nations
Educational, Scientific and Cultural Organization*)
UNESCO *f*

unethical [ʌn'eθɪkl] *adj* (*methods*) unlauter;
(*doctor's behaviour*) unethisch

uneven [ʌn'iːvn] *adj* (*teeth, road etc*) uneben;
(*performance*) ungleichmäßig

uneventful [ʌnɪ'ventful] *adj* ereignislos

unexceptional [ʌnɪk'sepʃənl] *adj*
durchschnittlich

unexciting [ʌnɪk'saɪtɪŋ] *adj* (*film, news*) wenig
aufregend

unexpected [ʌnɪks'pektɪd] *adj* unerwartet

unexpectedly [ʌnɪks'pektɪdlɪ] *adv* unerwartet

unexplained [ʌnɪks'pleɪnd] *adj* (*mystery, failure*)
ungeklärt

unexploded [ʌnɪks'pləudɪd] *adj* nicht
explodiert

unfailing [ʌn'feɪlɪŋ] *adj* (*support, energy*)
unerschöpflich

unfair [ʌn'feəʳ] *adj* unfair, ungerecht;
(*advantage*) ungerechtfertigt; **~ to** unfair *or*
ungerecht zu

unfair dismissal *n* ungerechtfertigte
Entlassung *f*

unfairly [ʌn'feəlɪ] *adv* (*treat*) unfair, ungerecht;
(*dismiss*) ungerechtfertigt

unfaithful [ʌn'feɪθful] *adj* (*lover, spouse*) untreu

unfamiliar [ʌnfə'mɪliəʳ] *adj* ungewohnt;
(*person*) fremd; **to be ~ with sth** mit etw nicht
vertraut sein

unfashionable [ʌn'fæʃnəbl] *adj* (*clothes, ideas*)
unmodern; (*place*) unbeliebt

unfasten [ʌn'faːsn] *vt* (*seat belt, strap*) lösen

unfathomable [ʌn'fæðəməbl] *adj*
unergründlich

unfavourable, (*US*) **unfavorable** [ʌn'feɪvrəbl]
adj (*circumstances, weather*) ungünstig; (*opinion,
report*) negativ

unfavourably, (*US*) **unfavorably** [ʌn'feɪvrəblɪ]
adv: **to compare ~ (with sth)** im Vergleich
(mit etw) ungünstig sein; **to compare ~
(with sb)** im Vergleich (mit jdm) schlechter
abschneiden; **to look ~ on** (*suggestion etc*)
ablehnend gegenüberstehen +*dat*

unfeeling [ʌn'fiːlɪŋ] *adj* gefühllos

unfinished [ʌn'fɪnɪʃt] *adj* unvollendet

unfit [ʌn'fɪt] *adj* (*physically*) nicht fit;
(*incompetent*) unfähig; **~ for work**
arbeitsunfähig; **~ for human consumption**
zum Verzehr ungeeignet

unflagging [ʌn'flægɪŋ] *adj* (*attention, energy*)
unermüdlich

unflappable [ʌn'flæpəbl] *adj* unerschütterlich

unflattering [ʌn'flætərɪŋ] *adj* (*dress, hairstyle*)
unvorteilhaft; (*remark*) wenig schmeichelhaft

unflinching [ʌn'flɪntʃɪŋ] *adj* unerschrocken

unfold [ʌn'fəuld] *vt* (*sheets, map*)
auseinanderfalten ▷ *vi* (*situation, story*) sich
entfalten

unforeseeable [ʌnfɔː'siːəbl] *adj*
unvorhersehbar

unforeseen ['ʌnfɔː'siːn] *adj* unvorhergesehen

unforgettable [ʌnfə'getəbl] *adj* unvergesslich

unforgivable [ʌnfə'gɪvəbl] *adj* unverzeihlich

unformatted [ʌn'fɔːmætɪd] *adj* (*disk, text*)
unformatiert

unfortunate [ʌn'fɔːtʃənət] *adj* (*unlucky*)
unglücklich; (*regrettable*) bedauerlich; **it is ~
that ...** es ist bedauerlich, dass ...

unfortunately [ʌn'fɔːtʃənətlɪ] *adv* leider

unfounded [ʌn'faundɪd] *adj* (*allegations, fears*)
unbegründet

unfriendly [ʌn'frendlɪ] *adj* unfreundlich

unfulfilled [ʌnful'fɪld] *adj* (*ambition, prophecy*)
unerfüllt; (*person*) unausgefüllt

unfurl [ʌn'fəːl] *vt* (*flag etc*) entrollen

unfurnished [ʌn'fəːnɪʃt] *adj* unmöbliert

ungainly [ʌn'geɪnlɪ] *adj* (*person*) unbeholfen

ungodly [ʌn'gɔdlɪ] *adj* (*annoying*) heillos; **at
some ~ hour** zu nachtschlafender Zeit

ungrateful [ʌn'greɪtful] *adj* undankbar

unguarded [ʌn'gɑːdɪd] *adj*: **in an ~ moment**
in einem unbedachten Augenblick

unhappily [ʌn'hæpɪlɪ] *adv* (*miserably*)
unglücklich; (*unfortunately*) leider

unhappiness [ʌn'hæpɪnɪs] *n* Traurigkeit
f

unhappy [ʌn'hæpɪ] *adj* unglücklich; **~ about/
with** (*dissatisfied*) unzufrieden über +*acc*/mit

unharmed [ʌn'hɑːmd] *adj* (*person, animal*)
unversehrt

UNHCR *n abbr* (= *United Nations High Commission
for Refugees*) Flüchtlingskommission der Vereinten
Nationen

unhealthy [ʌn'helθɪ] *adj* (*person*) nicht gesund;
(*place*) ungesund; (*fig: interest*) krankhaft

unheard-of [ʌn'həːdɔv] *adj* (*unknown*)
unbekannt; (*outrageous*) unerhört

unhelpful [ʌn'helpful] *adj* (*person*) nicht
hilfreich; (*advice*) nutzlos

u

843

unhesitating [ʌn'hezɪteɪtɪŋ] adj (loyalty) bereitwillig; (reply, offer) prompt

unholy [ʌn'həʊlɪ] (inf) adj (fig: alliance) übel; (: mess) heillos; (: row) furchtbar

unhook [ʌn'hʊk] vt (unfasten) losmachen

unhurt [ʌn'hɜːt] adj unverletzt

unhygienic ['ʌnhaɪ'dʒiːnɪk] adj unhygienisch

UNICEF ['juːnɪsɛf] n abbr (= United Nations International Children's Emergency Fund) UNICEF f

unicorn ['juːnɪkɔːn] n Einhorn nt

unidentified [ʌnaɪ'dɛntɪfaɪd] adj (unknown) unbekannt; (unnamed) ungenannt; see also **UFO**

unification [juːnɪfɪ'keɪʃən] n Vereinigung f

unification process n Einigungsprozess m

uniform ['juːnɪfɔːm] n Uniform f ▷ adj (length, width etc) einheitlich

uniformity [juːnɪ'fɔːmɪtɪ] n Einheitlichkeit f

unify ['juːnɪfaɪ] vt vereinigen

unilateral [juːnɪ'lætərəl] adj einseitig

unimaginable [ʌnɪ'mædʒɪnəbl] adj unvorstellbar

unimaginative [ʌnɪ'mædʒɪnətɪv] adj fantasielos

unimpaired [ʌnɪm'pɛəd] adj unbeeinträchtigt

unimportant [ʌnɪm'pɔːtənt] adj unwichtig

unimpressed [ʌnɪm'prɛst] adj unbeeindruckt

uninhabited [ʌnɪn'hæbɪtɪd] adj unbewohnt

uninhibited [ʌnɪn'hɪbɪtɪd] adj (person) ohne Hemmungen; (behaviour) hemmungslos

uninjured [ʌn'ɪndʒəd] adj unverletzt

uninspiring [ʌnɪn'spaɪərɪŋ] adj wenig aufregend; (person) trocken, nüchtern

unintelligent [ʌnɪn'tɛlɪdʒənt] adj unintelligent

unintentional [ʌnɪn'tɛnʃənəl] adj unbeabsichtigt

unintentionally [ʌnɪn'tɛnʃnəlɪ] adv unabsichtlich

uninvited [ʌnɪn'vaɪtɪd] adj (guest) ungeladen

uninviting [ʌnɪn'vaɪtɪŋ] adj (food) unappetitlich; (place) wenig einladend

union ['juːnjən] n (unification) Vereinigung f; (also: **trade union**) Gewerkschaft f ▷ cpd (activities, leader etc) Gewerkschafts-; **the U~** (US) die Vereinigten Staaten

unionize ['juːnjənaɪz] vt (employees) gewerkschaftlich organisieren

Union Jack n Union Jack m

union shop n gewerkschaftspflichtiger Betrieb m

unique [juː'niːk] adj (object etc) einmalig; (ability, skill) einzigartig; **to be ~ to** charakteristisch sein für

unisex ['juːnɪsɛks] adj (clothes) Unisex-; (hairdresser) für Damen und Herren

UNISON ['juːnɪsn] n Gewerkschaft der Angestellten im öffentlichen Dienst

unison ['juːnɪsn] n: **in ~** (say, sing) einstimmig; (act) in Übereinstimmung

unit ['juːnɪt] n Einheit f; **production ~** Produktionsabteilung f; **kitchen ~** Küchen-Einbauelement nt

unitary ['juːnɪtrɪ] adj (state, system etc)

unit cost n (Comm) Stückkosten pl

unite [juː'naɪt] vt vereinigen ▷ vi sich zusammenschließen

united [juː'naɪtɪd] adj (agreed) einig; (country, party) vereinigt

United Arab Emirates npl: **the ~** die Vereinigten Arabischen Emirate pl

United Kingdom n: **the ~** das Vereinigte Königreich

United Nations npl: **the ~** die Vereinten Nationen pl

United States n: **the ~ (of America)** die Vereinigten Staaten pl (von Amerika)

unit price n (Comm) Einzelpreis m

unit trust (Brit) n (Comm) Investmenttrust m

unity ['juːnɪtɪ] n Einheit f

Univ. abbr = **university**

universal [juːnɪ'vɜːsl] adj allgemein

universe ['juːnɪvɜːs] n Universum nt

university [juːnɪ'vɜːsɪtɪ] n Universität f ▷ cpd (student, professor) Universitäts-; (education, year) akademisch

university degree n Universitätsabschluss m

unjust [ʌn'dʒʌst] adj ungerecht; (society) unfair

unjustifiable ['ʌndʒʌstɪ'faɪəbl] adj nicht zu rechtfertigen

unjustified [ʌn'dʒʌstɪfaɪd] adj (belief, action) ungerechtfertigt; (text) nicht bündig

unkempt [ʌn'kɛmpt] adj ungepflegt

unkind [ʌn'kaɪnd] adj (person, comment etc) unfreundlich

unkindly [ʌn'kaɪndlɪ] adv unfreundlich

unknown [ʌn'nəʊn] adj unbekannt; **~ to me, ...** ohne dass ich es wusste, ...; **~ quantity** (fig) unbekannte Größe

unladen [ʌn'leɪdn] adj (ship) ohne Ladung; (weight) Leer-

unlawful [ʌn'lɔːfʊl] adj gesetzwidrig

unleaded ['ʌn'lɛdɪd] adj (petrol) bleifrei, unverbleit; **I use ~** ich fahre bleifrei

unleash [ʌn'liːʃ] vt (fig: feeling, forces etc) entfesseln

unleavened [ʌn'lɛvnd] adj (bread) ungesäuert

unless [ʌn'lɛs] conj es sei denn; **~ he comes** wenn er nicht kommt; **~ otherwise stated** wenn nicht anders angegeben; **~ I am mistaken** wenn ich mich nicht irre; **there will be a strike ~ ...** es wird zum Streik kommen, es sei denn, ...

unlicensed [ʌn'laɪsnst] (Brit) adj (restaurant) ohne Schankkonzession

unlike [ʌn'laɪk] adj (not alike) unähnlich ▷ prep (different from) verschieden von; **~ me, she is very tidy** im Gegensatz zu mir ist sie sehr ordentlich

unlikelihood [ʌn'laɪklɪhʊd] n Unwahrscheinlichkeit f

unlikely [ʌn'laɪklɪ] adj unwahrscheinlich; (combination etc) merkwürdig; **in the ~ event of/that ...** im unwahrscheinlichen Fall +gen/dass ...

unlimited [ʌn'lɪmɪtɪd] adj unbeschränkt

unlisted ['ʌn'lɪstɪd] adj (Stock Exchange) nicht notiert; (US: Tel): **to be ~** nicht im Telefonbuch stehen

unlit [ʌn'lɪt] adj (room etc) unbeleuchtet

unload [ʌn'ləud] vt (box etc) ausladen; (car etc) entladen

unlock [ʌn'lɔk] vt aufschließen

unlucky [ʌn'lʌkɪ] adj (object) Unglück bringend; (number) Unglücks-; **to be ~** (person) Pech haben

unmanageable [ʌn'mænɪdʒəbl] adj (tool, vehicle) kaum zu handhaben; (person, hair) widerspenstig; (situation) unkontrollierbar

unmanned [ʌn'mænd] adj (station, spacecraft etc) unbemannt

unmarked [ʌn'mɑ:kt] adj (unstained) fleckenlos; (unscarred) nicht gezeichnet; (unblemished) makellos; **~ police car** nicht gekennzeichneter Streifenwagen m

unmarried [ʌn'mærɪd] adj unverheiratet

unmarried mother n ledige Mutter f

unmask [ʌn'mɑ:sk] vt (reveal) enthüllen

unmatched [ʌn'mætʃt] adj unübertroffen

unmentionable [ʌn'menʃnəbl] adj (topic, word) Tabu-; **to be ~** tabu sein

unmerciful [ʌn'mə:sɪful] adj erbarmungslos

unmistakable, unmistakeable [ʌnmɪs'teɪkəbl] adj unverkennbar

unmistakably, unmistakeably [ʌnmɪs'teɪkəblɪ] adv unverkennbar

unmitigated [ʌn'mɪtɪgeɪtɪd] adj (disaster etc) total

unnamed [ʌn'neɪmd] adj (nameless) namenlos; (anonymous) ungenannt

unnatural [ʌn'nætʃrəl] adj unnatürlich; (against nature: habit) widernatürlich

unnecessarily [ʌn'nesəsərɪlɪ] adv (worry etc) unnötigerweise; (severe etc) übertrieben

unnecessary [ʌn'nesəsərɪ] adj unnötig

unnerve [ʌn'nə:v] vt entnerven

unnoticed [ʌn'nəutɪst] adj: **to go** or **pass ~** unbemerkt bleiben

UNO ['ju:nəu] n abbr (= United Nations Organization) UNO f

unobservant [ʌnəb'zə:vənt] adj unaufmerksam

unobtainable [ʌnəb'teɪnəbl] adj (item) nicht erhältlich; **this number is ~** (Tel) kein Anschluss unter dieser Nummer

unobtrusive [ʌnəb'tru:sɪv] adj unauffällig

unoccupied [ʌn'ɔkjupaɪd] adj (seat) frei; (house) leer (stehend)

unofficial [ʌnə'fɪʃl] adj inoffiziell

unopened [ʌn'əupənd] adj ungeöffnet

unopposed [ʌnə'pəuzd] adj: **to be ~** (suggestion) nicht auf Widerstand treffen; (motion, bill) ohne Gegenstimmen angenommen werden

unorthodox [ʌn'ɔ:θədɔks] adj (also Rel) unorthodox

unpack [ʌn'pæk] vt, vi auspacken

unpaid [ʌn'peɪd] adj unbezahlt

unpalatable [ʌn'pælətəbl] adj (meal) ungenießbar; (truth) bitter

unparalleled [ʌn'pærəlɛld] adj beispiellos

unpatriotic ['ʌnpætrɪ'ɔtɪk] adj unpatriotisch

unplanned [ʌn'plænd] adj ungeplant

unpleasant [ʌn'plɛznt] adj unangenehm; (person, manner) unfreundlich

unplug [ʌn'plʌg] vt (iron, record player etc) den Stecker herausziehen +gen

unpolluted [ʌnpə'lu:tɪd] adj unverschmutzt

unpopular [ʌn'pɔpjuləʳ] adj unpopulär; **to make o.s. ~ (with)** sich unbeliebt machen (bei)

unprecedented [ʌn'prɛsɪdɛntɪd] adj noch nie da gewesen; (decision) einmalig

unpredictable [ʌnprɪ'dɪktəbl] adj (person, weather) unberechenbar; (reaction) unvorhersehbar

unprejudiced [ʌn'prɛdʒudɪst] adj unvoreingenommen

unprepared [ʌnprɪ'pɛəd] adj unvorbereitet

unprepossessing ['ʌnpri:pə'zɛsɪŋ] adj (person, place) unattraktiv

unpretentious [ʌnprɪ'tɛnʃəs] adj (building, person) schlicht

unprincipled [ʌn'prɪnsɪpld] adj (person) charakterlos

unproductive [ʌnprə'dʌktɪv] adj (land) unfruchtbar, ertragsarm; (discussion) unproduktiv

unprofessional [ʌnprə'fɛʃənl] adj unprofessionell

unprofitable [ʌn'prɔfɪtəbl] adj nicht profitabel, unrentabel

UNPROFOR n abbr (= United Nations Protection Force) UNPROFOR f; **~ troops** UNPROFOR-Truppen, UNO-Schutztruppen

unprotected ['ʌnprə'tɛktɪd] adj ungeschützt

unprovoked [ʌnprə'vəukt] adj (attack) grundlos

unpunished [ʌn'pʌnɪʃt] adj: **to go ~** straflos bleiben

unqualified [ʌn'kwɔlɪfaɪd] adj unqualifiziert; (disaster, success) vollkommen

unquestionably [ʌn'kwɛstʃənəblɪ] adv fraglos

unquestioning [ʌn'kwɛstʃənɪŋ] adj bedingungslos

unravel [ʌn'rævl] vt (also fig) entwirren

unreal [ʌn'rɪəl] adj (artificial) unecht; (peculiar) unwirklich

unrealistic ['ʌnrɪə'lɪstɪk] adj unrealistisch

unreasonable [ʌn'ri:znəbl] adj (person, attitude) unvernünftig; (demand, length of time) unzumutbar

unrecognizable [ʌn'rɛkəgnaɪzəbl] adj nicht zu erkennen

unrecognized [ʌn'rɛkəgnaɪzd] adj (talent etc) unerkannt; (Pol: regime) nicht anerkannt

unreconstructed ['ʌnri:kən'strʌktɪd] (esp US) adj (unwilling to accept change) unverbesserlich

unrecorded [ʌnrə'kɔ:dɪd] adj (piece of music etc) nicht aufgenommen; (incident, statement) nicht schriftlich festgehalten

unrefined [ʌnrə'faɪnd] adj (sugar, petroleum) nicht raffiniert

unrehearsed [ʌnrɪ'hə:st] adj (Theat etc) nicht

geprobt; (*spontaneous*) spontan

unrelated [ʌnrɪ'leɪtɪd] *adj* (*incidents*) ohne Beziehung; (*people*) nicht verwandt

unrelenting [ʌnrɪ'lentɪŋ] *adj* (*person, behaviour etc*) unnachgiebig

unreliable [ʌnrɪ'laɪəbl] *adj* unzuverlässig

unrelieved [ʌnrɪ'liːvd] *adj* ungemindert

unremitting [ʌnrɪ'mɪtɪŋ] *adj* (*efforts, attempts*) unermüdlich

unrepeatable [ʌnrɪ'piːtəbl] *adj* (*offer*) einmalig; (*comment*) nicht wiederholbar

unrepentant [ʌnrɪ'pɛntənt] *adj*: **to be ~ about sth** etw nicht bereuen; **he's an ~ Marxist** er bereut es nicht, nach wie vor Marxist zu sein

unrepresentative ['ʌnrɛprɪ'zɛntətɪv] *adj*: **~ (of)** nicht repräsentativ (für)

unrepresented ['ʌnrɛprɪ'zɛntɪd] *adj* nicht vertreten

unreserved [ʌnrɪ'zɜːvd] *adj* (*seat*) unreserviert; (*approval etc*) uneingeschränkt, vorbehaltlos

unreservedly [ʌnrɪ'zɜːvɪdlɪ] *adv* ohne Vorbehalt

unresponsive [ʌnrɪs'pɒnsɪv] *adj* unempfänglich

unrest [ʌn'rɛst] *n* Unruhen *pl*

unrestricted [ʌnrɪ'strɪktɪd] *adj* unbeschränkt; **to have ~ access to** ungehinderten Zugang haben zu

unrewarded [ʌnrɪ'wɔːdɪd] *adj* unbelohnt

unripe [ʌn'raɪp] *adj* unreif

unrivalled, (*US*) **unrivaled** [ʌn'raɪvəld] *adj* unübertroffen

unroll [ʌn'rəʊl] *vt* entrollen ▷ *vi* sich entrollen

unruffled [ʌn'rʌfld] *adj* unbewegt; (*hair*) unzerzaust

unruly [ʌn'ruːlɪ] *adj* (*child, behaviour*) ungebärdig; (*hair*) widerspenstig

unsafe [ʌn'seɪf] *adj* unsicher; (*machine, bridge, car etc*) gefährlich; **~ to eat/drink** ungenießbar

unsaid [ʌn'sɛd] *adj*: **to leave sth ~** etw ungesagt lassen

unsaleable, (*US*) **unsalable** [ʌn'seɪləbl] *adj* unverkäuflich

unsatisfactory ['ʌnsætɪs'fæktərɪ] *adj* unbefriedigend

unsatisfied [ʌn'sætɪsfaɪd] *adj* unzufrieden

unsavoury, (*US*) **unsavory** [ʌn'seɪvərɪ] *adj* (*fig: person, place*) widerwärtig

unscathed [ʌn'skeɪðd] *adj* unversehrt

unscientific ['ʌnsaɪən'tɪfɪk] *adj* unwissenschaftlich

unscrew [ʌn'skruː] *vt* losschrauben

unscrupulous [ʌn'skruːpjʊləs] *adj* skrupellos

unseat [ʌn'siːt] *vt* (*rider*) abwerfen; (*from office*) aus dem Amt drängen

unsecured ['ʌnsɪ'kjʊəd] *adj*: **~ creditor** nicht gesicherter Gläubiger *m*; **~ loan** Blankokredit *m*

unseeded [ʌn'siːdɪd] *adj* (*player*) nicht gesetzt

unseemly [ʌn'siːmlɪ] *adj* unschicklich

unseen [ʌn'siːn] *adj* (*person, danger*) unsichtbar

unselfish [ʌn'sɛlfɪʃ] *adj* selbstlos

unsettled [ʌn'sɛtld] *adj* (*person*) unruhig; (*future*) unsicher; (*question*) ungeklärt; (*weather*) unbeständig

unsettling [ʌn'sɛtlɪŋ] *adj* beunruhigend

unshakable, unshakeable [ʌn'ʃeɪkəbl] *adj* unerschütterlich

unshaven [ʌn'ʃeɪvn] *adj* unrasiert

unsightly [ʌn'saɪtlɪ] *adj* unansehnlich

unskilled [ʌn'skɪld] *adj* (*work, worker*) ungelernt

unsociable [ʌn'səʊʃəbl] *adj* ungesellig

unsocial [ʌn'səʊʃl] *adj*: **to work ~ hours** außerhalb der normalen Arbeitszeit arbeiten

unsold [ʌn'səʊld] *adj* unverkauft

unsolicited [ʌnsə'lɪsɪtɪd] *adj* unerbeten

unsophisticated [ʌnsə'fɪstɪkeɪtɪd] *adj* (*person*) anspruchslos; (*method, device*) simpel

unsound [ʌn'saʊnd] *adj* (*floor, foundations*) unsicher; (*policy, advice*) unklug; **of ~ mind** unzurechnungsfähig

unspeakable [ʌn'spiːkəbl] *adj* (*indescribable*) unsagbar; (*awful*) abscheulich

unspoken [ʌn'spəʊkn] *adj* (*word*) unausgesprochen; (*agreement etc*) stillschweigend

unstable [ʌn'steɪbl] *adj* (*piece of furniture*) nicht stabil; (*government*) instabil; (*person: mentally*) labil

unsteady [ʌn'stɛdɪ] *adj* (*step, voice, legs*) unsicher; (*ladder*) wack(e)lig

unstinting [ʌn'stɪntɪŋ] *adj* (*support*) vorbehaltlos; (*generosity*) unbegrenzt

unstuck [ʌn'stʌk] *adj*: **to come ~** (*label etc*) sich lösen; (*fig: plan, idea etc*) versagen

unsubstantiated ['ʌnsəb'stænʃɪeɪtɪd] *adj* (*rumour*) unbestätigt; (*accusation*) unbegründet

unsuccessful [ʌnsək'sɛsful] *adj* erfolglos; (*marriage*) gescheitert; **to be ~** keinen Erfolg haben

unsuccessfully [ʌnsək'sɛsfəlɪ] *adv* ohne Erfolg vergeblich

unsuitable [ʌn'suːtəbl] *adj* (*time*) unpassend; (*clothes, person*) ungeeignet

unsuited [ʌn'suːtɪd] *adj*: **to be ~ for** *or* **to sth** für etw ungeeignet sein

unsung [ʌn'sʌŋ] *adj*: **an ~ hero** ein unbesungener Held

unsure [ʌn'ʃʊəʳ] *adj* unsicher; **to be ~ of o.s.** unsicher sein

unsuspecting [ʌnsəs'pɛktɪŋ] *adj* ahnungslos

unsweetened [ʌn'swiːtnd] *adj* ungesüßt

unswerving [ʌn'swɜːvɪŋ] *adj* unerschütterlich

unsympathetic ['ʌnsɪmpə'θɛtɪk] *adj* (*showing little understanding*) abweisend; (*unlikeable*) unsympathisch; **to be ~ to(wards) sth** einer Sache *dat* ablehnend gegenüberstehen

untangle [ʌn'tæŋgl] *vt* entwirren

untapped [ʌn'tæpt] *adj* (*resources*) ungenutzt

untaxed [ʌn'tækst] *adj* (*goods, income*) steuerfrei

unthinkable [ʌn'θɪŋkəbl] *adj* undenkbar

unthinking [ʌn'θɪŋkɪŋ] *adj* (*uncritical*) bedenkenlos; (*thoughtless*) gedankenlos

untidy [ʌn'taɪdɪ] *adj* unordentlich

untie [ʌn'taɪ] *vt* (*knot, parcel*) aufschnüren;

(*prisoner, dog*) losbinden

until [ən'tɪl] *prep* bis +*acc*; (*after negative*) vor +*dat*
▷ *conj* bis; (*after negative*) bevor; ~ **now** bis jetzt;
~ **then** bis dann; **from morning ~ night**
von morgens bis abends; ~ **he comes** bis er
kommt

untimely [ʌn'taɪmlɪ] *adj* (*moment*) unpassend;
(*arrival*) ungelegen; (*death*) vorzeitig

untold [ʌn'təuld] *adj* (*joy, suffering, wealth*)
unermesslich; **the ~ story** die Hintergründe

untouched [ʌn'tʌtʃt] *adj* unberührt;
(*undamaged*) unversehrt; ~ **by** (*unaffected*)
unberührt von

untoward [ʌntə'wɔ:d] *adj* (*events, effects etc*)
ungünstig

untrained ['ʌn'treɪnd] *adj* unausgebildet; (*eye,
hands*) ungeschult

untrammelled [ʌn'træmld] *adj* (*person*)
ungebunden; (*behaviour*) unbeschränkt

untranslatable [ʌntrænz'leɪtəbl] *adj*
unübersetzbar

untried [ʌn'traɪd] *adj* (*policy, remedy*) unerprobt;
(*prisoner*) noch nicht vor Gericht gestellt

untrue [ʌn'tru:] *adj* unwahr

untrustworthy [ʌn'trʌstwə:ðɪ] *adj*
unzuverlässig

unusable [ʌn'ju:zəbl] *adj* (*object*) unbrauchbar;
(*room*) nicht benutzbar

unused¹ [ʌn'ju:zd] *adj* (*new*) unbenutzt

unused² [ʌn'ju:st] *adj*: **to be ~ to sth** an etw
acc nicht gewöhnt sein; **to be ~ to doing sth**
nicht daran gewöhnt sein, etw zu tun

unusual [ʌn'ju:ʒuəl] *adj* ungewöhnlich;
(*exceptional*) außergewöhnlich

unusually [ʌn'ju:ʒuəlɪ] *adv* (*large, high etc*)
ungewöhnlich

unveil [ʌn'veɪl] *vt* (*also fig*) enthüllen

unwanted [ʌn'wɒntɪd] *adj* unerwünscht

unwarranted [ʌn'wɒrəntɪd] *adj*
ungerechtfertigt

unwary [ʌn'wɛərɪ] *adj* unachtsam

unwavering [ʌn'weɪvərɪŋ] *adj* (*faith, support*)
unerschütterlich; (*gaze*) fest

unwelcome [ʌn'wɛlkəm] *adj* (*guest*)
unwillkommen; (*news*) unerfreulich; **to feel ~**
sich nicht willkommen fühlen

unwell [ʌn'wɛl] *adj*: **to be ~, to feel ~** sich
nicht wohlfühlen

unwieldy [ʌn'wi:ldɪ] *adj* (*object*) unhandlich;
(*system*) schwerfällig

unwilling [ʌn'wɪlɪŋ] *adj*: **to be ~ to do sth** etw
nicht tun wollen

unwillingly [ʌn'wɪlɪŋlɪ] *adv* widerwillig

unwind [ʌn'waɪnd] (*irreg: like* **wind**) *vt*
abwickeln ▷ *vi* sich abwickeln; (*relax*) sich
entspannen

unwise [ʌn'waɪz] *adj* unklug

unwitting [ʌn'wɪtɪŋ] *adj* (*accomplice*)
unwissentlich; (*victim*) ahnungslos

unworkable [ʌn'wə:kəbl] *adj* (*plan*)
undurchführbar

unworthy [ʌn'wə:ðɪ] *adj* unwürdig; **to be ~
of sth** einer Sache *gen* nicht wert *or* würdig

sein; **to be ~ to do sth** es nicht wert sein,
etw zu tun; **that remark is ~ of you** diese
Bemerkung ist unter deiner Würde

unwrap [ʌn'ræp] *vt* auspacken

unwritten [ʌn'rɪtn] *adj* (*law*) ungeschrieben;
(*agreement*) stillschweigend

unzip [ʌn'zɪp] *vt* aufmachen

 KEYWORD

up [ʌp] *prep*: **to be up sth** (oben) auf etw *dat*
sein; **to go up sth** (auf) etw *acc* hinaufgehen;
go up that road and turn left gehen Sie die
Straße hinauf und biegen Sie links ab
▷ *adv* **1** (*upwards, higher*) oben; **put it a bit
higher up** stelle es etwas höher; **up there**
dort oben; **up above** hoch oben
2: **to be up** (*out of bed*) auf sein; (*prices, level*)
gestiegen sein; (*building, tent*) stehen; **time's
up** die Zeit ist um *or* vorbei
3: **up to** (*as far as*) bis; **up to now** bis jetzt
4: **to be up to** (*depending on*) abhängen von;
it's up to you das hängt von dir ab; **it's not
up to me to decide** es liegt nicht bei mir, das
zu entscheiden
5: **to be up to** (*equal to*) gewachsen sein +*dat*;
he's not up to it (*job, task etc*) er ist dem
nicht gewachsen; **his work is not up to the
required standard** seine Arbeit entspricht
nicht dem gewünschten Niveau
6: **to be up to** (*inf: be doing*) vorhaben; **what
is he up to?** (*showing disapproval, suspicion*) was
führt er im Schilde?
▷ *n*: **ups and downs** (*in life, career*) Höhen und
Tiefen *pl*
▷ *vi* (*inf*): **she upped and left** sie sprang auf
und rannte davon
▷ *vt* (*inf: price*) heraufsetzen

up-and-coming [ʌpənd'kʌmɪŋ] *adj* (*actor,
company etc*) kommend

upbeat ['ʌpbi:t] *n* (*Mus*) Auftakt *m*; (*in
economy etc*) Aufschwung *m* ▷ *adj* (*optimistic*)
optimistisch

upbraid [ʌp'breɪd] *vt* tadeln

upbringing ['ʌpbrɪŋɪŋ] *n* Erziehung *f*

upcoming ['ʌpkʌmɪŋ] (*esp US*) *adj* kommend

update [ʌp'deɪt] *vt* aktualisieren

upend [ʌp'ɛnd] *vt* auf den Kopf stellen

upfront [ʌp'frʌnt] *adj* (*person*) offen ▷ *adv*: **20%
~** 20% (als) Vorschuss, 20% im Voraus

upgrade [ʌp'greɪd] *vt* (*house*) Verbesserungen
durchführen in +*dat*; (*job*) verbessern;
(*employee*) befördern; (*Comput*) nachrüsten

upheaval [ʌp'hi:vl] *n* Unruhe *f*

uphill ['ʌp'hɪl] *adj* bergaufwärts (führend);
(*fig: task*) mühsam ▷ *adv* (*push, move*)
bergaufwärts; (*go*) bergauf

uphold [ʌp'həuld] (*irreg: like* **hold**) *vt* (*law,
principle*) wahren; (*decision*) unterstützen

upholstery [ʌp'həulstərɪ] *n* Polsterung *f*

upkeep ['ʌpki:p] *n* (*maintenance*)
Instandhaltung *f*

u

up-market [ʌp'mɑːkɪt] adj anspruchsvoll

upon [ə'pɔn] prep (position) auf +dat; (motion) auf +acc

upper ['ʌpəʳ] adj obere(r, s) ▷ n (of shoe) Oberleder nt

upper class n: **the ~** die Oberschicht

upper-class ['ʌpə'klɑːs] adj vornehm

uppercut ['ʌpəkʌt] n Uppercut m

upper hand n: **to have the ~** die Oberhand haben

Upper House n (Pol) Oberhaus nt

uppermost ['ʌpəməust] adj oberste(r, s); **what was ~ in my mind** woran ich in erster Linie dachte

Upper Volta [-'vɔltə] n (formerly) Obervolta nt

upright ['ʌpraɪt] adj (vertical) vertikal; (fig: honest) rechtschaffen ▷ adv (sit, stand) aufrecht ▷ n (Constr) Pfosten m

uprising ['ʌpraɪzɪŋ] n Aufstand m

uproar ['ʌprɔːʳ] n Aufruhr m

uproarious [ʌp'rɔːrɪəs] adj (laughter) brüllend; (joke) brüllend komisch; (mirth) überwältigend

uproot [ʌp'ruːt] vt (tree) entwurzeln; (fig: people) aus der gewohnten Umgebung reißen; (: in war etc) entwurzeln

upset [vt, adj ʌp'sɛt, n 'ʌpsɛt] (irreg: like **set**) vt (knock over) umstoßen; (person: offend, make unhappy) verletzen; (routine, plan) durcheinanderbringen ▷ adj (unhappy) aufgebracht; (stomach) verstimmt ▷ n: **to have/get a stomach ~** (Brit) eine Magenverstimmung haben/bekommen; **to get ~** sich aufregen

upset price (US, Scot) n Mindestpreis m

upsetting [ʌp'sɛtɪŋ] adj (distressing) erschütternd

upshot ['ʌpʃɔt] n Ergebnis nt; **the ~ of it all was that ...** es lief schließlich darauf hinaus, dass ...

upside down ['ʌpsaɪd-] adv verkehrt herum; **to turn a room ~** (fig) ein Zimmer auf den Kopf stellen

upstage ['ʌp'steɪdʒ] adv (Theat) im Bühnenhintergrund ▷ vt: **to ~ sb** (fig) jdn ausstechen, jdm die Schau stehlen (inf)

upstairs [ʌp'stɛəz] adv (be) oben; (go) nach oben ▷ adj (room) obere(r, s); (window) im oberen Stock ▷ n oberes Stockwerk nt; **there's no ~** das Haus hat kein Obergeschoss

upstart ['ʌpstɑːt] (pej) n Emporkömmling m

upstream [ʌp'striːm] adv, adj flussaufwärts

upsurge ['ʌpsəːdʒ] n (of enthusiasm etc) Schwall m

uptake ['ʌpteɪk] n: **to be quick on the ~** schnell kapieren; **to be slow on the ~** schwer von Begriff sein

uptight [ʌp'taɪt] (inf) adj nervös

up-to-date ['ʌptə'deɪt] adj (modern) modern; (person) up to date

upturn ['ʌptəːn] n (in economy) Aufschwung m

upturned ['ʌptəːnd] adj: **~ nose** Stupsnase f

upward ['ʌpwəd] adj (movement) Aufwärts-; (glance) nach oben gerichtet

upwardly mobile ['ʌpwədlɪ-] adj: **to be ~** ein Aufsteigertyp m sein

upwards ['ʌpwədz] adv (move) aufwärts; (glance) nach oben; **~ of** (more than) über +acc

URA (US) n abbr (= Urban Renewal Administration) Stadtsanierungsbehörde

Ural Mountains ['juərəl-] npl: **the ~** (also: **the Urals**) der Ural

uranium [juə'reɪnɪəm] n Uran nt

Uranus [juə'reɪnəs] n Uranus m

urban ['əːbən] adj städtisch; (unemployment) in den Städten

urbane [əː'beɪn] adj weltgewandt

urbanization ['əːbənaɪ'zeɪʃən] n Urbanisierung f, Verstädterung f

urchin ['əːtʃɪn] (pej) n Gassenkind nt

Urdu ['uəduː] n Urdu nt

urge [əːdʒ] n (need, desire) Verlangen nt ▷ vt: **to ~ sb to do sth** jdn eindringlich bitten, etw zu tun; **to ~ caution** zur Vorsicht mahnen
  ▶ **urge on** vt antreiben

urgency ['əːdʒənsɪ] n Dringlichkeit f

urgent ['əːdʒənt] adj dringend; (voice) eindringend

urgently ['əːdʒəntlɪ] adv dringend

urinal ['juərɪnl] n (building) Pissoir nt; (vessel) Urinal nt

urinate ['juərɪneɪt] vi urinieren

urine ['juərɪn] n Urin m

URL n abbr (Comput: = uniform resource locator) URL-Adresse f, Internetadresse f

urn [əːn] n Urne f; (also: **tea urn**) Teekessel m

Uruguay ['juərəgwaɪ] n Uruguay nt

Uruguayan [juərə'gwaɪən] adj uruguayisch ▷ n (person) Uruguayer(in) m(f)

US n abbr (= United States) USA pl

us [ʌs] pl pron uns; (emphatic) wir; see also **me**

USA n abbr (= United States of America) USA f; (Mil: = United States Army) US-Armee f

usable ['juːzəbl] adj brauchbar

USAF n abbr (= United States Air Force) US-Luftwaffe f

usage ['juːzɪdʒ] n (Ling) (Sprach)gebrauch m

USB abbr of **universal serial bus**

USCG n abbr (= United States Coast Guard) Küstenwache der USA

USDA n abbr (= United States Department of Agriculture) US-Landwirtschaftsministerium

USDAW ['ʌzdɔː] (Brit) n abbr (= Union of Shop, Distributive, and Allied Workers) Einzelhandelsgewerkschaft

USDI n abbr (= United States Department of the Interior) US-Innenministerium

use [n juːs, vt juːz] n (using) Gebrauch m, Verwendung f; (usefulness, purpose) Nutzen m ▷ vt benutzen, gebrauchen; (phrase) verwenden; **in ~** in Gebrauch; **out of ~** außer Gebrauch; **to be of ~** nützlich or von Nutzen sein; **to make ~ of sth** Gebrauch von etw machen; **it's no ~** es hat keinen Zweck; **to have the ~ of sth** über etw acc verfügen können; **what's this ~d for?** wofür wird das gebraucht?; **to be ~d to sth** etw gewohnt sein; **to get ~d to sth** sich an etw *acc* gewöhnen; **she ~d to do it** sie hat es früher gemacht

▶ **use up** *vt* (*food, leftovers*) aufbrauchen; (*money*) verbrauchen

used [ju:zd] *adj* gebraucht; (*car*) Gebraucht-

useful ['ju:sful] *adj* nützlich; **to come in ~** sich als nützlich erweisen

usefulness ['ju:sfəlnıs] *n* Nützlichkeit *f*

useless ['ju:slıs] *adj* nutzlos; (*person: hopeless*) hoffnungslos

user ['ju:zəʳ] *n* Benutzer(in) *m(f)*; (*of petrol, gas etc*) Verbraucher(in) *m(f)*

user-friendly ['ju:zə'frendlı] *adj* benutzerfreundlich

usher ['ʌʃəʳ] *n* (*at wedding*) Platzanweiser *m* ▷ *vt:* **to ~ sb in** jdn hineinführen

usherette [ʌʃə'rɛt] *n* Platzanweiserin *f*

USIA *n abbr* (= *United States Information Agency*) US-Informations- und Kulturinstitut

USM *n abbr* (= *United States Mint*) US-Münzanstalt; (= *United States Mail*) US-Postbehörde

USN *n abbr* (= *United States Navy*) US-Marine *f*

USPHS *n abbr* (= *United States Public Health Service*) US-Gesundheitsbehörde

USPO *n abbr* (= *United States Post Office*) US-Postbehörde

USS *abbr* (= *United States Ship*) Namensteil von Schiffen der Kriegsmarine

USSR *n abbr* (*formerly:* = *Union of Soviet Socialist Republics*) UdSSR *f*

usu. *abbr* = **usually**

usual ['ju:ʒuəl] *adj* üblich, gewöhnlich; **as ~** wie gewöhnlich

usually ['ju:ʒuəlı] *adv* gewöhnlich

usurer ['ju:ʒərəʳ] *n* Wucherer *m*

usurp [ju:'zə:p] *vt* (*title, position*) an sich *acc* reißen

usury ['ju:ʒurı] *n* Wucher *m*

UT (*US*) *abbr* (*Post*) = *Utah*

utensil [ju:'tensl] *n* Gerät *nt*; **kitchen ~s** Küchengeräte *pl*

uterus ['ju:tərəs] *n* Gebärmutter *f*, Uterus *m*

utilitarian [ju:tılı'tɛərıən] *adj* (*building, object*) praktisch; (*Philosophy*) utilitaristisch

utility [ju:'tılıtı] *n* (*usefulness*) Nützlichkeit *f*; (*public utility*) Versorgungsbetrieb *m*

utility room *n* = Hauswirtschaftsraum *m*

utilization [ju:tılaı'zeıʃən] *n* Verwendung *f*

utilize ['ju:tılaız] *vt* verwenden

utmost ['ʌtməust] *adj* äußerste(r, s) ▷ *n:* **to do one's ~** sein Möglichstes tun; **of the ~ importance** von äußerster Wichtigkeit

utter ['ʌtəʳ] *adj* (*amazement*) äußerste(r, s); (*rubbish, fool*) total ▷ *vt* (*sounds, words*) äußern

utterance ['ʌtərəns] *n* Äußerung *f*

utterly ['ʌtəlı] *adv* (*totally*) vollkommen

U-turn ['ju:'tə:n] *n* (*also fig*) Kehrtwendung *f*

Uzbekistan [ʌzbɛkı'sta:n] *n* Usbekistan *nt*

u

Vv

V¹, v [vi:] *n* (*letter*) V *nt*, v *nt*; **V for Victor** = V wie Viktor

V² *abbr* (= *volt*) V

v. *abbr* = **verse**; (= *versus*) vs.; (= *vide*) s.

VA (*US*) *abbr* (*Post*) = Virginia

vac [væk] (*Brit: inf*) *n* = **vacation**

vacancy ['veɪkənsɪ] *n* (*Brit: job*) freie Stelle *f*; (*room in hotel etc*) freies Zimmer *nt*; **"no vacancies"** „belegt"; **have you any vacancies?** (*hotel*) haben Sie Zimmer frei?; (*office*) haben Sie freie Stellen?

vacant ['veɪkənt] *adj* (*room, seat, job*) frei; (*look*) leer

vacant lot (*US*) *n* unbebautes Grundstück *nt*

vacate [və'keɪt] *vt* (*house*) räumen; (*one's seat*) frei machen; (*job*) aufgeben

vacation [və'keɪʃən] (*esp US*) *n* (*holiday*) Urlaub *m*; (*Scol*) Ferien *pl*; **to take a ~** Urlaub machen; **on ~** im Urlaub

vacation course *n* Ferienkurs *m*

vaccinate ['væksɪneɪt] *vt*: **to ~ sb (against sth)** jdn (gegen etw) impfen

vaccination [væksɪ'neɪʃən] *n* Impfung *f*

vaccine ['væksi:n] *n* Impfstoff *m*

vacuum ['vækjum] *n* (*empty space*) Vakuum *nt*

vacuum cleaner *n* Staubsauger *m*

vacuum flask (*Brit*) *n* Thermosflasche® *f*

vacuum-packed ['vækjum'pækt] *adj* vakuumverpackt

vagabond ['vægəbɒnd] *n* Vagabund *m*

vagary ['veɪgərɪ] *n*: **the vagaries of** die Launen +*gen*

vagina [və'dʒaɪnə] *n* Scheide *f*, Vagina *f*

vagrancy ['veɪgrənsɪ] *n* Landstreicherei *f*; (*in towns, cities*) Stadtstreicherei *f*

vagrant ['veɪgrənt] *n* Landstreicher(in) *m(f)*; (*in town, city*) Stadtstreicher(in) *m(f)*

vague [veɪg] *adj* (*memory*) vage; (*outline*) undeutlich; (*look, idea, instructions*) unbestimmt; (*person: not precise*) unsicher; (: *evasive*) unbestimmt; **to look ~** (*absent-minded*) zerstreut aussehen; **I haven't the ~st idea** ich habe nicht die leiseste Ahnung

vaguely ['veɪglɪ] *adv* (*unclearly*) vage, unbestimmt; (*slightly*) in etwa

vagueness ['veɪgnɪs] *n* Unbestimmtheit *f*

vain [veɪn] *adj* (*person*) eitel; (*attempt, action*) vergeblich; **in ~** vergebens; **to die in ~**

umsonst sterben

vainly ['veɪnlɪ] *adv* vergebens

valance ['væləns] *n* (*of bed*) Volant *m*

valedictorian [vælɪdɪk'tɔːrɪən] (*US*) *n* (*Scol*) Abschiedsredner(in) bei der Schulentlassungsfeier

valedictory [vælɪ'dɪktərɪ] *adj* (*speech*) Abschieds-; (*remarks*) zum Abschied

valentine ['væləntaɪn] *n* (*also*: **valentine card**) Valentinsgruß *m*; (*person*) Freund/Freundin, dem/der man am Valentinstag einen Gruß schickt

valet ['vælɪt] *n* Kammerdiener *m*

valet parking *n* Einparken *nt* (*durch Hotelangestellte etc*)

valet service *n* Reinigungsdienst *m*

valiant ['vælɪənt] *adj* (*effort*) tapfer

valid ['vælɪd] *adj* (*ticket, document*) gültig; (*argument, reason*) stichhaltig

validate ['vælɪdeɪt] *vt* (*contract, document*) für gültig erklären; (*argument, claim*) bestätigen

validity [və'lɪdɪtɪ] *n* (*soundness*) Gültigkeit *f*

valise [və'li:z] *n* kleiner Koffer *m*

valley ['vælɪ] *n* Tal *nt*

valour, (*US*) **valor** ['vælə'] *n* Tapferkeit *f*

valuable ['væljuəbl] *adj* wertvoll; (*time*) kostbar

valuables ['væljuəblz] *npl* Wertsachen *pl*

valuation [vælju'eɪʃən] *n* (*of house etc*) Schätzung *f*; (*judgement of quality*) Einschätzung *f*

value ['vælju:] *n* Wert *m*; (*usefulness*) Nutzen *m* ▷ *vt* schätzen; **values** *npl* (*principles, beliefs*) Werte *pl*; **you get good ~ (for money) in that shop** in dem Laden bekommt man etwas für sein Geld; **to lose (in) ~** an Wert verlieren; **to gain (in) ~** im Wert steigen; **to be of great ~ (to sb)** (*fig*) von großem Wert (für jdn) sein

value-added tax [vælju:'ædɪd-] (*Brit*) *n* Mehrwertsteuer *f*

valued ['vælju:d] *adj* (*customer, advice*) geschätzt

valuer ['væljuə'] *n* Schätzer(in) *m(f)*

valve [vælv] *n* Ventil *nt*; (*Med*) Klappe *f*

vampire ['væmpaɪə'] *n* Vampir *m*

van [væn] *n* (*Aut*) Lieferwagen *m*; (*Brit: Rail*) Wa(g)gon *m*

V and A (*Brit*) *n abbr* (= *Victoria and Albert Museum*) Londoner Museum

vandal ['vændl] *n* Rowdy *m*

vandalism ['vændəlɪzəm] *n* Vandalismus *m*

vandalize ['vændəlaɪz] *vt* mutwillig zerstören

vanguard ['vænga:d] n (fig): **in the ~ of** an der Spitze +gen

vanilla [və'nɪlə] n Vanille f

vanilla ice cream n Vanilleeis nt

vanish ['vænɪʃ] vi verschwinden

vanity ['vænɪtɪ] n (of person) Eitelkeit f

vanity case n Kosmetikkoffer m

vantage point ['va:ntɪdʒ-] n Aussichtspunkt m; (fig): **from our ~** aus unserer Sicht

vaporize ['veɪpəraɪz] vt verdampfen ▷ vi verdunsten

vapour, (US) **vapor** ['veɪpəʳ] n (gas, steam) Dampf m; (mist) Dunst m

vapour trail n (Aviat) Kondensstreifen m

variable ['vɛərɪəbl] adj (likely to change: mood, quality, weather) veränderlich, wechselhaft; (able to be changed: temperature, height, speed) variabel ▷ n veränderlicher Faktor m; (Math) Variable f

variance ['vɛərɪəns] n: **to be at ~ (with)** nicht übereinstimmen (mit)

variant ['vɛərɪənt] n Variante f

variation [vɛərɪ'eɪʃən] n (change) Veränderung f; (different form: of plot, theme etc) Variation f

varicose ['værɪkəus] adj: **~ veins** Krampfadern pl

varied ['vɛərɪd] adj (diverse) unterschiedlich; (full of changes) abwechslungsreich

variety [və'raɪətɪ] n (diversity) Vielfalt f; (varied collection) Auswahl f; (type) Sorte f; **a wide ~ of ...** eine Vielfalt an +acc ...; **for a ~ of reasons** aus verschiedenen Gründen

variety show n Varietévorführung f

various ['vɛərɪəs] adj (reasons, people) verschiedene; **at ~ times** (different) zu verschiedenen Zeiten; (several) mehrmals, mehrfach

varnish ['va:nɪʃ] n Lack m ▷ vt (wood, one's nails) lackieren

vary ['vɛərɪ] vt verändern ▷ vi (be different) variieren; **to ~ with** (weather, season etc) sich ändern mit

varying ['vɛərɪɪŋ] adj unterschiedlich

vase [va:z] n Vase f

vasectomy [væ'sɛktəmɪ] n Vasektomie f

Vaseline® ['væsɪli:n] n Vaseline f

vast [va:st] adj (knowledge) enorm; (expense, area) riesig

vastly ['va:stlɪ] adv (superior, improved) erheblich

vastness ['va:stnɪs] n ungeheure Größe f

VAT [væt] (Brit) n abbr (= value-added tax) MwSt f

vat [væt] n Fass nt

Vatican ['vætɪkən] n: **the ~** der Vatikan

vatman ['vætmæn] (inf: irreg: like **man**) n ≈ Fiskus m (bezüglich Einbehaltung der Mehrwertsteuer)

vaudeville ['vəudəvɪl] n Varieté nt

vault [vɔ:lt] n (of roof) Gewölbe nt; (tomb) Gruft f; (in bank) Tresorraum m; (jump) Sprung m ▷ vt (also: **vault over**) überspringen

vaunted ['vɔ:ntɪd] adj: **much-~** viel gepriesen

VC n abbr = **vice-chairman**; (Brit) = Victoria Cross) Viktoriakreuz nt, höchste britische

Tapferkeitsauszeichnung

VCR n abbr = **video cassette recorder**

VD n abbr = **venereal disease**

VDU n abbr (Comput) = **visual display unit**

veal [vi:l] n Kalbfleisch nt

veer [vɪəʳ] vi (wind) sich drehen; (vehicle) ausscheren

veg (Brit: inf) n abbr = **vegetable; vegetables**

vegan ['vi:gən] n Veganer(in) m(f) ▷ adj radikal vegetarisch

vegeburger ['vɛdʒɪbə:gəʳ] n vegetarischer Hamburger m

vegetable ['vɛdʒtəbl] n (plant) Gemüse nt; (plant life) Pflanzen pl ▷ cpd (oil etc) Pflanzen-; (garden, plot) Gemüse-

vegetarian [vɛdʒɪ'tɛərɪən] n Vegetarier(in) m(f) ▷ adj vegetarisch

vegetate ['vɛdʒɪteɪt] vi (fig: person) dahinvegetieren

vegetation [vɛdʒɪ'teɪʃən] n (plants) Vegetation f

vegetative ['vɛdʒɪtətɪv] adj vegetativ

veggieburger ['vɛdʒɪbə:gəʳ] n = **vegeburger**

vehemence ['vi:ɪməns] n Vehemenz f, Heftigkeit f

vehement ['vi:ɪmənt] adj heftig

vehicle ['vi:ɪkl] n (machine) Fahrzeug nt; (fig: means) Mittel nt

vehicular [vɪ'hɪkjuləʳ] adj: **"no ~ traffic"** „kein Fahrzeugverkehr"

veil [veɪl] n Schleier m ▷ vt (also fig) verschleiern; **under a ~ of secrecy** unter einem Schleier von Geheimnissen

veiled [veɪld] adj (also fig: threat) verschleiert

vein [veɪn] n Ader f; (fig: mood, style) Stimmung f

Velcro® ['vɛlkrəu] n (also: **Velcro fastener** or **fastening**) Klettverschluss m

vellum ['vɛləm] n (writing paper) Pergament nt

velocity [vɪ'lɒsɪtɪ] n Geschwindigkeit f

velours [və'luəʳ] n Velours m

velvet ['vɛlvɪt] n Samt m ▷ adj (skirt, jacket) Samt-

vendetta [vɛn'dɛtə] n Vendetta f; (between families) Blutrache f

vending machine ['vɛndɪŋ-] n Automat m

vendor ['vɛndəʳ] n Verkäufer(in) m(f); **street ~** Straßenhändler(in) m(f)

veneer [və'nɪəʳ] n (on furniture) Furnier nt; (fig) Anstrich m

venerable ['vɛnərəbl] adj ehrwürdig; (Rel) hochwürdig

venereal [vɪ'nɪərɪəl] adj: **~ disease** Geschlechtskrankheit f

Venetian [vɪ'ni:ʃən] adj (Geog) venezianisch ▷ n (person) Venezianer(in) m(f)

Venetian blind n Jalousie f

Venezuela [vɛnɛ'zweɪlə] n Venezuela nt

Venezuelan [vɛnɛ'zweɪlən] adj venezolanisch ▷ n (person) Venezolaner(in) m(f)

vengeance ['vɛndʒəns] n Rache f; **with a ~** (fig: fiercely) gewaltig; **he broke the rules with a ~** er verstieß die Regeln – und nicht zu knapp

vengeful ['vɛndʒful] adj rachsüchtig

V

Venice ['vɛnɪs] n Venedig nt
venison ['vɛnɪsn] n Rehfleisch nt
venom ['vɛnəm] n (poison) Gift nt; (bitterness, anger) Gehässigkeit f
venomous ['vɛnəməs] adj (snake, insect) giftig; (look) gehässig
vent [vɛnt] n (also: **air vent**) Abzug m; (in jacket) Schlitz m ▷ vt (fig: feelings) abreagieren
ventilate ['vɛntɪleɪt] vt (building) belüften; (room) lüften
ventilation [vɛntɪ'leɪʃən] n Belüftung f
ventilation shaft n Luftschacht m
ventilator ['vɛntɪleɪtəʳ] n (Tech) Ventilator m; (Med) Beatmungsgerät nt
ventriloquist [vɛn'trɪləkwɪst] n Bauchredner(in) m(f)
venture ['vɛntʃəʳ] n Unternehmung f ▷ vt (opinion) zu äußern wagen ▷ vi (dare to go) sich wagen; **a business ~** ein geschäftliches Unternehmen; **to ~ to do sth** es wagen, etw zu tun
venture capital n Risikokapital nt
venue ['vɛnjuː] n (for meeting) Treffpunkt m; (for big events) Austragungsort m
Venus ['viːnəs] n Venus f
veracity [və'ræsɪtɪ] n (of person) Aufrichtigkeit f; (of evidence etc) Richtigkeit f
veranda, verandah [və'rændə] n Veranda f
verb [vəːb] n Verb nt
verbal ['vəːbl] adj verbal; (skills) sprachlich; (translation) wörtlich
verbally ['vəːbəlɪ] adv (communicate etc) mündlich, verbal
verbatim [vəː'beɪtɪm] adj wörtlich ▷ adv Wort für Wort
verbose [vəː'bəʊs] adj (person) wortreich; (writing) weitschweifig
verdict ['vəːdɪkt] n (Law, fig) Urteil nt; **~ of guilty/not guilty** Schuld-/Freispruch m
verge [vəːdʒ] n (Brit) n (of road) Rand m, Bankett nt; **"soft ~s"** (Brit: Aut) „Seitenstreifen nicht befahrbar"; **to be on the ~ of doing sth** im Begriff sein, etw zu tun
▷ **verge on** vt fus grenzen an +acc
verger ['vəːdʒəʳ] n (Rel) Küster m
verification [vɛrɪfɪ'keɪʃən] n (see vt) Bestätigung f; Überprüfung f
verify ['vɛrɪfaɪ] vt (confirm) bestätigen; (check) überprüfen
veritable ['vɛrɪtəbl] adj (real) wahr
vermin ['vəːmɪn] npl Ungeziefer nt
vermouth ['vəːməθ] n Wermut m
vernacular [və'nækjʊləʳ] n (of country) Landessprache f; (of region) Dialekt m
versatile ['vəːsətaɪl] adj vielseitig
versatility [və:sə'tɪlɪtɪ] n Vielseitigkeit f
verse [vəːs] n (poetry) Poesie f; (stanza) Strophe f; (in bible) Vers m; **in ~** in Versform
versed [vəːst] adj: **(well-)~ in** (gut) bewandert in +dat
version ['vəːʃən] n Version f
versus ['vəːsəs] prep gegen
vertebra ['vəːtɪbrə] (pl **-e**) n Rückenwirbel m

vertebrae ['vəːtɪbriː] npl of **vertebra**
vertebrate ['vəːtɪbrɪt] n Wirbeltier nt
vertical ['vəːtɪkl] adj vertikal, senkrecht ▷ n Vertikale f
vertically ['vəːtɪklɪ] adv vertikal
vertigo ['vəːtɪgəʊ] n Schwindelgefühle pl; **to suffer from ~** leicht schwindlig werden
verve [vəːv] n Schwung m
very ['vɛrɪ] adv sehr ▷ adj: **the ~ book which …** genau das Buch, das …; **the ~ last** der/die/das Allerletzte; **at the ~ least** allerwenigstens; **~ well/little** sehr gut/wenig; **~ much** sehr viel; (like, hope) sehr; **the ~ thought (of it) alarms me** der bloße Gedanke (daran) beunruhigt mich; **at the ~ end** ganz am Ende
vespers ['vɛspəz] npl (Rel) Vesper f
vessel ['vɛsl] n Gefäß nt; (Naut) Schiff nt; see **blood**
vest [vɛst] n (Brit: underwear) Unterhemd nt; (US: waistcoat) Weste f ▷ vt: **to ~ sb with sth, ~ sth in sb** jdm etw verleihen
vested interest ['vɛstɪd-] n (Comm) finanzielles Interesse nt; **to have a ~ in doing sth** ein besonderes Interesse daran haben, etw zu tun
vestibule ['vɛstɪbjuːl] n Vorhalle f
vestige ['vɛstɪdʒ] n Spur f
vestment ['vɛstmənt] n (Rel) Ornat nt
vestry ['vɛstrɪ] n Sakristei f
Vesuvius [vɪ'suːvɪəs] n Vesuv m
vet [vɛt] (Brit) n = **veterinary surgeon**; (US) = **veteran** ▷ vt (examine) überprüfen
veteran ['vɛtərn] n Veteran(in) m(f) ▷ adj: **she's a ~ campaigner for …** sie ist eine altgediente Kämpferin für …
veteran car n Oldtimer m (vor 1919 gebaut)
veterinarian [vɛtrɪ'nɛərɪən] (US) n = **veterinary surgeon**
veterinary ['vɛtrɪnərɪ] adj (practice, medicine) Veterinär-; (care, training) tierärztlich
veterinary surgeon (Brit) n Tierarzt m, Tierärztin f
veto ['viːtəʊ] (pl **-es**) n Veto nt ▷ vt ein Veto einlegen gegen; **to put a ~ on sth** gegen etw ein Veto einlegen
vetting ['vɛtɪŋ] n Überprüfung f
vex [vɛks] vt (irritate, upset) ärgern
vexed [vɛkst] adj (upset) verärgert; (question) umstritten
VFD (US) n abbr (= volunteer fire department) ≈ freiwillige Feuerwehr f
VG (Brit) n abbr (Scol etc: = very good) ≈ "sehr gut"
VHF abbr (Radio: = very high frequency) VHF
VI (US) abbr (Post) = Virgin Islands
via ['vaɪə] prep über +acc
viability [vaɪə'bɪlɪtɪ] n (see adj) Durchführbarkeit f; Rentabilität f
viable ['vaɪəbl] adj (project) durchführbar; (company) rentabel
viaduct ['vaɪədʌkt] n Viadukt m
vial ['vaɪəl] n Fläschchen nt
vibes [vaɪbz] npl (Mus) see **vibraphone** (inf: vibrations): **I get good/bad ~ from it/him** das/er macht mich an/nicht an

vibrant ['vaɪbrnt] adj (lively) dynamisch; (bright) lebendig; (full of emotion: voice) volltönend

vibraphone ['vaɪbrəfəun] n Vibrafon nt

vibrate [vaɪ'breɪt] vi (house) zittern, beben; (machine, sound etc) vibrieren

vibration [vaɪ'breɪʃən] n (act of vibrating) Vibrieren nt; (instance) Vibration f

vibrator [vaɪ'breɪtər] n Vibrator m

vicar ['vɪkər] n Pfarrer m

vicarage ['vɪkərɪdʒ] n Pfarrhaus nt

vicarious [vɪ'kɛərɪəs] adj (pleasure, experience) indirekt

vice [vaɪs] n (moral fault) Laster nt; (Tech) Schraubstock m

vice- [vaɪs] pref Vize-

vice-chairman [vaɪs'tʃɛəmən] n stellvertretender Vorsitzender m

vice chancellor (Brit) n (of university) ≈ Rektor m

vice president n Vizepräsident(in) m(f)

viceroy ['vaɪsrɔɪ] n Vizekönig m

vice squad n (Police) Sittendezernat nt

vice versa ['vaɪsɪ'və:sə] adv umgekehrt

vicinity [vɪ'sɪnɪtɪ] n: **in the ~ (of)** in der Nähe or Umgebung (+gen)

vicious ['vɪʃəs] adj (attack, blow) brutal; (words, look) gemein; (horse, dog) bösartig

vicious circle n Teufelskreis m

viciousness ['vɪʃəsnɪs] n Bösartigkeit f, Gemeinheit f

vicissitudes [vɪ'sɪsɪtju:dz] npl Wechselfälle pl

victim ['vɪktɪm] n Opfer nt; **to be the ~ of an attack** einem Angriff zum Opfer fallen

victimization ['vɪktɪmaɪ'zeɪʃən] n Schikanierung f

victimize ['vɪktɪmaɪz] vt schikanieren

victor ['vɪktər] n Sieger(in) m(f)

Victorian [vɪk'tɔ:rɪən] adj viktorianisch

victorious [vɪk'tɔ:rɪəs] adj (team) siegreich; (shout) triumphierend

victory ['vɪktərɪ] n Sieg m; **to win a ~ over sb** einen Sieg über jdn erringen

video ['vɪdɪəu] n (film, cassette, recorder) Video nt ▷ vt auf Video aufnehmen ▷ cpd Video-

video camera n Videokamera f

video cassette n Videokassette f

video cassette recorder n Videorekorder m

videodisc, videodisk ['vɪdɪəudɪsk] n Bildplatte f

video game n Videospiel nt, Telespiel nt

video nasty n Video mit übertriebenen Gewaltszenen und/oder pornografischem Inhalt

videophone ['vɪdɪəufəun] n Bildtelefon nt

video recorder n Videorekorder m

video recording n Videoaufnahme f

video tape n Videoband nt

vie [vaɪ] vi: **to ~ with sb/for sth** mit jdm/um etw wetteifern

Vienna [vɪ'enə] n Wien nt

Viennese [vɪə'ni:z] adj Wiener

Vietnam ['vjɛt'næm] n Vietnam nt

Viet Nam ['vjɛt'næm] n = **Vietnam**

Vietnamese [vjɛtnə'mi:z] adj vietnamesisch ▷ n inv (person) Vietnamese m, Vietnamesin f;

(Ling) Vietnamesisch nt

view [vju:] n (from window etc) Aussicht f; (sight) Blick m; (outlook) Sicht f; (opinion) Ansicht f ▷ vt betrachten; (house) besichtigen; **to be on ~** (in museum etc) ausgestellt sein; **in full ~ of** vor den Augen +gen; **to take the ~ that ...** der Ansicht sein, dass ...; **in ~ of the weather/ the fact that** in Anbetracht des Wetters/der Tatsache, dass ...; **in my ~** meiner Ansicht nach; **an overall ~ of the situation** ein allgemeiner Überblick über die Lage; **with a ~ to doing sth** mit der Absicht, etw zu tun

viewdata® ['vju:deɪtə] (Brit) n Bildschirmtext m

viewer ['vju:ər] n (person) Zuschauer(in) m(f); (viewfinder) Sucher m

viewfinder ['vju:faɪndər] n Sucher m

viewpoint ['vju:pɔɪnt] n (attitude) Standpunkt m; (place) Aussichtspunkt m

vigil ['vɪdʒɪl] n Wache f; **to keep ~** Wache halten

vigilance ['vɪdʒɪləns] n Wachsamkeit f

vigilance committee (US) n Bürgerwehr f

vigilant ['vɪdʒɪlənt] adj wachsam

vigilante [vɪdʒɪ'læntɪ] n Mitglied einer Selbstschutzorganisation oder Bürgerwehr ▷ adj (group, patrol) Bürgerwehr-, Selbstschutz-

vigorous ['vɪgərəs] adj (action, campaign) energisch, dynamisch; (plant) kräftig

vigour, (US) **vigor** ['vɪgər] n (of person, campaign) Energie f, Dynamik f

vile [vaɪl] adj abscheulich

vilify ['vɪlɪfaɪ] vt diffamieren

villa ['vɪlə] n Villa f

village ['vɪlɪdʒ] n Dorf nt

villager ['vɪlɪdʒər] n Dorfbewohner(in) m(f)

villain ['vɪlən] n (scoundrel) Schurke m; (in novel etc) Bösewicht m; (Brit: criminal) Verbrecher(in) m(f)

VIN (US) n abbr (= vehicle identification number) amtliches Kennzeichen nt

vinaigrette [vɪneɪ'grɛt] n Vinaigrette f

vindicate ['vɪndɪkeɪt] vt (person) rehabilitieren; (action) rechtfertigen

vindication [vɪndɪ'keɪʃən] n Rechtfertigung f

vindictive [vɪn'dɪktɪv] adj (person) nachtragend; (action) aus Rache

vine [vaɪn] n (Bot: producing grapes) Weinrebe f; (: in jungle) Rebengewächs nt

vinegar ['vɪnɪgər] n Essig m

vine grower n Weinbauer m

vine-growing ['vaɪngrəuɪŋ] adj (region) Weinbau- ▷ n Weinbau m

vineyard ['vɪnjɑ:d] n Weinberg m

vintage ['vɪntɪdʒ] n (of wine) Jahrgang m ▷ cpd (classic) klassisch; **the 1980 ~** (of wine) der Jahrgang 1980

vintage car n Oldtimer m (zwischen 1919 und 1930 gebaut)

vintage wine n erlesener Wein m

vinyl ['vaɪnl] n Vinyl nt; (records) Schallplatten pl

viola [vɪ'əulə] n Bratsche f

853

violate ['vaɪəleɪt] vt (agreement) verletzen; (peace) stören; (graveyard) schänden

violation [vaɪə'leɪʃən] n (of agreement etc) Verletzung f; **in ~ of** (rule, law) unter Verletzung +gen

violence ['vaɪələns] n Gewalt f; (strength) Heftigkeit f

violent ['vaɪələnt] adj (behaviour) gewalttätig; (death) gewaltsam; (explosion, criticism, emotion) heftig; **a ~ dislike of sb/sth** eine heftige Abneigung gegen jdn/etw

violently ['vaɪələntlɪ] adv heftig; (ill) schwer; (angry) äußerst

violet ['vaɪələt] adj violett ▷ n (colour) Violett nt; (plant) Veilchen nt

violin [vaɪə'lɪn] n Geige f, Violine f

violinist [vaɪə'lɪnɪst] n Violinist(in) m(f), Geiger(in) m(f)

VIP n abbr (= very important person) VIP m

viper ['vaɪpə^r] n Viper f

viral ['vaɪərəl] adj (disease, infection) Virus-

virgin ['və:dʒɪn] n Jungfrau f ▷ adj (snow, forest etc) unberührt; **she is a ~** sie ist Jungfrau; **the Blessed V~** die Heilige Jungfrau

virgin birth n unbefleckte Empfängnis f; (Biol) Jungfernzeugung f

virginity [və:'dʒɪnɪtɪ] n (of person) Jungfräulichkeit f

Virgo ['və:gəu] n (sign) Jungfrau f; **to be ~** Jungfrau sein

virile ['vɪraɪl] adj (person) männlich

virility [vɪ'rɪlɪtɪ] n (masculine qualities) Männlichkeit f

virtual ['və:tjuəl] adj (Comput, Phys) virtuell; **it's a ~ impossibility** es ist so gut wie unmöglich; **to be the ~ leader** eigentlich or praktisch der Führer sein

virtually ['və:tjuəlɪ] adv praktisch, nahezu; **it is ~ impossible** es ist so gut wie unmöglich

virtual reality n virtuelle Realität f

virtue ['və:tju:] n Tugend f; (advantage) Vorzug m; **by ~ of** aufgrund +gen

virtuosi [və:tju'əuzi] npl of **virtuoso**

virtuosity [və:tju'ɔsɪtɪ] n Virtuosität f

virtuoso [və:tju'əuzəu] (pl **~s** or **virtuosi**) n Virtuose m

virtuous ['və:tjuəs] adj tugendhaft

virulence ['vɪruləns] n (of disease) Bösartigkeit f; (hatred) Feindseligkeit f

virulent ['vɪrulənt] adj (disease) bösartig; (actions, feelings) feindselig

virus ['vaɪərəs] n (Med, Comput) Virus m or nt

visa ['vi:zə] n Visum nt

vis-à-vis [vi:zə'vi:] prep gegenüber

viscose ['vɪskəus] n (also Chem) Viskose f

viscount ['vaɪkaunt] n Viscount m

viscous ['vɪskəs] adj zähflüssig

vise [vaɪs] (US) n (Tech) = **vice**

visibility [vɪzɪ'bɪlɪtɪ] n (range of vision) Sicht(weite) f

visible ['vɪzəbl] adj sichtbar; **~ exports/ imports** sichtbare Ausfuhren/Einfuhren

visibly ['vɪzəblɪ] adv sichtlich

vision ['vɪʒən] n (sight) Sicht f; (foresight) Weitblick m; (in dream) Vision f

visionary ['vɪʒənrɪ] adj (with foresight) vorausblickend

visit ['vɪzɪt] n Besuch m ▷ vt besuchen; **a private/official ~** ein privater/offizieller Besuch

visiting ['vɪzɪtɪŋ] adj (speaker, team) Gast-

visiting card n Visitenkarte f

visiting hours npl Besuchszeiten pl

visiting professor n Gastprofessor(in) m(f)

visitor ['vɪzɪtə^r] n Besucher(in) m(f)

visitors' book ['vɪzɪtəz-] n Gästebuch nt

visor ['vaɪzə^r] n (of helmet etc) Visier nt

VISTA ['vɪstə] (US) n abbr (= Volunteers In Service To America) staatliches Förderprogramm für strukturschwache Gebiete

vista ['vɪstə] n Aussicht f

visual ['vɪzjuəl] adj (image etc) visuell; **the ~ arts** die darstellenden Künste

visual aid n Anschauungsmaterial nt

visual display unit n (Daten)sichtgerät nt

visualize ['vɪzjuəlaɪz] vt sich dat vorstellen

visually ['vɪzjuəlɪ] adv visuell; **~ appealing** optisch ansprechend; **~ handicapped** sehbehindert

vital ['vaɪtl] adj (essential) unerlässlich; (organ) lebenswichtig; (full of life) vital; **of ~ importance (to sb/sth)** von größter Wichtigkeit (für jdn/etw)

vitality [vaɪ'tælɪtɪ] n (liveliness) Vitalität f

vitally ['vaɪtəlɪ] adv: **~ important** äußerst wichtig

vital statistics npl (fig: of woman) Körpermaße pl; (of population) Bevölkerungsstatistik f

vitamin ['vɪtəmɪn] n Vitamin nt ▷ cpd (pill, deficiencies) Vitamin-

vitiate ['vɪʃɪeɪt] vt (spoil) verunreinigen

vitreous ['vɪtrɪəs] adj: **~ china** Porzellanemail nt; **~ enamel** Glasemail nt

vitriolic [vɪtrɪ'ɔlɪk] adj (fig: language, behaviour) hasserfüllt

viva ['vaɪvə] n (Scol: also: **viva voce** [-'vəutʃɪ]) mündliche Prüfung f

vivacious [vɪ'veɪʃəs] adj lebhaft

vivacity [vɪ'væsɪtɪ] n Lebendigkeit f

vivid ['vɪvɪd] adj (description) lebendig; (memory, imagination) lebhaft; (colour) leuchtend; (light) hell

vividly ['vɪvɪdlɪ] adv (describe) lebendig; (remember) lebhaft

vivisection [vɪvɪ'sɛkʃən] n Vivisektion f

vixen ['vɪksn] n (Zool) Füchsin f; (pej: woman) Drachen m

viz [vɪz] abbr (= videlicet) nämlich

VLF abbr (Radio: = very low frequency) VLF

V-neck ['vi:nɛk] n (also: **V-neck jumper** or **pullover**) Pullover m mit V-Ausschnitt

VOA n abbr (= Voice of America) Stimme f Amerikas

vocabulary [vəu'kæbjuləri] n (words known) Vokabular nt, Wortschatz m

vocal ['vəukl] adj (of the voice) stimmlich;

(*articulate*) lautstark

vocal cords *npl* Stimmbänder *pl*

vocalist ['vəʊkəlɪst] *n* Sänger(in) *m(f)*

vocals ['vəʊklz] *npl* (*Mus*) Gesang *m*

vocation [vəʊ'keɪʃən] *n* (*calling*) Berufung *f*; (*profession*) Beruf *m*

vocational [vəʊ'keɪʃənl] *adj* (*training, guidance etc*) Berufs-

vociferous [və'sɪfərəs] *adj* (*protesters, demands*) lautstark

vodka ['vɒdkə] *n* Wodka *m*

vogue [vəʊg] *n* (*fashion*) Mode *f*; (*popularity*) Popularität *f*; **in ~** in Mode

voice [vɔɪs] *n* (*also fig*) Stimme *f* ▷ *vt* (*opinion*) zum Ausdruck bringen; **in a loud/soft ~** mit lauter/leiser Stimme; **to give ~ to** Ausdruck verleihen +*dat*

voice mail *n* (*Comput*) Voicemail *f*

voice-over ['vɔɪsəʊvəʳ] *n* (*Film*)kommentar *m*

void [vɔɪd] *n* (*hole*) Loch *nt*; (*fig: emptiness*) Leere *f* ▷ *adj* (*invalid*) ungültig; **~ of** (*empty*) ohne

voile [vɔɪl] *n* Voile *m*

vol. *abbr* (= *volume*) Bd.

volatile ['vɒlətaɪl] *adj* (*person*) impulsiv; (*situation*) unsicher; (*liquid etc*) flüchtig

volcanic [vɒl'kænɪk] *adj* (*rock, eruption*) vulkanisch, Vulkan-

volcano [vɒl'keɪnəʊ] (*pl* **~es**) *n* Vulkan *m*

volition [və'lɪʃən] *n*: **of one's own ~** aus freiem Willen

volley ['vɒlɪ] *n* (*of gunfire*) Salve *f*; (*of stones, questions*) Hagel *m*; (*Tennis etc*) Volley *m*

volleyball ['vɒlɪbɔːl] *n* Volleyball *m*

volt [vəʊlt] *n* Volt *nt*

voltage ['vəʊltɪdʒ] *n* Spannung *f*; **high/low ~** Hoch-/Niederspannung *f*

volte-face ['vɒlt'fɑːs] *n* Kehrtwendung *f*

voluble ['vɒljʊbl] *adj* (*person*) redselig; (*speech*) wortreich

volume ['vɒljuːm] *n* (*space*) Volumen *nt*; (*amount*) Umfang *m*, Ausmaß *nt*; (*book*) Band *m*; (*sound level*) Lautstärke *f*; **~ one/two** (*of book*) Band eins/zwei; **his expression spoke ~s** sein Gesichtsausdruck sprach Bände

volume control *n* (*Radio, TV*) Lautstärkeregler *m*

volume discount *n* (*Comm*) Mengenrabatt *m*

voluminous [və'luːmɪnəs] *adj* (*clothes*) sehr weit; (*correspondence, notes*) umfangreich

voluntarily ['vɒləntrɪlɪ] *adv* freiwillig

voluntary ['vɒləntərɪ] *adj* freiwillig

voluntary liquidation *n* freiwillige Liquidation *f*

volunteer [vɒlən'tɪəʳ] *n* Freiwillige(r) *f(m)* ▷ *vt* (*information*) vorbringen ▷ *vi* (*for army etc*) sich freiwillig melden; **to ~ to do sth** sich

anbieten, etw zu tun

voluptuous [və'lʌptjʊəs] *adj* sinnlich, wollüstig

vomit ['vɒmɪt] *n* Erbrochene(s) *nt* ▷ *vt* erbrechen ▷ *vi* sich übergeben

voracious [və'reɪʃəs] *adj* (*person*) gefräßig; **~ appetite** Riesenappetit *m*

vortal ['vɔːtl] *n* (*Comput*) Vortal *nt*

vote [vəʊt] *n* Stimme *f*; (*votes cast*) Stimmen *pl*; (*right to vote*) Wahlrecht *nt*; (*ballot*) Abstimmung *f* ▷ *vt* (*elect*): **to be ~d chairman** *etc* zum Vorsitzenden *etc* gewählt werden; (*propose*): **to ~ that** vorschlagen, dass ▷ *vi* (*in election etc*) wählen; **to put sth to the vote, (take a) ~ on sth** über etw *acc* abstimmen; **~ of censure** Tadelsantrag *m*; **to pass a ~ of confidence/no confidence** ein Vertrauens-/Misstrauensvotum annehmen; **to ~ to do sth** dafür stimmen, etw zu tun; **to ~ yes/no** mit Ja/Nein stimmen; **to ~ Labour/Green** *etc* Labour/die Grünen *etc* wählen; **to ~ for** *or* **in favour of sth/against sth** für/gegen etw stimmen

vote of thanks *n* Danksagung *f*

voter ['vəʊtəʳ] *n* Wähler(in) *m(f)*

voting ['vəʊtɪŋ] *n* Wahl *f*

voting paper (*Brit*) *n* Stimmzettel *m*

voting right *n* Stimmrecht *nt*

vouch [vaʊtʃ]: **~ for** *vt fus* bürgen für

voucher ['vaʊtʃəʳ] *n* Gutschein *m*; (*receipt*) Beleg *m*; **gift ~** Geschenkgutschein *m*; **luncheon ~** Essensmarke *f*; **travel ~** Reisegutschein *m*

vow [vaʊ] *n* Versprechen *nt* ▷ *vt*: **to ~ to do sth/that** geloben, etw zu tun/dass; **to take** *or* **make a ~ to do sth** geloben, etw zu tun

vowel ['vaʊəl] *n* Vokal *m*

voyage ['vɔɪdʒ] *n* Reise *f*

voyeur [vwɑː'jəːʳ] *n* Voyeur(in) *m(f)*

voyeurism [vwɑː'jəːrɪzəm] *n* Voyeurismus *m*

VP *n abbr* = **vice president**

vs *abbr* (= *versus*) vs.

V-sign ['viːsaɪn] (*Brit*) *n*: **to give sb the ~** ≈ jdm den Vogel zeigen

VSO (*Brit*) *n abbr* (= *Voluntary Service Overseas*) *britischer Entwicklungsdienst*

VT (*US*) *abbr* (*Post*) = *Vermont*

vulgar ['vʌlgəʳ] *adj* (*remarks, gestures*) vulgär; (*decor, ostentation*) geschmacklos

vulgarity [vʌl'gærɪtɪ] *n* (*see adj*) Vulgarität *f*; Geschmacklosigkeit *f*

vulnerability [vʌlnərə'bɪlɪtɪ] *n* Verletzlichkeit *f*

vulnerable ['vʌlnərəbl] *adj* (*person, position*) verletzlich

vulture ['vʌltʃəʳ] *n* (*also fig*) Geier *m*

vulva ['vʌlvə] *n* Vulva *f*

V

Ww

W¹, w [ˈdʌblju:] n (letter) W nt, w nt; **W for William** ≈ W wie Wilhelm

W² [ˈdʌblju:] abbr (Elec: = watt) W; (= west) W

WA abbr (US: Post) = Washington; (Australia) = Western Australia

wad [wɔd] n (of cotton wool) Bausch m; (of paper, banknotes) Bündel nt

wadding [ˈwɔdɪŋ] n Füllmaterial nt

waddle [ˈwɔdl] vi watscheln

wade [weɪd] vi: **to ~ across** (a river, stream) waten durch; **to ~ through** (fig: a book) sich durchkämpfen durch

wafer [ˈweɪfəʳ] n (biscuit) Waffel f

wafer-thin [ˈweɪfəˈθɪn] adj hauchdünn

waffle [ˈwɔfl] n (Culin) Waffel f; (inf: empty talk) Geschwafel nt ▷ vi (in speech etc) schwafeln

waffle iron n Waffeleisen nt

waft [wɔft] vt, vi wehen

wag [wæg] vt (tail) wedeln mit; (finger) drohen mit ▷ vi (tail) wedeln; **the dog ~ged its tail** der Hund wedelte mit dem Schwanz

wage [weɪdʒ] n (also: **wages**) Lohn m ▷ vt: **to ~ war** Krieg führen; **a day's ~s** ein Tageslohn

wage claim n Lohnforderung f

wage differential n Lohnunterschied m

wage earner [-ə:nəʳ] n Lohnempfänger(in) m(f)

wage freeze n Lohnstopp m

wage packet n Lohntüte f

wager [ˈweɪdʒəʳ] n Wette f ▷ vt wetten

waggle [ˈwægl] vt (ears etc) wackeln mit ▷ vi wackeln

wagon, waggon [ˈwægən] n (horse-drawn) Fuhrwerk nt; (Brit: Rail) Wa(g)gon m

wail [weɪl] n (of person) Jammern nt; (of siren) Heulen nt ▷ vi (person) jammern; (siren) heulen

waist [weɪst] n (Anat, of clothing) Taille f

waistcoat [ˈweɪskəut] (Brit) n Weste f

waistline [ˈweɪstlaɪn] n Taille f

wait [weɪt] n Wartezeit f ▷ vi warten; **to lie in ~ for sb** jdm auflauern; **to keep sb ~ing** jdn warten lassen; **I can't ~ to ...** (fig) ich kann es kaum erwarten, zu ...; **to ~ for sb/sth** auf jdn/etw warten; **~ a minute!** Moment mal!; **"repairs while you ~"** „Reparaturen sofort"
▶ **wait behind** vi zurückbleiben
▶ **wait on** vt fus (serve) bedienen
▶ **wait up** vi aufbleiben; **don't ~ up for me**

warte nicht auf mich

waiter [ˈweɪtəʳ] n Kellner m

waiting [ˈweɪtɪŋ] n: **"no ~"** (Brit: Aut) „Halten verboten"

waiting list n Warteliste f

waiting room n (in surgery) Wartezimmer nt; (in railway station) Wartesaal m

waitress [ˈweɪtrɪs] n Kellnerin f

waive [weɪv] vt (rule) verzichten auf +acc

waiver [ˈweɪvəʳ] n Verzicht m

wake [weɪk] (pt **woke, ~d**, pp **woken, ~d**) vt (also: **wake up**) wecken ▷ vi (also: **wake up**) aufwachen ▷ n (for dead person) Totenwache f; (Naut) Kielwasser nt; **to ~ up to** (fig) sich dat bewusst werden +gen; **in the ~ of** (fig) unmittelbar nach, im Gefolge +gen; **to follow in sb's ~** (fig) hinter jdm herziehen

waken [ˈweɪkn] vt = **wake**

Wales [weɪlz] n Wales nt; **the Prince of ~** der Prinz von Wales

walk [wɔ:k] n (hike) Wanderung f; (shorter) Spaziergang m; (gait) Gang m; (path) Weg m; (in park, along coast etc) (Spazier)weg m ▷ vi gehen; (instead of driving) zu Fuß gehen; (for pleasure, exercise) spazieren gehen ▷ vt (distance) gehen, laufen; (dog) ausführen; **it's 10 minutes' ~ from here** es ist 10 Minuten zu Fuß von hier; **to go for a ~** spazieren gehen; **to slow to a ~** im Schritttempo weitergehen; **people from all ~s of life** Leute aus allen Gesellschaftsschichten; **to ~ in one's sleep** schlafwandeln; **I'd rather ~ than take the bus** ich gehe lieber zu Fuß als mit dem Bus zu fahren; **I'll ~ you home** ich bringe dich nach Hause
▶ **walk out** vi (audience) den Saal verlassen; (workers) in Streik treten
▶ **walk out on** (inf) vt fus (family etc) verlassen

walkabout [ˈwɔ:kəbaut] n: **the Queen/president went on a ~** die Königin/der Präsident mischte sich unters Volk or nahm ein Bad in der Menge

walker [ˈwɔ:kəʳ] n (person) Spaziergänger(in) m(f)

walkie-talkie [ˈwɔ:kɪˈtɔ:kɪ] n Walkie-Talkie nt

walking [ˈwɔ:kɪŋ] n Wandern nt; **it's within ~ distance** es ist zu Fuß erreichbar

walking holiday n Wanderurlaub m

walking shoes *npl* Wanderschuhe *pl*

walking stick *n* Spazierstock *m*

Walkman® ['wɔːkmən] *n* Walkman® *m*

walk-on ['wɔːkɔn] *adj* (*Theat*): **~ part** Statistenrolle *f*

walkout ['wɔːkaut] *n* (*of workers*) Streik *m*

walkover ['wɔːkəuvəʳ] (*inf*) *n* (*competition, exam etc*) Kinderspiel *nt*

walkway ['wɔːkweɪ] *n* Fußweg *m*

wall [wɔːl] *n* Wand *f*; (*exterior, city wall etc*) Mauer *f*; **to go to the ~** (*fig: firm etc*) kaputtgehen
  ▸ **wall in** *vt* (*enclose*) ummauern

wall cupboard *n* Wandschrank *m*

walled [wɔːld] *adj* von Mauern umgeben

wallet ['wɔlɪt] *n* Brieftasche *f*

wallflower ['wɔːlflauəʳ] *n* (*Bot*) Goldlack *m*; **to be a ~** (*fig*) ein Mauerblümchen sein

wall hanging *n* Wandbehang *m*

wallop ['wɔləp] (*Brit: inf*) *vt* verprügeln

wallow ['wɔləu] *vi* (*in mud, water*) sich wälzen; (*in guilt, grief*) schwelgen

wallpaper ['wɔːlpeɪpəʳ] *n* Tapete *f* ▸ *vt* tapezieren

wall-to-wall ['wɔːltə'wɔːl] *adj*: **~ carpeting** Teppichboden *m*

wally [wɔlɪ] (*inf*) *n* Trottel *m*

walnut ['wɔːlnʌt] *n* (*nut*) Walnuss *f*; (*tree*) Walnussbaum *m*; (*wood*) Nussbaumholz *nt*

walrus ['wɔːlrəs] (*pl ~ or* **walruses**) *n* Walross *nt*

waltz [wɔːlts] *n* Walzer *m* ▸ *vi* Walzer tanzen

wan [wɔn] *adj* bleich; (*smile*) matt

wand [wɔnd] *n* (*also:* **magic wand**) Zauberstab *m*

wander ['wɔndəʳ] *vi* (*person*) herumlaufen; (*mind, thoughts*) wandern ▸ *vt* (*the streets, the hills etc*) durchstreifen

wanderer ['wɔndərəʳ] *n* Wandervogel *m*

wandering ['wɔndrɪŋ] *adj* (*tribe*) umherziehend; (*minstrel, actor*) fahrend

wane [weɪn] *vi* (*moon*) abnehmen; (*influence etc*) schwinden

wangle ['wæŋgl] (*Brit: inf*) *vt* sich *dat* verschaffen

wanker ['wæŋkəʳ] (*inf!*) *n* Wichser *m*

wannabe, wannabee ['wɔnəbiː] (*inf*) *n* Möchtegern *m*; **James Bond ~(e)** Möchtegern-James-Bond *m*

want [wɔnt] *vt* (*wish for*) wollen; (*need*) brauchen ▸ *n* (*lack*): **for ~ of** aus Mangel an +*dat*; **wants** *npl* (*needs*) Bedürfnisse *pl*; **to ~ to do sth** etw tun wollen; **to ~ sb to do sth** wollen, dass jd etw tut; **to ~ in/out** herein-/hinauswollen; **you're ~ed on the phone** Sie werden am Telefon verlangt; **he is ~ed by the police** er wird von der Polizei gesucht; **a ~ of foresight** ein Mangel *m* an Voraussicht

want ads (*US*) *npl* Kaufgesuche *pl*

wanted ['wɔntɪd] *adj* (*criminal etc*) gesucht; **"cook ~"** „Koch/Köchin gesucht"

wanting ['wɔntɪŋ] *adj*: **to be found ~** sich als unzulänglich erweisen

wanton ['wɔntn] *adj* (*violence*) mutwillig; (*promiscuous: woman*) schamlos

WAP [wæp] *n abbr* (*Comput*: = *wireless application protocol*) WAP *nt*

war [wɔːʳ] *n* Krieg *m*; **to go to ~** (*start*) einen Krieg anfangen; **to be at ~ (with)** sich im Kriegszustand befinden (mit); **to make ~ (on)** Krieg führen (gegen); **a ~ on drugs/crime** ein Feldzug gegen Drogen/das Verbrechen

warble ['wɔːbl] *n* Trällern *nt* ▸ *vi* trällern

war cry *n* Kriegsruf *m*; (*fig: slogan*) Schlachtruf *m*

ward [wɔːd] *n* (*in hospital*) Station *f*; (*Pol*) Wahlbezirk *m*; (*Law: also:* **ward of court**) Mündel *nt* unter Amtsvormundschaft
  ▸ **ward off** *vt* (*attack, enemy, illness*) abwehren

warden ['wɔːdn] *n* (*of park etc*) Aufseher(in) *m(f)*; (*of jail*) Wärter(in) *m(f)*; (*Brit: of youth hostel*) Herbergsvater *m*, Herbergsmutter *f*; (*: in university*) Wohnheimleiter(in) *m(f)*; (*: also:* **traffic warden**) Verkehrspolizist(in) *m(f)*

warder ['wɔːdəʳ] (*Brit*) *n* Gefängniswärter(in) *m(f)*

wardrobe ['wɔːdrəub] *n* (*for clothes*) Kleiderschrank *m*; (*collection of clothes*) Garderobe *f*; (*Cine, Theat*) Kostüme *pl*

warehouse ['wɛəhaus] *n* Lager *nt*

wares [wɛəz] *npl* Waren *pl*

warfare ['wɔːfɛəʳ] *n* Krieg *m*

war game *n* Kriegsspiel *nt*

warhead ['wɔːhed] *n* Sprengkopf *m*

warily ['wɛərɪlɪ] *adv* vorsichtig

Warks (*Brit*) *abbr* (*Post*) = **Warwickshire**

warlike ['wɔːlaɪk] *adj* kriegerisch

warm [wɔːm] *adj* warm; (*thanks, applause, welcome, person*) herzlich; **it's ~** es ist warm; **I'm ~** mir ist warm; **to keep sth ~** etw warm halten; **with my ~est thanks/congratulations** mit meinem herzlichsten Dank/meinen herzlichsten Glückwünschen
  ▸ **warm up** *vi* warm werden; (*athlete*) sich aufwärmen ▸ *vt* aufwärmen

warm-blooded ['wɔːm'blʌdɪd] *adj* warmblütig

war memorial *n* Kriegerdenkmal *nt*

warm-hearted [wɔːm'hɑːtɪd] *adj* warmherzig

warmly ['wɔːmlɪ] *adv* (*applaud, welcome*) herzlich; (*dress*) warm

warmonger ['wɔːmʌŋgəʳ] (*pej*) *n* Kriegshetzer *m*

warmongering ['wɔːmʌŋgrɪŋ] (*pej*) *n* Kriegshetze *f*

warmth [wɔːmθ] *n* Wärme *f*; (*friendliness*) Herzlichkeit *f*

warm-up ['wɔːmʌp] *n* Aufwärmen *nt*; **~ exercise** Aufwärmübung *f*

warn [wɔːn] *vt*: **to ~ sb that ...** jdn warnen, dass ...; **to ~ sb of sth** jdn vor etw *dat* warnen; **to ~ sb not to do sth** or **against doing sth** jdn davor warnen, etw zu tun

warning ['wɔːnɪŋ] *n* Warnung *f*; **without (any) ~** (*suddenly*) unerwartet; (*without notifying*) ohne Vorwarnung; **gale ~** Sturmwarnung *f*

warning light *n* Warnlicht *nt*

warning triangle *n* (*Aut*) Warndreieck *nt*

warp [wɔːp] *vi* (*wood etc*) sich verziehen ▸ *vt*

W

(*fig: character*) entstellen ▷ *n* (*Textiles*) Kette *f*

warpath ['wɔːpɑːθ] *n*: **to be on the ~** auf dem Kriegspfad sein

warped [wɔːpt] *adj* (*wood*) verzogen; (*fig: character, sense of humour etc*)

warrant ['wɔrnt] *n* (*Law: for arrest*) Haftbefehl *m*; (: *also*: **search warrant**) Durchsuchungsbefehl *m* ▷ *vt* (*justify, merit*) rechtfertigen

warrant officer *n* (*Mil*) *Dienstgrad zwischen Offizier und Unteroffizier*

warranty ['wɔrəntɪ] *n* Garantie *f*; **under ~** (*Comm*) unter Garantie

warren ['wɔrən] *n* (*of rabbits*) Bau *m*; (*fig: of passages, streets*) Labyrinth *nt*

warring ['wɔːrɪŋ] *adj* (*nations*) Krieg führend; (*interests*) gegensätzlich; (*factions*) verfeindet

warrior ['wɔrɪər] *n* Krieger *m*

Warsaw ['wɔːsɔː] *n* Warschau *nt*

warship ['wɔːʃɪp] *n* Kriegsschiff *nt*

wart [wɔːt] *n* Warze *f*

wartime ['wɔːtaɪm] *n*: **in ~** im Krieg

wary ['wɛərɪ] *adj* (*person*) vorsichtig; **to be ~ about** *or* **of doing sth** Bedenken haben, etw zu tun

was [wɔz] *pt of* **be**

wash [wɔʃ] *vt* waschen; (*dishes*) spülen, abwaschen; (*remove grease, paint etc*) ausspülen ▷ *vi* (*person*) sich waschen ▷ *n* (*clothes etc*) Wäsche *f*; (*washing programme*) Waschgang *m*; (*of ship*) Kielwasser *nt*; **he was ~ed overboard** er wurde über Bord gespült; **to ~ over/ against sth** (*sea etc*) über/gegen etw *acc* spülen; **to have a ~** sich waschen; **to give sth a ~** etw waschen

▶ **wash away** *vt* wegspülen

▶ **wash down** *vt* (*wall, car*) abwaschen; (*food: with wine etc*) hinunterspülen

▶ **wash off** *vi* sich herauswaschen ▷ *vt* abwaschen

▶ **wash out** *vt* (*stain*) herauswaschen

▶ **wash up** *vi* (*Brit: wash dishes*) spülen, abwaschen; (*US: have a wash*) sich waschen

Wash. (*US*) *abbr* (*Post*) = Washington

washable ['wɔʃəbl] *adj* (*fabric*) waschbar; (*wallpaper*) abwaschbar

washbasin ['wɔʃbeɪsn], (*US*) **washbowl** ['wɔʃbəul] *n* Waschbecken *nt*

washcloth ['wɔʃklɔθ] (*US*) *n* Waschlappen *m*

washer ['wɔʃər] *n* (*on tap etc*) Dichtungsring *m*

washing ['wɔʃɪŋ] *n* Wäsche *f*

washing line (*Brit*) *n* Wäscheleine *f*

washing machine *n* Waschmaschine *f*

washing powder (*Brit*) *n* Waschpulver *nt*

Washington ['wɔʃɪŋtən] *n* Washington *nt*

washing-up [wɔʃɪŋ'ʌp] *n* Abwasch *m*; **to do the ~** spülen, abwaschen

washing-up liquid (*Brit*) *n* (Geschirr)spülmittel *nt*

wash-out ['wɔʃaut] (*inf*) *n* (*failed event*) Reinfall *m*

washroom ['wɔʃrum] (*US*) *n* Waschraum *m*

wasn't ['wɔznt] = **was not**

WASP, Wasp [wɔsp] (*US: inf*) *n abbr* (= *White Anglo-Saxon Protestant*) weißer angelsächsischer Protestant *m*

wasp [wɔsp] *n* Wespe *f*

waspish ['wɔspɪʃ] *adj* giftig

wastage ['weɪstɪdʒ] *n* Verlust *m*; **natural ~** natürliche Personalreduzierung

waste [weɪst] *n* Verschwendung *f*; (*rubbish*) Abfall *m* ▷ *adj* (*material*) Abfall-; (*left over: paper etc*) ungenutzt ▷ *vt* verschwenden; (*opportunity*) vertun; **wastes** *npl* (*area of land*) Wildnis *f*; **it's a ~ of money** das ist Geldverschwendung; **to go to ~** umkommen; **to lay ~** (*area, town*) verwüsten

▶ **waste away** *vi* verkümmern

wastebasket ['weɪstbɑːskɪt] (*US*) *n* = **wastepaper basket**

waste disposal unit (*Brit*) *n* Müllschlucker *m*

wasteful ['weɪstful] *adj* (*person*) verschwenderisch; (*process*) aufwendig

waste ground (*Brit*) *n* unbebautes Grundstück *nt*

wasteland ['weɪstlənd] *n* Ödland *nt*; (*in town*) ödes Gebiet *nt*; (*fig*) Einöde *f*

wastepaper basket ['weɪstpeɪpə-] (*Brit*) *n* Papierkorb *m*

waste pipe *n* Abflussrohr *nt*

waste products *npl* Abfallprodukte *pl*

waster ['weɪstər] *n* Verschwender(in) *m(f)*; (*good-for-nothing*) Taugenichts *m*

watch [wɔtʃ] *n* (*also*: **wristwatch**) (Armband)uhr *f*; (*surveillance*) Bewachung *f*; (*Mil, Naut: group of guards*) Wachmannschaft *f*; (*Naut: spell of duty*) Wache *f* ▷ *vt* (*look at*) betrachten; (: *match, programme*) sich *dat* ansehen; (*spy on, guard*) beobachten; (*be careful of*) aufpassen auf +*acc* ▷ *vi* (*look*) zusehen; **to be on ~** Wache halten; **to keep a close ~ on sb/ sth** jdn/etw genau im Auge behalten; **to ~ TV** fernsehen; **~ what you're doing!** pass auf!; **~ how you drive!** fahr vorsichtig!

▶ **watch out** *vi* aufpassen; **~ out!** Vorsicht!

watchband ['wɔtʃbænd] (*US*) *n* = **watchstrap**

watchdog ['wɔtʃdɔg] *n* (*dog*) Wachhund *m*; (*fig*) Aufpasser(in) *m(f)*

watchful ['wɔtʃful] *adj* wachsam

watchmaker ['wɔtʃmeɪkər] *n* Uhrmacher(in) *m(f)*

watchman ['wɔtʃmən] (*irreg: like* **man**) *n see* **night watchman**

watch stem (*US*) *n* (*winder*) Krone *f*, Aufziehrädchen *nt*

watchstrap ['wɔtʃstræp] *n* Uhrarmband *nt*

watchword ['wɔtʃwəːd] *n* Parole *f*

water ['wɔːtər] *n* Wasser *nt* ▷ *vt* (*plant*) gießen; (*garden*) bewässern ▷ *vi* (*eyes*) tränen; **a drink of ~** ein Schluck Wasser; **in British ~s** in britischen (Hoheits)gewässern; **to pass ~** (*urinate*) Wasser lassen; **my mouth is ~ing** mir läuft das Wasser im Mund zusammen; **to make sb's mouth ~** jdm den Mund wässrig machen

▶ **water down** *vt* (*also fig*) verwässern

water biscuit *n* Cracker *m*

water cannon n Wasserwerfer m

water closet (Brit: old) n Wasserklosett nt

watercolour, (US) watercolor ['wɔːtəkʌləʳ] n (picture) Aquarell nt; **watercolours** npl (paints) Wasserfarben pl

water-cooled ['wɔːtəkuːld] adj wassergekühlt

water-cooler ['wɔːtəkuːləʳ] n Wasserkühler m; **~ talks** (inf) Flurfunk m

watercress ['wɔːtəkrɛs] n Brunnenkresse f

waterfall ['wɔːtəfɔːl] n Wasserfall m

waterfront ['wɔːtəfrʌnt] n (at seaside) Ufer nt; (at docks) Hafengegend f

water heater n Heißwassergerät nt

water hole n Wasserloch nt

water ice n Fruchteis nt (auf Wasserbasis)

watering can ['wɔːtərɪŋ-] n Gießkanne f

water level n Wasserstand m; (of flood) Pegelstand m

water lily n Seerose f

water line n Wasserlinie f

waterlogged ['wɔːtəlɔgd] adj (ground) unter Wasser

water main n Hauptwasserleitung f

watermark ['wɔːtəmaːk] n (on paper) Wasserzeichen nt

watermelon ['wɔːtəmɛlən] n Wassermelone f

waterproof ['wɔːtəpruːf] adj (trousers, jacket etc) wasserdicht

water-repellent ['wɔːtərɪ'pɛlnt] adj Wasser abstoßend

watershed ['wɔːtəʃɛd] n (Geog) Wasserscheide f; (fig) Wendepunkt m

water-skiing ['wɔːtəskiːɪŋ] n Wasserski nt

water softener n Wasserenthärter m

water tank n Wassertank m

watertight ['wɔːtətaɪt] adj wasserdicht; (fig: excuse, case, agreement etc) hieb- und stichfest

water vapour n Wasserdampf m

waterway ['wɔːtəweɪ] n Wasserstraße f

waterworks ['wɔːtəwəːks] n Wasserwerk nt; (inf: fig: bladder) Blase f

watery ['wɔːtərɪ] adj (coffee, soup etc) wässrig; (eyes) tränend

watt [wɔt] n Watt nt

wattage ['wɔtɪdʒ] n Wattleistung f

wattle ['wɔtl] n Flechtwerk nt

wattle and daub n Lehmgeflecht nt

wave [weɪv] n (also fig) Welle f; (of hand) Winken nt ▷ vi (signal) winken; (branches) sich hin und her bewegen; (grass) wogen; (flag) wehen ▷ vt (hand, flag etc) winken mit; (gun, stick) schwenken; (hair) wellen; **short/medium/long ~** (Radio) Kurz-/Mittel-/Langwelle f; **the new ~** (Cine, Mus) die neue Welle f; **he ~d us over to his table** er winkte uns zu seinem Tisch hinüber; **to ~ goodbye to sb** jdm zum Abschied winken

▶ **wave aside** vt (fig: suggestion etc) zurückweisen

waveband ['weɪvbænd] n (Radio) Wellenbereich m

wavelength ['weɪvlɛŋθ] n (Radio) Wellenlänge

f; **on the same ~** (fig) auf derselben Wellenlänge

waver ['weɪvəʳ] vi (voice) schwanken; (eyes) zucken; (love, person) wanken

wavy ['weɪvɪ] adj (line) wellenförmig; (hair) wellig

wax [wæks] n Wachs nt; (for sealing) Siegellack m; (in ear) Ohrenschmalz nt ▷ vt (floor) bohnern; (car, skis) wachsen ▷ vi (moon) zunehmen

waxed [wækst] adj (jacket) gewachst

waxen [wæksn] adj (face) wachsbleich

waxworks ['wækswəːks] npl (models) Wachsfiguren pl ▷ n (place) Wachsfigurenkabinett nt

way [weɪ] n Weg m; (distance) Strecke f; (direction) Richtung f; (manner) Art f; (method) Art und Weise f; (habit) Gewohnheit f; **which ~ to ...?** wo geht es zu ...?; **this ~, please** hier entlang, bitte; **on the ~** (en route) auf dem Weg, unterwegs; **to be on one's ~** auf dem Weg sein; **to fight one's ~ through a crowd** sich acc durch die Menge kämpfen; **to lie one's ~ out of sth** sich aus etw herauslügen; **to keep out of sb's ~** jdm aus dem Weg gehen; **it's a long ~ away** es ist weit entfernt; (event) das ist noch lange hin; **the village is rather out of the ~** das Dorf ist recht abgelegen; **to go out of one's ~ to do sth** sich sehr bemühen, etw zu tun; **to be in the ~** im Weg sein; **to lose one's ~** sich verirren; **under ~** (project etc) im Gang; **the ~ back** der Rückweg; **to make ~ (for sb/sth)** (für jdn/etw) Platz machen; **to get one's own ~** seinen Willen bekommen; **put it the right ~ up** (Brit) stell es richtig herum hin; **to be the wrong ~ round** verkehrt herum sein; **he's in a bad ~** ihm geht es schlecht; **in a ~** in gewisser Weise; **in some ~s** in mancher Hinsicht; **no ~!** (inf) kommt nicht infrage!; **by the ~ ...** übrigens ...; **"~ in"** (Brit) „Eingang"; **"~ out"** (Brit) „Ausgang"; **"give ~"** (Brit: Aut) „Vorfahrt beachten"; **~ of life** Lebensstil m

waybill ['weɪbɪl] n Frachtbrief m

waylay ['weɪ'leɪ] (irreg: like lay) vt auflauern +dat; **to get waylaid** (fig) abgefangen werden

wayside ['weɪsaɪd] adj am Straßenrand ▷ n Straßenrand m; **to fall by the ~** (fig) auf der Strecke bleiben

way station (US) n (Rail) kleiner Bahnhof m; (fig) Zwischenstation f

wayward ['weɪwəd] adj (behaviour) eigenwillig; (child) eigensinnig

WC (Brit) n abbr (= water closet) WC nt

WCC n abbr (= World Council of Churches) Weltkirchenrat m

we [wiː] pl pron wir; **here we are** (arriving) da sind wir; (finding sth) na bitte

weak [wiːk] adj schwach; (tea, coffee) dünn; **to grow ~(er)** schwächer werden

weaken ['wiːkn] vi (resolve, person) schwächer werden; (influence, power) nachlassen ▷ vt schwächen

w

weak-kneed ['wi:k'ni:d] *adj (fig)* schwächlich

weakling ['wi:klɪŋ] *n* Schwächling *m*

weakly ['wi:klɪ] *adv* schwach

weakness ['wi:knɪs] *n* Schwäche *f*; **to have a ~ for** eine Schwäche haben für

wealth [welθ] *n* Reichtum *m*; *(of details, knowledge etc)* Fülle *f*

wealth tax *n* Vermögenssteuer *f*

wealthy ['welθɪ] *adj* wohlhabend, reich

wean [wi:n] *vt (also fig)* entwöhnen

weapon ['wepən] *n* Waffe *f*; **~s of mass destruction** Massenvernichtungswaffen *pl*

wear [weəʳ] *(pt* **wore**, *pp* **worn**) *vt (clothes, shoes, beard)* tragen; *(put on)* anziehen ▷ *vi (last)* halten; *(become old: carpet, jeans)* sich abnutzen ▷ *n (damage)* Verschleiß *m*; *(use)*: **I got a lot of/very little ~ out of the coat** der Mantel hat lange/nicht sehr lange gehalten; **baby~** Babykleidung *f*; **sports~** Sportkleidung *f*; **evening ~** Kleidung für den Abend; **to ~ a hole in sth** *(coat etc)* etw durchwetzen
▸ **wear away** *vt* verschleißen ▷ *vi (inscription etc)* verwittern
▸ **wear down** *vt (heels)* abnutzen; *(person, strength)* zermürben
▸ **wear off** *vi (pain etc)* nachlassen
▸ **wear on** *vi* sich hinziehen
▸ **wear out** *vt (shoes, clothing)* verschleißen; *(person, strength)* erschöpfen

wearable ['weərəbl] *adj* tragbar

wear and tear [-teəʳ] *n* Verschleiß *m*

wearer ['weərəʳ] *n* Träger(in) *m(f)*

wearily ['wɪərɪlɪ] *adv (say, sit)* lustlos, müde

weariness ['wɪərɪnɪs] *n (tiredness)* Müdigkeit *f*

wearisome ['wɪərɪsəm] *adj (boring)* langweilig; *(tiring)* ermüdend

weary ['wɪərɪ] *adj (tired)* müde; *(dispirited)* lustlos ▷ *vi*: **to ~ of sb/sth** jds/etw *gen* überdrüssig werden

weasel ['wi:zl] *n* Wiesel *nt*

weather ['weðəʳ] *n* Wetter *nt* ▷ *vt (storm, crisis)* überstehen; *(rock, wood)* verwittern; **what's the ~ like?** wie ist das Wetter?; **under the ~** *(fig: ill)* angeschlagen

weather-beaten ['weðəbi:tn] *adj (face)* vom Wetter gegerbt; *(building, stone)* verwittert

weathercock ['weðəkɔk] *n* Wetterhahn *m*

weather forecast *n* Wettervorhersage *f*

weatherman ['weðəmæn] *(irreg: like* **man**) *n* Mann *m* vom Wetteramt, Wetterfrosch *m* *(hum inf)*

weatherproof ['weðəpru:f] *adj* wetterfest

weather report *n* Wetterbericht *m*

weather vane [-veɪn] *n* = **weathercock**

weave [wi:v] *(pt* **wove**, *pp* **woven**) *vt (cloth)* weben; *(basket)* flechten ▷ *vi (fig: pt, pp* **weaved**: *move in and out)* sich schlängeln

weaver ['wi:vəʳ] *n* Weber(in) *m(f)*

weaving ['wi:vɪŋ] *n* Weberei *f*

web [web] *n (also fig)* Netz *nt*; *(Comput)* **the Web** das Web, das Internet; *(on duck's foot)* Schwimmhaut *f*

webbed ['webd] *adj (foot)* Schwimm-

webbing ['webɪŋ] *n (on chair)* Gewebe *nt*

website ['websaɪt] *n (Comput)* Website *f*, Webseite *f*

wed [wed] *(pt, pp* **~ded**) *vt, vi* heiraten ▷ *n*: **the newly-~s** die Jungvermählten *pl*

Wed. *abbr (= Wednesday)* Mi.

we'd [wi:d] = **we had**; **we would**

wedded ['wedɪd] *pt, pp of* **wed** ▷ *adj*: **to be ~ to sth** *(idea etc)* mit etw eng verbunden sein

wedding ['wedɪŋ] *n* Hochzeit *f*; **silver/golden ~** silberne/goldene Hochzeit

wedding day *n* Hochzeitstag *m*

wedding dress *n* Hochzeitskleid *nt*

wedding present *n* Hochzeitsgeschenk *nt*

wedding ring *n* Trauring *m*

wedge [wedʒ] *n* Keil *m*; *(of cake)* Stück *nt* ▷ *vt (fasten)* festklemmen; *(pack tightly)* einkeilen

wedge-heeled shoes ['wedʒhi:ld-] *npl* Schuhe *pl* mit Keilabsätzen

wedlock ['wedlɔk] *n* Ehe *f*

Wednesday ['wednzdɪ] *n* Mittwoch *m*; *see also* **Tuesday**

wee [wi:] *(Scot) adj* klein

weed [wi:d] *n (Bot)* Unkraut *nt*; *(pej: person)* Schwächling *m* ▷ *vt (garden)* jäten
▸ **weed out** *vt (fig)* aussondern

weedkiller ['wi:dkɪləʳ] *n* Unkrautvertilger *m*

weedy ['wi:dɪ] *adj (person)* schwächlich

week [wi:k] *n* Woche *f*; **once/twice a ~** einmal/zweimal die Woche; **in two ~s' time** in zwei Wochen; **a ~ today/on Friday** heute/Freitag in einer Woche

weekday ['wi:kdeɪ] *n* Wochentag *m*; *(Comm: Monday to Saturday)* Werktag *m*; **on ~s** an Wochentagen/Werktagen

weekend [wi:k'end] *n* Wochenende *nt*; **this/next/last ~** an diesem/am nächsten/am letzten Wochenende; **what are you doing at the ~?** was machen Sie am Wochenende?; **open at ~s** an Wochenenden geöffnet

weekly ['wi:klɪ] *adv* wöchentlich ▷ *adj (newspaper)* Wochen- ▷ *n (newspaper)* Wochenzeitung *f*; *(magazine)* Wochenzeitschrift *f*

weep [wi:p] *(pt, pp* **wept**) *vi (person)* weinen; *(wound)* nässen

weeping willow ['wi:pɪŋ-] *n (tree)* Trauerweide *f*

weepy ['wi:pɪ] *adj (person)* weinerlich; *(film)* rührselig ▷ *n (film etc)* Schmachtfetzen *m*

weigh [weɪ] *vt* wiegen; *(fig: evidence, risks)* abwägen ▷ *vi* wiegen; **to ~ anchor** den Anker lichten
▸ **weigh down** *vt* niederdrücken
▸ **weigh out** *vt (goods)* auswiegen
▸ **weigh up** *vt (person, offer, risk)* abschätzen

weighbridge ['weɪbrɪdʒ] *n* Brückenwaage *f*

weighing machine ['weɪɪŋ-] *n* Waage *f*

weight [weɪt] *n* Gewicht *nt* ▷ *vt (fig)*: **to be ~ed in favour of sb/sth** jdn/etw begünstigen; **to be sold by ~** nach Gewicht verkauft werden; **to lose ~** abnehmen; **to put on ~** zunehmen; **~s and measures** Maße und Gewichte

weighting ['weɪtɪŋ] n (allowance) Zulage f
weightlessness ['weɪtlɪsnɪs] n
Schwerelosigkeit f
weightlifter ['weɪtlɪftə^r] n Gewichtheber m
weight limit n Gewichtsbeschränkung f
weight training n Krafttraining nt
weighty ['weɪtɪ] adj schwer; (fig: important)
gewichtig
weir [wɪə^r] n (in river) Wehr nt
weird [wɪəd] adj (object, situation, effect) komisch;
(person) seltsam
weirdo ['wɪədəu] (inf) n verrückter Typ m
welcome ['welkəm] adj willkommen ▷ n
Willkommen nt ▷ vt begrüßen, willkommen
heißen; **~ to London!** willkommen in
London!; **to make sb ~** jdn freundlich
aufnehmen; **you're ~ to try** du kannst es
gern versuchen; **thank you — you're ~!**
danke — nichts zu danken!
welcoming ['welkəmɪŋ] adj (smile, room)
einladend; (person) freundlich
weld [weld] n Schweißnaht f ▷ vt schweißen
welder ['weldə^r] n (person) Schweißer(in) m(f)
welding ['weldɪŋ] n Schweißen nt
welfare ['welfeə^r] n (well-being) Wohl nt; (social
aid) Sozialhilfe f
welfare state n Wohlfahrtsstaat m
welfare work n Fürsorgearbeit f
well [wel] n (for water) Brunnen m; (oil well)
Quelle f ▷ adv gut; (for emphasis with adj)
durchaus ▷ adj: **to be ~** (person) gesund sein
▷ excl nun!, na!; **as ~** (in addition) ebenfalls;
you might as ~ tell me sag es mir ruhig; **he
did as ~ as he could** er machte es so gut er
konnte; **pretty as ~ as rich** sowohl hübsch
als auch reich; **~ done!** gut gemacht!; **to
do ~** (person) gut vorankommen; (business)
gut gehen; **~ before dawn** lange vor
Tagesanbruch; **~ over 40** weit über 40; **I
don't feel ~** ich fühle mich nicht gut or wohl;
get ~ soon! gute Besserung!; **~, as I was
saying ...** also, wie ich bereits sagte, ...
▷ **well up** vi (tears, emotions) aufsteigen
we'll [wi:l] = **we will; we shall**
well-behaved ['welbɪ'heɪvd] adj wohlerzogen
well-being ['wel'bi:ɪŋ] n Wohl(ergehen) nt
well-bred ['wel'bred] adj (person) gut erzogen
well-built ['wel'bɪlt] adj gut gebaut
well-chosen ['wel'tʃəuzn] adj gut gewählt
well-deserved ['weldɪ'zə:vd] adj wohlverdient
well-developed ['weldɪ'veləpt] adj gut
entwickelt
well-disposed ['wel'dɪspəuzd] adj: **~ to(wards)**
freundlich gesonnen +dat
well-dressed ['wel'drest] adj gut gekleidet
well-earned ['wel'ə:nd] adj (rest) wohlverdient
well-groomed ['wel'gru:md] adj gepflegt
well-heeled ['wel'hi:ld] (inf) adj betucht
well-informed ['welɪn'fɔ:md] adj gut
informiert
Wellington ['welɪŋtən] n (Geog) Wellington nt
wellingtons ['welɪŋtənz] npl (also: **wellington
boots**) Gummistiefel pl

well-kept ['wel'kept] adj (house, grounds)
gepflegt; (secret) gut gehütet
well-known ['wel'nəun] adj wohlbekannt
well-mannered ['wel'mænəd] adj
wohlerzogen
well-meaning ['wel'mi:nɪŋ] adj (person)
wohlmeinend; (offer etc) gut gemeint
well-nigh ['wel'naɪ] adv: **~ impossible**
geradezu unmöglich
well-off ['wel'ɔf] adj (rich) begütert
well-read ['wel'red] adj belesen
well-spoken ['wel'spəukn] adj: **to be ~** sich gut
or gewandt ausdrücken
well-stocked ['wel'stɔkt] adj gut bestückt
well-timed ['wel'taɪmd] adj gut abgepasst
well-to-do ['weltə'du:] adj wohlhabend
well-wisher ['welwɪʃə^r] n (friend, admirer)
wohlmeinender Mensch m; **scores of ~s
had gathered** eine große Gefolgschaft hatte
sich versammelt; **letters from ~s** Briefe von
Leuten, die es gut meinen
well-woman clinic ['welwumən-] n ≈
Frauensprechstunde f
Welsh [welʃ] adj walisisch ▷ n (Ling) Walisisch
nt; **the Welsh** npl die Waliser pl
Welshman ['welʃmən] (irreg: like **man**) n
Waliser m
Welsh rarebit n überbackenes Käsebrot nt
Welshwoman ['welʃwumən] (irreg: like **woman**)
n Waliserin f
welter ['weltə^r] n: **a ~ of** eine Flut von
went [went] pt of **go**
wept [wept] pt, pp of **weep**
were [wə:^r] pt of **be**
we're [wɪə^r] = **we are**
weren't [wə:nt] = **were not**
werewolf ['wɪəwulf] (pl **werewolves**) n
Werwolf m
werewolves ['wɪəwulvz] npl of **werewolf**
west [west] n Westen m ▷ adj (wind, side, coast)
West-, westlich ▷ adv (to or towards the west)
westwärts; **the W~** (Pol) der Westen
westbound ['westbaund] adj (traffic,
carriageway) in Richtung Westen
West Country (Brit) n: **the ~** Südwestengland
nt
westerly ['westəlɪ] adj westlich
western ['westən] adj westlich ▷ n (Cine)
Western m
westerner ['westənə^r] n Abendländer(in) m(f)
westernized ['westənaɪzd] adj (society etc)
verwestlicht
West German adj westdeutsch ▷ n (person)
Westdeutsche(r) f(m)
West Germany n (formerly) Bundesrepublik f
Deutschland
West Indian adj westindisch ▷ n (person)
Westinder(in) m(f)
West Indies [-'ɪndɪz] npl: **the ~** Westindien nt
Westminster ['westmɪnstə^r] n Westminster
nt; (parliament) das britische Parlament
westward ['westwəd], **westwards**
['westwədz] adv westwärts

W

861

wet [wɛt] adj nass ▷ n (Brit: Pol) Gemäßigte(r) f(m), Waschlappen m (pej); **to get** ~ nass werden; **"~ paint"** „frisch gestrichen"; **to be a ~ blanket** (fig: pej: person) ein(e) Spielverderber(in) m(f) sein; **to ~ one's pants/o.s.** sich dat in die Hosen machen

wetness ['wɛtnɪs] n Nässe f; (of climate) Feuchtigkeit f

wet suit n Taucheranzug m

we've [wiːv] = **we have**

whack [wæk] vt schlagen

whacked [wækt] (Brit: inf) adj (exhausted) erschlagen

whale [weɪl] n Wal m

whaler ['weɪləʳ] n Walfänger m

whaling ['weɪlɪŋ] n Walfang m

wharf [wɔːf] (pl **wharves**) n Kai m

wharves [wɔːvz] npl of **wharf**

 KEYWORD

what [wɒt] adj **1** (in direct/indirect questions) welche(r, s); **what colour/shape is it?** welche Farbe/Form hat es?; **for what reason?** aus welchem Grund?
2 (in exclamations) was für ein(e); **what a mess!** was für ein Durcheinander!; **what a fool I am!** was bin ich doch (für) ein Idiot!
▷ pron (interrogative, relative) was; **what are you doing?** was machst du?; **what are you talking about?** wovon redest du?; **what is it called?** wie heißt das?; **what about me?** und ich?; **what about a cup of tea?** wie wärs mit einer Tasse Tee?; **what about going to the cinema?** sollen wir ins Kino gehen?; **I saw what you did/what was on the table** ich habe gesehen, was du getan hast/was auf dem Tisch war; **tell me what you're thinking about** sag mir, woran du denkst
▷ excl (disbelieving) was, wie; **what, no coffee!** was or wie, kein Kaffee?

whatever [wɒt'ɛvəʳ] adj: ~ **book** welches Buch auch immer ▷ pron: **do ~ is necessary/you want** tun Sie, was nötig ist/was immer Sie wollen; ~ **happens** was auch passiert; **no reason ~ or whatsoever** überhaupt kein Grund; **nothing ~ or whatsoever** überhaupt nichts

whatsoever [wɒtsəu'ɛvəʳ] adj = **whatever**

wheat [wiːt] n Weizen m

wheatgerm ['wiːtdʒɜːm] n Weizenkeim m

wheatmeal ['wiːtmiːl] n Weizenmehl nt

wheedle ['wiːdl] vt: **to ~ sb into doing sth** jdn beschwatzen, etw zu tun; **to ~ sth out of sb** jdm etw abluchsen

wheel [wiːl] n Rad nt; (also: **steering wheel**) Lenkrad nt; (Naut) Steuer nt ▷ vt (pram etc) schieben ▷ vi (birds) kreisen; (also: **wheel round**: person) sich herumdrehen

wheelbarrow ['wiːlbærəu] n Schubkarre f

wheelbase ['wiːlbeɪs] n Radstand m

wheelchair ['wiːltʃɛəʳ] n Rollstuhl m

wheel clamp n Parkkralle f

wheeler-dealer ['wiːlə'diːləʳ] (pej) n Geschäftemacher(in) m(f)

wheelie-bin ['wiːlɪbɪn] n Mülltonne f auf Rädern

wheeling ['wiːlɪŋ] n: ~ **and dealing** (pej) Geschäftemacherei f

wheeze [wiːz] vi (person) keuchen ▷ n (idea, joke etc) Scherz m

wheezy ['wiːzɪ] adj (person) mit pfeifendem Atem; (cough) keuchend; (breath) pfeifend; (laugh) asthmatisch

 KEYWORD

when [wɛn] adv wann
▷ conj **1** (at, during, after the time that) wenn; **she was reading when I came in** als ich hereinkam, las sie gerade; **be careful when you cross the road** sei vorsichtig, wenn du die Straße überquerst
2 (on, at which) als; **on the day when I met him** am Tag, als ich ihn traf
3 (whereas) wo ... doch, obwohl; **why did you buy that when you can't afford it?** warum hast du das gekauft, obwohl du es dir nicht leisten kannst?

whenever [wɛn'ɛvəʳ] adv, conj (any time that) wann immer; (every time that) (jedes Mal,) wenn; **I go ~ I can** ich gehe, wann immer ich kann

where [wɛəʳ] adv, conj wo; **this is ~ ...** hier ...; ~ **possible** so weit möglich; ~ **are you from?** woher kommen Sie?

whereabouts [wɛərə'bauts] adv wo
▷ n: **nobody knows his ~** keiner weiß, wo er ist

whereas [wɛər'æz] conj während

whereby [wɛə'baɪ] adv (form) wonach

whereupon [wɛərə'pɒn] conj worauf

wherever [wɛər'ɛvəʳ] conj (position) wo (auch) immer; (motion) wohin (auch) immer ▷ adv (surprise) wo (um alles in der Welt); **sit ~ you like** nehmen Sie Platz, wo immer Sie wollen

wherewithal ['wɛəwɪðɔːl] n: **the ~ (to do sth)** (money) das nötige Kleingeld(, um etw zu tun)

whet [wɛt] vt (appetite) anregen; (tool) schleifen

whether ['wɛðəʳ] conj ob; **I don't know ~ to accept or not** ich weiß nicht, ob ich annehmen soll oder nicht; ~ **you go or not** ob du gehst oder nicht; **it's doubtful ~ ...** es ist zweifelhaft, ob ...

whey ['weɪ] n Molke f

 KEYWORD

which [wɪtʃ] adj **1** (interrogative: direct, indirect) welche(r, s); **which picture?** welches Bild?; **which books?** welche Bücher?; **which one?** welche(r, s)?
2: in which case in diesem Fall; **by which time** zu dieser Zeit

▷ *pron* **1** (*interrogative*) welche(r, s); **which of you are coming?** wer von Ihnen kommt?; **I don't mind which** mir ist gleich, welche(r, s) **2** (*relative*) der/die/das; **the apple which you ate/which is on the table** der Apfel, den du gegessen hast/der auf dem Tisch liegt; **the chair on which you are sitting** der Stuhl, auf dem Sie sitzen; **the book of which you spoke** das Buch, wovon *or* von dem Sie sprachen; **he said he saw her, which is true** er sagte, er habe sie gesehen, was auch stimmt; **after which** wonach

whichever [wɪtʃˈɛvəʳ] *adj*: **take ~ book you want** nehmen Sie irgendein *or* ein beliebiges Buch; **~ book you take** welches Buch Sie auch nehmen

whiff [wɪf] *n* (*of perfume*) Hauch *m*; (*of petrol, smoke*) Geruch *m*; **to catch a ~ of sth** den Geruch von etw wahrnehmen

while [waɪl] *n* Weile *f* ▷ *conj* während; **for a ~** eine Weile (lang); **in a ~** gleich; **all the ~** die ganze Zeit (über); **I'll/we'll** *etc* **make it worth your ~** es wird sich für Sie lohnen
▶ **while away** *vt* (*time*) sich *dat* vertreiben

whilst [waɪlst] *conj* = **while**

whim [wɪm] *n* Laune *f*

whimper [ˈwɪmpəʳ] *n* (*cry, moan*) Wimmern *nt* ▷ *vi* wimmern

whimsical [ˈwɪmzɪkəl] *adj* wunderlich, seltsam; (*story*) kurios

whine [waɪn] *n* (*of pain*) Jammern *nt*; (*of engine, siren*) Heulen *nt* ▷ *vi* (*person*) jammern; (*dog*) jaulen; (*engine, siren*) heulen

whip [wɪp] *n* Peitsche *f*; (*Pol*) ≈ Fraktionsführer *m* ▷ *vt* (*person, animal*) peitschen; (*cream, eggs*) schlagen; (*move quickly*): **to ~ sth out/off** etw blitzschnell hervorholen/wegbringen
▶ **whip up** *vt* (*cream*) schlagen; (*inf: meal*) hinzaubern; (*arouse: support*) anheizen; (*: people*) mitreißen

⬤ **WHIP**

⬤ Der Ausdruck *whip* bezieht sich in der
⬤ Politik auf einen Abgeordneten, der für die
⬤ Einhaltung der Parteidisziplin zuständig
⬤ ist, besonders für die Anwesenheit und
⬤ das Wahlverhalten der Abgeordneten
⬤ im Unterhaus. Die whips fordern die
⬤ Abgeordneten ihrer Partei schriftlich
⬤ zur Anwesenheit auf und deuten
⬤ die Wichtigkeit der Abstimmungen
⬤ durch ein-, zwei-, oder dreimaliges
⬤ Unterstreichen an, wobei dreimaliges
⬤ Unterstreichen (3-line whip) strengsten
⬤ Fraktionszwang bedeutet.

whiplash [ˈwɪplæʃ] *n* (*Med: also*: **whiplash injury**) Schleudertrauma *nt*

whipped cream [wɪpt-] *n* Schlagsahne *f*

whipping boy [ˈwɪpɪŋ-] *n* (*fig*) Prügelknabe *m*

whip-round [ˈwɪpraund] (*Brit: inf*) *n* (Geld)

sammlung *f*

whirl [wəːl] *vt* (*arms, sword etc*) herumwirbeln ▷ *vi* wirbeln ▷ *n* (*of activity, pleasure*) Wirbel *m*; **to be in a ~** (*mind, person*) völlig verwirrt sein

whirlpool [ˈwəːlpuːl] *n* (*lit*) Strudel *m*

whirlwind [ˈwəːlwɪnd] *n* (*lit*) Wirbelwind *m*

whirr [wəːʳ] *vi* (*motor etc*) surren

whisk [wɪsk] *n* (*Culin*) Schneebesen *m* ▷ *vt* (*cream, eggs*) schlagen; **to ~ sb away** *or* **off** jdn in Windeseile wegbringen

whiskers [ˈwɪskəz] *npl* (*of animal*) Barthaare *pl*; (*of man*) Backenbart *m*

whisky, (*US, Ireland*) **whiskey** [ˈwɪskɪ] *n* Whisky *m*

whisper [ˈwɪspəʳ] *n* Flüstern *nt*; (*fig: of wind*) Wispern *nt* ▷ *vt, vi* flüstern; **to ~ sth to sb** jdm etw zuflüstern

whispering [ˈwɪspərɪŋ] *n* Geflüster *nt*

whist [wɪst] (*Brit*) *n* Whist *nt*

whistle [ˈwɪsl] *n* (*sound*) Pfiff *m*; (*object*) Pfeife *f* ▷ *vi, vt* pfeifen

whistle-stop [ˈwɪslstɔp] *adj*: **to make a ~ tour of** (*fig*) eine Rundreise machen durch; (*Pol*) eine Wahlkampfreise machen durch

Whit [wɪt] *n* = **Whitsun**

white [waɪt] *adj* weiß ▷ *n* (*colour*) Weiß *nt*; (*person*) Weiße(r) *f(m)*; (*of egg, eye*) Weiße(s) *nt*; **to turn** *or* **go ~** (*person: with fear*) weiß *or* bleich werden; (*: with age*) weiße Haare bekommen; (*hair*) weiß werden; **the ~s** (*washing*) die Weißwäsche *f*; **tennis/cricket ~s** weiße Tennis-/Krickettrikots

whitebait [ˈwaɪtbeɪt] *n* essbare Jungfische (Heringe, Sprotten etc)

whiteboard [ˈwaɪtbɔːd] *n* Weißwandtafel *f*; **interactive ~** interaktive Weißwandtafel

white coffee (*Brit*) *n* Kaffee *m* mit Milch

white-collar worker [ˈwaɪtkɔlə-] *n* Schreibtischarbeiter(in) *m(f)*

white elephant *n* (*fig: venture*) Fehlinvestition *f*

white food *n* weiße Lebensmittel *pl*, weißes Essen *nt*

white goods *npl* (*appliances*) große Haushaltsgeräte *pl*; (*linen etc*) Weißwaren *pl*

white-hot [waɪtˈhɔt] *adj* (*metal*) weiß glühend

⬤ **WHITE HOUSE**

⬤ *White House*, eine weiß gestrichene Villa in
⬤ Washington, ist der offizielle Wohnsitz
⬤ des amerikanischen Präsidenten. Im
⬤ weiteren Sinne bezieht sich dieser Begriff
⬤ auf die Exekutive der amerikanischen
⬤ Regierung.

white lie *n* Notlüge *f*

whiteness [ˈwaɪtnɪs] *n* Weiß *nt*

white noise *n* weißes Rauschen *nt*

whiteout [ˈwaɪtaut] *n* starkes Schneegestöber *nt*

white paper *n* (*Pol*) Weißbuch *nt*

whitewash [ˈwaɪtwɔʃ] *n* (*paint*) Tünche *f*; (*inf, Sport*) totale Niederlage *f* ▷ *vt* (*building*)

w

tünchen; (fig: incident, reputation) reinwaschen
white water n: **white-water rafting**
Wildwasserflößen nt
whiting ['waɪtɪŋ] n inv (fish) Weißling m
Whit Monday n Pfingstmontag m
Whitsun ['wɪtsn] n Pfingsten nt
whittle ['wɪtl] vt: **to ~ away** or **down** (costs etc)
verringern
whizz [wɪz] vi: **to ~ past** or **by** vorbeisausen
whizz kid (inf) n Senkrechtstarter(in) m(f)
WHO n abbr (= World Health Organization)
Weltgesundheitsorganisation f, WHO f

O KEYWORD

who [hu:] pron **1** (interrogative) wer; (: acc) wen;
(: dat) wem; **who is it?, who's there?** wer ist
da?; **who did you give it to?** wem hast du es
gegeben?
2 (relative) der/die/das; **the man/woman who
spoke to me** der Mann, der/die Frau, die mit
mir gesprochen hat

whodunit, whodunnit [hu:'dʌnɪt] (inf) n
Krimi m
whoever [hu:'ɛvəʳ] pron: **~ finds it** wer (auch
immer) es findet; **ask ~ you like** fragen Sie,
wen Sie wollen; **~ he marries** ganz gleich or
egal, wen er heiratet; **~ told you that?** wer
um alles in der Welt hat dir das erzählt?
whole [həʊl] adj (entire) ganz; (not broken) heil
▷ n Ganze(s) nt; **the ~ lot (of it)** alles; **the ~
lot (of them)** alle; **the ~ (of the) time** die
ganze Zeit; **~ villages were destroyed** ganze
Dörfer wurden zerstört; **the ~ of** der/die/
das ganze; **the ~ of Glasgow/Europe** ganz
Glasgow/Europa; **the ~ of the town** die
ganze Stadt; **on the ~** im Ganzen (gesehen)
wholefood ['həʊlfuːd] n, **wholefoods**
['həʊlfuːdz] ▷ npl Vollwertkost f
wholefood shop n ≈ Reformhaus nt
wholehearted [həʊl'hɑːtɪd] adj (agreement etc)
rückhaltlos
wholeheartedly [həʊl'hɑːtɪdlɪ] adv (agree etc)
rückhaltlos
wholemeal ['həʊlmiːl] (Brit) adj (bread, flour)
Vollkorn-
whole note (US) n ganze Note f
wholesale ['həʊlseɪl] n (business) Großhandel
m ▷ adj (price) Großhandels-; (destruction etc)
umfassend ▷ adv (buy, sell) im Großhandel
wholesaler ['həʊlseɪləʳ] n Großhändler m
wholesome ['həʊlsəm] adj (food) gesund;
(effect) zuträglich; (attitude) positiv
wholewheat ['həʊlwiːt] adj = **wholemeal**
wholly ['həʊlɪ] adv ganz und gar

O KEYWORD

whom [hu:m] pron **1** (interrogative: acc) wen;
(: dat) wem; **whom did you see?** wen hast du
gesehen?; **to whom did you give it?** wem
hast du es gegeben?

2 (relative: acc) den/die/das; (: dat) dem/der/
dem; **the man whom I saw/to whom I
spoke** der Mann, den ich gesehen habe/mit
dem ich gesprochen habe

whooping cough ['huːpɪŋ-] n Keuchhusten m
whoosh [wuʃ] vi: **to ~ along/past/down**
entlang-/vorbei-/hinuntersausen ▷ n Sausen
nt; **the skiers ~ed past, skiers came by with
a ~** die Skifahrer sausten vorbei
whopper ['wɔpəʳ] (inf) n (lie) faustdicke Lüge f;
(large thing) Mordsding nt
whopping ['wɔpɪŋ] adj Riesen-, riesig
whore [hɔːʳ] (inf: pej) n Hure f

O KEYWORD

whose [hu:z] adj **1** (possessive: interrogative)
wessen; **whose book is this?, whose is this
book?** wessen Buch ist das?, wem gehört das
Buch?; **I don't know whose it is** ich weiß
nicht, wem es gehört
2 (possessive: relative) dessen/deren/dessen;
the man whose son you rescued der Mann,
dessen Sohn du gerettet hast; **the woman
whose car was stolen** die Frau, deren Auto
gestohlen worden war
▷ pron: **whose is this?** wem gehört das?; **I
know whose it is** ich weiß, wem es gehört

Who's Who ['huːz'huː] n (book) Who's who nt

O KEYWORD

why [waɪ] adv warum; **why not?** warum
nicht?
▷ conj warum; **I wonder why he said that** ich
frage mich, warum er das gesagt hat; **that's
not why I'm here** ich bin nicht deswegen
hier; **the reason why** der Grund, warum or
weshalb
▷ excl (expressing surprise, shock) na so was;
(expressing annoyance) ach; **why, yes (of course)**
aber ja doch; **why, it's you!** na so was, du
bists!

WI n abbr (Brit: = Women's Institute) britischer
Frauenverband ▷ abbr = **West Indies**;
(US: Post) = Wisconsin
wick [wɪk] n Docht m; **he gets on my ~**
(Brit: inf) er geht mir auf den Geist
wicked ['wɪkɪd] adj (crime, person) böse; (smile,
wit) frech; (inf: prices) unverschämt; (: weather)
schrecklich
wicker ['wɪkəʳ] adj (chair etc) Korb-; (basket)
Weiden-
wickerwork ['wɪkəʳwəːk] adj (chair etc) Korb-;
(basket) Weiden- ▷ n (objects) Korbwaren pl
wicket ['wɪkɪt] n (Cricket: stumps) Tor nt, Wicket
nt; (: grass area) Spielbahn f
wicket-keeper ['wɪkɪtkiːpəʳ] n Torwächter m
wide [waɪd] adj breit; (area) weit; (publicity)
umfassend ▷ adv: **to open sth ~** etw weit

öffnen; **it is 3 metres ~** es ist 3 Meter breit; **to go ~** vorbeigehen

wide-angle lens [ˈwaɪdæŋgl-] n Weitwinkelobjektiv nt

wide-awake [waɪdəˈweɪk] adj hellwach

wide-eyed [waɪdˈaɪd] adj mit großen Augen; (fig) unschuldig, naiv

widely [ˈwaɪdlɪ] adv (differ, vary) erheblich; (travel) ausgiebig, viel; (spaced) weit; (believed, known) allgemein; **to be ~ read** (reader) sehr belesen sein

widen [ˈwaɪdn] vt (road, river) verbreitern; (one's experience) erweitern ▷ vi sich verbreitern

wideness [ˈwaɪdnɪs] n (of road, river, gap) Breite f

wide open adj weit geöffnet

wide-ranging [waɪdˈreɪndʒɪŋ] adj (effects) weitreichend; (interview, survey) umfassend

widespread [ˈwaɪdsprɛd] adj weitverbreitet

widget [ˈwɪdʒɪt] n (Comput) Minianwendung f, Widget nt

widow [ˈwɪdəu] n Witwe f

widowed [ˈwɪdəud] adj verwitwet

widower [ˈwɪdəuəʳ] n Witwer m

width [wɪdθ] n Breite f; (in swimming pool) (Quer)bahn f; **it's 7 metres in ~** es ist 7 Meter breit

widthways [ˈwɪdθweɪz] adv der Breite nach

wield [wiːld] vt (sword) schwingen; (power) ausüben

wife [waɪf] (pl **wives**) n Frau f

Wi-Fi [ˈwaɪfaɪ] n Wi-Fi nt

wig [wɪg] n Perücke f

wigging [ˈwɪgɪŋ] n (Brit: inf) Standpauke f

wiggle [ˈwɪgl] vt wackeln mit

wiggly [ˈwɪglɪ] adj: **~ line** Schlangenlinie f

wild [waɪld] adj wild; (weather) rau, stürmisch; (person, behaviour) ungestüm; (idea) weit hergeholt; (applause) stürmisch ▷ n: **the ~** (natural surroundings) die freie Natur f; **the wilds** npl die Wildnis; **I'm not ~ about it** ich bin nicht versessen or scharf darauf

wild card n (Comput) Wildcard f, Ersatzzeichen nt

wildcat [ˈwaɪldkæt] n Wildkatze f

wildcat strike n wilder Streik m

wilderness [ˈwɪldənɪs] n Wildnis f

wildfire [ˈwaɪldfaɪəʳ] n: **to spread like ~** sich wie ein Lauffeuer ausbreiten

wild-goose chase [waɪldˈguːs-] n aussichtslose Suche f

wildlife [ˈwaɪldlaɪf] n (animals) die Tierwelt f

wildly [ˈwaɪldlɪ] adv wild; (very: romantic) wild-; (: inefficient) furchtbar

wiles [waɪlz] npl List f

wilful, (US) **willful** [ˈwɪlful] adj (obstinate) eigensinnig; (deliberate) vorsätzlich

KEYWORD

will [wɪl] aux vb **1** (forming future tense): **I will finish it tomorrow** ich werde es morgen fertig machen, ich mache es morgen fertig; **will you do it? — yes I will/no I won't** machst du es? — ja/nein

2 (in conjectures, predictions): **that will be the postman** das ist bestimmt der Briefträger

3 (in commands, requests, offers): **will you sit down** (politely) bitte nehmen Sie Platz; (angrily) nun setz dich doch; **will you be quiet!** seid jetzt still!; **will you help me?** hilfst du mir?; **will you have a cup of tea?** möchten Sie eine Tasse Tee?; **I won't put up with it!** das lasse ich mir nicht gefallen!

▷ vt (pt, pp **willed**) **to will sb to do sth** jdn durch Willenskraft dazu bewegen, etw zu tun; **he willed himself to go on** er zwang sich dazu, weiterzumachen

▷ n (volition) Wille m; (testament) Testament nt; **he did it against his will** er tat es gegen seinen Willen

willful [ˈwɪlful] (US) adj = **wilful**

willing [ˈwɪlɪŋ] adj (having no objection) gewillt; (enthusiastic) bereitwillig; **he's ~ to do it** er ist bereit, es zu tun; **to show ~** guten Willen zeigen

willingly [ˈwɪlɪŋlɪ] adv bereitwillig

willingness [ˈwɪlɪŋnɪs] n (readiness) Bereitschaft f; (enthusiasm) Bereitwilligkeit f

will-o'-the-wisp [ˈwɪləðəˈwɪsp] n Irrlicht nt; (fig) Trugbild nt

willow [ˈwɪləu] n (tree) Weide f; (wood) Weidenholz nt

willpower [ˈwɪlˈpauəʳ] n Willenskraft f

willy-nilly [ˈwɪlɪˈnɪlɪ] adv (willingly or not) wohl oder übel

wilt [wɪlt] vi (plant) welken

Wilts [wɪlts] (Brit) abbr (Post) = **Wiltshire**

wily [ˈwaɪlɪ] adj listig, raffiniert

wimp [wɪmp] (inf: pej) n Waschlappen m

wimpish [ˈwɪmpɪʃ] (inf) adj weichlich

win [wɪn] (pt, pp **won**) n Sieg m ▷ vt gewinnen ▷ vi siegen, gewinnen
  ▶ **win over** vt (persuade) gewinnen
  ▶ **win round** (Brit) vt = **win over**

wince [wɪns] vi zusammenzucken

winch [wɪntʃ] n Winde f

Winchester disk [ˈwɪntʃɪstə-] n Winchesterplatte f

wind¹ [wɪnd] n (air) Wind m; (Med) Blähungen pl; (breath) Atem m ▷ vt (take breath away from) den Atem nehmen +dat; **the winds** npl (Mus) die Bläser pl; **into** or **against the ~** gegen den Wind; **to get ~ of sth** (fig) von etw Wind bekommen; **to break ~** Darmwind entweichen lassen

wind² [waɪnd] (pt, pp **wound**) vt (thread, rope, bandage) wickeln; (clock, toy) aufziehen ▷ vi (road, river) sich winden
  ▶ **wind down** vt (car window) herunterdrehen; (fig: production) zurückschrauben
  ▶ **wind up** vt (clock, toy) aufziehen; (debate) abschließen

windbreak [ˈwɪndbreɪk] n Windschutz m

windcheater [ˈwɪndtʃiːtəʳ], (US) **windbreaker** n Windjacke f

W

winder ['waɪndə'] (Brit) n (on watch) Krone f, Aufziehrädchen nt

windfall ['wɪndfɔːl] n (money) unverhoffter Glücksfall m; (apple) Fallobst nt

wind farm n Windpark m

winding ['waɪndɪŋ] adj gewunden

wind instrument ['wɪnd-] n Blasinstrument nt

windmill ['wɪndmɪl] n Windmühle f

window ['wɪndəu] n (also Comput) Fenster nt; (in shop) Schaufenster nt

window box n Blumenkasten m

window cleaner n Fensterputzer(in) m(f)

window dresser n Schaufensterdekorateur(in) m(f)

window envelope n Fensterumschlag m

window frame n Fensterrahmen m

window ledge n Fenstersims m

window pane n Fensterscheibe f

window-shopping ['wɪndəuʃɔpɪŋ] n Schaufensterbummel m; **to go ~** einen Schaufensterbummel machen

windowsill ['wɪndəusɪl] n Fensterbank f

windpipe ['wɪndpaɪp] n Luftröhre f

wind power ['wɪnd-] n Windkraft f, Windenergie f

windscreen ['wɪndskriːn] n Windschutzscheibe f

windscreen washer n Scheibenwaschanlage f

windscreen wiper n [-waɪpə'] n Scheibenwischer m

windshield ['wɪndʃiːld] (US) n = **windscreen**

windsurfing ['wɪndsəːfɪŋ] n Windsurfen nt

windswept ['wɪndswɛpt] adj (place) vom Wind gepeitscht; (person) vom Wind zerzaust

wind tunnel ['wɪnd-] n Windkanal m

windy ['wɪndɪ] adj windig; **it's ~** es ist windig

wine [waɪn] n Wein m ▷ vt: **to ~ and dine sb** jdm zu einem guten Essen ausführen

wine bar n Weinlokal nt

wine cellar n Weinkeller m

wine glass n Weinglas nt

wine list n Weinkarte f

wine merchant n Weinhändler(in) m(f)

wine tasting [-teɪstɪŋ] n Weinprobe f

wine waiter n Weinkellner m

wing [wɪŋ] n (of bird, insect, plane) Flügel m; (of building) Trakt m; (of car) Kotflügel m; **the wings** npl (Theat) die Kulissen pl

winger ['wɪŋə'] n (Sport) Flügelspieler(in) m(f)

wing mirror (Brit) n Seitenspiegel m

wing nut n Flügelmutter f

wingspan ['wɪŋspæn] n Flügelspannweite f

wingspread ['wɪŋsprɛd] n = **wingspan**

wink [wɪŋk] n (of eye) Zwinkern m ▷ vi (with eye) zwinkern; (light etc) blinken

winkle [wɪŋkl] n Strandschnecke f

winner ['wɪnə'] n (of race, competition) Sieger(in) m(f); (of prize) Gewinner(in) m(f)

winning ['wɪnɪŋ] adj (team, entry) siegreich; (shot, goal) entscheidend; (smile) einnehmend; see also **winnings**

winning post n (lit) Zielpfosten m; (fig) Ziel nt

winnings ['wɪnɪŋz] npl Gewinn m

winsome ['wɪnsəm] adj (expression) gewinnend;

(person) reizend

winter ['wɪntə'] n Winter m ▷ vi (birds) überwintern; **in ~** im Winter

winter sports npl Wintersport m

wintry ['wɪntrɪ] adj (weather, day) winterlich, Winter-

wipe [waɪp] vt wischen; (dry) abtrocknen; (clean) abwischen; (erase: tape) löschen; **to ~ one's nose** sich dat die Nase putzen ▷ n: **to give sth a ~** etw abwischen
  ▶ **wipe off** vt abwischen
  ▶ **wipe out** vt (destroy: city etc) auslöschen
  ▶ **wipe up** vt (mess) aufwischen

wire ['waɪə'] n Draht m; (US: telegram) Telegramm nt ▷ vt (US): **to ~ sb** jdm telegrafieren; (also: **wire up**: electrical fitting) anschließen

wire brush n Drahtbürste f

wire cutters npl Drahtschere f

wireless ['waɪəlɪs] (Brit: old) n Funk m; (set) Rundfunkgerät nt

wireless phone n schnurloses Telefon nt

wire netting n Maschendraht m

wire service (US) n Nachrichtenagentur f

wire-tapping ['waɪə'tæpɪŋ] n Anzapfen nt von Leitungen

wiring ['waɪərɪŋ] n elektrische Leitungen pl

wiry ['waɪərɪ] adj (person) drahtig; (hair) borstig

Wis. (US) abbr (Post) = Wisconsin

wisdom ['wɪzdəm] n (of person) Weisheit f; (of action, remark) Klugheit f

wisdom tooth n Weisheitszahn m

wise adj (person) weise; (action, remark) klug; **I'm none the ~r** ich bin genauso klug wie vorher
  ▶ **wise up** (inf) vi: **to ~ up to sth** hinter etw acc kommen

...wise [waɪz] suff: **timewise/moneywise** etc zeitmäßig/geldmäßig etc

wisecrack ['waɪzkræk] n Witzelei f

wisely ['waɪzlɪ] adv klug, weise

wish [wɪʃ] n Wunsch m ▷ vt wünschen; **best ~es** (for birthday etc) herzliche Grüße, alle guten Wünsche; **with best ~es** (in letter) mit den besten Wünschen or Grüßen; **give her my best ~es** grüßen Sie sie herzlich von mir; **to make a ~** sich dat etw wünschen; **to ~ sb goodbye** jdm Auf Wiedersehen sagen; **he ~ed me well** er wünschte mir alles Gute; **to ~ to do sth** etw tun wollen; **to ~ sth on sb** jdm etw wünschen; **to ~ for sth** sich dat etw wünschen

wishbone ['wɪʃbəun] n Gabelbein nt

wishful ['wɪʃful] adj: **it's ~ thinking** das ist reines Wunschdenken

wishy-washy ['wɪʃɪ'wɔʃɪ] (inf) adj (colour) verwaschen; (person) farblos; (ideas) nichtssagend

wisp [wɪsp] n (of grass) Büschel nt; (of hair) Strähne f; (of smoke) Fahne f

wistful ['wɪstful] adj wehmütig

wit [wɪt] n (wittiness) geistreiche Art f; (person) geistreicher Mensch m; (presence of mind) Verstand m; **wits** npl (intelligence) Verstand m;

to be at one's ~s' end mit seinem Latein am Ende sein; **to have one's ~s about one** einen klaren Kopf haben; **to ~** (*namely*) und zwar

witch [wɪtʃ] *n* Hexe *f*

witchcraft ['wɪtʃkrɑ:ft] *n* Hexerei *f*

witch doctor *n* Medizinmann *m*

witch-hunt ['wɪtʃhʌnt] *n* (*fig*) Hexenjagd *f*

🔵 **KEYWORD**

with [wɪð] *prep* **1** (*accompanying, in the company of*) mit; **we stayed with friends** wir wohnten bei Freunden; **I'll be with you in a minute** einen Augenblick, ich bin sofort da; **I'm with you** (*I understand*) ich verstehe; **to be with it** (*inf: up-to-date*) auf dem Laufenden sein; (: *alert*) da sein

2 (*descriptive, indicating manner*) mit; **the man with the grey hat/blue eyes** der Mann mit dem grauen Hut/den blauen Augen; **with tears in her eyes** mit Tränen in den Augen; **red with anger** rot vor Wut

---

withdraw [wɪð'drɔ:] (*irreg: like* **draw**) *vt* (*object, offer*) zurückziehen; (*remark*) zurücknehmen ▷ *vi* (*troops*) abziehen; (*person*) sich zurückziehen; **to ~ money** (*from bank*) Geld abheben; **to ~ into o.s.** sich in sich *acc* selbst zurückziehen

withdrawal [wɪð'drɔ:əl] *n* (*of offer, remark*) Zurücknahme *f*; (*of troops*) Abzug *m*; (*of participation*) Ausstieg *m*; (*of services*) Streichung *f*; (*of money*) Abhebung *f*

withdrawal symptoms *npl* Entzugserscheinungen *npl*

withdrawn [wɪð'drɔ:n] *pp of* **withdraw** ▷ *adj* (*person*) verschlossen

wither ['wɪðə*r*] *vi* (*plant*) verwelken

withered ['wɪðəd] *adj* (*plant*) verwelkt; (*limb*) verkümmert

withhold [wɪð'həʊld] (*irreg: like* **hold**) *vt* vorenthalten

within [wɪð'ɪn] *prep* (*place*) innerhalb +*gen*; (*time, distance*) innerhalb von ▷ *adv* innen; **~ reach** in Reichweite; **~ sight (of)** in Sichtweite (+*gen*); **~ the week** vor Ende der Woche; **~ a mile of** weniger als eine Meile entfernt von; **~ an hour** innerhalb einer Stunde; **~ the law** im Rahmen des Gesetzes

without [wɪð'aʊt] *prep* ohne; **~ a coat** ohne Mantel; **~ speaking** ohne zu sprechen; **it goes ~ saying** das versteht sich von selbst; **~ anyone knowing** ohne dass jemand davon wusste

withstand [wɪð'stænd] (*irreg: like* **stand**) *vt* widerstehen +*dat*

witness ['wɪtnɪs] *n* Zeuge *m*, Zeugin *f* ▷ *vt* (*event*) sehen, Zeuge/Zeugin sein +*gen*; (*fig*) miterleben; **to bear ~ to sth** Zeugnis für etw ablegen; **~ for the prosecution/defence** Zeuge/Zeugin der Anklage/Verteidigung; **to ~ to sth** etw bezeugen; **to ~ having seen sth** bezeugen, etw gesehen zu haben

witness box *n* Zeugenstand *m*

witness stand (*US*) *n* = **witness box**

witticism ['wɪtɪsɪzəm] *n* geistreiche Bemerkung *f*

witty ['wɪtɪ] *adj* geistreich

wives [waɪvz] *npl of* **wife**

wizard ['wɪzəd] *n* Zauberer *m*

wizened ['wɪznd] *adj* (*person*) verhutzelt; (*fruit, vegetable*) verschrumpelt

wk *abbr* = **week**

Wm. *abbr* = William

WO *n abbr* (*Mil*) = **warrant officer**

wobble ['wɒbl] *vi* wackeln; (*legs*) zittern

wobbly ['wɒblɪ] *adj* (*hand, voice*) zitt(e)rig; (*table, chair*) wack(e)lig; **to feel ~** sich wack(e)lig fühlen

woe [wəʊ] *n* (*sorrow*) Jammer *m*; (*misfortune*) Kummer *m*

woeful ['wəʊful] *adj* traurig

wok [wɒk] *n* Wok *m*

woke [wəʊk] *pt of* **wake**

woken ['wəʊkn] *pp of* **wake**

wolf [wʊlf] (*pl* **wolves**) *n* Wolf *m*

wolves [wʊlvz] *npl of* **wolf**

woman ['wʊmən] (*pl* **women**) *n* Frau *f*; **~ friend** Freundin *f*; **~ teacher** Lehrerin *f*; **young ~** junge Frau; **women's page** Frauenseite *f*

woman doctor *n* Ärztin *f*

womanize ['wʊmənaɪz] (*pej*) *vi* hinter Frauen her sein

womanly ['wʊmənlɪ] *adj* (*virtues etc*) weiblich

womb [wu:m] *n* Mutterleib *m*; (*Med*) Gebärmutter *f*

women ['wɪmɪn] *npl of* **woman**

women's lib ['wɪmɪnz-] (*inf*) *n* Frauenbefreiung *f*

Women's Liberation Movement, Women's Movement *n* Frauenbewegung *f*

won [wʌn] *pt, pp of* **win**

wonder ['wʌndə*r*] *n* (*miracle*) Wunder *nt*; (*awe*) Verwunderung *f* ▷ *vi*: **to ~ whether/why** *etc* sich fragen, ob/warum *etc*; **it's no ~ (that)** es ist kein Wunder(, dass); **to ~ at** (*marvel at*) staunen über +*acc*; **to ~ about** sich *dat* Gedanken machen über +*acc*; **I ~ if you could help me** könnten Sie mir vielleicht helfen

wonderful ['wʌndəful] *adj* wunderbar

wonderfully ['wʌndəfəlɪ] *adv* wunderbar

wonky ['wɒŋkɪ] (*Brit: inf*) *adj* wack(e)lig

wont [wəʊnt] *n*: **as is his ~** wie er zu tun pflegt

won't [wəʊnt] = **will not**

woo [wu:] *vt* (*woman, audience*) umwerben

wood [wʊd] *n* (*timber*) Holz *nt*; (*forest*) Wald *m* ▷ *cpd* Holz-

woodcarving ['wʊdkɑ:vɪŋ] *n* (*act, object*) Holzschnitzerei *f*

wooded ['wʊdɪd] *adj* bewaldet

wooden ['wʊdn] *adj* (*also fig*) hölzern

woodland ['wʊdlənd] *n* Waldland *nt*

woodpecker ['wʊdpekə*r*] *n* Specht *m*

wood pigeon *n* Ringeltaube *f*

woodwind ['wʊdwɪnd] *adj* (*instrument*)

W

867

Holzblasinstrument *nt*; **the ~** die Holzbläser *pl*

woodwork ['wʊdwə:k] *n (skill)* Holzarbeiten *pl*

woodworm ['wʊdwə:m] *n* Holzwurm *m*

woof [wʊf] *n (of dog)* Wau *nt* ▷ *vi* kläffen; **~, ~!** wau, wau!

wool [wʊl] *n* Wolle *f*; **to pull the ~ over sb's eyes** *(fig)* jdn hinters Licht führen

woollen, *(US)* **woolen** ['wʊlən] *adj (hat)* Woll-, wollen

woollens ['wʊlənz] *npl* Wollsachen *pl*

woolly, *(US)* **wooly** ['wʊlɪ] *adj (socks, hat etc)* Woll-; *(fig: ideas)* schwammig; *(person)* verworren ▷ *n (pullover)* Wollpullover *m*

woozy ['wu:zɪ] *(inf) adj* duselig

Worcs *(Brit) abbr (Post)* = **Worcestershire**

word [wə:d] *n* Wort *nt*; *(news)* Nachricht *f* ▷ *vt (letter, message)* formulieren; **~ for word** Wort für Wort, (wort)wörtlich; **what's the ~ for "pen" in German?** was heißt „pen" auf Deutsch?; **to put sth into ~s** etw in Worte fassen; **in other ~s** mit anderen Worten; **to break/keep one's ~** sein Wort brechen/halten; **to have ~s with sb** eine Auseinandersetzung mit jdm haben; **to have a ~ with sb** mit jdm sprechen; **I'll take your ~ for it** ich verlasse mich auf Sie; **to send ~ of sth** etw verlauten lassen; **to leave ~ (with sb/ for sb) that ...** (bei jdm/für jdn) die Nachricht hinterlassen, dass ...; **by ~ of mouth** durch mündliche Überlieferung

wording ['wə:dɪŋ] *n (of message, contract etc)* Wortlaut *m*, Formulierung *f*

word-perfect ['wə:d'pə:fɪkt] *adj:* **to be ~** den Text perfekt beherrschen

word processing *n* Textverarbeitung *f*

word processor [-'prəʊsɛsə'] *n* Textverarbeitungssystem *nt*

wordwrap ['wə:dræp] *n (Comput)* (automatischer) Zeilenumbruch *m*

wordy ['wə:dɪ] *adj (book)* langatmig; *(person)* wortreich

wore [wɔ:'] *pt of* **wear**

work [wə:k] *n* Arbeit *f*; *(Art, Liter)* Werk *nt* ▷ *vi* arbeiten; *(mechanism)* funktionieren; *(be successful: medicine etc)* wirken ▷ *vt (clay, wood, land)* bearbeiten; *(mine)* arbeiten in; *(machine)* bedienen; *(create: effect, miracle)* bewirken; **to go to ~** zur Arbeit gehen; **to set to ~, to start ~** sich an die Arbeit machen; **to be at ~ (on sth)** (an etw *dat*) arbeiten; **to be out of ~** arbeitslos sein; **to be in ~** eine Stelle haben; **to ~ hard** hart arbeiten; **to ~ loose** *(part, knot)* sich lösen; **to ~ on the assumption that ...** von der Annahme ausgehen, dass ...

▶ **work on** *vt fus (task)* arbeiten an +*dat*; *(person: influence)* bearbeiten; **he's ~ing on his car** er arbeitet an seinem Auto

▶ **work out** *vi (plans etc)* klappen; *(Sport)* trainieren ▷ *vt (problem)* lösen; *(plan)* ausarbeiten; **it ~s out at 100 pounds** es ergibt 100 Pfund

▶ **work up** *vt:* **to get ~ed up** sich aufregen

workable ['wə:kəbl] *adj (system)* durchführbar;

(solution) brauchbar

workaholic [wə:kə'hɒlɪk] *n* Arbeitstier *nt*

workbench ['wə:kbɛntʃ] *n* Werkbank *f*

worker ['wə:kə'] *n* Arbeiter(in) *m(f)*; **office ~** Büroarbeiter(in) *m(f)*

workforce ['wə:kfɔ:s] *n* Arbeiterschaft *f*

work-in ['wə:kɪn] *(Brit) n* Fabrikbesetzung *f*

working ['wə:kɪŋ] *adj (day, conditions)* Arbeits-; *(population)* arbeitend; *(mother)* berufstätig; **a ~ knowledge of English** *(adequate)* Grundkenntnisse in Englisch

working capital *n* Betriebskapital *nt*

working class *n* Arbeiterklasse *f*

working-class ['wə:kɪŋ'klɑ:s] *adj (family, town)* Arbeiter-

working man *n* Arbeiter *m*

working order *n:* **in ~** in betriebsfähigem Zustand

working party *(Brit) n* Ausschuss *m*

working relationship *n* Arbeitsbeziehung *f*

working week *n* Arbeitswoche *f*

work-in-progress ['wə:kɪn'prəʊgrɛs] *n* laufende Arbeiten *pl*

workload ['wə:kləʊd] *n* Arbeitsbelastung *f*

workman ['wə:kmən] *(irreg: like* **man**) *n* Arbeiter *m*

workmanship ['wə:kmənʃɪp] *n* Arbeitsqualität *f*

workmate ['wə:kmeɪt] *n* Arbeitskollege *m*, Arbeitskollegin *f*

workout ['wə:kaʊt] *n* Fitnesstraining *nt*

work permit *n* Arbeitserlaubnis *f*

works [wə:ks] *(Brit) n (factory)* Fabrik *f*, Werk *nt* ▷ *npl (of clock)* Uhrwerk *nt*; *(of machine)* Getriebe *nt*

work sheet *n* Arbeitsblatt *nt*

workshop ['wə:kʃɒp] *n (building)* Werkstatt *f*; *(practical session)* Workshop *nt*

work station *n* Arbeitsplatz *m*; *(Comput)* Workstation *f*

work-study ['wə:kstʌdɪ] *n* Arbeitsstudie *f*

worktop ['wə:ktɒp] *n* Arbeitsfläche *f*

work-to-rule ['wə:ktə'ru:l] *(Brit) n* Dienst *m* nach Vorschrift

world [wə:ld] *n* Welt *f* ▷ *cpd (champion, power, war)* Welt-; **all over the ~** auf der ganzen Welt; **to think the ~ of sb** große Stücke auf jdn halten; **what in the ~ is he doing?** was um alles in der Welt macht er?; **to do sb a** *or* **the ~ of good** jdm unwahrscheinlich guttun; **W~ War One/Two** der Erste/Zweite Weltkrieg; **out of this ~** fantastisch

World Cup *n:* **the ~** *(Football)* die Fußballweltmeisterschaft *f*

world-famous [wə:ld'feɪməs] *adj* weltberühmt

worldly ['wə:ldlɪ] *adj* weltlich; *(knowledgeable)* weltgewandt

world music *n* World Music *f*, Richtung der Popmusik, die musikalische Stilelemente der Dritten Welt verwendet

World Series *(US) n* Endrunde der Baseball-Weltmeisterschaft zwischen den Tabellenführern der Spitzenligen

worldwide ['wə:ld'waɪd] adj, adv weltweit
worm [wə:m] n Wurm m
 ▸ **worm out** vt: **to ~ sth out of sb** jdm etw entlocken
worn [wɔ:n] pp of **wear** ▷ adj (carpet) abgenutzt; (shoe) abgetragen
worn-out ['wɔ:naut] adj (object) abgenutzt; (person) erschöpft
worried ['wʌrɪd] adj besorgt; **to be ~ about sth** sich wegen etw Sorgen machen
worrier ['wʌrɪəʳ] n: **to be a ~** sich ständig Sorgen machen
worrisome ['wʌrɪsəm] adj besorgniserregend
worry ['wʌrɪ] n Sorge f ▷ vt beunruhigen ▷ vi sich dat Sorgen machen; **to ~ about** or **over sth/sb** sich um etw/jdn Sorgen machen
worrying ['wʌrɪɪŋ] adj beunruhigend
worse [wə:s] adj schlechter, schlimmer ▷ adv schlechter ▷ n Schlechtere(s) nt, Schlimmere(s) nt; **to get ~** (situation etc) sich verschlechtern or verschlimmern; **he is none the ~ for it** er hat keinen Schaden dabei erlitten; **so much the ~ for you!** um so schlimmer für dich!; **a change for the ~** eine Wendung zum Schlechten
worsen ['wə:sn] vt verschlimmern ▷ vi sich verschlechtern
worse off adj (also fig) schlechter dran; **he is now ~ than before** er ist jetzt schlechter dran als zuvor
worship ['wə:ʃɪp] n (act) Verehrung f ▷ vt (god) anbeten; (person, thing) verehren; **Your W~** (Brit: to mayor) verehrter Herr Bürgermeister; (: to judge) Euer Ehren
worshipper ['wə:ʃɪpəʳ] n (in church etc) Kirchgänger(in) m(f); (fig) Anbeter(in) m(f), Verehrer(in) m(f)
worst [wə:st] adj schlechteste(r, s), schlimmste(r, s) ▷ adv am schlimmsten ▷ n Schlimmste(s) nt; **at ~** schlimmstenfalls; **if the ~ comes to the worst** wenn alle Stricke reißen
worst-case scenario ['wə:stkeɪs-] n Schlimmstfallszenario nt
worsted ['wustɪd] n Kammgarn nt
worth [wə:θ] n Wert m ▷ adj: **to be ~** wert sein; **£2 ~ of apples** Äpfel für £2; **how much is it ~?** was or wie viel ist es wert?; **it's ~ it** (effort, time) es lohnt sich; **it's ~ every penny** es ist sein Geld wert
worthless ['wə:θlɪs] adj wertlos
worthwhile ['wə:θ'waɪl] adj lohnend
worthy [wə:ðɪ] adj (person) würdig; (motive) ehrenwert; **~ of** wert +gen

◯ KEYWORD

would [wud] aux vb **1** (conditional tense): **if you asked him he would do it** wenn du ihn fragtest, würde er es tun; **if you had asked him he would have done it** wenn du ihn gefragt hättest, hätte er es getan
2 (in offers, invitations, requests): **would you like a**

biscuit? möchten Sie ein Plätzchen?; **would you ask him to come in?** würden Sie ihn bitten hereinzukommen?
3 (in indirect speech): **I said I would do it** ich sagte, ich würde es tun
4 (emphatic): **it WOULD have to snow today!** ausgerechnet heute musste es schneien!
5 (insistence): **she wouldn't behave** sie wollte sich partout nicht benehmen
6 (conjecture): **it would have been midnight** es mochte etwa Mitternacht gewesen sein; **it would seem so** so scheint es wohl
7 (indicating habit): **he would go there on Mondays** er ging montags immer dorthin; **he would spend every day on the beach** er verbrachte jeden Tag am Strand

would-be ['wudbi:] adj (singer, writer) Möchtegern-
wouldn't ['wudnt] = **would not**
wound[1] [waund] pt, pp of **wind**[2]
wound[2] [wu:nd] n Wunde f ▷ vt verwunden; **~ed in the leg** am Bein verletzt
wove [wəuv] pt of **weave**
woven ['wəuvn] pp of **weave**
WP n abbr = **word processing; word processor** ▷ abbr (Brit: inf: = weather permitting) bei günstiger Witterung
WPC (Brit) n abbr (= woman police constable) Polizistin f
wpm abbr (= words per minute) Worte pro Minute (beim Maschineschreiben)
WRAC (Brit) n abbr (= Women's Royal Army Corps) Frauenkorps der Armee
WRAF (Brit) n abbr (= Women's Royal Air Force) Frauenkorps der Luftwaffe
wrangle ['ræŋgl] n Gerangel nt ▷ vi: **to ~ with sb over sth** sich mit jdm um etw zanken
wrap [ræp] n (shawl) Umhang m; (cape) Cape nt ▷ vt einwickeln; (also: **wrap up**: pack) einpacken; (wind: tape etc) wickeln; **under ~s** (fig: plan) geheim
wrapper ['ræpəʳ] n (on chocolate) Papier nt; (Brit: of book) Umschlag m
wrapping paper ['ræpɪŋ-] n (brown) Packpapier nt; (fancy) Geschenkpapier nt
wrath [rɒθ] n Zorn m
wreak [ri:k] vt: **to ~ havoc (on)** verheerenden Schaden anrichten (bei); **to ~ vengeance** or **revenge on sb** Rache an jdm üben
wreath [ri:θ] n (pl **~s**) n Kranz m
wreck [rɛk] n Wrack nt; (vehicle) Schrotthaufen m ▷ vt kaputt machen; (car) zu Schrott fahren; (chances) zerstören
wreckage ['rɛkɪdʒ] n (of car, plane, building) Trümmer pl; (of ship) Wrackteile pl
wrecker ['rɛkəʳ] (US) n (breakdown van) Abschleppwagen m
Wren (Brit) n abbr weibliches Mitglied der britischen Marine
wren [rɛn] n (Zool) Zaunkönig m
wrench [rɛntʃ] n (Tech) Schraubenschlüssel m; (tug) Ruck m; (fig) schmerzhaftes Erlebnis nt

W

wrest | WYSIWYG

▷ *vt* (*pull*) reißen; (*injure: arm, back*) verrenken;
to ~ sth from sb jdm etw entreißen
wrest [rest] *vt*: **to ~ sth from sb** jdm etw
abringen
wrestle ['rɛsl] *vi*: **to ~ (with sb)** (mit jdm)
ringen; **to ~ with a problem** mit einem
Problem kämpfen
wrestler ['rɛslə͡r] *n* Ringer(in) *m(f)*
wrestling ['rɛslɪŋ] *n* Ringen *nt*; (*also*: **all-in
wrestling**) Freistilringen *nt*
wrestling match *n* Ringkampf *m*
wretch [rɛtʃ] *n*: **poor ~** (*man*) armer Schlucker
m; (*woman*) armes Ding *nt*; **little ~!** (*often
humorous*) kleiner Schlingel!
wretched ['rɛtʃɪd] *adj* (*poor*) erbärmlich;
(*unhappy*) unglücklich; (*inf: damned*) elend
wriggle ['rɪgl] *vi* (*also*: **wriggle about**: *person*)
zappeln; (*fish*) sich winden; (*snake etc*) sich
schlängeln ▷ *n* Zappeln *nt*
wring [rɪŋ] (*pt, pp* **wrung**) *vt* (*wet clothes*)
auswringen; (*hands*) wringen; (*neck*)
umdrehen; **to ~ sth out of sth/sb** (*fig*) etw/
jdm etw abringen
wringer ['rɪŋə͡r] *n* Mangel *f*
wringing ['rɪŋɪŋ] *adj* (*also*: **wringing wet**)
tropfnass
wrinkle ['rɪŋkl] *n* Falte *f* ▷ *vt* (*nose, forehead etc*)
runzeln ▷ *vi* (*skin, paint etc*) sich runzeln
wrinkled ['rɪŋkld] *adj* (*fabric, paper*) zerknittert;
(*surface*) gekräuselt; (*skin*) runzlig
wrinkly ['rɪŋklɪ] *adj* = **wrinkled**
wrist [rɪst] *n* Handgelenk *nt*
wristband ['rɪstbænd] (*Brit*) *n* (*of shirt*)
Manschette *f*; (*of watch*) Armband *nt*
wristwatch ['rɪstwɔtʃ] *n* Armbanduhr *f*
writ [rɪt] *n* (*Law*) (gerichtliche) Verfügung *f*;
to issue a ~ against sb, serve a ~ on sb eine
Verfügung gegen jdn erlassen
write [raɪt] (*pt* **wrote**, *pp* **written**) *vt* schreiben;
(*cheque*) ausstellen ▷ *vi* schreiben; **to ~ to sb**
jdm schreiben
▸ **write away** *vi*: **to ~ away for sth** etw
anfordern
▸ **write down** *vt* aufschreiben
▸ **write off** *vt* (*debt, project*) abschreiben;
(*wreck: car etc*) zu Schrott fahren ▷ *vi* = **write
away**
▸ **write out** *vt* (*put in writing*) schreiben; (*cheque,
receipt etc*) ausstellen
▸ **write up** *vt* (*report etc*) schreiben
write-off ['raɪtɔf] *n* (*Aut*) Totalschaden *m*
write-protected ['raɪtprə'tɛktɪd] *adj* (*Comput*)

schreibgeschützt
writer ['raɪtə͡r] *n* (*author*) Schriftsteller(in) *m(f)*;
(*of report, document etc*) Verfasser(in) *m(f)*
write-up ['raɪtʌp] *n* (*review*) Kritik *f*
writhe [raɪð] *vi* sich krümmen
writing ['raɪtɪŋ] *n* Schrift *f*; (*of author*) Arbeiten
pl; (*activity*) Schreiben *nt*; **in ~** schriftlich; **in
my own ~** in meiner eigenen Handschrift
writing case *n* Schreibmappe *f*
writing desk *n* Schreibtisch *m*
writing paper *n* Schreibpapier *nt*
written ['rɪtn] *pp of* **write**
WRNS (*Brit*) *n abbr* (= *Women's Royal Naval Service*)
Frauenkorps der Marine
wrong [rɔŋ] *adj* falsch; (*morally bad*) unrecht;
(*unfair*) ungerecht ▷ *adv* falsch ▷ *n* (*injustice*)
Unrecht *nt*; (*evil*): **right and ~** Gut und Böse
▷ *vt* (*treat unfairly*) unrecht *or* ein Unrecht tun
+*dat*; **to be ~** (*answer*) falsch sein; (*in doing,
saying sth*) unrecht haben; **you are ~ to do it**
es ist ein Fehler von dir, das zu tun; **it's ~ to
steal, stealing is wrong** Stehlen ist unrecht;
you are ~ about that, you've got it wrong
da hast du unrecht; **what's ~?** wo fehlts?;
there's nothing ~ es ist alles in Ordnung;
to go ~ (*person*) einen Fehler machen; (*plan*)
schiefgehen; (*machine*) versagen; **to be in the
~** im Unrecht sein
wrongdoer ['rɔŋduːə͡r] *n* Übeltäter(in) *m(f)*
wrong-foot [rɔŋ'fut] *vt*: **to ~ sb** (*Sport*) jdn
auf dem falschen Fuß erwischen; (*fig*) jdn im
falschen Moment erwischen
wrongful ['rɔŋful] *adj* unrechtmäßig
wrongly ['rɔŋlɪ] *adv* falsch; (*unjustly*) zu
Unrecht
wrong number *n* (*Tel*): **you've got the ~** Sie
sind falsch verbunden
wrong side *n*: **the ~** (*of material*) die linke
Seite
wrote [rəut] *pt of* **write**
wrought [rɔːt] *adj*: **~ iron** Schmiedeeisen *nt*
wrung [rʌŋ] *pt, pp of* **wring**
WRVS (*Brit*) *n abbr* (= *Women's Royal Voluntary
Service*) *karitativer Frauenverband*
wry [raɪ] *adj* (*smile, humour*) trocken
wt. *abbr* = **weight**
WV (*US*) *abbr* (*Post*) = *West Virginia*
W.Va. (*US*) *abbr* (*Post*) = *West Virginia*
WWW *n abbr* (= *World Wide Web*) WWW *nt*
WY, Wyo. (*US*) *abbr* (*Post*) = *Wyoming*
WYSIWYG ['wɪzɪwɪg] *abbr* (*Comput*: = *what you see
is what you get*) WYSIWYG *nt*

Xx

X, x [ɛks] n (letter) X nt, x nt; (Brit: Cine: formerly) Klassifikation für nicht jugendfreie Filme; **X for Xmas** ≈ X wie Xanthippe

Xerox® ['zɪərɔks] n (also: **Xerox machine**) Xerokopierer m; (photocopy) Xerokopie f ▷ vt xerokopieren

XL abbr (= extra large) XL

Xmas ['ɛksməs] n abbr = **Christmas**

XML abbr (Comput: = extensible markup language) XML

X-rated ['ɛks'reɪtɪd] (US) adj (film) nicht jugendfrei

X-ray ['ɛksreɪ] n Röntgenstrahl m; (photo) Röntgenbild nt ▷ vt röntgen; **to have an ~** sich röntgen lassen

xylophone ['zaɪləfəun] n Xylofon nt

x

Yy

Y, y [waɪ] n (letter) Y nt, y nt; **Y for Yellow, Y for Yoke** (US) ≈ Y wie Ypsilon

yacht [jɔt] n Jacht f

yachting ['jɔtɪŋ] n Segeln nt

yachtsman ['jɔtsmən] (irreg: like **man**) n Segler m

yam [jæm] n Jamswurzel f, Yamswurzel f

Yank [jæŋk] (pej) n Ami m

yank [jæŋk] vt reißen ▷ n Ruck m; **to give sth a ~** mit einem Ruck an etw dat ziehen

Yankee ['jæŋkɪ] (pej) n = **Yank**

yap [jæp] vi (dog) kläffen

yard [jɑːd] n (of house etc) Hof m; (US: garden) Garten m; (measure) Yard nt (= 0,91 m); **builder's ~** Bauhof m

yardstick ['jɑːdstɪk] n (fig) Maßstab m

yarn [jɑːn] n (thread) Garn nt; (tale) Geschichte f

yawn [jɔːn] n Gähnen nt ▷ vi gähnen

yawning ['jɔːnɪŋ] adj (gap) gähnend

yd abbr = **yard**

yeah [jɛə] (inf) adv ja

year [jɪəʳ] n Jahr nt; (referring to wine) Jahrgang m; **every ~** jedes Jahr; **this ~** dieses Jahr; **a or per ~** pro Jahr; **~ in, ~ out** jahrein, jahraus; **to be 8 ~s old** 8 Jahre alt sein; **an eight-~-old child** ein achtjähriges Kind

yearbook ['jɪəbuk] n Jahrbuch nt

yearling ['jɪəlɪŋ] n (horse) Jährling m

yearly ['jɪəlɪ] adj, adv (once a year) jährlich; **twice ~** zweimal jährlich or im Jahr

yearn [jəːn] vi: **to ~ for sth** sich nach etwas sehnen; **to ~ to do sth** sich danach sehnen, etw zu tun

yearning ['jəːnɪŋ] n: **to have a ~ for sth** ein Verlangen nach etw haben; **to have a ~ to do sth** ein Verlangen danach haben, etw zu tun

yeast [jiːst] n Hefe f

yell [jɛl] n Schrei m ▷ vi schreien

yellow ['jɛləu] adj gelb ▷ n Gelb nt

yellow fever n Gelbfieber nt

yellowish ['jɛləuɪʃ] adj gelblich

Yellow Pages® npl: **the Yellow Pages** die gelben Seiten pl, das Branchenverzeichnis

Yellow Sea n: **the ~** das Gelbe Meer

yelp [jɛlp] n Jaulen nt ▷ vi jaulen

Yemen ['jɛmən] n: **(the) ~** (der) Jemen

Yemeni ['jɛmənɪ] adj jemenitisch ▷ n Jemenit(in) m(f)

yen [jɛn] n (currency) Yen m; (craving): **to have a ~ for** Lust auf etw haben; **to have a ~ to do sth** Lust darauf haben, etw zu tun

yeoman ['jəumən] (irreg: like **man**) n: **Y~ of the Guard** (königlicher) Leibgardist m

yes [jɛs] adv ja; (in reply to negative) doch ▷ n Ja nt; **to say ~** Ja sagen; **to answer ~** mit Ja antworten

yes-man ['jɛsmæn] (irreg: like **man**) (pej) n Jasager m

yesterday ['jɛstədɪ] adv gestern ▷ n Gestern nt; **~ morning/evening** gestern Morgen/Abend; **~'s paper** die Zeitung von gestern; **the day before ~** vorgestern; **all day ~** gestern den ganzen Tag (lang)

yet [jɛt] adv noch ▷ conj jedoch; **it is not finished** ~ es ist noch nicht fertig; **must you go just ~?** musst du schon gehen?; **the best ~** der/die/das bisher Beste; **as ~** bisher; **it'll be a few days ~** es wird noch ein paar Tage dauern; **not for a few days ~** nicht in den nächsten paar Tagen; **~ again** wiederum

yew [juː] n (tree) Eibe f; (wood) Eibenholz nt

Y-fronts® ['waɪfrʌnts] npl (Herren-)Slip m (mit y-förmiger Vorderseite)

YHA (Brit) n abbr (= Youth Hostels Association) britischer Jugendherbergsverband

Yiddish ['jɪdɪʃ] n Jiddisch nt

yield [jiːld] n (Agr) Ertrag m; (Comm) Gewinn m ▷ vt (surrender: control etc) abtreten; (produce: results, profit) hervorbringen ▷ vi (surrender, give way) nachgeben; (US: Aut) die Vorfahrt achten; **a ~ of 5%** ein Ertrag or Gewinn von 5%

YMCA n abbr (organization: = Young Men's Christian Association) CVJM m

yob ['jɔb], **yobbo** ['jɔbəu] (Brit: inf: pej) n Rowdy m

yodel ['jəudl] vi jodeln

yoga ['jəugə] n Yoga m or nt

yoghourt, yogourt ['jəugət] n = **yoghurt**

yoghurt, yogurt ['jəugət] n Joghurt m or nt

yoke [jəuk] n (also fig) Joch nt ▷ vt (also: **yoke together**: oxen) einspannen

yolk [jəuk] n (of egg) Dotter m, Eigelb nt

yonder ['jɔndəʳ] adv: **(over) ~** dort drüben ▷ adj: **from ~ house** von dem Haus dort drüben

yonks [jɔŋks] (*inf*) *n*: **for ~** seit einer Ewigkeit
Yorks [jɔ:ks] (*Brit*) *abbr* (*Post*) = *Yorkshire*

◯ KEYWORD

you [ju:] *pron* **1** (*subject: familiar: singular*) du;
(: *plural*) ihr; (: *polite*) Sie; **you Germans enjoy
your food** ihr Deutschen esst gern gut
2 (*object: direct: familiar: singular*) dich; (: *plural*)
euch; (: *polite*) Sie; (: *indirect: familiar: singular*)
dir; (: *plural*) euch; (: *polite*) Ihnen; **I know you**
ich kenne dich/euch/Sie; **I gave it to you** ich
habe es dir/euch/Ihnen gegeben; **if I were
you I would ...** an deiner/eurer/Ihrer Stelle
würde ich ...
3 (*after prep, in comparisons*): **it's for you** es ist für
dich/euch/Sie; **she's younger than you** sie
ist jünger als du/ihr/Sie
4 (*impersonal: one*) man; **you never know** man
weiß nie

you'd [ju:d] = **you had; you would**
you'll [ju:l] = **you will; you shall**
young [jʌŋ] *adj* jung; **the young** *npl* (*of animal*)
die Jungen *pl*; (*people*) die jungen Leute *pl*; **a
~ man** ein junger Mann; **a ~ lady** eine junge
Dame
younger [jʌŋgəʳ] *adj* jünger; **the ~ generation**
die jüngere Generation
youngish [ˈjʌŋɪʃ] *adj* recht jung
youngster [ˈjʌŋstəʳ] *n* Kind *nt*
your [jɔ:ʳ] *adj* (*familiar: sing*) dein/deine/dein;
(: *pl*) euer/eure/euer; (*polite*) Ihr/Ihre/Ihr;
(*one's*) sein; **you mustn't eat with ~ fingers**
man darf nicht mit den Fingern essen; *see
also* **my**
you're [juəʳ] = **you are**
yours [jɔ:z] *pron* (*familiar: sing*) deiner/deine/

dein(e)s; (: *pl*) eurer/eure/eures; (*polite*)
Ihrer/Ihre/Ihres; **a friend of ~** ein Freund
von dir/Ihnen; **is it ~?** gehört es dir/Ihnen?;
~ sincerely/faithfully mit freundlichen
Grüßen; *see also* **mine**[1]
yourself [jɔ:ˈsɛlf] *pron* (*reflexive: familiar: sing: acc*)
dich; (: *dat*) dir; (: *pl*) euch; (: *polite*) sich;
(*emphatic*) selbst; **you ~ told me** das haben Sie
mir selbst gesagt
yourselves [jɔ:ˈsɛlvz] *pl pron* (*reflexive: familiar*)
euch; (: *polite*) sich; (*emphatic*) selbst; *see also*
oneself
youth [ju:θ] *n* Jugend *f*; (*young man: pl youths*)
Jugendliche(r) *m*; **in my ~** in meiner Jugend
youth club *n* Jugendklub *m*
youthful [ˈjuːθful] *adj* jugendlich
youthfulness [ˈjuːθfəlnɪs] *n* Jugendlichkeit
f
youth hostel *n* Jugendherberge *f*
youth movement *n* Jugendbewegung *f*
you've [ju:v] = **you have**
yowl [jaul] *n* (*of animal*) Jaulen *nt*; (*of person*)
Heulen *nt*
yr *abbr* (= *year*) J.
YT (*Canada*) *abbr* = *Yukon Territory*
yuck factor [ˈjʌkfæktəʳ] *n* (*inf*) Igitt-Faktor *m*
Yugoslav [ˈjuːgəuslɑːv] (*formerly*) *adj*
jugoslawisch ▷ *n* Jugoslawe *m*, Jugoslawin *f*
Yugoslavia [ˈjuːgəuˈslɑːvɪə] (*formerly*) *n*
Jugoslawien *nt*
Yugoslavian [ˈjuːgəuˈslɑːvɪən] (*formerly*) *adj*
jugoslawisch
Yule log [juːl-] *n* Biskuitrolle mit Überzug, die zu
Weihnachten gegessen wird
yuppie [ˈjʌpɪ] (*inf*) *n* Yuppie *m* ▷ *adj* yuppiehaft;
(*job, car*) Yuppie-
YWCA *n abbr* (*organization*): = *Young Women's
Christian Association*) CVJF *m*

y

Zz

Z, z [zɛd, (US) ziː] n (letter) Z nt, z nt; **Z for Zebra**
≈ Z wie Zacharias
Zaire [zɑːˈiːər] n Zaire nt
Zambia [ˈzæmbɪə] n Sambia nt
Zambian [ˈzæmbɪən] adj sambisch ▷ n
Sambier(in) m(f)
zany [ˈzeɪnɪ] adj verrückt
zap [zæp] vt (Comput: delete) löschen
zeal [ziːl] n Eifer m
zealot [ˈzɛlət] n Fanatiker(in) m(f)
zealous [ˈzɛləs] adj eifrig
zebra [ˈziːbrə] n Zebra nt
zebra crossing (Brit) n Zebrastreifen m
zenith [ˈzɛnɪθ] n (also fig) Zenit m
zero [ˈzɪərəʊ] n (number) Null f ▷ vi: **to ~ in on**
sth (target) etw einkreisen; **5 degrees below ~**
5 Grad unter null
zero hour n die Stunde X
zero option n (esp Pol) Nulllösung f
zero-rated [ˈziːrəʊreɪtɪd] (Brit) adj (Tax)
mehrwertsteuerfrei
zest [zɛst] n (for life) Begeisterung f; (of orange)
Orangenschale f
zigzag [ˈzɪɡzæɡ] n Zickzack m ▷ vi sich im
Zickzack bewegen
Zimbabwe [zɪmˈbɑːbwɪ] n Zimbabwe nt
Zimbabwean [zɪmˈbɑːbwɪən] adj zimbabwisch
zimmer® [ˈzɪmər] n (also: **zimmer frame**)
Laufgestell nt

zinc [zɪŋk] n Zink nt
Zionism [ˈzaɪənɪzəm] n Zionismus m
Zionist [ˈzaɪənɪst] adj zionistisch ▷ n
Zionist(in) m(f)
zip [zɪp] n (also: **zip fastener**) Reißverschluss m
▷ vt (also: **zip up**: dress etc) den Reißverschluss
zumachen an +dat
zip code (US) n Postleitzahl f
zipper [ˈzɪpər] (US) n = **zip**
zither [ˈzɪðər] n Zither f
zodiac [ˈzəʊdɪæk] n Tierkreis m
zombie [ˈzɒmbɪ] n (fig) Schwachkopf m
zone [zəʊn] n (also Mil) Zone f, Gebiet nt; (in
town) Bezirk m
zonked [zɒŋkt] (inf) adj (tired) total geschafft;
(high on drugs) high; (drunk) voll
zoo [zuː] n Zoo m
zoological [zuəˈlɒdʒɪkl] adj zoologisch
zoologist [zuˈɒlədʒɪst] n Zoologe m, Zoologin
f
zoology [zuːˈɒlədʒɪ] n Zoologie f
zoom [zuːm] vi: **to ~ past** vorbeisausen; **to**
~ in (on sth/sb) (Phot, Cine) (etw/jdn) näher
heranholen
zoom lens n Zoomobjektiv nt
zucchini [zuːˈkiːnɪ] (US) n(pl) Zucchini pl
Zulu [ˈzuːluː] adj (tribe, culture) Zulu- ▷ n (person)
Zulu m/f; (Ling) Zulu nt
Zürich [ˈzjuərɪk] n Zürich nt

Grammar
Grammatik

Using the grammar

The Grammar section deals systematically and comprehensively with all the information you will need in order to communicate accurately in German. The user-friendly layout explains the grammar point on a left-hand page, leaving the facing page free for illustrative examples. The numbers, → ❶ etc, direct you to the relevant example in every case.

The Grammar section also provides invaluable guidance on the danger of translating English structures by identical structures in German. Use of Numbers and Punctuation are important areas covered towards the end of the section. Finally, the index lists the main words and grammatical terms in both English and German.

Abbreviations

acc	*feminine*
ctd	*continued*
dat	*dative*
fem	*feminine*
intr	*intransitive*
masc	*masculine*
neut	*neuter*
nom	*nominative*
tr.	*transitive*

Contents

Tense Formation

Tenses are either simple or compound. Once you know how to form the past participle, compound tenses are similar for all verbs (see pages 22–29). To form simple tenses you need to know whether a verb is weak, strong or mixed.

In German these are:

> Present indicative → ❶
> Imperfect indicative → ❷
> Present subjunctive → ❸
> Imperfect subjunctive → ❹

Subjunctive forms are widely used in German, especially for indirect or reported speech (see pages 66–67).

The simple tenses are formed by adding endings to a verb stem. The endings show the number, person and tense of the subject of the verb → ❺

The types of verb you need to know to form simple tenses are:

Strong verbs (pages 12–15), those whose vowel usually changes in forming the imperfect indicative → ❻

Weak verbs (pages 8–11), which are usually completely regular and have no vowel changes. Their endings differ from those of strong verbs → ❼

Mixed verbs (pages 16–17), which have a vowel change like strong verbs, but the endings of weak verbs → ❽

❶ ich hole

I fetch
I am fetching
I do fetch

❷ ich holte

I fetched
I was fetching
I used to fetch

❸ (dass) ich hole

(that) I fetch/I fetched

❹ (dass) ich holte

(that) I fetched

❺ ich hole
wir holen
du holtest

I fetch
we fetch
you fetched

❻ singen
er singt
er sang

to sing
he sings
he sang

❼ holen
er holt
er holte

to fetch
he fetches
he fetched

❽ bringen
er bringt
er bringte

to bring
he brings
he brought

Weak Verbs

Weak verbs are usually regular in conjugation. Their simple tenses are formed as follows:

Present and imperfect tenses are formed by adding the endings shown below to the verb stem. This stem is formed by removing the **–en** ending of the infinitive (the form found in the dictionary) → ❶

Where the infinitive of a weak verb ends in **–eln** or **–ern**, only the **–n** is removed to form the verb stem → ❷

The endings are as follows:

	PRESENT INDICATIVE	PRESENT SUBJUNCTIVE	
1st singular	-e	-e	
2nd	-st	-est	
3rd	-t	-e	→ ❸
1st plural	-en	-en	
2nd	-t	-et	
3rd	-en	-en	

	IMPERFECT INDICATIVE	IMPERFECT SUBJUNCTIVE	
1st singular	-te	-te	
2nd	-test	-test	
3rd	-te	-te	→ ❸
1st plural	-ten	-ten	
2nd	-tet	-tet	
3rd	-ten	-ten	

① INFINITIVE   STEM

holen	to fetch	**hol-**
machen	to make	**mach-**
kauen	to chew	**kau-**

② INFINITIVE   STEM

| wandern | to roam | **wander-** |
| handeln | to trade, to act | **handel-** |

③ holen to fetch

PRESENT INDICATIVE	PRESENT SUBJUNCTIVE	
ich hol**e**	ich hol**e**	I fetch
du hol**st**	du hol**est**	you fetch
er/sie/es hol**t**	er/sie/es hol**e**	he/she/it fetches
wir hol**en**	wir hol**en**	we fetch
ihr hol**t**	ihr hol**et**	you (*plural*) fetch
sie/Sie hol**en**	sie/Sie hol**en**	they/you (*polite*) fetch

IMPERFECT INDICATIVE AND IMPERFECT SUBJUNCTIVE
(*These tenses are identical for weak verbs*)

ich hol**te**	I fetched
du hol**test**	you fetched
er/sie/es hol**te**	he/she/it fetched
wir hol**ten**	we fetched
ihr hol**tet**	you (*plural*) fetched
sie/Sie hol**ten**	they/you (*polite*) fetched

Weak Verbs *continued*

Where the stem of a weak verb ends in **-d** or **-t**, an extra **-e-** is inserted before those endings where this will ease pronunciation → ❶

Weak verbs whose stems end in **-m** or **-n** may take this extra **-e-**, or not, depending on whether its addition is necessary for pronunciation. If the **-m** or **-n** is preceded by a consonant other than **l**, **r** or **h**, the **-e-** is inserted → ❷

Weak (and strong) verbs whose stem ends in a sibilant sound (**-s**, **-z**, **-ss**, **-ß**) normally lose the **-s-** of the second person singular ending (the **du** form) in the present indicative → ❸

NOTE: When this sibilant is **-sch**, the **-s-** of the ending remains → ❹

Examples

❶ reden to speak

arbeiten to work

PRESENT	IMPERFECT	PRESENT	IMPERFECT
ich rede	ich redete	ich arbeite	ich arbeitete
du redest	du redetest	du arbeitest	du arbeitetest
er redet	er redete	er arbeitet	er arbeitete
wir reden	wir redeten	wir arbeiten	wir arbeiteten
ihr redet	ihr redetet	ihr arbeitet	ihr arbeitetet
sie reden	sie redeten	sie arbeiten	sie arbeiteten

❷ atmen to breathe

segnen to bless

PRESENT	IMPERFECT	PRESENT	IMPERFECT
ich atme	ich atmete	ich segne	ich segnete
du atmest	du atmetest	du segnest	du segnetest
er atmet	er atmete	er segnet	er segnete
wir atmen	wir atmeten	wir segnen	wir segneten
ihr atmet	ihr atmetet	ihr segnet	ihr segnetet
sie atmen	sie atmeten	sie segnen	sie segneten

BUT:

umarmen to embrace

lernen to learn

PRESENT	IMPERFECT	PRESENT	IMPERFECT
ich umarme	ich umarmte	ich lerne	ich lernte
du umarmst	du umarmtest	du lernst	du lerntest
er umarmt	er umarmte	er lernt	er lernte
wir umarmen	wir umarmten	wir lernen	wir lernten
ihr umarmt	ihr umarmtet	ihr lernt	ihr lerntet
sie umarmen	sie umarmten	sie lernen	sie lernten

❸ grüßen to greet

❹ löschen to extinguish

PRESENT	PRESENT
ich grüße	ich lösche
du **grüßt**	du löschst
er grüßt	er löscht
wir grüßen	wir löschen
ihr grüßt	ihr löscht
sie grüßen	sie löschen

Strong Verbs

A table of the most useful strong verbs is given on pages 86–97.

What differentiates strong verbs from weak ones is that when forming their imperfect indicative tense, strong verbs undergo a vowel change and have a different set of endings → ①

Their past participles are also formed differently (see page 24).

To form the imperfect subjunctive of strong verbs, the endings from the appropriate table below are added to the stem of the imperfect indicative, but the vowel is modified by an umlaut where this is possible, i.e. **a ä, o ö, u ü**. Exceptions to this are clearly shown in the table of strong verbs → ②

The endings for the simple tenses of strong verbs are as follows:

	PRESENT INDICATIVE	PRESENT SUBJUNCTIVE	
1st singular	-e	-e	
2nd	-st	-est	
3rd	-t	-e	→ ③
1st plural	-en	-en	
2nd	-t	-et	
3rd	-en	-en	

	IMPERFECT INDICATIVE	IMPERFECT SUBJUNCTIVE	
1st singular	—	-e	
2nd	-st	-(e)st	
3rd	—	-e	→ ③
1st plural	-en	-en	
2nd	-t	-(e)t	
3rd	-en	-en	

Examples

❶   Compare:

	INFINITIVE	PRESENT	IMPERFECT
WEAK	sagen to say	er sagt	er sagte
STRONG	rufen to shout	er ruft	er rief

❷

	IMPERFECT INDICATIVE	IMPERFECT SUBJUNCTIVE
BUT:	er gab he gave	er gäbe (*umlaut added*)
	er rief he shouted	er riefe (*no umlaut possible*)

❸   singen to sing

PRESENT INDICATIVE	PRESENT SUBJUNCTIVE
ich singe	ich singe
du singst	du singest
er singt	er singe
wir singen	wir singen
ihr singt	ihr singet
sie singen	sie singen
Sie singen	Sie singen

IMPERFECT INDICATIVE	IMPERFECT SUBJUNCTIVE
ich sang	ich sänge
du sangst	du säng(e)st
er sang	er sänge
wir sangen	wir sängen
ihr sangt	ihr säng(e)t
sie sangen	sie sängen
Sie sangen	Sie sängen

Strong Verbs *continued*

In the present tense of strong verbs, the vowel also often changes for the second and third persons singular (the du and er/sie/es forms). The pattern of possible changes is as follows:

long **e** → **ie**
short **e** → **i**
a → **ä**
au → **äu**
o → **ö**

Verbs which undergo these changes are clearly shown in the table on page 86 → ❶

Strong (and weak) verbs whose stem ends with a sibilant sound (**-s**, **-z**, **-ss**, **-ß**) normally lose the **-s-** of the second person singular ending (the **du** form) in the *present indicative*, unless the sibilant is **-sch**, when it remains → ❷

In the second person singular of the *imperfect* tense of strong verbs whose stem ends in a sibilant sound (including **-sch**) the sibilant remains, and an **-e-** is inserted between it and the appropriate ending → ❸

1

sehen to see	helfen to help	fahren to drive
ich sehe	ich helfe	ich fahre
du **sie**hst	du **hi**lfst	du **fä**hrst
er/sie/es **sie**ht	er/sie/es **hi**lft	er **fä**hrt
wir sehen	wir helfen	wir fahren
ihr seht	ihr helft	ihr fahrt
sie sehen	sie helfen	sie fahren

saufen to booze	stoßen to push
ich saufe	ich stoße
du s**äu**fst	du st**ö**ßt
er s**äu**ft	er st**ö**ßt
wir saufen	wir stoßen
ihr sauft	ihr stoßt
sie saufen	sie stoßen

2

wachsen to grow	waschen to wash
ich wachse	ich wasche
du wächst	du wäsch**s**t
er wächst	er wäscht
wir wachsen	wir waschen
ihr wachst	ihr wascht
sie wachsen	sie waschen

3

lesen to read	schließen to close	waschen to wash
ich las	ich schloss	ich wusch
du las**es**t	du schloss**es**t	du wuschest
er las	er schloss	er wusch
wir lasen	wir schlossen	wir wuschen
ihr last	ihr schlosst	ihr wuscht
sie lasen	sie schlossen	sie wuschen

Mixed Verbs

There are nine mixed verbs in German, and, as their name implies, they are formed according to a mixture of the rules already outlined for weak and strong verbs.

The mixed verbs are:

brennen to burn	kennen to know	senden to send
bringen to bring	nennen to name	wenden to turn
denken to think	rennen to run	wissen to know

Full details of their principal parts are given in the verb table beginning on page 86.

Mixed verbs form their imperfect tense by adding the weak verb endings to a stem whose vowel has been changed as for a strong verb → ❶

NOTE: Bringen and denken have a consonant change too in their imperfect forms → ❷

The imperfect subjunctive forms of mixed verbs are unusual and should be noted → ❸

Other tenses of mixed verbs are formed as for strong verbs.

The past participle of mixed verbs has characteristics of both weak and strong verbs, as shown on page 24.

Examples

❶ IMPERFECT INDICATIVE

kennen to know	senden to send	wissen to know
ich kannte	ich sandte	ich wusste
du kanntest	du sandtest	du wusstest
er kannte	er sandte	er wusste
wir kannten	wir sandten	wir wussten
ihr kanntet	ihr sandtet	ihr wusstet
sie kannten	sie sandten	sie wussten

❷ IMPERFECT INDICATIVE

bringen to bring	denken to think
ich brachte	ich dachte
du brachtest	du dachtest
er brachte	er dachte
wir brachten	wir dachten
ihr brachtet	ihr dachtet
sie brachten	sie dachten

❸ IMPERFECT SUBJUNCTIVE

brennen	kennen	senden
ich brennte	ich kennte	ich sendete
du brenntest	du kenntest	du sendetest
er brennte *etc*	er kennte *etc*	er sendete *etc*

bringen	nennen	wenden
ich brächte	ich nennte	ich wendete
du brächtest	du nenntest	du wendetest
er brächte *etc*	er nennte *etc*	er wendete *etc*

denken	rennen	wissen
ich dächte	ich rennte	ich wüsste
du dächtest	du renntest	du wüsstest
er dächte *etc*	er rennte *etc*	er wüsste *etc*

The Imperative

Ths is the form of a verb used to give an order or a command, or to make a request:

> Come here/Stand up/Please bring me a beer → ❶

German has three main imperative forms. These correspond to the three ways of addressing people - Sie, du and ihr (see page 160)

	FORMATION	EXAMPLES	
SINGULAR	stem (+ e)	hol(e)!	fetch!
PLURAL	stem + t	holt	fetch!
POLITE (*sing* and *pl*)	stem + en Sie	holen Sie!	fetch!

The -e of the singular form is often dropped, BUT not where the verb stem ends in -chn, -ckn, -dn, -fn, -gn or -tm → ❷

Weak verbs ending in -eln or -ern take the -e ending in the singular form, but the additional -e- within the stem may be dropped → ❸

Any vowel change in the present tense of a strong verb (see page 14) occurs also in its singular imperative form and no -e is added → ❹

BUT: If the vowel modification in the present tense of a strong verb is the addition of an umlaut, this is not added in the singular form of the imperative → ❺

In the imperative form of a reflexive verb (see page 30) the pronoun is placed immediately after the verb → ❻

Separable prefixes (see page 72) are placed at the end of an imperative statement → ❼

Examples

①

SINGULAR	Komm mal her!	Come here!
PLURAL	Steht auf!	Stand up!
POLITE	Kommen Sie herein!	Do come in!

②

Hör zu!   Listen!
Hol es!   Fetch it!

BUT:
Öffne die Tür!   Open the door!

③

wandern to walk   handeln to act
wand(e)re! walk!   hand(e)le! act!

④

nehmen to take   helfen to help
du nimmst you take   du hilfst you help
nimm! take!   hilf! help!

BUT:
sehen to see
sieh(e)! see!

⑤

laufen to run   stoßen to push
du läufst you run   du stößt you push
lauf(e)! run!   stoß(e)! push!

⑥

sich setzen to sit down
Setz dich! Sit down!
Setzt euch! Sit down!
Setzen Sie sich! Do sit down!

⑦

zumachen to close   aufhören to stop
Mach die Tür zu!   Hör aber endlich auf!
Close the door!   Do stop it!

The Imperative *continued*

Imperatives are followed in German by an exclamation mark, unless the imperative is not intended as a command → ❶

Du and **ihr**, though not normally present in imperative forms, may be included for emphasis → ❷

An imperative form also exists for the **wir** form of the verb. It consists of the normal present tense form, but with the pronoun **wir** following the verb. It is used for making suggestions → ❸

The imperative forms of **sein** (to be) are irregular → ❹

The particles **auch**, **nur**, **mal**, **doch** are frequently used with imperatives. They heighten or soften the imperative effect, or add a note of encouragement to a request or command. Often they have no direct equivalent in English and are therefore not always translated → ❺

Some alternatives to the imperative in German

Infinitives are often used instead of the imperative in written instructions or public announcements → ❻

The impersonal passive (see page 34) may be used → ❼

Nouns, adjectives or adverbs can also be used with imperative effect → ❽

Some of these have become set expressions → ❾

1.   Lass ihn in Ruhe!
Leave him alone!
Sagen Sie mir bitte, wie spät es ist.
What's the time please?

2.   Geht ihr voran!   You go on ahead.
Sag du ihm, was los ist.   You tell him what's wrong.

3.   Nehmen wir an, dass ...
Let's assume that ...
Sagen wir mal, es habe 2.000 Euro gekostet.
Let's just say it cost 2,000 euros.

4.   sein to be
sei!
seid!
seien wir!
seien Sie!

5.   Geh doch!   Go on!/Get going!
Sag mal, ...   Tell me ...
Versuchen Sie es mal!   Do give it a try!
Komm schon!   Do come/Please come!
Mach es auch richtig!   Be sure to do it properly.

6.   Einsteigen!
All aboard!
Zwiebeln abziehen und in Ringe schneiden.
Peel the onions and slice them.

7.   Jetzt wird aufgeräumt!
You're going to clear up now!

8.   Ruhe!   Be quiet!/Silence!
Vorsicht!   Careful!/Look out!

9.   Achtung!   Listen!/Attention!
Rauchen verboten!   No smoking.

Compound Tenses

The present and imperfect tenses in German are simple tenses, as described on pages 6–17.

All other tenses, called compound tenses, are formed for all types of verb by using the appropriate tense of an auxiliary verb plus a part of the main verb.

There are three auxiliary verbs:

> haben   for past tenses
> sein   also for past tenses
> werden   for future and conditional tenses

The compound past tenses in German are:

> Perfect indicative → ❶
> Perfect subjunctive → ❷
> Pluperfect indicative → ❸
> Pluperfect subjunctive → ❹

These are dealt with on pages 24–27.

The future and conditional tenses in German are all compound tenses.

They are:

> Future indicative → ❺
> Future subjunctive → ❻
> Future perfect → ❼
> Conditional → ❽
> Conditional perfect → ❾

These are dealt with on pages 28–29.

Examples

	WITH haben	**WITH** sein
1	er hat geholt he (has) fetched	er ist gereist he (has) travelled
2	er habe geholt he (has) fetched	er sei gereist he (has) travelled
3	er hatte geholt he had fetched	er war gereist he had travelled
4	er hätte geholt he had fetched	er wäre gereist he had travelled
5	er wird holen he will fetch	er wird reisen he will travel
6	er werde holen he will fetch	er werde reisen he will travel
7	er wird geholt haben he will have fetched	er wird gereist sein he will have travelled
8	er würde holen he would fetch	er würde reisen he would travel
9	er würde geholt haben he would have fetched	er würde gereist sein he would have travelled

Compound Past Tenses: Formation

Compound past tenses are normally formed by using the auxiliary verb haben, plus the past participle of the main verb (see below) → ❶

Certain types of verb take sein instead of haben, and this is clearly indicated in the verb table starting on page 86. They fall into three main types:

- intransitive verbs (those that take no direct object, often showing a change of state or place) → ❷

- certain verbs meaning "to happen" → ❸

- miscellaneous others, including:
  begegnen to meet, bleiben to remain,
  gelingen to succeed, sein to be, werden to become → ❹

In some cases the verb can be conjugated with either haben or sein, depending on whether it is used transitively (with a direct object) or intransitively (where no direct object is possible) → ❺

The past participle: formation (see also page 50)

Weak verbs add the prefix ge- and suffix -t to the verb stem → ❻

Verbs ending in -ieren or -eien omit the ge- → ❼

Strong verbs add the prefix ge- and the suffix -en to the verb stem → ❽
The vowel of the stem may be modified (see verb table, page 86) → ❾

Mixed verbs add the prefix ge- and the "weak" suffix -t to the stem. The stem vowel is modified as for many strong verbs → ❿

Examples

1 Haben Sie gut geschlafen?
Did you sleep well?
Die Kinder hatten fleißig gearbeitet.
The children had worked hard.

2 Wir sind nach Bonn gefahren.
We went to Bonn.
Er ist schnell eingeschlafen.
He quickly fell asleep.

3 Was ist geschehen?
What happened?

4 Er ist zu Hause geblieben.
He stayed at home.
Es ist uns nicht gelungen.
We did not succeed.
Er ist einem Freund begegnet.
He met a friend.

Er ist krank gewesen.
He has been ill.
Sie ist krank geworden.
She became ill.

5 Er hat den Wagen nach Köln gefahren.
He drove the car to Cologne.
Er ist nach Köln gefahren.
He went to Cologne.

6 holen **to fetch**
geholt **fetched**

7 studieren **to study**
studiert **studied**
prophezeien **to prophesy**
prophezeit **prophesied**

8 laufen **to run**
gelaufen **run**

9 singen **to sing**
gesungen **sung**

10 enden **to send**
gesandt **sent**
bringen **to bring**
gebracht **brought**

For a full list of strong and mixed verbs see page 86.

Compound Past Tenses: Formation *continued*

The formation of past participles for weak, strong and mixed verbs is described on page 24, and a comprehensive list of the principal parts of the most commonly used strong and mixed verbs is provided for reference on pages 86–97.

How to form the compound past tenses:

Perfect indicative	the present tense of haben or sein plus the past participle of the verb → ❶
Perfect subjunctive	(used in indirect or reported speech) the present subjunctive of haben or sein plus the past participle → ❷
Pluperfect indicative	imperfect indicative of haben or sein plus the past participle → ❸
Pluperfect subjunctive	(for indirect or reported speech) imperfect subjunctive of haben or sein plus the past participle → ❹
	NOTE: The pluperfect subjunctive is a frequently used tense in German, since it can replace the much clumsier conditional perfect tense shown on page 28.

Examples

WITH haben	**WITH** sein

❶ PERFECT INDICATIVE

ich habe geholt	ich bin gereist
du hast geholt	du bist gereist
er/sie/es hat geholt	er/sie/es ist gereist
wir haben geholt	wir sind gereist
ihr habt geholt	ihr seid gereist
sie/Sie haben geholt	sie/Sie sind gereist

❷ PERFECT SUBJUNCTIVE

ich habe geholt	ich sei gereist
du habest geholt	du sei(e)st gereist
er/sie/es habe geholt	er/sie/es sei gereist
wir haben geholt	wir seien gereist
ihr habet geholt	ihr seiet gereist
sie/Sie haben geholt	sie/Sie seien gereist

❸ PLUPERFECT INDICATIVE

ich hatte geholt	ich war gereist
du hattest geholt	du warst gereist
er/sie/es hatte geholt	er/sie/es war gereist
wir hatten geholt	wir waren gereist
ihr hattet geholt	ihr wart gereist
sie/Sie hatten geholt	sie/Sie waren gereist

❹ PLUPERFECT SUBJUNCTIVE

ich hätte geholt	ich wäre gereist
du hättest geholt	du wär(e)st gereist
er/sie/es hätte geholt	er/sie/es wäre gereist
wir hätten geholt	wir wären gereist
ihr hättet geholt	ihr wär(e)t gereist
sie/Sie hätten geholt	sie/Sie wären gereist

Future and Conditional Tenses: Formation

The future and conditional tenses are formed in the same way for all verbs, whether weak, strong or mixed.

The auxiliary werden is used for all verbs together with the infinitive of the main verb.

The infinitive is usually placed at the end of the clause (see page 224).

How to form the future and conditional tenses:

Future indicative	present tense of werden plus the infinitive of the verb → ❶
Future subjunctive	present subjunctive of werden plus the infinitive → ❷
Future perfect	present indicative of werden plus the perfect infinitive (see below) → ❸
Conditional imperfect	subjunctive of werden plus the infinitive → ❹
Conditional perfect	imperfect subjunctive of werden plus the perfect infinitive (see below) → ❺

NOTE: The conditional perfect is often replaced by the pluperfect subjunctive.

The perfect infinitive consists of the infinitive of haben/sein plus the past participle of the verb.

1   **FUTURE INDICATIVE**

ich werde holen	wir werden holen
du wirst holen	ihr werdet holen
er/sie/es wird holen	sie/Sie werden holen

2   **FUTURE SUBJUNCTIVE**

ich werde holen	wir werden holen
du werdest holen	ihr werdet holen
er/sie/es werde holen	sie/Sie werden holen

3   **FUTURE PERFECT**

ich werde geholt haben	wir werden geholt haben
du wirst geholt haben	ihr werdet geholt haben
er wird geholt haben	sie/Sie werden geholt haben

4   **CONDITIONAL IMPERFECT**

ich würde holen	wir würden holen
du würdest holen	ihr würdet holen
er/sie/es würde holen	sie/Sie würden holen

5   **CONDITIONAL PERFECT**

ich würde geholt haben	wir würden geholt haben
du würdest geholt haben	ihr würdet geholt haben
er würde geholt haben	sie/Sie würden geholt haben

NOTE: The conditional perfect is often replaced by the pluperfect subjunctive (see page 26).

Reflexive Verbs

A verb whose action is reflected back to its subject may be termed reflexive:

> *she* washes *herself*

Reflexive verbs in German are recognized in the infinitive by the preceding reflexive pronoun sich → ❶

German has many reflexive verbs, a great number of which are not reflexive in English → ❶

Reflexive verbs are composed of the verb and a reflexive pronoun (see page 170). This pronoun may be either the direct object (and therefore in the accusative case) or the indirect object (and therefore in the dative case) → ❷

Many verbs in German which are not essentially reflexive may become reflexive by the addition of a reflexive pronoun → ❸
When a verb with an indirect object is made reflexive (see page 170) the pronoun is usually dative → ❹

A direct object reflexive pronoun changes to the dative if another direct object is present → ❺

In a main clause the reflexive pronoun follows the verb → ❻
After inversion (see page 226), or in a subordinate clause, the reflexive pronoun must come after the subject if the subject is a personal pronoun → ❼
It may precede or follow a noun subject → ❽

Reflexive verbs are always conjugated with haben *except* where the pronoun is used to mean *each other*. Then the verb is normally conjugated with sein.

The imperative forms are shown on page 19.

1 sich beeilen wir beeilen uns
to hurry we are hurrying

2 sich (*accusative*) erinnern to remember
ich erinnere mich wir erinnern uns
du erinnerst dich ihr erinnert euch
er/sie/es erinnert sich sie/Sie erinnern sich

sich (*dative*) erlauben to allow oneself
ich erlaube mir wir erlauben uns
du erlaubst dir ihr erlaubt euch
er/sie/es erlaubt sich sie/Sie erlauben sich

3 etwas melden to report something
sich melden Ich habe mich gemeldet.
to report/to volunteer I volunteered.

4 wehtun to hurt
sich wehtun Hast du dir wehgetan?
to get hurt Have you hurt yourself?

kaufen to buy
Er kaufte ihr einen Mantel. Er kaufte sich (*dative*)
He bought her a coat. einen neuen Mantel.
  He bought himself a new coat.

5 Ich wasche mich. Ich wasche mir die Hände.
I am having a wash. I am washing my hands.

6 Er wird sich darüber freuen.
He'll be pleased about that.

7 Darüber wird er sich freuen.
He'll be pleased about that.
Ich frage mich, ob er sich darüber freuen wird.
I wonder if he'll be pleased about that.

8 Langsam drehten sich die Kinder um. OR:
Langsam drehten die Kinder sich um.
The children slowly turned round.

Reflexive Verbs *continued*

Some examples of verbs which can be used with a reflexive pronoun in the accusative case:

> sich anziehen to get dressed → ❶
> sich aufregen to get excited → ❷
> sich beeilen to hurry → ❸
> sich beschäftigen mit[1] to be occupied with → ❹
> sich bewerben um[1] to apply for → ❺
> sich erinnern an[1] to remember → ❻
> sich freuen auf[1] to look forward to → ❼
> sich interessieren für[1] to be interested in → ❽
> sich irren to be wrong → ❾
> sich melden to report (for duty *etc*)/to volunteer
> sich rasieren to shave
> sich (hin)setzen to sit down → ❿
> sich trauen[2] to trust oneself
> sich umsehen to look around → ⓫

Some examples of verbs which can be used with a reflexive pronoun in the dative case:

> sich abgewöhnen to give up (something) → ⓬
> sich aneignen to appropriate
> sich ansehen to have a look at
> sich einbilden to imagine (wrongly) → ⓭
> sich erlauben to allow oneself → ⓮
> sich leisten to treat oneself → ⓯
> sich nähern to get close to
> sich vornehmen to plan to do → ⓰
> sich vorstellen to imagine → ⓱
> sich wünschen to want → ⓲

[1] For verbs normally followed by a preposition, see pages 76–79.

[2] trauen when non-reflexive takes the dative case.

1. Du sollst dich sofort anziehen.
   You are to get dressed immediately.
2. Reg dich doch nicht so auf!
   Calm down!
3. Wir müssen uns beeilen.
   We must hurry.
4. Sie beschäftigen sich sehr mit den Kindern.
   They spend a lot of time with the children.
5. Hast du dich um diese Stelle beworben?
   Have you applied for this post?
6. Ich erinnere mich nicht daran.
   I can't remember it.
7. Ich freue mich auf die Fahrt.
   I am looking forward to the journey.
8. Interessierst du dich für Musik?
   Are you interested in music?
9. Er hat sich geirrt.
   He was wrong.
10. Bitte, setzt euch hin!
    Please sit down!
11. Die Kinder sahen sich erstaunt um.
    The children looked around in amazement.
12. Eigentlich müsste man sich das Rauchen abgewöhnen.
    One really ought to give up smoking.
13. Bilde dir doch nichts ein!
    Don't kid yourself!
14. Eins könntest du dir doch erlauben.
    You could surely allow yourself one.
15. Wenn ich mir nur einen Mercedes leisten könnte!
    If only I could afford a Mercedes!
16. Du hast dir wieder zu viel vorgenommen!
    You've taken on too much again!
17. So hatte ich es mir oft vorgestellt.
    I had often imagined it like this.
18. Was wünscht ihr euch zu Weihnachten?
    What do you want for Christmas?

The Passive

In active tenses, the subject of a verb carries out the action of the verb, but in passive tenses the subject of the verb has something done to it.

Compare the following:

> Peter kicked the cat (subject: Peter)
> The cat was kicked by Peter (subject: the cat)

English uses the verb "to be" to form its passive tenses. German uses werden → ❶

A sample verb is conjugated in the passive on pages 39–41.

In English, the word "by" usually introduces the agent through which the action of a passive tense is performed. In German this agent is introduced by:

> von for the performer of the action
> durch for an inanimate cause → ❷

The passive can be used to add impersonality or distance to an event → ❸

It may also be used where the identity of the cause of the deed is unknown or not important → ❹

In general, however, the passive is used less in German than in English. The following are common replacements for the passive:

- an active tense with the impersonal pronoun man as subject (meaning they/one). This resembles the use of *on* in French, and man is not always translated as one or they → ❺

- sich lassen plus a verb in the infinitive → ❻

❶   Das Auto wurde gekauft.
The car was bought.

❷   Das ist von seinem Onkel geschickt worden.
It was sent by his uncle.

Das Kind wurde von einem Hund gebissen.
The child was bitten by a dog.

Seine Bewerbung ist von der Firma abgelehnt worden.
(*the firm is viewed as a human agent*)
His application was turned down by the firm.

Die Tür wurde durch den Wind geöffnet.
The door was opened by the wind.

Das Getreide wurde durch den Sturm niedergeschlagen.
The crop was flattened by the storm.

❸   Die Praxis ist von Dr. Disselkamp übernommen worden.
The practice has been taken over by Dr Disselkamp.

Anfang 1993 wurde ein weiterer Anschlag auf sein
Leben verübt.
Another attempt was made on his life early in 1993.

❹   In letzter Zeit sind neue Gesetze eingeführt worden.
New laws have recently been introduced.

❺   Man hatte es schon verkauft.
It had already been sold.

Man wird es verkauft haben.
It will have been sold.

❻   Das lässt sich schnell herausfinden.
We'll/You'll/One will be able to find that out quickly.

The Passive *continued*

In English the indirect object of an active tense can become the subject of a passive statement e.g.

> Peter gave *him* a car (*him* = to him)
> *He* was given a car by Peter

This is not possible in German, where the indirect object (*him*) must remain in the dative case (see page 110). There are two ways of handling this in German:

> 1 with the direct object (*car*) as the subject of a passive verb → ❶
> 2 by means of an impersonal passive construction, with or without the impersonal subject es → ❶

These constructions would however normally be avoided in favour of an active tense, when the agent of the action is known → ❷

Verbs which are normally followed by the dative case in German and so have only an indirect object (see page 80) should therefore be especially noted, as they can only adopt the impersonal or man-forms of the passive → ❸

Some passive tenses are avoided in German, as they are inelegant (and difficult to use!). For instance, the future perfect passives should be replaced by an active tense or a construction using man → ❹

The conditional perfect passives are also rarely used, past conditional being shown by the pluperfect subjunctives, either passive or active → ❺

English passive constructions such as

> he was heard whistling/they were thought to be dying

are not possible in German → ❻

❶   Ein Auto wurde ihm von Peter geschenkt.
OR:
Es wurde ihm von Peter ein Auto geschenkt.
OR:
Ihm wurde von Peter ein Auto geschenkt.
He was given a car by Peter.

❷   Peter schenkte ihm ein Auto.
Peter gave him a car.

❸   helfen (+ *dative*) to help
Sie half mir.   Mir wurde von ihr geholfen.
She helped me.   OR:
                        Es wurde mir von ihr geholfen.
                        I was helped by her.

❹   Er meint, es werde schon gesehen worden sein.
He thinks that it will already have been seen.

BETTER: Er meint, man werde es schon gesehen haben.

❺   Es würde geholt worden sein / Man würde es geholt haben.
It would have been fetched.

BETTER: Es wäre geholt worden / Man hätte es geholt.

❻   Man hörte ihn singen.
He was heard singing.
Man sah sie ankommen.
She was seen arriving.
Man glaubte, er sei betrunken.
He was thought to be drunk.

Passive Tenses: Conjugation

Simple tenses

Present passive indicative
e.g. *it is seen*

present indicative of
werden + past participle of the
verb → ❶

Present passive subjunctive

present subjunctive of
werden + past participle of the
verb → ❷

Imperfect passive indicative
e.g. *it was seen*

imperfect indicative of
werden + past participle of the
verb → ❸

Imperfect passive subjunctive

imperfect subjunctive of
werden + past participle of the
verb → ❹

Compound tenses

Perfect passive indicative
e.g. *it has been seen*

present indicative of sein
+ e.g. past participle of the
verb + worden → ❺

Perfect passive subjunctive

present subjunctive of sein
+ past participle of the verb
+ worden → ❻

Pluperfect passive indicative
e.g. *it had been seen*

imperfect indicative of sein
+ past participle of the verb
+ worden → ❼

Examples

❶ PRESENT PASSIVE INDICATIVE

ich werde gesehen
du wirst gesehen
er/sie/es wird gesehen
OR: man sieht mich/man sieht dich *etc*

wir werden gesehen
ihr werdet gesehen
sie/Sie werden gesehen

❷ PRESENT PASSIVE SUBJUNCTIVE

ich werde gesehen
du werdest gesehen
er/sie/es werde gesehen
OR: man sehe mich/man sehe dich *etc*

wir werden gesehen
ihr werdet gesehen
sie/Sie werden gesehen

❸ IMPERFECT PASSIVE INDICATIVE

ich wurde gesehen/wir wurden gesehen *etc*
OR: man sah mich/man sah uns *etc*

❹ IMPERFECT PASSIVE SUBJUNCTIVE

ich würde gesehen/wir würden gesehen *etc*
OR: man sähe mich/man sähe uns *etc*

❺ PERFECT PASSIVE INDICATIVE

ich bin gesehen worden/wir sind gesehen worden *etc*
OR: man hat mich/uns gesehen *etc*

❻ PERFECT PASSIVE SUBJUNCTIVE

ich sei gesehen worden/wir seien gesehen worden *etc*
OR: man habe mich/uns gesehen *etc*

❼ PLUPERFECT PASSIVE INDICATIVE

ich war gesehen worden/wir waren gesehen worden *etc*
OR: man hatte mich/uns gesehen *etc*

Passive Tenses: Conjugation *continued*

Pluperfect passive subjunctive	imperfect subjunctive of sein + past participle of the verb + worden → ①
Present passive infinitive e.g. *to be seen*	infinitive of werden + past participle of the verb → ②
Future passive indicative e.g. *it will be seen*	present indicative of werden + present passive infinitive of the verb → ③
Future passive subjunctive	present subjunctive of werden + present passive infinitive of the verb → ④
Perfect passive infinitive e.g. *to have been seen*	past participle of the verb + worden sein → ⑤
Future perfect passive e.g. *it will have been seen*	present indicative of werden + perfect passive infinitive of the verb → ⑥
Conditional passive e.g. *it would be seen*	imperfect subjunctive of werden + present passive infinitive of the verb → ⑦
Conditional perfect passive e.g. *it would have been seen*	imperfect subjunctive of werden + perfect passive infinitive of the verb → ⑧

① PLUPERFECT PASSIVE SUBJUNCTIVE

ich wäre gesehen worden/wir wären gesehen worden *etc*
OR: man hätte mich/uns gesehen *etc*

② PRESENT PASSIVE INFINITIVE

gesehen werden

③ FUTURE PASSIVE INDICATIVE

ich werde gesehen werden/wir werden gesehen werden *etc*
OR: man wird mich/uns sehen *etc*

④ FUTURE PASSIVE SUBJUNCTIVE

ich werde gesehen werden/wir werden gesehen werden *etc*
OR: man werde mich/uns sehen *etc*

⑤ PERFECT PASSIVE INFINITIVE

gesehen worden sein

⑥ FUTURE PERFECT PASSIVE

ich werde/wir werden gesehen worden sein *etc*
OR: man wird mich/uns gesehen haben *etc*

⑦ CONDITIONAL PASSIVE

ich würde gesehen werden/wir würden gesehen werden
OR: man würde mich/uns sehen *etc*

⑧ CONDITIONAL PERFECT PASSIVE

ich würde/wir würden gesehen worden sein *etc*
OR: man würde mich/uns gesehen haben *etc*
OR: pluperfect subjunctive: man hätte mich/uns gesehen *etc*

Impersonal Verbs

These verbs are used only in the third person singular, usually with the subject es meaning *it* → **1**

Intransitive verbs (verbs with no direct object) are often made impersonal in the passive to describe activity of a general nature → **2**

When the verb and subject are inverted (see page 226), the es is omitted → **3**

Impersonal verbs in the passive can also be used as an imperative form (see page 20) → **4**

In certain expressions in the active, the impersonal pronoun es can be omitted. In this case, a personal pronoun object begins the clause → **5**

In the following lists * indicates that es may be omitted in this way:

Some common impersonal verbs and expressions

es donnert	it's thundering
es fällt mir ein, dass/zu*	it occurs to me that/to → **6**
es fragt sich, ob	one wonders whether → **7**
es freut mich, dass/zu	I am glad that/to → **8**
es friert	it is freezing → **9**
es gefällt mir	I like it → **10**
es geht mir gut/schlecht	I'm fine/not too good
es geht nicht	it's not possible
es geht um	it's about
es gelingt mir (zu)	I succeed (in) → **11**
es geschieht	it happens → **12**
es gießt	it's pouring
es handelt sich um	it's a question of

Examples

❶   Es regnet.
It's raining.

❷   Es wurde viel gegessen und getrunken.
There was a lot of eating and drinking.

❸   Auf der Hochzeit wurde viel gegessen und getrunken.
There was a lot of eating and drinking at the wedding.

❹   Jetzt wird gearbeitet!
Now you're/we're going to work!

❺   Mir ist warm.
I'm warm.

❻   Nachher fiel (es) mir ein, dass der Mann ziemlich
komisch angezogen war.
Afterwards it occurred to me that the man was rather oddly
dressed.

❼   Es fragt sich, ob es sich lohnt, das zu machen.
One wonders if that's worth doing.

❽   Es freut mich sehr, dass du gekommen bist.
I'm so pleased that you have come.

❾   Heute Nacht hat es gefroren.
It was below freezing last night.

❿   Ihm hat es gar nicht gefallen.
He didn't like it at all.

⓫   Es war ihnen gelungen, die letzten Karten zu kriegen.
They had succeeded in getting the last tickets.

⓬   Und so geschah es, dass ...
And so it came about that ...

Impersonal Verbs and Expressions *continued*

es hängt davon ab	it depends
es hat keinen Zweck (zu)	there's no point (in) → ❶
es interessiert mich, dass/zu*	I am interested that/to
es ist mir egal (ob)*	it's all the same to me (if) → ❷
es ist möglich(, dass)	it's possible (that) → ❸
es ist nötig	it's necessary → ❹
es ist mir, als ob*	I feel as if
es ist mir gut/schlecht *etc* zumute	I feel good/bad *etc* → ❺
es ist schade(, dass)	it's a pity (that)
es ist (mir) wichtig*	it's important (to me)
es ist mir warm/kalt*	I'm warm/cold
es ist warm/kalt	it's *or* the weather is warm/cold
es ist zu hoffen/bedauern *etc**	it is to be hoped/regretted *etc*
es klingelt	someone's ringing the bell → ❻
es klopft	someone's knocking
es kommt darauf an(, ob)	it all depends (whether)
es kommt mir vor(, als ob)	it seems to me (as if)
es läutet	the bell is ringing → ❼
es liegt an	it is because of → ❽
es lohnt sich (nicht)	it's (not) worth it → ❾
es macht nichts	it doesn't matter
es macht nichts aus	it makes no difference → ❿
es macht mir (keinen) Spaß(, zu)	it's (no) fun (to) → ⓫
es passiert	it happens → ⓬
es regnet	it's raining → ⓭
es scheint mir, dass/als ob*	it seems to me that/as if
es schneit	it's snowing
es stellt sich heraus, dass	it turns out that
es stimmt (nicht), dass	it's (not) true that
es tut mir leid(, dass)	I'm sorry (that)
wie geht es (dir)?	how are you? → ⓮
mir wird schlecht	I feel sick

1 Es hat keinen Zweck, weiter darüber zu diskutieren.
There's no point in discussing this any further.

2 Es ist mir egal, ob du kommst oder nicht.
I don't care if you come or not.

3 Es ist doch möglich, dass der Zug Verspätung hat.
It's always possible the train has been delayed.

4 Es wird nicht nötig sein, uns darüber zu informieren.
It won't be necessary to inform us of it.

5 Mir ist heute seltsam zumute.
I feel strange today.

6 Es hat gerade geklingelt.
The bell just went/The phone just rang.

7 Es hat schon geläutet.   **8** Woran liegt es?
The bell has gone.   Why is that?

9 Ich weiß nicht, ob es sich lohnt oder nicht.
I don't know if it's worth it or not.

10 Mir macht es nichts aus.
It makes no difference to me.
Macht es Ihnen etwas aus, wenn ... ?
Would you mind if ... ?

11 Hauptsache, es macht Spaß.
The main thing is to enjoy yourself.

12 Ihm ist bestimmt etwas passiert.
Something must have happened to him.

13 Es hat den ganzen Tag geregnet.
It rained the whole day.

14 Wie gehts denn? — Danke, es geht.
How are things? — All right, thank you.

The Infinitive

Forms

There are four forms of the infinitive → ❶.
These forms are used in certain compound tenses (see page 28). The present active infinitive is the most widely used and is the form found in dictionaries.

Uses

Preceded by zu (*to*)

- as in English, after other verbs ("I tried *to come*") → ❷

- as in English, after adjectives ("it was easy *to see*") → ❸

- where the English equivalent is not always an infinitive:

- after nouns, where English may use an "-ing" form → ❹

- after sein, where the English equivalent may be a passive tense → ❺

Without zu, the infinitive is used after the following:

modal verbs → ❻
lassen → ❼
heißen → ❽
bleiben → ❾
gehen → ❿
verbs of perception → ⓫

NOTE: Verbs of perception can also be followed by a subordinate clause beginning with wie or dass, especially if the sentence is long or involved → ⓬

Examples

❶   INFINITIVES:

PRESENT ACTIVE holen **to fetch**	PERFECT ACTIVE geholt haben **to have fetched**
PRESENT PASSIVE geholt werden **to be fetched**	PERFECT PASSIVE geholt worden sein **to have been fetched**

❷   Ich versuchte zu kommen.   I tried to come.

❸   Es war leicht zu sehen.   It was easy to see.

❹   Ich liebe es, Musik zu hören.
     I love listening to music.

❺   Er ist zu bedauern.   He is to be pitied.

❻   Er kann schwimmen.   He can swim.

❼   Sie ließen uns warten.   They kept us waiting.

❽   Er hieß ihn kommen.   He bade him come.

❾   Er blieb sitzen.   He remained seated.

❿   Sie ging einkaufen.   She went shopping.

⓫   Ich sah ihn kommen.   I saw him coming.
     Er hörte sie singen.   He heard her singing.

⓬   Er sah, wie sie langsam auf und ab schlenderte.
     He watched her strolling slowly up and down.

The Infinitive *continued*

Used as an imperative

The infinitive can be used as an imperative (see page 20) → ❶

Used as a noun

The infinitive can be made into a noun by giving it a capital letter. Its gender is always neuter → ❷

Used with modal verbs (see page 52)

An infinitive used with a modal verb is always placed at the end of a clause (see page 56) → ❸

If the modal verb is in a compound tense, its auxiliary will follow the subject in a main clause in the normal way, and the modal participle comes after the infinitive.

BUT: In a subordinate clause, the auxiliary immediately precedes the infinitive and the modal participle, instead of coming at the end → ❹

An infinitive expressing change of place may be omitted entirely after a modal verb (see page 56) → ❺

Used in infinitive phrases

Infinitive phrases can be formed with:

zu	ohne … zu
um … zu	anstatt … zu → ❻

The infinitive comes at the end of its phrase → ❼

In separable verbs, zu is inserted *between* the verb and its prefix in the present infinitive → ❽

A reflexive pronoun comes first, immediately following an introductory word if there is one → ❾

Examples

1 Einsteigen und Türen schließen!
All aboard! Close the doors!

2 rauchen to smoke
Er hat das Rauchen aufgegeben.
He's given up smoking.

3 Wir müssen morgen einkaufen gehen.
We have to go shopping tomorrow.

4 Sie haben gestern aufräumen müssen.
They had to tidy up yesterday.

BUT:

Da sie gestern haben aufräumen müssen, durften sie nicht kommen.
They couldn't come as they had to tidy up yesterday.

5 Er will jetzt nach Hause.
He wants to go home now.

6
es zu tun	to do it
es getan zu haben	to have done it
um es zu tun	in order to do it
um es getan zu haben	in order to have done it
ohne es zu tun	without doing it
ohne es getan zu haben	without having done it
anstatt es zu tun	instead of doing it
anstatt es getan zu haben	instead of having done it

7 Ohne ein Wort zu sagen, verließ er das Haus.
He left the house without saying a word.
Er ging nach Hause, ohne mit ihr gesprochen zu haben.
He went home without having spoken to her.

8
aufgeben	to give up
um es aufzugeben	in order to give it up

9 Sie gingen weg, ohne sich zu verabschieden.
They left without saying goodbye.

The Present Participle

The present participle for all verbs is formed by adding **-d** to the infinitive form → ❶

The present participle may be used as an adjective. As with all adjectives, it is declined if used attributively (see page 140) → ❷

The present participle may also be used as an adjectival noun (see page 148) → ❸

The past participle

For weak verbs, the past participle is formed by prefixing **ge-** and adding **-t** to the verb stem → ❹

For strong verbs, the past participle is formed by adding the prefix **ge-** and the ending **-en** to the verb stem → ❺
The vowel is often modified too → ❻
(See table of strong and mixed verbs beginning on page 86)

Mixed verbs form their past participle by adding the **ge-** and **-t** of weak verbs, but they change their vowel as for strong verbs. (See table on page 86) → ❼

The past participles of *separable* verbs are formed according to the above rules and are joined on to the separable prefix → ❽

For *inseparable* verbs, past participles are formed without the **ge-** prefix → ❾

Many past participles can also be used as adjectives and adjectival nouns → ❿

Examples

1

lachen	to laugh	singen	to sing
lachend	laughing	singend	singing

2

ein lachendes Kind	a laughing child
mit klopfendem Herzen	with beating heart

3

der Vorsitzende/ein Vorsitzender	the/a chairman

4

machen	to do/make
gemacht	done/made

5

sehen	to see
gesehen	seen

6

singen	to sing
gesungen	sung

7

wissen	to know
gewusst	known

8

aufstehen	to get up	nachmachen	to copy/imitate
aufgestanden	got up	nachgemacht	copied/imitated

9

bestellen	to order	entscheiden	to decide
bestellt	ordered	entschieden	decided

10

seine verlorene Brille	his lost spectacles
Wir aßen Gebratenes.	We ate fried food.

Modal Auxiliary Verbs

Modal verbs, sometimes called modal auxiliaries, are used to modify other verbs (to show e.g. possibility, ability, willingness, permission, necessity) much as in English:

> he *can* swim
> *may* I come?
> we *shouldn't* go

In German the modal auxiliary verbs are: dürfen, können, mögen, müssen, sollen and wollen.

Modal verbs have some important differences in their uses and in their conjugation from other verbs, and these are clearly shown in the verb tables on pages 86–97.

Modal verbs have the following meanings:

dürfen	*to be allowed to/may* → ❶
	used negatively: *must not/may not* → ❷
	to show probability → ❸
	also used in some polite expressions → ❹
können	*to be able to/can* → ❺
	in its subjunctive forms:
	would be able to/could → ❻
	as an informal alternative to dürfen with the meaning:
	to be allowed to/can → ❼
	to show possibility → ❽
mögen	*to like/to like to* → ❾
	most common in its imperfect subjunctive form which
	expresses polite inquiry or request: *should like to/*
	would like to → ❿
	to show possibility or probability → ⓫

1 Darfst du mit ins Kino kommen?
Are you allowed to/can you come with us to the cinema?
Darf ich bitte mitkommen?
May I come with you please?
Ich dürfte schon, aber ich will nicht.
I could/would be allowed to, but I don't want to.

2 Hier darf man nicht rauchen.
Smoking is prohibited here.

3 Das dürfte wohl das Beste sein.
That's probably the best thing.

4 Was darf es sein?
Can I help you?/What would you like?

5 Wir konnten es nicht schaffen.
We couldn't/weren't able to do it.

6 Er könnte noch früher kommen.
He could/would be able to come even earlier.
Er meinte, er könne noch früher kommen.
He thought he could come earlier.
Wir könnten vielleicht morgen hinfahren?
Perhaps we could go there tomorrow?

7 Kann ich/darf ich ein Eis haben?
Can I/may I have an ice cream?

8 Wer könnte es gewesen sein?   Das kann sein.
Who could it have been?   **That may be so.**

BUT: Das kann nicht sein.
        That cannot be so.

9 Magst du Butter?
Do you like butter?

10 Wir möchten bitte etwas trinken.
We should like something to drink.
Möchtest du sie besuchen?
Would you like to visit her?

11 Wie alt mag sie sein?
How old might she be?

Modal Auxiliary Verbs *continued*

müssen
to have to/must/need to → ❶

certain idiomatic uses → ❷

NOTE: For *must have ...*, use the relevant tense of müssen + past participle of main verb + the auxiliary haben or sein → ❸

For *don't have to/need not*, a negative form of brauchen (*to need*) may be used instead of müssen → ❹

sollen
ought to/should → ❺

to be (supposed) to where the demand is not self-imposed → ❻

to be said to be → ❼

as a command, either direct or indirect → ❽

wollen
to want/want to → ❾

used as a less formal version of mögen to mean: *to want/wish* → ❿

to be willing to → ⓫

to show previous intention → ⓬

to claim or pretend → ⓭

①   Er hatte jeden Tag um sechs aufstehen müssen.
He had to get up at six o'clock every day.
Man musste lachen.
One had to laugh/One couldn't help laughing.

②   Muss das sein? **Is that really necessary?**
Ein Millionär müsste man sein! **Oh to be a millionaire!**
Den Film muss man gesehen haben.
That film is worth seeing.

③   Es muss geregnet haben. **It must have been raining.**
Er meinte, es müsse am vorigen Abend passiert sein.
He thought it must have happened the previous evening.

④   Das brauchtest du nicht zu sagen.
You didn't have to say that.

⑤   Man sollte immer die Wahrheit sagen.
One should always tell the truth.
Er wusste nicht, was er tun sollte.
He didn't know what to do. (*what he should do*)

⑥   Ich soll dir helfen.
I am to help you. (*I have been told to help you*)
Du sollst sofort deine Frau anrufen.
You are to phone your wife at once. (*She has left a message asking you to ring*)

⑦   Er soll sehr reich sein.
I've heard he's very rich/He is said to be very rich.

⑧   Es soll niemand sagen, dass die Schotten geizig sind!
Let no-one say the Scots are mean!
Sie sagte mir, ich solle damit aufhören.
She told me to stop it.

⑨   Das Kind will Lkw-Fahrer werden.
The child wants to become a lorry driver.

⑩   Willst du eins? **Do you want one?**
Willst du/möchtest du etwas trinken?
Do you want/would you like something to drink?

⑪   Er wollte nichts sagen. **He refused to say anything.**

⑫   Ich wollte gerade anrufen. **I was just about to phone.**

⑬   Keiner will es gewesen sein. **No-one admits to doing it.**

Modal Auxiliary Verbs *continued*

Conjugation and use

Modal verbs have unusual present tenses → ❶

Their principal parts are given in the verb tables on pages 86–97.

Each modal verb has two past participles.

The first, which is the more common, is the same as the infinitive form and is used where the modal is modifying a verb → ❷

The second resembles a normal weak past participle and is used only where no verb is being modified (see the verb tables on page 86) → ❸

The verb modified by the modal is placed in its infinitive form at the end of a clause → ❹

Where the modal is used in a compound tense, its past participle in the form of the infinitive is also placed at the end of a clause, immediately after the modified verb → ❺

If the modal verb is modifying a verb, and if the modal is used in a compound tense in a subordinate clause, then the normal word order for subordinate clauses (see p 228) does not apply. The auxiliary used to form the compound tense of the modal is not placed right at the end of the subordinate clause, but instead comes before both infinitives → ❻

Such constructions are usually avoided in German, by using a simple tense in place of a compound. (For notes on the use of tenses in German, see pages 58–61) → ❼

A modified verb which expresses motion may be omitted entirely if an adverb or adverbial phrase is present to indicate the movement or destination → ❽

Examples

❶

dürfen	können
ich/er/sie/es darf	ich/er/sie/es kann
du darfst	du kannst
wir/sie/Sie dürfen	wir/sie/Sie können
ihr dürft	ihr könnt

mögen	müssen
ich/er/sie/es mag	ich/er/sie/es muss
du magst	du musst
wir/sie/Sie mögen	wir/sie/Sie müssen
ihr mögt	ihr müsst

sollen	wollen
ich/er/sie/es soll	ich/er/sie/es will
du sollst	du willst
wir/sie/Sie sollen	wir/sie/Sie wollen
ihr sollt	ihr wollt

❷ wollen: past participle wollen
Er hat kommen wollen.
He wanted to come.

❸ wollen: past participle gewollt
Hast du es gewollt?
Did you want it?

❹ Er kann gut schwimmen.
He can swim well.

❺ Wir haben das Haus nicht kaufen wollen.
We didn't want to buy the house.
Sie wird dich bald sehen wollen.
She will want to see you soon.

❻ COMPARE:
Obwohl wir das Haus gekauft haben, ...
Although we bought the house ...
Obwohl wir das Haus haben kaufen wollen, ...
Although we wanted to buy the house ...

❼ Obwohl wir das Haus kaufen wollten ...
Although we wanted to buy the house ...

❽ Ich muss nach Hause.
I must go home.
Die Kinder sollen jetzt ins Bett.
The children have to go to bed now.

Use of Tenses

Continuous forms

Unlike English, the German verb does not distinguish between its
simple and continuous forms → ❶
To emphasize continuity, the following may be used:

       simple tense plus an adverb or adverbial phrase → ❷
       am or beim plus an infinitive used as a noun → ❸
       eben/gerade dabei sein zu plus an infinitive → ❹

The present

The present tense is used in German with seit or seitdem where English
uses a past tense to show an action which began in the past and still
continues → ❺
If the action is finished, or does not continue, a past tense is used → ❻
The present is commonly used with future meaning → ❼

The future

The present is often used as a future tense → ❼
The future tense is used however to:

       emphasize the future → ❽
       express doubt or supposition about the future → ❾
       express future intention → ❿

The future perfect

The future perfect is used as in English to mean *shall/will have done* → ⓫
It is used in German to express a supposition → ⓬
In conversation it is replaced by the perfect → ⓭

The conditional

The conditional may be used in place of the imperfect subjunctive to
express improbable condition (see page 62) → ⓮
It is used in indirect statements or questions to replace the future
subjunctive in conversation or where the subjunctive form is not
distinctive → ⓯

① ich tue I do (*simple form*) OR: I am doing (*continuous*)
er rauchte he smoked OR: he was smoking
sie hat gelesen she has read OR: she has been reading
es ist geschickt worden it is sent OR: it is being sent

② Er kochte gerade das Abendessen.
He was cooking the supper.
Nun spricht sie mit ihm.
Now she's talking to him.

③ Ich bin am Bügeln.
I am ironing.

④ Wir waren eben dabei, einige Briefe zu schreiben.
We were just writing a few letters.

⑤ Ich wohne seit drei Jahren hier.
I have been living here for three years.

⑥ Seit er krank ist, hat er uns nicht besucht.
He hasn't visited us since he's been ill.
Seit seiner Verlobung habe ich ihn nicht geehen.
I haven't seen him since his engagement.

⑦ Wir fahren nächstes Jahr nach Griechenland.
We're going to Greece next year.

⑧ Das werde ich erst nächstes Jahr machen können.
I won't be able to do that until next year.

⑨ Wenn er zurückkommt, wird er mir bestimmt helfen.
He's sure to help me when he returns.

⑩ Ich werde ihm helfen.
I'm going to help him.

⑪ Bis Sonntag wird er es gelesen haben.
He will have read it by Sunday.

⑫ Das wird Herr Keute gewesen sein.
That must have been Herr Keute.

⑬ Bis du zurückkommst, haben wir alles aufgeräumt.
We'll have tidied up by the time you get back.

⑭ Wenn ich eins hätte, würde ich es dir geben.
If I had one I would give it to you.
Wenn er jetzt bloß kommen würde!
If only he would get here!

⑮ Er fragte, ob wir fahren würden.
He asked if we were going to go.

Use of Tenses *continued*

The conditional perfect

May be used in place of the pluperfect subjunctive in a sentence
containing a wenn-clause → ❶
But the pluperfect subjunctive is preferred → ❷

The imperfect

Is used in German with seit or seitdem where the pluperfect is used
in English to show an action which began in the remote past and
continued to a point in the more recent past → ❸
For discontinued actions the pluperfect is used → ❹
Is used to describe past actions which have no link with the present as
far as the speaker is concerned → ❺
Is used for narrative purposes → ❻
Is used for repeated, habitual or prolonged past action → ❼
See also the NOTE on The perfect (below).

The perfect

Is used to translate the English perfect tense, eg:
  I have spoken, he has been reading → ❽
Describes past actions or events which still have a link with the present
or the speaker → ❾
Is used in conversation and similar communication → ❿

NOTE: In practice however the perfect and imperfect are often
interchangeable in German usage, and in spoken German a mixture of
both is common.

The pluperfect

Is used to translate *had done/had been doing*, except in conjunction with
seit/seitdem (see The imperfect above) → ⓫

The subjunctive

For uses of the subjunctive tenses, see pages 62–67.

❶   Wenn du es gesehen hättest, würdest dus geglaubt haben.
You would have believed it if you'd seen it.

❷   Hättest du es gesehen, so hättest du es geglaubt.
If you had seen it, you'd have believed it.
Wenn ich das nur nicht gemacht hätte!
If only I hadn't done it!
Wäre ich nur da gewesen!
If I'd only been there!

❸   Sie war seit ihrer Heirat als Lehrerin beschäftigt.
She had been working as a teacher since her marriage.

❹   Ihren Sohn hatten sie seit zwölf Jahren nicht gesehen.
They hadn't seen their son for twelve years.

❺   Er kam zu spät, um teilnehmen zu können.
He arrived too late to take part.

❻   Das Mädchen stand auf, wusch sich das Gesicht und verließ das Haus.
The girl got up, washed her face and went out.

❼   Wir machten jeden Tag einen kleinen Spaziergang.
We went/We used to go for a little walk every day.

❽   Ich habe ihn heute nicht gesehen.
I haven't seen him today.

❾   Ich habe ihr nichts davon erzählt.
I didn't tell her anything about it.
Gestern sind wir in die Stadt gefahren und haben uns ein
paar Sachen gekauft.
Yesterday we went into town and bought ourselves a few things.

❿   Hast du den Krimi gestern Abend im Fernsehen gesehen?
Did you see the thriller on television last night?

⓫   Sie waren schon weggefahren.
They had already left.
Diese Bücher hatten sie schon gelesen.
They had already read these books.

The Subjunctive: when to use it

The subjunctive form in English has almost died out, leaving only a few examples such as:

> if I *were* rich
> if only he *were* to come
> so *be* it

German however makes much wider use of subjunctive forms, especially in formal, educated or literary contexts. Although there is a growing tendency to use indicatives in spoken German, subjunctives are still very common.

The indicative tenses in German display fact or certainty. The subjunctives show unreality, uncertainty, speculation about a situation or any doubt in the speaker's mind → **1**

Subjunctives are also used in indirect speech, as shown on pages 66–67.

For how to form all tenses of the subjunctive, the reader is referred to the relevant sections on Simple Tenses (pages 6–17) and Compound Tenses (pages 22–29). See also the Subjunctive in Reported Speech (page 66).

The imperfect subjunctive is very common. It is important to note that the imperfect subjunctive form does not always represent actions performed in the past → **2**

Uses of the subjunctive in German

To show improbable condition (e.g. if he *came*, he would ...).

The wenn-clause has a verb in the imperfect subjunctive and the main clause can have either an imperfect subjunctive or a conditional → **3**

Examples

①   INDICATIVE

Das stimmt.   Es ist eine Unverschämtheit.
That's true.   It's a scandal.

SUBJUNCTIVE

Es könnte doch war sein.
It could well be true.
Sie meint, es sei eine Unverschämtheit.
She thinks it's a scandal.
(*speaker not necessarily in agreement with her*)

②   *imperfect subjunctive expressing the future:*
Wenn ich morgen nur da sein könnte!
If only I could be there tomorrow!

expressing the present/immediate future:
Wenn er jetzt nur käme!
If only he would come now!

speaker's opinion, referring to present or future:
Sie wäre die Beste.
She's the best.

③   Wenn du kämest, wäre ich froh.
OR:
Wenn du kämest, würde ich froh sein.
I should be happy if you came.

Wenn es mir nicht gefiele, würde ich es nicht bezahlen.
OR:
Wenn es mir nicht gefiele, bezahlte ich es nicht.
If I wasn't happy with it, I wouldn't pay for it.

(*The second form is less likely, as the imperfect subjunctive and imperfect indicative forms of* bezahlen *are identical*)

The Subjunctive: when to use it *continued*

The imperfect of sollen or wollen, or a conditional tense might be used in the wenn-clause to replace an uncommon imperfect subjunctive, or a subjunctive which is not distinct from the same tense of the indicative → ❶

To show unfulfilled condition (if he *had come*, he would have ...)

The wenn-clause requires a pluperfect subjunctive, the main clause a pluperfect subjunctive or conditional perfect → ❷

NOTE: The indicative is used to express a *probable* condition, as in English → ❸

Wenn can be omitted from conditional clauses. The verb must then follow the subject and dann or so usually begins the main clause → ❹

With selbst wenn (*even if/even though*) → ❺

With wenn ... nur (*if only ...*) → ❻

To speculate or make assumptions → ❼

After als (*as if/as though*) → ❽

Where there is uncertainty or doubt → ❾

To make a polite enquiry → ❿

To indicate theoretical possibility or unreality → ⓫

As an alternative to the conditional perfect → ⓬

① Wenn er mich so sehen würde, würde er mich für verrückt halten!

OR:

Wenn er mich so sehen würde, hielte er mich für verrückt!

OR:

Wenn er mich so sehen sollte, würde er mich für verrückt halten!

If he saw me like this, he would think I was mad!

(Wenn er mich so sähe *would sound rather stilted*)

② Wenn du pünktlich gekommen wärest, hättest du ihn gesehen.

OR:

③ Wenn du pünktlich gekommen wärest, würdest du ihn gesehen haben.

If you had been on time, you would have seen him.

Wenn ich ihn sehe, gebe ich es ihm.

If I see him I'll give him it.

④ Hättest du mich nicht gesehen, so wäre ich schon weg.

If you hadn't seen me, I would have been gone by now.

⑤ Selbst wenn er etwas wüsste, würde er nichts sagen.

Even if he knew about it, he wouldn't say anything.

⑥ Wenn wir nur erfolgreich wären!

If only we were successful!

⑦ Und wenn er recht hätte?

What if he were right?

Eine Frau, die das sagen würde (OR: die das sagte), müsste Feministin sein!

Any woman who would say that must be a feminist!

⑧ Er sah aus, als sei er krank.

He looked as if he were ill.

⑨ Er wusste nicht, wie es ihr jetzt ginge.

He didn't know how she was.

⑩ Wäre da sonst noch etwas?

Will there be anything else?

⑪ Er stellte sich vor, wie gut er in dem Anzug aussähe.

He imagined how good he would look in the suit.

⑫ Ich hätte ihn gesehen.

OR:

Ich würde ihn gesehen haben.

I would have seen him.

The Subjunctive in Indirect Speech

What a person asks or thinks can be reported in one of two ways, either directly:

>   *Tom said, "I have been on holiday"*

OR indirectly:

>   *Tom said (that) he had been on holiday*

In English, indirect (or reported) speech can be indicated by a change in tense of what has been reported:

>   He said, "*I know* your sister"
>   He said (that) *he knew* my sister

In German the change is not in tense, but from indicative to subjunctive → ❶

There are two ways of introducing indirect speech in German, similar to the parallel English constructions:

- The clause which reports what is said may be introduced by dass (*that*). The finite verb or auxiliary comes at the end of the clause → ❷

- dass may be omitted. The verb in this case must stand in second position in the clause, instead of being placed at the end → ❸

Forms of the subjunctive in indirect speech

For conjugation of verbs in the subjunctive, see pages 8–15 and 26–31. In indirect (or reported) speech, wherever the present subjunctive is identical to the present indicative form, the imperfect subjunctive is used instead → ❹

❶ Er sagte: „Sie kennt deine Schwester".
He said, "She knows your sister".

Er sagte, sie kenne meine Schwester.
He said she knew my sister.

„Habe ich zu viel gesagt?", fragte er.
"Have I said too much?", he asked.

Er fragte, ob er zu viel gesagt habe.
He asked if he had said too much.

❷ Er hat uns gesagt, dass er Italienisch spreche.
He told us that he spoke Italian.

❸ Er hat uns gesagt, er spreche Italienisch.
He told us he spoke Italian.

❹ PRESENT SUBJUNCTIVE IN INDIRECT SPEECH

WEAK VERBS

holen to fetch

ich holte	wir holten
du holest	ihr holet
er hole	sie holten

STRONG VERBS

singen to sing

ich sänge	wir sängen
du singest	ihr singet
er singe	sie sängen

Verbs with Prefixes

Many verbs in German begin with a prefix. A prefix is a word or part of a word which precedes the verb stem → ①

Often the addition of a prefix changes the meaning of the basic verb → ②

Prefixes may be found in strong, weak or mixed verbs. Adding a prefix may occasionally change the verb conjugation → ③

There are four kinds of prefix and each behaves in a slightly different way, as shown on the following pages. Prefixes may be inseparable, separable, double or variable (i.e. either separable or inseparable depending on the verb).

Inseparable prefixes

The eight inseparable prefixes are:

| be- | ent- | ge- | ver- | |
| emp- | er- | miss- | zer- | → ④ |

These exist only as prefixes, and cannot be words in their own right.

They are never separated from the verb stem, whatever tense of the verb is used → ⑤

Inseparable prefixes are always unstressed → ⑥

①

zu + geben = zugeben
an + ziehen = anziehen

②

nehmen   to take
zunehmen   to put on weight/to increase
sich benehmen   to behave

③

WEAK		STRONG	
suchen	to look for	stehen	to stand
versuchen	to try	verstehen	to understand
besuchen	to visit	aufstehen	to get up

WEAK		STRONG	
löschen	to extinguish	erlöschen	to go out

WEAK		STRONG	
fehlen	to be missing	empfehlen	to recommend

④

beschreiben   to describe
empfangen   to receive
enttäuschen   to disappoint
erhalten   to contain
gehören   to belong
misstrauen   to mistrust
verlieren   to lose
zerlegen   to dismantle

⑤

besuchen to visit
Er besucht uns regelmäßig.   He visits us regularly.
Er besuchte uns jeden Tag.   He used to visit us every day.
Er hat uns jeden Tag besucht.   He visited us every day.
Er wird uns morgen besuchen.   He will visit us tomorrow.
Besuche sofort deine Tante!   Visit your aunt at once!

⑥

erlauben, verstehen, empfangen, vergessen

Verbs with Prefixes *continued*

Separable prefixes

Some common examples are:

ab	fest	herunter	mit
an	frei	hervor	nach
auf	her	hin	nieder
aus	herab	hinab	vor
bei	heran	hinauf	vorbei
da(r)	herauf	hinaus	vorüber
davon	heraus	hindurch	weg
dazu	herbei	hinein	zu
ein	herein	hinüber	zurecht
empor	herüber	hinunter	zurück
entgegen	herum	los	zusammen

Unlike inseparable prefixes, separable prefixes may be words in their own right. Indeed, nouns, adjectives and adverbs are often used as separable prefixes → **❶**

The past participle of a verb with a separable prefix is formed with **ge-**. It comes between the verb and the prefix → **❷**

In main clauses, the prefix is placed at the end of the clause if the verb is in a simple tense (i.e. present, imperfect or imperative form) → **❸**

In subordinate clauses, whatever the tense of the verb, the prefix is attached to the verb and the resulting whole placed at the end of the clause → **❹**

Where an infinitive construction requiring zu is used (see page 48), the zu is placed between the infinitive and prefix to form one word → **❺**

❶

noun + verb:	teilnehmen	to take part
adjective + verb:	loswerden	to get free of
adverb + verb:	niederlegen	to lay down

❷

Er hat nicht teilgenommen.
He did not participate.
Wir sind an der Grenze zurückgewiesen worden.
We were turned back at the border.

❸ wegbringen to take for repair/to take away

PRESENT
Wir bringen das Auto weg

IMPERFECT
Wir brachten das Auto weg

IMPERATIVE
Bringt das Auto weg!

FUTURE
Wir werden das Auto wegbringen

CONDITIONAL
Wir würden das Auto wegbringen

PERFECT
Wir haben das Auto weggebracht

PERFECT PASSIVE
Das Auto ist weggebracht worden

PLUPERFECT SUBJUNCTIVE
Wir hätten das Auto weggebracht

❹ PRESENT
Weil wir das Auto wegbringen, ...

IMPERFECT
Dass wir das Auto wegbrachten, ...

PERFECT
Nachdem wir das Auto weggebracht haben, ...

PLUPERFECT SUBJUNCTIVE
Wenn wir das Auto weggebracht hätten, ...

FUTURE
Obwohl wir das Auto wegbringen werden, ...

❺ Um das Auto rechtzeitig wegzubringen, müssen wir morgen
früh aufstehen.
In order to take the car in on time we shall have to get up early
tomorrow.

Verbs with Prefixes *continued*

Variable prefixes

These are:

durch	über	unter	wider
hinter	um	voll	wieder

These can be separable or inseparable → ❶

Often they are used separably and inseparably with the same verb. In such cases the verb and prefix will tend to retain their basic meanings if the prefix is used separably, but adopt figurative meanings when the prefix is used inseparably → ❷

Variable prefixes behave as separable prefixes when used separably, and as inseparable prefixes when used inseparably → ❸

Double prefixes

These occur where a verb with an inseparable prefix is preceded by a separable prefix → ❹

The separable prefix behaves as described on page 70, the verb plus inseparable prefix representing the basic verb to which the separable prefix is attached → ❺

Unlike other separable verbs, however, verbs with double prefixes have no **ge-** in their past participles → ❻

Examples

1   unternehmen (*inseparable*) to undertake, take on
Wir haben in den Ferien vieles unternommen.
We did a great deal in the holidays.
Du unternimmst zu viel.
You take on too much.

untergehen (*separable*) to sink, go down
Die Sonne geht unter.
The sun is going down/is setting.
Die Sonne ist untergangen.
The sun has gone down/has set.

2   etwas wiederholen (*separable*)   to retrieve something
etwas wiederholen (*inseparable*)   to repeat something

3   Er holte ihr die Tasche wieder.
He brought her back her bag.
Er wiederholte den Satz.
He repeated the sentence.

4   ausverkaufen to sell off

5   Er verkauft alles aus.
He's selling everything off.
Um alles auszuverkaufen ...
In order to sell everything off ...
Er wird alles ausverkaufen.
He'll be selling everything off.

6   Aber er hat doch alles ausverkauft.
But he's sold everything off.

Verb Combinations

Noun + verb combinations are normally written separately → ❶

BUT: Compound verbs if they are written as one word are almost exclusively used in the infinitive or as participles → ❷

OR: if the noun element has lost its distinctive meaning → ❸

Infinitive + verb combinations are normally written separately but many may also be written as one word → ❹

Participle + verb combinations are normally written separately → ❺

Adjective/adverb + verb combinations are written as one word if the first component of the compound is not a word in its own right → ❻

Adjective + verb combinations are normally written separately but writing them as one word is also acceptable → ❼

BUT: In figurative usage, such combinations are always written as one word → ❽

Verb combinations with **-ander** are written as one word → ❾

Verb combinations with **-seits** and **-wärts** are written as one word → ❿

Verb combinations with sein are written separately → ⓫

1. Ski fahren, Schlange stehen, Klavier spielen

2. bergsteigen, brustschwimmen, kopfrechnen, sonnenbaden

3. eislaufen, kopfstehen, teilhaben

4. baden gehen, sitzen bleiben *or* sitzenbleiben, spazieren gehen *or* spazierengehen

5. gefangen nehmen, getrennt schreiben

6. abhandenkommen, fehlschlagen, kundgeben

7. bekannt machen *or* bekanntmachen, blau färben *or* blaufärben, klein schneiden *or* kleinschneiden

8. freihalten, leichtfallen, nahebringen, satthaben

9. aneinanderlegen, auseinanderlaufen, durcheinanderreden

10. abseitsstehen, abwärtsgehen

11. auf sein, zu sein

Verbs followed by Prepositions

Some verbs in English usage require a preposition (*for/with/by* etc) for their completion.

This also happens in German, though the prepositions used with German verbs may not be those expected from their English counterparts → ❶

The preposition used may significantly alter the meaning of a verb in German → ❷

Occasionally German verbs use a preposition where their English equivalents do not → ❸

Prepositions used with verbs behave as normal prepositions and affect the *case* of the following noun (see page 198).

A verb plus preposition may be followed by a clause containing another verb rather than by a noun or pronoun. This often corresponds to an *-ing* construction in English:

> Thank you for *coming*

In German, this is dealt with in two ways:

- Where the "verb-plus-preposition" construction has the same subject as the following verb, the preposition is preceded by **da-** or **dar-** and the following verb becomes an infinitive used with zu → ❹

- Where the subject of the "verb-plus-preposition" is not the same as for the following verb, a dass clause is used → ❺

Following clauses may also be introduced by interrogatives (ob, wie etc) if the meaning demands them → ❻

❶ COMPARE:

sich sehnen **nach**	to long *for*
warten **auf**	to wait *for*
bitten **um**	to ask *for*

❷

bestehen	to pass (an examination/a test *etc*)
bestehen aus	to consist of
bestehen auf	to insist on

sich freuen auf	to look forward to
sich freuen über	to be pleased about

❸

diskutieren über	to discuss

❹ Ich freue mich sehr darauf, mal wieder mit ihm zu arbeiten.
I am looking forward to working with him again.

❺ Ich freue mich sehr darauf, dass du morgen kommst.
I am looking forward to your coming tomorrow.

Er sorgte dafür, dass die Kinder immer gut gepflegt waren.
He saw to it that the children were always well cared for.

❻ Er dachte lange darüber nach, ob er es wirklich kaufen wollte.
He thought for ages about whether he really wanted to buy it.

Sie freut sich darüber, wie schnell ihre Schüler gelernt haben.
She is pleased at how quickly her students have learned.

Verbs followed by Prepositions *continued*

COMMON VERBS FOLLOWED BY PREPOSITION PLUS **ACCUSATIVE CASE**:

achten auf	to pay attention to, keep an eye on → ①
sich amüsieren über	to laugh at, smile about
sich ärgern über	to get annoyed about/with
sich bewerben um	to apply for → ②
bitten um	to ask for → ③
denken an	to be thinking of → ④
denken über	to hold an opinion of, think about → ⑤
sich erinnern an	to remember
sich freuen auf	to look forward to
sich freuen über	to be pleased about → ⑥
sich gewöhnen an	to get used to → ⑦
sich interessieren für	to be interested in → ⑧
kämpfen um	to fight for
sich kümmern um	to take care of, see to
nachdenken über	to ponder, reflect on → ⑨
sich unterhalten über	to talk about
sich verlassen auf	to rely on, depend on → ⑩
warten auf	to wait for

COMMON VERBS FOLLOWED BY PREPOSITION PLUS **DATIVE CASE**:

abhängen von ·	to be dependent on → ⑪
sich beschäftigen mit	to occupy oneself with → ⑫
bestehen aus	to consist of → ⑬
leiden an/unter	to suffer from → ⑭
neigen zu	to be inclined to
riechen nach	to smell of → ⑮
schmecken nach	to taste of
sich sehnen nach	to long for
sterben an	to die of
teilnehmen an	to take part in → ⑯
träumen von	to dream of → ⑰
sich verabschieden von	to say goodbye to
sich verstehen mit	to get along with, get on with
zittern vor	to tremble with → ⑱

Examples

1   Er musste auf die Kinder achten.
He had to keep an eye on the children.

2   Sie hat sich um die Stelle als Sekretärin beworben.
She applied for the post of secretary.

3   Die Kinder baten ihre Mutter um Plätzchen.
The children asked their mother for some biscuits.

4   Woran denkst du?
What are you thinking about?
Daran habe ich gar nicht mehr gedacht.
I'd forgotten about that.

5   Wie denkt ihr darüber?
What do you think about it?

6   Ich freute mich sehr darüber, Johannes besucht zu haben.
I was very glad I had visited Johannes.

7   Man gewöhnt sich an alles. One gets used to anything.

8   Sie interessiert sich sehr für Politik.
She is very interested in politics.

9   Er hatte schon lange darüber nachgedacht.
He had been thinking about it for a long time.

10   Er verlässt sich darauf, dass seine Frau alles tut.
He relies on his wife to do everything.

11   Das hängt davon ab.
It all depends.

12   Sie sind im Moment sehr damit beschäftigt, ihr neues Haus in Ordnung zu bringen.
They are very busy sorting out their new house at the moment.

13   Dieser Kuchen besteht aus Eiern, Mehl und Zucker.
This cake is made from eggs, flour and sugar.

14   Sie hat lange an dieser Krankheit gelitten.
She suffered from this illness for a long time.
Alte Leute können sehr unter der Einsamkeit leiden.
Old people can suffer from dreadful loneliness.

15   Der Kuchen roch nach Zimt.
The cake smelled of cinnamon.

16   Sie hat an der Bonner Tagung teilnehmen müssen.
She had to attend the Bonn conference.

17   Er hat von seinem Urlaub geträumt.
He dreamt of his holiday.

18   Er zitterte vor Freude.
He was trembling with joy.

Verbs followed by the Dative

Some verbs have a direct object and an indirect object. In the English sentence "*He gave me a book*", *a book* is the direct object of *gave* and would be in the accusative and *me* (= *to me*) is the indirect object and would appear in the dative case in German → **1**

In German, as in English, this type of verb is usually concerned with giving or telling something to someone, or with performing an action for someone → **2**

The normal word order after such verbs is for the direct object to follow the indirect, *except* where the direct object is a personal pronoun (see page 224) → **2**

This order may be reversed for emphasis → **3**

Some examples of verbs followed by the dative in this way:

anbieten	gönnen	schicken	
bringen	kaufen	schreiben	
beweisen	leihen	schulden	→ **4**
erzählen	mitteilen	verkaufen	
geben	schenken	zeigen	

Certain verbs in German however can be followed *only* by an indirect object in the dative case. These should be noted especially, since most of them are quite different from their English equivalents:

begegnen	gratulieren	schmeicheln	
danken	helfen	trauen	
fehlen	imponieren	trotzen	
gefallen	misstrauen	vorangehen	→ **5**
gehören	nachgehen	wehtun	
gelingen	schaden	widersprechen	
gleichen	schmecken	widerstehen	

For how to form the passive of such verbs, see page 36.

Examples

1   Er gab mir ein Buch.   He gave me a book.

2   Er wusch dem Kind (*indirect*) das Gesicht (*direct*).
He washed the child's face.
Er erzählte ihm (*indirect*) eine Geschichte (*direct*).
He told him a story.
BUT:
Er hat sie (*direct*) meiner Mutter (*indirect*) gezeigt.
He showed it to my mother.
Kaufst du es (*direct*) mir (*indirect*)?
Will you buy it for me?

3   Er wollte das Buch (*direct*) seiner Mutter (*indirect*) geben.
(*This emphasises* seiner Mutter)
He wanted to give the book to his mother.

4   Er bot ihr die Arbeitsstelle an.   He offered her the job.
Bringst du mir eins?   Will you bring me one?
Ich gönne dir das neue Kleid.
I want you to have the new dress.
Er hat ihr mitgeteilt, dass ...   He told her that ...
Ich schenke meiner Mutter Parfüm zum Geburtstag.
I am giving my mother perfume for her birthday.
Das schulde ich ihm.   I owe him that.
Zeig es mir!   Show me it!

5   Er ist seinem Freund in der Stadt begegnet.
He bumped into his friend in town.
Mir fehlt der Mut dazu.   I don't have the courage.
Es ist ihnen gelungen.   They succeeded.
Wem gehört dieses Buch?   Whose book is this?
Er wollte ihr nicht helfen.   He refused to help her.
Ich gratuliere dir!   Congratulations!
Rauchen schadet der Gesundheit.
Smoking is bad for your health.
Das Essen hat ihnen gut geschmeckt.
They enjoyed the meal.

There is/There are

There are three ways of expressing this in German:

Es gibt

This is always used in the singular form, and is followed by an accusative object which may be either singular or plural → ❶

Es gibt is used to refer to things of a general nature or location → ❷

It also has some idiomatic usages → ❸

Es ist/es sind

The es here merely introduces the real subject. The verb therefore becomes plural where the real subject is plural. The real subject is in the nominative case → ❹

The es is not required and is therefore omitted when the verb and real subject come together. This happens when inversion of subject and verb occurs (see page 226) and in subordinate clauses → ❺

Es ist or es sind are used to refer to:

- subjects with a specific and confined location.
  This location must always be mentioned either by name or by da, darauf, darin etc → ❻
- temporary existence → ❼
- as a beginning to a story → ❽

The passive voice

Often *there is/there are* in English will be rendered by a verb in the passive voice in German → ❾

Examples

1   Es gibt zu viele Probleme dabei.
There are too many problems with it.
Es gibt kein besseres Bier.
There's no better beer.

2   Es gibt bestimmt Regen.
It's definitely going to rain.
Ruhe hat es bei uns nie gegeben.
There has never been any peace here.

3   Was gibts (= gibt es) zum Essen?   What is there to eat?
Was gibts?   What's wrong?, What's up?
So was gibts doch nicht!   That's impossible!

4   Es waren zwei ältere Leute unten im Hof.
There were two elderly people down in the yard.
Es sind so viele Touristen da.
There are so many tourists there.

5   Unten im Hof waren zwei ältere Leute.
Down in the yard were two elderly people.
Wenn so viele Touristen da sind, ...
If there are so many tourists there, ...

6   Es waren viele Flaschen Sekt im Keller.
There were a lot of bottles of champagne in the cellar.
Ein Brief lag auf dem Tisch. Es waren auch zwei
Bücher darauf.
A letter lay on the table. There were also two books on it.

7   Es war niemand da.
There was no-one there.

8   Es war einmal ein König ...
Once upon a time there was a king ...

9   Es wurde auf der Party viel getrunken.
There was a lot of drinking at the party.

Use of "**es**" as an Anticipatory Object

Many verbs can have as their object a dass clause or an infinitive with zu
→ ❶

With some verbs es is used as an object to anticipate this clause or
infinitive phrase → ❷

When the clause or infinitive phrase begins the sentence, es is not used
in the main clause but its place may be taken by an optional das → ❸

COMMON VERBS WHICH *USUALLY* HAVE THE "**ES**" OBJECT:

es ablehnen, zu	to refuse to
es aushalten, zu tun/dass	to stand doing → ❹
es ertragen, zu tun/dass	to endure doing
es leicht haben, zu	to find it easy to → ❺
es nötig haben, zu	to need to → ❻
es satt haben, zu	to have had enough of (doing)
es verstehen, zu	to know how to → ❼

COMMON VERBS WHICH *OFTEN* HAVE THE "**ES**" OBJECT:

es jemandem anhören/ansehen, dass	to tell by listening to/ looking at someone that → ❽
es begreifen, dass/warum/wie	to understand that/why/ how
es bereuen, zu tun/dass	to regret having done/that
es leugnen, dass	to deny that → ❾
es unternehmen, zu	to undertake to
es jemandem verbieten, zu	to forbid someone to
es jemandem vergeben, dass	to forgive someone for (doing)
es jemandem verschweigen, dass	not to tell someone that
es jemandem verzeihen, dass	to forgive someone for (doing)
es wagen zu	to dare to

❶ Er wusste, dass wir pünktlich kommen würden.
He knew that we would come on time.
Sie fing an zu lachen.
She began to laugh.

❷ Er hatte es abgelehnt mitzufahren.
He had refused to come.

❸ Dass es Wolfgang war, das haben wir ihr verschwiegen.
OR:
Dass es Wolfgang war, haben wir ihr verschwiegen.
We didn't tell her that it was Wolfgang.

❹ Ich halte es nicht mehr aus, bei ihnen zu arbeiten.
I can't stand working for them any longer.

❺ Er hatte es nicht leicht, sie zu überreden.
He didn't have an easy job persuading them.

❻ Ich habe es nicht nötig, mit dir darüber zu reden.
I don't have to talk to you about it.

❼ Er versteht es, Autos zu reparieren.
He knows about repairing cars.

❽ Man hörte es ihm sofort an, dass er kein Deutscher war.
OR:
Dass er kein Deutscher war, (das) hörte man ihm sofort an.
One could tell immediately (from the way he spoke) that he
wasn't German.

Man sieht es ihm sofort an, dass er dein Bruder ist.
OR:
Dass er dein Bruder ist, (das) sieht man ihm sofort an.
One can tell at a glance that he's your brother.

❾ Er hat es nie geleugnet, das Geld genommen zu haben.
He has never denied taking the money.

Verb Table

Strong and Mixed Verbs – Principal Parts

INFINITIVE	TRANSLATION	3RD PERSON PRESENT
backen	to bake	er bäckt
befehlen	to command	er befiehlt
beginnen	to begin	er beginnt
beißen	to bite	er beißt
bergen	to rescue	er birgt
bersten	to burst *intr*	er birst
betrügen	to deceive	er betrügt
biegen	to bend *tr*/to turn *intr*	er biegt
bieten	to offer	er bietet
binden	to tie	er bindet
bitten	to ask for	er bittet
blasen	to blow	er bläst
bleiben	to remain	er bleibt
braten	to fry	er brät
brechen	to break	er bricht
brennen	to burn	er brennt
bringen	to bring	er bringt
denken	to think	er denkt
dreschen	to thresh	er drischt
dringen	to penetrate	er dringt
dürfen	to be allowed to	er darf
empfehlen	to recommend	er empfiehlt
erlöschen	to go out (*fire, light*)	er erlischt
erschallen	to resound	er erschallt
erschrecken[1]	to be startled	er erschrickt
erwägen	to weigh up	er erwägt
essen	to eat	er isst
fahren	to travel	er fährt

[1] erschrecken meaning "to frighten" is weak:
erschrecken, erschreckt, erschreckte, hat erschreckt

Verb Table

3RD PERSON IMPERFECT	PERFECT	IMPERFECT SUBJUNCTIVE
er backte	er hat gebacken	er backte
er befahl	er hat befohlen	er befähle
er begann	er hat begonnen	er begänne
er biss	er hat gebissen	er bisse
er barg	er hat geborgen	er bärge
er barst	er ist geborsten	er bärste
er betrog	er hat betrogen	er betröge
er bog	er hat/ist gebogen	er böge
er bot	er hat geboten	er böte
er band	er hat gebunden	er bände
er bat	er hat gebeten	er bäte
er blies	er hat geblasen	er bliese
er blieb	er ist geblieben	er bliebe
er briet	er hat gebraten	er briete
er brach	er hat/ist gebrochen	er bräche
er brannte	er hat gebrannt	er brennte
er brachte	er hat gebracht	er brächte
er dachte	er hat gedacht	er dächte
er drosch	er hat gedroschen	er drösche
er drang	er ist gedrungen	er dränge
er durfte	er hat gedurft/dürfen[1]	er dürfte
er empfahl	er hat empfohlen	er empfähle
er erlosch	er ist erloschen	er erlösche
er erschallte	er ist erschollen	er erschölle
er erschrak	er ist erschrocken	er erschräke
er erwog	er hat erwogen	er erwöge
er aß	er hat gegessen	er äße
er fuhr	er ist gefahren	er führe

[1] The second (infinitive) form is used when combined with an infinitive construction (see page 56).

Strong and Mixed Verbs *continued*

INFINITVE	TRANSLATION	3RD PERSON PRESENT
fallen	to fall	er fällt
fangen	to catch	er fängt
fechten	to fight	er ficht
finden	to find	er findet
fliegen	to fly	er fliegt
fliehen	to flee *tr/intr*	er flieht
fließen	to flow	er fließt
fressen	to eat (*of animals*)	er frisst
frieren	to be cold/to freeze over	er friert
gebären	to give birth to	sie gebärt
geben	to give	er gibt
gedeihen	to thrive	er gedeiht
gehen	to go	er geht
gelingen	to succeed	es gelingt
gelten	to be valid	er gilt
genesen	to get well	er genest
genießen	to enjoy	er genießt
geraten	to get into (*a state etc*)	er gerät
geschehen	to happen	es geschieht
gewinnen	to win	er gewinnt
gießen	to pour	er gießt
gleichen	to resemble/to equal	er gleicht
gleiten	to glide	er gleitet
glimmen	to glimmer	er glimmt
graben	to dig	er gräbt
greifen	to grip	er greift
haben	to have	er hat
halten	to hold/to stop	er hält
hängen[1]	to hang *intr*	er hängt
heben	to lift	er hebt
heißen	to be called	er heißt

[1] hängen is weak when used transitively:
hängen, hängt, hängte, hat gehängt

3RD PERSON IMPERFECT	PERFECT	IMPERFECT SUBJUNCTIVE
er fiel	er ist gefallen	er fiele
er fing	er hat gefangen	er finge
er focht	er hat gefochten	er föchte
er fand	er hat gefunden	er fände
er flog	er hat/ist geflogen	er flöge
er floh	er hat/ist geflohen	er flöhe
er floss	er ist geflossen	er flösse
er fraß	er hat gefressen	er fräße
er fror	er hat/ist gefroren	er fröre
sie gebar	sie hat geboren	sie gebäre
er gab	er hat gegeben	er gäbe
er gedieh	er ist gediehen	er gediehe
er ging	er ist gegangen	er ginge
es gelang	es ist gelungen	es gelänge
er galt	er hat gegolten	er gälte
er genas	er ist genesen	er genäse
er genoss	er hat genossen	er genösse
er geriet	er ist geraten	er geriete
es geschah	es ist geschehen	es geschähe
er gewann	er hat gewonnen	er gewönne
er goss	er hat gegossen	er gösse
er glich	er hat geglichen	er gliche
er glitt	er ist geglitten	er glitte
er glomm	er hat geglommen	er glömme
er grub	er hat gegraben	er grübe
er griff	er hat gegriffen	er griffe
er hatte	er hat gehabt	er hätte
er hielt	er hat gehalten	er hielte
er hing	er hat gehangen	er hinge
er hob	er hat gehoben	er höbe
er hieß	er hat geheißen	er hieße

Strong and Mixed Verbs *continued*

INFINITVE	TRANSLATION	3RD PERSON PRESENT
helfen	to help	er hilft
kennen	to know (*someone etc*)	er kennt
klingen	to sound	er klingt
kommen	to come	er kommt
kneifen	to pinch	er kneift
können	to be able to	er kann
kriechen	to crawl	er kriecht
laden	to load	er lädt
lassen	to allow	er lässt
laufen	to walk/to run	er läuft
leiden	to suffer	er leidet
leihen	to lend	er leiht
lesen	to read	er liest
liegen	to lie	er liegt
lügen	to tell a lie	er lügt
mahlen	to grind	er mahlt
messen	to measure	er misst
misslingen	to fail	es misslingt
mögen	to like to	er mag
müssen	to have to	er muss
nehmen	to take	er nimmt
nennen	to call	er nennt
pfeifen	to whistle	er pfeift
preisen	to praise	er preist
quellen	to gush	er quillt
raten	to advise/to guess	er rät
reiben	to rub	er reibt
reißen	to tear *tr/intr*	er reißt
reiten	to ride *tr/intr*	er reitet

3RD PERSON IMPERFECT	PERFECT	IMPERFECT SUBJUNCTIVE
er half	er hat geholfen	er hülfe
er kannte	er hat gekannt	er kennte
er klang	er hat geklungen	er klänge
er kam	er ist gekommen	er käme
er kniff	er hat gekniffen	er kniffe
er konnte	er hat gekonnt/können[1]	er könnte
er kroch	er ist gekrochen	er kröche
er lud	er hat geladen	er lüde
er ließ	er hat gelassen	er ließe
er lief	er ist gelaufen	er liefe
er litt	er hat gelitten	er litte
er lieh	er hat geliehen	er liehe
er las	er hat gelesen	er läse
er lag	er hat gelegen	er läge
er log	er hat gelogen	er löge
er mahlte	er hat gemahlen	er mahlte
er maß	er hat gemessen	er mäße
es misslang	es ist misslungen	es misslänge
er mochte	er hat gemocht/mögen[1]	er möchte
er musste	er hat gemusst/müssen[1]	er müsste
er nahm	er hat genommen	er nähme
er nannte	er hat genannt	er nennte
er pfiff	er hat gepfiffen	er pfiffe
er pries	er hat gepriesen	er priese
er quoll	er ist gequollen	er quölle
er riet	er hat geraten	er riete
er rieb	er hat gerieben	er riebe
er riss	er hat/ist gerissen	er risse
er ritt	er hat/ist geritten	er ritte

[1] The second (infinitive) form is used when combined with an infinitive construction (see page 56).

Strong and Mixed Verbs *continued*

INFINITVE	TRANSLATION	3RD PERSON PRESENT
rennen	to run	er rennt
riechen	to smell	er riecht
ringen	to wrestle	er ringt
rinnen	to flow	er rinnt
rufen	to shout	er ruft
salzen	to salt	er salzt
saufen	to booze/to drink	er säuft
saugen	to suck	er saugt
schaffen[1]	to create	er schafft
scheiden	to separate *tr/intr*	er scheidet
scheinen	to seem/to shine	er scheint
schelten	to scold	er schilt
scheren	to shear	er schert
schieben	to shove	er schiebt
schießen	to shoot	er schießt
schlafen	to sleep	er schläft
schlagen	to hit	er schlägt
schleichen	to creep	er schleicht
schleifen	to grind	er schleift
schließen	to close	er schließt
schlingen	to wind	er schlingt
schmeißen	to fling	er schmeißt
schmelzen	to melt *tr/intr*	er schmilzt
schneiden	to cut	er schneidet
schreiben	to write	er schreibt
schreien	to shout	er schreit
schreiten	to stride	er schreitet
schweigen	to be silent	er schweigt

[1]schaffen meaning "to work hard/to manage" is weak:
   schaffen, schafft, schaffte, hat geschafft

Verb Table

3RD PERSON IMPERFECT	PERFECT	IMPERFECT SUBJUNCTIVE
er rannte	er ist gerannt	er rennte
er roch	er hat gerochen	er röche
er rang	er hat gerungen	er ränge
er rann	er ist geronnen	er ränne
er rief	er hat gerufen	er riefe
er salzte	er hat gesalzen	er salzte
er soff	er hat gesoffen	er söffe
er sog	er hat gesogen	er söge
er schuf	er hat geschaffen	er schüfe
er schied	er hat/ist geschieden	er schiede
er schien	er hat geschienen	er schiene
er schalt	er hat gescholten	er schölte
er schor	er hat geschoren	er schöre
er schob	er hat geschoben	er schöbe
er schoss	er hat geschossen	er schösse
er schlief	er hat geschlafen	er schliefe
er schlug	er hat geschlagen	er schlüge
er schlich	er ist geschlichen	er schliche
er schliff	er hat geschliffen	er schliffe
er schloss	er hat geschlossen	er schlösse
er schlang	er hat geschlungen	er schlänge
er schmiss	er hat geschmissen	er schmisse
er schmolz	er hat/ist geschmolzen	er schmölze
er schnitt	er hat geschnitten	er schnitte
er schrieb	er hat geschrieben	er schriebe
er schrie	er hat geschrien	er schrie
er schritt	er ist geschritten	er schritte
er schwieg	er hat geschwiegen	er schwiege

Strong and Mixed Verbs *continued*

INFINITVE	TRANSLATION	3RD PERSON PRESENT
schwellen[1]	to swell *intr*	er schwillt
schwimmen	to swim	er schwimmt
schwingen	to swing	er schwingt
schwören	to vow	er schwört
sehen	to see	er sieht
sein	to be	er ist
senden[2]	to send	er sendet
singen	to sing	er singt
sinken	to sink	er sinkt
sinnen	to ponder	er sinnt
sitzen	to sit	er sitzt
sollen	to be supposed to be	er soll
spalten	to split *tr/intr*	er spaltet
speien	to spew	er speit
spinnen	to spin	er spinnt
sprechen	to speak	er spricht
sprießen	to sprout	er sprießt
springen	to jump	er springt
stechen	to sting/to prick	er sticht
stehen	to stand	er steht
stehlen	to steal	er stiehlt
steigen	to climb	er steigt
sterben	to die	er stirbt
stinken	to stink	er stinkt
stoßen	to push	er stößt
streichen	to stroke/to wander	er streicht
streiten	to quarrel	er streitet

[1] schwellen is weak when used transitively:
  schwellen, schwellt, schwellte, hat geschwellt
[2] senden meaning "to broadcast" is weak:
  senden, sendet, sendete, hat gesendet

Verb Table

3RD PERSON IMPERFECT	PERFECT	IMPERFECT SUBJUNCTIVE
er schwoll	er ist geschwollen	er schwölle
er schwamm	er ist geschwommen	er schwömme
er schwang	er hat geschwungen	er schwänge
er schwor	er hat geschworen	er schwüre
er sah	er hat gesehen	er sähe
er war	er ist gewesen	er wäre
er sandte	er hat gesandt	er sendete
er sang	er hat gesungen	er sänge
er sank	er ist gesunken	er sänke
er sann	er hat gesonnen	er sänne
er saß	er hat gesessen	er säße
er sollte	er hat gesollt/sollen[1]	er sollte
er spaltete	er hat/ist gespalten	er spaltete
er spie	er hat gespien	er spie
er spann	er hat gesponnen	er spönne
er sprach	er hat gesprochen	er spräche
er spross	er ist gesprossen	er sprösse
er sprang	er ist gesprungen	er spränge
er stach	er hat gestochen	er stäche
er stand	er hat gestanden	er stünde
er stahl	er hat gestohlen	er stähle
er stieg	er ist gestiegen	er stiege
er starb	er ist gestorben	er stürbe
er stank	er hat gestunken	er stänke
er stieß	er hat/ist gestoßen	er stieße
er strich	er hat/ist gestrichen	er striche
er stritt	er hat gestritten	er stritte

[1] The second (infinitive) form is used when combined with an infinitive construction (see page 56).

Strong and Mixed Verbs *continued*

INFINITVE	TRANSLATION	3RD PERSON PRESENT
tragen	to carry/to wear	er trägt
treffen	to meet	er trifft
treiben	to drive/to engage in	er treibt
treten	to kick/step	er tritt
trinken	to drink	er trinkt
tun	to do	er tut
verderben	to spoil/to go bad	er verdirbt
verdrießen	to irritate	er verdrießt
vergessen	to forget	er vergisst
verlieren	to lose	er verliert
vermeiden	to avoid	er vermeidet
verschwinden	to disappear	er verschwindet
verzeihen	to pardon	er verzeiht
wachsen	to grow	er wächst
waschen	to wash	er wäscht
weichen	to yield	er weicht
weisen	to point	er weist
wenden	to turn	er wendet
werben	to recruit	er wirbt
werden	to become	er wird
werfen	to throw	er wirft
wiegen[1]	to weigh	er wiegt
winden	to wind	er windet
wissen	to know	er weiß
wollen	to want to	er will
ziehen	to pull	er zieht
zwingen	to force	er zwingt

[1] wiegen meaning "to rock" is weak:
wiegen, wiegt, wiegte, hat gewiegt

3RD PERSON IMPERFECT	PERFECT	IMPERFECT SUBJUNCTIVE
er trug	er hat getragen	er trüge
er traf	er hat getroffen	er träfe
er trieb	er hat getrieben	er triebe
er trat	er hat/ist getreten	er träte
er trank	er hat getrunken	er tränke
er tat	er hat getan	er täte
er verdarb	er hat/ist verdorben	er verdürbe
er verdross	er hat verdrossen	er verdrösse
er vergaß	er hat vergessen	er vergäße
er verlor	er hat verloren	er verlöre
er vermied	er hat vermieden	er vermiede
er verschwand	er ist verschwunden	er verschwände
er verzieh	er hat verziehen	er verziehe
er wuchs	er ist gewachsen	er wüchse
er wusch	er hat gewaschen	er wüsche
er wich	er ist gewichen	er wiche
er wies	er hat gewiesen	er wiese
er wandte	er hat gewandt	er wendete
er warb	er hat geworben	er würbe
er wurde	er ist geworden	er würde
er warf	er hat geworfen	er würfe
er wog	er hat gewogen	er wöge
er wand	er hat gewunden	er wände
er wusste	er hat gewusst	er wüsste
er wollte	er hat gewollt/wollen[1]	er wollte
er zog	er hat gezogen	er zöge
er zwang	er hat gezwungen	er zwänge

[1] The second (infinitive) form is used when combined with an infinitive construction (see page 56).

The Declension of Nouns

In German, all nouns may be declined. This means that they may change their form according to their:

> *gender* (i.e. masculine, feminine or neuter) → ❶

> *case* (i.e. their function in the sentence) → ❷

> *number* (i.e. singular or plural) → ❸

Nearly all *feminine* nouns change in the *plural* form by adding **-n** or **-en**. Many *masculine* and *neuter* nouns also change → ❹

Masculine and *neuter* nouns, with a few exceptions, add **-s** (**-s** or **-es** for nouns of one syllable) in the *genitive singular* (but see page 110) → ❺

All nouns end in **-n** or **-en** in the *dative plural*. This is added to the nominative plural form, where this does not already end in **-n** → ❻

A good dictionary will provide guidance on how to decline a noun:

The nominative singular form is given in full, followed by the gender of the noun, then the genitive singular and nominative plural endings are shown where appropriate → ❼ .

Adjectives used as nouns are declined as adjectives rather than nouns. Their declension endings are therefore dictated by the preceding article, as well as by number, case and gender (see page 140) → ❽

❶   der Tisch (*masculine*)   the table
          die Gabel (*feminine*)   the fork
          das Mädchen (*neuter*)   the girl

❷   des Tisches   of the table
          auf den Tischen   on the tables

❸   die Tische   the tables
          die Gabeln   the forks
          die Mädchen   the girls

❹

	NOM SING	NOM PLURAL
MASC	der Apfel	die Äpfel
FEM	die Schule	die Schulen
NEUT	das Kind	die Kinder

❺

	NOM SING	GEN SING
MASC	der Apfel	des Apfels
FEM	die Schule	der Schule
NEUT	das Kind	des Kind(e)s

❻

	DAT PLURAL
MASC	den Äpfeln
FEM	den Schulen
NEUT	den Kindern

❼ Tiger *m* -**s**, -

NOM SING	der Tiger	the tiger
GEN SING	des Tigers	of the tiger, the tiger's
NOM PLURAL	die Tiger	the tigers

❽   der Angestellte   the employee
          ein Angestellter   an employee
          (die) Angestellten   (the) employees

The Gender of Nouns

In German a noun may be masculine, feminine or neuter. Gender is relatively unpredictable and has to be learned for each noun. This is best done by learning each noun with its definite article, i.e.

> der Teppich
> die Zeit
> das Bild

The following are intended therefore only as guidelines in helping decide the gender of a word:

Nouns denoting male people and animals are masculine → ❶

Nouns denoting the female of the species, as shown on page 104, are feminine → ❷

But nouns denoting an entire species can be of any gender → ❸

Makes of cars identify with der Wagen and so are usually masculine → ❹

Makes of aeroplane identify with die Maschine and so are usually feminine → ❺

Seasons, months, days of the week, weather features and points of the compass are masculine → ❻

Names of objects that perform an action are usually masculine → ❼

Foreign nouns ending in **-ant**, **-ast**, **-ismus**, **-or** are masculine → ❽

Nouns ending in **-ich**, **-ig**, **-ing**, **-ling** are masculine → ❾

❶
der Hörer	(male) listener
der Löwe	(male) lion
der Onkel	uncle
der Vetter	(male) cousin

❷
die Hörerin	(female) listener
die Löwin	lioness
die Tante	aunt
die Kusine	(female) cousin

❸
der Hund	dog
die Schlange	snake
das Vieh	cattle

❹
| der Mercedes | Mercedes |
| der VW | VW, Volkswagen |

❺
| die Boeing | Boeing |
| die Concorde | Concorde |

❻
der Sommer	summer
der Winter	winter
der August	August
der Freitag	Friday
der Wind	wind
der Schnee	snow
der Norden	north
der Osten	east

❼
| der Wecker | alarm clock |
| der Computer | computer |

❽
| der Ballast | ballast |
| der Chauvinismus | chauvinism |

❾
| der Essig | vinegar |
| der Schmetterling | butterfly |

The Gender of Nouns *continued*

Cardinal numbers are mostly feminine, but fractions are neuter → ➊

Most nouns ending in **-e** are feminine → ➋

> BUT: Male people or animals are masculine → ➌
> Nouns beginning with **Ge–** are normally neuter (*see below*)

Nouns ending in **-heit**, **-keit**, **-schaft**, **-ung**, **-ei** are feminine → ➍

Foreign nouns ending in **-anz**, **-enz**, **-ie**, **-ik**, **-ion**, **-tät**, **-ur** are generally feminine → ➎

Nouns denoting the young of a species are neuter → ➏

Infinitives used as nouns are neuter → ➐

Most nouns beginning with **Ge–** are neuter → ➑

-chen or **-lein** may be added to many words to give a diminutive form. These words are then neuter → ➒

NOTE: The vowel adds an umlaut where possible (i.e. on **a**, **o**, **u** or **au**) and a final **-e** is dropped before these endings → ➓

Nouns ending in **-nis** or **-tum** are neuter → ⑪

Foreign nouns ending in **-at**, **-ett**, **-fon**, **-ma**, **-ment**, **-um**, **-ium** are mainly neuter → ⑫

Adjectives and participles may be used as masculine, feminine or neuter nouns (see page 148) → ⑬

Examples

①   Er hat eine Drei gekriegt.   He got a three (*mark*).
         ein Drittel davon   a third of it

②   die Falte   crease, wrinkle
         die Brücke   bridge

③   der Löwe   lion
         der Matrose   sailor

④   die Eitelkeit   vanity
         die Gewerkschaft   trade union
         die Scheidung   divorce
         die Druckerei   printing works

⑤   die Distanz   distance
         die Konkurrenz   rivalry
         die Theorie   theory
         die Panik   panic
         die Union   union
         die Elektrizität   electricity
         die Partitur   score (*musical*)

⑥   das Baby   baby
         das Kind   child

⑦   das Schwimmen   swimming

⑧   das Geschirr   crockery, dishes
         das Geschöpf   creature

⑨   das Getreide   crop
         das Kindlein   child

⑩   das Bächlein (*from* der Bach)   (small) stream
         das Kätzchen (*from* die Katze)   kitten

⑪   das Ereignis   event
         das Altertum   antiquity

⑫   das Tablett   tray
         das Telefon   telephone
         das Testament   will
         das Podium   platform, podium

⑬   der Verwandte   (male) relative
         die Verwandte   (female) relative
         das Gehackte   minced meat

The Gender of Nouns *continued*

The following are some common exceptions to the gender guidelines shown on pages 100–103:

das Weib	woman, wife
die Person	person
die Waise	orphan
das Mitglied	member
das Genie	genius
die Wache	sentry, guard
das Restaurant	restaurant

The formation of feminine nouns

As in English, male and female forms are sometimes shown by two completely different words e.g.

mother/father

→ ❶

uncle/aunt etc

Where such separate forms do not exist, however, German often differentiates between male and female forms in one of two ways:

- The masculine form may sometimes be made feminine by the addition of **-in** in the singular and **-innen** in the plural → ❷

- An adjective may be used as a feminine noun (see page 148). It has feminine adjective endings which change according to the article which precedes it (see page 140) → ❸

❶

der Vater
father

die Mutter
mother

der Bulle
bull

die Kuh
cow

der Mann
man

die Frau
woman

❷

der Lehrer
(male) teacher

die Lehrerin
(female) teacher

der König
king

die Königin
queen

der Hörer
(male) listener

die Hörerin
(female) listener

Liebe Hörer und Hörerinnen!
Dear listeners!

unsere Leser und Leserinnen
our readers

❸

eine Deutsche
a German woman
Er ist mit einer Deutschen verheiratet.
He is married to a German.

die Abgeordnete
the female MP
Nur Abgeordnete durften dabei sein.
Only MPs were allowed in.

The Gender of Nouns: Miscellaneous Points

Compound nouns

Compound nouns, i.e. nouns composed of two or more nouns put together, are a regular feature of German.

They normally take their gender and declension from the last noun of the compound word → **1**

Exceptions to this are compounds ending in **-mut**, **-scheu** and **-wort**, which do not always have the same gender as the last word when it stands alone → **2**

Nouns with more than one gender

A few nouns have two genders, one of which may only be used in certain regions → **3**

Other nouns have two genders, each of which gives the noun a different meaning → **4**

Abbreviations

These take the gender of their principal noun → **5**

Examples

❶

die Armbanduhr (*from* die Uhr)	wristwatch
der Tomatensalat (*from* der Salat)	tomato salad
der Fußballspieler (*from* der Spieler)	footballer

❷

der Mut	courage
die Armut	poverty
die Demut	humility
die Scheu	fear, shyness, timidity
der Abscheu	repugnance, abhorrence
das Wort	word
die Antwort	reply

❸

das/der Marzipan	marzipan
das/der Keks	biscuit

❹

der Band	volume, book
das Band	ribbon, band, tape, bond
der See	lake
die See	sea
der Leiter	leader, manager
die Leiter	ladder
der Tau	dew
das Tau	rope, hawser

❺

der DGB (*from* der Deutsche Gewerkschaftsbund)	the Federation of German Trade Unions
die EU (*from* die Europäische Gemeinschaft)	the EU
das AKW (*from* das Atomkraftwerk)	nuclear power station

The Cases

There are four grammatical *cases* – nominative, accusative, genitive and dative – which are generally shown by the form of the article used before the noun (see page 118).

The nominative case

The nominative singular is the form shown in full in dictionary entries.

The nominative plural is formed as described on page 98.

The nominative case is used for:

- the subject of a verb → **❶**
- the complement of sein or werden → **❷**

The accusative case

The noun in the accusative case usually has the same form as in the nominative → **❸**

Exceptions to this are "weak" masculine nouns (see page 115) and adjectives used as nouns (see page 148).

It is used:

- for the direct object of the verb → **❹**
- after those prepositions which always take the accusative case (see pages 206–209) → **❺**
- to show change of location after prepositions of place (see page 210) → **❻**
- in many expressions of time and place which do not contain a preposition → **❼**
- in certain fixed expressions → **❽**

1. Das Mädchen singt.   The girl is singing.

2. Er ist ein guter Lehrer.   He's a good teacher.
   Das wird ein Pullover.   It's going to be a jumper.

3. das Lied   the song   (*nominative*)
   das Lied   the song   (*accusative*)

   der Wagen   the car   (*nominative*)
   den Wagen   the car   (*accusative*)

   die Dose   the tin   (*nominative*)
   die Dose   the tin   (*accusative*)

4. Er hat ein Lied gesungen.   He sang a song.

5. für seine Freundin   for his girlfriend
   ohne diesen Wagen   without this car
   durch das Rauchen   through smoking

6. in die Stadt (*accusative*)   into town
   BUT:
   in der Stadt (*dative*)   in town

7. Das macht sie jeden Donnerstag.
   She does that every Thursday.
   Die Schule ist einen Kilometer entfernt.
   The school is a kilometre away.

8. Guten Abend!   Good evening!
   Vielen Dank!   Thank you very much!

The Cases *continued*

The genitive case

In the genitive singular, *masculine* and *neuter* nouns take endings as follows:

- **-s** is added to nouns ending in **-en**, **-el**, **-er** → ❶
- **-es** is added to nouns ending in **-tz**, **-sch**, **-st**, **-ss** or **-ß** → ❷
- for nouns of one syllable, either **-s** or **-es** may be added → ❸

Feminine singular and all *plural* nouns have the same form as their nominative.

The genitive is used:

- to show possession → ❸
- after prepositions taking the genitive (see page 212) → ❹
- in expressions of time when the exact occasion is not specified → ❺

The dative case

Singular nouns in the dative have the same form as in the nominative → ❻
-e may be added to the dative singular of *masculine* and *neuter* nouns if the sentence rhythm needs it → ❼
This **-e** is always used in certain set phrases → ❽
Dative plural forms for all genders end in **-n** → ❾
The only exceptions to this are some nouns of foreign origin that end in **-s** in all plural forms, including the dative plural (see page 114) → ❿

The dative is used:

- as the indirect object → ⓫
- after verbs taking the dative (see page 80) → ⓬
- after prepositions taking the dative (see page 202) → ⓭
- in certain idiomatic expressions → ⓮
- instead of the possessive adjective to refer to parts of the body and items of clothing (see page 122) → ⓯

Examples

1

der Wagen car	▶ des Wagens of the car
das Rauchen smoking	▶ des Rauchens of smoking
der Computer computer	▶ des Computers of the computer
der Reiter rider	▶ des Reiters of the rider

2

der Sitz seat; residence	▶ des Sitzes of the seat/residence
der Arzt doctor	▶ des Arztes of the doctor
das Schloss castle	▶ des Schlosses of the castle

3

Die Zähne des Kindes waren faul geworden.
The child's teeth had decayed.
Der Name des Kinds war ihm unbekannt.
The child's name was not known to him.

4

wegen seiner Krankheit	because of his illness
trotz ihrer Bemühungen	despite her efforts

5

eines Tages	one day

6

dem Wagen	to the car
der Frau	to the woman
dem Mädchen	to the girl

7

zu welchem Zwecke?	to what purpose?

8

nach Hause   home

sich zu Tode trinken/arbeiten
to drink/work oneself to death

9

mit den Anwälten	with the lawyers
nach den Kindern	after the children

10

SINGULAR	PLURAL
das Auto	die Autos
das Auto	die Autos
des Autos	der Autos
dem Auto	den Autos

11 Er gab dem Mann das Buch.   He gave the man the book.

12 Sie half ihrer Mutter.   She helped her mother.

13 Nach dem Essen ...   After eating ...

14 Mir ist kalt   I'm cold

15 Ich habe mir die Hände gewaschen.   I've washed my hands.

The Formation of Plurals

The following pages show full noun declensions in all their singular and plural forms.
Those nouns shown represent the most common types of plural.

Most feminine nouns add **-n**, **-en** or **-nen** to form their plurals:

	SINGULAR	PLURAL
NOM	die Frau	die Frauen
ACC	die Frau	die Frauen
GEN	der Frau	der Frauen
DAT	der Frau	den Frauen

Many nouns have no plural ending.
These are mainly masculine or neuter nouns ending in **-en**, **-er**, **-el**:

	SINGULAR	PLURAL
NOM	der Onkel	die Onkel
ACC	den Onkel	die Onkel
GEN	des Onkels	der Onkel
DAT	dem Onkel	den Onkeln

An umlaut is sometimes added to the vowel in the plural forms:

	SINGULAR	PLURAL
NOM	der Apfel	die Äpfel
ACC	den Apfel	die Äpfel
GEN	des Apfels	der Äpfel
DAT	dem Apfel	die Äpfeln

The Formation of Plurals *continued*

Many nouns form their plurals by adding ⸚e:

	SINGULAR	PLURAL
NOM	der Stuhl	die Stühle
ACC	den Stuhl	die Stühle
GEN	des Stuhl(e)s	der Stühle
DAT	dem Stuhl	den Stühlen

	SINGULAR	PLURAL
NOM	die Angst	die Ängste
ACC	die Angst	die Ängste
GEN	der Angst	der Ängste
DAT	der Angst	den Ängsten

Masculine and neuter nouns often add **-e** in the plural:

	SINGULAR	PLURAL
NOM	das Schicksal	die Schicksale
ACC	das Schicksal	die Schicksale
GEN	des Schicksals	der Schicksale
DAT	dem Schicksal	den Schicksalen

Masculine and neuter nouns sometimes add ⸚**er** or **-er**:

	SINGULAR	PLURAL
NOM	das Dach	die Dächer
ACC	das Dach	die Dächer
GEN	des Dach(e)s	der Dächer
DAT	dem Dach	den Dächern

The Formation of Plurals *continued*

Some unusual plurals

SINGULAR	TRANSLATION	PLURAL
das Ministerium	department	die Ministerien
das Prinzip	principle	die Prinzipien
das Thema	theme, topic, subject	die Themen
das Drama	drama	die Dramen
der Firma	firm	die Firmen
das Konto	bank account	die Konten
das Risiko	risk	die Risiken
das Komma	comma/decimal point	die Kommas *or* Kommata
das Baby	baby	die Babys
der Klub	club	die Klubs
der Streik	strike	die Streiks
der Park	park	die Parks
der Chef	boss, chief, head	die Chefs
der Israeli	Israeli	die Israelis
das Restaurant	restaurant	die Restaurants
das Bonbon	sweet	die Bonbons
das Hotel	hotel	die Hotels
das Niveau	standard, level	die Niveaus

German singular/English plural nouns

Some nouns are always plural in English, but singular in German.

Some of the most common examples are:

eine Brille	glasses, spectacles
eine Schere	scissors
eine Hose	trousers

They are only used in the plural in German to mean more than one pair, e.g. zwei Hosen *two pairs of trousers*

The Declension of Nouns

"Weak" masculine nouns

Some masculine nouns have a weak declension, which means that in all cases apart from the nominative singular, they end in **-en** or, if the word ends in a vowel, in **-n**.

The dictionary will often show such nouns as:

>   Junge *m* **-n**, **-n** boy
>   Held *m* **-en**, **-en** hero

Weak masculine nouns are declined as follows:

	SINGULAR	PLURAL
NOM	der Junge	die Jungen
ACC	den Jungen	die Jungen
GEN	des Jungen	der Jungen
DAT	dem Jungen	den Jungen

Masculine nouns falling into this category include:

- those ending in **-og(e)** referring to males:
  der Psychologe, der Geologe, der Astrologe
- those ending in **-aph** (*in many cases now spelt* **-af**) or **-oph**:
  der Graph, der Paragraf, der Philosoph
- those ending in **-nom** referring to males:
  der Astronom, der Gastronom
- those ending in **-ant**:
  der Elefant, der Diamant
- those ending in **-t** referring to males:
  der Astronaut, der Komponist, der Architekt
- miscellaneous others:
  der Bauer, der Chirurg, der Franzose, der Katholik, der Kollege, der Mensch, der Ochse, der Spatz

der Name (*name*) has a different ending in the genitive singular, **-ns**: des Namens. Otherwise it is the same as der Junge shown above. Others in this category are: der Buchstabe, der Funke, der Gedanke, der Glaube.

The Declension of Proper Nouns

Names of people and places add **-s** in the genitive singular unless they are preceded by the definite article or a demonstrative → ❶

Where proper names end in a sibilant (**-s**, **-sch**, **-ss**, **-ß**, **-x**, **-z**, **-tz**) and this makes the genitive form with **-s** almost impossible to pronounce, they are best avoided altogether by using von followed by the dative case → ❷

Personal names can be given diminutive forms if desired. These may be used as a sign of affection as well as with diminutive meaning → ❸

Herr (*Mr*) is always declined where it occurs as part of a proper name → ❹

When articles or adjectives form part of a proper name (e.g. in the names of books, plays, hotels, restaurants etc), these are declined in the normal way (see pages 118 and 140) → ❺

Surnames usually form their plurals by adding **-s**, unless they end in a sibilant, in which case they sometimes add **-ens**. They are often preceded by the definite article → ❻

Nouns of measurement and quantity

These usually remain singular, even if preceded by a plural number → ❼

The substance which they measure follows in the same case as the noun of quantity, and not in the genitive case as in English → ❽

①

Annas Buch   Anna's book
Klaras Mantel   Klara's coat
die Werke Goethes   Goethe's works
BUT: die Versenkung der Bismarck
       the sinking of the Bismarck

②

das Buch von Hans   Hans' book
die Werke von Marx   the works of Marx
die Freundin von Klaus   Klaus's girlfriend

③

von deinem Sabinchen   from your Sabine
Das kleine Kläuschen hat uns dann ein Lied gesungen.
Then little Klaus sang us a song.

④

an Herrn Schmidt   to Mr Schmidt
Sehr geehrte Herren   Dear Sirs

⑤

im Weißen Schwan   in the White Swan
Er hat den „Zauberberg" schon gelesen.
He has already read "The Magic Mountain".

nach Karl dem Großen   after Charlemagne

⑥

Die Schmidts haben uns eingeladen.
The Schmidts have invited us.
Die Zeißens haben uns eingeladen.
Mr and Mrs Zeiß have invited us.

⑦

Möchten Sie zwei Stück?
Would you like two?

⑧

Er wollte zwei Kilo Kartoffeln.
He wanted two kilos of potatoes.
Sie hat drei Tassen Kaffee getrunken.
She drank three cups of coffee.
Drei Glas Weißwein, bitte!
Three glasses of white wine please.

The Definite Article

In English the definite article *the* always keeps the same form:

> *the* book
> *the* books
> with *the* books

In German, however, the definite article has many forms:

In its singular form it changes for masculine, feminine and neuter nouns → **①**

In its plural forms it is the same for all genders → **②**

The definite article is also used to show the function of the noun in the sentence by showing which case it is.

There are four cases, as explained more fully on page 108:

1. *nominative* for the subject or complement of the verb → **③**
2. *accusative* for the object of the verb and after some prepositions → **④**
3. *genitive* to show possession and after some prepositions → **⑤**
4. *dative* for an indirect object (*to* or *for*) and after some prepositions and certain verbs → **⑥**

The forms of the definite article are as follows:

	SINGULAR			PLURAL
	MASC	FEM	NEUT	ALL GENDERS
NOM	der	die	das	die
ACC	den	die	das	die
GEN	des	der	des	der
DAT	dem	der	dem	den

→ **⑦**

1

MASCULINE:	der Mann	the man
	der Wagen	the car
FEMININE:	die Frau	the wife/woman
	die Blume	the flower
NEUTER:	das Ding	the thing
	das Mädchen	the girl

2

die Männer	the men
die Frauen	the women
die Dinge	the things

3

Der Mann ist jung. — The man is young.
Die Frau/das Kind ist jung. — The woman/the child is young.

4

Ich kenne den Mann/die Frau/das Kind.
I know the man/the woman/the child.

5

der Kopf des Mannes/der Frau/des Kindes
the man's/woman's/child's head
wegen des Mannes/der Frau/des Kindes
because of the man/the woman/the child

6

Ich gab es dem Mann/der Frau/dem Kind.
I gave it to the man/to the woman/to the child.

7

SINGULAR

	MASC	FEM	NEUT
NOM	der Mann	die Frau	das Kind
ACC	den Mann	die Frau	das Kind
GEN	des Mann(e)s	der Frau	des Kind(e)s
DAT	dem Mann	der Frau	dem Kind

PLURAL

	MASC	FEM	NEUT
NOM	die Männer	die Frauen	die Kinder
ACC	die Männer	die Frauen	die Kinder
GEN	der Männer	der Frauen	der Kinder
DAT	den Männern	den Frauen	den Kindern

Uses of the Definite Article

When to use and when not to use the definite article in German is one of the most difficult areas for the learner. The following guidelines show where German practice varies from English.

The definite article is used with:

abstract and other nouns where something is being referred to as a whole or as a general idea → ❶

Where these nouns are quantified or modified, the article is not used → ❷

the genitive, unless the noun is a proper name or is acting as a proper name → ❸

occasionally with proper names to make the sex or case clearer → ❹

always with proper names preceded by an adjective → ❺

sometimes with proper names in familiar contexts or for slight emphasis → ❻

with masculine and feminine countries and districts → ❼

with geographical names preceded by an adjective → ❽

with names of seasons → ❾

often with meals → ❿

with the names of roads → ⓫

❶	Das Leben ist schön.	Life is wonderful.
❷	Es braucht Mut.	It needs (some) courage.
	Gibt es dort Leben?	Is there (any) life there?
❸	das Auto des Lehrers	the teacher's car
	Günters Auto	Günter's car
	Muttis Auto	Mummy's car

❹ Er hat es Frau Lehmann gegeben.
Er hat es der Frau Lehmann gegeben.
He gave it to Frau Lehmann.

❺ Der alte Herr Brockhaus ist gestorben.
Old Mr Brockhaus has died.

❻ Ich habe heute den Christoph gesehen.
I saw Christoph today.
Du hast es aber nicht der Petra geschenkt!
You haven't given it to *Petra*!

❼	Deutschland is sehr schön.	Germany is very beautiful.
	Die Schweiz ist auch schön.	Switzerland is also lovely.

❽ im (= in dem) heutigen Deutschland
in today's Germany

❾ Im (= in dem) Sommer gehen wir schwimmen.
We go swimming in summer.
Der Winter kommt bald.
Soon it will be winter.

❿ Das Abendessen wird ab acht Uhr serviert.
Dinner is served from eight o'clock.
Was gibts zum (= zu dem) Mittagessen?
What's for lunch?
BUT:
Um acht Uhr ist Frühstück.
Breakfast is at eight o'clock.

⓫ Sie wohnt jetzt in der Geisener Straße.
She lives in Geisener Road now.

Uses of the Definite Article *continued*

with months of the year except after seit/nach/vor → ①

instead of the possessive adjective to refer to parts of the body and items of clothing → ②

A reflexive pronoun or noun in the dative case is used if it is necessary to clarify to whom the parts of the body belong → ③

in expressions of price, to mean *each/per/a* → ④

with certain common expressions → ⑤

Other uses

The definite article can be used with demonstrative meaning → ⑥

After certain prepositions, forms of the definite article can be shortened (see pages 198–201).
Some of these forms are best used in informal situations → ⑦
Others are commonly and correctly used in formal contexts → ① → ⑤
→ ⑧

Omitting the definite article

The definite article may be omitted in German:

in certain set expressions → ⑨

in *preposition + adjective + noun* combinations → ⑩

For the declension of adjectives without the article see page 142.

Examples

1 Wir fahren im (= in dem) September weg.
We are going away in September.
Wir sind seit September hier.
We have been here since September.

2 Er legte den Hut auf den Tisch.
He laid his hat on the table.
Ich drücke Ihnen die Daumen.
I'm keeping my fingers crossed for you.

3 Er hat sich die Hände schon gewaschen.
He has already washed his hands.
Er hat dem Kind schon die Hände gewaschen.
He has already washed the child's hands.

4 Die kosten ...   They cost ...
... fünf Euro das Pfund   ... five euros a pound
... sechs Euro das Stück   ... six euros each

5 in die Stadt fahren   to go into town
zur (= zu der) Schule gehen   to go to school
mit der Post   by post
mit dem Zug/Bus/Auto   by train/bus/car
im (= in dem) Gefängnis   in prison

6 Du willst **das** Buch lesen!
You want to read *that* book!

7 für das ► fürs vor dem ► vorm um das ► ums *etc*

8 an dem ► am zu dem ► zum zu der ► zur *etc*

9 von Beruf   by profession
nach Wunsch   as desired
Nachrichten hören   to listen to the news

10 Mit gebeugtem Rücken ...   Bending his back, ...

The Indefinite Article

Like the definite article, the form of the indefinite article varies depending on the gender and case of the noun → ❶

It has no plural forms → ❷

The indefinite article is declined as follows:

	MASC	FEM	NEUT
NOM	ein	eine	ein
ACC	einen	eine	ein
GEN	eines	einer	eines
DAT	einem	einer	einem

→ ❸

The indefinite article is omitted in the following:

- descriptions of people by profession, religion, nationality etc → ❹

BUT: Note that the article is included when an adjective precedes the noun → ❺

- in certain fixed expressions → ❻

- after als (*as a*) → ❼

❶

Da ist ein Auto.
Er hat eine Wohnung.
Sie gab es einem Kind.

There's a car.
He has a flat.
She gave it to a child.

❷

Autos sind in letzter Zeit teurer geworden.
Cars have become more expensive recently.

❸

	SINGULAR		
	MASC	FEM	NEUT
NOM	ein Mann	eine Frau	ein Kind
ACC	einen Mann	eine Frau	ein Kind
GEN	eines Mann(e)s	einer Frau	eines Kind(e)s
DAT	einem Mann	einer Frau	einem Kind

❹

Sie ist Kinderärztin.
Sie ist Deutsche.

She's a paediatrician.
She's (a) German.

❺

Sie ist eine sehr geschickte Kinderärztin.
She's a very clever paediatrician.

❻

Es ist Geschmacksache .
Tatsache ist ...

It's a question of taste.
It's a fact ...

❼

Als Ausländer ist er hier nicht wahlberechtigt.
As a foreigner he doesn't have the vote here.

... und ich rede nun als Vater von vier Kindern
... and I'm talking now as a father of four

The Indefinite Article *continued*

In German, a separate negative form of the indefinite article exists. It is declined exactly like ein in the singular, and also has plural forms:

	SINGULAR			PLURAL
	MASC	FEM	NEUT	ALL GENDERS
NOM	kein	keine	kein	keine
ACC	keinen	keine	kein	keine
GEN	keines	keiner	keines	keiner
DAT	keinem	keiner	keinem	keinen

→ ❶

It has the meaning *no/not a/not one/not any* → ❷

It is used even where the equivalent *positive* phrase has no article → ❸

It is also used in many idiomatic expressions → ❹

Nicht ein may be used instead of kein where the ein is to be emphasized → ❺

Examples

❶

	SINGULAR		
	MASC	FEM	NEUT
NOM	kein Mann	keine Frau	kein Kind
ACC	keinen Mann	keine Frau	kein Kind
GEN	keines Mann(e)s	keiner Frau	keines Kind(e)s
DAT	keinem Mann	keiner Frau	keinem Kind

	PLURAL		
	MASC	FEM	NEUT
NOM	keine Männer	keine Frauen	keine Kinder
ACC	keine Männer	keine Frauen	keine Kinder
GEN	keiner Männer	keiner Frauen	keiner Kinder
DAT	keinen Männern	keinen Frauen	keinen Kindern

❷

Er hatte keine Geschwister.	He had no brothers or sisters.
Ich sehe keinen Unterschied.	I don't see any difference.
Das ist keine richtige Antwort.	That's no answer.
Kein Mensch hat es gesehen.	Not one person has seen it.

❸

Er hatte Angst davor.	He was frightened.
Er hatte keine Angst davor.	He wasn't frightened.

❹

Er hatte kein Geld mehr. All his money was gone.
Es waren keine drei Monate vergangen, als ...
It was less than three months later that ...
Es hat mich keine zehn Euro gekostet.
It cost me less than ten euros.

❺

Nicht ein Kind hat es singen können.
Not *one* child could sing it.

Words declined like the definite article

The following have endings similar to those of the definite article shown on page 118:

aller, alle, alles	all, all of them
beide	both (*plural only*)
dieser, diese, dieses	this, this one, these
einiger, einige, einiges	some, a few, a little
irgendwelcher, -e, -es	some or other
jeder, jede, jedes	each, each one, every
jener, jene, jenes	that, that one, those
mancher, manche, manches	many a/some
sämtliche	all, entire (*usually plural*)
solcher, solche, solches	such/such a
welcher, welche, welches	which, which one

These words can be used as:

- articles → ❶
- pronouns → ❷

They have the following endings:

	SINGULAR			PLURAL
	MASC	FEM	NEUT	ALL GENDERS
NOM	-er	-e	-es	-e
ACC	-en	-e	-es	-e
GEN	-es/-en	-er	-es/-en	-er
DAT	-em	-er	-em	-en

Example declensions are shown on pages 134–135.

einiger and irgendwelcher use the **-en** genitive ending before masculine or neuter nouns ending in **-s** → ❸

jeder, welcher, mancher and solcher may also do so → ❹

❶   Dieser Mann kommt aus Südamerika.
This man comes from South America.

Er geht jeden Tag ins Büro.
He goes to the office every day.

Manche Leute können das nicht.
A good many people can't do it.

❷   Willst du diesen?
Do you want this one?

In manchem hat er recht.
He's right about some things.

Man kann ja nicht alles wissen.
You can't know everything.

Es gibt manche, die keinen Alkohol mögen.
There are some people who don't like alcohol.

❸   wegen irgendwelchen Geredes
on account of some gossip

❹   der Besitz solchen Reichtums
the possession of such wealth

trotz jeden Versuchs
despite all attempts

Words declined like the definite article *continued*

Adjectives following these words have the weak declension (see page 140) → ❶

Exceptions are the plural forms of einige, which are followed by the strong declension (see page 142) → ❷

Further points

Solcher, beide, sämtliche may be used after another article or possessive adjective. They then take weak (see page 140) or mixed (see page 142) adjectival endings, as appropriate → ❸

Although beide generally has plural forms only, one singular form does exist. This is in the neuter nominative and accusative: beides → ❹

Dies often replaces the nominative and accusative dieses and diese when used as a pronoun → ❺

A fixed form all exists which is used together with other articles or possessive pronouns → ❻

Ganz can also be used to replace both the inflected form aller/alle/alles and the uninflected all das/dieses/sein *etc*. It is declined as a normal adjective (see page 140) → ❼

It must be used with collective nouns, in time phrases and geographical references → ❽

①

dieses alte Auto
this old car
aus irgendwelchem dummen Grund
for some stupid reason or other
Welche neuen Waren?
Which new goods?

②

Dies sind einige gute Freunde von mir.
These are some good friends of mine.

③

Ein solches Kleid habe ich früher auch getragen.
I used to wear a dress like that too.
Diese beiden Männer haben es gesehen.
Both of these men have seen it.

④

Beides ist richtig.
Both are right.
Sie hat beides genommen.
She took both.

⑤

Hast du dies schon gelesen?
Have you already read this?
Dies sind meine neuen Sachen.
These are my new things.

⑥

All sein Mut war verschwunden.
All his courage had vanished.
mit all diesem Geld
with all this money

⑦

mit dem ganzen Geld
with all the money

⑧

die ganze Gesellschaft
the entire company
Es hat den ganzen Tag geschneit.
It snowed the whole day long.
Im ganzen Land gab es keinen besseren Wein.
There wasn't a better wine in the whole country.

Words declined like the definite article *continued*

derjenige/diejenige/dasjenige (*the one*, *those*) is declined exactly as the definite article plus an adjective in the weak declension (see page 140) → **1**

derselbe/dieselbe/dasselbe (*the same*, *the same one*) is declined in the same way as derjenige → **2**

After prepositions, however, the normal contracted forms of the definite article are used for the appropriate parts of derselbe → **3**

Examples

1

SINGULAR

MASC FEM	NEUT	
derjenige Mann	**die**jenige Frau	**das**jenige Kind
denjenigen Mann	**die**jenige Frau	**das**jenige Kind
desjenigen Mann(e)s	**der**jenigen Frau	**des**jenigen Kind(e)s
demjenigen Mann	**der**jenigen Frau	**dem**jenigen Kind

PLURAL

MASC	FEM	NEUT
diejenigen Männer	**die**jenigen Frauen	**die**jenigen Kinder
diejenigen Männer	**die**jenigen Frauen	**die**jenigen Kinder
derjenigen Männer	**der**jenigen Frauen	**der**jenigen Kinder
denjenigen Männern	**den**jenigen Frauen	**den**jenigen Kindern

2

SINGULAR

MASC	FEM	NEUT
derselbe Mann	**die**selbe Frau	**das**selbe Kind
denselben Mann	**die**selbe Frau	**das**selbe Kind
desselben Mann(e)s	**der**selben Frau	**des**selben Kind(e)s
demselben Mann	**der**selben Frau	**dem**selben Kind

PLURAL

MASC	FEM	NEUT
dieselben Männer	**die**selben Frauen	**die**selben Kinder
dieselben Männer	**die**selben Frauen	**die**selben Kinder
derselben Männer	**der**selben Frauen	**der**selben Kinder
denselben Männern	**den**selben Frauen	**den**selben Kindern

3

zur selben (= zu derselben) Zeit	at the same time
im selben (= in demselben) Zimmer	in the same room

Words declined like the definite article *continued*

Sample declensions in full

dieser, diese, dieses this, this one:

	MASC	**FEM**	**NEUT**
		SINGULAR	
NOM	dieser Mann	diese Frau	dieses Kind
ACC	diesen Mann	diese Frau	dieses Kind
GEN	dieses Mann(e)s	dieser Frau	dieses Kind(e)s
DAT	diesem Mann	dieser Frau	diesem Kind

	MASC	**FEM**	**NEUT**
		PLURAL	
NOM	diese Männer	diese Frauen	diese Kinder
ACC	diese Männer	diese Frauen	diese Kinder
GEN	dieser Männer	dieser Frauen	dieser Kinder
DAT	diesen Männern	diesen Frauen	diesen Kindern

jener, jene, jenes that, that one:

	MASC	**FEM**	**NEUT**
		SINGULAR	
NOM	jener Mann	jene Frau	jenes Kind
ACC	jenen Mann	jene Frau	jenes Kind
GEN	jenes Mann(e)s	jener Frau	jenes Kind(e)s
DAT	jenem Mann	jener Frau	jenem Kind

	MASC	**FEM**	**NEUT**
		PLURAL	
NOM	jene Männer	jene Frauen	jene Kinder
ACC	jene Männer	jene Frauen	jene Kinder
GEN	jener Männer	jener Frauen	jener Kinder
DAT	jenen Männern	jenen Frauen	jenen Kindern

jeder, jede, jedes each, every, everybody:

SINGULAR

	MASC	FEM	NEUT
NOM	jeder Wagen	jede Minute	jedes Bild
ACC	jeden Wagen	jede Minute	jedes Bild
GEN	jedes Wagens	jeder Minute	jedes Bild(e)s
	(jeden Wagens)		(jeden Bild(e)s)
DAT	jedem Wagen	jeder Minute	jedem Bild

welcher, welche, welches which?, which:

SINGULAR

	MASC	FEM	NEUT
NOM	welcher Preis	welche Sorte	welches Mädchen
ACC	welchen Preis	welche Sorte	welches Mädchen
GEN	welches Preises	welcher Sorte	welches Mädchens
	(welchen Preises)		(welchen Mädchens)
DAT	welchem Preis	welcher Sorte	welchem Mädchen

PLURAL

	MASC	FEM	NEUT
NOM	welche Preise	welche Sorten	welche Mädchen
ACC	welche Preise	welche Sorten	welche Mädchen
GEN	welcher Preise	welcher Sorten	welcher Mädchen
DAT	welchen Preisen	welchen Sorten	welchen Mädchen

Words declined like the indefinite article

The following have the same declension pattern as the indefinite articles ein and kein (see pages 124 and 126):

The possessive adjectives

mein	my → ❶
dein	your (*singular familiar*)
sein	his/its
ihr	her/its → ❷
unser	our
euer	your (*plural familiar*)
ihr	their → ❸
Ihr	your (*polite singular and plural*)

These words are declined as follows:

	SINGULAR			PLURAL
	MASC	FEM	NEUT	ALL GENDERS
NOM	—	-e	—	-e
ACC	-en	-e	—	-e
GEN	-es	-er	-es	-er
DAT	-em	-er	-em	-en

Adjectives following these determiners have the mixed declension forms (see page 142), e.g.

sein altes Auto his old car

irgendein (*some … or other*) also follows this declension pattern in the singular. Its plural form is irgendwelche (see page 128).

Examples

❶   mein, meine, mein **my**

SINGULAR

	MASC	FEM	NEUT
NOM	mein Bruder	meine Schwester	mein Kind
ACC	meinen Bruder	meine Schwester	mein Kind
GEN	meines Bruders	meiner Schwester	meines Kind(e)s
DAT	meinem Bruder	meiner Schwester	meinem Kind

PLURAL

	MASC	FEM	NEUT
NOM	meine Brüder	meine Schwestern	meine Kinder
ACC	meine Brüder	meine Schwestern	meine Kinder
GEN	meiner Brüder	meiner Schwestern	meiner Kinder
DAT	meinen Brüdern	meinen Schwestern	meinen Kindern

❷   ihr, ihre, ihr **her/its/their**

SINGULAR

	MASC	FEM	NEUT
NOM	ihr Bruder	ihre Schwester	ihr Kind
ACC	ihren Bruder	ihre Schwester	ihr Kind
GEN	ihres Bruders	ihrer Schwester	ihres Kind(e)s
DAT	ihrem Bruder	ihrer Schwester	ihrem Kind

PLURAL

	MASC	FEM	NEUT
NOM	ihre Brüder	ihre Schwestern	ihre Kinder
ACC	ihre Brüder	ihre Schwestern	ihre Kinder
GEN	ihrer Brüder	ihrer Schwestern	ihrer Kinder
DAT	ihren Brüdern	ihren Schwestern	ihren Kindern

Indefinite Adjectives

These are adjectives used in place of, or together with, an article:

ander	other, different
mehrere (*plural only*)	several
viel	much, a lot, many
wenig	little, a little, few

After the definite article and words declined like it (see page 128) these adjectives have weak declension endings → ❶

Adjectives following the indefinite adjectives are also weak → ❷

After ein, kein, irgendein or the possessive adjectives they have mixed declension endings → ❸

Adjectives following the indefinite adjectives are also mixed in declension → ❹

When used without a preceding article, ander and mehrere have strong declension endings → ❺

When used without a preceding article, viel and wenig may be declined as follows, though in the singular they are usually undeclined → ❻

	SINGULAR			PLURAL
	MASC	FEM	NEUT	ALL GENDERS
NOM	viel	viel	viel	viele
ACC	viel	viel	viel	viele
GEN	vielen	vieler	vielen	vieler
DAT	viel(em)	vieler	viel(em)	vielen

Any adjective following viel or wenig has strong endings → ❼

①   Die wenigen Kuchen, die übrig geblieben waren ...
The few cakes which were left over ...

②   die vielen interessanten Ideen, die ans Licht kamen
the many interesting ideas which came to light

③   Ihr anderes Auto ist in der Werkstatt.
Their other car is in for repair.

④   Mehrere gute Freunde waren gekommen.
Several good friends had come.

⑤   Mehrere prominente Gäste sind eingeladen.
Various prominent guests are invited.

Er war anderer Meinung.
He was of a different opinion.

⑥   Es wurde viel Bier getrunken.
They drank a lot of beer.

Sie essen nur wenig Obst.
They don't eat a lot of fruit.

⑦   Er kaufte viele billige Sachen.
He bought a lot of cheap things.

Es wurde viel gutes Bier getrunken.
They drank a lot of good beer.

Sie essen wenig frisches Obst.
They don't eat a lot of fresh fruit.

The Declension of Adjectives

There are two ways of using adjectives:

- They can be used attributively, where the adjective comes before the noun: *the new book*

- They can be used non-attributively, where the adjective comes after the verb: *the book is new*

In English the adjective does not change its form no matter how it is used.

In German, however, adjectives remain unchanged only when used non-attributively → ❶

Used attributively, adjectives change to show the number, gender and case of the noun they precede → ❷

The endings also depend on the nature of the article which precedes them → ❸

There are three sets of endings:

1) The weak declension

These are the endings used after der and those words declined like it as shown on page 128 → ❹

	SINGULAR			PLURAL
	MASC	FEM	NEUT	ALL GENDERS
NOM	-e	-e	-e	-en
ACC	-en	-e	-e	-en
GEN	-en	-en	-en	-en
DAT	-en	-en	-en	-en

❶   Das Buch ist neu.
The book is new.
Der Vortrag war sehr langweilig.
The lecture was very boring.

❷   Das neue Buch ist da.
The new book has arrived.
Während des langweiligen Vortrags sind wir alle
eingeschlafen.
We all fell asleep during the boring lecture.

❸   der junge Rechtsanwalt
the young lawyer
ein junger Rechtsanwalt
a young lawyer
manch junger Rechtsanwalt
many a young lawyer

❹

SINGULAR

	MASC	FEM	NEUT
NOM	der alt**e** Mann	die alt**e** Frau	das alt**e** Haus
ACC	den alt**en** Mann	die alt**e** Frau	das alt**e** Haus
GEN	des alt**en** Mann(e)s	der alt**en** Frau	des alt**en** Hauses
DAT	dem alt**en** Mann	der alt**en** Frau	dem alt**en** Haus

PLURAL

	MASC	FEM	NEUT
NOM	die alt**en** Männer	die alt**en** Frauen	die alt**en** Häuser
ACC	die alt**en** Männer	die alt**en** Frauen	die alt**en** Häuser
GEN	der alt**en** Männer	der alt**en** Frauen	der alt**en** Häuser
DAT	den alt**en** Männern	den alt**en** Frauen	den alt**en** Häusern

141

The Declension of Adjectives *continued*

2) The mixed declension

These are the endings used after ein, kein, irgendein and the possessive adjectives (see page 136) → ❶

	SINGULAR			PLURAL
	MASC	FEM	NEUT	ALL GENDERS
NOM	-er	-e	-es	-en
ACC	-en	-e	-es	-en
GEN	-en	-en	-en	-en
DAT	-en	-en	-en	-en

→ ❷

3) The strong declension

Strong declension endings:

	SINGULAR			PLURAL
	MASC	FEM	NEUT	ALL GENDERS
NOM	-er	-e	-es	-e
ACC	-en	-e	-es	-e
GEN	-en	-er	-en	-er
DAT	-em	-er	-em	-en

→ ❸

These endings are used where there is no preceding article. The article is omitted more frequently in German than in English, especially in *preposition + adjective + noun* combinations (see page 122).

These endings enable the adjective to do the work of the missing article by showing case, number and gender → ❹

Examples

❶

Meine neue Stelle ist bei einer großen Druckerei.
My new job is with a large printing works.
Ihre frühere Theorie ist jetzt bestätigt worden.
Her earlier theory has now been proved true.

❷

SINGULAR

	MASC	FEM	NEUT
NOM	ein langer Weg	eine lange Reise	ein langes Spiel
ACC	einen langen Weg	eine lange Reise	ein langes Spiel
GEN	eines langen Weg(e)s	einer langen Reise	eines langen Spiel(e)s
DAT	einem langen Weg	einer langen Reise	einem langen Spiel

PLURAL

ALL GENDERS

NOM	ihre langen Wege/Reisen/Spiele
ACC	ihre langen Wege/Reisen/Spiele
GEN	ihrer langen Wege/Reisen/Spiele
DAT	ihren langen Wegen/Reisen/Spielen

❸

SINGULAR

	MASC	FEM	NEUT
NOM	guter Käse	gute Marmelade	gutes Bier
ACC	guten Käse	gute Marmelade	gutes Bier
GEN	guten Käses	guter Marmelade	guten Biers
DAT	gutem Käse	guter Marmelade	gutem Bier

PLURAL

ALL GENDERS

NOM	gute Käse/Marmeladen/Biere
ACC	gute Käse/Marmeladen/Biere
GEN	guter Käse/Marmeladen/Biere
DAT	guten Käsen/Marmeladen/Bieren

❹

nach kurzer Fahrt	after a short journey
mit gleichem Gehalt	with the same salary

The Declension of Adjectives *continued*

Strong declension endings are also used after any of the following where they are not preceded by an article or other determiner:

ein bisschen	a little, a bit of
ein wenig	a little
ein paar	a few, a couple → ❶
weniger	fewer, less
einige (*plural forms only*)	some
allerlei/allerhand	all kinds of, all sorts of
keinerlei	no ... whatsoever, no ... at all
mancherlei	various, a number of
etwas	some, any (*singular*) → ❷
mehr	more
lauter	nothing but, sheer, pure
solch	such
vielerlei	various, all sorts of, many different
mehrerlei	several kinds of
was für	what, what kind of
(NOTE: Was für ein takes the mixed declension)	
welcherlei	what kind of, what sort of
viel	much, many, a lot of
wievielerlei	how many kinds of
welch ...!	what ...! what a ...! → ❸
manch	many a
wenig	little, few, not much → ❹
zweierlei/dreierlei *etc*	two/three *etc* kinds of
zwei, drei *etc*	two, three *etc* → ❺
(NOTE: The mixed declension is used after ein)	

The strong declension is also required after possessives where no other word indicates the case, gender and number → ❻

1   ein paar gute Tipps (*strong declension*)
a couple of good tips

2   Etwas starken Pfeffer zugeben. (*strong*)
Add a little strong pepper.

3   Welch herrliches Wetter! (*strong*)
What splendid weather!

4   Es gab damals nur wenig frisches Obst. (*strong*)
At that time there was little fresh fruit.

BUT:

Das wenige frische Obst, das es damals gab … (*weak*)
The little fresh fruit that was then available …

5   Zwei große Jungen waren gekommen. (*strong*)
Two big boys had come along.

BUT:

die zwei großen Jungen, die gekommen waren (*weak*)
the two big boys who had come along

meine zwei großen Jungen (*mixed*)
my two big sons

6   Herberts altes Buch. (*strong*)
Herbert's old book.

Muttis neues Auto. (*strong*)
Mum's new car.

The Declension of Adjectives *continued*

Some spelling changes when adjectives are declined

When the adjective hoch (*high*) is declined, its stem changes to
hoh- → ❶

Adjectives ending in **-el** lose the **-e-** when inflected, i.e. when endings are
added → ❷

Adjectives with an **-er** ending often lose the **-e-** when inflected → ❸

The participles as adjectives

The present participle can be used as an adjective with normal adjectival
endings (pages 140–143) → ❹

The present participles of sein and haben cannot be used in this way.

The past participle can also be used as an adjective → ❺

Adjectives followed by the dative case

The *dative case* is required after many adjectives e.g.

ähnlich	similar to
bekannt	familiar to
dankbar	grateful to
fremd	alien to
gleich	all the same to/like → ❻
leicht	easy for
nah	close to
peinlich	painful for
unbekannt	unknown to

Examples

1 Das Gebäude ist hoch. BUT: ein hohes Gebäude
The building is high. a high building

2 Das Zimmer ist dunkel. BUT: in dem dunklen Zimmer
The room is dark. in the dark room

3 Das Auto war teuer. BUT: Er kaufte ein teures Auto.
The car was expensive. He bought an expensive car.

4 die werdende Mutter
the mother-to-be

ein lachendes Kind
a laughing child

5 meine verlorene Sachen
my lost things

die ausgebeuteten Arbeiter
the exploited workers

6 Ist dir das bekannt?
Do you know about it?

Ich wäre Ihnen dankbar, wenn ...
I should be grateful to you if ...

Diese Sache ist mir etwas peinlich.
This matter is somewhat embarrassing for me.

Solche Gedanken waren ihm fremd.
Such thoughts were alien to him.

Adjectives used as Nouns

All adjectives in German, and those participles used as adjectives, can also be used as nouns. These are often called adjectival nouns.

Adjectives and participles used as nouns have:

- a capital letter like other nouns → ❶

- declension endings like other adjectives, depending on the preceding article, if any (see below) → ❷

Declension endings for adjectives used as nouns

After der, dieser and words like it shown on page 128, the normal *weak* adjective endings apply (see page 140) → ❸
Der Junge (*the boy*) is an exception, and is declined like a weak masculine noun, as shown on page 115.

After ein, kein, irgendein and the possessive adjectives shown on page 136, the *mixed* adjective endings apply (see page 142) → ❹

Where no article is present, or after those words shown on page 144, the *strong* adjective endings are used (see page 142) → ❺

When another adjective precedes the adjectival noun, the *strong* endings become *weak* in two instances:

- in the *dative singular* → ❻

- in the *nominative* and *accusative plural* after a possessive, where the strong endings might cause confusion with the singular feminine form → ❼

❶   der Angestellte
the employee

❷   die Angestellte
the (female) employee
das Neue daran ist ...
the new thing about it is ...
Es bleibt beim Alten.
Things remain as they were.
Er hat den ersten Besten genommen.
He took the first that came to hand.

❸   für den Angeklagten
for the accused
mit dieser Bekannten
with this (*female*) friend

❹   Kein Angestellter darf hier rauchen.
No employee may smoke here.
Sie machten einen Ausflug mit ihren Bekannten zusammen.
They went on a trip with their friends.

❺   Etwas Besonderes ist geschehen.
Something special has happened.

❻   Ich hatte es Rudis jüngerem Verwandten versprochen.
I had promised it to Rudi's young relative.

❼   Rudis jüngere Verwandten wollten es haben.
Rudi's young relatives wanted to have it.

Miscellaneous Points

Adjectives of nationality

These are not spelt with a capital letter in German except in public or official names → ❶

However, when used as a noun to refer to the language, a capital letter is used → ❷

In German, for expressions like *he is English/he is German etc* a noun or adjectival noun is used instead of an adjective → ❸

Adjectives derived from place names

These are formed by adding -er to names of towns → ❹

They are never inflected → ❺

Adjectives from die Schweiz and from certain regions can also be formed in this way → ❻

Such adjectives may be used as nouns denoting the inhabitants of a town.
They are then declined as normal nouns (see pages 98–99) → ❼
The feminine form is made by adding -in in the singular and -innen in the plural → ❽

Certain names ending in **-en** drop the **-e-** or the **-en** of their ending before adding **-er** → ❾

A second type of adjective formed from place names exists, ending in **-isch** and spelt with a small letter. It is inflected as a normal adjective (see page 140).
It is used mainly where the speaker is referring to the mood of, or something typical of, that place → ❿ .

Examples

❶
die deutsche Sprache	das französische Volk
the German language	the French people
BUT:	
die Deutsche Bahn	
the German railways	

❷
Sie sprechen kein Englisch.
They don't speak English.

❸
Er ist Deutscher.	Sie ist Deutsche.
He is German.	She is German.

❹
Kölner, Frankfurter, Leipziger *etc*

❺
der Kölner Dom	ein Frankfurter Würstchen
Cologne cathedral	a frankfurter sausage

❻
Schweizer Käse
Swiss cheese

❼
Die Sprache des Kölners heißt Kölsch.
People from Cologne speak Kölsch.
von den Frankfurtern
of the people of Frankfurt

❽
die Kölnerin, die Kölnerinnen
die Londonerin, die Londonerinnen

❾
München	►	der Münchner
Bremen	►	der Bremer
Göttingen	►	der Göttinger

❿
ein echt frankfurterischer Ausdruck
a real Frankfurt expression
Er spricht etwas münchnerisch.
He has something of a Munich accent.

The Comparison of Adjectives

Adjectives have three basic forms of comparison:

1) The simple form is used to describe something or someone.

> e.g. a *little* house
> the house is *little*

This form is fully dealt with on pages 140–147.

Simple forms are used in *as … as / not as … as* comparisons → **1**

2) The comparative form is used to compare two things or persons.

> e.g. he is *bigger* than his brother

In German, comparatives are formed by adding **-er** to the simple form → **2**

Than in comparative statements is translated by als → **3**

Unlike English, the vast majority of German adjectives, including those of several syllables, form their comparatives in this way → **4**

Many adjectives modify the stem vowel when forming their comparatives → **5**

1 so ... wie as ... as
Er ist so gut wie sein Bruder.
He is as good as his brother.

ebenso ... wie just as ... as
Er war ebenso glücklich wie ich.
He was just as happy as I was.

zwei-/dreimal *etc* twice/three times *etc*
so ... wie as ... as

Er war zweimal so groß wie sein Bruder.
He was twice as big as his brother.

nicht so ... wie not as ... as
Er ist nicht so alt wie du
He is not as old as you

2 klein/kleiner   small/smaller
schön/schöner   lovely/lovelier

3 Er ist kleiner als seine Schwester.
He is smaller than his sister.

4 bequem/bequemer   comfortable/more comfortable
gebildet/gebildeter   educated/more educated
effektiv/effektiver   effective/more effective

5 alt/älter   old/older
stark/stärker   strong/stronger
schwach/schwächer   weak/weaker
scharf/schärfer   sharp/sharper
lang/länger   long/longer
kurz/kürzer   short/shorter
warm/wärmer   warm/warmer
kalt/kälter   cold/colder
hart/härter   hard/harder
groß/größer   big/bigger

The Comparison of Adjectives *continued*

Adjectives whose simple form ends in **-el** lose the **-e-** before adding the comparative ending **-er** → ❶

Adjectives with a diphthong followed by **-er** in their simple forms also drop the **-e-** before adding **-er** → ❷

Adjectives whose simple form ends in **-en** or **-er** may drop the **-e-** of the simple form when adjectival endings are added to their comparative forms → ❸

With a few adjectives, comparative forms may be used not only for comparison, but also to render the idea of "-ish" or "rather ..."
Some common examples are:

älter	elderly	jünger	youngish	
dünner	thinnish	kleiner	smallish	→ ❹
dicker	fattish	kürzer	shortish	
größer	largish	neuer	newish	

When used attributively (*before* the noun), comparative forms are declined in exactly the same way as simple adjectives (see pages 140–147) → ❹ → ❺

3) The superlative form is used to compare three or more persons or things.

> e.g. he is *the biggest/the best*

Superlatives are formed by adding **-st** to the simple adjective. The vowel is modified, as for comparative forms, where applicable.

Superlative forms are generally used with an article and take endings accordingly (see page 140) → ❻

❶ eitel/eitler   vain/vainer
dunkel/dunkler   dark/darker

❷ sauer/saurer   sour/more sour
die saurere Zitrone
the sourer lemon
Der Wein ist saurer geworden.
The wine has grown more sour.

teuer/teurer   expensive/more expensive
Das ist eine teurere Sorte.
That is a more expensive kind.
Die Neuen sind teurer.
The new ones are more expensive.

❸ finster/finsterer   dark/darker
ein finstreres Gesicht
OR:
ein finstereres Gesicht
a grimmer face

❹ ein älterer Herr
an elderly gentleman
eine größere Summe
a rather large sum
von jüngerem Aussehen
of youngish appearance

❺ Die jüngere Schwester ist größer als die ältere.
The younger sister is bigger than the older one.
Mein kleinerer Bruder geht jetzt zur Schule.
My younger brother goes to school now.

❻ Er ist der Jüngste.
He is the youngest.
Ihr erfolgreichster Versuch war im Herbst 2009.
Her most successful attempt was in the autumn of 2009.

The Comparison of Adjectives *continued*

Many adjectives form their superlative forms by adding **-est** instead of **-st** where pronunciation would otherwise be difficult or unaesthetic → ❶

The English superlative "*most*" meaning "*very*" can be shown in German by any of the following → ❷

> äußerst
>
> sehr
>
> besonders
>
> außerordentlich
>
> höchst (*not with monosyllabic words*)
>
> furchtbar (*conversational only*)
>
> richtig (*conversational only*)

Some irregular comparative and superlative forms

SIMPLE FORM	COMPARATIVE	SUPERLATIVE
gut	besser	der beste
hoch	höher	der höchste
viel	mehr	der meiste
nah	näher	der nächste

❶

der/die/das schlechteste
the worst

der/die/das schmerzhafteste
the most painful

der/die/das süßeste
the sweetest

der/die/das neueste
the newest

der/die/das stolzeste
the proudest

der/die/das frischeste
the freshest

❷

Er ist ein äußerst begabter Mensch.
He is a most gifted person.

Das Essen war besonders schlecht.
The food was really/most dreadful.

Der Wein war furchtbar teuer!
The wine was dreadfully/most expensive!

Das sieht richtig komisch aus.
That looks really/most funny.

Personal Pronouns

As in English, personal pronouns change their form depending on their function in the sentence:

> *I* saw *him*
> *He* saw *me*   → **1**
> *We* saw *her*

The personal pronouns are declined as follows:

NOMINATIVE		ACCUSATIVE		DATIVE	
ich	I	mich	me	mir	to/for me
du	you (*familiar*)	dich	you	dir	to/for you
er	he/it	ihn	him/it	ihm	to/for him/it
sie	she/it	sie	her/it	ihr	to/for her/it
es	it/he/she	es	it/him/her	ihm	to/for it/him/her → **2**
wir	we	uns	us	uns	to/for us
ihr	you (*plural*)	euch	you	euch	to/for you
sie	they	sie	them	ihnen	to/for them
Sie	you (*polite*)	Sie	you	Ihnen	to/for you
man	one	einen	one	einem	to/for one

As can be seen from the above table, there are three ways of addressing people in German – du, ihr or Sie.

All three forms are illustrated on page 160.

Personal pronouns in the dative require no preposition when acting as indirect object, i.e. *to* me, *to* him *etc* → **3**

❶

Ich sah ihn.
I saw him.

Er sah mich.
He saw me.

Wir sahen sie.
We saw her.

❷

Wir sind mit ihnen spazieren gegangen.
We went for a walk with them.

Sie haben uns eine tolle Geschichte erzählt.
They told us a great story.

Soll ich Ihnen etwas mitbringen?
Shall I bring something back for you?

❸

Er hat es ihr gegeben.
He gave it to her.

Ich habe ihm ein neues Buch gekauft.
I bought a new book for him.
OR:
I bought him a new book.

Personal Pronouns *continued*

Du is a singular form, used only when speaking to one person. It is used to talk to children, close friends and relatives, animals and objects of affection such as a toy, one's car etc.

When in doubt it is always best to use the more formal Sie form.

Ihr is simply the plural form of du and is used in exactly the same situations wherever more than one person is to be addressed → ❶

The familiar forms and their possessives are written with a small letter → ❷

Sie is the polite, or formal, way of addressing people. It is written in all its declined forms with a capital letter, including the possessive → ❸

Sie is used:

- by children talking to adults outside their immediate family.

- by adults talking to older children from mid-teens onwards. Teachers use it to their senior classes and bosses to their trainees etc.

- among adult strangers meeting for the first time.

- among colleagues, friends and acquaintances unless a suggestion has been formally made by one party and accepted by the other that the familiar forms should be used. Familiar forms must then continue to be used at all times, as a reversion to the formal might be considered insulting.

Examples

❶

Kinder, was wollt ihr essen?
Children, what do you want to eat?

❷

Er hat mir gesagt, du sollst deine Frau mitbringen.
He told me you were to bring your wife.

Gestern bin ich deinem Bruder begegnet.
I met your brother yesterday.

❸

Was haben Sie gesagt?
What did you say?

Ich habe es Ihnen schon gegeben.
I have already given it to you.

Ja, Ihre Sachen sind jetzt fertig.
Yes, your things are ready now.

Personal Pronouns *continued*

Er/sie/es

All German nouns are masculine, feminine or neuter → ❶

The personal pronoun must agree in number and in gender with the noun which it represents.

Es is used only for neuter nouns, and not for all inanimate objects → ❷

Inanimate objects which are masculine use the pronoun er → ❸

Feminine inanimate objects use the pronoun sie → ❹

Neuter nouns referring to people have the neuter pronoun es → ❺

NOTE: A common error for English speakers is to call all objects es.

Man

This is used in much the same way as the pronoun one in English, but it is much more commonly used in German → ❻

It is also used to make an alternative passive form (see page 34) → ❼

The genitive personal pronoun

Genitive forms of the personal pronouns do exist → ❽

In practice, however, these are rarely used. Wherever possible, alternative expressions are found which do not require the genitive personal pronoun.

Special genitive forms exist for use with the prepositions wegen and willen → ❾

❶

der Tisch	the table (*masculine*)
die Gardine	the curtain (*feminine*)
das Baby	the baby (*neuter*)

❷

Das Bild ist schön.	►	Es ist schön.
The picture is beautiful.	►	It is beautiful.

❸

Der Tisch ist groß.	►	Er ist groß.
The table is large.	►	It is large.

❹

Die Gardine ist weiß.	►	Sie ist weiß.
The curtain is white.	►	It is white.

❺

Das Kind stand auf.	►	Es stand auf.
The child stood up.	►	He/she stood up.

❻

Es tut einem gut.
It does one good.

❼

Man holt mich um sieben ab.
I am being picked up at seven.

❽

meiner	of me	unser	of us
deiner	of you	euer	of you (*plural*)
seiner	of him/it	ihrer	of them
ihrer	of her/it	Ihrer	of you (*polite*)

❾

meinetwegen	because of me, on my account
deinetwegen	because of you, on your account *etc*
seinetwegen	
ihretwegen	
unsertwegen	
euretwegen	
Ihretwegen	

meinetwillen	for my sake, for me *etc*
deinetwillen	
ihretwillen *etc*	

Personal Pronouns *continued*

The use of pronouns after prepositions

Personal pronouns used after prepositions and referring to a person are in the *case* required by the preposition in question (see pages 198–199) → ①

When, however, a *thing* rather than a person is referred to, the construction

>   *preposition + pronoun*

becomes

>   **da-** + *preposition* → ②

Before a preposition beginning with a vowel, the form **dar-** + *preposition* is used → ③

This affects the following prepositions:

an	bei	in	neben	
auf	durch	mit	über	zwischen
aus	für	nach	unter	

These contracted forms are used after verbs followed by a preposition (see pages 76–79) → ④

After prepositions used to express motion the form with **da(r)-** is not felt to be sufficiently strong. Forms with hin and her are used as follows:

aus:	heraus/hinaus
auf:	herauf/hinauf → ⑤
in:	herein/hinein

Examples

① Ich bin mit ihm spazieren gegangen.
I went for a walk with him.

② Klaus hatte ein Messer geholt und wollte damit den Kuchen schneiden.
Klaus had brought a knife and was about to cut the cake with it.

③ Lege es bitte darauf.
Put it there please.

④ Der Unterschied liegt darin, dass ...
The difference is that ...

Ich erinnere mich nicht daran.
I don't remember (it).

⑤ Er sah eine Treppe und ging leise hinauf.
He saw some stairs and went up them quietly.

Endlich fand er unser Zelt und kam herein.
He finally found our tent and came in.

Er öffnete den Koffer und legte das Hemd hinein.
He opened his suitcase and put in his shirt.

Possessive Pronouns

meiner	mine
deiner	yours (*familiar*)
seiner	his/its
ihrer	hers/its
uns(e)rer	ours
eu(e)rer	yours (*plural*)
ihrer	theirs
Ihrer	yours (*polite*)

These have the same endings as dieser. Their declension is therefore the same as for possessive adjectives (see page 136) except in the masculine nominative singular and the neuter nominative and accusative singular:

		SINGULAR		PLURAL
	MASC	FEM	NEUT	ALL GENDERS
NOM	-er	-e	-(e)s	-e
ACC	-en	-e	-(e)s	-e
GEN	-es	-er	-es	-er
DAT	-em	-er	-em	-en

The bracketed **(e)** is often omitted, especially in spoken German.

Possessive pronouns must agree in number, gender and case with the noun they replace → **❶**

Note the translation of *of mine*, *of yours* etc → **❷**

meiner is declined in full opposite → **❸**
Deiner, seiner and ihrer are declined like meiner.

Unserer and euerer are shown in full, since they have slightly different forms with an optional **-e-** → **❹**

Examples

1 Der Wagen da drüben ist meiner. Er ist kleiner als deiner.
   The car over there is mine. It is smaller than yours.

2 Er ist ein Bekannter von mir.
   He is an acquaintance of mine.

3 meiner mine

	MASC	SINGULAR FEM	NEUT	PLURAL ALL GENDERS
NOM	meiner	meine	mein(e)s	meine
ACC	meinen	meine	mein(e)s	meine
GEN	meines	meiner	meines	meiner
DAT	meinem	meiner	meinem	meinen

4 uns(e)rer ours

	MASC	SINGULAR FEM	NEUT	PLURAL ALL GENDERS
NOM	uns(e)rer	uns(e)re	uns(e)res	uns(e)re
ACC	uns(e)ren	uns(e)re	uns(e)res	uns(e)re
GEN	uns(e)res	uns(e)rer	uns(e)res	uns(e)rer
DAT	uns(e)rem	uns(e)rer	uns(e)rem	uns(e)ren

eu(e)rer yours (*plural*)

	MASC	SINGULAR FEM	NEUT	PLURAL ALL GENDERS
NOM	eu(e)rer	eu(e)re	eu(e)res	eu(e)re
ACC	eu(e)ren	eu(e)re	eu(e)res	eu(e)re
GEN	eu(e)res	eu(e)rer	eu(e)res	eu(e)rer
DAT	eu(e)rem	eu(e)rer	eu(e)rem	eu(e)ren

Possessive Pronouns *continued*

Alternative forms

There are two alternatives to the meiner/deiner *etc* forms shown on page 167:

der, die, das meinige *or* Meinige	mine
der, die, das deinige *or* Deinige	yours (*familiar*)
der, die, das seinige *or* Seinige	his/its
der, die, das ihrige *or* Ihrige	hers/its
der, die, das uns(e)rige *or* Uns(e)rige	ours
der, die, das eu(e)rige *or* Eu(e)rige	yours (*plural*)
der, die, das ihrige *or* Ihrige	theirs
der, die, das Ihrige	yours (*polite*)

These are not as common as the meiner/deiner *etc* forms → ❶

These forms are declined as the definite article followed by a weak adjective (see page 140) → ❷

The bracketed (e) of the first and second person plural is often omitted in spoken German.

der, die, das meine *or* Meine	mine
der, die, das deine *or* Deine	yours (*familiar*)
der, die, das seine *or* Seine	his/its
der, die, das ihre *or* Ihre	hers/its
der, die, das uns(e)re *or* Uns(e)re	ours
der, die, das eu(e)re *or* Eu(e)re	yours (*plural*)
der, die, das ihre *or* Ihre	theirs
der, die, das Ihre	yours (*polite*)

These forms are also less common than the meiner/deiner *etc* forms. They are declined as the definite article followed by a weak adjective (see page 140) → ❸

❶ Ihr Auto ist aber neuer als das meinige *or* Meinige.
Your car is newer than mine.
Paul hat seiner Freundin Blumen gekauft. Ich habe der
meinigen *or* Meinigen Parfüm geschenkt.
Paul bought his girlfriend some flowers. I bought mine perfume.

❷

	SINGULAR		
	MASC	FEM	NEUT
NOM	der meinige	die meinige	das meinige
ACC	den meinigen	die meinige	das meinige
GEN	des meinigen	der meinigen	des meinigen
DAT	dem meinigen	der meinigen	dem meinigen

	PLURAL ALL GENDERS
NOM	die meinigen
ACC	die meinigen
GEN	der meinigen
DAT	den meinigen

❸

	SINGULAR		
	MASC	FEM	NEUT
NOM	der meine	die meine	das meine
ACC	den meinen	die meine	das meine
GEN	des meinen	der meinen	des meinen
DAT	dem meinen	der meinen	dem meinen

	PLURAL ALL GENDERS
NOM	die meinen
ACC	die meinen
GEN	der meinen
DAT	den meinen

NOTE: Der/die/das meinige *etc* can also be spelt der/die/das Meinige *etc*
and der/die/das meine *etc* can also be spelt der/die/das Meine *etc*.

Reflexive Pronouns

Reflexive pronouns, used to form reflexive verbs, have two forms, accusative and dative, as follows → ①

ACCUSATIVE	DATIVE	
mich	mir	myself
dich	dir	yourself (*familiar*)
sich	sich	himself/herself/itself/themselves
uns	uns	ourselves
euch	euch	yourselves (*plural*)
sich	sich	yourself/yourselves (*polite*)

Unlike personal pronouns and possessives, the polite forms have no capital letter → ②

For the position of reflexive pronouns within a sentence see page 30 (reflexive verbs) and pages 224–235 (sentence structure).

Reflexive pronouns are also used after prepositions when the pronoun has the function of "reflecting back" to the subject of the sentence → ③

A further use of reflexive pronouns in German is with transitive verbs where the action is performed for the benefit of the subject, as in the English phrase:

> I bought *myself* a new hat

The pronoun is not always translated in English → ④

Examples

❶ Er hat sich rasiert.
He had a shave.

Du hast dich gebadet.
You had a bath.

Ich will es mir zuerst überlegen.
I'll have to think about it first.

❷ Setzen Sie sich bitte.
Please take a seat.

❸ Er hatte nicht genug Geld bei sich. (NOT: bei ihm)
He didn't have enough money on him.

❹ Ich hole mir ein Bier.
I'm going to get a beer (for myself).

Er hat sich einen neuen Anzug gekauft.
He bought (himself) a new suit.

Reflexive Pronouns *continued*

Reflexive pronouns may be used for *reciprocal* actions, usually rendered by "each other" in English → ❶

Reciprocal actions may also be expressed by einander. This does not change in form → ❷

Einander is always used in place of the reflexive pronoun after prepositions. Note that the preposition and einander come together to form one word → ❸

Emphatic reflexive pronouns

In English, these have the same forms as the normal reflexive pronouns:

> The queen *herself* had given the order

> I haven't read it *myself*, but ...

In German, this idea is expressed not by the reflexive pronouns, but by selbst or (in colloquial speech) selber placed at some point in the sentence after the noun or pronoun to which they refer → ❹

selbst/selber do not change their form, regardless of number and gender of the noun to which they refer → ❹

They are always stressed, regardless of their position in the sentence.

❶ Wir sind uns letzte Woche begegnet.
We met (each other) last week.

Sie hatten sich auf einer Tagung kennengelernt.
They had got to know each other at a conference.

❷ Wir kennen uns schon.
OR:
Wir kennen einander schon.
We already know each other.

Sie kennen sich schon.
OR:
Sie kennen einander schon.
They already know each other.

❸ Sie redeten miteinander.
They were talking to each other.

❹ Die Königin selbst hat es befohlen.
The queen herself has given the order.

Ich selbst habe es nicht gelesen, aber ...
I haven't read it myself, but ...

Relative Pronouns

These have the same forms as the definite article, except in the dative plural and genitive cases.

They are declined as follows:

| | SINGULAR | | | PLURAL |
	MASC	FEM	NEUT	ALL GENDERS
NOM	der	die	das	die
ACC	den	die	das	die
GEN	dessen	deren	dessen	deren
DAT	dem	der	dem	denen

Relative pronouns must agree in gender and number with the noun to which they refer. They take their case however from the function they have in their own relative clause → **1**

The relative pronoun cannot be omitted in German as it sometimes is in English → **2**

The genitive forms are used in relative clauses in much the same way as in English → **3**

NOTE, however, the translation of certain phrases → **4**

When a preposition introduces the relative clause, the relative pronoun may be replaced by **wo-** or **wor-** if the noun or pronoun it stands for refers to an inanimate object or abstract concept → **5**

The full form of relative pronoun plus preposition is however stylistically better.

Relative clauses are always divided off by commas from the rest of the sentence → **1** – **5**

Examples

❶   Der Mann, den ich gestern gesehen habe, kommt aus
Hamburg.
The man whom I saw yesterday comes from Hamburg.

❷   Die Frau, mit der ich gestern gesprochen habe, kennt deine
Mutter.
The woman I spoke to yesterday knows your mother.

❸   Das Kind, dessen Fahrrad gestohlen worden war, ...
The child whose bicycle had been stolen ...

❹   Die Kinder, von denen einige schon lesen konnten, ...
The children, some of whom could read, ...

Meine Freunde, von denen einer ...
My friends, one of whom ...

❺   Das Buch, woraus ich vorgelesen habe, ...
OR:
Das Buch, aus dem ich vorgelesen habe, ...
The book I read aloud from ...

Relative Pronouns *continued*

Welcher

A second relative pronoun exists. This has the same forms as the interrogative adjective welcher without the genitive forms:

		SINGULAR		PLURAL
	MASC	FEM	NEUT	ALL GENDERS
NOM	welcher	welche	welches	welche
ACC	welchen	welche	welches	welche
GEN	——	——	——	——
DAT	welchem	welcher	welchem	welchen

These forms are used only infrequently as relative pronouns, where sentence rhythm might benefit.

They are also useful used as articles or adjectives to connect a noun in the relative clause with the contents of the main clause → ❶

Wer, was

These are normally used as interrogative pronouns meaning *who?*, *what?* and are declined as such on page 178.

They may, however, also be used without interrogative meaning to replace both subject and relative pronoun in English:

> *he who*
> *a woman who*   → ❷
> *anyone who*
> *those who* etc

Was is the relative pronoun used in set expressions with certain neuter forms → ❸

① Er glaubte, mit der Hausarbeit nicht helfen zu brauchen, mit welcher Idee seine Mutter nicht einverstanden war!
He thought he didn't have to help in the house, an idea with which his mother was not in agreement!

② Wer das glaubt, ist verrückt.
Anyone who believes that is mad.

Was mich angeht, ...
For my part, ...

Was du gestern gekauft hast, steht dir ganz gut.
The things you bought yesterday suit you very well.

③

alles, was ...	everything which
allerlei, was ...	all kinds of things that
das, was ...	that which
dasjenige, was ...	that which
dasselbe, was ...	the same one that
einiges, was ...	some that
Folgendes, was ...	the following which
manches, was ...	some which
nichts, was ...	nothing that
vieles, was ...	a lot that
wenig, was ...	little that

Nichts, was er sagte, hat gestimmt.
Nothing that he said was right.

Das, was du jetzt machst, ist reiner Unsinn!
What you are doing now is sheer nonsense!

Mit allem, was du gesagt hast, sind wir einverstanden.
We agree with everything you said.

Interrogative Pronouns

These are the pronouns used to ask questions.

As in English, they have few forms, singular and plural being the same.

They are declined as follows:

	PERSONS	THINGS
NOM	wer?	was?
ACC	wen?	was?
GEN	wessen?	wessen?
DAT	wem?	—

They are used in direct questions → ❶

or in indirect questions → ❷

When used as the subject of a sentence, they are always followed by a singular verb → ❸

BUT: When followed by a verb and taking a noun complement, the verb may be plural if the sense demands it → ❹

The interrogative pronouns can be used in rhetorical questions or in exclamations → ❺

①   Wer hat es gemacht?
    Who did it?

    Mit wem bist du gekommen?
    Who did you come with?

②   Ich weiß nicht, wer es gemacht hat.
    I don't know who did it.

    Er wollte wissen, mit wem er fahren sollte.
    He wanted to know who he was to travel with.

③   Wer kommt heute?
    Who's coming today?

④   Wer sind diese Leute?
    Who are these people?

⑤   Was haben wir gelacht!
    How we laughed!

Interrogative Pronouns *continued*

When used with prepositions, was usually becomes wo- and is placed in front of the preposition to form one word → ❶

Where the preposition begins with a vowel, wor- is used instead → ❷

This construction is similar to da(r)- + *preposition* shown on page 164.

As with da(r)- + *preposition*, this construction is not used when the preposition is intended to convey movement.

Wohin (*where to*) and woher (*where from*) are used instead → ❸

Was für ein?, welcher?

These are used to mean *what kind of one?* and *which one?*

They are declined as shown on pages 124–128.

They are used to form either direct or indirect questions → ❹

They may refer either to persons or to things with the appropriate declension endings → ❺

❶   Wonach sehnst du dich?
        What do you long for?

        Wodurch ist es zerstört worden?
        How was it destroyed?

❷   Worauf kann man sich heutzutage noch verlassen?
        What is there left to rely on these days?

❸   Wohin fährst du?
        Where are you going?

        Woher kommt das?
        Where has this come from?/How has this come about?

❹   Was für eins hat er?
        What kind (of one) does he have?

        Welches hast du gewollt?
        Which one did you want?

❺   Für welchen hat sie sich entschieden?
        Which one (*man/hat etc*) did she choose?

Indefinite Pronouns

(irgend)jemand someone, somebody

NOM	(irgend)jemand
ACC	(irgend)jemanden, (irgend)jemand
GEN	(irgend)jemand(e)s
DAT	(irgend)jemandem, (irgend)jemand

→ **1**

niemand no-one, nobody

NOM	niemand
ACC	niemanden, niemand
GEN	niemand(e)s
DAT	niemandem, niemand

→ **2**

The forms without endings are used in conversational German, but the inflected forms are preferred in literary and written styles.

When niemand and (irgend)jemand are used with a following adjective, they are usually not declined, but the adjective takes a capital letter and is declined as follows:

NOM	(irgend)jemand/niemand Neues
ACC	(irgend)jemand/niemand Neues
GEN	—
DAT	(irgend)jemand/niemand Neuem

→ **3**

When (irgend)jemand and niemand are followed by ander(e)s, this is written with a small letter, e.g. (irgend)jemand/niemand ander(e)s.

❶ Ich habe es (irgend)jemandem (*dat*) gegeben.
I gave it to someone.

(Irgend)jemand (*nom*) hat es genommen.
Someone has stolen it.

❷ Er hat niemanden (*acc*) gesehen.
He didn't see anyone.

Er ist unterwegs niemandem (*dat*) begegnet.
He encountered no-one on the way.

❸ Diese Aufgabe erfordert (irgend)jemand Intelligentes.
Someone intelligent is needed for this task.

Indefinite Pronouns *continued*

keiner none

| | | SINGULAR | | PLURAL |
	MASC	FEM	NEUT	ALL GENDERS
NOM	keiner	keine	keins	keine
ACC	keinen	keine	keins	keine
GEN	keines	keiner	keines	keiner
DAT	keinem	keiner	keinem	keinen

It is declined like the article kein, keine, kein (see page 126) except in the nominative masculine and nominative and accusative neuter forms → ❶

It may be used to refer to people or things → ❶

einer one

| | | SINGULAR | |
	MASC	FEM	NEUT
NOM	einer	eine	ein(e)s
ACC	einen	eine	ein(e)s
GEN	eines	einer	eines
DAT	einem	einer	einem

This pronoun may be used to refer to either people or things → ❷

It exists only in the singular forms.

❶ Keiner von ihnen hat es tun können.
Not one of them was able to do it.

Gibst du mir eine Zigarette? — Tut mir leid, ich habe keine.
Will you give me a cigarette? — Sorry, I haven't got any.

❷ Sie ist mit einem meiner Verwandten verlobt.
She is engaged to one of my relatives.

Wo sind die anderen Kinder? Ich sehe hier nur eins.
Where are the rest of the children? I can only see one here.

Gibst du mir einen? (e.g. *einen Whisky, einen Zehner* etc) OR:
Gibst du mir eine? (e.g. *eine Zigarette, eine Blume* etc) OR:
Gibst du mir eins? (e.g. *ein Buch, ein Butterbrot* etc)
Will you give me one?

Indefinite Pronouns *continued*

Certain adjectives and articles can be used as pronouns.

The following are all declined to agree in gender and number with the noun or pronoun they represent → **1**

aller	all
ander	other
beide	both
derjenige	that one
derselbe	the same one
dieser	this one
einiger	some
irgendwelcher	someone or other/something or other
jeder	each (one), every one
jener	that one
mancher	some, quite a few
mehrere	several
sämtliche	all, the lot
solcher	such as that, such a one
welcher	which one

The following do not change whatever the gender or number of the noun or pronoun they represent → **2**

ein bisschen	a bit, a little
ein paar	a few
ein wenig	a little, a few
(irgend)etwas	some, something
mehr	more
nichts	nothing, none

When an adjective follows etwas or nichts, it takes a capital letter and declension endings, e.g. etwas/nichts Gutes

❶ Andere machen es besser. (e.g. *Leute, Waschmaschinen* etc)
Others do it better.

Mit einem solchen kommst du nicht bis nach Hause.
(e.g. *Wagen* etc)
You won't make it home in one like that.

Alles, was er ihr schenkte, schickte sie sofort zurück.
Everything that he gave her she sent back at once.

Er war mit beiden zufrieden. (e.g. *Computern, Autos* etc)
He was satisfied with both.

❷ Ich muss dir etwas sagen.
I must tell you something.

(Irgend)etwas ist herausgefallen.
Something fell out.

Nichts ist geschehen.
Nothing happened.

Er ist mit nichts zufrieden.
Nothing ever satisfies him.

Gibst du mir bitte ein paar?
Will you give me a few?

Er hatte ein wenig bei sich.
He had a little with him.

Er braucht immer mehr um zu überleben.
He needs more and more to survive.

Use of Adverbs

Adverbs, or phrases which are used as adverbs, may:

- modify a verb → **①**

- modify an adjective → **②**

- modify another adverb → **③**

- modify a conjunction → **④**

- ask a question → **⑤**

- form verb prefixes (see page 72) → **⑥**

Adverbs are also used, in much the same way as in English, to make the meaning of certain tenses more precise e.g.

- with continuous tenses → **⑦**

- to show a future meaning where the tense used is not future → **⑧**

① Er ging langsam über die Brücke.
He walked slowly over the bridge.

② Er ist ein ziemlich großer Kerl.
He's quite a big chap.

③ Sie arbeitet heute besonders tüchtig.
She's working exceptionally well today.

④ Wenn er es nur aufgeben wollte!
If only he would give it up!

⑤ Wann kommt er an?
When does he arrive?

⑥ falsch spielen
to cheat (*at cards*)

hintragen
to carry (*to a place*)

⑦ Er liest gerade die Zeitung.
He's just reading the paper.

⑧ Er wollte gerade aufstehen, als ...
He was just about to get up when ...

Wir fahren morgen nach Köln.
We're driving to Cologne tomorrow.

The Formation of Adverbs

Many German adverbs are simply adjectives used as adverbs. Used in this way, unlike adjectives, they are not declined → **1**

Some adverbs are formed by adding **-weise** or **-sweise** to a noun → **2**

Some adverbs are also formed by adding **-erweise** to an uninflected adjective.

Such adverbs are used mainly to show the speaker's opinion → **3**

There is also a class of adverbs which are not formed from other parts of speech e.g. unten, oben, leider → **4**

For the position of adverbs within a clause or sentence, see the section on sentence structure, pages 224–235.

The following are some common adverbs of time:

endlich	finally
heute	today
immer	always
morgen	tomorrow
morgens	in the mornings
sofort	at once

→ **5**

The following are some common adverbs of degree:

äußerst	extremely
besonders	especially
beträchtlich	considerably
ziemlich	fairly

→ **6**

① Habe ich das richtig gehört?
Is it true what I've heard?

Sie war modern angezogen.
She was fashionably dressed.

②

beispielsweise	for example
beziehungsweise	or/or rather/that is to say
schrittweise	step by step
zeitweise	at times
zwangsweise	compulsorily

③

erstaunlicherweise	astonishingly enough
glücklicherweise	fortunately
komischerweise	strangely enough

④ Unten wohnte Frau Schmidt.
Mrs Schmidt lived downstairs.

Leider können wir nicht kommen.
Unfortunately we cannot come.

⑤ Ich kann erst morgen kommen.
I can't come till tomorrow.

Das Kind hat immer Hunger.
The child is always hungry.

⑥ Das Paket war besonders schwer.
The parcel was unusually heavy.

Diese Übung ist ziemlich leicht.
This exercise is quite easy.

Adverbs of place

In certain respects German adverbs of place behave very differently from their English counterparts:

Where no movement, or merely a movement within the same place, is involved, the adverb is used in its simple dictionary form → **1**

Movement *away from the speaker* is shown by the presence of hin → **2**

The following compound adverbs are therefore often used when movement away from the original position is concerned, even though a simple adverb would be used in English:

dahin	(to) there
dorthin	there
hierhin	here
irgendwohin	(to) somewhere or other
überallhin	everywhere
wohin?	where (to)?

→ **3**

Movement *towards the speaker* or central person is shown by the presence of her.

The following compound adverbs are therefore often used to show movement towards a person:

daher	from there
hierher	here
irgendwoher	from somewhere or other
überallher	from all over
woher?	where from?

→ **4**

Examples

❶ Wo ist er?
Where is he?

Er ist nicht da.
He isn't there.

Hier darf man nicht parken.
You can't park here.

❷ Klaus und Ulli geben heute eine Party. Gehen wir hin?
Klaus and Ulli are having a party today. Shall we go?

❸ Wohin fährst du?
Where are you going?

Sie liefen überallhin.
They ran everywhere.

❹ Woher kommst du?
Where do you come from?

Woher hast du das?
Where did you get that from?

Das habe ich irgendwoher gekriegt.
I got that from somewhere or other.

Comparison of Adverbs

The comparative form of the adverb is obtained in exactly the same way as that of adjectives, i.e. by adding **-er** → **①**

The superlative form is produced as follows:

> am + *adverb* + **-sten/-esten**

It is not declined → **②**

Note the use of the comparative adverb with immer to show progression → **③**

the more … the more … is expressed in German by:

> je … desto … or je … umso … → **④**

Some adverbial superlatives are used to show the extent of a quality rather than a comparison with others. These are as follows:

bestens	very well/very warmly
höchstens	at the most/at best
meistens	mostly/most often
spätestens	at the latest
strengstens	strictly, absolutely
wenigstens	at least

→ **⑤**

Two irregular comparatives and superlatives:

gern	►	lieber	►	am liebsten (used with haben) → **⑥**
well	►	better	►	best
bald	►	eher	►	am ehesten
soon	►	sooner	►	soonest

❶ Er läuft schneller als seine Schwester.
He runs faster than his sister.

Ich sehe ihn seltener als früher.
I see him less often than before.

❷ Wer von ihnen arbeitet am schnellsten?
Which of them works fastest?

Er isst am meisten.
He eats most.

❸ Die Mädchen sprachen immer lauter.
The girls were talking more and more loudly.

Er fuhr immer langsamer.
He drove more and more slowly.

❹ Je eher, desto besser.
The sooner the better.

❺ Er kommt meistens zu spät an.
He usually arrives late.

Rauchen strengstens verboten!
Smoking strictly prohibited.

❻ Welches hast du am liebsten?
Which do you like best?

Emphasizers

These are words commonly used in German, as indeed in English, especially in the spoken language, to emphasize or modify in some way the meaning of the sentence. The following are some of the most common:

aber

Used to lend emphasis to a statement → ❶

denn

As well as its uses as a conjunction (see page 214), denn is widely used to emphasize the meaning. It often cannot be directly translated → ❷

doch

Used as a positive reply in order to correct negative assumptions or impressions → ❸
It can strengthen an imperative → ❹
It can make a question out of a statement → ❺

mal

May be used with imperatives → ❻
It also has several idiomatic uses → ❼

ja

Strengthens a statement → ❽
It also has several idiomatic uses → ❾

schon

Is used familiarly with an imperative → ❿
It is also used in various idiomatic ways → ⓫

1.   Das ist aber schön!   Aber ja!
   Oh that's pretty!   Yes indeed!

2.   Was ist denn hier los?   Wo denn?
   What's going on here then?   Where?

3.   Hat es dir nicht gefallen? — Doch!
   Didn't you like it? — Oh yes, I did!

4.   Lass ihn doch!
   Just leave him!

5.   Das schaffst du doch?
   You'll manage it, won't you?

6.   Komm mal her!   Moment mal!
   Come here!   Just a minute!

7.   Mal sehen.   Hören Sie mal …
   We'll see.   Look here now …
   Er soll es nur mal versuchen!
   Just let him try it!

8.   Er sieht ja wie seine Mutter aus.
   He looks like his mother.
   Das kann ja sein.
   That may well be.

9.   Ja und?   Das ist ja lächerlich.
   So what?/What then?   That's ridiculous.
   Das ist es ja.
   That's just it.

10.   Mach schon!
    Get on with it!

11.   schon wieder   Schon gut!
    again   Okay/Very well!

Prepositions

In English, a preposition does not affect the word or phrase which it introduces, e.g.

the women	a large meal	these events
with the women	*after* a large meal	*before* these events

In German, however, the noun following a preposition must be put in a certain *case*:

accusative → ❶

dative → ❷

genitive → ❸

It is therefore important to learn each preposition with the case, or cases, it governs.

The following guidelines will help you:

Prepositions which take the accusative or dative cases are much more common than those taking the genitive case.

Certain prepositions may take a dative or accusative case, depending on whether *movement* is involved or not. This is explained further on pages 202–211 → ❹

Prepositions are often used to complete the sense of certain verbs, as shown on pages 76–79 → ❺

After many prepositions, a shortened or *contracted* form of the definite article may be merged with the preposition to form one word, e.g.

auf + das	▶	aufs
bei + dem	▶	beim
zu + der	▶	zur

Examples

①
Es ist für dich.
It's for you.

Wir sind durch die ganze Welt gereist.
We travelled all over the world.

②
Er ist mit seiner Frau gekommen.
He came with his wife.

③
Es ist ihm trotz seiner Bemühungen nicht gelungen.
Despite his efforts, he still didn't succeed.

④
Es liegt auf dem Tisch.
It's on the table.
(*dative*: no movement implied)

Lege es bitte auf den Tisch.
Please put it on the table.
(*accusative*: movement *onto* the table)

⑤
Ich warte auf meinen Mann.
I'm waiting for my husband.

Contracted forms

Contractions are possible with the following prepositions:

PREPOSITION	+das	+den	+dem	+der
an	ans		am	
auf	aufs*			
bei			beim	
durch	durchs*			
für	fürs*			
hinter	hinters*	hintern*	hinterm*	
in	ins		im	
über	übers*	übern*	überm*	
um	ums*			
unter	unters*	untern*	unterm*	
vor	vors*		vorm*	
von			vom	
zu			zum	zur

* NOTE: Those forms marked with an asterisk are suitable only for use in colloquial, spoken German.
All other forms (not marked with an asterisk) may be safely used in any context, formal or informal → ❶

Contracted forms are not used where the article is to be stressed → ❷

Other contracted forms involving prepositions, as shown on pages 164 and 174, occur:

- in the introduction to relative clauses → ❸
- with personal pronouns representing inanimate objects → ❹

Examples

❶   Wir gehen heute Abend ins Theater.
        We are going to the theatre this evening.

        Er geht zur Schule.
        He goes to school.

        Das kommt vom Trinken.
        That comes from drinking.

❷   In dem Anzug kann ich mich nicht sehen lassen!
        I can't go out in that suit!

❸   Die Bank, worauf wir saßen, war etwas wackelig.
        The bench we were sitting on was rather wobbly.

❹   Er war damit zufrieden.
        He was satisfied with that.

        Er hat es darauf gesetzt.
        He put it on it.

Prepositions followed by the Dative Case

Some of the most common prepositions taking the dative case are:

aus	gegenüber	seit
außer	mit	von
bei	nach	zu

aus

as a preposition meaning:　　*out of/from* → ❶

as a separable verbal prefix (see page 72) → ❷

außer

as a preposition meaning:　　*out of* → ❸
　　　　　　　　　　　　　　except → ❹

bei

as a preposition meaning:　　*at the home/shop/work etc of* → ❺
　　　　　　　　　　　　　　near → ❻
　　　　　　　　　　　　　　in the course of/during → ❼

as a separable verbal prefix (see page 72) → ❽

gegenüber

as a preposition meaning:　　*opposite* → ❾
　　　　　　　　　　　　　　to(wards) → ❿

NOTE: When used as a preposition, gegenüber is placed *after a pronoun*, but may be placed *before or after a noun*.

as a separable verbal prefix → ⑪

1
Er trinkt aus der Flasche.
He is drinking out of the bottle.
Er kommt aus Essen.
He comes from Essen.

2
aushalten to endure
Ich halte es nicht mehr aus.
I can't stand it any longer.

3
außer Gefahr/Betrieb
out of danger/order

4
alle außer mir
all except me

5
bei uns in Schottland
at home in Scotland
Er wohnt immer noch bei seinen Eltern.
He still lives with his parents.

6
Er saß bei mir.
He was sitting next to me.

7
Ich singe immer beim Arbeiten.
I always sing when I'm working.
Bei unserer Ankunft ...
On our arrival ...

8
beistehen to stand by
Er stand seinem Freund bei.
He stood by his friend.

9
Er wohnt uns gegenüber.
He lives opposite us.

10
Er ist mir gegenüber immer sehr freundlich gewesen.
He has always been very friendly towards me.

11
gegenüberstehen to face/to have an attitude towards
Er steht ihnen kritisch gegenüber.
He takes a critical view of them.

Prepositions followed by the Dative Case *continued*

mit

as a preposition meaning: *with* → ❶

as a separable verbal prefix (see page 72) → ❷

nach

as a preposition meaning: *after* → ❸
to → ❹
according to (it can be placed after the noun
with this meaning) → ❺

as a separable verbal prefix (see page 72) → ❻

seit

as a preposition meaning: *since* → ❼
for (of time) → ❽
NOTE: Beware of the tense!

von

as a preposition meaning: *from* → ❾
about → ❿

as an alternative, often preferred, to the genitive case → ⓫

as a preposition meaning: *by* (to introduce the agent of a passive
action, see page 34) → ⓬

zu

as a preposition meaning: *to* → ⓭
for → ⓮

as a separable verbal prefix (see page 72) → ⓯

1 Er ging mit seinen Freunden spazieren.
He went walking with his friends.

2 jemanden mitnehmen to give someone a lift
Nimmst du mich bitte mit?
Will you give me a lift please?

3 Nach zwei Stunden kam er wieder.
He returned two hours later.

4 Er ist nach London gereist.
He went to London.

5 Ihrer Sprache nach ist sie Süddeutsche.
From the way she spoke I would say she is from southern Germany.

6 nachmachen to copy
Sie macht mir alles nach.
She copies everything I do.

7 Seit der Zeit …
Since then …

8 Ich wohne seit zwei Jahren in Frankfurt.
I've been living in Frankfurt for two years.

9 Von Frankfurt sind wir weiter nach München gefahren.
From Frankfurt we went on to Munich.

10 Ich weiß nichts von ihm.
I know nothing about him.

11 Die Mutter von diesen Mädchen …
The mother of these girls …
Sie ist eine Freundin von Horst.
She is a friend of Horst's.

12 Er ist von unseren Argumenten überzeugt worden.
He was convinced by our arguments.

13 Er ging zum Arzt.
He went to the doctor's.

14 Wir sind zum Essen eingeladen.
We're invited for dinner.

15 zumachen to shut
Mach die Tür zu!
Shut the door!

Prepositions followed by the Accusative Case

The most common of these are:

| durch | für | ohne | wider |
| entlang | gegen | um | |

durch

as a preposition meaning: *through* → **1**

preceding the inanimate agent of a passive action (see page 34) → **2**

as a separable verbal prefix

entlang

as a preposition meaning: *along* (it follows the noun with this meaning) → **3**

as a separable verbal prefix → **4**

für

as a preposition meaning: *for* → **5**
   to → **6**

in was für/was für ein *what kind of/what* (see pages 144 and 180) → **7**

gegen

as a preposition meaning: *against* → **8**
   towards/getting on for → **9**

as a separable verbal prefix

Examples

❶ durch das Fenster blicken
to look through the window

❷ Durch seine Bemühungen wurden alle gerettet.
Everyone was saved through his efforts.

❸ die Straße entlang
along the street

❹ entlanggehen to go along
Wir gingen die Straße entlang.
We went along the street.

❺ Ich habe es für dich getan.
I did it for you.

❻ Das ist für ihn sehr wichtig.
That is very important to him.

❼ Was für Äpfel sind das?
What kind of apples are they?

❽ Stelle es gegen die Mauer.
Put it against the wall.

Haben Sie ein Mittel gegen Schnupfen?
Have you something for colds?

Ich habe nichts dagegen.
I've got nothing against it.

❾ Wir sind gegen vier angekommen.
We arrived at getting on for/around four o'clock.

Prepositions followed by the Accusative Case *continued*

ohne

as a preposition meaning: *without* → ❶

um

as a preposition meaning: *(a)round/round about* → ❷

at (in time expressions) → ❸

for (after certain verbs) → ❹

about (after certain verbs) → ❺

by (in expressions of quantity) → ❻

as a variable verbal prefix (see page 74) → ❼

wider

as a preposition meaning: *contrary to/against* → ❽

as a variable verbal prefix (see page 74) → ❾

❶
Ohne ihn gehts nicht.
It won't work without him.

❷
um die Ecke
(a)round the corner

❸
Es fängt um neun Uhr an.
It begins at nine.

❹
Sie baten ihre Mutter um Kekse.
They asked their mother for some biscuits.

❺
Es handelt sich um dein Benehmen.
It's a question of your behaviour.

❻
Es ist um zehn Euro billiger.
It is cheaper by ten euros.

❼
umarmen to embrace (*inseparable*)
Er hat sie umarmt.
He gave her a hug.

umfallen to fall over (*separable*)
Er ist umgefallen.
He fell over.

❽
Das geht mir wider die Natur.
That's against my nature.

❾
widersprechen to go against (*inseparable*)
Das hat meinen Wünschen widersprochen.
That went against my wishes.

(sich) widerspiegeln to reflect (*separable*)
Der Baum spiegelt sich im Wasser wider.
The tree is reflected in the water.

Prepositions followed by the Accusative or the Dative Case

These prepositions are followed by:

- the accusative when *movement towards* a different place is involved.

- the dative when *position* is described as opposed to movement, or when the movement is *within* the same place.

The most common prepositions in this category are:

an	*on/at/to*
auf	*on/in/to/at*
hinter	*behind*
in	*in/into/to* → ❶
neben	*next to/beside*
über	*over/across/above*
unter	*under/among* → ❷
vor	*in front of/before*
zwischen	*between* → ❸

These prepositions may also be used with figurative meanings as part of a *verb + preposition* construction (see page 76).

The case following auf or an is then not the same after all verbs →

It is therefore best to learn such constructions together with the case which follows them.

Many of these prepositions are also used as verbal prefixes in the same way as the prepositions described on pages 202–209 → ❺

❶ Er ging ins Zimmer (*acc*).
He entered the room.

Im Zimmer (*dat*) warteten viele Leute auf ihn.
A lot of people were waiting for him in the room.

❷ Er stellte sich unter den Baum (*acc*).
He (came and) stood under the tree.

Er lebte dort unter Freunden (*dat*).
There he lived among friends.

❸ Er legte es zwischen die beiden Teller (*acc*).
He put it between the two plates.

Das Dorf liegt zwischen den Bergen (*dat*).
The village lies between the mountains.

❹
sich verlassen auf (+*acc*)	to depend on
bestehen auf (+*dat*)	to insist on
glauben an (+*acc*)	to believe in
leiden an (+*dat*)	to suffer from

❺ anrechnen to charge for (*separable*)
Das wird Ihnen später angerechnet.
You'll be charged for that later.

aufsetzen to put on (*separable*)
Sie setzte sich den Hut auf.
She put her hat on.

überqueren to cross (*inseparable*)
Sie hat die Straße überquert.
She crossed the street.

Prepositions followed by the Genitive Case

The following are some of the more common prepositions which take the genitive case:

außerhalb	*outside*
beiderseits	*on both sides of*
diesseits	*on this side of*
... halber	*for ... sake/because of ...*
hinsichtlich	*with regard to*
infolge	*as a result of*
innerhalb	*within/inside* → ❶
jenseits	*on the other side of* → ❷
statt*	*instead of*
trotz*	*in spite of* → ❸
um ... willen	*for ... sake/because of ...*
während*	*during* → ❹
wegen*	*on account of* → ❺

* NOTE: Those prepositions marked with an asterisk may also be followed by the dative case → ❻

NOTE: Special forms of the possessive and relative pronouns are used with wegen, halber and willen → ❼

Examples

1. innerhalb dieses Zeitraums
    within this period of time

2. jenseits der Grenze
    on the other side of the frontier

3. trotz seiner Befürchtungen
    despite his fears

4. während der Vorstellung
    during the performance

5. wegen der neuen Stelle
    because of the new job

6. trotz allem
    in spite of everything

    wegen mir
    because of me

7.

meinetwegen	on my account, because of me
deinetwegen	on your account, because of you (*familiar*)
seinetwegen	on his account, because of him
ihretwegen	on her/their account, because of her/them
unsertwegen	on our account, because of us
euertwegen	on your account, because of you (*plural*)
Ihretwegen	on your account, because of you (*polite*)
derentwegen	for whose sake, for her/their/its sake
dessentwegen	for whose sake, for his/its sake
meinethalben *etc*	on my *etc* account
derenthalben	on whose account, on her/their/its account
dessenthalben	on whose account, on his/its account
meinetwillen *etc*	for my *etc* sake
derentwillen	for whose sake, for her/its/their sake
dessentwillen	for whose sake, for his/its sake

Co-ordinating Conjunctions

These are used to link words, phrases or clauses.

These are the main co-ordinating conjunctions:

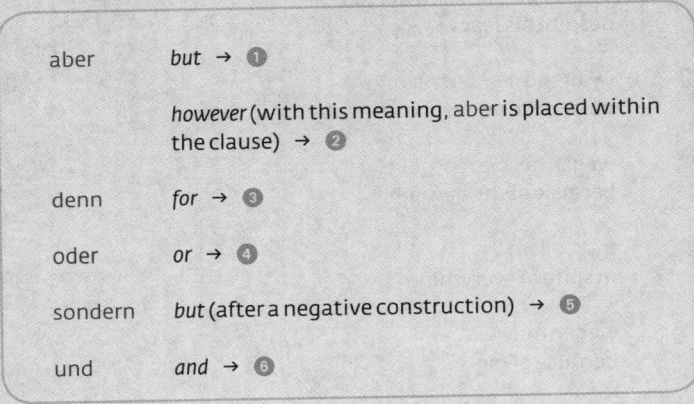

aber	*but* → ❶
	however (with this meaning, aber is placed within the clause) → ❷
denn	*for* → ❸
oder	*or* → ❹
sondern	*but* (after a negative construction) → ❺
und	*and* → ❻

These do not cause the inversion of subject and verb, i.e. the verb follows the subject in the normal way (see page 224) → ❶ – ❻

Inversion may however be caused by something other than the co-ordinating conjunction, e.g. dann, trotzdem, montags in the examples opposite → ❼

1 Wir wollten ins Kino, aber wir hatten kein Geld.
We wanted to go to the cinema but we had no money.

2 Ich wollte ins Theater; er aber wollte nicht mit.
I wanted to go to the theatre; however he wouldn't come.

3 Wir wollten heute fahren, denn montags ist weniger Verkehr.
We wanted to travel today because the traffic is lighter on Mondays.

4 Er hatte noch nie Whisky oder Schnaps getrunken.
He had never drunk whisky or schnapps.

Willst du eins oder hast du vielleicht keinen Hunger?
Do you want one or aren't you hungry?

5 Er ist nicht alt, sondern jung.
He isn't old, but young.

6 Horst und Veronika
Horst and Veronika

Er ging in die Stadt und kaufte sich ein neues Hemd.
He went into town and bought himself a new shirt.

7 Er hat sie besucht und dann ist er wieder nach Hause gegangen.
He paid her a visit and then went home again.

Wir wollten doch ins Kino, aber trotzdem sind wir zu Hause geblieben.
We wanted to go to the cinema, but even so we stayed at home.

Wir wollten heute fahren, denn montags ist der Verkehr geringer.
We wanted to travel today because there is less traffic on Mondays.

Double Co-ordinating Conjunctions

These conjunctions consist of two separate elements, like their English counterparts, e.g.

not only ... but also ...

The following are widely used:

> sowohl.. als auch
> *both ... and*

This may link words or phrases → **1**

The verb is usually plural, whether the subjects are singular or plural → **1**

> weder ... noch
> *neither ... nor*

This may link words or phrases → **2**

It may also link clauses, and inversion of subject and verb then takes place in both clauses → **3**

The verb is plural unless both subjects are singular → **4**

❶ Sowohl sein Vater als auch seine Mutter haben sich darüber gefreut.
Both his father and his mother were pleased about it.

Sowohl unser Lehrkörper als auch unsere Schüler haben teilgenommen.
Both our staff and our pupils took part.

❷ Weder Georg noch sein Bruder kannte das Mädchen.
Neither Georg nor his brother knew the girl.

❸ Weder mag ich ihn noch respektiere ich ihn.
I neither like nor respect him.

❹ Weder die Befürworter noch die Gegner haben recht.
Neither the supporters nor the opponents are right.

Weder du noch ich würde es schaffen.
Neither you nor I would be able to do it.

Double Co-ordinating Conjunctions *continued*

> nicht nur ... sondern auch
> *not only ... but also*

This is used to link clauses as well as words and phrases → ❶

The word order is: inversion of subject and verb in the first clause, and normal order in the second → ❷

However, if nicht nur does not begin the clause, normal order prevails → ❸

The verb agrees in number with the subject nearest to it → ❹

> entweder ... oder
> *either ... or*

The verb agrees with the subject nearest it → ❺

The normal word order is: inversion in the first clause, and normal order in the second → ❻

However, it is possible to use normal order in the first clause, and this may lend a more threatening tone to the statement → ❼

> teils ... teils
> *partly ... partly*

The verb is normally plural unless both subjects are singular → ❽

Inversion of subject and verb takes place in both clauses → ❾

❶ Er ist nicht nur geschickt, sondern auch intelligent. OR:
Nicht nur ist er geschickt, sondern er ist auch intelligent.
He is not only skilful but also intelligent.

❷ Nicht nur hat es die ganze Zeit geregnet, sondern ich habe mir
auch noch das Bein gebrochen.
Not only did it rain the whole time, but I also broke my leg.

❸ Es hat nicht nur die ganze Zeit geregnet, sondern ich habe mir
auch noch das Bein gebrochen.
Not only did it rain the whole time, but I also broke my leg.

❹ Nicht nur ich, sondern auch die Mädchen sind dafür
verantwortlich.
It's not just me, but it's also the girls who are also responsible.

Nicht nur sie, sondern auch ich habe es gehört.
They weren't the only ones to hear it — I heard it too.

❺ Entweder du oder Georg muss es getan haben.
It must have been either you or Georg who did it.

❻ Entweder komme ich morgen vorbei, oder ich rufe dich an.
I'll either drop in tomorrow or I'll give you a ring.

❼ Entweder du gibst das sofort auf, oder du kriegst kein
Taschengeld mehr.
Either you stop that immediately, or you get no more pocket
money.

❽ Die Studenten waren teils Deutsche, teils Ausländer.
The students were partly German and partly from abroad.

❾ Teils bin ich überzeugt, teils bleibe ich skeptisch.
Part of me is convinced, and part remains sceptical.

Subordinating Conjunctions

These are used to link clauses in such a way as to make one clause dependent on another for its meaning. The dependent clause is called a subordinate clause and the other a main clause.

The subordinate clause is always separated from the rest of the sentence by commas → ❶

The subordinate clause may precede the main clause. When this happens, the verb and subject of the main clause are inverted, i.e. they swap places, as shown on page 226 → ❷

The finite part of the verb (i.e. the conjugated part) is always at the end of a subordinate clause (see page 228) → ❸

For compound tenses in subordinate clauses, it is the auxiliary (the main part of the verb) which comes last, after the participle or infinitive used to form the compound tense (see pages 22–29) → ❹

Any modal verb (mögen, können etc, see pages 52–57) used in a subordinate clause is placed last in the clause → ❺

BUT: When the modal verb is in a compound tense, the order is as shown → ❻

MAIN CLAUSE   **SUBORDINATE CLAUSE**

Er ist zu Fuß gekommen, weil der Bus zu teuer ist.
He came on foot because the bus is too dear.

Ich trinke viel Bier, obwohl es nicht gesund ist.
I drink a lot of beer although it isn't good for me.

Wir haben weitergefeiert, nachdem sie gegangen waren.
We carried on with the party after they went.

SUBORDINATE CLAUSE   **MAIN CLAUSE**

Weil der Bus zu teuer ist, ist er zu Fuß gekommen.

Obwohl es nicht gesund ist, trinke ich viel Bier.

Nachdem sie gegangen waren, haben wir weitergefeiert.

Als er uns sah, ist er davongelaufen. **OR:**
Er ist davongelaufen, als er uns sah.
He ran away when he saw us.

Nachdem er gegessen hatte, ging er hinaus.
He went out after he had eaten.

Da er nicht mit uns sprechen wollte, ist er davongelaufen.
Since he didn't want to speak to us he ran away.

Da er nicht mit uns hat sprechen wollen, ist er davongelaufen.
Since he didn't want to speak to us he ran away.

Subordinating conjunctions *continued*

Here are some common examples of subordinating conjunctions and their uses:

als	when → ❶
als ob	as if, as though
bevor	before
bis	until → ❷
da	as, since → ❸
damit	so (that)
indem	while
inwiefern	to what extent
nachdem	after → ❹
ob	whether, if
obwohl	although
wann	when (*interrogative*) → ❺
während	while → ❻
weil	because → ❼
wenn	when, whenever/if → ❽
wie	as, like
wo	where
wohin	to where
worauf	whereupon/on which
worin	in which
seitdem	since
so dass, sodass	such that, so that
sobald	as soon as
soweit	as far as

1   Es regnete, als ich in Köln ankam. OR:
Als ich in Köln ankam, regnete es.
It was raining when I arrived in Cologne.

2   Ich warte, bis du zurückkommst.
I'll wait till you get back.

3   Da er nicht kommen wollte, ...
Since he didn't want to come ...

4   Er wird uns Bescheid sagen können, nachdem er angerufen
hat. OR:
Nachdem er angerufen hat, wird er uns Bescheid sagen
können.
He will be able to let us know for certain once he has phoned.

5   Er möchte wissen, wann der Zug ankommt.
He would like to know when the train is due to arrive.

6   Während seine Frau die Koffer auspackte, machte er das
Abendessen. OR:
Er machte das Abendessen, während seine Frau die Koffer
auspackte.
He made the supper while his wife unpacked the cases.

7   Wir haben den Hund nicht mitgenommen, weil im
Auto nicht genug Platz war. OR:
Weil im Auto nicht genug Platz war, haben wir den Hund nicht
mitgenommen.
**We didn't take the dog because there wasn't enough room in
the car.**

8   Wenn ich ins Kino gehe ...
When(ever) I go to the cinema ...

Ich komme, wenn du willst.
I'll come if you like.

Word Order: Main Clauses

In a main clause the subject comes first and is followed by the verb, as in English:

> His mother (*subject*) drinks (*verb*) whisky → **1**

If the verb is in a compound or passive tense, the auxiliary follows the subject and the past participle or infinitive goes to the end of the clause → **2**

The verb is the second concept in a main clause. The first concept may be a word, phrase or clause (see page 226) → **3**

Any reflexive pronoun follows the main verb in simple tenses and the auxiliary in compound tenses → **4**

The order for articles, adjectives and nouns is as in English: *article + adjective(s) + noun* → **5**

A direct object usually follows an indirect, except where the direct object is a personal pronoun.

BUT: The indirect object can be placed last for emphasis, providing it is not a pronoun → **6**

The position of adverbial expressions (see page 188) is not fixed. As a general rule they are placed close to the words to which they refer.

Adverbial items of *time* often come first in the clause, but this is flexible → **7**

Adverbial items of *place* can be placed at the beginning of a clause when emphasis is required → **8**

Adverbial items of *manner* are more likely to be within the clause, close to the word to which they refer → **9**

Where there is more than one adverb, a useful rule of thumb is: "time, manner, place" → **10**

Examples

❶
Seine Mutter trinkt Whisky.
His mother drinks whisky.

❷
Sie wird dir etwas sagen.   Sie hat mir nichts gesagt.
She will tell you something.   She told me nothing.
Es ist für ihn gekauft worden.
It was bought for him.

❸
1ST CONCEPT   2ND CONCEPT
Die neuen Waren   kommen   morgen
(The new goods are coming tomorrow)
Was du gesagt hast,   stimmt   nicht
(What you said isn't true)

❹
Er rasierte sich.   Er hat sich rasiert.
He shaved.   He (has) shaved.

❺
ein alter Mann   diese alten Sachen
an old man   these old things

❻
Ich gab dem Mann das Geld.
I gave the man the money.
Ich gab ihm das Geld.   Ich gab es ihm.
I gave him the money.   I gave him it/I gave it to him.
Er gab das Geld seiner Schwester.
He gave the money to his sister. (*not his brother*)

❼
Gestern gingen wir ins Theater. OR:
Wir gingen gestern ins Theater.
We went to the theatre yesterday.

❽
Dort haben sie Fußball gespielt. OR:
Sie haben dort Fußball gespielt.
They played football there.

❾
Sie spielen gut Fußball.
They play football well.
Das war furchtbar teuer.
It was terribly expensive.

❿
Wir haben gestern gut hierhin gefunden.
We found our way here all right yesterday.

Word Order: **Main Clauses** *continued*

A pronoun object precedes all adverbs → ❶

While the main verb must normally remain the second concept, the first concept need not always be the subject. Main clauses can begin with many things, including:

> an adverb → ❷
> a direct or indirect object → ❸
> an infinitive phrase → ❹
> a complement → ❺
> a past participle → ❻
> a prepositional phrase → ❼
> a clause acting as the object of the verb → ❽
> a subordinate clause → ❾

If the subject does not begin a main clause, the verb and subject must be turned around or "inverted" → ❷ ⁻ ❾

Beginning a sentence with something other than the subject is frequent in German.
It may however also be used for special effect to:

- *highlight* whatever is placed first in the clause → ❿

- *emphasize* the subject of the clause by forcing it from its initial position to the end of the clause → ⓫

After inversion, any reflexive pronoun precedes the subject, unless the subject is a pronoun → ⓬

The following do not cause inversion when placed at the beginning of a main clause, although inversion may be caused by something else placed after them:

> allein, denn, oder, sondern, und → ⓭
> ja and nein → ⓮
> certain exclamations: ach, also, nun *etc* → ⓯
> words or phrases qualifying the subject: auch, nur, sogar, *etc* → ⓰

Examples

① Sie haben es gestern sehr billig gekauft.
They bought it very cheaply yesterday.

② Gestern sind wir ins Theater gegangen.
We went to the theatre yesterday.

③ So ein Kind habe ich noch nie gesehen!
I've never seen such a child!

Seinen Freunden wollte er es nicht zeigen.
He wouldn't show it to his friends.

④ Seinen Freunden zu helfen, hat er nicht versucht.
He didn't try to help his friends.

⑤ Deine Schwester war es.　　**It was your sister.**

⑥ Geraucht hatte er nie.　　**He had never smoked.**

⑦ In diesem Haus ist Mozart auf die Welt gekommen.
Mozart was born in this house.

⑧ Was mit ihm los war, haben wir nicht herausgefunden.
We never discovered what was wrong with him.

⑨ Nachdem ich ihn gesehen hatte, ging ich nach Hause.
I went home after seeing him.

⑩ Dem würde ich nichts sagen!
I wouldn't tell *him* anything!

⑪ An der Ecke stand eine riesengroße Fabrik.
A huge factory stood on the corner.

⑫ Daran erinnerten sich die Zeugen nicht.
The witnesses didn't remember that.

Daran erinnerten sie sich nicht.
They didn't remember that.

⑬ Peter ging nach Hause und Elsa blieb auf der Party.
Peter went home and Elsa stayed at the party.

BUT: Peter ging nach Hause und unterwegs sah er Kurt.
Peter went home and on the way he saw Kurt.

⑭ Nein, ich will nicht.　　**No, I don't want to.**

BUT: Nein, das tue ich nicht.　**No, I won't do that.**

⑮ Also, wir fahren nach Hamburg.
So we'll go to Hamburg.

BUT: Also, nach Hamburg wollt ihr fahren.
So you want to go to Hamburg.

⑯ Sogar seine Mutter wollte es ihm nicht glauben.
Even his mother wouldn't believe him.

BUT: Sogar mit dem Zug ginge es nicht schneller.
It would be no faster even by train.

Word Order: Subordinate Clauses

A subordinate clause may be introduced by:

- a relative pronoun (see page 174) → **①**

- a subordinating conjunction (see page 222) → **②** − **③**

The subject follows the opening conjunction or relative pronoun – see wir and er → **①** − **③**

The main verb almost always goes to the end of a subordinate clause → **①** − **③**

The exceptions to this are:

- in a wenn clause where wenn is omitted (see page 64) → **④**

- in an indirect statement without dass (see page 64) → **⑤**

The order for articles, nouns, adjectives, adverbs, direct and indirect objects is the same as for main clauses (see page 224), but they are all placed between the subject of the clause and the verb → **⑥**

If the subject of a reflexive verb in a subordinate clause is a pronoun, the order is *subject pronoun + reflexive pronoun* → **⑦**

If the subject is a noun, the reflexive pronoun may follow or precede it → **⑧**

Where one subordinate clause lies inside another, both still obey the order rule for subordinate clauses → **⑨**

Examples

① Die Kinder, die wir gesehen haben ...
   The children whom we saw ...

② Da er nicht schwimmen wollte, ist er nicht mitgekommen.
   As he didn't want to swim he didn't come.

③ Ich weiß, dass er zur Zeit in London wohnt.
   I know he's living in London at the moment.
   Ich weiß nicht, ob er kommt.
   I don't know if he's coming.

④ Findest du meine Uhr, so ruf mich bitte an.
   (= Wenn du meine Uhr findest, ruf mich bitte an.)
   If you find my watch, please give me a ring.

⑤ Er meint, er werde es innerhalb einer Stunde schaffen.
   (= Er meint, dass er es innerhalb einer Stunde schaffen werde.)
   He thinks (that) he will manage it within an hour.

⑥ **MAIN CLAUSE**
   Er ist gestern mit seiner Mutter in die Stadt gefahren.
   He went to town with his mother yesterday.

   SUBORDINATE CLAUSES
   Da er gestern mit seiner Mutter in die Stadt gefahren ist, ...
   Since he went to town with his mother yesterday ...
   Der Junge, der gestern mit seiner Mutter in die Stadt gefahren ist, ...
   The boy who went to town with his mother yesterday ...
   Ich weiß, dass er gestern mit seiner Mutter in die Stadt gefahren ist.
   I know that he went to town with his mother yesterday.

⑦ Weil er sich nicht setzen wollte, ...
   Because he wouldn't sit down ...

⑧ Weil das Kind sich nicht setzen wollte, ... OR:
   Weil sich das Kind nicht setzen wollte, ...
   Because the child wouldn't sit down ...

⑨ Er wusste, dass der Mann, mit dem er gesprochen hatte, bei einer Baufirma arbeitete.
   He knew that the man he had been speaking to worked for a construction company.

Word Order

In the imperative

- normal order → **①**

- with reflexive verbs → **②**

- with separable verbs → **③**

- with separable reflexive verbs → **④**

In direct and indirect speech

The verb of saying ("he replied/he said") must be inverted if it is placed within a quotation → **⑤**

The position of the verb in indirect speech depends on whether or not dass (see page 66) is used → **⑥**

Verbs with separable prefixes (see pages 72–75)

In main clauses the verb and prefix are separated in simple tenses and imperative forms → **⑦**

For compound tenses of main clauses and all tenses of subordinate clauses, the verb and its prefix are united at the end of the clause → **⑧**

In a present infinitive phrase (see page 46), the verb and prefix are joined together by zu and placed at the end of the phrase → **⑨**

Examples

❶
Hol mir das Buch! (*singular*)
Holt mir das Buch! (*plural*)   Fetch me that book!
Holen Sie mir das Buch! (*polite*)

❷
Wasch dich sofort! (*singular*)
Wascht euch sofort! (*plural*)   Wash yourself/yourselves
Waschen Sie sich sofort! (*polite*) at once!

❸
Hör jetzt auf! (*singular*)
Hört jetzt auf! (*plural*)   Stop it!
Hören Sie jetzt auf! (*polite*)

❹
Dreh dich um! (*singular*)
Dreht euch um! (*plural*)   Turn round!
Drehen Sie sich um! (*polite*)

❺
„Meine Mutter" sagte er, „kommt erst morgen an".
"My mother", he said, "won't arrive till tomorrow".

❻
Er sagte, dass sie erst am nächsten Tag ankomme.
He said that she would not arrive until the next day.
Er sagte, sie komme erst am nächsten Tag an.
He said she would not arrive until the next day.

❼
Er machte die Tür zu.
He closed the door.
Ich räume zuerst auf.
I'll clean up first.
Hol mich um 7 ab!
Pick me up at 7!

❽
Er hat die Tür zugemacht.
He closed the door.
Ich werde zuerst aufräumen.
I'll clean up first.
Er wurde um 7 abgeholt.
He was picked up at 7.
Wenn du mich um 7 abholst, ...
If you pick me up at 7 ...
Nachdem du mich abgeholt hast, ...
After you've picked me up ...

❾
Um frühzeitig anzukommen, fuhren wir sofort ab.
In order to arrive early we left immediately.

Question Forms

Direct questions

In German, a direct question is formed by simply inverting the verb and subject → ❶

In compound tenses (see pages 22–27) the past participle or infinitive goes to the end of the clause → ❷

A statement can be made into a question by the addition of nicht, nicht wahr or doch, as with "isn't it" in English → ❸

Questions formed in this way normally expect the answer to be "yes".

When a question is put in the negative, doch can be used to answer it more positively than ja → ❹

Questions formed using interrogative words

When questions are formed with interrogative adverbs, the subject and verb are inverted → ❺

When questions are formed with interrogative pronouns and adjectives (see pages 144 and 176–178), the word order is that of direct statements:

* as the subject of the verb at the beginning of the clause they do not cause inversion → ❻
* if *not* the subject of the verb *and* at the beginning of the clause they do cause inversion → ❼

Indirect questions

These are questions following verbs of asking and wondering etc. The verb comes at the end of an indirect question → ❽

❶   Magst du ihn?
        Do you like him?

❷   Gehst du ins Kino?   Do you go to the cinema?
                              OR: Are you going to the cinema?

        Hast du ihn gesehen?   Did you see him?
                              OR: Have you seen him?

        Wird sie mit ihm kommen?
        Will she come with him?

❸   Das stimmt, nicht (wahr)?
        That's true, isn't it?

        Das schaffst du doch?
        You'll manage, won't you?

❹   Glaubst du mir nicht? — Doch!
        Don't you believe me? — Yes I do!

❺   Wann ist er gekommen?
        When did he come?

        Wo willst du hin?
        Where are you off to?

❻   Wer hat das gemacht?
        Who did this?

❼   Wem hast du es geschenkt?
        Who did you give it to?

❽   Er fragte, ob du mitkommen wolltest.
        He asked if you wanted to come.

        Er möchte wissen, warum du nicht gekommen bist.
        He would like to know why you didn't come.

Negatives

A statement or question is made negative by adding:

>   nicht (*not*) or nie (*never*)

The negative may be placed next to the phrase or word to which it refers. The negative meaning can be shifted from one element of the sentence to another in this way → ❶

nie can be placed at the beginning of a sentence for added emphasis, in which case the subject and verb are inverted → ❷

nicht comes at the end of a negative imperative, except when the verb is separable, in which case nicht *precedes* the separable prefix → ❸

The combination nicht ein is usually replaced by forms of kein (see page 126) → ❹

doch (see page 196) is used in place of ja to contradict a negative statement → ❺

Negative comparison is made with nicht ... sondern (*not ... but*).

This construction is used to correct a previous false impression or idea → ❻

❶ Mit ihr wollte er nicht sprechen.
He didn't want to speak to *her*.
Er wollte nicht mit ihr sprechen.
He didn't *want* to speak to her.

Er will nicht morgen nach Hause.
OR: Morgen will er nicht nach Hause.
He doesn't want to go home *tomorrow*.
Er will morgen nicht nach Hause.
He doesn't want to go *home* tomorrow.

Wohnen Sie nicht in Dortmund?
Don't you live in Dortmund?
Warum ist er nicht mitgekommen?
Why didn't he come with you?
Waren Sie nie in Dortmund?
Have you never been to Dortmund?

❷ Nie war sie glücklicher gewesen.
She had never been happier.

❸ Iss das nicht!
Don't eat that!
Beeilen Sie sich nicht!
Don't hurry!
BUT: Geh nicht weg!
Don't go away!

❹ Gibt es keine Plätzchen?
Aren't there any biscuits?
Kein einziges Kind hatte die Arbeit geschrieben.
Not a single child had done the work.

❺ Du kommst nicht mit. — Doch, ich komme mit.
You're not coming. — Yes I am.

❻ Nicht Joachim, sondern sein Bruder war es.
It wasn't Joachim, but his brother.

Cardinal
(one, two etc)

Ordinal
(first, second etc)

Cardinal		Ordinal	
null	0		
eins	1	der erste [2]	1.
zwei [1]	2	der zweite [1]	2.
drei	3	der dritte	3.
vier	4	der vierte	4.
fünf	5	der fünfte	5.
sechs	6	der sechste	6.
sieben	7	der siebte	7.
acht	8	der achte	8.
neun	9	der neunte	9.
zehn	10	der zehnte	10.
elf	11	der elfte	11.
zwölf	12	der zwölfte	12.
dreizehn	13	der dreizehnte	13.
vierzehn	14	der vierzehnte	14.
fünfzehn	15	der fünfzehnte	15.
sechzehn	16	der sechzehnte	16.
siebzehn	17	der siebzehnte	17.
achtzehn	18	der achtzehnte	18.
neunzehn	19	der neunzehnte	19.
zwanzig	20	der zwanzigste	20.
einundzwanzig	21	der einundzwanzigste	21.
zweiundzwanzig [1]	22	der zweiundzwanzigste [1]	22.
dreißig	30	der dreißigste	30.
vierzig	40	der vierzigste	40.
fünfzig	50	der fünfzigste	50.
sechzig	60	der sechzigste	60.

[1] zwo often replaces zwei in speech, to distinguish it clearly from drei: zwo, zwoundzwanzig *etc*.

[2] The ordinal number and the preceding definite article (and adjective if there is one) are declined, e.g.:

bei seinem dritten Versuch   at his third attempt

siebzig	70	der siebzigste	70.
achtzig	80	der achtzigste	80.
neunzig	90	der neunzigste	90.
hundert	a hundred	der hundertste	100.
einhundert	one hundred		
hunderteins	101	der hunderterste	101.
hundertzwei	102	der hundertzweite	102.
hunderteinundzwanzig	121	der hunderteinundzwanzigste	121.
zweihundert	200	der zweihundertste	200.
tausend	a thousand	der tausendste	1000.
eintausend	one thousand		
tausendeins	1001	der tausenderste	1001.
zweitausend	2000	der zweitausendste	2000.
hunderttausend	100 000	der hunderttausendste	100 000.
eine Million	1 000 000	der millionste	1 000 000.

With large numbers, spaces or full stops are used where English uses a comma, e.g.:

1.000.000 or 1 000 000 for 1,000,000 (*a million*)

Decimals are written with a comma instead of a full stop, e.g.:

7,5 (sieben Komma fünf) for 7.5 (*seven point five*)

When ordinal numbers are used as nouns, they are written with a capital letter, e.g.:

sie ist die Zehnte   she's the tenth

Fractions

halb	die Hälfte	eine halbe Stunde
half (a)	half (the)	half an hour
das Drittel	zwei Drittel	das Viertel
third	two thirds	quarter
drei viertel	anderthalb, eineinhalb	zweieinhalb
three quarters	one and a half	two and a half

Wie spät ist es? / Wie viel Uhr ist es?
What time is it?

Es ist ...
It's ...

00.00	Mitternacht / null Uhr / vierundzwanzig Uhr / zwölf Uhr
00.10	zehn (Minuten) nach zwölf / null Uhr zehn
00.15	Viertel nach zwölf / null Uhr fünfzehn
00.30	halb eins / null Uhr dreißig
00.40	zwanzig (Minuten) vor eins / null Uhr vierzig
00.45	Viertel vor eins / drei viertel eins / null Uhr fünfundvierzig
01.00	ein Uhr
01.10	zehn (Minuten) nach eins / ein Uhr zehn
01.15	Viertel nach eins / ein Uhr fünfzehn
01.30	halb zwei / ein Uhr dreißig
01.40	zwanzig (Minuten) vor zwei / ein Uhr vierzig
01.45	Viertel vor zwei / drei viertel zwei / ein Uhr fünfundvierzig
01.50	zehn (Minuten) vor zwei / ein Uhr fünfzig
12.00	zwölf Uhr
12.30	halb eins / zwölf Uhr dreißig
13.00	ein Uhr / dreizehn Uhr
16.30	halb fünf / sechzehn Uhr dreißig
22.00	zehn Uhr / zweiundzwanzig Uhr / zwoundzwanzig Uhr

morgen um halb drei
at half past two tomorrow

um drei Uhr (nachmittags)
at three (pm)

kurz vor zehn Uhr
just before ten o'clock

gegen vier Uhr (nachmittags)
towards four o'clock (in the afternoon)

erst um halb neun
not until half past eight

ab neun Uhr
from nine o'clock onwards

morgen früh/Abend
tomorrow morning/evening

Dates

Der Wievielte ist heute? / Welches Datum haben wir heute?
What's the date today?

Heute ist ...   It's ...
    der zwanzigste März   the twentieth of March
    der Zwanzigste   the twentieth

Heute haben wir ...   It's ...
    den zwanzigsten März   the twentieth of March
    den Zwanzigsten   the twentieth

Am Wievielten findet es statt?   When does it take place?

Es findet am ersten April statt ...   ... on the first of April

Es findet am Ersten statt   ... on the first

Es findet (am) Montag, den ersten April statt.
OR:
Es findet Montag, den 1. April statt.
It takes place on Monday, the first of April / April 1st.

Years

Er wurde 1980 geboren.   (im Jahre) 2010
He was born in 1980.   in 2010

Other expressions

im Dezember/Januar *etc*   im Winter/Sommer/Herbst/Frühling
in December/January *etc*   in winter/summer/autumn/spring

nächstes Jahr   Anfang September
next year   at the beginning of September

Punctuation

German punctuation differs from English in the following cases:

Commas

Decimal places are always shown by a comma → ①

Large numbers are separated off by means of a space or a full stop → ②

Subordinate clauses are always marked off from the rest of the sentence by a comma → ③

This applies to all types of subordinate clause, e.g.:

- clauses with an adverbial function → ③

- relative clauses → ④

- clauses containing indirect speech → ⑤

A comma is not required between two main clauses linked by und or oder → ⑥

Exclamation marks

Exclamation marks are used after imperative forms unless these are not intended as commands → ⑦

An exclamation mark is occasionally used after the name at the beginning of a letter, but this tends to be rather old-fashioned → ⑧

①
3.4 (drei Komma vier)
3.4 (three point four)

②
20 000
OR: 20.000 (zwanzigtausend)
20,000 (twenty thousand)

③
Als er nach Hause kam, war sie schon weg.
She had already gone when he came home.

Er bleibt gesund, obwohl er zu viel trinkt.
He stays healthy, even though he drinks too much.

④
Der Mann, mit dem sie verheiratet ist, soll sehr reich sein.
The man she is married to is said to be very rich.

⑤
Er sagt, es gefällt ihm nicht.
He says he doesn't like it.

⑥
Wir gehen ins Kino oder wir bleiben zu Hause.
We'll go to the cinema or stay at home.

⑦
Steh auf!
Get up!

Bitte nehmen Sie doch Platz.
Do please sit down.

⑧
Liebe Elke! ...
Dear Elke, ...

Sehr geehrter Herr Braun! ...
Dear Mr Braun, ...

Index

The following index lists comprehensively both grammatical terms and *key words* in **German** and English contained in this book.

Index

Index

Index